France

**Jeremy Gray
Steve Fallon
Paul Hellander
Daniel Robinson
Miles Roddis
Nicola Williams**

LONELY PLANET PUBLICATIONS
Melbourne • Oakland • London • Paris

FRANCE

BURGUNDY
Absorb Dijon's wealth of medieval and Renaissance architecture, visit Beaune's spectacular Hôtel-Dieu des Hospices and sample fine wines

PARIS
Bask in the art treasures of the Louvre or Musée d'Orsay and stroll along the banks of the romantic River Seine

AROUND PARIS
Relive the glory of Versailles, the kingdom of France in the 17th and 18th centuries

NORMANDY
Explore Mont St-Michel's fascinating network of narrow streets, and visit Claude Monet's famous house and gardens in Giverny

BRITTANY
Hike the rugged coastline, experience Celtic culture and forget time in the winding streets of St-Malo's walled city

LOIRE VALLEY
Gape at the magnificent castles of Chambord, Chaumont, Cheverny and Chenonceau

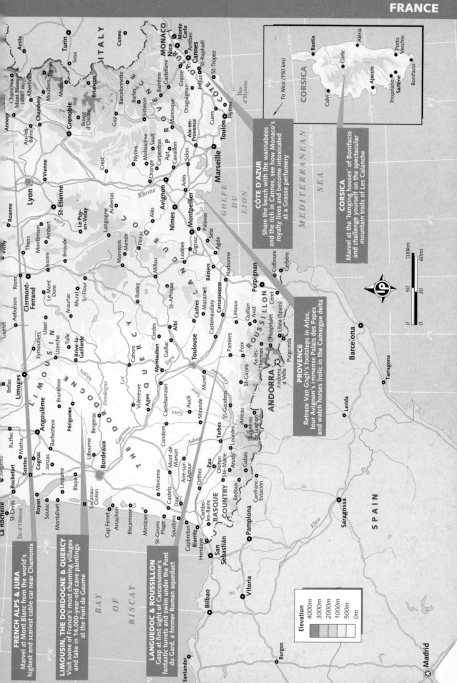

FRANCE

FRENCH ALPS & JURA
Marvel at Mont Blanc from the world's highest and scariest cable car near Chamonix

LIMOUSIN, THE DORDOGNE & QUERCY
Visit some of France's most charming villages and take in 14,000-year-old cave paintings at the Font de Gaume

LANGUEDOC & ROUSSILLON
Gasp at first sight of Carcassonne's fantastic turrets and swim under the Pont du Gard, a former Roman aqueduct

CÔTE D'AZUR
Share the beach with the wannabes and the rich in Cannes, see how Monaco's royalty lives and become intoxicated at a Grasse perfumery

CORSICA
Marvel at the 'hanging houses' of Bonifacio and challenge yourself on the spectacular mountain trails of Les Calanche

PROVENCE
Retrace Van Gogh's footsteps in Arles, tour Avignon's immense Palais des Papes and watch horses frolic in the Camargue delta

CORSICA

Elevation
4000m
3000m
2000m
1000m
500m
0m

France
4th edition – January 2001
First published – April 1994

Published by
Lonely Planet Publications Pty Ltd A.C.N. 005 607 983
90 Maribyrnong St, Footscray, Victoria 3011, Australia

Lonely Planet Offices
Australia Locked Bag 1, Footscray, Victoria 3011
USA 150 Linden St, Oakland, CA 94607
UK 10a Spring Place, London NW5 3BH
France 1 rue du Dahomey, 75011 Paris

Photographs
All of the images in this guide are available for licensing from
Lonely Planet Images.
email: lpi@lonelyplanet.com.au

Front cover photograph
Chalk drawing, Paris pavement: France is so packed with art that it
spills onto the streets (Rod Hyett).

ISBN 1 86450 151 0

text & maps © Lonely Planet 2001
photos © photographers as indicated 2001

GR and PR are trademarks of the FFRP (Fédération Française de la
Randonnée)

Printed by Colorcraft Ltd, Hong Kong

Although the authors and Lonely Planet try to make the information as accurate as possible, we accept no responsibility for any loss, injury or inconvenience sustained by anyone using this book.

Contents – Text

4 Contents – Text

Contents – Maps

8 Contents – Maps

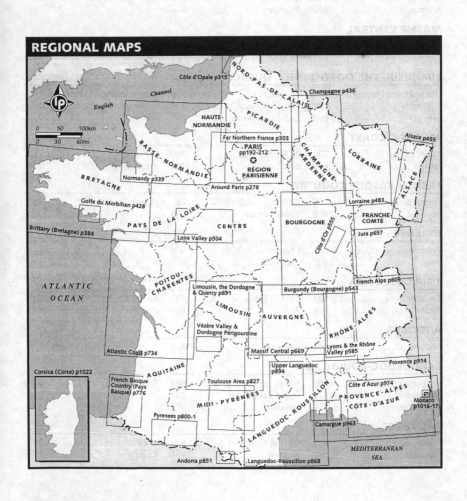

The Authors

Jeremy Gray
A Louisiana native, Jeremy studied literature and business in the wilds of Texas before taking a university scholarship to Germany in 1984. Infatuated with Europe, he chucked his MBA plans and embarked on a glittering career as an English teacher and clerk for the US Air Force in Wiesbaden (speciality: plumbing translations).

Next came a master's degree in politics at Canterbury and a string of jobs in the rough-and-tumble of financial journalism - in Woking, Surrey, and in equally lovely Frankfurt. While freelancing for the Financial Times in Holland he tumbled into Lonely Planet, and has worked on titles including Germany, The Netherlands and LP's city guides to Munich and Montreal. Jeremy currently resides in Amsterdam, a three-hour drive from the French border.

Steve Fallon
A native of Boston, Massachusetts, Steve graduated from Georgetown University with a Bachelor of Science in modern languages and then taught English at the University of Silesia near Katowice in Poland. After he had worked for several years for a Gannett newspaper, his fascination with the 'new' Asia took him to Hong Kong, where he lived and worked for 13 years for a variety of publications and owned a travel bookshop. Steve lived in Budapest for 2½ years from where he wrote Hungary and Slovenia before moving to London in 1994. He has written or contributed to a number of other Lonely Planet titles.

Paul Hellander
Paul has never really stopped travelling since he was born in England to a Norwegian father and English mother. He graduated with a degree in Greek before heading for Australia in 1977, via Greece and a number of other countries. He taught Modern Greek and trained interpreters and translators for thirteen years before throwing it all away for a life as a travel writer. Paul has contributed to over 20 LP titles among which are guides to Greece, Cyprus, Israel, Eastern Europe, Singapore and Central America. A long-standing francophile and francophone, Paul ate and drank his way around the tastiest parts of France for this edition of France. When not travelling he lives in Adelaide, South Australia, where he studies the history of espionage, listens to Neil Young, cooks Thai food and grows hot chillies. He was last spotted heading once more for Greece to write a regional guide to Rhodes & the Dodecanese.

Daniel Robinson
Daniel was raised in the USA (the San Francisco Bay area and Glen Ellyn, Illinois) and Israel. His passion for shoestring travel was kindled at age 17 with a trip to Cyprus, and since then he has spent several years on the road exploring some of the more remote parts of Asia, the Middle East and Europe. Over the past 12 years, Daniel's work for Lonely Planet has included the award-winning 1st editions of Vietnam,

9

researched one step ahead of the secret police (the story of his expulsion from Hanoi recently appeared in the anthology *Lonely Planet Unpacked*) and (with Tony Wheeler) *Cambodia*, at the time still in a state of civil war. He has worked on all four editions of *France*, covering virtually every region of the Hexagone.

Daniel holds a BA in Near Eastern Studies from Princeton University and is currently finishing up an MA in Israeli history at Tel Aviv University.

Miles Roddis

Miles' involvement with France began when, 15 and spotty, he noisily threw up the night's red wine in a Paris cafe. Undeterred by the subsequent monumental hangover, he mainlined in French at university, becoming seriously hooked and spending an idyllic sandwich year in Neuville-sur-Saône, a place quite rightly overlooked by the best guidebooks, including the one in your hand.

He now lives over the Pyrenees in Spain, from where he has contributed to *Africa on a Shoestring*, *West Africa*, *Lonely Planet Unpacked*, *Spain*, *Walking in Britain*, *Walking in Spain* and – perhaps most satisfyingly – *Walking in France*.

Nicola Williams

Nicola lives in Lyon, crossroads to the French Alps and Mediterranean. A journalist by training, she first hit the road in 1990 when she bussed and boated it from Jakarta to East Timor and back again. Following a two-year stint at the *North Wales Weekly News*, she moved to Latvia to bus it round the Baltics as Features Editor of the English-language *Baltic Times* newspaper. Following a happy 12 months exploring the Baltic region as editor-in-chief of the *In Your Pocket* city-guide series, she traded in Lithuanian *cepelinai* for Lyonnais *andouillette*.

Nicola graduated from Kent and completed an MA in Islamic Societies & Cultures at London's School of Oriental & African Studies. Previous titles she has written or updated for Lonely Planet include *Provence & the Côte d'Azur*, *The Loire*, *Romania & Moldova*, *Estonia, Latvia & Lithuania* and *Russia, Ukraine & Belarus*.

FROM THE AUTHORS

From Jeremy Gray The utterly lovely, charitable staff in the vast majority of tourist offices I visited deserve my boundless gratitude. Isabelle at Le Conquet (Brittany) deserves a very special mention – I never would have found those secret treasures without her. Thanks, too, to Jen Wabisabi for getting lost with me at all those confusing roundabouts, and to Jacques and Gi Veit for being the consummate hosts (I'll never forget the truffle-scented eggs). Fellow authors Steve Fallon, Paul Hellander, Daniel Robinson, Miles Roddis and Nicola Williams all earn a *palme d'or* for being sooo professional and for infusing this book with so much character. At Lonely Planet in London, editors Paul Bloomfield, Samantha Trafford and Claudia Martin, as well as designers Sara Yorke and Adam McCrow, provided a wealth of sound advice, while in Melbourne, culinary guru Martin Hughes gave of his tastebuds for the Food and Wine section.

From Steve Fallon Once again, my share of this guidebook is dedicated to Michael Rothschild (Cupid draw back our Bow).

A number of people helped in the updating of my portion of *France*. Paris resident Brenda Turnnidge provided invaluable support; her efficiency is unequalled, her enthusiasm for the City of Light and its people palpable. Thanks too to Emma Bland, Christine Coste, Rob Flynn, Jeremy Gray, Zahia Hafs, Daniel Robinson, Chew Terrière and Frank Viviano for assistance, ideas, hospitality and/or a few laughs along the way. It was a pleasure working with the editorial team in London; unflappable cartographer Angie Watts was a Rock of Gibraltar fiddling with all those map keys that will get you where you want to go. *Merci mille fois à tous!*

From Paul Hellander Re-visiting France after quite some time away was like a breath of fresh air. The task was made immeasurably easier by certain people and organisations who contributed to my work in one way or another. They deserve a mention. Thanks to the invariably co-operative and information-rich *Offices de Tourisme* around France that plied me with kilos of excellent data and to SNCM for excellent transport to and from Corsica. Thanks to my wife Stella for her unstinting assistance on the trip around France and for her excellent photography. Special mention also to the following individuals who helped in various ways: Louiza Maragozidis; Nicola Williams and Matthias Lüftkens; Stéphanie 4; Michel, Stella & Véronique le Petit; Iain & Liz Purce; Jean-Marie & Irène Casta and finally Deborah Palmer for 'tooling around' with us for a while. To sons Byron and Marcus in Greece – another title bites the dust for you.

From Daniel Robinson In storm-battered Champagne, thanks go to Martine Eluau and Cédric Baudouin of the Reims and Troyes tourist offices, Didier Carayon and Gilbert Picard.

My work in Alsace would not have been anywhere near as much fun were it not for my parents, Bernie and Yetta Robinson, who came to visit; Amand Stroh of Brasseries Kronenbourg; Martine Barth; Kiera Tchelistcheff; Mylène Neves; Ian Clayton (Bristol, England), Michelle Zoric (Pittsburgh, Pennsylvania), Amy McFarland (Arcanum, Ohio) and Sheetal Aiyer (Lubbock, Texas); and Corrine and Rachel of Radio Judaica, who helped me track down Salim Halali's unique Arabic version of the Yiddish classic 'Ma Yiddische Mama'.

In Dijon, the world of student nightlife was opened to me late one freezing winter's night by Emilie Desnouveaux, Amélie Peigneu and the staff of Coco-Loco. Warmth and hominess were contributed by Prof Bob Wiener, Albert and Myrna Huberfel, and the Tenenbaum family. Thanks, too, to Didier Renault of the tourist office.

In Limoges, valuable insights were provided by Christelle Prince and Fedia Mattarelli of Le Duc Étienne and University of Birmingham students Rob Coleridge, Simon Stephen and Rebecca Squires. In

Périgueux, Mike and Bev Vinnicombe welcomed me at The Star Inn.

In Bordeaux, I am indebted to the gracious proprietors of the Hôtel de la Tour Intendance and Armelle Lambert of the St Émilion tourist office. In Le Teich, Julie Cazabeil and Sonia Missoum were enthusiastic hosts.

My stay in Cognac would have been *much* duller if not for the boisterous antics of Paul Dell of the Hôtel Saint Martin and his merry gang of neighbourhood habitués, including Sandrine, Melanie, Madame Légume and little Julie, as well as Kim Wooseok of Songnam, South Korea. Nathalie Boucq updated me on Futuroscope's attractions while we careened around in a golf cart. In Nantes, thanks go to Bethan Morgan of Machynlleth, Wales, Kristen Rahn of Cincinnati, Ohio and Marc Paquereau of John McByrne Irish Pub.

In Paris, I am indebted to the staff of Lonely Planet's Paris bureau, including Arnot, Benjamin, Caroline, Didier, Rob and Zahia; SNCF staffers Fabrice Bartrolich, Barbara Grau and Philippe Kirsanow; Eliane, Pauline and Antoine Bebe and Tom Cohen; Diane Holt and Michael Feldman, who are always up for a weekend away from Naples; Harriet and Les Niss, who may never again arrive for dinner so wet; David Saliamonis; Irit Kleiman; my almost-cousin Miel de Botton; my real cousin Natasha Leland; and Kamal, Karim, Madame Sadou and the inimitable staff of the Hôtel Rivoli.

The Peugeot 106 that transported me for 7000 fault-free kilometres was arranged through Geoff Harvey of Australia's DriveAway Holidays.

From Miles Roddis To Ingrid, the world's best travelling companion, Damon for putting me wise about surfing and Tristan for resolving computer glitches and incipient heart attacks.

To countless tourist office staff for information cheerfully and patiently given – especially Marie Ange Pepin (Maison de la Lozère, Montpellier), Valerie (Nîmes), Lydia Tocchio and Christian Rivière (Albi), Helène Barrere (Bayonne) and Laurence Tapie and colleagues (Bedous). Thanks too to Robert and Jacqueline Pastor and Mike and Kate Nichols for hospitality and help in answering a number of niggling, left-until-last queries.

I also owe a big debt and several beers to Julia Wilkinson and John King, indefatigable researchers and writers of Lonely Planet's *South West France*.

From Nicola Williams In the Loire Valley, particular thanks to Catherine Leroi from Château d'Angers; Yveline Galand from Château de Chenonceau; Laurent de Froberville from the Domaine de Cheverny; Louis Hubert from the Domaine de Chambord; Jean Saint-Bris from Le Clos Lucé in Amboise; and Catherine Moulé from the École Nationale d'Équitation in equestrian Saumur. In France's culinary capital, a *grand merci* to Lyon's chefs for never failing to tickle those tastebuds and to foodie fanatic Matthias for making Lyon our home.

This Book

The 1st edition of Lonely Planet's guide to France was the work of Daniel Robinson and Leanne Logan. For the 2nd edition, Daniel teamed up with Steve Fallon, who was the coordinator, and Richard Nebeský. Daniel and Steve joined forces with Nicola Williams and Teresa Fisher for the 3rd edition. For this 4th edition, Daniel, Steve and Nicola were joined by Jeremy Gray, Miles Roddis and Paul Hellander.

Jeremy coordinated the project and updated the Introduction, Facts about France, Facts for the Visitor, Far Northern France, Normandy and Brittany chapters, and the Food & Wine special section. Steve updated the Paris and Around Paris chapters. Paul updated the French Alps & Jura, Provence, Côte d'Azur & Monaco and Corsica chapters. Daniel updated the Getting There & Away, Getting Around, Champagne, Alsace & Lorraine, Burgundy, Atlantic Coast, Massif Central, and Limousin, the Dordogne & Quercy chapters. Miles updated the Toulouse, French Basque County, Pyrenees, Andorra and Languedoc-Roussillon chapters. Finally, Nicola updated the Loire and Lyons & the Rhone Valley chapters.

From the Publisher

This book was produced in Lonely Planet's London office. Sam Trafford coordinated the editing, assisted by Abigail Hole, Amanda Canning, Claudia Martin, Emma Sangster, Heather Dickson, Imogen Franks and Michala Green. The book was proofread by Abigail and Michala with help from Tim Ryder and Sam. Paul Edmunds was responsible for mapping, design and layout. Angie Watts, David Wenk Ed Pickard, James Ellis, James Timmins, and Sara Yorke assisted with the mapping, Adam McCrow designed the cover and Jim Miller drew the back-cover map. Michala and Abigail produced the index with help from Finola Collins and Paul Bloomfield. Quentin Frayne used his linguistic expertise on the language chapter, and Jane Smith and Nicky Caven supplied the illustrations. Special thanks to Tim Fitzgerald, Tim Ryder and Adam who provided sound advice, calmness and last-minute Quark help.

The quotation on page 166 is from A Moveable Feast by Ernest Hemingway. Copyright © 1964 by Mary Hemingway. Copyright renewed © 1992 by John H Hemingway, Patrick Hemingway and Gregory Hemingway. Reprinted by permission of Scribner, a division of Simon & Schuster, publisher for the USA and Canada, and Jonathan Cape, publisher for the rest of the world.

THANKS

Many thanks to the travellers who used the last edition and wrote to us with helpful hints, advice and interesting anecdotes. Your names appear in the back of this book.

Foreword

ABOUT LONELY PLANET GUIDEBOOKS

The story begins with a classic travel adventure: Tony and Maureen Wheeler's 1972 journey across Europe and Asia to Australia. Useful information about the overland trail did not exist at that time, so Tony and Maureen published the first Lonely Planet guidebook to meet a growing need.

From a kitchen table, then from a tiny office in Melbourne (Australia), Lonely Planet has become the largest independent travel publisher in the world, an international company with offices in Melbourne, Oakland (USA), London (UK) and Paris (France).

Today Lonely Planet guidebooks cover the globe. There is an ever-growing list of books and there's information in a variety of forms and media. Some things haven't changed. The main aim is still to help make it possible for adventurous travellers to get out there – to explore and better understand the world.

At Lonely Planet we believe travellers can make a positive contribution to the countries they visit – if they respect their host communities and spend their money wisely. Since 1986 a percentage of the income from each book has been donated to aid projects and human rights campaigns.

Updates Lonely Planet thoroughly updates each guidebook as often as possible. This usually means there are around two years between editions, although for more unusual or more stable destinations the gap can be longer. Check the imprint page (following the colour map at the beginning of the book) for publication dates.

Between editions up-to-date information is available in two free newsletters – the paper *Planet Talk* and email *Comet* (to subscribe, contact any Lonely Planet office) – and on our Web site at www.lonelyplanet.com. The *Upgrades* section of the Web site covers a number of important and volatile destinations and is regularly updated by Lonely Planet authors. *Scoop* covers news and current affairs relevant to travellers. And, lastly, the *Thorn Tree* bulletin board and *Postcards* section of the site carry unverified, but fascinating, reports from travellers.

Correspondence The process of creating new editions begins with the letters, postcards and emails received from travellers. This correspondence often includes suggestions, criticisms and comments about the current editions. Interesting excerpts are immediately passed on via newsletters and the Web site, and everything goes to our authors to be verified when they're researching on the road. We're keen to get more feedback from organisations or individuals who represent communities visited by travellers.

Lonely Planet gathers information for everyone who's curious about the planet – and especially for those who explore it first-hand. Through guidebooks, phrasebooks, activity guides, maps, literature, newsletters, image library, TV series and Web site we act as an information exchange for a worldwide community of travellers.

Research Authors aim to gather sufficient practical information to enable travellers to make informed choices and to make the mechanics of a journey run smoothly. They also research historical and cultural background to help enrich the travel experience and allow travellers to understand and respond appropriately to cultural and environmental issues.

Authors don't stay in every hotel because that would mean spending a couple of months in each medium-sized city and, no, they don't eat at every restaurant because that would mean stretching belts beyond capacity. They do visit hotels and restaurants to check standards and prices, but feedback based on readers' direct experiences can be very helpful.

Many of our authors work undercover, others aren't so secretive. None of them accept freebies in exchange for positive write-ups. And none of our guidebooks contain any advertising.

Production Authors submit their raw manuscripts and maps to offices in Australia, USA, UK or France. Editors and cartographers – all experienced travellers themselves – then begin the process of assembling the pieces. When the book finally hits the shops, some things are already out of date, we start getting feedback from readers and the process begins again ...

WARNING & REQUEST

Things change – prices go up, schedules change, good places go bad and bad places go bankrupt – nothing stays the same. So, if you find things better or worse, recently opened or long since closed, please tell us and help make the next edition even more accurate and useful. We genuinely value all the feedback we receive. Julie Young coordinates a well travelled team that reads and acknowledges every letter, postcard and email and ensures that every morsel of information finds its way to the appropriate authors, editors and cartographers for verification.

Everyone who writes to us will find their name in the next edition of the appropriate guidebook. They will also receive the latest issue of *Planet Talk*, our quarterly printed newsletter, or *Comet*, our monthly email newsletter. Subscriptions to both newsletters are free. The very best contributions will be rewarded with a free guidebook.

Excerpts from your correspondence may appear in new editions of Lonely Planet guidebooks, the Lonely Planet Web site, *Planet Talk* or *Comet*, so please let us know if you *don't* want your letter published or your name acknowledged.

Send all correspondence to the Lonely Planet office closest to you:

Australia: Locked Bag 1, Footscray, Victoria 3011
USA: 150 Linden St, Oakland, CA 94607
UK: 10A Spring Place, London NW5 3BH
France: 1 rue du Dahomey, 75011 Paris

Or email us at: talk2us@lonelyplanet.com.au

For news, views and updates see our Web site: www.lonelyplanet.com

HOW TO USE A LONELY PLANET GUIDEBOOK

The best way to use a Lonely Planet guidebook is any way you choose. At Lonely Planet we believe the most memorable travel experiences are often those that are unexpected, and the finest discoveries are those you make yourself. Guidebooks are not intended to be used as if they provide a detailed set of infallible instructions!

Contents All Lonely Planet guidebooks follow roughly the same format. The Facts about the Destination chapters or sections give background information ranging from history to weather. Facts for the Visitor gives practical information on issues like visas and health. Getting There & Away gives a brief starting point for researching travel to and from the destination. Getting Around gives an overview of the transport options when you arrive.

The peculiar demands of each destination determine how subsequent chapters are broken up, but some things remain constant. We always start with background, then proceed to sights, places to stay, places to eat, entertainment, getting there and away, and getting around information – in that order.

Heading Hierarchy Lonely Planet headings are used in a strict hierarchical structure that can be visualised as a set of Russian dolls. Each heading (and its following text) is encompassed by any preceding heading that is higher on the hierarchical ladder.

Entry Points We do not assume guidebooks will be read from beginning to end, but that people will dip into them. The traditional entry points are the list of contents and the index. In addition, however, some books have a complete list of maps and an index map illustrating map coverage.

There may also be a colour map that shows highlights. These highlights are dealt with in greater detail in the Facts for the Visitor chapter, along with planning questions and suggested itineraries. Each chapter covering a geographical region usually begins with a locator map and another list of highlights. Once you find something of interest in a list of highlights, turn to the index.

Maps Maps play a crucial role in Lonely Planet guidebooks and include a huge amount of information. A legend is printed on the back page. We seek to have complete consistency between maps and text, and to have every important place in the text captured on a map. Map key numbers usually start in the top left corner.

Although inclusion in a guidebook usually implies a recommendation we cannot list every good place. Exclusion does not necessarily imply criticism. In fact there are a number of reasons why we might exclude a place – sometimes it is simply inappropriate to encourage an influx of travellers.

Introduction

The largest country in Western Europe, France's most salient characteristic is its exceptional diversity. It stretches from the rolling plains of the north to the jagged ridges of the Pyrenees, and from the rugged coastline of Brittany to the clear, blue lakes and icy crags of the Alps.

There are mountain peaks and glaciers here, dense forests and vineyards, cliff-lined canyons and endless sandy beaches. And with the country's superb train network, you can – throughout most of the year – ski one day and sunbathe the next. But unless you have a lifetime, you have to make some choices, and this book will help you decide whether it's the Alps or the Pyrenees for some skiing and the Atlantic or the Mediterranean for a swim.

France's cities and towns are especially alluring. In Paris, celebrated for centuries for its stunning architecture and romantic *joie de vivre*, as well as in other cities, you'll see people strolling along grand boulevards, picnicking in parks and watching the world go by from cafe terraces. All cities and even many small towns have exceptional museums and galleries devoted to art, regional culture or both. Shopping is generally better in the larger cities, but many a tiny village makes products that are consumed and praised throughout the country – a cheese, perhaps, or a particularly fine wine.

Over the centuries, France has absorbed more immigrants than any other country in Europe: from the Celtic Gauls and Romans to arrivals in this century from the nation's former colonies in Indochina and Africa.

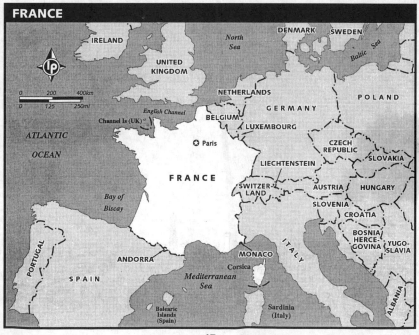

FRANCE

Elements of the culture, art and cuisine of these new citizens have been assimilated into French life, helping to create the unique and diverse civilisation that is modern France. Today, Vietnamese spring rolls are as French as baguettes, North African rai music as familiar to most people as *chansons françaises*.

Geographically France is on the western edge of the European continent, but with the unification of Europe, it is at the crossroads politically: between England and Italy, and girded by Belgium, Germany and Spain. Of course, this is just how the French have always viewed their nation – at the very centre of things.

Facts about France

HISTORY
Early Inhabitants

France has been inhabited at least since the Middle Palaeolithic period (about 90,000 to 40,000 BC) when Neanderthal people (thought to be early representatives of *Homo sapiens*) hunted animals, made crude flakestone tools and lived in caves. Several of their skeletons have been found in the caves at Le Moustier near Les Eyzies and at Le Bugue (both in modern-day Périgord). Mousterian people, who are associated with Neanderthals, have left the earliest evidence in Western Europe of the use of fire and the practice of burying their dead.

During a dramatic change of climate about 35,000 years ago, the Neanderthals disappeared. They were followed by Cro-Magnon people, a later variety of *Homo sapiens*. Much taller than their predecessors (over 170cm), Cro-Magnons had nimble hands, larger brains, long, narrow skulls and short, wide faces. They were skilful hunters, and with their improved tools and hunting techniques were able to kill reindeer, bison, horses and mammoths.

Prehistoric art began with the Cro-Magnon race. They started drawing, painting and sculpting, using a variety of different techniques. Their initial simplistic drawings and engravings of animals gradually became far more detailed and realistic, as at the Lascaux cave in the Vézère Valley of Périgord. They also decorated tools, played music, danced, performed assorted ceremonies (for example, magical rituals to enhance fertility) and had fairly complex social patterns.

In the Mesolithic period, which began about 13,000 years ago, hunting and fishing became very efficient and wild grains were harvested. The Neolithic period (about 7500 to 4000 years ago), also known as the New Stone Age, saw the advent of polished stone tools. Warmer weather caused great changes in flora and fauna, ushering in the practice of farming and stock rearing.

Cereals were grown, as were peas, beans and lentils. Communities were therefore more settled and villages were built. Pottery decorated with geometric patterns became common, as did woven fabric. This was also the time in which the first megalithic monuments were erected, such as the amazing menhirs and dolmens at Carnac in Brittany.

Indo-European tribes from the Aegean region started to use copper tools and weapons in the early 3rd millennium BC and by about 2500 BC, copper was being worked on both sides of the Alps. After the introduction of more durable bronze, forts were built and a military elite developed.

Over the next millennium, iron was introduced in various parts of Europe, but it was a scarce, precious metal and used only for ornaments and small knives. It did not come into common use until the arrival of the Celts.

The Gauls & the Romans

The Celtic Gauls moved into what is now France between 1500 and 500 BC. By about 600 BC, they had established trading links with the Greeks, whose colonies on the Mediterranean coast included Massilia (Marseilles). Some 300 years later, members of a Celtic tribe called the Parisii set up a few huts made of wattle and daub on what is now the Île de la Cité in Paris and engaged in fishing and trading.

Centuries of conflict between the Gauls and Romans ended in 52 BC, when Julius Caesar's legions crushed a revolt led by the Gallic chief Vercingétorix and took control of the territory. Christianity was introduced to Roman Gaul early in the 2nd century AD.

France remained under Roman rule until the 5th century, when the Franks (thus the name 'France') and the Alemanii overran the country from the east. These peoples adopted important elements of Gallo-Roman civilisation (including Christianity) and their eventual assimilation resulted in a fusion of Germanic culture with that of the Celts and the Romans.

The Merovingians & the Carolingians

Two Frankish dynasties, the Merovingians and the Carolingians, ruled from the 5th to the 10th century. The Frankish tradition by which the king was succeeded by *all* of his sons led to power struggles and the eventual disintegration of the kingdom into a collection of small feudal states. In 732, Charles Martel defeated the Moors at Poitiers, thus ensuring that France would not fall under Muslim rule as had Spain.

Charles Martel's grandson Charlemagne significantly extended the power and boundaries of the kingdom and was crowned Holy Roman Emperor (Emperor of the West) in 800. But during the 9th century, the Scandinavian Vikings (also known as the Norsemen, thus Normans) began raiding France's western coast. They eventually settled in the lower Seine Valley and formed the duchy of Normandy in the early 10th century.

The Middle Ages

The Capetian dynasty, which would last for the next 800 years, was founded in 987, when the nobles elected Hugh Capet as their king. The king's domains were then quite modest, consisting mostly of land around Paris and Orléans. At the time, no one could foresee that this dynasty would eventually rule one of the richest and most powerful countries in Europe.

In 1066 Norman forces under William the Conqueror, duke of Normandy, occupied England, making Normandy – and, later, Plantagenet-ruled England – a formidable rival of the kingdom of France. A further third of France came under the control of the English crown in 1152, when Eleanor of Aquitaine married Henry of Anjou (later King Henry II of England). The subsequent rivalry between France and England for control of Aquitaine and the vast English territories in France would last for three centuries.

France played a leading role in the Crusades (the First Crusade was preached at Clermont in 1095 by Pope Urban II), and most of France's major cathedrals were erected between the 12th and early 14th centuries. This was a heady period for the French monarchy: through a combination of economic growth, strategic marriages and clever deal-making, the Capetians were able to retake Normandy and much other English-held territory. By the early 14th century their acquisitions covered much of what is present-day France. In 1309, the French-born Pope Clement V fled the political turmoil in Rome and moved the Holy See to Avignon, where it remained until 1377, a useful tool of French policy.

The Hundred Years' War By the middle of the 14th century the struggle between the Capetians and England's King Edward III (a member of the Plantagenet family) over the powerful French throne degenerated into the Hundred Years' War, which was fought on and off from 1337 to 1453.

The bubonic plague (or Black Death) ravaged the country in 1348 and 1349, killing about a third of the population. In the meantime the Church was racked with division, and there were fears that the papacy might fall.

By the early 15th century, things were not going well for the Capetians. French forces were defeated at Agincourt in 1415, and the dukes of Burgundy, allied with the English, occupied Paris five years later. In 1422 John Plantagenet, duke of Bedford, was installed as regent of France for England's King Henry VI, then an infant. Henry was crowned as king of France at Notre Dame less than a decade later, and the English might have remained in power had a 17-year-old peasant girl not intervened.

In 1429, the teenage Jeanne d'Arc (Joan of Arc) persuaded the French legitimist Charles VII that she had a divine mission from God to expel the English from France and bring about Charles' coronation. She rallied the French troops to defeat the English near Orléans, and Charles was crowned at Reims. However, Joan of Arc failed in her attempt to take Paris, and in 1430 she was captured by the Burgundians and sold to the English. Convicted of witchcraft and heresy by a tribunal of French ecclesiastics, she burned at the stake two years later at Rouen. Charles VII returned to Paris in 1437, but it wasn't until 1453 that the English were entirely driven from French territory (with the exception of Calais).

The Renaissance

During the reign of François I in the early 16th century the culture of the Italian Renaissance (French for 'rebirth') arrived full swing in France after French troops returned from Italy laden with art and new cultural ideas. For the first time, the French aristocracy was exposed to Renaissance ideas of scientific and geographic scholarship and discovery, and the value of secular over religious life.

Writers such as Rabelais, Marot and Ronsard were influential, as were the architectural and artist disciples of Michelangelo and Raphael. Italian artists were recruited in droves by the French monarchy, and François I even imported Leonardo da Vinci, who died in glory at Amboise. The French arts shone with a new grace, and old palaces sprouted a Florentine wing or Italianate pilasters. François I's chateau at Fontainebleau and the Petit Château at Chantilly are prime examples of the shift away from Gothic styles.

This new architecture was meant to reflect the splendour of the monarchy, which was fast moving towards absolutism. But this grandeur and show of strength was not enough to stem the tide of Protestantism that was flowing into France.

The Reformation

By the 1530s the significance of the Reformation that was sweeping through Europe had been strengthened in France by the ideas of Jean (John) Calvin, a Frenchman exiled to Geneva. The Edict of January (1562), which afforded the Protestants certain rights, was met by violent opposition from ultra-Catholic nobles, whose fidelity to their religion was mixed with a desire to strengthen their power base in the provinces.

The Wars of Religion (1562–98) involved three groups: the Huguenots (French Protestants who received help from the English), the Catholic League (led by the House of Guise) and the Catholic monarchy. The fighting severely weakened the position of the king and brought the French state close to disintegration. The most deplorable massacre took place in Paris in 1572, when some 3000 Huguenots who had come to the capital to celebrate the wedding of the Protestant Henri of Navarre (the future Henri IV) were slaughtered in the St-Bartholomew's Day Massacre (23–24 August). In 1588, on the so-called Day of the Barricades, the Catholic League rose up against Henri III and forced him to flee the royal court at the Louvre; he was assassinated the following year.

Henri III was succeeded by Henri IV, starting the Bourbon dynasty. In 1598 Henri IV issued the Edict of Nantes, which guaranteed the Huguenots many civil and political rights and, most importantly, the freedom of conscience, but this was not universally accepted. Ultra-Catholic Paris refused to allow their new Protestant king entry to the city, and a siege of the capital continued for almost five years. Only when Henri IV embraced Catholicism at the cathedral in St-Denis – '*Paris vaut bien une messe*' (Paris is well worth a Mass), he is reputed to have said upon taking communion there – did the capital submit to him.

Henri IV was succeeded by Louis XIII in 1610. Throughout most of his undistinguished reign Louis XIII remained under the control of his ruthless chief minister, Cardinal Richelieu. Richelieu is best known for his untiring efforts to establish an all-powerful monarchy in France (opening the door to the absolutism of Louis XIV) and French supremacy in Europe, which would see France fighting Holland, Austria and England almost continuously throughout the 17th century.

Louis XIV & the Ancien Régime

In 1643, at the age of five, le Roi Soleil (the Sun King) ascended the throne as Louis XIV, and stayed ruler until 1715. Bolstered by claims of divine right, he sought to project the power of the French monarchy, both at home and abroad, throughout his long reign. He involved France in a long series of costly wars that gained it territory but terrified its neighbours and nearly bankrupted the treasury.

But Louis XIV – whose widely quoted saying 'L'État c'est moi' (I am the State) is often taken out of historical context – was able to quash the ambitious, feuding aristocracy and create the first centralised French state, elements of which can still be seen today. He poured huge sums of money into building his extravagant palace at Versailles, 23km south-west of Paris, but by doing so he was able to sidestep the endless intrigues of the capital, by then a city of 600,000 people. And by turning his nobles into courtiers, Louis XIV forced them to compete with each other for royal favour, reducing them to ineffectual sycophants. He also mercilessly persecuted the Protestant minority, which he considered a threat to the unity of the State (and thus his power). In 1685 he revoked the Edict of Nantes, which had guaranteed the Huguenots freedom of conscience.

Louis XIV's successor, his grandson Louis XV (ruled 1715–74), turned out to be an oafish buffoon. His regent, the duke of Orléans, managed however to move the court from Versailles back to Paris; in the Age of Enlightenment, the French capital had become, in effect, the centre of Europe. It was Louis XV who said 'Après moi, le deluge' (After me, the flood); in hindsight his words were more than prophetic. He was followed by the incompetent – and later universally despised and powerless – Louis XVI, who met an early demise.

As the 18th century progressed, new economic and social circumstances rendered the ancien régime (old order) dangerously out of step with the needs of the country. The regime was further weakened by the anti-establishment and anticlerical ideas of the Enlightenment, whose leading lights included Voltaire, Rousseau and Montesquieu. Entrenched vested interests, a cumbersome power structure and royal lassitude prevented change until the 1770s, by which time the monarchy's moment had passed.

The Seven Years' War (1756–63), fought by France and Austria against Britain and Prussia, was one of a series of ruinous wars pursued by Louis XV, and it led to the loss of France's flourishing colonies in Canada, the West Indies and India to the British. It was in part to avenge these losses that Louis XVI sided with the colonists in the American War of Independence. But the Seven Years' War cost a fortune and, even more ruinous for the monarchy, it helped to disseminate in France the radical democratic ideas that the American Revolution had thrust onto the world stage.

The French Revolution & the First Republic

By the late 1780s, the indecisive Louis XVI and Marie-Antoinette, his vain and overbearing queen, had managed to alienate virtually every segment of society – from enlightened groups to conservatives. Surrounded by incompetent advisors, the king failed to address the national debt, which had trebled in less than 15 years.

His finance minister, Calonne, finally proposed a tax reform to avert disaster. However, in doing so he attempted to bypass parliament, which retaliated by calling a meeting of the États Généraux (Estates General, which represented nobles, clergy and the bourgeoisie) to decide on the matter.

Reform-minded delegates of the Estates General finally banded together in July 1789 and declared themselves an Assemblée Nationale (National Assembly) – effectively replacing parliament – and the king reacted by sending in the troops. That was the final straw for the masses, whose confidence in the regime had already been shattered by soaring food prices and chronic unemployment. On 14 July, a Paris mob raided Invalides for weapons and then stormed the prison at Bastille, which represented the ultimate symbol of the despotism of the ancien régime.

At first, the Revolution was in the hands of relative moderates. France was declared a constitutional monarchy and various re-forms were enacted, including the adoption of the Declaration of the Rights of Man. But as the new government armed itself against the threat posed by Austria, Prussia and the many exiled French nobles, patriotism and nationalism mixed with revolutionary fervour. It wasn't long before the moderate republican Girondins lost power to the radical Jacobins, led by Robespierre, Danton and Marat. After Louis XVI proved unreliable as a constitutional monarch, the Jacobins abolished the monarchy and declared the First Republic in September

Republican Calendar

During the Revolution, the Convention adopted a new, more 'rational' calendar from which all 'superstitious' associations (such as saints' days) were removed. Year 1 began on 22 September 1792, the day the Republic had been proclaimed. The 12 months – renamed Vendémiaire, Brumaire, Frimaire, Nivôse, Pluviôse, Ventôse, Germinal, Floréal, Prairial, Messidor, Thermidor and Fructidor – were divided into three 10-day weeks called *décades*.

Based on the cult of nature, the poetically inspired names of the months were chosen according to the seasons: the autumn months, for instance, were Vendémiaire (derived from *vendange*, grape harvest or vintage), Brumaire (from *brume*, mist or fog) and Frimaire (from *frimas*, frost). The last day of each *décade* was a rest day, and the five or six remaining days of the year were used to celebrate Virtue, Genius, Labour, Opinion and Rewards. These festivals were initially called *sans-culottides* in honour of the *sans-culottes*, the extreme revolutionaries who wore pantaloons rather than the short breeches favoured by the upper classes.

While the Republican calendar worked well in theory, it caused no end of confusion for France in its communication and trade abroad since the months and days kept on changing in relation to those of the Gregorian calendar. Napoleon reintroduced the Gregorian calendar on 1 January 1806.

1792. The National Assembly was replaced by a 'Revolutionary Convention'.

In January 1793, Louis XVI, who had tried to flee the country with his family, was convicted of 'conspiring against the liberty of the nation' and guillotined at place de la Révolution (today's place de la Concorde). The unloved Marie-Antoinette – who, upon hearing of the deprivation of the common people, supposedly replied 'Let them eat cake' – met a similar fate the following October. In March, the Jacobins set up the notorious Committee of Public Safety. This body virtually had dictatorial control over the country during the Reign of Terror (September 1793 to July 1794), which saw religious freedoms revoked, churches desecrated and closed and cathedrals turned into 'Temples of Reason'.

By autumn, following Marat's assassination by a Girondin sympathiser, the Reign of Terror was in full swing. By the summer of 1794, some 17,000 people from all over France had been beheaded. In the end, the Revolution turned on itself, 'devouring its own children' in the words of the Jacobin St-Just: Robespierre sent Danton to the guillotine, and later St-Just and even Robespierre themselves died on the scaffold.

After the Terror, a five-man delegation of moderate republicans led by Paul Barras, who had seen to the arrests of, among others, Robespierre and St-Just, set themselves up as a Directoire (Directory) to rule the Republic. On 13 Vendémiaire in the year VI (5 October 1795; see the boxed text 'Republican Calendar'), a group of royalist rebels bent on overthrowing the Directory was intercepted in Paris by loyalist forces led by a dashing young Corsican general named Napoleon Bonaparte. His military tactics and skill were immediately recognised and Napoleon was put in command of the army in Italy, where he was particularly successful in the campaign against Austria. His victories soon turned him into an independent political force.

Napoleon & the First Empire

The post-Revolutionary government was extremely unstable, and when Napoleon returned to Paris in 1799, he found a chaotic republic in which few had any faith. In November, when it appeared that the Jacobins were again on the ascendancy in the legislature, Napoleon tricked the delegates into leaving Paris for St-Cloud to the southwest, 'for their own protection', overthrew the discredited Directory and assumed power himself.

At first, Napoleon took the title of first consul. In 1802, a referendum declared him consul for life and his birthday became a

MATT KING

As well as for his ego, Napoleon is remembered for strengthening the new republic.

national holiday. By 1804, when he had himself crowned emperor of the French by Pope Pius VII at Notre Dame Cathedral in Paris, the scope and nature of Napoleon's ambitions were all too obvious. But to consolidate and legitimise his authority, Napoleon needed more victories on the battlefield.

So began a seemingly endless series of wars in which France came to control most of Europe. In 1812, in an attempt to eliminate his last major rival on the continent, Napoleon invaded Russia. Although his Grande Armée captured Moscow, it was wiped out shortly thereafter by the brutal Russian winter. Prussia and Napoleon's other enemies quickly recovered from their earlier defeats, and less than two years after the fiasco in Russia, the allied armies entered Paris. Napoleon was exiled to rule the tiny Mediterranean island-kingdom of Elba.

At the Congress of Vienna (1814–15), the Allies restored the House of Bourbon to the French throne, installing Louis XVI's brother as Louis XVIII (the second son of Louis XVI had been declared Louis XVII by monarchist exiles and died in 1795). However, in March 1815, Napoleon escaped from Elba, landed in southern France and gathered a large army as he marched northwards towards Paris. His 'Hundred Days' back in power ended, however, when his forces were defeated by the English under the Duke of Wellington at Waterloo in Belgium. They exiled him to the remote South Atlantic island of St-Helena, where he died in 1821.

Although reactionary in some ways – he re-established slavery in the colonies, for instance – Napoleon instituted a number of important reforms, including a reorganisation of the judicial system, a new education system and the promulgation of a new legal code, the Code Napoléon (or civil code), which forms the basis of the French legal system (and many others in Europe) to this day. More importantly, he preserved the essence of the changes brought about by the Revolution. Napoleon is therefore remembered by the French as a great hero.

The Second Republic

The rule of Louis XVIII (1814–24) was dominated by the struggle between extreme monarchists who sought a return to the ancien régime, people who saw the changes wrought by the Revolution as irreversible, and the radicals of the poor working-class neighbourhoods of Paris. Charles X (ruled 1824–30) responded to the conflict with great ineptitude and was overthrown in the so-called July Revolution of 1830, when a motley group of revolutionaries seized the town hall in Paris. Those killed in the street battles that accompanied the Revolution are buried in vaults under the Colonne de Juillet, in the centre of the place de la Bastille.

Louis-Philippe (ruled 1830–48), a constitutional monarch of bourgeois sympathies and tastes, was then chosen by parliament to head what became known as the July Monarchy. Louis-Philippe was in turn ousted in the February Revolution of 1848, in whose wake the Second Republic was established.

The Second Empire

In presidential elections held in 1848, Napoleon's almost useless nephew, Louis Napoleon Bonaparte, was overwhelmingly elected. Legislative deadlock caused Louis Napoleon to lead a coup d'etat in 1851, after which he was proclaimed Emperor Napoleon III.

The Second Empire lasted from 1852 until 1870. During this period, France enjoyed significant economic growth and, under Baron Haussmann, Paris was transformed. But as his uncle had done before him, Napoleon III embroiled France in a number of conflicts, including the disastrous Crimean War (1853–6). It was the Prussians, however, who ended the Second Empire. In 1870, Prussian prime minister Otto von Bismarck goaded Napoleon III into declaring war on Prussia. Within months the thoroughly unprepared French army had been defeated and the emperor taken prisoner.

When news of the debacle reached the French capital, the Parisian masses took to the streets and demanded that a republic be declared.

The Third Republic & the Belle Époque

The Third Republic began as a provisional government of national defence in September 1870. The Prussians were, at the time, advancing on Paris and would subsequently lay siege to the capital, forcing its starving citizens to bake bread laced with sawdust and consume most of the animals in the zoo. In January 1871 the government negotiated an armistice with the Prussians, who demanded that National Assembly elections be held immediately. The republicans, who had called on the nation to continue to resist, lost to the monarchists, who had campaigned on a peace platform.

As expected, the monarchist-controlled assembly ratified the Treaty of Frankfurt (1871). However, when ordinary Parisians heard of its harsh terms – a five-billion-franc war indemnity and surrender of the provinces of Alsace and Lorraine – they revolted against the government.

The Communards, as supporters of the Paris Commune, a group of hard-core insurgents – were known, took over the city in March and the French government moved to Versailles. In May, the government launched a week-long offensive (now known as La Semaine Sanglante, Bloody Week) on the Commune in which several thousand rebels were killed. A further 20,000 or so Communards, mostly from the working class, were summarily executed. Karl Marx interpreted the Communard insurrection as the first great proletarian uprising against the bourgeoisie, and socialists came to see its victims as martyrs of the class struggle.

Despite this disastrous start, the Third Republic ushered in the glittering *belle époque* (beautiful age), with Art-Nouveau architecture, a whole field of artistic 'isms' from Impressionism onwards, and advances in science and engineering, including the construction of the first metro line in Paris. *Expositions universelles* (world exhibitions) were held in the capital in 1889 (showcased by the Eiffel Tower, much maligned at the time) and again in 1901 in the purpose-built Petit Palais. The Paris of nightclubs and artistic cafes made its first appearance around this time.

France was obsessed with a desire for revenge after its defeat by Germany in 1871, and jingoistic nationalism, scandals and accusations were the order of the day. The greatest moral and political crisis of the Third Republic was the infamous Dreyfus Affair, which began in 1894 when Captain Alfred Dreyfus, a Jewish army officer, was accused of betraying military secrets to Germany; he was court-martialled and sentenced to life imprisonment on Devil's Island, a French penal colony off the northern coast of South America. Despite bitter opposition from the army command, right-wing politicians and many Catholic groups, the case was eventually reopened and Dreyfus vindicated. The affair greatly discredited both the army and the Catholic Church. The result was more rigorous civilian control of the military and, in 1905, the legal separation of Church and State.

The Entente Cordiale (literally, 'Cordial Understanding') of 1904 ended colonial rivalry between France and Britain in Africa, beginning a period of cooperation that has, more or less, continued to this day.

WWI & the Interwar Period Central to France's entry into WWI was the desire to regain Alsace and Lorraine, lost to Germany in 1871. Indeed, Raymond Poincaré, president of the Third Republic from 1913 to 1920 and later prime minister, was a native of Lorraine and a firm supporter of war with Germany. However, when the heir to the Austrian throne, Archduke Franz Ferdinand, was assassinated by Serbian nationalists at Sarajevo on 28 June 1914, precipitating what would erupt into a global war, Germany jumped the gun. Within a month, it had declared war on Russia and France.

The defeat of Austria-Hungary and Germany in WWI, which regained Alsace and Lorraine for France, was achieved at unimaginable human cost. Of the eight million French men who were called to arms, 1.3 million were killed and almost one million crippled. The dead included two of every 10 Frenchmen aged between 20 and 45 years of age. At the 1916 Battle of Verdun alone, the French (led by General Philippe Pétain) and the Germans each lost about 400,000 men.

Because much of the war took place on French territory – including most of the trench warfare that used thousands of soldiers as cannon fodder to gain a few metres of territory – large parts of north-eastern France were devastated. Industrial production dropped by 40%, the value of the franc was seriously undermined, and the country faced a devastating financial crisis. The Treaty of Versailles in 1919, which officially ended the war, was heavily influenced by French Prime Minister Georges Clemenceau, the most uncompromising of the Allied leaders, who made sure that its harsh terms included a provision that Germany pay US$33 billion in reparations.

The 1920s and '30s saw France – and Paris in particular – as a centre of the avant-garde, with artists pushing into the new fields of Cubism and Surrealism, Le Corbusier rewriting the architectural textbook, foreign writers like Ernest Hemingway and F Scott Fitzgerald attracted by the city's liberal atmosphere, and nightlife establishing a cutting-edge reputation for everything from jazz to striptease. Too shocking in her native America, Josephine Baker's risqué shows found an enthusiastic audience in the nightclubs of the French capital.

France's promotion of a separatist movement in the Rhineland and its occupation of the Ruhr in 1923 to enforce reparations proved disastrous. But it did lead to almost a decade of accommodation and compromise with border guarantees and Germany's admission to the League of Nations. The naming of Adolf Hitler as chancellor in 1933, however, changed all that.

WWII During most of the 1930s, the French, like the British, had done their best to appease Hitler, but two days after Berlin's invasion of Poland in 1939, France joined the British in declaring war on Germany. By June of the following year, France had capitulated. The British expeditionary force sent to help the French barely managed to avoid capture by retreating to Dunkirk and crossing the English Channel in small boats. The very expensive Maginot Line, a supposedly impregnable wall of fortifications along the Franco-German border, had proved useless: the German armoured divisions had simply outflanked it by going through Belgium.

The Germans divided France into a zone under direct German occupation (in the north and along the western coast) and a puppet state based in the spa town of Vichy, which was led by the ageing WWI hero of the Battle of Verdun, General Pétain. His collaborationist government and supporters assumed that the Nazis were Europe's new masters and had to be accommodated, in hope of softening terms of an armistice, especially in regard to the release of prisoners (Hitler, of course, had no intention of making any such concessions).

The worst aspect of the Vichy regime was arguably the vicious anti-Semitism, which on occasion even exceeded German requirements. Local police were often very helpful to the Nazis in rounding up French Jews and others for deportation to Auschwitz and other death camps.

After the capitulation, General Charles de Gaulle, France's undersecretary of war, fled to London and, in a famous radio broadcast on 18 June 1940, appealed to French patriots to continue resisting the Germans. De Gaulle also set up a French government-in-exile and established the Forces Françaises Libres (Free French Forces), a military force dedicated to continuing the fight against the Germans. (Ironically, a French military court sentenced him to death for desertion, but the verdict was overturned after the war.)

The underground movement known as the Résistance (Resistance) didn't ever include more than perhaps 5% of the population – the other 95% either collaborated or did nothing, despite the myth of 'la France résistante'. The active members engaged in railway sabotage, collecting intelligence for the Allies, helping Allied airmen who had been shot down and publishing anti-German leaflets, among other activities. Although the impact of their pursuits was modest, the Resistance served as an enormous boost to French morale.

The liberation of France began with the US, British and Canadian landings in Normandy on D-Day (6 June 1944), and within two months most of Normandy and Brittany were free. On 15 August, Allied forces also landed in southern France, from where they drove up the Rhône Valley to Lyon. After a brief insurrection by the Resistance, Paris was liberated on 25 August by an Allied force spearheaded by Free French units, sent in ahead of the Americans, so the French would have the honour of liberating the capital.

The Fourth Republic

By the time of the liberation France lay in ruins. The damage to property was greater even than during WWI: nearly half a million buildings had been destroyed and the rail and road networks were devastated. De Gaulle returned to Paris and set up a provisional government, but in January 1946 he had already resigned as president, miscalculating that such a move would provoke a popular outcry for his return. A few months later, a new constitution was approved by referendum, and the omens for a rapid political renewal looked favourable – at first.

The Fourth Republic turned out to be a period of unstable coalition cabinets that followed one another with bewildering speed (on average, once every six months). On the other hand, economic recovery was fortunately swift, helped immeasurably by massive US aid, and France was able to play a leading role in the founding of the European Economic Community in 1957.

The 1950s also spelled the end of French colonialism. The eight-year war to reassert French control of Indochina ended in French defeat at Dien Bien Phu in 1954. France also tried to suppress an uprising by Arab nationalists in Algeria, whose population included over one million French settlers.

The Fifth Republic

The Fourth Republic came to an end in 1958, when extreme right-wingers, furious at what they saw as defeatism in dealing with the uprising in Algeria, began conspiring to overthrow the government. De Gaulle was brought back to power to prevent a military coup and possible civil war. He soon drafted a new constitution that gave considerable powers to the president at the expense of the National Assembly.

The Fifth Republic (which continues to this day) was rocked in 1961 by an attempted coup staged in Algiers by a group of right-wing military officers. When it failed, the Organisation de l'Armée Secrète (OAS; a group of French settlers and sympathisers opposed to Algerian independence) turned to terrorism, trying several times to assassinate de Gaulle. The book and film *The Day of the Jackal* portrayed a fictional OAS attempt on de Gaulle's life.

In 1962, de Gaulle negotiated an end to the war in Algeria. Some 750,000 *pieds noirs* (literally, 'black feet' – as Algerian-born French people are known in France) flooded into France. In the meantime, almost all of the other French colonies and protectorates in Africa had demanded and achieved independence. Shrewdly, the French government began a programme of economic and military aid to its former colonies in order to bolster France's waning international importance and create a bloc of French-speaking nations in the Third World.

However, the loss of the colonies, the surge in immigration and economic difficulties, including a big rise in unemployment, weakened the de Gaulle government. A large demonstration in Paris against the war in Vietnam in the spring of 1968, led by student Daniel Cohn-Bendit ('Danny the Red'), now a European parliament member representing the German Green Party, gave extra impetus to the student movement and protests were staged throughout the spring.

A seemingly insignificant incident in May 1968, in which police broke up yet another in a long series of demonstrations by Paris university students, sparked a violent reaction on the streets of the capital: students occupied the Sorbonne, barricades were erected in the Latin Quarter and unrest spread to other universities. Workers joined in the protests and about nine million people participated in a general strike, virtually paralysing the country. It was a period of much creativity and new ideas, with slogans appearing everywhere. Such slogans included '*L'Imagination au Pouvoir*' (literally, 'Power to the Imagination') and '*Sous les Pavés, la Plage*' ('Under the Cobblestones, the Beach'), a reference to Parisians' favoured material for building barricades and what they could expect to find beneath them.

The alliance between workers and students couldn't last long. While the former wanted a greater share of the consumer market, the latter wanted to destroy it. De Gaulle took advantage of this division and appealed to people's fear of anarchy. Just as the country seemed on the brink of revolution and an overthrow of the Fifth Republic, stability was restored. The government made a number of immediate changes, including the decentralisation of the higher education system. Reforms (such as lowering the voting age to 18, an abortion law, and self-management for workers) continued through the 1970s.

1969 to the Present In 1969 de Gaulle was succeeded as president by the Gaullist leader Georges Pompidou, who was in turn succeeded by Valéry Giscard d'Estaing in 1974. François Mitterrand, long-time head of the Parti Socialiste (PS; Socialist Party), was elected president in 1981 and, as the business community had feared, immediately set out to nationalise 36 privately owned banks, large industrial groups and various other parts of the economy. During the mid-1980s, however, Mitterrand followed a generally moderate economic policy and in 1988, at the age of 69, was re-elected for a second seven-year term. In the 1986 parliamentary elections, the right-wing opposition led by Jacques Chirac, mayor of Paris from 1977, received a majority in the National Assembly, and for the next two years Mitterrand was forced to work with a prime minister and cabinet from the opposition, an unprecedented arrangement known as *cohabitation*.

In the May 1995 presidential elections Chirac walked away with a comfortable electoral victory. The ailing Mitterrand, who would die in January 1996, had decided not to run again. In his first few months in office, Chirac received high marks for his direct words and actions in matters relating to the European Union (EU) and the war raging in Bosnia. His cabinet choices, including the selection of 'whizz-kid' foreign minister Alain Juppé as prime minister, were well received. But Chirac's decision to resume nuclear testing on the Polynesian island of Moruroa and a nearby atoll was met with outrage both in France and abroad. On the home front, Chirac's moves to restrict welfare payments – a move designed to bring France closer to meeting the criteria of European Monetary Union (EMU) – led to the largest protests since 1968.

In 1997 Chirac took a big gamble and called an early parliamentary election. The move backfired: Chirac remained president but his party, the Rassemblement pour la République (RPR; Rally for the Republic) lost support and a coalition of socialists, communists and greens came to power. Lionel Jospin, a former minister of education in the Mitterrand government became prime minister. France had once again entered into a period of cohabitation – with Chirac on the other side this time around.

Jospin and his government continue to enjoy the electorate's broad trust and approval, thanks largely to a recovery in economic growth and the introduction of a 35-hour working week, which has created hundreds of thousands of (primarily parttime) jobs. The prime minister remains the front-runner to succeed Chirac at the next national election, due at the latest in 2002 – especially if the right remains a factional shambles. Since the near-disaster of the 1997 ballot, the president's position has been undermined by the success of the Rassemblement Pour La France (RPF; Rally for France), a breakaway Gaullist party led by Charles Pasqua which scored 13% of the vote in the European elections of 1999.

GEOGRAPHY

France covers an area of 551,000 sq km and is the largest country in Europe after Russia and Ukraine. It is shaped like a hexagon and bordered, except for the north-eastern boundary, by either mountains or water. France has been invaded repeatedly across this relatively flat frontier, which abuts Germany, Luxembourg and Belgium.

France's coastline, which is some 3200km long, is remarkably diverse, ranging from the white chalk cliffs of Normandy and the treacherous promontories of Brittany to the fine-sand beaches along the Atlantic. The Mediterranean coast tends to have pebbly and even rocky beaches, though beaches in Languedoc and some in Roussillon are sandy.

France is drained by five major river systems:

The 775km-long Seine, used widely for navigation, passes through Paris on its way from Burgundy to the English Channel.
The Loire, the longest river in the country, stretches for 1020km from the Massif Central to the Atlantic. Its flow is eight times greater in December and January than at the end of summer.
The Rhône, which links Lake Geneva (Lac Léman) and the Alps with the Mediterranean, is joined by the Saône at Lyon.
The Garonne system, which includes the Rivers Tarn, Lot and Dordogne, drains the Pyrenees and the rest of the south-west, emptying into the Atlantic.
The Rhine, which flows into the North Sea, forms the eastern border of Alsace for about 200km. Its tributaries, including the Moselle and Meuse, drain much of the area north and east of Paris.

GEOLOGY

A significant proportion of France is covered by mountains, many of them among the most spectacular in Europe.

The French Alps, which include Mt Blanc (4807m), Europe's highest peak, run along France's eastern border from Lake Geneva to the Côte d'Azur. There is permanent snow cover above 2800m. The Jura Range, gentle limestone mountains north of the Alps that peak at just over 1700m, stretches along the Swiss frontier north of Lake Geneva. The Pyrenees run along France's entire 450km border with Spain, from the Atlantic to the Mediterranean. Though the loftiest peak is only 3404m high, the Pyrenees can be almost as rugged as the Alps.

The Alps, the Jura and the Pyrenees, though spectacular, are young ranges in comparison with France's ancient massifs, formed between 225 and 345 million years ago. The most spectacular is the Massif Central, a huge region in the middle of France whose 91,000 sq km cover one-sixth of the entire country. It is perhaps best known for its chain of extinct volcanoes, such as the Puy de Dôme (1465m).

France's other ancient massifs, worn down over the ages, include the Vosges, a forested upland in the country's north-eastern corner between Alsace and Lorraine; the Ardennes, most of which lies in Belgium and Germany and whose French part is on the northern edge of Champagne; and the Massif Armoricain, which stretches westwards from Normandy and forms the backbone of Brittany and Normandy.

CLIMATE

In general, France has a temperate climate with mild winters, except in mountainous areas and Alsace.

The Atlantic has a profound impact on the north-west, particularly Brittany, whose weather is characterised by high humidity and lots of rain (200 days per year compared to the national average of 164). The area is also subject to persistent and sometimes violent westerly winds.

France's north-east, especially Alsace, has a continental climate, with fairly hot summers and winters cold enough for snow to stay on the ground for weeks at a time. The wettest months in Alsace are June and July, when storms are common.

Midway between Brittany and Alsace – and affected by the climates of both – is the Paris basin. The region records the nation's lowest annual precipitation (about 575mm),

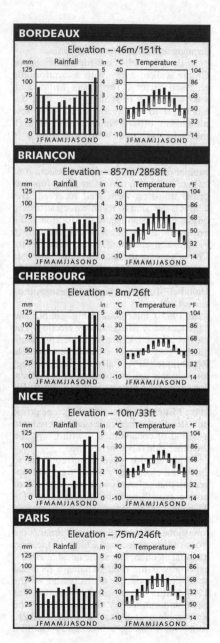

but rainfall patterns are erratic: you're just as likely to be caught in a heavy spring or autumn downpour as in a sudden summer cloudburst. Paris' average yearly temperature is 12°C, but the mercury sometimes drops below zero in January and can climb to the mid-30s or higher in August.

The southern coastal plains are subject to a Mediterranean climate as far inland as the southern Alps, the Massif Central and the eastern Pyrenees. If you like hot summers and mild winters, the south of France is for you: frost is rare, spring and autumn downpours are sudden but brief, and summer is virtually without rain. However, the south is also the region of the mistral, a cold, dry wind that blows down the Rhône Valley for about 100 days per year. Most relentless (and fierce) in spring, it is sometimes blamed for making people ill-tempered and even driving them mad.

ECOLOGY & ENVIRONMENT
Ecology

France may not have as many nuclear power stations as the USA but, while the USA ceased building new ones more than a decade ago, the French programme – the most ambitious in the world – is still going strong. Since the late 1980s, the State-owned electric company, Electricité de France (EDF), has produced about three-quarters of the country's electricity using nuclear power. Most of France's nuclear reactors are on main rivers or near the coast. France has also sought to export nuclear technology to various developing countries. Nuclear waste, which is becoming an increasingly important issue, is dumped on the Cotentin Peninsula in Normandy.

EDF also controls France's hydroelectric programme. By damming rivers to produce electricity, it has created huge recreational lakes but destroyed the traditional habitats of many animals. High-voltage power lines are a blight on much of the countryside and electrocute at least 1000 birds of prey each year. The EDF has announced that new lines will, as often as possible, run underground.

In July 1985, French agents blew up the Greenpeace ship *Rainbow Warrior* in Auckland harbour in an attempt to derail the organisation's campaign against nuclear testing on the Polynesian island of Moruroa and a nearby atoll. One person on board was killed. The French government took a positive step in 1992, when it finally agreed to suspend the tests, but just three years later President Jacques Chirac decided to conduct one last series of underground detonations before supporting a worldwide test-ban treaty. This round of tests concluded in January 1996, and France and the UK signed the treaty in April 1998.

Environment

The Office National des Forêts (ONF) manages most of the forests in France, but they are not protected reserves. French ecologists claim that the ONF runs them less to ensure the survival of their ecosystems than to bring in revenue from timber sales.

Summer forest fires are an annual hazard. Great tracts of land are burned each year, often because of careless day-trippers but sometimes, as is sometimes the case in the Maures and Esterel ranges in the Côte d'Azur, because they are intentionally set alight in order to get licences to build on the damaged lands. France's northern forests, particularly in the Vosges, have been affected by acid rain.

Wetlands, fantastically productive ecosystems that are essential for the survival of a great number of bird species, reptiles, fish and amphibians, are also shrinking. More than two million hectares – 3% of French territory – are considered important wetlands, but only 4% of this land is protected. The vulnerability of these areas was highlighted when the oil tanker Erika broke up off the coast of southern Brittany in December 1999, crippling bird and marine life by fouling more than 400km of shoreline.

FLORA & FAUNA

France is blessed with a rich variety of flora and fauna. Unfortunately, many fragile species are having a hard time surviving in the face of urbanisation, intensive agriculture, the draining of wetlands, hunting, pollution, the encroachment of industries and the expansion of the tourism infrastructure. Unfortunately, there are precious few established nature reserves so the long-term future of much of the fauna, in particular, appears bleak.

Flora
About 14 million hectares of forest – mostly beech, oak and pine – cover approximately 20% of France. There are some 4200 different species of plants and flowers.

Fauna
All told, France is home to 113 species of mammals (more than any other country in Europe), 363 species of birds, 30 kinds of amphibians, 36 varieties of reptiles and 72 kinds of fish.

Endangered Species
At least three kinds of mammals have disappeared in modern times, and the Pyrenean ibex, Corsican red deer, European mink and nine species of bats are among those on the critically endangered list. A quarter of the fish species are also in trouble. Few wolves are left; just 30 of these animals still roam the French Alps, according to recent reports. River otters, once abundant, have fallen victim to trappers.

The once-common brown bear disappeared from the Alps in the mid-1930s. At that time about 300 of the animals still lived in the Pyrenees but today the number has dwindled to six. Many birds, including vultures and storks, have all but disappeared from the skies, and Bonnelli's eagle is down to about two dozen pairs from 670 only 20 years ago.

Some animals still live in the wild thanks to reintroduction programmes based in certain national and regional parks. Storks are being bred in Alsace, vultures have also been reintroduced in Languedoc, and beavers, once nearly wiped out, are prospering in the Parc Naturel Régional d'Armorique in Brittany and in the Rhône Valley. Alpine creatures such as the chamois (a mountain antelope) and the larger bouquetin (a type of ibex) were

widely hunted until several national parks were established.

France counts some 1.7 million hunters, many of whom head to the forests and woodlands with their dogs as soon as the five-month season opens at the end of September. To safeguard the passage of migratory birds, long a target of hunters, the Brussels Directive was introduced in 1979 to protect wild birds, their eggs, nests and habitats; it applies to all member states of the EU.

The French government signed the directive but didn't bother to make its provisions part of French law, so birds that can safely fly over other countries may still be shot as they cross France. As a result, environmentalists have in the past rented entire mountain passes on birds' flight paths in order to keep hunters away.

National & Regional Parks
About 0.7% of France's land is within a *parc national* (national park), and another 7% within a *parc naturel régional* (regional park). There are also nearly 100 small *réserves naturelles* (nature reserves) and a few private reserves set up by environmental groups. The proportion of protected land is low relative to France's size.

The national parks, which are uninhabited, are under the direct control of the government and are fully protected by legislation: dogs, vehicles and hunting are banned and camping is restricted. However, the parks themselves are relatively small (all are under 1000 sq km) and the ecosystems they are supposed to protect spill over into what are called 'peripheral zones', populated areas around the parks in which tourism and other economic activities are permitted.

France has six national parks, all of them in the mountains except for the Parc National de Port Cros, an island marine park off the Côte d'Azur. Most national parkland is in the Alps, where the Vanoise, Écrins and Mercantour parks are hugely popular with nature lovers and hikers in summer. The Parc National des Pyrénées runs for 100km along the Spanish border and is a favourite with rock climbers. The wild Parc

National des Cévennes, which has a few inhabitants in its central zone, is on the border of the Massif Central and Languedoc (see the Languedoc-Roussellin chapter).

The country's almost three dozen regional parks and its nature reserves, most of which were established both to improve (or at least maintain) local ecosystems and to encourage economic development and tourism, all support human populations and are locally managed. The regional parks are mainly in areas with diminishing populations that are facing severe economic problems, such as the Massif Central and parts of Corsica.

GOVERNMENT & POLITICS

France has had 11 constitutions since 1789. The present one, which was instituted by de Gaulle in 1958, established what is known as the Fifth Republic. It gives considerable power to the president of the Republic. Jacques Chirac took over the presidency from François Mitterrand in May 1995.

The 577 members of the Assemblée Nationale (National Assembly) are directly elected in single-member constituencies for five-year terms. The 321 members of the rather powerless Sénat (Senate), who serve for nine years, are indirectly elected. The president of France is chosen by direct election for a five-year term (the people of France voted to change this from seven years in 2000). Women gained the right to vote in 1944. The voting age is 18.

Executive power is shared by the president and the Conseil des Ministres (Council of Ministers), whose members (including the prime minister) are appointed by the president but are responsible to parliament. The president, who resides in the Palais de l'Élysée (Élysée Palace) in Paris, serves as commander-in-chief of the armed forces and theoretically makes all major policy decisions. In periods of cohabitation, however, when the president and prime minister are not of the same party, the main policy-maker is the prime minister while the president is concerned with foreign affairs only (the office's *domaine reservé*). He or she can also dismiss the prime minister and has the power to dissolve the National Assembly in times of crises and no-confidence.

France is one of the five permanent members of the UN Security Council. It withdrew from NATO's joint military command in 1966 and has maintained an independent arsenal of nuclear weapons since 1960.

Local Administration

France has long been a highly centralised state. Before the Revolution, the country consisted of about two dozen major regions and a variety of smaller ones. Their names (and those of their long-extinct predecessors) are still widely used, but for administrative purposes the country has, since 1790, been divided into units of about 6100 sq km called *départements* (departments). There are 96 departments in metropolitan France – the mainland and Corsica – and another five in overseas territories. Most are named after geographical features, especially rivers, but are commonly known by their two-digit code, which appears as the first two digits of all postcodes in the department and as the last two numbers on number plates of cars registered there.

The national government is represented in each department by a *préfet* (prefect). A department's main town, where the government and the prefect are based, is known as a *préfecture* (prefecture). It is also the seat of an elected *conseil général* (general council). You can tell if a town is a prefecture because the last three digits of the postcode are zeros.

A department is subdivided into a number of *arrondissements* (for a national total of 324), each of whose main town is known as a *sous-préfecture* (subprefecture). The arrondissements are further divided into *cantons* and these are further split into *communes*, the basic administrative unit of local government. Each of France's 36,400 communes is presided over by a *maire* (mayor) based in a *mairie* (town hall). Almost one-third of the communes have populations of less than 200.

Departments are ill-suited for carrying out modern regional coordination, because of their small size. In 1972, the government divided France into 22 regions *(régions)* based roughly on the country's historical divisions. Each of these regions has an elected council and other organs, but its powers are limited and it plays no direct role in actual administration.

France's five *départements d'outre-mer* (overseas departments) include: the Caribbean islands of Guadeloupe and Martinique; French Guiana (Guyane), a 91,000 sq km territory on the northern coast of South America between Brazil and Suriname; the island of Réunion, which is in the Indian Ocean east of Madagascar; and St-Pierre-et-Miquelon in the Atlantic, just off the southern coast of the Canadian province of Newfoundland. The island of Mayotte, one of the Comoros Islands in the Indian Ocean, has quasi-departmental status.

In addition, France has three *territoires d'outre-mer* (overseas territories), all of which are in the South Pacific: French Polynesia, which includes Tahiti and 130 other islands; New Caledonia, which also includes a large tract of the Pacific and several island dependencies; and the Wallis and Futuna islands. France also claims a sizeable chunk of Antarctica. All of these far-

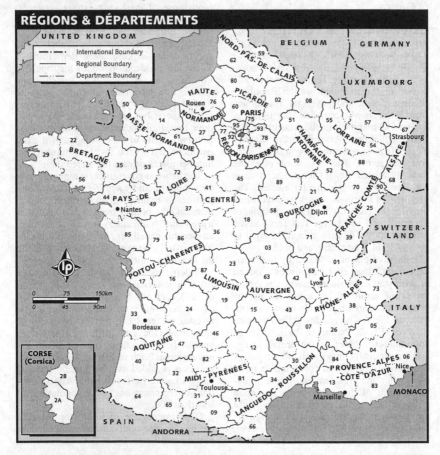

RÉGIONS & DÉPARTEMENTS

flung bits of territory are often referred to collectively as DOM-TOM, the acronym of the *départements d'outre-mer-territoires d'outre-mer*.

ECONOMY

France's economy may not be the power-house of Europe – Germany can lay claim

to that distinction – but French financial leaders have enough clout to help determine the course of European Monetary Union.

Although Frankfurt, not Paris, was cho-sen as the headquarters of the new Euro-pean Central Bank (ECB), the French won a victory in 1998 that was a surprise to many European observers: the ECB's chief,

RÉGIONS & DÉPARTEMENTS

ALSACE
67   Bas-Rhin
68   Haut-Rhin

AQUITAINE
24   Dordogne
33   Gironde
40   Landes
47   Lot-et-Garonne
64   Pyrées-Atlantiques

AUVERGNE
03   Allier
15   Cantal
43   Haute-Loire
63   Puy-de Dôme

BASSE-NORMANDIE
14   Calvados
50   Manche
61   Orne

BRETAGNE
22   Côtes d'Armor
29   Finistère
35   Ille-et-Vilaine
56   Morbihan

BOURGOGNE
21   Côte d'Or
58   Nièvre
71   Saône-et-Loire
89   Yonne

CENTRE
18   Cher
28   Eure-et-Loire
36   Indre
37   Indre-et-Loire
41   Loir-et-Cher
45   Loiret

CHAMPAGNE-ARDENNE
08   Ardennes
10   Aube
51   Marne
52   Haute-Marne

CORSE
2A   Corse-du-Sud
2B   Haute-Corse

FRANCHE-COMTÉ
25   Doubs
39   Jura
70   Haute-Saône
90   Territoire de Belfort

HAUTE-NORMANDIE
27   Eure
76   Seine-Maritime

LANGUEDOC-ROUSSILLON
11   Aude
30   Gard
34   Hérault
48   Lozère
66   Pyrénées-Orientales

LIMOUSIN
19   Corrèze
23   Creuse
87   Haute-Vienne

LORRAINE
54   Meurthe-et-Moselle
55   Meuse
57   Moselle
88   Vosges

MIDI-PYRÉNÉES
09   Ariège
12   Aveyron
31   Haute-Garonne
32   Gers
46   Lot
65   Hautes-Pyrénées
81   Tarn
82   Tarn-et-Garonne

NORD-PAS-DE-CALAIS
59   Nord
62   Pas-de-Calais

PAYS DE LA LOIRE
44   Loire-Atlantique
49   Maine-et-Loire
53   Mayenne
72   Sarthe
85   Vendée

PICARDIE
02   Aisne
60   Oise
80   Somme

POITOU-CHARENTES
16   Charente
17   Charente-Maritime
79   Deux-Sèvres
86   Vienne

PROVENCE-ALPES-CÔTE D'AZUR
04   Alpes-de-Haute-
       Provence
05   Hautes-Alpes
06   Alpes-Maritimes
13   Bouches-du-Rhône
83   Var
84   Vaucluse

RÉGION PARISIENNE
75   Ville de Paris
77   Seine-et-Marne
78   Yvelines
91   Essonne
92   Hauts-de-Seine
93   Seine-St-Denis
94   Val-de-Marne
95   Val-d'Oise

RHÔNE-ALPES
01   Ain
07   Ardèche
26   Drôme
38   Isère
42   Loire
69   Rhône
73   Savoie
74   Haute-Savoie

a Dutchman, would have a much shorter reign than originally envisaged, and its second head would be Jean-Claude Trichet, the governor of the Banque de France, the country's central bank. However, a recent investigation of Trichet's ties to a 1990s banking scandal has placed a question mark over his future role at the ECB.

For the traveller the most important consequence of EMU will be the disappearance of many of Europe's banknotes and bills in 2002, when the euro becomes the standard European Union currency (see the boxed text 'Adieu Franc, Bonjour Euro' in the Facts for the Visitor chapter).

To the surprise of many outsiders, the French *dirigiste* (interventionist) model of State ownership is still alive and well. More than 50% of GDP is spent by the government, which employs one in every four French workers despite a series of heavyweight privatisations during the 1990s. The 'family silver' – including Air France, France Telecom and Aerospatiale – may have been partly sold off, but enough other mammoth concerns such as car-maker Renault remain government-controlled.

Pragmatism had something to do with the socialists going back on their word and opting for privatisation, as it helped to plug holes in the State coffers. After the overtaxed, free-spending 1980s, the next decade brought sluggish growth and high unemployment as France curbed its deficit spending to qualify for a single European currency. The effort has paid off: the French economy is turning over nicely (with growth predicted at around 3.5% in 2001) and unemployment was expected to fall to below 9% by 2001, the lowest level in over a decade. Inflation is running at less than 1.5%.

France is one of the world's most industrialised nations, with some 40% of the workforce employed in the industrial sector. About half of the economy's earnings come from industrial production. However, there is poor coordination between academic research and companies that might turn good ideas into products, and the country has fewer large corporations – an important source of private capital and investment in research and development – than other industrialised nations of similar size.

France can also lay claim to being the largest agricultural producer and exporter in the EU. Its production of wheat, barley, maize (corn) and cheese is particularly significant. The country is to a great extent self-sufficient in food except for certain tropical products, for example, bananas and coffee.

POPULATION & PEOPLE

France has a population of 60.2 million, more than 20% of whom live in the greater metropolitan area of Paris. The number of people living in rural and mountain areas has been declining since the 1950s.

For much of the last two centuries, France has had a considerably lower rate of population growth than its neighbours. On the other hand, over that period the country has accepted more immigrants than any other European nation, including significant numbers of political refugees.

Between 1850 and WWI, the country received 4.3 million immigrants. A further three million immigrants arrived between the world wars, in part because the carnage of WWI had left France with a serious shortage of workers. Most immigrants came from other parts of Europe (especially Italy, Spain, Poland, Russia and Armenia), but the economic boom following WWII, also accompanied by a labour shortage, attracted several million workers – most of them unskilled – along with their families from North Africa and French-speaking sub-Saharan Africa.

During the late 1950s and early 60s, as the French colonial empire collapsed, over one million French settlers returned to metropolitan France from Algeria, other parts of Africa and Indochina. At the same time, millions of non-French immigrants from the same places were welcomed as much-needed manpower during France's '30 glorious years' of fast economic growth.

Large-scale immigration was stopped by a 1974 law banning all new foreign workers, but in recent years there has been a racist backlash against the country's non-white immigrant communities, especially Muslims from North Africa, who haven't assimilated into French society as quickly as their European predecessors. The extreme-right Front National (National Front) party has fanned these racist feelings in a bid to win more votes.

In 1993 the French government changed its immigration laws to make it harder for immigrants to get French citizenship or bring their families into the country. In 1997 the National Assembly approved (by a large margin) new legislation that legitimised the status of some illegal immigrants, but also implemented measures that made it easier to locate and repatriate others.

EDUCATION

France's education system has long been highly centralised, a fact reflected in teachers' status as civil servants. Its high standards have produced great intellectuals and almost universal literacy, but equal opportunities are still not available to people of all classes.

Private schools, most of which are Catholic (though Protestant and Jewish schools also exist), educate about 17% of students – and also account for almost a quarter of all students planning to attend university. The State pays staff salaries and some of the operating costs at most private schools provided they follow certain curriculum guidelines. Tuition fees are thus very low.

Primary

One third of all French children begin attending a *crèche* (day nursery), a *jardin d'enfants* (daycare centre) or an *école maternelle* (nursery school) at the age of two. By the age of three they are joined by virtually all of their peers. Until the age of 10 or 11, all children – rich or poor, gifted or slow – follow pretty much the same curriculum. In 1882 primary education became compulsory for all children between the ages of six and 13. Education is now obligatory until 16 years of age.

Secondary

Lycée (secondary school) studies are divided into two stages. The first cycle *(collège)*, attended by children aged 11 to 15, follows a curriculum of general studies that is more or less the same in all schools. During the second cycle, which is for those aged 15 to 18, pupils can choose between the academic track and the less highly regarded vocational track.

Only students in the academic track can sit for the university entrance exam, the *baccalauréat* (usually shortened to the *bac*). At present, 73% of high-school students take the matriculation exam, double the proportion in 1980 and considerably more than in other European countries. There is also a vocational baccalauréat.

Tertiary

Universities Anyone who has passed the bac is entitled to a free place at one of France's 77 universities, an option taken up by about one third of young people (again, the highest proportion in Western Europe). The catch is that after the first year of study, students must face a gruelling examination that only 30 to 40% of them end up passing (in medicine, one in six). Those who fail must make do with other options, such as attending a two-year *collège universitaire*. The dropout rate is exacerbated by the scarcity of government stipends, received by only one in eight students.

French university degrees are slightly different from their counterparts granted in English-speaking countries. A *licence*, awarded after three years, is similar to a bachelor's degree. It is followed by a *maîtrise*, roughly equivalent to a master's degree, which is in turn followed in some fields by a *diplôme d'études approfondies* (DEA) or a *diplôme d'études supérieures spécialisées* (DESS), taken before completing a PhD. The prestigious *doctorat*, which is necessary to become a full professor, takes many years of highly specialised research. The highest-level teaching qualification is known as an *agrégation*.

In 1793, the Revolutionary government abolished the universities, some of which had been founded in the Middle Ages. They were re-established by Napoleon in 1808. The Sorbonne, founded in the 13th century, was long the country's leading university. Now incorporated into the University of Paris system (part of which occupies the old Sorbonne buildings in the Latin Quarter), it has for centuries helped to draw many of France's most talented and energetic people to Paris, creating a serious provincial brain drain. Today, about one third of French students study in Paris.

Grandes Écoles Some of France's ablest and most ambitious young people do not attend the overcrowded universities. About 5% of students are enrolled in the country's 140 prestigious *grandes écoles*, institutions offering training in such fields as business management, engineering and the applied sciences. Students do not pay tuition and even receive salaries but they must work as civil servants after graduation – for up to 10 years in some cases. A high percentage of the top positions in the public sector, the traditionally less prestigious private sector and politics are filled by grandes écoles graduates.

PHILOSOPHY

René Descartes (1586–1650) was the founder of modern philosophy, and the greatest thinker since Aristotle. He was small in stature and poor in health, but an intellectual giant who used a rigorous method of wholesale doubt and sought mathematical-like certainty in all things. Descartes' famed phrase '*Cogito, ergo sum*' (I think, therefore I am) is the basis of modern philosophical thought, and his method and systems of thought came to be known as Cartesianism.

France has produced some other luminary thinkers, particularly in the late 19th and early 20th centuries, and these include Henri Louis Bergson, Jean-Paul Sartre (see the boxed text 'Jean-Paul Sartre & Existentialism'), Gabriel Honoré Marcel, Maurice Merleau-Ponty, Michel Foucault, Jacques Derrida (an Algerian) and Simone de Beauvoir, who headed the French feminist movement. They are collectively known as the French existentialists, although their influences were predominantly German. Their views differed widely, but the theme of human freedom was common to all.

ARTS
Dance

Ballet as we know it today originated in Italy but was brought to France in the late 16th century by Catherine de Médici. The first Ballet Comique de la Reine (a type of dramatic court ballet) in France was performed at an aristocratic wedding at the French court in 1581. It combined music, dance and poetic recitations (usually in praise of the monarchy) and was performed by male courtiers with women of the court forming the corps de ballet. Louis XIV so enjoyed the spectacle that he danced many leading roles himself at Versailles. In 1661 he founded the Académie Royale de Danse (Royal Dance Academy), from which ballet around the world developed.

By the end of the 18th-century ballet had developed into a fully fledged art form, and choreographers like Jean-Georges Noverre became more important than the musicians, poets and dancers themselves. In the early 19th century, Romantic ballets such as *La Sylphide* (1832) and *Giselle* (1841) were more popular than opera in Paris.

France was at the forefront of classical ballet until the end of the 19th century when the Imperial Russian Ballet was becoming the centre for innovation. This was exacerbated when Marius Petipa, a native of Marseilles, left France for Russia. Mixing the French dance tradition with Slavic sensibilities, folklore and music Petipa created such masterpieces as *La Bayadère* (1877) and *Le Lac des Cygnes* (Swan Lake; 1895).

France has lost its pre-eminent position in dance to countries such as the USA, Germany and even Japan in this century, though Roland Petit managed to shake French ballet out of its lethargy between 1945 and 1955, creating some innovative ballets such as *Turangalila*, with music composed by Olivier Messiaen. Another important figure was Maurice Béjart who shocked the public in 1955 with his *Ballet sur la Symphonie d'un Homme Seul* (Symphony for a Lonely Man), danced in black, *Le Sacre du Printemps* (The Rite of Spring; 1959) and *Le Marteau sans Maître* (The Hammer Without a Master; 1968), with music by Pierre Boulez.

After 1968 many dance centres were cre-ated outside Paris, mainly at Nancy, La Rochelle and Montpellier, but all have been heavily influenced from the outside by such choreographers as the American Merce Cunningham.

Today French dance seems to be moving in a new, more personal direction with per-formers such as Caroline Marcadé and

Jean-Paul Sartre & Existentialism

The 20th century's most famous French thinker was Jean-Paul Sartre, the quintessential Parisian in-tellectual who was born in Paris on 21 June 1905 and died there on 15 April 1980. For most peo-ple he embodied an obscure idea called existentialism. It's one of the great 'isms' of popular culture, but even philosophers have trouble explaining what existentialism really means.

Sartre was a novelist, a playwright, a critic and a brilliant philosopher. His father was a decorated naval officer, and his mother was the cousin of Albert Schweitzer, the famous Alsatian-German the-ologian and African missionary doctor. His father died when Sartre was young and he was raised by his grandfather. In 1938 he published his first novel, *La Nausée* (Nausea), which introduced many themes of his later philosophical works. He worked as a *lycée* (secondary school) teacher until the outbreak of WWII and spent a year as a prisoner of war. As a result of his war experiences he found a new political commitment and became a key figure in the French Resistance.

Sartre never used the term existentialism in his early defining works, but it came to represent a body of thought that he, in part, inherited from the German philosopher Edmund Husserl. It was also adopted by a Parisian cafe clique of writers, dramatists and intellectuals (which included life-long companion Simone de Beauvoir), and even painters and musicians. Jean-Paul's intellectual in-fluences were the German philosophers, in particular Martin Heidegger and Friedrich Nietzche, and he was also influenced by the Dane Søren Kierkegaard.

Sartre was an atheist, and the 'loss of God' was a phrase he used often. In the 1930s he wrote a series of analyses of human self-awareness that culminated in his most important philosophical work, *L'Etre et le Néant* (Being and Nothingness; 1943). The central idea of this long and difficult book is to distinguish between objective things and human consciousness, and to assert that consciousness is a 'non-thing'. Consciousness is made real by taking a point of view on things, on 'being'. He claimed that we are 'condemned to be free', and that even in indecision we choose not to choose, thus making freedom inescapable.

For all its lofty language and convoluted philosophical argument, *L'Etre et le Néant* is a treatise on a fairly simple way of life that embraces one's own autonomy and seeks to maximise one's choices (or one's awareness of them). Many read Sartre's message as a positive one, but for him this height-ened human awareness was characterised by emptiness, boredom and negativity.

The many literary works, essays, plays and political writings of Sartre were charged with his philo-sophical ideas. *Huis-clos* (No Exit; 1944), his most popular play, is an allegorical and unnerving story about three people who find themselves in a room together with no way out. This work includes Sartre's famous words 'Hell is other people'.

He remained politically active in later years, but his health deteriorated. Throughout his life he'd imbibed vast quantities of alcohol, tobacco and amphetamines, and this continued unabated – he ultimately went blind. Jean-Paul Sartre succumbed to lung cancer aged 74. Over 25,000 people at-tended his funeral procession.

Odile Duboc, Jean-Claude Gallotta and Jean-François Duroure.

Music

When French music comes to mind, most people hear accordions and *chansonniers* (cabaret singers) such as Edith Piaf and Jacques Brel. But they're only part of a much larger and more complex picture.

In the 17th and 18th centuries, French Baroque music influenced a great deal of the European musical output. Composers such as François Couperin (1668–1733), especially noted for his harpsichord studies, and Jean Phillipe Rameau (1683–1764), who played a pivotal role in the development of modern harmony, were two major players in this field. French harpsichord music set the precedent for much of the keyboard music that was later to evolve.

France produced a number of musical luminaries in the 19th century. Among these were Hector Berlioz (1803–69), Charles Gounod (1818–93), César Franck (1822–90), Camille Saint-Saëns (1835–1921) and Georges Bizet (1838–75). Nowadays Bizet is chiefly known for his operas *Carmen* and *Les Pêcheurs de Perles* (The Pearl Fishers), and Gounod for his operas *Faust* and *Roméo et Juliette*.

Berlioz is the greatest figure in the French Romantic movement and the founder of modern orchestration. As an orchestrator he demanded gargantuan forces: his ideal orchestra included 240 stringed instruments, 30 grand pianos and 30 harps.

Berlioz's operas and symphonies and Franck's organ compositions sparked a musical renaissance in France that would produce such greats as Gabriel Fauré and the Impressionists Claude Debussy and Maurice Ravel. Debussy revolutionised classical music with his *Prélude à l'Après-Midi d'un Faune* (Prelude to the Afternoon of a Faun), creating a light, almost Asian musical Impressionism, while Ravel's work, including *Boléro*, is often characterised by its sensuousness and tonal colour. Contemporary composers include Olivier Messiaen, who until his death in 1992 combined modern, almost mystical music with natural sounds

such as birdsong; and his student, the radical Pierre Boulez, who blends computer-generated sound in his compositions.

Jazz hit Paris with a bang in the 1920s and has remained popular, particularly among intellectuals, ever since. France's contribution to the world of jazz has been great: the violinist Stéfane Grappelli and the legendary three-fingered Roma guitarist Django Reinhardt from the 1930s, Claude Luter and his Dixieland Band in the 1950s. More recently, electric-violinist Jean-Luc Ponty and pianists Martial Solal and Michel Petrucciani have left their mark on the scene.

The most appreciated form of indigenous music is the *chanson française*, which has a tradition dating back to the troubadours of the Middle Ages. It was an important medium for conveying ideas and information to the illiterate masses. Such enduring greats as *La Marseillaise* and the socialist anthem *L'Internationale*, are rooted in this tradition.

French songs have always favoured lyrics over music and rhythm, which goes some way to explaining the enormous popularity of rap in France.

Eclipsed by the music halls and burlesque of the early 20th century, the chanson tradition was revived from the 1930s by such singers as Piaf (see the boxed text 'Edith Piaf, the Urchin Sparrow' on the next page) and Charles Trenet. In the 1950s the cabarets of the Left Bank gave young author-composers the opportunity to break new ground, and singers such as Léo Ferré, Georges Brassens, Claude Nougaro, Jacques Brel and Barbara became national stars.

Today's popular music has come a long way since the *yéyé* (imitative rock) of the 1960s sung by Johnny Halliday – watch out for rappers MC Solaar, Doc Gynéco, Alliance Ethnik, and I Am, from Marseilles. Evergreen balladeer-folksingers include Francis Cabrel, Julien Clerc, Jean-Jacques Goldman and Jacques Higelin, while the late Serge Gainsbourg remains enormously popular.

The controversial New Age space music of Jean-Michel Jarre has split audiences

Edith Piaf, the Urchin Sparrow

Like her contemporary, Judy Garland in the USA, Edith Piaf (1915–63) was not just a singer but a tragic, stoical figure who the nation took to its heart and never let go.

She was born Edith Giovanna Gassion to a street acrobat and his singer wife, who lived in the poor Belleville district of Paris. Her early childhood was spent with her maternal grandmother, an alcoholic who neglected her, and later her father's parents, who ran a local brothel in Normandy. When she was nine she toured with her father but left home at 15 to sing alone in the streets of Paris. Her first employer, Louis Leplée, called her '*la môme piaf*' (the urchin sparrow) and introduced her to the cabarets of Pigalle.

When Leplée was murdered in 1935, she faced the streets again. But along came Raymond Asso, an ex-Legionnaire who would become her Pygmalion, forcing her to break with her pimp and hustler friends, putting her in her signature black dress and inspiring her first big hit (*Mon Légionnaire*; 1937). When he succeeded in getting her a contract at one of the most famous Parisian music halls of the time, her career skyrocketed.

This frail women, who sang about street life, drugs, death and whores, seemed to embody all the miseries of the world yet sang in a husky, powerful voice with no self-pity. Her tumultuous love life earned her a reputation as *une dévoreuse d'hommes* (a man-eater), but she launched the careers of several stars, including Yves Montand and Charles Aznavour. Another one of her many lovers was the world middleweight boxing champion Marcel Cerdan; he was killed in a plane crash on his way to join her on her American tour in 1949. True to form, Piaf insisted that the show go on after learning of his death but fainted on stage in the middle of L'Hymne à l'Amour, a love song inspired by Cerdan.

After she was involved in a car accident in 1951, Piaf began drinking heavily and became addicted to morphine. Her health declined quickly but she continued to sing around the world (notably at New York's Carnegie Hall in 1956) and record some of her biggest hits, including *Je Ne Regrette Rien* (I Regret Nothing) and *Milord*. In 1962, frail and once again penniless, Piaf married a young hairdresser called Théo Sarapo, recorded the duet *À Quoi Ça Sert l'Amour?* (What Use Is Love?) with him and left Paris for southern France. But just a year later she returned to the capital, where she passed away. A crowd of some two million people attended her funeral in Paris, and the grave of the much-missed 'urchin sparrow' in Père Lachaise Cemetery (20e) is still visited and decorated by thousands of her loyal fans each year.

across the globe, but most agree that his laser-led stage shows are impressive.

France's main claim to fame over the past decade has been *sono mondial* (world music) – from Algerian rai and other North African music (artists include Cheb Khaled, Natacha Atlas, Jamel, Cheb Mami, Racid Taha) to Senegalese *mbalax* (Youssou N'Dour), West Indian zouk (Kassav, Zouk Machine) and Cuban salsa. Les Négresses Vertes and Mano Negra were two bands in the late 1980s that combined many of these elements – often with brilliant results. Etienne Daho continues to top the charts with trance numbers, and another recent, pretty bizarre development is Astérix rock, a homegrown folk-country sound based on the accordion.

Literature

Middle Ages The earliest work of French literature is the 11th-century *Chanson de Roland* (Song of Roland), an epic poem that recounts the heroic death of Charlemagne's nephew Roland, ambushed on the way back from a campaign against the Muslims in Spain in 778.

Lyric poems of courtly love composed by troubadours dominated medieval French literature, and there was the new genre of the *roman* (literally, 'the romance'), which often drew on Celtic stories such as King

Arthur and his court, the search for the Holy Grail, and Tristan and Iseult. The *Roman de la Rose*, a 22,000-line poem written by Guillaume de Lorris and Jean de Meung, was a new departure, manipulating allegorical figures such as Pleasure and Riches, Shame and Fear.

François Villon was condemned to death in 1462 for stabbing a lawyer, but the sentence was commuted to banishment from Paris. As well as a long police record, Villon left a body of poems charged with a highly personal lyricism, among them the *Ballade des Femmes du Temps Jadis* (Ballad of Dead Ladies).

Renaissance The great landmarks of French Renaissance literature are the works of La Pléaide, Rabelais and Montaigne. François Rabelais composed a farcical epic about the adventures of the giant Gargantua and his son Pantagruel. His highly exuberant narrative blends coarse humour with encyclopaedic erudition in a vast panorama that seems to include every kind of person, occupation and jargon found in mid-16th-century France.

La Pléaide was a group of poets active in the 1550s and '60s, of whom the best known is Pierre de Ronsard. They are chiefly remembered for their lyric poems. Michel de Montaigne wrote a long series of essays on all sorts of topics that constitutes a fascinating self-portrait.

Classicism The 17th century is known as '*le grand siècle*' (the great century) because it is the century of the great French classical writers. In poetry, François de Malherbe brought a new rigour to the treatment of rhythm. Transported by the perfection of Malherbe's verses, Jean de La Fontaine recognised his vocation and went on to write his charming *Fables* in the manner of Aesop.

Molière was an actor who became the most popular comic playwright of his time. Plays such as *Tartuffe* are staples of the classical repertoire, and they are still performed in translation around the world. The tragic playwrights Pierre Corneille and Jean

Racine, by contrast, drew their subjects from history and classical mythology. For instance, Racine's *Phèdre*, taken from Euripides, is a story of incest and suicide among the descendants of the Greek gods.

The mood of classical tragedy permeates *La Princesse de Clèves* by Marie de La Fayette, which is widely regarded as the first major French novel.

Enlightenment The literature of the 18th century is dominated by philosophers, among them Voltaire and Jean-Jacques Rousseau. The most durable of Voltaire's works have been his 'philosophical tales', such as *Candide*, which ironically recounts the improbable adventures of a simple soul who is convinced that he is living in the best of all possible worlds despite the many problems that befall him.

Rousseau, a Catholic convert from Protestantism, came from Switzerland and always considered himself a religious exile in France. Voltaire's political writings, in which it is argued that society is fundamentally opposed to nature, were to have a profound and lasting influence on him. Rousseau's sensitivity to landscape and its moods anticipates Romanticism, and the insistence on his own singularity in *Les Confessions* makes it the first modern autobiography.

19th Century Victor Hugo was a major literary force in the 19th century, widely acclaimed for his poetry as well as for his novels *Les Misérables* and *Notre Dame de Paris* (The Hunchback of Notre Dame). By virtue of his enormous output, the breadth of his interests and his technical innovations, Hugo is the key figure of French Romanticism. In 1885 some two million people followed his funeral procession.

Other 19th-century novelists include Stendhal, author of *Le Rouge et le Noir* (The Red and the Black), the story of the rise and fall of a poor young man from the provinces who models himself on Napoleon; Honoré de Balzac, whose vast series of novels, known under the general title of *La Comédie Humaine*, approaches a social history of France; Aurore Dupain, better known by the nom de plume George Sand, who combined the themes of social injustice and romantic love in her work; and of course Alexandre Dumas the elder, who wrote *Le Comte de Monte Cristo* (The Count of Monte Cristo), *Les Trois Mousquetaires* (The Three Musketeers) and other adventures, as well as several plays and poems.

By the mid-19th century, Romanticism was evolving into new movements, both in fiction and poetry. In 1857 two landmarks of French literature appeared: *Madame Bovary* by Gustave Flaubert and *Les Fleurs du Mal* (The Flowers of Evil) by Charles Baudelaire. Both writers were tried for the supposed immorality of their works. Flaubert won his case, and his novel was distributed without cuts. Less fortunate was Baudelaire (who moonlighted as a translator in Paris – he introduced the works of the American writer Edgar Allan Poe to Europe in translations that have since become French classics), who was obliged to cut several poems from *Les Fleurs du Mal*. He died an early and painful death, practically unknown, but his work influenced all the significant French poetry of the late 19th century and is reflected in much 20th-century verse as well.

The aim of Émile Zola, who claimed Flaubert as a precursor to his school of naturalism, was to convert novel-writing from an art to a science by the application of experimentation. His theory may seem naive, but his work (especially with regards the *Les Rougon-Macquart* series) was powerful and innovative.

Paul Verlaine and Stéphane Mallarmé created the symbolist movement, which strove to express states of mind rather than simply detail daily reality. Arthur Rimbaud had a great deal of influence on the symbolists, and apart from crowding an extraordinary amount of rugged, exotic travel into his 37 years and having a tempestuous homosexual relationship with Verlaine, produced two enduring pieces of work: *Illuminations* and *Une Saison en Enfer* (A Season in Hell).

20th Century Marcel Proust dominated the early 20th century with his giant seven-volume novel, *A la Recherche du Temps Perdu* (Remembrance of Things Past); it is largely autobiographical and explores in evocative detail the true meaning of past experience recovered from the unconscious by 'involuntary memory'.

André Gide found his voice in the celebration of homosexual sensuality and later in left-wing politics. *Les Faux-Monnayeurs* (The Counterfeiters) exposes the hypocrisy and self-deception with which people try to avoid sincerity – a common theme with Gide.

Surrealism was a vital force in French literature until WWII. André Breton ruled the group and wrote its three manifestoes, although the first use of the word 'Surrealist' is attributed to the writer Guillaume Apollinaire, a fellow traveller. Breton's autobiographical narratives, such as *Nadja*, capture the spirit of the movement: the fascination with dreams, divination and all manifestations of 'the marvellous'. As a poet, Breton was overshadowed by Paul Éluard and Louis Aragon, whose most famous Surrealist work was *Le Paysan de Paris* (The Nightwalker).

Colette enjoyed tweaking the nose of conventionally moral readers with titillating novels that detailed the amorous exploits of such heroines as the schoolgirl Claudine. One of her more interesting works concerned the German occupation of Paris, *Paris de Ma Fenêtre* (Paris from My Window).

After WWII, existentialism, a significant literary movement, developed around Jean-Paul Sartre, Simone de Beauvoir and Albert Camus, who worked and conversed in the cafes of St-Germain des Prés in Paris. All three stressed the importance of the writer's political engagement. Camus' best work on this theme is *L'Étranger* (The Outsider); he won a Nobel Prize for Literature in 1957.

De Beauvoir, author of *Le Deuxième Sexe* (The Second Sex), a ground-breaking study, had a profound influence on feminist thinking.

In the late 1950s, some younger novelists

began to look for new ways of organising the narrative. *Les Fruits d'Or* (The Golden Fruits) by Nathalie Sarraute, for example, does away with identifiable characters and has no plot as such. The so-called new novel *(nouveau roman)* refers to the works of Sarraute, Alain Robbe-Grillet, Boris Vian, Julien Gracq and Michel Butor, among others. However, these writers never formed a close-knit group, and their experiments have taken them in divergent directions. Today the nouveau roman is very much out of favour in France. Mention must also be made of *Histoire d'O*, the highly erotic sadomasochistic novel written by Dominique Aury under a pseudonym in 1954. The book sold more copies than any other contemporary French novel outside France.

In 1980 Marguerite Yourcenar, best known for memorable historical novels such as *Mémoires d'Hadrien*, became the first woman to be elected to the exclusive literary institution, the French Academy.

Marguerite Duras came to the notice of a larger public when she won the prestigious Prix Goncourt for her novel *L'Amant* (The Lover) in 1984. A prolific writer and filmmaker, she is also noted for the screenplays of *India Song* and *Hiroshima, Mon Amour*, described by one critic as part nouveau roman, part Mills & Boon.

Philippe Sollers was one of the editors of *Tel Quel*, a highbrow, then left-wing review that was very influential in the 1960s and early 70s. His 60s novels were forbiddingly experimental, but with *Femmes* (Women) he returned to a conventional narrative style.

Another of the editors of *Tel Quel* was Julia Kristeva, best known for theoretical writings on literature and psychoanalysis. Her book *Les Samuraï*, a fictionalised account of the heady days of *Tel Quel*, is an interesting document on the life of the Paris intelligentsia. Roland Barthes and Michel Foucault are other authors and philosophers associated with this period.

More accessible authors who enjoy a wide following include Françoise Sagan, Pascal Quignard, Jean Auel, Emmanuel Carrère and Stéphane Bourguignon. The *roman policier* (detective novel) has always been a great favourite with the French and among its greatest exponents has been the Belgian-born Georges Simenon, and his novels featuring Inspector Maigret, as well as Frédéric Dard (alias San Antonio), Léo Malet and Daniel Pennac, widely read for his witty crime fiction such as *Au Bonheur des Ogres* and *La Fée Carabine* (The Fairy Gunmother).

Architecture

Prehistoric The earliest monuments made by humans in France were stone mégaliths erected during the Neolithic period from about 4000 to 2400 BC. Although these prehistoric monuments are mainly found in Brittany, particularly around Carnac, there are others in northern Languedoc (for example, around the town of Mende) and on Corsica (for example, Filitosa).

Gallo-Roman From the 1st century BC the Romans constructed a large number of public works all over the country: aqueducts, fortifications, marketplaces, temples, amphitheatres, triumphal arches and bathhouses. They also established regular street grids at many settlements.

Southern France – especially Provence and the coastal plains of Languedoc – is the place to go in search of France's *gallo-romain* legacy. Testimony to the Romans' architectural brilliance includes the Pont du Gard aqueduct between Nîmes and Avignon, the colossal amphitheatres at Nîmes and Arles, the theatre at Orange, the Maison Carrée in Nîmes and the public buildings in Vaison-la-Romaine.

Dark Ages Although quite a few churches were built during the Merovingian and Carolingian periods (5th to 10th century), very little remains of them. However, traces of churches from this period can be seen at St-Denis (north of Paris) and in Auxerre's St-Germain abbey.

Romanesque A religious revival in the 11th century led to the construction of a large number of *roman* (Romanesque) churches, so-called because their architects adopted many architectural elements (such as vaulting) from Gallo-Roman buildings still standing at the time. Romanesque buildings typically have round arches, heavy walls whose few windows let in very little light, and a lack of ornamentation that borders on the austere.

Many of the most famous Romanesque churches – for instance the Basilica de St-Sernin in Toulouse – were built for pilgrims en route to Santiago de Compostela in Spain. Others, like Caen's two famous Romanesque abbeys, were erected by prominent benefactors. Chateaux built during this era tended to be massive, heavily fortified structures that afforded very few luxuries to their inhabitants. The Romanesque style remained popular until the mid-12th century.

Gothic The Gothic style originated in the mid-12th century in northern France, whose great wealth enabled it to attract the finest architects, engineers and artisans. Gothic structures are characterised by ribbed vaults carved with great precision, pointed arches, slender verticals, chapels (often built by rich people or guilds) along the nave and chancel, refined decoration and large stained-glass windows.

The first Gothic building was the basilica in St-Denis, which combined various late-Romanesque elements to create a new kind of structural support in which each arch counteracted and complemented the next. Gothic technology and the width and height it made possible subsequently spread to the rest of Western Europe.

Cathedrals built in the early-Gothic style, which lasted until about 1230, were majestic but lacked the lightness and airiness of most later works. Since the stained-glass windows could not support the roof, thick stone buttresses were placed between them. It was soon discovered that reducing the bulk of the buttresses and adding outer piers to carry the thrust created a lighter building without compromising structural integrity.

This discovery gave rise to flying buttresses, which helped lift the Gothic style to its greatest achievements, between 1230 and 1300. During this period, when French architecture dominated the European scene for the first time, Gothic masterpieces such as the seminal cathedral at Chartres and its successors at Reims and Amiens were decorated with ornate tracery (the delicate stone rib work on stained-glass windows) and huge, colourful rose windows.

Because of the fiascos at Beauvais cathedral, whose 48m vaults collapsed in 1272 and again in 1284, it became clear that Gothic technology had reached its limits. Architects became less interested in sheer size and put more energy into ornamentation.

In the 14th century, the Rayonnant (Radiant) Gothic style – named after the radiating tracery of the rose windows – developed, with interiors becoming even lighter thanks to broader windows and more translucent stained glass. One of the most influential Rayonnant buildings was the Ste-Chapelle in Paris, whose stained glass forms a sheer curtain of glazing.

By the 15th century, decorative extravagance led to Flamboyant Gothic, so named because its wavy stone carving was said to resemble flames. Beautifully lacy examples of Flamboyant architecture include the Clocher Neuf at Chartres, Rouen cathedral's Tour de Beurre, Rouen's Église St-Maclou and the spire of Strasbourg cathedral.

Renaissance The Renaissance, which began in Italy in the early 15th century, set out to realise a 'rebirth' of classical Greek and Roman culture. It had its first impact on France at the tail end of the 15th century, when Charles VIII began a series of invasions of Italy.

The French Renaissance is divided into two periods: early Renaissance and Mannerism. During the first period, a variety of classical components and decorative motifs (columns, tunnel vaults, round arches, domes) were blended with the rich decoration of Flamboyant Gothic, a synthesis best exemplified by the Château de Chambord in the Loire Valley. But the transition from late Gothic to Renaissance can be seen most clearly in the Château de Blois, whose Flamboyant section was built only 15 years before its early Renaissance wing.

Mannerism began around 1530, when François I (who had been so deeply impressed by what he'd seen in Italy that he brought Leonardo da Vinci to Amboise in 1516) hired Italian architects and artists – many of them disciples of Michelangelo or Raphael – to design and decorate his new chateau at Fontainebleau.

Over the next couple of decades, French architects who had studied in Italy took over from their Italian colleagues. In 1546 Pierre Lescot designed the richly decorated south-western corner of the Louvre's Cour Carrée. The Petit Château at Chantilly was built about a decade later.

Because French Renaissance architecture was very much the province of the aristocracy and was designed by imported artists, the middle classes – resentful French artisans among them – remained loyal to the indigenous Gothic style, and Gothic churches continued to be built throughout the 16th century. The Mannerist style lasted until the early 17th century.

PARTS OF A CATHEDRAL

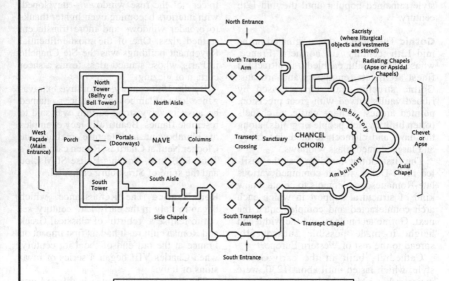

NOTE:
Very few churches incorporate all of the elements shown here, some of which are found only in Gothic cathedrals from certain periods. Romanesque churches have a much simpler layout.

Many French cathedrals are oriented roughly east to west so that the chancel faces more or less east towards Jerusalem. As a result, the main entrance is usually at the base of the west facade and the transept arms extend north and south from the transept crossing as shown here.

Baroque During the Baroque period, which lasted from the end of the 16th century to the late 18th century, painting, sculpture and classical architecture were integrated to create structures and interiors of great subtlety, refinement and elegance.

Salomon de Brosse, who designed Paris' Palais du Luxembourg (1615), set the stage for France's two most prominent early-Baroque architects: François Mansart, designer of the classical wing of the Château de Blois (1635), and his younger rival, Louis Le Vau, the first architect for Louis XIV's palace at Versailles and its predecessor and model, Vaux-le-Vicomte. Baroque elements are particularly in evidence in Versailles' lavish interiors, such as the Galerie des Glaces (Hall of Mirrors). Jules Hardouin-Mansart, Le Vau's successor at Versailles, also designed the Église du Dôme (1670s) at the Invalides in Paris, considered the finest church built in France during the 17th century.

Rococo A derivation of Baroque, rococo was popular during the Enlightenment (1700–80). In France, rococo was confined almost exclusively to the interiors of private

PARTS OF A CATHEDRAL

USEFUL TERMS:

Ambulatory
The ambulatory, a continuation of the aisles of the nave around the chancel, forms a processional path that allows pilgrims relatively easy access to radiating chapels, saints' relics and altars around the chancel and behind the altar.

Clerestory Windows
The clerestory windows, a row of tall windows above the triforium (see below), are often difficult to see because they're so high above the floor.

Cloister
The cloister (cloître), a four-sided enclosure surrounded by covered, colonnaded arcades, is often attached to a monastery church or a cathedral. In monasteries, the cloister served as the focal point of the monks' educational and recreational activities.

Crypt
The crypt (crypte) is a chamber under the church floor, usually at the eastern end, in which saints, martyrs, early church figures and worthy personages are buried. In many Gothic churches, the crypt is often one of the few extant parts of earlier, pre-Gothic structures on the site. A visit to the crypt, usually reached via stairs on one or both sides of the chancel, may involve a small fee.

Narthex
The narthex is an enclosed entrance vestibule just inside the west entrance. It was once reserved for penitents and the unbaptised.

Rood Screen
A rood screen, also known as a jube (jubé), is an often elaborate structure separating the chancel from the nave. Because rood screens made it difficult for worshippers to see religious ceremonies taking place in the chancel, most were removed in the 17th and 18th centuries.

Rose Window
The circular stained-glass windows commonly found in Gothic cathedrals over the west entrance and at the northern and southern ends of the transept arms are known as rose or wheel windows. The stained-glass panels are usually separated from each other by elaborate stone bar tracery, which people inside the church see in silhouette.

Treasury
A treasury (trésor) is a secure room for storing and displaying precious liturgical objects. It may be open shorter hours than the church itself. Visiting often involves a small entry fee.

Triforium
The triforium is an arcaded or colonnaded gallery above the aisle, choir or transept. Most triforia are directly above the columns that separate the aisles from the nave or the ambulatory from the chancel. From the late 13th century, larger clerestory windows often replaced the triforium.

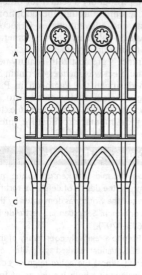

View of Nave Wall

A. Clerestory Windows

B. Triforium

C. Aisle (behind the columns)

residences and had a minimal impact on churches, chateaux and facades, which continued to follow the conventional rules of Baroque classicism. Rococo interiors, such as the oval rooms of the Archives Nationales building in Paris, were lighter, smoother and airier than their 17th-century predecessors and favoured pastels over vivid colours.

Neoclassicism Neoclassical architecture, which emerged around 1740 and remained popular in Paris until well into the 19th century, had its roots in the renewed interest in classical forms. Although it was in part a reaction against the excesses of rococo, it was more profoundly a search for order, reason and serenity through the adoption of the forms and conventions of Graeco-Roman antiquity: columns, simple geometric forms and traditional ornamentation.

France's greatest 18th-century neoclassical architect was Jacques-Germain Soufflot, who designed the Panthéon in Paris. But neoclassicism really came into its own under Napoleon, who used it extensively for monumental architecture intended to embody the grandeur of imperial France. Well-known Paris sights designed (though not necessarily completed) during the First Empire (1804–14) include the Arc de Triomphe, La Madeleine, the facade of the Palais Bourbon, the Arc du Carrousel at the Louvre, the Assemblée Nationale building and the Bourse.

Art Nouveau This style, which emerged in Europe and the USA in the second half of the 19th century but came to be seen as outdated by around 1910, is characterised by sinuous curves and flowing, asymmetrical forms reminiscent of tendrilous vines, water lilies, the patterns on insect wings and the flowering boughs of trees. It was influenced by the arrival of objets d'art from Japan, and its name comes from a Paris gallery that featured works in the new style.

Art Nouveau had a profound impact on all of the applied arts, including interior design, glasswork, wrought-iron work, furniture making and graphics. Art Nouveau combined a variety of materials – including iron, brick, glass and ceramics – in ways never before seen. France's major Art-Nouveau centres were Nancy and Paris; the latter is still graced by Hector Guimard's noodle-like metro entrances. There are some fine Art-Nouveau interiors in the Musée d'Orsay, an Art-Nouveau glass roof over the Grand Palais and, on rue Pavée in the Marais, a synagogue designed by Guimard.

Contemporary Architecture France's most celebrated architect this century, Le Corbusier, was born in Switzerland but settled in Paris in 1917 at the age of 30. A radical modernist, he tried to adapt buildings to suit their function in industrialised society without ignoring the human element. At the Cité Radieuse development (1952) in Marseilles, for example, he put buildings with related functions in a circular formation and constructed them in standard sizes based on the proportions of the human form. His chapel at Ronchamp (1955), in eastern France, is one of the most important works of modern French architecture.

Vauban's Citadels

From the mid-17th century to the mid-19th century, the design of defensive fortifications around the world was dominated by the work of one man: Sébastien le Prestre de Vauban (1633–1707).

Born to a relatively poor family of the petty nobility, Vauban worked as a military engineer during almost the entire reign of Louis XIV, revolutionising both the design of fortresses and siege techniques. To defend France's frontiers, he built 33 immense citadels, many of them star-shaped and surrounded by moats, and he rebuilt or refined over 100 more. Vauban's most famous citadel is situated at Lille, but his work can also be seen at Antibes, Belfort, Belle Île, Bensançon, Concarneau, Perpignan, St-Jean Pied de Port, St-Malo and Verdun.

France's leaders have long sought to immortalise themselves by erecting huge, public edifices – known as *grands projects* – in Paris. In recent years, the late President Georges Pompidou commissioned the once-reviled but now much-revered Centre Beaubourg (1977) and his successor, Giscard d'Estaing, was instrumental in transforming a derelict train station into the glorious Musée d'Orsay, which opened in 1986. But François Mitterrand managed to surpass them both with his monumental commissions.

Since the early 1980s, Paris has seen the construction of such projects as IM Pei's glass pyramid at the Louvre, an architectural cause celebre in the late 1980s; the Opéra-Bastille; the Grande Arche in the skyscraper district of La Défense; the huge science museum and park at La Villette; Parc André Citroën in the western corner of the 15e arrondissement; the new Finance Ministry offices in Bercy; and the controversial new home of the Bibliothèque Nationale (National Library), whose four sun-drenched skyscrapers house the stacks while readers peruse their books in rooms underground.

France's first new cathedral in more than a century was inaugurated in 1995 in Evry, a 'new town' 20km south of Paris. Designed by architect Mario Botta, the controversial Cathédrale de la Résurrection is a truncated red-brick cylinder whose sloping roof has two dozen lime trees planted around its rim to symbolise Christ's crown of thorns.

The most recent mega-project was the Stade de France, the lavish, futuristic stadium built especially for the 1998 football World Cup at a stunning cost of 2.7FF billion. Since the cup, its 80,000 seats are rarely more than half-filled.

Painting

16th Century & Before Sculpture and stained glass rather than paintings were the main adornments of the medieval Gothic cathedrals of northern France, in part because the many windows left little wall space. The Sienese, French and Spanish artists working at the papal court in Avignon in the 14th century, however, created an influential style of mural painting, examples of which can be seen in the city's Palais des Papes.

In the 15th century, France might have served as a meeting ground for the rich traditions of Italy and Flanders, but the Hundred Years' War got in the way. In the 16th century, the Wars of Religion further hampered the development of French painting. Most French Renaissance painters copied Italian models with little inspiration or passion.

17th Century Voltaire wrote that French painting began with Nicolas Poussin (1594–1665), a Baroque painter who frequently set scenes from classical mythology and the Bible in ordered landscapes bathed in golden light.

Poussin spent most of his working life in Rome. His main subject was the slanting light of the Roman countryside.

In 1648 Charles le Brun founded the Royal Academy and, as its head, dominated French painting until the arrival of Jean-Antoine Watteau. Watteau's scenes of concerts and picnics are set in gardens with the occasional presence of characters from the Italian commedia dell'arte.

18th Century In the 18th century, Jean-Baptiste Chardin brought the humbler domesticity of the Dutch masters to French art. He was the first painter to regard still life as an essay in composition rather than a show of skill in reproduction.

In 1785 the public reacted with enthusiasm to two large paintings by Jacques Louis David with clear republican messages, *Le Serment des Horaces* (The Oath of the Horatii) and *Brutus Condamne son Fils* (Brutus Condemning His Son). David became one of the leaders of the Revolution, and a virtual dictator in matters of art, where he advocated a precise, severe classicism. He was made official State painter by Napoleon and produced such vast pictures as *Le Sacre de Napoléon* (Coronation of Napoleon) in 1804. He is perhaps best remembered for the famous painting of Marat lying dead in his bath.

19th Century Jean Auguste Dominique Ingres, David's most gifted pupil, continued in the neoclassical tradition. The historical pictures to which he devoted most of his life are now generally regarded as inferior to his portraits.

The gripping *Le Radeau de la Méduse* (Raft of the Medusa) by Théodore Géricault is on the threshold of Romanticism; if Géricault had not died young, he would probably have become a leader of the movement along with his friend Eugène Delacroix. The latter searched through the histories and literatures of many countries to find subjects to suit his turbulent, dramatic style. His most famous picture, perhaps, is *La Liberté Conduisant le Peuple* (Freedom Leading the People), which commemorates the July Revolution of 1830.

While the Romantics revamped the subject picture, members of the Barbizon School effected a parallel transformation of landscape painting. The school derived its name from the village of Barbizon near the forest of Fontainebleau, where Camille Corot and Jean-François Millet, among others, gathered to paint in the open air. Corot is best known for his landscapes, while Millet took many of his subjects from peasant life and had a strong influence on van Gogh. Reproductions of his *L'Angélus* (The Angelus) still hang over many mantelpieces in rural France as well as on the walls of Catholic grammar schools around the world.

Millet anticipated the realist programme of Gustave Courbet, a prominent member of the Paris Commune, whose paintings show the drudgery of manual labour and the difficult lives of the working class.

Édouard Manet used realism to depict the life of the Parisian middle classes, yet he included in his pictures numerous references to the old masters. His *Le Déjeuner sur l'Herbe* (Luncheon on the Grass) and *Olympia* were considered scandalous, largely because they broke with the traditional treatment of their subject matter.

Impressionism, initially a term of derision, was taken from the title of an experimental painting by Claude Monet in 1874, *Impression: Soleil Levant* (Impression: Sunrise). Monet (see the boxed text 'Claude Monet' in the Normandy chapter) was the leading figure of the school, which counted among its members Alfred Sisley, Camille Pissarro, Berthe Morisot and Pierre-Auguste Renoir. The Impressionists' main aim was to capture fleeting light effects, and light came to dominate the content of their painting. For instance, Monet painted the same subjects – cathedrals, haystacks, trees, water lilies – many times to show the transient effect of light at different times of day.

Edgar Degas was a fellow traveller of the Impressionists, but he preferred his studio to open-air painting. He found his favourite subjects at the racecourse and the ballet. His superb draughtsmanship seized on gestures and movements ignored by earlier artists, and he invented new kinds of composition, such as depicting subjects from an oblique angle.

Henri de Toulouse-Lautrec was a great admirer of Degas and chose similar subjects: people in the bars, brothels and music halls of Montmartre in Paris. He is best known for his posters and lithographs in which the distortion of the figures is both caricature and decorative.

Paul Cézanne is celebrated for his still lifes and landscapes depicting the south of France, while the name of Paul Gauguin immediately conjures up the South Pacific and his studies of Tahitian women. Both he and Cézanne are usually referred to as Postimpressionists, something of a catch-all word for the diverse styles that flowed from Impressionism.

In the late 19th century, Gauguin worked for a time in Arles with the Dutch artist Vincent van Gogh, who spent most of his painting life in France. A brilliant and innovative artist, van Gogh produced haunting, intense self-portraits and landscapes in which colour assumes an expressive and emotive quality. His later technique foreshadowed pointillism, developed by

Georges Seurat, who applied paint in small dots or uniform brush strokes of unmixed colour, producing fine mosaics of warm and cool tones.

Henri Rousseau was a contemporary of the Postimpressionists, but his 'naive' art was totally unaffected by them. A customs official, he painted on Sundays, and his dreamlike pictures of the Paris suburbs, jungle and desert scenes have had a lasting influence on 20th-century art.

Gustave Moreau was a member of the symbolist school. His eerie treatment of mythological subjects can be seen in his old studio south-west of place Pigalle – now the Musée Gustave Moreau – in Paris.

20th Century French painting in the 20th century has been characterised by a bewildering diversity of styles, two of which are particularly significant: Fauvism and Cubism. Fauvism took its name from the slur of a critic who compared the exhibitors at the 1906 autumn salon with *fauves* (wildcats) because of their radical use of intensely bright colours. Among these 'wild' painters were Henri Matisse, André Derain and Maurice de Vlaminck.

Cubism was effectively launched in 1907 by the Spanish prodigy Pablo Picasso with his *Les Demoiselles d'Avignon*. Cubism, as developed by Picasso, Georges Braque and Juan Gris, deconstructed the subject into a system of intersecting planes and presented various aspects of it simultaneously. Collages incorporating bits of cloth, wood, string, newspaper and other things that happened to be lying around were a Cubist speciality.

After WWI, the School of Paris was formed by a group of expressionists, mostly foreign-born, such as Amedeo Modigliani from Italy and Russian-born Marc Chagall. The latter's pictures combine fantasy and folklore.

Dada, a literary and artistic movement of revolt, started in Germany and Switzerland during WWI. One of the principal French Dadaists was Marcel Duchamp, whose Mona Lisa with a moustache and goatee epitomises the spirit of the movement.

The German Dadaist Max Ernst moved to Paris in 1922 and was instrumental in starting Surrealism, an offshoot of Dada that flourished between the wars. Drawing on the theories of Freud, Surrealism attempted to reunite the conscious and unconscious realms, to permeate everyday life with fantasies and dreams. The most famous Surrealist painter, the Catalan Salvador Dalí, came relatively late to the movement in Paris.

WWII ended Paris' role as the world's artistic capital. Many artists left France, and though some returned after the war, the city never regained its old magnetism. Bernard Buffet, who died in 2000, was probably France's leading postwar painter (his sad, moving portraits hang in the Vatican and New York's Museum of Modern Art).

Sculpture

At the end of the 11th century, sculptors began to decorate the portals, capitals, altars and fonts of Romanesque churches, illustrating Bible stories and the lives of the saints for the illiterate.

Two centuries later, when the cathedral became the centre of monumental building, sculpture spread from the central portal to the whole facade, whose brightly painted and carved surface offered a symbolic summary of Christian doctrine. In the 14th century, the Dutchman Claus Sluter, working at the court of Burgundy, introduced a vigorous realism with his sculptures for the Chartreuse de Champnol monastery in Dijon.

As well as adorning cathedrals, sculpture was increasingly commissioned for the tombs of the nobility. The royal tombs in the basilica of St-Denis, near Paris, illustrate the progress in naturalism from the 13th to the 15th centuries.

In Renaissance France, Pierre Bontemps decorated the beautiful tomb of François I at St-Denis, and Jean Goujon created the Fontaine des Innocents near the Forum des Halles in Paris. The Baroque style is exemplified by Guillaume Coustou's *Horses of Marly* at the entrance to the ave des Champs-Élysées.

In the 19th century, memorial statues in

public places came to replace sculpted tombs. One of the best artists in the new mode was François Rude, who sculpted the statue of Marshall Ney outside the Closerie des Lilas in Paris and the bas-relief on the Arc de Triomphe. Jean-Baptiste Carpeaux began as a Romantic sculptor, but *La Danse* (The Dance) on the Opéra-Garnier in Paris and his fountain in the Luxembourg Gardens reflect the warmth and gaiety of the Baroque.

At the end of the 19th century, Auguste Rodin overcame the conflict of neoclassicism and Romanticism. His sumptuous bronze and marble figures of men and women, often intimately entwined, and often incomplete, did much to revitalise sculpture as an expressive medium.

Rodin is seen by some critics as the finest portraitist in the history of the art. Some of his best-known works include *Le Baiser* (The Kiss), *Le Penseur* (The Thinker) and *Les Bourgeois de Calais* (The Burghers of Calais). One of Rodin's most gifted pupils was Camille Claudel, whose work can also be seen in the Musée Rodin in Paris.

One of the most important French sculptors of the early 20th century was Aristide Maillol, whose voluptuous female nudes reveal his attachment to formal analysis, in direct contrast to Rodin's emotive style.

Braque and Picasso, who lived in Paris, experimented with sculpture, and in the spirit of Dada, Marcel Duchamp exhibited 'found objects', such as a urinal, which he titled *Fontaine* (Fountain) and signed. The Swiss-born sculptor Alberto Giacometti participated in the Surrealist movement in Paris during the 1930s. After WWII he produced a disturbing series of emaciated human figures in bronze.

One of the most influential sculptors to emerge after WWII was César Baldaccini (known as César to the world), who was born in Marseilles in 1921. He began using iron and scrap metal (most notably crushed cars) to create his imaginary insects and animals but later graduated to pliable plastics. Arguably his best-known work is the little statue handed to actors at the Césars, the French cinema awards equivalent to Hollywood's Oscars.

Cinema

Early Days to WWII France's place in the film history books was ensured by those cinematographic pioneers, the Lumière brothers, who invented 'moving pictures' and organised the world's first paying (1FF) public movie screening – a series of two-minute reels – in Paris' Grand Café on the blvd des Capucines on 28 December 1895. They went on to specialise in newsreels and documentaries, leaving Charles Pathé – often called the Napoleon of cinema – to monopolise and rapidly expand France's cinema scene prior to WWI.

The 1920s and '30s were innovative times for film in France, as such avant-garde directors as René Clair, Marcel Carné and the intensely productive Jean Renoir, son of the famous artist, searched for new forms and subjects. Clair created a world of fantasy in his films in which he gave free rein to his penchant for invention. Though Carné's films were visually stunning, he presented a pessimistic world in which violence and poverty dominate. Poetic realism, strong narrative and a strong sense of social satire mark the work of Jean Renoir.

New Wave After the war, however, ideas and techniques gradually lost innovation, and the big names tended to go somewhat stale. The industry stagnated until the late 1950s, when a large group of new directors burst onto the scene with a new genre, the so-called *nouvelle vague* (new wave).

This group included Jean-Luc Godard, François Truffaut, Claude Chabrol, Eric Rohmer, Jacques Rivette, Louis Malle and Alain Resnais. The one belief that united this disparate group was that a film should be the conception of the film-maker rather than the product of a studio or producer, hence giving rise to the term *film d'auteur*.

With small budgets, sometimes entirely self-financed, no extravagant sets or big-name stars, they made films like *Et Dieu Créa la Femme* (And God Created Woman; 1956), which brought sudden stardom to Brigitte Bardot, the little fishing village of St-Tropez and the young director Roger

Vadim. The film, which examined the amorality of modern youth, received international acclaim.

A ream of films followed, among them Alain Resnais' *Hiroshima, Mon Amour* (1959) and *L'Année Dernière à Marienbad* (Last Year in Marienbad; 1961), which explored the problems of time and memory. François Truffaut's *Les Quatre Cents Coups* (The 400 Blows; 1959) was partly based on his own rebellious adolescence. Jean-Luc Godard made such films as *À Bout de Souffle* (Breathless; 1960), *Alphaville* (1965) and *Pierrot le Fou* (Crazy Pete; 1965), which showed even less concern for sequence and narrative, with frequent jump-cutting and interruptions by pop-art images and actors' comments on the film itself. The new wave continued until the 1970s, by which time it had lost its experimental edge.

Other famous French directors making films at this time included Agnès Varda and Claude Chabrol. Of the non-new-wave directors of the 1950s and '60s, one of the most notable was Jacques Tati, who made many comic films based around the charming, bumbling figure of Monsieur Hulot and his struggles to adapt to the modern age.

Contemporary Cinema The most successful directors of the 1980s and '90s have produced both original and visually striking films featuring unusual locations, bizarre stories and unique characters. Well-regarded directors include Jean-Jacques Beineix, who made *Diva* in 1981, followed five years later by *Betty Blue* (the film's French title was the rather bizarre *37°2 le Matin*), and Luc Besson with *Subway* (1985) and *Le Grand Bleu* (The Big Blue; 1988). Some of Beineix's work, including *La Lune dans le Caniveau* (The Moon in the Gutter; 1983) with Nastassja Kinski and Gérard Depardieu, has been dismissed as self-indulgent twaddle. Besson's later films have become more commercial, including the action-packed *Nikita* (1990) and *Léon* (1994).

In 1986 Claude Berri came up with *Jean de Florette* followed by *Manon des Sources*, modern versions of writer/film-maker Marcel Pagnol's original works, which proved enormously popular both in France and abroad. Léos Carax, in his *Boy Meets Girl* (1983), created a kind of Parisian purgatory of souls lost in the eternal night.

Modern French cinema has a reputation for being intellectual, elitist and, frankly, boring. But French films aren't always so pat and serious. Light social comedies like *Trois Hommes et un Couffin* (Three Men and a Cradle; 1985) and *Romuald et Juliette* (1989) by Coline Serreau and *La Vie Est un Long Fleuve Tranquille* (Life is a Long Quiet River; 1988) by Étienne Chatiliez have been among the biggest hits in France in recent years.

Other well-regarded directors today include Olivier Assayas (*Les Destinées Sentimentales*; 2000), Catherine Breillat (*Romance*; 1999), Cédric Klapisch (*Un Air de Famille* or Family Resemblances; 1996) and Arnaud Desplechin (*Esther Kahn*; 2000). Alain Resnais' *On Connaît la Chanson* (Same Old Song), based on the life of the late British television playwright Dennis Potter, received international acclaim and six Césars in 1997. Bruno Dumont's *Humanité*, probably the slowest fictional murder investigation ever filmed, won several major awards in 1999.

Other film-makers to look out for include German-born Dominik Moll, whose delightful black comedy *Harry, un Ami Qui Vous Veut du Bien* (Harry, He's Here to Help) was selected at Cannes in 2000. Don't miss a showing of *Saint Cyr* (in English: The King's Daughters; 2000), a visually stunning historical drama directed by Patricia Mazuy.

Events & Stars The French film industry's main annual event is the Cannes Film Festival, which, since 1946, has awarded the coveted Palme d'Or and other prizes to French and foreign films. French movie stars, directors, technicians and so on are annually honoured with the Césars, created in 1976.

One of the nation's earliest screen heroes was the great comic Fernandel, who was nicknamed 'Horseface' because of his inimitable grin and who starred in the *Don*

Camillo series of the 1950s. Maurice Chevalier left for Hollywood in the 1930s, becoming the man who epitomised the dapper Frenchman in musicals such as *The Merry Widow*, *Gigi* and *Can-Can*. Two of France's best-loved thespians of the 1930s and '40s were Jean Gabin and Arletty. Gabin frequently portrayed strong-willed nonconformists; his most notable role was in Jean Renoir's *La Grande Illusion* (1937). Cast as the downtrodden prostitute in many films, Arletty is best remembered for her role in Carné's *Les Enfants du Paradis* (1945). Stars of the 1950s and '60s included Jean-Paul Belmondo, a kind of impertinent James Bond; the tall, dark and handsome Alain Delon; and the sexy Bardot.

More contemporary is Philippe Noiret, a veteran of over 100 French films whose hangdog face found international acclaim in 1989 as the Sicilian movie-loving projectionist in *Cinema Paradiso*.

The 1980s seemed to favour very masculine, almost macho, older characters with interesting and mysterious pasts, including Jean Reno (*Subway*; 1985) and Richard Bohringer (*Diva*; 1981). In recent years, however, less macho actors such as Daniel Auteuil (*Manon des Sources*; 1986), Hippolyte Girardot (*Un Monde sans Pitié*; 1989) and Fabrice Luchini (*La Discrète*, 1990; and *Beaumarchais*; 1996) have gained considerable followings.

However, it is Gérard Depardieu more than any other French actor who has reached worldwide audiences over the past two decades. Among his most powerful roles were those in François Truffaut's *Le Dernier Métro* (1980), *Jean de Florette* (1986; directed by Claude Berri), *Danton* (1982; by the Polish director Andrzej Wajda) and *Cyrano de Bergerac* (1990; by Jean-Paul Rappeneau). Starring next to Depardieu in *Le Dernier Métro* was the incomparable Catherine Deneuve, generally considered one of France's leading actresses.

Emmanuelle Béart, Isabelle Huppert, Sandrine Bonnaire, Carole Bouquet, Isabelle Adjani, Sophie Marceau and Oscar-winning Juliette Binoche are among the contemporary female stars of the French

cinema. Some up-and-comers include Emmanuel Schotte, Mathilde Seigner and Morgane Moré.

Humour
Though it may come as a surprise to some, French people do like to laugh. Such comedians as Bourvil, Fernandel, Bernard Blier, Louis de Funès, Francis Blanche, Jean Poiret and Michel Serrault have enjoyed enormous popularity over the years and their films (such as *La Grande Vadrouille*, *La Vache et le Prisonnier*, *Les Tontons Flingueurs*, *La Cage aux Folles*) have been among the most successful movies made over the past 40 years. Inexplicably, the American comedian Jerry Lewis is immensely popular in France, as is the neurotic film director Woody Allen.

Stand-up comics now considered classics include Fernand Raynaud, whose sketches were based on real characters and situations, and Pierre Dac, who broadcast to the Free French Forces on Radio Londres during WWII.

Among contemporary stars are the pieds-noirs comics Elie Kakou and Guy Bedos (the latter is left-wing, which, among this generally conservative group, is comical in itself) and the French-Arab comedian Smaïn. Raymond Devos, who builds up extravagant situations, plays with words and pushes logic to a Surrealistic extreme also has a large following as does the trio Les Nuls and Patrick Timsi. But one of the biggest phenomena of the past 20 years was Coluche, who began his career with Gérard Depardieu, Miou-Miou and Josiane Balasko in a small cafe-theatre near Beaubourg in Paris. He quickly became famous for his bizarre dress and crude humour, which sometimes bordered on the vulgar. As his humour became more and more political, he was censored and his 'alternative' nightly news on Canal+ was eventually cancelled. Sadly, he died in a motorcycle accident at the height of his fame in 1986.

Adult comic books (*bandes dessinées*) enjoy a following unimaginable in English-speaking countries, with the well-known *Astérix* paving the way for more recent publications such as *Rubrique à Brac* and the artists Marcel Gotlib and Cabu. The latter's signature character is Le Grand Duduche, a rebellious and lazy student fighting to integrate himself into post-1968 French society, and his racist, almost fascist *beau-frére* (brother-in-law). The word *beauf* has passed into the language to describe just such a man. In *Les Bidochon*, Alain Binet caricatures the life of average middle-class citizens who live in council flats, commute to work and go on organised holidays abroad.

One of the few women to have broken into this predominantly male domain is Claire Brétécher, who gently mocks feminist intellectuals in her *Les Mères*, a popular gift for women expecting a baby.

SOCIETY & CONDUCT
Interacting with the French
Some visitors to France conclude that it would be a lovely country if it weren't for the French. As in other countries, however, the more tourists a particular town or area attracts, the less patience the locals tend to have for them.

Making Friends & Avoiding Offence
By following a number of simple guidelines, you can usually win people over and avoid offending anyone.

Here are a few dos:

- The easiest way to improve the quality of your relations with the French is always to say *'Bonjour, monsieur/madame/mademoiselle.'* when you walk into a shop, and *'Merci, monsieur...au revoir.'* when you leave. 'Monsieur' means 'sir' and can be used with any male person who isn't a child. 'Madame' is used where 'Mrs' would apply in English, whereas 'mademoiselle' is used when talking to unmarried women. When in doubt, use 'madame'.
- It is customary for people who know each other to exchange kisses *(bises)* as a greeting, though this is rare between two men except in the south or if they are related. The usual ritual is one glancing peck on each cheek but, depending on the region (and the personalities involved), some people go for three or even four kisses. People who don't kiss each other will almost always shake hands.

- If invited to someone's home or a party, always bring some sort of gift, such as good wine (not some 10FF *vin de table*). Flowers are another good stand-by, but chrysanthemums are only brought to cemeteries.
- Many French people seem to feel that 'going Dutch' (splitting the bill) at restaurants is an uncivilised custom. In general, the person who did the inviting pays for dinner, though close friends and colleagues will sometimes share the cost.

And a few don'ts:

- When buying fruit, vegetables or flowers anywhere except at supermarkets, do not touch the produce or blossoms unless invited to do so. Show the shopkeeper what you want and he or she will choose for you.
- In a restaurant, do not summon the waiter by shouting *'garçon'*, which means 'boy'. Saying *'s'il vous plaît'* (please) is the way it's done nowadays.
- When you're being served cheese (for example, as the final course for dinner), remember two cardinal rules: never cut off the tip of the pie-shaped soft cheeses (such as Brie or Camembert); and cut cheese whose middle is the best part (for example, blue cheese) in such a way as to take your fair share of the crust. See also the Food and Wine special section.
- Money, particularly income, is a subject that is simply not discussed in France.
- In general, lawns in France are meant to be looked at and praised for their greenness, not sat upon; watch out for *'pelouse interdite'* (Keep off the Grass!) signs. This has been changing in recent years, with signs being removed and replaced with *'pelouse autorisée'*, meaning tourists and locals alike are permitted to sit, eat, play and walk on the grass of certain parks (with some exceptions, such as the Jardin des Tuileries and Jardin du Luxembourg in Paris).

RELIGION
Catholics
Some 80% of French people identify themselves as Catholic but, although most have been baptised, very few ever attend church. *Conversion*, such as that experienced by the poet Paul Claudel (1868–1955) and the novelist Henry de Montherlant (1896–1972), thus actually means 'reconversion' in English. The Catholic Church in France is generally very progressive and ecumenically minded. Cardinal Jean-Marie Lustiger,

archbishop of Paris since 1981, was born in Paris in 1926 to Jewish immigrants from Poland. He converted to Catholicism at age 14. His mother died in the Nazi concentration camp of Auschwitz in 1942.

Protestants

France's Protestants (Huguenots), who were severely persecuted during much of the 16th and 17th centuries, now number around one million. They are concentrated in Alsace, the Jura, the south-eastern part of the Massif Central and along the Atlantic coast.

Jean (John) Calvin (1509–64), a leader of the Protestant reformation in France and Switzerland, was born in Noyon in the far north of France and educated in Paris, Orléans and Bourges but spent much of his life in Geneva.

Muslims

France has between four and five million nominally Muslim residents, and they now make up the country's second-largest religious group. The vast majority are immigrants who came from North Africa during the 1950s and '60s, or their offspring.

In recent years, France's Muslim community has been the object of racist agitation by right-wing parties and extremist groups. The so-called Muslim scarf affair of 1994, when pupils were expelled from school for wearing scarves (considered 'ostentatious religious signs') brought the matter to the forefront but was more or less resolved two years later when the Conseil Constitutionnel (Constitutional Council, which is similar to the US Supreme Court) ruled that schools may not suspend pupils who wear scarves if no overt religious proselytising is involved. Many North Africans complain of discrimination by the police and employers.

Jews

There has been a Jewish community in France for most of the time since the Roman period. During the Middle Ages, the community suffered persecution and there were a number of mass expulsions. French Jews, the first in Europe to achieve emancipation, were granted full citizenship in 1790–91. Since 1808, the French Jewish community has had an umbrella organisation known as the Consistoire based in Paris.

The country's Jewish community, which now numbers some 650,000 (the largest in Europe), grew substantially during the 1960s as a result of immigration from Algeria, Tunisia and Morocco. France generally enjoys a favourable standing with the Jewish community, and there have been relatively few incidents of anti-Semitism reported in recent years. The national Jewish community's Web site is at www.col.fr.

A recent study, published by the Matteoli Commission in April 2000, caused a stir by claiming that Nazis and French collaborators stole far more from Jews during WWII than had been previously assumed. Headed by Jean Matteoli, a Resistance fighter, the report found that $1.3 billion worth of assets was taken in the form of frozen bank accounts, fines, businesses and other property. Some 90% had been repaid within a decade after the war, but the French government still holds unclaimed funds worth $2 billion.

Facts for the Visitor

HIGHLIGHTS

France has a wealth of wonderful places to visit, but some aspects of the country are so outstanding that they deserve special mention:

Art & Architecture
- Paris' wealth of gorgeous architecture
- The Loire Valley chateaux of Chambord, Chenonceau, and Cheverny
- The fortress-like Palais des Papes in Avignon
- The Pont du Gard Roman aqueduct near Nîmes
- The towering spires of Strasbourg's cathedral
- The Bayeux Tapestry with its 'living scenes' from history
- An afternoon in Paris' Louvre, Musée d'Orsay, Musée Rodin or Musée Picasso
- The stained glass of Chartres cathedral on a bright sunny day

Activities & Culture
- Cruising to idyllic Île d'Ouessant off Brittany
- Taking the waters in the *belle époque* spa town of Vichy
- Watching the birds and galloping horses of the Camargue delta
- Hiking in the Pyrenees
- Seeing the 'giants' dance at Arras' folk festivals
- Taking in a performance at Arles' Roman amphitheatre
- Wandering the aroma-filled streets of Grasse, the elegant squares of Lyons and the medieval quarter of Dijon

Beauty Spots
- Monet's gardens at Giverny in full blossom
- The breathtaking cliffs and rock formations at Étretat on the Normandy coast
- Mont Blanc seen from the western side of Chamonix Valley
- Cannes' alluring waterfront at dusk
- The spectacular Gorges du Verdon in Provence
- Corsica's lofty mountains seen rising up from the sea

SUGGESTED ITINERARIES

Depending on the length of your stay, you might want to see and do the following in France:

One week
Visit Paris – the most beautiful city in the world – and a nearby area, such as the Loire Valley, Champagne, Alsace or Normandy.
Two weeks
As above, plus one area in the west or south, such as Brittany, the Alps or Provence.
One month
As above but spend more time in each place and visit more of the west or south (for example, Brittany or the Côte d'Azur).
Two months
As above, plus hike in the Pyrenees or Alps; hang out at one of the beach areas on the Mediterranean or Atlantic coast; and spend some time in more remote areas (for example, the Basque Country or Corsica).

PLANNING
When to Go

France is at its very best in spring, though winter-like relapses aren't unknown and the beach resorts only begin to pick up sometime in May. Autumn is pleasant, too, but the days are fairly short and it gets a bit cool for sunbathing later on, even along the Côte d'Azur. Winter is great for skiing and other snow sports in the Alps, the Pyrenees and other mountain areas, but Christmas, New Year and the February–March school holiday periods create surges in domestic tourism that can make it very difficult and/or expensive to find accommodation. Paris has various cultural events on offer all winter long.

In July and August, the weather is warm and even hot, especially in the south, and France's beaches, resorts and camp sites are packed.

Small villages may be almost entirely shut down on Sundays and public holidays. Public transport is likely to be limited or suspended, and food shops – except a morning-only *boulangerie* – may be shut.

Domestic Tourism By law, all French wage-earners get five weeks of *congés payés* (paid holiday) each year. Most of them take advantage of their time off between mid-July and the end of August, when France's city-dwellers descend like a locust storm on the coasts, mountains and other areas.

Meanwhile, in the half-deserted cities of the interior – only partly refilled by foreign tourists – many shops, restaurants, cinemas, cultural institutions and even hotels simply shut down so the proprietors can head out of town along with their customers. A *congé annuel* (annual closure) sign in the window usually means 'come back in September'. Worse still, the people left behind to staff essential services tend to be even more irritable than usual.

The February–March school holiday is another period of mass domestic tourism, bringing huge numbers of people (and higher prices) to the Alps, the Pyrenees and Andorra.

School Holiday Periods The *vacances scolaires* (school holidays), during which millions of families take domestic breaks, generally fall during the following times of year:

Christmas–New Year
  Schools all over the country are closed from 20 December to 4 January.
February–March
  The 'February' holidays last from about 11 February to 11 March; pupils in each of three zones are off for overlapping 15-day periods.
Easter
  The month-long spring break, which begins around Easter, also means pupils have overlapping 15-day holidays.
Summer
  The nationwide summer holiday lasts from the tail end of June until very early September.

Weather Forecasts If you understand French (or know someone who does), you can find out the *météo* (weather forecast) by calling the following numbers:

National forecast	☎ 08 36 70 12 34
Regional forecasts	☎ 08 36 68 00 00
Mountain area	
& snow forecasts	☎ 08 36 68 04 04
Marine forecast	☎ 08 36 68 08 08

For departmental forecasts, dial ☎ 08 36 68 02 plus the two digit departmental number (for example, ☎ 08 36 68 02 75 for Paris). Each call costs five *télécarte* (phonecard) units or 2.23FF per minute. By Minitel, key in 3615 MET or 3617 METPLUS (for information on Minitel see Telephone later in the chapter).

What Kind of Trip

'If this is Tuesday, it must be Strasbourg.' Though often ridiculed, the mad dash that 'does' an entire country the size of France in a couple of weeks can have its merits. If you've never visited France before, you won't know which areas you'll like, and a quick 'scouting tour' will give an overview of the options. A rail pass that offers unlimited travel within a set period of time can be the best way to do this. For more information, see the boxed text 'Discount Train Tickets & Passes' in the Getting Around chapter.

But if you know where you want to go, or have found a place you like, the best advice is to stay put for a while, explore the area and discover some of the lesser-known sights, make a few local friends and settle in. It's also cheaper in the long run.

If you have specific interests such as walking or folk culture, the Activities and Organised Tours sections in the regional chapters offer a wealth of information on walking and hiking paths, guided tours and theme trips.

Maps

Road maps and city maps are available at Maisons de la Presse (large news agencies found all over France), bookshops, tourist offices, and even some newspaper kiosks. Where relevant, advice on maps and where to buy them is given under Orientation in a city or town listing.

In Paris, the best place to find a full selection of Institut Géographique National (IGN) maps is at the Espace IGN (☎ 01 43 98 85 00, metro Franklin D Roosevelt) at 107 rue La Boétie, 8e, open 9.30 am to 7 pm Monday to Friday and 12.30 to 6.30 pm Saturday.

Using Map Indexes

In French map indexes, place names that begin with a definite article (such as Le Mont St-Michel, La Rochelle, L'Île Rousse) may be listed either under Le/La/L' or under the rest of the name. Names that start with 'Saint' (abbreviated as St) appear before names that begin with 'Sainte' (Ste), a female saint. Streets named after people are listed either by the last name or, as Michelin seems to prefer, by the first name or title (Général, Maréchal and so on).

When more than one town bears the same name, each one is given a descriptive suffix. For instance, you'll find in various parts of the country Villefranche-sur-Cher (Villefranche on the Cher River), Villefranche-sur-Mer (Villefranche by the Sea) and Villefranche du Périgord (Villefranche in Périgord). Unless there's another Villefranche nearby, local people usually drop the suffix.

Road Maps A variety of *cartes routières* (road maps) are available, but if you're going to be driving a lot, the best road atlas to have in the car is Michelin's *Atlas Routier France*, which covers the whole country in 1:200,000 scale (1cm = 2km). It comes with either spiral or regular binding and costs 115FF.

Driving in and out of Paris can be confusing even with a map; without one, it's hopeless. The most useful road map of the greater Paris area is Michelin's 1:100,000 scale *Environs de Paris* (green map No 106, 26FF).

If you're concentrating on just a few regions, it's easier and cheaper to buy Michelin's yellow-jacketed 1:200,000-scale foldout maps, which come in two sizes: small (about 15FF for each of the 39 sheets), marked with two-digit identification numbers; and large (35FF), identified by three-digit numbers. The latter cover the country in only 17 sheets but are rather clumsy.

IGN covers France with 16 maps in 1:250,000 scale (46FF) and 74 1:100,000-scale maps (29FF), but both are more difficult to drive with than Michelin's maps.

To plot cross-country travel, you have two 1:1,000,000-scale maps to choose from: Michelin's red-series map No 911; and IGN's Map No 901, entitled *France – Routes, Autoroutes* (23FF). Both are updated annually.

Walking & Cycling Maps Didier et Richard publishes a series of 1:50,000 scale trail maps (67FF), perfect for walking or for off-road cycling.

IGN covers all of France with about 1100 1:50,000-scale topographical maps and 2200 1:25,000-scale maps. There are two varieties in the 1:25,000 scale: the old kind (46FF), which cover the entire country; and the more recent Top 25 series maps (58FF), which are available for the Mediterranean coast, the Alps, the Pyrenees, the Basque Country and a few other areas. Map No 1748OT (OT is short for *ouest*, west) covers an area slightly west of that covered by map No 1748ET (short for *est*, east).

IGN's 1:1,000,000 scale grey-jacketed Map No 903 (32FF), entitled *France – Grande Randonnée*, shows all of France's long-distance GR trails (see Walking later in the chapter). It is useful for the strategic planning of a cross-country trek.

IGN No 906 (29FF), known as *France – VTT & Randonnées Cyclos*, indicates dozens of suggested bicycle tours. Other IGN cycling maps include *90 Circuits Cyclos en Île de France* and various regional *cyclocartes* (cycle maps). See the Web site at www.ign.

City Maps Lonely Planet's *Paris City Map* is a handy, laminated product that covers the city at a scale of 1:16,000. It also features a Metro map, walking tour and a complete index of all streets and sights.

The *plans* (street maps) distributed free by tourist offices range from the superb to the virtually useless. Michelin's *Guide Rouge* (see Restaurant & Accommodation Guides later in the chapter) has over 500 city and town maps that show one-way streets and have numbered town entry points that are coordinated with Michelin's yellow-jacketed 1:200,000-scale road maps. Some of them also appear, in a slightly different form, in the company's *Guides Verts* (Green Guides). Michelin publishes an excellent 1:10,000-scale map of Lyon. Plans-Guides Blay offers orange-jacketed street maps of 125 French cities and towns.

Abbreviations commonly used on city maps include: *R* for *rue* (street); *Bd, Boul* or *Bould* for boulevard; *Av* for avenue; *Q* for *quai* (quay); *Cr* for *cours* (avenue); *Pl* for *place* (square); *Pte* for *porte* (gate); *Imp* for *impasse* (dead-end street); *St* for *saint* (masculine) and *Ste* for *sainte* (feminine).

What to Bring The cardinal rule in packing is to bring as little as possible. It's better to start off with too little rather than too much, as virtually everything you could possibly need is available locally. Sea mail services have been discontinued in France, so the only way to send packages overseas is by airmail, which can be very expensive, even for low-priority printed matter.

If you'll be doing any walking with your gear, a backpack is the only way to go. One of the most flexible models is an internal-frame travel pack whose straps can be zipped inside a flap, turning it into a nylon suitcase. Some have an exterior pouch that zips off to become a daypack.

If you're hostelling, pack a towel and a plastic soap container or buy them when you arrive. Bedding is always provided or available for hire, though you might want to take along your own sheet bag. You'll sleep easier with a padlock on your storage locker, which are usually provided at hostels.

Other optional items you might need include a torch (flashlight), an adapter plug for electrical appliances (such as a cup or coil immersion heater to make your own tea or instant coffee), a universal bath/sink plug (a plastic film canister sometimes works), sunglasses, a hat and a few clothes-pegs.

For a checklist of first-aid and pharmaceutical items, see the Health section later in the chapter.

RESPONSIBLE TOURISM

In France's nature reserves and national parks, be sure to follow the local code of ethics and common decency and pack up your litter. Minimise waste by taking minimal packaging and no more food than you will need. Don't use detergents or toothpaste, even if they are biodegradable, in or near watercourses. Bear in mind that sensitive biospheres, both for flora and fauna, may be seriously damaged if you depart from designated paths in protected areas. When camping in the wild (checking first with the landowners or a park ranger to see that it's allowed), bury human waste in catholes at least 15cm (6 inches) deep and at least 100m (320 feet) from any watercourse.

For further tips on how you can reduce your impact on the environment, contact Les Amis de la Nature (☎ 01 46 27 53 56), 197 rue Championnet, 75018 Paris.

TOURIST OFFICES
Local Tourist Offices

Every city, town, village and hamlet seems to have either an *office de tourisme* (a tourist office run by some unit of local government) or a *syndicat d'initiative* (a tourist office run by an organisation of local merchants). Both are an excellent resource and can almost always provide a local map at the very least. Some will also exchange foreign currency, especially when banks are closed, though the rate is rarely good. Many tourist offices will make local hotel reservations, usually for a small fee.

Details on local tourist offices appear under Information at the beginning of each city, town or area listing.

Tourist Offices Abroad

French government tourist offices (usually called Maisons de la France) can provide every imaginable sort of tourist information on France, most of it in the form of brochures. They include:

Australia (☎ 02-9231 5244, fax 9221 8682; @ ifrance@internetezy.com.au) 25 Bligh St, 22nd floor, Sydney, NSW 2000. Open from 9 am to 5 pm weekdays.

Belgium (☎ 02-513 5886, fax 514 3375, ✉ maisondelafrance@pophost.eunet.be) 21 ave de la Toison d'Or, 1050 Brussels. Open from 10 am to 5 pm weekdays.

Canada (☎ 514-288 4264, fax 845 4868, ✉ mfrance@mtl.net) 1981 McGill College Ave, Suite 490, Montreal, Que H3A 2W9. Open from 9 am to 4 pm weekdays.

Germany (☎ 069-580 131, fax 069-745 556, ✉ maison_de _la_France@t-online.de) West-endstrasse 47, D-60325 Frankfurt. Open from 9 am to 4.30 pm weekdays.

Ireland (☎ 01 679 0813, fax 679 0814, ✉ french touristoffice@tinet.ie) 10 Suffolk St, Dublin 2. Open from 9.30 am to 1.30 pm and 2 to 5 pm weekdays.

Italy (☎ 02 584 8657, fax 5848 6222, ✉ info@turismofrancese.it) Via Larga 7, 20122 Milan. Open from 9.30 am to 5.30 pm week-days.

Netherlands (☎ 0900 112 2332, fax 020-620 3339, ✉ informatie@fransverkeersbureau.nl) Prinsengracht 670, 1017 KX Amsterdam. Open from 1 pm to 5 pm weekdays.

Spain (☎ 91-541 8808; fax 541 2412; ✉ maisondelafrance@mad.sericom.es) Alcalá 63, 28014 Madrid. Open from 9 am to 1.30 pm and 4 to 7 pm weekdays (8 am to 3 pm in summer).

Switzerland

  Zurich: (☎ 01-211 3085, fax 212 1644, ✉ tourismefrance@bluewin.ch) Löwenstrasse 59, 8023 Zurich. Open from 10 am to 1 pm and 2 to 5.30 pm weekdays.

  Geneva: (☎ 022-90 8977, fax 909 8971, ✉ mdlfva@bluewin.ch) 2 rue Thalberg, 1201 Geneva. Open from 9 am to noon and 1 to 5.45 pm Monday to Thursday (to 5 pm on Friday).

UK (☎ 020-7399 3500, fax 7493 6594, ✉ piccadilly@mdlf.demon.co.uk) 178 Pic-cadilly, London W1V 0AL. Open from 10 am to 6 pm daily (to 5pm on Saturday, closed on Sunday).

USA

  New York: (☎ 212-838 7800, fax 838 7855, ✉ info@francetourism.com) 444 Madison Ave, 16th floor, New York, NY 10022-6903. Open 9 am to 5 pm weekdays.

  Los Angeles: (☎ 310-271 6665, fax 276 2835, ✉ fgto@gte.net) 9454 Wiltshire Blvd, Suite 715, Beverly Hills, CA 90212-2967. Open 9 am to 5 pm weekdays.

DOCUMENTS
Passport

By law, everyone in France, including tourists, must carry some sort of ID on them at all times. For foreign visitors, this means a passport (if you don't want to carry your passport for security reasons a photocopy should do, although you may be required to report to a police station later to verify your identity) or, for citizens of the European Union (EU), a national ID card.

Visas

Tourist EU nationals have no entry re-quirements, and citizens of Australia, the USA, Canada, New Zealand and Israel do not need visas to visit France as tourists for up to three months. Except for people from a handful of other European countries (in-cluding Switzerland and Poland), everyone else needs a so-called Schengen Visa, named after the Schengen Agreement that abol-ished passport controls between Austria, Belgium, France, Germany, Greece, Italy, Luxembourg, the Netherlands and Portugal. A visa for any of these countries should, in theory, be valid throughout the area, but it pays to double-check with the embassy or consulate of the countries you intend to visit.

Visa fees depend on the current exchange rate, but a transit visa costs about US$9, a visa valid for stays of up to 30 days costs around US$23, and a single or multiple-entry visa of up to three months costs about US$32. You will need your passport (valid for a period of three months beyond the date of your departure from France), a return ticket, proof of sufficient funds to support yourself, proof of pre-arranged accommo-dation (possibly), two passport-size photos and the visa fee in cash. South African visas take two days to process.

If all the forms are in order, your visa will be issued on the spot. You can also apply for a French visa after arriving in Europe – the fee is the same, but you may not have to pro-duce a return ticket. If you enter France overland, your visa may not be checked at the border, but major problems can arise if you don't have one later on (for example, at the airport as you leave the country).

Long-Stay & Student If you'd like to work or study in France or stay for over three months, apply to the French embassy or consulate nearest your residence for the appropriate sort of *long séjour* (long-stay) visa.

Unless you live in the EU, it's extremely difficult to get a visa that will allow you to work in France. For any sort of long-stay visa, begin the paperwork in your home country several months before you plan to leave. Applications cannot usually be made in a third country nor can tourist visas be turned into student visas after you arrive in France. People with student visas can apply for permission to work part-time (inquire at your place of study).

Au Pair There are visas especially for au pairs. These must be arranged *before* you leave home, unless you're an EU resident, in which case they can be obtained in France. See Work later in the chapter for more information on au pair work.

Carte de Séjour If you are issued a long-stay visa valid for six or more months, you'll probably have to apply for a *carte de séjour* (residence permit) within eight days of arrival in France. For details, ask at your place of study or the local *préfecture* (prefecture), *sous-préfecture* (subprefecture), *hôtel de ville* (town or city hall), *mairie* (town hall) or *commissariat* (police station).

In Paris, EU passport-holders should apply to the visa office in Salle Europe, which is on the ground floor next to *escalier* (stairway) C in the Préfecture de Police, 1 place Louis Lépine, 4e (☎ 01 53 71 51 68/ 0 836 67 22 22, metro Cité). By Minitel key in 3611 PREFECTURE DE POLICE. It opens 8.30 am to 4.30 pm weekdays (4 pm on Friday).

Foreigners with other passports who are staying in *arrondissements* (administrative district) 1er to 5e, 10e and 19e must go to the Hôtel de Police at 80 blvd de Sébastopol, 3e (metro Réaumur Sébastopol); those in arrondissements 6e and 7e and 13e to 16e should report to the Hôtel de Police at 114–116 ave du Maine, 14e (metro Gaîté);

for those in arrondissements 8e, 9e, 17e and 18e it's the Hôtel de Police at 19–21 rue Truffaut, 17e (metro place Clichy or La Fourche); and those in arrondissements 11e–12e and 20e should go to the Hôtel de Police at 163 rue de Charenton, 12e (metro Reuilly Didreot). All open 9 am to 4.30 pm weekdays (to 4 pm on Friday).

Students of all nationalities must apply for a carte de séjour at the Centre des Étudiants at 13 rue Miollis, 15e (metro Cambronne or Ségur). It opens from 8.45 am to 4.30 pm weekdays (to 4 pm on Friday).

Visa Extensions Tourist visas *cannot* be extended except in emergencies (such as medical problems). If you're in Paris and have an urgent problem, you should call the Préfecture de Police (☎ 01 53 71 51 68) for guidance.

If you don't need a visa to visit France, you'll almost certainly qualify for another automatic three-month stay if you take the train to Geneva or Brussels, say, and then re-enter France. The fewer recent French entry stamps you have in your passport the easier this is likely to be. If you needed a visa the first time around, one way to extend your stay is to go to a French consulate in a neighbouring country and apply for another one there.

People entering France by rail or road often don't have their passports checked, much less stamped, and even at airports don't be surprised if the official just glances at your passport and hands it back without stamping the date of entry. Fear not: you're in France legally, whether or not you had to apply for a visa before arriving (though at some point, to show your date of entry, you may be asked to produce the plane, train or ferry ticket you arrived with). If you prefer to have your passport stamped (because, for example, you expect to have to prove when you last entered the country), it may take a little bit of running around to find the right border official.

Travel Insurance

You should seriously consider taking out travel insurance. This not only covers you for medical expenses and luggage theft or loss but also for cancellation or delays in your travel arrangements. Cover depends on your insurance and type of airline ticket, so ask both your insurer and your ticket-issuing agency to explain where you stand. Ticket loss is also covered by travel insurance. EU citizens on public health insurance schemes should note that they're generally covered by reciprocal arrangements in France (see Health later in the chapter for more details).

Paying for your airline ticket with a credit card often provides limited travel accident insurance, and you may be able to reclaim the payment if the operator doesn't deliver. In the UK, for instance, institutions issuing credit cards are required by law to reimburse consumers if a company goes into liquidation and the amount in contention is more than UK£100. Ask your credit-card company what it's prepared to cover.

Driving Licence & Permits

Many non-European drivers licences are valid in France, but it's still a good idea to bring along an International Driving Permit, which can make life much simpler, especially when hiring cars and motorbikes. Basically a multilingual translation of the vehicle class and personal details noted on your local driver's licence, an IDP is not valid unless accompanied by your original licence. An IDP can be obtained for a small fee from your local automobile association – bring along a passport photo and a valid licence.

Hostel Cards

A Hostelling International (HI) card is necessary only at official *auberges de jeunesse* (youth hostels), but it may get you small discounts at other hostels. If you don't pick one up before leaving home, you can buy one at almost any official French hostel for 70/100FF if you're under 26 years of age/26 or older. One night's membership (where available) costs 19FF, and a family card is 150FF. See the HI Web site at www.iyhf.org for further details

Student, Youth & Teachers Cards

An International Student Identity Card (ISIC) can pay for itself through half-price admissions, discounted air and ferry tickets, and cheap meals in student cafeterias. Many places stipulate a maximum age, usually 24 or 25. In Paris, ISIC cards are issued by the Accueil des Jeunes en France (AJF) and other student travel agencies for 60FF (see Student Travel Agencies under Information in the Paris chapter). The ISIC Web site is at ww.istc.org.

If you're under 26 but not a student, you can apply for a GO25 card issued by the Federation of International Youth Travel Organisations (FIYTO; 60FF), which entitles you to much the same discounts as an ISIC and is also issued by student unions or student travel agencies.

A Carte Jeunes (120FF for one year) is available to anyone under 26 who has been in France for at least six months. It gets you discounts on things like air tickets, car rental, sports events, concerts and movies. In France, details are available from ☎ 08 03 00 12 26; by Minitel key in 3615 CARTE JEUNES. In Paris, qualifying young people can pick one up at AJF and other student travel agencies.

Teachers, professional artists, museum conservators and certain categories of students are admitted to some museums free. Bring along proof of affiliation, such as an International Teacher Identity Card (ITIC; 60FF).

Seniors Cards

Reduced entry prices are charged for people aged over 60 at most cultural centres, including museums, galleries and public theatres. Société Nationale des Chemins de Fer (SNCF) issues the Carte Senior (which replaces the Carte Vermeil) to those aged over 60, which gives reductions of 20% to 50% on train tickets. It costs 140FF for a card valid for purchasing four train tickets or 285FF for a card valid for one year.

Camping Card International

The Camping Card International (CCI; formerly the Camping Carnet; issued by the

Geneva-based Alliance Internationale de Tourisme) is a form of ID that can be used instead of a passport when checking into a camp site and includes third-party insurance (up to Sfr2.5 million) for damage you may cause. As a result, many camp sites offer a small discount if you sign in with one. CCIs are issued by automobile associations, camping federations and, sometimes, on the spot at camp sites. In the UK, the RAC issues them to its members for UK£4. You can also pick one up in Paris for 30FF at the Fédération Française de la Randonnée Pédestre (☎ 01 44 89 93 93), 14 rue Riquet.

Carte Musées et Monuments

The Carte Musées et Monuments (Museums & Monuments Card) can be used to gain quick entry (no queuing) to around 70 venues in Paris and the Île de France, including the Louvre and the Musée d'Orsay. One/three/five days costs 80/160/240FF. There is no reduced rate for students or senior travellers. In France details are available from ☎ 01 44 78 45 81, fax 01 44 78 12 22; or from the Web site, which is at www.intermusees.com.

Photocopies

The hassles brought on by losing your passport can be considerably reduced if you have a record of its number and issue date or, even better, photocopies of the relevant data pages. A photocopy of your birth certificate can also be useful. Remember that you can store and protect vital information that can be accessed while travelling in the Ekno 'virtual' travel vault (www.ekno .lonelyplanet.com).

Also record the serial numbers of your travellers cheques (cross them off as you cash them) and photocopies of your credit cards, airline ticket and other travel documents. Keep all this material separate from your passport, cheques and cash, and leave extra copies with someone you can rely on back home. Add some emergency money, say US$50 in cash, to this separate stash as well. If you do lose your passport, notify the police immediately to get a statement, and contact your nearest consulate.

EMBASSIES & CONSULATES
Your Own Embassy

It's important to realise what your own embassy – the embassy of the country of which you are a citizen – can and can't do to help you if you get into trouble. Generally speaking, it won't be much help in emergencies if the trouble you're in is remotely your own fault. Remember that you are bound by the laws of the country you are in. Your embassy will not be sympathetic if you end up in jail after committing a crime locally, even if such actions are legal in your own country.

In genuine emergencies you might get some assistance, but only if other channels have been exhausted. For example, if you need to get home urgently, a free ticket home is exceedingly unlikely – the embassy would expect you to have insurance. If you have all your money and documents stolen, it might assist with getting a new passport, but a loan for onward travel is out of the question.

French Embassies & Consulates

Don't expect France's diplomatic and consular representatives abroad to be helpful or even civil at times, though you do come across the odd exception. Almost all of them have information posted at Web site www.france.diplomatie.fr. Addresses include the following:

Australia
  Embassy: (☎ 02-621 60100, fax 621 60127, @ embassy@france.net.au) 6 Perth Ave, Yarralumla, ACT 2600
  Consulate: (☎ 03-982 00921, fax 982 09363, @ cgmelb@france.net.au) 492 St Kilda Rd, Level 4, Melbourne, Vic 3004
  Consulate: (☎ 02-926 15779, fax 928 31210, @ cgsydney@france.net.au) 20th floor, St Martin's Tower, 31 Market St, Sydney, NSW 2000
Belgium
  Embassy: (☎ 02-548 8711, fax 513 6871, @ amba@ambafrance.be) 65 rue Ducale, 1000 Brussels
  Consulate: (☎ 02-229 8500, fax 229 8510, @ consulat.france@skynet.bruxelles.be) 12A place de Louvain, 1000 Brussels 82
Canada
  Embassy: (☎ 613-789 1795, fax 562 3735,

@ consulat@amba-ottowa.fr) 42 Sussex Drive,
Ottawa, Ont K1M 2C9
Consulate: (☎ 514-878 4385, fax 878 3981,
@ fsltmral@cam.org) 26th floor, 1 place Ville
Marie, Montreal, Que H3B 4S3
Consulate: (☎ 416-925 8041, fax 925 3076,
@ fsltto@idirect.com) 130 Bloor St West,
Suite 400, Toronto, Ont M5S 1N5

Germany
Embassy: (☎ 030-20 639 000, fax 639 010)
Kochstrasse 6–7, D-10969 Berlin
Consulates: (☎ 030-885 902 43, fax 882
5295), Kurfürstendamm 211, 10719 Berlin
(☎ 089-419 4110, fax 419 41141)
Möhlstrasse 5, 81675 Munich

Ireland
(☎ 01-260 1666, fax 283 0178,
@ consul@ambafrance.ie) 36 Ailesbury Rd,
Ballsbridge, Dublin 4

Italy
Embassy: (☎ 06-686 011, fax 860 1360,
@ france-italia@france-italia.it) Piazza
Farnese 67, 00186 Rome
Consulate: (☎ 06-6880 6437, fax 6860 1260,
@ consulfrance-rome@iol.it) Via Giulia 251,
00186 Rome

Netherlands
Embassy: (☎ 070-312 5800, fax 312 5854)
Smidsplein 1, 2514 BT, The Hague
Consulate: (☎ 020-624 8346, fax 626 0841,
@ consulfr@euronet.nl) Vijzelgracht 2, 1000
HA, Amsterdam

New Zealand
(☎ 04-384 2555, fax 384 2577,
@ consulfrance@actrix.gen.nz) Rural Bank
Building, 34–42 Manners Street, Wellington

Spain
Embassy: (☎ 91-423 8900, fax 423 8901)
Calle de Salustiano, Olozaga 9, 28001 Madrid
Consulate: (☎ 91-700 7800, fax 700 7801,
@ creire@ConsulFrance-Madrid.org)
Calle Marques de la Enseñada 10, 28004
Madrid
Consulate: (☎ 93-270 3000, fax 270 0349,
@ info@consulat-france.org) Ronda Universi-
tat 22, 08007 Barcelona

Switzerland
Embassy: (☎ 031-359 2111, fax 352 2191,
@ ambassade.fr@iprolink.ch) Schosshalden-
strasse 46, 3006 Berne
Consulate: (☎ 022-319 0000, fax 319 0072,
@ consualt.France@ties.itu.int) 11 rue Imbert
Galloix, 1205 Geneva
Consulate: (☎ 01-268 8585, fax 268 8500,
@ consulat.france.zurich@swissonline.ch)
Mühlebachstrasse 7, 8008 Zurich

UK
Embassy: (☎ 020-7201 1000, fax 7201 1004,

@ press@ambafrance.org) 58 Knightsbridge,
London SW1X 7JT
Consulate: (☎ 020-7838 2000, fax 7838 2018)
21 Cromwell Rd, London SW7 2EN. The visa
section is at 6A Cromwell Place, London SW7
2EW (☎ 020-7838 2051).

USA
Embassy: (☎ 202-944 6000, fax 944 6166,
@ visas-washington@amb-wash.fr) 4101
Reservoir Rd NW, Washington DC 20007
Consulate: (☎ 212-606 3600/88, fax 606 3620,
@ visa@franceconsulatny.org) 934 Fifth Ave,
New York, NY 10021
Consulate: (☎ 415-397 4330, fax 433 8357,
@ consul-general@accueil-sfo.org) 540 Bush
St, San Francisco, CA 94108
Other consulates are located in Atlanta,
Boston, Chicago, Houston, Los Angeles,
Miami and New Orleans.

Embassies & Consulates in France

All foreign embassies can be found in Paris.
Canada, the UK and the USA also have
consulates in other major cities. The locations of some major embassies are indicated
by reference to the colour maps (Maps 1 to
8) that appear in the Paris chapter.

To find an embassy or consulate not
listed here, consult the *Yellow Pages* (*Pages
Jaunes*; look under Ambassades et Con-
sulats) in Paris.

Countries with representation in Paris include the following:

Australia
(Map 4, ☎ 01 40 59 33 00, metro Bir Hakeim)
4 rue Jean Rey, 15e. The consular section
opens 9.15 am to noon and 2 to 4.30 pm
weekdays.

Belgium
(☎ 01 44 09 39 39, metro Charles de Gaulle-
Étoile) 9 rue de Tilsitt, 17e

Canada
(Map 2, ☎ 01 44 43 29 00, metro Franklin D
Roosevelt) 35 ave Montaigne, 8e. Consular
services are available 9 am to noon and 2 to
5 pm weekdays.

Germany
Embassy: (Map 2, ☎ 01 53 83 45 00,
@ ambassade@amb-allemagne.fr, metro
Franklin D Roosevelt) 13–15 ave Franklin D
Roosevelt, 8e
Consulate: (☎ same, metro Iéna)
34 ave d'Iéna, 16e

Ireland
(Map 2, ☎ 01 44 17 67 00, ☎ 01 44 17 67 67 after hours, Minitel 3615 IRLANDE, metro Argentine) 4 rue Rude, 16e. The chancellery opens 9.30 am to noon weekdays or by appointment.

Italy
Embassy: (☎ 01 49 54 03 00, metro Rue du Bac) 51 rue de Varenne, 7e
Consulate: (☎ 01 44 30 47 00, metro La Muette) 5 blvd Émile Augier, 16e

Netherlands
(☎ 01 40 62 33 00, metro St-François Xavier) 7 rue Eblé, 7e

New Zealand
(Map 2, ☎ 01 45 01 43 43, metro Victor Hugo) 7 ter rue Léonard de Vinci, 16e. Consular services are available 9 am to 1 pm and 2 to 5.30 pm weekdays (8.30 am to 2 pm on Friday in July and August).

Spain
(☎ 01 44 43 18 00, metro Alma Marceau) 22 ave Marceau, 8e

Switzerland
(☎ 01 49 55 67 00, metro Varenne) 142 rue de Grenelle, 7e

UK
Embassy: (Map 2, ☎ 01 44 51 31 00, @ ambassade@amb-grandebretagne.fr, metro Concorde) 35 rue du Faubourg St-Honoré, 8e
Consulate: (Map 2, ☎ 01 44 51 31 02, metro Madeleine) 18 bis rue d'Anjou, 8e. The consulate opens 9 am to noon and 2.30 to 5 pm on weekdays.

USA
Embassy: (Map 2, ☎ 01 43 12 22 22, @ ambassade@amb-usa.fr, metro Concorde), 2 ave Gabriel, 8e
Consulate: (Map 2, ☎ 01 43 12 23 47, metro Concorde) 2 rue St-Florentin, 1er. The American Services section opens 9 am to 3 pm weekdays.

CUSTOMS

The usual allowances apply to duty-free goods purchased at airports or on ferries outside the EU (from June 1999): tobacco (200 cigarettes, 50 cigars, or 250g of loose tobacco), alcohol (1L of strong liquor or 2L of less than 22% alcohol by volume and 2L of wine), coffee (500g or 200g of extracts) and 100g of tea or 40g tea extracts; and perfume (50g of perfume and 0.25L of eau de toilette).

Do not confuse these with duty-paid items (including alcohol and tobacco) bought at normal shops and supermarkets in another EU country and brought into France, where certain goods might be more expensive. Then the allowances are more than generous: 800 cigarettes, 200 cigars, or 1kg of loose tobacco; 10L of spirits (more than 22% alcohol by volume), 20L of fortified wine or aperitif, 90L of wine or 110L of beer.

Note that duty-free shopping within the EU was abolished in mid-1999. This means that you can still enter an EU country with duty-free items from countries outside the EU, but you can't buy duty-free goods in, say, France and go to the UK.

MONEY
Currency

Until the euro is introduced (see the boxed text 'Bonjour Euro, Adieu Franc' on p68), the national currency is the French franc, abbreviated in this book by the letters 'FF'. One franc is divided into 100 centimes. French coins come in denominations of 5, 10, 20 and 50 centimes (0.5FF) and 1, 2, 5, 10 and 20FF. The two highest denominations have silvery centres and brass edges. It's a good idea to keep a supply of various coins for parking meters, laundrettes, tolls, etc.

Banknotes are issued in denominations of 20FF, 50FF, 100FF, 200FF and 500FF. It is often difficult to get change for a 500FF bill.

Exchange Rates

country	unit		franc
Australia	A$1	=	4.10FF
Canada	C$1	=	4.97FF
EU	€1	=	6.56FF
Germany	DM1	=	3.35FF
Japan	¥100	=	6.92FF
New Zealand	NZ$1	=	3.10FF
Spain	100pta	=	3.94FF
UK	UK£1	=	10.88FF
USA	US$1	=	7.43FF

Exchanging Money

Wherever you exchange money, you can tell how good the rate is by checking the spread between the rates for *achat* (buy rates, that is, what they'll give you for foreign cash or travellers cheques) and *vente* (sell rates, that is, the rate at which they sell foreign currency to people going abroad) – the greater the difference, the further each is from the inter-bank rate (printed daily in newspapers, including the *International Herald Tribune*).

Banks, exchange bureaux and post offices often give a better rate for travellers cheques than for cash. Major train stations and fancy hotels also have exchange facilities, which usually operate in the evening, at the weekend and during holidays, but the rates are generally poor.

Cash In general, cash is not a very good way to carry money. Not only can it be stolen, but in France you don't get an optimal exchange rate. The Banque de France, for instance, usually pays about 2.5% *more* for travellers cheques, which more than makes up for the 1% commission usually involved in buying cheques.

Bring along the equivalent of about US$100 in low-denomination notes, which makes it easier to exchange small sums of money if necessary (for example, at the end of your stay). Because of the risk of counterfeiting it may be difficult to exchange US$100 notes (even the new ones with the oversized picture of Benjamin Franklin).

Post offices often offer the best exchange rates in town, and accept banknotes in a variety of currencies as well as travellers cheques issued by American Express (Amex) or Visa. The commission for travellers cheques in French francs is 1.2% to 1.5%; minimum charges vary from 16FF to 25FF. Cheques in US dollars are cashed for free.

The Banque de France, France's central bank, used to offer the country's best exchange rates but nowadays the post offices are a better deal. Branches open Monday to Friday but only offer walk-in currency services in the morning.

Commercial banks usually charge a stiff 20FF to 35FF per foreign currency transaction. The rates offered vary, so it pays to compare. Hours are usually from 8 or 9 am to sometime between 11.30 and 1 pm, and 1.30 or 2 to 4.30 or 5 pm, Monday to Fri-

day or Tuesday to Saturday. Exchange services may end half an hour before closing time. See the Business Hours section later in the chapter for details of other standard opening times.

In big cities, exchange bureaux *(bureaux de change)* are faster and easier, open longer hours and give better rates than banks. Your best bet is to familiarise yourself with the rates offered by the post office and compare them with those on offer at exchange bureaux (which are not generally allowed to charge commissions). On small transactions, even exchange places with less-than-optimal rates may leave you with more francs in your pocket.

All major train stations have exchange bureaux – some run by Thomas Cook – but their rates are less than stellar.

Travellers Cheques & Eurocheques
Commercial banks charge something like 22FF to 35FF to cash travellers cheques. The post office will cash franc travellers cheques for 1.2% to 1.5% commission, with a minimum fee of 16FF to 25FF; dollar-denoted travellers cheques are cashed for free. Amex offices don't charge commission on their own travellers cheques (but 3% or at least 40FF on other brands).

The most flexible travellers cheques are issued by Amex (in US dollars or French francs) and Visa (in French francs) because they can be changed at many post offices.

Keep a record of cheque numbers, where they were purchased and which ones have been cashed, separate from the cheques themselves. If your Amex travellers cheques are lost or stolen in France, you can call ☎ 08 00 90 86 00, a 24-hour toll-free number.

In Paris, reimbursements can be made at the main Amex office (Map 2, ☎ 01 47 77 77 75, metro Auber or Opéra), 11 rue Scribe, 9e, from 9.30 am to 6.30 pm weekdays and from 10 am to 5.30 pm on Saturday. There are Amex branches in other large towns (see the Money sections of the regional chapters).

If you lose your Thomas Cook cheques, you can contact any Thomas Cook bureau

Bonjour Euro, Adieu Franc

You'll come across two sets of prices at hotels, restaurants, department stores and so on while visiting France. Since 1999 both the franc and Europe's new currency – the euro – have been legal tender, and businesses must now by law list prices in both currencies. Along with the franc, the currencies of 10 other EU members are being phased out to complete Europe's monetary union. The advent of the cash euro will end the 642-year reign of the franc, which began in 1360 when King Jean le Bon struck coins to signify that his part of France was *franc des anglois* (free of English domination).

Euro coins and banknotes will be introduced in January 2002; before that time payment in euros can only be made by credit card or cheque. Both the euro and the franc will remain in circulation until July 2002, when the franc will be withdrawn and prices displayed in euros only.

The scheme is open to abuse; a restaurant might, for example, print euro prices larger and more prominently on the menu than franc prices during the period of coexistence. Check your bill carefully, too – your total might have the amount in francs, but a credit card company may bill you in the euro equivalent.

Fortunately, the euro has many benefits – cross-border travel will become easier, and prices in the 11 'euro-zone' countries will be immediately comparable. Also, once euro notes and coins are issued, you won't need to change money when travelling within most of the EU. Indeed, even EU countries not participating (such as the UK) may price goods in euros and accept cash euros over shop counters.

The EU has a dedicated euro site, http://europa.eu.int/euro, and you can also check the currency converter at www.oanda.com for the latest rates.

Australia	A$1	=	€0.62
Canada	C$1	=	€0.76
France	1FF	=	€0.15
Germany	DM1	=	€0.51
Japan	¥100	=	€1.06
New Zealand	NZ$1	=	€0.47
Spain	100 pta	=	€0.60
United Kingdom	UK£1	=	€1.66
United States	US$1	=	€1.13

for example, in a major train station such as the Gare du Nord (Map 3, ☎ 01 42 80 11 50) or at 4 blvd St-Michel, 6e (Map 6), ☎ 01 46 34 23 81) – for replacements. Their customer service bureau can be contacted toll-free on ☎ 08 00 90 83 30.

Eurocheques, available if you have a European bank account, are guaranteed up to a certain limit. When cashing them (for example, at post offices), you'll be asked to show your Eurocheque card, and perhaps a passport or ID card.

Eurocheques are relatively unpopular with merchants and hotels because of the bank charges attached.

ATMs The cheapest way to change money abroad is probably via Automatic Teller Machines (ATMs) – known in French as DABs *(distributeurs automatiques de billets)* or *points d'argent* – which also draw on your home account at a superior exchange rate. Most ATMs will also give you a cash advance through your Visa or MasterCard (see Credit Cards later in the chapter). Some non-US ATMs won't accept PIN codes with more than four digits – ask your bank how to handle this. There are plenty of ATMs in France linked to the international Cirrus, Plus and Maestro networks. If you normally remember your PIN code as a string of letters, translate it back into numbers, as keyboards may not have letters indicated.

Credit Cards The next-cheapest way to pay during your trip is by credit or debit card. Visa (Carte Bleue) is the most widely accepted, followed by MasterCard (Access or Eurocard). Amex cards are useful at more upmarket establishments, allow you to get cash at certain ATMs and over a dozen Amex offices in France. In general, all three cards can be used for train travel, restaurant visits and cash advances.

When you get a cash advance against your Visa or MasterCard credit card account, your issuer charges a transaction fee which can be as high as US$10 *plus* interest. Also, many banks charge a commission of 30FF or more; over the past year, many credit-card issuers have started taking a 1% to 4% fee for transactions abroad, which is cheeky because it comes on top of the usual 1% foreign-currency charge. The moral here: check with your card issuer before leaving home.

You can avoid all this by depositing funds into your account ahead of time, effectively turning your credit card into an interest-bearing bank account – this method usually incurs the lowest fees.

It may be impossible to get a lost Visa or MasterCard reissued until you get home, so two different credit cards are safer than one. If your Visa card is lost or stolen, call Carte Bleue on ☎ 08 36 69 08 80 or 08 00 90 20 33, 24 hours a day. To get a replacement card you'll have to deal with the issuer.

Report a lost MasterCard, Eurocard or Access to Eurocard France (☎ 01 45 67 53 53) and, if you can, to your credit card issuer back home (for cards from the USA, call ☎ 314-275 6690). In Paris, Eurocard France at 16 rue Lecourbe, 15e (Map 4, metro Sèvres Lecourbe), opens 9.30 am to 5.30 pm, Monday to Friday.

If your Amex card is lost or stolen, call ☎ 01 47 77 70 00 or ☎ 01 47 77 72 00; both are staffed 24 hours a day. In an emergency, Amex card holders from the USA can call collect on ☎ 202-783 7474 or ☎ 202-677 2442. If necessary, on-the-spot replacements can be arranged at any Amex office (see Travellers Cheques & Eurocheques earlier in the chapter).

A lost Diners Club card should be reported on ☎ 01 47 62 75 75.

International Transfers Telegraphic transfers are not very expensive but, despite their name, can be quite slow. Be sure to specify the name of the bank and the name and address of the branch where you'd like to pick it up.

It's quicker and easier to have money wired via Amex (US$50 for US$1000). Western Union's Money Transfer system (☎ 01 43 54 46 12) and Thomas Cook's MoneyGram service (☎ 01 47 58 21 00) are also popular.

Security Don't carry more money than you need, and keep your credit cards in a concealed pouch or a hotel safe. Always keep some spare travellers cheques or cash on hand for an emergency. See also Dangers & Annoyances later in the chapter.

Costs

By staying in hostels or showerless, toilet-less rooms in budget hotels and having picnics rather than dining out, you can travel around France for about US$30 a day per person (US$35 in Paris). A couple staying in two-star hotels and eating one cheap restaurant meal each day should count on spending at least US$65 a day per person, not including car rental. Lots of moving from place to place, eating in restaurants, drinking wine or treating yourself to France's many little luxuries can increase these figures considerably.

Discounts Museums, cinemas, the SNCF, ferry companies and other institutions offer all sorts of price breaks to people under the age of either 25 or 26, students with ISIC cards (age limits may apply) and *le troisième age* (seniors, that is people over 60 or, in some cases, 65). Look for the words *demi-tarif* or *tarif réduit* (half-price tariff or reduced rate) on rate charts and then ask if you qualify.

euro currency converter €1 = 6.56FF

Those under 18 get an even wider range of discounts, including free admission to Musées Nationaux (museums run by the French government). For information on the Carte Musées et Monuments, which allows entry to around 70 venues in Paris, see that listing under Documents.

Ways to Save Money There are lots of things you can do to shave francs off your daily expenditures. A few suggestions:

• Travel with someone else – single rooms usually cost only marginally less than doubles. Triples and quads (often with only two beds) are even cheaper per person. Budget hotel rooms often cost less per person than hostel beds.
• You'll get the best exchange rate and low commissions at post offices and banks by using a credit card.
• Avoid travel in high season, when accommodation prices often go up (for example, in Corsica and the Côte d'Azur during July and August, and the Alps in February).
• Avail yourself of France's many free sights: bustling marketplaces, tree-lined avenues, cathedrals, churches, parks, canal towpaths, nature reserves and so on.
• Visit museums on days when admission is free or discounted. In Paris, for instance, the Louvre is more than 40% cheaper after 3 pm and free on the first Sunday of every month.
• When calling home, avoid France's pricey International Direct Dial (IDD) services – use a phonecard and ask to be rung back.
• Bring along a pocketknife and eating utensils so you can have picnics instead of restaurant meals. The cheapest food is sold at supermarkets and outdoor markets.
• Carry a water bottle so you don't have to pay for a pricey cold drink each time you're thirsty (there are few public drinking fountains in France).
• In restaurants, order the *menu* (set menu) and ask for tap water rather than soft drinks, mineral water or wine.
• Avoid taking trains which incur supplements or reservation fees. For information on rail passes and reduced-rate train tickets, see under Train in the Getting Around chapter.
• If you'll be hiring a car, arrange for rental before you leave home. If you'll be staying at least a month, hire a purchase-repurchase car (see Purchase-Repurchase Plans under Car & Motorbike in the Getting Around chapter).

• Buy discount bus/metro passes or carnets of reduced-price tickets rather than single tickets.

Tipping & Bargaining

French law requires that restaurant, cafe and hotel bills include the service charge (usually 10 to 15%), so a *pourboire* (tip) is neither necessary nor expected in most cases. However, most people leave a few francs in restaurants, unless the service was bad. They rarely tip in cafes and bars when they've just had a coffee or a drink.

In taxis, the usual tip is 2FF no matter what the fare, with the maximum about 5FF. People in France rarely bargain, except at flea markets.

Taxes & Refunds

France's VAT is 19.6% on most goods except food, medicine and books, for which it's 5.5%. It is as high as 33% on items such as watches, cameras and video cassettes. Prices that include VAT are often marked TTC (*toutes taxes comprises*, 'all taxes included').

If you're not an EU resident, you can get a refund of most of the VAT (TVA in French) provided that: you're over 15; you'll be spending less than six months in France; you purchase goods (not more than 10 of the same item) worth at least 1200FF (tax included) at a single shop; and the shop offers *vente en détaxe* (duty-free sales).

Present a passport at the time of purchase and ask for a *bordereau de détaxe* (export sales invoice). Some shops may refund less than the 17.1% of the purchase price you are entitled to in order to cover expenses involved in the refund procedure.

As you leave France or another EU country, have all three pages (yellow, pink and green) of the bordereau validated by the country's customs officials at the airport or border. Customs officials will take the yellow and pink sheets and the stamped self-addressed envelope provided by the store; the green sheet is your receipt. The pink sheet is then sent to the shop where you made your purchase, which will then make a *virement* (transfer of funds) in the form you have requested, such as by French-franc cheque or directly into your account. Be prepared for waits of up to three months.

For more information contact the customs information centre on ☎ 01 53 24 68 24.

Instant Refunds If you're flying out of Orly or Roissy Charles de Gaulle airports, certain stores can arrange for you to receive your refund as you're leaving the country. You must make arrangements for such at the time of purchase.

When you arrive at the airport you have to do three things:

- Up to three hours before your flight leaves, you need to take your bordereau, passport, air ticket and the things you purchased (don't put them in your checked luggage) to the *douane* (customs) office so they can stamp the three copies of the bordereau (one of which they'll keep).
- Go to an Aéroports de Paris (ADP) information counter, where they will check the figures and put another stamp on the documents.
- Go to the *douane de détaxe* (customs refund window) or the exchange bureau indicated on your bordereau to pick up your refund.

POST & COMMUNICATIONS

Postal services in France are fast, reliable, bureaucratic and expensive. About three-quarters of domestic letters arrive the day after they've been mailed.

Each of France's 17,000 post offices is marked with a yellow or brown sign reading 'La Poste'; older branches may also be marked with the letters PTT. To mail things, go to a postal window marked '*toutes opérations*'.

Hours are generally 8.30 or 9 am to 5 or 6 pm weekdays, maybe with a midday break, and Saturday mornings. See the Business Hours section later in this chapter for details of other standard opening times.

Postal Rates

Domestic letters up to 20g cost 3FF. Postcards and letters up to 20g cost 3FF within the EU; 3.80FF to most of the remainder of Europe; 3.90FF to Africa; 4.40FF to the USA, Canada and the Middle East; and 5.20FF to Australasia. Aerograms cost 5FF to all destinations.

Worldwide express mail delivery, called Chronopost (☎ 01 46 48 10 00, Minitel 3614 CHRONOPOST for information), costs a fortune.

Sea-mail services have stopped, so sending packages overseas sometimes costs almost as much as the exorbitant overweight fees charged by airlines, even if you use *économique* (discount) airmail. Packages weighing over 2kg may not be accepted at branch post offices – in Paris, they're handled by the *poste principale* of each arrondissement. Post offices sell smallish boxes in four different sizes (6.50FF to 12.50FF).

Sending Mail

All mail to France *must* include the five-digit postcode, which begins with the two-digit number of the department. In Paris, virtually all postcodes begin with 750 and end with the two-digit arrondissement number, for example 75004 for the 4e arrondissement. The local postcode is listed under the main heading of each city or town in this book.

Mail to France should be addressed as follows:

> John SMITH
> 8, rue de la Poste
> 75020 Paris
> FRANCE

The surname (family name) should be written in capital letters. As you'll notice, the French put a comma after the street number and don't capitalise 'rue', 'av', 'bd' (boulevard), and so on. The notation 'CEDEX' after a town name simply means that mail sent to that address is collected at the post office, rather than delivered to the door.

Receiving Mail

Poste Restante To have mail sent to you via poste restante (general delivery), available at all French post offices, have it addressed as follows:

> SMITH, John
> Poste Restante
> Recette Principale
> 76000 Rouen
> FRANCE

Write your *nom de famille* (surname or family name) first and in capital letters. In case your friends back home forget, always check under the first letter of your *prénom* (first name). There's a 3FF charge for every piece of poste-restante mail you pick up weighing less than 20g; for anything between 20g and 100g, the fee is 4FF. It's usually possible to forward *(faire suivre)* mail from one poste restante address to another. You'll need to present your passport or national ID card when you pick up your mail.

Poste-restante mail not addressed to a particular branch goes to the city's *recette principale* (main post office) whether or not you include the words Recette Principale in the address. If you want it sent to a specific branch post office mentioned in this book (most of which are generally centrally located and marked on the maps), write the street address mentioned in the text.

You can also receive mail (but not parcels or envelopes larger than an A4 sheet of paper) in care of Amex. If you don't have an Amex card or their travellers cheques, there's a 5FF charge each time you check to see if you've received something (some offices waive the fee if there's nothing for you). The office will hold mail for 30 days before returning it to the sender. After that, having them forward it to another Amex office costs 15FF for two months. Amex addresses are given under Money in the relevant city listings in the regional chapters.

Telephone

A quarter of a century ago, France had one of the worst telephone systems in Western Europe. But thanks to massive investment in the late 1970s and early '80s, the country now has one of the most modern and sophisticated telecommunications systems in the world.

International Dialling To call from outside France, dial your country's international access code, then dial 33 (France's country code), then omit the 0 at the beginning of the 10-digit local number.

To call someone outside France, dial the international access code (00), the country code, the area code (without the initial zero if there is one) and the local number. International Direct Dial (IDD) calls to almost anywhere in the world can be placed from public telephones. Useful country codes include:

Andorra	☎ 376
Australia	☎ 61
Canada	☎ 1
Germany	☎ 49
Hong Kong	☎ 852
India	☎ 91
Ireland	☎ 353
Japan	☎ 81
Monaco	☎ 377
New Zealand	☎ 64
Singapore	☎ 65
South Africa	☎ 27
UK	☎ 44
USA	☎ 1

If you don't know the country code *(indicatif pays)* and it's not posted in the telephone cabin, consult a telephone book or dial ☎ 12 (directory inquiries).

To make a reverse-charges (collect) call *(en PCV*, pronounced '**pey-sey-vey**') or a person-to-person call *(avec préavis*, pronounced 'ah-**vek** preh-ah-**vee**'), dial 00, and then dial 33 plus the country code of the place you're calling (for the USA and Canada, dial 11 instead of 1). Don't be surprised if you get a recording and have to wait a while. If you're using a public phone and want to place operator-assisted calls through the international operator, you must insert a phonecard (or, in the case of public coin telephones, 1FF).

For directory inquiries for numbers outside France, dial 00 then 3312 and finally the relevant country code (again, 11 instead of 1 for the USA and Canada). You may be put on hold for quite a while. In public phones, you can access this service without a télécarte, but from home phones the charge is a staggering 19.70FF per inquiry.

Toll-free 1-800 numbers in the USA and Canada cannot be called from overseas except through certain Country Direct services, in which case you bear the cost.

Urban Orienteering

When a building is put up in a location where they've run out of consecutive street numbers, a new address is formed by fusing the number of an adjacent building with the notations *bis* (twice), *ter* (thrice) or, rarely, *quater* (four times). Thus, the street numbers 17 bis or 89 ter are the equivalent of 17A or 89B.

In larger cities, especially Paris, the street doors of many apartment buildings can be opened only if someone has given you the entry code, which is changed periodically. Outside intercoms are more common in provincial cities. In some buildings, the entry code device is de-activated during the day, but to get in (or out) you still have to push a button (usually marked *porte*) to release the electric catch.

The doors of many French apartments are completely unmarked: not only are the occupants' names nowhere in sight, but there isn't even an apartment number. To know which door to knock on, you'll usually be given cryptic instructions, such as *cinquième étage, premier à gauche* (5th floor, first on the left) or *troisième étage, droite droite* (3rd floor, turn right twice). In France (and in this guidebook), the 1st floor is the floor above the *rez-de-chaussée* (ground floor).

International Rates Daytime calls to other parts of Europe cost from 1.64FF to 3.22FF per minute. Reduced tariffs (0.99FF to 2.28FF) generally apply from 7 pm to 8 am weekdays, at the weekend and on public holidays.

Nondiscount calls to continental USA and Canada are 1.64FF per minute from 1 to 7 pm weekdays. The price then drops to 0.99FF. The rate to Alaska, Hawaii and the Caribbean is a whopping 9.22FF per minute (7.34FF discount rate).

Full-price calls to Australia, Japan, New Zealand, Hong Kong and Singapore are 4.26FF per minute. A discount rate of 3.07FF per minute applies from 7 pm to 8 am daily, at the weekend and on public holidays.

Calls to other parts of Asia, South America and non-Francophone Africa are generally 5.45FF to 9.22FF per minute, though to some countries a rate of 4.26FF to 7.34FF will apply at certain times.

Country Direct Services Country Direct lets you phone home by billing the long-distance carrier you use at home. The numbers can be dialled from public phones without inserting a phonecard. Services include AT&T (☎ 08 00 99 00 11), MCI (☎ 08 00 99 00 19) Sprint (☎ 08 00 99 00 87) and Worldcom (☎ 08 00 99 00 13), all US-based; BT (☎ 08 00 99 02 44) and Mercury (☎ 08 00 99 09 44), both UK-based; and Telstra (☎ 0800 99 00 61) and Optus (☎ 08 00 99 20 61) in Australia.

Note that the rates aren't likely to be brilliant – you'll do better using a French phonecard (see Telephone Cards later in the chapter).

Domestic Dialling France has five telephone dialling areas. To make calls within any region, just dial the 10-digit number. The same applies for calls between regions and from metropolitan France to French overseas departments and vice versa. The five regional area codes are:

01	the Paris region
02	the north-west
03	the north-east
04	the south-east (including Corsica)
05	the south-west

For France Telecom's directory inquiries *(services des renseignements)*, dial ☎ 12. Not all operators speak English. The call is free from public phones but costs 4.46FF per call from private lines.

There is no way to make a domestic reverse-charges call. Instead, ask the person you're calling to ring you back (see Public Phones later in the chapter).

Domestic Tariffs Local calls are quite cheap, even at the peak tariff: one calling unit (0.81FF with a télécarte) lasts for three minutes. For calls anywhere in the country outside your local zone, one unit lasts 39 seconds.

The regular rate for calls within France, known as the *tarif rouge* (red tariff), applies 8 am to 7 pm Monday to Friday. The rest of the time, you enjoy 50% off with the *tarif bleu* (blue tariff).

Note that *numéros verts* (literally, 'green numbers') which all begin with '0 800' are toll-free, but others in the same series cost something (such as those beginning with '0 836', like the SNCF's national information number, which is always billed at 2.23FF per minute). Emergency numbers (see Emergency later in the chapter) and 0 800 numbers can be dialled from public telephones without inserting a télécarte or coins.

Public Phones Almost all public telephones in France require a télécarte, which can be purchased at post offices, *tabacs* (tobacconists), supermarket check-out counters, SNCF ticket windows, Paris metro stations, and anywhere that you see a blue sticker reading *télécarte en vente ici*. Cards worth 50/120 calling units cost 48.60/96.70FF.

To make a domestic or international phone call with a télécarte, follow the instructions on the LCD display. Most public phones have a button displaying two flags which you push for explanations in English. If not, when you see the words *introduire carte ou faire numéro libre* (insert the card or dial a toll-free number), insert the card chip-end first with the rectangle of electrical connectors facing upwards. *Patientez SVP* means 'please wait'.

When the top line of the display tells you your *crédit* or *solde* (how many units you have left), denominated in *unités* (units), the bottom line of the LCD screen will read *numérotez* (dial). As you press the keyboard, the *numéro appelé* (number being called) will appear on the display.

After you dial, you will hear a rapid beeping followed by long beeps (it's ringing) or short beeps (it's busy). To redial, push the button inscribed with a telephone receiver icon (not available on all public phones).

If something goes wrong, you'll be asked to *raccrochez SVP* (please hang up). *Crédit épuisé* means that your télécarte has run out of units.

All public phones can receive both domestic and international calls. If you want someone to call you back, just give them France's country code, the area code (where relevant) and the number, usually written after the words *ici le* or *no d'appel* on the tariff sheet or on a little sign inside the phone box.

You occasionally run across phones that take coins (1FF for a local call) rather than télécartes, especially in remote rural areas. Remember that coin phones don't give change.

Most coin phones let you hear the dial tone immediately, but with the very oldest models – the ones with windows down the front – you must deposit your money before you get the tone.

Many cafes and restaurants have privately owned and coin-operated Point Phones. To find a Point Phone, look for blue-on-white window stickers bearing the Point Phone emblem.

Mobile Phones France uses GSM 900/1800, which is compatible with the rest of Europe and Australia but not with the North American GSM 1900 or the totally different system in Japan (though some North Americans have GSM 1900/900 phones that do work here). If you have a GSM phone, check with your service provider about using it in France, and beware of calls being routed internationally (very expensive for a 'local' call).

A prepaid Mobicarte is a cheaper alternative. Sold by France Telecom, this package deal costs 270FF – probably cheaper by the time you read this – and includes a mobile phone, a local mobile phone number and 144FF of prepaid connection time. For more time you can buy a recharge card for

70FF, 140FF or 250FF (including 30FF extra talk time) from tabacs and other places you'd buy a télécarte. Per-minute costs depend which rate scheme you choose; the *classique* plan charges you 4.20FF per minute, 24 hours a day. There are also schemes geared towards heavy evening and weekend use. The Web site is at www.mobicarte.tm.fr.

Telephone Cards You can buy prepaid phonecards in France that make calling abroad cheaper than with a standard télécarte. France Telecom's Le Ticket de Téléphone, Carte Intercall Monde, Carte Astuce and Eagle Télécom International are among the more popular cards, and give up to 60% off standard French international call rates. They're available in 50FF and 100FF denominations from tabacs and other sales points.

Lonely Planet's eKno Communication Card is aimed specifically at independent travellers and provides budget international calls, a range of messaging services, free email and travel information – for local calls, you're usually better off with a local card. You can join online at www.ekno .lonelyplanet.com, or by phone from France by dialling 08 00 91 26 77. Once you have joined, to use eKno from France, dial 08 00 91 20 66.

Minitel Minitel is a screen-based information service peculiar to France, set up in the 1980s. It's useful but can be expensive to use, and the growing popularity of the Internet is giving the Minitel a run for its money. The most basic variety, with a B&W monitor and a clumsy keyboard, is free to telephone subscribers. Newer Minitel models have colour screens, and many people now access the system with a home computer and a modem.

Minitel numbers consist of four digits (for example, 3611, 3614 or 3615) and a string of letters. Home users pay a per-minute access charge, but consulting the *annuaire* (directory) is free. Most of the Minitels in post offices are also free for directory inquiries (though some require a

1FF or 2FF coin), and many of them can access pay-as-you-go online services.

Fax & Telegraph Virtually all large offices can send and receive domestic and international faxes *(télécopies or téléfaxes)*, telexes and telegrams. It costs about 60FF (12FF within France) to send a one-page fax.

Email & Internet Access Over the past few years, some 1000 post offices across France have been equipped with a Cyberposte, a modern, card-operated Internet terminal for public use. This is about the cheapest reliable way to check your email in France, and it allows you to set up a free email address. To use the Cyberposte – restricted to post office opening hours – buy a chip card at the counter for 50FF, worth an hour's connection time. When the card's exhausted you can recharge for 30FF, good for another hour. There is a list of post offices with a Cyberposte at www .cyberposte.com.

Otherwise you can seek out one of the growing ranks of cybercafes in French towns. They aren't cheap: expect to pay 20F to 30FF for a half-hour surf (note that some places charge by the minute, which might be useful if you just want to check your email).

See the Post & Communications sections under individual towns in this book for details of local Cyberpostes and Internet cafes.

INTERNET RESOURCES

The World Wide Web is a rich resource for travellers. You can research your trip, hunt down bargain air fares, book hotels, check on weather conditions or chat with locals and other travellers about the best places to visit (or avoid).

There's no better place to start your Web explorations than the Lonely Planet Web site (www.lonelyplanet.com). Here you'll find succinct summaries on travel to most places on earth, postcards from other travellers and the Thorn Tree bulletin board, where you can ask questions before you go or dispense advice when you get back. You can also find travel news and updates to many of our most

Accessing Email in France

While visiting France, it's possible to access your home email account (and the Web) without making expensive international calls on noisy lines, or stopping by the post office's Cyberposte or the relatively pricey cybercafes. But doing so takes the right equipment and a fair bit of patience.

Once you've got your laptop and a PC Card modem (be aware that some modems have trouble recognising European dial tones, and others will melt down if accidentally connected to a digital line), the next step is to get roaming Internet access. Your options are:

- Connecting through your service provider back home. Larger companies (such as AOL) have domestic access numbers around the world.
- Tapping into a network of local access numbers coordinated by companies such as Eunet (https://traveller.eu.net), which charge a monthly rate and a small fee for each connection. It may be necessary to configure your email program to present a dialogue box during login.
- Signing up with a French access provider. This can be time-consuming, require payment of a monthly fee of 50FF to 150FF *plus* per-hour fees, and involve dealing with technical instructions and customer support people in French.

In any case, you'll need to know your home account's POP user name and the addresses of your SMTP (outgoing mail) and POP (incoming mail) servers.

It can be tricky to get your modem to talk to the computer you're dialling – and not only because of configuration problems. French phones use a T-shaped jack particular to France and its former colonies. Modems, on the other hand, generally have wires equipped with the closest thing there is to an international standard, the RJ-11 (modular) plug of the type used in the USA and quite a few other countries. Linking the two requires an adapter, which you can get for about 30FF at larger Monoprix, Prisunic and Carrefour department stores.

Harder to find is an in-line coupler that turns one RJ-11 socket into two. (Your best bet is to buy up before leaving home – in France about the only place they're sold is at BHV and specialist telecoms shops.) Along with an extension phone cord equipped with RJ-11 plugs at both ends and a French adapter, it can connect both your modem and a telephone to the same line. This is often crucial, as getting past the hotel's automatic switchboard may require that you use their pulse-dial telephone. To do this you'll have to configure your network-connection program to work in manual dial mode. As soon as you hear the fax-like noise of the access provider, connect your computer and hang up the phone. Don't be surprised if it takes several attempts (perhaps trying different access numbers) to establish a connection.

Unless your server access is local or uses a national access number billed at local rates, be prepared for ruinously high phone bills, especially from hotel rooms, where each France Télécom billing unit – good for just 32 seconds of cross-country connection time at the highest daytime rate – costs around 2FF. The only way to connect a modem to a public phone (or any hard-wired phone, such as those in some hotel rooms) is to use an acoustic coupler, a bulky and slow gadget that costs about US$100.

An Internet site with useful information on connecting your modem to local phone lines while on the road is: at www.kropla.com/phones.htm. Companies that sell equipment to enable 'international modem connectivity' include TeleAdapt (www.teleadapt.com) and Road Warrior International (www.warrior.com).

popular guidebooks, and the subWWWay section links you to the most useful travel resources elsewhere on the Web.

Useful Web sites on France in English include:

Diplomatic & Visa Information
    www.france.diplomatie.fr
    (includes lists of consulates and embassies
    with visa information)
French Government Tourist Office
    www.francetourism.com
    (official tourist site with all manner of infor-
    mation on and about travel in France)
Gay & Lesbian Directory
    www.france.qrd.org
    ('queer resources directory' for gay and
    lesbian travellers)
Guide Web
    www.guideweb.com
    (good tourist site, but only on selected
    regions)
Maison de la France
    www.franceguide.com
    (the main tourist office site)
Paris Tourist Office
    www.paris-touristoffice.com
    (covers things to see and do in the capital)
Real France
    www.realfrance.com
    ('inside' information on arts and crafts,
    nature, leisure, food, restaurants, wine,
    museums, sights, events, hotels, guesthouses
    and chateaux)
Skiing
    www.skifrance.fr
    (ski resorts, services, conditions and so on)
Weather
    www.meteo.fr
    (two-day weather forecasts and current
    conditions)

BOOKS

Most books are published in different editions by different publishers in different countries, so a book might be a hardcover rarity in one country while it's readily available in paperback in another. Fortunately, bookshops and libraries search by title or author, so your local bookshop or library is best placed to advise you on the availability of the following recommendations.

There are so many excellent books on

France that it's hard to choose just a few to recommend, though the list has been shortened considerably by limiting the selection mainly to works available in paperback.

Lonely Planet

Lonely Planet's *Western Europe*, *Mediterranean Europe* and *Europe on a Shoestring* all have chapters dealing with France. It also publishes a *French phrasebook* and one for Western Europe as a whole.

Paris is a complete guide to the French capital, *Paris Condensed* is a pocket guide written for those on shorter visits and *Out to Eat – Paris* describes an enormous selection of the city's best eateries. The *Paris* video provides a visual picture of the city while *CitySync Paris* offers a digital guide specially designed for palmtop computers.

There are also regional guides to *Provence & the Côte d'Azur*, *The Loire*, *South-West France* and *Corsica*. French and Italian landscapes merge alluringly in the Mediterranean island video *Corsica, Sicily and Sardinia*.

For those who want to explore the great outdoors, *Walking in France* and *Cycling France* offer a wealth of lively description and practical information.

First-time travellers shouldn't miss *Read This First Europe*, the essential predeparture tool for exploring the continent. For a culinary tour of every area of France, *World Food France* is an ideal companion, and will tell you how to distinguish a Burgundy from a Bordeaux.

Travel Photography: A Guide to Taking Better Pictures is written by internationally renowned travel photographer, Richard I'Anson. It's full colour throughout and designed to take on the road.

Guidebooks

Large travel bookshops carry titles on virtually every aspect of visiting France.

Michelin, the huge rubber conglomerate, has been publishing guidebooks ever since the earliest days of motorcar touring, when the titles were intended to promote sales of its inflatable rubber tyres. Its *guides verts* (green guides, 69FF to 79FF each), which cover all of France in 24 regional volumes

– about a dozen of which are currently available in English – are full of historical information, although the editorial approach is very conservative and regional cultures tend to be given short shrift. The green guide to all of France (75FF) has brief entries on the most touristy sights.

Among the French-language guides, the best overall guidebooks are those published by Guide Bleu; its blue-jacketed all-France (198FF) and regional guides provide accurate, balanced information on matters historical, cultural and architectural.

Guide Bleu also publishes abridged guides called *Les Petits Bleus*, including one on Paris (49FF). Good walking guides to Paris include *Paris Step by Step* by Christopher Turner; *Walking Paris* by Gilles Desmons and *Paris Walks* by Alison & Sonia Landes. *Paris Pas Cher*, updated annually, lists inexpensive shopping options. Another source of information on penny-wise living in Paris is *Paris aux Meilleurs Prix*.

Restaurant & Accommodation Guides

Many people swear by Michelin's red-jacketed *Guide Rouge* to France (130FF), published each March, which has over 1200 pages of information on 3900 restaurants and 6400 mid- and upper-range hotels in every corner of the country. Accompanied by 521 detailed city maps, it's best known for rating France's greatest restaurants with one, two or three stars. Its reputation has suffered a bit in recent years, and the ratings don't quite carry the weight they used to (but still carry a lot). The icons used instead of text are explained in English at the front. The *Guide Rouge* to Paris costs 50FF.

The *Guide Gault Millau France* (189FF), published annually, awards up to four *toques rouges* (red chefs' caps) to restaurants with exceptionally good, creative cuisine; *toques blanches* (white chefs' caps) go to places with superb modern or traditional cuisine. *Gault Millau* is said to be quicker at picking up-and-coming restaurants than the *Guide Rouge*. The symbols used are explained in English and an English edition is also available. The *Food Lover's Guide*

to France, by the Paris-based American food reviewer Patricia Wells, is informative and a good read. *Le Guide des Hôtels-Restaurants Logis de France* (95FF) provides a complete listing of Logis de France affiliates in France (see Mid-Range Hotels under Accommodation later in the chapter).

The French *Guide du Routard* series is popular with youngish French people travelling around their own country. The restaurant tips generally offer good value, but rock-bottom hotels rarely make an appearance and there are few maps. Guide du Routard's *Hôtels & Restos de France* (105FF) lists mid-range hotels and restaurants all over the country; their *Restos & Bistrots de Paris* (45FF) deals with the capital.

The *Annuaire Vert* (Green Directory, 240FF), issued annually by Éditions OCEP (☎ 01 47 00 46 46, metro St-Amboise), 11 rue St-Amboise, 75011 Paris, lists organic and macrobiotic food shops, vegetarian restaurants, *pharmaciens-herboristes* (naturopathic pharmacies) and all sorts of relevant organisations. The listings are broken up by department.

Travel & Literature

France has long attracted writers from all over the world, in part because of its tolerance of those people who deviate from conventional social norms.

The Autobiography of Alice B Toklas, by Gertrude Stein. An autobiographical account of the author's years in Paris, her salon at 27 rue de Fleurus near the Luxembourg Gardens, and her friendships with Matisse, Picasso, Braque, Hemingway and others.

Down and Out in Paris and London, by George Orwell. Orwell's famous account of the time he spent living with tramps in Paris and London in the late 1920s.

Flaubert's Parrot, by Julian Barnes. A highly entertaining novel that pays witty homage to the great French writer.

A Moveable Feast, by Ernest Hemingway. Portrays bohemian life in Paris between the wars.

Tropic of Cancer and ***Tropic of Capricorn***, by Henry Miller. Steamy novels set in Paris, published in France in the 1930s but banned under obscenity laws in the UK and USA until the 1960s.

A Year in Provence and *Toujours Provence*, by Peter Mayle. Best-selling accounts of life in the Midi that take a witty look at the French through English eyes.

History, Politics & Society

A wide variety of excellent works on French history, politics and society are available in English.

The Age of the Cathedrals, by Georges Duby. An authoritative study of the relationship between art and society in medieval France.

Cross Channel, by Julian Barnes. A witty collection of key moments in shared Anglo-French history – from Joan of Arc to Eurostar.

Cultural Atlas of France, by John Ardagh. A superb illustrated synopsis of French culture and history with a short section on each region of the country.

Feminism in France, by Claire Duchen. A work that charts the progress of feminism in France from 1968 to the mid-1980s.

France – Fin de Siècle, by Eugene Weber. A wide-ranging social history portrait of late 19th-century France.

France Today, by John Ardagh. A good introduction to modern-day France, its politics, its people, and its idiosyncrasies.

The French, by Theodore Zeldin. A highly acclaimed and very insightful survey of French passions, peculiarities and perspectives. It's intelligent, informative and humorous.

A History of Modern France, by Alfred Cobban. A very readable, three-volume history that covers the period from Louis XIV to 1962.

The Identity of France, by Fernand Braudel. A very comprehensive (two-volume) look at the country and its people, though it is currently out of print.

Is Paris Burning?, by Dominique Lapierre and Larry Collins. A dramatic account of the liberation of Paris in 1944.

Past Imperfect: French Intellectuals, 1944–1956, by Tony Judt. An examination of the lively intellectual life of postwar France.

Pétain's Crime, by Paul Webster. Examines the collaborationist Vichy government that ruled France during WWII.

A Social History of the French Revolution, by Christopher Hibbert. A highly readable social account of the said period.

The Sun King, by Nancy Mitford. A classic work on Louis XIV and the country he ruled from Versailles.

NEWSPAPERS & MAGAZINES

France's main daily newspapers are *Le Figaro* (right wing; aimed at professionals, businesspeople and the bourgeoisie), *Le Monde* (centre-left; very popular with businesspeople, professionals and intellectuals), *Le Parisien* (centre; middle-class, easy to read if your French is basic), *France Soir* (right; working and middle-class), *Libération* (left; popular with students and intellectuals) and *L'Humanité* (communist; working-class). *L'Équipe* is a daily focussing exclusively on sport.

News weeklies with commentary include the left-leaning, comprehensive *Le Nouvel Observateur* and the more conservative *L'Express*. For investigative journalism blended with satire, pick up *Le Canard Enchaîné*. *Paris Match* is a gossipy, picture-heavy boulevard-style weekly seemingly devoted to the royal family in Monaco.

Entertainment listings magazines for Paris and its environs include *Pariscope* (3FF) and *L'Officiel des Spectacles* (2FF), both of which come out on Wednesday and are available at newsstands. The monthly *Les Inrockuptibles* (15FF) and *Nova* (20FF) are good sources for information on clubs and the music scene.

In larger towns, larger newsagents and those at railway stations usually carry English-language dailies including the *International Herald Tribune*, *Guardian*, *Financial Times*, *New York Times* and the colourful *USA Today*. Also readily available are *Newsweek*, the *Economist* and *Time*.

Paris-based *France USA Contacts* (or *FUSAC*), issued every fortnight, consists of hundreds of ads placed by both companies and individuals. It's distributed free at Paris' English-language bookshops, Anglophone embassies and the American Church (Map 4, ☎ 01 40 62 05 00, metro Pont de l'Alma) at 65 quai d'Orsay, 7e. It can be helpful if you're looking for au-pair work or short-term accommodation. To place an ad, contact FUSAC (☎/fax 01 56 53 54 55, metro Alésia) at 26 rue Bénard (14e), 10 am to 7 pm weekdays. You can also advertise via its Web site, www.fusac.fr.

FILMS

France has provided popular settings for scores of English-language films. Some of the better ones include:

Dangerous Liaisons (USA, 1988). An Oscar-winning, beautifully acted tale about two jaded aristocrats who play games of sexual intrigue.

The Hunchback of Notre Dame (USA, 1939). A superb remake of Victor Hugo's novel about a deformed bellringer who saves a gypsy girl from his master's evildoings.

Man in the Iron Mask (USA, 1939). Lots of swashbuckling as musketeers replace King Louis XIV with his imprisoned twin brother (a 1998 remake with Leonardo DiCaprio doesn't quite measure up).

Les Miserables (USA, 1934). Wrongly sentenced to years in the galleys, Jean Valjean emerges to rebuild his life but is tormented by a police officer. There's a less riveting British remake of this classic (1978).

'Round Midnight (USA, 1986). The last days of a black American jazz musician in Paris, with plenty of atmospheric club scenes.

Saving Private Ryan (USA, 1998). Stephen Spielberg's chillingly realistic, Oscar-winning account of the American landing at Omaha Beach in Normandy in June 1944.

The Three Musketeers (USA, 1948). D'Artagnan and his dashing cohorts save the throne of France, with duels and fights as musical numbers. The 1993 remake is eminently missable.

To Catch a Thief (USA, 1955). The French Riviera provides the scenic backdrop for an entertaining Hitchcock caper about a reformed cat burglar suspected in a new wave of jewel heists.

Victor/Victoria (USA, 1982). A girl singer poses as a female impersonator in a Paris nightclub of the 1930s, causing complications in her love life.

CD-ROMS

CD-Roms still tend to be awkward to use compared to conventional books. One notable exception is Choiceway Guide's *Paris* ($19.95) with virtual tours of the capital, interactive maps, bus and metro timetables and other useful resources. In France, FNAC bookshops sell the *Itineraires France et Europe* (99FF) by GT Interactive, which seeks out the most efficient travel routes and has a layout function even for tiny villages. Topography fans will get a kick out of Havas' *Vu de l'Espace: la France* (247FF), with hundreds of satellite maps that can be zoomed in to astonishing detail (for example, it has an accuracy of 3m in Paris).

RADIO

Public radio is grouped under the umbrella of Radio France, which broadcasts via a network of 53 radio stations, of which five are national: France Inter, France-Culture, France-Musique (which broadcasts over 1,000 concerts each year), Radio Bleue for over-50s listeners and France Info, a 24-hour news station, that broadcasts the news headlines in French every few minutes. In Paris, Franc Info is at 105.5 MHz FM.

Among the private networks, RTL is the leading general-interest station with over eight million listeners. The droves of FM pop-music stations include Fun Radio, Skyrock and Nostalgie, most of which follow the breakfast-time format with phone-ins and wisecracking DJs.

Radio France Internationale (RFI) has been France's voice abroad since 1931 and broadcasts in 17 languages (including English); in Paris the frequency is 738 kHz AM. You can pick up a mixture of the BBC World Service and BBC for Europe on 648 kHz AM. The Voice of America (VOA) is on 1197 kHz AM but reception is often poor.

By law, at least 40% of musical variety broadcasts must consist of songs in French (stations can be fined if they don't comply). This helps explain why so many English-language hits are re-recorded in French (which can be a real hoot).

Internet

Many local and international radio stations from every corner of the globe now 'broadcast' their programme via the Internet, to be picked up by surfers using software like RealAudio, which can be easily downloaded. Station Web sites often include write-ups of the latest news and are an excellent source of short-wave schedules. TRS Consultants' Hot Links (www.trsc.com) has dozens of hypertext links relevant to Internet radio, such as Radio France Internationale (www.rfi.fr).

TV

Half of France's six major national TV channels are public: France 2, France 3 and Arte (which splits the broadcast day with La Cinquième, 'the Fifth'). The major private stations are Canal+ (pronounced 'ka-**nahl** ploose'), TF1 and M6. There are also 25 or so French cable networks.

The strengths of the major channels lie in their consistently good selection of films, documentaries, cultural programmes and news. France 2 and 3 are general-interest stations designed to complement each other: the former focuses on news, entertainment and education, while the latter broadcasts regional programmes and news at certain times of the day. La Cinquiéme targets a daytime audience with a diet of cartoons, game shows and documentaries; at 7 pm it becomes Arte, a highbrow Franco-German cultural channel.

Canal+ is a pay channel which shows lots of films, both foreign and French – which isn't surprising, as it's the chief sponsor of the French cinema industry. In the private sector, TF1 focuses on news, sports and variety programmes, and, with about one-third of viewers, is the most popular station in France. M6 lures a youngish audience with its menu of drama, music and news programmes. One of the popular smaller stations is Canal Jimmy, a blast from the past with some fine films and US sitcoms such as *Friends*. MCM is France's answer to MTV.

Some good French programmes include *Le Vrai Journal* on Canal+ on Sunday afternoons, a popular, hard-hitting programme of investigative journalism hosted by one Karl Zéro (surely NOT his real name). Another great show is *Guignol* (with Spitting Image-type rubber puppets), which is part of the same channel's nightly Nulle Part Ailleur programme.

Weekend-to-weekend TV listings (such as *Tél' 7 jours* or *Télérama*) are sold at newsstands. Foreign movies that haven't been dubbed and are shown with subtitles are marked 'VO' or 'v.o.' (*version originale*).

Upmarket hotels often offer Canal+ and access to CNN, BBC Prime, Sky and other English-language networks.

VIDEO SYSTEMS

Unlike the rest of Western Europe and Australia, which use PAL (phase alternation line), French TV broadcasts are in SECAM (*système électronique couleur avec mémoire*). North America and Japan use a third incompatible system, NTSC (National Television Systems Committee). Non-SECAM TVs won't work in France, French videotapes can't be played on TVs and video recorders that lack a SECAM capability.

PHOTOGRAPHY & VIDEO
Film & Equipment

A good companion when on the road, *Travel Photography: A Guide to Taking Better Pictures*, is by internationally renowned travel photographer Richard I'Anson.

Colour-print film produced by Kodak and Fuji is widely available in supermarkets, photo shops and FNAC stores. Film is fairly expensive in France compared to a lot of other countries, so it pays to stock up ahead of time. At FNAC, a 36-exposure roll of Kodak Gold costs 35/44FF for 100/400 ASA or 41FF for 200 ASA (note that film is usually sold in packs of two). Developing costs are 20FF per roll plus 2.50FF per photo. Note that many smaller photography shops may charge less (for example, 1FF to 1.50FF per photo). One-hour developing is widely available.

For slides (*diapositives*), count on paying at least 46/54/68FF for a 36-exposure roll of Ektachrome rated at 100/200/400 ASA; developing costs 28/32FF for 24/36 exposures. Avoid Kodachrome: it's difficult to process quickly in France and can give you many a headache if not handled correctly.

Properly used, a video camera can give a fascinating record of your holiday. Unlike still photography, video 'flows' so, for example, you can shoot scenes of the countryside rolling past the train window, to give an overall impression that isn't possible with ordinary photos.

Video cameras these days have very sensitive microphones, which can present a problem if there is a lot of ambient noise – filming by the side of a busy road might seem OK at the time, but once you view the tape back home you may find your enjoyment ruined by a cacophony of traffic noise. One good rule for beginners is to try to film in long takes, and don't move the camera around too much. If your camera has a stabiliser, you can use it to obtain good footage while travelling on various means of transport, even on bumpy roads.

You can easily obtain video cartridges in large towns, but make sure you buy the correct format. It's usually worth buying a few cartridges duty-free to start off your trip.

Restrictions

Photography is rarely forbidden, except in museums and art galleries. Of course, taking snapshots of military installations is not appreciated in any country. When photographing people, it's basic courtesy to ask permission. If you don't know any French, just smile while pointing at your camera and they'll get the picture – as you probably will.

Security

Be prepared to have your camera and film run through x-ray machines at airports and the entrances to sensitive public buildings. The gadgets are ostensibly film-safe up to 1000 ASA, and laptops and computer disks appear to pass through without losing data, but there is always some degree of risk.

The police and gendarmes who run x-ray machines often seem to treat a request that they hand-check something as casting doubt on the power and glory of the French Republic. Arguing almost never works, and being polite is only slightly more effective (unless you can do it in French). You're most likely to get an affirmative response if you are deferential and your request is moderate: request that they hand-check your film, not your whole camera (which could, after all, conceal a bomb). They are usually happy to check computer disks by hand.

TIME

France uses the 24-hour clock, with the hours separated from the minutes by a lower-case letter 'h'. Thus, 15h30 is 3.30 pm, 21h50 is 9.50 pm, 00h30 is 12.30 am and so on.

France is on Central European Time, which is one hour ahead of (later than) GMT/UTC. During daylight-saving time, which runs from the last Sunday in March to the last Sunday in October, France is two hours ahead of GMT/UTC.

Without taking daylight-savings time into account, when it's noon in Paris it's 3 am in San Francisco, 6 am in New York, 11 am in London, 8 pm in Tokyo, 9 pm in Sydney and 11 pm in Auckland.

Note that the time difference to Melbourne and Sydney is complicated because daylight-saving time Down Under takes effect during the northern hemisphere's winter. The Australian eastern coast is between eight and 10 hours ahead of France.

ELECTRICITY
Voltage & Cycle

France and Monaco run on 220V at 50Hz AC. Andorra has a combination of 220V and 125V, both at 50Hz.

In the USA and Canada, the 120V electric supply is at 60Hz. While the usual travel transformers allow North American appliances to run in France without blowing out, they cannot change the Hz rate, which determines – among other things – the speed of electric motors. As a result, tape recorders not equipped with built-in adapters may function poorly.

There are two types of adapters; mixing them up will destroy either the transformer or your appliance, so be warned. The 'heavy' kind, usually able to handle 35 watts or less (see the tag) and often metal-clad, is designed for use with small electric devices such as radios, tape recorders and razors. The 'lighter' kind, rated for up to 1500 watts, is for use with appliances with heating elements, such as hairdryers and irons.

Plugs & Sockets

Old-type wall sockets, often rated at 600 watts, take two round prongs. The new kinds of sockets take fatter prongs and have a protruding earth (ground) prong.

Adapters to make new plugs fit into the old sockets are said to be illegal but are still available in electrical shops. In Paris, adapters and transformers of all sorts are available at the BHV department store (Map 8, ☎ 01 42 74 90 00, metro Hôtel de Ville) at 52–64 rue de Rivoli, 4e.

WEIGHTS & MEASURES
Metric System
France uses the metric system, which was invented by the French Academy of Sciences after the Revolution at the request of the National Assembly and adopted by the French government in 1795. Inspired by the same rationalist spirit in whose name churches were ransacked and turned into 'Temples of Reason', the metric system replaced a confusing welter of traditional units of measure, which lacked all logical basis and made conversion complicated and commerce chaotic.

For a conversion chart, see the inside back cover of this book.

Numbers
For numbers with four or more digits, the French use full stops or spaces where writers in English would use commas: so one million appears as 1.000.000 or 1 000 000. For decimals, on the other hand, the French use commas, so 1.75 is written 1,75.

LAUNDRY
Doing laundry while on the road in France is pretty straightforward. To find a *laverie libre-service* (self-service laundrette) near your accommodation, see Laundry under Information at the beginning of each city listing, or ask at your hotel or hostel.

French laundrettes are not cheap. They usually charge 18FF to 20FF for a 6 or 7kg machine and 2/5FF for five/12 minutes of drying. Some laundrettes have self-service *nettoyage à sec* (dry cleaning) for about 60FF per 6kg.

In general, you will deposit coins into a *monnayeur central* (central control box) – not the machine itself – and push a button that corresponds to the number of the machine you wish to operate. These gadgets are sometimes programmed to deactivate the washing machines an hour or so before closing time.

Except with the most modern systems, you're likely to need all sorts of peculiar coin combinations – change machines are often out of order, so come prepared. Coins, especially 2FF pieces, are handy for the *séchoirs* (dryers) and the *lessive* (laundry powder) dispenser.

You can choose between a number of washing cycles:

blanc – whites
couleur – colours
synthétique – synthetics
laine – woollens
prélavage – prewash cycle
lavage – wash cycle
rinçage – rinse cycle
essorage – spin-dry cycle

TOILETS
Public Toilets
Public toilets, signposted *toilettes* or *w.c.* (pronounced 'vey sey' or 'doo-bluh vey sey'), are few and far between, though small towns often have them near the town hall *(mairie)*. In Paris, there are a number of superb public toilets from the *belle époque* (for example, at place de la Madeleine), but you're more likely to find one of the tan, self-disinfecting toilet pods. Many public toilets cost 2FF or 2.50FF.

In a few cities and towns, you still find flushless, kerbside *urinoirs* (urinals) reeking with generations of urine. Failing that, there's always a fast-food outlet or a cafe (try saying '*Est-ce que je peux utiliser les toilettes, s'il vout plaît?*'). Some toilets are unisex: the washbasins and urinals are in a common area through which you pass to get to the closed toilet stalls.

In older cafes and even hotels, the amenities may consist of a *toilette à la turque* (Turkish-style toilet), a squat toilet with a high-pressure flushing mechanism that will soak your feet if you don't step back in time. In some older buildings, the toilets used by ground-floor businesses (for example, restaurants) are tiny affairs accessed via an interior courtyard. Many hall toilets are in a little room all of their own, with the nearest washbasin nowhere to be seen (in hotels, it's more than likely to be attached to the nearest shower).

Bidets

In many hotel rooms – even those without toilets or showers – you will find a bidet, a porcelain fixture that looks like a shallow toilet with a pop-up stopper in the base. Originally conceived to improve the personal hygiene of aristocratic women, its primary purpose is for washing the genitals and anal area, though its uses have expanded to include everything from handwashing laundry to soaking your feet.

HEALTH

France is a healthy place. Your main risks are likely to be sunburn, foot blisters, insect bites and an upset stomach from eating and drinking too much. You might experience mild stomach problems if you're not used to copious amounts of rich cream and olive-oil-based sauces, but you'll get used to it after a while.

See also Emergency later in the chapter.

Predeparture Planning

Immunisations No jabs are required to travel to France, but they may be necessary to visit other European countries if you're coming from an infected area – yellow fever is the most likely requirement. If you are travelling to France with stopovers in Africa, Latin America or Asia, check with your travel agency or the embassies of the countries you plan to visit at least six weeks before you depart.

However, there are a few routine vaccinations that are recommended whether you are travelling or not, and this Health section assumes that you've had them: polio (usually administered during childhood), tetanus and diphtheria (usually administered during childhood, with a booster shot every 10 years), and sometimes measles. Be aware that there is often a greater risk of disease with children and during pregnancy. For details, see your doctor.

All vaccinations should be recorded on an International Health Certificate, available from your doctor or government health department. Don't leave this till the last minute, since certain vaccinations have to be spread out over a period of time.

Health Insurance Make sure that you have adequate health insurance. See Travel Insurance under Documents earlier in the chapter for details.

Citizens of EU countries are covered for emergency medical treatment in France on presentation of an E111 form, though charges are likely for medications, dental work and secondary examinations including x-rays and laboratory tests. Ask about the E111 at your national health service or travel agent at least a few weeks before you go. In the UK you can get the forms at the post office. Claims must be submitted to a local *caisse primaire d'assurance-maladie* (sickness insurance office) before you leave France.

Travel Health Guides Lonely Planet's handy, pocket-sized Healthy Travel guides are packed with useful information, which includes pretrip planning, emergency first aid, immunisation and disease information and what to do if you get sick on the road. *Travel with Children* from Lonely Planet also has advice on the travel health of younger children.

There are also a number of excellent travel health sites on the Internet. From the Lonely Planet home page there are links at www.lonelyplanet.com/weblinks/wlheal.htm to the World Health Organization and the US Centers for Disease Control & Prevention.

Other Preparations Ensure that you're healthy before you start travelling. If you're going on a long trip make sure your teeth are OK. If you wear glasses take a spare pair and your prescription.

If you require a particular medication take an adequate supply, as it may not be available locally. Take part of the packaging showing the generic name; this will make getting replacements easier. It's a good idea to have a legible prescription or letter from your doctor to show that you legally use the medication to avoid any problems.

Medical Treatment

Public Health System France has an extensive public health care system. Anyone (including foreigners) who is sick, even mildly so, can receive treatment in the *service des urgences* (casualty ward or emergency room) of any public hospital. Hospitals try to have people who speak English in the casualty wards, but this is not done systematically. If necessary, the hospital will call in an interpreter. It's an excellent idea to ask for a copy of the diagnosis – in English, if possible – in case your doctor back home is interested.

Getting treated for illness or injury in a public hospital costs much less in France than in many other western countries, especially the USA: being seen by a doctor (a *consultation*) costs about 150FF (235FF to 250FF on Sunday and holidays, 275FF to 350FF from 8 pm to 8 am). Seeing a specialist is a bit more expensive. Blood tests and other procedures, each of which has a standard fee, will increase this figure. Full hospitalisation costs from 3000FF a day. Hospitals usually ask that visitors from abroad settle accounts right after receiving treatment (residents of France are sent a bill in the mail).

Dental Care Most major hospitals offer dental services. For details on dental care options in Paris, see Medical Services under Information in the Paris chapter.

Pharmacies French pharmacies are almost always marked by a green cross, the neon components of which are lit when it's open. *Pharmaciens* (pharmacists) can often suggest treatments for minor ailments.

If you are prescribed medication, make sure you understand the dosage, and how often and when you should take it. It's a good idea to ask for a copy of the *ordonnance* (prescription) for your records.

French pharmacies coordinate their days and hours of closure so that a town or district isn't left without a place to buy medication. For details on the nearest *pharmacie de garde* (pharmacy on weekend/night duty), consult the door of any pharmacy.

Medical Kit Check List

Following is a list of items you should consider including in your medical kit – consult your pharmacist for brands available in your country.

- ☐ **Aspirin or paracetamol** (acetaminophen in the USA) – for general pain or fever.
- ☐ **Antihistamine** – for allergies, for example hay fever; to ease the itch from insect bites of stings; and to prevent motion sickness.
- ☐ **Loperamide** or **Lomotil** for diarrhoea; **prochlorperazine** or **metaclopramide** for nausea and vomiting.
- ☐ **Rehydration mixture** – to prevent dehydration, which may occur during bouts of diarrhoea; particularly important when travelling with children.
- ☐ **Antiseptic**, such as povidone-iodine – for cuts and grazes.
- ☐ **Calamine lotion, sting relief spray or aluminium sulphate spray** – to ease irritation from bites or stings.
- ☐ **Bandages** and **Band-Aids**.
- ☐ **Scissors, tweezers** and a **thermometer** (note that mercury thermometers are prohibited by airlines).
- ☐ **Cold and flu tablets, throat lozenges** and nasal decongestant.
- ☐ **Insect repellent, sunscreen**, a **chapstick, eye drops** and **water purification tablets**.

Basic Rules

Everyday Health Normal body temperature is 37°C (98.6°F); more than 2°C (4°F) higher indicates a high fever. The normal adult pulse rate is 60 to 100 per minute (children 80 to 100, babies 100 to 140). As a general rule the pulse increases about 20 beats per minute for each 1°C (2°F) rise in fever.

Respiration (breathing) rate is also an indicator of illness. Count the number of breaths per minute: between 12 and 20 is normal for adults and older children (up to 30 for younger children, 40 for babies). People with a high fever or serious respiratory illness breathe more quickly than normal. More than 40 shallow breaths a minute may indicate pneumonia.

Water Tap water all over France is safe to drink. However, the water in most French fountains is not drinkable and – like the taps in some public toilets – may have a sign reading *eau non potable* (undrinkable water).

Always beware of natural sources of water. A burbling Alpine or Pyrenean stream may look crystal clear, but it's inadvisable to drink untreated water unless you're at the source and can see it coming out of the rocks.

It's very easy not to drink enough liquids, especially on hot days or at high altitudes – don't rely on feeling thirsty to indicate when you should drink. Not needing to urinate or very dark-yellow urine is a danger sign. France suffers from a singular lack of drinking fountains, so it's a good idea to carry a water bottle.

Water Purification The simplest way of purifying water is to boil it thoroughly. Vigorous boiling should be satisfactory, but at high altitude water boils at a lower temperature, so germs are less likely to be killed. You'll need to boil it for longer in these environments.

Simple filtering will not remove all dangerous organisms, so if you cannot boil water it should be treated chemically. Chlorine tablets (Puritabs, Steritabs or other brand names) will kill many pathogens, but not some parasites, like amoebic cysts and giardia. Iodine is more effective at purifying water and is available in tablet form (such as Potable Aqua). Follow the directions carefully and remember that too much iodine can be harmful.

Environmental Hazards

Altitude Sickness Lack of oxygen at high altitudes (over 2500m) affects most people to some extent. The affect may be mild or severe and occurs because less oxygen reaches the muscles and the brain at high altitude, requiring the heart and lungs to compensate by working harder. Symptoms of Acute Mountain Sickness (AMS) usually develop during the first 24 hours at altitude but may be delayed up to three weeks. Mild symptoms include headache, lethargy, dizziness, difficulty sleeping and loss of appetite.

AMS may become more severe without warning and can be fatal. Severe symptoms include breathlessness, severe headache, a dry, irritative cough (which may progress to the production of pink, frothy sputum), lack of coordination and balance, confusion, irrational behaviour, vomiting, drowsiness and unconsciousness. There is no hard-and-fast rule as to what is too high: AMS has been fatal at 3000m, although 3500 to 4500m is the usual range. Very few treks or ski runs in the Alps and Pyrenees reach heights of 3000m or more, so it's unlikely to be a major concern. Mild altitude problems will generally abate after a day or two, but if symptoms persist or become worse the only treatment is to descend – even 500m can help.

Fungal Infections Fungal infections occur more commonly in hot weather and are usually found on the scalp, between the toes or fingers, in the groin and on the body (ringworm). You get ringworm (which is a fungal infection, not a worm) from infected animals or other people. Moisture encourages these infections.

To prevent fungal infections wear loose, comfortable clothes, avoid artificial fibres, wash frequently and dry carefully. If you do get an infection, wash the infected area at least daily with a disinfectant or medicated soap and water, and rinse and dry well. Apply an antifungal cream or powder like tolnifate (Tinaderm). Try to expose the infected area to air or sunlight as much as possible and wash all towels and underwear in hot water, change them often and let them dry in the sun.

Heat Exhaustion Dehydration and salt deficiency can cause heat exhaustion. Take time to acclimatise to high temperatures, drink sufficient liquids and do not do anything too physically demanding.

Salt deficiency is characterised by fatigue,

lethargy, headaches, giddiness and muscle cramps; salt tablets may help, but adding extra salt to your food is better.

Hypothermia Too much cold can be just as dangerous as too much heat. If you are trekking at high altitudes, be prepared.

Hypothermia occurs when the body loses heat faster than it can produce it and the core temperature of the body falls. It is surprisingly easy to progress from very cold to dangerously cold due to a combination of wind, wet clothing, fatigue and hunger, even if the air temperature is above freezing. It is best to dress in layers: silk, wool and some of the new artificial fibres are all good insulating materials. A hat is important, as a lot of heat is lost through the head. A strong, waterproof outer layer and a 'space' blanket for emergencies are essential. Carry basic supplies, including food containing simple sugars to generate heat quickly and fluid to drink.

Symptoms of hypothermia are exhaustion, numb skin (particularly toes and fingers), shivering, slurred speech, irrational or violent behaviour, lethargy, stumbling, dizzy spells, muscle cramps and violent bursts of energy. Irrationality may take the form of sufferers claiming they are warm and trying to take off their clothes.

To treat mild hypothermia, first get the person out of the wind and/or rain, remove their clothing if it's wet and replace it with dry, warm clothing. Give them hot liquids – not alcohol – and some high-kilojoule, easily digestible food. Do not rub victims; instead allow them to warm themselves slowly. This should be enough to treat the early stages of hypothermia. The early recognition and treatment of mild hypothermia is the only way to prevent severe hypothermia, which is a critical condition.

Jet Lag Jet lag is experienced when a person travels by air across more than three time zones (each time zone usually represents a one-hour time difference). It occurs because many of the functions of the human body (such as temperature, pulse rate and emptying of the bladder and bowels) are regulated by internal 24-hour cycles. When we travel long distances rapidly, our bodies take time to adjust to the 'new time' of our destination, and we may experience fatigue, disorientation, insomnia, anxiety, impaired concentration and loss of appetite. These effects will usually be gone within three days, but to minimise the impact of jet lag:

- Rest for a couple of days prior to departure.
- Try to select flight schedules that minimise sleep deprivation; arriving late in the day means you can go to sleep soon after you arrive. For very long flights, try to organise a stopover.
- Avoid excessive eating (which bloats the stomach) and alcohol (which causes dehydration) during the flight. Instead, drink plenty of non-carbonated, non-alcoholic drinks such as fruit juice or water.
- Avoid smoking.
- Make yourself comfortable by wearing loose-fitting clothes and perhaps bringing an eye mask and earplugs to help you sleep.
- Reset your watch immediately on boarding and try to sleep at the appropriate time for the time zone to which you are travelling.

Motion Sickness Eating lightly before and during a trip will reduce the chances of motion sickness. If you are prone to motion sickness try to find a place that minimises movement – near the wing on aircraft, close to midships on boats, near the centre on buses. Fresh air usually helps; reading and cigarette smoke don't. Commercial motion-sickness preparations, which can cause drowsiness, have to be taken before the trip commences. Ginger (available in capsule form) and peppermint (including mint-flavoured sweets) are natural preventatives.

Prickly Heat This is an itchy rash caused by excessive perspiration trapped under the skin. It usually strikes people who have just arrived in a hot climate. Keeping cool, bathing often, drying the skin and using a mild talcum or prickly heat powder, or resorting to air-conditioning may help.

Sunburn You can get sunburned surprisingly quickly, even through cloud. Use a sunscreen, hat and barrier cream for your nose and lips. Calamine lotion or Stingose are good for mild sunburn. Protect your eyes with good-quality sunglasses, particularly if you will be near water, sand or snow.

Hay Fever Sufferers should be aware that the pollen count in certain parts of southern France, particularly Provence and Corsica, is very high in May and June.

Infectious Diseases

Diarrhoea Simple things such as a change of water, food or climate can cause a mild bout of diarrhoea, but a few rushed toilet trips with no other symptoms is not indicative of a major problem.

Dehydration is the main danger with any diarrhoea, particularly in children or the elderly as it can occur quite quickly. Fluid replacement (at least equal to the volume being lost) is the most important thing to remember. Weak black tea with a little sugar, soda water, or soft drinks allowed to go flat and diluted 50% with clean water are all good. Keep drinking small amounts often. Stick to a bland diet as you recover.

Hepatitis Hepatitis is a general term for inflammation of the liver. There are several different viruses that cause hepatitis; they differ in the way that they are transmitted.

There are almost 300 million chronic carriers of hepatitis B in the world. It is spread through contact with infected blood, blood products or body fluids, for example through sexual contact, unsterilised needles and blood transfusions, or contact with blood via small breaks in the skin. Other risk situations include having a shave, tattoo, or body piercing with contaminated equipment.

The symptoms are similar in all forms of the illness, and include fever, chills, headache, fatigue, feelings of weakness and aches and pains, followed by loss of appetite, nausea, vomiting, abdominal pain, dark urine, light-coloured faeces, jaundiced (yellow) skin and yellowing of the whites of the eyes. You should seek medical advice, but there is not much you can do apart from resting, drinking lots of fluids and eating lightly.

HIV & AIDS The Human Immunodeficiency Virus (HIV; VIH in French) may develop into Acquired Immune Deficiency Syndrome (AIDS; SIDA in French), which is a fatal disease. Any exposure to blood, blood products or body fluids may put the individual at risk. The disease is often transmitted through sexual contact or dirty needles – vaccinations, acupuncture, tattooing and body piercing can be potentially as dangerous as intravenous drug use. HIV/AIDS can also be spread through infected blood transfusions, but in France all blood products are safe.

Fear of HIV infection should never prevent you from seeking treatment for serious medical conditions.

For information on free and anonymous HIV-testing centres *(centres de dépistage)* in and around Paris, ring the SIDA Info Service toll-free, 24 hours, on ☎ 08 00 84 08 00. Its Web site is at www.sida-infoservice.org. Information is also available at Le Kiosque (☎ 01 44 78 00 00). There's one in the Marais district at 36 rue Geoffroy l'Asnier, 4e (metro St-Paul), and in the Latin Quarter at 6 rue Dante, 5e (metro Maubert Mutualité). Both open from 10 am to 12.30 pm and 1 to 7 pm weekdays and on Saturday from 2 to 7 pm.

The offices of AIDES (☎ 01 44 52 00 00; metro Télégraphe) at 247 rue de Belleville, 19e, an organisation that works for the prevention of AIDS and assists AIDS sufferers, are staffed 10 am to 13.30 pm and 2 to 6 pm weekdays (and again 7 to 10 pm on Thursday).

FACTS-Line (☎ 01 44 93 16 69), in operation 6 to 10 am Monday, Wednesday and Friday, is an English-language helpline for those with HIV or AIDS.

Sexually Transmitted Diseases Gonorrhoea, herpes and syphilis are among these diseases; sores, blisters or rashes around the genitals, pain when urinating or discharges are common symptoms. In some STDs, such as wart virus or chlamydia, symptoms may be less marked or not observed at all, especially in women. Syphilis symptoms eventually disappear completely but the disease continues and can cause severe problems in later years. While abstinence from sexual contact is the only 100% effective prevention, using condoms is also effective. The treatment of gonorrhoea and syphilis is with antibiotics. The different sexually transmitted diseases each require specific antibiotics. There is no cure for herpes.

All pharmacies carry condoms (*préservatifs*), and many have 24-hour automatic condom dispensers outside the door. Some brasseries, discotheques, metro stations and WCs in petrol stations and cafes are also equipped with condom machines. Condoms that conform to French government standards are always marked with the letters NF (*norme française*) in black on a white oval inside a red-and-blue rectangle.

Cuts, Bites & Stings

Rabies Rabies is a fatal viral infection found in many countries but is not widespread in France. Many animals can be infected and it is their saliva that is infectious. Any bite, scratch or even lick from a warm-blooded, furry animal should be cleaned immediately and thoroughly. Scrub with soap and running water, and then apply alcohol or iodine solution. If you suspect the animal is rabid, medical help should be sought promptly to receive a course of injections to prevent the onset of symptoms and death.

Bedbugs & Lice Bedbugs live in various places, but particularly in dirty mattresses and bedding, evidenced by spots of blood on bedclothes or on the wall. Bedbugs leave itchy bites in neat rows. Calamine lotion or a sting-relief spray may help.

All lice cause itching and discomfort. They make themselves at home in your hair (head lice), your clothing (body lice) or in your pubic hair (crabs). You catch lice through direct contact with infected people or by sharing combs, clothing and the like. Powder or shampoo treatment will kill the lice and infected clothing should then be washed in very hot, soapy water and left to dry in the sun.

Insect Bites & Stings Bee and wasp stings are usually painful rather than dangerous. However, in people who are allergic to them severe breathing difficulties may occur and the victim may require urgent medical care. Calamine lotion or sting-relief spray will give relief, and ice packs will reduce the pain and swelling. Various insect repellents can be useful against mosquitoes.

Jellyfish Local advice will help prevent your coming into contact with jellyfish (*méduses*) and their stinging tentacles, which are often found along the Mediterranean. Dousing the wound in vinegar will deactivate any stingers that have not 'fired'. Calamine lotion, antihistamines and analgesics may reduce the reaction and relieve the pain. The sting of the Portuguese man-of-war, which has a sail-like float and long tentacles, is painful but rarely fatal.

Leeches & Ticks You should check all over your body if you have been walking through a potentially tick-infested area, as ticks can cause skin infections and other more serious diseases. If a tick is found attached, press down around the tick's head with tweezers, grab the head and gently pull upwards. Avoid pulling the rear of the body as this may squeeze the tick's gut contents through the attached mouth parts into the skin, increasing the risk of infection and disease. Smearing chemicals on the tick will not make it let go and is not to be recommended.

Snakes To minimise your chances of being bitten always wear boots, socks and long trousers when walking through undergrowth where snakes may be present. Don't put your hands into holes or crevices, and be careful when collecting firewood.

Snake bites do not cause instantaneous death and antivenenes are usually available. Immediately wrap the bitten limb tightly, as you would for a sprained ankle, and then attach a splint to immobilise it. Keep the victim still and seek medical help, if possible with the dead snake for identification. Don't attempt to catch the snake if there is a possibility of being bitten again. The use of tourniquets to stop the poison and sucking it out have now been comprehensively discredited.

Women's Health

Gynaecological Problems Sexually transmitted diseases are a major cause of vaginal problems. Symptoms include a smelly discharge, painful intercourse and sometimes a burning sensation when urinating. Male sexual partners must also be treated. Medical attention should be sought and remember in addition to these diseases HIV or hepatitis B may also be acquired during exposure. Besides abstinence, the best thing is to practise safe sex using condoms.

Antibiotic use, synthetic underwear, sweating and contraceptive pills can lead to fungal vaginal infections in hot climates. Maintaining good personal hygiene and wearing loose-fitting clothes and cotton underwear will help to them.

Fungal infections, characterised by a rash, itch and discharge, can be treated with a vinegar or lemon-juice douche, or with yoghurt. Nystatin, miconazole or clotrimazole pessaries or vaginal cream are the usual treatment.

WOMEN TRAVELLERS
Attitudes Towards Women

Women were given the right to vote in 1945 by De Gaulle's short-lived postwar government, but until 1964 a woman needed her husband's permission to open a bank account or get a passport. Younger French women especially are quite outspoken and emancipated, but self-confidence has yet to translate into equality in the workplace, where women are often kept out of senior and management positions. Sexual harassment (*harcèlement sexuel*) in the workplace is more commonplace and tolerated here than in countries such as the USA and Australia.

Safety Precautions

Women tend to attract more unwanted attention than men, but female travellers need not walk around France in fear: people are rarely assaulted on the street. However, a number of French men (and some women) still persist in thinking that to stare suavely at a passing woman is to pay her a flattering compliment.

Physical attack is very unlikely but, of course, it does happen. As in any country, the best way to avoid being assaulted is to be conscious of your surroundings and aware of situations that could be potentially dangerous: deserted streets, lonely beaches, dark corners of large train stations and so on. Using the metros late at night is generally OK, as stations are rarely deserted, but there are a few to avoid. See Dangers & Annoyances under Information in the Paris chapter for details.

France's national rape-crisis hotline (☎ 08 00 05 95 95) can be reached toll-free from any telephone without using a phonecard. Staffed by volunteers 10 am to 6 pm Monday to Friday, it's run by a women's organisation called Viols Femmes Informations, whose Paris office is at 9 villa d'Este, 13e (metro Porte d'Ivry).

If you've been attacked, you can always call the police (☎ 17), who will take you to the hospital. In Paris, medical, psychological and legal services are available to people referred by the police at the 24-hour Service Médico-Judiciaire of the Hôtel Dieu (☎ 01 42 34 84 46/ 82 34).

Organisations

France's women's liberation movement flourished along with its counterparts in other western countries in the late 1960s and early 70s but by the mid-80s the movement was pretty moribund. For reasons that have more to do with French society than anything else, few women's groups function as the kind of supportive social institutions that have been formed in the USA, UK and Australia.

The women-only Maison des Femmes (Map 5, ☎ 01 43 43 41 13; metro Reuilly Diderot) at 163 Rue Charenton, 12e is the main meeting place for women of all ages and nationalities. It is staffed 4 to 7 pm on Wednesday and 3 to 6 pm on Saturday.

GAY & LESBIAN TRAVELLERS

France is one of Europe's most liberal countries when it comes to homosexuality, in part because of the long French tradition of public tolerance towards groups of people who choose not to live by conventional social codes. In addition to the large gay and lesbian communities in Paris, a thriving gay centre since the late 1970s, there are active communities in Cannes, Lyon, Marseilles, Nice, Toulouse and many other towns. Predictably, attitudes towards homosexuality tend to become more conservative in the countryside and villages. France's lesbian scene is much less public than its gay counterpart and is centred mainly around women's cafes and bars.

Gay Pride marches are held in Paris, Marseilles, Montpellier, Nantes, Rennes and other cities each June yearly. For details, contact Paris' Centre Gai et Lesbien (see Organisations below).

For information on AIDS and free, anonymous HIV tests, see HIV & AIDS in the Health section earlier in the chapter.

Organisations

Most of France's major gay and lesbian organisations are based in Paris and include the following:

Act Up-Paris (☎ 01 48 06 13 89/49 29 44 75, ✉ actup@actupp.org). Advice by phone is available 2 to 6 pm on Wednesday and meetings are held at 7 pm every Tuesday at the École des Beaux-Arts (Map 6, metro St-Germain des Prés), 14 rue Bonaparte, 6e.
Association des Médecins Gais (☎ 01 48 05 81 71). The Association of Gay Doctors, based in the Centre Gai et Lesbien, deals with gay-related health issues. It's staffed 6 to 8 pm on Wednesday and 2 to 4 pm on Saturday.
Centre Gai et Lesbien (CGL; Map 5, ☎ 01 43 57 21 47, metro Ledru Rollin), 3 rue Keller, 11e. The CGL normally opens 2 to 8 pm Monday to Saturday.
Écoute Gaie (☎ 01 44 93 01 02). This hotline for gays and lesbians is staffed 6 to 10 pm on weekdays and 6 to 8 pm on Saturday.
SOS Homophobie (☎ 01 48 06 42 41). This hotline accepts anonymous calls 8 to 10 pm weekdays concerning discriminatory acts against gays and lesbians.

Gay Publications

A monthly national magazine, *Têtu* is available at newsstands everywhere (30FF). Among the more serious gay publications are Act Up-Paris' monthly called *Action* (free) and the CGL's *3 Keller*, which appears about once a month. Be on the lookout for *e.m@le*, which has interviews, gossip and articles (in French) and among the best listings of gay clubs, bars and associations and personal classifieds. It is available free at gay venues or for 5FF at newsagents.

Guidebooks listing pubs, restaurants, discotheques, beaches, saunas, sex shops and cruising areas include those appearing below. Most of these titles are available from Les Mots à la Bouche in Paris (see Bookshops in the Paris chapter).

Guide Gai Pied A predominantly male, French and English-language annual guide (79FF) to France (about 80 pages on Paris) that is published by Les Éditions du Triangle Rose (☎ 01 43 14 73 00). Web site: www.gaipied.fr.
Spartacus International Gay Guide A male-only guide (190FF; US$34.95) to the world with more than 100 pages devoted to France and 28 pages on Paris.

Lesbian Publications

The monthly national magazine *Lesbia* (25FF) gives a rundown of what's happening around the country. *Les Nanas*, a freebie appearing every other month, is for women only. *Women's Traveller* is an English-language guide (109FF/US$17.95) for lesbians, published by Damron.

DISABLED TRAVELLERS

France is not particularly well equipped for *handicapés* (disabled people): kerb ramps are few and far between, older public facilities and budget hotels often lack lifts, cobblestone streets are a nightmare to navigate in a wheelchair, and the Paris metro, most of it built decades ago, is hopeless. But disabled people who would like to visit France can overcome these difficulties. Most hotels with two or more stars are equipped with lifts, and Michelin's *Guide Rouge* indicates those hotels with lifts and facilities for disabled people. In Paris both the Foyer International d'Accueil de Paris Jean Monnet and the Centre International de Séjour de Paris Kellermann have facilities for disabled travellers (see Hostels & Foyers under Places to Stay in the Paris chapter).

In recent years the SNCF has made efforts to make its trains more accessible to people with physical disabilities. A traveller in a wheelchair *(fauteuil roulant)* can travel in the wheelchair in both TGV and regular trains provided a reservation is made by phone or at a train station at least a few hours before departure. Details are available in SNCF's booklet *Guide du Voyageur à Mobilité Réduite*. You can also contact SNCF Accessibilité on toll-free ☎ 08 00 15 47 53.

Other general publications you might look for include:

Access in Paris A complete, 245-page guide to Paris for the disabled is published by Quiller Press (☎ 020-7499 6529), 46 Lilliue Rd, London SW6.

Gîtes Accessibles aux Personnes Handicapés A guide (60FF) to *gîtes ruraux* and *chambres d'hôtes* with disabled access. Published by Gîtes de France (see Gîtes Ruraux & B&Bs under Accommodation later in the chapter).

Organisations
The following organisations give information to disabled travellers:

Association des Paralysées de France (☎ 08 00 85 49 76/ 01 40 78 69 00), 17 blvd Auguste-Blanqui, 75013 Paris. Publishes brochures on wheelchair access for accommodation in Paris.

Comité Nationale Française de Liaison pour la Réadaptation des Handicapées (CNRH; ☎ 01 53 80 66 66), 236 bis rue de Tolbiac, 75013 Paris. An information centre that publishes guides for disabled travellers.

Groupement pour l'Insertion des Personnes Handicapées Physiques (☎ 01 41 83 15 15) at 98 rue de la Porte Jaune, 92210 St-Cloud. Provides vehicles outfitted for people in wheelchairs within the city.

SENIOR TRAVELLERS
Senior citizens are entitled to discounts in France on things like public transport, museum admission fees and so on, provided they show proof of their age. In some cases they might need a special pass. See Seniors Card under Documents earlier in the chapter for details.

TRAVEL WITH CHILDREN
Make sure the activities of the holiday include the kids – balance that day at the Louvre in Paris with a visit to the city's zoo in the Jardin des Plantes or even Disneyland Paris (see the Around Paris chapter). Include the kids in the trip planning; if they've helped to work out where you will be going, then they will be much more interested when they get there. Lonely Planet's *Travel with Children* is a good source of information.

Most car-rental firms in France have children's safety seats for hire at a nominal cost, but it is essential that you book them in advance. The same goes for highchairs and cots (cribs); they're standard in most restaurants and hotels but numbers are limited. The choice of baby food, infant formulas, soy and cow's milk, disposable nappies (diapers) and the like is as great in French supermarkets as it is back home, but the opening hours may be quite different. Run out of nappies on Saturday afternoon and you could be facing a long and messy weekend.

The weekly entertainment magazine *L'Officiel des Spectacles* (2FF) advertises baby-sitting services *(gardes d'enfants)* in Paris. It's out on Wednesday and is available at any newsstand.

DANGERS & ANNOYANCES
In general, France is a pretty safe place in which to live and travel. Though property crime – especially theft involving vehicles – is a *major* problem, it is extremely unlikely that you will be physically assaulted while walking down the street.

Theft
By far the biggest crime problem facing tourists in France is theft *(vol)*. Most thieves are after cash or valuables, but they often end up with passports, address books, personal mementoes and other items. You may

have to rush off to your nearest consulate to sort out the missing documents.

The problems you're most likely to encounter are thefts from – and of – cars, pickpocketing and the snatching of daypacks or women's handbags, particularly in dense crowds (for example, at busy train stations, on rush-hour public transport, in fast-food joints and in cinemas). A common ploy is for one person to distract you while another zips through your pockets. The south of France seems to have more crime than the north – the Côte d'Azur and Provence are notorious.

Although there's no need whatsoever to travel in fear, a few simple precautions will minimise your chances of being ripped off.

Before Leaving Home Photocopy your passport, credit cards, plane ticket, driver's licence, and other important documents, such as your address book and travellers cheques receipts – leave one copy of each document at home and keep another one with you, separate from the originals. Some people even bring along a photocopy of their birth certificate, which is useful if you have to replace a passport.

Write your name and address on the inside of your suitcase, backpack, daypack, address book, diary and so on. If such items are lost or stolen and later recovered, the police will have at least some chance of finding you.

Documents & Money Always keep your money, credit cards, tickets, passport, driver's licence and other important documents in a money belt worn *inside* your trousers or skirt. Never carry them around in a daypack or waist pouches, which are easy for thieves to grab (or slice off) and sprint away with. The same goes for those little pouches that you wear around your neck.

Keep enough money for a day's travel separate from your moneybelt (for example, in your daypack or suitcase). That way, you'll be penniless only if everything gets taken at once.

While theft from hotel rooms is pretty rare, it's a bad idea to leave cash or important documents in your room. Hostels are a fair bit riskier, since so many people are always passing through. If you don't want to carry your documents with you, ask the hotel or hostel's front desk to put them in the *coffre* (safe).

When going swimming, especially along the Côte d'Azur, try to leave valuables in the hotel or hostel safe. And while you're in the water, have members of your party take turns sitting with everyone's packs and clothes.

While on the Move Be especially careful with your passport and important documents at airports: pickpockets and professional passport thieves know that people are often careless when they first arrive in a foreign country.

When travelling by train, especially if you'll be sleeping, the safest place for small bags is under your seat. Large bags are best off in the overhead rack right above your head, and you may want to fasten them to the rack with the straps or even a small lock. Bags left in the luggage racks at the ends of the carriage are an easy target: as the train is pulling out of a station, a thief can grab your pack and hop off; the authors of this guide have seen it happen. In sleeping compartments, make sure to lock the door at night.

Keep an eagle eye on your bags in train stations, airports, fast-food outlets, cinemas and at the beach. Anything you can do to make your equipment easy to watch and clumsy to carry will make it more difficult to snatch. Some people lock, zip or tie their daypack to their main pack. Affixing tiny locks to the zips will help keep out prying fingers. When sitting in a cinema or outdoor cafe, you might also wrap one strap of your daypack around your leg (or the leg of your chair).

If you leave your bags at a left-luggage office or in a luggage locker (where available), treat your claim chit (or locker code) like cash: some audacious daypack-thieves have been known to take stolen chits back to the train station left luggage and thus claim possession of the rest of their victims' belongings.

While Travelling by Car Parked cars and motorbikes, as well as the contents of vehicles (especially those cars with rental company stickers or out-of-town, red-coloured purchase-repurchase or foreign plates) are favourite targets for thieves. The risk is especially high in the south of France, where theft victims – including one of the authors for this book – abound.

Never, ever leave anything valuable inside your car. Like other Europeans, many French people often carry their removable car radios with them whenever they park their vehicles. In fact, never leave anything at all in a parked car. Even a few old clothes, a handkerchief or an umbrella left lying in the backseat may attract the attention of a passing thief, who won't think twice about breaking a window or smashing a lock to see if there's a camera hidden underneath. Hiding your bags in the trunk is considered very risky; indeed, French people with hatchbacks often remove the plastic panel that covers the boot (trunk) so passing thieves can see that it's empty.

When you arrive in a new city or town, find a hotel and unload your belongings *before* doing any sightseeing that will involve leaving the car unattended. And on your last day in town, ask the hotel manager to store your luggage until after you've done any local touring, shopping or errands.

Racism

The rise in support for the extreme right-wing National Front in recent years reflects the growing racial intolerance in France, particularly against North African Muslims and, to a somewhat lesser extent, blacks from sub-Saharan Africa and France's former colonies and territories in the Caribbean. From time to time the friction erupts into violent demonstrations which are accompanied just as often by reports of police brutality.

In many parts of France, especially in the south (for example, Provence and the Côte

d'Azur), places of entertainment such as bars and discotheques are, for all intents and purposes, segregated: owners and their ferocious bouncers make it abundantly clear what sort of people are 'invited' to use their nominally private facilities and what sort are not. Such activities are possible in the land of *liberté*, *égalité* and *fraternité* because there is little civil rights enforcement.

Hunters

The hunting season usually runs from the end of September to the end of February. If you see signs reading *chasseurs* or *chasse gardé* strung up or tacked to trees, you might want to think twice about wandering into the area, especially if you're wearing anything that might make you resemble a deer. Unless the area is totally fenced off, it's not illegal to be there, but accidents do happen (50 French hunters die each year after being shot by other hunters).

Natural Dangers

There are strong undertows and currents along the Atlantic coast, particularly in south-western Brittany. If sleeping on a beach, always ensure you are above the high tidemark (especially on the northern coast of Brittany).

Thunderstorms in the mountains and hot southern plains can be extremely sudden, violent and dangerous. It's a good idea to check the weather report before you set out on a long walk. If you're heading into the high country of the Alps or Pyrenees it is important to be well prepared: take extra food and water and make sure that you have plenty of warm clothing.

Smoking

By nature many French people do not take seriously laws they consider stupid or intrusive; whether others feel the same is another matter. Laws banning smoking in public places do exist, for example, but no one pays much attention to them. In restaurants, diners will often smoke in the non-smoking sections – and the waiter will happily bring them an ashtray.

EMERGENCY
Emergency Numbers

The following toll-free numbers can be dialled 24 hours from any public phone or Point Phone in France without inserting a télécarte or coins:

SAMU (medical/ambulance
  services)   ☎ 15
Police   ☎ 17
Fire department *(pompiers)*   ☎ 18
Multilingual Europe-wide
  emergency   ☎ 115
Rape crisis hotline   ☎ 08 00 05 95 95

SOS Help

This Paris-based crisis hotline (☎ 01 47 23 80 80) is staffed from 3 to 11 pm daily. The volunteer staff – all of whom are native English-speakers – are there to talk with other English-speakers who are having difficulties and to make referrals for specific problems (such as on-the-spot emergency psychological counselling and referrals to medical services, through their links to sister organisations SOS Mèdecins and SOS Dentistes). They're also happy to give out practical information on less urgent matters.

SAMU

When you ring ☎ 15 (also ☎ 01 45 67 50 50 in Paris), the 24-hour dispatchers of the Service d'Aide Médicale d'Urgence (Emergency Medical Aid Service) will take down details of your problem (there's a duty person who speaks English) and then send out a private ambulance (250FF to 300FF) or, if necessary, a mobile intensive care unit.

For less serious problems, SAMU can also dispatch a doctor for a house call. If you prefer to be taken to a particular hospital, mention this to the ambulance crew, as usually they'll take you to the nearest one. In emergency cases (that is, those requiring intensive care units), billing will be taken care of later. Otherwise, you need to pay in cash at the time you receive assistance.

Highway Emergencies

There are *postes d'appel d'urgence* (emergency phones), mounted on bright orange posts, about every 4km along main highways and every 1.5 to 2km on motorways.

SOS Voyageurs

Many large train stations (for example, at Marseilles) have offices of SOS Voyageurs, an organisation of volunteers (mostly retirees) who try to help travellers having some sort of difficulty. If your pack has been stolen or your ticket lost, or if you just need somewhere to change your baby, they may be able to help. The staff can be sweet and helpful, but they are not very good in a crisis.

LEGAL MATTERS
Police

Thanks to the Napoleonic Code (on which the French legal system is based), the police can pretty much search anyone they want to at any time – whether or not there is probable cause. They have been known to stop and search chartered coaches for drugs just because they are coming from Amsterdam.

France has two separate police forces. The Police Nationale, under the command of departmental prefects (and, in Paris, the Préfet de Police), includes the Police de l'Air et des Frontières (PAF), the border police. The Gendarmerie Nationale, a paramilitary force under the control of the Ministry of Defence, handles airports, borders and so on, and are particularly important in rural areas.

The dreaded Compagnies Républicaines de Sécurité (CRS), riot-police heavies, are part of the Police Nationale. You often see hundreds of them, equipped with the latest riot gear, at strikes or demonstrations.

Police with shoulder patches reading 'Police Municipale' are under the control of the local mayor.

If asked a question, cops are likely to be correct and helpful but no more than that (though you may get a salute). If the police stop you for any reason, be polite and remain calm. They have wide powers of search and seizure and, if they take a dislike to you, they may choose to use them. The police can, without any particular reason, decide to examine your passport, visa, carte de séjour and so on.

French police are very strict about security, especially at airports. Do not leave baggage unattended: they're serious when they warn that suspicious objects will be summarily blown up.

Drinking & Driving

As elsewhere in the EU, the laws are very tough when it comes to drinking and driving, and for many years the slogan has been: *'Boire ou conduire, il faut choisir'* (To drink or to drive, you have to choose). The acceptable blood-alcohol limit is 0.05%, and drivers exceeding this amount face fines of up to 30,000FF plus up to two years in jail. Licences can also be immediately suspended.

Littering

The fine for littering is about 1000FF.

Drugs

Importing or exporting drugs can lead to a 10- to 30-year jail sentence. The fine for possession of drugs for personal use can be as high as 500,000FF.

BUSINESS HOURS

Most museums are closed on either Monday or Tuesday, though in summer some open daily. A few places (such as the Louvre in Paris) stay open until almost 10 pm on one or two nights a week.

Small businesses are open daily, except Sunday and often Monday. Hours are usually 9 or 10 am to 6.30 or 7 pm, with a midday break from noon or 1 pm to 2 or 3 pm.

Banks usually open from 8 or 9 am to sometime between 11.30 and 1 pm, and 1.30 or 2 to 4.30 or 5 pm, Monday to Friday or Tuesday to Saturday. Exchange services may end half an hour before closing time.

Post offices generally open 8.30 or 9 am to 5 or 6 pm on weekdays, perhaps with a one- to 1½-hour break at midday, and Saturday mornings.

Supermarkets and hypermarkets open Monday to Saturday; a few open on Sunday morning in July and August. Small food shops are mostly closed on Sunday morning or afternoon and Monday, so Saturday afternoon may be your last chance to stock up on provisions until Tuesday. Many restaurants in Paris are closed on Sunday.

In some parts of France, local laws require that most business establishments close for at least one day per week. Exceptions include family-run businesses, such as grocery stores and small restaurants, and places large enough to rotate staff so everyone gets to have a day off.

Since you can never tell which day of the week a certain merchant or restaurateur has chosen to take off, this book includes, where possible (summer times can be particularly unpredictable), details on weekly closures.

In July and August, loads of businesses tend to shut down, the owners and employees heading for the hills or the beaches for their annual vacation.

PUBLIC HOLIDAYS & SPECIAL EVENTS

The following *jours fériés* (public holidays) are observed in France:

New Year's Day *(Jour de l'An)* 1 January – parties in larger cities; fireworks tend to be subdued by international standards
Easter Sunday and Monday *(Pâques & lundi de Pâques)* Late March/April
May Day *(Fête du Travail)* 1 May – traditional parades
Victoire 1945 8 May – celebrates the Allied victory in Europe that ended WWII
Ascension Thursday *(L'Ascension)* May – celebrated on the 40th day after Easter
Pentecost/Whit Sunday and Whit Monday *(Pentecôte & lundi de Pentecôte)* Mid-May to mid-June – celebrated on the 7th Sunday after Easter
Bastille Day/National Day *(Fête Nationale)* 14 July – *the* national holiday
Assumption Day *(L'Assomption)* 15 August
All Saints' Day *(La Toussaint)* 1 November
Remembrance Day *(Le onze novembre)* 11 November – celebrates the WWI armistice
Christmas *(Noël)* 25 December

The following are *not* public holidays in France: Shrove Tuesday (Mardi Gras; the first day of Lent); Maundy (or Holy) Thursday *(jeudi saint)* and Good Friday *(vendredi saint)* just before Easter; and Boxing Day (26 December). Good Friday and Boxing Day, however, are holidays in Alsace.

Most museums and shops (but not cinemas, restaurants or most *boulangeries*) are closed on public holidays. When a holiday falls on a Tuesday or a Thursday, the French have a custom of making a *pont* (bridge) to the nearest weekend by taking off Monday or Friday as well. The doors of banks are a good place to look for announcements of upcoming long weekends.

France's national day, 14 July, commemorates the day in 1789 when defiant Parisians stormed the Bastille prison, thus beginning the French Revolution. Often called Bastille Day by English speakers, it is celebrated with great gusto in most of the country, and in many cities and towns it can seem as if every person and their poodle is out on the streets. In Paris and many provincial towns (for example, Carcassonne), Bastille Day ends with a fireworks' display.

On May Day, many people – including those marching in the traditional trade-union parades – buy *muguets* (lilies of the valley), said to bring good luck, to give to friends. French law allows anyone to sell wild muguet on 1 May without a permit. Mid-May brings the International Film Festival in Cannes, the epitome of see-and-be-seen cinema events in Europe, followed by the French Open, the Grand Slam tennis tournament held in Paris.

Most French cities have at least one major music, dance, theatre, cinema or art festival each year. Some villages hold *foires* (fairs) and *fêtes* (festivals) to honour anything from a local saint to the year's garlic crop. In this book, important annual events are listed under Special Events in many city and town listings; for precise details about dates, which change from year to year, contact the local tourist office. Remember that towns hosting the largest festivals get extremely busy, making it very difficult to find accommodation; make reservations as far in advance as possible.

ACTIVITIES

France's varied geography and climate make it a superb place for a wide range of outdoor pursuits. Some hostels, for example those run by the Fédération Unie des Auberges de Jeunesse (FUAJ; see Hostels & Foyers under Accommodation later in the chapter), offer week-long sports *stages* (training courses).

Little of France consists of pristine wilderness. Even the remotest regions are dotted with villages and crisscrossed by roads, power lines, hydroelectric projects and so on. Not that there aren't beautiful, unspoiled places, but they're not – as in Australia or North America – a three-day walk from the nearest road. On the other hand, to many travellers coming from built-up Britain (which supports roughly the same population) or other parts of continental Europe, parts of France will look almost empty.

Cycling

The French take their cycling very seriously, and whole parts of the country almost grind to a halt during the annual Tour de France.

A *vélo tout-terrain* (VTT, mountain bike) is a fantastic tool for exploring the countryside. Some GR and GRP trails (see Walking later in the chapter) are open to mountain bikers, but take care not to startle walkers. A *piste cyclable* is a bicycle path.

Mountain-bike enthusiasts who can read French should look for the books of *Les Guides VTT*, a series of cyclists topoguides published by Didier et Richard. Information on topoguides for cyclists can be found under Maps earlier in the chapter.

Lonely Planet's *Cycling France* is essential when touring and contains 35 mapped rides from one to nine days duration. As well as turn-by-turn directions, it includes information on places to stay and eat, details of attractions en route, and gives on-the-road bike maintainance tips and nutrition advice.

Some of the best areas for cycling (with varying grades of difficulty) are around the Alpine resorts of Annecy and Chambéry (see the French Alps & Jura chapter for details) and through the Pyrenees. In southwestern France, the Dordogne and Quercy offer a vast network of scenic, tranquil roads for cycle tourists, while the beautiful Mt Aigoual region has a huge network of paths (see the Languedoc-Roussillon chapter). The Loire Valley and coastal regions such as Brittany, Normandy and the Atlantic Coast offer a wealth of easier options.

For information on transporting your bicycle and bike rental, see Bicycle in the Getting Around chapter. Details on places that rent bikes appear at the end of each city or town listing under Getting Around.

Skiing

France has more than 400 ski resorts in the Alps, the Jura, the Pyrenees, the Vosges, the Massif Central and even the mountains of Corsica. The ski season generally lasts from December to March or April, though it's shorter at low altitudes and longer high up in the Alps. Snow conditions can vary greatly from year to year. January and February tend to have the best overall conditions, but the slopes can be very crowded during the February–March school holidays. Although prices differ from place to place, *ski de piste* or *ski alpin* (downhill skiing) ends up being quite expensive because of the cost of equipment, lift tickets, accommodation and the customary après-ski drinking sessions. *Ski de fond* (cross-country skiing) is a lot cheaper.

France can claim a fair few superlatives in the world of skiing. The largest ski area in the world is Les Portes du Soleil at Morzine-Avoriaz, north-west of Chamonix. The longest vertical drop (2500m) in France is at Les Arcs, near Bourg St-Maurice. The highest resort in Europe is Val Thorens (2300m), west of Méribel. Europe's largest skiable glacier, measuring almost 200 hectares, is at Les Deux Alpes in the spectacular Parc National des Écrins. One of the longest unofficial trails (20km) in France is in the Vallée Blanche at Chamonix; the longest official (groomed) one – some 16km – is the black-marked Sarenne Trail at Alpe d'Huez.

The Alps have some of Europe's finest – and priciest – ski facilities. In a few places, you can even ski on glaciers during the summer (for details, see the French Alps & the Jura chapter). The high-altitude down-

hill ski resorts in the Alps not only satisfy skiers at all levels but also offer good snowboarding and cross-country skiing. Two of the best ski areas are Les Trois Vallées (The Three Valleys), which include the resorts of Méribel, Courchevel, Val Thorens and Les Menuires, and L'Espace Killy, with Val d'Isère and Tignes. Almost as good – and cheaper – are the resorts of Les Arcs and Alpe d'Huez. In these resorts the snow is the most plentiful and tends to be more powdery, the runs are long and varied, and off-piste skiing is among the best in the world.

Smaller, low-altitude stations, more suited to beginners and intermediates, include quite a few of the resorts in the Pyrenees (for example, Andorra, Cauterets and Vallée d'Aspe) and the Massif Central (for example, Le Mont Dore). They are much cheaper and less glitzy than their classier, more vertically challenging counterparts. In the Alps, low-altitude skiing is popular on the Vercors massif (see Around Grenoble in the French Alps & Jura chapter).

Cross-country skiing is possible at high-altitude resorts but is usually much better in the valleys (for example, on the 200km of trails around Le Grand Bornand and La Clusaz near Annecy). Undoubtedly some of the best trails are in the Jura range, around resorts like Métabief and Les Rousses.

One of the cheapest ways to ski in France is to buy a package deal before leaving home. Ask your travel agency for details. Many hostels in the Alps offer affordable week-long packages in winter, including room, board, ski passes and sometimes equipment and lessons.

Outside France, French government tourist offices (see Tourist Offices Abroad earlier in the chapter for addresses) can supply you with the annual *France: The Largest Ski Domain in the World*, a brochure with details on more than 50 French ski resorts. It is published by the Association des Mairies des Stations Françaises de Sports d'Hiver et d'Été (Map 2, ☎ 01 47 42 23 32, fax 01 42 66 15 904, @ skifrance@laposte.fr, metro Havre Caumartin), better known as Ski France, based at 61 blvd Haussmann, 8me, 75008 Paris. It has a Web site at www.skifrance.fr. The Club Alpin Français office (see Walking below) may also be able to provide information.

During the snow season, the Thursday and Friday editions of the *International Herald Tribune* have a weekend ski report on the back page. By Minitel, information on snow conditions and some 100 ski stations is available on 3615 CORUS.

Walking

France is crisscrossed by a staggering 120,000km of *sentiers balisés* (marked walking paths), which pass through every imaginable kind of terrain in every region of the country. No permits are needed for hiking, but there are restrictions on where you can camp, especially in national parks.

Probably the best-known trails are the *sentiers de grande randonnée*, long-distance footpaths whose alphanumeric names begin with the letters GR and whose track indicators *(jalonnement or balisage)* consist of red and white stripes on trees, rocks, walls, posts and so on. Some are many hundreds of kilometres long, such as the GR5, which goes from the Netherlands through Belgium, Luxembourg and the spectacular Alpine scenery of eastern France, before ending up in Nice. Others include the GR1, which circumnavigates the Paris metropolitan area; the GR3, which passes through the Loire Valley; the GR4, which meanders through the Massif Central; the popular GR10, which runs along the Pyrenees from the Mediterranean to the Atlantic; and the stunning GR20, which takes you to some of Corsica's highest peaks.

The *grandes randonnées de pays* (GRP) trails, whose markings are yellow and red, usually go in some sort of loop. These 'country walks' are designed for intense exploration of one particular area and usually take from a few days to a week, though some are longer.

Other types of trails include *sentiers de promenade randonnée* (PR), walking paths whose trail markings are yellow; *drailles*, paths used by cattle to get to high-altitude summer pastures; and *chemins de halage*, towpaths built in the days when canal barges

were pulled by animals walking along the shore. Shorter day-hike trails are often known as *sentiers de petites randonnées* or *sentiers de pays*; many of them are circular so that you end up where you started.

If you are planning to explore some of France on foot, Lonely Planet's *Walking in France* is packed with lively detail and essential practical information.

The Fédération Française de la Randonnée Pédestre (FFRP, Map 1; French Ramblers' Association) has an information centre and bookshop in Paris at 14 rue Riquet, 19me (☎ 01 44 89 93 93, fax 01 40 35 85 67, Minitel 3615 RANDO, metro Pernety) open 10 am to 6 pm Monday to Saturday.

The FFRP publishes some 120 topoguides in French (75FF or 99FF), map-equipped booklets on GR, GRP and PR trails. Local organisations also produce topoguides, some of them in the form of a *pochette* (a folder filled with single-sheet itineraries). The information that topoguides provide includes details on trail conditions, flora, fauna, villages en route, camp sites, mountain shelters and so on. In many areas, bookshops and tourist offices stock a selection of titles with local relevance.

The UK publisher Robertson McCarta has translated quite a few topoguides into English. Issued in book form as part of the Footpaths of Europe series, regions covered include Normandy, Brittany, the Loire Valley, the Auvergne, the Dordogne, the Alps, the Pyrenees, Provence and Corsica. They're cheaper and easier to find in the UK than in France.

Hotel walks are unguided walks in which a walking company arranges for accommodation and hearty dinners, as well as transport for your pack so you can hike unencumbered from village to village. Headwater (☎ 0160-648 699), a company based in Cheshire (UK) that arranges such walks, is represented in Australia by Peregrine (☎ 03-9663 8611).

The Club Alpin Français (Map 3, ☎ 01 53 72 88 00, fax 01 42 02 24 18, Minitel 3615 CALPIN, metro Laumière), 24 ave de Laumière, 19e, 75019 Paris, generally provides its services (such as courses and group walks) only to members, though the shelters it maintains are open to everyone. Membership costs 486FF per year (285FF for people aged 18 to 24) and includes various kinds of insurance. Its Web site is at www.clubalpin-idf.com.

Wild France, edited by Douglas Botting and published by the Sierra Club in the USA, is a good general walking guide while *Walking in the Alps*, by Kev Reynolds, focuses on Alpine walks.

For details on *refuges* (mountain huts) and other overnight accommodation for walkers, such as *gîtes d'étape*, see Accommodation later in the chapter.

Mountaineering & Rock Climbing

If you're interested in *alpinisme* (mountaineering) or *escalade* (rock climbing), you can arrange climbs with professional guides through the Club Alpin Français (see the Walking section).

Swimming

France has lovely beaches along all of its coasts – the English Channel, the Atlantic and the Mediterranean (including the coast of Corsica) – as well as on lakes such as Lac d'Annecy and Lake Geneva. The fine, sandy beaches along the family-oriented Atlantic coast (for example, near La Rochelle) are much less crowded than their rather pebbly counterparts on the Côte d'Azur. Corsica is crowded only during July and August. Beaches along the Channel and in southern Brittany are cooler than those farther south. The public is free to use any beach not marked as private in France.

Topless bathing for women is pretty much the norm in France – if other people are doing it, you can assume it's OK. For information on nude bathing, see Naturism later in the chapter.

Surfing & Windsurfing

The best surfing in France is on the Atlantic coast around Biarritz, where waves can reach heights of 4m. Windsurfing is popular wherever there's water and a breeze, and renting equipment is often possible on lakes.

Rafting & Canoeing

White-water rafting, canoeing and kayaking are practised on many French rivers, including those that flow down from the Massif Central (for example, the Dordogne) and the Alps. Farther south, the Gorges du Verdon are popular for white-water rafting, while canoe and kayak enthusiasts tend to favour the Gorges du Tarn. The Fédération Française de Canoë-Kayak (FFCK; ☎ 01 45 11 08 50, fax 01 48 86 13 25), 87 quai de la Marne, 94340 Joinville-le-Pont, can supply information on canoeing and kayaking clubs around the country.

Canal Boating

One of the most relaxing ways to see France is to rent a houseboat for a leisurely cruise along canals and navigable rivers, whose slow-moving and often tree-lined channels pass through some of the most beautiful countryside in Europe. Changes in altitude are taken care of by a system of *écluses* (locks), where you can often hop ashore to meet the lock-keeper, who frequently sells local cheeses, wine and fruit as a sideline. There is no charge to pass through a lock, though some people leave a tip.

Generally, the boats available for hire can accommodate from four to 12 passengers and are outfitted with sleeping berths, a shower, a toilet, sheets, blankets, pillows, a fridge, a hotplate, an oven and kitchen utensils. Anyone over 18 can pilot a river boat without a special licence (though you do need a licence to fish). Before departure, first-time skippers are given instructions on relevant laws and how to operate the boat – learning the ropes takes only about a half-hour. The speed limit is 6km/h on canals and 10km/h on rivers.

Since the canals are usually quite wide (almost 40m in many cases), there's plenty of space to moor your craft (or stop for the night) pretty much wherever you please: for example, near a village, next to an interesting historical site, or in the middle of nowhere. Figure on covering about 20km to 25km a day. Personal equipment you might want to bring along includes binoculars, tennis shoes, wet-weather gear and bicycles (the last of which are available from many boat-rental companies).

Rental in France Canal boats can be rented for a weekend (late Friday afternoon to Monday morning), a short week (Monday afternoon to Friday morning), a week (Saturday afternoon to Saturday morning or Monday afternoon to Monday morning) or a number of weeks. From late June to early September, when demand is very high, the minimum rental period is generally one week.

For a four-person craft, the rates for a weekend or short week generally range from 2000FF (mid-October to mid-April) to 6000FF (in summer, if they're not already booked). Weekly rates, generally 3500FF to 4500FF in winter, start at 6000FF in July and August. These prices do not include fuel, for which you should figure on paying about 500FF a week, depending on how far you travel.

Although for much of the year rental can be arranged with only a day or two of advance notice, you're better off reserving well in advance, especially if you're not familiar with the exact dates of France's holiday weekends and overlapping school holiday periods. If you want a boat in July and August make your reservation several months ahead.

Many companies require that you pay 30% or 40% of the total at the time you make your reservation and the remainder four weeks before your scheduled holiday. Quite a few companies refuse payment by credit card but do accept personal cheques (even from overseas), bank transfers, bank cheques, Eurocheques and postal money orders. Before sailing away, you have to leave a deposit equal to the boat's insurance excess (deductible), usually somewhere between 2000FF and 5000FF.

For details on rental companies, see Activities in the Paris chapter, Redon in the Brittany chapter, Quercy in the Limousin, the Dordogne and Quercy chapter and the introduction to the Burgundy chapter. For a booklet listing boat rental companies, contact the Syndicat National des Loueurs de Bateaux de Plaisance (Map 4, ☎ 01 44 37 04 00, fax 01 45 77 21 88, metro Javel) at Port de Javel, 75015 Paris.

Rental from Abroad Crown Blue Line offers canal-boat rental in Brittany, Alsace, Languedoc and the Camargue area of Provence and along the Canal du Midi in the Toulouse area. Contact Crown Travel (☎ 01603-630513, fax 664298) at 8 Ber Street, Norwich NR1 3EJ, UK.

Fishing

Fishing in France requires not only the purchase of a licence but familiarity with conservation rules that differ from region to region and even from river to river. Dates when fishing is permitted are strictly controlled and, during part of the year, may be limited to certain days of the week. There are rules about the types of lures and hooks you can use, the minimum legal size for each species (that, too, can vary from stream to stream) and the number of fish you can catch in the course of a day. Most tackle shops should have details on any local (often department-based) fishing organisations.

Bird Watching

Places of ornithological interest include Le Teich (near Arcachon on the Atlantic Coast), Provence's spectacular Camargue delta, and the Parc National de Pyrénées.

Horse-Riding

Horse-riding (*équitation*) is popular in many park areas. The opportunities for riding and the variety of trails available are great, from Alpine paths to the trails that run through the Forêt de Fontainebleau. Some GR and GRP trails (see Walking earlier in the chapter) are open to horses. See the regional chapters for details or inquire at local tourist offices.

Hang-Gliding & Parapente

Deltaplane (hang-gliding) and *parapente* (paragliding) are all the rage in many parts of France, particularly in the Alps (see the Annecy and Chamonix listings), the Massif Central (see Le Mont Dore), Languedoc (see Millau) and the Pyrenees (see Bedous).

Paragliding involves running off the top of a mountain dragging a rectangular parachute behind you until it opens. The chute then fills with air and, acting like an aircraft wing, lifts you up off the ground. If the thermals are good you can stay up for hours, circling the area peacefully.

Newcomers can try out paragliding with a *baptême de l'air* (tandem introductory flight) for 250FF to 500FF. A five-day *stage d'initiation* (beginners course) costs 2000FF to 3500FF. See the Pyrenees, French Alps & Jura, Massif Central, Alsace & Lorraine and Languedoc-Roussillon chapters for more information.

Gliding

Vol à voile (gliding) is most popular in France's south, where the temperatures are warmer and the thermals better. Causse Méjean (for example, near Florac) in Languedoc is one of the most popular spots. For the addresses and details of gliding clubs around France, contact the Fédération Française de Vol à Voile (FFVV; ☎ 01 45 44 04 78, fax 01 45 44 71 93, metro Sèvres Babylone) at 29 rue de Sèvres, 75006 Paris.

Ballooning

For details on *montgolfière* (hot-air balloon) flights, see Hot-Air Ballooning under Activities at the beginning of the Burgundy chapter and the boxed text 'Hot-Air Ballooning' in the Loire Valley chapter.

Spelunking

Speleology, the scientific study of caves, was pioneered by the Frenchman Édouard-André Martel at the end of the nineteenth century, and France still has some great places for cave exploration. The Club Alpin Français (see Walking earlier in the chapter) supplies details about organised activities.

Spas & Thalassotherapy

For over a century, the French have been keen fans of *thermalisme* (water cures), for which visitors with ailments ranging from rheumatism to serious internal disorders flock to hot-spring resorts.

Once the domain of the wealthy, spa centres now offer fitness packages intended to appeal to a broad range of people of all ages. Many of the resorts are in the volcanic Massif Central – Vichy is the best known – but there are others along the shore of Lake Geneva (for example, Aix-les-Bains; see the French Alps & Jura chapter) and in the Pyrenees (for example, Cauterets and Luz St-Sauveur).

A salty variant of thermalisme is *thalassothérapie* (sea-water therapy). Centres dot the Côte d'Azur, the Atlantic Coast and the Brittany coast (for example, in Roscoff).

Naturism

France is one of Europe's most popular venues for *naturisme*. Naturist centres, most of them – not surprisingly – in the sunny south (Languedoc-Roussillon, Provence, the Côte d'Azur and the Gironde region of the Atlantic coast), range from small rural camp sites to large chalet villages with cinemas, tennis courts and shops. Their common denominator is water – virtually all have access to the sea, a lake, a river or, at the very least, a pool. Most are open from April to October, and all require that visitors have either a *carte associatif* (membership card) from a naturist club or an International Naturist Federation (INF) *passeport naturiste* (naturist passport). The latter is available at many naturist holiday centres for about 120FF. Nude bathing and sunbathing is also practised all over France on relatively isolated strips of beach.

The Fédération Française du Naturisme (French Naturist Federation, Map 2; ☎ 01 47 64 32 82, fax 01 47 64 32 63, Minitel 3615 NATURISM, metro Wagram), 65 rue de Tocqueville, 75017 Paris, has a variety of brochures on *au naturel* clubs and leisure activities, virtually all of them family-oriented. Their glossy magazine, *Nat-Info* (also known as *Les Nouvelles Vacances*, 30FF), published four times a year, has information on scores of naturist centres and is available from newsstands. Abroad, French government tourist offices (see Tourist Offices Abroad earlier in the chapter) can supply you with a copy of *Naturism in France*, which has details on 65 major holiday centres.

COURSES
Language

All manner of French courses, lasting from two weeks to nine months, are held in Paris and a variety of provincial cities and towns. A number of language schools start new courses at the beginning of every month. Many of the organisations detailed below can also arrange homestays or other accommodation.

The Service Culturel (French Cultural Service) has reams of information on studying in France, as do French government tourist offices and consulates. In Paris, you might also contact the Ministry of Tourism-sponsored International Cultural Organisation (ICO, Map 6; ☎ 01 42 36 47 18, fax 01 40 26 34 45, metro Châtelet) at 55 rue de Rivoli, 1er. The mailing address is 55 rue de Rivoli, BP 2701, 75027 Paris CEDEX.

Within France, lists of addresses are available from a Centre Régional Information Jeunesse (CRIJ), located in almost two dozen cities nationwide (see Employment Agencies under Work later in the chapter). The Paris tourist office has a list of programmes in Paris.

Among the offices of the French Cultural Service, many of them attached to embassies, are the following:

Australia (☎ 02-6216 0100, fax 6216 0127, ✆ *embassy*@france.net.au) 6 Perth Ave, Yarralumla, ACT 2600
Belgium (☎ 02-548 8711, fax 514 1772, ✆ ambafr@linkline.be) 42 blvd de Régent, 1000 Bruxelles
Canada (☎ 416-925 0025, fax 925 2560, ✆ kulto@idirect.com) 175 Bloor St East, Suite 606, Toronto, Ont M4W 3R8
Germany (☎ 030-885 9020, fax 030 882 1287, ✆ info@IF-Berlin.b.shuttle.de) Kurfüstendamm 211D, 10719 Berlin
Ireland (☎ 01-676 7116, fax 676 4077) 1 Kildare St, Dublin 2
Italy (☎ 06-686 011, fax 686 01331, ✆ france-italia@inet.it) 67 Piazza Farnese, 00186 Rome
Netherlands (☎ 020-622 4936, fax 020 623

3631, ✆ mdescart@ambafrance.nl) Vijzelgracht 2a, 1017 HR Amsterdam
New Zealand (☎ 09-524 9401, fax 524 9403) 27 Gilles Ave, Newmarket, PO Box 99, 382 Auckland
Spain (☎ 91-308 4958, fax 319 6401, ✆ institutofrances@mad.servicom.es) Calle Marques de la Ensenada 12, 28004 Madrid
Switzerland (☎ 031-359 2111, fax 359 2192, ✆ ambassade.fr@iprolink.ch) Schosshaldenstrasse 46, 3006 Berne
UK (☎ 020-7838 2055, fax 7838 2088, ✆ scientec@scientec.demon.co.uk) 23 Cromwell Rd, London SW7 2EL
USA (☎ 212-439 1400, fax 439 1455, ✆ new-york-culture@diplomatie.fr) 972 Fifth Ave, New York, NY 10021

Paris The many French-language schools in the capital include:

Alliance Française (Map 4, ☎ 01 42 84 90 00, ✆ info@alliancefrancaise.fr, metro St-Placide) 101 Blvd Raspail, 6e. This is the Paris headquarters of a venerable institution whose brief is to promote French language and civilisation around the world. Month-long French courses at all levels begin on the first working day of each month; registration (250FF) takes place five days before. If there's space, it's possible to enrol for just two weeks. *Intensif* courses, which meet for four hours per day, cost 3200FF per month; *extensif* courses, which involve two hours of class per day, cost 1600FF per month. The registration office opens 9 am to 5 pm on weekdays. Bring your passport and a passport-sized photo. Payment, which must be made in advance, can be done with travellers cheques or credit cards.

Cours de Langue et Civilisation Françaises de la Sorbonne (Map 6, ☎ 01 40 46 22 11, ✆ccfs@paris4sorbonne.fr, metro Cluny-La Sorbonne) 47 rue des Écoles, 5e. The Sorbonne's prestigious French Language & Civilisation Course, from which one of the authors graduated sometime in the early Middle Ages, has courses in French language and civilisation for students of all levels. Costs vary but a four-week summer course should cost from about 5300FF while 16 to 20 hours per week of lectures and tutorials costs between 7000FF and 8000FF per semester. The instructors take a very academic and stilted (though solid) approach to language teaching; don't expect to learn how to haggle in a market or swear at road hogs even after a year here.

Eurocentre (Map 6, ☎ 01 40 46 72 00, 🖃 parinfo@ ieurocentres.com, metro Odéon) 13 passage Dauphine, 6e, 75006. This is the Paris branch of the Zurich-based, non-profit-making Eurocentre chain, which has schools in 10 countries. Two-/four-week intensive courses with 12 to 15 participants, well reviewed by Lonely Planet readers, cost 3820/7640FF, including – each week – 25 50-minute lessons, three lectures and five to 10 hours in the multimedia learning centre. There are also intensive 12-week courses for 20,400FF. New courses begin every two weeks. Web site: www.eurocentres.com

Institut Parisien de Langue et de Civilisation Françaises (Map 4, ☎ 01 40 56 09 53, 🖃 institut .parisien@dial.oleane.com, metro Dupleix) 87 blvd de Grenelle, 15e. Four-week courses with a maximum of 12 students per class cost 2640/3960/6600FF for 10/15/25 hours a week; six-week courses are 3920/5880/9800FF. The office opens 8.30 am to 5 pm weekdays.

Langue Onze (Map 6, ☎ 01 43 38 22 87, 🖃 langue11@club-internet.fr, metro Parmentier) 15 rue Gambey, 11e. This small, independent language school gets good reports from readers. Two/four-week intensive courses of four hours' instruction a day cost 1900/3200FF (1900/3400 July to September), evening classes start at 2000FF a trimester (48 hours) and individual lessons are around 120FF an hour. Classes have a maximum of nine students.

Provinces There are also several language schools in the provinces, which can sometimes have cheaper accommodation options, including:

Aix-en-Provence
The American University Center (☎ 04 42 38 42 38, fax 04 42 38 95 66) 409 ave Jean-Paul Coste. It offers courses of varying length and intensity, which cost 2300FF for 30 hours of instruction and 2700FF for 40 hours spread over two weeks.

Université de Provence (☎ 04 42 95 32 18, fax 04 42 20 64 87, 🖃 scefee@newsup.univ-mrs.fr) 29 ave Robert Schumann. Organises cheaper summer courses (for example, 20 hours of instruction over one week for 1000FF) and offers accommodation for students costing 950FF per week.

Amboise
Eurocentre (☎ 02 47 23 10 60, fax 02 47 30 54 99,) 9 Mail St-Thomas, BP 214, 37402 Amboise CEDEX. A small school in the charming Loire Valley. www.eurocentres.com

Avignon
Centre d'Études Linguistiques d'Avignon (☎ 04 90 86 04 33, fax 04 90 85 92 01, 🖃 cela@ avignon-et-provence.com) 16 rue Ste-Catherine, 84000 Avignon. Has courses that start at 1600FF per week (from 1900FF in July). B&B accommodation can be arranged at 85FF per night per person.

Besançon
Centre de Linguistique Appliquée (☎ 03 81 66 52 00, fax 03 81 66 52 25, 🖃 cla@ univ-fcomte.fr) 6 rue Gabriel Plançon, 25000 Besançon. One of France's largest language schools offering a wide range of French courses at all levels. Four-week summer courses for beginners start at 4000FF.

Dijon
Centre International d'Études Françaises (☎ 03 80 39 35 60, fax 03 80 39 35 61, 🖃 cief@ u-bourgogne.fr) Esplanade Erasme, BP 87874, 21078 Dijon. Attached to Bourgogne university, the centre charges 1950/3450/4800/5900FF for 2/4/6/8 weeks of instruction.

La Rochelle
Eurocentre, Parc de la Francophonie (☎ 05 46 50 57 33, fax 05 46 44 24 77, 🖃 www .eurocentres.com) ave Marillac, 17024 La Rochelle CEDEX 01. Housed in facilities near the Université de La Rochelle's campus, this is a good but pricey school, and can provide accommodation.

Lyon
Alliance Française (☎ 04 78 95 24 72, fax 04 78 60 77 28) 11 rue Pierre Bourdan, 69003 Lyon. Charges 1600FF for 32 hours of instruction spread over 16 days (3200FF for an intensive 64-hour course).

Cooking Courses

The major cooking schools in Paris include École Le Cordon Bleu (☎ 01 53 68 22 50, fax 01 48 56 03 96, metro Vaugirard or Convention), 8 rue Léon Delhomme, 15e; École de Gastronomie Française Ritz Escoffier (☎ 01 43 16 30 50, 🖃 ecole@ritzparis .com, metro Concorde), 38 rue Cambon, 1er; and La Toque d'Or (☎ 01 45 44 86 51, 🖃 younggg@aol.com, metro Varenne), 55 rue de Varenne, 7e. Tuition varies widely (1300FF to 3400FF) but the highly popular Cours de Cuisine Françoise Meunier (☎ 01 40 26 14 00, 🖃 fmeunier@easynet.fr, metro Bourse), 7 rue Paul Lelong, 2e, offers three-hour courses at 10.30 am from Tuesday to

Saturday and at 7.30 pm on Wednesday for 450FF. 'Carnets' of 5/10/20 courses cost 2000/3800/7200FF.

WORK

Despite France's unemployment rate of nearly 10% and laws that forbid non-EU nationals from working in France, working 'in the black' (that is, without documents) is still possible. People without documents probably have their best chance of finding work during fruit harvests, at Alpine ski resorts in the ski season and in the Côte d'Azur's tourist industry. Au-pair work is also very popular and can be done legally even by non-EU citizens.

The national minimum wage for nonprofessionals (le SMIC, or *salaire minimum interprofessionel de croissance*) is 40.72FF per hour. However, employers willing to hire people in contravention of France's employment laws are also likely to ignore the minimum wage law. For practical information on employment in France, you might want to pick up *Living and Working in France: A Survival Handbook* by David Hampshire.

Residence Permits

To work legally in France you must have a residence permit known as a carte de séjour. Getting one is almost automatic for EU nationals and almost impossible for anyone else except full-time students (see Documents at the start of the chapter).

Non-EU nationals cannot work legally unless they obtain a work permit *(autorisation de travail)* before arriving in France. Obtaining a work permit is no easy matter, because a prospective employer has to convince the authorities that there is no French – and, increasingly these days, no EU – citizen who can do the job being offered to you.

Employment Agencies

France's national employment service, the Agence National pour l'Emploi (ANPE), has offices in the cities and most large towns. It has lists of job openings, but you're not likely to find much temporary or casual work except during the time of the fruit harvests, when certain ANPE offices allow special provisions for people interested in becoming temporary farmworkers. The ANPE has office branches throughout Paris; the one at 20 bis rue Ste-Croix de la Bretonnerie, 4e (Map 7; ☎ 01 42 71 24 68, metro Hôtel de Ville) deals with those people residing in the 1er, 2e and 12e arrondissements, for example.

The Centre Régional Information Jeunesse (CRIJ), which provides all sorts of information for young people on housing, professional training and educational options, also sometimes have noticeboards with work possibilities. The Paris headquarters (Map 4; ☎ 01 44 49 12 00, fax 01 40 65 02 61, metro Champ de Mars-Tour Eiffel) is at 101 quai Branly, 15e. Both these bodies are useless, however, if you don't have a carte de séjour.

Au Pair

Under the au-pair system, single young people (aged 18 to about 27) who are studying in France live with a French family and receive lodging, full board and a bit of pocket money in exchange for taking care of the kids, babysitting, doing light housework and perhaps teaching English to the children. Most families prefer young women, but a few positions are also available for young men. Many families want au pairs who are native English speakers, but being able to speak some French may be a prerequisite.

For practical information, pick up *The Au Pair and Nanny's Guide to Working Abroad* by Susan Griffith & Sharon Legg, published by Vacation Work Publications.

Depending on the family and the placement agency, the minimum commitment ranges from two to six months; the maximum initial stay is 12 months, extendable to 18 months. Many families prefer to hire an au pair for the entire school year (from September to late June).

In general, the family provides room and board and gives the au pair 400FF to 500FF per week of pocket money in exchange for up to 30 hours of work and two or three evenings of babysitting each week. By law, au pairs must have one full day off a week (usually Sunday).

Non-EU nationals must contact the placement agency from their home country at least three months in advance, but residents of the EU can apply after arriving in France. The publication *France USA Contacts* (see Newspapers & Magazines earlier in the chapter) is a useful source of want ads for au pairs. The Paris tourist office also has a list of placement agencies, including Accueil Familial des Jeunes Étrangers (Map 4, ☎ 01 42 22 50 34, fax 01 45 60 48, metro Sèvres Babylone), 23 rue du Cherche Midi, 6e, 75006 Paris. Note that most agencies charge the au pair 650FF (for the short summer period) to 800FF (in winter) and collect an additional 570FF to 1270FF from the family.

Agricultural Work
The French government seems to tolerate undocumented workers helping out with some agricultural work, especially during harvests. To find a field job, ask around in areas where harvesting is taking place – trees with almost-ripe fruit on them are a sure sign that pickers will soon be needed. Many farmers prefer hiring people who know at least a bit of French.

The *vendange* (grape harvest) is traditionally France's biggest employer of casual labour, requiring some 100,000 extra pairs of hands each year from about mid-September to mid or late October. Increasingly, vendange is being done by machine, though mechanical picking is forbidden in some areas (such as Champagne) and mechanisation is disdained by the most prestigious chateaux.

The dates of the vendange are set by the prefecture only a week (or less) before the start of the picking, which usually lasts a fortnight. Food is often supplied, but growers offering accommodation are getting harder to find.

Fruits and vegetables are harvested in France from mid-May straight through to November. Apples are grown nearly all over, with the harvest starting in the south (for example, Languedoc) in September and moving northwards to cooler regions (for example, Normandy) by October.

Ski Resorts
The Alps are the most promising of France's ski regions for picking up hospitality work in hotels and restaurants in ski resorts with lots of British holidaymakers. The season runs from about December to April.

If you speak only English, the fashionable resort of Méribel, in the Tarentaise Valley east of Chambéry, may be a good place to start looking, as a large number of British tour companies operate from there.

Côte d'Azur
The season on the Côte d'Azur runs from June to September. Selling goods or services on the beach is one way to make a few francs, though you've got to sell an awful lot of ice cream and wrap a lot of hair with coloured beads to make a living.

A tad more glam is working on a yacht. Cannes and Antibes are the places to start looking and March is the month, as many jobs are filled by mid-April.

ACCOMMODATION
France has accommodation of every sort and for every budget. For details – and, in many cases, help with reservations – contact the nearest tourist office.

In many parts of France, local authorities impose a *taxe de séjour* (tourist tax) on each visitor in their jurisdiction. The prices charged at camp sites, hotels and so on may therefore be as much as 1FF to 7FF per person higher than the posted rates.

Reservations
Advance reservations save you the hassle of looking for a place to stay each time you pull into a new town. During periods of heavy domestic or foreign tourism (for example, around Easter and Christmas–New Year's, during the February–March school holiday and, in some areas, in July and August), having a reservation can mean the difference between finding a room in your

price range and moving on. Many tourist offices will help travellers make local hotel reservations, usually for a small fee (2FF to 10FF). In some cases, you pay a deposit that is later deducted from the first night's bill. The staff may also have information on vacancies, but they will usually refuse to make specific recommendations. You cannot take advantage of reservation services by phone – you have to stop by the office.

Many hotels, particularly budget ones, accept reservations only if they are accompanied by *des arrhes* (pronounced 'dez **ar**'; a deposit) in French francs. Some places, especially those with two or more stars, don't ask for a deposit if you give them your credit-card number or send them confirmation of your plans by letter or fax in clear, simple English.

Even during the peak season, most hotels keep a few rooms unreserved, so that at least some of the people who happen by looking for a place can be accommodated. As a result, a hotel that was all booked up three days earlier may have space if you ring on the morning of your arrival. Except in Paris, you can almost always find a place to stay this way, even in August.

Most places will hold a room only until a set hour, rarely later than 6 or 7 pm (and sometimes earlier). If you're running late, let them know or they're liable to rent out the room to someone else.

Camping

Camping, either in tents or in caravans, is immensely popular in France, and the country has thousands of camp sites, many of them near streams, rivers, lakes or the ocean. Most of them close for at least a few months in winter, and some only open in summer. Hostels sometimes let travellers pitch tents in the back garden.

Rates are generally the same for tents and camping cars, except that the latter are charged an extra fee for electricity. Some places have *forfaits* (fixed price deals) for two or three people. Children up to about age 12 enjoy significant discounts. Few camp sites are close to any major sights, so campers without their own wheels may

spend a fair bit of money (and time) commuting.

Camping à la ferme (camping on the farm) is coordinated by Gîtes de France (see Gîtes Ruraux & B&Bs later in the chapter), publisher of the annual guide *Camping à la Ferme* (75FF). The sites – of which there are more than 1100 all over the country – are generally accessible only if you have a car or bicycle.

For details on camp sites not mentioned in the text, inquire at a local tourist office. If you'll be doing lots of car camping, you should pick up a copy of Michelin's *Camping-Caravanning France* (83FF), which lists 3500 camp sites.

In July and especially August, when most camp sites are completely packed, campers who arrive late in the day have a much better chance of getting a spot if they arrive on foot (that is, without a vehicle). Camp-site offices are often closed for most of the day – the best times to call for reservations are in the morning (before 10 or 11 am), late afternoon or early evening.

Freelance Camping If you'll be doing overnight backpacking, remember that camping is generally permitted only at designated camp sites. Pitching your tent anywhere else (for example, by a road or in a trailside meadow), known as *camping sauvage* in French, is usually illegal, though it's often tolerated to varying degrees. Except in Corsica, you probably won't have any problems if you're not on private land and are at least 1500m from a camp site (or, in a national park, at least an hour's walk from a road).

If you camp out on the beach, you'll be an easy target for thieves, so be careful where you put your valuables when sleeping. In areas with especially high tidal variations (for example, on the northern coast of Brittany and nearby parts of Normandy), sleeping on the beach is not a good idea.

Rental Accommodation

If you don't speak French or have a local person helping you, it may be very difficult to find a flat for long-term rental. In any case, don't sign any documents without having someone fluent in French legalese take a look at them.

The first hurdle is finding a landlord with a suitable apartment who's willing to entrust it to someone who isn't French. After you've exhausted your personal connections, places to look include the *petites annonces* (classified ads) in local newspapers – *De Particulier à Particulier* (15FF) and *La Centrale des Particuliers* (17FF), both issued each Thursday – *À Vendre à Louer* (7FF); and, for students, the CROUS office of the nearest university. Estate agents require lots of paperwork and charge commissions of up to one month's rent.

Competition for apartments can be fierce, especially in September and October, when lots of students are searching for places. However, at any time of year, finding an apartment is a matter of making your calls as soon as possible after the information becomes public.

Refuges & Gîtes d'Étape

A *refuge* (mountain hut or shelter, pronounced 'reh-**fuuzh**') is a very basic dorm room established and operated by national park authorities, the Club Alpin Français or other private organisations along trails in uninhabited mountainous areas that are frequented by hikers and mountain climbers. *Refuges*, some of which are open year-round, are generally marked on hiking and climbing maps.

In general, refuges are equipped with bunks (usually wall-to-wall), mattresses and blankets but not sheets, which you have to bring yourself or (sometimes) rent for 15FF to 20FF. Overnight charges average between 50FF to 70FF per night per person. Meals, prepared by the *gardien* (attendant), are sometimes available. Most refuges are equipped with a telephone, and it is often a good idea to call ahead and make a reservation.

For details on refuges, contact a tourist office near where you'll be hiking or consult the *Guide des Refuges et Gîtes des Alpes*, published by the Grenoble-based Glénat, which covers the Alps; or for the Pyrenees *Hébergement en Montagne*, published by the St-Girons-based Éditions Randonnées Pyrénéennes. Both should be available in bookshops or Maisons de la Presse.

Gîtes d'étape, which are usually better equipped and more comfortable than refuges (some even have showers), are situated in less remote areas, often in villages. They cost around 60FF or 70FF per person and are listed in *Gîtes d'Étape et de Séjour* (70FF), published annually by Gîtes de France.

Gîtes Ruraux & B&Bs

Several types of accommodation – often in charming, traditional-style houses with gardens – are available for people who would like to spend time in rural areas and have a vehicle. All are represented by Gîtes de France, an organisation that acts as a liaison between owners and renters.

A *gîte rural* – of which France has some 35,000 – is a holiday cottage (or part of a house) in a village or on a farm. Amenities always include a kitchenette and bathroom facilities.

A gîte rural owned by a *commune* (the smallest unit of local government) is known as a *gîte communal*. In most cases, there is a minimum rental period – often one week, but sometimes only a few days.

A *chambre d'hôte*, basically a B&B (bed and breakfast), is a room in a private house rented to travellers by the night. Breakfast is included. France has about 15,000 *chambres d'hôtes*.

Details on how to contact the nearest Gîtes de France office are available at any local tourist office, which may also be able to supply a brochure. You can also get in contact with the Fédération Nationale des Gîtes de France (Map 3, ☎ 01 49 70 75 75, fax 01 42 81 28 53, @ information@gites-de-france.fr, Minitel 3615 GITES DE FRANCE, metro Trinité) at 59 rue St-Lazare, 75009 Paris. It also publishes the guides: *Chambres et Tables d'Hôtes* (120FF) and *Nouveaux Gîtes Ruraux* (120FF).

Homestays

Under an arrangement known as *hôtes payants* (literally, 'paying guests') or *hébergement chez l'habitant* (lodging with the owners or occupants of private homes), students, young people and tourists can stay with French families. In general you rent a room and have access (sometimes limited) to the family's kitchen and telephone. Many language schools (see Courses earlier in the chapter) can arrange homestays for their students.

Students and tourists alike should count on paying 3000FF to 5200FF per month, 1200FF to 1500FF per week, or 130FF to 300FF per day for a single room, including breakfast.

Accueil Familial des Jeunes Étrangers (Map 4, ☎ 01 45 49 15 57, fax 01 45 44 60 48, metro Sèvres Babylone) 23 rue du Cherche Midi, 75006 Paris. They'll find you a room with a family for 3000FF to 3500FF per month, including breakfast. For stays of less than a month, expect to pay about 150FF per day. There's a subscription fee of 500FF for stays of less than a month.

France Lodge (Map 3, ☎ 01 53 20 09 09, fax 01 53 20 01 25; metro Le Peletier) 41 rue La Fayette, 75009. A non-profit-making organisation that arranges accommodation in private homes and apartments. In Paris, prices start at about 150FF per night per person (cheaper by the month). Annual membership costs 100FF, and payment must be made in French francs.

Hostels & Foyers

Official hostels that belong to one of the three hostel associations in France are known as *auberges de jeunesse* and are so indicated in this book. In university towns, you may also find *foyers* (pronounced 'fwayei'), student dormitories converted for use by travellers during the summer school holidays. In certain cities and towns, young workers are accommodated in dormitories called either *foyers de jeunes travailleurs* or *travailleuses*, and despite the names, most are now mixed sex. These places, which often take *passagères* and *passagers* (female and male short-term guests) when they have space, are relatively unknown to most travellers and very frequently have

space available when the other kinds of hostels are full. Information on hostels and foyers not mentioned in the text is available from local tourist offices.

In Paris, expect to pay 100FF to 130FF per night for a hostel bed, including breakfast. In the provinces, a bunk in the single-sex dorm room generally costs somewhere from 50FF (at an out-of-the-way place with basic facilities) to 70FF, which does not include a sometimes-optional continental breakfast (around 15FF).

Hostel Organisations Most of France's hostels belong to one of three major hostel associations:

Fédération Unie des Auberges de Jeunesse (FUAJ, Map 3; ☎ 01 44 89 87 27, fax 01 44 89 87 10, Minitel 3615 FUAJ, metro La Chapelle) 27 rue Pajol, 75018 Paris. Web site: www.fuaj.org

Ligue Française pour les Auberges de la Jeunesse (LFAJ, Map 1;☎ 01 44 16 78 78, fax 01 44 16 78 80, metro Glacière) 67 rue Vergniaud, 75013 Paris

Union des Centres de Rencontres Internationales de France (UCRIF, Map 6; ☎ 01 40 26 57 64, fax 01 40 26 58 20, Minitel 3615 UCRIF, ☎ ucrif@aol.com, metro Les Halles or Étienne Marcel) 27 rue de Turbigo, 75002 Paris

FUAJ and LFAJ affiliates will require Hostelling International or similar cards, available at any hostel for about 100FF (70FF if you're under 26). They also require that you either bring a sleeping sheet or rent one for 13FF to 17FF per stay.

Hotels

Most French hotels have between one and four stars; the fanciest places have four stars plus an L (for 'luxury'). A hotel that has no stars (that has not been rated) is known as *non-homologué*, sometimes abbreviated as NH. The letters 'NN' after the rating mean the establishment conforms to the *nouvelle norme* (new standards), introduced in 1992. Hotel ratings are based on certain objective criteria (for example, the size of the entry hall), not the quality of the service, the decor or cleanliness, so a one-star establishment may be more pleasant than some two- or three-star places. Prices often reflect these intangibles far more than they do the number of stars.

Most hotels offer a *petit déjeuner* (breakfast), consisting of a croissant, French rolls, butter, jam and either coffee or hot chocolate. The charge is usually 20FF to 40FF per person, a bit more than you would pay at a cafe. Some places in particularly tourist-heavy areas require guests to take breakfast.

Budget Hotels In general, hotels listed under 'budget' have doubles that cost less than two hostel beds, that is up to 180FF (270FF in Paris), quite a bit less than the budget options available in countries such as the UK or Germany. Most are equipped with a washbasin (and, usually, a bidet) but lack private bath or toilet. Almost all these places also have more expensive rooms equipped with shower, toilet and other amenities.

Most doubles, which generally cost only marginally more than singles, have only one double bed, though some places have rooms with two twin beds *(deux lits séparés)*; triples and quads usually have two or three beds. Taking a shower in the hall bathroom is sometimes free but is usually *payant*, which means there's a charge of 10FF to 25FF per person.

If you're in the market for truly rock-bottom accommodation, you may come across *hôtels de passe*, hotels whose rooms are rented out for use by prostitutes. Certain parts of central Marseilles and Paris' Pigalle and rue St-Denis areas are known to have such establishments, but so do other cities and towns. Of course, it's not that you can't get a good night's sleep in a *hôtel de passe* – if the walls are thick enough, that is.

Some cheap hotels have the unpleasant habit of refusing to refund the unused part of your deposit when you switch hotels or leave town earlier than planned. The moral of the story is not to prepay for those nights where there's a chance you won't be staying. In any case, the sooner you tell the manager, the better your chances of being reimbursed.

If you're travelling by car, you'll be able to take advantage of the remarkably cheap hotel chains on the outskirts of France's cities and towns, usually on a main access route. The best known, Formule 1, charges 120FF to 150FF for a ticky-tacky, toilet-equipped room with hall shower for up to three people; until 7 pm, there's no penalty to cancel a reservation prepaid by credit card. You can reserve on ☎ 08 36 68 56 85 or at www.hotelformule1.com.

Hôtel Meublé A small hotel that rents out rooms with *cuisinettes* (kitchenettes), generally by the week and often to the same holidaying clients year after year, is known as a *hôtel meublé*. They are common on the Côte d'Azur, especially in Nice.

Mid-Range Hotels Hotels with double rooms listed under 'mid-range' in this book come with showers and toilets (unless otherwise noted) and usually have doubles for 170FF to about 350FF. Many places listed under 'budget' have rooms that, from the point of view of amenities and price, fall into the mid-range category.

Some 4000 hotels – many of them family-run places in the countryside, by the sea or in the mountains – belong to Logis de France, an organisation whose affiliated establishments meet strict standards of service and amenities. They generally offer very good value. The Fédération Nationale des Logis de France (Map 1, ☎ 01 45 84 70 00, fax 01 45 83 59 66, ✆ info@logis-de-france.fr, Minitel 3615 LOGIS DE FRANCE, metro Tolbiac), based at 83 ave d'Italie, 13e, 75013 Paris, issues an annual guide with a detailed map of how to find each hotel.

MEALS IN FRANCE
Breakfast

In the Continental tradition, the French start the day with a petit déjeuner, comprising a croissant and a bread roll with butter and jam, followed by a *café au lait* (coffee with lots of hot milk), a small black coffee or hot chocolate. Buying rolls or pastries from a patisserie is quite a bit cheaper than eating at a hotel or cafe.

Lunch & Dinner

For many French people, especially in the provinces, lunch is still the main meal of the day. Restaurants generally serve lunch between noon and 2 or 2.30 pm and dinner from 7 or 7.30 pm to sometime between 9.30 and 10.30 pm. Very few restaurants (except for brasseries, cafes and fast-food places) open between lunch and dinner.

In big towns, most restaurants close on Sunday. In cities such as Paris, from where most locals flee for the beaches in August, many restaurateurs lock up and leave town along with their clients.

Traditional Meals

As the pace of French life becomes more hectic, the three-hour midday meal is becoming increasingly rare, at least on weekdays. Dinners, however, are still turned into elaborate affairs whenever time and finances permit. For visitors, the occasional splurge can be the perfect end to a day of sightseeing.

A fully fledged, traditional French meal is an awesome event, often comprising six courses and sometimes more. The meal is always served with wine (red, white or rosé, depending on what you're eating). The fare served at a traditional *déjeuner* (lunch), usually eaten around 1 pm, is largely indistinguishable from that served at *dîner* (dinner), usually begun around 8.30 pm.

TYPES OF EATERIES
Restaurants & Brasseries

There are lots of restaurants where you can get an excellent French meal for 150FF to 200FF – Michelin's *Guide Rouge* is filled with them – but good, inexpensive French restaurants are in short supply. In this book, we have tried to list restaurants that offer what the French call a *bon rapport qualité-prix* (good value for money).

Some of the best French restaurants in the country are attached to hotels, and those on the ground floor of budget hotels often have some of the best deals in town. Almost all are open to non-guests.

Routiers (truckers restaurants), usually found on the outskirts of towns and along

major roads, cater to truck drivers and can provide a quick, hearty break from cross-country driving.

Restaurants usually specialise in a particular variety of food (for example, regional, traditional, North African, Vietnamese), whereas brasseries – which look very much like cafes – serve more standard fare. This often includes *choucroute* (sauerkraut served with meat) because the brasserie, which actually means 'brewery', originated in Alsace. Unlike restaurants, which usually open only for lunch and dinner, brasseries keep going from morning until night and serve meals (or at least something solid) at all times of the day.

Ethnic Restaurants

France has a considerable population of immigrants from its former colonies and protectorates in North and West Africa, Indochina, the Middle East, India, the Caribbean and the South Pacific, as well as refugees from every corner of the globe, so a huge variety of reasonably priced ethnic food is available.

There are a number of good *cacher* (kosher) restaurants in Paris, Strasbourg and Marseilles (see the Paris, Alsace & Lorraine and Provence chapters).

Menus

Most restaurants offer at least one fixed-price, multicourse meal known in French as a *menu*, *menu à prix fixe* or *menu du jour* (menu of the day). A *menu* (not to be confused with a *carte* – throughout this book we italicise *menu* to distinguish it from the English word 'menu') almost always costs much less than ordering à la carte. In some places, you may also be able to order a *formule*, which usually has fewer choices but allows you to pick two of three courses. In many restaurants, the cheapest lunch *menu* is a much better deal than the equivalent one available at dinner.

When you order a three-course *menu*, you usually get to choose an entree, such as salad, paté or soup; a main dish (several meat, poultry or fish dishes, including the *plat du jour*, are generally on offer); and one or more final courses (usually cheese or dessert).

Boissons (drinks), including wine, cost extra unless the menu says *boisson comprise* (drink included), in which case you may get a beer or a glass of mineral water. If the *menu* has *vin compris* (wine included), you'll probably be served a small *pichet* (jug) of wine. The waiter will always ask if you would like coffee to end the meal, but this will almost always cost extra.

Cafes

See Entertainment later in the chapter for information on pubs, bars and cafes.

Vegetarian Eateries

Vegetarians form only a small minority in France and are not very well catered for, as specialised vegetarian restaurants are few and far between. Only the cities are likely to have vegetarian establishments, and these may often look more like laid-back cafes than restaurants. Other options include *saladeries*, casual restaurants that serve a long list of *salades composées* (mixed salads). For more information on vegetarian options in France, see Guidebooks under Books earlier in the chapter.

Salons de Thé

Salons de thé (tearooms) are trendy and somewhat pricey establishments that usually offer quiches, salads, cakes, tarts, pies and pastries in addition to tea and coffee.

Crêperies

Crêperies specialise in *crêpes*, ultra-thin pancakes cooked on a flat surface and then folded or rolled over a filling. In some parts of France, the word 'crêpe' is used to refer only to sweet crêpes made with *farine de froment* (regular wheat flour), whereas savoury crêpes, often made with *farine de sarrasin* (buckwheat flour) and filled with cheese, mushrooms and the like, are called *galettes*.

Cafeterias

Many cities have cafeteria restaurants offering a good selection of dishes you can see before ordering, a factor that can make life easier if you're travelling with kids. Cafeteria chains include Flunch, Mélodine and Casino.

University Restaurants

All French universities have student restaurants subsidised by the Ministry of Education and operated by the Centre Régional des Œuvres Universitaires et Scolaires, better known as CROUS. Meal tickets are sold at ticket windows, but each university seems to have its own policy on feeding students from out-of-town.

FOOD SHOPPING

Most people buy a good part of their food from a series of small neighbourhood shops, each with its own speciality. At first, having to go to four shops and stand in four queues to fill the fridge (or assemble a picnic) may seem rather a waste of time, but the whole ritual is an important part of the way many French people live their daily lives. Note that many food shops are closed on Sunday afternoon and Monday.

It's perfectly acceptable to purchase only meal-size amounts: a few *tranches* (slices) of meat to make a sandwich, perhaps, or a *petit bout* (small chunk) of sausage.

Boulangeries

Fresh bread is baked and sold at France's 36,000 boulangeries, which supply three-quarters of the country's bread.

All Parisian boulangeries have 250g baguettes, which are long and thin, and 400g fatter loaves of *pain* (bread), both of which should be eaten within four hours of baking. If you're not very hungry, ask for a *demi baguette* or *demi pain*. A *ficelle* is a thinner, crustier version of the baguette – really like very thick breadsticks.

Bread is baked at various times of day, so fresh bread is readily available as early as 6 am and also in the afternoon. Most boulangeries close one day a week, but the days are staggered so that you will always be able to find one establishment open somewhere (except, perhaps, on Sunday afternoon.)

FOOD & WINE

WALES
CARDIFF
Bristol
Oxford
ENGLAND
LONDON

WINE REGIONS
- Bordeaux
- Burgundy
- Beaujolais
- The Rhône
- The Loire
- Alsace
- Languedoc-Roussillon
- French Alps & Jura
- Champagne

NETHERLANDS
GERMANY

Dover
Straits of Dover
Dunkirk
Calais
St-Omer
Boulogne-sur-Mer
Béthune
Lille
BRUSSELS
BELGIUM
LUXEMBOURG
LUXEMBOURG

English Channel

Abbeville
Somme
Amiens
St-Quentin
Charleville-Mézières
Longwy
Thornville
Forbach
Haguenau

Fécamp
Côte d'Albâtre
Dieppe
Beauvais
Compiègne
Soissons
Laon
Reims
Épernay
Châlons-en-Champagne
Verdun
Bar-le-Duc
Nancy
Lunéville
Strasbourg
Molsheim
St-Dié
Colmar
Mulhouse

Cap de la Hague
Cherbourg
Le Havre
Rouen
Seine
Meaux
Marne
CHAMPAGNE
St-Dizier
Épinal
Belfort

Guernsey Island
Jersey Island
St-Helier
Golfe de St-Malo
St-Malo
Caen
Lisieux
Alençon
Chartres
Corbeil
Melun
Sens
Troyes
Chaumont
Besançon
BERN
SWITZERLAND

Île de Batz
Roscoff
Morlaix
St-Brieuc
Fougères
NORMANDY
PARIS
Seine
Montargis
Auxerre
Dijon
Saône
Doubs
Dole

Brest
Quimper
St-Guénolé
Île de Groix
Lorient
Vannes
Rennes
Laval
Le Mans
Sarthe
Orléans
BURGUNDY
Beaune
Chalon-sur-Saône
Lons-le-Saunier
Lake Geneva
Geneva
Thonon
Rhône
Mont Blanc (4807m)

BRITTANY
Belle Île
Île de Noirmoutier
Angers
Baugé
Blois
Loire
Cher
Vierzon
Bourges
Autun
Montceau
Bourg-en-Bresse
Nantua
Annecy
Albertville

St-Nazaire
Nantes
Cholet
Saumur
Tours
LOIRE VALLEY
Châteauroux
Vichy
Roanne
Lyon
Chambéry
Vienne
Grenoble
Briançon
ITALY

Bay of Biscay
La Roche-sur-Yon
Les Sables d'Olonne
Châtellerault
Poitiers
Vienne
Montluçon
Clermont-Ferrand
St-Étienne
Le Puy-en-Velay
MONACO

Île d'Yeu
Île de Ré
La Rochelle
Île d'Oléron
Niort
Limoges
LIMOUSIN
Rhône
PROVENCE
CÔTE D'AZUR
Nice
Cannes
St-Tropez

Saintes
Royan
Cognac
Angoulême
Périgueux
Brive-la-Gaillarde
Nyons
Avignon
Nîmes
Aix-en-Provence
Marseille
Toulon
Îles d'Hyères

Bordeaux
DORDOGNE
Dordogne
QUERCY
Lot
Agen
Montauban
Albi
LANGUEDOC
Montpellier
Golfe du Lion

St-Girons Plage
Bayonne
Biarritz
Hendaye
BASQUE COUNTRY
Pau
Tarbes
Garonne
Toulouse
Castres
Béziers
Carcassonne
ROUSSILLON
Perpignan
Mediterranean Sea

Bilbao
San Sebastián
Vitoria
Pamplona
SPAIN
ANDORRA LA VELLA
ANDORRA

Elevation
3000m	10,000ft
2000m	6500ft
1500m	5000ft
1000m	3000ft
500m	1500ft
0m	0ft

0   50   100km
0   30   60ml

To Nice (750 km)
Bastia
CORSICA
Corte
Ajaccio
Sartène

FOOD HIGHLIGHTS

NORMANDY
1 Apples & Cider
2 Camembert Cheese

ALSACE
3 Choucroute
4 Baeckeoffe

BURGUNDY
5 Mustard
6 Snails

LYON & THE RHÔNE
7 Boudin Blanc
8 Quenelles
9 Boeuf Bourguignon
10 Crème de Cassis

CENTRAL FRANCE: THE DORDOGNE, LIMOUSIN & THE AUVERGNE
11 Truffles
12 Goose Liver

PROVENCE
13 Olives & Olive Oil

14 Fresh Fruit, Vegetables & Herbs
15 Bouillabaisse

GASCONY & THE BASQUE COUNTRY
16 Garbure
17 Deep-Red Chilies
18 Jambon de Bayonne

LANGUEDOC
19 Cassoulet
20 Roquefort

GREG ELMS

'The French think mainly about two things – their two main meals,' a well-fed bon-vivant friend in Paris once told us. 'Everything else is in parentheses.'

And it's true. While not every French man, woman and child is a walking *Larousse Gastronomique*, eating and drinking well is still of prime importance to most people here, and the French continue to spend an inordinate amount of time thinking about, talking about and consuming food and wine.

FRENCH CUISINE

French cuisine is remarkably varied, with a great many differences based on the produce and gastronomy of each region. Culinary traditions that have been developed and perfected over the centuries have made French cooking a highly refined art. This is true of even the simplest peasant dishes, which require careful preparation and great attention to detail. However, the secret to success in a French kitchen is not so much elaborate techniques as the use of fresh ingredients that are locally produced and in season.

Even if you can't afford to eat in expensive restaurants, you can still enjoy France's epicurean delights by buying food at markets or speciality shops, trying the local delicacies of the particular region you're in, and avoiding the standard fare of tourist menus such as steak frites, creme caramel and so on.

For a full culinary tour of the country, including tips on how to prepare your own French banquet, pick up a copy of Lonely Planet's *World Food France*.

Regional Specialities

There are all sorts of reasons for the amazing variety of France's regional cuisine. Climatic and geographical factors have been particularly important: the hot south tends to favour olive oil, garlic and tomatoes, while the cooler, pastoral regions farther north suit the production of cream and butter. Areas near the coast specialise in mussels, oysters and saltwater fish, while those near lakes and rivers make use of freshwater fish.

Diverse though it is, French cuisine is typified by certain regions, most notably Normandy, Burgundy, the Dordogne, Lyons and, to a lesser extent, Provence, Alsace, the Basque Country and Languedoc.

Normandy This region is famous for the incredible richness and superior quality of its local produce, especially its dairy products. Every Norman cow produces an average of five tonnes of milk

JANE SMITH

annually, which is why the region supplies something like half of France's milk, butter, cream and cheese. Among the cheeses, Camembert (produced in Normandy since the time of William the Conqueror) is supreme, but there are a great many others including Neufchâtel (or Bondon), Pont l'Évêque and Livarot (see also Cheese later in the chapter). Cream and butter go into the creation of the many rich, thick sauces that accompany fish, meat and vegetable dishes in the region.

Charcuteries (delicatessens) abound in Normandy, their windows displaying various terrines, patés and tripe. Also common are *galantine*, a cold dish of boned, stuffed, pressed meat (especially pork) that is presented in its own jelly, often with truffles and pistachio nuts. One Norman dish that may not be to everyone's taste is *tripes à la mode de Caen*, tripe combined with ox or calf's trotters, cider or Calvados, carrots, leeks, onions and herbs, and slow-cooked in a clay pot.

Rouen is famous for its duck dishes. The ducks are slaughtered by choking in order to retain the blood, which is then used to make the accompanying sauces. A typical dish is *canard à la rouennaise*, but there are countless other duck dishes, and recipes vary from town to town.

Trouville and Honfleur are the places to go for fish and seafood; their markets are crammed with lobsters, crayfish, langoustines, prawns, tiny scallops, plump oysters, delicious small mussels and an endless variety of fish. Specialities include mussel soup, which is made with stock, white wine and cream, and *sole à la normande*.

Apples are another essential of Norman cuisine, and cider is used extensively in cooking, particularly in meat and poultry dishes. Apple *cidre* (cider) is bubbly, lightly alcoholic and refreshing. There are two kinds: *doux* (sweet) and *brut* (dry).

Calvados is to the apple what Cognac is to the grape. This strong apple brandy (whose most celebrated variety comes from the Vallée d'Auge) is sometimes augmented by adding cider to make *pommeau*, which is drunk as a strong (18% alcohol) aperitif. Calvados is used in the preparation of sauces and in desserts.

Burgundy
Burgundian cuisine is solid, substantial and served in generous portions. The region's best-known dish, *bœuf bourguignon*, is beef marinated and cooked in red wine with mushrooms, onions, carrots and bits of bacon. Any dish described as *à la bourguignonne* will be prepared with a similar sauce. Quite a few other Burgundian dishes are prepared with cream-based sauces,

GREG ELMS

Left: Apples feature strongly in Norman cuisine, including refreshing cider and warming Calvados.

although *andouillette de Mâcon* (a small raw pork sausage) comes with a mustard sauce.

The region's most famous condiment is mustard, which was introduced to Gaul by the Romans. Burgundy's speciality mustards are made with anything from tarragon to honey and range in taste from delicate to fiery.

Other traditional Burgundian products include gingerbread (which traditionally takes six to eight weeks to prepare), black *escargots* (snails) – those raised on grape leaves are reputed to be the tastiest in France – and blackcurrants. The latter are used to make both jams and *crème de cassis*, a sweet blackcurrant liqueur that is combined with white wine (traditionally Aligoté) to make the aperitif known as *kir*.

Périgord Regarded as one of the best regional cuisines of France, Périgord is famous for its truffles, foie gras and poultry. Most prized by chefs is goose, which is turned into *pâté de foie gras* (goose liver palé) but also stuffed with chestnuts or plums, roasted, boiled or turned into *confit d'oie* (cooked and stored in its own fat). Goose fat is used a lot in cooking, as is walnut oil. Also popular are ducks and pork, which are also turned into a confit. Regional dishes are usually called *à la périgourdine*, which may (or may not) mean it will come with périgourdine or *périgueux* sauce (a rich brown sauce with foie gras puree and truffles).

The region's cuisine is very diverse and also includes freshwater fish (which can be stuffed with foie gras or cooked with truffles, grilled, marinated or cooked in ashes), crayfish, rabbit and beef. One of the best desserts is chestnut gateau, but also look out for flans and tarts with plums, quinces, grapes, cherries or pears.

Truffles

Périgord is famed for its *truffes* (truffles), edible subterranean fungi that grow on the roots of certain oak and hazelnut trees and can sell for over 2000FF per 100g in exclusive Parisian shops. Specially trained dogs or pigs 'sniff' them out between November and March. The Périgord region's highly prized variety, renowned for its distinctive aroma, is black and rough in texture. Truffles are at their best when eaten fresh – they only keep for a week and lose some of their flavour when preserved. The precious fungus is traditionally added to a variety of sauces and dishes but is also delicious in omelettes and pasta.

JANE SMITH

Lyons The city of Lyons, at the crossroads of some of France's richest agricultural regions (Burgundy and its wines, Charollais and its cattle, Dauphiné and its dairy products), enjoys a supply of quality foodstuffs unequalled in France. Indeed, it is considered by most to be the country's *temple de gastronomie*; some of the world's most renowned chefs work here, including Paul Bocuse, Alain Chapel and Roger Roucou. The most typical dishes are *boudin blanc* (veal sausage) and *quenelles* (light dumplings made of fish or meat, poached and often served in a *sauce Nantua*, a creamy crayfish sauce). Surprisingly, in the very masculine world of French cuisine, Lyons owes most of its reputation to women, the famous *mères lyonnaises*, who have run traditional-style restaurants in that city for generations.

Alsace Most of the dishes on offer in traditional Alsatian restaurants are not found anywhere else in France – except in the brasserie, whose cuisine still reflects that venerable institution's Alsatian origins.

On the savoury side, you're likely to find *baeckeoffe* (baker's oven), a stew made of several kinds of meat (often pork, mutton and beef) and vegetables that have been marinated for two days. It is traditionally prepared at home before being cooked in the oven of a nearby bakery. *Choucroute alsacienne* (or *choucroute garnie*) is sauerkraut served hot with sausage, pork or ham – it is often accompanied by cold, frothy beer or a local wine. *Flammeküche*, a thin layer of pastry topped with cream, onion, bacon and sometimes cheese or mushrooms and cooked in a wood-fired oven, is known in French as *tarte flambée*. A *zwiebelküche* (or *tarte à l'oignon)* is an onion tart, while a *tourte* is a raised pie with ham, bacon or ground pork, eggs and leeks. Alsace produces some excellent *charcuterie*, products prepared from what is renowned in these parts as *le seigneur cochon* (the 'noble pig').

The white *asperges* (asparagus) of Alsace are prized throughout France and only available for a couple of weeks in late May.

Alsace's *patisseries* (pastry shops) are particularly well stocked with scrumptious pastries, including *kougelhopf* (or *kougloff*), a mildly sweet sultana and almond cake that is baked in a mould and is easily identified by its ribbed, dome-like shape. *Tarte alsacienne* is a custard tart made with local fruits, which also includes the wonderful Alsatian plums called *quetsches*.

Alsace also has its own kinds of eateries. *Winstub* (**veen**-shtub), warm and wood-panelled, serve wine by the glass or carafe as well as hearty Alsatian pork

JANE SMITH

dishes, many of them prepared, of course, with wine. Places to drink beer were once known as *bierstub* (**beer**-shtub), but these days the bierstub exists more in local myth than in day-to-day reality.

Provence Provençal cuisine is prepared with *huile d'olive* (olive oil) and *ail* (garlic). *Tomates* (tomatoes) are another common ingredient, and you can safely assume that any culinary delight described as *à la provençale* will be prepared with garlic-seasoned tomatoes. Other vegetables that frequently appear on local menus are aubergines (eggplant), summer squash or courgettes (zucchini) and onions. Tomatoes, aubergine and squash, stewed together along with green peppers, garlic and various aromatic herbs, produce that perennial Provençal favourite, ratatouille.

Aïoli is a sauce prepared by mixing mayonnaise (made with olive oil) with lots of freshly crushed garlic. It is spread generously on hot or cold vegetables, such as asparagus, eggs and especially *morue pochée* (poached codfish).

Provence's most famous soup is *bouillabaisse*, which is made with at least three kinds of fresh fish cooked for 10 minutes or so in broth with onions, tomatoes, saffron and various herbs, including bay leaves (laurel), sage and thyme. It is sometimes prepared with shellfish as well. Bouillabaisse, which is eaten as a main course, is usually served with toast and *rouille*, a spicy sauce that some people mix into the soup but which most spread on the crisp toast. The most renowned bouillabaisse is made in Marseille. A popular starter is *soupe au pistou*, a soup of vegetables, noodles, beans and basil, and a hearty winter meal is *daube de bœuf* (a beef stew cooked in red wine) with *pâtés fraîches* (cold paté).

Provence is sometimes called 'the garden of France' because of its superb spices, fruit and vegetables. The region is also famous for its locally pressed olive oil, honey and fresh goat cheese. Truffles are harvested from November to April. Depending on the season, all these

MARTIN MOOS

Right: Provençal cuisine, rich with garlic and onions, is guaranteed to wake the tastebuds.

Types of Cuisine

There are several different kinds of French cuisine:

Haute cuisine (high cuisine) Originating in the spectacular feasts of French kings, haute cuisine is typified by super-rich, elaborately prepared and beautifully presented multicourse meals.

Cuisine bourgeoise This is French home-cooking of the highest quality.

Cuisine des régions Also known as *cuisine campagnarde* (country cuisine), regional cuisine uses the finest ingredients and most refined techniques to prepare traditional rural dishes.

Nouvelle cuisine (new cuisine) This style of cuisine made a big splash at home and abroad in the diet-conscious 1970s and 80s. It features rather small portions served with light sauces. Nouvelle cuisine is prepared and presented in such a way as to emphasise the inherent textures and colours of the ingredients.

delicacies are available fresh at local food markets.

A favourite way to eat *crudités* (raw vegetables) is with *anchoïade* (*anchoyade* in Provençal), a dipping sauce of anchovy paste.

French Basque Country Among the essential ingredients of Basque cooking are the deep-red chillies you'll see hanging out to dry in summer, brightening up houses and adding that extra bite to many of the region's dishes. Equally characteristic is the goose fat that is used to cook almost everything – from eggs to *garbure*, a filling cabbage and bean soup. The paté de foie gras and the confit d'oie are also excellent. Fish dishes abound on the coast, with tuna and sardines being the speciality of St-Jean-de-Luz. A fish stew called *ttoro* may include scampi, hake, eel and monkfish as well as chillies, tomatoes and white wine. Other local delicacies include baby eels, trout and *salmis de palombe*, wood pigeon partially roasted then simmered in a rich sauce of wine and vegetable puree.

JANE SMITH

The locally cured *jambon de Bayonne* (Bayonne ham) is a salty staple of Basque cuisine, but its cheaper Spanish cousin *jamón serrano* is far more common on menus.

Languedoc As in Provence, food in Languedoc is cooked in and laced with liberal amounts of olive oil. France's most famous blue cheese is made at Roquefort, south of Millau. Other regional favourites include Bleu des Causses and Pélardon.

Languedoc's most celebrated dishes are *cassoulet* (a hearty stew of white beans and pork), mutton, confit d'oie and *confit de canard* (preserved duck). The term *à la languedocienne* usually means dishes served with a garlicky garnish of tomatoes, aubergines and ceps (boletus mushrooms).

GREG ELMS

Cheese

France has 500-plus varieties of cheese produced at farms, dairies, mountain huts and even monasteries. They're made of either cow's, goat's, or ewe's milk, which can be raw, pasteurised or petit-lait (the whey left over after the milk fats and solids have been curdled with rennet, an enzyme derived from the stomach of a calf or young goat).

The choice on offer at a *fromagerie* (cheese shop) can be overwhelming – even to the initiated. But *fromagers* (cheese merchants) always allow you to sample before you buy (see Fromageries under Food Shopping in the Facts for the Visitor chapter). The following list divides French cheeses into five main groups, including some excellent varieties and (where relevant) their regions of origin:

Fromage de chèvre (goat's-milk cheese) is usually creamy and both sweet and a little salty when fresh, but hardens and gets much saltier as it matures. Ste-Maure-de-Touraine is a creamy, mild cheese from the Loire region; Crottin-de-Chavignol from Burgundy is a classic variety that can get very salty after two weeks; Cabécou-de-Rocamadour from Midi-Pyrénées is often served warm with salad or marinated in oil and rosemary.

Fromage à pâte persillée (veined or blue cheese) is also called persillé because the veins often resemble parsley. Fourme-d'Ambert is a very mild cow's-milk cheese from Rhône-Alpes; Bresse Bleu is a pasteurised cow's-milk cheese from Rhône-Alpes; Roquefort is a ewe's-milk cheese that is to many the king of French cheese.

Fromage à pâte molle (soft cheese) is moulded or rind-washed. Camembert de normandie, a classic moulded cheese from Normandy – which for many is synonymous with French cheese – and the refined Brie de Meaux

Right: With 500-odd types of French cheese to try, it's best to go for smaller portions than this.

are both made from raw cow's milk; Munster is a rind-washed Alsatian cheese.

Fromage à pâte demi-dure (semi-hard cheese) is uncooked, pressed cheese. Tomme de Savoie is an outstanding cheese made from either raw or pasteurised cow's milk; Cantal is a cow's-milk cheese from Auvergne that tastes something like Cheddar; St-Nectaire is a strong-smelling pressed cheese of pink or reddish colour.

Serving & Wine

The ideal place to store cheese is in a cool, dark, well-ventilated room. The refrigerator is a second choice, but that's where most people in France keep it these days. Most cheese should be wrapped in foil – or waxed paper and then foil – before going into the fridge. Cheese removed from the fridge should warm up for a half-hour before serving to allow the flavour to develop.

When cutting cheese at the table, remember that a small circular cheese like a Camembert is cut in slices like a pie. If a cheese has been bought already sliced (for example, Brie), cut from the tip to the rind (never cut off the tip). Slice cheeses whose middle is the best part (for example, the blues) in such a way as to take your fair share of the rind. A flat piece of semi-hard cheese like Emmental is usually just cut horizontally in hunks.

Wine and cheese are a match made in heaven, and many regional vintages go well together with a certain cheese. Personal tastes vary, but in general, strong, pungent cheeses require a young, full-bodied red or a sweet wine, while soft cheeses with a refined flavour call for more quality and age in the wine.

Some classic pairings include Alsatian Gewürztraminer and Munster, a Rhône Valley red and Roquefort, a Côte d'Or red with a Brie or Camembert, and a mature Bordeaux with Emmental or Gruyère.

GREG ELMS

Left: French cheese etiquette: don't pinch all the good bits.

WINE

Grapes and the art of winemaking were introduced to Gaul by the Romans. In the Middle Ages, important vineyards developed around the monasteries, whose monks needed wine to celebrate Mass. Large-scale wine production later moved closer to the ports (for example, Bordeaux) for export.

In 1863, a kind of aphid known as phylloxera was accidentally brought to Europe from the USA. It ate through the roots of Europe's grapevines, destroying around 10,000 sq km of vineyards in France alone. It looked like European wine production was doomed until phylloxera-resistant root stocks were brought from California and had older varieties grafted onto them.

Winemaking is a complicated chemical process, but ultimately the taste and quality of the wine depends on four key factors: the type(s) of grape used, the climate, the soil, and the art of the winemaker.

LPP

Some viticulturists have honed their skills and techniques to such a degree that their wine is known as a *grand cru* (literally, 'great growth'). If this wine has been produced in a year of optimum climatic conditions it becomes a *millésime* (vintage). Grands crus are aged first in small oak barrels and then in bottles, sometimes for 20 years or more, before they develop their full taste and aroma. These are the memorable (and pricey) bottles that wine experts talk about with such passion.

There are dozens of wine-producing regions throughout France, but the eight principal regions are Alsace, the Loire Valley, Bordeaux, Burgundy, Champagne, Beaujolais, Languedoc-Roussillon and the Rhône. Wines in France are named after the location of the vineyard rather than the grape varietal, except in Alsace.

In addition to Champagne, which is world-renowned for its sparkling wine, two regions produce the most celebrated table wines in France: Bordeaux (St-Émilion and Pomerol are well known) and Burgundy (for example, Côte-de-Beaune, Côte-de-Nuits). Vintners can argue interminably about a wine's merits, but it seems that although a Burgundy of the right vintage can be extraordinary, Bordeaux is more reliable.

Wine Regions

Alsace Alsace has been producing wine since about AD 300. These days, the region produces almost exclusively white wines – mostly varieties produced nowhere else in France – that are known for their clean, fresh taste and compatibility with the often heavy local cuisine. Some of the fruity Alsatian whites also, unusually, go well with red meat.

Alsace's four most important varietal wines are Riesling, known for its subtlety; the more pungent and highly regarded Gewürztraminer; the robust, high-alcohol Tokay-Pinot Gris; and Muscat d'Alsace, which is

Wine Quality

Wine production in France is strictly supervised by the government. Under French law, wines are divided into four categories:

Appellation d'origine contrôlée (AOC) These wines have met stringent government regulations governing where, how and under what conditions they are grown, fermented and bottled. They are almost always, at the very least, good and may actually be superb. A bottle of AOC wine can cost from as little as 20FF to many hundreds of francs a bottle, depending on its origin and which label it bears. The makers of AOC wines are the elite of the French wine industry.

Vin délimité de qualité supérieure (VDQS) These are good wines from a specific place or region – the second rank of French quality control. Prices are similar to AOC wines.

Vin de pays Wines with this label, whose literal meaning is 'country wine', are of reasonable quality and are generally drinkable. They usually sell for between 10FF and 15FF per bottle.

Vin de table These table wines are also known as *vins ordinaires* (ordinary wines). You can buy 1L bottles from a supermarket for 9FF to 13FF, but if you buy directly from the producer, you'll pay as little as 5FF per litre (bring your own container). Spending an extra 5FF or 10FF can often make a big difference in quality, drinkability and the severity of your hangover.

not as sweet as that made with Muscat grapes grown farther south. Edelzwicker is light, premium wine made from a blend of different grapes.

Eaux de vie (brandies) are made and flavoured with locally grown fruit and nuts. Of the many varieties, kirsch, a cherry concoction, is the most famous.

Beaujolais Unlike their more subtle cousins from Burgundy and Bordeaux, the light but undistinguished reds of Beaujolais age poorly and are therefore drunk young – so young, in fact, that some are considered fit for consumption just a few weeks after the grape harvest. There are 13 different types of Beaujolais in all.

The first day on which the year's new Beaujolais wines – made with Gamay grapes – can officially be sold falls on the third Thursday in November. For many revellers, the chance to sample the year's new *crus* (vintages) provides the perfect excuse for a day and night of partying – and not just in France. Amid the media hype across Europe, bars and cafes hail the new stock's arrival with signs proclaiming '*le Beaujolais nouveau est arrivé!*' (the new Beaujolais has arrived!).

The bright, cherry-red wine, which should be drunk chilled (10°C), has as many detractors (who say it tastes like blackcurrant cordial) as supporters.

The region has 10 appellations: in addition to Nouveau, Chiroubles, St-Amour and Chénas also tend to age poorly; Régnié is only a new appellation and is still establishing its reputation; Juliénas has some backbone but should still be drunk within two to three years of its vintage; Fleurie is one of the most expensive and is especially renowned for its floral perfume; and Brouilly, Moulin-à-Vent and Morgon all tend to defy the region's reputation and age well.

Bordeaux Wines from this region have always enjoyed a favourable reputation, even from Roman times. Britons (who call the reds 'claret') have hungered for the wines of Bordeaux since the mid-12th century, when King Henry II, who controlled this region of France thanks to his marriage to Eleanor of Aquitaine, tried to gain favour with the citizens of Bordeaux by allowing them, among other concessions, tax-free trade with England. As a result, Bordeaux wine was the cheapest imported wine. This demand has remained ever since. Since those days, Bordeaux's wines have gained a worldwide reputation.

Bordeaux has the perfect climate for producing wine – it is halfway between the North Pole and the equator and its proximity to the Atlantic helps protect it from frosts and excessive heat.

As a result Bordeaux produces more fine wine than any other region in the world. From its 100,000 hectares of vineyards, the region typically produces around one-quarter of France's total *appellation contrôlée* wine, of which 75% is red.

The Bordeaux reds are often described as well-balanced, a quality achieved by blending several grape varieties. The grapes predominantly used are Merlot, Cabernet Sauvignon and Cabernet Franc.

Burgundy This famous wine-growing region is most noted for its great white and red wines. The red wines are produced with Pinot Noir grapes; although these are used in other areas they produce their best results in Burgundy. The best reds need 10 to 20 years to age and when mature produce a unique mix of aromas. White wine is made from the Chardonnay grape.

The four main wine-growing areas of Burgundy are Chablis, Côte d'Or, Chalonnais and Mâconnais.

Burgundy has produced wines since the days of the Celts (there is some evidence to suggest they introduced wine to the region before the Roman arrival), but developed its reputation in the reign of Charlemagne, when monks first began to produce wine. The Benedictines of Cluny were the first group of monks to gain a significant toehold in the region, but others followed. With cellars to mature the wine, the inclination to keep records and the organisation to make improvements, the monks' influence on wine in Burgundy has meant the region has enjoyed a reputation for great wine ever since.

The *vignerons* (vine growers) of Burgundy generally only have small vineyards (rarely more than 10 hectares and sometimes only a row or two), partly because the land has always been so valuable but largely because of the Napoleonic Code, which insists that every family member receives an equal inheritance. Often this sees vignerons produce small quantities of wine (sometimes just one barrel, enough for 25 cases), which merchants then buy and blend, sometimes with spectacular results, but sometimes not.

Champagne The late 17th century saw the appearance of Champagne on the French wine scene thanks to Dom Pierre Pérignon, the innovative cellar master of the Benedictine abbey at Hautvilliers (near Épernay). He perfected a technique for making sparkling wine of consistent quality (earlier attempts had proved remarkably – even explosively – unpredictable). He proceeded to put his product in strong, English-made bottles (the local bottles couldn't take the enormous pressure) and capped them, thereby sealing in the bubbles, with a new kind of bottle stopper – corks brought from Spain and forced into the mouth of the bottle under high pressure, creating a bulbous, mushroom shape.

Champagne is made using only three varieties of grapes: Chardonnay, Pinot Noir and Pinot Meunier. Each vine is vigorously pruned and trained to produce a small quantity of high-quality grapes. Indeed, to maintain exclusivity (and price), the amount of champagne that can be produced each year is limited to between 160 and 220 million bottles, most of which is consumed in France and the UK.

The process of making champagne – carried out by innumerable *maisons* (houses), both large and small – is a long, complex one. There are two fermentation processes, the first in casks and the second after the wine has been bottled and had sugar and yeast added. In years of an inferior vintage, older wines are blended to create what is known as 'nonvintage champagne'.

During the two months that the bottles are aged in cellars kept at 12°C, the wine turns effervescent. The sediment that forms in the bottle is removed by *remuage*, a painstakingly slow process in which each bottle – stored horizontally – is rotated slightly every day for weeks until the sludge works its way to the cork. Next comes *dégorgement*: the neck of the bottle is frozen, creating a blob of solidified champagne and sediment, which is then removed.

At this stage, the champagne's sweetness is determined by adding varying amounts of syrup dissolved in old champagne. If the final product is labelled *brut*, it is extra dry, with only 1.5% sugar content. *Extra-sec* means it's very dry (but not as dry as brut), *sec* is dry and *demi-sec* is slightly sweet. The sweetest champagne is labelled *doux*. There's also rosé, a blend of red and white wine that has long been snubbed by connoisseurs. Lastly, the bottles of young champagne are laid in a cellar. Ageing lasts between two and five years (and

Right: Champagne is made by a long and complex process which dates back to the 17th century – but its taste is worth all that effort.

ELLIOT DANIEL

sometimes longer), depending on the *cuvée* (vintage).

Some of the most famous champagnes are Möet et Chandon, Veuve Cliquot, Mercier, Mumm, Laurent-Perrier, Piper-Heidsieck, Dom Pérignon and Taittinger.

Languedoc-Roussillon This region is the country's most important wine-growing area. Up to 40% of France's wine, mainly cheap red vin de table, is produced here. About 300,000 hectares of the region is 'under vine', which represents one-third of France's total. And this is in spite of EU-led initiatives to reduce Europe's wine surplus by subsidising vignerons to cut down their vines and replant with better-quality AOC grapes.

About 10% of the wine produced now is AOC standard. In addition to the well-known Fitou label, the area's other AOC wines are Coteaux-du-Languedoc, Faugères, Corbières and Minervois. The region also produces about 70% of France's vin de pays, much of which is labelled as Vin de Pays d'Oc. Many vignerons are now also concentrating on producing more and higher-quality white wine. A dry rosé, mainly for local consumption, is also produced, as are a muscat and some sparkling wine.

The region's wine producers are also seen as France's most troublesome, often (and sometimes violently) protesting any change that affects their industry. This is especially true of the appellation laws. Many local vignerons, for instance, prefer to disregard the AOC categories and produce high-quality vin de pays instead.

Loire Valley The Loire produces the greatest variety of wines of any region in France: very dry wines to very tart; all manner of colours from the lightest white to the deepest purple; and all types of sparkling wines. A particular speciality of the region is rosé, the most noted of which is Rosé de Anjou.

Many of the Loire wines tend to be underrated by the experts, but obvious exceptions to this are the wines of Pouilly-Fumé, Sancerre, Bourgueil, Chinon and, in particular, Saumur.

Rhône The River Rhône is an important tributary for wine, not only in France but also in Switzerland; however, in wine circles the Rhône always means the area in south-western France.

The French Rhône is divided up into four areas, but the two most important are the northern and southern districts. The different soil, climate, topography and grapes used means there is a dramatic difference in the wines produced by each.

Set on steep hills beside the river, the northern vineyards make red wines exclusively from the Syrah grape, which is a deep ruby-red colour and produces rich wines. The aromatic Viognier grape is the most popular for white wines. The most prestigious wines come from this area, and several rival those of Bordeaux and Burgundy. The south is better known for the quantity of wine it produces. The vineyards are also more spread out and interspersed with fields of lavender and orchards of olives, pears and almonds. The Grenache grape, which ages well when blended, is used in the reds, while the whites use the Ugni Blanc grape.

Wine at Meals

The French nearly always drink wine with their meals. A fine meal will be accompanied by an equally fine *bouteille* (bottle) of wine – *rouge* (red), *blanc* (white) or rosé – chosen to complement the main course. Unfortunately, wines cost several times more in restaurants than in supermarkets, and the practice of Australian-style BYO (bring your own) is utterly unknown – indeed, the very idea strikes the French as being in unspeakably bad taste.

Ultimately, the taste of any wine is determined by the food with which it is drunk. As a rule, the stronger the food, the stronger the wine. Game is generally be eaten with a full-bodied red wine; beef and lamb with a lighter one; pork, veal and poultry with either a medium white or a light red; fish and shellfish with a dry white; and dessert with a

GREG ELMS

Right: Good bread and good wine – French meal basics.

Study, Swirl, Sniff, Sip, Swallow . . . hic

The art of wine tasting is a complex process that takes years to fully appreciate (and usually also requires an extensive vocabulary of adjectives, the more obscure the better), but here's our guide to help you bluff your way through it.

1. Colour Look through the wine towards a source of light. Then tilt the glass slightly and look through it towards a pale background. What you're looking for here is clarity and colour. Clarity is obvious (no good wines have particles floating around in them) but colour is more complex. A deep colour indicates a strong wine. The colour can also reveal the types of grapes used as well as the wine's age (in red wines a blue hue indicates youth, whereas an orange hue indicates age).

2. Smell Swirl the wine around and smell it in one inhalation. The agitation will release the wine's full bouquet. Close your eyes and concentrate: what do you smell? There are 11 main groups of smells associated with wine, ranging from fruits to plants, herbs and spices, and even toasted.

3. Taste Take a sip, swill it around in your mouth and then (here's the tough part) draw in some air to bring out the flavour. Our tastebuds can identify four sensations: bitter, acid, salty and sweet. After doing this swallow the wine. A fine wine should leave an aftertaste.

---

sweet white wine.

Except for champagne, for which the following terms are used a bit differently (see the boxed text 'The Art of Making Bubbly' in the Champagne chapter), brut is very dry, sec is dry, demi-sec is medium sweet, doux is very sweet, and *mousseux* is sparkling.

Wine Tasting

Wine tasting is an art and a tradition. The wine is poured into a small, shallow cup called a *taste-vin*. Tasters use a rich vocabulary to describe wines: wine can be nervous, elegant, fleshy, supple or round and taste of vanilla, strawberry, cherry, cinnamon and even cigars and cedar.

In most wine-growing regions, *caves* (wine cellars) provide an opportunity to purchase wine straight from the vigneron. Quite often, you'll be offered a *dégustation* (tasting), with the wine poured straight from enormous wood barrels or sparkling stainless-steel vats (you don't have to spit it out). It's usually free, but you won't be at all popular if you sample several vintages and then leave without buying. Cellars often require that you buy in bulk (*en vrac*) – a 5L minimum is common in some areas.

Wine Bars

Bars à vins, mostly an urban phenomenon, serve a dozen or more selected wines by the glass so you can taste and compare different varieties and vintages. Wines do not keep for very long after the bottle has been opened, but a few years back someone realised that wine in an uncorked bottle can be stabilised by replacing the air inside with a nonoxidising gas.

Wine Shops

Wine is sold by *marchands de vin* (or a *caviste*), such as the shops of the Nicolas chain. Wine shops in close proximity to the vineyards of Burgundy, Bordeaux, Chablis and other wine-growing areas may offer tastings.

The cheapest vintages can cost less than 10FF a bottle – less than a soft drink in a cafe! – but it's usually worth paying a bit more (at least 20FF) for something more refined. Of course, the better vintages can cost up to several thousand francs.

LEE FOSTER

GREG ELMS

ELLIOT DANIEL

This page: In France the ingredients are the freshest possible, while the wine is carefully aged.

Title page: Browsing round specialist shops is all part of the French gastronomic experience. (photograph: Greg Elms)

SIMON BRACKEN

JULIET COOMBE

GREG ELMS

CHRIS MELLOR

OLIVIER CIRENDINI

OLIVIER CIRENDINI

The flavours of France –
dijon mustard, steak
and oysters matched by
a fine array of wines –
mean hunger is one
thing you won't need
to worry about.

Patisseries

Mouth-watering pastries are available at patisseries (*pâtisseries* in French), which are often attached to boulangeries. Some of the most common pastries include *tarte aux fruits* (fruit tarts), *pain au chocolat* (similar to a croissant but filled with chocolate), *pain aux raisins* (a flat, spiral pastry made with custard and sultanas) and *religieuses* (eclairs with one cream puff perched on top of another to resemble a nun's headdress).

You can tell if a croissant has been made with margarine or butter by the shape: margarine croissants have their tips almost touching, while those made with butter have them pointing away from each other.

Confiseries

Chocolate and other sweets made with the finest ingredients can be found at *confiseries*, which are sometimes combined with boulangeries and patisseries.

Fromageries

If you buy your cheese in a supermarket, you'll end up with unripe and relatively tasteless products unless you know your stuff. Here's where a *fromagerie*, also known as a *crémerie*, comes in. The owners will advise you and usually let you taste before you decide what to buy. Just ask, *'Est-ce que je peux le goûter, s'il vous plaît?'* Most fromageries sell both whole and half-rounds of Camembert, so you don't have to buy more than you're likely to eat in a day or two.

Charcuteries

A *charcuterie* is a delicatessen offering sliced meats, seafood salads, patés, terrines and so on. Most supermarkets have a charcuterie counter. If the word *traiteur* (trader) is written on a sign, it means that the establishment sells ready-to-eat takeaway dishes.

Fruit & Vegetables

Fruits and *légumes* are sold by a *marchand de légumes et de fruits* (greengrocer) and at food markets and supermarkets. Most small groceries have only a limited selection. You can buy whatever quantity of produce suits you, even if it's just three carrots and a

peach. *Biologique* means grown organically (without chemicals).

Meat & Fish

A general butcher is a *boucherie*, but for specialised poultry you have to go to a *marchand de volaille*, where *poulet fermier* (free-range chicken) will cost much more than a regular chicken. A *boucherie chevaline*, easily identifiable by the gilded horse's head above the entrance, sells horse meat. Fresh fish and seafood are available from a *poissonnerie*.

Épiceries & Alimentations

A small grocery store with a little bit of everything is known as an *épicerie* (literally, 'spice shop') or an *alimentation générale*. Most *épiceries* are more expensive than supermarkets, especially in Paris, though some – such as those of the Casino chain – are more like minimarkets. Some épiceries open on days when other food shops are closed, and many family-run operations stay open until late at night.

Supermarkets

Both town and city centres usually have at least one department store with a large *supermarché* (supermarket) section. Places to look for include Monoprix, Prisunic and Nouvelles Galeries. In Paris, the cheapest edibles are sold at the no-frills supermarkets of Ed l'Épicier. Most larger supermarkets have charcuteric and cheese counters, and many also have in-house boulangeries.

The cheapest place to buy food is a *hypermarché* (hypermarket), such as those of the Auchan, Carrefour, Intermarché, E Leclerc and Rallye chains, where you'll pay up to 40% less for staples than at an épicerie. Unfortunately, they're nearly always on the outskirts of town.

Food Markets

In most towns and cities, many of the aforementioned products are available one or more days a week at *marchés en plein air* (open-air markets), also known as *marchés découverts*, and up to six days a week at *marchés couverts* (covered marketplaces), often known as *les halles*. Markets are cheaper than food shops and supermarkets and the merchandise, especially fruit and vegetables, is fresher and of better quality.

DRINKS

Although alcohol consumption has dropped by 20% since the war, the French drink more than any other national group in the world, except the people of Luxembourg. On average, the French consume 11L of pure alcohol a year, compared to 8.3L in the USA and 8.2L in the UK (and with the 18L they drank each year in 1960).

Nonalcoholic Drinks

Water All tap water in France is safe to drink, so there is no need to buy expensive bottled water. Tap water that is not drinkable (for example, at most public fountains or in some streams) will usually have a sign reading '*eau non potable*'.

If you prefer tap water rather than some pricey soft drink or wine, make sure you ask for *de l'eau* (some water), *une carafe d'eau* (a jug of water) or *de l'eau du robinet* (tap water). Otherwise you'll most likely get *eau de source* (mineral water), which comes *plate* (flat or noncarbonated) or *gazeuse* (fizzy or carbonated).

Soft Drinks Soft drinks are expensive in France. Don't be surprised if you're charged 20FF for a little bottle of Gini or Pschitt. A beer may be cheaper than a Coke. Even in the supermarket, soft drinks are only just cheaper than beer, milk and even some kinds of wine.

One relatively inexpensive cafe drink is *sirop* (squash, fruit syrup), served either *à l'eau* (mixed with water), with *soda* (carbonated water) or Perrier. A *citron pressé* is a glass of iced water (either flat or carbonated) with freshly squeezed lemon juice and sugar. The French are not particularly fond of drinking very cold things, so if you'd like ice cubes, ask for *des glaçons*.

Coffee The most ubiquitous form of coffee is espresso, made by forcing steam through ground coffee beans. A small espresso,

served without milk, is called *un café noir*, *un express* or simply *un café*. You can also ask for a *grand* (large) version.

Un café crème is espresso with steamed milk or cream. *Un café au lait* is lots of hot milk with a little coffee served in a large cup or, sometimes, a bowl. A small café crème is a *petit crème*. A *noisette* (literally, 'hazelnut') is an espresso with just a dash of milk. Decaffeinated coffee is *un café décaféiné* or *un déca*.

Tea & Hot Chocolate *Thé* (tea) is also widely available and will be served with milk if you ask for *un peu de lait frais*. Herbal tea, very popular as a treatment for minor ailments, is called *tisane* or *infusion*.

French *chocolat chaud* (hot chocolate) can be either excellent or completely undrinkable.

Alcoholic Drinks

Wine For information on wine, see the Food & Wine section earlier in the chapter.

Apéritifs Meals are often preceded by an appetite-stirring *apéritif* such as *kir* (white wine sweetened with cassis, blackcurrant syrup), *kir royale* (champagne with cassis) and *pineau* (cognac and grape juice). Port is drunk as an aperitif rather than after the meal in France.

Pastis is a 90-proof, anise-flavoured alcoholic drink that, as you mix it with water, turns cloudy. It's strong, refreshing and cheap. Although it's popular all over the country, it's a particular favourite in southern France, where people sip it as an apéritif. Popular brand names are Pernod and Ricard.

Digestifs After-dinner drinks are often ordered along with coffee. France's most famous brandies are Cognac and Armagnac, both of which are made from grapes in the regions of those names. The various other sorts of brandies, many of them very strong local products, are known collectively as *eaux de vie* (literally, 'waters of life').

Eaux de vie, such as the celebrated Marc de Champagne and Marc de Bourgogne, are made from grape skins and pulp left over after being pressed for wine. Calvados is an apple brandy that is made in Normandy; Poire William is a pear-based concoction. Yellow *mirabelle* plums and raspberries are used to make the fiery, highly perfumed *eau de vie de prune* or *eau de vie de framboise*.

Produced all over France, most liqueurs are made from grapes, eau de vie, sugar and either fruit or the essences of aromatic herbs. Well-known brands include Cointreau, Bénédictine and Chartreuse, all of which are elaborate blends of various ingredients, and the orange-spiced Grand Marnier.

Beer Beer, which is served by the *demi* (about 330mL), is usually either Alsatian (like Kronenbourg, 33 or Pelforth) or imported from Germany or Belgium.

In pubs, beer is cheaper *à la pression* (on draught/tap) than in a *bouteille* (bottle), but prices vary widely depending on what sort of an establishment you're in. At a decent but modest sort of place, count on paying 12FF to 16FF for a demi of Kronenbourg on tap. Prices often go up two or three francs as the night wears on. Strong Belgian brews such as Trappist beers or cherry-flavoured *kriek* are quite pricey, typically costing about 25FF a bottle.

ENTERTAINMENT

Local tourist offices are generally the best source of information about what's going on in their city or town. In larger towns, they'll usually have a free brochure listing the cultural events and entertainment planned for each week, fortnight or month.

Pubs, Bars & Cafes

French pubs and bars aren't quite the fixture that public houses are in Britain. But that doesn't mean they haven't got a lot going for them: many establishments ooze beautiful old Art-Deco trimmings and quirky paraphernalia, have canned or live music and provide for a fine night out. Their character runs the gamut in large towns, from dead chic to seedy to Irish pubs, the latest

foreign invasion. Many cafes are, in Anglo-Saxon terms, actually pubs but serve little to eat except, maybe, a baguette sandwich or a *croque-monsieur*.

Traditional cafes (the places that open from the morning) are an important focal point for social life in France. Sitting in a cafe to read, write, talk with friends or just daydream is an integral part of many people's day-to-day existence. Many people see cafe-sitting as a way of keeping in touch with their neighbourhood and maximising their chances of running into friends and acquaintances.

Three factors determine how much you'll pay in a cafe: where the cafe is situated, where you are sitting within the cafe, and what time of day it is. Ordering a cup of coffee (or anything else) earns you the right to sit there for as long as you like.

You usually pay the *addition* (bill) right before you leave, though if your waiter is going off duty you may be asked to pay up then and there.

In most towns you'll also come across slightly seedy bars which, in the Mediterranean tradition, seemingly attract only men. These places are typically glass-fronted and have lots of tall barstools occupied by swarthy, vaguely suspicious-looking locals slurping a brew or pastis.

Clubs

In French, a club or discotheque (also called a *boîte*) is any sort of establishment where music (live or recorded) leads to dancing. The music on offer ranges from jazz and rai to Latino and techno, and the crowd may be gay, lesbian, straight or mixed. The sign *'tenue correcte exigée'*, which you may see displayed at various venues, means 'appropriate dress required'. Most *boîtes* only begin to warm up after midnight (and sometimes much later).

An unfortunate fixture at many big-city clubs is the bouncer – the *videur* (literally 'emptier') who eyes you at the entrance. In some places, bouncers are encouraged to keep out 'undesirables', which, depending on the place, ranges from unaccompanied men who aren't dressed right to members of certain minority groups (for example, North Africans and blacks).

At some particularly exclusive discotheques, you have to be dressed in a manner appropriate to the night's theme. Although locals can find their night out abruptly reconfigured by a bouncer's snap decision, tourists aren't usually held to such strict standards. All discos, however, are very careful not to admit people who are drunk.

Gay & Lesbian Venues

France's relatively liberal attitudes on homosexuality make for a thriving pub and club scene. In Paris, the Marais quarter has been main centre of gay and lesbian nightlife since the early 1980s, catering to every possible taste and preference, from starched business types to the leather-Levi's crowd. Most of the larger towns have at least a few such bars, clubs or discos, and the regional chapters attempt to list some of the better ones; not surprisingly, few such venues exist in the more conservative villages and rural areas.

Cinema

If you don't want to hear your favourite actor dubbed into French, look in the film listings and on the theatre's billboard for the letters *VO* or *v.o. (version originale)* or *v.o.s.t. (version originale sous-titrée)*, all of which mean that the film has been given French subtitles. If v.o. is nowhere to be seen, or if you notice the letters *v.f. (version française)*, it means the film has been dubbed into French.

In Paris, the film listings in *Pariscope* and *L'Officiel des Spectacles* (see Listings in the Entertainment section in the Paris chapter) usually also include the original release names of some English-language movies. However, local newspapers, cinema billboards and cinema answering machines generally only use the French titles, which may be completely unrelated to the original English names.

Cinema schedules usually list two times for each film: one for the *séance* (when the prescreening ads and trailers begin) and the other, usually 10 to 25 minutes later, for the film itself. No self-respecting French *cinéphile* would dream of missing the ads, which are often creative and entertaining.

Film-going in France does not come cheap – count on paying 40FF to 50FF for a first-run film. Most French cinemas offer discounts to students, and people under 18 or over 60 usually get discounts of about 25%, but not on Friday, Saturday or Sunday nights. On Wednesday (and sometimes also on Monday), most cinemas give discounts to everyone.

Theatre

Long gone is French theatre's postwar golden age, when dramatists and directors such as Anouilh, Beckett, Camus, Genet, Ionesco and Montherlant held audiences spellbound with their innovative works.

These days, the French theatre scene is dominated by the revival of old favourites and the translation of foreign hits, especially in Paris. As it has since the time of Louis XIV, Paris' famous Comédie Française continues to produce French classics, though it has expanded its repertoire in recent years. Almost all of the country's major theatre productions, including those written in other languages, are performed in French (with a few exceptions in Paris).

Some of the cosier venues bill themselves as a *café-théâtres*, the hybrid outfits serving up popular or lowbrow productions while you wine and dine. They're generally infused with more local humour (and often, bawdiness) than you'd experience in a more formal theatre environment.

One of the highlights of the French theatre year is the Festival d'Avignon and the concurrent Festival Off (fringe festival), held in Avignon from mid-July to mid-August. Grenoble holds a week-long festival of European theatre in early July.

Cabaret

France's risqué cancan revues – featuring hundreds of performers and including female dancers both in and out of their elaborate costumes – are, of course, most common in Paris. But if you consult the listings guides, you'll run across cabaret performances in Lyon, Marseilles, Strasbourg and other large towns, often staged at local theatres or nightclubs, and perhaps with a *chanson* or two thrown in for good measure (see French Chansons later in the chapter). Be prepared for political satire mixed with clever monologues and short skits – and allusions to current trends or in-jokes which you may have trouble following even if you speak French. Some of the fancier establishments (such as Paris' legendary Moulin Rouge) offer shows in conjunction with a dinner.

Opera & Classical Music

The French opera and classical music scenes are very lively and less Paris-centric than you might think. The dozen or so non-Parisian orchestras include well-regarded organisations in Lille, Strasbourg and Toulouse. There are many classical music festivals all over France, especially during the summer; those held in Aix-en-Provence and Orange in July are especially popular.

All French cities and many towns put on at least one music festival each year, often with performances of opera, ballet and symphonic works. For details, see Special Events under specific city and town listings or contact the local tourist office. The nationwide Fête de la Musique brings live music to every corner of the country each 21 June.

Rock

French rock and pop music has experienced something of a revival in recent years, despite the ongoing dominance of Anglo-Saxon bands. That's due in part to France's leading role in the development of 'world music': in Paris and other large French towns, you'll just as likely be able to catch an Algerian rai concert as you would Johnny Halliday, France's ageing rock icon. Hip-hop acts are also popular, and techno is almost as widespread in Paris as it is in Berlin. Check with the local listings magazine for what's on at bars, cafes and clubs, which in Paris will charge anything from 20FF to 120FF for admission. The capital also has a number of venues which host acts

by international performers: it's often easier to see Anglophone acts in Paris than in their home countries.

Jazz

Paris established itself as Europe's most important jazz centre in the postwar period, and the city's better clubs still attract top international stars (consult the weekly *Pariscope* or *L'Officiel des Spectacles* for dates). You can count on paying upwards of 200FF to hear household names such as Wynton Marsalis or Chick Corea in larger concert halls, although some excellent artists also pop up in hole-in-the-wall venues. The apex of the Paris jazz season is the La Villette Jazz Festival, which sets toes tapping in early May. Some towns far removed from the capital also have vibrant jazz scenes – Juan-Les-Pins on the Côtes d'Azur, for instance, holds its own international jazzfest for two weeks in late July.

French Chansons

Any visit to France isn't complete without an evening of *chansons*, the half-spoken, heart-on-your-sleeve tunes popularised by Edith Piaf, Georges Brassens and Belgian-born Jacques Brel. They're usually sung with a single instrumental accompaniment such as an accordion. Paris, of course, has the greatest choice of venues, many of them intimate cafe-theatres that you'd imagine were packed with artists and intellectuals in the early 20th century. See French Chansons under Entertainment in the Paris chapter.

SPECTATOR SPORTS

Football and cycling are probably the most popular spectator sports, but the French are also particularly taken with tennis and rugby. Skiing is also popular though France hasn't produced any stars since Jean-Claude Killy and Marielle Goitchel in the 1960s. Champion figure-skaters Philippe Candeloro and Surya Bonnally have sparked interest in ice-skating in the past few years.

For details on upcoming sporting events, consult the sports daily *L'Équipe* (4.90FF) or the *Figaroscope*, published by *Le Figaro*, each Wednesday.

Football

France's greatest sporting moment came at the 1998 World Cup, which the country hosted and won, beating the reigning champions and tournament favourite, Brazil, in a one-sided final. This was crowned by France's victory in the 2000 European Championships, defeating Italy in the final in spectacular style.

The football-mad French had waited a long time for these successes. France's national teams had traditionally been hailed for their flair and imaginative play but had never progressed further than the World Cup semifinals. Not until 1984 did France win a major international football trophy – the European Championship.

At club level, in 1991 Marseilles became the first French side to win the European Champions League. Paris-St-Germain took the European Cup Winners' Cup in 1994.

The 1995 Bosman decision – allowing any European club to field as many European players as they wish – has resulted in a great exodus of French players (including Zidane and Petit) to clubs in Italy, Britain, Spain and Germany where they are better paid. This could have a great impact on the future of French club football at both national and European level.

France's home matches (friendlies and qualifiers for major championships) are held at the magnificent Stade de France at St-Denis, built especially for the World Cup. Check the sporting press for details on when and where individual club sides are playing.

Rugby

Rugby league has a strong following in the south and south-west of France with favourite teams being Toulouse, Montauban and St-Godens. Rugby union is more popular still, as the enduring success of the powerful Paris-St-Germain club testifies. The French national teams in both codes have always been notoriously difficult to beat at home.

France's home games in the Tournoi des Six Nations (Six Nations Tournament) are held in March and April and involve France, England, Scotland, Wales, Ireland and, since the year 2000, Italy. The finals of the Championnat de France de Rugby take place in late May and early June.

Tennis

The French Open, held in Paris's Roland Garros Stadium in late May and early June, is the second of the four Grand Slam tournaments. For more information, see Spectator Sports in the Paris chapter.

Cycling

The Tour de France is the world's most prestigious bicycle race. For three weeks in July, 189 of the world's top cyclists (in 21 teams of nine) take on a 3000km-plus route. The route changes each year, but three things remain constant – the inclusion of the Alps, Pyrenees and, since 1975, the race's finish on the Champs-Élysées in Paris. Frequently the race crosses the border into Switzerland, Spain, Italy and Andorra; in recent years it has even started in England and Ireland! Wherever it goes, the route is blocked off hours before the cyclists stream past.

The race itself is typically divided into 22 daily stages: it starts with a prologue, which is a short time trial used essentially to put a rider (the prologue's winner) in the leader's jersey for the first stage; two other time trials; five or six stages in the mountains; the rest are usually long flat stages; and, usually, there's at least one rest day. Each stage is timed and the race's overall winner is the rider with the lowest aggregate time – the smallest winning margin was in 1989, when Greg LeMond beat enigmatic Parisian Laurent Fignon by eight seconds after 23 days of racing and 3285km.

There are three special jerseys: the *maillot jaune* (yellow jersey) for race leader, *maillot vert* (green jersey) for points leader, and *maillot à pois rouges* (red polka dot jersey) for the king of the mountains. These jerseys are awarded after every stage in the race and to win one, especially the maillot jaune, even for a day, is certain to make headlines back home for that rider (see also the boxed text 'The Mondialisation of Le Tour').

France is also the world's top track cycling nation and has a formidable reputation in the developing sport of mountain biking.

For information on the Paris–Roubaix cycle race and the indoor Grand Prix des Nations competition, see Spectator Sports in the Paris chapter.

Traditional Sports

Pétanque France's most popular traditional games are *pétanque* and the similar, though more formal, *boules* (similar to lawn bowls but played on a hard surface). Unlike lawn bowls, whose white-clad players throw their woods on an immaculate strip of grass, pétanque and boules (which has a 70-page rule book) are usually played by village men in work clothes on a rough gravel or sandy pitch known as a *boulodrome*, scratched out wherever a bit of flat and shady ground can be found. Especially popular in the south, the games are often played in the cool of late afternoon, sometimes with a glass of pastis near to hand. The object is to get your boules (biased

The Mondialisation of Le Tour

During the halcyon days of French dominance of the Tour de France in the 1960s, '70s and early '80s, it used to be said that the government could fall, taxes double, trains strike, but there was only one thing the French public cared about in July: who was wearing the *maillot jaune* (yellow leader's jersey) in the Tour de France.

With no French winner in the Tour since voracious Breton Bernard Hinault won his fifth Tour crown in 1985, cycling has slipped in the national psyche and football is the nation's number one sporting love. The 1998 drugs scandal on the Tour didn't help, and embarrassingly, France didn't win a single *étape* (race segment) in the 1999 competition – the first time since 1926. However, the race itself continues in its march towards *mondialisation* (internationalisation).

From its humble beginnings in 1903, when newspaper publisher Henry Desgrange created the race to boost sales of *l'Auto*, Le Tour, as the race is more fondly known, is now the biggest annual sporting event in the world in terms of budget, worldwide TV audiences and spectators, and is only eclipsed in these areas by the World Cup of Football and the Olympic Games (both of which are only held every four years).

The mondialisation of Le Tour was inadvertently started by a core group of English-speaking cyclists in the 1980s (often referred to as the 'Foreign Legion'). These riders were very successful and the subsequent demand for TV coverage has now meant that the race (and the sport of cycling) is well known in the USA, Australia, Ireland and the UK. As a result, traditional French and European sponsors such as Fiat, Crédit Lyonnais and Champion have been joined by major multinationals such as Coca-Cola, Nike and Kawasaki.

The Foreign Legion (whose careers are detailed in Rupert Guinness' book of the same name) included the likes of Irishmen Stephen Roche (who won the race in 1987) and Sean Kelly, Brits Graeme Miller and Sean Yates, Australians Phil Anderson and Alan Pieper, and the most successful of them all, America's Greg LeMond, who won the race three times. Although the cyclists of the initial 'regiment' of the Foreign Legion have all retired now, another regiment – including German Erik Zabel, Italian Silvio Martinelli and American Lance Armstrong (a former cancer patient, who recovered and came back to win the 1999 and 2000 tours) – continues to make its mark on Le Tour.

However, it isn't just the English-speaking riders that inspire devotees of Le Tour these days. It's almost impossible to watch the action without appreciating the strength and panache (a highly regarded quality by the French public) of the likes of Marco Pantani, who broke the 32-year drought of wins by Italians in 1998, and French hero Richard Virenque.

metal balls) as close as possible to the 'jack', the small ball thrown at the start. World championships are held for both sports.

Pelote In the Basque Country, the racquet game of *pelote*, the fastest form of which is called *cesta punta*, is very popular. For details, see the boxed text 'Pelota' in the French Basque Country chapter.

SHOPPING
France is renowned for its luxury goods, particularly *haute couture*, high-quality clothing accessories (for example, Hermès scarves), lingerie and perfume. Obviously Paris has the largest selection on offer, but for local crafts and art (for example, colourful faïence from Quimper in Brittany, crystal and glassware from Baccarat in southern Lorraine, enamel and porcelain from Limoges in Limousin), it's best to go directly to the source.

This is especially true for wines (for example, Bordeaux, Burgundy, Alsace, Champagne) and other alcoholic beverages, (Bénédictine from Fécamp in Normandy), cheese (chèvre from Provence, Mont d'Or from the Jura, brocciu from Corsica) and exotic foodstuffs like the delectable black truffles harvested around Vaison-la-Romain in Provence, macaroons from St-Émilion (see the Atlantic Coast chapter) and candied fruit from Nice on the Côte d'Azur. For information on local shopping options, see Shopping under the individual towns and cities.

Non-EU residents may be able to get a rebate of some of the 19.6% value-added tax (VAT). See Taxes & Refunds under Money earlier in the chapter for details.

Clothing & Shoe Sizes
Clothes and footwear are sized differently in France than in the UK and USA. For the equivalents, see the tables below.

Clothing Sizes

| Women's Tops & Dresses | | | Men's Shirts | | | Men's Suits | | |
UK	USA	France	UK	USA	France	UK	USA	France
8	6	36	–	14	36	30	36	38
10	8	38	14½	14½	37	32	37	40
12	10	40	15	15	38	38	38	42–44
14	12	42	15½	15½	39	–	39	44
18	16	46–48	16	16½	41	38	42	48
20	18	50	16½	17	42			
22	20	52						

Shoe Sizes

| Women's Shoes | | | Men's Shoes | | |
UK	USA	France	UK	USA	France
3	4	35½	5½	6	39
3½	4½	36	6½	7	40
4	5	36½	7	7½	41
4½	5½	37	8	8½	42
5	6	37½	8½	9	43
5½	6½	38	9½	10	44
6	7½	39	10½	11	45

Getting There & Away

AIR
Airports & Airlines

Air France (www.airfrance.com and www.airfrance.co.uk), France's money-losing national carrier, and scores of other airlines link Paris with every part of the globe. Other French airports with significant international services (mainly within Europe) include Bordeaux, Lyon, Marseilles, Metz-Nancy-Lorraine, Mulhouse-Basel (also known as EuroAirport), Nantes, Nice, Strasbourg and Toulouse. Some of Europe's new budget carriers use minor provincial airports for flights from countries such as the UK and the Netherlands.

For details on Paris' two main international airports, Orly and Roissy Charles de Gaulle, and for the addresses of airline offices in the French capital, see Air under Getting There & Away in the Paris chapter. The various ways to travel between the airports and central Paris are covered under To/From the Airports in that chapter's Getting Around section.

Buying Tickets

A bit of research – talking to recent travellers, perusing the ads in the newspaper, checking Internet sites – can often save you quite a bit of money on your air ticket. Start early: some of the cheapest tickets have to be bought well in advance, and the most popular flights sell out early.

Cheap tickets are available in two distinct categories: official and unofficial. Official ones are sold under a variety of names, including advance purchase tickets, advance purchase excursion (Apex) and super-Apex. Unofficial tickets are released by the airlines through selected travel agencies and are not usually sold directly by the airline's offices. Since only a few travel agencies may be given access to a particular batch of discounted tickets, the best way to find the best deals is to phone around.

Return (round-trip) tickets are usually cheaper than two one-ways. In some cases,

the return fare may actually cost *less* than a one-way ticket. Inexpensive tickets often come with cumbersome restrictions: you may have to buy your ticket weeks in advance or pay heavy penalties for changing travel dates; the non-extendable period of validity may be very short; there may be a minimum stay or you may be required to spend a Saturday night at your destination (this weeds out the business travellers); the routing may involve time-consuming stopovers; and cancellation penalties of up to 100% may apply.

Round-the-world (RTW) tickets make it possible to combine a visit to the Alps with a trek in the Himalayas and backpacking in the Rockies. If you live in Australasia, they are often no more expensive than an ordinary return fare. In the UK, prices are pretty stable year round and start at an absolute minimum of UK£500, though UK£700 is probably more realistic. In Australia, count on paying A$2000 to A$3000 for a routing through Paris, depending on the season. In New Zealand, RTW tickets through Paris are available for NZ$2500. US prices for tickets with stops in Europe and South-East Asia start at about US$1200. The flight dates (but not the overall routing) are changeable en route. The departure date from your home country usually determines the fare (that is, whether you're charged high- or low-season rates). Validity usually lasts for a year.

As you phone around, you may discover that those impossibly cheap flights are 'fully booked, but we have another one that costs only a bit more...' Or that the flight is on an airline notorious for its poor safety record and will leave you for 14 hours in the world's least-favourite airport, where you'll be confined to the transit lounge unless you get an expensive visa... Or the agent may claim that the last two cheap seats until next autumn will be gone in two hours. Don't panic – keep ringing around.

If you are travelling from the USA or

Air Travel Glossary

Cancellation Penalties If you have to cancel or change a discounted ticket, there are often heavy penalties involved; insurance can sometimes be taken out against these penalties. Some airlines impose penalties on regular tickets as well, particularly against 'no-show' passengers.

Courier Fares Businesses often need to send urgent documents or freight securely and quickly. Courier companies hire people to accompany the package through customs and, in return, offer a discount ticket which is sometimes a phenomenal bargain. However, you may have to surrender all your baggage allowance and take only carry-on luggage.

Full Fares Airlines traditionally offer 1st class (coded F), business class (coded J) and economy class (coded Y) tickets. These days there are so many promotional and discounted fares available that few passengers pay full economy fare.

Lost Tickets If you lose your airline ticket an airline will usually treat it like a travellers cheque and, after inquiries, issue you with another one. Legally, however, an airline is entitled to treat it like cash and if you lose it then it's gone forever. Take good care of your tickets.

Onward Tickets An entry requirement for many countries is that you have a ticket out of the country. If you're unsure of your next move, the easiest solution is to buy the cheapest onward ticket to a neighbouring country or a ticket from a reliable airline which can later be refunded if you do not use it.

Open-Jaw Tickets These are return tickets where you fly out to one place but return from another. If available, this can save you backtracking to your arrival point.

Overbooking Since every flight has some passengers who fail to show up, airlines often book more passengers than they have seats. Usually excess passengers make up for the no-shows, but occasionally somebody gets 'bumped' onto the next available flight. Guess who it is most likely to be? The passengers who check in late.

Promotional Fares These are officially discounted fares, available from travel agencies or direct from the airline.

Reconfirmation If you don't reconfirm your flight at least 72 hours prior to departure, the airline may delete your name from the passenger list. Ring to find out if your airline requires reconfirmation.

Restrictions Discounted tickets often have various restrictions on them – such as needing to be paid for in advance and incurring a penalty to be altered. Others are restrictions on the minimum and maximum period you must be away.

Round-the-World Tickets RTW tickets give you a limited period (usually a year) in which to circumnavigate the globe. You can go anywhere the carrying airlines go, as long as you don't backtrack. The number of stopovers or total number of separate flights is decided before you set off and they usually cost a bit more than a basic return flight.

Transferred Tickets Airline tickets cannot be transferred from one person to another. Travellers sometimes try to sell the return half of their ticket, but officials can ask you to prove that you are the person named on the ticket. On an international flight tickets are compared with passports.

Travel Periods Ticket prices vary with the time of year. There is a low (off-peak) season and a high (peak) season, and often a low-shoulder season and a high-shoulder season as well. Usually the fare depends on your outward flight – if you depart in the high season and return in the low season, you pay the high-season fare.

South-East Asia, you will sometimes find that the cheapest flights are being advertised by obscure agencies whose names have yet to reach the telephone directory. Many such firms are honest and solvent, but there are a few rogues who will take your money and run – only to reopen elsewhere a month or two later under a new name. If you feel suspicious about a firm, don't give them all the money at once – leave a deposit of 20% or so and pay the balance when you get the ticket. If they insist on cash in advance, go somewhere else or take a very big risk. And once you have the ticket, ring the airline to confirm that you are indeed booked on the flight.

You may decide that it's worthwhile to pay a bit more than the rock-bottom fare in return for the safety of a better-known travel agency. We mention a number of such firms in this section under individual country headings.

In France, as elsewhere, the only way to find the best deal is to shop around. Prices and available dates vary greatly, and an agency with great prices to Bangkok may not be able to get you the lowest student fare to New York. Inexpensive flights offered by charter clearing houses can be booked through many regular travel agencies – look in agency windows for posters and pamphlets advertising flights from Go Voyages (☎ 01 53 40 44 29), with a Web site at www.govoyages.com; or Look Voyages (☎ 01 55 49 49 60, 0 803 31 36 13), whose Web site is at www.look-voyages.fr. Reliable travel agency chains include the French student travel company OTU (☎ 01 40 29 12 12), with a Web site at www.otu.fr; Nouvelles Frontières (☎ 0 803 33 33 33 costing 1.09FF a minute), whose Web site is at www.newfrontiers.com; and the Franco-Belgian company Wasteels (☎ 01 43 62 30 00), with a Web site at www.voyages-wasteels.fr. Some of the fares advertised in the Paris metro and the free Paris biweekly *France USA Contacts (FUSAC)* are too good to be true (for example, they may not include taxes and all sorts of 'handling fees').

Aventure du Bout du Monde (ABM; ☎ 01 45 45 29 29, fax 01 45 45 20 30),

based in Paris at 11 Rue de Coulmiers, 14e (metro: Alésia), is a non-profit-making organisation that facilitates the exchange of practical travel information (for example, advice on cheap flights) between travellers. Membership costs 190FF a year. Check out the Web site at www.abm.fr.

Travellers with Special Needs

If you have special needs of any sort – you're vegetarian or require a special diet, you are travelling in a wheelchair, taking a baby, terrified of flying – let the airline people know as soon as possible so that they can make the necessary arrangements. Remind them when you reconfirm your booking (at least 72 hours before departure) and again when you check in at the airport. It may also be worth calling several airlines before making your booking to find out how they can handle your particular needs.

In general, children aged under two travel for 10% of the standard fare (or, on some carriers, for free) as long as they don't occupy a seat. They do not get a luggage allowance. Skycots, baby food, formula, nappies (diapers) etc should be provided by the airline if requested in advance. Children aged between two and 12 can usually occupy a seat for half to two-thirds of the full fare and do get a luggage allowance.

Weight Limits

Unless you're flying to/from North America (across the Atlantic or the Pacific), in which case you can usually bring along two suitcases of fairly generous proportions, your checked luggage will be subject to a 20kg weight limit. On most flights (with the exception of certain cheapo charters) you won't be charged if you're only 3kg to 5kg over, but beyond that each kilogram will be assessed at 1% of the price of a full-fare, 1st-class, one-way ticket. This can work out to be very expensive indeed, for example, A\$40 to A\$60 per kilogram to/from Australia.

The single piece of hand luggage that you're technically allowed is supposed to be limited to 5kg. Of late, for safety reasons, there has been a tendency to enforce this limit, especially in the USA.

The UK

Increased deregulation has brought in new carriers whose fares are made all the more attractive by the small discounts available if you book online. Return fares on the London–Paris route can often be as low as UK£50, but with the larger companies expect to pay at least UK£90. For return travel from London to the south of France, UK£60 is the absolute minimum, but most fares range from UK£90 to UK£150.

Some of the best deals, especially to destinations other than Paris, are offered by Buzz (www.buzzaway.com), Ryanair (www.ryanair.ie) and easyJet (www.easyjet .co.uk). With fares that are often quite reasonable (especially for young people), Air France (www.airfrance.co.uk) and British Airways (BA; www.britishairways.com) link London and a variety of other British cities (for example, Birmingham, Edinburgh and Manchester) with Paris and France's major provincial cities. Other airlines that may have decent prices include

BritishMidland (www.britishmidland.com), Go (www.go-fly.com), KLM uk (www .klmuk.com) and Jersey European Airways (www.jea.co.uk).

Advertisements for travel agencies appear in the travel pages of the weekend broadsheet newspapers, as well as in *Time Out*, the *Evening Standard* and the free magazine *TNT*. Popular discount 'student' travel agencies include STA Travel (☎ 020-7361 6161), with Web sites at www .sta-travel.com and www.statravel.co.uk, whose offices around the UK include one at 86 Old Brompton Rd, London SW7; and Campus Travel (☎ 020-7730 3402), with a Web site at www.usitcampus.co.uk and one of many branches at 52 Grosvenor Gardens, London SW1. Other recommended travel agencies include: Trailfinders (☎ 020-7937 5400), 194 Kensington High St, London W8; Bridge the World (☎ 020-7734 7447), 4 Regent Place, London W1; and Flight-bookers (☎ 020-7757 2000), 177-178 Tottenham Court Rd, London W1. Have a look at their Web sites: www.trailfinders.co.uk, www.b-t-w.co.uk and www.ebookers.com, respectively.

The USA

The flight options across the North Atlantic, the world's busiest long-haul air corridor, are bewildering. The *New York Times*, *LA Times*, *Chicago Tribune* and *San Francisco Chronicle* all have weekly travel sections in which you'll find any number of travel agencies' ads. Independent periodicals such as the *San Francisco Guardian* and New York's *Village Voice* are another good place to check. Reliable discount travel chains include Council Travel (☎ 1-800-226 8624) and STA Travel (☎ 1-800-781 4040), whose Web sites are at www.counciltravel.com and www.sta-travel.com, respectively. San Francisco-based Ticket Planet (☎ 1-800-799 8888) is an online agency (www.ticket planet.com) with an excellent reputation and lots of RTW offerings.

You should be able to fly from New York to Paris and back for about US\$480 in the low season and US\$780 in the high season; sometimes even lower promotional fares are on offer. Tickets from the west coast are US$150 to US$250 higher. In Paris, one-way, off-season discount flights to New York start at about 1400FF. Return fares of 2300FF are sometimes available, but a more usual rock-bottom fare is 2600FF (3400FF around Christmas and in July and August). Return fares to the west coast are 600FF to 1000FF higher.

If your schedule is flexible, flying standby can work out to be very reasonable. Airhitch (☎ 1-800-326 2009 in New York, 310-574 0090 in Los Angeles, 01 47 00 16 30 in Paris) specialises in this sort of thing and can get you to Europe (but not necessarily Paris) for around US$170/220/250 each way from the Northeast/Midwest/West Coast, plus taxes of US$16 to US$46. Have a look at their Web site at www.airhitch.org.

Another very cheap option is a courier flight, which can cost as little as US$300 for a New York–Paris return arranged at the last minute. The drawbacks are that your stay in Europe may be limited to one or two weeks; your luggage is usually restricted to a carry-on; there is unlikely to be more than one courier ticket available for any given flight; and you may have to be a local resident and apply for an interview before they'll take you on.

You can find out more about courier flights and fares from the Colorado-based Air Courier Association (☎ 1-800-282 1202), which charges US$39 for a one-year membership and whose Web site is at www.airhitch.org; the International Association of Air Travel Couriers (☎ 561-582 8320, fax 582 1581), with a Web site at www.courier.org; and Now Voyager Travel (☎ 212-431 1616, fax 334 5243), with a Web site at www.nowvoyagertravel.com.

Canada

Travel CUTS (☎ 604-659 2887 in Vancouver, 416-614 2887 in Toronto), known as Voyages Campus in Quebec, has offices in all major cities. Check out their Web site at www.travelcuts.com. You might also scan the travel agencies' ads in the *Globe & Mail*, *Toronto Star* and *Vancouver Province*. From Toronto or Montreal, return flights to

Paris are available from about C$900 in the low season; prices are C$300 or C$400 more from Vancouver. From Paris, flights are often a bit cheaper to Montreal than to Toronto, with one-way/return fares starting at an absolute minimum of 1300/2400FF (double that in high season).

Continental Europe

Fares on some routes have been dropping as deregulation kicks in. Air France offers many of the best youth and student rates, available if you are either aged under 26 or are a student (maximum age somewhere between 29 and 32).

In Amsterdam, agencies with cheap tickets include the NBBS subsidiary Budget Air (☎ 020-627 1251), at Rokin 34. Check out their Web site at www.nbbs.nl. Youth and student flights to Paris cost from around f160/280 one-way/return. Adult return fares to Paris/Nice start at about f380/440.

In Belgium, Acotra Student Travel Agency (☎ 02-723 23 23), at rue de la Madeleine 51, Brussels, and WATS Reizen (☎ 03-233 70 20), at de Keyserlei 44, Antwerp, are both well-known agencies. A return youth ticket from Brussels to Nice costs about f7000.

In Switzerland, SSR Voyages (☎ 01-297 11 11 in Zurich), whose Web site is at www.ssr.ch, specialises in student, youth and budget fares. The branches in Zurich include one at Leonhardstrasse 10; there are also offices in other major cities. One-way/return youth and student fares from Zurich to Paris cost Sfr 90/170 on Air France.

In Stockholm, agencies such as Kilroy Travels (☎ 08-234 515), at Kungsgatan 4, can get young people and students to Paris for around 1200/2400 kr one-way/return. Their Web site is at www.kilroytravels.com.

In Copenhagen, STA Travel (☎ 33 141 501), with a Web site at www.sta-travel.com, is at Fiolstraede 18; and Kilroy Travels (☎ 33 110 044) is at Skindergarde 28. For those aged under 26 and students aged under 32, the one-way/return fare to Paris is around 740/1480 kr with Air France; the cheapest adult return costs about 1800 kr.

In Oslo, STA Travel (☎ 23 01 02 90) is at

Karl Johans Gt 33, while Kilroy Travels (☎ 47 23 10 23 10) is at Nedre Spottsgate 23. Youth and student flights to Paris on Air France cost around 1410/2650 kr one-way/return.

In Berlin, STA Travel (☎ 030-311 0950) has one of its many branches at Goethestrasse 73 (U2 stop: Ernst-Reuter-Platz). Return flights to Paris on Air France or Lufthansa start at DM460; students can get one-way fares of DM280.

In Rome, recommended travel agencies include CTS Viaggi, whose many offices around Italy include one at 16 Via Genova (☎ 06 462 04 31); and Passagi (☎ 06 474 09 23), which is at Stazione Termini FS, Galleria Di Tesla. Youth and student flights to Paris on Air France cost around L230,000/490,000 one-way/return; adult returns are sometimes available for L350,000.

In Madrid, usit Unlimited (☎ 90 225 25 75), with a Web site at www.unlimited.es, is at 3 Plaza de Callao; Barcelo Viajes (☎ 91 559 18 19) is at Princesa 3; and Nouvelles Frontières (☎ 91 547 42 00), with a Web site at www.nouvelles-frontieres.es, is at Plaza de España 18. A youth and student fare to Paris is around 16,000/31,000 ptas one-way/return; low-season adult return fares start at 25,000 ptas.

Ireland

Usit Voyages (☎ 01-602 1600 in Dublin, 01 42 34 56 90 in Paris) has changeable *and* refundable Dublin–Paris flights for students and those aged under 26 costing around IR£55/100 one-way/return (a bit more in summer). Have a look at their Web sites: www.usitnow.ie for the Irish Republic, www.usitnow.com for Northern Ireland. Ryanair (www.ryanair.ie) often has cheap promotional fares to Beauvais (80km north of Paris) and a number of minor regional airports. Belfast–Paris youth and student fares (for example, on British Airways or British Midland) start at around UK£50/90 for one-way/return.

Australia

STA Travel (☎ 131 776 Australiawide), with a Web site at www.statravel.com.au,

and Flight Centre (☎ 131 600 Australia wide), whose Web site is at www.flightcentre.com.au, are major dealers in cheap air tickets. Smaller agencies often advertise in the Saturday travel sections of the *Sydney Morning Herald* and the Melbourne *Age*.

From Melbourne or Sydney, one-way/return tickets to Paris range from A$980/1500 (low season) to A$1000/2100 (high season, which is June to August and around Christmas). Fares from Perth are about A$200 cheaper. Airlines offering good deals include Kuwait Airways, Qantas Airways, Thai Airways International, Royal Jordanian and Malaysian Airlines.

New Zealand

As in Australia, STA Travel (☎ 09-309 0458) and Flight Centre (☎ 09-309 6171) are popular travel agencies. Ads for other agencies can be found in the travel section of the *New Zealand Herald*.

The cheapest fares to Europe are routed through Asia. With Thai Airways International, one-way/return fares from Auckland (via Bangkok) range from NZ$1170/2020 (low season) to NZ$1320/2320 (high season, which is June to August and around Christmas). Other companies with attractive fares include Royal Jordanian, Kuwait Airways, Quantas and Malaysian Airlines.

North Africa

Charter fares to/from Morocco and Tunisia can be quite cheap if you're lucky enough to find a seat. From Paris, one-way/return charter flights to Tunis start at 800/1300FF, but popular dates can cost double that. Expect to pay at least 1100/1700FF to Marrakech.

LAND

Paris, France's main rail and road hub, is linked with every part of Europe. International rail travel to places in France outside Paris sometimes (though much less frequently than in the past) involves switching train stations in the French capital – for details on Paris' six major train stations, see Train under Getting There & Away in the Paris chapter.

The UK

The Channel Tunnel, inaugurated in 1994, is the first dry-land link between England and France since the last Ice Age. The three parallel tunnels – one for service access and two for trains – pass through a layer of impermeable chalk marl 25 to 45m below the floor of the English Channel.

For details on rail passes (such as Eurail) and other reduced-price train options, see the boxed text 'Discount Train Tickets & Passes' in the Getting Around chapter.

Bus Eurolines (☎ 01582-404 511 in Luton, 01 43 54 11 99 in Paris) runs coach services from London's Victoria coach station to various French cities. One-way/return fares to Paris (7½ hours), via Dover and Calais cost around UK£32/45 (a bit less if you qualify for a discount and a bit more in July and August). Eurolines has a Web site at www.eurolines.co.uk. For details on the Eurolines Pass, see Continental Europe later in this section. Bookings can be made at any office of National Express, whose buses also link London and other parts of the UK with the Channel ports. See the Web site at www.nationalexpress.co.uk.

From April to October, the UK company Busabout (☎ 020-7950 1661 ✆ info@busabout.co.uk), based in London at 258 Vauxhall Bridge Rd, offers a bus version of the Eurail pass. Electronic tickets (replaceable if lost), valid for a minimum of 15 days, let you travel around much of Western Europe (16 countries) for 30% to 40% less than a Eurail pass, though with less flexibility. Stops in France are in Paris, Tours, Bordeaux, Lyon, Avignon and Nice. One-/two-month passes, available through student travel agencies, cost UK£289/449 (around 3000/4670FF) or UK£259/399 (2700/4150FF) for those aged under 26, students and teachers; a Flexi Pass good for 21 days of travel over three months costs UK£445 (around 4630FF) or UK£399 (4150FF) for those aged under 26, students and teachers. Buses stop at each of the 70 cities served every two days. On-board guides can take care of hostel reservations. To find out more information or to book online, check out their Web site at www.busabout.com.

Eurostar Taking the Eurostar is an extraordinary experience that has changed the way many Britons see the Continent: you're on a sleek, ultra-modern train clickety-clicking through Kent, then it's dark for 20 minutes, and then you're whizzing silently across Flanders at 300km/h. The highly civilised Eurostar takes only three hours (not including the one-hour time difference) to get from London to Paris: 70 minutes from London's Waterloo station to Folkestone, 20 minutes inside the Channel Tunnel, and 90 minutes from Calais to Paris' Gare du Nord. The ride from London to Lille takes two hours.

There are direct services from London and Ashford to Paris and the three other stations in France: Calais-Fréthun, Lille and Disneyland Paris. In winter, ski trains link London with Bourg St-Maurice in the Alps.

A full-fare, 2nd-class one-way/return ticket from London to Paris costs a whopping UK£155/270, but prices for return travel drop precipitously if you stay over a Saturday night: UK£70/80 if you book 14/seven days ahead, UK£100 to UK£140 if you don't. Tickets for people aged under 26 cost UK£45/75 one-way/return. Kids aged under 12 pay UK£29/58 one-way/return. Student travel agencies (see The UK under Air earlier in this chapter) often have youth fares that are not available direct from Eurostar. With the cheapest tickets you cannot change your travel dates or get a reimbursement.

For information on Eurostar services, contact Eurostar UK (☎ 0990 186 186) or Rail Europe Direct (☎ 0990 848 848) in the UK or the Société Nationale des Chemins de Fer Français (SNCF; ☎ 0 836 35 35 39 for 2.23FF a minute) in France. Alternatively, have a look at the Web site www.eurostar.com.

Eurotunnel High-speed Eurotunnel shuttle trains (☎ 0990 353 535 in the UK, 03 21 00 61 00 in France) whisk cars, motorbikes, bicycles and coaches from Folkestone through the Channel Tunnel to Coquelles, 5km south-west of Calais, in soundproofed and air-conditioned comfort. Shuttles run 24 hours a day, every day of the year, with up to five departures an hour during peak periods (one an hour from 1 to 5 am). Details are available on their Web site: www.eurotunnel.com.

Prices vary with market demand, but the regular one-way fare for a passenger car, including all its passengers, ranges from around UK£110 (in February or March) to UK£175 (July or August); return passage costs twice as much. Return fares valid for less than five days cost UK£140 to UK£230. The fee for a bicycle, including its rider, is UK£15 return; advance reservations (☎ 01303-288 680) are mandatory. To take advantage of promotional fares you must book at least one day ahead.

Continental Europe

Bus Eurolines (☎ 01 43 54 11 99 in Paris or 0 836 69 52 52 at 2.23FF a minute), with a Web site at www.eurolines.fr, is an association of 31 bus companies that serves destinations in 26 countries and links Paris and numerous other French cities with points all over Western and Central Europe, Scandinavia and Morocco. Buses are slower and less comfortable than trains, but they are cheaper, especially if you qualify for the 10% discount available to those aged under 26 and over 60, or take advantage of the discount fares on offer from time to time.

Eurolines' direct buses link Paris with destinations including Amsterdam (200FF, 7½ hours), Barcelona (490FF, 15 hours), Berlin (450FF, 14 hours), Budapest (520FF, 23 hours), Madrid (530FF, 17 hours), Prague (400FF, 16 hours) and Rome (450FF, 23 hours). These are one-way fares for young people and seniors – adults pay about 10% more. Return tickets cost about 20% less than two one-ways. In summer, it's not a bad idea to make reservations at least two working days in advance.

The Eurolines Pass gives you unlimited bus travel between 48 major cities in 21 European countries (but not to other cities en route). Low/high-season tickets good for

30 days cost 1730/2220FF (those aged under 26 1400/1850FF); tickets good for 60 days cost 2140/2530FF (those aged under 26 1730/2320FF). High-season rates apply from June to September.

Eurolines-affiliated companies can be found across Europe, including Amsterdam (☎ 020-560 8787), Barcelona (☎ 93 490 40 00), Berlin (☎ 030-860 960), Brussels (☎ 02-203 07 07), Budapest (☎ 1-11 72 562, 1-31 72 562), Copenhagen (☎ 33 251 244, 99 344 488), Göteborg (☎ 031-100 240, 020-987 377), Hamburg (☎ 040-249 818, 040-247 106), Istanbul (☎ 212-696 9600), Lisbon (☎ 01-315 26 44), Madrid (☎ 91 528 11 05, 91 327 13 81), Prague (☎ 02-242 134 20, 02-231 23 55), Rome (☎ 06 44 23 39 28), Vienna (☎ 01-712 0453) and Warsaw (☎ 022-870 59 40 or 022-620 49 48). For details on Eurolines offices in France, see Bus under Getting There & Away in the listings for the relevant cities.

Eurolines' all-Europe Web site, www .eurolines.com, has links to each national company's site.

Intercars (☎ 01 42 19 99 35 in Paris), whose Paris office is at 139 bis rue de Vaugirard, 15e (metro: Falguière), links Paris with Berlin (490FF, 13 hours) and Eastern Europe (700FF from Nice to Warsaw, 29½ hours). From southern France, the company's buses serve Eastern Europe (810FF from Nice to Moscow, 50 hours), Italy (200FF from Nice to Rome, 16 hours), Spain (535FF from Nice to Madrid, 19 hours), Portugal and Morocco (925FF from Nice to Tangier, 30 hours plus the ferry). Return fares are 10% to 25% cheaper; discounts of 5% to 20% are available to people under 26 and over 60. Have a look at the Web site at www.intercars.fr.

See The UK section above for details on Busabout's passes for travel in France and Europe.

Train Services link France with every country in Europe; schedules are available from major train stations in France and abroad. See Train under Getting There & Away in the Paris chapter for sample international fares. Because of different track gauges and electrification systems, you sometimes have to change trains at the border (for example, when travelling to Spain).

The only international TGV service (except the Eurostar) is Thalys (www .thalys.com), which links Paris' Gare du Nord with Brussels-Midi (f2180, 85 minutes, 20 daily), Amsterdam (160f, 4¼ hours, five daily) and Cologne's Hauptbahnhof (DM130, four hours, seven daily). Youth fares are half (or less) of the regular adult fare; seniors also get discounts.

You can book tickets and get information from Rail Europe (www.raileurope.com) up to two months ahead. Ring ☎ 02-534 45 31 in Belgium, ☎ 069-975 846 41 in Germany, ☎ 02 725 44 370 in Italy, ☎ 01 547 84 42 in Spain, and ☎ 031-382 99 00 in Switzerland. In France, ticketing is handled by the SNCF. Telephone bookings with SNCF (☎ 0 836 35 35 35 in French, 0 836 35 35 39 in English) are possible, but they won't post tickets outside France.

For details on discount train passes and tickets, see the boxed text 'Discount Train Tickets & Passes' in the Getting Around chapter.

Hitching For information on Allostop and other organisations that help people looking for a ride link up with drivers, see Hitching in the Getting Around chapter.

East Asia

Thanks to the fabled Trans-Siberian Railway, it *is* possible to get to France overland from East Asia, though count on spending at least eight days doing it. Details are available from the Russian National Tourist Office (www.interknowledge.com/russia /trasib01.htm) and Helsinki-based Finnsov Tours (www.finnsov.fi).

SEA

Tickets for ferry travel to/from England, Ireland, Italy and North Africa are available from most travel agencies in France and the countries served. Children aged four to somewhere between 12 and 15 (depending on the company) travel for half to two-thirds of an adult fare. Food is relatively

expensive on ferries, so you might want to bring your own. If you're travelling with a vehicle, you are usually denied access to it during the voyage.

The UK

Fares vary widely according to demand, which depends on the season (July and August are especially popular) and the time of day (a Friday-night ferry can cost much more than a Sunday-morning one). The most expensive tickets can cost almost three times as much as the cheapest ones. Three- or five-day excursion (return) fares generally cost about the same as regular one-way tickets. Special promotional return fares, often requiring advance booking, are sometimes cheaper than a one-way. On some overnight sailings you have to pay extra for a mandatory reclining seat or sleeping berth.

Ferry companies may try to make it hard on people who use super-cheap one-day return tickets for one-way passage – a huge backpack is a dead giveaway that you're not out for an afternoon outing.

Eurail passes are *not* valid for ferry travel between England and France. Transporting bicycles is often (but not always) free.

Via Far Northern France The fastest way to cross the English Channel is between Dover (Douvres) and Calais. This route is occasionally served by Hoverspeed's Sea-Cats (Australian-designed catamarans), which take 50 minutes. For foot passengers, a one-way trip (or a return completed within five days) costs around UK£25. Depending on the season, a car with up to nine passengers pays around UK£110 to UK£175 one way, and UK£135 to UK£225 for a five-day return. All sorts of incredibly cheap promotional fares are often available, including return day-trip fares for pedestrians costing as little as UK£5 or UK£10.

Another quick crossing, handled by Hoverspeed's SeaCats, is the Folkestone–Boulogne route (55 minutes, four daily). Service may be suspended from Christmas to sometime in March. Foot passengers pay the same as for Dover–Calais; car crossings are a bit cheaper.

Ferry Companies

Brittany Ferries
UK Reservations	☎ 0870 536 0360
Ireland Reservations (Cork)	
	☎ 021-277 801
France Reservations (Roscoff)	
	☎ 02 98 29 28 00
Caen	☎ 02 31 36 36 36
Cherbourg	☎ 02 33 88 44 44
St-Malo	☎ 02 99 82 80 80
Santander	☎ 942 36 06 11
Web site:	www.brittany-ferries.com

Compagnie Marocaine de Navigation
Sète	☎ 04 99 57 21 21
Tanger	☎ 09-94 23 50

Compagnie Tunisienne de Navigation
Tunis	☎ 01-341 777

Condor Ferries
UK Reservations (Weymouth)	
	☎ 01305-761 551
France Reservations (St-Malo)	
	☎ 02 99 20 03 00
Poole	☎ 01202-207 215
	☎ 01202-207 207
St-Helier	☎ 01534-601 000
St-Peter Port	☎ 01481-729 666
Web site:	www.condorferries.co.uk

Émeraude Lines
General Reservations (Jersey)	
	☎ 01534-766 566
Guernsey	☎ 01481-711 414
Carteret	☎ 02 33 52 61 39
Granville	☎ 02 33 50 16 36
St-Malo	☎ 02 23 18 01 80
Web site:	www.emeraudelines.co.uk

Hoverspeed
UK Reservations (Dover)	
	☎ 0870 524 0241
France Reservations	☎ 082 0 00 35 55
Boulogne	☎ 03 21 30 27 26
Calais	☎ 03 21 46 14 00
Folkestone	☎ 01303-715 313
Web site:	www.hoverspeed.co.uk

Irish Ferries
Ireland Reservations	☎ 01-638 3333
UK Reservations	☎ 0870 517 1717
Cherbourg	☎ 02 33 23 44 44
Paris	☎ 01 44 94 20 40
Roscoff	☎ 02 98 61 17 17
Rosslare	☎ 053-33 158
Web site:	www.irish-ferries.com

P&O Irish Sea Ferries
Northern Ireland Reservations	
	☎ 0870 242 4777
Cherbourg	☎ 0 803 01 30 13
Web site:	www.poirishsea.com

P&O Portsmouth
UK Reservations	☎ 0870 598 0555
France Reservations	☎ 0 803 01 30 13
Bilbao	☎ 94 423 44 77
Web site:	www.poef.com

P&O Stena Line
UK Reservations (Dover)	
	☎ 0870 598 0980
	☎ 0870 600 0611
France Reservations	☎ 0 802 01 00 20
Calais	☎ 03 21 46 04 40
Web site:	www.posl.com

SeaFrance Sealink
UK Reservations (Dover)	
	☎ 0870 571 1711
France Reservations	☎ 0 804 04 40 45
Web site:	www.seafrance.com

SNCM
France Reservations (for Corsica and Sardinia)	
	☎ 0 836 67 95 00
France Reservations (for North Africa)	
	☎ 0 836 67 21 00
Ajaccio	☎ 04 95 29 66 99
Bastia (town)	☎ 04 95 54 66 99
Bastia (port)	☎ 04 95 54 66 60
Porto Torres	☎ 079-51 44 77
Sète	☎ 04 67 46 68 00
Toulon	☎ 04 94 16 66 66
Web site:	www.sncm.fr

The Dover–Calais crossing is also handled by car ferries, run by SeaFrance (1½ hours, 15 daily) and P&O Stena (one to 1¼ hours, 29 daily). With SeaFrance, foot passengers pay UK£15 for a one-way or five-day return ticket; day trips are sometimes available for just UK£5 or UK£10. A car with up to nine passengers pays around UK£120 to UK£170 one way, and double that for return. A five-day return costs UK£150 to UK215. Prices are a bit cheaper if you book via the Internet. If you don't book ahead there's a surcharge at the port. With P&O Stena, foot passengers pay UK£24 for a one-way or five-day return ticket; a car with up to nine people pays upwards of UK£120.

Via Normandy The Newhaven–Dieppe route is handled by Hoverspeed's SeaCats (2¼ hours, one to three daily). Pedestrians pay UK£28 one way; a car with up to nine occupants is charged from UK£140 to UK£200 one way.

Poole is linked to Cherbourg by Brittany Ferries' 4¼-hour crossing (one or two daily). Foot passengers pay UK£20 to UK£40 one way; a car with up to five passengers is charged UK£80 to UK£190 one way. On overnight sailings you have to book either a reclining seat (UK£3) or a sleeping berth (UK£14 to UK£21 for the cheapest variety).

On the Portsmouth–Cherbourg route, P&O Portsmouth runs three car ferries a day (five hours by day, eight hours overnight) and, from mid-March to mid-October, two faster catamarans a day. Foot passengers pay UK£20 to UK£35 one way; a non-mandatory overnight cabin for one or two people costs UK£32 to UK£46. Cars with up to eight passengers pay between UK£150 and UK£190 one way, not including a surcharge of up to UK£40 for some catamaran crossings.

The Portsmouth–Le Havre crossing (5½ hours by day, 7¾ hours overnight) is handled by P&O Portsmouth, which runs three car ferries a day (fewer in winter). Passage costs about the same as for Portsmouth–Cherbourg.

Brittany Ferries runs car ferries from Portsmouth to Caen (Ouistreham, six hours, three daily). Tickets cost a bit more than for Poole–Cherbourg.

Via Brittany From mid-March to mid-November, Plymouth is linked to Roscoff (six hours for day crossings; one to three daily) by Brittany Ferries. The one-way fare for foot passengers is around UK£25 to UK£40. Cars with up to five passengers pay around UK£100 to UK£180 one way. On overnight sailings you have to book either a reclining seat (UK£3) or a sleeping berth (UK£14 to UK£21 for the cheapest type).

Brittany Ferries links Portsmouth with St-Malo (8¾ hours by day, one daily); all sailings *to* St-Malo are overnight and require that you book either a reclining seat (UK£3) or a sleeping berth (at least UK£14 to UK£21). Pedestrians pay around UK£20 to UK£45 one way; a car with up to five passengers is charged UK£90 to UK£190 one way.

From late May to mid-October, Condor runs one catamaran a day linking Weymouth with St-Malo. The 4¼-hour crossing costs UK£26 one way for pedestrians; cars, including two passengers, cost UK£95 to UK£190. The company also links Poole with St-Malo.

Via Spain If you'd like to start your trip in south-western France (or return to England from there), a couple of ferry services from northern Spain are worth considering.

P&O Portsmouth links Portsmouth with Bilbao (Santurtzi port, 35 hours and two nights *to* Bilbao, 29 hours and one night *from* Bilbao), which is only about 150km west of Biarritz, twice a week (once a week from late October to late March; no service from early January to early February). Foot passengers pay UK£55 to UK£120 one way, not including a mandatory sleeping birth (at least UK£33 to UK£46). A car with up to five passengers costs UK£255 to UK£480 (not including sleeping berths).

From mid-March to mid-November, Brittany Ferries runs twice-weekly car-ferry services from Plymouth to Santander (24 hours), which is about 240km west of Biarritz. Foot passengers pay UK£60 to UK£100 one way; a car costs UK£165 to UK£300 one way. You have to book either a reclining seat (UK£3) or a cabin (upwards of UK£57 for one or two people).

The Channel Islands

From April to mid-October, Condor's high-speed catamarans (passengers only for licensing reasons) link the Channel Islands (Îles Anglo-Normandes) with St-Malo in Brittany. The one-way crossing from Jersey (70 minutes, one or two daily) or Guernsey (Guernesey in French; 70 minutes, one daily) costs UK£20 (230FF, or 160FF if you're aged 16 to 23). One-day return fares from St-Malo are around 300FF (200FF for those aged 16 to 23).

Émeraude Lines runs express car ferries from St-Malo to Jersey (1¼ hours; one daily, except on Tuesday and Thursday from November to March). The one-way pedestrian fare is UK£28; one-day return fares are UK£24 to UK£29. A car (not including the passengers) costs around UK£100 one way.

From mid-April to sometime in mid- to late October, Émeraude Lines' passengers-only catamarans link the Channel Islands with two small ports in Normandy, Granville and Carteret (one daily, with departures to/from the Channel Islands in the morning/evening). Fares are the same as for the St-Malo–Jersey run.

Ireland

Eurail pass holders pay 50% of the adult pedestrian fare for crossings between Ireland and France on Irish Ferries (make sure you book ahead).

Irish Ferries has overnight runs from Rosslare to either Cherbourg (18 hours) or Roscoff (16 hours) every other day (three times a week from mid-September to October, with a possible break in service from November to February). Pedestrians pay IR£40 to IR£80 (IR£32 to IR£66 for students and seniors) one way. A two-bed cabin costs IR£26 to IR£34. A car with two passengers costs around IR£130 to IR£320 one way.

From April to September, Brittany Ferries runs a car ferry every Saturday from Cork (Ringaskiddy) to Roscoff (14 hours), and every Friday in the other direction. Foot passengers pay IR£35 to IR£70 one way; a car with two adults costs IR£115 to IR£320 one way.

Freight ferries run by P&O Irish Sea link Rosslare with Cherbourg (18 hours, three a week). A car with two passengers pays IR£110 to IR£260 one way. Foot passengers are not accepted.

Italy

From late April to mid-October, the Société Nationale Maritime Corse Méditerranée (SNCM) has five to nine car ferries a month from Marseilles or Toulon to Porto Torres (and occasionally Olbia) on the island of Sardinia (Sardaigne in French). The one-way adult pedestrian fare is around 360FF to 410FF (seniors 260FF to 300FF, a bit less for those aged under 22).

A variety of ferry companies ply the waters between Corsica and Italy. For details, see the introductory Getting There & Away section of the Corsica chapter.

North Africa

The SNCM and the Compagnie Tunisienne de Navigation (CTN) link Marseilles with the Tunisian capital, Tunis (about 24 hours, three or four a week). The standard adult fare is 900/1620FF one-way/return, with 50FF or 100FF extra each way for the cheapest berth. The return fare is 1330FF if you're aged 16 to 21. In Tunis, CTN's office is at 5 Rue Dag Hammarskjoeld. In France, ticketing is handled by the SNCM.

The Compagnie Marocaine de Navigation (CoMaNav) links Sète, 29km (20 minutes by train) south-west of Montpellier, with the Moroccan port of Tangier (Tanger; 36 hours, five to seven a month). The cheapest berth costs 970FF (1390FF in August and for some other summer sailings) one way; return tickets cost 15% to 20% less than two one-ways. Discounts are available if you're aged under 26 or in a group of four or more. In France, ticketing is handled by SNCM.

The SNCM also links Marseilles with the capital of Algeria, Alger (20 hours, four to six a month). Foot passengers pay 1000/1830FF one-way/return; discounts are available for students and seniors.

The USA, Canada & Elsewhere

The days when you could earn your passage to Europe on a freighter have well and truly passed, but it's still possible to travel as a passenger on a cargo ship from North America (and ports further afield) to France's Atlantic coast. Such vessels typically carry five to 12 passengers (more than 12 would require a doctor on board) and charge an average of US$100 per person a day.

Details are available from: Travltips Cruise and Freighter Travel Association (☎ 1 800 872 8584 in the USA), who have a Web site at www.travltips.com; Freighter World Cruises (☎ 1 800 531 7774 in the USA), whose Web site is at www.freighter world.com; and The Cruise People (☎ 0800 526 313 in the UK, 416-444 2410 in Canada), who have a Web site at http://members.aol.com/CruiseAZ/home.htm.

ORGANISED TOURS

An extensive list of UK-based companies offering trips to France is available from the Web site of the Association of British Tour Operators to France, which is at www.holidayfrance.org.uk.

Cycling & Walking In North America, CBT Tours (☎ 800 736 BIKE, 773-404 1710), with a Web site at www.biketrip.net, runs group cycling tours in many regions of France for about US$190 a day, including breakfast and dinner.

Upmarket biking and walking holidays (about US$3500 for a week) are a speciality of Butterfield & Robinson (☎ 1 800 678 1147, 416-864 1354), based in Canada at 70 Bond St, Toronto M5B 1X3. For more details check out their Web site at www.butterfieldandrobinson.com.

In the UK, Cycling for Softies (☎ 0161-248 8282), at 2-4 Birch Polygon, Manchester M14 5HX, arranges unescorted cycling trips through rural France for . about UK£620 a week, including accommodation, breakfast and dinner. Have a look at their Web site at www.cycling-for-softies.co.uk.

Cycling and rambling holidays for independent travellers (from about UK£300 a week including breakfast), and guided group hiking tours (UK£1195 for eight days, including all meals), are available from ATG Oxford (☎ 01865-315 678), at 69–71 Banbury Road, Oxford OX2 6PE, England. The company has a Web site at www.atg-oxford.co.uk.

Ramblers Holidays (☎ 01707-331 133), Box 43, Welwyn Garden City, AL8 6PQ, England, organises guided walking tours (about UK£300 for a week, including half-board) as well as tours based on other outdoor activities (such as trekking and cross-country skiing). Have a look at their Web site at www.ramblersholidays.co.uk.

euro currency converter €1 = 6.56FF

Getting Around

France's domestic transport network, much of it owned or subsidised by the government, tends to be monopolistic: the state-owned Société Nationale des Chemins de Fer Français (SNCF) takes care of most inter-departmental land transport, and short-haul bus companies are either run by the *département* or grouped so each local company handles different destinations. To protect the SNCF, the pan-European long-haul bus companies Eurolines and Intercars are barred from carrying passengers on routes wholly within France. However, in recent years domestic air travel has been partly deregulated.

AIR

France's long-protected domestic airline industry is being opened up to competition, so a mode of transport once limited to businesspeople on expense accounts is now an option even for budget travellers. Carriers with domestic flights include Air Bretagne, Air France, Air Liberté (owned by British Airways), AOM, Air Littoral, Corsair (run by the Nouvelles Frontières travel agency), Corse Méditerranée and Proteus.

Thanks to the TGV, travel between some cities (for example, Paris to Lyons) is faster and easier by train than by air, particularly if you include the time and hassle involved in getting to and from the airports.

Any French travel agency can make bookings for domestic flights and supply details on the complicated fare options. Outside France, Air France representatives sell tickets for many domestic flights. For details on contacting carriers, see Airline Offices under Getting There & Away in the Paris chapter.

On most flights, each passenger is allowed one carry-on bag and 23kg of checked luggage. Excess baggage, including bikes and skis, costs just 10FF per kilogram on Air France.

Domestic Air Services

All of France's major cities – as well as many minor ones – have airports. Many are mentioned under Getting There & Away under relevant cities. Details about city-to-airport transport links – including the many options for getting to/from Orly and Roissy Charles de Gaulle near Paris – appear under To/From the Airports in the Getting Around section of each city listing.

The cheapest, off-season, one-way youth tickets on Air France (www.airfrance.fr) include the following fares: Paris–Ajaccio/Bastia (440FF), Paris–Bordeaux (440FF), Paris–Biarritz (290FF), Paris–Nice (325FF), Lille–Nice (440FF), Lyon–Toulouse (250FF) and Marseilles–Strasbourg (440FF). Adult tickets cost 1¼ to six times as much, depending on restrictions and when you fly. In general, the longer in advance that you book (for example, seven or 14 days ahead) the cheaper the fare, and the cheaper the ticket the more cumbersome the restrictions (for example, it may be impossible to change the date of travel or to get a refund).

Significant discounts are available to: children aged under 12; those aged 12 to 24; couples who are either married, have proof of cohabitation (a French government-issued *certificat de concubinage*), or who are *pacsé* (are in an official state of non-married couplehood); families, defined as at least one parent or grandparent travelling with one or more children aged 24 or under; and people aged over 60.

On many flights, everyone else can also fly for considerably less than the full fare. You can sometimes find last-minute promotional fares – travel agencies can provide details.

BUS

Because French transport policy is biased in favour of the excellent state-owned rail system, the country has only extremely limited inter-regional bus services. However, buses are used quite extensively for short-distance travel within départements, especially in rural areas with relatively few train lines (for example, Brittany and Normandy).

Over the years, certain uneconomical train lines have been replaced by SNCF buses – unlike regional buses, these are free for people with train passes. For details of bus services, see Getting There & Away sections throughout the book.

TRAIN

France's superb rail network, operated by the state-owned SNCF, reaches almost every part of the country. Many towns and villages not on the SNCF train and bus network are linked with nearby railheads by intra-departmental bus lines.

France's most important train lines radiate from Paris like the spokes of a wheel, making train travel between provincial towns situated on different spokes infrequent and rather slow. In some cases you have to transit through Paris, which sometimes (though these days less and less frequently) requires transferring from one of the capital's six train stations to another. For details, see the colour SNCF Trains & Ferries map, which shows the parts of France served by each of Paris' stations.

The pride and joy of the SNCF is the world-renowned TGV *(train à grande vitesse)*, whose name – pronounced '**teh-zheh-veh**' – means 'high-speed train'. There are now three TGV lines that go under a variety of names:

TGV Sud-Est & TGV Midi-Méditerranée
These link Paris' Gare de Lyon with the southeast, including Dijon, Lyons, Geneva, the Alps, Avignon, Marseilles, Nice and Montpellier.

TGV Atlantique Sud-Ouest & TGV Atlantique Ouest These link Paris' Gare Montparnasse with western and south-western France, including Brittany (Rennes, Quimper, Brest), Nantes, Tours, Poitiers, La Rochelle, Bordeaux, Biarritz and Toulouse.

TGV Nord, Thalys & Eurostar These link Paris' Gare du Nord with Arras, Lille, Calais, Brussels, Amsterdam, Cologne and, via the Channel Tunnel, Ashford and London Waterloo.

For details on Thalys and the Eurostar, see Land in the Getting There & Away chapter. A fourth line, the TGV Est, which will whizz from Paris to Strasbourg in just two hours, is planned. All three TGV lines are now connected to each other, making it possible to go directly from, say, Lyons to Nantes or Bordeaux to Lille, without switching trains (and stations) in Paris. Stops on the link-up, which runs east and south of Paris, include Roissy Charles de Gaulle airport and Disneyland Paris.

A train that is not a TGV is often referred to as a *corail*, a *classique* or a TER *(train express régional)*.

Classes

Most French trains, including the TGV, have both 1st- and 2nd-class sections. The 2nd-class couchette compartments have six berths, while those in 1st class have four. On some overnight trains a 2nd-class *siège inclinable* (reclining seat) costs 20FF.

Tickets & Reservations

At especially large stations (for example, those in Paris), there are separate ticket windows for travel on *international*, *grandes lignes* (long-haul) and *banlieue* (suburban) lines; some stations may also have separate windows for *achat à l'avance* (advance purchase) and *départ du jour* (same-day departure). You can almost always use MasterCard, Visa, Diners Club, Aurore or American Express credit cards. Tickets bought with cash can be reimbursed for cash (by you or a thief), so keep them in a safe place.

If you buy your ticket with a credit card via the SNCF's Web site (www.sncf.com), you can either have it sent to you by post or pick it up at any SNCF ticket office using your *numéro de dossier* (reference number). As a safety precaution, you will also be asked to show the credit card used to purchase the ticket.

Virtually every SNCF station in the country has at least one *billeterie automatique* (automatic ticket machine) that accepts credit cards for purchases of at least 10FF. To make the on-screen interface switch to English, touch the Union Jack (UK flag) in the upper right-hand corner of the *'Bonjour'* screen (if you see a different screen, try touching the screen or pushing the red *annulation* button).

Discount Train Tickets & Passes

Discount Tickets

These discounted fares and passes are available at all SNCF stations but are not applicable to travel wholly within the Paris Transport Region. There are no residency requirements.

Reduced-Price Tickets

Discounts of 25% on one-way or return travel within France are available at train station ticket windows for certain groups of travellers, subject to availability. Just show the ticket agent proof of eligibility and you'll get the reduction on the spot.

- If you're aged 12 to 25, you are eligible for a Découverte 12/25 fare.
- One to four adults travelling with a child aged four to 11 qualify for the Découverte Enfant Plus fare.
- People aged over 60 enjoy a fare called Découverte Senior.
- Any two people travelling together qualify for a Découverte À Deux fare, which gives you a 25% reduction in 1st or 2nd class, but only on return travel.
- Internationally, young people aged 12 to 25 get significant discounts on the Eurostar and Thalys; seniors enjoy special fares on Thalys.

Travel Passes

Discounts of 50% (25% if the cheapest seats are sold out) on travel within France are available to certain groups of travellers if they purchase a card valid for 12 months (passport photo required).

- Young people aged 12 to 25 qualify for the Carte 12/25 (270FF).
- One to four adults travelling with a child aged four to 11 can get the Carte Enfant Plus (350FF).
- People aged over 60 qualify for a Carte Senior, formerly known as the Carte Vermeil (285FF).

Découverte Séjour

You can get a 25% reduction for return travel within France if you meet two conditions: the total distance you'll be travelling is at least 200km, and you'll be spending a Saturday night at your destination.

Découverte J30 & J8

You can save significant sums if you buy a ticket for a specific train well in advance. The Découverte J30, which must be purchased 30 to 60 days before the date of travel, offers savings of 45% to 55%. The Découverte J8, which you must buy at least eight days ahead, gets you 20% to 30% off. A refund of 70% is available up to four days before departure; after that, it's use it or lose it.

BIJ (BIGE) Tickets

These venerable tickets – the acronym stands for Billets Internationaux de Jeunesse (International Youth Tickets) – are available to anyone aged under 26 and, except to Italy, save you at least 20% on international 2nd-class train travel (one way or return, but in some cases only on night trains). BIJ tickets are not sold at SNCF ticket windows. Rather, you have to go to an office of Voyages Wasteels (☎ 01 43 62 30 00) or a student travel agency. There's almost always at least one BIJ issuer in the vicinity of major train stations.

Discount Train Tickets & Passes

Rail Passes for Residents of Europe

These passes are available to people of all ages and nationalities provided they have been resident in Europe for at least six months. However, you cannot purchase a pass for use in your country of residence. Holders of these passes get discounts on the Eurostar, Thalys, SNCM ferries to Corsica, and SeaFrance ferries on the Dover–Calais route, but they must pay all SNCF reservation fees (and, with InterRail, supplements).

Euro Domino France

The new Euro Domino flexipass, sold at major train stations in most European countries (including France), gives you three to eight consecutive or non-consecutive days of midnight-to-midnight travel over a period of one month in one of the 28 participating countries. The pass also gets you 25% off on train travel from the place where it was purchased to the border of the country in which you'll be travelling. Euro Domino France – the version good for travel on the SNCF – comes in two versions: the youth version (for people aged under 26), which costs around 790FF for three days and 160FF for each additional day; and the adult version, costing about 990FF for three days and 200FF for each extra day.

InterRail Pass

With the InterRail Pass, you can travel in 29 European countries organised into eight zones; France is in Zone E, grouped with the Netherlands, Belgium and Luxembourg. For 22 days of unlimited 2nd-class travel in one zone, the cost is around 1800FF (1300FF if you're aged under 26). You also get 50% off on travel from your home country to your zone(s), and between non-adjacent zones.

Rail Passes for Non-Europeans

These passes do *not* cover SNCF reservation fees or *couchette* (sleeping berth) charges, but they do cover supplements and get you discounts on the Eurostar and Thalys. Most of them come in half-price versions for children aged four to 11. Contrary to popular belief, these passes *can* be purchased at a limited number of places in Europe provided you're not a resident of any European country. However, prices are about 10% higher than they are overseas. In France, passes are available from the SNCF offices at Orly and Roissy Charles de Gaulle airports; in Paris at Gare du Nord, Gare de Lyon and Gare St-Lazare; and at the main train stations in Marseilles and Nice.

Eurail

Eurail passes offer reasonable value if you plan to really clock up the kilometres and have not reached your 26th birthday on the first day of travel (people over that age can only get the pricey 1st-class versions). One/two months of unlimited travel with the Eurail Youthpass costs US$623/882. The Eurail Youth Flexipass, good for travel on any 10/15 days you select over a period of two months, costs US$458/599. Eurail passes are not valid in the UK or on cross-Channel ferries but they do get you half-price on Irish Ferries routes between the Irish Republic and France.

Europass

The Europass lets you travel in certain European countries for between five and 15 consecutive or non-consecutive days within a two-month period. Regular adult passes, good for 1st-class passage within France, Germany, Italy, Spain and Switzerland, range from US$348 for five days to US$728 for 15 days (20% less for two adults travelling together). The Europass Youth, available to people aged under 26, ranges from US$233 for five days to US$513 for 15.

euro currency converter €1 = 6.56FF

Discount Train Tickets & Passes (continued)

France Railpass

This flexipass entitles you to unlimited travel on the SNCF system for three to nine days over the course of a month. In 2nd class, the three-day version costs US$180 (US$145 each for two people travelling together); each additional day of travel costs US$30.

The France Youthpass, available if you're under 26, costs US$164 for four days of travel over two months; additional days (up to a maximum of 10) cost US$20.

Where to Buy Train Passes

Australia
Rail Plus ☎ 03-9642 8644
www.railplus.com.au

Canada
Rail Europe ☎ 1 800 361 7245
www.raileurope.com

New Zealand
Rail Plus ☎ 09-303 2484
www.railplus.com.au

UK
Rail Europe ☎ 0870 5848 848
www.raileurope.co.uk

USA
Rail Europe ☎ 1 800 456 7245
www.raileurope.com

Outside Europe, some train passes are also available from accredited travel agencies.

Tickets *can* be purchased on board the train but, unless the ticket window where you boarded was closed, prohibitive surcharges will apply: 50/100FF for journeys under/over 75km. If you search out the *contrôleur* (conductor) rather than letting yourself be discovered ticketless, the surcharge may be only 20/40FF. TGV tickets bought on board cost an extra 40FF regardless of distance.

Reserving in advance (20FF) is optional unless: you're travelling by TGV, Eurostar or Thalys; you want a couchette (sleeping berth; 90FF) or a bed; or you'll be travelling during holiday periods (for example, around Easter and 14 July), when trains may be full. Reservations can be made by telephone or via the SNCF's Web site.

Before departure time you can change your reservation by telephone. To pick up your new tickets, go to a ticket counter with the *numéro de dossier* (reference number) you've been given. Reservations can be changed for no charge up to one hour *after* your scheduled departure time, but only if you are actually at your departure station.

For full-fare SNCF tickets, getting a 90% reimbursement (100% before scheduled departure if you've got a reservation) is possible up to two months after purchase (up to six months for international tickets except for Eurostar and Thalys). The process is pretty straightforward – just go to any train station ticket window or, in a mainline station, a Service Clientèle office. Tickets purchased from a travel agency or outside France can be reimbursed only at the issuing office.

Schedules

SNCF's free, pocket-size *horaires* (timetables) can be a bit complicated to read, especially if you're not too familiar with French railway-speak. The numbers at the top of each column are *notes à consulter* (footnote references). Often a particular train *circule* (runs) only on Friday or only on certain dates. Alternatively, it may operate *tous les jours* (every day) *sauf* (except) Saturday, Sunday and/or *fêtes* (holidays). Of 20 trains listed on the schedule, only a few may be running on the day you'd like to travel.

If you'll be doing a lot of travel in one region of France, ask at a train station for a *Guide Régional des Transports*, an easy-to-use booklet of SNCF schedules published by some regional governments. For national coverage, you can purchase an *Indicateur Horaires Ville à Ville* (60FF for a book or a Windows-compatible CD-ROM), sold in train stations at Relay newsagents.

Some people swear by the *Thomas Cook European Timetable* (150FF), useful for figuring out which domestic and international routings are feasible so you can use train passes to their fullest. It is updated monthly and is available from Thomas Cook bureaux de change.

Validating Your Ticket
Before boarding the train you must validate your ticket by time-stamping it in a *composteur*, one of those orange posts situated somewhere between the ticket windows and the tracks. If you forget, find a conductor so they can punch it for you (if you wait for your crime to be discovered, you're likely to be fined).

Eurail and some other train passes must be validated at a train station ticket window before you begin your first journey, in order to begin the period of validity.

Costs
For 2nd-class travel, count on paying 50FF to 60FF per 100km for cross-country trips, and 70FF to 100FF per 100km for short hops. (By comparison, autoroute tolls come to from 36FF to 46FF per 100km, while petrol adds another 43FF.) Full-fare return (round-trip) passage costs twice as much as one-way. Travel in 1st class is 50% more expensive than 2nd class. Children aged under four travel free; those aged four to 11 pay 50% of the adult fare.

On certain trains to/from Paris, passengers travelling during *heures de pointe* (peak periods) have to pay a supplement of 45FF to 90FF in 2nd class. Supplements do not generally apply for travel from one provincial station to another but may be levied if you take an international train on a domestic segment. Departure boards at

How to Find Train Information
From 7 am to 10 pm daily, you can get schedule and fare information and make reservations for the SNCF's domestic and international services in a number of languages (2.23FF a minute):

English	☎ 0 836 35 35 39
French	☎ 0 836 35 35 35
German	☎ 0 836 35 35 36
Spanish	☎ 0 836 35 35 37
Italian	☎ 0 836 35 35 38

SNCF	www.sncf.com
Eurostar	www.eurostar.com
Thalys	www.thalys.com
Rail Europe (North America)	
	www.raileurope.com

train stations indicate which trains require supplements.

Left Luggage
Most larger SNCF stations have both a *consigne manuelle* (left-luggage office), where it costs 30FF or 35FF to store a bag, skis or a bicycle for 24 hours; and a *consigne automatique*, a computerised locker system that will issue you with a lock code or a magnetic ticket (good for 48 or 72 hours) in exchange for 15FF, 20FF or 30FF, depending on the size of the locker. At smaller stations you may be able to check your bag with the clerk at the ticket window (30FF). Some left-luggage facilities are open only for limited hours.

As we went to press many luggage lockers were out of service as part of a national programme to prevent terrorist attacks.

CAR & MOTORCYCLE
Having your own wheels gives you exceptional freedom. Unfortunately, it can be expensive, and cars are often inconvenient in city centres, where parking and traffic are frequently a major headache.

Motorcyclists will find France great for touring, with winding roads of good quality and lots of stunning scenery. Just make sure your wet-weather gear is up to scratch.

France (along with Belgium) has the densest highway network in Europe. There are four types of intercity roads:

Autoroutes These multilane divided highways/motorways, which usually require the payment of tolls, have alphanumeric designations that begin with A. Marked by blue signs depicting a divided highway receding into the distance, they often have lovely *aires de repos* (rest areas), some with restaurants and pricey petrol stations.

Routes Nationales These are main highways, some of them divided for short stretches, whose names begin with N (or, on older maps and signs, RN).

Routes Départementales These are local roads whose names begin with D.

Routes Communales These are minor rural roads whose names sometimes begin with C or V.

Road Rules

All drivers must carry at all times a national ID card or passport; a valid driver's licence (*permis de conduire*; many foreign licences can be used in France for up to a year); car ownership papers, known as a *carte grise* (grey card); and proof of third-party (liability) insurance, known as a *carte verte* (green card). Never leave your car ownership or insurance papers in the vehicle.

A right-hand-drive vehicle brought to France from the UK or Ireland must have deflectors fixed to the headlights to avoid dazzling oncoming traffic.

A motor vehicle entering a foreign country must display a sticker identifying its country of registration. In the UK, information on driving in France is available from the RAC (☎ 0800 550 055) and the AA (☎ 0870 550 0600). *Motoring in Europe* (UK£4.99), published in the UK by the RAC, gives an excellent summary of road regulations in each European country, including parking rules.

French law requires that all passengers, including those in the back seat, wear seat belts, and children who weigh less than 18kg must travel in backward-facing child seats. A passenger car is permitted to carry a maximum of five people. North American

Road Signs

On the green signs that show drivers how to get to various destinations, an arrow next to the words *toutes directions* (all directions) or *autres directions* (other directions) indicates where to head unless you're going to one of the destinations specifically mentioned elsewhere on the sign.

Sens unique means 'one way'. *Voie unique* means 'one-lane road' (eg, at a narrow bridge). *Allumez vos feux* means 'turn on your headlights'. If you come to a *route barrée* (a closed road), you'll usually also find a yellow panel with instructions for a *déviation* (detour) – following the arrows does not necessarily make you into a deviant. Signs for *poids lourds* (heavyweights) are meant for lorries (trucks), not automobiles. The words *sauf riverains* on a no-entry sign mean 'except residents'.

Road signs with the word *rappel* (remember) written on or under them are telling you something that you are already supposed to know (eg, the speed limit).

drivers should remember that turning right on a red light is illegal in France.

Unless otherwise posted, a speed limit of 50km/h applies in *all* areas designated as built-up, no matter how rural they may appear. On intercity roads, you must slow to 50km/h the moment you pass a white sign with red borders on which a place name is written. This limit remains in force until you arrive at the other edge of town, where you'll pass an identical sign with a red diagonal bar across the name.

Outside built-up areas, speed limits are: 90km/h (the limit is 80km/h if it's raining) on undivided N and D highways; 110km/h (100km/h if it's raining) on dual carriageways (divided highways) or on short sections of highway with a divider strip; and 130km/h (110km/h in the rain, 60km/h in icy conditions) on autoroutes. Speed limits are generally not posted unless they deviate from those mentioned above. If you drive at the speed limit, expect to have lots of cars coming to within a few metres of your rear bumper, flashing their lights, and then overtaking at the first opportunity.

For overseas drivers, the most confusing – and dangerous – traffic law in France is the notorious *priorité à droite* (priority to the right) rule, under which any car entering an intersection (including a T-junction) from a road on your right has right of way. At most larger roundabouts (traffic circles) – French road engineers *love* roundabouts – priorité à droite has been suspended so that the cars already on the roundabout have right of way. Look for signs reading either *'vous n'avez pas la priorité'* (you do not have right of way) or *'cédez le passage'* (give way), or for yield signs displaying a circle made out of three curved arrows.

Priorité à droite is also suspended on priority roads, which are marked by an up-ended yellow square with a black square in the middle. Such signs appear every few kilometres and at intersections. Priorité à droite is reinstated if you see the same sign with a diagonal bar through it.

French law is very tough on drunk drivers. To find drivers whose blood-alcohol concentration (BAC) is over 0.05% (0.5 grams per litre of blood) – the equivalent of two glasses of wine for a 75kg adult – the police sometimes conduct random breathalyser tests. Fines start at 900FF; you can also be arrested on the spot.

Riders of any type of two-wheeled vehicle with a motor (except motor-assisted bicycles) must wear a helmet. If you're caught bareheaded, you can be fined and have your bike confiscated until you get a helmet. Bikes of more than 125cc must have their headlights on during the day. No special licence is required to ride a motorbike whose engine is smaller than 50cc, which is why you often find places renting scooters rated at 49.9cc.

Costs

The convenience of having your own vehicle does not come cheap, but for two or more people a car may cost less than going by train (this depends in part on what rail discounts you qualify for). In addition, a car will allow you to avail yourself of less expensive camping grounds, hostels, hotels and B&Bs located on city outskirts and in the countryside.

By autoroute, the drive from Paris to Nice, a distance of about 950km (about eight hours of actual driving), costs around 420FF for petrol (at 16km per litre) and 360FF for autoroute tolls, making a total of about 780FF. This figure does not include wear and tear, depreciation, repairs, insurance or the risk of damage, theft or accident. By comparison, a regular, one-way, 2nd-class TGV ticket for the six-hour Paris–Nice run costs 445FF to 522FF.

Essence (petrol or gasoline), also known as *carburant* (fuel), is expensive in France, incredibly so if you're used to Australian or North American prices. At the time of writing, unleaded *(sans plomb)* petrol with an IOR octane rating of 98 cost 6.70FF to 7.70FF a litre (US$3.70 to US$4.30 per US gallon). Diesel fuel *(gazole)* costs 5FF to 6FF per litre (US$2.80 to US$3.30 per US gallon). Filling up *(faire le plein)* is most expensive at the rest stops along the autoroutes and cheapest at small rural petrol stations and at petrol stations attached to supermarkets. Petrol is cheaper in all the countries that have borders with France (except, perhaps, Italy) than in France itself; Luxembourg and Andorra are especially inexpensive.

Tolls are charged for travel on almost all autoroutes (except around major cities) and many bridges. On autoroutes, you're essentially paying for the right to drive faster and thus save time – and to maintain the profit margins of the private companies that built

euro currency converter €1 = 6.56FF

and maintain the infrastructure. Despite the high speed limits and the many lorries (trucks), such travel is much safer per kilometre than driving on regular highways. At the *péages* (toll booths), count on paying 36FF to 46FF per 100km, by credit card if you prefer. From Paris, autoroute destinations with hefty tolls include Bordeaux (262FF for passenger cars), Calais (99FF), Lyon (161FF), Marseilles (277FF), Nantes (176FF), Nice (360FF) and Strasbourg (184FF). Toll details are available from the Web site www.autoroutes.fr.

Dangers & Annoyances
Measured relative to the number of kilometres driven, the rate of fatalities on French roads – some 8000 a year – is almost double that of the UK or the USA.

Theft from and of cars is a *major* problem in France, especially in the south. For details, see Theft under Dangers & Annoyances in the Facts for the Visitor chapter.

If you are involved in a minor accident with no injuries, the easiest way for the drivers to sort things out with their respective insurance companies is to fill out a Constat Aimable d'Accident Automobile, known in English as a European Accident Statement, which has a standardised way of recording important details about what happened. In rental cars it is usually included in the packet of documents you are given.

If your French is not fluent, find someone who can explain exactly what each word of traffic jargon means. Never sign anything you don't understand – insist on a translation and sign that only if it's acceptable. Make sure you can read the other driver's handwriting. If problems crop up, it is usually not very hard to find a police officer. To alert the police, dial ☎ 17.

Make sure the report includes any information that will help you to prove that the accident was not your fault. For instance, if you were just sitting there and the other person backed into you, mention this under Observations (No 14 on the Constat). Remember, if you *did* cause the accident (or can't prove that you didn't) you may end up paying a hefty excess (deductible), dep-

---

Make Sense of the Spaghetti

On a map, the motorways leading in and out of Paris – looping under and over the Péripherique (ring road/beltway) and criss-crossing the inner and outer suburbs on their way to a maze of highways and autoroutes – look rather like a pile of spaghetti. Don't even think of driving in or out of the French capital without a good road map – get one whose scale is at least 1:250,000. Michelin and Institut Gèographique National (IGN) maps are available at bookshops.

---

ending on your insurance policy or rental contract.

If your car is *en panne* (breaks down), you'll have to find a garage that handles your *marque* (make of car). There are Peugeot, Renault and Citroën garages all over the place, but if you have a non-French car you may have trouble finding someone to service it in more remote areas. Michelin's *Guide Rouge* lists garages at the end of each entry.

Parking
If you will be spending time in France's cities, finding a place to park is likely to be the single greatest hassle you'll face. Your best bet is usually to ditch the car somewhere and then walk or take public transport.

Parking in city centres requires paying up to 10FF an hour and is subject to a time limit, often two hours. This lamentable circumstance, which requires that you keep running to the car to plug the metre, is generally indicated either by the word *payant* written on the asphalt or by an upright sign in French.

Payment is made using kerbside *horodateurs* (parking meters), into which you feed coins according to how long you want to park. When you press the correct button (usually the green one – the other ones are for local residents), the machine spits out a little ticket listing the precise time after which you'll be illegally parked. Take the ticket and place it on the dashboard so it's visible from the pavement.

Horodateurs in most cities (Bordeaux is an exception) are programmed to take into account periods when parking is free, so you can pay the night before for the first two hours after 9 am.

Parking on some streets is governed by an arrangement called *stationnement alterné semi-mensuel*, which means you can park on one side of the street from the 1st of the month until the evening of the 15th and on the other side from the 16th until the end of the month. Your clue to this circumstance: a no-parking sign with '1-15' (parking forbidden for the first half of the month) or '16-31' written on it.

Rental

Car The big international firms – Avis (☎ 08 02 05 05 05), Budget (☎ 08 00 10 00 01), Europcar (☎ 08 03 35 23 52), Hertz (☎ 01 39 38 38 38) and National-Citer (☎ 01 44 38 61 61, 08 00 20 21 21) – provide a very reliable service. Have a look at their Web sites at www.avis.com, www.budget.com, www.europcar.com, www.hertz.com and www.citer.com. Usually, you can arrange to return the car at a different outlet. Unfortunately, if you walk into an agency and ask for a car on the spot you'll pay a small fortune – up to 995FF for one day with Avis, and about 40% to 50% of that with most of the others. Under SNCF's pricey Train + Auto plan, you can reserve an Avis car when you book your train ticket and it will be waiting for you when you arrive at any of 195 train stations.

Even the French-based chains such as ADA (www.ada-sa.fr), Autop Rent (☎ 08 25 83 58 36), Rent A Car Système (☎ 08 36 69 46 95), with a Web site at www.rentacar.fr, and – for students – OTU Voyages (☎ 01 40 29 12 12), with a Web site at www.otu.fr, are not really cheap, but you can generally get a small car for about 270FF for one day (including 100km) or 570/1500FF for a weekend/week. Weekly rates with some of the big boys (for example, Europcar or National-Citer) may be only marginally more expensive. It's a good idea to reserve a few days in advance, especially during tourist high seasons.

Prebooked and prepaid rates, arranged before you leave home, are often a *much* better deal than on-the-spot rentals. You can often get a car for US$200 a week (including collision damage and theft waivers). Rentals in the countries bordering France, especially Belgium, can be up to 25% cheaper. Details on deals are available in newspaper travel sections, on the Internet, from local travel agencies and from companies such as US-based Auto Europe (☎ 1 888 223 5555), with a Web site at www.autoeurope.com, and UK-based Holiday Autos (☎ 0870 5300 400), whose US affiliate Kemwel Holiday Autos (☎ 1 800 576 1590), has a Web site at www.kemwel.com. If you'll be needing a car for more than three or four weeks, see Purchase-Repurchase Plans later in this section for details on some incredibly inexpensive options.

Assurance au tiers (third-party/liability insurance) is mandatory, but things like collision-damage waivers (CDWs) vary greatly from company to company. The contract offered by some no-name, cut-rate firm may leave you liable for up to 8000FF – when comparing rates, the most important thing to check is the *franchise* (excess/deductible), which is usually 2000FF for a small car. If you're in an accident in which you're at fault, or the car is damaged and the party at fault is unknown (for example, someone dents your car while it's parked), or the car is stolen, this is the amount that you are liable for before the CDW kicks in. Some US credit card companies have built-in CDW if you use their card to pay for the rental, but you may have to cover all expenses in the event of an accident and claim the damage back from the credit-card company later.

Most companies require that you be at least 21 (or, in some cases, over 25) and have had a driver's licence for a minimum of one year. Some may also require that you have a credit card. *Kilométrage illimité* means that there's no limit on how many kilometres you can drive. Airport tariffs may be higher than the rates charged in town.

The addresses of car rental companies appear in city listings under Getting There

& Away (in Paris, under Car & Motorbike in the Getting Around section). Virtually all are closed on Sunday, and some are also closed on Saturday afternoon.

Motorcycle Motorcycle and moped rental is popular in southern France, especially in beach resorts, but it is all too common to see inexperienced riders leap on bikes and very quickly fall off them again. Where relevant, details on rental options appear under Getting There & Away at the end of city and town listings.

To rent a moped, scooter or motorcycle you usually have to leave a *caution* (deposit) of several thousand francs, which you forfeit – up to the value of the damage – if you're in an accident and it's your fault, or if the bike is in some way damaged. You'll also lose the deposit if the bike is stolen. Most places accept deposits made by credit card, travellers cheques or Eurocheques.

Purchase-Repurchase Plans

If you'll be needing a car in Europe for 17 days to six months (one year if you're studying or teaching in France), by far your cheapest option is to 'purchase' a brand-new one from Peugeot or Renault and then, at the end of your trip, 'sell' it back to them. In reality, you pay only for the number of days you use the vehicle, but the tax-free, purchase-repurchase *(achat-rachat)* aspect of the paperwork (none of which is your responsibility) makes this uniquely French type of leasing *considerably* cheaper than renting, especially for longer periods. Eligibility is restricted to people who are not *residents* of the EU (citizens of EU countries are eligible provided they live outside the EU).

Everyone we know who's travelled with a purchase-repurchase car – including several Lonely Planet authors – has given Renault's Eurodrive and Peugeot's Vacation Plan (Sodexa) programmes rave reviews. Prices include unlimited kilometrage, 24-hour towing and breakdown service, and comprehensive insurance with – incredibly – no excess (deductible), so returning a damaged car is totally hassle free. Both

companies let you drive in about 30 countries in Western and Central Europe (not including Hungary and Poland for insurance reasons) as well as Morocco and Tunisia. The minimum age is 18. It's helpful but not obligatory to have a credit card.

One minor problem: the red number plates announce to all passing thieves that the car is being driven by someone from abroad (see Theft under Dangers & Annoyances in the Facts for the Visitor chapter).

Payment for the period for which you would like the car must be made in advance. If you return it early, you can usually get a refund for the unused time (seven days minimum). Extending your contract is possible (using a credit card) but you'll end up paying about double the prepaid per-day rate, in part because of the added paperwork – call Peugeot (☎ 01 49 04 81 19) or Renault (☎ 01 40 40 33 68) at least four working days before your original return date so insurance coverage can be extended.

Cars can be picked up in cities all over France, in many cases at the airport, and returned to any other purchase-repurchase centre. They can also be collected or dropped off outside France (for example, in Amsterdam, Frankfurt, London, Madrid or Rome) but this involves a hefty surcharge (with Renault, from 1250FF to 2350FF each for pick-up and return).

Renault You can order a Eurodrive car either from a travel agency or through the company representatives – contact details are listed in the boxed text 'Purchase-Repurchase Contacts'. One advantage of dealing directly with Renault's well-organised Special Export Sales Division (Map 1; metro: Porte de Pantin), 186 ave Jean Jaurès, 19e, Paris, is that at the absolute minimum they need only four days to arrange a vehicle for pickup in Paris. But it might be cheaper to order a car in your home country or on the Internet, where special offers may be available. From abroad, allow at least three weeks for paperwork.

Arranged from the USA, the cheapest

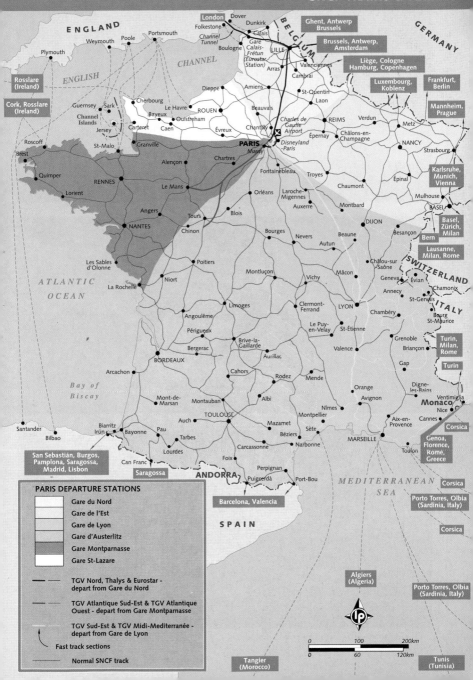

ELLIOT DANIEL

SIMON BRACKEN

MARK HONAN

SIMON BRACKEN

EDWARD SNIJDERS

Paris is dotted with squares where you can enjoy a coffee, chat with friends and rest weary legs.

Purchase-Repurchase Contacts

Renault Eurodrive Representatives

Have a look at the company Web site, at www.eurodrive.renault.com, or ring one of the following numbers:

France
☎ 01 40 40 32 32
fax 01 42 41 83 47

Australia
☎ 02-9299 3344
fax 02-9262 4590

Canada
☎ 450-461 1149
fax 450-461 0207

New Zealand
☎ 09-525 8800
fax 09-525 8818

South Africa
☎ 011-325 2345
fax 011-325 2840

USA
☎ 1 800 221 1052
☎ 212-532 1221
fax 212-725 5379

Peugeot Vacation Plan Representatives

Have a look at the company Web site, at www.sodexa.com, ring one of the following

numbers, or check out one of the individual Web sites:

France
☎ 01 49 04 81 56
fax 01 49 04 82 50

Australia
☎ 02-9976 3000
fax 02-9905 5874
www.driveaway.com.au

Canada
☎ 514-735 3083
fax 514-342 8802
www.europauto.qc.ca

New Zealand
☎ 09-914 91 00
fax 09-379 41 11

South Africa
☎ 011-458 1600
fax 011-455 2818

USA
Auto France   ☎ 1 800 572 9655
fax 201-934 75 01
www.auto-france.com
Europe by Car ☎ 1 800 223 1516
fax 212-246 1458
www.europebycar.com
Kemwel   ☎ 914-825 3000
fax 914-835 5449
www.kemwel.com

model available – a 1.2L, three-door, five-speed Twingo (most people will want something a bit more muscular) – costs around US$500 for the first 17 days and US$16 for each additional day. If arranged through Paris, a Twingo costs 3700FF for the first 17 days and 60FF for each day thereafter. For 45/90 days, the prices – as we go to press – come out to US$947/1667 in the USA, A$1270/1900 (US$759/1137) in Australia and 5400/8100FF (US$787/1183) in France.

Peugeot The Vacation Plan, also known as Sodexa, is smaller than its counterpart at Renault. The company prefers that reservations be made through its representatives

abroad (see the boxed text 'Purchase-Repurchase Contacts'), which in any case is cheaper than going through the Sodexa office in Courbevoie (near Paris).

Arranged from the USA, the least expensive model on offer, a Peugeot 106 with a 1.0L engine (the 206 is much peppier), costs about US$490 for the first 17 days and US$13 or US$14 for each additional day. For 45/90 days, that comes to about US$860/1450 (including discounts); as we go to press, the cheapest 45/90-day rates available in Australia come to around A$1300/2000 (US$798/1230). Start the paperwork at least a month before your pickup date (15 days if you deal directly with Sodexa's office in Paris).

euro currency converter €1 = 6.56FF

Car & Motorcycle Road Distances (km)

	Bayonne	Bordeaux	Brest	Caen	Cahors	Calais	Chambéry	Cherbourg	Clermont-Ferrand	Dijon	Grenoble	Lille	Lyons	Marseille	Nantes	Nice	Paris	Perpignon	Strasbourg	Toulouse	Tours
Bayonne	---																				
Bordeaux	184	---																			
Brest	811	623	---																		
Caen	764	568	376	---																	
Cahors	307	218	788	661	---																
Calais	164	876	710	339	875	---															
Chambéry	860	651	120	800	523	834	---														
Cherbourg	835	647	399	124	743	461	923	---													
Clermont-Ferrand	564	358	805	566	269	717	295	689	---												
Dijon	807	619	867	548	378	572	273	671	279	---											
Grenoble	827	657	1126	806	501	863	56	929	300	302	---										
Lille	997	809	725	353	808	112	767	476	650	505	798	---									
Lyons	831	528	1018	698	439	755	103	820	171	194	110	687	---								
Marseille	700	651	1271	1010	521	1067	344	1132	477	506	273	999	314	---							
Nantes	513	326	298	292	491	593	780	317	462	656	787	609	618	975	---						
Nice	858	810	1429	1168	679	1225	410	1291	636	664	337	1157	473	190	1131	---					
Paris	771	583	596	232	582	289	565	355	424	313	571	222	462	775	384	932	---				
Perpignon	499	451	1070	998	320	1149	478	1094	441	640	445	1081	448	319	773	476	857	---			
Strasbourg	1254	1066	1079	730	847	621	496	853	584	335	551	522	488	803	867	804	490	935	---		
Toulouse	300	247	866	865	116	991	565	890	890	727	533	923	536	407	568	564	699	205	1022	---	
Tours	536	348	490	246	413	531	611	369	369	418	618	463	449	795	197	952	238	795	721	593	---

Purchase

The hassle of buying a car and later selling it, the risk of losing your entire investment if something expensive goes wrong, and the cost of registration, insurance and taxes make purchasing your own vehicle worthwhile only if you'll be spending a lot of time in Europe. Because of regulations requiring that cars over four years old pass a regular safety test *(contrôle technique)*, dirt-cheap old beaters are a thing of the past. The book value of used cars up to eight years old is listed in *L'Argus* (15FF), available at newsagents and kiosks.

The seller should provide you with two copies of the *certificat de cession d'un véhicule* (certificate of transfer of a vehicle); the car's carte grise (the vehicle's registration certificate) marked with the words *vendu le* or *cédé le* (sold on) and the date; a contrôle technique form issued in the last six months; and a *certificat de situation administrative* (or *non-gage*; a certificate from the prefecture attesting that the car has not been pledged as collateral, such as for a loan).

The seller's liability insurance stays in force until midnight of the day you buy the car – after that it is illegal to drive it until you have a *carte verte* (a certificate of third-party/liability insurance), a small square of which you display on the lower right-hand side of the windscreen. In Paris, a reliable insurance agent with decent rates is BUSTA (Map 4; ☎ 01 47 05 05 04, fax 01 45 50 40 94; metro: Pont de l'Alma), 9 ave Rapp, 7e. It's a good idea to contact them a few days before you make your purchase.

Within 15 days of purchase, you must take care of *immatriculation* (vehicle registration) and get a new carte grise. This can be done at the nearest prefecture or, in Paris, the Préfecture de Police on Île de la Cité. Bring along *attestation* or a *justificatif* (written proof) of where you live (for example, an official receipt from your hotel or hostel that includes your full name and passport number). All cars are given new licence-plate numbers when they change hands, so when you get your carte grise you must drive to a garage and get them to punch out *plaques d'immatriculation* (number or registration plates) within 24 hours.

When you sell your car, cut off the upper right-hand corner of the carte grise, draw a diagonal line across it and write *vendu le* (sold on) plus the date. Take the little green insurance tag out of the sticker on the right-hand side of the windscreen. Make sure to have the buyer sign a *reçu d'achat de véhicule* (receipt for the purchase of a vehicle). Within 15 days, take one copy of the certificat de cession d'un véhicule (give two other copies to the purchaser) to the prefecture where the car was registered.

BICYCLE

France is an eminently cycleable country, thanks in part to its extensive network of secondary and tertiary roads, many of which carry relatively light traffic. Indeed, some connoisseurs consider such back roads – a good number of which date from the 19th century or earlier – the ideal vantage point from which to view France's celebrated rural landscapes. One pitfall: they rarely have proper shoulders (verges). Many French cities have a growing network of urban and suburban *pistes cyclables* (bicycle paths), and in some areas (for example, around Bordeaux) such paths link one town to the next.

Never leave your bicycle locked up outside overnight if you want to see it or most of its parts again. You can store it in train station left-luggage offices for 35FF a day.

More information of interest to cyclists can be found in the Facts for the Visitor chapter: general information on cycling appears under Activities; map options are discussed under Maps in the Planning section; information on cyclists' topoguides can be found under Walking and Cycling Maps in the Maps section; and the Tour de France is discussed under Spectator Sports.

Rental

Most towns have at least one shop that hires out *vélos tout-terrains* (mountain bikes), popularly known as VTTs (60FF to 100FF a day), or cheaper touring bikes. In general, they require a deposit of 1000FF or 2000FF which you forfeit if the bike is damaged or stolen. Some cities (for example, Strasbourg and La Rochelle) have remarkably inexpensive rental agencies run by the municipality.

For details on rental shops, see Getting Around in many of the city and town listings throughout this book.

Bringing Your Own

It is relatively easy to take your bicycle with you on an aircraft. You can either take it apart and pack everything in a bike bag or box, or simply wheel it to the check-in desk, where it will be treated as a piece of baggage (you may have to supply your own box, available from bike shops). It may be necessary to remove the pedals and turn the handlebars sideways so that it takes up less space in the aircraft's hold. Check all this (and weight limits) with the airline well in advance, preferably before you pay for your ticket.

Transporting a bicycle is free on many cross-Channel ferries, though a fee of UK£5 or 50FF may apply, especially from April to September. On Eurotunnel, the cross-Channel fee for a bicycle, including its rider, is UK£15 return; reservations (☎ 01303-288 680) are mandatory. Bikes are sometimes free on ferries to/from Ireland but may cost up to IR£15. Taking a bike to Corsica or Sardinia costs 85FF to 100FF.

European Bike Express (☎ 01642-251 440), with a Web site at www.bikeexpress.co.uk, transports cyclists and their bikes from the UK to places all over France. Depending on your destination, return fares cost around UK£140 to UK£170 (UK£10 less for members of the Cyclists' Touring Club).

Within France, a bicycle can be brought along free of charge as hand luggage on most trains, provided it is enclosed in a *housse* (cover) that measures no more than 1200cm by 90cm. You are responsible for loading and unloading your bicycle from the luggage section of your train car; the SNCF will accept no responsibility for its condition when it arrives. Special tariffs apply in Corsica.

HITCHING

Hitching is never entirely safe in any country in the world, and we don't recommend it. Travellers who decide to hitch should understand that they are taking a small but potentially serious risk. However, many people do choose to hitch, and the advice that follows should help to make their journeys as fast and safe as is possible. Dedicated hitchers may wish to invest in the slightly outdated *Europe: A Manual for Hitch-Hikers* by Simon Calder (Vacation Work; 1994; UK£4.95).

A woman hitching on her own is taking a risk, but two women should be reasonably safe. Two men together may have a harder time getting picked up than a man travelling alone. The best (and safest) combination is probably a man and a woman. In any case, never get in the car with someone you don't trust, even if you have no idea why. Keep your belongings with you on the seat rather than in the boot (trunk).

Hitching from city centres is pretty much hopeless: take public transport to the outskirts. It is illegal to hitch on autoroutes, but you can stand near the entrance ramps as long as you don't block traffic. Thumbing around the Côte d'Azur is nearly impossible. Remote rural areas are often an excellent bet, but once you get off the busier routes nationales there are few vehicles. If your itinerary includes a ferry crossing, it's worth trying to score a ride before the ferry rather than after, since vehicle tickets sometimes include a number of passengers free of charge. At dusk, give up and think about finding somewhere to stay.

To maximise your chances of being picked up, stand where it's convenient for drivers to stop; look cheerful, presentable and non-threatening; orient your backpack so it looks as small as possible to oncoming drivers; and make eye contact with the people driving by. It is an excellent idea to hold up a sign with your destination followed by the letters *s.v.p.* (short for *s'il vous plaît*, meaning, 'please') written on it. One traveller reported that a sign with the destination *'n'importe où'* ('anywhere') works well if you aren't heading to any particular place.

Ride Share Organisations

A number of organisations around France put people looking for rides in touch with drivers going to the same destination. The oldest and best known is Allostop Provoya (☎ 01 53 20 42 42, 01 53 20 42 43 from outside Paris, @ allostop@ecritel.fr; metro: Cadet), based in Paris at 8 rue Rochambeau, 9e. It opens until 6 or 6.30 pm (closed Sunday and holidays). Have a look at the Web site at www.ecritel.fr/allostop.

Travelling this way offers undeniable environmental advantages, but it requires a fair bit of advance planning (for example, contacting Allostop a few days ahead) and is far from free: each passenger pays 22 centimes a kilometre to the driver and a fee to cover administrative expenses: 30/45/60FF for trips under 200/300/500km, and 70FF for trips over 500km. If you buy an eight-trip *abonnement* (membership; 240FF), valid for up to two years, you pay only the per-kilometre charge. To arrange a trip, contact Allostop to get details of a driver going your way. The administrative fee can be paid for by telephone with a credit card.

Similar organisations exist in Dijon (La Clef de Contact on ☎ 03 80 66 31 31), Grenoble (Stop Pouce on ☎ 04 76 43 14 14), Lyon (Autopartage on ☎ 04 72 78 69 76), Montpellier (Autostop on ☎ 04 67 04 36 66), Nantes (Voyage au Fil on ☎ 03 51 72 94 60), Rennes (Autostop Bretagne on ☎ 02 99 67 34 67) and Toulouse (Autostop on ☎ 05 62 30 10 91).

BOAT

For information on touring France's waterways by boat, see Canal Boating under Activities in the Facts for the Visitor chapter.

LOCAL TRANSPORT
Public Transport
France's cities and larger towns generally have excellent public transport systems, including metros in Paris, Lyons, Marseilles, Lille and Toulouse, and ultra-modern trams in Paris, Grenoble, Nantes, Lille, Strasbourg, Nancy and (soon) Bordeaux. Details on routes, fares, tourist passes, etc are available at tourist offices and from local bus company information offices; in this book see Getting Around at the end of each city listing.

Taxi
All large and medium-sized train stations – and many small ones – have a taxi stand (rank) out front.

For details on the tariffs and regulations applicable in major cities, see Taxi in the Getting Around section of the Paris chapter. In small cities and towns, where taxi drivers are unlikely to find another fare anywhere near where they let you off, there are four kinds of tariffs, set locally by the prefecture:

Tariff A (about 3.50FF per kilometre) – for return trips taken from 7 am to 7 pm Monday to Saturday

Tariff B (about 5FF per kilometre) – for return trips taken from 7 pm to 7 am and all day on Sunday and holidays

Tariff C (about 7FF per kilometre) – for one-way travel undertaken during the day from Monday to Saturday

Tariff D (about 10FF per kilometre) – for one-way travel at night and on Sunday and holidays

Travel under 20km/h (or thereabouts) is calculated by time (about 95FF an hour) rather than distance. Since the *prise en charge* (flag fall) is about 14FF, a one-way, 4km trip taken on a weekday afternoon will cost about 42FF. There may be a surcharge of 5FF to get picked up at a train station or airport, a fee of 6FF per bag and a charge of 8FF for a fourth passenger.

ORGANISED TOURS
Local tourist offices, museums, wineries, chateaux and private minibus companies all over France offer a wide variety of guided tours that you arrange locally. Choices often include a museum tour with an art history expert (or with recorded commentary), a cathedral tour that highlights architectural features and the art of stained glass windows, an architecturally-orientated walk around a historic city centre (sometimes you'll listen to the commentary on a Walkman), a chateau tour that makes the medieval furnishings come alive, or a wine (or champagne, or cognac) cellar visit that ends with a tasting session.

Some tourist offices also offer tours to destinations outside of town – for instance wine tours in Bordeaux, St-Émilion, Dijon and Beaune. Chateau tours abound in the Loire Valley and the Dordogne. Details on tours – including when they're available in English – appear either under the relevant museum, winery and chateau listings, or under Organised Tours in city listings and at the beginning of regional chapters. Tourist offices can supply up-to-date details.

Details on canoe/kayak tours, guided hikes, cycling tours, horse riding and other organised outdoor activities appear in listings on natural sites (and nearby cities) under Activities. Regions with lots of things to do out-of-doors include Alsace, the Alps, Corsica, Burgundy, the Dordogne, the Massif Central and Quercy.

Some places are difficult to visit unless you have wheels, or are much more interesting with expert commentary. Where relevant (for example, the D-Day Beaches in Normandy), your options are mentioned under Organised Tours in city listings and at the beginning of regional chapters.

Paris

postcode 75000 • pop 2.2 million (urban area), 9.4 million (Île de France) • elevation 34m

Paris has almost exhausted the superlatives that can be reasonably applied to any world-class city. Notre Dame, the Eiffel Tower, ave des Champs-Élysées – at sunrise, at sunset, at night, in the snow – have been described innumerable times, as have the River Seine, and the subtle (and not-so-subtle) differences between the Left and Right Banks. But what writers have rarely been able to capture is the magic of strolling along the broad avenues that lead from impressive public buildings and exceptional museums to parks, gardens and esplanades.

Paris has more familiar landmarks and aspects than just about any other city in the world. As a result, first-time visitors often arrive in the French capital with all sorts of expectations: grand vistas, intellectuals pontificating at street cafes, romance along the Seine, naughty nightclub revues, rude people who won't speak English but who will rip you off. To be sure, if you look hard enough, you'll find all those things. But another approach is to set aside the preconceptions of Paris and to explore the city's avenues and backstreets as if the tip of the Eiffel Tower or the spire of Notre Dame weren't about to pop into view at any moment.

Paris is enchanting almost everywhere, in every season, at any time of day. And, like a good meal, it excites, it satisfies, and the memory lingers. In *A Moveable Feast*, his recollections of Paris in the early 1920s, Ernest Hemingway wrote: 'If you are lucky enough to have lived in Paris as a young man, then wherever you go for the rest of your life, it stays with you, for Paris is a moveable feast.'

Those of us who were able to take Mr Hemingway's advice in our salad days could not agree more. We're still dining out on the memories.

Highlights

- **Centre Pompidou** – enjoy the renovated centre's new video area, expanded exhibition space, cutting-edge cinema and spectacular rooftop view

- **Louvre** – visit one of the new collections along with old favourites such as the *Mona Lisa* and *Venus de Milo*

- **Musée d'Orsay** – marvel at this beautiful museum's incomparable collection of impressionist art

- **Ste-Chapelle** – admire the Holy Chapel's sublime stained glass on a sunny day

- **Notre Dame** – attend an organ concert

- **Marais** – check out the stately *hôtels particuliers* (private mansions) by day and the throbbing bars and clubs after dark

- **River Seine** – enjoy it on foot from the banks or on an evening cruise

- **Bercy** – see what's happening in the south-east with its new national library, Bercy Village, lovely park and floating clubs and restaurants

Paris maps p193-212

ORIENTATION

The city of Paris is relatively small: approximately 9.5km (north to south) by 11km (east to west). Not including the Bois de Boulogne and the Bois de Vincennes, its total area is 105 sq km. Within central Paris (which the French call *Intra-Muros* – meaning 'within the walls'), the Rive Droite (Right Bank) is north of the Seine, while the Rive Gauche (Left Bank) is south of it.

This chapter gives you three ways to find the addresses mentioned: by arrondissement, by map reference and by metro station.

Arrondissements

Paris is divided into 20 *arrondissements* (districts), which spiral out from the centre clockwise like a conch shell. Paris addresses always include the number of the arrondissement as streets with the same names exist in different districts.

In this chapter, arrondissement numbers are given after the street address using the usual French notation: 1er for *premier* (1st), 4e for *quatrième* (4th), 19e for *dix-neuvième* (19th), and so forth (on some signs or commercial maps, you will see the variation 4ème, 19ème, etc).

Maps & Map References

The exact location of every museum, hotel, restaurant, exchange bureau etc mentioned in this chapter is indicated on one of the colour maps (between pages 192 and 213). Each address includes the reference number of the relevant map, usually just before the telephone number.

The most useful map of Paris for sale is the 1:10,000 scale *Paris Plan* published by Michelin. It comes in booklet form (No 11 or 14) or by fold-out sheet (No 10 or 12) for 35FF or, under the name *Atlas Paris 15*, in large format (75FF). Lonely Planet's Paris

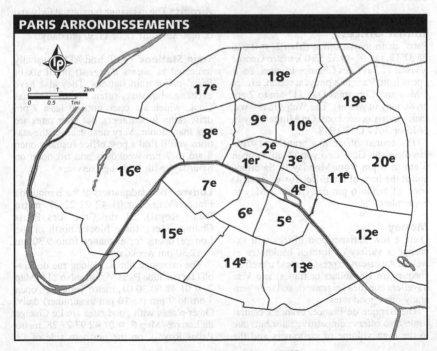

PARIS ARRONDISSEMENTS

17e 18e 19e 9e 10e 8e 2e 1er 3e 20e 16e 7e 11e 4e 6e 5e 15e 12e 14e 13e

0 1 2km
0 0.5 1mi

city map is available from good bookshops both in the UK and France (UK£3.99 or 39FF).

Many Parisians swear by *Paris par Arrondissement* (57FF), a pocket-sized book that has a double-page hand-drawn street plan of each arrondissement. Others find it confusing, though it does list the appropriate metro stop next to streets in the index. A more user-friendly choice is *Paris Practique par Arrondissement* (36FF), a slimmer pocket-sized atlas with a larger format.

Metro Stations

There is almost always a metro station within 500m of wherever you want to go in Paris, so all offices, museums, hotels and restaurants mentioned here have the nearest metro stop written immediately after the contact numbers. Metro stations usually have a useful *plan du quartier* (map of the neighbourhood) on the wall near the exits.

INFORMATION
Tourist Offices

Paris' main tourist office (Map 2, ☎ 0 836 68 31 12, fax 01 49 52 53 00, metro George V) is at 127 ave des Champs-Élysées, 8e. It opens from 9 am to 8 pm year round, except 1 May and Christmas Day, (11 am to 7 pm on Sunday in winter). The Web site is www.paris-touristoffice.com. On Minitel, key in 3615 or 3617 OTPARIS.

The tourist office has branches (☎/fax same) in the Gare de Lyon (Map 5) open 8 am to 8 pm from Monday to Saturday, and at the base of the Eiffel Tower (Map 4) open 11 am to 6 pm daily from 2 May to September.

Money

Quite a few Parisian post offices will exchange a variety of foreign banknotes as well as American Express (Amex) travellers cheques (in US dollars or francs) and Visa travellers cheques (in francs), and they generally offer good rates.

The Banque de France, France's central bank, also offers competitive rates but, due to the high volume of customers and the shortage of counter staff, some branches are limiting their exchange operations to the morning only, and very few accept US$100 notes.

The better exchange bureaux also offer good rates. Changing money at the big *bureau de change* chains like Chequepoint and Exact Change is crazy; they offer about 10% less than what could be considered a fair rate. Note that not all commercial bank branches handle foreign currency exchange.

American Express The Amex office (Map 2, ☎ 01 47 77 77 75, metro Auber or Opéra) is at 11 rue Scribe (9e), facing the western side of Opéra Garnier. Exchange services are available from 9.30 am to 6 pm (to 7 pm June to September) weekdays, and 10 am to 5 pm at the weekend. Cash advances, refunds and poste restante pick-up are available 9.30 am to 6.30 pm weekdays and 10 am to 5.30 pm on Saturday.

Airports The exchange bureaux at Orly and Charles de Gaulle airports are open from 6 or 6.30 am until 11 or 11.30 pm daily.

Train Stations You'll find ATMs (usually indicated as *points d'argent*) in all six of Paris' major train stations. They also have exchange bureaux, often run by Thomas Cook, which are open until at least 7 pm daily (later in summer), but their rates are less than stellar. Very near each of the stations you'll find a post office (usually open 8 am to 7 pm weekdays and till noon on Saturday) with exchange services.

Louvre The headquarters of the Banque de France (Map 6, ☎ 01 42 92 22 27, metro Palais Royal), 31 rue Croix des Petits Champs (1er), three blocks north of the Louvre, opens for exchange from 9.30 am to 12.30 pm weekdays.

The exchange bureaux along rue de Rivoli (1er) include Paris Vision at No 214 (Map 2, ☎ 01 42 60 30 01, metro Tuileries), open 7 am to 9 pm (to 10 pm in summer) daily. Other places with good rates are Le Change du Louvre (Map 6, ☎ 01 42 97 27 28, metro Palais Royal), on the northern side of Le

Louvre des Antiquaires at 151 rue St-Honoré (1er), open 10 am to 6 pm weekdays from 10.30 am to 4.30 pm on Saturday, and Le Change de Paris (Map 2, ☎ 01 42 60 30 84, metro Tuileries), 2 place Vendôme (1er), open 10 am to 6 pm Monday to Saturday.

Les Halles Best Change (Map 6, ☎ 01 42 21 46 05, metro Louvre-Rivoli) at 21 rue du Roule (1er), three blocks south-west of Forum des Halles, opens 10 am to 8 pm Monday to Saturday.

Bastille The Banque de France branch (Map 7, ☎ 01 44 61 15 30, metro Bastille), 3 bis place de la Bastille (4e), across from Opéra Bastille, opens for exchange 9 am to 12.15 pm weekdays.

Latin Quarter & 6e Arrondissement La Socíté Touristique de Service (STS) exchange office (Map 6, ☎ 01 43 54 76 55, metro St-Michel), 2 place St-Michel (6e), has some of the best rates in Paris and opens 9 am to 9 pm Monday to Saturday and 11 am to 8 pm on Sunday. Rates are only marginally lower at the nearby Change de Paris bureau (Map 6, ☎ 01 46 34 70 46) at 1 rue Hautefeuille (near the southern end of place St-Michel), open 9 am to 9 pm daily.

The Banque de France branch (Map 4, ☎ 01 49 54 27 27, metro Sèvres Babylone), 48 blvd Raspail, opens 8.45 am to 12.15 pm weekdays.

Champs-Élysées Area The bureau de change (Map 2, ☎ 01 42 25 38 14, metro Franklin D Roosevelt), 25 ave des Champs-Élysées (8e), has very good rates and is an especially good bet at the weekend. It opens 9 am to 8 pm daily.

Near La Madeleine, the Office de Change de Paris (Map 2, ☎ 01 42 66 25 33, metro Madeleine or Concorde), 13 rue Royale (8e), opens 9 am to 6 pm weekdays and from 10 am on Saturday.

Parc de Monceau Area The Banque de France branch (Map 2, ☎ 01 42 27 78 14, metro Monceau), 1 place du Général Catroux (17e), a block north of Parc de Monceau, opens for exchange from 8.45 am to noon weekdays.

Montmartre The bureau de change (Map 8, ☎ 01 42 52 67 19, metro Abbesses) at 6 rue Yvonne Le Tac (18e) usually has decent rates, and opens 10 am to 6.30 pm weekdays and 10.30 am to 6 pm on Saturday (the same hours on Sunday from June to September). The Thomas Cook bureau (Map 8) at place Blanche (18e), next to the Moulin Rouge, opens 9.30 am to 10 pm (10.30 pm in summer) daily.

Post
Most post offices in Paris are open 8 am to 7 pm weekdays and till noon on Saturday. *Tabacs* (tobacconists) usually sell postage stamps.

The main post office (Map 6, ☎ 01 40 28 20 00, metro Sentier or Les Halles), 52 rue du Louvre (1er), five blocks north of the eastern end of the Louvre, opens 24 hours a day, seven days a week, but only for sending mail, telegrams and domestic faxes, and picking up poste restante mail (window No 6, 3FF per letter). Other services, including currency exchange, are available only during regular post office hours. Be prepared for long queues after 7 pm. Poste restante mail not specifically addressed to a particular branch post office is delivered here.

The post office branch (Map 2, ☎ 01 53 89 05 80, metro George V) at 71 ave des Champs-Élysées (8e) has somewhat extended opening hours (8 am to 7.30 pm weekdays, and 10 am to 7 pm on Saturday), when you can send letters, telegrams and faxes and change money.

Each arrondissement has its own five digit postcode, formed by adding 750 or 7500 to the arrondissement number (eg, 75001 for the 1er arrondissement, 75019 for the 19e). The only exception is the 16e, which has two postcodes: 75016 and 75116. All mail to addresses in France *must* include the postcode. The notation CEDEX after the postcode and 'Paris' simply means that mail sent to that address is collected at the post office rather than delivered to the door.

Telephone

For information on how to use phones in France, see Telephone under the Post & Communications section in the Facts for the Visitor chapter. Télécartes are on sale at post offices, tabacs, supermarket check-out counters, metro stations, SNCF ticket windows and anywhere you see a blue sticker reading *télécartes en vente ici* (phonecards for sale here). Cards worth 50/120 units cost 49/97.50FF.

Fax

Most Paris post offices and telephone shops can send and receive domestic and international faxes. It costs 13FF to send a one-page fax within France. Prices vary for international faxes depending on the destinations, but count on it costing about 75FF per page.

Email & Internet Access

Some 80 post offices in Paris have Cyberposte Internet centres where a rechargeable chip card costing 50FF provides one hour's access; additional hours cost 30FF, including use of a printer. They are generally open from 9 am to 7 pm weekdays and till noon on Saturday, including the one at the main post office north of the Louvre (see Post earlier in this section). For a complete list check out their Web site at www.cyberposte .com.

Commercial cybercafes in Paris include the following:

Café Orbital (Map 5, ☎ 01 43 25 76 77, ✉ info@ orbital.fr, metro Luxembourg), 13 rue de Médicis (6e). Open 9 am to 10 pm Monday to Saturday, from noon on Sunday (1/55FF per minute/hour, 200/300FF for five/10 hours). Web site: www.cafeorbital.com

Cyberbe@ubourg Internet C@fé (Map 7, ☎/fax 01 42 71 49 89, metro Châtelet-Les Halles), 38 rue Quincampoix (4e). Open 9 am to 10 pm daily (1/48FF per minute/hour, 190/ 290FF for five/10 hours).

Village Web (Map 6, ☎ 01 44 07 20 15, ✉ infos@ village-web.net, metro St-Michel or Maubert Mutualité), 18 rue de la Bûcherie (5e). Open 10 am to 10 pm daily (1/45FF per minute/hour, 200/300FF for five/10 hours). Web site: www.village-web.net

Web Bar (Map 6, ☎ 01 42 72 66 55, ✉ web bar@webbar.fr, metro Temple or République), 32 rue de Picardie (3e). Open 8.30 am to 2 am weekdays, from 11 am at the weekend (25/45FF per half-hour/hour, 300FF for 10 hours). Web site www.webbar.fr

Internet Resources

For useful English-language Web sites on both Paris and France in general, see the Internet Resources section in the introductory Facts for the Visitor chapter.

Travel Agencies

General The following agencies are among the largest in Paris and offer the best services and deals:

Forum Voyages (☎ 0 803 83 38 03). Forum has 10 branches in Paris, including one at 11 ave de l'Opéra (Map 6, ☎ 01 42 61 20 20, metro Pyramides) in the 1er and another at 81 blvd St-Michel (Map 5, ☎ 01 43 25 80 58, metro Luxembourg) in the 5e. They are usually open 9.30 am to 7 pm weekdays and 10 am to 6 pm on Saturday. Their Web site is www.forum-voyages.fr. For Minitel, key in 3615 FV.

Nouvelles Frontières (☎ 0 825 00 08 25). This agency has 14 outlets around the city, including one at 13 ave de l'Opéra (Map 6, metro Pyramides) in the 1er open 9 am to 8 pm weekdays and to 7 pm on Saturday, and another at 66 blvd St-Michel (Map 5, metro Luxembourg) in the 5e open 9 am to 7 pm Monday to Saturday. Their Web site is www.nouvelles-frontieres.fr. For Minitel key in 3615 NF.

Voyageurs du Monde (Map 6, ☎ 01 42 86 16 00, metro Pyramides or Quatre Septembre), 55 rue Ste-Anne (2e). 'World Travellers' is an enormous agency with different departments dealing with specific destinations (eg, North America, China, South America, South-East Asia) open 9.30 am to 7 pm Monday to Saturday. There's also a good travel bookshop (☎ 01 42 86 17 38) here and the agency has its own restaurant next door (☎ 01 49 86 17 17) serving daily specialities from around the world at lunch only. Their Web site is www.vdm.com.fr and can be reached on Minitel at 3615 VOYAGEURS.

Student Paris travel agencies that cater to students and young people can supply discount tickets to travellers of all ages. Most issue ISIC student ID cards (60FF) and the Carte Jeunes (120FF), and sell Eurolines tickets.

OTU Voyages (☎ 01 40 29 12 12). Along with its branch opposite the Centre Pompidou (Map 7, see Accommodation Services in the Places to Stay section later in this chapter) the OTU French student travel agency has a branch at 39 ave Georges Bernanos (Map 5, ☎ 01 44 41 38 50, metro Port Royal) in the 5e, open 10 am to 6.30 pm weekdays.
Web site: www.otu.fr

usit Connect (☎ 0 825 08 25 25/01 42 44 14 00). Ireland's student travel agency has four branches in Paris: 6 rue de Vaugirard (Map 5, ☎ 01 42 34 56 90, metro Luxembourg) in the 6e, open 9.30 am (10 am on Tuesday) to 6.30 pm weekdays; 14 rue Vivienne (Map 6, ☎ 01 44 55 32 60, metro Bourse) in the 2e, open 9.30 am to 6 pm (to 8 pm on Thursday in summer) weekdays; 85 blvd St-Michel (Map 5, ☎ 01 43 29 69 50, metro Luxembourg) in the 5e, open 10 am to 6 pm Monday to Saturday; and 31 bis rue Linné (Map 5, ☎ 01 44 08 71 20, metro Jussieu) also in the 5e, open noon to 7 pm Monday to Saturday.
Web site: www.usitconnect.fr

Bookshops

Paris has a number of bookshops that cater for English speakers.

Abbey Bookshop (Map 6, ☎ 01 46 33 16 24, metro Cluny-La Sorbonne), 29 rue de la Parcheminerie (5e). A mellow place, not far from place St-Michel, and known for having free tea and coffee, a supply of Canadian newspapers and a good selection of new and used works of fiction. It opens 10 am to 7 pm Monday to Saturday and some Sundays according to the owner's whim.

Brentano's (Map 3, ☎ 01 42 61 52 50, metro Opéra), 37 ave de l'Opéra (2e). Midway between the Louvre and Opéra Garnier, this is a good shop for tracking down books from the USA, including fiction, business titles and magazines, as well as a good range of children's books. It opens 10 am to 7.30 pm Monday to Saturday.

Les Mots à la Bouche (Map 6, ☎ 01 42 78 88 30, metro Hôtel de Ville), 6 rue Ste-Croix de la Bretonnerie (4e). Paris' premier gay bookshop opens 11 am to 11 pm Monday to Saturday and 2 to 8 pm on Sunday. Most of the back wall is devoted to English-language books, including lots of novels.

Shakespeare & Company (Map 6, ☎ 01 43 26 96 50, metro St-Michel), 37 rue de la Bûcherie (5e). Paris' most famous English-language bookshop (but very much resting on its laurels)

has a varied and unpredictable collection of new and used books in English, including novels from as little as 10FF. It opens noon till midnight daily. Poetry readings are held at 8 pm on most Mondays, and there's a library on the 1st floor. This is *not* the original Shakespeare & Company owned by Sylvia Beach and made famous after she published James Joyce's *Ulysses* in 1922. That was at 12 rue de l'Odéon and was closed by the Germans in 1941.

WH Smith (Map 2, ☎ 01 44 77 88 99, metro Concorde), 248 rue de Rivoli (1er). One block east of place de la Concorde, WH Smith opens 9 am to 7.30 pm Monday to Saturday and from 1 pm on Sunday.

Village Voice (Map 6, ☎ 01 46 33 36 47, metro Mabillon), 6 rue Princesse (6e). A helpful shop with an excellent selection of contemporary North American fiction and European literature in translation. It opens 2 to 8 pm on Monday, from 10 am Tuesday to Saturday and 2 to 7 pm on Sunday.

Libraries

Both French and foreign libraries in Paris are open to foreigners.

American Library in Paris (Map 4, ☎ 01 53 59 12 61, metro École Militaire or Pont de l'Alma), 10 rue du Général Camou (7e). This is among the largest English-language lending libraries in Europe, with some 100,000 volumes of classic and contemporary fiction, nonfiction and some 450 magazines. Annual membership costs 570FF (460FF for students), 240/350FF for four/six months and 70FF a day (50FF for students; library reading privileges only). It opens 10 am to 7 pm Tuesday to Saturday, with limited hours in the summer.

Bibliothèque Nationale de France François Mitterrand (Map 1, ☎ 01 53 79 53 79, metro Bibliothèque François Mitterrand), 11 quai François Mauriac (13e). This national library contains some 10 million tomes stored on some 420km of shelves, and can accommodate 2000 readers and 2000 researchers. It opens to the public (20/200FF per day/year) from 10 am to 8 pm Tuesday to Saturday, and from noon to 7 pm on Sunday.

Bibliothèque Publique d'Information (BPI; Map 7, ☎ 01 44 78 12 33/47 86, metro Rambuteau), Centre Pompidou (4e). This huge, non-circulating (and free) library is spread over three floors of the Centre Pompidou, with its entrance on the mezzanine level. The 2500 periodicals include 150 daily newspapers (many of them in English) and 150 magazines from around the world. It opens noon to 10 pm on Monday and Wednesday to Friday, and from 11 am on Saturday and Sunday. Queues can be enormous; the best time to visit is between 1 and 1.30 pm and after 7 pm.

British Council (Map 4, ☎ 01 49 55 73 23, metro Invalides), 9–11 rue de Constantine (7e). The British Council has a lending library that costs 160/300FF to join for six months/a year (130/250FF with a student card); the reference library costs 30FF a day to use. It opens 11 am to 6 pm (to 7 pm on Wednesday) weekdays. For more information see the Cultural Centres Section below.

Cultural Centres
British Council The British Council (Map 4, ☎ 01 49 55 73 00, metro Invalides), 9–11 rue de Constantine (7e), has reference and lending libraries (see the previous Libraries section), and also runs language courses through the British Institute.

American Church The American Church (Map 4, ☎ 01 40 62 05 00, metro Pont de l'Alma or Invalides), 65 quai d'Orsay (7e), functions as a community centre for English-speakers and is an excellent source of information on accommodation and jobs. The reception is staffed from 9 am till noon and 1 to 10.30 pm Monday to Saturday, and to 8 pm on Sunday. The church has four bulletin boards: an informal board downstairs on which people post all sorts of announcements at no charge, and three identical official ones – one near reception, another outside and one downstairs – listing flats, items for sale and jobs, especially work for au pairs, baby-sitters and English-language teachers. The American Church sponsors a variety of classes, workshops, concerts (at 6 pm on Sunday) and other cultural activities.

Laundry
There are self-service laundrettes around every corner in Paris.

Louvre Area Near the BVJ hostel, the Laverie Libre Service (Map 6, metro Louvre-Rivoli), 7 rue Jean-Jacques Rousseau (1er), opens 7.30 am to 10 pm daily.

Marais The laundrette (Map 7, metro Hôtel de Ville) at 35 rue Ste-Croix de la Bretonnerie (4e) and the Laverie Libre Service (Map 7, metro St-Paul) at 25 rue des Rosiers (4e) are open from 7 or 7.30 am to 10 pm daily. You can start your washing at any time until 8.30 pm at the renovated Laverie (Map 7, metro St-Paul) at 40 rue du Roi de Sicile (4e).

Bastille Area The Miele laundrette (Map 6, metro Bastille) at 2 rue de Làppe (11e) opens 7 am to 10 pm daily.

Latin Quarter Three blocks south-west of the Panthéon, the laundrette (Map 5, metro Luxembourg) at 216 rue St-Jacques (5e) opens 7 am to 10 pm daily. Just south of the Arènes de Lutèce, the Lavomatique (Map 5, metro Monge) at 63 rue Monge (5e) opens 6.30 am to 10 pm daily. Near place de la Contrescarpe, Le Bateau Lavoir (Map 5, metro Cardinal Lemoine) at 1 rue Thouin (5e) opens 7 am to 10 pm daily.

6e Arrondissement The Julice Laverie (Map 6, metro Mabillon), 56 rue de Seine (6e), opens 7 am to 10.30 pm daily. There is a second Julice (Map 6, metro St-André des Arts) at 22 rue des Grands Augustins (6e,) which opens 7 am to 9 pm daily.

Gare de l'Est The Lav' Club (Map 3, metro Gare de l'Est), near the Franprix supermarket at 55 blvd de Magenta (10e), stays open until 10 pm daily. The Laverie (Map 3, metro Château d'Eau) at 6 rue des Petites Écuries (10e) opens 7 am to 10 pm daily.

Montmartre This area's plentiful laundrettes include one at 92 rue des Martyrs (Map 8, metro Abbesses), open 7.30 am to 10 pm daily.

West of the Butte de Montmartre, the Laverie Libre Service (Map 8, metro Blanche), 4 rue Burq (18e), also opens 7.30 am to 10 pm daily.

Toilets
The tan-coloured, self-cleaning cylindrical toilets you see on Paris pavements are open

24 hours a day and cost 2FF. In general, cafe owners do not appreciate you using their facilities if you are not a customer. If you're desperate try ducking into a fast-food place, a major department store, Forum des Halles or the underground toilets in front of Notre Dame.

Medical Services

There are some 50 *assistance publique* (public health service) hospitals in Paris. If you need an ambulance, call ☎ 15 or ☎ 01 45 67 50 50; the multilingual Europe-wide emergency number is ☎ 115. For emergency treatment, call Urgences Médicales on ☎ 01 53 94 94 94 or SOS Médecins on ☎ 01 47 07 77 77. Both offer 24-hour house calls. For information on free and anonymous HIV-testing centres and helplines in Paris, see Health in the Facts for the Visitor chapter.

Some hospitals in Paris include:

Hôtel Dieu (Map 6, ☎ 01 42 34 81 31, metro Cité), on the northern side of place du Parvis Notre Dame (4e). After 8 pm use the emergency entrance on rue de la Cité. The 24-hour emergency room can refer you to the hospital's emergency gynaecological services in cases of sexual assault.
American Hospital (Map 1, ☎ 01 46 41 27 37, metro Anatole France), 63 blvd Victor Hugo, 92202 Neuilly, offers emergency medical and dental care 24 hours a day.
Hôpital Franco-Britannique (Map 1, ☎ 01 46 39 22 22, metro Anatole France), 3 rue Barbès, 92300 Levallois-Perret, is a less expensive English-speaking option. People from outside the EU must pay up front.

Dental Care For emergency dental care contact:

Hôpital La Pitié-Salpêtrière (Map 1, ☎ 01 42 16 00 00/17 72 47 in an emergency, metro Chevaleret), on rue Bruant (13e), is the only dental hospital with extended hours. The night-time entrance (5.30 pm to 8.30 am) is at 83 blvd de l'Hôpital (Map 5, metro Gare d'Austerlitz) in the 13e.
SOS Dentistes (Map 5, ☎ 01 43 37 51 00, metro Port Royal), 87 blvd de Port Royal (14e), is a private dental office that offers services when most dentists are off duty: Monday to Friday

from 8.30 to 11 pm and at weekends from 9.30 am to 11 pm.

Pharmacies Some pharmacies with extended hours include:

Pharmacie Les Champs (Map 2, ☎ 01 45 62 02 41, metro George V), inside the shopping arcade at 84 ave des Champs-Élysées (8e), opens 24 hours a day year round.
Pharmacie Européenne (Map 2, ☎ 01 48 74 65 18, metro place de Clichy), 6 place de Clichy (17e), opens 24 hours a day year round.
Pharmacie des Halles (Map 6, ☎ 01 42 72 03 23, metro Châtelet), 10 blvd de Sébastopol (4e), opens 9 am (from noon on Sunday) to midnight.

Emergency

Emergency telephone numbers include:

Police	☎ 17
Fire brigade	☎ 18
Ambulance (SAMU)	☎ 15
	☎ 01 45 67 50 50
Urgences Médicales	
(24-hour house calls)	☎ 01 53 94 94 94
SOS Médecin	
(24-hour house calls)	☎ 01 47 07 77 77

Dangers & Annoyances

Crime In general, Paris is a safe city and occurrences of random street assault are rare. La Ville Lumière (the City of Light), as Paris is called, is generally well-lit, and there's no reason not to use the metro until it stops running sometime between 12.30 and 12.45 am. As you'll notice, women *do* travel alone on the metro late at night in most areas, though not all report feeling 100% comfortable.

Metro stations that you might wish to avoid at night include: Châtelet-Les Halles and its seemingly endless corridors; Château Rouge in Montmartre; Gare du Nord; Strasbourg St-Denis; Réaumur Sébastopol; and Montparnasse Bienvenüe. *Bornes d'alarme* (alarm boxes) are in the centre of each metro/RER platform and in some station corridors. Neither the Bois de Boulogne nor Bois de Vincennes are particularly safe places to be at night

Nonviolent crime such as pickpocketing and thefts from bags or rucksacks can be a problem wherever there are crowds, especially tourists. Places in which to be especially careful include Montmartre, Pigalle, around Forum des Halles and the Centre Pompidou, on the metro at rush hour and even the Latin Quarter.

Lost & Found All objects found anywhere in Paris – except those picked up on trains or in train stations – are eventually brought to the city's Bureau des Objets Trouvés (Lost Property Office; Map 1, ☎ 01 55 76 20 20, fax 01 40 02 40 45, metro Convention), 36 rue des Morillons (15e), run by the Préfecture de Police. Since telephone inquiries are impossible, the only way to find out if a lost item has been located is to go all the way down there and fill in the forms. The office opens 8.30 am to 5 pm on Monday, Wednesday and Friday, and to 8 pm on Tuesday and Thursday. The office closes at 3.45 pm on Wednesday and Friday and at 4.45 pm on Tuesday and Thursday in July and August.

Items lost in the metro (☎ 01 40 30 52 00 for information) are held by station agents for one day before being sent to the Bureau des Objets Trouvés. Anything found on trains or in train stations is taken to the *objets trouvés* bureau – usually attached to the left-luggage office – of the relevant station. Telephone inquiries (in French) are possible:

Gare d'Austerlitz	☎ 01 53 60 71 98
Gare de l'Est	☎ 01 40 18 88 73
Gare de Lyon	☎ 01 53 33 67 22
Gare Montparnasse	☎ 01 40 48 14 24
Gare du Nord	☎ 01 55 31 58 40
Gare St-Lazare	☎ 01 53 42 05 57

LOUVRE

The Louvre area of the 1er arrondissement contains some of the most important sights for visitors in Paris and has long been a chic residential area for people of means.

Musée du Louvre

The vast Louvre (Map 6, ☎ 01 40 20 53 17 or, for a recording, ☎ 01 40 20 51 51, metro Palais Royal) was constructed around 1200 as a fortress and rebuilt in the mid-16th century for use as a royal palace. It began its

career as a public museum in 1793. The museum's Web site is www.louvre.fr. By Minitel key in 3615 LOUVRE.

The paintings, sculptures and artefacts on display have been assembled by French governments over the past 50 years. Among them are works of art and artisanship from all over Europe and important collections of Assyrian, Etruscan, Greek, Coptic and Islamic art and antiquities. Traditionally the Louvre exists to present western art from the Middle Ages to the year 1848 (at which point the Musée d'Orsay picks up the ball) as well as the works of ancient civilisations at the origins of western art.

The Louvre may be the most actively avoided museum in the world. Daunted by the sheer size (the side facing the Seine is some 700m long) and richness of the place, both visitors and residents often find the prospect of an afternoon at a smaller museum far more inviting.

Eventually, most people do their duty and come, but many leave overwhelmed, unfulfilled, exhausted and frustrated at having got lost on their way to Da Vinci's *La Joconde*, better known to us as the *Mona Lisa*. Since it takes several serious visits to get anything more than a brief glimpse of the works on offer, your best bet – after checking out a few you really want to see – is to choose a period or section of the Louvre and pretend that the rest is in another museum somewhere across town.

The most famous works from antiquity include the *Seated Scribe*, the *Jewels of Rameses II* and that armless duo: the *Winged Victory of Samothrace* and the *Venus de Milo*. From the Renaissance, don't miss Michelangelo's *Slaves* and works by Raphael, Botticelli and Titian. French masterpieces of the 19th century include Ingres' *La Grande Odalisque*, Géricault's *The Raft of the Medusa* and the work of David and Delacroix.

When the museum opened in the late 18th century it contained 2500 paintings; today some 30,000 are on display. The seven billion franc *Grand Louvre* project inaugurated by the late President François Mitterrand in 1989 has doubled the museum's exhibition

Ah, la Carte!

La Carte Musées et Monuments (Museums & Monuments Card) is valid for entry to some 70 venues in Paris and the Île de France (see the Around Paris chapter), including the Louvre, Centre Pompidou and the Musée d'Orsay (but *not* the Jeu de Paume and a few other important places). The cost for one/three/five days is 80/160/240FF; there is no reduced tariff. The pass is available from the participating venues as well as the tourist office and its branches, Fnac outlets and certain metro stations and RATP information desks.

Note that national museums in Paris give a reduced rate for those aged 18 to 25 and over 60 and are free for those under 18 and, on the first Sunday of each month, for everyone.

The vast majority of museums in Paris close on Monday, though some (such as the Louvre and the Centre Pompidou) are closed on Tuesday. It is also important to remember that *all* museums and monuments in Paris shut their doors or gates between a half-hour and an hour before their actual closing times. If a museum or monument closes at 6 pm, for example, don't count on getting in much after 5 pm.

space, breathing new life into the museum, with many new and renovated galleries now open to the public. Seven new rooms containing furniture, silver, clocks and Sèvres porcelain opened in late 1999. In the spring of 2000 a controversial (and permanent) four-room exhibit devoted to primitive art forms collected from Africa, Asia, Australasia and the Americas was unveiled in the Pavillon des Sessions of the Denon wing.

Orientation The main entrance and ticket windows in the Cour Napoléon (1er) are covered by a 21m-high **glass pyramid** designed by China-born American architect IM Pei. You can avoid the queues outside the pyramid by entering the Louvre complex via the Carrousel du Louvre shopping area (Map 6), 99 rue de Rivoli, or by following the 'Louvre' exit from the Palais Royal-Musée du Louvre metro stop.

The Louvre is divided into four sections. **Sully** forms the four sides of the Cour Carrée (literally 'square courtyard') at the eastern end of the building. **Denon** stretches along the Seine to the south. **Richelieu** is the northern wing along rue de Rivoli. The centrepiece of the underground **Carrousel du Louvre** shopping mall (open 8.30 am to 11 pm daily), which stretches from the pyramid to the Arc du Triomphe du Carrousel (see later in this section), is an **inverted glass pyramid**, also by Pei.

The split-level public area under the glass pyramid is known as **Hall Napoléon**. It has an exhibit on the history of the Louvre, a bookshop, a restaurant, a cafe and auditoriums for concerts, lectures and films. Free maps in English of the complex (*Louvre Plan/Information*) are available at the information desk. The best publication for a general overview is *Louvre: First Visit* (20FF), which leads you past some 50 works of art including the Code of Hammurabi stele, Vermeer's *The Lacemaker*, and the Apollo Gallery with the French crown jewels as well as the *Winged Victory of Samothrace*, *Venus de Milo* and, of course, the *Mona Lisa*, who is soon to get her own private room. The more comprehensive *Louvre: The Visit* (60FF) illustrates and describes more than 160 works of art. Both publications are available in the museum gift shop.

Opening Hours & Tickets The Louvre opens from Wednesday to Monday and closes on certain public holidays. The hours are 9 am to 6 pm (last admission: 5.15 pm) from Thursday to Sunday, and from 9 am to 9.45 pm (last admission: 9.15 pm) on Monday and Wednesday. On Wednesday virtually the entire museum remains open after 5.15 pm but on Monday there's a *circuit court* (short tour) of selected galleries in the three wings. The Hall

Napoléon opens 9 am to 9.45 pm Wednesday to Monday.

Admission to the permanent collections costs 45FF (26FF after 3 pm and all day Sunday); the first Sunday of every month is free. There are no discounts for students or seniors, but those under 18 get in free. Admission to temporary exhibits varies. Tickets are valid for the whole day, so you can leave and re-enter as you please. Entry to just the Hall Napoléon costs 30FF for everyone. A *billet jumelé* (combination ticket) for the permanent collections and Hall Napoléon costs 60/40FF before 3 pm/after 3 pm and all day Sunday.

Those in the know buy their tickets in advance at the *billeteries* (ticket office) of Fnac (see Booking Agencies under Entertainment later in this chapter) or from any of the department stores listed for an extra 6FF and walk straight in without queuing at all.

Guided Tours English-language guided tours (☎ 01 40 20 52 63) lasting 1½ hours depart from the Accueil des Groupes area under the glass pyramid three to five times a day, depending on the season, but just once on Sunday at 11.30 am. Tickets cost 38FF (aged 13 to 18 22FF, free for children aged 12 and under) in addition to the regular admission. Groups are limited to 30 people, so it's a good idea to sign up at least 30 minutes before departure time.

Recorded audioguide tours in six languages, available until 4.30 pm, can be rented for 30FF under the pyramid, at the entrance to each wing. The tour lasts 1½ hours.

Palais du Louvre Museums
In addition to the Musée du Louvre, the Palais du Louvre contains three other museums (☎ 01 44 55 57 50 for all) revamped or created under the Grand Louvre scheme. All are at the western end of the Richelieu wing and can be entered at 107 rue de Rivoli, 1er (Map 6, metro Palais Royal).

The **Musée des Arts Décoratifs** (Museum of Applied Arts), on the 3rd floor, displays furniture, jewellery and such *objets d'art* as ceramics and glassware from the Middle Ages and the Renaissance through

to the Art Nouveau and Art Deco periods. The **Musée de la Publicité** (Advertising Museum), which shares the same floor, contains everything from 19th-century posters touting elixirs to electronic publicity. On the 1st and 2nd floors is the **Musée de la Mode et du Textile** (Museum of Fashion and Textile). The museums are open 11 am to 6 pm (to 9 pm on Wednesday) Tuesday to Friday and from 10 am to 6 pm at the weekend. Admission to all three costs 35FF (aged 18 to 25 25FF).

Arc de Triomphe du Carrousel
Built by Napoleon to celebrate his battlefield successes of 1805, this triumphal arch (Map 6), which is set in the Jardin du Carrousel at the eastern end of the Jardin des Tuileries, was once crowned by the *Horses of St Mark's*, stolen from Venice by Napoleon but returned after Waterloo. The quadriga (a two-wheeled chariot drawn by four horses) on the top, added in 1828, celebrates the return of the Bourbons to the French throne after Napoleon's downfall. The sides of the arch are adorned with depictions of Napoleonic victories and eight pink marble columns, atop each of which stands a soldier of the emperor's Grande Armée.

Jardin des Tuileries
The formal, 28-hectare Tuileries Garden (Maps 2 and 6), which begins just west of the Jardin du Carrousel, was laid out in its present form (more or less) in the mid-1600s by André Le Nôtre, who also created the gardens at Vaux-le-Vicomte and Versailles (see the Around Paris chapter). The Tuileries soon became the most fashionable spot in Paris for parading about in one's finery. The gardens are open from 7 am (7.30 am in winter) to between 7.30 and 9 pm daily, depending on the season.

The **Voie Triomphale** (also known as the **Grand Axe** or 'Great Axis'), the western continuation of the Tuileries' east–west axis, follows the ave des Champs-Élysées to the Arc de Triomphe and, ultimately, to the Grande Arche in the skyscraper district of La Défense (see the Around Paris chapter).

Enjoy a picnic with a view in Paris' many parks.

GREG ELMS

Napoleon's Arc de Triomphe du Carrousel

SIMON BRACKEN

Notre Dame, Paris' exceptional Gothic heart

RICHARD I'ANSON

The famous cemetery at Montmartre

JULIET COOMBE

Modern sculpture outside the Église St-Enstache

ELLIOT DANIEL

SIMON BRACKEN

Detail of the Panthéon

RICHARD I'ANSON

The Arc de Triomphe towers over place Charles de Gaulle.

CHRISTINE OSBORNE

The trendy 17th-century district of the Marais is the centre of Paris' gay life.

JULIET COOMBE

A way with the birds – feathered friends outside Notre Dame

ROD HYETT

The car to tour France in?

Orangerie

The Musée de l'Orangerie des Tuileries (Orangerie Museum; Map 4, ☎ 01 42 97 48 16, metro Concorde), in the south-west corner of the Jardin des Tuileries at place de la Concorde (1er), has important impressionist works, including a series of Monet's *Décorations des Nymphéas* (Water Lilies) and paintings by Cézanne, Matisse, Picasso, Renoir, Sisley, Soutine and Utrillo. The museum closed in the spring of 1999 for major structural renovations and will reopen at the end of 2001.

Jeu de Paume

The Galerie Nationale du Jeu de Paume (Map 2, ☎ 01 42 60 69 69, metro Concorde) is housed in an erstwhile *jeu de paume*, a real (or royal) tennis court built in 1861 during the reign of Napoleon III in the north-west corner of the Jardin des Tuileries. Once the home of a good part of France's national collection of impressionist works (now housed in the Musée d'Orsay), today it serves as a gallery for innovative short-term exhibitions of contemporary art and is the venue for exhibiting the work of artists invited to the Festival d'Automne (see Special Events later in this chapter). It opens noon to 9.30 pm on Tuesday, to 7 pm Wednesday to Friday and from 10 am to 7 pm at weekends. Admission costs 38FF (aged 13 to 18, students under 26 and people over 60 28FF).

Place Vendôme

Octagonal place Vendôme (Map 2, metro Tuileries) and the arcaded and colonnaded buildings around it were built between 1687 and 1721. In March 1796, Napoleon married Josephine in the building at No 3. The Ministry of Justice has been at Nos 11–13 since 1815.

Today, the buildings around the square house the posh Hôtel Ritz (see Places to Stay – Deluxe) and some of Paris' most fashionable and expensive boutiques, more of which can be found along nearby rue de Castiglione, rue St-Honoré and rue de la Paix (see the Shopping section later in this chapter).

The 43.5m-tall **Colonne Vendôme** in the centre of the square consists of a stone core wrapped in a 160m-long bronze spiral made from 1250 Austrian and Russian cannons captured by Napoleon at the Battle of Austerlitz in 1805. The bas-reliefs on the spiral depict Napoleon's victories between 1805 and 1807. The statue on top depicts Napoleon as a Roman emperor and dates from 1873.

Jardin du Palais Royal

The **Palais Royal** (Map 6, metro Palais Royal), which briefly housed a young Louis XIV in the 1640s, lies to the north of place du Palais Royal and the Louvre. Construction was begun in the 17th century by Cardinal Richelieu, though most of the present neoclassical complex dates from the latter part of the 18th century. It now contains the Conseil d'État (State Council) and is closed to the public. The colonnaded building facing place André Malraux is the **Comédie Française** (see Theatre in the Entertainment section later in this chapter), founded in 1680, and the world's oldest national theatre.

Just north of the palace is the Jardin du Palais Royal, a lovely park surrounded by arcades. **Galerie de Valois** on the eastern side shelters designer shops while **Galerie de Montpensier** on the west has a few old shops remaining that sell things like colourful Légion d'Honneur-style medals and lead soldiers. The park opens daily from 7 am (7.30 am from October to March) to between 8.30 pm in winter and 11 pm in summer.

Le Louvre des Antiquaires

This impressive building at 2 place du Palais Royal (Map 6, metro Palais Royal) houses some 250 elegant antique shops filled with objets d'art, furniture, clocks and classical antiquities available to anyone with a king's ransom to spare. It opens 11 am to 7 pm Tuesday to Sunday (Tuesday to Saturday in July and August).

LES HALLES

The huge pedestrian zone between the Centre Pompidou (1er) and the Forum des

Halles, with rue Étienne Marcel to the north and rue de Rivoli to the south, is always filled with people, just as it was for the 850-odd years when the area served as Paris' main marketplace (*les halles*).

Centre Pompidou

It's all change at the Centre Georges Pompidou (Map 7, ☎ 01 44 78 12 33, metro Rambuteau) following a massive renovation lasting more than two years that was completed in time for the start of the new millennium. The result is a stunning reworked facade on the western side – all bright white and light – and, inside, expanded exhibition space, a new cinema, CD and video centre, dance and theatre venues, a cybercafe, a rooftop restaurant, work and play areas for children and a panoramic view of Paris from the rooftop.

The Centre Pompidou, also known as the Centre Beaubourg, has amazed and delighted visitors since it was built in the mid-1970s, not just for its outstanding collection of modern art, but for its radical (at the time) architectural statement. It is the most popular attraction in the city and attracts upwards of 25,000 visitors a day. It's Web site is www.centrepompidou.fr. By Minitel key in 3615 BEAUBOURG.

In order to keep the exhibition halls as spacious and uncluttered as possible, the architects – the Italian Renzo Piano and Briton Richard Rogers – put the building's 'insides' on the outside. The purpose of each of the ducts, pipes and vents that enclosed the centre's glass walls could be divined from the paint job: escalators and lifts in red, electrical circuitry in yellow, the plumbing green and the air-conditioning system blue. But it all began to look somewhat *démodé* by the late 1990s and thus the refit.

Two floors of the centre are dedicated to exhibiting some of the 40,000-plus works of the **Musée National d'Art Moderne** (MNAM; National Museum of Modern Art), France's national collection of 20th-century art – including the work of the Fauvists, the Surrealists and Cubists as well as pop and op art and contemporary works.

The **Atelier Brancusi**, the studio of the Romanian-born sculptor Constantin Brancusi (1876–1957) on the piazza, contains almost 140 examples of his work as well as drawings, paintings and glass photographic plates. The centre also contains the Bibliothèque Publique d'Information (BPI); for details see Libraries in the Information section of this chapter.

Place Georges Pompidou, on the western side of the centre, and the nearby pedestrian streets attract buskers, street artists, musicians, jugglers and mime artists, and can be as much fun as the centre itself. The fanciful **mechanical fountains** (Map 7) of skeletons, dragons, G-clefs and a big pair of ruby-red lips, at **place Igor Stravinsky,** on the centre's southern side, were created by Jean Tinguely and Niki de Saint-Phalle. They are a positive delight.

The Forum of the Centre Pompidou (the open space at ground level with temporary exhibits and information desks) opens from 11 am to 10 pm Wednesday to Monday. Admission is free. The MNAM's permanent collection opens 11 am to 9 pm on the same days and costs 30FF (students, seniors and those aged 18 to 26 20FF, free for under 18s and for everyone on the first Sunday of the month). Admission to the Atelier Brancusi, open 1 to 9 pm Wednesday to Monday, costs 20FF. A combination ticket including access to the museum, atelier and rooftop costs 40/30FF while a 'passe-partout' valid for the day and allowing entry to the temporary exhibits as well costs 50/40FF. There's even an annual pass for 240/120FF.

Forum des Halles

Les Halles, Paris' main wholesale food market, occupied the area just south of Église St-Eustache from the early 12th century until 1969, when it was moved lock, stock and barrel to the suburb of Rungis near Orly. In its place, the unspeakable Forum des Halles (Map 6, ☎ 01 44 76 96 56 for information, metro Les Halles or Châtelet), a huge underground shopping mall, was constructed in the glass-and-chrome style of the early 1970s. It all looks a bit frayed more than 30 years on.

Église St-Eustache

This majestic church (Map 6, ☎ 01 42 36 31 05, metro Les Halles), one of the most beautiful in Paris, is just north of the gardens on top of Forum des Halles. Constructed between 1532 and 1640, St-Eustache's dominant style is Gothic, though a neoclassical facade was added on the western side in the mid-18th century. Inside, there are some exceptional Flamboyant Gothic arches holding up the ceiling of the chancel, though most of the interior ornamentation is Renaissance or classical. The gargantuan organ above the west entrance with 101 stops and 8000 pipes is used for concerts, long a tradition here. The church opens 9 am to 7 pm (to 8 pm in summer) Monday to Saturday and 9 am to 12.30 pm and 2.30 to 7 pm (to 8 pm in summer) on Sunday.

La Samaritaine Rooftop Terrace

For an amazing 360° panoramic view of central Paris, head to the roof of La Samaritaine department store's main building (Map 6, ☎ 01 40 41 20 20, metro Pont Neuf) on rue de la Monnaie (1er). The 11th-floor lookout opens from 9.30 am to 7 pm (10 pm on Thursday) Monday to Saturday. Access to the rooftop is free.

Tour St-Jacques

The 52m-tall Flamboyant Gothic Tower of St-James (Map 6, metro Châtelet) on the north-eastern side of place du Châtelet (4e) is all that remains of the Église St-Jacques la Boucherie, built by the powerful butchers' guild in 1523. The tower, topped by a weather station, is not open to the public.

Hôtel de Ville

After having been gutted by fighting during the Paris Commune of 1871, Paris' city hall (Map 7, ☎ 01 42 76 40 40, metro Hôtel de Ville) was rebuilt in the neo-Renaissance style (1874–82). The ornate facade is decorated with 108 statues of noteworthy Parisians. The visitors entrance is at 29 rue

de Rivoli (4e), where there's a hall used for temporary exhibitions (open 9.30 am to 6 pm Monday to Saturday).

The Hôtel de Ville faces the majestic **place de l'Hôtel de Ville**, used since the Middle Ages to stage many of Paris' celebrations, rebellions, book burnings and public executions.

MARAIS

The Marais (literally, 'marsh'), the area of the Right Bank directly north of Île St-Louis, was in fact a swamp until the 13th century when it was put to agricultural use. In the early 17th century, Henri IV built place des Vosges, turning the area into Paris' most fashionable residential district and attracting wealthy aristocrats who then erected their own luxurious but understated *hôtels particuliers* (private mansions). When the aristocracy moved out of Paris to Versailles and Faubourg St-Germain (7e) during the late 17th and 18th centuries, the Marais and its townhouses passed into the hands of ordinary Parisians. The 110-hectare area was given a major face-lift in the late 1960s and early 70s. Many of the hôtels particuliers now house museums and government institutions.

Today, the Marais is one of the few neighbourhoods of Paris that has most of its pre-Revolutionary architecture intact; indeed, the oldest house in Paris (1407), still intact, is at 51 rue de Montmorency (3e). In recent years the area has become trendy, but it's still home to a long-established Jewish community and is the centre of Paris' gay life.

Place des Vosges

Place des Vosges, 4e (Map 7, metro Bastille or Chemin Vert), inaugurated in 1612 as place Royale, is a square ensemble of 36 symmetrical houses with ground-floor arcades (now occupied by upmarket art galleries, antique shops and places to eat and drink), steep slate roofs and large dormer windows. Only the earliest houses were built of brick; to save time, the rest were given timber frames and faced with plaster, which was later painted to resemble brick.

The beloved author Victor Hugo lived at the Hôtel de Rohan-Guéménée, 6 place des Vosges, from 1832 to 1848, moving here a year after the publication of *Notre Dame de Paris* (The Hunchback of Notre Dame). **Maison de Victor Hugo** (☎ 01 42 72 10 16), now a municipal museum, opens from 10 am to 5.40 pm Tuesday to Sunday. Admission costs 22FF (students and seniors 15FF, free for those under 26).

Musée Carnavalet

Also known as the Musée de l'Histoire de Paris (Map 7, ☎ 01 44 59 58 58/42 72 21 13, metro St-Paul), 23 rue de Sévigné (3e), this museum of Parisian history is housed in two hôtels particuliers: the mid-16th-century, Renaissance-style Hôtel Carnavalet, once home to the 17th-century writer Madame de Sévigné, and the Hôtel Le Peletier de St-Fargeau, which dates from the late 17th century. The artefacts on display in the museum's sublime rooms chart the history of Paris from the Gallo-Roman period to the 20th century. Some of France's most important documents, paintings and other objects from the French Revolution are here as is Fouquet's Art Nouveau jewellery shop from the rue Royale and Marcel Proust's cork-lined bedroom from his apartment on blvd Haussmann.

The museum opens 10 am to 5.40 pm Tuesday to Sunday. Admission costs 30FF (students and seniors 20FF, free for those under 26 and for everyone from 10 am to 1 pm on Sunday).

Musée Picasso

The Picasso Museum (Map 7, ☎ 01 42 71 25 21, metro St-Paul or Chemin Vert), 5 rue de Thorigny (3e), housed in the mid-17th-century Hôtel Aubert de Fontenay (or Hôtel Salé), is one of Paris' best-loved art museums. Displays include more than 3500 of Picasso's engravings, paintings, ceramic works and drawings, and an unparalleled collection of sculptures.

You can also see part of Picasso's personal art collection, which includes works by Braque, Cézanne, Matisse and Degas. The museum opens 9.30 am to 6 pm (to 8 pm on Thursday) Wednesday to Monday; from October to March it closes at 5.30 pm. Admission costs 30FF (aged 18 to 25 20FF, free for under 18s and for everyone on the first Sunday of the month). When there are special exhibits (frequently), admission costs 38/28FF.

Maison Européenne de la Photographie

Housed in the Hôtel Hénault de Cantorbe dating from the early 1700s, the European House of Photography (Map 7, ☎ 01 44 78 75 00, metro St-Paul or Pont Marie), 5–7 rue de Fourcy (4e), has cutting-edge temporary exhibits (last seen: a retrospective of Brazilian photographer Sebastiaõ Salgado) and a permanent collection on the history of photography with particular reference to France. The museum opens 11 am to 8 pm Wednesday to Sunday; admission costs 30FF (those aged nine to 25 or over 60 15FF, free for children under eight and for everyone after 5 pm on Wednesday).

Musée d'Art et d'Histoire du Judaïsme

Recently transferred from their modest digs in Montmartre to the stunning Hôtel de St-Aignan (1650) in the heart of the Marais, the crafts, paintings and ritual objects from Eastern Europe and North Africa of the Musée d'Art Juif (Jewish Art Museum) have been combined with medieval Jewish artefacts from the Musée National du Moyen Age (see the Latin Quarter) to create the Art and History of Judaism Museum (Map 7, ☎ 01 53 01 86 60, metro Rambuteau), 71 rue du Temple (3e), which traces the evolution of Jewish communities from the Middles Ages to the present, with particular emphasis on the history of the Jews in France. Highlights include documents relating to the Dreyfus Affair and works by Chagall, Modigliani and Soutine. It opens 11 am to 6 pm on weekdays and from 10 am on Sunday. Admission (including audioguide) costs 40FF (students and those aged 18 to 26 25FF, free for under 18s).

Musée des Arts et Métiers

Recently reopened after a hiatus of six years, the Arts and Crafts Museum (Map 6, ☎ 01 53 01 82 00, metro Arts et Métiers), 60 rue de Réaumur (3e), is a must for anyone with a scientific leaning. Scientific instruments, machines and working models from the 18th to 20th centuries are displayed over three floors, with Foucault's original pendulum (1855), which he introduced to the world with the words: 'Come and see the world turn,' taking pride of place. The museum opens 10 am to 6 pm Tuesday to Sunday and costs 35FF (reduced rate 25FF).

BASTILLE

After years as a rundown immigrant neighbourhood notorious for its high crime rate, the Bastille area, which encompasses mostly the 11e and 12e arrondissements, but also the easternmost part of the 4e, has undergone a fair degree of gentrification, in large part because of the Opéra Bastille, which opened in 1989. The area east of place de la Bastille retains its lively atmosphere and ethnicity.

Bastille

The Bastille, built during the 14th century as a fortified royal residence, is the most famous monument in Paris that doesn't exist: the infamous prison – the quintessential symbol of monarchic despotism – was demolished shortly after a mob stormed it on 14 July 1789 and all seven prisoners were freed. The site where it once stood, place de la Bastille, 12e (Map 7, metro Bastille), is now a very busy traffic roundabout.

In the centre of place de la Bastille is the 52m-tall **Colonne de Juillet** (July Column), whose shaft of greenish bronze is topped by a gilded and winged figure of Liberty. It was erected in 1833 as a memorial to the people killed in the street battles that accompanied the July Revolution of 1830; they are buried in vaults under the column.

Opéra Bastille

Paris' 'second' opera house (Map 6, ☎ 0 836 69 78 68/01 44 73 13 99, metro Bastille), 2–6 place de la Bastille (12e), designed by the Canadian Carlos Ott, was inaugurated on 14 July 1989, the 200th anniversary of the storming of the Bastille. For details on the 1¼-hour guided tours of the building (50FF, students, seniors and children under 16 30FF), which depart most days at 1 or 7 pm, call ☎ 01 40 01 19 70. See the Entertainment section later in this chapter for information on buying tickets to performances.

ÎLE DE LA CITÉ

The site of the first settlement around the 3rd century BC and later the centre of the Roman town of Lutèce (Lutetia), the Île de la Cité remained the centre of royal and ecclesiastical power even after the city spread to both banks of the Seine during the Middle Ages. The middle part of the island was demolished and rebuilt during Baron Haussmann's great urban renewal scheme of the late 19th century.

Notre Dame

If Paris has a heart then the Cathédrale de Notre Dame de Paris (Cathedral of Our Lady of Paris; Map 6, ☎ 01 42 34 56 10, metro Cité), place du Parvis Notre Dame (4e), is it. Notre Dame is not only a masterpiece of French Gothic architecture but has also been Catholic Paris' ceremonial focus for seven centuries.

Built on a site occupied by earlier churches – and, some two millennia ago, a Gallo-Roman temple – it was begun in 1163 and completed around 1345. Viollet-le-Duc carried out extensive renovations in the 19th century. The interior is 130m long, 48m wide and 35m high, and can accommodate over 6000 worshippers. Some 12 million people visit the cathedral each year.

Notre Dame is known for its sublime balance, although if you look closely you'll see all sorts of minor asymmetrical elements introduced to avoid monotony, in accordance with standard Gothic practice. These include the slightly different shapes of each of the three main entrances. One of the best views of Notre Dame is from **square Jean XXIII**, the lovely little park south and east of the cathedral, where you

PARIS

The Hunchback of Notre Dame

The story of the Hunchback of Notre Dame as told by Victor Hugo in his romantic novel *Notre Dame de Paris* – and not some silly cartoon version with a happy ending – goes something like this...

It's 15th-century Paris during the reign of Louis XI. A Romany girl called Esmeralda is in love with Captain Phoebus, but the evil and jealous archdeacon, Claude Frollo, denounces her as a witch. The hunchbacked bell ringer, Quasimodo, is devoted to Esmeralda and saves her (for a while) when she seeks protection from the mob in the belfry of Notre Dame. We won't give the ending away but suffice it to say that everyone comes to a tragic end – including Captain Phoebus, who gets married to someone else.

Was *Notre Dame de Paris*, which is pure fiction, just a good story or a commentary on the times? Hugo began the book during the reign of the unpopular and reactionary Charles X who, with the guidance of his chief minister, had abolished freedom of the press and dissolved parliament. The ascent of Louis-Philippe, a bourgeois king with liberal leanings, in the July Revolution of 1830 took place shortly before the book was published. The novel can thus be seen as a condemnation of absolutism (ie of Charles X) and of a society that allows the likes of people like Frollo and Phoebus to heap scorn and misery on unfortunate characters like Esmeralda and Quasimodo.

Hugo's evocation of the colourful and intense life of the late 15th century is seen by some as a plea for the preservation of Gothic Paris and its decaying architecture. Indeed, the condition of Notre Dame in the early 19th century was so bad that artists, politicians and writers, including Hugo, beseeched Louis-Philippe to rectify it. Hugo was appointed to the new Commission for Monuments and the Arts, where he sat for 10 years. In 1845 the Gothic revivalist architect Viollet-Le-Duc began his renovation of Notre Dame, in which he added the steeple and gargoyles (among other things). The work continued for almost 20 years.

JANE SMITH

PARIS

can see the mass of ornate **flying buttresses** that encircle the chancel and support its walls and roof.

Inside, exceptional features include three spectacular **rose windows**, the most renowned of which is the window over the west facade, which is 10m across, and that on the northern side of the transept, which has remained virtually unchanged since the 13th century. The central choir with its carved wooden stalls and statues is also noteworthy. The 7800-pipe organ was restored between 1990 and 1992.

Notre Dame opens 8 am to 6.45 pm daily. The **trésor** (treasury) at south-east transept contains liturgical objects and works of art; it opens 9.30 to 11.30 am and 1 to 5.30 or 6.30 pm Monday to Saturday (15FF, students 15FF, children 5FF). There are free **guided tours** of the cathedral in English at noon on Wednesday and Thursday and at 2.30 pm on Saturday (daily in August).

North Tower The entrance to Notre Dame's north tower (Map 6, ☎ 01 44 32 16 72) is on rue du Cloître Notre Dame – to the right and around the corner as you walk out of the cathedral's main doorway. Climbing the 387 spiralling steps brings you to the top of the **west facade**, where you'll find yourself face to face with many of the cathedral's most frightening gargoyles – and a spectacular view of Paris. The tower opens from 9.30 am to 7.30 pm Monday to Thursday and from 10 am Friday, Saturday and Sunday from April to September. During the rest of the year it opens 10 am to 6 or 6.30 pm daily. Tickets cost 35FF (aged 12 to 25 23FF, free for children under 12).

Ste-Chapelle

The most exquisite of Paris' Gothic monuments, Ste-Chapelle (literally 'holy chapel'; Map 6, ☎ 01 53 73 78 51, metro Cité), 4 blvd du Palais (1er), is tucked away within the walls of the **Palais de Justice** (Law Courts). In stark contrast to the buttressed hulk of nearby Notre Dame, Ste-Chapelle is a masterpiece of delicacy and finesse. The 'walls' of the **upper chapel** (built for wor-

Notre Dame's Kestrels

Birdwatchers estimate that about 40 pairs of kestrels (*Falco tinnunculus*) currently nest in Paris, preferring tall old structures like the towers of Notre Dame. Four or five pairs of kestrels regularly breed in niches and cavities high up in the cathedral, and once a year (usually late June), local ornithologists set up a public kestrel-watching station behind the cathedral, with telescopes and even a camera transmitting close-up pictures of one of the kestrels' nesting sites. The birds form their partnerships in February, eggs are laid in April, the kestrel chicks hatch in May and are ready to depart by early July. In late June, birdwatchers may spot the adult kestrels returning to their young with a tasty mouse or sparrow. Unfortunately, Paris' pigeons – those dirty flying rats – are too large for a kestrel chick to handle.

ship by the king and his court) are sheer curtains of richly coloured and finely detailed **stained glass**, which bathe the chapel in an extraordinary light.

Built in just under three years (compared with nearly 200 for Notre Dame), Ste-Chapelle was consecrated in 1248. The chapel was conceived by Louis IX (St Louis) to house his collection of holy relics, including what was believed to be the Crown of Thorns and part of John the Baptist's skull – for which he paid several times the cost of building the chapel itself. The relics were relocated to Notre Dame after the Revolution.

Ste-Chapelle opens from 9.30 am to 6.30 pm daily from April to September and 10 am to 5 pm during the rest of the year. Admission costs 35FF (aged 12 to 25 23FF, free for children under 12). A ticket valid for both Ste-Chapelle and the Conciergerie costs 50/25FF.

Conciergerie

The Conciergerie (Map 6, ☎ 01 53 73 78 50, metro Cité), 1 quai de l'Horloge (1er), was a luxurious royal palace when it was built in the 14th century, but it later lost favour with the kings of France and was turned into a prison. During the Reign of Terror (1793–94), the Conciergerie was used to incarcerate alleged enemies of the Revolution before they were brought before the Revolutionary Tribunal, which met in the Palais de Justice next door. Among the 2600 prisoners held in the **cachots** (dungeons) here before being sent in tumbrels to the guillotine were Queen Marie-Antoinette and, as the Revolution began to turn on its own, the Revolutionary radicals Danton and Robespierre and, finally, the judges of the tribunal themselves.

The huge Gothic **Salle des Gens d'Armes** (Cavalrymen's Hall) dates from the 14th century and is a fine example of the Rayonnant Gothic style. It is the largest surviving medieval hall in Europe. **Tour de l'Horloge**, the tower on the corner of blvd du Palais and quai de l'Horloge, has held a public clock aloft since 1370, but the last time we looked it was still not working. Opening hours and admission fees at the Conciergerie are the same as those at Ste-Chapelle.

Mémorial des Martyrs de la Déportation

At the south-eastern tip of the Île de la Cité, behind Notre Dame, is the Memorial to the Deportation Victims (Map 6), erected in 1962. It's a haunting monument to the 200,000 residents of France – including 76,000 Jews – who were killed in Nazi concentration camps. A single barred 'window' separates the bleak, rough concrete courtyard from the waters of the Seine. The Tomb of the Unknown Deportee is flanked by 200,000 bits of back-lit glass and the walls are etched with inscriptions from celebrated writers and poets. The memorial opens from 10 am to noon and 2 to 5 pm (8 pm from April to September). Admission is free.

Pont Neuf

The now sparkling-white, stone spans of Paris' oldest bridge, Pont Neuf (literally 'new bridge'; Map 6), link the western end of the Île de la Cité with both banks of the Seine. Begun in 1578, Pont Neuf was completed in 1607, when the king inaugurated it by crossing the bridge on a white stallion – the occasion is commemorated by an equestrian **statue of Henri IV**. The arches are decorated with humorous and grotesque figures of street dentists, pickpockets, loiterers and the like.

ÎLE ST-LOUIS

The smaller of the Seine's two islands, Île St-Louis, 4e (Map 6) is just downstream from the Île de la Cité. Until the early 17th century it was actually two uninhabited islands – sometimes used for duels – when a building contractor and two financiers worked out a deal with Louis XIII to create one island out of the two and build two stone bridges to the mainland. In exchange they would receive the right to subdivide and sell the newly created real estate. This they did with great success, and between 1613 and 1664 the entire island was covered with fine new houses.

Today, the island's 17th-century, greystone houses and the small-town shops that line the streets and quays impart a village-like, provincial calm. The central thoroughfare, rue St-Louis en l'Île, is home to a number of upmarket art galleries, boutiques and tea rooms. The area around **Pont St-Louis**, the bridge linking the island with the Île de la Cité, and **Pont Louis Philippe**, the bridge to the Marais, is one of the most romantic spots in all of Paris.

JARDIN DES PLANTES

This picturesque area is due east of the Latin Quarter.

Jardin des Plantes

Paris' botanical garden (Map 5, ☎ 01 40 79 30 00, metro Gare d'Austerlitz or Jussieu), 57 rue Cuvier (5e), was founded in 1626 as a medicinal herb garden for Louis XIII. The first greenhouse, constructed in 1714, was home to an African coffee tree whose offspring helped establish coffee production in South America. The gardens are open daily from 7.30 am until some time between 5.30 and 8 pm, depending on the season.

Zoo The northern section of the Jardin des Plantes is taken up by the **Ménagerie du Jardin des Plantes** (☎ 01 40 79 37 94, metro Jussieu), a medium-sized zoo founded in 1794. During the Prussian siege of Paris in 1870, most of the animals were eaten by starving Parisians. The Microzoo, open to children older than 10, features microscopic animals. It opens 9 am to 6 pm Monday to Saturday, and to 6.30 pm on Sunday April to September, and to 5 pm the rest of the year. Admission costs 30FF (students, seniors and children six to 15 20FF).

Musée National d'Histoire Naturelle
The National Museum of Natural History (Map 5, ☎ 01 40 79 30 00, metro Censier Daubenton or Gare d'Austerlitz), created by a decree of the Convention in 1793, was the site of important scientific research in the 19th century. It is contained in four buildings along the southern edge of the Jardin des Plantes.

The five-level **Grande Galerie de l'Évolution**, 36 rue Geoffroy St-Hilaire (5e), has some imaginative exhibits on evolution and humankind's effect on the world's ecosystem; the African parade, as Noah would have lined up his cargo for the ark, is quite something. The Salle des Espèces Menacées et des Espèces Disparues, on level 2, displays extremely rare specimens of endangered and extinct species of animals. The Salles de Découverte (Discovery Rooms) house interactive exhibits for kids. They are all open from 10 am to 6 pm (to 10 pm on Thursday) Wednesday to Monday. Entry costs 40FF (students, seniors and those aged 18 to 26 30FF).

The **Galerie de Minéralogie, de Géologie et de Paléobotanie**, 36 rue Geoffroy St-Hilaire (5e), which covers mineralogy, geology and palaeobotany (fossilised plants), has an amazing exhibit of giant natural crystals and a basement display of precious objects made from minerals. It opens 10 am to 5 pm Wednesday to Monday (to 6 pm at the weekend from April to October) and costs 30/20FF.

The **Galerie d'Entomologie**, in a modern building opposite the park at 45 rue Buffon (5e), focuses on insects. It opens 1 to 5 pm on weekdays and costs 15/10FF. The **Galerie d'Anatomie Comparée et de Paléontologie**, 2 rue Buffon (5e), has displays on comparative anatomy and palaeontology. It opens the same hours and charges the same admission as the Galerie de Minéralogie.

Mosquée de Paris
Paris' central mosque (Map 5, ☎ 01 45 35 97 33, metro place Monge), place du Puits de l'Ermite (5e), was built in 1926 in the ornate Moorish style favoured at the time. Guided tours take place from 9 am to noon and 2 to 6 pm Saturday to Thursday and cost 15FF (students and children 10FF). Visitors must remove their shoes at the entrance to the prayer hall and be modestly dressed. The complex includes a North African-style *salon de thé* (tearoom), a restaurant (☎ 01 43 31 38 20) with excellent couscous and *tajines* (a meat and vegetable stew cooked in a domed earthenware pot) costing 60FF to 110FF, and a **hammam** (Turkish bath; ☎ 01 43 31 18 14), both of whose entrances are at 39 rue Geoffroy St-Hilaire. The hammam (85FF) opens to men from 2 to 9 pm on Tuesday and from 10 am to 9 pm on Sunday only; on other days (open 10 am to 9 pm) it is reserved for women.

LATIN QUARTER
Known as the Quartier Latin because all communication between students and professors here took place in Latin until the Revolution, this area has been the centre of Parisian higher education since the Middle Ages. It still has a large population of students and academics affiliated with the Sorbonne (now part of the University of Paris system), the Collège de France, the École Normale Supérieure and other institutions of higher learning, but it has become increasingly touristy in recent years.

Musée National du Moyen Âge
The National Museum of the Middle Ages (Map 6, ☎ 01 53 73 78 00, metro Cluny-La Sorbonne or St-Michel), also known as the Musée de Cluny, is housed in two structures:

the frigidarium and other remains of Gallo-Roman baths dating from around AD 200, and the late 15th-century Hôtel de Cluny, considered the finest example of medieval civil architecture in Paris. The spectacular displays include statuary, illuminated manuscripts, arms, furnishings and objects made of gold, ivory and enamel. A sublime series of late 15th-century tapestries from the southern Netherlands known as *La Dame à la Licorne* (The Lady with the Unicorn) is hung in a round room on the 1st floor. A medieval garden and wood has recently been laid out to the north and east of the museum.

The museum, whose entrance is at 6 place Paul Painlevé (5e), opens 9.15 am to 5.45 pm Wednesday to Monday. Admission costs 38FF (aged 18 to 25 and everyone on Sunday 28FF, free for under 18s and for everyone on the first Sunday of the month).

Sorbonne

Paris' most renowned university, the Sorbonne (Map 5) was founded in 1253 by Robert de Sorbon, confessor of King Louis IX, as a college for 16 impoverished theology students. Closed in 1792 by the Revolutionary government after operating for centuries as France's premier theological school, it reopened under Napoleon. Today, its main complex (bounded by rue de la Sorbonne, rue des Écoles, rue St-Jacques and rue Cujas) and other buildings in the vicinity, house most of the 13 autonomous universities that were created when the University of Paris was reorganised following the violent student protests of 1968.

Place de la Sorbonne links blvd St-Michel and **Chapelle de la Sorbonne** (Map 5), the university's gold-domed church built between 1635 and 1642.

Panthéon

The domed landmark now known as the Panthéon (Map 5, ☎ 01 44 32 18 00, metro Luxembourg), place du Panthéon (5e), was commissioned around 1750 as an abbey church, but because of financial problems wasn't completed until 1789, not a good year for churches to open in France. Two

years later, the Constituent Assembly converted it into a secular mausoleum for the *grands hommes de l'époque de la liberté française* (great men of the era of French liberty), removing all Christian symbols and references. The Panthéon's ornate marble interior is gloomy in the extreme and, while renovations to the nave have been completed, the upper levels remain closed. Permanent residents of the crypt include Voltaire, Louis Braille, Jean-Jacques Rousseau, Victor Hugo, Émile Zola, Jean Moulin and Nobel Prize-winner Marie Curie, who was reburied here (along with her husband, Pierre) in 1995.

The Panthéon opens 9.30 am to 6.30 pm daily from April to September, 10 am to 6.15 pm the rest of the year. Admission costs 35FF (aged 12 to 25 23FF, free for under 12s).

ST-GERMAIN & LUXEMBOURG

Centuries ago, Église St-Germain des Prés and its affiliated abbey owned most of today's 6e and 7e arrondissements. The neighbourhood around the church began to get built up in the late 1600s, and these days – under the name St-Germain des Prés – it is celebrated for its 19th-century charm. Cafes such as Les Deux Magots and Café de Flore (see St-Germain & Odéon under Pubs, Bars & Cafes in the Entertainment section later in this chapter) were favourite hang-outs of post-war Left Bank intellectuals, and are the places where existentialism was born. Indeed, in the spring of 2000 place St-Germain des Prés, the little square in front of the church and facing Les Deux Magots, was named place Sartre-Beauvoir.

Église St-Germain des Prés

The Romanesque-style Church of St-Germanus of the Fields (Map 6, metro St-Germain des Prés), the oldest (though hardly the most interesting) church in Paris, was built in the 11th century on the site of a 6th-century abbey. It has since been altered many times, but the **Chapelle de St-Symphorien** to the right as you enter was part of the original abbey and is the final resting place of St-Germanus (AD 496–576), the first bishop of Paris. The **bell tower** over the west entrance has changed little since AD 1000, apart from the addition of the spire in the 19th century.

The church opens from 8 am to 7 pm daily.

Institut de France

This august body was created in 1795 by bringing together five of France's academies of arts and sciences. The most famous of these is the **Académie Française**, founded in 1635, whose 40 members, known as the *Immortels*, or Immortals, are charged with the Herculean task of safeguarding the purity of the French language.

The domed building housing the Institut de France (Map 6, ☎ 01 44 41 44 41, metro Mabillon or Louvre-Rivoli), a masterpiece of French neoclassical architecture from the mid-17th century, is at 23 quai de Conti (6e), across the Seine from the eastern end of the Louvre.

The only part of the complex that is generally open to the public is the **Bibliothèque Mazarine** (Mazarine Library; ☎ 01 44 41 44 06), 25 quai de Conti (6e), founded in 1643 and the oldest public library in France. You can visit the bust-lined, late-17th-century reading room or consult the library's collection of 500,000 items from 10 am to 6 pm weekdays (closed during the first half of August). A two-day entry pass is free, but you must leave your ID at the office on the left-hand side of the entryway. Annual membership to borrow books costs 100FF or 50FF for 10 visits.

Musée de la Monnaie

The Museum of Coins and Medals (Map 6, ☎ 01 40 46 55 30, metro Pont Neuf), 11 quai de Conti (6e), traces the history of French coinage from antiquity to the present and, along with coins and medals, includes presses and other minting equipment. It opens 11 am to 5.30 pm Tuesday to Friday, from noon to 5.30 pm at the weekend. Admission costs 20FF (students and seniors 15FF, free for under 16s and for everyone on Sunday).

The Hôtel des Monnaies, which houses the museum, became a royal mint during the 18th century and is still used by the Ministry of Finance to produce commemorative medals. Except in August, French-language tours of the mint's workshops (☎ 01 40 46 55 35) leave at 2.15 pm on Wednesday and Friday (20FF).

Jardin du Luxembourg

When the weather is warm Parisians of all ages flock to the formal terraces and chestnut groves of the 23-hectare Luxembourg Gardens (Map 5, metro Luxembourg) to read, relax and sunbathe. They open 7 am to 9.30 pm in summer and from 8 am to sunset in winter.

Palais du Luxembourg Luxembourg Palace (Map 5), at the northern end of the Jardin du Luxembourg along rue de Vaugirard (5e) was built for Marie de Médicis (queen of France from 1600 to 1610) to assuage her longing for the Palazzo Pitti in Florence, where she spent her childhood. Just east of the palace is the Italianate **Fontaine des Médicis**, a long, ornate goldfish pond built around 1630. The palace has housed the Sénat (Senate), the upper house of the French parliament, since 1958. There are free tours of the interior (☎ 01 44 61 21 69 for reservations) at 10 am on the first Sunday of each month, but you must book by the preceding Wednesday.

Musée du Luxembourg The Luxembourg Museum (Map 5, ☎ 01 42 34 25 94, metro Luxembourg or St-Sulpice), 19 rue de Vaugirard (6e), opened at the end of the 19th century in the *orangerie* of the Palais du Luxembourg and was dedicated to presenting the work of artists still living; for many years it housed the work of the impressionists. It now hosts temporary art exhibitions, often from different regions of France. It opens 10 am to 7 pm daily; admission depends on the exhibit, but is sometimes free.

MONTPARNASSE

After WWI, writers, poets and artists of the avant-garde abandoned Montmartre and crossed the Seine, shifting the centre of artistic ferment to the area around blvd du Montparnasse. Chagall, Modigliani, Léger, Soutine, Miró, Picasso, Kandinsky, Stravinsky, Hemingway, Pound, Henry Miller and Cocteau, as well as such political exiles as Lenin and Trotsky, all used to hang out in the cafes and brasseries for which the quarter became famous. Montparnasse remained a creative centre of Paris until the mid-1930s.

Although the trendy Latin Quarter crowd considers the area hopelessly nondescript, blvd du Montparnasse (on the southern border of the 6e) and its many fashionable restaurants, cafes and cinemas attract large numbers of people in the evening.

Tour Montparnasse

The 209m-high Montparnasse Tower (Map 4, ☎ 01 45 38 52 56, metro Montparnasse Bienvenüe), 33 ave du Maine (15e), built in 1974 of steel and smoked glass, affords spectacular views of the city. The lift to the 56th-floor indoor observatory, with shops, an exhibition and a video about Paris, costs 40FF (students and seniors 35FF, under 14s 27FF). If you want to combine the lift trip with a hike up the stairs to the 59th-floor **open-air terrace**, the cost is 48/40/32FF. The tower opens 9.30 am to 11.30 pm daily from April to September, to 10.30 pm Sunday to Thursday and 11 pm Friday and Saturday and holidays during the rest of the year.

Cimetière du Montparnasse

Montparnasse Cemetery (Map 4, ☎ 01 44 10 86 50, metro Edgar Quinet or Raspail), accessible from blvd Edgar Quinet and from rue Froidevaux (14e), was opened in 1824. It contains the tombs of such illustrious personages as Charles Baudelaire, Guy de Maupassant, Samuel Beckett, François Rude, Frédéric August Bartholdi, Constantin Brancusi, Chaim Soutine, Man Ray, Camille Saint-Saëns, André Citroën, Alfred Dreyfus, Jean Seberg, Simone de Beauvoir and Jean-Paul Sartre. If Père Lachaise has Jim Morrison, Montparnasse has Serge Gainsbourg (division 1); fans leave metro tickets with their names inscribed on them on the late crooner's tombstone. Maps

showing the location of the tombs of the dead and famous are posted near the entrances and are available free from the conservation office at 3 blvd Edgar Quinet. The cemetery opens 8 am to 6 pm daily from April to October (to 5.30 pm the rest of the year). Admission is free.

FAUBOURG ST-GERMAIN

Faubourg St-Germain (7e), the area between the Musée d'Orsay and, 1km to the south, rue de Babylone, was Paris' most fashionable neighbourhood in the 18th century. Some of the most interesting mansions, many of which now serve as embassies, cultural centres and government ministries, are along three streets running east to west: rue de Lille, rue de Grenelle and rue de Varenne. The **Hôtel Matignon** (Map 4), the official residence of France's prime minister since the start of the Fifth Republic (1958), is at 57 rue de Varenne, 7e. The area also contains several major museums and monuments.

Musée d'Orsay

The Musée d'Orsay (Map 4, ☎ 01 40 49 48 48 or, for a recording, ☎ 01 45 49 11 11, metro Musée d'Orsay or Solférino), facing the Seine at 1 rue de la Légion d'Honneur (7e), displays France's national collection of paintings, sculptures, objets d'art and other works produced between 1848 and 1914, including the fruits of the impressionist, postimpressionist and Art Nouveau movements. It is spectacularly housed in a former train station built in 1900 and opened as a museum in 1986.

Many visitors head straight to the upper level (lit by a skylight) to see the famous **impressionist paintings** by Monet, Renoir, Pissarro, Sisley, Degas, Manet, Van Gogh and Cézanne, and the **postimpressionist works** by Seurat, Matisse and so on, but there's also a great deal to see on the ground floor, including some early works by Manet, Monet, Renoir and Pissarro. The middle level has some magnificent **Art Nouveau rooms**. The museums Web site is www.musee-orsay.fr. By Minitel key in 3615 ORSAY or 3615 CULTURE.

Opening Hours & Tickets The Musée d'Orsay opens 10 am (9 am on Sunday) to 6 pm (to 9.45 pm on Thursday) Tuesday to Sunday from late September to late June. In summer the museum opens at 9 am. Admission to the permanent exhibits cost 40FF (those aged 18 to 25, over 60 and everyone on Sunday 30FF, free for under 18s and everyone on the first Sunday of the month); tickets are valid all day so you can leave and re-enter the museum as you please. There are separate fees for rotating exhibitions.

Guided Tours General English-language tours begin at 11.30 am Tuesday to Saturday. There's an additional one at 7 pm on Thursday, and one focusing on the impressionists at 2.30 pm on Tuesday. Tickets (40FF in addition to the entry fee, no discounts) are sold at the information desk to the left as you enter the building. Audioguides (1½-hour cassette tours), available in six languages, point out 80 major works – many of which had a revolutionary impact on 19th-century art – that the uninitiated might easily miss. They can be rented for 30FF (no discounts) on the right just past the ticket windows. The excellent full-colour *Guide to the Musée d'Orsay* (95FF) is available in English.

Assemblée Nationale

The National Assembly, the lower house of the French parliament, meets in the 18th-century Palais Bourbon (Map 4, ☎ 01 40 63 60 00, metro Assemblée Nationale) at 33 quai d'Orsay (7e). There are free guided tours in French (☎ 01 46 36 41 13) at 2.15 pm every Saturday. Admission is on a first-come, first-served basis (each tour has only 30 places), so join the queue early. A national ID card or passport is required.

The Second Empire-style **Ministère des Affaires Étrangères** (Ministry of Foreign Affairs; Map 4), built between 1845 and 1855 and popularly referred to as the 'Quai d'Orsay', is next door at 37 quai d'Orsay.

Musée Rodin

The Musée Auguste Rodin (Map 4, ☎ 01 44 18 61 10, metro Varenne), 77 rue de Varenne (7e), often listed by visitors as their favourite Paris museum, is one of the most relaxing spots in the whole city. Rooms on two floors of this 18th-century residence display extraordinarily vital bronze and marble sculptures by Rodin and Camille Claudel, including casts of some of Rodin's most celebrated works: *The Hand of God*, *The Burghers of Calais*, *Cathedral*, that crowd-pleaser *The Thinker* and – we have tears in our eyes as we remember it – the incomparable *The Kiss*. There's a delightful rear **garden** filled with sculptures and shady trees.

The Musée Rodin opens 9.30 am to 5.45 pm daily from April to September (to 4.45 pm the rest of the year). Admission costs 28FF (aged 18 to 25, over 60 and for everyone on Sunday 18FF, free for under 18s and for all on the first Sunday of each month). Visiting just the garden, which closes at 5 pm, costs 5FF.

Hôtel des Invalides

The Hôtel des Invalides, 7e (Map 4, metro Varenne or La Tour Maubourg), was built in the 1670s by Louis XIV to provide housing for 4000 *invalides* (disabled war veterans). On 14 July 1789, a mob forced its way into the building and, after fierce fighting, seized 28,000 rifles before heading on to the prison at Bastille. The 500m-long **Esplanade des Invalides** (Map 4, metro Invalides), which stretches from the main building north to the Seine, was laid out between 1704 and 1720.

The **Église du Dôme** (Map 4, metro Varenne or La Tour Maubourg), with its sparkling dome, was built between 1677 and 1735 and is considered one of the finest religious edifices erected under Louis XIV. The church's career as a mausoleum for military leaders began in 1800, and in 1861 it received the remains of Napoleon, encased in six coffins that fit into one another like a Russian *matrushka* doll. The buildings on either side of the **Cour d'Honneur** (Map 4), the main courtyard, house the **Musée de l'Armée** (☎ 01 44 42 37 72), 129 rue de Grenelle (7e), a huge military museum. The Musée de l'Armée and the very extravagant **Tombeau de Napoléon** (Napoleon's Tomb), inside the church, are open from 10 am to 6 pm daily from April to September (to 5 pm the rest of the year). Admission costs 38FF (students and seniors 28FF, free for children under 12).

Musée des Égouts de Paris

The Paris Sewers Museum (Map 4, ☎ 01 47 05 10 29, metro Pont de l'Alma or Alma-Marceau) is a working museum whose entrance – a rectangular maintenance hole toped with a kiosk – is across the street from 93 quai d'Orsay (7e).

Raw sewage flows beneath your feet as you walk through 480m of odoriferous tunnels, passing artefacts illustrating the development of Paris' waste-water disposal system. The sewers are open from 11 am to 6 pm Saturday to Wednesday from May to September (to 5 pm the rest of the year) – except, God forbid, when rain threatens to flood the tunnels. Admission costs 25FF (students, seniors and children 20FF, free for children under five).

EIFFEL TOWER AREA

Paris' most prominent and recognisable landmark, the Eiffel Tower, is surrounded by open areas on both banks of the Seine, which take in both the 7e and 16e arrondissements. There are several outstanding museums in this part of the Right Bank.

Eiffel Tower

The Tour Eiffel (Map 4, ☎ 01 44 11 23 23, metro Champ de Mars-Tour Eiffel or Trocadéro) faced massive opposition from Paris' artistic and literary elite when it was built for the 1889 Exposition Universelle (World Fair), marking the centenary of the Revolution. It was almost torn down in 1909 but was spared for purely practical reasons: it proved an ideal platform for the transmitting antennas needed for the new science of radiotelegraphy. It was the world's tallest structure until the Chrysler building in New York was completed in 1930.

The Eiffel Tower, named after its designer, Gustave Eiffel, is 320m high, including the television antenna at the very tip. This figure can vary by as much as 15cm, however, as the tower's 7000 tonnes of iron, held together by 2.5 million rivets, expand in warm weather and contract when it's cold.

When you're done peering upwards through the girders, you can choose to visit any of the three levels open to the public. The lift at the west and north pillars, which follows a curved trajectory, costs 22FF for the 1st platform (57m above the ground), 44FF for the 2nd (115m) and 62FF for the 3rd (276m). Children aged four to 12 pay 13/23/32FF respectively; there are no youth or student discounts. You can avoid the lift queues by using the stairs and the escalator in the south pillar to the 1st and 2nd platforms for 18FF.

The tower lifts operate from 9.30 am to 11 pm (9 am till midnight from mid-June to August) daily; the escalators run from 9.30 am to 6.30 pm (to 9 pm May to June, 11 pm July and August).

Champ de Mars

Running south-east from the Eiffel Tower, the grassy 'Field of Mars' (Mars was the Roman god of war) was originally a parade ground for the cadets of the 18th-century **École Militaire** (Military Academy, Map 4), the vast, French classical-style building at the south-eastern end of the park, which counts Napoleon among its graduates.

Jardins du Trocadéro

The Trocadéro Gardens (Map 4, metro Trocadéro), whose fountains and statue garden are grandly illuminated at night, are across Pont d'Iéna from the Eiffel Tower in the posh 16e arrondissement. They are named after the Trocadéro, a Spanish stronghold near Cádiz captured by the French in 1823.

Palais de Chaillot

The two curved, colonnaded wings of the Palais de Chaillot, 16e (Map 4, metro Trocadéro), built for the 1937 World Exhibition here, and the terrace in between them, afford an exceptional panorama of the Jardins du Trocadéro, the Seine and the Eiffel Tower.

This vast complex houses a couple of interesting museums. The **Musée de l'Homme** (Museum of Mankind; ☎ 01 44 05 72 72), 17 place du Trocadéro (16e), contains anthropological and ethnographic exhibits from Africa, Asia, Europe, the Arctic, the Pacific and the Americas. It opens 9.45 am to 5.15 pm Wednesday to Monday; admission costs 30FF (concessions 20FF).

The **Musée de la Marine** (Maritime Museum; ☎ 01 53 65 69 69), known for its beautiful model ships, opens 10 am to 5.45 pm Wednesday to Monday. Admission costs 38FF (concessions 28FF).

At the far eastern tip of the Palais de Chaillot is the main branch of the **Cinémathèque Française** (see Cinema in the Entertainment section later in this chapter for details).

Musée Guimet

The Guimet Museum (Map 2, ☎ 01 47 23 88 11, metro Iéna), 6 place d'Iéna (16e), midway between the Eiffel Tower and the Arc de Triomphe, is Paris' foremost repository for Asian art and has sculptures, paintings, objets d'art and religious articles from Afghanistan, India, Nepal, Pakistan, Tibet, Cambodia, China, Japan and Korea. However, until massive renovations are completed at the end of 2000, part of the collection is housed at the **Musée du Panthéon Bouddhique** (Buddhist Pantheon Museum; Map 2, ☎ 01 40 73 88 11, metro Iéna), the Guimet annexe a short distance to the north at 19 ave d'Iéna (16e). It has Chinese and Japanese Buddhist paintings and sculptures brought to Paris in 1876 by collector Émile Guimet, and a wonderful Japanese garden. It opens 10.15 am to 1 pm and 2.30 to 6 pm Wednesday to Monday. Admission costs 16FF (students, seniors, those aged 18 to 25 and everyone on Sunday 12FF, free for under 18s).

Princess Diana Memorial

East of the two museums is place de l'Alma (Map 2, metro Alma-Marceau), an insignificant square that would go unnoticed by most travellers if not for the car accident that occurred in the underpass running parallel to the Seine on 31 August 1997, killing Diana, Princess of Wales, her companion, Dodi Fayed, and their chauffeur, Henri Paul. The only reminder of the tragedy surrounds the bronze **Flame of Liberty** (Map 2, metro Alma-Marceau), a replica of the one atop the torch of New York's Statue of Liberty that was placed here by American firms based in Paris in 1987 on the centenary of the *International Herald Tribune* newspaper as a symbol of friendship between France and the USA. It has become something of a memorial to Diana and is decorated with flowers, personal notes and graffiti.

PLACE DE LA CONCORDE AREA

The cobblestone expanses of place de la Concorde (8e) are sandwiched between the Jardin des Tuileries and the parks at the eastern end of ave des Champs-Élysées.

Place de la Concorde

Place de la Concorde (Map 2, metro Concorde) was laid out between 1755 and 1775. The 3300-year-old pink granite **obelisk** in the middle was given to France in 1831 by Muhammad Ali, viceroy and pasha of Egypt. Weighing 230 tonnes and towering 23m over the cobblestones, it once stood in the Temple of Ramses at Thebes (modern-day Luxor). The female statues adorning the four corners of the square represent France's eight largest cities.

In 1793, Louis XVI's head was lopped off by a guillotine set up in the north-west corner of the square, near the statue representing the city of Brest. During the next two years, another guillotine – this one near the entrance to the Jardin des Tuileries – was used to behead some 1343 more people, including Marie-Antoinette and, six months later, the Revolutionary leaders Danton and Robespierre. The square was given its present name after the Reign of Terror, in the hope that it would be a place of peace and harmony.

The two imposing buildings on the north side of place de la Concorde are the **Hôtel de la Marine** (Map 2), headquarters of the French navy, and the **Hôtel de Crillon**

(Map 2), one of Paris' most exclusive hotels (see the Places to Stay – Deluxe section).

Église de la Madeleine

The neoclassical Church of St Mary Magdalen (Map 2, metro Madeleine), known simply as La Madeleine, is 350m north of place de la Concorde along rue Royale. Built in the style of a Greek temple, it was consecrated in 1842 after almost a century of design changes and construction delays. It is surrounded by 52 Corinthian columns, each standing 20m tall. The marble and gilt interior, topped by three skylit cupolas, is open from 7.45 to 11 am and 12.25 to 6.30 pm Monday to Saturday, and 7.30 am to 1 or 1.30 pm and 3.30 to 7 pm on Sunday. You can hear the massive organ being played during Mass at 6 pm on Saturday and at 11 am, 12.30 and 6 pm on Sunday.

CHAMPS-ÉLYSÉES AREA

Ave des Champs-Élysées, 8e (Map 2), whose name means Elysian Fields (Elysium was where happy souls dwelt after death, according to Greek mythology), links place de la Concorde with the Arc de Triomphe. The avenue has symbolised the style and *joie de vivre* of Paris since the mid-19th century.

Ave des Champs-Élysées

Popular with the aristocracy of the mid-19th century as a stage on which to parade their wealth, the 2km-long ave des Champs-Élysées was, after WWII, taken over by airline offices, cinemas, car showrooms and fast-food restaurants. In recent years, however, the municipality's US$48 million investment to regain some of the 72m-wide avenue's former sparkle and prestige has paid off and the Champs-Élysées is a more popular destination than ever. In late July it plays host to the final stage of the Tour de France bicycle race (see Cycling in the Spectator Sports section later in this chapter).

Rue du Faubourg St-Honoré

Rue du Faubourg St-Honoré (8e), the western extension of rue St-Honoré some 400m

north of the Champs-Élysées, links rue Royale (metro Concorde) with place des Ternes (metro Ternes). It is home to some of Paris' most renowned couture houses, jewellers and antique shops.

The most remarkable of the avenue's 18th-century mansions is the **Palais de l'Élysée** (Map 2), at the intersection of rue du Faubourg St-Honoré and ave de Marigny (8e), which is now the official residence of the French president.

Musée du Petit Palais

The Little Palace (Map 2, ☎ 01 42 65 12 73, metro Champs-Élysées Clemenceau), ave Winston Churchill (8e), built for the 1900 Exposition Universelle, houses the **Musée des Beaux-Arts de la Ville de Paris**, the Paris municipality's Museum of Fine Arts, with medieval and Renaissance objets d'art (including porcelain and clocks), tapestries, drawings and 19th-century French painting and sculpture. It opens 10 am to 5.40 pm (to 8 pm on Thursday) Tuesday to Sunday and admission costs 30FF (reduced price 20FF), but it is expected to close for refurbishment in late 2000.

Grand Palais

West of the Petit Palais, the Great Palace (Map 2, ☎ 01 44 13 17 17, metro Champs-Élysées Clemenceau), 3 ave du Général Eisenhower (8e), houses the **Galeries Nationales du Grand Palais**, which hosts special exhibitions lasting three or four months. Also erected for the 1900 Exposition Universelle, the Grand Palais has an iron frame and an Art Nouveau-style glass roof. It is usually open from 10 am to 8 pm (to 10 pm on Wednesday) from Wednesday to Monday. Admission cost varies depending on the exhibition.

Palais de la Découverte

The Palace of Discovery (Map 2, ☎ 01 56 43 20 21, metro Champs-Élysées Clemenceau), ave Franklin D Roosevelt (8e), is a fascinating science museum with interactive exhibits on astronomy, biology and medicine, chemistry, mathematics and computer science, physics and earth sciences. It

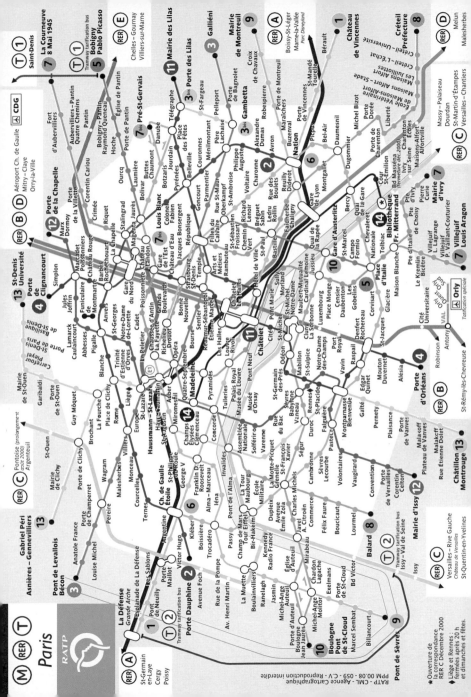

MAP 1

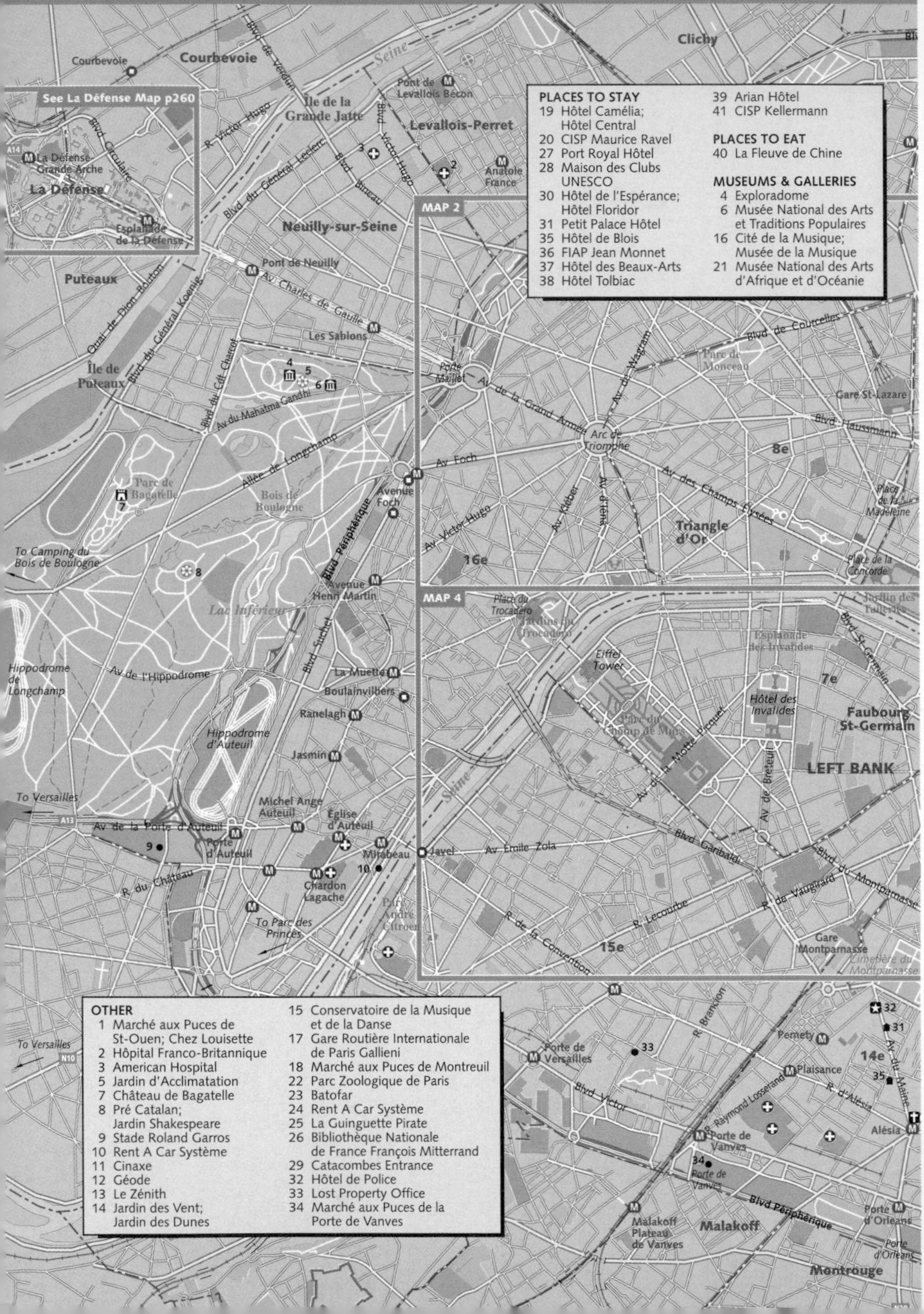

PLACES TO STAY
19 Hôtel Camélia; Hôtel Central
20 CISP Maurice Ravel
27 Port Royal Hôtel
28 Maison des Clubs UNESCO
30 Hôtel de l'Espérance; Hôtel Floridor
31 Petit Palace Hôtel
35 Hôtel de Blois
36 FIAP Jean Monnet
37 Hôtel des Beaux-Arts
38 Hôtel Tolbiac
39 Arian Hôtel
41 CISP Kellermann
PLACES TO EAT
40 La Fleuve de Chine
MUSEUMS & GALLERIES
4 Exploradome
6 Musée National des Arts et Traditions Populaires
16 Cité de la Musique; Musée de la Musique
21 Musée National des Arts d'Afrique et d'Océanie
OTHER
1 Marché aux Puces de St-Ouen; Chez Louisette
2 Hôpital Franco-Britannique
3 American Hospital
5 Jardin d'Acclimatation
7 Château de Bagatelle
8 Pré Catalan; Jardin Shakespeare
9 Stade Roland Garros
10 Rent A Car Système
11 Cinaxe
12 Géode
13 Le Zénith
14 Jardin des Vent; Jardin des Dunes
15 Conservatoire de la Musique et de la Danse
17 Gare Routière Internationale de Paris Gallieni
18 Marché aux Puces de Montreuil
22 Parc Zoologique de Paris
23 Batofar
24 Rent A Car Système
25 La Guinguette Pirate
26 Bibliothèque Nationale de France François Mitterrand
29 Catacombes Entrance
32 Hôtel de Police
33 Lost Property Office
34 Marché aux Puces de la Porte de Vanves
See La Défense Map p260
La Défense
La Défense Grande Arche
Esplanade de la Défense
Courbevoie
Clichy
Seine
Pont de Levallois Bécon
Île de la Grande Jatte
Levallois-Perret
Anatole France
Neuilly-sur-Seine
Pont de Neuilly
Puteaux
Île de Puteaux
Les Sablons
Porte Maillot
Av Charles de Gaulle
Blvd de Courcelles
Parc de Monceau
Gare St-Lazare
Av de la Grand Armée
Arc de Triomphe
Blvd Haussmann
8e
Av Foch
Avenue Foch
Allée de Longchamp
Parc de Bagatelle
Bois de Boulogne
Av Victor Hugo
Av des Champs Élysées
Triangle d'Or
16e
Place de la Madeleine
Place de la Concorde
To Camping du Bois de Boulogne
Lac Inférieur
Avenue Henri Martin
Blvd Périphérique
MAP 2
MAP 4
Place du Trocadéro
Jardins du Trocadéro
Jardin des Tuileries
Esplanade des Invalides
Eiffel Tower
Parc du Champ de Mars
Hôtel des Invalides
7e
Faubourg St-Germain
LEFT BANK
Hippodrome de Longchamp
Av de l'Hippodrome
La Muette
Boulainvilliers
Ranelagh
Jasmin
Hippodrome d'Auteuil
To Versailles
Michel Ange Auteuil
Église d'Auteuil
Av de la Porte d'Auteuil
Porte d'Auteuil
Mirabeau
Javel
Av Émile Zola
Blvd Garibaldi
Blvd du Montparnasse
R de Vaugirard
R du Château
Chardon Lagache
Parc André Citroën
To Parc des Princes
R Lecourbe
R de la Convention
15e
Gare Montparnasse
Cimetière du Montparnasse
Porte de Versailles
Blvd Victor
Pernety
Plaisance
14e
R d'Alésia
Alésia
Porte de Vanves
Malakoff Plateau de Vanves
Malakoff
Porte d'Orléans
Montrouge

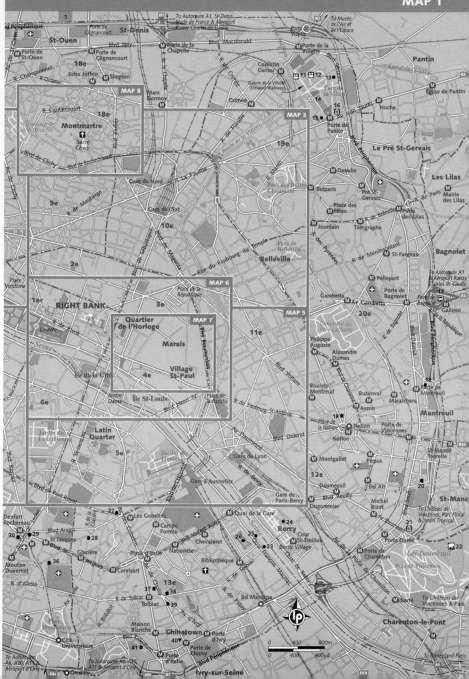

MAP 1

MAP 2

PLACES TO STAY
3 Résidence Cardinal
16 Atlantic Opéra Hôtel
17 Hôtel Britannia
37 Hôtel de Crillon
90 Hôtel Costes
93 Hôtel Ritz
99 Hôtel Brighton

PLACES TO EAT
1 Macis et Muscade
11 L'Étoile Verte
26 Fauchon
27 Hédiard
44 Monoprix Supermarket
49 Ladurée
54 Bistro Romain
78 Spoon, Food & Wine
89 L'Ardoise

MUSEUMS & GALLERIES
23 Palais Garnier; Bibliothèque-Musée de l'Opéra
59 Musée du Panthéon Bouddhique (Musée Guimet Annexe)
60 Musée Guimet
80 Palais de la Découverte
81 Grand Palais; Galeries Nationales du Grand Palais
82 Petit Palais; Musée des Beaux-Arts de la Ville de Paris
85 Jeu de Paume

OTHER
2 Pharmacie Européenne (24hrs)
4 ADA Car Rental
5 Banque de France
6 James Joyce Pub (Buses to Beauvais Airport)
7 Palais de Congrès de Paris
8 Fnac Étoile Store
9 Irish Embassy
10 Air France Buses
12 St Joseph's Church
13 American Express Office
14 Mariage Frères Tea Shop
15 Salle Pleyel
18 Fnac Department Store
19 Le Printemps Department Store (Men)
20 Le Printemps Department Store (Household Goods)
21 Le Printemps Department Store (Women)
22 Galeries Lafayette
24 Main American Express Office
25 La Maison du Miel
28 Kiosque Théâtre
29 Église de la Madeleine
30 UK Consulate
31 Guy Laroche
32 Comptoir Théâtral
33 Lolita Lempicka
34 Buddha Bar
35 Galerie Royale
36 Office de Change de Paris
38 US Embassy
39 Palais de l'Élysée
40 Théâtre Marigny
41 Christian Lacroix
42 Bureau de Change
43 Virgin Megastore
45 Montecristo Café
46 Pharmacie Les Champs (24 Hours)
47 Agence des Théâtres
48 Post Office
50 Hermès
51 Le Queen
52 Le Latina Café
53 Le Lido
55 Air France
56 Main Tourist Office
57 New Zealand Embassy
58 Rue Copernic Synagogue
60 American Cathedral in Paris
62 Givenchy
63 Liberty Flame; Princess Diana Memorial
64 US Consulate
65 Théâtre des Champs Élysées
66 Valentino

OTHER (continued)
67 Prada
68 Inès de la Fressange
69 Canadian Embassy
70 Nina Ricci
71 Christian Lacroix
72 Bateaux Mouches
73 Église Notre Dame de la Consolation
74 Armenian Church
75 Church of Scotland
76 Celine
77 Thierry Mugler
79 Chanel
83 Batobus Stop
84 Obelisk
86 Hôtel de la Marine
87 US Consulate
88 WH Smith Bookshop
91 Cour Vendôme
92 Cartier
94 Harry's New York Bar
95 Van Cleef & Arpels
96 Colonne Vendôme
97 Patek Philippe
98 Le Change de Paris
100 Cécile et Jeanne
101 Colette
102 Il Pour l'Homme
103 Paris Vision

MAP 3

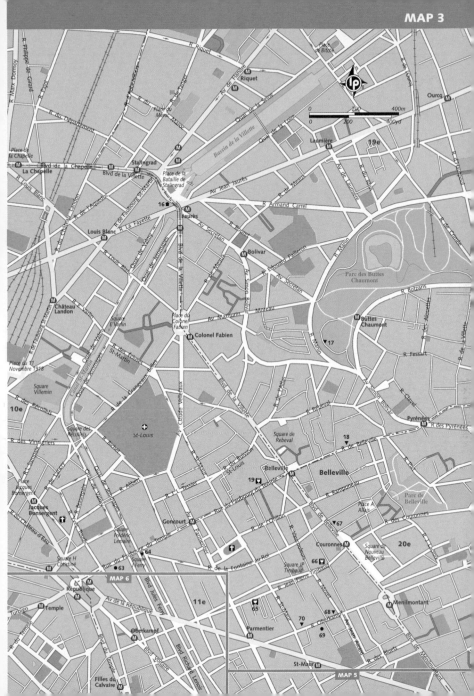

MAP 4

MAP 2

MAP 2

Av Georges Mandel
Trocadéro
Place du Trocadéro et du 11 Novembre
Cimetière de Passy
Av d'Eylau
Av d'Iéna
Iéna
Av d'Iéna
Alma-Marceau
Place de l'Alma
Rue de la Pompe
Av Decamps

Pont de l'Alma
Pont de l'Alma
Place de la Résistance

Square Yorktown
Jardins du Trocadéro
Place de Varsovie
Quai Branly
Av de New York

R Nicolo
R Paul Doumer
R de la Tour
R Raynouard
R de Passy
Place de Passy
Place de Costa Rica
Pont d'Iéna
Eiffel Tower
Tour Eiffel
Champ de Mars
Parc du Champ de Mars
Av de la Bourdonnais
Av Élysée Reclus
Place du Général Gouraud
École Militaire

16e
Passy
Champ de Mars Tour Eiffel
Stade Émile Anthoine
Av Gustave Eiffel
Av Charles Floquet
Place Jacques Rueff
Av de Suffren

Pont de Bir Hakeim
Place de Bolivie
Av de Lamballe
Bir Hakeim
Blvd de Grenelle
Place A Sauvy
Place Dupleix
Place Joffre

Maison de Radio-France
Av du President Kennedy
Quai de Grenelle
R du Docteur Finlay
Place Dupleix
Dupleix
La Motte Picquet Grenelle

Seine
Pont de Grenelle
Square Béla Bartók
Place de Brazzaville
Daniel Stern
Blvd de Grenelle
Square Cambronne
Cambronne

33
Place de Versailles
Place Clément Ader
Square Pablo Casals
Square St-Charles
Commerce
Avenue Émile Zola
Place du Commerce
Commerce
Place Étienne Pernet
Félix Faure
Square St-Lambert
R Mademoiselle
R Léon Lhermitte
R Lecourbe
Place Adolphe Chérioux
Vaugirard

PLACES TO STAY
16 Hôtel Lenox St-Germain
35 Flatôtel International
37 Three Ducks Hostel
39 Aloha Hostel
44 Pension Ladagnous;
   Pension Les Marroniers
48 Pension Au Palais
   Gourmand
51 Hôtel des Académies
53 Citadines Aparthôtel
   Raspail Montparnasse
57 Celtic Hôtel
59 Hôtel Miramar
65 Hôtel de l'Espérance

PLACES TO EAT
24 Boulangerie Poilâne
49 Le Select
50 Hippopotamus
52 Le Caméléon
54 Le Dôme
55 La Coupole
56 Mustang Café
58 Crêperies
59 Food Market
63 Inno Supermarket

OTHER
1 Musée de l'Homme;
   Musée de la Marine
2 Palais de Chaillot
3 Cinémathèque Française
4 Bateaux Parisiens

5 American Library in Paris
6 Musée des Égouts
   de Paris (Entrance)
7 American Church
8 Aérogare des Invalides
9 Air France Buses
10 British Council
11 Ministère des Affaires Étrangères
12 Assemblée Nationale
   (Palais Bourbon)
13 Orangerie
14 Batobus Stop
15 Musée d'Orsay
17 Madeleine Gély
18 Sonia Rykiel (Men)
19 Sonia Rykiel (Women)
20 Celine
21 Kenzo
22 Yves Saint Laurent
23 Il Bisonte
25 Banque de France
26 Au Bon Marché
27 Hôtel Matignon
28 Musée Rodin
29 Église du Dôme
30 Église Saint Louis des Invalides
31 Musée de l'Armée
32 Australian Embassy
33 Maison de Radio France
34 Statue of Liberty Replica
36 Institut Parisien de Langue
   et de Civilisation Françaises
38 Église Saint Jean Baptiste
40 Carte de Séjour Office (Students)

41 UNESCO Annexe
42 UNESCO Building
43 Clothing & Shoe Shops
45 Alliance Française
46 Fnac Montparnasse Store
47 Église Notre Dame des Champs
60 Tour Montparnasse
62 Kiosque Théâtre
64 Air France Buses

MAP 4

1er

Cours Albert 1er — Cours la Reine

MAP 2

Tuileries

Pont des
Invalides

Pont
Alexandre III

Pont de la
Concorde

Jardin des Tuileries

13

Quai d'Orsay

Quai d'Orsay

Place de
Finlande

8
9
10
11   12

Invalides

R. de l'Université

Seine

Pont de
Solférino

Assemblée
Nationale

Quai Anatole France

14

Musée
d'Orsay

15

Pont
Royal

Quai Voltaire

Quai des

R. de Lille

Place du Près
Herriot

Place du
Palais Bourbon

R. de l'Université

Quai d'Orsay

7

R. St-Dominique

Esplanade
des Invalides

R. St-Dominique

Square S
Rousseau

Solférino

R. Las Cases

Bd St-Germain

R. de l'Université

R. de Verneuil

Quai Voltaire

Place Santiago
du Chili

Square Santiago
du Chili

Place des
Invalides

La Tour
Maubourg

R. de Grenelle

Square
d'Ajaccio

7e

Place des
Invalides

Varenne

31   Cour
d'Honneur

R. de Grenelle

R. du Bac

16

Hôtel
des
Invalides

30
29

28

R. de Varenne

Faubourg
St-Germain

Rue du
Bac

17

18

Ecole
Militaire

Jardin de
l'Intendant

27

19

Place de
l'Ecole
Militaire

Av de Tourville

Square
Chaise
Récamier

20
21

R. du Four

Place
Vauban

Lycée
Victor
Duruy

Square des
Missions
Étrangères

Esplanade du
Souvenir
Français

Place André
Tardieu

R. de Babylone

Jardin
Catherine
Labouré

26

R. de Sèvres

24
22

St-Sulpice

St François
Xavier

Square
Boucicaut

23

Square de
l'Abbé Esquerré

Laennec

25

Sèvres
Babylone

42

Vaneau

43 Rennes

Place de
Fontenoy

Duroc

Place L P
Fargue

6e

St Placide

45

Ségur

R. de Vaugirard

46

Sèvres
Lecourbe

Necker

Place
Camille
Claudel

Falguière

Blvd du Montparnasse

Montparnasse
Bienvenüe

Notre-Dame
des Champs

Place
A Blanc

44

41

Lycée
Buffon

Pasteur

Place et T
Trefouel

Place du 18 Juin 1940

47

48

49

Vavin

56

50

Volontaires

Montparnasse
Bienvenüe

61

60

Place
Bienvenüe

59

57

55

54

Place
Picasso

51
52
53

Square
Blomet

58

Edgar Quinet

Square Max
Hymans

62

63

Square
Gaston Bati

Square
Necker

Gare Montparnasse

Blvd Edgar Quinet

Raspail

Jardin de
l'Atlantique

64

14e

Cimetière du
Montparnasse

Place des
Cinq Martyrs du
Lycée Buffon

Gaîté

65

Rue du Commandant
René Mouchotte

MAP 6

MAP 5

MAP 5

PLACES TO STAY
3 Hôtel Familial
4 Hôtel de Savoie
5 Hôtel de France
6 Résidence Bastille
11 Hôtel des alliés
14 Hôtel Pax
15 Vix Hôtel
16 Hôtel Baudin
21 Auberge Internationale des Jeunes
22 Hôtel St-Amand
24 Maison Internationale des Jeunes
27 Citadines Apart'hôtel Bastille Nation
28 Blue Planet Hostel
37 Hôtel Au Royal Cardinal
38 Familia Hôtel
39 Hôtel Minerve
40 Centre International BVJ
   Paris-Quartier Latin
41 Hôtel St-Jacques
49 Hôtel Cluny Sorbonne
50 Grand Hôtel St-Michel
62 Hôtel de Médicis
65 Hôtel Gay Lussac
67 Hôtel des Grands Écoles
72 Résidence Monge
75 Hôtel St-Christophe
78 Young & Happy Hostel
82 Grand Hôtel du Progrès
90 Hôtel de l'Espérance

PLACES TO EAT
1 La Piragua
2 Lire Entre Le Vignes
8 Crêpes Show
9 Chez Paul
12 Le Square Trousseau
13 Monoprix Supermarket
18 Suds
19 Le Réservoir
20 À la Banane Ivoirienne
23 Café Cannelle
25 Les Amognes
31 L'Encrier
44 Indonesia
53 Perraudin
54 Tashi Delek
56 Food Shops; Fromagerie
57 Assas University Restaurant
63 Douce France
64 Tao
68 Shopi Supermarket
69 Le Petit Légume
73 Jardin des Pâtes
76 Ed l'Épicier Supermarket
77 Le Vigneron
79 Franprix Supermarket
80 Châtelet University Restaurant
81 Chez Léna et Mimille
85 Bullier University Restaurant;
   OTU Voyages
89 Rue Mouffetard Food Market
91 Founti Agadir

MUSEUMS & GALLERIES
45 Musée du Luxembourg
94 Grande Galerie de l'Évolution
95 Galerie de Minéralogie' de
   Géologie et de Paléobotanie
96 Galerie d'Entomologie
98 Galerie d'Anatomie Comparée
   et de Paléontologie

OTHER
7 Centre Gai et Lesbien
10 Sanz Sans
17 Boca Chica
26 Marché d'Aligre
29 Le Viaduc Café
30 La Maison du Cerf-Volant
32 China Club
33 Capitainerie; Europ' Yachting
34 Rollerland Paris
35 Ménagerie Entrance
36 Ménagerie du Jardin des Plantes
42 Chapelle de la Sorbonne
43 usit connect
47 Grand Bassin
47 Fontaine des Médicis
48 Café Orbital
51 Église St-Étienne du Mont
52 Panthéon
55 Café Oz
59 Nouvelles Frontières
59 usit connect
60 Forum Voyages
61 Laundrette
66 Laundrette
70 usit connect
71 Arènes de Lutèce
73 Laundrette
83 Fontaine de l'Observatoire
84 La Closerie des Lilas
86 Jadis et Gourmande
87 Église Notre Dame du Val de Grace
88 SOS Dentistes
92 Paris Vélo
93 Mosquée de Paris
99 Hospital Night Entrance
99 Cour d'Arrivée
100 La Pitié-Salpêtrière Hospital
101 Cour de Départ
102 Ministry of Finance
103 Palais Omnisports de Paris-Bercy

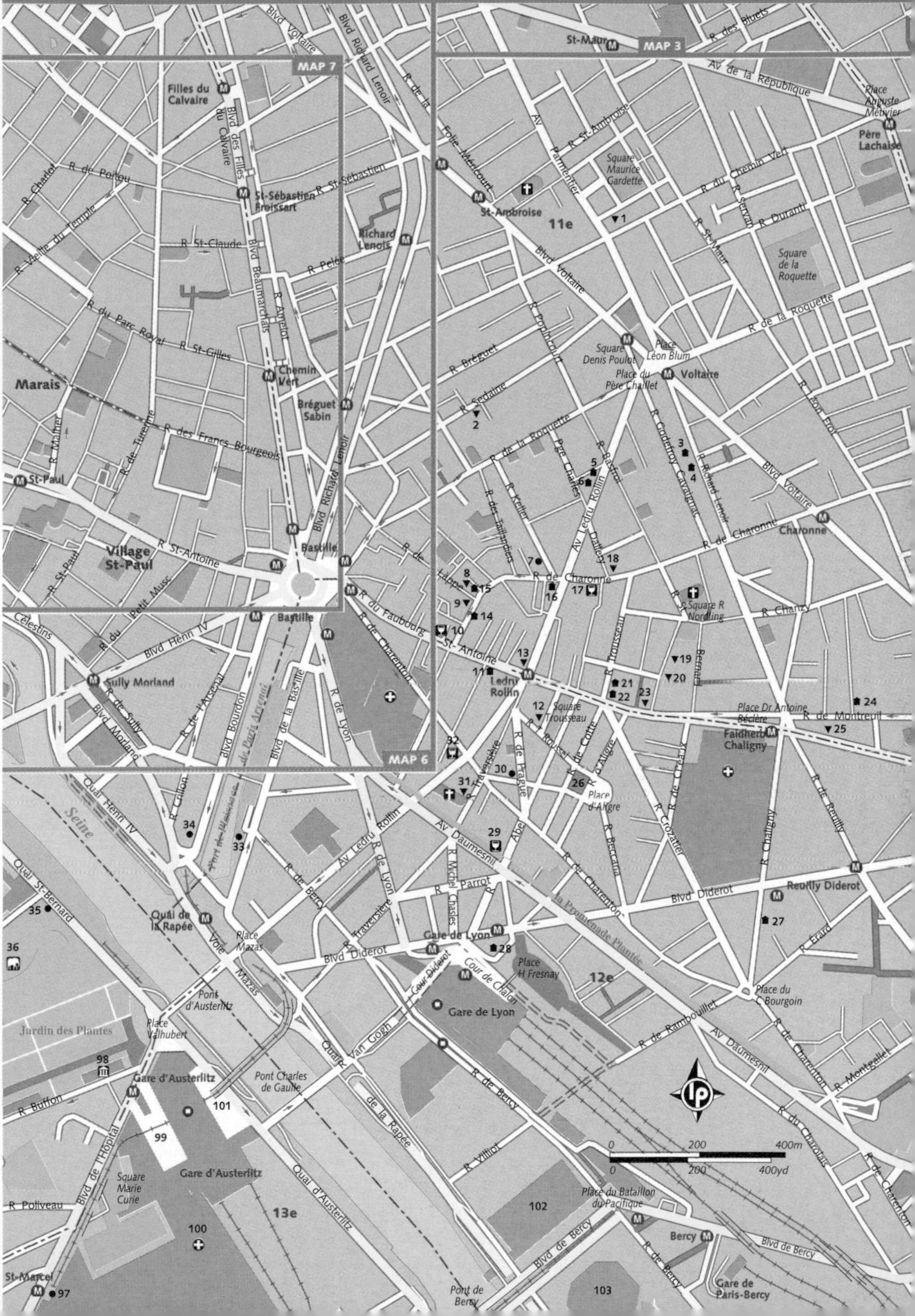

MAP 5

MAP 3

MAP 7

Filles du Calvaire

St-Sébastien Froissart

R. St-Sébastien

Richard Lenoir

Chemin Vert

Bréguet Sabin

Marais

Blvd Voltaire

St-Maur

Av de la République

Place Auguste Métivier

Père Lachaise

Square Maurice Gardette

St-Ambroise

11e

▼1

Square de la Roquette

R. de la Roquette

Square Denis Poulot

Place Léon Blum

Place du Père Chaillet

Voltaire

▼2

3
■
4

5
■■

▼18

7 ■ R. de Charonne

Charonne

8
9 ▼15
16

14

10

13

11 Ledru Rollin

12 Square Trousseau

Square R Nordling

R. de Charonne

▼19
▼20

21
22
23

Place Dr Antoine Béclère

▲24
▼25

Faidherbe Chaligny

26

Place d'Aligre

30
31

29

Reuilly Diderot

Blvd Diderot

27

32

34

33

35

36

Quai de la Rapée

Place Mazas

Gare de Lyon

28

Place H Fresnay

12e

Place du Bourgoin

Jardin des Plantes

98

Gare d'Austerlitz

Pont Charles de Gaulle

101

99

Place Valhubert

Square Marie Curie

100

Gare d'Austerlitz

13e

97

St-Marcel

102

Place du Bataillon du Pacifique

Bercy

103

Gare de Paris-Bercy

Blvd de Bercy

Pont de Bercy

0   200   400m
0   200   400yd

MAP 6

2e

MAP 3

MAP 2

Square
Louvois

R. de Cléry

R. d'Aboukir

R. du Caire

6

Bibliothèque
Nationale

1

R. des Petits Champs

R. du Mail

2

Sentier

R. Réaumur

R. J. Bellan

R. St-Sauveur

Réaumur
Sébastopol

7

Pyramides

R. d'Aboukir

35

Greneta

R. Montmartre

R. Tiquetonne

8

33

Place des
Victoires

34

36

R. Greneta

1er

Jardin
du
Palais
Royal

Banque
de
France

32 31 30 29

40 39

38 37

Étienne
Marcel

R. de Turbigo

48

Place
André
Malraux

41

28

R. J. J. Rousseau

R. Étienne Marcel

47

10

Palais
Royal

24

25

Place des
2 Écus

42

43

44

Les Halles

R. aux Ours

11

13

23

26

45

46

12

Place du
Palais Royal

22

21

27

Place
R. Cassin

Forum
des Halles

Châtelet
Les Halles

14

19

20

R. Berger

67

Place
Georges
Pompidou

Jardin du
Carrousel

Palais
Musée du Louvre

R. St-Honoré

80

Place
M Quentin

68

Square des
Innocents

Place
E. Michelet

15

18

Jardin de
l'Oratoire

81

69 70

71

Place Igor
Stravinsky

16

17

Cour
Napoléon

Louvre
Rivoli

82

Châtelet

72

73

Rue de la
Ferronnerie

Cour
Carrée

83

79

Place St-
Opportune

Place du
Louvre

85

Châtelet

78

Jardin de
l'Infante

84

74

Hôtel
de
Ville

Quai des Tuileries

Quai du Louvre

77

75

Place de
l'Hôtel
de Ville

Pont du
Carrousel

Seine

86

Pont
des Arts

Place de
l'École

Quai de la Mégisserie

76

Châtelet

Hôtel
de Ville

École
Nationale
Supérieure
des Beaux-Arts

Place de
l'Institut

Square du
Vert Galant

Pont
Neuf

91

Quai de l'Horloge

Av. Victoria
Place du
Châtelet

Pont
d'Arcole

87 88

Quai de Conti

90

92

Pont
Neuf

93

Place
Dauphine

Pont au
Change

Pont
Notre Dame

89

Palais
de
Justice

Conciergerie

Pont
Notre Dame

Quai de l'Hôtel

95

94

St-
Chapelle

Cité

135

Pont
d'Arcole

98 96

Place de
Fürstenberg

117

Place
Louis Lépine

136

99

116

123

Préfecture
de Police

St Michel-
Notre Dame

100

St-Germain
des Prés

122

124

126

Place du Parvis
Notre Dame

101

97

115

118 120 121

Pont St-
Michel

125

Place St-
Michel

137

102

Place A.
Copeau

114

119

R. St-André des Arts

St-Michel

Petit
Pont

Notre
Dame

103

Mabillon

113 112

Place St-André
des Arts

127

134

138

140 139

153

Pont au
Double

R. du Four

104

Odéon

R. Danton

133

141

Square
Jean XXIII

155

105

Blvd St-Germain

132

Square A.
Lefevre

142

152

151

106 107 110

Carrefour
de l'Odéon

111

Cluny-La
Sorbonne

143

154

Pont de
l'Archevêché

108

109

R. St-Sulpice

Medieval
Garden

144

148

Maubert
Mutualité

150

Place St-
Sulpice

R. de Tournon

131

145

147

Place Maubert

Place de
l'Odéon

128 129

130

R. Racine

R. des Écoles

146

149

6e

MAP 5

R. de Vaugirard

MAP 6

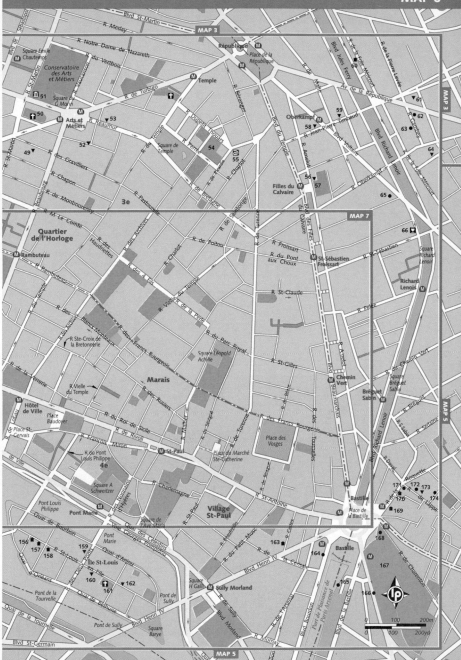

MAP 6

Boat trips are a perfect way to relax and enjoy the sights of Paris.

RICHARD I'ANSON

MAP 6

In warm weather you wouldn't find a seat spare in the Jardin de Luxembourg!

SIMON BRACKEN

MAP 7

R M Le Comte

Quartier
de l'Horloge

Rue des Haudriettes

Rue des 4 Fils

R St-Martin

R de Sébastopol

Rue Quincampoix

R Berger

Place E
Michelet

Place
Georges
Pompidou

Centre
Georges
Pompidou

1

2

3

4

5

6

17

Rue St-Merri

16

Place Igor
Stravinsky

18

R St-Martin

Rue Rambuteau

Rambuteau

R Rambuteau

Temple

Rue Ste-Croix-de-la-Bretonnerie

R des Blancs Manteaux

Rue des Francs Bourgeois

Rue des Archives

11

15

14

13

12

R du Renard

21

R de la Verrerie

R de Rivoli

Rue de Rivoli

19

Hôtel
de Ville

Hôtel
de Ville

Place de
l'Hôtel de Ville

Hôtel
de Ville

20

Av Victoria

22

23 24

Rue de Moussy

Rue Ste-Croix de la Bretonnerie

Rue du Bourg Tibourg

25

26

27

28

33

34

29

32

31

30

R Vielle du Temple

R du Trésor

R des Écouffes

R des Rosiers

47

46

48

R F Duval

35

36

43

45

44

R du Roi de Sicile

42

41

R de Rivoli

R du Lobau

Place
Baudoyer

Place St-
Gervais

Hôtel
de Ville

37

Rue François Miron

Rue des Barres

39

40

Rue du Pont Louis Philippe

Rue Geoffroy-l'Asnier

Rue des Nonnains d'Hyères

55

56

57

Rue de Fourcy

Quai de l'Hôtel de Ville

Q de Gesvres

Pont
d'Arcole

Quai de l'Hôtel de Ville

R d'Arcole

R du Cloître Notre-Dame

Notre
Dame

Seine

38

4e

Square A
Schweitzer

59

60

Rue de l'Hôtel de Ville

Pont
Marie

Pont Louis
Philippe

Quai de Bourbon

Quai des Célestins

Square de
l'Ave Maria

MAP 7

R. Pastourelle

R. de Poitou

R. de Saintonge

R de Bretagne

R de Turenne

R. Froissart

Blvd des Filles du Calvaire

St-Sébastien Froissart ⑧

R-St-Sébastien

R. du Pont aux Choux

R. Charlot

R. St-Claude

R. Pelée

Rue Vieille du Temple

Rue de la Perle

Rue de Thorigny

7 🏛

3e

R. du Parc Royal

Square Léopold Achille

R. St-Gilles

R. Amelot

Blvd Beaumarchais

⑨

Chemin Vert Ⓜ

Marais

10 🏛

▼ 49

50

51 ▼

R. Pelée

52

R des Francs Bourgeois

R. de Béarn

53 ♟

R. Mahler

R. de Sévigné

Rue de Jarente

54 ■

66

67 ●

R. Turenne

Rue des Francs Bourgeois

R. des Tournelles

Place des Vosges

Place du Marché Ste-Catherine

Ⓜ St-Paul

65 ■

64 ■

68 ●

58 ▼

72 🏛

R. Charlemagne

63 ▼

71 ■

R. de Birague

69 ■

R. St-Antoine

Blvd Richard-Lenoir

77 ■

Ⓜ Bastille

0   50   100m
0   50   100yd

76

Rue de la Bastille

75

78 ▼

73 ■

74 ■

62

70

Village St-Paul

R. Beautreillis

R. St-Paul

R. Charles V

61

R. Castex

Bastille

79 Ⓜ

Place de la Bastille

⚓ 80

MAP 7

RICHARD I'ANSON

The Louvre overwhelms the senses, starting with IM Pei's stunning glass pyramid at the main entrance.

MAP 8

MAP 3

Gare du Nord

MAP 3

MAP 2

Square Léon

Hospital

Château Rouge

Place du Château Rouge

Blvd Barbès

Barbès Rochechouart

Blvd de Magenta

R du Faubourg Poissonnière

18e

18e

Parc de la Turlure

Square Willette

Square d'Anvers

Anvers

Lycée J Decour

Montmartre

Place du Tertre

Cimetière St-Vincent

Abbesses

Pigalle

Place Pigalle

Square J Rictus

Square J Buisson

Square S Buisson

Place Constantin Pecqueur

Cimetière de Montmartre

Place Blanche

PLACES TO STAY
9 Hôtel de Carthage
10 Hôtel de Rohan
16 Timhôtel Montmartre
19 Hôtel Bonséjour
20 Hôtel des Arts
21 Hôtel Audran
22 Hôtel du Moulin;
   Hôtel des Capucines
   Montmartre; Hôtel Utrillo
25 Citadines Apart'hôtel
   Montmartre
37 Résidence Pierre &
   Vacances Paris Montmartre
39 Le Village Hostel
40 Hôtel Luxia
41 Hôtel St-Pierre
42 Hôtel Avenir

PLACES TO EAT
1 Franprix Supermarket
12 Le Refuge des Fondus
15 Il Duca
17 Le Bateau Lavoir
23 Le Mono
38 Ed l'Épicier
   Supermarket

OTHER
2 Windmill
3 Windmill
4 Musée de Montmartre
6 Au Lapin Agile
6 Église St-Pierre
   de Montmartre
7 Access to Dome & Crypt
8 Basilique du Sacré Cœur
11 Funicular
13 Bureau de Change
14 Laundrette
18 Laverie Libre Service
   Laundrette
24 Cemetery Entrance
26 La Locomotive
27 Moulin Rouge
28 Thomas Cook
   Exchange Office
29 Musée de l'Eroticisme
30 Folies Pigalle
31 Chao-Bà Café
32 Le Divan du Monde
33 La Fourmi
34 La Cigale
35 Théâtre de l'Atelier
36 L'Élysée-Montmartre

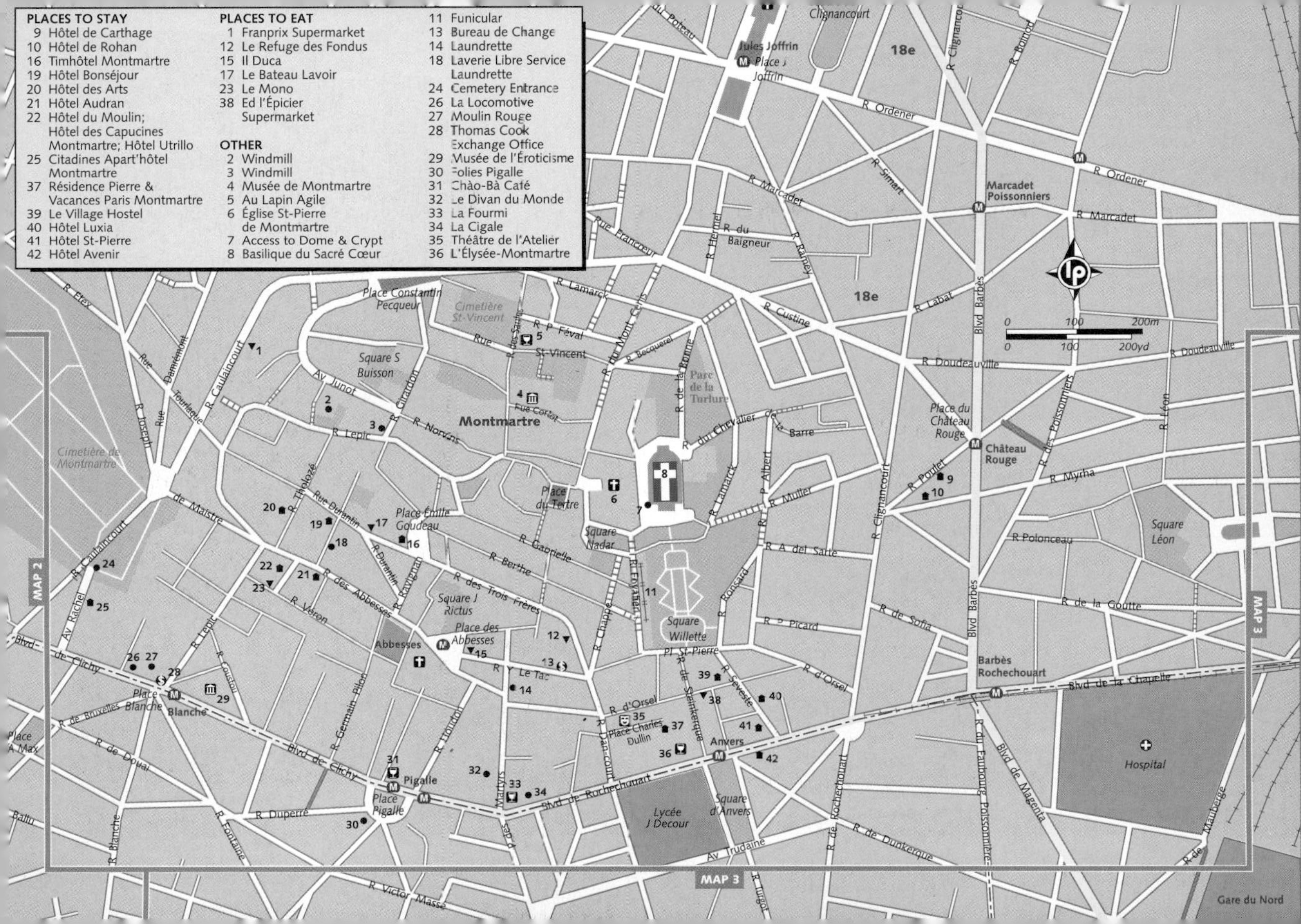

BETHUNE CARMICHAEL

Musée d'Orsay – not bad for an old train station

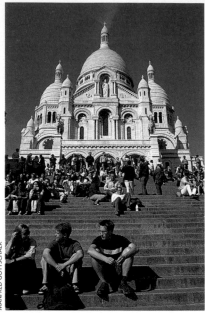

MANFRED GOTTSCHALK

Sacré Coeur, perched atop Montmartre Hill

MANFRED GOTTSCHALK

As if the view from the top of the Eiffel Tower wasn't enough to make your head spin.

opens 9.30 am to 6 pm Tuesday to Saturday, and 10 am to 7 pm on Sunday; admission costs 30FF (students, people under 18 or over 60 20FF, free for children under five). The **planetarium**, which has four shows a day in French, costs an extra 15FF.

Arc de Triomphe

The Arc de Triomphe (Map 2, ☎ 01 55 37 73 77, metro Charles de Gaulle-Étoile) is 2.2km north-west of place de la Concorde in the middle of place Charles de Gaulle (or place de l'Étoile), the world's largest traffic roundabout and the meeting point of a dozen different avenues. Commissioned in 1806 by Napoleon to commemorate his imperial victories, it remained unfinished when he started losing – first battles and then entire wars. It was finally completed in 1836.

Since 1920, the body of an **Unknown Soldier** from WWI taken from Verdun in Lorraine has lain beneath the arch; his fate and that of countless others is commemorated by a memorial flame that is rekindled each evening around 6.30 pm.

From the viewing platform on top of the arch (284 steps and well worth the climb) you can see the 12 avenues – many of them named after Napoleonic victories and illustrious generals – radiating towards every part of Paris. The platform can reached from 9.30 am to 11 pm daily from April to September, and from 10 am to 10.30 pm the rest of the year. Tickets cost 40FF (aged 12 to 25 25FF, free for children). Tickets are sold in the subway (underground passageway).

OPÉRA

The Palais Garnier (9e), which houses Paris' world-famous opera house, abuts the Grands Boulevards, broad thoroughfares whose *belle époque* elegance has only partially been compromised by the traffic and pedestrian tumult of modern Paris.

Palais Garnier

This renowned opera house (Map 2, metro Opéra) at place de l'Opéra (9e), designed in 1860 by Charles Garnier to showcase the splendour of Napoleon III's France, is one of the most impressive monuments erected

during the Second Empire. It contains the **Bibliothèque-Musée de l'Opéra** (Opera Library-Museum; ☎ 01 47 42 07 02), which opens 10 am to 5 pm daily and costs 30FF (students, seniors and those under 26 20FF, free for under 10s). It includes a visit to the opera house unless there's a daytime rehearsal or performance going on.

Grands Boulevards

The eight contiguous Grands Boulevards (Maps 2 and 3) – Madeleine, Capucines, Italiens, Montmartre, Poissonnière, Bonne Nouvelle, St-Denis and St-Martin – stretch from elegant place de la Madeleine (8e) eastward to the less-than-luxurious place de la République (3e and 10e), a distance of just under 3km. The Grands Boulevards were laid out in the 1600s on the site of obsolete fortifications and served as a centre of cafe and theatre life in the 18th and 19th centuries, reaching the height of fashion during the *belle époque*.

Shopping Arcades

Walking through the covered shopping arcades off blvd Montmartre is the best way to step back into early-19th-century Paris. The **Passage des Panoramas** (Map 3, metro Grands Boulevards), 11 blvd Montmartre (2e), which was opened in 1800 and received Paris' first gas lighting in 1817, was expanded in 1834 with the addition of four other interconnecting passages: Feydeau, Montmartre, St-Marc and Variétés. The arcades are open till about midnight daily.

On the northern side of blvd Montmartre (9e), between Nos 10 and 12, is **Passage Jouffroy** (Map 3, metro Grands Boulevards), which leads across rue de la Grange Batelière to **Passage Verdeau**. Both contain shops selling antiques, old postcards, used and antiquarian books, gifts, pet toys, imports from Asia and the like. The arcades are open until 10 pm.

10E ARRONDISSEMENT

The lively working-class area (metro Château d'Eau and Gare de l'Est) around blvd de Strasbourg and rue du Faubourg St-Denis (especially south of blvd de Magenta) is home to large communities of Indians, Bangladeshis, West Indians, Africans, Turks and Kurds. Strolling through **Passage Brady** (Map 3, metro Château d'Eau) is almost like stepping into a back alley in Mumbai.

Tranquil 4.5km-long Canal St-Martin (Map 3) links the 10e with Parc de la Villette (19e) via the Bassin de la Villette and Canal de l'Ourcq (see the later section La Villette). Rue de Paradis (Map 3, metro Château d'Eau) is famed for its crystal, glass and tableware shops.

Porte St-Denis & Porte St-Martin

Porte St-Denis (Map 3, metro Strasbourg St-Denis), the 24m-high triumphal arch at the intersection of rue du Faubourg St-Denis and blvd St-Denis, was built in 1672 to commemorate Louis XIV's campaign along the Rhine. On the northern side, carvings represent the fall of Maastricht in 1673.

Two blocks east, at the intersection of rue du Faubourg St-Martin and blvd St-Denis, is another triumphal arch, the 17m-high Porte St-Martin (Map 3), erected two years later to commemorate the capture of Besançon and the Franche-Comté region by Louis XIV's armies.

BERCY

Long cut off from the rest of the city by railway tracks and the Seine, but since 1996 joined with the Left Bank by the 240FF million (and frankly quite ordinary-looking) Pont Charles de Gaulle, Bercy (Map 5), in the 12e, has some of Paris' most important new buildings. These include the octagonal **Palais Omnisports de Paris-Bercy** (Map 5), blvd de Bercy, designed to serve as both an indoor sports arena and a concert, ballet and theatre venue, and the giant **Ministry of Finance** (Map 5), also on blvd de Bercy.

Across the Seine in the 13e is the new Bibliothèque Nationale de France François Mitterrand. At the same time the development of Bercy Village (Map 1, metro Cour St-Émilion), a series of former wine *chais* (warehouses) that now house wine bars and trendy restaurants, and the arrival of Seine *péniches* (barges) fitted out with more glitzy eateries and music clubs, has turned

the 12e arrondissement into a seriously happening district. Parc de Bercy, between the Palais Omnisports and Bercy Village, is particularly attractive.

13E & 14E ARRONDISSEMENTS

The 13e arrondissement begins a few blocks south of the Jardin des Plantes (5e) and is beginning to undergo something of a renaissance since the opening of the Bibliothèque Nationale de France François Mitterrand and the new high-speed, driverless Météor metro line (No 14). The less-than-thrilling 14e is best known for the Montparnasse Cemetery (see the Montparnasse section earlier in this chapter), but it also boasts one of Paris' more macabre attractions.

Bibliothèque Nationale de France François Mitterrand

Right across the river from Bercy are the four glass towers of the controversial, US$2 billion National Library of France (Map 1, ☎ 01 53 79 59 59/53 79, metro Bibliothèque), 11 quai François Mauriac (13e), which opened in 1998 and was conceived by the late President François Mitterrand as a 'wonder of the modern world'. No expense was spared to carry out a plan that many said defied logic. While many of the more than 10 million books and historical documents are shelved in the sun-drenched, 18-storey towers – shaped like half-open books – patrons sit in artificially lit basement halls built around a 'forest courtyard' of 140 50-year-old pines, trucked in from the countryside. For details on using the library, see Libraries in the Information section.

Chinatown

In the triangle bounded by ave de Choisy, ave d'Ivry and blvd Masséna, Paris' high-rise Chinatown (Map 1, metro Tolbiac, Porte d'Ivry or Porte de Choisy) has a distinctly Franco-Chinese ambience, thanks to the scores of Asian restaurants, shops and travel agencies.

Catacombes

In 1785, it was decided to solve the hygienic and aesthetic problems posed by Paris' overflowing cemeteries by exhuming the bones and storing them in the tunnels of three disused quarries. One ossuary created in 1810 is now known as the Catacombes (Map 1, ☎ 01 43 22 47 63, metro Denfert Rochereau) and without a doubt is the most macabre place in Paris. After descending 20m from street level, visitors follow 1.6km of underground corridors in which the bones and skulls of millions of Parisians are neatly stacked along the walls. During WWII, these tunnels were used by the Résistance as a headquarters.

The route through the Catacombes begins from the small green building at 1 place Denfert Rochereau. It opens 2 to 4 pm Tuesday to Friday, from 9 to 11 am and 2 to 4 pm at the weekend. Tickets cost 33FF (students and seniors 22FF, children 17FF). It's a good idea to bring along a torch (flashlight) and flash photography is allowed (no tripods).

The exit (metro Mouton Duvernet), where a guard will check your bag for stolen bones, is on rue Remy Dumoncel, 700m south-west of place Denfert Rochereau.

MONTMARTRE
During the 19th century the bohemian lifestyle of Montmartre (18e) attracted artists and writers whose presence turned the area into Paris' most important centre of creativity. Although the activity shifted to Montparnasse after WWI, Montmartre retains an upbeat ambience that all the tourists in the world couldn't spoil.

The RATP's sleek funicular (Map 8) travelling Montmartre's southern slope whisks visitors from square Willette (metro Anvers) to Sacré Cœur. It runs until 12.40 am daily and costs one metro/bus ticket each way. Weekly and monthly Carte Orange coupons as well as Paris Visite and Mobilis passes are also valid.

Montmartrobus, run by the RATP, takes a circuitous route all over Montmartre; their maps are posted at bus stops.

Sacré Cœur
Basilique du Sacré Cœur (Basilica of the Sacred Heart; Map 8, ☎ 01 53 41 89 00,

metro Anvers), 35 rue du Chevalier de la Barre (18e), perched at the very top of Butte de Montmartre (Montmartre Hill), was built from contributions pledged by Parisian Catholics as an act of contrition after the humiliating Franco-Prussian War of 1870–71. Construction began in 1873, but the basilica was not consecrated until 1919.

Some 234 spiralling steps lead you to the basilica's **dome**, which affords one of Paris' most spectacular panoramas; you can see as far away as 30km on a clear day. Admission to the dome costs 15FF (students under 25 and children 8FF). The chapel-lined **crypt** (same admission), down the stairs to the right as you exit the basilica, is huge but not very interesting.

The basilica opens 7 am to 11 pm daily; the dome and crypt open 9 am to 7 pm daily from April to September (to 6 pm the rest of the year).

Place du Tertre
Half a block west of the **Église St-Pierre de Montmartre** (Map 8), parts of which date from a 12th-century abbey, is place du Tertre (Map 8, metro Abbesses), once the main square of the village of Montmartre. These days it's filled with cafes, restaurants, portrait artists and tourists and is always animated. Look for the two **windmills** to the west on rue Lepic.

Musée de Montmartre
The Montmartre Museum (Map 8, ☎ 01 46 06 61 11, metro Lamarck Caulaincourt), 12 rue Cortot (18e), displays paintings, lithographs and documents mostly relating to the area's rebellious and bohemian/artistic past. It's hard to appreciate what the big deal is (and to justify the admission fee) unless you care about Montmartre's mythology – and can read French. There's a lush little garden out the back. The museum opens 11 am to 6 pm Tuesday to Sunday and admission costs 25FF (students and seniors 20FF).

Cimetière de Montmartre
Montmartre Cemetery (Maps 2 and 8, ☎ 01 43 87 64 24, metro place de Clichy or Blanche), established in 1798, is the most

famous cemetery in Paris after Père Lachaise. It contains the graves of Zola, Alexandre Dumas the younger, Stendhal and Heinrich Heine, Jacques Offenbach and Hector Berlioz, Degas, film director François Truffaut, and Vaslav Nijinsky.

The entrance nearest the Butte de Montmartre is at 20 ave Rachel, down the stairs from 10 rue Caulaincourt. The cemetery opens 9 am weekdays, 8.30 am on Saturday and 9 am on Sunday to 6 pm from mid-March to early November, and 8.30 am to 5.30 pm daily the rest of the year.

Pigalle

Only a few blocks south-west of the tranquil, residential streets of Montmartre is lively, neon-lit Pigalle, 9e and 18e (Map 8), one of Paris' two main sex districts; the other, much more low-rent, is along rue St-Denis (1er) north of Forum des Halles. But Pigalle is more than just a sleazy red-light district: though the area around blvd de Clichy between the Pigalle and Blanche metro stops is lined with erotica shops and striptease parlours and strip joints, there are also plenty of trendy nightspots, including La Locomotive and Élysée Montmartre clubs and the celebrated Moulin Rouge cabaret (see the Entertainment section for details).

The **Musée de l'Érotisme** (Museum of Erotic Art; Map 8, ☎ 01 42 58 28 73, metro Blanche), 72 blvd de Clichy (18e), tries to put some 2000 titillating statuary and stimulating sexual aids from days gone by on a loftier plane – with erotic art both antique and new from four continents spread over seven levels – but we know why we visited. The museum opens 10 am to 2 am daily and admission costs 40FF (students 30FF).

LA VILLETTE

The 19e arrondissement is of interest to visitors mainly because of the Parc de la Villette, with its wonderful museums and other attractions. You can go boating on Canal de l'Ourcq (see Organised Tours at the end of this section), which is the north-east extension of Canal St-Martin (see the earlier 10e Arrondissement section).

Parc de la Villette Cité des Sciences et de l'Industrie

The enormous City of Sciences and Industry (Map 1, ☎ 01 40 05 80 00 for information, ☎ 01 40 05 12 12 for reservations, metro Porte de la Villette), 30 ave Corentin Cariou (19e), at the northern end of Parc de la Villette, has all sorts of high-tech exhibits. You can find out more from the Web site at www.citesciences.fr. By Minitel, key in 3615 VILLETTE.

Musée Explora The huge, rather confusing main museum opens 10 am to 6 pm (to 7 pm on Sunday) Tuesday to Sunday. A ticket good for Explora, the planetarium, a 3D film and the French navy submarine *Argonaute* (commissioned in 1957) in the park costs 50FF (those aged eight to 25, seniors and teachers, and for everyone on Saturday 35FF, free for children under 7) and allows you to enter and exit up to four times during the day. Various combo tickets valid for the Cité des Sciences, the Géode and Cinaxe are available.

A free map-brochure in English and the detailed 80-page *Guide to the Permanent Exhibitions* are available from the round information counter at the Cité des Sciences' main entrance.

Cité des Enfants The highlight of the Cité des Sciences is the brilliant Cité des Enfants, whose colourful and imaginative hands-on demonstrations of basic scientific principles are divided into two sections: one for three to five-year-olds, the other for five to 12-year-olds. Younger kids can explore, among other things, the behaviour of water (waterproof lab ponchos provided), while older children can build toy houses with industrial robots and stage news broadcasts in a TV studio equipped with real video cameras.

Visits lasting 90 minutes begin four times a day at two-hour intervals from 9.30 am (Tuesday, Thursday and Friday) or 10.30 am (Wednesday, Saturday and Sunday). Each child is charged 25FF and must be accompanied by an adult. During school holiday periods it's a good idea to make reservations two or three days in advance by telephone, Internet or Minitel.

Géode

Just south of the Cité des Sciences at 26 ave Corentin Cariou is the Géode (Map 1, ☎ 01 40 05 12 12), a 36m-high sphere whose mirror-like surface made of thousands of polished, stainless-steel triangles has made it one of the architectural calling cards of modern-day Paris. Inside, high-resolution, 70mm films – virtual reality, special effects, nature, etc – lasting 45 minutes are projected onto a 180° screen that gives viewers a sense of being surrounded by the action. Films begin every hour on the hour from 9 am to 6 pm Tuesday to Sunday, with a special double feature at 6.30 pm. Headsets that pick up an English soundtrack are available for no extra charge.

Tickets to the Géode cost 57FF (the reduced tariff of 44FF for under 25s and seniors is not available during weekends and holidays from 2 to 5 pm); the double feature at 6.30 pm is 65FF.

Cinaxe

The Cinaxe (☎ 01 42 09 86 04 for information, ☎ 01 40 05 12 12 to book), a hydraulic cinema with seating for 60 people that moves in synchronisation with the action on the screen, is right across the walkway from the south-western side of the Cité des Sciences. This example of proto-virtual reality technology opens 11 am to 5 pm Tuesday to Sunday, and costs 34FF (students, seniors and those aged 12 to 17 29FF, under 12s 25FF). Shows begin every 15 minutes.

Cité de la Musique

On the southern edge of Parc de la Villette, the City of Music (Map 1, ☎ 01 44 84 44 84, metro Porte de Pantin), 221 ave Jean Jaurès (19e) is a striking triangular concert hall whose brief is to bring non-elitist music from around the world to Paris' multiethnic masses. Some 900 rare musical instruments are on display at its fascinating **Musée de la Musique** (Music Museum); you can hear many of them being played through the earphones included in the admission fee.

The museum opens from noon to 6 pm Tuesday to Thursday, to 7.30 pm Friday and Saturday, and 10 am to 6 pm on Sunday. Admission costs 35FF (students, seniors and those aged 18 to 25 25FF, aged six to 17 10FF).

MÉNILMONTANT & BELLEVILLE

The area of Ménilmontant in the 11e is growing trendier by the day, thanks to the surfeit of restaurants, bars and clubs, while Belleville (20e) remains for the most part unpretentious and working-class. Paris' most famous necropolis lies just south.

Belleville

This inner-city 'village', centred around blvd de Belleville (Map 3, metro Belleville), is home to large numbers of immigrants, especially Muslims and Jews from North Africa and Vietnamese and ethnic Chinese from Indochina. In recent years, the area's none-too-solid, late-19th-century workers' flats have become popular with artists in search of cheap housing and the cachet that comes with slumming it.

Cimetière du Père Lachaise

The world's most visited cemetery, Père Lachaise (Map 1, ☎ 01 43 70 70 33, metro Philippe Auguste, Père Lachaise or Gambetta), opened in 1805 and its 70,000 ornate (and even ostentatious) tombs of the rich and/or famous form a verdant, open-air sculpture garden. Among the one million people buried here are Chopin, Molière, Apollinaire, Oscar Wilde, Balzac, Proust, Gertrude Stein, Colette, David, Simone Signoret, Pissarro, Seurat, Modigliani, Sarah Bernhardt, Yves Montand, Delacroix, Edith Piaf, Isadora Duncan, and even those immortal 12th-century lovers, Abélard and Héloïse (see the boxed text 'Star-Crossed Lovers'). One particularly frequented (and now guarded) tomb is that of 1960s US rock star **Jim Morrison**, who died in an apartment at 17–19 rue Beautreillis (4e) in the Marais in 1971; he is buried in division 6.

The cemetery, which has five entrances (two of them on blvd de Ménilmontant), opens from 8 am (8.30 am on Saturday,

9 am on Sunday) to 6 pm from mid-March to early November (to 5.30 pm the rest of the year). Maps indicating the location of noteworthy graves are posted around the cemetery and can be obtained free at all the entrances, including the Conservation office at 16 rue du Repos (20e), on the western side of the cemetery. Newsstands and flower kiosks in the area sell the *Plan Illustré du Père Lachaise* (Illustrated Map of Père Lachaise; 10FF). Two-hour tours (☎ 01 40 71 75 60) of the cemetery in English leave from the Conservation office at 3 pm on Saturday from June to September; they cost 38FF (concessions 26FF). The tours are available in French (both themed and general) throughout the year at various times but usually at 2.30 pm on Saturday.

BOIS DE BOULOGNE

The 8.65 sq km Boulogne Wood (Map 1), on the western edge of the city in the 16e, owes its informal layout to its designer, Baron Haussmann (see the boxed text), who took his inspiration from London's Hyde Park instead of the more geometric French models.

The southern reaches of the wood take in **Stade Roland Garros** (Map 1), home of the French Open tennis tournament, and two horse-racing tracks, the **Hippodrome de Longchamp** for flat races and the **Hippodrome d'Auteuil** (Map 1) for steeplechase. For details, see Horse Racing in the Spectator Sports section later in this chapter.

Gardens

The enclosed **Parc de Bagatelle** (Map 1), in the north-western corner of the Bois de Boulogne, is renowned for its beautiful gardens, which surround the **Château de Bagatelle**, built in 1775. There are areas dedicated to irises (which bloom in May), roses (June to October) and water lilies (August).

The **Pré Catelan** (Map 1) includes a **Jardin Shakespeare** in which you can see plants, flowers and trees mentioned in Shakespeare's plays. It opens 8.30 am to 7 or 7.30 pm daily.

Rowboats & Bicycles Rowboats can be hired (☎ 01 42 88 04 69) at **Lac Inférieur** (Map 1, metro Avenue Henri Martin), the largest of the park's lakes and ponds, for 56FF an hour from 10 am to 6 pm (to 7 pm in summer). Paris Cycles (☎ 01 47 47 76 50

Star-Crossed Lovers

He was a brilliant 39-year-old philosopher and logician who had gained a reputation for his controversial ideas. She was the beautiful niece of a canon at Notre Dame. And like Bogart and Bergman in Casablanca and Romeo and Juliet in Verona, they had to fall in love in medieval Paris – of all damned places.

In 1118, the wandering scholar Pierre Abélard (1079–1142) went to Paris, having clashed with yet another theologian in the provinces. There he was employed by Canon Fulbert of Notre Dame to tutor his niece Héloïse (1098–1164). One thing led to another and a son, Astrolabe, was born. Abélard did the gentlemanly thing and married his sweetheart. But they wed in secret and when Fulbert learned of it he was outraged. The canon had Abélard castrated and sent Héloïse packing to a nunnery. Abélard took monastic vows at the abbey in St-Denis and continued his studies and controversial writings. Héloïse, meanwhile, was made abbess of a convent.

All the while, however, the star-crossed lovers continued to correspond: he sending tender advice on how to run the convent and she writing passionate, poetic letters to her lost lover. The two were reunited only in death; in 1817 their remains were disinterred and brought to Père Lachaise Cemetery (Map 1) in the 20e, where they lie today beneath a neo-Gothic tombstone. A sad – and timeless – story.

Baron Haussmann

Few town planners anywhere in the world have had as great an impact on the city of their birth as Baron Georges-Eugène Haussmann (1809–91) did on Paris. As prefect of the Seine département under Napoleon III for 17 years, Haussmann and his staff of architects and engineers completely rebuilt huge swathes of Paris. He is best known – and most bitterly attacked – for having demolished much of medieval Paris, replacing the chaotic narrow streets, which are easy to barricade in an uprising, with the handsome, arrow-straight thoroughfares for which the city is so famous. He also revolutionised Paris' water supply and sewerage systems and laid out many of the city's loveliest parks, including large areas of the Bois de Boulogne (16e) and Bois de Vincennes (12e).

for a recorded message or ☎ 01 47 47 22 37 to book) rents out bicycles at two locations: on ave du Mahatma Gandhi (Map 1, metro Les Sablons), across from the Porte Sablons entrance to the Jardin d'Acclimatation amusement park, and near the Pavillon Royal (metro avenue Foch) at the northern end of Lac Inférieur. Except when it rains, bicycles are available from 10 am to sundown daily from mid-April to mid-October, and the same hours on Wednesday, Saturday and Sunday only during the rest of the year. The rental cost is 20/30FF for a half-hour/hour and 60/80FF for a half-day/day.

Jardin d'Acclimatation

This kids-orientated amusement park (Map 1, ☎ 01 40 67 90 82, metro Les Sablons) on ave du Mahatma Gandhi now includes the high-tech **Exploradôme**, a tented structure in the western section devoted to science, the media and the Internet. The park opens 10 am to 6 pm daily and admission costs 13FF (reduced price 6.50FF). To visit the park and Exploradôme costs 30/20FF.

Musée National des Arts et Traditions Populaires

The National Museum of Popular Arts and Traditions (Map 1, ☎ 01 44 17 60 00, metro Les Sablons), 6 ave du Mahatma Gandhi (16e), near the Jardin d'Acclimatation, has displays illustrating life in rural France before and during the period of the Industrial Revolution. It opens 9.45 am to 5.15 pm Wednesday to Monday and admission costs 30FF (students, seniors and those aged 18 to 25 23FF, free for under 18s and everyone on the first Sunday of the month).

BOIS DE VINCENNES

Paris' other large English-style park, the 9.3 sq km Bois de Vincennes, 12e (Map 1), is in the far south-eastern corner of the city. The **Parc Floral** (Floral Park, metro Château de Vincennes), just south of the Château de Vincennes, is on Route de la Pyramide. The **Jardin Tropical** (Tropical Garden; RER stop Nogent-sur-Marne) is at the park's eastern edge on ave de la Belle Gabrielle.

Musée National des Arts d'Afrique et d'Océanie

The National Museum of African and Oceanic Art (Map 1, ☎ 01 44 74 84 80, metro Porte Dorée), 293 ave Daumesnil (12e), is devoted to the art of the South Pacific as well as North, West and Central Africa. It opens 10 am to 5.30 pm (to 6 pm at the weekend) Wednesday to Monday and costs 30FF (students, seniors and those aged 18 to 25 20FF, free for under 18s and everyone on the first Sunday of the month).

Zoo

The Parc Zoologique de Paris (Map 1, ☎ 01 44 75 20 10, metro Porte Dorée), 53 ave de St-Maurice, just east of blvd Périphérique (the Paris ring road), was founded in 1934. It opens 9 am to 6 pm (to 5 pm in winter) Monday to Saturday and to 6.30 pm (5.30 pm in winter) on Sunday. Admission costs 40FF (reduced tariff 30FF, students 10FF).

Château de Vincennes

The Château de Vincennes (☎ 01 48 08 31 20, metro Château de Vincennes), at the northern edge of the Bois de Vincennes, is a *bona fide* royal chateau complete with massive fortifications and a moat. Louis XIV spent his honeymoon at the mid-17th-century **Pavillon du Roi**, the westernmost of the two royal pavilions flanking the **Cour Royale** (Royal Courtyard). The 52m-high **dungeon**, completed in 1369, was used as a prison during the 17th and 18th centuries.

You can walk around the grounds for free, but the only way to see the Gothic **Chapelle Royale**, built between the 14th and 16th centuries, is to take a guided tour (in French, with an information booklet in English). Tickets cost 32FF (reduced price 21FF) for a long tour, and 25FF (15FF) for a short one; the tours are free for those under 18. There are five long and five short tours a day from April to September, when the chateau opens from 10 am till noon and 1.15 to 6 pm daily, and four of each the rest of the year from 10 am till noon and 1.15 to 5 pm.

ACTIVITIES

The entertainment weeklies *Pariscope* and *L'Officiel des Spectacles* (see Listings under Entertainment later in this chapter) have up-to-date information in French on every imaginable sort of activity.

Sports Facilities

For information (in French) on Paris' sporting activities and facilities (including its three dozen swimming pools), dial Allô Sports on ☎ 01 42 76 54 54 or Minitel 3615 PARIS. It is staffed from 10.30 am to 5 pm (4.30 pm on Friday) on weekdays only.

Boating

The Paris area's three rivers (the Seine, Marne and Oise) and its canals (St-Martin and Ourcq) offer a unique vantage point from which to enjoy the delights of Paris. A one or two week rental – less expensive than many hotels if there are four or more of you – can easily be split between quiet canal/river cruises and days spent moored in the city. Within Paris proper, the only places you can stay overnight are Bassin de

la Villette, 19e (Map 1), and Port de Plaisance de Paris Arsenal (Map 5) in the 4e and 12e, but it's possible to stop for an hour or two at a number of quays along the Seine.

Europ' Yachting (Map 5, ☎ 01 43 44 66 77, fax 01 43 44 74 18, metro Quai de la Rapée), 11 blvd de la Bastille (12e), on the ground floor of the Capitainerie of Port de Plaisance de Paris Arsenal, rents out boats for four to seven people. From mid-March to mid-October you can rent by the weekend (Friday night to Sunday night, costing from 2000FF to 5000FF), workweek (Monday to Friday, costing from 3000FF to 7000FF) or full week (Saturday night to Saturday morning, 4000FF to 9000FF). Hiring a pilot costs 4500FF for up to three hours, or 8500FF a day. Bookings should be made three weeks in advance, though boats are sometimes available at the last minute. The office opens from 10 am to 1 pm and 2.30 to 7 pm Monday to Saturday.

COURSES

For information on studying French and learning how to cook, see Courses in the Facts for the Visitor chapter.

ORGANISED TOURS

If you can't be bothered making your own way around Paris or don't have the time, consider a tour by bus, boat, bicycle or on foot.

Bus

From 1pm to just before 9 pm on Sunday from April to late September, RATP's Balabus follows a 50-minute route from Gare de Lyon to the Grande Arche in La Défense that passes by many of central Paris' most famous sights. Buses depart about every 20 minutes and cost one metro/bus ticket.

L'Open Tour (☎ 01 43 46 52 06, fax 01 43 46 53 06) runs open-deck buses along three circuits (central Paris, Montmartre and Bercy) year round, which allows you to jump on and off at more than 30 stops around the city. Tickets cost 135FF for a day (110FF if you're holding a Carte Orange, Paris Visite or Batobus pass) and 150FF for two consecutive days. Schedules vary, but on the Grand Tour of central Paris, with some 20 stops between Notre Dame and the Arc de Triomphe, buses depart every 15 to 25 minutes from 10 am to 6 or 6.30 pm.

Cityrama (Map 6, ☎ 01 44 55 61 00, metro Tuileries), 4 place des Pyramides (1er), opposite the western end of the Louvre, runs two-hour tours of the city daily (150FF), accompanied by taped commentary in a dozen or so languages. They also have day and half-day trips to Chartres (285FF), Versailles (200FF) and other places around Paris.

Boat
Be it on the Seine – 'la ligne de vie de Paris' (Paris' lifeline) as it's called – or the canals to the north-east, a boat cruise is the most relaxing way to watch the city glide by.

Seine Cruises From its base just north of the Eiffel Tower at Port de la Bourdonnais, 7e (Map 4, metro Pont de l'Alma), Bateaux Parisiens (☎ 01 44 11 33 44) runs one-hour river circuits costing 50FF (children under 12 25FF) and lunch/dinner cruises (300/580FF) year round. From May to October, boats also depart from the dock opposite Notre Dame (Map 6, metro Maubert Mutualité), on quai de Montebello, 5e.

Bateaux Mouches (Map 2, ☎ 01 42 25 96 10 or, for an English-language recording, ☎ 01 40 76 99 99, metro Alma-Marceau), based on the Right Bank just east of Pont de l'Alma (8e), runs 1000-seat tour boats, the biggest ones on the Seine. From mid-November to mid-March there are sailings daily at 11 am, 2.30 and 3.15 pm, and on the hour from 4 to 9 pm. Depending on demand, there are additional cruises at 1 and 9.30 pm. The rest of the year boats depart every half-hour from 10 am to 12.30 pm and 1.30 to 11.30 pm. A 1½ hour cruise with commentary costs 40FF (under 14s 20FF).

Vedettes du Pont Neuf (Map 6, ☎ 01 46 33 98 38, metro Pont Neuf), whose home dock is at the far western tip of Île de la Cité (1er), offers one-hour boat excursions year round. Between March and October, boats generally leave every half-hour between 10 am and noon and 1.30 to 8 pm; night cruises depart every 30 minutes from 9 to 10.30 pm. From November to February there are about a dozen cruises on weekdays (when night services stop at 10 pm) and up to 18 on Saturday and Sunday. A ticket costs 50FF (children under 12 25FF).

Canal Cruises From March to October, Canauxrama (Map 6, ☎ 01 42 39 15 00) barges travel between Port de Plaisance de Paris Arsenal (12e) and Parc de la Villette (19e) along the charming Canal St-Martin and Canal de l'Ourcq. Departures are at around 9.45 am and 2.30 pm from Bassin de la Villette, 13 quai de la Loire (19e) and at 9.45 am and 2.30 pm from Port de l'Arsenal, 50 blvd de la Bastille (12e). The cost is 80FF (students 60FF, children aged six to 11 50FF, except on Sunday and holidays when everyone pays 80FF).

Paris Canal Croisières (☎ 01 42 40 96 97) has daily three-hour cruises from late March to mid-November from quai Anatole France, just north-west of the Musée d'Orsay (Map 4), leaving at 9.30 am and departing back from Parc de la Villette at 2.30 pm. There are extra trips at 2.35 pm (from the museum) and 6.15 pm (from the park) from mid-July to August. The cost is 100FF for adults, 75FF for those aged 12 to 25 and over 60 (excluding Sunday afternoons and holidays when it's full price for all), and 55FF for children aged four to 11. In winter they run sporadic themed cruises: contact their Web site (www.pariscanal .com) for details.

Walking
Paris is a wonderful city to walk around and surprisingly pedestrian-friendly, in part because it's relatively compact. It's also a fairly level city, so apart from toiling up to Montmartre, there's no hill-climbing involved. Traffic can be a problem, though: cars will only stop for you if you absolutely assert your rights on pedestrian crossings. And then there's those damn dogs...

English-language tours of different areas and themes are run by Paris Walking Tours (☎ 01 48 09 21 40, fax 01 42 43 75 51,

Remembrance of Dogs Past & Present

The Paris municipality spends 75 million FF a year to keep the city's pavements relatively passable, and the technology it employs – most notably the 'distinktive' *moto-crotte* (pooper scooter) driven around by the city's *chevaliers du trottoir* (knights of the sidewalk) to keep the pavements free of dog mess – is undeniably impressive. But it would seem that repeated campaigns to get people to clean up after their pooches have been less than a howling success. Evidence to this effect takes the form of 'souvenirs' left by recently walked poodles and other breeds, often found smeared along the pavement by daydreaming strollers, one assumes, or guidebook writers absorbed in jotting down something important. And it gets more serious than that: more than 600 people are admitted to hospital each year after slipping on a *crotte*. Until that far-off day when Parisians – and their much loved canines – change their ways, the word on the streets remains the same: watch your step.

@ paris@pariswalkingtours.com), including tours of Montmartre at 10.30 am on Sunday and Wednesday (leaving from the Abbesses metro station) and of the Marais from the St-Paul metro at 2.30 pm on Sunday and Thursday and at 10.30 am on Tuesday. A tour called Hemingway's Paris departs the Cardinal Lemoine metro at 10 am on Tuesday. The tours costs 60FF (students under 25 40FF, children 30FF).

If your French is up to scratch, the sky's the limit on specialised and themed walking tours. Both *Pariscope* and *L'Officiel des Spectacles* (see Listings in the Entertainment section) list different organised walks and tours each week under the heading 'Conférences'. They are usually both informative *and* entertaining, particularly those run by Paris aux Cents Visages (☎ 01 44 67 92 33) and Paris Passé, Présent (☎ 01 42 58 95 99).

Bicycle

Both Roue Libre and Paris à Vélo, C'est Sympa! (see Bicycle in the Getting Around section at the end of this chapter for details) offer between seven and 10 bicycle tours of Paris lasting about three hours and departing between 10 am and 3 pm on Saturday and Sunday (tours during the week depend on demand). Paris à Vélo's cost 185FF (under 26s 160FF) while Roue Libre's are 135FF (children aged four to 12 85FF). Both include a guide, the bicycle and insurance. A short, 1½-hour tour run by Paris à Vélo at 11 am on Sunday costs 100/60FF.

An English-speaking outfit that gets good reports from readers is Bullfrog Bike Tours (mobile ☎ 06 09 98 08 60, @ bullfrogbikes @hotmail.com), which offers day tours of the city starting at 11 am and 3.30 pm from early May to late August (at 11 am only from late August to mid-September) departing from ave Gustave Eiffel (7e) just opposite the Eiffel Tower at the start of the Champ de Mars. The tours cost 150FF. Night bicycle tours depart from the same spot at 8 pm Sunday to Thursday during the same months and cost 170FF.

SPECIAL EVENTS

Innumerable cultural and sporting events take place in Paris throughout the year; weekly details appear in *Pariscope* and *L'Officiel des Spectacles* (see Listings in the Entertainment section later in this chapter). The mayor's office produces a *Progamme des Manifestions* each season with major events listed; check their Web site at www.paris-france.org. You can also find them listed on the tourist office's site at www.paris-touristoffice.com.

The following abbreviated list gives you a taste of what to expect:

31 December to 1 January
Blvd St-Michel (5e), place de la Bastille (11e), the Eiffel Tower (7e) and especially ave des Champs-Élysées (8e) are the places to be on New Year's Eve. La Grande Parade de Paris – the city's New Year's Day parade – originated in Montmartre but now takes place in different venues (eg, along the Grands Boulevards) each

year. Check the Web site at www.parisparade .com.

Late January/early February

Chinese New Year Dragon parades and other festivities are held in Chinatown, the area of the 13e between ave d'Ivry and ave de Choisy (metro Porte de Choisy or Tolbiac), with an abridged version along rue Au Maire (metro Arts et Métiers) in the 3e.

Late February/early March

Salon International de l'Agriculture This is a 10-day international agricultural fair with lots to eat, including dishes from all over France. It is held at the Parc des Expositions at Porte de Versailles in the 15e (metro Porte de Versailles).

Late February/March

Banlieues Bleues This 'Suburban Blues' jazz and blues festival held in St-Denis and other Paris suburbs attracts big-name talent.

Early March

Jumping International de Paris This show jumping tournament is held at the Palais Omnisports de Paris-Bercy in the 12e (metro Bercy).

Early April

Marathon International de Paris The Paris international marathon starts on place de la Concorde (1er) and finishes on ave Foch (16e).

Late April/early May

Foire de Paris This huge food and wine fair at the Parc des Expositions at Porte de Versailles in the 15e (metro Porte de Versailles) has a 10-day jazz festival held concurrently.

May to September

Paris Jazz festival Free jazz concerts are held every Saturday and Sunday afternoon in Parc Floral (metro Château de Vincennes), south of the Château de Vincennes on Route de la Pyramide (12e).

Late May/early June

Internationaux de France de Tennis (French Open Tennis Tournament) This glitzy tennis tournament is held at Stade Roland Garros (metro Porte d'Auteuil) at the southern edge of Bois de Boulogne (16e).

Late June/early July

La Course des Garçons et Serveuses de Café This Sunday afternoon race 8km along the Grands Boulevards and St-Germain des Prés has some 500 waiters and waitresses balancing a glass and a bottle on a small tray. Spilling or breaking anything results in disqualification.

Late June

Gay Pride The colourful, Saturday afternoon parade through the Marais (4e) is to celebrate Gay Pride Day. Various bars and clubs sponsor floats.

21 June

Fête de la Musique This music festival caters to a great diversity of tastes and features impromptu live performances all over the city.

Early July

La Goutte d'Or en Fête This is world music festival (raï, reggae, rap etc) at square de Léon in the 18e (metro Barbès Rochechouart).

14 July

Bastille Day Paris is *the* place to be on France's national day. Late on the night of the 13th, *bals des sapeurs-pompiers* (dances sponsored by Paris fire brigades, who are considered sex symbols in France) are held at fire stations around the city. At 10 am on the 14th, there's a military and fire brigade parade along ave des Champs-Élysées, accompanied by a fly-over of fighter aircraft and helicopters. In the evening, a huge display of *feux d'artifice* (fireworks) is held at around 11 pm at the Champ de Mars (7e).

Late July

Tour de France The last stage of the world's most prestigious cycling event ends with a dash up ave des Champs-Élysées on the 3rd or 4th Sunday of the month.

Mid-September to December

Festival d'Automne The 'Autumn Festival' of arts includes painting, music and theatre held in venues throughout the city.

September/October

Foire Internationale d'Art Contemporain (FIAC) This huge contemporary art fair has some 160 galleries represented. Usually held at the Grand Palais (metro Champs-Élysées Clemenceau) in the 8e.

24–25 December

Christmas Eve Mass This is celebrated at midnight on Christmas Eve at many Paris churches, including Notre Dame (4e), but get there by 11 pm to find a place in a pew.

PLACES TO STAY

Paris has a very wide choice of accommodation options available and, unlike London and even New York, they cater comfortably to all budgets in most sections of the city. When calculating accommodation costs in the French capital assume you'll spend close to 100FF per person per night in a hostel and at least 150FF for a washbasin-equipped double in a bottom-end hotel. Bear in mind that in budget hotel rooms without en-suite shower or bath, you may be charged from 10FF to as much as 30FF each time you use the hall shower. If you can't go without your daily ablutions it is often a false economy staying at such places.

PARIS

Mid-range places in Paris charge roughly between 300FF and 600FF for a double and offer excellent value, especially at the higher end. Top-range places will cost two people up to about 1200FF a night; anything over that falls into the deluxe category.

Accommodation Services

The main tourist office (Map 2, ☎ 0 836 68 31 12, fax 01 49 52 53 00, Minitel 3615 or 3617 OTPARIS, metro George V), 127 ave des Champs-Élysées (8e), and the annexe at the Gare de Lyon can find you a place to stay for the night of the day you stop by. It also has a number of brochures on homestays, including one on *pensions de famille*, which are similar to B&Bs. Recommended pensions de famille in Paris include:

Pension Ladagnous (Map 4, ☎ 01 43 26 79 32, 78 rue d'Assas, 6e, metro Vavin or Notre Dame des Champs). Singles/doubles with half-board cost 260/395FF.

Pension Les Marroniers (Map 4, ☎ 01 43 26 37 71, fax 01 43 26 07 72, 78 rue d'Assas, 6e, metro Vavin or Notre Dame des Champs). Half-board costs from 270/495FF. Monthly rates cost 20% less and vegetarian meals are available.

Pension Au Palais Gourmand (Map 4, ☎ 01 45 48 24 15, fax 01 42 22 33 41, 120 blvd Raspail, 6e, metro Vavin or Notre Dame des Champs). Half-board singles cost 290FF to 374FF; doubles cost 442FF to 495FF.

Résidence Cardinal (Map 2, ☎ 01 48 74 16 16, 4 rue Cardinal Mercier, 9e, metro Liège or Place de Clichy). Singles with breakfast cost 160FF to 190FF; doubles cost 260FF to 320FF.

Some travel agencies, especially student ones (see that section under Information in this chapter) can book you reasonably priced accommodation. OTU (Map 7, ☎ 01 40 29 12 12, @ otuvoyage@terranet.fr, metro Rambuteau), at 119 rue St-Martin (4e) directly across the square (parvis Beaubourg) from the Centre Pompidou, can *always* find you accommodation, even in summer. It works like this: you come in on the day (or the day before) you need a place to stay and pay for the accommodation (plus a 20FF fee). The staff then give you a voucher to take to the hotel. Prices for singles are around 270FF, doubles start at

about 300FF. This OTU branch opens 10 am to 6.30 pm weekdays, to 5 pm on Saturday. Be prepared for long queues.

Homestays

For more information on the arrangement known as *hôtes payants* (literally 'paying guests') or *hébergement chez l'habitant* (lodging with the occupants of a private home), see Homestays in the Accommodation section of the Facts for the Visitor chapter.

Apartments & Flats

For details on accommodation for longer stays, see Long-Term Rentals at the end of this section.

PLACES TO STAY – BUDGET
Camping

The only camping ground within the Paris city limits, *Camping du Bois de Boulogne* (☎ 01 45 24 30 81, fax 01 42 24 42 95, 2 allée du Bord de l'Eau, 16e) is along the Seine at the far western edge of the Bois de Boulogne opposite the Île de Puteaux. Two people with a tent pay 67FF to 88FF (105FF to 143FF with a vehicle), depending on the season; the reception at this seven-hectare site is staffed 24 hours a day. It's very crowded in summer, but there's always space for a small tent. Fully equipped caravans accommodating four people are available for rent for between 285FF and 399FF, depending on the size and the season. The Porte Maillot metro stop (Map 2), 4.5km to the north-east through the wood, is linked to the camping ground by RATP bus No 244 (which runs 6 am to 8.30 pm) and, from April to October, by privately operated shuttle bus (10FF).

Hostels & Foyers

Accommodation in hostels and *foyers* (student residence halls) doesn't come cheaply in Paris. Beds under 100FF are few and far between, so two people who don't mind sleeping in the same bed may find basic rooms in budget hotels a less expensive proposition. Groups of three or four willing to share two or three beds in a budget hotel will save even more. Showers are always free at hostels in Paris.

Some hostels allow guests to stay a maximum of three nights, particularly in summer, though places that have upper age limits (eg, 30) tend not to enforce them. Only the official *auberges de jeunesse* (youth hostels) require guests to present Hostelling International (HI) cards or equivalent. Curfew – if enforced – is generally at 1 or 2 am. Only a few hostels accept telephone reservations from individuals; those that do are noted in the text.

Louvre & Les Halles You can't get any more central than the 1er arrondissement between the Louvre and the Forum des Halles.

Centre International BVJ Paris-Louvre (Map 6, ☎ 01 53 00 90 90, fax 01 53 00 90 91, 20 rue Jean-Jacques Rousseau, 1er, metro Louvre-Rivoli). This modern, 200-bed hostel run by the Bureau des Voyages de la Jeunesse charges 130FF (including breakfast) for a bunk in a single-sex room for two to 10 people. Guests should be aged under 35. Rooms are accessible from 2.30 pm on the day you arrive and all day after that. There are no kitchen facilities. There is usually space in the morning, even in summer. The BVJ Web site for this hostel and its sister property in the Latin Quarter is www.bvjhotels.com.

Marais The Marais is one of the liveliest sections of the Right Bank and its hostels are among the city's finest. The Maison Internationale de la Jeunesse et des Étudiants (MIJE) runs three hostels in attractively renovated 17th- and 18th-century *hôtels particuliers* (private mansions) here.

Costs and phone details are the same for all three. A bed in a single-sex dorm room with shower for four to eight people costs 145FF (155FF in a triple, 175FF in a double, 240FF in a single), including breakfast. Rooms are closed from noon to 3 pm; curfew is from 1 to 7 am.

Individuals can make reservations for all three MIJE hostels by calling or faxing the central switchboard (☎ 01 42 74 23 45, fax 01 40 27 81 64); they'll hold you a bed till noon, and the maximum stay is seven

nights. During summer and other busy periods, there may not be space after about mid-morning. There's an annual membership fee of 15FF. The MIJE Web site is www.mije.com.

MIJE Fourcy (Map 7, 6 rue de Fourcy, 4e, metro St-Paul). This 207-bed branch is the largest of the three. There's a cheap restaurant here with a three course *menu* with a drink costing 60FF and a *plat du jour* plus drink for 50FF.

MIJE Fauconnier (Map 7, 11 rue du Fauconnier, 4e, metro St-Paul or Pont Marie). This 111-bed hostel is two blocks south of MIJE Fourcy.

MIJE Maubuisson (Map 7, 12 rue des Barres, metro Hôtel de Ville). This 114-bed place, the pick of the three in our opinion, is half a block south of the *mairie* (town hall) of the 4e arrondissement.

Latin Quarter The lively Latin Quarter, in the northern section of the 5e arrondissement and close to the Seine, is popular with students and young people.

Centre International BVJ Paris-Quartier Latin (Map 5, ☎ 01 43 29 34 80, fax 01 53 00 90 91, 44 rue des Bernardins, 5e, metro Maubert Mutualité). This 138-bed hostel has the same rules as the Centre International BVJ Paris-Louvre (see Louvre & Les Halles in this section) though rates are a bit different. Individuals pay 160/140/130FF per person in rooms with one/two/five beds.

Young & Happy Hostel (Map 5, ☎ 01 45 35 09 53, fax 01 47 07 22 24, ✆ smile@youngandhappy.fr, 80 rue Mouffetard, 5e, metro Place Monge). This friendly place is in the most happening centre of the Latin Quarter and very popular with a younger crowd. The rooms are closed from 11 am to 4 pm, but reception is always open. A bed in a smallish room with washbasin for three or four people costs 117FF, and 137FF per person in a double, including breakfast. The 2 am curfew is strictly enforced. In summer, the best way to get a bed is to stop by at about 9 am.

Bastille The relatively untouristy 11e arrondissement is made up generally of unpretentious, working-class areas and is a good way to see 'real' Paris up close.

Auberge de Jeunesse Jules Ferry (Map 6, ☎ 01 43 57 55 60, fax 01 43 14 89 09,✆ auberge @easynet.fr, 8 blvd Jules Ferry, 11e, metro

République or Goncourt). This official hostel, three blocks east of place de la République, is a bit institutional, but the atmosphere is fairly relaxed. Beds cost 115FF in a four or six-person room and 120FF in a double, including breakfast. Rooms are locked from 10.30 am to 2 pm. You must have an HI card to stay here or pay an extra 19FF per night. Internet access costs 5FF.

Auberge Internationale des Jeunes (Map 5, ☎ 01 47 00 62 00, fax 01 47 00 33 16, ✉ aij@ aijparis.com, 10 rue Trousseau, 11e, metro Ledru Rollin). This clean and very friendly hostel, 700m east of place de la Bastille, attracts a young, international crowd and gets very full in summer. Beds in dorms for two to six people cost 81FF from November to February and 91FF from March to October, including breakfast. Rooms are closed for cleaning between 10 am and 3 pm.

Maison Internationale des Jeunes pour la Culture et la Paix (Map 5, ☎ 01 43 71 99 21, fax 01 43 71 78 58, ✉ mij.cp@wanadoo.fr, 4 rue Titon, 11e, metro Faidherbe Chaligny). The 150-bed MIJCP, 1.3km east of place de la Bastille, charges 110FF for a bed in a spartan dorm room for up to eight people, including breakfast. Curfew is from 2 to 6 am. The upper age limit of 30 is not strictly enforced. Telephone reservations are accepted, but your chance of finding a bed is greatest if you call or stop by between 8 and 10 am. The maximum stay is theoretically three days, but you can usually stay for a week if there's room.

Résidence Bastille (Map 5, ☎ 01 43 79 53 86, fax 01 43 79 35 63, 151 ave Ledru Rollin, 11e, metro Voltaire). This 150-bed hostel is about 900m north-east of place de la Bastille. Beds in rooms for two to four people cost 125FF (110FF from November to February), including breakfast, and there are singles costing 175FF (160FF in the low season). Check-in is from 7 am to 12.30 pm and 2 to 10 pm. Curfew is at 1 am.

Gare du Nord & Gare de l'Est The areas east and north-east of these two train stations have always had a more than ample selection of hotels, but until recently there wasn't a hostel to be found in the quarter.

Peace & Love Hostel (Map 3, ☎ 01 46 07 65 11, fax 01 42 05 47 50, ✉ pl@paris-hostels.com, 245 rue La Fayette, 10e, metro Jaurès). This groovy hostel, which attracts a crowd that appreciates all the gifts of Mother Nature, is one of the cheapest around, with beds in rooms for two, three of four people costing a uniform

85FF in winter and 97FF in summer. Facilities are limited, but there's Internet access and a full bar on the ground floor open till 2 am that boasts the cheapest beer in Paris.

Gare de Lyon & Nation The development of Bercy Village (see the Bercy section) has done much to resuscitate the 12e arrondissement.

Blue Planet Hostel (Map 5, ☎ 01 43 42 06 18, fax 01 43 42 09 89, ✉ general@hostelblue planet.com, 5 rue Hector Malot, 12e, metro Gare de Lyon). If you like the idea of rolling out of bed directly onto your south-bound train, this new 43-room hostel is for you: you couldn't find a place closer to the Gare de Lyon. A bed in a room for two/three to five people costs 150/100FF per person, including breakfast. Rooms are locked between 11 am and 3 pm but there's no curfew. Internet access costs 1FF a minute.

Centre International de Séjour de Paris Maurice Ravel (Map 1, ☎ 01 44 75 60 06, fax 01 43 44 45 30, ✉ 100616.2215@compuserve.com, 4–6 ave Maurice Ravel, 12e, metro Porte de Vincennes). The 230-bed CISP Maurice Ravel, on the south-eastern edge of the city, charges 126FF in a room for two to four people, 156FF in a double and 206FF in a single, including breakfast. Meals cost 50FF to 55FF. If you stay more than a week the nightly rates are 116FF, 146FF and 196FF, respectively. There is no age limit. Reception opens from 6.30 am to 1.30 am. Individuals (as opposed to groups, which predominate) can make telephone reservations up to two days ahead. To get there from Porte de Vincennes metro station, walk south on blvd Soult, turn left onto rue Jules Lemaître and then right onto rue Maurice Ravel. Their Web site is www.cisp.asso.fr.

Chinatown & Montparnasse The southern 13e, 14e and 15e arrondissements are not particularly exciting quarters, but they're not too far from the Left Bank's major sights.

Aloha Hostel (Map 4, ☎ 01 42 73 03 03, fax 01 42 73 14 14, ✉ friends@aloha.fr, 1 rue Borromée, 15e, metro Volontaires). Run by the same people as the Three Ducks Hostel (see later in this section) and charging the same prices, the Aloha is much more laid-back and quiet than its sister hostel to the west. The rooms, which have two to six beds and sometimes showers, are closed from 11 am to 5 pm, but reception is always open. Curfew is at 2 am. Kitchen facilities and safe-deposit boxes are available.

Centre International de Séjour de Paris Keller-mann (Map 1, ☎ 01 44 16 37 38, fax 01 43 44 45 30, **@** 100616.2215@compuserve.com, 17 blvd Kellermann, 13e, metro Porte d'Italie). The 350-bed CISP Kellermann has beds in dorm rooms accommodating two to four people costing 126FF, and 101FF in those with eight beds. Basic singles cost 146FF or 196FF with shower and WC. A double with facilities costs 312FF. Except on Friday and Saturday nights, curfew is at 1.30 am. The maximum stay is five or six nights. There are no kitchen facilities. Telephone reservations can be made up to 48 hours before you arrive. Facilities for disabled people are available.

Foyer International d'Accueil de Paris Jean Monnet (Map 1, ☎ 01 43 13 17 00, fax 01 45 81 63 91, **@** fiapadmi@fiap.assoc.fr, 30 rue Caba-nis, 14e, metro Glacière). FIAP Jean Monnet, a few blocks south-east of place Denfert Rochereau, has modern, carpeted rooms for either five to eight, three to four or two people – pretty luxurious by hostel standards – for 139/172/194FF per person (including break-fast); singles cost 301FF. Rooms specially fitted for disabled people are available. Curfew is from 2 to 6 am. Telephone reservations are ac-cepted up to 15 days ahead, but priority is given to groups.

Maison des Clubs UNESCO (Map 1, ☎ 01 43 36 00 63, fax 01 45 35 05 96, **@** clubs.unesco .paris@wanadoo, 43 rue de la Glacière, 13e, metro Glacière). This rather institutional place charges 130FF for a bed in a large, unsurprising room for three or four people; singles/doubles cost 180/300FF. In the multi-bed rooms, prior-ity is given to 18 to 30-year-olds. Beds booked by telephone are usually held until 2 pm.

Three Ducks Hostel (Map 4, ☎ 01 48 42 04 05, fax 01 48 42 99 99, **@** backpack@3ducks.fr, 6 place Étienne Pernet, 15e, metro Félix Faure). Named after three ducks who used to live in the courtyard, this friendly, down-to-earth hostel at the southern end of rue du Com-merce is a favourite with young backpackers looking to party. It can apparently get pretty noisy at night (the new bar opens till 1 am) so if you're in Paris to sleep, stay somewhere else. A bunk bed in a very basic room for two to eight people costs 117FF (97FF from Novem-ber to April), including breakfast. Telephone reservations are accepted on the day of arrival. Kitchen facilities and Internet access are avail-able. Rooms are closed between noon and 5 pm

and there's a 2 am curfew. Their Web site is at www.3ducks.fr.

Montmartre & Pigalle Both the 9e and 18e arrondissements each have a fine hostel to choose from.

Le Village Hostel (Map 8, ☎ 01 42 64 22 02, fax 01 42 64 22 04, **@** bonjour@villagehostel.fr, 20 rue d'Orsel, 18e, metro Anvers). This fine 26-room hostel with beamed ceilings and views of Sacré Cœur has beds in rooms for two to six people costing 117FF (97FF from November to February) and doubles/triples/quads costing 147/137/127FF per person (137/127/117FF in winter), including breakfast. All rooms have showers and WC. Kitchen facilities are avail-able, and there is a bar and a lovely outside ter-race. Curfew is at 2 am.

Woodstock Hostel (Map 3, ☎ 01 48 78 87 76, fax 01 48 78 01 63, **@** flowers@woodstock.fr, 48 rue Rodier, 9e, metro Anvers). This hostel is just down the hill from raucous Pigalle in a quiet, residential quarter. A dorm bed in a room for four to six people costs 77FF off-season, and a bed in a double room costs 87FF; both tariffs include breakfast. In summer prices rise to 97FF and 107FF, respectively. There's a 2 am curfew and rooms are shut from noon to 4 pm. There's a kitchen and Internet access.

Hotels

Paris may not be able to boast the number of cheap hotels it did even a decade ago, but the choice is still more than ample, espe-cially in the Marais, around Bastille and near the major train stations off the Grands Boulevards. Places with one star or the des-ignation 'NN' (Nouvelle Norme), which signifies that a hotel is awaiting its rating but assures a certain standard of comfort, are much of a muchness and are usually be-yond our powers of description. Remember: the consideration at these places is cost – not quality.

Louvre & Les Halles This area of the 1er may be very central, but don't expect to find tranquillity or many bargains left. Both air-ports are linked to the Châtelet-Les Halles metro/RER station (Map 6) by Roissyrail and Orlyval.

Hôtel de Lille (Map 6, ☎ 01 42 33 33 42, 8 rue du Pélican, 1er, metro Palais Royal-Musée du

Louvre). Clean singles/doubles at this 13-room hotel down a quiet side street come with washbasin, bidet and cheap ceiling tiles and cost 210/240FF. Doubles with shower cost 290FF. A hall shower costs an expensive 30FF.

Marais
This district is one of the liveliest and trendiest in Paris and, despite gentrification, the Marais still has some cheapies left.

Hôtel de la Herse d'Or (Map 7, ☎ *01 48 87 84 09, fax 01 48 87 94 01, 20 rue St-Antoine, 4e, metro Bastille).* This friendly, 35-room place has unsurprising, serviceable singles with washbasin costing 170FF and with basin and toilet for 210FF; doubles with toilet and a small shower cost 290FF to 305FF. Hall showers cost 10FF.

Hôtel Moderne (Map 7, ☎ *01 48 87 97 05, 3 rue Caron, 4e, metro St-Paul).* The less-than-salubrious rooms at this small hotel off lovely place du Marché Ste-Catherine come with washbasin and start at 160FF; doubles with shower cost 260FF (300FF with shower and toilet). Triples cost 400FF. There's a shower (15FF) on the stairs halfway between each floor.

Hôtel Pratic (Map 7, ☎ *01 48 87 80 47, fax 01 48 87 40 04, 9 rue d'Ormesson, 4e, metro St-Paul).* This 23-room hotel around the corner from the Hôtel Moderne has renovated singles/doubles with washbasin and WC costing 250/305FF (370/390 with shower). Rooms with bath and toilet cost 420/450FF.

Hôtel Rivoli (Map 7, ☎ *01 42 72 08 41, 44 rue de Rivoli, 4e, metro Hôtel de Ville).* This hotel is no longer as cheap as it was but it's still a good deal. Basic and somewhat noisy rooms with washbasin start at 200FF. Singles with shower cost 210FF; doubles with bath but no toilet cost 230FF, and a double with bath and toilet costs 300FF. The hall shower (20FF) can be lukewarm. The front door is locked from 2 to 7 am.

Hôtel Sully (Map 7, ☎ *01 42 78 49 32, fax 01 44 61 76 50, 48 rue St-Antoine, 4e, metro Bastille).* You'll find basic doubles with washbasin for 230FF, 280FF with shower, and 300FF with shower and toilet here, only one block south of delightful place des Vosges. A two-bed triple with shower and toilet costs 320FF.

Île de la Cité
Believe it or not, the only hotel on Île de la Cité is a budget one.

Hôtel Henri IV (Map 6, ☎ *01 43 54 44 53, 25 place Dauphine, 1er, metro Pont Neuf or Cité).* This old-fashioned, very popular hotel is a bit tattered and worn, but has 21 adequate rooms. One-bed rooms with no facilities cost 125FF to 155FF, and with a sink cost from 170FF to 210FF; two-bed rooms with washbasin cost 215FF to 245FF; and a room for three to four people costs 295FF. Breakfast is included. Showers in the hall cost 15FF. The four rooms with their own showers cost 270FF to 295FF. Reception opens until 8 pm, but you should make reservations a month in advance.

Latin Quarter
Real cheapies have almost gone the way of the dodo in the Latin Quarter but a couple remain.

Hôtel de Médicis (Map 5, ☎ *01 43 54 14 66, 214 rue St-Jacques, 5e, metro Luxembourg).* This is exactly how a dilapidated Latin Quarter dive for impoverished students and travellers has always looked. Very basic singles cost 90FF to 100FF, but they're usually occupied; doubles/triples cost 180/250FF.

Port Royal Hôtel (Map 1, ☎ *01 43 31 70 06, fax 01 43 31 33 67, 8 blvd de Port Royal, 5e, metro Les Gobelins).* The clean, quiet and well-kept 46 singles/doubles at this older place start at 180/245FF (380FF with shower and toilet). Hall showers cost 15FF.

Gare du Nord
This may not be one of the city's most attractive districts, but it's not dangerous, unless you opt to spend the night in the train station. Gare du Nord is linked to Charles de Gaulle airport by Roissy-rail and RATP bus No 350 and to Orly airport by Orlyval. This area of Paris has some pretty good budget deals.

Hôtel Bonne Nouvelle (Map 3, ☎ *01 48 74 99 90, 125 blvd de Magenta, 10e, metro Gare du Nord).* The 'Good News' is a modest hotel with simple, clean, shower-equipped doubles which cost from 160FF to 240FF. Hall toilets are on the landing.

Grand Hôtel Magenta (Map 3, ☎ *01 48 78 03 65, fax 01 48 78 41 64, 129 blvd de Magenta, 10e, metro Gare du Nord).* Clean, spacious rooms are available with washbasin and bidet from 150FF to 190FF, with shower from 250FF, or with shower and toilet from 300FF. Larger rooms for three to five people cost 350FF to 450FF. Hall showers cost 20FF.

Hôtel de Milan (Map 3, ☎ *01 40 37 88 50, fax 01 46 07 89 48, 17–19 rue de St-Quentin, 10e, metro Gare du Nord).* This old-fashioned, friendly 50-room place is equipped with an ancient lift. Clean, quiet but basic singles cost from

160FF to 180FF, doubles cost 200FF. Doubles with toilet and shower cost from 280FF; triples cost from 430FF. Hall showers cost 18FF.

Hôtel La Vieille France (Map 3, ☎ 01 45 26 42 37, fax 01 45 26 99 07, 151 rue La Fayette, 10e, metro Gare du Nord). This is a 34-room place with spacious, pleasant and soundproofed doubles with washbasin and bidet costing 245FF, and with bath or shower and toilet from 355FF to 390FF. Triples cost 430FF to 480FF. Hall showers cost 15FF.

Gare de l'Est This lively, working-class area of the 10e has its own attractions even if your train doesn't pull into Gare de l'Est. RATP bus No 350 to/from Charles de Gaulle airport stops right in front of the station. The 10e has some of Paris' grungiest flophouses, but the few diamonds in the rough offer some bargains.

Hôtel d'Alsace, Strasbourg & Magenta (Map 3, ☎ 01 40 37 75 41, 85 blvd de Strasbourg, 10e, metro Gare de l'Est). This is an old, but well-maintained, 30-room hostelry with bright, clean singles/doubles/triples with washbasin costing 134/187/250FF. Doubles with shower cost 247FF. The fireplaces give the rooms a bit of old-time charm. Hall showers cost 10FF. The entrance is on the left of the passageway.

Hôtel Liberty (Map 3, ☎ 01 42 08 60 58, fax 01 42 40 12 59, 16 rue de Nancy, 10e, metro Château d'Eau). Clean, plain singles/doubles on this 1st-floor hotel start at 150/180FF (190/230FF with shower, 220/275FF with shower and toilet). Hall showers cost 10FF.

Hôtel Pacific (Map 3, ☎ 01 47 70 07 91, fax 01 47 70 98 43, 70 rue du Château d'Eau, 10e, metro Château d'Eau). An older place with 23 rooms, the Pacific has unpretentious but clean singles costing 153FF to 173FF; doubles/triples cost 186/259FF (276/309FF with shower). Hall showers cost 15FF.

Sibour Hôtel (Map 3, ☎ 01 46 07 20 74, fax 01 46 07 37 17, ✉ sibour.hotel@wanadoo.fr, 4 rue Sibour, 10e, metro Gare de l'Est). This friendly hotel has 45 well-kept rooms, including old-fashioned singles/doubles costing from 180/200FF (290/320FF with shower/bath, toilet and TV). Hall showers cost 15FF.

Bastille The area just east of place de la Bastille (ie around rue de Làppe) gets busy after dark since the arrival of the Opéra Bastille. Farther east is an ungentrified, typ-

ically Parisian working-class neighbourhood whose hotels cater mainly to French businesspeople of modest means. Place de la Nation (Map 1) is linked to Charles de Gaulle airport by RATP bus No 351.

The 11e has Paris' best selection of respectable, old-time cheapies. The best deals are away from place de la Bastille.

Hôtel des Alliés (Map 5, ☎ 01 44 73 01 17, 90 rue du Faubourg St-Antoine, 12e, metro Ledru Rollin). This uninspiring, 37-room place offers one of the better deals in the Bastille neighbourhood, with singles/doubles/triples/quads ranging from 90/150/195/240FF to 130/180/210/280FF in the high season. Some rooms have their own showers.

Hôtel Bastille Opéra (Map 6, ☎ 01 43 55 16 06, 6 rue de la Roquette, 11e, metro Bastille). This ageing, 20-room place, just off place de la Bastille, has basic singles costing 130FF to 140FF and doubles for 180FF. Showers are free. Reception, open 24 hours, is on the 1st floor. There are several other hotels along the same stretch of rue de la Roquette.

Hôtel Baudin (Map 5, ☎ 01 47 00 18 91, fax 01 48 07 04 66, 113 ave Ledru Rollin, 11e, metro Ledru Rollin). This once grand, old-fashioned hostelry has 17 partially renovated singles/doubles costing from 170/230FF (220/290FF with shower, 260/320FF with shower and toilet); triples cost 350FF to 470FF. Hall showers are free.

Hôtel Camélia (Map 1, ☎ 01 43 73 67 50, 6 ave Philippe Auguste, 11e, metro Nation). This family-run, 30-room establishment has well-kept rooms costing from 175/250FF. Doubles with shower/bath and toilet cost 280/350FF. Hall showers cost 20FF.

Hôtel Central (Map 1, ☎ 01 43 73 73 53, 16 ave Philippe Auguste, 11e, metro Nation). This quiet and clean place just north of place de la Nation has singles/doubles/quads with washbasin and bidet costing 165/185/270FF. Hall showers cost 20FF.

Hôtel Familial (Map 5, ☎ 01 43 67 48 24, 33 rue Richard Lenoir, 11e, metro Voltaire). This family-run, old-time cheapie has basic, rundown singles with washbasin costing 80FF to 100FF and doubles costing 115FF to 120FF. Hall showers cost 15FF.

Hôtel de France (Map 5, ☎ 01 43 79 53 22, 159 ave Ledru Rollin, 11e, metro Voltaire). Decent, well-maintained singles/doubles/triples with shower cost 150/220/280FF at this establishment. All the toilets are off the hall. Reception is in the Restaurant de France next door.

PARIS

Hôtel St-Amand (*Map 5*, ☎ *01 47 00 90 55, 6 rue Trousseau, 11e, metro Ledru Rollin*). The linoleum floored, washbasin-equipped rooms spread over six floors (there's no lift) are nothing fancy, but the prices begin at only 100/120FF (from 170FF with shower). Hall showers cost 20FF.

Hôtel de Savoie (*Map 5*, ☎ *01 43 72 96 47, 27 rue Richard Lenoir, 11e, metro Voltaire*). Nondescript but serviceable singles/doubles start at 150/180FF; showers are free. Rooms with shower cost 180/250FF. A sign on the door advertises a 15% discount for those with a copy of this book.

Vix Hôtel (*Map 5*, ☎ *01 48 05 12 58, fax 01 48 06 15 09, 19 rue de Charonne, 11e, metro Bastille or Ledru Rollin*). This place is a bit dreary and not exactly spotless, but it has plenty of basic rooms costing from 130/200FF; hall showers cost 15FF. Doubles with shower cost 220FF and 250FF with shower and toilet.

Chinatown Paris' original Chinatown (Belleville in the 20e has one too) is south of place d'Italie along ave d'Ivry and ave de Choisy. The 13e may not be electrifying, but it has some good deals and there are plenty of decent Chinese restaurants around.

Arian Hôtel (*Map 1*, ☎ *01 45 70 76 00, fax 01 45 70 85 53,* ✉ *arianhotel@aol.com, 102 ave de Choisy, 13e, metro Tolbiac*). This motel-like 30-room place has simple singles costing 170FF, with shower for 250FF. Doubles/triples with shower and toilet cost 300/400FF.

Hôtel des Beaux-Arts (*Map 1*, ☎ *01 44 24 22 60, 2 rue Toussaint-Féron, 13e, metro Tolbiac*). Singles/doubles at this 25-room hotel start at 160/190FF and go up to 250FF with shower and 390FF with bath and toilet.

Hôtel Tolbiac (*Map 1*, ☎ *01 44 24 25 54, fax 01 45 85 43 47,* ✉ *htolbiac@club-internet.fr, 122 rue de Tolbiac, 13e, metro Tolbiac*). Well-lit, quiet and spotlessly clean rooms with washbasin cost 140/170FF, or 270FF with shower and toilet. Hall showers are free.

Montparnasse Though untouristy and less than thrilling, the 14e and easternmost corner of the 15e arrondissements do have a number of good deals on offer. Gare Montparnasse is served by Air France buses from both airports. Place Denfert Rochereau is also linked to both airports by Orlybus, Orlyval and Roissyrail. The budget places in

the 14e don't usually see many foreign tourists.

Celtic Hôtel (*Map 4*, ☎ *01 43 20 93 53, fax 01 43 20 66 07, 15 rue d'Odessa, 14e, metro Edgar Quinet*). The 29-room Celtic is an old-fashioned hotel that has undergone only partial modernisation. It has bare singles/doubles costing 230/260FF, and doubles/triples with shower costing 300/410FF.

Hôtel de l'Espérance (*Map 4*, ☎ *01 43 21 63 84, 45 rue de la Gaîté, 14e, metro Gaîté*). This 14-room place along a street lined with sex shops has slightly frayed doubles with washbasin costing 170FF, with shower for 185FF to 215FF, and with shower and toilet for 220FF. A bed for a third person costs 50FF. Hall showers cost 15FF.

Hôtel de l'Espérance (*Map 1*, ☎ *01 43 21 41 04, fax 01 43 22 06 02, 1 rue de Grancey, 14e, metro Denfert Rochereau*). This similarly named but unrelated 17-room place has basic rooms from 200FF, and from 275FF with shower.

Montmartre & Pigalle Montmartre, encompassing the 18e and the northern part of the 9e, is one of the most charming neighbourhoods in Paris. The flat area around the base of the hill has some surprisingly good deals. The lively, ethnically mixed area east of Sacré Cœur can be a bit rough – some people say it's prudent to avoid the Château Rouge metro stop at night.

Hôtel Audran (*Map 7*, ☎ *01 42 58 79 59, fax 01 42 58 39 11, 7 rue Audran, 18e, metro Abbesses*). Basic rooms start at 120/160FF; doubles with shower start at 160FF, and 250FF with shower and toilet. The 1st and 3rd floors have showers (10FF).

Hôtel Bonséjour (*Map 7*, ☎ *01 42 54 22 53, fax 01 42 54 25 92, 11 rue Burq, 18e, metro Abbesses*). We've had quite a few letters from readers praising this hotel at the end of a quiet cul-de-sac in Montmartre, and we liked what we saw the last time we visited. Basic singles cost 120FF to 140FF, doubles 180FF, and a hall shower costs 10FF. Doubles/triples with shower are a bargain at 230/270FF and some rooms (Nos 14, 23, 33, 43 and 53) have little balconies.

Hôtel de Carthage (*Map 7*, ☎/*fax 01 46 06 27 03, 10 rue Poulet, 18e, metro Château Rouge*). This 40-room place has singles and twins with shower costing 250FF, and doubles with shower and toilet for 300FF. Doors are locked at 1 am.

Hôtel de Rohan (Map 7, ☎ 01 42 52 32 57, fax 01 55 79 79 63, 90 rue Myrha, 18e, metro Château Rouge). Basic, tidy rooms at this 25-room establishment cost 120/150FF. Doubles with shower and TV cost 220FF. Showers in the hall cost 20FF.

Hôtel St-Pierre (Map 7, ☎ 01 46 06 20 73, 3 rue Seveste, 18e, metro Anvers). This friendly, family-run establishment in a renovated 150-year-old building with 36 simple but serviceable rooms charges from 120/180FF for basic rooms (170/190FF with shower and toilet, 230FF with bath and toilet). With busy blvd de Rochechouart so close, it can be a bit noisy.

PLACES TO STAY – MID-RANGE

Mid-range hotels in Paris offer some of the best value for money in Europe.

Louvre & Les Halles

This area is more disposed to welcoming top-end travellers, but there are some mid-range places to choose from.

Hôtel St-Honoré (Map 6, ☎ 01 42 36 20 38, fax 01 42 21 44 08, 85 rue St-Honoré, 1er, metro Châtelet). This upgraded hotel at the eastern end of a very upmarket shopping street offers cramped doubles/quads from 290/480FF; more spacious doubles cost 380FF to 420FF.

Marais

There's an excellent choice of one- and two-star hotels in the buzzy Marais.

Hôtel Castex (Map 6, ☎ 01 42 72 31 52, fax 01 42 72 57 91. ✆ info@castexhotel.com, 5 rue Castex, 4e, metro Bastille). This cheery, 29-room establishment, equidistant from Bastille and the heart of the Marais, has been run by the same family since 1919. Quiet, old-fashioned but immaculate singles/doubles with shower cost 240/320FF (290FF to 360FF with toilet too). Triples/quads cost 460/530FF. Reserve well in advance.

Hôtel Le Compostelle (Map 7, ☎ 01 42 78 59 99, fax 01 40 29 05 18, 31 rue du Roi de Sicile, 4e, metro Hôtel de Ville). This tasteful 25-room place at the more tranquil end of the Marais has singles/doubles with shower, toilet and TV costing 330/490FF. Double rooms with bath cost 530FF.

Hôtel Jeanne d'Arc (Map 7, ☎ 01 48 87 62 11, fax 01 48 87 37 31, 3 rue de Jarente, 4e, metro St-Paul). This 36-room hotel near lovely Place du Marché Ste-Catherine is a great little *pied-à-terre* for your peregrinations among the museums, bars and restaurants of the Marais, Village St-Paul and Bastille. Small rooms cost 320/325FF; larger ones cost 410/425FF. Triples/quads cost 550/620FF.

Hôtel de Nice (Map 7, ☎ 01 42 78 55 29, fax 01 42 78 36 07, 42 bis rue de Rivoli, 4e, metro Hôtel de Ville). The English-speaking owner of this especially warm, family-run place has 23 comfortable singles/doubles/triples costing 380/550/680FF. Many rooms have balconies high above busy rue de Rivoli.

Hôtel de la Place des Vosges (Map 7, ☎ 01 42 72 60 46, fax 01 42 72 02 64 ✆ hotel.place.des .vosges@gofornet.fr, 12 rue de Birague, 4e, metro Bastille). Superbly situated due south of sublime place des Vosges, this 16-room place has rather average singles costing from 365FF (495FF in summer) and doubles with bathroom costing from 545FF to 690FF, including breakfast. There's a tiny lift from the 1st floor.

Hôtel du Septième Art (Map 7, ☎ 01 44 54 85 00, fax 01 42 77 69 10, 20 rue St-Paul, 4e, metro St-Paul). This is a fun place for movie buffs, with a black-and-white movie theme throughout, right down to the tiled floors and bathrooms. Basic singles cost 295FF; doubles with shower or bath and WC range from 430FF to 690FF.

Latin Quarter

There are dozens of two and three-star hotels, including a cluster near the Sorbonne and another group along the lively rue des Écoles. Mid-range hotels in the Latin Quarter are popular with visiting academics so rooms are hardest to find when conferences and seminars are scheduled: usually March to July and in October.

The Luxembourg and Port Royal metro/RER stations are linked to both airports by Roissyrail and Orlyval.

Hôtel Cluny Sorbonne (Map 5, ☎ 01 43 54 66 66, fax 01 43 29 68 07, ✆ cluny@club-internet.fr, 8 rue Victor Cousin, 5e, metro Luxembourg). The lift in this 23-room hotel, which has pleasant, well-kept singles/doubles/triples for 450/480/700FF, is the size of a telephone box but will accommodate most travellers and their hat boxes.

Hôtel de l'Espérance (Map 5, ☎ 01 47 07 10 99, fax 01 43 37 56 19, 15 rue Pascal, 5e, metro Censier Daubenton). Just a couple of minutes walk south of lively rue Mouffetard, this quiet and immaculately kept 38-room hotel has singles/doubles with shower and toilet costing

400/450FF. Larger rooms with two beds cost between 500FF and 600FF. Breakfast costs 38FF.

Hôtel Esmeralda (Map 6, ☎ 01 43 54 19 20, fax 01 40 51 00 68, 4 rue St-Julien le Pauvre, 5e, metro St-Michel). This 19-room gem, tucked away in a quiet street with full views of Notre Dame, has been everyone's secret 'find' for years now, with its resident cats and artistowner Mme Burel. A simple single with washbasin costs 180FF; doubles with shower and toilet cost 350FF, and with bath and toilet from 450FF to 520FF. Triples/quads start at 580/650FF. Book *well* in advance.

Familia Hôtel (Map 5, ☎ 01 43 54 55 27, fax 01 43 29 61 77, 11 rue des Écoles, 5e, metro Cardinal Lemoine). This exceptionally welcoming and well-situated hotel has 21 rooms attractively decorated with murals of Parisian landmarks. Eight have balconies, from which you can catch a glimpse of Notre Dame. Singles/doubles/triples/quads with shower or bath cost 385/465/615/765FF.

Hôtel Gay Lussac (Map 5, ☎ 01 43 54 23 96, fax 01 40 51 79 49, 29 rue Gay Lussac, 5e, metro Luxembourg). This family-run, 35-room hotel with lots of character and a lift has small singles costing as little as 170FF, but averaging 220FF. Rooms with toilet cost from 240FF to 260FF, and rooms with shower or bath and toilet from 310FF to 360FF. Fairly large doubles/quads with shower, toilet and high ceilings start at 360/450FF.

Grand Hôtel du Progrès (Map 5, ☎ 01 43 54 53 18, fax 01 56 24 87 80, 50 rue Gay Lussac, 5e, metro Luxembourg). Washbasin-equipped singles at this older, 26-room hotel cost 160FF to 180FF; large, old-fashioned doubles with a view and morning sun cost 240FF to 290FF (320FF to 350FF with shower and toilet), including breakfast. Hall showers are free.

Hôtel Marignan (Map 6, ☎ 01 43 54 63 81, 13 rue du Sommerard, 5e, metro Maubert Mutualité). This friendly, 30-room place has pleasant, old-fashioned singles/doubles/triples/quads with washbasin costing 250/320/460/500FF. Doubles with shower cost 490FF to 520FF, triples 530FF to 560FF and quads 600FF to 670FF. About half of the rooms have toilets. Guests also have free use of a fridge, microwave, washing machine and clothes dryer.

Hôtel Minerve (Map 5, ☎ 01 43 26 26 04, fax 01 44 07 01 96, 13 rue des Écoles, 5e, metro Cardinal Lemoine). Sister hotel to the Familia, the 54-room Minerve has been completely renovated and the reception area is kitted out in Oriental carpets and antique books, which owner/manager Erich collects, and some of the rooms have frescoes of French monuments and repro-

duction 18th-century wallpaper. Singles with shower and toilet cost 390FF to 540FF, doubles 460FF to 540FF and triples 620FF to 650FF. Some 10 rooms have small balconies, eight have views of Notre Dame and two have tiny courtyards that are swooningly romantic.

Hôtel St-Jacques (Map 5, ☎ 01 44 07 45 45, fax 01 43 25 65 50, ✉ hotelstjacques@wanadoo.fr, 35 rue des Écoles, 5e, metro Maubert Mutualité). Audrey Hepburn and Cary Grant, who filmed some scenes of *Charade* here, would commend the mod-cons that now complement the original 19th-century detailing (ornamented ceilings, iron staircase) of this adorable 35-room hotel, whose balconies overlook the Panthéon. Spacious singles cost 260FF to 480FF, doubles 450FF to 610FF and triples 680FF.

St-Germain & Odéon

St-Germain des Prés is a delightful area, but it is quite expensive given the modest comforts offered by most mid-range places. The places listed here are the least expensive mid-range hotels the 6e has to offer.

Hôtel des Académies (Map 4, ☎ 01 43 26 66 44, fax 01 43 26 03 72, 15 rue de la Grande Chaumière, 6e, metro Vavin). This truly charming 21-room hotel has been run by the same friendly family since 1920 and has immaculate singles with washbasin costing 230FF. Doubles with shower cost 315FF (360FF to 375FF with shower and toilet).

Delhy's Hôtel (Map 6, ☎ 01 43 26 58 25, fax 01 43 26 51 06, 22 rue de l'Hirondelle, 6e, metro St-Michel). This 21-room hotel, through the arch from 6 place St-Michel, has neat, simple washbasin-equipped singles/doubles cost 220/300FF; doubles with toilet cost 300FF and with shower cost 390FF. Hall showers cost 25FF. Breakfast (35FF) is usually obligatory during summer and holiday periods.

Hôtel du Globe (Map 6, ☎ 01 43 26 35 50, fax 01 46 33 62 69, 15 rue des Quatre Vents, 6e, metro Odéon). The 15 rooms in this eclectic hotel – each with their own theme – cost from 410FF to 495FF with shower and WC, and 595FF with bath and WC.

Hôtel de Nesle (Map 6, ☎ 01 43 54 62 41, 7 rue de Nesle, 6e, metro Odéon or Mabillon). The Nesle is a relaxed, colourfully decorated hotel (theme: Arabian Nights) in a quiet street west of place St-Michel. It is no longer the bargain it once was, but singles/doubles with shower cost 275/350FF; a double with shower/bath and toilet costs 400/450FF. Reservations are not accepted

– the only way to get a bed is to stop by in the morning.

Hôtel Petit Trianon *(Map 6, ☎ 01 43 54 94 64, 2 rue de l'Ancienne Comédie, 6e, metro Odéon)*. This less than sensitively redecorated 15-room hotel has basic singles with washbasin costing 180FF; the showers in the hall are free. Doubles with shower start at 380FF and with shower and toilet 450FF; triples cost 550FF. There's a discount after a stay of more than four nights.

Hôtel St-André des Arts *(Map 6, ☎ 01 43 26 96 16, fax 01 43 29 73 34, ✆ hsaintand@ minitel.net, 66 rue St-André des Arts, 6e, metro Odéon)*. Rooms at this 31-room hotel, on a lively, restaurant-lined thoroughfare, start at 380/490/600/670FF for one/two/three/four people, including breakfast.

Hôtel St-Michel *(Map 6, ☎ 01 43 26 98 70, fax 01 40 46 95 69, 17 rue Gît le Cœur, 6e, metro St-Michel)*. Comfortable but pretty standard, soundproofed singles/doubles cost from 228/ 256FF with washbasin, 328/356FF with shower, and 368/396FF with shower and toilet. The hall shower costs 12FF.

Gare St-Lazare & Grands Boulevards

The avenues around blvd Montmartre are a popular nightlife area. The better deals are away from Gare St-Lazare, but there are several places along rue d'Amsterdam beside the station including the hotels listed below.

Hôtel des Arts *(Map 3, ☎ 01 42 46 73 30, fax 01 48 00 94 42, 7 cité Bergère, off rue Bergère, 9e, metro Grands Boulevards)*. This cheap and funky 26-room hotel with loads of personality (and resident parrot) is situated in a little alley near the Grands Boulevards. Gay readers might like to know that the largest and most popular sauna in town is just around the corner. Singles with shower/bath cost 370/390FF, doubles cost 390/410FF and triples cost 550FF.

Hôtel Britannia *(Map 2, ☎ 01 42 85 36 36, fax 01 42 85 16 93, 24 rue d'Amsterdam, 9e, metro St-Lazare)*. This 46-room place with narrow hallways and pleasant, clean rooms has singles/ doubles with shower costing 395/490FF; doubles with bath cost 490FF. The triples (565/ 610FF with shower/bath) are a bit on the small side.

Hôtel Chopin *(Map 3, ☎ 01 47 70 58 10, fax 01 42 47 00 70, 46 passage Jouffroy, enter from 10 blvd Montmartre, 9e, metro Grands Boule-*

vards). This 36-room place is down one of Paris' most delightful 19th-century *passages* (covered shopping arcades). It may be a little faded around the edges, but it's still enormously evocative of the *belle époque*, and the welcome is always warm. The top floors are the most comfortable. Basic singles cost from 355FF; shower-equipped singles/doubles/triples cost from 405/450/595FF. After the arcade closes at 10 pm, ring the *sonnette de nuit* (the night doorbell).

Hôtel Peletier-Haussmann *(Map 3, ☎ 01 42 46 79 53, fax 01 48 24 12 01, ✆ peletier.haussman@ wanadoo.fr, 15 rue Le Peletier, 9e, metro Richelieu Drouot)*. This friendly 24-room hotel just off blvd Haussmann has shower-equipped singles/ doubles/triples/quads costing 405/460/575/ 620FF.

Gare du Nord & Gare de l'Est

There are quite a few two- and three-star places around the train stations in the 10e arrondissement.

Hôtel Français *(Map 3, ☎ 01 40 35 94 14, fax 01 40 35 55 40, 13 rue du 8 Mai 1945, 10e, metro Gare de l'Est)*. This is 71-room place with attractive, almost luxurious, singles/doubles/ triples (some with balconies) costing from 405/450/550FF. Parking in the hotel garage costs 40FF.

Grand Hôtel de Paris *(Map 3, ☎ 01 46 07 40 56, fax 01 42 05 99 18, 72 blvd de Strasbourg, 10e, metro Gare de l'Est)*. This well-run establishment has 49 pleasant, soundproofed singles/ doubles/triples/quads (320/380/500/620FF) and a tiny lift. If you stay at least four days in the off-season, they may throw in breakfast (30FF) for free.

Nord Hôtel *(Map 3, ☎ 01 45 26 43 40, fax 01 42 82 90 23, ✆ nordhotel@wanadoo.fr, 37 rue de St-Quentin, 10e, metro Gare du Nord)*. This 46-room hotel, right across from Gare du Nord, has clean and quiet singles/doubles/triples with shower or bath costing 320/410/620FF, including breakfast.

Bastille

Two-star comfort is less expensive in the 11e than in the inner arrondissements.

Hôtel Bastille *(Map 6, ☎ 01 47 00 06 71, fax 01 43 57 07 23, 24 rue de la Roquette, 11e, metro Bastille)*. The youthful staff at this friendly, 20-room hotel offer neat and modern singles/

doubles/triples costing 350/400/500FF, including breakfast. From June to September and around Christmas, a bed in a single-sex shared triple with shower and toilet costs 122FF, including breakfast.

Hôtel Lyon Mulhouse (Map 7, ☎ 01 47 00 91 50, fax 01 47 00 06 31,◙ hotelyonmulhouse @wanadoo.fr, 8 blvd Beaumarchais, 11e, metro Bastille). This renovated 40-room hotel offers quiet, though predictable singles costing from 340FF, and doubles with shower and toilet from 530FF; there are also triples (550FF to 580FF) and quads (600FF to 640FF) available.

Hôtel Pax (Map 5, ☎ 01 47 00 40 98, fax 01 43 38 57 81, 12 rue de Charonne, 11e, metro Bastille or Ledru Rollin). Large, spotless rooms with shower range from 250FF to 270FF (270FF to 450FF with toilet and shower).

Montparnasse

Just east of Gare Montparnasse, there are a number of two- and three-star places on rue Vandamme and rue de la Gaîté; the latter street is rife with sex shops.

Hôtel de Blois (Map 1, ☎ 01 45 40 99 48, fax 01 45 40 45 62, 5 rue des Plantes, 14e, metro Mouton Duvernet). This 25-room establishment offers smallish singles/doubles with washbasin and bidet costing 240/250FF. Doubles with shower cost 280FF, and 350FF with shower and toilet. Fully equipped triples cost 370FF.

Hôtel Floridor (Map 1, ☎ 01 43 21 35 53, fax 01 43 27 65 81, 28 place Denfert Rochereau, 14e, metro Denfert Rochereau). Shower-equipped singles/doubles cost 289/317FF (307/335FF with toilet as well), including breakfast. Triples cost 423FF.

Petit Palace Hôtel (Map 1, ☎ 01 43 22 05 25, fax 01 43 21 79 01, 131 ave du Maine, 14e, metro Gaîté). The same family has run this friendly, ambitiously named 44-room hotel for half a century. It has smallish but spotless doubles/triples costing 250/320FF with washbasin and bidet, and from 440FF with shower and toilet. Hall showers cost 20FF.

Montmartre & Pigalle

The attractive two-star places on rue Aristide Bruant are generally less full in July and August than in spring and autumn.

Hôtel des Arts (Map 8, ☎ 01 46 06 30 52, fax 01 46 06 10 83, 5 rue Tholozé, 18e, metro Abbesses). This is a friendly, attractive, 50-

room place with singles/doubles costing from 360/460FF (490FF with two twin beds). Breakfast costs 35FF.

Hôtel Avenir (Map 8, ☎ 01 48 78 21 37, fax 01 40 16 92 62, 39 blvd Rochechouart, 9e, metro Anvers). This 42-room place on noisy blvd Rochechouart has singles/doubles/triples costing from 300/420/460FF. All rooms have a bath or shower and the rates include breakfast.

Hôtel des Capucines Montmartre (Map 8, ☎ 01 42 52 89 80, fax 01 42 52 29 57,◙ capucines@ compuserve.com, 5 rue Aristide Bruant, 18e, metro Abbesses). Singles with TV and minibar cost from 250FF to 325FF, doubles cost from 300FF to 350FF and triples from 350FF to 420FF.

Hôtel Luxia (Map 8, ☎ 01 46 06 84 24, fax 01 46 06 10 14, 8 rue Seveste, 18e, metro Anvers). This 45-room hotel mainly takes groups, but at least a few rooms are almost always left for independent travellers. Plain, clean singles/doubles/triples with shower, toilet and TV cost 280/300/390FF.

Hôtel du Moulin (Map 8, ☎ 01 42 64 33 33, fax 01 46 06 42 66, ◙ moulin.hotel@worldnet.fr, 3 rue Aristide Bruant, 18e, metro Blanche or Abbesses). This 27-room place has rooms with toilet and bath or shower costing 250/300FF in winter and 350/440FF in summer.

Timhôtel Montmartre (Map 8, ☎ 01 42 55 74 79, fax 01 42 55 71 01, ◙ montmartre@timhotel.fr, 11 rue Ravignan and place Émile Goudeau, 18e, metro Abbesses). This is a good choice if you place more value on location than room size. The 60 neat, modern rooms of this branch of the Timhôtel chain cost 680FF for singles and doubles; triples cost 810FF. Some of the rooms on the 4th and 5th floors have stunning views of the city (100FF extra). Buffet breakfast costs 50FF.

Hôtel Utrillo (Map 8, ☎ 01 42 58 13 44, fax 01 42 23 93 88, ◙ adel.utrillo@wanadoo.fr, 7 rue Aristide Bruant, 18e, metro Abbesses). Singles/doubles at this 30-room hotel cost 305/380FF in the low season and 360/420FF in summer. A double with bath and toilet costs 420FF (450FF in summer). Breakfast costs 40FF.

Airports

Both airports have a wide selection of places, including mid-range Ibis hotels, and a rather unusual form of accommodation if you just need to rest.

Cocoon (☎ 01 48 62 06 16, fax 01 48 62 56 97, below departure level (Hall 36) at Aéroport Charles de Gaulle 1). This strange place has 60 'cabins' where you can sleep for up to 16 hours – but no longer than that. The single/double day rates (check in any time between 8 am and 6 pm) are 150/250FF, overnight they're 250/300FF. All cabins have TVs, telephones with fax and, most importantly, alarm clocks.

Hôtel Ibis CDG Aéroport (☎ *01 49 19 19 19, fax 01 49 19 19 21, next to Aéroport Charles de Gaulle 1 train station*). This large, modern, chain hotel with two stars and 556 rooms has singles and doubles costing from 455FF, and triples from 595FF. The hotel is linked to the terminals by shuttle bus.

Hôtel Ibis Orly Aéroport (☎ *01 46 87 33 50, fax 01 46 87 29 92, Orly airport*). This 299-room chain hotel is linked to both terminals by the Navette ADP (airport shuttle bus). Rooms for up to three people start at 415FF; quads start at 500FF.

PLACES TO STAY – TOP END

There's a big range in price at hotels bearing three and four stars in Paris.

Louvre & Les Halles

The 1er is the area to come to if you really want to blow the budget.

Hôtel Brighton (*Map 2*, ☎ *01 47 03 61 61, fax 01 42 60 41 78*, **☺** *hotel.brighton@wanadoo.fr, 218 rue de Rivoli, 1er, metro Tuileries*). This is a three-star, 70-room establishment with lovely singles/doubles/triples costing from 530/670/955FF and climbing to 875/905/1055FF, depending on the season and the room. The rooms that overlook Jardin des Tuileries are the most popular; those on the 4th and 5th floors afford views over the trees to the Seine.

Grand Hôtel de Champagne (*Map 6*, ☎ *01 42 36 60 00, fax 01 45 08 43 33, 17 rue Jean Lantier, 1er, metro Châtelet*). This very comfortable, three-star hotel has 42 rooms, with singles costing from 596FF to 920FF and doubles from 652FF to 1045FF, depending on the season.

Marais

There are top-end hotels in the heart of the Marais as well as in the vicinity of the elegant place des Vosges.

Hôtel Axial Beaubourg (*Map 7*, ☎ *01 42 72 72 22, fax 01 42 72 03 53, 11 rue du Temple, 4e, metro Hôtel de Ville*). The name of this place says it all: modern mixed with historic. It's in

the heart of the Marais and charges from 500/650FF for singles/doubles with shower.

Hôtel Central Marais (*Map 7*, ☎ *01 48 87 56 08, fax 01 42 77 06 27, 2 rue Ste-Croix de la Bretonnerie, 4e, metro Hôtel de Ville*). This seven-room, mostly gay male hotel also welcomes lesbians. Singles and doubles with one bathroom for every two rooms cost 535FF; suites for one or two/three or four cost 650/795FF. After 3 pm reception is around the corner in the bar at 33 rue Vieille du Temple. Reservations should be made four to six weeks ahead.

Grand Hôtel Malher (*Map 6*, ☎ *01 42 72 60 92, fax 01 42 72 25 37*, **☺** *ghmalher@yahoo.fr, 5 rue Malher, 4e, metro St-Paul*). The 31 nicely appointed rooms at this family-run establishment start at 490/590FF for singles/doubles (100FF more in the high season).

Île de St-Louis

The smaller of the two islands in the Seine is an easy walk from central Paris but the hotels are pricey.

Hôtel des Deux Îles (*Map 6*, ☎ *01 43 26 13 35, fax 01 43 29 60 25, 59 rue St-Louis en l'Île, 4e, metro Pont Marie*). This excellent 17-room hotel has small singles costing from 770FF and doubles from 890FF. Breakfast costs 55FF.

Hôtel de Lutèce (*Map 6*, ☎ *01 43 26 23 52, fax 01 43 29 60 25, 65 rue St Louis en l'Île, 4e, metro Pont Marie*). This exquisite 23-room hotel, more country than city, is under the same friendly and helpful management as the Hôtel des Deux Îles. The comfortable rooms are tastefully decorated, the staff are friendly and the location is probably the most desirable in all of France. Rates are similar to those at the Hôtel des Deux Îles.

Hôtel St-Louis (*Map 6*, ☎ *01 46 34 04 80, fax 01 46 34 02 13, 75 rue St-Louis en l'Île, 4e, metro Pont Marie*). Singles/doubles (costing from 695/895FF) at this 21-room establishment are appealing but unspectacular, though the public areas are lovely. The basement breakfast room dates from the early 1600s; breakfast costs 49FF.

Latin Quarter

The Latin Quarter generally offers better value than the nearby 6e arrondissement in the top-end category.

Hôtel des Grandes Écoles (*Map 5*, ☎ *01 43 26 79 23, fax 01 43 25 28 15*, **☺** *hotel.grandes. ecoles@wanadoo.fr, 75 rue du Cardinal*

Lemoine, 5e, metro Cardinal Lemoine). This wonderful 51-room hotel just north of place de la Contrescarpe has one of the loveliest situations in the Latin Quarter, tucked away in a courtyard at a medieval street with its own garden. Singles/doubles cost 550/720FF and an extra bed costs 100FF.

Grand Hôtel St-Michel (Map 5, ☎ 01 46 33 33 02, fax 01 40 46 96 33, @ grand.hotel .st.michel@wanadoo.fr, 19 rue Cujas, 5e, metro Luxembourg). This well-situated 45-room hotel is far enough away from the din of blvd St-Michel to make it feel almost remote. Rooms (some with balcony) cost 690/890FF, while triples cost 1290FF. The attached salon de thé is quite pleasant.

Hôtel Au Royal Cardinal (Map 5, ☎ 01 43 26 83 64, fax 01 44 07 22 32, @ royalcardinal@ multi.micro.com, 1 rue des Écoles, 5e, metro Cardinal Lemoine or Jussieu). We've heard good things about this very central, 36-room hotel near the Sorbonne. Singles cost 460FF to 510FF, doubles cost from 500FF to 550FF and triples cost from 735FF to 785FF.

Résidence Monge (Map 5, ☎ 01 43 26 87 90, fax 01 43 54 47 25, @ hotel-monge@gofornet.com, 55 rue Monge, 5e, metro Place Monge). This clean, well-managed hotel with 36 rooms right in the thick of things is an expensive choice if you're alone (singles cost from 380FF to 480FF) but a good deal if you've got a companion or two: doubles cost 500FF to 550FF and triples cost 600FF to 650FF.

Hôtel St-Christophe (Map 5, ☎ 01 43 31 81 54, fax 01 43 31 12 54, @ hotelstchristophe@ compouserve.com, 17 rue Lacépède, 5e, metro Place Monge). This classy small hotel has 31 well-equipped rooms costing 550/680FF, although discounts are often available.

St-Germain & Odéon

Many three-star hotels cluster around St-Germain des Prés.

Hôtel des Deux Continents (Map 6, ☎ 01 43 26 72 46, fax 01 43 25 67 80, 25 rue Jacob, 6e, metro St-Germain des Prés). This 41-room establishment has spacious singles costing 775FF, doubles from 845FF to 895FF and triples costing 1100FF. Breakfast costs 60FF.

Hôtel Lenox St-Germain (Map 4, ☎ 01 42 96 10 95, fax 01 42 61 52 83, @ hotel@lenoxsaint germain.com, 9 rue de l'Université, 7e, metro Rue du Bac). Simple, uncluttered and comfortable rooms upstairs and a late-opening 1930s-style bar downstairs attract a chic clientele. The

Art Deco decor is magnificent. Doubles with shower/bath start at 700/850FF.

Hôtel des Marronniers (Map 6, ☎ 01 43 25 30 60, fax 01 40 46 83 56, 21 rue Jacob, 6e, metro St-Germain des Prés). This 37-room place in the back of a small courtyard has less-than-huge singles/doubles/triples from 610/805/1100FF and a magical garden out the back.

Hôtel Michelet Odéon (Map 6, ☎ 01 53 10 05 60, fax 01 46 34 55 35, @ hotel@micheletodeon .com, 6 place de l'Odéon, 6e, metro Odéon). Opposite the Odéon Théâtre de l'Europe and just a minute's walk from Jardin du Luxembourg, this 42-room place has tasteful, generously proportioned singles costing 430FF, doubles with shower/bath costing 510/580FF, triples from 700FF and quads from 770FF.

Gare St-Lazare & Grands Boulevards

There are a few reasonably priced top-end hotels in this area.

Atlantic Opéra Hôtel (Map 2, ☎ 01 43 87 45 40, fax 01 42 93 06 26, 44 rue de Londres, 8e, metro St-Lazare or Europe). On the northern side of the train station, this stylishly renovated 85-room hotel has singles costing 580FF, doubles costing 780FF and triples for 995FF.

Montparnasse

The area around the Gare Montparnasse is better known for budget and mid-range accommodation but there are some top-end hotels.

Hôtel Miramar (Map 4, ☎ 01 45 48 62 94, fax 01 45 48 68 73, 3 Place Bienvenüe, 15e, metro Montparnasse Bienvenüe). Soundproofed, smallish and typically three-star singles/doubles/triples here cost 486/512/818FF.

Montmartre & Pigalle

There are a bunch of top-end hotels in this area, including one within easy reach of Pigalle.

Hôtel des Trois Poussins (Map 3, ☎ 01 53 32 81 81, fax 01 53 32 81 82, @ h3p@les3poussins .com, 15 rue Clauzel, 9e, metro St-Georges). This lovely hotel due south of place Pigalle has singles/doubles costing from 680/780FF (750/850FF in the high season), but more than half of its 40 rooms are small studios with their own cooking facilities. They cost from 780/880FF (850/950FF in the high season).

PLACES TO STAY – DELUXE

Paris' most opulent – and famous – four-star and four-star+ hotels are in the 1er arrondissement.

Hôtel Costes (*Map 2*, ☎ *01 42 44 50 00, fax 01 45 44 50 01, 239 rue St-Honoré, 1er, metro Concorde*). Jean-Louis Costes' eponymous 83-room hotel, which opened in 1995, offers a 'luxurious and immoderate home away from home' to the visiting style mafia. Outfitted by Jacques Garcia in camp Second Empire castoffs, it's the current darling of the richly famous. Doubles range from 2000FF to 3500FF (remember: size matters among the rich); suites start at 5500FF. Breakfast costs 170FF.

Hôtel de Crillon (*Map 2*, ☎ *01 44 71 15 00, fax 01 44 71 15 02*, ✉ *crillon@crillon-paris.com, 10 place de la Concorde, 8e, metro Concorde*). The colonnaded, 200-year old Crillon, whose sparkling public areas (including Les Ambassadeurs restaurant, with two Michelin stars) are sumptuously decorated with chandeliers, original sculptures, gilt mouldings, tapestries and inlaid furniture, is the epitome of French luxury. Spacious singles/doubles with pink marble bathrooms start at 2950/3500FF. The cheapest suites cost 4950FF, larger ones cost between 7300FF and 8300FF. Breakfast costs another 185FF (continental) or 275FF (American).

Hôtel Ritz (*Map 2*, ☎ *01 43 16 30 30, fax 01 43 16 36 68*, ✉ *resa@ritzparis.com, 15 place Vendôme, 1er, metro Opéra*). As one of the world's most celebrated and expensive hotels, the 142-room, 45-suite Ritz has sparkling rooms starting at 3000/3600FF (3300/4000FF in May–June and September–October). Junior suites begin at 5000FF (5400FF); regular suites start at 6500FF (7700FF). The hotel restaurant, L'Espadon, has two Michelin stars, and the renovated Hemingway Bar is where Papa imbibed once he'd made it.

LONG-TERM RENTALS

If you intend to stay in Paris for more than a week or so, consider staying in a serviced flat or even renting a furnished flat through one of the many agencies listed under the heading *Location Appartements Meublés* in sheets distributed by the Paris tourist office and on their Web site (see the Information section earlier in the chapter). For information about renting a flat for a longer period, see Rental Accommodation in the introductory Facts for the Visitor chapter.

The tourist office sheets entitled *Logements pour Étudiants* list organisations that can help find accommodation for students who will be in Paris for at least a term.

Serviced Flats

Serviced flats – like staying in a hotel without all the extras – are an excellent option for those on a budget, particularly those in small groups. There are several locations around Paris.

Citadines Apart'hôtels (✉ *res@citdines .com*) hotel chain, with studios and apartments, has some 18 properties in Paris, including the following four:

Bastille Nation (*Map 5*, ☎ *01 40 04 43 50, fax 01 40 04 43 99, 14–18 rue de Chaligny, 12e, metro Reuilly Diderot*)
Montmartre (*Map 8*, ☎ *01 44 70 45 50, fax 01 45 22 59 10, 16 ave Rachel, 18e, metro Blanche*)
Opéra Drouot (*Map 3*, ☎ *01 40 15 14 00, fax 01 40 15 14 15, 18 rue Favart, 2e, metro Richelieu Drouot*)
Raspail Montparnasse (*Map 4*, ☎ *01 43 35 46 35, fax 01 40 47 43 01, 121 blvd du Montparnasse, 6e, metro Vavin*)

Prices vary during the year and from property to property, but in general a small studio (or 'studette') for one person with cooking facilities ranges in price from 505FF to 875FF; a studio accommodating two people costs 600FF to 975FF and a one-bedroom flat sleeping four costs from 850FF to 1600FF. For stays longer than six days there's a discount of about 10%, and over a month of about 25%.

Flatôtel International (*Map 4*, ☎ *01 45 75 62 20, fax 01 45 79 73 30, 14 rue du Théâtre, 15e, metro Charles Michels*). Kitchen-equipped studios measuring 40 sq m cost from 680FF to 900FF a day and one-bedroom flats cost 980FF to 1300FF; rates are much lower by the month.
Résidence Pierre & Vacances Paris Montmartre (*Map 8*, ☎ *01 42 57 14 55, fax 01 42 54 48 87*, ✉ *ydarsa@pierre-vacances.fr, 10 place Charles Dullin, 18e, metro Anvers*). One of several branches of a new serviced flat chain, this one charges from 570FF to 910FF a night for a studio and 900FF to 1115FF for a one-bedroom flat. There's a 10% discount on stays of more than eight days, and 30% on stays of more than 28 days.

Rental Agencies

A nonprofit organisation that acts as a liason between flat owners and foreigners looking for furnished apartments for periods of one week to one year is Allô Logement Temporaire (Map 7, ☎ 01 42 72 00 06, fax 01 42 72 03 11, @ alt@claranet.fr, metro Rambuteau) at 64 rue du Temple, 3e.

Small furnished studios of about 25 to 30 sq m cost from 3000FF to 5000FF a month, depending on the location. October, when university classes resume, is the hardest month in which to find a place, but over summer it's usually possible to find something within a matter of days.

Before any deals are signed, the company will arrange for you to talk to the owner by phone, assisted by an interpreter if necessary. There is a 300FF annual membership fee and, in addition to the rent and one month deposit (paid directly to the owner), there is a charge of 200FF for each month you rent. The office opens noon to 8 pm weekdays only.

Another nonprofit organisation that can help you find a flat is France Lodge Locations (Map 3, ☎ 01 53 20 09 09, fax 01 53 20 01 25, metro Le Peletier), 41 rue La Fayette, 9e. Prices start at about 150FF per person (cheaper by the month) and annual membership costs 100FF.

PLACES TO EAT

'The French think mainly about two things – their two main meals,' one well-fed bon vivant friend in Paris told us. 'Everything else is in parentheses.' And it's true. Eating well is still of prime importance to Parisians, who spend an amazing amount of time thinking about, talking about and consuming food.

Restaurants & Brasseries

Parisian restaurants usually specialise in a particular variety of food (eg, traditional French, regional, North African, Vietnamese), whereas brasseries serve more standard French and Alsatian fare. Most restaurants open for lunch and dinner only (ie, they are closed between 2.30 or 3 and 7 pm) and shut on Sunday. Brasseries usu-

ally stay open from morning till late at night and many remain open on Sunday.

Except in really touristy areas, most of Paris' estimated 11,000 restaurants, brasseries and cafes offer pretty good value for money. Intense competition tends to rid the city quickly of places with bad food or prices that are out of line. Still, you can be unlucky. Study the posted menus carefully and check to see how full or empty the place is before entering.

University Restaurants Stodgy but rib-sticking cafeteria food is available in copious quantities at Paris' 15 *restaurants universitaires* (student cafeterias) run by the Centre Régional des Œuvres Universitaires et Scolaires (CROUS, ☎ 01 40 51 36 00). Tickets for three-course meals cost 14.50FF for students with ID, including an ISIC. Guests pay between 22FF and 26FF, depending on the CROUS branch. CROUS restaurants (usually called 'restos U') have variable opening times that change according to school holiday schedules and weekend rotational agreements; check the schedule posted outside any of the following:

Assas (Map 5, ☎ 01 46 33 61 25, 92 rue d'Assas, 6e, metro Port Royal or Notre Dame des Champs)
Bullier (Map 5, ☎ 01 43 54 93 38, 39 ave Georges Bernanos, 5e, metro Port Royal)
Châtelet (Map 5, ☎ 01 43 31 51 66, 8 rue Jean Calvin, just off rue Mouffetard, 5e, metro Censier Daubenton)
Mabillon (Map 6, ☎ 01 43 25 66 23, 3 rue Mabillon, 6e, metro Mabillon)

Cafes

The cafe is an integral part of many Parisians' day-to-day existence, but only basic foods like sandwiches are available at most traditional ones. Many of the pubs, bars and less-traditional cafes listed in the Entertainment section later in this chapter also serve snacks and light meals.

Fast Food & Chain Restaurants

American fast-food companies have busy branches all over Paris as does the local hamburger chain Quick.

A number of restaurants have several outlets around Paris with standard menus. They're a definite step up from fast-food places and can be good value in areas like the ave des Champs-Élysées, where restaurants tend to be expensive or bad value (or both).

Bistro Romain

This increasingly popular chain, with some 21 branches around the city, has *menus* available from 49FF (lunch) to 99FF. They are usually open from 11.30 am to 1 am, but the Champs-Élysées branch *(Map 2, ☎ 01 43 59 93 31, 122 ave des Champs-Élysées, 8e, metro George V)* opens later.

Buffalo Grill

This national newcomer took over many of the former Batifol restaurants and now counts 10 branches in Paris proper, including one opposite Gare du Nord *(Map 3, ☎ 01 40 16 47 81, 9 blvd de Denain, 10e, metro Gare du Nord)*. The emphasis is on steak – T-bone (93FF) and even ostrich (86FF). Set meals start at 63FF. The restaurants are open 11 am to 11 pm daily.

Hippopotamus

There are about 19 branches in Paris of this hugely popular national chain which specialises in solid, steak-based meals. *Menus* are available from 52FF (lunch) to 143FF and branches are typically open daily from 11.30 am to 1 am (1.30 am on Friday and Saturday). Five branches, however, are open till 5 am daily, including the one facing place de la Bastille *(Map 7, ☎ 01 44 61 90 40, 1 blvd Beaumarchais, 4e, metro Bastille)*.

Léon de Bruxelles

The 13 branches of this restaurant chain are dedicated to only one thing: *moules* (mussels). Meal-size bowls of the bivalves, served with chips and fresh bread, start at 50FF, there are *menus* available at 66FF, 70FF and 99FF. They're open daily from 11.30 am to 1 am (2 am on Saturday), including the one near Forum des Halles *(Map 6, ☎ 01 42 36 18 50, 120 rue Rambuteau, 1er, metro Châtelet-Les Halles)*.

Self-Catering

Buying your own food is one of the best ways to keep travel costs down. For details on how French food shops work and where one buys what, see Food Shopping section in the Facts for the Visitor chapter. Supermarkets like Franprix, Ed l'Épicier and those attached to department stores like Monoprix are much cheaper than *épiceries* (grocery stores). Many food shops are closed on Sunday and/or Monday and take a break between 12.30 or 1 pm and 3 or 4 pm.

Paris has an exceptional number of places perfect for picnicking: parks, the courtyards of public buildings, the quays along the Seine and so forth.

Food Markets Paris' neighbourhood food markets offer the freshest and best-quality fruits, vegetables, cheeses and prepared salads at the lowest prices in town.

The *marchés découverts* (open-air markets) – 57 of which pop up in public squares around the city two or three times a week – are open from about 7 am to 2 pm. The 18 *marchés couverts* (covered markets) are open from 8 am to about 1 pm and from 3.30 or 4 to 7 or 7.30 pm from Tuesday to Saturday and in the morning on Sunday. To find out when there's a market near your hotel or hostel, ask the staff or anyone who lives in the neighbourhood.

Louvre & Les Halles

The area between Forum des Halles and the Centre Pompidou is filled with scores of trendy restaurants, but few of them are particularly good or inexpensive. Streets lined with places to eat include rue des Lombards, the pedestrians-only rue Montorgueil, and the narrow streets north and east of Forum des Halles.

French The 1er and 4e arrondissements have a diverse selection of French eating establishments.

Café Marly (Map 6, ☎ 01 46 26 06 60, cour Napoléon, 93 rue de Rivoli, 1er, metro Palais Royal). Nibbling and sipping under the colonnades of the Louvre, overlooking the glowing pyramid on a warm spring evening – well, it ain't gonna get any better than this. The Marly serves contemporary French fare, tending towards white meats, fish and salad, with a great fruit salad to finish. It opens 11 am to 1 am daily.

Aux Crus de Bourgogne (Map 6, ☎ 01 42 33 48 24, 3 rue de Bachaumont, 2e, metro Les Halles or Sentier). Set on a pedestrianised street, this excellent bistro serves great seafood and has a 130FF *menu* (expect 200FF a la carte). It opens for lunch and dinner till 11.30 pm weekdays only.

L'Épi d'Or (Map 6, ☎ 01 42 36 38 12, 25 rue Jean-Jacques Rousseau, 1er, metro Louvre-Rivoli). This oh-so-Parisian bistro east of Les Halles serves classic, well-prepared dishes like *gigot d'agneau* (leg of lamb) cooked for seven hours to a surprisingly well-heeled crowd. There's a *menu* for 105FF (open for lunch and dinner Monday to Friday and Saturday evening).

Le Petit Mâchon (Map 6, ☎ 01 42 60 08 06, 158 rue St-Honoré, 1er, metro Palais Royal). This bistro has Lyons-inspired specialities, with starters costing from 39FF to 85FF, main courses from 68FF to 118FF and a 98FF *menu*. It opens for lunch and dinner Tuesday to Sunday to 11 pm.

Asian Japanese businesspeople in search of real sushi and soba flock to rue Ste-Anne and other streets of Paris' Japantown, which is just west of Jardin du Palais Royal. There's also some good-value restaurants serving other Asian cuisine.

Higuma (Map 6, ☎ 01 47 03 38 59, 32 bis rue Ste-Anne, 1er, metro Pyramides). Stepping into this place is like ducking into a corner noodle shop in Tokyo. A meal-sized bowl of soup noodles costs 40FF to 48FF and there are *menus* for 63FF to 70FF. It opens 11.30 am to 10 pm daily.

La Maison Savoureuse (Map 3, ☎ 01 42 60 03 22, 62 rue Ste-Anne, 2e, metro Quatre Septembre). This cheap and cheerful little place serves excellent value Vietnamese food to eat in (lunch/dinner *menus* from 37/46FF to 62FF) or you can take your spring rolls (from 10FF) and vermicelli noodles to square Louvois, a pretty little park just south-east of here, for a picnic.

Other This part of Paris is a fast-food-lovers' paradise, with a variety of chain outlets near Centre Pompidou and Les Halles.

Joe Allen (Map 6, ☎ 01 42 36 70 13, 30 rue Pierre Lescot, 1er, metro Étienne Marcel). A friendly American bar/restaurant with a great atmosphere and a good selection of Californian wines, Joe Allen has two/three course *menus* costing 112/140FF. It opens noon to 1.30 am daily; Sunday brunch (90FF to 105FF) is from noon to 4 pm.

Self-Catering There are a number of options along ave de l'Opéra and rue de Richelieu, as well as around Forum des Halles (Map 6), including *Monoprix* (21 ave de l'Opéra, 2e), open 9 am to 10 pm weekdays and to 9 pm Saturday; *Franprix* (35 rue Berger, 1er), open 8.30 am to 8 pm Monday to Saturday; and *Ed l'Épicier* inside the courtyard (80 rue de Rivoli, 4e), open 9 am to 8 pm Monday to Saturday. *Fine food shops* can be found on rue de Richelieu, 1er (Map 6), including a *fromagerie* at No 38 (open Tuesday to Saturday) and *Evrard*, a *traiteur* (delicatessen) across the street at No 41 (open to 7.30 pm weekdays).

Marais

The Marais, filled with small eateries of every imaginable kind, is one of Paris' premier neighbourhoods for eating out. Pretty little place du Marché Ste-Catherine is surrounded by small restaurants, some with outside seating.

French The French places in this area tend to be small and intimate.

Amadéo (Map 7, ☎ 01 48 87 01 02, 19 rue François Miron, 4e, metro St-Paul or Hôtel de Ville). This chic Mozart-mad restaurant is decidedly gay, although straight diners are very welcome. The food is stylish and delicious modern French with *entrée*/main courses/desserts at 55/105/45FF, lunch *menus* at 75FF and 95FF, and an evening one at 185FF (110FF on Tuesday evening, including a *kir* (white wine and crème de cassis). A highlight is the Thursday *dîner lyrique* with a live opera or operetta performance, with a *menu* at 285FF. It opens for lunch Tuesday to Friday and for dinner Monday to Saturday till 11 pm.

Au Bascou (Map 6, ☎ 01 42 72 69 25, 38 rue Réaumur, 3e, metro Arts et Métiers). This popular Basque eatery serves classics including *pipérade* (peppers, onions, tomatoes and ham cooked with scrambled eggs), *Ttoro* (Basque bouillabaisse) and Bayonne ham in all its guises. The 90FF lunch *menu* is good value; expect to pay about 180FF at dinner. It opens for lunch on weekdays and for dinner until 10.30 pm Monday to Saturday.

Le Petit Picard (Map 7, ☎ 01 42 78 54 03, 42 rue Ste-Croix de la Bretonnerie, 4e, metro Hôtel de

The Birth of Restoration

In 1765 a certain Monsieur A Boulanger opened a small business in Rue Bailleul (1er), just off Rue de Rivoli in Paris, selling soups, broths and later sheep's feet in white sauce. Above the door he hung a sign advertising these *restaurants* (restoratives, from the verb *se restaurer*, 'to feed oneself'). The world had its first restaurant as we know it today – and a new name for an eating place.

Before that time not everyone cooked at home every day of the year. Hostelries and inns existed, but they only served guests set meals at set times and prices from the *table d'hôte* (host's table) while cafes only offered drinks. Boulanger's restaurant is thought to have been the first public place where diners could order a meal from a menu offering a range of dishes.

Other restaurants opened in following decades, including a luxury one in Paris called La Grande Taverne de Londres in 1782. The 1789 Revolution at first stemmed the tide of new restaurants, but when corporations and privileges were abolished in the 1790s their numbers multiplied. By 1804 Paris alone counted some 500 restaurants, providing employment for many of the chefs and cooks who had once worked in the kitchens of the aristocracy. A typical menu at that time might have included 12 soups, two dozen hors d'œuvre, between 12 and 30 entrées of beef, veal, mutton, fowl and game, 24 fish dishes, 12 types of *pâtisseries* (pastries) and 50 desserts.

Ville). This popular restaurant serves very traditional French cuisine, with *menus* at 64FF (lunch) and 89FF; there's a *menu* of Picardy specialities for 129FF. It opens for lunch on weekdays and for dinner Tuesday to Sunday.

Robert et Louise (Map 7, ☎ 01 42 78 55 89, 64 *rue Vieille du Temple, 3e, metro St-Sébastien Froissart*). This authentic country inn in Paris – complete with red gingham curtains – offers delightful, unfussy and inexpensive French food prepared by a husband and wife team, including *côte de bœuf* (beef rib) cooked on an open fire (200FF for two). Starters cost 20FF to 60FF, main courses cost from 70FF to 120FF, with a *plat du jour* (daily special) costing 80FF. It opens for lunch on weekdays and for dinner till 10 pm Monday to Saturday.

Vins des Pyrénées (Map 7, ☎ 01 42 72 64 94, 25 *rue Beautreillis, 4e, metro Bastille*). In a former wine warehouse a couple of doors down from where US rock singer Jim Morrison of the Doors died in 1971 (No 17–19), this bistro is a good place to splurge on a French meal, with starters costing from 35FF to 60FF and main courses from around 70FF to 110FF; count on spending about 170FF. It is open for lunch daily and for dinner until 11.30 pm Monday to Saturday.

Jewish & Kosher The kosher and kosher-style restaurants along rue des Rosiers serve specialities from North Africa, Central Europe and Israel. Many are closed on Friday evening, Saturday and Jewish holidays. Takeaway falafel and *shwarma* (kebabs) are available at several places along the street.

Chez Marianne (Map 7, ☎ 01 42 72 18 86, 2 *rue des Hospitalières St-Gervais, 4e, metro St-Paul*). A Sephardic (Middle Eastern/North African Jewish) alternative to the Ashkenazic Jo Goldenberg (see later in this section). Plates with four/five/six different meze (such as falafel and hummus) cost 65/75/85FF; a *plat dégustation* (a selection of different dishes) costs 115FF. The window of the adjoining deli dispenses killer takeaway falafel sandwiches for 25FF. Chez Marianne opens 11 am till midnight daily.

Hammam Café (Map 7, ☎ 01 42 78 04 45, 4 *rue des Rosiers, 4e, metro St-Paul*). Positively the grooviest strictly kosher place we've ever eaten in (and our Lubavitch in-laws have dragged us to quite a few), the Hammam Café is bright and airy with original Art Nouveau mosaics of an old Turkish bar and designer furnishings. Dishes include kosher pizzas (45FF to 98FF), gratins (45FF to 65FF) and galettes (from 29FF). It opens for lunch Sunday to Friday and for dinner till midnight (to 2 am on Saturday) daily except Friday.

Jo Goldenberg (Map 7, ☎ 01 48 87 20 16, 7 rue des Rosiers, 4e, metro St-Paul). Founded in 1920, this kosher-style deli/restaurant is Paris' most famous Jewish eatery. The mixed starters (32FF) and apple strudel (30FF) are excellent, but the *plats du jour* (79FF to 89FF) don't measure up to even a generic New York deli. The restaurant opens noon till midnight daily.

Pitchi Poï (Map 7, ☎ 01 42 77 46 15, 7 Place du Marché Ste-Catherine, 4e, metro St-Paul). This Eastern European Jewish restaurant beamed down onto a picturesque little square on the edge of the Marais will delight with its trademark *tchoulent* (slow simmered duck with vegetables), *datcha* (smoked salmon served with a baked potato cream) and chopped liver. There's a *menu* for 119FF (open for lunch and dinner daily to 11 pm).

Vegetarian The Marais is one of the few neighbourhoods in Paris to actually offer a choice of meatless restaurants.

Aquarius (Map 7, ☎ 01 48 87 48 71, 54 rue Ste-Croix de la Bretonnerie, 4e, metro Rambuteau). The calming atmosphere of this healthy restaurant is perfect if you're in the mood for something light. The two-course lunch *menu* costs 64FF; at dinner it costs 95FF for three courses. It opens noon to 10.15 pm Monday to Saturday.

Piccolo Teatro (Map 6, ☎ 01 42 72 17 79, 6 rue des Écouffes, 4e, metro St-Paul). The *menus* at this intimate place with stone walls, beamed ceiling and cosy little tables cost 63FF and 85FF at lunch, and 90FF and 125FF at dinner; the tasty *assiette végétarienne* (vegetarian plate) costs 70FF. It opens for lunch and dinner Tuesday to Sunday.

Other The Marais has a good selection of ethnic places. If you're looking for authentic Chinese food but can't be bothered going all the way to Chinatown in the 13e or Belleville (20e), check out any of the small Wenzhou noodle shops and restaurants along rue Au Maire, 3e (Map 6, metro Arts et Métiers), which is south-east of Musée des Arts et Métiers.

404 (Map 6, ☎ 01 42 74 57 81, 69 rue des Gravilliers, 3e, metro Arts et Métiers). The upbeat 404, as comfortable a Maghrebi caravanserai as you'll find in Paris, has excellent couscous and *tajines* both from 85FF to 130FF. It also has excellent grills from 98FF to 135FF, aniseed bread and a lunch *menu* costing 89FF. The weekend

brunch berbère (Berber brunch; 120FF) is available from noon to 4 pm. The 404 opens for lunch/brunch and dinner till midnight daily.

Caves St-Gilles (Map 7, ☎ 01 48 87 22 62, 4 rue St-Gilles, 3e, metro Chemin Vert). This trendy Spanish wine bar north-east of place des Vosges is the best place for tapas (82FF for a platter) and sangria (130FF for 1L). It is always full and opens for lunch and dinner daily till midnight.

L'Enoteca (Map 7, ☎ 01 42 78 91 44, 25 rue Charles V, 4e, metro Pont Marie). This attractive place in the historic Village St-Paul quarter serves haute cuisine *à l'italienne*, and there's an excellent list of Italian wines by the glass (20FF to 48FF). The weekday lunch *menus* are good value at 75FF and 100FF; the *plat du jour* is around 60FF. Expect to pay from 160FF a la carte.

Minh Chau (Map 7, ☎ 01 42 71 13 30, 10 rue de la Verrerie, 4e, metro Hôtel de Ville). For a mere 26FF to 32FF you can enjoy tasty main dishes (grilled chicken with lemon grass, roast duck) at this tiny but welcoming Vietnamese place in the heart of the Maris. It opens for lunch and dinner till 11 pm Monday to Saturday.

Self-Catering There are several *food shops* and *Asian delicatessens* on the odd-numbered side of rue St-Antoine, 4e (Map 7), between the *Monoprix* supermarket (open 9 am to 9 pm Monday to Saturday) at No 71 and *Supermarché G20* (open 9 am to 8.30 pm Monday to Saturday) at No 115. There's a *Franprix* supermarket (open 8.30 am to 7.45 pm Monday to Saturday, 9 am to 12.45 pm Sunday) at No 135.

Flo Prestige (Map 7, ☎ 01 53 01 91 91, metro Bastille, 10 rue St-Antoine, 4e) is near the corner of rue des Tournelles. This branch of the famous traiteur, with a dozen branches around town, has picnic supplies and some of the most delectable pastries in Paris (open 8 am to 11 pm daily).

Île St-Louis

Famed for its ice cream as much as anything else, the Île St-Louis (4e) is generally an expensive place to eat. It's best suited to those looking for a light snack or ingredients for lunch beside the Seine.

French Rue St-Louis en l'Île has several *salons de thé* including the lovely *La Charlotte en Île* (☎ 01 43 54 25 83) at No 24, and there are lots of restaurants both on and just off this street.

euro currency converter 10FF = €1.52

La Ruelle de la Bactérie

One of Paris' largest concentration of ethnic restaurants is squeezed into a labyrinth of narrow streets in the 5e arrondissement across the Seine from Notre Dame. The Greek, North African and Middle Eastern restaurants between rue St-Jacques, blvd St-Germain and blvd St-Michel attract mainly foreign tourists, who appear to be unaware that some people refer to rue de la Huchette and nearby streets such as rue St-Séverin and rue de la Harpe as 'bacteria alley'. To add insult to injury, many of the poor souls who eat here are under the impression that this little maze is the famous Latin Quarter. You'll be better off avoiding these establishments that ripen their meat and seafood in the front window. Look for ethnic food elsewhere: blvd de Belleville in the 20e for Middle Eastern; nearby rue de Belleville in the 19e for Asian (especially Thai and Vietnamese); and Chinatown in the 13e for Chinese, especially ave de Choisy, ave d'Ivry and rue Baudricourt.

***Les Fous de l'Île** (Map 6, ☎ 01 43 25 76 67, 33 rue des Deux Ponts, 4e, metro Pont Marie).*This friendly and down-to-earth establishment has a lunch *menu* for 78FF and serves evening a la carte meals for between 120FF and 150FF per person. It opens noon to 11 pm Tuesday to Friday, from 3 pm on Saturday and noon to 7 pm on Sunday.

Self-Catering Along rue St-Louis en l'Île, 4e (Map 6, metro Pont Marie) there are a number of *fromageries* and *groceries* (usually closed Sunday afternoon and Monday). More *food shops* line rue des Deux Ponts.

***Berthillon** (Map 6, ☎ 01 43 54 31 61, 31 rue St-Louis en l'Île, 4e, metro Pont Marie).* This *glacier* (ice-cream shop) is reputed to have Paris' most delicious ice cream. While the fruit flavours are justifiably renowned, the chocolate, coffee, *marrons glacés* (candied chestnuts), *agenaise* (Armagnac and prunes) and *nougat au miel* (honey nougat) ones are much richer. The takeaway counter opens 10 am to 8 pm Wednesday to Sunday, with one/two/three small scoops costing 9/16/20FF. The *salon dégustation* (sit-down area) opens 1 pm (2 pm on weekends) to 8 pm on the same days.

Latin Quarter

Rue Mouffetard, 5e (metro Place Monge or Censier Daubenton) is filled with scores of places to eat. It's especially popular with students, in part because of the number of stands selling baguette sandwiches, *panini* (Italian toasted bread with fillings) and *crêpes* (pancakes). Rue Soufflot (metro Luxembourg) is lined with cafes.

Avoid rue de la Huchette (Map 6; see the boxed text 'La Ruelle de la Bactérie') unless you're after shwarma, available at several places, including Nos 14 and 17.

French The Latin Quarter is dotted with a good selection of reasonably priced French places.

***Les Bouchons de François Clerc** (Map 6, ☎ 01 43 54 15 34, 12 rue de l'Hôtel Colbert, 5e, metro Maubert Mutualité).* Along with excellently prepared French dishes (a two-course *formule* – similar to a *menu* but allows choice of whichever two of three courses you want – costs 137FF at lunch including wine, 227FF for four courses at dinner), the draws here are the wonderful wines sold at almost wholesale prices and an excellent cheese selection. It opens for lunch on weekdays and for dinner Monday to Saturday.

***Chez Léna et Mimille** (Map 5, ☎ 01 47 07 72 47, 32 rue Tournefort, 5e, metro Censier Daubenton).* The two/three-course lunch *menus* cost 98/138FF and the dinner one costs 198FF at this cosy but elegant French restaurant with live piano music most nights. The fabulous terrace overlooks a lovely little park. It opens for lunch and dinner to 11 pm (for lunch on weekdays and dinner Monday to Saturday in winter).

***Perraudin** (Map 5, ☎ 01 46 33 15 75, 157 rue St-Jacques, 5e, metro Luxembourg).* If you fancy classics like *bœuf bourguignon*, *gigot d'agneau* or *confit de canard* (preserved duck; all 59FF), try this reasonably priced traditional French restaurant, which hasn't changed much since the late 19th century. At lunchtime there's a 65FF *menu* and 25cL of wine costs 10FF. It opens for lunch on weekdays and for dinner to 10.15 pm Monday to Saturday.

***Le Vigneron** (Map 5, ☎ 01 47 07 29 99, 18–20 rue du Pot de Fer, 5e, metro place Monge).* Arguably the best French restaurant in the Mouffetard quarter, the 'Wine Grower' specialises in south-western cuisine, with lunch *menus* costing 60FF and 80FF and dinner ones costing 118FF and 158FF. A la carte prices range from

65FF to 110FF for starters, 95FF to 125FF for main dishes and 55FF to 75FF for desserts. It opens for lunch and dinner till midnight daily.

North African & Middle Eastern The Latin Quarter is a good area for couscous and tajines as well as meze.

Al Dar (Map 6, ☎ 01 43 25 17 15, 8–10 rue Frédéric Sauton, 5e, metro Maubert Mutualité). This Lebanese restaurant has lunch *menus* costing 89FF and 150FF; a la carte main courses cost 64FF to 75FF and the *plat du jour* costs 70FF. The restaurant's excellent deli section, with little pizzas (15FF), sandwiches (from 22FF) and stuffed grapevine leaves (5FF), opens 7 am to midnight daily. It opens for lunch and dinner till midnight daily.

Founti Agadir (Map 5, ☎ 01 43 37 85 10, 117 rue Monge, 5e, metro Censier Daubenton). This Moroccan restaurant has some of the best couscous and tajines (75FF to 89FF) and *pastillas* (meat or poultry baked in filo pastry; 40FF to 42FF) on the Left Bank, and there are lunch *menus* costing 75FF and 89FF. It opens for lunch and dinner to 11 pm Tuesday to Sunday.

Asian The Latin Quarter abounds with Asian restaurants of all types.

Tashi Delek (Map 5, ☎ 01 43 26 55 55, 4 rue des Fossés St-Jacques, 5e, metro Luxembourg). Paris abounds with Tibetan restaurants ('with yak butter, madame?') and while the food at this intimate little place (whose name means 'bonjour' in Tibetan) is not gourmet, it's cheap, with a lunch *menu* costing 65FF and a dinner one costing 105FF, including 25cL of wine. There are some seven vegetarian choices on the menu (37FF to 51FF). It opens for lunch and dinner to 11 pm Monday to Saturday.

Tao (Map 5, ☎ 01 43 26 75 92, 248 rue St-Jacques, 5e, metro Luxembourg). Decidedly upmarket with zen-ish décor, Tao serves some of the best Vietnamese cuisine in the Latin Quarter – try the warm beef noodle salad or grilled minced prawns – with dishes in the 60FF to 95FF range. It opens for lunch Monday to Saturday and for dinner till 11 pm Monday and Wednesday to Saturday.

Vegetarian The choice for vegetarians isn't as great in the Latin Quarter as in the Marais, but there are a couple of decent options.

Jardin des Pâtes (Map 5, ☎ 01 43 31 50 71, 4 rue Lacépède, 5e, metro Cardinal Lemoine). OK,

not strictly vegetarian but 100% *bio* (organic), the cosy 'Garden of Pastas' has as many types of pasta as you care to name (including wholewheat, buckwheat and chestnut) costing from 39FF to 77FF; fresh vegetable juice costs 17FF to 24FF. It opens for lunch and dinner to 11 pm daily.

Le Petit Légume (Map 5, ☎ 01 40 46 06 85, 36 rue des Boulangers, 5e, metro Cardinal Lemoine). This tiny place is a great choice for home-made vegetarian fare, with *menus* costing 50FF, 64FF and 75FF. It opens for lunch and dinner to 10 pm Monday to Saturday.

Self-Catering Place Maubert, 5e (Map 6, metro Maubert Mutualité), is transformed into a lively *food market* from 7 am to 1.30 pm on Tuesday, Thursday and Saturday. *Food shops* are also found around here, including a *fromagerie* at 47 blvd St-Germain.

There's a particularly lively *food market* along rue Mouffetard, at the southern end, around rue de l'Arbalète, 5e (Map 5, metro Censier Daubenton), open all day from Tuesday to Sunday. The *Franprix* supermarket (Map 5, metro Censier Daubenton or Place Monge) at 82 rue Mouffetard (5e) opens 9 am to 8 pm Monday to Saturday, and to 1 pm on Sunday.

The *food market* on Place Monge, 5e (Map 5, metro Place Monge), opens from about 7 am to 1 pm on Wednesday, Friday and Sunday. Nearby at 34 rue Monge there's a *Shopi* supermarket (open 8.30 am to 9 pm Monday to Saturday) and at 37 rue Lacépède an *Ed l'Épicier* supermarket (open 9 am to 7.30 pm Monday to Saturday).

For sandwiches to take to Jardin du Luxembourg for a picnic, try the popular hole-in-the-wall *Douce France* at 7 rue Royer Collard, 5e (Map 5, metro Luxembourg), where the lunchtime line of Sorbonne students is testament to the quality of the sandwiches (13.50FF) and fruit juices (6FF). It opens 11 am to 4 pm weekdays.

St-Germain & Odéon

Rue St-André des Arts (Map 6, metro St-Michel or Odéon) is lined with restaurants, including a few down the covered passage between Nos 59 and 61. There are lots of places between Église St-Sulpice and Église

On the Menu

We can thank Isabeau of Bavaria, consort to Charles VI (ruled 1380–1422) for the world's first written menu. Apparently until that century people attending banquets frequently had to guess at what dish they were being served or eating until *la reine* came up with the idea of writing it all down and called it an *escriteau*. It wasn't a true menu in the sense that people could pick and choose from it, but rather akin to a 'bill of fare'.

St-Germain des Prés, especially along rue des Canettes, rue Princesse and rue Guisarde. Place Carrefour de l'Odéon (Map 6, metro Odéon) has a cluster of lively bars, cafes and restaurants.

French Place St-Germain des Prés is home to famous cafes like Les Deux Magots and Café de Flore (see Pubs, Bars & Cafes in the Entertainment section) as well as a celebrated brasserie.

Brasserie Lipp (Map 6, ☎ 01 45 48 53 91, 151 blvd St-Germain, 6e, metro St-Germain des Prés). Politicians rub shoulders with intellectuals and editors at the Lipp, while tuxedoed waiters serve pricey a la carte dishes (*choucroute* – sauerkraut served with meat – costs 102FF). *Plats du jour* cost 115FF to 120FF) at this old-time, wood panelled cafe-brasserie. The *menu touristique* costs 196FF (including 25cL of wine). Many people make a big fuss about sitting downstairs rather than upstairs, which is the nonsmoking section and considered nowheresville (open 11.30 am to 1 am daily).

Cour de Rohan (Map 6, ☎ 01 43 25 79 67, 59–61 rue St-André des Arts, 6e, metro Mabillon). Local writers and publishers seek peace, quiet and home-made scones in this slightly faded tearoom, with its assortment of exquisite furniture and *objets*. Mixed salads and daily specials complement the aromatic teas, while three chefs keep the dessert cart piled with delicacies. It opens noon to 7.30 pm weekdays, and to 11 pm at the weekend.

Le Mâchon d'Henri (Map 6, ☎ 01 43 29 08 70, 8 rue Guisarde, 6e, metro St-Sulpice). This very

Parisian bistro in a street awash with bars serves up Lyons-inspired dishes like lentil salad, *rosette du mâconnais* (large pork slicing sausage prepared with red wine) and *clafoutis* (fruit covered with a thick batter and baked until puffy). Starters cost 35FF to 40FF, main courses cost from 60FF to 80FF and desserts cost 35FF to 40FF. It opens for lunch and dinner until 11.30 pm daily.

Le Petit Zinc (Map 6, ☎ 01 42 61 20 60, 11 rue St-Benoît, 6e, metro St-Germain des Prés). This wonderful (and expensive – *entrées* cost from 48FF to 119FF, main courses from 99FF to 170FF) place serves both traditional French and regional specialities from the south-west in true Art Nouveau splendour. There are *menus* costing 148FF and 188FF. It opens from noon to 2 am daily.

Polidor (Map 6, ☎ 01 43 26 95 34, 41 rue Monsieur le Prince, 6e, metro Odéon). A meal at this *crèmerie-restaurant* is like a quick trip back to Victor Hugo's Paris – the restaurant and its decor date from 1845 – but everyone knows about it, and the place is pretty touristy. *Menus* of tasty, family-style French cuisine are available for 55FF (lunch only) and 110FF. Specialities include *bœuf à la provençal* (60FF), *blanquette de veau* (veal in white sauce, 68FF) and the most famous *tarte Tatin* (caramelised apple pie, 25FF) in Paris. It opens for lunch and dinner to 12.30 am (11 pm on Sunday) daily.

Other The cuisine of southern Europe and Asia are well represented in the 6e.

Chez Albert (Map 6, ☎ 01 46 33 22 57, 43 rue Mazarine, 6e, metro Odéon). Authentic Portuguese food is not easy to come by in Paris, but this place has it in spades: *cataplana* (shellfish cooked with ham), numerous *bacalhau* (salt-dried cod) dishes and prawns sautéed in lots of garlic, plus a good selection of Portuguese wines. Booking is advisable. *Menus* cost 95FF for two courses till 8 pm; there's a three-course 135FF one at night. It opens for lunch Tuesday to Saturday and for dinner till 11.30 pm Monday to Saturday.

Le Golfe de Naples (Map 6, ☎ 01 43 26 98 11, 5 rue de Montfaucon, 6e, metro Mabillon). Italian residents say this restaurant/pizzeria has the best pizza and home-made pasta in Paris, which is not generally celebrated for its Italian food. Pizzas range from 49FF to 59FF, and don't forget to try the grilled fresh vegetables (85FF).

Indonesia (Map 5, ☎ 01 43 25 70 22, 12 rue de Vaugirard, 6e, metro Luxembourg). One of two

Indonesian restaurants in the city, this nonprofit cooperative has all the standards – from an elaborate, multicourse *rijsttafel* to *nasi goreng*, *rendang* (beef cooked in coconut) and *gado-gado* (salad with a peanut sauce). *Menus* (there are six) cost 49FF to 89FF at lunch, and 79FF to 129FF at dinner. The Indonesia opens for lunch and dinner to 11 pm daily.

Self-Catering With Jardin du Luxembourg nearby, the 6e is the perfect area for a picnic lunch. There is a large cluster of *food shops* on rue de Seine and rue de Buci, 6e (metro Mabillon). The covered *Marché St-Germain* (metro Mabillon) on rue Lobineau (6e), just north of the eastern end of Église St-Germain des Prés, has a huge array of produce and prepared foods.

Champion (Map 6, 79 rue de Seine, 6e, metro Mabillon). This supermarket opens 8.40 am to 9 pm Monday to Saturday and there's a superb *fromagerie* just next door.
Chez Jean-Mi (Map 6, ☎ 01 43 26 89 72, 10 rue de l'Ancienne Comédie, 6e, metro Odéon). This boulangerie (with a restaurant in the back) opens 24 hours a day, 365 days a year.
Monoprix (Map 6, 52 rue de Rennes, 6e, metro St-Germain des Prés). This department store's supermarket, at the back of the basement level, opens 9 am to 10 pm Monday to Saturday.

Champs-Élysées

Few places along touristy ave des Champs-Élysées offer good value, but some restaurants in the surrounding areas are excellent.

French Generally, you're unlikely to find cheap eats in this area, but there are more than a few places offering excellent food.

L'Ardoise (Map 2, ☎ 01 42 96 28 18, 28 rue du Mont Thabor, 1er, metro Concorde or Tuileries). This little bistro has no menu as such (*ardoise* means 'blackboard', which is all there is), but who cares? The food – rabbit and hazelnut terrine, and beef fillet with morels, prepared dexterously by chef Pierre Jay – is superb and the 175FF *menu* offers excellent value. It opens for lunch and dinner until 11.30 pm Tuesday to Sunday.
L'Étoile Verte (Map 2, ☎ 01 43 80 69 34, 13 rue Brey, 17e, metro Charles de Gaulle-Étoile). When one of us was a student in Paris, this was

the place for both Esperanto speakers (their symbol is a 'green star') and a splurge and it still feels like it did way back then. All the old classics remain – the onion soup, the snails, the rabbit – and there are *menus* costing 74FF (available at lunch weekdays), 110FF (with 25cL of wine) and 155FF (with aperitif, wine and coffee). A la carte soups/*entrées* start at 35/60FF, main courses average 90FF. It opens for lunch on weekdays and for dinner to 11 pm daily.

Ladurée (Map 2, ☎ 01 40 75 08 75, 75 ave des Champs Élysées, 8e, metro George V). The salons of this sumptuous *belle époque* tearoom, established in 1862, are named after the mistresses of Napoleon III: Mathilde, Castiglione and Paeva. But it's difficult to imagine any of them being as sweet as the pastries Ladurée is famous for. Mixed salads and light lunches round out the menu. There's a dinner *menu* costing 195FF. It opens daily from 7.30 am to 1 am.

Other The area boasts one of the city's most inventive new restaurants.

Spoon, Food & Wine (Map 2, ☎ 01 40 76 34 44, 14 rue de Marignan, 8e, metro Franklin D Roosevelt). Three-star Michelin chef Alain Ducasse invites diners to mix and match their own mains and sauces – grilled calamari, say, with a choice of satay, curry or béarnaise sauces. Controversially (this is France), the cellar features wines from the USA, Australia and other parts of Europe, with only a small proportion being French. SFW opens for lunch and dinner till midnight on weekdays.

Self-Catering Place de la Madeleine, 8e (Map 2, metro Madeleine) is the luxury food centre of one of the world's food capitals (see Food & Wine in the Shopping section later in this chapter). The delicacies on offer don't come cheap, but even travellers on a modest budget can turn a walk around La Madeleine into a gastronomic odyssey.

Monoprix (Map 2, 62 ave des Champs-Élysées, 8e, metro Franklin D Roosevelt). The supermarket section in the basement opens 9 am to midnight Monday to Saturday.

Gare St-Lazare & Grands Boulevards

This area has a number of fine restaurants. The neon-lit blvd Montmartre (Map 3, metro Grands Boulevards or Richelieu

Drouot) and nearby sections of rue du Faubourg Montmartre (neither of which are anywhere near the neighbourhood of Montmartre) form one of Paris' most animated cafe and dining districts.

French This area has one of the cheapest French restaurants in Paris.

Chartier (Map 3, ☎ 01 47 70 86 29, 7 rue du Faubourg Montmartre, 9e, metro Grands Boulevards). A real gem that is justifiably famous for its 330-seat *belle époque* dining room, virtually unaltered since 1896. With starters costing from 9FF to 33FF, mains from 34FF to 54FF and a bottle of cider/wine for 14/20FF, you should spend no more than 85FF per person, though there are more elaborate *menus* costing 74FF, 110FF and 190FF. Chartier opens for lunch and dinner to 10 pm daily. Reservations are not accepted, so don't be surprised if there's a queue.

Jewish & North African There's a large selection of kosher Jewish and North African restaurants on rue Richer, rue Cadet and rue Geoffroy Marie, 9e (Map 3) just south of the Cadet metro stop.

Les Ailes (Map 3, ☎ 01 47 70 62 53, next door to Folies Bergères at 34 rue Richer, 9e, metro Cadet). This kosher Tunisian place has superb couscous with meat or fish starting at about 100FF and a good selection of North African salads. Pre-ordered and pre-paid *shabbas* (Sabbath) meals taken at the restaurant cost 250FF per person. It opens for lunch from Sunday to Friday and for dinner till 11.30 Sunday to Thursday.

Wally le Saharien (Map 3, ☎ 01 42 85 51 90, 36 rue Rodier, 9e, metro St-Georges or Cadet). Wally's is a cut above most of Maghrebi restaurants in Paris, offering couscous in its pure Saharan form – without stock or vegetables, just a finely cooked grain served with a delicious sauce. The rich Moorish coffee is a fitting finish. It opens for lunch and dinner to 10.30 pm Tuesday to Saturday.

Other Down-home-American-style cooking can be found in this area.

Haynes Restaurant (Map 3, ☎ 01 48 78 40 63, 3 rue Clauzel, 9e, metro St-Georges). This legendary and very funky African-American-run

hangout dishes up genuine shrimp gumbo, fried chicken, barbecued ribs and cornbread (about 70FF for a main course). There's usually a lively crowd for the jazz sessions at 9 pm on Friday and Saturday. It opens for dinner to 12.30 am Tuesday to Saturday.

Gare du Nord & Gare de l'Est
This area offers all types of food but most notably Indian and Pakistani, usually elusive cuisines in Paris.

French There's a cluster of brasseries and bistros opposite the facade of Gare du Nord. They're decent options for a first or final meal in the City of Light.

Brasserie Terminus Nord (Map 3, ☎ 01 42 85 05 15, 23 rue de Dunkerque, 10e, metro Gare du Nord). The copper bar, white tablecloths, brass fixtures and mirrored walls look much as they did between the wars. Breakfast (39.50FF) is available from 8 to 11 am daily; full meals are served from 11 am to 12.30 am. The 138FF *faim de nuit* (night hunger) menu is available after 10 pm.

Other The tiny restaurants off blvd de Strasbourg, many open throughout the afternoon, serve the city's most authentic Indian and Pakistani food.

Passage Brady (Map 3, metro Château d'Eau), between 43 rue du Faubourg St-Denis and 58 blvd de Strasbourg (10e), could easily be in Calcutta. The incredibly cheap Indian, Pakistani and Bangladeshi places are generally open for one of the best lunch deals in Paris (meat curry, rice and a tiny salad from 30FF) and for dinner, with *menus* from 49FF to 65FF. Pick of the crop are *Pooja (☎ 01 48 24 00 83)* at No 91 and *Yasmin (☎ 01 45 23 04 25)* at No 71–73.

Self-Catering Rue du Faubourg St-Denis, 10e (Map 3, metro Strasbourg St-Denis or Château d'Eau), between blvd St-Denis and blvd de Magenta, is one of the cheapest places in Paris to buy food, especially fruit and vegetables. It has a distinctively Middle Eastern air, and quite a few of the groceries offer Turkish and North African specialities. Many of the *food shops*, including the *fromagerie* at No 54, are open Tuesday to midday Sunday. The *Franprix* supermarket,

7–9 rue des Petites Écuries, 10e (metro Château d'Eau), opens 9 am to 7.50 pm Monday to Saturday.

Farther north, **Marché St-Quentin** (Map 3, metro Gare de l'Est), opposite 88–92 blvd de Magenta (10e), at the start of rue de Chabrol, opens 8 am to 1 pm and 3.30 to 7.30 pm Tuesday to Sunday morning. The **Franprix** supermarket (Map 3, metro Gare de l'Est) at 57 blvd de Magenta (10e) opens 9 am to 8 pm Monday to Saturday.

Bastille

The area around Bastille is chock-a-block with restaurants. Narrow, scruffy rue de Làppe, 11e (Maps 5 and 6), may not look like much during the day, but it's one of the most popular streets for cafes and nightlife in Paris and attracts a young, alternative crowd.

French Traditional French food in all price ranges can be found in the Bastille area.

Le Bistrot du Dôme Bastille (Map 7, ☎ 01 48 04 88 44, 2 rue de la Bastille, 4e, metro Bastille). Opposite Bofinger (see the following), this superb restaurant, a distant cousin of Le Dôme in Montparnasse, specialises in superbly prepared (and pricey) fish dishes. The blackboard menu has starters from 55FF to 80FF, and main courses from 105FF to 130FF, so count on about 210FF a head. Wines all cost 99FF; it opens for lunch and dinner till 11.30 pm daily.

Bofinger (Map 7, ☎ 01 42 72 87 82, 5–7 rue de la Bastille, 4e, metro Bastille). This is reputedly the oldest brasserie in Paris (founded in 1864), with Art Nouveau brass, glass and mirrors throughout. Specialities include *choucroute* (86FF to 118FF) and seafood dishes (from 116FF). There are *menus* costing 119FF, 178FF and 189FF (the last include a half-bottle of wine). Bofinger opens noon to 3 pm and 6.30 pm to 1 am (no afternoon closure on Saturday and Sunday).

Chez Paul (Map 5, ☎ 01 47 00 34 57, 13 rue de Charonne, 11e, metro Ledru Rollin). This is a convivial and extremely popular bistro with traditional French main courses costing from 62FF to 95FF, so count on paying about 150FF for a meal. It opens for lunch and dinner to 12.30 am daily.

Crêpes Show (Map 5, ☎ 01 47 00 36 46, 51 rue de Làppe , 11e, metro Ledru Rollin). This small restaurant specialises in sweet Breton *crêpes* and savoury buckwheat *galettes* (18FF to 45FF). It has *menus* at 43FF (lunch), 55FF and 63FF; vegetarian dishes include salads and cost from 39FF. It opens for lunch on weekdays and for dinner to 1 or 2 am daily (closed on Sunday in winter).

L'Encrier (Map 5, ☎ 01 44 68 08 16, 55 rue Traversière, 12e, metro Ledru Rollin). If you're looking for lunch in the Bastille area, you couldn't do better than the 'Inkwell', which serves an excellent-value three-course lunch *menu* costing 65FF and dinner ones costing 78FF and 108FF. It opens for lunch on weekdays and for dinner to 11 pm Monday to Friday.

Le Square Trousseau (Map 5, ☎ 01 43 43 06 00, 1 rue Antoine Vollon, 12e, metro Ledru Rollin). This vintage bistro, with its etched glass, zinc bar and polished wood panelling, is comfortable rather than trendy and attracts a jolly and very mixed clientele. But most people come to enjoy the lovely terrace overlooking a small park. The two/three-course lunch *menus* cost 100/135FF; a la carte starters cost 40FF to 106FF and mains cost 88FF to 125FF at night, so expect to pay from 180FF a head. It opens for lunch and dinner until 11.30 pm daily.

Lire Entre les Vignes (Map 5, ☎ 01 43 55 69 49, 38 rue Sedaine, 11e, metro Bastille or Bréguet Sabin). Hidden away in a nondescript Bastille backstreet, 'Read between the Vines' is an oasis of conviviality, reminiscent of a comfortable and spacious country kitchen, and a great spot to dine with friends. The food is fresh, imaginative and tasty – prepared before your eyes in the corner kitchen. It opens for lunch and dinner till 10.30 pm on weekdays.

Other Cuisines from all over the world are found along rue de la Roquette and rue de Làppe , just east of place de la Bastille, but Tex-Mex (usually rather bland in Paris) and Latino is the major attraction.

Havanita Café (Map 6, ☎ 01 43 55 96 42, 11 rue de Làppe , 11e, metro Bastille). This restaurant/ bar is decorated with posters and murals inspired – like the food and drinks – by Cuba. Cocktails cost from 48FF, starters cost from 38FF to 57FF and excellent main courses are from 69FF to 94FF. Happy hour, when cocktails cost 28FF, is from 5 to 8 pm. Havanita opens from 5 pm (noon on Sunday) to 2 am daily.

Suds (Map 5, ☎ 01 43 14 06 36, 55 rue de Charonne, 11e, metro Ledru Rollin). No, not a groovy laundrette but a very *branché* (trendy) bar/restaurant with a name that means 'Souths' and has jazz in the basement. There is an eclectic mix of cuisine here, anything from Mexican and Peruvian to Portuguese and North African. There's a lunch *menu* costing 70FF, the *plat du jour* costs 72FF to 88FF and the vegetarian plate costs 52FF. A la carte starters range from 29FF to 45FF, main courses from 64FF to 88FF and desserts from 34FF to 39FF, so expect to pay about 150FF a head. It opens for lunch Tuesday to Friday and for dinner to 2 am Tuesday to Sunday.

Self-Catering There are lots of *food shops* along rue de la Roquette up towards place Léon Blum (metro Voltaire). There's a *Monoprix* (Map 5, metro Ledru Rollin) at 97 rue du Faubourg St-Antoine (11e), open 9 am to 9 pm Monday to Saturday.

Ménilmontant & Belleville

In the northern part of the 11e and into the 19e and 20e, rue Oberkampf and its extension, rue de Ménilmontant, are becoming increasingly popular with diners and denizens of the night. Rue de Belleville and the streets running off it are dotted with Chinese, South-East Asian and a few Turkish places; blvd de Belleville has loads of kosher couscous restaurants (closed on Saturday).

French From the sublime to the ridiculously cheap, French restaurants run the gamut here.

Le Charbon (Map 3, ☎ 01 43 57 55 13, 109 rue Oberkampf, 11e, metro Parmentier). With its remarkable distressed-retro-industrial ambience, the Charbon was the first – and arguably is still the best – of the hip new cafes and bars to sprout up in Ménilmontant. The *plat du jour* costs 66FF to 69FF. There's a 68FF lunch *menu* and brunch on Saturday and Sunday (11 am to 5 pm) costs 75FF. It opens 9 am to 2 am daily.

Le Clown Bar (Map 6, ☎ 01 43 55 87 35, 114 rue Amelot, 11e, metro Filles du Calvaire). This wonderful wine bar next to the Cirque d'Hiver is like a museum, with painted ceilings, mosaics on the wall and a lovely zinc bar. The food is simple and unpretentious traditional French, with starters costing from 38FF to 58FF and main courses from 65FF to 88FF so expect to pay from 150FF per person. It opens for lunch Monday to Saturday and for dinner till 11.30 pm daily.

Le Pavillon Puebla (Map 3, ☎ 01 42 08 92 62, *Parc des Buttes-Chaumont, 19e, metro Buttes-Chaumont*). Situated near the corner of ave Simon Bolivar and rue Manin, this exquisite – no, not Mexican but French Catalan – restaurant in a Second Empire-style pavilion attracts not so much for its wonderful seafood and fish dishes, but the wonderful terrace open in summer. *Menus* cost 180FF and 250FF. For dessert, don't miss the *millefeuille aux fraises* (strawberries in layers of flaky pastry). It opens for lunch and dinner to 10.30 pm Tuesday to Saturday.

Le Repaire de Cartouche (Map 7, ☎ 01 47 00 25 86, entrances at 8 blvd des Filles du Calvaire or 99 rue Amelot, 11e, metro St-Sébastien Froissart). This old-fashioned place takes a very modern approach to French food under the direction of a talented young chef. Innovative starters cost from 40FF to 60FF, main courses cost from 85FF to 120FF and desserts cost from 30FF to 40FF. Wines average about 160FF a bottle. It opens for lunch and dinner till 11 pm Tuesday to Saturday.

Au Trou Normand (Map 6, ☎ 01 48 05 80 23, 9 rue Jean-Pierre Timbaud, 11e, metro Oberkampf). Hosted by several grannies, this cosy, very French little restaurant has some of the lowest prices in Paris. Starters cost from 10FF to 12FF (the vegetable soup is particularly good), main courses cost from 29FF to 39FF, and desserts are under 10FF, so you won't spend a lot more than 60FF per person. It opens for lunch on weekdays and for dinner till 11 pm Monday to Saturday.

Le Villaret (Map 6, ☎ 01 43 57 89 76, 13 rue Ternaux, 11e, metro Parmentier). This excellent neighbourhood bistro, an easy walk from the great food market on blvd Richard Lenoir, has diners coming from across Paris till late to sample the house specialities. Starters cost from 45FF to 55FF, main courses from 85FF to 110FF and desserts from 45FF. The lunch *menus* cost 120/150FF for two/three courses, and the *plat du jour* costs 90FF. Le Villaret opens for lunch on weekdays and for dinner to 1 am Monday to Saturday.

Other The cuisines of southern Europe, North Africa and Asia are well represented.

Chez Lalou (Map 3, ☎ 01 43 58 35 28, 78 blvd de Belleville, 20e, metro Couronnes). The pick of the kosher couscous crop on blvd de Belleville, Chez Lalou has killer steamed semolina plus unusual stews and tajines from 65FF to 80FF, grills from 65FF to 75FF, *brick à l'oeuf* (egg fritter) for 25FF and salads from 20FF to 40FF. The terrace is a lovely – and lively – place to dine in the warm weather.

PARIS

Café Florentin (Map 6, ☎ 01 43 55 57 00, 40 rue Jean-Pierre Timbaud, 11e, metro Parmentier). Excellent Italian fare can be had here in cosy surroundings. The lunch *menu* costs 65FF (including wine), a la carte starters cost 24FF to 75FF and main courses cost 60FF to 90FF. The two dozen pasta dishes range in price from 45FF to 75FF. Café Florentin opens for lunch weekdays and for dinner till 11 pm Monday to Saturday.

Favela Chic (Map 3, ☎ 01 43 57 15 47, 131 rue Oberkampf, 11e, metro Ménilmontant). The day job of the people who co-host the hotter-than-hot Brazilian evenings at the Élysée Montmartre in Pigalle on certain Saturdays (see the boxed text 'Salsa City' later in the chapter) is preparing authentic Brazilian dishes at this cosy restaurant. Main courses, including a massive *feijoada* (Brazilian stew), cost 50FF to 70FF. It opens noon to 2 am (from 7 pm on Saturday).

La Piragua (Map 5, ☎ 01 40 21 35 98, 6 rue Rochebrune, 11e, metro St-Ambroise). Colombian food and good Latino music feature at this small, brightly coloured eatery. There are *menus* costing 99FF and 112FF, a la carte starters like *empañadas* (meat-filled dumplings) and fried plantains for 25FF to 40FF, and mains from 60FF to 98FF. La Piragua opens for lunch and dinner to 10.30 pm Monday to Saturday.

Thai Classic (Map 3, ☎ 01 42 40 78 10, 41 rue de Belleville, 19e, metro Belleville). One of the most authentic Thai eateries we've found in Paris, Thai Classic offers soups for 40FF to 45FF and all the favourite Thai dishes (and a few Laotian ones too) for 45FF to 50FF. About a half-dozen of the choices are vegetarian. It opens for lunch and dinner to 11.30 pm Monday to Saturday.

Self-Catering There's a *Franprix* supermarket (Map 6, metro Oberkampf) at 23 rue Jean-Pierre Timbaud (11e), open 8 am to 8 pm Monday to Saturday and also one at 28 blvd Jules Ferry (Map 3, metro République or Goncourt) open the same hours.

Nation
There are loads of decent restaurants on the roads fanning out from place de la Nation.

French The French restaurants in this area tend to be real finds.

Les Amognes (Map 5, ☎ 01 43 72 73 05, 243 rue du Faubourg St-Antoine, 11e, metro Faidherbe Chaligny). A meal at Les Amognes is a quin-

tessentially French (rather than Parisian) experience: haute cuisine at a reasonable 180FF set price, discreet service, an atmosphere that is *correct*, even a little provincial. The wines aren't cheap though – from 200FF for a Burgundy. It opens for lunch Tuesday to Friday and for dinner to 10.30 pm (11.30 pm at the weekend) Monday to Saturday.

Other The area around place de la Nation has a large number of restaurants specialising in cuisines other than French.

À La Banane Ivoirienne (Map 5, ☎ 01 43 70 49 90, 10 rue de la Forge Royale, 11e, metro Ledru Rollin). This friendly place serves West African specialities, with *entrées* costing from 20FF to 38FF and main courses in the 60FF to 90FF region. There's live African-Brazilian music from 10 pm on Friday. À La Banane Ivoirienne opens 7 pm till midnight Tuesday to Saturday.

Café Cannelle (Map 5, ☎ 01 43 70 48 25, 1 bis rue de la Forge Royale, 11e, metro Ledru Rollin). This festive Moroccan restaurant is run by Algerians who do couscous with a twist. How does it sound flavoured with cinnamon, orange-blossom water and almonds for dessert? Couscous and *tajines* cost 79FF to 95FF; *pastilla* costs 79FF. It opens 8 pm to 12.30 am Tuesday to Sunday.

Le Réservoir (Map 5, ☎ 01 43 56 39 60, 16 rue de la Forge Royale, 11e, metro Ledru Rollin). This warehouse turned bar/restaurant done up in modern kitsch serves Mediterranean dishes to celebrities and their hangers-on. Count on at least 200FF a head. The restaurant opens 8 pm till midnight daily, the bar to 2 am.

Chinatown
Dozens of East Asian restaurants line the main streets of Paris' Chinatown (13e), including ave de Choisy, ave d'Ivry and rue Baudricourt. The cheapest *menus*, which cost about 50FF, are usually only available at lunch on weekdays.

La Fleuve de Chine (Map 1, ☎ 01 45 82 06 88, 15 ave de Choisy, or through Tour Bergame housing estate at 130 blvd Masséna, 13e, metro Porte de Choisy). Take it from the experts, this place has the most authentic Cantonese and Hakka food in Paris and, as is typical, both the surrounds and the service are as forgettable as the 1997 Hong Kong handover. Main courses cost from 40FF to 95FF, but settle in at around 40FF to 50FF for chicken, prawn and superb claypot dishes; expect to pay about 120FF a head. It opens for lunch and dinner to 11 pm Friday to Wednesday.

Montparnasse

Since the 1920s, the area around blvd du Montparnasse has been one of the city's premier avenues for enjoying that most Parisian of pastimes: sitting in a cafe and checking out the passers-by. Many younger Parisians, however, now consider the area *démodé* (unfashionable).

As Gare Montparnasse is where Bretons looking for work in Paris would disembark (and apparently venture no farther), there is no shortage of *crêperies* in the area. There are three alone at 20 rue d'Odessa, 14e (Map 4), and many, many more around the corner on rue du Montparnasse. *Mustang Café (Map 4, ☎ 01 43 35 36 12, 84 blvd du Montparnasse, 14e, metro Montparnasse Bienvenüe)*, has passable Tex-Mex (platters and chilli from 47FF to 78FF, *fajitas* for 99FF) available to 5 am.

French Blvd du Montparnasse, around the Vavin metro stop, is home to a number of legendary places, made famous between the wars by writers (such as Ernest Hemingway and F Scott Fitzgerald) and avant-garde artists (Dalí, Cocteau). Before the Russian Revolution, these cafes attracted the exiled revolutionaries Lenin and Trotsky.

La Coupole (Map 4, ☎ 01 43 20 14 20, 102 blvd du Montparnasse, 14e, metro Vavin). La Coupole's famous mural-covered columns (decorated by such artists as Brancusi and Chagall), dark wood panelling and indirect lighting have hardly changed since the days of Sartre, Soutine, Man Ray and Josephine Baker. Starters at this 450-seat brasserie, which opened in 1927, cost 29FF to 50FF and mains cost 78FF to 92FF so count on spending about 200FF for a full meal. A lunchtime express *menu* costs 98.50FF including 25cL of wine; evening *menus* cost 138FF to 189FF. La Coupole opens noon to 1 or 1.30 am daily. There's dancing on some nights and tea dances at the weekend (see Clubs in the Entertainment section for details).
Le Select (Map 4, ☎ 01 42 22 65 27, 99 blvd du Montparnasse, 6e, metro Vavin). Another Montparnasse legend, the Select's decor has changed very little since 1923. The *menu* costs 90FF,

and *tartines* (buttered bread with toppings) made with Poilâne bread start at 30FF. Breakfast/brunch costs 55/80FF. Meals are served at Le Select daily from 11 am to 3 am (4 am on Friday and Saturday).
Le Caméléon (Map 4, ☎ 01 43 20 63 43, 6 rue de Chevreuse, 6e, metro Vavin). If you want to eat at a 'nouveau' bistro or brasserie – the distinction isn't that clear even to the French any more – that serves fresh, innovative food in a traditional setting, you couldn't do better than Le Caméléon; their lobster ravioli (92FF) alone is worth a visit. Starters cost from 35FF to 90FF, main courses from 88FF to 120FF, and there's a lunchtime *menu* costing 120FF. It opens for lunch weekdays and for dinner to 10.30 pm Monday to Saturday.

Self-Catering There's an *Inno* supermarket (Map 4, metro Montparnasse Bienvenüe) on rue du Départ opposite the Tour Montparnasse open 9 am to 10 pm weekdays and to 9 pm on Saturday. The nearby *food market* on blvd Edgar Quinet (Map 4) opens Wednesday and Saturday mornings until about 1 pm.

Montmartre & Pigalle

The restaurants along rue des Trois Frères, 18e (Map 8), are a much better bet than their touristy counterparts at place du Tertre.

French Some of Montmartre's French restaurants, like almost everything else on the Butte, are slightly offbeat.

Le Bateau Lavoir (Map 8, ☎ 01 42 54 23 12, 8 rue Garreau, 18e, metro Abbesses). Named after the studio behind it on Place Émile Goudeau where Picasso & Co made art at the beginning of the 20th century, this wonderful old-style bistro has good-value salads (50FF), lunch/dinner *menus* costing 98/140FF, and makes its own foie gras and *confit de canard*. It opens for lunch and dinner to about 11 pm Thursday to Tuesday.
Le Refuge des Fondus (Map 8, ☎ 01 42 55 22 65, 17 rue des Trois Frères, 18e, metro Abbesses or Anvers). This establishment has been a Montmartre favourite since 1966. For 92FF you get an aperitif, hors d'œuvre, red wine (or beer or soft drink) in a baby bottle and a good quantity of either fondue savoyarde (cheese) or bourguignonne (meat; minimum order for two). It opens 7 pm to 2 am daily with the last seating at midnight or 12.30 am.

PARIS

Macis et Muscade (Map 2, ☎ *01 42 26 62 26, 110 rue Legendre, 17e, metro La Fourche*). This is another example of an excellent *restaurant du quartier* (neighbourhood restaurant), with a lunch-time *menu* costing 75FF and a dinner one costing 130FF. A la carte *entrées* cost from 37FF to 44FF and mains cost 68FF to 85FF. It opens for lunch from Sunday to Friday and for dinner till 11 pm Tuesday to Sunday.

Other French cuisine is not the only option in Montmartre.

Il Duca (Map 8, ☎ *01 46 06 71 98, 26 rue Yvonne le Tac, 18e, metro Abbesses*). This is an intimate little Italian restaurant with good, straightforward food including a three-course *menu* costing 89FF and main courses from 80FF to 90FF. Home-made pasta dishes cost 55FF to 76FF. It opens for lunch and dinner to 11 pm daily.

Le Mono (Map 8, ☎ *01 46 06 99 20, 40 rue Véron, 18e, metro Abbesses or Blanche*). West African specialities at Le Mono include *lélé* (flat, steamed cakes of white beans and shrimp and served with a tomato sauce; 25FF), *maffé* (beef or chicken served with a peanut sauce; 50FF), *gbekui* (a sort of goulash made with spinach, onions, beef, fish and shrimp; 55FF) and *djenkoumé* (grilled chicken with semolina noodles; 60FF). It opens for dinner from 7 to about 11.30 pm Thursday to Tuesday.

Self-Catering Towards Pigalle there are lots of *groceries*, many of them open until late at night – try the side streets leading off blvd de Clichy (for example rue Lepic). Heading south from the junction of blvd de Clichy and blvd de Rochechouart, rue des Martyrs, 9e (Map 3), is lined with food shops almost all the way to the Notre Dame de Lorette metro stop. There's a *Franprix* supermarket (Map 8, metro Lamarck Caulaincourt) at 44 rue Caulaincourt (18e) open 8.30 am to 7.25 pm (7.45 pm on Friday and Saturday) daily except Sunday. The *Ed l'Épicier* supermarket (Map 7, metro Anvers), a block south of the bottom of the funicular at 31 rue d'Orsel (18e), opens 9 am to 8 pm Monday to Saturday.

ENTERTAINMENT
Listings
It's virtually impossible to sample the richness of Paris' entertainment scene without first perusing *Pariscope* (3FF) or *L'Officiel des Spectacles* (2FF), both of which come out on Wednesday and are available at any newsstand. *Pariscope* includes a six-page insert in English courtesy of London's *Time Out* weekly events magazine and can be found online (in French) at www.pariscope.fr.

For up-to-date information on clubs and the music scene pick up a copy of *LYLO* (an acronym for Les Yeux, Les Oreilles, literally 'eyes and ears'), a free magazine with excellent listings of rock concerts and other live music, available at certain cafes, bars and on Minitel at 3615 LYLO. The monthly magazines *Les Inrockuptibles* (15FF) and *Nova* (20FF) are good sources for information on clubs and the music scene; the latter's *Hot Guide* insert of listings is particularly useful. Check out any of the Fnac (rhymes with 'snack') outlets (see the following Booking Agencies section), especially the ones in the Forum des Halles shopping mall and Bastille, for free flyers and programmes.

Two other excellent sources for what's on are Radio FG on 98.2 MHz FM and Radio Nova on 101.5 MHz FM.

Booking Agencies
You can buy tickets for many (but not all) cultural events at several ticket outlets, among them Fnacs and Virgin Megastores. Both accept reservations and ticketing by phone and take most credit cards. Tickets cannot be returned or exchanged unless a performance is cancelled. Reservations for a variety of theatre and opera productions can be made using Minitel 3615 THEA.

Fnac (☎ *0 803 80 88 03*). Fnac has outlets with *billeteries* (ticket offices) throughout Paris (usually open 10 am to 7.30 pm Monday to Saturday) including Fnac Forum des Halles on the 3rd underground level of the Forum des Halles department store (Map 6, ☎ 01 40 41 40 00, 1–7 rue Pierre Lescot, 1er, metro Châtelet-Les Halles); Fnac Montparnasse (Map 4, ☎ 01 49 54 30 00, 136 rue de Rennes, 6e, metro St-Placide); Fnac Musique Bastille (Map 6, ☎ 01 43 42 04 04, 4 place de la Bastille, 12e, metro Bastille), open 10 am to 8 pm (10 pm on Wednesday and Friday) Monday to Saturday; and Fnac Étoile (Map 2, ☎ 01 44 09 18 00, 26–30 ave des Ternes, 17e, metro Ternes). You can purchase tickets via the Web at www.fnac.com or using Minitel (3615 FNAC) with your credit card (commission: 10FF to 20FF), and the tickets will be sent to you by post.

Virgin Megastore *(Map 2, ☎ 01 49 53 50 00, metro Franklin D Roosevelt)*, 52–60 ave des Champs-Élysées, 8e. The ticket office (☎ 01 49 53 52 09) in the basement opens 10 am (noon on Sunday) to midnight daily. Virgin has another store (☎ 01 49 53 52 90, metro Palais Royal) with a box office next to the inverted glass pyramid in the Carrousel du Louvre shopping mall, 99 rue de Rivoli, 1er. It opens 11 am to 8 pm (to 10 pm Wednesday to Saturday) daily.

Other booking agencies include:

Agence des Théâtres *(Map 2, ☎ 01 43 59 24 60, 78 Champs-Élysées, 8e, metro Franklin D Roosevelt)*

Agence des Théâtres Marivaux *(Map 3, ☎ 01 42 97 46 70, 7 rue de Marivaux, 2e, metro Quatre Septembre)*

Comptoir Théâtral *(Map 2, ☎ 01 42 60 58 31, 6 place de la Madeleine, 8e, metro Madeleine)*

Discount Tickets On the day of a performance, ***Kiosque Théâtre*** outlets (there is no telephone number) sell theatre tickets for 50% off the usual price (plus a commission of 16FF). The seats are almost always the most expensive ones in the orchestra or 1st balcony. Tickets to concerts, operas and ballets might also be available.

Both outlets – one across from 15 place de la Madeleine (Map 2, metro Madeleine) in the 8e and the other on the parvis Montparnasse, halfway between Gare Montparnasse and the nearby Tour Montparnasse (Map 4, metro Montparnasse Bienvenüe) in the 15e – are open 12.30 to 8 pm Tuesday to Saturday, and to 4 pm on Sunday.

Pubs, Bars & Cafes

Like most other cities in Europe, Paris has been invaded by Irish pubs, which though much of a muchness, have helped to bring the price of a pint of beer down to merely expensive rather than extortionate levels. But you'll be able to find those on your own.

Les Halles The area around Forum des Halles has many attractive places to drink.

Café Beaubourg *(Map 7, ☎ 01 48 87 63 96, 43 rue St-Merri, 4e, metro Châtelet-Les Halles)* is just opposite the Centre Pompidou. This minimalist cafe draws an arty crowd, and there's always free entertainment on the *parvis* (large square) in front. Breakfast (70FF) and Sunday brunch (120FF) on the terrace is excellent. It's open 8 am to 1 am Monday to Thursday and Sunday (to 2 am on Friday and Saturday).

Café Oz *(Map 6, ☎ 01 40 39 00 18, 18 rue St-Denis, 1er, metro Châtelet)*. An Aussie pub bubbling with the same Down Under (well, let's just call it) enthusiasm as the original across the river on rue St-Jacques in the 5e (see the Latin Quarter section for details). It opens noon to 2 am daily (happy hour 6 to 8 pm).

Marais The 4e has quite a few lively places for daytime and after-hours drinks.

La Chaise au Plafond *(Map 7, ☎ 01 42 76 03 22, 10 rue du Trésor, 4e, metro Hôtel de Ville)*. Owned by the same people as Au Petit Fer à Cheval (below), la Chaise is a warm place with tables outside on a pedestrian-only backstreet. It opens 9 am to 2 am daily.

Au Petit Fer à Cheval *(Map 7, ☎ 01 42 72 47 47, 30 rue Vieille du Temple, 4e, metro Hôtel de Ville or St-Paul)*. A slightly offbeat bar/restaurant named after its horseshoe-shaped counter, often overflowing with friendly, mostly straight young regulars. The stainless-steel bathroom is straight out of a Flash Gordon film. This place opens 9 am (11 am at the weekend) to 2 am. Food (*plat du jour* 60FF, sandwiches from 32FF) is available nonstop from noon to about 1.15 am. Happy hour is 6 to 8 pm.

Stolly's *(Map 7, ☎ 01 42 76 06 76, 16 rue de la Cloche Percée, 4e, metro Hôtel de Ville)*. On a tiny street just off rue de Rivoli, this Anglophone bar is always crowded, particularly during the 4.30 to 8 pm happy hour, when a 1.6L pitcher of cheap *blonde* (house lager) costs 55FF. It opens 4.30 pm to 1.30 am daily.

Île de la Cité The island is not exactly hopping after dark, but has a good wine bar.

Taverne Henri IV *(Map 6 , ☎ 01 43 54 27 90, 13 place du Pont Neuf, 1er, metro Pont Neuf)*. A decent restaurant as well as a serious wine bar with a choice of 14 *tartines* (open sandwiches) costing 40FF, this place attracts lots of people in the legal profession from the nearby Palais de Justice. It opens noon to 9 pm weekdays and to 4 pm on Saturday.

Latin Quarter The Latin Quarter has Paris' highest concentration of bars catering to Anglophones.

Café Oz (Map 5, ☎ 01 43 54 30 48, 184 rue St-Jacques, 5e, metro Luxembourg). A casual, friendly Australian pub with Foster's on tap for 22FF (35FF for a 'schooner' or 400mL), and VB, Coopers, Cascade and Redback as other amber options, plus Australian wines costing from 20FF a glass. Pies start at 30FF. It opens 4 pm to 2 am Sunday to Thursday, to 3 am on Friday and noon to 3 am on Saturday. Happy hour is from to 9.30 pm.

Le Cloître (Map 6, ☎ 01 43 25 19 92, 19 rue St-Jacques, 5e, metro St-Michel). An unpretentious, relaxed place where the mellow background music goes down well with the students who congregate here. It opens 3 pm to 2 am daily.

Polly Magoo (Map 6, ☎ 01 46 33 33 64, 11 rue St-Jacques, 5e, metro St-Michel). An informal, friendly bar founded in 1967 and still spinning disks from the 60s. The regulars include English-speakers resident in Paris. Beer starts at 13FF (19.50FF after 10 pm). It opens noon to 4 am, and to 6 am on Friday and Saturday.

St-Germain & Odéon The 6e has some of Paris' most famous cafes and quite a few decent newcomers.

Café de Flore (Map 6, ☎ 01 45 48 55 26, 172 blvd St-Germain, 6e, metro St-Germain des Prés). An Art Deco-style cafe less touristy than Les Deux Magots (see below) where the red banquettes, mirrors and marble walls haven't changed since the days when Sartre, de Beauvoir, Albert Camus and Picasso imbibed here. The terrace is a sought-after place to sip beer (42FF for 400mL), the house Pouilly Fumé wine (33FF) or coffee (23FF). It opens 7 am to 1.30 am daily.

Les Deux Magots (Map 6, ☎ 01 45 48 55 25, 170 blvd St-Germain, 6e, metro St-Germain des Prés). There's been a cafe here since 1881, but the present one – whose name derives from the two *magots* (grotesque figurines) of Chinese dignitaries at the entrance – dates from 1914. It is perhaps best known as the haunt of Sartre, Hemingway and André Breton. Coffee costs 23FF, beer on tap costs 30FF and the famous home-made hot chocolate served in steaming porcelain jugs costs 33FF. It opens 7.30 am to 2 am daily.

La Palette (Map 6, ☎ 01 43 26 68 15, 43 rue de Seine, 6e, metro Mabillon). This *fin de siècle* cafe, erstwhile stomping ground of Cézanne and Braque, attracts art dealers and collectors from the nearby galleries. It opens 8 am to 2 am Monday to Saturday.

Champs-Élysées Once considered *très démodé* (very out of fashion), the ave des Champs-Élysées and the area around it have had a new lease of life since their costly renovation in the mid-1990s.

Buddha Bar (Map 2, ☎ 01 53 05 90 00, 8 rue Boissy d'Anglais, 8e, metro Concorde). At centre stage in the cavernous dining room of this bar/restaurant frequented by suits, supermodels and their hangers-on is an enormous bronze Buddha. Everyone should go at least once for a look, but stick with the drinks (cocktails cost from 60FF); a Pacific Rim-style meal costs upwards of 300FF. The bar opens 6 pm to 2 am daily

Grands Boulevards The bars and cafes on and just off the Grands Boulevards are some of the best venues for a night on the town on the Right Bank.

Café Noir (Map 6, ☎ 01 40 39 07 36, 65 rue Montmartre, 2e, metro Sentier). It may be a bit out of the way on the edge of the Sentier garment district, but this funky cafe/bar draws a crowd of Anglo and Francophones well into the night, attracted by the friendly ambience and reasonable prices. It opens 8 am to 2 am weekdays and 4 pm to 2 am on Saturday.

Harry's New York Bar (Map 2, ☎ 01 42 61 71 14, 5 rue Daunou, 2e, metro Opéra). Back in the pre-war years, when there were several dozen American-style bars in Paris, Harry's was one of the most popular; regulars included US writers F Scott Fitzgerald and Hemingway. The Cuban mahogany interior dates from the mid-19th century and was brought over lock, stock and barrel from Manhattan's Third Avenue in 1911. Beer costs 30FF (38FF after 10 pm). Drinks at the basement piano bar (soft jazz from 10 pm to 2 or 3 am) cost 53FF to 77FF. Harry's opens 10.30 am to 4 am daily.

Bastille The area just north-east of place de la Bastille is enormously popular for dining, drinking and dancing all night long. Southeast of the square are a number of excellent after-dark venues.

Boca Chica (Map 5, ☎ 01 43 57 93 13, 58 rue de Charonne, 11e, metro Ledru Rollin). This is an enormous, almost industrial, place with three large bars on two floors and a friendly, lively crowd. Happy hour is 4 to 8 pm daily when 1L of sangria costs 45FF and cocktails are half-price. It opens 11 am to 2 am daily.

China Club (Map 5, ☎ 01 43 43 82 02, 50 rue du Charenton, 12e, metro Ledru Rollin). If you've got a rich uncle (he's the 'American uncle' in French) or aunt in tow, have them take you to this stylish establishment behind the Opéra Bastille. It's got a huge bar with high ceilings on the ground floor, a *fumoir* for smoking cigars on the 1st floor, and a jazz club called Le Sing Song done up to look like Shanghai circa 1930 in the cellar. Happy hour is from 7 to 9 pm daily when all drinks cost 35FF. It opens 7 pm to 2 am (to 3 am on Friday and Saturday).

Sanz Sans (Map 5, ☎ 01 44 75 78 78, 49 rue du Faubourg St-Antoine, 11e, metro Bastille). By night this full-on watering hole is one of the liveliest (OK, read rowdiest) drinking spots on the Bastille beat: dress (or undress) to impress. By day the red velvet decor seems a tad overdone. It opens 9 am to 2 am daily.

Le Viaduc Café (Map 5, ☎ 01 44 74 70 70, 43 ave Daumesnil, 12e, metro Gare de Lyon). The terrace of this *branché* (trendy) cafe in one of the glassed-in arches of the Viaduc des Arts is an excellent spot to while away the hours, and the jazz brunch on Sunday (*menus* cost 95FF to 135FF) is very popular. It opens 9 am to 4 am daily.

Ménilmontant South of place de la République, rue Oberkampf and its eastern extension, rue Ménilmontant, are among the hottest areas in Paris at the moment, with a number of interesting cafes and bars.

L'Autre Café (Map 3, ☎ 01 40 21 03 07, 62 rue Jean Pierre Timbaud, 11e, metro Parmentier). This popular venue has already begun to move the centre of after-dark activity north of rue Oberkampf. With its long bar, open spaces, relaxed environment and reasonable prices, it attracts a mixed young crowd of locals, artists and party-goers. It opens 9 am to 2 am daily.

Café Cannibale (Map 3, ☎ 01 49 29 95 59, 93 rue Jean-Pierre Timbaud, 11e, metro Couronnes). A laid-back alternative to the pubs and bars of rue Oberkampf, the 'Cannibal' is the place to linger over a coffee (10FF) or grab a quick beer at the bar (13FF) or *à table* (17FF). It opens 8 am (9 am at the weekend) to 2 am daily.

Montparnasse The most popular places to while away the hours over a drink or coffee in Montparnasse are the large restaurant/

cafes like *La Coupole* and *Le Select* on blvd du Montparnasse (Map 4; see the Places to Eat section earlier in this chapter).

La Closerie des Lilas (Map 5, ☎ 01 40 51 34 50, 171 blvd du Montparnasse, 6e, metro Port Royal). Anybody who has read Hemingway knows he did a lot of writing, drinking and eating of oysters here; little brass tags on the tables tell you exactly where he (and other luminaries such as Picasso and Apollinaire) whiled away the hours making art, gossiping and/or bickering. It opens 11.30 am to 1 am.

Montmartre & Pigalle In between the sleaze there are some interesting bars at the bottom of the Butte de Montmartre (Montmartre Hill).

Chào-Bà Café (Map 8, ☎ 01 46 06 72 90, 22 blvd de Clichy, 18e, metro Pigalle). This restaurant/cafe, transformed from the old-style Café Pigalle into something straight out of Indochina, opens 9 am to 2 am Sunday to Wednesday, to 4 am Thursday and 5 am Friday and Saturday.

La Fourmi (Map 8, ☎ 01 42 64 70 35, 74 rue des Martyrs, 18e, metro Pigalle). This trendy Pigalle hangout buzzes all day and night and is a convenient place to meet before heading for Le Divan du Monde (see the Rock section) just opposite. It opens 8.30 am (10 am on Sunday) to 2 am.

Clubs

The clubs and other dancing venues favoured by the Parisian 'in' crowd change frequently, and many are officially private. Single men may not be admitted, even if their clothes are subculturally appropriate, simply because they're single men. Women, on the other hand, get in for free on some nights. It's always easier to get into the club of your choice during the week, when things may be hopping even more than they are at the weekend. The truly trendy crowd considers showing up before 1 am a serious breach of good taste.

Paris is a great music town (though techno lingers on, sadly) and there are some fine DJs based here. Latino and Cuban salsa and merengue are also particularly hot (see the boxed text 'Salsa City'). Theme nights are also common; for more details consult any of the sources mentioned under Listings at the start of this section.

Salsa City

Ay, que rico! Whether you're a Latin music aficionado, a salsa and merengue enthusiast or just a Hemingway wannabe in search of that perfect *mojito* (rum cocktail), you'll soon discover that Paris boasts enough sizzling and tropical bars and *boîtes* (clubs) to more than rival its Hispanic neighbour to the south and some say even Havana itself.

What's more, the Latino vibes don't stop when the temperatures drop. New clubs are opening up all the time, established venues are adding salsa nights and virtually anyone who's anyone in the Latin world makes it to Paris eventually, including the Cuban *Buena Vista* veterans. So don your dancing shoes and *bailamos* till dawn.

For a who and what is *caliente* (hot) in Latino music, tune into Radio Latina 99 FM, *'la radio officielle de la fiesta'* (the official fiesta radio station), with listings from 6 and 10 am and 5 and 8 pm weekdays and 5 to 11 pm on Saturday. You can also check out their Web site at www.latina.fr. By Minitel, key in 3615 LATINA. *Pariscope* and *L'Officiel des Spectacles* (see Listings at the start of the Entertainment section) also list concerts.

The following is an A to Z listing of the hottest, most happening Latin dance venues in Paris at the moment. Be sure to check with the clubs specified in advance as schedules and times may have changed. The price of admission often includes the first drink. Many clubs offer salsa and merengue classes in the early evening; call ahead if you're interested.

Les Bains (Map 6, ☎ 01 48 87 01 80, 7 rue du Bourg l'Abbé, 3e, metro Étienne Marcel). This club, in refitted old Turkish baths, is still renowned for its surly, selective bouncers on the outside and both celebrity and star-struck revellers inside, and it's hard to get in at the weekend. Music is house, garage and techno. It opens 11.30 pm to 6 am daily; admission costs 100FF to 130FF.

Batofar (Map 1, ☎ 01 56 29 10 00, opposite 11 quai François Mauriac, 13e, metro Bibliothèque). What looks like a mild-mannered tugboat moored near the imposing Bibliothèque Nationale de France François Mitterrand is a rollicking dancing spot open 6 pm to 2 am Tuesday to Sunday which attracts some top international DJ talent. Admission costs up to 100FF.

Le Balajo (Map 6, ☎ 01 47 00 07 87, 9 rue de Làppe, 11e, metro Bastille). This vintage place has been a mainstay of Parisian nightlife since 1936. Wednesday (9 pm to 2 am) is mambo night, Thursday is salsa (10 pm to 5 am) and DJs play rock, 1970s disco and funk on Friday and Saturday from 11.30 pm to 5 am. Admission costs 100FF (50FF on Wednesday) and includes one drink. From 2.30 to 6.30 pm on Thursday and 3 to 7 pm on Sunday, DJs play old-fashioned *musette* (accordion music) – waltz, tango, cha-cha – for aficionados of retro tea dancing (50FF).

Cithéa (Map 3, ☎ 01 40 21 70 95, 114 rue

Salsa City

Le Balajo (Map 6, ☎ 01 47 00 07 87, 9 rue de Lappe, 11e, metro Bastille). Live salsa music and dancing are featured at this old ballroom from 10 pm to 5 am on Thursday (100FF).

La Casa 128 (Map 3, ☎ 01 48 01 05 71, 128 rue La Fayette, 10e, metro Gare du Nord). This club has an excellent ambiance and salsa from 8 pm to 2 am Thursday to Sunday (50FF).

La Chapelle des Lombards (Map 6, ☎ 01 43 57 24 24, 19 rue de Lappe, 11e, metro Bastille). This place has tropical and Latin nights Thursday to Saturday (100FF).

La Coupole (Map 4, ☎ 01 43 20 14 20, 102 blvd du Montparnasse, 14e, metro Vavin). The epidemic of Latin fever can be traced to 1993 and La Coupole when the now (in)famous Tuesday salsa night (8.30 pm to 3 am) with live big bands was launched. Admission costs 100FF, or 140FF for admission plus a dance class from 8.30 to 9.30 pm.

Le Divan du Monde (Map 8, ☎ 01 44 92 77 66/43 38 70 76, 75 rue des Martyrs, 18e, metro Pigalle). World-music nights are featured with at least one salsa night a week. Admission varies.

L'Élysé-Montmartre (Map 8, ☎ 01 44 92 45 45/55 06 07 00, 72 blvd de Rochechouart, 18e, metro Anvers). On certain Saturdays this place co-hosts special Brazilian evenings (80FF) with the Favela Chic restaurant (see Ménilmontant & Belleville in the Places to Eat section); check Pariscope for details. On other Saturdays it becomes a salsa venue as the Bal de l' Élysée-Montmartre.

Les Étoiles (Map 3, ☎ 01 47 70 60 56, 61 rue du Château d'Eau, 10e, metro Château d'Eau). Paris' first music hall (open in 1856) features live Latin bands and an ambiente popular from 9 pm to 4 am Thursday to Saturday (60FF to 100FF).

La Java (Map 3, ☎ 01 42 02 20 52, 105 rue du Faubourg du Temple, 10e, metro Belleville). The dance hall where Piaf got her first break now reverberates to the sound of salsa from 11 pm to 5 am Thursday to Saturday and 2 to 7 pm Sunday (80FF to 100FF).

Le Latina Café (Map 2, ☎ 01 42 89 98 89, 114 ave des Champs-Élysées, 8e, metro George V). This recently opened restaurant/music club has something for everyone – from novices to well-honed Latino lovers. There's a bodeguita (little bar) and tapas bar on the ground floor, a restaurant and the Bar Hacienda on the 1st floor, and in the basement a club with a stage and live bands. Radio Latina broadcasts from here live every Thursday. It opens from 10 am to 5 am daily.

Los Latinos (Map 3, ☎ 01 43 55 55 12 45, 45 rue de St-Sébastien, 11e, metro Richard Lenoir). This Latin restaurant has a small but intimate dance floor and tropical atmosphere. Live bands play Thursday to Saturday nights (180FF including dinner and concert).

Montecristo Café (Map 2, ☎ 01 45 62 30 86, 68 ave des Champs-Élysées, 8e, metro Franklin D Roosevelt). This bar/restaurant brings Latino mainstream to the Right Bank and the tourists love it. The music is decent, there's a great bar and the place never closes – it opens 24 hours a day, seven days a week. There's a DJ and salsa music from 10 pm (60FF to 100FF).

Oberkampf, 11e, metro Parmentier). This ever-hopping place has bands playing soul, acid jazz, Latin and funk. Wine and beer cost 30FF and cocktails cost from 70FF. It opens 10 am to 6 pm daily.

La Coupole (Map 4, ☎ 01 43 27 56 00/20 14 20, 102 blvd du Montparnasse, 14e, metro Vavin). La Coupole hosts one of the best salsa sessions in town on Tuesday night (see the boxed text 'Salsa City'); on Friday and Saturday from 9.30 pm to 4 am there's a retro disco (100FF) and tea dances from 3 to 7 pm on Saturday and 3 to 9 pm on Sunday (40FF).

Folies Pigalle (Map 8, ☎ 01 48 78 25 56 or 01 40 36 71 58, 11 place Pigalle, 9e, metro Pigalle). A heaving, mixed place that is great for cruising from the balcony above the dance floor. It opens midnight till dawn Thursday to Saturday with concerts at 2 am. Admission costs 150FF.

Le Gibus (Map 3, ☎ 01 47 00 78 88, 18 rue du Faubourg du Temple, 11e, metro République). A former cathedral of rock, this cave-like place has metamorphosed itself, with Wednesday devoted to techno and trance, and house at the weekend. It opens midnight to dawn Wednesday to Sunday; admission costs 20FF in the week and 100FF at the weekend.

La Guinguette Pirate (Map 1, ☎ 01 56 29 10 20, opposite 11 quai François Mitterrand, 13e, metro Bibliothèque). Another barge-based boîte (club), this time in a three-masted Chinese junk.

There's usually a concert of some sort at 9 or 10.30 pm (admission costs 40FF), *and the* crowd is young and energetic. It opens from about noon to 2 am daily.

La Locomotive (Map 8, ☎ 0 836 69 69 28/01 53 41 88 88, 90 blvd de Clichy, 18e, metro Blanche). An enormous ever-popular disco on three levels that has long been one of the favourite dancing venues for teenage out-of-towners. It opens 11 pm (midnight on Monday) to 6 or 7 am. Admission costs 70/55FF with/without a drink on weekdays, and women get in free before 12.30 am. On Friday and Saturday admission costs 60FF without a drink before midnight and 100FF with one after that.

Le Queen (Map 2, ☎ 01 53 89 08 90, 102 ave des Champs-Élysées, 8e, metro George V). The king (as it were) of gay discos in Paris now reigns even more supreme with special theme parties open to all (eg, the mixed Respect night on Wednesday), if they can get past the bouncers. Queen opens midnight to 6 am daily; admission (Friday and Saturday nights only) costs 100FF.

Rex Club (Map 3, ☎ 01 42 36 83 98, 5 blvd Poissonnière, 2e, metro Bonne Nouvelle). This huge club is the undisputed hottest place in town for techno and attracts Paris' top DJ talent. It opens 11 pm till dawn Wednesday to Sunday and admission costs 60FF to 100FF, depending on the night.

La Scala de Paris (Map 6, ☎ 01 42 60 45 64, 188 bis rue de Rivoli, 1er, metro Palais Royal or Pyramides). A large, touristy disco whose three dance floors (all playing the same music) and five bars are lit by laser lights. The patrons are mostly Eurotrash in the 18–30 age group and come from all over Euroland and provincial France. It opens 10.30 pm to dawn daily. Admission costs 80FF (100FF on Friday and Saturday nights), including one drink. Women get in free from Sunday to Thursday except on the eve of public holidays.

Gay & Lesbian Venues

The Marais, especially those areas around the intersection of rue Ste-Croix de la Bretonnerie, rue des Archives and westwards to rue Vieille du Temple, has been Paris' main centre of gay and lesbian nightlife since the early 1980s. There are also a few bars and clubs in walking distance west of blvd de Sébastopol.

Amnésia Café (Map 7, ☎ 01 42 72 16 94, 42 rue Vieille du Temple, 4e, metro Hôtel de Ville). This is a cosy, warmly lit and very popular place, with cosy sofas and a mixed clientele.

Beers start at 19FF, cocktails at 45FF. Breakfast costs 75FF and brunch (daily from noon to 4 pm) costs 95FF and 135FF. It opens 9.30 am to 2 am daily.

Banana Café (Map 6, ☎ 01 42 33 35 31, 13 rue de la Ferronerie, 1er, metro Châtelet). This ever-popular cruise bar on two levels has a nice enclosed terrace with stand-up tables and attracts a young, buffed-up crowd. Happy hour (drinks half-price) is between 4 and 9 pm. It opens 4.30 pm to 6 am daily.

La Champmeslé (Map 6, ☎ 01 42 96 85 20, 4 rue Chabanais, 2e, metro Pyramides). A relaxed, long-established place that plays mellow music for its patrons, about 75% of whom are lesbians (the rest are mostly gay men). The back room is reserved for women only. Beer or fruit juice costs 20FF to 30FF. La Champmeslé opens 5 pm to 5 am Monday to Saturday, and there's a cabaret of French *chansons* at 10 pm on Thursday.

Open Bar (Map 7, ☎ 01 42 72 26 18, 17 rue des Archives, 4e, metro Hôtel de Ville). This is where most people head after work or where they start the evening. It's packed but more social than cruisy. Open Bar opens 11 am to 2 am (happy hour is 6 to 8 pm) and its small *coffee shop* next door serves food from noon to 11 pm.

Quetzal Bar (Map 7, ☎ 01 48 87 99 07, 10 rue de la Verrerie, 4e, metro Hôtel de Ville). The Quetzal, just opposite rue des Mauvais Garçons (literally 'Street of Bad Boys', its name since the 16th century when brigands congregated here) is a dimly lit, modern bar popular with 30-something gay men and is still the cruisiest place in the Marais. It opens 5 pm to 3 am (5 am on Friday and Saturday). Happy hour is from 5 to 8 pm.

Les Scandaleuses (Map 6, ☎ 01 48 87 39 26, 8 rue des Écouffes, 4e, metro Hôtel de Ville). A glossy and lively women-only bar in the Marais, popular with artists and designers. It opens 6 pm to 2 am daily.

Cinemas

Pariscope and *L'Officiel des Spectacles* list the cinematic offerings alphabetically by their French title followed by the English (or German, Italian or Spanish) one. Going to the movies in Paris does not come cheaply: expect to pay around 50FF for a ticket. Students and people aged under 18 and over 60 usually get discounts of about 25% except on Friday, Saturday and Sunday nights. On Wednesday (and sometimes

Monday) most cinemas give discounts to everyone.

Cinémathèque Française (☎ *01 53 65 74 74/56 26 01 01 for a recording*). This cultural institution almost always leaves its foreign offerings – often seldom-screened classics – in their original versions. There are two cinemas: one at the Palais de Chaillot (Map 4, metro Trocadéro or Iéna), 7 ave Albert de Mun, 16e, and the other at 42 blvd Bonne Nouvelle, 10e (Map 3, metro Bonne Nouvelle). Screenings take place Tuesday to Sunday; check *Pariscope* and *L'Officiel des Spectacles* for exact times. Tickets cost 29FF (reduced price 18FF). The Web site (in French) is www.cinematheque.tm.fr.

Theatre

Almost all of Paris' theatre productions, including those written in other languages, are performed in French. There are a few English-speaking troupes around, though – look for ads on metro poster boards and in English-language periodicals like *France USA Contacts* (or *FUSAC*; see Newspapers & Magazines in the Facts for the Visitor chapter for details).

Comédie Française (*Map 6, ☎ 01 44 58 15 15, 2 rue de Richelieu, 1er, metro Palais Royal*). Founded under Louis XIV, the Comédie Française bases its repertoire around the works of the classic French playwrights (including Corneille, Molière and Racine) though contemporary and even – shock, horror! – non-French works have been staged in recent years. The box office (same telephone number) is open from 11 am to 6 pm daily. Tickets for regular seats cost from 70FF to 190FF; tickets for places near the ceiling (30FF) go on sale one hour before curtain time (8.30 pm), which is when those aged under 25 and students under 27 can purchase any of the better seats remaining for around 60FF. Tickets to Thursday's performance are a uniform 50FF (except for the 30FF cheapies). The discount tickets are available from the window around the corner from the main entrance and facing rue de Montpensier. The Web site (in French) is www.comedie-francaise.fr.

Odéon Théâtre de l'Europe (*Map 6, 01 44 41 36 00, place de L'Odéon, 6e, metro Odéon*). This huge, ornate theatre, built in the early 1780s, often puts on foreign plays in their original languages (subtitled in French) and hosts theatre troupes from abroad (seats cost 30FF to 180FF). The box office (☎ *01 44 41 36 36*) opens 11 am to 6 pm Monday to Saturday. People aged over

60 get a discount on the pricier tickets, while students and people under 26 with a Carte Jeune can get good reserved seats for as little as 30FF to 50FF. On Thursday and Sunday 50 seats are sold to all for 20FF 1½ hours before curtain time. The Web site (in French) is www.theatre-odeon.fr.

Point Virgule (*Map 7, ☎ 01 42 78 67 03/39 91 62 10, 7 rue Ste-Croix de la Bretonnerie, 4e, metro Hôtel de Ville*). This popular spot in the Marais offers cafe-theatre at its best, with stand-up comics, performance artists, musical acts – you name it. The quality is variable, but it's great fun nevertheless. There are three shows daily at 8, 9.15 and 10.15 pm. Entry costs 90/130/150FF for one/two/three shows (students 70FF).

Cabaret

Paris' risqué cancan revues – those dazzling, pseudo-bohemian productions featuring hundreds of performers, including female dancers both in and out of their elaborate costumes – are about as representative of the Paris of the 21st century as crocodile-wrestling is of Australia or bronco-busting of the USA. But they do keep on drawing in the crowds...

Le Lido (*Map 2, ☎ 01 40 76 56 10, 116 bis ave des Champs-Élysées, 8e, metro George V*). The floor show of this cabaret (founded in 1946) gets top marks for its ambitious sets and lavish costumes. Nightly shows including a half-bottle of champagne cost 560FF at 10 pm and 460FF (560FF on Friday and Saturday) at midnight, 375FF to watch from the bar with two drinks and 815FF, 915FF and 1015FF for the show and dinner, depending on the *menu* chosen.

Moulin Rouge (*Map 8, ☎ 01 53 09 82 82, 82 blvd de Clichy, 18e, metro Blanche*). This legendary cabaret, whose dancers appeared in Toulouse-Lautrec's famous posters, sits under its trademark red windmill (a 1925 copy). The champagne dinner show (at 7 or 8 pm, depending on the season) costs 790FF, 890FF or 990FF. The show at 9 or 10 pm with a drink costs 560FF; at 11 pm or midnight it drops to 500FF.

Opera & Classical Music

The Opéra National de Paris now splits its performances between Palais Garnier, its original home built in 1875, and the modern Opéra Bastille, which opened in 1989. Both opera houses also stage ballets and concerts put on by the Opéra National's affiliated orchestra and ballet company. The opera season runs from September to July. The Web site is www.opera-de-paris.fr. On Minitel key in 3615 OPERAPARIS.

Opéra Bastille (Map 6, ☎ 0 836 69 78 68 or 01 44 73 13 99, 2–6 place de la Bastille, 12e, metro Bastille). The box office, which is at 120 rue de Lyon (11e), opens from 11 am to 6.30 pm Monday to Saturday. Ticket sales begin 14 days before the date of the performance, but according to local opera buffs, the only way to ensure a booking is by post some two months in advance (120 rue de Lyon, 75576 Paris Cedex 12). Opera tickets cost 90FF to 670FF. To have a shot at the cheapest (ie, worst) seats in the house (45FF to 60FF), you have to stop by the ticket office the day tickets go on sale – exactly 14 days before the performance (on a Monday if the performance is on a Sunday). Ballets cost 70FF to 420FF (45FF to 50FF for the cheapest seats), concerts 85FF to 255FF (45FF). If there are unsold tickets, people aged under 25 or over 65 and students can get excellent seats for about 100FF only 15 minutes before the curtain goes up (tarif spécial).

Opéra Comique (Map 3, ☎ 01 42 44 45 46 for reservations, 5 rue Favart, 2e, metro Richelieu Drouot). This is a century-old hall that plays host to classic and less-well-known works of opera. The season lasts from late October to early July. Tickets, available from Fnac or Virgin, cost 100FF to 610FF; 50FF tickets with limited or no visibility are available up to 12 hours before the performance at the box office (opposite the theatre at 14 rue Favart), which opens 11 am to 6 pm Monday to Saturday and one hour before any performance. Subject to availability, students and those under 26 can purchase unsold tickets for around 50FF.

Palais Garnier (Map 2, ☎ 0 836 69 78 68 for information and reservations, place de l'Opéra, 9e, metro Opéra). Ticket prices and conditions (including last-minute discounts) are almost exactly the same as those at Opéra Bastille.

In addition to opera, Paris plays host to dozens of orchestral, organ and chamber music concerts each week.

Salle Pleyel (Map 2, ☎ 01 45 61 53 01, 252 rue du Faubourg St-Honoré, 8e, metro Ternes). This is a highly regarded, 1920s-era hall that hosts many of Paris' finest classical-music concerts

and recitals. The box office opens 11 am to 6 pm Monday to Saturday. Tickets cost 80FF to 410FF.

Théâtre des Champs-Élysées (Map 2, ☎ 01 49 52 50 50, 15 Ave Montaigne, 8e, metro Alma-Marceau). A prestigious Right Bank orchestral and recital hall with popular Sunday concerts (100FF) held most of the year at 11 am. The box office opens from 1 to 7 pm Monday to Saturday.

Théâtre Musical de Paris (Map 6, ☎ 01 40 28 28 00/40 for information and reservations, 2 rue Édouard Colonne, 1er, metro Châtelet). On the western side of place du Châtelet, this hall – also called Théâtre du Châtelet – hosts operas (200FF to 750FF for the better seats, 50FF to 80FF for seats with limited visibility), ballets (90FF to 200FF), concerts (including by the excellent Orchestre de Paris) and theatre performances. Classical music is performed at 11 am on Sunday (120FF) and at 12.45 pm on Monday, Wednesday and Friday (55FF). The ticket office opens 11 am to 7 pm (8 pm on performance nights) daily; tickets go on sale 14 days before the performance date. Subject to availability, anyone under 26 or over 65 can get reduced-price tickets (opera 100FF, ballet 60FF, concerts 50FF) starting 15 minutes before curtain time. There are no performances in July and August. You can also book via the theatre's Web site at www.chatelet-theatre.com or try Minitel 3615 CHATELET.

Church Venues The churches of Paris are popular venues for classical music concerts and organ recitals. The concerts held at Notre Dame Cathedral (Map 6, ☎ 01 42 34 56 10) don't keep to any particular schedule but are advertised on posters around town and usually cost 100/80FF for the full/reduced tariff. From April to October, classical concerts are also held in Ste-Chapelle (Map 6, ☎ 01 42 77 65 65/53 73 78 51) on Île de la Cité (1er); the cheapest seats cost about 110FF (students under 25 80FF).

Other noted concert venues with similar admission fees are Église St-Eustache (Map 6) in the 1er; Église Notre Dame du Val de Grâce, Église St-Étienne du Mont (Map 5) and Église St-Julien le Pauvre (Map 6) in the 5e; Église St-Germain des Prés (Map 6) in the 6e; the American Church (Map 4) in the 7e; and Église de la Madeleine (Map 2) in the 8e.

Rock

There's rock at numerous bars, cafes and clubs around Paris, plus a number of venues regularly host acts by international performers. It's often easier to see Anglophone acts in Paris than in their home countries. The most popular stadium venues for international acts include the *Palais Omnisports de Paris-Bercy* (Map 8, ☎ 01 44 68 44 68) in the 12e; *Stade de France* (☎ 01 55 93 00 00/44 68 44 44) in St-Denis (see the Around Paris chapter); and *Le Zénith* (☎ 01 42 08 60 00), at the Cité de la Musique (Map 1) in the 19e.

Other venues – though not exclusively for rock – include the following:

Le Bataclan (Map 6, ☎ 01 43 14 35 35/0 826 02 12 12, 50 blvd Voltaire, 11e, metro St-Ambroise). A small concert venue attracting some big names (eg, Oasis), Le Bataclan also masquerades as a theatre and dancehall. It opens 8.30 pm for concerts.

Café de la Danse (Map 6, ☎ 01 47 00 57 59, 5 Passage Louis Philippe, 11e, metro Bastille). This auditorium, with 300 to 500 seats, is only a few metres from 23 rue de Làppe. Almost every evening at 7.30 or 8.30 pm, it plays host to rock and world-music concerts, dance performances, musical theatre and poetry readings. Tickets (60FF to 120FF) are available from Fnac.

La Cigale (Map 8, ☎ 01 49 25 89 99, 102 blvd de Rochechouart, 18e, metro Pigalle). This enormous old music hall hosts international rock acts and occasionally jazz and folk groups. There's seating in the balcony and dancing up at the front. Admission costs from 80FF to 170FF.

Le Divan du Monde (Map 8, ☎ 01 44 92 77 66/43 38 70 76, 75 rue des Martyrs, 18e, metro Pigalle). One of the best concert venues in town with good visibility and sound, Latino figures at least once a week (see the boxed text 'Salsa City'). It's also a popular club open most evenings from 11.30 pm till dawn.

L'Élysée-Montmartre (Map 8, ☎ 01 44 92 45 45, 72 blvd de Rochechouart, 18e, metro Anvers). This huge, old music hall is one of the better venues for one-off rock and indie concerts. For details about Brazilian and salsa nights see the boxed text 'Salsa City'.

Jazz

After WWII, Paris was Europe's most important jazz centre and is again very much

à la mode these days; the city's better clubs attract top international stars. The Banlieues Bleues (☎ 01 49 22 10 10 for information), a jazz festival held in St-Denis and other Paris suburbs in late February and March, attracts big-name talent.

Le Caveau de la Huchette (Map 6, ☎ 01 43 26 65 05, 5 rue de la Huchette, 5e, metro St-Michel). The medieval *caveau* (cellar) – used as a courtroom and torture chamber during the Revolution – is where virtually all the jazz greats have played since 1946. It's touristy, no doubt about that, but the atmosphere can often be more electric than at the more 'serious' jazz clubs. It opens 9.30 pm to 2.30 am (3.30 am on Friday and 4 am on Saturday); sessions begin at 10.30 pm. The cover charge is 60FF (55FF for students) during the week, and 70FF (no discounts) at the weekend.

Au Duc des Lombards (Map 6, ☎ 01 42 33 22 88, 42 rue des Lombards, 1er, metro Châtelet). This cool venue decorated with posters of past jazz greats (such as the Duke himself) attracts a far more relaxed (and less reverent) crowd than other jazz venues in the area. The ground-floor bar vibrates nightly from 9 pm to 4 am, with sets starting at 10 pm. The cover charge is 80FF to 100FF, depending on what's on.

New Morning (Map 3, ☎ 01 45 23 51 41, 7–9 rue des Petites Écuries, 10e, metro Château d'Eau). This informal auditorium that hosts concerts of jazz as well as blues, rock, funk, salsa, Afro-Cuban and Brazilian music three to seven nights a week at 9 pm. The second set ends at about 1 am. Tickets (120FF to 150FF), available from the box office (4.30 to 7.30 pm) as well as Fnac and Virgin, can usually be purchased at the door.

Le Sunset (Map 6, ☎ 01 40 26 46 60, 60 rue des Lombards, 1er, metro Châtelet). Musicians and actors (cinema and theatre) are among the jazz fans who hang out at this trendy club, whose cellar hosts live concerts of funk, Latino, bebop and the like at 9 pm and 2 am daily. Admission costs 50FF to 120FF, depending on who's playing.

French Chansons

For details on accordion music at Le Balajo's tea dances, see the earlier Clubs section.

Chez Louisette (Map 1, ☎ 01 40 12 10 14, in the Marché aux Puces de St-Ouen, metro Porte de Clignancourt). This is one of the highlights of a visit to Paris' largest flea market. Market-goers crowd around little tables to eat lunch and hear an old-time *chanteuse* belt out Piaf numbers accompanied by accordion music. It opens noon to 6 pm on Saturday, Sunday and Monday. Main dishes cost 65FF to 135FF; count on 200FF per person. Chez Louisette is inside the maze of Marché Vernaison not far from 130 ave Michelet, the boulevard on the other side of the highway from the Porte de Clignancourt metro stop, 18e.

Le Croquenote (Map 3, ☎ 01 42 33 60 70, 22 Passage des Panoramas, 2e, metro Grands Boulevards). An intimate French restaurant with dinner (180FF) at 8 pm and *chansons* – in the styles of Brel, Brassens, Léo Ferré and Félix Leclerc – at around 10 pm. It opens Monday to Saturday (closed in August).

Au Lapin Agile (Map 8, ☎ 01 46 06 85 87, 22 rue des Saules, 18e, metro Lamarck Caulaincourt). A rustic cabaret venue favoured by artists and intellectuals in the early 20th century. These days, *chansons* are performed and poetry read nightly from 9 pm to 2 am Tuesday to Sunday. Entry costs 130FF (90FF for students, except on Saturday and holidays), including a drink.

SPECTATOR SPORTS

Parisians are mad about sport. For details of upcoming sporting events, consult the sports daily *L'Équipe* (4FF) or *Figaroscope* published by *Le Figaro* each Wednesday.

Football & Rugby

Le foot (football or soccer) has gained even more popularity since France won the FIFA World Cup at home in 1998, and Paris hosts its fair share of international events. The Paris-St-Germain football team plays its home games at the *Parc des Princes (Map 1, 24 rue du Commandant Guilbaud, 16e, metro Porte de St-Cloud)*. Tickets (50FF to 600FF) are available through Fnac and Virgin Megastores (see Booking Agencies in the Entertainment section), as well as at the Parc des Princes box office (☎ 01 49 87 29 29), which opens 9 am to 8 pm weekdays and 10 am to 5 pm on Saturday.

The 80,000-seat *Stade de France (☎ 01 55 93 00 00/44 68 44 44, metro St-Denis-Porte de Paris)*, rue Francis de Pressensé in St-Denis, hosted the 1998 World Cup finals and is the major venue for soccer and rugby alike.

Rugby is popular in South-West France and Paris-based Le Racing Club de France are the reigning champions. Their home ground is *Stade Yves du Manoir (☎ 01 45 67 55 86)* in Colombes.

Tennis

In late May/early June the tennis world focuses on the clay surface of *Stade Roland Garros (Map 1, ☎ 01 47 43 48 00, 2 ave Gordon Bennett in Bois de Boulogne, 16e, metro Porte d'Auteuil)*, for Les Internationaux de France de Tennis (French Open), the second of the four Grand Slam tournaments. The capacity of the stadium's main section, Le Central, is about 16,500. Tickets are expensive and hard to come by; bookings must usually be made by March at the latest.

The top indoor tournament is the Open de Tennis de la Ville de Paris (Paris Tennis Open), which usually takes place sometime in late October/early November at the *Palais Omnisports de Paris-Bercy (Map 5, ☎ 01 44 68 44 68, 8–12 blvd de Bercy, 12e, metro Bercy)*.

Cycling

Since 1974 the final stage of the Tour de France, the world's most prestigious cycling event, has ended on the ave des Champs-Élysées. The final day varies from year to year but is usually the 3rd or 4th Sunday in July, sometime in the afternoon. If you want to see this exciting event, find a spot at the barricades before midday.

The second biggest 'Parisian' event on the cycling calendar does not even begin in Paris any more. Held on the first Sunday after Easter, the gruelling, one-day Paris-Roubaix road race actually begins in Compiègne (see the Around Paris chapter), 82km north-east of Paris, and continues for 267km over 27 different sections (totalling 50km) of *pavé* (cobblestone) before reaching the velodrome at Roubaix, north-east of Lille.

The biggest indoor cycling event is the Grand Prix des Nations, held in October, which pits the best cyclists from the world's eight best nations against one another on a

250m velodrome at the *Palais Omnisports de Paris-Bercy*.

Horse Racing

A cheap way to spend a relaxing afternoon in the company of Parisians of all ages, backgrounds and walks of life is to go to the races. The most accessible of Paris' six racecourses is *Hippodrome d'Auteuil (Map 1, ☎ 01 40 71 47 47/45 27 12 25, metro Porte d'Auteuil)* in the south-east corner of the Bois de Boulogne (16e), which hosts steeplechases from February to early July and from early September to early December.

Races are held on Sunday as well as some other days of the week, with half a dozen or so heats scheduled between 2 and 5.30 pm. There's no charge to stand on the *pelouse* (lawn) in the middle of the track; a seat in the *tribune* (stands) costs 25FF (40FF on Sunday and holidays, 50FF during special events). Race schedules are published in almost all national newspapers. If you can read a bit of French, pick up a copy of *Paris Turf*, the horse-racing daily available at newsstands for 7FF.

Show jumping is all the rage in Paris and the Jumping International de Paris held in March at the *Palais Omnisports de Paris-Bercy* attracts thousands of fans.

SHOPPING

Paris is a superb place to shop, whether you're someone who can afford an original Cartier diamond bracelet or you're an impoverished *lèche-vitrine* (literally 'window licker'). From the ultra-chic couture houses of ave Montaigne to the flea-market bargains at St-Ouen, the vast underground shopping mall at Les Halles to the cubbyhole boutiques of the Marais, Paris is a city that knows how to make it, present it and charge for it.

Certain streets in Paris still specialise in certain products. Rue du Pont Louis Philippe, 4e (Map 6, metro Pont Marie), for example, has all manner of paper goods and stationery, while rue de Paradis, 10e (Map 3, metro Château d'Eau), is famed for its crystal, glass and tableware shops. If you're in the market for a sewing machine, turn

south from rue de Paradis onto rue Martel – it's chock-a-block with the things. In the nearby passage de l'Industrie, shops specialise in equipment and tools for *coiffeurs* (hairdressers). Walk along rue Victor Massé, 9e (Map 3, metro Pigalle), and you'll see more musical instruments than you thought existed. The shops on rue Drouot in the 9e (Map 3, metro Le Peletier) sell almost nothing but old postage stamps.

Opening Hours

Opening hours in Paris are notoriously anarchic, with each store setting its own hours according to some ancient black art. Most stores will be open at least 10 am to 6 pm five days a week (including Saturday), but they may open earlier, close later, close for lunch (usually 1 to 2.30 pm) or for a full or half-day on Monday or Tuesday. Many larger stores also have a *nocturne* – one late night a week (up to 10pm).

Department Stores

Paris boasts a number of *grands magasins* (department stores) including the following. *Soldes* (sales) are generally held in January and June/July.

Bazar de l'Hôtel de Ville (BHV; Map 7, ☎ 01 42 74 90 00, metro Hôtel de Ville), 52–64 rue de Rivoli, 4e. BHV is a straightforward department store – apart from its enormous but hopelessly chaotic hardware/DIY department in the basement, with every type of hammer, power tool, nail, plug or hinge you could ask for (which is what you'll have to do since you'll never find it on your own). It opens 9.30 am to 7 pm (to 10 pm on Wednesday) Monday to Saturday.

Galeries Lafayette (Map 2, ☎ 01 42 82 34 56, metro Auber), 40 blvd Haussmann, 9e. This vast store, in two adjacent buildings linked by a pedestrian bridge over rue de Mogador, features over 75,000 brand-name items, and has a wide selection of fashion and accessories. There's a fine view from the rooftop restaurant. It opens 9.30 am to 7 pm (9 pm on Thursday) Monday to Saturday.

Le Printemps (Map 2, ☎ 01 42 82 50 00, metro Havre Caumartin), 64 blvd Haussmann, 9e. Actually three separate stores – one each for women's and men's fashion and one for household goods – Le Printemps offers a staggering display of perfume, cosmetics and accessories, as well as established and up-and-coming designer wear. There's a fashion show at 10 am on Tuesday (and on Friday from March to October) on the 7th floor under the cupola. Printemps opens 9.35 am to 7 pm (10 pm on Thursday) Monday to Saturday.

La Samaritaine (Map 6, ☎ 01 40 41 20 20, metro Pont Neuf) is in three buildings between Pont Neuf and 142 rue de Rivoli, 1er. The arrowhead-shaped building on rue de Rivoli is devoted solely to sports and games; the men's building has a big supermarket in the basement. The main store's biggest draw is the outstanding view from the rooftop. La Samaritaine is 9.30 am to 7 pm (10 pm on Thursday) Monday to Saturday.

Clothing & Fashion Accessories

All of the Parisian couturiers have their own boutiques in the capital – some, like Yves Saint Laurent (YSL) have several – but it's also possible to see impressive designer collections at major department stores such as Le Printemps, Galeries Lafayette and Au Bon Marché (Map 4). The Right Bank is traditionally the epicentre of Parisian fashion. New collections are released twice a year – for spring/summer and autumn/winter.

Triangle d'Or Some of the fanciest clothes in Paris are sold by the *haute couture* houses of the Triangle d'Or (1er and 8e), an ultra-chic neighbourhood whose corners are at place de la Concorde, the Arc de Triomphe and place de l'Alma (Map 2). Along the even-numbered side of ave Montaigne (1er, metro Franklin D Roosevelt or Alma-Marceau) you'll find Prada at No 10, Inès de la Fressange at No 14, Christian Lacroix at No 26 and Celine at No 38. On the odd side you'll pass Valentino at No 17, Nina Ricci at No 39 and Thierry Mugler at No 49. Givenchy (metro Alma-Marceau) is nearby at 3 ave George V (8e); Hermès is at No 42 of the same street.

Rue du Faubourg St-Honoré & Rue St-Honoré There is another grouping of couture houses, exclusive clothing shops and accessories stores just north of place de la Concorde along rue du Faubourg St-

Honoré, 8e (Map 2, metro Madeleine or Concorde), and its eastern extension, rue St-Honoré (metro Tuileries). Lolita Lempicka is at 14 rue du Faubourg St-Honoré, Guy Laroche at No 28 and Christian Lacroix at No 73.

Place des Victoires Trendy designer boutiques at place des Victoires, 1er and 2e (Map 6, metro Bourse or Sentier), include Kenzo at No 3, Cacharel at No 5 and Stephane Kélian at No 6. The postmodern designs of Jean-Paul Gaultier are on sale a few blocks north-west of place des Victoires at 6 rue Vivienne (metro Bourse) in the 2e.

Rue Étienne Marcel, which runs to the east of place des Victoires, is home to Comme des Garçons at No 40 (for men) and No 42 (for women), Yohji Yamamoto at Nos 45 and 47, Chevignon at No 49, Kenzo at No 51 and Junko Shimada at No 54. Farther east towards Forum des Halles and near Église St-Eustache on rue du Jour (1er), the modern, casual styles of Agnès B (Map 6, metro Les Halles) are available at No 3 (for men) and No 6 (for women).

Marais Rue des Rosiers, 4e (Map 7, metro St-Paul) is attracting a growing number of fashionable clothing shops, including Tehen at No 5 bis and Martin Grant at No 32. Under the exclusive arcades of place des Vosges (4e), Issey Miyake is tucked away at No 5. There are other interesting shops along rue des Francs Bourgeois (3e and 4e), leading out of place des Vosges. For more everyday clothing, there are lots of shops along rue de Rivoli, which gets less expensive as you move east from the 1er into the 4e.

6e Arrondissement For the largest grouping of chic clothing boutiques in the fashionable 6e – many of them run by younger and more daring designers – head northwest of place St-Sulpice (Maps 4 and 6, metro St-Sulpice or St-Germain des Prés). Ultra-chic clothing, footwear and leathergoods shops along rue du Cherche Midi include YSL at No 13 and Il Bisonte at No 17

(Map 4). Along blvd St-Germain, Sonia Rykiel has shops at No 175 (for women) and No 194 (for men). Rue de Rennes has Celine at No 58 and Kenzo at No 60 (Map 4). At place St-Sulpice, you can pop into YSL Rive Gauche at No 6 and its Rive Gauche Homme at No 12 (Map 6).

To the south-west, just south of Au Bon Marché department store, rue St-Placide (Map 4, metro Sèvres Babylone) has lots of attractive shops selling clothes and shoes, mainly (but not exclusively) for women.

Reasonably priced clothing and shoe shops are legion along the southern half of rue de Rennes (Map 4, metro Rennes or St-Placide).

Fashion shops offering creations and accessories from a variety of cutting-edge designers include:

Colette (Map 2, ☎ 01 55 35 33 90, metro Tuileries), 213 rue St-Honoré, 1er. Probably the most talked about shop in Paris in the last few years, Japanese-inspired Colette is an ode to style over all else. Its selection and display of clothes, accessories and odds and ends is exquisite. Featured designers include Alexander McQueen, Alberta Ferretti and Lulu Guinness. It opens 10.30 am to 7.30 pm daily.

Kiliwatch (Map 6, ☎ 01 42 21 17 37, metro Étienne Marcel), 64 rue Tiquetonne, 2e. This enormous shop is filled with rack after rack of colourfully original street and clubwear, plus a startling range of quality second-hand clothes and accessories. It opens from 1 to 7 pm on Monday, and 10.30 am to 9 pm Tuesday to Saturday.

Spleen (Map 7, ☎ 01 42 74 65 66, metro St-Paul), 3 bis rue des Rosiers, 4e. This is a stunning showcase for a range of new *créateurs*, many from Italy and the UK, among them John Richmond, Lawrence Steele, Emilio Cavallini and Joerg Hartmann. It opens 3 to 7 pm on Monday, 11 am to 7 pm Tuesday to Saturday, and 2 to 7 pm on Sunday.

Jewellery

Around place Vendôme, 1er (Map 2, metro Tuileries), Cartier has a shop at No 7, Patek Philippe is at No 10 and Van Cleef & Arpels is at No 22. There are more expensive jewellery shops along nearby rue de Castiglione (1er) and rue de la Paix, 2e.

Less expensive jewellery is sold at various places around the city. Funky items, many of them imported, can be found in the Marais, including along rue des Francs Bourgeois, 3e and 4e (Map 7). Costume jewellery can be found at the flea markets.

Cécile et Jeanne (Map 2, ☎ 01 42 61 68 68, metro Tuileries), 215 rue St-Honoré, 1er. Cécile and Jeanne are two young jewellery designers making a splash in Paris with their colourful and arty jewellery and accessories. They have several locations in the city and open 11 am to 7 pm Monday to Saturday.

Galerie d'Amon (Map 6, ☎ 01 43 26 96 60, metro St-Sulpice), 28 place St-Sulpice, 6e. This shop specialises in modern glass and jewellery with a medieval twist. It opens 11 am to 6.45 pm Tuesday to Saturday.

Sic Amor (Map 7, ☎ 01 42 76 02 37, metro Pont Marie), 20 rue du Pont Louis Philippe, 4e. Sic Amor sells contemporary jewellery by local designers. It opens 10.30 am to 7.30 pm Monday to Saturday, and from noon on Sunday.

Antiques

For details on Le Louvre des Antiquaires (Map 6), see the earlier section on the Louvre. In the 6e there are a number of shops selling antique maps and antiquarian books around rue Bonaparte and rue Jacob (Map 6, metro St-Germain des Prés).

Food & Wine

The food and wine shops of Paris are legendary and well worth seeking out.

Cacao et Chocolat (Map 6, ☎ 01 46 33 77 63, metro Mabillon), 29 rue de Buci, 6e. Here's a contemporary exotic take on chocolate, showcasing the bean in all its lustful guises, both solid and liquid. The added citrus notes, spices and even chilli are guaranteed to tease you back for more. It opens 10.30 am to 7.30 pm Tuesday to Saturday.

Fauchon (Map 2, ☎ 01 47 62 60 11, metro Madeleine), 26–30 place de la Madeleine, 8e. Six departments sell the most incredibly mouth-watering (and expensive) delicacies, such as foie gras for 1000FF to 2000FF per kilogram. Fruit – the most perfect you've ever seen – includes exotic items from South-East Asia (such as mangosteens and rambutans). It opens 9.30 am to 7 pm Monday to Saturday.

Hédiard (Map 2, ☎ 02 43 12 88 88, metro Madeleine), 21 place de la Madeleine, 8e. This famous luxury food shop consists of two adjacent sections selling prepared dishes, tea, coffee, jams, wine, pastries, fruit and vegetables. It opens 9.30 am to 9.30 pm Monday to Saturday.

Jadis et Gourmande (Map 5, ☎ 01 43 26 17 75, metro Port Royal), 88 blvd de Port Royal, 5e. One of four branches selling chocolate, chocolate and more chocolate. It opens 1 to 7 pm on Monday, and 9.30 am to 7 pm Tuesday to Saturday.

La Maison du Miel (Map 2, ☎ 01 47 42 26 70, metro Madeleine), 24 rue Vignon, 9e. This store stocks over 40 kinds of honey costing from 19FF to 45FF for 500g. It opens 9.15 am to 7 pm Monday to Saturday.

Mariage Frères (Map 7, ☎ 01 42 72 28 11, metro Hôtel de Ville), 30 rue du Bourg Tibourg, 4e. Paris' first (founded in 1854) and arguably finest tea shop, with 500 varieties from more than 30 countries; the most expensive is a variety of Japanese *thé vert* (green tea) that costs about 50FF for 100g. Mariage Frères has a branch (Map 6, ☎ 01 40 51 82 50, metro Odéon) at 13 rue des Grands Augustins (6e) and another one (Map 2, ☎ 01 46 22 18 54, metro Tuileries) at 260 rue du Faubourg St-Honoré, 8e. All are open 10.30 am to 7.30 pm daily.

À l'Olivier (Map 7 ☎ 01 48 04 86 59, metro St-Paul), 23 rue de Rivoli, 4e. *The* place in Paris for oil – from olive to walnut – with a good selection of vinegars and olives too. It opens 9.30 am to 1 pm and 2 to 7 pm Tuesday to Saturday.

Boulangerie Poilâne (Map 4, ☎ 01 45 48 42 59, metro Sèvres Babylone), 8 rue du Cherche Midi, 6e. Truly a legend in his own lunchtime, Poilâne – the most famous *boulangerie* in Paris – bakes perfect wholegrain bread (21.50FF for a small loaf) using traditional sourdough leavening and sea salt. Every loaf is an original. It opens 7.15 am to 8.15 pm Monday to Saturday.

Gifts & Souvenirs

Paris has a huge number of speciality shops offering gift items.

Album (Map 6, ☎ 01 43 25 85 19, metro Maubert Mutualité), 8 rue Dante, 5e. This shop specialises in *bandes dessinées* (comic books), which have an enormous following in France, with everything from Tintin to erotic comics and French editions of the latest Japanese *manga*. It opens 10 am to 8 pm Monday to Saturday.

E Dehillerin (Map 6, ☎ 01 42 36 53 13, metro Les Halles), 18–20 rue Coquillère, 1er. This shop (founded in 1820) carries the most incredible selection of professional-quality cookware – you're sure to find something even the most

well-equipped kitchen is lacking. It opens 8 am to 12.30 pm and 2 to 6 pm Monday, and 8 am to 6 pm Tuesday to Saturday.

EOL' Modelisme (Map 6, ☎ 01 43 54 01 43, metro Maubert Mutualité), 62 blvd St Germain (5e) with branches at Nos 55 and 70 of the same street. This shop sells expensive toys for big boys and girls, including every sort model imaginable, from radio-controlled aircraft to large wooden yachts. The main shop opens 1 to 7 pm Monday, 11 am to 1 pm and 2 to 7 pm Tuesday to Saturday.

Il Pour l'Homme (Map 2, ☎ 01 42 60 43 56, metro Tuileries), 209 rue St-Honoré, 1er. Housed in an old paint shop with 19th-century display counters and chests of drawers, 'It for the Man' has everything a man (or boy) could want or not need – from tie clips and cigar cutters to DIY tools and designer tweezers. It opens 10.30 am to 7 pm Monday to Saturday.

La Maison du Cerf-Volant (Map 5, ☎ 01 44 68 00 75, metro Ledru Rollin), 7 rue de Prague, 12e. This shop sells kites of every conceivable size, shape and colour. It opens 10 am to 7 pm Monday to Saturday.

Madeleine Gély (Map 4, ☎ 01 42 22 63 35; metro St-Germain des Prés), 218 blvd St-Germain, 7e. If you're in the market for a bespoke cane or umbrella, this shop (founded in 1834) will supply. It opens 10 am to 7 pm Tuesday to Saturday.

Mélodies Graphiques (Map 7, ☎ 01 42 74 57 68, metro Pont Marie), 10 rue du Pont Louis Philippe, 4e. This shop carries all sorts of items made from exquisite Florentine *papier à cuve* (paper hand-decorated with marbled designs). It opens 2 to 7 pm on Monday and 11 am to 7 pm Tuesday to Saturday.

Robin des Bois (Map 7, ☎ 01 48 04 09 36, metro St-Paul), 15 rue Fernand Duval, 4e. A shop for environmentalists, this place sells everything and anything made from recycled things – from jewellery to stationery. It opens 10.30 am to 7.30 pm Monday to Saturday, and from 2 pm on Sunday.

Flea Markets

Paris' *marchés aux puces* (flea markets), easily accessible by metro, can be great fun if you're in the mood to browse for unexpected treasures among the *brocante* (secondhand goods) and bric-a-brac on display. Some new goods are also available, and a bit of bargaining is expected.

Marché d'Aligre (Map 5, metro Ledru Rollin), place d'Aligre, 12e. Smaller but more central than the other flea markets listed here, marché d'Aligre is one of the best places in Paris to rummage through boxes filled with old clothes and one-of-a-kind accessories worn decades ago by fashionable (and not-so-fashionable) Parisians. It opens early in the morning to 1 pm Tuesday to Sunday.

Marché aux Puces de Montreuil (Map 1, metro Porte de Montreuil), ave de la Porte de Montreuil, 20e. Established in the 19th century, this market is known for having good-quality, second-hand clothes and designer seconds. The 500 stalls also sell engravings, jewellery, linen, crockery, old furniture and appliances. It opens 7 am to about 7 pm Saturday, Sunday and Monday.

Marché aux Puces de la Porte de Vanves (Map 1, metro Porte de Vanves), ave Georges Lafenestre and ave Marc Sangnier, 14e. This market is known for its fine selection of junk. Ave Georges Lafenestre looks like a giant car-boot sale, with lots of 'curios' that aren't quite old (or classy) enough to qualify as antiques. Ave Marc Sangnier is lined with stalls selling new clothes, shoes, handbags and household items. It opens 7 am to 6 pm on Saturday and Sunday.

Marché aux Puces de St-Ouen (Map 1, metro Porte de Clignancourt), rue des Rosiers, ave Michelet, rue Voltaire, rue Paul Bert and rue Jean-Henri Fabre, 18e. This vast flea market, founded in the late 19th century and said to be Europe's largest, has 2000-odd stalls grouped into nine *marchés* (market areas), each with its own speciality (for example antiques and cheap clothing). It opens 7.30 am to 7 pm on Saturday, Sunday and Monday.

GETTING THERE & AWAY

For information on transport options between the city and the airports, see To/From the Airports in the following Getting Around section. For information on air links to Paris, see Air in the introductory Getting There & Away chapter.

Air

Orly Airport Aéroport d'Orly, the older and smaller of Paris' two major international airports, is 18km south of the city. Air France and some other international carriers (such as Iberia and TAP Air Portugal) use Orly-Ouest (the west terminal), so the traditional division of responsibilities – Orly-Sud (the south terminal) for international flights, Orly-Ouest for domestic services – no longer holds. A driverless overhead rail

line linking Orly-Ouest with Orly-Sud – part of the Orlyval system – functions as a free shuttle between the terminals.

For flight and other information call ☎ 01 49 75 15 15 or 0 836 25 05 05. By Minitel, dial 3615 HORAV.

Roissy Charles de Gaulle Airport Aéroport Roissy Charles de Gaulle, 30km northeast of the city centre in the suburb of Roissy, consists of three terminal complexes. Aérogare 2 has five semicircular terminals that face each other in pairs (2A, 2B, 2C, 2D and 2F); a 6th – terminal 2E – is expected to open in 2003. Aérogare 2 is used by Air France for international and domestic flights and a number of foreign carriers, but the majority of international carriers use the cylindrical Aérogare 1. Aérogare T9 is used by charter companies and domestic airlines.

Airport shuttle buses link Aérogare 1 with both train stations and Aérogare 2 (see To/From the Airports in the following Getting Around section). Shuttle buses also go to Aérogare T9.

Flight and other information is available in English or French 24 hours a day on ☎ 01 48 62 22 80 or 0 836 25 05 05. By Minitel, you can get flight information on 3615 HORAV.

Beauvais Airport The city of Beauvais is 80km north of Paris; its airport is used by charter flight companies and discount airline Ryanair for its Paris–Dublin flights.

Airline Offices The following is a list of selected airlines. Airline offices can also be found in the Paris Yellow Pages under *Transports aériens*.

Air Canada	☎ 01 44 50 20 20
Air France	☎ 0 802 80 28 02
	(information and
	reservations)
	☎ 0 836 68 10 48
	(recorded information on
	arrivals and departures)
	Minitel 3615 or 3616 AF
	Web site: www.airfrance.fr

Air Liberté	☎ 0 803 80 58 05
	Minitel 3615 AIR
	LIBERTE
	Web site: www.air-liberte.fr
Air Littoral	☎ 0 803 83 48 34
Air New Zealand	☎ 01 40 53 82 23
Air UK	☎ 01 44 56 18 08
	Minitel 3615 AIR UK
American Airlines	☎ 0 801 87 28 72
	(toll-free)
British Airways	☎ 0 825 82 54 00
British Midland	☎ 01 48 62 55 52 or
	☎ 01 41 91 87 04
Continental	
Airlines	☎ 01 42 99 09 09
	Minitel 3615
	CONTINENTAL
Delta Air Lines	☎ 01 47 68 92 92
easyJet	☎ 0 825 08 25 08
KLM-Royal	
Dutch Airlines	☎ 01 44 56 18 18
Lufthansa Airlines	☎ 0 802 02 00 30
Northwest	
Airlines	☎ 01 42 66 90 00
Qantas Airways	☎ 0 803 84 68 46
Ryanair	☎ 03 44 11 41 41
Scandinavian	
Airlines (SAS)	☎ 0 801 25 25 25
	Minitel 3615 FLY SAS
Singapore Airlines	☎ 01 53 65 79 00
South African	
Airways	☎ 01 49 27 05 50
Thai Airways	
International	☎ 01 44 20 70 80
United Airlines	☎ 0 801 72 72 72
	Minitel 3615
	UNITED
	Web site: www.ualfrance.fr

Bus

Domestic Because the French government prefers to avoid competition with the state-owned rail system (SNCF) and the heavily regulated domestic airlines, there is no domestic intercity bus service to or from Paris.

International Eurolines runs buses from Paris to cities all over Europe, including London (see Bus under Land in the introductory Getting There & Away chapter). The company's Gare Routière Internationale de Paris-Gallieni (international bus terminal; Map 1, ☎ 0 836 69 52 52, metro Gallieni) is at 28 ave du Général de Gaulle (20e) in the inner suburb of Bagnolet.

The Eurolines ticket office (Map 6, ☎ 01 43 54 11 99, metro Cluny-La Sorbonne), 55 rue St-Jacques (5e), opens 9.30 am to 6.30 pm weekdays and 10 am to 5 pm on Saturday. In summer, you should reserve a few days in advance. The Web site is at www.eurolines.fr. On Minitel, key in 3615 EUROLINES.

Train

SNCF train information is available for mainline services on ☎ 0 836 35 35 35 and for suburban services on ☎ 01 53 90 20 20 or 0 836 67 68 69. The Web site is www.sncf.fr. By Minitel, key in 3615 SNCF (3615 SNCFIDF for suburban services).

Paris has six major train stations, each of which handles passenger traffic to different parts of France and Europe. For more information on the breakdown of regional responsibility of trains from each station, see the SNCF Railways & Ferries map between pages 112 and 113.

Gare d'Austerlitz (Map 5, metro Gare d'Austerlitz), blvd de l'Hôpital, 13e. Handles trains for the Loire Valley, Spain and Portugal and non-TGV trains to south-western France (Bordeaux and the Basque Country).

Gare de l'Est (Map 3, metro Gare de l'Est), blvd de Strasbourg, 10e. Responsible for trains to parts of France east of Paris (Champagne, Alsace and Lorraine), Luxembourg, parts of Switzerland (Basel, Lucerne, Zürich), southern Germany (Frankfurt, Munich) and points farther east.

Gare de Lyon (Map 5, metro Gare de Lyon), blvd Diderot, 12e. Has regular and TGV Sud-Est trains to places south-east of Paris, including Dijon, Lyons, Provence, the Côte d'Azur, the Alps, parts of Switzerland (Bern, Geneva, Lausanne), Italy and points beyond.

Gare Montparnasse (Map 4, metro Montparnasse Bienvenüe), ave du Maine and blvd de Vaugirard, 15e. Handles train to Brittany and places between (Chartres, Angers, Nantes) and is the terminus of the TGV Atlantique serving Tours, Nantes, Bordeaux and other destinations in south-western France.

Gare du Nord (Map 3, metro Gare du Nord), rue de Dunkerque, 10e. Takes care of trains to the northern suburbs of Paris, northern France, the UK, Belgium, northern Germany, Scandinavia, Moscow etc; terminus of the TGV Nord (Lille and Calais) and the Eurostar to London.

Gare St-Lazare (Map 2, metro St-Lazare), rue St-Lazare and rue d'Amsterdam, 8e. Responsible for traffic to Normandy, including Dieppe, Le Havre and Cherbourg.

Fares One-way, 2nd-class fares to destinations around France and abroad include:

Destination	fare (FF)	duration (hours)
Amsterdam	385	5
Aneecy	363	3½
Berlin	1084	11
Copenhagen	1132	16
Geneva	420	3½*
Lille	208	1*
Lyons	318	2*
Madrid	647	16
Marseille	379	4¼*
Nantes	297	2*
Nice	455	6*
Prague	1066	16
Rome	660	12
Strasbourg	220	4
Toulouse	455	5½*

*by TGV

Hitching

Getting out of Paris by hitching near highway entrance ramps or at petrol stations doesn't work very well. Your best bet is probably to take an RER train out to the suburbs and try from there. Le Shuttle motorists can take a car full of passengers through the Channel Tunnel without extra charge so you can hitch to/from France for nothing. Channel ferry services sometimes also include a number of passengers free with each car carried, but usually in the low or shoulder seasons only.

An organisation in Paris that matches travellers and drivers heading in the same destination is Âllostop Provoya (Map 3, ☎ 01 53 20 42 42, metro Cadet), 8 rue Rochambeau, 9e. They can also be reached on the Internet at www.ecritel.fr/allostop and on Minitel at 3615 ALLOSTOP. Sample fares are Paris to

Rennes (75FF), Marseille (169FF), Hamburg (195FF) and Berlin (300FF). Annual membership costs 40FF. The office opens 9 am to 6.30 pm weekdays and 9 am to 1 pm and 2 to 6 pm on Saturday.

GETTING AROUND

Paris' public transit system, most of which is operated by the RATP (Régie Autonome des Transports Parisians; ☎ 0 836 68 77 14), is one of the most efficient and cheapest in the western world. For information in English call ☎ 0 836 68 41 14. Their Web site is www.ratp.fr and you can contact them on Minitel at 3615 RATP. The *Plan de Paris*, RATP's map No 1 showing metro, RER and bus routes (available free at most metro station ticket windows and RATP information desks) will meet most travellers' requirements.

To/From the Airports

Orly Airport Most of the half-dozen public transport options linking Orly with Paris run every 15 minutes or so (less frequently late at night) from some time between 5.30 and 6.30 am to 11 or 11.30 pm seven days a week. Tickets are sold on board the buses. With certain exceptions, children aged four or five and between 10 and 12 pay half fare.

Orlybus
An RATP-run bus (☎ 01 44 36 32 74, 35FF, 30 minutes) to/from the Denfert Rochereau metro station, in the heart of the 14e near place Denfert Rochereau (Map 1). It runs every 12 minutes from 6.30 am to 11.30 pm and makes several stops in the eastern 14e in each direction.

Jetbus
The cheapest way to get into the city (☎ 01 69 01 00 09, 26.50FF, 20 minutes). A bus, running every 12 to 15 minutes from about 6 am to about 10 pm, links both terminals with the Villejuif-Louis Aragon metro stop, which is south of the 13e on the city's southern fringe. From there a regular metro ticket will get you into the city.

Air France Bus
Air France bus (☎ 01 41 56 89 00) No 1 goes to/from Orly and the eastern side of Gare Montparnasse in the 15e (Map 4, metro Montparnasse Bienvenüe) along rue du Commandant René Mouchotte and Aérogare des Invalides in the 7e (Map 4, metro Invalides). The trip costs

PARIS

45FF (children aged two to 11 half-price), runs every 12 minutes from 5.45 am to 11 pm and takes 30 to 45 minutes. On your way into the city, you can request to get off at the Porte d'Orléans or Duroc metro stops.

RATP Bus No 183

A slow public bus that links Orly-Sud (only) with the Porte de Choisy metro station (Map 1), at the southern edge of the 13e. It costs just 8FF or one bus/metro ticket. It runs daily from 5.35 am to 12.30 am every 35 minutes or so.

Orlyval

Orlyval (☎ 0 836 68 77 14) links the airport with the city centre via the RER and a shuttle train (57FF, 35 minutes). A completely automated shuttle train connects both Orly terminals with the Antony RER station on RER line B in eight minutes; to get to Antony from the city, take line B4 towards Saint-Rémy lès Chevreuse. Tickets are valid for 1st-class passage on the RER and metro travel within the city. Orlyval runs 6 am to 10.30 pm Monday to Saturday and 7 am to 11 pm on Sunday.

Orlyrail

It links the airport with RER line C (32.50FF, 50 minutes to the city centre). An airport shuttle bus, which runs every 15 minutes from 5.30 am to 9 pm and then every half-hour to 11.30 pm, takes you to/from the Pont de Rungis-Aéroport d'Orly RER station; to get there from the city, take a C2 train code-named ROMI or MONA towards Pont de Rungis or Massy-Palaiseau. Tickets are valid for onward travel on the metro.

Shuttle Van

PariShuttle (☎ 01 43 90 91 91, @ parishuttle @aol.com), Paris Airports Service (☎ 01 49 62 78 78, @ pas@magic.fr) and Airport Shuttle (☎ 01 45 38 55 72) all provide door-to-door service for around 125FF single, or 75FF per person for two or more people. Book in advance and allow for numerous pick-ups and drop-offs.

Taxi

A standard taxi to/from central Paris will cost between 120FF and 175FF (plus 6FF per piece of luggage over 5kg) and take 20 to 30 minutes, depending on traffic conditions.

Roissy Charles de Gaulle Airport Paris' main international airport has two train stations: Aéroport Charles de Gaulle 1 (CDG1), linked to other parts of the airport complex by free shuttle bus, and the sleek Aéroport Charles de Gaulle 2 (CDG2), at Aérogare 2. Both are served by commuter trains on RER line B3 (ie Roissyrail); the latter is on the TGV link that connects the

TGV Nord line with the TGV Sud-Est line and is also connected with the TGV Atlantique line.

There are six public transport options for travel between Aéroport Charles de Gaulle and Paris. Unless otherwise indicated, they run from some time between 5 and 6.30 am until 11 or 11.30 pm. Tickets are sold on board the buses. With certain exceptions, children aged four or five and between 10 and 12 pay half fare.

Roissybus

An RATP-run bus (☎ 01 48 04 18 24, 48FF, 45 minutes) that links the *aérogares* with place de l'Opéra (Maps 2 and 3, metro Opéra) in 9e arrondissement.

Air France Buses

Air France bus No 2 (☎ 01 41 56 89 00, 60FF, 35 to 50 minutes) links the airport with two locations on the Right Bank: outside 1 ave Carnot near the Arc de Triomphe (Map 2, metro Charles de Gaulle-Étoile) in the 17e and the Palais des Congrès de Paris at blvd Gouvion St-Cyr at Porte Maillot (Map 2, metro Porte Maillot) also in the 17e. Buses run every 12 to 20 minutes from 5.45 am to 11 pm. Air France bus No 4 (70FF, 45 to 55 minutes) links the airport with Gare de Lyon (Map 5) at 20 bis blvd Diderot, and Gare Montparnasse (Map 4, metro Montparnasse Bienvenüe) in the 15e. Buses leave the airport every hour on the half-hour from 7 am to 9 pm; there are departures from the city every half-hour from 7 am to 9.30 pm.

RATP Buses

RATP bus No 350 (24FF or three bus/metro tickets) links both aérogares with Porte de la Chapelle (18e) and stops at Gare du Nord (Map 3) at 184 rue du Faubourg St-Denis (10e) and Gare de l'Est (Map 3) on rue du 8 Mai 1945, 10e. The trip takes 50 minutes (60 to 70 minutes during rush hour). RATP bus No 351 goes to ave du Trône, on the eastern side of Place de la Nation (Map 1, metro Nation) in the 11e and runs every half-hour or so until 8.20 pm (9.30 pm from the airport to the city). The trip costs 24FF or three bus/metro tickets.

Roissyrail

Links the city with both of the airport's train stations (49FF, 35 minutes). To get to the airport, take any line B train whose four letter destination code begins with E (eg, EIRE). Regular metro ticket windows can't always sell these tickets, so you may have to buy one at the RER station where you board. Trains run every 15 minutes from 5.30 am to around 11 pm.

Shuttle Van

PariShuttle (☎ 01 43 90 91 91, ✉ parishuttle @aol.com), Paris Airports Service (☎ 01 49 62 78 78, ✉ pas@magic.fr) and Airport Shuttle (☎ 01 45 38 55 72) all will take you to/from your hotel for about 150FF single (85FF per person for two or more people). Book in advance.

Taxi

Taxis to the city centre should cost 200FF to 280FF, depending on the traffic and time of day. Luggage costs 6FF per bag weighing over 5kg.

Between Orly & Roissy Air France bus No 3 (☎ 01 41 56 89 00, 75FF) runs between the two airports every 20 to 30 minutes from 6 am to 11 or 11.30 pm; the service is free for Air France passengers making flight connections. When traffic is not heavy, the ride takes 50 to 60 minutes.

Taking a combination of Roissyrail and Orlyval costs 106FF and takes about an hour. A taxi from one airport to the other should cost around 350FF.

Beauvais Airport An express bus, which leaves and picks up from beside the James Joyce Pub (Map 2, ☎ 01 44 09 70 32, metro Porte Maillot), 71 blvd Gouvion St-Cyr (17e), departs 2½ hours prior to each Ryanair departure and leaves the airport 20 minutes after arrival. Tickets (50FF one way) can be purchased at the Ryanair terminal and the James Joyce Pub (open 7 am to 2 am). The trip takes about one hour.

Bus

Regular bus services operate from between 5.45 and 7 am to 12.30 am daily. Services are drastically reduced on Sunday and holidays and after 8.30 pm, when a system of night buses is put into operation.

Night Buses After the metro closes (between 12.25 and 12.45 am), the Noctambus network links the area just west of Hôtel de Ville (Map 6) in the 4e with most parts of the city. Look for the symbol of a little black owl silhouetted against a yellow quarter moon. All 18 lines depart every hour on the half-hour from 1 to 5.30 am seven days a week.

Noctambus services are free if you have a Carte Orange, Mobilis or Paris Visite pass

(see the following Travel Passes and Tourist Passes sections) for zones in which you are travelling. Otherwise, a single ride costs 15FF and allows one immediate change/transfer onto another Noctambus.

Tickets & Fares Short bus rides (ie rides in one or two bus zones) cost one bus/metro ticket; longer rides within the city require two tickets. Transfers to other buses or the metro are not allowed on the same ticket. Travel to the suburbs costs up to three tickets, depending on the zone. Special tickets valid only on the bus can be purchased from the driver.

Whatever kind of single-journey ticket you have, you must cancel (*oblitérer*) it in the *composteur* (cancelling machine) next to the driver. If you have a Carte Orange, Mobilis or Paris Visite pass, just flash it at the driver when you board. Do *not* cancel your magnetic *coupon*.

Metro & RER

Paris' underground network consists of two separate but linked systems: the Métropolitain, known as the *métro*, (which now has 14 lines with the opening of the ultra-modern, driverless Météor linking the Madeleine stop with the Bibliothèque Nationale de France François Mitterrand in the 13e and RER line C) with over 300 stations, and the RER, a network of suburban services that pass through the city centre. The term 'metro' is used in this chapter to refer to the Métropolitain as well as any station of the RER system within Paris proper.

For a list of the metro stations you might want to avoid late at night, see the Dangers & Annoyances entry under Information at the start of this chapter.

Information Metro maps of varying sizes and detail are available for free at metro ticket windows. For information on the metro, RER and bus system, call RATP's 24-hour inquiries number (☎ 0 836 68 77 14 in French, or 0 836 68 41 14 in English) It costs 2.23FF a minute. Their Web site is www.ratp.fr; by Minitel, key in 3615 RATP. A useful tool is 3615 SITU on Minitel. Key

PARIS

Art in the Metro

There are more modern subway systems than the Paris metro but few are as convenient, reasonably priced or, at the better stations, more elegant. To mark what was both the start of the new millennium *and* the centenary of the Métropolitain, the RATP staged themed displays in nine different stations – from Health at Pasteur and Cinema at Bonne Nouvelle to Creation at St-Germain des Prés and Europe at (where else?) Europe. Many of the displays are meant to last (and evolve) over several years.

At the same time some 175 metro stations have been given a spring cleaning, with their lighting improved and their permanent decorations spruced up and/or rearranged. The following list is just a sample of the most interesting stations from an artistic point of view. The true train (station) spotters among you – and we know you're out there – will want to pick up a copy of *Promenades dans le Métro* (Journeys in the Metro), which highlights some 17 of the best stations.

Abbesses (Map 8, line No 12). The noodle-like pale-green metalwork and glass canopy of the station entrance is one of the finest examples of the work of Henri Guimard (1867–1942), the best known of French Art Nouveau architects, whose signature style once graced most metro stations. Another fine example can be found at the Porte Dauphine station entrance (Map 1, Line 2).

Arts et Métiers (Map 6, line No 11, platform). The copper panelling, portholes and mechanisms recall Jules Verne, Captain Nemo and the nearby Musée des Arts et Métiers.

Bastille (Map 6, line No 5, platform). An enormous ceramic fresco illustrates scenes taken from newspaper engravings published during the Revolution.

Bibliothèque François Mitterrand (Map 1, line No 14). This enormous new (1998) station, all screens, steel and glass and the terminus of the driverless Météor metro train, resembles a high-tech cathedral.

Champs-Élysées Clemenceau (Map 2, transfer corridor between line Nos 1 and 13). The elegant frescoes done in blue enamelled faïence recall Portuguese *azulejos* tiles and so they should; they were done by Manuel Cargaleiro as part of a cultural exchange between Paris and Lisbon.

Cluny-La Sorbonne (Map 6, line No 10, platform). A large ceramic mosaic replicates the signatures of intellectuals, artists and scientists from the Quartier Latin.

Concorde (Map 2, line No 12, platform). On the walls of the station, what look like children's building blocks in white and blue ceramic spell out the text of the *Déclarations des Droits de l'Homme et du Citoyen* (Declaration of the Rights of Man), the document setting forth the principles of the French Revolution.

Louvre-Rivoli (Map 6, line No 1, platform and corridor). Statues, bas-reliefs and photographs offer a small taste of what's to come at the nearby Musée du Louvre.

in your destination in Paris or the Île de France and you'll get an immediate response on the quickest and easiest route to follow on public transport.

Information on SNCF's suburban services (including certain RER lines) is available on ☎ 01 53 90 20 20 or 0 836 67 68 69). Their Web site is www.sncf.fr. By Minitel, type 3615 SNCFIDF.

Metro Network Each Métropolitain train is known by the name of its terminus, which means that trains on the same line

have different names depending on the direction in which they are travelling. Each line is also officially known by a number (1 to 14), and these are being used more and more by Parisians these days.

Though there are plans afoot to change the colour schemes, at present blue-on-white *direction* signs in metro and RER stations indicate the way to the correct platform. On lines that split into several branches the terminus served by each train is indicated on the cars with back-lit panels.

Black-on-orange *correspondance* (change

or transfer) signs show how to get to connecting trains. In general, the more lines that stop at a station, the longer the *correspondances* will be – and some (eg, those at Châtelet) are *very* long.

White-on-blue *sortie* signs indicate the station 'exit' you have to choose from.

The last metro train on each line begins its final run of the night some time between 12.25 and 12.45 am. Metro travel is free after midnight and the barriers are left open. The metro starts up again around 5.30 am.

RER Network The RER is faster than the Métropolitain, but the stops are more widely spaced apart. Some parts of the city, such as the Musée d'Orsay, the Eiffel Tower and the Panthéon, can be reached far more conveniently by RER than by metro.

RER lines are known by an alphanumeric combination – the letter (A to E) refers to the line, the number to the spur it will follow somewhere out in the suburbs. As a rule of thumb, even-numbered RER lines head for Paris' southern or eastern suburbs while odd-numbered ones go north or west. All trains whose code begins with the same letter have the same terminus. Stations served are usually indicated on electronic destination boards above the platform. Unlike the metro, the RER has both 2nd-class and 1st-class cars.

Suburban Services The RER and the SNCF's commuter lines serve destinations outside the city (ie those in zones 2 to 8). Purchase a special ticket *before* you board the train or you won't be able to get out of the station when you arrive. You are not allowed to pay the additional fare when you get there.

If you are issued a full-sized SNCF ticket for travel to the suburbs, validate it in one of the orange time-stamp pillars before boarding the train. You may also be given a *contremarque magnétique* (magnetic ticket) to get through any metro/RER-type turnstiles you'll have to go through on the way to/from the platform. If you are travelling on a multi-zone Carte Orange, Paris Visite or Mobilis pass, do *not* punch the magnetic coupon in SNCF's orange time-stamp machines. Some – but not all – RER/SNCF tickets purchased in the suburbs for travel to the city allow you to continue your journey by metro; if in doubt, ask.

For some destinations, tickets can be purchased at any metro ticket window, but for others you'll have to go to an RER station on the line you need in order to buy a ticket. If you're trying to save every franc and have a Carte Orange, Paris Visite or Mobilis, you could get off the train at the last station covered by your coupon and then purchase a separate ticket for the rest of your journey.

Tickets & Fares The same RATP tickets are valid on the metro, the RER (for travel within the city limits) and buses as well as trams (eg, in the northern suburb of St-Denis) and the Montmartre funicular. They cost 8FF if bought individually and 55FF for a *carnet* of 10. Children aged four to 11 pay half the fare. Tickets are sold at every metro station, though not always at each and every entrance. At some stations, you can pay by credit card if the bill comes to at least 35FF and vending machines accept most cards.

One bus/metro ticket lets you travel between any two metro stations for a period of two hours, no matter how many transfers are required. You can also use it on the RER commuter rail system for travel within Paris (that is, within zone 1). However, a single ticket cannot be used to transfer from the metro to a bus, from a bus to the metro or between buses. Always keep your ticket until you exit from your station.

Travel Passes The cheapest and easiest way to travel the metro is to get a Carte Orange, a bus/metro/RER pass whose accompanying magnetic coupon comes in weekly and monthly versions. You can get tickets for travel in two to eight urban and suburban zones, but unless you'll be using the suburban commuter lines daily, the basic ticket – valid for zones 1 and 2 – will be sufficient.

A weekly ticket costs 82FF for zones 1 and 2 and is valid from Monday to Sunday. Even if you'll be in Paris for only three or four days, it may work out cheaper than purchasing a carnet (you'll break even at 15 rides) and it will certainly cost less than buying a daily Mobilis or Paris Visite pass (see the following Tourist Passes section). The monthly Carte Orange ticket (279FF for zones 1 and 2) begins on the first day of each calendar month. Both are on sale in metro and RER stations from 6.30 am to 10 pm and at certain bus terminals. You can also buy your Carte Orange coupon by machine and even via the Internet.

To get a Carte Orange, bring a passport-size photograph of yourself to any metro or RER ticket window (four photos for 25FF are available from automatic booths in the train stations and many metro stations). Request a Carte Orange (which is free) and the kind of coupon you'd like. To prevent tickets from being used by more than one person, you must write your surname (*nom*) and given name (*prénom*) on the Carte Orange, and the number of your Carte Orange on each weekly or monthly coupon you buy (next to the words *Carte No*).

Tourist Passes The rather pricey Mobilis and Paris Visite passes allow unlimited travel on the metro, the RER, SNCF's suburban lines, buses, the Noctambus night-bus system, trams and the Montmartre funicular railway. They do not require a photo, though you should write your card number on the ticket.

The Mobilis card and its coupon allows unlimited travel for one day in two to eight zones (32FF to 110FF). It is on sale at all metro and RER ticket windows and all SNCF stations in the Paris region, but you would have to make at least six metro trips in a day with a carnet of tickets to break even on this pass.

Paris Visite passes, which allow you discounts on admission to some museums and activities as well as transport, are valid for one/two/three/five consecutive days of travel in three, five or eight zones. The version covering one to three zones costs 55/90/120/175FF for one/two/three/five days. Children aged four to 11 pay half-price. Passes can be purchased at larger metro and RER stations, at SNCF bureaux in Paris and at the airports.

Car & Motorcycle

Driving in Paris is nerve-wracking but not impossible, except for the faint-hearted or indecisive. The fastest way to get across Paris is usually via the *boulevard Périphérique* (Map 1), the ring road or beltway that encircles the city.

In many parts of Paris you have to pay 10FF or 15FF an hour to park your car on the street. Large municipal parking garages usually charge 15FF an hour, 130FF for up to 10 hours and 200FF for 24 hours. Parking fines are 75FF or 230FF, and parking attendants dispense them with great abandon. You pay them by purchasing a *timbre amende* (fine stamp) for the amount written on the ticket from any *tabac* (tobacconist), affixing the stamp on the ticket pre-addressed coupon and dropping it in a letter box. We know – we've been there.

Rental The easiest (if not cheapest) way to turn a stay in Paris into an uninterrupted series of hassles is to rent a car. If driving the car doesn't destroy your holiday sense of spontaneity, parking the damn thing will. A small car (eg, Peugeot 106) costs 290FF from Hertz for one day without insurance and no kilometres , but there are deals from smaller agencies from as little as 269FF a day with 100km, 569FF for a weekend with 800km and 999FF for five days with 1000km.

Most of the larger companies listed below have offices at the airports, and several are also represented at Aérogare des Invalides in the 7e (Map 4, metro Invalides). Higher rates may apply for airport rental, and you may have to return the car there.

Avis	☎ 0 802 05 05 05
	☎ 01 42 66 67 58
Budget	☎ 0 800 10 00 01
Europcar	☎ 0 803 35 23 52
Hertz	☎ 01 39 38 38 38
National/Citer	☎ 01 42 06 06 06
Thrifty	☎ 0 801 45 45 45

For other rental operators check the Yellow Pages under *Location d'automobiles: tourisme et utilitaires*. A number of national and local companies offer more reasonable rates. It's a good idea to reserve at least three days ahead, especially for holiday weekends and during the summer.

ADA (☎ 0 836 68 40 02). ADA has about 18 bureaux in Paris including ones at 72 rue de Rome, 8e (Map 2, ☎ 01 42 93 65 13, metro Rome); 97 blvd Magenta, 10e (Map 3, ☎ 01 47 70 06 06, metro Gare du Nord); and 34 ave de la République, 11e (Map 6, ☎ 01 48 06 58 13, metro Parmentier). ADA's Web site is www.ada-location.com.

Rent A Car Système (☎ 0 836 69 46 95, Minitel 3615 RENTACAR). Rent A Car has a dozen branches in Paris, including ones at 115 blvd Magenta, 10e (Map 3, ☎ 01 42 80 31 31, metro Gare du Nord); 79 rue de Bercy, 12e (Map 1, ☎ 01 43 45 98 99, metro Bercy); and 84 ave de Versailles, 16e (Map 1, ☎ 01 42 88 40 04, metro Mirabeau). Their Web site is at www.rentacar.fr.

Rollerland Paris (@ rollerland@wanadoo.fr) with a branch near Bastille (Map 5, ☎ 01 40 27 96 97, metro Bastille) at 3 blvd Bourdon (4e), rents electric-powered mini-scooters for 299FF a day. It is open from 10 am to 6 pm daily.

Taxi

The *prise en charge* (flag fall) is 13FF. Within the city limits, it costs 3.53FF per kilometre for travel from 7 am to 7 pm Monday to Saturday (tariff A). At night and on Sunday and holidays (tariff B), it's 5.83FF per kilometre.

There's an extra 8FF charge for taking a fourth passenger, but most drivers refuse to take more than three people because of insurance constraints. Each piece of baggage over 5kg costs 6FF extra, and for pick-up from SNCF mainline stations there's a 5FF supplement. The usual tip is 2FF no matter what the fare, with the maximum about 5FF.

Radio-dispatched taxi companies, on call 24 hours, include:

Alpha Taxis	☎ 01 45 85 85 85
Artaxi	☎ 01 42 03 50 50
Taxis 7000	☎ 01 42 70 00 42
Taxis Bleus	☎ 01 49 36 10 10
Taxis-Radio Étoile	☎ 01 42 70 41 41
Taxis G7	☎ 01 47 39 47 39

Bicycle

Paris now has some 130km of bicycle lanes running throughout the city and a lane running parallel to the Périphérique is being planned. Many are not particularly attractive or safe, but cyclists can be fined about 250FF for failing to use them. The tourist office distributes a free brochure-map produced by the mayor's office called *Paris à Vélo*.

There's plenty of space for cyclists in the Bois de Boulogne (16e), the Bois de Vincennes (12e), along Canal St-Martin (10e) to Parc de la Villette (19e) and then along the south bank of the 108km Canal de l'Ourcq. The quays along the Seine on the Right Bank and the quai d'Orsay on the Left Bank are closed to motor vehicles from 9 am and 4 pm on Sunday.

The best place to rent bicycles is the RATP-sponsored Roue Libre (Map 6, ☎ 01 53 46 43 77, fax 01 40 28 01 00, metro Les Halles) at the Forum des Halles, 95 bis rue Rambuteau, 1er. Bicycles cost a mere 20/75FF per hour/day or 115/225FF for a weekend/week, insurance included. The deposit is 1000FF and some form of identification is required. They also offer bicycle tours; see the earlier Organised Tours section earlier in this chapter. The office opens 9 am to 7 pm daily. On Sunday from March to October bikes can also be rented from Cyclobus, parked in a half-dozen locations around Paris including place de la Concorde (8e) and place Denfert Rochereau (14e).

Other places renting bikes (usually 80FF a day) include the following:

Bike 'n' Roller
(Map 6, ☎ 01 44 07 35 89, metro St-Michel), 6 rue St-Julien le Pauvre, 5e.

Paris Cycles
(Map 1, ☎ 01 47 47 76 50 for a recorded message, ☎ 01 47 47 22 37 for bookings). This outfit rents bicycles from two locations in the Bois de Boulogne, 16e (see that section for details).

Paris à Vélo, C'est Sympa!
(Map 6, ☎ 01 48 87 60 01, @ info@parisvel osympa.com, metro Bastille), 37 blvd Bourdon, 4e.

Paris Vélo
(Map 5, ☎ 01 43 37 59 22, metro Censier Daubenton), 2 rue du Fer à Moulin, 5e.

PARIS

Bicycles are not allowed on the metro. You can take your bicycle for free on some RER lines out to the suburbs on weekends and holidays (all day), and on weekdays before 6.30 am, between 9 am and 4.30 pm, and after 7 pm (ie outside peak travel times). More lenient rules apply to SNCF commuter services. For details, call the SNCF or RATP or stop by one of their information offices.

Boat

From mid-April to early November, the Batobus river shuttle (Map 4, ☎ 01 44 11 33 99, fax 01 45 56 07 88) docks at these stops:

Eiffel Tower (Map 4, Port de la Bourdonnais next to the Pont d'Iéna, 7e)

Musée d'Orsay (Map 4, Port de Solférino, 7e)

St-Germain des Prés (Map 6, quai Malaquais, 6e)

Notre Dame (Map 6, quai Montebello, 5e)

Hôtel de Ville (Map 6, quai de l'Hôtel de Ville, 4e)

Musée du Louvre (Map 6, quai du Louvre, 1er)

Champs-Élysées (Map 2, Port des Champs-Élysées, 8e)

Boats come by every 25 minutes from about 10 am to 7 pm (9 pm in July and August). A one/two-day pass costs 60/80FF (children under 12 35/40FF). A seasonal pass costs 250FF.

Around Paris

Paris is encircled by the Île de France, the 12,000-sq-km 'Island of France' shaped by five rivers: the Epte (to the north-west), the Aisne (north-east), the Eure (south-west), the Yonne (south-east) and the Marne (east). It was from this small kernel that, starting about AD 1100, the kingdom of France began to grow.

Today, the region's excellent rail and road links with the French capital and its exceptional sights – the cathedrals of St-Denis and Chartres; the chateaux of Versailles, Fontainebleau and Chantilly; and, of course, every kid's favourite, Disneyland Paris – make it especially popular with day-trippers from Paris. The many woodland areas around the city, including the forests of Fontainebleau and Chantilly, offer unlimited outdoor activities. For information about other destinations within easy striking distance of Paris, including Beauvais and Compiègne in far northern France and Giverny in Normandy, see the Far Northern France and Normandy chapters.

Information

The Espace du Tourisme d'Île de France (☎ 0 803 81 80 00, 01 44 50 19 98 from abroad, ✉ info@paris-ile-de-france.com), which is in the lower level of the Carrousel du Louvre shopping mall (enter from 99 rue de Rivoli, 1er), opens 10 am to 7 pm Wednesday to Monday You can also visit the bilingual Web site at www.paris-ile-de-france.com. If you're under your own steam, pick up a copy of Michelin's 1:200,000-scale *Île de France* map (No 237; 35FF) or the 1:100,000-scale *Environs de Paris* (No 106; 26FF).

LA DÉFENSE

postcode 92080 • pop 35,000 • elevation 34m

La Défense, Paris' skyscraper district, is 3km west of the 17th arrondissement. Set on the sloping western bank of the Seine, its ultramodern architecture and multi-storey

Highlights

- **Versailles** – relive the glory that was the kingdom of France in the 17th and 18th centuries
- **Stade de France** – marvel at one of Europe's most technically advanced sports stadia
- **Chartres** – learn about the cathedral's awesome stained glass and spires on one of the excellent tours
- **Disneyland Paris** – become a child again (for a day, at least)
- **Château de Chantilly** – wonder at the colour and richness of the 15th-century *Très Riches Heures du Duc de Berry* illuminated manuscript
- **Forêt de Fontainebleau** – go for a walk or ride in the Île de France's loveliest forest

office blocks are so strikingly different from the rest of centuries-old Paris that it's well worth a brief visit.

The development of La Défense, one of

AROUND PARIS

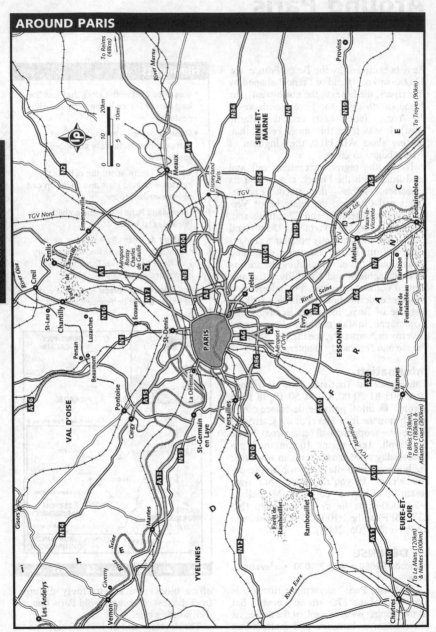

the world's most ambitious civil engineering projects, began in the late 1950s. Its first major structure was the triangular-shaped Centre des Nouvelles Industries et Technologies (Centre for New Industries & Technologies, better known as the CNIT), inaugurated in 1958 and renovated some three decades later. During the mid-1970s, when skyscrapers fell out of fashion, office space in La Défense became hard to sell or lease: buildings stood empty and the whole project appeared doomed.

Things picked up in the 1980s and 90s, and today La Défense has some 60 buildings, the highest of which is the 45-storey, 178m-tall Framatome. The head offices of more than half of France's 20 largest corporations are housed here, and a total of 1200 companies of all sizes employ some 150,000 people.

Information

Just north-west of the computer-controlled Agam fountain, Info-Défense (☎ 01 47 74 84 24, fax 01 47 78 17 93) at 15 place de la Défense (open 10 am to 6 pm daily) has a guide to the area's monumental art (15FF), a *Guide to Architecture* (35FF) and details on cultural activities. It also contains a museum of the development of La Défense through the years with drawings, architectural plans and scale models.

There are banks with ATMs everywhere in La Défense, including BNP (☎ 0 801 63 06 06, 19 place des Reflets), open 9 am to 5.15 pm weekdays, and CIC (☎ 0 836 68 75 20, 11 place de la Défense), open 8.45 am to 4.45 pm weekdays. There's a post office at the south-eastern corner of the CNIT building.

Grande Arche de la Défense

The remarkable Grande Arche (☎ 01 49 07 27 57), designed by Danish architect Otto von Spreckelsen and housing government and business offices, is a hollow cube of white marble and glass measuring 112m on each side. Inaugurated on 14 July 1989, it marks the western end of the 8km-long **Grand Axe**, the 'Great Axis', stretching from the Louvre's glass pyramid through

In Defence of Paris

La Défense is named after *La Défense de Paris*, a sculpture erected here in 1883 to commemorate the defence of Paris during the Franco-Prussian War of 1870–71. Removed in 1971 to facilitate construction work, it was placed on a round pedestal just west of the Agam fountain in 1983.

Many people don't like the name La Défense, which sounds rather militaristic, and it has caused some peculiar misunderstandings over the years. A high-ranking official of the authority that manages the project was once denied entry into Egypt because his passport indicated he was the 'managing director of La Défense', which Egyptian officials apparently assumed was part of France's military-industrial complex. And a visiting Soviet general expressed admiration at how well the area's military installations had been camouflaged

the Jardin des Tuileries and along the ave des Champs-Élysées to the Arc de Triomphe, Porte Maillot and finally the fountains, shaded squares and plazas of La Défense's Esplanade du Général de Gaulle. The structure, which symbolises a window open to the world, is ever so slightly out of alignment with the Grand Axe.

Neither the view from the rooftop nor the temporary exhibitions relating to human rights housed in the top storey justify the ticket price of 46FF (students, those aged six to 18 and seniors 33FF). Both are open 10 am to 7 pm daily (last admission 6 pm).

Parvis & Esplanade

The Parvis, place de la Défense and Esplanade du Général de Gaulle, which together form a pleasant, kilometre-long pedestrian walkway, have been turned into a **garden of contemporary art**. The nearly 70 monumental sculptures and murals here – and west of the Grande Arche in the **Quartier du Parc** and **Jardins de l'Arche**, a 2km-long westward extension of the Grand

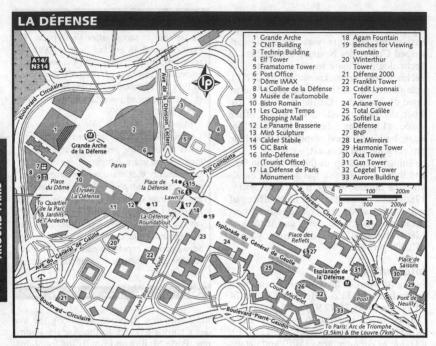

LA DÉFENSE

1 Grande Arche
2 CNIT Building
3 Technip Building
4 Elf Tower
5 Framatome Tower
6 Post Office
7 Dôme IMAX
8 La Colline de la Défense
9 Musée de l'automobile
10 Bistro Romain
11 Les Quatre Temps Shopping Mall
12 Le Paname Brasserie
13 Miró Sculpture
14 Calder Stabile
15 CIC Bank
16 Info-Défense (Tourist Office)
17 La Défense de Paris Monument
18 Agam Fountain
19 Benches for Viewing Fountain
20 Winterthur Tower
21 Défense 2000
22 Franklin Tower
23 Crédit Lyonnais Tower
24 Ariane Tower
25 Total Galilée
26 Sofitel La Défense
27 BNP
28 Les Miroirs
29 Harmonie Tower
30 Axa Tower
31 Gan Tower
32 Cegetel Tower
33 Aurore Building

Axe – include colourful and imaginative works by Calder, Miró, Agam, Torricini and others.

In the south-eastern corner of place de la Défense and opposite the Info-Défense office is a much older monument honouring the defence of Paris during the Franco-Prussian War of 1870-71 (see the boxed text 'In Defence of Paris').

Colline de la Défense

This complex, just south of the Grande Arche and west of Les Quatre Temps shopping mall, houses the huge **Dôme IMAX** (☎ 01 46 92 45 50), a 460-seat, 180° cinema that screens the usual 2D and IMAX 3D films – documentaries about travel, space and wildlife that thrill and shock and frighten for a while and then get rather dull and repetitive. Tickets cost 57FF (students, seniors and under 16s 44FF) and 40FF for the second film. On Saturday a double feature costs 80/70FF. Screenings start every

hour from 12.30 pm to 5.45 pm (10.45 am to 7.30 pm at the weekend).

Of more conventional interest is the **Musée de l'Automobile** (☎ 01 46 92 71 71), 1 place du Dôme, whose outstanding collection of 110 vintage motorcars includes lots of very early French models. It opens 12.15 to 7 pm daily (last admission 6 pm) and admission costs 40FF (reduced price 30FF).

Places to Eat

In Les Quatre Temps shopping mall, there are some 30 restaurants, including *Le Paname Brasserie* (☎ 01 47 73 50 60), with pizzas from 54FF to 66FF and *menus* at 92FF and 125FF, and yet another *Bistro Romain* (☎ 01 40 81 08 08), which can be entered from 37 Le Parvis.

Getting There & Away

The Grande Arche de la Défense metro station is the western terminus of metro line

No 1; the ride from the Louvre takes about 15 minutes. If you take the faster RER (line A), remember that La Défense is in zone 3 and you must pay a supplement (11.50FF) if carrying a travel pass for zones 1 & 2.

ST-DENIS
postcode 93200 • pop 85,800 • elevation 33m

For 1200 years, St-Denis was the burial place of the kings of France; today it is a quiet suburb just north of Paris' 18th arrondissement. The ornate royal tombs, adorned with some truly remarkable statuary, and the basilica that contains them (the world's first major Gothic structure) are an easy half-day excursion by metro. St-Denis' more recent claim to fame is the Stade de France just south of the Canal de St-Denis, the futuristic stadium where France beat Brazil to win the World Cup in July 1998. It is now open to visitors.

Information
The tourist office (☎ 01 55 87 08 70, fax 01 48 20 24 11), 1 rue de la République, opens 9.30 am to 1 pm and 2 to 6 pm Monday to Saturday and 10 am to 1.30 pm on Sunday. The hours are 9.30 am to 1 pm and 2.30 to 6.30 pm on Monday to Saturday and 2 to 5.30 pm on Sunday April to September. Visit the bilingual Web site at www.ville-saint-denis.fr. The office offers guided tours of the city in French at 3 pm on Saturday and at 4 pm on Sunday from June to September (40FF, students and under 18s 30FF).

Banks with ATMs include the Société Générale (☎ 01 43 20 86 39) at 11 place Jean Jaurès, which opens 9 am to 12.30 pm and 2 to 5 pm Tuesday to Saturday, and the BNP (☎ 01 48 13 53 49) near the St-Denis-Porte de Paris metro at 6 blvd Anatole France (open 9.30 am to 6.15 pm Monday to Friday).

Basilique St-Denis
The basilica of St-Denis (☎ 01 48 09 83 54), 1 rue de la Légion d'Honneur, served as the burial place for all but a handful of France's kings from Dagobert I (ruled 629–39) to Louis XVIII (ruled 1814–24). Their tombs and mausoleums constitute one of Europe's most important collections of funerary sculpture.

The present basilica, construction of which began in around 1135, changed the face of western architecture. It was the first major structure to be built in the Gothic style, and it served as a model for many other 12th-century French cathedrals, including the one at Chartres. Features illustrating the transition from Romanesque to Gothic can be seen in the **choir** and **ambulatory**, which are adorned with a number of 12th-century **stained-glass windows**. The **narthex** (the portico running along the western end of the basilica) also dates from this period. The nave and transept were built in the 13th century.

During the Revolution and the Reign of Terror, the basilica was devastated; the royal tombs were emptied of their human remains, which were then dumped into two pits outside the church, but the mausoleums, put into storage in Paris, survived. They were brought back in 1816, and the royal bones were reburied in the crypt a year later. Restoration of the structure began under Napoleon, but most of the work was carried out by Viollet-le-Duc from 1858 until his death in 1879.

Tombs The tombs (now empty) are decorated with life-size figures of the deceased. The ones built before the Renaissance are adorned with *gisants* (recumbent figures). Those made after 1285 were carved from death masks and are thus fairly, well, lifelike; those made before under Louis IX (St-Louis; 1214–70) are depictions of how the sculptors thought the rulers might have looked. The oldest tombs (dating from around 1230) are those of **Clovis I** (died 511) and his son **Childebert I** (died 558), brought to St-Denis during the early 19th century.

Opening Hours & Tickets You can visit the nave for free, but there's an admission charge of 32FF (aged 12 to 25, students and seniors 21FF, free for those under 12) to

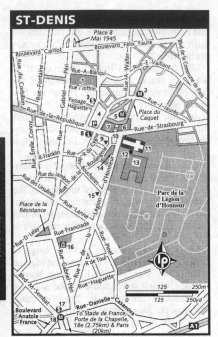

ST-DENIS

1 Halle du Marché
2 Basilique de St-Denis Metro Station
3 Société Générale Bank
4 Place Jean Jaurès; Food Market
5 Basiliquede St-Denis Metro Station
6 Town Hall Annexe
7 Town Hall
8 Tourist Office
9 Les Mets du Roy
10 Place Victor Hugo
11 Basilique St-Denis
12 Entrance to Royal Tombs
13 Maison de l'Éducation de la Légion d'Honneur
14 Place de la Légion d'Honneur
15 Au Petit Breton
16 Musée d'Art et d'Histoire
17 BNP
18 St-Denis-Porte de Paris Metro Station

visit the transept and crypt. The basilica opens 10 am (noon on Sunday) to 5 pm (7 pm from April to September) daily; ticket counters close 30 minutes before. Self-paced 1¼-hour tours on CD-ROM headsets cost 25FF (two people sharing 35FF).

Stade de France
The 80,000-seat Stadium of France (☎ 01 55 93 00 00, fax 01 55 93 00 49), rue Francis de Pressensé, due south of central St-Denis and in full view from rue Gabriel Péri, was built for the 1998 FIFA World Cup, which France won after miraculously defeating Brazil 3-0. The futuristic and quite beautiful structure, with a roof the size of place de la Concorde, is now used for football and rugby matches as well as big-ticket music concerts (last seen performing: Tina Turner). It can be visited on a self-guided tour (38FF, children aged six to 17 30FF) from 10 am to 6 pm daily or on a

more elaborate 1½-hour guided one called Les Coulisses du Stade (Behind the Scenes of the Stadium; 90/65FF), with departures from 10 am to 4.30 pm in French and an English-language tour at 2.30 pm. The bilingual Web site is at www.stadefrance .com; by Minitel it's 3615 STADE DE FRANCE.

Musée d'Art et d'Histoire
St-Denis' excellent Museum of Art and History (☎ 01 42 43 05 10), 22 bis rue Gabriel Péri, occupies a restored Carmelite convent founded in 1625 and later presided over by Louise de France, the youngest daughter of Louis XV. Displays include reconstructions of the Carmelites' cells, an 18th-century apothecary and, in the archaeology section, fascinating items found during excavations around St-Denis. There's also a section on modern art as well as politically charged posters, cartoons, lithographs and paintings from the 1871 Paris Commune. The museum opens 10 am to 5.30 pm Monday and Wednesday to Saturday and 2 to 6.30 pm on Sunday. Admission costs 20FF (students, teachers and seniors 10FF, free for under 16s).

Places to Eat
There are a number of restaurants in the modern shopping area around the Basilique

de St-Denis metro stop and along rue de la Légion d'Honneur, including *Au Petit Breton* (☎ *01 48 20 11 58*) at No 18, with a *menu* for 65FF (open for lunch and dinner till 9 pm from Monday to Saturday afternoon). A more expensive choice is *Les Mets du Roy* (☎ *01 48 20 89 74*), opposite the basilica at 4 rue de la Boulangerie, with an a la carte meal costing about 250FF. It opens for lunch weekdays and for dinner Monday to Saturday.

From 7 am to 1 pm on Tuesday, Friday and Sunday, there's a large, multi-ethnic *food market* – known in particular for its selection of spices – at place Jean Jaurès, across the street from the tourist office, and in the *Halle du Marché*, the large covered market to the north-west.

Getting There & Away

Take metro line No 13 to the penultimate stop, Basilique de St-Denis, for the basilica and tourist office, or St-Denis-Porte de Paris for the Museum of Art and History and the Stade de France; the latter can also be reached via RER line D1 (station: Stade de France-St-Denis). When taking line No 13, make sure you board a train heading for St-Denis Université and not Gabriel Péri/Asnières-Gennevilliers. The line splits at La Fourche station.

DISNEYLAND PARIS
postcode 77777

It took some US$4.4 billion and five years of work to turn the beet fields 32km east of Paris into Disneyland Paris, which opened in 1992 amid much fanfare and controversy. Although Disney stockholders were less than thrilled with the park's performance for the first few years, what was originally known as EuroDisney is now in the black, and the many visitors – mostly families with young children – seem to be having a great time. The park is the single most popular paid tourist attraction in Europe, having welcomed some 12.5 million visitors in 1998.

Orientation

Disneyland Paris consists of two main areas: the commercial Disney Village, with shops, restaurants and clubs, and Disneyland Paris Theme Park. The two are separated by the RER and TGV train stations. Moving walkways whisk visitors from the far-flung car park.

Information

There are information booths scattered around the park, including one next to the RER station and another one in City Hall, which can also make hostel reservations. In France, information is available (and hotel reservations can be made) on ☎ 01 60 30 60 30, fax 01 60 30 30 99. In the UK ring ☎ 08705 030303 and in the USA ☎ 407-WDISNEY. The park's Web-site address is www.disney.fr; by Minitel key in 3615 DISNEYLAND.

There are several American Express (Amex) exchange bureaux, including one in the wing of the Disneyland Hôtel nearest the main ticket office to the Theme Park, usually open from 10 am to 6.30 pm daily, and another in Disney Village open 9.30 am to 9.30 pm weekdays and 9 am to 10 pm at the weekend (shorter hours in the low and shoulder seasons).

The post office in Disney Village opens 12.30 to 7 pm weekdays, 9.45 am to 6 pm on Saturday and 1 to 7 pm on Sunday. Summer hours are 8.30 am to 10.30 pm Monday to Saturday and 1 to 7 pm on Sunday.

Disneyland Paris Theme Park

The theme park, isolated from the outside world by a clever layout and grassy embankments, is divided into five *pays* (lands). **Main Street, USA**, just inside the main entrance and behind the Disneyland Hotel, is a spotless avenue reminiscent of Norman Rockwell's idealised small-town America, circa 1900. The adjoining **Frontierland** is a recreation of the 'rugged, untamed American West'.

Adventureland, intended to evoke the 1001 Arabian Nights and the wilds of Africa (among other exotic lands portrayed in Disney films), is home to that old favourite, Pirates of the Caribbean, as well as the Indiana Jones and the Temple of Doom roller coaster. **Fantasyland** brings fairy-tale characters such as Sleeping Beauty, Pinocchio, Peter Pan and Snow White to life. And in **Discoveryland**, the high-tech rides (including Space Mountain and Orbitron) and futuristic movies pay homage to Leonardo da Vinci, George Lucas and – for a bit of local colour – Jules Verne.

Opening Hours & Tickets Disneyland Paris opens 365 days a year. The hours are 10 am to 6 pm (to 8 pm on Saturdays, some Sundays and perhaps during school holiday periods) daily from early September to March; 9 am to 8 pm (to 11 pm at the weekend) daily in spring and early summer; and 9 am to 11 pm daily from early July to early September.

The one-day admission fee, which includes unlimited access to all rides and activities (except the shooting gallery and the video games arcade), costs 220FF (children aged three to 11 170FF) from April to early November. The rest of the year, except during the Christmas holidays, prices drop to 165/135FF. Multiple-day passes are also available (two- and three-day passes in high season for adults/children at 425/330FF and 595/460FF.

Places to Stay

Camping & Bungalows The *Davy Crockett Ranch* (☎ 01 60 45 69 000), a lovely forested area whose entrance is 7km southwest of the theme park, opens year round. It costs 300FF to 450FF to park a caravan or pitch a tent, depending on the season. There are also some 500 bungalows with kitchenettes for from two to six people; doubles start from 755FF to 1038FF, depending on the season, and there's an extra charge of 335FF for children aged three to 11.

Hotels Each of the park's six enormous hotels has its own all-American theme, reflected in the architecture, landscaping, decor, restaurants and entertainment. All the rooms have two double beds (or, in the case of the Hôtel Cheyenne, one double bed and two bunk beds) and can sleep up to four people.

Rates depend on the dates of stay. Prices

are highest during July and August and around Christmas; on Friday and Saturday nights and during holiday periods from April to October; and on Saturday nights from mid-February to March. The least expensive rates are available on most week nights (Sunday to Thursday or, sometimes, Friday) from January to mid-February; from mid-May to June; for most of September; and from November to mid-December.

The cheapest hotel is the 1000-room, New Mexico-style *Hôtel Santa Fe* (☎ 01 60 45 78 00, fax 01 60 45 78 33), which charges 1380FF to 1760FF for a double room (335FF extra per child). The 14 buildings of the 1000-room *Hôtel Cheyenne* (☎ 01 60 45 62 00, fax 01 60 45 62 33) – each with its own hokey name – are arranged to resemble a Wild West frontier town. Rooms cost 740FF to 955FF per person in a double.

Places to Eat

There are some 50 restaurants at Disneyland Paris, including *Planet Hollywood* (☎ 01 60 43 78 27) in Disney Village, which opens daily from 11 or 11.30 am to about midnight. Burgers, pasta and sandwiches are in the 74FF to 89FF range. You are not allowed to picnic inside the Theme Park.

Getting There & Away

Marne-la-Vallée-Chessy (Disneyland's RER station) is served by RER line A4, which runs every 15 minutes or so. Tickets, available at metro stations, cost 38FF (35 to 40 minutes). Trains that go all the way to Marne-la-Vallée-Chessy have four-letter codes beginning with the letter 'Q'. The last train back to Paris leaves Disneyland around 12.20 am. A taxi to/from the centre of Paris costs about 350FF (about 450FF from 7 pm to 8 am and on Sunday and holidays).

VERSAILLES
postcode 78000 • pop 85,700 • elevation 130m

The prosperous, leafy and very bourgeois suburb of Versailles, 23km south-west of Paris, is the site of the grandest and most famous chateau in France. It served as the kingdom's political capital and the seat of the royal court for almost the entire period between 1682 and 1789, the year in which revolutionary mobs massacred the palace guard and dragged Louis XVI and Marie-Antoinette back to Paris, where they eventually had their heads lopped off.

Because so many people consider Versailles a must-see destination, the chateau attracts more than three million visitors a year. The best way to avoid the queues is to arrive first thing in the morning; if you're interested in just the Grands Appartements, another good time to come is around 3.30 to 4 pm.

Information

The tourist office (☎ 01 39 24 88 88, ℮ tourisme@ot-versailles.fr) is at 2 bis ave de Paris, just north of the Versailles-Rive Gauche train station and east of the chateau. It opens 9 am to 7 pm daily from April to October and to 6 pm the rest of the year.

The Banque de France (☎ 01 39 24 55 49), 50 blvd de la Reine, opens for exchange 8.45 am till noon on weekdays. The main post office, on the opposite side of ave de Paris from the tourist office, opens 8.30 am to 7 pm weekdays and to 12.30 pm on Saturday.

Château de Versailles

This enormous palace (☎ 01 30 83 78 00 or 01 30 83 77 77) was built in the mid-17th century during the reign of Louis XIV – the Roi Soleil (Sun King) – to project both at home and abroad the absolute power of the French monarchy, then at the height of its glory. Its scale and decor also reflect Louis XIV's taste for profligate luxury and his near boundless appetite for self-glorification. Some 30,000 workers and soldiers toiled on the structure, whose construction bills wrought havoc on the kingdom's finances.

The chateau complex consists of four main parts: the palace building, a 580m-long structure with innumerable wings, grand halls and sumptuous bedchambers (only parts of which are open to the public); the vast gardens, canals and pools west of the palace; and two outbuildings, the Grand Trianon and, a few hundred metres to the east, the Petit Trianon. The chateau has undergone relatively few alterations since its construction, though almost all the interior furnishings disappeared during the Revolution and many of the rooms were rebuilt by Louis-Philippe (ruled 1830–48).

History About two decades into his long reign (1643–1715), Louis XIV decided to enlarge the hunting lodge his father had built at Versailles and turn it into a palace big enough for the entire court, which numbered some 6000 people. To accomplish this task he hired four supremely talented men: the architect Louis Le Vau; his successor, Jules Hardouin-Mansart, who took over in the mid-1670s; the painter and interior designer Charles Le Brun; and the landscape artist André Le Nôtre, whose workers flattened hills, drained marshes and relocated forests as they laid out the seemingly endless gardens, ponds and fountains.

Le Brun and his hundreds of artisans decorated every moulding, cornice, ceiling and door of the interior with the most luxurious and ostentatious of appointments: frescoes, marble, gilt, woodcarvings, many of whose themes and symbols are drawn from Greek and Roman mythology. The **Grand Appartement du Roi** (King's Suite), for example, includes rooms dedicated to Hercules, Venus, Diana, Mars and Mercury. The opulence reaches its peak in the **Galerie des Glaces** (Hall of Mirrors), a 75m-long ballroom with 17 huge mirrors on one side and, on the other, an equal number of windows looking out on the gardens and the setting sun.

Gardens & Fountains The section of the vast gardens nearest the palace, laid out between 1661 and 1700 in the formal French style, is famed for its geometrically aligned terraces, flower beds, tree-lined paths, ponds and fountains. The many statues of marble, bronze and lead were made by finest sculptors of the period. The English-style **Jardins du Petit Trianon** are more pastoral and have meandering, sheltered paths.

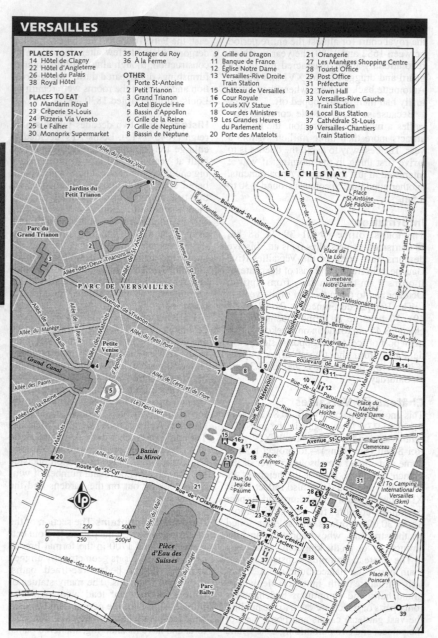

VERSAILLES

PLACES TO STAY
14 Hôtel de Clagny
22 Hôtel d'Angleterre
26 Hôtel du Palais
38 Royal Hôtel

PLACES TO EAT
10 Mandarin Royal
23 Crêperie St-Louis
24 Pizzeria Via Veneto
25 Le Falher
30 Monoprix Supermarket

35 Potager du Roy
36 À la Ferme

OTHER
1 Porte St-Antoine
2 Petit Trianon
3 Grand Trianon
4 Astel Bicycle Hire
5 Bassin d'Appollon
6 Grille de la Reine
7 Grille de Neptune
8 Bassin de Neptune

9 Grille du Dragon
11 Banque de France
12 Église Notre Dame
13 Versailles-Rive Droite
   Train Station
15 Château de Versailles
16 Cour Royale
17 Louis XIV Statue
18 Cour des Ministres
19 Les Grandes Heures
   du Parlement
20 Porte des Matelots

21 Orangerie
27 Les Manèges Shopping Centre
28 Tourist Office
29 Post Office
31 Préfecture
32 Town Hall
33 Versailles-Rive Gauche
   Train Station
34 Local Bus Station
37 Cathédrale St-Louis
39 Versailles-Chantiers
   Train Station

The **Grand Canal**, 1.6km long and 62m wide, is oriented to reflect the setting sun. It is traversed by the kilometre-long **Petit Canal**, creating a cross-shaped body of water with a perimeter of over 5.5km. Louis XIV used to hold boating parties here. From May to mid-October, you too can paddle around the Grand Canal: four-person rowing boats (☎ 01 39 54 22 00) cost 72FF per hour. The dock is at the canal's eastern end. The **Orangerie**, built under the Parterre du Midi (flower bed) on the south side of the palace, is used to store exotic plants in winter.

The gardens' largest fountains are the 17th-century **Bassin de Neptune** (Neptune Fountain), 300m north of the main palace building, whose straight side abuts a small, round pond graced by a winged dragon; and, at the eastern end of the Grand Canal, the **Bassin d'Apollon**, in whose centre Apollo's chariot, pulled by rearing horses, emerges from the water.

On Saturday from July to September and on Sunday from early April to early October, the fountains are turned on at 11 am for the hour-long **Grande Perspective** and from 3.30 to 5 pm for the longer and more elaborate **Grandes Eaux**. The Bassin de Neptun flows for 10 minutes from 5.20 pm. All the performances, which cost 30FF (students 20FF) are accompanied by taped classical music.

The Trianons In the middle of the park, about 1.5km north-west of the main building, are Versailles' two smaller palaces, each surrounded by neatly tended flower beds. The pink-colonnaded **Grand Trianon** was built in 1687 for Louis XIV and his family, who used it as a place of escape from the rigid etiquette of the court. Napoleon I had it redone in the Empire style. The much smaller, ochre-coloured **Petit Trianon**, built in the 1760s, was redecorated in 1867 by the Empress Eugénie, who added Louis XVI-style furnishings similar to the uninspiring pieces that now fill its 1st-floor rooms.

A bit farther north is the **Hameau de la Reine** (Queen's Hamlet), a mock rural village of thatch-roofed cottages constructed from 1775 to 1784 for the amusement of Marie-Antoinette.

Opening Hours & Tickets The **Grands Appartements** (State Apartments), the main section of the palace that can be visited without a guided tour, include the **Galerie des Glaces**, the **Muséee de l'Histoire de France** (Museum of French History) and the **Appartement de la Reine** (Queen's Suite). They are open 9 am to 5.30 pm (to 6.30 pm from May to September) Tuesday to Sunday; the ticket windows close 30 minutes earlier. Admission costs 45FF (after 3.30 pm 35FF, free for under 18s). Tickets are on sale at Entrée A (Entrance A), which is off to the right from the equestrian statue of Louis XIV as you approach the palace. The queues are worst on Tuesday, when many Paris museums are closed, and on Sunday. The chateau's Web site is at www.chateauversailles.fr. You can also contact them by Minitel at 3615 VERSAILLES.

The Tennis Court Oath

In May 1789, in an effort to deal with the huge national debt and to moderate dissent by reforming the tax system, Louis XVI convened at Versailles the États-Généraux (States General), a body made up of over 1000 deputies representing the three estates: the nobility, the clergy (most of whom were exempted from paying taxes) and the Third Estate, representing the middle classes. When the Third Estate, whose members constituted a majority of the delegates, was denied entry to the usual meeting place of the States General, they met separately in the Salle de Jeu de Paume (Royal Tennis Court), where they constituted themselves as the National Assembly on 17 June. Three days later they took the famous Tennis Court Oath, swearing not to dissolve the Assembly until Louis XVI had accepted a new constitution. This act of defiance sparked demonstrations of support and, less than a month later, a mob in Paris would storm the Bastille prison.

AROUND PARIS

A rather esoteric exhibit called **Les Grandes Heures du Parlement** (Landmarks in the History of the French Parliament; ☎ 01 39 67 07 73), which focuses on the history of France's Assemblée Nationale (National Assembly; see also the boxed text 'The Tennis Court Oath'), is in the chateau's southern wing. It keeps the same hours as the chateau though the ticket office closes one hour earlier. Admission costs 20FF (aged 18 to 25 15FF, free for under 18s). Admission includes a taped commentary.

The Grand Trianon (25FF, reduced price 15FF, free for under 18s) opens noon to 6.30 pm daily from April to October. It closes at 5.30 pm during the rest of the year. The last admission is 30 minutes before closing time. The Petit Trianon, open the same days and hours, costs 15FF (reduced price 10FF, free for under 18s). A combined ticket for both will set you back 30FF (reduced price 20FF).

The gardens are open daily (unless it's snowing) from 7 am (8 am in winter) to dusk (between 5.30 and 9.30 pm, depending on the season). Admission is free except when the fountains are in operation (see Gardens & Fountains earlier in the section).

If you have a Carte Musées et Monuments (see the boxed text 'Ah, la Carte!' in the Paris chapter), you don't have to wait in the queue – go straight to Entrée A2.

Guided Tours One of the best ways to get a sense of the Grands Appartements is to rent the audioguide recorded tour available for 30FF at Entrée A, from just behind the ticket booths. The excellent commentary lasts 80 minutes.

The **Appartement de Louis XIV** and the **Appartements du Dauphin et de la Dauphine** can be toured with a one-hour audioguide, available at Entrée C, for 25FF (free for children aged under 10). You can begin your visit between 9 am and 3.30 pm (4.15 pm from May to September). This is also a good way to avoid the queues at Entrée A.

Several different guided tours are available in English from 9 am to 3.30 pm (4 pm from May to September). They last one, 1½

and two hours and cost 25FF, 37FF and 50FF respectively (17/26/34 FF for those aged 10 to 17). Tickets are sold at Entrée D; tours begin across the courtyard at Entrée F. For information ring ☎ 01 30 83 77 88.

All the tours require that you also purchase a ticket to the Grands Appartements. If you buy it at Entrée C or Entrée D when paying for your tour, you can later avoid the Grands Appartements queue at Entrée A by going straight to Entrée A2. The entrance for disabled visitors is Entrée H, just northwest of Entrée A.

Places to Stay

About 3km south-east of the centre at 31 rue Berthelot, **Camping International de Versailles** (☎ 01 39 51 23 61, fax 01 39 53 68 29) is 400m from the Versailles-Porchefontaine train station (on RER line C4) and in the Parc Forestier des Nouettes. It charges 65FF to 75FF for two people with a tent and 100FF to 130FF for two people with caravan, depending on the season.

Across the street from the Versailles-Rive Gauche station and in front of the bus station on the 2nd floor of 6 place Lyautay is the **Hôtel du Palais** (☎ 01 39 50 39 29, fax 01 39 50 80 41), a well-kept 24-room place that has doubles with washbasin for 180FF, and with shower for 250FF to 280FF. Another central but somewhat overpriced choice is the 38-room **Royal Hôtel** (☎ 01 39 50 67 31, ✆ royalhotel@post.club-internet .fr, 23 rue Royale), with basic doubles for 260FF and ones with shower and toilet for 290FF. Triples cost 380FF. Around the corner from the Jeu de Paume, the charming 18-room **Hôtel d'Angleterre** (☎ 01 39 51 43 50, ✆ hotel.angleterre@volia.fr, 2 bis rue de Fontenay) has attractive rooms with washbasin and toilet from 200FF and with shower and toilet from 300FF to 350FF.

Farther afield, the **Hôtel de Clagny** (☎ 01 39 50 18 09, fax 01 39 50 85 17, 6 Impasse de Clagny), is a block east of 81 blvd de la Reine and behind the Versailles-Rive Droite station. Singles with washbasin and toilet at this 21-room place are 200FF. Doubles with shower and toilet cost 280FF (300FF with bath and toilet) and triples cost 330/350FF.

Places to Eat

Restaurants The quiet and elegant *Le Falher* (☎ *01 39 50 57 43, 22 rue de Satory*) has French gastronomic *menus* for 138FF and 175FF (including wine) at lunch and 168FF and 210FF at dinner. It opens for lunch Tuesday to Friday and for dinner Monday to Saturday.

Traditional French *menus* at the refined *Potager du Roy* (☎ *01 39 50 35 34, 1 rue du Maréchal Joffre*) go for 135FF (weekday lunch only) and 178FF. There's also a four-course *menu dégustation* with wine for 280FF. It opens for lunch Tuesday to Friday and on Sunday and for dinner Tuesday to Saturday. Next door the much cheaper and more relaxed *À la Ferme* (☎ *01 39 53 10 81, 3 rue du Maréchal Joffre*) specialises in grilled meats and the cuisine of south-western France. Two-course *formules* and *menus* cost 60FF to 93FF at lunch and 88FF to 118FF at dinner. It opens for lunch Wednesday to Sunday and for dinner Tuesday to Sunday.

The Breton specialities served at the cosy *Crêperie St-Louis* (☎ *01 39 53 40 12, 33 rue du Vieux Versailles*) include sweet and savoury crepes and galettes (18FF to 46FF), and there are *menus* for 52FF, 58FF and 75FF. It opens daily. There are lots of other restaurants in the immediate vicinity, including *Pizzeria Via Veneto* (☎ *01 39 51 03 89, 20 rue de Satory*), which has pizzas (39FF to 53FF) and pasta dishes (50FF to 63FF) and opens daily.

Just west of the Église Notre Dame, the *Mandarin Royal* (☎ *01 39 50 48 03, 5 rue de Ste-Geneviève*), a Chinese restaurant with some Vietnamese dishes, has lunch *menus* for 49FF and 58FF and dinner ones for 68FF, 88FF and 118FF. It's open for lunch Tuesday to Sunday and dinner Monday to Saturday.

Self-Catering The outdoor *food market* (*place du Marché Notre Dame*) opens 7.30 am to 2 pm on Tuesday, Friday and Sunday; if coming from the tourist office, enter via the passage Saladin at 33 ave de St-Cloud. The *food stalls* in the adjoining covered market are open 7 am to 7.30 pm daily (to 2 pm on Sunday).

The *Monoprix* (*9 rue Georges Clemenceau*), north of ave de Paris, opens 8.30 am to 9 pm Monday to Saturday.

Getting There & Away

Bus No 171 (8FF or one metro/bus ticket, 35 minutes) links Pont de Sèvres, 15e, in Paris with the place d'Armes and the chateau in Versailles, but it's quicker to go by train. Each of Versailles' three train stations is served by RER and/or SNCF trains coming from a different group of Paris stations.

RER line C4 takes you from Paris' Left Bank RER stations to Versailles-Rive Gauche station (14.50FF), which is only 700m south-east of the chateau and close to the tourist office. From Paris, catch any train whose four-letter code begins with the letter 'V'. There are up to 70 trains a day (half that number on Sunday), and the last train back to Paris leaves shortly before midnight.

RER line C5 links Paris' Left Bank with Versailles-Chantiers station (14.50FF), a 1300m walk from the chateau. From Paris, take any train whose code begins with 'S'. Versailles-Chantiers is also served by some three dozen SNCF trains a day (20 on Sunday) from Gare Montparnasse (14.50FF, 15 minutes); all trains on this line continue on to Chartres.

From Paris' Gare St-Lazare (20FF) and La Défense (12FF), the SNCF has about 70 trains a day to Versailles-Rive Droite, which is 1200m from the chateau. The last train to Paris leaves a bit past midnight.

Getting Around

From late February to December, a company called Astel (☎ 01 39 66 97 66) hires out bicycles for 32/64FF per half/full day from kiosks at the Petite Venise area at the eastern end of the Grand Canal and from next to Grille de la Reine Opening hours are 10 am to at least 5 pm (later as the days get longer).

FONTAINEBLEAU

postcode 77300 • pop 15,900 • elevation 75m

The town of Fontainebleau, 65km southeast of Paris, is renowned for its elegant

Renaissance chateau – one of France's largest royal residences – whose splendid furnishings make it particularly worth visiting. It's much less crowded and pressured than Versailles. The town itself has a number of nice restaurants and night spots – we always have a fine time in Fontainebleau – and is surrounded by the beautiful Forêt de Fontainebleau, a favourite hunting ground of a long line of French kings.

Information

The tourist office (☎ 01 60 74 99 99, fax 01 60 74 80 22) in a converted petrol station at 4 rue Royale opens 10 am to 6.30 pm Monday to Saturday and to 4 pm on Sunday. It rents bicycles (see Getting Around later in this section) and self-paced audioguide tours of the city in English lasting 1½ hours (20FF). The Web-site address is www.fontainebleau.org. On Minitel key in 3615 FONTAINEBLEAU.

The Banque de France at 192 rue Grande exchanges money 8.30 to noon on weekdays. The main post office, 2 rue de la Chancellerie, opens 8.15 am to 7 pm weekdays and to noon on Saturday.

Château de Fontainebleau

The enormous, 1900-room Château de Fontainebleau (☎ 01 60 71 50 70), whose list of former tenants reads like a who's who of French royal history, is one of the most beautifully ornamented and furnished chateaux in France. Every centimetre of the wall and ceiling space is richly adorned with wood panelling, gilded carvings, frescoes, tapestries and paintings. The parquet floors are of the finest woods, the fireplaces ornamented with exceptional carvings, and many of the pieces of furniture are Renaissance originals.

History The first chateau on this site was built sometime in the early 12th century and enlarged by Louis IX a century later. Only a single medieval tower survived the energetic Renaissance-style reconstruction undertaken by François I (ruled 1515–47), whose superb artisans, many of them brought from Italy, blended Italian and

French styles to create what is known as the First School of Fontainebleau. During this period, the *Mona Lisa* hung here amidst other fine works of art in the royal collection.

During the latter half of the 16th century, the chateau was further enlarged by Henri II, Catherine de Médicis and Henri IV, whose Flemish and French artists created the Second School of Fontainebleau.

Even Louis XIV got in on the act: it was he who hired Le Nôtre to redesign the gardens. But his most (in)famous act at Fontainebleau was the revocation in 1685 of the Edict of Nantes, which had guaranteed freedom of conscience for France's Protestants since 1598.

Fontainebleau, which was not damaged during the Revolution (though its furniture was stolen or destroyed), was beloved by Napoleon, who did a fair bit of restoration work. Napoleon III also visited the chateau frequently.

During WWII, the chateau was turned into a German headquarters. Liberated in 1944 by US General George Patton, part of the complex served as Allied and then NATO headquarters from 1945 to 1965.

Courtyards & Rooms As successive monarchs added their own wings to the chateau, five irregularly shaped courtyards were created. The oldest and most interesting is the U-shaped **Cour Ovale** (Oval Courtyard), no longer oval due to Henri IV's construction work. It incorporates the keep, the sole remnant of the medieval castle. The largest courtyard is the **Cour du Cheval Blanc** (Courtyard of the White Horse), also known as the Cour des Adieux (Farewell Courtyard). The second name dates from 1814 when Napoleon, about to be exiled to Elba, bid farewell to his guards from the magnificent **double-horseshoe staircase**, built under Louis XIII in 1634.

The **Grands Appartements** (State Apartments) include a number of outstanding rooms. The spectacular **Chapelle de la Trinité** (Trinity Chapel), whose ornamentation dates from the first half of the 17th century, is where Louis XV married Marie

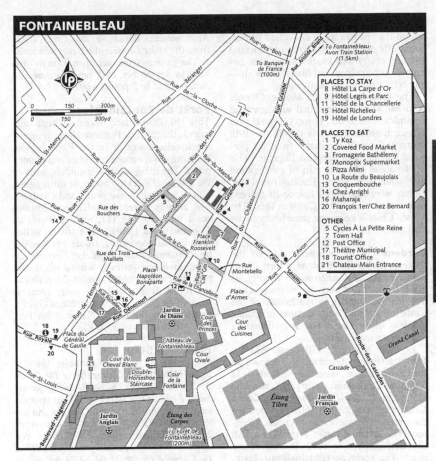

FONTAINEBLEAU

0   150   300m
0   150   300yd

To Fontainebleau-
Avon Train Station
(1.5km)

To Banque
de France
(100m)

Rue-des-Bois

Rue-Aristide-Briand

Rue Grande

Rue-Béranger

Rue-de-la-Cloche

Rue-de-la-Paroisse

Rue-des-Pins

Rue-St-Merry

Rue Guérin

Rue-du-Marché

Rue Marrier

Rue-St-Honoré

Rue des
Bouchers

Rue-des-Sablons

Rue Conv. Geoffroy

Rue Grande

Rue-du-Château

Rue—de—France

Rue de la Corne

Rue Paul

Rue du

Rue des Trois
Maillets

Place
Franklin
Roosevelt

Rue
Montebello

d'Avon

Rue Séramy

Passage-Ronsin

Place
Napoléon
Bonaparte

Rue-du-
Coq-Gris

Rue de la Chancellerie

Place
d'Armes

Route-des-Cascades

Rue-de-Ferrare

Rue Richelieu

Rue Dénecourt

Jardin
de Diane

Cour
des
Princes

Cour
des
Cuisines

Grand Canal

Place du
Général
de Gaulle

Château de
Fontainebleau

Cour
Ovale

Rue-Royale

Cour du
Cheval Blanc

Double-
Horseshoe
Staircase

Cour
de la
Fontaine

Cascade

Rue-St-Louis

Boulevard-Magenta

Jardin
Anglais

Étang des
Carpes

Étang
Tibre

Jardin
Français

To Forêt de
Fontainebleau
(200m)

PLACES TO STAY
8 Hôtel La Carpe d'Or
9 Hôtel Legris et Parc
11 Hôtel de la Chancellerie
15 Hôtel Richelieu
19 Hôtel de Londres

PLACES TO EAT
1 Ty Koz
2 Covered Food Market
3 Fromagerie Bathélemy
4 Monoprix Supermarket
6 Pizza Mimi
10 La Route du Beaujolais
13 Croquembouche
14 Chez Arrighi
16 Maharaja
20 François 1er/Chez Bernard

OTHER
5 Cycles À La Petite Reine
7 Town Hall
12 Post Office
17 Théâtre Municipal
18 Tourist Office
21 Chateau Main Entrance

AROUND PARIS

Leczinska in 1725 and where the future Napoleon III was christened in 1810. **Galerie François 1er**, a gem of Renaissance architecture, was decorated from 1533 to 1540 by Il Rosso, a Florentine follower of Michelangelo. In the wood panelling, François I's monogram appears repeatedly along with his emblem, a dragon-like salamander.

The mid-16th-century **Salle de Bal**, a ballroom 30m long that was also used for receptions and banquets, is renowned for its mythological frescoes, marquetry floor and Italian-inspired coffered ceiling. The large windows afford views of the Cour

Ovale and the gardens. The gilded bed in the 17th- and 18th-century **Chambre de l'Impératrice** was never used by Marie-Antoinette, for whom it was built in 1787. The gilding in the **Salle du Trône**, the royal bedroom before the Napoleonic period, is in three shades: yellowish, greenish and golden.

The **Petits Appartements** were the private apartments of the emperor and empress. They do not have fixed opening hours but are usually open 9 am to 5 pm on Monday. There may be a separate admission fee to view them.

Museums The Musée Napoléon 1er within the chateau has a collection of personal effects (uniforms, hats, ornamented swords, coats) and knick-knacks that belonged to Napoleon and his relatives. It is currently undergoing renovation.

The four rooms of the **Musée Chinois** (Chinese Museum) are filled with beautiful ceramics and other objects brought to France from eastern Asia during the 19th century. Some of the items, from the personal collection of Empress Eugénie (wife of Napoleon III), were gifts of a delegation that came from Siam (Thailand) in 1861. Others were stolen by a Franco-British expeditionary force sent to China in 1860. The Musée Chinois keeps the same hours as the chateau.

Gardens On the northern side of the chateau, the **Jardin de Diane**, a formal garden created by Catherine de Médici, is home to a flock of noisy *paons* (peacocks). The marble fountain in the middle of the garden, decorated with a statue of Diana, goddess of the hunt, and four urinating dogs, dates from 1603.

Le Nôtre's formal, 17th-century **Jardin Français** (French Garden), also known as the Grand Parterre, is east of the **Cour de la Fontaine** (Fountain Courtyard) and the **Étang des Carpes** (Carp Pond). The **Grand Canal** was excavated in 1609 and predates the canals at Versailles by over half a century. The informal **Jardin Anglais** (English Garden), laid out in 1812, is west of the pond. The **Forêt de Fontainebleau**, crisscrossed by paths, begins 500m south of the chateau.

Opening Hours & Tickets The interior of the chateau (enter from the Cour du Cheval Blanc) opens 9.30 am to 12.30 pm and 2 to 5 pm Wednesday to Monday (no midday closure from June to September and until 6 pm in July and August). The last visitors are admitted an hour before closing time. Tickets for the Grands Appartements and the Musée Chinois, valid for the day, cost 35FF (those aged 18 to 25 and, on Sunday, for everyone 23FF, free for under 18s).

Conducted tours in English of the Grands Appartements depart several times a day from the staircase near the ticket windows.

The gardens (free) are open 9 am to 7 pm May to September, to 5 pm in spring and autumn, and to 5 pm in winter.

Forêt de Fontainebleau

This 20,000-hectare forest, which surrounds the town of Fontainebleau, is one of the loveliest woods in the Paris region, boasting oaks, beeches, birches and planted pines. The many trails – including parts of the GR1 and GR11 – are great for jogging, hiking, cycling, horse riding and climbing. The area is covered by IGN's 1:25,000-scale map No 2417OT, entitled *Forêt de Fontainebleau* (58FF). The tourist office sells a small topoguide, *Guide des Sentiers de Promenades dans le Massif Forestier de Fontainebleau* (60FF), whose maps and text (in French) cover almost 20 walks in the forest. It also sells the more comprehensive *La Forêt de Fontainebleau* (79FF), published by the Office National des Foretes, with details of 33 walks.

Places to Stay

Old-fashioned but comfortable, the 25-room *Hôtel de la Chancellerie* (☎ 01 64 22 21 70,✉ hotel.chancellerie@gofornet .com, 1 rue de la Chancellerie) has spotless singles/doubles/triples with shower and toilet for 220/280/320FF; prices between April and October are roughly 50FF more. You might also try the partially renovated *Hôtel La Carpe d'Or* (☎ 01 64 22 28 64, fax 01 64 22 39 95, 7 rue d'Avon) with 16 rooms. Singles/doubles with showers cost 225/ 295FF and there are larger rooms for three or four for 370FF. It costs 35FF to park in their garage.

The 18-room *Hôtel Richelieu* (☎ 01 64 22 26 46, fax 01 64 23 40 17, 4 rue Richelieu), just north of the chateau, has singles with shower from 260FF to 310FF, depending on the season, and doubles from 290FF to 340FF. It's part of the Logis de France group – always a sign of quality.

If you want to splurge, Fontainebleau can oblige. First choice should be the lovely

32-room *Hôtel Legris et Parc* (☎ *01 64 22 24 24, fax 01 64 22 22 05, 36 rue Paul Seramy*), which abuts the palace park and an old synagogue. Singles start at 300FF, doubles cost 350FF to 570FF and triples 570FF to 620FF.

Another fine choice is the 12-room *Hôtel de Londres* (☎ *01 64 22 20 21, fax 01 60 72 39 16, 1 place du Général de Gaulle*) opposite the chateau's main entrance. Singles/doubles with everything go for 450FF in winter and 650/750FF in summer.

Places to Eat
Restaurants Two excellent choices on rue de France are *Chez Arrighi* (☎ *01 64 22 29 43*) at No 53, whose Corsican two-course formule are 120FF and 148FF and three-course *menus* 98FF, 145FF and 195FF (open lunch and dinner Tuesday to Sunday), and *Croquembouche* (☎ *01 64 22 01 57*) at No 43, where the *menus* go for 88FF and 125FF (at lunch), 135FF (till 10 pm) and 210FF. The latter is open for lunch Friday to Tuesday and for dinner Thursday to Tuesday. The *François 1er/Chez Bernard* (☎ *01 64 22 24 68, 3 rue Royale*) has excellent specialities from Normandy and Brittany (especially seafood) and *menus* at 98FF and 160FF. Expect to pay about 220FF per person if ordering a la carte.

La Route du Beaujolais (☎ *01 64 22 27 98, 3 rue Montebello*) is no great shakes but it's central, reliable and open daily. Lyon-inspired *menus* are 75FF at lunch and 85FF and 130FF at dinner; expect to pay about 180FF if ordering à la carte.

The *Maharaja* (☎ *01 64 22 14 64, 15 rue Dénecourt*) has curries (46FF to 65FF) and tandoori dishes (35FF to 48FF) as well as standard starters like pakoras and samosas for 22FF to 26FF. There are lunchtime *menus* for 59FF and 89FF and one at dinner for 99FF. It's open for lunch and dinner Monday to Saturday.

For Breton crepes and galettes (15FF to 45FF), head for *Ty Koz* (☎ *01 64 22 00 55*) down a little alleyway from 18 rue de la Cloche. It opens noon to 10 pm daily. *Pizza Mimi* (☎ *01 64 22 70 77, 17 rue des Trois Maillets*) has pizzas (44FF to 56FF), pasta

(40FF to 57FF) and more elaborate Italian main courses (69FF to 75FF) available at lunch and dinner daily.

Self-Catering The covered *food market* on rue des Pins opens dawn to 4 pm Tuesday, Friday and Sunday. The *Monoprix (58 rue Grande)* opens from 8.45 am to 7.45 pm Monday to Saturday; the food section is on the 1st floor. The *Fromagerie Bathélemy* (☎ *01 64 22 21 64, 92 rue Grande*) a few doors north is one of the finest cheese shops in the Île de France. It's open 8 or 8.30 am to 12.30 or 1 pm and 3.30 to 7.30 Tuesday to Saturday and on Sunday morning.

Getting There & Away
Up to three dozen daily commuter trains link Fontainebleau-Avon with Paris' Gare de Lyon (48FF, 40 to 60 minutes); in off-peak periods, there's about one train an hour. The last train back to Paris leaves Fontainebleau a bit after 9.45 pm (just after 10.30 pm on Sunday and holidays). SNCF has a package that includes return transport to and from Paris, bus transfers to the chateau and admission for 125/100/50FF for adults/children aged 10 to 17/children under 10).

Getting Around
The tourist office rents bikes for 80/100FF per half/full day. Cycles À La Petite Reine (☎ *01 60 74 57 57*), 32 rue des Sablons, rents mountain bikes year round for 30FF per hour and 60/80FF per half/full day (80/100FF at the weekend). The weekly tariff is 350FF. A 2000FF deposit is required. The shop opens 9 am to 7.30 pm Monday to Saturday and to 6 pm on Sunday.

CHANTILLY
postcode 60500 • pop 10,900 • elevation 59m
The elegant town of Chantilly, 48km north of Paris, is best known for its heavily restored but imposing chateau, surrounded by gardens, lakes and a vast forest. The chateau is just over 2km east of the train station. The most direct route is to walk

through the Forêt de Chantilly along ave de la Plaine des Aigles, but you will get a better sense of the town by taking ave du Maréchal Joffre onto rue de Paris to connect with rue du Connétable, Chantilly's main thoroughfare.

Information

The tourist office (☎ 03 44 57 08 58, fax 03 44 57 74 64), 60 ave du Maréchal Joffre, opens 9 am to 7 pm daily May to September. It opens 9.30 am to 12.30 pm and 2.15 to 6 pm Monday to Saturday during the rest of the year. The tourist office Web site is at www.ville-chantilly.fr.

Société Générale bank (☎ 03 44 62 57 00), 1 ave du Maréchal Joffre, opens 8.30 am to 12.15 pm and 1.45 to 5.25 pm on weekdays and to 4.15 pm on Saturday. There's a post office at 26 ave du Maréchal Joffre open 9 am to 12.15 pm and 1.45 to 6 pm weekdays, and on Saturday from 9 am to 12.30 pm.

Château de Chantilly

The chateau (☎ 03 44 62 62 62), left in a shambles after the Revolution, is of interest mainly because of its gardens and a number of superb paintings. It consists of two attached buildings entered through the same vestibule. The **Petit Château** was built around 1560 for Anne de Montmorency (1492–1567), who served six French kings as *connétable* (high constable), diplomat and warrior and died in battle against the Protestants. The attached Renaissance-style **Grand Château**, completely demolished during the Revolution, was rebuilt by the Duke of Aumale, son of King Louis-Philippe, in the late 1870s. It served as a French military headquarters during WWI.

The Grand Château, to the right as you enter the vestibule, contains the **Musée Condé**. Its unremarkable 19th-century rooms are adorned with furnishings, paintings and sculptures haphazardly arranged according to the whims of the duke, who

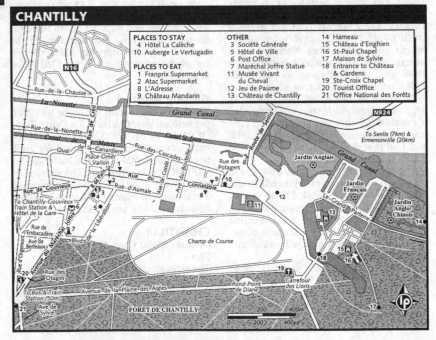

CHANTILLY

PLACES TO STAY
4 Hôtel La Calèche
10 Auberge Le Vertugadin

PLACES TO EAT
1 Franprix Supermarket
2 Atac Supermarket
8 L'Adresse
9 Château Mandarin

OTHER
3 Société Générale
5 Hôtel de Ville
6 Post Office
7 Maréchal Joffre Statue
11 Musée Vivant du Cheval
12 Jeu de Paume
13 Château de Chantilly

14 Hameau
15 Château d'Enghien
16 St-Paul Chapel
17 Maison de Sylvie
18 Entrance to Château & Gardens
19 Ste-Croix Chapel
20 Tourist Office
21 Office National des Forêts

donated the chateau to the Institut de France at the end of the 19th century on condition that the exhibits not be reorganised. The most remarkable works are hidden away in a small room called the **Sanctuaire**, including paintings by Raphael (1483–1520), Filippino Lippi (1457–1504) and Jean Fouquet (1415–80).

The Petit Château contains the **Appartements des Princes** (Princes' Apartments), which are straight ahead from the entrance. The highlight here is the **Cabinet des Livres**, a repository of 700 manuscripts and over 12,000 volumes including a Gutenberg Bible and a facsimile of the *Très Riches Heures du Duc de Berry*, an illuminated manuscript dating from the 15th century that illustrates the calendar year for the peasantry and the nobility. The chapel, to the left as you walk into the vestibule, is made up of mid-16th-century woodwork and windows assembled by the Duke of Aumale in 1882.

Gardens The chateau's excellent but long-neglected gardens were once among the most spectacular in France. The formal **Jardin Français**, whose flower beds, lakes and Grand Canal were laid out by Le Nôtre in the mid-17th century, is north-east of the main building. To the west, the 'wilder' **Jardin Anglais** was begun in 1817. East of the Jardin Français is the rustic **Jardin Anglo-Chinois** (Anglo-Chinese Garden), created in the 1770s. Its foliage and silted-up waterways surround the **hameau** (hamlet), a mock rural village whose mill and half-timbered buildings, built in 1774, inspired the hameau at Versailles. Crème Chantilly, cream beaten with icing and vanilla sugar and dolloped on everything sweet that doesn't move in France, was born here (see the boxed text 'Château de Whipped Cream').

Activities There are a couple of attractions in the gardens that will keep the kids (and maybe even you) happy. The **Áerophile**, the world's largest hot-air balloon, takes on passengers and soars 150m up into the sky (it's attached to a cable), offering views as far as Paris (they say) on a clear day. The **Hydrophile**, an electric boat, silently slips along the Grand Canal. Admission to the Áerophile and park costs 66FF (those aged 12 to 17 60FF, children aged three to 11 38FF). The **Hydrophile** and park cost 52/47/30FF. Both are open from 10 am to 7 pm March to October. Combination tickets including admission to the chateau, the Musée Vivant du Cheval (see the following) and rides on either the balloon or the boat are available. For information ring ☎ 03 44 57 35 35.

Musée Vivant du Cheval The chateau's **Grandes Écuries** (Great Stables), built from 1719 to 1740 to house 240 horses and over 400 hunting hounds, are next to Chantilly's famous **Champ de Course** (racecourse), inaugurated in 1834. They house the Living Horse Museum (☎ 03 44 57 40 40), whose equines live in luxurious **wooden stalls** built by Louis-Henri de Bourbon, the seventh prince de Condé. Displays, in 31

Château de Whipped Cream

Like every self-respecting French chateau of the 18th century, the one at Chantilly had its own *hameau* (hamlet), a mock rural village complete with *laitier* (dairy) where the lady of the household and her guests could play at being milkmaid. But the cows at Chantilly's dairy took their job rather seriously, and news of the sweet cream served at the hamlet's teas became the talk (and envy) of aristocratic Europe. The future Habsburg emperor Joseph II visited this *temple de marbre* (marble temple) incognito in 1777, and when the Baroness of Oberkirch tasted the goods she cried: 'Never have I eaten such good cream, so appetising, so well-prepared.'

Not to be outdone, the Château de Fontainebleau has lent its name to yet another sweet dairy product. Take some *fromage frais* (curds or cottage cheese), fold in Chantilly and – *voilà!* – you've got Fontainebleau, a triple-cream cheese.

---

rooms, include everything from riding equipment to horse toys and paintings of famous nags. The museum opens 10.30 am to 5.30 pm (6 pm at the weekend) April to October; it's closed on Tuesday except in May and June (open on Tuesday afternoons in July and August). From November to March it opens 2 to 5 pm Wednesday to Monday; it's open from 10.30 am to 5.30 pm at the weekend. Admission costs 50FF (aged 12 to 17 40FF, children aged three to 11 35FF).

The 30-minute **Présentation Équestre Pédagogique** (Introduction to Dressage Riding), included in the admission price, generally takes place at 11.30 am, 3.30 and 5.15 pm (3.30 pm only from November to March). More elaborate, hour-long demonstrations of dressage riding (100FF, children aged four to 12 90FF) are held on the first Sunday of the month at 3.30 pm from February to November.

Opening Hours & Tickets The chateau and Musée Condé are open 10 am to 6 pm Wednesday to Monday. The hours are 10.30 am to 12.45 pm and 2 to 5 pm on the same days from November to February. Ticket sales end 45 minutes before closing time. Admission to the chateau and its park, which opens daily, costs 42FF (those aged 12 to 17 37FF, children aged three to 11 15FF). Admission to just the park costs 17FF (10FF).

Forêt de Chantilly

The Chantilly Forest, once a royal hunting estate, covers some 15,000 hectares. Its tree cover, patchy in places because of poor soil and overgrazing by deer, includes beeches, oaks, chestnuts, limes and pines.

The forest is crisscrossed by a variety of walking and riding trails. In some areas, straight paths laid out centuries ago meet at multi-angled *carrefours* (crossroads). Long-distance trails that pass through the Forêt de Chantilly include the **GR11**, which links the chateau with the town of Senlis and its wonderful cathedral; the **GR1**, which goes from Luzarches (famed for its 16th-century cathedral) to Ermenonville; and the **GR12**, which goes north-eastwards from four lakes known as the **Étangs de Commelles** to the Forêt d'Halatte.

The area is covered by IGN's 1:25,000-scale map No 2412OT (58FF), which is entitled *Forêts de Chantilly, d'Halatte and d'Ermenonville*. The *Carte de Découverte des Milieux Naturels et du Patrimoine Bâti* (40FF), a 1:100,000-scale map available at the tourist office, indicates sites of historic and tourist interest (for example, churches, chateaux, museums and ruins). The Office National des Forêts (ONF; ☎ 03 44 57 03 88, fax 03 44 57 91 67), south of the tourist office at the start of Route de l'Aigle, publishes a good walking guide for families titled *Promenons-nous dans les forêts de Picardie* (49FF). It also organises forest walks departing at 3 pm on Sunday from June to September.

Places to Stay

The friendly (since the management and name changed) *Auberge Le Vertugadin* (☎ 03 44 57 03 19, fax 03 44 57 92 31, 44 rue du Connétable), with seven rooms, has large and cheery singles and doubles with shower for 230FF and triples for 290FF. Reception is in the restaurant (see Places to Eat below).

Hôtel La Calèche (☎ 03 44 57 02 55, 3 ave du Maréchal Joffre) has rooms for up to three people uniformly priced at 240FF. *Hôtel de la Gare* (☎ 03 44 62 56 90, fax 03 44 62 56 99), just opposite the train station on place de la Gare, is a surprisingly pleasant place with shower-equipped doubles for 290FF.

Places to Eat

The restaurant at the *Auberge Le Vertugadin*, with starters for around 50FF, main courses for 85FF and *menus* for 98FF and 150FF, is highly recommended. Other restaurants on the rue du Connétable include the bistro-like *L'Adresse* (☎ 03 44 57 27 74) at No 49, and the *Château Mandarin* (☎ 03 44 57 00 29), a Chinese restaurant at No 62. L'Adresse has starters from 40FF to 48FF, mains for 75FF to 98FF, two-course formules at 98FF and a *menu* for 145FF. It's open from noon to 2 pm Tuesday to Sunday and 7 to 10 pm Tuesday to Saturday. The Château Mandarin has starters in the 25FF to 35FF range, main courses for 40FF to 96FF and a 76FF lunch *menu*. It opens for lunch and dinner to 9.30pm Tuesday to Sunday.

Midway between the train station and the chateau, the *Atac* supermarket *(place Omer Vallon)* opens 8.30 am to 7.30 pm from Monday to Saturday. There's a *Franprix (132 rue du Connétable)* open 8.30 am to 7.30 pm Tuesday to Saturday and from 8.45 am to 12.45 pm on Sunday.

Getting There & Away
Paris' Gare du Nord is linked to Chantilly-Gouvieux train station (42FF, 30 to 45 minutes) by a mixture of RER and SNCF commuter trains; there's a total of almost 40 a day (about two dozen on Sunday). In the morning, there are departures from Gare du Nord at least twice an hour; in the evening, there are generally trains back to Paris every hour or so until just before midnight.

The two dozen weekday trains (signposted for a variety of destinations, including Compiègne, St-Quentin, Amiens and Creil) start at Gare du Nord, where Chantilly-bound trains use both the Grandes Lignes and Banlieues platforms. The bus station is next to the train station.

CHARTRES
postcode 28000 • pop 40,300 • elevation 142m
The magnificent 13th-century cathedral of Chartres, crowned by two very different spires – one Gothic, the other Romanesque – rises from rich farmland 88km south-west of Paris and dominates the medieval town around its base.

The cathedral's varied collection of relics (particularly the Ste-Chemise, a piece of cloth claimed to have been worn by the Virgin Mary when she gave birth to Jesus) attracted many pilgrims during the Middle Ages. Indeed, the town of Chartres has been attracting pilgrims for over 2000 years: Gallic Druids may have had a sanctuary here, and the Romans apparently built themselves a temple dedicated to the Dea Mater (mother goddess), later interpreted by Christian missionaries as prefiguring the Virgin Mary.

Information
The tourist office (☎ 02 37 18 26 26, @ chartres.tourism@wanadoo.fr) is across place de la Cathédrale from the cathedral's main entrance. It opens 9 am to 7 pm Monday to Saturday and 9.30 am to 5.30 pm on Sunday from April to September. The hours are 10 am to 6 pm Monday to Saturday and 10 am to 1 pm and 2.30 to 4.30 pm on Sunday during the rest of the year.

The Banque de France, 32 rue du Docteur Maunoury, opens for exchange from 9 am to 12.30 pm weekdays. There's a BNP (☎ 0 802 35 63 91) at 9 place des Épars; it opens 8.30 am till noon and 1.30 to 5.30 pm Tuesday to Friday and to 4.30 pm on Saturday. The impressive neo-Gothic main post office on place des Épars opens 8.30 am to 7 pm weekdays and from 8.30 am to noon on Saturday.

Cathédrale Notre Dame
Chartres' 130m-long cathedral (☎ 02 37 21 75 02), one of the crowning architectural achievements of western civilisation, was built in the Gothic style during the first quarter of the 13th century to replace a Romanesque cathedral that had been devastated – along with much of the town – by fire on the night of 10 June 1194. Because of effective fundraising among the aristocracy and donations of labour by the common folk, construction took only 30 years, resulting in a high degree of architectural unity. It is France's best-preserved medieval cathedral, having been spared both post-medieval modifications and the ravages of war and the Revolution (see the boxed text 'Saved by Red Tape' later in this section).

Opening Hours & Guided Tours The cathedral opens 7.30 am (8.30 am on Sunday) to 7.15 pm daily, except during Mass, weddings and funerals. There are wonderful 1½ hour English-language tours (35FF, students 25FF) conducted by Chartres expert

CHARTRES

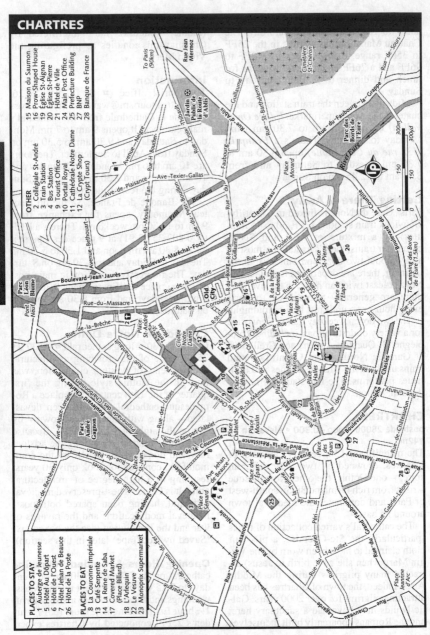

PLACES TO STAY
1 Auberge de Jeunesse
5 Hôtel Au Départ
6 Hôtel de l'Ouest
7 Hôtel Jehan de Beauce
26 Hôtel de la Poste

PLACES TO EAT
8 La Couronne Impériale
13 Café Serpente
16 La Reine de Saba
17 Covered Market
18 L'Arlequin
22 Le Vesuve
23 Monoprix Supermarket

OTHER
2 Collégiale St-André
3 Train Station
4 Bus Station
9 Tourist Office
10 Portail Royal
11 Cathédrale Notre Dame
12 La Crypte Shop (Crypt Tours)
15 Maison du Saumon
16 Prow-Shaped House
19 Église St-Aignan
20 Église St-Pierre
21 Hôtel de Ville
24 Main Post Office
25 Prefecture Building
27 BNP
28 Banque de France

AROUND PARIS

Malcolm Miller (☎ 02 37 28 15 58, fax 02 37 28 33 03) that depart at noon and 2.45 pm Monday to Saturday from Easter to sometime in November. If you miss one of his tours, buy one of Miller's books at the cathedral gift shop: *Chartres* (30FF) or *Chartres Cathedral* (110FF; hard-bound 150FF). Audioguide tours in English lasting 25 to 70 minutes (15FF to 30FF) can be hired from the cathedral bookshop.

Portals & Towers All three of the cathedral's entrances have superbly ornamented triple portals, but the west entrance, known as the **Portail Royal** (Royal Portal), is the only one that predates the fire. Carved from 1145 to 1155, its superb statues, whose features are elongated in the Romanesque style, represent the glory of Christ in the centre and the Nativity and Ascension to the right and the left.

The structure's other main Romanesque feature is the 105m **Clocher Vieux** (Old Bell Tower), also known as the Tour Sud (South Tower), which was begun in the 1140s. It is the tallest Romanesque steeple still standing.

A visit to the 112m-high **Clocher Neuf** (New Bell Tower) – also known as the Tour Nord (North Tower) – is well worth the ticket price and the long, spiral climb. Access is via the northern transept. A 70m-high platform on the lacy, Flamboyant Gothic spire, built from 1507 to 1513 by Jehan de Beauce after an earlier wooden spire burned down, affords superb views of the three-tiered flying buttresses and the 19th-century copper roof, turned green by verdigris. The Clocher Neuf opens 9.30 or 10 to 11.30 am and 2 to 4 pm Monday to Saturday, and 1 to 2 pm on Sunday from November to February (to 5 pm on Sunday in March, April, September and October). It opens 9 am to 6 pm Monday to Saturday and from 1 to 6.30 pm on Sunday from May to August. Admission costs 25FF (those aged 12 to 25 15FF, free for children under 12 and on certain Sundays).

Stained-Glass Windows The cathedral's extraordinary 172 stained-glass windows,

almost all of which are 13th-century originals, form one of the most important ensembles of medieval stained glass in Europe. The three most important windows dating from before the 13th century are in the wall above the west entrance, below the rose window. Survivors of the fire of 1194 (they were made around 1150), the windows are renowned for the depth and intensity of their blue tones, a colour known as Chartres blue.

Trésor & Crypte Chapelle St-Piat, up the stairs at the far end of the choir, houses the cathedral's treasury, including the Ste-Chemise, which is also known as the Voile de Notre Dame (Veil of Our Lady). It is currently undergoing renovation.

The cathedral's 110m-long crypt, a tombless Romanesque structure built circa 1024 around a 9th-century crypt, is the largest in France. Guided tours in French (with a written English translation) lasting 30 minutes start at La Crypte (☎ 02 37 21 56 33), the cathedral-run shop selling religious items at 18 Cloître Notre Dame. There are four or five tours a day (two a day from November to March); year round, there are departures at 11 am and 4.15 or 4.30 pm. Tickets cost 15FF (students and seniors 10FF, free for those under seven).

Old City

Chartres' carefully preserved old city is north-east and east of the cathedral along the narrow western channel of the River Eure, which is spanned by a number of footbridges. From rue du Cardinal Pie, the stairway called **Tertre St-Nicolas** and **rue Chantault** – the latter is lined with old houses – lead down to the empty shell of the 12th-century **Collégiale St-André**, a Romanesque collegiate church closed in 1791 and severely damaged in the early 19th century and again in 1944.

Rue de la Tannerie, and its continuation **rue de la Foulerie**, along the river's eastern bank, are lined with flower gardens, mill-races and the restored remnants of riverside trades: wash houses, tanneries and the like. **Rue aux Juifs** (Street of the Jews) has been extensively renovated. Half a block down the hill there's a riverside promenade and up the hill **rue des Écuyers** has many houses from around the 16th century, including a prow-shaped, half-timbered structure at No 26 with its upper section supported by beams. **Rue du Bourg** and **rue de la Poissonerie** also have some old half-timbered houses; look for the magnificent **Maison du Saumon** (Salmon House) built in 1500.

From **place St-Pierre**, you get a good view of the flying buttresses holding up the 12th- and 13th-century **Église St-Pierre**. Once part of a Benedictine monastery founded in the 7th century, it was outside the city walls and was vulnerable to attack; the fortress-like, pre-Romanesque **bell tower** attached to it was used as a refuge by monks and dates from around 1000. The fine, brightly coloured **clerestory windows** in the nave, choir and apse are from the mid-13th and early 14th centuries. It opens 10 am to noon and 2 to 5 pm daily.

Église St-Aignan, on place St-Aignan and built in the early 16th century, is interesting for its wooden barrel-vault roof (1625) and its painted interior of faded blue and gold floral motifs (circa 1870). The stained glass and the Renaissance Chapelle de St-Michel date from the 16th century. It's open 9 am to noon and 2 to 6.30 pm daily.

Places to Stay

Camping About 2.5km south-east of the train station, *Camping des Bords de l'Eure* (☎ 02 37 28 79 43, 9 rue de Launay) opens from May to early September. From the train station or place des Épars take bus No 8 (direction Hôpital) to the Launay stop.

Hostel The 70-bed *Auberge de Jeunesse* (☎ 02 37 34 27 64, fax 02 37 35 75 85, 23 ave Neigre) is about 1.5km east of the train station via blvd Charles Péguy and blvd Jean Jaurès. A bed in this pleasant hostel costs about 68FF, including breakfast (sheets: 17FF). Reception opens from 2 to 10 pm daily. Curfew is 10.30 pm in winter and 11.30 pm in summer. To get there from the train station, take bus No 5 (direction Mare aux Moines) to the Rouliers stop.

Hotels The 29-room *Hôtel de l'Ouest* (☎ 02 37 21 43 27, 3 place Pierre Sémard) has somewhat dingy rooms with washbasin for 120FF, with shower and toilet for 190FF and with bath, toilet and TV from 210FF to 260FF. The hall shower costs 10FF.

Almost next door is the *Hôtel Jehan de Beauce* (☎ 02 37 21 01 41, fax 02 37 21 59 10), on the 1st floor of 19 ave Jehan de Beauce. This 46-room hotel has clean, decent singles/doubles from 160/180FF (200/240FF with shower and toilet). Triples are also available for 315FF.

You might also try the eight-room *Hôtel Au Départ* (☎ 02 37 36 80 43, 1 rue Nicole), where singles/doubles/triples with washbasin and bidet are 120/190/300FF. Reception (at the Brasserie L'Ouest at 9 place Pierre Sémard) is closed on Sunday. The Near place des Épars *Hôtel de la Poste* (☎ 02 37 21 04 27, fax 02 37 36 42 3, rue du Général Koenig 17), with 57 rooms, has singles with shower/shower and toilet for 250/290FF, doubles with shower/shower and toilet for 320/350FF and triples/quads for 380/450FF.

Places to Eat

Restaurants *L'Arlequin* (☎ 02 37 34 88 57, 8 rue de la Porte Cendreuse), features freshly caught fish dishes for 72FF to 85FF, with starters for 33FF to 75FF and a lunchtime *menu* at 95FF. Evening *menus* are 120FF and 150FF. It's open for lunch Tuesday to Friday and on Sunday and dinner till 11 pm from Tuesday to Saturday.

The *Café Serpente* (☎ 02 37 21 68 81, 2 Cloître Notre Dame), a brasserie and *salon de thé*, serves meals from 10 am to 1 am daily. The plat du jour is 78FF to 98FF, salads are 69FF to 79FF. *La Reine de Saba* (☎ 02 37 21 89 16, 8 Cloître Notre Dame), has lunch *menus* for 69FF and 99FF. This casual French restaurant opens from 11.30 am to 8 pm daily (to 9.30 or 10 pm at the weekend and from July to mid-September).

At *Le Vesuve* (☎ 02 37 21 56 35, 30 place des Halles), pizzas (35FF to 60FF), salads (42FF to 48FF) and light meals are served noon to 3 pm and 7 to 11 pm daily. *La Couronne Impériale* (☎ 02 37 21 87 59, 7–9 rue de la Couronne) has Chinese and Vietnamese starters for 25FF to 50FF, main courses for 40FF to 66FF and dim sum for 26FF to 33FF. *Menus* are available at 60FF and 82FF. It's open for lunch and dinner Tuesday to Sunday.

Self-Catering There are a number of *food shops* around the *covered market* on rue des Changes (open until about 1 pm Saturday). The *Monoprix (21 rue Noël Ballay)* opens 9 am to 7.30 pm Monday to Saturday.

Getting There & Away

There are some three dozen trains a day (20 on Sunday) to/from Paris' Gare Montparnasse (72FF, 55 to 70 minutes) that also stop at Versailles' Chantiers station (61FF, 45 minutes). The last train back to Paris leaves Chartres a bit after 9 pm (7.40 pm on Saturday, sometime after 10 pm on Sunday and holidays).

Far Northern France

Travellers coming from the UK or Belgium usually first set foot on French soil in the far north, an area made up of three historical regions: Flanders (Flandre or Flandres), Artois and Picardy (Picardie). Le Nord de France – densely populated and laden with rust belt industry: its major heavy industries in decline – is not one of the more fabled corners of France but, if you're just making a short trip from the UK or inclined to do a little exploring, the region offers lots to do and some excellent dining.

In the Middle Ages the region nearest the Belgian border, together with much of Belgium and part of the Netherlands, made up a feudal principality known as Flanders. Many people in the area still speak Flemish, which is essentially Dutch with some variances in pronunciation and vocabulary. Unlike elsewhere in France, the locals drink more beer than wine, especially during the carnivals or annual fairs known as *braderies*, when 'giants' come out of hiding (see the boxed text 'The Giants' later in this chapter).

Lille, the region's commercial and cultural capital, is only two hours from London by Eurostar. Some 50km to the south, the 17th- and 18th-century, Flemish-style buildings that surround the central squares in picturesque Arras have no equal anywhere in France. Amiens, not far from a number of sobering battlefield memorials from WWI, is graced by one of France's most magnificent Gothic cathedrals.

Calais' prosperity as the premier trans-Channel port has come partly at the expense of nearby Boulogne-sur-Mer and Dunkirk (Dunkerque). The spectacular Côte d'Opale stretches from Calais to Boulogne along the Straits of Dover (Pas de Calais), the narrowest bit of the English Channel (La Manche).

In the south of the region Beauvais, with its elegant cathedral, and Compiègne, a one-time royal hunting retreat, are popular with Paris day-trippers.

Highlights

- **Côte d'Opale** – gaze across at the white cliffs of Dover in England from this spectacular coastline
- **Sangatte and Wissant** – lounge in the sun on sandy Channel beaches
- **Lille** – visit the city's superb museums; explore its old town, restaurants and lively nightlife
- **Arras** – stroll among the Flemish-style arcades of the Grand' place and place des Héros
- **Compiègne** – try to feel sporting at the grand Château de Compiègne, where Napoleon III threw his hunting parties
- **Beauvais** – marvel at Cathédrale St-Pierre, with the highest Gothic vaults ever built

NETHERLANDS

BELGIUM

Far Northern France p303

Côte d'Opale p315

Calais p310

Boulogne-sur-Mer p317

NORD-PAS-DE-CALAIS

Lille p304

Arras p322

Amiens p329

Battle of the Somme Memorials p325

HAUTE-NORMANDIE

PICARDIE

Beauvais p333

Compiègne p335

CHAMPAGNE

LILLE

postcodes 59800 (east) 59000 (west)
● pop 1.1 million ● elevation 10m

Thanks to Eurostar and other fast rail links, Lille – France's northernmost metropolis –

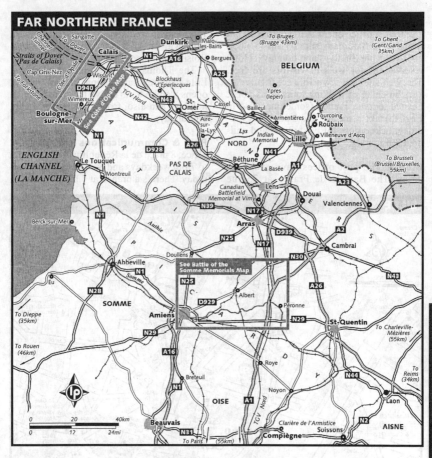

FAR NORTHERN FRANCE

is a popular first stop for visitors coming from across the Channel and Belgium. Long a major industrial centre, today's Lille is a lively, forward-looking place, with two renowned art museums and an attractive old town graced with ornate Flemish-style buildings. Charles de Gaulle was born in Lille in 1890.

Orientation

Lille is centred around three public squares: place du Général de Gaulle (also known as the Grand' place), place du Théâtre and place Rihour. Vieux Lille (old Lille) is on the northern side, while the imposing Citadelle lies north-west of the centre.

Gare Lille-Flandres is about 400m south-east of place du Général de Gaulle; the ultra-modern Gare Lille-Europe is 500m farther east. The cavernous Euralille shopping centre lies between the two stations.

Information

Tourist Offices The tourist office (☎ 03 20 21 94 21, fax 03 20 21 94 20, ☻ ot.lille@ wanadoo.fr), place Rihour, occupies a remnant of 15th-century Palais Rihour, a former residence of the dukes of Burgundy; a war memorial forms the structure's eastern side. The tourist office opens 9.30 am to 6.30 pm Monday to Saturday; and 10 am to noon and 2 to 5 pm Sundays and holidays. Hotel reservations for walk-in visitors are free. The Web site is at www.lille.cci.fr.

A brochure of walking tours costs 10FF. Guided tours in French (sometimes also in English) take place at 3 and 5 pm every Saturday; tickets cost 45FF (students and children 30FF).

Money The post offices have exchange desks. The Banque de France at 75 rue

Royale exchanges money from 8.30 am to 12.15 pm on weekdays. There's a Credit du Nord with an ATM at the corner of rue Jean Roisin and place Rihour.

The Thomas Cook exchange bureau at Lille-Flandres train station, behind track 8, opens 8 am to 8 pm daily (10 am to 6 pm on holidays and also, from October to March, on Sunday).

Post & Communications The main post office, 8 place de la République, opens 8 am to 7 pm weekdays and 8 am to noon on Saturday. There's a branch at 1 blvd Carnot, in

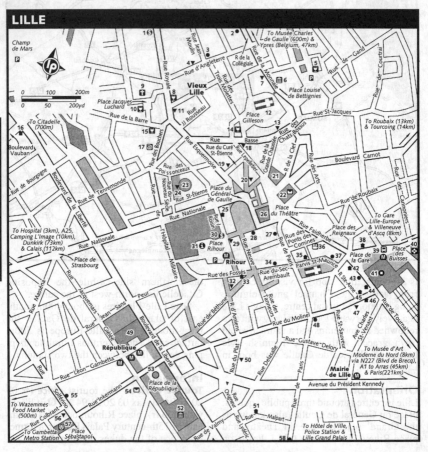

the Chambre de Commerce. Both have Cyberposte terminals. The city has two postcodes: the area east of blvd de la Liberté is 59800; to the west is 59000.

Net Arena Games (☎ 03 28 38 09 20), 10 rue des Bouchers, charges 20FF per half-hour of Web surfing.

Laundry Laverie O'Claire at 57 rue du Molinel lets you begin your last wash as late as 8 pm and your last dry cycle at 8.30 pm.

Medical Services The Cité Hospitalière (☎ 03 20 44 59 62, metro CHR Oscar Lambret), 3.5km south-west of the city centre, is a large hospital at place de Verdun. SOS Médecins (☎ 03 20 29 91 91) can send a doctor 24 hours.

Around the Centre

On place du Général de Gaulle, the ornate, Flemish Renaissance **Vieille Bourse** (Old Stock Exchange; 1652) consists of 24 separate buildings around a courtyard. A book market is held here daily except Sunday. On the southern side of the square, the Art

Deco home of **La Voix du Nord** (1932), the leading regional daily, has a gilded sculpture of three graces on top. The goddess-topped **column** (1845) in the fountain commemorates the Austrian siege of Lille in 1792.

Nearby, place du Théâtre is dominated by the neoclassical **Opéra** and the tower-topped neo-Flemish **Chambre de Commerce**, both of which were built in the early 20th century.

North of place du Général de Gaulle, **Vieux Lille** gleams with nicely restored 17th- and 18th-century houses. The old residences along rue de la Monnaie now house chic shops. Other streets with note-worthy buildings include rue de la Grande Chaussée and rue Esquermoise.

South of the centre on rue de Paris, the **Porte de Paris** is a triumphal arch (1685–92) celebrating the capture of Lille by Louis XIV in 1667. At place Roger Salengro, the vast, Art-Deco-style **town hall** (1924–32), has a slender *beffroi* (belfry). You can climb it from 9 to 11 am and 2 to 4 pm weekdays and from 9.30 am to noon on Sunday and holidays (closed

LILLE

PLACES TO STAY		47	Monoprix Supermarket	26	Vieille Bourse
16	Hôtel Le Globe	50	La Source	27	Le 30
25	Grand Hôtel Bellevue	56	Food Market	28	La Voix du Nord Building
33	Hôtel de France			30	Credit du Nord Bank; ATM
35	Hôtel Breughel	**OTHER**		31	Tourist Office
38	Hôtel Flandre-	1	Banque de France	34	FNAC Ticket Agency
	Angleterre	2	Lavarie Libre Service	36	Cinéma Metropole
42	Hôtel des Voyageurs		Laundrette	37	Eurolines Office
44	Hôtel Faidherbe	3	L'Angle Saxo	39	Gare Lille-Flandres
45	Hôtel Floréal	5	Café Oz		Metro Station; Thomas
46	Hôtel Moulin d'Or	6	Musée de l'Hospice		Cook Bureau; Local-
51	Auberge de Jeunesse		Comtesse		Suburban Bus Terminal
		8	L'Illustration Café	40	Euralille Shopping Centre
PLACES TO EAT		9	Église Ste-Catherine	41	Gare de Lille-Flandres
4	Plat Net Africa	10	Bar Rocambole	43	Europcar
7	La Pâte Brisée	12	Cathédrale Notre Dame	48	Laverie O'Claire
11	Moroccan Restaurant		de la Treille		Laundrette
13	À l'Huîtrière	14	Au Lieu d'Elles	49	Prefecture
18	Boulangerie	15	Le Balatum	52	Palais des Beaux-Arts
19	Fromagerie	17	Net Arena Games	53	Fountain
20	La Tarterie de la Voûte	21	Opéra	54	Main Post Office
24	Le Hochepot	22	Chambre de Commerce; Post	55	Laundrette
29	Brasserie La Chicorée		Office	57	Théâtre Sébastopol
32	Aux Moules	23	Palais de la Musique	58	Porte de Paris

Braderie de Lille

During the first weekend in September, Vieux Lille (Old Lille) and surrounding avenues are transformed into an enormous flea market – with stands selling antiques, local delicacies, handicrafts and more – called the Braderie de Lille. The 48-hour extravaganza, which has been expanded considerably over the years, is believed to date from the Middle Ages when the Lillois were allowed to hawk old garments from sundown to sun-up for extra cash.

It's the biggest bash of the year, running from Saturday evening to midnight and again from Sunday afternoon till the wee hours of the morning, when the street-sweepers emerge to tackle the mounds of mussel shells and old *frites* left behind by the hordes of merry-makers. Before the festivities, you can make room for all those extra calories by joining in the inner-city marathon held on Saturday morning (usually at 9 am). A free map of the market, *Braderie – le Plan*, is available from the tourist office.

Saturday), early April to September Admission costs 15FF (those aged 12 to 25, 5FF).

Museums

South of place de la République, Lille's outstanding **Palais des Beaux-Arts** (Fine Arts Museum; ☎ 03 20 06 78 17, metro République) possesses a superb collection of 15th- to 20th-century paintings and exhibits of archaeology, medieval sculpture and ceramics. It opens noon (2 pm on Monday) to 6 pm (8 pm on Friday); it's closed Tuesday and bank holidays. Tickets, valid the whole day, cost 30FF (students and children 20FF).

The **Musée de l'Hospice Comtesse** (☎ 03 20 49 50 90), 32 rue de la Monnaie, is housed in a lovely 17th-century former home for the poor (1236). The wood ceiling of the **Salle des Malades** (Hospital Hall) is decorated with Lille tapestries from 1704. Displays include ceramics, faïence wall tiles, 17th- and 18th-century paintings, furniture and religious art. It opens 10 am to 12.30 pm and 2 to 6 pm (closed Tuesday and most holidays). Admission costs 15FF (those aged 12 to 25, 5FF).

A few blocks north of Vieux Lille at 9 rue Princesse is the **Musée Charles de Gaulle** (☎ 03 20 31 96 03), in the house where the premier-to-be was born in 1890. Displays include photos, a dainty baptismal robe, and the Citroën in which de Gaulle narrowly escaped an assassination attempt in 1961. It opens 10 am to noon and 2 to 5 pm (closed

Monday, Tuesday and holidays). Admission costs 15FF (children aged under 12, 5FF).

The renowned **Musée d'Art Moderne du Nord** (☎ 03 20 19 68 68), 8km east of Lille in Villeneuve-d'Ascq, displays works by artists including Braque, Calder, Léger, Miró, Modigliani and Picasso. It opens 10 am to 6 pm daily (closed Tuesday); admission costs 25FF (students 15FF). Take metro line No 1 (towards 4 Cantons) to Pont de Bois, then bus No 41 to Parc Urbain-Musée.

Citadel

The world's greatest 17th-century military architect, Sébastien Le Prestre de Vauban (see the boxed text 'Vauban's Citadels' in the Facts about France chapter), constructed this massive star-shaped fortress after the capture of Lille by French forces in 1667. It still functions as a military base, but the outer ramparts are open to the public. There's a large, tree-shaded **park**, a **mini-amusement park** and a **children's play area** on the south-eastern side.

The tourist office runs two-hour tours (45FF) in French at 3 pm on Sunday, May to October; they begin at Porte Royale, the citadel's main gate.

Special Events

The Fêtes de Lille, a street theatre festival, takes place during the third weekend of June. The Braderie, which is an enormous flea market extraordinaire, is held on the first weekend of September (see the boxed text 'Braderie de Lille').

The Festival de Lille is a series of concerts and other cultural events that take place over four weeks in September and October.

The Festival Mozart, a programme of orchestral works, ballets and operas composed mainly by Wolfgang Amadeus, runs from November to late March. Tickets are sold at FNAC (see Entertainment later in this chapter). Contact the Lille tourist office for exact dates and details of all these events.

Christmas decorations and the like are on offer at the Marché de Noël (Christmas market) from late November to 31 December.

Places to Stay – Budget

Camping Ten kilometres north-west of Lille in the suburb of Houplines, *Camping L'Image* (☎ 03 20 35 69 42, 140 rue Brune) is open year-round. It charges 11/18FF per adult/tent. By car, take the A25 towards Dunkirk and get off at exit No 8 (Chapelle d'Armentières).

Hostels The modern, 170-bed *Auberge de Jeunesse* (☎ 03 20 57 08 94, fax 03 20 63 98 93, ✉ lille@fuaj.org, 12 rue Malpart, metro République or Mairie de Lille), is in a former maternity hospital. Dorm beds start at 73FF, including breakfast. Reception opens 8 am to noon and 2 pm to 2 am. It's closed from 20 December to the end of January.

Hotels The two-star *Hôtel de France* (☎ 03 20 57 14 78, fax 03 20 57 06 01, 10 Rue de Béthune) has airy singles/doubles with washbasin for 150/170FF (200/240FF with shower and toilet). Hall showers are free. Drivers unloading luggage should take rue des Fossés; if the barrier is down, push the hotel's button on the barrier's intercom.

There are several hotels on place de la Gare. *Hôtel des Voyageurs* (☎ 03 20 06 43 14, fax 03 20 74 19 01) at No 10 has simple and clean singles/doubles, reached via a vintage lift, starting at 130/160FF (205 /250FF with shower and toilet). A hall shower costs 20FF. *Hôtel Faidherbe* (☎ 03

20 06 27 93, fax 03 20 55 95 38) at No 42 has singles/doubles starting at 160FF (260FF with shower and toilet). There's no hall shower.

At the quiet *Hôtel Floréal* (☎ 03 20 06 36 21, fax 03 20 21 10 76, 21 rue Ste-Anne), ordinary singles/doubles start at 150FF (250FF with shower and toilet); there's no hall shower. The one-star *Hôtel Moulin d'Or* (☎ 03 20 06 12 67, fax 03 20 06 33 50, 15 rue du Molinel) has very simple, linoleum-floored doubles from 160FF (280FF with shower and 300FF with shower and toilet). There are no hall showers. Curfew is midnight.

Hôtel Le Globe (☎ 03 20 57 29 58, 1 blvd Vauban) has doubles from 155FF (195FF with shower and toilet). There's free parking next to the Citadel.

Places to Stay – Mid-Range & Top End

The friendly, two-star *Hôtel Breughel* (☎ 03 20 06 06 69, fax 03 20 63 25 27, 5 parvis St-Maurice) has a range of decent, modern doubles for 180FF (345FF with shower and toilet). The wood and wrought-iron lift is from the 1920s. Enclosed parking costs 26FF a night.

You might try *Hôtel Flandre-Angleterre* (☎ 03 20 06 04 12, fax 03 20 06 37 76, 13 place de la Gare), which has doubles from 380FF (less at weekends). Two rooms with shower are available for 190FF.

The three-star, Best Western *Grand Hôtel Bellevue* (☎ 03 20 57 45 64, fax 03 20 40 07 93, 5 rue Jean Roisin), built in the early 20th century, has very comfortable singles or doubles from 590FF. Enclosed parking costs 40FF.

Places to Eat

Restaurants Lille has an excellent and varied selection of restaurants. Most are closed on Sunday.

Vieux Lille Relaxed *La Pâte Brisée* (☎ 03 20 74 29 00, 63–65 rue de la Monnaie) has savoury and sweet *tartes*, salads, meat dishes and *gratin* in one/two/three-course *menus* costing 47/69/84FF, including a drink. Try the great regional *menu*, costing 89FF, at intimate *La Tarterie de la Voûte* (☎ *03 20 42 12 16, 4 rue des Débris St-Étienne*) which is closed Monday night and Sunday.

Elegant *Le Hochepot* (☎ *03 20 54 17 59, 6 rue du Nouveau Siècle*) serves Flemish dishes such as *coq à la bière* and *carbonade* (a beef stew cooked in beer). The *menus* cost 125FF, including drinks. It's closed Saturday lunchtime and Sunday.

À l'Huîtrière (☎ *03 20 55 43 41, 3 rue des Chats Bossus*), decorated with mosaics dating from 1928, has great seafood and traditional French cuisine. It doubles as a fish shop and delicatessen. The lunch *menu* costs 245FF; mains cost about 170FF. It opens noon to 2.30 pm and 7 to 9.30 pm (closed Sunday evening and late July to late August). Book ahead.

Rue Royale is *the* place for ethnic cuisine, including the *Moroccan Restaurant* at No 16. For African specialities, *Plat Net Africa* (☎ *03 20 06 14 54, 44 rue d'Angleterre*) has *menus* costing from 100FF to 150FF. Kangaroo meat and other down-under specialities are on offer noon to 3 pm daily (except Sunday) at *Café Oz* (see Bars & Pubs under Entertainment later in this chapter).

South of Place du Général de Gaulle The rue d'Amiens area is full of restaurants and pizzerias. The brasserie-style *Aux Moules* (☎ *03 20 57 12 46, 34 rue de Béthune*) serves Flemish dishes such as rabbit in *Kriek* beer sauce and potatoes (53FF) and, of course, mussels (51FF). It opens noon to midnight.

Brasserie La Chicorée (☎ *03 20 54 81 52, 15 place Rihour*) serves meals (including seafood) 10 am to 4.30 am daily (until 6 am Saturday and Sunday mornings). *Menus* start at 68FF. There are other brasseries close by.

La Source (☎ *03 20 57 53 07, 13 rue du Plat*) is an organic food shop with a vegetarian eatery out back. Lunch is served noon to 2 pm, Monday to Saturday; dinner is available Friday night only from 7 to 9 pm. *Menus* cost from 57FF to 75FF.

Self-Catering The lively *Wazemmes food market* (*place Nouvelle Aventure, metro Gambetta*) 1.2km south-west of the centre, opens early morning to 7 pm (closed Monday). The city's largest *outdoor market* is held nearby on the square outside the covered market on Tuesday, Thursday and Sunday mornings (until 1.30 or 2 pm); Sunday is also flea-market day. There's a *food market* on place Sébastopol Wednesday and Saturday mornings.

The *Monoprix supermarket* (*31 rue du Molinel*) opens 8.30 am to 8 pm Monday to Saturday. The *Carrefour hypermarket* in the Euralille shopping centre opens until 10 pm (closed Sunday).

In Vieux Lille, the *fromagerie* at (*3 rue du Curé St-Étienne*) opens Tuesday to Saturday. There's a good *boulangerie* opposite 26 rue Basse (closed Sunday afternoon).

Entertainment

Tickets for cultural events are available at the FNAC ticket agency (*billetterie*); ☎ 03 20 15 58 15) opposite 15 rue du Sec-Arembault. It opens 10 am to 7.30 pm, Monday to Saturday.

Cinema Nondubbed films are shown daily at *Cinéma Metropole* (☎ *03 20 15 92 23, 26 rue des Ponts des Comines*).

Classical Music & Jazz The very well-regarded Orchestre National de Lille plays in the *Palais de la Musique* (☎ *03 20 54 78 75*). *Le 30* (☎ *03 20 30 15 54, 30 rue de Paris*), has live jazz nightly from 10 pm to 4 am (except Sunday). The audience sits on soft, modular couches in what looks like a 1960s airport VIP lounge. There's more live jazz – 10 pm to 2 am on Friday and Saturday, and sometimes during the week – in the cellars of *L'Angle Saxo* (☎ *03 20 51 88 89, 36 rue d'Angleterre*).

Pubs & Bars A branch of Paris' famous Australian bar, *Café Oz* (☎ *03 20 55 15 15, 33 place Louise de Bettignies*) has Foster's on tap (18FF for 250mL) as well as good cocktails (45FF). It opens 11 am (6 pm on Sunday) to 2 am daily; from noon to 3 pm it's a restaurant (except Sunday). There are lots of pubs and restaurants nearby on rue de Gand.

In Vieux Lille, laid-back *Le Balatum* (*☎ 03 20 57 41 81, 13 rue de la Barre*) has numerous beers from 13FF. *L'Illustration Café* (*☎ 03 20 12 00 90, 18 rue Royale*) is a mellow Art-Nouveau-style bar. Both open until 2 am.

Bar Rocambole (11 place Jacques Luchard) is a dark, trendy bar for gay men, open Monday to Saturday nights. The intimate *Au Lieu d'Elles* (*☎ 03 20 51 54 88 or ☎ 03 20 06 61 04, 19 rue du Cirque),* on the 1st floor, is a lesbian *cafette* (mini-cafe) open Wednesday evenings and closed in August and late July.

Getting There & Away
Bus The Eurolines office (*☎ 03 20 78 18 88*), 23 parvis St-Maurice, has direct buses to Paris (350FF, 7¼ hours), Amsterdam (250FF, 6½ hours), Brussels (50FF, 2½ hours), London (250FF, five hours) and other destinations. It opens 9 am to 6 or 8 pm (closed on Sunday and from noon to 2 pm Monday to Wednesday).

Train Lille has frequent rail links to almost everywhere in France. Its two train stations (*☎ 08 36 35 35 35*) are linked by metro line No 2.

Gare Lille-Flandres handles almost all regional services and most TGVs to Paris' Gare du Nord (208FF to 278FF, one hour, one to two hourly). The information office opens from 9 am to 7 pm (closed Sunday and holidays).

Gare Lille-Europe is served by Eurostar trains to London (700FF at weekends, 1050FF on weekdays, two hours) and TGVs and Eurostars to Brussels (85FF to 98FF, 38 minutes, 15 daily). TGVs also run to Disneyland-Paris (from 228FF to 298FF, 45 minutes to 1¼ hours, 15 daily), Roissy Charles de Gaulle airport (278FF, one to 1¾ hours, over 15 daily), Lyons (from 402FF to 476FF, four hours, three daily) and Nice (590FF, nine hours).

Other options include Calais (84FF, 1½ hours, eight to 15 daily), Boulogne (106,

2¼ hours, 10 daily on weekdays, three at weekends), Arras (53FF, 40 minutes, hourly) and Amiens (96FF, 1½ hours, four direct daily).

Car & Motorcycle There's free parking at the Champ de Mars, the huge car park north of the Citadel; along the streets south-west of rue Solférino; and around Musée Charles de Gaulle.

Europcar (*☎ 03 20 78 18 18*) is at 32 place de la Gare; it's closed Sunday.

Getting Around
Transpole (*☎ 03 20 40 40 40*), which has an information window in Gare Lille-Flandres metro station, runs Lille's two metro lines, two tram lines and municipal buses, several of which cross into Belgium. Tickets (7.50FF) are sold on the bus but must be purchased (and validated in the orange posts) before boarding the metro or tram. A carnet of 10 costs 64FF and a weekly pass 71FF, valid Monday to Sunday.

CALAIS
postcode 62100 • pop 78,000
Calais, only 34km from the English town of Dover (Douvres in French), has long been a popular port for passenger travel between the UK and continental Europe. Its dominance of trans-Channel transport was sealed in 1994 when the Channel Tunnel was opened at Coquelles, 5km south-west of the town centre.

Over 20 million people pass through Calais each year, but few tarry: except for several decent museums and Rodin's *The Burghers of Calais*, there's little to see here other than the vast Cité Europe shopping centre that's designed to lure British daytrippers.

The English king Richard I (the Lion-Heart) passed through Calais on his way to the Third Crusade in 1190. The English later so coveted Calais – in part to control its audacious pirates – that King Edward III captured the town in 1346, thus beginning over two centuries of English rule. In mid-1944 the Germans launched flying bombs against Britain from the Calais area.

FAR NORTHERN FRANCE

CALAIS

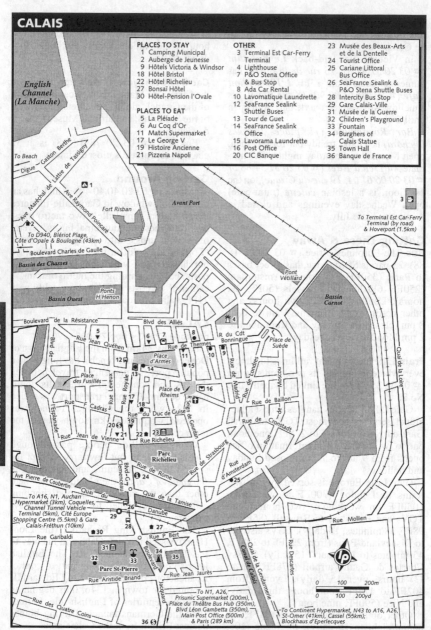

PLACES TO STAY
1 Camping Municipal
2 Auberge de Jeunesse
9 Hôtels Victoria & Windsor
18 Hôtel Bristol
22 Hôtel Richelieu
27 Bonsaï Hôtel
30 Hôtel-Pension l'Ovale

PLACES TO EAT
5 La Pléiade
6 Au Coq d'Or
11 Match Supermarket
17 Le George V
19 Histoire Ancienne
21 Pizzeria Napoli

OTHER
3 Terminal Est Car-Ferry Terminal
4 Lighthouse
7 P&O Stena Office & Bus Stop
8 Ada Car Rental
10 Lavomatique Laundrette
12 SeaFrance Sealink Shuttle Buses
13 Tour de Guet
14 SeaFrance Sealink Office
15 Lavorama Laundrette
16 Post Office
20 CIC Banque

23 Musée des Beaux-Arts et de la Dentelle
24 Tourist Office
25 Cariane Littoral Bus Office
26 SeaFrance Sealink & P&O Stena Shuttle Buses
28 Intercity Bus Stop
29 Gare Calais-Ville
31 Musée de la Guerre
32 Children's Playground
33 Fountain
34 Burghers of Calais Statue
35 Town Hall
36 Banque de France

English Channel (La Manche)

To Beach

Digue – Gaston Berthe

Ave Marechal de Lattre de Tassigny

Ave Raymond Poincaré

Fort Risban

Avant Port

To D940, Blériot Plage, Côte d'Opale & Boulogne (43km)

Boulevard Charles de Gaulle

Bassin des Chasses

To Terminal Est Car-Ferry Terminal (by road) & Hoverport (1.5km)

Pont Vétillard

Bassin Ouest

Ponts H Hénon

Bassin Carnot

Boulevard de la Résistance

Blvd des Alliés

Quai de la Loire

Blvd de...

Rue Jean Quéhen

Rue de Thermes

R du Cdt Bonningue

Place de Suède

Place d'Armes

Rue de Londres

Place des Fusillés

Rue Leveux

Rue Royale

Place de Rheims

Rue de Madrid

R Seigr de Gourdan

Rue de Baillon

Esplanade

Rue Cadras

Rue du Duc de Guise

Rue de Cronstadt

Rue Jean de Vienne

Rue Richelieu

Parc Richelieu

Rue de Strasbourg

Rue d'Amsterdam

Ave Pierre de Coubertin

Rue de Rome

Quai du Clemenceau

Blvd Gco Clemenceau

Quai de la Tamise

Danube

To A16, N1, Auchan Hypermarket (3km), Coquelles, Channel Tunnel Vehicle Terminal (5km), Cité Europe Shopping Centre (5.5km) & Gare Calais-Fréthun (10km)

Rue Garibaldi

Rue P Bert

Rue Mollien

Parc St-Pierre

Rue Aristide Briand

Rue Jean Jaurès

Quai de la Commanderie

Rue Descartes

Canal de Calais

Jacquard

Boulevard

Rue des Quatre Coins

To N1, A26, Prisunic Supermarket (200m), Place du Théâtre Bus Hub (350m), Blvd Léon Gambetta (350m), Main Post Office (500m) & Paris (289 km)

To Continent Hypermarket, N43 to A16, A26, St-Omer (41km), Cassel (55km); Blockhaus d'Eperlecques

0   100   200m
0   100   200yd

euro currency converter 10FF = €1.52

Orientation

The centre of Calais, whose main square is place d'Armes, is encircled by canals and harbour basins, with Gare Calais-Ville 650m to the south. The untouristed part of town is 700m farther south along blvd Jacquard, around blvd Léon Gambetta and the place du Théâtre bus hub.

The car ferry terminal is 1.7km north-east of place d'Armes; the hoverport (for hovercraft and SeaCats) is another 1.5km farther out.

Information

Tourist Offices The tourist office (☎ 03 21 96 62 40, fax 03 21 96 01 92, ✉ ot@ ot-calais.fr), 12 blvd Georges Clemenceau, opens 9 am to 7 pm Monday to Saturday and 10 am to 1 pm on Sundays and holidays. Hotel reservations for the Calais area are free. The Web site is at www.ot-calais.fr.

Money The Banque de France at 77 blvd Jacquard exchanges money from 8.30 am to 12.10 pm weekdays. The post office exchanges currency and there are commercial banks along rue Royale, including a CIC Banque at No 4.

Post & Communications The post office on place de Rheims opens 8 am to 6 pm weekdays and until noon on Saturday. It has a Cyberposte terminal.

Laundry The Lavorama on the eastern side of place d'Armes opens 7 am to 9 pm.

Things to See

The 13th-century **Tour de Guet** (watch-tower), place d'Armes, is a rare pre-20th-century remnant of Calais – the rest was virtually demolished during WWII. About 400m to the north-east, the 53m **lighthouse** (☎ 03 21 34 33 34) on blvd des Alliés, built in 1848, affords superb panoramas. For 15FF (children 7.50FF) you can climb its 271 stairs 2 to 5.30 pm on Wednesday, and 10 am to noon and 2 to 5 pm at weekends. From June to September it opens 2 to 6.30 pm weekdays and 10 am to noon at weekends.

A cast of Auguste Rodin's famous bronze statue of six emaciated but proud figures, known in English as *The Burghers of Calais* (see the boxed text below), stands in front of the Flemish Renaissance-style town hall (1911–25) which is topped with an ornate 75m clock tower.

Across the street in Parc St-Pierre, next to a *boules* ground and near a **children's playground**, is the **Musée de la Guerre** (☎ 03 21 34 21 57), an intriguing WWII museum housed in a 94m-long concrete bunker (once a German naval headquarters). You can begin your visit from 11 am to 4.15 pm (10 am to 5.15 pm from April to September); it's closed on Tuesday and in December and January. Admission costs 25FF (children and students 20FF).

The newly renovated **Musée des Beaux-Arts et de la Dentelle** (Museum of Fine Arts and Lace; ☎ 03 21 46 48 40), 25 rue Richelieu, has exhibits on mechanised lace-making (the first machines were smuggled to Calais from England in 1816), some fine 15th- to 20th-century paintings, ceramics and sculpture, including pieces by Rodin. It opens 10 am to noon and 2 or 2.30 to 5.30 pm daily (6.30 pm at weekends; closed Tuesday). Admission costs 15FF (students 10FF) but is free on Wednesday.

Calais' sandy, cabin-lined **beach**, where you can watch huge car ferries sailing towards the white cliffs of Dover, is nearly 1km north-west of place d'Armes. Take bus No 3 from Gare Calais-Ville, which

The Burghers of Calais

Rodin sculpted *Les Bourgeois de Calais* in 1895 to honour six local citizens who, in 1347, after eight months of holding off the besieging English forces, surrendered themselves and the keys to the starving city to Edward III. Their hope was that by sacrificing themselves they might save the town and its people. Moved by his wife Philippa's entreaties, Edward eventually spared both the Calaisiens and their six brave leaders.

continues along the coast westwards to 8km-long **Blériot Plage**. It's named after the pioneer French aviator Louis Blériot who took off from here in 1909 for the first trans-Channel flight.

Places to Stay
Camping The grassy but soulless *Camping Municipal* (☎ *03 21 97 89 79, ave Raymond Poincaré*) opens year round. It charges 18.90/13.20FF per adult/tent or caravan site. From Gare Calais-Ville, take bus No 3 to the Pluviose stop.

Hostels The modern, nicely furnished *Auberge de Jeunesse* (☎ *03 21 34 70 20, fax 03 21 96 87 80, ave Maréchal de Lattre de Tassigny*), also called the Centre Européen de Séjour, is 200m from the beach. A spot in a two-bed double costs 94FF and a single costs 136FF, including breakfast. It opens 24 hours. From Gare Calais-Ville take bus No 3 to the Pluviose stop.

Hotels Near Gare Calais-Ville, the nicely renovated *Hôtel-Pension l'Ovale* (☎/*fax 03 21 97 57 00, 38–40 ave du Président Wilson*) has bright, cheery rooms with high ceilings and sparkling new TVs. Singles or doubles cost 160FF, triples 180FF (all with private shower). Breakfast costs 20FF.

The welcoming *Hôtel Windsor* (☎ *03 21 34 59 40, fax 03 21 97 68 59, 2 rue du Commandant Bonningue*), run by an Englishman and his French wife, has decent doubles from 170FF (265FF with shower and toilet). Enclosed parking costs 30FF. At No 8, the two-star *Hôtel Victoria* (☎ *03 21 34 38 32, fax 03 21 97 12 13*) has comfortable singles/doubles that start at 160FF (200 /260FF with shower and toilet).

The central and friendly *Hôtel Bristol* (☎/*fax 03 21 34 53 24, 15 rue du Duc de Guise*) has cosy singles/doubles from 150/160FF (180/220FF with shower and toilet); hall showers are free. Rooms for four and five people are also available.

The family-run *Hôtel Richelieu* (☎ *03 21 34 61 60, fax 03 21 85 89 28, 17 rue Richelieu*) is a very quiet place. It has singles/ doubles/quads with soft beds and a range of

amenities for 250/254/314FF, including breakfast.

Right across the road from Gare Calais-Ville, the prefab *Bonsaï Hôtel* (☎ *03 21 96 10 10, fax 03 21 96 60 00, quai du Danube*) has cheap but crumbling and utterly characterless rooms sleeping one to three people for 149FF.

Places to Eat
Restaurants For a first/last-day splurge in France try family-run *La Pléiade* (☎ *03 21 34 03 70, 32 rue Jean Quéhen*), an elegant, mainly seafood restaurant whose *menus* cost from 85FF to 160FF, plus dessert. It opens at lunchtime and evenings from 7.30 pm (closed Saturday midday and Monday). Another fine French restaurant is *Le George V* (☎ *03 21 97 68 00, 36 rue Royale*) where three-course *menus* range from 95FF to 285FF (closed Saturday lunch, Sunday and holiday evenings).

Histoire Ancienne (☎ *03 21 34 11 20, 20 rue Royale*) is a Paris-style bistro specialising in meat dishes grilled over a wood fire. *Menus* cost 98FF to 158FF (closed Monday night and Sunday). Show a ferry or shuttle ticket and get a free bottle of takeaway wine.

The rustic *Au Coq d'Or* (☎ *03 21 34 79 05, 31 place d'Armes*) serves grilled meat dishes and seafood daily. *Menus* run from 64FF to 245FF (closed Wednesday).

Pizzeria Napoli (☎ *03 21 34 49 39, 2 rue Jean de Vienne*) serves generous portions of pasta and pizza costing from 34FF to 49FF. It's closed Monday.

Self-Catering Place d'Armes hosts a *food market* on Wednesday and Saturday mornings. There's a *Match supermarket* (*place d'Armes*) that also opens Sunday morning in July and August. The *Prisunic supermarket* (*17 blvd Jacquard*) opens Monday to Saturday and all day Sunday from April to December.

Getting There & Away
For details of Channel Tunnel and ferry fares and schedules, see To/From The UK under Land and Sea in the Getting There & Away chapter.

Shop Till You Drop in Calais

Although duty-free discounts within the EU ended in June 1999, Calais' onshore shops and hypermarkets still supply day-tripping *rosbifs* (Britons) with everything except, perhaps, roast beef. Items worth picking up 'on the Continent' include delicious edibles (fresh oysters, foie gras, cheeses, gourmet-prepared dishes) and drinks (wine, champagne, beer and spirits) that are hard to find – or much more expensive – in the land of the pound sterling.

The enormous steel-and-glass **Cité Europe** shopping centre (☎ 03 21 46 47 48) is right next to the vehicle loading area for the Channel Tunnel. Its 150 shops include a vast Carrefour hypermarket (open 9 am to 10 pm Monday to Friday) and wine shops such as **Tesco Vin Plus** and **Oddbins**, where buying in bulk to carry home in the car is easy. Most places open 10 am to 8 pm to 9 pm on Friday; closed on Sunday except for the bars, restaurants and cinemas).

By car, follow the signs to the 'Tunnel sous La Manche' and then to the Centre Commercial; by public transport, take bus No 7 (8FF) from the central train station, Gare Calais-Ville.

Bus Inglard (☎ 03 21 96 49 54) runs buses (marked 'Colvert') three times daily, except Sunday, from Gare Calais-Ville and place du Théâtre to Boulogne's blvd Daunou (27FF, 1¼ hours), via the beautiful Côte d'Opale (along the D940). Cariane Littoral (☎ 03 21 34 74 40), 10 rue d'Amsterdam, has buses from the train station to St-Omer and express BCD services to Boulogne (38FF, 35 minutes, six on weekdays and two on Saturday) and Dunkirk (40FF, 30 minutes, 11 on weekdays and three on Saturday).

Train Calais has two train stations: Gare Calais-Ville (also known as Gare Centrale) in the city centre and Gare Calais-Fréthun, 10km south-west of town near the Channel Tunnel entrance.

At Gare Calais-Ville (☎ 08 36 35 35 35) the information office opens 9 am to 6.30 pm daily (5.30 pm on Saturday, closed Sunday). It has direct, non-TGV trains to Paris' Gare du Nord (182FF, 3½ hours, three to six daily), Boulogne (41FF, 35 minutes, hourly), Amiens (118FF, two hours, six to nine daily), Arras (101FF, two hours, six to eight daily) and Lille-Flandres (84FF, 1½ hours, seven to 15 daily). The last train to Paris (via Amiens) is 7.05 pm (6.15 pm on Sunday).

Calais-Fréthun is served by most TGVs to Paris' Gare du Nord (215FF, 1½ hours, two daily) as well as the Eurostar to London

(700FF to 1050FF, 1¾ hours, three daily). The last Eurostar to Paris departs at 8.28 pm. Calais-Fréthun is linked to Gare Calais-Ville station by Opale Bus No 7 (7.20FF).

Car & Motorcycle To reach the Channel Tunnel's vehicle loading area at Coquelles, follow the road signs on the A16 to the 'Tunnel Sous La Manche' (tunnel under the Channel).

Car rental firms in Calais include ADA (☎ 08 36 68 40 041), 14 rue de Thermes, which charges competitive rates (closed on Sunday). Eurorent, Hertz, Avis, Budget and Europcar have agencies at place d'Armes and at the car-ferry terminal (though the latter aren't always staffed). Their desks at the hoverport are staffed only if you've reserved.

Boat P&O Stena and SeaFrance Sealink car ferries to/from Dover dock at the busy Terminal Est, just over 1km north-east of place d'Armes.

P&O Stena's office (☎ 08 02 01 00 20), 41 place d'Armes, opens 8.30 am to 6 pm weekdays and until noon on Saturday. Nearby at No 2 is SeaFrance Sealink's office (☎ 08 03 04 40 45), open 9.30 am to 6 pm (5.30 pm on Friday and to noon on Saturday). Both companies' ferry terminal bureaux (☎ 03 21 46 10 10 for P&O Stena, ☎ 03 21 46 80 00 for SeaFrance Sealink) open 24 hours.

FAR NORTHERN FRANCE

SeaCats to/from Dover use the hoverport, which is 3km north-east of the town centre.

Getting Around

Bus To reach the car-ferry terminal, take a free shuttle operated by SeaFrance Sealink and P&O Stena – buses stop at Gare Calais-Ville and near each company's office at place d'Armes. Times, coordinated with the arrival and departure of boats, are posted.

Local buses, operated by Opale Bus (☎ 03 21 00 75 75), run from a hub at place du Théâtre, which is 700m south of the train station, near the intersection of blvd Jacquard and blvd Gambetta. Almost all the lines stop at Gare Calais-Ville.

Taxi To order a cab call Eurotaxi (☎ 03 21 97 35 35) or TRL (☎ 03 21 97 13 14). A taxi from the train station to the hoverport costs about 45FF (55FF at night).

AROUND CALAIS

The hilltop village of **Cassel** (population 2200), 29km south of Dunkirk, affords panoramic views of the verdant Flanders plain. It served as Maréchal Ferdinand Foch's headquarters from 1914 to 1915 and, in 1940, was the site of intensive rearguard resistance by British troops defending Dunkirk during the evacuation.

Taverne Flamande (☎ 03 28 42 42 59, *34 Grand' place*) serves tasty *menus* from 68FF to 99FF in a pseudo-medieval atmosphere (closed Tuesday). *Hôtel Le Foch* (☎ 03 28 42 47 73, 41 Grand' place) has just two doubles with shower for 250FF.

The quiet town of **St-Omer** (population 14,400) is known for its **basilica**, the only large Gothic church in the region. *Hotel-Restaurant Le Vivier* (☎ 03 21 95 76 00, fax 03 21 95 42 20, 22 rue Louis Martel), just off place Victor Hugo, has pleasant doubles for 310FF and a good seafood restaurant downstairs.

The 22m-high **Blockhaus d'Eperlecques** (☎ 03 21 88 44 22), off the D600 between Dunkirk and St-Omer, was built by the Nazis in 1943 as a V2 rocket assembly and launching site. Construction was carried out by 3000 forced labourers, many of whom

were killed in the 25 Allied air raids that prevented the site from becoming operational. It opens 2.15 to 6 pm at weekends in March and daily in April, May, October and November; and 10 am to noon and 2.15 to 7 pm daily, June to September.

CÔTE D'OPALE

The 40km of cliffs, sand dunes and beaches between Calais and Boulogne, known as the Opal Coast, are a stunningly beautiful introduction to France. The coastal peaks (which are frequently buffeted by gale-force winds) are dotted with the remains of Nazi Germany's Atlantic Wall, a chain of fortifications and gun emplacements built to prevent an Allied invasion.

Part of the **Parc Naturel Régional Nord Pas de Calais**, the Côte d'Opale area is criss-crossed by hiking paths, including the GR Littoral trail that follows the coast; some routes are also suitable for mountain biking and horse riding (for details, pick up the free French-language booklet *Randonnées en Côte d'Opale* at a tourist office). Each town along the Côte d'Opale has at least one camping ground.

If you arrive in Calais by car, the Côte d'Opale's main highway, the D940, offers some spectacular vistas. All the sights and villages mentioned below are served by the Calais–Boulogne bus line operated by Inglard (☎ 03 21 96 49 54).

Sangatte

The village of Sangatte, 8km west of Calais, sits right on top of where the Channel Tunnel slips under the Straits of Dover. It is known for its long, dune-lined beach.

Cap Blanc-Nez

The windswept, 134m-high Cap Blanc-Nez affords truly spectacular views of the Bay of Wissant, Cap Gris-Nez, the port of Calais, the verdant Flemish countryside and the cliffs of Kent. The road leading up to the grey **obelisk** honouring the WWI Dover Patrol passes by scrubland dotted with German fortifications and Allied bomb craters.

Atop the bomb-pocked hill across the highway is the **Musée du Transmanche**

(☎ 03 21 85 57 42) with exhibits on the many attempts to cross the Channel by balloon, biplane, bridge, tunnel and the like. It opens 10 am to 5.30 pm Tuesday to Friday, and 1.30 to 6.30 pm at weekends; in July and August it opens 11 am to 7 pm daily. Admission costs 20FF (students and those aged under 18, 15FF).

Wissant

The cute, upmarket seaside resort of Wissant is midway between Cap Blanc-Nez and Cap Gris-Nez on a vast, fine-sand beach. In 55 BC, Julius Caesar launched his invasion of Britain from here.

Places to Stay Just 200m from the beach, Wissant's municipal *Camping de la Source* (☎ 03 21 35 92 46) charges 19/18/10FF per adult/tent site/car and opens mid-March to November.

Hôtel Le Vivier (☎ 03 21 35 93 61, fax 03 21 82 10 99, place de l'Église) has singles/doubles with shower from 220/260FF, and rooms in a separate annex with washbasin and a sea view for 180FF. Prices include breakfast.

Audinghen

The inland village of Audinghen, 3km south-east of Cap Gris-Nez, was rebuilt after being completely destroyed in 1944.

Audinghen has one of the Côte d'Opale's cheapest hotels, the five-room *Hôtel Chez Monique* (☎ 03 21 87 30 09, 98 Grand' place), across the highway from the striking, post-war church. Doubles cost 120FF with washbasin (160FF with shower). There are no hall showers. Breakfast costs 30FF.

Cap Gris-Nez

Topped by a lighthouse and a radar station serving the 500 ships that pass each day, the 45m-high cliffs of Cap Gris-Nez – the name 'Grey Nose' being a corruption of the archaic English 'craig ness', which means 'rocky promontory' – are only 28km from the English coast. The area is a favourite stopping-off point for millions of migrating birds.

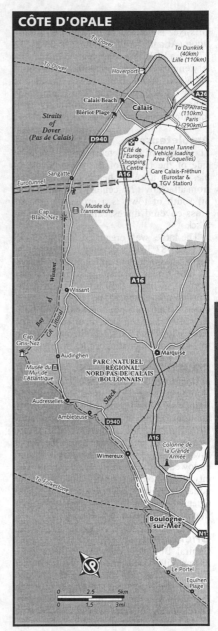

COTE D'OPALE

To Dover

To Dover

To Dover

Hoverport

To Dunkirk
(40km)
Lille (110km)

To Arras
(110km)
Paris
(290km)

Calais Beach

Bloriot Plage

Calais

Straits
of
Dover
(Pas de Calais)

D940

Cité de
l'Europe
Shopping
Centre

Channel Tunnel
Vehicle loading
Area (Coquelles)

Gare Calais-Fréthun
(Eurostar &
TGV Station)

Sangatte

A16

Eurotunnel

Musée du
Transmanche

Cap
Blanc-Nez

Bay
of

Wissant

A16

Wissant

Cap
Gris-Nez

CR Littoral

Audinghen

Marquise

Musée du
Mur de
l'Atlantique

PARC NATUREL
RÉGIONAL
NORD-PAS-DE-CALAIS
(BOULONNAIS)

Audresselles

Slack

Ambleteuse

D940

A16

Wimereux

Colonne de
la Grande
Armée

To Folkestone

Boulogne-
sur-Mer

N1

Le Portel

Equihen
Plage

0   2.5   5km
0   1.5   3mi

FAR NORTHERN FRANCE

About 500m south of the turn-off to Cap Gris-Nez is the **Musée du Mur de l'Atlantique** (Atlantic Wall Museum; ☎ 03 21 32 97 33), a WWII museum housed in an artillery emplacement whose 380mm gun could lob 800kg shells all the way to England. It opens 9 am to noon and 2 to 6 pm, mid-February to October. Admission costs 30FF (children aged eight to 14, 12FF).

Ambleteuse

The village of Ambleteuse, on the northern side of the mouth of the River Slack, is blessed by a lovely **beach** once defended from attack by 17th-century **Fort Mahon**. A bit south of town is a protected area of grass-covered dunes called **Dunes de la Slack**.

The large, well-organised **Musée 39–45** (☎ 03 21 87 33 01), devoted to the wartime period, has oodles of authentic paraphernalia (don't miss the displays of field rations – yum). It opens 9.30 am to 7 pm daily, April to mid-October. The rest of the year it opens 10 am to 6 pm, weekends and holidays. It's closed in December and January. Admission costs 33FF (children aged seven to 14, 22FF), including a film in English.

BOULOGNE-SUR-MER
postcode 62200 • pop 44,000

Boulogne is by far the most interesting of France's Channel ports. Most of the city is an uninspiring mass of post-war reconstruction, but the attractive Ville Haute (Upper City), perched high above the rest of town, is girded by a 13th-century wall and endowed with a surprising museum. The city is also home to one of France's premier aquariums. In recent years most trans-Channel vehicle and passenger traffic has moved up the coast to Calais.

Orientation

Central Boulogne consists of the walled, hilltop Ville Haute, the Basse Ville (Lower City), and the port area. The commercial district stretches from the tourist office to the Ville Haute. The main train station, Gare Boulogne-Ville, is 1200m south-east of the tourist office along blvd Daunou.

Information

Tourist Offices The tourist office (☎ 03 21 31 68 38, fax 03 21 33 81 09, @ boulogne@ tourisme.norsys.fr) is on quai de la Poste and opens 8.45 am to 12.30 pm and 1.30 to 6.15 pm Monday to Saturday; and 10 am to 12.30 pm and 2.30 to 5 pm on Sunday; and 9am to 7 pm daily in July and August. Local hotel reservations are free, as is a brochure (in French) on nearby walking, cycling and equestrian trails.

Money The post office has an exchange desk. The Banque de France at 1 place Angleterre changes money from 8.45 am to noon on weekdays. There are several commercial banks on or near rue Victor Hugo. Thomas Cook has exchange bureaux aboard the SeaCats.

Post & Communications The main post office, next to the bus hub at place de France, opens 8 am to 6 pm weekdays and 8.30 am to noon on Saturday. It has a Cyberposte.

Laundry The Lavomatique at 235 rue Nationale opens 5.30 am to 9.30 pm daily.

Ville Haute

The Upper City is an island of centuries-old buildings and cobblestone streets perched high above the bustle of the Basse Ville. You can walk completely around the Ville Haute atop the rectangular, tree-shaded **ramparts**, a distance of just under 1.5km.

The square, medieval **belfry** of the 18th-century town hall (☎ 03 21 87 80 80), opens from 8 am to 6 pm (closed Saturday afternoon and Sunday) and affords spectacular views of the city; access (free) is from place Godefroy de Bouillon, named after a local lord crowned King of Jerusalem during the First Crusade. Among the impressive buildings around the square is the neoclassical **Hôtel Desandrouin**, built in the 1780s and later used by Napoleon.

The dominant feature here is the 19th-century **Basilique Notre Dame** (☎ 03 21 99 75 98) whose towering, Italianate dome is visible all over town. It opens 8 am to noon

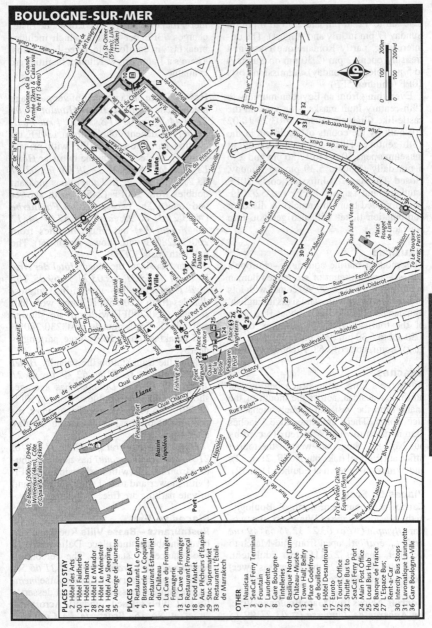

BOULOGNE-SUR-MER

PLACES TO STAY
2 Hôtel des Arts
20 Hôtel Faidherbe
21 Hôtel Hamiot
28 Hôtel Le Mirador
32 Hôtel Le Ménestrel
34 Hôtel Au Sleeping
35 Auberge de Jeunesse

PLACES TO EAT
4 Restaurant Le Cyrano
5 Brasserie Le Coquelin
11 Restaurant Estaminet
   du Château
12 La Cave du Fromager
   Fromagerie
13 La Cave du Fromager
16 Restaurant Provençal
18 Food Market
29 Stoc Supermarket
33 Restaurant L'Étoile
   de Marrakech

OTHER
1 Nausicaa
3 SeaCat Ferry Terminal
6 Fountain
7 Laundrette
8 Gare Boulogne-
   Tintelleries
9 Basilique Notre Dame
10 Château-Musée
13 Town Hall; Belfry
14 Place Godefroy
   de Bouillon
15 Hôtel Desandrouin
17 Euroto
22 Tourist Office
23 Shuttle Bus to
   SeaCat Ferry Port
24 Main Post Office
25 Local Bus Hub
26 Banque de France
27 L'Espace Bus;
   Rent-a-Car
30 Intercity Bus Stops
31 Lavomatique Laundrette
36 Gare Boulogne-Ville

FAR NORTHERN FRANCE

euro currency converter €1 = 6.56FF

and 2 to 7 pm Monday to Saturday, and 8.30 am to 12.30 pm and 2.30 to 6 pm on Sunday (7 pm in July and August). The uninteresting, partly Romanesque **crypt** and **treasury** opens 2 pm (2.30 pm on Sunday) to 5 pm (closed Monday). Admission costs 10FF (children 5FF).

Everything from an Egyptian mummy to 19th-century Inuit masks is on view in the castle-like **Château-Musée** (☎ 03 21 10 02 20) built by the counts of Boulogne in the 13th century. This eclectic but excellent museum opens 10 am to 12.30 pm and 2 to 5 pm daily (2.30 to 5.30 pm on Sunday, closed Tuesday). Admission costs 20FF (students and seniors 13FF) and 32/20FF with a guided tour (in French). A discount combination ticket will also get you into Nausicaa.

Nausicaa

This modern marine aquarium – Europe's largest – and museum of sea-related human activities (☎ 03 21 30 99 99) comes with lots of kid-friendly activities and signs in English. Situated on blvd Ste-Beuve about 1km north of the tourist office, the complex opens 9.30 am to 6.30 pm (to 8 pm in July and August). Admission costs 68FF (children 48FF).

Beaches

Boulogne's long, wide beach begins just north of Nausicaa, across the mouth of the Liane from the vast and vaguely menacing steelworks. There are other nice beaches 4km north of town at Wimereux (served by bus No 1); 2.5km south-west of the tourist office at Le Portel (take bus No 17, 21 or 23); and 5km south of town at Equihen 11 or 12).

Places to Stay

Camping About 4km north of Boulogne in the seaside village of Wimereux, the two-star *Olympic* (☎/fax 03 21 32 45 63, 49 rue de la Libération), open from mid-March to October, charges 22/11FF per adult/tent. Take bus No 1 or 2 (the latter is slower) from place de France.

Hostels Across from Gare Boulogne-Ville, the *Auberge de Jeunesse* (☎ 03 21 99 15 30, fax 03 21 80 45 62, ℮ boulogne-sur-mer@fuaj.org, 56 place de Rouget de Lisle) charges 73FF per person, which includes breakfast, in comfortable, three-bed rooms. There's a 1 am curfew. Kitchen facilities are available.

Hotels There are a number of very average places near the river. *Hôtel Hamiot* (☎ 03 21 31 44 20, fax 03 21 83 71 56, 1 rue Faidherbe) has decent doubles from 130FF, including hall shower (200FF with private shower). A block south, the two-star *Hôtel Le Mirador* (☎ 03 21 31 38 08, fax 03 21 83 21 79, 4 rue de la Lampe) has pleasant doubles from 200FF (245FF with shower and toilet). The two-star *Hôtel Faidherbe* (☎ 03 21 31 60 93, fax 03 21 87 01 14, 12 rue Faidherbe) has plush doubles from 200FF (280FF with shower and toilet). The hall bath costs 30FF.

Near Nausicaa, the faded *Hôtel des Arts* (☎ 03 21 31 53 31, fax 03 21 33 69 05, 102 blvd Gambetta) has unexciting singles/doubles from 120/150FF, some with hall shower (150/200FF with private shower and toilet). Triples/quads cost 230/280FF and breakfast costs 26FF. Free parking is nearby.

Near the train station the friendly *Hôtel Au Sleeping* (☎ 03 21 80 62 79, fax 03 21 10 63 97, 18 blvd Daunou) has average, shower-equipped doubles from 150FF (200FF with toilet). Except in summer, reception (at the bar) is closed on Sunday after 1 pm.

Hôtel Le Ménestrel (☎ 03 21 31 60 16, 21 rue de Bréquerecque) has no-frills doubles from 140FF (with washbasin) to 185FF (with shower and toilet). Hall showers and private parking are free.

Places to Eat

Restaurants – Basse Ville Rue Coquelin, blvd Gambetta and place Dalton have a good choice of restaurants. The welcoming *Restaurant Le Cyrano* (☎ 03 21 31 66 57, 9 rue Coquelin) serves a three-course *menu* – for example, mussels, steak and dessert – for just 49FF (closed Sunday). Across the street at No 16, *Brasserie Le Coquelin*

(☎ 03 21 30 01 88) has pizza from 30FF and *menus* from 50FF (closed Sunday for lunch).

Walk past the fresh fish on ice at *Aux Pêcheurs d'Étaples* (☎ 03 21 30 29 29, 31 Grande rue) into the fine seafood restaurant. The 95FF and 130FF *menus* are available noon to 2 pm and 7 to 10 pm (closed Sunday evening).

For a steaming portion of couscous (from 69FF) before heading to England try *Restaurant L'Étoile de Marrakech* (☎ 03 21 31 38 42, 228 rue Nationale). It's closed Wednesday.

Restaurants – Ville Haute The restaurants along rue de Lille include *La Cave du Fromager* (☎ 03 21 80 49 69) at No 30, a cheese restaurant offering *raclette* (a Swiss cheese dish), Welsh rarebit, fondue Savoyarde and more. *Menus* are available from 80FF (closed Tuesday). *Restaurant Estaminet du Château* (☎ 03 21 91 49 66, 2 rue du Château) has fish and meat *menus* which cost from 70FF to 170FF (closed Wednesday night and Thursday).

Restaurant Provençal (☎ 03 21 80 49 03, 107 rue Porte Gayole), outside the ramparts, serves tasty Moroccan couscous (from 65FF) amid exaggerated Oriental décor.

Self-Catering In the Basse Ville, there's a *food market* at place Dalton on Wednesday and Saturday mornings. The *Stoc supermarket* in the Centre Commercial La Liane at 53 blvd Daunou opens 8 am to 8 pm Monday to Saturday. There are *food shops* along rue de la Lampe.

In the Ville Haute, *food shops* on rue de Lille include *La Cave du Fromager*, a fromagerie at No 23 open 9 am to 7 pm (closed Sunday after 4 pm and Tuesdays).

Getting There & Away

Bus Buses to the Côte d'Opale and Calais stop across the street from 75 blvd Daunou. For details see Getting There & Away under Calais.

Dumont (☎ 03 21 31 77 48) has four or five buses daily (except Sunday and holidays) from blvd Daunou southwards to the beach resorts of Le Touquet (17FF, 40 minutes) and Berck-sur-Mer (28FF, 1¼ hours).

Train Boulogne has two train stations: Gare Boulogne-Ville on blvd Voltaire and the small, poorly served Gare Boulogne-Tintelleries on rue de Belterre. The Gare Maritime (ferry terminal station) is no longer used.

Gare Boulogne-Ville's information office (☎ 08 36 35 35 35) opens 9.15 am to noon and 2 to 6.45 pm (closed Sunday). Paris' Gare du Nord is served by regular train (164FF, 2¾ hours, eight daily), TGV (215FF to 288FF, one direct on weekdays) and, from Calais-Fréthun (linked to Calais by SNCF bus), by Eurostar (215FF, 1½ hours, four daily). The Eurostar also goes to London. Other destinations include Lille-Flandres (105FF, 2¼ hours, 10 daily on weekdays, three at weekends), Amiens (93FF, 1¼ hours, up to nine daily), Arras (96FF, two hours, eight on weekdays, three at weekends) and Calais (41FF, 40 minutes, hourly).

Car Rent-a-Car (☎ 03 21 80 97 34), 26 rue de la Lampe, may be cheaper than Euroto (☎ 03 21 30 32 23) at 96 rue Nationale.

Boat Boulogne is linked only to Folkestone (45km away) by Hoverspeed's SeaCats (☎ 08 20 03 55 55 at the ferry terminal). For details on fares and schedules see To/From The UK under Sea in the Getting There & Away chapter.

Getting Around

Bus The local bus company, TCRB, has an information office called L'Espace Bus (☎ 03 21 83 51 51) at 14 rue de la Lampe. Most lines stop at the main bus hub on place de France opposite the tourist office. A single ride to the old town costs 4FF (6.40FF for the entire centre).

Shuttle buses coordinated with ferry sailings link the pleasure port side of the main post office with the SeaCat port, a distance of about 600m.

Taxi To order a taxi, ring ☎ 03 21 91 25 00. Count on paying 38FF (48FF at night) to get from the ferry terminal to the Gare Boulogne-Ville.

DUNKIRK
postcode 59140 • pop 209,000
Dunkirk was flattened shortly before one of the most uninspired periods in the whole of western architecture – 1950s brick low-rise. Unless you're planning to spend time on the beach or join in the colourful pre-Lent carnival there's little reason to spend the night here.

Under Louis XIV, Dunkirk – whose name means 'church of the dunes' in Flemish – served as a base for French privateers, including the infamous Jean Bart (1650–1702), whose daring attacks on English and Dutch ships have ensured his status as a local hero. The city centre's main square, suitably adorned with a dashing statue, bears his name.

These days, Dunkirk is no longer linked to England by ferry.

Orientation
The train station is 600m south-west of Dunkirk's main square, place Jean Bart. The beach and its waterfront esplanade, Digue de Mer, are 2km north-east of the centre – via ave des Bains – in the suburb of Malo-les-Bains, whose main square is place Turenne.

Tourist Offices In the medieval belfry on rue de l'Amiral Ronarc'h, the **tourist office** (☎ 03 28 26 27 28, fax 03 28 63 38 40, ✉ dunkerque@tourism.norsys.fr) is open 9 am to 12.30 pm and 1.30 to 6.30 pm (no midday closure on Saturday, or in July and August); and 10 am to noon and 2 to 5 pm on Sunday. Hotel reservations in the Flanders region are free.

Money Banks just east of place Jean Bart include a CIC Banque at 5 blvd Ste-Barbe. The Banque de France exchanges currency from 8.45 am to noon on weekdays. The post office also changes money.

Post & Communications The main post office at 20 rue Poincaré (200m east of the

The Evacuation of Dunkirk

In May and June, 1940, Dunkirk (Dunkerque) earned a place in the history books when the British Expeditionary Force and French and Belgian units found themselves almost completely surrounded by Hitler's armies, which had advanced into far northern France.

In an effort to salvage what it could, Churchill's government ordered British units to make their way to Dunkirk, where naval vessels and hundreds of fishing boats and pleasure craft, many manned by civilian volunteers, braved intense German artillery and air attacks to ferry 340,000 men to the safety of England. Conducted in the difficult first year of WWII, this unplanned and chaotic evacuation – dubbed Operation Dynamo – failed to save any of the units' heavy equipment but was however seen as an important demonstration of Britain's resourcefulness and determination.

tourist office) opens 8.30 am to 6.30 pm on weekdays and to 1 pm on Saturday. It has a Cyberposte.

Things to See & Do
The **Musée Portuaire** (Harbour Museum, ☎ 03 28 63 33 39), 9 quai de la Citadelle, housed in a former tobacco warehouse, has splendid ship models and exhibits on the history of Dunkirk as a port. It opens 10 am to 12.45 pm and 1.30 to 6 pm daily (closed Tuesday; no lunchtime break in July and August). Admission costs 25FF (those aged under 18 and students 20FF).

One-hour **boat tours** (☎ 03 28 58 85 12 for reservations) depart from place du Minck and afford views of the huge port and some of France's most important steel and petroleum works. Tickets cost 35FF (children 27FF).

Dunkirk's wide, promenade-lined beach, **Plage des Alliés**, is about 2km north-east of the city centre at Malo-les-Bains, a faded turn-of-the-century seaside resort. The tourist office has a map-brochure on walking trails in the **Dewulf and Marchand dunes**,

5km north-east of Malo-les-Bains near Bray-Dunes. To get there, take bus No 2 or 2AM.

Special Events
Dunkirk's carnival, held at the beginning of Lent, was effectively started by cod fishermen as a final fling before setting out for their month-long shifts in the Icelandic waters. The most colourful celebrations of the carnival take place on the Sundays before and after Mardi Gras – on the first Sunday costumed locals gather at the town hall, where the mayor and other dignitaries stand on the balcony and pelt the crowd with herrings.

Places to Stay & Eat
The *Auberge de Jeunesse* (☎ 03 28 63 36 34, fax 03 28 63 24 54, place Paul Asseman) is on the beach 3km north of the train station. Spots in eight-bed dorm rooms cost 48FF, plus 19FF for breakfast. There's an 11 pm curfew. Take bus No 3 to the 'Piscine' stop, walk past the pool and the hostel's on your right.

Across from the tourist office, the two-star *Hôtel du Tigre* (☎/fax 03 28 66 75 17, 8 rue Clemenceau) has singles/doubles from 90/130FF (190/240FF with shower and toilet).

Kim Thanh Restaurant (☎ 03 28 51 22 98, 14 place Roger Salengro), 100m north-west of the tourist office, does Chinese-Vietnamese lunch menus (with oodles of chicken) for 55FF. Evening mains cost from 35FF (closed Tuesday and Saturday lunch). The *Crêmerie* (☎ 03 28 59 22 25, 22 rue Poincaire) is a fantastic cheese shop that sells crêpes and meat-and-cheese platters from just 10FF.

Getting There & Away
BCD (☎ 03 21 83 51 51) runs buses to/from Dunkirk train station to Calais (40FF, 45 minutes, 11 on weekdays and three on Saturday), and Boulogne (60FF, 1¼ hours).

Dunkirk has frequent train links to Lille (73FF, 1¼ hours, 16 daily) Boulogne (94FF, 1½ hour, three daily), Calais (83FF, 1¼ to 1¾ hours, 13 daily) and Paris Gare du Nord by TGV (280FF to 320FF, 1½ hours, hourly).

ARRAS
postcode 62000 • pop 40,000
• elevation 72m
Arras (the final 's' is pronounced), former capital of Artois, is renowned for its harmonious, picturesque ensemble of 17th- and 18th-century Flemish-style buildings in the town centre. The rest of the city, seriously damaged during both world wars, is nothing to write home about.

Orientation
Arras is centred around the Grand' place and almost-adjoining place des Héros (the Petite place), where you'll find the town hall. The train station is 600m south-east of place des Héros. The commercial centre is around rue Ronville in the pedestrianised area south-east of place des Héros.

Information
Tourist Offices The tourist office (☎ 03 21 51 26 95, fax 03 21 71 07 34, ☻ arras .tourisme@wanadoo.fr), inside the town hall at place des Héros, opens 9 am to noon and 2 to 6 pm Monday to Saturday, and 10 am to 12.30 pm and 3 to 6.30 pm Sundays and holidays. From late April to late September it opens 9 am (10 am on Sunday and holidays) to 6.30 pm, with a break from 1 to 2.30 pm on Sunday and holidays. You can visit its Web site at www.ot-arras.fr.

The discount City-Pass (65FF; students and children 40FF) covers visits to the subterranean tunnels, a historical slide show, the Fine Arts Museum and a self-guided audio tour around town (see Things to See & Do later in this chapter).

Money The Banque de France at 1 rue Ernestale changes money from 9 am to noon Monday to Friday. There are lots of commercial banks along rue Gambetta and its continuation, rue Ernestale. The post office also changes money.

Post & Communications The post office on rue Gambetta opens 8 am to 6.30 pm

ARRAS

PLACES TO STAY
3 Hôtel des 3 Luppars
4 Auberge de Jeunesse
14 Hôtel Diamant
18 Hôtel du Beffroi
26 Le Passe Temps
29 Hôtel Carnot Astoria

PLACES TO EAT
2 La Faisanderie
5 La Rapière
6 Aux Grandes Arcades
9 Le Pain Helios
10 Arcades Fraicheur
11 Fromagerie
12 Café-Brasserie Georget
15 Pizzéria Le Vidocq
23 Monoprix Supermarket

OTHER
1 Cathedral
7 Super-Lav Laundrette
8 Le Louisiane
13 Dan Foley's Irish Pub
16 Tourist Office
17 Town Hall
19 Musée des Beaux-Arts
20 Robespierre's House
21 Théâtre
22 Banque de France
24 Post Office
25 Citer-Eurodollar Car Rental
27 War Memorial
28 Train Station
30 ADA Car Rental
31 Bus Station

weekdays and until noon on Saturday. It has a Cyberposte.

Laundry The Super-Lav at 17 place d'Ipswich opens 7 am to 8 pm daily.

Things to See & Do
The 11th-century market squares, **place des Héros** and **Grand' place**, are flanked by Flemish baroque houses from the 17th and 18th centuries. They vary in detail, but their 345 sandstone columns form a common arcade.

The Flemish Gothic **town hall** at place des Héros dates from the 16th century but was completely rebuilt after WWI. Two giants (see the boxed text 'The Giants'), Colas and Jacqueline, are on display in the lobby.

From the basement you can take a lift to the top of the 75m **belfry**, open daily until 6 pm; admission costs 14FF (students 10FF). A 40-minute guided tour with English translation of the slimy *souterrains* (tunnels) – also known as *boves* (cellars) – under place des Héros, which were turned into British command posts, hospitals and barracks during WWI. Tours generally begin at 11 am, 3 and 4.30 pm daily. Admission costs 22FF (students and children 14FF); tickets including the **Historama**, a 20-minute slide show covering the city's past, cost 37FF (students and children 24FF).

The **Musée des Beaux-Arts** (☎ 03 21 71 26 43), 22 rue Paul Doumer, is housed in a neoclassical former Benedictine abbey. Displays include the original copper lion from the town hall belfry, Gallo-Roman artefacts, medieval sculpture (including a skeletal, recumbent figure from 1446 whose stomach cavity is being devoured by worms), tapestries and paintings. It opens 10 am to noon and 2 to 6 pm daily (to 5 pm October to March, closed Tuesday), and 10 am to noon and 3 to 6 pm on Sunday. Admission costs 20FF (children, students and seniors 10FF; free the first Sunday and Wednesday of the month).

The neoclassical, cruciform **cathedral** (1773–1833), just north of the museum, is graced with two rows of huge Corinthian columns. It opens 2.15 to 6.30 pm daily (to 6 pm in winter).

Just before the Revolution, the Arras-born lawyer and Jacobin radical **Robespierre** lived in the bourgeois, 18th-century house (built 1730) at 9 rue Maximilien Robespierre. The house contains reams of letters, some dramatic-looking garments, and a few pieces of well-kept period furniture from its former owner. It opens 2 to 5.30 pm Monday and Tuesday, and 3.30 to 6.30 pm weekends (free).

Places to Stay

Camping The *Camping Municipal* (☎ 03 21 71 55 06, 138 rue du Temple) is a 10-minute, signposted walk south of the train station along ave du Maréchal Leclerc. Charges are 15/8.50/8FF per adult/tent/car. It opens April to September.

Hostels The central, 53-bed *Auberge de Jeunesse* (☎ 03 21 22 70 02, fax 03 21 07 46 15, 59 Grand' place) charges 48FF for a bed and 19FF for breakfast. Reception opens 8 am to noon and 5 to 11 pm. Curfew is 11 pm. It is closed in December and January.

Hotels Close to the train station, *Le Passe Temps* (☎ 03 21 71 58 38, 1 place du Maréchal Foch) has faded but spacious singles/doubles which start at 130/150FF (210FF with bath and toilet).

The two-star *Hôtel Carnot Astoria* (☎ 03 21 71 08 14, fax 03 21 71 60 95, 10 place du Maréchal Foch) has singles/doubles/triples in contemporary style for 260/290/320FF, plus 20FF for breakfast.

The charming *Hôtel des 3 Luppars* (☎ 03 21 07 41 41, fax 03 21 24 24 80, 47 Grand' place) occupies the only non-Flemish-style building on the square. Very comfortable singles/doubles/triples start at 200/270/360FF and there's a sauna.

The 12-room, two-star *Hôtel Diamant* (☎ 03 21 71 23 23, fax 03 21 71 84 13, 5 place des Héros) has pleasant but generic singles/doubles with shower and toilet costing from 280/300FF.

The central *Hôtel du Beffroi* (☎ 03 21 23

The Giants

In far northern France, *géants* (giants) – huge wickerwork body-masks up to 8.5m tall and animated by a person inside – emerge to dance and add to the general merrymaking of local carnivals and feast days. Each has a name and a personality, usually based either on characters from legends or local history. The giants marry and have children, creating, over the years, complicated family relationships. When they get old and tatty they die, and all the locals to turn out for the 'cremation'.

The giants have been a tradition in this region (though nowhere else in France) since the 16th century; nearly 200 of the creatures now 'live' in towns including Dunkerque, Douai, Bailleul, Aire-sur-la-Lys and Cassel. Your best chance to see them is at pre-Lenten carnivals, during Easter and at summer festivals – dates and places appear in the annual brochure *L'Année des Géants – Fêtes et Sorties*, available at tourist offices.

FAR NORTHERN FRANCE

13 78, fax 03 21 23 03 08, 28 place de la Vacquerie) has renovated singles/doubles from 170/220FF (200/250FF with shower and toilet).

Places to Eat

Restaurants For traditional French and regional cuisine try *La Rapière (☎ 03 21 55 09 92, 44 Grand' place)* which has *menus* from 88FF to 195FF (closed Sunday night).

For a splurge, try *La Faisanderie (☎ 03 21 48 20 76, 45 Grand' place)*, a French restaurant under vaulted ceilings with *menus* from 145FF to 315FF. It opens 12.50 to 2 pm and 7.30 to 9.15 pm (closed Sunday night and Monday). The brasserie-style *Aux Grandes Arcades (☎ 03 21 23 30 89, 10 Grand' place)* has *menus* starting at 86FF and *plats du jour* for 65FF (open October to April, closed on Sunday night).

The unpretentious *Café-Brasserie Georget (☎ 03 21 71 13 07, 42 place des Héros)*, offers a simple, home-made *plat du jour* for 48FF (closed evenings).

The popular *Pizzéria Le Vidocq (☎ 03 21 23 79 50, 24 rue des Trois Visages)* has pasta dishes and pizzas (from 39FF to 66FF) baked in a wood-fired oven. It opens noon to 2 pm and 7 to 10 pm (closed Saturday lunch and on Sunday).

Self-Catering On Wednesday and Saturday mornings *food markets* are held around the town hall and at Grand' place. The *Monoprix* supermarket *(30 rue Gambetta)* opens 8.30 am to 8 pm Monday to Saturday. *Le Pain Helios* is a huge, well-stocked bakery *(29 Grand' place)*; it's closed Monday.

There's a stunning *fromagerie* at 37 place des Héros that opens 9 am to 1 pm and 2.30 to 6 pm daily except Sunday and Monday. Fruit and vegetables are available just down the street at *Arcades Fraicheur (33 rue de la Taillerie)*; it's closed on Sunday.

Entertainment

Cafes and pubs line the northern side of place des Héros and rue de la Taillerie. *Dan Foley's Irish Pub (☎ 03 21 71 46 08, 7 place des Héros)* opens to 1 am daily.

Live music on Thursday, Friday and Saturday nights starts at 10 pm. *Le Louisiane (☎ 03 21 23 18 00, 12 rue de la Taillerie)* often has live music (especially piano and jazz) and opens until 1 or 2 am daily.

Getting There & Away

Bus The information office at the modern bus station (☎ 03 21 51 34 64) on rue Abel Bergaigne opens until 7 pm (until noon on Saturday; closed Sunday). It serves mainly local destinations within 10km.

Train Arras, on the main Lille–Paris line and other secondary lines, has direct trains to destinations including Paris' Gare du Nord (from 162FF to 250FF by TGV, 50 to 90 minutes, one to two hourly), Albert (40FF, 25 minutes, six to eight daily), Amiens (59FF, 45 minutes, four to six daily), Boulogne (96FF, two hours, seven on weekdays, three to four at weekends), Calais (101FF, two hours, four to eight daily) and Lille–Flandres (53FF, 40 minutes, 11 to 14 daily).

Car ADA (☎ 03 21 24 04 33, fax 03 21 71 05 99) is at 60 blvd Carnot (closed Sunday). Citer-Eurodollar (☎ 03 21 71 49 14, fax 03 21 71 81 15) is at 14 blvd Faidherbe (closed Saturday afternoon and Sunday).

Taxi Alliance Taxi (☎ 03 21 23 69 69), available 24 hours, can take you around town as well as to nearby battlefield sites.

BATTLE OF THE SOMME MEMORIALS

The First Battle of the Somme, the WWI Allied offensive waged in the villages and woodlands north-east of Amiens, was designed to relieve pressure on the beleaguered French troops at Verdun (for more details see the Alsace & Lorraine chapter). On 1 July 1916, British, Commonwealth and French troops 'went over the top' in a massive assault along a 34km front. But German positions proved virtually unbreachable and on the first day of the battle an astounding 20,000 British troops were killed and another 40,000 were wounded.

Most casualties were infantrymen mowed down by German machine guns.

By the time the offensive was called off in mid-November, some 1.2 million lives had been lost on both sides. The British had advanced 12km, the French only 8km. The Battle of the Somme has become a metaphor for the meaningless slaughter of war and its killing fields are a site of pilgrimage.

Commonwealth Cemeteries & Memorials

Over 750,000 soldiers from Canada, Australia, New Zealand, South Africa, the Indian subcontinent, the West Indies and other parts of the British Empire died on the Western Front, two-thirds of them in France. By Commonwealth tradition, they were buried where they fell, in over 1000 military cemeteries and 2000 civilian cemeteries. Today, hundreds of neatly tended Commonwealth plots dot the landscape along a wide line running roughly from Albert and Cambrai north via Arras and Béthune to Armentières and Ypres (Ieper) in Belgium. Many of the Commonwealth headstones bear inscriptions composed by

family members. Some 26 memorials (20 of them in France) bear the names of over 300,000 Commonwealth soldiers whose bodies were never recovered or identified. The French, Americans and Germans reburied their dead in large war cemeteries after the war.

Except where noted, all the monuments listed here are always open. Larger Commonwealth cemeteries usually have a plaque (often inside a little marble pavilion) with historical information in English. Touring the area is only really feasible by car or bicycle.

Maps & Brochures All of the memorials and cemeteries mentioned here (and hundreds of others) are indicated on Michelin's 1:200,000 scale maps. For more information, pick up Michelin's yellow maps Nos 51 and/or 52 overprinted by the Commonwealth War Graves Commission (☎ 03 21 21 77 00 in Beaurains) with all the Commonwealth cemeteries in the region (25FF). The brochure *The Somme – Remembrance Tour of the Great War* (5FF) is on offer at area tourist offices.

To visit WWI sites farther north, in the

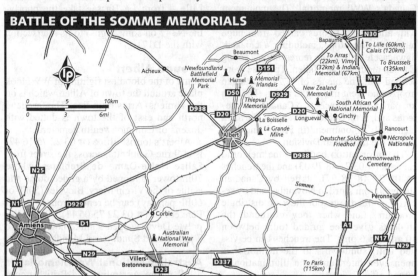

BATTLE OF THE SOMME MEMORIALS

departments of Nord and Pas de Calais, you might want to pick up *Along the Track of the First World War* (35FF), available at tourist offices (eg in Lille). It provides driving instructions for a car tour.

North of Arras

The area north of Arras has a couple of noteworthy memorials and numerous military cemeteries.

Canadian Battlefield Memorial Park

Whereas the French have attempted to erase all signs of the war and return the Somme region to agriculture and normalcy, the Canadians decided that the most apt way to remember their fallen was to preserve bits of the crater-pocked battlefields. As a result, the best place in the area to get some sense of the unimaginable hell known as the Western Front, is the Canadian Battlefield Memorial Park at Vimy, with its chilling, eerie moonscape and reconstructed trenches.

Of the 66,655 Canadians killed in WWI, 3589 died in August 1917 taking Vimy Ridge, a German defensive line whose highest point was later chosen as the site of Canada's WWI memorial. The monument (which took 25 years to build) is covered with allegorical figures carved from huge blocks of limestone, including a cloaked, downcast female figure representing a young Canada mourning her fallen. The base is inscribed with the names of 11,285 Canadian troops who went missing in action. The 1 sq km park also embraces two Canadian cemeteries and, at the vehicle entrance to the main memorial, a monument (in French and Arabic) to the Moroccan Division.

The information booths at the memorial car park (☎ 03 21 48 79 03) and the trenches (☎ 03 21 48 98 97), staffed by Canadian students from April to November and by security guards the rest of the year, distribute brochures (and when they're around, the students give free guided tours between 10 am and 6 pm). The trenches can be visited until sundown and the memorial is open even later, until the illumination is turned off.

The Canadian Memorial is 10km north of Arras – take the N17 and follow the signs. From Arras, trains go to the town of Vimy (15FF, eight daily and one on Sundays and holidays), 6km east of the memorial. You can also take bus No 91 towards Lens from Arras bus station (13FF, 20 minutes, seven daily but no service on Sunday) – ask the driver to stop at Vimy Ridge, 3km from the memorial. A taxi from Arras costs about 110FF return (140FF on Sunday).

Indian Memorial

The fascinating and seldom-visited Mémorial Indien, vaguely Moghul in architecture, records the names of Commonwealth soldiers from the Indian subcontinent who 'have no known grave'. The units (31st Punjabis, 11th Rajputs, 2nd King Edward's Own Gurkha Rifles) and the ranks of the fallen (sepoy, havildar, naik, sowar, labourer, follower) engraved on the walls evoke the pride, pomp and exploitation on which the British Empire was built. About 200m to the south is a Cemeterio Militar Português (Portuguese Military Cemetery).

The Indian Memorial is about 35km north of Arras and 20km south-west of Lille – from La Bassée take the poorly-signposted northbound D947 (marked as the N347 on some signs) to its intersection with the D171.

Around Albert

Some of the bloodiest fighting of WWI took place around the town of Albert which is on the Amiens–Arras train line. The farmland north and east of the town is dotted with dozens of Commonwealth cemeteries.

Albert's tourist office (☎ 03 22 75 16 42) is at 9 rue Gambetta, across the street from Église Notre-Dame de Brebières, whose 70m tower is topped by a gilded dome and statue of the Virgin Mary. Bicycles (50FF or 60FF per day) can be rented from Brasselet Père et Fils (☎ 03 22 75 05 11), 10 rue Hippolyte Devaux, open 9 am to noon and 2 to 7 pm (closed Sunday and Monday).

Australian National War Memorial

On a hill where Australian and British troops

repulsed a German assault on 24 April 1918, Australia's National War Memorial at Villers-Bretonneux is a 32m tower engraved with the names of 10,982 soldiers who went missing in action. It was dedicated in 1938; only two years later its stone walls were scarred by the guns of Hitler's invading armies. During WWI, 313,000 Aussies (out of a total population of 4.5 million) volunteered for military service; of the 60,000 men who never returned, 46,000 met their deaths on the Western Front.

In the **Commonwealth military cemetery** between the road and the monument there are Australian and Canadian sections. Many of the headstones are marked simply 'A Soldier of the Great War/Known Unto God' from 'An Australian Regiment'.

The Australian memorial is 16km southwest of Albert and 15km east of Amiens – from the latter take the N29 or D1, then the D23. The Villers-Bretonneux train station, linked to Amiens (20FF, 12 minutes, five to seven daily), is 3km south of the memorial.

Newfoundland Battlefield Memorial Park The evocative Parc Terre-Neuvien is the site of an infantry assault on German trenches in which the volunteer Royal Newfoundland Regiment was nearly wiped out on 1 July 1916. It preserves part of the Western Front as it looked at fighting's end. The zigzag trench system (which still fills with mud in winter) is clearly visible, as are countless shell craters and the remains of barbed-wire barriers. You can survey the whole battlefield from the **caribou statue** – in 1918, hundreds of square kilometres of northern France looked like this. Opened in 1925, the memorial sits on land 'purchased with funds subscribed by the government and women of Newfoundland' (as a sign explains).

The park is 8km north of Albert along the D50.

Thiepval Memorial Dedicated to 'the Missing of the Somme', this memorial was built in the early 1930s on the site of a German stronghold that was stormed on 1 July 1916 with unimaginable casualties.

The columns of the arches are inscribed with the names of 73,367 British and South African soldiers whose remains were never found. When two or more soldiers have the same surname and first initial, their serial numbers are indicated. Locals still dig up shrapnel from the nearby fields.

In the **Thiepval Anglo-French cemetery** behind the memorial, most of the gravestones are marked either 'Inconnu' or 'A Soldier of the Great War/Known Unto God'.

Thiepval is about 8km north-east of Albert along the D929, the D20 and finally the D151. These roads pass a number of Commonwealth cemeteries.

Mémorial Irlandais Built on a German frontline position assaulted by the 36th (Ulster) Division on 1 July 1916, the **Tour d'Ulster** (Ulster Tower), dedicated in 1921 and something of a Unionist pilgrimage site, is a replica of Helen's Tower near Bangor, County Down in Northern Ireland, where the unit did its training. The **memorial room** inside the tower and the gardens are especially well tended. A black obelisk known as the **Orange Memorial to Fallen Brethren** stands near the entrance.

The Mémorial Irlandais is about 1km north of Thiepval.

La Grande Mine Officially known as the Lochnagar Crater Memorial, this enormous crater – one of many made by tunnelling under enemy (in this case German) trenches and planting vast quantities of explosives – looks like a meteor hit it. It was made at 7.30 am on 1 July 1916. The nearby grassy area is pocked with smaller craters.

To get there from Albert, take the D929 north-eastwards for about 3km to its intersection with the D20 (at La Boisselle). Then turn south-eastwards for 500m along the C9 (also known as Route de la Grande Mine).

South African National Memorial The Mémorial Sud-Africain, founded in 1920, is in the middle of shell-pocked **Delville Wood**, which was almost captured by a South African brigade in the third week of

July 1916. The avenues through the trees are named after streets in London and Edinburgh. The star-shaped **museum** (☎ 03 22 85 02 17) opens 10 am to 3.45 pm (5.45 pm April to mid-October); it's closed on Monday, holidays and in December and January. There's a **Commonwealth cemetery** across the street.

To get to Delville Wood, which is about 15km east of Albert between the villages of Longueval and Ginchy, take the D20. The **New Zealand Memorial** is 1.5km due north of Longueval.

Rancourt This village, 20km east of Albert, is the site of three military cemeteries. The French **Nécropole Nationale** (National Necropolis), on the N17 just south of the edge of town, has 54,665 graves marked with double rows of cement crosses and, for Muslims, Jews and *libre-penseurs* (freethinkers), tablet-shaped markers. The **chapel**, built with private donations, is lined with memorial plaques marked *mort pour la patrie* (meaning 'died for the homeland'); some include heroic descriptions of battlefield valour. There's a small **Commonwealth cemetery** across the street.

The **Deutscher Soldaten Friedhof** (Cimetière Militaire Allemand or German Military Cemetery), 500m due west of the French cemetery (near the intersection of the N17 and the D20), contains the remains of 11,422 German soldiers, many of whom are buried in the mass graves at the top of the slope.

Péronne About 25km south-east of Albert in the town of Péronne is informative **Historial de la Grande Guerre** (☎ 03 22 83 14 18), which examines the origins and consequences of WWI from the perspective of France, Germany and Great Britain and their respective soldiers and civilians. It opens 10 am to 5.30 pm daily, except Monday, (6 pm from May to September). It's closed mid-December to mid-January. Admission costs 39FF (those aged under 18, students, teachers, ex-servicemen or veterans 20FF).

AMIENS
postcode 80000 • pop 132,000
• elevation 34m
Amiens, the friendly if austere former capital of Picardy, is home to one of France's most magnificent cathedrals. The city's 23,000 students give the city a young, lively feel. Seriously damaged during both world wars, it is a good base for visits to the Battle of the Somme memorials.

Orientation
The centre of the partly pedestrianised commercial district is two blocks west of the cathedral around grassy place Gambetta. The main shopping street is rue des Vergeaux and the train station is about 1km south-east of place Gambetta.

Information
Tourist Offices The main tourist office (☎ 03 22 71 60 50, fax 03 22 71 60 51 ✉ OT@amiens.com), 6 bis rue Dusevel, opens 9.30 am to 7 pm Monday to Saturday; it closes at 6 pm from October to March. It opens 2 to 5 pm on Sunday. Hotel reservations cost 20FF. Brochures on the Somme war monuments are available. The Web site is at www.amiens.com/tourisme.

Money The post office exchanges currency. The Banque de France on rue de la République exchanges currency from 9 am to noon. There are several commercial banks around place René Goblet and a Caisse d'Épargne across place Alphonse Fiquet from the train station; many open Tuesday to Saturday.

Post & Communications The main post office, 7 rue des Vergeaux, opens 8 am to 7 pm weekdays and until noon on Saturday. It has a Cyberposte.

Laundry NET Express at 10 rue André opens 7 am to 9 pm daily.

Cathédrale Notre Dame
This spectacular Gothic cathedral, the largest in France, was begun in 1220 to house what was purported to be the head of

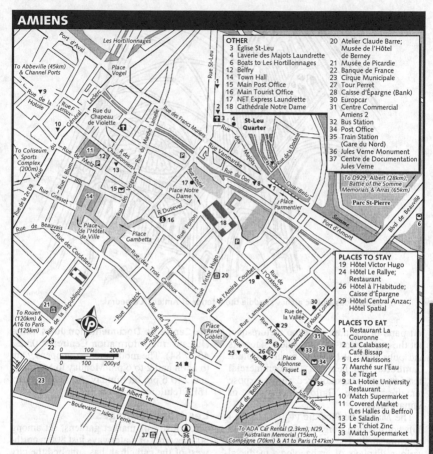

AMIENS

St-John the Baptist. It's noted for its soaring Gothic arches, unity of style and immense interior: 145m long, 70m wide at the transept and up to 43m high.

The nave, lined with beautifully decorated chapels, is graced by the 13th-century bronze **recumbent figures** of the bishops who built the cathedral. The choir, with its 110 sumptuously carved oak **choir stalls** (1508–22), is separated from the ambulatory by wrought-iron grates (1761–62) and choir screens whose painted stone figures illustrate the lives of St-Firmin (1495), the first bishop of Amiens and patron saint of

Picardy, and St-John the Baptist (1531). Note the black and white, 234m-long **maze** embedded in the floor of the nave.

The cathedral opens 8.30 am to noon and 2 pm (2.30 pm on Sunday) to 5 pm daily (7 pm from April to October, when there's no midday closure). The **treasury** is on the southern side of the ambulatory around the choir.

Other Sights

The medieval **St-Leu Quarter**, north of the cathedral, is the best place in town for a riverside stroll. Post-war renovations have

JANE SMITH

Vertiginous Gothic arches straddle the interior of Amiens Cathedral.

left parts of the area a bit too picturesque, but the many neon-lit, riverside restaurants and pubs make it lively at night. At **place Gambetta**, the heart of the commercial district, two glass-covered shafts expose remains of the Gallo-Roman city of Samarobriva.

The **Musée de Picardie** (☎ 03 22 97 14 00), housed in a gorgeous Second Empire building at 48 rue de la République, has various displays of archaeology, medieval art, 18th-century French paintings and Revolutionary-era ceramics. It opens 10 am to 12.30 pm and 2 to 6 pm (closed Monday). Admission costs 20FF (those aged under 18, 10FF).

From Monday to Saturday at 3 pm you can visit a private collection of 13th- to 20th-century stained glass at the workshop **Atelier Claude Barre** (☎ 03 22 91 81 18), 40 rue Victor Hugo. Admission costs 20FF (children and students 5FF).

Jules Verne (1828–1905) wrote many famous works during his two decades in the turreted house at 2 rue Charles Dubois, now

the **Centre de Documentation Jules Verne** (Jules Verne Information Centre; ☎ 03 22 45 37 84). The modest museum opens 9 am to noon and 2 to 6 pm Monday to Saturday, and 2 to 6 pm on Sunday. Admission costs 15FF (children/students 10/5FF).

Les Hortillonnages

This cluster of market gardens, set among 300 hectares of waterways just 800m north-west of the cathedral, has supplied the city with vegetables and flowers since the Middle Ages. From April to October, one-hour cruises of the peaceful canals depart from the small kiosk (☎ 03 22 92 12 18) at 54 blvd de Beauvillé. Tickets cost 30FF (children aged four to 10/those aged under 16, 15/25FF). Boats depart daily from 2 pm, but only if enough people show up. In summer, cruises usually begin until at least 6 pm.

Places to Stay

The lovely and central *Hôtel Victor Hugo* (☎ 03 22 91 57 91, fax 03 22 92 74 02, 2 rue *de l'Oratoire)* has modern, stylish doubles from 135FF (205FF with shower and toilet). Reception opens 24 hours.

The two-star **Hôtel Central Anzac** (☎ 03 22 91 34 08, fax 03 22 91 36 02, 17 rue Alexandre Fatton) was started decades ago by an Australian ex-serviceman. It has clean and comfortable (if small) singles /doubles from 155/180FF (225/250FF with shower and toilet). **Hôtel Spatial** (☎ 03 22 91 53 23, fax 03 22 92 27 87), next door at No 15, has renovated, modern singles/ doubles from 160/180FF (230/255FF with shower and toilet). Free, enclosed parking is available. **Hôtel à l'Habitude** (☎ 03 22 91 69 78, fax 03 22 91 84 48, 7 place Alphonse Fiquet) has doubles with private facilities from 195FF to 230FF.

The **Hôtel Le Rallye** (☎ 03 22 91 76 03, fax 03 22 91 16 77, 24 rue des Otages), built in the 1920s, has slightly tatty doubles from 120FF (180FF with shower and toilet).

Places to Eat
Restaurants The elegant *Les Marissons* (☎ 03 22 92 96 66, Pont de la Dodane) is in a 14th-century boatwright's workshop, and offers *menus* of Picardy cuisine from 120FF to 295FF (closed Saturday lunch and Sunday). French and regional *menus* are on offer at **Restaurant La Couronne** (☎ 03 22 91 88 57, 64 rue St-Leu), for 92FF and 135FF. It's closed Saturday and Sunday night.

The restaurant in **Hôtel Le Rallye** (see Places to Stay above) has *menus* from 60FF to 170FF (closed Saturday evening and Sunday). **Le T'chiot Zinc** (☎ 03 22 91 43 79, 18 rue de Noyon) is an inviting bistro with Picardy-style *menus* costing from 69FF to 159FF (closed Monday lunch and Sunday).

Hot and cold salads (from 49FF to 83FF) are the speciality of **Le Saladin** (☎ 03 22 92 05 15, rue des Chaudronniers) which is closed Sunday.

Algerian Berber-style couscous (from 60FF to 135FF) is on offer at **Le Tizgirt** (☎ 03 22 91 42 55, 60 rue Vanmarcke) (closed Saturday lunch, Monday night and Sunday). **La Calabesse** (☎ 03 22 91 28 00, 48 rue St-Leu), serves Afro-Antillean dishes (closed Saturday for lunch and on Sunday).

La Hotoie (☎ 03 22 91 30 35, 4 rue de la Hotoie) is a large university cafeteria open 11.35 am to 11.15 pm and 6.35 to 8 pm on weekdays during the academic year.

Self-Catering Fruits and vegetables grown in the hortillonnages are on offer at the *marché sur l'eau* (floating market), now held on dry land at place Parmentier on Saturday morning.

The modern *covered market* in the eastern bit of Les Halles du Beffroi, a shopping centre on rue de Metz, opens 8 am to 7 pm Tuesday to Saturday (from 12.30 pm on Saturday). Outside, there's also a *food market* from 9 am to 6 pm on Wednesday and Saturday. The *Match supermarket* inside the Amiens 2 Centre Commercial by the train station opens 8 am to 8 pm Monday to Saturday.

Entertainment
A mellow bar with African décor and a world music ambience, *Café Bissap* (☎ 03 22 92 36 41, 50 rue St-Leu) opens 4 pm to 3 am Monday to Saturday.

Getting There & Away
Bus The bus station (☎ 03 22 92 27 03) in the basement of the Centre Commercial has services to Beauvais (61FF or 68FF, 1¼ hours, 11 weekdays, five on Saturdays), Albert (28FF, 45 to 60 minutes, four daily except Sunday, the first at noon) and Arras (46.50FF, two hours, two daily except Sunday).

Train The Gare du Nord (☎ 03 36 35 35 35), the city's main train station, has an information office open 8.45 am to 6.20 pm (closed Sunday and holidays).

Destinations served include Paris' Gare du Nord (98FF, 1¼ to two hours, hourly), Lille (96FF, 1½ hours, four direct daily), Arras (59FF, 45 minutes, six daily) via Albert (34FF, 25 minutes, hourly, five to eight at weekends), Villers-Bretonneux (20FF, 12 minutes, five to seven daily), Calais (118FF,

FAR NORTHERN FRANCE

two hours, up to eight daily) via Boulogne (93FF, 1¼ hours, five to eight daily) and Rouen (92FF, 1½ to two hours, three or four daily). SNCF buses, timed with the TGVs, link Amiens with the Haute Picardie TGV station (43FF).

Car & Motorcycle ADA car rental (☎ 03 22 46 49 49) is 2.5km south-east of the train station at 387 chaussée Jules Ferry (closed Sunday). By bus, take line No 1 or 16. Europcar (☎ 03 22 72 32 48) is at 3 blvd Alsace Lorraine.

There's free parking beyond Jules Barni west of the train station.

BEAUVAIS
postcode 60000 • pop 57,000
• elevation 67m
The soaring Cathédrale St-Pierre and the town's fine museums make Beauvais a great day trip from Paris – or a fine stopover on your way between northern France and the French capital. Beauvais, prefecture (*préfecture*) of the Oise département, is 81km north of Paris.

Information
The tourist office (☎ 03 44 15 30 30, fax 03 44 15 30 31, ✉ ot.bvsis@wanadoo.fr), 1 rue Beauregard, opens 9.30 am to 7 pm Tuesday to Saturday, and 10 am to 5 pm on Sunday, mid-April to September. The rest of the year it opens 10 am to 1 pm and 2 to 6 pm on Monday, 9.30 am to 6.30 pm Tuesday to Saturday, and 10 am to 1.30 pm on Sunday.

The Banque de France, 31 rue du Dr Gérard, exchanges currency from 9.15 am to noon Monday to Friday. The post office, 1 rue Gambetta, opens 8 am to 7 pm on weekdays and to noon on Saturday. It has a Cyberposte terminal.

Cathédrale St-Pierre
To enthusiasts, Beauvais' unfinished Gothic cathedral (☎ 03 44 48 11 60) is a bit like the Venus de Milo: a beautiful work with key extremities missi''ng (in this case the nave). When the town's Carolingian cathedral was partly destroyed by fire in 1225, ambitious

local bishops and noblemen decided that its replacement should surpass anything ever built. Unfortunately, their richly adorned creation also surpassed the limits of technology and in 1272 (and again in 1284) the 48m-high vaults – the highest ever built – collapsed.

The cathedral opens 9 am to 12.15 pm and 2 to 6.15 pm May to October (to 5.30 pm the rest of the year). The **astronomical clock** (built 1868) sounds at 10.40 and 11.40 am, and at 2.40, 3.40 and 4.40 pm Monday to Saturday. Admission costs 22FF (students 15FF; children aged four to 14, 5FF).

Église St-Étienne
This church on rue Engrand Leprince, begun in the 12th century but dating mostly from the 16th century, has a Romanesque nave and a Gothic choir, which some historians believe was the birthplace of that style. The church contains some superb 16th-century stained glass (notably *L'Arbre de Jessé*). It opens 9.30 to 11.30 am and 2 to 5 pm April to October (4 pm the rest of the year).

Museums
The outstanding **Musée Départemental de l'Oise** (☎ 03 44 11 43 83), 1 rue du Musée, is just west of the cathedral in the former Bishops' Palace. Its sections include medieval wood carvings, Art Nouveau, ceramics and French and Italian paintings (including some gruesome 16th-century works of decapitations). It opens 10 am to noon and 2 to 6 pm (closed Tuesday). Admission costs 10FF, but those aged under 18 get in free (and on Wednesday, everyone does).

The **Galerie Nationale de la Tapisserie** (☎ 03 44 05 14 28), rue St-Pierre, has exhibitions of tapestry, a craft for which Beauvais is famous. It opens 9.30 to 11.30 am and 2 to 6 pm (closed Monday) April to September, and 10 to 11.30 am and 2.30 to 4.30 pm the rest of the year. Admission costs 25FF (seniors and those aged 18 to 25 15FF, those aged under 18 free).

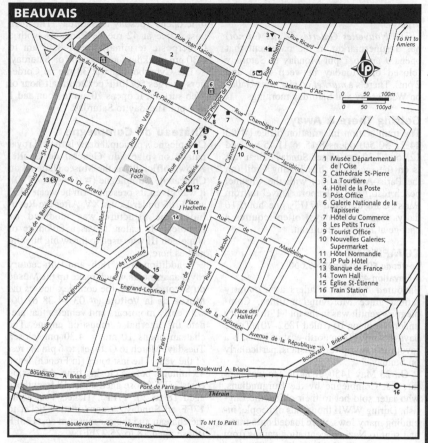

BEAUVAIS

1 Musée Départemental de l'Oise
2 Cathédrale St-Pierre
3 La Tourtière
4 Hôtel de la Poste
5 Post Office
6 Galerie Nationale de la Tapisserie
7 Hôtel du Commerce
8 Les Petits Trucs
9 Tourist Office
10 Nouvelles Galeries; Supermarket
11 Hôtel Normandie
12 JP Pub Hôtel
13 Banque de France
14 Town Hall
15 Église St-Étienne
16 Train Station

FAR NORTHERN FRANCE

Places to Stay

The *Hôtel Normandie* (☎ 03 44 45 07 61, 19 rue Beauregard) has utilitarian doubles from 120FF (140FF with toilet). Reception is closed on Monday. The cheap but cheerful *Hôtel du Commerce* (☎ 03 44 48 17 84, 11–13 rue Chambiges) has basic singles/doubles with washbasin for 110/120FF (150/165FF with shower).

More central is the *JP Pub Hôtel* (☎ 03 44 45 07 51, fax 03 44 45 71 25, 15 place Jeanne Hachette) (120/180FF with shower). *Hôtel de la Poste* (☎ 03 44 45 14 97, fax 03 44 45 02 31, 19 rue Gambetta) has rooms

with washbasin and toilet for 145/195FF (155/205FF with shower).

Places to Eat

Les Petits Trucs (☎ 03 44 48 31 31, 6 rue Philippe de Dreux) is a creperie serving galettes and crepes from 15FF to 49FF and *menus* at 58FF (weekday lunch only) and 70FF. It opens daily, except Sunday, to 10 pm.

La Tourtière (☎ 03 44 45 86 32, 3 rue Ricard), has savoury and sweet *tartes* (from 21FF to 23FF) as well as salads from 33FF. Takeaways are cheaper. It opens 11.30 am

euro currency converter €1 = 6.56FF

to 2 pm Monday to Saturday (to 9 pm on Friday).

The *Nouvelles Galeries (2 rue Carnot)* has a supermarket in the basement that opens 9 am to 7 pm Monday to Saturday (closed on Monday between noon and 2 pm). There's a *market* on place des Halles on Wednesday and Saturday mornings.

Getting There & Away

The train station information office (☎ 03 44 21 50 50) opens 8.15 to 11.45 am and 12.15 to 7.30 pm (closed Sunday). Beauvais is on the secondary line linking Creil (on the Paris–Amiens line) with the Channel beach resort of Le Tréport. Travel to/from Paris' Gare du Nord (71FF, one hour, 16 daily, nine on Sundays) often requires a change at Persan-Beaumont.

COMPIÈGNE
postcode 60200 • pop 45,000
• elevation 41m

Favoured by French rulers as a country retreat since Merovingian times, Compiègne's zenith was in the mid-19th century under Napoleon III (ruled 1852–70). These days the city, 80km north-east of Paris, is a favourite day trip for Parisians, particularly on Sunday.

On 23 May 1430, Joan of Arc was captured at Compiègne by the Burgundians, who later sold her to their allies, the English. During WWII thousands of people, including many Jews, were loaded onto trains and sent to Nazi concentration camps from a transit camp in the Compiègne suburb of Royallieu.

Information

Tourist Offices The tourist office (☎ 03 44 40 01 00, fax 03 44 40 23 28, @ glg@mairie-compiègne.fr) is in the 15th-century Gothic town hall opposite the statue of Jeanne d'Arc. It opens 9.15 am to 12.15 pm and 1.45 to 6.15 pm Monday to Saturday, November to March; and to 6.30 pm, and also 10 am to 1 pm and 2.30 to 5 pm on Sunday, the rest of the year. Staff make local hotel reservations for 10FF.

The Société Générale (☎ 03 44 38 57 00)

at the corner of rue Magenta and rue de l'Étoile opens Tuesday to Saturday. The main post office at 42 rue de Capucins (with a Cyberposte terminal) opens 8.30 am to 6.30 pm weekdays and to noon on Saturday.

The Cyberboutique at 33 rue de Cordeliers charges 50/30FF per hour/half-hour of Web surfing. It opens 10 am to noon and 1 to 7 pm Tuesday to Saturday.

Château de Compiègne

Compiègne's principal draw is the old royal palace on place du Général de Gaulle. Known officially as the Musée National du Château de Compiègne (☎ 03 44 38 47 00), it was given its present form between 1752 and 1786 under Louis XV. After the Revolution the structure was modified by Napoleon I. Later it was a favourite of Napoleon III who used to throw big hunting parties here.

In addition to the 18th- and 19th-century royal apartments which make up the **Musée du Second Empire**, the complex houses the **Musée de la Voiture** (☎ 03 44 38 67 00) with early motorcars and vehicles that predate the internal combustion engine. The chateau opens 10 am to 4.30 pm (closed Tuesday) March to October; to 6 pm the rest of the year. The last tours (in French) leave 45 minutes before closing time. Admission costs 25FF (those aged under 18 free; those aged 18 to 25, 17FF). Tickets cost a flat 17FF on Sunday. A combination ticket to the chateau and the car museum costs 35FF (those aged 18 to 25 22FF).

Forêt de Compiègne

The 220 sq km Forêt de Compiègne, one of the most attractive forest areas in the Île de France, abuts the southern and eastern outskirts of Compiègne. The area is covered by IGN's 1:25,000 scale map *Forêts de Compiègne et de Laigue* (58FF).

Clairière de l'Armistice The Armistice Clearing where WWI was officially ended is 7km north-east of Compiègne (towards Soissons), not far from the River Aisne. Early on the morning of 11 November 1918 – a date still commemorated in many

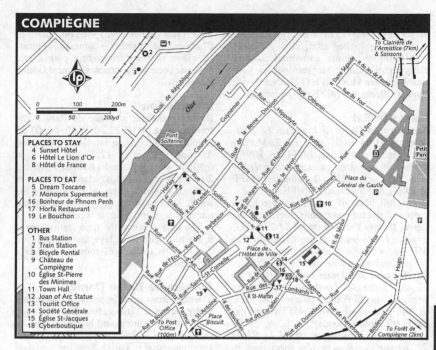

COMPIÈGNE

PLACES TO STAY
4 Sunset Hôtel
6 Hôtel Le Lion d'Or
8 Hôtel de France

PLACES TO EAT
5 Dream Toscane
7 Monoprix Supermarket
16 Bonheur de Phnom Penh
17 Horfa Restaurant
19 Le Bouchon

OTHER
1 Bus Station
2 Train Station
3 Bicycle Rental
9 Château de
   Compiègne
10 Église St-Pierre
   des Minimes
11 Town Hall
12 Joan of Arc Statue
13 Tourist Office
14 Société Générale
15 Église St-Jacques
18 Cyberboutique

countries – in the railway carriage of the Allied supreme commander, Maréchal Ferdinand Foch, German representatives and Foch signed an armistice to come into force on 'the 11th hour of the 11th day of the 11th month'.

On 22 June 1940 in the same railway car, the French were forced to sign the armistice that recognised the German conquest of France. The carriage was later taken for exhibition to Berlin where it was destroyed by Allied bombing in 1943. A replica of the original carriage, placed here to commemorate the first signing ceremony (most French guidebooks prefer to forget about the second one), opens 9 am to noon and 2 to 5.30 pm, except Tuesday, mid-October to February. The rest of the year it opens to 6.30 pm. Admission costs 12FF.

Special Events

Paris–Roubaix, one of the world's toughest one-day cycling races, starts in Compiègne on the first Sunday after Easter. What's gruelling isn't so much the 267km of course to Roubaix velodrome, but the 27 energy-sapping, bone-jarring sections of old *pavé* (cobblestone) roads totalling 50km spread throughout its length. Tens of thousands of spectators line the race's route every year, especially the 2.4km pavé section through the Fôret d'Arenberg. Buy a copy of *L'Équipe* a day or so prior for details.

Places to Stay

Compiègne has several decent options. The one-star *Hôtel le Lion d'Or* (☎ 03 44 23 32 17, fax 03 44 86 06 23, 4 rue Général Leclerc) is an old-fashioned place with basic singles/doubles with sink costing 140/150FF (160/180FF with shower). Rooms with bath cost 190/210FF.

The soulless but clean *Sunset Hôtel* (☎ 03 44 20 47 47, 4 rue Solférino) offers singles starting at 170FF and doubles/triples for 180FF. All rooms have a shower.

The *Hôtel de France* (☎ 03 44 40 02 74, fax 03 44 40 48 37, 17 rue Eugène Floquet) is a lovingly looked-after, 20-room hotel with antiques, chintz and dried flowers everywhere. Simple singles/doubles with washbasin are 110/160FF (175/250FF with shower). Breakfast (48FF) is overpriced.

Places to Eat
Restaurants Old-style brasserie *Le Bouchon* (☎ 03 44 40 05 32, 5 rue St-Martin) has starters and salads (40FF to 80FF), stick-to-the-ribs main courses such as *tête de veau*, duck *cassoulet* and *andouilles* (48FF to 80FF), and a *formule* at 69FF.

The left bank of the River Oise has a couple of decent restaurants, including the Italian *Dream Toscane* (☎ 03 44 23 31 33, 5 rue de Harlay) with pizzas (from 40FF to 55FF) cooked in a wood-burning oven.

For Cambodian food the friendly, family-run *Bonheur de Phnom Penh* (☎ 03 44 40 09 45, 13 rue des Lombards) has starters costing from 20FF, main courses cost 32FF to 70FF and *menus* start at 45FF (lunch) to 98FF. It's closed Monday lunch.

The *Horfa Restaurant* (☎ 03 44 97 03 27, 10 rue des Boucheries) specialises in meat dishes (particularly *entrocôte* recipes) from its in-house butcher. *Menus* start at 52FF. It opens for lunch and dinner.

Self-Catering The *Monoprix* (37 rue Solférino) opens 8.30 am to 8 pm Monday to Saturday.

Getting There & Around
Compiègne enjoys frequent rail service from Paris' Gare du Nord (70FF, one hour), Amiens (64FF, 1½ to two hours) and Beauvais (60FF via Creil, 1¼ hours).

Bicycles are for rent about 50m to the right as you exit the train station in front of the Brasserie du Nord. Ring ☎ 06 07 54 99 26 for information.

LAON
postcode 02000 • pop 26,300
• elevation 181m
About 63km north-east of Compiègne lies Laon, the capital of the Carolingian Empire

in the 9th and 10th centuries. Its medieval *Ville Haute* (upper town) – the birthplace of Charlemagne's mother – commands fantastic views of the surrounding plains, and possesses one of the country's finest Gothic cathedrals.

Information
By the cathedral at place du Parvis, the **tourist office** (☎ 03 23 20 28 62, fax 03 23 20 68 11, @ tourisme.info.laon@wanadoo.fr) opens 9 am to 12.30 pm and 2 to 6.30 pm weekdays, and 11 am to 1 pm and 2 to 6 pm at weekends, March to June; in July and August it closes at 7 pm during the week. The rest of the year it closes at 6 pm on weekdays and 5 pm at weekends.

The post office at the train station opens 8 am to 7 pm weekdays and to noon on Saturday. It exchanges money and has a Cyberposte.

Cathédrale Notre Dame
The main draw is the impressive **Cathédrale Notre Dame**, a 12th-century Gothic design blended with Roman and Norman styles of the day (you'll find similar arcades on its sister cathedral in Paris). Near the top of its five 60m towers, look for the carved statues of oxen which supposedly heaved the masonry up the hill. The interior is remarkable for its dimensions – 110m in length and 30m in width – as well as its medieval stained glass, through which the sun splashes a dark, fascinating mosaic. The cathedral opens 8 am to 6.30 pm daily. Two-hour guided tours (in French) take place at 3 pm at weekends and holidays; meet at the tourist office. Tickets cost 35FF (students and children 20FF).

Places to Stay & Eat
About 100m north of the train station, *Hotel Welcome* (☎ 03 23 23 06 11, 2 ave Carnot) charges 130FF for basic singles/doubles with washbasin (150FF with shower). In the Haute Ville, the two-star *Hôtel Les Chevaliers* (☎ 03 23 27 17 50, fax 02 23 23 40 71, 3-5 rue Sérurer) has comfortable doubles with hall shower starting at 155FF and ones with private facilities costing from 220FF,

including breakfast. It's closed from mid-November to mid-March.

L'Agora (☎ *03 23 20 29 21, 16 rue des Cordeliers*) in the Ville Haute has galettes costing from 18FF to 54FF and Breton *menus* starting at 48FF (closed Monday).

Getting There & Around

Frequent train services include Reims (48FF, 45 minutes, six daily), Paris Gare du Nord (104FF, 1¾ hours, eight daily), Amiens (84FF, 1½ hours, five daily) and Compiègne (64FF, 1½ hours, six daily).

To reach the Ville Haute, it's a steep 20-minute walk from the end of ave Carnot near the train station. More fun is the automated Poma 2000 mini-metro, which departs 50m north-east of the train station and drops you 3½ minutes later in the upper town (single 6.40FF).

Normandy

Often compared with the countryside of southern England, Normandy (Normandie) is the land of the *bocage*, farmland subdivided by hedges and trees. The hedgerows *(haies)* made fighting difficult in WWII, and for the past half century there has been a trend to cut them down.

In many areas, however, they still break the landscape up into a patchwork of enclosed fields. Winding through these hedgerows are sunken lanes, whose grassy sides are covered with yellow primroses and gorse. At various points, the lanes are deep enough to hide the half-timbered houses.

Set among this peaceful, pastoral landscape are Normandy's cities and towns. Rouen is well endowed with medieval architecture, including a spectacular cathedral; Caen boasts some fine Norman Romanesque abbeys; Bayeux, home to the 11th-century Bayeux Tapestry, is only a dozen kilometres from the D-day landing beaches. Between Rouen and Paris is Giverny, the home and garden of Claude Monet. In Normandy's south-western corner, on the border with Brittany, is the celebrated island abbey of Mont St-Michel. Normandy's most important port cities are Cherbourg and Le Havre.

Along the Côte d'Albâtre (Alabaster Coast), the area south-west of Dieppe, dramatic chalk cliffs rise above the pebble beaches. Farther west, the coastline is padded with sand.

Because it's only a couple of hours by train from Paris, much of Normandy's coast is lined with seaside resorts, including those at Fécamp, Honfleur, and the fashionable twin towns of Deauville and Trouville. During the second half of the 19th century, the Norman coast attracted a number of impressionist painters.

The Battle of Normandy (1944) left its mark on the region. It is most evident in cities such as Le Havre and Caen, where post-war architecture predominates.

Highlights

- **Mont St-Michel** – explore this fascinating island's myriad network of narrow streets
- **Bayeux** – marvel at the magnificent Bayeux Tapestry
- **Giverny** – visit the Musée Claude Monet, Monet's famous house and diverse gardens
- **D-day landing beaches** – pay homage to those who fell during Operation Overlord in WWII
- **Honfleur** – linger at the scenic old harbour where explorers set sail for the New World
- **Étretat** – view the stunning Manneport rock arch from the top of the white cliffs
- **Coutances** – picnic in the beautiful Jardin des Plantes among the ornamental trees

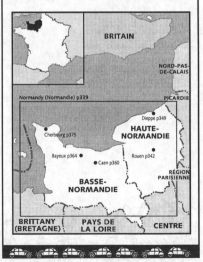

History

Normandy's evolution as a historical entity began with the invasions by the Vikings in the 9th century. Originally made up of

NORMANDY (NORMANDIE)

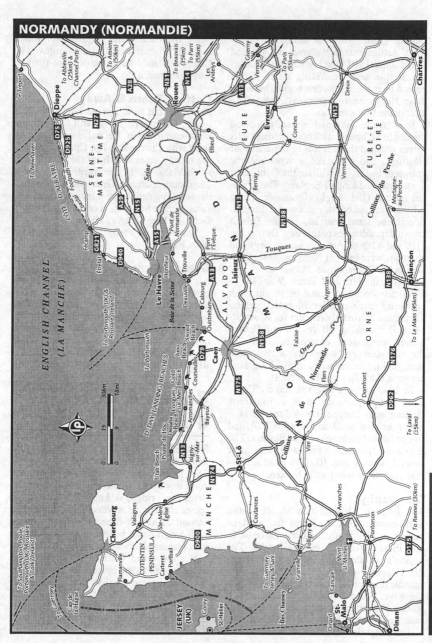

bands of plundering pirates, many of these raiding groups from Scandinavia established settlements in the area and adopted Christianity. In 911 the French king Charles the Simple and the Viking chief Hrölfr agreed to make the Rouen region home to these Norsemen (or Normans), who gave their name to the region.

In 1066 the duke of Normandy crossed the English Channel with 6000 soldiers. His forces crushed the English in the Battle of Hastings, and the duke – who became known to history as William the Conqueror – was crowned king of England. The Channel Islands (Îles Anglo-Normandes), just off the Norman coast, came under English rule in the same year and remain British crown dependencies to this day. During the 11th and 12th centuries, many abbeys and churches were built in Normandy and England in the Romanesque style.

During the Hundred Years' War (1337–1453) the duchy switched back and forth between French and English rule. England dominated Normandy (except for Mont St-Michel) for about 30 years until France gained permanent control in 1450. In the 16th century Normandy, a Protestant stronghold, was the scene of much fighting between Catholics and Huguenots.

In 1942, a force of 6000, mostly Canadian, troops participated in a disastrous landing near Dieppe. On 6 June 1944 – better known as D-day – 45,000 Allied troops landed on beaches near Bayeux. The Battle of Normandy followed, and after several months and 100,000 deaths, German resistance was finally broken.

Geography

The English Channel (La Manche) and north-eastern Brittany form the western border of Normandy, and the Paris basin and Picardy form its eastern border. The region's two divisions are Haute Normandie (Upper Normandy) and Basse Normandie (Lower Normandy), through which the River Seine flows from Paris through Rouen before emptying into the Channel near Le Havre at the Baie de la Seine.

The Cotentin Peninsula, with Cherbourg at its northern tip, divides the Baie de la Seine from the Golfe de St-Malo, which is famed for its extraordinary tides. The Channel Islands lie to the west of the Cotentin peninsula.

Getting There & Away

Ferries to and from England dock at Cherbourg, Dieppe, Le Havre and Ouistreham, north-east of Caen. Ireland is connected by ferry with Cherbourg. The Channel Islands are mostly accessible from the Breton port of St-Malo, but in the warm season from Cherbourg, Carteret, Granville and Portbail as well. For details on ferry schedules and fares, see the Sea section of the introductory Getting There & Away chapter.

Normandy is easily accessible by train from Paris.

Getting Around

All major towns in Normandy are well-connected by rail, but the buses between smaller towns and villages are somewhat infrequent. Visitors who would like to explore Normandy's rural areas might well consider renting a car. See Getting There & Away under D-day Beaches, Caen and Rouen for information on rental companies.

Rouen & Côte d'Albâtre

ROUEN
postcode 76000 • pop 107,000

The city of Rouen, for centuries the farthest point downriver where you could cross the Seine by bridge, is known for its many spires and church towers. The old city has around 2000 half-timbered houses, many with rough-hewn beams, posts and diagonals leaning this way and that. Rouen also has a renowned Gothic cathedral and a number of excellent museums. The city was occupied by the English during the Hundred Years' War when the young French heroine Joan of Arc (Jeanne d'Arc) was tried for heresy and burned at the stake in Rouen.

NORMANDY

Rouen can be visited on an overnight or even a day trip from Paris. It's an excellent base for visiting Monet's home in Giverny.

Orientation

The main train station (Gare Rouen-Rive Droite) is at the northern end of rue Jeanne d'Arc, the main thoroughfare running south to the Seine. The old city is centred around rue du Gros Horloge between the place du Vieux Marché and the cathedral.

Information

Tourist Offices The tourist office (☎ 02 32 08 32 40, fax 02 32 08 32 44, ✉ otrouen@ mcom.fr) is in a lovely, early 16th-century building at 25 place de la Cathédrale, opposite the western facade of the Cathédrale Notre Dame. The office opens 9 am to 7 pm Monday to Saturday, and 9.30 am to 12.30 pm and 2.30 to 6 pm on Sunday, May to September; and 9 am to 6 pm Monday to Saturday, and 10 am to 1 pm on Sunday the rest of the year. Staff make hotel reservations in the area for 15FF.

The tourist office conducts two-hour guided tours (French only) of the city at 10.30 am and 3 pm daily in July and August, and at weekends only the rest of the year for 35FF (children 25FF). The Web site is at www.mairie-rouen.fr.

Money The Banque de France at 32 rue Jean Lecanuet exchanges money from 8.45 am to noon Monday to Friday. The Bureau de Change at 7–9 rue des Bonnetiers has decent exchange rates, no commission and opens 10 am to 7 pm (closed Sunday). Banks line rue Jeanne d'Arc between the Théâtre des Arts and place Maréchal Foch, in front of the Palais de Justice.

American Express (☎ 02 35 89 48 60) has a branch in the tourist office at 25 place de la Cathédrale. It opens 9 am to 1 pm and 2 to 6 pm Monday to Saturday, and 9.30 am to 12.30 pm and 2.30 to 6 pm on Sunday.

The main post office also exchanges currency.

Post & Communications The main post office is at 45 rue Jeanne d'Arc and opens 8 am to 7 pm weekdays and to noon on Saturday. It has a Cyberposte terminal.

PlaceNet (☎ 02 32 76 02 22), 37 rue de la République, charges 32FF per hour of Internet use. It opens 1 to 9 pm on Monday and 11 am to 9 pm Tuesday to Saturday.

Travel Agencies Voyages Wasteels (☎ 02 35 71 92 56), 111 bis rue Jeanne d'Arc, sells discount air tickets. It opens 9 am to noon and 2 to 7 pm Monday to Friday and to 6 pm on Saturday.

Bookshops For English-language books, the ABC Bookshop (☎ 02 35 71 08 67), 11 rue des Faulx, opens 10 am and 6 pm Tuesday to Saturday.

Laundry Among several options, the laundrette diagonally opposite 44 rue d'Amiens opens 7 am to 9 pm daily.

Old City

Rouen's old city suffered enormous damage during WWII but has been painstakingly restored. The main street is **rue du Gros Horloge**, which runs from the cathedral to **place du Vieux Marché**, where 19-year-old Joan of Arc was executed for heresy in 1431. The striking **Église Jeanne d'Arc** marking the site was completed in 1979; you'll learn more about her life from its stained-glass windows than at the tacky **Musée Jeanne d'Arc** across the square at No 33. The church opens 10 am to 12.30 pm and 2 to 6 pm, except Friday and Sunday mornings. Admission to the museum costs 25FF (students 13FF).

The pedestrianised rue du Gros Horloge is spanned by an early 16th-century gatehouse holding aloft the **Gros Horloge**, a large medieval clock with only one hand. Visits to the late 14th-century belfry have been suspended until 2001 due to renovations.

The ornate **Palais de Justice** (Law Courts), which was left a shell at the end of WWII, has been restored to its early 16th-century Gothic glory, though the 19th-century western facade that faces place Maréchal Foch still shows extensive bullet

NORMANDY

ROUEN

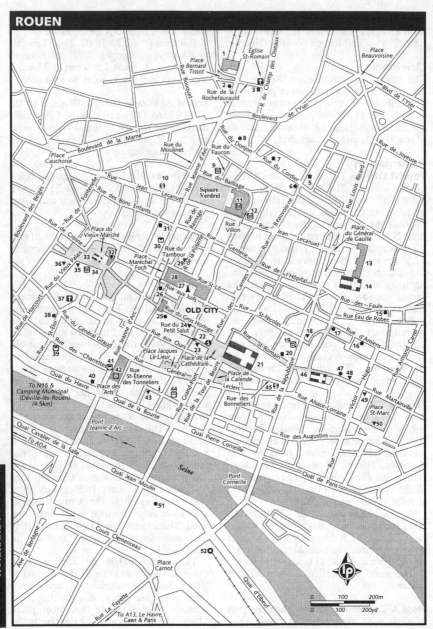

Place Bernard Tissot
Rue Bouquet
Église St-Romain
Place Beauvoisine
Blvd de l'Yser
Rue de la Rochefaucauld
R. du Champ des Oiseaux
Boulevard de l'Yser
Rue de Joyeuse
Place Cauchoise
Boulevard de la Marne
Rue du Moulinet
Rue du Faucon
Rue du Donjon
Rue du Cordier
Rue Louis Ricard
Rue Jeanne d'Arc
Rue du Bailliage
Place du Général de Gaulle
Square Verdrel
Rue des Bons Enfants
Rue Jean Lecanuet
Rue de Fontenelle
Boulevard des Belges
Rue de Crosne
Place du Vieux-Marché
Rue Villon
Rue de Baragnie
Rue de la Poterie
Rue Beauvoisine
Rue Jean Lecanuet
Rue du Vieux Palais
Place Maréchal Foch
Rue du Tambour
Ganterie
Rue de l'Hôpital
Rue de Harcourt
Rue aux Ours
Rue aux Juifs
Rue St-Lô
Rue des Carmes
Rue des Faulx
Rue du Gros Horloge
Rue St-Nicolas
Rue Eau de Robec
Rue d'Amiens
OLD CITY
Rue du Général Giraud
Rue du Petit Salut
Rue St-Romain
Rue d'Amiens
Rue St-Éloi
Rue des Charrettes
Rue Jeanne d'Arc
Place Jacques Le Lieur
Place de la Cathédrale
Rue St-Romain
Rue de la République
Victor Hugo
Rue Martainville
Quai du Havre
Place des Arts
Rue St-Étienne des Tonneliers
Rue du Général Leclerc
Place de la Calende
Rue Alsace-Lorraine
Place St-Marc
To N15 & Camping Municipal (Déville-lès-Rouen) (4.5km)
Quai de la Bourse
Rue Grand-Pont
Rue de la Tour de Beurre
Rue des Bonnetiers
Pont Jeanne d'Arc
Quai Pierre Corneille
Rue des Augustins
Quai Cavalier de la Salle
To ADA
Pont Corneille
Quai de Paris
Seine
Quai Jean Moulin
Ave de Bretagne
Cours Clemenceau
Rue de Paris
Place Carnot
Quai d'Elbeuf
Rue La Fayette
To A13, Le Havre, Caen & Paris

NORMANDY

| 0 | 100 | 200m |
| 0 | 100 | 200yd |

euro currency converter 10FF = €1.52

and shell damage. During construction of the city's underground (subway) system, archaeologists discovered a 3rd-century Gallo-Roman settlement.

The courtyard of the Palais de Justice, which you can enter through a gate on rue aux Juifs, is worth a look for its spires, gargoyles and statuary. Under the courtyard is the **Monument Juif**, a stone building used as a synagogue by Rouen's Jewish community in the early 12th century. Hour-long guided visits (in French; book a day ahead at the tourist office) take place at 2.30 pm on Saturday. Admission costs 35FF (students 25FF).

Cathédrale Notre Dame

Rouen's cathedral, which was the subject of a series of paintings by the impressionist artist Claude Monet, is considered a masterpiece of French Gothic architecture. Erected between 1201 and 1514, it suffered severe damage during WWII and has been undergoing restoration and cleaning for decades. The Romanesque **crypt** was part of a cathedral completed in 1062 and destroyed by fire in 1200. Note also the Flamboyant Gothic **Tour de Beurre**, with its apt yellow stonework, paid for out of the alms donated by various members of the congregation who wanted to eat butter during Lent. There are several guided visits a day to the crypt, ambulatory and **Chapel of the Virgin** during Easter, July and August, but only at weekends the rest of the year. Admission costs 15FF (students 10FF). The cathedral opens 8 am to 7 pm Monday to Saturday and to 6 pm on Sunday. Access is restricted during Sunday morning masses.

Museums

The fascinating **Musée Le Secq des Tournelles** (☎ 02 35 71 28 40), devoted to the blacksmith's craft, displays some 12,000 locks, keys, scissors, tongs and other wrought-iron utensils made between the 3rd and 19th centuries. It's located in a desanctified 16th-century church at 2 rue Jacques Villon (opposite 27 rue Jean Lecanuet). Admission costs 13FF (students 9FF).

The **Musée des Beaux-Arts** (Fine Arts Museum, ☎ 02 35 71 28 40), 26 bis rue Jean Lecanuet, features paintings from the 15th to the 20th centuries on two floors. Admission costs 20FF (students 13FF).

The **Musée de la Céramique** (☎ 02 35 07 31 74), whose speciality is 16th to 19th century faïence (decorated earthenware), is

ROUEN

NORMANDY

up a flight of steps at 1 rue du Faucon. The building it occupies, with a fine courtyard, dates from 1657. Admission costs 15FF (students 10FF). All these museums open from 10 am to 1 pm and 2 to 6 pm (closed on Tuesday).

Churches

The **Église St-Maclou** (entrance next to 56 rue de la République) is a Flamboyant Gothic church built between 1437 and 1521, but much of the decoration dates from the Renaissance. It opens 10 am to noon and 2 to 6 pm (3 to 5.30 pm on Sunday).

The **Église St-Ouen**, a 14th-century abbey church, is a refined example of the High Gothic style. The entrance is through a lovely garden along rue des Faulx. It opens from 10 am to 12.30 pm and 2 to 4.30 pm, and to 6.30 pm in summer (closed all day Tuesday).

Aître St-Maclou

This curious ensemble of half-timbered buildings, built between 1526 and 1533, is decorated with macabre carvings of skulls, crossbones, grave-diggers' tools and hourglasses reminding visitors of their mortality. The courtyard was used as a burial ground for victims of the plague as late as 1781 and is now the municipal École des Beaux-Arts. It can be visited from 8 am to 8 pm (free); enter at 186 rue Martainville, behind the Église St-Maclou.

La Tour Jeanne d'Arc

This tower (☎ 02 35 98 16 21) in rue du Donjon is the sole survivor of eight that once ringed a huge chateau built by Philippe Auguste in the 13th century. Joan of Arc was imprisoned here before her execution. The tower and its two exhibition rooms are open 10 am to noon and 2 to 5 pm, and to 5.30 pm in summer (closed on Tuesday). Admission costs 10FF (students free).

Places to Stay

If you're staying over a weekend, ask the tourist office about its 'Bon Week-end' offer of two nights for the price of one in some hotels. But you'll have to reserve eight days in advance.

Camping The *Camping Municipal* (☎ 02 35 74 07 59), in Déville-lès-Rouen, is 5km north-west of the train station on rue Jules Ferry. From the Théâtre des Arts or the bus station, take bus No 2 (last bus at 11 pm) and get off at the *mairie* of Déville-lès-Rouen. Open year-round, it charges 25FF per adult with tent, 6FF per child and 8.50FF per car.

Hotels – North of the Centre Across from the train station, the welcoming *Hôtel de la Rochefaucauld* (☎ 02 35 71 86 58) offers simple singles/doubles for one or two people from 120/150FF, including breakfast. Showers cost 15FF.

Spotless *Hôtel Normandya* (☎ 02 35 71 46 15, 32 rue du Cordier), is a pleasant, family-run place. Single rooms (some with shower) cost 110FF to 140FF, doubles cost 10FF to 20FF more and a hall shower costs 10FF.

The *Hôtel Sphinx* (☎ 02 35 71 35 86, 130 rue Beauvoisine), is a cosy, friendly place with some timbered rooms. Doubles range from 100FF to 110FF; an extra bed is 60FF. Showers cost 10FF.

Hotels – City Centre The *Hôtel des Flandres* (☎ 02 35 71 56 88, 5 rue des Bons Enfants), is probably the pick of the centre budget options, with comfy, newly renovated doubles costing 150FF with shower (170FF with shower and toilet).

The *Hôtel Le Palais* (☎ 02 35 71 41 40, 12 rue du Tambour), well-situated near the Palais de Justice and the Gros Horloge, has singles/doubles starting at 140FF. The pricier *Hôtel Viking* (☎ 02 35 70 34 95, 21 quai du Havre) has singles/doubles with shower overlooking the river for 200/220FF.

The upmarket, two-star *Hôtel de la Cathédrale* (☎ 02 35 71 57 95, fax 02 35 70 15 54, 12 rue St-Romain) is just the ticket for a splurge, next to the cathedral in a 17th-century house. Singles/doubles cost 210/250FF with hall facilities, 260/310FF with

NORMANDY

private shower and toilet. Ask for a room looking onto the inner courtyard.

Places to Eat

Restaurants The pick of the Vieux Marché's many restaurants has to be *Paris-Maraîchers* (☎ 02 35 71 57 73, *37 place du Vieux Marché*) with its lively pavement terrace and varied *menus* (from 69FF for lunch, 89FF for dinner).

For hybrid Japanese/Korean/Chinese food, try *Kyoto* (☎ 02 35 07 76 77, *35 rue du Vieux Palais*), which opens for lunch and dinner (closed Sunday and Monday lunch).

Gourmand'grain (☎ 02 35 98 15 74, *3 rue du Petit Salut*), is a lunchtime vegetarian cafe with good salads and health-food *menus* for 45FF and 69FF.

Chez Zaza (☎ 02 35 71 33 57, *85 rue Martainville*) specialises in couscous (from 45FF) and opens for lunch and dinner.

Kim Ngoc (☎ 02 35 98 76 33, *166 rue Martainville*) is a friendly Vietnamese restaurant with *menus* for 69FF and 89FF. It opens for lunch and dinner (closed Monday).

Hostellerie du Vieux Logis (see Places to Stay) is reminiscent of the 1920s, with a massive candelabra of melting wax, and an ageing *patron* softly padding between the tables. A multicourse *menu* costs 65FF.

Pascaline (☎ 02 35 89 67 44, *5 rue de la Poterne*) is an old-time bistro with a piano player and some wonderful duck dishes. It opens for lunch and dinner with two- and three-course *menus* for 69FF and 99FF. The intimate *La Vieille Auberge* (☎ 02 35 70 56 65, *37 rue St-Étienne des Tonneliers*) has an enticing 98FF *menu* including fish dishes such as *trout almandine* or *filet of whiting* (closed Monday).

Self-Catering Dairy products, fish and fresh produce are on sale from 6 am to 1.30 pm at the *covered market* at place du Vieux Marché (closed Monday). But Thursday to Sunday there's a more lively food and clothing *market* on place St-Marc.

The *Alimentation Générale* (*78 rue de la République*) opens 8 am to 10.30 pm. The supermarket in the Monoprix at 65 rue du Gros Horloge opens 8.30 to 9 pm (closed Sunday).

Entertainment

Cinéma Le Melville (☎ 02 35 98 79 79, *12 rue St-Étienne des Tonneliers*) occasionally runs undubbed English-language films. Tickets cost a flat 30FF. From May or June to September, concerts are frequently held in Rouen's cathedral and churches. The *Théâtre des Arts* (☎ 02 35 71 41 36, *place des Arts*), is home to the Opéra de Normandie. Inquire at the tourist office for listings.

Getting There & Away

Bus Four bus companies, represented by SATAR, serve Dieppe (68FF, two hours, three daily) and towns along the coast west of Dieppe, including Fécamp (93FF, 3¼ hours, one daily) and Le Havre (84FF, three hours, five daily). The buses to Dieppe and Le Havre are much slower than the train and are more expensive.

Train Trains to Paris and other far-flung destinations depart from the Art Nouveau Gare Rouen-Rive Droite, built between 1912 and 1928. The Gare Rouen-Rive Gauche south of the river has mainly regional services.

From Gare Rouen-Rive Droite, there's a frequent express train to/from Paris' Gare St-Lazare (124FF, 70 minutes). Other frequent services include Amiens (96FF, 1¼ hours) Caen (116FF, two hours), Dieppe (55FF, 45 minutes), Le Havre (92FF, one hour) and, via Paris, Lyon (392FF, four hours).

Car For rental, try ADA (☎ 02 35 72 25 88), 34 ave Jean Rondeaux. Avis (☎ 02 35 53 17 20) and Hertz (☎ 02 35 70 70 71) have offices in the Gare Rouen Rive Droite train station.

Getting Around

Bus & Metro TCAR (also known as Espace Métrobus) operates Rouen's extensive local bus network as well as its metro line. The metro runs between 5 am (6 am on Sunday) and 11.30 pm. Tickets, valid for an

NORMANDY

hour of unlimited travel, cost 8FF or 63FF for a magnetic card for 10 rides. A Carte Découverte, for one/two/three days, is available at the tourist office for 20/30/40FF.

Taxi To order a taxi 24 hours, ring Radio Taxi (☎ 02 35 88 50 50).

Bicycle Rouen Cycles (☎ 02 35 71 34 30), 45 rue St-Éloi, rents mountain bikes for 120FF a day with a deposit of 2000FF to 3000FF, depending on the model. It opens 8.30 am to 12.15 pm and 2 to 7.15 pm Tuesday to Saturday.

LES ANDELYS
postcode 27700 • pop 8500
Some 39km south-east of Rouen lies Les Andelys, a small, elongated town at the confluence of the Seine and the tiny Le Gambon rivers. The main reason for coming is to visit the ruins of Château Gaillard, a 12th-century stronghold of English king Richard the Lion-Heart.

Information & Orientation
The town is split into two parts: Grand Andely, whose main square is place Poussin, and to the west, the older Petit Andely which lies on the banks of the mighty Seine. The tiny tourist office (☎ 02 32 54 41 93) is at 24 rue Philippe-Auguste in Petit Andely at the foot of the cliffs which form the base of the chateau. The office opens 9.30 am to noon and 2 to 6 pm Monday to Saturday (to 5.30 pm on Sunday), June to September; and 2 to 5.30 pm daily the rest of the year.

Château Gaillard
Built in 1196–97, the chateau secured the western border of English territory along the Seine until Henry IV ordered its destruction in 1603. More impressive than the ruins themselves is the fantastic outlook over the Seine, whose white cliffs are best seen from the viewing platform just north of the castle. You're free to wander about year-round, but guided tours (in French) of the stark interior are held from 9 am to noon and 2 to 6 pm, mid-March to mid-

November (18FF, students and children 9FF). The chateau is a stiff 20-minute climb via a path which begins about 100m north of the tourist office. By car, take the turn-off opposite Église Notre Dame in Grand Andelys and follow the signs.

Places to Stay & Eat
Camping Château Gaillard (☎ 02 32 54 18 20, fax 02 32 54 32 66, route de la Mare) is 800m south-east of the chateau and 200m from the Seine. It charges 28/26FF per adult/tent, including use of the pool. It's closed in January.

Hotels are expensive in Les Andelys, but the tourist office has a list of *chambres d'hotes* with doubles from about 130FF. *Hôtel Normandie* (☎ 02 32 54 10 52, fax 02 32 54 11 28, 1 rue Grande) has nicely equipped doubles with shower from 220FF.

In Petit Andelys, *Villa du Vieux Château* (☎ 02 32 54 30 10, 78 rue G Nicolle) does excellent fish *menus* for 89FF (closed Monday and Tuesday). There are restaurants around place Poussin in Grand Andelys.

Getting There & Away
There's no train station in Les Andelys. SATAR buses link Grand Andelys (place Poussin) and Rouen at least twice daily (52FF, 1¼ hours).

GIVERNY
postcode 27620 • pop 548
Between Paris and Rouen and an ideal day trip from either, this small village contains the Musée Claude Monet, the home and flower-filled garden, from 1883 to 1926, of one of France's leading impressionist painters. Here Monet painted some of his most famous series of works, including *Décorations des Nymphéas* (Water Lilies).

First opened to the public in 1980, the museum attracts almost 500,000 visitors annually, many of whom also come to view the fine impressionist collection of the Musée Américain.

Musée Claude Monet
Monet's home (☎ 02 32 51 28 21) opens 10 am to 6 pm, except Monday, April to

NORMANDY

Claude Monet

One of the most important figures in modern art, Claude Monet, born in Paris in 1840, was the undisputed leader of the impressionists. He grew up near Le Havre, where in his late teens he started painting nature in the open air, a practice that was to affect his work throughout the rest of his career.

By the time he was 17, Monet was studying in Paris at the Académie Suisse with such artists as Pissarro. Influenced by the intensity of the light and colours of Algeria, where he spent some time during his military service, Monet concentrated on painting landscapes, developing an individual style that aimed to capture on canvas the immediate impression of the scene before him, rather than precise detail.

During the Franco-Prussian War of 1870–1, Monet travelled to London where he discovered the works of Turner and Constable. Consequently, painting from his houseboat on the Seine at Argenteuil, he focused on the effects of air and light, and in particular on the latter's effect on the water's surface. He also began using the undisguised, broken brush strokes that best characterise the impressionist style.

It was in the late 1870s that Monet first began painting pictures in series, in order to study the effects of the changing conditions of light and the atmosphere. The best known of these include the Rouen cathedral series, which were painted in the 1890s. In 1883, four years after the death of his first wife Camille, he moved to Giverny with Alice Hoschedé, his two sons and her five children from a previous marriage. Here he set about creating an environment where he could study and paint the subtle effects and changes of colour that varying tones of sunlight had on nature.

Alice died in 1911, followed three years later by Monet's eldest son Jean. Soon after, the portly, bearded artist built a new studio and started painting the *Nymphéas* (Water Lilies) series. The huge dimensions of some of these works, together with the fact that the pond's surface takes up the entire canvas, meant the abandonment of composition in the traditional sense and the virtual disintegration of form. Monet completed the series just before his death in 1926.

October. Admission to the house and gardens costs 35FF (students/children 25/20FF). Seasons have an enormous effect on the gardens at Giverny. From early to late spring, daffodils, tulips, rhododendrons, wisteria and irises appear, followed by poppies and lilies. By June, nasturtiums, roses and sweet peas are in flower. Around September, there are dahlias, sunflowers and hollyhocks.

The hectare of land that Monet owned has become two distinct areas cut by the Chemin du Roy, a small railway line that was unfortunately converted into what is now the busy D5 road.

The northern part is the **Clos Normand** where Monet's famous pastel pink and green house and the Water Lily studio stand. These days the studio is the entrance hall, adorned with precise reproductions of his works and ringing with cash register bells from busy souvenir stands. Outside are the symmetrically laid-out gardens.

From the Clos Normand's far corner, a tunnel leads under the D5 to the **Jardin d'Eau** (Water Garden). Having bought this piece of land in 1895 after his reputation had been established, Monet dug a pool (fed by the Epte, a tributary of the nearby Seine), planted water lilies and constructed the Japanese bridge, which has since been rebuilt. Draped with purple wisteria, the bridge blends into the asymmetrical foreground and background, creating the intimate atmosphere for which the 'Painter of Light' was famous.

Musée Américain

The American Impressionist Museum (☎ 02 32 51 94 65) contains works of American impressionist painters who flocked to

NORMANDY

France in the late 19th and early 20th centuries. It's housed in a garish building at 99 rue Claude Monet, 100m down the road from Musée Claude Monet, but has the same opening hours. Admission costs 35FF (students 20FF; children aged seven to 12, 15FF).

Getting There & Away

Giverny is 76km north-west of Paris and 66km south-east of Rouen. The nearest town is Vernon, nearly 7km to the north-west on the Paris–Rouen train line.

From Paris' Gare St-Lazare (66FF, 50 minutes) there are two early-morning trains to Vernon. For the return trip there's roughly one train an hour between 5 and 9 pm. From Rouen (54FF, 40 minutes), four trains leave before noon; to get back, there's about one train every hour between 5 and 10 pm.

Once in Vernon it's still a hike to Giverny. Buses (☎ 02 35 71 32 99) meet most trains and cost 14/22FF for a single/return, but bikes can be hired from the train station for 55FF a day. A 1000FF deposit is required.

DIEPPE

postcode 76200 • pop 35,000

Dieppe is an ancient seaside town and long a favourite among British weekend visitors. It's not the prettiest place in Normandy, but its location – set between two limestone cliffs – and its medieval castle are dramatic. Dieppe also has the attractive, gritty appeal of an old-fashioned port. It's also the closest Channel port to Paris (171km). Privateers based in Dieppe pillaged Southampton in 1338 and blockaded Lisbon two centuries later. The first European settlers in Canada included many Dieppois. The town was one of France's most important ports during the 16th century, when ships regularly sailed from Dieppe to West Africa and Brazil.

Orientation

The town centre is largely surrounded by water. Blvd de Verdun runs along the lawns – a favourite spot for kite-flyers – that border the beach. Most of the Grande rue

and rue de la Barre has been turned into a pedestrian mall. Quai Duquesne and its continuation quai Henri IV follow the western and northern sides of the port area. Ferries dock at the terminal on the north-eastern side of the port, just under 2km on foot from the tourist office.

Information

Tourist Offices On the western side of the port area, the tourist office (☎ 02 32 14 40 60, fax 02 32 14 40 61, @ officetour.dieppe@wanadoo.fr) is on Pont Jehan Ango. It opens 9 am to 1 pm and 2 to 7 pm Monday to Saturday, and 10 am to 1 pm and 3 to 6 pm Sunday, May to September; and 9 am to noon and 2 to 6 pm Monday to Saturday, the rest of the year (to 8pm in July and August). Hotel reservations in the Dieppe area cost 20FF.

Money The banks in Dieppe are closed on Monday, except the Crédit Maritime Mutuel, at 3 rue Guillaume Terrien. The Banque de France is at 4 rue Claude Groulard. Several other banks are around place Nationale, including a Banque Populaire at No 15.

Post & Communications The main post office, 2 blvd Maréchal Joffre, opens from 8.30 am to 6 pm on weekdays and until noon on Saturday. It has a Cyberposte.

The Cybercabine (☎ 02 35 84 64 36), 46 rue de l'Épée, charges 60FF per hour of Web surfing. It opens noon to 7 pm Monday to Saturday and 2 to 6 pm on Sunday.

Laundry The laundrette at 44 rue de l'Épée opens 7 am to 9 pm.

Things to See & Do

Though the white cliffs on either side of Dieppe have been compared to those at Dover, the **beach** is gravelly and at times very windy.

The vast **lawns** between blvd de Verdun and the beach were laid out in the 1860s by that seashore-loving imperial duo, Napoleon III and his wife, Eugénie. **Église St-Jacques**, a Norman Gothic church at

NORMANDY

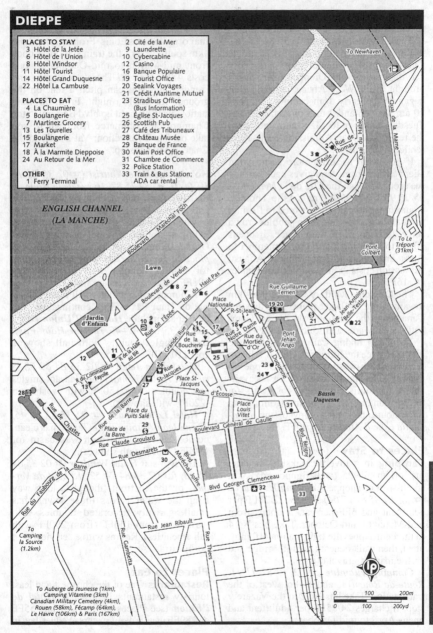

place St-Jacques, has been reconstructed several times since the early 13th century.

The **Château-Musée** (☎ 02 35 84 19 76), in the castle perched on the cliff at rue de Chastes, displays model ships and ivory carvings made in Dieppe from tusks brought from West Africa, a trade that began in the early 16th century. It opens 10 am to noon and 2 to 5 pm daily except Tuesday, October to May; and until 6pm the rest of the year. Admission costs 13FF (children 7.50FF).

If you want to learn more about what Dieppe takes from – and gives back to – the sea around it, visit the **Cité de la Mer** (☎ 02 35 06 93 20) at 37 rue de l'Asile Thomas. Aquariums and exhibits devoted to fishing, shipbuilding, cliffs and even pebbles crowd some 1650 sq m of floor space. It opens 10 am to noon and 2 to 6 pm, September to April; and 10 am to 7 pm, May to August. Admission costs 28FF (children aged under 16, 16FF).

The **Canadian Military Cemetery** is 4km towards Rouen. To get there, take ave des Canadiens (the continuation of rue Gambetta) southwards and follow the signs.

The **GR21 hiking trail** follows the Côte d'Albâtre (see the following Côte d'Albâtre section) south-westwards from Dieppe all the way to Le Havre. A map (35FF) is available at the tourist office. For easy walks in the surrounding areas ranging from one to three hours, pick up a copy of the *Topo-Guide Côte d'Albâtre* for 90FF.

Places to Stay

Camping In a lovely creekside location just off the D925 (well-signposted), 3km south-west of Dieppe, *Camping La Source* (☎/fax 02 35 84 27 04) charges 22/28FF per adult/tent and 6FF per car. It opens from mid-March to mid-October. Take bus No 4 to the Petit-Appeville train station (10 minutes), then walk beneath the rail bridge and up the marked gravel drive.

Camping Vitamine (☎ 02 35 82 11 11, Route de Rouen) is about 3km west of the train station. Take bus No 2 to the Vazarely stop. It charges 24/25FF per adult/tent and opens April to mid-October.

Hostels The *Auberge de Jeunesse* (☎ 02 35 84 85 73, fax 02 35 84 89 62, **@** dieppe@ fuaj.org, 48 rue Louis Fromager), about 4km south-west of the train station, is open from mid-March to mid-October. A bed costs 48FF a night. There's a kitchen and laundry, and you can pitch a tent on the grounds for 25FF a night. From the train station, walk straight up blvd Bérigny to the Chambre de Commerce from where you take bus No 2 (direction: Val Druel) to the Château Michel stop.

Hotels The *Hôtel Tourist* (☎ 02 35 06 10 10, fax 02 35 84 15 87, 16 rue de la Halle au Blé) has plain but modern singles/doubles with shower for 135/165FF (doubles with private facilities 225FF).

For a hint of bygone glamour, *Hôtel Grand Duquesne* (☎ 02 32 14 61 10, 15 place St-Jacques), has shower-less rooms for 175FF (doubles with all amenities 198FF). Hall showers are free.

A number of popular small hotels along rue du Haut Pas and its continuation, rue de l'Épée, include *Hôtel de l'Union* (☎ 02 35 84 35 52, 47–49 rue du Haut Pas). Basic singles/doubles with hall showers cost 110/150FF.

Hôtel de la Jetée (☎ 02 35 84 89 98, 5 rue de l'Asile Thomas) has pleasant singles and doubles from 150FF with washbasin (220FF with shower).

Hôtel La Cambuse (☎ 02 35 84 19 46, 42 rue Jean-Antoine Belle-Teste), has clean, no-nonsense doubles with washbasin for 180FF (200FF with shower).

The two-star *Hôtel Windsor* (☎ 02 35 84 15 23, fax 02 35 84 74 52, 18 blvd de Verdun) on the seafront (though a long way from the water across those lawns) has small, garishly decorated doubles with washbasin from 150FF (from 290FF with full amenities). Rooms with a sea view cost 50FF extra.

Places to Eat

Restaurants One of the cheapest and least touristy restaurants in town is *Hôtel de l'Union* (see Places to Stay). It has 55FF and 89FF *menus* daily, except Wednesday. In

NORMANDY

summer it's only available for dinner. *Au Retour de la Mer* (☎ *02 35 84 04 81, 31 place Louis Vitet*) has a standard *menu* for 65FF.

Just behind the Casino, *Les Tourelles* (☎ *02 35 84 15 88, 43 rue du Commandant Fayolle*) serves good-value *menus* from 59FF and generous paellas from 85FF (must be ordered 24 hours in advance).

Friendly *La Chaumière* (☎ *02 35 40 18 54, 1 quai du Hâble*) on the waterfront has an excellent 68FF seafood *menu*, but if you really want to taste Dieppe's *fruits de la mer* at their best, head for the intimate *À la Marmite Dieppoise* (☎ *02 35 84 24 26, 8 rue St-Jean*) in the old city. *Menus* cost from 85FF to a whopping 215FF (closed Sunday evening and Monday).

Self-Catering The *food market* between place St-Jacques and place Nationale opens Tuesday and Thursday mornings and all day Saturday. The *boulangerie* at 15 quai Henri IV opens 7 am to 7.30 pm daily except Monday. There's another bakery at 14 rue de la Boucherie (closed Wednesday). The *Martinez grocery*, 44 rue du Haut Pas, opens 7.30 am to 8.30 pm (closed Monday).

Entertainment

Dieppe has loads of pubs and bars full of interesting characters, but don't be surprised if you have to buzz to be let in. The *Scottish Pub* (*12 rue St-Jacques*), is a good place to start a crawl and the friendly bar staff will point you in the right direction. *Café des Tribunaux* (*place du Puits Salé*) is an inviting place in a sprawling 18th-century building.

Getting There & Away

Bus The bus station is in the same cavernous building as the train station. There are services to Fécamp (75FF, 2¼ hours, at least two daily), Le Tréport (41FF, 1¼ hours, four daily) and Rouen (72FF, two hours, three daily). No buses run on Saturday or Sunday afternoon.

Train The paucity of direct trains to Paris' Gare St-Lazare (126FF, 2¼ hours, four daily) is offset by frequent services to

Rouen (55FF, 45 to 60 minutes, 10 daily), where there's a connecting service to Le Havre (110FF, two hours from Dieppe). The last train from Dieppe to Paris (via Rouen) leaves just before 7 pm daily.

Boat The first ferry service from Dieppe to England (Brighton, to be exact) began in 1790. These days, Stena Sealink (☎ 02 35 06 39 03) and Hoverspeed (☎ 08 20 00 35 55) operate car and pedestrian ferries between Dieppe and Newhaven. Boats depart from the ferry terminal on the north-eastern side of the port area at the end of quai de la Marne. For details on prices and schedules, see The UK section under Sea in the Getting There & Away chapter.

Getting Around

Bus The local bus network, Stradibus, operates 13 lines which run to either 6 or 8 pm. All buses stop at either the train station or the nearby Chambre de Commerce on quai Duquesne. A single ticket costs 6.40FF, a 10-ticket carnet 42FF.

A bus timed to meet incoming and outgoing ferries shuttles foot passengers between the terminal and the tourist office (12FF).

Taxi Taxis can be called on ☎ 02 35 84 20 05. The fare from the ferry pier to the city centre is about 35FF.

Car ADA car rental (☎ 02 35 84 32 28) has an office in the train station.

CÔTE D'ALBÂTRE

Stretching 100km from Dieppe south to Étretat, the tall, white cliffs and stony beaches of the Côte d'Albâtre (Alabaster Coast) are reminiscent of the coast of southern England. Small villages and a few resorts nestle in the dry valleys leading down from the Pays de Caux, a chalky inland plateau.

Without a car, the Côte d'Albâtre is rather inaccessible. However, walkers can follow the coastal GR21 from Dieppe to Le Havre. If you are driving, take the coastal road, which starts as the D75 west

NORMANDY

of Dieppe, and not the inland D925. The Côte d'Albâtre's two main centres are Fécamp and Étretat, both of which are at the southern end.

FÉCAMP

postcode 76400 • pop 21,000

Fécamp was little more than a fishing village until the 6th century, when a few drops of Christ's blood miraculously found their way here and attracted hordes of pilgrims. Benedictine monks soon established a monastery and the 'medicinal elixir' concocted there in the early 16th century helped keep Fécamp on the map. The recipe, lost during the Revolution, was rediscovered in the 19th century and the after-dinner liqueur was produced commercially. Today, Bénédictine is one of the most widely marketed *digestifs* in the world.

Information

Tourist Offices The tourist office (☎ 02 35 28 51 01, fax 02 35 27 07 77, @ fecamp tourisime@wanadoo.fr) is at 113 rue Alexandre Le Grand. It opens 9 am to 12.15 pm and 1.45 to 6 pm daily (10 am to 6 pm in July and August). The Web site is at www.fecamp.com.

Palais Bénédictine The Bénédictine Distillery (☎ 02 35 10 26 10) is at 110 rue Alexandre Le Grand in an ornate building (1900) mixing Flamboyant Gothic and eclectic styles, inspired by the 15th-century Hôtel de Cluny in Paris. It's geared up to tell you everything about the history and making of its aromatic liqueur – except the exact recipe. Tours start in the Art Museum, which houses the private collection of founder Alexandre Le Grand, and continues through a hall where hundreds of bottles of bootlegged Bénédictine are proudly displayed. In the fragrant Plant & Spice Room, you can smell a handful of some of the ingredients used to make the potent drink. The tour ends in the attractive Modern Art Gallery, which has changing exhibits.

The Palais opens 10 am to noon and 2 to 5.30 pm, mid-March to June and early September to mid-November; and 9.30 am

to 6 pm, July to early September; and 10 to 11.15 am and 2 to 5 pm, mid-November to mid-March. Admission costs 29FF (students/children 22/14.50FF) and includes a free shot of Bénédictine.

Getting There & Away Fécamp is accessible by bus from Dieppe, Le Havre and Rouen, and by train from Le Havre. See those sections for more information.

Getting Around Mountain bikes and 10-speeds (80FF a day) are available for rent from Location Vélo-VTT (☎ 02 35 28 45 09), north-east of the tourist office and Palais Bénédictine at 2 ave Gambetta.

Étretat

postcode 76280 • pop 1600

The small village of Étretat, which is 20km south-west of Fécamp, is renowned for its two cliffs: the Falaise d'Amont and the Falaise d'Aval. Featuring the most unusual rock formations in the area, you'll see them long before you arrive, appearing somewhat deceivingly to be one rock.

Beyond the Falaise d'Aval to the south-west of the village is the stunning Manneporte rock arch and the 70m-high Aiguille (Needle), which pierces the surface of the water behind the arch. From the western end of Étretat's stony beach, a steep path leads to the top of the cliff, which affords a fine view of the rocks. On the Falaise d'Amont opposite, a memorial marks the spot where two aviators were last seen before their attempt to cross the Atlantic in 1927. Do *not* try to explore the base of the cliffs outside low tide.

Information The tourist office (☎ 02 35 27 05 21, fax 02 35 29 39 79), in the centre of the village on place Maurice Guillard, has accommodation lists for the area posted on the door for inspection outside opening hours. It opens 10 am to noon and 2 to 6 pm daily. It also has a map of the cliff trails.

Getting There & Away The easiest way to reach Étretat is by bus from Le Havre,

28km to the south. For details see Getting There & Away in the next section.

LE HAVRE

postcode 76600 • pop 193,000

Le Havre, France's second-most important port, is also a bustling gateway for ferries to Britain and Ireland, but there's not much more to recommend this city at the mouth of the Seine. All but obliterated by WWII bombing raids, Le Havre was rebuilt around its historical remains by Auguste Perret, the architect who also designed the city's 100m-high 'Stalinist baroque' Église St-Joseph, which is, unfortunately, visible from all points. The result is a regimented grid of wide, straight central streets – there are more roads per inhabitant here than anywhere else in France – lined with row upon row of three-storey, reinforced-concrete buildings.

Orientation

The main square is the enormous place de l'Hôtel de Ville. Ave Foch runs westwards to the sea and the Port de Plaisance recreational area; blvd de Strasbourg goes eastwards to the train and bus stations. Rue de Paris cuts southwards past the Espace Oscar Niemeyer, a square named after the Brazilian who designed two cultural centre buildings (which have been compared to a truncated cooling tower and a toilet bowl).

Rue de Paris ends at the quai de Southampton and the Bassin de la Manche, from where ferries to Britain set sail out of the Terminal de la Citadelle, south-east of the central square. Within easy walking distance of the terminal is the Quartier St-François, Le Havre's restaurant-filled 'old city'.

Information

Tourist Offices The tourist office (☎ 02 32 74 04 04, fax 02 35 42 38 39, ℮ office .du.tourisme.havre@wanadoo.fr, 186 blvd Clemenceau on the waterfront about 1km south of the town hall, opens 9 am to noon and 1.30 to 6 pm Monday to Saturday and 10 am to 1 pm on Sunday, October to April; 8.45 am to 6 pm Monday to Saturday and

10 am to 1 pm on Sunday, October to April; and 8.45 am to 7 pm Monday to Saturday and 10 am to 12.30 pm and 2.30 to 6 pm on Sunday, May to September. Staff reserve local accommodation for free.

Money The Banque de France, 22 ave Ren' Coty, changes money 8.45 to noon, Monday to Friday. A Société Générale is at 2 place Léon Meyer and there are more banks on blvd de Strasbourg. An exchange bureau opposite the old Irish Ferries terminal at 41 blvd Kennedy opens 8 am to 12.30 pm and 1.30 to 7 pm, Monday to Saturday (8 am to 7.30 pm in July and August).

American Express (☎ 02 32 74 75 76), 57 quai Georges V, opens 8.45am to noon and 1.30 to 6 pm on weekdays.

Post & Communications Le Havre's main post office, 62 rue Jules Siegfried, opens 8 am to 7 pm weekdays and noon on Saturday, and has a Cyberposte. Cyber-metro (☎ 02 32 73 04 28), 15 cours de la République opposite the train station, charges 30/45FF (students 20/35FF) per half-hour/hour of Internet use. It opens 9 am to midnight daily.

Laundry The laundrette at rue Georges Braque 5, three blocks west of the town hall, opens 8 am to 10 pm daily.

Musée Malraux

The one thing really worth seeing in Le Havre is the newly remodelled Musée Malraux (☎ 02 35 19 62 62) at 2 blvd Clemenceau, about 200m west of the old Irish Ferries terminal. Noted for its excellent collection of impressionist paintings, including some by Monet and Eugène Boudin (who spent part of his youth here), it also displays works by Raoul Dufy, a native of Le Havre.

Places to Stay

Camping The closest camping ground is *Camping de la Forêt de Montgeon* (☎ 02 35 46 52 39), nearly 3km north of town in a 250-hectare forest. It opens April to September and charges 55FF for one/two

NORMANDY

people and tent and 12FF per car. From the station, take bus No 11 and alight after the 700m-long Jenner Tunnel. Then walk north through the park another 1.5km.

Hotels Hidden down an alley opposite the train station (to the right of the Hertz office) is *Hôtel d'Yport* (☎ 02 35 25 21 08, fax 02 35 24 06 34, 27 cours de la République), a friendly place with a range of rooms including basic singles/doubles/triples from 120/170/210FF. A hall shower costs 25FF extra. Rooms with a shower cost 180/200/243FF. The hotel has a private garage (35FF).

Also close to the station is the *Grand Hôtel Parisien* (☎ 02 35 25 23 83, fax 02 35 25 05 06, 1 cours de la République). Clean and pleasant, it has singles/doubles starting at 210/260FF with shower and TV.

Near the old Irish Ferries terminal, *Hôtel Le Monaco* (☎ 02 35 42 21 01, fax 02 35 42 01 01, 16 rue de Paris) (turn right as you leave the ferry building and take the first left), has shipshape rooms from 150/190FF. Nearby, the tiny *Le Ferry Boat* (☎ 02 35 42 29 55, 11 quai de Southampton) has seven rooms, which cost from 160/180FF for singles/doubles. Hall showers are free.

At the eastern end of the Bassin du Commerce is Best Western *Hôtel Le Bordeaux* (☎ 02 35 22 69 44, fax 02 35 42 09 27, 147 rue Louis Brindeau). Rooms cost 385/470FF (discounted rates at weekends).

Places to Eat

Around the train station are several decently priced restaurants, including *Flunch* (☎ 02 35 46 59 82), a cheap, cheerful self-service place attached to Auchan hypermarket in the Mont Gaillard shopping centre (clearly signposted from the station). Another budget option is the restaurant at the *YMCA* (☎ 02 35 19 87 87, 153 blvd de Strasbourg), about 400m west of the train station, with *menus* starting at 39FF.

The Quartier St-François is the best place to eat, with creperies and couscous restaurants in abundance. For the former try *Au Petit Breton* (☎ 02 35 21 44 14, 11 rue Dauphine). Couscous starts at 60FF.

The restaurant at *Hôtel Le Monaco* (see Places to Stay) has excellent seafood *menus* from 69FF.

Getting There & Away

Bus Caen-based Bus Verts du Calvados (☎ 08 01 21 42 14) and Rouen's CNA (☎ 02 35 52 92 00) operate frequent services from the bus station to Caen (102.50FF), Honfleur (42.40FF), Rouen (84FF) and Deauville-Trouville (59FF). Auto-Cars Gris (☎ 02 35 27 04 25) has 10 buses daily to Fécamp (45FF, 1½ hours) via Étretat and five on Sunday.

Train Le Havre's train station (☎ 08 36 35 35 35) is about 1km east of the city centre on cours de la République. Chief destinations are Rouen (72FF, one hour, 15 daily) and Paris' Gare St-Lazare (151FF, 2¼ hours, 10 daily). A secondary line goes north to Fécamp (43FF, 1¼ hours, five daily) with a change at Bréauté-Beuzeville.

Boat P&O European Ferries (☎ 08 02 01 30 13), which links Le Havre with Portsmouth, uses the new Terminal de la Citadelle on ave Lucien Corbeaux just over a kilometre south-west of the train station. The information desk opens 9 am to 7 pm. A special bus (8FF) takes passengers from the terminal to the tourist office and the train station 15 minutes after each ferry arrives. For schedules and prices, see the Sea section in the Getting There & Away chapter.

Getting Around

Bus Fourteen lines in Le Havre are operated by Bus Océane as well as a small funicular linking place Thiers with rue Félix Faure near the hilltop Fort de Tournville. Bus Océane's information office (☎ 02 35 43 46 00), in a kiosk on place de l'Hôtel de Ville, opens 7 am to 7 pm Monday to Saturday. Single tickets cost 8FF, a carnet of 10 is 55FF and a 'Ticket Ville' day ticket costs 18FF. The three-minute funicular ride costs 2FF up and 1FF down.

Taxi To order a taxi, ring ☎ 02 35 25 81 81 or ☎ 02 35 25 81 00. A two-hour taxi tour

NORMANDY

(in English) of Le Havre costs 300FF (book on ☎ 02 35 25 81 81) for up to four people.

Calvados

The department of Calvados stretches from Honfleur in the east to Isigny-sur-Mer in the west. It's famed for its rich pastures and farm products: butter, cheese, cider and an apple-flavoured brandy called Calvados. The D-day beaches extend along almost the entire coast of Calvados.

HONFLEUR
postcode 14600 • pop 8200
The picturesque seaside town of Honfleur sits opposite Le Havre at the mouth of the Seine. Because it's only about 200km north-west of Paris – closer to the capital than almost any other point on the coast – multitudes of Parisian day-trippers flock to the town. There are no beaches in Honfleur, but there are some fine stretches of sand not far away. Just 15km south-west are the up-market coastal resorts of Deauville and Trouville.

In the 19th century Honfleur attracted a steady stream of artists, among them many impressionists. Because of extensive silta-tion, centuries-old wooden houses that once lined the seafront quay now lie several hundred metres inland. The graceful 2km-long Pont de Normandie over the Seine, linking Honfleur with Le Havre for the first time, opened to great fanfare in January 1995.

History
Honfleur's seafaring tradition dates back over a millennium. After the Norman inva-sion of England in 1066, goods bound for the conquered territory were shipped across the Channel from Honfleur.

In 1608, Samuel de Champlain set sail from here on his way to found Quebec City. In 1681, Cavelier de la Salle started out from Honfleur to explore what is now the USA. He reached the mouth of the Mis-sissippi and named the area Louisiana in honour of King Louis XIV, ruler of France at the time. During the 17th and 18th centuries, Honfleur achieved a certain degree of prosperity through trade with the West Indies, the Azores and the colonies on the western coast of Africa.

Orientation
Honfleur is centred around the Vieux Bassin (old harbour). To the east is the heart of the old city, known as the Enclos because it was once enclosed by fortifications. To the north is the Avant Port (outer harbour) where the fishing fleet is based. Quai Ste-Catherine fronts the Vieux Bassin on the west, while rue de la République runs southwards from it. The Plateau de Grâce, with Chapelle Notre Dame de Grâce on top, is west of town.

Information
Tourist Offices The tourist office (☎ 02 31 89 23 30, fax 02 31 89 31 82) is in the En-clos at place Arthur Boudin, a couple of blocks south-east of the Vieux Bassin. It opens 9.30 am to 12.30 pm and 2 to 6 pm Monday to Saturday; and also 10 am to 1 pm on Sunday, Easter to September. In July and August it opens 9.30 am to 7 pm daily.

From July to September the tourist office runs two-hour guided tours of Honfleur on Wednesday at 3 pm. The cost is 32FF (students/children 28FF). The Web site is at www.ville-honfleur.fr.

Post & Communications The main post office is south-west of the centre on rue de la République, just past place Albert Sorel. It has a Cyberposte terminal.

Église Ste-Catherine
This wooden church, whose stone prede-cessor was destroyed during the Hundred Years' War, was built by the people of Hon-fleur during the second half of the 15th and the early 16th centuries. It is thought that they chose wood, which could be worked by local shipwrights, in an effort to save money in order to strengthen the fortifica-tions of the Enclos. The structure that the town's ship's carpenters created, which was intended to be temporary, has a vaulted roof

that looks like an overturned ship's hull. The church is also remarkable for its twin naves. Église Ste-Catherine opens 10 am to noon and 2 to 6 pm to visitors, except during services.

Clocher Ste-Catherine

The church's free-standing wooden bell tower, Clocher Ste-Catherine (☎ 02 31 89 54 00), dates from the second half of the 15th century. It was built apart from the church for both structural reasons (so the church roof would not be subject to the bells' weight and vibrations) and for safety (a high tower was more likely to be hit by lightning). The former bell-ringer's residence at the base of the tower houses a small museum of liturgical objects, but the huge, rough-hewn beams are of more interest.

The bell tower opens 10 am to noon and 2 to 6 pm daily, except Tuesday, mid-March to September; and 2.30 to 5 pm on weekdays and 10 am to noon and 2.30 to 5 pm at weekends, the rest of the year. Admission costs 30FF (students 25FF), and also gets you into the Musée Eugène Boudin. Admission costs 10FF for Clocher Ste-Catherine only.

Musée Eugène Boudin

Named in honour of the early impressionist painter born here in 1824, this museum (☎ 02 31 89 54 00), on rue de l'Homme de Bois at place Erik Satie, has an excellent collection of impressionist paintings from Normandy, including works by Boudin, Dubourg, Dufy and Monet. It has the same opening hours as the Clocher Ste-Catherine.

Harbours

The **Vieux Bassin**, from where ships bound for the New World once set sail, now shelters mainly pleasure boats. The nearby quays and streets, especially **quai Ste-Catherine**, are lined with tall, narrow houses – many faced with bluish-grey slate shingles – dating from the 16th to 18th centuries. The **Lieutenance**, once the residence of the town's royal governor, is at the mouth of the old harbour.

The **Avant Port**, on the other side of the Lieutenance, is home to Honfleur's 50 or so

fishing vessels. Farther north, dikes line both sides of the entrance to the port.

Either harbour makes a pleasant route for a walk to the seashore. One-hour **boat tours** of the Vieux Bassin and the port area are available on the *Calypso* for 20FF. Ask at the tourist office where to board.

Musée de la Marine

Honfleur's small Maritime Museum (☎ 02 31 89 14 12) is on the eastern side of the Vieux Bassin in the deconsecrated Église St-Étienne, which was begun in 1369 and enlarged during the English occupation of Honfleur (1415–50). Displays include assorted model ships, ship's carpenters' tools and engravings.

It opens 10 am to noon and 2 to 6 pm, except Monday, April to late September; and 2 to 6 pm on weekdays and 10 am to noon and 2 to 6 pm on weekends, from late September to mid-November and mid-February to March (closed mid-November to mid-February). Admission to both the Musée de la Marine and the Musée d'Ethnographie et d'Art Populaire Normand costs 25FF (students 15FF).

Musée d'Ethnographie et d'Art Populaire Normand

Next to the Musée de la Marine on rue de la Prison, the Museum of Ethnography & Norman Folk Art (☎ 02 31 89 14 12) occupies a couple of houses and a former prison dating from the 16th and 17th centuries. It contains 12 furnished rooms of the sort you would have found in the shops and wealthy homes of Honfleur between the 16th and 19th centuries.

It can be visited only by guided tour (in French), which leaves about once an hour. It opens 2 to 5.30 pm weekdays and 10 am to noon and 2 to 5.30 pm weekends. Admission is the same as to the Musée de la Marine.

Greniers à Sel

The two huge salt stores (☎ 02 31 89 02 30) on rue de la Ville, down the block from the tourist office, were built in the late 17th century to store the salt needed by the

NORMANDY

fishing fleet to cure its catch of herring and cod. For most of the year, the only way to see the Greniers à Sel is to take a guided tour (inquire at the tourist office). During July and August the stores host art exhibitions and concerts.

Chapelle Notre Dame de Grâce

This chapel, built between 1600 and 1613, is at the top of the Plateau de Grâce, a wooded, 100m-high hill about 1km west of the Vieux Bassin. There's a great view of the town and port.

Places to Stay

Camping About 500m north-west of the Vieux Bassin, *Camping du Phare (☎ 02 31 89 10 26, blvd Charles V)* opens April to September. It costs 28FF per person and 35FF for a tent site and car. To reach it from the centre of town follow rue Haute.

Hotels *Bar de la Salle des Fêtes (☎ 02 31 89 19 69, 8 place Albert Sorel)*, 400m south-west of the Vieux Bassin along rue de la République, charges 160FF (including breakfast) for each of its four double rooms. The *Auberge de la Claire (☎ 02 31 89 05 95, fax 02 31 89 11 37, 77 cours Albert Manuel)*, 700m south-west, has apartments starting at 250FF.

More centrally, *Hôtel Le Hamelin (☎ 02 31 89 16 25, fax 02 31 89 16 25, 16 place Hamelin)* near the Église Ste-Catherine, has doubles with shower from 180FF. *Hôtel des Cascades (☎ 02 31 89 05 83, fax 02 31 89 32 13, 17 place Thiers)* has rooms from 200FF.

Hôtel Le Moderne (☎ 02 31 89 44 11, 20 quai Lepaulmier) has very simple singles/doubles for 125/190FF as well as doubles with shower for 255FF.

Places to Eat

Restaurants Places to dine are abundant (especially along quai Ste-Catherine) but they don't come cheaply: *menus* start at about 85FF. *Hôtel Le Moderne* is one of the less expensive places with *menus* from 70FF. One highly recommended spot is cosy *La Tortue (☎ 02 31 89 04 93, 36 rue de l'Homme de Bois)* whose succulent

seafood *menus* start at 100FF. It also does a vegetarian *menu* for 77FF.

Self-Catering The Saturday *market* at place Ste-Catherine runs from 9 am to 1 pm. There's a *Champion* supermarket just west of rue de la République, near place Albert Sorel. It opens 8.30 am to 12.30 pm and 2.30 to 7.30 pm Monday to Friday, and 8.30 am to 7.30 pm on Saturday.

Getting There & Away

Bus The bus station (☎ 02 31 89 28 41) is south-east of the Vieux Bassin on rue des Vases. Bus Verts (☎ 02 31 44 77 44 in Caen) No 20 bus runs via Deauville-Trouville (21.20FF, 30 minutes, five daily) to Caen (68.90FF or 86FF by express bus). The same line goes northwards to Le Havre (42.40FF, 30 minutes, five daily) via the Pont de Normandie. Line No 50 goes to Lisieux (one hour). Bus Verts offers a 12% discount for those aged under 26 on Wednesday, Saturday afternoon and Sunday.

TROUVILLE & DEAUVILLE

postcode 14360 • pop 5600 (Trouville)
postcode 14800 • pop 4300 (Deauville)

Some 15km south-west of Honfleur lie two seaside resorts that couldn't be much different from each other: Trouville and Deauville. The latter has been a playground of the wealthy ever since it was founded by Napoleon III's cousin, the Duke of Morny, in 1861. Tattier but unpretentious, Trouville offers cheaper accommodation and a range of decent restaurants.

Orientation

The towns are separated only by the River Touques, with Trouville on the east and Deauville on the western bank respectively, and linked by the Pont des Belges. The combined train and bus station is just west of the bridge. Beaches line the coast to the north of both towns on either side of the port.

Information

Tourist Offices Deauville's **tourist office** (☎ 02 31 14 40 00, fax 02 32 88 78 88,

NORMANDY

@ info-deauville@deauville.org) is at the place de la Mairie, at the north-western end of rue Desire-Le-Hoc from the central place Morny. It opens 9 am to 12.30 pm and 2 to 6.30 pm Monday to Saturday, from mid-September to April; in May and June there's no midday break. From July to September it opens 9 am to 7 pm, Monday to Saturday, and 10 am to 1 pm and 2 to 5 pm on Sunday (to 6 pm in July and August). You can pick up a copy of the disgusting, glossy tourist magazine *Deauville Passions* for an overview of annual events. The Web site is at www.deauville.org.

The smaller Trouville tourist office is at 32 quai Fernand Moureaux (☎ 02 31 14 60 70, fax 02 31 14 60 71, @ o.t.trouville@ wanadoo.fr). It opens 9 am to noon and 1.30 to 6 pm daily, September to April, and 9 am to 7 pm from May to August.

Money Banks in Deauville include a Crédit du Nord at 84 rue Eugene Colas and a Société Générale at 9 place Morny. The post office also exchanges currency.

Post & Communications The post office on rue Robert Fossorier in Deauville opens 9 am to 6 pm Monday to Friday, and Saturday mornings. It has a Cyberposte.

Things to See & Do
In Deauville, the rich, famous and assorted wannabes strut along the beachside **Promenade des Planches**, a 500m-long boardwalk lined with private swimming huts, before losing a wad at the **Casino de Deauville** (☎ 02 31 14 31 14), 200m to the south on ave Lucien Barrière. Dress is formal, but men can borrow a jacket and tie from reception. The casino opens 11 am to 2 am Monday to Friday, and 10 am to 4 am at weekends (3 am on Sunday). Trouville's casino, **Louisiane Follies** (☎ 02 31 87 75 00) at place du Maréchal Foch on the beachfront, is a more relaxed affair with an adjoining cinema and nightclub. It opens from 10 am daily.

About 1.5km north-east of Trouville's tourist office stands the magnificent **Villa Montebello** (☎ 02 31 88 16 26), 64 rue du Général Leclerc. This former summer residence of Napoleon III holds regular exhibits of local artists and opens 2 to 6 pm daily (except Tuesday), April to September. Admission varies.

On Trouville beach ('La Plage') is the remarkably varied **Aquarium Vivarium de Trouville** (☎ 02 31 88 46 04) which, aside from wild and wonderfully colourful fish, also houses some fearsome reptiles (snakes, crocodiles and iguanas among them) and weird insects. It opens 10 am to noon and 2 to 7 pm daily, from Easter to June and in September and October; 10 am to 7.30 pm in July and August; and 2 pm to 6.30 pm November to May. Admission costs 35FF (students 30FF).

Special Events
Deauville's answer to Cannes is the **American Film Festival**, which is open to all and attracts a procession of Hollywood stars the first week of September.

A much more down-to-earth event is Trouville's **Festival Folkorique**, which fills the streets with colourfully clad musicians and dancers the third week of June.

Deauville is renowned for its equestrian tradition. The **horseracing season**, which runs from early July to mid-October, is held at two local racetracks: Hippodrome La Touques (300m south-west of the train station) for gallop races and Hippodrome Clairfontaine (2km farther west) with galloping, trotting and steeplechase.

Places to Stay
In a large field near the local hospital, *Camping Hamel* (☎ 02 31 88 15 56, 55 rue des Soeurs de l'Hopital) charges 12/6FF per adult/tent. From the Pont des Belges, walk five minutes east through rue Biesta and its continuations.

The cheaper hotels are all in Trouville. *Hôtel Paix* (☎ 02 31 88 35 15, fax 02 31 88 28 44, 4 place Fernand-Moureaux) charges 150FF for cheerful singles/doubles with washbasin (230FF for doubles with private shower and toilet).

About 100m east of Trouville casino, *Hôtel La Reynita* (☎ 02 31 88 15 13, fax 02

31 87 86 85, 29 rue Carnot) has spacious, newly renovated doubles for 195FF (265FF in high season).

Places to Eat
Among the waterfront eateries in Trouville, the *Bistrot Sur Le Quai (☎ 02 31 81 28 85, 68 blvd Fernand Moureaux)* has seafood *menus* from 65FF served on its pleasant front terrace.

Just off the pedestrianised rue des Bains, *Le Relais des Diligences (☎ 02 31 81 44 40, 7 rue du Dr Leneveu)* is a cosy place offering filling two-course seafood *menus* for 55FF and 85FF. *La Petite Auberge (☎ 02 31 88 11 07, 7 rue Carnot)* is another good bet.

There's a big *Monoprix* supermarket at the northern end of blvd Fernand Mou reaux. A *market* is held on place Maréchal Foch on Wednesday and Saturday mornings.

In Deauville, the popular *Mamy Crêpe (55 rue Eugene Colas)* is a fine takeaway option for quiche and sandwiches (from 12FF to 22FF) and crêpes (from 9FF to 21FF).

Getting There & Away
Bus The bus is generally faster and cheaper than the train. Bus Verts (☎ 08 01 21 42 14) has very frequent services to Caen (53FF, 1¼ hours), Honfleur (21.20FF, 30 minutes) and via Honfleur, Le Havre (59FF, one hour).

Train Most train services from Deauville-Trouville require changes at Lisieux (31FF, 20 minutes, 10 daily). There are trains to Caen (65FF, 1 to 1½ hours, 13 daily), Rouen (105FF, 3¼ hours, four daily) and via Rouen, Dieppe (138FF, 3 to 3½ hours, four daily).

CAEN
postcode 14000 • pop 114,000 • elevation 25m
Caen, the capital of Basse Normandie, was one of the many Norman cities to suffer heavily in WWII. Bombed on D-day, the city burned for over a week before being liberated by the Canadians – only to be then

shelled by the Germans. The only vestiges of the past to survive are the ramparts around the chateau and the two great abbeys, all built by William the Conqueror when he founded the city in the 11th century. Much of the medieval city was built from 'Caen stone', a creamy local limestone exported for centuries over the channel to England.

Linked to the sea by a canal running parallel to the River Orne, Caen has seen rapid expansion in recent years and these days is a bustling university city. It is also the gateway for Ouistreham, a minor passenger port for ferries to England.

Orientation
Caen's modern heart is made up of a few pedestrianised shopping streets and some busy boulevards. The largest, ave du 6 Juin, links the centre, which is based around the southern end of the chateau, with the canal and train station to the south-east. What's left of the old city is centred around rue du Vaugueux, a short distance south-east of the chateau.

Information
Tourist Offices The modern tourist office (☎ 02 31 27 14 14, fax 02 31 27 14 18, ✉ tourisminfo@ville-caen.fr) on place St-Pierre opens 10 am to 1 pm and 2 to 6 pm Monday to Saturday, and 10 am to 1 pm on Sunday. In July and August it opens 10 am to 7 pm Monday to Saturday, and 10 am to 1 pm and 2 to 5 pm on Sunday. Hotel reservations within the city cost 10FF. The office sells various maps including one to the D-day beaches (39FF).

Money The Banque de France, 14 ave de Verdun, exchanges money from 8.45 am to 12.15 pm. There's an exchange bureau run by Crédit Agricole at 1 blvd Maréchal Leclerc. From May to September the tourist office offers exchange services.

Post & Communications The main post office, place Gambetta, opens 8 am to 7 pm weekdays and to noon on Saturday. It has a Cyberposte.

CAEN

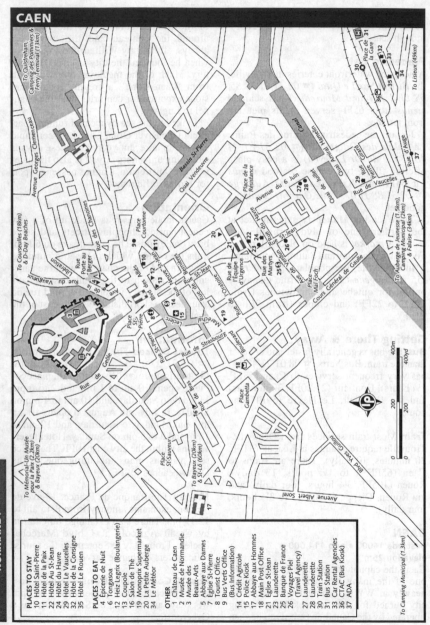

To Quistreham,
Camping des Pommiers &
Ferry Terminal (13km)

To Courseulles (18km)
& D-Day Beaches

To Mémorial-Un Musée
pour la Paix (2.2km)
& Bayeux (20km)

To Bayeux (20km)
& St-Lô (60km)

To Camping Municipal (1.3km)

To Lisieux (49km)

To Auberge de Jeunesse (1.5km),
Camping Municipal (2km)
& Falaise (34km)

Bassin St-Pierre

Quai Vendeuvre

Place de la
Résistance

Place
Courtonne

Avenue du 6 Juin

Canal

Quai Amiral Hamelin

Rue de Vaucelles

Place
Mal Foch

Cours Général de Gaulle

Place
Gambetta

Place
St-Sauveur

Avenue Albert Sorel

Blvd Yves Guillou

PLACES TO STAY
10 Hôtel Saint-Pierre
11 Hôtel de la Paix
22 Hôtel Au St-Jean
24 Hôtel du Havre
29 Hôtel Le Vaucelles
32 Hôtel de la Consigne
35 Hôtel Le Rouen

PLACES TO EAT
4   Épicerie de Nuit
6   Tongasoa
12 Heiz Legrix (Boulangerie)
13 Coupole
16 Salon de Thé
19 Monopix Supermarket
20 La Petite Auberge
34 Le Météor

OTHER
1   Château de Caen
2   Musée de Normandie
3   Musée des
    Beaux-Arts
5   Abbaye aux Dames
7   Église St-Pierre
8   Tourist Office
9   Bus Verts Office
    (Bus Information)
14 Crédit Agricole
15 Police Kiosk
17 Abbaye aux Hommes
18 Main Post Office
21 Église St-Jean
23 Launderette
25 Banque de France
26 Voyages Piel
    (Travel Agency)
27 Launderette
28 Launderette
30 Train Station
31 Bus Station
33 Car Rental Agencies
36 CTAC (Bus Kiosk)
37 ADA

NORMANDY

Laundry The laundrette at 127 rue St-Jean opens 7 am to 8 pm daily.

Mémorial – Un Musée pour la Paix

Caen's best-known museum is the Memorial – A Museum for Peace (☎ 02 31 06 06 44), whose aim is to promote world peace by focusing on the horrors of WWII. The exhibits may well help visitors to 'reflect on the scourge of war', as one brochure puts it, but the hordes of noisy school children who pass through the museum daily (except at the height of summer) certainly won't. All signs are in French, English and German.

The exhibits consist of three distinct parts:

- A history of Europe's descent into total war, tracing events from the end of WWI through the rise of Fascism to the Battle of Normandy in 1944.
- Three segments of unnarrated film footage (50 minutes in total) taken from the archives of both sides. This documentary material is further enlivened by scenes from the fictional film *The Longest Day*. The last film of the day begins at 6 pm (8 pm from mid-May to early September).
- An exhibit on Nobel Peace Prize laureates, housed in a former German command post underneath the main building and reached via a futuristic tunnel.

The Mémorial is about 3km north-west of the tourist office on Esplanade Dwight Eisenhower. Tickets are sold 9 am to 7 pm daily (9 pm in summer and 6 pm from November to mid-February). Admission costs 74FF (students 65FF). WWII veterans get in free.

To reach the museum, take bus No 17 from opposite the tourist office at place St-Pierre; the last bus back departs at 8.45 pm (earlier on Sunday). By car, follow the multitude of signs with the word 'Mémorial'.

Château de Caen

This enormous fortress surrounded by a dry moat opens 6 am to 7.30 pm daily (10 pm from May to September).

Visitors can walk around the **ramparts** and visit the 12th-century **Chapelle de St-Georges** and the **Échiquier (Exchequer)**, dating from about AD 1100 and one of the oldest civic buildings in Normandy. Of special interest is the **Jardin des Simples**, a garden of medicinal and aromatic herbs cultivated during the Middle Ages – some of which are poisonous. A book (in French) on the garden is on sale for 30FF inside the **Musée de Normandie** (☎ 02 31 30 47 50), which contains historical artefacts illustrating life in Normandy. There are explanatory signs in English. The museum opens 9.30 am to 12.30 pm and 2 to 6 pm daily (closed Tuesday). Admission costs 10FF (students 5FF), but it's free on Wednesday.

The **Musée des Beaux-Arts** (☎ 02 31 30 47 70), in an extravagant modern building nearby, houses an extensive collection of paintings dating from the 15th to 20th centuries (including the wonderful *Marriage of the Virgin* painted by Pietro Vannucci in 1504), ceramics, etchings and engravings. It opens 10 am to 6 pm except Tuesday. Admission costs 25FF (students 15FF, free for everyone on Wednesday).

Abbeys

Caen's two Romanesque abbeys were built on opposite sides of town by William the Conqueror and his wife, Matilda of Flanders, after the distant cousins had been absolved by the Roman Catholic church for marrying. The **Abbaye aux Hommes** (Abbey for Men, ☎ 02 31 30 42 81), with its multi-turreted Église St-Étienne, is at the end of rue St-Pierre and once contained William's mortal remains. Today it's home to the town hall and can be visited by guided tour at 9.30 and 11 am and 2.30 and 4 pm. Admission costs 10FF but entry is free to the church which opens 8.15 am to noon and 2 to 7.30 pm.

The starker **Abbaye aux Dames** (Abbey for Women; ☎ 02 31 06 98 98), at the eastern end of rue des Chanoines, incorporates the Église de la Trinité; look for Matilda's tomb behind the main altar. Access to the abbey, which houses regional government offices, is by guided tour daily at 2.30 and 4 pm. Admission is free.

NORMANDY

Places to Stay

Camping On the bank of the River Orne, *Camping Municipal* (☎ 02 31 73 60 92, *route de Louvigny*), 2.5km south-west of the train station, opens May to September. It charges 20/14/11FF per person/tent/car. Take bus No 13 to the Camping stop (last bus at 8 pm).

Near the coast at Ouistreham, *Camping des Pommiers* (☎ 02 31 97 12 66, fax 02 31 96 87 33, rue de la Haie Breton) opens all year except mid-December to mid-February. Prices are 21.20FF per person and the same for a tent site.

Hostels The *Auberge de Jeunesse* (☎ 02 31 52 19 96, fax 02 31 84 29 49, 68 rue Eustache Restout) charges 62FF (plus 10FF for breakfast) but opens only June to September. It's 2km south-west of the train station – take bus No 5 or 17 (the last one is at 9 pm) to the Cimetière de Vaucelles stop.

Hotels The *Hôtel de la Paix* (☎/fax 02 31 86 18 99, 14 rue Neuve St-Jean) has plain, medium-sized singles/doubles starting at 140/170FF with private shower and toilet.

Hôtel du Havre (☎ 02 31 86 19 80, 11 rue du Havre) has average rooms of above-average size from 150FF with washbasin or toilet (210/230FF with shower). *Hôtel Au St-Jean* (☎ 02 31 86 23 35, fax 02 31 86 74 15, 20 rue des Martyrs) has nicely done singles or doubles for 150FF (with shower) or 190FF (with full bathroom). There's free enclosed parking.

Hôtel Le Vaucelles (☎ 02 31 82 23 14, 13 rue de Vaucelles) has rooms starting at 115FF (140FF with shower and TV). Hall showers are free. The hard-to-miss yellow and green *Hôtel de la Consigne* (☎ 02 31 82 23 59, 48-50 place de la Gare) has decent doubles from 140FF.

Hôtel Le Rouen (☎ 02 31 34 06 03, fax 02 31 34 05 16, 8 place de la Gare) has decent singles/doubles with washbasin for 130/150FF (200/220FF with shower). In the city centre, *Hôtel St-Pierre* (☎ 02 31 86 28 20, fax 02 31 85 17 21, 40 blvd des Alliés) has basic but comfortable rooms from 120/130FF (155FF with private shower).

Places to Eat

Restaurants The pedestrianised quarter around rue du Vaugueux is a popular dining area. Lots of little, mid-priced restaurants serve a vast range of cuisines: North African, Chinese and even Malagasy at *Tongasoa* (☎ 02 31 43 87 15, 7 rue du Vaugueux). The diverse range of main courses start at 58FF and *menus* at 79FF (closed Sunday lunch).

Coupole (☎ 02 31 86 37 75, 6 blvd des Alliés) has a good-value *menu* for 63FF, salads from 38FF and a selection of local dishes including *tripes à la mode de Caen*.

La Petite Auberge (☎ 02 31 86 43 30, 17 rue de l'Équipe d'Urgence) is a homely little place with *menus* of home-cooked food from 68FF and *plats du jour* from 55FF. Near the train station is *Le Météor* (☎ 02 31 82 31 35, 55 rue d'Auge), a tiny haunt charging only 48FF for a three-course *menu*, including a glass of wine. The cheery *Salon de Thé* (153 rue St-Pierre) has salads from 28FF, quiche from 12FF and sandwiches from 15.50FF. It opens 6 am to 8 pm daily.

Self-Catering *Monoprix* (45 blvd Maréchal Leclerc) has a downstairs supermarket that opens 8.30 am to 8.30 pm Monday to Saturday. Late-night purchases can be made at *Épicerie de Nuit* (23 rue Porte au Berger), open 8 pm to 2 am from Tuesday to Sunday.

Exquisite gateaux and dozens of types of bread are available at *Heiz Legrix* (8 blvd des Alliés), open 7 am to 7.30 pm daily, except Monday.

For *food markets* head to place St-Sauveur on Friday, blvd Leroy (behind the train station) on Saturday and place Courtonne on Sunday.

Getting There & Away

Bus The entire Calvados department is served by Bus Verts, including Bayeux (36FF, 50 minutes), the eastern D-day beaches, Deauville-Trouville (53FF), Honfleur (67FF via Cabourg and Deauville, or 86FF by express bus), the ferry port at Ouistreham (21FF, 25 minutes), Falaise,

Lisieux and Vire. It also runs two buses daily to Le Havre (1½ hours).

Most buses stop both at the bus station and in the centre of town at place Courtonne, where there's a Bus Verts information kiosk. During the summer school holidays (July and August, more or less), the Ligne Côte du Nacre goes to Bayeux (one hour and 20 minutes) twice daily via Ouistreham and the eastern D-day beaches. A line (No 44) to Bayeux takes in the Mémorial, Arromanches, Pointe du Hoc and the American Military Cemetery.

If you arrive in Caen by bus, your ticket is valid on CTAC city buses for one hour. If you purchase your intercity ticket in advance, your ride *to* the bus station to catch your bus is free.

Train Caen is on the Paris–Cherbourg line. There are connections to Paris' Gare St-Lazare (156FF, 2½ hours, 13 daily), Bayeux (31FF, 20 minutes), Cherbourg (99FF, 1½ hours, four daily), Pontorson (122FF, six daily), Rennes (167FF, three hours, two daily), Rouen (116FF, two hours, 10 daily), and Tours (169FF, 3¾ hours, five daily) via Le Mans.

Car Rental agencies on place de la Gare include Hertz (☎ 02 31 84 64 50) at No 34, Europcar (☎ 02 31 84 61 61) at No 36 and Avis (☎ 02 31 84 73 80) at No 44. ADA (☎ 02 31 34 88 89) is at 26 rue Auge.

Boat Brittany Ferries (☎ 02 31 36 36 36) sails from Ouistreham, 14km north-east of Caen, to Portsmouth in England. For more information, see the Sea section in the Getting There & Away chapter.

Getting Around
Bus CTAC (02 31 15 55 55) runs city bus No 7 and the more direct No 15 between the train station and the tourist office (stop: St-Pierre). A single ride costs 6.20FF, and a carnet of 10 costs 50.50FF. Services end between 6 and 8 pm.

Taxi To order a taxi, ring ☎ 02 31 26 62 00 or ☎ 02 31 52 17 89.

BAYEUX
postcode 14400 • pop 15,000 • elevation 50m

Bayeux is celebrated for two trans-Channel invasions: the conquest of England by the Normans under William the Conqueror in 1066 (an event chronicled in the celebrated Bayeux Tapestry) and the Allied D-day landings of 6 June 1944, which launched the liberation of Nazi-occupied France. Bayeux was the first town in France to be freed and, remarkably, survived virtually unscathed.

Bayeux is a very attractive – though fairly touristy – town with several excellent museums. It also serves as a base for visits to the D-day beaches.

Orientation
The Cathédrale Notre Dame, the major landmark in the centre of Bayeux and visible throughout the town, is 1km north-west of the train station. The River Aure, with several attractive little mills along its banks, flows northwards on the eastern side of the centre.

Information
Tourist Offices The tourist office (☎ 02 31 51 28 28, fax 02 31 51 28 29) is at Pont St-Jean, just off the northern end of rue Larcher. It opens 9 am to noon and 2 to 6 pm, Monday to Saturday, and 9.30 am to noon and 2.30 to 6 pm on Sunday in July and August. Staff reserve accommodation for a 10FF fee.

A *billet jumelé* (multipass ticket), valid for four of the five museums listed in this section (excluding the Musée Mémorial) and available at each, costs 38FF (students 22FF).

Money There's a Société Générale at 26 rue St-Malo and a Caisse d'Épargne at No 59 on the same street. The tourist office will change money when the banks are closed (Monday and public holidays). The post office also exchanges currency.

Post & Communications The main post office, opposite the town hall at 14 rue

NORMANDY

BAYEUX

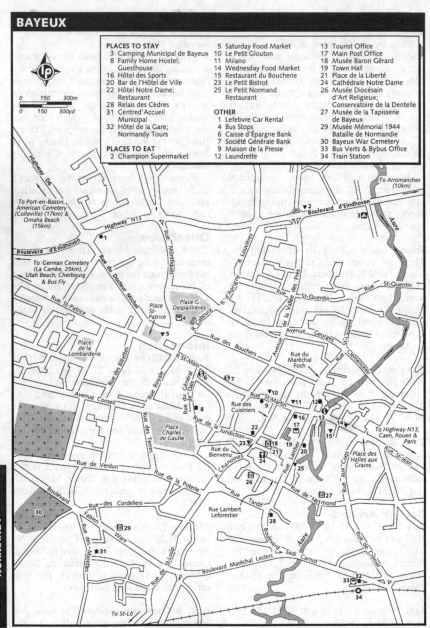

PLACES TO STAY
3 Camping Municipal de Bayeux
8 Family Home Hostel;
   Guesthouse
16 Hôtel des Sports
20 Bar de l'Hôtel de Ville
22 Hôtel Notre Dame;
   Restaurant
28 Relais des Cèdres
31 Centred'Accueil
   Municipal
32 Hôtel de la Gare;
   Normandy Tours

PLACES TO EAT
2 Champion Supermarket

5 Saturday Food Market
10 Le Petit Glouton
11 Milano
14 Wednesday Food Market
15 Restaurant du Boucherie
23 Le Petit Bistrot
25 Le Petit Normand
   Restaurant

OTHER
1 Lefebvre Car Rental
4 Bus Stops
6 Caisse d'Épargne Bank
7 Société Générale Bank
9 Maison de la Presse
12 Laundrette

13 Tourist Office
17 Main Post Office
18 Musée Baron Gérard
19 Town Hall
21 Place de la Liberté
24 Cathédrale Notre Dame
26 Musée Diocésain
   d'Art Religieux;
   Conservatoire de la Dentelle
27 Musée de la Tapisserie
   de Bayeux
29 Musée Mémorial 1944
   Bataille de Normandie
30 Bayeux War Cemetery
33 Bus Verts & Bybus Office
34 Train Station

euro currency converter 10FF = €1.52

Larcher, opens 8 am to 6.30 pm weekdays and to noon on Saturday, and has a Cyberposte. You can also surf at the tourist office (25FF per 15 minutes, with a Cyberis card bought from the counter).

Laundry The laundrette at 13 rue du Maréchal Foch opens 7 am to 10 pm daily.

Bayeux Tapestry

The world-famous Bayeux Tapestry – actually a 70m-long strip of coarse embroidered linen – was commissioned by Bishop Odo of Bayeux, half-brother to William the Conqueror, sometime between the successful Norman invasion of England in 1066 and 1082.

The tapestry, which was probably made in England, recounts the dramatic story of the Norman invasion and the events that led up to it – from the Norman perspective. The story is told in 58 panels, with vivid, action-packed scenes following each other in quick succession. The events are accompanied by written commentary in dog Latin. The scenes are filled with depictions of 11th-century Norman and Saxon dress, food, tools, cooking utensils and weapons. The Saxons are depicted with moustaches and the backs of the Norman soldiers' heads are shaved. Halley's Comet, which passed through our part of the solar system in 1066, also makes an appearance.

The tapestry is housed in the **Musée de la Tapisserie de Bayeux** (☎ 02 31 51 25 50) on rue de Nesmond. It opens 9 or 9.30 am to 12.30 pm and 2 to 6 pm, mid-September to April; the museum stays open to 7 pm without a midday break, the rest of the year. Admission covers four other attractions, too: the Cathédrale Notre Dame, the Musée Diocésain d'Art Religieux, the Conservatoire de la Dentelle and the Musée Baron Gérard, costs 40FF (students 16FF). The excellent taped commentary (5FF) makes viewing the upstairs exhibits a bit unnecessary. A 14-minute film is screened eight to 13 times daily in English on the 2nd floor (last showing 5.15 pm, or 5.45 pm May to mid-September).

Cathédrale Notre Dame

Most of Bayeux's spectacular cathedral, a fine example of Norman Gothic architecture, dates from the 13th century, though the crypt, the arches of the nave and the lower portions of the towers on either side of the main entrance are late 11th-century Romanesque. The central tower was added in the 15th century; the copper dome

JANE SMITH

A medieval masterpiece: 70m of stitching depict the 1066 Norman invasion of England.

NORMANDY

dates from the 1860s. The cathedral opens 8.30 am to 6 pm daily (8 am to 7 pm in July and August).

Musée Diocésain d'Art Religieux

The Diocesan Museum of Religious Art (☎ 02 31 92 14 21), an Aladdin's cave of vestments and liturgical objects, is just south of the cathedral at 6 rue Lambert Leforestier. It opens 10 am to 12.30 pm and 2 to 6 pm daily (9 am to 7 pm from July to September). Admission costs the same as for the Musée de la Tapisserie de Bayeux.

Conservatoire de la Dentelle

The fascinating Lace Conservatory (☎ 02 31 92 73 80) is dedicated to the preservation of traditional Norman lacemaking. This is claimed to be the only place where you can watch some of France's most celebrated lacemakers, who are creating the intricate designs using dozens of bobbins and hundreds of pins.

The Conservatoire also gives lacemaking classes and sells materials (pins, bobbins, thread etc). Small lace objects, the product of something like 50 hours' work, are on sale for around 750FF. The museum opens 10 am to 12.30 pm and 2 to 6 pm daily, October to June; and 9 am to 7 pm the rest of the year. Admission costs the same as for the Musée de la Tapisserie de Bayeux.

Musée Baron Gérard

This pleasant museum (☎ 02 31 92 14 21), next to the cathedral at place de la Liberté, specialises in local porcelain, lace and 15th- to 19th-century paintings (Italian, Flemish, impressionist). Out front there is a huge plane tree known as the Arbre de la Liberté, which, like many such 'Freedom Trees', was planted in the years after the Revolution. It is one of only nine left in France. The museum opens 10 am to 12.30 pm and 2 to 6 pm daily, mid-September to May; 9 am to 7 pm the rest of the year. Admission costs the same as for the Musée de la Tapisserie de Bayeux.

Musée Mémorial 1944 Bataille de Normandie

Bayeux's huge war museum (☎ 02 31 92 93 41), blvd Fabien Ware, rather haphazardly displays thousands of photos, uniforms, weapons, newspaper clippings and lifelike scenes associated with D-day and the Battle of Normandy. It opens 10 am to 12.30 pm and 2 to 6 pm daily, mid-September to April and 9.30 am to 6.30 pm May to mid-September. Admission costs 33FF (students 16FF). A 30-minute film in English is screened two to five times daily (always at 10.45 am and 5 pm).

Bayeux War Cemetery

This peaceful cemetery, on blvd Fabien Ware a few hundred metres west of the war museum, is the largest of the 18 Commonwealth military cemeteries in Normandy. It contains 4868 graves of soldiers from the UK and 10 other countries. Many of the 466 Germans buried here were never identified and the headstones are simply marked 'Ein Deutscher Soldat' (A German Soldier). There is an explanatory plaque in the small chapel to the right as you enter the grounds. The structure across blvd Fabien Ware commemorates the 1807 Commonwealth soldiers missing in action.

Places to Stay

Camping About 2km north of the town centre, just south of blvd d'Eindhoven, is *Camping Municipal de Bayeux* (☎ 02 31 92 08 43). It opens mid-March to mid-November and you can check in from 8 to 9 am and 5 to 7 pm (7 am to 9 pm in July and August). A tent site costs 9.20FF, adults pay 17.10FF and children aged under seven pay 9.20FF.

A few tents can be pitched in the back garden of the *Family Home* hostel (see the following section) for about 30FF per person, including breakfast.

Hostels The *Family Home* (☎ 02 31 92 15 22, fax 02 31 92 55 72, 39 rue du Général de Dais) is an excellent old hostel and a great place to meet other travellers. A bed in a dorm room costs 105FF (95FF if

NORMANDY

William Conquers England

From an unpromising beginning, William the Conqueror (1027–87) became one of the most powerful men of the early Middle Ages and ruler of two kingdoms. The son of Robert I of Normandy and his concubine Arlette (during his lifetime, he was commonly referred to as 'William the Bastard'), William ascended the throne of Normandy at the age of five. In spite of several attempts by rivals – including members of his own family – to kill him and his advisers, William took over the running of Normandy aged 15. He managed to retain power, and then, for a period of about five years from when he was about 20, set about regaining his lost territory and feudal rights, quashing several rebellions along the way. These tasks accomplished, he began to think of expanding Norman influence.

In England, King Ethelred II (William's relative) had apparently promised William that upon his death the throne would pass to the young Norman ruler. And when the most powerful Saxon lord in England, Harold Godwinson of Wessex, was shipwrecked on the Norman coast, he was obliged to swear to William that the English crown would pass to Normandy.

In January 1066 Ethelred died without an heir. The great nobles of England (and very likely the majority of the Saxon people) supported Harold's claim to the throne, and he was crowned on 5 January. He immediately faced several pretenders to his throne, William being the most obvious one. But while William was preparing to send an invasion fleet across the Channel, a rival army consisting of an alliance between Harold's estranged brother Tostig and Harold Hardrada of Norway landed in the north of England. Harold marched north and engaged them in battle at Stamford Bridge, near York, on 25 September. He was victorious, and both Harold Hardrada and Tostig were killed.

Meanwhile, William had crossed the Channel unopposed with an army of about 6000 men, including a large cavalry force. They landed at Pevensey before marching to Hastings. Making remarkably quick time southwards from York, Harold faced William with about 7000 men from a strong defensive position on 13 October. William put his army into an offensive position and the battle began the next day.

Although William's archers scored many hits among the densely packed and ill-trained Saxon peasants, the latter's ferocious defence terminated a charge by the Norman cavalry and drove them back in disarray. For a while William faced the real possibility of losing the battle. However, summoning all the knowledge and tactical ability he had gained in numerous campaigns against his rivals in Normandy, he used the cavalry's rout to draw the Saxon infantry out from their defensive positions, whereupon the Norman infantry turned and caused heavy casualties on the undisciplined Saxon troops. The battle started to turn against Harold – his two other brothers were slain, and he himself was killed (by an arrow through the eye, according to the Bayeux Tapestry) late in the afternoon. The embattled Saxons fought on until sunset and then fled, leaving the Normans effectively in charge of England. William immediately marched to London, ruthlessly quelled the opposition, and was crowned king of England on Christmas Day.

William thus became king of two realms and entrenched England's feudal system of government under the control of Norman nobles. However, ongoing unrest among the Saxon peasantry soured his opinion of the country and he spent most of the rest of his life after 1072 in Normandy, only going to England when compelled to do so. He left most of the governance of the country to the bishops.

In Normandy William continued to expand his influence by military campaigns or by strategic marriages. In 1077, he took control of the Maine region, but then fought Philip I of France over several towns on their mutual border. In 1087 he was injured during an attack on Mantes. He died at Rouen a few weeks later and was buried at Caen.

you've got a Hostelling International card), including breakfast. Singles are 160FF. The hostel opens all day, but the curfew is (theoretically) at 11 pm; just ask for a key to the main door. Multicourse French dinners cost 65FF, including wine. Vegetarian dishes are available on request or you can cook for yourself. There's a laundry, too.

The *Centre d'Accueil Municipal* (☎ 02 31 92 08 19, 21 rue des Marettes) in a large, modern building 1km south-west of the cathedral. Antiseptic but comfy singles (all that's available) are a great deal at 90FF, including breakfast. Telephone reservations are usually accepted.

Chambres d'Hôtes The tourist office has a list of chambres d'hôtes in the Bayeux area. The cheapest cost about 150FF for two people, with breakfast.

Hotels The old but well-maintained *Hôtel de la Gare* (☎ 02 31 92 10 70, fax 02 31 51 95 99, 26 place de la Gare) has singles/doubles from 85/100FF. Two-bed triples/quads are 160FF and showers are free. There are no late trains so it's usually pretty quiet at night.

The *Bar de l'Hôtel de Ville* (☎ 02 31 92 30 08, 31ter rue Larcher) has large, quiet singles/doubles for 140/160FF including free showers. An extra bed costs 50FF. Telephone reservations aren't accepted.

Hôtel des Sports (☎ 02 31 92 28 53, 19 rue St-Martin) is a cut above, with tastefully appointed rooms (most with shower or free use of those in the hall) starting at 160/200FF.

The *Relais des Cèdres* (☎ 02 31 21 98 07, 1 blvd Sadi Carnot) is an old mansion done up in 'French country' style. Doubles cost 150FF with washbasin and toilet, 200FF with shower and 250FF with shower or bath and toilet. Showers are free.

If you're flush, try *Hôtel Notre Dame* (☎ 02 31 92 87 24, fax 02 31 92 67 11, 44 rue des Cuisiniers) a one-star place opposite the western facade of the cathedral. Doubles cost from 250FF to 270FF with shower or bath, but they have cheaper rooms without shower for 160FF. Hall showers cost 20FF.

Places to Eat

Restaurants *Le Petit Normand* (☎ 02 31 22 88 66, 35 rue Larcher) serves traditional Norman food prepared with apple cider and is popular with English tourists. Simple fixed-price *menus* start at 58FF; more expensive *menus* cost 78/98/128FF. The restaurant opens for lunch and dinner (closed Wednesday and Sunday night). It opens daily in July and August.

Milano (☎ 02 31 92 15 10, 18 rue St-Martin), serves very good pizza. It opens 11.30 am to 10 pm Monday to Saturday (Sunday, too, in June and August).

The food at the *Hôtel Notre Dame* (see Places to Stay) is Norman at its finest; count on 60FF for a lunch *menu* and 95FF per person minimum at dinner. It's closed for Sunday lunch and all day Monday from November to March.

Le Petit Bistrot (☎ 02 31 51 85 40, 2 rue du Bienvenu) is a charming little eatery with excellent fish and duck *menus* starting at 98FF (closed Sunday and Monday).

Meat is king at the *Restaurant du Boucherie* (☎ 02 31 92 05 53, Alleé de l'Orangerie) with excellent Norman-style *menus* from 60FF. It opens for lunch and dinner (closed Sunday evening and Monday).

Self-Catering There are lots of takeaway shops along or near rue St-Martin and rue St-Jean, including *Le Petit Glouton* (42 rue St-Martin). Rue St-Jean has an open-air *food market* on Wednesday morning, as does place St-Patrice on Saturday morning. Don't miss *Teurgoule*, a sweet, cinnamon-flavoured rice pudding typical of the Bayeux region.

The *Champion* supermarket across the road from the Camping Municipal is open Monday to Saturday from 9 am to 8 pm.

Getting There & Away

Bus A rather infrequent service is offered by Bus Verts (☎ 02 31 92 02 92, 02 31 44 77 44 in Caen) from the train station and place St-Patrice to Caen, the D-day beaches (see Getting There & Away in the following section), Vire and elsewhere in the Calvados department.

NORMANDY

The schedules are arranged for school children coming into Bayeux in the morning and going home in the afternoon. The Bus Verts office, across the car park from the train station, opens 10 am to noon and 3 to 6 pm weekdays (closed most of July).

Train Services include Paris' Gare St-Lazare (171FF) via Caen (31FF, 20 minutes, 15 daily) as well as Cherbourg (81FF, one hour, 10 daily). There's a service to Quimper (266FF, 5¾ hours, three daily) via Rennes.

Getting Around

Bus The local bus line, Bybus (☎ 02 31 92 02 92), which shares an office with Bus Verts, has two routes traversing Bayeux, all of which end up at place St-Patrice. From the train station, take bus No 3 (direction J. Cocteau).

Bicycle Family Home (see Places to Stay) rents out 10-speeds for 60FF/day, plus 100FF deposit.

Taxi Taxis can be ordered 24 hours on ☎ 02 31 92 92 40 or ☎ 02 31 92 04 10.

D-DAY BEACHES

The D-day landings, codenamed 'Operation Overlord', were the largest military operation in history. Early on the morning of 6 June 1944, swarms of landing craft – part of a flotilla of almost 7000 boats – hit the beaches, and tens of thousands of soldiers from the USA, UK, Canada and elsewhere began pouring onto French soil.

Most of the 135,000 Allied troops stormed ashore along 80km of beach north of Bayeux codenamed (from west to east) Utah and Omaha (in the US sector) and Gold, Juno and Sword (in the British and Canadian ones). The landings on D-day – called Jour J in French – were followed by the Battle of Normandy, which would lead to the liberation of Europe from Nazi occupation. In the 76 days of fighting, the Allies suffered 210,000 casualties, including 37,000 troops killed. German casualties are believed to be around 200,000; and another 200,000 German soldiers were taken prisoner. Caen's Memorial museum provides the best introduction to the history of what took place here and also attempts to explain the rationale behind each event. Once on the coast, travellers can take a well marked circuit that links the battle sites, close to where holiday-makers sunbathe.

Fat Norman cows with udders the size of beach balls use the bombed-out bunkers to shield themselves from the wind. Many of the villages near the D-day beaches have small museums with war memorabilia on display collected by local people after the fighting.

Information

Maps of the D-day beaches are available at *tabacs* (tobacconists), newsagents and bookshops in Bayeux and elsewhere. The best one is called *D-day 6.6.44 Jour J* and sells for 29FF. The area is also known as the Côte du Nacre (Mother-of-Pearl Coast).

Arromanches

To make it possible to unload the quantities of cargo necessary, the Allies established two prefabricated ports code-named **Mulberry Harbours**.

The harbour established at Omaha Beach was completely destroyed by a ferocious gale just two weeks after D-day, but one of them, Port Winston, can still be viewed at Arromanches, a seaside town 10km north-east of Bayeux.

The harbour consists of 146 massive cement caissons towed from England and sunk to form a semicircular breakwater in which floating bridge spans were moored. In the three months after D-day, 2.5 million men, four million tonnes of equipment and 500,000 vehicles were unloaded there. At low tide you can walk out to many of the caissons. The best view of Port Winston is from the hill, east of town, topped with a statue of the Virgin Mary.

The well regarded **Musée du Débarquement** (Invasion Museum; ☎ 02 31 22 34 31), on place de 6 Juin right in the centre of Arromanches by the sea, explains the logistics and importance of Port Winston and

NORMANDY

The Battle of Normandy

In early 1944 an Allied invasion of continental Europe seemed inevitable. Hitler's folly on the Russian front and the Luftwaffe's inability to control the skies had left Germany vulnerable.

Normandy was to be the spearhead into Europe. Codenamed Operation Overlord, the invasion entailed an assault by three paratroop divisions and five seaborne divisions, along with 1000 planes, 300 gliders and countless ships and boats. The total invasion force was 45,000, and 15 divisions were to follow once successful beachheads had been established.

Allied intelligence confused the Germans about the landing site. The narrow Channel crossing to Calais seemed more likely, although Hitler and Field Marshal Rommel both felt that Normandy would be the choice. As a result, fortifications were much stronger around Calais than in Normandy.

Because of the tides and unpredictable weather patterns, Allied planners had only a few days available each month to launch the invasion. On 4 June, the date chosen, very bad weather set in, delaying the operation. The weather had only improved slightly the next day, but General Dwight D Eisenhower, Allied commander-in-chief, gave the go-ahead: 6 June would be D-day.

In the very early hours of 6 June the first troops were on the ground. British commandos captured key bridges and destroyed German communications, while the paratroops weren't far behind them. Although the paratroops' tactical victories were few, they caused enormous confusion in German ranks. More importantly, because of their relatively small numbers, at first, the German high command didn't believe that the real invasion had begun.

Sword, Juno & Gold Beaches These beaches, stretching for about 35km from Ouistreham to Arromanches, were attacked by the British 2nd Army which included sizeable detachments of Canadians and smaller groups of Commonwealth, Free French and Polish forces.

At Sword Beach, initial German resistance was quickly overcome and the beach was secured after about two hours. Infantry pushed inland from Ouistreham to link up with paratroops around Ranville, but soon suffered heavy casualties as their supporting armour fell behind, trapped in a huge traffic jam on the narrow coastal roads. Nevertheless, they were within 5km of Caen by 4 pm, but a heavy German armoured counterattack forced them to dig in. Thus, in spite of the Allies' successes, Caen was not taken on the first day as planned, one of the prime D-day objectives.

At Juno Beach, Canadian brigades cleared the beach in 15 minutes and headed inland. Mines took a heavy toll on the infantry, but by noon they were south and east of Creuilly. Late in the afternoon, the German armoured divisions that had halted the British from Sword were deflected towards the coast and held Douvres, thus threatening to drive a wedge between the Sword and Juno forces. However, the threat of encirclement caused them to withdraw by the next day.

At Gold Beach, the attack by the British forces was at first chaotic; the initial ferocious bombardment of German positions by air and sea hadn't silenced enough of the defenders' big guns. By 9 am though, Allied armoured divisions were on the beach and several brigades pushed inland. By afternoon they had joined up with the Juno forces and were only 3km from Bayeux.

On all three beaches, odd-looking 'Funnies' – specially designed armoured amphibious vehicles designed to clear minefields, breach walls and wire entanglements and provide support and protection for the infantry – proved their worth. Their construction and successful deployment was due to the ingenuity and foresight of British Major-General Hobart.

Omaha & Utah Beaches For some reason, US General Omar Bradley decided that his US 1st Army didn't need the Funnies – a mistake that was to cost his men dearly at Omaha. It was compounded by the loss of 27 tanks that been launched from landing craft too far out from the beach. Thus, the US 5th Corps had to land on a well defended beach with virtually no armoured cover at

The Battle of Normandy

all. The landing itself was close to a shambles; troops had to struggle though deep water to the beach where they collected in exhausted little groups, facing devastating fire from enemy positions and with little prospect of support. Eventually, a precarious toehold was gained; the Germans, lacking reserves, were forced to fall back a short distance. Nevertheless, 1000 Allied soldiers were killed at Omaha on D-day, out of a total of 2500.

At Utah, US forces faced little resistance, and got off the beach after two hours. By noon, the beach had been cleared with the loss of only 12 men. Pockets of troops held large tracts of territory to the west of the landing site, and the town of Ste-Mère Église was captured.

Four days later, the Allies held a coastal strip about 100km long and 10km deep. British Field Marshal Montgomery's plan successfully drew the weight of German armour towards Caen, where fierce fighting continued for more than a month and reduced the city to rubble, thus leaving the US army farther west to consolidate and push northwards up the Cotentin Peninsula.

The port of Cherbourg was a major prize; after a series of fierce battles it fell to the Allies on 29 June. However, its valuable facilities were blown up by the Germans so it remained out of service until autumn. To overcome likely logistical problems, the Allies had devised the remarkable 'Mulberry Harbours'. These were enormous floating harbours that were towed from England, and set up off the Norman coast. They were indispensable in allowing large amounts of supplies to be taken quickly off ships and onto the roads leading to the front. A big storm from 19 to 22 June, however, destroyed the harbour stationed at Omaha Beach and damaged the Gold Beach installation.

The fierce Battle of the Hedgerows was fought mainly by the Americans up and down the Cotentin Peninsula. The land of the *bocage*, divided into countless fields bordered by walled roads and hedgerows, made ideal territory for defending. Nevertheless, once the Allies finally broke out from the beachheads their superior numbers meant the end was nigh for the Germans in Normandy.

By the end of July, US army units had smashed through to the border of Brittany. By mid-August, two German armies had been surrounded and destroyed near Falaise and Argentan, and on 20 August, US forces crossed the Seine at several points about 40km north and south of Paris.

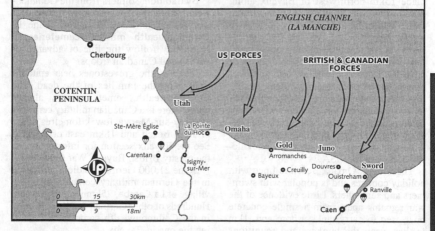

makes a good first stop before visiting the beaches. The museum opens 9 am to 6 pm in April, 9 am to 7 pm May to September, 9.30 am to 5 pm October to December and February to March. It's closed on Monday and throughout January. Admission costs 35FF (students 20FF). The last guided tour (in French, with a written text in English) leaves 45 minutes before closing time. An unimpressive seven-minute diorama/slide show in English is held throughout the day.

Longues-sur-Mer

The massive 152mm German guns on the coast near Longues-sur-Mer, 6km west of Arromanches, were designed to hit targets some 20km away, which in June 1944 included both Gold Beach (to the east) and Omaha Beach (to the west). Half a century later, the mammoth artillery pieces are still sitting in their colossal concrete emplacements. (In wartime they were covered with camouflage nets and tufts of grass.)

Parts of an American film about D-day, *The Longest Day* (1962), were filmed both here and at Pointe du Hoc. On clear days, Bayeux's cathedral, 8km away, is visible to the south.

Omaha & Juno Beaches

The most brutal fighting on D-day took place 15km north-west of Bayeux along 7km of coastline known as Omaha Beach, which had to be abandoned in storms two weeks later.

As you stand on the gently sloping sand, try to imagine how the US soldiers must have felt running inland towards the German positions on the nearby ridge.

A memorial marks the site of the first US military cemetery on French soil, where soldiers killed on the beach were buried. Their remains were later reinterred at the American Military Cemetery at Colleville-sur-Mer or in the USA.

These days, Omaha Beach is lined with holiday cottages and is popular with swimmers and sunbathers. Little evidence of the war remains apart from a single concrete boat used to carry tanks ashore and, 1km farther west, the bunkers and munitions

sites of a German fortified point (look for the tall obelisk on the hill).

Dune-lined Juno Beach, 12km east of Arromanches, was stormed by Canadian troops on D-day. A Cross of Lorraine marks the spot where General Charles de Gaulle came ashore shortly after the landings.

Military Cemeteries

The bodies of the American soldiers who lost their lives during the pivotal Battle of Normandy were either sent back to the USA (if their families so requested) or buried in the **American Military Cemetery** (☎ 02 31 51 62 00) at Colleville-sur-Mer, 17km north-west of Bayeux. The cemetery contains the graves of 9386 American soldiers and a memorial to 1557 others whose remains were never found.

The huge, immaculately tended expanse of lawn, with white crosses and Stars of David and set on a hill overlooking Omaha Beach, testifies to the extent of the killings that took place around here in 1944. There's a large colonnaded memorial, a reflecting pond and chapel for silent meditation. The cemetery opens 8 am to 5 pm (9 am to 6 pm mid-April to mid-October). From Bayeux, it can be reached by Bus Verts' line No 70, but service is infrequent. Bus No 44 from Caen will also drop you off here.

By tradition, soldiers from the Commonwealth killed in the war were buried near where they fell. And as a result, the 18 **Commonwealth military cemeteries** in Normandy follow the line of advance of British and Canadian troops.

Many of the gravestones bear epitaphs written by the families of the dead. The Commonwealth cemeteries are always open. There is a Canadian military cemetery at **Bény-sur-Mer**, a few kilometres south of Juno Beach and 18km east of Bayeux. See the Bayeux section for information on the mostly British Bayeux War Cemetery.

Some 21,000 German soldiers are buried in the German military cemetery near the village of **La Cambe**, 25km west of Bayeux. Hundreds of other German dead were buried in the Commonwealth cemeteries, including the one in Bayeux.

Pointe du Hoc Ranger Memorial

At 7.10 am on 6 June 1944, 225 US Army Rangers scaled the 30m cliffs at Pointe du Hoc, where the Germans had emplaced a battery of huge artillery guns.

The guns, as it turned out, had been transferred elsewhere, but the Americans captured the gun emplacements (the two huge circular cement structures) and the German command post (next to the two flag poles), and then fought off German counterattacks for two days. By the time they were relieved on 8 June, 81 of the rangers had been killed and 58 more had been wounded.

Today, the site, which France turned over in perpetuity to the US government in 1979, looks much as it did half a century ago.

The ground is still pockmarked with 3m bomb craters. Visitors can walk among and inside the German fortifications, but they are warned not to dig: there may still be mines and explosive materials below the surface. In the German command post, you can see where the wooden ceilings were charred by American flame-throwers. As you face the sea, Utah Beach, which runs roughly perpendicular to the cliffs here, is 14km to the left. Pointe du Hoc, which is 12km west of the American cemetery, is always open. The command post is open the same hours as the American Military Cemetery.

Organised Tours

A bus tour is an excellent way to see the D-day beaches. Normandy Tours (☎ 02 31 92 10 70), based at the Hôtel de la Gare in Bayeux, has four-hour tours stopping at Longues-sur-Mer, Arromanches, Omaha Beach, the American Military Cemetery and Pointe du Hoc for 200FF (students/children 150FF). The times and itineraries are flexible.

Bus Fly (☎ 02 31 22 00 08), 25 rue des Cuisiniers in Bayeux, is best booked through the Family Home hostel (see Places to Stay for Bayeux). An afternoon tour to major D-day sites costs 200FF (students 180FF), including museum admission fees. They'll collect you from your hotel or the tourist office in Bayeux.

Getting There & Away

Bus Line No 70 operated by Bus Verts (☎ 02 31 92 02 92 in Bayeux, 02 31 44 77 44 in Caen) goes westwards to the American Military Cemetery at Colleville-sur-Mer and Omaha Beach, and on to Pointe du Hoc and the town of Grandcamp-Maisy. Bus No 74 (No 75 during summer) serves Arromanches, Gold and Juno beaches, and Courseulles. During July and August only, the Côte du Nacre line goes to Caen via Arromanches, Gold, Juno and Sword beaches, and Ouistreham; and Circuit 44 links Bayeux and Caen via Pointe du Hoc, the American Military Cemetery, Arromanches and the Mémorial museum.

Car For three or more people, renting a car can be cheaper than a tour. Lefebvre Car Rental (☎ 02 31 92 05 96), on blvd d'Eindhoven (at the Esso petrol station) in Bayeux, charges 350FF per day with 200km free (more than enough for a circuit to the beaches along coastal route D514) and 699FF for two days with 400km free. The office opens 8 am to 8 pm daily.

Manche

The Manche department, surrounded on three sides by the English Channel (La Manche), includes the entire Cotentin Peninsula. Its 320km of coastline stretches from Utah Beach north-westwards to the port city of Cherbourg and then south to the magnificent Mont St-Michel. The fertile inland areas, crisscrossed with hedgerows, produce an abundance of cattle, dairy products and apples.

The Cotentin Peninsula's north-west corner is especially lovely, with unspoiled stretches of rocky coastline sheltering tranquil bays and villages. Due west lie the Channel Islands of Jersey (25km from the coast) and Guernsey (45km), accessible by ferry from St-Malo in Brittany and, in season, from the Norman towns of Carteret, Portbail and Granville.

Very sadly, over the past two decades, the Manche region has become known as

'Europe's nuclear dump'. On the peninsula's western tip at Cap de la Hague is France's first uranium waste treatment plant which is well hidden until you reach its heavily fortified perimeter. Farther south at Flamanville is a sprawling power plant, and at the Cherbourg shipyards the latest nuclear submarines are built.

Getting Around

Trains run to and from Cherbourg, but local buses are few and far between in the Manche region.

CHERBOURG
postcode 50100 • pop 25,000

At the very tip of the Cotentin Peninsula sits Cherbourg, the largest but hardly the most appealing town in this part of Normandy. A port city and naval base, it's too busy with transatlantic cargo ships and passenger ferries crossing to England and Ireland to think about much else. Don't expect to find any of the romance portrayed in Jacques Demy's 1964 classic film *Les Parapluies de Cherbourg* (The Umbrellas of Cherbourg) here.

Orientation

The Bassin du Commerce, a wide central waterway, separates the 'living' half of Cherbourg to the west from the deserted streets of the Basin de Commerce to the east. The attractive Avant Port (Outer Harbour) lies to the north.

Information

Tourist Offices The tourist office (☎ 02 33 93 52 02, fax 02 33 53 66 97), 2 quai Alexandre III, opens 9 am to noon and 2 to 6 pm weekdays and on Saturday morning; and 9 am to 6.30 pm Monday to Saturday, July and August. The annexe (☎ 02 33 44 39 92) at the ferry terminal opens 7 to 9 am and 2 to 3 pm daily. The tourist office makes hotel reservations for 10FF.

Money The Banque de France, 22 quai Alexandre III, exchanges money from 9 am to noon. A Crédit Lyonnais is at 16 rue Maréchal Foch. The post office also exchanges currency.

Post & Communications The main post office, 1 rue de l'Ancien Quai, opens 8 am to 7 pm weekdays and until noon on Saturday, and has a Cyberposte.

The Cybercafe in the upper floor of the Forum Espace Culture bookshop charges 15FF per half-hour. It opens 2 to 7 pm on Monday, and 10 am to 7 pm Tuesday to Saturday.

Laundry The laundrette at 62 rue au Blé opens 7 am to 8 pm daily.

Musée Thomas Henry

This museum (☎ 02 33 23 02 23), upstairs in the cultural centre on rue Vastel, has 200 works by French, Flemish, Italian and other artists, but the 30 paintings by Jean-François Millet alone make it worth the visit. The museum opens 9 am (10 am Sunday) to noon and 2 to 6 pm daily (closed Monday). Admission costs 15FF (students 7FF).

Nuclear Tours

Those who might like to glow in the dark can take free guided tours of the Cogemauranium waste **reprocessing plant** (☎ 02 33 02 61 04) at Cap de La Hague or the **Flamanville nuclear power plant** (☎ 02 33 04 12 99). Each tour lasts about three hours and you must present your passport or national ID card. The facility at la Hague opens 10 am to 6 pm daily, April and September, and on weekends only during the rest of the year. The Flamanville station opens 9 am to noon and 2 to 6.30 pm Monday to Saturday.

Walking

The tourist office organises walks of 12km or more in the surrounding countryside some Saturdays from April to October, and every Saturday in July and August.

Places to Stay

Camping The nearest camping ground is *Camping Collignon* (☎ 02 33 20 16 88) in Tourlaville, on the coast about 5km northeast of town. It opens from June to September. Adults pay 20FF each and a tent site costs 29FF. Bus No 5 makes two runs daily

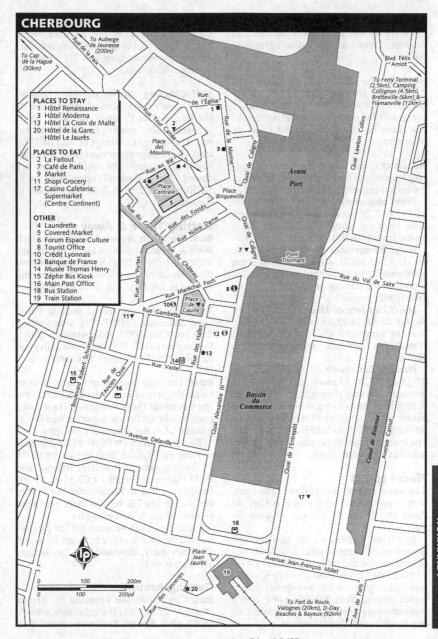

CHERBOURG

PLACES TO STAY
1 Hôtel Renaissance
3 Hôtel Moderna
13 Hôtel La Croix de Malte
20 Hôtel de la Gare;
   Hôtel Le Jaurès

PLACES TO EAT
2 La Faitout
7 Café de Paris
9 Market
11 Shopi Grocery
17 Casino Cafeteria;
   Supermarket
   (Centre Continent)

OTHER
4 Laundrette
5 Covered Market
6 Forum Espace Culture
8 Tourist Office
10 Crédit Lyonnais
12 Banque de France
14 Musée Thomas Henry
15 Zéphir Bus Kiosk
16 Main Post Office
18 Bus Station
19 Train Station

To Auberge de Jeunesse (200m)
To Cap de la Hague (30km)
Rue de la Paix
Rue Tour Carrée
Rue de l'Église
Rue de la Marine
Blvd Fèlix Amiot
To Ferry Terminal (2.5km), Camping Collignon (4.5km), Brètteville (6km) & Flamanville (12km)
Quai Lawton Collins
Quai de Caligny
Place des Moulins
Rue au Blé
Place Centrale
Place Briqueville
Avant Port
Rue du Commerce
Rue des Fossés
Rue Notre Dame
Rue du Château
Rue des Portes
Pont Tournant
Rue du Val de Saire
Rue Maréchal Foch
Place de Gaulle
Rue Gambetta
Rue des Halles
Rue Vastel
Boulevard Robert Schuman
Rue de l'Ancien Quai
Bassin du Commerce
Quai Alexandre III
Canal de Retenue
Avenue Carnot
Avenue Delaville
Quai de l'Entrepôt
Place Jean Jaurès
Avenue Jean-François Millet
Rue des Tanneries
To Fort du Roule, Valognes (20km), D-Day Beaches & Bayeux (92km)
Ave de Paris

0   100   200m
0   100   200yd

NORMANDY

euro currency converter €1 = 6.56FF

Monday to Saturday from the train station and there are frequent shuttles (*navettes*) in summer. There's a large indoor swimming pool nearby.

Hostels The comfortable, ultra-modern *Auberge de Jeunesse* (☎ 02 33 78 15 15, fax 02 33 78 15 16, 55 rue de l'Abbaye) charges 70FF per night, including breakfast. Take bus No 3 or 5 to the Hôtel de Ville stop.

Hotels Quai de Caligny has plenty of midrange options. There are cheaper places in the backstreets north of the tourist office.

Hôtel Moderna (☎ 02 33 43 05 30, fax 02 33 43 97 37, 28 rue de la Marine), one block back from the harbour, has decent, basic rooms from 140FF (190FF with shower).

Hôtel Renaissance (☎ 02 33 43 23 90, fax 02 33 43 96 10, 4 rue de l'Église), has comfortable, well-equipped rooms (ask for a port view) starting at 140/160FF (160/180FF with shower).

Hôtel La Croix de Malte (☎ 02 33 43 19 16, fax 02 33 43 65 66, 5 rue des Halles), near the sumptuous Théâtre de Cherbourg (1882), has well equipped doubles from 160FF.

Hôtel de la Gare (☎ 02 33 43 06 81, fax 02 33 43 12 20, 10 place Jean Jaurès) has decent rooms with shower from 160/180FF. A couple of doors along at No 4, *Hôtel Le Jaurès* (☎ 02 33 43 06 35) has basic rooms for 120/130FF (150/170FF with shower). The hotel is closed on Sunday. The brasserie below can get pretty lively.

Places to Eat

Restaurants One fine seafood restaurant, with *menus* from around 110FF, is *Café de Paris* (☎ 02 33 43 12 36, 40 quai de Caligny).

Rue Tour Carrée, rue de la Paix and around place Centrale offer a wide choice of both cuisine and price. *La Faitout* (☎ 02 33 04 25 04, 25 rue Tour Carreé) is an atmospheric place with wonderful lunch dishes costing from 55FF to 60FF and a show-stopping *menu* for 115FF (closed all day Sunday, and Monday lunch).

If you can forgo the atmosphere, the *Casino Cafeteria*, on the 1st floor of the Centre Continent at quai de l'Entrepôt, has two-course *menus* from just 29FF and lots of other cheap eats.

Self-Catering *Market* days are Tuesday and Thursday until about 5 pm at place de Gaulle and place Centrale. The latter, which is covered, also operates on Saturday morning. The Centre Continent at quai de l'Entrepôt has a huge *supermarket* open all day, seven days a week. The little *Shopi grocery store* (57 rue Gambetta) opens 8.30 am to 12.30 pm and 2.30 to 7.30 pm Monday to Saturday.

Getting There & Away

Bus The main regional bus line (which stops at the bus station on ave Jean-François Millet) is STN (☎ 02 33 88 51 00 in Tourlaville) which has services to the camping ground in Bretteville-en-Saire (12.80FF).

Train Destinations served include Paris' Gare St-Lazare (218FF, 3½ hours, seven daily) via Caen (99FF, 1½ hours, eight daily), Pontorson (131FF, 2½ hours, two daily) and Rennes (175FF, 3½ hours, two daily).

Boat The three companies with services to either England or Ireland have offices in the ferry terminal (*gare maritime*). Their desks open two hours before departure and for 30 minutes after the arrival of each ferry.

Brittany Ferries (☎ 08 03 82 88 28) goes to Poole in England; Irish Ferries (☎ 02 35 19 24 00) sails to Rosslare, Ireland; and P&O European Ferries (☎ 02 33 88 65 70) handles the link to Portsmouth. For further details, see The UK section under Sea of the Getting There & Away chapter.

Local buses run between the ferry terminal and the tourist office between three and 10 times daily, depending on the season. The fare is 6FF.

Getting Around

Bus City buses are operated by Zéphir (☎ 02 33 22 40 58). The information kiosk at 40 blvd Robert Schuman opens 9 to

NORMANDY

11.45 am and 1.30 to 6.30 pm on weekdays, and 9.30 to 11.45 am on Saturday. Buses leave from either outside the kiosk or at various points around place Jean Jaurès, in front of the train station. Single tickets cost 6FF, and a carnet of 10 costs 51FF.

Taxi Taxis can be called on ☎ 02 33 53 36 38. The trip between the train station and the ferry terminal costs about 40FF.

COUTANCES
postcode 50200 • pop 9700 • elevation 91m
The medieval hilltop town of Coutances, 77km south of Cherbourg, has two major sights: a remarkable cathedral and – as if to encourage daily strolls among the clerics – a stunning landscape garden. Together they justify a day trip from Bayeux, or a pleasant stopover on the road to Mont St-Michel further south.

Information
Tourist Offices The tourist office (☎ 02 33 19 08 10, fax 02 33 19 08 19) is at places Georges Leclerc behind the town hall. It opens 10 am to 12.30 pm and 2 to 6 pm Monday to Friday, and to 5 pm on Saturday, September to June; and 10 am to 12.30 pm and 1.30 to 7 pm Monday to Saturday, and 3 to 7 pm on Sunday, in July and August. The train station is about one mile southeast of the town centre.

There's a Société Générale opposite the tourist office at 8 rue Daniel. The post office at 10 rue St-Dominique opens 8 am to 6.30 pm on weekdays and also Saturday morning; it exchanges money and has a Cyberposte terminal.

Things to See & Do
The lofty 13th-century Gothic **Cathédrale de Coutances** is one of France's finest, prompting Victor Hugo to call it the prettiest he'd seen after the one at Chartres. Its airy Norman-Romanesque design is enhanced by the use of light-hued limestone, which gives the massive colonnades (supporting a 90m-high nave) an almost dainty character. There are several frescos worth a look, including a 13th-century St-George

slaying the beast. Tours in English are held at 3.30 pm on weekdays in summer (adults 30FF, those aged between 12 and 18, 20FF), and afford sweeping views from the galleries in the lantern tower. In summer, the steeple lights up during an effective sound-and-light show.

Opposite place Leclerc lies the splendid **Jardin des Plantes**, a grand 19th-century landscape garden. Conceived by a civil engineer and painter, the garden tastefully blends symmetrical French lines with Italianate terraces, English-style copses, a maze and fountains. Its varied stock of ornamental trees includes giant redwood, cedar of Lebanon, New Zealand beech and Canadian nut. Like the cathedral, the grounds are illuminated on summer nights; during the day it's ideal for picnics (there's a good spot near the old cider press). The garden opens 9 am to 8 pm daily (5 pm from October to March, 11.30 pm from July to mid-September).

Places to Stay & Eat
About 1.2km north-west of town on the D44, *Camping Municipal Les Vignettes* (*☎ 02 33 45 43 13, route de Coutainville*) charges 16FF per adult/tent/car.

Hôtel de Normandie (*☎ 02 33 45 01 40, fax 02 33 46 74 54, 2 place Général du Gaulle*) is an old-fashioned place with a homey atmosphere. It charges 120/160FF for roomy singles/doubles with TV and hall shower, some with a cathedral view. The restaurant does great fish *menus* for 53FF (except Sundays) and *bouillabaisse* (90FF).

Hôtel des Trois Piliers (*☎ 02 33 45 01 31, 11 rue des Halles*) has smallish but well-equipped singles/doubles for 125FF with washbasin (135FF with private shower). The bar downstairs draws a noisy, pubescent crowd.

The *Restaurant le Vieux Coutances* (*☎ 02 33 47 94 78, 55 rue Geoffroy de Montbray*) is a small, intimate Norman eatery with excellent fish or meat *menus* for 70FF or 85FF. It's closed Sunday.

Getting There & Away STN (☎ 02 33 50 77 89) runs buses to Granville (41FF, 30

NORMANDY

minutes, up to five daily). Regular train services include Cherbourg (94FF, two hours, six daily), Caen (83FF, 1½ hours, six daily) and Paris Gare du Nord (from 210FF to 243FF, four hours, twice daily).

MONT ST-MICHEL
postcode 51016 • pop 42

It's difficult not to be impressed with your first sighting of Mont St-Michel. Covering the summit is the massive abbey, a soaring ensemble of buildings in a hotchpotch of architectural styles. The abbey (80m above the sea) is topped by a slender spire with a gilded copper statue of Michael the Archangel slaying a dragon. Around the base are the ancient ramparts and a jumble of buildings that house the handful of true residents. At night the whole structure is brilliantly illuminated.

Mont St-Michel's fame derives equally from the bay's extraordinary tides. Depending on the orbits of the moon and, to a lesser extent, the sun, the difference between low and high tides can reach 15m. The Mont either looks out on bare sand stretching many kilometres into the distance or, at high tide – only about six hours later – the same expanse under water (though the Mont and its causeway are completely surrounded by the sea only at the highest of tides, which occur at seasonal equinoxes).

History

According to Celtic mythology, Mont St-Michel was one of the sea tombs to which the souls of the dead were sent. In AD 708 the saint appeared to Bishop Aubert of Avranches and told him to build a devotional chapel at the summit. In 966, Richard I, duke of Normandy, gave Mont St-Michel to the Benedictines, who turned it into an important centre of learning and, in the 11th century, into something of an ecclesiastical fortress, with a military garrison at the disposal of the abbot and the king.

In the early 15th century, during the Hundred Years' War, the English blockaded and besieged Mont St-Michel three times. But the fortified abbey withstood these assaults; it was the only place in western and northern France not to fall into English hands. After the Revolution, Mont St-Michel was turned into a prison. In 1966 the abbey was symbolically returned to the Benedictines as part of the celebrations marking its millennium.

Orientation

There is only one opening in the ramparts, Porte de l'Avancée, immediately to the left as you walk down the causeway. The Mont's single street – Grande rue – is lined with restaurants, a few hotels, souvenir shops and entrances to some rather tacky exhibits in the crypts below. There are several large car parks (15FF) close to the Mont.

Pontorson (population 4100), the nearest town to Mont St-Michel, is 9km south and the base for most travellers. Route D976 from Mont St-Michel runs right into Pontorson's main thoroughfare, rue du Couësnon.

Information

Tourist Offices The tourist office (☎ 02 33 60 14 30, fax 02 33 60 06 75, ☻ OT.Mont .Saint.Michel@wanadoo.fr) is up the stairs to the left as you enter Porte de l'Avancée. It opens 9 am to noon and 2 to 5.45 pm Monday to Saturday; 9.30 am to noon and 1 to 6.30 pm daily, Easter to September; and 9 am to 7 pm daily, July and August.

If you're interested what in the tides will be doing, look for the table of tides (horaire des marées) posted outside. In July and August – when up to 9000 people a day visit – children under eight can be left with a gardien (baby-sitter) near the abbey church. A detailed map of the Mont is available at the tourist office for 20FF.

The friendly staff at Pontorson's tourist office (☎ 02 33 60 20 65, fax 02 33 60 85 67, ☻ mont.st.michel.pontorson@wanadoo .fr), in the place de l'Église just west of the town hall, are on duty from 9.30 am to 6 pm Tuesday to Friday (7 pm daily mid-June to mid-September). It opens from 10 am to noon and 2 to 5 pm (6 pm in summer) on Saturday and from 10 am to noon on Sunday.

NORMANDY

Money There's a Société Générale ATM just inside the Porte de l'Avancée. You can change money at Mont St-Michel, but for a better rate try the CIN bank, 98 rue du Couësnon in Pontorson (closed Sunday and Monday). There are more banks on rue du Couësnon and place de l'Hôtel de Ville.

Post The Pontorson post office (☎ 02 33 60 01 66) on the eastern side of the place de l'Hôtel de Ville opens 8.30am to noon and 2 to 5.30 pm on weekdays, and on Saturday morning. The Mont St-Michel post office on Grand rue keeps similar hours.

Books *The Mont St-Michel*, a booklet written by Lucien Bély and published by Éditions Ouest-France, is a surprisingly readable history of the abbey and its inhabitants. Souvenir shops along the Grande rue sell it for 50FF.

Walking Tour
When the tide is out, you can walk all the way around Mont St-Michel, a distance of about 1km. Straying too far from the Mont could be risky: you might get stuck in wet sand – from which Norman soldiers are depicted being rescued in one scene of the Bayeux Tapestry.

Abbaye du Mont St-Michel
The Mont's major attraction is the renowned abbey (☎ 02 33 89 80 00), open 9.30 am to 5.30 pm daily (5 pm from October to April). To reach it, walk to the top of the Grande rue and then climb the stairway. From mid-May to September (except Sunday) there are self-paced night-time illuminated visits (60FF; 35FF for those aged under 25) of Mont St-Michel complete with music starting at 9.30 or 10 pm and lasting for three hours.

Most rooms can be visited without a guide, but it's worthwhile taking the guided tour included in the ticket price of 40FF (children free; students and those aged between 18 and 25, 22FF). One-hour tours in English depart three to eight times daily (the last leaves about half an hour before closing).

The **Église Abbatiale** (Abbey Church) was built at the rocky tip of the mountain cone. The transept rests on solid rock while the nave, choir and transept arms are supported by the massive rooms below. The church is famous for its mixture of architectural styles: the nave and south transept (11th and 12th centuries) are Norman Romanesque, while the choir (late 15th century) is Flamboyant Gothic. Mass is said here daily at 12.15 pm.

The buildings on the northern side of the Mont are known as **La Merveille** (literally, 'the marvel'). The famous **cloître** (cloister) is an ambulatory surrounded by a double row of delicately carved arches resting on granite pillars. The early 13th-century **réfectoire** (dining hall) is illuminated by a wall of recessed windows – remarkable, given that the sheer drop precluded the use of flying buttresses – which diffuses the light beautifully. The Gothic **Salle des Hôtes** (Guest Hall), which dates from 1213, has two giant fireplaces. Watch out for the **promenoire** (ambulatory), with one of the oldest ribbed vaulted ceilings in Europe, and **La Chapelle de Notre de Dame sous Terre** (Underground Chapel of Our Lady), one of the earliest rooms built in the abbey and rediscovered in 1903.

The masonry used to build the abbey was brought to the Mont by boat and then pulled up the hillside using ropes. What looks like a treadmill for gargantuan gerbils was in fact powered in the 19th century by half a dozen prisoners who, by turning the wheel, hoisted the supply sledge up the side of the abbey.

Museums
The Grande rue at times resembles a fair, with touts trying to rope you into visiting the 20-minute **Archéoscope** (☎ 02 33 48 09 37) multimedia show or the **Musée Grévin** (☎ 02 33 60 14 09), a wax museum with a mish-mash of pseudo-historical exhibits. The **Musée Maritime** (☎ 02 33 60 14 09) is a bit more serious with explanations about the bay. A combined ticket for the three venues costs 75FF (students 60FF, children 45FF); individually they're 45FF (students

and children 30FF). The museums open 9 am to 6 pm daily.

Église Notre Dame de Pontorson

Though no match for its dramatic sister to the north, the 12th-century Church of Our Lady in Pontorson is a good example of the Norman Romanesque style of architecture. To the left of the main altar is a 15th-century relief of Christ's Passion, which was mutilated during the Religious Wars and again during the Revolution.

Places to Stay

Camping On the shop-lined D976 to Pontorson, only 2km from the Mont, is *Camping du Mont St-Michel* (☎ 02 33 60 09 33, fax 02 33 68 22 09). This grassy camping ground opens early February to October and charges 22FF per person and 20FF for a tent and car. It also has bungalows with shower and toilet for two people for 220FF.

There are several other camping grounds – one called *Camping sous les Pommiers* (☎ 02 33 60 11 36, fax 02 33 60 25 81) – a couple of kilometres farther south towards Pontorson. It opens April to mid-October and charges 13FF per person and 23FF for car and tent.

Hostels *Centre Duguesclin* (☎/fax 02 33 60 18 65, ✆ aj@ville-pontorson.fr, blvd du Général Patton) in Pontorson, is about 1km west of the train station in an old three-storey stone building opposite No 26. This modern, newly renovated hostel with kitchen facilities opens Easter to mid-September and charges 48FF per night in a four- to six-bed room. The hostel closes 10 am to 6 pm, but there's no curfew.

Gîtes d'Étape The Pontorson tourist office can arrange private accommodation or farm stays costing from 140FF to 250FF per double, including breakfast.

Hotels Mont St-Michel has plenty of hotels but most are expensive. *Hôtel de la Mère Poulard* (☎ 02 33 60 14 01, fax 02 33 48 52 31, ✆ hotel.mere.poulard@wanadoo.fr, Grand rue) is a pretty museum-piece hotel

on your left as you enter town, offering doubles starting at 300FF with shower.

Your best bet is to stay in Pontorson. Across place de la Gare from the train station are a couple of cheap hotels. *Hôtel de l'Arrivée* (☎ 02 33 60 01 57, 14 rue du Docteur Tizon) has doubles for 95FF with washbasin, 120FF with washbasin and toilet, and 165FF with shower. Triples/quads with washbasin or toilet cost 170/190FF and from 220FF with shower. Hall showers are 15FF.

Hôtel Le Rénové (☎ 02 33 60 00 21, 4 rue de Rennes), has simple doubles with washbasin for 160FF (180FF with shower and toilet). Triples or quads cost 230/250FF. Hall showers are free.

Hôtel La Tour de Brette (☎ 02 33 60 10 69, fax 02 33 48 59 66, 8 rue du Couësnon) is an excellent deal. Its cheerful rooms – all with shower and TV – cost 169FF (220FF in summer).

At the top end, there is *Hôtel Montgomery* (☎ 02 33 60 00 09, fax 02 33 60 37 66, ✆ Hotel.Montgomery@wanadoo.fr, 13 rue du Couësnon), which is in a lovely 16th-century townhouse, and has rooms from 250FF with shower and toilet.

Places to Eat

Restaurants The tourist restaurants around the base of the Mont have lovely views, but they aren't bargains; *menus* start at about 80FF and quality can be mediocre.

In Pontorson, *La Squadra* (☎ 02 33 68 31 17, 102 rue Couësnon) has decent pizza from 36FF, salads from 16FF and pasta for lunch and dinner (closed Monday and Tuesday). For crepes and savoury galettes (10FF to 30FF), try *La Crêperie du Couësnon* (☎ 02 33 60 16 67, 21 rue du Couësnon). The splendid restaurant at *Hôtel La Tour de Brette* (see Places to Stay) offers *menus* for 60FF, 80FF and 95FF.

For something a little more formal, try the dining room of *Hôtel de Bretagne* (☎ 02 33 60 10 55, 59 rue du Couësnon) with excellent food (*menus* from 80FF) and service.

Self-Catering The *supermarket* nearest the Mont is next to the Camping du Mont

St-Michel on the D976. It opens 8 am to 8 pm (10 pm in July and August), except for Sunday, mid-February to October. In Pontorson, the *8 à 8*, 5 rue du Couësnon, opens 8.30 am to 12.45 pm and 2.30 to 7.30 pm Monday to Saturday, and 9 am to 12.30 pm on Sunday.

Getting There & Away

Bus STN runs bus No 15 (☎ 02 33 58 03 07 in Avranches) which goes from Pontorson train station to Mont St-Michel (14.10/22.60FF for singles/returns). There are nine buses daily in July and August (six on weekends) and three or four during the rest of the year. Most buses connect with trains to/from Paris, Rennes and Caen.

For details of bus transport to/from St-Malo, 54km to the west, or Rennes, see Getting There & Away in those sections. The Pontorson office of the Courriers Bretons bus company (☎ 02 33 60 11 43) is 50m west of the train station at 2 rue du Docteur Bailleul. Courriers Bretons buses on their way *to* Mont St-Michel from St-Malo do *not* pick up passengers in Pontorson but do so in the opposite direction.

Train Services to/from Pontorson include Caen (125FF, 2¼ hours, two daily) via Folligny; Rennes (69FF, 50 minutes, two daily) via Dol; and Cherbourg (131FF, 2½ hours, two daily). From Paris, take the train to Caen (from Gare St-Lazare), to Rennes (from Gare Montparnasse) or travel directly to Pontorson via Folligny (from Gare Montparnasse, 210FF). The train station has a left-luggage service for 30FF.

Getting Around

Bicycle Bikes can be rented at the train station (55FF per day plus 1000FF deposit) and from E Videloup (☎ 02 33 60 11 40) at 1 bis rue du Couësnon, which charges 50FF per day for city bicycles and 80FF for mountain bikes. E Videloup opens 8.30 am to 12.30 pm and 2 to 7 pm, Monday to Saturday (closed Monday morning).

Taxi Call a taxi on ☎ 02 33 60 33 23 or ☎ 02 33 60 26 89.

ALENÇON

**postcode 61000 • pop 30,000 •
elevation 135m**

In the far south of Normandy, on the edge of the Normandie-Maine nature reserve, lies the former lacemaking hub of Alençon. The town exudes an aura of genteel wealth – harking back to its days as a Norman tax-collecting centre in the 17th century – and makes a nice breather en route to/from Paris, 193km to the south.

Orientation

The old town and its sights are about 1.5km south-west of the train station, via ave du Président Wilson and rue St-Blaise. The River Sarthe snakes past the old quarter to the south.

Information

Tourist Offices The tourist office (☎ 02 33 80 60 33, fax 02 33 80 60 32, ✉ alencon .tourisme@wanadoo.fr) is in the turreted Maison d'Ozé on place La Magdelaine. It opens 9.30 am to noon and 2 to 6.30 pm Monday to Saturday, and 10 am to 12.30 pm and 2.30 to 5.30 pm on Sunday in July and August; the rest of the year it opens 9.30 am to noon and 2 to 6.30 pm Monday to Saturday. It books accommodation for free and has a free English-language brochure, *Alençon on Foot*, showing a walking tour of town. See the Web site at www.ville-alencon.fr.

Money The Banque de France on rue Docteur du Becquembois exchanges money from 8.40 am to noon Monday to Friday. There is a Crédit Mutuel at 89 bis rue aux Sieurs. The post office has a currency window.

Post & Communications The post office at 16 rue du Jeudi opens 8.15 am to 7 pm Monday to Friday, and Saturday mornings. It has a Cyberposte.

Things to See & Do

The old town, especially along the **Grande rue**, is full of atmospheric Second Empire houses and wrought-iron balconies dating

NORMANDY

from the 18th century. To the south-east looms the crowned turret of the **Château des Ducs**, which was used by the Nazis as a prison during WWII (closed to the public).

The **Musée des Beaux-Arts et de la Dentelle** (☎ 02 33 32 40 07) occupies a restored Jesuit school building at 12 rue Charles Aveline. It houses a so-so collection of Flemish, Dutch and French artworks from the 17th to 19th centuries and upstairs, an exhaustive (some might say exhausting) exhibit on the history of lacemaking and its techniques. There's also an unexpected section of Cambodian artefacts – including buddhas, spears and tiger skulls – donated by a former (French) governor of Cambodia. It opens 10 am to noon and 2 to 6 pm daily (closed Monday); admission costs 18FF (students 15FF).

The **Église Notre Dame** on rue St-Blaise has a stunning Flamboyant Gothic portal from the 16th century and some superb stained glass in the chapel where St-Theresa was baptised. It opens 8.30 am to noon and 2 to 5.30 pm daily. The house where St-Theresa was born is next door; admission is free.

The **Musée Leclerc** (☎ 02 33 26 27 26) at 33 rue du Pont Neuf details the history of Alençon during WWII, including some fascinating wartime photos. The town was liberated in August 1944 by General Leclerc, whose statue stands guard out front. It opens 10 am to noon and 2 to 6 pm Monday to Saturday. Admission costs 15FF (those aged between 12 and 18, 8FF).

Places to Stay & Eat

The *Camping Municipal* (☎ 02 33 26 34 95, 69 rue de Guéramé), in the south-west of town on the River Sarthe, charges 12/13FF per adult/tent site. It's open all year.

Hôtel de Paris (☎ 02 33 29 01 64, fax 02 33 29 44 87, 26 rue Denis Papin) just east of the train station has basic singles/doubles with washbasin for 130/140FF (180/200FF with private shower and toilet).

Two-star *Le Grand Cerf* (☎ 02 33 26 00 51, fax 02 33 26 63 07, 21 rue St-Blaise) on the edge of the old town offers more luxury, with plush singles/doubles costing 250/290FF. It also has a good French restaurant with three-course *menus* costing 80FF.

Le Madras (☎ 02 33 26 19 30, 7 rue des Filles Notre Dame) does Antillian specialities with filling *menus* for 49FF and 59FF.

Getting There & Away

Bus TIS (☎ 02 43 39 97 30) runs buses between Alençon and Le Mans (55FF, 1¾ hours, three to four daily). Buses depart from the bus station on the Square des Déportés just east of the Église Notre Dame. There are also regular services to small towns throughout the Orne department.

Train Alençon has frequent train services to Paris Gare Montparnasse (from 213FF to 278FF, 1¾ hours) Caen (86FF, 1¾ hours), Pontorson (136FF, two hours) and Le Mans (50FF, 45 minutes), among other destinations.

Brittany

Brittany (Bretagne in French, Breizh in Breton) commands the rugged western tip of France. Centuries of independence followed by relative isolation from the rest of the country have forged a distinctive Breton culture, language and way of life.

Many people say that there are two Brittanys: the 1100km-long coast, known as Armor (meaning 'Land of the Sea'), and the secretive interior, Argoat (meaning 'Land of the Woods'). The coastline, swept by the rough Atlantic Ocean and the somewhat calmer waters of the English Channel, is dotted with lighthouses and is characterised by rocky coves that shelter tiny port villages and tidal inlets. Unfortunately, much of the coastline is lined with holiday houses. The offshore islands, some of which are protected areas for sea birds, can get quite overcrowded by tourists during summer.

Inland, paths lead to ruined castles, legendary forests and farms built in pink, grey and black local stone. However, the sea is never more than 60km away from even the remotest parts of the interior. Though many of the villages are picturesque and easily accessible, Argoat remains relatively unfrequented by tourists. On the whole, they tend to stick to the main cities such as Quimper and St-Malo and to towns such as Vannes or Dinan, all proud of their rich historical and architectural heritage. The mysterious megaliths which dot the land, especially around Carnac, are even older.

History

Brittany was first inhabited by Neolithic tribes whose menhirs and dolmens are still scattered throughout the region (see the boxed text 'The Megaliths of Carnac later in this chapter). Around the 6th century BC, they were joined by the region's first wave of Celts. Julius Caesar conquered the region in 56 BC and it remained in Roman hands until the 5th century AD.

Following the departure of the Romans,

Highlights

- **Quimper** – take in the Festival de Cornouaille (late July)
- **Île d'Ouessant** – explore this or one of Brittany's other rugged islands
- **Carnac** – marvel at the extraordinary standing stones
- **Forêt de Paimpont** – trace the legends of King Arthur and Merlin the magician
- **St-Malo** – wander the quaint, winding streets of the old walled city
- **Presqu'île de Crozon** – walk or cycle around this peninsula's many natural wonders

a second wave of Celts – driven from what is now Britain and Ireland by the Anglo-Saxon invasions – crossed the Channel and settled in Brittany. In the 5th and 6th centuries, the region was gradually Christianised by Celtic missionaries, after whom many Breton towns (eg St-Malo and St-Brieuc) are named.

BRITTANY (BRETAGNE)

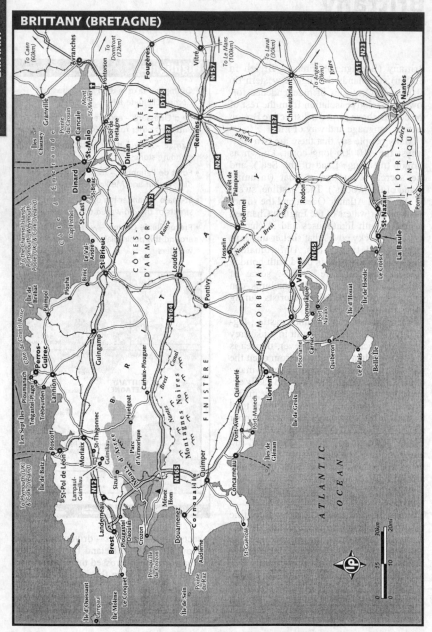

King Arthur

While Breton culture abounds in legends, the most famous is the story of King Arthur, linked to both Brittany and, via Cornwall, England since the Middle Ages. In Brittany many sites are tied to Arthur, Lancelot, Merlin, the fairies Vivian and Morgan le Fay and others.

The Île Grande and Île d'Aval, close to Perros-Guirec, are both said to be the island of Avalon where Morgan le Fay (the sister of Arthur according to Chrétien de Troyes' version of the tale) lived and where Arthur was buried. Hidden in the last stronghold of the old inland forest, the Forêt d'Huelgoat is the place where Arthur should have found the Holy Grail. The Forêt de Paimpont (or Brocéliande) south-west of Rennes contains Merlin's spring of eternal youth and was home to his mistress, Vivian, the mysterious Lady of the Lake. Vannes was the capital of the kingdom ruled by Ban, the father of Lancelot, while Nantes appears in many versions of the myth as the court of King Arthur himself.

In the 9th century, Brittany's national hero, Nominoë, revolted against French rule, taking control of both Rennes and Nantes. Shortly thereafter, his successors managed to repulse the Normans (Vikings). Because of its location, the duchy of Brittany was contested by the kings of both France and England throughout the Middle Ages. After a series of royal weddings, the region became part of France in 1532.

Over the centuries, Brittany has retained a separate regional identity and has become far less assimilated into the French mainstream than most areas of the country. Recently, there has been a drive for cultural and linguistic renewal, and stronger ties have been established with the Celtic cultures of Ireland, Wales, Scotland, Cornwall and Galicia in Spain.

To this day, some Bretons have not abandoned the hope that their region will one day regain its independence. In the late 1960s and '70s, Breton separatists carried out a violent campaign for an independent Breton state, culminating in a bomb attack on the palace at Versailles in 1978. There are still isolated incidents, such as the bomb that killed a restaurant employee near Dinan in April 2000.

Geography

Brittany largely occupies the ancient Massif Armoricain, but 300 million years of erosion have turned most of the region into low-lying plains and gentle uplands. The only exceptions are the north-western Monts d'Arrée and the south-central Montagnes Noires.

White, sandy beaches and pleasant inlets leading to picturesque small ports are commonplace along the coast. Spectacular rocky cliffs can be found in many areas, particularly at the end of the westernmost peninsulas and on the Île d'Ouessant. Deep tidal inlets or gorges, called *abers*, are common on the northern coast.

Brittany is divided into four departments. Finistère occupies the far western quarter of the peninsula. The central section is divided between the Côtes d'Armor (to the north) and Morbihan (to the south). In the east and north-east, next to Normandy, is the mainly inland département of Ille-et-Vilaine, which includes the regional capital, Rennes.

Climate

Brittany's coast is washed by the Gulf Stream, a warm ocean current flowing from the Gulf of Mexico towards north-western Europe. As a result, the region enjoys a very mild climate. Brittany does record France's highest annual precipitation, but it rarely rains for many days, even during the wettest months (from January to May).

Society & Conduct

Breton customs – such as the Breton language – are most evident in Basse Bretagne (lower Brittany), the western half of the peninsula, and particularly in Cornouaille, the south-western tip. Haute Bretagne (upper

Brittany), the eastern half of the peninsula (which includes St-Malo), has retained little of its traditional way of life.

Traditional costumes, including the tall lace headdresses of the women, can sometimes still be seen at *fest-noz* (night-time dance and music festivals) and *pardons* (colourful religious celebrations). The region's two major cultural festivals are Quimper's Festival de Cornouaille in late July and the Festival Interceltique, which takes place in Lorient in early August.

Religious Art

The stone *calvaires* (calvaries) at Lampaul-Guimiliau, St-Thégonnec and Sizun, with their sculpted stories of saints and other figures, speak eloquently of the strong Celtic influence which is evident in Breton religious art. Brittany has a long list of saints unrecognised by Rome.

Also typically Breton is the *enclos paroissial* (enclosed parish), which consists of a walled enclosure containing a church, an ossuary and a calvary. Good examples can be found at Lampaul-Guimiliau, St-Thégonnec and Plougastel-Daoulas.

Language

The indigenous language of Brittany is Breton (Breiz), a Celtic language related to Cornish and Welsh and, more distantly, to Irish and Scottish Gaelic. Breton can sometimes still be heard in western Brittany (especially in Cornouaille), where as many as 600,000 people have some degree of fluency. However, the number of Breton-speaking households is diminishing.

After the Revolution, the new government made a concerted effort to suppress the Breton language and replace it with French. Even 20 years ago, if school children spoke Breton in the classroom they were punished. Things have changed, however, and about 20 privately subsidised schools now teach in Breton, several at the secondary level.

A few helpful Breton expressions are:

Breton	French	English
demad, demat	bonjour	hello
d'ur wech all	à une autre fois	see you again
kenavo	au revoir	goodbye
trugarez	merci	thank you
yehed mad, yec'hed mat	à votre santé	cheers

The following are some Breton words you may come across, especially in place names. Note that the spelling may vary.

aber	embouchure	mouth
ar	le, la	the

The Breton Flag & Emblems

The flag of Brittany consists of nine horizontal black and white stripes representing each of the nine ancient *évêchés* (bishoprics) of Upper and Lower Brittany. In the top left-hand corner of the flag is a field of stylised ermines, stoats with black and white fur that symbolise the duchy of Brittany. You'll see ermines on many city and town flags and seals in the region.

A symbol also often encountered is the *triskelion* (from the Greek *triskelês* – 'three-legged'), a decorative motif consisting of three curved branches, arms or legs radiating from a centre. It was first used by the Celts around 450 BC and remains an important symbol in Celtic countries, evoking images of the sun or the eternal wheel of life and death.

MATT KING

aven	rivière, fleuve	river
bae	baie	bay
bed	monde	world
bihan	petit	little
deiz	jour	day
dol	table	table
douar	terre	earth
dour	eau	water
du	noir	black
enez	île	island
fao, faou	hêtre	beech tree
fest-noz	fête de nuit	night festival
gall	français	French
gwenn	blanc	white
hir	long	long
...ig, ic	-ette	diminutive suffix
iliz	église	church
izel	bas	low
kember, kemper	confluent	confluence
ker	cher	dear
koad, goat	forêt	forest
koan	dîner	dinner
kromm, crom	courbé	curved
men/mein	pierre	stone
menez	montagne	mountain
mor	mer	sea
nant	vallée	valley
pen	tête, bout	head, end
plou, plo, ple...	paroisse	parish
(used only as a prefix in place names)		
poull	mare	pond
pred	déjeuner	lunch
raz	détroit	strait
roz, ros	tertre	hillock, mound
ster, stêr, steir	rivière, fleuve	river
stif, stivell	source	spring
tann	chêne	oak tree
telenn	harpe	Celticharp
ti, ty	maison	house
trev, tre, treo	trêve	parish division
trez	sable	sand
uhel	haut	high

Activities

Sailing and windsurfing are very popular in Brittany. Scuba diving around the rocky archipelagos is among the best in France.

The wonderful sandy beaches south-east of the Gulf of Morbihan, which were fouled by a huge oil spill in late 1999, have been cleaned up and reopened to the public.

A leisurely way to tour the region is by canal boat along the canals and waterways from Brest or Dinan to Nantes. See Canal Boats under Activities in the Facts for the Visitor chapter for details. For information on canal boats, moorings and locks contact the Service de la Navigation (☎ 02 99 59 20 60 in Rennes, ☎ 02 97 64 85 20 in Lorient).

Getting There & Away

Ferries of various sorts link St-Malo with the Channel Islands; the English ports of Weymouth, Portsmouth and Poole; and Cork in Ireland. From Roscoff, there are ferries to Plymouth (England) and Cork (Ireland). For more information, see The UK and Ireland under Sea in the Getting There & Away chapter as well as the Getting There & Away listings under St-Malo and Roscoff.

Getting Around

Brittany's major towns and cities are linked by rail, but the tracks basically follow the coast and leave the interior poorly served. The bus network is extensive, but services are often infrequent.

The lack of convenient intercity public transport and the appeal of exploring out-of-the-way destinations make renting a car or motorbike worth considering. Brittany – especially Cornouaille – is an excellent area for cycling, and bike-rental places are never hard to find.

North Coast

The central part of Brittany's northern coast belongs to the Côtes d'Armor département, which stretches from Perros-Guirec, near the north-eastern corner of Finistère, to St-Briac, just west of Dinard, a swish beach resort. Dinard, ever popular St-Malo, the oyster-producing town of Cancale and other points along the Baie du Mont St-Michel are in the département of Ille-et-Vilaine.

The rugged coast between Le Val André in the west and Pointe du Grouin in the east is known as the Côte d'Émeraude (Emerald Coast). The area, which includes Dinard, St-Malo and the Rance Estuary, is famous for its numerous peninsulas and promontories, many of which have spectacular sea views.

The best way to explore the Côte d'Émeraude is on foot along the GR34 trail, which runs along the entire coast of both departments. The largest offshore islands are Île de Bréhat, 8km north of the port town of Paimpol, and Les Sept Îles, 18km north of Perros-Guirec. The medieval town of Dinan, about 20km from the coast, is on the River Rance south of St-Malo.

ST-MALO
postcode 35400 • pop 52,300
The Channel port of St-Malo is one of the most popular tourist destinations in Brittany – and with good reason. Situated at the mouth of the River Rance, it is famed for its walled city, nearby beaches and some of the highest tidal variations in the world.

St-Malo was a key French port during the 17th and 18th centuries, serving as a base for both merchant ships and government-sanctioned pirates, known more politely as privateers. Although fortification of the city was begun in the 12th century, the most imposing military architecture dates from the 17th and 18th centuries, when the English – the favourite targets of Malouin privateers – posed a constant threat.

Orientation
St-Malo consists of the resort towns of St-Servan, St-Malo, Paramé and Rothéneuf. St-Malo's old city, signposted as Intra-Muros (meaning 'within the walls') and also known as the Ville Close, is connected to Paramé by the Sillon Isthmus.

Information
Tourist Offices The tourist office (☎ 02 99 56 64 48, fax 02 99 56 67 00, 🖂 office .de.tourisme.saint-malo@wanadoo.fr) is on Esplanade St-Vincent. It opens 2 to 6 pm on Monday, and 9.30 am to 12.30 and 2 to

6 pm, Tuesday to Friday and 9.30 to 1 pm and 2 to 5 pm on Saturday. In July and August it opens 8.30 am to 8 pm Monday to Saturday, and 10 am to 7 pm on Sunday.

Money There are many banks near the train station along blvd de la République and at place de Rocabey. In the old city, the Banque de France at 7 rue d'Asfeld changes money from 8.45 am to noon, and a Caisse d'Épargne is at 14 rue de Dinan. The post office also exchanges currency.

Post & Communications The main post office, 1 blvd de la Tour d'Auvergne, opens 8 am to 7 pm weekdays and to noon on Saturday and has a Cyberposte terminal. Cop Imprimu, 29 blvd des Talards, charges 30FF per half-hour of Web surfing and opens 9 am to 7 pm Monday to Friday, and 9 am to noon on Saturday.

Laundry The laundrette at 25 blvd de la Tour d'Auvergne opens 7 am to 9 pm daily.

Old City
During the fighting of August 1944, which drove the Germans from St-Malo, 80% of the old city was destroyed. The main historical monuments were faithfully reconstructed, but the rest of the area was rebuilt in the style of the 17th and 18th centuries. **Cathédrale St-Vincent**, begun in the 11th century, is noted for its medieval stained-glass windows. The striking modern altar in bronze reveals a Celtic influence. It opens 8 am to noon and 2 to 7 pm, September to May (no midday closure in July and August).

There is free access to the **ramparts walk** at Porte de Dinan, the Grande Porte, Porte St-Vincent and elsewhere. The remains of the 17th-century **Fort National** (☎ 02 99 46 91 25), built by Vauban and long used as a prison, are just beyond the northern stretch. They can be visited 10 am to 5.30 pm daily, Easter to late October.

Museums
The **Musée de la Ville** (☎ 02 99 40 71 57), in the Château de St-Malo at Porte

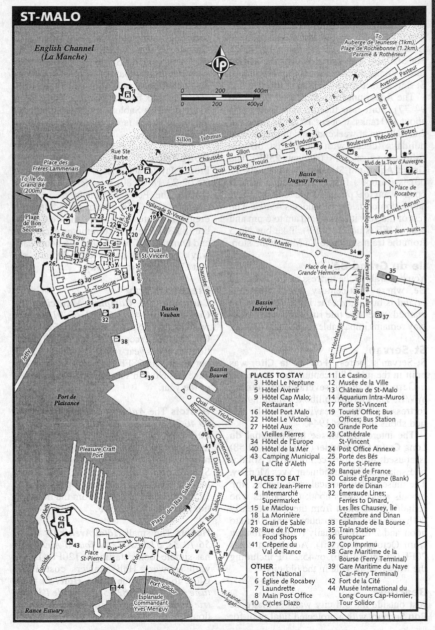

ST-MALO

English Channel (La Manche)

To
Auberge de Jeunesse (1km),
Plage de Rochebonne (1.2km),
Paramé & Rothéneuf

Avenue Pasteur

Rue du Cakaie

Grande Plage

Avenue Théodore Botrel

Boulevard Théodore Botrel

Blvd de la Tour d'Auvergne

Sillon Isthmus

Chaussée du Sillon

Quai Duguay Trouin

Rue Ste Barbe

Place des Frères Lammenais

To l'Île du Grand Bé (200m)

Plage de Bon Secours

R du Boyer

Bassin Duguay Trouin

Place de Rocabey

Rue Ernest-Renan

Avenue Jean-Jaurès

Esplanade St-Vincent

Avenue Louis Martin

Quai St-Vincent

Chaussée des Corsaires

Place de la Grande Hermine

Bassin Intérieur

Boulevard des Talards

Rue de Toulouse

Quai St-Louis

Bassin Vauban

R Alphonse Thébault

Rue Hochelage

Jetty

Bassin Bouvet

Port de Plaisance

Quai de Trichet

Rue Georges

Clémenceau

R Dauphine

Pleasure Craft Port

Rue des Bas Sablons

Plage des Bas Sablons

Rue des Bas

Rue-Pré-Brécel

Rue Jeanne-Jugan

Gare Maritime du Naye (Car-Ferry Terminal)

Fort de la Cité

Place St-Pierre

Corniche

Rue-de-la-Cité

R du Dick

R Gervat

Quai-Solidor

Port Solidor

Esplanade Commandant Yves Menguy

Rance Estuary

0   200   400m
0   200   400yd

PLACES TO STAY
3 Hôtel Le Neptune
5 Hôtel Avenir
9 Hôtel Cap Malo; Restaurant
16 Hôtel Port Malo
22 Hôtel Le Victoria
27 Hôtel Aux Vieilles Pierres
34 Hôtel de l'Europe
40 Hôtel de la Mer
43 Camping Municipal La Cité d'Aleth

PLACES TO EAT
2 Chez Jean-Pierre
4 Intermarché Supermarket
15 Le Maclou
18 La Morinière
21 Grain de Sable
28 Rue de l'Orme Food Shops
41 Crêperie du Val de Rance

OTHER
1 Fort National
6 Église de Rocabey
7 Laundrette
8 Main Post Office
10 Cycles Diazo

11 Le Casino
12 Musée de la Ville
13 Château de St-Malo
14 Aquarium Intra-Muros
17 Porte St-Vincent
19 Tourist Office; Bus Offices; Bus Station
20 Grande Porte
23 Cathédrale St-Vincent
24 Post Office Annexe
25 Porte des Bés
26 Porte St-Pierre
29 Banque de France
30 Caisse d'Épargne (Bank)
31 Porte de Dinan
32 Émeraude Lines; Ferries to Dinard, Les Îles Chausey, Île Cézembre and Dinan
33 Esplanade de la Bourse
35 Train Station
36 Europcar
37 Cop Imprimu
38 Gare Maritime de la Bourse (Ferry Terminal)
39 Gare Maritime du Naye (Car-Ferry Terminal)
42 Fort de la Cité
44 Musée International du Long Cours Cap-Hornier; Tour Solidor

euro currency converter €1 = 6.56FF

St-Vincent, covers the history of the city and the St-Malo area. It opens 10 am to noon and 2 to 6 pm daily (closed Monday in winter). Admission costs 27FF (students 13.50FF). For 50/25FF, you can also visit the Musée International du Long Cours Cap-Hornier in St-Servan (see the St-Servan section).

The **Aquarium Intra-Muros** (☎ 02 99 56 94 77), built into the old city walls, has about 100 tanks. It opens 10 am to 1 pm and 2 to 6.30 pm at weekends and during school holidays (check with the tourist office). Admission costs 30FF (students 25FF). The **Grand Aquarium St-Malo** (☎ 02 99 21 19 00) is Europe's first circular aquarium. It opens 9 am to 9 pm mid-June to September; admission costs 56FF (students 45FF). The rest of the year it opens 9.30 am to 6 pm and costs 44FF (students 30FF). Take bus No 5 from the train station to La Madeleine stop.

Île du Grand Bé

You can walk to the fortress on Île du Grand Bé, where 18th-century writer Chateaubriand is buried, via the Porte des Bés. Be warned: when the tide rushes in, the causeway remains impassable for about six hours.

St-Servan

St-Servan's fortress, **Fort de la Cité**, was built in the mid-18th century and served as a German base for several years during WWII. The German pillboxes flanking the fortress walls were heavily scarred by Allied shells in August 1944.

The interesting **Musée International du Long Cours Cap-Hornier** (☎ 02 99 40 71 58) is housed in the 14th-century Tour Solidor on Esplanade Commandment Yves Menguy. The museum has nautical instruments, ship models and exhibits about the sailors who rounded Cape Horn from the 17th to early 20th centuries. The museum opens 10 am to noon and 2 to 6 pm daily (closed Monday from October to April). Admission costs 20FF (students 10FF), or 45/25FF including the Musée de la Ville in the old city.

Beaches

Just outside the old city walls is **Plage de Bon Secours** with a protected tidal pool for bathing. St-Servan's **Plage des Bas Sablons** has a cement wall that keeps the sea from receding completely at low tide. The **Grande Plage**, which stretches north-eastwards from the Sillon Isthmus, is spiked with tree trunks that act as breakers. **Plage de Rochebonne** is 1km or so to the north-east. The walk from the Grande Plage to the Plage des Bas Sablons via the ramparts of the Intra-Muros is especially enjoyable at sunset.

Boat Trips

From May to September, Émeraude Lines (☎ 02 23 18 01 80) runs ferries from just outside the Porte de Dinan to Les Îles Chausey (125/75FF return for adults/children, 90 minutes each way), the Île Cézembre (55/30FF return, 20 minutes each way) and Dinan (130/75FF return, 2½ hours each way). For details of ferries to Dinard, see that Getting There & Away.

Places to Stay

Camping The *Camping Municipal La Cité d'Aleth* (☎ 02 99 81 60 91), at the western tip of St-Servan next to Fort de la Cité, has an exceptional view in all directions. It opens year-round and charges 21FF per adult, and 28FF for a tent site and car. Take bus No 1 in summer and No 6 the rest of the year.

Hostels The *Auberge de Jeunesse* (☎ 02 99 40 29 80, fax 02 99 40 29 02, 37 ave du Père Umbricht) is about 2km north-east of the train station. A spot in a four- to six-bed room costs 72FF and doubles cost 85FF. Singles with washbasin cost 114FF. Prices include breakfast. Reception opens 9 am to 12.30 pm and 2 to 8 pm. From the train station, take bus Nos 2 or 5.

Hotels The small *Hôtel Avenir* (☎ 02 99 56 13 33, 31 blvd de la Tour d'Auvergne) has simple rooms starting at 120FF (160FF with shower). Hall showers cost 15FF. Close to the Grande Plage, *Hôtel Le Neptune* (☎ 02 99 56 82 15, 21 rue de l'Industrie) is an older, family-run place. Adequate doubles with washbasin start at 130FF

(180FF with shower and toilet). Hall showers cost 15FF.

The cheerful *Hôtel Cap Malo* (☎/*fax 02 99 40 39 58, 53 quai Duguay Trouin*) has decent doubles for 120FF (160FF with twin beds). Showers cost 10FF.

In the noisy train station area, *Hôtel de l'Europe* (☎ *02 99 56 13 42, 44 blvd de la République*) has modern, nondescript doubles from 180FF. Rooms with a shower and without/with a toilet cost 240/260FF. There are no hall showers.

In the old city, the friendly, family-run *Hôtel Aux Vieilles Pierres* (☎ *02 99 56 46 80, 4 rue des Lauriers*) has rooms starting at 140FF (170FF with shower, 240FF with shower and toilet). Hall showers are free.

More in the thick of things is *Hôtel Le Victoria* (☎ *02 99 56 34 01, fax 02 99 40 32 78, 4 rue des Orbettes*) with doubles with hall shower costing from 150FF (185FF with private shower).

Hôtel Port Malo (☎ *02 99 20 52 99, fax 02 99 40 29 53, 15 rue Ste-Barbe*) is a cool, medium-sized place 150m from Porte St-Vincent. Singles/doubles with shower and toilet cost 145/175FF (175/220FF in July and August).

Hôtel de la Mer (☎ *02 99 81 61 05, 3 rue Dauphine*) is next to Plage des Bas Sablons in St-Servan. Singles/doubles start at 165FF (190FF in summer). If you call after arriving in St-Malo, they'll hold a room for an hour or so. Take bus No 2 or 3 to rue Georges Clemenceau.

Places to Eat

Restaurants The old city has lots of *tourist restaurants*, creperies and pizzerias in the area between Porte St-Vincent, the cathedral and the Grande Porte.

La Morinière (☎ *02 99 40 85 77, 9 rue Jacques Cartier*) has good seafood *menus* for 70FF and 90FF (closed Wednesday). The intimate *Grain de Sable* (☎ *02 99 56 68 72, 2 rue Jacques Cartier*), serves an excellent crepe *menu* with cider for 45FF. For takeaway sandwiches till 1 am, head for *Le Maclow* (☎ *02 99 56 50 41, 22 rue Ste-Barbe*). It's closed from 2.30 to 5.30 pm.

Chez Jean-Pierre (☎ *02 99 40 40 48, 60*

chaussée du Sillon) is popular for pizza and pasta (*menus* for 55FF including wine). The restaurant at *Hôtel Cap Malo* (see Places to Stay), a one-time dock workers hang-out, has excellent-value *menus* for 65FF and 80FF.

In St-Servan, *Crêperie du Val de Rance* (☎ *02 99 81 64 68, 11 rue Dauphine*) serves Breton-style crepes and galettes (from 8FF to 42FF) all day. Order a dry Val de Rance cider and quaff – as they all do here – from a teacup.

Self-Catering There are *food shops* along rue de l'Orme, including an excellent cheese shop (closed Sunday and Monday) at No 9, a fruit and vegetable shop (closed Sunday) at No 8 and two boulangeries. The *Intermarché* supermarket on blvd Théodore Botrel opens 9 am to 7.15 pm Monday to Saturday (also Sunday morning in July and August).

Entertainment

In summer, classical music concerts are held in Cathédrale St-Vincent and elsewhere in the city. Ask the tourist office for details.

For nightlife, try *Le Casino* (☎ *02 99 40 64 00, quai Duguay Trouin*) with its bars, brasserie, pizzeria, slot machines and disco.

Getting There & Away

Bus Courriers Bretons (☎ *02 99 19 70 70*) has regular services to Cancale (some via Pointe du Grouin, 21.50FF), Fougères (81FF, Monday to Saturday only), Pontorson (48.50FF, one hour) and Mont St-Michel (55FF, 1¼ hours). The daily bus to Mont St-Michel leaves at 9.50 am and returns around 4.30 pm.

TIV (☎ *02 99 40 82 67*) has buses to Cancale (21FF), Dinan (35FF), Dinard (20FF) and Rennes (56.50FF).

Pansart Voyages (☎ *02 99 40 85 96*) offers all-day tours to Mont St-Michel for 126FF (children 65FF, students 115FF). They're twice a week from April to October, three times in July and August.

Train There is a direct service to Paris' Gare Montparnasse (315FF, 4¼ hours, eight to 10 daily), Rennes (70FF, one hour, eight daily), Dinan (47FF, one hour, five daily) and to Lannion (165FF, four hours, seven daily).

Car You can reach ADA on ☎ 02 99 56 06 15. Avis (☎ 02 99 40 58 68) and Budget (☎ 02 99 40 15 10) have desks at the Gare Maritime du Naye. Europcar (☎ 02 99 56 75 17) is near the train station at 16 blvd des Talards.

Boat Ferries, hydrofoils or catamarans link St-Malo with the Channel Islands (Îles Anglo-Normandes), Weymouth and Portsmouth. For fares and schedules, see the Sea section in the Getting There & Away chapter.

Hydrofoils and catamarans depart from the Gare Maritime de la Bourse; car ferries leave from the Gare Maritime du Naye.

Getting Around
Bus Tickets for the St-Malo bus cost 7FF and are valid for one hour. A carnet of 10 costs 50FF and a pass costs 20FF. In summer tickets are also valid on Courriers Bretons buses for travel within St-Malo. Buses usually operate until about 8.30 pm, but in the summer some lines run until about midnight.

From Esplanade St-Vincent to the train station, take bus Nos 1, 2, 3 or 4.

Taxi Taxis can be ordered on ☎ 02 99 81 30 30.

Bicycle Cycles Diazo (☎ 02 99 40 31 63), 47 quai Duguay Trouin, opens 8.15 am to noon and 2 to 6 pm Monday to Saturday. Three-speeds cost 55FF and mountain bikes 85FF daily, plus a passport or 1000FF deposit.

DINARD
postcode 35800 • pop 10,400
Dinard has attracted a well-heeled clientele (especially from the UK) since the mid-19th century. Indeed, it has the feel of a turn-of-the-century beach resort, especially in summer, with its striped bathing tents, beachside carnival rides and spike-roofed *belle époque* mansions perched above the

water. A festival of British film is held in Dinard in early October – note the statue of director Alfred Hitchcock, two seagulls perched on his shoulders, near the entrance to Plage de l'Écluse.

Staying in Dinard can strain the budget, but you can easily come over by bus or boat for the day from St-Malo (12km by road).

Orientation and Information
Plage de l'Écluse (also called Grand Plage), which is right down the hill from the tourist office, runs along the northern edge of town between Pointe du Moulinet and Pointe de la Malouine. To get there from the Embarcadère (the pier where boats from St-Malo dock) climb the stairs and walk 200m north-west along rue Georges Clemenceau. Place de Newquay, where there are a couple of budget hotels, is 1km south-west of the tourist office.

The tourist office (☎ 02 99 46 94 12, fax 02 99 88 21 07, ✉ dinard.office.de. tourisme@wanadoo.fr) is in a round, colonnaded building at 2 blvd Féart. It opens 9 am to noon and 2 to 6 pm Monday to Saturday (9.30 am to 7.30 pm with no midday break in July and August). Staff reserve accommodation in the area for free.

Money There are banks on rue Levavasseur and a Caisse d'Épargne at 30 blvd Féart.

Post & Communications The main post office at place Rochaid opens 8 am to noon and 1.30 to 6.30 pm weekdays and on Saturday morning, and has a Cyberposte terminal. The funky Rock Fish Café, 3 rue Dumont, charges 30FF per half-hour of Internet use. It opens 4 to 10 pm daily.

St-Bartholomew Church
This Anglican church (☎ 02 99 46 77 00), built from contributions in 1871, is at 3 rue Faber, 50m up the hill from 25 ave George V. The church and its library open 10 am to 6 pm daily.

Musée du Site Balnéaire
The town's only real museum (☎ 02 99 46 81 05), at 12 rue des Français Libres,

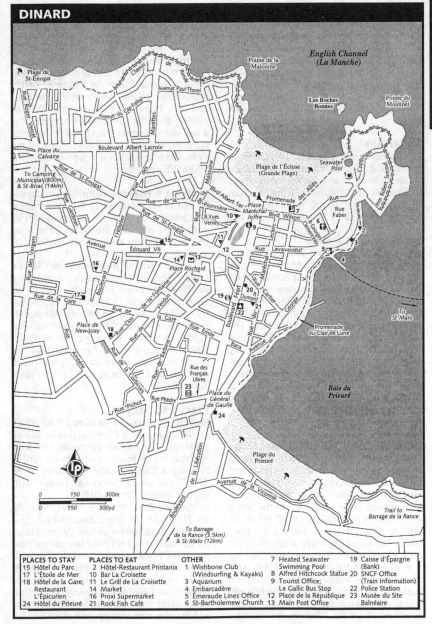

DINARD

English Channel
(La Manche)

Pointe de la
Malouine

Les Roches
Bonnes

Pointe du
Moulinet

Plage de
St-Enogat

Chemin de Ronde

Avenue Paul Thorel

Avenue du Cap Fréhel

Place du
Calvaire

Boulevard Albert Lacroix

To Camping
Municipal (800m)
& St-Briac (14km)

Rue de St-Enogat

Rue de la

Rue de St-Enogat

Seawater
Pool

Plage de l'Écluse
(Grande Plage)

Promenade des Allées

8 Place
Maréchal
Joffre

Rue Faber

St-Pionnière

10

R. Yves
Verney

9

6

7

Blvd Albert 1er

Blvd Wilson

R. Georges Clemenceau

Rue Levavasseur

Édouard VII

14   13

Place Rochaid

16

11

12

To
St-Malo

15

17

Rue de la Gare

19

20

22

21

R. Dumont

Place de
Newquay

18

Rue Clos

Rue de la Gare

Rue Émile

Rue de Verdun

Rue de la Fontaine

Boulevard Féart

Rue du Maréchal Leclerc

Rue Cartier

Rue George

Promenade
du Clair de Lune

Baie du
Prieuré

Rue des
Français
Libres

23

Place du
Général
de Gaulle

24

Rue Phédre

Rue Pichot

Baie du
Prieuré

Plage du
Prieuré

0   150   300m
0   150   300yd

Boulevard de la Libération

Avenue de la Vicomté

Trail to
Barrage de la Rance

To Barrage
de la Rance (3.5km)
& St-Malo (12km)

PLACES TO STAY	PLACES TO EAT	OTHER		
15 Hôtel du Parc	2 Hôtel-Restaurant Printania	1 Wishbone Club	7 Heated Seawater	19 Caisse d'Épargne
17 L'Étoile de Mer	10 Bar La Croisette	(Windsurfing & Kayaks)	Swimming Pool	(Bank)
18 Hôtel de la Gare;	11 Le Grill de La Croisette	3 Aquarium	8 Alfred Hitchcock Statue	20 SNCF Office
Restaurant	14 Market	4 Embarcadère	9 Tourist Office;	(Train Information)
L'Épicurien	16 Proxi Supermarket	5 Émeraude Lines Office	Le Gallic Bus Stop	22 Police Station
24 Hôtel du Prieuré	21 Rock Fish Café	6 St-Bartholemew Church	12 Place de la République	23 Musée du Site
			13 Main Post Office	Balnéaire

focuses on the history of the area and, in particular, Dinard's development as a seaside resort. But it's really more interesting as a building than a museum. The Villa Eugénie was built in 1868 for the wife of Napoleon III who – alas – never got to stay here. It opens 2 to 6 pm daily, April to June; and 10 am to noon and 2 to 7 pm, July and August. Admission costs 16FF (students 10FF).

Aquarium
The unspectacular aquarium (☎ 02 99 46 13 90) of the Muséum National d'Histoire Naturelle is at 17 ave George V. It opens 10.30 am to 12.30 pm and 3.30 pm (2.30 pm on Sunday) to 7.30 pm. Admission costs 10FF (students up to the age of 25, 5FF).

Barrage de la Rance
Between St-Malo and Dinard along the D168, you'll see the Usine Marémotrice de la Rance (Rance Tidal Power Station, ☎ 02 99 16 37 00), a hydroelectric dam across the estuary of the River Rance that uses St-Malo's extraordinarily high tides to generate nearly 10% of Brittany's electricity. The 750m-long dam, built between 1963 and 1967, has 24 turbines that turn on the rising and falling tides. Near the lock on the Dinard side is a small, subterranean visitors centre that opens 8.30 am to 8 pm daily. It runs a good film in English on how the power station works. Admission is free.

Activities
Swimming Wide, sandy **Plage de l'Écluse** is surrounded by fashionable hotels, a casino and changing cubicles. Picasso used the beach as the setting for his tableaux in the 1920s, and you'll see reproductions of them planted in the sand. Next to the beach is the **Piscine Olympique** (☎ 02 99 46 22 77), an Olympic-sized swimming pool filled with heated sea water. It opens 10 am to 12.30 pm and 3 to 7.30 pm daily (Sunday to 6.30 pm). Admission costs 13FF (students 11FF) on weekdays and 25/16FF on weekends and holidays. **Plage du Prieuré**, 1km to the south along Blvd Féart, isn't as smart as Plage de l'Écluse but is less crowded. **Plage de St-Énogat** is 1km west of Plage de l'Écluse on the other side of Pointe de la Malouine.

Windsurfing & Kayaking The Wishbone Club (☎ 02 99 88 15 20), next to the swimming pool on Plage de l'Écluse, offers windsurfing instruction for 180FF per hour and also hires out boards from 70FF to 1200FF per hour (from 180FF to 250FF for a half-day). It opens 9 am to 10 pm daily in summer, and only weekends the rest of the year. Catamarans/kayaks are on offer for 190/65FF per hour.

Walking & Hiking Beautiful seaside trails extend along the coast in both directions. The tourist office sells a topoguide (5FF) with maps and information in French on five coastal paths entitled *Sentiers du Littoral du Canton de Dinard*.

Dinard's famous **promenade du Clair de Lune** (Moonlight promenade) runs along the Baie du Prieuré just north of place du Général de Gaulle to Plage de l'Écluse via the rocky coast of **Pointe du Moulinet**, from where St-Malo's old city can be seen across the water. Bikes are not allowed. Ask the tourist office for details of the sound-and-light show on the promenade du Clair de Lune from mid-June to mid-September.

Places to Stay
Hotels The *Hôtel de la Gare* (☎ 02 99 46 10 84, 28 rue de la Corbinais) is as dull as a waiting room but has decent doubles with washbasin and bidet costing from 120FF. Friendly *L'Étoile de Mer* (☎ 02 99 46 11 19, 52 rue de la Gare) has rooms with shower starting from 250FF.

Hôtel du Parc (☎ 02 99 46 11 39, fax 02 99 88 10 58, 20 ave Édouard VII), is a medium-sized hotel with half a dozen cheap rooms starting at 150FF for one or two people (170FF with shower and 240FF with shower and TV). *Hôtel du Prieuré* (☎ 02 99 46 13 74, fax 02 99 46 81 90, 1 place du Général de Gaulle) is a lovely little place overlooking the beach and St-Malo. Singles and doubles with shower start at 230FF.

Places to Eat

Restaurants Crepe eateries abound near the tourist office. *L'Épicurien* at the Hôtel de la Gare (see Places to Stay) is a family-style restaurant with a good-value lunch *menu* costing 50FF which includes a choice from the salad bar.

Bar La Croisette (☎ 02 99 46 43 32, *4 rue Yves Verney*), easily spotted by the blond shop-window dummy on the roof, has a good, four-course *menu* for 65FF (closed Monday evening and Tuesday). It has a branch close by at 4 place de la République.

Hôtel-Restaurant Printania (☎ 02 99 46 13 07, 5 ave George V) isn't cheap (*menus* start at 90FF) but has a sunny terrace with views of St-Malo.

Self-Catering The *Proxi* supermarket at 45 rue Gardiner opens 8.30 am to 12.30 pm and 2.30 to 8 pm Monday to Saturday and 9 am to 12.30 pm on Sunday. There's a large *covered market* west of the post office on place Rochaid.

Getting There & Away

Bus There's no train station in Dinard, but TIV buses (☎ 02 99 40 82 67) leave Esplanade St-Vincent in St-Malo and stop at the Barrage de la Rance in Dinard and the tourist office (stop: Le Gallic). Buses run almost hourly till 6 pm (to St-Malo) and 7 pm (to Dinard). The one-way fare is 20FF. TAE (☎ 02 99 16 93 06) also runs buses to Rennes (65FF, two hours, five daily).

Boat From April to late September, the Bus de Mer (Sea Bus) operated by Émeraude Lines (☎ 02 99 46 10 45) links St-Malo's Porte de Dinan with Dinard's Embarcadère at 27 ave George V. This frequent ferry costs 20/30FF one way/return (12/20FF for children aged under 12) and takes 10 minutes. Bicycles cost 15FF one way.

Getting Around

Call taxis on ☎ 02 99 46 88 80 or ☎ 02 99 88 15 15.

POINTE DU GROUIN DOMAINE NATUREL DÉPARTEMENTAL

This nature reserve lies on the beautiful and wild coast between St-Malo and Cancale. Île des Landes, just off the coast, is home to a large number of giant black cormorants – which are among the largest sea birds in Europe, some 90cm long and with a wingspan of 170cm. The tourist office in Cancale has a basic map of the area and French-language brochures that describe the local flora and fauna.

Getting There & Away

Via the GR34 coastal trail (also called the Chemin des Douaniers in this area), Pointe du Grouin is 7km from Cancale and 18km from St-Malo. Count on about five hours of walking from St-Malo. By road (the D201), it's 4km from Cancale and 18km from St-Malo.

There is a bus service from St-Malo and Cancale during the summer school holidays (roughly July and August). Daily during the rest of the year, at least one of nine Courriers Bretons buses (☎ 02 99 56 79 09 in St-Malo) on the St-Malo–Cancale run (21FF) stops at the reserve.

CANCALE

postcode 35260 • pop 5200

Cancale, a relaxed fishing port 14km east of St-Malo, is famed for its offshore *parcs à huîtres* (oyster beds). The town even has a museum dedicated to oyster farming and shellfish, the **Ferme Marine** (☎ 02 99 89 69 99), on the Corniche de l'Aurore southwest of the port. It opens daily from mid-February to October and charges 38FF (students/children 30/18FF).

Orientation & Information

Port de la Houle occupies one side of a small bay. Cancale's fleet of small fishing boats moors just off the sandy bathing beach to the north-east within sight of the oyster beds. The town overlooks Port de la Houle from the north. Its centre is Place de l'Église.

The tourist office (☎ 02 99 89 63 72, fax 02 99 89 75 08, @ ot.cancale@wanadoo.fr) is south-west of place de l'Église at 44 rue du Port. It opens 9 am to 12.30 pm and 2 to 6 pm Monday to Saturday, from October to May; to 6.30 pm in June and September; and 9 am to 8 pm daily in July and August. Sunday hours are 10 am to 1 pm, September to June. The Web site is at www.villecancale.fr.

There's also a tourist office annexe at Port de la Houle, which opens 10 am to 1 pm and 5 to 8.30 pm daily in July and August and 3 to 7 pm at weekends in June and September.

Money There are several banks around place de la République, including the Banque Populaire, which opens weekdays.

Post The main post office north-west of the tourist office on ave du Général de Gaulle opens 8 am to noon and 2.30 to 5.30 pm weekdays and 9 am to noon on Saturday.

Places to Stay
Camping The *Camping Municipal Le Grouin* (☎ 02 99 89 63 79) 6km north of Cancale near Pointe du Grouin, has a fine beach. It opens early March to October and charges 62.50FF for two people, tent and car. There are several other private camp sites in the area.

Hotels The *Hôtel La Cotriade* (☎ 02 99 89 61 78, 23 quai Gambetta) has doubles with washbasin/shower starting at 150/190FF (closed mid-November to March). A block inland from the water, *Hôtel de l'Arrivée* (☎ 02 99 89 80 46, 28 rue Victor Hugo) has doubles/triples for 160/210FF. *La Vague* (☎ 02 99 89 60 04, 1 quai Thomas) charges 180FF per double in season, with hall shower and great sea views.

Places to Eat
Most restaurants at Port de la Houle specialise in oysters, which cost a minimum 65FF a dozen. *Le Pêcheur* (☎ 02 99 89 61 58, 1 place de la Chapelle) at the southern end of rue du Port is a good choice. It has *menus* starting at 75FF.

Ty Breizh (☎ 02 99 89 60 26, 13 quai Gambetta) is a lovely little Breton place with top-notch *menus* for 89.50FF. It's open for lunch and dinner.

If you prefer your oysters direct from the source, walk 100m east towards the Pointe des Crolles lighthouse. Along the quay are kiosks selling different types of oyster (numbered according to size and quality) and only costing from 16FF to 35FF a dozen.

The *Marché Plus* supermarket at place de la République opens 7 am to 9 pm Monday to Saturday, and Sunday morning.

Getting There & Away
Cancale has two bus stops, one behind the church on place Lucidas and another a few hundred metres down the hill at Port de la Houle next to the pungent Halle des Poissons (fish market). Courriers Bretons (☎ 02 99 56 79 09 in St-Malo) and TIV (☎ 02 99 40 82 67 in St-Malo) have year-round services to/from St-Malo (21FF).

DINAN
postcode 22100 • pop 11,000 • elevation 92m
Perched above the River Rance about 22km south of Dinard, the medieval town of Dinan was once surrounded by ramparts and more than a dozen stone towers. A good portion of the walls still stands today, as do some beautiful 15th-century half-timbered houses. During the Fête des Remparts in late September, Dinannais dressed in medieval garb are joined by some 40,000 visitors for a rollicking, two-day festival in the tiny old city.

Orientation & Information
Nearly everything of interest – except the picturesque port area on the River Rance – is within the tight confines of the old city, which is centred around place des Cordeliers and place des Merciers. Place Duclos is the centre of the modern town.

The tourist office (☎ 02 96 39 75 40, fax 02 96 39 01 64, @ infos@dinan-tourisme.com) at 6 rue de l'Horloge opens 9 am to 7 pm Monday to Saturday, and 10 am to

12.30 pm and 3 to 5.30 pm on Sunday, mid-June to September; and 9 am to 12.30 pm and 2 to 6.15 pm Monday to Saturday, the rest of the year. The tourist office sells an excellent map and guide to Dinan (15FF).

Money The Banque de France on rue Thiers changes currency from 9 am to noon on weekdays. There's a Crédit Mutuel de Bretagne with ATMs at 13 place du 11 Novembre 1918 across from the train station.

Post & Communications The main post office at 7 place Duclos opens 8.30 am to

6.30 pm weekdays and to noon on Saturday, and has a Cyberposte terminal. At 9 rue de la Choux, @rospace charges 20FF per half-hour of Internet use and opens 10 am to 7 pm Tuesday to Saturday.

Old City

The cobbled streets of the old city are Dinan's main attraction. Two streets not to miss – particularly if you're heading down to the port – are **rue du Jerzual** and its continuation, the steep **rue du Petit Fort**. They both have an endless number of galleries, expensive shops and some restaurants. The

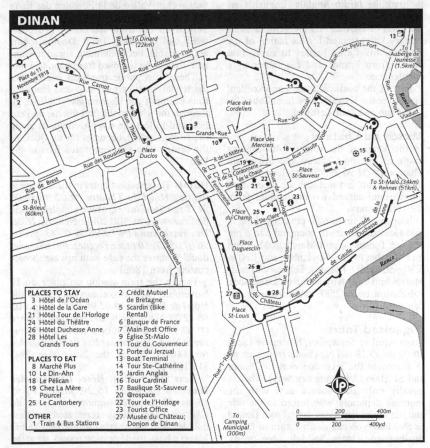

DINAN

PLACES TO STAY
3 Hôtel de l'Océan
4 Hôtel de la Gare
21 Hôtel Tour de l'Horloge
24 Hôtel du Théâtre
26 Hôtel Duchesse Anne
28 Hôtel Les
   Grands Tours

PLACES TO EAT
8 Marché Plus
10 Le Din-Ahn
18 Le Pélican
19 Chez La Mère
   Pourcel
25 Le Cantorbery

OTHER
1 Train & Bus Stations

2 Crédit Mutuel
   de Bretagne
5 Scardin (Bike
   Rental)
6 Banque de France
7 Main Post Office
9 Église St-Malo
11 Tour du Gouverneur
12 Porte du Jerzual
13 Boat Terminal
14 Tour Ste-Catherine
15 Jardin Anglais
16 Tour Cardinal
17 Basilique St-Sauveur
20 @rospace
22 Tour de l'Horloge
23 Tourist Office
27 Musée du Château;
   Donjon de Dinan

latter ends with a neck-craning view of the Viaduct de Dinan over the Rance.

Back in the old city, the most attractive half-timbered houses hang over the central **place des Merciers**. A few paces south, the **Tour de l'Horloge**, a clock tower whose tinny chimes rattle every quarter-hour, rises from rue de l'Horloge. From June to September, you can climb up to its tiny balcony for 16FF (those aged under 18, 10FF). **Église St-Malo**, opposite 33 Grande rue, dates from the late 15th century.

Pride of Dinan is the **Basilique St-Sauveur**, on the same-named square west of the parklike **Jardin Anglais** (English Garden). Inside you'll find a crypt containing the heart of Bertrand du Guesclin, a 14th-century knight noted for his hatred of the English, his fierce battles to expel that nation from France and his rather ugly countenance.

East of the basilica, there's an excellent view over the Rance valley from **Tour Ste-Cathérine** and **Tour Cardinal**.

Musée du Château

In the keep of the ruined 14th-century castle on rue du Château, the Musée du Château (☎ 02 96 39 45 20) relates the history of Dinan and includes a collection of polychrome carved wooden statues from the 16th century.

It opens 10 am to 6.30 pm daily, June to mid-October; 10 am to noon and 2 to 6 pm (closed Tuesday), mid-March to May and mid-October to mid-November; and 1.30 to 5.30 pm, except Tuesday, February to mid-March and mid-November to December. Admission costs 25FF (children and students 10FF).

Organised Tours

From April to September, Émeraude Lines (☎ 02 96 39 18 04) runs boats from quai de la Rance at the riverside port to Dinard and St-Malo (2½ hours one way). There's usually only one boat a day, with the morning departure time linked to the tide and the return trip a day later. From Dinard or St-Malo, you can easily return to Dinan by bus (or, from St-Malo, by train).

Tickets cost 95FF (children 60FF) one way and 135FF return (children 80FF).

Places to Stay

Camping The nearest camping ground is the two-star *Camping Municipal* (☎ 02 96 39 11 96, fax 02 96 85 06 97, 103 rue Chateaubriand), which is just 2km south of place Duclos. It opens June to September and charges 13/14/10FF per person/tent-site/car.

Hostels The *Auberge de Jeunesse* (☎ 02 96 39 10 83, fax 02 96 39 10 62, ✉ dinan@fuaj.org) at Vallée de la Fontaine des Eaux sits by a stream in a cool, green valley about 3km from the train station. A bed costs 49FF and breakfast, 19FF. Double rooms are available, but book them ahead in summer. Reception is closed from noon to 3 pm.

There's no public transport nearby, but the hostel shuttles guests to and from the train station if you phone ahead. On foot, go through the town to the port via rue du Petit Fort and follow the river northwards along rue du Port, which becomes rue du Quai. At the bridge take the signposted lane to the left.

Hotels The cheapest hotel in the old city is the tiny *Hôtel du Théâtre* (☎ 02 96 39 06 91, 2 rue Ste-Claire), where simple singles/doubles start at 80/120FF. Nearby, *Hôtel Duchesse Anne* (☎ 02 96 39 09 43, fax 02 96 87 05 27, 10 place Duguesclin) has quiet doubles above the cafe with private shower costing from 180FF.

Facing the train station on place du 11 Novembre 1918, two cheap options are the *Hôtel de l'Océan* (☎ 02 96 39 21 51, fax 02 96 87 05 27), at No 9, and *Hôtel de la Gare* (☎ 02 96 39 04 57), on a rather noisy corner at No 1. The former has singles/doubles for 140/170FF; at the latter they cost 115/155FF.

Near the chateau, *Hôtel Les Grandes Tours* (☎ 02 96 85 16 20, fax 02 96 85 16 04, ✉ carregi@wanadoo.fr, 6 rue du Château) has nicely renovated singles/doubles with washbasin costing 180/200FF. It's on a busy road but most rooms are at the back of the building. There's private parking (25FF).

Hôtel Tour de l'Horloge (☎ 02 96 39 96 92, fax 02 96 85 06 99, 5 rue de la Chaux) is in a charming 18th-century house on a cobbled, pedestrianised lane. Its large doubles start at 270FF; the top floor has a splendid view of the clock tower.

Places to Eat
Restaurants Tr*Le Din-Ahn* (☎ 02 96 39 56 95, 3 Grande rue) for inexpensive *menus*, crepes, salads and sandwiches. East of place des Merciers, *Le Pélican* (☎ 02 96 39 47 05, 3 rue Haute Voie) has good seafood *menus* for 80/120FF (closed Monday). Elegant *Le Cantorbery* (☎ 02 96 39 02 52, 6 rue Ste-Claire) serves a tasty, three-course *menu* from 75FF. If you want to try a snazzier place, head for *Chez La Mère Pourcel* (☎ 02 96 39 03 80, 3 place des Merciers). *Menus* start at 97FF.

Self-Catering The big *Marché Plus* supermarket, 28 place Duclos, opens 7 am to 9 pm Monday to Saturday and 9 am to 1 pm on Sunday. *Market* mornings are Thursday at place Duguesclin and the adjoining place du Champ, and Saturday on rue Carnot.

Getting There & Away
Bus Buses leave from place Duclos and the bus station. Services to Dinard (25FF, 30 minutes) and St-Malo (33.50FF, 40 minutes) are operated by CAT (☎ 02 96 39 21 05). The services to Rennes (49FF, 1¼ hours) are operated by TAE (02 99 26 16 00).

Train Trains to Paris' Gare Montparnasse (316FF, 3¼ hours, up to seven daily) go via Rennes (72FF, one hour). There are also frequent services to St-Malo (46FF, one hour) and Dol (29FF, 25 minutes).

Getting Around
Taxi Call taxis on ☎ 02 96 39 06 00 or ☎ 02 96 39 10 60.

Bicycle Scardin (☎ 02 96 39 21 94), 30 rue Carnot, rents out city bikes for 50/300FF per day/week.

The 'Real' Brittany

Le Goëlo is the region marking the northern end of an imaginary line running from north to south separating 'Breton Brittany' to the west from what the local people call 'Gallic Brittany' to the east. The demarcation line makes its way from Plouha (between Paimpol and Binic) south to Vannes in Morbihan. Someone from Paimpol then, is a 'real' Breton, whereas a neighbour from Binic, a mere 25km south-east, is a 'Gallo-Breton' (in Breton, 'gal' means 'abroad'). Gallic Brittany (also known as Haute Bretagne or Upper Brittany) is predominantly French-speaking, while in Breton Brittany (Bretagne Basse or Lower Brittany) many people still speak the regional tongue, heard these days mainly in Finistère.

PAIMPOL
postcode 22500 • pop 7900
Paimpol (Pempoull in Breton) is a charming port on the Côte du Goëlo, the border region between the 'real' Brittany and the rest of the region (see the boxed text). Until early this century, many fishermen would set sail from here to Iceland for seven months at a stretch. Many never returned, the victims of storms and disease and now the subjects of folk tales and *chants de marins* (sea ditties).

Paimpol is the closest port to Île de Bréhat (Enez Vriad in Breton), a tiny island 8km north of town whose local population of 450 is virtually overwhelmed by sun-worshipping tourists in summer.

Orientation & Information
The centre of Paimpol is place du Martray. A short distance to the east and north-east are the two *bassins* of the Port de Plaisance and the Baie de Paimpol. Place de la République lies between the train station and the port.

The tourist office (☎ 02 96 20 83 16, fax 02 96 55 11 12) in place de la République opens 10 am to 12.30 pm and 2.30 to 6 pm Tuesday to Saturday, September to June; and 9 am to 7.30 pm Monday to Saturday, and Sunday from 10 am to 1.30 pm in July and August.

Money There's a Banque de Bretagne on place du Martray (closed Monday). The post office also has exchange services.

Post & Communications The main post office is north-east of the train station on ave du Général de Gaulle. It opens 9 am to noon and 1 to 5.30 pm on weekdays, and 8 am to noon on Saturday.

The Cybercommune in the Centre Micarmor, 1 Gardenn Rohou about ½km northwest of the train station, charges 20FF per hour (0.33FF per minute) of Internet use. It opens 9 am to noon and 3 to 8 pm Monday to Friday, and 2 to 6 pm on Saturday.

Laundry The laundrette at 23 rue 18 June just north of the train station opens 8 am to 8 pm daily.

Places to Stay
The quiet, two-star *Camping Municipal de Cruckin* (☎ 02 96 20 78 47, rue de Cruckin) is on the beautiful Baie de Kérity, 2km south-east of town off the road to Plouha. It opens Easter to September and costs 71.65FF for up to three people plus tent and car.

The *Auberge de Jeunesse* (☎ 02 96 20 83 60, fax 02 96 20 96 46, ✉ paimpol@fuaj .org) is at the Château de Kerraoul, 1.5km north-west of the centre. A dorm bed with breakfast at the hostel costs 67FF and it stays open all year.

A few inexpensive hotels front the port. *Hôtel Le Goëlo* (☎ 02 96 20 82 74, fax 02 96 20 58 93, quai Duguay Trouin) has simple singles for 160FF and doubles from 220FF with shower and toilet. *Hôtel Le Berthelot* (☎ 02 96 20 88 66, 1 rue du Port) is slightly pricier: nicely-done rooms with washbasin cost 160FF (230FF with private bath).

Places to Eat
The port restaurants are fairly touristy and expensive. Instead, try the popular *Crêperie-Restaurant Morel* (☎ 02 96 20 86 34, 11 place du Martray), with savoury galettes costing from 19FF to 33FF.

The *Intermarché* supermarket on ave du Général de Gaulle, just west of the train station, opens 8.30 am to 12.15 pm and 2.30 to 7.15 pm weekdays. On Saturday there's no midday break.

A **market** is held on Tuesday morning at place Gambetta. There are *oyster vendors* selling freshly-shucked bivalves at quai Duguay Trouin at weekends.

Getting There & Away
Bus & Train Buses to St-Brieuc operated by CAT (☎ 02 96 68 31 20) cost 45FF and take 1½ hours from Paimpol train station. To reach the tourist office, head north up rue du 18 Juin, turn left into rue de l'Église, take the first right, then turn left on rue Sylvain Bertho. The tourist office is at the end.

The closest rail junction to Paimpol is Guingamp, which you can reach by frequent bus (39FF, 40 minutes) from where there are trains west to Brest (119FF) and east to Dinan (104FF).

Boat Ferries to Île de Bréhat, operated by Vedettes de Bréhat (☎ 02 96 55 79 50), leave from the port at Pointe de l'Arcouest, 6km north of town. The trip takes 10 minutes and costs 40FF for a return (children aged under 11, 34FF). Taking a bicycle along costs 50FF return. There are hourly sailings in summer between 8.30 am and 8 pm.

Getting Around
Bus CAT buses leave six or seven times daily in summer from Paimpol train station (13FF one way) to Pointe de l'Arcouest to connect with the Île de Bréhat ferries.

Bicycle Bikes can be hired for 70FF per day from Cycles du Vieux Clocher (☎ 02 96 20 83 58) at place de Verdun. It's south of the tourist office near the Vieux Tour (old tower).

PERROS-GUIREC
postcode 22700 • pop 7600
A venerable resort on the Côte de Granit Rose (Pink Granite Coast), Perros-Guirec

(Perroz Gireg in Breton) sits at the point of Brittany's northernmost peninsula. It's an exclusive town, flanked by a sheltered new marina to the south-east and the old fishing port of Ploumanach about 2km to the north-west; in between lies a coastline of rose-coloured granite, beaches and coves where sea otters still feel at home. The town of Lannion (Lannuon in Breton; population 18,400), 12km inland and the nearest town served by train, has a decent hostel.

Orientation

Perros has two distinct parts: the main upper town on the hill and the marina area at its base. They're about 1km apart if you make your way up along the small roads, or double that distance if you instead follow the coastal blvd de la Mer and blvd Clemenceau around Pointe du Château, the peninsula that extends eastwards from town.

Information

Tourist Offices The tourist office (☎ 02 96 23 21 15, fax 02 96 23 04 72, ☻ infos@perros-guirec.com) is in the upper town at 21 place de l'Hôtel de Ville. It opens 9 am to 12.30 pm and 2 to 6.30 pm Monday to Saturday in winter, and 9 am to 7.30 pm in summer (when it also opens 10 am to 12.30 pm and 4 to 6.30 pm on Sunday).

Money The Crédit Maritime Mutuel at 20 place de l'Hôtel de Ville has exchange services, as does the Société Général at 4 rue de la Poste.

Post & Communications The main post office is east of the tourist office on rue de la Poste. It opens 9 am to noon and 2 to 5.30 pm on weekdays and 9 am to noon on Saturday, and has a Cyberposte.

Swimming & Walking

Of several beaches close to Perros, the main one is **Plage de Trestraou**, to the north about 1km from the tourist office. The others, attractive **Plage de Trestrignel** and **Plage du Château** on either side of Pointe du Château, are smaller and more isolated.

For a fantastic walk along the coast, follow the GR34 from Plage de Trestraou along the pink rocks to the Port de Ploumanach. It's about 5km each way.

Places to Stay

Camping Four camping grounds dot the area. The four-star *Camping Le Ranolien* (☎ 02 96 91 43 58, fax 02 96 91 41 90) has the best location: close to the sea, between the rocks just off the road to Ploumanach. It opens April to mid-November and charges 75FF for two people with a tent (130FF in high season).

Hostels There are two year-round youth hostels outside of Perros. Inland at Lannion (12km), *Les Korrigans* (☎ 02 96 37 91 28, fax 02 96 37 02 06, ☻ lannion@fuaj.org, 6 rue du 73 Territorial) is a two-minute walk from the train station. It charges 72FF a night plus 19FF for breakfast, and has a few tent sites.

The other hostel, *Le Toëno* (☎ 02 96 23 52 22, fax 02 96 15 44 34, route de la Corniche) is on the coast, 10km west of Perros near the town of Trébeurden. It charges 67FF for a bed and breakfast. Take CAT bus No 15 from the train station in Lannion or from Perros' mairie.

Hotels In Perros' upper town, *Hôtel Les Violettes* (☎ 02 96 23 21 33, 19 rue du Calvaire), a Victorian-style house south-west of the tourist office, has rooms with washbasin/shower starting at 130FF (175FF with shower and toilet). *Hôtel de la Mairie* (☎ 02 96 23 22 41, fax 02 96 23 33 04, 28 place de l'Hôtel de Ville) offers doubles with washbasin for 170FF (220FF with shower and toilet).

Places to Eat

The Perros hotels listed have decent *menus* from 55FF (at Hôtel Les Violettes) to 79FF.

Self-caterers will find a *Marché Plus* supermarket just south-west of the tourist office on blvd Aristide Briand. It opens from 8.30 am to 12.30 pm and 3 to 7.30 pm Monday to Saturday, and 9 am to 1 pm on Sunday.

Getting There & Away

Buses operated by CAT (☎ 02 96 46 76 70) shuttle between Lannion's train station and Perros (17FF), where they stop at the marina and place de l'Hôtel de Ville.

From Lannion train station, there are rail links via Plouaret Trégor eastwards to Guingamp and on to St-Brieuc; and westwards via Morlaix (45FF, 1½ hours) to Roscoff (64FF, three hours) and Brest (84FF, 2½ hours, six daily).

Getting Around

Bus CAT bus No 15 runs from Lannion train station to Perros, before continuing on north-west to Ploumanach and then on to Trébeurden and Trégastel. There are up to nine buses daily on weekdays, fewer on Saturday and none on Sunday.

Taxi Call taxis in Lannion on ☎ 02 96 48 09 50.

Bicycle Perros-Cycles (☎ 02 96 23 18 08, 12 blvd Aristide Briand, charges 50/70FF per day for touring bikes, with passport or 1500FF deposit.

Finistère

Brittany's westernmost region, Finistère (Land's End) is also the most Breton in character. It's known for its many calvaries and *pardons*, especially in Cornouaille, the area of southern Finistère whose name commemorates the early Celts who sailed from Cornwall and other parts of Britain to settle here. This is where you're most likely to hear people speaking Breton. The area's major city, Quimper, stages an annual summer festival celebrating Celtic culture.

Brest, Finistère's other main city, is at the far western tip of the peninsula. Along the southern coast there are numerous fishing ports, including the engaging town of Concarneau.

Finistère is surrounded by the sea, which pounds the rocky cliffs and deep inlets making up much of the rugged coastline. The sea breeze sweeps as far inland as the Monts d'Arrée, the eastern frontier of the Parc Naturel Régional d'Armorique. Islands off the coastlike Ouessant, Molène and Sein are buffeted by very strong currents. Some 350 lighthouses, beacons, buoys and radar installations make the area's busy and treacherous sea routes more navigable.

ROSCOFF

postcode 29680 • pop 3600

Protected from the furious seas by the little offshore island of Batz, the town of Roscoff (Rosko in Breton), whose 16th-century granite houses surround a small bay, is the southernmost – and arguably the most attractive – Channel port for entering France by ferry from Britain or Ireland.

Nearby areas of the Channel are home to a wide variety of algae, some of which are used in *thalassothérapie*, a health treatment using sea water. Roscoff's hinterland is known for its *primeurs* (early fruits and vegetables), such as cauliflower, onions, tomatoes, new potatoes and artichokes, which flourish here. Before the advent of large vehicular ferries, Roscoff farmers, known as 'Johnnies', would load up boats with the small pink onions grown locally, sail to England and deliver them to markets by bicycle.

Orientation & Information

Roscoff is arrayed around the fishing and pleasure craft port. Place de la République lies to the west of quai d'Auxerre, where there are several restaurants. The town's focal point, though, is rue Amiral Réveillère leading north-westwards to place Lacaze-Duthiers and Église Notre Dame de Kroaz-Batz.

The **tourist office** (☎ 02 98 61 12 13, fax 02 98 69 75 75) is in a fine old stone building just north of place de la République at 46 rue Gambetta. It opens 9 am to noon and 2 to 6 pm Monday to Saturday (though in winter it may open an hour later and close an hour earlier). In July and August it opens 9 am to 12.30 pm and 1.30 to 7 pm Monday to Saturday, and on Sunday from 10 am to 12.30 pm.

Money There's a Caisse d'Épargne near the tourist office at 9 rue Gambetta, and a 24-hour banknote exchange and ATM in the ferry terminal.

Post & Communications The post office at 19 rue Gambetta opens 9 am to noon and 2 to 5 pm weekdays and on Saturday morning.

System D Plus, 5 rue Gambetta, charges 1FF per minute of Internet use. It opens 9 am to 12.30 pm and 1.30 to 6 pm Monday to Friday (to 5 pm on Saturday).

Laundry The Ferry Laverie, 23 rue Jules Ferry south of the tourist office, opens 8 am to 8 pm daily.

Things to See & Do
Of Roscoff's few historical sites, the Flamboyant Gothic **Église Notre Dame de Kroaz-Batz** and its 16th-century Renaissance belfry are worth a look.

The Station Biologique de Roscoff (☎ 02 98 29 23 25 49), at place Georges Teissier just north-west of the church, contains both an **aquarium** and **marine museum**. It opens 10 am to noon and 1 to 6 pm (7 pm in June to August) and afternoons only in April, May, September and October (closed in winter). Admission costs 26FF (students 22FF).

Next to the tourist office, the desanctified **Chapelle de Ste-Anne**, which was turned into a Temple of Reason during the Revolution, houses the **Maison des Johnnies** (☎ 02 98 61 12 13). This museum is devoted to the onion growers and sellers, who are much revered and earn almost hero status in these parts.

The Centre Nautique on quai d'Auxerre (☎ 02 98 69 72 79) rents **sailboards** and **catamarans** for 150FF and 350FF for three hours.

You can also take a thalassotherapy cure at Roc Kroum (☎ 02 98 29 20 00) on the Anse inlet west of the centre on ave Victor Hugo. This fitness temple also has a large pool (40FF) as well as a Jacuzzi (50FF) and sauna (70FF). It opens 12.45 to 2.30 pm and 5.30 to 8.30 pm weekdays (1.30 to 2.30 pm

on Thursday), and 9.30 am to noon and 3 to 6 pm on Sunday.

Places to Stay
Camping *Camping de Kérestat* (☎/fax 02 98 69 71 92), 2.5km south of Roscoff, charges 24/12FF per adult/child and 40/14FF for a tent site/car. It opens all year.

Camping Municipal de Perharidy (☎ 02 98 69 70 86, fax 02 98 61 15 74) is on the grounds of a lovely 19th-century mansion about 6km south-west of the centre on the south-western side of the Anse inlet. It charges 10/7FF per adult/child or 15/9FF, depending on the season, while a tent site/parking place costs 9/6FF or 13/7FF. Showers are free. Bungalows sleeping four cost 850FF to 1600FF a week.

Both camp sites are close to sandy beaches, but neither is served by public transport.

Hotels Hotels are relatively expensive in Roscoff and most raise their prices in July and August. Be advised that many shut down in winter.

The two-star *Hôtel Les Arcades* (☎ 02 98 69 70 45, fax 02 98 61 12 34, 15 rue Amiral Réveillère) is great deal, with simple but modern singles/doubles starting at 180/205FF (270/285FF with shower). Hall showers are free. Les Arcades closes in winter.

Hôtel Le Centre (☎ 02 98 61 24 25, fax 02 98 61 15 43, 5 rue Gambetta) near the tourist office, has simple doubles without/with showers for 220/240FF and charming old photos of Johnnies in the bar. Pleasant doubles with shower at *Hôtel Les Alizés* (☎ 02 98 69 72 22, fax 02 98 61 11 40, quai d'Auxerre) cost 190FF or 260FF, depending on the season.

Places to Eat
There are pizzerias and creperies everywhere, but seafood reigns in Roscoff, France's premier crabbing port. Many restaurants close in winter.

L'Écume du Jour (☎ 02 98 61 22 83, quai D'Auxerre) overlooking the port and the Île de Batz, is a good choice for fish, with *menus* costing from 92FF (closed Wednesday). On the same quay, *Les Korrigans* (☎ 02 98 61 22 15) serves all manner of crepes and galettes and has seafood *menus* for 74FF and 96FF.

Chez Gaston (☎ 02 98 69 75 65, *rue Joseph Barra*) south-east of the port is an intimate little restaurant, but seafood *menus* are cheaper (and the views better) at *Hôtel Les Arcades restaurant* (see Places to Stay).

Getting There & Away
Bus & Train The combined bus and train station is on rue Ropartz Morvan. To get to the tourist office, turn right into rue Vloche as you leave the station, then right onto rue Brizeux. Follow it until it curves around to the left into rue Jules Ferry, which leads to place de la République, rue Gambetta and the tourist office.

There are trains to Morlaix (29FF, one hour), from where you can make connections to Brest (72FF, 1½ hours), south to Quimper (114FF, 1¾ hours) and east to Lannion (65FF, three hours, five daily) and St-Brieuc (89FF, 99FF via TGV, 1¾ hours, five daily). Bus destinations include Huelgoat (34FF, one hour, four daily).

Boat Brittany Ferries (☎ 02 98 29 28 28) sails to Plymouth in England and Cork in Ireland. Boats leave from the Gare Maritime de Bloscon, which opens 9 am to midnight. It's about 2km east of the tourist office; to get to town, head straight up the hill as you leave the ferry terminal, turn right and then take the first left into rue de Plymouth. This leads down to quai d'Auxerre.

Getting Around
Cycles Desbordes (☎ 02 98 69 72 44), near the train station at 13 rue Brizeux, rents touring bikes for 40FF per day (mountain bikes 60FF).

AROUND ROSCOFF
Île de Batz
postcode 29253 • pop 575 • elevation 5m
Just 2km offshore, the 4-sq-km Île de Batz (Enez Vaz in Breton) is a charming

island with some good beaches, a lovely garden (Jardins Georges Delaselle, open daily in summer, 20FF) and lots of seaweed. The *Auberge de Jeunesse* (☎ 02 98 61 77 69, *fax 02 98 61 78 85*) on the island opens April to October and charges 67FF per person, including breakfast.

Getting There & Away Boats to Île de Batz take 15 minutes and are operated by CFTM Vedettes (☎ 02 98 61 78 87). At high tide, they leave from the pier running eastwards into the old port; at low tide, cross the long, narrow footbridge to the north of the port. Return tickets cost 34FF (children 17FF). In July and August boats sail every 15 minutes between 8 am and 8 pm; during the rest of the year, services are less frequent, with about eight sailings daily.

BREST
postcode 29200 • pop 149,600
Sheltered by a wide natural harbour, rainy Brest is one of France's most important naval ports. Flattened by air attacks during WWII, it was rebuilt as a modern, not particularly attractive, city. The medieval port area and its narrow streets, where Jean Genet set his homoerotic novel *Querelle* (and his film *Fassbinder*), are long gone. You'll still see the starched white uniforms of French sailors everywhere, though, lurching and staggering about on shore leave.

Orientation
The centre of Brest lies north of the harbour (known as the Rade) and the Port de Commerce; to the west are the Arsenal Maritime and the River Penfeld. From place de la Liberté, the main square, rue de Siam runs south-west and rue de Jean Jaurès northeast. Both are lined with restaurants, cafes and bars. The Château de Brest lies to the south-west.

Information
Tourist Offices The tourist office (☎ 02 98 44 24 96, fax 02 98 44 53 73, **☻** Office .de.Tourisme.Brest@wanadoo.fr) is south of place de la Liberté at 8 ave Georges

Clemenceau, next to the modern Quartz cultural and convention centre. It opens 10 am to 12.30 pm and 2 to 6 pm Monday to Saturday, mid-September to mid-June; and 9.30 am to 6 pm Monday to Saturday, and 10 am to noon and 2 to 6 pm on Sunday, mid-June to mid-September.

Hikers and walkers should pick up a copy of *30 Circuits Pédestres autour de Brest* (50FF) from the tourist office.

Money The Banque de France, south-west of the tourist office at 39 rue du Château, changes money 8.45 am to 12.15 pm. There's a Crédit Mutuel de Bretagne at 2 place de la Liberté and lots more banks along rue de Siam. The post office also has exchange services.

Post & Communications The main post office is south-west of place de la Liberté at place Général Leclerc. It opens 8 am to 7 pm weekdays and 8 am to noon on Saturday, and has a Cyberposte.

Le Cyber Jeux, 129 rue Jean de Jean Jaurès, charges 30FF per half-hour of Internet use. It opens 1.30 to 10 pm on weekdays (midnight on Friday and Saturday), and 2.30 to 10 pm on Sunday.

Laundry The laundrette at 8 place de la Liberté opens 7 am to 8.30 pm daily.

Océanopolis

The ultramodern Océanopolis (☎ 02 98 34 40 40) at the Port de Plaisance, about 3km east of the city centre, has lovely aquariums with algae forests, seals, crabs, anemones, sea urchins and Brest's famed scallops. There are also exhibitions on all aspects of sea life and even a section on cooking with seaweed. It opens 9 am to 7 pm daily; admission costs 90FF (children aged between 4 and 12, 70FF). Take bus No 7 from the tourist office.

Musée de la Marine

The Maritime Museum (☎ 02 98 22 12 39) is housed in the fortified, 13th-century Château de Brest, which is one of the city's few buildings to survive WWII bombing.

The rather feeble exhibits examine the city's maritime tradition, but the views of the Rade and the naval port from the thick walls are striking. The museum opens 10 am to 6.30 pm daily, April to September; and 10 am to noon and 2 to 6 pm the rest of the year (closed Tuesday). Admission costs 29FF (those aged under 19, 19FF).

Tour Tanguy

The paintings, photographs and dioramas in this round 14th-century tower (☎ 02 98 00 88 60), which is across the River Penfeld on place Pierre Péron, trace the history of Brest with emphasis on how the city looked on the eve of WWII. Don't miss the documented visit of three Siamese ambassadors in 1686 who presented the court of Louis XIV with gifts of gold, silver and lacquer; rue de Siam was renamed to commemorate the occasion. Tour Tanguy opens 2 to 5 pm Wednesday and Thursday, and 2 to 6 pm at weekends, October to May; and 10 am to noon and 2 to 7 pm, June to September. Admission is free.

Places to Stay

Camping The *Camping du Goulet* (☎/fax 02 98 45 86 84) is a huge, hilly facility in Ste-Anne du Portzic, 6km west of Brest and 400m from the sea. It charges 18FF per adult and 21FF per tent. Take bus No 14 from the train station to Le Cosquer stop.

Hostels The *Auberge de Jeunesse* (☎ 02 98 41 90 41, fax 02 98 41 82 66, @ BREST.AJ.CIS@wanadoo.fr, rue de Kerbriant) is near Océanopolis and a stone's throw from the artificial beach at Moulin Blanc. It charges 71FF (breakfast included) per person and opens year-round. Take bus No 7 from the train station to Port de Plaisance, the last stop.

Hotels The *Hôtel Vauban* (☎ 02 98 46 06 88, fax 02 98 44 87 54, 17 ave Georges Clemenceau,) is a fairly grand place south-east of the tourist office with simple doubles for 140FF (from 230FF with shower, toilet and TV). Overall, it's an excellent deal.

Hôtel Abalis (☎ 02 98 44 21 86, fax 02 98 43 68 32, 7 ave Georges Clemenceau) charges 195/225FF for a single/double with shower and TV. Simple rooms with wash-basin cost 140/160FF.

Places to Eat

Alsatian may seem out of place in Brittany, but *La Taverne St-Martin* (☎ 02 98 80 48 17, 92 rue Jean Jaurès) has generous *menus* starting at 85FF (50FF for lunch), six beers (including Belgian cherry-flavoured *kriek*) on tap and opens till midnight every day.

The *Brasserie Le Palais* at Hôtel Vauban (see Places to Stay) has a 60FF *menu* and plats du jour for 47FF.

Ma Petite Folie (☎ 02 98 42 44 42), an old lobster boat beached at Moulin Blanc near the hostel, does a fantastic fish *menu* for 110FF.

The *Monoprix* supermarket, 49 rue de Siam, has a large grocery section in the basement. It opens 8.30 am to 7.30 pm Monday to Saturday.

Getting There & Away

Bus Brest's bus station is south-east of the tourist office on place du 19ème Régiment d'Infanterie. CAT (☎ 02 98 44 32 19) has up to seven buses daily to Quimper (84FF, 1¼ hours). Les Cars de St Mathieu (☎ 02 98 89 12 02) links Brest with Le Conquet (26FF, 45 minutes, six daily and three on Sunday) and Roscoff (55FF, 1½ hours, up to four times daily).

Train There area services to Quimper (83FF, one hour 20 minutes) or to Morlaix (53FF, 40 minutes), from where there are connections to Roscoff (71FF to 80FF, 1¼ hours by TGV). There are also TGV trains to Paris' Gare Montparnasse (375FF, 4½ hours) and Rennes (165FF, two hours).

Car ADA (☎ 02 98 44 44 88) has an office next to Hôtel Abalis at 9 ave Georges Clemenceau. Avis (☎ 02 98 44 63 02) is at 20 bis rue de Siam.

Boat Ferries to the Île d'Ouessant leave from the Port de Commerce east of the

chateau. See Getting There & Away in the Île d'Ouessant section for details.

Getting Around

Bus The local bus network, Bibus, has an information kiosk on place de la Liberté. Single tickets cost 6FF, a carnet of 10 is 51FF and day passes cost 18FF.

Taxi Call a taxi at ☎ 02 98 80 43 43.

Bicycle Torch VTT (☎ 02 98 41 93 71) at 87 rue de Paris rents mountain bikes for 90FF a day and 65FF for half a day (70FF and 45FF October to May).

LE CONQUET
postcode 29217 • pop 2150

Perched on the westernmost tip of Brittany, the pretty fishing village of **Le Conquet** lies close to some pristine beaches and lovely coastal paths. It's largely ignored by tourists, who generally leave their cars here to pile onto the ferries headed for Île d'Ouessant.

Information

The tourist office (☎ 02 98 89 11 31, fax 02 98 89 08 20, @ ot.conquet@wanadoo.fr) is in the town hall in the Parc de Beauséjour. Staff will give you a free brochure detailing walks of the town and coastline (1½ to three hours). One of them leads to the **Phare de Kermorvan** (☎ 02 98 89 00 17), a 37m-high lighthouse on the Kermorvan peninsula which shelters the port of Le Conquet. You can climb it from 3.30 to 6 pm in July and August (10FF). The lovely **Plage des Blancs Sablons** is a wide, sandy beach running to the north.

Places to Stay & Eat

The *Camping Municipal le Thévan* (☎ 02 98 89 06 90) lies 400m east of the Plage des Blancs Sablons. Open April to September, it charges 16/16FF per adult/tent site. From the Parc de Beauséjour, take the footbridge *Passerelle de Croaë* and walk 4km north (it's signposted).

The modern **Hôtel de la Pointe Ste-Barbe** (☎ 02 98 89 00 26, fax 02 98 89 14 81,

Pointe Ste-Barbe) has comfortable singles/doubles with shower and a sea view for 201FF. **Le Relais du Vieux Port** (☎ 02 98 89 15 91, fax 02 98 89 19 06, 1 quai du Drellac'h) has very pretty doubles for 210FF (270FF with a view) and a cosy restaurant (daily specials for 35FF and crepes from 15FF).

Getting There & Away
Buses operated by Les Cars de St-Mathieu (☎ 02 98 89 12 02) link Brest with Parc de Beauséjour in Le Conquet (26FF, 45 minutes, six daily and three on Sunday).

ÎLE D'OUESSANT
postcode 29242 • pop 1060 • elevation 24m
Île d'Ouessant (in Breton, Enez Eusa meaning 'Island of Terror', Ushant in English) a wild but hauntingly beautiful island 20km from the mainland, epitomises the ruggedness of the Breton coast. About 7km long and 4km wide, it serves as a beacon for more than 50,000 ships entering the Channel each year.

Traditionally, the sea played a pivotal role in the everyday life of the islanders, providing them with both a livelihood and resources. The interiors of the houses, partitioned by little more than wooden panels, resembled the insides of a boat and had furniture made from driftwood. Outside, the houses were painted in symbolic colours: blue and white for the Virgin Mary, green and white for hope.

Although the island is no longer as isolated as it once was, some particular traditions and customs remain. Old women still make lace crosses in memory of the husbands who never returned from the sea; little black sheep are free to roam about; and local favourite *ragoût de mouton* (lamb baked for five hours under a layer of roots and herbs) retains its popularity.

Orientation & Information
The only village of any size is Lampaul, 3km from where the ferries dock. It has a handful of hotels and shops.

On place de l'Église is the tiny tourist office (☎ 02 98 48 85 83, fax 02 98 48

87 09), open 10.30 am to noon and 2 to 5 pm Monday to Saturday, and 10 am to 12.30 pm on Sunday. It sells brochures (10FF, in French) with maps outlining four walks of between 10 and 17km in length.

Lighthouses
Standing tall on the western side of Ouessant is the striped **Phare de Créac'h**, the world's most powerful lighthouse. Just north of the ferry dock on the opposite side, 7km east, is the **Phare du Stiff**.

The entire island is ideal for (very windy) walks. A 45km path follows the craggy, rocky coastline, passing some very grand scenery.

Museums
Heading west from Lampaul, the **Écomusée d'Ouessant** (☎ 02 98 48 86 37), also known as the Maison du Niou, has simple but moving displays on local life arranged in two colourful houses furnished in the traditional style. It opens 10 am to noon and 2 to 4 pm, October to April (6.30 pm in April and May) and 10.30 am to 6.30 pm, June to September. It's closed Monday year-round. Admission costs 25FF (children 15FF).

Musée des Phares et des Balises (☎ 02 98 48 80 70), a lighthouse and beacon museum beneath the Phare de Créac'h, tells the intriguing story of these vital installations. A 30-minute walk west of Lampaul, the museum opens 2 to 4 pm daily, except Monday, October and March (2 to 6.30 pm in April and May) and 10.30 am to 6.30 pm the rest of the year. Admission costs 25FF (children 15FF).

Places to Stay & Eat
The *Camping Municipal* (☎ 02 98 48 84 65) in Lampaul looks more like a football field than a camping ground. It opens March to November and costs 14/14FF per person/tent site.

The smart *Hôtel L'Océan* (☎ 02 98 48 80 03) opens all year. It has bay-view rooms and a lively bar underneath. Singles/doubles with shower cost 325/575FF for half-board. In the warmer summer months, a cheaper option is the *Duchesse Anne* (☎ 02 98 48 80 25), which offers rooms starting at 140/180FF.

The hotels, notably the Duchesse Anne, have decent restaurants specialising in lamb and stingray. There's a small *supermarket* in town.

Getting There & Away

Air If time (but not money) is a concern, Finist'air (☎ 02 98 84 64 87) will fly you from the Aéroport International de Brest-Guipavas, about 9km north-east of Brest, to Ouessant in 15 minutes. There are two return flights daily. The one-way fare is 320FF (children aged between two and 12, 160FF).

Boat Year-round ferries to Ouessant are operated by Penn Ar Bed (meaning 'End of the World', ☎ 02 98 80 80 80), which sails from Brest's Port de Commerce (2½ hours) or from Le Conquet (1½ hours). Most boats call at tiny Île Molène en route.

From May to September there are two to five boats daily, with the first sailing at 7.45 or 8.30 am. In July and August, daily boats leave Brest at 8 am and from Le Conquet at 8, 9.45 and 10.40 am and at 5.45 pm. Returning from Ouessant, there are five boats daily bound for Le Conquet (last at 7.45 pm). A return adult ticket costs 186/157FF from Brest/Le Conquet (those aged up to 16, 112/94FF).

Finist'mer (☎ 02 98 89 16 61 in Le Conquet) runs faster boats up to eight times daily between Le Conquet and Ouessant from May to September. The crossing takes 40 minutes and costs 142FF (children 80FF).

Getting Around

Bus A shuttle bus covers the 3km from the ferry terminal to Lampaul (12FF).

Bicycle OuessanCycles (☎ 02 98 48 83 44), which has a kiosk at the ferry terminal on the island's eastern side, rents bicycles/mountain bikes for 65/85FF a day. Locacycles (☎ 02 98 48 80 44), also at the ferry terminal, charges similar rates.

PARC NATUREL RÉGIONAL D'ARMORIQUE

Of France's almost three dozen regional parks, the 1100 sq km Armorique Regional Park (Park An Arvorig in Breton) is among the most diverse. Taking in the Monts d'Arrée and the unspoiled forests around Huelgoat, it stretches westwards for some 70km along the Presqu'île de Crozon (Crozon Peninsula) and includes the reserves of Île d'Ouessant and the Molène archipelago.

The Crozon Peninsula is particularly well-endowed with natural wonders, many of which can be reached only via foot and bicycle paths. Some highlights include:

- Menez Horn, a 330m summit in the Montagnes Noires (Black Mountains) at the eastern end of the peninsula, which offers a panorama over the Bay of Douarnenez
- Étang du Fret, an isolated 18-hectare pond some 5km north of Crozon which serves as a fish nursery and bird sanctuary
- Pointe de Pen-Hir, high white sandstone cliffs extending into the sea by Camaret-sur-Mer, with a protected bird sanctuary
- Cap de la Chèvre, the rugged, heath-covered southern spit of the peninsula, dotted with traditional villages and windmills

For more information, contact the park's head office (☎ 02 98 21 90 69) at Ménez-Meur near Hanvec, 50km north of Quimper on the D18.

CROZON & MORGAT

postcode 29160 • pop 7700

Crozon, the largest town on the same-named peninsula, is unremarkable in itself but incorporates the much more alluring beach resort of **Morgat** a few kilometres to the south. The towns make a good base for exploring this outstandingly beautiful region.

Information

Crozon's tourist office (☎ 02 98 27 07 92, fax 02 98 27 24 89) is in the former train station on blvd Pralognan. It sells the Topoguide hiking and walking maps of the region (75FF), and books regional accommodation for 2FF. The office opens 9.15 am to noon and 1.30 to 6 pm Monday to Saturday; there's no midday break in July and

August, when it also opens Sunday mornings. There's also an office annexe at Morgat Plage in summer. The Web site is at www.crozon-morgat.com.

The post office on rue Alsace-Lorraine opens 9 am to noon and 2 to 5 pm, and Saturday mornings. It has a currency desk and a Cyberposte. There's a BNP bank on the square opposite the tourist office (closed Monday).

Cave Tours

Several Morgat-based companies operate **boat tours** of the colourful **grottos** along the Cap de la Chèvre, including Vedettes Rosmeur (☎ 02 98 27 10 71), Vedettes Sirènes (☎ 02 98 26 20 10) and Vedettes Tertu (☎ 02 98 26 26 90). Tours cost around 45FF and boats depart from Morgat harbour several times an hour from May to September.

Places to Stay & Eat

There are hundreds of campsites on the peninsula. The *Plage de Goulien (☎ 02 98 27 17 10)* on the coast 4km west of Crozat (along the D308) has a charming beachside location. It charges 22/22/12FF per adult /tent/car and opens from mid-June to mid-September. There's no bus link to the camp site.

The tourist office has a list of *chambres chez l'habitant* (B&Bs) starting at 130FF per double. In Morgat, *Hôtel de la Baie (☎ 02 98 27 07 51, fax 02 98 26 29 65, 46 blvd de la Plage)* is one of the cheapest deals in town, charging 150/180FF for nice singles/doubles with private shower (170/ 220FF with a sea view).

Toul-Boss (☎ 02 98 27 17 95, 2 rue de la Fontaine) by the Morgat tourist annexe serves good seafood *menus* (79FF) and crepes (from 15FF) in its grassy inner courtyard. It's open for lunch and dinner.

There's a *Shopi* supermarket in Crozon on rue Alsace-Lorraine (open all day Saturday and Sunday morning).

Getting There & Around

Bus SCETA (☎ 02 98 93 06 98) runs buses to Crozon from Quimper (60FF, 1¼ hours, up to five daily), while Pouget (☎ 02 98 27

02 02) has a service from Camaret and Crozon to Brest (71FF, 1¼ hours, up to three daily). Buses also run between Morgat, Crozon and Camaret several times daily (11FF).

Bicycle Presqu'îles Loisirs (☎ 02 98 27 07 92) opposite Crozon tourist office rents out bikes for 40/60FF per half-day/day.

Car One of the cheaper car rental agencies is Car Go (☎ 02 98 16 00 92) at 7 route de Camaret in Crozon.

HUELGOAT

postcode 29690 • pop 1687 • elevation 149m
Huelgoat (An Uhelgoat in Breton) is an excellent base for exploring what's left of the forested Argoat. The village borders the unspoiled Forêt d'Huelgoat – where King Arthur's treasure is said to be buried – with its unusual rock formations, caves, menhirs and abandoned silver and lead mines. To the east and north-east, are the Forêt de St-Ambroise and the Forêt de Fréau. All have a good network of walking trails.

Orientation & Information

Huelgoat lies to the east of a small wishbone-shaped lake which empties into the River Argent. The tourist office (☎ 02 98 99 72 32, fax 02 98 99 75 72) is in the Moulin du Chaos on the main road about 1km east of town. It opens 11 am to noon and 2 to 5.30 pm Tuesday to Saturday, September to June; and 9.30 am to noon and 2 to 5.30 pm Monday to Saturday, in July and August.

Things to See & Do

The **Moulin du Chaos** (☎ 02 98 99 77 83) on the River Argent takes its name from the steady erosion of the forest's granite base. It has regular exhibits on the archaeology, geology, flora and fauna of the Argoat (open 1.30 to 6.30 pm daily except Monday, July and August).

Most of the **walking trails** fan out from the end of rue du Lac. Pick up a free map from the tourist office (and a brochure about the precarious Trembling Rock).

Places to Stay & Eat

Camping Municipal du Lac (☎ 02 98 99 78 80), 500m west of the centre on rue du Général de Gaulle, opens from mid-June to mid-September and charges 17/19FF per person/tent. There's a swimming pool.

The sole hotel is *Hôtel du Lac* (☎ 02 98 99 71 14, fax 02 98 99 70 91, *9 rue du Général de Gaulle*). This is a top-notch place, charging from 250/280FF for singles/doubles, all with shower, toilet and TV. Its popular restaurant has pizza costing from 40FF and salads from 28FF.

A bit further out is *Hôtel-Restaurant Le Sénéchal* (☎ 02 98 78 23 13, *Le Bourg*) in nearby Scrignac. Rustic but comfortable singles/doubles with bath and toilet go for 140/160FF. Take the CAT bus from Huelgoat to the 'Bourg' stop (4.50FF, 17 minutes).

Restaurants on place Aristide Briand include the *Crêperie des Myrtilles* with crepes from 10FF to 37FF and *menus* from 49FF. *La Chouette Bleue* (☎ 02 98 99 78 19) at 1 rue du Lac is a safe option for crepes and quiches.

Getting There & Away

SCETA buses (☎ 02 98 93 06 98 in Carhaix-Plouguer) link Huelgoat with Morlaix to the north (24km) and Carhaix-Plouguer to the south-east (17km). There are up to four buses daily to Morlaix (53FF, one hour) but only one on Sunday (at 5.05 pm). Count on three to Carhaix-Plouguer (24FF, 30 minutes) from Monday to Saturday and one on Sunday (at 7.15 pm). Buses stop in front of the Chapelle de Notre Dame at place Aristide Briand.

QUIMPER

postcode 29000 • pop 59,400 • elevation 41m

At the confluence of the Rivers Odet and Steïr, Quimper (Kemper in Breton) has preserved its Breton architecture and atmosphere and is considered the cultural and artistic capital of the region. Some even refer to Quimper (pronounced 'kam-**pair**') as the 'soul of Brittany'.

Orientation & Information

The old city, much of it for pedestrians only, is to the west and north-west of the cathedral. The train and bus stations are nearly 1km east of the old city. Mont Frugy overlooks the centre from the southern bank of the River Odet.

The **tourist office** (☎ 02 98 53 04 05, fax 02 98 53 31 33, @ office.tourisme .quimper@ouest-mediacap.com) at place de la Résistance, opens 9 am to noon and 1.30 to 6 pm Monday to Saturday (7 pm in July and August), and 10 am to 1 pm and 3 to 7 pm on Sunday, mid-June to September. A tour of the city in English leaves the tourist office at 2 pm every Tuesday in July and August.

Money The Banque de France at 29 ave de la Gare exchanges money from 8.45 am to noon. There's a Crédit Lyonnais at place St-Corentin and a Banque de Bretagne at 18 quai de l'Odet (both closed Monday). The post office also changes currency.

Post & Communications The main post office at 37 blvd Amiral de Kerguélen opens 8 am to 6.30 pm weekdays and on Saturday until noon, and has a Cyberposte terminal. Cyber Video, 51 blvd Amiral de Kerguélen, charges 20/30FF per half-hour/hour of Internet use (open 10 am to 8 pm weekdays, to 6 pm on Saturday).

Laundry The Lav' Seul laundrette, 9 rue de Locronan, opens 7 am to 9 pm daily.

Walking Tour

Strolling along the quays along the Odet is a fine way to get a feel for the city. The old city is known for its centuries-old houses, which are especially in evidence on **rue Kéréon** and around **place au Beurre**. To climb 72m-high **Mont Frugy**, which offers great views of the city, follow the switch-back **promenade du Mont Frugy**, which starts just east of the tourist office.

Cathédrale St-Corentin

Built between 1239 and 1515 (with spires added in the 1850s), Quimper's cathedral

QUIMPER

PLACES TO STAY
3 Hôtel Le Celtic
22 Hôtel La Tour d'Auvergne
27 Hôtel Café Nantais
28 Hôtel Pascal
30 Hôtel de l'Ouest
36 Hôtel Dupleix

PLACES TO EAT
7 Monoprix Supermarket
8 La Mie Celine
9 Covered Market
19 Le Jardin de l'Odet

21 Trattoria Mario
31 Le Lotus d'Or
33 Casino Grocery
38 Crêperie du Frugy

OTHER
1 Torch VTT (Bicycle Rental)
2 Laundrette
4 Église St-Mathieu
5 Banque de Bretagne
6 QUB Office (Bus Information)
10 Crédit Lyonnais
11 Place St-Corentin

12 Ar Bed Keltiek; François le Villec Shops
13 Musée Départemental Breton
14 Cathédrale St-Corentin
15 Musée des Beaux-Arts; Town Hall
16 Cafe/Coffeeshop
17 Jardin l'Évêché
18 Cyber Video
20 Main Post Office
23 Lennez (Bicycle Rental)

24 Laundrette
25 Bus Station
26 Train Station
29 Europcar
32 Banque de France
34 Theatre
35 Police Station
37 Prefecture
39 Promenade du Mont Frugy
40 Tourist Office
41 Musée de la Faïence
42 Faïenceries HB Henriot Factory

embraces many Breton elements, including – on the western facade between the spires – an equestrian statue of King Gradlon, the city's mythical 5th-century founder. The loaf of bread in the southern transept before a relic of St-Jean Discalcéat (1279–1349) will have been left by one of the faithful for the really poor (not you, that is). Mass in Breton is said on the first Sunday of every month.

Museums

The **Musée Départemental Breton** (☎ 02 98 95 21 60), or Mirdi Breizat An Départemant in Breton, is housed in the former bishop's palace at 1 rue du Roi Gradlon with exhibits on the history, furniture, costumes, crafts and archaeology of the area. It opens 9 am to noon and 2 to 5 pm daily, except Sunday morning and Monday, October to May; and 9 am to 6 pm, June to September. Admission costs 25FF (students 15FF). Adjoining the museum is the **Jardin de l'Évêché** (Bishop's Palace Garden), open 9 am to 5 or 6 pm.

The **Musée des Beaux-Arts** (☎ 02 98 95 45 20), in the town hall at 40 place St-Corentin, has a decent collection of European paintings from the 16th to early 20th centuries. It opens 10 am to noon and 2 to 6 pm daily except Tuesday (10 am to 7 pm daily in July and August). Admission costs 25FF (students 15FF).

The **Musée de la Faïence** (☎ 02 98 90 12 72) behind the Faïenceries HB Henriot factory at 14 rue Jean-Baptiste Bousquet has more than 500 pieces on display. It opens 10 am to 6 pm Monday to Saturday, mid-April to October. Admission costs 26FF (students 21FF). The factory itself (☎ 02 98 90 09 36) runs organised tours from 9 to 11.15 am and 1.30 to 4.15 pm on weekdays (4.45 pm in July and August). Tickets cost 20FF.

Walking

The topoguide *Balades en Pays de Quimper*, on sale at the tourist office for about 30FF, has details on 21 walks in the Quimper area. It includes excellent maps and an explanatory text in French.

Special Events

The Festival de Cornouaille, a showcase for traditional Breton music, costumes and culture, takes place between the third and fourth Sundays of July. After the traditional festival, classical music concerts are held at different venues around town. Ask the tourist office for details of a local *fest-noz*.

Places to Stay

Local accommodation gets scarce during the Festival de Cornouaille. The tourist office will make bookings for you anytime for 2FF in Quimper, 5FF elsewhere in Brittany and 10FF outside the region. Ask also for its list of B&Bs and *chambres d'hôtes*.

Camping About 1km west of the old city, *Camping Municipal* (☎ 02 98 55 61 09, ave des Oiseaux) is cheap – 17.70/8.70FF per adult/child, 3.90FF for a tent site, 6.70FF for a car – and opens all year. Take rue de Pont l'Abbé north-west from quai de l'Odet and walk straight ahead when rue de Pont l'Abbé veers left. From the train station, take bus Nos 1 or 8 to the Chaptal stop.

Hostels The *Auberge de Jeunesse* (☎ 02 98 64 97 97, fax 02 98 55 38 37, 6 ave des Oiseaux), about 1km west of the old city, charges 67FF per dorm-room bed, including breakfast. Take bus Nos 1 or 8 to the Chaptal stop.

Hotels Spotless *Hôtel de l'Ouest* (☎ 02 98 90 28 35, 63 Rue Le Déan) has large, pleasant singles/doubles/triples/quads starting at 100/150/220/250FF. Hall showers cost 15FF, and singles/doubles with shower 180/190FF.

The slightly down-at-heel *Hôtel Pascal* (☎ 02 98 90 00 81, fax 02 98 53 21 81, 17 ave de la Gare) offers singles/doubles with showers for 150/180FF.

Hôtel Derby (☎ 02 98 52 06 91, fax 02 98 53 39 04, 13 ave de la Gare) has good-sized rooms with shower, toilet and TV from 150/200FF – if you don't mind the betting shop downstairs. You could also try *Hôtel Café Nantaïs* (☎ 02 98 90 07 84, 23 ave de la Gare), which has rooms with washbasin and bidet at 128FF, including hall shower.

The rather noisy *Hôtel Le Celtic* (☎ *02 98 55 59 35, 13 rue de Douarnenez)* has doubles for 125FF, or for 165FF with shower (starting at 205FF with shower and toilet).

The modern *Hôtel Dupleix* (☎ *02 98 90 53 35, fax 02 98 52 05 31, 34 blvd Dupleix)* has modern doubles with private amenities from 230FF.

Charming *Hôtel La Tour d'Auvergne* (☎ *02 98 95 08 70, fax 02 98 95 17 31, 13 rue des Réguaires)* in a quiet area, has doubles with washbasin and toilet starting at 320FF.

Places to Eat
Restaurants *Crêperie du Frugy* (☎ *02 98 90 32 49, 9 rue Ste-Thérèse)* opens lunch and dinner except Sunday lunchtime and Monday. Crepes range from 7.50FF to 35FF.

Trattoria Mario (☎ *02 98 95 42 15, 35 rue des Réguaires)* docs great pizza and grilled dishes from 11 am to 2 pm and 7 to 11.30 pm (closed Monday).

For a splurge, try *Le Jardin de l'Odet* (☎ *02 98 95 76 76, 39 blvd Amiral de Kerguélen)* that looks onto part of the Jardin l'Évêché It specialises in Breton and French cuisine (*menus* from 95FF) and opens for lunch and dinner (closed Sunday).

Le Lotus d'Or (☎ *02 98 53 02 54, 53 rue Le Déan)* serves up great Vietnamese-Chinese cuisine for both lunch and dinner.

Self-Catering The *Monoprix* supermarket on quai du Port au Vin opens 9 am to 7 pm daily except Sunday. There's also a *Casino* grocery at 39 ave de la Gare. *La Mie Celîne* is a popular bakery at 14 quai du Steir; get a huge filled baguette, dessert pastry and soft drink for 30FF (open Sunday).

Entertainment
From late June to the first week in September, traditional Breton music is performed every Thursday evening at 9 pm in the Jardin de l'Évêché. Tickets cost about 25FF.

Rue du Frout near the cathedral has a couple of small pubs that attract a Breton-speaking clientele. The Café/Coffee Shop at No 26 is a popular gay venue open 6 pm to 1 am nightly.

Shopping
Ar Bed Keltiek (Celtic World, ☎ 02 98 95 42 82) at 2 rue du Roi Gradlon has a wide selection of Celtic books, music, pottery and jewellery. The store opens 10 am to noon and 2 to 7 pm Tuesday to Saturday (8 am to 8 pm daily in July and August).

For faïence and textiles with traditional Breton designs, visit the excellent shop of François Le Villec (☎ 02 98 95 31 54) at 4 rue du Roi Gradlon. It opens 9.30 am to 12.30 pm and 2 to 7 pm Monday to Saturday (daily with no midday break in summer). The shop behind the Faïenceries HB Henriot factory at place Bérardier has a large selection of Quimperware plates, cups, bowls etc. It opens 9.30 am to 6 pm Monday to Saturday.

Getting There & Away
Bus The bus station is served by half a dozen bus companies, including SCETA (☎ 02 98 93 06 98), Castric (☎ 02 98 56 33 03) and Le Cœur (☎ 02 98 54 40 15). Service is reduced on Sunday and during the off-season.

Another bus company, CAT (☎ 02 98 90 68 40), has buses to Brest (84FF), Pointe du Raz (France's westernmost point, 47FF), Roscoff (118FF) and other destinations.

Caoudal (☎ 02 98 56 96 72) serves Concarneau (26FF) and Quimperlé (45.50FF).

Train There are services to Paris' Gare Montparnasse (384FF, four hours, eight daily). Destinations within Brittany include Brest (83FF, 1½ hours, six to eight daily), Vannes (100FF, 1½ hours, seven daily) and St-Malo (202FF, three hours, four daily) via Rennes (168FF, 2½ hours, five daily). The station has luggage lockers (15FF to 30FF).

Car ADA (☎ 02 98 52 25 25) has an office at 2 ave de la Gare. Europcar (☎ 02 98 90 00 68) is nearby at 12 rue de Concarneau.

Getting Around
Bus QUB has an information office (☎ 02 98 95 26 27) opposite the tourist office at 2 quai de l'Odet. Tickets are 6FF each or 49FF for a carnet of 10. Buses stop running

around 7 pm and don't operate on Sunday except for bus No 8. To reach the old city from the station take bus No 1 or 6.

Taxi Taxis can be called on ☎ 02 98 90 21 21 or ☎ 02 98 90 16 45.

Bicycle Torch VTT (☎ 02 98 53 84 41) at 58 rue de la Providence rents out mountain bikes for 65/90FF a half-day/day (70/45FF from October to April). The shop, which opens 9.30 am to 12.30 pm and 2 to 7 pm, is a good source of information on cycling routes (closed Sunday and Monday, and Thursday morning).

CONCARNEAU
postcode 29900 • pop 18,600
Concarneau (Konk-Kerne in Breton) is France's third most important trawler port, and is 24km south-east of Quimper. Much of the tuna brought ashore here is caught in the Indian Ocean or off the coast of Africa; you'll see handbills announcing the size of the incoming fleet's catch all around town. Concarneau is slightly scruffy but refreshingly unpretentious, and decent beaches are nearby.

Orientation & Information
Concarneau curls around the protected harbour that houses the Port de Plaisance and the busy fisheries area, Port de Pêche. Quai d'Aiguillon runs from north to south along the harbour, turning into quai Peneroff as it passes the Ville Close, the walled town.

The tourist office (☎ 02 98 97 01 44, fax 02 98 50 88 81, **@** OTSI.concarneau@wanadoo.fr) is on quai d'Aiguillon. It opens 9 am to noon and 2 to 6 pm Monday to Saturday, September to June; and 9 am to 8 pm in July and August. From April to June, it also opens 9 am to noon on Sunday. The Web site is at www.concarneau.org.

Money There's a Société Générale at 10 rue du Général Morvan, half a block west of the tourist office, and a Caisse d'Épargne on rue Charles Linement (closed Monday). The post office also exchanges currency.

Post & Communications The post office at 14 quai Carnot opens 8 am to 12.15 pm and 1.30 to 6 pm weekdays and 8 am to noon on Saturday. It has a Cyberposte terminal.

Laundry The Lavomatique at 21 ave Alain Le Lay opens 7 am to 9 pm daily.

Ville Close
The walled city, built on a small island measuring just 350m by 100m and fortified between the 14th and 17th centuries, is linked frm place Jean Jaurès by a footbridge. By the entrance, notice the sundial warning us all that 'Time passes like a shadow'. Ville Close is packed with shops, restaurants and galleries, but there are nice views of the town, port and bay from the **ramparts**, which open 10 am to 6 pm daily (9 am to 7 pm in summer).

Museums
The **Musée de la Pêche** (☎ 02 98 97 10 20), on rue Vauban just beyond the gate of the Ville Close, has four aquariums and exhibits on everything you could possibly want to know about Concarneau's fishing industry. It opens 10 am to noon and 2 to 6 pm daily (9.30 am to 7 pm in July and August). Admission costs 36FF (those aged under 16, 24FF). At No 36 is an interesting little church called **Chapelle de la Trinité**, which now houses a theatre.

The more serious **Marinarium** (☎ 02 98 97 06 59) next to the hostel at quai de la Croix, has aquariums as well as exhibits on oceanography and marine biology. It opens 10 am to noon and 2 to 6.30 pm, Easter to September. Admission costs 20FF (children 12FF).

Activities
Plage des Sables Blancs 'White Sands Beach' is on Baie de la Forêt, 1.5km northwest of the tourist office. To get there, take bus No 2. For **Plage du Cabellou**, several kilometres south of town, take bus No 1.

The **fish auction**, known as *la criée* in French, takes place weekdays at 6 am in the warehouses along the Port de Pêche. To pull in a few of your own, four-hour **fishing trips** are available daily in summer on the

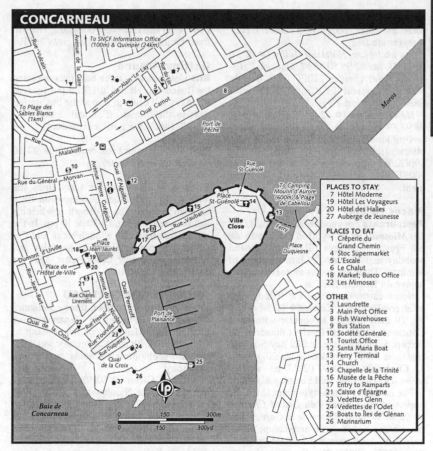

CONCARNEAU

PLACES TO STAY
7 Hôtel Moderne
19 Hôtel Les Voyageurs
20 Hôtel des Halles
27 Auberge de Jeunesse

PLACES TO EAT
1 Crêperie du Grand Chemin
4 Stoc Supermarket
5 L'Escale
6 Le Chalut
18 Market; Busco Office
22 Les Mimosas

OTHER
2 Laundrette
3 Main Post Office
8 Fish Warehouses
9 Bus Station
10 Société Générale
11 Tourist Office
12 Santa Maria Boat
13 Ferry Terminal
14 Church
15 Chapelle de la Trinité
16 Musée de la Pêche
17 Entry to Ramparts
21 Caisse d'Épargne
23 Vedettes Glenn
24 Vedettes de l'Odet
25 Boats to Îles de Glénan
26 Marinarium

Santa Maria (☎ 02 98 50 69 01), a boat that is moored along quai d'Aiguillon near the tourist office. It sails at 8 am, 1.30pm and 6 pm. The trip costs 200FF, including all equipment (children 100FF).

Places to Stay

Camping Concarneau's half a dozen camping grounds include *Camping Moulin d'Aurore* (☎ 02 98 50 53 08, 49 rue de Tregunc), which is 600m south-east of the Ville Close. It opens April to September and costs 22FF per person plus 20FF for a tent site and a place to park. Take bus No 1 or 2

(stop: Le Rouz) or the little ferry from Ville Close to place Duquesne and walk south along rue Mauduit Duplessis.

Hostels The *Auberge de Jeunesse* (☎ 02 98 97 03 47, fax 02 98 50 87 57, quai de la Croix) is right on the water next to the Marinarium. A bed costs 48FF and breakfast 19FF. Reception opens 9 am to noon and 6 to 8 pm, but you can leave your bags in the dining room which is unlocked all day.

Hotels The *Hôtel Les Voyageurs* (☎ 02 98 97 08 06, 9 place Jean Jaurès) has slightly

BRITTANY

overpriced doubles for 175FF with washbasin and bidet (200FF with shower). Hall showers are free.

For a bit more, *Hôtel des Halles* (☎ *02 98 97 11 41, fax 02 98 50 58 54, place de l'Hôtel de Ville*) charges 220FF for a double with shower and TV (from 260FF with shower, toilet and TV).

Hôtel Modern (☎ *02 98 97 03 36, fax 02 98 97 89 06, 5 rue du Lin*), a cosy, put-your-feet-up kind of place in a quiet backstreet, offers singles/doubles with washbasin for 190/220FF (doubles with shower start at 300FF). The private garage costs 50FF per night.

Places to Eat

Restaurants For good pizzas and pasta try *Les Mimosas* (☎ *02 98 50 66 61*), in narrow rue Fresnel; it opens till 11 pm (closed Monday and Sunday for lunch except in summer). There are oodles more restaurants on ave du Docteur Nicolas.

Some eateries north of the fishing port offer good value. *L'Escale* (☎ *02 98 97 03 31, 19 quai Carnot*) is popular with local Concarnois – a hearty lunch or dinner *menu* (except Saturday night and all day Sunday) costs just 51FF. Next door at No 20, similar *Le Chalut* (☎ *02 98 97 02 12*) has a 52FF *menu* (closed Friday and Saturday nights).

For excellent home-style crepes, try the unpretentious *Crêperie du Grand Chemin* (☎ *02 98 97 36 57, 17 ave de la Gare*). Your basic *crêpe au beurre* (buttered crepe) costs only 7FF – and more extravagant varieties from 15FF to 23FF. They're much cheaper by the pair.

Self-Catering There's a *covered market* on place Jean Jaurès open until 1 pm daily. The big market day is Friday.

The *Stoc* supermarket on quai Carnot next to the post office is open Monday to Saturday from 8.45 am to 7.30 pm (8 pm in July and August).

Getting There & Away

Bus There's no train station in Concarneau. Caoudal (☎ *02 98 56 96 72*) runs up to four buses daily (three on Sunday) between Quimper and Quimperlé via Concarneau, Pont Aven and La Forêt Fouësnant. The trip from Quimper to Concarneau costs 26FF.

Getting Around

Bus Concarneau's three bus lines operated by Busco run all day till 7.20 pm (except Sunday). All of them stop at the bus station next to the tourist office and tickets cost 5.50FF (46FF for a 10-ticket carnet).

Taxi You can ring taxis on ☎ 02 98 97 10 93 or ☎ 02 98 97 06 06.

Boat A small passenger ferry links the Ville Close with place Duquesne on Concarneau's eastern shore, departing when it's full between 8 am and 8.30 or 10 pm. In the off-season, they take a lunch break and finish at 6.20 pm (7.20 pm on Saturday and Sunday). One-way tickets cost 4FF (or 25FF for 10 tickets).

AROUND CONCARNEAU

From April to September, three companies offer excursions to Îles de Glénan, a group of nine little islands about 20km south of Concarneau with an 18th-century fort, sailing and scuba-diving schools, and a bird sanctuary.

Vedettes Glenn (☎ 02 98 97 10 31), 17 ave du Docteur Nicolas, and Vedette Taxi (☎ 02 98 97 25 25), based in Quimper, charge 105FF return (children 52.50FF). A return trip with Vedettes de l'Odet (☎ 02 98 50 72 12) costs 110FF (children 60FF).

LORIENT
postcode 56100 • pop 59,000
In the 17th century the Compagnie des Indes (the French East India Company) founded the Port de l'Orient; the name was later abbreviated to Lorient. Ever since, it has been one of the most important ports in France. In WWII, it held U-boat pens; during fierce fighting in 1945, the city was almost entirely destroyed.

Lorient (An Oriant in Breton) has few specific attractions, but its tidy streets, upbeat atmosphere and large student community make it well worth a visit. Fans of

The attractive seaside town of Honfleur is popular with day-trippers from Paris.

The towering chalk cliffs of the Côte d'Albâtre

Traditional half-timbered house, Normandy

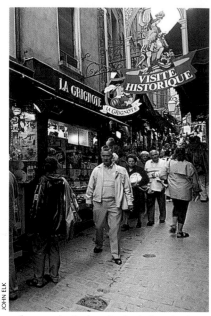

Admire the striking view of the Mont St-Michel...   ...then wander its shop-lined, winding streets.

The medieval town of Dinan, Brittany: original city walls, half-timbered houses and cobbled streets

Celtic culture will enjoy the Festival Interceltique, which takes the city by storm every summer.

Orientation & Information

Lorient is set on a large natural harbour and the River Scorff. The centre of town is about 1km south of the train and bus stations near the narrow Port de Plaisance. You can reach it by walking down cours de Chazelles and its continuation, rue Maréchal Foch.

The tourist office (☎ 02 97 21 07 84, fax 02 97 21 99 44) is on quai de Rohan on the southern side of the Port de Plaisance. It opens 9 am to 7 pm on weekdays, and 9 am to noon and 2 to 7 pm on Saturday; and also 10 am to noon and 2 to 5 pm Sundays in July and August. The rest of the year it opens 9 am to 12.30 pm and 1.30 to 6 pm weekdays, and 9 am to noon and 2 to 6 pm on Saturday.

Money There are several banks along cours de Chazelles, including the Société Générale at No 24 (also open Saturday).

Post & Communications The main post office is in the centre of town at 9 quai des Indes. It opens 8 am to 7 pm weekdays and till noon on Saturday, and has a Cyberposte terminal.

Laundry The Cleanfil laundrette at 2 rue George Gaigneux, just off rue Maréchal Foch, opens 8 am to 9 pm daily.

Musée de la Compagnie des Indes

This fascinating museum (☎ 02 97 82 19 13) is housed in a 17th-century citadel in the Port Louis area, south-east of Lorient's centre. Its exhibitions trace the history of the French East India Company and its extremely lucrative trade with India, China, Africa and the New World from 1660 to the end of the 18th century. The museum opens 10 am to 7 pm daily, except Tuesday, from April to September; and 1.30 to 6 pm the rest of the year. Admission costs 30FF (students 20FF).

To reach Port Louis and the museum, take the 10-minute ferry from the Embarcadère de la Rade (☎ 02 97 33 40 55) at the end of quai des Indes and opposite the tourist office. Ferries run every half-hour from Monday to Saturday between 7 am and 7.20 pm (10.30 am to 6.30 pm on Sunday). The one-way fare is 7FF and a bike costs an extra 6.50FF.

Special Events

For 10 days in early August, Lorient holds a celebration of Celtic culture, especially music, literature and dance, called the Festival Interceltique. People from the Celtic countries or regions (*broiou keltiek* in Breton) – Ireland, Scotland, Wales, Cornwall, Isle of Man and certain parts of northwestern Spain – join the Bretons to pay homage to their common heritage.

Places to Stay

Hostels The *Auberge de Jeunesse* (☎ 02 97 37 11 65, fax 02 97 87 95 49, 41 rue Victor Schoelcher) is 3km out of town. Dorm beds cost 70FF, breakfast included. There's a laundry and cooking facilities. Take bus B2 or C1 from the train station and alight at the Auberge de Jeunesse stop.

Hotels The one-star *Hôtel d'Arvor* (☎ 02 97 21 07 55, 104 rue Lazare Carnot) is a small, friendly place about 600m southwest of quai de Rohan. Rooms, some with antique furnishings, cost from 170FF (with washbasin) to 190FF (with shower and toilet). From the train station, take bus D (direction: Nouvelle Ville) and get off at the Carnot stop.

Hotel Les Pecheurs (☎ 02 97 21 19 24, fax 02 97 21 13 19, 7 rue Jean Lagarde) about 200m west of the tourist office, has basic rooms without/with shower for 90FF/130FF. The bar downstairs can get pretty noisy.

The two-star *Hôtel Victor Hugo* (☎ 02 97 21 16 24, fax 02 97 84 95 13, 36 rue Lazare Carnot) charges 250FF for comfortable singles/doubles with shower and TV. There are also a few doubles with washbasin that cost 170FF.

Places to Eat

Restaurants The *Hôtel d'Arvor* has a very good restaurant with *menus* for 85FF and 120FF (closed Sunday). *Menus* at **Hôtel Victor Hugo** start at 85FF (see Places to Stay).

The *Royal Couscous* (☎ 02 97 64 45 78, 65 rue Lazare Carnot) serves North African specialities, including tajines (from 60FF), for lunch and dinner.

Intimate *Le St-Louis* (☎ 02 97 21 50 45, 48 rue Jules Le Grand) has two good *menus* for 65FF and 105FF (closed Tuesday night and Wednesday), but an even better bet is the *Bistrot du Yachtman* (☎ 02 97 21 31 91, 14 rue Poissonière) north of the tourist office where *Menus* start at 79FF.

Self-Catering *Le Garde Manger*, a small grocery at 79 rue Lazare Carnot, opens 8.30 am to 1 pm and 4 to 9 pm (closed Sunday).

Getting There & Away

Bus The bus station (☎ 02 97 21 28 29) is next to the train station. Destinations, among many others in the Morbihan département, include Josselin (60FF) and Carnac (35FF).

Train Lorient's enormous Gare d'Échanges is at 7 cours de Chazelles. Frequent services include Brest (135FF, 2¼ hours), Quimper (62FF, 45 minutes), Vannes (51FF, 35 minutes), and Rennes (131FF, 1½ hours). Lorient is also served by TGVs from Paris' Gare Montparnasse (358FF, 3½ hours).

Boat Car ferries operated by CMN (☎ 02 97 64 77 64) depart frequently in summer for Île de Groix, an 8km-long island with some fine beaches and accommodation south-west of Lorient. They leave from the Embarcadère Île de Groix, about 150m south-east of the tourist office on blvd Adolphe Pierre. The return fare is 107FF (children aged up to 12 and students aged up to 25, 66FF). Bicycles cost 52FF return, but you can also rent a bicycle/mountain bike/scooter there from Loca Loisirs, quai de Port Tudy (☎ 02 97 86 80 03). In July

and August, passenger ferries go to Belle Île on Tuesday, Thursday and Friday (see the previous section) from Lorient, but you'll have to book well ahead.

Getting Around

Bus Tickets for Vitaville city buses cost 7FF each or 58FF for a carnet of 10. A daily pass is 22FF. Bus D links the train station with the quai de Rohan and the tourist office. Most of the city's 11 lines run till 8 pm; service is greatly reduced on Sunday.

Taxi Taxis in Lorient can be reached on ☎ 02 97 21 29 29.

Morbihan Coast

Morbihan, the département which covers Brittany's south-central section, stretches from Lorient near the Finistère border to Redon in the east.

Naturally enough, it is the coast – particularly around the regional capital, Vannes – that attracts most visitors. The Golfe du Morbihan (Morbihan Gulf), enclosed by arms of land which leave only a narrow outlet to the Atlantic, is virtually an inland sea (*mor bihan* means 'little sea' in Breton). About 40 of its islands are inhabited. Oysters are cultivated around the gulf, which is also a bird sanctuary of international importance.

West of the gulf, the Presqu'île de Quiberon, a narrow, claw-shaped peninsula, makes it about halfway to Belle Île, an island 12km from the town of Quiberon.

The whole Morbihan région is a showcase of Neolithic landmarks. At nearly every crossroads, you'll see signs pointing to megalithic sites, of which the ones at Carnac are the most famous.

CARNAC
postcode 56340 • pop 4600

Carnac (Garnag in Breton) is home to some of the world's foremost megalithic sites. Located about 32km west of Vannes, the town consists of an attractive old village, Carnac Ville, and a more modern seaside resort, Carnac Plage, with a 2km-long sandy beach (Grande Plage) on the sheltered Baie de Quiberon.

Orientation & Information

Carnac Ville and Carnac Plage are 500m apart. They're joined by ave de Salines and ave de l'Atlantique, which head south to the beachfront blvd de la Plage.

The efficient main tourist office (☎ 02 97 52 13 52, fax 02 97 52 86 10, ☻ ot .carnac@ot-carnac.fr) is in Carnac Plage at 74 ave des Druides, two blocks north of the beach. It opens 9 am to noon and 2 to 6 pm Monday to Saturday, September to June; and 9 am to 7 pm, July and August. It also opens 3 to 7 pm on Sunday in summer. There's a computer screen with accommodation options out front.

The tourist office annexe (same telephone number) in Carnac Ville is behind the church on the central place de l'Église. It opens 9.30 am to 12.30 pm and 2 to 6 pm Monday to Saturday, April to November; and 9.30 am to 12.30 pm and 2.30 to 7 pm and 10 am to 1 pm, July and August.

Money Banks on rue St-Cornély, west of place de l'Église, include Crédit Mutuel de Bretagne at No 27. Société Générale has an ATM at the main tourist office in Carnac Plage.

Post & Communications The main post office, with exchange services, is opposite 27 rue de la Poste (south from place de l'Église). It opens 9 am to noon and 2 to 5 pm on weekdays and Saturday mornings. Le BaoBab, 3 allée du Parc in Carnac-Plage, is a bar charging 1FF/minute on its one slow Internet terminal.

Megaliths

Carnac's megalithic sites stretch 13km north from Carnac Ville and east as far as the village of Locmariaquer. Don't expect Stonehenge, though; most of the menhirs are no more than 1m high. To see inside many of the dolmens, you'll need a torch (flashlight).

In Carnac, **Tumulus St-Michel**, 200m

north-east of place de l'Église at the end of rue du Tumulus, dates back to at least 5000 BC and is topped with a 16th-century cross and the **Chapelle St-Michel**.

The closest and largest line of menhirs is the **Alignements du Ménec**, 1km north of Carnac Ville; from place de l'Église, head straight up rue de Courdiec, which is a block north-west of the church. The area is fenced off to protect these 1100 ancient monuments from damage, but they're easily seen from the road or the roof of the nearby Archéoscope.

From here, route de Kerlescan heads east for about 1.5km to the impressive **Alignements de Kermario** (1029 menhirs in 10 lines), a protected site with a specially-built viewing platform. Another 500m farther is the **Alignements de Kerlescan**, a smaller grouping but the only one where you're free to wander.

Between the two alignments is the **Géant de Manio**, a huge dolmen that apparently points the way to the **Quadrilatère**, a group of menhirs arranged in a square. South of the Géant is the small **Tumulus de Kercado** in the grounds of a chateau with the same name. It dates from 3800 BC and was the burial ground of a Neolithic chieftain. During the Revolution it became a hiding place for Breton royalists.

Near Locmariaquer, the big monuments are the **Table des Marchands**, a 30m-long dolmen, and the **Grand Menhir Brisé**, the region's largest menhir, which once stood 20m high but is now lying broken on its side. These two are off the D781 just before the village. The site opens 10 am to 1 pm and 2 to 6 pm, April and May; 10 am to 7 pm, June to September; and 2 to 5 pm, October to mid-December. Admission costs 32FF in July and August, and 25FF the rest of the year (students 15FF year-round).

Just south of Locmariaquer by the sea is the **Dolmen des Pierres Plates**, a 24m-long chamber whose rocky walls are decorated with impressive, multi-shaped engravings.

No buses run to Locmariaquer from Carnac (there's a very infrequent service from Auray in the late morning and late

The Megaliths of Carnac

Megalithic culture arose during the Neolithic period between 4500 and 2000 BC, created by people whose lives were based on agriculture and herding – a radical change from the hunting and gathering of the earlier Palaeolithic era.

The most enduring monuments left by this culture include: menhirs, stones between 1m and 20m high, weighing between two and 200 tonnes and planted upright in the ground (in Breton, 'men' means 'stone' and 'hir' means 'long'); dolmens ('dol' meaning 'table'), stone burial chambers, standing on their own or accessed by a narrow passage, often engraved with symmetrical designs; and tumuli, earth mounds which covered the dolmens. The most spectacularly decorated dolmens and the largest tumuli are on Gavrinis, an island in the Golfe du Morbihan.

While menhirs and dolmens are found in other parts of France and the rest of Europe, their concentration around Carnac has made this region famous. There's a wealth of sites, from solitary menhirs protruding from a field to the most impressive feature, the alignements, which are parallel lines of menhirs running for several kilometres and capped by a cromlech, a semicircle of stones.

The meaning of menhirs – unlike that of dolmens – has not been deciphered, though theories abound. Solitary rocks have been interpreted as being everything from phallic symbols to signposts indicating that a burial ground is nearby. It has been suggested that the alignements have astronomical and religious significance, though the mystery remains unsolved.

afternoon), but it's cyclable and not an impossible hitch along the D781.

Musée de Préhistoire

The Museum of Prehistory (☎ 02 97 52 22 04), 10 place de la Chapelle in Carnac Ville, a block north-east of place de l'Église, chronicles life in and around Carnac from the Palaeolithic and Neolithic eras to the Middle Ages. A free English-language booklet guides you through the two floors.

The museum opens 10 am to noon and 2 to 5 pm daily, October to March; and 10 am to noon and 2 to 6 pm in June and September. In July and August hours are 10 am to 6 pm (closed noon to 2 pm on weekends). Admission costs 30FF (students and children, 15FF) and 25/15FF from October to March.

Archéoscope

Opposite the Alignements du Ménec on route des Alignements is the Archéoscope (☎ 02 97 52 07 49). The glitzy 25-minute show uses special effects to take you back to Neolithic times. It opens 10 am to noon and 2 to 5 pm daily, October to April; and from 10 am to 6.30 pm, May to September. There are English-language shows

at 10.30 am and 2.30 pm. Admission costs 45FF (students/children 30/25FF). A viewing stand on top of the building gives a good view of the menhirs.

Places to Stay

Camping There's a cluster of campgrounds about 2km north of Carnac Ville – head straight up rue de Courdiec past the menhirs until you see the signs. The three-star *Les Pins* (☎ 02 97 52 18 90) opens April to mid-November and charges 22/13FF for adults/children aged under seven plus 42FF for a tent site and parking. Prices rocket in July and August.

In Carnac Plage, the three-star *Camping Nicolas* (☎ 02 97 52 95 42, fax 02 97 52 22 28, blvd de Légenèse), west of the tourist office one block from the sea, opens April to October. Besides the usual facilities it has a laundry. Adults/children pay 27/16FF. A tent site and car cost 33FF.

Hotels Hotels are no bargain in Carnac Ville. About the cheapest is the lovely little *Chez Nous* (☎ 02 97 52 07 28, 5 place de la Chapelle) where a double with shower costs 220FF (240FF in summer). *Auberge Le Râtelier* (☎ 02 97 52 05 04, fax 02 97 52

76 11, 4 Chemin du Douet), a quiet street one block south-west of place de l'Église, has rustic charm, low ceilings and timber furnishings. Doubles with/without shower start at 230/200FF (250FF in summer).

In Carnac Plage, *Hôtel Hoty (*☎ *02 97 52 11 12, fax 02 97 52 80 03, 15 ave de Kermario)*, two blocks east of the tourist office, opens year-round with rooms from 170FF (190FF in summer).

Another cheapie is *La Frégate (*☎ *02 97 52 97 90, 14 allée des Alignements)* (next to the tourist office). It offers rooms at 175FF from April to September.

For a fine ocean view, try *Hôtel Bord de Mer (*☎ *02 97 52 10 84, fax 02 97 52 87 63)* on the beach at 13 blvd de la Plage. It opens Easter to October with singles/doubles with shower from 295/350FF.

Places to Eat
Restaurants In Carnac Ville, *Auberge Le Râtelier* (see Places to Stay) has gourmet *menus*, served in a dining room illuminated by stained-glass windows, for 95/138/185FF (closed February). *Ty-Gwelig (*☎ *02 97 52 92 05, 8 rue de Colary)* has snacks and standard *menus* costing from 52FF while, just south of place de l'Église, *Chez Yannick (*☎ *02 97 52 08 67, 8 rue du Tumulus)* is a lush garden creperie serving galettes priced from 16FF to 49FF. *La Frégate* (see Places to Stay) is very popular, with a lunch *menu* (including wine) for 65FF and dinner ones from 75FF.

Self-Catering On Wednesday and Sunday there's a *produce market* just off place de l'Église in Carnac Ville.

On route de Plouharnel as you enter Carnac Ville, the *Intermarché* opens from 8.30 am to 12.30 pm and 3 to 7 pm (in summer, to 8 pm and Sunday mornings). In Carnac Plage, the *Super U*, 188 ave des Druides about 1km east of the tourist office, keeps similar hours.

Getting There & Away
Bus Cariane Atlantique buses (☎ 02 97 47 29 64) go to Vannes (39FF) and Quiberon (22FF) and stop in Carnac Ville just outside

the *gendarmerie* (police station) on rue St-Cornély, leading into place de l'Église. In Carnac Plage they stop in front of the tourist office. There are also daily buses to Auray (22FF) and Plouharnel (10FF).

Train The nearest train station is in Plouharnel, 4km north-west of Carnac Ville. Plouharnel is on the Auray–Quiberon line which runs in summer only (see Getting There & Away under Quiberon for details). Otherwise you'll have to make your way by bus to/from Auray, 12km to the north-east. SNCF has an office on the 1st floor of the main tourist office in Carnac Plage.

Getting Around
In summer, bikes can be hired in Carnac Ville from Lorcy (☎ 02 97 52 09 73) at 6 rue de Courdiec. In Carnac Plage, a few blocks from the tourist office, you can rent three-speeds for 37FF daily (27/165FF per half-day/week) at Le Randonneur (☎ 02 97 52 02 55), 20 ave des Druides. Cycling on the beach is *interdit* (prohibited).

QUIBERON
postcode 56170 • pop 4600
At the end of a narrow, 14km-long peninsula south-west of Carnac lies Quiberon (Kiberen in Breton), a popular seaside town surrounded by sandy beaches and a wild coastline swept by enormous seas. It's also the port for ferries to Belle Île.

Orientation & Information
One main road, the D768, leads into Quiberon; at the end of it is the train station. From here rue de Verdun winds down to a sheltered bay (Port Maria), which is lined by the town's main beach, the Grande Plage.

The tourist office (☎ 02 97 50 07 84, fax 02 97 30 58 22, @ quiberon@ quiberon.com) is at 14 rue de Verdun, between the train station and the Grande Plage. It opens 9 am to 12.30 pm and 1.30 to 6.30 pm Monday to Saturday, September to June; and 9 am to 8 pm Monday to Saturday, and 10 am to noon and 5 to 8 pm on Sunday, in July and August.

Money There's a Banque CIO just north of the tourist office on rue de Verdun, and a Caisse d'Épargne at place Hoche and rue de Verdun (the latter's open all day Saturday).

Post & Communications The main post office is north-west of the tourist office on place Duchesse Anne. It opens 9 am to noon and 2 to 6 pm weekdays and on Saturday morning, and has a Cyberposte terminal.

Beaches

The wide, sandy beach is *the* attraction in and around Quiberon. The Grande Plage attracts families while bathing spots towards the peninsula's tip are larger and less crowded. The peninsula's rocky western side is known as the Côte Sauvage (Wild Coast). It's great for a windy cycle but too rough for swimming. The spooky, Gothic-style mansion perched on the rocks is the privately-owned Château de Turpault.

Places to Stay

Many hotels and other accommodation in Quiberon close between November and March or April.

Camping The peninsula's 14 camping grounds are very close to the shore, mostly on the east and south-eastern coasts. The closest public site is *Camping Municipal du Rohu* (☎ 02 97 50 27 85, fax 02 97 30 87 20) in Le Petit Rohu, about 4km north-east of the centre. It charges 46FF (including tent, two people and car) or 50FF for a site by the sea (open April to September).

The closer *Camping du Conguel* (☎ 02 97 50 19 11, fax 02 97 30 46 66, blvd de la Teignouse) is south-east of the centre. It opens from April to October and costs 22/15.50FF per adult/child and 81.50FF for a tent site. Prices double in July and August.

Hostels The *Auberge de Jeunesse* (☎ 02 97 50 15 54, fax 02 97 36 90 83, 45 rue du Roch Priol) is in a quiet part of town south-east of the train station. Open May to September, it charges 68FF for a dorm bed and breakfast. A bed in a tent for two in the back garden costs 42FF and you can pitch your own tent for 35FF. The hostel closes 10 am to 6 pm.

Hotels The *Hôtel Bon Accueil* (☎ 02 97 50 07 92, 6 quai de l'Houat) along the waterfront to the west has spacious, well-kept rooms with washbasin/shower costing from 165/195FF. The more upmarket *Hôtel L'Océan* (☎ 02 97 50 07 58, fax 02 97 50 27 81, 7 quai de l'Océan) has rooms with washbasin/shower from 170/240FF in low season and 180/250FF in summer.

Facing the ferry pier, *Hôtel Albatros* (☎ 02 97 50 15 05, fax 02 97 50 27 61, 19 rue de Port Maria) has rooms with shower starting at 270/290FF in low/high season.

Hôtel L'Idéal (☎ 02 97 50 12 72, fax 02 97 50 39 99, 43 rue de Port Haliguen) several blocks south-east of the train station, has singles/doubles starting at 230/250FF.

Places to Eat

Restaurants Creperies, pizzerias and snack stands line quai de Belle Île and rue de Port Maria, while the restaurants in *Hôtel Bon Accueil* and *Hôtel Albatros* (see Places to Stay) have *menus* starting at 82FF and 79FF respectively. The quaint little *Crêperie Duchesse Anne* (☎ 02 97 30 49 33, place Duchesse Anne) does galettes for 10FF to 40FF as well as soups and salads.

Self-Catering The *Stoc* supermarket on rue de Verdun south of the tourist office opens 8.45 am to 12.30 pm and 3 to 7.15 pm Monday to Saturday, and Sunday mornings.

Getting There & Away

Bus Cariane Atlantique buses (☎ 02 97 47 29 64) connect Quiberon with Carnac (22FF), Auray (37FF) and Vannes (55FF, 1¾ hours). Buses stop at the train station and place Hoche near the tourist office and beach.

Train Trains run to/from Quiberon only in July and August. The nearest major train station is Auray, 23km north-east on the Lorient–Paris rail line. In summer, a normal SNCF train to Auray from Quiberon takes 40 minutes and costs 35FF. There's also the much slower *tire-buchon* (corkscrew) train, which costs a flat 15FF between any two stations.

Boat For boats to Belle Île and the smaller islands of Houat and Hoëdic, see Getting There & Away in the following Belle Île section.

Getting Around
Taxi To order a taxi in Quiberon, ring ☎ 02 97 50 11 11.

Bicycle Cycles Lenoble (☎ 02 97 50 18 11), 4 rue de la Poste leading east from place Duchesse Anne, charges 46/65FF per day for touring/mountain bikes, with a deposit of 400/1000FF.

BELLE ÎLE
postcode 56360 • pop 4300 • elevation 45m

Belle Île, about 15km south of Quiberon, is what its name says: a beautiful island. Vauban built a citadel here, but it is far less impressive than the island's natural rock formations.

About 20km long and 9km wide, Belle Île is bounded by relatively calm waters to the east and by the crashing force of the Atlantic to the west. The population swells to 35,000 in summer, but the place rarely feels crowded.

Information
The tourist office (☎ 02 97 31 81 93, fax 02 97 31 56 17, ☺ belle.ile.infos@belle-ile-en.mer.com) is in Le Palais, the main village, on quai Bonnelle to the left as you get off the ferry. It opens 9 am to 7.30 pm Monday to Saturday, July to mid-September. The rest of the year it opens 9.30 am to 6.30 pm. It opens 9 or 10 am to noon or 1 pm on Sunday, year-round.

Things to See & Do
Le Palais is a cosy port dominated by the citadel, which Vauban strengthened in 1682 after centuries of Anglo-French disputes over control of the area. The citadel now houses the **Musée Historique** (☎ 02 97 31

84 17), which examines Belle Île's past. It opens 9.30 am to 6 pm daily, May to October; the rest of the year there's a two-hour break at noon. Admission costs 35FF (students 25FF).

Belle Île's wild southern side has spectacular rock formations, a few small, natural ports and a number of caves. The most famous, **Grotte de l'Apothicairerie** (Cave of the Apothecary's Shop), is an awesome cavern into which the waves roll from two sides.

A pedestrians-only track follows the island's entire coastline. Cyclists can pick up the tourist office's brochure of *sentiers côtiers* (coastal paths).

Places to Stay
Camping There are 11 camping grounds dotted around Belle Île; most are two-star places open only from April or May to September or October. Municipal *Les Glacis* (☎ 02 97 31 41 76) in Le Palais at the base of the citadel charges 18/12FF for adults/children and 12FF for a tent site, and opens April to September.

Hostels & Gîtes d'Étape The *Auberge de Jeunesse* (☎ 02 97 31 81 33, fax 02 97 31 58 38) in Le Palais charges 51FF per person in doubles (70FF with breakfast). For walkers, there's a *gîtes d'étape* along the coast at Port Gouen about 1km south of Le Palais (☎ 02 97 31 55 88, 45FF) and another in Locmaria (☎ 02 97 31 70 48). The latter charges 36FF for a dorm bed and 136FF for a room with three beds.

Hotels & B&Bs The cheapest is *Hôtel La Frégate* (☎ 02 97 31 54 16) open from April to October, facing the dock at quai de l'Acadie, with simple singles/doubles for 120/170FF (230FF with private amenities). The local *chambres chez l'habitant* (B&Bs) are better – ask at the tourist office for a list. Prices average about 250FF for a double room with breakfast.

Places to Eat
For a sumptuous seafood meal, try highly recommended *La Saline* (☎ 02 97 31 84 70, route du Phare) heading out of Le Palais.

Traou-Mad (☎ 02 97 31 84 84, place de la Resistance) is the best place for galettes and crepes.

Getting There & Away

Ferries from Quiberon to Le Palais (on Belle Île) and the smaller islands of Houat and Hoëdic are operated by CMN (☎ 02 97 31 80 01 in Quiberon). The trip to Belle Île takes 45 minutes. Ferries run at least six times daily. Return fares are 107FF (children aged under 12, 66FF); 52FF for bicycles; and from 418FF to 798FF for cars. Passenger prices are the same to Houat and Hoëdic, but services to these car-free islands are less frequent (sometimes only one a day in the low season). The return trip between Houat and Hoëdic costs 50FF (children 33FF).

You can also reach Belle Île from Vannes by boat in summer. Navix (☎ 02 97 46 60 00) charges 155FF for a return (children under 14, 90FF).

Getting Around

In Le Palais, Les Cars Verts (☎ 02 97 31 81 88) on quai de Lysère rents 2CV Citroën *décapotables* (convertibles) for 370FF per day. There are bicycle and scooter rental places near Le Palais' port.

VANNES

postcode 56000 • pop 51,800

Gateway to the islands of the Golfe du Morbihan, Vannes (Gwened in Breton) is a lovely town – small enough to feel intimate, close enough to the sea to taste the salt air and old enough to have an interesting history. The medieval heart of town, full of students from the Vannes branch of the Université de Rennes, is almost as lively as it was centuries ago.

History

In pre-Roman times Vannes was the capital of the Veneti, a Gallic tribe of intrepid sailors who fortified their town with a sturdy wall (a long section of which remains) and built a formidable fleet of sailing ships. The Veneti were conquered by Julius Caesar after a Roman fleet defeated

them in a battle off Brittany's south-eastern coast in the 1st century BC. Under the 9th-century Breton hero Nominoë, the town became the centre of Breton unity. In 1532 the union of the duchy of Brittany with France – achieved through a series of royal marriages – was proclaimed in Vannes.

Orientation

Vannes' small, yacht-filled port sits at the end of a canal-like waterway 1.5km from the gulf's entrance. The Île de Conleau, about 3.5km south of town, is linked to the mainland by a causeway and is sometimes called Presqu'île de Conleau (Conleau Peninsula).

Information

Tourist Offices The tourist office (☎ 02 97 47 24 34, fax 02 97 47 29 49, ✉ office .tourisme.vannes@wanadoo.fr) in a lovely 17th-century half-timbered house at 1 rue Thiers, opens 9 am to 12.30 pm and 2 to 6 pm Monday to Saturday, October to May; and from 9 am to 7 pm the same days, June to September. On Sunday it opens 10 am to 6 pm. Its cheerful staff will book accommodation in the area for a 5FF fee. Its Web site is at www.vannes-bretagne-sud.com.

The tourist office conducts city walks on Wednesday and Saturday at 3 pm, May to mid-September (10.30 am and 3 pm daily in July and August). The tour, which costs 30FF (students 16FF) leaves from the Musée de la Cohue. The office also sells a guide of 36 walks and hikes in the Golfe du Morbihan area (25FF).

Money The Banque de France at 55 ave Victor Hugo exchanges money 8.45 am to 12.15 pm. Banks in the centre include a Société Générale at 25 rue Thiers and a Banque CIO at 2 place du Maréchal Joffre.

Post & Communications The main post office, 2 place de la République, opens 8 am to 7 pm weekdays and on Saturday until noon, and has a Cyberposte terminal. Cyber Café 7, 15 place Général de Gaulle, charges 12.50FF per 15 minutes of Web surfing

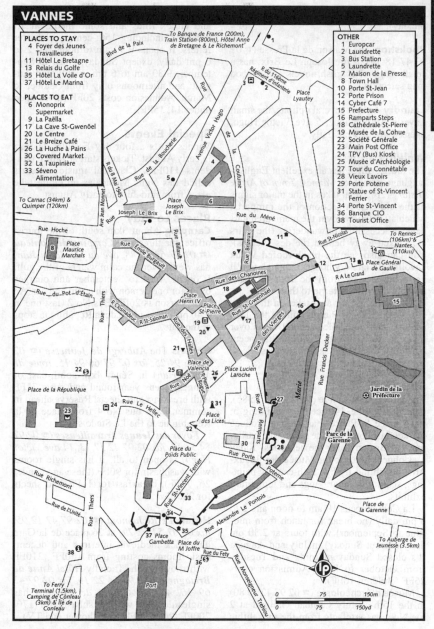

VANNES

PLACES TO STAY
4 Foyer des Jeunes
  Travailleuses
11 Hôtel Le Bretagne
13 Relais du Golfe
35 Hôtel La Voile d'Or
37 Hôtel Le Marina

PLACES TO EAT
6 Monoprix
  Supermarket
9 La Paëlla
17 La Cave St-Gwenöel
20 Le Centre
21 Le Breize Café
26 La Huche à Pains
30 Covered Market
32 La Taupinière
33 Séveno
  Alimentation

OTHER
1 Europcar
2 Laundrette
3 Bus Station
5 Laundrette
7 Maison de la Presse
8 Town Hall
10 Porte St-Jean
12 Porte Prison
14 Cyber Café 7
15 Prefecture
16 Ramparts Steps
18 Cathédrale St-Pierre
19 Musée de la Cohue
22 Société Générale
23 Main Post Office
24 TPV (Bus) Kiosk
25 Musée d'Archéologie
27 Tour du Connétable
28 Vieux Lavoirs
29 Porte Poterne
31 Statue of St-Vincent
  Ferrier
34 Porte St-Vincent
36 Banque CIO
38 Tourist Office

and opens 4 to 11 pm daily (6 to 11 pm on Sunday).

Bookshop The Maison de la Presse (☎ 02 97 47 18 79), 6 rue Joseph Le Brix, has a small range of English novels and a good map selection.

Laundry Among several options, the small Laverie Automatique, 5 ave Victor Hugo, opens 7 am to 9 pm daily.

Walking Tour
The tourist office has an excellent English-language pamphlet, *Vannes: Town of Art & History* (2FF), that takes in the major sights of the **old city**. A section of the **ramparts**, which afford views over the manicured gardens, is accessible for wandering (the stairs are tucked away behind rue des Vierges). You can also see the black-roofed **Vieux Lavoirs** (old laundry houses), though you'll get a better view from the **Tour du Connétable** or **Porte Poterne** to the south.

The walking tour also takes in the massive **Cathédrale St-Pierre**, built in the 13th century and remodeled several times over the centuries. The city's patron, St-Vincent Ferrier, whose statue is in place des Lices, is buried in the northern transept.

Museums
The **Musée de la Cohue** (☎ 02 97 47 35 86), named after the 14th-century building at 9–15 place St-Pierre, has been a produce market, law court and the seat of the parliament of Brittany over the centuries. Today La Cohue is home to the **Musée des Beaux-Arts**, which mostly has 19th-century paintings, sculptures, engravings and temporary exhibits.

La Cohue opens 10 am to noon and 2 to 6 pm daily (no break for lunch from mid-June to September) with tours at 2.30 pm daily (except Sunday) in July and August. It's closed Sunday morning and Tuesday from October to May. Admission costs 26FF (children 16FF).

Musée d'Archéologie (☎ 02 97 42 59 80) in the 15th-century Château Gaillard at 2 rue Noë, has artefacts from the megalithic

sites at Carnac and Locmariaquer, Roman and Greek finds and some medieval art treasures, including 15th-century alabaster reliefs. It opens 9.30 am to noon and 2 to 6 pm daily, except Sunday, April to September; 9.30 am to 6 pm in July and August; and afternoons only from October to March. Admission costs 20FF (those aged under 14, 15FF).

Special Events
Vannes hosts a four-day Festival de Jazz in early August. Tickets start at 140FF (students 110FF). Classical music concerts called Les Nuits Musicales du Golfe take place from mid-July to early August.

Places to Stay
Camping About 3km south of the tourist office, the three-star *Camping de Conleau* (☎ 02 97 63 13 88, ave du Maréchal Juin) has views over the calm waters of the gulf. It opens April to September and charges 69FF for one person with a tent and car. An extra person is 26FF. Bus No 2 (last one at 7.40 pm) from place de la République stops at the gate.

Hostels The *Auberge de Jeunesse* (☎ 02 97 66 94 25, fax 02 97 66 94 15, route de Moustérian) in Séné, 4km south-east of Vannes, opens year-round and costs 71FF with breakfast and sheets. Reserve ahead in summer. Take bus No 4 from place de la République to the Le Stade stop.

Foyer des Jeunes Travailleuses (☎ 02 97 54 33 13, fax 02 97 42 57 73, 14 ave Victor Hugo) is open to all. It has single rooms with washbasin for 90FF (those aged under 26, 75FF), breakfast for 14FF, and sheets for 28FF.

Hotels *Le Richemont* (☎ 02 97 47 12 95, fax 02 97 54 92 79) at 26 place de la Gare has mock medieval interiors and decent, basic rooms costing from 160FF (210FF with shower). The friendly *Hôtel Anne de Bretagne* (☎ 02 97 54 22 19, fax 02 97 42 69 10, 42 rue Olivier de Clisson) has singles/doubles with washbasin for 170/200FF (240/290FF with shower and TV).

The comfortable *Hôtel Le Marina* (☎ 02 97 47 22 81, fax 02 97 47 00 34, 4 place Gambetta) has relaxing, modern rooms with views over the marina and the crowded cafes below. Singles/doubles start at 190FF (260/280FF with private shower and toilet). *Hôtel La Voile d'Or* (☎ 02 97 42 71 81, fax 02 97 42 42 95, 1 place Gambetta) has doubles with washbasin for 160FF (220FF with shower).

Outside the old city walls, the very tidy *Hôtel Le Bretagne* (☎ 02 97 47 20 21, fax 02 97 47 90 78, 36 rue du Méné) has singles/doubles with shower from 180FF. The *Relais du Golfe* (☎ 02 97 47 14 74, fax 02 97 42 52 28, place Général de Gaulle) has rooms from 150FF with washbasin (from 180FF with shower).

Places to Eat

Restaurants Hidden under a medieval turret, popular *La Taupinière* (☎ 02 97 42 57 82, 9 place des Lices) offers crepes and galettes from 8FF to 40FF (closed on Monday).

The warm atmosphere and the crepes of *La Cave St-Gwenöel* (☎ 02 97 47 47 94, 23 rue St-Gwenhael) come highly recommended. It opens lunch and dinner (closed Sunday and Monday).

Popular *La Paëlla* (☎ 02 97 40 70 75, 7 rue Brizeux) in the ancient townhouse, serves plates of its namesake (starting at 47FF) and jugs of sangria (from 32FF). It's closed Sunday and Monday.

Le Centre (☎ 02 97 54 25 14, 7 place St-Pierre), has a standard, three-course menu that's great value at 56FF. **Le Breizh Caffé** (13 rue des Halles) goes way beyond crepes and galettes, with Breton specialities starting at 50FF.

Self-Catering On Wednesday and Saturday mornings, a *produce market* takes over place du Poids Public and the surrounding area. Fresh meat and fish are sold in the *covered market* round the corner.

The *Monoprix (1 place Joseph Le Brix)* has a *boulangerie* and an upstairs grocery section. It opens 8.35 am to 8.30 pm Monday to Saturday. *Séveno Alimentation (12 rue St-Vincent Ferrier)* also opens 10 am to noon on Sunday.

La Huche à Pains (☎ 02 97 47 23 76, 23 place des Lices) is a popular patisserie for Breton pastries such as *kouign amman*.

Getting There & Away

Bus CTM buses (☎ 02 97 01 22 10) cover destinations in Morbihan including Port Navalo (35FF), Ploërmel (47FF) and Pontivy (48FF) . They leave from the parking lot opposite the train station.

Cariane Atlantique buses Nos 23 and 24 go via Auray to Carnac (39FF, 1¼ hours, four daily) and on to Plouharnel (42FF) and Quiberon (52FF, 1¾ hours). The train is cheaper on some routes (eg, Auray or Nantes).

Train Destinations from Vannes include Rennes (98FF, 1½ hours) to Paris' Gare Montparnasse (335FF, 3½ hours, three daily), Auray (21FF, 12 minutes), Nantes (101FF, 1¼ hours, six daily and Quimper (94FF, 1¼ hours, six daily). For details on trains to Quiberon, see Getting There & Away in that section.

Car ADA (☎ 02 97 42 59 10) and Europcar (☎ 02 97 42 43 43) both have offices in the train station.

Getting Around

Bus TPV runs seven city bus lines till 8.15 pm, with limited service on Sunday. A single ticket costs 6.90FF (48FF for a carnet of 10). Bus Nos 3 and 4 link the train station with place de la République.

Taxi To order a taxi, ring ☎ 02 97 54 34 34.

Bicycle Bikes can be hired in summer from the train station luggage office for 45FF a day (slightly more in July and August) plus a 500FF deposit.

AROUND VANNES
Golfe du Morbihan Islands

There are about 40 inhabited islands in the Golfe du Morbihan, most privately owned by artists, actors and the like.

BRITTANY

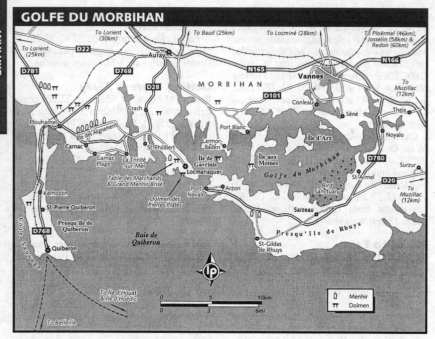

GOLFE DU MORBIHAN

The two largest islands, **Île d'Arz** and **Île aux Moines**, are home to several small villages. Though there's little on them apart from palm groves and beaches, they're popular day trips from Vannes.

Between Easter and October, two boats daily (at 10 and 11.30 am) operated by Navix (☎ 02 97 46 60 00) and stopping at both islands leave from the ferry terminal at the end of ave Maréchal de Lattre de Tassigny in Vannes (take bus No 2 to Parc du Golfe). Return fare is 160FF (those aged under 14, 105FF). Boats calling at just one island sail at 9.30 and 10 am and cost 125/80FF. La Compagnie des Îles (☎ 02 97 46 18 19) charges similar fares.

Navix also runs boats to Belle Île south of Quiberon (see Belle Île later in this chapter). Return fare is 155FF (children 95FF). There are regular ferries to both islands year-round. To Île d'Arz, boats operated by Le Didroux (☎ 02 97 66 92 06) leave from Île de Conleau at least 11 times daily. To Île

aux Moines, boats owned by Société Izenah (☎ 02 97 26 31 45) sail from Port Blanc, 13km south-west of Vannes, about every half an hour between 7 am and 10 pm in summer (8 pm at other times). The fare to Île aux Moines is 21FF (children aged up to 10, 11FF).

Eastern & Central Brittany

Eastern Brittany, encompassing the inland portion of the département of Ille-et-Vilaine, has retained little of the region's traditional way of life. Rennes, the capital of Ille-et-Vilaine and of Brittany as a whole, hardly feels Breton but serves as a useful transport centre.

Parts of central Brittany, split between the departments of Côtes d'Armor (to the north) and Morbihan (to the south), are no more Breton than Rennes. But the Forêt de Paimpont (or Brocéliande), where King Arthur and his court once held sway (see the boxed text 'King Arthur' earlier in this chapter), is a wonderful place to explore.

To the south-west is Josselin, a picturesque little town with a stunning 14th-century chateau.

JOSSELIN

postcode 56120 • pop 2400 • elevation 58m
The picturesque if somewhat touristy town of Josselin, 43km north-east of Vannes, was the seat of a dynastic line of counts for several centuries in the Middle Ages. They built the large chateau, which hosted many of the dukes of Brittany during their wanderings through the duchy. The best time to visit Josselin is Bastille Day (14 July), when the entire town dresses up for the Festival Médiéval.

Orientation & Information

Josselin lies on the River Oust. The centre of the village is place Notre Dame, a beautiful square of 16th-century half-timbered houses. The shop-lined rue Olivier de Clisson runs north from the square.

The tourist office (☎ 02 97 22 36 43, fax 02 97 22 20 44, @ ot.josselin@wanadoo.fr) on place de la Congrégation opens 10 am to noon and 2 to 6 pm daily (closed Monday morning and Saturday afternoon from November to March).

There's a Caisse d'Épargne at 14 rue Olivier de Clisson (closed Monday). The main post office, a few doors down at No 10, opens 8 am to noon and 2 to 5 pm weekdays, and on Saturday morning.

Things to See & Do

The **Basilique Notre Dame du Roncier**, parts of which date from the 12th century, is on place Notre Dame. It contains some superb 15th- and 16th-century stained glass on the southern wall. In the chapel on the north-eastern side of the choir is the tomb of Olivier de Clisson, high constable (*connétable*) of France who fortified the chateau during the Hundred Years' War in the late 14th century.

The **Château de Josselin** (☎ 02 97 22 36 45), south-west of the tourist office down rue du Château, was built in the 12th century and retains four of its original round towers. The chateau's rooms, most of which were restored in the 19th century, are open 10 am to 6 pm daily in July and August, and 2 to 6 pm in June and September. In April, May and October it opens afternoons only on Wednesday, Saturday and Sunday. Admission costs 33FF (students and those aged up to 14 years, 18FF).

Places to Stay & Eat

The *Camping du Bas de la Lande* (☎ 02 97 22 22 20, fax 02 97 73 93 85), about 2km south-west of the centre and open May to September, charges 20/10/18/13FF per adult/child/tent/car. There's no hostel in Josselin, but the village-run *gîte d'étape* (☎ 02 97 22 21 69) south-east of the chateau by the River Oust has dormitory beds for 45FF and stays open all year.

Hôtel de France (☎ 02 97 22 23 06, fax 02 97 22 35 78, 6 place Notre Dame) has doubles with shower costing from 220FF (270FF in summer).

Menus at *Hôtel de France* start at 81FF. The *Crêperie Grill Sarrazine* (☎ 02 97 22 37 80, 51 rue Glatinier) really packs in the locals. Lunch and dinner *menus* start at 59FF, galettes at 37FF and salads at 37FF.

Getting There & Away

Cariane Atlantique buses (☎ 02 97 47 29 64) has two to four buses daily to/from Rennes (58FF, 1½ hours) and Vannes (44FF, one hour). Buses to/from Rennes also call at Ploërmel (17FF, 20 minutes), 13km south-east, which has the closest train station to Josselin.

FORÊT DE PAIMPONT

The Paimpont Forest is about 40km south-west of Rennes. It was here that the young Arthur supposedly received the sword Excalibur from the fairy Vivian, the mysterious Lady of the Lake and later Merlin's mistress. Visitors still come here in search of the spring of eternal youth, where the magician first met his lover.

The best base for exploring the Forêt de Paimpont is the village of **Paimpont**, whose tourist office (☎ 02 99 07 84 23) is next to the 12th-century **Église Abbatiale** (Abbey Church). The office opens 10 am to noon and 2 to 6 pm daily, except Tuesday, from February to September. It has a free annotated walking/cycling map of the forest (62km of trails) or you can buy the more complete *Tour de Brocéliande* topoguide covering 162km of trails. On Thursday and Saturday in July and August, there are guided tours of the lower forest (10 am, 15FF) and upper forest (2 pm, 25FF). A guided tour for the whole day costs 35FF.

Places to Stay & Eat

The small *Camping Municipal de Paimpont* (☎ 02 99 07 89 16) near the lake opens from mid-April to September and charges 15/13/5FF per person/tent/car. Two *gîtes d'étape* just outside the village – **Les Forges** (☎ 02 99 06 81 59) and **Trudeau** (☎ 02 99 07 81 40) – charge 50/46FF per person respectively. Trudeau also offers hotel accommodation, with a double including breakfast costing 210FF.

For more comfort, the central *Relais de Brocéliande* (☎ 02 99 07 81 07, fax 02 99 07 80 60) has nice rooms starting at 200FF (250FF with shower) and excellent *menus* from 75FF. For crepes and galettes, try the *Crêperie du Porche* (☎ 04 91 07 81 88).

Getting There & Around

TIV (☎ 02 99 30 87 80) runs buses to/from from Rennes (17FF, one hour, up to seven daily from Monday to Saturday). You can rent bikes for about 50FF per day from Trudeau (see Places to Stay & Eat) or mountain bikes (90FF per day) from Le Brécilien (☎ 02 99 07 81 13), a bar next to the tourist office.

REDON

postcode 35600 • pop 9300 • elevation 10m
Some 65km east of Vannes lies the former inland port of Redon, a sleepy old town bathed by canals at the confluence of the Rivers Oust and Vilaine. Its glory days are past, as indicated by its largely defunct industrial docks, but Redon remains a good launch point for boaters who want to laze their way up and down the Nantes-Brest canal.

Information

The tourist office (☎ 02 99 71 06 04, fax 02 99 71 01 59,✉ tourisme.redon@wanadoo .fr) is at place de la République. It opens 9 am to noon and 2 to 6 pm Monday to Saturday (also Sunday in July and August).

The chief historical draw is the **Abbey St-Sauveur**, a Gothic-Romanesque structure with a curious four-storey belfry, which has stood separate since a fire destroyed the church in the Middle Ages. It houses the tomb of Gilles de Rais, the judge who tried the notorious pirate known as Bluebeard.

Canal Boating

Brittany has some 600km of navigable waterways. The tourist office has a brochure *Les Rivières Océanes* describing 30 canal and river stops in southern Brittany and which details on-shore lodging, restaurants, canoe and bicycle rentals, hikes and other activities.

Among local rental companies, Bretagne Croiseires (☎/fax 02 99 7 108 05), 71 rue de Vannes, lets two- to four-cabin motorboats and barges for six to 12 passengers. Prices range from 2591FF per week in low season (for a two-cabin 9.3m sleeper with cooking and sanitary facilities) to a staggering 12,398FF in high season (for a deluxe 4-cabin, 13m-long vessel). See Canal Boating in the Facts for the Visitor chapter for general details (rental conditions, deposits, boating rules and more).

Those on tighter budgets might try L'île aux Pies (☎ 02 99 91 21 15, fax 02 99 91 32 26) in St-Vincent-sur-Oust, 8km north-west of Redon. It rents out one-person kayaks from 100FF/day and two- to three-person canoes for 155FF/day.

Places to Stay & Eat

The *Hôtel Le France* (☎ 02 99 71 06 11, fax 02 99 72 17 92, quai de Brest) has simple but welcoming singles/doubles overlooking the canal for 100FF (160FF with washbasin, 190FF for nicer ones with private shower)

In the old town south of quai de Brest, *L'Abene* (☎ *02 99 71 25 15, 10 rue du Jeu de Paume)* is a cute little place selling crepes from 9.50FF to 36FF (closed Tuesday). The restaurant in the *Asther Hotel (☎ 99 71 10 91, 14 rue de Douves)* does decent *flammenküches* (Alsatian pizzas), which cost from 41FF.

Getting There & Away

Bus services to Vannes or Rennes are fiddly and involve several changes. Redon has frequent train links to/from Nantes (69FF, 45 minutes), Vannes (51FF, 1¼ hours), Rennes (66FF, 50 minutes) and Paris Gare Montparnasse (317FF, three to four hours via Nantes).

RENNES
postcode 35000 • pop 203,500
• elevation 40m
Rennes, a university centre, has sat at an important crossroads since Roman times. Capital of Brittany since its incorporation into France in the 16th century, the city developed at the junction of the highways linking the northern and western ports of St-Malo and Brest with the former capital, Nantes (see the Atlantic Coast chapter), and the inland city of Le Mans.

Orientation

The city centre is divided by La Vilaine, a river channelled into a cement-lined canal which disappears underground just before the central square, place de la République. The northern area includes the pretty, pedestrianised old city, while the south is garishly modern.

Information

Tourist Offices The main tourist office (☎ 02 99 67 11 11, fax 02 99 67 11 10, ℮ infos@tourisme-rennes.com) is at 11 rue St-Yves. It opens 9 am to 7 pm Monday to Saturday and 11 am to 6 pm on Sunday, April to September. The rest of the year hours are the same, except that it closes at 6 pm Monday to Saturday. Staff will book

local accommodation for a 10FF fee. It's Web site is at www.ville-rennes.fr.

Money The Banque de France at 25 rue de la Visitation changes currency from 8.45 am to noon. There's a Crédit Agricole inside the train station (also open Saturday). The post office also exchanges money.

Post & Communications The main post office at 27 blvd du Colombier opens 8 am to 7 pm weekdays and 8 am to noon on Saturday, and has a Cyberposte terminal.

Cyberspirit, 22 rue de la Visitation, charges 1FF/minute or 50FF/hour of Internet use. It opens 2 to 9 pm on Monday, noon to 9 pm on Tuesday, noon to midnight on Wednesday to Friday and 2 pm to midnight on Saturday.

Laundry Of several options, the laundrette at 23 rue de Penhoët opens from 7 am to 8 pm daily.

Old City

Much of medieval Rennes was gutted by *le grand incendie*, the great fire of 1720 started by a drunken carpenter who accidentally set a pile of shavings alight. The half-timbered houses that survived now make up the old city, Rennes' most picturesque quarter.

Among the prettiest streets are **rue St-Michel** and **rue St-Georges**. The latter intersects the enormous place de la Mairie and place du Palais, site of the 17th-century **Palais du Parlement de Bretagne**, the former seat of the rebellious Breton parliament and more recently, the Palais de Justice. In 1994 the building was destroyed by fire caused by the maritime flares fired by angry fishermen during a protest over income tax rates. It has since been lovingly restored at great expense.

On **rue St-Guillaume**, the superbly carved but crumbling **Maison Du Guesclin** at No 3 was named after a 14th-century Breton warrior. Nearby is the outwardly reserved 17th-century **Cathédrale St-Pierre**, whose golden neoclassical interior comes as a warm surprise. It opens 9 am to noon and 2 to 7 pm.

BRITTANY

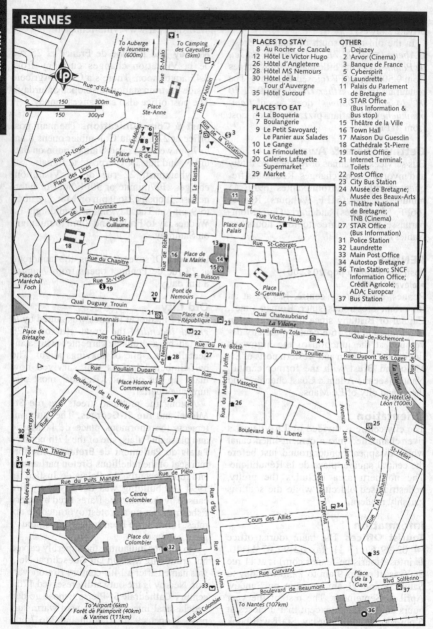

RENNES

To Auberge
de Jeunesse
(600m)

To Camping
des Gayeulles
(3km)

Rue St-Malo

Rue-d'Échange

Rue d'Antrain

Place
Ste-Anne

Rue de la Visitation

0   150   300m
0   150   300yd

Rue-St-Louis

R St-Michel

R de Penhoët

Place
St-Michel

Rue des Lices

Rue Le Bastard

Rue de la Monnaie

Rue St-
Guillaume

Rue R Hoche

Rue Victor Hugo

Place du
Palais

Rue St-Georges

Rue du Chapitre

Rue de Rohan

Place de
la Mairie

Place du
Maréchal
Foch

Rue St-Yves

Rue F Buisson

Place
St-Germain

Quai Duguay Trouin

Pont de
Nemours

Quai Chateaubriand

Quai-Lamennais

Place de la
République

Quai Émile Zola

La Vilaine

Place de
Bretagne

Rue Châlotais

Rue du Pré Botté

Rue Toullier

Rue Dupont des Loges

Rue de Nemours

Poullain Duparc

Rue Jules Simon

Rue Maréchal Joffre

Vasselot

To Hôtel de
Léon (100m)

Boulevard de la Liberté

Place Honoré
Commeurec

Boulevard de la Liberté

Rue Chicogné

Rue de la Tour d'Auvergne

Rue Thiers

Avenue Jean Janvier

Rue St-Hélier

Rue Du Puits Manger

Rue de Plélo

Rue d'Isly

Boulevard Magenta

Rue J M Duhamel

Centre
Colombier

Cours des Alliés

Place du
Colombier

Rue de l'Alma

Rue Gurvand

Place
(de la
Gare)

Blvd Solférino

Boulevard de Beaumont

To Airport (6km)
Forêt de Paimpont (40km)
& Vannes (111km)

To Nantes (107km)

Blvd du Colombier

PLACES TO STAY	OTHER
8 Au Rocher de Cancale	1 Dejazey
12 Hôtel Le Victor Hugo	2 Arvor (Cinema)
26 Hôtel d'Angleterre	3 Banque de France
28 Hôtel MS Nemours	5 Cyberspirit
30 Hôtel de la	6 Laundrette
Tour d'Auvergne	11 Palais du Parlement
35 Hôtel Surcouf	de Bretagne
	13 STAR Office
PLACES TO EAT	(Bus Information &
4 La Boqueria	Bus stop)
7 Boulangerie	15 Théâtre de la Ville
9 Le Petit Savoyard;	16 Town Hall
Le Panier aux Salades	17 Maison Du Guesclin
10 Le Gange	18 Cathédrale St-Pierre
14 La Frimoulette	19 Tourist Office
20 Galeries Lafayette	21 Internet Terminal;
Supermarket	Toilets
29 Market	22 Post Office
	23 City Bus Station
	24 Musée de Bretagne;
	Musée des Beaux-Arts
	25 Théâtre National
	de Bretagne;
	TNB (Cinema)
	27 STAR Office
	(Bus Information)
	31 Police Station
	32 Laundrette
	33 Main Post Office
	34 Autostop Bretagne
	36 Train Station; SNCF
	Information Office;
	Crédit Agricole;
	ADA; Europcar
	37 Bus Station

euro currency converter 10FF = €1.52

Museums

Jointly housed in the city's old university at 20 quai Émile Zola are the **Musée de Bretagne** (☎ 02 99 28 55 84) and the **Musée des Beaux-Arts** (☎ 02 99 28 55 85). The former, with insightful displays on Breton history and culture, is closed for extensive renovation until 2003. Upstairs, the Fine Arts Museum is unexceptional apart from the room devoted to Picasso. It opens 10 am to noon and 2 to 6 pm (closed Tuesday). Admission costs 20FF (children 10FF).

Special Events

Rennes is at its most lively in the first week of July during the Tombées de la Nuit, when the old city is filled with music, theatre and people in medieval costume.

Places to Stay

Camping Rennes' only camping ground is the municipal *Camping des Gayeulles* (☎ 02 99 36 91 22, *rue du Professeur Maurice Audin*) in the Parc des Bois, about 4.5km north-east of the station. It opens April to September and charges 14/12/6FF per person/tent/car. From place de la Mairie, take bus No 3 to the Gayeulles stop.

Hostels The bustling *Auberge de Jeunesse* (☎ 02 99 33 22 33, fax 02 99 59 06 21, *10–12 Canal St-Martin*) is 2.5km northwest of the train station. A bed in a room for three costs 72FF, including breakfast. A single/double costs 118/156FF. Take bus Nos 20 and 18 from the train station or place de la Mairie (last one at about 8 pm); get off at the Pont St-Martin stop.

Hotels The *Hôtel Surcouf* (☎ 02 99 30 59 79, fax 02 99 31 72 71, *13 place de la Gare*) has basic rooms starting at 130FF and 209FF with shower (the latter cost 180FF at weekends). *Hôtel d'Angleterre* (☎ 02 99 79 38 61, fax 02 99 79 43 85, *19 rue du Maréchal-Joffre*) is well-placed between the river and the station with singles/doubles costing from 135/160FF (190/225FF with shower).

Of the few options in the old city, *Au Rocher de Cancale* (☎ 02 99 79 20 83,

10 rue St-Michel), in a half-timbered house in a lively neighbourhood, has rooms from 220FF. It's closed at weekends.

East of the old city, *Hôtel Le Victor Hugo* (☎ *02 99 38 85 33, fax 02 99 36 54 95, 14 rue Victor Hugo)* has a good location with generic-looking singles/doubles with washbasin for 140/180FF and with shower for 220/230FF. The shipshape *Hôtel MS Nemours* (☎ *02 99 78 26 26, fax 02 99 78 25 40, 5 rue de Nemours)* has particularly neat singles/doubles with shower and TV from 240/265FF.

Warm, inviting *Hôtel de la Tour d'Auvergne* (☎ *02 99 30 84 16, 20 blvd de la Tour d'Auvergne)* has basic rooms for 140FF (175FF with shower). Hall showers cost 15FF. *Hôtel de Léon* (☎/fax *02 99 30 55 28, 15 rue de Léon)* is a quirky, art-bedecked place in a quiet part of town. It offers simple but large singles/doubles for 135/165FF (180/190FF with shower). Hall showers cost 18FF.

Places to Eat

Restaurants In the old city, *Le Petit Savoyard* (☎ *02 99 78 21 29, 13 rue de Penhoët)* does fondues and a lunch-only *menu* for 56FF. *Le Panier aux Salades* (☎ *02 99 79 20 97)*, next door at No 15, has salads starting at 36FF.

La Boqueria (☎ *02 99 84 02 02, 34 rue de la Visitation)* does tasty tapas for 10FF and 15FF, paella from 35FF and a variety of seafood dishes. Wash it all down with Spanish beer or Breton cider.

In the corridor behind the Théâtre de la Ville on place de la Mairie, *La Frimoulette* (☎ *02 99 79 44 63)* has 16 types of mussels and *menus* of these crustaceans for 55FF and 71FF (closed Sunday and Monday evening). Indian restaurant *Le Gange* (☎ *02 99 30 18 37, 34 place des Lices)*, serves highly-touted *menus* from 85FF and a wide variety of vegetarian dishes.

Lovely rue St-Georges is *the* street for indulging in crepes, pizza and ethnic food from Indian to Brazilian.

Self-Catering There's a large covered *market hall* on place Honoré Commeurec that operates 7 am to 6.30 pm Monday to Saturday. A *market* is held at place des Lices on Saturday morning.

The *Galeries Lafayette* on quai Duguay Trouin has a grocery section open 9am to 8pm Monday to Saturday. For fresh bread on Sunday, the *boulangerie* on rue St-Michel opens 7 am to 1 pm and 2 to 8 pm.

Entertainment
Cinema Nondubbed films are screened at both *Arvor* (☎ *02 99 38 72 40, 29 rue d'Antrain*) and *TNB* (☎ *02 99 30 88 88, 1 rue St-Hélier*) at the Théâtre National de Bretagne. *Ciné Spectacles* is the free weekly cinema guide.

Rue St-Malo has lots of music bars and cafes, including *Dejazey* (☎ *02 99 38 70 72*) at No 54, which has live jazz several nights a week.

Getting There & Away
Air Rennes' St-Jacques airport (☎ 02 99 29 60 00) is about 6km south-west of town.

Bus Several lines operate from Rennes. Cariane Atlantique offers services to Nantes (95FF, two hours) and Josselin (58FF, 1¼ hours). TAE buses go to Dinan (50FF, 1¼ hours) and Dinard (67FF, 1¾ hours); Courriers Bretons has buses to Pontorson (58.50FF, one hour) and Mont St-Michel (64FF, 1¼ hours). TIV serves Fougères (50FF, one hour) and Paimpont (17FF, 25 minutes).

Train Rennes' modern train station has banks, shops and a large SNCF information office. Destinations with frequent services include Paris' Gare Montparnasse by TGV (289FF, two hours), St-Malo (70FF, one hour), Vannes (98FF, one hour), Nantes (140FF, two hours), Brest (165FF, 2½ hours) and Quimper (168FF, 2½ hours).

Car Both ADA (☎ 02 99 38 59 88) and Europcar (☎ 02 99 51 60 61) have offices at the train station.

Hitching Autostop Bretagne (☎ 02 99 67 34 67), 6 cours des Alliés, matches up hitchers and drivers for a fee. It opens 10 am to 6 pm Monday to Saturday. Regular offers include Paris (100FF) and Amsterdam (214FF), plus the per-kilometre charge of 0.23FF.

Getting Around
To/From the Airport St-Jacques airport is connected to the city by bus No 57, which stops at place de la République.

Bus Tickets for local STAR buses cost 6.50FF and a carnet of 10 is 49.50FF. To reach place de la République from the station, take bus No 1, 17 or 20. From 2002 a new metro line, VAL, will link the northwest of the city to the south-east via place de la République and the train station.

Taxi Ring (☎ 02 99 30 79 79) for a taxi.

Champagne

Champagne, known in Roman times as Campania (literally, 'Land of Plains'), is a largely agricultural region famed around the world for the sparkling wines that have been made here since the days of Dom Pérignon. According to French law, only bubbly from very limited parts of the region – grown, aged and bottled according to the strictest standards – can be labelled as champagne.

The production of the celebrated wine takes place mainly in two departments: Marne, whose metropolis is the 'Coronation City' of Reims; and the less prestigious Aube, whose prefecture is the ancient and picturesque city of Troyes. The town of Épernay, a bit south of Reims, is the de facto capital of champagne (the drink) and is the best place to head for *dégustation* (tasting). The Route Touristique du Champagne (Champagne Tourist Route) wends its way through the many vineyards of the region.

For a different way to see the region, Champagne Air Show (☎ 03 26 87 89 12, fax 03 26 87 89 14), based at 9 rue Thiers in Reims, runs hot-air balloon flights all over Champagne.

REIMS
postcode 51100 • pop 206,000
• elevation 85m

Meticulously reconstructed after the first and second world wars, Reims is a neat and orderly city with wide avenues and well-tended parks. Together with Épernay, it is the most important centre of champagne production.

After Clovis I, founder of the Frankish kingdom, was baptised here in AD 496, Reims (rhymes with the French pronunciation of *prince*; often anglicised as Rheims) became the traditional site of French coronations. From 816 to 1825, 34 sovereigns, among them 25 kings – including Charles VII, crowned here on 17 July 1429 with Joan of Arc at his side – began their reigns

Highlights

- **Reims and Épernay** – inhale the potent odours of maturing champagne (and mould) on a cellar tour
- **Route Touristique du Champagne** – explore the region's vineyards on this scenic drive
- **Verzy** – consider the contortions of the dwarf-mutant beech trees
- **Troyes** – admire the handtools and modern art in the medieval old city's museums.

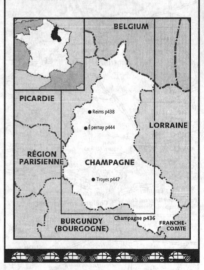

as Christian rulers in the city's famed cathedral.

The main streets of Reims' commercial centre, the area north-west of the cathedral, are rue Carnot, rue de Vesle, rue Condorcet and, for shopping, rue de Talleyrand. The train station is about 1km north-west of the cathedral, across Square Colbert from place Drouet d'Erlon, the city's major nightlife centre. Virtually every street in the city centre is one way.

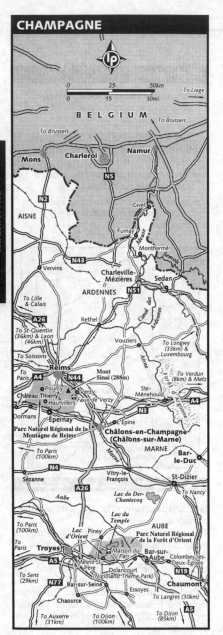

Information

Tourist Office The tourist office (☎ 03 26 77 45 25, fax 03 26 77 45 27, ✉ visitreims @netvia.net), at 2 rue Guillaume de Machault, opens from 9 am to 6 pm (10 am to 5 pm on Sunday and holidays). From mid-April to mid-October, closing time is one hour later. Same-day reservations at local hotels are free. You can pick up brochures on Champagne and, usually, the free weekly *Les Rendez-Vous Rémois*, which lists concerts, films and other cultural events. See the Web site at www .tourisme.fr/reims.

Money The Banque de France, on rue Docteur Jacquin (opposite the building marked 'Galeries Rémoises'), changes money on weekdays from 8.45 am to 12.20 pm. There's a cluster of commercial banks, most open Monday to Friday, on rue Carnot; several more can be found at the southern end of place Drouet d'Erlon. The tourist office changes money on Saturday, Sunday and holidays.

Post & Communications The branch post office at 2 rue Cérès, through the arches on the east side of place Royale, is open weekdays from 8.30 am to 6 pm and Saturday from 8 am to noon. Currency exchange and a Cyberposte are available.

Laundry The laundrettes at 59 rue Chanzy and 129 rue de Vesle are both open from 7 am to at least 9 pm.

Public Squares

Reims' main nightlife centre is **place Drouet d'Erlon**, a huge pedestrianised square that has runway lights down the middle and places to eat and drink along the sides. Just south-east of the **fountain** is a shopping arcade. At rue Condorcet, the 12th- to 14th-century **Église St-Jacques** has some pretty awful post-war stained glass.

The **Porte de Mars**, a Roman triumphal arch from the 3rd century AD, is in a small park at **place de la République**.

In the town centre, the mid-18th-century **place Royale**, graced by a statue of Louis XV and still crisscrossed by the old tram tracks, is surrounded by neoclassical arcades.

At **place du Forum**, excavations have uncovered the **Cryptoportique**, a Roman 3rd-century gallery that was used for grain storage. The interior can be visited from mid-June to mid-September; hours are 2 to 5 pm (closed Monday).

Churches & Museums

For centuries the traditional site of French coronations, **Cathédrale Notre Dame** was begun in 1211 on a site occupied by churches since the 5th century and was mostly completed 100 years later. Badly damaged (like the whole city) by artillery and fire during WWI, it was restored with funds donated largely by John D Rockefeller; reconsecration took place in 1938, just in time for the next war. The long (138m) and relatively narrow structure is noted for its lightness, elegance and harmony, but can hardly be called sublime and is more interesting for its history than for its heavily restored architectural features. The finest stained glass is in the western facade's 12-petalled **great rose window** and its smaller downstairs neighbour. There's a window by Chagall in the axial chapel (directly behind the high altar) and, two chapels to the left, a statue of Joan of Arc. Along the north aisle, near the Flamboyant Gothic organ case (15th and 18th centuries), is a 15th-century **astronomical clock**, restored after WWI. The interior of the western facade is decorated with 120 statues in niches, some of them badly damaged. The cathedral opens 7.30 am to 7.30 pm, except during services. In July (at 11 pm) and August (at 10 pm) there is an impressive (and free) 30-minute sound-and-light show inside the cathedral on Friday and Saturday nights.

The **Palais du Tau** (☎ 03 26 47 81 79), a former archbishop's residence constructed in 1690, was once the abode of princes about to be crowned king. It is now a museum housing exceptional statues, ritual objects and tapestries (some displayed in the impressive Salle du Tau) from the cathedral. Opening hours are 9.30 am to 12.30 pm and

2 to 6 pm (to 6.30 pm in July and August, when there's no midday closure). From mid-November to mid-March, hours are 10 am to noon and 2 to 5 pm (6 pm at weekends). Admission costs 32FF (those aged 17 or under free, teachers and those aged 18 to 25 21FF). The entrance is inside the cathedral, to the right of the high altar (during Mass entry is via the courtyard).

Named after Remigius, the bishop who baptised Clovis and 3000 Frankish warriors in the 5th century, the 121m-long **Basilique St-Rémi** is worn but stunning. Once a Benedictine abbey church, its Romanesque nave and transept date mainly from the mid-11th century. The choir (1162–90) is in the early Gothic style, with a large triforium gallery and tiny clerestory windows. The 12th-century-style chandelier has 96 candles, one for each year of the life of St Rémi, whose tomb (in the choir) is marked by a mausoleum from the mid-17th century. The basilica is about 1.5km south-east of the tourist office at place St Rémi; to get there take bus A, F or I to the St-Rémi or St-Timothée stops.

Just 100m from the western facade of Basilique St-Rémi, **Musée St-Rémi** (☎ 03 26 85 23 36), 53 rue Simon, displays archaeological items, tapestries and 16th- to 19th-century weapons. It is open daily from 2 to 6 pm (7 pm on weekends). Admission costs 10FF (students free).

Nazi Germany capitulated on 7 May 1945 in US General Dwight D Eisenhower's war room, now a museum (☎ 03 26 47 84 19) known as the **Salle de Reddition** (Surrender Room). The original battle maps are still affixed to the walls. Located inside a school at 12 rue Franklin Roosevelt, it is open from 10 am to noon and 2 to 6 pm (closed Tuesday). Admission costs 10FF (students free).

The **Musée des Beaux-Arts** (☎ 03 26 47 28 44), 8 rue Chanzy, has an interesting collection of paintings from the Renaissance onward. It opens 10.30 am (10 am at the weekend) to noon and 2 to 6 pm (closed Tuesday). Admission costs 10FF (students free). The **Musée-Hôtel Le Vergeur** (☎ 03 26 47 20 75), 36 place du Forum, houses a

CHAMPAGNE

collection of furniture and art objects. It opens 2 to 6 pm (closed Monday), and admission costs 25FF.

The **Chapelle Foujita** (☎ 03 26 40 06 96), 33 rue du Champ de Mars, is a small church set in a garden, whose neo-Romanesque frescoes were created in 1966 by the Japanese-born artist Léonard Foujita. It can be visited from May to October; it is open 2 to 6 pm daily except Wednesday. Admission costs 10FF (free on Saturday).

About 1.5km south-east of the cathedral, the **Musée d'Automobiles** (☎ 03 26 82 83 84), 84 ave Georges Clemenceau, displays 140 motor vehicles from the 1920s to the 1970s. It opens 10 am to noon and 2 to 6 pm (no midday closure at the weekend; closed Tuesday). Admission costs 35FF (25FF for those aged 12 to 18, 15FF for children aged under 12). To get there, take bus D to the Boussinesq stop.

Fort de la Pompelle, a WWI fortress about 5km south-east of Reims on the N44 (towards Châlons-en-Champagne), now houses a military museum (☎ 03 26 49 11 85). Admission costs 20FF (students 10FF).

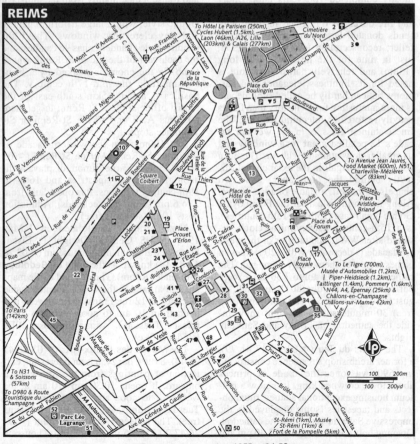

REIMS

It is open daily except Tuesday from 10 am to 5 pm (7 pm from April to October; closed for two weeks around New Year).

Champagne Cellars

The musty *caves* (cellars) and dusty bottles of about a dozen Reims-area champagne houses can be visited on guided tours that include explanations of how champagne is made – details are available at the tourist office. Places that charge fees generally don't require advance reservations except for groups. Tours listed below all include a tasting session at the end.

Mumm (☎ 03 26 49 59 70), 34 rue du Champ de Mars, is one of the largest producers in Reims, with an output of some 7.8 million bottles a year. Its 45-minute cellar tours (25FF, those aged under 16 free), often held in English, begin daily, year-round, from 9 to 11 am and 2 to 5 pm (closed weekend mornings from November to February). To get there, take bus K to the Justice stop.

Taittinger (☎ 03 26 85 84 33), 9 place St-Niçaise, is 1.5km south-east of the cathedral. The one-hour tours (35FF, children aged under 12 free), in English when there's demand, include a video and a visit to the 13th-century cellars. They begin on weekdays from 10 to 11.50 am and 2.20 to 4.20 pm, and on weekends from 9.30 to 10.50 am and 2.20 to 4.50 pm (closed on weekends from December to February). To get there, take bus A to the St-Timothée stop.

Pommery (☎ 03 26 61 62 56) is headquartered on a hilltop at 5 place du Général Gouraud, 1.8km south-east of the cathedral. From April to mid-November, 45-minute tours (in English approximately once an hour – call for details) depart daily every 20 or 30 minutes from 10.20 am to 6 pm. The rest of the year they take place Monday to Friday from 10.20 am to about 5 pm. The charge is 40FF (20FF for students but without the tasting session; free for children 13 and under). Weekends can get crowded so you might want to make reservations. Bus A will take you to the St-Timothée stop, from where you can either take bus R to the Gouraud stop or walk east about 600m.

Champagne meets Disneyland at **Piper-Heidsieck** (☎ 03 26 84 43 44), 51 blvd Henry Vasnier, which is 1.2km south-east of the cathedral. For 40FF (children aged seven to 16, 20FF), you get a 20-minute tour

CHAMPAGNE

REIMS

PLACES TO STAY		OTHER		25	Fountain
8	Hôtel Alsace	49	Le Chamois; Cactus Café	26	Shopping Arcade
12	Grand Hôtel de l'Univers			27	Merry-Go-Round
21	Grand Hôtel du Nord	**OTHER**		29	La Boutique TUR
43	Hôtel Thillois	1	Salle de la Reddition		(Bus Information)
44	Hôtel Au Bon Accueil	2	Chapelle Foujita	30	Grand Théâtre
47	Le Bon Moine	3	Mumm Champagne Cellar	31	Théâtre Bus Hub
48	Hôtel de la Cathédral	4	Main Post Office	32	Palais de Justice
51	Centre International de	6	Porte de Mars	33	Tourist Office
	Séjour	9	ADA; National-Citer; Rent-a-	34	Cathédrale Notre Dame
			Car Système	35	Palais du Tau
PLACES TO EAT		10	Train Station	36	Laundrette
5	Food Market	11	Intercity Bus Stops	38	Bibliothèque Médiathèque
7	Brasserie Le Boulingrin	13	Town Hall		(Library)
20	Le Continental	14	Banque de France	39	Musée des Beaux-Arts
23	L'Apostrophe	15	Musée-Hôtel Le Vergeur	40	Église St-Jacques
24	The Glue Pot	16	Cryptoportique	45	Centre des Congrès
28	Monoprix Supermarket	17	Branch Post Office		(Convention Centre)
37	Le Bouchon Champenois	18	Intercity Bus Stops	46	Laundrette
41	Waïda	19	Cinéma Gaumont	50	Synagogue (1879)
42	Il Colosseo	22	Le Cirque (Cultural Events	52	Comédie de Reims (Theatre)
			Venue)		

euro currency converter €1 = 6.56FF

with automated commentary (in English). There are regular tours from 9 to 11.45 am and 2 to 5.15 pm. To get there by bus, take line A to the St-Timothée stop and either walk about 500m north-east or take bus R to the Henry Vasnier stop.

Organised Tours

The tourist office's three-hour Walkman tour of the area around the cathedral, available in six languages, costs 50FF for one or two people. In July and August there are often English-language guided tours of the cathedral (35FF) at 2.30 pm.

Special Events

During the first or second week of June, the four-day Les Sacres du Folklore, one of northern France's most colourful folk festivals, takes place concurrently with Les Fêtes Johanniques, a medieval celebration that re-enacts Joan of Arc's arrival in Reims.

In July and August, Les Flâneries Musicales d'Été brings over 120 concerts (most free) to historic venues all over town.

Places to Stay – Budget

Reims' hotels, at their fullest in July and August, offer good value for money.

Hostels The 150-bed *Centre International de Séjour (CIS;* ☎ 03 26 40 52 60, fax 03 26 47 35 70, allée Polonceau) is in Parc Léo Lagrange, a bit over 1km west of the cathedral (just over the canal). Beds in rooms sleeping two to four cost 59FF (79FF with shower and toilet); singles are 89FF (129FF with shower and toilet). Breakfast costs 18FF. Reception is open 24 hours. To get there take bus B, K or N to the Comédie stop or bus H to the Pont De Gaulle stop.

Hotels The friendly *Hôtel Alsace* (☎ 03 26 47 44 08, fax 03 26 47 44 52, 6 rue du Général Sarrail) has large and pleasant singles/doubles/triples starting at 130/145/160FF (185/205/255FF with shower and toilet). Reception is closed on Sunday after noon.

The 29-room *Hôtel Au Bon Accueil* (☎ 03 26 88 55 74, 31 rue de Thillois) doesn't quite live up to its name, but it does offer clean, decent singles/doubles from 80/140FF (200FF with shower and toilet). Hall showers are 10FF. At the quiet, 19-room *Hôtel Thillois* (☎ 03 26 40 65 65, 17 rue de Thillois), singles/doubles that are nothing to write home about start at 125/145FF (155/175FF with shower and toilet). There are no hall showers; toilets are on the landing. Reception is closed on Sunday morning and, sometimes, on Sunday afternoon. To get to both these places by car, take rue Buirette and turn south onto rue Jeanne d'Arc.

About 900m north-east of the train station, the quiet, 22-room *Hôtel Le Parisien* (☎ 03 26 47 32 89, fax 03 26 86 81 39, 3 rue Périn) – next to 73 ave de Laon – has clean, serviceable doubles from 130FF (180FF with shower). By bus, take line A or C to the St-Thomas stop. Free street parking is available.

Places to Stay – Mid-Range

The family-run, two-star *Hôtel de la Cathédrale* (☎ 03 26 47 28 46, fax 03 26 88 65 81, 20 rue Libergier), 250m west of the cathedral, has 17 tidy, tasteful rooms with high ceilings starting at 305/450FF for two/four people. The recently remodelled singles/doubles of the two-star, 10-room *Le Bon Moine* (☎ 03 26 47 33 64, fax 03 26 40 43 87, 14 rue des Capucins) go for 250/320FF. Except in July and August, reception is closed on Sunday from noon to 4 pm and after 8 pm.

The two- and three-star hotels on lively place Drouet d'Erlon include the old-time *Grand Hôtel du Nord* (☎ 03 26 47 39 03, fax 03 26 40 92 26, 75 place Drouet d'Erlon), a 50-room establishment whose spacious doubles – some with great views – go for 295FF. Directly opposite the train station, the 42-room, three-star *Grand Hôtel de l'Univers* (☎ 03 26 88 68 08, fax 03 26 40 95 61, ✉ hotel-univers@ebc.net, 41 blvd Foch) has spacious, modern doubles starting at 375FF (415FF from mid-April to October).

Places to Eat

Place Drouet d'Erlon is lined with pizzerias, brasseries, cafés, pubs and sandwich places.

Restaurants – French Locals flock to the *Hôtel Alsace* (see Places to Stay) for one of the best lunch deals in town: a generous, four-course, bistro-style *menu* for just 58FF (available Monday to Saturday).

Le Bouchon Champenois (☎ 03 26 88 50 35, 45 rue Chanzy) specialises in the cuisine of Champagne, often prepared with sauces based on champagne or ratafia (an almond-flavoured aperitif). The *menus* start at 75FF (closed Sunday and Monday). At *Le Bon Moine* (☎ 03 26 47 33 64, 14 rue des Capucins), traditional French and Champenois *menus* cost 59FF, 85FF and 135FF (closed Sunday).

Le Chamois (☎ 03 26 88 69 75, 45 rue des Capucins) serves salads (45FF) and Savoyard specialities, including *pierre à feu* (meat you cook yourself on a hot volcanic rock; 75FF) and fondue (67FF for cheese, 82FF for beef) amid rustic Alpine décor (closed Sunday lunchtime and Wednesday).

The original 1920s décor, including an old-time zinc bar, make a meal at *Brasserie Le Boulingrin* (☎ 03 26 40 96 22, 48 rue de Mars) a mini-trip back in time. Fish and meat mains cost 69FF to 99FF (closed Sunday). *Le Continental* (☎ 03 26 47 01 47, 95 place Drouet d'Erlon), built in the early 20th century, has panoramic views. Its French, regional and seafood *menus* cost from 79FF to 198FF. It's open daily, with dinner service until 11.30 pm. Down the block, *L'Apostrophe* (☎ 03 26 79 19 89, 59 place Drouet d'Erlon) is a cafe-brasserie that serves generous portions of very French intellectual pretension along with its very French mains (82FF to 105FF) and salads (44FF to 88FF).

Restaurants – Other Reached through an ornate, dilapidated former theatre facade, *Il Colosseo* (☎ 03 26 47 68 50, 9 rue de Thillois) serves pizzas and pastas for 40FF to 63FF as well as salads for 45FF to 56FF. It is closed Sunday and Monday.

Only the French genius for eclecticism could have created *The Glue Pot* (☎ 03 26

47 36 46, 49 place Drouet d'Erlon), an Irish pub and Tex-Mex restaurant that serves pizzas to patrons seated on purple banquettes. There are several *East-Asian restaurants* on rue de Thillois (near Hôtel Au Bon Accueil) and the parallel rue de Vesle (near the laundrette).

For something light, you might try *Waïda* (☎ 03 26 47 44 49, 5 place Drouet d'Erlon), a pâtisserie and tea room.

Self-Catering There are *food markets* at place du Boulingrin on Wednesday and Saturday (until 2 pm) and on ave Jean Jaurès (east of place Aristide Briand) on Sunday (until 1 pm).

The *Monoprix* supermarket (1 rue de Talleyrand) opens 8.30 am to 9 pm Monday to Saturday.

Entertainment

Brasseries and cafes with terraces line brightly lit place Drouet d'Erlon, the focal point of Reims' nightlife; some places stay open as late as 3 am. *Cinéma Gaumont* (☎ 03 26 47 32 02, 72 place Drouet d'Erlon) screens a nondubbed film every Tuesday.

Le Tigre (☎ 03 26 82 64 00, 2 bis ave Georges Clemenceau), a funky, student-oriented bar-disco about 1km east of the cathedral, has live bands (20FF) on Friday and Saturday starting at 9 pm. At about midnight from Tuesday to Saturday, Le Tigre becomes a disco (free except Friday and Saturday, when admission, including a drink, costs 30/70FF for women/men, 30/60FF for students). It opens until 4 or 5 am (closed Sunday).

The *Cactus Café* (☎ 03 26 88 16 99, 47 rue des Capucins) is a mellow Tex-Mex bar-restaurant that's popular with students. It's open from 11 am (4 pm on Saturday) to 12.30 am (1.30 am on Friday and Saturday nights; closed Sunday).

Getting There & Away

Bus TransChampagne (STDM; ☎ 03 26 65 17 07) runs two to four buses a day (one on Sunday except during university holiday periods, none on bank holidays) to Châlons-en-Champagne (45 minutes) and Troyes

(113FF, 2 hours). Stops are at place du Forum and next to the train station (hours posted at both).

Train Reims' train station (☎ 08 36 35 35 35) is on the secondary Paris-Longwy line. Destinations with direct services include Paris' Gare de l'Est (120FF, 1½ hours, seven to 13 daily), Épernay (33FF, 25 minutes, 13 to 21 daily) and Dijon (189FF, 3¾ hours, four daily). There are also services to Nancy (154FF, 2½ hours, two or three daily), Metz (154FF via Bar-le-Duc), Verdun (121FF) and Strasbourg (223FF). The best way to reach Troyes is by bus.

Car ADA (☎ 03 26 50 08 40), Rent-a-Car Système (☎ 03 26 78 87 77) and National Citer (03 26 40 43 38) have offices facing the train station car park.

Getting Around
Bus The local bus company's information office, La Boutique TUR (☎ 03 26 88 25 38; closed Sunday and holidays), 6 rue Chanzy, is next to the Théâtre bus hub. Most lines begin their last runs at about 8.50 pm. The five night lines (A, B, C, G and H) make their last pass by the Théâtre bus hub at about 10.35 pm (11.50 pm on Saturday, Sunday and holidays). A single ticket, available from drivers, costs 5FF; a *carnet* of 10 (35FF) is available at La Boutique TUR and from *tabacs* (tobacconists).

Taxi For a taxi, call ☎ 03 26 47 05 05.

Bicycle Bikes can be rented for 50FF a day at Cycles Hubert (☎ 03 26 09 16 93), 82 rue de Neufchâtel, which is about 1.5km due north of place de la République (by bus take line C towards Orgeval). It opens 9 am to noon and 2 to 7 pm (closed Sunday and Monday).

AROUND REIMS
The signposted tertiary roads that make up the **Route Touristique du Champagne** (Champagne Tourist Route) – 600km in all, divided into seven circuits – meander through the region's three most important wine-growing areas: the **Montagne de Reims**, between Reims and Épernay; the **Côte des Blancs**, south of Épernay towards Sézanne; and the **Vallée de la Marne**, west of Épernay towards **Dormans**, where there's a WWI memorial, and Château Thierry. The picturesque town of **Hautvillers**, where Dom Pérignon created champagne three centuries ago, is about 6km north of Épernay.

The Route Touristique weaves its way among the neatly tended vines that cover the slopes between very average-looking villages, some with notable churches or small speciality museums. All along the route, beautiful panoramas abound and small *producteurs* (champagne producers) welcome travellers in search of bubbly; brown (or black) and white signs indicate how to find each one. Tourist offices can supply you with the colour-coded brochure *La Route Touristique du Champagne – Visites de Caves*, available in English, which includes addresses and opening hours.

For details on the Route Touristique's Côtes des Bar section, see Around Troyes later in this chapter.

Parc Naturel Régional de la Montagne de Reims
The section of the Route Touristique nearest Reims skirts the Montagne de Reims Regional Park, endowed with lush forests and a botanical curiosity, the mutant beech trees known as **Faux de Verzy** (see the boxed text 'Dwarf-Mutant Beech Trees'). To get to the faux from the village of Verzy, follow the signs up the D34; the first trees can be seen about 1km from 'Les Faux' parking lot. Across the D34, a short trail leads through the forest to the *point de vue* (panoramic viewpoint) atop 288m-high **Mont Sinaï**.

Brochures (some in English) on the park and its many hiking trails (including the GR14), and details on outdoor activities, are available from area tourist offices and the Maison du Parc (visitors centre; ☎ 03 26 59 44 44), in the village of Pourcy (next to Marfaux), which is open on weekdays until at least 6 pm (closed from noon to 1.30 pm). From mid-April to October it also

Dwarf-Mutant Beech Trees

No-one knows why the forests near the village of Verzy are home to 800-odd bizarrely malformed beech trees, but their presence has been documented since at least the 6th century. Scientists have determined that the phenomenon is genetic, but that hardly explains why so many of these so-called *faux* are to be found in the same small area (similar mutants sometimes grow elsewhere in ones and twos) – or why the vertically challenged beeches have as neighbours two dwarf-mutant oaks. One thing is certain though: the faux, whose gnarled and contorted branches droop towards the ground to form an umbrella-shaped dome, suffer in the competition for light with their nonmutant companions and need to be protected.

Some of the mutant trees, which grow slowly and live a very long time, are fertile and can reproduce sexually, but to help nature along and ensure the survival of these botanical curiosities, experts from the University of Reims carry out in-vitro fertilisation of the trees. City-dwelling faux, transplanted from Verzy, can often be seen around France in public parks.

opens 2.30 to 6.30 pm at the weekend and on holidays.

Épernay-based Argos CFE (☎ 03 26 51 95 36) publishes colour-coded cycling maps, available for 2FF each at tourist offices (eg, in Épernay).

South-East of Reims

Châlons-en-Champagne (also known as Châlons-sur-Marne; population 48,000), the regional capital, is about 20km south-east of the Parc Naturel Régional de la Montagne de Reims. It is known for the 12th-century, Champenois-Gothic **Église Notre Dame-en-Vaux** and **Cathédrale St-Étienne**, whose 17th-century neoclassical facade leads to a 12th-century triple nave.

About 8km farther east, the village of **l'Épine** (population 630) is home to a huge, Flamboyant Gothic basilica (1410–1524) with a lovely rood screen and noteworthy statues of the Virgin and the Entombment.

The flight of Louis XVI from Paris in 1791 ended at **Ste-Ménehould** (pronounced Saint Menoo), 79km east of Reims, when the soon-to-be-beheaded monarch and Marie-Antoinette were recognised by the postmaster thanks to the king's portrait printed on a banknote. The town, birthplace of Dom Pérignon (in 1639), has a fine ensemble of 18th-century buildings and is on the western edge of the **Forêt d'Argonne (Argonne Forest)**.

ÉPERNAY
postcode 51200 • pop 27,000
• elevation 75m
Épernay, a prosperous (and traffic-clogged) provincial town 25km south of Reims, is home to some of the world's most famous champagne houses. Underneath the streets, in some 100km of subterranean cellars, tens of millions of bottles of champagne, just waiting to be popped open for some sparkling celebration, are being aged. In 1950, one such cellar – owned by the irrepressible Mercier – hosted a car rally without the loss of a single bottle!

The town, set amid the gentle vineyard-covered slopes of the Marne valley, is the best place in Champagne to tour cellars and sample fizzy wine. It can easily be visited as a day trip from Reims.

Orientation
The mansion-lined ave de Champagne, where many of Épernay's champagne houses are based, stretches eastward from the town's commercial heart (around place des Arcades), whose liveliest streets are rue Général Leclerc and rue St-Thibault. The area south of place de la République is given over to car parks.

Information
Tourist Offices The helpful and well-equipped tourist office (☎ 03 26 53 33 00, fax 03 26 51 95 22), 7 ave de Champagne,

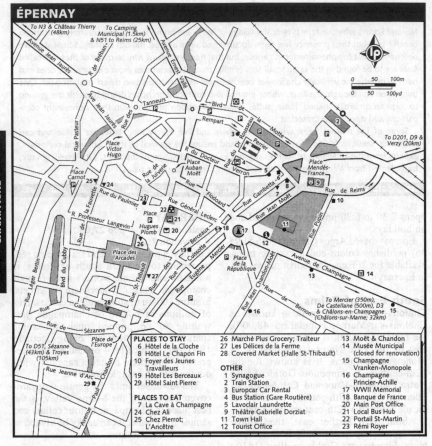

ÉPERNAY

PLACES TO STAY	26 Marché Plus Grocery; Traiteur	13 Moët & Chandon
6 Hôtel de la Cloche	27 Les Délices de la Ferme	14 Musée Municipal
8 Hôtel Le Chapon Fin	28 Covered Market (Halle St-Thibault)	(closed for renovation)
10 Foyer des Jeunes		15 Champagne
Travailleurs	OTHER	Vranken-Monopole
19 Hôtel Les Berceaux	1 Synagogue	16 Champagne
29 Hôtel Saint Pierre	2 Train Station	Princier-Achille
	3 Europcar Car Rental	17 WWII Memorial
PLACES TO EAT	4 Bus Station (Gare Routière)	18 Banque de France
7 La Cave à Champagne	5 Lavoclair Laundrette	20 Main Post Office
24 Chez Ali	9 Théâtre Gabrielle Dorziat	21 Local Bus Hub
25 Chez Pierrot;	11 Town Hall	22 Portail St-Martin
L'Ancêtre	12 Tourist Office	23 Rémi Royer

can supply you with details of cellar visits as well as walking and cycling information and maps. It opens 9.30 am to 12.30 pm and 1.30 to 5.30 pm Monday to Saturday (to 7 pm from mid-April to mid-October, when it's also open on Sunday and holidays from 11 am to 4 pm).

Money The Banque de France at place de la République changes money from 8.45 am to noon weekdays.

Post & Communications The main post office, on place Hugues Plomb, opens 8 am

to 7 pm weekdays and until noon on Saturday. Currency exchange and a Cyberposte are available.

Laundry The Lavoclair at 40 rue du Docteur Verron opens 9.30 am (2 pm in winter) to 6 pm (closed Thursday).

Champagne Houses
Épernay's champagne houses cannot be accused of cowering behind excessive modesty or aristocratic understatement. When it comes to PR for brand-name bubbly, dignified razzle-dazzle is the name of the game.

Many of the well-touristed maisons on or near ave de Champagne offer interesting, informative tours, followed by a visit to the factory-outlet bubbly shop. Reservations are not necessary for those listed below, all of whose tours end with a tasting.

Moët & Chandon (☎ 03 26 51 20 20), 18 ave de Champagne, offers 45- to 60-minute tours (40FF; those aged 12 to 16, 25FF), many in English, that are among the region's most interesting and informative. They depart every 15 or 20 minutes from 9.30 to 11.30 am and 2 to 4.30 pm (closed weekends from November to March). You can sample and compare two/three different champagnes for 65/100FF. See the Web site at www.champagne.com.

Just down the hill from 64 ave de Champagne, **De Castellane** (☎ 03 26 51 19 19) has 45-minute cellar tours in English (30FF; children under 10, 20FF) pretty much whenever Anglophone visitors arrive. The circuit includes a visit to an informative **museum**. Tours begin 10 to 11.15 am and 2 to 5.15 pm daily from early April to October; come on a weekday to see the production lines in action. The 60m-high tower, reached via 237 steps, affords panoramic views.

The most popular brand in France, **Mercier** (☎ 03 26 51 22 22), based at 68–70 ave de Champagne, has thrived on unabashed self-promotion since it was founded in 1847 by Eugène Mercier, a trailblazer in the field of eye-catching publicity stunts and the virtual creator of the cellar tour. Everything here is flashy, including the 160,000L barrel that took two decades to build and the lift that transports you 30m underground to a laser-guided train that – yes, there's a glitch in the glitz – gets confused by camera flashes and has been known to veer into the bottles that line its route. Entertaining, 45-minute tours (30FF, those aged 12 to 16 20FF) begin daily from 9.30 to 11.30 am and 2 to 4.30 pm (5 pm on weekends and holidays); closed on Tuesday and Wednesday from December to February. From April to November there are tours in English about once an hour; the rest of the year phone ahead for times.

Places to Stay

Overall, Reims offers better value than Épernay.

Camping The *Camping Municipal* (☎ 03 26 55 32 14, allée de Cumières), 2km northwest of the train station near the River Marne, is open between mid-April and mid-September.

Hostels The *Foyer des Jeunes Travailleurs (FJT;* ☎ 03 26 51 62 51, fax 03 26 54 15 60, 2 rue Pupin), also known as the Centre International de Séjour, has beds for 70FF in two- to six-person rooms. Reception opens 2 to 8 pm Monday to Saturday. It's a good idea to reserve in advance by phone.

Hotels The best (and most atmospheric) deal in town is the 15-room *Hôtel St Pierre* (☎ 03 26 54 40 80, fax 03 26 57 88 68, 1 rue Jeanne d'Arc), which occupies an elegant, early-20th-century mansion on the southern edge of town. Charming singles/doubles start at 118/130FF; shower- and toilet-equipped doubles are 186FF. Reception may be closed on Sunday from 2 to 6 pm. Private parking is available.

The 11-room *Hôtel Le Chapon Fin* (☎ 03 26 55 40 03, fax 03 26 54 94 17, @ lechaponfin@wanadoo.fr, 2 place Mendès-France) has unexciting, linoleum-floored doubles with shower and toilet for 190FF. The two-star, 19-room *Hôtel de la Cloche* (☎ 03 26 55 15 15, fax 03 26 55 64 88, 5 place Mendès-France) has doubles with shower and toilet from 195FF.

In the three-star category, the veteran, 29-room *Hôtel Les Berceaux* (☎ 03 26 55 28 84, fax 03 26 55 10 36, 13 rue des Berceaux) has comfortable but fairly ordinary doubles from 390FF.

Places to Eat

Restaurants The intimate, rustic *L'Ancêtre* (☎ 03 26 55 57 56, 20 rue de la Fauvette) serves traditional French cuisine. Fish and meat mains cost 66FF to 135FF; the *menus* range from 78FF to 99FF (closed Wednesday and, from November to March, on

Tuesday evening). Another good bet is the elegant **Chez Pierrot** (☎ 03 26 55 16 93, 16 rue de la Fauvette), which serves bourgeois-style French cuisine; *menus* start at 110FF (130FF in the evening; closed Saturday at midday and Sunday). **Chez Ali** (☎ 03 26 51 80 82, 27 rue de la Fauvette) offers couscous dishes costing from 65FF to 100FF (closed Monday).

Rue Gambetta is home to several restaurants, including four pizzerias, a Tunisian couscous place (next to No 31) and **La Cave à Champagne** (☎ 03 26 55 50 70, 16 rue Gambetta), which specialises in Champenois cuisine and has *menus* for 79FF and 140FF (sometimes closed Wednesday evening).

Rustic **Hôtel Le Chapon Fin** has a reasonably priced French restaurant; the 'gastronomique' restaurant attached to **Hôtel de la Cloche** is slightly more expensive. The **Hôtel Les Berceaux** has an elegant restaurant with one Michelin star, where French gastronomique *menus* start at 180FF (closed Sunday night and Monday); and a cosy wine bar with *menus* for 90FF and 135FF (closed for Saturday lunch). See Places to Stay for more details of the above places.

Self-Catering The **covered market** (*rue Gallice*) springs to life from 8 am to noon on Wednesday and Saturday. On Sunday mornings there's a small **open-air market** (*place Auban Moët*).

Marché Plus grocery (*13 place Hugues Plomb*) opens from 7 am to 9 pm (9 am to 1 pm on Sunday). Next door, the **traiteur** (delicatessen or takeaway; *9 place Hugues Plomb*) sells scrumptious prepared dishes (open 8 am to 12.45 pm and 3 to 7.30 pm, closed on Sunday afternoon and Wednesday). **Les Délices de la Ferme** (*19 rue St-Thibault*), a *fromagerie*, opens until 7.30 pm (closed from 12.30 to 3 pm) Tuesday to Saturday.

Getting There & Away
The train station (☎ 08 36 35 35 35), at place Mendès-France, is linked by direct trains to Paris' Gare de l'Est (106FF, 1¼ hours, 16 daily), Reims (33FF, 25 minutes, 13 to 21 daily), Metz (143FF) and Nancy

(143FF, two hours, five daily). Other destinations include Strasbourg (direct or via Nancy; 215FF) and Verdun (via Châlons-en-Champagne, 109FF).

Getting Around
Europcar (☎ 03 26 54 90 61) is at 20 Rempart Perrier (closed Sunday).

Mountain bikes can be rented for 70/110FF per half-day/day at Rémi Royer (☎ 03 26 55 29 61), 10 place Hugues Plomb, open 9 am to noon and 2 to 7 pm (closed Sunday and Monday).

TROYES
postcode 10000 • pop 123,000
• elevation 113m

Troyes – like Reims, one of the historic capitals of Champagne – has a lively commercial district that is graced with one of France's finest ensembles of medieval and Renaissance half-timbered houses. Several unique and very worthwhile museums and a number of ancient churches provide further reasons to spend a couple of days here.

Troyes does not have any champagne cellars. However, if you have shopping on your mind, you can shop till you drop in its scores of cut-price outlet stores specialising in brand-name clothing and accessories.

Orientation
Although Troyes hardly benefits from the champagne trade, the medieval city centre – bounded by blvd Gambetta, blvd Victor Hugo, blvd du 14 Juillet and the Seine – is, ironically, shaped like a champagne cork (*bouchon*). The main commercial street is rue Émile Zola.

The train station and the tourist office are at the cork's westernmost extremity. Most of the city's sights and activities are in the square part of the cork 'below' (south-west of) the bulbous cap. However, the cathedral and the Musée d'Art Moderne are in the 'cap', in a district known as Quartier de la Cité. The old town is centred around the 17th-century town hall and nearby Église St-Jean.

CHAMPAGNE

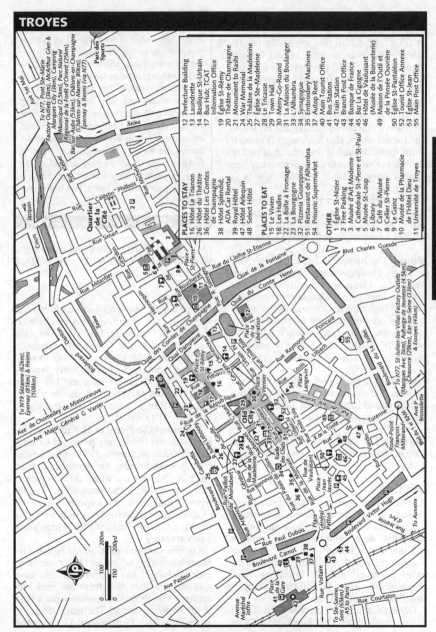

TROYES

PLACES TO STAY
16 Hôtel Le Trianon
36 Hôtel du Théâtre
38 Hôtel Les Comtes de Champagne; ADA Car Rental
39 Hôtel Splendid; Royal Hôtel
47 Hôtel Arlequin
48 Select Hôtel

PLACES TO EAT
15 Le Vivien
18 Les Halles
22 La Boîte à Fromage
23 La Bourgogne
32 Pizzeria Giuseppino
51 Restaurant de l'Alhambra
54 Prisunic Supermarket

OTHER
1 Église St-Nizier
2 Free Parking
3 Musée d'Art Moderne
4 Cathédrale St-Pierre et St-Paul
5 Musée St-Loup
6 Library
7 Café du Musée
8 Cellier St-Pierre
9 Le Gainz
10 Musée de la Pharmacie de l'Hôtel Dieu
11 Université de Troyes
12 Prefecture Building
13 Laundrette
14 Basilique St-Urbain
17 Bus Hub; TCAT Information Office
19 Église St-Rémy
20 Théâtre de Champagne
21 Monument to Rashi
24 War Memorial
25 Théâtre de la Madeleine
27 Église Ste-Madeleine
28 Le Tricasse
29 Town Hall
30 Merry-Go-Round
31 La Maison du Boulanger
33 L'Alhambra
34 Synagogue
35 Embroidery Machines
37 Autop Rent
40 Main Tourist Office
41 Bus Station
42 Train Station
43 Branch Post Office
44 Banque de France
45 Bar La Cigogne
46 Hôtel de Vauluisant (Musée de la Bonneterie)
49 Maison de l'Outil et de la Pensée Ouvrière
50 Église St-Pantaléon
52 Tourist Office Annexe
53 Église St-Jean
55 Main Post Office

CHAMPAGNE

Information

Tourist Offices The main tourist office (☎ 03 25 82 62 70, fax 03 25 73 06 71, 📧 troyes@club-internet.fr), 16 blvd Carnot, opens 9 am to 12.30 pm and 2 to 6.30 pm Monday to Saturday (closed holidays). The tourist office annexe (☎ 03 25 73 36 88), on rue Mignard opposite Église St-Jean, opens the same hours and is also staffed 10 am to noon and 2 to 5 pm on Sunday and holidays. The tourist office also has *points d'accueil* (information tables) at five churches (seven churches from June to early September; see Churches for details). The Web site is at www.ot-troyes.fr.

The tourist office can provide free bus maps, brochures on factory outlets and details of outdoor activities in the nearby Parc Naturel Régional de la Forêt d'Orient.

Money The Banque de France, 6 blvd Victor Hugo, changes money 9 am to 12.30 pm weekdays. There are several commercial banks – open either Monday to Friday or Tuesday to Saturday – around the town hall.

The tourist office's rue Mignard annexe will exchange foreign currency when the banks are closed but the rate is not very good.

Post The branch post office at place Général Patton opens 8 am to 6.30 pm weekdays and until noon on Saturday. Currency exchange is possible.

Laundry The laundrette at 9 rue Georges Clemenceau opens daily from 7.30 am to 8 pm.

Old City

Half-timbered houses line the streets of Troyes' old city, rebuilt after a devastating fire in 1524 – good places to look include **rue Paillot de Montabert**, **rue Champeaux** and **rue de Vauluisant**. An effort is being made to uncover the many half-timbered facades plastered over as buildings were 'modernised' after WWII (for example, along rue Émile Zola).

Off rue Champeaux (between No 30 and 32), a stroll along tiny **Ruelle des Chats**

The Troyes Ounce

In the 12th and 13th centuries, Troyes grew exceptionally prosperous thanks to its three-month trade fairs, which attracted artisans and merchants from as far afield as Scotland and Constantinople. The fairs' bureaux de change were kept very busy exchanging ducats for dinars and crowns for pounds, and the standards of measurement that were established eventually spread throughout Europe and the world. That's why, to this day, precious metals such as gold and silver are measured in units known as troy weight (one pound equals 12 troy ounces, one troy ounce equals 31.1g).

(Alley of the Cats), as dark and narrow as it was four centuries ago, is like stepping back into the Middle Ages.

Churches

Except during Mass, the tourist office is responsible for opening Troyes' historic churches to the public. Five churches – the four detailed in the following paragraphs plus Église St-Jean – open 10 am to noon and 2 to 5 pm. From June to early September, hours are 9 am to noon and 1 to 7 pm, and two other churches can also be visited: Église St-Rémy (9 am to noon) and Église St-Nizier (1 to 7 pm).

Cathédrale St-Pierre et St-Paul incorporates elements from every period of Champenois Gothic architecture. The Flamboyant Gothic **west facade**, for instance, is from the mid-16th century, whereas the choir and transepts are over 250 years older. The interior is illuminated by a spectacular series of about 180 **stained-glass windows** dating from the 13th to 17th centuries. There's also a tiny **treasury**.

On rue Général de Gaulle, **Église Ste-Madeleine**, Troyes' oldest (and most interesting) church, has an early Gothic nave and transept that date from the mid-12th century; the choir and tower weren't built until the Renaissance. The main attraction is the splendid Flamboyant Gothic **rood**

Eguisheim, Alsace, and its gabled, geranium-adorned houses

Notre Dame, Strasbourg

The Nécropole National, Rancourt, is one of hundreds of war cemeteries across Far Northern France.

Musee d'Unterlinden, Colmar

Reims is ideal for tours and tastings at local champagne cellars.

The 16th-century gardens of Chenonceau, The Loire, created by Diane de Poitiers, mistress of Henri II

The 'revolutionary' staircase at Château de Blois

Bouchard's 'Grape Picker' at Vougeot, Burgundy

screen, which dates from the early 1500s. In the nave, the statue of a deadly serious **Ste-Marthe** (St-Martha), around the pillar from the wooden pulpit, is considered a masterpiece of the 15th-century Troyes School.

Other churches in Troyes include the Renaissance-style **Église St-Pantaléon** on rue de Turenne, which was built from 1508 to 1672 on the one-time site of a synagogue. The interior is decorated with dozens of 16th-century statues, most of them carved locally. The Gothic **Basilique St-Urbain**, at place Vernier, was begun in 1262 by Pope Urban IV, who was born in Troyes and whose father's shoemaking shop once stood on this spot. Its 13th-century stained-glass windows were recently remounted after restoration work. In the choir is **La Vierge au Raisin**, a graceful, early-15th-century stone carving of the Virgin.

Museums

A combined ticket (*billet groupé*), valid for admission to all the museums mentioned below except the Maison de l'Outil et de la Pensée Ouvrière, costs 60FF (those under 18 10FF) and is sold at museum ticket counters. These same four museums are free on Wednesday.

The once-time bishop's palace at place St-Pierre is now home to the superb **Musée d'Art Moderne** (☎ 03 25 76 26 80), whose outstanding collection consists of French paintings (including lots of fauvist works), glass and ceramics, created between 1850 and 1950. Artists represented include Modigliani, Derain, Matisse, Picasso, Cézanne, Soutine and local favourite Maurice Marinot. It opens from 11 am to 6 pm (closed Monday and holidays). Admission costs 30FF (students and those aged under 18, 5FF).

Musée St-Loup (☎ 03 25 76 21 68), next to 83 rue de la Cité, has a varied, worthwhile and sometimes surprising collection of medieval sculpture, enamels, archaeology and natural history – don't let the stuffed mammals and birds at the entrance put you off. Hours are 10 am to noon and 2 to 6 pm (closed Tuesday and holidays); admission costs 30FF (students and those aged under 18, 5FF).

At the **Maison de l'Outil et de la Pensée Ouvrière** (Museum of Tools and Crafts; ☎ 03 25 73 28 26), 7 rue de la Trinité, thousands of hand tools, worn to a sensuous smoothness, bring to life a world of manual skills now largely lost. Housed in the mid-16th-century, Renaissance-style Hôtel de Mauroy and run by a national crafts guild, it opens 9 am (10 am on weekends and holidays) to 1 pm and 2 to 6.30 pm (6 pm on weekends and holidays); admission costs 40FF (children and students 30FF).

The 16th-century Renaissance-style **Hôtel de Vauluisant**, 4 rue de Vauluisant, houses a museum of local history as well as the less-than-scintillating **Musée de la Bonneterie** (Hosiery & Knitwear Museum; ☎ 03 25 42 33 33). It opens 10 am to noon

CHAMPAGNE

Rashi

During the 11th and 12th centuries, a small Jewish community was established in Troyes under the protection of the counts of Champagne. Its most illustrious member was Rabbi Shlomo Yitzhaki (1040–1105), who is better known by his acronym, Rashi (Rachi in French).

His commentaries on the Bible and the Talmud, which combine literal and nonliteral methods of interpretation and make extensive use of allegory, symbolism and parable, are still vastly important to Jews; they have also had an impact on Christian Bible interpretation. Rashi's habit of explaining difficult words and passages in the local vernacular – written in Hebrew characters, of course – has made his writings an important source for scholars of Old French. In 1475 (a mere 30 years after Gutenberg) Rashi's Bible commentary became one of the first books to be printed in Hebrew.

In Troyes there's a striking monument to Rashi next to the Théâtre de Champagne.

---

and 2 to 6 pm (closed Monday, Tuesday and holidays). Admission costs 30FF (children and students 5FF).

On Quai des Comtes de Champagne, part of a former hospital founded in the 12th century has been turned into the **Musée de la Pharmacie de l'Hôtel Dieu** (☎ 03 25 80 98 97), a fully outfitted, wood-panelled pharmacy from the early 1700s. It opens 2 to 6 pm on Wednesday, Saturday and Sunday; from June to September, hours are 10 am to noon and 2 to 6 pm (closed Tuesday). Admission costs 20FF (children and students 5FF).

Special Events

La Ville en Musique brings music of all sorts (classical, jazz, rock, organ, etc) to Troyes from late June to late August. The annual Nuits de Champagne, a colourful music festival usually held in late October, is created by a celebrity performer who chooses which other musicians to invite. For details and tickets contact the tourist office or the Théâtres de Troyes (☎ 03 25 76 27 60).

Places to Stay – Budget

Camping The three-star *Camping Municipal* (☎ 03 25 81 02 64, 7 rue Roger Salengro in Pont Ste-Marie), open from around April to 15 October, is about 3.5km northeast of the train station. To get there, take bus No 1 (towards Pont Ste-Marie) to the Stade de l'Aube stop.

You can also camp at the Auberge de Jeunesse (see Hostels) for 27FF per person.

Hostels The 102-bed *Auberge de Jeunesse* (☎ 03 25 82 00 65, fax 03 25 72 93 78, at 2 rue Jules Ferry) is about 5.5km south of the train station in the Troyes suburb of Rosières. A bed costs 47FF; breakfast is 20FF. Check-in is from 8 am to 10 pm. To get there take bus No 8 (towards Rosières-Château) to the Liberté stop.

Hotels The superbly situated, eight-room *Hôtel Le Trianon* (☎ 03 25 73 18 52, 2 rue Pithou) has doubles with washbasin from 130FF (there *may* be a hall shower installed

by the time you read this); shower-equipped rooms for two/four people cost 220/250FF. Reception closes at 9 pm (at noon or 1 pm on Sunday).

The welcoming, 35-room *Hôtel Les Comtes de Champagne* (☎ 03 25 73 11 70, fax 03 25 73 06 02, 56 rue de la Monnaie) is an excellent bet, with decent doubles starting at 140FF (200FF with shower and toilet). The rooms away from the street are quietest. Hall showers are free. Enclosed parking costs 30FF.

The friendly, nine-room *Hôtel du Théâtre* (☎ 03 25 73 18 47, fax 03 25 73 85 73, 35 rue Jules Lebocey) has recently-remodelled singles/doubles with bath for 150/170FF. Reception (at the bar) is closed after 4 pm on Sunday.

The *Select Hôtel* (☎/fax 03 25 73 36 16, 1 rue de Vauluisant), in a rather ugly, half-timbered building, has basic but serviceable singles/doubles/quads from 80/110/205FF. Half-board costs 50FF extra per person. On Sunday, reception is closed until 6 pm.

The newly refurbished, 16-room *Hôtel Splendid* (☎ 03 25 73 08 52, fax 03 25 73 41 04, 44 blvd Carnot) has cheery singles/doubles from 140/155FF (230/245FF with shower and toilet).

Places to Stay – Mid-Range

The 22-room, two-star *Hôtel Arlequin* (☎ 03 25 83 12 70, fax 03 25 83 12 99, ✉ arlequin@pem.net, 50 rue de Turenne) is one of the best deals in town. Its charming singles/doubles/triples with antique furnishings and high ceilings – each different – start at 220/250/320FF.

The three-star *Royal Hôtel* (☎ 03 25 73 19 99, fax 03 25 73 47 85, ✉ royal.hotel@infonie.fr, 22 blvd Carnot), run by a friendly and welcoming couple, has large, delightful doubles from 395FF; for 50FF you can add a third person. It's closed for three weeks at Christmas.

Places to Eat

Restaurants – French The family-run *Le Vivien* (☎ 03 25 73 70 70, 7 place St-Rémy), an elegant but relaxed French and Champenois restaurant, has *menus* for 115FF and

175FF (closed Sunday evening and Monday). The elegant **Restaurant du Royal Hôtel** (see Places to Stay – Mid-Range) serves traditional French *menus* for 125FF and 165FF; all ingredients are fresh and home made (closed Saturday and Monday lunchtime and Sunday evening). **Le Bourgogne** (☎ *03 25 73 02 67, 40 rue Général de Gaulle*) also serves classic French cuisine, with a *menu* that usually costs 170FF (closed Sunday night and Monday).

Le Théâtre, a bar-brasserie-restaurant affiliated with the hotel of the same name (see Places to Stay – Budget), has decent *menus* from 68FF (closed Sunday evening).

Restaurants – Other The chummy **Pizzeria Giuseppino** (☎ *03 25 73 92 44, 26 rue Paillot de Montabert*), on a narrow medieval street, serves pasta and ultra-thin, crispy pizzas for 35FF to 48FF. It is hugely popular with students (closed Monday for lunch and Sunday).

Restaurant de l'Alhambra (☎ *03 25 73 18 41, 31 rue Champeaux*) serves Algerian couscous (65FF to 85FF) amid Moorish-style décor. The many other restaurants along the same street include two *crêperies* (*9 and 29 rue Champeaux*).

A number of mainly student-oriented takeaways, cafes and ethnic restaurants can be found along rue de la Cité just west of the cathedral.

Self-Catering Ideal picnicking spots include the park along blvd Carnot (near the train station) and the flowery place de la Libération.

Les Halles, just off rue de la République, a lively 19th-century marketplace, opens until 7 pm (closed from 12.45 to 3.30 pm and on Sunday afternoon). The food shops nearby include **La Boîte à Fromage** (*18 rue Général de Gaulle*), a cheese shop that stays open until 7.30 pm (closed 12.30 to 3 pm, and on Sunday and Monday), and a couple of **Asian groceries** (*14 and 30 rue Général de Gaulle*).

The **Prisunic** supermarket (*71 rue Émile Zola*) opens 8.30 am to 8 pm Monday to Saturday.

Entertainment

Nondubbed films are screened each Tuesday at **L'Alhambra** (☎ *03 25 73 09 24, 20 rue Champeaux*).

Le Tricasse (☎ *03 25 73 14 80, 16 rue Paillot de Montabert*) and its two billiard tables have long been a favourite of students, local and foreign alike. It opens 3 pm to 3 am, Monday to Saturday. **Bar La Cigogne** (☎ *03 25 73 06 04, 33 place Jean Jaurès*) is a welcoming and very popular bar run by four brothers from Salamanca, Spain. Hours are 8 am to 1.30 am (closed Sunday).

The relaxed **Café du Musée** (☎ *03 25 80 58 64, 59 rue de la Cité*), popular with students, opens 11 am to 3 am Monday to Saturday. Down the block, **Le Gainz** (☎ *03 25 80 60 76, 39 rue de la Cité*) is a totally unpretentious student hang-out with beer for just 10FF. It opens 9 am to 3 am, Monday to Saturday.

Shopping

The 500 wines on offer at **Cellier St-Pierre** (*1 place St-Pierre*) include Champagne's own non-sparkling rosé (closed noon to 2.30 pm, and Sunday and Monday).

Troyes is known for its *magasins d'usine* (factory outlets), whose discounted (and perhaps delabelled) brand-name sportswear, underwear, baby clothes, shoes and so on, attract bargain-hunting French people by the coachload. They are generally open 10 am to 7 pm (closed Monday morning and Sunday). Most are situated in two main zones:

St-Julien-les-Villas is about 3km south of the city centre on blvd de Dijon (the N71 to Dijon). Some 86 shops occupy the five buildings of Marques Avenue (☎ 03 25 82 00 72), centred around 114 blvd de Dijon. By bus, take line No 2 towards Bréviandes.

Pont Ste-Marie is about 3km north-east of the city centre along rue Marc Verdier, which links ave Jean Jaurès (the N77 to Châlons-en-Champagne) with ave Jules Guesde (the D960 to Nancy). McArthur Glen (☎ 03 25 70 47 10) is a strip mall with 62 shops; there are more stores at nearby Marques City. By bus take line No 1 towards Pont Ste-Marie.

CHAMPAGNE

Getting There & Away

Bus Coach services fill some of the gaping holes left by Troyes' rather pathetic rail services. The bus station office (☎ 03 25 71 28 42), run by Courriers de l'Aube, is in a corner of the train station building and opens 8.30 am to noon and 2 to 6.15 pm weekdays. Schedules are posted on the uprights next to each bus berth.

TransChampagne (STDM; ☎ 03 26 65 17 07) runs two to four buses a day (one on Sunday except during university holiday periods, none on holidays) to Reims (113FF, 2 hours). From Monday to Thursday, Les Rapides de Bourgogne (03 86 94 95 00) has a 4 pm service to Auxerre in Burgundy (74FF, 2¼ hours). The company also runs SNCF buses to Laroche–Migennes (62FF, one to 1¾ hours, four daily on weekdays, one daily at the weekend), a stop on the Paris–Dijon rail line.

Train Troyes (☎ 08 36 35 35 35) is on the rather isolated Paris–Basel line. Destinations include Paris' Gare de l'Est (117FF, 1½ hours, up to 13 a day) and Basel (Bâle in French, 207FF, 3½ hours, three to five daily). To get to Dijon (143FF, 3½ hours, five a day) and Lyon (233FF) you have to change train/bus. The best way to get to northern Champagne (including Reims) and to Burgundy is by bus.

Car ADA (☎ 03 25 73 41 68) is at 36 blvd Carnot; Autop Rent (☎ 03 25 73 27 66) is around the corner at 2 rue Voltaire.

Getting Around

There's a large, free car park two blocks east of the cathedral.

Bus The main bus hub (known as Halle) of the TCAT system (☎ 03 25 70 49 00) is on rue de la République near Les Halles. The eight regular lines run every 10 or 20 minutes (30 to 60 minutes on Sunday) until 7.30 or 8 pm; schedules are posted at each stop. Magnetic tickets valid for one/three rides are available from drivers for 7/17FF.

Taxi To order a taxi, call ☎ 03 25 78 30 30.

AROUND TROYES
Parc Naturel Régional de la Forêt d'Orient

The Parc Naturel Régional de la Forêt d'Orient, 700 sq km of forests, fields, villages and water, begins less than 10km east of Troyes. In the warm season, you can swim, fish, sail, windsurf, kayak, waterski and jet ski on two large lakes, the **Lac d'Orient** and the **Lac du Temple**, both 20 to 30km from the city. The Maison du Parc (park headquarters; ☎ 03 25 43 81 90), on the D79 just east of the Lac d'Orient's **Réserve Ornithologique** (bird reserve), is open daily until at least 5.30 pm.

Les Courriers de l'Aube (☎ 03 25 71 28 42) runs buses from Troyes' train station to villages including the lakeside Mesnil St-Père (35 minutes, two on weekdays, one on Saturday) and Piney (30 minutes, two or three a day), as well as Bar-sur-Aube (70 minutes, two on weekdays, one on Saturday). From late June to late August, the company's buses link Troyes with the Lac d'Orient and the **Nigloland Theme Park** (☎ 03 25 27 94 52) at Dolancourt (☎ 03 25 27 94 52), open from April until September (83FF; those under 12/over 60, 73FF). See the Web site at www.nigloland.fr.

About 30 km north-east of the Forêt d'Orient is France's largest lake, the 48-sq-km **Lac du Der-Chantecoq**, whose Celtic name refers to the area's many oak trees. The area is a favourite with migrating birds.

South of Troyes

Chaource, famed for its eponymous cheese, is 30 km south of Troyes. The crypt of Église St-Jean-Baptiste shelters a superb, 16th-century entombment.

Langres, too, is a cheese, as well as a walled, hilltop town. Situated some 120km south-east of Troyes, its noteworthy sights include the 12th-century cathedral, given a new facade in the 18th century, and some Renaissance-style houses.

Route Touristique du Champagne

Although the Aube department, of which Troyes is the capital, is a major producer of champagne (about 20 million bottles a year), it gets little of the recognition accorded the Marne department and the big maisons around Reims and Épernay. Much of the acrimony dates to 1909, when the Aube growers were excluded from the growing area for Champagne's Appellation d'Origine Contrôlée (AOC). Two years later, they were also forbidden to sell their grapes to producers up north, resulting in months of strikes and chaos; eventually, the army was called in. It was another 16 years before the Aube wine growers could again display the prestigious (and lucrative) AOC tag on their labels, but by then the produc-

ers in the north had come to dominate the market.

Today, champagne production in the Troyes area is modest in scale, though the reputation of the area's wines has been on an upward trajectory in recent years. The Aube's own section of the Route Touristique du Champagne, the **Côtes des Bar**, passes through **Bar-sur-Seine** (about 33km south-east of Troyes) and **Bar-sur-Aube** (about 35km north-east of Bar-sur-Seine).

Charles de Gaulle is buried in **Colombey-les-Deux-Églises**, 16km east of Bar-sur-Aube, where he lived out his final years. His estate, **La Boisserie**, is now a museum.

CHAMPAGNE

Alsace & Lorraine

Though often spoken of as if they were one, Alsace and Lorraine, neighbouring regions in France's north-eastern corner, are linked by little more than a common border through the Vosges Mountains and the imperial ambitions of late-19th-century Germany: in 1871 the newly created German Reich annexed Alsace and part of Lorraine, making the regions a focal point of French nationalism.

Alsace

The charming and beautiful region of Alsace, long a meeting place of Europe's Latin and Germanic cultures, is nestled between the Vosges Mountains and the River Rhine – along which the long-disputed Franco-German border has finally found a resting place. Popularly known as a land of storks' nests and colourful, half-timbered houses sprouting geraniums, Alsace also offers a wide variety of outdoor activities – including hiking, mountain-biking and skiing – in and around its gentle, forested mountains. Throughout France, the people of Alsace have a reputation for being hardworking, well organised and tax-paying.

Alsace, which occupies an area 190km long and no more than 50km wide, is made up of just two departments: Bas-Rhin (Lower Rhine), the area around the dynamic regional capital, Strasbourg; and Haut-Rhin (Upper Rhine), which covers the region's more southerly reaches, including the department's picturesque capital, Colmar, and the industrial city of Mulhouse. Germany is just across the busy, barge-laden Rhine, whose western bank is Alsatian as far south as the Swiss city of Basel.

History

French influence in Alsace began at the end of the 1500s during the Wars of Religion (1562–98) and increased during the Thirty Years' War (1618–48), when Alsatian

Highlights

- Gaze up at the rose-coloured spires and stained glass of Strasbourg's Gothic cathedral
- Watch the storks clacking their beaks in Munster or Hunawihr
- Marvel at the Issenheim Altarpiece in Colmar
- Head up to the Grand Ballon or Ballon d'Alsace for panoramic views of the Rhine, the Black Forest and the Alps
- In Nancy, admire the gilded grillwork at Place Stanislas and the curvaceous Art-Nouveau furniture at the Musée de l'École de Nancy

cities, caught between opposing Catholic and Protestant factions, turned to France for assistance. Most of the region was attached to France in 1648 under the Treaty of Westphalia. Today about one-fifth of Alsatians are Protestants.

By the time of the French Revolution, the Alsatians felt far more connected to

France than to Germany. Indeed, the upper classes had already begun to adopt the French language. But more than two centuries of French rule did little to dampen 19th-century Germany's enthusiasm for a foothold on the western bank of the southern Rhine. The Franco-Prussian War of 1870–71, a supremely humiliating episode in French history, ended with the Treaty of Frankfurt (1871), by which an embittered France was forced to cede Alsace and the northern part of the present-day region of Lorraine to the Second Reich.

Following Germany's defeat in WWI, Alsace and Lorraine were returned to France, but the French government's program to reassimilate the area (for example, by banning German-language newspapers) gave rise to a strong home-rule movement. These days, similar sentiments fuel support for the far-right Front National party.

Germany's second annexation of Alsace and Lorraine in 1940 (and indeed the occupation of all of France) was supposed to have been made impossible by the state-of-the-art Maginot Line (see the boxed text 'The Maginot Line' later in the chapter). Immediately after Nazi Germany took over the area, about half a million Alsatian people fled to occupied France. This time, the Germanisation campaign was particularly harsh: anyone caught speaking French was imprisoned, and even the Alsatian language was banned.

After the war, Alsace was once again returned to France. Intra-Alsatian tensions ran high, however, as those who had left came back and confronted former neighbours whom they suspected of having collaborated with the Germans (many Alsatians, as annexed citizens of the Third Reich, were drafted into Hitler's armies). To make Alsace a symbol of hope for future Franco-German (and pan-European) cooperation, Strasbourg was chosen as the seat of the Council of Europe (in 1949) and, later, of the European Parliament.

Language

Alsatian, the language of Alsace, is an Alemannic dialect of German not unlike the

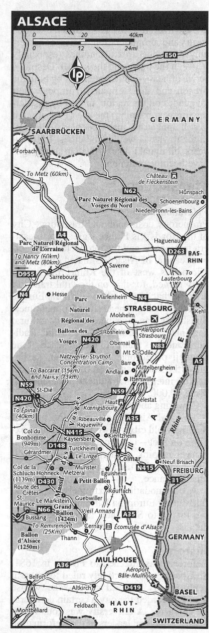

dialects spoken in nearby parts of Germany and Switzerland. It has no official written form, and pronunciation varies considerably from one area to another (especially between the north and the south). Despite a series of heavy-handed attempts by both the French and the Germans to impose their languages on the region, in part by restricting (or even banning) the use of Alsatian, it is still spoken by many people of all ages, in the towns as well as the cities. In recent years, bilingual French-Alsatian street signs have become common.

STRASBOURG
postcode 67000 • pop 423,000
• elevation 143m

Prosperous, cosmopolitan Strasbourg ('City of the Roads') is France's great north-eastern metropolis and the intellectual and cultural capital of Alsace. Situated only a few kilometres west of the Rhine, the city is aptly named, for it is on the vital transport arteries that have linked northern Europe with the Mediterranean since Roman times. Strasbourg has long been a lively cultural and intellectual crossroads, and this tradition continues thanks to the presence of the Council of Europe, the European Parliament, the European Court of Human Rights and an international student population of some 40,000.

Towering above the restaurants, *winstubs* (traditional Alsatian eateries) and pubs of the lively old city – a wonderful area to explore on foot – is the cathedral, a medieval marvel in pink sandstone. Nearby you'll find one of the finest ensembles of museums in France.

Accommodation is extremely difficult to find during European Parliament sessions – see Places to Stay later in the chapter for details.

History
Before it was attached to France in 1681, Strasbourg was effectively ruled for several centuries by a guild of citizens whose tenure accorded the city a certain democratic character. A university was founded in 1566 and several leaders of the Reformation

took up residence here. Johann Gutenberg worked in Strasbourg from about 1434 to 1444, perfecting his printing press and the moveable metal type that made it so revolutionary. Three centuries later, the German poet, playwright, novelist and philosopher Johann Wolfgang von Goethe (1749–1832) studied law here.

Orientation
The city centre is about 3.5km west of Pont de l'Europe, the bridge that links the French bank of the Rhine with the German city of Kehl.

Strasbourg's train station is about 400m west of the Grande Île (Big Island), the core of ancient and modern Strasbourg. Over half of the Grande Île, which is surrounded by the River Ill and its branch, the Fossé du Faux Rempart, is pedestrianised.

The Grande Île's main squares are place Kléber, place Broglie (pronounced **broag**-lee), place Gutenberg and place du Château. They are linked by a number of relatively narrow streets, including, east to west, rue du Vieux Marché aux Vins (and its eastward continuation) and the pedestrianised Grand' Rue; and, north to south, rue des Francs Bourgeois (with a tramline down the middle) and rue des Grandes Arcades. The cathedral's spire is visible from all over town. The quaint Petite France area in the Grande Île's south-western corner is subdivided by canals.

The new European Parliament building and Palais de l'Europe are about 2km northeast of the cathedral.

Information
Tourist Offices The main tourist office (☎ 03 88 52 28 28, fax 03 88 52 28 29, ⓔ otsr@strasbourg.com) is at 17 place de la Cathédrale, right next to the ornate, 16th-century Maison Kammerzell. It opens from 9 am to 7 pm daily. The train station annexe (☎ 03 88 32 51 49), in the subterranean Galerie de l'En-Verre (underneath place de la Gare), opens from 9 am to 6 pm (to 7 pm from June to September; closed on Sunday from January to March). The Web site is at www.strasbourg.com.

At both bureaux, same-day reservations for tourist office-affiliated hotels anywhere in Alsace cost 10FF. Bus/tram tickets and passes are available, as are free route maps. Also on offer: cycling maps and *Strasbourg Actualités*, a free, French-language monthly listing concerts, expositions etc. The 'Strasbourg Pass' (58FF), valid for three days, gets you a variety of discounts.

Strassbuch, put out each March by local students and available for free from the tourist office and bookshops until stocks run out, has details on virtually every sort of establishment, including places to eat and shop.

The Agence de Développement Touristique en Bas-Rhin (☎ 03 88 15 45 80), 9 rue du Dôme, can supply you with information on the Alsace region (open weekdays and, from May to September, on Saturday). Its Web site is at www.tourisme-alsace.com.

Money The Banque de France, 3 place Broglie, exchanges money 9 am to 12.30 pm weekdays. The first performance of the French national anthem, 'La Marseillaise' (see the boxed text 'La Marseillaise' on p461), was held on this spot in 1792.

The American Express office (☎ 03 88 21 96 59), 19 rue des Francs Bourgeois, opens 9 am to noon and 1.30 to 6 pm weekdays (2 to 5.30 pm from October to March); it also opens on Saturday from about May to September.

The seven-day-a-week CIC Banque CIAL window in the train station's Arrivée (arrival) area, open 9 am to 7.30 pm (closed from 1 to 2 pm), charges a 25FF commission and has poor rates. There are a couple of 24-hour currency exchange machines at place Gutenberg (outside the Sogenal and CCF banks).

Post & Communications The main post office, a neo-Gothic structure at 5 ave de la Marseillaise, was built by the Germans in 1899. It opens 8 am to 7 pm weekdays and until noon on Saturday. The branch at place de la Cathédrale closes at 6.30 pm (noon on Saturday). Both have exchange services; the former has Cyberposte.

The Best Coffee Shop (☎ 03 88 35 79 47), 10 quai des Pêcheurs, offers cheap email access from 10 am (2 pm at the weekend) to 11.30 pm. NeT SuR CouR (☎ 03 88 35 66 76), in the narrow courtyard at 18 quai des Pêcheurs, charges 0.75FF per minute for email (students 0.65FF). Hours are 11.30 am (2.30 pm at the weekend) to 9 pm.

In front of the train station in the Galerie à l'En-Verre, the municipality's Cybercentre (☎ 03 88 22 40 32) lets you access your email for free for up to 20 minutes, but hours are limited (open mainly in the afternoon; closed Sunday).

Bookshops The Bookworm (☎ 03 88 32 26 99), an English-language bookshop at 3 rue de Pâques, has a wide selection of new and used books, including Lonely Planet guides. Hours are 10 am (1.30 pm on Monday) to 6.30 pm (6 pm on Saturday; closed Sunday).

Maps and topoguides are available from Géorama (☎ 03 88 75 01 95), 20–22 rue du Fossé des Tanneurs (closed Monday morning and Sunday), and the Club Vosgien walking organisation (☎ 03 88 32 57 96), 16 rue Ste-Hélène (closed Sunday).

Laundry On the Grande Île, there are laundrettes at 29 Grand' Rue (open until 8 pm), 8 rue de la Nuée Bleue (open until 9 pm) and 15 rue des Veaux (open until 9 pm). The Laverie Libre Service at 2 quai Finkwiller affords the finest view from a laundrette you'll fine anywhere in France (open until 9 pm).

Medical Services The Hôpital Civil (☎ 03 88 11 67 68, Porte de l'Hôpital tram stop), 1 place de l'Hôpital, accepts patients 24 hours a day.

Emergency The Police Nationale's Hôtel de Police (☎ 03 88 15 37 37), 11 rue de la Nuée Bleue, is open 24 hours a day.

Grande Île Walking Tour

With its bustling public squares, busy pedestrianised areas and upmarket shopping streets, the Grande Île is a great place

ALSACE

STRASBOURG

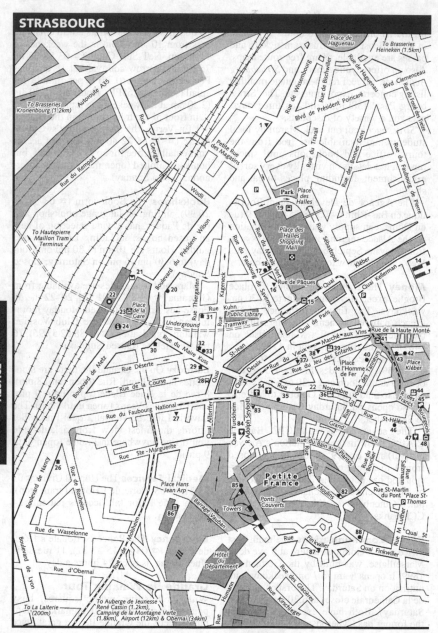

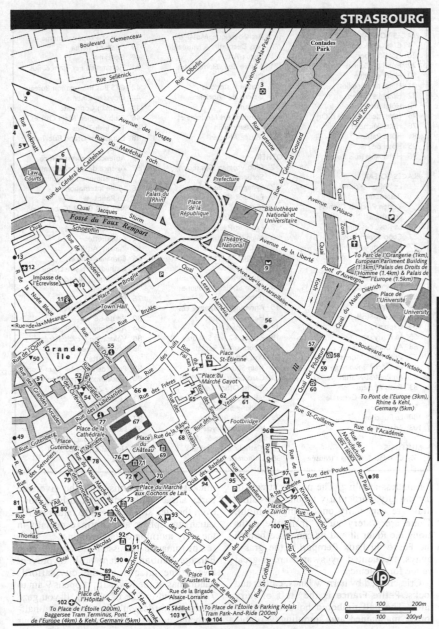

STRASBOURG

Contades Park

Boulevard Clemenceau

Rue Sellénick

Rue Oberlin

Avenue de la Paix

3

Quai Zorn

Avenue des Vosges

Rue Turenne

Rue du Maréchal Foch

Rue du Général de Castelnau

Rue Finkmatt

2

4

5

6

Law Courts

Rue du Général Gourand

Prefecture

Avenue d'Alsace

Quai Zorn

Palais du Rhin

Place de la République

Bibliothèque National et Universitaire

7

Quai Jacques Sturm

Quai Schoepflin

Fossé du Faux Rempart

Rue de la Fonderie

Théâtre National

Avenue de la Liberté

8

13

12

Impasse de l'Écrevisse

Rue de la Nuée Bleue

Place Broglie

Quai

Lezay - Marnésia

Ave de la Marseillaise

Pont d'Auvergne

Quai du Maire Diétrich

Place de l'Université

University

To Parc de l'Orangerie (1km), European Parliament Building (1.3km), Palais des Droits de l'Homme (1.4km) & Palais de l'Europe (1.5km)

10

11

Town Hall

Rue Brûlée

9

Rue de la Mésange

Grande Île

Rue du Dôme

55

Rue des Juifs

56

Quai Koch

Rue de l'Outre

50

Rue des Frères

Place St-Étienne

57

58

59

Boulevard de la Victoire

Rue des Grandes Arcades

51

52

53

54

Rue Sédillot

Rue des Hallebardes

66

63

64

Place du Marché Gayot

62

61

Veaux

60

Quai des Pêcheurs

To Pont de l'Europe (3km), Rhine & Kehl, Germany (5km)

49

Place de la Cathédrale

65

68

Footbridge

Rue St-Guillaume

Rue de l'Académie

Rue Mercière

67

Place du Château

69

96

Rue de la Manufacture des Tabacs

Rue des Serruriers

Rue du Vieux Marché aux Poissons

76

71

72

70

Rue des Bateliers

97

Rue de Zurich

Rue des Poules

98

Rue Paul Janet

78

79

73

94

95

Place de Zurich

99

Ste Catherine Kniténau

81

'Ail

80

75

74

93

Rue des Couples

Rue de Zurich

100

Rue du Jeu de Paume

Rue de la Division Leclerc

Rue Thomas

92

91

90

Rue des Bouchers

Rue d'Austerlitz

Rue des Orphelins

Rue St-Gothard

101

Place d'Austerlitz

Rue de Berne

89

Rue des Tête Armée

Place de l'Hôpital

Rue de la Brigade Alsace-Lorraine

102

To Place de l'Étoile (200m), Baggersee Tram Terminus, Pont de l'Europe (4km) & Kehl, Germany (5km)

R Sédillot

103

104

To Place de l'Étoile & Parking Relais Tram Park-And-Ride (200m)

0   100   200m

0   100   200yd

ALSACE

euro currency converter €1 = 6.56FF

STRASBOURG

PLACES TO STAY
4   CIARUS Hostel
26   Hôtel Weber
29   Hôtel Le Colmar
30   Hôtel du Rhin
31   Hôtel de Bruxelles
32   Hôtel Le Grillon
43   Hôtel Kléber
75   Hôtel de la Cruche d'Or
78   Hôtel Michelet
81   Hôtel Patricia
95   Hôtel de l'Ill
96   Hôtel Aux Trois Roses

PLACES TO EAT
1   Le Wilson (Kosher Restaurant)
5   Yarden Produits Cachers
16   Le Sahara
18   La Rose des Vins
27   Coop Supermarket
37   Rojas Empanaderia
38   Sidi Bou Saïd
50   Au Crocodile
51   Atac Supermarket
52   Winstub Le Clou
53   Chez Yvonne
54   St-Sépulchre
59   Broc-en-Stock
64   Geppetto
65   La Korrygane
68   Au Coin du Feu
72   Winstubs s'Muensterstuewel
79   La Cloche á Fromage
82   Au Pont St-Martin
83   Toros Alimentation
87   Alimentation Générale
99   Au Càdre
100 Le Bouchon
103 Adan

MUSEUMS
69   Château des Rohan (Musée Archéologique, Musée des Arts Décoratifs & Musée des Beaux-Arts)
71   Musée de l'Œuvre Notre Dame
73   Musée Historique
74   Galerie de l'Ancienne Douane
86   Musée d'Art Moderne et Contemporain
92   Musée Alsacien

OTHER
2   Club Vosgien (Strasbourg Section)
3   Synagogue de la Paix
6   Église St-Pierre-le-Jeune (Catholic)
7   US Consulate
8   Église St-Paul
9   Main Post Office
10   Le Griot
11   Banque de France
12   Hôtel de Police
13   Laundrette
14   Église St-Pierre-le-Jeune (Protestant)
15   Ancienne Synagogue Les Halles Tram Stop
17   The Bookworm
19   Réseau 67 Bus Station
20   Europcar Car Rental
21   Post Office
22   Train Station
23   Gare Centrale Tram Stop
24   Tourist Office Annexe
25   Vélocation Bicycle Rental (Parking St-Aurélie)
28   Pont Kuss Bus Stop
33   Vélocation Bicycle Rental
34   Église St-Pierre-le-Vieux (Catholic & Protestant)
35   Laundrette
36   Star St-Exupéry Cinema
39   Le Star Cinema
40   Géorama
41   Homme de Fer Tram & Bus Hub
42   CTS Bus Information Bureau
44   Odyssée Cinema
45   German Consulate
46   Club Vosgien Main Office
47   The Irish Times
48   Langstross Grand'Rue Tram Stop
49   American Express Office
55   Agence de Développement-Touristique en Bas-Rhin
56   Lycée International
57   Le Rafiot
58   NeT SuR CouR (Cybercafe)
60   Best Coffee Shop (Cybercafe)
61   Les Trois Brasseurs
62   Laundrette
63   Zanzib' Art Bar
66   Eurolines Office
67   Cathédrale Notre Dame
70   Strasbourg Fluvial Boat Excursions
76   Post Office
77   Main Tourist Office
80   Route 66
84   Académie de la Bière
85   Vélocation Bicycle Rental
88   Laverie Libre Service Laundrette
89   Porte de l'Hôpital Tram Stop
90   Vélocation Bicycle Rental
91   Bar Le Zoo
93   Le Trou
94   Gehol
97   Café des Anges
98   La Salamandre
101 Eurolines Coach Stop
102 Hôpital Civil (Hospital)
104 Espace Cycles

for aimless ambling. The narrow streets of the **old city**, particularly around the cathedral, are especially enchanting at night. There are watery views from the paths along the **River Ill** and its canalised branch the **Fossé du Faux Rempart** – the grassy quays, frequented by swans, are a great venue for a picnic.

Crisscrossed by narrow lanes, canals and locks, **Petite France** is the stuff of fairy tales. The half-timbered houses, meticulously maintained and sprouting veritable thickets of geraniums, and the riverside parks attract multitudes of tourists. However, the area still manages to retain its Alsatian atmosphere and charm, especially in the early morning or late evening.

The romantic Terrasse Panoramique atop **Barrage Vauban**, a dam built to prevent river-borne attacks on the city, affords panoramas of the River Ill; it opens 9 am to 7.30 pm and is free of charge. If you gaze north-eastwards you'll see the quaint, half-timbered houses of Petite France and four

La Marseillaise

Though you'd never know it from the name, France's stirring national anthem, 'La Marseillaise', was written in Strasbourg. In April 1792, at the beginning of the war with Austria, the mayor of Strasbourg – in whose city a garrison was getting ready for battle – suggested that the revolutionary army could use a catchy and patriotic tune to sing while marching off to spread the blessings of liberty throughout Europe. He approached Claude Rouget de Lisle, a young army engineer with a minor reputation as a composer, who after a furious all-night effort came up with a marching song entitled 'Chant de Guerre de l'Armée du Rhin' (War Song of the Rhine Army). It was first performed in the mayor's house (on the site of the present-day Banque de France building) by the mayor himself. The soul-stirring tune and its bloody lyrics became popular immediately, and by August was on the lips of volunteer troops from Marseille as they marched northwards to defend the Revolution.

13th-century fortified towers; turn around and the ultramodern Musée d'Art Moderne et Contemporain will be reflected in the river.

Cathédrale Notre Dame

The western facade of Strasbourg's lacy, almost fragile-looking Gothic cathedral – viewed to best advantage from rue Mercière – was completed in 1284, but the 142m spire, the tallest of its time, was not in place until 1439; its southern companion was never built.

On a bright day, the 12th- to 14th-century **stained-glass windows**, especially the rose window over the western portal, shine like jewels. The colourful **organ case** on the northern side dates from the 14th century, while the 30m-high Gothic and Renaissance contraption just inside the southern entrance is the **horloge astronomique** (astronomical clock), a late-16th-century clock (though the mechanism dates from 1842) that strikes solar noon every day at 12.30 pm. There's a 5FF charge to see the carved wooden figures whirl through their paces, which is why only the cathedral's southern entrance is open between 11.55 am and the end of the show. The cathedral can be visited until 7 pm daily.

The 66m-high platform above the facade (from which the **tower** and its Gothic open-work **spire** soar another 76m) affords a stork's-eye view of Strasbourg. The 330 spiral steps up to the platform can be climbed daily from 9 am to between 4.30 pm (No-

vember to February) and 7 pm (July and August). The entrance (☎ 03 88 43 60 40) is at the base of the bell tower that was never built. Tickets cost 20FF (students 10FF).

The cathedral plays host to organ concerts (35FF) at 8.30 pm on Friday and Saturday between May and September.

Museums

Except for the Musée de l'Œuvre Notre-Dame and the new Musée d'Art Moderne et Contemporain, which close on Monday, all of the city's museums are open daily except Tuesday. Opening hours (except for the Musée d'Art Moderne et Contemporain) are 10 am to noon and 1.30 to 6 pm (10 am to 5 pm on Sunday). Most museums charge 20FF (students up to age 25 and seniors 10FF); admission is free if you're under 15 or disabled. All the museums are free before noon on Sunday between November and March. Unless otherwise noted, the telephone number for Strasbourg's museums is ☎ 03 88 52 50 00. The French-language Web site is at www.musees-strasbourg.org.

The **Musée de l'Œuvre Notre-Dame**, housed in a group of 14th- and 16th-century buildings at 3 place du Château, displays a magnificent collection of Romanesque, Gothic and Renaissance sculptures, including a number of the cathedral's original statues. The **Tête du Christ** (Head of Christ), part of a stained-glass window from the mid-11th century – the oldest work of its kind in France – is in Room II. The celebrated figures of a downcast and blindfolded *Synagoga* (representing Judaism) and a serenely victorious *Église* (the Church), which date from around 1230 and once flanked the southern entrance to the cathedral (the statues there now are copies), are in Room VI.

The **Château des Rohan**, 2 place du Château, also known as the Palais Rohan, was built between 1732 and 1742 as a residence for the city's princely bishops. Today, it houses three museums, each with a separate 20FF admission fee. The whole place can be visited for 40FF (students and seniors 20FF). In the basement, the reasonably interesting **Musée Archéologique** covers the period from the Paleolithic to AD 800. On the ground floor is the **Musée des Arts Décoratifs**, which includes a series of lavish rooms that illustrate the lifestyle of the rich and powerful during the 18th century. Louis XV and Marie-Antoinette once slept here (in 1744 and 1770, respectively). On the 1st floor, the **Musée des Beaux-Arts** has a rather staid collection of French, Spanish, Italian, Dutch and Flemish masters from the 14th to the 19th centuries.

The outstanding **Musée d'Art Moderne et Contemporain** (Museum of Modern and Contemporary Art; ☎ 03 88 23 31 31) at place Hans Jean Arp, inaugurated in November 1998, has an exceptionally diverse collection of works representing every major art movement of the past century or so, including Impressionism, Symbolism, Fauvism, Cubism, Dada and Surrealism. An audioguide tour costs 20FF. Laminated cards in each room (except those given over to temporary contemporary installations) provide background in English. It opens 11 am to 7 pm daily except Monday (noon to 10 pm on Thursday). Admission costs 30FF.

The **Musée Alsacien** (☎ 03 88 35 55 36), 23 quai St-Nicolas, housed in three 16th- and 17th-century houses, affords a fascinating glimpse of Alsatian life over the centuries. Displays in the two dozen rooms include kitchen equipment (stoves, ceramics, biscuit cutters), colourful furniture, children's toys and even a tiny, 18th-century synagogue.

The **Musée Historique** (☎ 03 88 32 25 63), housed in a Renaissance-style abattoir (1588) at 3 place de la Grande Boucherie, traces the history of Strasbourg. It is closed for renovations until at least early 2001.

North-East of the Grande Île

The new – and hugely expensive – chamber of the 626-member **European Parliament** (Parlement Européen; ☎ 03 88 17 20 07), inaugurated in 1999, is 2km north-east of the cathedral on rue Lucien Fèbvre. Used 12 times a year for five-day 'part-sessions' (plenary sessions), it can be visited on weekdays. During sessions, you can sit in on debates for up to an hour; the best times to come are 9 am to noon and 3 to 6 pm Tuesday to Thursday. The rest of the time, there are free guided tours of the building at 2.30 pm (in French) and 4 pm (in either English or German). Make reservations a few days ahead. The Web site is at www .europarl.eu.int.

Across the Ill, the Council of Europe's **Palais de l'Europe** (☎ 03 90 21 49 40), opened in 1977 and once used by the European Parliament, can also be visited. Free tours begin at the Centre de la Presse from 8.30 to 11 am and 2 to 4.30 pm weekdays; for security reasons advance reservations are obligatory. During the four annual sessions of the 41-country Council's *assemblée parliamentaire* you can sit in on debates. To get there by bus, take No 23, 30 or 72.

Just across the Canal de la Marne, the **Palais des Droits de l'Homme**, home of the European Court of Human Rights since 1995, completes the city's ensemble of major European institutions.

Across ave de l'Europe from Palais de l'Europe, the flowerbeds, playgrounds, shaded paths and swan-dotted lake of **Parc de l'Orangerie** are hugely popular with local families, especially on sunny Sunday afternoons. In the warm months you can rent **rowboats** on Lac de l'Orangerie. The **bowling alley** (☎ 03 88 61 36 24), which also has billiard tables, is open until at least midnight daily (to 3 am on Saturday night). To get there by bus, take No 23, 30 or 72.

ALSACE

Many of Strasbourg's most impressive (and German-built) public buildings are just north-east of the Grande Île around **place de la République**. From there eastwards to Parc de l'Orangerie stretches a neighbourhood of solid, stone buildings inspired by late-19th-century Prussian tastes. Most are some sort of 'neo' – Romantic, Gothic or Renaissance – and you can see that some had the initials RF (République Française) hastily added after 1918 to replace the original German insignia.

Organised Tours

City The tourist office runs 90-minute, English-language tours (38FF, students 19FF) of the cathedral and the old city at 2.30 pm on Tuesday, Wednesday and Friday from May to December (daily at 10.30 am in July and August).

Boat Strasbourg Fluvial (☎ 03 88 84 13 13/ 32 75 25) runs 75-minute boat excursions that take in Petite France and Palais de l'Europe (41/20.50FF for adults/students; 1¼ hours). The dock (*embarcadère*) is behind the Château des Rohan.

Breweries Two of Strasbourg's largest *brasseries* (breweries) offer guided tours of their production facilities.

Brasseries Kronenbourg (☎ 03 88 27 41 59, Ducs d'Alsace tram stop), which sells 1 billion litres of beer in France each year (that's enough beer to fill over 300 Olympic swimming pools!), has a brewery 2.5km north-west of the Grande Île at 68 route d'Oberhausbergen in the suburb of Cronenbourg. Free tours in French, German and/or English (depending on group reservations) are usually conducted at 9 and 10 am and 2 and 3 pm weekdays (and at 11 am, and 4 and 5 pm from June to September); there are also tours on Saturday from early May to September and in December. Call ahead to reserve a place. By bus, take No 7 to the Jacob stop.

Brasseries Heineken (☎ 03 88 19 59 53) is 2.5km north of the Grande Île at 4 rue St-Charles (near the corner of Route de Bischwiller) in Schiltigheim. There are free,

1½-hour tours in French, German and/or English (depending on group bookings) at various times during the week; reservations are mandatory. Take the No 4 bus (northbound) to the Schiltigheim Mairie stop.

Walking The Strasbourg section of the Club Vosgien, a regional walking organisation founded in 1872, runs group walks and ski trips in the Vosges (and other parts of Alsace) on Sunday and, for seniors, Thursday. Visitors are welcome; the cost is 65FF, plus 25FF for insurance. Reservations should be made a few days ahead through their office (☎ 03 88 35 30 76) at 71 ave des Vosges, staffed 4 to 6.30 pm weekdays and 10 am to noon on Saturday. Bus trips leave from in front of the Palais du Rhin at place de la République.

Special Events

Strasbourg's summer season is enlivened by a variety of cultural events, including the Festival International de Musique (☎ 03 88 15 44 66), which takes place from early June to early July, and the Festival Jazz (☎ 03 88 32 43 10) in early July. Musica (☎ 03 88 23 47 23), a festival of contemporary music, is held from mid-September to early October.

The city's huge and justifiably renowned Marché de Noël (Christmas Market) is held at place Kléber, place de la Cathédrale, place Broglie and place de la Gare from the last weekend in November until 31 December (until 24 December at place Broglie).

Places to Stay

It is *extremely* difficult to find last-minute weekday accommodation when the European Parliament is in plenary session (for one week each month except August; there are two sessions in October) – contact the tourist office for dates. Because of the Christmas Market, weekends in December are also a problem. If you're stuck, the tourist office can provide details on same-night room availability.

Most of the hotels mentioned under Grande Île are not far from a tram stop.

Reservations for some hotels can be

ALSACE

made on-line at www.strasbourg.com/hotels and http://tourism-alsace.worldres.com.

Places to Stay – Budget

Camping The grassy, municipal *Camping de la Montagne Verte* (☎ *03 88 30 25 46, 2 rue Robert Forrer)* is open from mid-March to October. It is next to the *Auberge de Jeunesse René Cassin* (see Hostels), where you can pitch a tent for 42FF per person, including breakfast.

Hostels The stylish *Centre International d'Accueil et de Rencontre Unioniste de Strasbourg (CIARUS; ☎ 03 88 15 27 88, fax 03 88 15 27 89, 7 rue Finkmatt)* is a 285-bed, Protestant-run hostel that welcomes people of all ages and faiths. No hostelling card is necessary. Per-person tariffs (including breakfast) range from 92FF (in a room with up to eight beds) to 124FF (in a double, sometimes with a bunk bed). Facilities for the disabled are available. Curfew is at 1 am. This place is so attractive that at least a few European MPs choose to stay here. By bus, take No 4, 10, 20 or 72 to the place de Pierre stop.

The *Auberge de Jeunesse René Cassin* (☎ *03 88 30 26 46, fax 03 88 30 35 16, 9 rue de l'Auberge de Jeunesse)* is about 2.5km south-west of the train station. A bed in a room for three to six costs 73FF (100FF for a bed in a double), including breakfast. A HI card is mandatory. Take bus No 3 or 23 to the Auberge de Jeunesse stop; the nearest bus stop to the train station is Pont Kuss.

Hotels – Train Station Area The 15-room *Hôtel Le Colmar* (☎ *03 88 32 16 89, fax 03 88 21 97 17, 1 rue du Maire Kuss)* isn't stylish, but it's cheap and convenient. Airy, spotless doubles/triples start at 167/218FF; doubles with shower and toilet start at 212FF. Hall showers cost 15FF. Reception may be closed 2 to 5.30 pm on Sunday.

The *Hôtel Weber* (☎ *03 88 32 36 47, 22 blvd de Nancy)* is hardly in the most attractive part of town, but clean, quiet doubles start at 140FF; doubles/triples with shower and toilet cost 220/320FF. Hall showers cost 12FF. Unmetered parking is available

if you drive south on blvd de Nancy to rue de Kœnigshoffen and turn right under the railroad tracks.

Hotels – Grande Île An excellent bet is the *Hôtel Patricia* (☎ *03 88 32 14 60, fax 03 88 32 19 08,* ✉ *hotelpatricia@hotmail.com, 1a rue du Puits)*, whose generally dark, rustic interior (the 16th-century building was once a convent) fits in well with the local ambience. Ordinary but spacious doubles with great views start at 180FF (240FF with shower and toilet). The hall shower costs 12FF. Reception closes at 8 pm (2 pm on Sunday).

The 16-room *Hôtel Michelet* (☎ *03 88 32 47 38, 48 rue du Vieux Marché aux Poissons)*, a family-run establishment on the 'Street of the Old Fish Market', has simple singles/doubles costing from 145/170FF (220/270FF with shower and toilet).

Places to Stay – Mid-Range to Top End

Train Station Area The informal *Hôtel Le Grillon* (☎ *03 88 32 71 88, fax 03 88 32 22 01,* ✉ *grillon@compuserve.com, 2 rue Thiergarten)*, a 35-room, two-star place, has singles/doubles from 180/230FF (230/270FF with shower and toilet). Extra beds (up to a total of five people per room) are 70FF each.

The slightly tattered, 32-room, two-star *Hôtel de Bruxelles* (☎ *03 88 32 45 31, fax 03 88 32 06 22, 13 rue Kuhn)* has dull but fairly large doubles from 155FF (265FF with shower and toilet); quads cost 380FF.

Among the cheapest of the tourist-class hotels arrayed around place de la Gare is the 61-room *Hôtel du Rhin* (☎ *03 88 32 35 00, fax 03 88 23 51 92,* ✉ *hotel-rhin@ strasbourg.com, 7–8 place de la Gare)*, which has doubles with washbasin starting at 200FF (360FF with shower and toilet).

Grande Île The 14-room, two-star *Hôtel de la Cruche d'Or* (☎ *03 88 32 11 23, fax 03 88 21 94 78, 6 rue des Tonneliers)* has modern singles/doubles from 190/310FF. An extra bed costs 80FF. Reception closes at noon on Sunday.

The 31-room, two-star *Hôtel Kléber* (☎ *03 88 32 09 53, fax 03 88 32 50 41,* **@** *hotel.kleber@gofornet.com, 29 place Kléber)* is distinguished by its classic 1970s decor in atrociously bad taste. Cramped doubles with awful plaster-panel walls start at 216FF (276FF with shower and toilet); more spacious rooms are available from 360FF. Look on the bright side: the location couldn't be better.

On the right (southern) bank of the Ill, the 27-room, two-star *Hôtel de l'Ill* (☎ *03 88 36 20 01, fax 03 88 35 30 03, 8 rue des Bate-liers)* has tasteful singles/doubles with shower for 190/250FF (275/295FF with toilet, too). The 33-room, two-star *Hôtel Aux Trois Roses* (☎ *03 88 36 56 95, fax 03 88 35 06 14,* **@** *hotel-aux-trois-roses@ wanadoo.fr, 7 rue de Zurich)* has a free private sauna and comfortable but rather small singles/doubles with minibar for 295/ 398FF. Two rooms are outfitted for disabled guests. Free parking is sometimes available.

Places to Eat

In recent years, more and more of Strasbourg's restaurants have started calling themselves *winstubs* (literally 'wine rooms'), but most are just restaurants with Alsatian dishes. The winstubs mentioned below are as authentic as they come.

Restaurants – Winstubs & Alsatian

The narrow streets north of the cathedral are home to three excellent, intimate winstubs. *St-Sépulchre* (☎ *03 88 32 39 97, 15 rue des Orfèvres)* is exalted by some locals as the city's last authentic winstub. Solid everyday dishes such as *jambonneau* (knuckle of ham) and *jambon en croûte* (ham wrapped in a crust) cost 80FF. Hours are 11 am to 1.30 pm and 4 to 9.30 pm (closed Sunday and Monday). *Winstub Le Clou* (☎ *03 88 32 11 67, 3 rue du Chaudron)* seats diners together at long tables. Specialities include *baeckeoffe* (meat stew; 97FF) and *wädele braisé au pinot noir* (ham knuckles in wine; 86FF). Meals are served from 11.45 am to 2 pm and 5.30 pm to 12.30 am (closed Wednesday for lunch and on Sunday and holidays). The upmarket *Chez Yvonne* (☎ *03*

88 32 84 15, 10 rue du Sanglier) has baeckeoffe for 100FF. Frequented by Jacques Chirac and other politicos, it opens from 11.45 am to 2 pm and 6 pm to midnight (closed Monday for lunch and on Sunday).

Just south of the cathedral, a good bet is *Winstub s'Muensterstuewel* (☎ *03 88 32 17 63, 8 place du Marché aux Cochons de Lait),* closed Sunday and Monday.

Petite France's many tourist-oriented restaurants include *Au Pont St-Martin* (☎ *03 88 32 45 13, 15 rue des Moulins),* a reasonably priced restaurant that specialises in Alsatian dishes such as *choucroute* (cabbage with pork and potatoes; 69FF) and baeckeoffe (89FF). Vegetarians can select the *fricassée de champignons* (mushroom fricassee; 48FF) and one or two other dishes. The lunch *menu* costs 60FF. Regional specialities can be sampled by the fireplace at *Au Coin du Feu* (☎ *03 88 35 44 85, 10 rue de la Râpe),* which has *menus* for 58FF (weekday lunch only) and 135FF. It's closed Monday.

Restaurants – French

Lively, atmospheric *Le Bouchon* (☎ *03 88 37 32 40, 6 rue Ste-Catherine)* offers excellent French cuisine at reasonable prices (69FF to 125FF for mains). The proprietor, a *chansonnière* of local repute, performs most nights from about 9 or 9.30 pm onwards. Hours are 7 pm to 2 am (4 am for the bar; closed Sunday and Monday). *La Rose des Vins* (☎ *03 88 32 74 40, 5 rue de Pâques)* is a French restaurant that offers good value for money, with mains for 50FF to 90FF and a 98FF *menu* (closed Saturday and Sunday).

The world's largest cheese platter is on offer at *La Cloche à Fromage* (☎ *03 88 23 13 19, 27 rue des Tonneliers).* Cheese plates start at 91FF, *fondue Savoyarde* (cheese fondue) costs 118FF. For Breton crepes in a relaxed atmosphere, try *La Korrygane* (☎ *03 88 37 07 34, 12 place du Marché Gayot),* open daily. The same courtyard is home to several other small restaurants.

For all-out indulgence, *the* place to go is *Au Crocodile* (☎ *03 88 32 13 02, 10 rue de l'Outre),* which boasts three Michelin stars and often plays host to visiting heads of

ALSACE

state. The *menus* start at 410FF (including wine) for lunch on weekdays, 460FF the rest of the time (closed Sunday and Monday).

Restaurants – Other Copious portions of *tajines* (65FF) and couscous (44FF to 95FF) are on offer at **Le Sahara** (☎ 03 88 22 64 50, 3 rue du Marais Vert). **Sidi Bou Saïd** (☎ 03 88 22 17 17, 22 rue du Vieux Marché aux Vins) has Tunisian couscous for 60FF to 75FF (closed Monday). **Au Càdre** (☎ 03 88 25 14 69, 1 rue St-Gothard), on place de Zurich, is a hugely popular Lebanese place with a 110FF *menu*.

Broc-en-Stock (☎ 03 88 24 06 09, 15 quai des Pêcheurs) is an Italian place with *menus* for 45FF (lunch only), 85FF and 100FF (closed at midday at the weekend). **Rojas Empanaderia** (☎ 03 88 75 05 43, 6 place du Vieux Marché aux Vins) serves tasty and inexpensive Argentine food 11 am to 7 pm weekdays.

Inexpensive student restaurants, including several pizzerias, can be found along rue des Frères, especially towards place St-Étienne. **Geppetto** (☎ 03 88 36 91 05, 1 place St-Étienne) is a well-regarded pizzeria open 6 pm to 1 am daily.

Just south of place Gutenberg, pedestrianised rue des Tonneliers is lined with midrange restaurants of all sorts, both French and ethnic.

Restaurants – Vegetarian & Kosher Self-service vegetarian-organic food is on offer at **Adan** (☎ 03 88 35 70 84, 6 rue Sédillot); the *menu* costs 62FF. It is open for lunch (noon to 2 pm) from Monday to Saturday.

Le Wilson (☎ 03 88 52 06 66, 25 blvd du Président Wilson) is a kosher restaurant with *menus* from 95FF; the plat du jour is 48FF (closed Friday night and Saturday).

Self-Catering Strasbourg's 20 weekly markets include a large *food market* at either place Kléber or place Broglie (as we go to press the municipality has yet to decide) open until at least 4 pm on Wednesday and Friday.

The **Atac** supermarket *(47 rue des Grandes Arcades)* is open 8.30 am to 8 pm Monday to Saturday. **Toros Alimentation** *(8 Grand' Rue)* opens 8 am to 8 pm daily. Near the train station, the **Coop** supermarket *(19 rue du Faubourg National)* is open 8 am to 12.30 pm and 3 to 7 pm weekdays, and 8 am to 6 pm on Saturday.

A few blocks south of the cathedral, pedestrianised rue d'Austerlitz is home to quite a few *food shops*. In Petite France, the **Alimentation Générale** *(12 rue Finkwiller)* is open Monday to Saturday.

Yarden Produits Cachers *(3 rue Finkmatt)* is a kosher grocery that's closed from 12.30 to 3 pm and on Friday evening, Sunday afternoon and Saturday.

Entertainment

Pubs & Bars Popular with students, **Les Trois Brasseurs** *(☎ 03 88 36 12 13, 22 rue des Veaux)* is a warm, dimly lit pub that brews four varieties of beer on the premises (from 12FF, 15FF after 9.30 pm). Alsatian snacks and brasserie meals are served at the downstairs picnic tables. It opens 11 am to 1 am daily.

Also popular with students, **Académie de la Bière** *(☎ 03 88 32 61 08, 17 rue Adolphe Seyboth)* is a perennial favourite. You can sit amid rough-hewn wooden beams – or, if you prefer, in the cellar below – and choose from among 80 beers (from 10FF, 15FF after 9 pm). It opens 9 am to 4 am daily. At **Le Trou** *(☎ 03 88 36 91 04, 5 rue des Couples)*, in a vaulted brick cellar, you can sip 40 kinds of beer (from 15FF) at small wooden tables. A largely student crowd gathers from 8.30 pm (9.30 pm in summer) to 3.30 am daily.

Look for the Guinness sign to find **The Irish Times** *(☎ 03 88 32 04 02, 19 rue St-Barbe)*, a congenial pub that has live music from about 9 pm on Tuesday, Friday and Saturday. Hours are 2 pm (noon on Sunday) to 1 or 2 am. The friendly, laid-back **Zanzib' Art Bar** *(☎ 03 88 36 66 18, 1 place St-Étienne)* has live music from 10 pm on Friday and Saturday nights (open 5 pm until as late as 4 am daily; closed Sunday). Beers start at 10FF (15FF after 9 pm).

The friendly, down-to-earth *Route 66* (☎ *03 88 32 89 79, 15 rue de la Division Leclerc*) attracts lots of English-speakers. As for the background music, almost anything goes except techno and rap (open noon to 4 am daily, except Monday). Another favourite of English-speakers is the *Best Coffee Shop* (see Post & Communications earlier in the chapter), which is pretty hopping at night, especially on Friday and Sunday.

Discos & Clubs From 9 pm to 3 am Wednesday to Saturday, *La Salamandre* (☎ *03 88 25 79 42, 3 rue Paul Janet*), an informal dance club, has either live bands playing salsa, 70s music, *chansons* and so on (60FF to 100FF) or themed DJ nights (40FF). There's a *bal musette* (dancing to French accordion music) from 5 to 10 pm on Sunday between October and early May. The ever-popular, easygoing *Café des Anges* (☎ *03 88 37 12 67, 5 rue Ste-Catherine*) has dancing to soul, R&B, funk and so on in the cellar Thursday to Saturday; on the ground floor, bods move to salsa Tuesday to Saturday and merengue on Thursday. Hours are 9 pm to 4 am (closed on Sunday and Monday except on holidays). There's no admission fee; drinks start at 20FF. At both these places dress is informal and things only really get going after 11 pm.

The soul, funk, salsa and African music at the very informal *Le Griot* (☎ *03 88 52 00 52, 6 impasse de l'Écrevisse*) attracts a racially and ethnically mixed crowd (sadly a rare sight at French nightspots). Hours are 9 pm to 4 am (closed Sunday and Monday); dancing starts very late on Thursday, Friday and Saturday nights. There's no cover charge except for the live jazz concerts (80FF, students 60FF), held in the vaulted cellar at 10.30 pm on many Thursdays and Fridays. The free Tuesday-night jam sessions start at about 10 pm.

Le Rafiot (☎ *03 88 36 36 16, across the street from 16 quai des Pêcheurs*), which occupies the cargo hold of a one-time coal barge, is a *bar ambiance* with dancing. Amid nautical decor, the DJs play every-thing from reggae to disco for a mixed-age crowd. There's no cover charge. Hours are 8 pm to 3 or 4 am nightly (except Monday) during winter; the terrace opens early every afternoon during the summer.

Gay Venues The friendly, mostly gay *Bar Le Zoo* (☎ *03 88 24 55 33,* ✉ *lezoobar@ yahoo.com, 6 rue de Bouchers*), has a mellow lounge with giant wing chairs in the cellar. It opens from 6 pm to 1.30 am (4 pm to midnight on Sunday). Starting at 9 pm each Wednesday there's a *soirée poste*, during which patrons post letters to each other. *Kfé Kuchen*, a coffee and cake combo, is served from 4 pm on Sunday.

Cinemas Nondubbed films can be seen at the *Odyssée* (☎ *03 88 75 10 47, 3 rue des Francs Bourgeois*), an art cinema; the *Star St-Exupéry* (☎ *03 88 32 34 82, 18 rue du 22 Novembre*); and the six-screen *Le Star* (☎ *03 88 22 33 95, 27 rue du Jeu des Enfants*).

Concerts Strasbourg's most vibrant venue for live music is *La Laiterie* (☎ *03 88 23 72 37, 11–13 rue du Hohwald; Laiterie tram stop*), about 1km south-west of the train station. Concert tickets (50FF to 150FF) are available either at the door (telephone bookings are not accepted) or, for a slight surcharge, at a FNAC or Virgin ticket outlet. At midnight on Friday nights La Laiterie turns into a disco (50FF for a compulsory one-year membership).

Shopping

The city's most elegant shopping is around rue des Hallebards, lined with beautiful window displays.

At Gehol (Génération Holographie; ☎ 03 88 52 17 16), 28 quai des Bateliers, a 3D holographic portrait of yourself costs 250FF (for the 12 by 18cm version; by appointment). The studio is open 1 to 7.30 pm Wednesday to Saturday.

Getting There & Away

Air Strasbourg airport (☎ 03 88 64 67 67) is 12km south-west of the city centre

ALSACE

(towards Molsheim) near the village of Entzheim. Its Web site is at www.strasbourg .aeroport.fr.

Bus Réseau 67 (☎ 03 88 23 43 23), the departmental bus network, has few services of interest to tourists except one to Obernai (21FF). The station, just north of the place des Halles shopping mall, has an office open 6 am to 7 pm Monday to Saturday.

Eurolines (☎ 03 88 22 73 74) has an office at 5 rue des Frères (closed on Thursday morning and at the weekend), but its coaches arrive and depart from place d'Austerlitz.

Strasbourg city bus No 21 links place Gutenberg with the Stadthalle in Kehl (7FF), the German town just across the Rhine.

Train The train station (☎ 08 36 35 35 35), built in 1883, is open 24 hours. Destinations include Paris' Gare de l'Est (215FF, four to five hours, eight to 13 a day), Lille (273FF, five hours), Metz (113FF, 1¼ hours, 12 a day, seven at weekends) and Nancy (109FF, 70 to 95 minutes, eight to 13 a day); and, internationally, Basel (Bâle; 103FF, 1½ hours, nine to 14 direct a day; bicycle transport possible), Frankfurt (218FF, at least two hours) and Budapest (882FF, 14 hours, nightly).

Route du Vin destinations include Colmar (56FF, 30 to 95 minutes, 37 a day, 23 at weekends; bicycle transport possible), Molsheim (21FF, 15 to 35 minutes, 40 a day, 10 to 14 at weekends) and Sélestat (42FF, one to 1½ hours, 49 a day, 25 at weekends; bicycle transport possible). Rosheim (25FF, 25 to 40 minutes) and Obernai (29FF, 30 to 50 minutes) have 20 services a day (four to seven at weekends). About 11 trains a day (four to six at weekends) go to Barr (40 to 60 minutes) and Dambach (60 to 80 minutes).

Car Europcar (☎ 03 88 15 55 66) is at 16 place de la Gare.

Getting Around
To/From the Airport The CTS *navette* (shuttle; ☎ 03 88 77 70 70) links the Baggersee tram terminus with the airport (27FF; 12 minutes). It runs every 15 minutes until 11.15 pm (to 9.40 pm on Saturday).

Bus & Tram Three highly civilised tramlines form the centrepiece of Strasbourg's excellent public transport network, run by CTS (☎ 03 88 77 70 70). The main hub is at place de l'Homme de Fer. Buses from the city centre run until about 11.30 pm, trams until a bit after midnight.

Single bus/tram tickets, sold by bus drivers and the ticket machines at tram stops, cost 7FF. The Tourpass (20FF), valid for 24 hours from the moment you time-stamp it, is sold at tourist offices and ticket machines. The weekly Hebdopass (64FF) is good from Monday to Sunday.

Parking Virtually the whole city centre is pedestrianised, so don't even think of driving around the Grande Île – or parking there for more than a couple of hours.

About 500m south of the cathedral, at the 'Parking Relais Tram' lot at place de l'Étoile (Étoile Bourse tram stop), the 15FF all-day parking fee gets the driver and each passenger a free round-trip tram ride into the city centre.

Taxi Try Alsace Taxi (☎ 03 88 22 19 19) or Taxi Treize (☎ 03 88 36 13 13), which operate round the clock.

Bicycle & Electric Car Strasbourg has an extensive *réseau cyclable* (network of cycling paths); free maps are available at the tourist office.

The city government's Vélocation system (☎ 03 88 52 01 01) can supply you with a well-maintained bike for a mere 20/30FF per half-day/day or 150FF for 10 days (and just 100FF a month for students!). Offices, open daily until 7 pm, can be found two blocks east of the train station at 4 rue du Maire Kuss; in the northernmost tower of the Ponts Couverts in Petite France; and just south of the old city at 10 rue des Bouchers.

Espace Cycles (☎ 03 88 35 33 81), 17 rue de la Brigade Alsace-Lorraine, rents mountain bikes for 100/20FF for the first/subsequent days (closed Sunday and Monday).

Vélocation's agencies at Parking St-Aurélie and on rue des Bouchers hire out four-seat electric cars, which run for a bit

ALSACE

over 50km on a single charge (100FF per half-day; 1000FF deposit).

ROUTE DU VIN D'ALSACE

Meandering for some 120km along the eastern foothills of the Vosges, the Route du Vin d'Alsace (Alsace Wine Route) passes through villages guarded by ruined hilltop castles, surrounded by vine-clad slopes and brightened by colourful half-timbered houses. Combine such charms with numerous roadside *caves* (wine cellars), where you can sample Alsace's crisp white wines (Riesling and Gewürztraminer in particular), and you have one of France's busiest tourist tracks. Local tourist offices can supply you with an English-language map-brochure, *The Alsace Wine Route*.

The Route du Vin, at places twee and touristy, stretches from Marlenheim, about 20km west of Strasbourg, southwards to Thann, about 35km south-west of Colmar. En route are some of Alsace's most picturesque villages (and some very ordinary ones, too), many extensively rebuilt after being flattened in WWII. Ramblers can take advantage of the area's *sentiers viticoles* (signposted vineyard trails).

Some of the slightly less touristy places include (north to south) Mittelbergheim, Andlau, Itterswiller, Turckheim and Eguisheim. Also worth visiting are the very popular Ribeauvillé, Riquewihr, Kientzheim, Kaysersberg and the chateau at Haut Kœnigsbourg, all of which can easily be seen on a day trip from Colmar.

The villages mentioned below – listed from north to south – all have plenty of hotels, camp sites and restaurants. *Chambres d'hôtes* (B&Bs) can cost as little as 160FF for a double – tourist offices can provide details on local options.

Organised Tours

LCA Top Tour (☎ 03 89 41 90 88, 🖻 lca-toptour@alsace-travel.com), based at 6 place de la Gare (next to the train station) in Colmar, offers minibus tours of the Route du Vin (275FF per person for a half-day). Reservations can be made at the Colmar tourist office (see Colmar later in the chapter).

Getting There & Away

The Route du Vin, which is not just one road but a composite of several (the D422, D35, D1 bis and so on), can be followed by either car or bicycle (local cycling maps are available at tourist offices). It is well signposted but drivers might want to pick up a copy of Blay's colour-coded map, *Alsace Touristique* (40FF at tourist offices). Parking can be a nightmare in the high season, especially in Ribeauvillé and Riquewihr.

Getting to and around the Route du Vin by public transport can be a bit tricky but is eminently possible, and most of the towns mentioned below are served by train and/or bus – for details see Getting There & Away under Colmar and Strasbourg.

Obernai

This picturesque town, 35km south of Strasbourg, is centred around place du Marché, a market square that's still put to use each Thursday morning. In the square you'll find the newly reroofed **Halle aux Blés** (Corn Exchange; 1554); the mainly 16th-century **town hall**, decorated with Baroque trompe l'œil; and, across rue du Général Gouraud (the main street), a Renaissance well known as the **Puits aux Six Seaux** (Well of the Six Buckets).

The cool, flower-bedecked courtyards and alleyways (such as tiny ruelle des Juifs next to the tourist office) are fun to explore, as are the 1.75km-long, 13th-century **ramparts**. A number of wine cellars are just a short walk out of town (contact the tourist office for details).

The tourist office (☎ 03 88 95 64 13, fax 03 88 49 90 84, 🖻 obernai@sdv.fr) is on place du Beffroi (behind the town hall) opposite the 59m-high **Kapellturm** (belfry; 1280). It opens until 5 pm (7 pm from May to October; closed from noon or 12.30 to 2 pm and, from November to April, on Sunday).

The cheapest hotel in town is the nine-room *Maison du Vin d'Obernai* (☎ 03 88 95 46 82, fax 03 88 95 54 00, 1 rue de la Paille), across rue du Marché from the Halle aux Blés. Doubles costs 160FF to 210FF. The newly renovated, 25-room

ALSACE

Hôtel Le Gouverneur (☎ 03 88 95 63 72, *fax 03 88 49 91 04, 13 rue de Sélestat)* has doubles from 320FF.

The train station is a few hundred metres east of the walled town centre.

Mont St-Odile

Occupied by a convent founded in the 8th century (and destroyed several times), the 763m-high summit of Mont St-Odile, surrounded by conifer forests, affords spectacular views of Alsace's wine country and, nearer the Rhine, the fields of white cabbage (for sauerkraut) around Krautergersheim. It can be reached on foot via a network of trails that come from every direction, including Obernai (12km).

Vestiges of the 10km-long **Mur Païen** (Pagan Wall), built by the Celts around 1000 BC and fixed up by the Romans, can be seen nearby.

Some of the monastery buildings have been converted into a 140-room guest house, *Hostellerie du Mont St-Odile* (☎ 03 88 95 80 53, *fax 03 88 95 82 96)*, run by the Strasbourg archdiocese, where singles/doubles start at 125/170FF (270FF with shower and toilet).

Réseau 67 bus No 210 links Mont St-Odile with Strasbourg's bus station daily in July and August (and on Sunday and holidays between Easter and 1 November). There is ample parking at the summit.

Mittelbergheim & Andlau

Some 10km south-west of Obernai and 2km apart, these two villages are – refreshingly – not as geared up for tourism as their flashier siblings to the north and south. Mittelbergheim is a hilly village with no real centre.

It's awash with vines and its tiny streets are lined with Renaissance houses. Private accommodation is easy to come by – '*chambres/zimmer*' signs are in windows all over town.

Andlau is at the bottom of a forested valley along a stream. **Église Ste-Richarde**, a former abbey church, has a celebrated Romanesque frieze and an eerie, 11th-century crypt. The two dilapidated chateaux above

town, **Haut Andlau** (1337) and **Spesbourg** (1247), are accessible on foot via a three hour circuit. Trails, including the GR5, lead in every direction. The *grand cru* (top-quality vintage) labels to try here are Kastelberg, Mœnchberg and Wiebelsberg.

The tourist office (☎ 03 88 08 22 57, fax 03 88 08 42 22, @ otandlau@netcourrier .com), 5 rue du Général de Gaulle, opens in the afternoon (except Sunday and holidays).

Haut Kœnigsbourg

Perched on a forested promontory high above the town of St-Hippolyte, the imposing, red-sandstone **Château du Haut Kœnigsbourg** (☎ 03 88 82 50 60) was reconstructed early this century by Germany's Kaiser Wilhelm II (ruled 1888–1918) on the site of a 12th-century fortress that was home to the powerful Hohenstaufen family. Hours are 9 or 9.30 am to noon and 1 pm to sometime between 4.30 pm (November to February) and 6.30 pm (in July and August; no midday closure from May to September). Admission costs 40FF (students 25FF, free for under 18s).

Ribeauvillé

Some 19km north-west of Colmar, Ribeauvillé is arguably the most heavily touristed of all the villages on the Route du Vin. It's easy to see why: the little village, nestled in a valley and brimming with 18th-century overhanging houses and narrow alleys, is picture-perfect.

Don't miss the 13th- and 16th-century **Tour des Bouchers** (Butchers' Belltower), the **town hall** and its Renaissance fountain, or the 17th-century **Pfifferhüs** (Fifers' House) at 14 Grand' Rue, which once housed the town's fife-playing minstrels and is now home to a friendly winstub. The ruins of three 12th- and 13th-century **castles** west and north-west of Ribeauvillé can be reached on foot in three hours. One of them, **Château du Haut Ribeaupierre**, is visible from the village centre.

The tourist office (☎ 03 89 73 62 22, fax 03 89 73 36 61) is at No 1 on the pedestrianised Grand' Rue (open Monday to Saturday).

Riquewihr

This partially walled, largely pedestrianised village is every bit as popular with visitors as Ribeauvillé, 5km to the north, but somehow feels just a tad more authentic. The 16th-century **ramparts** are great for exploring, as are the alleys and courtyards. Sights include the **château**, built in 1540 and now housing a **postal museum** (open daily except Tuesday from early April to early November; 34FF); and the **Dolder** (1291), a stone and half-timbered gate with a bell tower and, inside, a small museum. From there, rue des Juifs leads to the **Tour des Voleurs** (Thieves' Tower; 10FF), a former dungeon containing some extremely efficient-looking implements of torture (open from Easter to 1 November).

The tourist office (☎ 03 89 49 08 40, fax 03 89 49 08 49), 2 rue de la Première Armée, is open year round (closed Sunday and holidays).

At the two-star *Hôtel St-Nicolas* (☎ 03 89 49 01 51, fax 03 89 49 04 36, 2 rue St-Nicolas), 100m from the Dolder, singles/doubles/quads start at 210/300/420FF.

Kaysersberg

The picture-perfect town centre, 10km north-west of Colmar (and surrounded by mall sprawl) is known for its squat, **fortified bridge** over the River Weiss and its 12th- to 15th-century, red-sandstone **church**, which has a Renaissance **fountain** on one side and the ornate, Renaissance **town hall** (1605) on the other. The house where the musicologist, medical doctor and 1952 Nobel-Peace-Prize winner **Albert Schweitzer** (1875–1965) was born, at 126 rue du Général de Gaulle, is now a museum (☎ 03 89 47 36 55). It opens May to October and admission costs 10FF. The remains of a massive, crenellated **château** stand above town, surrounded by vines. Footpaths lead in all directions from town; possible destinations include Riquewihr (1½ hours), Labaroche (2½ hours) and Ribeauvillé (three hours).

The tourist office (☎ 03 89 78 22 78, fax 03 89 78 27 44, ℮ ot.kaysersberg@ rmcnet.fr) is inside the town hall at 37 rue du Général de Gaulle (formerly the Grand' Rue). It is closed Saturday afternoon and Sunday except in July and August.

The two-star *Hôtel Arbre Vert* (☎ 03 89 47 11 51, next to 135 rue du Général de Gaulle), at the western edge of the town centre, has doubles from 350FF.

Eguisheim

Just 5km south-west of Colmar, the village of Eguisheim has a circular town centre in whose middle sits the **chateau**, founded in the 8th century, where Pope Leo IX was born in 1002. Bisected by the Grand' Rue, the village is known for its geranium-adorned, gabled houses, two **Renaissance-style fountains** and, on a hill above the town, three square **donjons** (fortified towers) made of red sandstone. The latter are linked to the town by a variety of walking trails that also go to neighbouring villages. The area's most famous *grands crus* are Eichberg and Pfersigberg, whose vineyards are north-west of town.

The tourist office (☎ 03 89 23 40 33), at 22a Grand' Rue, is open Tuesday to Saturday, except holidays (daily in July and August).

NATZWEILER-STRUTHOF

The only Nazi concentration camp on French soil, Natzweiler-Struthof was established about 30km west of Obernai in late 1940. The site was chosen because of the nearby granite quarries (**La Grande Carrière**), in which many of the inmates were worked to death as slave labourers. In all, some 10,000 to 12,000 of the camp's prisoners, most of them Jews and French Resistance fighters, died or were executed here. In April 1944, as the Allies approached Alsace, the surviving inmates were sent to Dachau.

The camp provided the Reich University in Strasbourg with inmates (including many Roma people) for use in often lethal pseudo-medical experiments involving chemical warfare agents and infectious diseases such as hepatitis and typhus. In April 1943, about 130 prisoners, most of them Jews specially brought from Auschwitz, were gassed here to supply the university's anatomical institute with skeletons for its anthropological and racial skeleton collection.

Today, visitors can see the remains of the camp (☎ 03 88 97 04 49), still surrounded by guard towers and two rows of barbed wire, including the **four crématoire** (crematorium). One of the *baraques* (barracks) has been turned into a **museum**. The ordinary-looking building that served as a **chambre à gaz** (gas chamber) is 1.7km down the D130 from the camp gate.

Struthof can be visited from 10 am to noon and 2 to 5 or 5.30 pm daily from March to 24 December (10 am to 6 pm in July and August). Admission costs 8FF. To get there from Obernai, take the D426, D214 and D130, following the signs to Le Struthof or Camp du Struthof.

COLMAR
postcode 68000 • pop 64,000
• elevation 194m

The centre of the harmonious town of Colmar, capital of Haut-Rhin, is a maze of cobbled pedestrian malls and restored, Alsatian-style buildings from the late Middle Ages and the Renaissance. Many of the half-timbered houses are painted in bold pastel tones of blue, orange, red or green. The Musée d'Unterlinden is world-renowned for the spectacular Issenheim Altarpiece.

The Route du Vin can easily be explored by bike, car and even bus using Colmar as a base (see also the Route du Vin d'Alsace section earlier in the chapter).

Orientation

Ave de la République links the train station and bus terminal with the Musée d'Unterlinden and the nearby tourist office, a distance of about 1km. The old city, much of it pedestrianised, is south-east of the Musée d'Unterlinden. The Petite Venise quarter runs along the River Lauch, at the southern edge of the old city.

Information

Tourist Office The efficient tourist office (☎ 03 89 20 68 92, fax 03 89 41 34 13,

ⓔ accueil@ot-colmar.fr), 4 rue des Unterlinden, is open from 9 am to noon and 2 to 6 pm Monday to Saturday (no midday closure from April to October; open until 7 pm in July and August); and from 10 am to 2 pm on Sunday and holidays. The staff can supply you with brochures on day hikes and cycling around Colmar and in the Massif des Vosges, and the local *Calendrier des Manifestations* (Calendar of Events), published every month or two. On-the-spot hotel reservations are free. See the Web site (in French) at www.ot-colmar.fr.

Money The Banque de France, 46 ave de la République, changes money from 8.45 am to noon on weekdays. The tourist office's exchange rate is pathetic. There's a 24-hour banknote-exchange machine at the Sogenal bank, 17 rue des Têtes.

Post & Communications The main post office, 36 ave de la République, is open from 8 am to 6.30 pm on weekdays and from 8.30 am to noon on Saturday. Exchange services and a Cyberposte are available.

Laundry The Point Laverie at 1 rue Ruest is open from 7 am to 9 pm daily.

Medical Services Hôpital Pasteur (☎ 03 89 12 40 00, 24 hours a day) is 700m west of the train station at 39 ave de la Liberté. It is served by bus lines 1, 3, A or C.

Old City

The medieval streets of the old city, including **rue des Clefs**, the **Grand' Rue** and **rue des Marchands**, are lined with dozens of restored, half-timbered houses. **Maison Pfister** (1537), which is opposite 36 rue des Marchands, is remarkable for its exterior decoration, including delicately painted panels, an elaborate oriel window and a carved wooden balcony. The house next door at 9 rue des Marchands, which dates from 1419, has a wooden sculpture of a sombre-looking *marchand* (merchant) on the corner. The **Maison des Têtes** (House of the Heads; 1609), 19 rue des Têtes, has

ALSACE

a fantastic facade crowded with 106 grimacing stone faces and animal heads.

Colmar has a number of small **quartiers** (quarters, or neighbourhoods) – not much more than single streets in a few cases – which preserve some of the ambience that existed back when each was home to a specific guild. At the south-eastern end of rue des Marchands, near the **Quartier des Tanneurs** (Tanners' District), is the **Ancienne Douane** (or Koïfhus in Alsatian; Old Customs House), built in 1480. Now used for temporary exhibitions and concerts, it is the town's best example of late-medieval civil architecture.

Rue des Tanneurs, with its tall houses and rooftop verandas for drying hides, intersects **quai de la Poissonnerie**, the former fishers' quarter, which runs along the River Lauch. The river provides the delightful **Petite Venise** (Little Venice) area – also known as Quartier de la Krutenau – with its rather fanciful appellation. It's best appreciated from the **rue de Turenne bridge**.

On Friday and Saturday and during holiday and festival periods, Colmar's historic sites are lit up at night by special computer-controlled spotlights of different colours and varying intensities.

Museums

The most renowned work in the **Musée d'Unterlinden** (☎ 03 89 20 15 50) is the **Issenheim Altarpiece** (Rétable d'Issenheim), which has been acclaimed as one of the most dramatic and moving works of art ever created. Other displays include an Alsatian wine cellar, armour, weapons, Strasbourg faïence and Revolutionary memorabilia. Hours are 10 am to 5 pm (9 am to 6 pm from April to October; closed on Tuesday from November to March). Admission costs 35FF (25FF if you're aged 12 to 25).

Dedicated to the life and work of the Colmar native who created New York's Statue of Liberty, the **Musée Bartholdi** (☎ 03 89 41 90 60), 30 rue des Marchands, displays some of the work and personal memorabilia of Frédéric Auguste Bartholdi (1834–1904) in the house where he was

born. It opens 10 am to noon and 2 to 6 pm daily except Tuesday (closed in January and February). Admission costs 23FF (students 15FF). The **Musée du Jouet** (☎ 03 89 41 93 10), 40 rue Vauban, has an impressive collection of wind-up antique toys and trains. It opens the same hours and days as Musée Bartholdi (no midday closure in July and August). Admission costs 25FF.

Churches

The 13th- and 14th-century **Collégiale St-Martin**, an unusually intimate Gothic basilica on place de la Cathédrale, is commonly referred to as the cathedral (though Colmar is not a bishopric). It is known for its peculiar, Mongol-style copper spire (1572) and its sombre ambulatory. It is open from 8 am to 6 or 7 pm daily.

The celebrated triptych *La Vierge au Buisson de Roses* (The Virgin in the Rose Bush), painted by Martin Schongauer in 1473, is on display inside the desanctified, Gothic **Église des Dominicains**, whose stained glass is from the 14th and 15th centuries. The church is open from 10 am to 1 pm and 3 to 6 pm (closed from January to mid-March). Admission costs 8FF.

At the northern end of Grand' Rue, the Protestant **Temple St-Mathieu** – until 1937 both a Catholic *and* Protestant church – has a rare medieval *jubé* (rood screen). It can be visited from 10 am to noon and 3 to 5 pm daily (except Sunday morning) around Easter and most of the time between mid-June and mid-October.

Organised Tours

From April to October and throughout December, the tourist office runs 1¼-hour tours of the Musée d'Unterlinden at 10.15 am (55FF) and the old city (25FF). Night-time tours lasting 1½ hours are held three or four times a weekend from late November to late December, and cost 25FF. Call ahead to see if an English-speaking guide is available.

Special Events

From mid-May to mid-September, Soirées Folkloriques (free performances of Alsatian

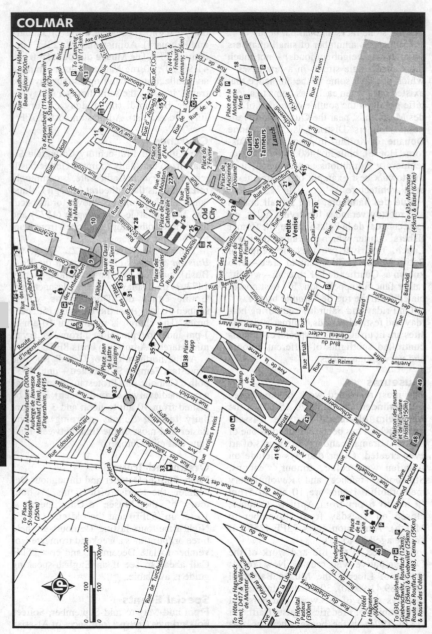

COLMAR

COLMAR

PLACES TO STAY		OTHER			
2	Hôtel Primo	1	Free Parking	29	Sogenal Bank
35	Hôtel Kempf	3	Eden Café	30	Église des Dominicains
43	Hôtel La Chaumière	4	Tourist Office	31	Maison des Têtes; Restaurant
45	Grand Hôtel Bristol	5	Unterlinden/Point Central		Maison des Têtes
			Bus Hub	32	ADA Car Rental
PLACES TO EAT		6	Theatre	33	Rock Café; Captain
9	Monoprix Supermarket	7	Musée d'Unterlinden		Café
13	Atac Supermarket	8	TRACE Bus Information	36	Cycles Geiswiller
14	Le Temps des		Office	37	Metal Café
	Delices	10	Town Hall	38	Entrance to Underground
15	Les Gourmets d'Asie	11	Point Laverie Laundrette		Parking
19	Aux Trois Poissons	12	Musée du Jouet	39	Merry-Go-Round
20	Le Petit Gourmand	16	Temple St-Mathieu	40	Main Post Office
21	Old Covered Market	17	Synagogue	41	Banque de France
22	La Maison Rouge	18	Free Parking	42	Prefecture Building
27	Djerba La Douce	23	Ancienne Douane	44	Autop Car Rental
28	Fromagerie	24	Musée Bartholdi	46	Train Station
	St-Nicolas	25	Maison Pfister	47	Bus Terminal
34	Flunch Cafeteria	26	Collégiale St-Martin	48	Cour d'Appel
				49	Water Tower

music and dancing) are held every Tuesday at 8.30 pm at place de l'Ancienne Douane.

Vintners display their wines at the Foire Régionale des Vins d'Alsace (Regional Wine Fair of Alsace), which attracts large numbers of visitors from the weekend before 15 August until the following weekend. Local food specialities are also on offer. During the summer, villages all over Alsace hold Fêtes du Vin (Wine Festivals) with food, wine and music – the tourist office has details.

From July to mid-September, Colmar plays host to a number of music festivals, including the Western-classical Festival International de Colmar, held during the first half of July. The Festival de Jazz takes place in early September.

The Marché de Noël (Christmas Market) lasts from the last weekend in November to 24 December, with some bits open until 31 December.

Places to Stay

In December, around Easter and from mid-July to mid-August (especially during the wine fair) most hotels are booked up in advance.

Camping The three-star *Camping de l'Ill* (☎ 03 89 41 15 94, on Route de Neuf Brisach *in Horbourg-Wihr*), open from February to November, is just over 3km east of Colmar. By bus, take No 1 to the Plage de l'Ill stop.

Hostels The 110-bed *Auberge de Jeunesse Mittelhart* (☎ 03 89 80 57 39, fax 03 89 80 76 16, *2 rue Pasteur*), just off Route d'Ingersheim, is 2km north-west of the train station. A bed costs 69FF, including breakfast. Reception is open from 7 to 10 am and 5 pm to midnight; curfew is midnight (11 pm in winter). By bus, take No 4 to the Pont Rouge stop.

The 41-bed *Maison des Jeunes et de la Culture (MJC; ☎ 03 89 41 26 87, fax 03 89 23 20 16, 17 rue Camille Schlumberger)* accepts only groups, with a minimum of six people. A bed costs 45FF. Reception, staffed until 10 pm, is closed after 12 noon on Saturday and all day Sunday.

Hotels Near the train station, the cosy, 18-room *Hôtel La Chaumière (☎ 03 89 41 08 99, 74 ave de la République)* has simple and rather small doubles from 180FF (240FF with shower and toilet). Reception is closed from 1 to 5 pm on Sunday. The three-star *Grand Hôtel Bristol (☎ 03 89 23 59 59, fax 03 89 23 92 26, ✆ reservation @grand-hotel-bristol.fr, 7 place de la Gare)* was built in 1925. Unsurprising doubles with lovely bathrooms go for 430FF (295FF for a few small rooms).

More centrally, the 23-room *Hôtel Kempf* (☎ *03 89 41 21 72, fax 03 89 23 06 94, 1 ave de la République*) has slightly tattered doubles from 180FF (250FF with shower and toilet). The blush-pink (but fading) *Hôtel Primo* (☎ *03 89 24 22 24, fax 03 89 24 55 96,* @ *hotel-primo-99@ rmcnet.fr, 5 rue des Ancêtres*) has rooms with washbasin for up to three people for 159FF; singles/doubles/quads with shower and toilet cost 269/329/399FF. There's a free car park just down the street.

About 1km north-east of the centre, the venerable *Hôtel Beau Séjour* (☎ *03 89 41 37 16, fax 03 89 41 43 07, 25 rue du Ladhof*) has been at this location since 1913. Doubles with all the amenities start at 380FF.

The 10-room *Hôtel Le Hagueneck* (☎ *03 89 80 68 98, fax 03 89 79 55 29, 83 ave du Général de Gaulle*) is about 700m southwest of the train station. Singles/doubles/ quads with shower and toilet start at 160/230/350FF. Reception is closed on Sunday. On foot take the pedestrian tunnel under the train tracks. By bus, take No 2 to the Hohnack stop.

Places to Eat

There are restaurants all over the old town, especially around place de l'Ancienne Douane.

Restaurants – Alsatian & French A variety of Alsatian specialities, including spit-roasted ham (60FF), are served at *La Maison Rouge* (☎ *03 89 23 53 22, 9 rue des Écoles*). The basic four course Alsatian *menu* costs 84FF. It is closed on Sunday and Wednesday. Alsatian dishes with Italian touches are on the menu at *Le Temps des Délices* (☎ *03 89 23 45 57, 11 rue d'Alspach*), closed Sunday night and Monday.

The tiny, intimate *Le Petit Gourmand* (☎ *03 89 41 09 32, 9 quai de la Poissonnerie*) has terrace seating along the River Lauch in the warm months. The *menu* costs 120FF and the restaurant is closed Monday

night and Tuesday. *Aux Trois Poissons* (☎ *03 89 41 25 21, 15 quai de la Poissonnerie*), an elegant fish restaurant, has *menus* from 135FF to 230FF as well as frogs' legs (95FF). It is closed on Sunday night, Tuesday evening and Wednesday.

The very classy *Restaurant La Maison des Têtes* (☎ *03 89 24 43 43, 19 rue des Têtes*), in the spectacular Maison des Têtes, has a superb wine list and gourmet *menus* for 169FF to 340FF. It is closed Sunday evening and Monday.

Restaurants – Other Authentic Vietnamese cuisine, served with exceptional elegance, awaits you at *Les Gourmets d'Asie* (☎ *03 89 41 75 10, 20b rue d'Alspach*). The cheapest *menus* (not available on Saturday night) cost 70FF and 80FF. It is closed on Monday. *Djerba La Douce* (☎ *03 89 24 17 12, 10 rue du Mouton*) has Tunisian couscous for 53FF to 95FF. It is closed on Sunday.

Self-Catering Place de l'Ancienne Douane and the old covered market (1865) on rue des Écoles play host to a *food market* on Thursday morning until 1 pm.

The *Monoprix* supermarket, across the square from the Musée d'Unterlinden, is open from 8 am to 8.25 pm Monday to Saturday (to 7.55 pm on Saturday). Just northeast of the old city on route de Neuf Brisach, the large *Atac* supermarket opens 8.30 am to 7.30 pm Monday to Saturday. Parking is available.

Fromagerie St-Nicolas (18 rue St-Nicolas) sells only traditionally made, non-pasteurised products. It is closed Monday morning and Sunday.

Entertainment

The sprawling *Rock Café* (☎ *03 89 24 05 36, 6 rue des Trois Épis*), facing the railway tracks, is a relaxed, American-themed bar with live rock and DJs on alternate weekends (Friday and Saturday) at 10 pm. Hours are 7 pm to 3 am daily. In the same complex, the mainly gay *Captain Café* is open the same hours from Thursday to Sunday.

The *Metal Café* (☎ *03 89 24 24 44, 15 bis*

blvd du Champ de Mars) has futuristic, outer-space-style decor with lots of blue neon. From about 10 pm on Friday and Saturday, it becomes a techno club (no cover charge). Hours are 5 or 6 pm to 1.30 am (3 am from Friday to Sunday).

The **Eden Café** (☎ *03 89 23 31 57, 17 rue du Rempart)* is an American-style bar with diner overtones. Beer (from 15FF) and light meals (including salads) are served daily from 11.30 am (1.30 or 2 pm in winter) to 1 am.

Colmar's main concert and theatre venues are La Manufacture (☎ 03 89 24 31 78), a one-time factory at 6 rue de Ingersheim, and the newly renovated Théâtre (☎ 03 89 20 29 02) next to the Musée d'Unterlinden.

Getting There & Away

Bus The bus terminal – little more than a parking lot – is to the right as you exit the train station. Hours are posted but the route numbers mentioned below don't necessarily appear. Service is severely reduced on Sunday and holidays. The tourist office can supply bus schedules.

Route du Vin Public bus may not be the quickest way to explore Alsace's Route du Vin (see Route du Vin d'Alsace earlier in the chapter), but it *is* a viable option.

From Monday to Saturday, Pauli's line 502 goes to Riquewihr (14.30FF, 35 minutes) and Ribeauvillé (15.30FF, 50 minutes) five or six times a day. The first bus leaves Colmar at 8.10 am; the last one back begins its run at 5 pm. Martinken's line 506 also links Colmar with Ribeauvillé (30 minutes, six a day except Sunday). On school days, Martinken's line 505 has two runs a day to Riquewihr (30 minutes) and Hunawihr (35 minutes) but only one service coming back, at 7 am.

STAHV's line 509 goes to Kienzheim (10.60FF, 25 minutes) and Kaysersberg (12.60FF, 30 minutes) 17 times a day (once on Sunday).

Line 303, shared by Kunegel and Sodag, serves points south of Colmar six or seven times a day (except Sunday), including

Eguisheim (10FF, 5 minutes), Gueberschwihr (13.20FF, 15 minutes), Rouffach (19.20FF, 25 minutes) and Guebwiller (27.50FF, 35 to 55 minutes). Eguisheim can also be reached by Pauli's line 514.

The Vosges STAHV's line 510, which runs twice a day, goes to Gunsbach (35 minutes), Munster (20.20FF, 40 minutes), Col de la Schlucht (31FF, 1¼ hours), Gérardmer (42FF, 1½ hours), Remiremont (63FF, 2¼ hours) and the Lorraine town of Épinal (three hours, 80FF).

STAHV's line 509 goes to Col du Bonhomme (one hour) and St-Dié (1¾ hours) four times a day, except Sunday.

Sodag has services to Cernay, starting point of the Route des Crêtes, via Guebwiller (lines 303 and 304).

Germany Kunegel (☎ 03 89 24 65 65) and SüdbadenBus (SBG; ☎ 0761-36172 in Freiburg) have seven buses a day (three or four at the weekend and holidays) from Colmar's train station, across the Rhine to the German university city of Freiburg, where stops include the bus station (ZOB) and the Moosweiher tram terminus (34FF or 10DM, 65 minutes).

Train The train station (☎ 0 836 35 35 35) is linked to Paris' Gare de l'Est (243FF, six hours) via Strasbourg. Bicycles can be carried on almost all trains to Strasbourg (56FF, 30 to 95 minutes, 37 a day, 23 at the weekend), Mulhouse (42FF, 25 minutes, 24 to 36 a day) and Basel (63FF, 50 minutes, eight to 12 a day). Four to seven trains go to Besançon daily (127FF, 2¼ hours).

To get to Obernai (43FF) you have to change trains at Sélestat (24FF, 15 minutes, 14 to 21 a day). About a dozen daily autorails or buses (five on Sunday and holidays) link Colmar with the Vallée de Munster towns of Gunsbach (18FF, 25 minutes), Munster (20FF, 30 minutes) and Metzeral (25FF, 45 minutes). The last train back begins its run at 7.15 pm.

Car Autop (☎ 03 89 41 30 26) at 80 ave de la République and ADA (☎ 03 89 23 90 30)

at 22 bis rue Stanislas are closed on Saturday afternoon and Sunday.

Getting Around

To/From the Airport EuroAir'Bus (☎ 03 89 90 25 11) links Bâle-Mulhouse airport (EuroAirport) with Colmar's train station (45 minutes, six a day).

Bus Colmar's local buses, some of which run on natural gas, are operated by TRACE (☎ 03 89 20 80 80), which has an office around the corner from the tourist office in Galerie du Rempart. All 10 lines, which run until sometime between 6 and 8 pm from Monday to Saturday, stop at the Unterlinden/Point Central hub; most also stop at the train station. A Billet Pass, available at the tourist office, is valid for from one day (16FF) to seven days (43FF).

Parking Unmetred street parking is available a couple of blocks east of the train station and just north of the Hôtel Primo.

Taxi Try Radios Taxis (☎ 03 89 80 71 71) or Taxi Gare (☎ 03 89 41 40 19).

Bicycle Cycles Geisswiller (☎ 03 89 41 30 59), 4–6 blvd du Champ de Mars, has mountain bikes for 100FF a day. It is open Tuesday to Saturday.

MASSIF DES VOSGES

The delightful and sublime Parc Naturel Régional des Ballons des Vosges covers about 3000 sq km in the southern part of the Vosges range. Roughly speaking, it is bounded by Sélestat and Cernay in Alsace, Belfort in Franche-Comté and Remiremont and St-Dié in Lorraine.

In the warm months, the gentle, rounded mountains, deep forests, glacial lakes, rolling pastureland and tiny villages are a walkers paradise, with an astounding 7000km of marked trails, including a variety of GRs and their variants (the GR5, GR7, GR53 etc). Cyclists also have hundreds of kilometres of idyllic trails. For details of group walks sponsored by the Club Vosgien, see Walking under Organised Tours in the Strasbourg section.

The Massif des Vosges has 36 modest skiing areas with 170 ski lifts (mostly tow lines) and 1000km of cross-country trails, which cost 22FF to 40FF a day. Lift tickets cost from 65FF to 100FF a day, depending on the season. Information on snow conditions is available on ☎ 03 89 41 34 76 (for a recording in French).

For details on bus and train services to Cernay, the Vallée de Munster and Col de la Schlucht, see Getting There & Away in the Colmar section earlier in the chapter.

Vallée de Munster

This lush, verdant river valley – its pastureland dotted with tiny villages, its upper slopes thickly forested – is one of the loveliest in the Vosges range. Walking and cycling trails abound. Nearby slopes are home to six small downhill ski stations.

Munster The town of Munster (population 4700; the name means 'monastery'), famed for its eponymous cheese, grew up around Abbaye St-Grégoire, a Benedictine abbey founded in AD 660 by monks from Ireland. At place du Marché, the roof and chimneys of the Maison du Prélat (former prelate's quarters) are the year-round home of a half-dozen pairs of storks. About 250m behind the Renaissance town hall (1550), the Hunawihr-based stork reintroduction centre (see the boxed text 'Storks') has an Enclos Cigognes (stork enclosure), in which a dozen frisky young birds dine mainly on fish and day-old male chicks (sorry cuddly-chick lovers, but storks are avid carnivores).

The tourist office (☎ 03 89 77 31 80, fax 03 89 77 07 17, ✆ tourisme.munster@ wanadoo.fr) at 1 rue du Couvent (through the arch of the Maison du Prélat) is open from 9.30 am to 12.30 pm and 2 to 6 pm (4 pm on Saturday; 6.30 pm in July and August). It is open from 10 am to noon on Sunday in July and August.

Information on the Parc Régional is available from the Maison du Parc (☎ 03 89 77 90 20, fax 03 89 77 90 30, ✆ info@ parc-ballons-vosges.fr), which is in the same building as the tourist office but

ALSACE

Storks

White storks (cigognes), long a feature of Alsatian folklore, are one of the region's most beloved symbols. Believed to bring luck (as well as babies), they spend the winter in Africa and then migrate to Europe for the warmer months, feeding from marshes (their favourite delicacies include small rodents, moles, lizards, all sorts of insects and even frogs) and building their nests of twigs and sticks on church steeples, rooftops and tall trees. Since about 1960, however, the draining of the marshes along the Rhine, hunting in Africa, chemical poisons and – most lethal of all – high-tension lines have reduced stork numbers catastrophically. By the early 1980s there were only three pairs left in all of Alsace.

When cold weather arrives, instinct tells young storks – at the age of just a few months – to fly south for a two- or three-year, 12,000km-trek to sub-Saharan Africa, from which they return to Alsace ready to breed – if they return at all. Research has shown that 90% die en route because of electrocution, hunting, exhaustion and dehydration. In subsequent years, the adult storks – 1m long, with a 2m wingspan and weighing 3.5kg – make only a short trek south for the winter, returning to Alsace to breed after a few months in Africa.

In the 1980s, research and breeding centres were set up with the goal of establishing a permanent, year-round Alsatian stork population. The young birds spend the first three years of their lives in captivity, which causes them to lose their migratory instinct and thus avoid the rigours and dangers of migration. The program has been a huge success, and today Alsace – the western extremity of the storks' range – is home to some 700 of these majestic birds. The **Centre de Réintroduction des Cigognes** (☎ 03 89 73 72 62) is in Hunawihr, just south of Ribeauvillé; its 200 storks can be visited 10 am to noon and 2 pm to sometime between 5 and 7 pm daily from April to 11 November. Admission costs 45FF (30FF for children aged five to 14). Storks can also be seen in the town of Munster (see Massif des Vosges for details) and along the Route du Vin (if you're lucky).

around the other side. Hours are 10 am to noon and 2 to 6 pm (closed on Monday morning and, except from May to mid-September, at the weekend).

The family-run, 13-room *Hôtel des Vosges* (☎ 03 89 77 31 41, fax 03 89 77 59 86, 58 Grand' Rue), on the main commercial street, has spacious, simply furnished doubles from 200FF (260FF with shower and toilet). Hall showers cost 10FF. Reception is closed on Sunday afternoon except in July and August.

Soultzbach-les-Bains This untouristed hamlet, whose houses and market gardens straddle a creek called the River Kresbach, is 5km east of Munster in a lovely valley surrounded by forested hillsides. The only hotel, the 10-room, one-star *Hôtel St-Christophe* (☎ 03 89 71 13 09, fax 03 89 71 06 84, 4 rue de l'Église), on the D43, has

singles/doubles from 135/155FF; doubles/triples with shower and toilet cost 250/280FF.

Le Linge The German fortifications at Le Linge (986m), carved into the sandstone hilltop, were the object of a French offensive launched in July 1915. Some 10,000 French troops and 7000 Germans died in the assaults and subsequent hand-to-hand warfare between trenches only metres apart. The battle site, which has one of the best preserved WWI trench networks in France, is still surrounded by rusted tangles of the original barbed wire, areas that have yet to be cleared of live munitions, and never-exhumed human remains. The forested memorial site, on the D11-VI, affords gorgeous views of tree-covered hills and pastoral hamlets – these contrast jarringly with the trenches and rifle slits. The small

ALSACE

museum (12FF) is open from 15 April to 1 November.

About 500m south-east of Le Linge, at the intersection of the D11-VI and the D5 bis-I, is a **Deutscher Soldatenfriedhof 1914–18** (WWI German military cemetery).

Route des Crêtes

The Route of the Crests, part of it built during WWI to supply French frontline troops, takes you to (or near) the Vosges' highest *ballons* (bald, rounded mountain peaks), as well as to several WWI sites. Mountaintop lookouts afford spectacular views of the Alsace plain, the Schwartzwald (Black Forest) across the Rhine in Germany, the Jura and, on clear days, the Alps.

Beginning in Cernay, the Route des Crêtes continues north-east and then north along the D431, D430, D61 and D148 to the Col du Bonhomme (949m). During the winter months and early spring it is often impassable due to snow. The sites mentioned below are listed from south to north.

Site of the bloodiest WWI fighting in Alsace, Hartmannswillerkopf – renamed **Vieil Armand** by the French troops – saw the deaths of some 30,000 French and German soldiers as the strategic hilltop fortress changed hands several times. The remains of trenches and fortifications, most of them German, can be seen near the hilltop fortress (956m), marked by a 22m-high white cross.

At the dramatic, windblown summit of the 1424m-high **Grand Ballon**, the highest point in the Vosges, a trail takes you to a radar ball and a weather station. If the unsurpassed panorama doesn't blow you away, the howling wind just might. At the top of the road pass (1325m), you'll find the chalet-style *Grand Hôtel Ballon* (☎ 03 89 48 77 99), run by the Club Vosgien, which is open year round (as is the attached *restaurant*). Doubles start at 190FF (255FF with shower and toilet).

The tiny, low-budget ski station of **Le Markstein** (1260m; ☎ 03 89 82 14 46 at the ski lift) consists of a number of scattered hotels, sandwich bars and lifts. The D430 to

Guebwiller is kept open year round. The *Hôtel Wolf* (☎ 03 89 82 64 36, fax 03 89 38 72 06) is a 20-room, two-star place with unadorned doubles from 185FF (with washbasin) to 325FF. It is closed from early November to mid-December.

Col de la Schlucht, a 1139m-high mountain pass on the D417 about 36km west of Colmar, is home to a small ski station and a modern church. Trails lead in various directions; walking north along the GR5 will take you to three lakes with colours for names: **Lac Vert**, **Lac Noir** and **Lac Blanc**.

The 1250m-high **Ballon d'Alsace**, 20km west of the Grand Ballon as the crow flies (by road, take the D465 from St-Maurice), is the meeting point of four departments (Haut-Rhin, Territoire de Belfort, Haute-Saône and Vosges) and three regions (Alsace, Franche-Comté and Lorraine). Between 1871 and WWI, the border between France and Germany passed by here, attracting French tourists eager to catch a glimpse of France's 'lost province' of Alsace. During WWI the mountaintop was heavily fortified, but the trenches, whose shallow remains can still be seen, were never used in battle. The 25-room, two-star *Grand Hôtel du Sommet* (☎ 03 84 29 30 60, fax 03 84 23 95 60) has doubles/quads for 240/300FF. The attached *restaurant* has *menus* for 80FF to 130FF.

The Ballon d'Alsace is a good base for day walks. The GR5 passes by here, as do other walking trails; possible destinations include a number of lakes, including the **Lac des Perches**. In winter, the area has snowshoeing and cross-country skiing. For information on parapente lessons and introductory flights, contact Centre École Pent'Air (☎ 03 84 23 20 40).

The riverside town of **Bussang** (population 1800), north of the Ballon d'Alsace near the source of the River Moselle, is another good base for walkers, cyclists and skiers of both the downhill and cross-country variety. The two-star, 19-room *Hôtel Le Tremplin* (☎ 03 29 61 50 30, fax 03 29 61 50 89), on the N66 (the main road through town), has doubles from 160FF (260FF with shower and toilet); quads with all the amenities cost 340FF. It is closed in November. The attached *restaurant* has *menus* from 80FF. It is closed Monday except during school holiday periods.

MULHOUSE
**postcode 68100 • pop 108,000
• elevation 240m**

The industrial city of Mulhouse (pronounced 'moo-**looze**'), 43km south of Colmar, has little of the quaint Alsatian charm that typifies its northern neighbours. In fact, in recent years it has made the news mainly because of ethnic tensions and urban violence. However, the city's dozen museums, several of them world class, are well worth a stop even if you're not a particular fan of the industrial technologies that they highlight.

Information
The tourist office (☎ 03 89 35 48 48, fax 03 89 45 66 16, ✉ ot@ville-mulhouse.fr) is 200m north of the train station at 9 ave du Maréchal Foch. It is open from 9 am to 7 pm Monday to Saturday (to 5 pm on Saturday except in July and August) and, except in December, from 10 am to noon on Sunday (to 1 pm in summer). The staff can provide you with two excellent pamphlets (in English) for self-guided walking tours.

Museums
A gricer's dream, the **Musée Français du Chemin de Fer** (☎ 03 89 42 25 67 for a recording), 2 rue Alfred de Glehn, displays locomotives, carriages and switching equipment of all types and periods. It shares its space – a disused railway station – with the **Musée du Sapeur-Pompier** (Firefighters' Museum).

Both are open from 9 am to 5 pm daily (to 6 pm from April to September); admission costs 46FF (students and children 20FF). By car, take the A36 to the Mulhouse Ouest exit. By bus, take the hourly line No 17 from the train station.

The **Musée National de l'Automobile** (☎ 03 89 33 23 23), 192 ave de Colmar, displays 500 rare and historic motorcars made since 1878 by over 100 different compa-

---

The Continental Divide

The Massif des Vosges serves as a *ligne de partage des eaux* (continental divide). A raindrop that falls on the range's eastern slopes will flow to the Rhine and eventually make its way to the icy waters of the North Sea, while a drop of rain that lands on the western slopes of the Vosges – perhaps only a few metres from its Rhine-bound counterpart – will eventually end up in the Rhône before merging with the warm waters of the Mediterranean.

---

nies, including Bugatti, whose factory was in nearby Molsheim. It is open from 9 or 10 am to 6 pm daily (to 6.30 pm in July and August). The admission fee is as upmarket as the cars: 60FF (students 46FF, children aged seven to 17 27FF). By car, get off the A36 at the Mulhouse Centre exit. By bus, take the hourly line No 17 from the train station.

The **Musée de l'Impression sur Étoffes** (Museum of Textile Printing; ☎ 03 89 46 83 00), across from the train station at 14 rue Jean-Jacques Henner, has a collection (assembled since 1833) of over three million printed fabric samples from all over the world. It opens 10 am to 6 pm daily and admission costs 36FF (students 18FF).

The delightful **Musée du Papier Peint** (Wallpaper Museum; ☎ 03 89 64 24 56), at 28 rue Zuber in Rixheim (a couple of kilometres south-east of Mulhouse on the D66), is open from 9 or 10 am to noon and 2 to 6 pm daily (closed on Tuesday from October to May). Admission costs 35FF (children aged 12 to 16, students and seniors 25FF). By car, take the A36 towards Basel (Bâle) and get off at Rixheim. By bus, take the No 10 to the Commanderie stop.

Getting There & Away
The train station (☎ 0 836 35 35 35) is south of the city centre at 10 ave du Général Leclerc. There are direct services to Colmar (42FF, 25 minutes, 24 to 36 a day), Strasbourg (85FF, one hour, 24 to 37 a day) and

euro currency converter €1 = 6.56FF

ALSACE

Besançon (110FF, 1¾ hours, five or six a day).

Buses, which leave from the terminus next to the train station, serve towns and villages north, west and south of Mulhouse, including Colmar.

ÉCOMUSÉE D'ALSACE

The largest open-air museum in France, the Écomusée d'Alsace (☎ 03 89 74 44 56) at Ungersheim (about 17km north-west of Mulhouse off the A35 to Colmar), is a 'living museum' in which traditional artisans and craftspeople do their thing in and among traditional Alsatian buildings brought here from around the region. Opening time is 9 or 9.30 am (10 or 10.30 am from October to March); closing time ranges from 4.30 pm (November to February) to 7 pm (July and August). Admission costs 78/65/48FF for adults/students/children (54/48/33FF from November to March).

Lorraine

Lorraine, popularly associated with quiche and de Gaulle's double-barred cross (croix de Lorraine), has little of the picturesque quaintness of Alsace. But the region – fed by the rivers Meurthe, Moselle and Meuse – is home to two handsome cities, both former capitals. Nancy, one of France's most refined and attractive cities, is famed for its Art Nouveau architecture, while Metz, 54km to the north, is an attractive, dynamic city known for the stunning stained glass of its cathedral. The town of Verdun bears silent testimony to the destruction and insanity of WWI.

History

Lorraine was the birthplace of Joan of Arc (1412–31), who became France's national heroine during the Hundred Years' War by stirring the French royalist army to resist the English and their allies. Lorraine became part of France in 1766 upon the death of Stanislaw I, the former king of Poland and father-in-law of Louis XV, who had been given Lorraine in 1738 by the treaties that ended the War of the Polish Succession (1733–38).

During the 17th century, Lorraine was fortified by the construction of a number of massive fortresses designed by the foremost military architect of the period, Vauban (see the boxed text 'Vauban's Citadels' in the Facts about France chapter). Along with the Verdun battlefields and the Maginot Line, these fortifications are a major draw for those interested in military history.

NANCY

**postcode 54000 • pop 329,000
• elevation 206m**

Delightful Nancy has an air of refinement found nowhere else in Lorraine. With a stunning, gilded central square, several fine museums and shop windows filled with fine chocolates and fragile works of glass, the former capital of the dukes of Lorraine seems as opulent today as it did during the 16th to 18th centuries, when much of the city centre was built.

Nancy thrives on a combination of innovation and sophistication. The Musée de l'École de Nancy, the city's premier museum, houses many of the dream-like, sinuous works of the Art Nouveau movement that flourished here (as the Nancy School) thanks to the rebellious spirit of local artists, including Émile Gallé. Further examples of their work can be found at the Musée des Beaux-Arts and throughout the city: look for the stained-glass windows and elaborate grillwork that grace the entrances to many banks, shops and private homes.

Orientation

In the heart of Nancy is beautifully proportioned, 18th-century place Stanislas and adjoining place de la Carrière. These grand public spaces connect the narrow, twisting streets of the medieval Vieille Ville (Old Town), centred around the Grande Rue, with the rigid right angles of the 16th-century Ville Neuve (New Town) to the south, whose main thoroughfares are rue St-Dizier, rue St-Jean and rue St-Georges. The train station, at the bottom of busy rue

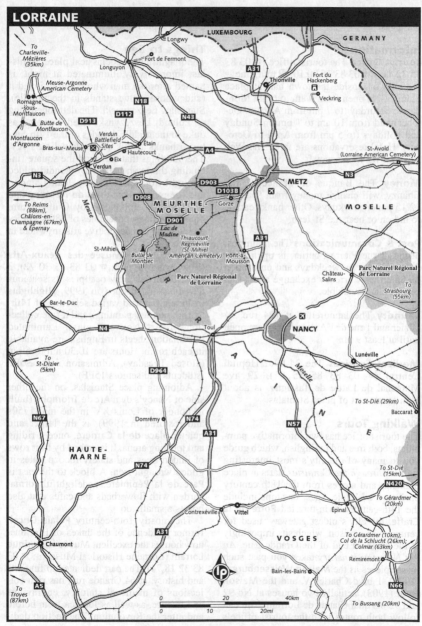

Stanislas, is 800m south-west of place Stanislas.

Information

Tourist Office The tourist office (☎ 03 83 35 22 41, fax 03 83 35 90 10, ✆ tourisme@ ot-nancy.fr), inside the town hall at place Stanislas, is open from 9 am to 6 pm Monday to Saturday (to 7 pm from April to October) and from 10 am to 1 pm on Sunday and holidays (to 5 pm from April to October). Hotel reservations are free. The Web site is at www.ot-nancy.fr.

Money The Banque de France, 2 rue Chanzy, will change money from 9 am to 12.15 pm on weekdays. Other banks can be found on or near rue St-Jean.

Post & Communications The main post office, 8 rue Pierre Fourier, is open from 8 am to 7 pm on weekdays and until noon on Saturday. Currency exchange and a Cyberposte are available.

Laundry The laundrettes at 124 rue St-Dizier and 1 rue de l'Armée Patton are open until at least 9 pm.

Medical Services The 24-hour Hôpital Central (☎ 03 83 85 85 85), 29 ave Maréchal de Lattre de Tassigny, is about 1km south-east of place Stanislas.

Walking Tours

The tourist office has two informative pamphlets, both free and in English, which guide you to many of the city's most interesting sights. *Through the Centuries* starts at place Stanislas and moves from the 18th century back to the Middle Ages. Its stops include the 14th-century, twin-turreted **Porte de la Craffe**, the city's oldest gateway, used for centuries as a prison, which sits imposingly at the northern end of the Grande Rue. *An Art Nouveau Itinerary* takes you past such masterpieces as the **Maison Weissenburger** (1904), 1 blvd Charles V, and the **Maison Huot** (1903), actually two houses at No 92 and 92 bis quai Claude de Lorrain. You can follow both routes with the tourist office's

visites audioguidées (Walkman tours) which cost 35FF plus a 300FF deposit.

Things to See

The magnificent neoclassical **place Stanislas**, impressively illuminated at night, is named after the man who commissioned it (and whose statue stands in the middle), Stanislaw Leszczynski. The dethroned king of Poland, Leszczynski ruled Lorraine as duke in the middle decades of the 17th century, thanks to his son-in-law Louis XV. The buildings that surround the square (including the **town hall**), the splendid gilded **wrought-iron gateways** by Jean Lamour, and the rococo **Fontaines de Neptune** and **d'Amphitrite** (fountains) by Guibal, form one of the finest ensembles of 18th-century architecture and decorative arts anywhere in France.

The excellent **Musée des Beaux-Arts** (Fine Arts Museum; ☎ 03 83 85 30 72), 3 place Stanislas, now occupies its spacious new quarters, opened in 1999. Highlights include a rich and varied selection of 14th- to 18th-century paintings and a fine collection of Art Nouveau glass. Laminated information sheets in English are available in each room. Hours are 10.30 am to 6 pm (closed Tuesday). Admission costs 30FF (students and seniors 15FF).

Adjoining place Stanislas, on the other side of Nancy's own **Arc de Triomphe** (built in honour of Louis XV in the mid-1750s and restored in 1999), is the larger and quieter **place de la Carrière**, once a riding and jousting arena. It is graced by four rows of linden trees and stately rococo gates in gilded wrought iron. A block to the east is **Parc de la Pépinière**, a delightful formal garden with flowerbeds and cafes that also boasts a small zoo.

The mostly 16th-century **Palais Ducal**, former residence of the dukes of Lorraine, now houses the excellent **Musée Historique Lorrain** (Lorraine Historical Museum; ☎ 03 83 32 18 74). The part dedicated to fine arts and history, at 64 Grande rue, has rich collections of medieval statuary, engravings and faïence, as well as Judaica from before and after the Revolution. The section dedicated to Arts et Traditions Populaires (Regional Art and Folklore), at 66 Grande rue, is housed in the 15th-century **Couvent des Cordeliers**, a former Franciscan monastery. Inside, the late-15th-century Gothic **Église des Cordeliers** and the adjacent **Chapelle Ducale** (Ducal Chapel; 1607), modelled on the Medici Chapel in Florence, served as the burial place of the dukes of Lorraine. The whole museum is open from 10 am to noon and 2 to 5 pm daily except Tuesday. Closing time is 6 pm on Sunday and holidays, and from May to September, when there's no midday closure. Admission to each museum costs 20FF (children and students 15FF); the Église des Cordeliers costs an additional 10FF. A ticket good for all three costs 30FF.

The interior of the domed, 18th-century **Cathédrale**, on rue St-Georges, is a mixture of neoclassical and Baroque. The organ loft dates from 1757.

Housed in a 19th-century villa about 2km south-west of the city centre, the outstanding **Musée de l'École de Nancy** (School of Nancy Museum; ☎ 03 83 40 14 86), 36–38 rue du Sergent Blandan, brings together a heady collection of colourful, curvaceous pieces produced by the turn-of-the-century Art Nouveau movement (see Architecture under Arts in the Facts about France chapter). It is open from 10.30 am to 6 pm daily except Tuesday (from 2 pm on Monday). Admission costs 30FF (children and students 15FF). By bus, take No 5 or 25 to the Nancy Thermal stop or No 6, 16 or 46 to the Painlevé stop and walk south for 200m.

For something completely different, you might visit the extravagantly coloured fish at the **Aquarium Tropical** (☎ 03 83 32 99 97), north-east of the centre at 34 rue Ste-Catherine. The stuffed animals and birds of the upstairs **Musée de Zoologie** are more interesting than they sound. Both are open from 10 am to noon and 2 to 6 pm daily. Admission costs 30FF (students 20FF).

Places to Stay

Camping The leafy *Camping de Brabois* (☎ 03 83 27 18 28, ave Paul Muller), open from April to mid-October, is on a hill about

5km south-west of the centre. By bus, take No 26 or 46 to the Camping stop.

Hostels The 60-bed *Auberge de Jeunesse Remicourt* (☎ 03 83 27 73 67, fax 03 83 41 41 35, 149 rue de Vandœuvre in Villers-lès-Nancy), in a fantastic old chateau surrounded by a peaceful park, is 4km south of the centre. A bed costs 80FF (95FF for a double with shower), including breakfast. reception is closed from 9.30 am to 5.30 pm on Sunday and holidays, but there's almost always someone around. By bus, take No 26 to the St-Fiacre stop.

Hotels The (formerly Grand) *Hôtel de la Poste* (☎ 03 83 32 11 52, fax 03 83 37 58 74, 56 place Monseigneur Ruch) was once a classy establishment. These days its large, if simple and tattered, doubles start at 165FF with shower (185FF with toilet as well). The welcoming and slightly off-beat, 29-room *Hôtel de l'Académie* (☎ 03 83 35 52 31, fax 03 83 32 55 78, 7 bis rue des Michottes) offers excellent value: singles/doubles with shower start at 110/160FF (from 175FF with toilet, too). Some rooms can take an extra bed for 30FF.

The 24-room, two-star *Hôtel Poincaré* (☎ 03 83 40 25 99, fax 03 83 27 22 43, 81 rue Raymond Poincaré) has decent singles from 110FF; doubles cost 160FF with toilet, 200FF with shower, too. Sunday night is free if you stay Friday and Saturday. The spotless, friendly, 18-room *Hôtel de la Croix de Bourgogne* (☎ 03 83 40 01 86, 68bis rue Jeanne d'Arc) has cheery doubles from 130FF (170FF with shower and toilet). To get there, take bus No 7, 8, 17 or 44 to the Croix de Bourgogne stop. There's plenty of free parking near both of these places.

The friendly, two-star, 20-room *Hôtel des Portes d'Or* (☎ 03 83 35 42 34, fax 03 83 32 51 41, 21 rue Stanislas) has charming and very well kept doubles with upholstered doors from 280FF. The *Hôtel Le Grenier à Sel* (☎ 03 83 32 31 98, fax 03 83 35 32 88, 28 rue Gustave Simon) has rustic rooms with low, beamed roofs. Basic doubles with bath start at 220FF. Reception is closed on Sunday and Monday.

LORRAINE

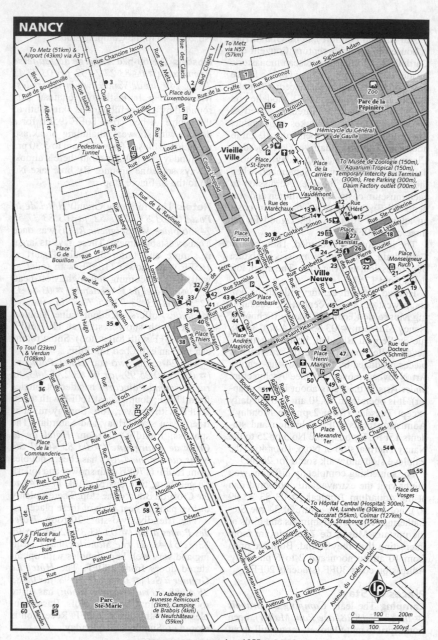

NANCY

PLACES TO STAY					
19	Hôtel de la Poste	3	Maison Huot	29	Musée des Beaux-Arts
24	Hôtel des Portes d'Or	4	Théâtre de la Manufacture	32	Europcar Car Rental
30	Hôtel Le Grenier à Sel	5	Mémorial Désilles	33	Bus No 26 to Auberge de
31	Hôtel de l'Académie; Blue	6	Couvent des Cordeliers;		Jeunesse
	Note Club		Musée Historique Lorrain	35	Laundrette
34	Hôtel Piroux; Hôtel de Flore		(Arts et Traditions Populaires	37	Caméo Cinema
36	Hôtel Poincaré		Section)	38	Train Station
57	Hôtel de la Croix de	7	Palais Ducal; Musée	39	Aérolor Airport Bus
	Bourgogne		Historique Lorrain (Fine Arts	40	Discothèque Le Cinquième
			& History Section)		Élément
PLACES TO EAT		8	Palais du Gouvernement	42	Porte Stanislas
11	Chez Bagot-Le Chardon Bleu	9	Le Ch'timi	43	Chambre de Commerce
13	Aux Croustillants	10	Basilique St-Epvre		Building
14	Restaurant Le Gastrolâtre	12	Arc de Triomphe	44	Banque de France
28	Au Petit Cochon	15	L'Arquebuse	45	Point Central Bus-Tram Hub
41	Brasserie Excelsior	16	Cristallerie Daum	48	CGFTE Bus Information
46	La Cigogne	17	Wrought-Iron Gateway		Office
47	Covered Market	18	Prefecture Buildings	52	Synagogue
49	La Bocca	20	Cathédral	53	Laundrette
50	Casino Supermarket	21	Musée du Téléphone	54	ADA Car Rental
51	Match Supermarket	22	Main Post Office	55	Porte St-Nicolas
		23	Baccarat Crystal Shop;	56	Michenon Bike Rentals
OTHER			Espace 54	58	Laundrette
1	Porte de la Craffe	25	Tourist Office	59	Piscine Louison Bobet
2	Maison Weissenburger	26	Town Hall	60	Musée de l'École de
		27	Statue of Stanislaw Leszczynski		Nancy

Near the train station, the 22-room, two-star *Hôtel Piroux* (☎ 03 83 32 01 10, fax 03 83 35 44 92, 12 rue Raymond Poincaré) has doubles with shower starting at 160FF (200FF with bath and toilet). Reception closes on Saturday and Sunday. You might also try the 13-room, two-star *Hôtel de Flore* (☎ 03 83 37 63 28, fax 03 83 37 86 89, 8 rue Raymond Poincaré); serviceable singles/doubles start at 160/220FF.

Places to Eat

Restaurants Innovative French cuisine is on offer at *Chez Bagot-Le Chardon Bleu* (☎ 03 83 37 42 43, 45 Grande rue) and fish is a speciality. The *menus* cost 82FF for lunch (except on Sunday) and 132FF to 195FF for dinner. It is closed on Tuesday at midday and Monday. The convivial *Au Petit Cochon* (☎ 03 83 32 21 43, 5 rue Stanislas)* serves the cuisine of Lorraine and Alsace, including *porcelet grillé* (grilled piglet; 85FF). *Menus* cost 88FF to 149FF. There are a number of other restaurants, including pizzerias, nearby along rue Stanislas and rue Gambetta.

Restaurant Le Gastrolâtre (☎ 03 83 35 51 94, 1 place Vaudémont) has long been a favourite for Lorraine and Provençal cuisine. Its *menus* run from 95FF (lunch only) to 195FF. It is closed on Monday at midday and on Sunday. Around the corner, rue des Maréchaux is lined with about a dozen restaurants of all sorts; *menus* start at just 52FF.

If you'd like to dine amid Art Nouveau and Art Deco elegance, try *Brasserie Excelsior* (☎ 03 83 35 24 57, 50 rue Henri Poincaré), which opened in 1910. The *menus* cost 119FF to 169FF. Hours are 7.30 am to 12.30 am; full meals are served from noon to 3 pm and 7 pm to closing time.

For those on a budget, *La Cigogne* (☎ 03 83 32 11 13, 4 bis rue des Ponts), a neighbourhood-style brasserie-cafe, has *menus* from 68FF. It is closed on Sunday. *La Bocca* (☎ 03 83 32 74 47, 33 rue des Ponts) lets you compose your own pizzas (48FF) from a selection of 34 toppings (closed Sunday).

Self-Catering The *covered market (place Henri Mangin)* is open from 7 am to 6 pm

euro currency converter €1 = 6.56FF

LORRAINE

Tuesday to Saturday. On the other side of place Henri Mangin, inside the St-Sébastien shopping centre, the *Casino* supermarket is open until 8.30 pm daily except Sunday. The *Match* supermarket (*rue du Grand Rabbin Haguenauer*) is open until 10 pm daily except Sunday.

Aux Croustillants (*10 rue des Maréchaux*), a boulangerie, is open 24 hours a day, except from 10 pm on Sunday to 5.30 am on Tuesday.

Entertainment

Discos, Clubs & Bars An underground place with plenty of flashing lights and varied music, *Discothèque Le Cinquième Élément* (☎ 03 83 32 20 30, rue Mazagrin) is open from 11 pm to 4 am Tuesday to Sunday. Thursday is student night. Admission costs 30FF (50FF on Friday and Saturday), including a drink.

The *Blue Note Club* (☎ 03 83 30 31 18, 3 rue des Michottes), a vaulted, subterranean bar, becomes a disco on Friday and Saturday nights (60FF, including a drink). Sunday is karaoke night. Hours are 9.30 pm to 4 am (5 am at the weekend). It is closed on Tuesday.

At the unpretentious, three-level *Le Ch'timi* (☎ 03 83 32 82 76, 17 place St-Epvre) you can sample almost 200 different beers from 10 am to 2 am (8 pm on Sunday). *L'Arquebuse* (☎ 03 83 32 11 99, 13 rue Héré) is a very stylish bar with modern, nautical decor and a small area for late-night dancing. Hours are 6 pm to 4 am (5 am at the weekend). It is closed Sunday and Monday.

Cinema There's a good selection of non-dubbed films at the *Caméo* (☎ 03 83 40 35 68, 16 rue de la Commanderie), a four-screen art cinema.

Shopping

The Baccarat shop (☎ 03 83 30 55 11), where a basic wine glass can cost 600FF, is at 2 rue des Dominicains. Espace 54 (☎ 03 83 32 34 00), next door at 3 rue Gambetta, specialises in truly stunning glasswork by contemporary French artists. Cristallerie

Daum has a shop (☎ 03 83 32 21 65) at 14 place Stanislas. All three are closed on Monday morning and Sunday.

Daum's factory outlet (☎ 03 83 32 14 55), about 1km north-east of place Stanislas at 17 rue des Cristalleries, sells discontinued designs and seconds. Hours are 9.30 am to 12.30 pm and 2.30 to 5 pm (6 pm on Saturday). It is closed on Sunday. By bus, take lines 26, 33, 40, 43 or 46 to Le Digue stop.

Getting There & Away

Air The Metz-Nancy-Lorraine airport (☎ 03 87 56 70 00) is 43km north of Nancy off the A31.

Bus The temporary intercity bus terminal is in a parking lot 500m north-east of place Stanislas, at the end of rue Ste-Catherine, but at some point it's supposed to move to the vicinity of the train station. Les Rapides de Lorraine (☎ 03 83 32 80 00), which serves Verdun (95FF, 2¾ hours, five a day, one on Sunday and holidays), is staffed from 2 to 6.15 pm. Les Courriers Mosellans (☎ 03 83 32 23 58), open from 8 am to noon on weekdays, handles Eurolines ticketing.

Train The train station (☎ 0 836 35 35 35), on place Thiers, is linked with Paris' Gare de l'Est (206FF, three hours, about 15 a day), Baccarat (52FF, 45 minutes, about 10 a day), Épinal (62FF, one hour, 10 to 16 a day), Metz (51FF, 40 to 70 minutes, 15 to 34 a day), Remiremont (82FF, 1¼ to two hours, four to six a day), Épernay (143FF, two hours, four to six a day), and Strasbourg (109FF, 70 to 95 minutes, eight to 13 a day).

Car Europcar (☎ 03 83 37 57 24) is at 18 rue de Serre, while ADA (☎ 03 83 36 53 09) is at 138 rue St-Dizier. Both are closed on Sunday.

Getting Around

To/From the Airport Aérolor Shuttles (☎ 03 87 34 60 12) links the train station (the Hôtel Mercure tower) with Metz-Nancy-Lorraine airport (40FF, 40 minutes, six times a day on weekdays).

euro currency converter 10FF = €1.52

Bus The local public transport company, CGFTE (☎ 03 83 35 54 54), has an office at 3 rue du Docteur Schmitt, open daily except Sunday. Most lines stop at the Point Central, which is around the intersections of rue St-Dizier with rue St-Georges (north-east bound) and rue Stanislas (south-west bound). The first of three planned tramlines is supposed to be functional in 2001.

Parking There's ample free parking 500m north-east of place Stanislas in the lots along the canal, and in the working-class neighbourhoods west of the railway tracks.

Taxi To order a taxi, call ☎ 03 83 37 65 37.

Bicycle VTTs (110/340FF a day/week) can be rented from Michenon (☎ 03 83 17 59 59), 91 rue des Quatre Églises, which is open Tuesday to Saturday from 9 am to noon and 2 to 7 pm.

BACCARAT
postcode 54120 • pop 5000
• elevation 260m
For centuries Nancy and southern Lorraine have produced some of the world's finest crystal and glassware. The most famous *cristallerie* (crystal glassworks) of all, founded in 1764, is at Baccarat, 55km south-east of Nancy. At the **Musée du Cristal** (☎ 03 83 76 61 37), on the grounds of the Baccarat glassworks, you can admire some 1100 exquisite pieces. It is open until 6 or 6.30 pm daily, and admission costs 15FF. The company shop, out front at 2 rue des Cristalleries, sells discontinued, first-quality items at 25% to 40% off. It is open daily.

Across the River Meurthe, the concrete **Église St-Rémy**, built in the mid-1950s to replace an earlier church destroyed by Allied bombing in 1944, is decorated with over 4000 panels of coloured Baccarat crystal.

The tourist office (☎ 03 83 75 13 37), in the parking lot behind the church, is open until 5.30 pm Monday to Saturday and, from March to November, on Sunday morning. The two-star *Hôtel Renaissance* (☎ 03 83 75 11 31, fax 03 83 75 21 09, 31 rue des Cristalleries) has doubles from 295FF.

Baccarat's train station, a few hundred metres north of the Musée du Cristal, is linked to Nancy by train (52FF, 45 minutes, about 10 a day).

METZ
postcode 57000 • pop 193,000
• elevation 173m
Metz, present-day capital of the Lorraine region, is a dignified, cosmopolitan city with stately public squares, shaded riverside parks, a large university and a historic commercial centre. Many of the most impressive buildings date from the period when Metz was part of the German Empire. The magnificent Gothic cathedral, with its stunning stained glass, is the most outstanding attraction.

Metz became part of France in 1648. When the city was annexed by Germany in 1871, a quarter of the population fled to French territory. Many went to nearby Nancy, in the unoccupied part of Lorraine.

Orientation
The cathedral, on a hill above the River Moselle, is a bit over 1km due north of the train station. The city centre's most important public squares are place d'Armes, next to the cathedral; place St-Jacques, in the heart of the pedestrianised commercial district; place de la République, linked to place St-Jacques by rue Serpenoise, once a Roman highway; and, 400 metres to the east, triangular place St-Louis. The main university campus is 600m west of the cathedral on the Île de Saulcy.

Information
Tourist Offices The highly professional tourist office (☎ 03 87 55 53 76, fax 03 87 36 59 43, @ tourisme@ot.mairie-metz.fr) is across place d'Armes from the cathedral. It opens 9 am to 6.30 pm Monday to Saturday (to 9 pm in July and August) and 11 am to 5 pm on Sunday and holidays. The free monthly *Carnet de Rendez-Vous* lists cultural events. Hotel reservations cost 10FF.

Money The Banque de France, 12 ave Robert Schuman, changes money from

LORRAINE

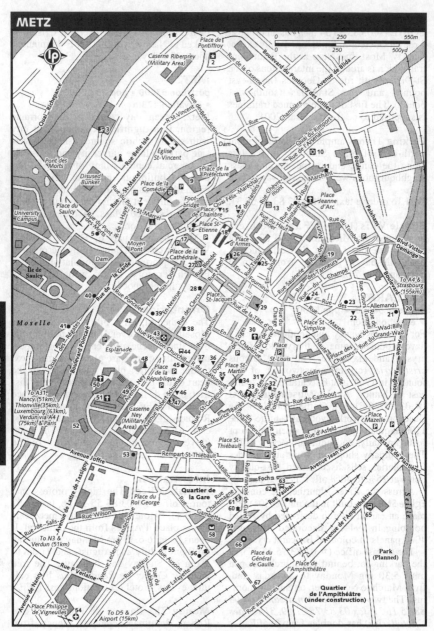

METZ

	PLACES TO STAY		OTHER			
1	Auberge de Jeunesse Metz-Plage	2	Hôtel de Police	43	Galeries Lafayette
		3	Swimming Pool	44	Intercity Bus Stops
11	Auberge de Jeunesse Carrefour	4	Bell Tower	45	TCRM Bus Information Office
16	Hôtel de la Cathédrale	5	Laundrette	47	Banque de France
28	Grand Hôtel de Metz	6	Temple Neuf	48	Statue of Marshall Ney
34	Hôtel Chez Françoise	8	Théâtre	49	Arsenal Cultural Centre
38	Hôtel Lafayette	9	Prefecture Building	50	Église St-Pierre-aux-Nonains
55	Cécil Hôtel	10	Synagogue		
57	Hôtel Moderne	12	Salle des Trinitaires	51	Ancienne Chapelle des Templiers
60	Hôtel Métropole	13	Musée d'Art et d'Histoire		
		18	Cathédrale St-Étienne	52	Palais du Gouverneur
	PLACES TO EAT	20	Panorama	53	Porte Serpenoise
7	Restaurant du Pont St-Marcel	20	Porte des Allemands	54	Notre Dame de Bonsecours (Hospital)
14	Taj Mahal	21	Peugeot Cycles		
15	À La Ville de Lyon	23	Laundrette	56	Bailly (Sixt) Car Rental
17	Covered Market	24	Laundrette	58	Main Post Office
22	Tâm Traiteur	25	Laundrette	59	Aérolor Airport Shuttle
29	Atac Supermarket (Centre St-Jacques Shopping Mall)	26	Tourist Office; Town Hall	61	Banque Populaire de Lorraine
		27	Net Café		
31	L'Étoile du Maroc	30	Église Notre Dame	62	Discothèque Le Retro
35	Au Pied de Vigne	32	Laundrette	63	Intercity Bus Stops
36	Pizzerias	33	Église St-Martin	64	Water Tower
37	Au Gourmet Alsacien; Le Tiffany	39	Le Privilège	65	Bus Station
		40	Boat Hire	66	Train Station
46	L'Etude	41	Pleasure Boat Dock	67	New Train Station Entrance
		42	Palais de Justice		

8.30 am to 12.30 pm on weekdays. The Banque Populaire de Lorraine at 3 rue François de Curel is open from 8.30 am to 6 pm on weekdays. There are several banks at place St-Louis. The tourist office also has an exchange service.

Post & Communications The imposing main post office at 9 rue Gambetta is open from 8 am to 7 pm on weekdays and until noon on Saturday. Foreign exchange services and a Cyberposte are available.

The tourist office has a free Internet and email terminal. Net Café (☎ 03 87 76 30 64), in the courtyard at 11 place de la Cathédrale, charges 1FF a minute. It is open from 1 to 6 pm Monday to Saturday.

Laundry The laundrettes at 4 rue des Allemands, 11 rue de la Fontaine and 22 rue du Pont des Morts are open from 7 am to 8 pm daily.

Medical Services Notre Dame de Bonsecours CHR (☎ 03 87 55 31 31), a huge

hospital at 1 place Philippe de Vigneulles, is open 24 hours a day.

Emergency The Police Nationale's Hôtel de Police (☎ 03 87 16 17 17) at 6 rue Belle Isle is staffed 24 hours a day.

Things to See & Do
The spectacular, Gothic **Cathédrale St-Étienne**, built between 1220 and 1522, is famed for its veritable curtains of 13th- to 20th-century stained glass, considered among the finest in France. The superb **Flamboyant Gothic windows** (1504), on the main wall of the left-hand transept arm, provide a remarkable stylistic contrast with the magnificent **Renaissance windows** on the main wall of the right-hand transept arm, created a mere two decades later. Visits are possible from 7 am to noon and 1.30 to 6 pm daily (to 7 pm from June to September, when there's no midday closure). Visits to the **treasury** and 15th-century **crypt** (below the altar), from whose ceiling hangs a legendary monster known as the Graoully

('**Grau**-lee' or '**Grau** -yee'), cost 12FF. Try to come on a bright day.

The neoclassical **place de la Comédie**, bounded by one of the channels of the River Moselle, is home to the city's **Théâtre** (1738–53), the oldest theatre building in France that's still in use. During the Revolution, place de l'Égalité (as it was then known) was the site of a guillotine that lopped off the heads of 63 'enemies of the people'. The Rhenish-style, neo-Romanesque **Temple Neuf** (Protestant Church), just south-west, was built under the Germans in 1903.

The excellent **Musée d'Art et d'Histoire** (Art & History Museum; ☎ 03 87 68 25 00), 2 rue du Haut Poirier, has an outstanding collection of Gallo-Roman antiquities, paintings and early-medieval religious art and stonework. Housed in a maze-like series of 60 rooms that were originally part of a 15th-century granary and a 17th-century convent, it is open from 10 am to noon and 2 to 6 pm daily. Admission costs 30FF (students 15FF, seniors 22FF, free for children under 12 and, on Wednesday and Sunday mornings, for everyone).

On the eastern edge of the city centre, **place St-Louis** is surrounded by medieval arcades and merchants' houses dating from the 14th to 16th centuries.

The formal flowerbeds of the **esplanade** – and its statue of a gallant-looking Marshall Ney, sword dangling at his side (1859) – are flanked by imposing public buildings, including the **Arsenal** (Cultural Centre; 1863), now a concert hall, and the sober, neoclassical **Palais de Justice** (late 18th century).

Église St-Pierre-aux-Nonains was originally built between AD 380 and 400 as part of a Gallo-Roman spa complex (the parts of the walls that have horizontal red-brick stripes are Roman originals). From the 6th to 16th centuries, the structure served as the abbey church of a women's monastery. Hours are 2 to 6.30 pm daily except Monday from April to September. The rest of the year it only opens at the weekend.

West and north-west of the Esplanade, on both sides of blvd Poincaré, is a lovely

riverside park, graced with statues, ponds, swans, ducks and a fountain. **Boats** can be rented on quai des Régates in the warm months.

Just north of the train station, the solid, bourgeois buildings and broad avenues of the handsome **Quartier de la Gare**, including rue Gambetta and ave Foch, were constructed at the end of the 19th and beginning of the 20th century. Intended to Germanise the city by emphasising its post-1871 status as an inalienable part of the German Empire, the neo-Romanesque and neo-Renaissance buildings are made of dark-hued sandstone, granite and basalt, rather than the yellow-tan Jaumont limestone characteristic of French-built neoclassical structures.

The huge, grey-sandstone **train station**, completed in 1908 and decorated with sculptures whose common theme is German imperial might, was designed with military needs in mind. With a length of 300m, it can load or unload 20,000 troops and their equipment in 24 hours. The massive **main post office**, built in 1911 of red Vosges sandstone, is as solid and heavy as the cathedral is light and lacy.

On the other side of the tracks from the train station, a wasteland of abandoned hangars and depots is being turned into a huge new neighbourhood, the **Quartier de l'Amphithéâtre**.

First erected around 1230 when a wall to surround this part of the city was constructed, the crenellated Porte des Allemands (Gate of the Germans) owes its name to the brothers of Notre-Dame-des-Allemands, who ran a hospital near here in the Middle Ages. Overlooking the River Seille, the gate was severely damaged during the liberation of the city by Allied forces in November 1944.

Organised Tours The tourist office's 1½-hour *visites audioguidées* (Walkman tours) of the city, available in six languages, cost 45FF. In July and August (and the rest of there year if there are at least three people – call ahead to reserve), guided tours of the city (in English if there's demand) leave the tourist office at 3 pm daily except Sunday and holidays. Tours cost 50FF.

Places to Stay

Several of the city's two-star places have a few cheap rooms on offer.

Hostels The *Auberge de Jeunesse Carrefour* (☎ 03 87 75 07 26, fax 03 87 36 71 44, **☻** ascarrefour@wanadoo.fr, 6 rue Marchant) charges 83FF per person in a plain but well-maintained single or double, 72FF per person in a room for three, four or eight, including breakfast. Kitchen facilities are available, rooms are accessible all day, and there's no curfew. From the train station, take minibus B to the St-Ségolène stop.

The *Auberge de Jeunesse Metz-Plage* (☎ 03 87 30 44 02, fax 03 87 33 19 80, just off place du Pontiffroy), on the river, charges 68FF, including breakfast. Reception is open from 7.30 to 10 am and 5 to 10 pm; there's no curfew. Kitchen facilities are available, and the hostel loans out bicycles for free. By bus, take No 3 or 11 to the Pontiffroy stop.

Hotels – Train Station Area Metz' cheapest hotel is the nine-room *Hôtel Chez Françoise* (☎ 03 87 75 29 79, 8 rue des Parmentiers), where doubles with washbasin cost 130FF. Reception (at the bar) is closed on Sunday. Many of the rooms are let by the week (700FF) or month (2400FF), so it's often full.

The 80-room, two-star *Hôtel Métropole* (☎ 03 87 66 26 22, fax 03 87 66 29 91, 5 place du Général de Gaulle) has clean, modern singles with washbasin for 130FF (no hall shower available); doubles with shower and toilet start at 185FF. The 43-room, two-star *Hôtel Moderne* (☎ 03 87 66 57 33, fax 03 87 55 98 59, 1 rue Lafayette) has functional doubles from 160FF (255FF with shower and toilet). The two-star, 39-room *Cécil Hôtel* (☎ 03 87 66 66 13, fax 03 87 56 96 02, 14 rue Pasteur) has comfortable doubles for 305FF.

Hotels – City Centre In the pedestrianised commercial centre, the 18-room *Hôtel Lafayette* (☎ 03 87 75 21 09, 24 rue des Clercs) has simple doubles with old-fashioned touches for 145FF; doubles/triples with shower and toilet are 200/250FF. A hall shower is 20FF. The two-star, 62-room *Grand Hôtel de Metz* (☎ 03 87 36 16 33, fax 03 87 74 17 04, 3 rue des Clercs) has doubles/triples from 350/425FF; enormous rooms with Jacuzzis go for 480FF. By car, take rue Fabert from the cathedral.

The three-star, 20-room *Hôtel de la Cathédrale* (☎ 03 87 75 00 02, fax 03 87 75 40 75, **☻** hotel-cathedrale.metz@wanadoo. fr, 25 place de Chambre), in a 17th-century townhouse, has charming – even romantic – doubles for 300FF to 450FF (490FF for a suite).

Places to Eat

Place St-Jacques is taken over by cafes in the warmer months.

Restaurants – French The hugely popular *L'Étude* (☎ 03 87 36 35 32, 11 ave Robert Schuman) is a typically French mixture of the intellectual (book-lined walls) and the gastronomic, with two/three course *menus* for 98/120FF (126/148FF on evenings when there's live music, which starts at 8 or 8.30 pm; reservations are recommended).

At *Restaurant du Pont St-Marcel* (☎ 03 87 30 12 29, 1 rue du Pont St-Marcel), everything is typical of Lorraine, from the succulent dishes to the billowy cotton shirts and black trousers worn by the waiters. The *menus* cost 98FF and 168FF. Traditional French gastronomic fare is on offer at *Au Pied de Vigne* (☎ 03 87 21 01 07, 34 rue du Coëtlosquet), where *menus* cost 80FF to 195FF. It is closed Sunday night and Monday. The intimate, family-run *Au Gourmet Alsacien* (☎ 03 87 36 00 62, 22 rue du Coëtlosquet) has French and Alsatian cuisine, with *menus* from 89FF. It is closed Sunday evening.

For a splurge, an excellent bet is the formal *À la Ville de Lyon* (☎ 03 87 36 07 01, next to 13 rue des Piques), whose traditional French *menus* start at 115FF. It is closed on Sunday evening and on Monday.

LORRAINE

Restaurants – Other   A block east of place de la République, rue Dupont des Loges is home to a number of *pizzerias*. Couscous and tajines (60FF to 90FF) are the speciality of *L'Étoile du Maroc* (☎ 03 87 76 33 66, *5 rue des Huiliers*). *Taj Mahal* (☎ 03 87 74 33 23, *16 rue des Jardins*) has a weekday buffet for just 45FF; vegetarian mains are also about 45FF.

Self-Catering   The old *covered market* (*place de la Cathédrale*) is open from 6 am to 6 pm daily except Sunday and Monday. On Saturday morning, there's a large, outdoor *food market* at either place d'Armes (July to September) or place St-Jacques (the rest of the year).

The *Atac* supermarket (*place St-Jacques*), on the lowest level of the Centre St-Jacques shopping mall, is open from 8.30 am to 7.30 pm Monday to Saturday. *Tâm Traiteur* (☎ 03 87 74 96 93, *39 rue des Allemands*) has inexpensive Vietnamese takeaway dishes. It is open until 8 pm daily except Sunday.

Entertainment
The city's main concert venues are the *Arsenal cultural centre* (☎ 03 87 39 92 00, *next to the Esplanade*) and the smaller *Salle des Trinitaires* (☎ 03 87 75 75 87, *place Jeanne d'Arc*). Free outdoor concerts are held next to the latter every Thursday evening from late June to early September. Free summertime concerts also take place at other venues around town.

The pulsating, gyrating bodies and ultra-modern decor would have knocked the socks off the medieval people who built the vaulted cellar that houses *Le Tiffany* (☎ 03 87 75 23 32, *24 rue du Coëtlosquet*), a discotheque whose hours are 11.30 pm to 5 am daily except Tuesday. Admission is free except on Friday (50FF) and Saturday (60FF). Sports shoes are forbidden. *Discothèque Le Rétro* (☎ 03 87 74 77 47, *11 rue des Augustins*) attracts over 25s from Wednesday to Sunday. Admission costs 50FF to 80FF (free for women before midnight except on Saturday and holidays).

Le Privilège (☎ 03 87 36 29 29, *20 rue aux Ours*), a friendly gay bar and techno club, is open 11 pm to 5 am on Tuesday (just as a bar), Friday (admission free), Saturday (60FF) and Sunday (with a *spectacle transformiste*; 60FF after 1 am).

Getting There & Away
Air   Metz-Nancy-Lorraine airport (☎ 03 87 56 70 00) is 16km south of the city centre off the A31.

Bus   The bus station is on ave de l'Amphithéâtre (some lines also stop near the train station). Les Rapides de Lorraine (☎ 03 87 63 65 65) links Metz with Veckring (lines 49 and 107 via Thionville; about two hours, two to five a day, none on Sunday) and Verdun (line 69; 69.10FF, 1¾ hours, seven a day except Sunday and holidays). Les Courriers Mosellans (☎ 03 87 34 60 12), which handles Eurolines ticketing, has buses to Gorze (line 78; 26.60FF, 50 minutes) at 11.15 am and 6.15 pm on weekdays and Saturday, but there's no way to get back the same day. Both companies' offices are open until at least 5 pm on weekdays (to 4 pm on Friday; closed from noon to 2 pm).

Train   Metz' train station (☎ 0 836 35 35 35) has direct services to cities including Paris' Gare de l'Est (206FF, 2¾ hours, six to eight a day), Nancy (51FF, 40 to 70 minutes, 15 to 34 a day), Verdun (72FF, 1¼ hours, one or two a day) and Strasbourg (113FF, 1¼ hours, 12 a day, seven at the weekend).

Car   Bailly (Sixt; ☎ 03 87 66 36 31), 5 rue Lafayette, and National-Citer (☎ 03 87 76 14 44), in the train station's arrival hall, are both closed on Saturday afternoon and Sunday.

Getting Around
To/From the Airport   Aérolor shuttles (☎ 03 87 34 60 12) link the train station with Metz-Nancy-Lorraine airport (40FF, 25 minutes, six times a day on weekdays).

Bus   TCRM (☎ 03 87 76 31 11) has an information office at 1 ave Robert Schuman. It is closed Sunday. Most lines operate from

6 am to about 8 pm daily, though bus No 11 also has runs at about 10 and 11 pm and midnight nightly.

Parking Near the train station, there's free parking under the trees on ave Foch.

Taxi For a cab, ring ☎ 03 87 56 91 92 day or night.

Bicycle Bikes can be hired for 50FF to 80FF a day at Peugeot Cycles (☎ 03 87 74 13 14), 23 boulevard André Maginot, open from 9 am to noon and 2 to 7 pm daily except Monday morning and Sunday.

AROUND METZ
Parc Naturel Régional de Lorraine

The 2000 sq km Lorraine Regional Park, created in 1974, covers areas both southwest and south-east of Metz. Its forests, streams and lakes attract fishers and families on holiday.

Gorze The **Val de Metz** area of the park contains some of Lorraine's most picturesque villages, including **Gorze** (population 1390), 20km south-west of Metz. Its Benedictine abbey, founded in 749 by St-Chrodegang, played a role in creating the Gregorian chant. The tourist office (☎ 03 87 52 04 57) is open daily except Monday from mid-June to September. When it is closed, brochures are available next door in the town hall (1st floor), which is open weekdays. The many footpaths around Gorze include the GR5.

The 12th- and 13th-century **Église St-Étienne** has an austere, Romanesque exterior, a Lorraine-style Gothic interior and a mid-18th-century choir. There's a formal garden at the back of the **Palais Abbatial** (1696), now a retirement home. The tourist office building houses a small **museum**, open from April to October.

The two-star, 18-room *Hostellerie du Lion d'Or* (☎ 03 87 52 00 90, 103 rue du Commerce) has doubles from 170FF to 330FF. It is closed on Monday.

For details on bus services, see Getting

There & Away under Metz. The D903 and D103B from Metz to Gorze pass by a number of German memorials from the Franco-Prussian War of 1870–71.

Fort du Hackenberg

The Metz area was heavily fortified by the Germans before WWI and, as part of the Maginot Line (see the boxed text), by the French between the wars. The largest single Maginot Line bastion in the area was the 1000-man Hackenberg fort (☎ 03 82 82 30 08), 30km north-east of Metz near the village of Veckring, whose 10km of galleries were designed to be self-sufficient for three months and, in battle, to fire four tonnes of shells a minute. Two-hour tours begin between 2 and 3.30 pm on Saturday, Sunday and holidays (at 3 pm in July and August) from April to October. An electric trolley takes visitors along 4km of the fortress' underground tunnels, past such subterranean installations as a kitchen, a hospital, a generating plant and ammunition stores. For information on buses to Veckring, see Getting There & Away under Metz.

VERDUN
postcode 55100 • pop 20,700
• elevation 198m

The horrific events that took place in and around Verdun between February 1916 and August 1917 – *l'enfer de Verdun* (the hell of Verdun) – have turned the town's name into a byword for wartime slaughter. During the last two years of WWI, over 800,000 soldiers – some 400,000 French and almost as many Germans, along with thousands of the Americans who arrived in 1918 – lost their lives here.

After the annexation of Alsace and part of Lorraine by Germany in 1871, Verdun became a frontline outpost. Over the next four decades, it was turned into the most important – and most heavily fortified – element in France's eastern defensive line. During WWI, Verdun itself was never taken by the Germans, but the evacuated town was almost totally destroyed by artillery bombardments. In the hills to the north and east of Verdun, where most of the fighting took

LORRAINE

place, the brutal combat (carried out with artillery, flame-throwers and poison gas) completely wiped out nine villages.

These days, Verdun is an economically depressed and profoundly provincial (and sometimes even unfriendly) backwater, though the recent dispatch of Verdun-based French troops to peacekeeping missions abroad has made world politics a very local – and for some, personal – affair. Recent investments in pavements, trees and lighting around quai de Londres have brightened the city centre a bit.

Orientation

Central Verdun straddles the River Meuse and its two canals but the livelier Ville Haute (Upper Town) is on the river's left (western) bank, which rises to the cathedral. The train station is 700m north-west of the cathedral. Verdun's wide streets, such as main drag rue Mazel and rue St-Paul, were laid out in the years following WWI.

Information

Tourist Office Verdun's unreliable tourist office (☎ 03 29 86 14 18, fax 03 29 84 22

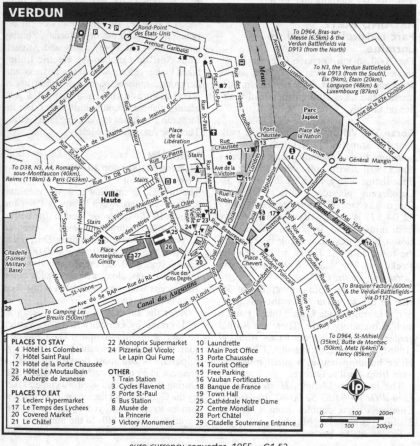

PLACES TO STAY
4 Hôtel Les Colombes
7 Hôtel Saint Paul
12 Hôtel de la Porte Chaussée
23 Hôtel Le Moutaulbain
26 Auberge de Jeunesse

PLACES TO EAT
2 Leclerc Hypermarket
17 Le Temps des Lychees
20 Covered Market
21 Le Châtel

22 Monoprix Supermarket
24 Pizzeria Del Vicolo;
   Le Lapin Qui Fume

OTHER
1 Train Station
3 Cycles Flavenot
5 Porte St-Paul
6 Bus Station
8 Musée de
   la Princerie
9 Victory Monument

10 Laundrette
11 Main Post Office
13 Porte Chaussée
14 Tourist Office
15 Free Parking
16 Vauban Fortifications
18 Banque de France
19 Town Hall
25 Cathédrale Notre Dame
27 Centre Mondial
28 Port Châtel
29 Citadelle Souterraine Entrance

euro currency converter 10FF = €1.52

42), at place de la Nation, is open from 8.30 or 9 am to noon and 2 to 5.30 or 6 pm Monday to Saturday. There's no midday break and closing time is 6.30 pm (7.30 pm in July and August) from May to September. Hours are 9 or 10 am to 1 pm (5 pm from April to September) on Sunday and holidays. The tourist office manages the main battlefield sites.

Money The Banque de France, 12 quai de la République, changes money between 8.30 and 11.55 am on weekdays. There are also several banks around the intersection of rue Mazel and rue Beaurepaire. The tourist office can exchange foreign cash.

Post & Communications The main post office, on ave de la Victoire, is open from 8 am to 7 pm on weekdays and until noon on Saturday. Currency exchange and a Cyberposte are available.

Laundry The laundrette on ave de la Victoire is open from 6.30 am to 10 pm daily.

Things to See & Do

Verdun's huge **Citadelle Souterraine** (Underground Citadel; ☎ 03 29 86 62 02), whose visitors entrance is on ave du 5e RAP, was designed by Vauban in the 17th century and completed in 1838. In 1916, its 7km of underground galleries were turned into an impregnable command centre in which 10,000 *poilus* (French WWI soldiers) lived, many while waiting to be dispatched to the front. About 10% of the galleries have been converted into an imaginative audiovisual re-enactment of Verdun in 1916, making this the best introduction to the WWI history of the area. Half-hour tours available in six languages, in battery-powered cars, depart every five minutes from 9 am (10 am in February and March) to noon and 2 to 5 or 5.30 pm (6 or 7 pm from April to September, when there's no

---

The Maginot Line

The famed Maginot Line, named after France's minister of war from 1929 to 1931, was one of the most spectacular blunders of WWII. This elaborate, mostly subterranean defence network, built between 1930 and 1940, was the pride of pre-war France. It included everything France's finest military architects thought would be needed to defend the nation in a 'modern war' of poison gas, tanks and aeroplanes: reinforced concrete bunkers, subterranean lines of supply and communication, minefields, antitank canals, floodable basins and even artillery emplacements that popped out of the ground to fire and then disappeared. The only things visible above ground were firing posts and lookout towers. The line stretched along the Franco-German frontier from the Swiss border all the way to Belgium where, for political and budgetary reasons, it stopped. The Maginot Line even had a slogan: '*Ils ne passeront pas*' (They won't get through).

'They' – the Germans – never did. Rather than attack the Maginot Line straight on, Hitler's armoured divisions simply circled around through Belgium and invaded France across its unprotected northern frontier. They then attacked the Maginot Line from the rear. Against all the odds – and with most of northern France already in German hands – some of the fortifications held out for a few weeks. When resistance became hopeless, thousands of French troops managed to escape to Switzerland, where the Swiss promptly interned them (they were freed the following year).

Parts of the Maginot Line are open to visitors, but without your own wheels they're a bit hard to get to. In Lorraine, visitors can tour Fort du Hackenberg and Fort de Fermont (see the Lorraine section of this chapter). In Alsace, it's possible to visit Schœnenbourg (☎ 03 88 80 59 39 for the Hunspach tourist office), which is about 45km north of Strasbourg. From April to October there are tours from 9.30 to 11 am and 2 to 4 pm on Sunday; from May and September it's also open 2 to 4 pm Monday to Saturday. Admission costs 30FF (20FF for under 18s).

LORRAINE

midday closure). In January it is closed in the morning. Admission costs 35FF (children aged 15 and under 15FF). Bring a sweater – the temperature below is a constant 7°C.

The innovative **Centre Mondial de la Paix** (World Centre for Peace; ☎ 03 29 86 55 00) at place Monseigneur Ginisty, part of which you visit with an infrared headset, has imaginative and moving exhibits on the themes of peace and human rights in light of the horrific carnage of WWI. English documentation is available. The centre can be visited from 10 am to 1 pm and 2 to 6 pm daily (9.30 am to 7 pm from June to mid-September; closed in January). Admission costs 35FF (20FF if you're aged 12 to 17).

Next door, **Cathédrale Notre Dame** incorporates Romanesque, Gothic and baroque elements. Some of the most colourful stained glass is from the inter-war period.

Verdun's remaining city gates include the imposing, riverside **Porte Chaussée**, built in the 14th century as part of the city walls and later used as a prison.

Across from the bus station, the drawbridge-equipped **Porte St-Paul** was built in 1877 and rebuilt between 1919 and 1929. The Rodin bronze was given to the city by the Netherlands.

The municipal **Musée de la Princerie** (☎ 03 29 86 10 62), 16 rue de la Belle Vierge, displays sculptures, furnishings and medieval bits and bobs. It opens from 9.30 am to noon and 2 to 6 pm daily except Tuesday, from April to October. Admission costs 10FF.

Overlooking rue Mazel is the colossal, almost Fascist-looking **Monument à la Victoire** (Victory Monument; 1920–29), which portrays a warrior and is flanked by two cannons.

Dragées (pronounced 'dra-**zhay**'; sugared almonds) – not to be confused with *draguer* ('dra-**gay**'), which means to chat up – have long been a Verdun speciality. There are tours (10FF) of the **Braquier factory**, east of the centre at 50 rue du Fort de Vaux, at 9.30 and 10.30 am and 2.30 and 3.30 pm on weekdays. Reservations and ticketing are handled by the tourist office.

Places to Stay

Camping The three-star *Camping Les Breuils* (☎ 03 29 86 15 31, *Allée des Breuils*), open from April to mid-October, is about 500m west of the Citadelle Souterraine. By bus, take No 3 to the Cité Verte École stop.

Hostels The 69-bed *Auberge de Jeunesse* (☎ 03 29 86 28 28, fax 03 29 86 28 82, *place Monseigneur Ginisty*), situated behind the cathedral, is affiliated with the Centre Mondial de la Paix. Reception is staffed from 8 am to noon (10 am at the weekend) and 5 to 11 pm. A modern bunk of generous proportions costs 51FF. Rooms are accessible all day long. A kitchenette is available.

Hotels The one-star, 34-room *Hôtel Les Colombes* (☎ 03 29 86 05 46, fax 03 29 83 75 25, 📧 linda.jacquot@wanadoo.fr, *9 ave Garibaldi*) has simple singles/doubles from 130/150FF (160FF with shower and toilet); triples and quads are 190FF to 250FF.

The attractive, two-star *Hôtel Le Montaulbain* (☎ 03 29 86 00 47, fax 03 29 84 75 70, *4 rue de la Vieille Prison*) has spacious and cheerful doubles with shower from 170FF (200FF with toilet, too). A quad costs 260FF. The 17-room *Hôtel de la Porte Chaussée* (☎ 03 29 86 00 78, *67 quai de Londres*) has plain but spacious and newly renovated doubles from 170FF (200FF with shower). Hall showers cost 15FF.

The 31-room *Hôtel St-Paul* (☎/fax 03 29 86 02 16, *12 place St-Paul*) has dull but well lit rooms from 165FF (235FF with shower and toilet).

Places to Eat

There are quite a few brasseries and fast-food joints along the pedestrianised, riverside quai de Londres and nearby streets.

Restaurants Three-course Lorraine-style *menus* start at 60FF at *Le Châtel* (☎ 03 29 86 20 14, *opposite 34 rue des Gros Degrés*), a real *restaurant du quartier* (neighbourhood restaurant). It is closed on Saturday for lunch and Sunday. *Pizzeria Del Vicolo* (☎ 03 29 86 43 14, *33 rue des Gros Degrés*) has decent pizzas for 32FF to 61FF. It is closed on Monday at midday and on Sunday.

Le Temps des Lychees (☎ 03 29 86 26 26, 8 rue du Puty) is a Chinese place with *menus* from 55FF for weekday lunches, 90FF the rest of the time.

Self-Catering On Friday from 7 am to 12.30 pm there's a *food market (rue Victor Hugo)* in and around the old covered market.

The *Monoprix* supermarket at the southern end of rue Mazel is open from 9 am to noon and 2 to 7 pm Monday to Saturday. Across the parking lot from the train station, the cavernous *Leclerc* hypermarket is open from 9 am to 8 pm (8.30 pm on Friday, closed on Sunday).

Entertainment
Le Lapin Qui Fume (☎ 03 29 86 15 84, 31 rue des Gros Degrés) is a friendly neighbourhood bar that opens from 10 am (3 pm on Sunday) until as late as 2 am if there's demand. It is closed on Monday. Beers start at 11FF.

Getting There & Away
Bus At the bus station, Les Rapides de la Meuse (☎ 03 29 86 02 71) has an information desk that opens from 5.30 am to 7 pm (closed on Saturday after 12.30 pm and on Sunday). Destinations served include Metz (69.10FF, 1¾ hours, seven a day, except Sunday and holidays) and Nancy (95FF, 2¾ hours, five a day, one on Sunday and holidays).

Train Verdun's poorly served little train station (☎ 0 836 35 35 35) is linked to Paris' Gare de l'Est (179FF via Châlons-en-Champagne, three to four hours, two or three a day), Metz (72FF, 1¼ hours, one or two direct a day), Nancy (89FF, 1½ to 2¼ hours, one to three non-direct a day), Reims (100FF via Châlons-en-Champagne) and Strasbourg (163FF via Metz).

Getting Around
Parking There's free parking two blocks east of the tourist office in the giant lot on ave du 8 Mai 1945.

Taxi To order a taxi, ring ☎ 03 29 84 53 59 or ☎ 03 29 86 05 22.

Bicycle Cycles Flavenot (☎ 03 29 86 12 43), Rond-point des États-Unis, the local Cannondale dealer, rents mountain bikes for 100FF a day and can supply information on local group rides. It opens from 9 am to noon and 2 to 7 pm (closed on Sunday and, sometimes, Monday morning).

VERDUN BATTLEFIELDS
The outbreak of WWI in August 1914 was followed, on the Western Front, by a long period of trench warfare in which neither side made any significant gains. To break the stalemate, the Germans decided to change tactics, attacking a target so vital for both military and symbolic reasons that the French would throw every man they had into its defence. These troops would then be slaughtered, 'bleeding France white' and causing the French people to lose their will to resist. The target selected for this bloody plan by the German general staff was the heavily fortified city of Verdun.

The Battle of Verdun began on the morning of 21 February 1916. After the heaviest shelling of the war to that date (something like two million shells were fired in 10 hours), German forces went on the attack and advanced with little opposition for four days, capturing, among other unprepared French positions, the Fort de Douaumont. Thus began a 300-day battle fought by hundreds of thousands of cold, wet, miserable and ill-fed men, sheltering in their muddy trenches and foxholes amid a moonscape of craters.

French forces were regrouped and rallied by General Philippe Pétain (later the leader of the collaborationist Vichy government during WWII), who slowed the German advance by launching several French counterattacks. He also oversaw the massive resupply of Verdun via the **Voie Sacrée** (Sacred Way), the 75km road from Bar-le-Duc, which was maintained by territorial troops from Senegal. The Germans were not pushed back beyond their positions of February

LORRAINE

1916 until American troops and French forces launched a coordinated offensive in September 1918.

By car, you can easily visit the area on a day trip from Metz or even Nancy.

Information

Most of the battle sites detailed below are managed by the Verdun tourist office, which can supply historical and practical information on the battlefields, including Alistaire Horne's *The Price of Glory: Verdun 1916* (99FF). The area and its trails are covered in detail by the IGN Top 25 map No 3112 ET (*Forêts de Verdun et du Mort-Homme*; 58FF).

Organised Tours

The Verdun tourist office runs guided minibus tours of the five main battlefield sites from 2 to 6 pm daily from May to September. Tours cost 145FF for adults, including admission fees. Printed or recorded commentary is available in English.

Mémorial de Verdun

The village of Fleury, wiped off the face of the earth in the course of being captured and recaptured 16 times, is now the site of the Verdun Memorial (☎ 03 29 84 35 34), also known as the Musée Mémorial de Fleury. The story of the battle is told using evocative photos, documents, weapons and other objects. Downstairs is a re-creation of the battlefield as it looked on the day the guns finally fell silent. Some of the signs are in English.

The museum opens from 9 am to noon and 2 to 5 or 6 pm daily from about mid-September to March (except from mid-December to January, when it's closed). The rest of the year, hours are 9 am to 6 pm. Admission costs 30FF (children aged 11 to 16 15FF) and includes a film on the Battle of Verdun, available in English.

Fleury

The Mémorial de Verdun actually sits atop Fleury's former train station – the town centre was a few hundred metres down the road. Today, a memorial chapel known as

Notre Dame de l'Europe (Our Lady of Europe) marks the grassy, crater-pocked site, surrounded by low ruins and signs indicating the layout of the village.

Mémorial Ossuaire

The 137m-long Ossuary Memorial (☎ 03 29 84 54 81), inaugurated in 1932 and also known as the Ossuaire de Douaumont, contains the remains of about 130,000 unidentified French and German soldiers, collected from the battlefields after the war. The excellent, 20-minute audiovisual presentation on the battle and its participants costs 17FF (children 11FF). Except from December to February, screenings begin every 30 minutes from 9 to 11.30 am and 2 pm to sometime between 4.30 pm (in November) and 6 pm (from May to early September); there's no midday closure from April to early September. The 46m-high **bell tower** can be climbed for 6FF. The memorial itself is open year round.

Out front, the 15,000 cement crosses (and a few non-Christian markers) of the **Nécropole Nationale** (French military cemetery) extend down the hill. The **Mémorial Israélite** (Jewish Memorial), inscribed with the Ten Commandments in Hebrew, is nearby.

Fort de Douaumont

About 2km north-east of the Ossuary Memorial on the highest of the area's hills stands Douaumont (☎ 03 29 84 41 91), the strongest of the 39 forts and bastions built along a 45km front to protect Verdun. Because the French high command disregarded warnings of an impending German offensive, Douaumont had only a skeleton crew when the Battle of Verdun began. By the fourth day it had been captured easily, and was not recaptured until October 1916, when colonial troops from Morocco retook it.

The 3km network of cold, dripping galleries inside Douaumont, built between 1885 and 1912, can be visited from 10 am to 1 pm and 2 to 5 pm daily (to 6 or 7 pm from April to September, when there's no midday closure). It is closed in January.

Admission costs 16FF (children aged eight to 16 8FF).

Tranchée des Baïonnettes

On 12 June 1916, two companies of the 137th Infantry Regiment of the French army were sheltering in their *tranchées* (trenches), *baïonnettes* (bayonets) fixed, waiting for a ferocious artillery bombardment to end. It never did – the incoming shells covered their positions with mud and debris, burying them alive. They weren't found until three years later, when several hundred bayonet tips sticking through the ground were spotted. The victims were left where they died, their bayonets still poking through the soil. The site is always open.

The tree-filled valley across the D913 is known as the **Ravin de la Mort** (Ravine of Death).

Fort de Vaux

On 1 June 1916 German troops managed to enter the tunnel system of the Vaux Fortress (☎ 03 29 88 32 88 or ☎ 03 29 84 18 85), attacking the French defenders from inside their own ramparts. After six days and seven nights of brutal, metre-by-metre combat along the narrow passageways (the most effective weapons were grenades, flame throwers and poison gas) the steadfast French defenders, dying of thirst (licking drops of moisture off the walls had become their only source of water), were forced to surrender. The fort was recaptured by the French five months later.

The interior of Vaux, built between 1881 and 1912 and encased in 2.5m of concrete, is smaller, more reconstructed and less dreary – and thus less interesting – than Douaumont. It can be visited from 9 or 9.30 am to noon and 1 to 5 pm (6 or 6.30 pm from April to September, when there's no midday closure). It is closed in January. Tickets cost 16FF (children aged eight to 16 8FF).

Fort de Souville

This unrestored fort (built 1875–77), some of whose underground galleries have collapsed, sits in the middle of the Forêt Do-maniale de Verdun (Verdun Forest) on a gravel track linked to the D112 and D913. All around, postwar trees and undergrowth sprout from still-visible shell craters and traces of the trench lines.

American Memorials

The largest US military cemetery in Europe, the WWI **Meuse-Argonne American Cemetery**, is at Romagne-sous-Montfaucon, 41km north-west of Verdun along the D38 and D123. Just east of Montfaucon d'Argonne (about 10km south-east of the cemetery), a 58m-high column atop the 336m-high **Butte de Montfaucon** commemorates the US 1st Army's Meuse-Argonne offensive of 1918.

About 40km south-east of Verdun, the WWI **St-Mihiel American Cemetery** is on the outskirts of Thiaucourt-Regniéville. From there, a 15km drive to the south-west takes you to the 375m-high **Butte de Montsec**, site of a US monument with a bronze relief map surrounded by a round, neoclassical colonnade.

The WWII **Lorraine American Cemetery** is 45km east of Metz just outside of St-Avold. The Web site of the American Battle Monuments Commission is at www .abmc.gov.

Getting Around

The battle sites, which are well signposted (follow the signs to the 'Champ de Bataille 14–18'), are about 5 to 8km (as the crow flies) north-east of Verdun in a forested area served by the D913 and D112.

Les Rapides de la Meuse (☎ 03 29 86 02 71) can get you from Verdun's bus station to both ends of the D913, the highway along which most of the monuments are situated. You could also take a taxi from Verdun.

FORT DE FERMONT

One of the larger underground fortresses of the Maginot Line (see the earlier boxed text 'The Maginot Line'), Fermont (☎ 03 82 39 35 34) is about 56km north of Verdun. Around 30m deep, it withstood three days of heavy bombardment when the Germans attacked on 21 June 1940 but surrendered a few days later. You can take a 2½ hour tour, in English for Anglophone groups (the rest of the time a written translation is available), during which a small electric trolley transports you from one subterranean army block to another. From April to September there are tours at the weekend and on holidays beginning at 2 and 3.30 pm and, in June, on weekdays at 3 pm. In July and August tours begin daily from 2 to 4 pm. They cost 30FF (children aged six to 12, 20FF.

The Loire

The Loire is France's longest, most regal river. From its source in the Massif Central, it follows a 1020km-long course through Bourgogne, Orléanais, Blésois, Touraine, Anjou, into the Atlantic.

From the 15th to the 18th century, the fabled Loire Valley – generally understood to be the western stretch of the river, from Orléans, south-west of Paris, to the city of Nantes (see the Atlantic Coast chapter) – served as the playground of kings, princes, dukes and nobles, who expended family fortunes and the wealth of the nation to turn it into a vast neighbourhood of lavish (and not-so-lavish) chateaux.

Today, this region is a favourite destination of tourists seeking architectural testimony to the glories of the Middle Ages and the Renaissance.

The earliest chateaux were medieval *châteaux forts* (fortresses), thrown up in the 9th century to fend off marauding Vikings. By the 11th century, massive walls topped with battlements, fortified keeps, arrow slits and moats spanned by drawbridges were all the rage.

As the threat of invasion diminished – and the cannon, introduced in the mid-15th century, rendered castles almost useless for defence – chateaux architecture changed: defensive fortresses were superseded by pleasure palaces as the Renaissance (whose innovations were introduced to France from Italy at the end of the 15th century) ushered in whimsical, decorative features. Chambord, Chaumont, Chenonceau and Azay-le-Rideau remain the most resplendent of these creature-comfort extravaganzas. From the 17th century, grand country houses – built in the neoclassical style and set amidst formal gardens – took centre stage instead.

The Loire, no more than an hour or two away by train from Paris' Gare d'Austerlitz (for regular trains) and Gare Montparnasse (for TGVs), is easily accessible from the capital.

Once in the region, cycling through its

Highlights

- Gaze in awe at the magnificent castles of Chambord, Chaumont, Cheverny and Chenonceau
- Be bewitched by a son-et-lumière at Château de Blois
- See Leonardo da Vinci's fabulous flying machines in Amboise
- Discover the world's largest medieval tapestry at Château d'Angers
- Take to the skies in a hot-air balloon for an aerial Loire Valley view

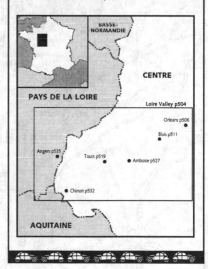

beautiful (and beautifully flat) countryside is an invigorating means of getting around, although amateur cyclists should be aware that up to 50km can be clocked up for a return trip to just one chateau. Details on bicycle hire and cycling routes are listed in the respective Getting Around sections. For regional SNCF train information call ☎ 08 36 35 35 39 or visit their Web site at http://ter.sncf.fr/centre.

THE LOIRE

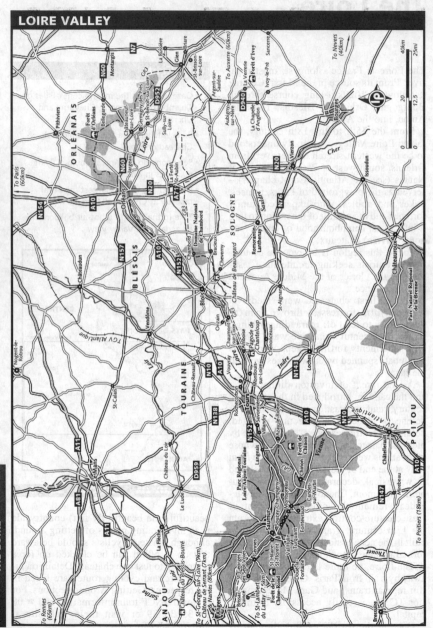

LOIRE VALLEY

Orléanais

The historical region of Orléanais is the gateway to the Loire Valley. Orléans, an ancient Roman city and the region's capital, had its place in history secured by a simple French peasant girl, Joan of Arc, in 1429. Upstream, the sand-bank-strewn River Loire twists past a rash of ecclesiastical treasures to the vineyards of Sancerre, source of the region's most prized white wine.

ORLÉANS

postcode 45000 • pop 112,600
• elevation 100m

Despite being heavily bombed during WWII, the historic heart of Orléans survived more or less intact. Following Pope Honorius' ban on the teaching of law in Paris (but not Orléans) in 1219, the city blossomed as a centre of learning. In May 1429, Joan of Arc stormed the city, smashed English forces who had besieged it for seven months, and marched Charles VII north to Reims be crowned king of France. This was the turning point in the Hundred Years' War (1337–1453), bitterly fought between the Capetians and the English.

Today Orléans has a reputation for innovation. South of the city, in the modern university district of La Source, is Parc Floral de la Source, a lovely park in which the Loiret, a tributary of the River Loire, springs.

Orientation

The Loire snakes along the southern fringe of the city centre. Place du Martroi, the main square, links rue de la République with the central train station (Gare d'Orléans), 400m to the north. The historic quarter is east of place du Martroi, along rue Jeanne d'Arc. The station for trains to/from Paris (Gare des Aubrais-Orléans) is 2km north.

Information

Tourist Offices The tourist office (☎ 02 38 24 05 05, fax 02 38 54 49 84, ✉ office-de-tourisme.orleans@wanadoo.fr), place Albert 1er, opens 10 am to 7 pm Monday and 9 am to 6 pm Tuesday to Saturday.

Money There are several commercial banks on place du Martroi. Banque de France at 30 rue de la République operates an exchange service mornings only.

Post & Communications The post office, place du Général de Gaulle, opens from

---

Hot-Air Ballooning

Hop aboard a hot-air balloon to view the Loire Valley from an aerial perspective.

France Montgolfière (☎ 02 54 71 75 40, fax 02 54 71 75 78, ✉ dlabeaume@teaser.fr) is run by a group of English, Welsh and Americans and is based at La Roulière in Monthou-sur-Cher (about 30km south of Blois). Weather permitting, they run hot-air balloon flights year round from almost anywhere in the Loire Valley. A one- to 1½-hour flight, including a round of champagne at the end, costs 1600FF per person (children aged six to 12, 1100FF) for a fully flexible ticket which can be reimbursed should your flight be cancelled due to adverse weather conditions; cheaper non-refundable weekday/weekend fares (cancelled flights can only be rescheduled) cost 1250/1450FF, and a ticket for a stand-by flight (48-hours notice) costs 950FF. They also offer a variety of other deals. Make reservations several days ahead for weekday flights, four weeks ahead for weekend (especially Saturday night) flights. France Montgolfière accepts reservations via its Web site at www.franceballoons.com.

Between mid-March and mid-October you can sail in a helium-filled balloon without any advance reservation at Château de Cheverny (☎ 02 54 79 25 05). A balloon takes to the skies every 20 minutes or so during chateau opening hours. The 10-minute flight costs 47FF (84FF including admission to the chateau).

THE LOIRE

ORLÉANS

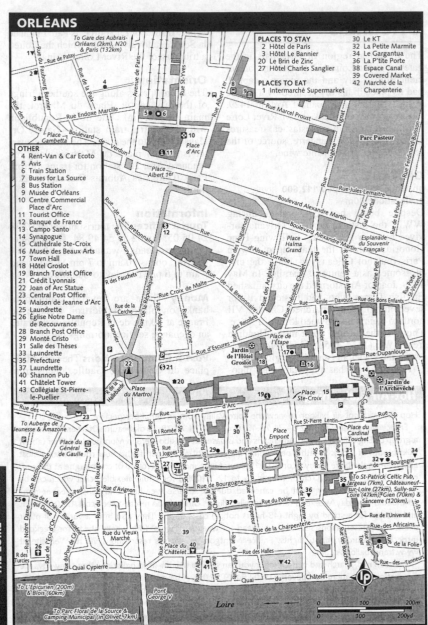

euro currency converter 10FF = €1.52

8 am to 7 pm on weekdays and 8 am to noon on Saturday.

The Monté Cristo cyberclub (☎ 02 38 53 86 99), 42 rue Etienne Dolet, charges 1FF per minute for Internet access. It opens 9 pm to 3 am Wednesday and Thursday, and 8 pm to 3 am Friday to Sunday.

Laundry There are laundrettes at 26 rue du Poirier, 176 rue de Bourgogne and 132 rue de Bourgogne, all open 7 or 7.30 am to 10 pm.

Hôtel Groslot
This flamboyant, Renaissance-style *hôtel particulier* (private mansion) on place de l'Étape was built in 1550–52 for Jacques Groslot, a city bailiff whose family lived here until 1790 when the French Revolution turned it into the town hall. Its lavish interior dates from 1850–54. The bedroom in which the 17-year-old king of France, François II (ruled 1559–60), died is used as a marriage hall today. Hôtel Groslot can be visited 9 am to 7 pm on weekdays, and 5 to 9 pm on Saturday (free admission).

Musée des Beaux Arts
The Musée des Beaux Arts (Museum of Fine Arts; ☎ 02 38 79 21 55), 1 rue Fernand Rabier, houses an impressive collection of European art from the 15th to 20th centuries. Numerous religious works of art and treasures from surrounding chateaux that were seized during the French Revolution are among the displays. The museum opens 11 am to 6 pm Tuesday and Sunday, 10 am to 8 pm on Wednesday, and 10 am to 6 pm Thursday to Saturday.

Cathédrale Ste-Croix
Orléans' Flamboyant Gothic cathedral was built under Henri IV from 1601. Louis XIII (1610–43) had the choir and nave restored, Louis XIV (1638–1715) built the transept, and the next two Louis (1715–74) rebuilt the western facade and its towers. The spire (1858) completed the project. **Stained-glass windows** (1895) in the lower nave depict the life of Joan of Arc, France's patron saint who was canonised in 1920.

Cathédrale Ste-Croix opens 9.15 am to 6.45 pm. The 81.84m-tall cathedral towers can be guided with a guided tour (25FF) at 3, 4 and 5 pm, July to September; and at 3.30 and 4.30 pm, Saturday, May and June.

Maison de Jeanne d'Arc
The timber-framed Maison de Jeanne d'Arc (☎ 02 38 52 99 89), 3 place du Général de Gaulle, is a reconstruction of the 15th-century house where Joan of Arc stayed for a few days in April–May 1429. The original building – put on rails in 1909 and moved 3.5m to widen the street – was destroyed during WWII. Timber beams from another house, dating from the same era, were used to build the current edifice in 1965. Inside, the exhibition dedicated to the 17-year-old virgin warrior opens 10 am to noon and 2 to 6 pm Tuesday to Saturday, April to October, 10 am to noon Tuesday to Sunday the rest of the year. Admission costs 13FF (seniors and students 6.50FF).

Special Events
Since 1430 the Orléanais have celebrated the annual Fête Johanniques which falls around 8 May and commemorates Joan of Arc's liberation of the city. A week of street parties, medieval costume parades and concerts climaxes with a solemn mass at the cathedral.

Places to Stay
Camping Seven kilometres south of Orléans in Olivet, *Camping Municipal* (☎ 02 38 63 53 94, rue du Pont Bouchet) charges 40FF for a tent, two people and a car. The site opens April to mid-October.

Hostels The *Auberge de Jeunesse* (☎ 02 38 53 60 06, fax 03 38 52 96 39, 1 blvd de la Motte Sanguin) in the town centre opens year round. A bed in a two-, three- or four-bedded room costs 55FF (45FF to HI card holders); single rooms cost 70FF (60FF) a night. Breakfast costs an extra 21FF. Reception opens 8 am to 9 pm.

Hotels The cheapest, most cheerful bet for budget travellers content to share a loo is

THE LOIRE

Hôtel de Paris (☎ 02 38 53 39 58, 29 rue du Faubourg Bannier), five minutes' walk from the central train station. The 13-room hotel above a busy bar-brasserie provides singles/doubles with washbasin costing 130/145FF, or 140/165FF with shower and 150/180FF with washbasin and bath).

Nearby, zero-star *Hôtel Le Bannier* (☎ 02 38 53 25 86, 13 rue du Faubourg Bannier), above a ground-floor games bar, has mediocre rooms with shower for 145/165FF.

In the town centre, chaotically run but endearing *Hôtel Charles Sanglier* (☎ 02 38 53 38 50, 8 rue Charles Sanglier) has singles/doubles costing 200/230FF. *Le Brin de Zinc* (☎ 02 38 53 38 77, fax 02 38 62 81 18, 62 rue Ste-Catherine) is an eclectic place. Its six doubles with shared/private bathroom cost 150/170FF each.

Places to Eat

Students from the 1st-floor catering school run *Le KT* (☎ 02 38 64 16 55, 13 rue des Pastoureaux) and dish up cheap 35FF *menus*. The canteen opens 11.30 am to 2 pm Monday to Saturday.

La P'tite Porte (02 38 62 28 00, 28 rue de la Poterne) is small, snug and serves a delicious 48FF *plat du jour* (dish of the day), concocted from fresh market produce and served on a peaceful terrace.

The stretch of rue du Bourgogne between the préfecture and rue St-Etienne is loaded with places to eat. Venues inside charming timber-framed houses and serving regional fare include *La Petite Marmite* (☎ 02 38 54 23 83, 178 rue Ste-Catherine) and *Le Gargantua* at No 134 on the same street. The former is one of France's few no-smoking restaurants.

Near the river, lobsters paddle around in a fish tank waiting to turn red at *L'Épicurien* (☎ 02 38 68 01 10, 54 rue Turcies). Fishy *menus* cost 130FF, 160FF and 190FF.

Espace Canal (☎ 02 38 62 04 30, 6 rue Ducerceau) is a unique cellar restaurant where you can swirl, sip and swallow or spit local wines.

Self-Catering The outdoor *Marché de la Charpenterie* (rue des Halles), opens 4 to 10.30 am on Tuesday, Thursday and Saturday. There is an *Intermarché* supermarket on rue du Faubourg Bannier.

Entertainment

What's-on listings fill *Orléans Poche*, a free pocket-sized events magazine published monthly. Busy drinking holes include the Irish *Shannon Pub* (place du Châtelet), *St-Patrick Celtic Pub* (☎ 02 38 54 53 50, 1 rue de Bourgogne), and *Amazone* (☎ 02 38 70 58 38, 105 bis rue du Faubourg Madeleine), a Creole disco, stumbling distance from the Auberge de Jeunesse.

Getting There & Away

Bus From the bus station (☎ 02 38 53 94 75) at 1 rue Marcel Proust, Les Rapides du Val de Loire operates buses to/from Châteauneuf-sur-Loire (33FF, 35 minutes, four to six daily), Gien (70FF, 1¾ hours, one daily) and Jargeau (27FF, ¾ hour, three daily).

Train Shuttle trains (every eight minutes) link the central train station called Gare d'Orléans (☎ 02 38 79 91 00, ❷ ter@cr-centre.fr) at 1 rue St-Yves with Gare des Aubrais-Orléans, 2km north.

From Orléans, most westbound trains along the Loire Valley stop at both train stations, including trains to/from Blois (52FF, 50 minutes, about 20 trains daily), St-Pierre des Corps (86FF, 50 minutes to 1¾ hours, four daily), Tours (88FF, 1¼ to 1¾ hours, four daily), and Nantes (186FF, 2½ hours, three daily). Trains to/from Paris' Gare d'Austerlitz use Gare des Aubrais-Orléans (91FF, 1¾ hours, 10 to 15 daily).

Getting Around

Car Avis has an office inside the central train station (open 8 am to noon). Rent-Van & Car Ecoto (☎ 02 38 77 92 92), behind the Ibis hotel at 19 ave de Paris, offers competitive rates.

Tram The first line of a new two-line tramway will be open by September 2000. The 18km-long, north-south line will link Gare des Aubrais-Orléans with the central train station, rue de la République and place du Général de Gaulle in the centre of town.

ORLÉANS TO SULLY-SUR-LOIRE

Medieval chateaux are overshadowed by ecclesiastical treasures along the eastern stretch of the River Loire between Orléans and Sully-sur-Loire. Its northern bank is flanked by the elk-rich **Forêt d'Orléans**, 38,234 hectares large and the only place in France to shelter nesting osprey.

Riverside **Jargeau** (population 3561), 20km east of Orléans, is home to the Confrèrie des Chevaliers du Goûte Andouille, a tripe sausage brotherhood dedicated to *andouille* – a fat tripe sausage, typical to the region, and sold at Monsieur Guibet's *charcuterie* at 14 place du Matroi. Delicate constitutions should nibble a *langues de femme* (literally 'tongues of woman' – a type of sweet wafer) instead.

The history of trade on the River Loire comes alive in the **Musée de la Marine** (☎ 02 38 46 84 46, fax 02 38 46 41 01), a marine museum housed in an 11th- to 17th-century chateau at 1 place Aristide Briand in **Châteauneuf-sur-Loire**, 7km east. The tourist office (☎ 02 38 58 44 79) has information on **cycling routes** in the area.

In **Germigny des Prés**, 6km east, the **Église de Germigny des Prés** is a rare example of Carolingian architecture and dates to AD 806. The church's Greek-cross-shaped floor plan and 9th-century mosaic in its eastern apse are unique. The 11th-century Romanesque basilica in **St-Benoît-sur-Loire**, 12km farther east, shelters the relics of St Benedict (480–547). The heavily ornamented capitals supporting the monumental porch tower illustrate the Book of Revelations.

Château de Sully-sur-Loire (☎ 02 38 36 36 86) sports thickset towers, fairytale moats and is a quintessential medieval fortress. It was built at the end of the 14th century to defend one of the River Loire's few crossings.

Places to Stay & Eat

The tourist office in Sully-sur-Loire (☎ 02 38 36 23 70, fax 02 38 36 32 21), place du Général de Gaulle, has accommodation details. Riverside *Camping Sully-sur-Loire* (☎ 02 38 36 23 93), next to the chateau, charges 7.40/11.90/5.40FF per tent/person/car. In the village, *Hôtel de la Poste* (☎ 02 38 36 26 22, fax 02 38 36 39 35, 11 rue Faubourg St-Germain)* has doubles from 240FF and a courtyard restaurant that dishes up memorable cuisine.

La Ferme des Châtaigniers (☎ 02 38 36 51 98, chemin des Châtaigniers), 2.5km west of Sully-sur-Loire off the D951, is run by a young couple who enthusiastically welcome guests to their old chestnut farm. *Menus* cost 120FF and 160FF and advance bookings are essential.

GIEN TO SANCERRE

Corn fields and asparagus crops line the southern banks of the River Loire between Sully-sur-Loire and the picture-postcard town of **Gien** (population 16,477), known for its distinctive *blue de Gien* earthenware, which is 23km east. Bridal paths, ideal for **cycling**, skirt the riverbanks here.

From Gien, the **GR3** shadows the river on its course to Briare, 15km east. Privately owned 17th-century **Château de la Bussière** (☎ 02 38 35 93 35), which showcases fishing memorabilia and a 13th-century vegetable garden, and **Château de St-Brisson** (☎ 02 38 36 71 29) known for its display of medieval stone-fed war machines, can be visited on route.

The industrial town of **Briare**, 15km east of Gien, is of little interest beyond its magnificent Art Nouveau canal bridge that spans the River Loire. Built from iron in 1604–42, the 662m-long canal bridge is Europe's longest and can traversed afloat. Cruises (39FF, 1½ hours) depart, April to November, from Port de Commerce (☎ 02 38 37 12 75) in Briare.

The vineyards around **Sancerre** produce the region's best known white wine. The tourist office (☎ 02 48 54 08 21, fax 02 48 78 03 58, @ ot.sancerre.cher@en-france .com), on Nouvelle place in the village, has a list of places where you can taste and buy the local vintage.

THE LOIRE

Places to Stay & Eat

The lower Loire Valley offers two remarkable places to stay and eat. *Château d'Ivoy* (☎ 02 48 58 85 01, 𝕰 *chateau.diovoy@wanadoo.fr*), 30km west of Sancerre in Ivoy-le-Pré, is a 16th-century chateau with dreamy doubles costing 700FF to 1000FF, including breakfast.

The Scottish Stuart clan had its summer house 8km north in La Verrerie. *Château de la Verrerie* (☎ 02 48 81 51 60, fax 02 48 58 21 25, 𝕰 *laverrerie@wanadoo.fr*) has 12 doubles from 950FF each. A 1.6km hiking trail encircles its lake.

Blésois

Blésois is graced with a rash of fine chateaux, including spectacular and stunning Chambord, magnificently furnished Cheverny, romantic Chaumont, and modest Beauregard. Blois tourist office has information on *son-et-lumières* (sound-and-light shows) hosted by these and other chateaux. Information on chateaux tours is listed under Organised Tours in the Blois section. Additional transport details are included under Getting There & Away at the end of each chateau listing. All times quoted are approximate and should be verified before you make plans.

BLOIS

postcode 41000 • pop 49,300 • elevation 73m

Medieval Blois (pronounced 'blwah') was once the seat of the powerful counts of Blois, from whom France's Capetian kings were descended. From the 15th to the 17th century, Blois was a hub of court intrigue, and during the 16th century it served as a second capital of France. Several dramatic events – involving some of the most important personages in French history such as the kings Louis XII, François I and Henri III – took place inside the city's outstanding attraction, Château de Blois.

The old city, seriously damaged by German attacks in 1940, retains its steep, twisting medieval streets.

Orientation

Blois, on the northern bank of the River Loire, is a compact town – almost everything is within 10 minutes' walk of the train station. The old city is the area south and east of Château de Blois, which towers over place Victor Hugo. Blois' modern commercial centre is focused around pedestrianised rue du Commerce, rue Porte Chartraine and rue Denis Papin, which is connected to rue du Palais by a monumental staircase built in the 19th century.

Information

Tourist Offices The tourist office (☎ 02 54 90 41 41, fax 02 54 90 41 49, 𝕰 blois.tourism@wanadoo.fr), 3 ave Dr Jean Laigret, opens 9 am (10 am on Sunday) to 7 pm, May to September; and 9 am to 12.30 pm and 2 to 6 pm Monday to Saturday, and 9.30 am to 12.30 pm on Sunday, the rest of the year.

Money Banque de France, 4 ave Dr Jean Laigret, opens 9 am to 12.15 pm and 1.45 to 3.30 pm weekdays. Several commercial banks face the river along quai de la Saussaye near place de la Résistance.

Post & Communications The post office on rue Gallois opens 8.30 am to 7 pm on weekdays and 8 am to noon on Saturday. It has Cyberposte. L'Étoile Tex (☎ 02 54 78 46 93, 𝕰 etoiletex.cybercafe@caramail.com), in the hotel of the same name at 7 rue du Bourg Neuf, is a busy bar with one computer. Internet access costs 1FF per minute.

Laundry The laundrette at 1 rue Jeanne d'Arc opens 7 am to 9 pm.

Medical Services The hospital (Centre Hospitalier de Blois; ☎ 02 54 55 66 33) is 2km north-east of the town centre on mail Pierre Charlot. Take bus No 1 from the train station or bus No 4 from place de la République.

Château de Blois

The Château de Blois (☎ 02 54 74 16 06) has a compelling and bloody history.

THE LOIRE

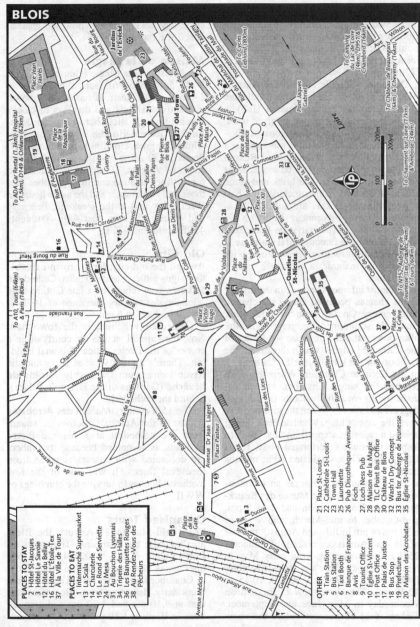

BLOIS

PLACES TO STAY
2 Hôtel St-Jacques
3 Hôtel Le Savoie
12 Hôtel du Bellay
16 Hôtel L'Étoile Tex
17 À la Ville de Tours

PLACES TO EAT
13 La Scala
14 Charcuterie
15 Le Rond de Serviette
24 La Mesa
31 Au Bouchon Lyonnais
34 Triperie des Halles
36 Les Banquettes Rouges
38 Au Rendez-Vous des Pêcheurs

OTHER
1 Intermarché Supermarket
4 Train Station
5 Bus Station
6 Taxi Booth
7 Banque de France
8 Avis
9 Tourist Office
10 Église St-Vincent
11 Post Office
18 Bus Stop
19 Prefecture
20 Maison des Acrobates
21 Place St-Louis
22 Cathédrale St-Louis
23 Town Hall
26 Pub Discothèque Avenue
27 Loch Ness Pub
28 Maison de la Magie
29 TLC Point Bus Office
30 Château de Blois
32 Wash'n Dry Concept
33 Bus for Auberge de Jeunesse
35 Église St-Nicolas

THE LOIRE

Architecturally, it has four distinct sections: medieval (13th century); Flamboyant Gothic (1498–1503), from the reign of Louis XII; early Renaissance (1515–24), from the reign of François I; and Classical (17th century).

During the Middle Ages, the counts of Blois meted out justice in the huge **Salle des États Généraux** (Estates General Hall), a part of the feudal castle that survived wars, rebuilding and – most dangerous of all – changes in style and taste. It was used as a film set by French film director Luc Besson for the trial scene in his box office hit *Jeanne d'Arc* (1999). The brick-and-stone **Louis XII section**, which includes the hall where entrance tickets are sold, is ornamented with porcupines, Louis XII's heraldic symbol. The Italianate **François I wing** includes the famous **spiral staircase**, a magnificent structure decorated with François I's insignia, a capital 'F' and a salamander.

The most infamous episode in the history of the chateau occurred during the chaotic 16th century. On 23 December 1588, King Henri III summoned his great rival, the ultra-powerful duke of Guise – a leader of the Catholic League (which threatened the authority of the king, himself a Catholic) – to his Counsel Chamber. When the duke reached the king's Chamber, he was set upon by 20 royal bodyguards armed with daggers and swords. When the violence was over, the joyous king, who had been hiding behind a tapestry, stepped into the room to inspect the duke's perforated body. Henri III was himself assassinated eight months later.

The chateau today houses an **archaeological museum** and the **Musée des Beaux-Arts**, open 9 am to noon and 2 to 5 pm, mid-October to mid-March; and 9 am to 6.30 pm (8 pm in July and August), the rest of the year. Admission costs 35FF (students 25FF). Every evening from early May to mid-September there's a *son-et-lumière* (☎ 02 54 78 72 76) at 9.30, 10, 10.15 or 10.30 pm. There's a show in English on Wednesday in May, June and September. Tickets, sold 30 minutes before the show

starts, cost 60FF (students 30FF). Combined same-day tickets for the show and chateau cost 75FF (students 55FF).

Maison de la Magie

The Maison de la Magie (House of Magic; ☎ 02 54 55 26 26) faces the chateau at 1 place du Château. It has magic shows, interactive exhibits and displays of clocks invented by the Blois-born magician Jean-Eugène Robert-Houdin (1805–71), after whom the great Houdini named himself. It opens 10.30 am to noon and 2 to 6.30 pm, July and August; 10 am to noon and 2 to 6 pm, April to June and in September, October and November; and the same hours on Wednesday and at the weekend, February and March. Tickets cost 48FF (students 42FF, children 34FF).

Old City

Around the old city, large brown explanatory signs indicate tourist sights. **Cathédrale St-Louis** was rebuilt in a late Gothic style after the devastating hurricane of 1678. It opens 7.30 am to 6 pm.

Immediately behind is the **town hall**. Note the **sundial**, across the courtyard in a corner of the Ecclesiastical Tribunal building. There's a great view of Blois and the River Loire from the lovely **Jardins de l'Évêché** (Gardens of the Bishop's Palace), behind the cathedral.

The 15th-century **Maison des Acrobates** (House of the Acrobats), across the square from the cathedral at 3 bis rue Pierre de Blois, is so-named because its timbers are decorated with characters taken from medieval farces. It was one of the few medieval houses to survive the bombings of WWII.

Organised Tours

From mid-May to 31 August, the Blois area's public bus company, Transports du Loir-et-Cher (TLC; ☎ 02 54 58 55 55) operates a chateau excursion from Blois to Chambord and Cheverny. There are two tours daily, departing from Blois train station at 9.10 am and 1.20 pm and arriving back in Blois at 1.10 pm and 6 pm respectively. Buses pick up passengers at TLC's Point Bus information office (☎ 02 54 78 15 66), at 2 place Victor Hugo, in Blois. The tours cost 65FF (students and children 50FF); admission fees to the two chateaux are not included but tour participants are eligible for reduced tariffs. Tickets are sold on the bus and, in advance, from the tourist office.

Places to Stay

Camping Two-star *Camping du Lac de Loire* (☎ 02 54 78 82 05), open April to mid-October, is in Vineuil, about 4km south of Blois. Two people with a tent are charged 49FF. There is no bus service from town except in July and August (phone the camp site or the tourist office for details).

Hostels The *Auberge de Jeunesse* (☎/fax 02 54 78 27 21, 18 rue de l'Hôtel Pasquier) in Les Grouëts, is 4.5km south-west of Blois train station. It opens March to mid-November, but call before arriving as it's often full. Beds in two large, single-sex dorms cost 68FF (not including breakfast). Rooms are locked from 10 am to 6 pm, but it's often possible to drop off your bags during the day.

To get to the hostel, take local TUB bus No 4 (runs until 7 pm) from place de la République (linked to the train station by TUB bus Nos 1, 2, 3 and 6) or – if you prefer to avoid a long detour – from 13 quai de la Saussaye, along the river.

Hotels One-star *Hôtel St-Jacques* (☎ 02 54 78 04 15, fax 02 54 78 33 05, 7 rue Ducoux) has singles/doubles with washbasin and bidet for 130/140FF (170/190FF with shower and toilet). Rates are lower out of season and it has bicycles to rent for 80FF per day. Opposite, family-run *Hôtel Le Savoie* (☎ 02 54 74 32 21, fax 02 54 74 29 58, 6 rue Ducoux) has well-kept singles/doubles with shower, toilet and TV costing from 180/200FF.

À la Ville de Tours (☎ 02 54 78 07 86, fax 02 54 56 87 33, 2 place de la Grève) has singles/doubles/triples/quads costing 150/180/250/300FF.

Twelve-room *Hôtel du Bellay* (☎ 02 54 78 23 62, fax 02 54 78 52 04, 12 rue des Minimes) touts doubles costing 135FF to 160FF (185FF with bath or shower). Triples/quads with private shower and toilet cost 240/280FF.

Hôtel L'Étoile Tex (☎ 02 54 78 46 93, ✆ etoiletex.cybercafe@caramail.com, 7 rue du Bourg Neuf) has nine rooms, some with private bathroom, costing from 150FF to 180FF. Reception is in the ground-floor bar.

Places to Eat

Restaurants Popular restaurants line rue Foulerie and several cafe-brasseries dot place de la Résistance. Cosy *Les Banquettes Rouges* (☎ 02 54 78 74 92, 16 rue des Trois Marchands) serves traditional French cuisine and has 89FF, 119FF and 159FF *menus*.

Splurging crowds make for *Au Bouchon Lyonnais* (☎ 02 54 74 12 87, 25 rue des Violettes). Main dishes of traditional French and Lyon-style cuisine cost from 78FF to 128FF; *menus* are 118FF and 165FF.

Au Rendez-Vous des Pêcheurs (☎ 02 54 74 67 48, 27 rue du Foix) specialises in fish (96FF to 140FF) from the River Loire and the sea. The handwritten menu adds a homely touch to this cottage style restaurant, refreshingly off the beaten tourist track.

Pasta and pizzas are dished up at *La Scala* (☎ 02 54 74 88 19, 8 rue des Minimes). Its summer terrace beneath trees gets full fast. *Le Rond de Serviette* (☎ 02 54 74 48 04, 18 rue Beauvoir) markets itself as Blois' cheapest and most humorous restaurant; its 49FF *menu* is certainly unbeatable.

La Mesa (☎ 02 54 78 70 70, 11 rue Vauvert) is a busy Franco-Italian joint, up an alleyway from 44 rue Foulerie. Its lovely courtyard is perfect for dining alfresco.

Self-Catering The *Intermarché* supermarket on ave Gambetta opens 9 am to 12.30 pm and 3 to 7.15 pm Monday to Saturday. In the old city, a *food market* fills rue Anne de Bretagne on Tuesday, Thursday and Saturday until 1 pm. The *charcuterie* (57 rue du Bourg Neuf) has a fine selection

THE LOIRE

of prepared dishes. For tasty tripe, try the *Triperie des Halles* (*5 rue Anne de Bretagne*).

Entertainment
Pub Discothèque Avenue Foch (☎ 02 54 90 00 00, 3 rue du Puits Châtel) opens from 10 pm. Several pubs overlook place Ave Maria. The *Loch Ness Pub*, at the intersection of rue des Juifs and rue Pierre de Bois, is another watering hole.

Getting There & Away
For information on transport to/from Blésois chateaux, see the Organised Tours section. Further details appear under each chateau listing.

Bus The TLC bus network is set up to transport school kids into Blois in the morning and to get them home in the afternoon. As a result, afternoon services to Blois are limited (reduced service during the holidays and on Sunday).

TLC buses to destinations around Blois leave from place Victor Hugo and the bus station – a patch of car park with schedules posted – next to the train station. To Chambord (No 2, 18.50FF, 45 minutes), there are three buses on weekdays, two on Saturday and one on Sunday during the school year. In July and August, your only option is TLC's tourist bus (see the Organised Tours section). Check schedules to avoid getting stranded.

Train The train station is at the western end of ave Dr Jean Laigret. The information office opens 9 am to 6.30 pm Monday to Saturday (closed holidays).

There are frequent trains to/from Tours (51FF, 40 minutes, 11 to 17 daily) and its TGV station, St-Pierre des Corps (49FF, 25 to 35 minutes, hourly). About three-quarters of trains on the Blois–Tours line stop at Amboise (34FF, 20 minutes).

There are four direct trains daily from Blois to Paris' Gare d'Austerlitz (123FF, 1½ to two hours), plus several more if you change trains in Orléans. Switch trains at Tours or St-Pierre des Corps to get to

Nantes (159FF, two hours) and Bordeaux (241FF, 3¼ to four hours, about 10 daily).

Car ADA (☎ 02 54 74 02 47) is 3km northeast of the train station at 108 ave du Maréchal Maunoury (D149). Take bus No 1 from the train station or bus No 4 from place de la République to the Cornillettes stop. Avis (☎ 02 54 74 48 15) has its office at 6 rue Jean Moulin.

Getting Around
Bicycle Hire two wheels from Cycles Leblond (☎ 02 54 74 30 13), 44 levée des Tuileries, which charges from 30/180FF per day/week and opens 9 am to 9 pm. To get there, walk eastwards along promenade du Mail for approximately 800m; levée des Tuileries is the continuation of promenade du Mail.

Château de Chambord
The pinprick village of Chambord is dominated by the spectacular Château de Chambord which François I had built from 1519 as a base for hunting game in the Sologne forests. Ironically the king, who chose the site for its easy two-day ride by horse and carriage from Paris, stayed here only 42 days during his 32-year reign (1515–47).

The Renaissance chateau has a feudal ground plan. The king's emblems – the royal monogram (a letter 'F') and salamanders of a particularly fierce disposition – adorn many parts of the building. Though forced by liquidity problems to leave his two sons unransomed in Spain and to help himself to both the wealth of his churches and his subjects' silver, François I kept 1800 workers and artisans busy for 15 years.

The chateau's famed **double-helix staircase**, attributed by some to Leonardo da Vinci who lived in Amboise (34km southwest of here) at the invitation of François I from 1516 until his death three years later, consists of two spiral staircases that wind around a central axis but never meet. The ornamentation is early French Renaissance.

The double-helix staircase leads up to the Italianate **rooftop terrace**. Standing here, surrounded by towers, cupolas, domes, chimneys, mosaic slate roofs and lightning rods, is rather like standing on an over-crowded chessboard. It was on the terrace that the royal court assembled to watch military exercises, tournaments and the hounds and hunters returning from a day of stalking deer.

Tickets to the chateau (☎ 02 54 50 50 02) are sold 9.30 am to 4.45 pm, July and August; 9.30 am to 5.45 pm, April, May, June and September; and 9.30 am to 4.45 pm, October to March. Visitors already in the chateau can stay for 45 minutes after ticket sales end. Admission costs 40FF (students aged 12 to 25, 25FF). There are explanatory signs in English. Free guided tours (1½ hours) are available, or you can rent an audio-guide (20FF).

Domaine National de Chambord The chateau is in the middle of the Domaine National de Chambord, a 54-sq-km hunting preserve reserved solely for the use of the president of France (a right that Jacques Chirac has chosen not to exercise) and larger than the whole of central Paris. A 32km-long stone wall built in 1542–1645 surrounds the estate. **Walking and moun-tain bike trails** criss cross 12 sq km on its western side and there's **aires de vision** (observation towers) where you can spot animals.

During the rutting season between mid-September and early October, the estate (☎ 02 54 50 50 00) organises forest expeditions (150FF), every evening except Friday, and week-long animal-photography courses (1000FF). It also runs 4WD forest tours (80FF), April to September.

Entertainment The chateau is lit up with a variety of images and scenes, with music playing in the background, every night from mid-July to mid-October. Visitors are then free to wander around at their own leisure. Tickets costing 80FF (students 50FF) are sold from 10.30 pm until midnight in July, from 10 to 11.30 pm in August, and from 8.30 to 9.30 or 10 pm between September and mid-October. A combination ticket

covering show and chateau admission costs 100F (a saving of 20FF).

Getting There & Away Chambord is 16km east of Blois and 20km north-east of Cheverny. To/from Blois there are TLC buses during the school year (see Getting There & Away in the earlier Blois section) and coach tours to Chambord and Cheverny between mid-May and 31 August (see Organised Tours in the Blois section).

In Chambord, TLC public buses use the stop on the westbound D33.

Getting Around Bicycles, perfect for exploring Forêt de Chambord and around, can be rented in Chambord from the Echapée Belle kiosk next to Pont St-Michel in the castle grounds. It costs 25/70/120FF per hour/day/weekend. The estate authorities (see the Domaine National de Chambord section above) organise cycling trips (120/160FF with/without your own bicycle).

Château de Cheverny

Château de Cheverny, the region's most magnificently furnished chateau, was built in 1625–34. Sitting like a sparkling white ship amid a sea of beautifully manicured gardens, the chateau is graced with a finely proportioned neoclassical facade. Inside, visitors are treated to room after sumptuous room fitted out with the finest of period appointments. The most richly furnished rooms are the **Chambre du Roi** (in which no king ever slept because no king ever stayed at Cheverny) and the **Grand Salon**. In the 1st-floor dining room, three-dozen panels illustrate the story of *Don Quixote*.

The grounds shelter the 18th-century **Orangerie** where Leonardo da Vinci's *Mona Lisa* was hidden during WWII. Near the lake, there's a **balloon pad** (☎ 02 54 79 25 05) where a helium-filled balloon takes off, mid-March to mid-October. The 10- to 12-minute ascent costs 47FF (students 43FF, children 30FF).

Château de Cheverny (☎ 02 54 79 96 29, @ chateau.cheverny@wanadoo.fr) opens 9.15 or 9.30 am to 6.15 pm April to September (to 6.30 pm July and August), and

THE LOIRE

La Soupe des Chiens

As was the custom among the nobility of centuries past, the viscount de Sigalas – whose family has owned Cheverny since it was built – hunts with hounds. His 90 dogs, most a cross between English fox terriers and French Poitevins (the white ones are pure English hounds), are quite beautiful, no matter what you think of the practice of using them to kill stags.

Each dog has a name, posing a fantastic memory feat for the two dog trainers who do, indeed, know every dog and its name. The *soupe des chiens* (feeding of the dogs) is an awe-inspiring demonstration of the exact control they exercise over the pack.

A massive 90kg of animal parts (a sight not recommended for the faint-hearted) is brought by wheelbarrow into the cement enclosure each day and methodically arranged in a 2m-wide mountain. Not until the dog master gives the word (or crack of the whip) does the pack of hungry, barking dogs dare do so much as sniff at their daily 1kg ration. The stinking offal is ripped to shreds and gobbled up in minutes. Double portions are doled out after the twice-weekly winter hunt.

The soupe des chiens takes place in the kennels *(chenils)* at 5 pm daily in summer. In January, February and between mid-September and December, the dogs are fed at 3 pm on Monday, Wednesday, Thursday and Friday only. The pack hunts every Tuesday and Saturday between September and March, departing from the majestic front entrance of the chateau if hunting in the Fôret de Cheverny.

9.15 or 9.30 am to noon and 2.15 to 5.30 pm the rest of the year (to 5 pm November to February). Admission costs 35FF (students 24FF, children 17FF). A combination ticket covering the chateau and balloon flight costs 84FF.

Getting There & Away Cheverny is 16km south-east of Blois and 20km south-west of Chambord. The TLC bus from Blois to Villefranche-sur-Cher stops at Cheverny (14.60FF). Buses leave Blois at 6.50 am and 12.25 pm Monday to Saturday. Returning to Blois, the last bus leaves Cheverny at 6.58 pm. Departure times vary on Sundays and holidays; check with TLC (☎ 02 54 58 55 55). Between mid-May and 31 August, TLC operates coach tours from Blois (see the Organised Tours section under Blois, earlier in this chapter).

Château de Chaumont

Château de Chaumont, set on a bluff overlooking the Loire, resembles a feudal castle. Its most famous feature is its luxurious **stables**, from where horse-drawn carriages take visitors on a short tour of the chateau's cedar-rich grounds (30FF, 20 minutes) in summer.

In 1560, Catherine de Médicis (France's powerful queen mother) took revenge on Diane de Poitiers, the mistress of her late husband, Henry II, by forcing her to accept Chaumont in exchange for her much more favoured residence, Château de Chenonceau (see Tours Area Chateaux in the later Touraine section). During the years after America won independence, Benjamin Franklin, at the time US ambassador to France, was a frequent guest at Chaumont.

Tickets to this state-owned chateau (☎ 02 54 51 26 26) are sold from 9.30 am to 6 pm, mid-March to September; and 10 am to 4.30 pm, the rest of the year; the chateau itself closes 30 minutes later. Admission costs 33FF (children 21FF). From mid-June to mid-October, its grounds host a **Festival International des Jardins** (International Garden Festival; ☎ 02 54 20 99 22).

Getting There & Away Chaumont-sur-Loire is 17km south-west of Blois and 20km north-east of Amboise, on the Loire's southern bank. The path leading to the park and chateau starts at the intersection of rue du Village Neuf and rue Maréchal Leclerc (D751).

THE LOIRE

By public transport, the only way to get to Chaumont-sur-Loire is via a local train on the Orléans–Tours line. Get off at Onzain (10 minutes, eight or more daily), from where it is a 2km walk across the river to the chateau. Single rail fares are 36/41/62FF to Onzain from Blois/Tours/Orléans.

By bicycle, the quiet back roads on the southern bank of the river are a tranquil option. The Chaumont-sur-Loire tourist office (☎ 02 54 20 91 73, fax 02 54 20 90 34), rue du Maréchal Leclerc, rents bicycles for 60FF per day.

Château de Beauregard

Built in the early 16th century to serve as a hunting lodge for François I, the most famous feature of Château de Beauregard is its **Galerie des Portraits**, the walls of which are plastered with 327 portraits of notable faces from the 14th to 17th centuries.

Beauregard (☎ 02 54 70 36 74) opens 9.30 am to noon and 2 to 5 or 6.30 pm,

April to September (no break in July and August); and the same hours Thursday to Tuesday in February, March and October to January. Admission costs 40FF (students and children 30FF).

Getting There & Away Beauregard is 6km south of Blois or can be reached via a pleasant 15km cycle ride through the forest from Chambord. There is road access to the chateau from the Blois–Cheverny D765 and the D956 (turn left at the village of Cellettes).

The TLC bus from Blois to St-Aignan stops at Cellettes (8.80FF), 1km south-west of the chateau, on Wednesday, Friday and Saturday; the first bus from Blois to Cellettes leaves at 12.25 pm. Unfortunately, there's no afternoon bus back except for the Châteauroux–Blois line operated by Transports Boutet (☎ 02 54 34 43 95), which passes through Cellettes around 6.15 pm Monday to Saturday, and – except during August – at about 6 pm on Sunday.

Ladies of the Loire

Countless ladies of the Loire – whether peasant, mistress, seductress or queen – made an indelible mark on history.

Without the beautiful and wealthy Eleanor of Aquitaine, the Hundred Years' War between England and France would never have happened. Initially married to King Louis VII of France, in 1152 she married Henry of Anjou who became Henry II of England, bringing to the throne her dowry – one-third of France.

In 1429, Joan of Arc rode into Chinon to roust the young Dauphin Charles VII into regaining his throne. Agnès Sorel was to become his favourite mistress and he set her up at Château de Loches. The first officially recognised royal mistress, she was a provocative woman, posing bare-breasted for Jean Fouquet's famous portrait of her as the Virgin Mary. She died pregnant, allegedly poisoned, in 1450.

Henri II's mistress, Diane de Poitiers, was given Chaumont on his death in 1559, while his wife, Queen Catherine de Médicis, took Chenonceau. Catherine's secret weapon to further her ambitions was a group of beautiful, scantily clad women called the *Escadron Volant* (Flying Squad), who enlivened festivities at the chateau by leaping out from behind bushes and seducing Catherine's opponents.

JANE SMITH

Loire luminary, Joan of Arc

THE LOIRE

Touraine

With the exception of the medieval fortresses at Chinon and Loches, the castles of Touraine date to the Renaissance: Azay-le-Rideau, Chenonceau, Langeais and Villandry were designed purely to pamper the soul and pander to the physical pleasures of the queen, king and his multitude of royal mistresses.

Tours, the historical capital of Touraine, is a cheap base from which to explore the region's castles and wine cellars that linger in ancient tufa cliffs north-east of the city. Southern Touraine is drained by River Vienne and has been protected by the Parc Naturel Régional Loire-Anjou-Touraine since 1996.

TOURS

postcode 37000 • pop 270,000 • elevation 108m

Lively Tours has the cosmopolitan and bourgeois air of a miniature Paris, with wide 18th-century avenues, formal public gardens, cafe-lined boulevards and a thriving university home to 30,000 students. The French spoken in Tours is said to be the purest in France.

Twice in its history Tours briefly hosted the French government – in 1870 during the Franco-Prussian war and again in 1940, with the onset on WWII. Since then, it has become better known for its crisp white Vouvray and Montlouis wines.

Orientation

Thanks to the spirit of the 18th century, Tours is efficiently laid out. Its focal point is place Jean Jaurès, where the city's major thoroughfares – rue Nationale, blvd Heurteloup, ave de Grammont and blvd Béranger – meet. The train station is 300m east of place Jean Jaurès.

The old city is centred on place Plumereau, which is about 400m west of rue Nationale. The northern boundary of the city is demarcated by the River Loire, which flows roughly parallel to the River Cher, 3km south.

Information

Tourist Offices The tourist office (☎ 02 47 70 37 37, fax 02 47 61 14 22, ℮ info@ligeris.com), 78–82 rue Bernard Palissy, opens 8.30 am to 7 pm Monday to Saturday and 10 am to 12.30 pm and 2.30 to 5 pm on Sunday, May to October; and 9 am to 12.30 pm and 1.30 to 6 pm Monday to Saturday, and 10 am to 1 pm on Sunday, the rest of the year.

Money Banque de France, 2 rue Chanoineau, has an exchange service open from 8.45 am to noon on weekdays. Commercial banks overlook place Jean Jaurès.

Post & Communications Tours' post office, 1 blvd Béranger, opens 8 am to 7 pm on weekdays and 8 am to noon on Saturday. It has Cyberposte.

Alli@nce Micro (☎ 02 47 05 49 50, ℮ alliance-micro@wanadoo.fr), 7ter rue de la Monnaie, charges 25FF/hour and opens 9 am to 8 pm Monday to Saturday, and 2 to 8 pm on Sunday.

Le Cyberspace (☎ 02 47 66 29 96, ℮ cyberspace@creaweb.fr), at 13 rue Lavoisier, is an Internet pub charging 1/20/30FF per minute/30 minutes/hour. It opens 2 pm to 5 am.

Bookshops La Boîte à Livres de l'Étranger (☎ 02 47 05 67 29), 2 rue du Commerce, stocks English-language fiction and nonfiction. Maps and guides are sold at Géothèque, (☎ 02 47 05 23 56), a travel bookshop at 6 rue Michelet.

Laundry The laundrette at 22 rue Bernard Palissy opens 7 am to 8.30 pm.

Emergency The police station (☎ 02 47 60 70 69) at 70–72 rue Marceau opens 24 hours.

Musée des Beaux-Arts

The Musée des Beaux-Arts (☎ 02 47 05 68 73), housed in a 17th- to 18th-century archbishops' palace at 18 place François Sicard, has an excellent collection of paintings, furniture and *objets d'art* from the 14th to the

THE LOIRE

TOURS

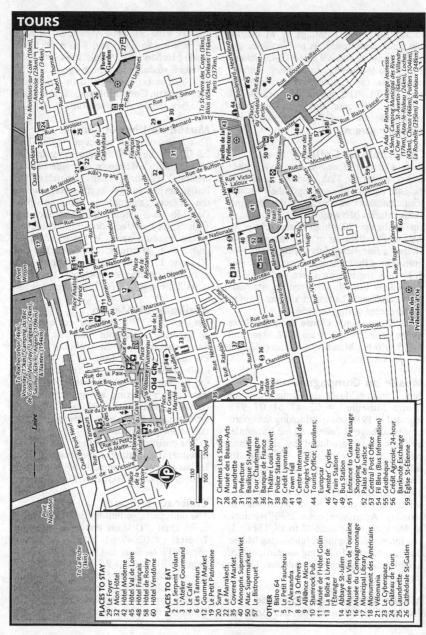

PLACES TO STAY
29 Le Foyer
32 Mon Hôtel
42 Hôtel Moderne
45 Hôtel Val de Loire
48 Hôtel Français
58 Hôtel de Rosiny
60 Hôtel Vendôme

PLACES TO EAT
2 Le Serpent Volant
3 L'Atelier Gourmand
4 Le Café
6 Les Tanneurs
12 Gourmet Market
19 Le Petit Patrimoine
20 Surya
22 Le Marrakech
35 Covered Market
40 Monoprix Supermarket
50 Atac Supermarket
57 Le Bistroquet

OTHER
1 Bistro 64
5 Le Petit Faucheux
7 L'Alexandra
8 Les 3 Orfèvres
9 Alliånce Micro
10 Shamrock Pub
11 Musée de l'Hôtel Goüin
13 La Boîte à Livres de
   l'Etranger
14 Abbaye St-Julien
15 Musée des Vins de Touraine
16 Musée du Compagnonnage
17 Municipal Library
18 Monument des Américains
21 Velomania
23 Le Cyberspace
24 Château de Tours
25 Laundrette
26 Cathédrale St-Gatien
27 Cinémas Les Studio
28 Musée des Beaux-Arts
30 Laundrette
31 Prefecture
33 Basilique St-Martin
34 Tour Charlemagne
36 Banque de France
37 Théâtre Louis Jouvet
38 Police Station
39 Crédit Lyonnais
41 Town Hall
43 Centre International de
   Congrès Vinci
44 Tourist Office; Eurolines;
   Europcar
46 Amster' Cycles
47 Train Station
49 Bus Station
51 Entrance to Grand Passage
   Shopping Centre
52 Palais de Justice
53 Central Post Office
54 Fil Bleu (Bus Information)
55 Géothèque
56 Crédit Agricole; 24-hour
   Banknote Exchange
59 Église St-Etienne

euro currency converter €1 = 6.56FF

20th centuries. It is especially proud of two 15th-century altar paintings by Mantegna that were taken from Italy by Napoleon.

The museum opens 9 am to 12.45 pm and 2 to 6 pm Wednesday to Monday. Admissions costs 30FF (seniors, students and children 15FF). The magnificent **cedar of Lebanon** in the courtyard was planted during Napoleon's reign. Behind it is a charming **flower garden**.

Cathédrale St-Gatien

Various parts of Tours' Gothic-style cathedral represent the 13th century (the choir), the 14th century (the transept), the 14th and 15th centuries (the nave) and the 15th and 16th centuries (the west facade). The domed tops of the two 70m-high **towers** (closed to the public) date from the Renaissance. There's a fine view of the **flying buttresses** from behind the cathedral. Spectacular exterior aside, the interior is renowned for its marvellous 13th- to 15th-century **stained-glass windows**. The cathedral opens 9 am to 7 pm (except during services).

The Renaissance **Cloître de la Psallette** can be visited from 8.30 am to 12.30 pm and 2 to 5 or 6 pm Monday to Saturday, 2 to 5 or 6 pm on Sunday.

Musée du Compagnonnage

Tours' unique Musée du Compagnonnage (Guild Museum; ☎ 02 47 61 07 93), founded in 1910 and overlooking the courtyard of **Abbaye St-Julien** at 8 rue Nationale, displays crafts produced by the French chapter of the freemasons – skilful crafts still practised today, from stone sculpting to horseshoeing. The museum opens 9 am to noon (12.30 pm from mid-June to mid-September) and 2 to 6 pm Wednesday to Monday. Admission costs 25FF (seniors, students and those aged 12 to 18, 15FF). If you intend visiting the neighbouring Musée des Vins (see the following section), opt for a 30FF ticket that covers admission to both the museums.

Musée des Vins de Touraine

The Musée des Vins de Touraine (Touraine Wine Museum; ☎ 02 47 61 07 93), 16 rue Nationale, occupies the vaulted, 13th-century wine cellars of Abbaye St-Julien. It opens 9 am to noon and 2 to 6 pm Wednesday to Monday. Admission costs 16FF (seniors, students and those aged 12 to 18, 10FF). A ticket (30FF) allowing access to the Musée du Compagnonnage is also available (see the previous section).

Musée de l'Hôtel Goüin

This archaeological museum (☎ 02 47 66 22 32), 25 rue du Commerce, is housed in Hôtel Goüin, a Renaissance residence built around 1510 for a wealthy merchant. Its Italian-style facade is worth seeing, even if the eclectic assemblage of prehistoric, Gallo-Roman, medieval, Renaissance and 18th-century artefacts doesn't interest you.

The museum opens 10 am to 12.30 pm and 2 to 6.30 pm, July and August; and 10 am to 12.30 pm and to 6.30 pm, March to June, September and October. Admission costs 21FF (seniors 16FF, children 12FF).

Basilique St-Martin

Fans of late 19th-century ecclesiastical architecture should not miss this extravagant, pseudo-Byzantine church on rue Descartes, built in 1886–1924. The crypt shelters the tomb of St-Martin, a soldier in the Roman army who converted to Christianity after meeting a beggar in Amiens (Picardy) who inspired him to slash his cloak coat in half with his sword and give half to the poor man.

The basilica usually opens 8 am to 7 pm; in winter it sometimes closes noon to 2 pm. In November, a fragment of St-Martin's skull is displayed above the high altar.

Château de Tours

The unimpressive buildings of this chateau at 25 Quai d'Orléans house an **Aquarium Tropical** (☎ 02 47 64 29 52). Admission costs 33FF (seniors and students 30FF, children 18FF). It opens 9.30 am to noon and 2 to 6 pm Monday to Saturday (9.30 am to 7 pm in July and August); and 2 to 6 pm on Sunday, April to mid-November, and 1 to 6 pm, the rest of the year.

The **Historial de Touraine** (☎ 02 47 61 02

95), a wax museum in the same building, requires a separate 35FF ticket (students 24FF, children 20FF). The 3rd floor of the chateau houses changing art exhibitions (free admission).

Organised Tours
For details on chateaux tours, see the Organised Tours at the start of the Tours Area Chateaux section.

Places to Stay
Camping Five kilometres south of Tours, *Camping Municipal des Rives du Cher* (☎ 02 47 27 27 60, 63 rue de Rochpinard, St-Avertin), opens April to mid-October and charges 14/14/8/8FF per tent/person/child/car. Take bus No 5 from place Jean Jaurès to the St-Avertin bus terminal, then follow the signs.

About 10km north-east of Tours in Vouvray (see the Around Tours section later in this chapter), pool-equipped *Camping du Bec de Cisse* (☎ 02 47 52 68 81) is across the N152 and 200m downhill from the tourist office. Open mid-May to September, it charges 26FF for tent and car, plus 16/9FF per adult/child.

Hostels Normally a dormitory for workers of both sexes aged 16 to 25, *Le Foyer* (☎ 02 47 60 51 51, fax 02 47 20 75 20 *@* fjt.tours @wanadoo.fr, 16 rue Bernard Palissy) accepts travellers of all ages in the summer if it has space. A single/double room costs 100/160FF and reception opens 9 am to 6 pm on weekdays, 8.30 to 11 am on Saturday.

Tours' *Auberge de Jeunesse* (☎ 02 47 25 14 45, ave d'Arsonval) is 5km south of the train station in Parc de Grandmont. A place in a four- or six-bedded room costs 48FF. Until 8.30 or 8.45 pm, you can take bus No 1 or No 6 from place Jean Jaurès; between 9.20 pm and about midnight, take Bleu de Nuit line N1 (southbound). Advance bookings are essential.

Hotels Looking almost as it did when it was a turn-of-the-century bourgeois home, *Hôtel Val de Loire* (☎ 02 47 05 37 86, 33

blvd Heurteloup) has basic singles/doubles with washbasin and bidet costing 100/150FF (130/180FF with shower, 200/250FF with bath and toilet). Hall showers cost 15FF.

Mon Hôtel (☎ 02 47 05 67 53, 40 rue de la Préfecture) provides one-star singles/doubles for 100/115FF (170/200FF with shower and toilet). Showers cost 15FF. Unremarkable *Hôtel de Rosiny* (☎ 02 47 05 23 54, fax 02 47 05 12 45, 12–19 rue Blaise Pascal) has singles/doubles from 110/160FF and it claims to offer discounted rates for stays of a week or more.

Hôtel Français (☎ 02 47 05 59 12, 11 rue de Nantes) provides a cold welcome but might be of interest to penny-pinchers: singles/doubles/triples/quads with washbasin and bidet are cheap at 120/140/150/170FF (140/160/170/180FF with shower or 155/190/220/250FF with shower and toilet). A hall shower/breakfast costs 10/28FF.

A fine choice is cheerful *Hôtel Vendôme* (☎ 02 47 64 33 54, *@* hotelvendome .tours@wanadoo.fr, 24 rue Roger Salengro), run by an exceptionally friendly couple. Simple but decent singles/doubles start at 140/170FF (150/185FF with shower and toilet).

Warm, family-run *Hôtel Moderne* (☎ 02 47 05 32 81, fax 02 47 05 71 50, 1–3 rue Victor Laloux) has doubles with high ceilings costing 188/230/255FF with basin/shower/shower and toilet.

Places to Eat
In the old city, place Plumereau and nearby rue du Grand Marché and rue de la Rôtisserie are loaded with restaurants, cafes, creperies and boulangeries – many of which have lovely street terraces. Another tasty cluster graces semi-pedestrianised rue Colbert.

Restaurants A small but sweet, cheap option is *Le Petit Patrimoine* (☎ 02 47 66 05 81, 58 rue Colbert). Tempting 50FF and 70FF lunchtime *menus* are served amid sunflooded stone walls and a wood-beamed ceiling; don't miss the cheese board crammed with *chèvres* (goat cheeses).

THE LOIRE

L'Atelier Gourmand (☎ 02 47 38 59 87, 37 rue Étienne Marcel) boasts the city's most romantic courtyard terrace. It has a 49FF plat du jour (weekday lunches only) and a 100FF *menu*.

Simple but attractive *Le Bistroquet* (☎ 02 47 05 12 76, 17 rue Blaise Pascal) specialises in paella but has French food *menus* for 44FF, 51FF and 62FF.

Le Marrakech (☎ 02 47 66 64 65, 111 rue Colbert) dishes up tasty Moroccan couscous and tajines from 65FF to 95FF a plateful. For those who like it hot hot hot, spicy *Surya* (☎ 02 47 64 34 04, 65 rue Colbert) serves North Indian dishes (lunch/dinner *menu* costing 59/85FF).

Cafes An old town highlight is *Le Serpent Volant* (54 rue du Grand Marché), a quintessential French cafe. A contemporary funky favourite is *Le Café* (39 rue du Dr Bretonneau).

Budget travellers can try sweet-talking their way into *Les Tanneurs*, the university resto-cum-cafe near the main university building on rue des Tanneurs. To dine you need a student ticket.

Sandwich stalls sell well-filled baguettes and pastries in the Grand Passage shopping centre at 18 rue de Bordeaux.

Self-Catering Tours' large *covered market* is on place Gaston Pailhou. An open-air *gourmet market* fills place de la Résistance on the first Friday of the month.

Atac (5 place du Général Leclerc) supermarket opens 8.30 am to 8 pm Monday to Saturday and 9.30 am to 12.30 pm on Sunday.

Entertainment

Nondubbed films are screened at *Cinémas Les Studio* (☎ 02 47 64 42 61, or for a recorded message, ☎ 08 36 68 20 15, 2 rue des Ursulines).

In the old city, cafe night-life is centred around place Plumereau. Les 3 Orfèvres (% 02 47 64 02 73, 6 rue des Orfèvres) has live music from Tuesday or Wednesday to Saturday starting at 11 pm. Student nightlife comes to life down tiny rue de la Longue

Echelle and the southern strip of adjoining rue Dr Bretonneau. L'Alexandra (106 rue Commerce) and Shamrock Pub (12 rue de Constantine) are mainstream pubs.

Live jazz venues include alternative cafe-theatre *Le Petit Faucheux* (☎ 02 47 38 67 62, 23 rue des Cerisiers) and brilliant *Bistro 64* (☎ 02 47 38 47 40, 64 rue du Grand Marché) which plays Latin, Blues and *musique Française* in a 16th-century interior.

Getting There & Away

Bus Eurolines' ticket office (☎ 02 47 66 45 56), 74 rue Bernard Palissy, opens 2 to 6 pm on Monday, 9 am to noon and 1.30 to 6.30 pm Tuesday to Friday; and 9 am to noon and 1.30 to 5.30 pm on Saturday (closed Sunday). See the introductory Getting There & Away chapter for route information.

Buses to destinations around Tours leave from the bus station (☎ 02 47 05 30 49) on place du Général Leclerc. The information desk (☎ 02 47 05 30 49) opens 7.30 am to noon and 2 to 6.30 pm Monday to Saturday. Tickets are sold on board.

In summer, you can make an all-day circuit by public bus from Tours to Chenonceaux and Amboise by taking CAT (Compagnies des Autocars de Touraine) bus No 10 for the hour-long ride to Chenonceaux (13FF) at around 10 am; catching the bus from Chenonceaux to Amboise (6.60FF, 35 minutes) at around noon (during July and August, there's also an afternoon bus); then returning to Tours by bus (at around 5 or 6 pm, 13FF) or by train (see the Getting There & Away section under Amboise, later in this chapter). Double-check times and schedules before departing.

Train The train station is off blvd Heurteloup, overlooking place du Général Leclerc. The information office opens 8.30 am to 6.30 pm Monday to Saturday, except on public holidays. Tours is linked to St-Pierre des Corps – Tours' TGV train station – by shuttle trains.

Local trains run between Tours and Orléans at least hourly (88FF, 1¼ hours).

Stops on this route include St-Pierre des Corps (eight minutes), Montlouis-sur-Loire (12 minutes), Amboise (28FF, 20 minutes) and Blois (51FF, 35 minutes). There are trains southbound to Loches (44FF, 45 minutes, two daily) and westbound to Saumur (56FF, 40 minutes, eight daily).

To get from Paris to Tours by rail take a TGV from Gare Montparnasse (from 211FF to 277FF, 1¼ hours, 10 to 15 daily), which often requires a change of trains at St-Pierre des Corps; or a direct non-TGV from Gare d'Austerlitz (154FF; two to three hours, five to eight daily). There are TGV and non-TGV services to Bordeaux (about 224FF, 2¾ hours by TGV), Poitiers (95FF, 50 to one hour 10 minutes, hourly) and Nantes (135FF, 1½ to two hours, four to eight daily). Change trains in Poitiers to get to/from La Rochelle (169FF, 3¼ to 4½ hours).

Car ADA (☎ 02 47 64 94 94) is south of the centre at 49 blvd Thiers, 250m west of the huge Hôtel Altéa at place Thiers (the intersection of ave de Grammont and blvd Thiers). Take bus No 3 or 6 from the train station or bus No 1, 2, 3, 5 or 9 (southbound) from place Jean Jaurès to the Thiers stop. Europcar (☎ 02 47 64 47 76) has an office at 76 blvd Bernard Palissy.

Getting Around

Bus The bus network serving Tours and its suburbs is run by Fil Bleu (☎ 02 47 66 70 70),which has an information office at 5 bis rue de la Dolve. Most lines stop around the periphery of place Jean Jaurès. Tickets, valid for one hour after being time-stamped, cost 6.50FF.

Bicycle From May to September, Amster' Cycles (☎ 02 47 61 22 23, fax 02 47 61 28 48), 5 rue du Rempart, rents road and mountain bikes for 80/125/330/450FF for 24 hours/two days/one week/two weeks. Staff provide cyclists with a puncture repair kit and map.

Vélomania (☎ 02 47 05 10 11, fax 02 47 05 79 77), 109 rue Colbert, is another rental outlet.

AROUND TOURS

Vineyards carpet **Vouvray** (population 2900) and **Montlouis-sur-Loire** (population 8000), 10km east of Tours, on the northern and southern bank respectively of the River Loire. For centuries, wine growers have stored their wines in *caves* (wine cellars), hewn out of the white tufaceous cliffs that line this stretch. Neither village is an overly attractive place, but each offers ample opportunity to taste and buy Appellation d'Origine Contrôlée (AOC) Vouvray and AOC Montlouis wines.

The Vouvray tourist office (☎ 02 47 52 68 73, fax 02 47 52 67 76), on the corner of route du Vignoble (N152) and ave Brulé (D46), has information on wine-tasting options and rents bicycles for 70/300FF per day/week. Opposite, the Maison du Vouvray (☎ 02 47 52 72 51), 24 ave Brulé, is a good place to kick off a *dégustation* (tasting) spree.

In Montlouis-sur-Loire, the tourist office (☎ 02 47 45 00 16, fax 02 47 45 10 87) on place de la Mairie, and the Maison de la Loire (☎ 02 47 50 97 52), 60 quai Albert Baillet, stock information.

A unique spot to stay in the surrounds is *Les Hautes Roches* (☎ *02 47 52 81 30, fax 02 47 52 81 30,* @ *hautes-roches@ wanadoo.fr, 86 quai de la Loire)* in the northern Tourangeau suburb of Rochecorbon. Dug by monks as a safe haven during the Wars of Religion, the caves form part of a four-star hotel today. Doubles cost from 520FF; bath tubs are of the enamel (rather than rock) variety. (See Saumur & Troglodyte Valley in the Anjou section, later in this chapter, for more troglomania).

Getting There & Away Fil Bleu's bus No 61 links Tours' place Jean Jaurès with Vouvray (20 minutes). Montlouis-sur-Loire is served by bus line C2 which is operated by Fil Vert.

TOURS AREA CHATEAUX

A number of the most interesting Loire chateaux make an easy day trip from Tours. Those accessible by train or SNCF bus from Tours include Chenonceau, Villandry,

THE LOIRE

Azay-le-Rideau, Langeais, Amboise (see the Amboise section later in this chapter), Chaumont (see Chaumont-sur-Loire in the Blésois section, earlier in this chapter), Chinon and Saumur. Transport details are listed under Getting There & Away at the end of each chateau listing.

The tourist office in Tours has details of son-et-lumières, medieval re-enactments, and other spectacles performed at the chateaux during the summer.

Organised Tours

Touring chateaux by public transport can be horribly slow and expensive, so even veteran backpackers should consider taking an organised bus tour. Far from being a regimental, sergeant-major affair, these interesting English-language tours are surprisingly relaxed and informal. Most allow you between 45 minutes and one hour at each chateau on the agenda. Prices often include entrance fees or entitle you to discounts. If you can get five to seven people together, you can design your own minibus itinerary.

See Organised Tours in the Blois section, earlier in this chapter, for information on tours departing from Blois. Reservations for the following can be made at the Tours tourist office:

St-Eloi Excursions (☎ 02 47 37 08 04, fax 02 47 39 34 67, ❺ excursions@saint-eloi.com) operates minibus trips for two to eight people, costing 100FF (children 50FF) for a half-day and from 135FF to 180FF (children 75FF to 90FF) for a full day trip.
Web site: www.saint-eloi.com

Services Touristiques de Touraine (STT; ☎/fax 02 47 05 46 09, ❺ info@stt-millet.fr) runs full-sized coaches aimed at individuals rather than groups from April to mid-October. Many tours include wine tasting in Vouvray or Montlouis-sur-Loire. Afternoon/day tours taking in three/four or five chateaux cost 190/300FF, including admission fees.
Web site: www.stt-millet.fr

Château de Chenonceau

With its stylised moat, drawbridge, towers and turrets, the 16th-century Château de Chenonceau is everything a fairy-tale castle should be, although its interior – crammed with period furniture, tourists, paintings, tourists, tapestries and tourists – is only of moderate interest.

Chenonceau's vast park, landscaped gardens and forests covering 70 hectares either side of the River Cher, afford stunning vistas of the chateau exterior. One of the series of remarkable women who created Chenonceau, Diane de Poitiers, mistress of King Henri II, planted the garden to the left (east) as you approach the chateau. After Henri's death in 1559, she was forced to give up Chenonceau by the vengeful Catherine de Médicis, Henri II's widow, who applied her own energies to the chateau and laid out the garden to the right (west) as you approach the castle.

In the 18th century, Madame Dupin, the chateau's owner at the time, brought Jean-Jacques Rousseau to Chenonceau as a tutor for her son. During the French Revolution, the affection with which the peasantry regarded Mme Dupin saved the chateau from the violent fate of its neighbours.

The 60m-long **gallery** crossing the River Cher was converted into a hospital during WWI. Between 1940 and 1942, the demarcation line between Vichy-ruled France and the German-occupied zone ran down the middle of the Cher: the castle itself was under direct German occupation, but the Galerie's southern entrance was in the area controlled by Marshal Pétain. For many trying to escape to the Vichy zone, this room served as a crossing point.

Chenonceau (☎ 02 47 23 90 07, ❺ chateau .de.chenonceau@wanadoo.fr) opens 9 am until sometime between 4.30 pm (mid-November to January) and 7 pm (mid-March to mid-September). Admission to the chateau costs 50FF (students and children 40FF).

Getting There & Away Château de Chenonceau, in the town of Chenonceaux (the village has an 'x' at the end), is 34km east of Tours, 10km south-east of Amboise and 40km south-west of Blois.

Chenonceaux SNCF train station is in

THE LOIRE

front of the chateau. Between Tours and Chenonceaux there are two or three trains daily (32FF, 30 minutes). Less appealing are trains serving the Tours–Vierzon line which stop at Chisseaux (33FF, 24 minutes, six daily), 2km east of Chenonceaux.

In summer, CAT bus No 10 leaves Tours for Chenonceaux (13FF one way, one hour) at 10 am; a bus back to Tours departs at 4.45 pm. There are no Sunday buses.

Château de Villandry

Château de Villandry has some of the most spectacular formal gardens in France. Its **Jardin d'Ornement** (Ornamental Garden) comprises intricate, geometrically pruned hedges and flowerbeds loaded with romantic symbolism so abstract that you can tour the entire garden without comprehending its true meaning (even with the aid of the free English-language brochure and map available at the entrance). Between the chateau and the village church, the **potager** (kitchen garden) is a cross between the vegetable plots in which medieval monks grew their food and the formal gardens so beloved in 16th-century France.

All told, Villandry's gardens occupy five hectares and include over 1150 lime trees, hundreds of grape trellises, and 52km of landscaped plant rows. Villandry is at its most colourful from May to mid-June and from August to October, but is worth a visit year round.

The chateau itself was completed in 1536, making it the last of the major Renaissance chateaux to be built in this area. The interior, whose sparsely furnished, 18th-century rooms and hallways are adorned with mediocre paintings, can be skipped, though the 13th-century Moorish **mosque ceiling** from Spain is of interest. The view from the tower – from which the intricate gardens can be seen in their entirety, as can the parallel Rivers Loire and Cher – is only slightly better than the magnificent one that can be had for no extra cost from the terraced hill east of the chateau.

Villandry's gardens open 9 am to dusk (last tickets sold at 7 or 7.30 pm in summer). The chateau (☎ 02 47 50 02 09) itself

– which, unlike the gardens, only opens mid-February to mid-November – can be visited from 9 or 9.30 am to 5 or 6.30 pm. Admission to the gardens costs 33FF (students and children 22FF). A combination ticket for the gardens and chateau costs 45FF (students and children 32FF).

Getting There & Away Villandry is 17km south-west of Tours, 31km north-east of Chinon and 11km north-east of Azay-le-Rideau. By road, the shortest route from Tours is the D7, but cyclists will find less traffic on the D88 (which runs along the southern bank of the Loire) and the D288 (which links the D88 with Savonnières). If heading south-westwards from Villandry towards Langeais, the best bike route is the D16, which has no verges but has light traffic.

Villandry is included on most organised tour circuits; see the Organised Tours earlier in this section for details. By public transport the only way of travelling between Tours and Villandry is by train to Savonnières (17FF, 10 minutes, two or three daily), about 4km east of Villandry. The first train from Tours is at 12.28 pm (noon on Sunday and holidays); the last train back to Tours is early at 1.39 pm (5.30 pm on Saturday).

Château d'Azay-le-Rideau

Azay-le-Rideau, built on an island in the River Indre and surrounded by a quiet pool and park, is harmonious and elegant. It is adorned with stylised fortifications and turrets intended both as decoration and to indicate the rank of the owners. Inside, seven rooms are open to the public which, beyond a few 16th-century Flemish tapestries, are disappointing. It is one of the few chateaux which freely allows visitors to picnic in the grounds.

The bloodiest incident in the chateau's history occurred in 1418. During a visit to Azay, then a fortified castle, the crown prince (later King Charles VII) was insulted by the Burgundian guard. Enraged, he had the town burned and executed some 350 soldiers and officers. The present chateau was begun exactly a century later by Giles Berthelot, one of François I's less-than-selfless financiers. When the prospect of being audited and hanged drew near, Berthelot fled abroad. The finishing touches were added in the 19th century.

The chateau (☎ 02 47 45 42 04) opens 9.30 am to 6 pm, April to June and September; 9 am to 7 pm, July and August; and 9.30 am to 12.30 pm and to 5.30 pm, October to March. Admission costs 35FF (those aged 18 to 25, 23FF).

Getting There & Away Château d'Azay-le-Rideau, 26km south-west of Tours, features on most tour itineraries from Tours (see the Organised Tours earlier in this section). The D84 and D17, either side of the River Indre, are a delight to cycle along.

Azay-le-Rideau is on SNCF's Tours–Chinon line (four or five daily Monday to Saturday and one on Sunday). From Tours, the 30-minute trip (50 minutes by SNCF bus) costs 27FF; the station is 2.5km from the chateau. The last train/bus to Tours leaves Azay at about 6.35 pm (8 pm on Sunday).

Château de Langeais

Built in the late 1460s to cut the most likely invasion route from Brittany, Château de Langeais (☎ 02 47 96 72 60), in flowery Langeais, presents two faces to the world. From the town it appears a 15th-century fortified castle – nearly windowless, machicolated ramparts (ie walls from which missiles and boiling liquids could be dropped on attackers) rising forbiddingly from the drawbridge. The sections facing the courtyard, however, are outfitted with the large windows, dormers and decorative stonework characteristic of later chateaux designed for more refined living. The **ruined dungeon** in its grounds dates from around 944 and is the oldest such structure in France.

Langeais has a truly interesting interior. The unmodernised configuration of the rooms and the **period furnishings** give you a pretty good idea of what the place looked like during the 15th and 16th centuries. The walls are decorated with fine but somewhat faded Flemish and Aubusson **tapestries**, many of which are in the millefleurs (thousand flowers) style.

In one room, wax figures re-enact the marriage of King Charles VIII and Duchess Anne of Brittany, held here on 6 December 1491. The event brought about the final union of France and Brittany.

Château de Langeais opens 9 am to 12.30 pm and 2 to 6.30 pm in October; and 9 am to noon and 2 to 5 pm the rest of the year. Admission costs 40FF (seniors, students and children 35FF).

Getting There & Away Langeais is 24km south-west of Tours and 14km west of Villandry. Its train station (☎ 02 47 96 82 19), 400m from Château de Langeais, is on the Tours–Savonnières–Saumur line. The last train back to Tours (27FF, 15 to 25 minutes, three to six daily) is at 6.37 pm (5.30 pm on Saturday, 7.15 or 8.20 pm on Sunday and holidays). Tickets cost 14FF to Savonnières (4km from Villandry) and 39FF to Saumur (25 minutes).

AMBOISE
postcode 37400 • pop 11,000
• elevation 112m

The picturesque town of Amboise, nestling under its fortified chateau on the southern bank of the Loire, reached its peak during the decades around 1500, when the luxury-loving King Charles VIII enlarged it and King François I held raucous parties here. These days, the town makes the most of its association with Leonardo da Vinci, who lived his last years here under the patronage of François I.

Amboise is protected from the river by a dike, whose flower-covered heights are a fine place for a riverside promenade. Tours, 23km downstream, and Blois, 34km upstream, are easy day trips from here. Amboise is a good base for visiting the chateaux east of Tours (see the chateaux listings in the Blésois section, earlier in this chapter).

Orientation

Amboise train station, across the river from the town centre, is about 800m from the

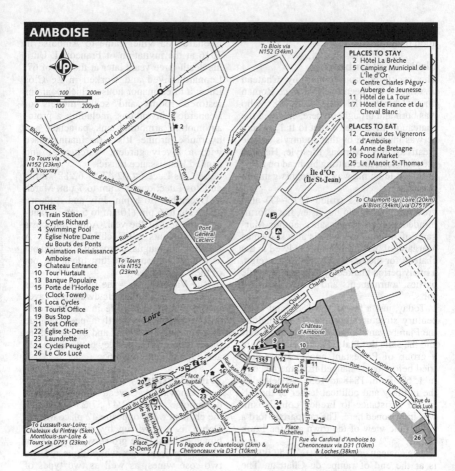

AMBOISE

0   100   200m
0   100   200yds

To Blois via
N152 (34km)

To Tours via
N152 (23km)
& Vouvray

Boulevard Gambetta
Blvd des Platanes
Rue d'Amboise
Rue de Nazelles
Rue Jules Ferry
Rue de Blois
Rue des Blois

Île d'Or
(Île St-Jean)

To Chaumont-sur-Loire (20km)
& Blois (34km) via D751

Pont
Général
Leclerc

To Tours
via N152
(23km)

Loire

Quai Charles Guinot

Château
d'Amboise

Quai de la Concorde

Rue de la Tour

Rue Léonard-Perrault

Rue Victor Hugo

Rue du Clos Lucé

Place Michel Debré

Place Chaptal
Place du Général de Gaulle
Ave de la Résistance
Quai du Général de Gaulle
Rue des Martyrs de la Résistance
Rue Nationale
Rue R Chateau
Rue Jean-Jacques Rousseau
Quai des Marais
Rue Joyeuse
Rue du Général Foy

Place
Richelieu

Place
St-Denis

To Lussault-sur-Loire;
Chateaux du Pintray (5km);
Montlouis-sur-Loire &
Tours via D751 (23km)

To Pagode de Chanteloup (2km) &
Chenonceaux via D31 (10km)

Rue Rabelais

Rue du Cardinal d'Amboise to
Chenonceaux via D31 (10km)
& Loches (38km)

PLACES TO STAY
2 Hôtel La Brèche
5 Camping Municipal de L'Île d'Or
6 Centre Charles Péguy-Auberge de Jeunesse
11 Hôtel de La Tour
17 Hôtel de France et du Cheval Blanc

PLACES TO EAT
12 Caveau des Vignerons d'Amboise
14 Anne de Bretagne
20 Food Market
25 Le Manoir St-Thomas

OTHER
1 Train Station
3 Cycles Richard
4 Swimming Pool
7 Église Notre Dame du Bouts des Ponts
8 Animation Renaissance Amboise
9 Chateau Entrance
10 Tour Hurtault
13 Banque Populaire
15 Porte de l'Horloge (Clock Tower)
16 Loca Cycles
18 Tourist Office
19 Bus Stop
21 Post Office
22 Église St-Denis
23 Laundrette
24 Cycles Peugeot
26 Le Clos Lucé

chateau. Le Clos Lucé, Leonardo da Vinci's former home, is 500m south-east of the chateau along rue Victor Hugo. The island in the middle of the Loire is called Île d'Or.

Place Michel Debré – effectively an extension of rue Victor Hugo and sometimes called place du Château – stretches westwards from the northern end of rue de la Tour to pedestrian rue Nationale, Amboise's main commercial and touristy street.

Information

Tourist Offices The tourist office (☎ 02 47 57 09 28, fax 02 47 57 14 35, ✆ tourisme .amboise@wanadoo.fr), in a pavillion opposite 7 quai du Général de Gaulle, stocks walking and cycling maps, and supplies a free English-language brochure for walking around Amboise. Opening hours are 9 am to 12.30 pm and 2 pm to 6.30 pm Monday to Saturday, November to Easter; the rest of the year it also opens 10 am to noon on Sunday. See the Web site is at www .amboise-valdeloire.com.

Money and Post Several banks dot rue Nationale, and the post office at 20 Quai du Général de Gaulle, opens 8.30 am to noon

THE LOIRE

and 1.30 to 6 pm on weekdays, 8.30 am to noon on Saturday.

Château d'Amboise

The rocky outcrop topped by Château d'Amboise has been fortified since Roman times. Charles VIII (ruled 1483–98), who was born and brought up here, enlarged the chateau in 1492 after a visit to Italy, where he was impressed by that country's artistic creativity and luxurious lifestyle. He died six years later after hitting his head on a low lintel while on his way to a tennis game in the moat.

King François I (ruled 1515–47) also grew up here, as did his sister, the reform-minded French Renaissance author Margaret of Angoulême, who is also known as Margaret of Navarre. François I lived in the chateau for the first few years of his reign, a lively period marked by balls, masquerade parties, tournaments and festivities of all sorts.

Today, just a few of the 15th- and 16th-century structures survive. These include the Flamboyant Gothic **Chapelle St-Hubert** and the **Salle des États** (Estates Hall), where a group of Protestant conspirators were tried before being hanged from the balcony in 1560. From 1848 to 1852, Abdelkader, the military and political leader of the Algerian resistance to French colonialism, was imprisoned here. The **ramparts** afford a panoramic view of the town and the Loire Valley.

The chateau entrance (☎ 02 47 57 00 98) is at the end of rampe du Château. The chateau opens 9 am to 6.30 pm, April to October (to 8 pm in July and August) and 9 am to noon and 2 to 5 or 5.30 pm; the rest of the year. Admission costs 40FF (students 33FF, children 21FF). On Wednesday and Saturday evening, from mid-June to end August, it stages an evening show (a re-enactment of the life and times of François I) in its courtyard. Tickets cost 75FF to 100FF and can be bought in advance from Animation Renaissance Amboise (☎ 02 47 57 14 47, fax 02 47 57 70 38), 7 rampe du Château. It opens 9 am to 12.30 pm and 1.30 to 5 or 6 pm Monday to Friday.

Le Clos Lucé

Leonardo da Vinci came to Amboise in 1516 at the invitation of François I. Until his death three years later at the age of 67, Leonardo lived and worked in Le Clos Lucé, a brick manor house which contains restored rooms and scale models of Leonardo's inventions, including a proto-automobile, armoured tank, parachute and hydraulic turbine. It's a fascinating place with a lovely garden, watchtower and canned Renaissance music.

Le Clos Lucé (☎ 02 47 57 62 88), 2 rue du Clos Lucé, opens 9 am to 7 pm, March to December (to 8 pm, July and August); and 9 am to 6 pm (10 am to 5 pm in January), the rest of the year. Admission costs 39FF (students 32FF, children 20FF). A free English-language brochure is doled out as you twirl through the turnstile at the foot of the watch tower.

Rue Victor Hugo – the road to Le Clos Lucé – passes **troglodytic dwellings**, caves in the limestone hillside in which people still live. Abodes worth a peek include those at Nos 31, 59, 81 and 83; as well as those at the end of the alley between Nos 27 and 29, and next to No 65.

Wine Tasting

The innovative Caveau des Vignerons d'Amboise (☎/fax 02 47 57 23 69), inside the chateau walls opposite 42 place Michel Debré, is a *cave* run by an enterprising bunch of local wine growers. Here you can taste – for free – six white, three red and two rosé wines, as well as two types of Touraine Crémant de Loire (a sparkling drink likened to champagne). To ensure the most untickled of tastebuds are titillated, the wine growers offer different local foods to taste. The *cave* (wine cellar) opens 10 am to 7 pm, Easter to October.

Places to Stay

Camping The 420-pitch *Camping Municipal de l'Île d'Or* (☎ 02 47 57 23 37, 02 47 23 47 23) on Île d'Or, opens April to September. It costs 24FF for a tent and car, plus 13/7.30FF per adult/child aged under 12. Admission to the neighbouring swimming

THE LOIRE

pool costs 12.50FF. There's also mini-golf, a mountain bike circuit and tennis courts on site.

Hostels Also on Île d'Or is *Centre Charles Péguy-Auberge de Jeunesse* (☎ 02 47 57 06 36, fax 02 47 23 15 80). Beds cost 52FF and breakfast 15FF. Reception opens 3 to 9 pm on weekdays, and 6 to 8 pm at the weekend; if you arrive when it's closed, screech into the intercom.

Chambres d'Hôtes The tourist office has a list of homes offering B&B around Amboise. *Château du Pintray* (☎ 02 47 23 22 84, fax 02 47 57 64 27), 5km west in Lussault-sur-Loire, is a 16th-century chateau with five gorgeous doubles costing 550FF, including breakfast. You can taste and buy AOC Montlouis wines produced on the estate here.

Hotels Charming *Hôtel La Brèche* (☎ 02 47 57 00 79, rue Jules Ferry) has doubles with washbasin/shower/shower and toilet costing 170/220/270FF. On warm days, guests breakfast (35FF) outside on a tree-shaded terrace.

Hôtel de France et du Cheval Blanc (☎ 02 47 57 02 44, fax 02 47 57 69 54, 6–7 quai du Général de Gaulle) has cheap rooms and is always packed. Doubles cost upwards of 155FF. The hotel opens mid-March to mid-November.

Hôtel de la Tour (☎ 02 47 57 25 04, 32 rue Victor Hugo), above a bar, has eight singles/doubles/triples with washbasin and bidet for 120/175/230FF. Reception (at the bar) is closed on Thursday except during July and August; the hotel closes for two weeks in March and three weeks in September.

Places to Eat

The southern side of place Michel Debré is lined with light, lunchtime-snack spots. Foodies seeking a taste of Touraine should munch on a 40FF lunchtime platter (and a free glass of wine) in the *Caveau des Vignerons d'Amboise* (see the Wine Tasting section earlier in this chapter). *Anne de*

Bretagne (☎ 02 47 57 05 46, 1 rampe du Château) serves a 54FF *menu* and a host of tempting, alcohol-soaked crepes.

Four-star *Le Manoir St-Thomas* (☎ 02 47 57 22 52, 1 mail St-Thomas) is housed in a sumptuous mansion and has 175FF, 265FF and 295FF *menus*.

Sandwich shops, fast food outlets, boulangeries and *creperies* line rue Nationale. An open-air *food market* spills across quai du Général de Gaulle on Friday and Sunday morning.

Getting There & Around

Bus Buses to/from Amboise stop at the bus shelter across the car park lot from the tourist office.

CAT's line No 10 links the town with Tours' bus terminal (19.60FF one way, 30 to 50 minutes, eight daily Monday to Saturday and six daily during the summer holidays). There are likewise round trips, Monday to Friday, between Amboise and Château de Chenonceau (see that section, earlier in this chapter).

Train The train station, on blvd Gambetta across the river from the centre of town, is served by trains from Paris' Gare d'Austerlitz (1/42FF, 2¼ to three hours, five or six daily).

About three-quarters of the trains on the Blois–Tours line (11 to 17 daily) stop here. Fares are 34FF to Blois (20 minutes) and 28FF to Tours (20 minutes).

Bicycle Cycles Richard (☎ 02 47 57 01 79), 2 rue de Nazelles, has mountain bikes to hire for 80FF per day. It opens 9 am to noon and 2.30 to 9 pm Monday to Saturday. Cycles Peugeot (☎ 02 47 57 00 17) at 5 rue Joyeuse and Loca Cycles (☎ 02 47 57 00 28) at 2 bis rue Jean-Jacques Rousseau, share similar rates and opening hours.

AROUND AMBOISE
Pagode de Chanteloup

This 44m-high, Chinese-style pagoda is one of the 18th century's more pleasing follies. Built between 1775 and 1778, it combines contemporary French architectural fashions

THE LOIRE

with elements from China, a subject of great fascination at the time. From the top of the pagoda, visitors are rewarded with an impressive view of the Loire Valley. Also visible are the overgrown outlines of the once splendid pools, gardens and forest paths that surrounded the estate's 18th-century chateau, torn down in 1823.

This eccentric pagoda is a delightful picnic venue. Hampers bursting with regional treats are sold at the entrance (50FF). You can hire a boat to row your sweetheart around the lake (40FF per hour) and there is a fun collection of old-fashioned games to play (free).

The Pagode de Chanteloup (☎ 02 47 57 20 97) opens 10 am to 6 pm in May; 10 am to 7 pm in June and September; 9.30 am to 8 pm in July and August; and 10 am to noon and 2 to 5 or 5.30 pm in March, April and October. Admission costs 35FF (students 30FF, children 25FF).

Getting There & Away The pagoda is about 2.5km south of Amboise. Head south on rue Bretonneau and follow the plentiful signs to 'La Pagode'. Public buses between Amboise and Tours stop at the 'Pagode' stop (see Bus under the Getting There & Away sections under Amboise and Tours for details).

LOCHES
postcode 37600 • pop 6550 • elevation 80m

Medieval Loches, with its cobbled streets and imposing keep perched on a rocky spur, could be a film set. Its 11th-century keep was built by Foulques Nerra (Falcon the Black; ruled 987–1040) while its feudal chateau witnessed Joan of Arc persuade Charles VII to march north in June 1429 to be crowned. The royal court that he consequently established here was notorious for its wild banquets, thrown primarily to woo the scandalously wicked yet stunningly beautiful Agnès Sorel, a royal mistress who died aged 28. Her tomb lies in Loches. The town's golden age ended in 1461 with the ascension of Louis XI to the throne who turned the keep into a state prison.

Orientation & Information
The citadel sits south of the old town, on the western bank of the River Indre. The train and bus stations are across Pont Pierre Senard on the eastern bank of the river.

The tourist office (☎ 02 47 59 07 98, fax 02 47 91 61 50), place de la Marne, is wedged between Pont Pierre Senard and rue de la République, the main commercial street. Its opens 9.30 am to 7 pm Monday to Saturday, and 9.30 am to 1 pm and 2 to 7 pm on Sunday. See the Web site at www.lochesentouraine.com.

Citadel
The 11th-century **Porte Royale** (Royal Gate), up the hill on rue de la Porte, is flanked by two 13th-century towers and remains the only opening in the sturdy 2km wall that encircles the citadel. Inside, the **Donjon** (Castle Keep; 1010–35), at the southernmost point of the rocky promontory, is the oldest structure within the citadel. The notorious **Round Tower** and **Martelet** were built under Louis XI as prisons. Inmates were tortured in a cage that weighed 2.5 tons, a replica of which is on display.

The northern end of the citadel contains the **Logis Royal** (Royal Residence). The 15th-century funerary urn of Agnès Sorel is in the northern wing of the residence, built for Charles VIII and Anne de Bretagne in the 16th century. The Logis Royal and Donjon open 9 am to 7 pm, July to September; and 9 am to noon and 2 to 5 or 6 pm, the rest of the year. Admission costs 23FF (children 13FF). A combination ticket for the two sights costs 31FF.

In summer, **son-et-lumières** (☎ 02 47 59 01 76) are held in the citadel at 10 pm Friday and Saturday. The terrace offers a fine panorama of Loches village tumbling down the hillside towards the Indre Valley.

Places to Stay & Eat
At *Camping La Citadelle* (☎ 02 47 59 05 91, ✉ camping@lacitadelle.com, ave Aristide Briand), open mid-March to mid-November, it costs 72FF for a tent site, car and two adults. To get here, head south along rue Quintefol (N143) for 1km.

Hôtel de la Tour St-Antoine (☎ 02 47 59 01 06, fax 02 47 59 13 80, 2 rue des Moulins) has basic doubles with washbasin for 150FF (180FF with shower, 230FF with shower and toilet). Nearby *Hôtel de France* (☎ 02 47 59 00 32, fax 02 47 59 28 66, 6 rue Piçois) has a courtyard restaurant, private parking and rooms for two starting at 295FF.

Out of town in St-Jean-St-Germain, 5km south on the N143, is *Le Moulin* (☎ 02 47 94 70 12), an 18th-century water mill on the banks of the Indre, now run as a charming chambre d'hôte by its British proprietors. It has six doubles costing 350FF each, including breakfast.

A fruit, vegetable, sausage and cheese *market* fills place du Marché and rue St-Antoine on Wednesday morning.

Getting There & Around

Loches is on the Tours-Châteauroux rail line. The train and bus stations are across Pont Pierre Senard on place des Cordeliers. There are trains to/from Tours (44FF, 45 minutes, two daily) and SNCF buses (44FF, 50 minutes, three or four daily).

Peugeot Cycles-JM Jourdain (☎ 02 47 59 02 15), 7 rue des Moulins, rents road/mountain bikes for 50/80FF per day or 300/500FF a week.

CHINON
postcode 37500 • pop 8627 • elevation 40m

Chinon's massive, 400m-long fortress looms above the town's medieval quarter. The uneven, cobblestone streets are lined with ancient houses, some built of decaying tufa stone, others half-timbered and brick. The contrast between the triangular, black slate roofs and the whitish-tan tufa gives the town its distinctive appearance.

Villandry, Azay-le-Rideau and Langeais can easily be visited from Chinon if you have your own transport. The Forêt de Chinon (Chinon Forest), a wooded area ideal for walking and cycling, begins a few kilometres north-east of town and stretches along the D751 all the way to Azay-le-Rideau.

Orientation & Information

Rue Haute St-Maurice, the main street in the medieval quarter, becomes rue Voltaire as you move east. The train station is 1km east of the town's commercial hub, place du Général de Gaulle, also called place de l'Hôtel de Ville.

The tourist office (☎ 02 47 93 17 85, fax 02 47 93 93 05), place de Hofheïm, opens 9 am to 6.30 or 7 pm Monday to Saturday year round; plus 10 am to 12.30 pm on Sunday in summer. There are several banks near the post office on quai Jeanne d'Arc.

Château de Chinon

Perched atop a rocky spur high above the River Vienne, this huge, mostly ruined medieval fortress consists of three parts separated by waterless moats: little remains of the 12th-century **Fort St-Georges**, which protected the chateau's vulnerable eastern flank; the **Château du Milieu** (the Middle Castle); and, at the western tip, the **Château du Coudray**. From the ramparts there are great views in all directions. The chateau is illuminated at night during the summer months.

After crossing the moat (once spanned by a drawbridge) and entering Château du Milieu, you pass under the **Tour de l'Horloge** (Clock Tower). The four rooms inside are dedicated to the career of Joan of Arc, who picked out Charles VII from among a crowd of courtiers in 1429 in the castle's **Salle du Trône** (Throne Room). Other parts of the almost undecorated **Grand Logis Royal** (Royal Apartments), built during the 12th, 14th and 15th centuries, are in slightly better condition.

Château de Chinon (☎ 02 47 93 13 45) opens 9 am to 6 pm, mid-March to October (to 7 pm in July and August, and 5 pm in October); and 9 am to noon and 2 to 5 pm, the rest of the year. Admission costs 28FF (seniors 19FF, children 16FF).

To get to the chateau, walk up the hill to rue du Puits des Bancs and turn left. By car, route de Tours (the continuation of the D751 from Tours) takes you to the rear of the chateau.

THE LOIRE

CHINON

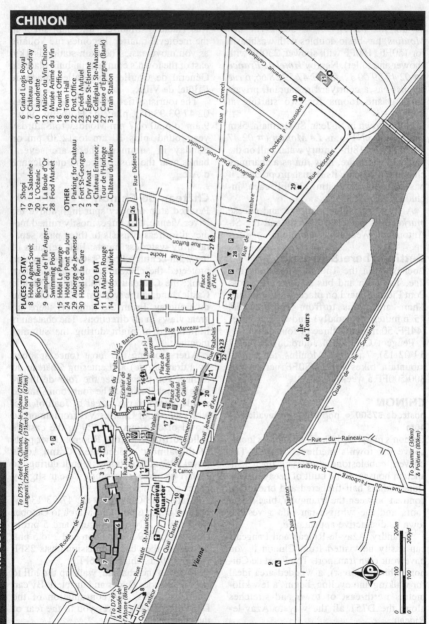

PLACES TO STAY
8 Hôtel Agnès Sorel;
9 Camping de l'Île Auger;
Bicycle Rental
Swimming Pool
15 Hôtel Le Panurge
24 Hôtel du Pont du Jour
29 Auberge de Jeunesse
30 Hôtel de la Gare

PLACES TO EAT
11 La Maison Rouge
14 Outdoor Market

17 Shopi
19 La Saladerie
20 L'Océanic
21 La Boule d'Or
28 Food Market

OTHER
1 Parking for Chateau
2 Fort St-Georges
3 Dry Moat
4 Chateau Entrance;
Tour de l'Horloge
5 Chateau du Milieu
6 Grand Logis Royal
7 Château du Coudray
10 Laundrette
12 Maison du Vin Chinon
13 Musée Animé du Vin
16 Tourist Office
18 Town Hall
22 Post Office
23 Crédit Mutuel
25 Collégiale Ste-Maxime
26 Église St-Etienne
27 Caisse d'épargne (Bank)
31 Train Station

Musée Animé du Vin

The kitsch Musée Animé du Vin (Animated Wine Museum; ☎ 02 47 93 25 63), 12 rue Voltaire, has life-sized mechanical figures that demonstrate how wine and wine barrels are made, accompanied by piped commentary in English. It opens 10.30 am to 12.30 pm and 2 to 7 pm, April and September. The 25FF admission fee (children 21FF) includes a sample of local wine and *confiture de vin* (sweet wine jam or jelly).

Serious vinophiles seeking hardcore information should try the **Maison du Vin de Chinon**, a block west on impasse des Caves Peintres. The local Syndicat des Vins de Chinon (☎ 02 47 93 30 44), based here, has a list of wine growers who sell wine and offer dégustation. Chinon's vineyards stretch north, south and east of the town, on both banks of the River Vienne.

Musée de l'Atome

The Musée de l'Atome (Atom Museum; ☎ 02 47 98 77 77) is housed in France's first commercial reactor, erected between 1957 and 1963 on the Loire's southern bank. The station, 8km north-west of Chinon in Avoine, has two decommissioned units and four active, pressurised water reactors rated at 900 megawatts.

To arrange a free visit (1½ hours) call the station a few days ahead (a day ahead in July and August) and take along some form of ID. The working reactors can only be visited weekdays, when there are four tours daily from May to September (less frequently the rest of the year). The tourist office (☎/fax 02 47 58 45 40) opposite the main entrance to the plant on the D749, can help arrange visits. It opens 10 am to 7 pm Monday to Saturday, and 2 to 7 pm Sunday, April to September.

Special Events

On the first weekend in August, musicians, dancers and locals dress up in period costume for the Marché Rabelais, held in the medieval quarter. Two weeks later, wines and traditional food products from the Loire region are sold at the Marché à l'Ancienne, which is a re-creation of a 19th-century farmers' market.

Places to Stay

Camping Riverside *Camping de l'Île Auger* (☎ 02 47 93 08 35), open April to October, is on the southern bank of the River Vienne and charges 11FF per tent/car/adult.

Hostels The friendly *Auberge de Jeunesse* (☎ 02 47 93 10 48, fax 02 47 98 44 98, 60 rue Descartes) has dorm beds costing 51FF. You can reserve a place and leave your bags there all day long, but check-in is only on weekdays between 6 to 10 pm; curfew is 10 pm. Guests can use the laundry facilities, kitchen and TV room.

Hotels In the centre, overlooking a leafy cafe-filled square is *Hôtel Le Panurge* (☎ 02 47 93 09 84, 45 place du Général de Gaulle). Doubles cost 135FF (160/185FF with shower/shower and toilet).

Hôtel du Pont du Jour (☎ 02 47 93 07 20, place Jeanne d'Arc) is above a simple bar-cum-cafe. Doubles with washbasin/shower/shower and toilet are good value at 120/150/170FF. It also has apartments and a *gîte rural* to let on a weekly/monthly basis.

Two-star *Hôtel de la Gare* (☎ 02 47 93 00 86, fax 02 47 93 36 38, 14 ave Gambetta), also called Gar' Hôtel, has large plain doubles/quads with shower and toilet for 280/340FF.

The small but sweet *Hôtel Agnès Sorel* (☎ 02 47 93 04 37, fax 02 47 93 06 37, ✉ catherine.rogereck@wanadoo.fr, 4 quai Pasteur) is a riverside spot run by a friendly family. It has six rooms, costing 220/300FF without/with private shower and toilet, and has bicycles to rent.

Places to Eat

In summer, tree-shaded place du Général de Gaulle becomes one huge outdoor cafe. Among the many eateries along rue Rabelais is *La Saladerie* (☎ 02 47 93 99 93) at No 5, which has meal-sized salads (about 45FF), meat dishes (50FF to 63FF) and, except in summer, *chaud' patats* (baked

THE LOIRE

potato dishes) and *gratins* (dishes made with cheese), both 40FF to 50FF.

L'Océanic (☎ 02 47 93 44 55) at No 13 specialises in seafood with *menus* swimming in at 110FF and 160FF. Similarly priced is *La Boule d'Or* (☎ 02 47 98 40 88) at No 21 with a 99FF and 148FF *menu du terroir* (literally 'menu of the soil', meaning a *menu* comprising local products). Its fish terrine with pistachio nuts is a speciality.

La Maison Rouge (☎ 02 47 98 43 65, 38 rue Voltaire), at the foot of the steep cobbled street leading to the chateau, serves *assiettes Rabelaisiennes* (Rabelaisian dishes) of local specialities (69FF, 79FF or 98FF) and 50cl jugs of Chinon wine (43FF).

Self-Catering A handy supermarket is *Shopi* (22 place du Général de Gaulle). At the northern end of place du Général de Gaulle, there's an *outdoor market* until 1 pm on Thursday, Saturday and Sunday mornings. Place Jeanne d'Arc plays host to a *food market* on Thursday morning.

Getting There & Around
Chinon is 47km south-west of Tours, 21km south-west of Azay-le-Rideau and 80km north of Poitiers.

The train station (☎ 02 47 93 11 04), 1km east of the medieval quarter, is linked by a tertiary line with Tours (48FF, 50 minutes, eight trains or SNCF buses on weekdays, five on Saturday and two on Sunday and holidays) and Azay-le-Rideau (21FF, 20–30 minutes, eight to 12 trains or SNCF buses daily). There is only one SNCF bus for Poitiers per day (one hour) from Chinon to St-Pierre des Corps, from where there are eight trains to Poitiers daily. The total journey time is two hours.

Hire a bicycle at the outlet (☎ 02 47 93 04 37) at 4 quai Pasteur, inside Hôtel Agnès Sorel. It costs 90/150FF per day/weekend.

Anjou

Renaissance chateaux peter out in Anjou where chalky-white tufa cliffs conceal an astonishing underworld of wine cellars, mushroom farms and monumental art sculptures. Above ground, black slate roofs pepper the vine-rich land. Outstanding architectural gems in Anjou's crown include the cathedral in Angers and the Romanesque Abbaye de Fontevraud east of Saumur.

Angers, the capital of Anjou, showcases the world-famous medieval *L'Apocalypse* tapestry. Saumur, 50km downstream, is a centre of equestrian sport and home to the prestigious Cadre Noir (see the boxed text 'Cadre Noir' later in this chapter). Europe's highest concentration of troglodyte dwellings dot the Loire riverbanks east and west of Saumur. South-eastern Anjou is protected by the Parc Naturel Régional Loire-Anjou-Touraine.

ANGERS
postcode 49000 • pop 141,500
• elevation 41m

Angers, 70km west of Chinon, straddles the River Maine. The city was settled by the Andes Celtic tribe and became an administrative capital under the Romans. In the 9th century, it served as the seat of the powerful counts of Anjou who controlled a vast territory embracing most of south-western France by the 12th century. Much of the city was bombed during WWII; the city housed an exiled Polish government in 1940 and the regional headquarters of the Gestapo in 1942.

Angers is pleasantly walkable. Its richest treasure, displayed inside its mighty chateau, is a medieval tapestry depicting the Apocalypse.

The city hosted the royal court until the 12th century when Henri II shifted it to Chinon.

Orientation
Angers' historic quarter lies on the eastern bank of the River Maine, bordered by blvd Ayrault and its continuation, blvd Carnot, to the north; blvd du Maréchal Foch to the east; and blvd du Roi René to the south.

The train station is 800m south of place du Président Kennedy, the square at the

THE LOIRE

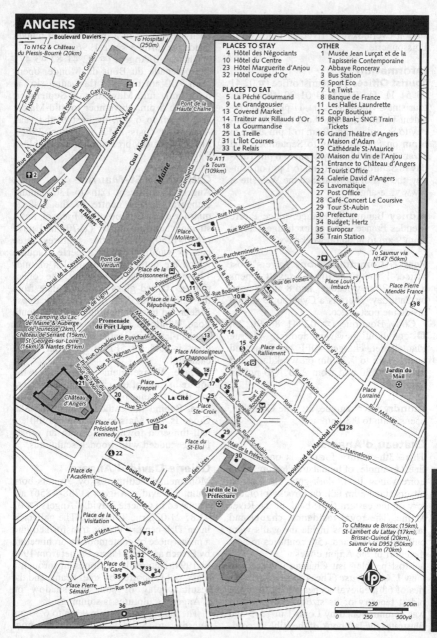

ANGERS

PLACES TO STAY
4 Hôtel des Négociants
10 Hôtel du Centre
23 Hôtel Marguerite d'Anjou
32 Hôtel Coupe d'Or

PLACES TO EAT
5 La Péché Gourmand
9 Le Grandgousier
13 Covered Market
14 Traiteur aux Rillauds d'Or
18 La Gourmandise
25 La Treille
31 L'Îlot Courses
33 Le Relais

OTHER
1 Musée Jean Lurçat et de la Tapisserie Contemporaine
2 Abbaye Ronceray
3 Bus Station
6 Sport Eco
7 Le Twist
8 Banque de France
11 Les Halles Laundrette
12 Copy Boutique
15 BNP Bank; SNCF Train Tickets
16 Grand Théâtre d'Angers
17 Maison d'Adam
19 Cathédrale St-Maurice
20 Maison du Vin de l'Anjou
21 Entrance to Château d'Angers
22 Tourist Office
24 Galerie David d'Angers
26 Lavomatique
27 Post Office
28 Café-Concert Le Coursive
29 Tour St-Aubin
30 Prefecture
34 Budget; Hertz
35 Europcar
36 Train Station

THE LOIRE

euro currency converter €1 = 6.56FF

western end of blvd du Roi René. The bus station overlooks the river on place de la Poissonnerie.

Information

Tourist Offices The tourist office (☎ 02 41 23 51 11, fax 02 41 24 01 20, @ angers. tourisme@ville-angers.fr), 11 place du Président Kennedy, opens 9 am to 7 pm Monday to Saturday and 10 am to 1 pm and 2 to 6 pm on Sunday, May to September; and 11 am to 6 pm Monday, 9 am to 6 pm Tuesday to Saturday, and 10 am to 1 pm on Sunday, the rest of the year. See the Web site at www.ville-angers.fr.

Money Banque de France, place Pierre Mendès France, runs an exchange service from 9 am to noon on weekdays.

Post & Communications Angers' post office, 1 rue Franklin Roosevelt, opens 8 am to 7 pm weekdays and 8 am to noon on Saturday. There is a Cyberposte station inside the post office.

Copy Boutique (☎ 02 41 88 96 26, @ copyboutique@wanadoo.fr), 48 rue Plantagenêt, charges 40FF per hour and opens 9 am to 7.30 pm on weekdays, and 9 am to 12.30 and from 2 to 7.30 pm on Saturday.

Laundry Lavomatique, at 3 rue Corneille, opens 7 am to 9.30 pm.

Château d'Angers

This 13th-century fortress is one of the finest examples of feudal architecture in the Loire Valley. Its 17 dark-grey, black schist towers stand 30m tall, on a rocky promontory on the eastern (left) bank of the River Maine. The **royal residence**, **chapel** and **landscaped gardens** inside the walls were built in the 14th and 15th centuries to host the court of the Anjou dukes.

Most people visit Château d'Angers to view *L'Apocalypse* (The Apocalypse), a series of 68 medieval scenes which form the oldest tapestry of its size in the world. It was commissioned by Louis I in 1375 and illustrates the last book of the Bible according to St-John. The 103m-long tapestry has been showcased in a purpose-built bunker inside the fortress since 1996.

Château d'Angers (☎ 02 41 87 43 47), 2 promenade du Bout du Monde, opens from 9.30 am to 7 pm (last admission at 6.15 pm), mid-May to mid-September; 10 am to 5 pm, November to mid-March; and 10 am to 6 pm, the rest of the year. Admission costs 35FF (children 25FF). Free explanatory brochures are available in English.

Cathédrale St-Maurice

Angers' magnificent 12th- to 13th-century cathedral, in the centre of the historic **quartier de la Cité** on place Freppel, has a striking Norman porch (1170) and nave (1150–1250). The latter features three convex vaults forming a perfect square which are outstanding examples of mid-12th-century Angevin vaulting. The collection of **stained-glass windows** date from the 12th to 16th centuries. The apocalypse is depicted in the stunning north and south **Rose Windows** in the transepts and an English-language leaflet detailing the windows is sold for 5FF at the front of the cathedral.

Place Monseigneur Chappoulie, the square in front of the cathedral, is linked to the River Maine by a **monumental staircase**. Behind the cathedral on place Ste-Croix is the **Maison d'Adam** (1500), a half-timbered town house with an ornate facade studded with wooden sculptures.

Galerie David d'Angers

Monumental sculptures by Angers-born sculptor David d'Angers (1788–1856) are displayed in Galerie David d'Angers (☎ 02 41 87 21 03), rue Toussaint. The gallery is in an 11th-century abbey, transformed into a masterpiece of contemporary architecture by French architect Pierre Prunet from 1980 to 1994. Natural light floods in through a glass roof supported by steel beams and the resultant play of sun and shadow on d'Angers' sculptures is stunning.

The gallery opens from 9 am to 6.30 pm Tuesday to Sunday, mid-June to mid-

THE LOIRE

September; and 10 am to noon and 2 to 6 pm Tuesday to Sunday, the rest of the year. Admission costs 10FF (students and children 5FF).

Musée Jean Lurçat et de la Tapisserie Contemporaine

This museum (☎ 02 41 24 18 45), 6 blvd Arago, housed in the Gothic-vaulted sick wards of a former hospital (1180–1865), showcases a series of 10 monumental tapestries woven in the 1960s by French-born artist Jean Lurçat (1892–1966). Entitled *Le Chant du Monde* (The Song of the World), the hangings illustrate the horror story of human destruction. A disturbing green skeleton depicts 'Hiroshima Man'.

The museum opens 9 am to 6.30 pm, mid-June to mid-September; and 10 am to noon and 2 to 6 pm Tuesday to Sunday, the rest of the year. Admission costs 20FF (students 10FF).

Wine Tasting

The Maison du Vin de l'Anjou (☎ 02 41 88 81 13, fax 02 41 86 71 84), across from the chateau at 5 bis place du Président Kennedy, is the perfect spot to sample Anjou and Saumur wines. It opens 9 am to 1 pm and 3 to 6.30 pm Tuesday to Sunday (closed Sunday October to March).

Places to Stay

Camping Overlooking a lake is *Camping du Lac de Maine* (☎ 02 41 73 05 03, fax 02 41 73 02 20, ave du Lac de Maine) some 2.5km south-west of the city. The 162-pitch site opens mid-March to mid-October and charges 80FF per day for a tent pitch, car and two people. To get here from the centre, take bus No 16 from the train station to the Perussaie stop on rue de la Chambre aux Deniers, a 500m walk from the lake shore.

Hostels The lakeside *Auberge de Jeunesse* (☎ 02 41 22 32 10, fax 02 41 22 32 11, 49 ave du Lac de Maine) has doubles (with two beds) for 170FF, including breakfast. To get here from the centre of Angers, follow the same instructions as for Camping du Lac de Maine earlier.

Hotels Within spitting distance (almost) of the chateau, *Hôtel Marguerite d'Anjou* (☎ 02 41 88 11 61, fax 02 41 87 37 62, 13 place du Président Kennedy) has eight rooms costing 180/220/260FF for one/two/three people. Reception is in the adjoining bar-brasserie.

Hôtel du Centre (☎ 02 41 87 45 07, 12 rue St-Laud), above a pub of the same name, has singles/doubles starting at 110/130FF.

Among the many hotels near the train station, nine-room *Hôtel Coupe d'Or* (☎ 02 41 88 45 02, fax 02 41 86 01 58, 5 rue de la Gare) sports the best-value, basic singles/doubles for 120/135FF (150/175FF with shower). Near the bus station, *Hôtel des Négociants* (☎ 02 41 88 24 08, 2 rue de la Roë) has cheap, shower-equipped doubles costing 155FF and triples/quads with two large beds costing 185/220FF.

Places to Eat

Restaurants Touting a terrace opposite Maison d'Adam, *La Treille* (☎ 02 41 88 45 51, 12 rue Montault) offers a 55FF lunchtime *menu*. There's another busy terrace on place Ste-Croix.

Grilled meats are cooked on a wood fire at *Le Grandgousier* (☎ 02 41 87 87 47, 7 rue St-Laud). *Crottin de Chavignol* (a type of goat cheese) served with raspberry coulis is among its local specialities. Seafood is the dish of the day at *Le Péché Gourmand* (☎ 02 41 81 04 76, 48 rue Parcheminerie) which serves up a good value 68FF *menu* until 9 pm on weekdays.

Close to the train station, *Le Relais* (☎ 02 41 88 42 51, 9 rue de la Gare) is run by a friendly apron-clad patron who takes enormous pride in the excellent cuisine his chef cooks up. *Menus* cost from 98FF and a 25cl jug of local Anjou Villages wine costs 36FF.

La Gourmandise, on the corner of place Ste-Croix and rue St-Aubin, sells top rate sandwiches, filled baguettes and other satisfying lunchtime bites; count on a long queue.

Self-Catering Near the train station, *L'Îlot Courses*, place de la Visitation, is a small

THE LOIRE

grocery store open from 8 am to 9 pm (9 am to 1 pm on Sunday). Meaty treats such as *rillons* (fat-fried pork cubes) are sold at *Traiteur aux Rillauds d'Or* (☎ 02 41 88 03 13, 59 rue St-Laud).

Entertainment

Pubs and bars bespeckle the southern end of rue St-Laud. Irish bars dot the pedestrian section of nearby rue des Poeliers. *Le Twist (8 rue St-Étienne)* is a fun 50s-style American bar where you can slam tequila shots. For live jazz, try *Café-Concert Le Coursive* (☎ 02 41 25 13 87, 7 bis blvd du Maréchal Foch), open 5 pm to 2 am Monday to Saturday.

Getting There & Away

Bus Eurolines buses depart from quai H at Angers bus station on place de la Poissonnerie.

Regional services are operated by Anjou Bus (☎ 02 41 88 59 25). Destinations include Brissac-Quincé (18.50FF, 25 minutes, six daily), St-Georges-sur-Loire (No 18 or 18B, 19.50FF, 40 minutes, about five daily); Saumur (No 5 or 11, 47FF, 1¼ to 1½ hours, about 10 daily).

Train Angers SNCF train station (listed as Angers St-Laud on timetables) is on place de la Gare. There is at least one train hourly to/from Tours (83/103FF for a non-TGV/TGV, 50 minutes to 1½ hours), Saumur (42FF, 20 minutes) and St-Pierre des Corps (83/103FF for a non-TGV/TGV, 55 minutes). Change trains in Tours or St-Pierre des Corps to get to/from Blois, Orléans and various other eastern Loire destinations.

There are TGV services between Angers and Paris' Gare Montparnasse (from 243FF to 302FF, 1½ hours, 10 to 15 daily) and non-TGV trains to/from Paris' Gare d'Austerlitz (243FF, 1¾ hours, at least eight daily). Other daily services to/from Angers include trains to/from Nantes (71/81FF, 40 minutes/one hour by TGV/non-TGV, at least half-hourly), from where there are connecting southbound rail services to La Rochelle, Bordeaux and Toulouse.

Getting Around

Car Europcar (☎ 02 41 87 87 10) has an office on place de la Gare. Budget (☎ 02 41 88 23 16), 16 rue Denis Papin, is opposite the station, as is Hertz (☎ 02 41 88 15 16) next door.

Bicycle & Rollerblades Sport ECO (☎ 02 41 87 07 77), 45 rue Maillé, has bikes and rollerblades to rent. Bicycles cost 70/130/295FF per day/weekend/week, and rollerblades cost 70/130/295FF. The shop opens from 10 am to noon and 2 to 7 pm Tuesday to Saturday.

AROUND ANGERS

South of Angers, the River Maine joins the Loire for the final leg of its journey to the Atlantic. The riverbanks immediately west of this confluence remain the source of some of the valley's most noble wines – Savennières, Coteaux du Layon and so on. The **Musée de la Vigne et du Vin d'Anjou**, (Museum of Anjou Wine and Vines), 17km south of Angers in St-Lambert du Lattay, is the best place to learn more about these wines.

A delightful place to stay (and eat) for wine lovers is *Prieuré de l'Epinay* (☎/fax 02 41 39 14 44, ✉ bgaultier@compuserve .com), a 13th-century priory in St-Georges-sur-Loire, 1km south-west of Serrant. The chambre d'hôte, open Easter to September, is run by a wine connoisseur who takes guests on tours of surrounding wine cellars. Doubles cost 400FF, including breakfast. The priory has bicycles to rent.

Château de Serrant

Château de Serrant, 15km west of Angers, is a perfect example of Renaissance architecture and has an unusually well-furnished interior. Its library houses over 12,000 books. The 17th-century ebony cabinet in the drawing room conceals 33 secret drawers and is one of four known to exist in the world (the others are in Windsor Castle, Château de Fontainebleau and the Rijksmuseum in Amsterdam). A hand-operated lift was installed in the chateau in 1900, followed by electricity in 1905 and running

THE LOIRE

water in 1920 (the bath water still flows into the moat today).

Serrant (☎ 02 41 39 13 01) can be visited with a guided tour from April to mid-November. Tours depart at 20 minutes past the hour from 10.20 am to 5.20 pm, with extra tours at 10 minutes to the hour in July and August (no tours run between 11.20 am and 2.20 pm). Admission costs 45FF (those aged under 18, 25FF).

Getting There & Away Château de Serrant is an easy cycle ride from Angers. Bus Nos 18 and 18B to St-Georges-sur-Loire (40 minutes, about five daily) stop near the chateau.

Château de Brissac

This highly ornate chocolate box folly, home to the Dukes of Brissac since 1502, is seven storeys high and sits royally amid grounds studded with cedar trees and stretching across 800 hectares. Inside, flamboyant furnishings and ornamentation coat its 203 rooms. The theatre, lit with chandeliers, was the whimsical creation of the Vicomtesse de Trèdene, a soprano with a passion for the arts.

Château de Brissac (☎ 02 41 91 22 21), 15km south of Angers in Brissac-Quincé, can be visited with a guided tour at 10 and 11 am, and 2.15, 3.15, 4.15 and 5.15 pm Wednesday to Sunday, April, May, June and September; and 10 am to 5.45 pm, July and August. Admission costs 45FF (students and children 35FF).

Getting There & Away From Angers, Brissac-Quincé can be reached via the D748 and its continuation, the D761. Bus Nos 9 and 9B link Angers bus station with Brissac-Quincé (25 minutes, about six times daily); the village bus stop is on place de la République, in front of the chateau.

Château du Plessis-Bourré

This medieval fortress – safe-guarded by a moat, double drawbridge and 2m-thick surrounding wall – was built between 1468 and 1473. Contrary to its defensive facade, its interior is Renaissance-inspired (although

most furnishings actually date to 1911 when the current proprietors moved in). The 24 painted ceiling panels in the **Salle des Gardes** (Guards' Hall) date to the 15th century and feature allegorical and alchemy motifs such as a wolf who only eats virgins (thus its thin state), and a young girl peeing into a hat to make gold out of urine.

Château du Plessis-Bourré (☎ 02 41 32 06 01) opens 10 am to 6 pm, July and August; 10 am to noon and 2 to 6 pm Thursday afternoon to Tuesday, May, June and September; and 2 to 6 pm Thursday to Tuesday in March, April, October and November. Admission costs 45FF (students 40FF, children 30FF).

Getting There & Away Château du Plessis-Bourré, some 20km north of Angers, is inaccessible by public transport. By car from Angers, follow the D106 and D768 to La Croix de Beauvais, then head east on the D74 to Ecullé. Continue through the village, then bear south on the narrow D508 to Plessis-Bourré.

SAUMUR & TROGLODYTE VALLEY

The notability of small-town Saumur (population 30,100), 70km south-east of Angers, rides on the renowned National Equestrian School, stabled in St-Hilaire-St-Florent on its western outskirts. In the town centre, military personnel from the calvary school – stationed here since 1599 – buzz around town on bicycles, creating a pleasant old-fashioned atmosphere.

During the French Revolution, *troglodytes* – Swiss-cheese-like caves hollowed in the chalky buffs which dominate the riverbanks around Saumur – provided a refuge for 75% of the populations of Angers and Saumur.

Information

Tourist Offices Saumur tourist office (☎ 02 41 40 20 60, fax 02 41 40 20 69, @ off.tourisme.saumur@interliger.fr), near the chateau on place de la Bilange, opens 9.15 am to 7 pm Monday to Saturday, and

THE LOIRE

10.30 am to 12.30 pm and 3.30 to 6.30 pm on Sunday. Its Web site is at www.saumur-tourisme.com.

In Doué-la-Fontane, the tourist office (☎ 02 41 59 20 49, fax 02 41 59 93 85, ☎ tourisme@ville-douelafontaine.fr) is on the central square at 30 place du Champ de Foire.

Saumur

The historic heart of Saumur, on the southern bank of the River Loire, is dominated by **Château de Saumur** (☎ 02 41 40 24 40), built under Louis XI from 1246. It houses two museums, dedicated to horses and decorative arts, today.

The **École Nationale d'Équitation** (National Equestrian School; ☎ 02 41 53 50 60, ☎ enecadrenoir@symphonie-fai.fr), 3km west of the town centre in St-Hilaire-St-Florent, trains instructors and riders at competition level, prepares teams for the Olympic Games and is home to the elite Cadre Noir (see the boxed text 'Cadre Noir' below). The school sports Europe's largest indoor riding arena. Guided tours (25FF or 35FF, one to 1½ hours) depart at 9.30 am Tuesday to Saturday, and between 2 and 4 pm on weekdays, April to September.

Surrounding **mushroom farms** recycle the 10 tonnes of droppings, dumped daily by the 400 horses at the school. The **Musée du Champignon** (Mushroom Museum; ☎ 02 41 50 31 55), tucked in a cave in St-Hilaire-St-Florent, is a living example of the area's thriving button mushroom industry which occupies 800km of Saumurois caves and accounts for 65% of national production.

West of Saumur

Caves riddle this stretch, dubbed 'Troglodyte Valley'. **St-George des Sept Voies**, 23km west of Saumur, is home to the **Hélice Terrestre de l'Orbière**, a startling piece of monumental art, sculpted underground by local artist Jacques Warminski (1946–96). The screw-shaped subterranean gallery, duplicated in reverse above ground, can be explored on foot from 11 am to 8 pm, May to September; and 2 to 6 pm, the rest of the year. Admission costs 25FF.

In **Gennes**, 8km south-east, there's a **Gallo-Roman amphitheatre** which hosts lively (bloodless) re-enactments of the bloody spectacles once staged by the Romans in summer. From here, the **scenic D69** cuts southwards through the green **Forêt de le Chêne-Rond** to **Doué-la-Fontaine** (population 7200), an ideal base for exploring troglodyte valley. In the town zoo (☎ 02 41 59 18 58), off route de Cholet (D960), giraffes hang out in former falun pits and crocodiles bathe in water pools inside clammy caves. Other troglodytic sites here include **Les Perrières** where falun rock was quarried in the 18th century; and the **Cave aux Sarcophages** (☎ 02 41 59 24 95) at

---

Cadre Noir

Three moves set the Cadre Noir apart from its equestrian counterparts in Vienna: the *croupade*, which requires the horse to stretch its hind legs 45° into the air while its front legs stay on the ground; the *courbette*, which sees its front legs raised and tucked firmly into its body; and the demanding *cabriole*, which elevates the horse into the air in a powerful four-legged leap. These acrobatic feats, far from being crude or cruel, are considered the height of grace, elegance and Classicism. They are achieved after 5½ years of training which starts when a horse is three years old. Daily training sessions last 1½ hours, following which the horse is untacked, washed down, dried, and boxed for the remaining 22 hours of the day.

A black cap and jacket, gold spurs and three golden wings on the rider's whip are the distinctive trademarks of an elite, Cadre Noir rider. The lone female in today's otherwise exclusively-male Cadre Noir – traditionally made up of 24 members – is the third woman to have been awarded this status; the first woman was accepted in 1984.

---

1 rue Croix Mordret, an ancient Merovingian mine where 35,000-odd Monolithic sarcophagi were manufactured from the 6th to 9th centuries. The abandoned troglodytic village of **Rouchemenier**, 6km north of Doué via the D761, is also open to visitors.

East of Saumur
Saumur's eastern troglodyte valley is dominated by underground wine cellars. Fruity Saumur-Champigny red wine, the most respected Saumurois appellation, can be sampled at various cave cellars in **Souzay-Champigny**, 6km east of Saumur.

In **Val Hulin**, 3km farther east along the riverside D947, the subterranean **Musée de la Pomme Tapée** (Museum of Tapped Apples; ☎ 02 41 51 48 30) demonstrates how apples were dried, squashed and rehydrated with spiced mulled wine in the 19th century. Button mushrooms are the gastronomic speciality of the **Cave à Champignons** in **Le Saut aux Loups**, a few kilometres farther east.

The neighbouring medieval villages of **Montsoreau** (population 560) and **Candes-sur-Martin** (population 240) are a harmonious blend of mellow-hued rooftops, snug on the confluence of the Rivers Loire and Vienne.

The breathtaking, 12th-century Romanesque **Abbaye de Fontevraud** (☎ 02 41 51 71 41), 4km south of Montsoreau, forms the largest monastic ensemble in France and, until it closed in 1793, was unique in that its nuns and monks were governed by a woman: the abbess. It consequently became one of France's harshest prisons (1804–1963).

Places to Stay & Eat
In Saumur, *Camping Caravaning l'Île d'Offard* (☎ 02 41 40 30 00, fax 02 41 67 *37 81, rue de Verden*) charges 37/46FF to pitch a tent in the low/high season, plus 22.50/26FF per adult and 11.50/13.50FF per child. The adjoining *Centre International de Séjour l'Île d'Offard* has hostel beds in two/four/eight-bedded rooms with shower for 106/106/82.50FF per person, including breakfast. It has mountain bikes to rent (70FF per day) and opens mid-January to mid-December.

A particularly memorable, more upmarket choice is *Prieuré St-Lazare* (☎ 02 41 51 73 16, fax 02 41 51 75 50, ⓔ abbaye-fontevraud.prieure@wanadoo.fr), a converted priory in the grounds of Abbaye de Fontevraud. Singles/doubles cost 310/440FF.

Eating spots worth a nibble include *Le Caveau* (☎ 02 41 59 98 28, fax 02 41 59 85 79, 4 bis place du Champ de Foire), a highly atmospheric cave restaurant in Doué-la-Fontaine which offers a 110FF *menu* of regional fare and includes as much red Anjou wine as you can drink. *Auberge de la Route d'Or* (☎ 02 41 95 81 10, 2 place de l'Église), in Candes-sur-Martin, has a roaring fire in winter, terrace in summer and delicious 85FF (lunch), 120FF and 150FF *menus*.

Getting There & Away
From Angers, Anjou Bus (☎ 02 41 88 59) operates regular daily buses to/from Saumur (1¼ to 1½ hours) and Doué-la-Fontaine (13FF, 55 minutes, about six daily). From Saumur, there are daily buses to/from Doué-la-Fontaine (30 minutes, eight to 10 daily) and Fontevraud (13.50FF, 25 minutes, three daily).

Saumur is on the rail line between Tours (56FF, 30 to 50 minutes) and Angers (42FF, 30 minutes) with regular trains – at least hourly – in both directions.

THE LOIRE

Burgundy

The dukedom of Burgundy (Bourgogne), situated on the great trade route between the Mediterranean and northern Europe, waxed wealthier and more powerful than the Kingdom of France during the 14th and 15th centuries. It was also larger, and at its height counted Holland, Flanders, Luxembourg and much of what is now Belgium and far northern France (Picardy, Artois) among its noncontiguous territories. Some of the finest musicians, artists and architects from these lands were brought to the Burgundian capital, Dijon, where their artistic legacy still graces the city. Six centuries ago, it seemed that France might one day find itself absorbed into Burgundy (it was the Burgundians who took Joan of Arc prisoner before selling her to the English), but in the end Burgundy became part of France, in 1477.

These days, Burgundy is renowned for its superb wines, excellent gastronomy and rich architectural heritage, including a large number of medieval and Renaissance-era homes, churches (many topped by colourful tile roofs) and monasteries. In the Middle Ages, most of the latter belonged to one of two Burgundy-based orders: the ascetic Cistercians headquartered at Cîteaux, or their bitter rivals, the powerful and wealthy Benedictines, based at Cluny.

Activities

Burgundy has hundreds of kilometres of walking and cycling trails, including sections of the GR2, GR7 and GR76. A number of these trails take you through some of France's most beautiful wine-growing areas.

The Comité Régional de Tourisme de Bourgogne (Regional Tourism Board; ☎ 03 80 50 90 00, fax 03 80 30 59 45), whose mailing address is BP 1602, 21035 Dijon CEDEX, publishes some excellent English-language brochures on outdoor activities of all sorts, including canal boating. They are available at many area tourist offices and the Web site at www.burgundy-tourism.com.

Highlights

- **Dijon** – wander among the city's medieval and Renaissance churches and townhouses
- **Beaune** – visit the spectacular Hôtel-Dieu des Hospices de Beaune and sample fine wines
- **Autun** – admire the Roman gates and other ancient sites
- **Noyers-sur-Serein** – ramble around this tiny walled village
- **Canals** – cruise peacefully along one of Burgundy's many waterways in a canal boat

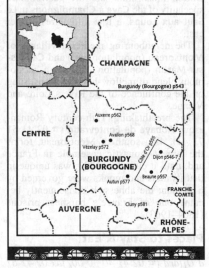

Hot-Air Ballooning From April to October (and perhaps through mid-November), you can take a *montgolfière* (hot-air balloon) ride over Burgundy for 1300FF per person (50% off for children aged under 12, 650FF). Two of the best-known companies are Air Escargot (☎ 03 85 87 12 30, fax 03 85 87 08 84, ✆ air-escargot@wanadoo.fr),

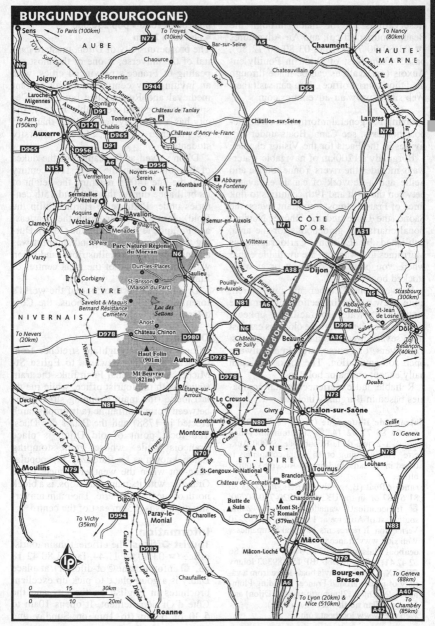

BURGUNDY (BOURGOGNE)

To Paris (100km)
Sens
TGV Sud-Est
N6
Joigny
Laroche-
Migennes
Canal
To Paris
(150km)
Auxerre
D965
D124
D965
N151
D956
A6
N77
St-Florentin
Pontigny
D91
Chablis
D956
D91
Tonnerre
Tonnerrois
Vermenton
Noyers-sur-
Serein
Y O N N E
To Troyes
(10km)
Chaource
Château de Tanlay
Château d'Ancy-le-Franc
D944
Bar-sur-Seine
A5
Chateauvillain
Châtillon-sur-Seine
Montbard
Abbaye
de Fontenay
Chaumont
HAUTE-
MARNE
Langres
N74
D65
D6
Canal de la Marne à la Saône

Sermizelles
Vézelay
Asquins
Vézelay
Clamecy
St-Père
Pontaubert
Avallon
Magny
Menades
Semur-en-Auxois
Vitteaux
C Ô T E
D ' O R
N71
A31
Varzy
Corbigny
N I È V R E
Parc Naturel Régional
du Morvan
Dun-les-Places
St-Brisson
(Maison du Parc)
Anost
Saulieu
Pouilly-
en-Auxois
N81
A6
Canal de Bourgogne
A38
Dijon
To
Strasbourg
(300km)
N5
N I V E R N A I S
Savelot & Maquis
Bernard Résistance
Cemetery
Lac des
Settons
Abbaye de
Cîteaux
St-Jean
de-Losne
Saône
To Nevers
(20km)
D978
Château Chinon
D980
N6
Château
de Sully
Beaune
D996
A36
Dôle
To
Besançon
(40km)
Haut Folin
(901m)
Mt Beuvray
(821m)
Autun
D973
Chagny
N73
Doubs
Decize
N81
Etang-sur-
Arroux
D978
Luzy
Le Creusot
Givry
Chalon-sur-Saône
Seille
To Geneva
Montchanin
N80
Le Creusot
Montceau
Centre
S A Ô N E -
E T - L O I R E
N78
Loûhans
Moulins
N79
Digoin
St-Gengoux-le-National
Château de Cormatin
Brancion
Chardonnay
Tournus
Butte de
Suin
Cluny
Mont St-
Romain
(579m)
TGV Sud-Est
N83
To Vichy
(35km)
D994
Paray-le-
Monial
Charolles
D982
Mâcon
Mâcon-Loché
N79
To Geneva
(88km)
Chaufailles
A6
To Lyon (20km) &
Nice (510km)
Bourg-en-
Bresse
A40
To
Chambéry
(85km)
A42
Roanne

See Côte d'Or Map PS55

Canal Latéral à la Loire
Loire
Canal de Roanne à Digoin
Loire
Arroux
Nivernais

0   15   30km
0   10   20mi

euro currency converter €1 = 6.56FF

based 16km south of Beaune in Remigny (reservations can be made through the Beaune tourist office); and Air Adventures (☎ 03 80 90 74 23, fax 03 80 90 72 86), based 43km west of Dijon in Pouilly-en-Auxois (reservations can be made through the Dijon tourist office). You can visit their Web site at www.air-adventures.com.

Boating For general information on houseboat holidays, see Canal Boats under Activities in the Facts for the Visitor chapter.

Burgundy's 1200km of navigable waterways includes the rivers Yonne, Saône and Seille and a network of canals excavated between the 17th and 19th centuries to link three of France's most important rivers: the Saône, the Loire and the Rhône. Navigational charts and guidebooks for the area, published by Éditions Cartographiques Maritimes and Vagnon, are available either where you pick up your boat or at well-stocked bookshops.

Between mid-October and mid-March, quite a few canals (or sections of them) are emptied of water to facilitate upkeep. Known as *chômages*, these closures can last from several weeks to a couple of months. The rivers, of course, are almost always open for navigation. The locks are open daily except on major holidays.

Reliable and experienced rental companies based in Burgundy include:

Bateaux de Bourgogne (☎ 03 86 72 92 10, fax 03 86 72 92 14, @ sla@tourismeyonne .com), 1-2 quai de la République, 89000 Auxerre. This grouping of 16 rental companies is based in the same building as Auxerre's tourist office.

France Afloat (Burgundy Cruisers, ☎/fax 03 86 81 67 87 or, in the UK, ☎/fax 020-7704 0700, @ france.afloat@wanadoo.fr), based 23km south-east of Auxerre at 1 quai du Port, 89270 Vermenton. It represents 11 rental companies. Web site: www.franceafloat.com

Locaboat Plaisance (☎ 03 86 91 72 72, fax 03 86 62 42 41) at Port au Bois, BP 150, 89303 Joigny CEDEX. This company's boats leave from a variety of places around France, including Plombières-lès-Dijon (7km north-west of Dijon) and Joigny (27km north-west of Auxerre). Web site: www.locaboat.com

DIJON
postcode 21000 • pop 230,000
• elevation 245m

The prosperous city of Dijon, mustard capital of the universe, is one of the most appealing of France's provincial cities, with an inviting city centre graced by elegant medieval and Renaissance buildings. Despite its long and venerable history, the city has a distinctly youthful air, thanks to the presence of some 24,000 university students.

Dijon served as the capital of the dukes of Burgundy from the early 11th century until the late 1400s, reaching the height of its brilliance during the 14th and 15th centuries under Philippe le Hardi (Philip the Bold), Jean sans Peur (John the Fearless) and Philippe le Bon (Philip the Good). During their reigns, the Burgundian court was among Europe's most illustrious, and Dijon was turned into one of the great centres of European art.

Dijon is just north of one of the world's foremost wine-growing regions, the Côte d'Or.

Orientation

Dijon's main thoroughfare stretches from the train station eastwards to Église St-Michel: ave Maréchal Foch links the train station with the tourist office, while rue de la Liberté (the main shopping street) runs between Porte Guillaume (a triumphal arch erected in 1788) and the Palais des Ducs. The focal point of old Dijon is place François Rude, whose grape-stomping statue, known as Le Bareuzay, is a popular hang-out when the weather is nice. Place Grangier, with its many bus stops, is a block north of rue de la Liberté. The main university campus is 2.3km east of the centre.

Information

Tourist Offices The efficient main tourist office (☎ 03 80 44 11 44, fax 03 80 42 18 83, @ infotourisme@ot-dijon.fr) at place Darcy is a good place to pick up excellent brochures in English on the city and the Côte d'Or département. It opens 10am to 5.30 or 6 pm (to 1pm on Sunday and holidays) from mid-October to April, and 9am to 8pm daily for the rest of the year. Hotel reservations in the Dijon area cost 15FF plus a 10% deposit. The Web site is at www.ot-dijon.fr.

The tourist office annexe, 34 rue des Forges, occupies the magnificent Hôtel Chambellan. It opens 10 am to noon and 2 to 5 pm weekdays (except holidays), mid-October to April; and 10 am to 1 pm and 2 to 6 pm, Monday to Saturday, the rest of the year.

La Clé de la Ville combination ticket (45FF) is a really great deal, gaining you access to all of Dijon's museums and to one of the tourist office's tours.

Money The Banque de France, 2 place de la Banque, changes money on weekdays from 8.45 to 11.45 am. Commercial banks can be found at place Darcy (near the tourist office), along rue de la Liberté and around place du Théâtre. The tourist office will change money – at poor rates – whenever it's open.

Post & Communications The main post office, at place Grangier, opens 8 am to 7 pm weekdays and to noon on Saturday. Exchange services and a Cyberposte are available.

Laundry The laundrettes at 41 rue Auguste Comte, 28 rue Berbisey, 55 rue Berbisey and 8 place de la Banque open until 8.30 or 9 pm daily.

Medical Services The Hôpital Général (☎ 03 80 29 30 31 for the 24-hour switchboard) is at 3 rue du Faubourg Raines.

Emergency The Hôtel de Police (police station; ☎ 03 80 44 55 00), 2 place Suquet, opens 24 hours (use the side entrance on rue du Petit Cîteaux from 6 pm to 7.30 am).

Medieval & Renaissance Architecture
The **Palais des Ducs et des États de Bourgogne** (Palace of the Dukes and States General of Burgundy), remodelled in the neoclassical style in the 17th and 18th centuries, was once the home of the powerful dukes of Burgundy. The 46m-high, 15th-century **Tour Philippe le Bon** (Tower of Philip the Good) affords great views of the city but, as of this writing, is closed to the public as part of a national anti-terrorism campaign. Tickets, when available, are sold at the municipal Accueil-Information office (☎ 03 80 74 52 71) in the Cour d'Honneur, open until 5.30 or 6 pm daily.

Most of the complex's western section is occupied by Dijon's city hall. The eastern wing, completed in 1852, houses the Musée des Beaux-Arts (see Museums), whose entrance is next to the **Tour de Bar**, a squat, four-storey tower built by Philip the Bold in the 1360s.

The palace faces the semicircular **place de la Libération**, a gracious, arcaded public square laid out by Jules Hardouin Mansart (one of the architects of Versailles) in 1686.

Some of Dijon's finest medieval and Renaissance *hôtels particuliers* (aristocratic townhouses) are just north of the Palais des Ducs on **rue Verrerie** and **rue des Forges** (check out Nos 38, 40 and 50), Dijon's main street until the 18th century. The splendid, Flamboyant Gothic style **Hôtel Chambellan** (1490), 34 rue des Forges, is now home to the tourist office annexe. There's a remarkable bit of vaulting at the top of the spiral stone staircase. Nearby **rue de la Chouette** is named for the small, stone *chouette* (owl) – said to grant happiness and wisdom to passers-by who stroke it – carved into the corner of one of the chapels on the northern side of the Église Notre Dame (see Churches). The **Hôtel de Vogüé** (1614), 8 rue de la Chouette, is known for its ornate Renaissance-style courtyard. The **Maison des Cariatides**, 28 rue Chaudronnerie, built in the early 17th century, has a facade decorated with stone caryatids and faces.

Churches
Dijon's major churches are open until a bit after sundown (until about 8 pm in summer) daily.

One block north of the Palais des Ducs, the **Église Notre Dame** was built in the

DIJON

PLACES TO STAY
5 Hôtel Clarine
6 Hôtel Châteaubriand
21 Hôtel République
24 Hôtel du Lycée
40 Hôtel Le Chambellan

45 Hôtel Confort
54 Hostellerie du Chapeau
    Rouge
58 Hôtel Monge
59 Hôtel Le Sauvage
71 Hôtel Philippe le Bon

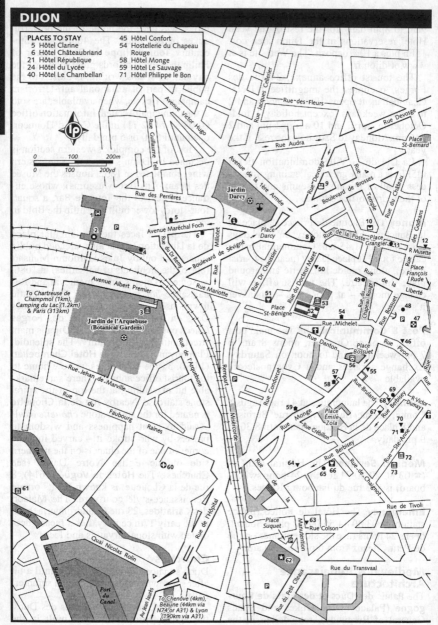

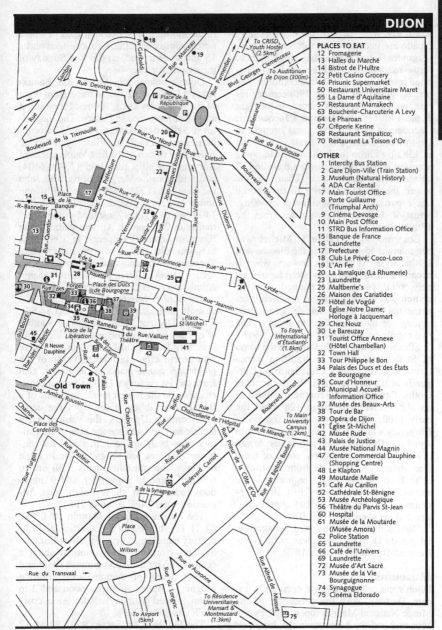

DIJON

PLACES TO EAT
12 Fromagerie
13 Halles du Marché
14 Bistrot de l'Huître
22 Petit Casino Grocery
46 Prisunic Supermarket
50 Restaurant Universitaire Maret
55 La Dame d'Aquitaine
57 Restaurant Marrakech
63 Boucherie-Charcuterie A Levy
64 Le Pharoan
67 Crêperie Kerine
68 Restaurant Simpatico;
70 Restaurant La Toison d'Or

OTHER
1 Intercity Bus Station
2 Gare Dijon-Ville (Train Station)
3 Muséum (Natural History)
4 ADA Car Rental
7 Main Tourist Office
8 Porte Guillaume (Triumphal Arch)
9 Cinéma Devosge
10 Main Post Office
11 STRD Bus Information Office
15 Banque de France
16 Laundrette
17 Prefecture
18 Club Le Privé; Coco-Loco
19 L'An Fer
20 La Jamaïque (La Rhumerie)
23 Laundrette
25 Maltberrie's
26 Maison des Cariatides
27 Hôtel de Vogüé
28 Église Notre Dame; Horloge à Jacquemart
29 Chez Nouz
30 Le Bareuzay
31 Tourist Office Annexe (Hôtel Chambellan)
32 Town Hall
33 Tour Philippe le Bon
34 Palais des Ducs et des États de Bourgogne
35 Cour d'Honneur
36 Municipal Accueil-Information Office
37 Musée des Beaux-Arts
38 Tour de Bar
39 Opéra de Dijon
41 Église St-Michel
42 Musée Rude
43 Palais de Justice
44 Musée National Magnin
47 Centre Commercial Dauphine (Shopping Centre)
48 Le Klapton
49 Moutarde Maille
51 Café Au Carillon
52 Cathédrale St-Bénigne
53 Musée Archéologique
56 Théâtre du Parvis St-Jean
60 Hospital
61 Musée de la Moutarde (Musée Amora)
62 Police Station
65 Laundrette
66 Café de l'Univers
69 Laundrette
72 Musée d'Art Sacré
73 Musée de la Vie Bourguignonne
74 Synagogue
75 Cinéma Eldorado

euro currency converter €1 = 6.56FF

Burgundian Gothic style between 1220 and 1240. The three tiers of the extraordinary facade are decorated with dozens of false gargoyles (false because they aren't there to throw rainwater clear of the building) separated by two rows of tall, thin columns. The present gargoyles are late 19th-century replacements. On top of the facade to the right is the 14th-century **Horloge à Jacquemart** (Jacquemart Clock), which was brought to Dijon from Kortrijk (Courtrai) in Flanders in 1382 by Philip the Bold, who had come across it while putting down a rebellion. It chimes every quarter hour. Thanks to the tower, the graceful interior of the church has a particularly high transept crossing. Some of the stained glass dates from the 13th century.

Construction of **Église St-Michel** was begun in the 15th century in the Flamboyant Gothic style. By the 16th century, when it became time to build the western facade, architectural tastes had changed and the church was given an impressive, richly ornamented Renaissance facade, considered among the most beautiful in France. The two cupola-topped towers date from 1667.

Situated on top of what may be the tomb of St-Benignus (who by tradition is believed to have brought Christianity to Burgundy in the 2nd century), the Burgundian Gothic **Cathédrale St-Bénigne** was built as an abbey church between 1280 and the early 1300s. Many of the great figures of Burgundy's history are buried inside. From April to October, the enormous **organ** (1743) is used for concerts, some of them free (details are available from the tourist office). To the right of the high altar is the entrance to the large **crypt** (7FF), all that remains of a Romanesque abbey church constructed between 1001 and 1026.

Dijon's domed and turreted **Synagogue**, on rue de la Synagogue, was built in the Romano-Byzantine style in 1879.

Museums

Dijon's major museums are open daily except Tuesday, with the exception of the Musée National Magnin (open daily except Monday) and the Museum in the Jardin de l'Arquebuse (open daily except Tuesday and in the morning at weekends). Except where noted, admission is free for those aged under 18 and students and, on the first Sunday of the month, for everyone.

Dijon's outstanding **Musée des Beaux-Arts** (☎ 03 80 74 52 70), in the eastern wing of the Palais des Ducs, is one of the richest and most renowned in France. The magnificent **Salle des Gardes** (Guards' Room) houses the extraordinary Flamboyant Gothic sepulchres of two of the first Valois dukes of Burgundy: Philip the Bold (1342–1404) and, with his wife Margaret of Bavaria, John the Fearless (1371–1419). The tombs and some amazing gilded altarpieces (circa 1400) were originally installed in the Chartreuse de Champmol. A room dedicated to Egyptian antiquities opened in 1999. The museum opens 10 am to 6 pm daily except Tuesday; the modern and contemporary art section closes between 11.30 am to 1.45 pm. Admission costs 22FF (seniors 10FF).

The superb **Musée Archéologique** (Archaeological Museum; ☎ 03 80 30 88 54), 5 rue du Docteur Maret, displays a number of extremely rare Celtic artefacts, including jewellery from 950 BC, 1st-century votive figures and a bronze representation of the goddess Sequana standing on a boat, also from the 1st century AD. The Romanesque chamber on the lowest level, once part of a Benedictine abbey, dates from the early 11th century. Upstairs, the vaulted early Gothic hall, at one time the abbey's dormitory, was built in the 12th and 13th centuries. Except on Tuesday and some holidays, the museum opens 9.30 am to 6.30 pm, June to September, and 9 am to noon and 2 to 6 pm, the rest of the year. Admission costs 14FF (seniors 7FF).

The **Musée National Magnin** (☎ 03 80 67 11 10), housed in a magnificent, 17th-century mansion at 4 rue des Bons Enfants, displays works of art assembled about a century ago by the magnanimous sister and brother team of Jeanne and Maurice Magnin. It opens 10 am to noon and 2 to 6 pm (closed Monday). Admission costs 16FF (students 12FF).

The **Musée d'Art Sacré** (☎ 03 80 44 12

69) at 15 rue Ste-Anne, housed in the copper-domed rotunda and chapels of a neoclassical church (1709), displays ecclesiastical objects from the 12th to 19th centuries. Almost next door at 17 rue Ste-Anne, the period rooms of the **Musée de la Vie Bourguignonne** (☎ 03 80 44 12 69) – installed in a 17th-century Cistercian convent – illustrate how the rural people of Burgundy lived in centuries past. A detailed brochure in English can be borrowed at the ticket counter. The opening hours for both museums are 9 am to noon and 2 to 6 pm (closed Tuesday); admission to both costs 18FF (seniors 10FF).

The small **Musée Rude** (☎ 03 80 66 87 95), in a desanctified church on rue Vaillant, displays works (and copies of works) by the Dijon-born sculptor François Rude (1784–1855), creator of the *Marseillaise* panel on the Arc de Triomphe in Paris. It opens 10 am to noon and 2 to 5.45 pm (closed Tuesday), June to September (free admission).

In the north-eastern corner of **Jardin de l'Arquebuse**, Dijon's delightful botanical gardens, is the **Muséum** (☎ 03 80 76 82 76) on ave Albert Premier, which features natural history. It opens 9 am to noon and 2 to 6 pm (closed in the morning on Saturday, Sunday and Tuesday). Admission costs 14FF (seniors 7FF). Nearby, you'll find a stream, a pond and a formal garden with hundreds of plants – some of them aquatic – labelled in botanical Latin. Along the park's southern edge, children frolic in two **playgrounds**, and locals match their skills and wits in games of boules.

A must for the mustard fan: tours (in French and English) of the **Musée de la Moutarde** (Mustard Museum), 48 quai Nicolas Rolin, also known as the Musée Amora. They take place on Wednesday and Saturday at 3 pm (Monday to Saturday at 3 pm from mid-June to mid-September). Admission costs 15FF (children aged under 12, free); tickets can be picked up at the tourist office.

Chartreuse de Champmol

This one-time *chartreuse* (charterhouse, ie, Carthusian monastery), founded in 1383,

was almost completely destroyed during the Revolution. The famous **Puits de Moïse** (Well of Moses; 1395–1405), a hexagonal grouping of six Old Testament figures by Claus Sluter, may finally be open to the public after years of restoration work. Nearby is another Sluter work, the **Portail de la Chapelle** (Chapel Doorway). Although the site, 1.2km west of the train station at 1 blvd Chanoine Kir, is now occupied by a psychiatric hospital, it can be visited all day, every day. To get there, follow the directions to Camping du Lac (see Places to Stay).

Organised Tours

The tourist office's two-hour Visite Audioguidée (Walkman tour; 39FF) of the city is very informative.

In July and August daily at 10 pm, the tourist office runs bilingual French and English tours of Dijon's floodlit monuments. These cost 40FF/70FF for adults/couples (students and seniors 30FF), and are free for kids aged under 12. The many other walking tours on offer are mostly in French.

The tourist office's Circuits des Châteaux bus tours, which take you to the region's chateaux, churches and abbeys, are held almost every Sunday from late June to mid or late September; destinations change each week. Commentary is in French. The tours cost 220/260FF for a half/whole day, not including the optional meal. The tourist office also offers two- or three-day themed tours around Burgundy (starting at 450FF).

Wine & Voyages (☎ 03 80 61 15 15, ✉ info@wineandvoyages.com) runs minibus tours in French and English, including two or three-hour circuits to the Côte de Nuits vineyards. Tours cost 270FF or 310FF and are held daily in both the morning and afternoon from mid-March to mid-December. Ticketing is handled by the tourist office. You can check out their Web site at www.wineandvoyages.com.

Special Events

Troupes come from around the world to participate in the Folkloriades Internationales et Fêtes de la Vigne, a week-long folkloric dance festival held each year in late August or early September. The Foire Internationale et Gastronomique, held at the Parc des Expositions during the first 12 days of November, gives visitors the chance to sample cuisines from Burgundy and around the world. From May to July, Dijon hosts L'Estivade, which brings a wide variety of cultural events (theatre, ballet, jazz, concerts) to town.

Places to Stay – Budget

Many of Dijon's smaller hotels are closed on Sunday afternoon.

Camping The two-star *Camping du Lac* (☎ 03 80 43 54 72, 3 blvd Chanoine Kir), open from April to mid-October, is 1.4km west of the train station behind the psychiatric hospital. By bus, take No 12 (towards Fontaine d'Ouche) to the Hôpital des Chartreux stop; services stop at around 8 pm.

Hostels The *Foyer International d'Étudiants* (☎ 03 80 71 70 00, 6 rue Maréchal Leclerc), a student dorm 2.5km east of the centre, accepts travellers year-round if there's space, though rooms (90FF for a single) are *least* likely to be available from October to December. By bus, take No 4 (towards St-Apollinaire) to the Vélodrome stop; at night take line A to Billardon.

The institutional, 260-bed *Centre de Rencontres Internationales et de Séjour de Dijon (CRISD; ☎ 03 80 72 95 20, fax 03 80 70 00 61, 1 blvd Champollion)* is 2.5km north-east of the centre. In rooms for four/eight people, a bed costs 78/72FF, including breakfast (there's an 8FF surcharge for the first four nights if you don't have a student or hostelling card); a room for three costs 140FF, not including breakfast. Amenities include washing machines and, next door, a municipal swimming pool. Check-in is possible 24 hours. By bus, take No 5 (towards Épirey) from place Grangier; at night take line A to the Épirey Centre Commercial stop.

From May to September (and during the rest of the year if there's space), travellers can stay at the *Résidence Universitaire Mansart (☎ 03 80 68 27 68, 94 rue Mansart)*, a university dorm 2.2km southeast of the centre (Mansart can also be spelled Mansard). The *secrétariat* (reception) opens 9 am to noon and 1.30 to 4.30 pm weekdays; the rest of the time there's a concierge or night watchperson. New guests can register any time before 9 pm. If you have an ISIC card, the charge is 68.80FF per person; otherwise, it's 87.20FF. By bus, take No 9 (towards Campus) or line C to the Mansart stop. The nearby *Résidence Universitaire Montmuzard (☎ 03 80 39 68 01, 8 ave Alain Savary)*, behind the Faculté de Droit (Law Faculty), has the same hours, prices and conditions. To get there, take bus No 9 or line C to the RU Montmuzard stop.

Hotels The friendly and accommodating, 24-room *Hôtel Monge (☎ 03 80 30 55 41, fax 03 80 30 30 15, 20 rue Monge)* has doubles/quads costing from 135/240FF (210/340FF with shower and toilet). Some of the mattresses are very soft. Hall showers cost 15FF. Students with ID get a 5% discount (10% for a stay of four or more days). It may be possible to park in the tiny courtyard. You might also try the 14-room *Hôtel Confort (☎ 03 80 30 37 47, fax 03 80 30 03 43, 12 rue Jules Mercier)* which has plain doubles with shower starting at 180FF (210FF with toilet as well); an extra bed costs 70FF. To get there by car, drive slowly along the pedestrianised rue du Bourg to rue Neuve Dauphine. The nearest bus stop is Liberation, served by six lines, including Nos 9 and 12.

The two-star, 23-room *Hôtel Le Chambellan (☎ 03 80 67 12 67, fax 03 80 38 00 39, 92 rue Vannerie)* has antique-style doubles from 140FF (220FF with shower and toilet). Breakfast (35FF) can be taken in the 17th-century courtyard. The nearest bus stop is Théâtre Vaillant, served by line No 12. The slightly tattered, 16-room *Hôtel du Lycée (☎ 03 80 67 12 35, fax 03 80 63 84 69, 28 rue du Lycée)* has ordinary doubles starting at 120FF (150FF with shower, 175FF with toilet as well). For 240FF you get a room with shower and toilet for up to five people. Reception is closed on Sunday from noon to 5 pm. Free parking is available on rue Diderot north of rue du Lycée. The nearest bus stop is Théâtre Vaillant, served by line No 12.

Near the train station, the 25-room *Hôtel Châteaubriand* (☎ *03 80 41 42 18, fax 03 80 59 16 28, 3 ave Maréchal Foch)* has simple, functional doubles for 165FF to 182FF (206FF to 251FF with shower and toilet). The whole atmosphere here is reminiscent of the cheap dives of postwar Paris.

There's a cluster of cheap chain hotels including a *Formule 1* (☎ *03 80 52 08 52)*, *Fimotel* (☎ *03 80 51 70 70)* and *One Star Plus* (☎ *03 80 52 15 11)* – 4km south of Dijon in Chenôve, on rue de Longvic near the E Leclerc hypermarket. If you're driving from the city centre, follow the signs to Lyon via the A31. The area is linked to the train station by bus No 7.

Places to Stay – Mid-Range
The two-star, 21-room *Hôtel Le Sauvage (Hostellerie du Sauvage;* ☎ *03 80 41 31 21, fax 03 80 42 06 07, 64 rue Monge)* occupies an old *relais de poste* (relay posthouse), parts of which date from the 15th century. The quiet doubles, decorated with old fashioned furniture, start at 240FF and are good value.

The quiet, 22-room, two-star *Hôtel République* (☎ *03 80 73 36 76, fax 03 80 72 46 04, 3 rue du Nord)* has ordinary but fairly large doubles/triples/quins for 240/310/450FF (a bit less from January to March). Reception closes at 6 pm on Sunday (2 pm December to March). By bus, take line Nos 5, 6 or 7 to the République Rousseau stop.

Near the train station, the two- and three-star hotels along ave Maréchal Foch include the 45-room, two-star *Hôtel Clarine* (☎ *03 80 43 53 78, fax 03 80 42 84 17, 22 ave Maréchal Foch)*, whose enormous and very comfortable doubles/quads go for 315/420FF.

Places to Stay – Top End
The 29-room, three-star *Hôtel Philippe le Bon* (☎ *03 80 30 73 52, fax 03 80 30 95 51,*

❷ *hotel-philippe-le-bon@wanadoo.fr, 18 rue Ste-Anne)* has contemporary doubles starting at 452FF. Private parking is free. The four-star, 30-room *Hostellerie du Chapeau Rouge* (☎ *03 80 50 88 88, fax 03 80 50 88 89,* ❷ *chapeau.rouge@wanadoo.fr, 5 rue Michelet)* has been at this site since 1847. Most of the jacuzzi-equipped doubles, commodious but hardly stunning, cost from 750FF to 870FF.

Places to Eat
Many of Dijon's restaurants, including quite a few small places with reasonably priced *menus*, are clustered in three main areas: on and around rue Berbisey (southwest of the Palais des Ducs); along the streets facing the Halles du Marché, especially rue Bannelier and rue Quentin; and north of the city centre around place de la République.

Restaurants – French The restaurant attached to the *Hostellerie du Chapeau Rouge* (see Places to Stay) features a new generation of bolder, more creative French cuisine, made with top-quality products brought direct from family-run farms. The *menus* cost about 250FF. *La Dame d'Aquitaine* (☎ *03 80 30 45 65, 23 place Bossuet)* purveys Burgundian and southwestern French cuisine under the soaring arches of a 13th-century cellar. The *menus*, served to the accompaniment of classical music, cost from 138FF (including wine; lunch only) to 245FF. It is closed Monday at midday and Sunday. *La Toison d'Or* (☎ *03 80 30 73 52, 18 rue Ste-Anne)* serves up traditional Burgundian and French cuisine in a rustic medieval setting. Two/three-course *menus* cost 215/270FF (125/170FF for lunch). It opens noon to 1.30 pm and 7 to 9.30 pm (closed Sunday).

The restaurants facing the Halles du Marché include a number offering reasonably priced *menus*. Oysters (from 47FF to 70FF for six) and foie gras (95FF) are featured at *Bistrot de l'Huître* (☎ *03 80 30 00 30, 12 rue Bannelier)*. The 130FF *menu* includes both delicacies; wine costs from 10FF to 18FF a glass. Nearby at *Chez Nous* (see Pubs & Bars under Entertainment), the copious, Burgundian plat du jour, served from noon to 2.15 pm, costs 60FF.

Restaurants – Other Copious portions of excellent tajines and couscous (from 70FF to 115FF) are on offer at *Restaurant Marrakech* (☎ 03 80 30 82 69, 20 rue Monge). It opens noon to 2 pm and 7 to 11 pm (to midnight on Friday and Saturday; closed Monday for lunch). *Le Pharaon* (☎ 03 80 30 11 36, 116 rue Berbisey) is one of France's few Egyptian restaurants (Lebanese fare is also on offer). *Menus* cost 58FF (weekday lunch only), 70FF (vegetarian), 75FF, 90FF and 110FF (closed Sunday at midday and Monday).

The attractive, modern *Restaurant Simpatico* (☎ 03 80 30 53 33, 30 rue Berbisey) has reasonably priced Italian cuisine, but no pizza (closed on Monday at midday and Sunday). Breton crepes are the speciality of *Crêperie Kerine* (☎ 03 80 30 35 45, 36 rue Berbisey). There are *Brazilian and Tunisian places* on the same street at Nos 42 and 44.

University Restaurant The *Restaurant Universitaire Maret* (☎ 03 80 40 40 34, 3 rue du Docteur Maret) opens 11.40 am to 1.15 pm and 6.40 am to 8 pm weekdays and one weekend a month (closed during university holidays). Tickets (students 14.90FF) are on sale on the ground floor at lunchtime (weekdays only) and during dinner on Monday.

Self-Catering Parks perfect for picnics include the fountain-adorned Jardin Darcy (next to the tourist office), Jardin de l'Arquebuse, place des Ducs de Bourgogne (just north of the Palais des Ducs) and place St-Michel (next to Église St-Michel).

Until 1 pm on Tuesday, Thursday, Friday and Saturday, the 19th-century *Halles du Marché* (covered market) fills with food stalls. Nearby is a *fromagerie (28 rue Musette)*.

The upstairs *Prisunic* supermarket *(11–13 rue Piron)* opens 8.30am to 8 pm Monday to Saturday. North of the Palais des Ducs

there are a number of food shops along rue Jean-Jacques Rousseau, including a *Petit Casino* épicerie *(16 rue Jean-Jacques Rousseau)* that opens until 7.45 pm (closed 12.45 to 3.15 pm daily, on Sunday afternoon and on Monday morning).

Kosher items are available until 7.30 pm at *Boucherie-Charcuterie A Levy (25 rue de la Manutention)*, closed Friday evening and Saturday.

Entertainment

For details (in French) on Dijon's lively cultural scene, pick up a copy of *Dijon Nuit et Jour*, published every three months (except in summer), or the monthly *Dijon Culture*. Published by the municipality, both are free and available at the tourist office.

Renowned for its superb acoustics, the new *Auditorium de Dijon* (☎ 03 80 60 44 44, 11 blvd de Verdun), 600m north-east of place de la République, has opera, dance and concert performances from September to June. The auditorium's Web site is at www.auditorium-dijon.com.

Dijon's city centre club and bar scene is centred around place de la République, especially along its northern side. There are a number of convivial cafes on and around rue Berbisey.

Discos Converted, factory-style *L'An-Fer* (☎ 03 80 70 03 69, 8 rue Marceau) achieved fame for pioneering techno music, now presented on the spacious main floor on Friday and Saturday nights. Especially popular with the university crowd – there are student nights on Wednesday, Thursday and, sometimes, Tuesday – it becomes mainly gay on Sunday. It opens 11 pm to 5 am (closed on Monday and, from mid-July to mid-September, on Tuesday and Wednesday). Admission costs 50FF or 60FF from Friday to Sunday, 40FF the rest of the week (25FF without a drink). Things start to take off at around 1 am.

At *Le Klapton* (☎ 03 80 50 06 54) you can rest at the 18m-long guitar-shaped bar between sessions of dancing to everything from rock to disco to techno. The dance floor has two raised platforms for those who are exhibitionally minded. It opens 10 or 11 pm to 5 am (closed Sunday); things really get going at about 2 am (midnight on Friday and Saturday). Admission costs just 20FF. This place is inside the Centre Commercial Dauphine shopping centre – to get there go through the door above, and to the left of, the underground parking entrance next to 19 rue Bossuet.

The flashing lights, pulsating speakers and leopard-skin banquettes of *Club Le Privé* (☎ 03 80 73 39 57, 20 ave Garibaldi), attract people in the 25 to 45 age bracket as well as some students. It opens 10 or 11 pm to 5 am nightly, but things tend to be slow until midnight or 1 am. Admission costs 30FF, including a non-alcoholic drink or a beer (50FF including a cocktail). An older crowd waltzes and tangos on Sunday and Monday from 3 to 8.30 pm (30FF).

Pubs & Bars A popular bar that attracts legions of students, especially late at night from Thursday to Saturday, is the friendly *Coco-Loco* (☎ 03 80 73 29 44, 18 ave Garibaldi). The background music, some of it salsa, is loudly danceable, so don't come here to discuss Sartre. Attacks of the munchies can be quenched with tapas (30FF) and frites (15FF). It opens 6 pm to 2 am (closed Sunday and Monday).

For something completely different, *Chez Nous* (☎ 03 80 50 12 98, 8 Impasse Quentin) is a small, welcoming neighbourhood bar down the alley from 6 rue Quentin. It opens 10 am to 2 am (closed Sunday and Monday). Beer starts at 11FF. The informal *Café Au Carillon* (☎ 03 80 30 63 71, 2 rue Mariotte), popular with a younger crowd, opens 6.30 am to 2 am (closed on Sunday from about October to May).

La Jamaïque (☎ 03 80 73 52 19, 14 place de la République) – also known as La Rhumerie – is a large bar with Caribbean-inspired décor. On Thursday, Friday and Saturday nights, there's live music from about 10.30 pm to 2 am. It opens 3 pm to 4 am (closed Sunday). *Maltberrie's* (☎ 03 80 67 51 14, 70 rue Vannerie), a vaguely Irish-style pub, hosts a jam session each

Tuesday at 10.30 pm and live jazz one Tuesday or Wednesday a month. It opens until 2 am daily.

The mainly gay and lesbian cellar of *Café de l'Univers* (☎ 03 80 30 98 29, 47 rue Berbisey) has a small dance floor and opens 9 or 10 pm to 2 am nightly. This is a good place to pick up *RDV*, which lists gay-oriented venues in and around Dijon.

Cinema Non-dubbed films flicker nightly on the three screens of *Cinéma Eldorado* (☎ 03 80 66 51 89 or 03 80 66 12 34, 21 rue Alfred de Musset), an art cinema that's closed from mid-July to mid-August. *Cinéma Devosge* (☎ 03 80 30 74 79, 6 rue Devosge) almost always has at least one non-dubbed Hollywood film.

Shopping
Moutarde Maille (☎ 03 80 30 41 02) at 32 rue de la Liberté, the factory shop of the company that makes Grey Poupon, sells nothing but fancy mustard (from 10FF), balsamic vinegar and faïence mustard pots (from 135FF to 1700FF). It opens 9 am to noon and 2.15 to 7 pm (no lunchtime closure from April to October; closed Sunday).

Getting There & Away
Air Dijon-Bourgogne airport (☎ 03 80 67 67 67) is 6km south-east of the city centre.

Bus The intercity bus station is part of the train station complex. The Transco information counter (☎ 03 80 42 11 00) is staffed on weekdays from 7.30 am to 6.30 pm and on Saturday until 12.30 pm; the *chef de gare* (station master), in an office facing the departure platforms, will gladly answer questions on weekdays from 6.30 to 7 pm, on Saturday from 4.30 to 7 pm, and on Sunday from 11 am to 12.30 pm and 5 to 7.45 pm. Schedules are posted on the platforms.

Lines serving the Côte d'Or winemaking area include the No 44 to Beaune (40FF, one hour), which stops at lots of winemaking villages (see the Beaune section for details), and the No 60 to Gevrey-Chambertin (30 minutes, a dozen daily, two on Sunday and holidays) via Fixin and Marsannay-la-Côte (the latter is also served by Dijon city bus No 24). Other destinations include Autun (81.50FF, 2¼ hours, one daily), Ava-llon (92.40FF, two hours, three daily, one on Sunday) and Saulieu (line No 48, 1½ hours, one daily except Sunday and holidays).

Train The Dijon-Ville train station (☎ 0 836 35 35 35) was built to replace a structure destroyed in 1944. Getting to/from Paris' Gare de Lyon takes 1¾ hours by TGV (from 227FF to 275FF, nine to 16 daily) and 2¾ hours by non-TGV (192FF, five to seven daily). Trains to Lyon's Gare de la Part-Dieu and/or Gare de Perrache (1½ to two hours, 12 to 17 daily) cost 133FF (153FF by TGV). Non-TGV trains also serve Nice (380FF, eight hours, one direct daily) and Strasbourg (205FF, four hours). For details on services to Beaune (38FF), Autun (95FF via Étang), Auxerre (124FF), Avallon (92FF via Montbard) and Vézelay, see each town's section in this chapter.

Car At the eastern tip of the train station building you'll find the offices of the international rental companies as well as ADA (☎ 03 80 52 33 14, staffed on demand).

Getting Around
To/From the Airport Take local bus No 1 (towards Longvic) and get off at the Longvic Mairie stop, from where it's a 500m walk to the airport.

Bus Dijon's extensive urban bus network is operated by STRD (☎ 03 80 30 60 90). A Forfait Journée ticket, valid all day, costs 16FF. STRD's office at place Grangier, L'Espace Bus, opens 7.15 am to 7.15 pm (closed 12.15 to 2.15 pm on Saturday, and on Sunday).

Bus lines are known by their number and the name of the terminus station. In the city centre, seven different lines stop along rue de la Liberté, and five more have stops around place Grangier. Most lines operate until 8 or 8.30 pm; after that, until 12.15 am, the six lines of the Réseau du Soir (A, B, C,

D, E and F) run every 30 minutes or so. The train station (rue du Docteur Remy) is linked with the city centre (rue de la Liberté) by bus Nos 1, 9 and 12.

Car & Motorcycle All city centre parking is metered. Free spots are available (clockwise from the train station): north-west of rue Devosge, north-east of blvd Thiers, south-east of blvd Carnot and south of rue du Transvaal. There's a big free car park at place Suquet, just south of the police station.

Taxi To order a taxi 24 hours, call ☎ 03 80 41 41 12.

ABBAYE DE CÎTEAUX
It was largely due to St-Bernard of Clairvaux (1090–1153) that the Abbey of Cîteaux (Cistercium in Latin; ☎ 03 80 61 32 58), founded in 1098, became the headquarters of a vast monastic order, the Cistercians, who at their height had 600 abbeys stretching from Sweden to the Near East. In contrast with the showy Benedictines, whose sumptuous centre of power was at Cluny, the austere Cistercian order was known for its rigid discipline and humility. The requirement that monks engage in manual labour, part of the order's ascetic ethos, had a revolutionary impact on economic development in medieval Europe, largely because the abbeys' economic activity fell outside the purview of feudal rules and prerogatives.

Cîteaux was largely destroyed during and after the Revolution (the monks didn't return to the abbey until 1898) so there are few historic buildings to be seen. From mid-May to mid-October, you can visit part of the monastery compound on a 1½ hour guided tour (in French or German) described as 'more spiritual than architectural'; a 30 minute audiovisual presentation (possibly available in English) provides details on the life of the abbey's 35 modern-day monks. Tours (45FF; children and students 25FF) take place every half-hour from 10 to 11 am and 2.15 to 4.45 pm Tuesday to Saturday and from 12.30 to 4.45pm on Sunday and on holidays. Groups are limited to 25 people so calling ahead is recommended.

The rest of the year there's not much to do here except visit the very modern church and the giftshop, and walk around the serene fields outside the compound walls. The Pavillon d'Accueil (reception pavilion), next to the car park, has some explanatory signs in English. You can visit the Web site at www.citeaux-abbaye.com.

CÔTE D'OR

Burgundy's finest vintages come from the vine-carpeted Côte d'Or (Golden Hillside), the narrow, eastern slopes of a limestone, flint and clay escarpment that runs south from Dijon for about 60km. The northern section, the **Côte de Nuits**, stretches from the village of Fixin south to Corgoloin and produces reds known for their full-bodied, robust character. The southern section, the **Côte de Beaune**, lies between Aloxe-Corton and Santenay and produces both great reds and great whites.

The Côte d'Or's most outstanding wine-making villages include (going from north to south): Marsannay-la-Côte, Fixin, Brochon, Gevrey-Chambertin, Vougeot, Vosne-Romanée, Nuits St-Georges, Pernand Vergelesses, Aloxe-Corton and Savigny-lès-Beaune, all north of Beaune; and Pommard, Volnay, St-Romain, Auxey-Duresses, Meursault, Puligny-Montrachet, Rochepot and Santenay, all south of Beaune. Just hearing these names makes the œnophile salivate.... See Bus under Beaune for details on bus services.

A good source of information on the region's vines and vintages is *The Wines of Burgundy* (10th edition; 84FF) by Sylvain Pitiot & Jean-Charles Servant, published by Presses Universitaires de France and available in Beaune at the tourist office and the Athenaeum bookshop.

Wine-Tasting

The villages of the Côte d'Or offer innumerable opportunities to sample excellent wines and purchase them where (or very near) they've been grown and aged. Just

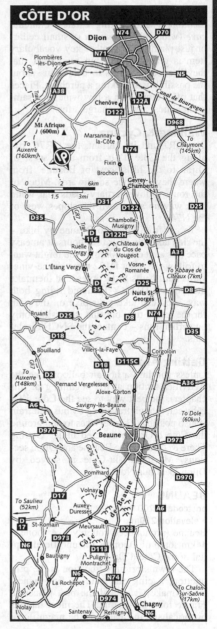

look for signs reading *dégustation* (tasting), *domaine* (wine-making estate), chateau, *cave* (wine cellar), *caveau* (a small cellar) or just plain *vins*. Another key vocabulary item is *gratuit* (free), but remember that they'll expect visitors to be serious about the possibility of making a purchase. Places that offer more than a few wines for sampling almost always charge a fee.

Walking & Cycling

The GR7 and its variant, the GR76, run along the Côte d'Or from a bit west of Dijon to the hills west of Beaune, from where they continue southwards. Much of the route follows tertiary roads that wend their way up and down the slopes west of the N74.

To get from Dijon to Beaune by bike – the ride takes three or four hours at an easy pace (it's a bit over 40km) – you might want to follow the quiet D122 through the vineyards until Nuits St-Georges, and then take the D8 and D115C. To avoid riding both ways, you can take your bike on the train for the return trip, but this is possible only on certain runs – contact the SNCF for details.

Getting Around

Unless you hire a hot-air balloon (see the Activities section at the beginning of this chapter), the best way to see the Côte d'Or is by car, though travelling by bus and train is also possible. Bus services to and around the Côte d'Or are covered under Getting There & Away in the Beaune and Dijon sections. Marsannay-la-Côte is served by Dijon local bus No 24.

BEAUNE

postcode 21200 • pop 22,000
• elevation 220m

Beaune (pronounced roughly like 'bone'), 44km south of Dijon, is the unofficial capital of the Côte d'Or.

The town's primary vocation is the production, ageing and sale of fine wines, which makes it one of the best places in France for wine-tasting. The most famous historical site in Beaune is the magnificent

Hôtel-Dieu, France's most fascinating medieval charity hospital.

Beaune makes an excellent day trip from Dijon. The best time to visit is in spring. The town is pretty dead from December to February.

Orientation

The amoeba-shaped old city, partly enclosed by ramparts and a stream, is encircled by a one-way boulevard with seven names. The tourist office and most of the town's sights are about 1km west of the train station. Rue Monge and rue Carnot are pedestrianised.

Information

Tourist Offices Beaune's tourist office (☎ 03 80 26 21 30, fax 03 80 26 21 39), rue de l'Hôtel-Dieu 1, opens 9 am (10 am in winter) to sometime between 6 pm (in winter) and 8 pm (from mid-June to late September, 7 pm on Sunday) daily. Staff can supply you with a free map and lists of wine cellars in Beaune and its environs. The Web site is at www.ot-beaune.fr.

Money The Banque de France, 26 place Monge, will change money on weekdays from 8.45 am to noon. There are several commercial banks nearby. The tourist office will change money on Saturday afternoon, Sunday (usually until 5 pm) and holidays (until at least 5 pm).

Post & Communications The post office at 7 blvd St-Jacques opens 8 am to 7 pm weekdays and 8 am to noon Saturday. Currency exchange and a Cyberposte are available.

Bookshops Athenaeum de la Vigne et du Vin (☎ 03 80 25 08 30) carries thousands of titles, including some in English, on *œnologie* (the art and science of wine-making), the Burgundy région and Burgundian cuisine. It opens 10 am to 7 pm daily.

Laundry The laundrette at 19 rue du Faubourg St-Jean opens 6.30 am to 9 pm daily.

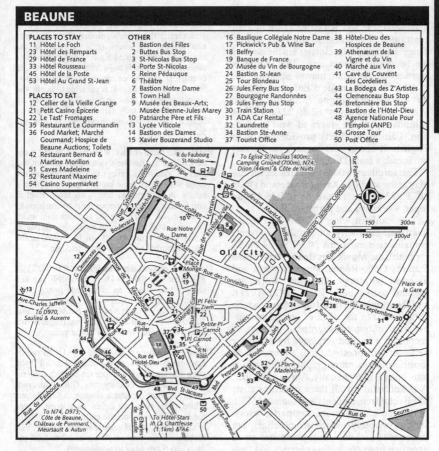

BEAUNE

PLACES TO STAY
11 Hôtel Le Foch
23 Hôtel des Remparts
29 Hôtel de France
33 Hôtel Rousseau
45 Hôtel de la Poste
53 Hôtel Au Grand St-Jean

PLACES TO EAT
12 Cellier de la Vieille Grange
21 Petit Casino Épicerie
22 'Le Tast' Fromages
35 Restaurant Le Gourmandin
36 Food Market; Marché Gourmand; Hospice de Beaune Auctions; Toilets
42 Restaurant Bernard & Martine Morillon
51 Caves Madeleine
52 Restaurant Maxime
54 Casino Supermarket

OTHER
1 Bastion des Filles
2 Buttes Bus Stop
3 St-Nicolas Bus Stop
4 Porte St-Nicolas
5 Reine Pédauque
6 Théâtre
7 Bastion Notre Dame
8 Town Hall
9 Musée des Beaux-Arts; Musée Étienne-Jules Marey
10 Patriarche Père et Fils
13 Lycée Viticole
14 Bastion des Dames
15 Xavier Bouzerand Studio

16 Basilique Collégiale Notre Dame
17 Pickwick's Pub & Wine Bar
18 Belfry
19 Banque de France
20 Musée du Vin de Bourgogne
24 Bastion St-Jean
25 Tour Blondeau
26 Jules Ferry Bus Stop
27 Bourgogne Randonnées
28 Jules Ferry Bus Stop
30 Train Station
32 ADA Car Rental
34 Bastion Ste-Anne
37 Tourist Office

38 Hôtel-Dieu des Hospices de Beaune
39 Athenæum de la Vigne et du Vin
40 Marché aux Vins
41 Cave du Couvent des Cordeliers
43 La Bodega des Z'Artistes
44 Clemenceau Bus Stop
46 Bretonnière Bus Stop
47 Bastion de l'Hôtel-Dieu
48 Agence Nationale Pour l'Emploi (ANPE)
49 Grosse Tour
50 Post Office

Things to See & Do

The celebrated **Hôtel-Dieu des Hospices de Beaune** (☎ 03 80 24 45 00), a charity hospital founded in 1443 by Nicolas Rolin (chancellor to Philip the Good) and his wife Guigone de Salins, is one of France's great architectural highlights. It is a Flemish-Burgundian Gothic-style structure, topped by a roof of multicoloured glazed tiles, and is home to the brilliant *Polyptych of the Last Judgement* (1443), which depicts a very literal interpretation of the Last Judgement: on the left, naked dead people climb out of their graves and are welcomed into heaven

(a golden cathedral), while on the right the terror-stricken damned are dragged into the fires of hell.

Hôtel-Dieu opens 9 am to 6.30 pm, from a week before Easter to mid-November; and 9 to 11.30 am and 2 to 5.30 pm, the rest of the year. Admission costs 32FF (students and children aged 10 to 17, 25FF). An excellent English-language brochure is available at the ticket window.

Basilique Collégiale Notre Dame, a collegiate church once affiliated with the Benedictine monastery at Cluny, was begun in 1120. The ambulatory, nave and apsidal chapels are all Burgundian-style Romanesque; the rest is Gothic (13th to 15th centuries). It opens 8.30 am to 6.45 pm. There's access to the cloister via the door of the southern transept arm. The church is surrounded by quaint, narrow streets.

A block away on rue d'Enfer, the **Musée du Vin de Bourgogne** (Museum of the Wines of Burgundy; ☎ 03 80 22 08 19) has exhibits on all the stages of wine production. Laminated sheets provide details in English. It opens 9.30 am to 6 pm (closed on Tuesday from December to March).

Extraordinary wood sculptures are on display at the studio of **Xavier Bouzerand** (☎ 03 80 21 23 00) at 12 ave de la République (open weekdays and perhaps Saturday).

The southern wing of the 17th-century town hall (formerly an Ursuline convent) contains two museums (☎ 03 80 24 56 98 for both): the **Musée des Beaux-Arts**, which features Gallo-Roman stone carvings and assorted paintings, including works by Beaune native Félix Ziem (1821–1911); and the **Musée Étienne-Jules Marey**, which is dedicated to the work of one of the pioneers of *chronophotographie* (the art of recording an action sequence by making a series of still photographs), a precursor of motion-picture photography. Both museums open 2 to 6 pm daily, April to October. A ticket valid for all three museums costs 25FF (children, students and seniors 15FF).

Beaune's thick stone **ramparts**, which shelter privately owned wine cellars, are surrounded by a wild, overgrown area given over in part to cultivating cherries and vegetables. The walls can easily be circumnavigated on foot.

Wine-Tasting

Under Beaune's buildings, streets and ramparts, millions of dusty bottles of wine are, at this very moment, being aged to perfection in cool, dark, cobweb-lined cellars. A number of places present an excellent opportunity to sample and compare different Burgundy wines.

Marché aux Vins (☎ 03 80 25 08 20), on rue Nicolas Rolin 30m south of the tourist office.

For 50FF, you get a *taste-vin* (a flat metal cup whose shiny convex and concave surfaces help you admire the wine's colour) with which you can sample 18 wines (mainly reds) in the candle-lit, barrel-lined Église des Cordeliers (a desanctified church built from the 13th to 15th centuries) and the cellars beneath it. The best reds are near the exit. It is possible to begin visits, which last at least an hour, 9.30 to 11.30 am and 2 to 6 pm daily (from late November to March the last visits begin at 11 am and 5.30 pm).

Patriarche Père et Fils (☎ 03 80 24 53 78), 6 rue du Collège. Patriarche's vast cellars are a lot like Paris' Catacombs except that the corridors are lined with dusty wine bottles instead of human bones. A self-guided tour with taped English commentary, and the opportunity to compare 13 wines, costs 50FF (free for accompanied under 18s who won't be sipping anything). One-hour visits begin from 10.30 am (9.30 am in the warm months) to 11 am and 2 to 5 pm.

Cave du Couvent des Cordeliers (☎ 03 80 25 08 85), 6 rue de l'Hôtel-Dieu. For 30FF you can sample two whites and four reds in the 13th-century cellar of a one-time convent. It opens 9.30 am to 7 pm, April to September; and 10.30 am to noon and 2 to 6 pm (slightly different on Sunday), the rest of the year.

Reine Pédauque (☎ 03 80 22 23 11), on rue de Lorraine next to Porte St-Nicolas. For 30FF you get a 45-minute guided tour (in English upon request) of an 18th-century cave, filled with crud-encrusted bottles, and a chance to sample one white, three reds and Belen, an apéritif. Given the thick cobwebs on the ceiling, you wouldn't want to be in here if gravity reversed itself. Visits begin from 9 to 11.30 am and 2 to 5.30 pm daily (to 6 pm May to September).

Lycée Viticole (☎ 03 80 26 35 81), 16 ave Charles Jaffelin, is one of 14 French secondary schools that train young people to plant and grow vines and ferment, age and bottle wine. From 8 am to noon and 2 to 5.30 pm (closed on Saturday afternoon and Sunday), you can visit the cellars as well as taste and purchase the excellent, relatively inexpensive wines made by the students as part of their studies; proceeds are reinvested in the school.

Organised Tours

From July to mid-September every day at noon, the tourist office runs English-language tours of the town (40/65FF for an individual/couple). The tourist office handles ticketing for year-round, two-hour minibus tours of the Côte (190FF) and for hot-air balloon rides.

Special Events

From late June to early August, the Festival International de Musique Baroque brings concerts and operas to the courtyard of the Hôtel-Dieu (Friday to Sunday at 9 pm). On the third Sunday in November in the covered market, the Hospices de Beaune auctions the wines from its endowment – 58 hectares of prime vineyards bequeathed by Rolin – to raise money for medical care and research.

Places to Stay

Beaune's hotels are often full in September and October, especially during the grape harvest. The tourist office can supply details on some accommodation options in nearby villages.

Camping The four-star *camping ground* (☎ 03 80 22 03 91, 10 rue Auguste Dubois), open from mid-March to October, charges 65FF for two adults with a tent. To get there from the town centre, go north on rue du Faubourg St-Nicolas for 1km and turn left at Église St-Nicolas.

Hotels – Budget The best deal in town is 12-room *Hôtel Rousseau* (☎ 03 80 22 13 59, 11 place Madeleine). Run by a friendly older woman, it has large, old-fashioned singles/doubles that cost from 140/185FF; a room for five costs 380FF. All prices include breakfast. Some of the rooms have a shower or toilet; the hall shower costs 20FF. Reception is sometimes closed for a couple of hours. Another good bet is nine-room *Hôtel Le Foch* (☎ 03 80 24 05 65, fax 03 80 24 75 59, 24 blvd Maréchal Foch), which has newly renovated doubles starting at 175FF (230FF with shower and toilet).

There are a half-a-dozen cheap chain hotels around rue Burgalat in La Chartreuse, an area a bit over 1km south of the old city near the Beaune exit of the A6 (the Paris-Lyon autoroute). These include the 38-room *Hôtel Stars* (☎ 03 80 22 53 17, fax 03 80 24 10 14, 8 rue André-Marie Ampère), where 175FF gets you a smallish double with pressboard walls, shower and toilet.

Hotels – Mid-Range & Top End The quiet, two-star, 22-room *Hôtel de France* (☎ 03 80 24 10 34, fax 03 80 24 96 78, 35 ave du 8 Septembre) has large, spotless doubles/quads starting at 275/460FF. The impersonal, 106-room, two-star *Hôtel Au Grand St-Jean* (☎ 03 80 24 12 22, fax 03 80 24 15 43, ✉ hotel.saint.jean@netclic.fr, 18 rue du Faubourg Madeleine) has garish hallways but decent doubles/quads costing from 235/295FF (closed from 20 November to 20 January). There are several other two- and three-star hotels nearby at place Madeleine.

The three-star *Hôtel des Remparts* (☎ 03 80 24 94 94, fax 03 80 24 97 08, ✉ hotel .des.remparts@wanadoo.fr, 48 rue Thiers), in a 17th-century mansion, has huge doubles, some with beam ceilings, from 290FF to 470FF, and quads from 570FF; prices may be a bit lower in winter. The luxurious, four-star *Hôtel de la Poste* (☎ 03 80 22 08 11, fax 03 80 24 19 71, ✉ françoise .stratigos@wanadoo.fr, 5 blvd Georges Clemenceau) has double rooms and suites ranging from 600FF to 1500FF.

Places to Eat

Restaurants A good choice for a splurge is the refined *Restaurant Bernard & Martine Morillon* (☎ 03 80 24 12 06, 31 rue Maufoux), which has traditional French *menus* costing from 180FF to 480FF (closed Monday, Tuesday at midday, and in January).

Caves Madeleine (☎ 03 80 22 93 30, 8 rue du Faubourg Madeleine) is a cosy wine bar that serves family-style Burgundian *menus* for 69FF and 115FF (closed on Thursday and Sunday). *Restaurant Maxime* (☎ 03 80 22 17 82, 3 place Madeleine) offers reasonably priced Burgundian cuisine in a rustic but elegant dining room; *menus* range from 76FF to 150FF (closed Sunday night, Monday and, except from June to September, on Thursday night).

There are a number of other restaurants nearby on rue du Faubourg Madeleine.

The intimate **Restaurant Le Gourmandin** (☎ 03 80 24 07 88, *8 place Carnot*), whose French and regional specialities include bœuf bourguignon (75FF), has *menus* for 120FF to 170FF (and 85FF for weekday lunches). It is closed on Wednesday and Thursday, except from April to September. There are a number of cafes and restaurants – many with warm-weather terraces – nearby, especially around place Carnot, Petite place Carnot and place Félix Ziem.

Self-Catering The covered market plays host to a *food market* on Saturday (until 12.30 or 1 pm) and a smaller *marché gourmand* (gourmet market) on Wednesday morning.

There's a cluster of *food shops* along the pedestrianised rue Monge (including a *Petit Casino* grocery at No 14) and rue Carnot. The nearest fromagerie is *Le Tast' Fromages* (*23 rue Carnot*).

The *Casino* supermarket (*28 rue du Faubourg Madeleine*) opens 8.30 am to 7.30 pm Monday to Saturday.

Wine is sold *en vrac* (in bulk) for as little as 6.70FF a litre, not including the container, at *Cellier de la Vieille Grange* (*27 blvd Georges Clemenceau*), which is closed Sunday afternoon.

Entertainment

Two Saturdays a month, from 9.30 pm to 2 am, *Pickwick's Pub & Wine Bar* (☎ 03 80 24 72 59, *2 rue Notre Dame*) hosts live music and has a convincingly English, pub-style ground floor. Hand-rolled cigars cost from 50FF to 200FF. It opens 11 am to 3 pm and 5 pm to 2 am (to 8.30 pm on Sunday). *La Bodega des Z'Artistes* (☎ 03 80 22 07 57, *44 rue Mafoux*), furnished with metal lawn chairs, has live music on Friday and Saturday from 10 pm and, on other nights, karaoke from 9 pm. It opens until 3 am (10 pm on Sunday; closed Monday).

Getting There & Away

Bus Transco bus No 44 (seven to nine daily, two on Sunday and holidays) links Beaune with Dijon (40FF, one hour), stopping at wine-growing villages such as Vougeot, Nuits St-Georges and Aloxe-Corton along the way. Certain buses on the No 44 run also serve villages south of Beaune (such as Pommard, Volnay, Meursault and Rochepot) and, once a day, Autun (1¼ hours). Buses stop at several places along the boulevards that encircle the old city, using different stops depending on what direction they're headed (see the Beaune map). The tourist office has schedules.

Train Beaune's train station (☎ 0 836 35 35 35), whose ticket windows are open daily until 8.30 pm, has frequent services to Dijon (38FF, 20 to 25 minutes, 18 to 24 daily) and Nuits St-Georges (10 minutes, 13 to 19 daily); the last train from Beaune to Dijon leaves at about 11.20 pm. Other destinations include Paris' Gare de Lyon (from 209FF to 294FF, one or two direct TGVs daily, one non-TGV daily), Autun (73FF via Étang, 1½ hours, two to four daily) and one or both of Lyon's train stations (115FF, 1½ to 2¼ hours, nine daily).

Car ADA car rental (☎ 03 80 22 72 90), 26 ave du 8 Septembre, is closed Sunday.

Getting Around

Parking is free outside the town walls.

To order a taxi, ring ☎ 06 09 42 36 80 or ☎ 06 09 43 12 08.

From April to October, Bourgogne Randonnées (☎ 03 80 22 06 03) at 7 ave du 8 Septembre rents hybrid bikes for 90FF a day, including printed information on route options. It opens until 7 pm daily (closed noon to 1.30 or 2 pm). Reservations can be made at the tourist office. Check out the Web site at www.terroirs-b.com/br.

AUXERRE

postcode 89000 ● pop 38,800
● elevation 130m

Auxerre (pronounced 'oh-SAIR') grew up around its attractive old city, whose slopes – graced by belfries, spires and steep-roofed, half-timbered houses – overlook the still waters of the River Yonne. Noteworthy sights include the cathedral and a 9th-century Carolingian crypt.

Auxerre, famed for its first-rate football teams, is a good base for visiting northern Burgundy, including the Chablis area. The city's pleasure-boat port makes this an excellent place to rent a canal boat (see Activities at the beginning of this chapter).

Orientation

The old city is on the left (western) bank of the River Yonne; the train station is on the right bank, 700m east of the river. The commercial centre is between the cathedral and the main post office; the liveliest bits are around the pedestrianised rue de l'Horloge and place Charles Surugue.

Information

Tourist Offices The efficient and helpful tourist office (☎ 03 86 52 06 19, fax 03 86 51 23 27), 1–2 quai de la République, opens 9 am to 1 pm and 2 to 7 pm (9.30 am to 1 pm and 3 to 6.30 pm on Sunday and holidays), mid-June to late September; 9 am to 12.30 pm and 2 to 6.30 pm (10 am to 1 pm on Sunday), the rest of the year. It has a Web site at www.auxerre.com.

Money The Banque de France, 1 rue de la Banque, changes money on weekdays from 8.30 am to noon. A number of banks, open either Monday to Friday or Tuesday to Saturday, can be found between place Charles Surugue and place Charles Lepère. The tourist office will change money on Sunday and holidays.

Post & Communications The main post office, at place Charles Surugue, opens 8 am to 7 pm weekdays and until 12.15 pm Saturday. Currency exchange and a Cyberposte are available.

Media 2 (☎ 03 86 51 04 35) at 17 blvd Vauban charges 1FF a minute for Internet access (opens 9 am to noon and 2 to 7 pm weekdays, to 6 pm Friday).

Laundry There are laundrettes at 138 rue de Paris (open until 8.30 pm) and ave Jean Jaurès (open until 9 pm).

Things to See & Do

Fine panoramas of the old city area are afforded from **Pont Paul Bert** (1857). A bridge has stood on this site for much of the period since Roman times. Great views are also on offer from the arched **footbridge** in front of the tourist office, which can provide details on warm-season **boat excursions** along the river. The old city's narrow streets are easily explored on foot.

The medium-sized, Gothic **Cathédrale St-Étienne**, constructed between the 13th and 16th centuries, has a Flamboyant-Gothic western front topped by a 68m-high **bell tower**, completed in the mid-1500s. Inside, the choir, the ambulatory and the vivid **stained-glass windows** around the ambulatory are from the 1200s. The 11th- to 13th-century frescoes in the Romanesque **crypt** (15FF), on the southern side of the building, include a scene of Jesus on horseback that is unlike any other known in Western art (open 9 am to noon and 2 to 6 pm; closed Sunday morning). The **treasury** (10FF) is open the same hours. The cathedral can be visited from 7.30 am until sometime between 5.30 pm (winter) and 7 pm (summer). From June to September, there is a 75-minute sound-and-light show (30FF) with English translation, nightly at 10 pm (9.30 pm in September). In July and August, one-hour organ concerts (30FF) are held every Sunday at 5 pm.

Abbaye St-Germain (☎ 03 86 51 09 74), a Benedictine abbey founded in the 6th century, rose to great prominence in the Middle Ages, when it attracted students and pilgrims from all over Europe. The extensive **Carolingian crypts** are decorated with exceptional 9th-century frescoes that are among the oldest in France. The area between the mostly Gothic **abbey church** (13th and 15th centuries) and the 51m-high **belfry**, once occupied by part of the nave (razed in 1812), has been excavated, revealing sarcophagi and architectural features – left in situ – from as far back as the Merovingian period (6th century). The 14th- to 17th-century monastery buildings around the cloister now house the **Musée d'Art et d'Histoire**, featuring prehistoric

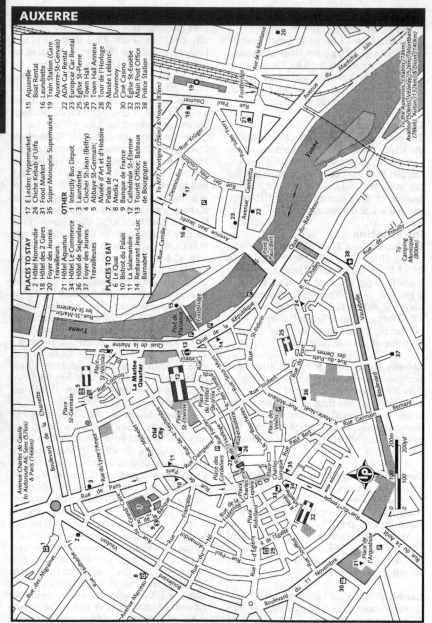

AUXERRE

PLACES TO STAY
2 Hôtel Normandie
18 Hôtel des 2 Gares
20 Foyer des Jeunes Travailleurs
21 Hôtel Aquarius
34 Hôtel Le Commerce
36 Hôtel de Seignelay
37 Foyer des Jeunes Travailleuses

PLACES TO EAT
6 Le Quai
10 Bistrot du Palais
11 La Salamandre
14 Restaurant Jean-Luc Barnabet

15 Aquarelle
16 Boat Rental
    Laundrette
19 Train Station (Gare Auxerre-St-Gervais)
22 ADA Car Rental
23 Europcar Car Rental
25 Église St-Pierre
26 Town Hall
27 Town Hall Annexe
28 Tour de l'Horloge
29 Musée Leblanc-Duvernoy
30 Ciné Casino
32 Église St-Eusèbe
33 Main Post Office
38 Police Station

17 E Leclerc Hypermarket
24 Chiche Kebab d'Urfa
31 Food Market
35 Super Monoprix Supermarket

OTHER
1 Interdity Bus Depot
3 Laundrette
4 Clocher St-Jean (Belfry)
5 Abbaye St-Germain; Musée d'Art et d'Histoire
7 Palais de Justice
8 Media 2
9 Banque de France
12 Cathédrale St-Étienne
13 Tourist Office; Bateaux de Bourgogne

euro currency converter 10FF = €1.52

stone implements, Gallo-Roman antiquities, paintings, sculpture and contemporary art.

The abbey complex opens 10 am to 6.30 pm, May to September; and 10 am to noon and 2 to 6 pm (closed Tuesday and some holidays), the rest of the year. The crypts must be visited with a guide – tours (with printed information in English) begin every hour (every half-hour in summer); the last one leaves at 5 pm (5.30 pm in summer). Admission costs 25FF but is free for those aged under 16, students and, on the first Sunday of the month, everyone. The same ticket is valid for the **Musée Leblanc-Duvernoy** (☎ 03 86 51 09 74), 9 bis rue d'Églény, which displays tapestries, faïence and paintings. It opens 2 to 6 pm, except on Tuesday and some holidays; separate admission costs 13FF.

In the animated, pedestrianised centre of the city stands the spire-topped **Tour de l'Horloge** (clock tower) over rue de l'Horloge, built in 1483 as part of the city's fortifications. On the 17th-century clock faces (one on each side), the hand with a sun on one end indicates the time of day. The other hand, decorated with an orb, shows what day of the lunar month it is, making a complete rotation every 29½ days.

Special Events

From 21 to 27 June, the Festival de Jazz brings to town about a dozen concerts, most of them free. The Festival de Piano lasts for a week in early or mid-September.

Places to Stay – Budget

Camping The shaded, grassy *Camping Municipal* (☎ 03 86 52 11 15, 8 Route de Vaux), open April to September, is 1.5km south of the train station, across the street from the football stadium. By bus, take line A to the Stades Arbre Sec stop.

Hostels Two co-ed dormitories for young working people offer travellers basic singles for 80FF, including breakfast; doubles (available only at ave de la Résistance) are 135FF. Rooms are open all day, and there's no curfew. The 135-room *Foyer des Jeunes*

Travailleuses (☎ 03 86 52 45 38, 16 blvd Vaulabelle) is served by bus line B or D; get off at the Vaulabelle stop. The 150-room *Foyer des Jeunes Travailleurs* (☎ 03 86 46 95 11, 16 ave de la Résistance) is across the tracks from the train station.

Hotels At the *Hôtel de Seignelay* (see Mid-Range), the handful of singles/doubles with washbasin go for 150/180FF. The 12-room *Hôtel des 2 Gares* (☎ 03 86 46 90 06, 10 rue Paul Doumer), opposite the train station, has basic doubles with shower and toilet for 140FF. Reception (at the bar) opens Monday to Saturday.

Places to Stay – Mid-Range

The two-star, 47-room *Hôtel Normandie* (☎ 03 86 52 57 80, fax 03 86 51 54 33, ❷ normandie@acom.fr, 41 blvd Vauban), a gem of a hotel on the northern edge of the old city, has elegant doubles starting at 295FF. Microwaved light meals, a billiard table, the bar and the sauna (30FF) are available 24 hours.

The pleasant, 21-room, two-star *Hôtel de Seignelay* (☎ 03 86 52 03 48, fax 03 86 52 32 39, 2 rue du Pont), centred around a quiet courtyard, has spacious doubles/quads for 280/370FF. The 20-room *Hôtel Le Commerce* (☎ 03 86 52 03 16, fax 03 86 52 42 37, ❷ hotel_du_commerce@ipoint.fr, 5 rue René Schaeffer) provides attractive doubles/triples for 230/290FF; rooms for five are 360FF. Reception is closed on Sunday after 3 or 3.30 pm.

The two-star, 13-room *Hôtel Aquarius* (☎ 03 86 46 95 02, fax 03 86 51 29 80, 33 ave Gambetta) has small, newly renovated doubles/triples for 230/290FF. Reception (at the bar) is closed 3 to 5 pm daily and on Sunday after 3 pm.

Places to Eat

Restaurants Deliciously innovative versions of traditional French cuisine – and, from October to March, dishes made with truffles – have earned one Michelin star for *Restaurant Jean-Luc Barnabet* (☎ 03 86 51 68 88, 14 quai de la République). The *menus* range from 180FF (not available on

Saturday night or Sunday) to 305FF (children 95FF). It closes on Sunday evening and Monday.

The restaurant in the *Hôtel de Seignelay* (see Places to Stay – Mid-Range) serves home-made French and Burgundian cuisine in a rustic dining room that has been much upgraded since it served as a stable in the 17th century. The four *menus* cost between 70FF (weekday lunches only) and 150FF (closed Monday and, from late October to late May, on Sunday night).

The friendly, old-time *Bistrot du Palais* (☎ 03 86 51 47 02, *69 rue de Paris*) serves Lyon-style meat mains for 60FF (closed Sunday and Monday). *La Salamandre* (☎ 03 86 52 87 87, *84 rue de Paris*) is a refined restaurant that specialises in fish (from 95FF to 188FF) and seafood. The *menus* start at 188FF (118FF for lunch and, before 9 pm, on non-weekend evenings). It closes on Saturday at midday and Sunday. There are several other intimate restaurants along the same street.

Le Quai (☎ 03 86 51 66 67, *4 place St-Nicolas*), a restaurant/bar with a large terrace, is on a picturesque public square in La Marine, once Auxerre's commercial quarter. The plat du jour costs from 65FF to 75FF, the *menus* go for 65FF (weekday lunch only) to 130FF. Pizzas are also on offer.

For a cheap kebab and frites, a good option is *Chiche Kebab d'Urfa* (*78 rue du Pont*) which is closed Monday.

Self-Catering The large *food market* (*place de l'Arquebuse*), a few blocks southwest of the old city, springs to life on Tuesday and Friday mornings. North of the centre, there are quite a few food shops along rue de Paris.

The *Super Monoprix* supermarket (*place Charles Surugue*) opens 8.30 am to 8 pm (closed Sunday). The vast *E Leclerc* hypermarket (*14 ave Jean Jaurès*) opens 9 am to 8 pm Monday to Saturday (8.30 pm on Friday).

Entertainment

The eight-screen *Ciné Casino* (☎ 03 86 52 36 80, *1 blvd du 11 Novembre*) has non-dubbed art films from Saturday to Tuesday, except during school holidays.

Getting There & Away

Bus The intercity bus depot (no office) on rue des Migraines is linked to the old city and the train station by local bus line B. Some intercity lines also stop at the train station and/or place de l'Arquebuse. Schedules can be consulted (and perhaps photocopied) at the Information desk (☎ 03 86 72 43 00) in the tourist office annexe at 14 place de l'Hôtel de Ville, open on weekdays until 5.30 pm and on Saturday until noon.

Les Rapides de Bourgogne (☎ 03 86 94 95 00) has buses to Chablis (26FF, 30 minutes, two daily on weekdays) and Pontigny (one daily except on Sunday and, during school holidays, Saturday). From Monday to Thursday, there's a direct bus to Troyes (74FF, 2¼ hours) at 8.40 am.

Train The Auxerre-St-Gervais train station (☎ 0 836 35 35 35) on rue Paul Doumer has regular connections to mainline Laroche-Migennes station (20 minutes, 12 to 15 daily), from where there are services to Paris' Gare de Lyon (123FF, 1½ to two hours, 12 to 15 daily), Dijon (124FF, 1½ hours, six to eight daily), Montbard (near the Abbaye de Fontenay; 83FF, 25 minutes, four to six daily) and, by SNCF bus, Troyes (62FF plus the Auxerre–Laroche fare, one to 1¾ hours, four/one daily on weekdays/weekends). There are also trains to Sermizelles-Vézelay (41FF, 45 minutes, three to five daily) and Avallon (50FF, one hour, three to five daily).

Car On ave Gambetta, ADA (☎ 03 86 46 01 02) is at 6 bis and Europcar (☎ 03 86 46 99 08) is at No 9.

Getting Around

Bus Local bus lines B, D and E (☎ 03 86 46 90 90 for Le Bus), which run once or twice hourly until about 7 pm, link the train station with the city centre.

Car & Motorcycle Free parking is available along the river near the tourist office and on the boulevards that ring the old city: blvd Vauban, blvd du 11 Novembre and blvd Vaulabelle.

Taxi To order a taxi, ring ☎ 03 86 46 91 61 or ☎ 03 86 46 78 78.

EAST OF AUXERRE
Between the River Yonne and the Canal de Bourgogne lie the Auxerrois and the Tonnerrois, rural areas whose rolling hills are dotted with farmhouses and hay bales and carpeted with forests, fields, pastures and – especially around Chablis – meticulously tended vineyards. The area has lots of quiet back roads, such as the D124, and walking trails that can be cycled; brochures, topoguides and maps are available at local tourist offices.

Chablis
postcode 89800 • pop 2600
• elevation 135m
The well-to-do but sleepy town of Chablis, 19km east of Auxerre, has made its fortune growing, ageing and marketing the delicate, dry white wines that bear its name.

Almost all the town's shops are closed on Monday and from about noon to 3 pm. From mid-December to February most (but not all) the Chablis area's cellars and domaines close down.

Orientation & Information Chablis' main commercial streets, both of which link up to the D965, are rue Auxerroise (west of the main square, place Charles de Gaulle) and rue du Maréchal de Lattre de Tassigny (east of place Charles de Gaulle).

The tourist office (☎ 03 86 42 80 80, fax 03 86 42 49 71, ✉ ot-chablis@chablis .net) is two blocks east of place Charles de Gaulle at 1 quai du Biez. It opens 10 am to 12.30 pm and 1.30 to 6 pm (closed on Sunday afternoon from December to mid-April). A topoguide for local walks costs 35FF.

Walking Tour The 12th- and 13th-century, early Gothic **Église St-Martin**, founded in the 9th century by monks fleeing the

---

A Knight in Shining Petticoats

Speculation about the cross-dressing habits of the French secret agent Charles Chevalier d'Éon de Beaumont (1728–1810), born 15km east of Chablis in Tonnerre, has been rife for centuries, especially in sex-obsessed England, where he spent a good part of his life wearing the latest in women's fashion and spying for Louis XV. The locals, at least, have no doubt about the brave chevalier's suitability as a role model for contemporary youth: they've named the local secondary school after him.

Norman attacks on Tours, is two short blocks north of place Charles de Gaulle. Two blocks south of place Charles de Gaulle – follow rue Porte Noël – you'll come upon the two round bastions of **Porte Noël** (1778). Around the corner, at 12 rue des Juifs, is the shell of a 16th-century building known (inaccurately) as the **synagogue**. On rue de Chichée, **Petit Pontigny** was once used by the Cistercian monks of Pontigny as a fermentation cellar.

Wine-Tasting Chablis, which is made from Chardonnay grapes, is divided into four Appellations d'Origine Contrôlées (AOC): Petit Chablis, Chablis, Premier Cru and, most prestigious of all, Grand Cru.

Chablis can be sampled and bought at dozens of places in and around town – the tourist office has a list with a map. One of the largest is **La Chablisienne** (☎ 03 86 42 89 89), a cooperative cellar owned by about 300 small producers that's about 1km south of town on blvd Pasteur (the D91 towards Noyers). Free dégustation is possible year-round. The cellar's Web site is at www .chablisienne.com.

Places to Stay The friendly, two-star, 15-room *Hôtel de l'Étoile* (☎ 03 86 42 10 50, fax 03 86 42 81 21, 4 rue des Moulins), just east of place Charles de Gaulle, has large, cheery doubles starting at 190FF (290FF with shower and toilet). From December to March reception closes on Sunday night and Monday. The six-room *Hôtel de la Poste* (☎ 03 86 42 11 94, 24 rue Auxerroise) has singles/doubles/triples with washbasin for 120/140/160FF. Reception closes on Sunday night.

Three-star *Hostellerie des Clos* (☎ 03 86 42 10 63, fax 03 86 42 17 11, ✆ host.clos@ wanadoo.fr, place Général Gras) – follow the signs – has refined doubles from 310FF (closed mid-December to mid-January).

Places to Eat The restaurant of the *Hôtel de l'Étoile* (see Places to Stay) serves traditional French and Burgundian cuisine, with *menus* starting at 85FF (120FF on Saturday and Sunday). From December to March it's closed on Sunday night and Monday. Many locals dine or down a pint at the unpretentious pub-restaurant attached to the *Hôtel de la Poste* (see Places to Stay). The lunch *menu* costs 65FF.

Popular *Le Syracuse* (☎ 03 86 42 19 45, 19 rue du Maréchal de Lattre de Tassigny) offers regional foods and pizzas (from 45FF) in a vaulted, 13th-century dining room. The *menus* range from 79FF to 149FF (closed Sunday night and Monday). There are other restaurants in the immediate vicinity.

The restaurant of the *Hostellerie des Clos* (see Places to Stay), bearer of one Michelin star, has 'gastronomique' *menus* from 198FF to 430FF. *La Table de Hôte de William Fèvre* (☎ 03 86 42 12 06, 8 rue Jules Rathier), four blocks south of place Charles de Gaulle via rue Porte Noël, specialises in both traditional and creative French cuisine. *Menus* range from 98FF (weekday lunch only) to 230FF. It opens Tuesday to Sunday for lunch, Friday and Saturday for dinner.

On Sunday until 1 pm, there's an *outdoor market* at place Charles de Gaulle. Except for the *Casino* grocery (across from 3 rue du Maréchal Leclerc), just east of place Charles de Gaulle, which closes on Sunday, all the *food shops* around place Charles de Gaulle are closed on Monday.

Getting There & Away Two buses run by Les Rapides de Bourgogne (☎ 03 86 94 95

The English Connection

Three archbishops of Canterbury played a role in the medieval history of Pontigny's abbey: Thomas à Becket spent the first three years of his exile here (1164–6); Stephen Langton, a refugee from political turmoil in England, lived here for six years (1207–13); and Edmund Rich, who fell ill and died at Soissy in 1240 while on his way to the Vatican, was brought here for burial.

00) link Chablis' place Charles de Gaulle with Auxerre (26FF, 40 minutes) on weekdays.

Pontigny
postcode 89230 • pop 825
• elevation 113m

The quiet village of Pontigny, on the River Serein 25km north-east of Auxerre, is best known for its superbly preserved **Abbatiale** (abbey church, ☎ 03 86 47 54 99), whose harmonious Gothic sanctuary, 108m long and lined with 23 chapels, was built in the mid-12th century. The simplicity of its lines and the lack of ornamentation (except for the choir screen, stalls and organ loft, added in the 17th and 18th centuries) reflect the Cistercian order's rigorous austerity. Monks from the abbey (open until sometime between 5 and 7 pm daily, depending on the season) were the first to perfect the production of Chablis wine.

The tourist office (☎ 03 86 47 47 03), across from the entrance to the Abbatiale at 22 rue Paul Desjardins (the N77), has information on accommodation and walking trails in the area (closed Sunday from November to March).

The six-room *Hôtel St-Vincent* (☎ 03 86 47 42 61, 40 rue Paul Desjardins) has doubles with washbasin costing from 120FF to 150FF. Except from May to October, reception closes on Sunday. The *Proximarché* grocery (43 rue Paul Desjardins) opens daily except Sunday afternoon.

On weekdays (and on Saturday when

school's in session), the No 18 bus operated by Les Rapides de Bourgogne (☎ 03 86 94 95 00) links Pontigny with Auxerre (45 minutes, once daily).

Noyers-sur-Serein
postcode 89310 • pop 809
• elevation 185m

In the centre of this tiny, medieval village (pronounced 'nwa-YER'), reached via fortified stone gates, narrow streets wind past 15th- and 16th-century stone and half-timbered houses.

Lines carved into the facade of the 18th-century **village hall**, right next to the ancient stone arcade of the library building, mark the level at which historic floods crested. Inside the village hall, tourist information, including a topo-guide with three local circuits, is available from the *point d'accueil* (reception counter; Easter to October) or the *secretariat*.

The **Musée de Noyers** (☎ 03 86 82 89 09; 20FF), not far from the 15th-century church on rue de l'Église, displays 100 or so works of naive art. It opens 2.30 to 6.30 pm weekends and holidays, October to May, except January; and 11 am to 6.30 pm, the rest of the year.

Just outside the clock-adorned southern gate, Chemin des Fossés leads eastwards to the Serein and a **riverside walk** around Noyers' 13th-century **walls**, affording views of fields and rolling, tree-covered hills.

Places to Stay & Eat Welcoming, B&B-style, 10-room *Hôtel de la Vieille Tour* (☎ 03 86 82 87 69, fax 03 86 82 66 04, 59 place du Grenier à Sel) is the perfect place for a truly relaxing break. It opens from April to sometime in October (and for part of the winter – call for details). Doubles start at 200FF (250FF with shower and toilet); the optional table-d'hôte dinner – in the garden when the weather is warm – costs 85FF. The best time to phone is between 8 and 10 am and in the evening after it gets dark.

At least one of the two *groceries* just inside the village's southern gate opens daily except Sunday afternoon.

Getting There & Away Bus No 28 operated by Les Rapides de Bourgogne (☎ 03 86 34 00 00) links Noyers with Avallon (30FF, one hour, one daily on weekdays, except on Wednesdays during school holidays).

ABBAYE DE FONTENAY
The Abbey of Fontenay (☎ 03 80 92 15 00), founded in 1118 and restored to its medieval glory over the past century, offers a fascinating glimpse of how the Cistercians used to live. One-hour guided tours begin on the hour from 10 am to noon and 2 to 5 pm daily. Admission costs 47FF (children and students 24FF). The 6km taxi ride (☎ 06 08 82 20 61 or ☎ 06 08 26 61 55) from the Montbard train station – served four to six times daily from Dijon (40 minutes) and three times daily from Paris' Gare de Lyon (2¼ hours) – costs 55FF.

AVALLON
postcode 89200 • pop 9500
• elevation 250m

The once-strategic walled town of Avallon, set on a picturesque hilltop overlooking the River Cousin, is at its most animated during the popular Saturday morning market. It is a good base for visits to the northern section of Parc Naturel Régional du Morvan, including Vézelay.

Orientation & Information
The train station is 900m north-east of place Vauban, which is just north of the walled old city, built on a roughly triangular, granite hilltop with ravines to the east and west. The old city's main commercial thoroughfare is Grande Rue Aristide Briand.

The tourist office (☎ 03 86 34 14 19, fax 03 86 34 28 29, ✉ avallon.otsi@ wanadoo.fr), in a 15th-century house at 4 rue Bocquillot, opens 9.30 am to 7.30 pm, in July and August; and 9.30 am to noon (1 pm on Saturday) and 2 to 6 pm (closed Monday morning and, except from April to September, on Sunday), the rest of the year. Free brochures in English detail a self-guided tour of the old city and an 8km *boucle pédestre* (walking loop) to nearby hillsides and valleys.

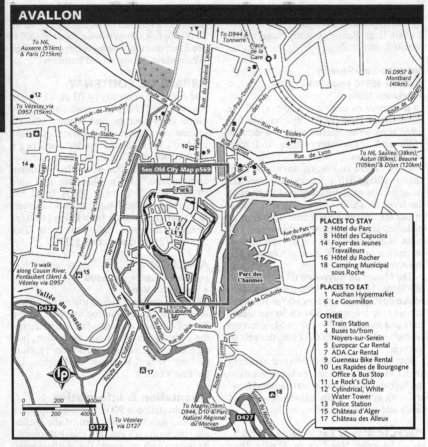

AVALLON

To N6,
Auxerre (51km)
& Paris (215km)

To Vézelay via
D957 (15km)

To D944 &
Tonnerre

Place
de la
Gare

To D957 &
Montbard
(40km)

Route de Paris

Rue du Général Leclerc

Avenue-de-Pepinster

Rue -du-Stade

Avenue -Victor -Hugo

Avenue -de-la-République

Avenue -de-la-Montande

Chemin -Cambon

Rue -de-l'Hôpital

Rue-de-Paris

Avenue-Paul-Doumer

Rue -des--Prés

Rue Carnot

Rue-des--Écoles

Rue de Lyon

To N6, Saulieu (38km);
Autun (80km), Beaune
(105km) & Dijon (120km)

Route -des--Lormes

See Old City Map p569

Park

Old
City

Ave du Parc
des Chaumes

Parc des
Chaumes

To walk
along Cousin River,
Pontaubert (3km) &
Vézelay via D957

Vallée du Cousin

Route de Cousin le Pont

R lles Labaume

R St-Martin

Rue des-deux-Cousins

Cousin

Route des Châtelaines

Chemin -de-la-Goulotte

Route des Lormes

Route du Moulison

To Magny (5km),
D944, D10 & Parc
Naturel Régional
du Morvan

To Vézelay
via D127

PLACES TO STAY		
2	Hôtel du Parc	
8	Hôtel des Capucins	
14	Foyer des Jeunes Travailleurs	
16	Hôtel du Rocher	
18	Camping Municipal sous Roche	
PLACES TO EAT		
1	Auchan Hypermarket	
6	Le Gourmillon	
OTHER		
3	Train Station	
4	Buses to/from Noyers-sur-Serein	
5	Europcar Car Rental	
7	ADA Car Rental	
9	Gueneau Bike Rental	
10	Les Rapides de Bourgogne Office & Bus Stop	
11	Le Rock's Club	
12	Cylindrical, White Water Tower	
13	Police Station	
15	Château d'Alger	
17	Château des Alleux	

Topoguides and maps of the Morvan are available at the tourist office and the Maison de la Presse at 19 place Vauban (closed on Sunday and holidays).

Money Avallon's banks, several of which can be found around place Vauban, open Tuesday to Saturday.

Post & Communications The post office, at 9 place des Odebert, opens 8 am to noon and 1.30 to 6 pm weekdays and on Saturday until noon. Currency exchange and a Cyberposte are available.

At the tourist office, a few minutes of Internet access is available for the cost of a phone call.

Walking Tour

Construction of Avallon's fortifications, which tower over the lush, terraced slopes of two tiny tributaries of the River Cousin, was begun in the 9th century following devastating attacks on the town by Muslim armies from Moorish Spain (731) and the Normans (843). A walk around the walls, with their many 15th- to 18th-century towers and bastions, is a fine way to get a sense of the town's geography. *Intra-muros* (literally, 'within the walls'), medieval and Renaissance houses grace many streets. **Tour de l'Horloge** is a clock tower built in the mid-15th century.

Soon after **Église St-Lazare** (open daily from Easter to late November) was completed at the start of the 12th century, the huge numbers of pilgrims drawn here by a piece of the skull of St Lazarus (believed to provide protection from leprosy) rendered the structure inadequate. As a result, in the mid-12th century the nave was made larger (though somewhat crooked) by moving the facade 20m to the west. The church's two remaining **portals** (a third was crushed when the northern belfry collapsed in 1633) are magnificently decorated in the Burgundian Romanesque style. From mid-June to mid-September (and perhaps May), temporary expositions are held next door in **Église St-Pierre**. Across the street in the 18th-century **Grenier à Sel** (salt store), products made by local artisans are on sale during July and August.

The **Musée de l'Avallonnais** (☎ 03 86 34 03 19) at place de la Collégiale, founded in 1862, has a little bit of everything: fossils, archaeology, armaments, religious art and paintings, including 58 expressionist sketches by Georges Rouault (1871–1958). It opens 10 am to noon and 2 to 6 pm daily except Tuesday, from May or June to October. Admission costs 20FF (students 15FF; those aged under 16, free).

About 100 costumes from the 18th to 20th centuries are displayed in period tableaux at the **Musée du Costume** (☎ 03 86 34 19 95) at 6 rue Belgrand (20FF, students 12FF). It opens 10.30 am to 12.30 pm and 1.30 to 5.30 pm (a bit later in summer) daily, from mid-April to October.

Walking & Cycling
A lovely route for a walk or bike ride in the **Vallée du Cousin** is the shaded, one-lane D427, which follows the gentle rapids of the River Cousin as it flows through dense forests and lush meadows. From the Hôtel du Rocher (see the main Avallon map), you can head either west towards Pontaubert

(cross under the viaduct; 3km) and Vézelay, or east towards Magny.

Places to Stay – Budget
Camping Set in the middle of a forest on the banks of the shallow River Cousin, the grassy and very attractive *Camping Municipal sous Roche* (☎/fax 03 86 34 10 39), 2km south-east of the old city (3km south of the train station), opens mid-March to mid-October.

Hostels If you'll be staying at least a week, you might try the Spartan, 150-room *Foyer des Jeunes Travailleurs* (☎ 03 86 34 01 88, fax 03 86 34 10 95, 10 ave Victor Hugo), in an area of 1970s apartment blocks. A single is 82FF. Phone before dropping by.

Hotels The 10-room *Hôtel du Parc* (☎ 03 86 34 17 00, fax 03 86 34 28 48), across the street from the train station, has ordinary but serviceable doubles starting at 130FF

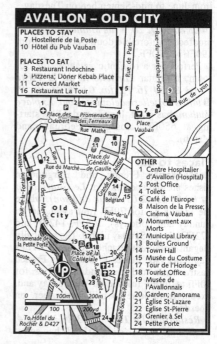

AVALLON – OLD CITY

PLACES TO STAY
7 Hostellerie de la Poste
10 Hôtel du Pub Vauban

PLACES TO EAT
3 Restaurant Indochine
5 Pizzeria; Döner Kebab Place
11 Covered Market
16 Restaurant La Tour

OTHER
1 Centre Hospitalier d'Avallon (Hospital)
2 Post Office
4 Toilets
6 Café de l'Europe
8 Maison de la Presse; Cinéma Vauban
9 Monument aux Morts
12 Municipal Library
13 Boules Ground
14 Town Hall
15 Musée du Costume
17 Tour de l'Horloge
18 Tourist Office
19 Musée de l'Avallonnais
20 Garden; Panorama
21 Église St-Lazare
22 Église St-Pierre
23 Grenier à Sel
24 Petite Porte

(149FF with shower). There are no hall showers. Reception is closed on Sunday.

The 14-room *Hôtel du Rocher* (☎ 03 86 34 19 03, 11 rue des Îles Labaume), in the Vallée du Cousin about 2.5km south-west of the train station (from place des Odebert take rue de la Fontaine Neuve), is the best deal in town. Plain, old-fashioned, wood-panelled doubles/quads with washbasin cost 120/170FF. One or two 2FF coins get you a shower. Reception closes on Monday unless it's a holiday; the hotel closes from late December to late January.

Places to Stay – Mid-Range & Top End

The pleasant, eight-room *Hôtel des Capucins* (☎ 03 86 34 06 52, fax 03 86 34 58 47, 6 ave Paul Doumer) has modern, quiet doubles for 300FF. The owners prefer that guests take their dinner at the hotel's elegant restaurant (see Places to Eat). Reception is closed on Wednesday and, except from June to mid-September, on Tuesday.

The five-room *Hôtel du Pub Vauban* (☎ 03 86 34 02 20, 3 rue Mathé) has sound-proofed, comfortable doubles costing from 190FF to 220FF.

Perfect for a romantic getaway, the 30-room, four-star *Hostellerie de la Poste* (☎ 03 86 34 16 16, fax 03 86 34 19 19, ℮ info@hostelleriedelaposte.com, 13 place Vauban) has giant, luxurious doubles starting at 650FF (closed in February and March).

Places to Eat

Restaurants French and Burgundian dishes are the speciality at *Le Gourmillon* (☎ 03 86 31 62 01, 8 rue de Lyon), where the *menus* go for 79FF (not available on Sunday and holidays), 108FF, 142FF and 172FF (closed Sunday night). The rustically elegant restaurant attached to the *Hôtel des Capucins* (see Places to Stay) has French gastronomic and Burgundian *menus* for 90FF to 260FF (closed on Wednesday and, except from June to mid-September, on Tuesday).

Restaurant La Tour (☎ 03 86 34 24 84, 84 Grande rue Aristide Briand) has sweet crepes, pasta and pizzas (35FF to 53FF). *Restaurant Indochine* (☎ 03 86 34 51 24, 3 rue des Odebert) serves Chinese and Vietnamese cuisine, with mains from 40FF to 52FF (closed Monday at midday).

There are several inexpensive restaurants along rue de Paris, including a *pizzeria (13 rue de Paris)* with salads, closed Tuesday at midday and Monday; and a *doner kebab place (15 rue de Paris)*.

Self-Catering Good places for a picnic include the garden behind Église St-Lazare, and promenade de la Petite Porte, just outside the southern end of the old city.

On Saturday morning until 1 pm (a bit earlier in winter), the *marché couvert* (covered market) and nearby place du Général de Gaulle fill with food stalls. There are several *food shops* nearby.

The vast *Auchan* hypermarket/shopping centre *(rue du Général Leclerc)* opens 8.30 am to 9 pm Monday to Saturday.

Entertainment

The often-crowded *Café de l'Europe* (☎ 03 86 34 04 45, 7 place Vauban) is a typical provincial cafe-bar-brasserie, with cheap coffee and beer, billiards, off-track betting, lottery tickets and meals available at any hour (open until 2 am daily).

Le Rock's Club (☎ 03 86 34 30 61, 13 rue de l'Hôpital), a bona fide discothèque, opens 11 pm to 4 am Friday and Saturday (free on Friday, 35FF on Saturday, when there's live music).

Getting There & Away

Bus Transco bus No 49 (☎ 03 80 42 11 00) goes to Dijon (92.40FF, two hours, three daily, once on Sunday) faster and more cheaply than the train. Les Rapides de Bourgogne (☎ 03 86 34 00 00) at 39 rue de Paris opens until at least 5 pm Monday to Saturday (closed from noon to 3 pm and on Saturday after 11.30 am). The company has services to Noyers-sur-Serein (30FF, one hour, one daily on weekdays except on Wednesdays during school holidays). Schedules *may* be available at the tourist office.

Train Three to five trains daily link Avallon's train station (☎ 03 86 34 01 01 or ☎ 0 836 35 35 35) with Auxerre (50FF, one hour) and the mainline Laroche-Migennes station (63FF, 1½ hours), from where there are services to Paris' Gare de Lyon (171FF from Avallon, 1½ to two hours, 12 to 15 daily) and Dijon (92FF from Avallon, 1½ hours, six to eight daily). SNCF buses go to Montbard (46FF, 50 minutes, three daily), also on the Paris–Dijon line (and very near the Abbaye de Fontenay). Trains/buses serve Saulieu (41FF, 50 to 60 minutes, three or four daily) and Autun (72FF, 1¾ hours, two daily, one on Sunday and holidays).

Car ADA (☎ 03 86 34 20 38) is at 25 rue de Lyon; Europcar (☎ 03 86 34 39 36) is at 28 rue de Lyon.

Getting Around

Gueneau (☎ 03 86 34 28 11) at 26 rue de Paris rents mountain bikes for 50/100FF for a half/whole day. It opens 8 am to noon and 2 to 7 pm (closed Sunday unless you call ahead).

VÉZELAY

postcode 89450 • pop 570
• elevation 285m

Despite the hordes of tourists who descend on Vézelay during the warm season, this tiny, fortified village is one of France's architectural gems and is surrounded by some of the most beautiful countryside in Burgundy, a patchwork of vineyards, sunflower fields, hay and grazing sheep. It is pretty dead in winter, though a few things do open at weekends.

Thanks to the relics of St-Mary Magdalene, to which great miracles were attributed, Vézelay's Benedictine monastery became an important pilgrimage site in the 11th and 12th centuries; it also served as the starting point for one of the four pilgrimage routes to St-Jacques de Compostelle (Santiago de Compostela) in Spain. The town reached the height of its renown and power in the 12th century, when St-Bernard of Clairvaux, leader of the Cistercian order, preached the Second Crusade here, and

King Philip Augustus of France and King Richard the Lion-Heart of England met up here before setting out on the Third Crusade.

Orientation

Place du Champ-de-Foire, recently spruced up, is linked to the hilltop basilica by touristy rue St-Étienne and its continuation, rue St-Pierre.

Information

The tourist office (☎ 03 86 33 23 69, fax 03 86 33 34 00), at the top of rue St-Pierre, is supposed to move to place du Champ de Foire in 2001. It opens 10 am to 1 pm and 2 to 6 pm, later in July and August (closed on Thursday except from mid-June to October).

Walking Tour

Although founded in the 880s, **Basilique Ste-Madeleine** was completely rebuilt between the 11th and 13th centuries. Later trashed by the Huguenots (1569), desecrated during the Revolution and, to top off the human ravages, repeatedly struck by lightning, it was, by the mid-1800s, on the point of collapse. In 1840, the restoration architect Viollet-le-Duc undertook the daunting task of rescuing the structure. His work, which included reconstructing significant parts of the building, such as the western facade and its doorways, helped Vézelay – previously a ghost town – spring back to life.

On the 12th-century **tympanum**, located between the mid-12th-century narthex and the nave, superb Burgundian-style Romanesque carvings show Jesus seated on a throne, radiating his holy spirit to the Apostles. The basilica's interior is a study in comparative architecture: the Romanesque **nave**, rebuilt in the decade and a half following the great fire of 1120, is endowed with round arches and very small windows, features typical of the Romanesque style; the transept and choir (1185) have ogival arches and much larger windows, two of the hallmarks of Gothic architecture. There's a mid-12th-century **crypt** under the transept crossing.

euro currency converter €1 = 6.56FF

BURGUNDY

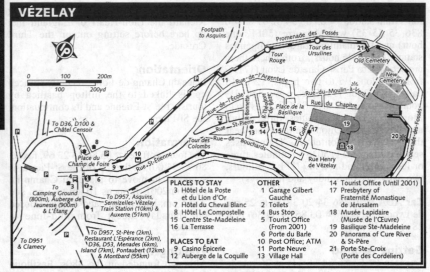

VÉZELAY

Footpath to Asquins

Promenade des Fossés

Tour Rouge

Tour des Ursulines

Old Cemetery

New Cemetery

Rue-de-l'Argenterie

Rue-du-Moulin-à-Vent

Rue du Chapitre

Rue-de-l'École

Place de la Basilique

R. Théodore de Bèze

R. Bonnette

Rue St-Pierre

Rue-de-Bouchards

R. Guidin

Tour des Colombs

Rue-St-Étienne

Place du Champ de Foire

Rue Henry de Vézelay

Promenade-des-Fossés

0   100   200m
0   100   200yd

To D36, D100 & Châtel Censoir

To Camping Ground (800m), Auberge de Jeunesse (900m) & L'Étang

To D957, Asquins, Sermizelles-Vézelay Train Station (10km) & Auxerre (51km)

To D957, St-Père (2km), Restaurant L'Espérance (2km), D36, D53, Menades (6km), Island (7km), Pontaubert (12km) & Montbard (55km)

To D951 & Clamecy

PLACES TO STAY	OTHER	14 Tourist Office (Until 2001)
3 Hôtel de la Poste et du Lion d'Or	1 Garage Gilbert Gauché	17 Presbytery of Fraternité Monastique de Jérusalem
7 Hôtel du Cheval Blanc	2 Toilets	18 Musée Lapidaire (Musée de l'Œuvre)
8 Hôtel Le Compostelle	4 Bus Stop	19 Basilique Ste-Madeleine
15 Centre Ste-Madeleine	5 Tourist Office (From 2001)	20 Panorama of Cure River & St-Père
16 La Terrasse	6 Porte du Barle	21 Porte Ste-Croix (Porte des Cordeliers)
	10 Post Office; ATM	
PLACES TO EAT	11 Porte Neuve	
9 Casino Épicerie	13 Village Hall	
12 Auberge de la Coquille		

The basilica can be visited all day, every day except during prayers (sometimes held in the cloister chapel), which visitors are welcome to attend or observe. On Sunday at 8 and 11 am, on Monday at 6.30 pm and Tuesday to Saturday at 7 am (8 am on Saturday and on holidays), 12.30 and 6 pm, services are sung in hauntingly beautiful four-voice polyphony by the monks and nuns of the Fraternité Monastique de Jérusalem; the prayers last 30 minutes (1¼ hours for the 6 pm Mass and, on Sunday, the 11 am Mass). During the warmer months the basilica's exterior is illuminated at night.

The small **Musée Lapidaire** (☎ 03 86 33 24 62; 10FF), also known as the Musée de l'Oeuvre, in the basilica's chapterhouse, displays medieval stonework removed from the basilica during the 19th-century repairs. From July to mid-September (and perhaps in June), it opens 10 am to noon and 2 to 6.30 pm daily.

The **park** behind the basilica affords wonderful views of the River Cure valley and nearby villages, including St-Père. From the northern side of the basilica, a dirt road leads northwards down to the **old cemetery**

(on the left) and the new cemetery (on the right). The walk around Vézelay's medieval ramparts is called the **Promenade des Fossés**.

You can set off from Vézelay in almost any direction and find yourself, almost instantly, far from the madding crowd and in the midst of the gorgeous countryside of the Morvan. A footpath links the Promenade des Fossés with the village of **Asquins**, from where trails lead to the River Cure. The tourist office sells brochures on mountain bike and walking trails around Vézelay.

Places to Stay

Camping & Hostels The very basic, 40-bed *auberge de jeunesse* (☎/fax 03 86 33 24 18), open year-round (in the dead of winter only for groups), is on a grassy hillside 900m south-west of place du Champ-de-Foire along the road towards Étang. A bunk costs 46FF (56FF without a hostelling card), 6FF extra in winter to cover heating. Kitchen facilities are available. Guests are asked to help with the cleaning. There's a *camping ground*, open April to mid-October, at the same site.

Friendly, 50-bed *Centre Ste-Madeleine*

(☎ *03 86 33 22 14, at the top of rue St-Pierre*) is a basic hostel run by four very with-it Franciscan nuns. A bed in a double or dorm room – co-ed if you prefer – costs 55FF; a single, 85FF. Kitchen facilities are available.

Hotels Seven-room *La Terrasse (☎ 03 86 33 25 50, place de la Basilique)*, open from April to October, has doubles starting at 190FF (220FF with shower; for some rooms toilets are across the garden). *Hôtel du Cheval Blanc (☎ 03 86 33 22 12, fax 03 86 33 34 29, place du Champ-de-Foire)* has eight modern rooms costing from 160FF to 250FF (closed from November to January).

The two-star, 18-room *Hôtel Le Compostelle (☎ 03 86 33 28 63, fax 03 86 33 34 34, 1 place du Champ-de-Foire)* has modern, spotless doubles/quads from 280/450FF; the pricier rooms have a more inspiring view (closed for most of January). The three-star *Hôtel de la Poste et du Lion d'Or (☎ 03 86 33 21 23, fax 03 86 32 30 92, place du Champ-de-Foire)* has attractive doubles from 330FF to 650FF (open from late March to October).

Places to Eat
The eateries along rue St-Pierre include *Auberge de la Coquille (☎ 03 86 33 35 57, 81 rue St-Pierre)*, which serves traditional French cuisine as well as crepes; *menus* cost from 60FF to 120FF. It opens daily from March to early November, and at weekends and during school holiday periods the rest of the year. Most of the hotels around place du Champ-de-Foire have restaurants.

The *Casino (rue St-Étienne)* opens until 7 pm (closed from 12.30 to 4 pm and in the afternoon on Monday, Wednesday and Sunday). In July and August it opens daily, except perhaps Sunday afternoon.

Getting There & Away
Vézelay is 15km from Avallon (19km if you take the gorgeous D427 to Pontaubert). By bike, it's a good idea to avoid the heavy traffic on the D957 – the less direct (and somewhat hilly) D53 and the D36 (via Island and Menades) are much quieter and

more scenic. For cars, there's a free car park 250m from place du Champ de Foire just off the road to Clamecy.

From June to early September, one SNCF bus daily links Vézelay with Avallon (20 minutes) and Montbard (on the Paris–Dijon line; 70 minutes). Three to five trains daily connect Sermizelles-Vézelay (☎ 03 86 33 41 78), about 10km north of Vézelay, with Avallon (17FF, 15 minutes), Auxerre (41FF, 50 minutes) and Laroche-Migennes (on the Paris–Dijon line; 70 minutes).

To order a taxi – expect to pay about 85FF (100FF at night) to/from Sermizelles-Vézelay – call ☎ 03 86 33 41 08, ☎ 03 86 32 31 88 or ☎ 06 85 77 89 36.

From March to November, Garage Gilbert Gauché (☎ 03 86 33 30 17), at the entrance to Vézelay's old city, rents mountain bikes for 90FF a day (closed Monday).

PARC NATUREL RÉGIONAL DU MORVAN
The 2304 sq km Morvan Regional Park, a sparsely populated granite plateau bounded by Vézelay, Avallon, Saulieu, Autun and Château Chinon, includes 700 sq km of dense woodland, 13 sq km of lakes and lots of rolling farmland subdivided by hedgerows, stone walls and stands of trees: beech, hornbeam, oak and, at higher elevations, conifers. Many of the area's 36,000 residents earn a living from such pursuits as farming, ranching, clear-cut logging and even growing Christmas trees. The time when the impoverished Morvan (the name, of Celtic origin, means 'Black Mountain') supplied wet nurses to rich Parisians and took in the capital's orphans has long passed.

Visitors to the park can enjoy walking (eg, along the GR13), mountain biking, horse riding, rock climbing, fishing and, on the lakes, water sports. Rafting, canoeing and kayaking are possible on the rivers Chalaux, Cousin, Cure and Yonne.

The Institut Géographique National (IGN) has just published new Top 25 maps of the park. The 1:50,000 scale Morvan map (48FF) in the IGN's Culture & Environment series is perfect for activities such as walking, cycling and horse-riding. *Le Morvan en Vélo Tout Terrain* (40FF) is a packet of colour-coded map sheets detailing 1400km of marked cycling itineraries.

St-Brisson

Surrounded by rolling hills, forests and small lakes, the Parc Régional's **Maison du Parc** (visitors' centre; ☎ 03 86 78 79 00, fax 03 86 78 74 22), 14km west of Saulieu in St-Brisson, is an excellent place to begin a visit to the area. Half a dozen trails pass by here; the 1km **Sentier Pédagogique** (educational trail) starts at the **children's playground** and follows the lakefront.

The **Écomusée du Morvan**, which presents the Morvan and its inhabitants in the past, present and future, has five sites around the park, and four more are planned. The main one, at the Maison du Park, opens 10.30 am to 6 pm daily, April to mid-October. The **Musée de la Résistance en Morvan** (☎ 03 86 78 72 99) chronicles the heroism that made the Morvan a Résistance stronghold during WWII; opening hours are the same as for the Écomusée. Admission costs 25FF (children 5FF).

The **Verger Conservatoire**, established in 1995, is an orchard that preserves some 200 varieties of fruit trees that are no longer commercially grown, many of them local. The **Herbularium**, a garden of 170 local plant species (some with medicinal properties), is open year-round.

Information on the park, including topoguides and details on guided walks (held in July and August), is available either in the new Accueil building (open 10.15 am to 6 pm daily) or, from 12 November to Easter, in the building marked *administration* (open 8.45 am to noon and 1.30 to 5.30 pm weekdays, to 5 pm on Friday). Take a look at the Web site at www.parcdumorvan.org.

Saulieu

postcode 21210 • pop 2900
• elevation 535m

Once an overnight stop on the Paris–Lyon coach road, the village of Saulieu – about 40 km from both Avallon and Autun – learned centuries ago to cater to visitors with high culinary expectations. Today it remains something of a gastronomic centre.

Orientation & Information The N6 is known as rue d'Argentine as it passes through town. From the Auberge du Relais at 8 rue d'Argentine, the tourist office is 100m north, the basilica is 200m up the hill (south-west) and the train station is 400m down the hill (north-east).

The well-equipped tourist office (☎ 03 80 64 00 21, fax 03 80 64 21 96, ✉ saulieu .tourisme@wanadoo.fr), at 24 rue d'Argentine, can supply you with lots of information on the Parc du Morvan. It opens 9.30 am to noon and 2 to 6 pm Tuesday to Saturday, May to October; and 10 am to noon on Sunday and holidays. It opens until 7 pm daily (5 pm on Sunday) in July and August.

Things to See The Burgundian Romanesque **Basilique St-Andoche** is known for its 60 vividly sculpted capitals depicting flora, fauna and Biblical stories. Next door, the well-conceived **Musée François Pompon** (☎ 03 80 64 19 51) at 3 rue du Docteur Roclore displays Gallo-Roman steles, medieval statuary and sleek sculptures by the noted animal sculptor François Pompon (1855-1933). It opens 10 am to 12.30 pm and 2 to 5.30 or 6 pm daily except Tuesday (5 pm on Sunday and holidays). Admission costs 20FF (children 15FF); closed in January and February except at the weekends.

Places to Eat Most of Saulieu's restaurants are open seven days a week.

The *Auberge du Relais* (☎ *03 80 64 13 16, 8 rue d'Argentine*) serves 'gastronomique' and Burgundian *menus* for 98FF to 165FF (children 62FF).

Restaurant Bernard Loiseau-La Côte d'Or (☎ *03 80 90 53 53, fax 03 80 64 08 92, 2 rue d'Argentine*), proud bearer of three Michelin stars, serves *menus* of fine country cuisine for 490FF (weekday lunches only), 680FF (not available on Friday, Saturday and Sunday nights) and 980FF (for the *menu dégustation*). Reservations are necessary on Saturday night. Look at the restaurant's Web site at www.bernard-loiseau.com.

The *Atac* supermarket, 300m down rue Jean Bertin (the D26) from Restaurant Bernard Loiseau, opens 8.45 am to 12.15 pm and 2.45 to 7 pm, Monday to Saturday.

Getting There & Away SNCF buses link Saulieu's train station with Montbard (on the Paris–Dijon line and very near the Abbaye de Fontenay; 56 minutes) three times daily (twice on Sunday and holidays). Other SNCF services go to Autun (43FF, one hour, four daily, two on Sunday and holidays) and Avallon (41FF, 50 to 60 minutes, three or four daily). Hours are posted inside the terminal building.

Transco bus No 48 serves Dijon (1½ hours) once daily except on Sunday and holidays.

Château Chinon

A rather ordinary town (population 2719), 37km north-west of Autun, Chateau Chinon is best known for having had François Mitterand as its mayor from 1959 to 1981. It makes a good base for exploring the Morvan area.

Orientation & Information The Hôtel Le Vieux Morvan is 200m up blvd de la République from place Notre Dame, the roundabout on the D978; the two museums are 500m farther up the street.

The tourist office (☎/fax 03 86 85 06 58), at place Notre Dame, has a good supply of brochures, maps and topoguides. It opens 2 or 2.30 pm to 6 or 6.30 pm Monday to Saturday; and daily in both the morning and afternoon during July and August and the February and Easter school holidays.

Things to See Jean Tinguely and Nikki de St-Phalle's playful, kinetic **fountain** in front of the neoclassical town hall is similar to the one at the Centre Pompidou in Paris.

The **Musée du Septennat** (☎ 03 86 85 19 23), 6 rue du Château, displays all sorts of official trinkets presented to Mitterand during his two *septennats* (seven-year terms as President of France). It opens from early

February to December (closed on Tuesday except in July and August). Admission costs 27FF (children and students 13.50FF). **Musée du Costume** (☎ 03 86 85 18 55; 25FF), next door at No 4, covers French fashion since the 18th century (open daily, May to September).

To get a 360° view of the area, go 250m up the residents-only road opposite the Musée du Septennat – follow the signs to the *table d'orientation* (viewpoint indicator).

Places to Stay & Eat Mitterand's official residence as mayor was a room in the 27-room, two-star *Hôtel Le Vieux Morvan* (☎ 03 86 85 05 01, fax 03 86 85 02 78, 8 place Gudin), where doubles start at 270FF (closed from 20 December to late January). The *restaurant* has *menus* of French and local cuisine starting at 95FF (Saturday night, Sunday and holidays 130FF; children 65FF).

Slightly tattered *Hôtel Lion d'Or* (☎ 03 86 85 13 56, fax 03 86 79 42 22, 10 rue des Fossés), through the arch from place Notre Dame, has plain doubles from 150FF (250FF with shower and toilet). Reception closes Sunday after 5 pm and Monday.

On blvd de la République, either the *Proximarché* grocery across from No 8 or the *Petit Casino* grocery at No 32 opens until 7 or 7.30 pm daily, except from 12.15 to 3 pm and on Sunday afternoon.

Getting There & Away From Monday to Friday (and Saturday when school is in session), RSL (☎ 03 85 52 30 02) has a daily bus from Château Chinon's tourist office to Autun (35.50FF, 50 minutes) via Roussillon-en-Morvan, Anost and Arleuf.

Maquis Bernard Résistance Cemetery

Seven RAF airmen – the crew of a bomber shot down near here in 1944 – and 21 *résistants* are buried in this neatly tended cemetery, surrounded by the dense forests in which a battalion of British paratroops operated jointly with Free French forces. The nearby **drop zone** is marked with bilingual signs.

The cemetery (*cimetière Franco-Anglais*), close to the tiny hamlet of Savelot, is about 8km south-west of Montsauche-les-Settons (along the D977) and 5.6km east of Oroux-en-Morvan (along the D12). From the D977 bis, go 2.8km along the one-lane dirt road to Savelot.

AUTUN
postcode 71400 • pop 18,000
• elevation 326m

Autun, an attractive town 85km south-west of Dijon, is now a quiet subprefecture, but almost two millennia ago – under the name Augustodunum – it was one of the most important cities in Roman Gaul, endowed with all the infrastructure typical of a Roman metropolis, including 6km of ramparts, two theatres, an amphitheatre and a system of aqueducts. Beginning in AD 269 the city was repeatedly sacked by Barbarian tribes, but its fortunes revived in the Middle Ages, when an impressive cathedral was erected. Many of the buildings in the city centre date from the 17th and 18th centuries.

Autun is a good base for exploring the southern reaches of the Parc Naturel Régional du Morvan.

Orientation

The train station, on ave de la République, is linked to Autun's common-turned-car park, the Champ de Mars, by the town's main thoroughfare, ave Charles de Gaulle. The hilly area around the cathedral, reached via narrow, twisting cobblestone streets, is known as the Old City. The main shopping area is around rue St-Saulge.

Information

Tourist Offices The tourist office (☎ 03 85 86 80 38, fax 03 85 86 80 39), 2 ave Charles de Gaulle, opens 9 am to noon or 12.30 pm and 2 to 6 pm (5.30 pm on Saturday, 7 pm in May; closed Sunday). From June to September, daily hours are 9 am to 7 pm. It has very little information on the Morvan park. Visit the Web site at www.autun.com.

The tourist office annexe (☎ 03 85 52 56 03) at 5 place du Terreau opens 9 am to 7 pm daily, June to October.

Maps and topoguides are available at Librairie À La Page (☎ 03 85 52 24 72), 17 bis ave Charles de Gaulle (closed Monday morning and Sunday).

Money The Banque de France at 38 ave Charles de Gaulle will change money from 8.45 am to noon Monday to Friday. Commercial banks (some of them open on Saturday morning) can be found along the southern section of ave Charles de Gaulle and around the perimeter of the Champ de Mars.

Post & Communications The post office, opposite 8 rue Pernette, opens 8.30 am to 6.30 pm Monday to Friday and on Saturday until noon. Currency exchange is possible.

In the afternoon it may be possible to use Internet computers at the Bibliothèque (library), which is inside the town hall (☎ 03 85 86 80 00) at the Champ de Mars.

Laundry There are laundrettes at 1 rue Guérin (open until 8 pm) and 18 rue de l'Arquebuse (open until 9 pm).

Emergency There's a 24-hour police station (☎ 03 85 52 14 22) at 29 ter ave Charles de Gaulle.

Walking Tour

Built during the reign of Constantine, **Porte d'Arroux**, one of Augustodunum's four gates, is particularly well preserved. Constructed without mortar, it has four arches: two large ones for vehicular traffic and two smaller ones for pedestrians. The 1st-century **Porte St-André** is similar in design.

The **Théâtre Romain** (Roman Theatre), designed to hold 16,000 people, was severely damaged in the Middle Ages (much of its stone was hauled off for new buildings), but thanks to 19th-century restorations it's possible to imagine the place filled with cheering (or jeering) spectators. From the top of the theatre, you can see to the south-west the **Pierre de Couhard** (Rock of Couhard), the 27m-high remains of a Gallo-Roman pyramid that was probably either a tomb or a cenotaph.

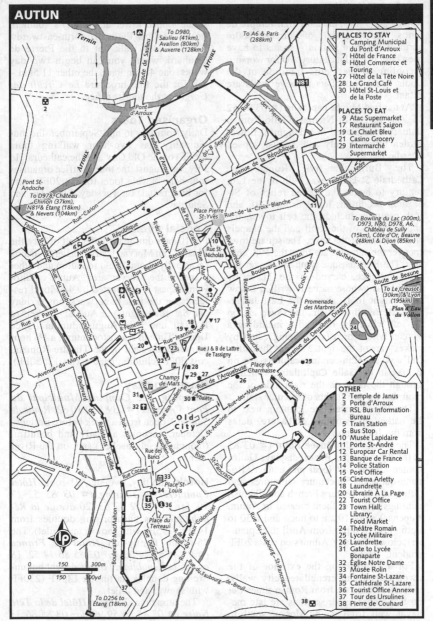

AUTUN

To D980,
Saulieu (41km),
Avallon (80km)
& Auxerre (128km)

To A6 & Paris
(288km)

N81

Ternin

Route de Saulieu

Arroux

Pont
d'Arroux

Arroux

Rue des-Pierres

Faubourg d'Arroux

Rue du 8 Septembre

Avenue de la République

Rue du Faubourg St-André

Pont St-
Andoche
To D978, Château
Chinon (37km),
N81 & Étang (18km)
& Nevers (104km)

Faubourg St-Andoche

Rue Carion

Rue de Paris

Place Pierre
St-Yves

Rue-de-la-Croix-Blanche

To Bowling du Lac (300m),
D973, N80, D978, A6,
Château de Sully
(15km), Côte-d'Or, Beaune
(48km) & Dijon (85km)

Rue du Théâtre-Romain

Route de Beaune

To Le Creusot
(30km) & Lyon
(195km)

Plan d'Eau
du Vallon

Avenue de la République

Rue Renault

Grand Rue

Rue St-Nicholas

Blvd Lattreu

Boulevard Mazagran

Croix-Vette

Boulevard Frédéric-Latouche

Rue du Faubourg St-Andoche

Avenue de la République

Rue Bernard

Rue des Clefs

Chares de Guille

Rue Marchaux

Rue Guérin

Promenade
des Marbres

Rue de Parpas

R. Pernette

Rue-Jeannin

Rue J & B de Lattre
de Tassigny

Avenue du Deuxième Dragon

Rue-Gaston

Joliet

Rue-St-Sauleuf

Place de
Charmasse

Place
de l'Arquebuse

Rue-des-Marbres

Rue-St-Antoine

Rue St-Pancrace

Rue St-Pancrace

Avenue-du-Morvan

Boulevard des Résistants Fusillés

Rue-aux-Raz

Champs
de Mars

R. de l'Arbalète

Old
City

Rue Cocand

Grand Rue
Chauchien

Rue des
Bancs

Place St-
Louis

Place du
Terreau

Boulevard MacMahon

Rue Differière

Rue du-Vieux-Colombier

Rue du-Faubourg-St-Pancrace

Faubourg Talus

Rue du Faubourg-de-Breuil

To D256 to
Étang (18km)

0   150   300m
0   150   300yd

euro currency converter €1 = 6.56FF

PLACES TO STAY
1 Camping Municipal
   du Pont d'Arroux
7 Hôtel de France
8 Hôtel Commerce et
   Touring
27 Hôtel de la Tête Noire
28 Le Grand Café
30 Hôtel St-Louis et
   de la Poste

PLACES TO EAT
9 Atac Supermarket
17 Restaurant Saigon
19 Le Chalet Bleu
21 Casino Grocery
29 Intermarché
   Supermarket

OTHER
2 Temple de Janus
3 Porte d'Arroux
4 RSL Bus Information
   Bureau
5 Train Station
6 Bus Stop
10 Musée Lapidaire
11 Porte St-André
12 Europcar Car Rental
13 Banque de France
14 Police Station
15 Post Office
16 Cinéma Arletty
18 Laundrette
20 Librairie À La Page
22 Tourist Office
23 Town Hall;
   Library;
   Food Market
24 Théâtre Romain
25 Lycée Militaire
26 Laundrette
31 Gate to Lycée
   Bonaparte
32 Église Notre Dame
33 Musée Rolin
34 Fontaine St-Lazare
35 Cathédrale St-Lazare
36 Tourist Office Annexe
37 Tour des Ursulines
38 Pierre de Couhard

Long associated (incorrectly) with the Roman god Janus, the 24m high **Temple de Janus** – in the middle of farmland 800m north of the train station – seems to have been built in the 1st century AD for worship according to the Celtic tradition of the Gauls. Only two of its massive walls are extant.

At the free **Musée Lapidaire** (☎ 03 85 52 35 71), 10 rue St-Nicolas, Gallo-Roman statuary is displayed in a delightful flower garden (open in July and August; closed Tuesday).

The Burgundian-style Romanesque **Cathédrale St-Lazare** was built in the 12th century to house the sacred relics of St-Lazarus. Additions made in the 15th and 16th centuries include the bell tower, the upper section of the choir and the chapels on both sides of the nave. The square towers over the entrance are from the 19th century. The Romanesque **tympanum** over the main entrance, carved in the 1130s by Gislebertus (whose name is written below Jesus' right foot), shows the Last Judgement. Across the bottom, the saved are on the left while the damned – including a woman whose breasts are being eaten by snakes – are on the right. Many of the cathedral's vivid, 12th-century **capitals** are on display in the **Salle Capitulaire**, which is through the door on the right side of the choir and up two flights of circular stairs.

The Renaissance-style fountain next to the cathedral, **Fontaine St-Lazare**, dates from the 16th century.

The worthwhile **Musée Rolin** (☎ 03 85 52 09 76), 5 rue des Bancs, displays Gallo-Roman artefacts of local provenance, Romanesque and 15th-century sculptures, and 15th- and 16th-century French and Flemish paintings, many of them created in Autun. It opens 9.30 or 10 am to noon and 2.30 to 5 pm (1.30 to 6 pm from April to September); closed Tuesday. Admission costs 20FF (students 10FF).

For a **stroll** along the exterior of the tower-topped and crenellated city walls, parts of which date from Roman times but most of whose upper sections are late medieval, walk from ave du Morvan south to the 12th-century **Tour des Ursulines** (the statue-topped tower at the city's southern tip) and follow the walls north-eastwards. You can also walk out to the Pierre de Couhard, where you can begin **two day walks**, one 4.7km long, the other 11.5km – ask for the free brochure *Le Circuit des Gorges* at the tourist office.

Organised Tours

Daily from July to mid-September, the municipality has two-hour walking tours (35FF) of the Old City and the cathedral. In July and August, the tourist office organises four-hour bicycle tours (65FF; 20FF extra for bike rental) on Tuesday, Thursday and Saturday.

Special Events

For 10 days during the latter half of July, the Musique en Morvan festival brings concerts (especially choral ones) to Autun and other places in the Morvan area. Autun's Gallo-Roman past is re-enacted by 400 local residents on the first three weekends (Friday and Saturday nights) in August – tickets to Il Était une Fois Augustodunum (Once Upon a Time in Augustodunum), a 1¾ hour extravaganza held in the Théâtre Romain, cost 80FF (children aged six to 12, 50FF).

Places to Stay

Camping The *Camping Municipal du Pont d'Arroux* (☎ 03 85 52 10 82; *Route de Saulieu*), open from a week before Easter to October, occupies a shady and beautiful (though densely packed) spot on the River Ternin.

Hotels The tidy, two-star, 21-room *Hôtel Commerce et Touring* (☎ 03 85 52 17 90, fax 03 85 52 37 63, 20 ave de la République*) has unsurprising doubles from 145FF (195FF with shower and toilet). The 26-room, family-run *Hôtel de France* (☎ 03 85 52 14 00, fax 03 85 86 14 52, 18 ave de la République*) offers decent but unexciting doubles starting at 130FF (230FF with shower and toilet).

The attractive, 27-room *Hôtel de la Tête Noire* (☎ 03 85 86 59 99, fax 03 85 86 33

90, **@** *welcome@hoteltetenoire.fr, 3 rue de l'Arquebuse*), is two-star, lift-equipped, and has comfortable rooms for one to four people costing from 270FF to 400FF.

The nine-room hotel attached to *Le Grand Café* (**☎** *03 85 52 27 66, 19 rue J & B de Lattre de Tassigny*), on the Champ de Mars, has doubles with shower for 180FF (245FF with bath and toilet). Reception (at the bar) is closed every other Sunday and on holidays.

Napoleon once slept at the four-star *Hôtel St-Louis et de la Poste* (**☎** *03 85 52 01 01, fax 03 85 86 32 54,* **@** *louisposte@aol.com, 6 rue de l'Arbalète*), and you can, too, from 450FF.

Places to Eat

Restaurants For Burgundian and creative French cuisine, *Le Chalet Bleu* (**☎** *03 85 86 27 30, 3 rue Jeannin*) is an excellent choice. The *menus* start at 85FF (135FF on Saturday night, Sunday and holidays). It opens daily except Monday evening and Tuesday. The Burgundian and French restaurant attached to the *Hôtel Commerce et Touring* and the traditional French restaurant at the *Hôtel de la Tête Noire* have *menus* from about 65FF to 160FF – see Places to Stay for addresses.

At *Restaurant Saigon* (**☎** *03 85 86 37 95, 12 rue Guérin*), *menus* of authentic Vietnamese cuisine cost from 65FF (weekday lunches only) to 130FF (closed Monday at midday).

Self-Catering The street level of the town hall, and the square that surrounds the building, are brought to life by a *food market* on Wed-nesday and Friday until noon or 12.30 pm.

The *Intermarché* supermarket (*21 rue J & B de Lattre de Tassigny*) and the *Atac* supermarket (*opposite 35 ave Charles de Gaulle*) open Monday to Saturday. The *Casino* grocery (*6 ave Charles de Gaulle*) opens every day except Monday. All three close for two hours or so at midday. North of the Champ de Mars, there are a number of *food shops* along rue Guérin and Grande Rue Marchaux.

Entertainment

Local young people flock to the eight-lane, restaurant-equipped *Bowling du Lac* (*bowling alley;* **☎** *03 85 86 90 25, on Route de Chalon*), next to the McDonald's, which is 700m north-east of the Théâtre Romain on the other side of Plan d'Eau du Vallon (lake). It opens 11 am to 1 am (4 am on Friday and Saturday nights).

Every Friday from 6 to 10 pm, spirited locals pack *Le Grand Café* (see Hotels) for a live concert, often of French *chansons*. There's no cover charge.

Cinéma Arletty (**☎** *03 85 52 05 54, 5 rue Pernette*) sometimes has non-dubbed films.

Getting There & Away

Bus RSL (**☎** *03 85 86 92 55*) links the bus stop (hours posted) next to the train station with destinations including Château Chinon (35.50FF, 50 minutes, one daily Monday to Friday and, when school is in session, Saturday). The company's information bureau, 13 ave de la République, opens 8 am to noon and 2 to 6 pm weekdays (to 5 pm on Friday). Bus schedules are also available at the tourist office.

Transco (**☎** *03 80 42 11 00*) runs daily to Dijon (81.50FF, 2¼ hours) via Beaune and the Côte d'Or wine making villages.

Train Autun's train station (**☎** *0 836 35 35 35*) on ave de la République and staffed until 7.30 pm (6.30 pm on Saturday), is on a very slow, autorail-only SNCF line that requires a change of train (or bus) to get almost anywhere except Saulieu (43FF, one hour, four daily, two on Sunday and holidays) and Avallon (72FF, 1¾ hours, two daily, one on Sunday and holidays). One train daily goes to Auxerre (105FF, 2¾ hours, one daily) and Sermizelles-Vézelay (79FF).

The fastest way to get to/from Lyon (142FF, 1¾ hours, five daily) and Paris' Gare de Lyon (259FF to 337FF, 2½ hours, five daily) is to take an RSL bus (49FF in addition to the train fare; those aged under 25, 42FF; 45 minutes; four or five daily) to Le Creusot. However, to Paris' Gare de Lyon it's much cheaper to take a non-TGV

(216FF, 4½ hours) via Étang or Nevers. Four trains daily (two at weekends) go to Dijon (95FF, two hours) and Beaune (73FF, 1½ hours) via Étang.

Car Europcar (☎ 03 85 52 13 31) is at 3 Grande Rue Marchaux.

AROUND AUTUN

The **Château de Sully** (☎ 03 85 82 10 27), a 16th-century Renaissance-style chateau whose northern facade was rebuilt in the 18th-century, is 15km east of Autun on the outskirts of the quiet village of Sully. The interior and the gardens can be visited at weekends and holidays from April to November, and daily from June to September. Hours are 2 to 6 pm and admission costs 36FF (just the gardens 15FF). Wine is produced on the estate and can be purchased from the concierge. The chateau makes a good cycling destination if you're feeling energetic. The village is served by SNCF buses (30 minutes, four daily, one on Sunday and holidays).

CLUNY

**postcode 71250 ● pop 4400
● elevation 248m**

The remains of Cluny's great abbey – Christendom's largest church until the construction of St-Peter's Basilica in the Vatican – are fragmentary and scattered, barely discernible among the medieval houses and green spaces of the tourist-oriented, modern-day town (which, by the way, has the same number of residents as it did 900 years ago). But with a bit of imagination, it's possible to picture how things looked in the 12th century, when Cluny's Benedictine abbey, renowned for its wealth and power – and answerable only to the Pope – held sway over 1100 Cluniac priories and monasteries stretching from Poland to Portugal.

Orientation & Information

Cluny's tourist-oriented main drag is known (from south-east to north-west) as place du Commerce, rue Filaterie, rue Lamartine and rue Mercière.

MATT KING

The impressive Château de Sully is complemented by vast gardens.

The very professional tourist office (☎ 03 85 59 05 34, fax 03 85 59 06 95, ✉ cluny@ wanadoo.fr) at 6 rue Mercière has several excellent English brochures. It opens 10 am to 12.30 pm and 2.30 to 5 pm Monday to Saturday (6 pm in October; to 7 pm from April to September, when it's also open the same hours on Sunday); there's no midday closure in July and August.

There are a number of banks (open Tuesday to Saturday) along rue Lamartine, including the Crédit Agricole opposite No 28.

Walking Tour

Cluny's truly vast **Église Abbatiale** (☎ 03 85 59 12 79), built between 1088 and 1130, once stretched from the narthex – now marked by a **map table** (in front of the Musée Ochier) – all the way to the line of tall trees on the other side of the octagonal 62m-high **Clocher de l'Eau Bénite** (Tower of the Holy Water) and its smaller neighbour, the square **Tour de l'Horloge**, a distance of 187m (almost two football pitches!). Much of the site, including the **southern transept arm** and the mid-18th-century **cloister**, is now occupied by one of the campuses of the École Nationale Supérieure d'Arts et Métiers (ENSAM), an institute for training mechanical and industrial engineers.

A visit to the abbey begins at the **Musée Ochier** (☎ 03 85 59 23 97), whose displays include a fascinating model of the Cluny complex, superb Romanesque carvings from the abbey, and a high-tech video presentation. Tickets good for both the museum and the ENSAM campus (32FF; those aged under 25, 21FF; those aged under 18, free) are sold daily (except on five major holidays) from 9 or 9.30 am to noon and 2 to 6 pm (to 7 pm in July and August; no midday closure from July to September). From October to March, it opens 10 am to noon and 2 to 4 or 5 pm.

The entrance to the ENSAM campus is through a small door in the restored 13th-century facade at place du 11 Août. Semi-officially you can wander around the institute grounds at midday and for an hour or so after closing time as long as you enter during opening hours. An explanatory sheet in English is available at the entrance. Free 90-minute guided tours in English take place on most days in July and August.

Cluny's many Romanesque houses – built when the abbey, humming with activity, brought prosperity to the town – can be admired from atop the solid **Tour des Fromages** (Tower of Cheeses). So named because it was once used to ripen and sell

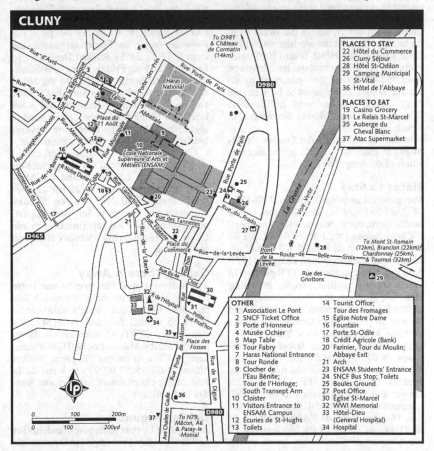

CLUNY

PLACES TO STAY
22 Hôtel du Commerce
26 Cluny Séjour
28 Hôtel St-Odilon
29 Camping Municipal St-Vital
36 Hôtel de l'Abbaye

PLACES TO EAT
19 Casino Grocery
31 Le Relais St-Marcel
35 Auberge du Cheval Blanc
37 Atac Supermarket

OTHER
1 Association Le Pont
2 SNCF Ticket Office
3 Porte d'Honneur
4 Musée Ochier
5 Map Table
6 Tour Fabry
7 Haras National Entrance
8 Tour Ronde
9 Clocher de l'Eau Bénite; Tour de l'Horloge; South Transept Arm
10 Cloister
11 Visitors Entrance to ENSAM Campus
12 Écuries de St-Hughs
13 Toilets
14 Tourist Office; Tour des Fromages
15 Église Notre Dame
16 Fountain
17 Porte St-Odile
18 Crédit Agricole (Bank)
20 Farinier, Tour du Moulin; Abbaye Exit
21 Arch
23 ENSAM Students' Entrance
24 SNCF Bus Stop; Toilets
25 Boules Ground
27 Post Office
30 Église St-Marcel
32 WWI Memorial
33 Hôtel-Dieu (General Hospital)
34 Hospital

euro currency converter €1 = 6.56FF

cheeses, its steep staircases are accessible whenever the tourist office is open (6FF, students 4FF).

The **Haras National** (National Stud Farm) at 2 rue Porte des Prés, founded by Napoleon in 1806, is a laid-back place: visitors are welcome to wander through the five spacious stables, built in the 1800s, and admire some of France's finest stallions (thoroughbreds, ponies and draught horses). It opens 9 am to 7 pm daily.

Cluny has two other churches of note: the late Romanesque **Église St-Marcel** (closed to the public) on rue Prud'hon, topped by an octagonal three-storey belfry; and the late 13th-century **Église Notre Dame** (open daily), across the street from the tourist office. At the southern end of rue de la Liberté, the **Hôtel Dieu** (10FF; students 5FF), a charity hospital built between 1683 and 1715 (and now occupied by an old-age home), is supposed to be visitable daily except Sunday and holidays at 2.30 pm (and, from May to September, at 4 pm).

In July and August, the **Écuries de St-Hughs** at place du 11 Août house an exhibition of contemporary art.

Places to Stay

The grassy *Camping Municipal St-Vital* (☎ 03 85 59 08 34, rue des Griottons), a bit east of town, opens May to early October.

Cluny Séjour (☎ 03 85 59 08 83, fax 03 85 59 26 27, rue du Prado), a 71-bed hostel run by the municipality, charges 117FF for a functional single and 76FF per bed in rooms for two to four people, including breakfast (but not towels). Reception is staffed from 9 am to noon and 3 to 7.30 pm (to 9 or 10 pm April to October). It closes for three weeks around New Year.

The central, 17-room *Hôtel du Commerce* (☎ 03 85 59 03 09, fax 03 85 59 00 87, 8 place du Commerce) has singles/doubles from 115/145FF (240FF with shower and toilet). Unless you call ahead, reception closes noon to 4.30 pm. The two-star, 16-room *Hôtel de l'Abbaye* (☎ 03 85 59 11 14, fax 03 85 59 09 76, opposite 17 ave Charles de Gaulle) has small rooms

costing from 190FF (rooms with shower and toilet for one to five people cost from 285FF to 450FF). The hotel completely closes on Sunday night; on Monday, reception reopens at 5 pm.

The new, 36-room, two-star *Hôtel St-Odilon* (☎ 03 85 59 25 00, fax 03 85 59 06 18, on Route de Belle Croix) has comfortable doubles for 290FF (closed from mid-December to mid-January).

Places to Eat

Burgundian specialities are on offer at *Le Relais St-Marcel* (☎ 03 85 59 76 19, opposite 5 rue Prud'hon) daily except Tuesday; the lunch *menu* costs 68FF. The *Auberge du Cheval Blanc* (☎ 03 85 59 01 13 1 rue Porte de Mâcon) has French *menus* ranging from 85FF to 205FF (closed December to February and on Friday night and Saturday). The restaurant attached to the *Hôtel de l'Abbaye* (see Places to Stay) has French and regional *menus* starting at 85FF for lunch and 105FF for dinner (closed Sunday night and Monday). There are several touristy eateries along Cluny's main drag.

Cluny's *food shops* – virtually all closed on Monday – are spread out along place du Commerce, rue Lamartine and rue Mercière. The *Casino* grocery (29 rue Lamartine) closes 12.30 to 3 pm, on Sunday afternoon and, except in July and August, on Monday. The *Atac* supermarket (on ave Charles de Gaulle) closes Sunday afternoon and Monday.

Getting There & Away

The toilet-equipped bus stop on rue Porte de Paris is served by the SNCF coach line that links Chalon-sur-Saône's train station (47FF, 85 minutes, four daily) with Mâcon's train station (25FF, 45 minutes, six daily) and the nearby Mâcon-Loché TGV station. The SNCF's Boutique Voyages (ticket office; ☎ 03 85 59 07 72) at 9 rue de la République closes Saturday afternoon, Sunday and holidays.

Getting Around

Association Le Pont rents bikes/tandems for 45/50FF per day. From April to October, it's based at Camping Municipal St-Vital (see Places to Stay) and closes Tuesday and Thursday mornings and on Sunday. The rest of the year it's at 27 rue du Merle – call ahead on ☎ 03 85 59 03 97.

AROUND CLUNY
North of Cluny

An old railway line stretching 44km from Cluny to Givry (7km west of Chalon-sur-Saône), has been turned into the flat **Voie Verte** (Green Road), which is perfect for walking, cycling and roller-skating.

Tournus, known for its 9th- to 12th-century church, is 33 km north-east of Cluny. The scenic roads linking the two towns, including the D14, D15, D82 and D56, pass through lots of tiny villages, many with charming churches. The medieval village of **Brancion** sits at the base of its chateau, while **Chardonnay** is surrounded by vineyards. There's a panoramic view from 579m **Mont St-Romain**.

The Renaissance-style **Château de Cormatin** (☎ 03 85 50 16 55), 14 km north of Cluny, is renowned for its Louis XIII-style interiors. It opens 10 am to noon and 2 to 5 pm daily, late March to mid-November (to

6.30 pm, June to September). Cormatin is linked to Cluny by seven SNCF buses daily (25 minutes).

Paray-le-Monial

This flower-filled town's well-preserved Burgundian Romanesque **basilica**, built in the 11th and 12th centuries, is very similar in design to Cluny's lost abbey church. The tourist office (☎ 03 85 81 10 92, fax 03 85 81 36 61), next to the basilica, opens until sometime between 5.30 and 7 pm (closed Sunday from November to March).

Two-star, 56-room *Grand Hôtel de la Basilique* (☎ *03 85 81 11 13, 18 rue de la Visitation*), run by the same family since 1904, opens from April to October; singles/doubles start at 230/290FF. Near the train station, *Hôtel du Nord* (☎ *03 85 81 05 12, 1 ave de la Gare*) has doubles costing from 150FF (240FF with shower and toilet). Except during school holiday periods, reception usually closes on Saturday. The hotel is closed for a month after Christmas.

Paray-le-Monial, 40km west of Cluny, is on the secondary train line between Moulins and Montchanin. There are limited services to Dijon (98FF) and Vichy (90FF).

Lyons & the Rhône Valley

For centuries, the Rhône Valley has profited from its enviable position at the crossroads between central Europe and the Atlantic, the Rhineland and the Mediterranean. During the Bronze Age (around 2000 BC), it was a prime trade route for amber and tin, and it became a viticulture stronghold under the Romans from the 1st century BC. Vineyards around Hermitage and St-Joseph in the northern Rhône Valley, and Châteauneuf-du-Pape in the southern part of the valley, rank among France's better known today.

The River Rhône, which slices down the valley, has its source in the Swiss Alps and links Lake Geneva and the French Alps with the Mediterranean. In Lyons – the gateway to the Rhône Valley proper – the Rhône is joined by the River Saône for the last leg of its 813km-long seabound journey.

Lyons is a majestic city with treasures that never cease to surprise the first-time visitor. Southbound lie the Gallo-Roman remains at Vienne; the terraced vineyards of Côtes du Rhône wines, the unassuming town of Valence; and charmingly-sweet Montélimar, famed for its nutty nougat. The Gorges de l'Ardèche, through which the River Ardèche (the only major tributary of the Rhône) saunters, provide a dramatic finale to the northern section of the Rhône Valley; its southern half is in Provence (see the Provence & Côte d'Azur chapter).

LYONS
postcode 69000 • pop 453,187
• elevation 175m

The grand city of Lyons (Lyon in French) has spent the last 500 years as a commercial, industrial and banking powerhouse. Despite its reputation for being staid and austere, modern-day Lyons – the focal point of a prosperous urban area of almost two million people, the second largest conurbation in France – is endowed with outstanding museums, a dynamic cultural life, a

Highlights

- Live like a Lyonnais: eat piggy parts and swill *pots* in a traditional *bouchon*
- Follow in the footsteps of a 19th-century silk weaver, from their subterranean world of passages and courtyards to the Maison des Canuts, an old-fashioned house where they lived and worked
- Explore the Renaissance face of Vieux Lyon, then ride the funicular railway up Fourvière hill for a superb panorama of Lyons and the French Alps
- Discover the hills and vineyards of Beaujolais by pedal-power; taste wine at a chateau en route
- Sail down the Rhône to Vienne, a Roman city with a legendary jazz festival
- Twist your way through the magnificent Gorges de l'Ardèche then head north to the land of chestnuts

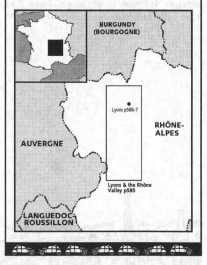

BURGUNDY (BOURGOGNE)

Lyons p586-7

RHÔNE-ALPES

AUVERGNE

Lyons & the Rhône Valley p585

LANGUEDOC-ROUSSILLON

university, classy shopping and lively pedestrian malls. Since 1989 the international police agency Interpol has had its headquarters here. Its Renaissance old town is one of UNESCO's heritage treasures.

More importantly, Lyons is renowned for its cuisine: it is one of France's great gastronomic capitals, with pleasures to sample for those on the tightest – or loosest – of budgets.

History

Lyons, founded in 43 BC as the Roman military colony of Lugdunum, served as the capital of the Roman territories known as the Three Gauls under Augustus. Christianity was introduced in AD 2 when the city was at the height of its Roman glory.

Lyons' extraordinary prosperity began in the 16th century. Moveable type printing arrived in 1473, a mere two decades after its invention, and within 50 years Lyons was one of Europe's foremost publishing centres, with several hundred resident printers. By the mid-18th century the city, a textiles stronghold since the 15th century, was Europe's silk-weaving capital.

The city's famous *traboules* (see the boxed text 'Traboules' later in this chapter) proved extremely useful to the Resistance during WWII. On 2 September 1944, the retreating Germans blew up all but two of Lyons' 28 road, rail and pedestrian bridges.

Lyons has been an important centre of scientific research since the 18th century and has produced such eminent scientists as the physicist André-Marie Ampère (1775–1836), after whom the basic unit of electric current was named, and the Lumière brothers, Auguste (1862–1954) and Louis (1864–1948), photographic pioneers and creators of the world's first motion picture in 1895.

Orientation

Lyons' bustling city centre is on the Presqu'île, a 500 to 800m-wide peninsula bounded by the Rivers Rhône and Saône. The line of impressive public squares running down the middle of the peninsula includes (from north to south): place de la Croix Rousse, in the hilltop neighbourhood of Croix Rousse; place Louis Pradel, just

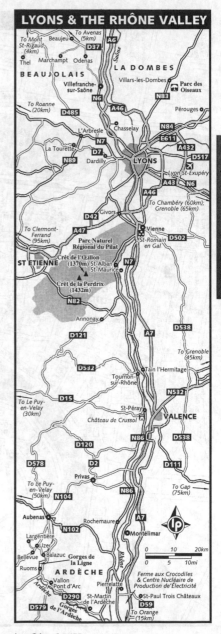

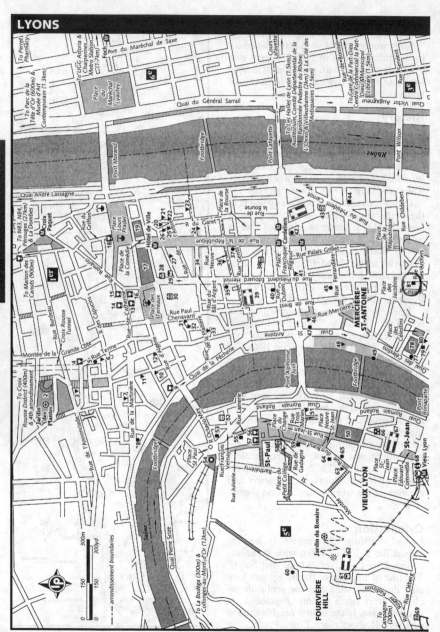

LYONS

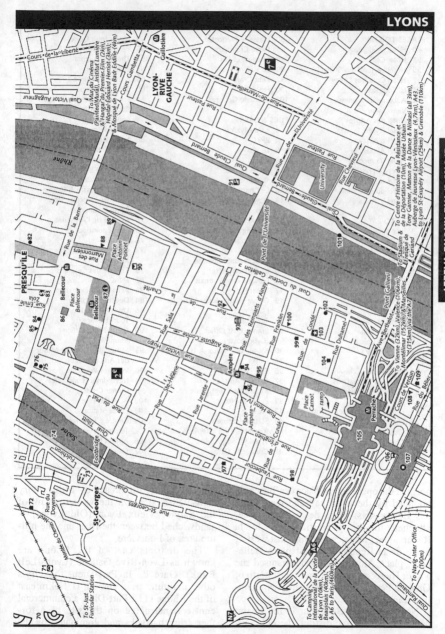

LYONS

LYONS & THE RHÔNE VALLEY

LYONS & THE RHÔNE VALLEY

LYONS

PLACES TO STAY
40 Hôtel Moderne
53 Hôtel Celtic
55 Hôtel Le Terminus St-Paul
59 Hôtel Cour des Loges
64 La Tour Rose
72 Auberge de Jeunesse du
   Vieux Lyon
79 Hotel des Artistes
81 Hôtel Élysée
94 Hôtel d'Ainay
95 Hôtel Alexandra
97 Hôtel Vaubecour
98 Gîtes de France
99 Hôtel de Vichy
104 Hôtel du Dauphiné
109 Hôtel Victoria

PLACES TO EAT
3 La Mangue Amère
6 La Randonnée
7 La Halle de la Martinière
10 Mushic
11 La Table d'Hippolyte
12 La Vieille Reserve
20 Chez Georges
21 Le Garet
22 Café 203
23 Alyssaar
24 La Mamounia
25 La Case Créole
26 Bistro Pizay
27 Chez Hugon
31 La Table des Échevins
32 Café des Fédérations
33 Moinon Charcuterie
36 La Meunière
41 Grand Café des Negociants
46 Lolo Quoi
48 Outdoor Food Market
51 Chez Chabert
63 Sol Café

80 Brasserie Francotte
85 Pierre Champion
88 Chabert et Fils
89 Le Sud
92 Petit Grain
100 Fromagerie
108 Brasserie Georges

PUBS & BARS
1 Kafé Myzik
4 2P+C
9 Le Voxx
13 Albion
14 Barrel House
15 Shamrock
16 Le Chantier
18 Down Under Australian
   Pub
56 Smoking Dog
57 Fleming's Irish Pub

OTHER
2 Roman Amphitheatre
5 Lav+ (laundrette)
8 Fresque des Lyonnais
17 Town Hall
19 Opera House & Les Musesde
   l'Opéra
28 Taxi Rank
29 Branch Post Office
   (Cyberposte)
30 Musée des Beaux-Arts
34 Banks
35 CNP-Terreaux
37 Cinéma Ambiance
38 Musée de l'Imprimerie
39 Église St-Nizier
42 Prisunic
43 Station Internet
44 Raconte-Moi La Terre
45 Whisky Lodge
47 Connectik Café

49 Navig-Inter Dock
50 Palais de Justice
52 Théâtre Guignol
54 Gare St-Paul
58 Musée Gadagne
60 Tour Métallique
61 Fourvière Funicular Station
62 Basilique Notre Dame de
   Fourvière
65 Le Cyclotouriste
66 Jardin Archéologique
67 Cathédrale St-Jean
68 Vieux Lyon Tourist Office
69 Musée de la Civilisation
   Gallo-Romaine
70 Roman Theatre & Odeon
71 Minimes Funicular Stop
73 Église St-Georges
74 Marché de l'Artisanat
75 Eton Bookshop
76 Rich Art
77 Centre Régional Information
   Jeunesse
78 Théâtre des Célestins
82 FNAC
83 Achat d'Or Exchange
84 Decitre Bookshop
86 Louis XIV Statue
87 Tourist Office
90 Central Post Office
91 Swimming Pool
93 Musée des Tissus et Musée
   des Arts Décoratifs
96 Voyages Wasteels
101 Navig-Inter (Lunch and
   Dinner Cruises)
102 ADA Car Hire
103 Police Station
105 Centre d'Échange; Bus
   Terminal
106 Airport bus
107 Gare de Perrache

north of the opera house; place des Terreaux, bounded by the town hall and the Musée des Beaux-Arts; place de la République, attached to the pedestrian rue de la République; place des Jacobins, just west of place de la République; vast place Bellecour; place Ampère, on pedestrianised rue Victor Hugo; and place Carnot, just north of Gare de Perrache, one of Lyons' two mainline train stations.

North of place Bellecour is the quaint Mercière-St-Antoine district, the old com-mercial quarter dominated by 14th-century Église St-Nizier. On the western bank of the Saône, Vieux Lyon (Old Lyons) is sandwiched between the river and the hill-top area of Fourvière.

The districts east of the Rhône are known as Lyon-Rive Gauche (Lyons-Left Bank). Gare de la Part-Dieu, the city's other mainline train station, is 1.5km east of the Rhône in La Part-Dieu, a commercial centre constructed on the site of a for-mer army barracks and dominated by the

The Butcher of Lyons

Klaus Barbie (1913–91) – better known as 'the butcher of Lyons' – served as Lyons' Gestapo commander from 1942 to 1944. He was responsible for ordering the deaths of some 4000 people (including Resistance leader Jean Moulin) and deporting 7500 others to Nazi death camps.

After the war, Barbie worked for US counter-intelligence (1947–51), then settled in Bolivia with his family under the name Klaus Altmann. In 1952 and again in 1954, he was sentenced to death in absentia by a Lyonnais court but it was not until 1987, following his extradition from Bolivia in 1983, that he was tried in person for crimes against humanity. Barbie was sentenced to life imprisonment but died of leukaemia in prison three years later.

The life and times of Klaus Barbie was the subject of the 4½-hour-long epic film *Hôtel Terminus*, which was awarded the International Critics' Prize at Cannes in 1988.

pencil-shaped Crédit Lyonnais building – a reddish cylindrical tower topped with a pyramid.

Arrondissements Lyons proper is divided into nine arrondissements. The area of the Presqu'île south of rue Neuve forms the 2nd arrondissement; the area north of rue Neuve is in the 1st arrondissement. Vieux Lyon and Fourvière are in the 5th arrondissement, and Croix Rousse is in the 4th. The left (east) bank of the Rhône is covered by the 6th, 3rd and 7th arrondissements.

The arrondissement number (1er for the 1st arrondissement, 2e for the 2nd arrondissement, and so on) of each place mentioned in the text is written in parentheses after the address.

Maps & Guides The tourist office sells a city map (5FF) which includes historical explanations (in English) on its reverse side. It also sells Michelin's 1:10,000 scale map (No 30, or No 31 with a street index) entitled *Lyon, Villeurbanne et son agglomération*, the only street map to show one-way streets (35FF); and Blay-Foldex's 1:16,000 scale *Lyon et son agglomération*, which has a 1:8800 scale inset of the centre and street index (65FF).

Le Petit Paumé is a fabulous French-language city guide to Lyons written by local university students. Unfortunately, it is only distributed (for free) for one day in October, meaning most visitors never get to see it. *Breaking the Ice* by Isabelle Corbett (95FF) is an English-language guide aimed at those intending to stay longer than a few days in the city; bookshops sell it.

Information

Tourist Offices Lyons' tourist office (☎ 04 72 77 69 69, fax 04 78 42 04 32, @ lyoncvb@lyon-france.com, metro Bellecour), in the south-eastern corner of place Bellecour (2e), opens 10 am to 7 pm May to October and 10 am to 7 pm the rest of the year. It has a Web site at www.lyon-france.com. The same building houses an SNCF information and reservations desk, open 10 am to 6 pm Monday to Saturday.

The tourist office annex in Vieux Lyon (metro Vieux Lyon), next to the lower funicular station on ave Adolphe Max, does not dole out tourist information; it only organises city tours for groups of 20 people or more. Individuals wanting to join a tour have to go to the Bellecour tourist office. See Organised Tours later in this chapter for details.

Money Commercial banks abound on rue Victor Hugo (north of place Ampère) and, just south of place des Terreaux, along rue du Bât d'Argent and nearby sections of rue de la République. There is a Thomas Cook exchange office at both mainline train stations. The Achat d'Or exchange (metro Bellecour) at 20 rue Gasparin (2e) opens 9.30 am to 6.30 pm Monday to Saturday.

LYONS & THE RHÔNE VALLEY

Passes

The **Lyons City Card** costs 90/160/200FF for one/two/three days and allows the card holder one 'free' entry per day to every museum in Lyons, including access to the observatory at Fourvière. It also allows you to freely join any city tour organised by the tourist office or take an audio-guided tour, and – between April and October – covers the cost of one river excursion too. Last but not least, the Lyons City Card gives you unlimited travel on the bus and metro. The tourist office sells it.

Those travelling further afield should consider a **Carte Rhône Musées**. It costs 100FF, is valid for one year, and showers you with unlimited entry to several museums, including the Musée de la Civilisation Gallo-Romaine and the Museum d'Histoire Naturelle in Lyon, and the Musée et Sites Archéologiques de St-Romain en Gal in Vienne.

Post The central post office (metro Bellecour), 10 place Antonin Poncet (2e), opens 8 am to 7 pm, Monday to Friday and until noon on Saturday.

Email & Internet Access The Centre Régional Information Jeunesse (see Travel Agencies immediately following) charges 10FF for 30 minutes to subscription holders (a one-year subscription, available to people of all ages, costs 10FF).

France Telecom's Station Internet (metro Cordeliers), 4 rue du Président Carnot (2e), opens 10 am to 7 pm, Monday to Saturday. Log in for 50FF per hour or buy a 200FF, five-hour card.

Raconte-Moi La Terre (see Bookshops later) has an 1st-floor Internet cafe. Rates are 130/200/350FF per three/five/10 hours.

Connectik Café (☎ 04 72 77 98 85, ✉ info@connectik.fr, metro Cordeliers), 19 quai St-Antoine (2e), charges 20/75/250FF for 10 minutes/one hour/five hours online and opens 11 am to 7 pm, Monday to Saturday.

Travel Agencies The Centre Régional Information Jeunesse (☎ 04 72 77 00 66, fax 04 72 77 04 39, metro Bellecour), 9 quai des Célestins (2e), opens noon to 6 pm Monday, 10 am to 6 pm Tuesday to Friday, 10 am to 5 pm on Saturday.

Voyages Wasteels (☎ 08 03 88 70 44, metro Perrache) has an office on the upper level of the Centre d'Échange, next to Gare de Perrache, and at 5 place Ampère (metro Ampère; 2e).

Bookshops The Eton English-language bookshop (☎ 04 78 92 92 36, metro Bellecour), 1 rue du Plat (2e), opens 9.30 am to 7 pm, Monday to Saturday. Decitre (☎ 04 72 40 54 54), 6 place Bellecour, has a good English-language section too and stocks maps.

Raconte-Moi La Terre (☎ 04 78 92 60 20, ✉ internet@raconte-moi.com, metro Cordeliers), 38 rue Thomassin (2e), is an excellent travel bookshop, open 9.30 am to 7.30 pm, Monday to Saturday.

Library The municipal library (Bibliothèque Municipale; ☎ 04 78 62 85 20, metro Part-Dieu), 30 blvd Vivier Merle (3e), has English-language newspapers, books and periodicals for your perusal.

Laundry Lav+ (metro Hôtel de Ville), rue Terme (1er), opens 6 am to 9 pm.

Medical Services Hôpital Édouard Herriot (☎ 04 72 11 73 11, metro Grange Blanche), 5 place d'Arsonval (3e), 4km south-east of place Bellecour, has a 24-hour emergency room. The Perret pharmacy (☎ 04 78 93 70 96, metro Foch), 30 rue Dusquene (6e) opens 24 hours.

Emergency The police station (Commissariat de Police; ☎ 04 78 42 26 56, metro Perrache or Ampère), 47 rue de la Charité (2e), covers the 2nd arrondissement. There is a different police station for each of the nine arrondissements.

Vieux Lyon

Old Lyons, whose narrow cobble streets are lined with a picture-postcard ensemble of over 300 meticulously restored **medieval and Renaissance houses**, lies at the foot of Fourvière hill. It embraces three districts: St-Paul at the northern end, St-Jean in the middle and St-Georges in the south. The ensemble is fronted by the 19th-century **Palais de Justice** (Law Courts) on quai Romain Rolland.

Many interesting historic buildings are on rue du Bœuf, rue St-Jean and rue des Trois Maries. Crane your neck upwards to see the fantastic gargoyles and other cheeky characters, carved from stone, that sit on the window ledges along the length of rue Juiverie.

Cathédrale St-Jean Built in 1180–1480, this mainly Romanesque cathedral has a Flamboyant Gothic facade whose portals are decorated with 368 square, stone medallions from the early 14th century. The 14th-century **astronomical clock** in the northern transept chimes at noon, 1, 2 and 3 pm. The cathedral (☎ 04 78 37 74 12) opens 8 am to noon and 2 to 7.30 pm (5 pm at weekends). Admission to both the clock and cathedral is free. Organ concerts are held at 5 pm on the third Sunday of each month and admission is free.

Musée Gadagne This museum (☎ 04 78 42 03 61, ✆ gadagne@marie-lyon.fr, metro Vieux Lyon), on place du Petit Collège, is housed in a 16th-century mansion once owned by two rich Florentine bankers. It has two sections: the **Musée de la Marionnette** (Puppet Museum) and the **Musée Historique**. The former was founded by Laurent Mourguet (1769–1844), creator of the Punch-and-Judy-type puppet Guignol, one of Lyons' symbols. Both museums open 10.45 am to 6 pm, Wednesday to Monday. Admission costs 25FF (students 13FF, free to those aged under 18).

Fourvière

Two millennia ago, the Romans built the city of Lugdunum on the slopes of Fourvière. Today, Lyons' 'hill of prayer' (topped by a basilica and the **Tour Métallique**, a grey, Eiffel Tower-like structure erected in 1893 and used as a TV transmitter) affords spectacular views of Lyons and its two rivers. Several footpaths lead up the slope. The easiest way to the top is to take the funicular railway from place Édouard Commette Jean in Vieux Lyon (metro Vieux Lyon). The Fourvière line, whose upper terminus is opposite the main entrance to the basilica, operates from 6 am to 10 pm. Use a bus/metro ticket or buy a 12.50FF funicular return ticket.

Basilique Notre Dame de Fourvière Like Sacré Cœur in Paris, this ungainly basilica, completed in 1896, was built by subscription to fulfil a vow taken by local Catholics during the disastrous Franco-Prussian War of 1870–71. Its ornamentation is a superb example of the exaggerated enthusiasm for embellishment that dominated French ecclesiastical architecture during the late 19th century. If overwrought marble and gilded mosaics are not your cup of tea, the **panoramic view** from the nearby terrace still merits a visit; Mont Blanc's snowy cap can be seen on clear days.

Rewarding views can also be enjoyed from the top of the cathedral's **Tour de l'Observatoire**, open 2 to 6 pm, Monday and Tuesday, 10 am to noon and 2 to 6.30 pm, Wednesday and Sunday. Admission to the tower costs 10FF (children 5FF).

The basilica itself opens 6 am to 7 pm. Mass is held in English at 9.30 am on the first Sunday of the month. Guided tours (☎ 04 78 25 13 01) depart from the door to the right of the main entrance, at 2.30 and 4 pm, Wednesday and Sunday. Tours (1¼ hours) cost 25FF (those aged under 26, 15FF).

Musée de la Civilisation Gallo-Romaine Among the extraordinary artefacts – almost all found in the Rhône Valley – displayed at the exceptional Museum of Gallo-Roman Civilisation (☎ 04 72 38 81 90, Fourvière funicular station), 17 rue Cléberg, are the remains of a four-wheeled vehicle from

Painted Walls

Trompe l'oeil reigns in Lyons where numerous building facades have been painted with realistic scenes over the centuries to reflect the face of Lyons.

Some 25 Lyonnais personalities peer out of the seven-storey, **Fresque des Lyonnais**, at the intersection of rue de la Martinière and quai de la Pêcherie on the Saône riverbank. Among the better-known faces are chef Paul Bocuse, loom inventor Joseph-Marie Jacquard (1752–1834), Renaissance poet Maurice Scève (1599–1560) and 16th-century explorer Giovanni da Verrazzano, a Florentine shipmaster navigator from Lyons who discovered what is now New York in 1524 (he left it untouched, enabling the Dutch to settle it a century later). The yellow-haired 'little prince' painted on the wall is a tribute to his creator, author Antoine de St-Exupéry, born in Lyons in 1900.

Heading uphill, the **Mur des Canuts** in Croix-Rousse, on the corner of blvd des Canuts and rue Denfert-Rochereau, celebrates the quarter's silk-weaving tradition. It is one of a clutch of painted walls created by the Lyons-based Cité de la Création, set up in the early 1980s. Other works of monumental dimensions, painted by this dedicated team of artists, include the **Bibliothèque de la Cité**, on the corner of quai de la Pêcherie and rue de la Platière (1er), which features five storeys of shelved books; the **Mur du Cinéma** on the corner of cours Gambetta and Grand Rue de la Guillotière (7e) which illustrates the city's marvellous cinematic history; and the **Fresque de Gerland**, near the stadium at 18 rue Pierre de Coubertin (7e).

---

around 700 BC, several sumptuous mosaics and lots of Latin inscriptions. It opens 9 am to noon and 2 to 6 pm, Wednesday to Sunday. Admission costs 20FF (students 10FF, free to children aged under 12).

The rebuilt **Roman theatre** and **odeon** next to the museum were discovered in 1933. The theatre, built around 15 BC, was enlarged in AD 120 to seat an audience of 10,000. The Romans held poetry readings and musical recitals in the smaller odeon. Both open 7 am to 9 pm (until 7 pm from mid-September to mid-April). Concerts are held here in summer.

Presqu'île

The centrepiece of beautiful **place des Terreaux** (metro Hôtel de Ville) is a 19th-century fountain incorporating 21 tonnes of lead and sculpted by Frédéric-Auguste Bartholdi, also responsible for New York's Statue of Liberty. The four horses pulling the chariot symbolise rivers galloping seaward. Fronting the square is the **town hall**, built in 1655 but given its present facade in 1702. The contemporary fountains dotting the remaining area of the square were designed by Burden.

Lyons' neoclassical glass-topped **opera house**, to the east of the town hall on place de la Comédie, was built in 1832 and remodelled in 1993. Skateboarders and rollerbladers buzz around the fountains of riverside **place Louis Pradel**, guarded by a **statue** of a *Homme de la Liberté* (man of freedom) on rollerskates, sculpted from scrap metal by Marseilles-born César (1921–98).

To the south, shop-lined **rue de la République** is known for its 19th-century buildings. Two blocks west is the **Mercière-St-Antoine quarter**, a web of narrow streets bearing the names of Lyons' traditional traders and crammed with outside cafes and restaurants.

Pedestrianised **rue Victor Hugo** runs southwards from **place Bellecour** (metro Bellecour), one of the largest public squares in Europe. Laid out in the 17th century, it has an equestrian statue of Louis XIV in the middle. Adjacent areas were razed during the Reign of Terror (1793–94) by Revolutionary radicals furious at the city's resistance to the Convention. Thousands of Lyonnais were executed before Robespierre's downfall spared the city from even greater devastation. The area was rebuilt in the early 19th century.

Musée des Beaux-Arts The 70 rooms of Lyons' Musée des Beaux-Arts (Museum of Fine Arts; ☎ 04 72 10 17 40, metro Hôtel de Ville), 20 place des Terreaux (1er), showcase an outstanding collection of sculptures and paintings from every period of European art. It opens 10.30 am to 6 pm, Wednesday to Sunday. Admission costs 25FF (students 13FF, free to those aged under 18). The museum's statue- and bench-clad cloister garden opens 7 am to 7 pm (6 pm in winter).

Musée des Tissus et Musée des Arts Décoratifs The Lyonnais are especially proud of their Musée des Tissus (Textile Museum; ☎ 04 78 38 42 00, metro Ampère), housed in a luxurious, 18th-century former private residence at 34 rue de la Charité (2e). Its collections include extraordinary Lyonnais silks, French and Asian textiles and carpets. The same building also houses the Musée des Arts Décoratifs (Museum of Decorative Arts) which showcases 18th-century furniture, tapestries, wallpaper, ceramics, silver and so forth. Both open 10 am to 5.30 pm, Tuesday to Sunday; the Museum of Decorative Arts closes noon to 2 pm. A ticket valid for both costs 30FF (students aged 25 or under, 15FF, free to those aged under 18).

Musée de l'Imprimerie The Printing Museum (☎ 04 78 37 65 98, metro Cordeliers), 37 rue de la Poulaillerie (2e), focuses on the history of a technology that had firmly established itself in Lyons by the 1480s. Among the exhibits are some of the first books ever printed, including a page of a Gutenberg Bible (1450s) and several incunabula (books printed before the year 1500). Don't miss the fantastic Renaissance courtyard. Museum hours are 9.30 am to noon and 2 to 6 pm, Wednesday to Sunday. Admission costs 25FF (students 13FF, free to those aged under 18).

Croix Rousse

The hilltop neighbourhood of Croix Rousse (literally 'russet cross'), just north of Lyons centre, is known for its bustling outdoor market and bohemian inhabitants. In sum-

mer, films are screened on place Colbert, halfway up the slopes (pentes) that lead to Croix Rousse plateau. By day, old men gather here to play boules lyonnaises (Lyonnais bowls) and chess.

In 1805, following the introduction of the mechanical Jacquard weaving loom, it was in Croix Rousse that Lyonnais silk weavers (canuts) built new workshops equipped with high, beamed ceilings to accommodate the new 3.9m-tall loom. During the bitter 1830–31 canut uprisings, prompted by bad pay and dire working conditions, hundreds were killed.

The history of Croix Rousse's canuts is painted on the **Mur des Canuts** (see the boxed text 'Painted Walls'). For an insight into a silk weaver's workshop visit the **Maison des Canuts** (☎ 04 78 28 62 04, metro Croix Rousse), 10–12 rue d'Ivry (4e) where the history of Lyons' silk weaving industry is traced. It opens 8.30 am to noon and 2 to 6.30 pm on weekdays, and 9 am to noon and 2 to 6 pm on Saturday. Admission costs 15FF (students 10FF).

Left Bank

Parc de la Tête d'Or This 105-hectare English-style park (☎ 04 78 89 53 52, metro Masséna, 6e), landscaped in the 1860s, is graced by a lake, botanical garden, zoo and rose garden. You can rent boats and play miniature golf. Take bus No 71 from the Rhône-side quay of the Presqu'île and across the river by the Churchill Bridge, or No 41 or 47 from Gare de la Part-Dieu.

The park opens 6 am to 9 pm, September to April, and 6 am to 11 pm the rest of the year. The open-air section of the **Jardin Botanique** (☎ 04 72 82 35 00), in the park's south-eastern corner, opens 9 to 11.30 am and 1.30 to 5 pm; the greenhouses, including one with carnivorous plants, open slightly shorter hours. From March to October, the **Jardin Alpin** (Alpine Garden) opens 8 to 11.30 am. **Guignol puppet shows** (☎ 04 78 93 71 75) are often held in the park on place de l'Observatoire (weather permitting).

Musée d'Art Contemporain The Museum of Contemporary Art (☎ 04 72 69 17 17,

Traboules

There's more to Lyons that meets the eye. Beneath the city facade of chic shopping malls and crowded cafes, there is a maze of *traboules* (secret passages) – 50km long with 315 passages linking 230 streets – which winds its way through apartment blocks, under streets and into courtyards.

Some of Vieux Lyon's traboules date from Roman times. Many of the 140 traboules that snake their way up the *pentes* (slopes) to the Croix Rousse plateau were constructed by *canuts* (silk weavers) in the 19th century to facilitate the transport of silk in inclement weather. Resistance fighters found them equally handy during WWII.

Genuine traboules (derived from the Latin *trans ambulare* meaning 'to pass through') cut from one street to another, often wending their way up fabulous spiral staircases en route. Passages that fan out into a courtyard or lead into a cul de sac are not traboules, but rather *miraboules*.

Lyons' most celebrated traboules link 24 rue St-Jean in Vieux Lyon to 1 rue du Bœuf, and 10 quai Romain Rolland to 2 place du Governement. In Croix Rousse, you can step into the city's underworld at 9 place Colbert, crossing cours des Voraces renowned for its monumental staircase that zigzags up seven floors, and emerging at 29 rue Imbert Colomès.

info@moca-lyon.org), which specialises in works created after 1960, hosts an excellent choice of temporary exhibitions. Digital art is explored in its Espace Culture Multimédia where aspiring surfers can freely access the Internet. The museum is housed in the Cité Internationale overlooking Parc de la Tête d'Or at 81 quai Charles de Gaulle (not far from the Interpol headquarters). Take bus No 47 from Gare de la Part-Dieu to the Musée d'Art Contemporain bus stop or bus No 4 from the Saxe Gambetta metro station. The museum opens noon to 7 pm, Wednesday to Sunday. Admission costs 25FF (students 13FF, free to those aged under 18).

Centre d'Histoire de la Résistance et de la Déportation
The WWII headquarters of Lyons' notorious Gestapo chief, Klaus Barbie, at 14 ave Berthelot (7e), has been transformed into an evocative, multimedia museum (☎ 04 78 72 23 11, metro Perrache or Jean Macé) which commemorates Nazi atrocities (including torture and executions planned or carried out in this building) and the heroism of French Resistance fighters.

The centre opens from 9 am to 5.30 pm, Wednesday to Sunday. Admission costs 25FF (students 13FF, free to those aged under 18).

Mosqué de Lyon Badr Eddine
This dazzling mosque (☎ 04 78 76 00 23, metro Laënnec), 5km east of the Presqu'île at 146 blvd Pinel (8e), fuses traditional North African architecture and calligraphy with late-20th-century western aesthetics. A religious focal point for Lyons' 130,000-strong Muslim community, it opens to modestly dressed visitors from 9 am to noon and 2 to 6 pm, Monday to Thursday. Admission costs 10FF. Leave shoes in the *vestiaire chaussures* (shoe storage area).

Institut Lumière
Lyons is the birthplace of cinema, the glorious beginnings of which are unravelled in the Institut Lumière (☎ 04 78 78 18 95, ✉ contact@institut-lumiere.org, metro Monplaisir Lumière), 25 rue du Premier Film (8e), 3km south-east of place Bellecour along cours Gambetta. The institute is in the family home of Antoine Lumière who, together with his sons Auguste and Louis, shot the first reels of the pioneering motion picture *La Sortie des Usines Lumières (The Exit of the Lumières' factories)* on 19 March 1885. The exhibition includes a model of the workshop that once stood opposite the family house. It opens 9 am to 12.30 pm and 2 to 6 pm, Tuesday to Sunday. Admission costs 25FF (students 20FF).

In the grounds is the **Hangar du Premier**

Film, a cinema where classic and cult films are screened (see Cinema under Entertainment later in this chapter).

Musée Urbain Tony Garnier This open-air museum – the only one of its kind in France – pays homage to Lyonnais architect Tony Garnier (1869–1948) who designed the low-cost council housing estate, in which this urban museum is housed, in the 1930s. A tour of the 50 seven-storey apartment blocks reveals 24 fantastic wall murals illustrating different aspects of Garnier's 'ideal city'.

Given the Musée Urbain Tony Garnier is a rejuvenated housing estate, you can stroll its streets any time. For information contact the Atelier Tony Garnier (☎ 04 78 75 16 15), 4 rue des Serpollières (8e), open 2 to 6 pm, Tuesday to Saturday.

Bus No 53 from Gare de Perrache stops outside the museum.

Boating, Bicycling & Walking
Between April and October Navig-Inter (☎ 04 78 42 96 81, fax 04 78 42 11 09), 13 bis quai Rambaud, conducts one- and 1½-hour **river excursions** from the dock by 3 quai des Célestins (metro Bellecour or Vieux Lyon, 2e). Tickets cost 42FF (children aged under 10, 32FF). Its one-hour evening cruise, departing at 9.30 pm on Saturday from mid-July to mid-August, is particularly pleasant (54FF; children aged under 10, 42FF), as are its year-round lunch and dinner cruises, which depart from the left bank, next to 23 quai Claude Bernard (7e). Advance bookings for these dine-afloat tours (2½ to 2¾ hours) are vital. Tickets cost upwards of 210FF. Navig-Inter also runs river trips to Vienne (see 'Downstream along the Rhône' later in this chapter).

Cycling aficionados can participate in the **bike rides** of Le Cyclotouriste (☎ 04 78 42 44 08, metro Vieux Lyon), a cycling club at 19 rue du Bœuf (5e). The office opens 4 to 7 pm, Tuesday, Thursday and Friday.

The Comité Départemental de la Randonnée Pédestre du Rhône (☎ 04 72 75 09 02, fax 04 72 74 20 54), 39 rue Germain (6e) organises **hikes in the Rhône Valley** most Sundays. Details are posted on its Web site at www.rhone-en-decouverte.com. Its office is staffed 3 to 7 pm Tuesday and Thursday, September to July.

Organised Tours
The tourist office offers a mind-boggling choice of thematic city tours costing 50FF per person (students and children 25FF). Alternatively, hire a set of headphones (40FF) to guide yourself, or hop aboard a bus (☎ 04 78 98 56 98, ✉ escapades@philibert.fr) for a 1½-hour tour (100FF).

Between December and April, SLD Voyages (☎ 04 72 40 28 28, fax 04 72 40 24 08, ✉ sldinfos@sldvoyages.com, metro Perrache), 14 place Carnot (2e), organises one-day skiing excursions to Alpine ski resorts. Departing by coach from Lyons at 7.30 am and returning around 8 pm, trips cost 155FF to 210FF per person, including breakfast and ski pass. Details are posted on its Web site at www.sldvoyages.com.

Special Events
Vieux Lyon rings with the sound of street entertainers and musical festivals in summer. Les Nuits de Fourvière, from mid-June to mid-September, bring a rash of open-air concerts to the Roman amphitheatres in Fourvière; tickets and program details are available at FNAC (see Entertainment).

Vieux Lyon hosts the two-day Vieux Lyon Tupiniers (Old Lyons Pottery Festival) during the second weekend in September, and from the end of November to mid-December it celebrates the Festival de Musique du Vieux Lyon. On 8 December, the city is lit up with the Fête des Lumières (Festival of Lights), marking the Feast of the Immaculate Conception. Around 8 pm, a procession of people carrying candles wends its way from place St-Jean in Vieux Lyon to Basilique Notre Dame de Fourvière. The faithful not in the procession place candles in the windows of their homes.

From mid-September in even-numbered years, there is the month-long dance festival, Biennale de la Danse (Dance Biennial), and in odd-numbered years during the same

LYONS & THE RHÔNE VALLEY

period, the Biennale d'Art Contemporain (Contemporary Art Biennial).

Places to Stay – Budget

Camping Some 10km north-west of Lyons in Dardilly is *Camping International de la Porte de Lyon* (☎ 04 78 35 64 55). It charges 80FF for two people with a tent and car. Reception opens 8 am to 12.30 pm and 4 to 8.30 pm. Bus No 3 or 19 (towards Ecully-Dardilly) from the Hôtel de Ville metro station stops right out front. By car, take the A6 towards Paris.

Hostels The superbly located *Auberge de Jeunesse* (☎ 04 78 15 05 50, fax 04 78 15 05 51, ✉ lyon@fuaj.org, *40–45 montée du Chemin Neuf, metro Vieux Lyon, 5e*) in Vieux Lyon has 180 dorm beds in two-, four-, five-, six- or seven-bedded rooms. A bed costs 71FF, including breakfast. Sheets cost 17FF. Non-HI members must buy a welcome stamp (19FF). The reception opens 24 hours.

There's another *Auberge de Jeunesse* (☎ 04 78 76 39 23, fax 04 78 77 51 11, ✉ lyonvenissieux@fuaj.fr, *51 rue Roger Salengro*) in Vénissieux, 5.5km south-east of Gare de Perrache. A dorm bed costs 68FF, including breakfast. Reception opens 7.30 to 12.30 am. Take bus No 35 from next to the central post office to the Georges Lévy stop. From Gare de la Part-Dieu, take bus No 36 (towards Minguettes) and get off at the Viviani-Joliot-Curie stop. From Gare de Perrache, take bus No 53 to the États-Unis-Viviani stop, 500m north of the hostel.

Chambres d'Hôtes B&B in family homes around Lyons and the Rhône Valley is arranged by *Gîtes de France* (☎ 04 72 77 17 55, fax 04 78 38 21 15, ✉ gites.rhone. alpes@wanadoo.fr, *1 rue Général Plessier, metro Perrache, 2e*) arranges. It also has *gîtes* (self-catering farms and cottages) to rent on a weekly basis. The office opens 9 am to noon and 1 to 6 pm, Monday to Friday, and 10 am to 1 pm on Saturday.

Hotels – Presqu'île Presqu'île's cheap hotels are scattered. Friendly *Hôtel Vaube-cour* (☎ 04 78 37 44 91, fax 04 78 42 90 17, *28 rue Vaubecour, metro Ampère, 2e*) is a spotless place with basic singles/doubles costing 130/150FF (150/175F with shower) and rooms for three or four people with shower for 380FF.

Hôtel de Vichy (☎ 04 78 37 42 58, *60 bis rue de la Charité, metro Perrache, 2e*) has rock-bottom rooms costing 140/150FF with washbasin (180/200FF with shower).

Hôtel d'Ainay (☎ 04 78 42 43 42, fax 04 72 77 51 90, *14 rue des Remparts d'Ainay, metro Ampère, 2e*) has rooms costing upwards of 165/175FF (205/215FF with shower and TV, 225/235FF with shower and toilet).

Hôtel Alexandra (☎ 04 78 37 75 79, fax 04 72 40 94 34, *49 rue Victor Hugo, metro Ampère, 2e*) has shower-equipped doubles costing upwards of 190FF, plus private parking.

Hôtel Victoria (☎ 04 78 37 57 61, fax 04 78 42 91 07, *3 rue Delandine, metro Perrache or Ampère, 2e*) is a two-star, lift-equipped place with a whole range of rooms, costing 160FF for a double with washbasin (180FF with washbasin and bidet, 190FF with shower, 200FF with shower and toilet).

Hotels – Vieux Lyon The *Hôtel Celtic* (☎ 04 78 28 01 12, fax 04 78 28 01 34, *10 rue François Vernay, metro Vieux Lyon, 5e*) is shabby but clean. Singles/doubles with shared shower cost 135/160FF (170/200FF with private shower).

Spitting distance away, *Hôtel Le Terminus St-Paul* (☎ 04 78 28 13 29, fax 04 72 00 97 27, *6 rue Lainerie, metro Vieux Lyon, 5e*) charges 200FF for doubles with shower (240FF with shower and toilet).

Hotels – Croix Rousse Friendly *Hôtel Croix Rousse* (☎ 04 78 28 29 85, fax 04 78 27 00 26, *157 blvd de la Croix Rousse, metro Croix Rousse, 4e*) has spotlessly clean doubles with shower and toilet for 220FF.

Round the corner, cheaper but less cosy *Hôtel de la Poste* (☎ 04 78 28 62 67, *1 rue Victor Fort, metro Croix Rousse, 4e*) has bargain-basement rooms for one/two people costing 100/139FF. Doubles/triples with private shower cost 180/250FF.

Places to Stay – Mid-Range

Presqu'île Cheaper two-star places in Lyons' commercial centre include classy, hostelry-style *Hôtel Élysée* (☎ *04 78 42 03 15, fax 04 78 37 76 49, 92 rue du Président Édouard Herriot, metro Bellecour, 2e*). Singles/doubles cost upwards of 340/360FF.

Very red, charming, three-star *Hotel des Artistes* (☎ *04 78 42 04 88, fax 04 78 42 93 76, 8 rue Gaspard André, metro Bellecour or Cordeliers, 2e*) has theatrically furnished, regal singles costing 390FF to 470FF and doubles for 450FF to 510FF. Prices reflect what is in the bathroom (shower or bath) and the view (Théâtre des Célestins being the most expensive).

Five blocks south of place des Terreaux is *Hôtel Moderne* (☎ *04 78 42 21 83, fax 04 72 41 04 40, 13 rue Dubois, metro Cordeliers, 1er*) has neither net curtains and touting basic singles/doubles/triples costing 200/240/410FF (290/315/440FF with shower).

Near Gare de Perrache Hotels next to Perrache train station include two-star *Hôtel du Dauphiné* (☎ *04 78 37 24 19, fax 04 78 92 81 52, 3 rue Duhamel, metro Perrache, 2e*). Small, functional singles/doubles with shower start at 135/270FF; quads with shower and toilet cost 287FF.

There are several other two- and three-star hotels in the immediate vicinity.

Places to Stay – Top End

Lyons has plenty of upmarket hotels geared to a corporate bank account rather than a backpacker's back pocket. Lavish *Hôtel Cour des Loges* (☎ *04 72 77 44 44, fax 04 72 40 93 61,* @ *contact@courdesloges.com, 2–8 rue du Bœuf, metro Vieux Lyon, 5e*) is housed in four adjoining 14th- to 17th-century mansions wrapped around a traboule. Modern, split-level duplex suites with sunken baths and avant-garde paintings cost upwards of 1200FF.

Equally historic is *La Tour Rose* (☎ *04 78 37 25 90, fax 04 78 42 26 02,* @ *chavent*

@asi.fr, 22 rue du Bœuf, metro Vieux Lyon, 5e), named after the pink, 17th-century tower in the nearby courtyard at 16 rue du Bœuf. Lushly furnished suites honour Lyons' silky past while the hotel restaurant is in a former chapel topped with a glass and steel roof. You pay at least 950/1400FF a single/double for the privilege.

Places to Eat

Bouchons Reservations are essential. See the 'Bouchons' boxed text later in this section for what to expect from Lyons' most quintessential establishment.

Café des Fédérations (☎ *04 78 28 26 00, 8 rue Major Martin, metro Hôtel de Ville, 1er*) is among Lyons' most splendid. And it's always packed, despite the entertaining apron-clad patron offering evening diners no choice beyond one 145FF *menu*. His Croix Rousse caviar (lentils dressed in a creamy sauce) is not to be missed.

Another buzzing place is *Le Garet* (☎ *04 78 28 16 94, 7 rue du Garet, metro Hôtel de Ville, 1er*), a warm and convivial bouchon where old friends have been meeting for years. *Menus* range from 98FF (lunch only) to 128FF. Opposite, *Chez Georges* (☎ *04 78 28 30 46, 8 rue du Garet, metro Hôtel de Ville, 1er*) has house specialities such as *cervelle d'agneau* (lamb's brains), with a handwritten menu featuring 89FF and 120FF *menus*.

As with many bouchons, the decor at *Chez Hugon* (☎ *04 78 28 10 94, 12 rue Pizay, metro Hôtel de Ville, 1er*) is a blast from the past by a good 40 years which, depending on your viewpoint, can seem superbly retro or horribly outdated. A shuffling, slipper and apron-clad Madame Hugon offers diners a 145FF *menu*, starring meaty treats such as *boudin aux pommes* (blood sausage with apples) or *tablier de sapeur* (breaded, fried stomach).

Typical Lyonnais specialities are laid out for all to see at unpretentious *La Meunière* (☎ *04 78 28 62 91, 11 rue Neuve, metro Cordeliers, 1er*). Cold dishes are displayed on a large banquet-style table that dominates this elegant 1920s bouchon. *Menus* start at 120FF.

LYONS & THE RHÔNE VALLEY

Bistro Pizay (☎ 04 78 28 37 26, 4 rue Verdi, metro Hôtel de Ville, 1er) has a terrace around the back in summer and touts good-value lunchtime *formules* costing 50FF, 65FF and 75FF.

Chabert et Fils (☎ 04 78 37 01 94, 11 rue des Marronniers, metro Hôtel de Ville, 1er) is a largish place touting 99FF, 139FF and 169FF *menus* crammed with *cochonnaille* (pork) treats. Come lunchtime, Monsieur Chabert serves a 55FF *plat du jour* (dish of the day).

Not to be confused with the latter is *Chez Chabert* (☎ 04 78 42 99 65, 14 quai Romain Rolland, metro Vieux Lyon, 5e). Liver lovers will adore the succulent *foie* (liver) here. It is one of the few bouchons to open seven days a week. Count on paying around 130FF a head, excluding drinks.

Brasseries Famed among European brasseries, *Brasserie Georges* (☎ 04 72 56 54 54, 30 cours de Verdun, metro Perrache, 2e) sees over 500 people dine amid ornate 1920s ceiling murals, floor tiles and upholstered red banquettes. The brasserie, which dates from 1836, set world records in 1986 for dishing up the largest dish of *choucroute* (sauerkraut) weighing a grotesque 1.5 tonnes and, 10 years on, for producing the longest baked Alaska (34m). Its sauerkraut dishes cost 79FF to 115FF today, and lunchtime/evening *menus* start at 71/102FF.

Brasserie Francotte (☎ 04 78 37 38 64, 8 place des Célestins, metro Bellecour, 2e) is popular with the theatre crowd as well as early risers in search of breakfast (35FF). It opens 8 am to midnight, has a 98FF *menu du jour* and sporadically hosts live jazz.

Equally refined is *Grand Café des Négociants* (☎ 04 78 42 50 05, 2 place Francisque Regaud, metro Cordeliers, 2e). The walls are lined with mirrors and the service, by charming waiters, is impeccable. It serves lovely light fish dishes among other things.

Other Restaurants Cheap, cheerful and favoured for its elephant-sized portions is *La Randonnée* (☎ 04 78 27 86 81, 4 rue Terme, metro Hôtel de Ville, 1er). It has a vegetarian plate costing 50FF, numerous

lunchtime/evening *formules* costing upwards of 32/38FF and *menus* for 49/65FF.

Two summertime hot spots, favoured as much for their terraces as their Provençal-inspired *cuisine du soleil* (cuisine of the sun) are *Le Sud* (☎ 04 72 77 80 00, 11 place Antonin Poncet, metro Bellecour, 2e) whose spicy tajine and couscous dishes start at 98FF and *Campagne* (☎ 04 78 36 73 85, 20 rue Cardinal Gerlier; Fourvière funicular station, 5e), up top in Fourvière.

Rue Mercière (2e) is likewise crammed with outside restaurants in summer: *Lolo Quoi* (☎ 04 72 77 60 90, metro Cordeliers) at No 40–42 is a hugely popular and highly chic spot, dressed in funky furnishings. The budget-conscious should stick to a delicious bowl of pasta (50FF).

Harking back in history, *La Table des Échevins* (☎ 04 78 39 98 33, 12 rue Major Martin, metro Hôtel de Ville, 1er) specialises in medieval Lyonnais cuisine.

La Table d'Hippolyte (☎ 04 78 27 75 59, 22 rue Hippolyte Flandrin) is as much a feast for the eyes as for the stomach. It has few tables, however, so reserve in advance. Count on paying around 120FF a head, excluding wine.

About 12km north of the city, famous chef Paul Bocuse presides over his three-Michelin-star restaurant *Paul Bocuse* (☎ 04 72 42 90 90, 50 quai de la Plage, Collonges-au-Mont-d'Or) where you can treat yourself to truffle soup, chicken baked and served inside a sealed pig's bladder and a host of other Bocuse wonders. *Menus* cost 540FF to 780FF; reservations are mandatory. Take bus No 184 from Gare de Perrache; a taxi from the centre of Lyons costs around 150FF.

Ethnic Cuisines For an oriental snack standing up, stroll rue Ste-Marie des Terreaux and rue Ste-Catherine (metro Hôtel de Ville). Both streets are lined with Chinese, Turkish and other types of quick-eating joints.

Heading towards Croix Rousse is small and cosy African *La Mangue Amère* (☎ 04 78 39 15 42, 7 montée de l'Amphithéâtre, metro Croix Paquet, 1er). *Menus* at the

Bouchons

In the world of Lyonnais gastronomy, a *bouchon* is a small, friendly, unpretentious restaurant that serves traditional Lyonnais cuisine. In the rest of France, the strict definition of the word conjures up the more prosaic meanings of 'bottle stopper', 'cork' or 'traffic jam'.

Kick-start your bouchon dining experience with a *communard*, a Lyonnais aperitif of red wine and crème de cassis (blackcurrant liqueur) – a mix considered completely criminal elsewhere in France. Blood-red in colour, it is named after the Paris Commune supporters, killed during the first great proletarian uprising against the bourgeoisie in 1871.

When ordering wine in a bouchon, always ask for a *pot*, a 46cl glass bottle with a solid 3cm-thick glass bottom and adorned with an elastic band round its neck to prevent wine drips when pouring. Pots cost around 45FF and are filled with red Côtes du Rhône or Beaujolais. Menus are invariably handwritten and tough to decipher for even the most fluent of French speakers.

Contrary to what your mother taught you as a child, you might well be required to keep your knife and fork for the duration of the meal; wiping your eating gadgets clean with a piece of bread between courses is allowed. If the table cloth is of the paper variety, the chances are that is where your final bill *(addition)* will be added up.

Bouchon fare is not for the faint hearted. Meaty dishes worth sinking your teeth into include *boudin blanc* (veal sausage), *quenelles* (lighter-than-light flour, egg and cream dumplings), *quenelles de brochet* (pike quenelles, usually served in a creamy crayfish sauce), and *andouillette* (sausages made from pigs' intestines). *Cervelle de canut* – a type of cream cheese mixed with chives and garlic – is another standard feature. Literally 'brains of the silk weaver', cervelle de canut originated in Croix Rousse and accompanied breakfast, lunch and dinner – day in, day out – for most weavers in the 19th century.

In keeping with tradition, many bouchons are closed in July and August. Most are typically closed at weekends too.

'Bitter Mango' cost 108FF and its *mousse d'avocat* (avocado mousse) melts in your mouth.

La Case Créole (☎ *04 78 29 41 70, 4 rue Verdi, metro Hôtel de Ville, 1er*) is a young and trendy Creole place with *menus* for 89FF, 98FF and 145FF. *La Mamounia* (☎ *04 78 28 68 44, 20 rue du Bât d'Argent, metro Hôtel de Ville, 1er*) is a Moroccan place where entrées and desserts costs 28FF and main dishes 99FF.

Syrian *Alyssaar* (☎ *04 78 29 57 66, 29 rue du Bât d'Argent, metro Hôtel de Ville, 1er*) specialises in the cuisine of Aleppo, 'the gastronomic capital of the Middle East' as far as the Syrian-born owner is concerned. *Menus* clock in at 78FF, 87FF and 105FF.

Cafes Outside cafes spill across every square and empty patch of street in Vieux Lyon on sunny days. Fountain-flooded place des Terreaux is likewise one big cafe

in summer. For an awe-inspiring bird's eye view of Lyons, ride the elevator to *Les Muses de l'Opéra* (☎ *04 72 00 45 58*), an upmarket restaurant (105FF *menu*) on the 7th floor of the opera house, which has a sun-drenched cafe-terrace tucked at the feet of the eight sculpted muses fronting the opera. Round the corner, artsy *Café 203* (☎ *04 78 28 66 65, 9 rue Garet, metro Hôtel de Ville, 1er*) is favoured by the opera crowd for its good-value 55FF *menu* that includes a glass of wine, served noon to 3 pm. Trendy *Mushic* (☎ *04 72 98 80 96, 26 rue Hippolyte Flandrin, metro Hôtel de Ville, 1er*) is decorated minimalist-style.

Handy for a quick nibble after a museum tour is the small but packed Vietnamese *Petit Grain* (☎ *04 72 41 77 85, 19 rue de la Charité, metro Ampère, 2e*), close to the Textile Museum. The 'Little Grain' has salads, spicy meats and vegetarian platters starting at 43FF.

In Vieux Lyon, tasteful *Sol Café (☎ 04 72 77 66 69, 28 rue du Bœuf, metro Vieux Lyon, 5e)* is adorned with sunflowers and serves light tapas-style snacks.

Self-Catering A colourful *outdoor food market* is held each morning, except Monday, on blvd de la Croix Rousse (metro Croix Rousse, 4e) and on quai St-Antoine (metro Bellecour, 2e).

The largest indoor food markets are *Les Halles de Lyon (102 cours Lafayette, metro Part-Dieu, 3e)*, east of the centre, open 7 am to 12.30 pm and 3 to 7 pm Tuesday to Thursday, 7 am to 7 pm Friday and Saturday and 7 am to 2 pm Sunday; and *La Halle de la Martinière (24 rue de la Martinière, metro Hôtel de Ville, 1er)*, open 6.30 am to 12.30 pm and 4 to 7.30 pm, Tuesday to Sunday lunchtime.

There's a *Carrefour* supermarket (metro Part-Dieu) in the Centre Commercial la Part-Dieu (see Shopping).

Seeking a taste-bud tickle? Head for expensive and exclusive *La Vieille Réserve* for wine (metro Hôtel de Ville) at 1 place Tobbie Robatel (1er); *Pierre Champion* for *foies gras* (duck liver pâté) at 4 place Bellecour (2e) and *Rich Art* for designer chocolate (metro Bellecour), 1 rue du Plat (2e); *Fromagerie* for cheese (metro Perrache or Ampère), 39 rue de la Charité (2e); *Moinon Charcuterie* at 18 rue de la Plaitière for Lyonnais boudins, andouillettes and other sausages and meats; or the *Whisky Lodge* for 118 types of whisky (metro Bellecour), 7 rue Ferrandière (2e).

Entertainment

The tourist office has details of Lyons' rich and varied entertainment scene, also detailed in the weekly *Lyon Poche* (8FF at newsagents) or free fortnightly *Le Petit Bulletin*. You can find comprehensive online cinema, theatre and other entertainment listings at www.webcity.fr.

Tickets for most events are sold at FNAC, which has branches at 85 rue de la République (☎ 04 72 40 49 49, ✆ lyon. bellecour@fnac.tm.fr, metro Bellecour, 2e) and inside the Centre Commercial la Part-Dieu (☎ 04 78 71 87 00, ✆ lyon.part-dieu@ fnac.tm.fr, metro Part-Dieu, 3e).

Pubs & Clubs Mainstream drinking holes include the Irish *Shamrock (15 rue Ste-Catherine, metro Hôtel de Ville, 1er)*; *Barrel House (13 rue Ste-Catherine)*; and *Albion (12 rue Ste-Catherine)*. For a touch of Oz try *Down Under Australian Pub (12 rue du Griffon, metro Hôtel de Ville, 1er)*.

In Vieux Lyon, *Smoking Dog (16 rue Lainerie, metro Vieux Lyon, 5e)* hosts a weekly pub quiz and happy hour, screens sports events on TV, and has British newspapers for punters' perusal. Live music is a feature of *Fleming's Irish Pub (2 rue de la Loge, 5e)* around the corner. A pint of Guinness here costs 28FF (34FF in the evening). *La Bodéga (☎ 04 78 29 42 35, 35 quai Pierre Scize, metro Vieux Lyon, 5e)*, west of place St-Paul, is a rocking late-night, quayside bar.

On the Presqu'île, trendy *Le Voxx (☎ 04 78 28 33 87, 1 rue d'Algérie, metro Hôtel de Ville, 1er)* boasts River Saône views, sunny outside seating, designer chairs, occasional live bands and a boisterous drinking crowd. Equally chic is *2P+C (☎ 04 78 30 02 01, 3 rue Terme, metro Hôtel de Ville or Croix Paquet, 1er)* where a designer-dressed crowd sips cocktails in the bath; 2P+C is an acronym for *deux pièces plus cuisine* (two rooms plus kitchen). Face control prevails at the door.

At funky *Le Chantier (☎ 04 78 39 05 56, 20 rue Ste-Catherine, metro Hôtel de Ville, 1er)* clubbers slide down bum-first courtesy of a metal slide to the basement dance floor. Alternatively, dance afloat at *Fish (☎ 04 72 84 98 98, 21 quai Victor Augagneur, metro Place Guichard, Foch or Cordeliers, 3e)*, an ultra-trendy nightclub on a boat moored on the Rhône's left bank.

In Croix Rousse, the very local *Whisky Ping Pong (4 ter rue Belfort, metro Croix Rousse, 4e)* is also packed thanks to its house specialities – *cassoulet* (a hearty stew), whisky and backgammon. Heading downhill, *Kafé Myzik (☎ 04 72 07 04 26, ✆ kafe.myzik@mailperso.com, 20 montée St-Sébastien, metro Croix Paquet, 1er)* is a hole-in-the-wall bar-cum-club that frequently hosts live bands.

Farther afield, crowded *Ninkasi* (☎ 04 72 76 89 09, ✉ ninkasi@free.fr, 267 rue Marcel Mérieux, 7e), a micro-brewery next to the stadium that serves its own beer, runs a great-value food bar and has local bands playing most evenings. Take bus No 17, 32, 47 or 96 from the centre to the stadium (*stade*) stop.

In the student quarter of Villeurbanne, directly east of the centre, *L'Oxxo* (☎ 04 78 93 62 03, 7 ave Albert Einstein) sports an eclectic decor of recycled aeroplanes and cable cars, a predominantly student clientele, and is known for its theme nights and rock bands.

Cinemas Lyons has some 15 cinemas. Tickets cost around 45FF. For English-language film screenings try *Cinéma Ambiance* (☎ 08 36 68 20 15, 12 rue de la République, metro Cordeliers, 2e); *CNP-Terreaux* (☎ 08 36 68 69 33, 40 rue du Président Édouard Herriot, metro Hôtel de Ville, 1er); or *UGC Astoria* (☎ 08 36 68 68 58, 31 cours Vitton, metro Charpennes, 6e).

For art films, B&W classics and other French and foreign 'cult-following' movies, look no further than the *Hangar du Premier Film* at the *Institut Lumière* (☎ 08 36 68 88 79, 25 rue du Premier Film, metro Monplaisir Lumière, 8e). There are two or three screenings daily and tickets cost 35FF (seniors aged over 60, students and those aged under 18, 29FF). Films are shown on the square in front of the institute in summer. Program details are posted online at www.institut-lumiere.org.

In Croix Rousse, films are screened under the trees on place Colbert (metro Croix Paquet, 1er) in summer.

Theatre, Opera & Classical Music
From mid-September to early July, opera, ballet, classical concerts and recitals are staged at the *opera house* (☎ 04 72 00 45 45, ✉ rpublic@opera-lyon.org, place de la Comédie, metro Hôtel de Ville, 1er). Opera tickets cost 70FF to 380FF depending on seating. The box office opens 11 am to

7 pm, Monday to Saturday. The *Auditorium* (☎ 04 78 95 95 95, 149 rue Garibaldi, metro Garibaldi, 1er), is a fine venue for classical concerts.

The box office at *Théâtre des Célestins* (☎ 04 72 77 40 00, place des Célestins, metro Cordeliers, 2e), dating from 1877, opens 11 am to 6 pm, Monday to Saturday. It shows mainstream plays.

In Vieux Lyon, puppet shows grace the stage at *Théâtre Guignol* (☎ 04 78 28 92 57, 2 rue Louis Carrand, metro Vieux Lyon, 5e).

Dance Contemporary dance, cabarets and occasional rock concerts take place at the *Maison de la Dance* (☎ 04 72 78 18 00, 8 ave Jean Mermoz, metro Grange Blanche, 8e). Its box office opens 11.45 am to 6.45 pm, Monday to Friday, and 2 to 6.45 pm on Saturday.

Shopping
From 7 am to 1 pm on Sunday morning, head for the Marché de l'Artisanat (Artists' Market) along quai Fulchiron in Vieux Lyon. Books (old and new) can be browsed through and bought at the outdoor book market that fills the length of quai de la Pêcherie (metro Hôtel de Ville, 1er) from 10 am to 6 pm Saturday and Sunday.

La Cité des Antiquaires (☎ 04 72 44 91 98), 117 blvd Stalingrad (6e), in the Villeurbanne suburb east of the centre, is the third largest antique market in Europe. It opens 9.30 am to 12.30 pm and 2.30 to 7 pm, Thursday, Saturday and Sunday (closed Sunday afternoon from 1 May to 31 August). In town, rue Auguste Comte (metro Perrache or Bellecour, 2e) is lined with antique shops.

The Centre Commercial la Part-Dieu (metro Part-Dieu) is a huge indoor shopping centre, open 9.30 am to 7.30 pm, Monday to Saturday.

Getting There & Away
Air Lyon-St-Exupéry airport (formerly Lyon Satolas; ☎ 04 72 22 76 91 for information, ☎ 04 72 22 72 21 for the switchboard) is 25km east of the city. Flight

schedules are posted on the airport Web site at www.lyon.aeroport.fr.

Some no-frills airlines fly to/from St-Étienne airport (☎ 04 77 55 71 71), from where there are shuttle buses to/from Lyons, 60km south-west. See the introductory Getting There & Away chapter for details.

Bus Most intercity buses to destinations north, east and south of Lyons (such as Annecy, Chambéry, Grenoble, Pérouges, Valence, St-Étienne) depart from the bus terminal under the Centre d'Échange, next to Gare de Perrache. Timetables are available from the information office of Lyons' mass transit authority, TCL (☎ 04 78 71 70 00) which has a Web site at www.tcl.fr. Tickets are sold by the driver. Buses to places west of Lyons (☎ 04 78 43 40 74) leave from outside the Gorge de Loup metro station.

Eurolines (☎ 04 72 56 95 30; buses to/from Belgium, Germany, Italy, Spain and the UK), Linebús (☎ 04 72 41 72 27; buses to/from Spain) and Intercars (☎ 04 78 37 20 80; buses to/from Poland) each have an office on the bus station level of the Centre d'Échange (follow the 'Lignes Internationales' signs), all open 8 or 9 am to noon and 2 to 6, 6.30 or 8.30 pm, Monday to Saturday.

Train Lyons has two mainline train stations (☎ 0 836 35 35 35 for both): Gare de Perrache, on the Presqu'île, and Gare de la Part-Dieu, about 1.5km east of the Rhône. Only a handful of local trains use Gare St-Paul in Vieux Lyon.

In general, trains that begin or end their journey in Lyons (including most short-haul lines) use Perrache, while trains passing through the city (including trains to southern France and TGVs to Roissy Charles de Gaulle airport and Lille) stop at Part-Dieu. Some trains – such as TGVs to/from Paris and most trains to/from the Alps and Geneva – stop at both.

TGV travel to/from Paris' Gare de Lyon (two hours, half-hourly) costs 318FF to 398FF. Lyons has direct rail links to *all* parts of France and Europe. Destinations accessible by direct TGV include Roissy Charles de Gaulle airport (338FF to 418FF, 2¼ hours), Lille-Europe (410FF to 476FF, three hours), Nantes (401FF to 462FF, five hours) and St-Pierre des Corps (Tours; 334FF to 395FF, three hours).

Following the completion of the new high-speed railway southbound (see TGV in the Getting Around chapter), Lyons will have direct TGV links to Avignon, Marseille and Montpelier.

Gare de Perrache The complex that includes Gare de Perrache (metro Perrache) consists of two main buildings: the Centre d'Échange, whose lower levels serve as a bus terminal and metro station, and the train station itself, southward across the pedestrian bridge called 'Le Mail'.

There is an SNCF information office (☎ 04 72 40 10 65), signposted 'Accueil', on the station's upper level. At least one ticket counter is staffed 24 hours a day, as are the public conveniences – down the half-flight of stairs near the Thomas Cook bureau – where you can take a shower (15.20FF/20 minutes).

Left luggage lockers, accessible 6.15 am to 9.45 pm, can be reached via platform A. Small/medium/large lockers cost 15/20/30FF for up to three days.

Gare de la Part-Dieu The information office of the Part-Dieu train station (metro Part-Dieu; ☎ 0 836 35 35 35), on the courtyard reached via the Vivier Merle exit, opens 9 am to 7.30 pm, Monday to Friday, and 9 am to 6.30 pm on Saturday. The Service Clientèle office, which handles reimbursements, is in the same building. It opens 10 am to 12.15 pm and 1.45 to 6.15 pm, Monday to Friday.

SOS Voyageurs (☎ 04 72 34 12 16), at the foot of the stairs up to platforms I and J, opens 8 am to 8 pm, Monday to Saturday, and 9 am to 8 pm on Sunday. Luggage lockers (30FF per two pieces of luggage/24 hours) are round the corner next to the Avis car rental office and can be accessed between 7 am and 10.15 pm. The showers under the stairs to platforms A and B open

4.45 am to 12.45 am (15.20/2.30FF to shower/pee).

Car ADA (☎ 04 78 37 93 93, metro Perrache) has an office at 42 quai du Docteur Gailleton (2e). All the major car rental companies have an office at Gare de la Part-Dieu, on the courtyard accessed by the Porte Villette exit.

Getting Around

To/From the Airport Buses (Satobus; ☎ 04 72 68 72 17, 04 72 35 94 96) from the city to Lyons St-Exupéry airport cost 49.50FF one-way (37/25FF for people aged 13 to 25/children aged four to 12) and take 45 minutes from Gare de Perrache (the stop is signposted 'Navette Aéroport', accessed via the international bus hall on the middle level of the Centre d'Échange) and 35 minutes from Gare de la Part-Dieu (the stop is across the plaza from the Vivier Merle exit). A return ticket valid for two months (88FF) is also available, as is a Ticket Rhône Pass (54FF) that entitles you to a one-way trip to/from the airport plus a one-hour ride in town on the metro.

Buses depart every 20 minutes (every 30 minutes on Saturday afternoon, Sunday and holidays) from the city centre from 5 am to 9 pm (from 6 am to 11 pm from the airport). Between mid-December and mid-April there are also regular weekly buses (Satobus-Alpes; ☎ 04 72 35 94 96) between Lyons St-Exupéry and Bourg St-Maurice (250/375FF for a single/return), Cluses (290/435FF), Grenoble (130/195FF), and Moutiers (230/345FF), from where there are bus connections to most French Alpine ski resorts. Schedules are posted on the Satobus Web site at www.satobus-alps.com.

Avoid taking a taxi between the town centre and the airport. The 30-minute trip into town can cost up to 350FF.

Shuttle buses to/from St-Étienne airport depart from in front of Gare de la Part-Dieu. Tickets (100FF one way) are sold on the bus.

Metro & Tram Lyons' metro system is run by TCL. Its four fast, quiet metro lines are known as A, B, C and D; the last is driverless. The two funicular railway lines that link Vieux Lyon with Fourvière and St-Just are known by their initials F and SJ. The metro runs from 5 am to midnight. Tickets must be time-stamped before proceeding to the platforms, which incidentally, have no turnstiles.

As of December 2000, Lyons will be graced with a two-line tramway (☎ 04 72 84 58 13 for information), estimated to cost 2,425 million FF. The northbound Perrache-La Doua line (8.7km) will link Gare de Perrache with Gare de Part-Dieu, while the eastbound Perrache-St Priest (10km) will connect Gare de Perrache with place Jean Macé, Grange-Blanche and beyond.

Tickets Tickets cost 8/68FF for a single/carnet of 10 and are valid for one-way travel on buses, trolley buses, the metro and the funicular. They can be used for an hour after being time-stamped for the first time. Up to three transfers are allowed but return trips are not.

The Ticket Liberté (24FF), good for a day of unlimited travel, can be bought on or before the day you use it at metro ticket machines, on buses and at TCL information offices. Its two-hour equivalent, the Ticket Liberté 2h (10FF), gives you two hours of unlimited travel between 9 am and 4 pm. Before using either ticket, you must fill in your name in the space provided on the ticket.

TCL Offices Near Gare de la Part-Dieu, TCL's information and sales bureau (☎ 04 78 71 70 00, metro Part-Dieu), 19 blvd Vivier Merle (3e), opens 8 am to 6.30 pm, Monday to Friday, and 9 am to 5 pm on Saturday. At Gare de Perrache, there's a TCL office on the middle level of the Centre d'Échange, open 7.30 am to 6.30 pm, Monday to Friday, and 7.30 am to 5 pm on Saturday. There are other TCL offices in or next to the Bellecour, Vieux Lyon, Croix Rousse and Gorge de Loup metro stations.

Taxi To order a taxi, call Allo Taxi (☎ 04 78 28 23 23), Taxis Lyonnais (☎ 04 78 26 81 81) or Télé-Taxi (☎ 04 78 28 13 14). You can get a taxi from rue du Président Édouard Herriot's northern end (metro Hôtel de Ville).

AROUND LYONS

Hills, lakes and vineyards are but a short ride away from cosmopolitan Lyons. Those intent on exploring the city's surrounds should invest in Blay Foldex's map (31FF) entitled *60km autour de Lyon* (60km around Lyons) or Michelin's 1:200,000 scale *Rhône-Alpes* (35FF). Buy a copy from the tourist office or a bookshop before leaving town.

Couvent Ste-Marie de la Tourette

The modernistic convent, 30km west of Lyons in La Tourette, is the next best thing after the chapel at Ronchamp (see the French Alps & Jura chapter) for dedicated fans of the architect Le Corbusier (1887–1965), renowned for his stark, concrete building and innovative furniture designs. Those unfamiliar with the work of the 20th-century architectural god are likely to perceive the convent building – home to 20 white-robed Dominican monks today – as nothing short of ugly.

Guided tours run at 10 and 11 am (no tour at 11 am on Sunday) and hourly from 2 to 6 pm, 15 June to 15 September. In winter, afternoon tours depart hourly at weekends only. Admission costs 30FF (students 20FF). Year round, you can stay at the convent and breakfast with the monks for 105FF. Full-board costs 235FF. Advance reservations (☎ 04 74 26 79 70, fax 04 74 26 79 99) are essential.

From Lyons' Gare St-Paul (metro Vieux Lyon, 5e) there are regular trains to L'Arbresle (25FF, 45 minutes, eight to 10 daily), 1.5km north of La Tourette. From L'Arbresle follow the 'Evreux' signs. By car follow the westbound N7 out of Lyons; cyclists should opt for the more scenic D7.

Pérouges & La Dombes

The heavily restored medieval village of **Pérouges** (population 850), perched on a hill 27km north-east of Lyons, is linked to Lyons by bus. Day-trippers flock here to stroll its cobbled streets and munch on *galettes de Perouges* (sweet tarts, served warm and crusted with sugar) and cider, the traditional Pérougien feast.

South-west is **La Dombes**, a marshy area whose hundreds of shallow lakes, created over the past six centuries by local farmers, are first used primarily as fish ponds, then drained so crops can be grown on the fertile lake bed. The area, bisected by the N83, attracts lots of wildlife, particularly waterfowl. Feathered species from different continents can be observed at the **Parc des Oiseaux** (bird park; ☎ 04 74 98 05 54) just outside Villars-les-Dombes.

Beaujolais

The hilly Beaujolais region, 40km north of Lyons, is a land of rivers (all tributaries of the Saône), granite peaks (the highest is the 1012m Mont St-Rigaud), pastures, farms and forests. The region is most famous, however, for its wines (see the Food & Wine section at the front of this book). It boasts some 150 sq km of terraced vineyards occupying a narrow, 60km-long strip along the right bank of the Saône. For a list of chateaux where you can taste and buy wine, contact Le Pays Beaujolais (☎ 04 74 02 22 00, fax 04 74 02 22 09) at 172 blvd Vermorel in **Villefranche-sur-Saône**, or the tourist office (☎ 04 74 69 22 88) in Beaujeu.

Beaujolais' other gastronomic wonders include its fine virgin oils – such as pecan nut oil, almond oil and pine kernel oil – available at the Huilerie Beaujolaise (☎ 04 74 69 28 06) at 29 rue des Echarmeaux in **Beaujeu**; the annual Chestnut Fair (☎ 04 74 64 85 14) held the last Sunday of October in **Thel**; and the delicious pots of prize-winning honey sold at the Miellerie du Fût (☎/fax 04 74 69 92 03) in **Avenas**.

Exploring Beaujolais by **mountain bike** is invigorating and uplifting, its gentle hills being suited to the least experienced of cyclists. Fifteen routes (230km) for two-wheelers are detailed in the Topoguide entitled *Le Beaujolais à VTT*. IGN's *Beau-*

jolais map (45FF) is also invaluable. The VTT Centre (☎ 04 74 02 06 84) in Marchampt, 10km south of Beaujeu, rents bicycles and maps out thematic circuits for cyclists.

Rewarding spots to sleep, wine and dine include *Anne de Beaujeu* (☎ 04 74 04 87 58, 28 rue de la République), a charming hotel and restaurant in Beaujeu with doubles costing upwards of 310FF, and upmarket *Restaurant Christian Mabeau* (☎ 04 74 03 41 79) in Odenas, 10km south of Beaujeu via the D37. Unextraordinary from the front, this place has the most extraordinary terrace overlooking a vineyard out back.

DOWNSTREAM ALONG THE RHÔNE

Downstream along the River Rhône, vineyards meet nuclear power plants – not the most obvious tourist destination but worth a stop for Lyons day-trippers or the Provence-bound. Rhône Valley flora and fauna comes to life in the **Maison du Rhône** (☎ 04 78 73 70 37) at 1 place de la Liberté in **Givors**, 20km south of Lyons on the right bank.

Vienne
postcode 38200 • pop 29,500
• elevation 160m

The former Roman colony of Vienne straddles the River Rhône, 32km south of Lyons. One of the largest settlements in Gaul, the city served as capital of Burgundy in the 9th century and enjoyed considerable power until its absorption by the French crown in 1450.

Contemporary Vienne is famed for its annual two-week jazz festival, held at the end of June in the city's open-air **Théâtre Antique** (Roman amphitheatre). Central place Charles de Gaulle is dominated by the **Temple d'Auguste et de Livie**, a superb Roman temple built around 10 BC to honour Emperor Augustus and his wife, Livia. Across the river on the right bank, the remains of the Gallo-Roman city of **St-Romain en Gal** (☎ 04 74 53 74 01), 2 chemin de la Plaine, have been excavated.

Vienne's tourist office (☎ 04 74 53 80 30,

fax 04 74 53 80 31) is at 3 cours Brillier. The *Auberge de Jeunesse* (☎ 04 74 53 21 97, fax 04 74 31 98 93, 11 quai Riondet), 50m south along riverside blvd du Rhône Sud, has dorm beds costing 67FF, including breakfast. Reception opens 6 to 9 pm.

Getting There & Away Cars VFD (☎ 04 74 85 18 51) operates a couple of buses daily to/from Grenoble (1¾ hours). Vienne is served by trains to/from Lyon-Perrache (33FF, 35 minutes, hourly) and Valence (62FF, 50 minutes, eight or so daily), from where there are connecting southbound trains.

Between April and October Navig-Inter (see Boating, Bicycling & Walking in the Lyons section, earlier in this chapter) runs river excursions, Monday or Tuesday to Saturday, between Vienne and Lyons, stopping at Givors to visit the Maison du Rhône. A singe/return ticket costs 75/140FF (children aged under 10, 50/65FF). Compagnie Resto Rhône (☎ 04 75 60 69 22) organises lunch cruises (290FF) from Vienne to Tournon-sur-Rhône; boats depart from the pier opposite the Vienne tourist office.

Towards Valence

The **Parc Naturel Régional du Pilat** spills across 65,000 hectares south-west of Vienne and offers breathtaking panoramas of the Rhône Valley from its highest peaks, Crêt de l'Œillon (1370m), and Crêt de la Perdrix (1432m). The Montgolfière brothers – inventors of the hot air balloon in 1783 – were born in **Annonay**, 50km north of Valence, on the park's south-eastern boundary.

South of Vienne vineyards sprout. Two of the most respected Côtes du Rhône *appellations*, St-Joseph and Hermitage, are harvested on the steep, terraced hills around **Tournon-sur-Rhône**. St-Joseph reds are lighter and drunk at an earlier age than their fuller-bodied counterpart, Hermitage. Hermitage is grown on a single granite hill behind **Tain l'Hermitage**, on the left bank of the Rhône. The tourist office here (☎ 04 75 08 06 81) has a list of *caves* (wine cellars) – such as Cave des Vignerons de Tain l'Hermitage (☎ 04 75 08 20 87) on route de

Larnage – where you can taste and buy wine. The village hosts a wine festival on the last weekend in February and on the third Sunday in September.

Valence

postcode 26000 • pop 63,500
• elevation 126m

Viewed by most travellers through the window of a TGV, Valence is a train hub between northern and southern France. Named Valentia by the Romans in 2 BC, the city has been graced with a university since 1452. Napoleon Bonaparte attended artillery school here from the age of 16, risking his life (so legend claims) to scale the white cliffs of Crussol which guard Valence from the opposite side of the river. The 12th-century **Château de Crussol** that crowns these cliffs (accessible from St-Péray, 5km north via the N532) is ruined today.

Vieux Valence (Old Valence) is dominated by **Cathédrale St-Apollinaire**, dating to 1057 and rebuilt in the 16th century. Nearby, the Flamboyant Gothic facade of **Maison des Têtes** (1530) at 57 Grande Rue is adorned with sculpted heads including those of the winds, Time and Fortune.

Valence tourist office (☎ 04 75 44 90 40, ℮ info@tourisme-valence.com) is next to the train and bus stations. Information is posted on its Web site at www.tourisme-valence.com. The riverside *Auberge de Jeunesse* (☎ *04 75 42 32 00, fax 04 75 56 20 67, chemin de l'Epervière*) has beds in three/six-bedded dorms costing 48/63FF a night, plus 13FF for sheets.

Getting There & Away Valence is 74km south of Vienne and 126km north of Avignon. Valence has direct non-TGV/TGV rail links with Lyons (82/122FF, 1¼ hours/40 minutes, about 10 daily) and has train connections to most parts of southern France, including to Avignon (172FF, one hour, about 10 daily), Montpellier (227FF, 2¼ hours, eight daily) and Nice (324FF, 4¾ hours, five or six daily). Local trains yo-yo between Valence and Montélimar (44FF, 20 minutes).

Between April and October, Compagnie Resto Rhône (see the Vienne section) runs Rhône river cruises to/from Tournon-sur-Rhône and Avignon.

Montélimar

postcode 26200 • pop 30,000
• elevation 90m

Sweet-toothed Montélimar, 46km south of Valence on the left bank, prides itself on its nutty nougat which has been produced here since the 16th century. The town has no less than 15 nougat factories that can be visited. Ask for a list at the tourist office (☎ 04 75 01 00 20, fax 04 75 52 33 69, ℮ montelimar.tourisme@wanadoo.fr) on allées Provençales.

Montélimar's origins lie in the 11th- to 16th-century **Château des Adhémar** (☎ 04 75 00 62 30), built atop Mont Adhémar after which the town was named. The castle served as a prison between 1790 and 1929 and is the valley's most important example of feudal architecture.

The ruined **Château de Rochemaure** which crowns the pretty village of Rochemaure, 7km north on the right bank of the Rhône, is also worth visiting.

Getting There & Away Montélimar is on the Valence–Avignon rail line. See Getting There & Away under Valence.

Gorges de l'Ardèche

The River Rhône's voyage through the northern Rhône Valley (the southern section from just north of Orange to the Mediterranean is part of Provence; see that chapter) crescendos at the Gorges de l'Ardèche. These gorges cut dramatically eastwards through a terrain of calcareous rock and herbal-scented *garrigue* (a type of scrub) from **Vallon Pont d'Arc** to **St-Martin de l'Ardèche** and are protected as a nature reserve. Eagles nest in the cliffs and there are numerous caves (*grottes*) to explore. Six kilometres south of Vallon Pont d'Arc, the rock forms a natural bridge across the River Ardèche which gushes into the Rhône at **Pont St-Espirit**, marking the end of its 120km journey.

Nuclear Tourism

No less than five nuclear power plants stud the Rhône Valley's riverbanks, making Rhône-Alpes the highest nuclear-energy producing *région* in France.

The plant at **St-Alban**, built 25km south of Vienne on the River Rhône's left bank between 1978 and 1985, touts two pressurised water reactors. Each is rated at 1300 megawatts and boasts a combined annual production of 15 billion kilowatts – sufficient electricity to power the city of Lyons 10 times over. The Centre Nucléaire de Production d'Électricité de St-Alban-St-Maurice (☎ 04 74 29 33 66) can be visited daily; its information centre opens 2 to 5.30 pm, but free tours of the plant must be booked in advance. Bring some ID with you.

Farther downstream at **St-Paul Trois Châteaux**, nuclear tourism enjoys an added twist. At the **Ferme aux Crocodiles** (☎ 04 75 04 33 73, ✉ fermecroco@enprovence.com), grouchy crocodiles slumber in tropical pools of 30°C water, heated by the nuclear power plant next door. Both places welcome visitors. The Crocodile Farm opens 9.30 am to 6 pm (45FF), while the neighbouring Centre Nucléaire de Production d'Électricité de Tricastin (☎ 04 75 50 37 10) can be visited by guided 'tour (2½ hours) Monday to Friday. Tours must be booked in advance and, again, you need some ID. Children aged under 10 are not allowed on site.

In addition to keeping 350 crocodiles warm, the four 915-megawatt reactors at the plant – which produce 24 billion kilowatts annually – heat 42 hectares of greenhouses and 2400 homes in **Pierrelatte**, 2km north.

From Vallon Pont d'Arc, the northbound D579 takes scenic-seeking cyclists and motorists to **Ruoms**. Across the river, the D4 (signposted 'Largentière') snakes wildly along the **Défilé de Ruoms** (a narrow tunnel of rock) and the **Gorges de la Ligne** for 8km to Bellevue. At Bellevue, bear north on the D104 for 2km to Uzer, then east on the D294 to **Balazuc**, one of France's *plus beaux* (prettiest) villages.

From Balazuc the D579 leads to **Aubenas**, from where a multitude of scenic roads fan out into the surrounding countryside. This is the land of chestnuts where the dark brown fruit is turned into everything from *crème de châtaigne* (a sweet puree served with ice cream, crepes or cake) to *bière aux marrons* (chestnut beer). Unique to the region is *liqueur de châtaigne*, a 21% vol liqueur which makes a sweet aperitif when mixed with white wine. The Palais du Marron (☎ 04 75 64 35 16) at 10 cours de l'Esplanade in **Privas** sells it.

The Ardèche is perfect to explore by bicycle, foot or **canoe**. There are several canoe rental outlets which organise half-day and day river expeditions in Vallon Pont'Arc and St-Martin de l'Ardèche. Both sport a couple of camping grounds too. In northern Ardèche, the tourist office in Privas (☎ 04 75 64 33 35, fax 04 74 64 73 95), overlooking cours de l'Esplanade, is the best information source. *Château de Liviers* (☎ *04 75 64 64 00*, ✉ *chateauliviers@ wanadoo.fr*), 2km from Privas signposted off the northbound D2, is a lovely place to stay. You can camp in the castle grounds, stay in a six- or eight-person gîte (55FF per person/night) or opt for a single/ double chambre d'hôte (250/290FF including breakfast).

Getting There & Around Buses from Valence to/from Aubenas (55.50FF, 1½ hours, five or six daily) and Privas (31.50FF, 55 minutes, at least 10 daily) are operated by Autocars Charrière (☎ 04 75 64 10 19 in Privas, ☎ 04 75 35 68 60 in Aubenas). The rest of the region is impossible to explore by public transport.

French Alps & the Jura

'Lances des glaciers fiers, rois blancs' (Lances of proud glaciers, white kings)

Arthur Rimbaud

The French Alps, where fertile, green valleys meet soaring peaks topped with craggy, snowbound summits, form one of the most awesome mountain ranges in the world. In summer, visitors take advantage of hundreds of kilometres of magnificent hiking trails and engage in all sorts of warm-weather sporting activities. In winter, the area's fine ski resorts attract cross-country and downhill enthusiasts from around the globe.

The first half of this chapter covers mountainous areas where you can hike and ski, including the mountains and valleys around Mont Blanc. During the warm months, Annecy, Thonon-les-Bains and Chambéry offer the best of the French Alps' lowland delights: swimming, hiking, *parapente* (paragliding) and the like. Grenoble, capital of the historical region of Dauphiné, provides big-city amenities and hiking opportunities, while nearby there are less expensive low-altitude ski stations. North of Lake Geneva, in the Jura, Besançon and the towns of Métabief Mont d'Or and Les Rousses offer a taste of the refreshingly untouched Franche-Comté region.

Geography

The Alps – whose name is derived from the Ligurian word for pasture – have served as a barrier between Europe's peoples and nations since ancient times. Formed some 44 million years ago, the peaks and valleys have been sculpted by erosion and, especially over the past 1.6 million years, massive glaciers. Both these factors have endowed the Alpine river valleys with mild climates and rich soils, making them very suitable for human settlement. The Alps stretch for 370km from Lake Geneva (Lac Léman) in the north, almost to Provence in the south. France's border with Italy follows the Alps' highest ridges and peaks.

Highlights

- **Chamonix** – marvel at Mont Blanc from the world's highest and scariest cable car
- **Annecy** – stroll around enticing cobbled streets; relax by its dreamy lake
- **Besançon** – learn French in Besançon – a relaxed, student-oriented town
- **Baume-les-Messieurs** – explore the caves and waterfalls near this timeless village
- **Ronchamp** – visit Le Corbusier's dramatically situated, futuristic chapel

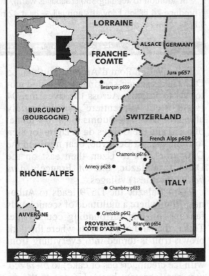

The Alps' two major historic regions are Savoy and Dauphiné. Savoy covers the northern portion of the Alps and culminates in Europe's highest mountain, Mont Blanc (4808m), with the town of Chamonix at its base. To the west, Annecy acts as the gateway to much of Savoy, while farther south sits the region's historic capital, Chambéry. Dauphiné, which is south of Savoy and stretches eastwards all the way to Briançon and the Italian

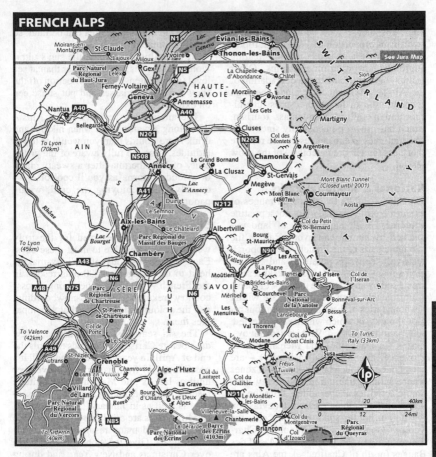

FRENCH ALPS

border, is home to Grenoble, the capital of the Alps.

North of Lake Geneva, the Jura Mountains form an arc that extends northwards along the River Doubs towards Alsace.

Climate

The Alps are characterised by extreme climatic diversity. As you would expect, the southern slopes are warmer than areas with northern exposure.

There's enough snow most years from December to April for skiing even at lower-altitude stations. In spring (late spring and

summer at higher elevations), carpets of flowers bloom next to and within the magnificent forests. Throughout the year, weather conditions can change rapidly.

For weather information, call the *météo* (weather bureau information) on ☎ 0 836 68 00 00 for the regional report, or ☎ 0 836 68 04 04 for the snow and mountain report. For the departmental report, dial ☎ 0 836 68 02 followed by the two-digit departmental number (see the Regions & Départments map in the Facts about France chapter). Year round, daily weather bulletins are pinned outside the tourist office in ski resorts.

euro currency converter €1 = 6.56FF

Ecology & Environment

The Alps' dense road network handles a significant proportion of Western Europe's motor vehicle and goods traffic, creating enormous air-pollution problems. Other factors that contribute to the degradation of the Alpine environment include the high concentration of heavy industries (chemicals and metallurgy) and mass tourism, which has grown tremendously since 1960 and continues to expand despite the relative shortness (and unpredictability) of the snow season.

National & Regional Parks

The Alps – unlike the mountain ranges of western North America – are not a pristine wilderness with huge tracts of land untouched by human endeavour. Rather, the habitable parts of the French Alps support a relatively dense population, and the region's many villages, towns and ski resorts are linked by an extensive network of roads.

Fortunately, parts of the Alps are within the boundaries of three national and four regional parks, in which wildlife is protected. The national parks – Vanoise (in Savoy), Écrins (in Dauphiné) and Mercantour (in Provence, along the Italian border) – are surrounded by much larger peripheral zones where human habitation and many economic activities are permitted. With the addition of the regional parks of Queyras (on the Italian border south of Briançon), the Vercors (south-west of Grenoble), Chartreuse (north of the Vercors) and Massif des Bauges (north of Chartreuse), the Alps are endowed with the greatest concentration of parks in France. The Jura is home to the Parc Naturel Régional du Haut-Jura.

Dangers & Annoyances

Despite precautions such as expensive anti-avalanche fences and tunnels, avalanches pose a very real danger in snowbound areas. Each year many people die as a result of these disasters, and whole valleys can be cut off for days. All avalanche warning signs should be strictly obeyed, whether they are along roads or on ski slopes. They are there for a reason.

On glaciers, be careful of crevasses. An accident in an isolated area can be fatal, so never ski, hike or climb alone.

At high altitudes, where the sun's ultraviolet radiation is much stronger than at sea level (and is intensified by reflection off the snow), wear sunglasses and put sunscreen on exposed skin.

The air is often very dry in the Alps – take along a water bottle when hiking, and drink more liquids than you would at lower altitudes. Also, be fully aware of the possibility of hypothermia after a sweaty climb or a sudden storm, as you'll cool off very quickly while enjoying the cold, windy panorama.

Skiing

Snow sports, once reserved for the truly wealthy, are accessible to most these days. Each winter millions of holiday-makers head to the staggering 200-plus resorts in the French Alps for Alpine skiing, cross-country treks, ski touring, snowboarding, and the colour and spectacle that accompanies them.

The ski season starts in earnest a few days before Christmas and ends towards the end of April. In years of heavy snowfall, it's possible to ski from as early as November until as late as mid-May in higher-altitude resorts. At the beginning and end of the season, as well as in January, accommodation and lift tickets are available at considerable discounts, and many resorts offer promotional deals. Give the slopes a wide berth over Christmas and New Year, and during school holidays in late February and early March, when prices are sky-high and most accommodation is scarce.

Summer skiing on high-altitude glaciers is usually possible in July and August in some areas. Most resorts typically have a combination of both cross-country and Alpine (downhill) runs. Some also have snowparks for snowboarders.

Ski Information Every ski station and nearby town has a tourist office providing exhaustive information on skiing, indoor and outdoor activities, and public transport.

FRENCH ALPS

The local accommodation service, ski school and Bureau des Guides are often in the same building. All resorts have post offices, banks, bakeries and supermarkets.

SkiFrance (☎ 01 47 42 23 32, fax 01 47 66 15 94, ✆ skifrance@laposte.fr), 61 blvd Haussmann, F-75008 Paris, and the Fédération Française de Ski (☎ 04 50 51 40 34, fax 04 50 51 75 90, ✆ ski@ffs.fr), 50 rue des Marguisats, BP 2451, F-74011 Annecy, can both provide information on all French ski resorts.

Alpine Skiing Downhill runs range in length from a few hundred metres to 20km and are colour-coded to indicate the level of difficulty: green (beginners), blue (intermediate), red (advanced) and black (very advanced). Summer skiing on glaciers tends to be on short green or blue runs.

Off-Piste Skiing Off-piste skiing, known in French as *hors piste* (skiing outside groomed trails on fresh or powder snow), is popular. However, off-piste skiers should always exercise extreme caution as these areas usually do not have any warning signs. Take a guide with you.

Cross-Country Skiing Known in French as *ski de fond*, cross-country skiing is most popular in the Jura. Cross-country stations are more relaxed and casual than the higher downhill ski resorts, with prices reflecting the lower altitudes, smaller snowfalls and shorter ski season.

Cross-country ski trails are designated as easy or difficult. Resorts charge fees for the upkeep of the trails. Cross-country ski passes cost around 38/150FF per day/week.

Snowboarding Snowboards and boots can be hired from ski rental shops, while the École de Ski Français (ESF; see Ski Schools) offers group or private snowboarding lessons that cost approximately the same as skiing lessons. Chamonix, Chamrousse, Les Arcs, Les Deux Alpes, La Plagne, Méribel and Espace Killy all have large snowparks equipped with half-pipes, quarters, gaps, tables and other tricky delights.

Ski Equipment Skis, boots and poles can be hired on a daily or weekly basis from ski shops in every resort. Alpine equipment starts at 100/300FF per day/week depending on the resort and the type of skis you hire. Cross-country equipment ranges from 40/200FF to 75/380FF per day/week, and snowboards and boots from around 100/750FF to 760/1200FF. You can hire mono-skis and telemark skis in most resorts too.

Take a note of the serial number marked on your skis. If you lose them, you have to pay for a replacement pair (take out insurance to cover this cost – see Insurance below). Most ski shops have a locker room where you can leave your skis free of charge overnight.

Always equip yourself with sunglasses, gloves, a *plan des pistes* (free from tourist offices), warm and water-resistant clothing, and sunscreen.

Lifts & Ski Passes A daunting range of contraptions (*remontées mecaniques*) cover the slopes to whisk skiers uphill. Lifts include *téléskis* (drag lifts), *télésièges* (chair lifts), *télécabines* (gondolas), *téléphériques* (cable cars) and *funiculaires* (funicular railways).

Daily, weekly, monthly or seasonal ski passes – *forfaits* – are the best way to use the above. Passes give access to a group of lifts, the lifts in one sector of the resort or the station's entire skiable domain, plus that of neighbouring resorts.

Passes are cheaper for children and seniors. Many resorts offer a cheaper package deal covering a six-day ski pass and six half-day group lessons. Others offer packages incorporating a six-day ski pass and accommodation or ski school.

Ski Schools France's leading ski school, the École de Ski Français, has branches in most stations and generally offers private or group tuition at better rates than the smaller, independent ski schools that are in some resorts.

A six-day course (three hours of group tuition daily) costs between 420FF and 920FF depending on the resort. Private

FRENCH ALPS

one-hour lessons cost between 200FF and 220FF. All resorts offer lessons for children; some have snow gardens for toddlers aged from three to five.

Ski Touring Experienced off-piste skiers can ski tour – skiing and climbing some of the less accessible peaks, ridges and glaciers outside resort areas. Tours require mountaineering and ice-climbing skills, are for one or several days, and include accommodation in mountain *refuges*. Seven-day tours start at 4000FF. Experienced guides – essential for these tours – can be contacted in most resorts at the Bureau des Guides or ESF.

Package Deals Package deals are the cheapest way to ski. Most resorts offer excellent-value discount packages that typically include a week's accommodation, a ski pass, and sometimes equipment hire and lessons.

The FUAJ (see Accommodation in the Facts for the Visitor chapter) has 17 hostels in the French Alps and offers good-value package deals in winter, starting from 1450/2950FF in the low/high season for six days' hostel accommodation, meals, ski pass and equipment hire.

Insurance Most package deals include insurance. If you don't have a package deal, take out Carré Neige insurance when you buy your ski pass. It covers mountain rescue costs, breakage or theft of skis, and costs 16FF per day.

Some resorts offer discounts on lift tickets and lessons if you have a Carte Neige – an annual insurance plan sold at all resorts costing 230/135FF for Alpine/cross-country skiers.

Warm-Weather Activities

Fantastic hiking trails wend their way up and around the mountains near Mont Blanc and crisscross the national parks; the GR5 traverses the entire Alps. Rafting, canoeing and mountain biking are also popular, as are the more gentle pastimes of horse riding and ice-skating. Warm-weather activities such as these can be enjoyed at most larger ski resorts.

A particularly popular Alpine activity is *parapente* (paragliding), the sport of floating

Skiing in the Alps

Resort	Trademarks	Alpine Runs
Chamonix-Mont Blanc	High in altitude and attitude. Young, trendy and full of fun.	162km
Portes du Soleil	Exclusive resort attracting a more sedate crowd.	650km
St-Gervais & Megève	Pricey, chic and full of Alpine charm.	300km
La Clusaz	A cheaper spot. Popular locally.	132km
Le Grand Bornand	A day trip from Annecy.	65km
Trois Vallées	Méribel: heavy traffic and heaving bars and clubs.	600km
La Plagne	The family choice. Olympic bobsleigh run.	210km
Les Arcs	Top skiing and snowboarding. Car-free but little charm.	200km
Val d'Isère	Unrivalled alpine skiing. Dizzying nightlife.	300km
Les Deux Alpes	Snowboarders' delight. Summer skiing and lively bar scene.	200km
Alpe d'Huez	Snowboarding park, longest black run and summer skiing.	220km
Le Grand Serre Chevalier	Strung-out resort with door-to-door skiing.	250km
Métabief Mont d'Or	Low altitude village. Snow not guaranteed.	42km
Les Rousses	Popular with French and Swiss day-trippers.	40km

euro currency converter 10FF = €1.52

down from somewhere high suspended from a wing-shaped, steerable parachute that allows you (if you're lucky and skilled) to catch updraughts and fly around for quite a while. The ESF in most resorts offers courses: an initiation flight) cost from 350FF to 500FF. A five-day beginners' course costs from 2000FF to 3250FF. A second five-day course, which prepares you to pursue the sport on your own, costs the same.

Skydiving will cost you a lot more: 900FF for a day of instruction and a first jump from 1200m (or 1900FF from a heart-destroying 3500m).

Places to Stay & Eat

Most resorts have a central reservation service that books accommodation in hotels, studios, apartments and chalets. Prices vary drastically between the low and high seasons. Hotels generally offer full- or half-board. Most apartments and studios have a self-catering kitchenette – the cheapest option for budget travellers. Gîtes de France (see Gîtes Ruraux & B&Bs under Accommodation in the Facts for the Visitor chapter) publishes the annual Gîtes de Neige guide.

The Club Alpin Français (CAF) has numerous mountain refuges in the Alps. Full details are available from the CAF offices listed in this chapter. Advance reservations are required for most refuges.

Restaurants in ski resorts tend to offer poor-quality cuisine at rip-off prices. On the slopes, you'll ski past plenty of restaurants with prices to reflect the altitude.

Getting There & Away

The Alps' closest international airports are Genève-Cointrin airport near Geneva, Switzerland, and Lyon-Satolas airport, just outside Lyons. On a clear day and with the right flight path, the view through the plane window is the best introduction to the Alps you can get. In winter there are direct bus connections from both airports to numerous ski resorts with Geneva's Aeroski bus (☎ 022-798 20 00) and Lyon's Satobus-Alpes (☎ 04 72 35 94 96, ✉ mail@satobus-alps.com.

The Eurostar speeds its way through the Channel Tunnel from London-Waterloo to Moûtiers (8¾ hours) and Bourg St-Maurice (9½ hours) on Saturday during the ski

Skiing in the Alps

Cross-Country Runs	Skiing Expertise Required	Ski Lifts	Ski Pass (6 days)
42km	Intermediate, advanced, off-piste	64	984/1181FF
40km	All abilities, off-piste	220	964FF
84km	Beginners, intermediate	81	880FF
70km	Beginners, intermediate	56	800FF
56km	Beginners, intermediate	39	663FF
90km	All abilities	200	1130FF
90km	Beginners, intermediate	110	1045FF
45km	All abilities, off-piste	77	1040FF
24km	Intermediate, advanced, off-piste	102	1047FF
20km	Intermediate, advanced	63	945FF
50km	All abilities	86	1030FF
45km	All abilities, off-piste	72	933FF
120km	Predominantly cross-country	33	552FF
220km	Predominantly cross-country	40	623FF

euro currency converter €1 = 6.56FF

FRENCH ALPS

season. Train services within France to many parts of the Alps are excellent. Full details are published in the SNCF's *La Neige en Direct* brochure.

To get to some ski resorts by car you may need snow chains after heavy snowfalls. In the high season, traffic on the high mountain passes leading to the resorts can be hellish. The Fréjus road tunnel connects the French Alps with Italy, as do a number of major passes: Petit St-Bernard (2188m), near Bourg St-Maurice; Mont Cénis (2083m), in the Haute Maurienne Valley; and Mont-Genèvre (1850m), near Briançon. Certain mountain passes, such as the Col du Galibier (2558m) and the Col de l'Iseran (2770m), are usually closed between November and June, depending on snowfall. Road signs indicate if passes are blocked well in advance. The Mont Blanc road tunnel is currently closed following an accident in March 1999.

Savoy

Bordered by Switzerland and Italy, Savoy (Savoie – pronounced 'sav-**wa**') rises from the southern shores of Lake Geneva and keeps rising until it reaches the massive Mont Blanc, which dominates the town of Chamonix. Farther south, long U-shaped valleys are obvious relics of ancient glaciers that created lakes such as Lac d'Annecy, as well as France's largest natural lake, Lac Bourget, near Aix-les-Bains.

Savoy is divided into two departments, Haute-Savoie and Savoie, and the people of the whole region are known as Savoyards. Despite centuries of French cultural influence, they have managed to keep their identity, and often speak their own dialect, which reveals Provençal influences. In the remote valleys, such as in the Haute Maurienne, rural life goes on as it has for centuries, and the people continue to struggle with the harsh climate and the ever present threat of avalanches.

History

Savoy was long ruled by the House of Savoy, which was founded by Humbert I (or the

Whitehanded, as he was known) in the mid-11th century. During the Middle Ages, the dukes of Savoy extended their territory eastwards to other areas of the western Alps, including the Piedmont region of what is now Italy.

In the 16th century, the dukes of Savoy began to shift their interest from Savoy to their Italian territories; in 1563 they moved their capital from Chambéry to Turin. However, they continued to rule Savoy and managed to resist repeated French attempts to take over the mostly French-speaking region. Savoy was annexed by France in 1792 but was returned 23 years later.

In 1720, Victor Amadeus II, duke of Savoy, became king of Sardinia, and over the next century important territories in northern Italy, including Genoa, came under Savoyard control. In the mid-19th century, the House of Savoy worked to bring about the unification of Italy under Piedmontese leadership, a goal they achieved in 1861 with the formation of the Kingdom of Italy under King Victor Emmanuel II of the House of Savoy. However, in exchange for Napoleon III's acceptance of the new arrangement and the international agreements that led up to it, Savoy – along with the area around Nice – was ceded to France.

CHAMONIX
postcode 74400 • pop 97,000
• elevation 1037m

The town of Chamonix sits in a valley surrounded by the most spectacular scenery in the French Alps. The area, a leading mountaineering centre, is almost Himalayan: tongues of deeply crevassed glaciers point towards the valley from the icy spikes and needles of Mont Blanc, which soars 3.8km above the valley floor. Chamonix has been a summer resort since the late 18th century and a winter one from 1903. Since 1965, when the 11.6km-long Mont Blanc tunnel – the world's highest rock-covered tunnel (2480m) – opened, Chamonix has been linked by road to Courmayeur in Italy. Unfortunately, the tunnel was closed in March 1999 following a major road accident and is not likely to open until Autumn 2001.

FRENCH ALPS

Orientation

Chamonix runs along the River l'Arve for about 2km and is a relatively easy town to navigate. The bus and train stations are conveniently located 500m east of the main streets, rue du Docteur Paccard and rue Joseph Vallot. These two central streets, which run into one another, follow the western bank of the Arve. Most shops, restaurants and services are along them. From the train/bus station walk west along ave Michel Croz to reach the main streets.

Information

Tourist Offices Chamonix' tourist office (☎ 04 50 53 00 24, fax 04 50 53 58 90, ℮ info@chamonix.com), 85 place du Triangle de l'Amitié, opens 8.30 am to 12.30 pm and 2 to 7 pm. It has useful brochures on ski-lift hours and costs, *refuges* and camping grounds, and the town's many recreational activities. Ski passes are also sold here. Upstairs, the Centrale de Réservation (☎ 04 50 53 23 33, fax 04 50 53 58 90, ℮ reservation@chamonix.com) takes accommodation bookings for stays of three nights and more only.

The CAF (☎ 04 50 53 16 03, fax 04 50 53 27 52), 136 ave Michel Croz, usually opens 3 to 7 pm (3 to 6.15 pm on Thursday and 9 am to noon on Saturday); it is closed Wednesday and Sunday.

Maison de la Montagne The Maison de la Montagne is near the tourist office at 109 place de l'Église. On the ground floor is the Compagnie des Guides (☎ 04 50 53 00 88, fax 04 50 53 48 04, ℮ chamonix.guides@ mont-blanc.com), where mountain guides can be hired year round. In winter it opens 8 am to noon and 3 to 7 pm, and 6 am to 5 pm during July and August. A guide costs from 1220FF per day for up to four people. The 1st floor is home to the ESF (☎ 04 50 53 22 57, fax 04 50 53 65 30), open 8.15 am to 7 pm in winter.

On the 2nd floor, the Office de Haute Montagne (☎ 04 50 53 22 08), which serves walkers, hikers and mountain climbers, has maps and information on trails, hiking conditions, the weather and *refuges* (they can

help non-French speakers make reservations). It opens 9 am to 12.30 pm and 2.30 to 6.30 pm Monday to Saturday.

Money There are several places to change money between the tourist and post offices. Le Change at 21 place Balmat offers a decent rate and usually opens 9 am to 1 pm and 3 to 7 pm (8 am to 8 pm from July to early September and December to April). Outside is a 24-hour exchange machine that accepts banknotes of 15 different currencies. The Banque Laydernier, opposite the post office, does not charge commission for exchanging French franc travellers cheques. The majority of banks sport an ATM accepting most credit cards.

Post & Communications The post office on place Balmat opens 8 am to noon and 2 to 6 pm weekdays, and until noon on Saturday. During July and August, weekday hours are 8 am to 7 pm.

Try the busy CyBar (☎ 04 50 53 64 80, ℮ cybarchamonix@hotmail.com), 81 rue Whymper, for Internet access. It opens from 10 am to 11 pm. You can also bring your own laptop to connect. The sometimes noisy Santa Fe Bar & Restaurant (☎ 04 50 53 99 14), 148 rue du Docteur Paccard, has eight terminals. The Club Cantina (see Entertainment) also has a couple of terminals open from 11 am to 10.30 pm and charges the same as the Santa Fe. Login also at the Gîte Vagabond (see Places to Stay). Access rates are all about 1FF a minute.

Bookshop English books are sold at Librairie VO, 20 ave Ravanel-le-Rouge. It opens 9 am to noon and 2 to 7.30 pm Monday to Saturday.

Laundry The Lav' Matic, 40 ave du Mont Blanc, is one convenient laundrette, and there is another at 174 ave de l'Aiguille du Midi. Both open 9 am to 8 pm.

Medical Services The Centre Hospitalier (☎ 04 50 53 84 00) is at Route des Pélerins in Les Favrands about 2km south of Chamonix centre.

FRENCH ALPS

FRENCH ALPS

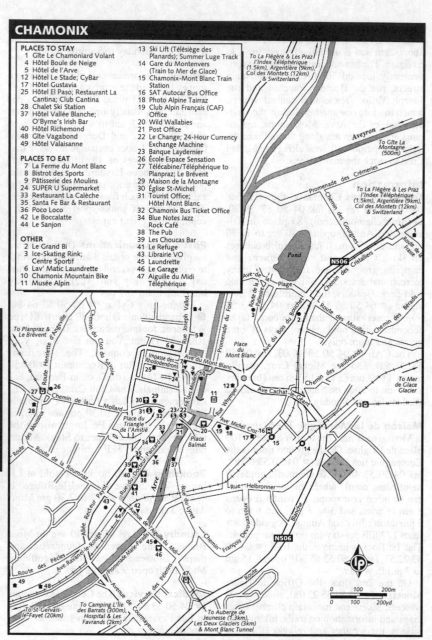

CHAMONIX

PLACES TO STAY
1 Gîte Le Chamoniard Volant
4 Hôtel Boule de Neige
5 Hôtel de l'Arve
12 Hôtel Le Stade; CyBar
17 Hôtel Gustavia
25 Hôtel El Paso; Restaurant La Cantina; Club Cantina
28 Chalet Ski Station
37 Hôtel Vallée Blanche; O'Byrne's Irish Bar
40 Hôtel Richemond
48 Gîte Vagabond
49 Hôtel Valaisanne

PLACES TO EAT
7 La Ferme du Mont Blanc
8 Bistrot des Sports
9 Pâtisserie des Moulins
24 SUPER U Supermarket
33 Restaurant La Calèche
35 Santa Fe Bar & Restaurant
42 Poco Loco
42 Le Boccalatte
44 Le Sanjon

OTHER
2 Le Grand Bi
3 Ice-Skating Rink; Centre Sportif
6 Lav' Matic Laundrette
10 Chamonix Mountain Bike
11 Musée Alpin

13 Ski Lift (Télésiège des Planards); Summer Luge Track
14 Gare du Montenvers (Train to Mer de Glace)
15 Chamonix-Mont Blanc Train Station
16 SAT Autocar Bus Office
18 Photo Alpine Tairraz
19 Club Alpin Français (CAF) Office
20 Wild Wallabies
21 Post Office
22 Le Change; 24-Hour Currency Exchange Machine
23 Banque Laydernier
26 École Espace Sensation
27 Télécabine/Téléphérique to Planpraz; Le Brévent
29 Maison de la Montagne
30 Église St-Michel
31 Tourist Office; Hôtel Mont Blanc
32 Chamonix Bus Ticket Office
34 Blue Notes Jazz Rock Café
38 The Pub
39 Les Choucas Bar
41 Le Refuge
43 Librairie VO
45 Laundrette
46 Le Garage
47 Aiguille du Midi Téléphérique

euro currency converter 10FF = €1.52

Aiguille du Midi

The Aiguille du Midi, a lone spire of rock looming across glaciers, snowfields and rocky crags, 8km from the summit of Mont Blanc, is unique in its accessibility to people interested in scaling sheer cliffs. The views in all directions are truly breathtaking and should not be missed (there is a lift for those not into climbing).

The téléphérique (☎ 04 50 53 30 80) from Chamonix to the Aiguille du Midi (3842m) is the highest and probably most scary cable car in Europe. From the Aiguille du Midi, between April and September, you can make the 5km transglacial ride (30 minutes) in the Panoramic Mont Blanc cable car to **Pointe Helbronner** (3466m) on the Italian border, where there's some summer skiing. The Italian ski resort of Courmayeur is accessible via téléphérique from here too. The views from the cable car alone are worth the trip.

Return tickets from Chamonix to the Aiguille du Midi cost 200FF; it's an extra 98FF return to Pointe Helbronner. One-way tickets are only 20% less than a return. A ride to the téléphérique's halfway point, Plan de l'Aiguille (2308m) – an excellent place to start hikes in summer – costs 66/85FF one way/return.

The téléphérique, which you can board at the station south of town at the end of ave de l'Aiguille du Midi, runs year round from 8 am (6 am between 5 July and 24 August). The last ride up is at 3.45 pm (4.45 pm in summer). It takes 40 minutes to get all the way to Italy. Be prepared for long queues – the earlier in the morning you get there, the better. You can make advance reservations 24 hours a day by calling ☎ 04 50 53 40 00.

Le Brévent

Le Brévent (2525m), the highest peak on the western side of the valley, is known for its great views of Mont Blanc and the rest of the eastern side of the valley. It can be reached by a combination of the télécabine and téléphérique (☎ 04 50 53 13 18), which costs 57/84FF one way/return. To reach it from the tourist office, walk west on Chemin de la Mollard. Service begins at 8 am

(9 am in winter); the last trips up/down are at 5/5.45 pm in summer and an hour or so earlier in winter. Quite a few hiking trails (including various routes back to the valley) can be picked up either at Le Brévent or at the télécabine's midway station, Planpraz (1999m; 48/58FF one way/return). There is a great restaurant at the summit of Le Brévent (see Places to Eat).

Mer de Glace

The heavily crevassed Mer de Glace (Sea of Ice), the second largest glacier in the Alps, is 14km long, 1800m wide and up to 400m deep. It moves 45m a year at the edges and up to 90m a year in the middle. It has become a popular tourist attraction thanks to a cogwheel rail line built between 1897 and 1908. In the 17th century, the Mer de Glace – like other glaciers in the area – reached the bottom of the valley, destroying houses and burying cultivated land.

The **Grotte de la Mer de Glace**, an ice cave that lets you get a look at the glacier from the inside for 14FF, is open from the end of May to the end of September. The interior temperature is -2 to -5°C. Since 1946, the cave has been carved anew each spring – the work is begun in February and takes just over three months. Look down the slope for last year's cave to see how far the glacier has moved.

With avalanche-proofing over parts of the railway tracks, the train – which leaves from Gare du Montenvers (☎ 04 50 53 12 54) in Chamonix and takes you to Montenvers (1913m) – runs year round. The last train up departs at 5.30 or 6 pm (earlier after mid-September) and comes down a half-hour later. The 20-minute trip costs 42/79FF one way/return. From Montenvers, a téléphérique (15FF return) takes tourists to the cave. A combined ticket valid for the train, téléphérique, and admission to the cave itself costs 116FF (children 70FF).

The Mer de Glace can also be reached on foot via the Grand Balcon Nord trail from Plan de l'Aiguille. The uphill trail from Chamonix (two hours) begins near the summer luge track. Traversing the glacier and its many crevasses is dangerous without proper equipment and a guide.

FRENCH ALPS

Musée Alpin

The Musée Alpin (☎ 04 50 53 25 93), just off ave Michel Croz in Chamonix, displays artefacts, lithographs and photos illustrating the history of mountain climbing and other Alpine sports. It opens 2 to 7 pm, June to mid-October; between Christmas and Easter its hours are 3 to 7 pm. It's closed during the rest of the year. Admission costs 20FF.

Skiing

Of Chamonix' nine skiing areas, the best areas for beginners are Le Tour, Les Planards, Le Brévent and La Flégère. The latter two are connected by téléphérique. Les Chosalets and Les Grands Montets, accessible from Argentière 9km north of Chamonix, offer intermediate and advanced skiers the most challenging skiing. Les Grands Montets also has a snowpark equipped with a half-pipe for snowboarders.

The region also has a number of marked but ungroomed trails suitable for advanced skiers in search of some off-piste thrills. The famous off-piste 20km-long Vallée Blanche descent, which leads from the top of the Aiguille du Midi over the Mer de Glace and through the forests back to Chamonix, should *only* be tackled with a guide. It takes four to five hours to complete and a guide costs 1220FF for up to four people. Contact the ESF or Compagnie des Guides for full details.

Ski Passes The tourist office sells a variety of ski passes, the most popular being the Cham' Ski pass, valid for all the lifts in the valley and entitles pass holders to one day's skiing in Courmayeur in Italy and free bus transport in the Chamonix region. Family and beginners' passes are available too.

The more expensive Ski Pass Mont Blanc covers the Megève–St-Gervais ski area as well as the Chamonix Valley.

Ski Touring In spring, ski touring is superb around Mont Blanc, but is not restricted to that area. It is possible to go for a week or longer and ski to Switzerland or Italy, staying in *refuges* or tents along the way. A four-day trip with an experienced local

guide costs 2650FF per person. During winter, it is against the law to make overnight trips in the Chamonix–Mont Blanc area without the permission of the Compagnie des Guides, due to the danger of avalanches and crevasses.

The king of ski tours is the classic six-day Haute Route between Chamonix and Zermatt in Switzerland. The trail is skiable from March until early May and costs 4250FF per person. It should only be attempted with an experienced local guide. Skiers should be at an advanced to expert level in off-piste skiing and have a high level of fitness, as the trail is quite physically demanding.

Heli-skiing is also possible. Contact Chamonix Mont Blanc Helicopters (☎ 04 50 54 13 82), SAF Chamonix Helicopters (☎ 04 50 54 07 86), or the Compagnie des Guides for details. A 10-minute panoramic helicopter flight costs 350FF per person.

In summer, there is limited (and expensive) skiing from Pointe Helbronner (see Aiguille du Midi) on the Italian frontier. The runs, which are down a glacier, are only about 800m long and are served by four téléskis.

Warm-Weather Activities

Walking In late spring and summer (more or less from mid-June to October), the Chamonix area has 310km of walking trails, some of the most spectacular anywhere in the Alps. The more rewarding trails are at higher elevations, which can be reached in minutes by cable car. The téléphériques shut down in the late afternoon, but in June and July there is enough light to walk until 9 pm or even later.

The combined map and guide, *Carte des Sentiers du Mont Blanc* (Mountain Trail Map; 75FF), is ideal for straightforward day walks. The most useful map of the area is the 1:25,000 scale IGN map entitled *Chamonix-Massif du Mont Blanc* (No 3630OT; 58FF). Both are sold at Photo Alpine Tairraz (☎ 04 50 53 14 23), 162 ave Michel Croz. *The Most Beautiful Hikes for Everyone* (Editions Aio; 25FF) maps out easy day hikes in the Mont Blanc region.

The fairly flat **Grand Balcon Sud** trail along the Aiguilles Rouges (western) side of the valley stays up around 2000m and affords great views of Mont Blanc and nearby glaciers. On foot, it can be reached from behind Le Brévent's télécabine station. If you want to avoid a lot of uphill walking, take either the Planpraz (46FF) or La Flégère (43FF) lifts.

From Plan de l'Aiguille (64FF), the **Grand Balcon Nord** trail takes you to the Mer de Glace, from where you can walk or take the cogwheel train down to Chamonix. There are a number of other trails from Plan de l'Aiguille.

There are trails to **Lac Blanc** (White Lake) at 2350m, a turquoise lake (despite its name) surrounded by mountains, from either the top of the Les Praz–l'Index cable car (61FF) or La Flégère (43FF), the line's midway transfer point.

Canyoning The Compagnie des Guides organises canyoning expeditions from April to October. A half-day/day initiation course costs 350/750FF.

Summer Luge The summer luge track (☎ 04 50 53 08 97), near the télésiège des Planards, opens 1.30 to 6 pm at the weekend in June. During July and August it opens 10 am to 7.30 pm. If there is no snow the luge also opens in May. It costs 32FF a ride.

Cycling Many of the trails around the bottom of the valley (eg the Petit Balcon Sud) are perfect for mountain biking. See Getting Around for information on bike rental.

In season, Chamonix' Club de Cyclotourisme has a group ride every Sunday. It begins sometime between 7 and 8 am at Le Grand Bi ski rental shop, 240 ave du Bois du Bouchet.

The Compagnie des Guides (see Maison de la Montagne under Information) can arrange one-day mountain bike tours for 1700FF (children 1300FF) It also offers three-, four- or five-day tours of the Mont Blanc region costing 1140FF for three days and 300FF for each additional day.

Parapente The sky above Chamonix is often dotted with colourful paragliders floating slowly down from the snowy heights. Initiation flights, with an instructor, from Planpraz (2000m) cost 500FF (1400FF from the Aiguille du Midi and 3600FF from Mont Blanc). A five-day course costs 2960FF. For details, contact Parapente Azur (☎ 04 50 53 50 14, @ pazur@club-internet.fr), 128 rue des Moulins, or Chamonix Parapente (☎ 04 50 55 99 22), 16 cours du Bartavel. École Espace Sensation (☎ 04 50 55 99 49), another parapente school, is at 8 Route Henriette d'Angeville.

Ice-Skating The indoor ice-skating rink in the Centre Sportif (☎ 04 50 53 12 36), Route de la Patinoire, opens 10 am to noon and 3 to 6 pm (9 to 11 pm on Wednesday). Admission costs 23FF (children 18FF); skate rental *(location patins)* costs 16FF.

The Centre Sportif's Club des Sports (☎ 04 50 53 11 57) has information on other activities available in the valley.

Places to Stay

During July, August and the ski season, hotels are heavily booked. Many prefer guests who take full or half-board. Book all accommodation in advance through the Centrale de Réservation (see Information earlier). *Les Carnets de l'Hébergement*, published annually by the tourist office, contains a comprehensive list of the region's camp sites, *refuges*, *gîtes d'étape*, *chambres d'hôtes*, apartment rental agencies and hotels. Expect to pay at least 1000/1800FF a week for a two-person studio in the low/high season.

Places to Stay – Budget

Camping There are some 13 camp sites in the Chamonix region. In general, camping costs 25FF per person and from 12FF to 26FF for a tent site. Because of the altitude, it's often chilly at night.

L'Île des Barrats (☎ 04 50 53 51 44), near the base of the Aiguille du Midi téléphérique, opens mid-April to mid-October. Three-star *Les Deux Glaciers* (☎ 04 50 53 15 84, Route des Tissières), in Les Bossons,

FRENCH ALPS

3km south of Chamonix, opens year round (except from mid-November to mid-December). To get there, take the train to Les Bossons or the Chamonix Bus (see Getting Around) to the Tremplin-le-Mont stop.

Hostels Two kilometres south-west of Chamonix in Les Pélerins, the *Auberge de Jeunesse* (☎ 04 50 53 14 52, fax 04 50 55 92 34, ❷ chamonix@fuaj.org, 127 montée Jacques Balmat) can be reached by bus. Take the Chamonix–Les Houches line and get off at the Pélerins École stop. In winter, only weekly packages are available, including bed, food, ski pass and ski hire for six days starting at 1450/2990FF in the low/high season. In summer a bed in a room of four or six costs 74FF, including breakfast. There's no kitchen and meals cost 50FF. You can check in between 8 am and 12 pm and 5 to 10 pm. The hostel is closed from October to mid-December.

Refuges Most mountain *refuges*, which cost 90FF to 100FF a night, are accessible to hikers, though a few can be reached only by mountain climbers. Breakfast and dinner, prepared by the warden, are often available for an extra fee. Call ahead to reserve a place. For information on *refuges*, contact the CAF (see Tourist Offices under Information). When the office is closed, pick up a list detailing CAF *refuges* and access routes from outside the office.

There are two easier to reach *refuges*: one at *Plan de l'Aiguille* (2308m; ☎ 04 50 53 55 60), which is the intermediate stop on the Aiguille du Midi téléphérique, and another at *La Flégère* (1877m; ☎ 04 50 53 06 13), the midway station on the Les Praz–l'Index cable car.

Gîtes d'Étape Near the Planpraz and Le Brévent télécabine station, *Chalet Ski Station* (☎ 04 50 53 20 25, 6 Route des Moussoux), has beds costing 60FF a night. Sheet hire costs 15FF and showers cost 5FF. It closes mid-May to late June and mid-September to mid-December.

The semi-rustic *Gîte Le Chamoniard Volant* (☎ 04 50 53 14 09, fax 04 50 53 23 25, 45 Route de la Frasse) is on the north-eastern outskirts of town. A bunk in a cramped, functional room for four, six or eight people costs 66FF; sheet hire costs 20FF, breakfast 27FF and dinner 66FF. The nearest bus stop is La Frasse.

Gîte La Montagne (☎ 04 50 53 11 60, 789 promenade des Crémeries), by far the most attractive of Chamonix' three gîtes, is on a beautiful, forested site, 1.5km north of the train station (if arriving by bus, get off at La Frasse stop). A bunk in a jam-packed room costs 65FF (including use of the kitchen). This place is closed from 11 November to 20 December.

The *Gîte Vagabond* (☎ 04 50 53 15 43, fax 04 53 68 21, 365 avenue Ravanel-le-Rouge) is a neat little hostelry with a guest kitchen, bar/restaurant with Internet access, BBQ area, climbing wall and parking. A bed in a four- or six-person dorm costs 70FF a night or 149FF for half-board.

Hotels At the small, family-owned *Hôtel Valaisanne* (☎ 04 50 53 17 98, 454 ave Ravanel-le-Rouge), 900m south-west of Chamonix town centre, doubles cost 170/270FF in the low/high season.

Lively *Hôtel El Paso* (☎ 04 50 53 64 20, fax 04 50 53 64 22, ❷ cantina@cantina.fr, 37 impasse des Rhododendrons), is great value. Doubles with shared bath in the low/high season cost 166/224FF, triples 236/306FF. In summer a bed in a dorm costs 90FF. *Hôtel Le Stade* (☎ 04 50 53 05 44, 83 rue Whymper (the entrance is around the back on the 1st floor), has simple but pleasant singles/doubles starting at 149/245FF.

Places to Stay – Mid-Range & Top End

Off a quiet lane farther north, pleasant, local-style *Hôtel de l'Arve* (☎ 04 50 53 02 31, fax 04 50 53 56 92, 60 impasse des Anémones), offers singles/doubles costing 219FF to 338FF in the high season. Cosy, anglophone *Hôtel Vallée Blanche* (☎ 04 50 53 04 50, fax 04 50 55 97 85, ❷ savoie@ europe.com, 36 rue du Lyret) sits practically on top of the River l'Arve, and its airy double rooms on the riverside are a delight.

FRENCH ALPS

Rates for double rooms in low/high season are range from 369FF to 745FF. There is even parking for a few cars.

Little *Hôtel Boule de Neige* (☎ *04 50 53 04 48, 362 rue Joseph Vallot*), has a lively bar and singles/doubles starting at 160/205FF with shared bathroom. Enormous *Hôtel Richemond* (☎ *04 50 53 08 85, fax 04 50 55 91 69, 228 rue du Docteur Paccard*) charges 265/385FF for singles/doubles.

Three-star, chalet-style *Hôtel Gustavia* (☎ *04 50 53 00 31, fax 04 50 55 86 39, 272 ave Michel Croz*) has attractive double rooms for 440/720FF in the low/high season. Four-star *Hôtel Mont Blanc* (☎ *04 50 53 05 64, fax 04 50 55 89 44, 62 allée Majestic*), just south of the tourist office, has luxurious doubles costing 530/837FF half-board per person in the low/high season.

Places to Eat

Restaurants Always packed is *Le Boccalatte* (☎ *04 50 53 52 14, 59 ave de l'Aiguille du Midi*), which has a happy hour between 5 and 7 pm and serves hearty portions of fondue (61FF), *tarte flambée* (39FF), and the like. Advance bookings are recommended. *Restaurant La Calèche* (☎ *04 50 55 94 68, 18 rue du Docteur Paccard*), dishes out fondue and folklore shows to undiscriminating tourists. Evening *menus* start at 99FF.

Popular locally is *Bistro des Sports* (☎ *04 50 53 00 46, 182 rue Joseph Vallot*), which has *menus* from 69FF. The sometimes crowded *Santa Fe* (☎ *04 50 53 88 14, 148 rue du Docteur Paccard*) is a popular eating as well as meeting place, abuzz with hungry diners looking for salads, pizzas, vegetarian platters and Tex Mex specialities.

There are lots of restaurants offering pizza and fondue in the streets leading off from place Balmat. Nearby *Poco Loco* (☎ *04 50 53 43 03, 47 rue du Docteur Paccard*) has pizzas from 33FF to 45FF and *menus* from 50FF. It also serves great hot sandwiches (from 23FF), sweet crepes (from 8FF), and burgers to eat in or take away.

For Mexican food, try cosy *La Cantina* (☎ *04 50 53 83 80, 37 impasse des Rhododendrons*) at the small Hôtel El Paso, which

is run by an Australian. *Le Sanjon* (☎ *04 50 53 56 44, 5 ave Ravanel-le-Rouge*), is a picturesque wooden chalet restaurant serving *raclette* – a block of melted cheese, usually eaten with potatoes and cold meats (99FF), and fondue (69F). A favourite is *pierrade* – three different meats that you prepare yourself on a small grill, with six sauces (98FF).

For a lofty lunch with an incredible view of Mont Blanc on a clear day, head for *Le Panoramic* (☎/fax *04 50 53 44 11*) at the Le Brévent cable station. A *menu* that includes local cheese, cured meat, potatoes and salad, costs 100FF. A warming glass of *vin chaud* (20FF) will perk you up on a snowy winter's day.

Cafes Snacks and the greatest cakes, pastries and hot chocolate in town are served at *Pâtisserie des Moulins* (☎ *04 50 53 58 95, 95 rue des Moulins*). It also offers a lunchtime *menu* for 50FF.

Self-Catering The *SUPER U Supermarket* (*117 rue Joseph Vallot*), opens 8.15 am to 7.30 pm (8.15 am to 12.45 pm on Sunday in winter). *Le Refuge Payot* (*166 rue Joseph Vallot*) opposite the supermarket, and *Le Ferme du Mont Blanc* (*202 rue Joseph Vallot*) both stock an excellent range of cheeses, meats and other local products.

Entertainment

Nightlife is plentiful and good. A popular après-ski place is the cafe-bar of *Hôtel Gustavia* (see Places to Stay), which has a happy hour until 7 pm most evenings. *Club Cantina*, beneath La Cantina (see Places to Eat) at Hôtel El Paso, hosts regular bands. Next to Hôtel Richemond is *Les Choucas* (*rue du Docteur Paccard*), which plays loud music and shows snowboard and ski videos to a packed crowd. *The Pub* (*rue du Docteur Paccard*), opposite, is another good bet. It does great Murphy's stout and is usually less crowded than other places, while *Wild Wallabies* (*1 rue de la Tour*) offers pool, table football and bar snacks. *O'Byrne's Irish Bar* at Hôtel Vallée Blanche (see Places to Stay) also does a very decent Murphy's and pulls a friendly crowd.

FRENCH ALPS

Most nightclubs have cover charges, although *Le Refuge* (275 *rue du Docteur Paccard*) does not. *Blue Notes Jazz Rock Café* (32 *rue du Docteur Paccard*) is free Sunday to Wednesday but charges 70FF admission on other nights. Chamonix' largest and flashiest disco is *Le Garage* (200 *ave de l'Aiguille du Midi*) where patrons can dance to classics.

Getting There & Away

Bus The bus station is in the train station building. The office of SAT Autocar (☎ 04 50 53 01 15) has opening hours posted on the door, but in general it opens 8.45 to 11.30 am and 1.45 to 5.30 pm weekdays, and 6.45 to 7.05 am, 8.45 to 11.05 am and 1.45 to 5.35 pm at the weekend. Buses also run to Annecy (95.30FF, two hours), Grenoble (161FF, three hours), Geneva bus station (170FF, 1½ to two hours) and Geneva airport (195FF, two to 2¼ hours). There are currently no services to Italy until the Mont Blanc tunnel re-opens.

Tickets to Lyon-Satolas airport (340FF, 3¼ hours) are sold at the ticket office outside the tourist office on place du Triangle de l'Amitié. There are two buses daily on weekdays and three daily at the weekend.

Train The Chamonix–Mont Blanc train station (☎ 04 50 53 00 44) is in the middle of town at the end of ave Michel Croz. Ticket counters are staffed from 6 am to 8 pm. The left-luggage counter opens 6.45 am to 8.45 pm (20FF for the first piece of luggage, 10FF for each additional piece).

Major destinations include Paris' Gare de Lyon (469FF, six to seven hours, five daily), Lyon (186FF, four to 4½ hours, four to five daily), Geneva (100FF, two to 2½ hours via St-Gervais, longer via Martigny), and Annecy (105FF, 2½ hours). There's an overnight train to Paris daily year round.

The narrow-gauge train line from St-Gervais-le-Fayet (23km west of Chamonix) to Martigny, Switzerland (42km north of Chamonix), stops at 11 towns in the valley including Argentière. There are nine to 12 return trips a day. To enter Switzerland you have to switch trains at the border (at Châte-

lard or Vallorcine) because the track gauge changes. From St-Gervais-le-Fayet, there are trains to all parts of France.

Getting Around

Bus Bus transport in the valley is handled by Chamonix Bus (☎ 04 50 53 05 55), place du Triangle de l'Amitié. In it winter opens 8 am to 7 pm, and 8 am to noon and 2 to 6.30 pm the rest of the year (7 pm from June to August).

Bus stops are marked by black-on-yellow roadside signs. From mid-December to mid-May, there are 13 lines to all the ski lifts in the area. During the rest of the year there are only two lines, both leaving from place de l'Église (which adjoins place du Triangle de l'Amitié) and pass by the Chamonix Sud stop. One line goes south to Les Houches via either Les Moussoux (nine a day) or Les Pélerins (eight a day). The other goes north via Argentière to Col des Montets. Buses do not run after 7 pm (6 or 6.30 pm in June and September). In winter, buses are free for holders of ski passes; all others pay 7.50FF for one sector, 15FF for a second sector.

Taxi There's a taxi stand (☎ 04 50 53 13 94) outside the train station. Tariffs for long-distance rides are posted inside the station.

Bicycle Between April and October, Le Grand Bi (☎ 04 50 53 14 16), 240 ave du Bois du Bouchet, has three and 10-speed bicycles for 65FF daily, and mountain bikes for 100FF. It opens 8.30 am to noon and 2 to 7 pm, Monday to Saturday.

Chamonix Mountain Bike (☎ 04 50 53 54 76), 138 rue des Moulins, opens 9 am to noon and 2 to 7 pm (no midday break during summer and winter holidays). The tariff is 50/95FF for two hours/day.

MEGÈVE & ST-GERVAIS

Megève (population 4700, elevation 1113m), 36km south-west of Chamonix, and neighbouring St-Gervais (population 5000, elevation 810m), sit below Mont Blanc and are connected by a common network of ski lifts. These tiny ski villages are among the oldest in the Alps: Megève was developed as a resort in the 1920s for a French baroness following her disillusionment with Switzerland's crowded St-Moritz. Today it remains an expensive, trendy resort with a charming old square from which old narrow medieval-style streets and lanes fan out. On the eastern outskirts of the village are chapels and oratories that trace the Stations of the Cross in baroque, rococo, and Tuscan-style wood carvings.

Summer hiking trails in the Mont d'Arbois, Bettex and Mont Joly areas are accessible from both villages. Mountain biking is equally popular; some of the best terrain is found along marked trails between Val d'Arly, Mont Blanc and Beaufortain.

Information

Tourist Offices Megève's tourist office (☎ 04 50 21 27 28, fax 04 50 93 03 09, ✆ megeve@megeve.com), rue de Monseigneur Conseil, opens in season from 9 am to 12.30 pm and 2 (4 pm on Sunday) to 7 pm. The accommodation service (☎ 04 50 21 29 52, fax 04 50 91 85 67, ✆ reservation@ megeve.com) is based here too. Megève's ESF (☎ 04 50 21 00 97) and the Bureau des Guides (☎ 04 50 21 55 11) are inside the Maison de la Montagne, 76 rue Ambroise Martin. Megève's International Ski School (ESI, ☎ 04 50 58 78 88) is at the bottom of the Mont d'Arbois cable car.

In St-Gervais the tourist office (☎ 04 50 47 76 08, fax 04 50 47 75 69), 115 ave Mont Paccard, opens 9 am to 12 pm and 2.30 to 7.30 pm (9 am to noon and 2 to 6 pm in the low season). It also has an accommodation service (☎ 04 50 93 53 63). The ESF (☎ 04 50 47 76 21) is on promenade du Mont Blanc and the Bureau des Guides (☎ 04 50 47 76 55) is at place du Mont Blanc.

Places to Stay

Both tourist offices stock lists of all types of accommodation available. Bookings for CAF *refuges* in St-Gervais and Megève can be made through the CAF office in Chamonix (see Information in the Chamonix section) or through the Refuge du Val-Monjoie (☎ 04 50 47 76 70, fax 04 50 47 76 71), 73 ave de Miage, St-Gervais.

Studios for two people start at 1500/2000FF per week in the low/high season. In Megève the family-run *La Marmotte* (☎ 04 50 21 24 49, Route du Jaillet) has smallish wood-lined singles/doubles from 190/250FF, including breakfast. The three-star *Hôtel Au Coeur de Megève* (☎ 04 50 21 25 30, fax 04 50 91 91 27, rue Charles Feige) has rooms from 460FF.

In St-Gervais, the one-star *Hôtel Les Capucines* (☎ 04 50 47 75 87, 138 rue du Mont Blanc) has older rooms with washbasin for 140/210FF for a single/double and with shower for 175/260FF, including breakfast. A notch up is the *Hôtel Maison Blanche* (☎ 04 50 47 75 81, fax 04 50 93 68 36), a two star hotel (in a lane behind the tourist office), with doubles starting at 180FF.

Getting There & Away

There's a SAT bus and SNCF office (☎ 04 50 47 73 88) opposite the tourist office in St-Gervais, and in Megève (☎ 04 50 21 23 42) a couple of blocks south-west of the tourist office.

Many trains to/from Paris via Annecy stop at Sallanches (13km from Megève) and St-Gervais-le-Fayet (16km from Megève and 2km from St-Gervais). All trains terminate in St-Gervais le Fayet.

There are four buses daily between St-Gervais, Megève and Chamonix (49FF, 55 minutes). Seven buses daily link Megève and St-Gervais with St-Gervais-le-Fayet and Sallanches train stations. There are also four buses daily in winter to/from Geneva airport (210FF, 1½ hours).

From St-Gervais-le-Fayet and St-Gervais, the Mont Blanc tramway (☎ 04 50 47 51 83) rattles its way up to Bellevue (1800m), offering staggering mountain views en route. A return ticket costs 90FF.

LES PORTES DU SOLEIL

The dozen villages linked by lifts along the French/Swiss border in the northern Chablais area – dubbed the Portes du Soleil (Gates of the Sun) – is the largest ski area in France. Some 650km of slopes and cross-country trails crisscross the region. You can buy a ski pass covering some or all of them.

Morzine (population 3000, elevation 1000m) in Haute Savoie is the largest village, retaining something (but not a lot) of its traditional Alpine village atmosphere. Accommodation can be booked through the central accommodation service (☎ 04 50 79 11 57, fax 04 50 79 03 48) inside the tourist office (☎ 04 50 74 72 72, fax 04 50 79 03 48). A bed in the *Auberge de Jeunesse* (☎ *04 50 79 14 86*) costs 70FF in summer. The hostel opens from Christmas to 22 April and from 14 June to 12 September.

Avoriaz (1800m), a few kilometres up the valley from Morzine, is among the most expensive of the French ski resorts. Built in the 1960s, it is made up almost entirely of high-rise apartment blocks that, surprisingly, blend into their surroundings because each one is covered with wooden shingles. Apart from two four-star hotels and *Club Méditerranée* (☎ *04 50 74 28 70*), all other accommodation is in studios or apartments, which can be booked through the tourist office (☎ 04 50 74 02 11, fax 04 50 74 24 29, ✉ avoriaz@wanadoo.fr). Avoriaz is a car-free resort but there are outdoor and covered car parks. Transport is by horse and sleigh in winter. There's a special course for mountain bikes (with jumps and other obstacles) where those inclined can practise. It's free, but only open in summer.

If you're arriving by road via Cluses, **Les Gets** (population 1300, elevation 1172m) is the first village of the Portes du Soleil. Quieter than Morzine and cheaper than Avoriaz, it has plenty of accommodation. Contact the tourist office (☎ 04 50 75 80 80, fax 04 50 79 76 90) or the accommodation booking office (☎ 04 50 75 80 51, fax 04 50 75 85 13). The *Auberge de Jeunesse* (☎ *04 50 79 14 86*) is open year round. Dorm beds cost 48FF.

Getting There & Away
Free ski shuttle buses take skiers from Morzine to the lifts of Télécabine Super Morzine, Télécabine du Pléney and Téléphérique Avoriaz.

During the ski season, Morzine is linked by bus to Lyon-Satolas (390FF) and Geneva airport (185FF). Geneva airport, 50km north of Morzine, is closer.

From Morzine there are frequent daily SAT buses (☎ 04 50 79 15 69) to Les Gets and Avoriaz. There are also buses from Morzine to its closest train stations: Thonon (34km to the north) and Cluses (31km to the south).

THONON-LES-BAINS
postcode 74202 • pop 30,000
• elevation 430m
Thonon-les-Bains is the main town on the French side of Lake Geneva. The Chablais peaks are behind the city and just across the water is the Swiss city of Lausanne. Geneva is 33km south-east of Thonon.

A residence of the dukes of Savoy in the Middle Ages, today Thonon makes for a peaceful overnight stop in summer, with serene lake cruises to keep you occupied during the day. Winter is pretty quiet, though hotels and restaurants are still operating normally.

Orientation
The centre of town, built up above the lake, is between place de l'Hôtel de Ville and the train station, just south of the main square, place des Arts. Ave du Général Leclerc is the main road down to the lake and the boat docks at port des Rives. From the port, quai de Ripaille follows the lake east around to the duke's chateau about 1km away.

Information
Tourist Offices The tourist office (☎ 04 50 71 55 55, fax 04 50 26 68 33, ✉ thonon@ thononlesbains.com), place du Marché, opens 8.30 am to noon and 2 to 6.30 pm, Monday to Saturday. In July and August there's a one-hour midday break, and it opens 10 am to noon on Sunday. To get there from the train station, head straight up ave de la Gare to blvd du Canal. Turn right and follow it past the next big intersection into ave Jules Ferry. The first street to the left leads onto place du Marché. Between June and September, the lakeside tourist office annexe (☎ 04 50 26 19 94) at port des Rives opens 10 am to 7 pm. Boat tickets for Lake Geneva cruises are also sold here (see the Getting There & Away section).

The Bureau Information Jeunesse (☎ 04 50 26 22 23, fax 04 50 81 74 45), 67 Grande Rue, only opens weekdays, from 1.30 to 6.30 pm.

Places to Stay & Eat

Its lakeside location means that Thonon's accommodation is fairly expensive though cheaper in winter. Cheaper options include *Camping Le St-Disdille* (☎ 04 50 26 13 59), 3km north-east of town near port Ripaille, which charges 84FF for up to three people with a tent or caravan. The site opens 1 April to 30 September. Take bus No 4 from place des Arts to the St-Disdille bus stop.

Centre International de Séjour (☎ 04 50 71 77 80, fax 04 50 26 68 57), 1.5km south-west of town off the N5 to Geneva at La Grangette, has beds in single or twin rooms for 120FF. Take bus A from place des Arts to La Grangette bus stop.

Hotel *Formule 1* (☎ 04 50 26 22 11, fax 04 50 81 93 49, pont de Dranse), a little way out of town, is a cheap option. Rooms go from 129FF to 149FF per night. Central *Hôtel de la Renovation* (☎ 04 50 71 11 27, 4 place du Château) has comfortable singles/doubles from 220/269FF, while *Hôtel Ibis* (☎ 04 50 71 24 24, fax 04 50 71 87 76, 2 ter, ave d'Évian) is very central and a good deal for two or three people at 305/340FF per night.

A good, filling Turkish meal can be had at the *Mosaïque* (☎ 04 50 71 99 34, 5 bis ave d'Évian) 100m from Hôtel Ibis. The doner kebab at 40FF is recommended.

Getting There & Away

Bus The SAT bus company (☎ 04 50 71 00 88), 11 ave Jules Ferry, has regular lines to Évian and into the Chablais Mountains, including to Morzine.

Train The train station (☎ 04 36 35 35 35) is a block south-west of place des Arts on place de la Gare. Trains go south-west to Geneva (40FF) and Bellegarde (59FF, 1¼ hours), where you can pick up the TGV connection to Paris' Gare de Lyon (354FF, 5½ hours). Most days there are six trains daily to Évian (12FF, 10 minutes).

Boat The Swiss CGN company (☎ 04 50 71 14 71 in summer only, or ☎ 021-614 04 44, fax 614 04 45 in Lausanne) serves the main cities and towns around the lake, hopping from one port to another. In Thonon, boats leave from port des Rives (☎ 04 50 71 44 00), stopping in Yvoire before continuing via several Swiss villages to Geneva. Boats heading in the other direction go to Évian then across to Lausanne or east to Montreux. Passengers aged between 16 and 25 years are entitled to a 50% discount on all regular tickets. One-day passes for unlimited travel are available for 200FF.

A local cruise company, Navirives (☎/fax 04 50 71 52 42), runs cruises within the French sector of the lake on a small cruiser, *Le Colibri,* which cost 52FF.

Getting Around

Local buses are run by BUT (☎ 04 50 26 35 35) and depart from place des Arts. Bus No 8 (July and August only) goes to port des Rives. A funicular (☎ 04 50 71 21 54) links place du Château, near the town hall, with port des Rives for 7/12FF one way/return; from 8 am to noon and 1.30 to 6.30 pm daily and 8 to 12 am in summer.

Taxis (☎ 04 50 71 07 00) can be picked up at place des Arts.

AROUND THONON-LES-BAINS

At the northern tip of a blunt peninsula 16km west of Thonon is **Yvoire**, a medieval stone village with a small port, pebbled coves and a multitude of geraniums. In the other direction is **Évian-les-Bains**, a more luxurious and exclusive version of Thonon (9km east), whose spring waters are famed worldwide. Known as the 'Pearl of Lake Geneva', it was in this town that the Accord d'Évian – recognising Algerian independence – was signed in 1962. It is possible to visit the Évian water bottling factory; ask at the tourist office (☎ 04 50 75 04 26, fax 04 50 75 61 08), place d'Allinges, for details or go to the factory's public relations office (☎ 04 50 26 80 80) at 22 ave des Sources for advance bookings for the free tours.

FRENCH ALPS

ANNECY

postcode 74000 • pop 50,000
• elevation 448m

Annecy, the rather chic but friendly capital of the Haute-Savoie department, is the perfect place to spend a relaxing holiday – discounting the bumper to bumper traffic that can be a touch troublesome in July and August. Visitors in a sedentary mood can sit along the lakefront and feed the swans or mosey around the canals of the old city in full view of the Alps. It is an unquestionably pretty town and has successfully managed to retain an old world feel. Its colonnaded streets and gurgling, geranium-shrouded canals blend magically into an enticing mix.

The town is at the most northern tip of the blue-green, 15km-long Lac d'Annecy and is an excellent base for water sports, as well as hiking, gliding, cycling and rollerblading.

Orientation

The train and bus stations are 500m northwest of the Vieille Ville (Old City), which is centred around the River Thiou (split into Canal du Thiou to the south and Canal du Vassé to the north). The modern town centre is between the main post office and the Centre Bonlieu. The tourist office is located here, close to the confluence of the lake and the canals. To get to the Vieille Ville from the station follow rue de la Gare 500m south and enter by the Porte du Sépulcre (Sepulchre Gate) to your left.

Information

Tourist Offices The tourist office (☎ 04 50 45 00 33, fax 04 50 51 87 20, ✉ ancytour@cybercable.tm.fr), is at 1 rue Jean Jaurès inside the Centre Bonlieu. It opens 9 am to 12.30 pm and 1.45 to 6 pm from 15 September to 15 May, and 9 am to 6.30 pm from May to September. Sunday openings vary: the office closes from 1 November to 31 March, it opens 10 am to 1 pm in April, May and October and 9 am to 12 pm and 1.45 to 6 pm June to September.

The Bureau Information Jeunesse (☎ 04 50 33 87 40) and Annecy Sport Information

(☎ 04 50 33 88 31), also in the Centre Bonlieu, open 3 to 7 pm on Monday, 2.30 to 7 pm Tuesday to Friday, and 10 am to noon on Saturday.

Money The Banque de France at 9 bis ave de Chambéry opens 8.45 am to noon and 1.45 to 3.45 pm weekdays. However, the foreign exchange service is only open in the morning. There's a 24-hour currency exchange machine in the Crédit Lyonnais, Centre Bonlieu, which accepts 15 different currencies. ATM machines can be found at most banks with a convenient Banque Populaire ATM and currency exchange machine at the western end of rue Faubourg Ste- Claire in the Vieille Ville.

Post & Communications The main post office, 4 bis rue des Glières, opens 8 am to 7 pm weekdays (until noon on Saturday).

There are two Internet centres in Annecy. The better of the two is Emailerie (☎ 04 50 10 18 91, ✉ message@emailerie.com) on Faubourg des Annonciades, open 10 am to 10 pm daily (June to October) and 2 to 10 pm Monday to Saturday at other times of the year. Access charges to their modern and fast machines are 25/45FF per half hour/hour.

The Syndrome Cybercafé (☎ 04 50 45 39 75, fax 04 50 45 85 65, ✉ infos@syndrome .com), 3 bis ave de Chevêne, opens 12 pm to midnight. This place is mainly used by young game players. One hour of Internet access costs 40FF.

Laundry The Lav' Confort Express at 4 rue de la Gare opens 7 am to 9 pm daily. A small wash load will cost you 25FF.

Walking Tour

Walking around and taking in the lake, flowers and quaint buildings is the essence of a visit to Annecy. Just east of the Vieille Ville, behind the town hall, are the flowery **Jardins de l'Europe**, shaded by giant redwoods from California. **Champ de Mars**, a grassy expanse across the Canal du Vassé from the redwoods, is a popular park. Both are linked by the evocatively named pont des Amours.

FRENCH ALPS

A fine stroll can be had by walking from the Jardins de l'Europe along quai de Bayreuth and quai de la Tournette to the Base Nautique des Marquisats (see Water Sports) and beyond. Another fine promenade begins at Champ de Mars and goes eastwards around the lake towards Annecy-le-Vieux.

Vieille Ville

The Vieille Ville, an area of narrow streets on either side of the Canal du Thiou, retains much of its 17th-century appearance despite efforts to make it quaint for tourists. On the island in the middle, **Palais de l'Isle** (☎ 04 50 33 87 31), a former prison, houses a display of the city and region's history and culture. It opens 10 am to noon and 2 to 6 pm daily, except Tuesday (10 am to 6 pm daily from June to September). Admission costs 20FF (students 5FF).

From mid-June to September there are guided tours in English around Vieille Ville (32FF). The tourist office has details.

Château d'Annecy

Musée Château (☎ 04 50 33 87 30), housed in the 13th- to 16th-century chateau overlooking the town, has a permanent collection that includes examples of local artisanship and miscellaneous objects about the region's natural history. It also puts on innovative temporary exhibitions. It opens 10 am to noon and 2 to 6 pm (closed Tuesday in winter). Admission costs 30FF (students 10FF), but is free on Wednesday to all (except during school holidays). The climb up to the chateau is worth it just for the view.

Carillon Concert

From mid-June to mid-September, a carillon concert is held at the **Basilique de la Visitation** (☎ 04 50 66 17 37) every Saturday. At 4 pm, immediately preceding the concert, there is a guided visit (20FF) of the 37-bell chromatic carillon and various displays about carillon playing. The basilica is south of (ie straight up the hill from) the Vieille Ville at the top of ave de la Visitation.

Sunbathing & Swimming

There are all sorts of grassy areas along the lakefront where, in the warm months, you can hang out, have a picnic, sunbathe and swim. There is a free beach, **Plage d'Annecy-le-Vieux**, 1km east of the Champ de Mars. Slightly closer to town is **Plage Impérial**, which costs 18FF and is equipped with changing rooms and other amenities.

Perhaps Annecy's most pleasant stretch of lawn-lined swimming beach is free **Plage des Marquisats**, 1km south of the Vieille Ville along rue des Marquisats. The beaches are officially open from June to September. **Base Nautique des Marquisats** (☎ 04 50 45 39 18), 29 rue des Marquisats, has three outdoor swimming pools and plenty of lawn. From 1 May to 1 September, the complex opens 9 am (10 am on Sunday and holidays) to 7 pm (7.30 pm from July to early September). Admission costs 20FF (those aged under 18 15FF).

Walking & Climbing

Forêt du Crêt du Maure, south of Annecy, has many walking trails but is hardly a pristine wilderness. There are better walking areas in and around two nature reserves: **Bout du Lac** (20km from Annecy on the southern tip of the lake) and **Roc de Chère** (10km from town on the eastern coast of the lake). Both can be reached by Voyages Crolard buses (see Getting There & Away).

Maps and topoguides can be purchased at La Maison de la Presse, 13 rue Vaugelas, and the tourist office. One of the better walking maps is the 1:25,000 scale Top 25 IGN map entitled *Lac d'Annecy* (No 3431OT; 58FF) while the larger scale 1:50,000 Bourne Bouges map (57FF) covers a wider area.

The CAF (☎ 04 50 09 82 09 or ☎ 04 50 27 29 45) has an office at 77 rue du Mont Blanc, about 1.5km north-east of the train station. Takamaka (see Water Sports) arranges guided hikes and climbs.

Cycling & Rollerblading

There's a *piste cyclable* (bicycle path), suitable for rollerbladers as well, along the western coast of the lake. It starts 1.5km

FRENCH ALPS

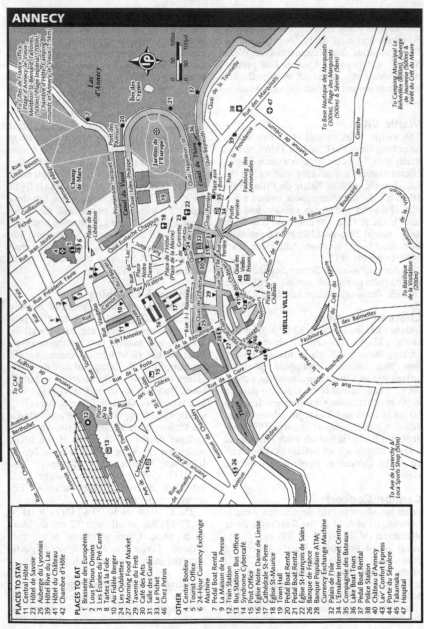

ANNECY

PLACES TO STAY
11 Central Hôtel
23 Hôtel de Savoie
25 Auberge du Lyonnais
39 Hôtel Rive du Lac
42 Chambre d'Hôte

PLACES TO EAT
1 Brasserie des Européens
2 Lous P'tious Onions
3 Les Écuries du Pré Carré
10 Tartes à la Folie
18 Au Fidèle Berger
24 Les Oubliettes
27 Morning Food Market
29 Taverne du Freti
31 Café des Arts
35 Salle des Gardes
36 Le Pichet
46 Chez Petros

OTHER
4 Centre Bonlieu
5 Tourist Office
6 24-Hour Currency Exchange
   Machine
7 Pedal Boat Rental
9 La Maison de la Presse
12 Train Station
13 Bus Station; Bus Offices
14 Syndrome Cybercafé
15 Post Office
16 Église Notre Dame de Liesse
17 Cathédrale St-Pierre
18 Église St-Maurice
19 Town Hall
20 Pedal Boat Rental
21 Pedal Boat Rental
22 Église St-François de Sales
26 Banque de France
28 Banque Populaire ATM;
   Currency Exchange Machine
32 Palais de l'Isle
34 L'Émailerie Internet Centre
35 Compagnie des Bateaux
36 Lake Boat Tours
37 Pedal Boat Rental
38 Police Station
40 Château d'Annecy
43 LaV' Confort Express
45 Porte du Sepulcre
47 Hospital

FRENCH ALPS

south of Annecy (on rue des Marquisats) and goes all the way to Duingt, 12km farther south. See Getting Around for information on bicycle and rollerblade rental.

Water Sports
The Base Nautique des Marquisats, 31 rue des Marquisats, is a centre for aquatic activities. One-person kayaks and canoes for two can be rented from their Canoë-Kayak Club d'Annecy (☎ 04 50 45 03 98). The office opens 9 am to noon and 1 to 5 pm June to September.

Between June and mid-September, the Société des Régates à Voile d'Annecy (SRVA; ☎ 04 50 45 48 39, fax 04 50 45 64 64) next door rents all sorts of sailing boats (Laser X4s, catamarans etc) and *planches à voile* (sailboards). The office opens weekdays 9 am to noon and 2 to 5 pm. From late March to late October, pedal boats and small boats with outboard motors can be hired along the quays of the Canal du Thiou and Canal du Vassé.

Takamaka (☎ 04 50 45 60 61, fax 04 50 51 87 20), 17 rue Faubourg Ste-Claire, arranges rafting, kayaking and canyoning expeditions.

Boat Excursions
Compagnie des Bateaux (☎ 04 50 51 08 40), 2 place aux Bois, has one-hour boat tours of the lake in summer costing 60/46FF for adults/children. Boats leave from the south bank of Canal du Thiou on quai Bayreuth. Tickets have to be bought one hour before departure from the blue wooden huts on the lakeside or direct from the Compagnie des Bateaux office. In summer there are also boat trips across the lake to Menthon-St-Bernard and Talloires (see Around Annecy).

Places to Stay – Budget
Camping Located in the Forêt du Crêt du Maure, *Camping Municipal Le Belvédère* (☎ 04 50 45 48 30, fax 04 50 45 55 56) is 2.5km south of the train station. It costs about 47/67FF for one/two people. To get there, turn off rue des Marquisats onto ave de Trésum, take the first left and follow

blvd de la Corniche. From mid-June to early September take bus No 91 (Ligne des Vacances, meaning 'Holiday Line') from the train station.

There are several other camping grounds near the lake in Annecy-le-Vieux.

Hostels Situated about 1km away, the *Auberge de Jeunesse* (☎ 04 50 45 33 19, fax 04 50 52 77 52, 4 Route du Semnoz) is south of town in the Forêt du Semnoz. A bed costs 72FF, including breakfast. Sheet hire costs 17FF. From mid-June to early September only, bus No 91 (the Ligne des Vacances) runs from the train station and town hall to the hostel between 9 am and 7 pm. The rest of the year, take bus No 1 to the Marquisats stop.

Chambres d'Hôte The regional Gîtes de France accommodation office (☎ 04 50 23 92 74, fax 04 79 86 71 32) overlooks the lake at 17 ave d'Albigny.

At the *chambre d'hôte* (☎ 04 50 23 34 43, 2 ave de la Mavéria) overlooking the lake next to the Impérial Palace doubles with shower/bath cost 210/280FF; breakfast costs 32FF. Also brilliantly located is another *chambre d'hôte* in a private home (☎ 04 50 45 72 28, rampe du Château), next to Hôtel du Château.

Hotels Cheap hotels are hard to find from mid-July to mid-August. Book in advance.

Small *Hôtel Rive du Lac* (☎ 04 50 51 32 85, fax 04 50 45 77 40, 6 rue des Marquisats), conveniently located near both the Vieille Ville and the lake, has one or two-bed rooms with shower for 146FF. Breakfast costs an extra 24FF.

One of the cheapest places close to the Vieille Ville is *Central Hôtel* (☎ 04 50 45 05 37, 6 bis rue Royale) in a quiet courtyard. Doubles start at 160FF. Triples/quads cost 220/230FF.

In the heart of the old city, *Auberge du Lyonnais* (☎ 04 50 51 26 10, fax 04 50 51 05 04, 14 quai de l'Évêché), occupies an idyllic setting next to the canal. Singles/doubles with toilet cost 170/240FF. Rooms with shower and toilet cost 240/290FF.

FRENCH ALPS

However, it only has nine rooms so be quick.

Places to Stay – Mid-Range & Top End

For a serene view over Annecy's lantern-lit lanes it's hard to beat *Hôtel du Château* (☎ 04 50 45 27 66, fax 04 50 52 75 26, 16 rampe du Château), just below one of the towers of its namesake. Cosy singles/doubles start at 250/330FF with shower and toilet. There's a large terrace and plenty of private parking.

The oddly placed *Hôtel de Savoie* (☎ 04 50 45 15 45, fax 04 50 45 11 99, **e** hotel .savoie@mail.dotcom.fr, 1 place de St-François) has its entrance on the left side of Église St-François de Sales…spooky. Simple rooms with washbasin cost from 150/220FF.

Places to Eat

Restaurants Annecy is endowed with an abundance of good restaurants. In the Vieille Ville, the streets on both sides of Canal du Thiou are lined with touristy establishments, most of which are remarkably similar to each other.

In the new town centre, there are good pizzas (starting at 38FF), large salads (19FF to 43FF) and a children's menu (42FF) at *Lous P'tious Onions* (☎ 04 50 51 34 41, 36 rue Sommeiller) in the Grand Passage. *Menus* start at 65FF. There are also a number of inexpensive places to eat along rue du Pâquier.

Nearby and popular with the local crowd is *Brasserie des Européens (23 rue Sommeiller)*, which specialises in *moules* (mussels) for 92FF; try the *Moules Spéciales Brasserie* at 104FF. They also have a fresh seafood takeaway counter.

A block further south and in a small courtyard off rue Vaugelas, is excellent *Les Écuries du Pré Carré* (☎ 04 50 45 55 62, 10 rue Vaugelas). The *plat du jour* costs 55FF; there are *menus* from 98FF to 118FF and the service is top-class.

Les Oubliettes (☎ 04 50 45 39 78, 10 quai de l'Isle), right next to the canal, has pizzas from 40FF to 55FF and a wide choice of other main courses such as an expansive *Menu Savoyard* (99FF). Just across the canal, *Le Pichet* (☎ 04 50 45 32 41, 13 rue Perrière), has a big terrace and three-course *menus* for 66FF and 78FF.

Rather touristy *Salle des Gardes* (☎ 04 50 51 52 00, quai des Vieilles Prisons), facing the old prison, has Savoyard specialities, such as fondue and *tartiflette* (sliced potatoes and reblochon cheese baked in the oven), as does the *Taverne du Freti* (☎ 04 50 51 29 52, 12 rue Faubourg Ste-Claire). Its authentic *raclette* is worth every centime at 68FF per person. Book in advance.

Chez Petros (☎ 04 50 45 50 26, 13 rue Faubourg Ste-Claire) is a small but busy Greek restaurant with classic Greek *menus* costing from 65FF to 115FF, as well as excellent vegetarian dishes such as stuffed aubergines or peppers (40FF), haricot beans (42FF) or okra (54FF).

Cafes Rue Perrière and rue de l'Isle have several cheap, hole-in-the-wall sandwich shops. Exquisite sweet and savoury tarts can be had at *Tartes à la Folie* (7–9 rue Vaugelas). There is a 39FF lunchtime *menu*, comprising a savoury tart, salad and soft drink. Don't miss out on the scrumptiously sweet rhubarb and nut tarts.

Heavenly hot chocolate is served at *Au Fidèle Berger (on the corner of rue Royale and rue Carnot)*, a traditional tea room and chocolate shop. *Café des Arts (4 passage de l'Isle)* is a small, dimly lit and intimate cafe, popular for its bohemian touch and emotive setting in the middle of the canal. It opens 9 to 1 am.

Self-Catering In the Vieille Ville, there's a popular *food market* held along rue Faubourg Ste-Claire 6 am to 12.30 pm Sunday, Tuesday and Friday.

Getting There & Away

Air Annecy's small airport (☎ 04 50 27 30 06) is north of the city at 8 Route Côte Merle in Meythet just west of the autoroute to Geneva. The airport has daily flights to Paris Orly Sud, Lilles, Nantes, Bordeaux and Toulouse.

Bus The bus station, Gare Routière Sud, is next to the train station on rue de l'Industrie. Exits from the train station platforms lead directly to the bus station.

Three companies offer a wide range of schedules. Voyages Crolard (☎ 04 50 45 08 12) open 7.45 am to 12 pm and 2 to 7.15 pm (Monday to Friday), 7.45 am to 12 pm (Saturday) and from 7.30 to 11 am and 1.45 to 7 pm on Sunday. They have regular services to various points around Lake Annecy, including Menthon, Talloires and Roc de Chère on the eastern shore; Sévrier on the western shore; and Bout du Lac on the southern tip. Other services include to/from the ski stations east of Annecy, including La Clusaz (56FF, 50 minutes), Le Grand Bornand (56FF, one hour), Albertville (44FF, 1¼ hours) and Chamonix (95FF, two hours).

Autocars Frossard (☎ 04 50 45 73 90) opens 7.45 am to 12 pm and 2 to 7.15 pm Monday to Friday, and 7.45am to 12pm on Saturday. They sell tickets to Annemasse, Chambéry, Évian, Geneva, Grenoble, Nice and Thonon.

Autocars Francony (☎ 04 50 45 02 43) has buses to destinations including Chamonix, Chambéry and Megève (57FF). Most do not run on Sunday or holidays. Its office opens 7.15 to 11 am and 2.15 to 6.15 pm weekdays.

Train The train station (☎ 04 36 35 35 35) is on place de la Gare. The information counters open 9 am to noon and 2 to 7 pm. The ticket windows open 4.45 am to 9.20 pm on Monday, 6.10 am to 9.20 pm Tuesday to Saturday, and 6.40 am to 10.40 pm on Sunday.

There are frequent trains to Paris' Gare de Lyon (451FF by TGV, 3¾ hours), Nice (404FF via Lyon, 352FF via Aix-les-Bains, eight to nine hours, faster with a change of train), Lyon (115FF, two hours), Chamonix (105FF, 2½ to three hours), Aix-les-Bains (39FF, 30 to 45 minutes) and Chambéry (49FF, one hour).

The night train to Paris (eight hours), often full on Friday and Saturday, leaves at 10.30 or 11.20 pm. Couchettes cost 90FF extra.

Getting Around
Bus The municipal bus company SIBRA (☎ 04 50 51 72 72) has an information bureau (☎ 04 50 51 70 33) inside the Centre Bonlieu. It opens 9 am to 7 pm Monday to Saturday.

Buses run 6 am to 8 pm Monday to Saturday. On Sunday, 20-seat minibuses – identified by letters rather than numbers – provide a limited service. Bus No 91 (the Ligne des Vacances), which serves the hostel, runs only from mid-June to early September. Bus tickets cost 8FF; a carnet for eight rides costs 39FF. Weekly coupons cost 50FF.

Taxi For taxis based at the bus station call ☎ 04 50 45 05 67. For Taxi Plus call ☎ 04 50 68 93 33.

Bicycle & Rollerblades Bikes can be hired from Loca Sports (☎ 04 50 45 44 33), south-west of the Vieille Ville at 37 ave de Loverchy. Sévrier Sport Location (☎ 04 50 52 42 68), 65 place de la Mairie, rents out tandems, mountain bikes and rollerblades.

AROUND ANNECY
When the sun shines, the charming villages of **Sévrier**, 5km south of Annecy on Lake Annecy's western shore, and **Menthon-St-Bernard**, 7km south on its eastern shore, are well worth a day trip. **Talloires**, just a few kilometres south of Menthon, is Annecy's most exclusive lakeside spot. Romantic, luxurious and delightful if you can afford it, is four-star *Auberge du Père Bise* (☎ 04 50 60 71 10, fax 04 50 60 73 05, ✆ bise@ silicone.fr), which overlooks Talloires' picturesque little harbour on Route du Port. The former Haitian dictator Jean Claude Duvalier (better known as Baby Doc) stayed in the 18th-century Abbaye hotel for three weeks following his overthrow and subsequent exile in 1986.

Skiing is the Annéciens' main weekend activity in winter. Just 18km south of the city is the predominantly cross-country resort of **Le Semnoz** (1700m), which also has a couple of tame downhill slopes for beginners. Farther afield are the larger village resorts of **La Clusaz** (1100m), 32km east of

FRENCH ALPS

Annecy, and **Le Grand Bornand** (1000m), 34km north-east of Annecy. Accommodation in La Clusaz is conveniently handled by the tourist office (☎ 04 50 32 65 00, fax 04 50 32 65 01, **@** infos@laclusaz.com). There is an *Auberge de Jeunesse* (☎ *04 50 02 41 73, fax 04 50 02 65 85,* **@** *la-clusaz@ fuaj.org, BP 47, 74220 La Clusaz)* 3km up the valley from La Clusaz at Route du Col de Croix Fry, Le Marcoret. It opens year round, but only accepts group bookings from 26 September to 20 December. A bed costs 51FF per night. Daily buses to and from Annecy serve all three resorts.

CHAMBÉRY
postcode 73000 • pop 55,000
• elevation 270m

Charming Chambéry, which lies in a wide valley between Annecy and Grenoble, has long served as one of the principal gateways between France and Italy. Occupying the entrance to the valleys that lead to the main Alpine passes, the town was the capital of Savoy from the 13th century until 1563. Its charming old quarter, crammed with unexplored courtyards and narrow cobbled streets, was built around the castle of one of the dukes of Savoy.

Orientation

Busy dual carriageways along a narrow canal separate the town's compact old section and the northern sprawl, which starts near the train station at the northern end of rue Sommeiller. Place des Éléphants – the old city's focal point – is at the north-eastern end of rue de Boigne.

Information

Tourist Offices The tourist office (☎ 04 79 33 42 47, fax 04 79 85 71 39, **@** ot-chambery@wanadoo.fr) in the Maison du Tourisme, 24 blvd de la Colonne, opens 9 am to noon and 1.30 to 6 pm Monday to Saturday. Mid-June to mid-September, it opens 9 am to 12.30 pm and 1.30 to 6.30 pm (10 am to 12.30 pm on Sunday).

It sells a myriad of useful maps and guides of the surrounding areas, including *Promenades autour de Chambéry* (50FF), which details 16 city walks. In July and August the tourist office arranges city walking tours (25 to 30FF) daily at 4 pm, with an additional one at 9 pm from 15 July. It also organises fun theme tours that take in everything from Chambéry's meandering alleyways to its colourful trompe l'oeil wall paintings.

The Chambéry Tourist Office has a Web site at www.mairie-chambery.fr.

Savoie Information Jeunesse (☎ 04 79 62 66 87), 79 place de la Gare, has information on hostels, sports, transport and housing. It opens 9 am to 12.30 pm and 1.30 to 6 pm on Monday, Wednesday and Thursday. It opens 9 am to 5 pm on Tuesday and Friday.

National Park Office The Parc National de la Vanoise headquarters (☎ 04 79 62 30 54, fax 04 79 96 37 18), 135 rue du Docteur Julliand, opens 9 am to noon weekdays. Travellers can stop by in the afternoon if they telephone ahead.

Walking & Touring Information The Bureau des Guides et Accompagnateurs de Montagne (☎ 04 79 62 62 48) has an information desk inside the tourist office, open 5.30 to 6.30 pm in July and August. It arranges canyoning, rock and ice climbing, skiing and caving expeditions, as well as walks in the region. Alternatively, contact the CAF (☎ 04 79 33 05 52), just south of the cathedral at 70 rue Croix d'Or, open from 5.30 to 7.30 pm Tuesday to Friday, and 10 am to noon on Saturday.

The tourist office sells the invaluable guidebooks *Cyclotourisme VTT* and *Escalade via Ferrata Canyoning*, each of which lists some 70-plus cycling and climbing routes in the Savoy region. It stocks walking maps of the Chartreuse and Vanoise parks too, as does La Piste Verte, 172 rue Croix d'Or, and La Maison de la Presse, 139 place St-Léger.

Money The Crédit Lyonnais next to the tourist office at 26 blvd de la Colonne opens 8.15 am to 12.55 pm and 1.30 to 5.15 pm daily, except Sunday (3.45 pm on Saturday). Banque de Savoie, 6 Blvd du Théâtre, opens 8.10 am to noon and 1.35 to 5.20 pm weekdays (Saturday until 4.20 pm; closed Sunday).

The post office at place de l'Hôtel de Ville has an ATM, as do most banks in the city centre.

Post The main post office, on square Paul Vidal, opens 8 am to 7 pm weekdays and on Saturday until noon. There is a more convenient post office at place de l'Hôtel de Ville with similar opening hours.

Laundry The Laverie Automatique laundrette at 1 rue Doppet opens 7.30 am to

8 pm. The Lavomatique at 37 place Monge opens 7 am to 10 pm. Both charge around 18FF for a small load.

Château des Ducs de Savoie

The chateau around which the town was built is an opulent 14th-century castle on place du Château. It houses the region's Conseil Général (County Council). The grounds open 7.30 am to 7 pm, but the chateau itself can only be visited on a guided one-hour tour that costs 30FF (students 20FF) organised by the tourist office. Tours take place daily at 10.30 am, 2.30,

CHAMBÉRY

PLACES TO STAY
1 Le Revard
2 Hôtel du Lion d'Or
7 Hôtel Art
15 Hôtel des Princes
18 Hôtel La Banche
22 Hôtel du Château
23 Hôtel Le Mauriennais
36 City Hotel

PLACES TO EAT
17 Prisunic Supermarket
19 Food Market
21 Twist Again Café
24 Au Fidèle Berger
25 La Spaghetteria
26 Le Saint Réal
27 Le Rest' aux Crêpes
32 Pr.Al.It
33 Hong Kong
34 Laiterie des Alpes
35 Théâtre Café
42 Café de l'Horloge
43 La Guérande

45 La Table de Marie
47 Hôtel Savoyard Restaurant
48 Café de Lyon

OTHER
3 Train Station
4 Main Post Office
5 Bus Station
6 Savoie Information Jeunesse
8 Musée des Beaux-Arts
9 Laverie Automatique
10 Crédit Lyonnais
11 Tourist Office
12 STAC Kiosk
13 Fountain
14 Banque de Savoie
16 Branch Post Office
20 Université de Savoie
28 Musée Savoisien
29 Cathédrale Métropole
30 CAF Office
31 Théâtre Charles Dullin
37 La Maison de la Presse
38 Accueil des Guides Office
39 Hôtel Montfalcon
40 Ste-Chapelle
41 Château des Ducs de Savoie
44 La Piste Verte
46 Lavomatique

FRENCH ALPS

3.30, 4.30 and 5.30 pm in July and August. There is one tour daily at 2.30 pm in April, May, June, September and October. Tours start – and they should be booked in advance – at the tourist office. Between January and March, tours (Saturday and Sunday at 2.30 pm in January and March; daily in February) start outside the Accueil des Guides office (☎ 04 79 85 93 73), beneath the 18th-century Hôtel Montfalcon, 6 place du Château. The office is open from 1.30 to 5.30 pm (closed Wednesday and at the weekend).

Tours take in the adjoining **Ste-Chapelle**, built in the 15th century to house what later became known as the Shroud of Turin (the sacred cloth believed to have been used to wrap the crucified Christ before burial). The shroud was taken to Turin in 1860, when Savoy became part of France. You can visit the 70-bell **Grand Carillon** in Ste-Chapelle – Europe's largest bell chamber – on a guided tour (30FF) on Saturday at 11 am and 6 pm between May and September and at 4 pm from October to April.

Fontaine des Éléphants

Splendidly dominating place des Éléphants at the intersection of blvd de la Colonne and rue de Boigne, this fountain, which could be the model for an Indian postage stamp with its four great elephants, was sculpted in 1838 in honour of Général de Boigne (1751–1830), a local who made a fortune in the East Indies. When he returned home, he bestowed some of his wealth on the town and was honoured posthumously with this monument. The arcaded street that leads from the fountain to the Château des Ducs and bears his name was one of his most important local projects.

Museums

Chambéry's three museums each cost 20FF (students 10FF). A block south of the elephant fountain and just north of the 15th- and 16th-century Cathédrale Métropole is **Musée Savoisien** (☎ 04 79 33 44 48), just off blvd du Théâtre on square de Lannoy de Bissy. Occupying a 13th-century Franciscan monastery, it exhibits local archaeolog-

ical finds, including a gallery of 13th-century wall paintings that had been hidden by a false roof inside a local mansion. Exhibits of traditional Savoyard mountain life are displayed on the 2nd floor. The museum opens 10 am to noon and 2 to 6 pm (closed Tuesday). **Musée des Beaux-Arts** (☎ 04 79 33 75 03), place du Palais de Justice, houses a rich collection of 14th- to 18th-century Italian works. It opens the same hours as the Musée Savoisien.

Musée des Charmettes (☎ 04 79 33 39 44), 1.5km south-east of the town, occupies the country house of philosopher and writer Jean-Jacques Rousseau, who lived here in bliss from 1736 to 1742 with his lover, Baronne Louise Éléonore de Warens. It opens 10 am to noon and 2 to 6 pm (closed Tuesday) from April to September. The rest of the year it closes at 4.30 pm. In July and August *only*, a special bus leaves from the tourist office at 2.30 pm on Monday, Thursday, Friday and Saturday. It returns at 4 pm. A bus ticket costs 6.50FF and admission to the museum costs 20FF.

Musical evenings are also held here on Wednesday and Friday in summer. Book in advance at the tourist office.

Places to Stay

Camping There are several camping grounds outside Chambéry, all open from May to September.

The closest is two-star *Camping Le Nivolet* (☎ 04 79 85 47 79) in Bassens, 3km north-east of the centre. The fees are 15/15/8FF per person/tent/car. To get there take bus C. Heading north from Chambéry, you might try three-star *L'Île aux Cygnes* (☎ 04 79 25 01 76, Le Bourget du Lac). Take bus H from the Éléphants stop or the train station to the terminus, from where it's a 400m walk.

To the south-east at Challes-les-Eaux, the two star *Le Mont St-Michel* (☎ 04 79 72 84 45, chemin St-Vincent), charges 15/12/8FF for a caravan/tent/car. It costs 15FF per person (children 8FF). Take bus G from the train station or the Éléphants stop to the Centre Challes stop, from where it's a 15-minute walk.

Hostels In Chambéry there are several *foyers* that take people under 25 – the tourist office has details. *Maison des Jeunes et de la Culture (MJC;* ☎ 04 79 85 05 84, 311 Faubourg Montmélian), opens year round and charges 75FF per person. There's a shower in the hallway.

The nearest *Auberge de Jeunesse* is in Aix-les-Bains (see Around Chambéry).

Hotels Just outside the old city to the west, *Hôtel Le Mauriennais* (☎ 04 79 69 42 78, fax 04 79 69 46 86, 2 rue Ste-Barbe), offers a chateau view and no-frills singles/doubles starting at 90/120FF.

Rather glum-looking *Hôtel du Château* (☎ 04 79 69 48 78, 37 rue Jean-Pierre Veyrat), is cheap with rooms with washbasin costing 90/130FF. Both hotels are on or near a busy road.

In the old city, *Hôtel La Banche* (☎ 04 79 33 15 62, 10 place de l'Hôtel de Ville), is quiet, with average rooms costing 130/200FF. Rooms with shower start at 220FF. South-east of the centre, the *City Hotel* (☎ 04 79 85 76 79, fax 04 79 85 86 11, 9 rue Denfert Rochereau), has rooms with washbasin for 170/210FF, and rooms with shower for 195/260FF. Private parking costs 30FF.

Directly opposite the train station, *Hôtel du Lion d'Or* (☎ 04 79 69 04 96, fax 04 79 96 93 20, 13 ave de la Boisse), provides decent rooms with toilet starting at 140/165FF or 200/235FF with shower. Breakfast costs 34FF, and there's a busy brasserie adjoining the hotel.

Le Revard (☎ 04 79 62 04 64, fax 04 79 96 37 26, 41 ave de la Boisse), close by, has basic rooms starting at 170/200FF.

Modern *Hôtel Art* (☎ 04 79 62 37 26, fax 04 79 62 49 98, 154 rue Sommeiller), is directly opposite the bus station. It has beautifully furnished rooms with bath and TV that start at 250/290FF; breakfast costs 35FF.

Close to the centre, the upmarket *Hôtel des Princes* (☎ 04 79 33 45 36, fax 04 79 70 31 47, 4 rue de Boigne), in one of the arcaded buildings, offers rooms with all mod-cons for 340/390FF. Breakfast costs 40FF as does private car parking.

Places to Eat

Restaurants In a side street near the Fontaine des Éléphants, *Le Rest' aux Crêpes* (☎ 04 79 75 00 07, 35 rue du Verger), specialises in Breton *crêpes* and *galettes* – hardly Alpine treats. However, the 48FF lunch-only *menu* is good value and includes a glass of *kir*. It opens Monday evening to Saturday.

For Italian-inspired cuisine, try *La Spaghetteria* (☎ 04 79 33 27 62, 43 rue St-Réal), which boasts 19 pizza and 21 pasta variations, as well as good-value *menus* for 70FF and 102FF, and a 40FF children's *menu*.

If you want to sample local Savoyard specialities, try the restaurant at *Hôtel Savoyard* (☎ 04 79 33 36 55, 35 place Monge). Its *tartiflette* (oven-cooked potatoes and reblochon cheese) and *gratin de crozets* (Savoyard pasta with cheese) are out of this world. *Menus* start at 79FF; the four-course *menu Savoyard* is excellent value at 130FF. It also has a children's *menu* for 48FF. Have a glass or two of Mondeuse (47FF a half-bottle), Savoy's almost berry-like red wine. *La Table de Marie* (☎ 04 79 85 99 76, 193 Croix d'Or), serves Savoyarde dishes daily until 11 pm. *Menus* start at 59FF.

The best restaurant in Chambéry is *Le St-Réal* (☎ 04 79 70 09 33, 10 rue St-Réal). *Menus* range from four-course ones for 180FF (220FF with wine and coffee) to six- and seven-course *séduction* and *passion menus* for 390FF. It opens Monday to Saturday.

Cafes Modern *Twist Again Café* (31 rue Jean-Pierre Veyrat) has a little terrace backing onto the marketplace. *Théâtre Café* (place du Théâtre), opposite the Théâtre Charles Dullin, has a popular terrace, that is lively until very late on summer nights.

Café de Lyon, on place Monge, is always packed. It has a lunch *menu* for 59FF and the cafe-bar opens 8 to 1.30 am. Hot spots in summer include *La Guérande* (7 place St-Léger) and *Café de l'Horloge* (11 place St-Léger), which offers 200 brands of bottled beer, 30 brands of whisky and nine draft beers. It's a great old world place with real atmosphere.

FRENCH ALPS

Self-Catering On Saturday morning a *food market* is held on place de Genève. *Prisunic (place du 8 Mai 1945)* supermarket opens 8.15 am to 7.30 pm Monday to Saturday. *Laiterie des Alpes (88 rue d'Italie)* stocks a good range of local cheeses and dairy products. Italian products are sold at *Pr.Al.It (67 rue d'Italie)*, while *Hong Kong (71 rue d'Italie)* is the place to go for Vietnamese and Chinese supplies.

Getting There & Away

Bus The ticket office at Chambéry bus station (☎ 04 79 69 11 88), south of the train station on place de la Gare, opens 6.15 am to 7.15 pm. From here there are buses to Aix-les-Bains (15.50FF, 35 minutes, five daily), Annecy (47FF, 50 minutes, seven daily), Grenoble (49FF, 1½ hours, 10 daily) and Voiron (55FF, 1¼ hours, six a day). There is one bus to Geneva and Nice daily, and six daily to Lyon-Satolas airport (130FF, one hour).

Train Chambéry's train station (☎ 0 836 35 35 35) is 400m north-west of the tourist office at the end of rue Sommeiller on place de la Gare. The information office opens 8.30 am to 7 pm (Monday to Friday) and 9 am to 6 pm on Saturday.

There are major rail connections to Paris' Gare de Lyon (446FF by TGV via Lyon, 3¼ hours, six daily), Lyon (84FF, 1¼ hours, 10 daily), Annecy (49FF, one hour, 10 daily) and Grenoble (51FF, one hour, 14 daily).

There are also trains up the Maurienne Valley to Modane (81FF, 1¾ hours, five daily), which continue on to Turin, Rome and Naples in Italy.

Getting Around

Bus The main hub for local buses run by STAC (☎ 04 79 68 67 00) is along blvd de la Colonne near the Fontaine des Éléphants, where the company has an information kiosk (☎ 04 79 70 26 27), open 7.15 am to 12.45 pm and 1 to 7.15 pm Monday to Friday, and 7.20 am to 12.20 pm and 2.20 to 5.40 pm on Saturday. Many buses also stop at the train station. In general, they run Monday to Saturday until about 8 pm.

Single tickets cost 6.50FF and a carnet of 10 costs 37.70FF.

AROUND CHAMBÉRY

Chambéry is wedged neatly between two regional parks – **Parc Naturel Régional de Chartreuse** in the south-west (see Around Grenoble) and **Parc Naturel Régional du Massif des Bauges**, to the north-east. Covering an area of 80,000 hectares, the Massif des Bauges offers unlimited hiking opportunities. The nature reserve in the north of the park is home to more than 600 chamois and mouflon. The park headquarters (☎ 04 79 54 86 40) is in Le Châtelard.

From the thermal spa of **Aix-les-Bains**, 11km north-west of Chambéry, you can tour **Lac Bourget** – France's largest natural lake – by boat. Contact Bateaux d'Aix-les-Bains (☎ 04 79 88 92 09) at the Grand Port or Aix-les-Bains tourist office (☎ 04 79 35 05 92, fax 04 79 88 88 01), next to the port on ave du Grand Rue. Aix-les-Bains' *Auberge de Jeunesse (☎ 04 79 88 32 88, fax 04 79 61 14 05,* @ *aix-les-bains@fuaj.org, Promenade du Sierroz)*, overlooks the lake. It opens 7 am to 10 am and 6 to 10 pm, for most of the year. **Albertville**, 39km from Chambéry on the eastern park boundary, played host to the 1992 Winter Olympics. The Olympic highs and lows are colourfully told at the Maison des Jeux Olympiques (☎ 04 79 37 75 71), 11 rue Pargoud.

MÉRIBEL

postcode 73500 • elevation 1450m

Méribel lies at the heart of one of the largest skiable areas in the world – the Trois Vallées (Three Valleys). The wealthy purpose-built ski station – 42km south-east of Albertville and 88km from Annecy and Chambéry – was established in 1938 by Scotsman Colonel Peter Lindsay, and today remains one of France's most 'British' resorts. Despite the circus of British pubs and grocery stores that have cropped up in recent years to appease its predominantly British clientele, Méribel has retained in part an Alpine village atmosphere, thanks to a decision made in the mid-1940s to employ only traditional Savoyard architectural styles.

Information

Tourist Office Méribel's central Maison du Tourisme houses the tourist office (☎ 04 79 08 60 01, fax 04 79 00 59 61, ✉ info@meribel.net), the accommodation service (☎ 04 79 00 50 00, fax 04 79 00 31 19, ✉ reservation@meribel.net), the ESF (☎ 04 79 08 60 31, fax 04 79 08 60 80) and a transport information counter. The Maison du Tourisme opens 9 am to 7 pm.

The glossy, bilingual (French–English) *Méribel – Very Belle!* booklet is available free from the tourist office and has a full listing of all the resort's facilities.

Méribel's Maison du Tourisme Web site is at www.meribel.net. Accommodation options can also be viewed here.

Skiing & Snowboarding

Skiing is between 1300m and 3200m. One of the best skiing resorts in France, the vast area can satisfy skiers all levels. Above Val Thorens, there is summer skiing on the Glacier de Péclet.

Méribel Valley alone has 73 Alpine ski runs (150km), 47 ski lifts, two snowboarding parks, a slalom stadium, and two Olympic downhill runs built for the 1992 Games. Many of these start or pass through Mottaret, a transit point 300m above the town, from where the valley's highest lift (2910m) climbs Mont Vallon. Cheaper ski passes that only cover Méribel Valley (ideal for beginners) are available. For more competent skiers, there is the Trois Vallées pass, which allows use of all area lifts. Passes valid for more than six days also allow one day of skiing at Espace Killy, La Plagne, Les Arcs, Peisey Vallandry, Pralognan la Vanoise or Les Saisies.

Summer Activities

The *Guide des Sentiers*, costing 35FF at the tourist office, details 20 marked walking trails in Méribel Valley. Particularly enticing is the botanical trail marked around Lake Tueda in the Réserve Naturelle de Tueda (Tueda Nature Reserve).

The Bureau des Guides organises rock climbing, walking and mountain biking expeditions. Contact Chardon Loisirs (☎ 04 79 24 08 84) for white-water rafting courses.

Places to Stay

Of the seven hotels built for the 1992 Olympics, all but two have three or four stars – one-star hotels became almost extinct in Méribel long ago. Accommodation prices are pretty high, but studio and apartment prices are bearable – from 2000FF to 2500FF per week for two people, or from 1600FF to 2100FF for four in the skiing season.

Contact the reservation service (see Information) for a bigger picture since there are too many options to list adequately here.

If you're intent on staying in Méribel, no-star *Hôtel du Moulin* (☎ 04 79 00 52 23, fax 04 79 00 58 84) has seven double rooms from 440FF to 550FF a night, including breakfast. No-star *Hôtel Le Doron* (☎ 04 79 08 60 02, fax 04 79 00 59 95, ✉ hotel-doron@wanadoo.fr), in the heart of the village near the tourist office, has thirteen doubles from 415FF to 540FF, also including breakfast.

One of Méribel's best hotels is the four-star *Hôtel Mont Vallon* (☎ 04 79 00 44 00, fax 04 79 00 46 93, ✉ montvallon-meribel@laposte.fr) where rooms with half-board start at 790FF and reach 3100FF a night for a suite.

Getting There & Away

Vehicle access to Méribel has been made easier thanks to the four-lane A43, built for the Olympics, which links Chambéry (88km north-west) with the nearest town, Moûtiers, 18km north of Méribel.

Geneva and Lyon-Satolas airports are connected to Méribel by shuttle bus services. There's an SNCF information bureau (☎ 04 79 00 53 28) at the tourist office. The closest train station is in Moûtiers (☎ 0 836 35 35 35), from where there are connections to Paris (486FF, five hours) and Chambéry (66FF, 1¼ hours).

Regional buses are operated by Transavoie (☎ 04 79 24 21 58) and run between Méribel and Moûtiers (62FF, four daily on weekdays, more at the weekend).

FRENCH ALPS

Getting Around

Bus Méribel provides a free shuttle bus service. Buses to Courchevel cost 52FF and a taxi about 260FF.

VAL D'ISÈRE

postcode 73150 • pop 1738
• elevation 1850m

It's hip to be seen in Val d'Isère, a trendy resort in the upper reaches of the Tarentaise Valley, 31km south-east of Bourg St-Maurice, and close to the Italian border. It's extremely popular with the British and Scandinavians; French is almost a second language here. Along with **Tignes** (2100m), Val d'Isère and four other small villages combine to form **Espace Killy**.

Val d'Isère – a former hunting ground for the dukes of Savoy – has grown from a village since 1932, when skiing was introduced to the region, but a settlement in the valley goes back thousands of years. The oldest building still standing is the 11th-century church, with the rest of the village being a mixture of traditional Savoyard stone homes, chalet-type hotels and apartment blocks.

The resort is home to the infamous *La Face de Bellevarde*, a 63% black ski slope peaking at 2809m and used for the men's downhill skiing events in the 1992 Winter Olympics. Anyone daring or reckless enough to do it can. One LP author at least has done it and moreover, survived to tell the tale. Olympic gold medallist, Austrian Patrick Ortlieb completed the enormous run in 1 minute 50.37 seconds.

The nearby Lac du Chevril is completely drained every 10 years exposing the valley floor (see boxed text 'The Disappearing Lake').

Information

Tourist Offices The Val d'Isère tourist office (☎ 04 79 06 06 60, fax 04 79 06 04 56, ✉ info@valdisere.com), place Jacques Mouflier, opens 8.30 am to 7.30 pm. Their Web site is at www.valdisere.com. The Bureau des Guides has a (summer) desk inside the tourist office and the Val Hôtel accommodation service (☎ 04 79 06 18 90, fax 04

79 06 11 88 ✉ valhotel@valdisere.com) is based there as well. However, they will only make bookings for a minimum of four days.

Money There are at least four ATMs in the village and a couple of Le Change exchange offices that keep long hours.

Winter Activities

Espace Killy offers some of the best skiing in the country – between 1550m and 3450m. Ski touring is also excellent in Espace Killy, especially in the Parc National de la Vanoise. The snowboarders' Snowspace Park in La Deille has a half-pipe, tables, gaps, quarters and hips. In July and August you can ski on the glacier.

Val d'Isère has no less than four ski schools and seven independent instructors. The ESF (☎ 04 79 06 02 34, fax 04 79 41 15 80) is housed in a large building off place Jacques Mouflier. Hors Limites (☎/fax 04 79 41 97 02, ✉ lionel@hors-limites.com) specialises in snowboarding. A six-day Espace Killy ski pass also entitles skiers to one day of skiing in La Plagne, Les Arcs or Les Trois Vallées.

Heli-skiing, ice diving, ice climbing, snowshoeing, sledging and husky-drawn sledge rides are also available. The tourist offices have details.

Summer Activities

One of the more popular walks is from Val d'Isère to the village of Tignes along the Gorges de la Daille or the high road along Vallon de la Tovière. Other possibilities are to Col de l'Iseran or Glacier des Sources d'Isère, but many other routes in the Parc National de la Vanoise are possible. The valleys and gentle walking trails also offer many possibilities for mountain biking and fishing.

The Bureau des Guides organises, among other things, visits to a local farm where you can see cheese being made, and Alpine bird-watching treks. Safaris Vanoise (☎ 04 79 06 00 03, fax 04 79 06 10 28) organises animal photography and filming expeditions. The ESF runs parapente lessons in summer.

The Disappearing Lake

As you head south along the winding road up towards your date with skis in the mountains, look out for the shimmering expanse of the Lac du Chevril to your right as you approach Val d'Isère. It was created amidst much controversy between 1947 and 1955 and the dam that created the lake is used by the French Electricity monopoly EDF to create hydroelectric power. The village of Tignes-le-Lac, once a thriving community of 500 people, was abandoned as a result of the project and now lies at the bottom of the deep lake. You can hardly miss Lac du Chevril – that is, if it is there…

Every 10 years the EDF drain the lake completely in order to carry out maintenance to the dam. When this happens there is no lake, just a huge hole where the lake used to be. In among the mud you can still spot the remains of the doomed Tignes-le-Lac – houses, tree trunks and even an old car, and on the southern side you should be able to make out the remains of a couple of bridges. Sightseers flock to the muddy floor of Lac du Chevril to wander among the debris of this bizarre spectacle and a solemn commemorative Mass is held on the lake floor before the lake is re-filled, a process that takes two months. The lake was last emptied in March 2000 and, like the 10 year performance cycle of the Oberammergau Passion Play in Germany, the emptying of the lake will not be undertaken again until 2010.

Places to Stay & Eat

Accommodation is, on the whole, expensive in Val d'Isère and is geared to the skier on a package rather than individual travellers. Advance bookings are imperative throughout the ski season and can be made through the accommodation service (see Tourist Office). Two-person studios and apartments start at 1600/3100FF a week in the low/high season, but prices do vary widely so shop around.

One of the more affordable hotels is *Relais du Ski* (☎ 04 79 06 02 06, fax 04 79 41 10 64), 200m south of the tourist office, where basic double rooms cost 280/390FF in the low/high season. Two star *Hôtel l'Avancher* (☎ 04 79 06 02 00, fax 04 79 41 16 07, Route Fornet), east of the tourist office, has double rooms with half-board from 440/610FF in low/high season.

Another reasonably priced place is the 27-room *Chardons* (☎ 04 79 06 00 15, fax 04 79 41 90 59) where half-board goes for 310/380FF in the low/high season.

With over 70 restaurants and eateries in the village catering to a mainly anglophone clientele, dining out can be a hit and miss experience. Nonetheless, try the central *Samovar* (☎ 04 79 06 13 51) for French and Savoyard dishes, or *Bananas* (☎ 04 79 06 04 23) for a selection of Tex Mex food.

Restaurant prices tend to be somewhat high overall in Val d'Isère.

At the southern end of the village near the Relais du Ski is a *Casino Supermarket* with a well-stocked wine cellar and plenty of DIY meal items.

Entertainment

There's no shortage of bars in this village. Serious après-skiers should head for anglophone *Dick's Tea Bar* (☎ 04 79 06 14 87) complete with 'coma night' on Wednesday and 'chalet girl showers' on other nights. *Café Face* (☎ 04 79 06 29 80, opposite Dick's) is a hot spot for the few French that make it up here, while *Victor's* (04 79 06 67 00) is always jam packed with a mixed bunch of imbibers. *La Banane* is a great little cellar bar.

Getting There & Away

Autocars Martin (☎ 04 79 06 00 42) runs four buses daily to Val d'Isère and Tignes (65FF) from Bourg St-Maurice, the nearest train station. It's essential to book your seat back to Bourg St-Maurice. The office opens 9 am to noon and 2 to 7.30 pm weekdays, 7 am to 1 pm and 1.45 to 9 pm on Saturday, and 7.30 am to noon and 2 to 7.30 pm on Sunday. There is an SNCF counter here too, open 9 am to noon and 3 to 7 pm.

FRENCH ALPS

Satobus-Alpes (☎ 04 72 35 94 96) runs four buses daily (three on Sunday) from Val d'Isère to Lyon-Satolas airport via Bourg St-Maurice. A single ticket costs 250FF. There are also buses to Geneva airport (285FF, five hours, three daily and eight at the weekend).

Getting Around

Val d'Isère runs complimentary buses around the resort centre. The *train rouge* (red train) – a network of 23 shuttle buses – connects Val d'Isère with Tignes and other neighbouring villages, including Les Boisses and the Grand Motte funicular. Timetables are posted at the bus stops.

PARC NATIONAL DE LA VANOISE

A wild mix of high mountains, steep valleys and glaciers, the Parc National de la Vanoise became France's first national park in 1963. It covers 530 sq km – basically the eastern part of the massif between the Tarentaise Valley to the north and the Maurienne Valley to the south. It's a hiker's heaven, with nearly 500km of marked trails (including the GR5 and GR55) and 42 *refuges* dotted around the rugged terrain. The scenery is spectacular – snowcapped peaks mirrored in icy lakes are just the start. Marmots and chamois, as well as France's largest colony of Alpine ibex *(bouquetin)*, graze free and undisturbed among the larch trees, and over them all reigns the eagle.

Orientation & Information

The Parc National de la Vanoise administration office (☎ 04 79 62 30 54, fax 04 79 96 37 18) in Chambéry has information on the park and a list of *refuges*, which cost 68FF per night. To book one in June, July or August call ☎ 04 79 08 71 49. The park newspaper, *Estive*, published seasonally and freely distributed in tourist offices, contains a full listing of all *refuges* complete with direct contact numbers.

Park information is also available at the tourist office (☎ 04 79 05 95 95, fax 04 79 05 86 87) in Bonneval-sur-Arc and the Maison du Val Cénis (☎ 04 79 05 23 66, fax 04 79 05 82 17) in Lanslebourg. A good map

of the region is the 1:50,000 scale IGN map *Parc de la Vanoise* (No 11).

Skiing

Lanslebourg and Bonneval-sur-Arc are popular cross-country skiing resorts. Both offer limited Alpine skiing as well. The ESF (☎ 04 79 05 95 70) is inside the Bonneval-sur-Arc tourist office.

In summer it's possible to ski on the Grand Pissaillas glacier at Col de l'Iseran, 23km north-east of Lanslebourg. The best skiing is between March and early May.

Walking

Walkers have a fine network of small trails to choose from – the Maison du Val Cénis has a walking trails booklet, which details, with maps, a dozen half-day or day treks. The Bureau des Guides (☎ 04 79 05 95 70 or ☎ 04 79 05 96 33) inside the Bonneval-sur-Arc tourist office and Guide de Haute-Montagne (☎ 04 79 05 94 74) both organise guided walks and climbs.

The trail from Lanslebourg up to the Turra Fort (2500m), from where there are great views over the Lac du Mont Cénis, generally takes about three hours. To really take in the region, you can follow all or part of Le Grand Tour de Haute Maurienne – a hike of five days or more around the upper reaches of the valley. There are 15 *refuges* or gîtes d'étape en route.

The GR5 and GR55 pass through the park and there are also paths linked to the Écrins National Park to the south and the Grand Paradiso National Park in Italy. Tracks are usually passable from June to the end of October.

Places to Stay

In Lanslebourg, *Camping Les Balmasses* (☎ 04 79 05 82 83) opens June to September. The *Auberge de Jeunesse Hameau des Champs* (☎ 04 79 05 90 96, fax 04 79 05 82 52) is in the hamlet of Les Champs, which is on the eastern side of Lanslevillard. It opens mid-December to September (closed in May) and costs 48FF per night.

There are five hotels in Lanslebourg. The warm and welcoming two-star *Hôtel La*

The Alpine village of Argentière, near Chamonix

Looks like a long walk home...

Parapente: soar effortlessly over the Alps.

Certainly beats walking uphill: cable cars over the famous Vallée Blanche, the Alps.

RICHARD NEBESKÝ

Swishing towards Briançon

RICHARD NEBESKÝ

Visitors first started flocking to Chamonix in the late 18th century.

RICHARD NEBESKÝ

The former prison of the Palais de l'Isle, Annecy, is now a museum of history and culture.

GARETH McCORMACK

Chamonix Valley is home to beautiful fauna such as this Capra ibex.

GARETH McCORMACK

Grand Balcon Sud, Chamonix

Vieille Poste (☎ *04 79 05 93 47, fax 04 79 05 86 85)*, on the main road through town, has doubles with shower from 250FF. It closes for a fortnight in April and again from November to Christmas. In Bonneval-sur-Arc the *Hôtel du Glacier des Evettes* (☎ *04 79 05 94 06, fax 04 79 05 85 00)* has doubles with shower/bath for 280/300FF. Bonneval also has plenty of delightful old stone cottages for rent. The tourist office has details.

Getting There & Away

The trains serving the valley leave from Chambéry and run as far as the Modane train station (☎ 0 836 35 35 35), 23km south-west of Lanslebourg.

From Modane, Transavoie buses (☎ 04 79 05 01 32) go to Lanslebourg (one hour). Once daily (in the evening) they continue to Bessans and Bonneval-sur-Arc. In winter a shuttle bus runs four times daily between Lanslebourg and Bonneval-sur-Arc.

Dauphiné

Dauphiné, which encompasses the territories south and south-west of Savoy, stretches from the River Rhône in the west to the Italian border in the east. It includes the city of Grenoble and, a little farther east, the mountainous Écrins National Park. The gentler terrain of the western part of Dauphiné is typified by the Vercors Regional Park, much loved by cross-country skiers. In the east, the town of Briançon stands guard like a sentinel near the Italian frontier.

History

The area now known as Dauphiné was inhabited by the Celts and then the Romans. By the 11th century it was under the rule of Guigues I, the count of Albon, whose great-grandson Guigues IV (ruled 1133–42) was the first local count to bear the name of 'dauphin'. By the end of the 13th century, the name 'dauphin' had been transformed into a title and the fiefs held by the region's ruling house, La Tour du Pin, were known collectively as Dauphiné. The rulers of Dauphiné continued to expand their territories, which gave them control of all the passes through the southern Alps.

In 1339, Humbert II established a university at Grenoble. A decade later, however, lacking both money and a successor, he sold Dauphiné to the French king, Charles V, who started the tradition whereby the eldest son of the king of France (the crown prince) ruled Dauphiné and bore the title 'dauphin'. The region was annexed to France by Charles VII in 1457.

GRENOBLE

postcode 38000 ● pop 155,000
● elevation 213m

Grenoble, site of the 1968 Winter Olympics, is the intellectual and economic capital of the French Alps. It's also the centre of the Dauphiné region, spectacularly sitting in a broad valley surrounded by mountains – the Chartreuse to the north, the Vercors to the south-west and Alpine peaks stretching east to Italy.

Grenoble gained a reputation for progress in the 1960s, when the Socialist Hubert Dubedout served as mayor. People from all over France flocked here, attracted by social, artistic and technological innovations, and eventually came to outnumber the native Grenoblois. The large university serves a student body of 36,000 and has a thriving foreign student exchange program.

Grenoble also has important facilities for nuclear and microelectronic research and is home to many large foreign companies.

The city hosts a jazz festival in March, a rock festival in April, and a European theatre festival in June and July. Given Grenoble is the capital of Dauphiné, this is *the* place to sample the popular French dish, *gratin Dauphinois*. *Noix de Grenoble* (a sweet walnut candy) and *gâteau aux noix* (walnut cake) are the local specialities for those with a sweet tooth.

Orientation

Grenoble can be a particularly difficult city to negotiate, especially from behind the wheel, since you can be unwittingly diverted down one-way streets from which it can be

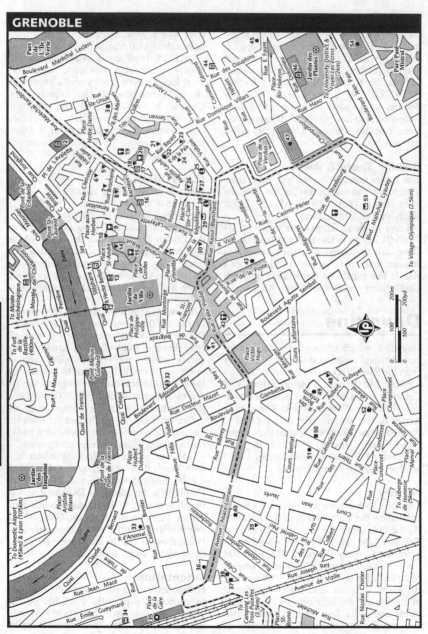

GRENOBLE

	PLACES TO STAY	21	Le Mal Assis	17	Cybernet
3	Foyer de l'Étudiante	23	La Panse	19	Notre Dame
22	Hôtel du Moucherotte	24	Ciao a Te		Cathedral;Bishop's Palace
37	Hôtel Alizé	26	Les Halles	20	Barberousse
38	Hôtel Lux	27	La Forêt Noire	25	Centre InformationJeunesse
40	Hôtel Royal	30	Prisunic Supermarket	28	Maison du Tourisme
43	Hôtel de la Poste	31	La Mère Ticket	29	Post Office
49	Hôtel Beau Soleil	39	Tchou Tchoura	32	Banque de France
50	Hôtel Victoria	41	Les Archers	33	Grenoble Université Club
52	Hôtel Lakanal	48	Subway	34	Bus Station
				35	Train Station
	PLACES TO EAT		OTHER	36	Voyages Wasteels
4	La Galerie Rome	1	Musée Dauphinois	42	Église St-Louis
5	Le Tonneau de Diogène	2	Musée de Grenoble	44	Musée de la Résistance
6	L'Amphitryon	9	Le Couche Tard	45	Maison de la Nature etde
7	Chorus Café	11	Théâtre de Grenoble		l'Environment
8	Restaurant des	12	Téléphérique to Fort de la	46	Musée d'HistoireNaturelle
	Montagnes		Bastille	47	Prefecture
10	Café Tamara	13	Musée Stendhal	51	Lavomatique Laundrette
14	Café de la Table Ronde	15	Le Saxo Pub	53	Main Post Office
18	Le Valgo	16	Le New Age Cyber Café	54	Town Hall

hard to escape without a good map. The old city is centred around place Grenette and place Notre Dame, both of which are about 1km east of the train and bus stations. The main university campus is a couple of kilometres east of the old centre on the southern side of the River Isère.

Information

Tourist Office The ground floor of the Maison du Tourisme, 14 rue de la République, houses the tourist office (☎ 04 76 42 41 41, fax 04 76 00 18 98, ☻ office-de-tourism-de-grenoble@wanadoo.fr), an SNCF counter, a kiosk for tickets to all forms of entertainment, an office of the local bus company (TAG) and the Bureau des Guides (☎/fax 04 76 03 28 63). The first three open 9 am to 12.30 pm and 1.30 to 6 pm Monday to Saturday. The tourist office opens 10 am to noon on Sunday from June to mid-September. The TAG counter opens 8.30 am to 6.30 pm Monday to Friday (Saturday from 9 am to 6 pm). The Bureau des Guides opens on Thursday between 2 and 6 pm (telephone or fax at other times).

Walking Information Info-Montagne (☎ 04 76 42 45 90, fax 04 76 15 3 91), on the 1st floor of the Maison du Tourisme, is

the place to go for first-hand information from dedicated outdoor enthusiasts on walking, climbing, mountain biking and every other imaginable mountain activity *except* skiing. It sells hiking maps and has info on gîtes d'étape and *refuges*. The office opens 9 am to noon and 2 to 6 pm Monday to Friday (from 10 am on Saturday).

The CAF (☎ 04 76 42 49 92), 1 rue Hauquelin, provides information on its *refuges* and organises walking, mountain-bike and skiing trips. It opens 2.30 pm to 7.30 pm Tuesday, to 8.30 pm on Thursday, and to 8 pm on Friday. Other friendly walking clubs include Mountain Wilderness (☎ 04 76 84 54 42, fax 04 76 84 54 44), Maison de la Nature et de l'Environment, 5 place Bir-Hakeim; and Grenoble Amitié Nature (☎ 04 76 51 32 36), 5 passage du Palais de Justice.

Skiing Information The tourist office has comprehensive information, including accommodation lists, for all of Grenoble's surrounding ski resorts (see Around Grenoble). Grenoble Université Club (☎ 04 76 57 47 72), near the train station at 25 rue Casimir Brenier, offers inexpensive skiing for students and nonstudents of all ages. There's a 295FF membership fee that includes insurance. The FUAJ ski club, based in the Auberge de Jeunesse (see Hostels under Places to Stay) also offers cheap skiing deals. Its office opens 10 am to 6 pm in season.

Money The Banque de France, on the corner of blvd Édouard Rey and ave Félix Viallet, opens 8.45 am to 12.15 pm and 1.30 to 3.30 pm weekdays.

Post The main post office, inconveniently located at 7 blvd Maréchal Lyautey, opens 8 am to 6.45 pm weekdays (Saturday until noon). More central is the post office next to the tourist office, open 8 am to 6.30 pm Tuesday to Saturday.

Email & Internet Access Surf the Internet and send emails at Cybernet (☎ 04 76 63 63 94, fax 04 76 03 20 33, ✆ services@ neptune.fr), 8 rue Hache. A 30-minute/one-hour connection costs 30/47FF. It opens noon to 2 pm and 10 pm to 1 am. Le New Age Cyber Café (☎ 04 76 51 94 43) charges the same rates and opens 9.30 am to 9 pm.

Travel Agencies Voyages Wasteels (☎ 04 76 47 34 54, fax 04 76 85 31 78), 50 ave Alsace Lorraine, sells air tickets. It opens 9 am to noon and 2 to 7 pm weekdays (until 6 pm on Saturday).

Laundry The Lavomatique opposite Hôtel Victoria, 14 rue Thiers, opens 7 am to 10 pm.

Museum Pass Museum buffs planning to visit all of Grenoble's museums should consider a *Pass' Musées*. It costs 50FF, is valid for a year, and entitles you to admission to 14 museums in and around Grenoble. The pass is sold at the Musée Dauphinois.

Fort de la Bastille

Fort de la Bastille, built in the 16th century (and expanded in the 19th) to control the approaches to the city, sits on the northern side of the Isère, 263m above the old city. It affords spectacular views, including Mont Blanc on clear days.

Three viewpoint indicators – one just west of the téléphérique station, the other two on the roof of the building just east of it – explain what you're looking at. A sign near the disused Mont Jalla chair lift (300m beyond the arch next to the bathrooms) indicates the hiking trails that pass by here.

To get to the fort, a téléphérique (☎ 04 76 44 33 65) leaves from Quai Stéphane Jay between the Marius Gontard and St-Laurent bridges. One-way/return tickets cost 24/ 35FF (students 19/28FF).

The téléphérique runs from 10.30 am to 6.30 pm (from 11 am on Monday) from November to March. The rest of the year the last trip up is at 11.30 pm and the last trip down is at 11.45 pm – except on Sunday (9 am to 7.15 pm) and Monday (11 am to 7.15 pm) from April to June and September and October. A variety of trails and a road lead up the hillside to the fort.

Musée Dauphinois

Occupying a beautiful 17th-century convent, this museum (☎ 04 76 85 19 01) at 30 rue Maurice Gignoux sits near the foot of the hill that is topped by Fort de la Bastille. From the city centre, it is most easily reached by the pont St-Laurent footbridge. The museum has good displays on the crafts and history of the Dauphiné region, with a particular focus on the mountain people's traditional way of life. It opens 10 am to 7 pm (closed Tuesday), and until 6 pm between November and April. Admission costs 20FF (students 10FF).

East of the museum, also in the historic St-Laurent quarter of town, is the excellent **Musée Archéologique** (☎ 04 76 44 78 68), housed in a church dating from the 12th century. It opens 10 am to noon and 2 to 6 pm (closed Tuesday).

Musée de Grenoble

Also called the Musée des Beaux-Arts, Musée de Grenoble (☎ 04 76 63 44 44), 5 place de Lavalette, is known for its outstanding collection of paintings and sculpture. Exhibits include an enormous work by the Flemish artist Pierre-Paul Rubens, as well as a renowned modern collection that features pieces by Chagall, Léger, Matisse, Modigliani, Monet, Picasso, Sisley and many others.

The museum opens 11 am to 7 pm (until 10 pm on Wednesday), except Tuesday. Admission costs 25FF (students 15FF). There are 1½-hour guided tours (25FF) on Saturday and Sunday at 3 pm

Musée de l'Ancien Évêché, Patrimoines de l'Isère et Baptistère de Grenoble

The double Notre Dame and St-Hugues Cathedral on place Notre Dame and the adjoining 14th-century Bishop's Palace (☎ 04 76 03 15 25) at 3 rue Très Cloîtres have had complete face-lifts and now contain three museums: the **crypte archéologique**, with its Roman-era walls and baptistery dating from the 4th to 10th century; the **Musée d'Art Sacré**, containing liturgical and other religious objects; and the **Centre Jean Achard**, with exhibits of art from the Dauphiné region. Admission costs 20FF.

Musée de la Résistance et de la Déportation de l'Isère

This museum (☎ 04 76 42 38 53) at 14 rue Hébert examines the deportation of Jews and others from Grenoble to Nazi concentration and labour camps during WWII and the role of the Vercors region in the Resistance. Captions are in French, English and German. It opens 9 am to noon and 2 to 6 pm (closed Tuesday). Admission costs 20FF (students 10FF).

Musée Stendhal

Stendhal, author of *Le Rouge et le Noir*, was born in Grenoble in 1783. The tourist office distributes a free brochure called *Route Historique – Stendhal*, which traces the life and works of the French writer from his birthplace and home where he lived for 18 years through to outlying villages that inspired him.

The Musée Stendhal (☎ 04 76 54 44 14), overlooking the Jardin de Ville at 1 rue Hector Berlioz, opens 10 am to noon and 2 to 6 pm (afternoons only in winter; closed Sunday).

Musée d'Histoire Naturelle

Various Alpine flora and fauna typical to the French Alps as well as a 'carnival of insects' and an aquarium is housed in the natural history museum (☎ 04 76 44 05 35), 1 rue Dolomieu, overlooking the Jardin des Plantes. There is a botanical garden in its grounds. The complex opens 9.30 am to noon and 1.30 to 5.30 pm, except Tuesday. On Sunday it is only open in the afternoon, from 2 to 6 pm). Admission costs 15FF (students 10FF).

Places to Stay

Camping Open year round, *Camping Les Trois Pucelles* (☎ 04 76 96 45 73, 58 rue des Allobroges), is one block west of the River Drac in Grenoble's western suburb of Seyssins. From the train station, take the tram towards Fontaine and get off at the Maisonnat stop. Then take bus No 51 (the last one goes at around 9 pm) to Mas des Îles and walk east on rue du Dauphiné. A place to camp and park costs 32/45FF for one/two people.

Hostels The *Auberge de Jeunesse* (☎ 04 76 09 33 52, fax 04 76 09 38 99, ✆ grenoble-echirolles@fuaj.org, 10 ave du Grésivaudan), 5km south of the train station in the Echirolles district, charges 68FF per person including breakfast; reception opens 7.30 am to 11 pm. From Cours Jean Jaurès, take bus No 8 (direction Pont de Claix; last one is at about 9 pm) to the Quinzaine stop (look for the Casino supermarket).

Friendly and central *Foyer de l'Étudiante* (☎ 04 76 42 00 84, 4 rue Ste-Ursule) accepts travellers of both sexes from the end of June to the end of September. Singles/doubles cost 90/130FF a day and, for those who want to stay put, 450/700FF a week. It opens 7 to 12.30 am.

Hotels – Train Station Area Good-value, no-star *Hôtel Royal* (☎ 04 76 46 18 92, fax 04 76 87 15 37, ✆ PRoyalhote@aol.com, 2 rue Gabriel Péri), has doubles with shower and toilet for 215FF.

One-star *Hôtel Alizé* (☎ 04 76 43 12 91, fax 04 76 47 62 79, 1 rue Amiral Courbet),

FRENCH ALPS

has modern singles/doubles with washbasin for 138/202FF and doubles with shower for 162/212FF. Two-star *Hôtel Lux* (☎ *04 76 46 41 89, fax 04 76 46 51 61, 6 rue Crépu*), a quiet back street south of the station, is tidy and friendly. Single rooms cost 147/220FF, and doubles with shower start at 188FF.

Hotels – Place Condorcet Area There are lots of inexpensive hotels in this vicinity. One of the best is *Hôtel Lakanal* (☎ *04 76 46 03 42, fax 04 76 17 21 24, 26 rue des Bergers*) 1km south-east of the station off place Championnet. It attracts a young and friendly crowd and has simple singles/doubles with toilet for just 100/120FF. Rooms with shower and toilet cost 140/180FF. Breakfast costs 20FF.

Quiet, comfortable, one-star *Hôtel Victoria* (☎ *04 76 46 06 36, 17 rue Thiers*) in a courtyard, has rooms with shower and TV for 170/195FF and with toilet as well for 190/215FF. The hotel is closed in August. Relaxed but no-star *Hôtel Beau Soleil* (☎ *04 76 46 29 40, 9 rue des Bons Enfants*), has rooms from 140FF (150FF with shower).

Hotels – City Centre Dark, rather old-fashioned *Hôtel du Moucherotte* (☎ *04 76 54 61 40, fax 04 76 44 62 52, 1 rue Auguste Gaché*), has huge, clean rooms. Singles/doubles with shower start at 145/178FF. Breakfast costs 30FF extra. Try to avoid the noisier front rooms.

Pleasant and friendly, family-run *Hôtel de la Poste* (☎ *04 76 46 67 25, 25 rue de la Poste*), has eight basic rooms for 100/160FF; showers are free and a traditional English breakfast costs 30FF.

Places to Eat

Grenoble has a fine array of funky restaurants and bistros serving traditional as well as foreign cuisine. North African places are scattered along and around rue Renauldon and rue Chenoise; while place Condorcet and rue de la Poste are the hot spots for Chinese fare. There are 20 or more pizza joints on quai Perrière, bang next door to each other.

Restaurants For good food at reasonable prices, try *Le Tonneau de Diogène* (☎ *04 76 42 38 40, 6 place Notre Dame*), which attracts a young, lively crowd. The *plat du jour* is 55FF, salads cost from 15FF to 38FF. It opens 8.30 am to 1 am.

Le Mal Assis (☎ *04 76 54 75 93, 9 rue Bayard*), is a cosy upmarket restaurant serving delicious and authentic *cuisine bourgeoise*. Its evening menu costs 138FF and reservations are recommended. It opens until 11 pm Tuesday to Saturday. *Le Valgo* (☎ *04 76 51 38 85, 2 rue St-Hugues*), close by, has many *menus* starting from 45FF to 125FF. *Pieds paquets* (lamb tripe) is the house speciality.

La Mère Ticket (*rue Jean-Jacques Rousseau*) serves astonishingly delicious *poulet aux écrevisses* (chicken with crayfish) on its 85FF *menu*. This tiny, homely restaurant opens until 11 pm. *La Panse* (☎ *04 76 54 09 54, 7 rue de la Paix*) offers a 50FF and 76FF lunch *menu* and a 100FF day and evening *menu* that are especially good value. It opens noon to 1.30 pm and 7.15 to 10 pm (closed Sunday).

For local fondue and tartiflette look no further than *Restaurant des Montagnes* (☎ *04 76 15 20 72, 5 rue Brocherie*). Salads start at 34FF, and there are 13 types of fondue (59FF to 100FF per person – minimum two persons). It opens 7 am to midnight. Credit cards not accepted.

Les Archers (☎ *04 76 46 27 76, 2 rue Docteur Bailly*) is a brasserie-style restaurant with great outside seating in summer. The *plat du jour* costs 57FF, oysters cost 106FF a dozen, and it opens 10 am to 10 pm.

Taking a more modern approach is *La Galerie Rome* (☎ *04 76 42 82 01, corner of rue du Vieux Temple and rue Très Cloîtres*) housed inside a smart art gallery. It opens 10 am to 10 pm (closed Sunday and Monday). *Menus* cost 58F and 90FF.

Ciao a Te (☎ *04 76 42 54 41, 2 rue de la Paix*), is a trendy Italian place, serving great pasta *menus* from 65FF. It opens from 7.45 pm (closed Sunday). Ultramodern *L'Amphitryon* (☎ *04 76 51 38 07, 9 rue Chenoise*) is the place for couscous (55FF to 77FF) – and has the funkiest entrance in

FRENCH ALPS

town. *Tchou Tchoura* (☎ 04 76 47 35 95, *16 rue Gabriel Péri*) is a Bulgarian restaurant with a 95FF *menu*.

Cafes The best breakfast option in town is trendy *Subway* (☎ 04 76 87 31 67, *corner of rue Lakanal and blvd Gambetta*), a five-minute walk from the train station. Salads, with or without meat, range from 22FF to 38FF. It opens 7 to 1 am (Sunday from 5 pm).

Great for afternoon tea is *La Forêt Noire* (*place Ste-Claire*). This delightful *salon de thé* serves a good range of salads, creamy cakes and a *menu minceur* (slimmers menu) for 47FF.

Café Tamara (*1 rue du Palais*), is a chic place for a cup of coffee. Graffiti covers the walls of the fun, jukebox playing *Chorus Café* (*8 rue Brocherie*) opposite Restaurant des Montagnes.

Dating from 1739 and an old haunt of Stendhal and Rousseau is historic *Café de la Table Ronde* (☎ 04 76 44 51 41, *7 place St-André*). The lunch *menu* costs 75FF. It closes at midnight.

Self-Catering Near the tourist office, lovely old *Les Halles* covered market opens 6 am to 1 pm (closed Monday). There's a *food market* on place Ste-Claire daily, except Tuesday.

Prisunic supermarket, on the corner of rue de la République and rue Lafayette, has a basement grocery section and an in-house *boulangerie*. It opens 8.30 am to 7.30 pm (closed Sunday).

Entertainment

Hip night-time bars include the small, dimly-lit *Barberousse* (☎ 04 76 57 14 53, *8 rue Hache*), which has 33 sorts of aromatic rum fermenting in giant glass flasks behind the bar. Down a shot of cherry, apple, papaya or other fruit-flavoured liquor for 12FF. The bar opens 5 pm to 1 am.

Le Couche Tard (☎ 04 76 44 18 79, *1 rue du Palais*), open 4 pm to 1 am, and *Le Saxo Pub* (☎ 04 76 51 06 01, *7 rue d'Agier*), open 6 pm to 2 am, are Grenoble's most popular late-night drinking spots.

Getting There & Away

Air Grenoble-St-Geoirs airport (☎ 04 76 65 48 48), 45km north of Grenoble, is for domestic flights only. International flights operate to/from Lyon-Satolas airport (☎ 04 72 22 72 21), 95km north-west of the city off the A43 to Lyons.

Bus The bus station (☎ 04 76 87 90 31) is next to the train station on rue Émile Gueymard. Numerous bus companies operate services from here. VFD (☎ 04 76 47 77 77) runs buses to Geneva (151FF, 2½ hours), Nice via Castellane, near the Gorges du Verdon (311FF, five hours) and most Alpine destinations including Annecy (99FF, 1¾ hours), Bourg d'Oisans (51FF, 50 minutes), Les Deux Alpes (102FF, 1¾ hours), Chamonix (161FF, three hours) and the ski stations on the Vercors range.

Intercars (☎ 04 76 46 19 77, fax 04 76 47 96 34) handles long-haul destinations such as Budapest (580FF), Madrid (540FF), Lisbon (830FF), London (550FF), Prague (520FF) and Venice (260FF). It operates buses departing from Annecy, Chamonix and Lyons too. Its office opens 9 am to noon and 2 to 6 pm (until noon on Saturday; closed Sunday). Their Web site is at www.intercars.fr.

Train The huge, modern train station (☎ 08 36 35 35 35), rue Émile Gueymard, is next to the Gare Europole tram stop, which is served by both tram lines (see Getting Around). The information office opens 9 am to noon and 2 to 5.30 pm. The station, and at least one ticket window, opens 4.30 am to 2 am.

Destinations served include Paris' Gare de Lyon (from 371FF, 3½ hours by TGV), Chambéry (55FF, one hour, 14 daily) and Lyons (97FF, 1½ hours, five daily). Change in Lyons for trains to Nice and Monaco. There are three trains daily to Turin (246FF) and Milan (321FF) in Italy, and two trains daily to Geneva (118FF, two hours). For Rome and Naples, change in Chambéry.

Getting Around

To/From the Airport The bus to Lyon-Satolas airport (130/195FF one way/return,

FRENCH ALPS

65 minutes), operated by Valencin-based Cars Faure (☎ 04 78 96 11 44), stops at the bus station. Buses to the Grenoble-St-Geoirs airport depart from the bus station (75/113FF one way/return, 45 minutes).

Bus & Tram The local mass transit company, TAG, has two ultramodern tram lines – called A and B. Both stop at the tourist office and the train station. Bus and tram tickets cost 7.50FF and are available from ticket machines at tram stops or from bus drivers. They must be time-stamped in the little blue machines located at each tram stop before boarding. Tickets are valid for transfers – but not return trips – within one hour of being time-stamped.

A carnet of 10 tickets costs 56FF. Daily/weekly passes – Visitag and Avantag – are available for 20/70FF at the TAG information desk (☎ 04 76 20 66 66) at the tourist office, or from the TAG office next to the post office outside the train station.

Most of the buses on the 20 different lines cease functioning rather early, sometime between 6 and 9 pm. Trams run daily from 5 am (6.15 am on Sunday) to midnight.

Taxi Radio-dispatched taxis can be ordered by calling ☎ 04 76 54 42 54.

AROUND GRENOBLE

Grenoble's surrounding low-altitude regions attract a relaxed crowd in search of cheap winter skiing or summer walking rather than the hard-core experts and flashy fluoro crowds drawn to the more expensive, higher-altitude resorts farther north.

Stations better known for their good cross-country skiing include Lans-en-Vercors and Villard de Lans, south-west of Grenoble in the Vercors range; and Col de Porte and Le Sappey, north of Grenoble in the Chartreuse range. Chamrousse, the nearest resort to Grenoble in the Belledonne range to the east, was built for the 1968 Winter Olympics. Skiers keen to take to the slopes in summer have to head farther east (see Les Deux Alpes and Alpe d'Huez sections).

Chamrousse

City dwellers flock to Chamrousse (elevation 1400m), 30km east of Grenoble, in winter. The family resort, popular for its wide and gentle slopes, has a snowpark too and attracts more snowboarders than the average resort. The snowboarding World Cup and the French freestyle ski championships are held here each year in March.

The tourist office (☎ 04 76 89 92 65, fax 04 76 89 98 06), in the centre of the resort, has full accommodation lists. The FUAJ ski club in Grenoble (see Skiing Information in the Grenoble section) arranges six-day skiing trips to Chamrousse from 2100FF, including ski pass, ski hire and full-board hostel accommodation at the *Auberge de Jeunesse* (☎ 04 76 89 91 31, fax 04 76 89 96 66, ✉ chamrousse@fuaj.org) in Chamrousse. The CAF also has a *refuge* here: contact the *Chalet du CAF* (☎ 04 76 87 03 73, fax 04 76 85 26 77) in Chamrousse.

There are four VFD buses daily from Grenoble to Chamrousse (1¼ hours).

Parc Naturel Régional du Vercors

The Parc Naturel Régional du Vercors (175,000 hectares), immediately south-west of Grenoble, is a large cross-country skiing, caving and hiking area. During WWII it became a stronghold of the Resistance movement and was dubbed the 'fortresse de la Résistance'.

Lans-en-Vercors (population 1450, elevation 1020m), 25km south-west of Grenoble, is the leading ski village on the Vercors plateau. There's none of the adrenalin of high-Alpine descents here, nor is there a bustling nightlife. Families abound and, outside school holidays, the hotels often have *non complet* (vacancy) signs up. From Lans-en-Vercors, hourly shuttle buses run to the Stade de Neige (Snow Stadium), an area of moderate, wooded slopes crowned by Le Grand Cheval (1807m), about 4km east.

The equally sedate village of **Villard de Lans** (population 3350, elevation 1050m), 9km up the valley from Lans-en-Vercors, is linked by ski lifts and roads to neighbouring resort **Corrençon-en-Vercors** (1111m).

Information The park headquarters (☎ 04 76 94 38 26, fax 04 76 94 38 39, @ info@pnr-vercors.fr) is inside the Maison du Parc at Chemin des Fusillés in Lans-en-Vercors. The tourist offices in Lans-en-Vercors (☎ 04 76 95 42 62, fax 04 76 95 49 70), place de l'Église, and in Villard de Lans (☎ 04 76 95 10 38, fax 04 76 95 98 39, @ villard.correncon@wanadoo.fr), place Mure Ravaud, can both provide extensive information on activities in the park. The free brochure entitled *Welcome to Vercors* lists numerous walks in the park as well as driving and caving tours; *Site National Historique de la Résistance en Vercors* traces the footsteps of the Resistance movement in the region.

The park's Web site is www.pnr-vercors.fr while the Lans-en-Vercors tourist office can be found at www.ot-lans-en-vercors.fr.

Places to Stay The tourist offices in both villages can help with accommodation bookings. In Lans-en-Vercors, *Vercors Immobilier Montagne* (☎ 04 76 95 41 64, fax 04 76 95 48 33), place du Village, arranges accommodation in chalets for two to 11 people. In the high season expect to pay from 2300FF to 3390FF for a four-person studio.

There are numerous gîtes d'étape in the region, the most central being *Chalet de la Piste de Luge* (☎ 04 76 94 10 66, fax 04 76 94 11 55), on the eastern edge of Villard de Lans, which costs 60FF per person. A bed for the night costs 50FF at the *Refuge Garde les Hauts Plateaux* (☎ 04 76 95 83 51) in Corrençon-en-Vercors.

Getting There & Away From Lans-en-Vercors, VFD (☎ 04 76 95 11 24) runs four buses daily (fewer at the weekend) to and from Grenoble (32.50FF, 50 minutes), Villard de Lans (10FF, 20 minutes) and Corrençon (15FF, 35 minutes).

Shuttle buses (11FF) run every half-hour between Lans-en-Vercors and Villard de Lans.

PARC NATIONAL DES ÉCRINS

The spectacular Parc National des Écrins was created in 1973 and is France's second largest national park, taking in nearly everything between the towns of Bourg d'Oisans, Briançon and Gap. The park's 917 sq km of fully protected land are surrounded by 1770 sq km of peripheral areas, most of which are largely unspoiled thanks to their relative inaccessibility. The area is enclosed by steep narrow valleys, sculpted by the Romanche, Durance and Drac rivers and their erstwhile glaciers. The overhanging cliffs look like battle-scarred layered cakes.

Bourg d'Oisans (population 3000, elevation 720m), 50km south-east of Grenoble in the Romanche Valley, and Briançon, another 67km in the same direction, make great bases for exploring the park.

Information

Several Maisons du Parc, open year round, provide detailed information. The park headquarters (☎ 04 92 40 20 10, fax 04 92 52 38 34) is at the Domaine de la Charance, F-05000 Gap. There's a large park office in Briançon (☎ 04 92 21 42 55).

In Bourg d'Oisans, the Maison du Parc (☎ 04 76 80 00 51), rue Gambetta, opens 9 am to noon and 3 to 7 pm in summer. It sells detailed guides (in French), topoguides and walking maps, including the invaluable IGN 1:25,000 *Les Deux Alpes-Le Parc National des Écrins* (No 3336ET) and *Bourg d'Oisans-Alpe d'Huez* (No 3335ET).

The town's tourist office (☎ 04 76 80 03 25, fax 04 76 80 10 38), on the main road just before the River Romanche at quai Girard, is well stocked with park information too. It opens from 9 am to noon and 2 to 6 pm Monday to Saturday.

Walking

There are plenty of zigzagging paths used for centuries by shepherds and smugglers from points all along the Romanche Valley. From Bourg d'Oisans there is a path to Villard Notre Dame (1525m, two hours). From Venosc, a tiny mountain village in the Vénéon Valley, 12km south-east of Bourg d'Oisans, there's a trail to the popular ski

FRENCH ALPS

resort of Les Deux Alpes (1660m, 1½ hours). The national park French-only publication *Dix Itinéraires* is a good companion for 10 different treks and climbs of up to seven hours. *Venosc/Vallée de Vénéon* (10FF) is another good publication. The Bourg d'Oisans tourist office sells six different walking maps (in English and French) entitled *Oisans au Bout des Pieds* (Oisans under Your Feet).

Other Activities

Bureau des Guides (☎ 04 76 80 11 27) in front of the Maison du Parc in Bourg d'Oisans organises rafting (150FF for a half-day), rock climbing (130FF for 2½ hours), parapente (670FF for a half-day), hot dogging (170FF for two or three people in an inflatable canoe) and other summer activities in the park. Air Écrins Club de Parapente de l'Oisans (☎/fax 04 76 11 00 35), 23 rue Général de Gaulle, Bourg d'Oisans, runs canoeing, kayaking and parapente schools.

At St-Christophe, near Venosc, Vénéon Eaux Vives (☎ 04 76 80 23 99) organises similar activities. It also hires out mountain bikes for 100FF a day.

Places to Stay & Eat

Within the park's central zone there are about 32 *refuges*, most of them run by the CAF. The charge is 65FF a night.

A handful of *gîtes d'étape* are on the outskirts of the park, many open year round. Expect to pay about 68FF a night. For a full listing, ask at the Bourg d'Oisans tourist office for the free brochure entitled *Guide des Hébergements*.

There are plenty of camping grounds in Bourg d'Oisans, including a cluster just down from the tourist office, on the road to Alpe d'Huez. Four-star *La Cascade* (☎ 04 76 80 02 42, fax 04 76 80 22 63) opens from mid-December to September. It charges 120FF for two people. Most of the cheaper camp sites are only open from June to September.

In Bourg d'Oisans, the *Maison des Jeunes Le Paradis* (☎ 04 76 80 01 76, 50 rue Thiers) charges 65FF for a dorm bed in rooms for 12 people and can also arrange

mountain biking, kayaking, canoeing etc. It is closed in May and October.

The town also has about 10 hotels, the cheaper ones being around the bus station on rue de la Gare. Simple doubles cost from 140FF at *Le Moulin des Fruites Bleues* (☎ 04 76 80 00 26), 155FF at *Hôtel Le Rocher* (☎ 04 76 80 01 53, fax 04 76 79 11 94), and from 200FF at *Hôtel de l'Oberland Français* (☎ 04 76 80 24 24).

More upmarket is cosy *Hôtel Beau Rivage* (☎ 04 76 80 03 19, fax 04 76 80 00 77, rue des Maquis de l'Oisans), the road running behind the tourist office. Doubles with washbasin cost from 185FF, and from 255FF with TV, shower and toilet. *Hôtel Le Réghaia* (☎ 04 76 80 03 37, ave Aristide Briand) has rooms with washbasin/shower for 160/195FF. It closes between 5 May and 5 June and in November. These two hotels also have excellent *restaurants*.

There are plenty of small *supermarkets* and grocery stores in Bourg d'Oisans to stock up on supplies.

Getting There & Away

VFD buses (☎ 04 76 80 00 90 in Bourg d'Oisans) serve the Romanche Valley and Briançon. They operate from the bus station on Ave de la Gare, the main road into Bourg d'Oisans.

From Grenoble, VFD bus No 300 goes to Bourg d'Oisans (68FF, 80 minutes) eight times a day, while the No 303 and the No 302 from Grenoble stop in Bourg d'Oisans on their way to Les Deux Alpes (48FF, 40 minutes) and Alpe d'Huez (47FF, 45 minutes) respectively. From Briançon, VFD's bus No 306 stops in Bourg d'Oisans (74FF, 1¾ hours, two daily).

LES DEUX ALPES

postcode 38860 • elevation 1600m

Les Deux Alpes, 28km south-east of Bourg d'Oisans, has the largest summer skiing area in Europe. From mid-June to early September, you can ski on the Glacier du Mont de Lans (3200m to 3425m), which, year round, offers good panoramic views of Mont Blanc (east), Massif Central (west) and Mont Ventoux (south).

Les Deux Alpes is a popular winter skiing resort too, as well as one of the top spots in France for snowboarding. The never-ending stream of traffic clogging up the entire length of Les Deux Alpes' 1.5km-long main street (D213) belies its lowly beginnings as a mountain pasture for the flocks of Mont de Lans and Venosc, villages neighbouring the resort to the north and south, respectively.

Information

Tourist Offices Everything in town revolves around the Maison des Deux Alpes on place des Deux Alpes. It houses the tourist office (☎ 04 76 79 22 00, fax 04 76 79 01 38, ✉ les2alp@icor.fr), the accommodation service (see Internet Resources and Places to Stay), the ESF (see Skiing & Snowboarding), and the Bureau des Guides (☎ 04 76 80 52 72, fax 04 76 79 58 42). The Bureau des Guides (☎ 06 11 32 71 88) inside the Maison de la Montagne, ave de la Muzelle, arranges ice climbing on frozen waterfalls, rock climbing, walking, rafting and mountain bike expeditions with experienced guides.

The *les2alpes Magazine* and the annual *Winter Guide,* both available free from the tourist office, have a stack of useful information in English about the resort.

Internet Resources Accommodation bookings for Les Deux Alpes can be made by the accommodation service's Web site at www.les2alpes.com.

Skiing & Snowboarding

The main skiing domain lies below La Meije (3983m), one of the highest peaks in the Parc National des Écrins. There's some 200km of marked pistes, 20km of cross-country trails, and in the snowpark (2600m), a 600m-long axe pipe, 110m-long half-pipe and numerous jumps for snowboarders (all to the blare of pop music).

The ESF (☎ 04 76 79 21 21, fax 04 76 79 22 07, ✉ esf.les2alpes@laposte.fr) and the École de Ski International St Christophe (☎ 04 76 79 04 21, fax 04 76 79 29 14, ✉ ecole.ski.internationale@wanadoo.fr),

close to place des Deux Alpes on ave de la Muzelle, both run ski and snowboarding schools.

Grotte de Glace A 6m-tall dinosaur, Alpine flowers and shepherds are just some of the fantastic ice sculptures exhibited inside the *grotte de glace* (ice cave) cut inside the Glacier du Mont de Lans at Dôme de Puy Salié (3421m). The cave opens 9.30 am to 4.30 pm year round. Admission costs 20FF (children 15FF). Nonskiers can access the glacier too. Take the Jandri Express télécabine to 3200m (change of télécabine at 2600m), from where you can take the underground Dôme Express funicular to 3400m. A return ticket costs 110FF.

Museums

For a glimpse of traditional Alpine life the way it was before mass tourism swallowed it, visit the **Maison de la Montagne** (☎ 04 76 79 53 15), at the western end of ave de la Muzelle. Traditional 19th-century dwellings as well as the history of wool farming are displayed in the village museum in Mont de Lans, **Le Chasal Lento** (☎ 04 76 80 23 97). In Venosc, a permanent arts and crafts exhibition is held in the tourist office.

The museums open 10 am to noon and 3 to 7 pm in summer, and 2 to 6 pm in winter. Admission to both costs 20FF. A free shuttle bus to Mont de Lans departs daily from outside the Maison de la Montagne at 2 pm and returns to Les Deux Alpes at 4 pm. You can also take a télésiège. To get to Venosc, take a télécabine from the eastern end of Les Deux Alpes. A return ticket for either costs 40FF.

Warm-Weather Activities

Numerous walks are listed in the free brochure *Le Guide des Randonnées Pédestres au Départ des Deux Alpes* available at the tourist office.

Parapente ESF (☎ 06 97 72 26 60), inside the Maison des Deux Alpes, offers five-day paragliding courses in summer costing 2300FF. A morning/afternoon session costs 300/350FF (380FF in winter). Its office opens 6 to 7.30 pm.

FRENCH ALPS

Places to Stay

The *Auberge de Jeunesse* (☎ 04 76 79 22 80, fax 04 76 79 26 15, ✉ les-deux-alpes@ fuaj.org) is in the heart of town at Les Brûleurs de Loups. A dorm bed in rooms for up to six people costs 48FF per person in summer. In winter only weekly packages are available, including seven days accommodation, food and a ski-lift pass. Prices start at 2000/3110FF in the low/high season.

The accommodation service (☎ 04 76 79 24 38, fax 04 76 79 01 38, ✉ res2alp@ icor.fr) inside the Maison des Deux Alpes takes bookings for all types of accommodation. Two-person studios and apartments can be found from 1600/3250FF a week in the low/high season. All hotel reservations should be made well in advance.

Off-piste skiers wishing to tackle the challenge of the fearsome La Grave descent should consider basing themselves in the village of La Grave 21km to the east. The *Auberge Edelweiss* (☎ 04 76 79 90 93, fax 04 76 79 92 64, ✉ edelweiss@waw.com) is a homely little hotel that caters to individual and small groups. Cosy single/double rooms go for 250/350FF in high season. There is also a restaurant and a jacuzzi to thaw out tired skiers.

Getting There & Away

VFD runs buses to Les Deux Alpes from Grenoble (102FF, 1¾ hours, six daily), 77km north-west. In Les Deux Alpes, reserve tickets in advance from the VFD office (☎ 04 76 80 51 22) on place de Mont de Lans or rue de l'Irarde. Buses stop at Bourg d'Oisans (40 minutes) en route. There are also services to Briançon, Alpe d'Huez, Lyon-Satolas and Geneva airports.

ALPE D'HUEZ

postcode 38750 • elevation 1860m

The ski resort of Alpe d'Huez sits just above Bourg d'Oisans, 13km away by a steep, twisting road (*La Montée de l'Alpe d'Huez*) best known as one of the 'classic' gruelling ascents often included in the Tour de France cycle race.

Alpe d'Huez has excellent winter runs for skiers and snowboarders of all abilities.

At 16km, La Sarenne is the longest black run in the French Alps. Experienced skiers can also ski here in July and part of August on glaciers (ranging from 2530m to 3330m). The panoramic view from Pic du Lac Blanc (3330m), the highest point accessible year round from the village by the Tronçon télécabines, is particularly impressive and well worth the effort.

Information

The tourist office (☎ 04 76 11 44 44, fax 04 76 80 69 54, ✉ info@alpdehuez.com), accommodation centre, and ESF (☎ 04 76 80 31 69, fax 04 76 80 49 33) are inside the Maison de l'Alpe, place Joseph Paganon and open 9 am to 7pm. The Bureau des Guides (☎ 04 76 80 42 55) and the Taburle École du Snowboard Français (☎ 04 76 80 95 82) are both off place du Cognet at the Rond Point des Pistes, the northernmost point of the village. The annual *Le Guide de l'Alpe* booklet, free from the tourist office, has a full listing of all facilities in the resort.

Places to Stay

The accommodation centre (☎ 04 76 11 44 44, fax 04 76 80 98 96, ✉ resa@alpdehuez. com) takes bookings for all types of accommodation. Expect to pay 1300/2000FF in the low/high season for a small, self-contained studio for two. With some 28 hotels and another 27 rental places, accommodation is plentiful but demand is high in season. Book well in advance, if possible.

One of the least expensive hotels in town is the one-star *Gai Vallon* (☎ 04 76 80 98 37, rue de l'Église); it has neat rooms costing from 220FF to 270FF or half-board starting at 240FF to 280FF. The friendly, helpful two-star *Hôtel Alp'Azur* (☎ 04 76 80 34 02, place Jean Molin), has doubles from 370FF to 540FF including breakfast.

Getting There & Away

There are some seven VFD buses (☎ 04 76 80 31 61) a day from Grenoble via Bourg d'Oisans to Alpe d'Huez 102FF, 2¾ hours). On Wednesday there is a shuttle bus between Les Deux Alpes and Alpe d'Huez (80FF, one hour).

FRENCH ALPS

BRIANÇON

postcode 05100 • **pop 11,000**
• **elevation 1026m**

Briançon is a town of mixed delights. Sitting on a rocky outcrop at the meeting of five valleys, it is one of the highest cities in Europe and boasts 300 days of sunshine a year. Long a frontier post, its beautiful fortified old city guards the road to the Col de Montgenèvre (1850m), a Roman mountain pass leading to Italy, 20km north-east.

In the late 17th century, the famous military architect Vauban was called in to make the town impregnable after it was razed during a regional war. Since then, the population has expanded and the town has crept down the slopes to encompass the Durance Valley. The modern lower town, which has a lift station (Briançon-Serre-Chevalier 1200) to the neighbouring ski resort of Le Grand Serre Chevalier, is functional if not exactly pretty.

Briançon is sandwiched between the awesome terrain of the Parc National des Écrins to the west and the Parc Naturel Régional du Queyras to the south, making it an excellent base to partake in all sorts of outdoor activities.

Orientation

The town is split into two sections. The upper Vieille Ville, with its quaint pedestrianised streets, sits high above its counterpart, the new Ville Basse (Lower Town). The train station is to the south in the suburb of Ste-Catherine. The upper and lower towns are connected by ave de la République. Entry to the Vieille Ville is either from place du Champ de Mars (on the old city's northern side) or, if you're walking up the hill from the lower town, through the Porte d'Embrun.

Information

Tourist Offices The tourist office (☎ 04 92 21 08 50, fax 04 92 20 56 45), in the Vieille Ville at 1 place du Temple, opens 8.30 am to noon and 1.30 to 6 pm Monday to Saturday. From mid-June to September it also opens on Sunday from 9 am to noon and 1.30 to 5 pm. City tours are organised by the Service du Patrimoine (☎ 04 92 20 29 49, fax 04 92 21 38 45), which is located beneath the Porte de Pignerol.

For information on the Parc National des Écrins, go to the Maison du Parc (☎ 04 92 20 29 29), which is at the southern end of Grande Rue in the Vieille Ville. It opens 10 am to noon and 2 to 7 pm year round. The CAF (☎ 04 92 20 16 52), 6 ave René Froger, opens 4 to 7 pm (closed Sunday and Monday).

Money The nearest bank to the train station is Crédit Agricole in Le Moulin shopping mall, just beyond the small bridge as you walk north on ave du Général de Gaulle. There's a foreign currency exchange machine at 20 ave Maurice Petsche.

The Vieille Ville has a Crédit Agricole branch at 10 Grande rue. It opens 8 am to noon and 1.55 to 5 pm weekdays, and on Saturday until 4.30 pm.

Post The main post office, place du Champ de Mars, opens 8.30 am to 6 pm (Saturday until noon; closed Sunday). There's also a branch just off ave du 159 RIA in Parc Chancel.

Laundry The LavPlus in Central Parc opens 7 am to 7 pm daily.

Vieille Ville

While the Vieille Ville's narrow streets are an ambler's delight, there's not all that much to see. The main street, Grande Rue, is also known as the Grande Gargouille (Great Gargoyle) because of the drain that gushes down the middle of it. There are fountains spurting everywhere in the old part of town. Ave Vauban affords some fine views of the snowcapped peaks of the Écrins park.

The **Collégiale** – or the Church of Our Lady & St Nicholas – was built by Vauban in the early 18th century and is characteristically heavy and fortified, its twin towers dominating the Vieille Ville skyline. The baroque paintings and gilt chapels around a circular choir are worth a look. The church is open daily.

FRENCH ALPS

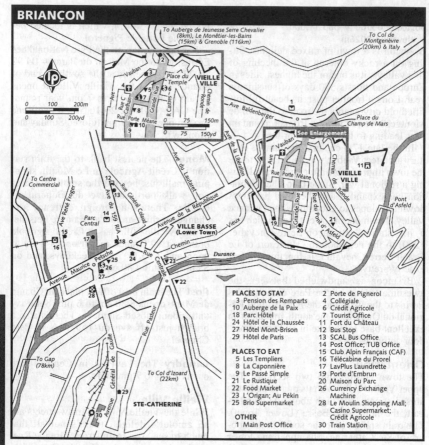

BRIANÇON

PLACES TO STAY
3 Pension des Remparts
10 Auberge de la Paix
18 Parc Hôtel
24 Hôtel de la Chaussée
27 Hôtel Mont-Brison
29 Hôtel de Paris

PLACES TO EAT
5 Les Templiers
8 La Caponnière
9 Le Passé Simple
21 Le Rustique
22 Food Market
23 L'Origan; Au Pékin
25 Brio Supermarket

OTHER
1 Main Post Office

2 Porte de Pignerol
4 Collégiale
6 Crédit Agricole
7 Tourist Office
11 Fort du Château
12 Bus Stop
13 SCAL Bus Office
14 Post Office; TUB Office
15 Club Alpin Français (CAF)
16 Télécabine du Prorel
17 LavPlus Laundrette
19 Porte d'Embrun
20 Maison du Parc
26 Currency Exchange Machine
28 Le Moulin Shopping Mall; Casino Supermarket; Crédit Agricole
30 Train Station

The 18th-century **Fort du Château** (Castle Fort) sits imposingly above the Vieille Ville. You can visit it daily in July and August and on Wednesday and Saturday in September, but only on a guided tour organised by the tourist office. The tour costs 22FF (students 15FF).

Télécabine du Prorel

The télécabine du Prorel, which leaves from the Briançon-Serre-Chevalier 1200 station in the centre of the lower town at 7 ave René Froger, goes up to Le Prorel (2566m), one of the highest points of Le Grand Serre Chevalier mountain range. It runs 8.30 am to 4.15 pm (Friday until 4.45 pm and Saturday until 5.15 pm) during the ski season and in summer from mid-June to mid-September. A one-way/return ticket costs 44/66FF (children under 12 27/33FF). It costs 52FF to take a mountain bike on board in summer and that includes the lift up.

Activities

In winter there's plenty of skiing down the slopes of Le Grand Serre Chevalier (see Around Briançon), the range that stretches from Briançon to Le Monêtier-les-Bains,

15km north-west. The ESF (☎ 04 92 20 30 57) and various ski hire shops are inside the télécabine du Prorel station.

In winter, ice climbing and ski tours are arranged by the Bureau des Guides (☎ 04 92 20 15 73, fax 04 92 20 46 49) in Central Parc. In summer it organises treks, parapente, rafting, cycling and canyoning. Every Monday and Wednesday year round it runs animal-spotting day treks led by an experienced nature photographer (125FF). The office opens 5 to 7 pm, and 9 am to 7 pm in July and August.

The Maison du Parc sells the useful *Promenades* booklets (37FF), which detail numerous walks and hikes in the Briançon, Oisans and Vanoise region. It only opens between June and August.

Places to Stay

Hostels The nearest hostel is *Auberge de Jeunesse Serre Chevalier* (☎ 04 92 24 74 54, fax 04 92 24 83 39, ✪ serre-chevalier@ fuaj.org, BP 2, 05240 Serre-Chevalier Cedex), about 8km north-west at Serre Chevalier-le-Bez near Villeneuve-la-Salle. It charges 48FF a night and 19FF for breakfast. In winter, when it's a popular skiing base, only seven-day packages are available, costing 2155/2880FF in the low/high season including board, meals, a ski pass and equipment rental. To get to the hostel from the train station or place du Champ de Mars, take the Rignon bus (every two hours; last one at 6.45 pm) in the direction of Le Monêtier-les-Bains to Villeneuve-la-Salle, from where it's a 500m walk.

Hotels The hotels in the Vieille Ville are the best in town but a bit away from any action Briançon has to offer. One of the cheapest is *Pension des Remparts* (☎ 04 92 21 08 73, 14 ave Vauban). The rooms at the front bask in the afternoon sun and have a good view of the mountains. Prices range from 156FF to 225FF, and breakfast is available for 28FF. *Auberge de la Paix* (☎ 04 92 21 37 43, fax 04 92 20 44 45, 3 rue Porte Méane), has comfortable single rooms with modern furnishings from 220FF to 260FF and doubles from 200FF to 260FF.

In the lower town, *Hôtel de la Chaussée* (☎ 04 92 21 10 37, fax 04 92 20 03 94, 4 rue Centrale), has upmarket doubles with shower from 260FF. *Hôtel Mont-Brison* (☎ 04 92 21 14 55, ave du Général de Gaulle) has doubles without/with shower for 250/260FF.

Other inexpensive options in the lower town and Ste-Catherine include *Hôtel de Paris* (☎ 04 92 20 15 30, fax 04 92 20 30 82, 41 ave Général de Gaulle), which offers singles with washbasin/shower starting at 190FF to 235FF. Doubles with washbasin/ shower cost from 220FF to 265FF. Prices rise by 30FF in the high season.

The central *Parc Hôtel* (☎ 04 92 20 37 47, fax 04 92 20 53 74, corner of ave Maurice Petsche and ave du 159 RIA), has singles/doubles with all mod cons starting at 450/490FF. Breakfast costs a hefty 45FF.

Places to Eat

Restaurants As with hotels, the higher up the hill you are, the more you pay to eat. Nightlife revolves around the few bars along rue Centrale.

Pension des Remparts (see Places to Stay) has some of the least expensive *menus* around – 59FF for three courses or 69FF for four. Good Savoyard fondues from 75FF to 120FF per person simmer at *Les Templiers* (☎ 04 92 20 29 04, 20 place du Temple).

For a pricier fondue and a variety of other local dishes, try the cavernous *Le Rustique* (☎ 04 92 21 00 10, 36 rue du Pont d'Asfeld), a steep climb up a hill if you walk from the lower town. It is open until 11 pm, has a nonsmoking room, and specialises in trout. Don't miss out on its delicious apple tart with *foie gras* or quail roasted in honey.

La Caponnière (☎ 04 92 20 36 77, 12 rue Commandant Carlhan), in the Vieille Ville, has *menus* oozing with local and Italian delicacies for 78FF, 89FF, 98FF or 125FF. *Le Passé Simple* (3 rue Porte Méane), adjoining the Auberge de la Paix, is another traditional place recommended locally. Prices range from 66FF to 118FF for a *menu*.

In the lower town, *L'Origan* (☎ 04 92 20 10 09, 25 rue Centrale), has 16 varieties of pizza starting at 34FF, as well as 32

FRENCH ALPS

different varieties of sweet and savoury crepes. Upstairs in the same building, *Au Pékin* (☎ *04 92 21 24 22*) has *menus* starting at 55FF and opens 11 am to 2 pm and 6 to 11 pm. The duck with five-spice powder is acceptable but portions are small, and if the owner offers you a glass of sake at the end of your meal, expect to pay for it.

Self-Catering On Wednesday there's a *food market* in the car park next to the fire station just off rue Centrale. Numerous quaint *food shops* line Grande Rue in the Vieille Ville. On ave Maurice Petsche, *Brio* supermarket opens 8.30 am to 12.30 pm and 2.15 to 7.30 pm (no break on Saturday; closed Sunday). There is a huge *Casino* supermarket in Le Moulin shopping mall.

Getting There & Away

Bus The so-called bus station – a simple bus stop marked Autocar Arrêt – is at the intersection of ave du 159 RIA and rue Général Colaud. SCAL (☎ 04 92 21 12 00) has an office next door at 14 ave du 159 RIA that opens 8 am to 12 pm and 2 to 6 pm weekdays. It runs a daily bus to Gap (53FF, two hours), Digne (105FF, 3¼ hours, no bus on Sunday), Marseille (160FF, 5¾ hours), Aix-en-Provence (144FF, five hours), and Oulx (53FF, 1½ hours) in Italy. VFD buses (☎ 04 76 47 77 77 in Grenoble) travel via Bourg d'Oisans (74FF, 1¾ hours) to Grenoble (142FF, 2¼ hours, two daily).

Train Briançon's station (☎ 04 92 51 50 50, 04 92 25 66 00), at the end of the line from Gap, is at the southern end of ave du Général de Gaulle, about 1.5km from the Vieille Ville. The ticket windows are open 5.30 am to 11.15 pm (until 10 pm on Saturday). Left luggage costs 10FF per piece.

To Paris' Gare de Lyon (400FF, 10½ hours) there's a direct overnight train leaving at 8.20 pm. Two quicker daytime services (seven hours) go via Grenoble or Valence, where they connect with the TGV (508FF). Other major destinations include Gap (69FF, 1¼ hours, five daily), Grenoble (144FF, 4½ hours, four daily) and Marseille (192FF, four hours, three daily).

Getting Around

Bus Two local bus lines run by TUB – the No 1 and the D – both go from the train station to place du Champ de Mars, 6.40 am to 6.40 pm Monday to Saturday and 9 am to noon on Sunday. A single ticket costs 6FF and a carnet of 10 41FF. The TUB office (☎ 04 92 20 34 91) is on place de Suze in parc Chancel, north of Central Parc.

Taxi To summon a taxi in Briançon, ring ☎ 04 92 21 14 42.

AROUND BRIANÇON
Le Grand Serre Chevalier

Le Grand Serre Chevalier is the name given to a large ski area that rises above the Serre Chevalier Valley in the Hautes Alpes region. There are 13 villages that spread out along the valley floor from the town of Briançon to the village of Le Monêtier-les-Bains, 14.5km to the north-west. The skiing is below the peaks and down the slopes of Serre Chevalier to the valley floor, but the lift system only reaches Briançon and the three villages of Chantemerle, Villeneuve-la-Salle and Le Monêtier-les-Bains.

Chantemerle (1350m) and Villeneuve-la-Salle (1400m) are the two central resorts with all the facilities and better nightlife. Le Monêtier-les-Bains (1500m) retains a quieter atmosphere while Briançon has the cheapest accommodation.

The main tourist office is in Briançon, but there are small offices in Chantemerle (☎ 04 92 98 97), Villeneuve-La Salle les Alpes (☎ 04 92 24 98 98) and Le Monêtier-les-Bains (☎ 04 92 24 98 99). Accommodation can be booked in advance through the central reservation office (☎ 04 92 24 98 90, fax 04 92 24 98 84). Ski touring for a day or overnight in the Parc National des Écrins is particularly rewarding. The Bureau des Guides in Briançon (see Activities in the Briançon section) and the Maison de la Montagne (☎ 04 92 24 75 90) in Villeneuve-la-Salle offer various winter ski tours and summer mountaineering trips.

Getting Around There are up to 10 buses a day from Briançon (23FF, 20 minutes) to

Villeneuve-la-Salle. In winter, lifts operate and free shuttle buses ply the route between Le Monêtier-les-Bains and Briançon.

The Jura

The Jura Mountains, a range of dark, wooded hills and undulating plateaus, stretch for 360km along the Franco-Swiss border from the Rhine to the Rhône (ie from near Basel to just north of Geneva). Part of the historic Franche-Comté region, the French Jura is one of the least explored regions in France and hence a fine retreat for people in search of tranquillity away from the tourist crowd. Franche-Comté's capital is Besançon. Le Corbusier's chapel near Ronchamp (see Belfort & Around) has long been a place of pilgrimage for architecture buffs worldwide, while the little-known Saugeais Republic close to the Swiss border (see Around Métabief Mont d'Or) is a must for anyone seeking a glimpse at the region's rich ethnographical treasures.

The Jura – from a Gaulish word meaning 'forest' – is also France's premier cross-country skiing area. The range is dotted with ski stations from north of Pontarlier all the way south to Bellegarde. Métabief Mont d'Or, north of the Parc Naturel Régional du Haut-Jura, is one of the better known stations, as popular for its superb hiking and nature trails as for its gentle slopes.

Although not as well-known as other wine-growing regions in France, the Jura produces several fine appellations. Because of the altitude, the vintners use rarer, sturdier grape varieties, and as a result the area produces some unique wines.

BESANÇON
postcode 25000 • pop 114,000
• elevation 250m
Besançon, capital of the Franche-Comté region, is surrounded by hills on the northern reaches of the Jura range. First settled in Gallo-Roman times, it later became an important stop on the early trade routes between Italy, the Alps and the Rhine. Since the 18th century, it has been a noted clock-making centre. Victor Hugo, author of *Les Misérables*, and the film-pioneering Lumière brothers, were born within a stone's throw of each other on the eponymous place Victor Hugo in Besançon's old town.

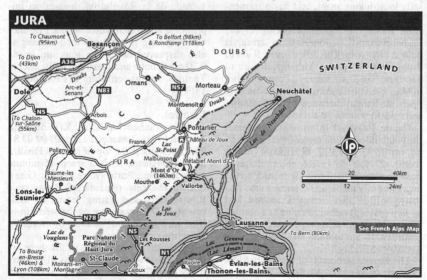

Noted for its vast parks, clean streets and few tourists, Besançon is considered one of the 'greenest' and most liveable cities in France. It has one of the country's largest foreign student populations and the old town's cobbled streets hum with fun bars and bistros. Besançon's charming Battant quarter, originally settled by wine-makers, is the most historic area of town.

Orientation

Besançon's old city is neatly encased by the horseshoe-shaped curve of the River Doubs called the Boucle du Doubs. The tourist office and train station are both just outside this loop to the north-west and north. The Battant quarter straddles the north-west bank of the river around rue Battant. Grande Rue, the pedestrianised main street, slices right through the old city from the river to the gates of the citadel.

Information

Tourist Offices Near the river and a park, the tourist office (☎ 03 81 80 92 55, fax 03 81 80 58 30, ✉ besancon@caramail.com), 2 place de la 1ère Armée Française, has an exchange service, books accommodation, sells local hiking maps, and has a tremendous amount of free material on everything from fishing to mountain biking in the Franche-Comté region. It also arranges guided city tours. The office opens 9 am to 7 pm (from 10 am on Monday; 10 am to noon and 3 to 5 pm Sunday). From October to March the office shuts at 6 pm and is only open on Sunday between mid-September and mid-June from 10 am to noon.

Centre Régional Information Jeunesse, the youth information centre (☎ 03 81 21 16 16, fax 03 81 82 83 17, ✉ crij@top-jeunes .com), 27 rue de la République, has a travel/accommodation noticeboard, gives away free city maps, and is home to the Autostop office that arranges shared and *payant* (paying) rides in France and abroad. The centre opens 1.30 to 6 pm Monday and Saturday, 10 am to noon and 1.30 to 6 pm Tuesday to Friday.

The Besançon branch of the Club Alpin Français (CAF; ☎ 03 81 81 02 77), 14 rue Luc Breton, has information on walking, skiing and mountain biking, and sells useful topoguides and maps. It opens 5 to 7 pm Tuesday to Friday.

Money The Banque de France is at 19 rue de la Préfecture. Foreign currency can also be changed at the tourist office, post office and the train station information office. Most banks around town have ATMs.

Post & Communications The main post office is the most convenient at 23 rue Proudhon in the old city. There is also a branch on rue Battant. For email access try Rom Collection, (☎ 03 81 81 65 00), 23 rue du Lycée, open 10 am to 12.30 pm and 2 to 7.30 pm. Frate (☎ 03 81 83 50 30), 44 Grande Rue, also offers access and opens 8 am to 12 pm and 2 to 6 pm.

Laundry The Blanc-Matic laundrette at 14 rue de la Madeleine opens 7 am to 8 pm.

Musée des Beaux-Arts et d'Archéologie

Thought to be France's oldest museum, the Musée des Beaux-Arts (☎ 03 81 82 39 92), 1 place de la Révolution, houses an impressive collection of paintings, including primitive and Renaissance works. Franche-Comté's long history of clock-making is also displayed here. The museum opens 9.30 am to noon and 2 to 6 pm daily, except Tuesday. Admission costs 21FF (students 13FF).

Citadel

Built by Vauban for Louis XIV between 1688 and 1711, Besançon's citadel (☎ 03 81 65 07 50) sits at the top of rue des Fusillés de la Résistance. It is a steep 15-minute walk from the **Porte Noire** (Black Gate), one of the few remains of Besançon's Roman days and dating from the 2nd-century AD. Get a sense of the strength of this well-preserved citadel by walking along the ramparts.

Within the 15–20m-thick walls there are three museums focusing on local culture: the **Musée Comtois**, the **Musée d'Histoire**

THE JURA

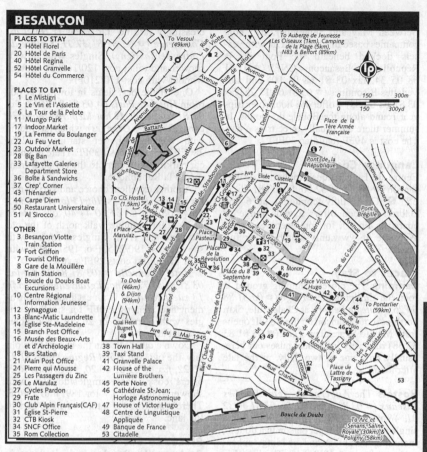

BESANÇON

PLACES TO STAY
2 Hôtel Florel
20 Hôtel de Paris
40 Hôtel Regina
52 Hôtel Granvelle
54 Hôtel du Commerce

PLACES TO EAT
1 Le Mistigri
5 Le Vin et l'Assiette
6 La Tour de la Pelote
11 Mungo Park
17 Indoor Market
19 La Femme du Boulanger
22 Au Feu Vert
23 Outdoor Market
28 Big Ban
33 Lafayette Galeries
     Department Store
36 Boîte à Sandwichs
37 Crep' Corner
43 Thénardier
44 Carpe Diem
50 Restaurant Universitaire
51 Al Sirocco

OTHER
3 Besançon Viotte
    Train Station
4 Fort Griffon
7 Tourist Office
8 Gare de la Mouillère
    Train Station
9 Boucle du Doubs Boat
    Excursions
10 Centre Régional
     Information Jeunesse
12 Synagogue
13 Blanc-Matic Laundrette
14 Église Ste-Madeleine
15 Branch Post Office
16 Musée des Beaux-Arts
     et d'Archéologie
18 Bus Station
21 Main Post Office
24 Pierre qui Mousse
25 Les Passagers du Zinc
26 Le Marulaz
27 Cycles Pardon
29 Frate
30 Club Alpin Français(CAF)
31 Église St-Pierre
32 CTB Kiosk
34 SNCF Office
35 Rom Collection
38 Town Hall
39 Taxi Stand
41 Granvelle Palace
42 House of the
     Lumière Brothers
45 Porte Noire
46 Cathédrale St-Jean;
     Horloge Astronomique
47 House of Victor Hugo
48 Centre de Linguistique
     Appliquée
49 Banque de France
53 Citadelle

THE JURA

Naturelle (Natural History Museum) and the **Musée de la Résistance et de la Déportation**, which examines the rise of Nazism and fascism and the French Resistance movement.

Less sobering are the colourful collections of insects, fish and nocturnal rodents exhibited in the **insectarium**, **aquarium** and **noctarium**. Siberian tigers prowl the **parc zoologique**.

The citadel opens 9 am to 7 pm; 9 am to 6 pm from Easter to June; and 10 am to 5 pm from November to March. Admission costs 40FF (children 30FF) and includes admission to all the museums. It is closed on Tuesday.

Horloge Astronomique

Housed in the predominantly 18th-century **Cathédrale St-Jean**, just below the citadel on rue de la Convention, this astronomical clock isn't a patch on Strasbourg's version, but there are 30,000 moving parts inside. There are seven guided tours of the cathedral every day from 9.50 am to 5.50 pm, except in January and on Tuesday; it closes Tuesday and Wednesday from October to March. Admission costs 15FF.

euro currency converter €1 = 6.56FF

Boat Excursions

Between May and September, two boat companies based in Villers-le-Lac with vessels docked beneath the Pont de la République in Besançon – CNFS (☎ 03 81 68 05 34, fax 03 81 68 01 00) and Les Vedettes Bisontines (☎ 03 81 68 13 25, fax 03 81 68 09 85) – offer 1¼-hour river trips year round along the Boucle du Doubs. In summer there are usually three trips a day. The cost is 49FF (children 39FF).

Language Courses

Centre de Linguistique Appliquée de Besançon (☎ 03 81 66 52 00, fax 03 81 66 52 25, ✉ CLA@univ-fcomte.fr) at 6 rue Gabriel-Plançon offers a wide range of course in French for foreigners. See their Web site at www.univ-fcomte.fr for full details.

Places to Stay

Camping The closest camping ground is four-star *Camping de la Plage* (☎ 03 81 88 04 26, *Route de Belfort*) at Chalezeule, 5km north-east of Besançon on the N83. It opens from May to September. TGB (☎ 03 81 83 37 38) runs very infrequent buses out here, usually only one or two daily, in the late afternoon.

Hostels The *Auberge de Jeunesse Les Oiseaux* (☎ 03 81 40 32 00, fax 03 81 40 32 01, 48 rue des Cras), charges 90FF for a single room or 80FF per person in a double, including breakfast and bedding; subsequent nights cost 10FF less. The hostel is 2km east of the train station. Alternatively take bus No 7 from the tourist office in the direction of Orchamps and get off at Les Oiseaux.

Centre International de Séjour (CIS; ☎ 03 81 50 07 54, fax 03 81 53 11 79, 19 rue Martin du Gard*)* charges 97/120FF for singles/doubles with toilet; with private shower rooms cost 154/180FF. Breakfast costs 22FF and other meals range from 34FF to 57FF. Take bus No 8 from the train station in the Campus direction, get off at the Intermarché stop. The hostel is nearby.

Hotels Dirt-cheap and one of France's increasingly rare no-star hotels is *Hôtel du Commerce* (☎ 03 81 81 37 11, 8 place de Lattre de Tassigny). Singles without/with shower and toilet cost 120/160FF; doubles without/with cost 170/210FF.

One of the best deals in town is at 60-room *Hôtel de Paris* (☎ 03 81 81 36 56, fax 03 81 61 94 90, ✉ hoteldeparis@hotmail. com, 33 rue des Granges), which has rooms with washbasin/shower starting at 205/280FF. Breakfast costs 39FF. There is ample car parking with entry to the car park from rue de la République.

Another excellent choice and very handy for the train station is *Hôtel Florel* (☎ 03 81 80 41 08, fax 03 81 50 44 40, 6 rue de la Viotte), a 10-minute walk north of the old city and the river. Singles/doubles with shower cost 190/215FF or 195/225FF with bath. Breakfast costs 29FF extra.

Hotel Granvelle (☎ 03 81 81 33 92, fax 03 81 81 31 77, ✉ hotel.granvelle@fc-net.fr, 13 rue Lecourbe) is a neat little establishment and charges 190FF for smallish singles with a shower or 265FF for doubles with a bath.

Down a quiet alley in the heart of the old city, the two-star *Hôtel Regina* (☎ 03 81 81 50 22, fax 03 81 81 60 20, 91 Grande Rue) offers cosy, floral singles/doubles with shower, toilet and TV for 189FF to 259FF. There's parking for a total of three cars in the lane.

Places to Eat

Restaurants Popular with students is *Boîte à Sandwichs* (21 rue du Lycée), which offers cheap, filling sandwiches ranging in price from 18FF to 28FF. Equally cheap and cheerful is *Au Feu Vert* (☎ 03 81 82 17 20, 11 place de la Révolution. It's a simple place with *menus* starting at 50FF and seven types of couscous starting at 55FF. It opens from noon to 2 am. For late-night snacks, try *Big Ban* (13 quai Veil Picard), which slaps out hot dogs, steaks and salads (around 22FF) from 11.30 am to 1 am.

Popular for its large tasty portions of local cuisine at favourable prices, *Le Mistigri (1a rue Général Roland)* is a five-minute walk

THE JURA

from the train station. Its *menu* and its house speciality, *jambon de montagne* (mountain ham), both cost 65FF. It opens 10 am to 2 pm and 5 to 10 pm (closed Monday).

Thénardier (☎ *03 81 82 06 18, 11 rue Victor Hugo)* is great for lunch. *Menus* start at 45FF and service is speedy. If the 1st floor is full, ask to sit in the cosy cellar. Thénardier opens 10 am to 2 pm and 5 to 11 pm. Vegetarians might want to check out *Crep' Corner (1 rue Mégevand)* where salads range in price from 40FF to 46FF. Crepes and *galettes* are house specialities.

Rue Bersot overflows with *pizzerias*. The best pizza in town, however, is served at *Al Sirocco* (☎ *03 81 82 24 05, 1 rue Chifflet)*, which also has a takeaway service. Its 24 varieties of pizza start at 46FF. It opens most days noon to 2 pm and 7.30 to 11 pm.

Popular with tourists is *La Tour de la Pelote* (☎ *03 81 82 14 58, 41 quai de Strasbourg)*, which is housed inside a 16th-century stone tower. *Menus* start at 140FF. It opens noon to 2 pm and 5 pm to 12.30 am (closed Monday).

Housed above the Caves Marcellin (Marcellin wine cellars) is *Le Vin et l'Assiette* (☎ *03 81 81 48 18, 97 rue Battant)*. This intimate bistro and wine bar has a *menu* for 95FF and opens noon to 2 pm and 5 to 11 pm (closed Sunday and Monday).

Mungo Park (☎ *03 81 81 28 01, 11 rue Jean Petit)*, which is named after a Scottish explorer, is *the* place for a splurge. *Menus* start at 250FF with the ultimate gourmand *menu* satisfying the appetite for 490FF. The restaurant opens noon to 3.30 pm and 5.30 to 9.30 pm (closed Sunday and Monday).

Almost broke? A cheap but tasteless meal (about 17FF for three courses) is available at the *Restaurant Universitaire (36 rue Mégevand)*, which opens 7.30 to 10.30 am and 2.30 to 5 pm.

Cafes Lost bohemians in search of a hangout are guaranteed to dig *Carpe Diem* (☎ *03 81 83 11 18, 2 place Jean Gigoux)*. This small and simple cafe-restaurant serves a good range of salads starting at 12FF; the plat du jour costs 45FF. Newspapers are free for customers to peruse. It opens 7 to 2 am.

Delicious homemade breads, sweet and savoury tarts, and healthy breakfasts are served with finesse at *La Femme du Boulanger* (☎ *03 81 82 86 93, 6 rue Morand)*, which specialises in local artisan produce. The plat du jour costs 67FF; don't miss its scrumptious apple bread. There is no obvious sign, so look for the blackboard and the bread displays.

Self-Catering Fresh fish, meat, vegetables and dairy products are sold at the large *indoor market* on the corner of rue Paris and rue Claude Goudimel. The nearby *outdoor market* on place de la Révolution sells mainly fruit and vegetables.

Lafayette Galeries, entered from 69 Grande Rue or opposite the Hôtel de Paris on rue des Granges, has a grocery section in the basement. It opens 9 am to 7 pm Monday to Saturday.

Entertainment

Perhaps the most popular brasserie is *Pierre qui Mousse* (☎ *03 81 81 15 25, 1 place Jouffrey)*. Under funky low, wooden beams you can sup Belgian beer (22FF) and munch on various sandwich concoctions (26FF to 36FF). Happy hour is from 6 to 7 pm.

Besançon's hip brigade can be found by night at *Les Passagers du Zinc* (☎ *03 81 81 54 70, 5 rue de Vignier)*, a grungy bar and club that hosts tapas nights, live bands, a host of eclectic 'worst record' competitions and other kitsch delights. Step through the bonnet of an old Citröen DS to reach the cellar. It opens 5 pm to 1 am (2 am on weekends; closed Monday). Small, packed, and equally fun is *Le Marulaz* jazz bar (☎ *03 81 01 40 30, 2 place Marulaz)*, open 11 am to 1 am.

Getting There & Away

Bus Buses operated by Monts Jura (☎ 03 81 21 22 00) depart from the bus station (☎ 03 81 83 06 11), 9 rue Proudhon, open 8 am to 6.30 pm weekdays, and 8 am to 1 pm and 2.30 to 5.30 pm on Saturday. There are daily connections to Ornans (20.50FF) Grey (42.50FF) and Pontarlier (45.50FF).

THE JURA

Train Besançon Gare Viotte (☎ 08 36 35 35 35) is 800m up the hill from the city centre at the north-western end of ave Maréchal Foch. The ticket office opens 4.30 am to 10.30 pm. Train tickets can be bought in advance at the SNCF office, 44 Grande Rue.

Major connections include Paris' Gare de Lyon (from 268FF, 2½ hours, five daily), Dijon (74FF, one hour, 20 daily), Lyons (145FF, 2½ hours, five daily), Belfort (78FF, 1¼ hours, four daily) and Arc-et-Senans (35FF, 35 minutes, four daily). To get to Frasne (near Métabief), change trains in Mouchard or Dole (68FF, two hours).

Getting Around

Bus Local buses are run by CTB (☎ 03 81 48 12 12), which has a ticket/information kiosk on place du 8 Septembre, open 9 am to 12.30 pm and 1 to 7 pm Monday to Saturday. A single ticket/carnet of 10 costs 6/50FF. Bus Nos 8 and 24 link the train station with the centre.

Taxi To order a taxi, call ☎ 03 81 88 80 80. Taxis can be picked up next to the town hall.

Bicycle If you have strong leg muscles, why not tackle Besançon's hilly terrain with a mountain bike hired from Cycles Pardon (☎ 03 81 81 08 79), 31 rue d'Arènes. It costs 65/105FF for a half-day/day (plus 3000FF deposit). The shop opens 9 am to noon and from 2 to 7 pm (closed on Sunday and Monday).

AROUND BESANÇON
Saline Royal

Envisaged by its late 18th-century designer, Claude-Nicolas Ledoux, as the 'ideal city', the Saline Royale (Royal Salt Works; ☎ 03 81 54 45 45, fax 03 81 54 45 46) at Arc-et-Senans, 30km south-west of town off the N83 to Chalezeule, is a showpiece of early Industrial Age town planning. Although his dream was never realised, Ledoux' semi-circular saltworks is listed as a UNESCO World Heritage List sight and is a must for anyone interested in town planning.

Opening hours and prices vary depending on the month, but it usually opens 9 or 10 am to noon and 2 to 5 or 6 pm (9 am to 7 pm in July and August). Admission costs 38/30/15FF for adults/students/children.

Family-run **Hotel Relais** (☎ 03 81 57 40 60, fax 03 81 57 46 17), in the centre of Arc-et-Senans village, has 10 cosy double rooms costing 180FF. Its lunchtime *menu* at 55FF is excellent value. Campers can pitch their tents at **Camping des Bords de Loue** (☎ 03 81 57 42 20, or 03 81 57 43 21), a 1.5km-hike signposted off the main road (open May to October). There are four trains daily from Besançon (33FF, 35 minutes) to Arc-et-Senans.

Ornans

postcode 25290 • pop 4015

Ornans, 25km south-west of Besançon, is Franche-Comté's 'Little Venice'. The River Loue cuts through the heart of the old town, above which towers the **Château d'Ornans**. The birthplace of Gustave Courbet (1819–77), an 18th-century house on the banks of the Loue, today houses a museum dedicated to the realist painter. Exhibits include works by Courbet. *Musée Courbet* (☎ 03 81 62 23 30) opens 10 am to noon and 2 to 6 pm (closed Tuesday in winter). Admission costs 40/20FF in summer/winter.

Ornan's surrounding **Vallée de la Loue** (Loue Valley) is a popular spot for mountain biking, canoeing and kayaking. Contact the Syratu sports club (☎ 03 81 57 10 82, fax 03 81 57 18 49), 2 Route de Montgesoye. Ornans tourist office (☎/fax 03 81 61 21 50), 7 rue Pierre Vernier, distributes the excellent free brochure *VTT et Cyclotourisme en Franche-Comté*.

There are eight buses daily (25FF, 45 minutes) from Besançon to Ornans.

Route Pasteur & Route du Vin

Louis Pasteur (1822–95) was born in **Dole**, 20km north-west of Arc-et-Senans along the D472. His childhood home, La Maison Natale de Pasteur (☎ 03 84 72 20 61), overlooking the Canal des Tanneurs in the old town, houses a museum dedicated to the man who invented both pasteurisation and the first rabies vaccine. The Pasteur family later moved to **Arbois**, 35km east of Dole.

euro currency converter 10FF = €1.52

Pasteur's former laboratory and workshops in Arbois inside Pasteur's house (☎ 03 84 66 11 72), 83 rue de Courcelles, open 9.45 am to 5.15 pm between May and September. Admission costs 30FF.

No visit to Arbois, the wine capital of Jura, is complete without sampling a glass of local *vin jaune*. The history of wine-making and of this nutty 'yellow wine', which is matured for six years in oak casks, is recounted in the **Musée de la Vigne et du Vin** (☎ 03 84 66 26 14, ✉ percee@jura.vins .com) inside Arbois' medieval Château Pécauld. The museum opens daily, except Tuesday, from 10 am to noon and 2 to 6 pm between February and September (no lunchbreak in July and August). The tourist office (☎ 03 84 37 47 37, fax 03 84 66 25 50), rue de l'Hôtel de Ville, arranges guided tours and accommodation. To get to Arbois from Besançon (45km) take a train to Mouchard, 8km north of Arbois.

For the ultimate *dégustation* experience, head 3km south along the Route du Vin to **Pupillin**, a beautifully quaint, yellow-brick village (population 220) brimming with wealth from its wine production. Some 10 different *caves* are open to visitors who can taste (and buy) Arbois-Pupillin wines. Pupillin is not served by public transport, but it is a pleasant 2.5km (uphill) walk from Arbois and very easy to walk back after tasting a few *vins jaunes*.

Poligny & Baume-les-Messieurs

Poligny, 10km south of Arbois, lies at the heart of France's lucrative Comté cheese-making industry, the history of which is displayed in the town's **Maison du Comté** (☎ 03 84 37 23 51), ave de la Résistance. Some 40 million tonnes of Comté cheese are produced each year, much of which is made by *fruitières* (cheese dairies) in the Franche-Comté region. Museum staff run five daily guided tours in summer between 10 am and 4.30 pm (15FF); from October to June the museum opens 9 to 11 am and 2 to 5 pm (admission free). Poligny's tourist office (☎ 03 84 37 24 21, fax 03 84 37 22 37), rue Victor Hugo, has a list of local cheese shops that visitors can tour.

Traditional Jurassien life is still firmly intact in **Baume-les-Messieurs** (population 200), an extraordinarily pretty village sunk between three valleys 20km south of Poligny. Its Benedictine abbey (☎ 03 84 44 61 41), established by Irish monk St Columban at the end of the 14th century, opens between 10 am and 6 pm from mid-June to mid-September. Admission costs 20FF. Equally spectacular is the **Grottes de Baume** (Baume caves), accessible by road from the foot of the 10m-tall **Cascade de Baume** (Baume waterfall). Guided tours of the 30 million-year-old caves (☎ 03 84 44 61 58) are available from 9 am to 6 pm between April and September.

Immediately east of Baume-les-Messieurs is the Jura's **Région des Lacs** (Lakes District).

Places to Stay & Eat Opposite Baume-les-Messieurs abbey, *Le Grand Jardin* (☎ 03 84 44 68 37) has quaint double rooms for 200FF. Book well in advance in summer. *Le Comptois* (☎/fax 03 84 25 71 21), some 5km east in Doucier, has singles/doubles with shower for 170/295FF. Rooms with shared bathroom are 140/220FF. Don't miss out on its restaurant's delicious Jurassien fondue, served between March and November to appease tourists hungry for a dip into the region's best known winter speciality (the French only eat fondue in winter). Le Comptois also organises gastronomic tours of the region.

BELFORT & AROUND

Belfort (population 50,125), just across the border from Germany and Switzerland, is as Alsatian as it is Jurassien. Historically part of Alsace, it became part of the Franche-Comté region in 1921. Today, the city is best known as the manufacturer of the TGV train.

Musée d'Art et d'Histoire (☎ 03 84 54 25 51), inside the **Vauban citadel**, opens 10 am to 7 pm (closed on Tuesday between October and April). Open-air concerts are held on Wednesday in summer. At the foot of the citadel stands **Le Lion de Belfort**, created by sculptor Frédéric-Auguste Bartholdi, who also designed the Statue of Liberty in New

THE JURA

York. The 11m-tall lion commemorates Belfort's resistance to the Prussians in 1870–71, following which all of Alsace – except Belfort – was annexed by Germany.

In July, Belfort hosts **Les Eurockéennes** (☎ 03 84 57 01 92, fax 03 84 28 15 12), a three-day open-air rock festival that, in the past, has attracted the likes of David Bowie, Garbage and the Red Hot Chili Peppers. A one/three day ticket costs 180/440FF and includes use of the festival camp site that overlooks Malsaucy lake.

In Sochaux, near Montbéliard 12km south of Belfort, car enthusiasts can visit the **Musée Peugeot** (☎ 03 81 94 48 21). Guided tours of the car factory are available Monday to Thursday at 8.30 am and 4 pm. The modernist **Église Audicourt** (Audin-court Church), 2km south-east, is a must for architecture buffs. The **Massif du Ballon d'Alsace** (1247m), 20km north of Belfort in the southern part of the Vosges Mountains, provides ample opportunity for winter skiing, summer walking, mountain biking, kayaking and hot-air ballooning.

Ronchamp

La Chapelle de Notre-Dame du Haut (the Chapel of our Lady of the Height; ☎ 03 81 20 65 13), on a hill overlooking the old mining town of Ronchamp (population 3000), 20km west of Belfort, is considered one of the 20th century's architectural master-pieces – making it a pilgrimage site for thousands of architects every year. The white chapel, unique for its surreal, sculpture-like form, was designed between 1950 and 1955 by France's most celebrated architect, Le Corbusier. Its sweeping, concrete roof is said to have been inspired by a hermit crab shell.

The chapel (☎ 03 84 20 65 13) is open from 9 am to 7 pm (to 4 pm between November and March). Admission costs 10FF. In summer, Sunday service takes place at 11 am. Over 3000 pilgrims gather here each year on 8 September. A 15-minute walking trail leads uphill from the centre of Ronchamp to the chapel.

Ronchamp tourist office (☎ 03 84 63 50 82), 14 place du 14 Juillet, is open between

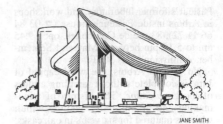
JANE SMITH

Le Corbusier's surreal church near Ronchamp is an icon of modern architecture

June and October on Monday, Friday and Saturday from 9 am to noon and 2 to 6 pm (5 pm on Saturday).

Places to Stay & Eat

Belfort tourist office (☎ 03 84 55 90 90, fax 03 84 55 90 99), 2 rue Clémenceau, has the free *Accommodation and Restaurant* brochure containing a city map and a comprehensive list of hotels and camp sites in and around Belfort.

In Belfort, a bed at the *Auberge de Jeunesse* (☎ 03 84 21 39 16, fax 03 84 28 58 95, 6 rue de Madrid), costs 72FF a night including breakfast.

In Ronchamp, *Hôtel à la Pomme d'Or* (☎ 03 84 20 62 12, fax 03 84 63 59 45), at the foot of the hill leading up to the chapel, has doubles starting at 210FF. More idyllic is *Hôtel Carrer* (☎ 03 84 20 62 32, fax 03 84 63 57 08), 2km north of Ronchamp in Le Rhien. Singles/doubles start at 170/280FF.

Don't leave Belfort without biting into a local Belfore, a scrumptious almond-flavoured pastry filled with raspberries and topped with hazelnuts.

Getting There & Away

Major connections from Belfort train station include Paris' Gare de Lyon via Besançon (278FF, five hours, three daily), Besançon (77FF, 1¼ hours, four daily) and Montbéliard (20FF, 15 minutes, 20 daily).

From Belfort there are one or two trains a day to/from Ronchamp (25FF, 25 minutes). On weekdays there are also two buses a day to/from Ronchamp (25FF, 35 minutes).

MÉTABIEF MONT D'OR
postcode 25370 ● pop 500
● elevation 1000m

Métabief Mont d'Or, 18km south of Pontarlier on the main road to Lausanne in the central part of the Jura range, is the region's leading cross-country ski resort. year round, lifts take you almost to the top of Mont d'Or (1463m), the area's highest peak, from where a fantastic 180° panorama stretches over the foggy Swiss plain to Lake Geneva and from the Matterhorn to Mont Blanc.

Métabief is famed for its unique *vacherin Mont d'Or* cheese.

Orientation & Information

The resort comprises six traditional villages. The main lift station for downhill skiers is in Métabief. There are smaller lifts in Les Hôpitaux Neufs, 2km north-east.

In Métabief, the tourist office (☎ 03 81 49 16 79, ✉ ot@metabief-montdor.com) and École du Ski Français (ESF; ☎ 03 81 49 04 21) are inside the Centre d'Accueil, 6 place du Xavier. Both open 9 am to noon and 2 to 5 pm. The tourist office (☎ 03 81 49 13 81, fax 03 81 49 09 27), 1 place de la Mairie, Les Hôpitaux Neufs, opens until 6 pm.

Fromagerie du Mont d'Or

Comté, *morbier* and vacherin Mont d'Or cheese have been made by the Sancey-Richard family in Métabief since 1953. The Fromagerie du Mont d'Or (☎ 03 81 49 02 36, fax 03 81 49 25 07), rue Moulin, which produces over 200 tonnes of cheese a year, opens year round to visitors. Guided tours include a visit to the dairy's salting rooms, where the vacherin Mont d'Or cheeses are washed daily with salt water, and the maturing cellars where the hefty 45kg-rounds of Comté cheese are turned by hand twice weekly for up to 12 months.

The cheese shop opens from 9 am to 12.15 pm and 3 to 7 pm (Sundays 9 am to midday). Arrive here with the milk lorry

---

Hot Box, Christmas Ice & Jesus

It's hot, it's soft and it's packed in a box. *Vacherin Mont d'Or* is the only French cheese to be eaten with a spoon – hot (or cold for that matter). Made between 15 August and 15 March with unpasteurised milk (*lait cru*) from red cows grazing above an altitude of 800m, it derives its unique nutty taste from the spruce bark in which it's wrapped.

Louis XV adored it. In the 18th century it was called fat cheese, wood cheese or box cheese. Today, vacherin Mont d'Or is named after the mountain village from which it originates. Connoisseurs top the soft-crusted cheese with chopped onions, garlic and white wine, then wrap it in aluminium foil and cook it in the oven for 45 minutes to create a *boîte chaude* (hot box).

Just 11 factories in the Jura are licensed to produce vacherin Mont d'Or, which ironically, has sold like hot cakes since 1987 when 10 people in Switzerland died from listeriosis after consuming the Swiss version of Mont d'Or, made just a few kilometres across the border. Old-fashioned cheese buffs are quite frank about the Swiss scandal's popularisation of their own centuries-old cheese. They believe the bacterial tragedy, which claimed 34 lives in total between 1983 and 1987, only happened because the Swiss copycats pasteurised their milk.

Mouthe, 15km south of Métabief Mont d'Or, is the mother of *liqueur de sapin* (fir tree liqueur). *Glace de sapin* (fir tree ice cream) also comes from this village, known as the North Pole of France due to its seasonal sub-zero temperatures (record low -38°). Sampling either is rather like ingesting a Christmas tree. Then there's Jesus. *Jésus* – a fat little version of regular *saucisse de Morteau* (Morteau sausage) – is the village of Morteau's gastronomic delight. Jesus is easily identified by the wooden peg on its back end, attached after being smoked with pine-wood sawdust in a traditional *tuyé* (mountain hut) above 600m. Morteau residents claim their sausage is bigger and better than any other French sausage. They host a sausage festival (☎ 03 81 50 69 43) each year in August.

before 10.30 am if you want to see cheese being made. Admission is free.

Places to Stay & Eat

Both tourist offices have comprehensive lists of hotels and apartments to rent.

In Métabief, family-run *Hôtel Étoile des Neiges* (☎ 03 81 49 11 21, fax 03 81 49 26 91), rue du Village, charges 160FF to 215FF for singles/doubles. Breakfast costs 33FF. Strictly local dishes such as raclette, fondue Comtoise, *Mont d'Or chaud* and *la saucisse Jésus de Morteau* are served in its excellent restaurant, also open to nonguests. Tickle your tastebuds first though with a hearty shot of *anis de Pontarlier* (a liquorice-flavoured aperitif), the Jura's answer to Provençal *pastis*.

Getting There & Away

The closest train station is at Frasne (☎ 0 836 35 35 35), 25km north-west on the rail line between Dijon, Arc-et-Senans and Vallorbe (9km east in Switzerland). From Frasne, there are six buses daily that pass through both Métabief and Les Hôpitaux Neufs (23FF, 50 minutes). You can reach both Métabief Ville (23FF) and the ski station (23FF) from Besançon, 78km to the north-west, in about two hours.

AROUND MÉTABIEF MONT D'OR

Winter skiers keen for a break from the slopes should head a few kilometres south to the **l'Odyssée Blanche – Parc du Chien Polaire** (White Odyssey Polar Dog Park; ☎ 03 81 69 20 20, fax 03 81 69 13 02) in Chaux Neuve. Try your hand at 'mushing' – that is exploring the region by dog-drawn sledge – or simply tour the kennels and coo over the Siberian huskies and Alaskan malamutes instead. White Odyssey opens 10 am to 5 pm. between 20 December and 31 March. A half-day/day expedition costs 470/920FF.

The **Château de Joux** (☎ 03 81 69 47 95), 10km north of Métabief on the Route de Pontarlier, guards the entrance from Switzerland into north and central France. It sits atop Mont Larmont (922m), overlooking a dramatic *cluse* (transverse valley) that cuts through the mountain to form a passage just wide enough for the road to snake between. Part of *Les Misérables* (1995) was filmed here. During the First Empire, the castle was a state prison. Today it houses France's most impressive arms museum. The chateau opens 9 am to 6 pm in summer, and from 10 to 11.15 am and 2 to 3.30 pm between October and February. Admission costs 32/27/16FF for adults/students/children. The music and theatre festival, **Festival des Nuits de Joux**, takes place here in mid-July.

Montbenoît (population 230), 20km farther north, is the capital of the tiny **Saugeais Republic**. The folkloric republic, declared in 1947, has its own flag, national anthem, postage stamp and a 92-year-old president, Gabrielle Pourchet, who is featured on the Saugeais banknote. In summer a Sauget customs officer greets tourists as they enter the town.

PARC NATUREL RÉGIONAL DU HAUT-JURA

The Haut-Jura regional park covers an area of 75,672 hectares, stretching from Chapelle-des-Bois in the north and almost to the western tip of Lake Geneva in the south. Each year in February, its abundant lakes, mountains and low-lying valleys play host to the Transjurassienne, the world's second longest cross-country skiing race (see the boxed text 'Grande Traversée du Jura'). Exploring this region is difficult without private transport.

The largest town in the park, **Ste-Claude** (population 12,704), is best known for its illustrious wooden pipe-making and diamond-cutting tradition, the history of which unfolds in the local pipe and diamond museum. The CAF (☎ 03 84 45 58 62, fax 03 84 60 36 88), 8 blvd de la République, provides information on its *refuges* in the Jura. Dubbed the French capital of wooden toys, **Moirans-en-Montagne**, 14km west, is an apt home for the playful **Musée du Jouet** (Toy Museum).

Les Rousses (population 2850, elevation 1100m), on the north-eastern edge of the park, is the main centre for winter sports, walking and mountain biking. Three of its

Grande Traversée du Jura

The Grande Traversée du Jura (GTJ) – the Grand Jura Crossing – is a 210km cross-country skiing track from Villers-le-Lac (north of Pontarlier) to Hauteville-Lompnes (south-west of Bellegarde). The path peaks at 1500m near the town of Mouthe (south of Métabief) and follows one of the coldest valleys in France. After the first 20km the route briefly crosses into Switzerland, but most of the time it runs close to the border on the French side. Well maintained and very popular, the crossing takes 10 full days of skiing to cover – a feat for the ultrafit and dedicated.

Part of the GTJ – the 76km from Lamoura to Mouthe – is traversed each year during the world's second largest cross-country skiing competition, the Transjurassienne. Held in late February, the challenge is taken up by more than 4000 skiers, who charge off in an incredible blaze of colour.

For information on the GTJ and accommodation possibilities along the route, contact Relais de Randonnée Étapes Jura (☎ 03 84 41 20 34), F-39310 Lajoux; or GTJ-Espace Nordique Jurassien (☎ 03 84 52 58 10; fax 03 84 52 35 56), Rue Baronne-Delort, F-39300 Champagnole. The best map of the area is the IGN 1:50,000 scale map entitled *Ski de Fond – Massif du Jura*.

four small, gently-sloped downhill ski areas – Les Jouvencelles, Le Noirmont and La Serra – are in France; the fourth – La Dole – is in Switzerland. Extensive cross-country trails take skiers as far north as Métabief Mont d'Or as well as eastwards across the border. The tourist office (☎ 03 84 60 02 55), SNCF bureau (☎ 03 84 60 01 90) and the Club des Sports (☎ 03 84 60 35 14) are inside the Maison du Tourisme, next to the bus station on Route Blanche.

The Jura's most staggering view can be savoured from the **Col de la Faucille**, 20km south of Les Rousses. As the N5 twists and turns its way down the Jura Mountains past the small ski resort of **Mijoux**, the panoramic view of Lake Geneva embraced by the French Alps and Mont Blanc beyond is startling. By sunset, it is a sight never

forgotten – easily rivalling Paris in the romantic spot stakes. Take a télécabine from Mijoux or gaze in the warmth from the terrace bar of the classy **La Mainaz** hotel-restaurant (☎ 04 50 41 31 10, fax 04 50 41 31 77) on the Col de la Faucille. Half-board starts at 405FF per person.

Continuing a farther 25km south-east you arrive at the French-Swiss border, passing through **Ferney-Voltaire**, 5km north of Geneva en Route. Following his banishment from Switzerland in 1759, Voltaire lived in Ferney until his return to Paris and death in 1778. Guided tours of his estate – chateau, chapel and 17-acre park – are available in July and August on Saturday at 3, 4 and 5 pm. Past visitors include Auden, Blake and Flaubert, all of whom wrote about the philosopher's home in exile.

THE JURA

Massif Central

The striking mountain landscape of the Massif Central, dimpled with the cones of extinct volcanoes, attracts outdoor sports enthusiasts of all sorts. The area is also known for its spa towns, among them Vichy and Le Mont Dore.

Except in the few small cities and the regional capital, Clermont-Ferrand, life is primarily rural. At higher elevations, cows and sheep produce some of the country's most popular (and cheapest) cheeses – you'll come across the powerful *bleu d'Auvergne* and the slightly sour-tasting *Cantal* everywhere in France.

Two large regional parks, the dramatic Parc Naturel Régional des Volcans d'Auvergne and its tamer eastern neighbour, the Parc Naturel Régional du Livradois-Forez, make up France's largest environmentally protected area.

Geography

Formed millions of years before the Alps or Pyrenees, the volcanic landscape of the Massif Central is best known for its *puys* (pronounced 'pwee'), or volcanic cones. The Puy de Dôme (west of Clermont-Ferrand) is one of the most spectacular, but there are many more, most notably in the Parc des Volcans d'Auvergne. Some puys are actually just the lava 'plugs' that remained when the surrounding cones eroded away – St-Michel d'Aiguilhe chapel in Le Puy-en-Velay is perched atop a particularly steep plug.

The Massif Central, which gives rise to some of France's great rivers (including the Dordogne, Allier and Loire), is roughly coextensive with the Auvergne, an administrative region comprised of the departments of Allier, Puy de Dôme, Cantal and Haute-Loire.

Activities

Walking is the most popular activity in the Massif Central, which is crossed by 13 GR tracks (including the GR4) and hundreds of

Highlights

- **Orcival** – admire the Romanesque basilica in this delightful mountain hamlet
- **Col de Guéry** – marvel at the spectacular view of the surrounding mountains
- **Mont Mézenc** – take in the whole of south-western France from Mont Blanc to Mont Ventoux
- **Puy Mary** – walk up to the summit
- **Vichy** – absorb the old-time atmosphere of this remarkably inexpensive spa town

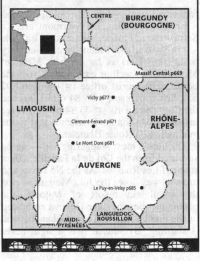

other footpaths. Some of these trails are also suitable for mountain biking. Chamina publishes a series of topoguides for the region.

Several ski resorts, particularly Le Mont Dore, Super Besse and Super Lioran (near Murat), provide full Alpine skiing facilities, including lifts. The Massif Central's undulating terrain is great for cross-country skiing.

The region's topography and thermal currents make it ideal for hang-gliding and *parapente* (paragliding) flights, for which the puys are used as take-off platforms. For

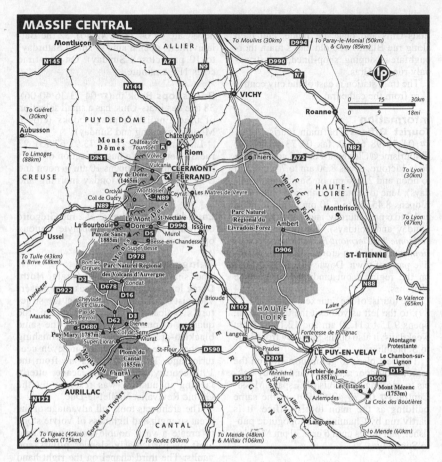

MASSIF CENTRAL

Montluçon
ALLIER
To Moulins (30km)
To Paray-le-Monial (50km)
& Cluny (85km)
D994
N145
A71
N9
D990
N7
N144
VICHY
To Guéret
(30km)
Roanne
PUY DE DÔME
Aubusson
Châtelguyon
To Limoges
(88km)
Monts
Dômes
Château de
Tournoël
Riom
D941
Volvic
Vulcania
N82
CREUSE
Puy de Dôme
(1465m)
CLERMONT-
FERRAND
To Lyon
(30km)
Thiers
A72
Orcival
Montlosier
N89
Ceyrat
Les Matres de Veyre
HAUTE-
LOIRE
Col de Guéry
N89
Montbrison
Ussel
Le Mont
Dore
St-Nectaire
Issoire
D996
Murol
Parc Naturel
Régional du
Livradois-Forez
To Lyon
(47km)
La Bourboule
Puy de Sancy
(1885m)
D5
Besse-en-Chandesse
Super Besse
Ambert
D906
ST-ÉTIENNE
To Tulle (43km)
& Brive (68km)
Bort-les-
Orgues
D978
Parc Naturel Régional
des Volcans d'Auvergne
N88
D922
D3
D678
Condat
D16
To Valence
(65km)
Mauriac
Cheylade
& Le Claux
Pas de
Peyrol
Salers
D62
Dienne
D3
Brioude
N102
HAUTE-
LOIRE
Loire
Forteresse de Polignac
D680
Col de Serre
Puy Mary (1787m)
Super Lioran
Murat
A75
Langeac
Montagne
Protestante
Plomb du
Cantal
(1855m)
St-Flour
D590
Prades
LE PUY-EN-VELAY
Le Chambon-sur-
Lignon
D301
D500
D15
AURILLAC
N122
D589
Ministrol
d'Allier
Gerbier de Jonc
(1551m)
Les Estables
Mont Mézenc
(1753m)
La Croix des Boutières
Arlempdes
CANTAL
N9
To Figeac (45km)
& Cahors (115km)
To Rodez (80km)
To Mende (48km)
& Millau (106km)
Langogne
To Mende (60km)
0   15   30km
0   9   18mi

details, see the Puy de Dôme listing and Outdoor Activities under Le Mont Dore later in the chapter.

CLERMONT-FERRAND
postcode 63000 • pop 254,000
• elevation 401m

The lively city of Clermont-Ferrand, the Massif Central's principal urban centre, is a good base for exploring the northern part of the region. The town centre, built on top of a long-extinct volcano, is considerably enlivened by a student population of some 34,000.

Clermont-Ferrand is the hub of France's rubber industry, better known to the rest of the world as the Michelin tyre empire. The company got into the sideline of guidebook publishing in 1898 in an effort to promote motorcar tourism – and thus the use of its pneumatic tyres.

Orientation

Clermont-Ferrand's cathedral is situated on the highest point in the old city, which is bounded by ave des États-Unis, rue André Moinier and blvd Trudaine. The partly pedestrianised commercial centre stretches

MASSIF CENTRAL

from the cathedral westwards to blvd des États-Unis and place de Jaude, and then along rue Blatin. The old city's main thoroughfare is sloping, shop-lined, pedestrian-only rue des Gras.

The train station is east of the city centre, 1km from the cathedral.

Information

Tourist Offices The main tourist office (☎ 04 73 98 65 00, fax 04 73 90 04 11, ⓔ tourisme@Clermont-Ferrand.com), place de la Victoire, opens 8.30 am to 7 pm (9 am to noon and 2 to 6 pm on Sunday and holidays), June to September; the rest of the year it opens 8.45 am to 6.30 pm (9 am to noon and 2 to 6 pm Saturday, and 9 am to 1 pm on Sunday and holidays). The free brochures *Welcome to Clermont-Ferrand* and *Tour of Fountains* take you around the more attractive parts of town. Downstairs is an exhibit on the region's outstanding Romanesque churches.

The tourist office annexe (☎ 04 73 91 87 89), to the left as you exit the train station, opens 9.15 to 11.30 am and 12.15 to 5 pm weekdays; it also opens Saturday from June to September.

The best place to get information on the region's outdoor activities (and to buy tickets to sporting events) is the Espace Massif Central (☎ 04 73 42 60 00), in the same building as the main tourist office. It is partly run by Chamina, the topoguide publisher, and opens until 6 or 6.30 pm Monday to Saturday.

Money The Banque de France, 15 cours Sablon, exchanges money from 9 am to 12.30 pm weekdays. Commercial banks are at the northern end of place de Jaude and 300m farther north at place Gilbert Gaillard. The Crédit Agricole, 3 ave de la Libération, opens 8.15 am to 6.30 pm weekdays and until noon on Saturday.

Post & Communications The main post office, rue Maurice Busset, opens 8 am to 7 pm weekdays and until noon on Saturday. Currency exchange and a Cyberposte are available.

Stainless steel predominates at the Internet@Café (☎ 04 73 92 42 80), 32 rue Ballainvilliers, open 8 am (11 am on Saturday) to 10 pm (closed Sunday). On-line time costs 1FF a minute.

Bookshops Book'in (☎ 04 73 36 40 06), 38 ave des États-Unis, has a small selection of used English-language books (closed Monday morning and Sunday).

La Cartographie (☎ 04 73 91 67 75), 23 rue St-Genès, has a huge selection of maps and topoguides. It opens 10 am to noon and 2 to 7 pm (closed Monday morning and Sunday).

Laundry The laundrettes at 2 rue Grégoire de Tours and 6 place Hippolyte Renoux open 7 am to 8 pm daily.

Things to See

The soaring, Gothic **Cathédrale Notre Dame** looks like a smog-blackened preservationist's nightmare, but in fact the structure's volcanic stones, dug from the quarries of nearby Volvic, were the same blackish-grey hue the day the finishing touches were put on the choir seven centuries ago. The twin towers are from the 19th century; the western facade, utterly lacking in nuance, was restored by the Gothic Revivalist Viollet-le-Duc.

The architects took full advantage of the great strength and lightness of Volvic stone to create a vast, double-aisled nave held aloft by particularly slender pillars and vaults. The third chapel on the right-hand side of the choir is decorated with **15th-century frescoes**. A number of windows in the choir and chapels date from the 13th and 14th centuries. It opens 8 or 9 am to 6 pm daily; closed noon to 2 pm except in July and August.

The early 16th-century **Fontaine d'Amboise**, two blocks north of the cathedral at place de la Poterne, affords a fine view of the Puy de Dôme and nearby peaks.

The narrow, shop-lined streets east of the cathedral are home to some of the city's most interesting 17th- and 18th-century townhouses, including the **Hôtel**

CLERMONT-FERRAND

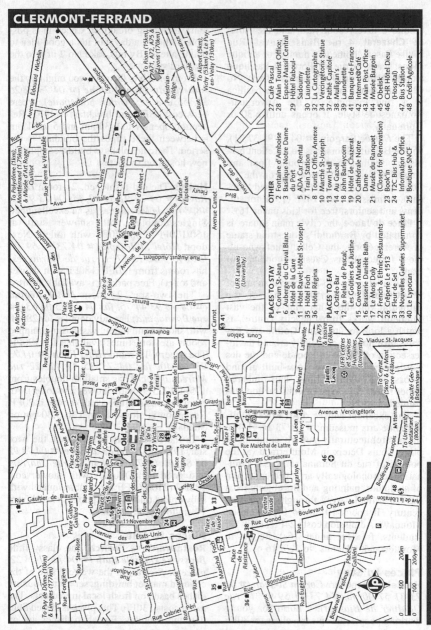

PLACES TO STAY
6 Corum St-Jean
7 Auberge du Cheval Blanc
9 Hôtel de la Gare
11 Hôtel Ravel; Hôtel St-Joseph
35 Hôtel Foch
36 Hôtel Régina

PLACES TO EAT
4 Ostréo Bar
12 Le Relais de Pascal;
   Les Goûtiers de Justine
15 Covered Market
16 Brasserie Danièle Bath
17 Le Moss Doly
26 Crêperie Le 1513
31 Fleur de Sel
33 Nouvelles Galeries Supermarket
40 Le Lypocan

OTHER
2 Fontaine d'Amboise
3 Basilique Notre Dame
   du Port
5 ADA Car Rental
8 Train Station
10 Tourist Office Annexe
10 Marché St-Joseph
13 Town Hall
14 Au Gazoil
18 John Barleycom
19 Hôtel de Chazerat
20 Cathédrale Notre
   Dame
21 Musée du Ranquet
   (Closed for Renovation)
23 Book'in
24 T2C Bus Hub &
   Information Office
25 Boutique SNCF
27 Café Pascal
28 Main Tourist Office
29 Espace Massif Central
   Hôtel Raboul-
   Sadoury
30 Laundrette
32 La Cartographie
34 Vercingétorix Statue
37 Pathé Capitole
38 Mulligan's
39 Laundrette
41 Banque de France
42 Internet@Café
43 Main Post Office
44 Musée Bargoin
45 Obelisk
46 CHR Hôtel Dieu
   (Hospital)
47 Bus Station
48 Crédit Agricole

Raboul-Sadourny, 9 rue Savaron, built around a lovely courtyard, and the **Hôtel de Chazerat**, 4 rue Blaise Pascal. Rue Blaise Pascal, home to a number of antique shops, leads to rue du Port and **Basilique Notre Dame du Port**, across from No 42. Constructed in the 1100s, the basilica is a fine example of the Auvergnat-Romanesque style. It opens until 6.30 or 7 pm daily.

The **Musée Bargoin** (☎ 04 73 91 37 31), 45 rue Ballainvilliers, has an excellent prehistory section on the ground floor and colourful Near Eastern carpets on the 1st floor. It opens 10 am to 6 pm (closed Monday). Admission costs 24FF (13FF for students and seniors, free for kids under 16).

Place de Jaude, the city's main square, is dominated by Bartholdi's equestrian statue of Vercingétorix, the Celtic chief who almost foiled Julius Caesar's conquest of Gaul.

The quiet, none-too-prosperous suburb of **Montferrand**, 2.5km north-east of the cathedral (on the other side of the vast Michelin works from the city centre), is worth a look for its many **Gothic and Renaissance houses**, especially around the intersection of rue de la Rocade and rue des Cordeliers. Many have stone-built ground floors and overhanging, half-timbered upper floors (this type of construction was banned in 1508).

The excellent **Musée d'Art Roget Quilliot** (fine arts museum; ☎ 04 73 16 11 30), in an architecturally superb complex at place Louis Deteix in Montferrand (at the bottom of rue du Seminaire), has a fascinating, chronologically arranged collection of sculpture, painting and art objects from the late Middle Ages through to the 20th century. It opens 10 am to 6 pm (closed Monday). Admission costs 24FF (13FF for students, free for under 16s). To get to Montferrand, take bus No 1, 9, 16 or 17.

Places to Stay

Hostels The modern *Corum St-Jean* (☎ 04 73 31 57 00, fax 04 73 31 59 99, 17 rue Gaultier de Biauzat), a dorm for young working people, accepts travellers for 80FF (10FF more without a HI card or equivalent), including breakfast. Check-in is possible 24 hours a day, but it's a good idea to phone ahead. By bus, take No 2 or 4 to the Gaillard stop.

From March to October, you might try the *Auberge du Cheval Blanc* (☎ 04 73 92 26 39, 55 ave de l'Union Soviétique), where beds cost 48FF and breakfast is 19FF. Reception opens 7 to 9.30 am and 5 to 11 pm – between these times the building is deserted. There are plans to build a completely new hostel on this site.

Hotels The old-fashioned, 21-room *Hôtel Ravel* (☎ 04 73 91 51 33, fax 04 73 92 28 48, 8 rue de Maringues) is an excellent bet. Singles/doubles with shower start at 150/170FF (200/220FF with toilet). Next door, *Hôtel St-Joseph* (☎ 04 73 92 69 71, fax 04 73 92 15 17, 10 rue de Maringues) has rooms from 120FF (180FF with shower and toilet). Free parking is available nearby.

The two-star, 23-room *Hôtel Régina* (☎ 04 73 93 44 76, fax 04 73 35 04 63, 14 rue Bonnabaud) has tidy doubles for 280FF with shower and toilet; washbasin-equipped rooms are sometimes available for 190FF. The cheery, 19-room *Hôtel Foch* (☎ 04 73 93 48 40, fax 04 73 35 47 41, 22 rue Maréchal Foch) has smallish doubles from 175FF (225FF with shower and toilet). An extra bed costs 45FF; a hall shower is 20FF. Reception is closed from 1 to 5.30 pm on Sunday.

In the seedy train station area, the two-star, 19-room *Hôtel de la Gare* (☎ 04 73 92 07 82, fax 04 73 90 74 36, 76 rue Charras) is a good bet. Doubles with shower cost 185FF (210/260FF for doubles/quads with shower and toilet). Reception is closed from 11 am to 5 pm Saturday.

Places to Eat

Restaurants – French The classy little *Brasserie Danièle Bath* (☎ 04 73 31 23 22, place St-Pierre), in the western side of the covered market building, serves top-quality dishes based on fresh local ingredients. The *menu* costs 130FF. This place is closed Sunday and Monday. Fine fish dishes are on

You want oysters? Exactly which type would you like...?

Tasting the latest Bordeaux

The lush landscape of Gascony rolls from west of Toulouse to the Atlantic Coast.

There's excellent surf on the beautiful, if rather chilly, Atlantic Coast.

JULIA WILKINSON

Drifting in the Dordogne

NEIL IRVINE

The graceful Pont d'Arc, Gorges de L'Ardèche, Languedoc

INGRID RODDIS

Puy de Sancy, the highest point in Massif Central, is an ideal base for exploring the volcanic landscape.

JULIA WILKINSON

Cahors' open-air market is laden with fresh produce.

JULIA WILKINSON

Fortress in the Limestone, Lot

offer at *Fleur de Sel* (☎ *04 73 90 30 59, 8 rue Abbé Girard)*, a small, elegant place where *menu* prices range from 95FF (lunch only) to 190FF. It's closed Saturday at midday and Sunday.

Le Relais de Pascal (☎ *04 73 92 21 04, 15 rue Blaise Pascal)* is an intimate bar-*restaurant du quartier* whose pork-based Auvergnat dishes are served on marble tables. Weekday lunch *menus* cost 50FF to 65FF. It's closed Sunday and Monday.

The cosy *Crêperie Le 1513* (☎ *04 73 92 37 46, 3 rue des Chaussetiers)*, housed in a sumptuous mansion built in 1513, serves savoury and sweet crepes and large salads noon to 3 pm and 6 pm to midnight daily.

From October to February, oysters (58FF a dozen) are on offer from 7.30 am to 8 pm at *Ostréo Bar* (☎ *04 73 91 58 28, 63 bis rue du Port)*, open Monday to Saturday.

Les Goûtiers de Justine (☎ *04 73 92 26 53, 11 bis rue Blaise Pascal)* is a tea room that's an island of calm and mellowness. It opens noon to 7 pm (closed Sunday).

Restaurants – Other Tasty rice-based Senegalese *menus* cost 59FF (lunch only) to 115FF at *Le Moss Doly* (☎ *04 73 14 20 17, 10 rue de la Coifferie)*, open Tuesday to Saturday.

There are several other eateries in the immediate vicinity. Pizzas are on offer at the informal *Le Lypocan* (☎ *04 73 92 07 24, 16 place Renoux)*, closed midday Saturday, Sunday and Monday night.

Two blocks north of place de Jaude, rue St-Dominique and nearby rue St-Adjutor, are home to quite a few reasonably priced *French and ethnic restaurants* (including Tunisian, Indian, Vietnamese, Italian, Tex-Mex, Portuguese and Cuban).

University Restaurant The university restaurant *(25 rue Étienne Dolet)*, 800m south from the bus station, serves student meals (15FF with a ticket, 16FF in cash) daily, year round for lunch and dinner (closed on holidays and, in July and August, on Saturday night and Sunday). Hours are 11.30 am to 1.30 pm (12.45 pm at the weekend) and 6.30 to 7.45 pm.

Self-Catering The jumble of blue, yellow and grey cubes that fill place St-Pierre is the city's *covered market*, open 6 am to 7 pm (closed Sunday).

The basement supermarket in the *Nouvelles Galeries* department store *(place de Jaude)* opens Monday to Saturday. There are a number of food shops on ave Charras, near the train station.

Entertainment

Clermont-Ferrand has a remarkably lively nightlife scene. The pubs and bars scattered in the area between the southern side of place de Jaude and place Gilbert Gaillard include *Mulligan's* (☎ *04 73 93 36 70, 2 place de la Résistance)*, an Irish-style pub open 8 am to 2 am (closed Sunday).

The hangout for exchange students, including many English-speakers, is the hopping *Café Pascal* (☎ *04 73 91 86 08, 4 place de la Victoire)*. It opens 10 am to 1.30 am; meals are available at lunchtime. Liquids made with both barley and corn are available at *John Barleycorn* (☎ *04 73 92 31 67, 9 rue du Terrail)*, a Celtic-style pub open 5 pm (2 pm from May to August) to 2 am (closed Sunday).

Au Gazoil (☎ *04 73 14 11 11, 14–16 rue des Deux Marchés)* is a rough-hewn bar-discotheque popular with students. It opens 8 pm to 4 am Tuesday to Saturday; the downstairs dance floor only fills up after 11 pm. Admission usually costs 10FF.

There are non-dubbed films at the five-screen *Pathé Capitole* (☎ *08 36 68 22 88, 32 place de Jaude)*.

The city's striking new conference centre, the *Polydôme* (☎ *04 73 14 41 44, place du Premier Mai)*, 2km north-east of the city centre, plays host to concerts. It is served by buses Nos 8 and 15.

Getting There & Away

Air The Clermont-Ferrand-Aulnat airport (☎ 04 73 62 71 00) is 7km east of the city.

Bus Inside the bus station, 69 blvd François Mitterrand, the efficient information office (☎ 04 73 93 13 61) opens 8.30 am to 6.30 pm Monday to Saturday. The bus to St-Nectaire

(45FF, one hour), Murol (50FF, one hour, not served some days during school holidays), Besse-en-Chandesse (50FF, 60 to 80 minutes) and Super Besse (60FF, 1½ hours) departs 5.10 pm most days (except Sunday), returning to Clermont-Ferrand the next day in the late morning. The Interlines office (☎ 04 73 29 70 05) handles Eurolines ticketing. It's generally closed Sunday.

Train Clermont-Ferrand's train station (☎ 0 836 35 35 35) is the most important rail junction in the Massif Central. In town, the Boutique SNCF (ticketing office), 43 rue du 11 Novembre, opens 10 am (11.50 am Monday) to 7 pm. It's closed Sunday and holidays.

Destinations include Paris' Gare de Lyon (239FF to 289FF, three hours, six to nine a day) and Lyon (138FF via St-Étienne, three hours, seven to 10 a day). The route through the Gorges de l'Allier to Nîmes (187FF, 4½ hours, two or three a day) via Langeac (81FF) and Monistrol d'Allier (96FF), known as Le Cévenol, is one of the most scenic in France.

There are short-haul SNCF services to La Bourboule (62FF), Le Mont Dore (66FF, 1½ hours, four or five a day), Le Puy-en-Velay (108FF, 2¼ hours, four or five daily), Murat (92FF, 1½ hours, five or six daily), Riom (18FF, 10 minutes, 19 to 40 daily) and Vichy (50FF, 40 minutes, 14 to 27 daily).

Car ADA car rental (☎ 04 73 91 66 07), 79 ave de l'Union Soviétique, is open Monday to Saturday.

Getting Around
The local bus company, T2C (☎ 04 73 28 56 56), has an information office at the northern end of place de Jaude, next to the city's main bus hub.

To order a taxi, call Taxi Radio on ☎ 04 73 19 53 53.

AROUND CLERMONT-FERRAND
Puy de Dôme
Covered in snow in winter and outdoor adventurers in summer, the balding Puy de Dôme (1465m) affords a panoramic view of

Clermont-Ferrand and scores of volcanoes. The Celts and later the Romans worshipped gods from the summit, nowadays dominated by a TV transmission tower that looks like a giant rectal thermometer.

Parapente and hang-gliding enthusiasts use the summit as a launching platform. Introductory flights with an instructor cost about 350FF; five-day courses are about 1600FF. Several companies organise flights – the tourist office in Clermont-Ferrand has details.

The summit can be reached either by the 'mule track' – an hour's climb starting at the Col de Ceyssat, 4km off the D941A – or by the 4km toll road (30FF; ☎ 04 73 62 12 18), open from 8am until between 7 and 10 pm, March to November and on weekends in December. The road is closed to private cars from 10 am to 6 pm daily in July and August and on weekend afternoons in May, June and September – at these times you're required to take a shuttle bus (21FF return, 7FF for kids aged 14 and under).

Vulcania
The Parc Européen du Volcanisme (European Volcanic Park; ☎ 04 73 31 85 65), better known as Vulcania, is a vast visitors centre that explains the workings of volcanoes in an architecturally innovative – some would say megalomaniacal – complex, most of which is underground. The site, 15km west of Clermont-Ferrand on the D941B, is set to open by mid-2001. It may close for two months every winter. Visit their Web site at www.vulcania.tm.fr.

Riom
postcode 63200 • pop 18,800
• elevation 363m
Riom, 15km north of Clermont-Ferrand on the train line to Vichy, was the capital of the Auvergne in the Middle Ages. The streets of the austere old city are lined with magistrates' mansions built of dark Volvic stone.

Orientation & Information The main streets of the old city, surrounded by tree-lined boulevards, are north–south rue du

Commerce (and its northern extension, rue de l'Horloge) and east–west rue de l'Hôtel de Ville. The train station is 400m south-east of the old city at the end of ave Virlogeux.

The tourist office (☎ 04 73 38 59 45, fax 04 73 38 25 15), 16 rue du Commerce (100m south of rue de l'Hôtel de Ville), can supply you with an English-language walking-tour brochure.

It opens 9.30 am to noon and 2 to 6.30 pm daily (4 pm on Sunday) in July to August; and to 5.30 pm (5 pm on Saturday; closed Monday morning and Sunday) during the rest of the year. Visit their Web site at www.riom-auvergne.com.

Things to See About 200m down rue du Commerce from the tourist office, you will find the 15th-century **Église Notre Dame du Marthuret**, famous for its 14th-century statue known as the *Vierge à l'Oiseau* (Virgin with Bird). The figure over the entrance is a copy – the original is inside, in the first chapel to the right.

The **Musée F Mandet** (☎ 04 73 38 18 53), 14 rue de l'Hôtel de Ville, has a collection of classical antiquities, medieval sculptures and 17th- to 19th-century paintings. About 200m down rue Delille is the excellent **Musée d'Auvergne** (☎ 04 73 38 17 31), where displays document rural life in Auvergne in past centuries. Both open 10 am to noon and 2 or 2.30 to 5.30 or 6 pm (closed Tuesday). Admission costs 26FF (10FF for students) for each museum or 36FF for both (free on Wednesday).

About 7km south-west of Riom is the town of **Volvic**, famous for its spring water and quarries, which provided the light-weight but strong volcanic stone used in so many buildings in the area, including Clermont-Ferrand's cathedral. The ruins of the nearby **Château de Tournoël** dominate the countryside and are worth visiting.

Places to Stay The *Hôtel Le Terminus* (☎ 04 73 38 01 26, 8 rue Gregoire de Tours), across the street from the train station, has 10 basic doubles/quads with washbasin and bidet for 120/170FF.

Parc Naturel Régional des Volcans d'Auvergne

The 3950 sq km, 120km-long Parc des Volcans d'Auvergne (☎ 04 73 65 64 00 for the park headquarters in Montlosier) is ideal for walking. The region's volcanic activity started about 20 million years ago, with the last eruptions petering out about 5000 years ago.

The **Monts Dômes**, the northernmost range, consists of a chain of 80 'recent' cinder cones, the best known being the Puy de Dôme (see the Around Clermont-Ferrand section earlier in the chapter). Three million years older, the **Monts Dore** culminate in the Puy de Sancy (1885m), the Massif Central's highest point. In winter it's a popular downhill ski station. At its foot lies the spa town of Le Mont Dore, an ideal summer and winter base for exploring the area. For more information, see the Orcival and Le Mont Dore sections later in the chapter.

The south of the park, one of the Massif Central's wildest areas, is dominated by the bald slopes of the rugged **Monts du Cantal**, the remains of a super-volcano worn down over the millennia. The highest point is the Plomb du Cantal (1855m), a lonely, desolate peak which is often shrouded in heavy, swirling clouds, even in summer. For details, see the sections on Puy Mary and Murat later in the chapter.

VICHY
postcode 03200 • pop 28,000
• elevation 340m
The spa resort of Vichy is one of the best places in France to see faded *belle époque* charm. The town became enormously fashionable following visits by Napoleon III in the 1860s, but these days the average age of *curistes* (patients taking the waters) is roughly that of Brezhnev's last Politburo. Most come seeking relief from rheumatism, arthritis and digestive ailments under France's generous social security system.

MASSIF CENTRAL

Thanks to the town's difficult economic situation – and the many centime-wise pensioners who make sure that every *sou* is well-spent – Vichy is a remarkably cheap place for a holiday.

Since July 1940, Vichy has been known around the world as the capital of Marshal Philippe Pétain's collaborationist 'Vichy French' government. The town, of course, had no role in its selection – Pétain's government was attracted by the availability of hotel rooms and phone lines. These days, Vichy retains very few explicit reminders of the period between July 1940 and August 1944, when Pétain's militias helped the Gestapo terrorise France.

Orientation

Vichy is centred around triangular Parc des Sources, 800m west of the train station along rue de Paris. Rue Georges Clemenceau, the main shopping thoroughfare, crosses the partly pedestrianised city centre.

Information

Tourist Office The building from which Pétain's 'État Français' (French State) ruled, 19 rue du Parc, now houses the overly spacious tourist office (☎ 04 70 98 71 94, fax 04 70 31 06 00, ✉ tourisme@ville-vichy.fr). It opens until 6.30 pm daily (closes earlier winter weekends) with a 1½ hour closure starting at noon or 12.30 pm (midday closure on Sunday only in July and August). It is closed Sunday morning from October to March. The staff can supply you with a photocopied map of WWII Vichy. Visit their Web site at www.ville-vichy.fr.

Money The Banque de France, 7 rue de Paris, exchanges money from 8.40 am to noon weekdays. Most commercial banks open Monday to Friday.

Post The main post office, place Charles de Gaulle, opens 8 am to 7 pm weekdays and until noon Saturday. Exchange services and a Cyberposte are available.

Laundry The Lavomatique, 37 rue d'Alsace, opens 7 am to 9 pm daily.

Things to See & Do

The bench-lined walkways of **Parc des Sources**, created in 1812 on the orders of Napoleon, are enclosed by a *belle époque*-style covered promenade (1900). At the park's northern end is the glass-enclosed **Hall des Sources**, built in 1903, whose taps deliver six types of mineral water, three of them hot (up to 43.3°C). There's no charge to sit in the metal chairs but taking a drink costs 10FF from April to October. A graduated, urine sample-style cup is included in the price. The site opens until 8.30 pm daily (6 pm in winter).

Across the path is the newly restored, Indo-Moorish-style **Grand Établissement Thermal**, adorned with tiled domes and towers. Established in 1903 and enlarged in 1933, it is now a shopping arcade.

The taps of **Source de l'Hôpital**, in a round pavilion at the southern end of Parc des Sources, dispense unlimited quantities of the warmish, odoriferous and rather bitter mineral waters of the Hôpital and Célestins springs. If you're sick they may make you well, but if you're well they're just as likely to make you sick. Bring a corrosion-resistant cup. The taps are open until 8.30 pm daily.

At **Source des Célestins**, in an ornate, oval pavilion on blvd du Président Kennedy, you can drink your fill of the bitter, slightly saline mineral water, which is bottled and sold in supermarkets all over France. It opens until 6 pm daily (8.30 pm from April to September); the taps are shut in winter to prevent the pipes from freezing.

Église St-Blaise, on rue de la Tour, built between 1925 and 1936 in the Art-Deco style often associated with fascism, is enlivened by neo-Byzantine mosaics and stained-glass windows depicting angular, muscle-bound figures. The small, free **Musée de Vichy** (☎ 04 70 32 12 97), in an Art-Deco theatre, 15 rue du Maréchal Foch, displays paintings, sculpture, archaeology and postage stamps. It opens 2 to 6 pm (closed Monday).

The flowery **Parcs de l'Allier** border the River Allier – now a lake – on Vichy's western and southern flanks.

MASSIF CENTRAL

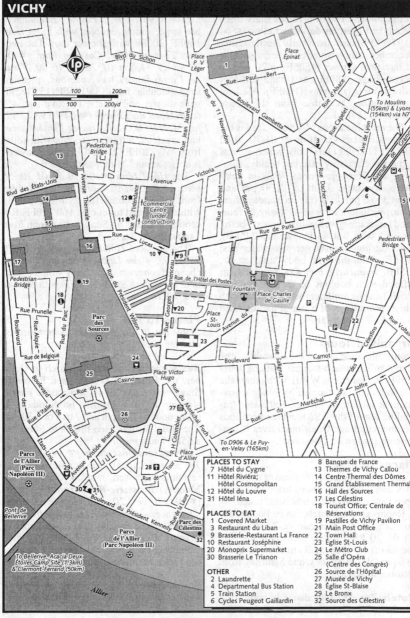

VICHY

0   100   200m
0   100   200yd

To Moulins
(55km) & Lyons
(154km) via N7

To D906 & Le Puy-
en-Velay (165km)

To Bellerive, Acacia Deux
Étoiles Camp Site (1.3km)
& Clermont-Ferrand (50km)

PLACES TO STAY
7 Hôtel du Cygne
11 Hôtel Riviéra;
    Hôtel Cosmopolitan
12 Hôtel du Louvre
31 Hôtel Iéna

PLACES TO EAT
1 Covered Market
3 Restaurant du Liban
9 Brasserie-Restaurant La France
10 Restaurant Joséphine
20 Monoprix Supermarket
30 Brasserie Le Trianon

OTHER
2 Laundrette
4 Departmental Bus Station
5 Train Station
6 Cycles Peugeot Gaillardin

8 Banque de France
13 Thermes de Vichy Callou
14 Centre Thermal des Dômes
15 Grand Établissement Thermal
16 Hall des Sources
17 Les Célestins
18 Tourist Office; Centrale de
    Réservations
19 Pastilles de Vichy Pavilion
21 Main Post Office
22 Town Hall
23 Église St-Louis
24 Le Métro Club
25 Salle d'Opéra
    (Centre des Congrès)
26 Source de l'Hôpital
27 Musée de Vichy
28 Église St-Blaise
29 Le Bronx
32 Source des Célestins

MASSIF CENTRAL

Thermal Baths

At the northern end of blvd des États-Unis, the modern **Thermes de Vichy Callou** (☎ 04 70 97 39 59), open from early April to early December, offers water treatments such as an intestinal shower (150FF), a 20-minute wet massage (180FF) and hand-and-foot *pulvérisation* (spraying; 163FF). Medical authorisation, available from the house doctor, is required.

The most luxurious of Vichy's spas is the ultramodern **Les Célestins** (☎ 04 70 30 82 00), 111 blvd des États-Unis, which attracts upmarket clients by offering beauty, slimming and fitness programs. Walk-in treatments, available 9 am to 12.30 pm and about 3 to 6 pm daily (except Sunday afternoon), include a *douche de Vichy* (a four-hand massage given while you're being sprayed with hot spring water; 245FF), *hydromassage* (a massage with water jets; 165FF), *illutation* (a body mud mask; 245FF), *bain carbo-bulles* (a bath in water infused with bubbles of carbon dioxide; 165FF) and *jet tonifiant* (being sprayed with a high-powered jet of water of the sort used to disperse riots; 165FF).

Organised Tours

From mid-June to mid-September, the tourist office runs historical walking tours (25FF; in French) of WWII Vichy that take you to buildings occupied by Pétain's government ministries, foreign embassies (including that of the USA) and the notorious Commissariat aux Questions Juives (Commission for Jewish Questions).

Places to Stay

Vichy's many hotels offer some of the country's best deals. The places listed below are open year round unless otherwise noted.

Rooms at some hotels can be booked for no charge at the Centrale de Réservations (☎ 04 70 98 23 83), located inside the tourist office. It opens 9 am to noon and 2 to 6 pm (closed Sunday, and Saturday from October to April).

Hotels Rue de l'Intendance is home to a number of hotels offering good value. The one-star **Hôtel Riviéra** (☎ 04 70 98 22 32, fax 04 70 96 14 09, 5 rue de l'Intendance) has large, simple doubles with toilet from 160FF (200FF with shower too). The two-star, 27-room **Hôtel Cosmopolitan** (☎ 04 70 98 29 14, fax 04 70 98 46 00, 7 rue de l'Intendance) has spacious, pleasant singles/doubles from 135/145FF (155/185FF with shower and toilet). The two-star, 45-room **Hôtel du Louvre** (☎ 04 70 98 27 71, fax 04 70 98 86 85, 15 rue de l'Intendance) has spacious, attractive rooms with toilet from 190/220FF (220/240FF with shower). It opens around March to October.

The **Hôtel Iéna** (☎ 04 70 32 01 20, 56 blvd du Président Kennedy) has doubles from 130FF; rooms for two/four people with shower and toilet cost 160/210FF. Reception is closed on Sunday afternoon from September to April.

The 26-room **Hôtel du Cygne** (☎ 04 70 98 21 03, 4 rue Dacher) has some of the cheapest rooms in town: very simple, clean doubles start at 90FF (140FF with shower and toilet).

Places to Eat

Many hotels also function as restaurants, offering reasonably priced *menus*.

Restaurants From about March to October, the **Hôtel du Louvre** (see Places to Stay) serves copious four-course *menus* starting at 70FF (100FF on Sunday). It opens noon to 1.30 pm and 7 to 8 or 8.30 pm. The **Hôtel Riviéra** (see Places to Stay) has a 65FF lunch *menu*.

Restaurant Joséphine (☎ 04 70 98 08 14, 30 rue Lucas) is a popular creperie-restaurant (closed midday Sunday and Monday). **Brasserie-Restaurant La France** (☎ 04 70 98 20 16, 34 rue Georges Clemenceau) has *menus* from 62FF to 149FF (closed Sunday from November to March). **Restaurant du Liban** (51 blvd Gambetta) has reasonably priced Lebanese food (closed midday Monday).

Self-Catering The cavernous *covered market* (place P V Léger), built in the mid-1930s, opens until 1 pm (closed Monday).

The *Monoprix* supermarket *(16 rue Georges Clemenceau)* opens 8.30 am to 7.30 pm daily (9.30 am to 12.30 pm and 3 pm to 7 pm on Sunday).

Entertainment

Vichy was once known as the 'French Bayreuth', and even today operas, operettas, dance performances and concerts are staged about once a week (less frequently in winter) in the ornate *Salle d'Opéra* (1902) in the Centre des Congrès (formerly the Grand Casino; ☎ *04 70 30 50 50, rue du Casino*).

Le Bronx bar *(☎ 04 70 98 17 75, 3 ave Aristide Briand)* has live music from 8 or 9 pm on Friday and Saturday. The disco, *Le Métro Club (☎ 04 70 97 16 46, near place Victor Hugo)*, opens from 11.30 pm Thursday to Sunday. Admission costs 50FF.

Shopping

The octagonal mint, aniseed and lemon lozenges known as *pastilles de Vichy*, pride of the city since 1825, can be sampled and purchased in the sweets pavilion in the Parc des Sources (open daily from April to October).

Getting There & Away

The train station (☎ 0 836 35 35 35) is linked to cities including Paris' Gare de Lyon (215FF, three hours, six to eight a day), Clermont-Ferrand (50FF, 40 minutes, 14 to 27 a day), Riom (42FF, 25 minutes, one to 24 a day), Dijon (162FF, at least three hours, one direct a day) and Lyons (122FF, 2½ hours, five to seven a day).

ORCIVAL

postcode 63210 • pop 283
• elevation 860m

The delightful, slate-roofed village of Orcival, about midway between the Puy de Dôme and Le Mont Dore, is surrounded by some of the region's most spectacular forests and pastureland. Situated along the gurgling River Sioulet, it's a perfect base for day hikes – and, despite the coachloads of tourists, a lovely spot to spend a few soothing days. Walking trails that pass through Orcival include the GR30; maps

are on sale at the *tabac* (tobacconist) next to the *boulangerie* (bakery).

The very fine Auvergnat-Romanesque **basilica**, built in the 1100s, has prisoners' balls and chains hanging above the entrance. Inside is a 12th-century statue of the Virgin made of gilded silver on wood. About 2.5km to the north, the 15th- and 17th-century **Château de Cordès** (☎ 04 73 65 81 34), known for its French-style gardens and 18th-century furnishings, can be visited daily from Easter to October (20FF).

The tourist office (☎ 04 73 65 89 77), in the village hall, opens from 10 am to noon and 2 to 5 pm weekdays (6 pm from Easter to September, when it's also open at the weekend).

Places to Stay

The reasonably priced one- and two-star hotels around the church include the seven-room *Les Bourelles* (☎ 04 73 65 82 28), which has a lovely, flowery terrace. Simple doubles/triples with washbasins, bidets and beautiful views cost 140/180FF (closed from about November to a bit before Easter). The seven-room *Hôtel Notre Dame* (☎ 04 73 65 82 02), open year round, has doubles with shower and toilet for 190FF. The two-star, eight-room *Hôtel des Touristes* (☎ 04 73 65 82 55, fax 04 73 65 91 11) has doubles/quads with shower and toilet from 220/280FF (closed in November, December and, except for weekends, in January).

Getting There & Away

Two buses a day (one on Sunday) link Clermont-Ferrand with Rochefort-Montagne (43FF, 40 minutes), a town 4km west of Orcival.

COL DE GUÉRY

The D27 from Orcival to the Col de Guéry (1268m), 8.5km to the south, passes through some really spectacular mountain scenery.

From mid-June to mid-September, the **Maison des Fleurs d'Auvergne** (☎ 04 73 65 20 09) functions as a visitors centre for people interested in the area's flora (open daily). Whenever there's snow (usually from January to March, but sometimes as early as

MASSIF CENTRAL

mid-November), it becomes the **Foyer Ski de Fond Orcival Guéry**, a cross-country skiing centre (open daily) with up to 30km of pistes. Cross-country equipment costs 50FF a day; snowshoes are 35FF a day.

On the far shore of the **Lac de Guéry**, the 17-room, two-star *Auberge de Guéry* (☎ 04 73 65 02 76, fax 04 73 65 08 78), open mid-January to October, has plain, functional doubles/quads for 290/440FF. Visit on-line at www.auberge-lac-guery.fr.

LE MONT DORE
postcode 63240 • pop 2000
• elevation 1050m

The lovely little spa town of Le Mont Dore is brilliantly situated for exploring the Puy de Sancy area on foot, by bicycle or with a car. It lies in a narrow, wooded valley along the Dordogne, not far from its source. Built from the dark local stone, the town bustles with skiers in winter and hikers, hanggliders and curistes (attracted by the hot springs) in summer.

Orientation & Information

The centre of town is around place du Panthéon and place de la République. The train station is about 500m to the north.

The tourist office (☎ 04 73 65 20 21, fax 04 73 65 05 71), ave de la Libération, is at the southern end of the complex housing the ice-skating rink and bowling alley. It opens 9 am to 12.30 pm and 2 to 6.30 pm Monday to Saturday; Sunday hours are variable. Loads of information on scenic walks and drives in the area, including a free brochure on cycling options, is available. Hotel reservations (☎ 04 73 65 36 00) are free. Visit the Web site at www.mont-dore.com.

The main post office, place Charles de Gaulle, opens 8.30 am to noon and 2 to 5 pm weekdays (until noon on Saturday). Currency exchange is available.

Maps and topoguides are available at the Maison de la Presse, 21 place du Panthéon, open 7.30 am to 7 pm (closed Sunday morning and from 12.30 to 2 or 3 pm); open until 8 pm in July and August.

The laundrette, place de la République, opens 9 am to 7 pm daily.

Things to See & Do

The huge **Établissement Thermal** (hot springs complex; ☎ 04 73 65 05 10), place du Panthéon, where the waters (37–40°C) are said to cure respiratory ailments (particularly asthma), offers a wide range of hydrotherapies from early May to late October. Half-hour guided tours (15FF) of the sumptuous, neo-Byzantine interior, which dates from the early and mid-19th century (with vestiges from the Gallo-Roman period), begin year round on weekdays at 4 pm; when the spa is open there are tours daily, except Sunday, from 2.30 to 5.30 pm.

From early May to September, the best way to get to the **Pic du Capucin**, the 1270m-high wooded plateau above the town, is to take the **Funiculaire du Capucin** (funicular railway; ☎ 04 73 65 01 25), ave René Cassin, built in 1898. One-way/return tariffs for adults are 20/26FF. From the upper station, you can link up with the GR30, which wends its way southwards to the Puy de Sancy, or walk back to town.

The **Téléphérique du Sancy** (cable car lift; ☎ 04 73 65 02 73), about 3.5km south of town, swings dramatically to the summit of the Puy de Sancy (also known as the Pic de Sancy), where you can take in the stunning panorama of the northern puys and the southern Monts du Cantal before starting a hike or, in winter, slip-sliding down the slopes.

Except sometimes in October and November, it operates from 9 am to 5 pm daily (to 5.50 pm in July and August), with a closure from 12.30 to 1.30 pm in May, June and September. One-way/return tickets for adults cost 31/38FF.

In winter, a free skiers shuttle bus *(navette)* links Le Mont Dore's train station and tourist office with the cable car. From mid-May to September, the bus runs five times a day (17FF return).

Outdoor Activities

Le Mont Dore is a pleasant and relatively cheap **ski resort**, with 42km of runs on the northern side of the spectacular Puy de Sancy, a few kilometres south of town. Another 40km of runs are found over the hill

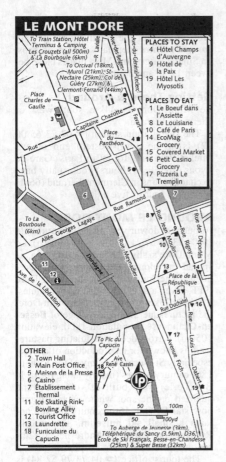

LE MONT DORE

PLACES TO STAY
4 Hôtel Champs d'Auvergne
9 Hôtel de la Paix
19 Hôtel Les Myosotis

PLACES TO EAT
1 Le Boeuf dans l'Assiette
8 Le Louisiane
10 Café de Paris
14 EcoMag Grocery
15 Covered Market
16 Petit Casino Grocery
17 Pizzeria Le Tremplin

OTHER
2 Town Hall
3 Main Post Office
5 Maison de la Presse
6 Casino
7 Établissement Thermal
11 Ice Skating Rink; Bowling Alley
12 Tourist Office
13 Laundrette
18 Funiculaire du Capucin

To Train Station, Hôtel Terminus & Camping Les Crouzets (all 500m) & La Bourboule (6km)

To Orcival (18km), Murol (21km), St-Nectaire (25km), Col de Guéry (27km) & Clermont-Ferrand (44km)

Place Charles de Gaulle

Place du Panthéon

To La Bourboule (6km)

To Pic du Capucin

To Auberge de Jeunesse (3km), Téléphérique du Sancy (3.5km), D36, École de Ski Français, Besse-en-Chandesse (25km) & Super Besse (32km)

at **Super Besse** (☎ 04 73 79 52 84), on the mountain's south-eastern slopes; generally sunnier, this area tends to have less snow. The cross-country network around Le Mont Dore is excellent, with 39km of runs (284km in the whole Sancy-Ouest area).

A lift ticket, good for both Le Mont Dore and Super Besse, costs just 110/283FF (78/195FF for kids under 11) for one/three days.

Renting downhill skis, including boots, at the many ski shops costs 70FF to 110FF a day; cross-country skis are about 45FF. A monoski is about 90FF.

FUAJ (the hostel association) offers week-long skiing packages that include bed, board, equipment and a lift pass – contact the hostel for details.

The forests, lakes, streams and peaks around the Puy de Sancy provide an ideal environment for **walking** and **cycling**. Trails GR4 and GR30 pass by the summit; various other trails are accessible from the top of the Téléphérique du Sancy and the Funiculaire du Capucin (see Things to See & Do earlier in the chapter). Chamina's new topoguide *Massif du Sancy* (45FF) covers the area.

École Ailes Libres (☎ 04 73 39 72 72, fax 04 73 69 40 27) has tandem *bi-place parapente* **flights** for about 400FF. Five-day introductory courses cost 1800FF (2000FF in July and August). The company is based at Camping La Font de Bleix in Les Martres de Veyre, 15km east of Clermont-Ferrand. Visit them on-line at www.ailes.libres .est-ici.org.

Places to Stay
Le Mont Dore has lots of inexpensive accommodation. Book ahead for July and August.

Camping The municipal, two-star *Les Crouzets* (☎ 04 73 65 21 60), across the river from the train station, closes from November to mid-December.

Hostels The *Auberge de Jeunesse* (☎ 04 73 65 03 53, fax 04 73 65 26 39), ideally situated for summer and winter activities, sits in the shadow of Puy de Sancy about 3.5km uphill from the town on Route du Sancy. It opens year round, except perhaps in November and early December. Beds cost 51FF; breakfast is 19FF. Advance reservations are always necessary. For details on the shuttle bus that passes by here, see Things to See & Do earlier in the chapter.

Hotels The two-star *Hôtel de la Paix* (☎ 04 73 65 00 17, fax 04 73 65 00 31, 8 rue Rigny) still has some of its *fin de siècle* grandeur, though the comfortable doubles (200FF to 260FF) are rather nondescript.

MASSIF CENTRAL

It's closed from mid-October until just before Christmas.

The homey, 23-room *Hôtel Champs d'Auvergne* (☎ 04 73 65 00 37, fax 04 73 65 00 30, 18 rue Favart) has basic singles/doubles from 105/135FF (180/210FF with shower and toilet); it's closed from mid-October to 25 December.

The modest, 26-room *Hôtel Terminus* (☎ 04 73 65 00 23, ave Guyot Dessaigne) has average doubles starting at 110FF (175FF with bath). It opens from mid-May to September and mid-December to mid-April.

The slightly fraying but very cheap *Hôtel Les Myosotis* (☎ 04 73 65 01 35, 31 rue Louis Dabert) has basic doubles from 100FF (170FF with shower and toilet); very basic studios with kitchenette cost 120FF to 250FF a night, less by the week.

Places to Eat

Restaurants Hotels with moderately priced *menus* include the restaurant in the *Hôtel Champs d'Auvergne* (see Places to Stay), which specialises in Auvergnat cuisine such as *truffade* (potatoes prepared with very young Cantal cheese) and *fondue Auvergnate* (Cantal cheese fondue; for more information see the special French Cuisine section); the four *menus* cost 58FF to 95FF. Meal times are noon to 1 pm and 7 to 8.30 pm (later in summer).

Fresh regional fare, including fish (such as trout), is the speciality of *Le Louisiane* (☎ 04 73 65 03 14, 2 rue Jean Moulin); *menus* cost 85FF to 150FF. It's closed Wednesday except from May to mid-October.

Le Bœuf dans l'Assiette (☎ 04 73 65 01 23, 9 place Charles de Gaulle) is a wood-panelled place with hearty beef and mutton dishes for 72FF to 92FF; *menus* cost 68FF and 89FF. It's closed Monday except during school holidays.

Pizzeria Le Tremplin (☎ 04 73 65 25 90, 3 ave Foch) opens for dinner (closed on off-season Mondays).

The *Café de Paris* (8 rue Jean Moulin) is a convivial, old-time cafe with beer for 12FF.

Self-Catering The best place to purchase edibles is place de la République, where

either the *Petit Casino* grocery, the *Eco-Mag* grocery or the small, mornings-only *covered market* open daily except, perhaps, on Sunday afternoon. Most places close between 12.30 and 3 pm.

Getting There & Around

Le Mont Dore is 44km south-west of Clermont-Ferrand.

The sleepy train station (☎ 04 73 65 00 02) is at the north-western end of ave Michel Bertrand. To get to Paris' Gare de Lyons (265FF, 5½ hours) you usually have to change trains in Clermont-Ferrand (66FF, 1½ hours, four or five a day).

AROUND LE MONT DORE

About 5km downriver (west), **La Bourboule** (☎ 04 73 65 57 71 for the tourist office), Le Mont Dore's slightly larger sister spa, is spread out along both banks of the Dordogne. The train trip from Le Mont Dore (9FF, seven a day) takes just eight minutes.

About 25km south-east of Le Mont Dore, the picturesque medieval village of **Besse-en-Chandesse** (population 1800, elevation 1050m), surrounded by undulating pastureland, is known for its production of cheese, especially St-Nectaire. Many of the 15th- to 18th-century houses (mainly along rue de la Boucherie) were built of volcanic stone quarried on the spot where each structure now stands. One 15th-century house contains a small **ski museum**. The mostly Romanesque **Église St-André** has a 12th-century nave with carved capitals.

The tourist office (☎ 04 73 79 52 84) is in the centre of the village at place du Docteur Pipet.

The ski station of **Super Besse** (see Outdoor Activities under Le Mont Dore earlier in the chapter), which looks like it was founded in 1962 (it was), is 7km to the west.

About 10km east of Le Mont Dore, the rather ordinary town of **Murol** is known for its squat, almost round **chateau** (☎ 04 73 88 67 11), which has been perched on a hilltop since the 12th century; from April to September actors in period costume recreate scenes from the Middle Ages (45FF, children 30FF). The tourist office (☎ 04 73 88

62 62), rue de Jassaguet, is just up the hill from the *food shops* (*rue George Sand*). See the Web site at www.grandevallee.com.

Lac Chambon, an inexpensive beach resort 1.5 km west of town, has a bunch of hotels, including the two-star, 15-room *Hôtel La Mouteroun* (☎ 04 73 88 63 18), where simple doubles with shower go for 180FF (200FF with toilet). It is open year round.

The spa town of **St-Nectaire**, a few kilometres east of Murol, is best known for its eponymous cheese, its 40 springs and its 12th-century Romanesque church, topped by an octagonal belfry.

For details on bus services to St-Nectaire, Murol, Besse-en-Chandess and Super Besse, see Bus under Getting There & Away in the Clermont-Ferrand section.

PUY MARY

The majestic Puy Mary (1787m), near the southern edge of the Parc des Volcans d'Auvergne, remains snowcapped until late July or early August. In summer, it's an easy, 30-minute climb to the summit – where there's an astounding view – from the **Pas de Peyrol**, a 1582m pass on the D680 that's blocked by snowdrifts between late October and late May. Trails here include the GR4 and GR400.

North of Puy Mary, the D62 follows the verdant River Cheylade valley, passing through rich pastures, deciduous forests and the hamlets of **Cheylade** and **Le Claux**. A tortuously serpentine drive takes you up to the 1364m **Col de Serre** (open year round), a pass 3km north-east of the Pas de Peyrol.

From the Col de Serre, the D680 follows the gentle Santoire Valley eastwards to the tidy village of **Dienne** and the town of Murat.

Places to Stay & Eat

In Dienne, the 10-room *Hôtel de la Poste* (☎ 04 71 20 80 40), opposite the post office on the D680, has doubles/triples/quads with shower and toilet for 250/300/350FF. It's closed December and January.

Right at the Col de Serre, the friendly *Chalet du Col de Serre* (☎ 04 71 78 93 97) serves tasty Auvergnat cuisine daily (except

from mid-November to mid-December). The *menus* cost 75FF to 195FF (49FF for children).

MURAT

postcode 15300 ● **pop 2400**
● **elevation 930m**

The town of Murat, situated in a natural amphitheatre at the foot of a basaltic crag that's topped by a statue of the Virgin Mary, is a good base for exploring the southern reaches of the Parc des Volcans d'Auvergne, including Puy Mary, the 1855m **Plomb du Cantal** (six hours on foot via Prat de Bouc) and the ski station of **Super Lioran**, 10km south-west. Trails passing through Murat include the GR4 and GR400.

The **Maison de la Faune** (☎ 04 71 20 00 52), in the turreted stone building up the stairs to the left as you face the town hall, is a better-than-average museum of stuffed and mounted wildlife. Admission costs 25FF (18FF for students); it opens 10 am to noon and 2 to 5 or 6 pm daily (7 pm in July and August).

The tourist office (☎ 04 71 20 09 47), next to the town hall at the top end of place du Balat, opens daily except perhaps Sunday. Banks open Tuesday to Saturday.

Places to Stay

The *Camping Municipal* (☎ 04 71 20 01 83, rue de la Stade), south of town, opens May to September.

The friendly, five-room *Hôtel du Stade* (☎ 04 71 20 04 73, 35 rue du Faubourg Notre Dame), 300m to the right as you exit the train station, has doubles with washbasin from 120FF. It opens year round. The two-star, 38-room *Hôtel Les Messageries* (☎ 04 71 20 04 04, fax 04 71 20 02 81, 18 ave du Docteur Mallet), across from the train station, has doubles/quads for 260/370FF. It's closed from early November to Christmas.

Getting There & Away

The train station (☎ 04 71 20 07 20) is linked to Clermont-Ferrand (92FF, 1½ hours, five or six a day) and Aurillac (46FF, 45 minutes). One or two direct trains a day serve Toulouse (172FF, 4½ hours).

MASSIF CENTRAL

LE PUY-EN-VELAY
postcode 43000 • pop 25,500
• elevation 629m

Le Puy-en-Velay, capital of the Haute-Loire department, sits amid striking volcanic plugs in a fertile valley near the source of the Loire. The city is very proud of its green lentils, which have earned AOC classification thanks to the area's uniquely rich volcanic soil.

Each of Le Puy-en-Velay's three lava pinnacles is topped by a religious edifice: the largest, on which the old city is built, by the cathedral; the highest, a bit north of the cathedral, by a giant statue of the Virgin; and the steepest, a few hundred metres farther north, by a 10th-century chapel.

The 1600km GR65 footpath begins here, following the medieval Via Podiensis to Santiago de Compostella in Spain.

Orientation
North of the main square, place du Breuil, lies the pedestrianised old city, whose narrow streets head up the hill to the cathedral. Le Puy-en-Velay's commercial centre is around the town hall and between blvd Maréchal Fayolle and rue Chaussade. The train and bus stations are 600m east of place du Breuil.

Information
Tourist Offices The main tourist office (☎ 04 71 09 38 41, fax 04 71 05 22 62), place du Breuil, opens every day of the year from 8.30 am to noon and 1.30 to 6.15 pm (from October to Easter, Sunday hours are 10 am to noon). In July and August hours are 8.30 am to 7.30 pm (9 am to noon and 2 to 6.15 pm on Sunday). A free walking tour brochure is available in English.

The tourist office Web site is at www.otlepuyenvelay.fr.

La Croisée des Chemins (☎ 04 71 04 15 95), the department's walking information office, is across from 14 rue Chèvrerie. It opens 9 am to noon and 1.30 to 6.30 pm (closed Sunday).

From February to October, you can get into Le Puy-en-Velay's four major sights – the cathedral's cloister, Rocher Corneille,

Chapelle St-Michel d'Aiguilhe and the Musée Crozatier – with a discount combination ticket (45FF), available at the tourist office and the sites.

Money The Banque de France, 30 blvd Alexandre Clair, exchanges money from 8.15 am to noon weekdays. Commercial banks – many open Tuesday to Saturday – can be found around the perimeter of place du Breuil.

Post & Communications The main post office, 8 ave de la Dentelle, opens 8 am to 7 pm weekdays and until noon on Saturday. Exchange services and a Cyberposte are available.

You can access the Internet at Logipro. com (☎ 04 71 09 15 53), 8 rue Pierre Farigoule, open 8.30 am to 12.30 pm and 1.30 to 7 pm. It's closed Saturday afternoon, Sunday and Monday.

Bookshop An extensive collection of maps and topoguides are available at the Maison de la Presse, 5 blvd St-Louis. It opens 7.45 am to 12.30 pm and 1.45 to 7.30 pm (closed after 12.15 pm on Sunday and holidays).

Laundry There are laundrettes at 24 rue Portail d'Avignon (open until 8 pm; till 6.30 pm on Sunday and holidays) and 12 rue Chèvrerie (open 7.30 am to noon and 1 to 7.30 or 8 pm).

Things to See & Do
If you picture today's tourists as pilgrims (which they are, in a way), the narrow, cobbled streets of the **old city** look much as they did 800 years ago. Medieval, Gothic and Renaissance houses made of dark volcanic stone can be found along (from east to west) rue Chaussade, rue du Collège, rue Porte Aiguière and rue Pannessac.

The most impressive way to enter **Cathédrale Notre Dame**, a heavily restored Romanesque cathedral begun in the 11th century, is by passing through the massive arches at the top of stone-paved rue des Tables. The structure's Byzantine and

MASSIF CENTRAL

LE PUY-EN-VELAY

PLACES TO STAY
1 Camping de Bouthézard
14 Auberge de Jeunesse (Centre Pierre Cardinal)
26 Hôtel St-Jacques
31 Etap Hôtel
35 Hôtel Le Régional
36 Dyke Hôtel
48 Hôtel Bristol

PLACES TO EAT
18 Restaurant Le Poivrier
19 La Farandole
22 Chantal Paul
24 Le Croco
38 Restaurant Bateau Ivre
40 Les Palmiers
46 Casino Supermarket

OTHER
2 Chapelle St-Michel d'Aiguilhe
3 Temple de Diane (Chapelle St-Clair)

4 Atelier-Conservatoire National de la Dentelle (Temporary Location)
5 Notre Dame de France Statue
6 Entrance to Rocher Corneille
7 Comité Départementale du Tourism
8 Chapelle des Pénitents
9 Cloister
10 Tourist Office Summer Annexe
11 Fountain
12 Cathédrale Notre Dame

13 Toilets
15 ADA Car Rental
16 Centre d'Enseignement de la Dentelle au Fuseau
17 Harry's Bar
20 Les Portraits du Velay
21 Town Hall
23 Municipal Library
25 La Croisée des Chemins
27 Toilets
28 Verveine du Velay Building
29 Le Clandestin
30 Bus Station
32 Train Station
33 Main Post Office
34 Budget Car Rental
37 Laundrette
39 Laundrette
41 Maison de la Presse
42 Bar de l'Aviation
43 Fontaine Crozatier
44 Main Tourist Office
45 Local Bus Hub
47 Logipro.com
49 Palais de Justice
50 Prefecture Building
51 Zoo
52 Childrens Play Areas
53 Musée Crozatier
54 Banque de France

MASSIF CENTRAL

Moorish elements include the six domes over the nave and the ornately patterned stonework. A 17th-century **Vierge Noire** (Black Madonna) takes pride of place on the Baroque high altar. The **11th-century frescoes** in the northern transept arm, and the **stairway** (open on some days from Easter to October) linking the western front directly with the nave, have recently undergone extensive restoration. The cathedral opens 8 am to 6 pm daily (8 pm from Easter to October).

The beautiful **cloister**, built in the 11th and 12th centuries, would look right at home in southern Spain. It can be visited from 9.30 am to noon or 12.30 pm and 2 to 6 pm (4.30 pm from October to March; 6.30 pm in July and August, when there's no midday closure). Admission costs 25FF (15FF if you're aged 12 to 25).

The Renaissance ceiling panels of the richly decorated **Chapelle des Pénitents** (1584), across the alley from the entrance to the cloister, date from 1630.

The massive **Rocher Corneille**, just north of the cathedral and accessible via rue du Cloître, was crowned in 1860 by a jarringly red, 16m-high statue of **Notre Dame de France** made from melted-down cannons captured in the Crimean War. The view – from 130m above place du Breuil – is superb. It opens 9 am until between 5 pm (October to March) and 7.30 pm (July and August). In December and January, it is closed except during school holiday periods and on Sunday afternoons, when opening hours are 2 to 5 pm. Admission costs 20FF (10FF for children and students).

You can admire antique and modern lace and take lacemaking classes (50FF for one hour) at the **Centre d'Enseignement de la Dentelle au Fuseau** (☎ 04 71 02 01 68), 38 rue Raphaël, a non-profit museum and educational centre that seeks to preserve what was once an important local industry (in 1900 the Haute-Loire department had 5000 lace workshops). It opens 10 am to noon and 2 to 5.30 pm weekdays; from mid-June to mid-September, it also opens Saturday from 10 am to 5 pm. Admission costs 12FF. Lace fans may also want to take a look

at the state-owned **Atelier-Conservatoire National de la Dentelle** (☎ 04 71 09 74 41), just west of place Carnot on rue Duguesclin, which is where the French government orders some of the prestigious gifts it gives to visiting heads of state. Free visits start from 10 to 10.45 am and 2 to 2.45 pm on Monday, Tuesday, Thursday and Friday. There are plans to move the atelier to new quarters.

The dark, silent and very medieval **Chapelle St-Michel d'Aiguilhe** (15FF) is perched at the summit of an 85m-high volcanic plug. The 10th-century choir is pre-Romanesque; you can still see traces of the 12th-century murals. The stained glass was installed in 1955. It opens 9 or 10 am to noon and 2 pm to sometime between 5 pm (late March) and 7 pm (mid-June to mid-September, when there's no midday closure). From mid-November to mid-March, it only opens between 2 and 4 pm (closed from mid-November to January, except around Christmas). To get there take bus No 6.

Jardin Henri Vinay is a lovely park with a swan lake, neat flower patches, a small zoo, two creative **children's play areas** and lots of benches. At its southern end you'll find the worthwhile **Musée Crozatier** (☎ 04 71 09 38 90). Exhibits include Gallo-Roman archaeology, folk art, local lace, paintings and some clever mechanical devices from the late 19th century. It opens daily, except Tuesday, from 10 am to noon and 2 to 6 pm (4 pm from October to April, when it's also closed on Sunday morning. Admission costs 20FF (10FF for children and students; free on Sunday afternoon from October to April).

La Distillerie de la Verveine du Velay (☎ 04 71 03 04 11), 6km to the east in St-Germain Laprade (take the N88 then the C150), is famous for its bright green firewater, first brewed in 1859. Tours of the production facilities (45 minutes) run from 10 am to noon and 1.30 to 6.30 pm weekdays (and Saturdays from June to September). Admission costs 28FF (children 10FF).

Places to Stay

Camping The impressively situated, riverside *Camping de Bouthézard* (☎ 04 71 09

55 09), a few hundred metres west of Chapelle St-Michel d'Aiguilhe, opens from a week before Easter until mid-October. Bus No 6 stops outside.

Hostels The 72-bed *Auberge de Jeunesse* (☎ *04 71 05 52 40, fax 04 71 05 61 24, 9 rue Jules Vallès)*, in the old city's Centre Pierre Cardinal (a municipal cultural centre), has beds for 42FF a night. Reception generally opens from 8 am to noon and 2 to 11.30 pm; Sunday hours are 8 to 10 am and 8 to 10 pm (closed weekends and holidays from October to March). If no one is around during opening hours, dial 9 on the wall phone inside the building marked 'Auberge de Jeunesse'. Kitchen facilities are available.

Hotels At *Hôtel Le Régional* (☎ *04 71 09 37 74, 36 blvd Maréchal Fayolle)* adequate doubles cost 130FF (165FF with shower and toilet). Reception closes at noon Sunday (it reopens at 6.30 pm in July and August).

The two-star, 12-room *Hôtel St-Jacques* (☎ *04 71 09 07 74, 7 place Cadelade)*, completely rebuilt in 2000, has doubles with disabled access for 240FF. Another good two-star option is the garden-equipped, 40-room *Hôtel Bristol* (☎ *04 71 09 13 38, fax 04 71 09 51 70, 7 ave Maréchal Foch)*. Comfortable but pretty standard doubles start at 250FF. The modern *Dyke Hôtel* (☎ *04 71 09 05 30, fax 04 71 02 58 66, 37 blvd Maréchal Fayolle)* – a *dyke* (pronounced 'deek') is a volcanic spire – has 15 singles/doubles, some with balconies, from 190/230FF. Reception closes 1 to 5 pm on Sunday from December to February.

The *Etap Hôtel* (☎ *04 71 02 46 22, fax 04 71 02 14 28, 25 ave Charles Dupuy)* has an automatic check-in machine that takes credit cards when reception is closed (after 10 pm). Functional triples start at 230FF (less from November to March).

Places to Eat

Restaurants Four-course lunch *menus* are served at *Chantal Paul* (☎ *04 71 09 09 16, place de la Halle)* for 60FF from 12.15 to 3 pm daily. Another lunch place (closed

Sunday and Monday) open for dinner on Friday and Saturday (daily from about July to September) is *La Farandole* (☎ *04 71 09 71 78, 29 rue Pannesac)*. The *plat du jour* costs 48FF; the *menu* costs 75FF.

The rustically elegant *Restaurant Bateau Ivre* (☎ *04 71 09 67 20, 5 rue Portail d'Avignon)* specialises in classic French and Auvergnat cuisine; *menus* cost 105FF to 185FF. It opens noon to 1.30 pm and 7 to 9 pm (closed Sunday and Monday).

Restaurant Le Poivrier (☎ *04 71 02 41 30, 69 rue Pannessac)* has French and regional *menus* for 79FF to 150FF (closed Monday). In the old city, there are a number of restaurants on or around rue Chenebouterie and rue Raphaël.

Le Croco (☎ *04 71 02 40 13, 5 rue Chaussade)*, a cheery and very popular eatery with meat as well as lighter fare (large salads and baked potato dishes), is closed Monday night and Sunday. Tunisian couscous (55FF to 75FF) is on offer at *Les Palmiers* (☎ *04 71 05 57 60, 66 rue Chaussade)*. It opens daily.

Self-Catering Behind the town hall, there's a Saturday morning *food market* (*place du Plot and place de la Halle)*. A few *food shops* can be found nearby, especially along rue Pannessac. The *Casino* supermarket *(2 ave de la Dentelle)* opens 8.30 am to 8 pm Monday to Saturday.

Entertainment

Cosy and welcoming, *Harry's Bar* (☎ *04 71 02 23 02, 37 rue Raphaël)*, opens 5 pm to 1 am (closed Sunday). The popular *Bar l'Aviation* (*opposite 1 blvd du Breuil)* opens 7 am to 1 am daily.

Le Puy-en-Velay's only discotheque, *Le Clandestin* (☎ *04 71 05 77 53, 20 rue de la Gazelle)* opens Friday and Saturday nights until 5 am and sometimes on Wednesday and Thursday nights.

Shopping

A number of shops around town sell handmade lace. Pieces marked *dentelle du Puy* were made in Le Puy-en-Velay many years ago (there's no longer any commercial lace production here); lace marked *fait main* (handmade) has probably been imported from China.

Les Portraits du Velay (☎ 04 71 02 82 08), a lace shop at 10 rue Raphaël, has lace-making demonstrations from June to August. It opens daily from Easter to September; the rest of the year it only opens in the afternoon (closed Sunday). Visit online at www.dentelledupuy.com.

Lacemaking books and equipment are on sale in the bookshop of the Centre d'Enseignement de la Dentelle au Fuseau.

Getting There & Away

Bus The bus station information office (☎ 04 71 09 25 60), next to the train station, is staffed from 7.30 am to 12.30 pm and 2 to 7 pm (closed Saturday afternoon and Sunday). From Monday to Friday there's one bus a day to Clermont-Ferrand (69FF, 3¼ hours) via Langeac (53.50FF, 40 minutes). On weekdays, during the school term, one bus a day goes to Le Chambon-sur-Lignon (1½ hours).

Train Le Puy-en-Velay's sleepy train station (☎ 0 836 35 35 35), at the eastern end of ave Charles Dupuy, has limited rail services.

Destinations include Lyons (108FF, 2½ hours, seven to nine a day), Nîmes (167FF; a beautiful trip via the Gorges de l'Allier) and Clermont-Ferrand (108FF, 2¼ hours, four or five a day).

Car ADA (☎ 04 71 05 23 17) is at 34 rue du Faubourg St-Jean; Budget (☎ 04 71 09 06 24) is at 3 ave de la Dentelle.

Getting Around

Information on the local bus network, run by TUDIP, is available at the tourist office. All six lines pass by the tourist office (place Michelet). Parking in the city centre is metred. In a *zone verte* (green zone) you can park all day for 20FF; *zones oranges* (orange zones) are more restrictive.

AROUND LE PUY-EN-VELAY

The roads around Le Puy-en-Velay offer plenty of scenic drives.

Le Chambon-sur-Lignon

This quiet, neat village (population 2900) 45km east of Le Puy-en-Velay, belatedly known for its WWII heroism (see the boxed text 'Quiet Heroism in Le Chambon-sur-Lignon' later in the chapter), is surrounded by pastureland and forests that are neither spectacular nor flashy, which is part of the area's charm. Warm-weather activities in and around the village include walking, cycling, swimming, windsurfing, horse riding, golf and go-carting. Across the street from the Protestant **temple** is a bronze **plaque** erected in Chambon's honour by Jews saved here as children; the small Catholic church is two blocks away. In July and August there may be an exposition on the town's WWII history.

The tourist office (☎ 04 71 59 71 56, fax 04 71 65 88 78), in the old town hall on rue de la Mairie, opens 9 am to 12.05 pm and 3 to 6 pm Monday to Saturday (2.30 to 6.30 pm June to September, when it also opens at least 11 am to noon on Sunday).

The two-star, 17-room *Hôtel Beau Soleil* (*☎ 04 71 59 72 77, 39 rue de Tence*) has spotless, simply furnished singles/doubles with shower and toilet from 160/200FF (20FF to 30FF more between April and September). The *Eco Service* supermarket, just down the hill from the central place de la Fontaine, opens daily except Sunday afternoon.

On weekdays during the school term, one bus a day links Chambon with Le Puy (1½ hours). There are two buses a day (one on Sunday and holidays) to/from the bus station in Valence (2½ hours).

Mont Mézenc

South of Le Chambon-sur-Lignon, the D500 and D262 take you to the scenic D410, from which the D400 – or, if you're coming from Les Estables (☎ 04 71 08 31 08 for the tourist office), the D631 – winds its way up to the 1508m col known as La Croix des Boutières. Here you can link up with the GR7 and GR73 for the half-hour hike to the summit of 1753m Mont Mézenc (pronounced 'meh-**zah**', rhymes with *fin*), marked by two viewpoint indicators. On a clear day, the view is absolutely stunning:

Quiet Heroism in Le Chambon-sur-Lignon

The village of Le Chambon-sur-Lignon, east of Le Puy-en-Velay in the Montagne Protestante (a remote highland area with a long-standing Protestant majority), has a tradition of sheltering the persecuted dating back to the 17th century, when the Huguenots fled here. Throughout WWII, Chambon and nearby hamlets 'hid, protected and saved' some 2500 or 3000 refugees, including many Jews (and hundreds of Jewish children) being hunted by French police and the Gestapo. A crucial role in this nonviolent – and very dangerous – resistance to the Nazis was played by the local religious leadership, led by Pastor André Trocmé. The town's relatively unknown 'conspiracy of goodness' was featured in Pierre Sauvage's award-winning documentary 'Weapons of the Spirit' (1989), Phillip P Hallie's nonfiction work *Lest Innocent Blood Be Shed* (1989) and Robert Daley's recent novel *The Innocents Within*.

Today, Chambon continues its venerable tradition of welcoming the disadvantaged by taking in orphans and children from troubled families, both in institutions (such as the Collège-Lycée International Cévenol) and in local homes.

you can see literally the entire south-eastern quarter of France, from Mont Blanc (200km to the north-east) to Mont Ventoux (140km to the south-east).

The River Loire begins near the **Gerbier de Jonc**, a 1551m stone outcrop with a *gîte d'étape* (☎ 04 75 38 81 51) at its base. Beds cost 50FF; the family-run *restaurant* serves cuisine of the Ardèche region with *menus* for 68FF to 105FF. Both close from mid-November to early January.

Forteresse de Polignac

On the outskirts of Le Puy-en-Velay, about 5km north-west of the town centre, the remains of this 9th- to 15th-century fortress (also known as the Château and the Donjon de Polignac; ☎ 04 71 02 46 57) sit on a volcanic plateau formed as the surrounding countryside eroded away. It was once home to the powerful Polignac family, who virtually ruled Velay from the 11th to the 14th centuries. From Easter to October it can be visited daily; it opens 2 to 6.30 pm in May and from 10 am to 7 pm June to September. Admission costs 15FF.

Gorges de l'Allier

About 30km west of Le Puy-en-Velay, the salmon-filled River Allier – paralleled by the scenic Langeac–Langogne (Paris–Nîmes) rail line (two to six trains a day) – weaves between rocky, scrub-covered hills hun-dreds of metres high. Above the river's right (eastern) bank, the narrow **D301** affords some fine panoramas as it passes through wild countryside and a number of remote, mud-puddle hamlets. Several villages in the area – including **Prades**, which also has a small sand beach – have Romanesque churches. Just north of Prades is the two-star, 18-room *Chalet de la Source* (☎ 04 71 74 02 39, on the D48), open April to October; doubles start at 230FF. In scenic **Monistrol d'Allier**, AN Rafting (☎ 04 71 57 23 90) organises river trips by raft, canoe and kayak. Visit their Web site at www.an-rafting.com. Other outdoor options include walking, cycling and rock climbing.

In tidy **Langeac** (population 4500), the largest town in the area, sights include Collégiale St-Gal, a 15th-century Gothic church, and the Renaissance-style Maison du Jacquemart, which houses a small museum. The well-equipped tourist office (☎ 04 71 77 05 41), place Aristide Briand, opens Tuesday to Saturday (open daily except Sunday afternoon from June to September). The one-star, 12-room *Hôtel Central* (☎ 04 71 77 05 99), next to the tourist office, has upbeat doubles from 150FF (200FF with bath and toilet).

From Monday to Friday, one bus a day links Langeac with Clermont-Ferrand (2½ hours) and Le Puy (40 mintues). Two or three trains go daily to Clermont-Ferrand (81FF, 1½ hours) and Nîmes (3¼ hours).

Limousin, the Dordogne & Quercy

The adjacent regions of Limousin, the Dordogne (Périgord) and Quercy are tucked away in south-western France between the Massif Central and the vineyard-covered lowlands around Bordeaux. Although they share similar histories and are firmly steeped in rural life, each has its own distinctive landscape, ambience and cuisine.

Limousin

The tranquil, green hills of Limousin, dotted with old churches and castles, present the quintessential image of rural France. Long overlooked by tourists, the region's many rivers, springs and lakes now attract visitors interested in such outdoor pursuits as sailing, canoeing, kayaking and fishing. The local economy is based on agriculture, in particular cattle and sheep farming.

The least densely populated region of France, Limousin is made up of three departments: Haute-Vienne, in the west, whose prefecture is the city of Limoges; the rural Creuse, in the north-east; and, in the south-east, the Corrèze, blessed with many of the region's most beautiful sights.

LIMOGES
**postcode 87000 • pop 221,000
• elevation 300m**
The pleasant though hardly compelling city of Limoges has long been acclaimed for its production of enamel and fine porcelain – museums and galleries dedicated to these arts are one of the city's main attractions. Known around Europe for its top-flight basketball team, Limoges also has a small but animated nightlife scene, thanks largely to the presence of some 17,000 students.

Orientation
The train station is 500m north-east of place

Highlights

- **Vézère Valley** – take in the 14,000-year-old cave paintings at the Font de Gaume or Combarelles caves
- **Sarlat-la-Canéda** – wander around the beautiful, stone-built old town
- **Limoges** – view the outstanding porcelain and enamel collections
- **Pretty Villages** – explore some of France's most charming villages (Gimel-les-Cascades, Collonges-la-Rouge) and bastides (Domme, Monpazier and Najac)
- **Cahors Area** – bask in the glorious Midi sunshine along the River Lot
- **Gouffre de Padirac** – take a boat ride along an underground river

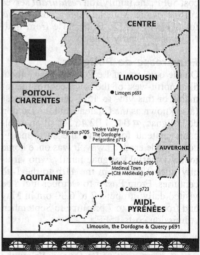

Jourdan. The Cité Quarter and its cathedral are south of place Jourdan and east of the partly pedestrianised commercial centre, the chateau-less Château Quarter.

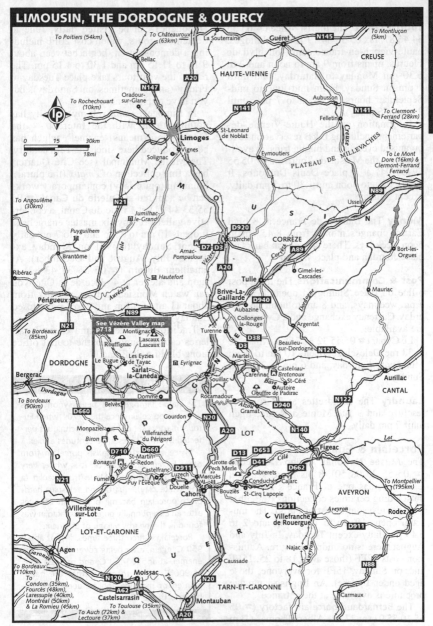

LIMOUSIN, THE DORDOGNE & QUERCY

Information

Tourist Office The tourist office (☎ 05 55 34 46 87, fax 05 55 34 19 12, ☻ otlimoges. haute-vienne-en-france.com), on blvd de Fleurus, opens from 9 am to noon and 2 to 6.30 pm Monday to Saturday, and until 1 pm on Sunday. From mid-June to mid-September hours are 9 am to 7 pm (until 2 pm on Sunday).

Information on the Haute-Vienne département, including B&B reservations and organised cycling and hiking trips, is available from the Maison du Tourisme (☎ 05 55 79 04 04) at 4 place Denis Dussoubs. It opens 9 am to noon and 1.30 to 5 pm daily, except Sunday.

Money The Banque de France at 8 blvd Carnot changes money from 8.45 am to noon weekdays. There are several banks on place Jourdan and place Wilson.

Post & Communications The main post office on place Stalingrad opens 8 am to 7 pm weekdays, and 8 am to noon on Saturday. Currency exchange and a Cyberposte are available.

Le Cybar (☎ 05 55 32 31 71), a cybercafe at 33 rue Delescluze, opens 10 am to 2 am Monday to Saturday, and 6 pm to 2 am on Sunday.

Laundry The laundrettes at 28 rue Delescluze and 9 rue Monte a Regret open until 9 pm daily.

Porcelain & Enamel

The **Musée National Adrien Dubouché** (☎ 05 55 33 08 50), 8 bis place Winston Churchill, has one of France's two most outstanding ceramics collections (the other is in Sèvres, south-west of Paris). The museum opens 10 am to 12.30 pm and 2 to 5.45 pm daily except Tuesday. In July and August there is no midday closure. Admission costs 22FF (those aged 18 to 25, 15FF and, on Sunday, 15FF for everyone; those aged under 18 free). An English-language brochure is available at the entrance.

The **Bernardaud porcelain factory** (☎ 05 55 10 55 91) at 27 ave Albert Thomas (1km north-west of the Musée National Adrien Dubouché) can be visited daily, June to September; tours, which cost 20FF including a demonstration, begin between about 9.15 to 11.15 am and 1.30 to 4.15 pm. The rest of the year tours take place Tuesday to Friday (and sometimes on Saturday), but you have to phone ahead.

In Limoges, *émail* (eh-**my**) usually has nothing to do with the Internet – the French word means 'enamel', which has been produced here since the 12th century. The Musée Municipal (see Cité Quarter) has a fine collection of *émaux* (the plural). Stunning (but pricey) contemporary works can be admired at **Galerie du Canal** (☎ 05 55 33 14 11) at 15 rue du Canal, a cooperative gallery run by six master enamelists. It opens 10 am to noon and 2 to 7 pm daily except Sunday (closed on Monday except in July, August and December). At **Émailleur Buforn** (☎ 05 55 32 43 82), a shop and atelier at 4 place de la Cité, you can watch Monsieur Buforn at work from about 11 am to 1 pm and 2 to 7 pm (closed Sunday).

Traditional porcelain and enamel galleries can be found near the tourist office along blvd Louis Blanc.

Porcelain

The name Limoges has been synonymous with fine porcelain since the 1770s, when European artists set out to copy techniques perfected by the Chinese five centuries earlier.

Three factors distinguish porcelain from other baked-clay ceramics: it is white, very hard and translucent. Made from kaolin (a fine white clay), quartz and feldspar, hard-paste porcelain became popular in Limoges after an exceptionally pure form of kaolin was found in the nearby village of St-Yrieix.

Porcelain is fired three times: first at about 950°C; again, after being covered with liquid enamel, at about 1450°C; and one last time, at 900°C or so, to ensure that the hand-painted or machine-applied decoration adheres to the surface.

LIMOUSIN

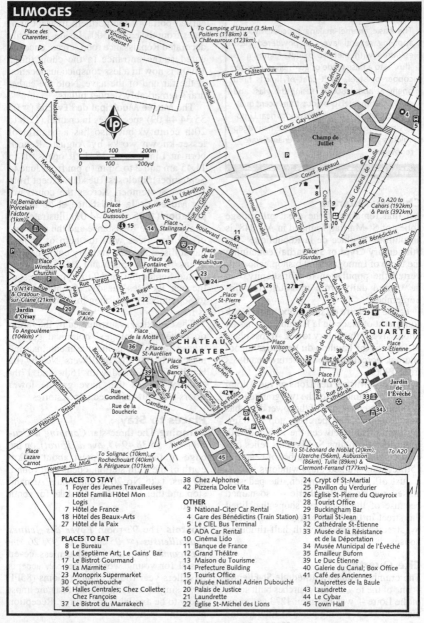

LIMOGES

LIMOUSIN

euro currency converter €1 = 6.56FF

PLACES TO STAY	38 Chez Alphonse	24 Crypt of St-Martial
1 Foyer des Jeunes Travailleuses	42 Pizzeria Dolce Vita	25 Pavillon du Verdurier
2 Hôtel Familia Hôtel Mon		26 Église St-Pierre du Queyroix
Logis	**OTHER**	28 Tourist Office
7 Hôtel de France	3 National-Citer Car Rental	29 Buckingham Bar
18 Hôtel des Beaux-Arts	4 Gare des Bénédictins (Train Station)	31 Pavillon St-Jean
27 Hôtel de la Paix	5 Le CIEL Bus Terminal	32 Cathédrale St-Étienne
	6 ADA Car Rental	33 Musée de la Résistance
PLACES TO EAT	10 Cinéma Lido	et de la Déportation
8 Le Bureau	11 Banque de France	34 Musée Municipal de l'Évêché
9 Le Septième Art; Le Gains' Bar	12 Grand Théâtre	35 Émailleur Buforn
19 La Marmite	13 Maison du Tourisme	39 Le Duc Étienne
23 Monoprix Supermarket	14 Prefecture Building	40 Galerie du Canal; Box Office
30 Croquembouche	15 Tourist Office	41 Café des Anciennes
36 Halles Centrales; Chez Collette;	16 Musée National Adrien Dubouché	Majorettes de la Baule
Chez Françoise	20 Palais de Justice	43 Laundrette
37 Le Bistrot du Marrakech	21 Laundrette	44 Le Cybar
	22 Église St-Michel des Lions	45 Town Hall

The Art of Enamel

The basic enamel-making process involves applying several layers of powdered glass coloured with metallic oxides – known as 'flux' – to a base made of gold, silver, bronze, copper or steel. Each coat of flux is fired briefly at about 800°C, fusing the glass and giving the enamel its unique translucent quality. Deposits of rare metallic oxides near Limoges make it possible to create the rich, deep colours for which the city's enamelware is renowned.

Château Quarter

All that remains of the great pilgrimage abbey of St-Martial, founded in AD 848, is an outline on place de la République. The 9th-century **Crypt of St-Martial**, containing the tomb of Limoges' first bishop, who converted the population to Christianity, can be visited daily from mid-June to mid-September.

Église St-Pierre du Queyroix, half a block south-east of place de la République, has an impressive 13th-century tower. Across place St-Pierre is the **Pavillon du Verdurier**, an octagonal, porcelain-faced structure that dates from 1900.

Église St-Michel des Lions on rue Adrien Dubouché, named after the two granite lions standing on either side of the tower door, has a huge copper ball perched atop its 65m-high spire. Built between the 14th and 16th centuries, it contains St-Martial's relics (including his head) and a number of beautiful 15th-century stained-glass windows.

Just off place St-Aurélien, the pedestrianised **rue de la Boucherie** – so named because of the butchers' shops that lined the street in the Middle Ages – and nearby streets are graced with half-timbered houses.

Cité Quarter

The crumbly granite **Cathédrale St-Étienne** – one of the few Gothic churches built south of the Loire – was begun in 1273 and completed in 1888. Facing place St-Étienne, the

Flamboyant Gothic **Portail St-Jean** (the carved portal of the northern transept arm) dates from the early 1500s. Inside, the richly decorated Renaissance rood screen, once situated at the entrance to the choir (circa 1300), is now in a less conspicuous location at the far end of the nave. Note the cathedral's remarkably slender pillars.

The **Musée Municipal de l'Évêché** (☎ 05 55 34 44 09) specialises in enamel (12th to 20th century) but also has a handful of lesser-known works by Auguste Renoir, born in Limoges in 1841. It opens 10 to 11.45 am and 2 to 5 pm (6 pm from June to September); it closes Tuesday, except from July to September. Across the courtyard, the **Musée de la Résistance et de la Déportation** (☎ 05 55 34 44 09) illustrates the exploits of the Resistance and the suffering of the deportees with the help of photos, handbills, maps and military equipment. It opens 10 to 11.45 am and 2 to 6 pm, June to mid-September; and 2 to 5 pm, the rest of the year. It closes Tuesday, except from July to September. Admission to both museums is free.

The cathedral is surrounded by the **Jardin de l'Évêché**, Limoges' botanical garden, whose formal beds include medicinal and toxic herbs and lots of flowers. Nearby **rue Haute Cité** is lined with 16th- and 17th-century houses that have granite lower floors and half-timbered upper stories.

Places to Stay

Camping The three-star *Camping d'Uzurat* (☎ 05 55 38 49 43, ave d'Uzurat), on the edge of the Bastide forest about 3.5km north of the train station, opens year round. By bus, take No 20 to the Louis Armand stop and then walk along the lake for about 600m.

Hostels The 93-room *Foyer des Jeunes Travailleuses* (☎ 05 55 77 63 97, 20 rue d'Encombe Vineuse), a charmless co-ed hostel for young working people, accepts travellers year round, though rooms (85FF for a single, including breakfast) are most likely to be available in summer. Reception is staffed 24 hours.

Hotels The 14-room, one-star *Hôtel Mon Logis* (☎ 05 55 77 41 43, *16 rue du Général du Bessol*) has singles/doubles with shower for 130/158FF (187/240FF for doubles/ quads with shower and toilet). Next door, the 14-room, two-star *Hôtel Familia* (☎ 05 55 77 51 40, *18 rue du Général du Bessol*) has quiet doubles with shower and toilet from 215FF.

The welcoming, 17-room *Hôtel de France* (☎ 05 55 77 78 92, *fax 05 55 77 71 75, 23 cours Bugeaud*) has small, basic, pastel-toned singles/doubles from 150/ 170FF (205/230FF for larger rooms with shower and toilet). The 21-room, one-star *Hôtel des Beaux-Arts* (☎ 05 55 79 42 20, *fax 05 55 79 29 13, 28 blvd Victor Hugo*) has rugs that are showing their age and somewhat tacky doubles starting at 140FF (215FF with shower and toilet).

The 31-room *Hôtel de la Paix* (☎ 05 55 34 36 00, *fax 05 55 32 37 06, 25 place Jourdan*) has a fantastic collection of 250 museum-quality gramophones (worth a visit even if you're staying elsewhere) and comfortable shower-equipped doubles for 210FF (270FF with toilet). There's free parking out front.

Places to Eat

Restaurants Inside the Halles Centrales (see Self-Catering), a couple of inexpensive, lunch-only restaurants – *Chez Colette* (closed Sunday and Monday) and *Chez Françoise* (closed Sunday and holidays) – cater to people who work nearby. *Chez Alphonse* (☎ 05 55 34 34 14, *5 place de la Motte*), an old-time bistro, has a *menu* for 79FF (closed Sunday). *Le Bistrot du Marrakech* (☎ 05 55 34 49 68, *11 place de la Motte*) serves *tajines*, *pastillas* (round, poultry-filled pastries) and – at their adjacent bistro – couscous. It is open daily.

Périgord specialities are on offer at intimate *La Marmite* (☎ 05 55 33 38 34, *1 place Fontaine des Barres*) which occupies a rustic, 17th-century house. *Menus* start at 90FF (70FF for a two-course lunch). It is closed Monday at midday and Sunday. *Le Bistrot Gourmand* (☎ 05 55 10 29 29, *5 place Winston Churchill*) serves tasty,

bistro-style cuisine from noon to 3 pm and 7 pm to midnight daily except Sunday; fish and meat mains cost from 49FF to 84FF.

The popular and reasonably priced eateries along cours Jourdan include *Le Septième Art* (☎ 05 55 10 71 70, *4 cours Jourdan*), a brasserie that opens 11 am to 1 am daily, and the spacious *Au Bureau* (☎ 05 55 79 88 55, *25 cours Jourdan*), which also opens daily.

Near the cathedral, there are a number of small restaurants on and around rue Haute Cité. A good bet for a light lunch is *Le Croquembouche* (☎ 05 55 33 17 54, *14 rue Haute Cité*), a *salon de thé* that serves meals from noon to 4 pm and tea until 7 pm. It is closed at the weekend.

Pizzeria Dolce Vita (☎ 05 55 32 92 80, *4 rue des Petites Pousses*) serves pizzas baked in a wood-fired oven; it opens daily, except – in winter – Sunday at midday.

Self-Catering The *Halles Centrales* (covered marked), on place de la Motte, opens every morning until 1 pm. The *Monoprix* supermarket (*42 rue Jean Jaurès*) opens 8.30 am to 8 pm Monday to Saturday.

Entertainment

Tickets for cultural events all over south-west France are available from *Box Office* (☎ 05 55 33 28 16, *3 place St-Aurelien*), which is closed Sunday and Monday. *Cinéma Lido* (☎ 05 55 77 26 71, *3 ave du Général de Gaulle*) screens non dubbed films.

The *Café des Anciènnes Majorettes de la Baule* (☎ 05 55 34 34 16), near the top of rue Haute Vienne, is a rambling, wood-floored cafe with book-lined walls (the second-hand books, some in English, are for sale) and live music on Friday at 10 pm. It opens 10 am to 2 am Tuesday to Saturday. *Le Duc Étienne* (*place St-Aurélien*) is a small, mellow bar popular with students; beers start at 10FF. It opens 2 pm (6 pm on Sunday) to 2 am daily.

The pubs along cours Jourdan include *Le Gains' Bar*, attached to Le Septième Art (see Restaurants) and named after Serge Gainsbourg, dubbed the French Bob Dillon by some. Popular with students (and not just because beer starts at just 10FF), it opens 11 am to 3 am, and, except in summer, there is live music a couple of times a month. *Au Bureau* (see Restaurants), open as a bar until 2 am, has music (either live or DJ) from 11 pm on Thursday and Friday.

Buckingham (☎ 05 55 33 66 73, *23 blvd St-Maurice*) is popular with students, especially as a late-night last stop, and has a dancefloor. It opens 8 pm to 2 am Monday to Wednesday nights, to 3 am on Thursday and Friday, and 4 am on Saturday. There is no cover charge.

Because of its several apparently quenching pubs, rue Charles Michels (near Pizzeria Dolce Vita) has been nicknamed 'rue de la Soif' (Thirst Street) by local students.

Getting There & Away

Bus Buses to destinations such as Oradour-sur-Glane (16.50FF), St-Léonard de Noblat (25FF by SNCF bus), Solignac and Rochechouart depart from Le CIEL (Centre Intermodal d'Échanges de Limoges; ☎ 05 55 10 91 95), the brand-new bus terminal situated right across the tracks from the train station.

Train The green-domed, Art Deco-style Gare des Bénédictins (☎ 0 836 35 35 35), completed in 1929, is one of the most striking train stations in all of France. Destinations include Paris' Gare d'Austerlitz (231FF, three hours, four or five daily), Aubusson (73FF, 1¾ hours, two daily except Sunday), Cahors (136FF, 2¼ hours, four or five daily), Périgueux (81FF, one hour, seven to 11 daily, four on Saturday), Tulle (99FF, two hours, two direct daily except Sunday) and Uzerche (55FF, 40 minutes, four to eight daily).

Car ADA (☎ 05 55 79 61 12) is at 27 ave du Général de Gaulle; National-Citer (☎ 05 55 77 10 10) is at 8 cours Gay-Lussac.

AROUND LIMOGES
Oradour-sur-Glane

This village (see the boxed text 'Silence Bears Witness'), site of a horrific SS massacre in 1944, has been turned into a moving and evocative memorial.

Four buses daily link Le CIEL in Limoges with Oradour-sur-Glane (16.50FF, 30 minutes). By car, take the D9 and follow the road signs to the *village martyr* (martyred village).

Solignac

The medieval village of Solignac (population 1350), 10km south of Limoges on the River Briance, owes its outsized, 75m-long granite **church** to its popularity as a stopover on the pilgrimage route to Santiago de Compostela (Spain). Built during the 2nd quarter of the 1100s in the Limousin-Romanesque style, the sober, one-time abbey church is – thanks to the domed roof – remarkably wide (14m) and (considering that it's pre-Gothic) pretty well-lit. The **stalls** in the nave, made for the Benedictines in the late 1400s, are decorated with carved human heads and bizarre animals – and a monk mooning the world. Above the stalls, the **capitals** of the columns – intended to further the moral education of the faithful – are decorated with human figures being devoured by dragons and serpents. There's a 15th-century **fresco** of St-Christophe on the southern (right-hand) wall of the choir. One of the transept arms is crowned with a dome, the other by a barrel arch.

The 12km-long **Sentier de la Briance**, with yellow trail markings, takes you through the surrounding countryside, much of it forested. The **Parc du Reynou**, a free-run animal park a few kilometres away in Le Vigen, was devastated by storms in December 1999.

The tourist office (☎ 05 55 00 42 31) on the car park across the street from the church, opens in the afternoon Wednesday to Sunday, and in the morning on Thursday and Saturday, as well as on holidays. When it's closed, brochures are available from the Secrétariat on the 1st floor of the Mairie (village hall) at 57 ave St-Eloi, 150m west of the church.

Hôtel Le St-Eloi (☎ 05 55 00 44 52, *fax 05 55 00 55 56, 66 ave St-Eloi*), 150m from the church's western front, has Provençal-style rooms from 280FF. The attached *restaurant* has *menus* from 78FF (closed Sunday night and Monday at midday).

Silence Bears Witness

Oradour-sur-Glane, 21km north-west of Limoges, was an unexceptional Limousin town until the afternoon of 10 June 1944, when German lorries bearing an SS detachment rumbled into town.

The town's entire population was ordered to assemble at the market square. The men were divided into groups and forced into *granges* (barns), where they were gunned down before the structures were set alight. Several hundred women and children were herded into the church, inside which a bomb was detonated; those who tried to escape through the windows were shot before the building was set on fire. The Nazi troops then burned down the entire town; inside the 328 buildings left smouldering that evening were the corpses of dozens of civilians who had hidden to avoid capture. Of the people rounded up that day – among them refugees from Paris and a couple of Jewish families living under assumed names – only one woman and five men survived; 642 people, including 205 children, were killed.

Since these events, the entire village has been left untouched to serve as a memorial (open 24 hours; no admission charge). The cafe still has its tables and chairs, two rusting vehicles are still parked inside the ruins of the garage, and the houses are furnished with moss-covered bedposts, bicycles and treadle sewing machines. The tram tracks and overhead wires, the prewar-style electricity lines and the rusting hulks of 1930s automobiles give a pretty good idea of what the town must have looked like on the morning of the massacre. The crypt-like **Mémorial**, under the altar-shaped platform next to the cemetery, displays personal effects found in the debris.

After the war, a larger Oradour was built a few hundred metres west of the ruins.

When school is in session, one bus daily (except Sunday) links Le CIEL in Limoges with Solignac (25 minutes); and year-round buses link Limoges with the neighbouring hamlet of Le Vigen (two or three daily). The Solignac-Le Vigen train station is linked to Limoges (15FF, 10 minutes) and Uzerche (46FF, 40 minutes) by one or two trains daily.

AUBUSSON
postcode 23200 • pop 5100
• elevation 300m

Aubusson, about 90km from both Limoges and Clermont-Ferrand, has been acclaimed for its exquisite tapestries and carpets for over 500 years. These days the town, in something of an economic slump, and nearby Felletin (10km to the south) are home to about 30 tapestry workshops, whose products – both traditional and contemporary in style – are on display from June to September at the **Forum de la Tapisserie** (15FF). Held inside the town hall on the Grande Rue (the main drag), it opens until 6.30 or 7 pm daily (5.30 pm on Sundays in early June and late September).

Across the curvaceous River Creuse, on the other side of the hill (on top of which sit the ruins of the chateau), is the modest **Musée Départemental de la Tapisserie** (☎ 05 55 66 33 06). The changing exhibits of antique and modern tapestries can be visited from 9.30 am to noon and 2 to 6 pm (closed Tuesday; no midday closure in July and August). Admission costs 20FF (children, students and seniors 15FF). The town's tapestry workshops include the large **Manufacture St-Jean** (☎ 05 55 66 10 08) on ave des Lissiers, 200m from the Musée Départemental, which can be toured for 35FF from 9 am to noon and 2 to 5 pm on weekdays.

The tourist office (☎ 05 55 66 32 12), down the alley from 65 Grande Rue, can provide details on visiting many of the area's other tapestry ateliers, most of which have no admission fee. It opens 10 am to 7 pm (10 am to noon and 2.30 to 5.30 pm on Sunday and holidays), mid-June to mid-September; and 9.30 am to noon or 12.30 pm and 2.30 to 5.30 pm Monday to Saturday, mid-September to Easter (6.30 pm from Easter to mid-June, when it also opens on Sunday until 5.30 pm). Next door, the

LIMOUSIN

16th-century **Maison du Tapissier** houses a museum of the history of tapestry-making. Opening hours are the same as those of the tourist office, which handles ticket sales; admission costs 17FF.

Places to Stay

The *Hôtel du Lissier* (☎ 05 55 66 14 18, 84 Grande Rue) has plain but serviceable singles/doubles from 120/150FF (220/250FF with shower and toilet). Reception is closed on Sunday and, in winter, on Monday night. At the 12-room *Hôtel Le Chapitre* (☎ 05 55 66 18 54, 53 Grande Rue) doubles with shower and toilet cost 190FF.

Getting There & Away

Aubusson is linked to Limoges (73FF, 1¾ hours) by two SNCF buses daily, except Sunday.

UZERCHE

postcode 19140 • pop 3270
• elevation 450m

Set on a promontory high above the River Vézère, the picturesque town of Uzerche – much quieter since the A20 began diverting most traffic around the town – is known for its 15th- and 16th-century **Maisons à Tourelles**, which look like small castles thanks to their turrets. Some fine examples can be seen around **Porte Bécharie**, a 14th-century town gate near place Marie Colein.

At the top of the hill, high above the steep, dark grey slate rooftops, is **Église St-Pierre**, a barrel-vaulted, Romanesque abbey church with a typically Limousin-style belfry and an 11th-century crypt, reached through a squat door in the outside wall of the choir. It opens daily, all day long. From July to September, there's an exhibition of Limousin archaeology in the 17th-century **Hôtel du Sénéchal** at 14 rue de la Justice.

Take the D3 under the railway viaduct to get a panoramic view of the town.

Orientation & Information

The old city is perched on a hill almost entirely surrounded by a hairpin curve in the Vézère. The only street into the old city is at shop-lined place Marie Colein, which is

about 500m up the D920 (ave de Paris) from the D3.

The tourist office (☎ 05 55 73 15 71), behind the church, opens 9 am to 12.30 pm and 2 to 6.30 pm daily, mid-June to September; and 8 am to noon and 12.30 to 5.30 pm on weekdays and 10 am to 1 pm on Saturday the rest of the year.

Places to Stay & Eat

The attractive, 14-room, two-star *Hôtel Jean Teyssier* (☎ 05 55 73 10 05, fax 05 55 98 43 31, at the intersection of the N20 and the D3) has doubles from 300FF. Reception is closed on Wednesday (open on Wednesday evening from 5 pm between mid-July and mid-September). The attached *restaurant* (closed Wednesday and, except in summer, on Tuesday at midday) has *menus* from 100FF to 250FF.

You might also try the 21-room *Hôtel Bellevue* (☎ 05 55 73 14 43, place Marie Colein), next to the post office, where doubles start at 120FF (200FF with shower and toilet). Reception is closed from about 3 to 5 pm.

Getting There & Away

Uzerche is linked to Limoges, 56km to the north, by train (55FF, 40 minutes, five to nine daily). The train station is 2km north of the old city along the N20.

BRIVE-LA-GAILLARDE

postcode 19100 • pop 50,000
• elevation 320m

Brive-La-Gaillarde, known for its champion rugby team, is a hole: sprawling, ugly and of virtually no interest. However, nearby areas of the Corrèze département include some of Limousin's most attractive towns and villages. A major rail junction, it can be used as a transport, provisioning and accommodation base.

Information

The tourist office (☎ 05 55 24 08 80, fax 05 55 24 58 24, **℮** tourisme.brive@wanadoo .fr), housed in a 19th-century water tower on place du 14 Juillet, opens 9 am to 7 pm Monday to Saturday and 10 am to 1 pm

Sunday during July and August. The rest of the year it opens 9 am to noon and 2 to 6 pm Monday to Saturday, except holidays.

Places to Stay

Near the train station, the cluster of cheap hotels along ave Jean Jaurès includes the 32-room *Hôtel Majestic et Voyageurs* (☎ *05 55 24 10 20, 67 ave Jean Jaurès*), where rooms with a bit of old-time charm start at 90FF (120FF with shower and toilet). Another decent hotel that has hardly changed in decades is the *Grand Hôtel Terminus* (☎ *05 55 74 21 14*), facing the train station, which is marginally more expensive.

Getting There & Around

Brive is the region's major rail and bus hub – see the relevant town and city listings for details. The bus station (☎ 05 55 74 20 13), on place du 14 Juillet (next to the tourist office), is staffed from 8.15 am to noon and 2 to 6.30 pm Monday to Saturday. Local and intercity buses do not run on Sunday or holidays.

The train station is linked to the tourist office and the nearby bus station, 1.3 km to the south-west, by the hourly bus No 5, which runs until a bit before 7 pm.

NORTH-EAST OF BRIVE
Aubazine

The restful, idyllic village of Aubazine sits on a hilltop surrounded by forests, sloping pastureland and verdant valleys. The tourist office (☎ 05 55 25 79 93) is in the village hall on place de l'Église, the main square.

The 12th-century, Romanesque **church** contains an extremely rare **armoire liturgique** (liturgical chest), made of oak in the late 1100s; and the elaborately carved, 13th-century limestone **tomb** of Étienne d'Obazine, founder of the Cistercian abbey to which the church once belonged. About 300m north of the church, along route de Tulle, the small, Greek Melchite (Catholic) monastery has a modern, Byzantine-style **Chapelle Grecque** (Greek Chapel; open all day).

One of the area's footpaths heads up the hill to the **Puy de Paulliac** (or Pauliat; 520m), which has a *cromlech* (dolmen) at

the top and affords fine views. For part of the way it follows the abbey's one-time aqueduct, the **Canal des Moines**.

The 24-room, two-star *Hôtel de la Tour* (☎ *05 55 25 71 17, fax 05 55 84 61 83, place de l'Église*) has spotless, pastel doubles with shower from 170FF (290FF with shower and toilet). Its rustically elegant **restaurant** serves Limousin-style *menus* from 85FF to 170FF (closed Sunday night and Monday at midday from October to April).

Tulle

The town of Tulle (with a long 'U'; population 15,500), prefecture of the Corrèze département and home of France's last accordion factory, stretches along both banks of the River Corrèze for some 3km. The train station is 2km south-west of the cathedral.

Facing the cathedral (and next to the ornate **Maison de Loyac**), the tourist office (☎ 05 55 26 59 61) opens 9.30 am to noon and 2 to 6 pm daily except Sunday afternoon in July and August. The rest of the year it is closed Monday morning and Sunday.

Next door to the Romanesque and Gothic **cathedral**, which consists of just a nave (the transept collapsed in 1796), a 13th-century cloister leads to the **Musée du Cloître** (☎ 05 55 26 22 05), which has an eclectic collection that includes lace, ceramics and religious sculpture. Admission costs 15FF and it is closed on Wednesday and Saturday mornings. Along the river a block south of the cathedral, the free **Musée de la Résistance et de la Déportation** (☎ 05 55 26 24 36), 2 quai Edmond Perrier (2nd floor), presents details on local events during WWII. It opens 9 am to noon and 2 to 6 pm weekdays.

At the other end of town, across the river from the train station, **Musée des Armes Anciennes** (Armaments Museum; ☎ 05 55 26 22 15), at 1 rue du 9 Juin 1944, displays firearms collected over the last two centuries by the city's national armaments manufactory, founded in 1777 and now known as GIAT. It opens 9 am to noon and 2 to 5 pm daily except Wednesday morning, Saturday morning and Sunday. Down the block at 8 rue du 9 Juin 1944, the **Musée de** l'Accordéon (Accordion Museum) is set to open in late 2001.

Right across the river from the cathedral, the 12-room, one-star *Hôtel Le Bon Accueil* (☎ 05 55 26 70 57, 8–10 rue du Canton) has average doubles with showefrom 170FF (190FF with shower and toilet). Reception is usually closed on Saturday night and Sunday. The attached *restaurant* has hearty, family-style French *menus* from 78FF. The cheapest of the four hotels across the street from the train station is the 11-room *Hôtel des Voyageurs* (☎ 05 55 26 95 51, 17 ave Winston Churchill) where basic doubles start at 100FF.

Tulle is linked by train and SNCF bus to Brive (29FF, 25 minutes, nine to 15 daily) and Clermont-Ferrand (106FF, three hours, three to seven daily).

Gimel-les-Cascades

This tiny (population 650), flower-filled village, 37km north-east of Brive-la-Gaillarde, is set amid some of the most spectacular scenery in Limousin. A few hundred metres down the hill from the late 15th-century Église St-Pardoux, known for its late 12th-century enamel reliquary, are the Cascades, three waterfalls that drop 143m into a gorge aptly named the Inferno. In a privately-owned park (☎ 05 55 21 26 49), they can be visited between 10am and 6 pm daily, March to October. Admission costs 20FF (those aged six to 14, 12FF).

Other sights in and around Gimel include the Pont de Péage, a medieval toll bridge rebuilt in the 1700s; the ruins of the Château de Roche Haute; the remains of the Romanesque Église St-Étienne de Braguse; and the Big Dipper-shaped, 20-hectare Étang de Ruffaud, a lake that offers a refreshing dip and a shady retreat for a picnic. Walking options include the trails along the Gorges de la Vallée de la Montane. Details are available at the tourist office (☎ 05 55 21 44 32), 50m up the hill from the church, which opens until 6 or 7 pm Wednesday to Sunday (until 7 pm daily in July and August). From October to March it opens until 6 pm daily except Monday morning and Sunday.

The nine-room, two-star *Hostellerie de la Vallée* (☎ 05 55 21 40 60, fax 05 55 21 38 74), between the tourist office and the church, opens April to October. It has doubles with shower and toilet for 240FF. The attached *restaurant*, overlooking the gorge, has *menus* for 85FF to 150FF (open daily).

SOUTH-EAST OF BRIVE

This part of Limousin is very near Carennac, the Château de Castelnau-Bretenoux, Rocamadour and the Gouffre de Padirac – for details see the Northern Quercy section.

TURENNE

postcode 19500 • pop 755
• elevation 480m

The pretty hilltop village of Turenne, 11km west of Collonges-la-Rouge on the D8, enjoyed considerable independence – under a viscount – from about 1000 until 1738, when it was sold to Louis XV, whose taxation sent the town into precipitous decline as the artisan class fled. Dominating the village is the Château, built on a sheer limestone outcrop that affords superb panoramas of the surrounding countryside. It opens 10 am to noon and 2 to 6 pm, April to October (7 pm in July and August, when there's no midday closure); the rest of the year it only opens on Sunday afternoon from 2 to 5pm. Admission costs 18FF (those aged under 18, 12FF). The massive 17th-century Collégiale (collegiate church) is in the style of the Counter Reformation. Turenne is on the GR46 footpath.

The tourist office (☎ 05 55 85 94 38), a few metres from place du Foirail (on the D8), opens at weekends and holidays from mid-April to sometime in September (daily from mid-June to early September). The rest of the time, brochures can be picked up at the village hall, 200m to the west, on weekday and Saturday mornings and in the afternoon on Tuesday, Thursday and Friday.

Surrounded by 15th- to 18th-century, slate-roofed houses, *La Maison des Chanoines* (☎ 05 55 85 93 43), a charming, six-room hotel in the centre of the village, has stylish doubles from 350FF. It opens April to early November. The attached

LIMOUSIN

restaurant, with its tree-shaded terrace, has *menus* from 160FF.

Turenne Gare, 3km south-east of the village, is served by trains from Brive (14 minutes, two daily). From Monday to Saturday there are buses from Brive (13.50FF, 25 minutes, one or two daily).

COLLONGES-LA-ROUGE
postcode 19500 • pop 50 • elevation 400m
On a gently angled slope above a tributary of the Dordogne, the narrow alleyways of 'Collonges-the-Red' – built entirely of bright red sandstone – squeeze between wisteria-covered houses topped with round turrets. Surrounded by lush greenery – and, in the spring, flowers of every colour – this tiny hamlet is a delightful place for a stroll.

The partly Romanesque **church**, built from the 11th to the 15th centuries on the foundations of an 8th-century Benedictine priory, was once an important resting place on the pilgrimage to Santiago de Compostela. In the late 16th century, local Protestants held prayers in the southern nave and their Catholic neighbours prayed in the northern nave, where a gilded wood retable erected in the 17th century still stands. Nearby, the ancient wood and slate roof of the **old covered market**, held up by stone columns, shelters an ancient baker's oven.

The tourist office (☎ 05 55 25 47 57), housed in a little wooden building on the D38, opens 2 to 5 pm Monday to Saturday, April to September and 10.30 am to 12.30 pm and 2.30 pm to 7 pm daily in July and August.

The only place to stay (closed from mid-November to mid-March) is the 16-room *Relais de St-Jacques de Compostelle* (☎ 05 55 25 41 02, fax 05 55 84 08 51), in a partly medieval building in the centre of the village (doubles with shower and toilet start at 310FF).

The attached *restaurant* opens daily and has regional *menus* from 85FF.

Collonges is linked with Brive – 18km to the north-west along the D38 – by buses (16FF, 30 minutes, four on weekdays and one on Saturday).

BEAULIEU-SUR-DORDOGNE
postcode 19120 • pop 1300
• elevation 140m
The verdant, aptly-named town of Beaulieu (literally, 'beautiful place'), one of the most attractive medieval villages along the upper Dordogne, is famed for the majestic **Abbatiale St-Pierre**, a 12th-century Romanesque abbey church that was once a stop on the pilgrimage to Santiago de Compostela. The southern portal's brilliant **tympanum** (circa 1130), based on prophecies from the books of Daniel and the Apocalypse, illustrates the Last Judgement with vivid scenes including monsters devouring the condemned. As we go to press, the **treasury**, with its 12th-century gilded Virgin and 13th-century enamel reliquary, is closed for security reasons. However, there are plans to reopen it, at least in the summer. Nearby streets have picturesque houses that date from the 14th and 15th centuries.

Lovely areas for a stroll include **Faubourg de la Chapelle**, a neighbourhood of 17th- and 18th-century houses on the banks of the Dordogne, especially up towards **Chapelle des Pénitents**, a Romanesque chapel. The river can be crossed on foot at the dam. The GR480, a spur of the GR46, passes by here.

Information
The tourist office (☎ 05 55 91 09 94), on place Marbot (which is on the D940), has an English-language brochure detailing walking trails. It opens until 5 pm (7 pm from mid-June to mid-September) Monday to Saturday (and on Sunday from April to mid-September), with a break from 12.30 pm to 2.30 or 3 pm.

Places to Stay
The lovely, shaded *Camping des Îles* (☎ 05 55 91 02 65) is on the other side of the old city from the tourist office, on an island sandwiched between two branches of the Dordogne. It opens May to about 20 September.

The homey, 28-bed *Auberge de Jeunesse de la Riviera Limousine* (☎ 05 55 91 13 82, fax 05 55 91 26 06, place du Monturu), idyllically situated along the river, occupies a partly 14th-century building. A basic bunk costs 48FF. Kitchen facilities are available. Staff are generally around from 8 to 11 am and 6 to 8.30 pm, but bags can be left during the day.

The eight-room *Auberge Les Charmilles* (☎ 05 55 91 29 29, fax 05 55 91 29 30, 20 blvd Rodolphe de Turenne), overlooking a branch of the river, has delightful doubles/quads with large bathrooms from 310/440FF.

The welcoming 18-room, one-star *Hôtel L'Étape Fleurie* (☎ 05 55 91 11 04, 17 place du Champ de Mars) has bright, modern doubles from 150FF (200FF with shower and toilet). The cosy, two-star, 27-room *Central Hôtel Fournié* (☎ 05 55 91 01 34, fax 05 55 91 23 57, 4 place du Champ de Mars), opens April to mid-November and has large, pleasant doubles from 200FF (260FF with shower and toilet).

Places to Eat
The rustic restaurant at the *Hôtel L'Étape Fleurie* (see Places to Stay) serves family-style regional specialities; *menus* cost 60FF (weekday lunch only), 78FF, 98FF and 150FF. Delicious, classic French cuisine is on offer at the *Auberge Les Charmilles* (see Places to Stay), where *menus* go from 95FF to 225FF (and 65FF for lunch except Sunday). It is closed on Tuesday and Wednesday, October to April.

Au Beau Lieu Breton (☎ 05 55 91 20 46, rue du Presbytère), on an alley behind (west of) the church, serves sweet and savoury crepes as well as omelettes and salads. It is closed on Monday night, Tuesday and Wednesday except from June to August.

On Wednesday and Saturday mornings, there's an *open-air market* next to the church. At least one of the two groceries on place Marbot – the *Suprette* and the *Casino* – are open daily (closed on Sunday afternoon except in July and August); midday closure for both lasts from 12.30 to 2.30 or 3 pm.

Getting There & Away
Beaulieu is 70km east of Sarlat-la-Canéda and 47km north-east of the Gouffre de Padirac (see the Quercy section).

From Monday to Saturday, there are buses linking Beaulieu with Brive (35FF, one hour, one to three a day, zero to two daily during school holiday periods). Schedules are posted at the bus shelter on place du Champ de Mars (opposite the Hôtel L'Étape Fleurie) and outside the tourist office.

The Dordogne

Known to the French as Périgord, the Dordogne département – named after the most important of the region's seven rivers – was one of the prehistoric cradles of human civilisation. The remains of Neanderthal and Cro-Magnon people have been discovered throughout the region, and quite a number of local caves – including the world-famous Lascaux – are decorated with extraordinary works of prehistoric art. Périgord's numerous hilltop chateaux and bastides (see the relevant boxed texts) bear witness to the bloody battles waged here during the Middle Ages and the Hundred Years' War.

Bastides

In the early 1200s, the population of south-western France was growing, as was a certain discontent with feudalism. Local suzerains and bishops, seeing in the new demographics an opportunity to enhance their authority and increase their income from rents, tolls and tariffs, turned to ancient Roman models of urban planning. They established – over the next century-and-a-half – more than 300 towns and villages known as bastides. Generally surrounded by a defensive wall, these 'new towns' had a regular street grid (terrain permitting), numbered building lots of uniform shape and size (to facilitate tax collection) and a charter granting various privileges to the inhabitants; the arcaded market square – the centre of commercial life – often had a church in one corner. Bastides covered in this chapter include Villefranche de Rouergue, Najac, Monpazier and Domme.

Chateaux

The Dordogne and Quercy aren't in the same league as the Loire Valley, but they do have quite a few impressive chateaux, many of them massive fortresses built in the Middle Ages. This chapter provides details on visiting the chateaux of Beynac, Biron, Bonaguil, Carennac, Castelnau-Bretenoux, Castelnaud, Milandes and Najac, as well as Turenne in southern Limousin.

Other chateaux in the region include:

The turreted 15th- to 17th-century **Jumilhac-le-Grand** (☎ 05 53 52 42 97), about 50km north-east of Périgueux along the N21 and D78 (opens daily June to September, and at weekends and holidays in May and from October to mid-November)

The Renaissance-influenced **Puyguilhem** (☎ 05 53 54 82 18), some 30km north of Périgueux near Villars (opens daily, except Monday in the off-season)

The imposing neoclassical **Hautefort** (☎ 05 53 50 51 23), 40km east of Périgueux, with its English-style garden and French flower terraces (opens daily from late March to October, on Sunday afternoons the rest of the year; closed mid-December to mid-January)

Eyrignac (☎ 05 53 28 99 71), 13km north-east of Sarlat, famed for its exquisite 18th-century French-style gardens (opens daily, year-round)

The castle-like, partly furnished **Puymartin** (☎ 05 53 59 29 97), 8km north-west of Sarlat (opens daily, April to November)

Losse (☎ 05 53 50 80 08), in the Vézère Valley 5km south-west of Montignac, which is decorated with 16th- and 17th-century tapestries and furniture (opens daily from Easter to October)

To make the region's attractions more accessible to visitors, Périgord has been divided into four areas, each assigned a colour according to its most prominent feature. The fields and forests to the north and north-west are known as Périgord Vert (green). In the centre, the area of limestone surrounding the capital, Périgueux, and along the River Isle is known as Périgord Blanc (white). The wine-growing area of Périgord Pourpre (purple) lies to the south-west, around Bergerac. Périgord Noir (black), known for its dark forests and many chateaux, encompasses the Vézère valley and, to the south, part of the Dordogne valley; between the two valleys lies the attractive medieval town of Sarlat-la-Canéda.

Warm-season sports popular in the region include canoeing, kayaking, fishing, rock climbing, horse riding and cycling. Tourist offices have details and can supply you with informative, English-language brochures.

During the warmer months, the Dordogne – famed for its rich cuisine – attracts vast numbers of tourists, including many from the UK. In winter, the region goes into deep hibernation, and many hotels, restaurants and tourist sites close.

PÉRIGUEUX
postcode 24000 • pop 33,294
• elevation 106m

Périgueux, prefecture of the Dordogne département, has a restored medieval and Renaissance quarter – much of it built of dazzling white limestone – and one of France's best museums of prehistory. Founded over 2000 years ago on a hill bounded by a curve in the gentle River Isle, the city is at its liveliest during the Wednesday and Saturday truffle and *foie gras* markets (see Self-Catering).

Périgueux is 45km north-west of the Vézère Valley.

Orientation

The medieval and Renaissance old city, known as Puy St-Front, is on the hillside between the Isle (to the east) and blvd Michel Montaigne and place Bugeaud (to the west). On the other side of place Bugeaud is the old city's historic rival, the largely residential Cité Quarter, centred around the ruins of a Roman amphitheatre. The train station is about 1km north-west of the old city.

Information

Tourist Offices The main tourist office (☎ 05 53 53 10 63, fax 05 53 09 02 50, @ tourisme.perigueux@perigord.tm.fr), 26 place Francheville, opens 9 am to 7 pm Monday to Saturday and 10 am to 6 pm Sunday and holidays, mid-June to mid-September; and 9 am to 6 pm daily, except Sunday, the rest of the year.

Information on the Dordogne département is available at Espace Tourisme Périgord (☎ 05 53 35 50 24), 25 rue du Président Wilson, which opens from 9 am to noon and 2 to 5 pm weekdays.

Money The Banque de France, 1 place du Président Roosevelt, changes money from 8.45 am to 12.15 pm weekdays. Several banks can be found on place Bugeaud.

Post & Communications The main post office, 1 rue du 4 Septembre, opens 8 am to 7 pm weekdays and 8 am to noon Saturday. Exchange operations and a Cyberposte are available.

Internet access is available at Cybertek (☎ 05 53 06 89 65) at 14 cours Fénelon, which opens Tuesday to Saturday.

Laundry There are laundrettes on place Hoche (open 8 am to 8 pm), 18 rue des Mobiles de Coulm (open 8 am to 9 pm) and 61 rue Gambetta (open 8 am to 9 pm; to 8 pm Saturday).

Emergency The Hôtel de Police (Police Station; ☎ 05 53 06 44 44), across from 20 rue du 4 Septembre, opens 24 hours.

Puy St-Front

The **Musée du Périgord** (☎ 05 53 06 40 70), 22 cours Tourny, is renowned for its rich collection of prehistoric tools and implements; Gallo-Roman and medieval artefacts are also on display. It opens 10 am to 5 pm weekdays (11 am to 6 pm from April to September), and 1 to 6 pm at weekends. It is closed Tues-

day and holidays. Admission costs 20FF (students 10FF, those aged under 18 free).

When seen against the evening sky, **Cathédrale St-Front**, topped with five bump-studded domes and many more equally bumpy domelets, looks like something you might come across in Istanbul. But by day, the sprawling structure, 'restored' by Abadie (the creator of Paris' Sacré Cœur) in the late 19th century, looks contrived and over-wrought in the finest pseudo-Byzantine tradition. The carillon sounds the same hour chime as Big Ben. The Greek cross shaped interior – whose entrance faces the southern end of rue St-Front – is noteworthy only for the 17th-century baroque **retable** in the choir. It generally opens 8 am to 12.30 pm and 2.30 to 7.30 pm. The eclectic **cloister**, accessible from place de la Clautre, is unexceptional. The best views of the cathedral (and the town) are from **Pont des Barris**.

The ancient cobblestone streets north of the cathedral, lined with centuries-old limestone houses, include **rue du Plantier**. A few short blocks to the west, the area's main thoroughfare, **rue Limogeanne**, has graceful Renaissance buildings at Nos 3 and 12. There are more such structures on nearby streets, including **rue Éguillerie** (such as the Renaissance-style **Maison du Pâtisser** at place St-Louis) and **rue de la Miséricorde**. The 15th- and 16th-century houses along **rue Aubergerie** include the **Hôtel d'Abzac de Ladouze** (across from No 19), with its two octagonal towers.

The **Musée Militaire** (☎ 05 53 53 47 36), 32 rue des Farges, founded right after WWI, has a particularly varied collection of swords, firearms, uniforms and insignia from the Napoleonic wars and the two world wars. It opens 10 am to noon and 2 to 6 pm daily except Sunday and holidays, April to September; afternoons only from October to December; and just Wednesday and Saturday afternoons from January to March. Admission costs 20FF.

Of the 28 towers that once formed Puy St-Front's medieval fortifications, only **Tour Mataguerre**, a stout, round bastion next to the main tourist office, remains. It was given its present form in the late 15th century.

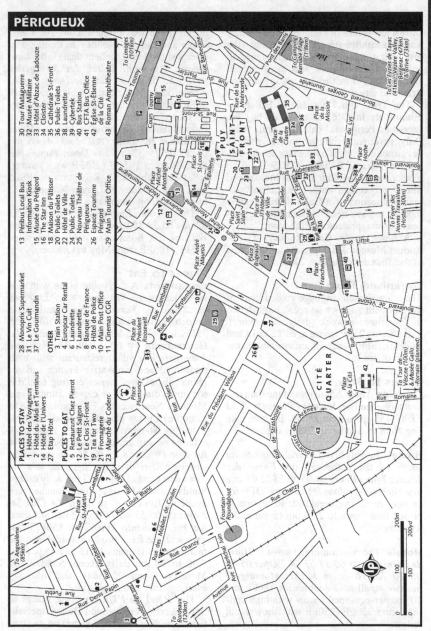

PÉRIGUEUX

PLACES TO STAY
1 Hôtel des Voyageurs
14 Hôtel du Midi et Terminus
14 Hôtel de l'Univers
27 Etap Hôtel

PLACES TO EAT
5 Restaurant Chez Pierrot
12 Le Petit Saigon
17 Le Clos St-Front
19 Tea for Two
21 Fromagerie
23 Marché du Coderc

28 Monoprix Supermarket
31 Le Vin Cuit
37 Le Gourmandin

OTHER
3 Train Station
4 Europcar Car Rental
6 Laundrette
7 Laundrette
8 Banque de France
9 Hôtel de Police
10 Main Post Office
11 Cinemas CGR

13 Péribus Local Bus
15 Information Kiosk
15 Musée du Périgord
16 The Star Inn
18 Maison du Pâtisser
20 Public Toilets
22 Hôtel de Ville
24 Public Toilets
25 Nouveau Théâtre de
   Périgueux
26 Espace Tourisme
   Périgord
29 Main Tourist Office

30 Tour Mataguerre
32 Musée Militaire
33 Hôtel d'Abzac de Ladouze
34 Cloister
35 Cathédrale St-Front
36 Public Toilets
38 Laundrette
39 Cybertek
40 Bus Station
41 CFTA Bus Office
42 Eglise St-Etienne
   de la Cité
43 Roman Amphitheatre

euro currency converter €1 = 6.56FF

Cité Quarter

Only a few arches of Périgueux' 1st-century **Roman amphitheatre** are still standing – the rest of the massive structure, designed to hold 30,000 spectators, was disassembled and carried off in the 3rd century to construct the city walls.

The 11th- and 12th-century **Église St-Étienne de la Cité**, on place de la Cité, served as Périgueux' cathedral until 1669. Only two cupolas and two bays survived the devastation wrought by the Huguenots during the Wars of Religion (1562–98). Two blocks south, the **Tour de Vésone**, shaped like a gargantuan anklet, is the only remaining section of a Gallo-Roman temple thought to have been dedicated to the goddess Vesuna, protector of the town.

A new **Musée Gallo-Romain** (Gallo-Roman Museum) is supposed to open next to the Tour de Vésone in 2002.

Organised Tours

There are French language guided tours of the city with guides who speak English two to four times a week (daily in summer). Tickets cost 25FF (those aged 12 to 18 and students 18FF) – details are available at the tourist office.

Places to Stay

Camping About 2.5km east of the train station along the Isle, *Barnabé Plage* (☎ 05 53 53 41 45) opens year round. By bus, take line No 8 to the rue des Bains stop.

Hostels Just off blvd Lakanal, about 600m south of the cathedral, the *Foyer des Jeunes Travailleurs* (☎ 05 53 53 52 05, rue des Thermes Prolongée) charges 73FF for a bed, including breakfast. Reception is closed from noon to 2.30 pm (5 pm at the weekend).

Hotels The welcoming, two-star *Hôtel de l'Univers* (☎ 05 53 53 34 79, fax 05 53 06 70 76, 18 cours Michel Montaigne) has two small attic doubles for 180FF and 10 shower-equipped rooms with high ceilings from 220FF (250FF with shower and toilet).

Near the train station, there are half a dozen inexpensive hotels along rue Denis Papin and rue des Mobiles de Coulm. The cheapest (and an excellent deal) is the family-run, 16-room *Hôtel des Voyageurs* (☎ 05 53 53 17 44, 26 rue Denis Papin) where basic but clean doubles cost only 80FF (100FF with shower). Reception may be closed in the afternoon at weekends (hours posted). The amiable, two-star *Hôtel du Midi et Terminus* (☎ 05 53 53 41 06, fax 05 53 08 19 32, 18 rue Denis Papin) has doubles from 145FF (215FF with shower, toilet and cable TV). Reception is closed until 6 pm Sunday and, from November to mid-March, on Saturday.

The 47-room *Etap Hôtel* (☎ 05 53 05 53 82, fax 05 53 35 93 42, 33 rue du Président Wilson) has hotel-chain-style triples for 175FF (195FF from May to October).

Places to Eat

Restaurants A convivial place with just seven tables, *Le Vin Cuit* (☎ 05 53 09 48 90, 7 rue des Farges) serves family-style French dishes, with *menus* for 50FF and 75FF. It is closed Sunday and holidays. *Le Gourmandin* (☎ 05 53 06 31 08, 3 rue Aubergerie), a small restaurant with both traditional and innovative French and regional dishes, has *menus* costing 68/95FF for lunch/dinner. It is closed Sunday and Monday. Nearby cours Fénelon is home to a couple of pizza places and small eateries.

In Puy St-Front, there are a number of eateries on and around place St-Louis. *Tea for Two* (☎ 05 53 53 92 86), in the southeastern corner of place St-Louis, is a tea room that opens 10 am to 7 pm daily except Sunday and Monday; light lunches are available from noon to 3 pm. *Le Clos St-Front* (☎ 05 53 46 78 58, 12 rue St-Front) has French *menus* (110FF to 150FF) that vary with the fresh produce available in the marketplace. It opens 12.15 to 1.45 pm and 7.30 to 10 pm daily except Sunday and Monday (opens Sunday and Monday evenings July and August).

The *Hôtel de l'Univers* (see Places to Stay) serves Périgord and Breton specialities (including fish and lobster) on its vine-covered terrace; *menus* are available for 90FF to 220FF. It is closed Sunday night and Monday.

A few hotels around the train station have very reasonable *menus*. *Restaurant Chez Pierrot* (☎ 05 53 53 43 22, 78 rue Chanzy) has hearty *menus* (from 50FF to 70FF) that come with 500mL of wine. It is closed Saturday at midday and Sunday. The *Hôtel du Midi et Terminus* (see Places to Stay), a favourite with locals, has Périgord-style *menus* from 75FF. It's closed at midday from Monday to Wednesday in July and August.

A good bet for East Asian cuisine is *Le Petit Saïgon* (☎ 05 53 09 51 99, 1 place du Général Leclerc) which has *menus* from 75FF. It opens daily except Sunday.

Self-Catering On Wednesday and Saturday mornings from about mid-November to mid-March, black truffles, wild mushrooms, *foie gras*, *confits* (duck or goose conserve), cheeses and other delicacies are sold at the *Marché de Gras* on place St-Louis in Puy St-Front.

On Wednesday and Saturday mornings year round, there's a *food market* on place de la Clautre, near the cathedral. Not far from the southern end of rue Limogeanne, the *Marché du Coderc* (covered market) opens until about 1.30 pm daily. Across the square, *Fromagerie du Coderc* opens daily except Sunday afternoon and Monday.

The upstairs *Monoprix* supermarket, between place Bugeaud and place Francheville, opens 8.30 am to 8 pm Monday to Saturday.

Entertainment

A welcoming pub run by a British couple, *The Star Inn* (☎ 05 53 08 56 83), across from 23 rue St-Front, is something of a hangout for English speakers, including students. You can borrow the English books from the wall rack. It opens 8 pm to 1 am Monday to Saturday (to 2 am from May to September).

The seven-screen *Cinémas CGR* (☎ 05 53 09 40 99, 19 cours Michel Montaigne) screens non-dubbed films, except during school holiday periods.

Getting There & Away

Bus The bus station is on the southern side of place Francheville; hours are posted at the bus stops. One of the carriers, CFTA (☎ 05 53 08 43 13), has an office (open weekdays) on the storey overlooking the waiting room. The tourist office and the train station information office can supply you with schedules.

Except on Sunday and holidays, destinations served include Bergerac (41FF, 70 minutes, three daily), Ribérac (31FF, one hour, four daily, one on Saturday), Hautefort (two hours, one daily on weekdays) and Sarlat-la-Canéda (50.50FF, 1½ hours, one or two daily, fewer in July and August) via the Vézère Valley town of Montignac (35FF, 55 minutes). You can also get to Le Bugue (45FF, one hour, one daily on weekdays when school is in session).

Train The train station, on rue Denis Papin, is served by local bus Nos 1, 4 and 5. Destinations with direct services include Bordeaux (99FF, 1¼ hours, nine to 13 daily), Brive-la-Gaillarde (65FF, one hour, three to five daily), Les Eyzies de Tayac (41FF, 30 minutes, two to four daily) and Limoges (81FF, one hour, seven to 11 daily, four on Saturday).

Services to Paris' Gare d'Austerlitz (268FF, four to five hours, 12 to 16 daily) are via Limoges. To get to Sarlat-la-Canéda (75FF) you have to change at Le Buisson.

Car Europcar (☎ 05 53 08 15 72) is at 7 rue Denis Papin (closed Sunday).

Getting Around

Allo Taxi (☎ 05 53 09 09 09) is available 24 hours.

SARLAT-LA-CANÉDA
postcode 24200 • pop 10,000
• elevation 173m

The beautiful, well-restored town of Sarlat, administratively twinned with nearby La Canéda, is the capital of Périgord Noir. Its medieval and Renaissance townscape – much of it built of tan sandstone in the 16th and 17th centuries – attracts large numbers of tourists, especially for the year-round Saturday market.

Sarlat is an excellent base for car trips to the prehistoric sites of the Vézère Valley and to the Dordogne Périgourdine.

Orientation

The heart-shaped Medieval Town (Cité Médiévale) is bisected by the ruler-straight rue de la République (La Traverse), which (along with its continuations) stretches for 2km from the viaduct (and the nearby train station) to the Auberge de Jeunesse. The medieval town is centred around place de la Liberté, rue de la Liberté and place du Peyrou.

Information

Tourist Offices The main tourist office (☎ 05 53 31 45 45, fax 05 53 59 19 44, ✉ ot24.sarlat@perigord.tm.fr), on place de la Liberté, occupies the beautiful Hôtel de Maleville, made up of three 15th- and 16th-century Gothic houses. Staff can supply you with the *Visitors' Map of the Medieval Town*, which takes you on a walking tour of the historic centre, and brochures on hikes and car tours in the area. In summer, there is a 10FF charge for making hotel and B&B bookings. The office opens 9 am to noon and 2 to 6 pm Monday to Saturday, November to April; during school holiday periods it may also be open on Sunday and holidays. The rest of the year it opens 9 am to 7 pm Monday to Saturday and 10 am to noon and 2 to 6 pm Sunday and holidays.

During July and August, the tourist office annexe (☎ 05 53 59 18 87) on ave du Général de Gaulle opens 9 am to noon and 2 to 6 pm Monday to Saturday.

Money There are several banks, open Tuesday to Saturday, along rue de la République.

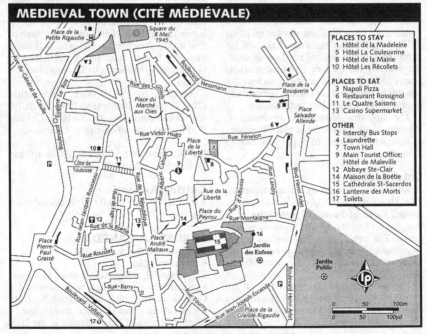

MEDIEVAL TOWN (CITÉ MÉDIÉVALE)

PLACES TO STAY
1 Hôtel de la Madeleine
5 Hôtel La Couleuvrine
8 Hôtel de la Mairie
10 Hôtel Les Récollets

PLACES TO EAT
3 Napoli Pizza
6 Restaurant Rossignol
11 Le Quatre Saisons
13 Casino Supermarket

OTHER
2 Intercity Bus Stops
4 Laundrette
7 Town Hall
9 Main Tourist Office;
   Hôtel de Maleville
12 Abbaye Ste-Clair
14 Maison de la Boétie
15 Cathédrale St-Sacerdos
16 Lanterne des Morts
17 Toilets

Post & Communications The main post office, on place du 14 Juillet, opens 9 am to 6 pm weekdays and until noon Saturday. Currency exchange and a Cyberposte are available.

Gamenet (☎ 05 53 31 45 91), down a small alley off place du Maréchal de Lattre de Tassigny (across from the Shell station), offers Internet access from 11 am to 7 pm daily.

Laundry There are laundrettes at 10 place de la Bouquerie (open 6 am to 10 pm) and 74 ave de Selves (open 7 am to 9 pm).

Things to See & Do

Once part of Sarlat's Cluniac abbey, **Cathédrale St-Sacerdos** is a hotchpotch of styles. The wide, airy nave and its chapels date from the 17th century; the cruciform chevet (at the far end from the entrance) is from the 14th century; and the western entrance and much of the belfry above it are 12th-century Romanesque. The organ dates from 1752.

Behind the cathedral is the **Jardin des Enfeus**, Sarlat's first cemetery, and the 12th-century **Lanterne des Morts** (Lantern of the Dead), a short tower that looks like the top of a missile. It may have been built to commemorate St-Bernard, who visited Sarlat in 1147 and whose relics were given to the abbey.

Across the square from the front of the cathedral is the ornate facade of the Renaissance **Maison de la Boétie**, birthplace of the writer Étienne de la Boétie (1530–63).

The alleyways of the quiet, largely residential area west of rue de la République, many of them lined with centuries-old stone houses, are also worth exploring. **Rue Jean-Jacques Rousseau** makes a good starting point.

From April to October, the vintage motor vehicles on display at the **Musée de l'Automobile** (☎ 05 53 31 62 81), 17 ave Thiers, can be viewed from 2.30 to 6.30 pm daily except Monday and, in April, Tuesday. In July and August, the museum opens 10.30 am to 7 pm daily. Admission costs 35FF (children aged eight to 12, 15FF).

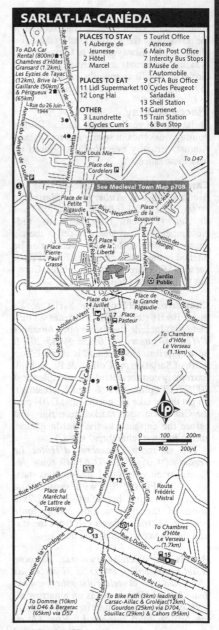

SARLAT-LA-CANÉDA

PLACES TO STAY	5 Tourist Office
1 Auberge de Jeunesse	Annexe
	6 Main Post Office
2 Hôtel Marcel	7 Intercity Bus Stops
	8 Musée de l'Automobile
PLACES TO EAT	9 CFTA Bus Office
11 Lidl Supermarket	10 Cycles Peugeot
12 Long Hai	Sarladais
	13 Shell Station
OTHER	14 Gamenet
3 Laundrette	15 Train Station
4 Cycles Cum's	& Bus Stop

See Medieval Town Map p708

A *piste cyclable* (bicycle path) begins 3km south-east of Sarlat (near the intersection of the D704 and the D704A), and takes you along an old railway grade to Carsac-Aillac (12km from Sarlat) and, across the river, to Groléjac. It will eventually go all the way to Souillac (about 30 km from Sarlat).

Places to Stay

Sarlat has no really cheap hotels. During holiday weekends in spring and in July and August, virtually everything is booked up way in advance.

Camping & Hostels The modest but friendly, 15-bed *Auberge de Jeunesse* (☎ 05 53 59 47 59 *or* 05 53 30 21 27, 77 ave de Selves) opens mid-March to mid-November, but call ahead to see if there's space. A bed costs 50FF; tents can be pitched in the tiny back garden for 30FF per person (5FF more for the first night). Cooking facilities are available.

Chambres d'Hôtes The Sarlat area's many B&Bs (the tourist office has a complete list) include the five-room *Chambres d'Hôtes Gransard* (☎ 05 53 59 35 20). It opens April to October and is about 1.2km north of Sarlat on the Colline de Péchauriol. Extremely comfortable doubles/triples cost 200/270FF, plus 28FF for each breakfast. To get there, take the northbound D704 past the Champion supermarket, turn right just before the entrance to the Mazda garage, and follow the 'chambres' signs.

The six-room *Chambres d'Hôtes Le Verseau* (☎ 05 53 31 02 63, 49 route des Pechs), open year round, has doubles starting at 150FF (210FF with shower and toilet), including breakfast. It is 2.2km north of the train station along route Frédéric Mistral – if you call from the station the owner will pick you up.

Hotels The friendly, two-star, 18-room *Hôtel Les Récollets* (☎ 05 53 31 36 00, fax 05 53 30 32 62, @ otelrecol@aol.com, 4 rue Jean-Jacques Rousseau) is on a narrow alleyway – the nearest parking is a block up the hill on blvd Eugène Le Roy. Quiet,

modern doubles start at 250FF. Near the tourist office, the seven-room, two-star *Hôtel de la Mairie* (☎ 05 53 59 05 71, 13 place de la Liberté) has fairly basic doubles with shower from 250FF. It opens March to December.

The rustic, two-star, 14-room *Hôtel Marcel* (☎ 05 53 59 21 98, fax 05 53 30 27 77, 50 ave de Selves) has spacious, cheerful doubles with shower and toilet from 220FF to 300FF. It is closed mid-November to mid-February.

The chateau-like, two-star *Hôtel La Couleuvrine* (☎ 05 53 59 27 80, fax 05 53 31 26 83, 1 place de la Bouquerie), parts of which date from the 13th to 15th centuries, has beautifully furnished doubles/quads from 265/420FF.

For three-star comfort, a good bet is the elegant, 39-room *Hôtel de la Madeleine* (☎ 05 53 59 10 41, fax 05 53 31 03 62, @ hotel.madeleine@wanadoo.fr, 1 place de la Petite Rigaudie) which has spacious doubles/triples from 370/515FF (a bit less in winter). It is closed in January.

Places to Eat

Restaurants There are quite a few tourist-oriented restaurants along the streets north, north-west and south of the cathedral.

Périgord's famous gastronomy can be sampled at a number of establishments. *Restaurant Rossignol* (☎ 05 53 31 02 30, 15 rue Fénelon) has *menus* of French and local dishes (including fish) from 87FF to 290FF. It opens noon to 1.30 pm and 7 to 8.30 pm daily except Wednesday. Another good bet is *Le Quatre Saisons* (☎ 05 53 29 48 59, 2 côte de Toulouse) where the *menus* range from 65FF (95FF in the evening) to 260FF. It is closed on Wednesday except in July and August. The elegant restaurant attached to the *Hôtel de la Madeleine* (see Places to Stay) has gastronomic *menus* from 115FF to 215FF. It is open daily from mid-March to mid-November (closed Monday at midday, except in July and August).

Napoli Pizza (☎ 05 53 31 26 93, 2 blvd Eugène Le Roy) serves pizzas, pasta and meat dishes in a rustic, informal ambience. It opens noon to 2 pm and 7 to 11 pm daily (closed Sunday at midday and, except in July and August, on Tuesday). *Long Hai* (☎ 05 53 29 61 94, 7 ave Aristide Briand) has Chinese and Vietnamese *menus* from 65FF (85FF in the evening). It is closed Monday.

Self-Catering Long a driving force in the local economy, the *Saturday market*, on place de la Liberté and along rue de la République, offers edibles in the morning (and, all day long, durables such as clothing). Depending on the season, Périgord delicacies on offer include truffles, *foie gras*, mushrooms and goose-based products. A smaller *fruit and vegetable market* is held on place de la Liberté on Wednesday morning. Quite a few shops around town sell *foie gras* and other pricey regional specialities.

The *Casino* supermarket (*32 rue de la République*) opens 8 am to 12.15 pm and 2.30 to 7.15 pm Tuesday to Saturday, and 8.30 am to 12.15 pm Sunday; hours are longer in July and August. The *Lidl* supermarket at the southern end of ave Aristide Briand opens 9 am to 12.30 pm and 2.30 to 7.30 pm Monday to Friday (to 7 pm on Saturday, when there's no midday closure).

Getting There & Away
Bus Bus services are very limited; schedules are available at the tourist office. There's no bus station – departures are from the train station, place Pasteur or place de la Petite Rigaudie, depending on where you're going.

There are one or two buses daily (fewer in July and August) to Périgueux (50.50FF, 1½ hours) via the Vézère Valley town of Montignac.

Train The train station (☎ 05 53 59 00 21 or 0 836 35 35 35), 1.3km south of the old city at the southern end of ave de la Gare, is poorly linked with the rest of the region. The ticket windows are staffed until 7 pm.

Destinations served include Bordeaux (119FF, 2½ hours, two to four direct daily) which is on the same line as Bergerac; Périgueux (change at Le Buisson, 75FF, 1½ hours, two daily); and Les Eyzies de Tayac

(change at Le Buisson, 47FF, 50 minutes, two daily). The SNCF bus to Souillac (28.50FF, 40 minutes, three daily) passes through Carsac-Aillac (on the scenic D703) and links up with trains on the Paris (Gare d'Austerlitz)-Limoges-Toulouse line.

Getting Around
Car & Motorcycle Free parking is available around the perimeter of the Cité Médiéval – along blvd Nessmann, blvd Voltaire and blvd Henri Arlet. Cars are banned from the Cité Médiéval from June to September, and rue de la République is pedestrianised in July and August.

Bicycle The Sarlat area has nine bike-rental outlets, including Cycles Cum's (☎ 05 53 31 28 40) at 8 ave Gambetta (open Tuesday to Saturday) and Cycles Peugeot Sarladais (☎ 05 53 28 51 87) at 36 ave Thiers.

PREHISTORIC SITES & THE VÉZÈRE VALLEY
Of the Vézère Valley's 175 known prehistoric sites, the most famous ones, including the world-renowned cave paintings in Lascaux, are situated between **Le Bugue** (near where the Vézère conflows with the Dordogne) and, 25km to the north-east, Montignac. The sites mentioned here are just the highlights and are listed roughly from south-west to north-east.

Many of the villages in the area, including Les Eyzies de Tayac and Montignac, have one or more hotels. Other bases from which the area can be explored include Sarlat (20km south-east of Les Eyzies de Tayac) and Périgueux (45km to the north-west). Most of the valley's sites are closed in winter – the best time to visit is in spring or autumn, when the sites are open but the crowds are not overwhelming.

Getting Around
The Vézère Valley is well signposted, and arrows at every crossroads direct you to sights major and minor. Public transport in the area is limited – for details, see Getting There & Away under Les Eyzies de Tayac, Périgueux and Sarlat-la-Canéda.

Les Eyzies de Tayac

postcode 24620 • pop 850 • elevation 70m
The two museums in the dull, touristy village of Les Eyzies provide an excellent introduction to the valley's prehistoric legacy.

Information The tourist office (☎ 05 53 06 97 05, fax 05 53 06 90 79, 🖂 ot.les.eyzies@ perigord.tm.fr) is on Les Eyzies' main street, the D47, right below the most prominent part of the cliff. It opens 9 am to noon and 2 to 6 pm daily, except on Sunday from October to February; July and August hours are 9 am to 7 pm (10 am to noon and 2 to 6 pm on Sunday).

IGN maps and topoguides are on sale across from the tourist office at Librairie de la Préhistoire, open 8.30 am to 12.30 pm and 3 to 7 or 7.30 pm daily (no midday closure from June to August; closed in the afternoon from December to February).

Things to See The very interesting **Musée National de Préhistoire** (National Museum of Prehistory; ☎ 05 53 06 45 45), built into the cliff above the tourist office (and in the process of being expanded), provides a great introduction to the area's prehistoric human habitation. Its well-presented collection of artefacts can be visited 9.30 am to noon and 2 to 5 pm (6 pm from mid-March to mid-November) daily except Tuesday; in July and August, there's no midday closure and it opens every day until 7 pm. Admission costs 22FF (those aged 18 to 25 and, on Sunday, for everyone, 15FF; free for those aged under 18 and, on the first Sunday of the month, for everyone).

About 250m north of Musée National de Préhistoire along the cliff face is the **Abri Pataud** (☎ 05 53 06 92 46), a Cro-Magnon shelter inhabited over a period of 15,000 years starting some 37,000 years ago; bones and other artefacts discovered during the excavations are on display. The ibex carved into the ceiling dates from about 19,000 BC. The site opens Tuesday to Sunday (daily in July and August); admission, including a one-hour guided tour (the guides generally know some English), costs 30FF (children aged 6 to 12, 15FF).

Places to Stay & Eat In the minuscule hamlet of Le Queylou (population 6), *Camping à la Ferme/Gîtes Le Queylou* (☎ 05 53 06 94 71) is in the middle of a forest 2.8 km south-west of Les Eyzies (and 800m off the D706). You can camp here from April to October; rustic cottages, sleeping up to five people, are available year round starting at 140/850FF per night/week (1600FF a week in July and August). If you call from the train station, the English-speaking owners will pick you up.

The reasonably priced, 14-room *Hôtel des Falaises* (☎ 05 53 06 97 35), almost across the street from the Abri Pataud, opens year round and has unremarkable doubles with shower and toilet from 170FF. The two-star, 19-room *Hôtel du Centre* (☎ 05 53 06 97 13, fax 05 53 06 91 63), on the square next to the tourist office, has charming doubles from 290FF (closed November to early February); the *restaurant* (closed Tuesday) has Périgord and French *menus* from 100FF to 225FF.

Getting There & Away The train station (☎ 05 53 06 97 22) is 700m north of the tourist office (and 200m off the D47). The ticket windows are staffed until at least 6 pm (closed until noon at the weekend).

Destinations served include Bordeaux (change at Le Buisson; 110FF, two to three hours, two or three daily), Périgueux (38FF, 30 minutes, four or five daily), Sarlat (change at Le Buisson; 47FF, 50 minutes, two daily) and Paris' Gare d'Austerlitz (289FF, 5½ hours, usually three daily including one direct).

Getting Around Bicycles can be rented at the tourist office.

Limeuil

This charming walled village, perched high above the confluence of the Rivers Vézère and Dordogne, is known for its municipal gardens. The 10-room *Hôtel Au Bon Accueil* (☎ 05 53 63 30 97), just down the one-way street from place des Fosses, opens Easter to October and has doubles from 150FF (180FF with shower). The attached

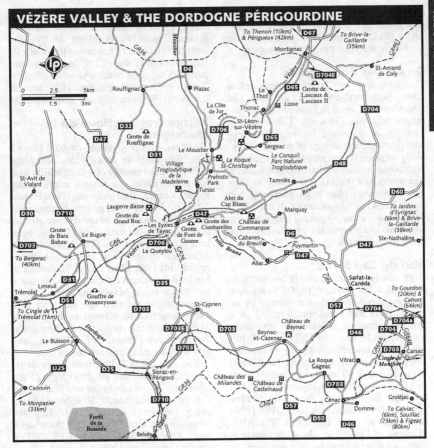

VÉZÈRE VALLEY & THE DORDOGNE PÉRIGOURDINE

restaurant, open year round, serves traditional Périgord-style *menus* from 82FF to 160FF. It is closed in the evening from November to Easter.

Grotte de Font de Gaume

This cave, just over 1km north-east of Les Eyzies on the D47, has one of the most astounding collections of prehistoric paintings still open to the public. About two dozen of its 230 remarkably sophisticated polychrome figures of bison, reindeer, horses, bears, mammoths and other creatures, created by Cro-Magnon people 14,000

years ago, can be visited. A number of the animals, engraved and/or painted in red and black, are depicted in movement or in three dimensions.

To protect the cave, discovered in 1901, the number of visitors is limited to 200 daily, and the 45-minute group tours (explanatory sheets in English available) are limited to 20 participants and must be reserved a few days ahead (a week or two ahead from July to September) by calling ☎ 05 53 06 86 00. Tours begin 9 am (9.30 or 10 am from October to March) to 11 am and 2 to 5 pm (4 or 4.30 pm from October

euro currency converter €1 = 6.56FF

to March) daily except Wednesday. Admission costs 35FF (those aged 18 to 25, 23FF; under 18s free). The site may be closed for a while in the spring of 2001 for repairs.

Grotte des Combarelles

The long and very narrow Combarelles Cave, 3km north-east of Les Eyzies and 1.6km east of Grotte de Font de Gaume, averages only 80cm in width. Discovered in 1894, it is renowned for its 600 often-superimposed engravings of animals, especially reindeer, bison and horses; there are also some human or half-human figures. The works date from 12,000 to 14,000 years ago. To reserve a place in a six person group (tours last 45 to 60 minutes), call the Grotte de Font de Gaume – opening hours, admission costs and reservation guidelines are the same for both sites.

Abri du Cap Blanc

High- and low-relief figures of horses, reindeer and bison, created 14,000 years ago, decorate this natural shelter, formed by an overhanging rocky outcrop. Situated on a pristine, forested hillside, the privately owned Abri (☎ 05 53 59 21 74) opens April to October; guided tours lasting 45 minutes (English explanatory sheets available) begin 10 am (9.30 am in July and August) to 11.15 am and 2 to 5.15 pm (6.15 pm in July and August, when there's no midday closure) daily. Admission costs 31FF (children aged seven to 15, 16FF). The Abri, 8km east of Les Eyzies along the beautiful D48, is a fine place to begin a day hike.

Grotte du Grand Roc

The Grand Roc Cave (☎ 05 53 06 92 70), known for its masses of delicate, translucent stalactites and stalagmites, is a few kilometres north-west of Les Eyzies along the D47. Nearby is the prehistoric site of **Laugerie Basse** and a still-inhabited troglodytic hamlet. Admission to both sites costs 48FF (children aged six to 12, 25FF); both open 10 am to 5 pm daily, November to February (closed January); and 9.30 am to 6 pm (7 pm in July and August) daily, the rest of the year.

Grotte de Rouffignac

About 15km north of Les Eyzies, the cave at Rouffignac (☎ 05 53 05 41 71), the largest in the area (it has some 10km of galleries), is known for its 250 engravings and paintings of mammoths and other animals. Tours (in French) begin 9 to 11.30 am and 2 to 5 pm (6 pm in July and August) daily.

Village Troglodytique de la Madeleine

This cave-dwelling village (☎ 05 53 06 92 49), 8km north of Les Eyzies along the D706, is in the middle of a delightfully lush forest overlooking a hairpin curve in the River Vézère. The site has two levels: 10,000 to 14,000 years ago, prehistoric people lived on the bank of the river in an area now closed to the public; and five to seven centuries ago, medieval French people built a fortified village – now in ruins – halfway up the cliff face. Their chapel, dedicated to Ste-Madeleine, gave its name to the site – and to the entire Magdelenian era. On the plateau above the cliff are the ruins of a 14th-century castle (closed to the public). Many of the artefacts discovered here are at the prehistory museum in Les Eyzies. Several walking trails pass by here.

The site opens 9.30 am to 7 pm daily, July and August; and 10 am to 6 pm (5 pm in deepest winter) daily the rest of the year. Guided tours (in French; 50 minutes) begin every half hour or so; a free English-language brochure is available. Admission costs 30FF (children aged 5 to 12, 17FF; a family ticket costs 100FF).

La Roque St-Christophe

This 900m-long series of terraces and caves (☎ 05 53 50 70 45), on a sheer cliff face 30m above the Vézère, has had an extraordinary history as a natural bastion, serving Mousterian (Neanderthal) people some 50,000 years ago, enemies of the Normans in the 10th century, the English from 1401 to 1416, and Protestants in the late 16th century.

La Roque St-Christophe is on the D706, 9km north-east of Les Eyzies. It opens 11 am to 5 pm daily from about November to March; and 10 am to 6.30 pm (7 pm in July and August) daily the rest of the year. Admission costs 35FF (children aged five to 13, 18FF; older children and students, 27FF). At the ticket kiosk, you can borrow an informative brochure that makes a valiant effort to make the now-empty caverns come alive.

Le Moustier

Across the River Vézère from La Roque St-Christophe is Le Moustier – the findings here gave the Mousterian era its name.

Dhagpo Kagyu-Ling (☎ 05 53 50 70 75, ✉ accueil@dhagpo-kagyu.org), a centre for Tibetan Buddhist studies and meditation that was founded in 1975, is 1km up the hill from the church – you'll know you've found it when you see the gold-topped stupa, the small, Tibetan-style temple, a row of prayer wheels and lots of fluttering prayer flags. The centre offers weekend (and longer) courses on Buddhist philosophy and meditation, many in English, and also hosts inter-religious dialogue. Expect to pay about 150FF per person per night in a dorm room (200FF in a double), including meals. The centre's Web site is www .dhagpo-kagyu.org.

Along the D706, the two-star, seven-room *Hôtel La Roque St-Christophe* (☎ 05 53 50 70 61) opens March to December and has doubles with shower and toilet from 180FF.

St-Léon-sur-Vézère

This quiet, one-time river port (population 427), on a picturesque loop of the River Vézère 10km south-west of Montignac, is a good base for day hikes. It has two small castles (closed to the public): the 14th-century **Manoir de la Salle**, with its squat, square donjon; and the more refined, 16th-century **Château de Clérens**, adorned with Renaissance turrets. The interior of the 11th- and 12th-century Romanesque **church** has a wooden ceiling; the half-dome above the choir shows remnants of medieval frescoes.

The 22-room *Auberge du Pont* (☎ 05 53 50 73 07), opens from just before Easter to mid-November (and the rest of the year if you phone ahead) and has doubles with shower and toilet from 230FF. The *restaurant* has *menus* from 68FF.

Le Thot

The museum and animal park known as Le Thot – Espace Cro-Magnon (☎ 05 53 50 70 44), intended as an introduction to the world of prehistoric people, has models of animals that appear in prehistoric art, live specimens of similar animals, and exhibits on the creation of Lascaux II. Admission costs 30FF (children aged six to 12, 15FF) but is almost free if you buy a Lascaux II ticket with a special add-on. It opens 10 am to 7 pm (5.30 pm from October to March, when it's closed on Monday and there's a midday break from noon to 1.30 pm). It is closed in January.

Montignac

postcode 24290 • pop 3101
• elevation 300m

The relaxing and picturesque town of Montignac, on the Vézère 25km north-east of Les Eyzies, achieved sudden fame after the discovery of the nearby Grotte de Lascaux. The attractive old city and commercial centre is on the river's right bank, but of more use for touristic logistics is the left bank area around place Tourny. Rue du Quatre Septembre links the D65 with the D704 and the D704E to Lascaux.

Orientation & Information The tourist office (☎ 05 53 51 82 60, fax 05 53 50 49 72), 200m west of place Tourny at 22 rue du Quatre Septembre, is next to the 14th-century Église St-Georges le Prieuré. It opens 9 am to 7 pm daily, July to September; and 9 am to noon and 2 to 6 pm (closed Sunday) the rest of the year. IGN maps and topoguides are sold at the Maison de la Presse just across the street (closed on Sunday afternoon except in July and August).

The banks, including three right around the tourist office, open Tuesday to Saturday. The post office on place Tourny opens 8.30 am to noon and 1.45 to 4.45 pm weekdays, and until noon on Saturday. Currency exchange is available.

Places to Stay & Eat The 10-room *Hôtel de la Grotte* (☎ 05 53 51 80 48, fax 05 53 51 05 96), 200m east of the tourist office at place Tourny, has very comfortable doubles/triples for 165/195FF (235/350FF for doubles/quads with shower and toilet). Its restaurant opens daily and has traditional and creative Périgord-style *menus* from 90FF (61FF at lunch) to 195FF.

Le Tourny (☎ 05 53 51 59 95, place Tourny) is both a brasserie (the three-course *menu* costs 65FF) and a bar. It usually opens 7.30 am to 1 am, but stays open to 5 am when there's a live concert, which is generally on Saturday night and, from April to September, on Friday night 10 pm to 2 am. The *Casino* supermarket (*place Tourny*), next to the post office, closes from 12.30 to 3 pm and on Sunday afternoon and Monday.

Entertainment *Cinéma Vox* (☎ 05 53 51 87 24), across the car park from the tourist office, screens non-dubbed films.

Getting There & Away For information on buses to/from Montignac, see Getting There & Away in the Sarlat-la-Canéda and Périgueux sections. There's a bus stop (hours posted) at place Tourny.

Grotte de Lascaux & Lascaux II

Lascaux Cave, 2km south-east of Montignac at the end of the D704E, is adorned with some of the most extraordinary prehistoric paintings ever found. Discovered in 1940 by four teenage boys who, it is said, were out searching for their dog, the cave's main room and a number of steep galleries are decorated with figures of wild oxen, deer, horses, reindeer and other creatures depicted in vivid reds, blacks, yellows and browns. The drawings and paintings, shown by carbon dating to be between 15,000 and 17,000 years old, are thought to have been done by members of a hunting cult.

The cave – in pristine condition when found – was opened to the public in 1948 but was closed 15 years later when it became clear that human breath and the resulting carbon dioxide and condensation were causing the colours to fade and a green

fungus – and even tiny stalactites – to grow over the paintings.

In response to massive public curiosity about prehistoric art, a precise replica of the most famous section of the original was meticulously re-created a few hundred metres away. Lascaux II (☎ 05 53 51 95 03) opened in 1983, and although the idea sounds kitschy, the reproductions are surprisingly evocative and well worth a look.

The 40m-long Lascaux II, which can handle 2000 visitors daily (in guided groups of 40), opens 10 am to 12.30 pm and 1.30 to 6 pm (no midday closure from April to October; until 8 pm in July and August) daily (except on Monday from November to March). It is closed for three weeks in January. The last tour begins about an hour before closing time, both in the morning and the afternoon. Tickets, which from April to October are sold *only* in Montignac (next to the tourist office), cost 50FF (children aged 6 to 12, 20FF), or marginally more if you'd also like to visit Le Thot. Reservations are not necessary except for groups.

St-Amand de Coly

The golden-hued limestone houses of St-Amand de Coly (population 30), in a bucolic little valley 8km east of Montignac, are dominated by the audaciously tall **Église Monastique** (abbey church). It was built in the early 1100s; the massive fortifications date from the mid-1300s. A footpath goes all the way around the building.

The 10-room *Hôtel Gardette* (☎/fax 05 53 51 68 50) opens April to mid-October and has doubles with shower for 175FF (220FF with shower and toilet).

DORDOGNE PÉRIGOURDINE

The term Dordogne Périgourdine is used to describe the part of Périgord that stretches along the River Dordogne.

Domme

postcode 24250 • pop 1030
• elevation 150m
Set on a steep promontory high above the Dordogne, the trapezoid-shaped walled village of Domme is one of the few bastides to

have retained most of its 13th-century ramparts, including three fortified gates. A bit too perfectly restored, it attracts more than its share of coach tours, but they in no way spoil the stunning panorama from the cliff-side **Esplanade du Belvédère** and the adjacent **Promenade de la Barre**, which stretches west along the forested slope to the Jardin Public (a public park).

The tourist office (☎ 05 53 31 71 00), on place de la Halle, opens 10 am to noon and 2 to 6 pm daily (to 7 pm in July and August, when there's no midday closure; to 5 pm from 12 November to early February, when it opens only on weekday afternoons).

Across from the tourist office, the 19th-century reconstruction of a 16th-century *halle* (covered market) houses the entrance to the **grottes**, 450m of stalactite-filled galleries underneath the village; a lift whisks you back up at the end of the 30-minute tour. Except in January, tours take place whenever the tourist office – which sells tickets – is open; the last tour leaves 30 minutes before closing time in the morning and the afternoon. Admission costs 35FF (those aged five to 14, 20FF; students 30FF).

On the far side of the square from the tourist office, the **Musée d'Arts et Traditions Populaires** (18FF) has nine rooms of artefacts such as clothing, toys and tools (mainly from the 19th century). It opens daily April to September.

Activities From March to September or mid-October (unless the river is too high), **canoe and kayak trips** can be arranged through local organisation Randonnée Dordogne (☎ 05 53 28 22 01, fax 05 53 28 53 00, ❷ randodordogne@wanadoo.fr), a highly professional, English-speaking outfit whose base is in Cénac, 300m to the right as you approach the D46 bridge over the River Dordogne from the south (ie, from Domme). Day trips cost 120FF per person, including transport.

Places to Stay The 15-room, two-star *Nouvel' Hôtel* (☎ 05 53 28 38 67, fax 05 53 28 27 13, place de la Halle), two buildings

The River Dordogne

The mighty Dordogne rises on the Puy de Sancy high in the Massif Central, flowing south-westwards and then due west for 472km – through five dams – to a point about 20km north of Bordeaux, where it joins the River Garonne to form the Gironde Estuary. Towns and chateaux along (or very near) the Dordogne with entries in this book include Le Mont Dore and La Bourboule (see the Massif Central chapter); Beaulieu-sur-Dordogne (see the Limousin section in this chapter); Castelnau-Bretenoux, Autoire, Carennac and Martel (see the Quercy section in this chapter); Domme, La Roque Gageac, Castelnaud, Beynac, Milandes, Limeuil and Bergerac (see the Dordogne section in this chapter); and St-Émilion (see the Atlantic Coast chapter).

down the hill from the tourist office, has doubles with shower and toilet for 230FF. It *might* be closed from about December to March.

Château de Castelnaud

The 12th- to 16th-century Château de Castelnaud (☎ 05 53 31 30 00), 11km west of Domme along the D50 and D57, has everything you'd expect from a cliff-top castle: walls up to 2m thick (as you can see from the loopholes, some designed for crossbows, others for small cannons); a superb panorama of the meandering Dordogne; and fine views of the fortified chateaux (including arch rival Château de Beynac) that dot the nearby hilltops. The interior rooms are occupied by a **museum of medieval warfare**, whose displays range from daggers and spiked halberds to huge catapults. The houses of the medieval village of Castelnaud cling to the steep slopes below the fortress.

From March to mid-November, the chateau opens 10 am to 6 pm (7 pm in May, June and September; 9 am to 8 pm in July and August) daily (including holidays). The rest of the year it opens 2 to 5 pm (closed Saturday). Admission costs 30FF (those aged 10 to 17, 16FF). An English-language guidebook can be borrowed at the ticket counter.

La Roque Gageac

This hamlet of tan stone houses is built half-way up the cliff face on the right bank of one of the *cingles* (hairpin curves) in the River Dordogne. The tiny tourist office shed (☎ 05 53 29 17 01) in the car park opens 10 am to noon and 3 to 7 pm daily, Easter to October; the rest of the year, brochures can be picked up at the post office.

The **Fort Troglodyte** (☎ 05 53 31 61 94), which consists of a number of medieval military positions built into the cliff, costs 25FF and opens April to 11 November (and, usually, in the off-season too). There's some tropical foliage in the small, free **Jardin Exotique** (Exotic Garden), next to the tiny **church**. Down below, the **quay** serves as a launch point for short river cruises (☎ 05 53 29 40 44 for Gabares Norbert). Canoes (120/150/190FF for two people travelling 7/14/21km) can be rented from Canoë Dordogne (☎ 05 53 29 58 50), next to the car park, which also offers rock climbing and spelunking daily from April to October (often booked out in July and August).

East of La Roque Gageac, the beautiful **D703** follows the northern bank of the serpentine Dordogne, passing by the **Cingle de Montfort** (a particularly sharp hairpin curve). Unfortunately, it's too narrow and busy for cycling – bikers are much better off taking the old railroad tracks, sections of which have been turned into a bike path (look for signs to the *piste cyclable*).

The place with the sign reading *Bar-Hôtel* (☎ 05 53 29 51 63), open from Easter to October, has doubles with shower for 180FF. The 16-room, two-star *Hôtel La Belle Étoile* (☎ 05 53 29 51 44, fax 05 53 29 45 63) has doubles from 280FF (and one room for 200FF without toilet). It opens from approximately April to October.

Château de Beynac

This dramatic fortress (☎ 05 53 29 50 40), dominating a strategic bend in the Dordogne, is perched atop a sheer cliff. A steep trail links it to the centre of the village of Beynac-et-Cazenac, 150m below on the river bank (and the D703).

Loyal to the king of France, the fort – built from the 12th to 14th centuries (and later modified) – was long a rival of Castelnaud, just across the river, which owed its allegiance to the king of England. The interior is architecturally interesting – you get a good idea of the layout of medieval fortresses – but is only partly furnished. It opens 10 am (noon from December to February) to 6 pm (6.30 pm from June to September; until nightfall from October to February) daily. From mid-March to mid-November, one-hour guided tours (in French) take place every half hour. Admission costs a steep 40FF (children aged five to 11, 17FF).

The two-star, 18-room *Hôtel-Restaurant du Château* (☎ 05 53 29 50 13, fax 05 53 28 53 05), overlooking the river on the main road through Beynac, has comfortable doubles with shower for 280FF. It is closed early December to early February. The attached *restaurant* (open daily), specialises in traditional Périgord cuisine and has *menus* from 83FF to 140FF.

Château des Milandes

The claim to fame of the smallish, late-15th-century Château des Milandes (☎ 05 53 59 31 21) is its post-war role as the home of the African-American dancer and music-hall star Josephine Baker (1906–75), who helped bring black American culture to Paris in the 1920s with her *Revue Nègre* and created a sensation by appearing on stage wearing nothing but a skirt of bananas.

Awarded the Croix de Guerre and the Legion of Honour for her work with the French Resistance during WWII and later active in the US civil rights movement, Baker established her Rainbow Tribe here in 1949, adopting 12 children from around the world as 'an experiment in brotherhood'.

The chateau opens 10 am to 6 pm (7.30 pm in July and August; 5 pm in October, when it's closed from 10 am to noon) daily, April to October. The last obligatory, bilingual guided tour (lasting about 60 minutes) begins about an hour before closing time. The fierce-looking birds of prey in the courtyard are the stars of falconry displays several times a day (only in the afternoon in April, September and October). Admission costs 48FF (students 40FF, children aged 4 to 15, 35FF).

MONPAZIER
postcode 24540 • pop 530
• elevation 180m

Of all the bastides in south-western France, Monpazier (about 45km from both Sarlat and Bergerac), founded by a representative of the king of England in 1284, is one of the most attractive – and popular with warm season tourists. The arcaded market square, **place des Cornières** (place Centrale), is surrounded by a motley assemblage of well-preserved stone houses that reflect centuries of building and rebuilding. The rectangular street grid is no longer enclosed by ramparts, but three of the town **gates** still stand. Thursday is market day, as it has been since the Middle Ages.

The tourist office (☎ 05 53 22 68 59, @ ot.monpazier@perigord.tm.fr), in the south-eastern corner of place des Cornières, opens 9.30 am to 12.30 pm and 2.30 to 5.30 pm (nonstop until 6.30 pm June to September) daily. It has an informative historical brochure in English.

The 10-room, one-star *Hôtel de France* (☎ 05 53 22 66 01, fax 05 53 22 07 27, 10 rue St-Jacques), through the arch from place des Cornières, has spacious, slightly tacky doubles with shower and toilet for 220FF. Reception is closed Monday night and Tuesday, except May to October. The attached *restaurant* has traditional French and Périgord *menus* from 90FF to 160FF.

The *Casino* grocery, on the northern side of the place des Cornières, opens 8 am to 12.30 pm and 2.30 to 7 pm (closed on Sunday afternoon and, except in July and August, on Monday).

CHÂTEAU DE BIRON
Over the course of eight centuries, the Gontaud (or Gontaut) Biron family built, expanded and rebuilt this castle (☎ 05 53 63 13 39) until, in the early 1900s, it was sold off – along with its contents – to pay for the extravagant lifestyle of a particularly irre-

sponsible heritor. The gloriously eclectic mixture of architectural styles, the oldest from the 12th century, is a bit hard to fathom if you don't take one of the free, French-language tours (a sheet in English is available). The realistic recreations of medieval life that fill some of the rooms were once movie sets (the chateau itself is frequently used as a backdrop for films). The GR36 links Biron with Monpazier, 8km to the north.

The chateau opens 10 am to 12.30 pm and 2 to 5.30 pm (9 am to 7 pm from mid-June to August) daily, except Monday and throughout January. Admission costs 30FF (children and students 15FF).

BERGERAC
postcode 24100 • pop 27,000
• elevation 37m

The less-than-thrilling town of Bergerac, the capital of the Périgord Pourpre wine-growing area, is surrounded by 125 sq km of vineyards. A Protestant stronghold in the 16th century, it sustained heavy damage during the Wars of Religion, but the old city and the old harbour quarter have retained some of their old-time ambience and are worth a stroll. Bergerac makes a convenient stopover on the way from Périgueux (47km to the north-east) to Bordeaux (93km to the west).

The dramatist and satirist Savinien Cyrano de Bergerac (1619–55) may have put the town on the map, but his connection with his namesake is extremely tenuous: it is believed that during his entire life he stayed here a few nights at most.

Information
The tourist office (☎ 05 53 57 03 11, fax 05 53 61 11 04), 97 rue Neuve d'Argenson, has useful brochures in English. It opens 9.30 am to 1 pm and 2 to 7 pm (closed Sunday except from June to September, where there's no midday closure). You can visit its Web site at www.bergerac-tourisme.com.

Things to See
Bergerac has long been an important tobacco-growing centre, which is why it has the **Musée du Tabac** (Tobacco Museum;

☎ 05 53 63 04 13), housed in the elegant, early 17th-century Maison Peyrarède at 10 rue de l'Ancien Port. It is closed Sunday morning and Monday. The **Musée de la Batellerie et de la Tonnellerie** (☎ 05 53 57 80 92), place de la Mirpe, showcases local winemaking and the historic role of the river as a vital transport artery (closed Saturday afternoon, Sunday and Monday; open Sunday afternoon from mid-March to mid-November). **Cloître des Récollets** (☎ 05 53 63 57 55), a 16th-century cloister along the river, is occupied by the local Maison des Vins, which offers free wine tasting from 10 am to 1 pm and 2 to 6 pm daily except Sunday, May to September.

Places to Stay
Near the train station, you'll find two small hotels offering good value: the friendly, 19-room *L'Ovale* (☎ 05 53 57 78 75, fax 05 53 57 81 07, 27–29 ave du 108e RI), with doubles from 140FF (230FF with shower and toilet); and the two-star, 11-room *Le Moderne* (☎ 05 53 57 19 62, 19 ave du 108e RI), where doubles start at 160FF (220FF with shower and toilet).

Getting There & Away
Bergerac is on the tertiary rail line that links Bordeaux and St-Émilion with Sarlat.

Quercy

South-east of the Dordogne département lies the warm, unmistakably southern region of Quercy, many of whose residents still speak Occitan (Provençal). The dry limestone plateau in the north-east is covered with oak trees and cut by dramatic canyons created by the serpentine River Lot and its tributaries. The main city, Cahors, is not far from some of the region's finest vineyards.

Boating
One of the most relaxing ways to see the cliffs and villages along the 64km-long, navigable stretch of the Lot between St-Cirq Lapopie and Luzech – Cahors is about mid-

way between the two – is to rent a houseboat. Over the next few years, there are plans to open up more of the River Lot to navigation, making it possible to sail downstream to Fumel and upstream to Cajarc.

For detailed information, contact the Centrale de Réservation Loisirs Accueil (see Organised Tours under Cahors) or Les Bateaux Safaraid (☎ 05 65 35 98 88, fax 05 65 35 98 89) in Bouziès; Baboumarine (☎ 05 65 30 08 99, fax 05 65 23 92 59) in Cahors; Crown Blue Line (☎ 05 65 20 08 79, fax 05 65 30 97 96) in Douelle; or Locaboat Plaisance (for their head office ☎ 03 86 91 72 72, fax 03 86 62 42 41) in Luzech.

For general information on boating in France, see Canal Boating under Activities in the Facts for the Visitor chapter.

Walking & Cycling
In addition to the GR36 and the GR65, both of which pass through Cahors, Quercy has numerous marked trails for day walks. Other Grande Randonnée trails that cross the Lot département include the GR6, GR46 and GR652. A variety of topoguides for walkers and cyclists are available from tourist offices.

CAHORS
postcode 46000 • pop 21,432
• elevation 128m
Cahors, former capital of the Quercy region, is a quiet town with a relaxed Midi atmosphere. Surrounded on three sides by a bend in the River Lot and ringed by hills, it is endowed with a famous medieval bridge, a large (if unspectacular) medieval quarter and a couple of minor Roman sites. The weather is mild in winter, hot and dry in summer and generally delightful in the spring and autumn. Cahors makes an excellent base for exploring Quercy.

Orientation
The main commercial thoroughfare, the north-south oriented blvd Léon Gambetta, is named after Cahors-born Léon Gambetta (1838–82), one of the founders of the Third Republic and briefly premier of France (1881–82). It divides Vieux Cahors (old Cahors), to the east, from the new quarters, to

the west. At its northern end is place Charles de Gaulle, essentially a giant car park; about 500m south is place François Mitterrand, home of the tourist office. An even-numbered street address is often blocks away from a similar odd-numbered one.

Information

Tourist Offices The efficient tourist office (☎ 05 65 53 20 65, fax 05 65 53 20 74, ✆ cahors@wanadoo.fr) is on place François Mitterrand. It opens 9 am to 12.30 pm and 1.30 to 6.30 pm Monday to Saturday (6 pm on Saturday); and, in July and August, on Sunday and holidays from 10 am to noon. Several excellent brochures in English are on offer.

For information on the Lot département, call, write or visit the Comité Départemental du Tourisme (☎ 05 65 35 07 09, fax 05 65 23 92 76, ✆ le-lot@wanadoo.fr) at 107 quai Eugène Cavaignac (1st floor). It opens 8 am to 12.30 pm and 1.30 to 5.30 pm weekdays (4.30 pm on Friday). Its Web site is www.tourisme-lot.com.

Money The Banque de France, 318 rue Président Wilson, changes money from 8.45 am to noon weekdays. The banks along blvd Léon Gambetta open either Tuesday to Saturday or Monday to Friday.

Post & Communications The main post office, 257 rue Président Wilson, opens 8 am to 7 pm Monday to Friday and until noon Saturday. Exchange services and a Cyberposte are available.

At Les Docks (see Entertainment), you can use the Internet from about 2 to 8 pm (6 pm at weekends, 10 or 11 pm Wednesday to Friday).

Laundry The laundrettes on place de la Libération and at 208 rue Georges Clemenceau are open 7 am to 9 pm daily.

Medical Services The ramp to the 24-hour Urgences (casualty ward) of the Centre Hospitalier Jean Rougier (hospital; ☎ 05 65 20 50 50) is across from 428 rue Président Wilson.

Things to See

It is possible to walk around three sides of Cahors by following the **quays** along the town's riverside perimeter. Sights below are listed more or less anticlockwise from the bridge.

Pont Valentré, one of France's finest fortified medieval bridges, consists of six arches and three tall towers, two of them outfitted with machicolations (projecting parapets equipped with openings that allow defenders to drop missiles on the attackers below). Built in the 14th century (the towers were added later), it was designed as part of the town's defences rather than as a traffic bridge.

Two millennia ago, the **Fontaine des Chartreux** was used in the worship of Divona, the namesake of Gallo-Roman Cahors. A large number of coins, minted between 27 BC and AD 54 and apparently thrown into the water as offerings, were discovered by archaeologists a few years back. The flooded cavern under the pool has been explored by divers to a depth of 137m.

In the Middle Ages Cahors was a prosperous commercial and financial centre and to this day **Vieux Cahors**, the medieval quarter east of blvd Léon Gambetta, is densely packed with old (though not necessarily picturesque) four-storey houses linked by streets and alleyways so narrow you can almost touch both walls. At place St-Urcisse, there's a fascinating **mechanical clock** (1997) that drops metal balls through a series of improbable contraptions.

In 1580, during the Wars of Religion, the Protestant Henri of Navarre (later to become the Catholic King Henri IV) captured the Catholic stronghold of Cahors and spent a night in the **Hôtel des Roaldès** (☎ 05 65 22 95 98) at 271 quai Champollion, open daily (except Sunday morning) from April to 20 September.

The cavernous nave of the Romanesque-style **Cathédrale St-Étienne**, consecrated in 1119, is crowned with two 18m-wide cupolas (the largest in France) that were inspired by the architecture of the Near East. The chapels along the nave (repainted in the 19th century) are Gothic, as are the choir and the massive western facade. The wall paintings between the organ and the interior of the western facade are early 14th-century originals.

The heavily mutilated, Flamboyant Gothic **cloître** (cloister), open May to September and accessible from the cathedral's choir or through the arched entrance opposite 59 rue de la Chantrerie, is in the Flamboyant Gothic style of the early 16th century. Off the cloister, **Chapelle St-Gausbert** (named after a late 9th-century bishop of Cahors) houses a small collection of liturgical objects. Admission to the chapel costs 15FF. The frescoes of the Final Judgement date from around 1500.

The **Musée Henri Martin** (☎ 05 65 30 15 13) at 792 rue Émile Zola, also known as the Musée Municipal, has some archaeological artefacts and a collection of works by the Cahors-born pointillist painter Henri Martin (1893–1972). It opens only when there are temporary exhibitions, usually from June to September. It is closed on Tuesday.

To get to the **Fontaine Musicale** (Musical Fountain, 1989), go down the alley next to 70 rue Louis Deloncle.

The **Tour du Pape Jean XXII**, a square, crenellated tower at 1–3 blvd Léon Gambetta – at 34m the tallest structure in town – was built in the 14th century as part of the home of Jacques Duèse, later Pope John XXII (1316–34). The second of the Avignon popes, he established a university in Cahors in 1331. The interior is closed to the public. Across the street is the 14th-century **Église St-Barthélémy**, with its massive brick and stone belfry.

The small **Musée de la Résistance** (☎ 05 65 22 14 25), on the northern side of place Charles de Gaulle, has illustrated exhibits on the Resistance, the concentration camps and the liberation of France. It opens 2 to 6 pm daily. Admission is free.

Die-hard fans of Roman architecture might want to visit the **Arc de Diane**, a stone archway with red-brick stripes that once formed part of a Gallo-Roman bathhouse. It is opposite 24 ave Charles de Freycinet.

Walking
Mont St-Cyr This 264m-high antenna-topped hill, across the river from Vieux Cahors, affords excellent views of the town and the surrounding countryside. It can easily be climbed on foot – the trail begins near the southern end of Pont Louis-Philippe (1838).

Organised Tours
The Centrale de Réservation Loisirs Accueil (☎ 05 65 53 20 90, fax 05 65 30 20 94, ✉ loisirs.accueil.lot@wanadoo.fr) in the tourist office building at place François Mitterrand, opens 8 am to 12.30 pm and 1.30 to 5.30 pm weekdays (and on Saturday from January to June). It can arrange canoe, bicycle and horse-riding excursions, cookery courses and houseboat rental. If you want a hassle-free walk, they can provide an itinerary and arrange for accommodation, meals and even the transport of your bags. Activities can often be booked at short notice.

Special Events
Le Printemps de Cahors, a three-week exhibition of photography and the visual arts, is held in June. Around Bastille Day (14 July), the week-long Festival de Blues brings big-name jazz stars to town.

Places to Stay
Rooms are hardest to come by in July and August. Many cheapies do not register new guests on Sunday unless you make advance arrangement by phone.

The Centrale de Réservation Loisirs Accueil (see Organised Tours) can arrange accommodation in the area's many chambres d'hôtes and gîtes.

Camping The three-star *Camping Rivière de Cassebut* (☎ 05 65 30 06 30), on the left bank of the Lot about 1km north of Pont de Cabessut (the bridge just east of Vieux Cahors), opens April to October.

Hostels The 40-bed *Auberge de Jeunesse* (☎ 05 65 35 64 71, fax 05 65 35 95 92, 20 rue Frédéric Suisse) is in the same building as the Foyer des Jeunes Travailleurs. Staying

CAHORS

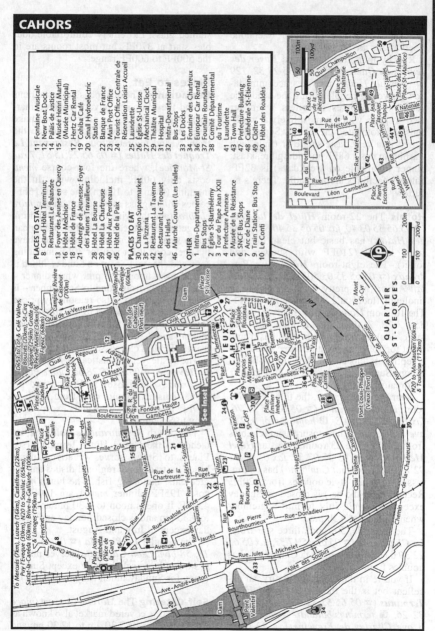

PLACES TO STAY
8 Grand Hôtel Terminus;
   Restaurant Le Balandre
13 Foyer des Jeunes en Quercy
16 Hôtel Melchior
18 Hôtel de France
21 Auberge de Jeunesse; Foyer
   des Jeunes Travailleurs
28 Hôtel La Bourse
39 Hôtel La Chartreuse
40 Hôtel Aux Perdreaux
45 Hôtel de la Paix

PLACES TO EAT
30 Champion Supermarket
35 La Pizzeria
42 Restaurant La Taverne
44 Restaurant Le Troquet
46 Marché Couvert (Les Halles)

11 Fontaine Musicale
12 New Boat Dock
14 Palais de Justice
15 Musée Henri Martin
   (Musée Municipal)
17 Hertz Car Rental
19 Cohiba Café
20 Small Hydroelectric
   Station
22 Banque de France
23 Main Post Office
24 Tourist Office; Centrale de
   Réservation Loisirs Accueil
25 Laundrette
26 Église St-Urcisse
27 Mechanical Clock
29 Théâtre Municipal
31 Hospital
32 Intra-Departmental
   Bus Stops
33 Les Docks
34 Fontaine des Chartreux
36 Europcar Car Rental
37 Fountain Roundabout
38 Comité Départemental
   du Tourisme
41 Laundrette
43 Town Hall
47 Prefecture Building
48 Cathédrale St-Etienne
49 Cloître
50 Hôtel des Roaldès

OTHER
1 Intra-Departmental
  Bus Stops
2 Église St-Barthélémy
3 Tour du Pape Jean XXII
4 Prefecture Annexe
5 Musée de la Résistance
6 SNCF Bus Stops
7 Arc de Diane
9 Train Station; Bus Stop
10 Le Conti

in a room with four to 11 beds costs 51FF. Check-in is possible 24 hours. Telephone reservations are advisable.

Run by nuns, the antiquated *Foyer des Jeunes en Quercy* (☎ 05 65 35 29 32, 129 rue Fondue Haute) provides accommodation for young people during the academic year but welcomes travellers whenever there's space, which is most likely at weekends and from late June to early September. A bed in a very basic single or triple with washbasin costs 68FF, including breakfast; dinner (available on weekdays) is 32FF. Kitchen facilities are available. There's no curfew.

Hotels The 22-room *Hôtel de la Paix* (☎ 05 65 35 03 40, fax 05 65 35 40 88, place des Halles) has basic but clean doubles from 160FF (210FF with shower and toilet). The eight-room *Hôtel Aux Per-dreaux* (☎ 05 65 35 03 50, 137 rue du Por-tail Alban) has pretty basic doubles with linoleum floors and a shower for 170FF. The 10-room *Hôtel La Bourse* (☎/fax 05 65 35 17 78, 7 place Claude Rousseau) has large doubles/quads with washbasin and bidet for 150/190FF. At all three places the reception is closed Sunday and holidays, except Sunday in July and August at Aux Perdreaux.

Near the train station, the three-star, 79-room *Hôtel de France* (☎ 05 65 35 16 76, fax 05 65 22 01 08, ✉ hdf46@crdi.fr, 252 ave Jean Jaurès) has unsurprising doubles from 245FF. The 23-room, two-star *Hôtel Melchior* (☎ 05 65 35 03 38, fax 05 65 23 92 75, place Jouinot Gambetta) has charmless, hotel chain-style doubles from 220FF. Reception (at the bar) is closed on Sunday except from mid-July to mid-September when it opens at 5.30 pm.

The riverside, 50-room, three-star *Hôtel La Chartreuse* (☎ 05 65 35 17 37, fax 05 65 22 30 03), on Chemin de la Chartreuse, has doubles from 260FF.

If you're in the mood for luxury, an excellent bet is the three-star *Grand Hôtel Terminus* (☎ 05 65 53 32 00, fax 05 65 53 32 26, ✉ terminus.balandre@wanadoo.fr, 5 ave Charles de Freycinet), a 22-room

place built around 1920 and decorated with stained glass. Extremely comfortable doubles start at 370FF, but most rooms are in the 500FF to 600FF range.

Places to Eat

Restaurants The inexpensive restaurants around the Marché Couvert (covered market), popular with the people who make their living in Vieux Cahors, include the friendly and unpretentious *Restaurant Le Troquet des Halles* (☎ 05 65 22 15 81, 7 rue St-Maurice), where the four-course *menu* costs only 60FF, including wine. In the morning (from 7 to 10 am), the soup (16FF) comes with a glass of wine so you can *faire chabrot* (add the wine to the soup and drink it together); for breakfast or lunch, you can buy a steak at the nearby market and have the chef cook it for you for 30FF, including soup and cheese. Except on Sunday, lunch is served from noon to 2 pm, while dinner – available only from June to September – is from 7 to 9.30 pm. Also reasonably priced is the restaurant attached to the *Hôtel de la Paix* (see Places to Stay) which opens noon to 2 pm and 7.30 to 9 pm, and serves *menus* from 68FF. It is closed Sunday and holidays.

The rustic yet sophisticated *Restaurant La Taverne* (☎ 05 65 35 28 66, place Pierre Escorbiac) specialises in French and regional cuisine. *Menus* cost from 75FF to 149FF. Its closed at weekends except from May to September.

The superb *Restaurant Le Balandre*, attached to the Grand Hôtel Terminus (see Places to Stay), serves creative cuisine based on traditional regional dishes and ingredients, including fish. The lunch *menu* costs 195FF; dinner *menus* are 180FF to 450FF. It opens noon to 1.30 pm and 7.30 to 9.30 pm and is closed Sunday and Monday except in July and August.

The popular *La Pizzeria* (☎ 05 65 35 12 18, 58 blvd Léon Gambetta) serves pizzas, pasta and large salads daily except Sunday (open for Sunday lunch May to October).

Self-Catering The *Marché Couvert* (place des Halles), a covered market also known as Les Halles, opens 7.30 am to 12.30 pm and

3 to 7 pm Tuesday to Saturday, and 9 am to noon on Sunday and most holidays. There's an *open-air market* around the covered market and on place Jean-Jaques Chapou on Wednesday and Saturday mornings. Nearby, *food shops* can be found around place des Halles and along rue de la Préfecture.

The *Champion* supermarket, down the street that's across from 109 blvd Léon Gambetta, opens 9.30 am to 12.30 pm and 2 to 7 pm daily, except Monday morning and Sunday.

Entertainment
Les Docks (☎ 05 65 22 36 38, 430 allée des Soupirs), a one-time warehouse, has recently been turned into a municipal cultural centre, with a concert hall, a venue for small-scale theatre productions, practice rooms for young musicians (5FF an hour), a free skatepark (for fans of in-line skates and skateboards) and a cybercafe (see Post & Communications).

The new, bi-level, Cuban-style *Cohiba Café* (☎ 05 65 53 95 83, 216 ave Jean Jaurès) opens 7 pm to 2 am (4 am when there is a live concert of Latin American music starting at 11 pm) Tuesday to Sunday. Another popular bar is *Le Conti* (☎ 05 65 35 22 60, 9 place Charles de Gaulle), which opens 7 am to 1 am daily. The cellar becomes a pub in summer.

Getting There & Away
Bus The bus services linking Cahors with destinations around the Lot département, designed primarily to transport school children, are a mess. To check into your limited options, ask at the tourist office.

For details of the daily SNCF bus services from Cahors' train station and place Charles de Gaulle to Bouziès, Tour de Faure (St-Cirq Lapopie) and Figeac, see those sections under East of Cahors. Details on SNCF buses to Mercuès, Castelfranc, Luzech and Puy l'Évêque appear under West of Cahors.

Train The train station (☎ 0 836 35 35 35), on place Jouinot Gambetta (place de la Gare), is on the main SNCF line (four to nine

daily) linking Paris' Gare d'Austerlitz (314FF, 5¼ hours) with Limoges (136FF, 2¼ hours), Souillac (56FF, 1¾ hours), Brive-la-Gaillarde (80FF, 70 minutes), Montauban (55FF, 45 minutes) and Toulouse (87FF, 1¼ hours). To get to Sarlat-la-Canéda, take a train to Souillac and an SNCF bus from there (28.50FF, 40 minutes, three daily).

Car Europcar (☎ 05 65 22 35 55) is at 68 blvd Léon Gambetta (closed Saturday afternoon and Sunday). Hertz (☎ 05 65 35 34 69) is opposite the train station at 385 rue Anatole France.

Free parking is available all along the river and in the westernmost sections of the car parks along allées Fénelon (behind the tourist office) and at place Charles de Gaulle.

EAST OF CAHORS
The limestone hills between Cahors and Figeac are cut by the dramatic, cliff-flanked Rivers Lot and Célé. The narrow, winding and supremely scenic D662 (signposted 'Vallée du Lot') follows the River Lot, while the even narrower and more spectacular D41 (signposted 'Vallée du Célé') follows the tortuous route of the River Célé.

Bouziès
The quiet hamlet of Bouziès (population 70), on the left bank of the River Lot between the cliffs and the riverbank, is home to the welcoming, 39-room, two-star *Hôtel Les Falaises* (☎ 05 65 31 26 83, fax 05 65 30 23 87, ✉ falaises@crdi.fr). Doubles cost from 262FF to 355FF, depending on the season. It is closed from November to early April. Mountain bikes, canoes and kayaks are rented out to guests and non-guests alike. The attached *restaurant* (open daily) serves regional *menus* from 82FF. Check out its Web site at www.crdi.fr/falaises.

Les Bateaux Safaraid (see Activities at the beginning of the Quercy section) rents out *gabarres* (flat-bottomed river boats) and six-person houseboats.

The SNCF bus (four to six daily) that links Cahors (27FF, 25 minutes) with Figeac (45FF, 70 minutes) stops on the D662 across

QUERCY

the narrow suspension bridge from Bouziès. If you make advance reservations, the hotel will send its minivan to pick you up at Cahors' train station or drop you off at the starting point of a hike.

Cabrerets

The verdant hamlet of Cabrerets (population 190), on the River Célé 3km upriver from where it joins the River Lot, is about midway between Bouziès and the Grotte de Pech Merle.

The 21-room, two-star *Hôtel des Grottes* (☎ 05 65 31 27 02, fax 05 65 31 20 15), on the D41 overlooking the river, has doubles with shower from 250FF (290FF with shower and toilet); 40FF more in July and August. It opens April to October. The attached *restaurant* serves hearty Quercynoise *menus* for 89FF and 120FF. It is closed on Sunday night and Monday in April and May.

SNCF buses on the Cahors–Figeac route stop just under 4km south of Cabrerets at the intersection of the D662 and the D41.

Grotte de Pech Merle

The spectacular, 1200m-long Pech Merle Cave (☎ 05 65 31 27 05), 30km east of Cahors, is first and foremost a natural wonder, with thousands of stalactites and stalagmites of all varieties and shapes. It also has dozens of paintings of mammoths, horses and 'negative' human handprints, drawn by Cro-Magnon people 16,000 to 20,000 years ago in red, black, blue and dark grey. Prehistoric artefacts found in the area are on display in the museum.

From about a week before Easter to October, one-hour guided tours (English text available) take place every 45 minutes (every 15 minutes in summer) from 9.30 am to noon and 1.30 to 5 pm daily. Tickets – well worth the price – cost 38FF (44FF from mid-June to mid-September); children aged five to 18, pay 25FF (30FF in summer). During the months when there are lots of tourists around (especially July and August), get there early as only 700 people daily are allowed to visit. Telephone reservations are accepted.

The Grotte de Pech Merle is 8km from the Bouziès bridge and 3km from Cabrerets along the D41, D13 and D198. On foot, the cave is about 3km from Bouziès via the GR651.

Conduché

Year round (weather permitting), Le Bureau des Sports Nature (☎ 05 65 24 21 01, ✉ bureau-sports-nature@wanadoo.fr), based in the village of Conduché (near the confluence of the rivers Lot and Célé), offers guided rock climbing and spelunking (200FF per person a day), guided walks (140FF per person a day), canoe trips (230FF for a 22km descent for two people) and mountain bike rental (100FF a day). The office opens Monday to Friday (and at weekends in July and August). You can visit their Web site at perso.wanadoo.fr/bureau-sports-nature.

St-Cirq Lapopie

postcode 46330 • pop 50 • elevation 147m
St-Cirq Lapopie, 25km east of Cahors and 44km south-west of Figeac, is perched on a cliff top 100m above the River Lot. The spectacular views and the area's natural beauty make up for the village's self-conscious charm.

The fortified, early 16th-century **Gothic church** is of no special interest except for its stunning location. The ruins of the 13th-century **chateau**, at the top of the hill, also afford a fine panorama. Below, along the narrow alleyways, the restored stone and half-timbered houses – topped with steep, red-tile roofs – shelter **artisans' studios** offering leather goods, pottery, jewellery and items made of wood. The **Musée Rignault** (10FF) has a delightful garden and an eclectic collection of French furniture and art from Africa and China. From April to November it opens daily from 10 or 11 am to 7 pm (8 pm in July and August, 6 pm in April and November), with a siesta at the weekend from 1 to 3 pm. The rest of the year it opens six days a week.

The tourist office (☎/fax 05 65 31 29 06) in the village hall, can supply you with an English-language brochure. It opens 10 or 11 am to 7 pm (8 pm in July and August,

6 pm in April and November) daily, April to November, with a siesta at the weekend from 1 to 3 pm. It opens six days a week the rest of the year.

The riverside *Camping de la Plage* (☎ 05 65 30 29 51), on the left bank of the Lot at the bridge linking the D662 (Tour de Faure) with the road up to St-Cirq Lapopie, opens year round. The eight-room *Auberge du Sombral* (☎ 05 65 31 26 08, fax 05 65 30 26 37), across the square from the tourist office, has rooms from 275FF to 400FF. It opens April to mid-November (reception is closed on Tuesday night and Wednesday, except from July to September).

St-Cirq Lapopie is 2km across the river and up the hill from Tour de Faure (on the D662), from where SNCF buses go to Cahors (28FF, 35 minutes, four to six daily) and Figeac (44FF, one hour, four daily).

Figeac
postcode 46100 • pop 9500
• elevation 250m

The harmonious riverside town of Figeac, on the River Célé 70km north-east of Cahors, has a picturesque **old city**, with many houses dating from the 12th to 18th centuries. Founded in the 9th century by Benedictine monks, it became a prosperous medieval market town, an important stopping place for pilgrims travelling to Santiago de Compostela and, later, a Protestant stronghold (1576–1623).

Orientation & Information The main commercial thoroughfare is the north–south blvd Docteur G Juskiewenski, which runs perpendicular to the Célé and its right-bank quays. Pedestrianised rue Gambetta, four short blocks east, is also perpendicular to the river. The train station, about 600m to the south-east, is across the river from the centre of town, at the end of ave Georges Clemenceau.

The tourist office (☎ 05 65 34 06 25), on place Vival (one block north of the river and two blocks east of blvd Docteur G Juskiewenski) opens 10 am to noon and 2.30 to 6 pm Monday to Saturday and, in May and June, 10 am to 1 pm Sunday. From July to mid-September it opens 10 am to 1 pm and 2 to 7 pm daily.

The post office, a block west of blvd Docteur G Juskiewenski at 8 ave Fernand Pezet, opens 8.30 am to 5.30 pm weekdays and until noon Saturday. Currency exchange is available. There are a couple of banks along the same street.

The Allo Laverie laundrette next to the tourist office opens 6 am to 10 pm daily.

Things to See The tourist office is housed in a handsome, 13th-century building known as the **Hôtel de la Monnaie** (Mint; in Occitan: Oustal de la Mounédo), though coins were never actually minted here. Upstairs is the **Musée du Vieux Figeac** (adults/children, 10/5FF), which has a varied collection of antique clocks, coins, minerals and a propeller blade made by a local aerospace firm. It opens the same hours as the tourist office.

Figeac's most illustrious son is the brilliant linguist and founder of the science of Egyptology, Jean-François Champollion (1790–1832), who managed to decipher the written language of the pharaohs by studying the Rosetta Stone, an edict issued in 196 BC in Greek and two Egyptian scripts, demotic and hieroglyphic. Discovered by Napoleon's forces in 1799 during their abortive invasion of Egypt, the stone was captured by the English in 1801 and taken to the British Museum, where it remains to this day; an enlarged copy fills the ancient courtyard next to Champollion's childhood home, now the **Musée Champollion** (☎ 05 65 50 31 08) on tiny rue des Frères Champollion (four blocks north of the tourist office along pedestrianised rue de la République). The small collection of Egyptian antiquities can be visited from 10 am to noon and 2.30 to 6.30 pm (closed Monday, except in July and August); from November to February, hours are 2 to 6 pm. Admission costs 20FF (children and students, 12FF). Some of the explanatory signs are in English.

North of the Musée Champollion and place Champollion, **rue de Colomb**, favoured by the local aristocracy in the 18th century, is lined with centuries-old mansions in sandstone, half-timbers and brick. Near the river on rue du Chapitre, the musty **Église St-Sauveur**, a Benedictine abbey church built from the 12th to 14th centuries, features stained glass installed during the last half of the 19th century.

Places to Stay Directly across the square from the train station, the 12-room, two-star **Hôtel Le Terminus** (✆ 05 65 34 00 43, fax 05 65 50 00 94, 27 ave Georges Clemenceau) has newly remodelled doubles with shower and toilet for 245FF. About 300m west of the train station on the other side of the tracks, the eight-room **Hôtel Le Toulouse** (✆/fax 05 65 34 22 95, 4 ave de Toulouse), on the D922, has ordinary doubles with shower and toilet from 180FF.

In the old city, the two-star, 10-room **Hôtel-Café Champollion** (✆ 05 65 34 04 37, fax 05 65 34 61 69, 3 place Champollion) has double/triples with bathroom for 260/290FF.

Places to Eat The friendly **À l'Escargot** (✆ 05 65 34 23 84, 2 ave Jean Jaurès), just across Pont Gambetta from the centre of town, has been run by the same family since 1950. Menus of traditional, family-style Quercy cuisine cost 90FF, 110FF and 165FF. The restaurant attached to the **Hôtel Le Terminus** (see Places to Stay) has Quercy and Périgord-style menus from 100FF to 250FF. It is closed midday Saturday.

Cambodian, Vietnamese and Chinese food is available at **Restaurant Vimean Ekreach** (✆ 05 65 34 79 65, 10 rue Baduel), a bit south of place Champollion; menus cost 58FF (lunch only), 85FF and 125FF. There are pizzerias at 30 bis rue Gambetta and, down the block, at 9 rue Ortabadial.

The **Centre L Gambetta** (Leclerc) supermarket (32 rue Gambetta) opens 8.30 am to 12.30 pm and 2 to 7.30 pm daily except Sunday. Place Carnot has a food market on Saturday morning.

Getting There & Away Four SNCF buses daily go to Cahors (62FF, 1¾ hours) via Bouziès and Tour de Faure (St-Cirq Lapopie). Stops are at Figeac's train station

and on ave Maréchal Joffre (which runs along the river) behind Lycée Champollion.

The train station (✆ 05 65 80 28 55) is on two major rail lines: the one that links Clermont-Ferrand (153FF, at least 3½ hours, one or two direct daily) with Villefranche de Rouergue (36FF, 35 minutes, four or five daily), Najac de la Vallée (45FF, 55 minutes, four or five daily) and Toulouse (114FF, 2½ hours, four or five daily); and the one from Paris' Gare d'Austerlitz (309FF, about 5½ hours, four or five daily) to Limoges (129FF, 2½ hours), Brive (72FF, 1½ hours), Rocamadour-Padirac (42FF, 40 minutes) and Rodez (62FF, 1¼ hours).

Villefranche de Rouergue
postcode 12200 • pop 12,300
• elevation 230m

Villefranche, 61km east of Cahors, is – like most bastides – centred around an arcaded central square, **place Notre Dame**. In one corner is the Languedoc-Gothic-style **Collégiale Notre Dame**, a flying buttress-less structure built in the 14th and 15th centuries, whose never-completed belfry is held aloft by massive supports. The 15th-century **choir stalls** are ornamented with humorous figures.

A few blocks to the south-west along streets lined with stone and half-timbered houses, the **Musée Urbain Cabrol** (✆ 05 65 45 44 37), on rue de la Fontaine, has an eclectic but fascinating collection of prehistory, religious art, local folk art and 19th-century medical equipment. It is closed Sunday and, except from June to mid-September, Saturday. The **fountain** at the front, decorated with stone carvings from 1336, gushes naturally.

About 500m towards Najac from the train station, the **Chartreuse St-Sauveur**, a 15th-century monastery once affiliated with the austere Carthusian order, now houses a hospital. Of interest are the vaulted Gothic **cloister** (always open) and the **chapel** (open 2 to 5 pm on weekdays and on Sunday from 9 to 11 am), topped by a square belfry.

The tourist office (✆ 05 65 45 13 18), next to the town hall on promenade du Guiraudet, has a walking tour brochure in

English. It opens 9 am to noon and 2 to 6 pm but is closed Saturday afternoon and Sunday except in summer, when opening hours are longer. Its Web site is at www.villefranche.com.

The 15-room, two-star *Hôtel Lagarrigue* (☎ 05 65 45 01 12, place Bernard Lhez), one block north of the tourist office, has decent but unexciting doubles from 240FF. The attached *restaurant* serves French gastronomique and local specialities daily, except from mid-October to March when it is closed Sunday night and Monday. *Menus* cost from 70FF to 185FF.

The unpretentious, family-run *Restaurant Bellerive* (☎ 05 65 45 23 17), at the intersection of the D922 and the D911, across the tracks and half-a-block up the hill from the train station, serves only the freshest home-made French cuisine; *menus* go from 80FF to 280FF (closed on Monday at midday and Sunday, except in July and August). The attached eight-room *hotel* has simple doubles with shower and toilet for 150FF (170FF from June to September).

Tasty, inexpensive pizza is on offer at the tiny *Pizza Vival* (☎ 05 65 45 78 60, on the southern side of place Notre Dame), open daily. There are several other informal restaurants nearby.

Buses link Villefranche's train station (across the river from the tourist office) with the train stations in Cahors (46FF, 1¼ hours, one daily except Sunday and holidays), Figeac (35FF, 40 minutes, one SNCF bus daily) and Montauban (50FF, 1¾ hours, two daily except Sunday and holidays). See Getting There & Away under Figeac for train details.

Najac

The charming bastide village of Najac (population 250) grew in the 13th century around the **Fortresse Royal** (Royal Fortress; ☎ 05 65 29 71 65; open daily, April to September), also known as the Château Fort, built on a rocky, easily defensible hill high above a hairpin curve in the River Aveyron. A bit to the west is the massive, Midi-Gothic-style **Église St-Jean l'Évangéliste**, which the locals were forced to construct by

the Inquisition in 1258 as punishment for their Catharist tendencies.

The medieval parts of Najac are spread out along one, east–west oriented street that runs 1.2km along the crest of the hill; it links the church with the sloping **place du Faubourg**, a charming, bastide-style central square surrounded by houses – each unique – from as early as the 13th century. The tourist office (☎ 05 65 29 72 05), on the southern side of place du Faubourg, opens 9 am to noon and 2.30 to 5 pm weekdays and Saturday morning (6 pm from April to September, when it's also open on Saturday afternoon); in July and August it also opens 10 am to noon Sunday.

Najac makes a good base for kayaking, rafting, cycling and hiking (a topoguide is available at the tourist office). **Najac de la Vallée**, along the river, is 3km (by road) down the hill near the train station (see Getting There & Away under Figeac for train information).

The 20-room, two-star *Oustal del Barry* (☎ 05 65 29 74 32, fax 05 65 29 75 32, place du Faubourg), just up the hill from the tourist office, opens late March to mid-November; doubles start at 310FF. The attached *restaurant* has *menus* made with fresh local products from 140FF to 260FF. It is closed Tuesday at midday and Monday, except from July to September. You can visit its Web site at www.oustaldelbarry.com.

The most scenic way to get to Villefranche de Rouergue, 23km to the north, is via the twisting, one-lane D638, which intersects the D339 about 5km north-east of Najac.

WEST OF CAHORS

Downstream from Cahors, the lower River Lot follows an impossibly serpentine route through the rich vineyards of the Cahors AOC, passing by the dams at **Luzech**, whose medieval section sits at the base of a donjon, and **Castelfranc**, with its suspension bridge. Along (and above) the river's right bank, the **D9** – too narrow and heavily trafficked for cycling – affords superb views of the vines and the river's many hairpin curves. For details on the nearby

QUERCY

Château de Biron and Monpazier, see the Dordogne section of this chapter.

Four to seven SNCF buses a day link Cahors with Mercuès (10 minutes), Luzech and Puy l'Évêque (34 FF, 50 minutes).

Mercuès

About 7km north-west of Cahors in the village of Mercuès, *Le Mas Azemar* (☎ *05 65 30 96 85*), on rue du Mas de Vinssou, is a delightful, six-room chambre d'hôte establishment in an 18th-century house. Doubles go from 390FF to 490FF, including breakfast. It opens year round by reservation only.

On the hilltop above the village, the **Château de Mercuès** is home to a one-star Michelin restaurant.

Puy l'Évêque

The once-important river port of Puy l'Évêque (population 2200), on a rocky hillside above the right bank of the Lot, has an intimate, stone centre with numerous, centuries-old stone houses. It is a good base for exploring the lower Lot area, including the Cahors AOC wineries. The town is 31 km from Cahors.

The tourist office (☎/fax 05 65 21 37 63), in the golden-hued village hall building – at the base of a square, 13th-century **donjon** – opens 8.30 am to 12.30 pm and 2 to 6 pm Monday to Saturday (5 pm on Saturday; open Sunday morning in July and August). It can supply you with an English-language brochure on day hikes.

About 4km north up the hill and through the forest, the austere **Église de Martignac**, topped by a peculiar half-timbered belfry, is decorated with 15th-century frescoes, protected for centuries by layers of whitewash. It opens 10 am to 7 pm daily. The surrounding area is perfect for quiet walks.

The 16-room, two-star *Hôtel Henry* (☎ *05 65 21 32 24, fax 05 65 30 85 18, 23 rue du Docteur Roumat*), very near the old town, opens year round; doubles go for about 200FF to 300 FF. The attached *restaurant* has French and Quercy-style *menus* from 75FF to 180FF. It is closed Sunday night and, in winter, perhaps Saturday. The Web site is at www.hotel-henry.com.

Château de Bonaguil

This imposing feudal fortress (☎ 05 53 71 90 33) is a superb example of late 15th-century military architecture, featuring the artful integration of cliffs, outcrops, towers, bastions, loopholes, machicolations and crenellations. Situated about 15km west of Puy l'Évêque (and on the GR36 footpath), it opens 10 or 10.30 am to noon and 2 or 2.30 to 4.30 pm (5 pm in June; 6 pm in July and August, when there's no midday closure); it is closed from December to early February except during the Christmas school break. Optional guided tours (1½ hours), in English three times daily in July and August, generally take place on the hour, with the last one about an hour before closing time. Admission costs 30FF (students 25FF, those aged seven to 16, 20FF).

About 5km to the south-east is the attractive village of **St-Martin-le-Redon**, in a quiet little valley along the River Thèze (and just off the D673).

NORTHERN QUERCY

The northern edge of Quercy is not far from Collonges-la-Rouge, Beaulieu-sur-Dordogne and Turenne (see South-East of Brive in the Limousin section).

Rocamadour
postcode 46500 • pop 630
• elevation 250m

Except in winter, when it's nearly dead, the spectacularly situated pilgrimage centre of Rocamadour, 59km north of Cahors and 51km east of Sarlat, is a touristic nightmare, overrun with coaches and crammed with tacky souvenir shops.

Perched on a 150m-high cliff face above the River Alzou, the old city – known as the **Cité** – was, from the 12th to 14th centuries, an important stop on one of the pilgrimage routes to Santiago de Compostela. These days, coach tourists with glazed eyes obediently plod through a number of over-restored Gothic chapels, including **Chapelle Notre Dame**, home to a 12th-century Black Madonna said to have miraculous powers. Other sights in the Cité include the **Musée du Jouet Ancien Automobile** (☎ 05 65 33

60 75), which displays over 100 kiddie cars with pedals (opens daily, mid-March to mid-November).

The Cité's only street is connected to the chapels and the plateau above, known as **L'Hospitalet**, by the **Grand Escalier** (Great Staircase) – once climbed by the pious on their knees – and a path whose switchbacks are marked with graphic Stations of the Cross. At the top is the 14th-century **chateau** (15FF for a view from the ramparts).

Sights in L'Hospitalet include the **Grotte des Merveilles** (☎ 05 65 33 67 92), a one-room cave with some mediocre stalactites and prehistoric cave paintings (open April to mid-November).

The tourist offices in the Cité (☎ 05 65 33 62 59), on the main street, and L'Hospitalet (☎ 05 65 33 22 00), next to the Grotte des Merveilles, are open daily, year round.

Gouffre de Padirac
The truly spectacular Padirac Cave (☎ 05 65 33 64 56), 15km north-east of Rocamadour and 10km south-east of Carennac, offers the closest thing – at least in *this* world – to a cruise to Hades across the River Styx. Discovered in 1889, the cave's navigable river – 103m below ground level – is reached through a 75m-deep, 33m-wide chasm. Boat pilots, who speak only Occitan and Midi-accented French, ferry visitors along a 500m stretch of the subterranean waterway, guiding them up and down a series of stairways to otherworldly pools and vast, floodlit caverns. The whole operation is unashamedly mass-market, but it retains an innocence and style reminiscent of the 1930s, when the first lifts were installed. The temperature inside the cave is a constant 13°C.

From April to the 2nd Sunday in October, 1¼ hour visits take place from 9 am to noon and 2 to 6 pm; hours are extended in July (9 am to 6.30 pm) and August (8 am to 7 pm). Admission costs 48FF (children aged 6 to 9, 27FF).

Autoire
No other village in Quercy boasts as many towers and turrets as Autoire, situated in a deep gorge in what was once an important wine-growing area. The many Renaissance-style manor houses were built by wealthy *vignerons*. At the top of the cliffs behind the village, it is just possible to make out the ruins of the **Château des Anglais**.

Château de Castelnau-Bretenoux
A stunning hilltop silhouette greets you as you approach this feudal fortress es (☎ 05 65 10 98 00), one of France's most impressive, which is 9km east of Carennac. Dominating the valleys of the rivers Dordogne, Cère and Bave, it is built of sandy limestone in hues ranging from golden yellow to deep red; most of the complex – which, mercifully, has not been over-restored – dates from the 12th to 15th centuries. The site has signs in English.

Château de Castelnau-Bretenoux can be visited daily (except Tuesday from October to March) from 9.30 or 10 am to 12.15 pm and 2 to 5.15 pm (6.15 pm from April to September; 6.45 pm in July and August, when there's no midday closure). Ticket sales stop 45 minutes before closing time, both in the morning and the afternoon. Admission costs 32FF (those aged 18 to 25, 21FF; those aged under 18 free). The seven eclectically furnished rooms must be visited with a guide (English information sheet available).

Carennac
The narrow alleyways of this delightful medieval village (population 370), on the left bank of the Dordogne, meander among tile-roofed houses made of golden-hued stone, some built as early as the 10th century (and most occupied only in the summer). An arched stone gate leads to the 16th-century **Château du Doyen** which houses a museum of regional history and wildlife, the **Maison de la Dordogne Quercynoise** (☎ 05 65 10 91 56). The museum opens daily, April to October. Above is the square **Tour de Télémaque**, named after the hero of Fénelon's *Les Aventures de Télémaque*, written here in 1699.

Next to the chateau is the **priory**, reached via the same stone gate. Over the entrance to the Romanesque **Église St-Pierre** is an exceptional **tympanum** depicting Jesus in majesty, carved in the Languedoc Romanesque style in the mid-12th century. Just off the **cloître** (cloister; 10FF), heavily damaged in the Revolution, is a remarkable, late 15th-century **Mise au Tombeau** (statue of the Entombment), once brightly painted. Its opening hours are the same as the tourist office (☎ 05 65 10 97 01) next door, which opens 10 am to 7 pm daily, mid-June to September; and 10 am to noon and 1.30 to 5.30 pm (closed at weekend mornings), the rest of the year.

Walking options include the **GR652**, which links the village of Mézels (on the river to the north-west) with the Gouffre de Padirac (to the south-east). For a lovely drive, follow the D30 south-eastwards along the Dordogne.

The lovely, 11-room *Hôtel des Touristes* (☎ *05 65 10 94 31, fax 05 65 39 79 85)*, run by the same family for four generations and open pretty much year round, has doubles (don't let the mosquito nets unnerve you) from 200FF. Half-pension (from 230FF per person, including the room) may be required in July and August. The *restaurant*, where *menus* of traditional regional cuisine cost from 80FF to 100FF, opens daily except Friday night and Saturday from October to mid-April.

The only place to buy food is the small *grocery* next to the post office, closed from 12.30 to 3 pm and in the afternoon on Sunday and Monday.

Martel

Known as the 'Town of the Seven Towers', this charming village (population 1460) – 24km north of Rocamadour – was named after Charles Martel, who built an abbey here in 632. For centuries it has been the centre of the regional nut trade, and the ancient weighing measures can still be seen at the 18th-century **halle** (market). The fortified Gothic **church** has a Romanesque tympanum. Many of the houses date from the 14th to 16th centuries.

The tourist office (☎ 05 65 37 43 44), at place de la Halle, generally opens 10 am to noon and 3 to 6 pm Monday to Saturday (daily in July and August when hours are longer).

Atlantic Coast

Pristine beaches, sand dunes, pine forests and salt marshes line France's unpretentious Atlantic coast from the English Channel all the way to the Spanish frontier. The region's major attractions include (from north to south) the commodious city of Nantes; Poitiers, famed for its superb Romanesque churches; the picturesque port of La Rochelle; the beach-fringed Île de Ré; the brandy town of Cognac; the lively metropolis of Bordeaux, surrounded by one of the world's most renowned wine-growing regions; and the coastal resort of Arcachon, where you'll find Europe's largest sand dune.

The northern part of the Atlantic seaboard is covered in the Brittany chapter; details on the far south are in the French Basque Country chapter.

NANTES

postcode 44000 • pop 496,000

The lively and relaxed university city of Nantes, historically part of Brittany, is France's sixth largest metropolis. It has a mild (if rainy) Atlantic climate, several fine museums, carefully tended parks and an unbelievable number of inexpensive cafes and restaurants. The Edict of Nantes, a landmark royal charter guaranteeing civil rights and freedom of conscience and worship to France's Protestants, was signed here by Henri IV in 1598.

Orientation

The city centre's two main arteries, both served by tram lines, are the north–south, partly pedestrianised cours des 50 Otages (named in memory of 50 people taken hostage and shot by the Germans in 1941), and an east–west boulevard that connects the train station (to the east) with quai de la Fosse (to the west).

The commercial centre runs from the Gare Centrale bus/tram hub north-east to rue de la Marne and north-west to rue du Calvaire; it includes place Royale, which is

Highlights

- **Nantes** – stroll through the lively centre and around the exquisite Jardin des Plantes
- **La Rochelle** – take in the atmosphere, at low tide and high, day and night, around the picturesque Vieux Port
- **Île de Ré & The Médoc** – lounge around on the fine-sand beaches
- **Bordeaux** – take advantage of the superb museums and lively nightlife
- **St-Émilion** – explore the medieval town centre and visit nearby vineyards and wineries
- **Arcachon** – climb the giant dune and visit the bird sanctuary at Le Teich

linked to cours des 50 Otages by rue d'Orléans. The old city is to the east, between cours des 50 Otages and the chateau. The small streets that run along the sides of many major thoroughfares are known as *allées*.

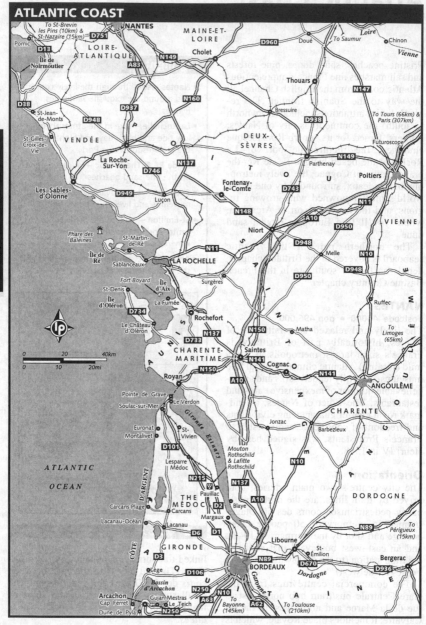

ATLANTIC COAST

euro currency converter 10FF = €1.52

Information

Tourist Offices The tourist office (☎ 02 40 20 60 00, fax 02 40 89 11 99) is on place du Commerce in the Palais de la Bourse. It opens 10 am to 7 pm Monday to Saturday. This is a good place to pick up bus/tram and city maps.

Money The Banque de France at 14 rue La Fayette opens 8.45 am to 12.30 pm Monday to Friday. Change Graslin, an exchange bureau at 17 rue Jean-Jacques Rousseau, opens until 6 pm (5 pm on Saturday, closed Sunday and holidays and from noon to 2 pm). The tourist office will also change money.

Post & Communications The main post office, at place de Bretagne, opens 8 am to 7 pm Monday to Friday and on Saturday until noon. Currency exchange and a Cyberposte are available.

Internet access is available at CyberNova (☎ 02 40 12 07 07), 14 rue Jean Jaurès, which opens 10 am to 9 or 10 pm (closed Sunday and holidays), and Cyber House Café Internet (☎ 02 40 12 11 84), 8 Quai de Versailles, open 2 pm (3 pm on Saturday) to 2 am. It is closed on Sunday.

Laundry The laundrettes at 8 allée des Tanneurs and 3 allée Duguay open daily from 7 am to 8.30 pm. The full-service Laverie du Bouffay at 3 rue du Bouffay, which costs about the same as self-service, opens 9 am to 7 pm Monday to Saturday.

Medical Services The 24-hour Service d'Urgence (emergency room ☎ 02 40 08 38 95) of the vast CHR de Nantes is along the river on Quai Moncousu.

Emergency The Police Nationale's 24-hour Hôtel de Police (☎ 02 40 37 21 21, tram stop Motte Rouge) is 1km north-east of the Monument des 50 Otages at place Waldeck Rousseau.

Things to See

From the outside, the **Château des Ducs de Bretagne** (Chateau of the Dukes of Brittany; ☎ 02 40 41 56 56) looks like your standard medieval castle, with a moat, high walls and crenellated towers. Inside, however, the parts facing the courtyard are in the style of a Renaissance pleasure palace. Admission to the courtyard is free, as is walking along part of the ramparts (both open daily from 10 am to noon and 2 to 6 pm; no midday closure in July and August). The building opposite the entrance arch often houses temporary exhibitions (closed Tuesday).

Inside the Flamboyant Gothic **Cathédrale St-Pierre et St-Paul** at place St-Pierre, the **tomb of François II** (ruled 1458–88), duke of Brittany, and his second wife, Marguerite de Foix, is considered a masterpiece of Renaissance art. The statue facing the nave, which represents **Prudence**, has a female body and face on one side and a bearded male face on the other.

The **Jardin des Plantes**, across blvd de Stalingrad from the train station, is one of the most exquisite botanical gardens in France. Founded in the early 19th century, it has beautiful flower beds, duck ponds, fountains and even a few California redwoods (sequoias). There are **hothouses** and a **children's playground** at the northern end.

The channels of the Loire that once surrounded **Île Feydeau** (the neighbourhood south of the Gare Centrale) were filled in after WWII, but you can still see the area's 18th-century mansions, built by rich merchants from the ill-gotten profits of the slave trade. Some are adorned with stone carvings of the heads of African slaves.

Two blocks north-west of Île Feydeau is **Passage Pommeray**, a delightful shopping arcade that opened in 1843. Nearby are **place Royale**, laid out in 1790, and **place Graslin**, on the northern side of which stands the **Théâtre Graslin**, built in 1788.

Promenade de l'Erdre is a network of riverside paths that follows both banks of the River Erdre from the Monument des 50 Otages north for about 7km. On the **Île de Versailles**, an island 500m north of the monument, you'll find a Japanese garden and, at the northern end, a children's playground.

ATLANTIC COAST

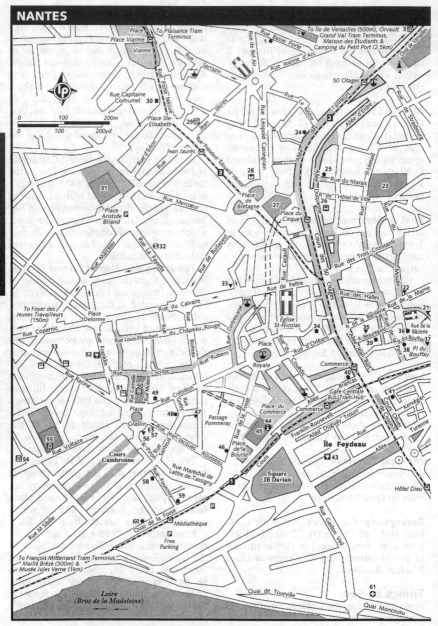

NANTES

NANTES

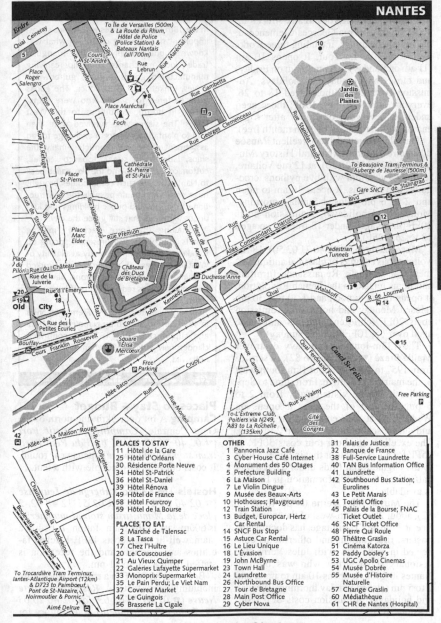

ATLANTIC COAST

PLACES TO STAY
11 Hôtel de la Gare
25 Hôtel d'Orléans
30 Résidence Porte Neuve
34 Hôtel St-Patrick
36 Hôtel St-Daniel
39 Hôtel Rénova
49 Hôtel de France
58 Hôtel Fourcroy
59 Hôtel de la Bourse

PLACES TO EAT
2 Marché de Talensac
8 La Tasca
17 Chez l'Huître
20 Le Couscousier
21 Au Vieux Quimper
22 Galeries Lafayette Supermarket
33 Monoprix Supermarket
35 Le Pain Perdu; Le Viet Nam
37 Covered Market
47 Le Guingois
56 Brasserie La Cigale

OTHER
1 Pannonica Jazz Café
3 Cyber House Café Internet
4 Monument des 50 Otages
5 Prefecture Building
6 La Maison
7 Le Violin Dingue
9 Musée des Beaux-Arts
10 Hothouses; Playground
12 Train Station
13 Budget, Europcar, Hertz
   Car Rental
14 SNCF Bus Stop
15 Astuce Car Rental
16 Le Lieu Unique
18 L'Évasion
19 John McByrne
23 Town Hall
24 Laundrette
26 Northbound Bus Office
27 Tour de Bretagne
28 Main Post Office
29 Cyber Nova

31 Palais de Justice
32 Banque de France
38 Full-Service Laundrette
40 TAN Bus Information Office
41 Laundrette
42 Southbound Bus Station;
   Eurolines
43 Le Petit Marais
44 Tourist Office
45 Palais de la Bourse; FNAC
   Ticket Outlet
46 SNCF Ticket Office
48 Pierre Qui Roule
50 Théâtre Graslin
51 Cinéma Katorza
52 Paddy Dooley's
53 UGC Apollo Cinemas
54 Musée Dobrée
55 Musée d'Histoire
   Naturelle
57 Change Graslin
60 Médiathèque
61 CHR de Nantes (Hospital)

Museums

The renowned **Musée des Beaux-Arts** (☎ 02 40 41 65 65), 10 rue Georges Clemenceau, has mainly paintings, including three works by Georges de La Tour. It opens 10 am (11 am on Sunday) to 6 pm (9 pm on Friday) and closes on Tuesday and holidays. Admission costs 20FF (those aged 18 to 26, everyone after 4.30 pm, 10FF; those aged under 18 , everyone on Friday after 6 pm and on the first Sunday of each month free).

The old-fashioned but excellent **Musée d'Histoire Naturelle** (Natural History Museum; ☎ 02 40 99 26 20), at 12 rue Voltaire, features a **vivarium** with live pythons, crocodiles and iguanas. It opens 10 am to noon and 2 to 6 pm (closed Sunday morning, Monday and holidays). Admission costs 20FF (those aged under 18 free; those aged 18 to 26, 10FF).

Musée Dobrée (☎ 02 40 71 03 50), 18 rue Voltaire, has exhibits of classical antiquities, medieval artefacts, Renaissance furniture and items related to the French Revolution. It opens 10 am to noon and 1.30 to 5.30 pm (closed Monday and holidays). Admission costs 20FF (children, students and those aged over 65, 10FF; free on Sunday).

The 133m-long French navy destroyer **Maillé Brézé** (☎ 02 40 69 56 82), in service from 1957 to 1988, is about 1km south-west of the main tourist office. From June to September it can be visited daily from 2 to 6 pm; the rest of the year it opens on Wednesday, at weekends and on holidays and during school holidays from 2 to 5 pm. The excellent one-hour tour costs 30FF, or 45FF for a 1½-hour tour that includes a visit to the engine room (kids under 12 roughly half-price). Written information in English is available.

The **Musée Jules Verne** (☎ 02 40 69 72 52), about 2km south-west of the tourist office at 3 rue de l'Hermitage, has documents, posters, first-editions and other items connected in some way with Jules Verne, the visionary sci-fi writer who was born in Nantes in 1828. It opens 10 am to noon and 2 to 5 pm (closed Sunday morning, Tuesday and holidays). Admission costs 8FF (concessions 4FF).

Nantes & the Slave Trade

In the 18th century, Nantes was France's most important slave-trading centre. In what was known euphemistically as 'the triangular trade', local merchants sent ships carrying manufactured goods – guns, gunpowder, knives, trinkets – to West Africa. The goods were bartered for slaves who were transported in horrific conditions to the West Indies. The slaves who survived were then sold to plantation owners in exchange for an assortment of tropical products. Finally, the ships, laden with sugar, tobacco, coffee, cotton, cocoa, indigo and the like, sailed back to Nantes, where such commodities brought huge profits and made possible the construction of the splendid public buildings and luxurious mansions that still grace the city.

All along the Loire, factories making sweets, chocolates and preserves sprang up to take advantage of the ready availability of West Indian sugar. Nearby, ironsmiths worked overtime to produce the leg irons, handcuffs and spiked collars required to outfit the slave ships.

Slavery was abolished in French colonies in 1794, re-established by Napoleon in 1802 and suppressed after 1827. It continued clandestinely until 1848, when it was finally outlawed.

Places to Stay – Budget

Camping A bit over 3km due north of the Gare Centrale, *Camping du Petit Port* (☎ 02 40 74 47 94, *21 blvd du Petit Port; tram stop Morrhonnière*) opens year round. It costs 66FF for two people with a tent.

Hostels The 82-bed *Auberge de Jeunesse* (☎ 02 40 29 29 20, fax 02 51 12 48 42, *2 place de la Manu; tram stop Moutonnerie*) is 600m east of the train station. A bed in a plain, well-lit room costs 48FF. Kitchen facilities are available and the reception is staffed from 8 am to 11 pm.

Beds cost 80/95FF in a triple/single room, including breakfast, at *Résidence Porte Neuve* (☎ 02 40 20 63 63, fax 02 40 20 63 79, *7 place Ste-Elisabeth*), a dormitory for young people. Places may be hard to come by on weekdays when school is in session.

Hotels Nantes' many excellent cheap hotels include the 22-room *Hôtel Rénova* (☎ 02 40 47 57 03, fax 02 51 82 06 39, *11 rue Beauregard*) where comfortable doubles cost from 130FF (180FF with shower and toilet). There are no hall showers and reception often closes noon to 7 pm on Sunday. Another great deal is the *Hôtel de la Bourse* (☎ 02 40 69 51 55, fax 02 40 71 73 89, *19 Quai de la Fosse*) whose tidy doubles cost from 109FF (149FF with shower and toilet). Hall showers cost 18FF. The reception closes 1 to 7 pm on Sunday.

The friendly, 15-room *Hôtel d'Orléans* (☎ 02 40 47 69 32, fax 02 51 82 34 66, *12 rue du Marais*) has bright, quiet doubles costing from 160FF; rooms with shower and toilet cost 185/250FF for two/four people. Reception closes on Saturday from noon to 6 pm and on Sunday from noon to 7.30 pm. The 24-room *Hôtel St-Patrick* (☎ 02 40 48 48 80, *7 rue St-Nicolas*) has decent, recently renovated doubles costing from 140FF (170FF with shower and toilet). Reception is on the 3rd floor (no lift).

The 19-room *Hôtel Fourcroy* (☎ 02 40 44 68 00, *11 rue Fourcroy*) has exceptionally well-kept doubles with upholstered doors, costing 137FF (with shower) and 157FF (with shower and toilet). Reception closes at 9 pm.

Hôtel St-Daniel (☎ 02 40 47 41 25, fax 02 51 72 03 99, *4 rue du Bouffay*), has ordinary but spacious doubles costing 150FF (with shower) and 170FF (with shower and toilet). Reception closes on Sunday from noon to 9 pm.

Places to Stay – Mid-Range

Hotels in the charmless area near the train station include the two-star, 31-room *Hôtel de la Gare* (☎ 02 40 74 37 25, fax 02 40 93 33 71, *5 allée Commandant Charcot*), which has small doubles/triples costing from 225/270FF. The three doubles with toilet cost 170FF.

Venerable, three-star *Hôtel de France* (☎ 02 40 73 57 91, fax 02 40 69 75 75, *24 rue Crébillon*), offers bath-equipped doubles with high ceilings costing from 350FF (480FF for an absolutely huge room).

Places to Eat

Nantes has an exceptionally varied selection of restaurants. Great deals (around 50FF for a *menu*) are on offer at lunchtime.

There are dozens of cafes, bars and small restaurants, many of them French-regional or ethnic, a couple of blocks west of the chateau in the lively area around rue de la Juiverie, rue des Petites Écuries and rue de la Bâclerie. West of cours des 50 Otages, you'll find eateries along rue Jean-Jacques Rousseau and rue Santeuil.

Restaurants – French The exquisite *Brasserie La Cigale* (☎ 02 51 84 94 94, *4 place Graslin*) is grandly decorated with 1890s tilework and painted ceilings that mix Baroque with Art Nouveau. Breakfast is served daily from 7.30 to 11 am; lunch and dinner are available from 11.45 am straight through to 12.30 am. The *menus* cost 75FF and 135FF at lunch, a bit more for dinner.

Le Guingois (☎ 02 40 73 36 49, *3 bis rue de Santeuil*), a real old-time bistro, has hearty *menus* costing from 68FF (lunch only) to 156FF (closed Sunday and Monday). *Le Pain Perdu* (☎ 02 40 47 74 21, *12 rue Beauregard*) has tasty, family-style French *menus* costing 60FF (lunch, except weekends and holidays), 89FF and 119FF; it closes on Monday. The same block has several other eateries.

There are great crepes on offer at *Au Vieux Quimper* (☎ 02 40 35 63 99, *10 rue de la Bâclerie*), open daily until 11 pm. Oysters, smoked fish and wine by the glass are the specialities at *Chez l'Huître* (☎ 02 51 82 02 02, *5 rue des Petites Écuries*), which is closed on Sunday.

Restaurants – Other For couscous, a good bet is *Le Couscousier* (☎ 02 40 48 14 49, *6 rue de la Juiverie*), closed Wednesday at midday and Tuesday. *Le Viet Nam* (☎ 02 40 20 06 26, *14 rue Beauregard*) has a lunch *menu* costing 40FF (closed on

ATLANTIC COAST

Sunday and holidays). At *La Tasca* (☎ 02 40 74 23 40, 91 rue Maréchal Joffre), Latin American cuisine and tapas are on offer from 7.30 pm to 3 am (closed Sunday and Monday).

Self-Catering The small *covered market* at place du Bouffay and the huge *Marché de Talensac* on rue Talensac are open until about 1 pm (closed Monday).

The *Monoprix* supermarket (2 rue du Calvaire) opens Monday to Saturday from 9 am to 9 pm. The huge *Galeries Lafayette* department store (rue de la Marne) has a basement food section that opens 9 am to 7.30 pm Monday to Saturday.

Entertainment

Listings of cultural events appear in *Nantes Poche* and *Pil'* (both 3FF). *Le Mois Nantais*, available at the tourist office, has day-by-day details of cultural events. Tickets are available across the hall from the tourist office at the *FNAC billeterie* (ticket outlet; ☎ 02 51 72 47 23), open 10 am to 8 pm Monday to Saturday.

Le Lieu Unique (☎ 02 40 12 14 34, Quai Ferdinand Faure), the city's new, industrial chic-style concert venue, occupies the one-time Lu biscuit factory.

Cinemas Non-dubbed films are on offer at the six-screen *Cinéma Katorza* (☎ 02 51 84 90 60/0 836 68 06 66, 3 rue Corneille). The *UGC Apollo cinemas* (Nos 20 and 21 rue Racine), where tickets cost just 10FF (13FF on Sunday), often show nondubbed films.

Clubs & Bars One of Nantes' main hangouts for English speakers is *Paddy Dooley's* (☎ 02 40 48 29 00, 9 rue Franklin), a spacious Irish-owned pub that has live music about twice a month. It opens 6 pm to 2 am. The bars in the area to the west of the chateau include *John McByrne* (☎ 02 40 89 64 46, 21 rue des Petites Écuries), an exceptionally friendly Irish-style bar that has live Irish music on Sunday starting at 6.30 pm. It opens noon to 2 am.

Pannonica Jazz Café (☎ 02 51 72 10 10, 9 rue Basse Porte) is open only during live jazz performances (35FF to 100F), which generally take place on Thursday and Friday at 9.30 pm. It is closed during school holiday periods, including mid-June to September.

At *La Tasca* (see Places to Eat), popular with students, you can dance the salsa and the merengue downstairs on Thursday, Friday and Saturday nights starting at 11 pm. Live Latin American-style bands play on the third Thursday of the month from 10 pm to 3 am. The tapas bar hours are 7.30 pm to 4 am (closed Monday).

Le Violin Dingue (☎ 02 40 74 09 29, 1 rue Lebrun) is a mellow bar with live music about twice a month on Saturday from 6.30 to 10 pm. Hours are 7 pm to 2 am (closed Monday). *La Maison* (☎ 02 40 37 04 12, 4 rue Lebrun) is a hilarious send-up of a home furnished in very bad taste circa 1970. A perfect place for a chat (and thus popular with loquacious students), this convivial bar is open daily from 3 pm to 2 am.

La Route du Rhum (☎ 02 40 74 48 57; tram stop Motte Rouge), on a two-storey houseboat a bit under 1km north-east of the Monument des 50 Otages, has jam sessions at 11 pm on Wednesdays and Thursdays, and concerts of blues, rock and reggae on Fridays and Saturdays from 11 pm to 3 am (30FF). The bar opens 8 pm to 4 am (closed Monday).

Another disco that has received good reviews from students is *L'Évasion* (☎ 02 40 47 99 84, 3 rue de l'Emery). Admission is free on Wednesday but costs 30FF to 50FF on Thursday and 80FF on Friday and Saturday; it is closed Sunday to Tuesday. Opening hours are 11 pm to 5 am.

Gay & Lesbian Venues A friendly, mainly gay bar, *Le Petit Marais* (☎ 02 40 20 15 25, 15 rue Kervégan) is open daily from 6 pm to 2 am. *L'Extrem' Club* (☎ 02 28 00 11 46), south of the Loire in Les Landes Bigots (about 10 minutes south by car from Nantes' chateau), is currently the area's hottest gay disco. It opens Friday, Saturday and Sunday nights from midnight to 5 am. Admission is free (except Saturday; 50FF).

Getting There & Away

Air Nantes-Atlantique airport (☎ 02 40 84 80 00) is about 12km south-east of the city centre.

Bus The southbound bus station (☎ 0 825 08 71 56), across from 13 allée de la Maison Rouge, is used by CTA buses serving areas of the Loire-Atlantique department south of the Loire River, including the seaside town of St-Brévin-les-Pins (60FF, 1½ hours). The information office opens weekdays from 6.45 to 10.30 am and 3.45 to 6.30 pm, and 10 am to 12.45 pm on Saturday.

The Eurolines office (☎ 02 51 72 02 03) opens weekdays until 6 pm and Saturday until 12.30 pm.

The northbound bus office (same telephone number) at 1 allée Duquesne (on cours des 50 Otages), run by Cariane Atlantique, handles buses to destinations north of the Loire.

Train The train station (☎ 0 836 35 35 35), 27 blvd de Stalingrad, is well connected to most of France. Destinations include Paris' Gare Montparnasse (297FF to 360FF, 2¼ hours by TGV, 20 a day, 10–12 at the weekend), Bordeaux (220FF, four hours, five or six a day) and La Rochelle (125FF, 1¾ hours, five or six a day).

The SNCF also serves the beach resort of Les Sables d'Olonne (90FF, 1½ hours, 10 a day, four at the weekend). SNCF bus stops are across the street from the train station's southern entrance on rue de Lourmel.

Tickets and information are also available at three SNCF ticket offices in the city centre, including one at 12 place de la Bourse, open 9 am (noon on Monday) to 7 pm (closed Sunday and holidays).

Car Budget, Europcar and Hertz have offices right outside the train station's southern entrance. Astuce (☎ 02 51 25 26 27), nearby at 45 Quai Malakoff, has cars costing from 170FF a day with a deductible/excess of 3500FF (closed Saturday afternoon and Sunday).

Getting Around

To/From the Airport A public bus known as TAN-Air links the airport with the Gare Centrale bus/tram hub and the train station's southern entrance (38FF, 20 minutes).

Bus & Tram The TAN network (☎ 0 801 44 44 44), whose information office is at 2 allée Brancas (closed Sunday), includes three modern tram lines that intersect at the Gare Centrale (Commerce), the main bus/tram transfer point. At night, the trams run at least twice an hour until about midnight.

Bus/tram tickets, sold individually (8FF) by bus (but not tram) drivers and at tram stop ticket machines, are valid for one hour after being time-stamped for travel in any direction. A *ticket journalier*, good for 24 hours, costs 21FF; time-stamp it only the first time you use it.

Parking You'll find free parking in the car park 200m east of the southbound bus station; in the one across the street from the Médiathèque tram stop (except for the first few rows, marked *payant*); and south of the train station along the southern section of Quai Malakoff.

Taxi To order a taxi, call ☎ 02 40 69 22 22.

Bicycle Pierre Qui Roule (☎ 02 40 69 51 01) at 1 rue Gretry rents out Dutch-style/mountain bikes for 45/65FF per day; in-line skates cost 50FF per day, or 30FF per half-day. It opens 10 am to 12.30 pm and 2 to 7 pm (closed Monday morning and Sunday). From late June to August, you can hire bikes from the tourist office (10FF per hour, minimum two hours).

POITIERS

postcode 86000 • pop 120,000
• elevation 116m

Poitiers, the former capital of Poitou, is home to some of France's most remarkable Romanesque churches. It is not a particularly fetching city – it fits very tightly into its hilltop site – but the pedestrian-only shopping precinct has its charms.

ATLANTIC COAST

ATLANTIC COAST

In AD 732, somewhere near Poitiers (the exact site is not known), the cavalry of Charles Martel defeated the Muslim forces of Abd ar-Rahman, governor of Córdoba, thus ending Muslim attempts to conquer France.

Orientation

The train station is about 600m west – and down the slope – from the old city and commercial centre, which begins just north of Poitiers' main square, place du Maréchal Leclerc, and stretches north-east to Église Notre Dame la Grande. Rue Carnot heads south from place du Maréchal Leclerc.

Information

The tourist office (☎ 05 49 41 21 24, fax 05 49 88 65 84, ✉ accueil-tourisme@interpc.fr), 150m north of place du Maréchal Leclerc at 8 rue des Grandes Écoles, opens 9 or 9.30 am to noon and 1.30 to 6 pm (closed Sunday and some bank holidays). From late June to late September, it opens all day until 7 pm (6 pm on Sunday and holidays). City maps are on sale for 1FF or 3FF.

The Banque de France, a block east of the tourist office at 1 rue Henri Oudin, changes money on weekdays from 9 am to 12.15 pm. Commercial banks can be found around place du Maréchal Leclerc.

Things to See

The renowned, Romanesque **Église Notre Dame la Grande** is at place Charles de Gaulle in the pedestrianised old city, 300m north-east of the tourist office. It dates from the 11th and 12th centuries – except for three of the five choir chapels (added in the 15th century) and all six chapels along the northern wall of the nave (added in the 16th century). The atrociously painted decoration in the nave is from the mid-19th century; the only original **frescoes** are the faint 12th or 13th-century works that adorn the U-shaped dome above the choir. The celebrated **west facade** is decorated with three layers of stone carvings based on the Old and New Testaments (open 8 am to 7 pm).

At the north-eastern end of rue Gambetta, the Palais de Justice (law courts) occupies a

one-time palace of the counts of Poitou and the dukes of Aquitaine. Inside, you can visit the **Salle des Pas-Perdus**, a vast, partly 14th-century hall with three huge fireplaces. It opens weekdays (daily in July and August) from 9 am to 6 pm.

At the bottom of rue de la Cathédrale (500m east of Église Notre Dame la Grande), the vast, Angevin (or Plantagenet) Gothic-style **Cathédrale St-Pierre** – so unlike its Gothic cousins to the north – was built from 1162 to 1271; the west facade and the towers date from the 14th and 15th centuries. At the far end of the choir, the stained-glass window of the Crucifixion and the Ascension is among the oldest in France. The choir stalls date from the mid-13th century. It opens daily from 8 am to 7.30 pm (6 pm in winter).

Constructed in the 4th and 6th centuries on Roman foundations, **Baptistère St-Jean** on rue Jean Jaurès (one block south of the cathedral) was rebuilt in the 10th century and used as a parish church. The octagonal hole under the 11th and 12th-century frescoes was used for total-immersion baptisms, practised until the 7th century. Now a museum of Merovingian (5th to 7th century) sarcophagi, it opens 10.30 am to 12.30 pm and 3 to 6 pm daily. From November to March, it opens 2.30 to 4.30 pm (closed Tuesday). Admission costs 4FF.

Across the lawn, the worthwhile **Musée Ste-Croix** (☎ 05 49 41 07 53), 3 rue Jean Jaurès, built atop Gallo-Roman walls that were excavated and left *in situ*, has exhibits on the history of Poitou from prehistoric times to the 19th century. It opens 10 am to noon and 1.15 to 5 pm weekdays (closed Monday morning) and 2 to 6 pm at the weekend. From June to September, it also opens weekend mornings, and closing time is 6 pm. Admission costs 20FF (those aged under 18 and students free) and also affords access to the **Musée Rupert de Chièvre** (☎ 05 49 41 07 53), 9 rue Victor Hugo, which displays furniture, paintings and art objects assembled in the 19th century.

The 11th- and 12th-century **Église St-Hilaire** is 600m south-west of place du Maréchal Leclerc, across the street from

20 rue St-Hilaire. The transept, the choir (decorated with late 11th-century frescoes) and the five apsidal chapels are 3m higher than the nave (mostly rebuilt in the 19th century), which is covered by three cupolas and has three rows of columns on each side. It opens daily from 9 or 10 am to 7 pm.

Places to Stay
In the unappealing area around the train station, the nine-room hotel above *Bistrot de la Gare* (☎ 05 49 58 56 30, 131 blvd du Grand Cerf) has mid-sized, Spartan doubles/triples with shower costing from 145/195FF. From November to February, reception (at the bar) closes on Sunday. In the two-star category, a good bet in this area is the *Hôtel Le Terminus* (☎ 05 49 62 92 30, fax 05 49 62 92 40, 3 blvd Pont Achard), which offers spacious, shower-equipped doubles costing from 250FF (280FF with toilet).

Half a block north of place du Maréchal Leclerc (through the arch next to the theatre), the two-star, 24-room *Hôtel du Plat d'Étain* (☎ 05 49 41 04 80, fax 05 49 52 25 84, 7–9 rue du Plat d'Étain) has uninspiring doubles starting at 150FF (260FF with shower and toilet). Hall showers cost 20FF.

The best deal in town is the family-run, 25-room *Hôtel Jules Ferry* (☎ 05 49 37 80 14, fax 05 49 53 15 02, 27 rue Jules Ferry), which is about 1km south of the train station (go up blvd du Pont Achard and then, if on foot, left up the ramp known as rue Jean Brunet) and the same distance southwest of place du Maréchal Leclerc (by car take rue Carnot to the very end and turn right twice). It has clean, simply furnished doubles costing from 140FF (210FF with shower and toilet). From June to September, reception closes on Sunday from about 1 to 7 pm.

Places to Eat
The most promising area for dining or sipping a beer is south of place du Maréchal Leclerc, especially along rue Carnot. *Le St-Nicolas* (☎ 05 49 41 44 48, down the alleyway at 7 rue Carnot), serves traditional French and regional cuisine. *Menus* cost 94FF and 119FF (closed at midday on Sunday and holidays, and on Wednesday). A bit farther south, *Le Poitevin* (☎ 05 49 88 35 04, 76 rue Carnot), serves Poitou-style cuisine, including lots of fish dishes. The *menus* cost 100FF to 230FF (closed Sunday).

The cement-roofed *Marché Notre Dame*, right next to Église Notre Dame la Grande, opens Tuesday to Saturday until 1 or 1.30 pm. About 200m to the south, the *Monoprix supermarket* across from 29 rue du Marché Notre Dame (behind the Palais de Justice) opens from 9 am to 7.30 pm Monday to Saturday.

Entertainment
The bars and cafes along rue Carnot include the *Blues Rock Café* (☎ 05 49 50 55 58, 17 rue Carnot), open 5.45 pm to 1.45 am (closed Sunday). There are several more pubs one block north of place du Maréchal Leclerc along rue du Chaudron d'Or.

Getting There & Away
The modern train station (☎ 0 836 35 35 35) on blvd du Grand Cerf has direct links to Bordeaux (172FF), La Rochelle (118FF), Tours (79FF) and many other cities. TGV tickets from Paris' Gare Montparnasse (1½ hours, 12 daily) cost 260FF to 320FF. The SNCF bus to Nantes (137FF, 3¼ hours) leaves daily at 7.35 am.

AROUND POITIERS
Futuroscope
Futuroscope (☎ 05 49 49 30 80) is a unique cinema theme park whose 21 innovative and visually striking pavilions (more are being added every year) make for a hugely entertaining day for the whole family. Its Web site is at www.futuroscope.com.

Attractions include the **Tapis Magique** (Magic Carpet), which shows action underfoot – from a bird's-eye perspective – as well as in front of you. At **Le Solido**, the rounded 180° images appear in colour 3-D thanks to special liquid-crystal glasses. **Le 360°** is a round projection hall whose nine screens give you a 360° view from the centre of the action. At the **Cinéma Dynamique**, the hydraulic seats shake and tilt

ATLANTIC COAST

to create a virtual-reality roller coaster ride that lasts just four minutes but seems like an eternity. The newest attraction is the **IMAX 3D Dynamique**, whose seats tilt and lurch while you watch computer-generated, full-colour action in 3-D.

The films, which last four to 40 minutes, are specially ordered to showcase the park's various cinematic technologies, so don't come expecting convincing acting or intelligent plots. A couple are unabashed propaganda flicks for the Vienne department – this is more about technological wizardry than about film-making as an art. Many of the attractions use stunningly sharp 70mm IMAX technology. A free infrared headset lets you pick up soundtracks in English and Spanish.

Futuroscope opens 9 am to 6 pm daily, but at the weekend from March to early November and daily from April to August there are lakeside laser and firework shows at night – as a result, closing time ranges from 9.30 pm to 1 am. The park may be closed in January.

All-day admission costs 145FF (kids aged five to 12, 100FF). On days when there are laser and fireworks shows, a ticket costs 210FF (children 145FF), 100FF (children 60FF) if you arrive after 6 pm.

There's an *Auchan* hypermarket a few hundred metres from the main entrance.

Futuroscope is a little over 10km north of Poitiers in Jaunay-Clan. Thanks to the park's new TGV station, Paris' Gare Montparnasse is only 80 minutes away.

Local buses No 16 and 17 (8FF) link Futuroscope with Poitiers' train station and place du Maréchal Leclerc; one or the other runs two to four times an hour (four times daily on Sunday and holidays) until 7.30 or 8 pm, with a few more late at night.

LA ROCHELLE
postcode 17000 • pop 120,000
The lively (and increasingly chic) port city of La Rochelle, midway down France's Atlantic seaboard, gets lots of tourists, especially in July and August, but most of them are still of the domestic, middle-class variety: unpretentious families or young

people out to have fun. The ever expanding Université de La Rochelle, opened in 1993, has added to the city's attraction for young people. La Rochelle's focal point is the cafe- and restaurant-lined old port, which basks in the bright Atlantic sunlight by day and is grandly illuminated by night.

Although the city centre does not have a beach, the nearby Île de Ré is ringed by kilometres of fine-sand beaches.

Orientation
La Rochelle is centred around the Vieux Port (old port), to the north of which lies the old city. The tourist office is on the southern side of the Vieux Port in an area known as Le Gabut. The train station is linked to the Vieux Port by the 500m-long ave du Général de Gaulle. Place du Marché and place de Verdun are at the northern edge of the old city.

The university campus is midway between the Vieux Port and the seaside neighbourhood of Les Minimes, 3km south-west of the city centre.

Information
Tourist Offices The tourist office (☎ 05 46 41 14 68, fax 05 46 41 99 85), in Le Gabut, opens10 am to noon and 2 to 6 pm Monday to Saturday (9 am to 7 pm in June and September, to 8 pm in July and August). It opens 10 am to noon (11 am to 5 pm in June and September, 9 am to 8 pm in July and August).

Money The Banque de France, 22 rue Réaumur, changes money 8.30 am to noon Monday to Friday. In the old city, there are a number of banks on rue du Palais.

Post & Communications The branch post office across from the city hall opens Monday to Friday until 6.30 pm and on Saturday until noon. Exchange services and a Cyberposte are available.

Laundry There are laundrettes at 4 rue des Dames (open until 7.30 pm, sometimes later in summer) and on Quai Louis Durand (open 8.30 am to 8.30 pm).

Emergency The Hôtel de Police (police station; ☎ 05 46 51 36 36) at 2 place de Verdun is staffed 24 hours a day.

Things to See & Do

To protect the harbour at night and defend it in times of war, an enormous chain used to be stretched between the two 14th-century stone towers at the harbour entrance. **Tour de la Chaîne** (☎ 05 46 34 11 81) affords fine views from the top and has displays on the history of the local Protestant community in the basement. Across the harbour you can also climb to the top of the 36m-high, pentagonal **Tour St-Nicolas**.

West of Tour de la Chaîne, the medieval walls lead to the steeple-topped, mid-15th-century **Tour de la Lanterne** (☎ 05 46 41 56 04), also known as Tour des Quatre Sergents in memory of four sergeants from the local garrison who were executed in 1822 for plotting to overthrow the newly reinstated monarchy. The English-language graffiti on the walls was carved by English privateers held here during the 18th century.

All three towers are can be visited daily, except Tuesday and holidays, from 10 am to 12.30 pm and 2 to 5.30 pm. From April to September it opens 10 am to 7 pm. Admission to each costs 25FF (those aged 12–25,

15FF); a ticket good for all three, as well as the Musée d'Orbigny-Bernon, costs 46FF (concessions 30FF).

Tour de la Grosse Horloge, the imposing Gothic-style clock tower on Quai Duperré, has a 14th-century base and an 18th-century top. The arch leads to arcaded **rue du Palais**, La Rochelle's main shopping street, which is lined with 17th- and 18th-century shipowners' homes. Two blocks to the east, **rue des Merciers** is also lined with arcades.

The Flamboyant Gothic outer wall of the city hall (☎ 05 46 41 14 68), place de l'Hôtel de Ville, was built in the late 15th century; the Renaissance-style courtyard dates from the last half of the 16th century. There are guided tours costing 20FF (students 10FF) at the weekend and on holidays at 3 pm (daily at 3 and 4 pm in July and August and during school holiday periods).

The **Musée du Nouveau Monde** (Museum of the New World; ☎ 05 46 41 46 50), 10 rue Fleuriau, has a large collection of material on early French exploration and settlement of the Americas, including Quebec and Louisiana. It opens 10.30 am to 12.30 pm and 1.30 pm (3 pm on Sunday) to 6 pm; it is closed Sunday morning and Tuesday. Admission costs 22FF (those aged under 18, students free). Just a block away

---

A Brief History of La Rochelle

La Rochelle was one of France's foremost seaports from the 14th to 17th centuries, and local shipowners were among the first to establish trade links with the New World. Many of the early French settlers in Canada – including the founders of Montreal – set sail from here in the 17th century.

During the 16th century, La Rochelle, whose spirit of mercantile independence made it fertile ground for Protestant ideas, incurred the wrath of Catholic loyalists, especially during the Wars of Religion. After the notorious St-Bartholomew's Day Massacre of 1572, many of the Huguenots who survived took refuge here.

In 1627, La Rochelle – by that time an established Huguenot stronghold – was besieged by Louis XIII's forces under the personal command of his principal minister, Cardinal Richelieu. When they surrendered after 15 months of resistance, all but 1500 of the city's 20,000 residents had died of starvation. The city recovered, albeit slowly, but was dealt further blows by the revocation of the Edict of Nantes in 1685 and the loss of French Canada – and the right to trade with North America – to the English in 1763.

During WWII, the German submarine base here was repeatedly attacked by Allied aircraft, devastating the town. The so-called La Rochelle Pocket did not surrender to the Allies until V-E Day, 8 May 1945, making it the last city in France to be liberated.

ATLANTIC COAST

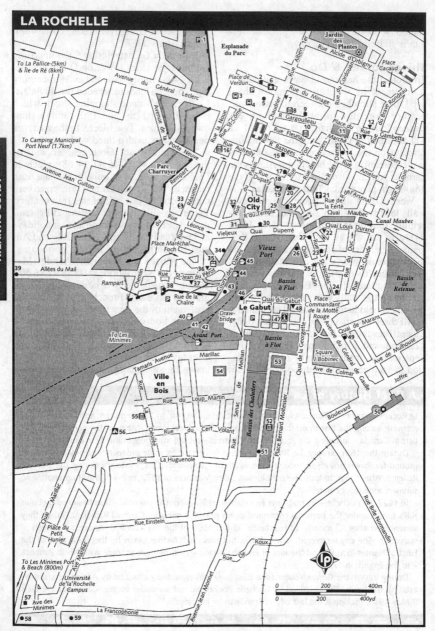

LA ROCHELLE

Jardin des Plantes
Esplanade du Parc
Place des Plantes
Rue Alcide d'Orbigny
Place Cacaud
To La Pallice (5km) & Île de Ré (8km)
Avenue du Général Leclerc
Place de Verdun
Rue du Minage
Rue du Brave Rondeau
To Camping Municipal Port Neuf (1.7km)
Chaudrier
R Gargoulleau
Place du Marché
Gambetta
Rue Fleuriau
Thiers
R Bazoges
Rue St-Yon
Rue des Merciers
Amelot
Avenue Jean Guiton
Parc Charruyer
Rampart
Rue de la Porte Neuve
Rue la Noue
Rue Ste-Côme
Rue Aufredy
Rue du Palais
Rue Dupaty
Rue des Dames
R des Augustins
Rue de la Ferté
Rue de l'Arsenal
Rue St-Louis
Réaumur
Old City
R du Temple
Rue du
Quai Maubec
Canal Maubec
Rue Léonce Vieljeux
Quai Duperré
Quai Louis Durand
Place Maréchal Foch
Vieux Port
Quai
Bassin de Retenue
Allées du Mail
St-Jean du Pérot
Rue des Dames
Bassin à Flot
Rampart
Chemin
Rue
Bassin de Retenue
Rue de la Chaîne
Le Gabut
Quai du Gabut
Place Commandant de la Motte Rouge
To Les Minimes
Drawbridge
Avant Port
Quai de la Georgette
Square J Bobinec
Avenue du Général de Gaulle
Quai de Marans
Ave de Mulhouse
Tamaris Avenue
Marillac
Ville en Bois
Rue de Meihan
Bassin à Flot
Ave de Colmar
Joffre
Rue
Rue du Loup Martin
Senac
Bassin des Chalutiers
Place Bernard Moitessier
Rue du Cert Volant
Rue La Huguenole
Boulevard
Rue Brie Normandin
Rue Einstein
Place du Petit Hunier
Quai Marillac
Ave Marillac
Roux
To Les Minimes Port & Beach (800m)
Rue Ozé
Université de la Rochelle Campus
Ave des Minimes
La Francophonie
Avenue Jean Monnet

0   200   400m
0   200   400yd

euro currency converter 10FF = €1.52

LA ROCHELLE

PLACES TO STAY		OTHER		35	La Coursive
2	Hôtel Le Commerce	1	Free Parking		(Concert Hall & Cinema)
9	Hôtel de la Paix;	3	Bus Station;	38	Tour de la Lanterne
	Hôtel de Paris		Océcars Bus Office	39	Club Oxford;
15	Hôtel François 1er	4	Autoplus Bus Information;		Club Papagayo
17	Bar de l'Hôtel de Ville		Electrique Autoplus Offices;	40	Croisières Inter-Îles Dock
23	Hôtel de Bordeaux		Bus Hub	41	Bus de Mer (Ferry)
24	Terminus Hôtel	5	Merry-Go-Round	42	Le Passeur (Shuttle Ferry)
28	Hôtel Henri IV	6	Police Station	43	Tour de la Chaîne
30	Hôtel La Marine	8	Musée des Beaux-Arts	44	Bus de Mer & Le Passeur-
56	Camping du Soleil	10	Musée du Nouveau Monde		Dock
57	Centre International de	14	Laundrette	45	Croisières Océanes
	Séjour-Auberge de Jeunesse	16	Musée d'Orbigny-Bernon	46	Tour St-Nicolas
		18	Place de l'Hôtel de Ville	47	Tourist Office
PLACES TO EAT		19	Branch Post Office	49	ADA Car Rental;
7	Café de la Paix	20	Town Hall		Rent-a-Car Système
11	Covered Market	21	Temple Protestant;	50	Train Station
12	Shéhérazade		Musée Protestant	51	Entrance to Musée Maritime
13	Boulangeries; East Asian	25	Lighthouse	52	Musée Maritime Neptunea
	Takeaway Places	26	Les Vélos Autoplus	53	Aquarium
22	Boulangerie Fillon	27	Laundrette	54	Médiathèque (Library)
32	Prisunic Supermarket	29	Place de la Caille	55	Musée des Modèles Réduits;
36	Bistrot l'Entracte	31	Tour de la Grosse Horloge		Musée des Automates
37	La Galathée	33	Banque de France	58	Bowling Alley
48	Loan Phuong	34	Eurolines (Citram Littoral)	59	Eurocentre Language School

ATLANTIC COAST

on rue Gargoulleau, the **Musée des Beaux-Arts** (☎ 05 46 41 64 65) opens 2 to 5 pm (closed Tuesday). The **Musée d'Orbigny-Bernon** (☎ 05 46 41 18 83) at 2 rue St-Côme has exhibits on local history, ceramics and East Asian art (closed Sunday morning and Tuesday). Admission costs 21FF.

The austere **Temple Protestant** (church) at 2 rue St-Michel was built in the late 17th century, though it became a Protestant church only after the Revolution; the interior took on its present form during the last 75 years of the 19th century. The small **Musée Protestant** (☎ 05 46 50 88 03) is open 2.30 to 6 pm July to mid-September (closed Sunday). Admission costs 10FF.

South of Le Gabut, the vast, new **aquarium** (☎ 05 46 34 00 00) is scheduled to open in January 2001. Opening hours are 9 am (10 am from October to March) to 8 pm (11 pm in July and August); admission costs 65FF (children and students 50FF).

The innovative **Musée Maritime Neptunea** (maritime museum; ☎ 05 46 28 03 00) at Bassin des Chalutiers is the permanent home of Jacques Cousteau's research ship the *Calypso*, presently awaiting repairs. The

admission fee of 50FF (those aged under 16, students 35FF) includes tours of a *chalutier* (fishing boat) and a meteorological research vessel. From October to March, it opens 2 to 6.30 pm (closed in December and January except during school holiday periods). The rest of the year it opens 10 am to 6.30 pm (to 7.30 pm in July and August). Ticket sales end 90 minutes before closing time.

About midway between the Vieux Port and Les Minimes is the **Musée des Automates** (☎ 05 46 41 68 08), 14 rue La Désirée, which displays – in action – some 300 automated dolls from the last two centuries. Next door at the **Musée des Modèles Réduits** (☎ 05 46 41 64 51), children of all ages can marvel at the miniature cars, ships (including a naval version of Vietnamese water puppetry) and railroad villages. Both open 10 am to noon and 2 to 6 pm daily (only in the afternoon from November to January; until 7 pm from June to August, when there's no midday closure). Admission to each museum costs a steep 40FF (children aged three to 10 25FF); a ticket good for both costs 65FF (small children 35FF).

euro currency converter €1 = 6.56FF

The modern resort neighbourhood of **Les Minimes**, 3km south-west of the city centre, has a small **beach** and the largest pleasure craft port on Europe's Atlantic coast.

Special Events

The Francofolies, a six-day festival held each year in mid-July, brings together vocalists and performing artists from all over La Francophonie (the French-speaking world) and attract lots of young people. The 10-day Festival International du Film runs from the end of June to early July.

Places to Stay

La Rochelle has a shortage of cheap hotels. Most places charge high-season rates from sometime in the spring until September or October. During July and August, virtually all the hotels are full before noon.

Camping During the warmer months, dozens of camping grounds open up around La Rochelle and on the Île de Ré. In July and August, many are so full that even walkers with small tents are turned away.

The camping ground nearest the city centre is *Camping du Soleil* (☎ 05 46 44 42 53, ave Marillac), open from mid-May to mid-September. It is often completely full. To get there, take bus No 10.

Hostels The *Centre International de Séjour-Auberge de Jeunesse* (☎ 05 46 44 43 11, fax 05 46 45 41 48, ave des Minimes) is 2km south-west of the train station in Les Minimes. A dorm bed/double room costs 72/179FF, including breakfast. Check-in is possible from 8 am to midnight. To get there, take bus No 10.

Hotels The two-star, 63-room *Hôtel Le Commerce* (☎ 05 46 41 08 22, fax 05 46 41 74 85, 6–10 place de Verdun), has doubles/quads with shower and toilet costing 235/245FF (290/335FF from May to September). The 11 rather plain doubles with washbasin cost 135FF (165F in the high season). In summer, breakfast (33FF) may be obligatory. In July and August, the nine-room hotel attached to the *Bar de l'Hôtel de*

Ville (☎ 05 46 41 30 25, 5 rue St-Yon) has doubles costing from 190FF (220FF with shower and toilet).

The friendly, 24-room *Hôtel Henri IV* (☎ 05 46 41 25 79, fax 05 46 41 78 64, place de la Caille) occupies a late-16th-century building in the middle of the pedestrianised old city. Spacious doubles cost from 170FF (220FF with shower and toilet). You can only drive into (or out of) the pedestrian zone from 6 to 10.30 am.

The welcoming, 22-room *Hôtel de Bordeaux* (☎ 05 46 41 31 22, fax 05 46 41 24 43, @ hbordeaux@free.fr, 43 rue St-Nicolas), has quiet, pastel doubles costing from 175FF (285FF from June to September, including breakfast); doubles with shower and toilet cost 225FF (345FF in the high season, including breakfast).

The 32-room *Terminus Hôtel* (☎ 05 46 50 69 69, fax 05 46 41 73 12, @ terminus@cdl-lr.com, 7 rue de la Fabrique) has comfortable doubles from 260FF to 300FF, depending on the season.

The two-star, 25-room *Hôtel de Paris* (☎ 05 46 41 03 59, fax 05 46 41 03 24, 18 rue Gargoulleau) provides clean and tidy doubles/quads for between 220/320FF (November to March) and 290/370FF (July to September). The newly renovated, 19-room *Hôtel de la Paix* (☎ 05 46 41 33 44, fax 05 46 50 51 28, @ herve.pannetier@wanadoo.fr, 14 rue Gargoulleau), in an 18th-century building, has pretty standard doubles costing 250FF (360FF from May to September). A huge, old-fashioned room for five people with a fireplace costs 490FF (550FF in high season).

In the 15th and 16th centuries, a number of French kings stayed in the building that houses the 39-room *Hôtel François 1er* (☎ 05 46 41 28 46, fax 05 46 41 35 01, @ hotelfrancois@multi-micro.com, 15 rue Bazoges). Decent but smallish doubles go for 390FF to 475FF (less from October to March); there are also a couple of rooms with a washbasin for 215FF.

The two-star, 13-room *Hôtel La Marine* (☎ 05 46 50 51 63, fax 05 46 44 02 69, 30 Quai Duperré), a friendly, family-run place on the 2nd floor, has passable doubles/quads with shower and toilet starting at 250/350FF (330/430FF late June to late September). Rooms with a port view cost 50FF more.

Places to Eat

According to local people, La Rochelle has so many restaurants that you could stay in town for a whole year, dining out every day, and never have dinner at the same place twice. Dozens of eateries can be found along the northern side of the Vieux Port, especially on Quai Duperré, cours des Dames, rue de la Chaîne and rue St-Jean du Pérot. The place du Marché area has several inexpensive restaurants and pizzerias.

Restaurants Traditional French cuisine, including fish dishes, is served at elegantly rustic *La Galathée* (☎ 05 46 41 17 06, 45 rue St-Jean du Pérot), whose *menus* cost 65FF (weekday lunch), 85FF and 130FF (closed Tuesday and Wednesday except in July and August). The stylish *Bistrot l'Entracte* (☎ 05 46 50 62 60, 22 rue St-Jean du Pérot), specialises in fish and seafood; the four-course *menu* costs 160FF (closed Sunday). There are several other seafood eateries on the same block.

Café de la Paix (☎ 05 46 41 39 79, 54 rue Chaudrier), a turn-of-the-century brasserie-bar, has *menus* for 83FF and 105FF. It opens daily from 7 am to 9.30 pm.

An all-you-can-eat Chinese and Vietnamese lunch/dinner buffet costs 69/75FF (39/45FF for children under 12) at *Loan Phuong* (☎ 05 46 41 90 20, Quai du Gabut). Couscous is on offer at *Shéhérazade* (☎ 05 46 27 07 17, 35 rue Gambetta), closed Monday at midday.

Self-Catering The best place to pick up edibles is the lively, 19th-century *covered market (place du Marché)*, open daily from 7 am to 1 pm. Food shops in the vicinity include two cheap East Asian *takeaway places (Nos 4 and 10 rue Gambetta)*. At least one of the *boulangeries (Nos 8 and 29 rue Gambetta)* opens daily until 8.30 pm.

In the old city, the *Prisunic* supermarket *(across from 55 rue du Palais)* opens 8.15 am to 8 pm Monday to Saturday.

Boulangerie Fillon (18 Quai Louis Durand) opens all day until at least 2 am (8 pm on Tuesday; closed Sunday afternoon and Wednesday).

Entertainment

The discos *Club Oxford* and *Club Papagayo* (☎ 05 46 41 51 81 for both), on the waterfront about 500m west of Tour de la Lanterne, are open Tuesday to Sunday nights (and on Monday in July and August) from 11 pm to 5 am. Admission costs 60FF, including a drink. In Les Minimes, the *bowling alley* (☎ 05 46 45 40 40), next to the hostel, opens daily from 10 am to 2 am.

The two auditoriums of *La Coursive* (☎ 05 46 51 54 00, 4 rue St-Jean du Pérot) host concerts and nondubbed art films (closed from late July to early September).

Getting There & Away

Bus The bus station (☎ 05 46 00 21 01 for the Océcars office) is at place de Verdun. See Getting There & Around under Île de Ré for details on bus services to the island.

Eurolines ticketing is handled by Citram Littoral (☎ 05 46 50 53 57) at 30 cours des Dames (closed Saturday afternoon, Monday morning and Sunday).

Train The train station (☎ 0 836 35 35 35) is linked by TGV to Paris' Gare Montparnasse (320FF to 380FF, three hours, five or six direct daily); a few non-TGV trains still use Paris' Gare d'Austerlitz (264FF). Other destinations served by direct trains include Nantes (125FF, 1¾ hours, five or six daily), Poitiers (108FF, 1½ hours, seven to 10 daily), Rochefort (30FF, 20 minutes, five to seven daily) and Bordeaux (134FF, two hours, five to seven daily).

Car On ave du Général de Gaulle, ADA (☎ 05 46 41 02 17) is at No 19 and Rent A Car Système (☎ 05 46 27 27 27) is at No 27. Other companies have offices along the same block or facing the train station.

Getting Around

Bus The innovative local transport system, Autoplus (☎ 05 46 34 02 22), has its main bus hub and an information office (open Monday to Saturday 7 am to 7.30 pm) at place de Verdun. Most lines run until sometime between 7.15 and 8 pm.

Bus No 10 links place de Verdun, the Vieux Port (Quai Valin) and the train station with the youth hostel and Les Minimes.

Electric Car & Scooter The Electric Autoplus office at place de Verdun (see Bicycle) rents electrically powered motorcars with a range of 50km for 60/100FF per half-day/day. Electric Barigo scooters that can go up to 30km cost 40/70FF. Both require a 2500FF cash or credit card deposit.

Parking & Traffic There is free parking on the side streets north of place de Verdun; at Esplanade des Parcs, which is a few hundred metres north-west of place de Verdun; and around Neptunea. There's an underground garage at place de Verdun.

The city centre, an impossible maze of one-way streets, turns into a giant traffic jam in summer; this is worst on market mornings (Wednesday and Saturday).

Taxi Taxis can be ordered 24 hours a day on ☎ 05 46 41 55 55 or ☎ 05 46 42 22 00.

Bicycle Les Vélos Autoplus (☎ 05 46 34 02 22), a branch of the public transport company, will furnish you with a bike (lock included; children's sizes available) for free for the first two hours; after that the charge is 6FF per hour. You must leave some sort of ID as a deposit. Child seats – but not bike helmets – are available for no extra charge. Bikes are available daily at the Electrique Autoplus office at place de Verdun, open from 6.45 am (1 pm on Sunday) to 7 pm. From May to September, they can also be picked up at the Vieux Port (across the street from 11 Quai Valin).

Boat Autoplus' *Le Passeur* (4FF) is a ferry service that links Tour de la Chaîne with the Avant Port. It runs when there are passengers – just press the red button on the board at the top of the gangplank. It opens 7.45 am to 8 pm (midnight July and August).

The *Bus de Mer* (10FF), also run by Autoplus, links Tour de la Chaîne with Les Minimes (20 minutes). It runs at the weekend, holidays and during school holiday periods and, from April to September, daily. Boats from the Vieux Port depart every hour on the hour (except at 1 pm) from 10 am to 7 pm (twice an hour and until 11.30 pm in July and August).

ÎLE DE RÉ
pop 16,000

This flat island, whose eastern tip is 9km west of the centre of La Rochelle, gets more hours of sunshine than any part of France away from the Mediterranean coast. In summer, its many beaches and seasonal camping grounds are a favourite destination for families with young children; the water is shallow and safe and the sun is bright and warming, but less harsh than along the Mediterranean. People in their teens and 20s also flock here, helping to increase the island's population 12-fold in August. The island can easily be visited as a day trip from La Rochelle.

Île de Ré's main town is the fishing port of St-Martin de Ré, on the northern coast about 12km from the toll bridge. In most villages, the houses are traditional in design: one or two-storey whitewashed buildings with green shutters and red Spanish tile roofs.

The Île de Ré boasts 70km of coastline, including 20km or 30km of fine-sand beaches. Most of the northern coast is taken up by mudflats and oyster farms. The island's western half curves around a bay known as the Fier d'Ars, which is lined with *marais salants* (salt evaporation pools), saltwater marshes and a nature reserve for birds, **Lilleau des Niges**.

There are virtually no budget hotels on the island. Every hotel and camping ground on the island is *totally* full from 14 July to 25 August.

St-Martin de Ré
postcode 17410 • pop 2500

This picturesque fishing village, entirely surrounded by Vauban's 17th-century fortifications, is especially attractive when the white houses and sailboats are bathed in the bright coastal sun. You can stroll along most of the ramparts but the **citadel** (1681), which has been a prison for over two centuries (Alfred Dreyfus was held here before being shipped to Devil's Island), is closed to the law-abiding public.

The fortified, mostly Gothic **church**, three blocks south of the port along rue de Sully, was damaged in 1692 in artillery attacks launched by an Anglo-Dutch fleet. There's a great view from the neoclassical **bell and clock tower**.

Information In St-Martin, the tourist office (☎ 05 46 09 20 06, fax 05 46 09 06 18, 🅮 ot.st.martin@wanadoo.fr) is a block east of the port on ave Victor Bouthillier (across the street from the Rébus bus stop). This is a good place to pick up maps of the island. It opens Monday to Saturday from 10 am to noon and 3 pm to sometime between 5.30 pm (winter) and 7 pm (in July and August, when the midday closure only lasts from 1 to 2 pm and the office also opens on Sunday morning).

In summer, almost every village has its own tourist office.

Places to Stay The grassy, shaded *Camping Municipal* (☎ 05 46 09 21 96), a few hundred metres south of the church, opens from March to mid-October. Pitching your tent anywhere but in a camp site is strictly forbidden.

The one-star, 15-room *Hôtel de Sully* (☎ 05 46 09 26 94, rue Jean Jaurès), 150m south of the port, has double rooms with shower costing from 190FF (240FF with toilet), 50FF more in summer. If it looks closed, enquire at the two-star, 35-room *Hôtel du Port* (☎ 05 46 09 21 21, fax 05 46 09 06 85, Quai de la Poithevinière), on the southern side of the port, where comfortable doubles/quins with shower and toilet cost from 310/480FF (380/550FF from July to September). Both open year round.

Two-star, 30-room *Hôtel des Colonnes* (☎ 05 46 09 21 58, fax 05 46 09 21 49, 19 Quai Job Foran), on the southern side of

the port, has doubles costing from 350FF (480FF in July and August); it closes from mid-December to January.

Places to Eat You can find touristy restaurants in the port area.

It's a lot cheaper to buy food in La Rochelle than on the island. In St-Martin, the *covered market (rue Jean Jaurès)*, on the southern side of the port, opens daily from 8.30 am to 1 pm. There is a cluster of *food shops* nearby.

Phare des Baleines
At the western tip of the island is the 57m Phare des Baleines (Lighthouse of the Whales), built of stone in 1854 and still operating. You can climb the 257 steps to the top (10FF) daily from 9.30 am to sometime between 5 pm (in winter, when it also closes from 12.30 to 2 pm) and 7.30 pm (summer). Behind you'll find an old lighthouse (1679), a shady garden and tidal pools. The pines and cypresses of the **Forêt du Lizay** stretch along the coast north-west of here.

Beaches
The best beaches on the Île de Ré are along the southern edge of the island (east and west of La Couarde) and around the island's western tip (north-east and south-east of Phare des Baleines). Near Sablanceaux, there are sandy beaches along the south coast towards Ste-Marie. Many of the beaches are bordered by dunes that have been fenced off to protect the vegetation.

Scenes from *The Longest Day* (1962), a Hollywood film about the D-day landings, were shot at **Plage de la Conche des Baleines**, on the north-western coast between Phare des Baleines and the town of Les Portes. There's an unofficial **naturist beach** near the outskirts of Les Portes; access is via the Forêt du Lizay.

Getting There & Away
For automobiles, the bridge toll (paid on your way *to* the island) is 60FF (a whopping 110FF from mid-June to mid-September).

Year round, excruciatingly slow buses run by Rébus (☎ 05 46 09 20 15) link La

Rochelle (the train station car park, Tour de la Grosse Horloge and place de Verdun) with Sablanceaux (15.50FF), La Flotte (23.50FF, 45 minutes) and St-Martin de Ré (28FF, 55 minutes) nine times daily (thrice on Sundays and holidays, more frequently in July and August). The company also covers intra-island routes.

In July and August, and on Wednesdays, holidays and at weekends in June, La Rochelle's Autoplus buses Nos 1 or 50 (known as No 21 between the train station and place de Verdun) go to Sablanceaux (10FF, 25 minutes).

Getting Around

Cycling is an extremely popular way to get around the island, which is flat and has an extensive network of paved bicycle paths. A biking map is available at tourist offices. In summer, practically every hamlet has somewhere to hire bikes.

At Sablanceaux, bikes can be hired at Cycland, in a kiosk in one of the little buildings to the left as you come off the bridge. Three-speeds/mountain bikes/tandems cost 45/75/100FF a day; helmets are usually available for no extra charge. The kiosk is staffed daily in July and August; the rest of the time, call Cycland's year-round office in La Flotte (☎ 05 46 09 65 27; open daily) and they'll deliver a bike to the bridge in about 15 minutes.

SOUTH OF LA ROCHELLE
Offshore Islands

The crescent-shaped Île d'Aix (pronounced 'eel day'), a 1.33 sq km, car-less island 16km due south of La Rochelle, was fortified by Vauban and later used as a prison. It has some nice beaches and is served by regular ferries from La Fumée (see Rochefort for information on getting to La Fumée by bus). Fort Boyard, built during the first half of the 19th century (and used as a venue for adventure TV game shows in the 1990s), is an oval-shaped island/fortress situated between the Île d'Aix and the Île d'Oléron – the latter is a larger and less picturesque version of the Île de Ré. There are buses to the Île d'Oléron from Rochefort.

Companies offering cruises include Croisières Océanes (☎ 05 46 50 68 44) on cours des Dames in La Rochelle, which has daily sailings from Easter to early November. Options include a trip around Fort Boyard (65FF, 1½ hours), an all-day trip to the Île d'Aix (110FF) and, from April to late September, an all-day trip to the Île d'Oléron (110FF to either St-Denis or Boyardville). Children aged four to 12 get a big discount. Another company with similar offerings is Croisières Inter-Îles (☎ 05 46 50 51 88), whose La Rochelle pier is just south-west of Tour de la Chaîne.

Rochefort

About 30 km south-east of La Rochelle, Rochefort (population 25,500), founded as a fortified town in the late 1600s – that's why the streets are arranged in a grid pattern – has several interesting museums. Just south of town is a 176m-long **pont transbordeur** (transporter bridge) built in 1890.

Along the Charente River, the restored, 17th-century **Corderie Royale** (Royal Rope-making Factory; ☎ 05 46 87 01 90), 370m long so that ropes of great length could plaited without splicing, hosts expositions with a maritime theme. It opens daily until 6 pm (7 pm from May to September); admission costs 30FF.

The **Maison Pierre Loti** (☎ 05 46 99 16 88), 141 rue Pierre Loti, is 'orientalism' incarnate: the late 19th-century novelist lavishly furnished his home with purchases from all over Asia, turning it into an idealised – and stunningly eclectic – version of the 'exotic and romantic East'. Guided tours (written text in English available), which cost 45FF (reduced price 25FF), begin at 10.30 and 11.30 am and 2, 3 and 4 pm (closed Sunday morning, Tuesday and holidays); from July to mid-September, they begin daily, every half hour, until 5 pm.

Les Métiers de Mercure (☎ 05 46 83 91 50), 12 rue Lesson, reconstitutes – down to the most minute detail – the shops and workshops that an average French person would have encountered in their day-to-day life between 1890 and 1940. It opens daily, except Sunday morning and Tuesday, from

10 am to noon and 2 to 6 or 7 pm (8 pm in July and August, when there is no midday closure); admission costs 30FF.

The tourist office (☎ 05 46 99 08 60), on ave Sadi Carnot, opens Monday to Saturday from October to March; hours are 9 or 9.30 am to noon or 12.30 pm and 2 to 6 or 6.30 pm (8 pm in July and August, when there's no midday closure).

The 60-bed *Auberge de Jeunesse* (☎ 05 46 99 74 62, 20 ave de la République), open year round, charges 48FF for a bed and 27FF to pitch a tent in the courtyard. Reception closes at 6.30 pm (5.30 pm on Saturday, later in July and August) and closes on Saturday morning and Sunday, except in July and August. The 16-room, two-star *Hôtel Roca Fortis* (☎ 05 46 99 26 32, 14 rue de la République) has doubles with shower costing from 230FF (245FF with toilet).

Citram Littoral buses (☎ 05 46 82 31 31) link Roquefort's bus station (place de Verdun) and train station with Le Château d'Oléron on the Île d'Oléron (40FF, six daily, one on Sunday and holidays) and La Fumée (16.50FF), from where there are ferries year round to the Île d'Aix. Five to seven trains daily go to/from La Rochelle (30FF, 20 minutes) and Bordeaux (two hours).

Royan

About 40km south of Rochefort is Royan (population 16,800), flattened by Allied bombing in early 1945 and rebuilt after the war in the modernist style of the early 1950s. **Église Notre Dame** (1958), topped by a 65m spire, is made of reinforced concrete. The 2km-long beach, **Front de Mer**, fronts a protected bay, the **Grande Conche**.

Royan is a good place to start a visit to the Médoc thanks to the ferry to Pointe de Grave (see Getting There & Away under The Médoc section later in this chapter). Trains go to Cognac (40 minutes) and, via Saints, to Nantes and Bordeaux.

COGNAC

postcode 16100 • pop 19,500
• elevation 25m

Cognac, surrounded by rolling vineyards and quiet villages, is famed round the world for the double-distilled spirit that bears the town's name – and on which the local economy is based.

Orientation

The train station is on the southern edge of the town centre, while the four cognac distilleries mentioned below are on the other side of town, about 1.5km to the north, near the Charente River. Place François 1er, 200m north-east of the tourist office (follow rue du 14 Juillet), is linked to the river by blvd Denfert Rochereau.

Information

The tourist office (☎ 05 45 82 10 71, fax 05 45 82 34 47), 16 rue du 14 Juillet, can supply you with a town map. It opens from 9 am to 12.30 pm and 2 to 6.15 pm (closed on Sunday and holidays). During July and August it opens from 9 am to 8 pm (10.30 am to 4 pm on Sunday and holidays).

The Banque de France, 39 blvd Denfert Rochereau, changes money weekdays from 8.45 am to noon.

Things to See

The narrow streets of the **Vieille Ville** (old city), between the partly Romanesque **Église St-Léger** (rue Aristide Briand) and the Charente River, are graced by 15th- to 17th-century buildings, some of them half-timbered.

The **Musée de Cognac** (☎ 05 45 32 07 25), 48 blvd Denfert-Rochereau, has a varied collection that covers fine arts, local folk traditions and, in the basement, Cognac production. It opens daily, except Tuesday, 10 am to noon and 2 to 6 pm (5.30 pm from October to May, when it closes in the morning). Admission costs 13FF (students 6.50FF).

The Musée de Cognac is in the southern corner of the **Jardin Public** (public park), most of whose trees were blown down in the great storm of December 1999. The small zoo is home to a few deer. To the north-east, surrounded on two sides by a bend in the Charente, is the larger **Parc François 1er**.

ATLANTIC COAST

Cognac Houses

The most famous cognac distilleries offer tours of their *chais* (cellars; pronounced shay) and production facilities that end with a tasting session. Reservations are only necessary for groups.

The only Cognac tour that is still free is run by Camus (☎ 05 45 32 28 28) at 29 rue Marguerite de Navarre, which is 250m north-east of the Jardin Public. From May to October, 1¾-hour tours begin on weekdays at 10 or 10.30 am, 2 pm and 4 pm. The rest of the year phone them in advance.

The informative tours (25FF; those aged under 16 free) of the sprawling **Martell** complex (☎ 05 45 36 33 33) at place Édouard Martell (250m north-west of the tourist office) last one hour and are sometimes in English. At the end, participants are given a tiny bottle of VSOP. Except from November to January, when you need to reserve in advance, tours begin on weekdays (except Friday afternoon) at 9.30 and 11 am and 2.30, 3.45 and 5 pm. From June to September, tours begin 9.30 am to 5 pm daily.

The Château de Cognac at 127 blvd Denfert Rochereau (650m north of place François 1er) was the birthplace in 1494 of King François I and has been home to **Otard** (☎ 05 45 36 88 88) since 1795. From April to October, the well-conducted, one-hour tours (printed English translation available) begin daily at 10 and 11 am and 2, 3, 4 and 5 pm. In November and December, tours begin on weekdays at 11 am and 2.30, 3.45 and 5 pm (4 pm on Friday). Phone ahead from January to March, or to find out when English tours are scheduled. Tickets cost 15FF (those aged under 18, 10FF).

The 1¼-hour tours of the **Hennessey** facilities (☎ 05 45 35 72 68) at 8 rue Richonne (100m up the hill from Quai des Flamands, which runs along the river) include a film (in English) and a boat trip across the Charente to visit the cellars. From March to December, they begin daily from 10 am to 5 pm (to 6 pm from June to September). The cost is 30FF (those aged under 16 free).

The tourist office can supply you with a list of smaller cognac houses near town;

The Production of Cognac

Cognac is made of grape *eaux de vie* (brandies) of various vintages, aged in oak barrels and then blended by an experienced *maître de chai* (cellar master). Each year, some 3% of the volume of the casks – *la part des anges* (the angels' share) – evaporates through the pores in the wood, nourishing the tiny black mushrooms that thrive on the walls of cognac warehouses.

Since the mid-18th century – when the process for turning 9L of mediocre, low-alcohol wine into 1L of fine cognac was invented – many of the key figures in the cognac trade have been Anglophones: Jean Martell was born on Jersey, Richard Hennessey hailed from County Cork in Ireland and Baron Otard was of Scottish descent. To this day, several of the most common cognac classifications are in English: VS (very special), aged for five to seven years; VSOP (very special old pale), aged for eight to 12 years; Napoleon, aged for 15 to 25 years; and XO (extra old), aged for about 40 years.

JANE SMITH

The lion's share of cognac is exported – mainly to the UK and Japan.

most are closed from October to mid-March. **Rémy Martin** (☎ 05 45 35 76 66), whose mini-train tours run from April to October (except on Sunday in April and October), is a few kilometres south-west of town towards Pons. Tickets cost 25FF (those aged under 18 free). Their Web site is at www.remy.com.

Places to Stay
The seven-room *Hôtel St-Martin* (☎ 05 45 35 01 29, 112 rue Paul Firino Martell) is 650m south-west of the tourist office (towards the D732 and Pons) and about 500m north-west of the train station. Run by an Englishman, it has singles/doubles with washbasin costing 155/175FF.

The two-star, 21-room *Hôtel Le Cheval Blanc* (☎ 05 45 82 09 55, fax 05 45 82 14 82, 6 place Bayard), 100m west of the tourist office, reopened in 2000 after being totally refurbished. It has modern and very practical doubles costing from 230FF.

The three-star, 28-room *Hôtel François 1er* (☎ 05 45 32 07 18, fax 05 45 35 33 89, 3 place François 1er), built in the mid-19th century, has spacious but plain rooms for two/four people costing 270/420FF.

Places to Eat
Restaurants & Pubs There are a number of restaurants and bars in the immediate vicinity of place François 1er and the tourist office.

Local Charentaise dishes such as *escargots*, frogs' legs and tripe are on offer for reasonable prices at the *Bar-Restaurant de la Presse* (☎ 05 45 82 06 37, 42 allée de la Corderie), across the square from the Martell complex. The *menus* start at 65FF, including wine and coffee. It opens daily except, from October to April, on Sunday.

Wellington Pub (☎ 05 45 82 43 43, 23 rue du 14 Juillet), across the street from the tourist office, is popular with local rugby players and has karaoke on Wednesday and Friday. It opens 7 pm to 2 or 3 am (closed Sunday).

Self-Catering The *Casa* supermarket (place François 1er) opens until 7 pm

(closed Monday morning and Sunday). About 300m to the north, the *covered market (57 blvd Denfert Rochereau)*, across from the Musée de Cognac, opens daily until 1 pm; only a handful of stalls are staffed on Monday.

Over 250 different cognacs costing up to 9500FF a bottle are available at Cognathèque (☎ 05 45 82 43 31), 100m from the tourist office at 10 place Jean Monnet (closed Sunday except in July and August).

Getting There & Away
Cognac's train station (☎ 0 836 35 35 35), at the southern end of ave du Maréchal Leclerc, is on the line that links Angoulême with Royan (40 minutes). There's one direct train a day from La Rochelle (77FF).

BORDEAUX
postcode 33000 • pop 650,000
Bordeaux is known for its neoclassical architecture, wide avenues and well tended parks, all of which give the city a certain 18th-century grandeur. The grimy state of the some of the buildings may give the impression that the city has seen better days, but don't let this put you off: Bordeaux has excellent museums, a vibrant night life, an ethnically diverse population and a lively university community that includes some 60,000 students.

About 100km from the Atlantic at the lowest bridging point on the Garonne River, Bordeaux was founded by the Romans in the 3rd century BC. From 1154 to 1453, it prospered under the rule of the English, whose fondness for the region's red wine – known across the Channel as claret (with the final T pronounced) – provided the impetus for the eventual creation of Bordeaux' international reputation for quality wines.

Orientation
The city centre lies between place Gambetta and the 350m- to 500m-wide Garonne, which is usually a muddy brown as it flows either towards the sea or inland, depending on the tides. From place Gambetta, place de Tourny is 500m north-east, and the tourist office is 400m to the east.

ATLANTIC COAST

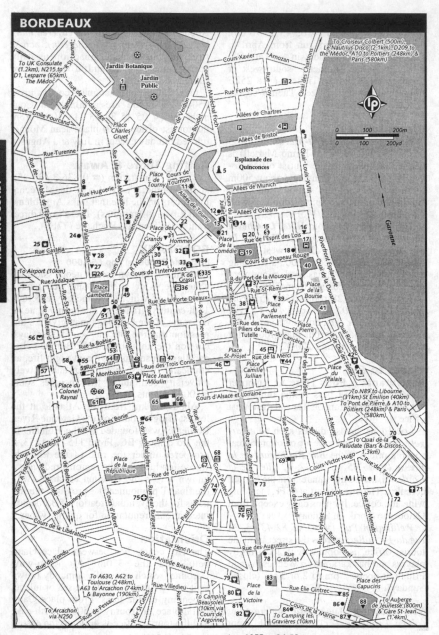

BORDEAUX

To Croiseur Colbert (500m);
Le Nautilus Disco (2.1km), D209 to
the Médoc, A10 to Poitiers (248km) &
Paris (580km)

To UK Consulate
(1.2km), N215 to
D1, Lesparre (65km),
The Médoc

Jardin Botanique

Jardin
Public

Cours Xavier

Arnozan

Rue Ferrère

Cours du Maréchal Foch

Allées de Chartres

Esplanade des
Quinconces

Allées de Bristol

Allées de Munich

Allées d'Orléans

Place
de la
Comédie

Rue de l'Esprit des Lois

Cours du Chapeau Rouge

Place
de la
Bourse

To Airport (10km)

Rue de l'Intendance

Place
Gambetta

Rue de la Porte-Dijeaux

Place
du
Parlement

Place
St-Pierre

Place
St-Projet

Rue des
Piliers de
Tutelle

Place
de la Merci

Place
Camille
Jullian

Place
du
Palais

Place Jean-
Moulin

To N89 to Libourne
(31km); St Émilion (40km)

To Pont de Pierre & A10 to
Poitiers (248km) & Paris
(580km)

Place du
Colonel
Raynal

Cours d'Alsace et Lorraine

To Quai de la
Paludate (Bars & Discos;
1.3km)

Place
de la
République

St-Michel

To A630, A62 to
Toulouse (248km),
A63 to Arcachon (74km)
& Bayonne (190km)

Place
de la
Victoire

Place des
Capucins

To Arcachon
via N250

To Camping
Beausoleil
(10km via
Cours
d'Argonne)

To Camping les
Gravières (10km)

To Auberge
de Jeunesse (800m)
& Gare St-Jean
(1.4km)

Garonne

euro currency converter 10FF = €1.52

BORDEAUX

PLACES TO STAY		47	Centre National Jean Moulin	40	Bourse du Commerce
8	Hôtel Dauphin	54	Musée des Arts Décoratifs	41	Hôtel de la Douane
9	Hôtel Touring;	61	Musée des Beaux-Arts	42	La Reine Carotte
	Hôtel Studio	68	Musée d'Aquitaine	43	Porte Cailhau
10	Hôtel de Famille			45	Cinéma Utopia
11	Hôtel Royal Médoc	**OTHER**		46	Post Office Branch
23	Hôtel Balzac; Laundrette	3	Bord'Eaux Vélos Loisirs	48	Seven Café
49	Hôtel de la Tour Intendance	4	Halte Routière	50	Porte Dijeaux
52	Hôtel Bristol		(Bus Station)	51	Virgin Megastore
53	Hôtel La Boëtie	5	Girondins Fountain-	55	Bradley's Bookshop
59	Hôtel Boulan		Monument	56	Main Post Office
		6	Laundrette	58	Galerie des Beaux-Arts
PLACES TO EAT		12	Bordeaux Magnum	60	Jardin de la Mairie
7	Restaurant Baud et Millet	13	Maison du Vin de Bordeaux	62	City Hall
16	Restaurant Jean Ramet	14	Tourist Office	63	Bar de l'Hôtel de Ville
22	Le Mably	15	Banque de France	64	Tribunal de Grande Instance
27	Restaurant Agadir	17	Bus Hub		(Court; 1998)
28	Cassolette Café	18	CGFTE Bus Information	65	Cathédrale St-André
30	Fromagerie		Office	66	Tour Pey-Berland
31	Champion Supermarket	19	Grand Théâtre	67	Cyberstation
34	La Chanterelle	20	Jet'Bus	69	Porte de la Grosse Cloche
39	Chez Édouard		(Airport Bus)	70	Porte des Salinières
44	Claret's	21	Merry-Go-Round	71	Église St-Michel
57	Auchan Supermarket	24	Laundrette	72	Tour St-Michel
73	Champion Supermarket	25	Police Station	75	Hôpital St-André
74	La Fournaise	26	Jet'Bus (Airport Bus)	76	Synagogue
81	Cassolette Café	29	Centre Jean Vigo	77	Net Zone
85	Fruit & Veggie Stalls	32	Église Notre Dame	78	Laundrette
87	Le Fournil des Capucins	33	Maison du Tourisme de la	79	The Down Under
88	Marché des Capucins		Gironde	80	Le Plana
		35	American Express	82	Café des Sports
MUSEUMS		36	Théâtre Femina	83	Porte d'Aquitaine
1	Musée d'Histoire Naturelle	37	Bodega Bodega	84	Laundrette
2	Musée d'Art Contemporain	38	Calle Ocho	86	La Lune dans le Caniveau

ATLANTIC COAST

The train station, Gare St-Jean, is in a seedy area about 3km south-east of the city centre. Cours de la Marne stretches from the train station to place de la Victoire, which is linked to place de la Comédie by rue Ste-Catherine.

Information

Tourist Offices The helpful and well-informed tourist office (☎ 05 56 00 66 00, fax 05 56 00 66 01) at 12 cours du 30 Juillet is open 9 am to 7 pm Monday to Saturday and 9.45 am to 4.30 pm on Sunday. From May to September or October, it opens until 8 pm (7 pm on Sunday). The *Plan Guide du Patrimoine* has information on the city's architectural heritage and suggests a walking itinerary. See the Web site at www.bordeaux-tourisme.com.

The tourist office annexe at the train station opens 9 am to noon and 1 to 6 pm Monday to Saturday. From May to September or October, it opens daily until 7 pm (6 pm on Sunday).

For brochures on the Gironde department, contact or visit the Maison du Tourisme de la Gironde (☎ 05 56 52 61 40, fax 05 56 81 09 99) at 21 cours de l'Intendance, open Monday to Saturday until 6 pm (7 pm from April to October). Its Web site is at www.tourisme-gironde.cg33.fr.

Money The Banque de France, 15 rue de l'Esprit des Lois, will change money on weekdays from 9 am to noon.

Most commercial banks open weekdays, though a few also open on Saturday. Lots of them can be found near the tourist office on cours de l'Intendance, rue de l'Esprit des Lois and cours du Chapeau Rouge.

American Express (☎ 05 56 00 63 36), 14 cours de l'Intendance, opens 9 am to noon and 1.30 to 5 pm Monday to Friday (5.30 pm from April to September) and, from June to September, on Saturday from 9.30 am to 12.30 pm.

Post & Communications The main post office, 37 rue du Château d'Eau, opens weekdays from 8.30 am to 6.30 pm, and until 12.30 pm on Saturday. The branch post office at place St-Projet opens until 6.30 pm (noon on Saturday). Currency exchange and Cyberpostes are available at both.

Cyberstation (☎ 05 56 01 15 15), 23 Cour Pasteur, is open from 11 am to 2 am (2 pm to midnight on Sunday). Five minutes on-line costs 5FF. NetZone (☎ 05 57 59 01 25), 209 rue Ste-Catherine, opens daily from 10 am to 8 pm.

Bookshops Bradley's Bookshop (☎ 05 56 52 10 57), 8 cours d'Albret, has a wide selection of English books, including some Lonely Planet titles. It opens 9.30 am to 12.30 pm and 2 to 7 pm (closed Monday morning and Sunday).

Laundry The laundrettes at 5 rue de Fondaudège and 8 rue Lafaurie de Monbadon open 7 am to 9 pm.

Medical Services & Emergency Hôpital St-André (☎ 05 56 79 56 79 ext 43230 for the 24-hour casualty ward) is at 1 rue Jean Burguet.

The police station (☎ 05 56 99 77 77), 29 rue Castéja, is staffed 24 hours a day.

Walking Tours

The sights mentioned below appear pretty much from north to south.

The **Croiseur Colbert** (☎ 05 56 44 96 11), a 180m-long French navy missile cruiser, was in service from 1957 to 1991. Now permanently docked at Quai des Chartrons, 500m north of the Musée d'Art Contemporain, it can be visited from 10 am to 6 or 7 pm (8 pm from June to August; closed on

Museum Hours & Prices

Bordeaux' museums are open daily, except Monday and holidays (daily except Tuesday and holidays for the Beaux-Arts, Arts Décoratifs and Histoire Naturelle). They open at 11 am (2 pm for the Arts Décoratifs and, at the weekend, for the Centre National Jean Moulin and Histoire Naturelle) and close at 6 pm. On Wednesday, the Art Contemporain stays open until 8 pm.

The Centre National Jean Moulin is free, but the others cost 25FF (people aged under 25 or over 60, 15FF). All are free for students and, on the first Sunday of each month, for everyone. Expect to pay 10FF more when special exhibitions are on.

With the free Carte Bordeaux Découverte, available at the tourist office, you pay full price for the first museum you visit (or walking tour you take) and then, for visits to other museums, you qualify for the reduced-price fee usually reserved for under 25s and over 60s – a great deal!

weekday mornings and on Monday from October to March). Admission costs 47FF (children and students 37FF).

Entrepôts Lainé was built in 1824 as a warehouse for the rare and exotic products of France's colonies (such as coffee, cocoa, peanuts and vanilla). Its capacious spaces now house the **Musée d'Art Contemporain** (Museum of Contemporary Art; ☎ 05 56 00 81 50), whose entrance is opposite 16 rue Ferrère. Most of the exhibits and installations are temporary.

The beautifully landscaped **Jardin Public** along cours de Verdun, established in 1755 and laid out in the English style a century later, includes the meticulously catalogued **Jardin Botanique**, founded in 1629 and at its present site since 1855 (open from 8 am to 6 pm), and the nearby **Musée d'Histoire Naturelle** (Natural History Museum; ☎ 05 56 48 29 86). There's a **children's playground** on the island.

The most prominent feature of **Esplanade des Quinconces**, a vast square laid out in 1820, is the fountain monument to the

Girondins, a group of moderate, bourgeois National Assembly deputies during the French Revolution, 22 of whom were executed in 1793 – convicted of counter-Revolutionary activities. The entire 50m-high ensemble, completed in 1902, was dismantled in 1943 by the Germans so the statues could be melted down for their 52 tonnes of bronze; restoration work was not completed until 1983.

Bordeaux' neoclassical **Grand Théâtre** (see Classical Music under Entertainment) on place de la Comédie, built in the 1770s, is surrounded by a Corinthian colonnade decorated with 12 figures of the Muses and Graces. City hall is *finally* getting its act together and turning the long-neglected, 4km-long **riverfront esplanade** – long little more than an ugly series of car parks and dilapidated hangars – into a park with trees, playgrounds and bicycle paths (see Bicycle under Getting Around).

Nowadays, **place Gambetta** is an island of calm and flowers in the midst of the city centre's hustle and bustle, but during the Reign of Terror that followed the Revolution, a guillotine placed here severed the heads of 300 alleged counter-Revolutionaries.

The city's main shopping area is east of place Gambetta along the pedestrianised **rue de la Porte Dijeaux** (named after **Porte Dijeaux**, a former city gate built in 1748), the upscale and boutique-lined **cours de l'Intendance**, and the 1.2km-long, mostly pedestrianised **rue Ste-Catherine**, where you'll find several major department stores. **Galerie Bordelaise**, a 19th-century shopping arcade, is at the intersection of rue de la Porte Dijeaux and rue Ste-Catherine.

A few blocks south of place Gambetta, the **Musée des Arts Décoratifs** (Museum of Decorative Arts; ☎ 05 56 00 72 50), 39 rue Bouffard, specialises in faïence, porcelain, silverwork, glasswork, furniture and the like.

The **Musée des Beaux-Arts** (☎ 05 56 10 20 56), 20 cours d'Albret, occupies two wings of the Hôtel de Ville (city hall) complex (built in the 1770s); between them is a verdant public park, the **Jardin de la Mairie**. Founded in 1801, the museum has a large

---

Bordeaux, Capital of France

Bordeaux served briefly as the capital of France on three occasions when the country was on the verge of defeat: during the Franco-Prussian War of 1870–71; at the beginning of WWI (1914); and for two weeks in 1940, just before the Vichy government was proclaimed.

---

collection of paintings, including Flemish, Dutch and Italian works from the 17th century and a particularly important work by Delacroix. At nearby place du Colonel Raynal, the museum's annexe, the newly renovated **Galerie des Beaux-Arts** hosts short-term exhibitions.

The **Centre National Jean Moulin** (Jean Moulin Documentation Centre; ☎ 05 56 79 66 00), facing the northern side of the cathedral, has exhibits on France during WWII: the occupation, Resistance and liberation.

In 1137, the future King Louis VII married Eleanor of Aquitaine in **Cathédrale St-André**. The exterior wall of the nave dates from 1096; most of the rest of the structure was built in the 13th and 14th centuries. The interior, reached via the newly cleaned north portal, is much more attractive than the stained, crumbling exterior; you should be able to visit it daily until 5.30 or 6 pm, but it may close from 11.30 am to 2 or 2.30 pm. Behind the choir, the 50m-high belfry, 15th-century **Tour Pey-Berland**, can be climbed for 25FF (concessions 15FF) from 10 am to noon and 2 to 5 pm (closed Monday).

The outstanding **Musée d'Aquitaine** (Museum of Aquitaine; ☎ 05 56 01 51 00), 20 cours Pasteur, illustrates 25,000 years of Bordeaux' history and ethnography. The prehistoric period is represented by a number of exceptional artefacts, including several stone carvings of women. A detailed, English-language catalogue can be borrowed at the ticket counter (10FF deposit).

Porte de la Grosse Cloche spans rue St-James. It is a 15th-century clock tower, and was once the city hall's belfry. It was restored in the 19th century.

ATLANTIC COAST

The architecture of the **Synagogue** (☎ 05 56 91 79 39) on rue du Grand Rabbin Joseph Cohen, inaugurated in 1882, is a mixture of Sephardic and Byzantine styles. Ripped apart and turned into a prison by the Nazis, it was painstakingly rebuilt after the war. Visits are generally possible Monday to Thursday from 9 am to noon and 2 to 4 pm – just ring the bell marked *gardien* at 213 rue Ste-Catherine.

Organised Tours

The tourist office runs bilingual, two-hour walking tours of the city every day – except on Wednesday and Saturday from May to October – at 10 am. The tour costs 40FF (students, those aged over 65, 35FF).

The tourist office also offers two-hour, bilingual 'Introduction to Wine Tasting' courses every Thursday at 4.30 pm (and, from mid-July to mid-August, on Saturday). The cost is 125FF (students and seniors 110FF). The Maison du Vin de Bordeaux (☎ 05 56 00 22 88) at 3 cours du 30 Juillet (see Bordeaux Wine-growing Region) has similar courses costing 100FF, held from mid-June to mid-September on Tuesday, Wednesday and Thursday at 3 pm.

Places to Stay – Budget

Bordeaux has lots of good-value hotels. If possible, don't stay in the seedy area around the train station.

Camping The 150-spot *Camping Les Gravières* (☎ 05 56 87 00 36, place de Courréjean in Villenave d'Ornon), open year round, is 10km south-east of the city centre. By bus, take line B from place de la Victoire towards Corréjean and get off at the terminus. By car, get off the ring road at exit No 20 (Bègles) and follow the signs to Corréjean.

Hostels The *Auberge de Jeunesse* (☎ 05 56 91 59 51, 22 cours Barbey) is being completely renovated and is scheduled to reopen in April 2001.

Hotels – City Centre The quiet, 16-room *Hôtel Boulan* (☎ 05 56 52 23 62, fax 05 56

44 91 65, 28 rue Boulan), offers excellent value. Decent singles/doubles with high ceilings cost 100/110FF (120/140FF with shower). Toilets are on the half-floor; hall showers cost 10FF.

The 27-room *Hôtel de Famille* (☎ 05 56 52 11 28, fax 05 56 51 94 43, 76 cours Georges Clemenceau), has rather ordinary but homey doubles costing from 120FF (185FF with shower and toilet). There's no lift. The one-star, 14-room *Hôtel Dauphin* (☎ 05 56 52 24 62, fax 05 56 01 10 91, 82 rue du Palais Gallien), has uninspiring, shower-equipped rooms costing 159FF (199FF for enormous rooms with toilet); singles cost 20FF less.

Hôtel Studio (☎ 05 56 48 00 14, fax 05 56 81 25 71, 26 rue Huguerie) is the headquarters of Bordeaux' cheap hotel empire – the same family owns three other places in the same neighbourhood. All of them offer charmless but newly renovated single and double rooms with shower, toilet and (in most cases) cable TV from 135FF. However, you're more likely to find a larger room for 150FF (250FF for a three-bed quad). The hotel's mini-cybercafe charges hotel guests 10FF an hour. Its Web site is at www.hotel-bordeaux.com.

The 18-room *Hôtel La Boëtie* (☎ 05 56 81 76 68, 4 rue la Boëtie), pronounced bo-eh-**see**, also part of the Hôtel Studio group, has doubles/quins costing 135/250FF. Reception is at the nearby Hôtel Bristol (see Places to Stay – Mid-Range).

You might also try the *Hôtel Balzac* (☎ 05 56 81 85 12, 14 rue Lafaurie de Monbadon), which has six large, pastel-coloured doubles with shower and toilet for 185FF (the other seven rooms are rented out by the month).

Hotels – Train Station Area The few budget places in this seedy area tend to be grungy and depressing. Your best bet is the turn-of-the-century *Hôtel Regina* (☎ 05 56 91 66 07, fax 05 56 91 32 88, 34 rue Charles Domercq), a friendly, 40-room place across from the train station's Arrivée (arrival) section. Well-kept, cheery singles/doubles with shower start at 145/185FF

(185/205FF with toilet). From mid-June to mid-September, it's a good idea to phone ahead.

You might also try the 17-room, two-star **Hôtel St-Martin** (☎ 05 56 91 55 40, *2 rue St-Vincent de Paul*), where joyless doubles cost from 140FF (180FF with shower and toilet).

Places to Stay – Mid-Range

You're assured of a warm welcome at the 20-room, two-star **Hôtel de la Tour Intendance** (☎ 05 56 81 46 27, fax 05 56 81 60 90, *16 rue de la Vieille Tour*). Ordinary doubles/triples cost 250/320FF. Another excellent deal is the 12-room, two-star **Hôtel Touring** (☎ 05 56 81 56 73, fax 05 56 81 24 55, *16 rue Huguerie*), which has gigantic and spotless singles/doubles with shower costing 180/220FF (220/240FF with toilet, too). Some of the rooms have fireplaces.

The two-star, 27-room **Hôtel Bristol** (☎ 05 56 81 85 01, fax 05 56 51 24 06, *2 rue Bouffard*), part of the Hôtel Studio group (see Places to Stay – Budget), has cheerful and very comfortable doubles/triples with 4m-high ceilings, bathroom, toilet and minibar costing from 210/300FF.

The three-star, 69-room **Hôtel Royal Médoc** (☎ 05 56 81 72 42, fax 05 56 48 98 00, *3 rue de Sèze*), offers comfortable doubles/triples costing 260/325FF.

Places to Eat

Quite a few restaurants offer reasonably priced lunch *menus*.

Restaurants – French Moderately priced traditional French and regional cuisine is served at **La Chanterelle** (☎ 05 56 81 75 43, *3 rue de Martignac*), including *menus* for 75FF (lunch only) and 98FF. It is closed Wednesday night and Sunday.

Bistro-style cuisine and south-western French specialities are on offer at **Claret's** (☎ 05 56 01 21 21, *place Camille Jullian*). The *menus* cost 65FF (lunch only), 98FF and 160FF (closed Saturday at lunchtime and Sunday).There are a number of other intimate restaurants, several of them French, in the immediate vicinity.

For classic bistro fare, try atmospheric **Le Mably** (☎ 05 56 44 30 10, *12 rue Mably*), where *menus* cost 125FF (not available on Friday and Saturday nights) and 172FF.

Chez Édouard (☎ 05 56 81 48 87, *16 place du Parlement*) serves French bistro-style meat and fish dishes; *menus* cost 59FF (lunch except Sunday), 70FF and 99FF. There are lots of other *cafes* and *restaurants*, some with terraces, at place du Parlement and along nearby rue du Parlement Ste-Catherine, rue des Piliers de Tutelle and rue St-Rémi.

Restaurant Baud et Millet (☎ 05 56 79 05 77, *19 rue Huguerie*), serves cheese-based cuisine (most dishes are vegetarian, including *raclette* (melted cheese with cold cuts of meat and pickles; 110FF for all-you-can-eat) and *fondue Savoyarde* (cheese fondue; 95FF); the *menus* cost 140FF to 170FF. The basement buffet has 150 to 200 different cheeses. It opens 11 am to midnight (closed Sunday). The same street is home to a number of reasonably priced eateries.

Restaurant Jean Ramet (☎ 05 56 44 12 51, *7 place Jean Jaurès*), serves classic French and Bordelais cuisine amid mirrors, white tablecloths and sparkling tableware. *Menus* cost 170FF (lunch only), 270FF and 340FF. It is closed Sunday and Monday.

The inexpensive cafes and restaurants around place de la Victoire – an area hugely popular with students – include the **Cassolette Café** (☎ 05 56 92 94 96, *20 place de la Victoire*), which offers great value by serving family-style French food in a unique way: each small/large *cassolette* (terracotta plate) that you order using a check-off form costs 13/39FF. Daily hours are noon to 2.30 pm and 7 to 11.30 pm. The second **Cassolette Café** (*26 rue du Palais Gallien*) is closed on Sunday at midday.

Restaurants – Other *La Fournaise* (☎ 05 56 91 04 71, *23 rue de Lalande*) is a welcoming place that serves the delicious cuisine of Réunion, which has strong Indian, Chinese, Basque and Breton elements. The *menus* cost 80FF to 140FF. It opens Tuesday to Saturday from 7 to 11 pm.

Richly ornamented *Restaurant Agadir* (☎ 05 56 52 28 04, *14 rue du Palais Gallien*), has generous portions of Moroccan couscous and *tajines* costing from 68FF to 100FF. There are quite a few restaurants and sandwich joints on the same street.

There are lots of East Asian restaurants on rue St-Rémi (a block north of place du Parlement).

Self-Catering The *Marché des Capucins*, a one-time wholesale market a few blocks east of place de la Victoire, opens Tuesday to Sunday from 6 am to 1 pm. Nearby rue Élie Gintrec has super-cheap *fruit and veggie stalls* on weekdays and Saturday until 1 or 1.30 pm.

The *Champion* supermarket (*place des Grands Hommes*), in the basement of the modern, mirror-plated Marché des Grands Hommes – visited by Queen Elizabeth II in 1992 – opens Monday to Saturday from 8.30 am to 7.30 pm. Nearby, there's a *fromagerie* (*2 rue Montesquieu*) that's closed Monday morning and Sunday.

Vast, cheap *Auchan* supermarket (*opposite 58 rue du Château d'Eau*), in the Centre Commercial Mériadeck, opens 8.30 am to 10 pm Monday to Saturday. The *Champion* supermarket (*190 rue Ste-Catherine*) opens daily 8.30 am to 8 pm, except Sunday.

Near place de la Victoire, *Le Fournil des Capucins* (*62–64 cours de la Marne*) is a 24-hour boulangerie.

Entertainment

Bordeaux has a really hopping nightlife scene; details on events appear in *Bordeaux Plus* and *Clubs & Concerts*, both free and available at the tourist office. Student nightlife is centred around place de la Victoire.

Tickets for events such as concerts and bullfights are available from the *Virgin Megastore billeterie* (☎ 05 56 56 05 55, *17 place Gambetta*), open 10 am to 7.30 pm (9.30 pm on Friday and Saturday); Sunday hours are 3 to 6.30 pm.

Cinemas Nondubbed films are screened at two art cinemas, *Centre Jean Vigo* (☎ 05 56

44 35 17, 6 rue Franklin), and the new, five-screen *Cinéma Utopia* (☎ 05 56 52 00 03, *3 place Camille Jullian*).

Classical Music Except in August, the 18th-century *Grand Théâtre* (☎ 05 56 00 85 95, *place de la Comédie*), stages operas, ballets and concerts of orchestral and chamber music. The ticket office, which also handles ticketing for the operettas, plays, dance performances and variety shows held at *Théâtre Femina* (*rue de Grassi*), is open Monday to Saturday from 11 am to 6 pm.

Bars Run by an ex-Aucklander, *The Down Under* (☎ 05 56 94 52 48, *104 cours Aristide Briand*) is a favourite of Aussie and Kiwi rugby players and other Anglophones. Daily opening hours are 7 or 8 pm to 2 am.

One of the hottest places in town is a Cuban-style bar called *Calle Ocho* (☎ 05 56 48 08 68, *24 rue des Piliers de Tutelle*), open 5 pm to 2 am (closed Sunday). The house speciality (the *mojito* (a mint drink made with lemon and rum), costs 25FF. Down the road, *Bodega Bodega* (☎ 05 56 01 24 24, *4 rue des Piliers de Tutelle*) is a hugely popular tapas bar that opens from noon to 3.15 pm and 7 pm to 2 am (closed for lunch on Sunday and holidays).

Clubs For zoning reasons, many of the city's late-late dance venues are a few blocks north-east of Gare St-Jean along the river, on Quai de Paludate (just south of the railway bridge) and perpendicular rue du Commerce. Most places are bars with dancing (they can't quite be called discos) and have deafening, pulsating music and large, selective bouncers but no cover charge (except where indicated). They can get incredibly crowded, especially just after 2 am, statutory closing time for most of the city's regular bars.

Among the best of the dancing bars is tropical beach-themed *La Plage* (☎ 05 56 49 02 46, *40 Quai de la Paludate*), whose patrons tend to be in the 24–35 age group (open Wednesday to Saturday nights). Similar places include *Le Bistro* (*50 Quai de la Paludate*), open Monday to Saturday nights, and **Quai Sud** (*37 Quai de la Paludate*), open Wednesday to Saturday nights. Hours for all three are midnight to 5 am.

A real disco with two floors and a capacity of 1000, **Le Duplex** (☎ *05 56 85 71 85, 18 rue du Commerce*), is a favourite with the 18–25 age group. It opens Thursday (20FF), Friday (free) and Saturday (50FF including a drink; free for women and students) from midnight to 5 am. Next door (and under the same management), **Le Living Room** (*14 rue du Commerce*) is a dancing bar that attracts a slightly older crowd. At the back there's a relatively quiet Oriental-style corner with rugs and couches. Opening hours are midnight to 5 am.

One of the most hopping student venues at place de la Victoire is **Le Plana** (☎ *05 56 91 73 23, 22 place de la Victoire*). Except in July and August, it has live jazz every Sunday at about 10.30 pm and concerts of funk and soul – some of them jam sessions – on some Mondays, Tuesdays and Wednesdays at 10.30 pm. It opens 7 am to 2 am. Across the street, **Café des Sports** (*5 cours de l'Argonne*) is also pumping.

Pierced eyebrows are recommended at **La Lune dans le Caniveau** (☎ *05 56 31 95 92, 39 place des Capucins*), a hardcore disco whose down-and-out surroundings and nonpop soundtrack (punk rock, 'hard', reggae, ska) attract some of the grungiest members of the student counter-culture scene. It opens Wednesday to Saturday from midnight (1 am on Wednesday and Thursday) to 5 am, but things don't get going until about 2 am. There's no cover charge.

Le Nautilus (☎ *05 56 505 596, 122 Quai de Bacalan*), along the river 2.4km north of Esplanade des Quinconces, hosts live bands each weekend, generally from midnight to 5 am. It occupies a cavernous old warehouse so there's plenty of space to boogie.

Gay & Lesbian Venues The spirited (and often crowded), 95% gay **Bar de l'Hôtel de Ville** (☎ *05 56 44 05 08, 4 rue de l'Hôtel de Ville*) opens 6 pm to 2 am. Around the corner, **Seven Café** (☎ *05 56 48 13 79, 73 rue des Trois Conils*) is a dimly-lit bar whose hours are also 6 pm to 2 am. The mixed

disco in the basement opens Saturday, Sunday and holiday mornings from 5 am (when the late discos close) until at least 9 am.

La Reine Carotte (☎ *05 56 01 26 68, 32 rue du Chai des Farines*), a mellow place that's about 50% lesbian, opens Tuesday and Saturday from 7 pm to 2 am.

Shopping

Bordeaux wine in all price ranges is on sale at several speciality shops near the tourist office, including Bordeaux Magnum (☎ 05 56 48 00 06) at 3 rue Gobineau, open Monday to Saturday until 7.30 pm.

There are antique shops along rue Bouffard, near the Musée des Arts Décoratifs.

Getting There & Away

Air Bordeaux airport (☎ 05 56 34 50 50) is in Mérignac, 10km west of the city centre.

Bus Buses to places all over the Gironde (and parts of nearby departments) leave from the Halte Routière on allées de Chartres (in the north-east corner of Esplanade des Quinconces); schedules are posted. The information kiosk (☎ 05 56 43 68 43) opens 7 to 8.30 am and 1 to 8.30 pm weekdays, 9 am to 12.30 pm and 5 to 8.30 pm on Saturday, and 8.30 to 10.30 am and 5 to 8.30 pm on Sunday. For details on buses to the Médoc and St-Émilion, see those listings.

Eurolines (☎ 05 56 92 50 42), facing the train station at 32 rue Charles Domercq, is open Monday to Saturday.

Train Bordeaux is one of France's most important rail transit points. The station, Gare St-Jean (☎ 0 836 35 35 35), is about 3km from the city centre at the southern terminus of cours de la Marne. The showers (20FF), on Quai 1 at Gate 42, are open daily from 5 am to midnight. Be extra careful with your bags here.

Destinations include Paris' Gare Montparnasse (352FF to 399FF, three hours, at least 16 daily), Bayonne (135FF, 1¾ hours, eight daily), Nantes (220FF, four hours, five or six daily), Poitiers (172FF, 1¾ hours, nine daily), La Rochelle (134FF, two hours, five to seven daily) and Toulouse (165FF, 2¼ hours, nine to 14 daily). For information on getting to the Médoc, St-Émilion and Arcachon, see those sections.

Car Inexpensive rental companies include AA Location (☎ 05 56 92 84 78) at 185 cours de la Marne (about 400m from the train station) and Rent A Car Système (☎ 05 56 33 60 75) at 204 cours de la Marne (both closed Sunday). The big boys have offices in the train station building, all the way to the left as you exit.

Getting Around
To/From the Airport Jet'Bus (☎ 05 56 34 50 50) links the train station, the Grand Théâtre and place Gambetta with the airport (35FF, 35 minutes, every 30/45 minutes at the weekend) until at least 9.30 pm.

Bus Bordeaux' urban buses, run by CGFTE (☎ 05 57 57 88 88), are to be joined by three tram lines, the first of which is supposed to begin service in 2002. The company has information bureaux at the train station, place de la Victoire and place Gambetta.

The train station is linked with the city centre by buses No 7 and 8; line No 1 runs along the waterfront from the train station north to Le Croiseur Colbert and beyond. Single tickets, sold on board, cost 7.50FF and are *not* valid for transfers. The Bordeaux Découverte card, available at the tourist office, allows unlimited travel for one day (23.50FF) to six days (77FF). Time-stamp it only the first time you use it.

Parking Parking in the city centre is hard to find and pricey (up to 10FF an hour), and the metres won't allow you to pay the night before for parking after 9 am. Places to look for free spaces include the side streets north of the Musée d'Art Contemporain and west of the Jardin Public.

Taxi To order a taxi 24 hours a day, call ☎ 05 56 96 00 34.

Bicycle Bord'Eaux Vélos Loisirs (☎ 05 56 44 77 31), on the waterfront at Quai Louis

XVIII, rents out bicycles and in-line skates (both 20/90FF for one/eight hours), talking bikes that take you on a tour of the city, kids' pedal-cars, and electric-powered bicycles and *trottinnettes* (scooters you ride standing up). From April to mid-October, it opens daily from 9.30 am to 8 pm; the rest of the year, it opens Wednesday and Sunday from 9.30 am to 6.30 pm and Monday, Friday and Sunday from 2.30 to 6.30 pm.

BORDEAUX WINE-GROWING REGION
The 1000 sq km wine-growing area around the city of Bordeaux is – along with Burgundy – France's most important producer of top-quality wines. The region is divided into 57 *appellations* (production areas whose soil and microclimate impart distinctive characteristics upon the wine produced there) that are grouped into six *familles* and subdivided into a hierarchy of designations (eg, *premier grand cru classé*, the most prestigious) that often vary from appellation to appellation.

The majority of the region's many wines – reds, rosés, sweet and dry whites and sparkling wines – have earned the right to include the abbreviation AOC (Appellation d'Origine Contrôlée) on their labels, indicating that the contents have been grown, fermented and aged according to strict regulations governing such matters as the number of vines permitted per hectare and acceptable pruning methods. In 1998, the region produced some 870 million bottles of wine.

Bordeaux has over 5000 *châteaux* (also known as *domaines*, *crus* or *clos*), a term that in this context refers not to palatial residences but rather to the properties where grapes are raised, picked, fermented and then matured as wine. The smaller chateaux sometimes accept walk-in visitors, but at many places – especially the better-known ones – you have to make advance reservations by phone. Many chateaux are closed during the *vendange* (grape harvest) in October.

Traditionally, Bordelais wine-makers have dealt with city-based *négociants* (merchants) to market their wine rather than selling direct from source, which may explain why some chateaux – even ones 'open to the public' – seem less-than-welcoming to casual visitors.

Information

In Bordeaux, the Maison du Vin de Bordeaux (☎ 05 56 00 22 88, fax 05 56 00 99 30), 3 cours du 30 Juillet (across the street from the tourist office), can supply you with a free, colour-coded map of production areas, details on chateau visits, and the addresses of local *maisons du vin* (tourist offices that deal mainly with winery visits). It is open weekdays from 10 am to 5.15 pm (9.30 am to 5.30 pm in summer, when it also opens on Saturday until 3 pm).

Organised Tours

On Wednesday and Saturday (daily from May to October) at about 1.15 pm, the Bordeaux tourist office runs five-hour bus tours in French and English to wine chateaux in the area (160FF; students, those aged over 65, 140FF). From May to October, all-day trips (290FF; concessions 255FF) start at 9.15 am on Wednesday and Saturday.

More information on winery tours appears under Activities in the St-Émilion section later in this chapter.

THE MÉDOC

North-west of Bordeaux, along the western shore of the Gironde Estuary – formed by the confluence of the Garonne and the Dordogne rivers – lie some of Bordeaux' most celebrated vineyards, those of Haut Médoc, Margaux and neighbouring appellations. To the west, fine-sand beaches, bordered by dunes and *étangs* (lagoons), stretch for some 200km from Pointe de Grave south along the **Côte d'Argent** (silver coast) to the Bassin d'Arcachon and beyond; seaside resorts include **Soulac-sur-Mer** (see following section), **Carcans Plage, Lacanau-Océan** and **Cap Ferret**. The coastal dunes abut a vast pine forest planted in the 19th century to stabilise the drifting sands and prevent them from encroaching on areas farther inland.

Vineyards & Chateaux

The gravelly soil of the Médoc's gently rolling hills supports orderly rows of meticulously tended grape vines (mainly Cabernet Sauvignon) that produce some of the world's most sought-after red wines. The rose bushes at the end of each row serve a purpose similar to that of canaries in coal mines: they're more susceptible to disease (especially mildew) than the vines, and tell the grower when prophylactic treatment is necessary. The most beautiful part of this renowned wine-growing area is north of **Pauillac**, along the D2 and the D204 (towards Lesparre). To the north, the vines give way to evergreen forests.

Chateaux in the Pauillac appellation that welcome visitors include the beautifully landscaped **Château Lafitte Rothschild** (☎ 01 53 89 78 00 in Paris), famed for its premier *grand cru classé*, whose free, bilingual, one-hour tours (including a tasting session) take place on weekdays (closed on holidays and from August to October); and the equally illustrious **Château Mouton Rothschild** (☎ 05 56 73 21 29), whose tours, frequently in English, take place daily (closed at weekends from November to March) and cost 30FF (80FF or 150FF including a tasting session). Both places require that you make advance reservations.

In the nearby St-Julien appellation, the impressive **Château Beychevelle** (☎ 05 56 73 20 70) has free tours (without a tasting session) on weekdays (and, from June to mid-October, on Saturday); it opens 10 am to noon and 1.30 to 5 pm. Phone ahead from late October to early May.

About 20km to the south in Margaux, you can visit the celebrated **Château Margaux** (☎ 05 57 88 83 83) on weekdays (closed in August and during the grape harvest); admission is free. **Château Palmer** (☎ 05 57 88 72 72), on the D2 3km south of Margaux in Issan, has one-hour tours (30FF) on weekdays (daily from April to September). Both chateaux require advance reservations.

Information on visiting the Médoc, and help with reservations for chateau visits, is available at the Maison du Tourisme et du Vin (☎ 05 56 59 03 08) in Pauillac, open daily until 6 pm year round.

Soulac-sur-Mer

Soulac (population 2800), which is 9km south of Pointe de Grave and 90km north of Bordeaux, is a lively seaside resort in summer and an almost dead seaside town the rest of the year. The beach, fronted by a promenade, is wide and safe.

Orientation & Information The commercial centre is along pedestrianised rue de la Plage, which runs perpendicular to the beach. The railway station is 700m south of the town's Romanesque church, buried by drifting dunes in 1757 and dug out a century later.

The tourist office (☎ 05 56 09 86 61, fax 05 56 73 63 76), across from 68 rue de la Plage, is next to the *marché municipal* (a covered food market that opens every morning). It opens Monday to Saturday from 9 am to 12.30 pm and 2 to 5.30 pm and, from May to mid-September, on Sunday morning; daily hours in July and August are 9 am to 7 pm.

The post office, which does currency exchange, is down the street at 81 rue de la Plage.

Places to Stay & Eat Rooms and camping grounds are nearly impossible to come by in July and August.

The two-star, 13-room *Hôtel La Dame de Cœur* (☎ 05 56 09 80 80, fax 05 56 09 97 47, ✉ la.dame.de.coeur@wanadoo.fr, 103 rue de la Plage), open throughout the year, has fairly ordinary singles/doubles/quads costing 200/250/350FF. Reception is closed from 2 to 6 pm in the low season.

The 11-room, two-star *Hôtel L'Hacienda* (☎ 05 56 09 81 34, fax 05 56 73 65 57, rue des Lacs), 150m south of the church, is open year round. Fairly basic doubles start at 230FF (in winter) and 300FF (June to September). Half-board (255FF or, in summer, 290FF per person) in the hotel *restaurant* (closed Sunday night in winter) – just about the only place in Soulac to eat in

winter – may be obligatory, especially in July and August

Euronat

The relaxed naturist village of Euronat (☎ 05 56 09 33 33, fax 05 56 09 30 27), open year round, is about 80km north of Bordeaux. The facilities, which can accommodate up to 7500 people, cover 3.3 sq km of pine forest and broom, and include 1.5km of dune-lined beachfront dotted with German pillboxes from WWII. The *restaurants* and commercial centre are open from about April to October.

The least expensive four-person *bungalows* range from 210FF a night (in winter) to 390FF a night (July and August), with a minimum stay of three nights. Advance reservations are necessary only in July and August. Tent sites for two people cost 44FF to 121FF, depending on the season. Their Web site is at www.euronat.fr.

For general information on naturism, see Naturism under Activities in the Facts for the Visitor chapter.

Getting There & Away

The northern tip of the Médoc, Pointe de Grave, is linked to Royan by car ferries (☎ 05 46 38 35 15; 25 minutes) that run six times daily in winter and every 40 minutes in summer. Fees are 9FF for bicycles, 56FF for motorcycles and 126FF for cars, plus 18FF per person. The service runs until sometime between 6.30 and 8.30 pm (7.15 and 9.30 pm from Royan), depending on the season.

Three to five Citram Aquitaine buses a day link Bordeaux with Lesparre, Soulac-sur-Mer (two hours) and Point de Grave (76FF, 2¼ hours). SNCF bus-train combos linking Bordeaux with Margaux, Pauillac (54FF, one hour), Lesparre, Soulac (83FF, two hours) and Pointe de Grave (or nearby Le Verdon; 89FF) run five times daily (twice at the weekend); bikes can be brought along on some runs.

Buses from Bordeaux also serve Carcans (1¾ hours, at least two to four daily), Lacanau and Cap Ferret (two hours, at least four or five daily).

ST-ÉMILION
postcode 33330 • pop 400
• elevation 30m

The medieval village of St-Émilion, 39km east of Bordeaux, is surrounded by vineyards renowned for their full-bodied, deeply coloured red wines. Situated on two limestone hills that look out over the Dordogne River valley, its ramparts (begun in the 13th century) and the rest of the town take on a luscious golden hue as the sun sets. Not even the vast numbers of tourists who flock here can spoil the charm.

Information
The tourist office (☎ 05 57 55 28 28, fax 05 57 55 28 29) at place des Créneaux has brochures in English and details on visiting almost 100 nearby chateaux. It opens daily from 9.30 am to 12.30 pm and 1.45 to 6 or 6.30 pm. In July and August, it opens 9.30 am to 7 pm. Its Web site is at www.saint-emilion.org.

Things to See
St-Émilion's most interesting historical sites – including the **Église Monolithe**, carved out of solid limestone from the 9th to the 12th centuries – can be visited only if you take one of the tourist office's 45-minute guided tours (in French, with printed English text). They depart every 45 minutes from 10 to 11.30 am and 2 to 5 pm (5.45 pm from April to October). The cost is 33FF (students 20FF; children aged 13 to 17, 16FF).

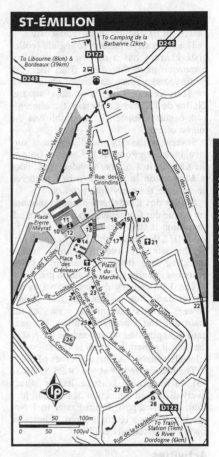

ATLANTIC COAST

ST-ÉMILION

PLACES TO STAY		3	Grandes Murailles	16	Chapelle de la Trinité;
7	Logis des Remparts	4	Douves du Palais Cardinal		Grotte de l'Ermitage;
20	Auberge de la Commanderie	5	Porte Bourgeoise		Catacombes
		6	Post Office;	18	Porte de la Cadène
PLACES TO EAT			Macaroon Bakery	19	Maison de la Cadène
1	Utile Grocery	9	Collégiale	21	Cloître des Cordeliers;
8	L'Envers du Décor	10	Maison du Vin		Les Cordeliers Winery
17	Boulangerie	11	Cloître de l'Église Collégiale	22	Porte Brunet
23	Restaurant Dominique	12	Tourist Office	25	Old Washhouse
24	Boulangerie	13	Fabrique des Macarons-	26	Castel daou Rey
			Matthieu Mouliérac		(King's Tower)
OTHER		14	Clocher (Bell Tower)	27	Musée de la Poterie
2	Intercity Bus Stop	15	Église Monolithe	28	Toilets

euro currency converter €1 = 6.56FF

To climb the **clocher** (bell tower) above the church (6FF), enquire in the tourist office.

The impressive former **Collégiale** (collegiate church) has a narrow, domed, Romanesque nave that dates from the 12th century, and a spacious vaulted choir (14th to 16th century) that's almost square. **Cloître de l'Église Collégiale**, the church's 14th-century cloister, is accessible via the tourist office.

Several of the city's medieval gates survive, including **Porte de la Cadène** (Gate of the Chain), just off rue Guadet. Next door is **Maison de la Cadène**, a half-timbered house from the early 16th century.

Cloître des Cordeliers, a ruined monastery on rue des Cordeliers, opens year round; admission is free. Les Cordeliers (☎ 05 57 24 72 07), the winery that has occupied part of the site for over a century makes sparkling wine; interesting (and free) **cellar tours** begin daily at 3, 4, 5 and 6 pm.

The 13th-century donjon known as the **Castel daou Rey** (or Tour du Roi; King's Tower) affords exceptional views of the town and the Dordogne Valley. It opens until 8.30 pm June to September; the rest of the year it generally opens in the afternoon (closed January). Admission costs 6FF.

The **Musée de la Poterie** (☎ 05 57 55 51 65), 21 rue André Loiseau, has an attractively displayed collection of pots and jugs from centuries past. From Easter to 1 November, it opens 10 am to 7 pm. Admission costs 20FF (students 10FF).

Activities

From mid-July to mid-September, the Maison du Vin (see the following Shopping section) offers bilingual, 1½-hour introductory wine-tasting classes daily at 11 am (110FF).

Daily (except Sunday) from May to September, St-Émilion's tourist office organises two-hour afternoon chateau visits in French and English. They cost 51FF (children aged 12 to 17, 31FF).

Places to Stay

The three-star *Camping de la Barbanne* (☎ 05 57 24 75 80, on the D122), about 2km

north of St-Émilion, opens from April to September.

The tourist office has a list of nearby *chambres d'hôtes*, which generally charge 200FF to 300FF for a double.

The two-star, 18-room *Auberge de la Commanderie* (☎ 05 57 24 70 19, fax 05 57 74 44 53, rue des Cordeliers) has spacious, flowery doubles/quads costing from 380/550FF (280/490FF from November to a week before Easter). It is closed from mid-January to February. The 17-room, three-star *Logis des Remparts* (☎ 05 57 24 70 43, fax 05 57 74 47 44, ✉ logis-des-remparts@saint-emilion.org, rue Guadet) has a 12m swimming pool and pleasant doubles costing from 400FF (closed mid-December to early February).

Places to Eat

Restaurants Serving a variety of regional specialities, *Restaurant Dominique* (☎ 05 57 24 71 00, rue de la Petite Fontaine) has *menus* costing 68FF, 89FF and 135FF. It closes on Sunday night and Monday (except in July and August) and mid-December to early February. *L'Envers du Décor* (☎ 05 57 74 48 31, rue du Clocher) has tasty, bistro-style cuisine and fine wine by the glass (20FF to 50FF).

Self-Catering The *Utile* grocery (*on the D122*), 150m north of town, opens daily until 7.30 pm (1 pm on Sunday and holidays; closed from 12.45 to 3 pm except from April to October).

At least one of the two *boulangeries* – one on rue Guadet, the other on rue de la Grande Fontaine – opens daily, all day long until at least 7 pm (from October to April, both are closed on Monday from 1 to 4 pm).

Shopping

St-Émilion's quaint streets and squares are lined with wine shops – about 50 of them, one for every eight residents! The cooperative Maison du Vin (☎ 05 57 55 50 55) at place Pierre Meyrat, owned by the 250 chateaux whose wines it sells, opens daily from 9.30 am to 12.30 pm and 2 to 6.30 pm.

The recipe for *macarons* (macaroons) was brought to St-Émilion in the 17th century by Ursuline nuns. Fabrique des Macarons Matthieu Mouliérac on Tertre de la Tente charges 30FF per two dozen (open daily, closed in the morning from January to March). There's another macaroon bakery next to the post office.

Getting There & Around

St-Émilion can be visited as a day trip from Bordeaux by bus and/or train. Buses to/from Bordeaux' Halte Routière (44FF) run at least once daily (except on Sundays and holidays from October to April), usually with a change at Libourne. The SNCF has three autorails daily (two on Sundays and holidays) *from* Bordeaux (44FF, 35 minutes); the last train back usually departs at 6.27 pm.

Year round, the tourist office rents out bicycles for 60/90FF per half-day/day.

ARCACHON

postcode 33120 • pop 11,800

The beach resort of Arcachon became popular with bourgeois residents of Bordeaux at the end of the 19th century. Its major attractions are the sandy seashore and the extraordinary Dune de Pyla (see the Around Arcachon section later in this chapter), Europe's highest sand dune. Arcachon, which is somnolent in winter and extremely crowded in summer, is well served by trains and makes an easy day trip from Bordeaux.

Orientation

Arcachon is on the southern side of the triangular Bassin d'Arcachon (Arcachon Bay), which is linked to the Atlantic by a 3km-wide channel just west of town. The narrow peninsula of Cap Ferret is on the other side of the outlet. The Dune de Pyla begins 8km south of Arcachon along the D218.

Arcachon's main commercial streets run parallel to the beach: blvd de la Plage, cours Lamarque de Plaisance and cours Héricart de Thury. Perpendicular to the beach, busy streets include ave Gambetta and rue du Maréchal de Lattre de Tassigny.

Information

Tourist Offices The tourist office (☎ 05 57 52 97 97, fax 05 57 52 97 77, ✉ tourisme@ arcachon.com), at place Président Roosevelt, opens 9 am to 12.30 pm and 2 to 5 pm Monday to Saturday (6 pm from April to September; 7 pm in July and August, when there's no midday closure). From April to September, it also opens on Sunday and holidays from 10 am to 1 pm.

Money The Banque de France, 55 blvd Général Leclerc, will change money Monday to Friday from 9 am to noon. There are a number of banks right around the Mairie (town hall) and along blvd de la Plage.

Post & Communications The main post office, at place Président Roosevelt, opens 8 am to 6.15 pm Monday to Friday, and on Saturday until noon. Exchange services and a Cyberposte are available.

Laundry The Laverie at the corner of blvd Général Leclerc and rue Molière opens daily from 7 am to 10 pm.

Central Arcachon

The flat area that abuts the **Plage d'Arcachon** (the town's beach) is known as the **Ville d'Été** (Summer Quarter). The liveliest section is around **Jetée Thiers**, one of the two piers.

The uninspiring **Aquarium et Musée** (☎ 05 56 54 89 28), 2 rue du Professeur Jolyet, opens 10 am to 12.30 pm and 2 to 7 pm daily from mid-March to early November (11 pm in July and August). Admission costs 25FF (children aged four to 10 and students 15FF).

The **Ville d'Hiver** (Winter Quarter), on the tree-covered hillside south of the Ville d'Été, dates from about a century ago. Its over 300 villas, many decorated with delicate wood tracery, range in style from neogothic to colonial.

A lovely **pedestrian promenade** lined with trees and playgrounds runs west and then south from Plage d'Arcachon to **Plage Péreire**, **Plage des Abatilles** and **Pyla-sur-Mer**.

ATLANTIC COAST

Activities

High-quality **cycle paths** links Arcachon with the Dune de Pyla and Biscarosse (30km to the south), and go all the way around the Bassin d'Arcachon to Cap Ferret. From Lège, at the northern tip of the Bassin, a cycleable path parallels the beach all the way to Pointe de Grave.

Centre Nautique d'Arcachon (☎ 05 56 22 36 83, @ arcachon.port@wanadoo.fr) on Quai Goslar, about 1.5km east of the Jetée d'Eyrac at the Port de Plaisance (Pleasure Boat Port), rents sea kayaks, windsurfing and diving equipment and offers courses.

Boat Excursions

Les Bateliers Arcachonnais (UBA; ☎ 05 57 72 28 28) runs ferries from Jetée Thiers to the pine-shaded town of **Cap Ferret**, across the mouth of the Bassin d'Arcachon. From April to October, boats run four to 20 times daily, depending on the season; the rest of the year there are four sailings daily on Monday, Wednesday, Friday and Sunday. A return fare costs 60FF (children aged four to 12, 40FF).

The company also runs daily, year-round cruises around the Île aux Oiseaux (Bird Island, in the Bassin d'Arcachon) at 3 pm

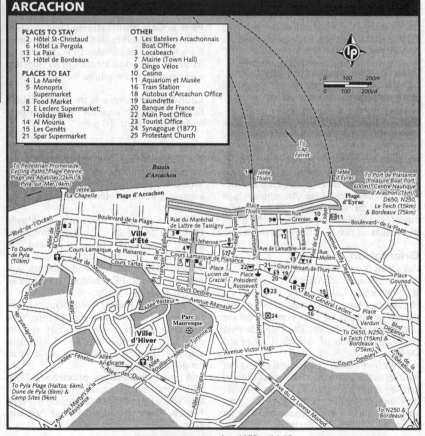

ARCACHON

PLACES TO STAY
2 Hôtel St-Christaud
6 Hôtel La Pergola
13 La Paix
17 Hôtel de Bordeaux

PLACES TO EAT
4 La Marée
5 Monoprix Supermarket
8 Food Market
12 E Leclerc Supermarket; Holiday Bikes
14 Al Mounia
15 Les Genêts
21 Spar Supermarket

OTHER
1 Les Bateliers Arcachonnais Boat Office
3 Locabeach
7 Mairie (Town Hall)
9 Dingo Vélos
10 Casino
11 Aquarium et Musée
16 Train Station
18 Autobus d'Arcachon Office
19 Laundrette
20 Banque de France
22 Main Post Office
23 Tourist Office
24 Synagogue (1877)
25 Protestant Church

(75FF, four times daily in July and August). Daily in July and August, and perhaps in June at the weekend, there are all-day excursions to the Banc d'Arguin (the sand bank off the Dune de Pyla, 75FF, daily at 10 or 11 am). During especially high tides it is possible to sail up the Leyre River.

Places to Stay

During July and August, prices go up dramatically and it is extremely difficult to find accommodation. Some hotels require that you take half-board.

Camping The steep, inland side of the Dune de Pyla (see Around Arcachon) is gradually burying five large and rather pricey camping grounds, most of them half hidden in a forest of pine trees. *La Forêt* (☎ 05 56 22 73 28, fax 05 56 22 70 50, 📧 camping.foret@wanadoo.fr), open early April to mid-October, charges 79FF to 140FF for two adults with a tent, depending on the season.

Hotels Friendly, down-to-earth *La Paix* (☎ 05 56 83 05 65, 8 ave de Lamartine) opens from late May to September. Simple doubles/quads start at 171/283FF (216/356FF with shower and toilet), including breakfast; prices are 25% higher from mid-June to early September. From March to October, studio apartments are available for 1000FF to 2000FF per week, depending on the season.

The 15-room *Hôtel St-Christaud* (☎/fax 05 56 83 38 53, 8 allée de la Chapelle), open year round, has neat, modern doubles costing 99FF to 200FF (129FF to 300FF with shower and toilet), depending on the season. Half-board (about 100FF extra per person) is obligatory in July and August.

The two-star, 20-room *Hôtel La Pergola* (☎ 05 56 83 07 89, fax 05 56 83 14 21, 40 cours Lamarque de Plaisance), has modern doubles with shower and toilet for between 230FF (from October to May) and 390FF (in July and August). The two rooms with washbasin cost 150FF to 250FF. Studios go for 1000FF to 2600FF per week.

Across from the train station, the 14-room *Hôtel de Bordeaux* (☎ 05 56 83 80 30, fax 05 56 83 69 02, 39 blvd Général Leclerc) has ordinary singles/doubles/triples with shower and toilet for between 180/250/330FF (in winter) and 250/350/430FF (summer).

Places to Eat

Restaurants The beachfront promenade between Jetée Thiers and Jetée d'Eyrac is lined with *tourist restaurants* and places offering pizza and crepes.

La Marée (☎ 05 56 83 24 05, 21 rue du Maréchal de Lattre de Tassigny), is a popular seafood restaurant where you can get six/12 No 3 oysters for 35/62FF; the fresh, home-made *menus* cost 55FF (weekday lunch), 99FF and 135FF. It is closed from December to mid-January and, except during school holiday periods, on Monday and Tuesday. There are several other restaurants (including pizzerias) in the immediate vicinity.

From June to mid-September, *La Paix* (see Places to Stay) serves traditional French *menus* for 60FF and 90FF in a delightful glass-enclosed terrace.

Les Genêts (☎ 05 56 83 40 28, 25 blvd Général Leclerc) specialises in seafood and fresh dishes made with local produce. It is closed on Monday and, except from July to September, on Sunday night.

The beautifully tiled *Al Mounia* (☎ 05 56 83 76 03, 43 cours Héricart de Thury) serves Moroccan couscous and *tajines* from 75FF.

Self-Catering The lively *food market* (rue Roger Expert), just north of the Mairie on the ground floor of a parking garage, is open daily from 8 am to 1 pm.

The *Spar* supermarket (57 blvd Général Leclerc) opens until 8 pm (closed from about 12.30 to 3.30 pm and on Sunday afternoon). Other supermarkets include *E Leclerc* (224 blvd de la Plage) and *Monoprix* (46 cours Lamarque de Plaisance).

Getting There & Away

Some of the trains from Bordeaux to Arcachon (54FF, 55 minutes, 11 to 18 daily) are coordinated with TGVs from Paris' Gare Montparnasse. The last train back to Bordeaux leaves Arcachon at 8 pm (9.50 pm on Sundays and holidays, around 9 pm on weeknights in July and August).

Getting Around

There is unmetered parking south of the casino along ave de Gaulle.

Locabeach (☎ 05 56 83 39 64) at 326 blvd de la Plage, which may be closed in December and January, and Holiday Bikes (☎ 05 56 22 45 15) at 218 blvd de la Plage rent out scooters and motorcycles starting at about 190FF a day; the deductible/excess is at least 4000FF. Both are open daily.

To order a cab, call ☎ 05 56 83 88 88, 24 hours a day.

Bicycle Daily from April to October, Dingo Vélos (☎ 05 56 83 44 09) on rue Grenier rents tandems, *triplos*, *quatros* and *quintuplos* (bikes with places for two to five riders) and pushme-pullyous (tandems whose riders face in opposite directions) for 30/50FF per person per half-hour/hour. Regular five-speeds/mountain bikes start at 50/80FF per day.

Locabeach and Holiday Bikes also rent out mountain bikes for 80FF per day; the former has five-speeds for 50FF per day.

AROUND ARCACHON
Dune de Pyla

This remarkable sand dune, also known as the Dune du Pilat, stretches from the mouth of the Bassin d'Arcachon southward for almost 3km. Studies have shown it to be creeping eastwards at about 4.5m a year – it has already swallowed trees, a road junction and even an entire hotel, and at this rate the camp sites at the base of the dune's steep eastern side appear to have a limited lifespan. The slope facing the Atlantic, dotted with tufts of grass, is much gentler.

The view from the top – approximately 114m above sea level – is magnificent. To the west you can see the sandy shoals at the mouth of the Bassin d'Arcachon, including the **Banc d'Arguin bird reserve** and **Cap**

Ferret. In the other direction, dense pine forests stretch from the base of the dune eastwards almost as far as the eye can see. The GR8 passes not far from here.

Caution is advised while swimming in this area: powerful currents swirl out to sea from the deceptively tranquil *baïnes* (baylets) that jut into the beach.

Getting There & Away The car park at the northern end of the dune charges 20FF for the whole day.

The local bus company, Autobus d'Arcachon (☎ 05 56 83 07 60), based at 47 blvd du Général Leclerc, has daily buses to Pyla Plage (Haïtza), 1km north of the dune (11FF). From mid-June to mid-September, buses continue south to the dune's parking lot (16FF) and the camping grounds.

Gujan Mestras

A bit east of Arcachon, the oyster port of Gujan Mestras sprawls along 9km of coastline. The tourist office (☎ 05 56 66 12 65) at 19 ave De Lattre de Tassigny (the D650), at the western edge of town, opens 8.30 am to noon or 12.30 pm and 2.30 to 6 pm Monday to Saturday (7.30 pm from June to mid-September, when it also opens Sunday and holidays from 9 am to noon).

About 4km to the east, **Port de Larros**, the largest of the town's seven oyster ports, is lined with weathered wood shacks, flat-bottom oystering boats moored out front. The small **Maison de l'Huître** (☎ 05 56 66 23 71) has exhibits on oyster farming (closed on Sunday from October to February). Admission costs 16FF (children aged under 12, students 10FF).

Just 100m away at **Cap Noroit** (☎ 05 56 66 04 15), you can buy superfresh Banc d'Arguin oysters (the area's finest) direct from the growers starting at just 13FF a dozen (plus 3FF a dozen to have them *écaillés*, ie, shucked); 30FF gets you a dozen so huge that they fall outside the accepted scale of oyster size and weight. It opens daily until 6 pm (1 pm on Sunday; closed from noon to 2 pm). The four seafood restaurants right near Port de Larros include *Les Viviers* (at the

Oyster Farming

Ostréiculture – the farming of the bivalve molluscs known as *huîtres* (oysters) – is practised in France in Normandy, Brittany and along the Atlantic coast. Prime oystering ground can be round on the Île de Ré and Île d'Oléron and around the Bassin d'Arcachon, where the main oyster farming centre is Gujan Mestras.

In the Arcachon area, oysters – some species of which are either hermaphroditic or change sex over the course of their lives – breed in June or July, each female releasing tens of millions of eggs. A few days later, *ostréiculteurs* (oyster farmers) provide the microscopic spat (larvae) with exactly what they're looking for: a nice, clean surface to which they can attach themselves. At the age of eight months, when they are 3cm or 4cm long, the young oysters – still very fragile – are transferred to plastic mesh bags and placed in special, protected beds. A second transfer, to larger beds with plenty of phytoplankton-rich water (a single oyster may filter eight to 12 litres of seawater an hour), takes place 10 months later.

Crassostrea gigas, the species of Japanese origin that is grown commercially around Arcachon, is harvested at the age of three or four years. Before being sent to market, the oysters are placed in special basins for two to four days so that any sand or seaweed left inside is washed out. The lack of tidal action ensures that the molluscs, filled with sea water, clamp themselves tightly shut, ensuring that they stay alive on the way to market.

Oysters are usually eaten raw (ie, live), either plain, with lemon juice or with a dash of balsamic vinegar. The ideal accompaniment is bread, butter and a chilled, dry white wine. You can dine on incredibly cheap oysters, purchased direct from the farmers, at Gujan Mestras and other oyster ports.

All types of oysters can produce pearls when a bit of foreign matter (such as a grain of sand) gets lodged inside the shell and is covered with layers of nacre (the material that lines the inside of the shell), but those that grow in the edible varieties are lustreless and thus valueless.

port) and *L'Escalumade* (facing the railway line).

Port de la Hume, near the tourist office, has a beach.

Family-oriented attractions in the **Parc de Loisirs**, which is just off the N250, include **Aqualand** (☎ 05 56 66 39 39), a water park (aquatic funfair; 98FF, children aged under 12 83FF) open from mid-June to mid-September; the **Village Mediéval** (☎ 05 56 66 16 76), open from late June to August, in which artisans demonstrate the crafts of the Middle Ages (40FF, children aged five to 11 20FF); **La Coccinelle** (☎ 05 56 66 30 41), an amusement park and petting zoo for children (35FF, children aged two to 14 36FF) that opens late May to August; **Les Jardins du Bassin** (☎ 05 56 66 00 71), a botanical park open from June to September (30FF, children aged six to 12 20FF); and the new giant playground **Kid Parc** (☎ 05 56 66 06 90), open mid-May to October (35FF; children aged two to 12 12.69FF).

Places to Stay The 23-room *Hôtel La Coquille* (☎ 05 56 66 08 60, fax 05 56 66 09 09, 55 cours de Verdun), 3km east of the tourist office on the D650, opens year round (except Sunday night and Monday from December to February). Bungalow-like doubles with washbasin/shower and-toilet cost 140/180FF (180/270FF from June to September).

Getting There & Away The Gujan Mestras station, not far from Port de Larros, is on the rail line linking Bordeaux (47FF) with Arcachon (12FF, nine minutes). The railway station in La Hume is not far from the tourist office.

Le Teich Parc Ornithologique

Only 29% of the shallow Bassin d'Arcachon, a 155 sq km tidal bay, is underwater at low tide, making it an ideal habitat for birds. Indeed, some 260 species, both migratory and non-migratory, visit the area each year.

The idyllic Parc Ornithologique (bird reserve; ☎ 05 56 22 80 93) at Le Teich, in the south-east corner of the bay at the mouth of the multi-channelled Leyre (l'Eyre) River, is an outstanding place to see some of Europe's rarest and most beautiful birds, such as the spoonbill, little egret, blue throat and black kite, as well as 30 nesting pairs of storks. Two walking circuits – the 2.5km Petit Parcours and the 6km Grand Boucle – take you along dike-topped paths to a series of observation hides (blinds).

It's easiest to observe the birds at high tide (at low tide the waders are out eating). Tidal schedules, available at local tourist offices, appear on the back page of the regional daily *Sud Ouest*; *pleine* means high tide; *basse* means low tide.

The Parc opens daily, year round, from 10 am to 6 pm (to 7 pm from mid-April to mid-September, 8 pm in July and August). Admission costs 36FF (children aged five to 14 25FF). *Jumelles* (binoculars) can be hired for 20FF; *graines* (bird food) costs 4FF a bag.

The **Jardin des Papillons** (☎ 05 57 52 33 51), Europe's largest butterfly garden, is a few hundred metres from the Parc Ornithologique. It opens from about April to September and admission costs 48FF (children aged four to 11, 35FF).

Activities The **Sentier du Littoral** footpath follows the vegetation-lined Leyre River to Lamothe, 4.5km to the south-east, and also goes 5km west to Gujan Mestras.

The Maison de la Nature du Bassin d'Arcachon (☎ 05 56 22 80 93) at the Parc runs nature discovery trips, including guided sea kayak tours (100FF per person for two hours) and unguided canoe cruises. Excursions are most frequent during the Easter and summer school holidays. For reservations, ring them two to four of days ahead (a week ahead in summer).

Places to Stay The 11-room *Hôtel Le Central* (☎ /fax 05 56 22 65 64, 61 ave de la Côte d'Argent*, on the D650 in Le Teich (across the street from the church) opens year round. It has bright doubles/triples with washbasin and shower (170/200FF).

Getting There & Away The Parc Ornithologique is 15km east of Arcachon on the D650. Le Teich's train station, 1200m south of the Parc, is on the line that links Bordeaux (44FF) with Arcachon (16FF).

French Basque Country

The Pyrénées-Atlantiques département in France's far south-western corner is the only part of the Basque Country (Euskadi in Basque) located north of the Pyrenees. Known in French as the Pays Basque, the region is a good base for day trips to the green western Pyrenees and the Spanish Basque Country (País Vasco), both less than 25km south of the region's two main cities, the cultural capital of Bayonne and the glitzy beach resort of Biarritz.

History

The early history of the Basques, who live in a region on the Bay of Biscay that straddles the French–Spanish border, is largely unknown. Roman sources mention a tribe called the Vascones living in the area. The Basques took over what is now south-western France in the 6th century.

Converted to Christianity in the 10th century, they are still known for their strong devotion to Catholicism.

After resisting invasions by Visigoths, Franks, Normans and Moors, the Basques on both sides of the Pyrenees emerged from the turbulent Middle Ages with a fair degree of local autonomy, which they lost in France during the Revolution. The French Basque Country, part of the duchy of Aquitaine, was under English rule from the mid-12th century until the mid-15th century.

Basque nationalism flourished before and during the Spanish Civil War (1936–39), when German aircraft flying for Francisco Franco's fascists destroyed the Spanish city of Guernica (1937), symbol of the Basque nation. Until Franco's death in 1975, many Spanish Basque nationalists and anti-Franco guerrillas sheltered in France. Some Basques still dream of carving an Euskadi state out of the Basque areas of Spain and France, and a few support the terrorist organisation ETA (Euskadi ta Azkatasuna, which means Basque Nation and Liberty). Bombings and other violent activities are not uncommon in the Spanish

Highlights

- Marvelling at the speed of *pelota*, the Basques' souped-up equivalent of squash
- Watching surfers ride the world-class waves off Anglet beach
- Creeping up the mountainside on Le Petit Train de la Rhune
- Walking the GR65 in the footsteps of centuries of Santiago-bound pilgrims near St-Jean Pied de Port

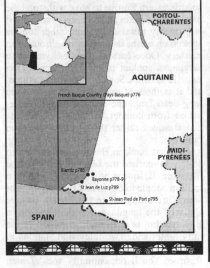

Basque Country. Hundreds of thousands of Basques live in South America and the USA, especially in the south-west.

Basque Symbols

The Basque flag is similar in layout to the UK flag, but the field is red, the arms of the vertical cross are white and the arms of the diagonal cross are green. Another common Basque symbol – the *laubura* – resembles a swastika but is perhaps best described as looking like a skinny Greek cross with the head of a golf club attached to each end.

The laubura – a symbol of Basque identity

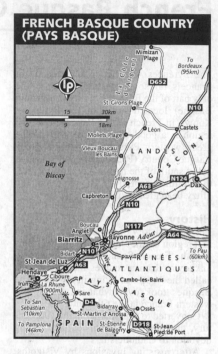

Language

Basque (Euskara) is the only language in south-western Europe to have withstood the onslaught of Latin and its derivatives, and it is probably unrelated to any other tongue spoken on earth. Its origins are shrouded in mystery. Once-current theories tying it to languages spoken in the Caucasus region east of the Black Sea have been discredited, and it is thought that similarities with the long-dead language Iberian may have resulted from contact between the Iberians and Basques rather than from a common origin.

The first book in Basque was printed in 1545 and marked the beginning of Basque literature. Basque is now spoken by about a million people in Spain and France, most of whom are bilingual. In the French Basque Country, the language is widely spoken in Bayonne but is even more common in the hilly hinterland. Two television stations in Spain and one in France now broadcast in Basque. You'll occasionally see '*Hemen Euskara emaiten dugu*' on shop doors, which means 'Basque spoken here'.

Spectator Sports

For a canter through the various kinds of *pelote Basque* see the boxed text 'Pelota' later in this chapter. For information about where to see them played, turn to the Spectator Sports section within each town.

Corrida, Spanish-style bullfighting in which the bull is killed, has devotees all over the Basque Country. Corridas are held about half a dozen times each summer and advance reservations are usually necessary; inquire at the Bayonne or Biarritz tourist offices.

Places to Stay

In coastal resorts, many holidaymakers return to the same hotel year after year, so it can be extremely difficult to find a room in July and August, when room prices rise substantially and some hotels insist on half-board.

Getting There & Away

Train For train timetables and fares throughout the region, ring ☎ 06 36 35 35 35. Calls are charged at 2.25FF per minute and waiting time, once you're connected, can be long.

Spain For rail travel to Spain, you have to switch trains at the frontier because the Spanish track gauge is narrower. Take an SNCF train to Hendaye, where you can pick up El Topo, a shuttle train that runs to San

Sebastián (150 ptas, 40 minutes) every half-hour until 10.30 pm.

Year round, the Spanish company Sema runs twice daily buses between Bayonne and San Sebastián via St-Jean de Luz, while ATCRB (see each town's Getting There & Away sections) has a summer-only service.

BAYONNE
postcode 64100 • pop 40,000

Bayonne (Baiona in Basque, meaning 'the good river') is the cultural and economic capital of the French Basque Country. Unlike the upmarket seaside resort of Biarritz, a short bus ride away, Bayonne retains much of its Basqueness: the riverside buildings with their red and green shutters are typical of the region and you'll hear almost as much Euskara as French in certain quarters. Most of the graffiti around town are the work of nationalist groups seeking an independent Basque state.

The city, founded as Lapurdum by the Romans, is known for its smoked ham, chocolate and marzipan. According to tradition, the *baïonnette* (bayonet) was developed here in the early 17th century.

Bayonne reached the height of its commercial prosperity in the 18th century, when Basque pirate ships landed cargoes much more valuable than the cod caught by the Basque fishing fleet off the coast of Newfoundland.

Orientation

The Rivers Adour and Nive split Bayonne into three: St-Esprit, the area north of the Adour; Grand Bayonne, on the western bank of the Nive and the oldest part of the city; and the very Basque Petit Bayonne quarter to its east.

Nondescript Anglet (the final 't' is pronounced) squeezes between Bayonne and Biarritz, 8km to the west. The urban area of Bayonne, Anglet and Biarritz (population 120,000) is sometimes abbreviated as BAB. Local bus company STAB's free local bus map gives a stylised overview of the conurbation. For something more detailed, buy Éditions Grafocarte's *Bayonne Anglet Biarritz*.

Information
Tourist Offices

The tourist office (☎ 05 59 46 01 46, fax 05 59 59 37 55, @ bayonne. tourisme@wanadoo.fr), place des Basques, opens 9 am to 7 pm daily (10 am to 1 pm Sunday) July and August; and 9 am to 6.30 pm weekdays and 10 am to 6 pm Saturday the rest of the year.

Among its useful free brochures are *Fêtes*, listing French Basque Country cultural and sporting events; *Guide Loisirs*, for hiking, biking and other activities; and *Promenades and Discoveries*, in English, detailing a self-guided walk around town.

In summer, it organises guided tours of the city (35FF) in French at 10 am, Monday to Saturday (in English on Thursday). During July and August it has an annexe (☎ 05 59 55 20 45) at the train station.

Post & Communications

The main post office is on rue de la Nouvelle Poste, about 1km north-west of the city centre.

You can log on at Cyber Net Café (☎ 05 59 55 78 98) on place de la République. It opens 7 am to 2 am daily (from midday on Sunday) and it charges 1FF per minute or 45FF per hour.

Bookshops

Mattin Megadenda (☎ 05 59 59 35 14), at place de l'Arsenal, is Bayonne's best source for texts on Basque history and culture; walking in the Basque Country; maps and CDs of Basque music. Librairie Celhay, 12 rue de la Salie, stocks a modest selection of guidebooks. Both have very little in English.

Laundry

Laverie St-Esprit at 16 blvd Alsace-Lorraine opens 8 am to 8 pm daily.

Ramparts

Thanks to Vauban's 17th-century fortifications (see the boxed text 'Vauban's Citadels' in the Facts about France chapter), now grass-covered and dotted with trees, the city centre is surrounded by a slim green belt. You can walk the stretches of the old ramparts, which rise above rue du Rempart Lachepaillet and rue Tour de Sault.

FRENCH BASQUE COUNTRY

BAYONNE

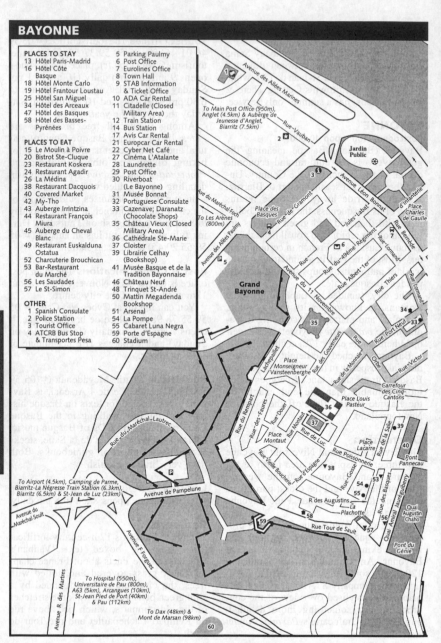

PLACES TO STAY
- 13 Hôtel Paris-Madrid
- 16 Hôtel Côte Basque
- 18 Hôtel Monte Carlo
- 19 Hôtel Frantour Loustau
- 25 Hôtel San Miguel
- 34 Hôtel des Arceaux
- 47 Hôtel des Basques
- 58 Hôtel des Basses-Pyrénées

PLACES TO EAT
- 15 Le Moulin à Poivre
- 20 Bistrot Ste-Cluque
- 23 Restaurant Koskera
- 24 Restaurant Agadir
- 26 La Médina
- 38 Restaurant Dacquois
- 40 Covered Market
- 43 My-Tho
- 43 Auberge Irrintzina
- 44 Restaurant François Miura
- 45 Auberge du Cheval Blanc
- 49 Restaurant Euskalduna Ostatua
- 52 Charcuterie Brouchican
- 53 Bar-Restaurant du Marché
- 56 Les Saudades
- 57 Le St-Simon

OTHER
- 1 Spanish Consulate
- 2 Police Station
- 3 Tourist Office
- 4 ATCRB Bus Stop & Transportes Pesa

- 5 Parking Paulmy
- 6 Post Office
- 7 Eurolines Office
- 8 Town Hall
- 9 STAB Information & Ticket Office
- 10 ADA Car Rental
- 11 Citadelle (Closed Military Area)
- 12 Train Station
- 14 Bus Station
- 17 Avis Car Rental
- 21 Europcar Car Rental
- 22 Cyber Net Café
- 27 Cinéma L'Atalante
- 28 Laundrette
- 29 Post Office
- 30 Riverboat (Le Bayonne)
- 31 Musée Bonnat
- 32 Portuguese Consulate
- 33 Cazenave; Daranatz (Chocolate Shops)
- 35 Château Vieux (Closed Military Area)
- 36 Cathédrale Ste-Marie
- 37 Cloister
- 39 Librairie Celhay (Bookshop)
- 41 Musée Basque et de la Tradition Bayonnaise
- 46 Château Neuf
- 48 Trinquet St-André
- 50 Mattin Megadenda Bookshop
- 51 Arsenal
- 54 La Pompe
- 55 Cabaret Luna Negra
- 59 Porte d'Espagne
- 60 Stadium

To Main Post Office (950m), Anglet (4.5km) & Auberge de Jeunesse d'Anglet, Biarritz (7.5km)

To Les Arènes (800m)

Avenue des Allées Marines

Rue Vauban

Jardin Public

Avenue Léon Bonnat

d'Infanterie

Place Charles de Gaulle

Ave du Maréchal Foch

Place des Basques

Rue de Gramont

Jules-Labat

Rue Remede

Rue Lormand

Rue du-49ème Régiment

Rue Albert-1er

Rue Thiers

Rue Lormand

Avenue du 11 Novembre

Grand Bayonne

Rue Port Neuf

Rue Victor

Lachepaillet

Place Monseigneur Vansteenberghe

Rue des Gouverneurs

Rue de la Monnaie

Orbe

Carrefour des Cinq-Cantons

Rue du-Maréchal-Lautrec

Rue du Rempart

Rue-des-Faures

Rue Douer

Place Louis Pasteur

Rue Montaut

Rue de Luc

Place Lacarre

Rue de la Salle

Pont Pannecau

To Airport (4.5km), Camping de Parme, Biarritz-La Négresse Train Station (6.3km), Biarritz (6.5km) & St-Jean de Luz (23km)

Place Montaut

Rue Vieille Boucherie – Rue d'Espagne

Rue Poissonnerie

Rue Gosse

Rue des Basques

Avenue de Pampelune

R des Augustins

La Plachotte

Quai Augustin Chaho

Avenue du Maréchal Soult

Avenue F Forgues

Avenue R des Martres

Rue Tour de Sault

Quai Amiral Jaurèguiberry

Pont du Génie

To Hospital (550m), Universitaire de Pau (800m), A63 (5km), Arcangues (10km), St-Jean Pied de Port (40km) & Pau (112km)

To Dax (48km) & Mont de Marsan (98km)

FRENCH BASQUE COUNTRY

euro currency converter 10FF = €1.52

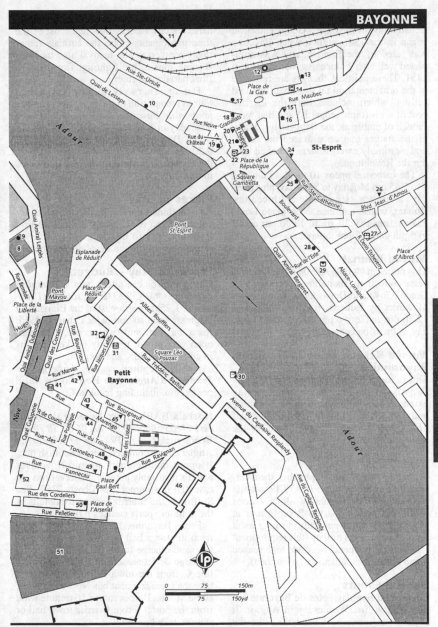

BAYONNE

Adour

Quai de Lesseps

Rue Ste-Ursule

Place de la Gare

Rue Maubec

St-Esprit

Rue Neuve-Graoullats

Rue du Château

R. Hugues

Place de la République

Square Gambetta

Rue Ste-Catherine

Boulevard

Blvd Jean d'Amou

R. Louis Etcheverry

Place d'Albret

Quai Amiral Bergeret

Rue de l'Este

Alsace-Lorraine

Quai Amiral Lesseps

Rue Bernède

Rue Hugo

Quai Amiral Dubourdieu

Place de la Liberté

Pont Mayou

Pont St-Esprit

Esplanade de Réduit

Place du Réduit

Allées Bouffiers

Square Léo Pouzac

Rue Frédéric Bastiat

Rue Jacques Laffitte

Rue Bourgneuf

Quai des Corsaires

Petit Bayonne

Rue Marsan

Rue

R de Coursic

Quai Galuperie

Rue des

Nive

Rue Pannecau

Rue Kimque

Rue du Trinquet

Rue Marengo

Rue Bourgneuf

Rue des Lisses

Rue Ravignan

Tonneliers

Place Paul Bert

Rue des Cordeliers

Place de l'Arsenal

Rue Pelletier

Avenue du Capitaine Resplandy

Ave du Capitaine Resplandy

Adour

0   75   150m
0   75   150yd

FRENCH BASQUE COUNTRY

Cathédrale Ste-Marie

Construction of Bayonne's Gothic cathedral began in the 13th century, when Bayonne was ruled by the English, and was completed well after France assumed control in 1451. These political changes are reflected in the ornamentation on the nave's vaulted ceiling, which includes both the English coat of arms (three leopards) and that most French of emblems, the fleur-de-lys. Many of the statues that once graced the cathedral's crumbly exterior were smashed during the Revolution.

The cathedral opens 10 to 11.45 am and 3 to 5.45 pm Monday to Saturday, plus Sunday afternoon. Its stately 13th-century **cloister,** whose entrance is on place Louis Pasteur, opens 9.30 am to 12.30 pm and 2 to 6 pm daily (5 pm in winter).

Musée Bonnat

This museum (☎ 05 59 59 08 52) houses diverse collections, including paintings by El Greco, Goya and Degas and a whole room of works by Rubens. It opens 10 am to 12.30 pm and 2 to 6 pm daily except Tuesday. Admission costs 20FF.

Musée Basque et de la Tradition Bayonnaise

This museum of Basque culture (☎ 05 59 59 08 98), at 1 rue Marengo, was undergoing extensive renovations at the time of writing and is expected to reopen in the second half of 2001. Contact the tourist office for the latest information.

River Trips

From mid-June to mid-September, the riverboat Le Bayonne (☎ 05 59 47 77 17, mobile ☎ 06 80 74 21 51) runs two-hour cruises (80FF per person) on the River Adour at 10 am, 2.45 and 5 pm daily, so long as at least 15 passengers turn up (this requirement means it rarely operates outside high season – and sometimes fails to sail even then).

Special Events

The annual five-day **Fêtes de Bayonne** begins on the first Wednesday in August. It includes a 'running of the bulls' like the one in Pamplona, Spain, only more benign; here, it's cows not bulls – and most of the time participants chase the animals rather than vice versa. The festival also includes Basque music, bullfighting, fireworks, a float parade and rugby.

During Easter week, the city hosts a Ham Fair in recognition of the justifiably famous *jambon de Bayonne*, the local ham. Every Thursday in July and August, there's traditional Basque music (admission free) at 9.30 pm in place Charles de Gaulle. Jazz on the Ramparts is six days of jazz and blues in mid-July.

Places to Stay

As mentioned earlier in this chapter, accommodation is extremely difficult to find from mid-July to mid-August – and near-impossible during the Fêtes de Bayonne.

Places to Stay – Budget

Camping You can pitch a tent at *Camping de Parme* (☎ 05 59 23 03 00, route de l'Aviation), 1.25km north-east of the Biarritz-La Négresse train station, which charges 79FF for a car, tent and two people. Although open year round, it's fully booked months in advance for July and August.

Another option is the *Auberge de Jeunesse d'Anglet* (see Hostels) for 48FF per person, including breakfast.

Hostels BAB's lively *Auberge de Jeunesse* (☎ 05 59 58 70 00, fax 05 59 58 70 07, @ biarritz@fuaj.fr, 19 route des Vignes) in Anglet comes complete with a Scottish pub. It opens mid-February to mid-November and it's justifiably popular. Reservations are essential in summer. B&B costs 73FF. See Surfing in the Biarritz section for details of the outdoor sports courses it offers.

From Bayonne, take STAB bus No 4 from the town hall to La Barre, the terminus, and change to No 9, alighting at the Auberge de Jeunesse stop (on Sunday take line C from the town hall). Alternatively, take the more frequent bus No 7 and get off at the Moulin Barbot stop, a 10 minute walk from the hostel. From Biarritz town hall or station, take bus No 9.

Hotels You can tumble off the train into the friendly *Hôtel Paris-Madrid* (☎ 05 59 55 13 98, fax 05 59 55 07 22), just beside the station, where owners Patrique and Sylvie speak excellent English. The cheapest singles are 95FF, and large, pleasant doubles without/with shower start at 130/160FF. Rooms with bathroom and cable TV, which can accommodate up to four, cost from 210FF to 260FF.

Nearby, *Hôtel Monte Carlo* (☎ 05 59 55 02 68, 1 rue Ste-Ursule) has simple rooms from 90FF and larger ones with bathroom for two to four people (170FF to 250FF). At *Hôtel San Miguel* (☎ 05 59 55 17 82, fax 05 59 50 15 22, 8 rue Ste-Catherine), generous doubles without/with shower cost 170/190FF while doubles/triples/quads with bathroom cost 220/260/300FF.

In Grand Bayonne the welcome is warm at *Hôtel des Arceaux* (☎ 05 59 59 15 53, 26 rue Port Neuf). Wood-panelled basic doubles/triples are from 130/210FF and doubles with bathroom are from 190FF (40FF per extra person up to four).

In Petit Bayonne, *Hôtel des Basques* (☎ 05 59 59 08 02, place Paul Bert), has large, pleasant rooms with washbasin and toilet from 135FF to 180FF and ones with full bathroom from 170FF to 230FF. Showers cost 10FF and paying parking is available in the square just outside.

Places to Stay – Mid-Range & Top End

Hôtel Côte Basque (☎ 05 59 55 10 21, fax 05 59 55 39 85, 2 rue Maubec) has doubles with bathroom for 300FF to 330FF and rooms for three/four/five at 330/360/390FF.

Hôtel des Basses-Pyrénées (☎ 05 59 59 00 29, fax 05 59 59 42 02, 12 rue Tour de Sault) is built around a 17th-century tower. Doubles/triples/quads with bathroom start at 300/330/350FF. It also has a few rooms with washbasin from 150FF to 170FF and private parking (30FF). It is closed January.

The three-star *Hôtel Frantour Loustau* (☎ 05 59 55 08 08, fax 05 59 55 69 36, @ loustau@aol.com, 1 place de la République) occupies an attractive 18th-century building overlooking the Adour. Doubles/

triples with bathroom cost 430/475FF and private parking costs 50FF.

Places to Eat

Restaurants – French Juicy sandwiches at the cheerful *Restaurant Dacquois* (☎ 05 59 59 29 61, 48 rue d'Espagne) cost from 12FF, while its 65FF *menu* provides a good choice of main dishes and hors d'œuvres.

Two other excellent choices in this category are the postmodern *Restaurant François Miura* (☎ 05 59 59 49 89, 24 rue Marengo) in Petit Bayonne with *menus* at 115FF and 185FF and, in Grand Bayonne, *Le St-Simon* (☎ 05 59 59 27 71, 1 rue des Basques) where the award-winning chef creates superb dishes. *Menus*, all excellent value, start at 100FF.

The elegant *Auberge du Cheval Blanc* (☎ 05 59 59 01 33, 68 rue Bourgneuf), which boasts a Michelin star, has *menus* at 118/185/260FF. From September to June it closes Sunday evening and Monday.

Restaurants – Basque It's not just the food; you'll walk out feeling more buoyant after lunch at *Bar-Restaurant du Marché* (☎ 05 59 59 22 66, 39 rue des Basques) where the cooking's homely and the owner's wife mothers everyone. Open only at midday and closed on Sunday, it will fill you to bursting point for under 100FF.

There's nowhere in town more authentically Basque than *Restaurant Euskalduna Ostatua* (☎ 05 59 59 28 02, 61 rue Pannecau) in Petit Bayonne, where most of the clients are local and eyebrows may rise as you walk in. But the welcome is warm and main dishes are a bargain from 35FF to 50FF. It opens for lunch, weekdays only.

A couple of blocks away, the cosy, cheerful *Auberge Irrintzina* (☎ 05 59 59 02 51, 9 rue Marengo) is another budget place to sample Basque hospitality. It is closed Monday lunchtime and Sunday.

In St-Esprit, *Restaurant Koskera* (☎ 05 59 55 20 79, 2 rue Hugues) is a six-days-a-week, lunchtime-only joint (plus dinner, from mid-June to September). It has inexpensive daily specials of hearty Basque fare and *menus* for 70FF and 95FF. At homely

FRENCH BASQUE COUNTRY

Le Moulin à Poivre (☎ 05 59 50 19 10, 4 *rue Maubec*), Basque and French dishes are in the 42FF to 70FF range. There's a good-value special menu for 90FF. It is closed Wednesday.

Restaurants – Other The Vietnamese-Chinese restaurant *My-Tho* (☎ 05 59 59 15 07, 40 *rue Bourgneuf*) in Petit Bayonne has excellent value *menus* from 70FF including wine. It opens daily except Tuesday and Wednesday lunchtime. *Restaurant Agadir* (☎ 05 59 55 66 56, 3 *rue Ste-Catherine*) in St-Esprit has southern Moroccan-style couscous from 60FF to 80FF and a *menu* at 100FF. Tunisian restaurant *La Médina* (☎ 05 59 55 85 17, 13 *blvd Jean d'Amou*) serves good couscous from 65FF to 75FF, and grills from 65FF. Beside the River Nive, *Les Saudades* (☎ 05 59 25 60 13, 15 *quai Amiral Jauréguiberry*) is a Portuguese restaurant with *menus* from 75FF and delicious fish dishes between 25FF and 80FF. *Bistrot Ste-Cluque* (☎ 05 59 55 82 43, 9 *rue Hugues*) specialises in paella (60FF) and offers *menus* from 55FF.

Self-Catering The covered market, *Les Halles*, occupies an imposing building on quai Amiral Jauréguiberry. It opens until 1.30 pm every morning except Sunday. On Friday and Saturday it reopens from 3.30 to 7 pm. There are a number of tempting *food shops and delicatessens* along rue Port Neuf and rue d'Espagne.

Entertainment
Pubs & Bars The greatest concentration is in Petit Bayonne, especially along rue Pannecau and quai Galuperie. In Grand Bayonne, *La Pompe* (☎ 05 59 25 48 12, 7 *rue des Augustins*), a lively discotheque, throbs from 10 pm to dawn, Thursday to Sunday. The enterprising *Cabaret Luna Negra* (☎ 05 59 25 78 05) on the same street offers cabaret, jazz, improvisational theatre and even puppet shows.

Cinema Nondubbed films are screened at *Cinéma L'Atalante* (☎ 05 59 55 76 63, 7 *rue Denis Etcheverry*). Admission costs 37FF.

Spectator Sports
Pelota Trinquet St-André (☎ 05 59 59 18 69), at the eastern end of rue des Tonneliers, has *main nue* matches every Thursday – beginning at 4.10 pm sharp – between October and June. Tickets cost 50FF. See also the boxed text 'Pelota'.

Bullfights In summer, corridas are held from time to time at *les arènes* (the arena) on ave du Maréchal Foch, 1km west of the city centre. The tourist office will have details of upcoming corridas and sells tickets (from 80FF to 450FF).

Shopping
Bayonne is famous throughout France for its ham. For the best prices, visit the food market (see Self-Catering under Places to Eat); or you can go to a specialist shop such as Charcuterie Brouchican (☎ 05 59 59 27 18) at 20 quai Augustin Chaho.

The town's other claim to gastronomic fame is its chocolate. Two traditional *chocolateries* are Daranatz (☎ 05 59 59 03 05), 15 rue Port Neuf, and Cazenave (☎ 05 59 59 03 16) at No 19, where you can also sit and sip a cup of their fine drinking chocolate, topped with a rich swirl of Chantilly cream.

Getting There & Away
Air The small Biarritz airport (☎ 05 59 43 83 83) is 5km south-west of central Bayonne and 2.5km south-east of the centre of Biarritz. Air France flies to/from Paris Orly about eight times daily. Ryanair (☎ 03 44 11 41 41) has a flight to/from London Stansted, daily except Sunday.

Bus From place des Basques, ATCRB buses (☎ 05 59 26 06 99) follow the coast to the Spanish border. There are 10 services daily to St-Jean de Luz (22FF, 40 minutes) with connections for Hendaye (36FF, one hour). Summer beach traffic can double journey times. Transportes Pesa buses leave also from place des Basques at noon and 6.30 pm Monday to Saturday, for Irún and San Sebastián in Spain (38FF, 1¾ hours).

From the train station car park, RDTL (☎ 05 59 55 17 59) runs services north-

Pelota

Pelota (*pelote basque* in French) is the generic name for a group of games native to the Basque Country, all played using a hard ball with a rubber core (a *pelote*) and either *mains nues* (bare hands) or a scoop-like racquet made of wicker, leather or wood.

Cesta punta, also known as *jaï alaï*, the world's fastest ball game and the most popular variety of pelota, became faster and faster after the introduction of rubber made it possible to produce balls with more bounce. In the 1920s and '30s, cesta punta was a big hit in Chicago and New Orleans but lost popularity when betting on it was outlawed. Introduced to Cuba in 1900, the game was banned after the 1959 Revolution.

Cesta punta is played with a *chistera*, a curved wicker scoop strapped to the wrist, with which players catch the ball and hurl it back with great force. Matches take place in a jaï alaï, or *cancha*, a three-walled court, usually a precise 53m long.

NICKY CAVEN

High-speed pelota is the Basque Country's national game.

The walls and floor are made of materials that can withstand the repeated impact of the ball, which can reach speeds of 300km/h. A cancha and its tiers of balconies for spectators constitute a *fronton*. Other types of pelota (such as *joko-garbi*, main nue, *pala, paleta, pasaka, rebot* and *xare*) are played in outdoor, one-wall courts, also known as frontons, and in enclosed structures called *trinquets*.

For information on pelota matches, see Spectator Sports under each town. Expect to pay anything from 40FF to 150FF for a ticket.

---

wards into the Landes (see the Atlantic Coast chapter). For beaches north of Bayonne, such as Mimizan Plage and Moliets Plage, get off at Vieux Boucau (39FF, 1¼ hours). TPR (☎ 05 59 27 45 98) has three buses daily to Pau (85FF, 2¼ hours).

Bayonne is one of three hubs in southwest France for Eurolines, whose buses stop in place Charles de Gaulle, opposite the company office (☎ 05 59 59 19 33) at No 3.

Train TGVs to/from Paris' Gare Montparnasse (428FF) take five hours. Non-TGV trains go overnight to Paris' Gare d'Austerlitz (401FF or 471FF with couchette, about eight hours, two daily).

Within the Basque Country, there are fairly frequent trains to Biarritz (13FF, 10 minutes), St-Jean de Luz (26FF, 25 minutes) and St-

Jean Pied de Port (47FF, one hour), plus the Franco-Spanish border towns of Hendaye (37FF, 40 minutes) and Irún (45 minutes).

There are also trains to Dax (48FF, 40 minutes, up to 10 daily), Bordeaux (145FF, 2¼ hours, about a dozen daily), Lourdes (126FF, 1¾ hours, six daily), Pau (82FF, 1¼ hours, eight daily) and Toulouse (216FF, 3¾ hours, at least four daily).

Car & Motorcycle There are three rental agencies within an easy walk of the train station: ADA (☎ 05 59 50 37 10, 11 quai de Lesseps), Europcar (☎ 05 59 55 38 20, 5 rue Hugues) and Avis (☎ 05 59 55 06 56, 1 rue Ste-Ursule). All are open daily except Sunday.

Parking Paulmy, within easy walking distance of the tourist office, is free.

FRENCH BASQUE COUNTRY

Getting Around

To/From the Airport There's no regular bus service to the airport. A taxi from the city centre costs about 60FF.

Bus STAB buses link Bayonne, Biarritz and Anglet. Tickets cost 7.50FF (62FF for a carnet of 10). STAB's information and ticket office (☎ 05 59 59 04 61) is in the northeastern corner of the town hall. It opens 8 am to noon and 1.30 to 6 pm weekdays.

Bus Nos 1 and 2 run between Bayonne and Biarritz with a major stop at their respective town halls.

Taxi To order a taxi, call ☎ 05 59 59 48 48. There's a large rank in front of the train station.

BIARRITZ

postcode 64200 • pop 30,000

The coastal town of Biarritz is more elegant than its clunky English slogan, 'Day or Night, Just Right'. In fact, it's downright stylish. Only 8km west of Bayonne, it took off as a resort in the mid-19th century when Napoleon III and his Spanish-born wife, Eugénie, began staying here. Later, it became popular with wealthy Brits and was visited by Queen Victoria and King Edward VII, who both have streets named in their honour. These days, the Biarritz area is known for its fine beaches and some of Europe's best surfing.

Biarritz can be a real budget-buster, however. Consider staying in Bayonne and travelling through, as many French holiday-makers do. Many surfers camp or stay at one of the two excellent youth hostels in Biarritz and in Anglet.

Orientation

Place Clemenceau, at the heart of Biarritz, is just south of the main beach (Grande Plage). Pointe St-Martin, topped with a lighthouse, rounds off Plage Miramar, the northern continuation of the Grande Plage, which is bounded on its southern side by Pointe Atalaye.

Both the train station and airport are about 3km south-east of the centre.

Information

The **tourist office** (☎ 05 59 22 37 10, fax 05 59 24 14 19, ✉ biarritz.tourisme@biarritz.tm.fr), at 1 square d'Ixelles, opens 9 am to 6.45 pm daily. In July and August, when it opens 8 am to 8 pm, it has a small annexe at the train station. It publishes *Biarritzcope*, a free monthly guide to what's on.

For surfing of the electronic kind, visit Génius Informatique (☎ 05 59 24 39 07, ✉ marlene-dif@hotmail.com), 60 ave Édouard VII. On-line time costs 1FF per minute or 50FF per hour. It opens 9.30 am to 7.30 pm Monday to Saturday (9am to 8 pm daily, June to mid-September).

The Bookstore (☎ 05 59 24 48 00) on place Georges Clemenceau has a small selection of English books.

For laundry, Laverie du Port Vieux at 7 rue Perspective de la Côte des Basques, opens 8.30 am to 9 pm daily.

Musée de la Mer

Biarritz's Sea Museum (☎ 05 59 24 02 59) overlooks Rocher de la Vierge (see Other Things to See later in this section). The ground floor aquarium has 24 tanks seething with underwater beasties from the Bay of Biscay (Golfe de Gascogne). On the 1st floor are exhibits on commercial fishing and whaling, recalling Biarritz's whaling past. Above, it's feeding time for a pair of seals at 10.30 am and 5 pm. A nearby pool holds a couple of sleek sharks while the top floor has a mournful display of stuffed birds.

The Sea Museum opens 9.30 am to 12.30 pm and 2 to 6 pm daily (continuously during school holidays). From July to mid-August, it stays open until midnight. Admission costs 45FF (students and children 30FF) – 5FF cheaper if you buy your ticket at the tourist office.

Musée Historique de Biarritz

The Biarritz History Museum (☎ 05 59 24 86 28), in a deconsecrated Anglican church (Église St-Andrew) on rue Broquedis, portrays the town's development from its origins as a small fishing port. It opens 10 am to noon and 2.30 to 6.30 pm daily Tuesday to Saturday. Admission costs 15FF.

Other Things to See

Stroll over the footbridge at the end of Pointe Atalaye to **Rocher de la Vierge** (Rock of the Virgin), named after the white statue of the Virgin and child. From this impressive outcrop, there are views of the Landes coastline stretching northwards and, far to the south, the mountains of the Spanish Basque Country.

Port des Pêcheurs, once a lively fishing port, is nowadays a haven only to pleasure craft. Above it, the Byzantine and Moorish-style **Église Ste-Eugénie** was built in 1864 for – who else? – Empress Eugénie.

Dominating the northern end of the Grande Plage is the stately **Hôtel du Palais**, also built for Empress Eugénie in 1854, and now a luxury hotel. Opposite, on ave de l'Impératrice, is **Église Alexandre Newsky**, a Russian Orthodox church constructed by and for the Russian aristocrats who frequented Biarritz until the Soviet Revolution. Eugénie was also the inspiration for the doll's house **Chapelle Impériale** (1864), nearby on ave de la Marne. It opens 3 to 7 pm, Tuesday, Thursday and Saturday, mid-April to mid-October (daily except Sunday, mid-July to mid-September).

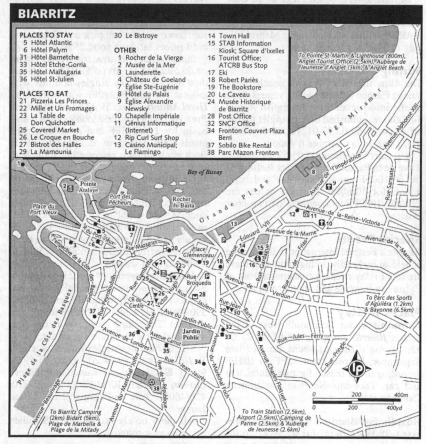

BIARRITZ

PLACES TO STAY
5 Hôtel Atlantic
6 Hôtel Palym
31 Hôtel Barnetche
33 Hôtel Etche-Gorria
35 Hôtel Maïtagaria
36 Hôtel St-Julien

PLACES TO EAT
21 Pizzeria Les Princes
22 Mille et Un Fromages
23 La Table de Don Quichotte
25 Covered Market
26 Le Croque en Bouche
27 Bistrot des Halles
29 La Mamounia
30 Le Bistroye

OTHER
1 Rocher de la Vierge
2 Musée de la Mer
3 Launderette
4 Château de Goeland
7 Église Ste-Eugénie
8 Hôtel du Palais
9 Église Alexandre Newsky
10 Chapelle Impériale
11 Génius Informatique (Internet)
12 Rip Curl Surf Shop
13 Casino Municipal; Le Flamingo
14 Town Hall
15 STAB Information Kiosk; Square d'Ixelles
16 Tourist Office; ATCRB Bus Stop
17 Eki
18 Robert Pariès
19 The Bookstore
20 Le Caveau
24 Musée Historique de Biarritz
28 Post Office
32 SNCF Office
34 Fronton Couvert Plaza Berri
37 Sobilo Bike Rental
38 Parc Mazon Fronton

FRENCH BASQUE COUNTRY

To the north on Pointe St-Martin is the **Phare de Biarritz**, the town's 73m-high lighthouse, erected in 1834.

Beaches
Biarritz's fashionable beaches are wall-to-wall humanity on hot summer days. In season, the **Grande Plage** is lined with striped bathing tents. To its north is **Plage Miramar**, with nude bathing beyond the boulders at its northern end. Beyond Pointe St-Martin, the superb surfing beaches of **Anglet** stretch northwards for 4km. Take bus No 9 from place Clemenceau.

Beyond long, exposed **Plage de la Côte des Basques**, some 500m south of Port Vieux, are **Plage de Marbella** and **Plage de la Milady**. Take bus No 9 to the Madrid Milady or Thermes Marins stop.

Surfing
The 4km stretch of Anglet beach ranks among Europe's finest surfing venues. Pick up the info-packed French-English *Anglet Surf Guide*, published by the Anglet tourist office (☎ 05 59 03 77 01, fax 05 59 03 55 91), 1 ave de la Chambre d'Amour.

Rip Curl Surf Shop (☎ 05 59 24 38 40), 2 ave de la Reine Victoria, rents surfboards for 60/100FF per half-day/day and body boards for 50/80FF. Instruction fees are 220/550/1000FF for one/three/six two-hour sessions.

Special Events
Biarritz's Festival International de Folklore is held in early July. In high summer, there are free Friday evening concerts in front of Église Ste-Eugénie and at other venues.

Places to Stay
Camping About 3km south-west of the centre, *Biarritz Camping* (☎ 05 59 23 00 12, 28 rue d'Harcet) opens June to late September. It costs from 75FF to 105FF according to the season for two adults, tent and car. Take bus No 9 to the Biarritz Camping stop.

Hostels For Biarritz's *Auberge de Jeunesse* (05 59 41 76 00, fax 05 59 41 76 07,

@ *aubergejeune.biarritz@wanadoo.fr, 8 rue Chiquito de Cambo)* follow the railway westwards from the train station for 800m. B&B in dorms or small rooms costs 76/85FF in winter/summer; half-board is 120FF. Like the Auberge de Jeunesse d'Anglet (see Places to Stay in Bayonne), it offers a host of outdoor activities and opens year round except mid-December to mid-January.

The otherwise expensive *Hôtel Barnetche* (☎ 05 59 24 22 25, fax 05 59 24 98 71, 5 avenue Charles Floquet) has dorm bunks for 100FF.

Hotels Inexpensive hotels are rare in Biarritz and any kind of room is at a premium in July and August. Outside this high season, however, you can pick and choose and most prices fall by a good 25%.

In the Vieux Port area, trim *Hôtel Palym* (☎ 05 59 24 16 56, fax 05 59 24 96 12, 7 rue du Port Vieux) has singles/doubles with toilet at 170/220FF (290FF with bathroom). *Hôtel Atlantic* (☎ 05 59 24 34 08, 10 rue du Port Vieux) has singles/doubles with washbasin for 195/215FF and doubles/triples/quads with bathroom at 295/330/350FF. Both hitch up their prices a bit in the high summer.

Up in town, *Hôtel Etche-Gorria* (☎ 05 59 24 00 74, 21 ave du Maréchal Foch) occupies a stylishly converted villa. Its simple doubles with washbasin and bidet cost between 150FF and 200FF (200FF to 250FF in July and August). Rooms with full bathroom range from 250FF to 350FF (250FF to 490FF in high season).

Hôtel Maïtagaria (☎ 05 59 24 26 65, 34 ave Carnot) has large, fully equipped singles/doubles/triples/quads for 240/290/390/450FF (270/340/450/500FF in July and August). The sitting room has a cosy fireplace and there's an intimate garden.

Singles/doubles/triples/quads at *Hôtel St-Julien* (☎ 05 59 24 20 39, fax 05 59 24 96 90, @ saint-julien@wanadoo.fr, 20 ave Carnot) are 285/310/330/360FF (325/370/420/460FF, July and August). It's closed January.

All these hotels except Hôtel St-Julien are open year round.

Places to Eat

Restaurants There are quite a few decent little restaurants scattered around Les Halles.

A three-course meal with wine from the chalkboard menu at *Bistrot des Halles* (☎ 05 59 24 21 22, 1 rue du Centre) will set you back about 150FF. At No 5, *Le Croque en Bouche* (☎ 05 59 22 06 57) serves quality regional dishes from 75FF and *menus* at 90FF and 125FF. It is closed Sunday evening and Monday. *Pizzeria Les Princes* (☎ 05 59 24 21 78, 13 rue Gambetta) has above average pizzas from 40FF to 50FF and pasta for around 40FF. It's closed Sunday.

Le Bistroye (☎ 05 59 22 01 02, 6 rue Jean Bart), low ceilinged and popular, has delicious main dishes for between 75FF and 95FF. It is closed Wednesday evening and all Sunday. Next door, *La Mamounia* (☎ 05 59 24 76 08) doles out couscous from 80FF and other Moroccan specialities from 95FF.

For a gourmet meal in sumptuous surroundings, with a spectacular seascape thrown in, indulge yourself at the *restaurant* of Hôtel du Palais (refer to the Other Things to See section), where the set menu costs 290FF.

Self-Catering Biarritz's covered market opens 7 am to 1.30 pm daily. Just downhill at 12 ave Victor Hugo, *La Table de Don Quichotte* sells all sorts of Spanish hams, sausages and wines, while at No 8 you'll find a tempting array of cheeses, wines and pâtés at *Mille et Un Fromages*.

Entertainment

Popular bar areas include the streets on both sides of rue du Port Vieux, the central food market area and around place Clemenceau. Two discos near the town centre are *Le Caveau* (☎ 05 59 24 16 17, 4 rue Gambetta) and *Le Flamingo* (☎ 05 59 22 77 59) in the Casino Municipal.

If you fancy frittering away your travel money, step into Biarritz's white slab of a *casino*, constructed in 1928. Fruit machines whirr and chink from 10 am to 3 am (4 am at the weekend). To lose your shirt as well, try the big-time gambling in the main casino (from 6 pm).

Spectator Sports

At the Fronton Couvert Plaza Berri (☎ 05 59 22 15 72), 42 ave du Maréchal Foch, there's pelota (see the boxed text 'Pelota' earlier in this chapter) at 9.15 pm every Tuesday and Friday, June to early September. Various other tournaments are held here year round, often on Sunday afternoons.

From July to mid-September, the open-air *fronton* at Parc Mazon has regular *chistera* matches at 9 pm on Monday.

Between mid-June and mid-September, Euskal-Jaï (☎ 05 59 23 91 09) in the Parc des Sports d'Aguilera complex, 2km east of central Biarritz on ave Henri Haget, has professional *cesta punta* matches at 9 pm every Wednesday and Saturday.

Admission for each costs about 50FF.

Shopping

For Basque music, crafts and guidebooks, visit Eki (☎ 05 59 24 79 64), 21 ave de Verdun. For scrumptious chocolates and Basque sweets, call by Robert Pariès, 27 place Clemenceau.

Getting There & Away

Air See Air under Getting There & Away in the Bayonne section.

Bus ATCRB buses (☎ 05 59 26 06 99) stop outside the tourist office. Nine daily follow the coast southwards to Bidart, St-Jean de Luz and Hendaye. For other destinations, it's better to go from Bayonne – not least in order to ensure a seat in high season.

Train Biarritz-La Négresse train station is about 3km from the town centre. Bus Nos 2 and 9 connect the two. SNCF has a downtown office (☎ 05 59 24 00 94), open weekdays, at 13 ave du Maréchal Foch. Times, fares and destinations are much the same as those detailed in the Bayonne Getting There & Away section.

Getting Around

To/From the Airport Take STAB bus No 6 or, on Sunday, line C to/from Biarritz's town hall. Each runs once or twice hourly until about 7 pm.

Bus Most services stop beside the town hall, from where routes Nos 1 and 2 go to Bayonne's town hall and station. STAB has an information kiosk (☎ 05 59 24 26 53) behind the tourist office. See also Getting Around in the Bayonne section.

Taxi Call Taxis Biarritz on ☎ 05 59 23 05 50.

Motorcycle & Bicycle Sobilo (☎ 05 59 24 94 47), 24 rue Peyroloubilh, hires mountain bikes (70FF a day), scooters (from 200FF) – and even in-line skates (80FF). It opens 9 am to 1 pm and 3 to 7 pm daily in July and August (from 10 am, and closed Sunday, March to November).

ST-JEAN DE LUZ
postcode 64500 • pop 13,600
St-Jean de Luz (Donibane Lohizune in Basque), 24km south-west of Bayonne at the mouth of the River Nivelle, is the most Basque of the region's beach resorts. Hugging one side of a sheltered bay, it has a colourful history of whaling and piracy. Together with its twin town of Ciboure, it makes a pleasant day trip from Bayonne or Biarritz.

St-Jean de Luz is still an active fishing port, renowned for large catches of sardines (from the waters off Portugal and Morocco), tuna (from the Bay of Biscay and West Africa) and anchovies (from the Bay of Biscay).

Orientation
The small town and its long beach occupy the eastern side – and smaller Ciboure the western curve – of the Baie de St-Jean de Luz, protected from the open sea by three breakwaters, stretched between the headlands of Socoa and Pointe Ste-Barbe. A small but active fishing harbour nestles at the mouth of the River Nivelle, dividing the two towns and spanned by Pont Charles de Gaulle.

The axis of St-Jean de Luz is its pedestrianised shopping precinct, rue Gambetta, 200m inland from the beach, with bustling place Louis XIV at its south-western end.

Information
The tourist office (☎ 05 59 26 03 16, fax 05 59 26 21 47) on place Maréchal Foch opens 9 am to 12.30 pm and 2 to 6.30 pm Monday to Saturday, plus 10am to 1 pm on Sunday. In July and August it opens continuously until 8 pm (10 am to 1 pm and 3 to 7 pm on Sunday).

The post office is at the junction of blvd Victor Hugo and rue Salagoity. Ciboure's post office is on quai Maurice Ravel.

Surfing at Cyber-Café (☎ 05 59 51 22 50, @ aldin-s@wanadoo.fr), 8 blvd Thiers, costs 10FF for up to 10 minutes and 40FF per hour.

Laverie du Port, a launderette on place Maréchal Foch, opens 7 am to 9 pm daily.

Place Louis XIV
Beside this pleasant, pedestrianised square sits **Maison Louis XIV** (☎ 05 59 26 01 56), built in 1643 by a wealthy shipowner. Here, Louis XIV lived the last days of his bachelorhood before his marriage to Maria Teresa (Marie Thérèse) of Spain (perhaps as a reaction against this monarchical connection, a guillotine was set up nearby during the French Revolution). This arranged marriage between Louis XIV, the French monarch, and the daughter of King Philip IV of Spain marked the end of 24 years of war between the two nations.

Still furnished in period style, it opens 10.30 am to noon and 2.30 to 5.30 pm (to 6.30 pm in July and August) daily (except Sunday morning) from June to September. Admission is free while guided tours (with English text) cost 25FF (students and children 20FF). Beside it, and rather dwarfed by its more imposing neighbour, is St-Jean de Luz's **town hall**, built in 1657.

Maison de l'Infante In the days immediately before her marriage to Louis XIV, Maria Teresa stayed in another shipowner's mansion, the brick-and-stone Maison Joanoenia, just off place Louis XIV and now called the **Maison de l'Infante**. It opens 11 am to 12.30 pm and 2.30 and 6.30 pm between mid-June and mid-October. Admission costs 15FF.

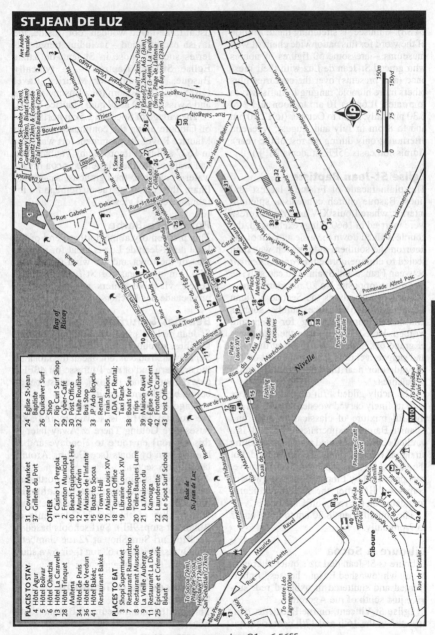

ST-JEAN DE LUZ

PLACES TO STAY
4 Hôtel Agur
5 Hôtel Bolívar
6 Hôtel Ohartzia
13 Hôtel La Caravelle
28 Hôtel Trinquet
34 Maïtena
34 Hôtel de Paris
36 Hôtel de Verdun
41 Hôtel Bakéa;
   Restaurant Bakéa

PLACES TO EAT
3 Shopi Supermarket
7 Restaurant Ramuntcho
8 Restaurant Muscade
9 La Vieille Auberge
11 Campement La Diva
   Kanouga
22 Launderette
23 Le Spot Surf School
25 Épicerie et Crèmerie
   Bidart

24 Covered Market
31 Grillerie du Port

OTHER
1 Casino La Pergola
2 Fronton Municipal
10 Beach Equipment Hire
12 Musée Grévin
14 Maison de l'Infante
15 Boats to Socoa
16 Town Hall
17 Maison Louis XIV
18 Tourist Office
19 Librairie Louis XIV
   Bookshop
20 Toiles Basques Larre
21 La Maison du
24 Église St-Jean
   Baptiste
26 Quiksilver Surf
   Shop
27 Rip Curl Surf Shop
29 Cyber-Café
30 Post Office
32 Halte Routière
   Bus Stop
33 JP Ado Bicycle
   Rental
35 Train Station;
   ADA Car Rental;
   Taxi Rank
38 Boats for Sea
   Trips
39 Maison Ravel
40 Église St-Vincent
42 Fronton Court
43 Post Office

Next door at **Musée Grévin** (☎ 05 59 51 24 88) – 'musée' is stretching the definition of the word for this nationwide chain of wax museums – are some 50 figures of nobles who graced St-Jean de Luz with their presence (and presents) over the centuries plus others more humble, ranging from fishwives to pirates. It opens 10 am to noon and 2 to 6.30 pm daily, April to October (to 12.30 pm and to 8 pm in July and August; weekend afternoons only during the rest of the year). Admission costs 35FF (students 28FF).

Église St-Jean Baptiste

The plain facade of France's largest and finest Basque church conceals a splendid interior, where Louis XIV and Maria Teresa were married in 1660. Rings exchanged, the couple walked down the aisle and out of the door on the southern side, which was then sealed to commemorate the *rapprochement* between France and Spain. You can still see its outline, opposite No 20 rue Gambetta.

Until as recently as the Second Vatican Council (1962–5), Basque churches such as this had separate seating for men and women. Here the men sat in the three tiers of grand oak galleries (five tiers at the rear) and sang as a chorus. The women sat on the ground floor near the underground family sepulchres.

The richly gilded 17th-century altarpiece with its finely carved wooden statues is a delightful mixture of classical severity and Spanish Baroque exuberance. Above all is a vaulted ceiling of painted panels, resembling an upturned ship's hull. The votive model of the ship, *L'Aigle*, suspended over the nave, was presented by Empress Eugénie (wife of Napoleon III) after the real thing nearly foundered on the rocks off Ciboure.

The church opens 8.30 am to noon and 2 to 7 pm daily.

Ciboure & Socoa

Ciboure is St-Jean de Luz's quiet alter ego. Many whitewashed Basque houses, timber-framed and shuttered in oxblood red, survive just south of rue Agorette.

Église St-Vincent, on rue Pocalette, constructed in the 16th and 17th centuries, has an octagonal bell tower, topped by an unusual three-tiered wooden roof. Inside, the lavish use of wood – including tiered galleries such as those in St-Jean de Luz's Église St-Jean Baptiste – is typically Basque. The composer Maurice Ravel (1875–1937) was born (of a Basque mother and Swiss father) at 27 quai Maurice Ravel.

The village of Socoa is 2.5km north-west of Ciboure along the continuation of quai Maurice Ravel. Its prominent fort was built in 1627 and later improved by Vauban. You can walk out to the **Digue de Socoa** breakwater or climb to the lighthouse via rue du Phare, then out along rue du Sémaphore for fabulous coastal views.

Pointe Ste-Barbe

This promontory at the northern end of the Baie de St-Jean de Luz is great for panoramas of the town and the wind-tossed sea. It's 1km north-east of St-Jean de Luz's beach, via blvd Thiers and the seaside promenade des Rochers.

Beaches & Surfing

St-Jean de Luz's sandy beach, popular with families, sprouts bathing tents from June to September. You can rent one at the kiosk by the northern end of rue Tourasse for 40FF a day. Ciboure has its own modest beach below blvd Pierre Benoît.

Plage de Socoa, 2km west of Socoa on the coastal D912, is served by ATCRB buses (see Getting There & Away later in this section) en route to Hendaye and in high season by boats (see Getting Around later in this section).

For prime surfing, head 4.5km north-east of St-Jean de Luz to **plage de Lafitenia**; ATCRB's Biarritz and Bayonne buses pass within 1km of the beach (Martienia or Bubonnet stop, 9FF). Surf schools based in the Rip Curl Surf Shop at 72 rue Gambetta and Quiksilver at No 68 run their own shuttle buses.

Écomusée de la Tradition Basque

This multimedia museum of Basque tradition (☎ 05 59 51 06 06) beside the N10,

2km north of St-Jean de Luz, will tell you all you want to know about Basque life – and probably a good deal more; once you've embarked upon the 1½ hour guided tour, there's no way of escape. It opens 10 am to 5 pm Monday to Saturday (9 am to 6 pm daily, July and August). Admission costs 35/30FF for adults/students.

Other Activities
From Easter to September, École de Voile International (☎ 05 59 47 06 32) in Socoa offers windsurfing lessons at 60/100/150FF for one/two/three hours. Tech Ocean (☎ 05 59 47 96 75) below Socoa Fort is a year-round diving school with introductory dives at 280FF, including equipment, plus longer courses.

Sea Trips From May to mid-September, a couple of boats leave quai du Maréchal Leclerc for morning deep-sea fishing trips (150FF) and afternoon cruises (70FF).

Special Events
The **Fêtes de la St-Jean** in honour of St-Jean Baptiste (St John the Baptist) are celebrated on the weekend nearest 24 June, the saint's day and midsummer's eve. The festivities include a choral concert at Église St-Jean Baptiste, bonfires, music and dancing.

La Nuit de la Sardine (Night of the Sardine) is not a horror movie but rather a night of music, folklore and dancing held twice each summer: on the first Saturday in early July and the Saturday nearest 14 August. It's held outdoors next to the pelota court on ave André Ithurralde and each of the 2000 places costs from 45FF to 90FF. Doors open at 7 pm and the fun starts an hour or so later.

La Fête du Thon (Tuna Festival), on the first Saturday in July, brings buskers to place des Corsaires, quai du Maréchal Leclerc and Ciboure; Basque music and rock to place Maréchal Foch; and midnight fireworks. Local organisations set up stands and sell tuna dishes. There are also two dances: at place Maréchal Foch a local orchestra plays traditional Basque music and rock, while a larger orchestra plays in a more formal venue.

Folk dancers from all over the Spanish and French Basque Country congregate for **Danses des 7 Provinces Basques** in late May or early June, while **Régates de Traînières** is a weekend of whale-boat races on the first weekend in July.

Places to Stay
It's essential to reserve your stay – ideally, well in advance – if you plan to visit between July and mid-September. We quote high season prices, which are generally at least 50% above the low season rate. There are no budget hotels, although low season prices can drop within this range.

Places to Stay – Budget
Camping Between St-Jean de Luz and Guéthary, 7km northwards up the coast, are no fewer than 16 camping grounds. ATCRB's Biarritz and Bayonne buses (see Getting There & Away later in this section) stop within 1km of them all. *Camping Luz Europ* (☎ 05 59 26 51 90) in Acotz, opens April to September and charges 94FF for two people with tent and car. *Le Maya* (☎ 05 59 26 54 91), also in Acotz, opens mid-June to September and charges 83FF.

Hostels At the *Centre Léo Lagrange* (☎/fax 05 59 47 04 79, 8 rue Simone Menez) in Ciboure a bed costs 50FF, including breakfast.

Places to Stay – Mid-Range
St-Jean de Luz Opposite the train station, *Hôtel de Verdun* (☎ 05 59 26 02 55, 13 Ave de Verdun) has large, plain doubles for 155FF with washbasin and bidet (170FF with shower and 195FF with bathroom). In July and August half-board (375FF for one person, 480FF for two) is obligatory.

At the cheerful *Hôtel Trinquet Maïtena* (☎ 05 59 26 05 13, fax 05 59 26 09 90, 42 rue du Midi), you can watch trinquet being played on the adjacent indoor court. Doubles start at 220FF and triples/quads at 320FF. It's normally fully booked between mid-June and September, when, if you manage to squeeze in, you have to take half-board.

At *Hôtel Bolivar* (☎ *05 59 26 02 00, 18 rue Sopite)*, open mid-May to September, singles/doubles cost 200/225FF with washbasin and toilet (280/330FF with full bathroom).

Handy for the train station, *Hôtel de Paris* (☎ *05 59 26 00 62, fax 05 59 26 90 02, 1 blvd du Commandant)*, has unexceptional singles/doubles/triples/quads with bathroom for 320/390/510/570FF.

Ciboure Friendly, central *Hôtel Bakéa* (☎ *05 59 47 34 40, 9 place Camille Julian)* has doubles with bathroom from 250FF to 280FF. It opens mid-February to mid-December.

Hôtel La Caravelle (☎ *05 59 47 18 05, fax 05 59 47 30 43, blvd Pierre Benoît)* is another cosy, friendly place. Its doubles/triples/quads with bathroom cost 280/380/490FF.

Places to Stay – Top End

Modern rooms at *Hôtel Agur* (☎ *05 59 51 91 11, fax 05 59 51 91 21, @ hotel.agur@ wanadoo.fr, 96 rue Gambetta)* are 425FF (495FF for triples). Scottish-owned, it opens mid-March to mid-November.

At *Hôtel Ohartzia* (☎ *05 59 26 00 06, fax 05 59 26 74 75, 28 rue Garat)*, pleasant rooms cost 470/530FF with shower/bath, including breakfast.

Places to Eat

There are a number of fancy restaurants along rue de la République and more interspersed with the cafes around place Louis XIV.

St-Jean de Luz Join the crowds gorging themselves on fresh sardines, tuna and omelette (and that's it, that's the menu!) at the informal, enormously popular *Grillerie du Port* (☎ *05 59 51 18 29)*, in an old quayside shack just off place Maréchal Foch. It opens daily, mid-June to mid-September. There's often a queue in the evening.

Less hearty but still firmly fishy, *Restaurant La Diva* (☎ *05 59 51 14 01, 7 rue de la République)* has good value *menus* at 70FF, 85FF and 115FF. It opens March to October.

La Vieille Auberge (☎ *05 59 26 19 61, 22 rue Tourasse)* serves generous portions of traditional French and Basque cuisine, including *ttoro* (Basque fish casserole). *Menus* begin at 75FF. It opens daily except Tuesday evening and Wednesday, April to October; and daily except Tuesday lunchtime, July and August.

Since the owner comes from Normandy, *Restaurant Ramuntcho* (☎ *05 59 26 03 89, 24 rue Garat)* has a special mix of northern and south-western French dishes. Specialities include duck and fish; *menus* start at 90FF. It's closed off-season on Monday. At No 20, *Restaurant Muscade* (☎ *05 59 26 96 73)* specialises in generous mixed salads and tasty pies and tarts, both savoury and sweet. It's closed in January.

Ciboure With magnificent fish and seafood, the *restaurant* of Hôtel Bakéa (see Places to Stay) is a superb choice for a splurge. Try their *plateau de fruits de mer* (seafood platter, 150FF) brimming with over a dozen kinds of edible sea creatures. There are also *menus* at 90/120/155FF. It opens daily except Tuesday night and Wednesday (daily in July and August).

Self-Catering There's a *food market* every Tuesday and Friday morning (plus Saturday in July and August) at the covered market and spilling over into blvd Victor Hugo. *Épicerie et Crémerie Bidart* (*29 rue Gambetta)* sells a fine selection of cold meats and cheeses.

Entertainment

Although swarming in summer, St-Jean de Luz has only two discos: *El Paseo* (☎ *05 59 26 38 60, 48 ave André Ithurralde)*, 2km east of the train station, and *La Tupiña* (☎ *05 59 54 73 23)*, 5km east on the N10.

Bang on the beach, *Casino La Pergola* opens until 3 am, with slot machines from 11 am daily and gaming from 9 pm daily except Monday.

Spectator Sports

In July and August, there's cesta punta at the Jaï Alaï Compos Berri (☎ *05 59 51 65 30)*

FRENCH BASQUE COUNTRY

on route de Bayonne (the N10), 1km north-east of the train station. Matches start at 9 pm every Tuesday and Friday and half-time is spiced up with music or dancing. Tickets cost from 50FF to 120FF, depending on the crowd-pulling capacity of the players.

In Ciboure, there is an outdoor fronton on rue Ramiro Arrue.

Shopping

Agonise over the rich choice of high-calorie Basque pastries and sweets at La Maison du Kanouga, 9 rue Gambetta. The *mouchous* or maybe *gochuak* (biscuits made with almonds and hazelnuts, respectively)? Or *kanouga* (cubes of chewy chocolate or coffee candy invented by the owner's grandfather)? Perhaps the *gâteau Basque*? And they have more kinds of marzipan than you've imagined in your sweetest dreams.

St-Jean de Luz is also a good place to buy Basque linen – for example at Toiles Basques Larre, 4 rue de la République. In summer, Basque linen woven by local manufacturers, Créations Jean-Vier, is on show and sale at Maison de l'Infante.

Getting There & Away

Bus Over 10 ATCRB (☎ 05 59 26 06 99) buses daily (six on Sunday) go north to Biarritz (17FF, 30 minutes) and Bayonne (22FF, 40 minutes) via Bidart. Southwards, there are around 15 services daily to Hendaye (17FF, 25 minutes), of which three to six follow the coast (continuing, in summer, to Irún in Spain).

The Spanish company Pesa has twice-daily trans-border buses to San Sebastián (22FF, one hour), to which ATCRB runs a summer-only service.

Train There are frequent trains to Bayonne (26FF, 25 minutes) via Biarritz (17FF, 15 minutes) and to Hendaye (17FF, 15 minutes), which has connections to San Sebastián.

Getting Around

Bus There are five local buses daily from the Halte Routière bus stop to Socoa (7FF) via Ciboure.

Taxi The train station has a taxi rank. To order a cab by phone, call ☎ 05 59 26 10 11.

Car ADA (☎ 05 59 26 26 22) has a rental office at the station. There's a parking area north of Shopi supermarket and another east of place Maréchal Foch.

Bicycle & Motorcycle JP Ado (☎ 05 59 26 14 95), 7 ave Labrouche, rents tourers for 60/294FF per day/week, mountain bikes for 80/365FF, and 50cc motorbikes for 535FF per week. They both open daily except Sunday afternoon, July and August; and Tuesday to Saturday, the rest of the year.

Boat Between June and September, a boat (single fare 12FF) plies between quai de l'Infante and Socoa.

LA RHUNE

La Rhune (Larrun in Basque), a 905m-high, antenna-topped mountain, lies 10km south-east of St-Jean de Luz. Half in France and half in Spain, it's something of a Basque symbol. Views are spectacular from its peak, which is best approached from **Col de St-Ignace**, 3km north-west of Sare on the D4 (the St-Jean de Luz road). From here, you can take a pleasant if fairly strenuous walk or hop onto Le Petit Train de la Rhune (☎ 05 59 54 20 26). This charming little train takes 30 minutes to haul itself up the 4km from col to summit. It runs from Easter to mid-November with departures roughly every half hour from 9 am (8.30 am in July and August) depending on the crowds (be prepared for a wait of up to an hour in high summer). The single/return fare is 45/60FF.

ST-JEAN PIED DE PORT
postcode 64220 • pop 1500
• elevation 160m

The walled Pyrenean town of St-Jean Pied de Port (Donibane Garazi in Basque), 53km south-east of Bayonne, was once the last stop in France for pilgrims who converged here from all over France. Refreshed, they headed south over the Spanish border, a mere 8km away, and on to Santiago de Compostela in western Spain. Nowadays the town is a popular departure point for latter day hikers and bikers attempting the trail.

St-Jean Pied de Port makes a pleasant day trip from Bayonne. Half the reason for coming here is the scenic journey south of Cambo-les-Bains as both railway and road (the D918) pass through rocky hills, forests and lush meadows dotted with white farmhouses, their signs announcing *ardi* ('cheese' in Basque) for sale.

The town can be hideously crowded in summer. Consider staying the night and exploring before breakfast or come in the low-season. Even better, to leave it all behind, rent a bike or pull on your boots and head for the surrounding hills.

Information

The tourist office (☎ 05 59 37 03 57, fax 05 59 37 34 91) on place Charles de Gaulle opens 9.30 am to noon and 2 to 6.30 pm Monday to Saturday. In Summer it opens 9 am to 12.30 pm and 2 to 7pm (plus 10 am to noon and 3 to 6 pm Sunday).

The Old Town

The church of **Notre Dame du Bout du Pont**, with foundations as old as the town itself, was thoroughly rebuilt in the 17th century. Beyond **Porte Notre Dame**, which abuts it, is the **Vieux Pont** (old bridge) from where there's a fine view of whitewashed houses with balconies leaning out above the water. Fishing is forbidden where the River Nive passes through town, and the fat, gulping trout seem to know it. Over the bridge is the commercial artery of rue d'Espagne. A pleasant 500m riverbank stroll upstream brings you to the steeply arched so-called Pont Romain (meaning Roman Bridge but in fact 17th-century).

Rue de la Citadelle is bordered by substantial pink granite 16th- to 18th-century houses. Look for the construction date on door lintels (the oldest we found was 1510). A common motif is the scallop shell, symbol of St-Jacques (St James or Santiago) and of the Santiago de Compostela pilgrims and perhaps an early example of come-hither advertising by the boarding house keepers of the time. Pilgrims would enter the town

through the porte de St-Jacques on the northern side of town then, refreshed and probably a little poorer, head for Spain through the porte d'Espagne, south of the river.

La Citadelle

From the top of rue de la Citadelle, a rough cobblestone path ascends to the massive Citadelle itself, offering fine views of the town, the Nive and the surrounding hills. Constructed in 1628, the fort was rebuilt around 1680 by military engineers of the Vauban school. During the Spanish civil war (1936–39), it was home to 500 Basque refugee children from Spanish Navarra. Nowadays it serves as a secondary school.

If you've a head for heights, descend by the steps signed *escalier poterne* (rear stairway). Steep and slippery after rain, they plunge beside the moss-covered ramparts to **Porte de l'Échauguette** (Watchtower Gate).

Prison des Évêques

The so-called Bishops' Prison (admission 10FF), a claustrophobic vaulted cellar at 41 rue de la Citadelle, gets its history muddled. It indeed served as the town jail from 1795, as a military lock-up in the 19th century, then as a place of internment during WWII for those caught trying to flee to Spain. And the lower part dates from the 13th century when St-Jean Pied de Port was a bishopric of the Avignon papacy. But the building above it dates from the 16th century, by which time the bishops were long gone. It opens 10 am to 12.15 pm and 3 to 6.15 pm daily, Easter to mid-October.

Walking & Cycling

St-Jean Pied de Port is a fine place from which to walk or cycle into the Pyrenean foothills, where the loudest sounds you'll hear are cowbells and the wind. Both the GR10, the trans-Pyrenean long distance trail from the Atlantic to the Mediterranean, and the GR65, the Chemin de St-Jacques pilgrim route, pass through town. Maison de la Presse, on place Charles de Gaulle, carries a reasonable selection of walking maps.

Pick up a copy of *25 Randonnées en Pays Basque* (40FF) from the tourist office. In

French but with explicit maps, it gives enough ideas for walking or mountain bike routes to keep you active and happy for a good two weeks or more.

To cycle the easy way while enjoying the best of the views of the Nive Valley, load your bike on the train in Bayonne – they're carried free – and roll back down the valley from St-Jean Pied de Port. If you find the ride all the way back to the coast daunting, rejoin the train at Pont-Noblia, for example, or Cambo-les-Bains. For local bike hire, see Getting Around at the end of this section.

Guided Tours
In summer, the tourist office conducts tours of the old town in French (10FF) at 10.30 am on Tuesday and Friday.

Places to Stay
Camping Riverside *Camping Municipal Plaza Berri* (☎ 05 59 37 11 19, ave du Fronton) opens Easter to early October and charges 42FF for two adults, car and tent. *Camping de l'Arraddy* (☎ 05 59 37 11 75, 4 chemin de Zalikarte) opens March to September and costs 36FF.

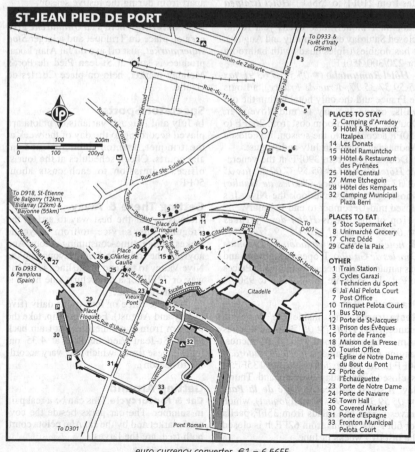

ST-JEAN PIED DE PORT

To D933 & Forêt d'Iraty (25km)

To D918, St-Étienne de Baïgorry (12km), Bidarray (22km) & Bayonne (55km)

To D933 & Pamplona (Spain)

To D301

Pont Romain

Vieux Pont

Citadelle

PLACES TO STAY
2 Camping d'Arraddy
9 Hôtel & Restaurant Itzalpea
14 Les Donats
15 Hôtel Ramuntcho
19 Hôtel & Restaurant des Pyrénées
25 Hôtel Central
27 Mme Etchegoin
28 Hôtel des Remparts
32 Camping Municipal Plaza Berri

PLACES TO EAT
5 Stoc Supermarket
8 Unimarché Grocery
17 Chez Dédé
29 Café de la Paix

OTHER
1 Train Station
3 Cycles Garazi
4 Technicien du Sport
6 Jaï Alaï Pelota Court
7 Post Office
10 Trinquet Pelota Court
11 Bus Stop
12 Porte de St-Jacques
13 Prison des Évêques
16 Porte de France
18 Maison de la Presse
20 Tourist Office
21 Église de Notre Dame du Bout du Pont
22 Porte de l'Échauguette
23 Porte de Notre Dame
24 Porte de Navarre
26 Town Hall
30 Covered Market
31 Porte d'Espagne
33 Fronton Municipal Pelota Court

FRENCH BASQUE COUNTRY

Gîtes d'Étape & Chambres d'Hôtes The tourist office has details of the wide choice of non-hotel accommodation, primarily but not exclusively for walkers and pilgrims. Two good gîtes d'étape for walkers, opens May to October and charging about 50FF per bed are *Les Donats* (☎ *05 59 37 15 64, 40 rue de la Citadelle*) and *Mme Etchegoin* (☎ *05 59 37 12 08, 9 route d'Uhart*).

Hotels At the cheerful *Hôtel des Remparts* (☎ *05 59 37 13 79, fax 05 59 37 33 44, 16 place Floquet*), smallish singles with bathroom range from 205FF and 240FF (doubles from 210FF to 255FF). *Hôtel Itzalpea* (☎ *05 59 37 03 66, fax 05 59 37 33 18, 5 place du Trinquet*), also opens year round (closed Saturday except in July and August). It has doubles/triples/quads with bathroom for 220/300/350FF.

Hôtel Ramuntcho (☎ *05 59 37 03 91, fax 05 59 37 35 17, 1 rue de France*), a Logis de France and the only hotel within the old walls, opens January to mid-November. Doubles with bathroom cost from 265FF to 350FF according to the season. It is closed Wednesday except in July and August.

Doubles cost from 390FF at the venerable *Hôtel Central* (☎ *05 59 37 00 22, fax 05 59 37 27 79, 1 place Charles de Gaulle*) whose rear rooms overlook the Nive. It's closed mid-December to end-February.

Top of the line is *Hôtel des Pyrénées* (☎ *05 59 37 01 01, fax 05 59 37 18 97,* @ *hotel.pyrenees@wanadoo.fr, 19 place Charles de Gaulle*). It opens year round and has a much acclaimed restaurant (see Places to Eat). Doubles are from 580FF to 950FF.

Places to Eat

Restaurants Just inside the porte de France, *Chez Dédé* (☎ *05 59 37 16 40*) has as many as seven good value, tasty menus, ranging from the modest *menu du routard* at 50FF to the *suggestion du chef* at 135FF. It is closed Wednesday evening and Thursday. Also economical is *Café de la Paix* (☎ *05 59 37 00 99, 4 place Floquet*), which serves pizzas and salads from 35FF, paella for 60FF and menus from 62FF. It is closed the last two weeks in June.

Two hotel restaurants are well worth a visit. *Hôtel Itzalpea* (see Places to Stay) serves family-style regional cuisine, with menus from 75FF. The one at *Hôtel Ramuntcho* offers first-rate menus from 66FF to 100FF.

Top of the line again is the restaurant at *Hôtel des Pyrénées*. Sporting two Michelin stars, it has menus of classical French and Basque cuisine ranging from 250FF to 550FF. It opens daily except Monday evening or Tuesday in January to March and Tuesday between April and June). It closes mid-November plus most of January, apart from during the festive season.

Self-Catering There's an *Unimarché grocery* on place du Trinquet and a larger *Stoc supermarket*, just off ave du Jaï Alaï. Local produce is sold at St-Jean Pied de Port's Monday market, held on place Charles de Gaulle.

Spectator Sports

In July and August, variants of pelota are played according to the day of the week at the trinquet, fronton municipal and jaï alaï courts. Check schedules at the tourist office. Admission to each costs about 50FF.

Getting There & Away

Train is by far the best way to arrive; the irregular bus service to/from Bayonne makes a huge, time-consuming detour. And anyway, the train trip from Bayonne up the Nive Valley to the end of the line (47FF one way or 72FF for a day return, one hour) is just plain beautiful.

There are three or four trains daily (five in July and August). For a day trip, take the 9.03 am from Bayonne; the last train back leaves St-Jean Pied de Port at 4.35 pm (check these times, which may vary according to season).

Getting Around

Car & Motorcycle This can be a real pain in summer. The car parks beside the covered market and by the Jaï Alaï pelota court, both free, are the largest.

Taxi To order a taxi, call ☎ 05 59 37 05 00 or ☎ 05 59 37 02 92.

Bicycles and Motorcycles Friendly Cycles Garazi (☎ 05 59 37 21 79), 32 ave du Jaï Alaï, rents two-wheelers year round. VTTs cost 50/80/450FF for per half day/day/week, scooters are 110/190/1140FF and 125cc motorbikes, 210/290/1700FF. The shop opens 8.30 am to noon and 2 to 7 pm daily. Nearby, Technicien du Sport (☎ 05 59 37 15 98) at No 18 has a smaller stock of VTTs at comparable prices.

AROUND ST-JEAN PIED DE PORT
St-Étienne de Baïgorry
The village of St-Étienne de Baïgorry and its outlying hamlets straggle satisfyingly across the Vallée de Baïgorry. Stretched thin along a branch of the Nive, it has, like so many Basque settlements, two focal points: the church and the fronton court.

At the eastern end of its mainly 17th-century **church** is an ornate, if not particularly subtle, gilded altarpiece (to illuminate it, press the button to the left of the main, western entrance) while the western wall of the interior is taken up by a giant organ. Nothing exceptional there – except that, in an era when churches are crumbling and closing for want of funds, it was installed, brand-new, in 1999. Note also the fine three-tier wooden balconies where the men used to sit.

The **Château d'Etchauz** (☎ 05 59 37 48 58), mainly 17th-century but with traces of an 11th-century original, dominates the village. Gleaming white and flanked by out-riding witches' hat towers, it opens 10 am to midday and 2 to 5.30 pm, Tuesday to Sunday (daily in summer), March to November. Admission costs 30FF.

Irouléguy is the French Basque country's only *appellation contrôlée* wine – and most of it comes from the Baïgorry Valley. The wine growers' cooperative just north of town organises vineyard visits (10FF) at 10 am and 4.30 pm, Monday to Saturday from June to September, and opens year round for sales and tasting.

Both St-Étienne de Baïgorry and its near-neighbour, Bidarray, farther down the valley (see the next section), make excellent bases for walking. Pick up a copy of *Randonnée dans la Vallée de Baïgorry* (40FF), a loose-leaf folder describing 33 walks in the valley. Even if your French isn't too hot, it gives useful pointers – and every walk is signposted. It's on sale at the tourist office (☎ 05 59 37 47 28), opposite the church.

An SNCF bus to/from the village connects with all trains running between Bayonne and St-Jean Pied de Port at the small station of Ossès-St-Martin d'Arrossa, 8km away (for details, see Getting There & Away in the St-Jean Pied de Port section). The municipal **Camping Irouléguy**, down a lane beside the wine co-op, charges 45FF for two people plus car and tent.

Bidarray
Typical of rural Basque settlements, Bidarray, like St-Étienne de Baïgorry, is not so much a village as a scattering of farmsteads and hamlets, perched on a plateau where the River Bastan joins the Nive. Its small tourist office (☎/fax 05 59 37 74 60) is beside the church.

La Maison du Pottok (☎ 05 59 52 21 14, ✉ pottok@aol.com), a private venture in the hills above the village, plays its role in the preservation of the pottok, the tiny, shaggy pony of the Basque Country. There are guided visits from 10 am to 6 pm daily, July and August. Admission costs 40FF. The reserve is signposted along a road about 5km from the D918 and train station.

Bidarray is a 1.5km walk from the nearest train station, Pont-Noblia, on the line between Bayonne and St-Jean Pied de Port (for details, see Getting There & Away in the St-Jean Pied de Port section).

The Pyrenees

The Pyrenees (Pyrénées) stretch laterally for 430km from the Bay of Biscay on the Atlantic coast to the Mediterranean Sea, forming a natural boundary between France and Spain.

There are three broad geographical zones. In the damper west, the Pyrénées-Atlantiques rise steadily from the Atlantic through the lush Basque forests to France's westernmost summits and valleys. This area features in the French Basque Country chapter.

The Hautes Pyrénées, the focus of much of this chapter, is a wild, mostly treeless, high country of rugged peaks and ridges, deep valleys, high cols and well over 100 lakes. Much of the most spectacular scenery lies within the long, skinny Parc National des Pyrénées. It runs along the border for about 100km from the Vallée d'Aspe in the west to the Vallée d'Aure in the east, its width never exceeding 15km. Pau is the nearest sizeable town to the Vallée d'Aspe and Vallée d'Ossau, while the pilgrimage city of Lourdes has bus links to the mountain town of Cauterets.

In the Pyrénées Orientales, the mountain chain gradually tapers towards the Mediterranean and the climate becomes warmer and drier. Its eastern end is in Roussillon, described in the Languedoc-Roussillon chapter. The Catalan-speaking principality of Andorra is in the middle of the Pyrenees, between France and Spain; for more information, see the Andorra chapter.

Information

In Paris, information on the Pyrenees région is available from the Maison des Pyrénées (☎ 01 42 86 51 86, métro Quatre Septembre), 15 rue St-Augustin (2e).

Getting Around

For train timetables and fares throughout the region, call ☎ 06 36 35 35 35. Calls are charged at 2.25FF per minute and waiting time, once you're connected, can be long.

Highlights

- **Pau** – the first glimpse of snow-capped mountains from stylish blvd des Pyrénées
- **Lourdes** – one of the world's most important pilgrimage sites
- **Parc National des Pyrénées** – trekking in western Europe's wildest area
- **Gavarnie** – the magnificent wraparound sweep of the Cirque de Gavarnie

PAU

postcode 64000 • pop 82,000
• elevation 207m

Pau (pronounced), capital of both the Béarn région and the Pyrénées-Atlantiques département, is famed for its mild climate, flower-filled public parks and magnificent views of the Pyrenees. In the 19th century it was a favourite wintering spot for wealthy English and Americans. Nowadays, the city owes its prosperity to a high-tech industrial base; the huge natural gas field at Lacq, 20km to the north-west; and an abundance of Spanish tourists and shoppers.

If you have a car, Pau – well supplied with cheap hotels – makes a good base for forays into the Pyrenees.

Orientation

The town centre sits atop a small hill with the railway and the River Pau (Gave de Pau) at its base. Stretched along its crest is blvd des Pyrénées, its wide promenade offering panoramic views of the mountains to the south. The town's east–west axis is the thoroughfare of rue Maréchal Joffre, rue Maréchal Foch and cours Bosquet with place Georges Clemenceau, through which every local bus line threads, at its heart. The minuscule Vieille Ville (old town) nestles around the chateau.

Information

Tourist Offices The tourist office (☎ 05 59 27 27 08, fax 05 59 27 03 21, ✉ omt@ ville-pau.fr) on place Royale opens 9 am to 12.30 pm and 1.30 to 6 pm Monday to Saturday (with a longer lunch break on Saturday); and 9 am to 6.45 pm daily, July and August (with shorter Sunday hours). Good free resources here are *Béarn: Guide Loisirs* in French, a detailed summary of almost everything there is to do in the region, and the brochure in English *Pau: an Authentic Town* which has practical information about the city.

Post & Communications The main post office at 21 cours Bosquet, has Cyberposte. Log on in more comfort and with a glass by your side at l'Arob@se (☎ 05 59 98 44 16), 5 rue Mathieu Lalanne. It opens 11am to 2 am Monday to Saturday (between 2 and 8 pm Sunday) and charges a bargain 5FF for 10 minutes or 30FF per hour.

Bookshops Librairie des Pyrénées (☎ 05 59 27 78 75), 14 rue St-Louis, carries an excellent selection of walking maps and guidebooks in French. Should you feel the call of the mountains, among the few titles in English it stocks are Lonely Planet's *Walking in France* and *Walking in Spain*, both of which give extensive treatment to the Pyrenees.

Laundry Laverie Automatique, 66 rue Émile Garet opens 7 am to 10 pm daily.

Pyrénées Panorama

From majestic blvd des Pyrénées, there's a breathtaking panorama of Pyrenean summits on clear days, which mostly come in autumn and winter. Opposite No 20 is an orientation table to tell you your position and what you're looking at.

Vieille Ville

Little remains of Pau's labyrinthine old centre – an area no more than 300m in diameter and rich in restored medieval and Renaissance buildings.

Chateau

The original 14th-century castle, residence of the monarchs of Navarre, was transformed into a Renaissance chateau, bedecked with gardens, by Marguerite d'Angoulême (also known as Margaret of Navarre) in the 16th century. Marguerite's grandson, the future Henri IV, was born here – cradled, so the story goes, in an upturned tortoise shell.

Neglected in the 18th century and used as barracks after the Revolution, the chateau was in a sorry state by 1838, when King Louis-Philippe ordered a complete interior renovation, completed by Napoleon III. The result is a rather soulless pastiche of medieval and Renaissance architecture.

The chateau holds one of Europe's richest collections of 16th- to 18th-century Gobelins tapestries and some fine Sèvres porcelain. These items apart, most of the ornamentation and furniture, including an oak dining table that can seat 100, dates from Louis-Philippe's intervention. In the room where Henry IV was born is what's claimed to be that tortoise-shell cradle.

Within the brick-and-stone Tour de la Monnaie below the main chateau, a free modern lift hauls you from river to chateau level.

The chateau (☎ 05 59 82 38 19) opens 9.30 am to 12.15 pm and 1.30 to 5.45 pm daily, July and August; and 9.30 to 11.45 am and 2 to 4.15 pm daily, the rest of

PYRENEES

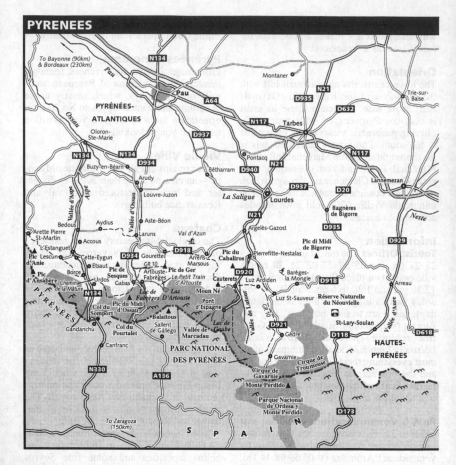

PYRENEES

the year. Admission costs 27FF (those aged under 18 free; 18 to 26, 18FF) and includes an obligatory and less than arresting guided tour in rapid-fire French or Spanish (though a printed narrative in English is available).

Musée Bernadotte

The Bernadotte Museum (☎ 05 59 27 48 42), 8 rue Tran, has exhibits illustrating the improbable yet true story of how a French general, born in this very building, became king of Sweden and Norway (see the boxed text 'France's Swedish King' later in this section). Displays include letters, documents,

engravings, paintings and memorabilia. The museum, which flies both Swedish and French flags, opens 10 am to noon and 2 to 6 pm Tuesday to Sunday. Admission costs 10FF (children and students 5FF).

Musée des Beaux-Arts

Pau's Fine Arts Museum is one of the south-west's better provincial museums. Among works on display are 17th- to 20th-century European paintings, including works by Rubens, El Greco and Degas. The museum (☎ 05 59 27 33 02), entered from rue Mathieu Lalanne, opens 10 am to noon

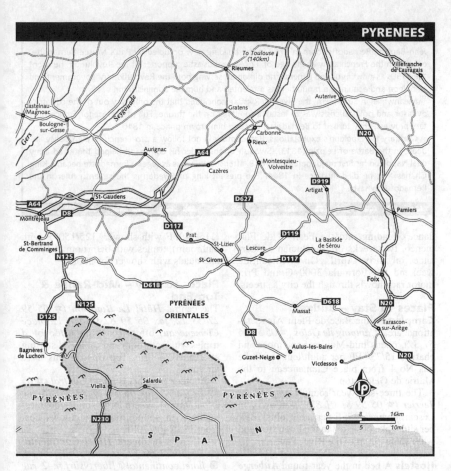

PYRENEES

and 2 to 6 pm daily except Tuesday. Admission costs 10FF (children and students 5FF).

Activities

Compagnie du Sud (☎ 05 59 27 04 24, fax 05 59 27 63 25), 27 rue Maréchal Joffre, offers small-group treks led by English-speaking guides in the French and Spanish Pyrenees between May and October. It can also arrange food, lodging or other support for unaccompanied trips, from 1500FF to 2200FF per person for four to seven days.

Romano Sport (☎/fax 05 59 98 48 56),

1 rue Jean Réveil, rents equipment for a whole range of outdoor activities: walking (boots 35FF per day), mountain climbing (gear minus ropes 65FF per day), skiing (50FF per day), canyon clambering (100FF) and also bikes (see Getting Around Pau).

Special Events

The Festival de Pau, a three-week extravaganza of dance, music and theatre, is held from mid-June to early July at the Théâtre St-Louis and in the chateau courtyard. March sees both Carnival week and the month-long Festival de Dance (modern

PYRENEES

France's Swedish King

Jean-Baptiste Bernadotte, born in 1763 in the building now occupied by Pau's Musée Bernadotte, enlisted in the French army at the age of 17. An enthusiastic supporter of the Revolution, he spent the 1790s as a distinguished general and diplomat, serving both the Revolutionary government and Napoleon and acquiring a reputation as a talented and humane administrator.

Meanwhile, in Stockholm, the Swedish Riksdag concluded that the only way out of the country's dynastic and political crisis was to install a foreigner on the throne. Full of respect for French military prowess, they turned to Bernadotte, electing him crown prince in 1810.

Contrary to Napoleon's expectations, Bernadotte did not follow a pro-French foreign policy. Indeed, in the Battle of Leipzig (1813), Swedish troops under his command helped the allied army deal Napoleon his first major defeat. In 1818, after several years as regent, Bernadotte became King Charles XIV; he died in office in 1844. The present king of Sweden is the seventh ruler in the Bernadotte dynasty.

dance), leading into the Festival de Flamenco, two weeks of Andalucían exuberance in early April. On Whitsuntide weekend the Formula 3000 Grand Prix motor race howls through the city's streets.

Places to Stay – Budget

Camping At the Base de Plein Air recreational area, *Camping de Gelos* (☎ 05 59 06 57 37), opens mid-May to September and charges 15/23/5FF per adult/tent/car. Take bus No 1 from place Clemenceau to the Mairie de Gelos stop.

The three-star, year-round *Camping Le Terrier* (☎ 05 59 81 01 82), 7km away in Lescar, charges 25FF per adult plus 32FF per site. Take bus No 8 to the Laou stop and walk some 800m to the River Pau.

Hostels A bed in the year-round *Auberge de Jeunesse* (☎ 05 59 06 69 35) at the Base de Plein Air in Gelos (see Camping) costs 54FF.

Hotels The friendly, family-run, *Hôtel d'Albret* (☎ 05 59 27 81 58, 11 rue Jeanne d'Albret) has clean doubles with washbasin and bidet for only 90FF (120FF with shower, 155FF with bathroom). Hall showers cost 10FF.

Hôtel de la Pomme d'Or (☎ 05 59 11 23 23, fax 05 59 11 23 24, 11 rue Maréchal Foch), on the 1st floor of a former coaching inn, has basic singles/doubles for 90/110FF

(115/140FF with shower, 125/150FF with bathroom), triples with bathroom at 195FF and quads with shower for 200FF.

Places to Stay – Mid-Range & Top End

The central *Hôtel Le Bourbon* (☎ 05 59 27 53 12, fax 05 59 82 90 99, 12 place Clemenceau) offers cosy singles/doubles/triples with bathroom and cable TV starting at 215/310/360FF. Top-floor rooms have air-con.

Another good bet is *Hôtel Central* (☎ 05 59 27 72 75, fax 05 59 27 33 28, 15 rue Léon Daran), where large singles/doubles/quads with soundproofed windows cost from 185/240/270FF.

At Pau's landmark *Hôtel Continental* (☎ 05 59 27 69 31, fax 05 59 27 99 84, ✉ hotel.continental@libertysurf.fr, 2 rue Maréchal Foch), singles/doubles/triples start at 350/400/550FF.

Places to Eat

Restaurants Restaurants cluster around the small pedestrianised area east of the chateau and there are a number of brasseries and cafes along blvd des Pyrénées and around square George V.

Restaurants – French Top value among Pau's brasseries is *Brasserie Le Berry* (☎ 05 59 27 42 95, 4 rue Gachet), with Béarnaise specialities under 100FF, lots of

PYRENEES

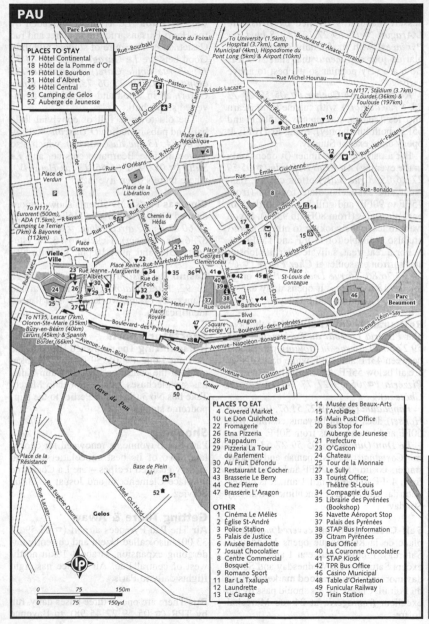

PAU

PLACES TO STAY
- 17 Hôtel Continental
- 18 Hôtel de la Pomme d'Or
- 19 Hôtel Le Bourbon
- 31 Hôtel d'Albret
- 45 Hôtel Central
- 51 Camping de Gelos
- 52 Auberge de Jeunesse

Parc Lawrence

Place du Foirail / To University (1.5km), / Hospital (3.7km), Camp / Municipal (4km), Hippodrome du / Pont Long (5km) & Airport (10km)

Boulevard d'Alsace-Lorraine

Rue-Bourbaki

Rue-Pasteur

Rue Michel-Hounau

To N117, Stadium (3.7km), / Lourdes (36km) & / Toulouse (197km)

Rue Michel-Hounau

Rue-Carnot

R-Louis Lacaze

Rue-Jean-Réveil

Rue Castetnau

Rue-Henri-Faisans

Place de la République

Rue Lespy

Rue-Émile-Guichenné

Rue-Bonado

Place de Verdun

Place de la Libération

Rue-d'Orléans

Rue Samonzet

Cours Bosquet

Place Gramont

Vieille Ville

Place Reine-Rue Maréchal Joffre

Place Jeanne d'Albret

Rue de Foix

Place Georges Clemenceau

Blvd-Barbanègre

Place St-Louis de Gonzague

Parc Beaumont

To N117, / Eurorent (500m), / ADA (1.5km), / Camping Le Terrier / (7km) & Bayonne / (112km)

To N135, Lescar (7km), / Oloron-Ste-Marie (35km), / Buzy-en-Béarn (40km), / Laruns (45km) & Spanish / Border (66km)

Place Royale

Henri-IV

Rue Louis

Blvd Aragon

Square George V

Boulevard-des-Pyrénées

Avenue-Napoléon-Bonaparte

Avenue-Jean-Biray

Avenue / Gaston-Lacoste

Canal Heid

Avenue-Léon-Say

Place de la Résistance

Gave de Pau

Base de Plein Air

Gelos

Rue Eugène Daure

Allée Oct Heid

0 75 150m
0 75 150yd

LP

PLACES TO EAT
- 4 Covered Market
- 10 Le Don Quichotte
- 22 Fromagerie
- 26 Etna Pizzeria
- 28 Pappadum
- 29 Pizzeria La Tour du Parlement
- 30 Au Fruit Défondu
- 32 Restaurant Le Cocher
- 43 Brasserie Le Berry
- 44 Chez Pierre
- 45 Brasserie L'Aragon

OTHER
- 1 Cinéma Le Méliès
- 2 Église St-André
- 3 Police Station
- 5 Palais de Justice
- 6 Musée Bernadotte
- 7 Josuat Chocolatier
- 9 Centre Commercial Bosquet
- 9 Romano Sport
- 11 Bar La Txalupa
- 12 Laundrette
- 13 Le Garage

- 14 Musée des Beaux-Arts
- 15 l'Arob@se
- 16 Main Post Office
- 20 Bus Stop for Auberge de Jeunesse
- 21 Prefecture
- 23 O'Gascon
- 24 Chateau
- 25 Tour de la Monnaie
- 27 Le Sully
- 33 Tourist Office; Théâtre St-Louis
- 34 Compagnie du Sud
- 35 Librairie des Pyrénées (Bookshop)
- 36 Navette Aéroport Stop
- 37 Palais des Pyrénées
- 38 STAP Bus Information
- 39 Citram Pyrénées Bus Office
- 40 La Couronne Chocolatier
- 41 STAP Kiosk
- 42 TPR Bus Office
- 46 Casino Municipal
- 48 Table d'Orientation
- 49 Funicular Railway
- 50 Train Station

PYRENEES

euro currency converter €1 = 6.56FF

fish dishes under 80FF and an immense dessert menu. It's rivalled by *Brasserie L'Aragon* (☎ *05 59 27 12 43, 18 blvd des Pyrénées*) with its friendly service, 50FF plat du jour and *menus* that start at 90FF. Both are very popular so it's best to arrive early.

Restaurant Le Cocher (☎ *05 59 27 72 83, 8 rue de Foix),* with cuisine from Béarn and les Landes, has *menus* at 50FF and 65FF (both lunch only), rising to 110FF. It opens daily except Sunday.

For a participatory dinner (it opens only in the evening) *Au Fruit Défondu* (☎ *05 59 27 26 05, 3 rue Sully)* offers cheese, fish, meat and even chocolate fondues (from 75FF to 90FF) and grill-it-yourself duck or beef *pierrades* (from 80FF to 93FF). If you want to leave the cooking to others, *menus* are also available for 110FF and 150FF.

For a real treat, salivate over the lobster and saffron cassoulet at *Chez Pierre* (☎ *05 59 27 76 86, 16 rue Louis Barthou)* or go for the 185FF *menu.* It opens daily except Saturday lunchtime and Sunday.

Restaurants – International At the popular *Pizzeria La Tour du Parlement* (☎ *05 59 27 38 29, 36 rue du Moulin),* pizzas cost between 43FF and 60FF while pasta dishes are all below 55FF. Alternatively, visit *Etna Pizzeria* (☎ *05 59 27 77 94, 16 rue du Château).*

Pappadum (☎ *05 59 27 51 67, 9 impasse Honset)* does Indian biryanis costing from 60FF and lunch menus from 50FF.

Le Don Quichotte (*05 59 27 63 08, 30 rue Castetnau)* serves Spanish and Basque starters costing from 28FF and main dishes from 45FF to 60FF until 1 am. It is closed Saturday and Monday lunchtime and all day Sunday.

Self-Catering The big *covered market* on place de la République opens Monday to Saturday. It closes between 1 and 3.30 pm except Saturday. On Wednesday and Saturday mornings there's a **food market** at place du Foirail. Cheese lovers should pass by the excellent *fromagerie* at 24 rue Maréchal Joffre.

Entertainment

Bars & Pubs 'Le Triangle', bounded by rue Henri Faisans, rue Émile Garet and rue Castetnau is the centre of student nightlife. Good bets are *Le Garage* (☎ *05 59 83 75 17, 49 rue Émile Garet)* and *Bar La Txalupa* (☎ *05 59 98 06 73, 34 rue Émile Garet),* all in wood and shaped like an inverted ship's hull.

The old town is full of convivial little bars and pubs including *O'Gascon* (☎ *05 59 27 64 74, 13 rue du Château),* which also serves up fine Béarnaise cuisine, and *Le Sully* (☎ *05 59 82 86 56, 13 rue Henri IV),* where there's often live jazz.

Cinemas Pau's only cinema showing non-dubbed films is **Cinéma Le Méliès** (☎ *05 59 27 60 52 or, for a recording,* ☎ *0 836 68 68 87, 6 rue Bargoin).* Tickets cost 35FF (students 35FF and, after 10 pm, 22FF for all).

Casino The *Casino Municipal* (☎ *05 59 27 06 92, Parc Beaumont)* opens 10 am to 3 am daily (4 am, weekends). You'll need identification.

Spectator Sports

Horse Racing The renowned Hippodrome du Pont Long (☎ 05 59 32 07 93), 5km north of the centre on blvd du Cami-Salié, has steeplechases from October to March. Take bus No 3 (direction Perlic) to the Hippodrome stop.

Shopping

Pau, like Bayonne, is renowned for chocolate. Two of its best chocolatiers – with closely guarded recipes – are La Couronne on place Clemenceau and Josuat at 23 rue Serviez.

Getting There & Away

Air The Pau-Pyrénées airport (☎ 05 59 33 33 00), also called Uzein and currently undergoing expansion, is about 10km northwest of central Pau. Air France has eight flights daily to Paris.

Bus There are one to three buses daily, run by TPR (☎ 05 59 27 45 98), to Bayonne

(86FF, 2¼ hours), continuing to Biarritz (92FF, 2½ hours). TPR also serves Lourdes (32FF, 1¼ hours, four to six daily).

Buses of Citram Pyrénées (☎ 05 59 27 22 22) roll up the Vallée d'Ossau as far as Laruns (46FF, one hour, up to four daily; Sunday service in July and August only).

Both companies have their offices and bus stands on rue Gachet.

Train Up to 10 trains or SNCF buses daily link Pau and Oloron-Ste-Marie (38FF, 40 minutes) via Buzy-en-Béarn. From Buzy, there are onward bus connections into the Vallée d'Ossau and from Oloron-Ste-Marie into the Vallée d'Aspe. A few of the latter continue to the Spanish railhead of Canfranc, from where trains run to Zaragoza (Saragossa). There are frequent trains to Lourdes (43FF, 30 minutes).

Direct medium- and long-haul destinations include Bayonne (82FF, 1¼ hours, up to 10 daily), Bordeaux (155FF, 2¼ hours by TGV, six daily) and Toulouse (143FF, 2¾ hours, up to 10 daily). There are six daily TGVs to Paris' Gare Montparnasse (436FF, five hours).

Getting Around
To/From the Airport You can pick up the Navette Aéroport (airport shuttle; ☎ 05 59 02 45 45) at the train station or in the south-western corner of place Clemenceau, from where there are departures at 10 am (weekdays) and 2 and 6 pm daily. Buses leave the airport at 10.30 am weekdays and 2.40, 6.50 and 10.50 pm daily. The shuttle costs 30FF.

A taxi to the airport costs about 120FF (150FF on Sunday).

Bus The local bus company, STAP (☎ 05 59 27 69 78), has an office on rue Gachet and a kiosk at the south-eastern corner of place Clemenceau. Both provide route maps (also available at the tourist office), information and tickets, but on weekdays only.

All nine local lines run from about 6 am to 7.30 pm Monday to Saturday, and stop somewhere on place Clemenceau (consult the map at the kiosk). Single tickets, sold on

board, cost 6FF while a carnet for eight rides costs 32FF and a daily pass costs 15FF.

Funicular Railway The train station is linked to blvd des Pyrénées by a free **funicular railway**, a funny little contraption built in 1908 by the hotels along the boulevard. Cars leave about every five minutes until 9 pm. However, unless you're heavily laden or a railway freak, it's scarcely worth the wait; the walk itself, even uphill, takes less time.

Car & Motorcycle There's extensive free parking on place de Verdun. Rental agencies in town include Eurorent (☎ 05 59 27 44 41), ADA (☎ 05 59 72 94 40) and Europcar (☎ 05 59 92 09 09).

Taxi There's a taxi stand (☎ 05 59 02 22 22) on place Clemenceau.

Bicycle Romano Sport (☎ 05 59 98 48 56), 1 rue Jean Réveil, rents bikes and other sporting equipment. It opens 9 am to noon and 3 to 7 pm Monday to Saturday (daily between December and March).

LOURDES
postcode 65100 • pop 15,000
• elevation 400m
Lourdes, 43km south-east of Pau, was just a sleepy market town on the edge of the snow-capped Pyrenees until 1858, when Bernadette Soubirous (1844–79), a near-illiterate, 14-year-old peasant girl, saw the Virgin Mary in a series of 18 visions that took place in a grotto near the town. The girl's account was eventually investigated by the Vatican, which confirmed them as bona fide apparitions. Bernadette, who lived out her short life as a nun, was canonised as St-Bernadette in 1933.

These events set Lourdes on the path to becoming one of the world's most important pilgrimage sites. Some five million visitors from all over the world converge here annually. Well over half are pilgrims, including many sick people seeking cures. Nowadays, 45% come from beyond France's frontiers – and two-thirds are over 45 years old.

PYRENEES

LOURDES

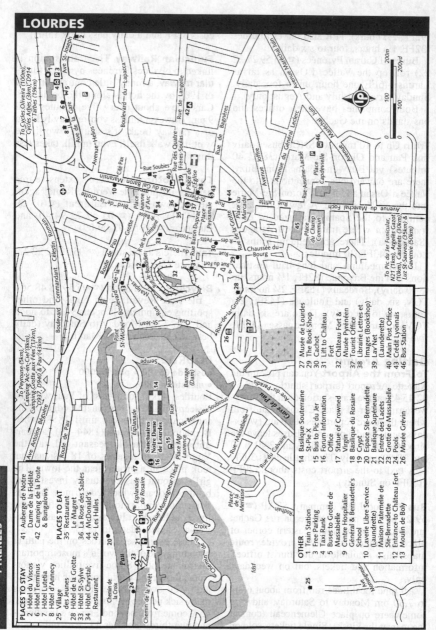

PLACES TO STAY
2 Hôtel du Viscos
6 Hôtel Terminus
7 Hôtel Lutelia
8 Hôtel d'Annecy
25 Village
  des Jeunes
28 Hôtel de la Grotte
33 Hôtel St-Sylve
34 Hôtel Chrystal;
  Restaurant
41 Auberge de Notre
  Dame de la Fidélité
42 Camping de la Poste
  & Bungalows

PLACES TO EAT
35 Restaurant
  Le Magret
36 La Rose des Sables
44 McDonald's
45 Les Halles

OTHER
1 Train Station
3 Free Parking
4 Taxi Rank
5 Buses to Grotte de
  Massabielle
9 Centre Hospitalier
  Général & Bernadette's
  School
10 Laverie Libre Service
  (Launderette)
11 Maison Paternelle de
  Ste-Bernadette
12 Entrance to Château Fort
13 Moulin de Boly
14 Basilique Souterraine
  St-Pie X
15 Bus to Pic du Jer
16 Forum Information
  Office
17 Statue of Crowned
  Virgin
18 Basilique du Rosaire
19 Crypt
20 Espace Ste-Bernadette
21 Basilique Supérieure
22 Entrée des Lacets
23 Grotte de Massabielle
24 Pools
26 Musée Grévin

27 Musée de Lourdes
29 The Book Shop
30 Cachot
31 Lift to Château
  Fort
32 Château Fort &
  Musée Pyrénéen
37 Tourist Office
38 Librairie Lettres et
  Images (Bookshop)
39 Lav'Net
  (Launderette)
40 Main Post Office
43 Crédit Lyonnais
46 Bus Station

PYRENEES

But accompanying the fervent, almost medieval piety of the pilgrims is an astounding display of unspeakably tacky commercial exuberance: wall thermometers, shake-up snow domes and plastic bottles in the shape of the Virgin (just add holy water at the shrine) are but a sample. It's dead easy to mock. Yet remember: some people have spent their life savings to come here; for many of the Catholic faithful, Lourdes is as sacred a place as the Wailing Wall in Jerusalem for Jews, Mecca for Muslims or the Ganges to Hindus.

Orientation

Lourdes' two main east-west streets are rue de la Grotte and, 300m north, blvd de la Grotte. Both lead to the Sanctuaires Notre Dame de Lourdes, the latter taking you over Pont St-Michel to the main entrance. The principal north–south thoroughfare, known as Chaussée Maransin when it passes above blvd de la Grotte, connects the train station with place Peyramale, where the tourist office is.

The huge religious complex that has grown up around the original cave where Bernadette's visions took place, is across the River Pau, west of the town centre.

Information

Tourist Offices The horseshoe-shaped glass-and-steel tourist office (☎ 05 62 42 77 40, fax 05 62 94 60 95, ☻ lourdes@sudfr.com) on place Peyramale opens 9 am to noon and 2 to 6 pm Monday to Saturday (7 pm between Easter and mid-October, when it also opens 10 am to 6 pm Sunday). There is no midday closure from June to September. The office sells a pass called Visa Passeport Touristique for 169FF (children under 12, 85FF) allowing admission to five museums in Lourdes and rides on the Pic du Jer funicular and the little train that circumnavigates the town.

Sanctuaries For information on the Sanctuaires Notre Dame de Lourdes, including brochures in a variety of languages, drop by the Forum Information office (☎ 05 62 42 78 78, ☻ saccueil@lourdes-france.com) on the Esplanade des Processions. It opens 8.30 am to 12.30 pm and 1.30 to 7.00 pm daily, April to mid-October; and 9 am to noon and 2 to 6 pm daily, the rest of the year. Visitors to the Sanctuaires should dress modestly – don't, for example, wear very short skirts or even shorts and a T-shirt. Smoking is strictly forbidden throughout the complex.

Post & Communications The main post office at 1 rue de Langelle has a Cyberposte and changes money.

Bookshops The Book Shop (☎/fax 05 62 42 27 94, ☻ lourdesbks@aol.com), at 5 rue du Bourg, carries a large stock of books in English relating to Lourdes plus novels, travel titles and a good stock of maps for walking the town's Pyrenean hinterland. Some walking maps are also available at Librairie Lettres et Images (☎ 05 62 94 00 29) at 7 rue St-Pierre.

Laundry The little Lav' Net, in an arcade opposite the post office, opens 8 am to 7 pm Monday to Saturday. Laverie Libre Service, opposite Hôtel Ibis, functions from 7 am to 7 pm daily.

Sanctuaires Notre Dame de Lourdes

The site of The Sanctuaries of Our Lady of Lourdes started to be developed within a decade of the events of 1858 (see the introduction to this section) and expansion has gone on ever since. You won't be alone if you find it difficult to understand how the gaudy late 19th-century architecture, more reminiscent of Disneyland than of the majesty of a Gothic cathedral, inspires awe and devotion, but clearly it does. The grounds can be entered 24 hours via the Entrée des Lacets on rue Monseigneur Theas. The Pont St-Michel entrance opens 5 am to midnight.

The most revered site in the complex is known variously as the **Grotte de Massabielle** (Massabielle Cave or Grotto), the Grotte Miraculeuse (Miraculous Cave) and the Grotte des Apparitions (Cave of the

Apparitions). Open round the clock, its walls are worn smooth by the touch of millions of hands over the years. Nearby are 17 **pools** – six for men, 11 for women – in which 400,000 people seeking to be healed immerse themselves each year. Miraculous cures are becoming rarer and rarer; the last medically certifiable case took place in 1987 and, after exhaustive investigation, was recognised by the church as a miracle in 1999.

The main 19th-century section of the Sanctuaries has three parts. On the western side of Esplanade du Rosaire, between the two ramps, is the neo-Byzantine **Basilique du Rosaire** (Basilica of the Rosary), inaugurated in 1889.

One level up is the **crypt**, opened in 1866 and reserved for silent worship. Above that is the spire-topped, neo-Gothic **Basilique Supérieure** (Upper Basilica), completed in 1876.

From Palm Sunday (the Sunday before Easter) to at least mid-October there are solemn **torch-light processions** nightly at 9.15pm from the Massabielle Grotto. The Procession Eucharistique (Blessed Sacrament Procession), in which groups of pilgrims carrying banners march along the Esplanade des Processions, takes place daily at 5 pm during the same period. When it's wet, the ceremony is held inside the bunker-like **Basilique Souterraine St-Pie X** (Underground Basilica of St Pius X), a bleak cave once described as a cross between a football stadium and an underground car park. With a length of 200m and 80m wide, it can hold 20,000 people. Built in 1959 in the fallout shelter-style then all the rage, it's redeemed to some extent by some fine, vibrantly warm back-lit works of *gemmail* – superimposed pieces of coloured glass embedded in colourless enamel.

All four places of worship open 6 am to 7 pm, between Easter and October; and 8 am to 6 pm, the rest of the year.

The modern complex north of the Massabielle Grotto, the **Espace Ste-Bernadette**, is where the sick and ailing receive assistance and have access to the distinctive covered wheelchairs in which volunteers convey them to the shrine.

Chemin de la Croix Also known as the Chemin du Calvaire (Way of Calvary), the 1.5km Way of the Cross leads up the forested hillside from near the Basilique Supérieure. Inaugurated in 1912, it is lined with life-size versions of the 14 Stations of the Cross. The especially devout mount the stairs to the first station on their knees. The path opens 6 to 8 am and 9.45 am to 6 pm in winter months; and 6 to 8.45 am and 9.45 am to 7pm, the rest of the year.

Other Bernadette Sites

Four other places that figured largely in the life of St-Bernadette are open to the public and charge no admission. Her birthplace, the **Moulin de Boly** (Boly Mill), is at 12 rue Bernadette Soubirous, reached by taking an alley beside 55 blvd de la Grotte. On the same road, the **Maison Paternelle de Ste-Bernadette** is the house that the town of Lourdes bought for the Soubirous family after the apparitions. The **Cachot**, a former prison at 15 rue des Petits Fossés, is where Bernadette lived during the apparitions. **Bernadette's school**, where she studied and lived from 1860 to 1866 with the Sœurs de Notre Dame de Nevers (Sisters of Our Lady of Nevers), is now part of the town's Centre Hospitalier Général. West of the train station on Chaussée Maransin, it contains some of her personal effects.

Musée Grévin

This commercial wax museum (☎ 05 62 94 33 74), at 87 rue de la Grotte, has life-size dioramas of important events in the lives of both Jesus Christ and Bernadette Soubirous. It opens 9 to 11.30 am and 1.30 to 6.30 pm daily, April to mid-November (also 8 to 10 pm during July and August). Admission costs 35FF (students 18FF).

Musée de Lourdes

The Lourdes Museum (☎ 05 62 94 28 00), due west of the Cinéma Pax in the Parking de l'Égalité, portrays the life of St-Bernadette as well as the general history of

Lourdes. It opens daily 9 am to noon and 1.30 to 6.45 pm. Admission costs 30FF (students 20FF).

Château Fort

The eyrie-like medieval Château Fort (Fortified Castle; ☎ 05 62 42 37 37), most of whose buildings date from the 17th and 18th centuries, houses a small **Musée Pyrénéen**. Both castle and museum open 9 am to noon and 2 to 6 pm Wednesday to Monday (longer afternoon hours in summer).

To take a lift up to the Château Fort, go to the entrance on rue Le Bondidier, opposite 42 rue du Fort. Otherwise, walk up the ramp at the northern end of rue du Bourg.

Pic du Jer

The Pic du Jer, whose 948m summit affords a splendid panoramic view of Lourdes and the central Pyrenees, can be reached by a six minute ride in a funicular. Its lower station is on blvd d'Espagne about 1.5km due south of the tourist office and is served by bus No 2. The funicular operates from 9.30 am to noon and 1.30 to 6.30 pm, April and October (afternoons only in April and October, continuously in July and August). A return ticket costs 44FF (children 22FF).

Alternatively, the walk (three hours return) to the top of Pic du Jer is quite pleasant. The trail starts near the lower station. You can get a bus to the base of the funicular from the stop on place Monseigneur Laurence.

Places to Stay

Since Lourdes has over 350 hotels – more than any other city in France but Paris – you shouldn't need our help to find one of the 32,000 available beds. This said, you may have to scout around during Easter, Whitsuntide, Ascension Day, during May and from August to the first week of October. Rooms are most difficult to find from about 12 to 17 August, when France's Pèlerinage Nationale (national pilgrimage) is held in honour of Assumption Day (15 August). In winter the town is very, very quiet and most hotels shut down.

Central streets with plenty of hotels include blvd de la Grotte, rue Basse, rue de la Fontaine, rue du Bourg, rue Baron Duprat and Chaussée du Bourg. Near the train station, there's a profusion along ave de la Gare, ave Helios and ave Maransin.

Places to Stay – Budget

Camping The tiny, friendly *Camping de la Poste* (☎ *05 62 94 40 35, 26 rue de Langelle)* is in the heart of town and consequently often full in summer. Open Easter to mid-October, it charges 15FF per person and 21FF for a tent site. It also rents a small number of excellent value rooms with bathroom for 150FF.

Camping Arc-en-Ciel (☎ *05 62 41 81 54)* in Peyrouse, 8km west of town along the D937, opens June to September and charges 45FF for two adults, tent and car. A farther 3km brings you to *Camping Grotte aux Fées* (☎ *05 62 41 81 63)* in St-Pé de Bigorre, which opens May to October and charges 26FF for the same package.

Between March and September (plus Christmas and in February, if you're hardy enough) pilgrims – but not curious tourists – can pitch a tent at *Village des Jeunes* (☎ *05 62 42 79 95,* 🄴 *village.jeunes@ lourdes france.com)*. This Youth Village, about 1km south-west of the Sanctuaries off ave Monseigneur Rodhain, charges 17FF per person.

Hostels Young pilgrims can stay at the *Village des Jeunes* (see Camping), which runs all sorts of group religious activities for young people. A dorm bed costs 27FF and one in a room, 35FF. Bring your own sheets or sleeping bag. Reception is staffed 24 hours.

Auberge de Notre Dame de la Fidélité (☎ *05 62 42 14 91, 15 rue Soubies)* offers B&B from 50FF to 75FF. Showers cost 8FF and the auberge's doors shut sharp at 9 pm.

Hotels Lourdes has a wide selection of cheap hotel rooms. Near the train station, the family-run *Hôtel du Viscos* (☎ *05 62 94 08 06, fax 05 62 94 26 74, 6 bis ave St-Joseph)* opens February to mid-December.

PYRENEES

Unadorned singles/doubles cost 100/160FF with washbasin and bidet and 130/200FF with bathroom. Hall showers are free.

The friendly *Hôtel d'Annecy* (☎ 05 62 94 13 75, 13 ave de la Gare) opens from the week before Easter to late October. Spruce and set back from the road, it charges 95/ 152/176/198FF for plain singles/doubles/ triples/quads with washbasin (140/195/ 215/223FF for ones with shower and toilet). Hall showers cost 10FF.

Nearby, *Hôtel Lutetia* (☎ 05 62 94 22 85, fax 05 62 94 11 10, 19, ave de la Gare) opens mid-March to mid-November. Ordinary singles/doubles cost 100/135FF with washbasin (from 200/218FF with bathroom). Hall showers cost 18FF.

On the same street, *Hôtel Terminus* (☎ 05 62 94 68 00, fax 05 62 42 23 89, 31 ave de la Gare) opens Easter to mid-November. Singles/doubles cost 140/170FF with washbasin and bidet (170/190FF with shower and toilet). There are also a few triples at 220FF.

In the town centre, *Hôtel St-Sylve* (☎/fax 05 62 94 63 48, 9 rue de la Fontaine) has large singles/doubles with washbasin for 75/140FF (100/160FF with shower). It opens April to October.

Places to Stay – Mid-Range & Top End

In the town centre, *Hôtel Chrystal* (☎ 05 62 94 00 36, fax 05 62 94 80 32, 16 rue Basse) has singles/doubles/triples for 130/140/ 200FF with shower (140/160/210FF with full bathroom). It opens from February to October.

One of the more stylish places in town (and priced accordingly) is the *fin de siècle Hôtel de la Grotte* (☎ 05 62 94 58 87, fax 05 62 94 20 50, 66 rue de la Grotte) with balconies and a gorgeous garden. Singles/doubles with all mod-cons start at 390/420FF and it opens April to October.

Places to Eat

Restaurants Most hotels offer pilgrims half- or full-board; some even require guests to stay on those terms, especially in the high season. It usually works out

cheaper than eating outside but the food is seldom very inspiring. Restaurants close early in this pious town; even *McDonald's* (7 place du Marcadal) is slammed shut at 10.30 pm.

Restaurant le Magret (☎ 05 62 94 20 55, 10 rue des Quatre Frères Soulas), opposite the tourist office, has versatile a la carte dishes and *menus* at 80FF and 150FF, both excellent value for money. It opens daily except Monday. Next door *La Rose des Sables* (☎ 05 62 42 06 82), a North African restaurant – and a bold Muslim presence in this fervently Catholic town – specialises in couscous (from 78FF). It opens daily except Monday. For something even more exotic, try a spicy dish from the Indian Ocean island of La Réunion at the restaurant of *Hôtel Chrystal* (see Places to Stay), which also serves French cuisine. Count on about 100FF for a three-course meal.

Self-Catering The *covered market* (place du Champ Commun), south of the tourist office, opens 7 am to 1 pm Monday to Saturday (daily, Easter to October).

Getting There & Away

Bus The bus station, down rue Anselme Lacadé east of the covered market, has services northwards to Pau (32FF, 1¼ hours, four to six daily) and Tarbes (22FF, 30 minutes, over 10 daily) and south to Argelès-Gazost (14FF, 20 minutes, over 10 daily), on the way to the Pyrenean communities of Cauterets, Luz-St-Sauveur and Gavarnie.

SNCF buses to Cauterets (39FF, one hour, five daily), and to Luz-St-Sauveur (40FF, one hour, six daily) leave from the train station. Some services require a change in Pierrefitte-Nestelas.

Train The train station is about 1km east of the Sanctuaries.

Since so many pilgrims arrive by rail, Lourdes is well connected by train to cities all over France, including Bayonne (106FF, three to four daily, 1¾ hours), Bordeaux (172FF, six daily, 2½ hours), Pau (39FF, 30 minutes, over 10 daily) and Toulouse (125FF, 2¼ hours, seven daily). There are five TGVs daily to Paris' Gare Montparnasse (478FF, six hours) and one overnight train to the capital's Gare d'Austerlitz (409FF, nine hours).

Getting Around

Bus From 1 April to mid-October, local bus No 1 links the train station (the stop is beside Hôtel Terminus) with the Grotte de Massabielle. A ride costs 11FF (6FF from the station to the centre of town). Buses run every 15 minutes from 7.30 to noon and 1.30 to 6.30 pm.

Car & Motorcycle Lourdes is one big, fuming traffic jam in summer. If you have a vehicle, your best bet is to leave it near either the train or bus station, where there's free parking, and walk.

Taxi There's a taxi stand (☎ 05 62 94 31 30) outside the train station.

Bicycle Between May and August, Cycles Oliveira (☎ 05 62 42 24 24) at 14 ave Alexandre Marqui rents VTTs for 70/110/450FF per half-day/day/week and town bikes for 60/100/400FF. Opposite Leclerc supermarket at 51 bis ave Alexandre Marqui, Cycles Arbes (☎ 05 62 94 05 51) hires out VTTs at identical rates and town bikes for 35/50/100FF, year round.

ARREAU

postcode 65240 • pop 840 • elevation 750m
Arreau snuggles at the confluence of the Rivers Neste du Louron and Neste d'Aure. Equidistant from the Mediterranean and the Atlantic and straddling a former trade route with Spain, it prospered as the ancient capital of four valleys. Buildings such as the Renaissance **Maison des Lys** and the Romanesque **Church of St-Exupère** recall this wealth. In the **Château de Nestes** are the tourist office (☎ 05 62 98 63 15) and a small, free museum of Pyrenean craftwork. Both open 9.30 am to noon and 2 to 5.30 pm Tuesday to Saturday (daily except Sunday afternoon in July and August).

There are two to three SNCF buses daily between Lannezan and Arreau.

GAVARNIE

postcode 65120 • pop 165
• elevation 1360m
In winter, Gavarnie, 52km south of Lourdes at the end of the D921, offers limited downhill and cross-country skiing plus snowshoe treks. In summer, it's a popular take-off point for walkers. And take off they do, as quickly as their feet will carry them: by 10 am the village and its tawdry souvenir stalls are overrun. Consult the IGN Top 25 map *Gavarnie, Luz-St-Sauveur* (59FF) or the national park booklet *Randonnées dans le Parc National des Pyrénées: Vallée de Luz* (40FF) for the rich menu of routes.

The most frequented trail, accessible to all, leads to the Cirque de Gavarnie, a breathtaking rock amphitheatre, 1500m high, dominated by ice-capped peaks and measuring 14km around the crest line. The round-trip walk to its foot takes around two hours (or hire a horse or donkey for 100FF). In mid-July Gavarnie hosts an arts festival in the dramatic setting of the Cirque.

The tourist office and National Park office (☎ for both 05 62 92 49 10) open 9 am to midday and 1.30 to 6.30 pm Monday to Saturday (shorter hours on Sunday).

Camping Le Pain de Sucre (☎ 05 62 92 47 55) opens mid-December to mid-April and June to September. It charges 45FF for car, tent and two people.

Two buses daily operate between Lourdes and Gavarnie (70FF) in summer only.

AROUND GAVARNIE
Cirque de Troumouse

From Gèdre, 6.5km north of Gavarnie, a winding toll road (25FF per vehicle) heads south-east up a desolate valley back into the Pyrenees. It leads to the base of the Cirque de Troumouse, wilder, infinitely less trodden and almost as stunning as the Cirque de Gavarnie. Snows permitting, the road is open between May and October.

Luz-St-Sauveur

postcode 65120 • pop 1200
• elevation 711m
Luz-St-Sauveur, on the D921 and 12km north of Gèdre, developed as a spa town in

PYRENEES

the 19th century. Nowadays, it's a small, bustling winter and summer vacation centre. Its bastion-like late 12th-century Templar church is enclosed by a 14th-century crenellated defensive wall constructed by the Knights of St-John of Jerusalem. Between May and October, Les Thermes health spa (☎ 05 62 92 81 58) offers a variety of sybaritic relaxation and fitness programmes (from 40FF). The tourist office (☎ 05 62 92 30 30) is on place du 8 mai at the heart of the village.

PARC NATIONAL DES PYRÉNÉES

The Pyrenees National Park stretches for about 100km along the Franco-Spanish border from the Vallée d'Aspe in the west to the Vallée d'Aure in the east. Its width varies from 1.5 to 15km. Created in 1967, it covers an area of 457 sq km, within which are 230 lakes and Vignemale, whose summit, at 3298m, is the highest in the French Pyrenees. To the south, over the border, is Spain's 156 sq km Parque Nacional de Ordesa y Monte Perdido, with whom the park collaborates closely.

Its many streams are fed by both springs and some 2000mm of annual precipitation, much of which falls as snow. The French slopes, especially the western section, are much wetter and greener than the dun-coloured Spanish side.

The vast and varied park is exceptionally rich in both fauna and plant life (over 150 species of flora are endemic). Keep glancing up; its wilder reaches rank among the best places in Europe to see large birds of prey such as golden eagles, griffon and bearded vultures, booted eagles, buzzards and falcons.

The animal population includes 42 of France's 110 species of mammal. Particularly look out for marmots – or rather listen out for their distinctive whistle. Having become extinct in the Pyrenees, they were successfully reintroduced from the Alps, where they thrive, in the 1950s. Another success story is that of the izard, a close relative of the chamois which was all but blasted out of existence half a century ago, in the main by firearms left over from

---

A Degrading Process

Decomposition, always slow, is even more protracted in the high mountains. Typical times are:

paper handkerchief: 3 months
apple core: up to 6 months
cigarette butt: 3 to 5 years
wad of chewing gum: 5 years
lighter: 100 years
plastic bag: 450 years
aluminium can: up to 500 years
plastic bottle: up to 1000 years
glass bottle: up to 4000 years

Make sure that whatever you bring to the mountains leaves with you.

WWII. Nowadays, thanks to careful control and monitoring, the park is home to about 5000 and numbers on both sides of the Pyrenees chain exceed 20,000. By contrast, brown bears (see the boxed text 'Pyrenean Bears' later in this chapter), once numerous, are now extremely scarce; indeed, it's possible that the last survivors may have disappeared by the time you read this.

Each year, the park receives over two million visitors, 80% of whom increase the pressure upon three beleaguered sites: the Cirque de Gavarnie, Pont d'Espagne above Cauterets and the Réserve Naturelle de Néouvielle in the eastern sector.

Park boundaries are marked by paintings (on rocks, trees etc) of a red *izard* (chamois) head on a white background.

Information

National Park Offices There are national park offices with visitors centres at Arrens-Marsous, Cauterets, Etsaut, Laruns (due to open in 2001), Gavarnie, Luz-St-Sauveur and St-Lary-Soulon. Most – though not the Cauterets or Gavarnie ones – are closed during the cold half of the year. The park headquarters (☎ 05 62 44 36 60, fax 05 62 44 36 70) is at 59 route de Pau, 65000 Tarbes.

PYRENEES

Maps & Books Each of the six valleys of the national park is covered by a folder containing 10 to 15 walking itineraries in French entitled *Randonnées dans le Parc National des Pyrénées*. Costing 42FF and worthwhile for the route maps alone, they're on sale at local park and tourist offices.

The park is covered by IGN 1:25,000 maps Nos 1547OT (*Ossau*), 1647OT (*Vignemale*), 1748OT (*Gavarnie*) and 1748ET (*Néouvielle*). Each costs 59FF.

The Pyrenees chapter in Lonely Planet's *Walking in France* centres upon the Vallée d'Aspe and Vallée de Cauterets. It describes in detail a variety of day walks plus a three-day tour in and around the valleys and gives suggestions for more extended treks in the Pyrenees.

Fleurs des Pyrénées Faciles à Reconnaître (Easily Recognised Flowers of the Pyrenees; 49FF) by Philippe Mayoux, published by Rando Éditions, is a handy, well-illustrated pocket guide in French.

Walking
The Parc National des Pyrénées is crisscrossed by 350km of waymarked trails (including the Mediterranean to Atlantic GR10), some of which link up with trails in Spain. For walking suggestions, see the Walking sections within both Cauterets and Vallée d'Aspe in this chapter.

The park has about 20 *refuges* (mountain huts or lodges), five belonging to the park and the majority run by the Club Alpin Français (CAF). Most are staffed only from July to September but retain a small wing open year round.

Skiing
The Pyrenees receive less snow than the much higher Alps, and what snow falls is generally wetter and heavier. Despite this, there's reasonable alpine skiing and snowboarding for beginners and intermediates. The potential for cross-country skiing, ski touring and, increasingly, snowshoeing, is also quite good. The ski season normally lasts from December to early April, depending upon snow conditions.

Ski Resorts Ski resorts dot both sides of the Pyrenees. France alone has over 20 downhill ski stations – most of them quite modest – and more than 10 cross-country areas.

One of the oldest resorts is Cauterets, which usually has the longest season and most reliable snow conditions. The largest is the combined resort of Barèges-La Mongie (tourist office ☎ 05 62 92 16 00), 39km south-east of Lourdes, with 64 runs and over 50 lifts.

For some of the best cross-country skiing, head for Val d'Azun (tourist office ☎ 05 62 97 49 49 in Arrens-Marsous), about 30km south-west of Lourdes. It has 110km of trails between 1350m and 1600m.

CAUTERETS
postcode 65110 • pop 1200
• elevation 930m

The attractive thermal spa and ski resort of Cauterets nestles in a tight valley, crowded in by steep slopes rising to 2800m. In summer, it makes a superb base for exploring the forests, meadows, lakes and streams of Parc National des Pyrénées – though in July and August the trails nearer town can be very crowded. In winter, Cauterets is blessed with an abundance of snow; it's usually the first of France's Pyrenean ski stations to open and the last to close. Lourdes, the gateway to Cauterets, is less than 30km to the north.

Orientation
Cauterets spreads for about 1km alongside its slim river, the Gave de Cauterets. The main road from Lourdes, the D920, becomes Route de Pierrefitte as it enters town, taking you straight to place de la Gare, bordered by the bus station and national park office with, just above it, Téléphérique du Lys, the cable car that rises 1850m to the Cirque du Lys.

Information
Tourist Offices The tourist office (☎ 05 62 92 50 27, fax 05 62 92 59 12, ✉ espaces .cauterets@cauterets.com) on place Maréchal Foch opens 9 am to 12.30 pm and 2 to

6.30 pm Monday to Saturday (daily and longer afternoon hours in July and August). There's also a small branch office (☎ 05 62 92 52 19) at Pont d'Espagne (see the Walking section), open year round except mid-October to mid-November.

National Park Office The Maison du Parc National des Pyrénées (☎ 05 62 92 52 56), place de la Gare, opens 9.30 am till noon and 3.30 to 6.30 pm daily except Thursday and Sunday afternoons and all Wednesday. Afternoon hours are 3 to 7 pm daily from June to September. One of the few park offices that doesn't close in the off season, it also houses an impressive free exhibition on Pyrenean flora and fauna and shows films on the park at 5.30 pm daily except Wednesday and Sunday. In July and August it arranges guided walks (100FF).

Maps The area west of Cauterets is covered by IGN's 1:25,000 scale Top 25 map No 1647OT, *Vignemale, Ossau, Arrens, Cauterets*; the area east of town features on No 1748OT, *Gavarnie, Luz-St-Sauveur*. Each costs 59FF. Rando Éditions' map No 4, *Bigorre*, also covers the area at 1:50,000. You can pick up these and more at Maison du Parc National or Maison de la Presse, 8 place Maréchal Foch, opposite the tourist office.

The Maison du Parc also sells *Promenades dans le Parc National des Pyrénées: Vallée de Cauterets* (42FF), an excellent pack describing, in French, 15 walking itineraries. You can consult it for free and the friendly staff are knowledgeable about local trails. The tourist office carries *Cauterets à Deux Pas* (35FF), a slim volume describing eight short, easy walks around Cauterets.

Laundry The laundrette at 19 rue Richelieu opens 7 am to 10 pm daily. The one opposite Hôtel César opens 9 am to 8 pm Monday to Saturday.

Walking

Cauterets makes a particularly good base for day walks since so many start right from town or from Pont d'Espagne at the end of the spectacular D920 road, 8km south, 600m higher and accessible in season by bus.

For a week's worth of stimulating walking in the area, consult Lonely Planet's *Walking in France* (see Maps & Books under Parc National des Pyrénées earlier in this chapter).

Around Cauterets To gain height painlessly from Cauterets, take one of the cabin lifts that continue to run in summer. For information on the Téléphérique du Lys, see the Getting Around section.

One of the most stimulating lower level walks is along the steep Val de Jéret between Cauterets and Pont d'Espagne. From Cauterets follow Chemin des Pères to the hamlet of La Raillère, then strike southwest up chemin des Cascades, which passes by a series of spectacular waterfalls. Allow two to three hours, uphill – or do it the easy way by taking the shuttle bus from Cauterets to Pont d'Espagne and walking downhill.

For a pleasant day trip, follow the GR10 south-westwards as far as **Lac d'Ilhéou** (1988m) with its *refuge* (☎ 05 62 92 75 07) which is staffed late May to mid October. A walk southwards from town, up the Vallée du Lutour as far as the waterfalls at **Cascades de Lutour**, makes an enjoyable half-dayer.

From Pont d'Espagne From the giant car park at Pont d'Espagne (for information about bus access see Getting Around later in this section) you've a choice of two valleys, each different in character.

Following the Gave de Gaube upstream through a pine wood brings you to the popular **Lac de Gaube** and, nearby, *Hôtellerie de Gaube* which does drinks, snacks and midday *menus*. Three hours, not counting breaks, is generous for this out-and-back walk.

Alternatively, a longer trek up the gentler, more open **Vallée de Marcadau** leads to *Refuge Wallon* (1866m, ☎ 05 62 92 64 28), staffed March to early November. Allow about five hours for the round trip.

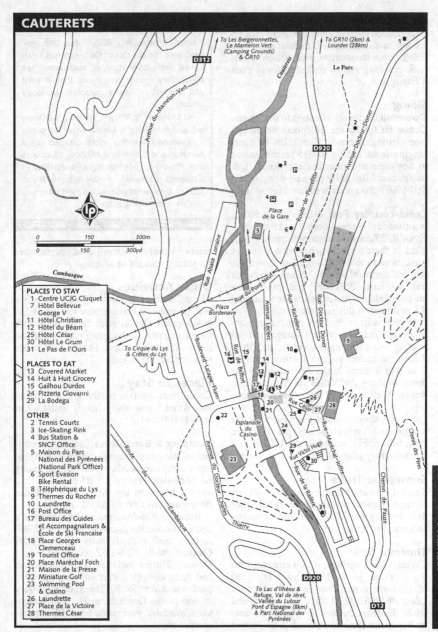

CAUTERETS

To Les Bergeronnettes,
Le Mamelon Vert
(Camping Grounds)
& GR10

To GR10 (2km) &
Lourdes (28km)

Le Parc

D312

D920

Avenue du Mamelon-Vert

Cauterets

Avenue-Docteur-Domer

Route-de-Pierrefitte

Place de la Gare

Cambasque

Rue Alsace Lorraine

Rue du Pont Neuf

Rue Richelieu

Rue Docteur Domer

PLACES TO STAY
1 Centre UCJG Cluquet
7 Hôtel Bellevue George V
11 Hôtel Christian
12 Hôtel du Béarn
25 Hôtel César
30 Hôtel Le Grum
31 Le Pas de l'Ours

PLACES TO EAT
13 Covered Market
14 Huit à Huit Grocery
15 Gailhou Durdos
24 Pizzeria Giovanni
29 La Bodega

OTHER
2 Tennis Courts
3 Ice-Skating Rink
4 Bus Station & SNCF Office
5 Maison du Parc National des Pyrénées (National Park Office)
6 Sport Évasion Bike Rental
8 Téléphérique du Lys
9 Thermes du Rocher
10 Laundrette
16 Post Office
17 Bureau des Guides et Accompagnateurs & École de Ski Francaise
18 Place Georges Clemenceau
19 Tourist Office
20 Place Maréchal Foch
21 Place Maréchal Foch
22 Miniature Golf
23 Swimming Pool & Casino
26 Laundrette
27 Place de la Victoire
28 Thermes César

Place Bordenave

To Cirque du Lys & Crêtes du Lys

Boulevard-Lacappe-Flumn

Rue de Belfort

Avenue Leclerc

Rue Césaire

Rue-Maréchal-Joffre

Chemin des Pères

Esplanade du Casino

Route du Cambasque

Avenue du Docteur Charles

Rue Victor Hugo

L'Aure-de-la-Raillère

Chemin de Pauze

Thierry

D920

D12

To Lac d'Ilhéou &
Refuge, Val de Jéret,
Vallée du Lutour
Pont d'Espagne (8km)
& Parc National des
Pyrénées

0   150   300m
0   150   300yd

PYRENEES

Rock Climbing

Experienced climbers might want to pick up a copy of *Cauterets – L'Escalade en Tête* (30FF) from the tourist office, which details rock climbing routes up the cliffs at Pont d'Espagne.

Skiing

Downhill Cauterets is linked to the 23-run **Cirque du Lys** by the Téléphérique du Lys (see Getting Around). The 36km of runs, ranging from 1850m to 2350m, are suited to beginner and intermediate skiers. Lift passes cost 110/135FF per half-day/day and 560/690FF for six days in low/high season.

Cross-country Pont d'Espagne (1500m) is primarily a cross-country skiing area. From it, 37km of maintained trails, paralleled in their lower reaches by a piste for walkers and snowshoers, lead up the attractive Vallée du Marcadau. A one-day/week trail pass costs 35/170FF. For information on bus links with Cauterets, see Getting Around later in this section.

In the valleys and on the ridges surrounding Cauterets there's some good ski touring for experienced skiers and Pont d'Espagne makes a good starting point. A 7km tour – three hours up and one hour down – along the Vallée de Marcadau to Refuge Wallon makes a good introductory trip.

Several shops around town hire out ski equipment. Typical prices per day are downhill 55FF, snowboards 100FF and cross-country gear 50FF.

Snowshoe Treks

Several mountain guides organise winter outings. Typical prices are 110/150FF per half day/day plus 30FF for hire of snowshoes and poles.

Thermal Spa

Cauterets' hot springs, which emerge from the earth at 36 to 53°C, have attracted *curistes* since the 19th century. Thermes César (☎ 05 62 92 51 60) opens year round while Thermes du Rocher (same tel) normally opens June to August. The former

A Little Sweetener

Halitosis is never fun. Back in the 19th century, once the *curistes* of Cauterets had swallowed their daily dose of sulphurous spa water, they – and, even more, their nearest and dearest – would complain of dog's breath.

An enterprising villager, spotting a chance, set about making a boiled sweet or candy that would mask the odour. Shaped like a humbug and made in a rainbow of colours and flavours, *berlingots*, a speciality of Cauterets, are readily on sale in town. If you happen by a sweet shop at the right time, you can see them being made.

offers a variety of water-based programmes for weary walkers or skiers.

Other Activities

About 200m south-west of the tourist office is Esplanade du Casino, also known as Esplanade des Oeufs, with cafes, an indoor swimming pool, a miniature golf course and the town's large casino. There's also an ice rink at place de la Gare.

Places to Stay

Cheap beds are thin on the ground in July and August and many hotels insist on at least half-board.

Camping & Bungalows There are a number of camping grounds slightly north of town along ave du Mamelon Vert, including *Le Mamelon Vert* (☎/fax 05 62 92 51 56), open January to late September and *Les Bergeronnettes* (☎ 05 62 92 50 69).

Between mid-June and mid-September, a bed in a dormitory tent costs 40FF (50FF under a roof) at the friendly *Centre UCJG Cluquet* (☎ 05 62 92 52 95, Ave Docteur Domer). The fee includes use of the shower and fully equipped kitchen. You can also pitch a tent here for 20FF per person or stay in one of the five extremely basic bungalows, available year round for 55FF per person per night.

PYRENEES

Gîtes d'Étape The welcoming *Pas de l'Ours* (☎ 05 62 92 58 07, fax 05 62 92 06 49, **@** le.pas.de.l-ours@wanadoo.fr, *21 rue de la Raillère*) is both hotel and gîte. Both wings open May to mid-October and December to mid-April. A dorm bed costs 70FF, including use of the kitchen, while, on the hotel side, doubles with bathroom start at 240FF. All guests can use the sauna (45FF).

Hotels At *Hôtel du Béarn* (☎ 05 62 92 53 54, *4 ave Leclerc*), has plain but large basic doubles for 140FF (165FF with bathroom) and triples for 215FF. Hall showers cost 6FF. It closes October to mid-December.

The friendly *Hôtel Le Grum* (☎ 05 62 92 53 01, fax 05 62 92 64 99, *4 rue Victor Hugo*) offers rooms for one/two/three/four people, all with bathroom, for 150/190/210/240FF. It closes November to mid-December.

Hôtel Christian (☎ 05 62 92 50 04, fax 05 62 92 05 67, *10 rue Richelieu*) opens February to September and has big singles/doubles for 185/220FF with washbasin and bidet (215/225FF with shower and 241/302FF with bathroom). Triples/quads with bathroom are also available for 400/482FF. All prices include breakfast and use of hall showers.

At *Hôtel César* (☎ 05 62 92 52 57, fax 05 62 92 08 19, *3 rue César*), attractive rooms, all with bathroom and TV, start at 230FF. It opens year round except May and October. The venerable *Hôtel Bellevue Georges V* (☎ 05 62 92 50 21, fax 05 62 92 62 54, *place de la Gare*) has singles/doubles/triples costing from 210/260/335FF.

Places to Eat

Restaurants Good areas for restaurant-hunting are rue de la Raillère, place Maréchal Foch and rue Richelieu.

Pizzeria Giovanni (☎ 05 62 92 57 80, *5 rue de la Raillère*) opens mid-June to early November and mid-December to mid-May. Except during school holidays, it often opens evenings only. Pizzas cost between 44FF and 53FF, there's a *menu* for 85FF and the home-cooked desserts are a dream.

A nice touch is clients being able to check out their emails for free. Up the road at No 12, *La Bodega* (☎ 05 62 92 60 21) does tapas starting at 45FF and excellent value *menus* at 65FF and 85FF.

Self-Catering The covered market on ave Leclerc opens 7 am to 12.30 pm and 4 pm (3.30 pm in summer) to 7.30 pm daily except Sunday afternoon. Just inside, a stall does tasty takeaway regional dishes such as *garbure* (a local pork-based soup so thick with vegetables and pulses that your spoon can almost stand vertical), cassoulet and Basque chicken – plus 30 kinds of pizza. Just follow your nose. *Gailhou Durdos*, opposite the post office, has a rich selection of local wines and specialities.

Getting There & Away

The last train steamed out of Cauterets' grand all-wood station in 1947. Looking like a cross between a western movie set and a giant cuckoo clock, it now serves as the bus station (☎ 05 62 92 53 70). SNCF buses run between it and Lourdes train station (39FF, one hour) six times daily (nine during school holidays). The last bus for Lourdes leaves at 7.25 pm (5.50 pm on Sunday).

Getting Around

Bus Navettes Pont d'Espagne is a shuttle service between Cauterets' bus station and Pont d'Espagne (20FF one way, 35FF return). During the ski season, buses leave Cauterets at 9.30 and 10.30 am plus 2 pm. The last bus descends from Pont d'Espagne at 5.30 pm. In summer, there are six departures from each end daily, starting at 8 am from Cauterets and finishing with a 7 pm departure from Pont d'Espagne.

Taxi For a taxi, call Monsieur Houssat on ☎ 05 62 92 61 62 or ☎ 06 12 91 83 19. Excursions Bordenave (☎ 05 62 92 53 68) also runs a taxi service. The one-way fare is 70FF to Pont d'Espagne, 230FF to Lourdes and 400FF to Gavarnie.

Bicycle Year round, the friendly folk at Sport Évasion (☎ 05 62 92 05 85), 3 route

PYRENEES

de Pierrefitte, rent both VTTs and tourers for 78/98/450FF per half-day/day/week.

Cable Car The Téléphérique du Lys cable car operates from mid-June to mid-September and from December to the end of the ski season. It rises over 900m to the Cirque du Lys, where you can catch the Grand Barbat chair lift up to Crêtes du Lys (2400m). The one-way/return trip costs 46/56FF to Crêtes du Lys or 30/40FF as far as Cirque du Lys. Transporting a mountain bike to the top costs 45FF one way. The last ascent allowing you to get back to Cauterets by nightfall is at 4.30 pm.

VALLÉE D'ASPE

The River Aspe (Gave d'Aspe) flows for some 60km from the Col du Somport, which marks the frontier with Spain, down to Oloron-Ste-Marie. Fewer than 3000 people live in the 13 villages of the valley, whose upper reaches have always been among the remotest corners of the French Pyrenees and one of the final refuges of their more timid wildlife.

The Vallée d'Aspe has been a trans-Pyrenean passage ever since Julius Caesar's Roman legionaries marched through. Completed in 1928, a railway line, a small masterpiece of engineering, forged its way up the valley before tunnelling through to meet the Spanish railhead at Canfranc. Services stopped abruptly when a bridge collapsed one day in 1970 and the railway, still visible for most of its length, has been allowed to rust away.

These days, the valley is an environmental battleground. From the Col du Somport, the ever busier N134 highway runs along its length. European Union (EU) planners have designated it the E7 and both they and powerful commercial interests see it becoming a major road link between Spain and France. Opposition has been intense, both locally and nationally. Local resistance is spearheaded by a cooperative, La Goutte d'Eau (the Drop of Water), headed by eco-activist Éric Petetin, which also functions as a gîte d'étape (see Lescun later in this section). Members occupy, appropriately and

with the grudging consent of SNCF, the train station at Cette-Eygun, 2km south of the ill-fated bridge at l'Estanguet.

Information

Tourist Offices The friendly and well-informed tourist office in Bedous (☎ 05 59 34 71 48, fax 05 59 34 52 51, ✉ aspe .tourisme@wanadoo.fr) covers the whole of the valley. In the main square, place François Sarraillé, it shares premises with the town hall and opens 9.30 am to 12.30 pm and 2 to 6 pm Monday to Saturday. In July and August, it maintains a subsidiary office, open daily except Sunday afternoon, in the town hall of Urdos, higher up the valley.

National Parks Office Refer to Etsaut, later in this section.

Maps The 1:50,000 scale *Béarn: Pyrénées* sheet No 3, published by Rando Éditions, is a practical general walking map of the area. A more detailed option is IGN's 1:25,000 scale Top 25 map No 1547OT *Ossau, Vallée d'Aspe* (59FF).

There are two handy trekking titles, useful for their maps alone even if your French reading skills aren't too hot. The tourist office in Bedous has *Paysage de Lumière sur les Sentiers de la Vallée d'Aspe* (the name may change with the publication of a new edition that's being prepared as we write). Costing 30FF, it describes 40 walks of varying difficulty within the Vallée d'Aspe. The National Park's *Randonnées dans le Parc National des Pyrénées: Aspe* (40FF) is a pack of information sheets on 10 more demanding treks, varying from 1½ to eight hours, in and around the valley. Although they're rich in information, you need to have one of the above maps in your pack to navigate with confidence.

Getting There & Away

SNCF buses and trains connect Pau and Oloron-Ste-Marie about six times daily (see Getting There & Away in the Pau section). From the latter, there are onward bus connections into the valley, via Bedous (28FF) to Estout (33FF, 50 minutes, three to four daily), most of which continue to Somport and the Spanish railhead of Canfranc (78FF, 1¼ hours). The last bus down the valley leaves Etsaut at 8.10 pm on weekdays (5.30 pm at weekends).

Bedous

Bedous, the valley's biggest village – with, despite this superlative, under 600 inhabitants – is 25km south of Oloron-Ste-Marie. Confidently planted where the valley's still wide, it's the starting point for some good lower-elevation walks and a good place to stock up on food. Librairie d'Aspe on rue de la Caserne has a good selection of walking maps.

Walking & Cycling The prettiest short walk from Bedous is eastwards, following the lightly trafficked D237 upstream beside the tumbling River Gabarret to tiny Aydius, 7km to the east. From there, follow signs to Plateau d'Ourdinse for excellent views up and down the valley, then descend steeply to return to your starting point. Aydius has a gîte d'étape and a good restaurant which makes an excellent lunch stop (see Places to Stay & Eat).

Prefer hands-in-pockets walking? The folk at Le Choucas Blanc (see Places to Stay & Eat) rent donkeys for 200FF per day and can advise on the best of the local trails.

VTT Nature (☎ 05 59 34 75 25, fax 05 59 34 75 77), on the N134 just south of town, rents VTTs for 60/100/300FF per half-day/day/week and are also knowledgeable about mountain bike routes in and around the valley. Guided trips with/without your own bike cost 180/250FF per day, including transport to start and from finish.

Places to Stay & Eat About 300m west of the N134, *Camping Municipal de Carolle* (☎ 05 59 34 70 45 or ☎ 05 59 34 59 19 in July and August), opens March to November and charges 38FF for two adults, tent and car.

The friendly gîte d'étape *Le Choucas Blanc* (☎ 05 59 34 53 71, fax 05 59 34 50 86, ✉ choucas.blanc@wanadoo.fr, 4 rue *Gambetta)* has beds for 48FF (plus 5FF on the first night for an obligatory six-month membership card). Half-board costs 110FF, a packed lunch costs 30FF and use of the kitchen is free. Another gîte d'étape, *Le Mandragot* (☎ 05 59 34 59 33) on the main square, charges 50FF per bed or 140FF half-board. Both are open year-round. *Chez Michel* on rue Gambetta does a hearty *menu* for 55FF.

It would be worth making a 50km detour to dig into the sumptuous 60FF *menu* at *Restaurant des Cols* (☎ 05 59 34 70 25) – happily a mere 6km east of Bedous in the hamlet of Aydius (see Walking & Cycling earlier in this section). Try their hearty garbure. They also have simple double rooms including breakfast for 210FF.

Accous

Accous, 2.5km south of Bedous and 800m to the east of the highway, sits at the yawning mouth of the Vallée Berthe with a splendid backdrop of 2000m-plus peaks. North of here, the Vallée d'Aspe is broad and fertile. To the south, it closes in dramatically.

Beside the N134 is the Fermiers Basco-Bernais cheese centre (☎ 05 59 34 76 06), at once museum and interpretive centre, farmers' cooperative and thriving from agerie. It has a free audiovisual presentation and sampling plus the opportunity to buy the best of local ewe, goat and cows' milk cheeses. It opens 9 am to midday and 2 to 6 pm on weekdays (afternoons only at weekends).

Activities Tiny Accous has not one but two parapente schools. École de Parapente Ascendance (☎ 05 59 34 52 07, fax 05 59 34 53 33) offers accompanied introductory flights for 350FF and five-day induction courses for 2200FF plus board and lodging. From October to June it opens at weekends only. Abelio (☎/fax 05 59 34 58 07, ✉ abelio@abelio.com) has similar prices and opens year round.

From Easter to November, hiring a horse at the Auberge Cavalière (see Places to Stay & Eat) costs 260/415FF for a half-day/day ride. The auberge also offers walking

PYRENEES

holidays, supplying detailed maps for circular day walks.

Places to Stay & Eat Behind the Fermiers Basco-Béarnais cheese museum and just off the N134, *Camping Despourrins* (☎ 05 59 34 71 16) opens March to October and costs 15FF per adult and 17FF per site. At the gîte d'étape *Maison Despourrins* (☎ 05 59 34 53 50), open year round, beds are 60FF and half-board is 160FF.

Hôtel Le Permayou (☎ 05 59 34 72 15, fax 05 59 34 72 68) opens April to October and offers doubles with bathroom from 230FF and good *menus* from 70FF. About 3km south of Accous and just off the highway, the well-established *Auberge Cavalière* (☎ 05 59 34 72 30, fax 05 59 34 51 97) opens year-round. It has doubles with bathroom for 240FF and a cosy restaurant where *menus* start at about 100FF.

Lescun
About 4km south of Bedous is the bridge at l'Estanguet whose collapse in 1970 finished off the valley's train traffic. Here also is the junction with the D340 and a chance to take a steeply hairpinned 5.5km detour south west, up and out of the main valley, to the mountain village of Lescun (900m), whose slate roofs once sheltered a leper colony. It's worth a touch of vertigo on the ascent for the breathtaking, photogenic view westwards of the Cirque de Lescun, an amphitheatre of jagged limestone mountains, backed by the 2504m Pic d'Anie.

Walking Several fine walks radiate from Lescun. For spectacular views back over the Lescun Valley and the distinctive Pic du Midi d'Ossau, follow the GR10 north-west via the Refuge de Labérouat and along the base of Les Orgues de Camplong (the Camplong Organ Pipes) up to the Cabane du Cap de la Baigt, a summertime fromagerie. To be comfortable, allow a whole day for the out-and-back trip.

Lonely Planet's *Walking in France* has suggestions for other day walks from Lescun – and also from Estaut, higher up the Vallée d'Aspe.

Places to Stay At the junction of the D340 and the main N134 valley road is *La Goutte d'Eau* (☎ 05 59 34 78 83, ✉ lagoutte68@hotmail.com), at once cooperative (see the introduction to this section), cafe and gîte d'étape. A bed costs 35FF plus a once-off annual subscription of 10FF, and meals are 20FF. Since it's a cooperative, you may want to give more than these minimum rates.

The *Gîte and Camping du Lauzart* (☎/fax 05 59 34 51 77) is 1.5km south-west of Lescun. A bed in the gîte, which is open year round except October, costs 55FF between May and late September (59FF at other times). The camping area, open mid-April to September, charges 57FF for two people, car and tent.

In the village itself, *Hôtel du Pic d'Anie* (☎ 05 59 34 71 54, fax 05 59 34 53 22) has rooms with bathroom for 260FF and does half-board (dinner is particularly hearty) for 245FF per person. It opens only between Easter and mid-September – but a couple of doors away is its year-round *gîte d'étape*, where a bed in a dorm or a room for two or four costs 60FF. Round the corner is a cosy new gîte d'étape, *Maison de la Montagne* (☎ 05 59 34 79 14), adapted from an old barn, with beds for 60FF and half-board at 155FF.

Etsaut and Borce
Etsaut, about 12km south of Bedous, and Borce, which overlooks it from the southwest, are popular bases for higher-elevation walks.

The National Park office (☎ 05 59 34 88 30) in Etsaut's old train station at the northern end of town opens 9.30 am to 12.30 pm and 2 to 6.30 pm daily, mid-May to late September. It has a free exhibition on the rapidly disappearing Pyrenean brown bear.

Up the hill in **Borce** is the altogether more impressive bear centre, the **Clos aux Ours** (☎ 05 59 34 88 88) with a film plus audiovisual display and poor old Jojo, stuffed and in pride of place (see the boxed text 'Pyrenean Bears'). It opens from 10 am to noon and 2 to 7 pm daily, mid-June to mid-September; plus 2 to 6 pm at weekends and

Pyrenean Bears

The upper reaches of the Vallée d'Aspe and Vallée d'Ossau, near the Franco-Spanish border, are the last Pyrenean home of the brown bear (*Ursos arctos*). Tourism, roadbuilding and forest management, plus a long (two-year) breeding cycle, have driven numbers relentlessly down. From 2000 in 1967, there are now only *six* adult bears known to remain in the National Park, including just one female.

The tiny village of Borce would have remained firmly off the map had two young boys not returned from a picnic in 1971 carrying a tiny bear cub, its mother presumably shot by poachers. Named Jojo, it became a popular tourist attraction and remained the village mascot until its death 20 years later.

The exhibition at Le Clos aux Ours – Jojo's former home, now inhabited by two resident bears, Antoine and Ségolène and their frisky cub, Myrtille – portrays the life of Pyrenean bears and their bleak future – if indeed they have one.

LISA BORG

during other school holidays. Admission costs 19FF.

Medieval pilgrims heading for Santiago de Compostela crossed the Pyrenees into Spain by two routes – the dominant one via St-Jean-Pied-de-Port (see the French Basque Country chapter) and also up Vallée d'Aspe, through Borce and over the Col de Somport (the GR653). In Bource is **Hospital St-Jacques de Compostelle** (☎ 05 59 34 88 999), a small free museum housed in a former pilgrims' lodging.

Walking For a great day walk, pick up the GR10 in Bource and follow it southwards to **Fort du Portalet**, a 19th-century fortress which was used as a prison in WWII by the Germans and Vichy government. Here, head east towards **Chemin de la Mâture**. This 1km mule path, partly hacked into the vertical cliff face, is not for those who suffer from vertigo. Either retrace your steps to Etsaut or stay overnight at a brand-new refuge, *La Borde Passete* (☎ 05 59 34 58

07). It opens mid-June to mid-September and a bed in rooms for two or four costs 80FF. Half-board costs 180FF.

Places to Stay & Eat Take the alleyway next to the church to reach Etsaut's *Auberge de Jeunesse* (☎ 05 59 34 88 98, fax 05 59 34 86 91) (also known as the Centre International de Séjour). It offers 55FF beds in dorms or rooms and does half-board for 120FF. There's also a kitchen for self-caterers, a washing machine and they rent skiing, climbing and camping equipment at very reasonable rates. The wardens are very knowledgeable about local walks.

Maison de l'Ours (☎ 05 59 34 86 38), a gîte d'étape in the village square, is also known as the Centre d'Hébergement Léo Lagrange. B&B costs 95FF or pay 130FF for excellent value half-board. The centre organises bike trips and other activities for guests.

Hôtel des Pyrénées (☎ 05 59 34 88 62, fax 05 59 34 86 96) has doubles without/

euro currency converter €1 = 6.56FF

PYRENEES

with shower and toilet for 150/260FF, and a restaurant with menus from 70FF.

All, except the Aire Naturelle complex, open year round.

VALLÉE D'OSSAU

The River Ossau makes a 60km journey from the watershed at Col du Pourtalet (1794m) to its confluence with the River Aspe at Oloron-Ste-Marie. The Vallée d'Ossau, through which it cuts a swathe, is a schizophrenic place. The valley's lower, northern reaches as far as Laruns are broad, green and pastoral. Then, as it cuts more deeply and more steeply into the Pyrenees, it becomes narrow, confined, wooded and looming before broadening out again before the hamlet of Gabas.

Getting There & Around

SNCF goes to Buzy-en-Béarn (20 minutes, three to six daily) on the line between Pau and Oloron-Ste-Marie. From Buzy there are onward bus connections into the valley as far as Laruns (40 minutes, three or four daily). Citram Pyrénées (☎ 05 59 27 22 22) runs up to four buses daily from Pau to Laruns (Sunday service only in July and August).

In July and August, and during school holidays, SARL Canonge (☎ Laruns 05 59 05 30 31) runs a morning and an evening bus between Laruns and Artouste-Fabrège (25FF, 35 minutes, daily). The summer service continues as far as Col du Pourtalet (50FF).

Information

Tourist and National Park Office The friendly valley tourist office, La Maison de la Vallée d'Ossau (☎ 05 59 05 31 41, fax 05 59 05 35 49, ☻ ossau.tourisme@wanadoo .fr), is on place de La Mairie, Laruns' main square. It opens 9.30 am to 12.30 pm and 2 to 6.30 pm daily, July and August and 9 am to noon plus 2 to 5 pm, daily except Sunday morning, the rest of the year. Next door, a National Park visitor centre is under construction. Scheduled for late 2001, it will supersede the smaller office in Gabas which opens mid-June to mid-September.

Maps The most practical general walking map of the area is the 1:50,000 scale *Béarn: Pyrénées Carte No 3*, published by Rando Éditions. For more detail, consult IGN 1:25,000 scale Top 25 map Nos 1547OT *Ossau, Vallée d'Aspe*, 1647OT *Vignemale* and 1546ET *Laruns*.

Activities

Ask at the tourist office for its free English brochure, *Four Seasons in the Ossau Valley*, and check out their booklets on mountain biking, *Circuits VTT en Vallée d'Ossau* (15FF), and short walks, *32 Randonnées Faciles* (30FF). *Promenades dans le Parc National des Pyrénées: Vallée d'Ossau* (42FF) describes 14 more challenging walks.

There's also a seasonal tourist office (☎ 05 59 05 34 00) beside the cable car in Artouste-Fabrèges.

Falaise aux Vautours

The gliding flight of the griffon vulture (*Gyps folvus*) is again once more a familiar sight over the Pyrenees. It feeds exclusively on carrion, which nowadays means mainly livestock killed by predators, disease or age – thus acting as a kind of 'alpine dustman'.

In 1974, locals established an 82-hectare reserve to protect around 10 griffon vulture pairs nesting in the limestone cliffs above the villages. Just 25 years later, there were 108 nesting pairs, plus various other raptors and five pairs of migratory Egyptian vultures.

La Falaise aux Vautours (Cliff of the Vultures) (☎ 05 59 82 65 49) in Aste-Béon shows round-the-clock live, big screen images from griffon vulture nests up on the cliffs. Time it right and you can peek in on nesting, hatching and feeding in real time. There's also an interactive museum about vultures with captions in English.

The museum is free and the 'vulture show' costs 37FF. The centre opens 10 am to 1 pm and 2 to 7 pm daily, April, July and August, but keeps more limited hours at other times. It's closed to the public for much of the winter.

At *L'Étape du Berger* (☎ 05 59 82 65

58), a short walk from La Falaise aux Vautours, try the filling *casse-croûte du berger* (shepherd's snack; 56FF) – a bowl of thick gruel, ham, a couple of fried eggs and ewe's milk cheese, all of it local produce. There are also good-value *menus* of Béarnaise specialities from 79FF. The restaurant closes Sunday and Monday evenings, except in July and August.

Laruns
postcode 64440 • pop 1500
• elevation 536m
Laruns, 6km south of Aste-Béon and 37km from Pau, is the valley's principal village and a good base for exploring its upper reaches.

The year-round *Camping Pont Lauguère* (☎ 05 59 05 35 99), beside the river 1km south of Laruns, charges 16/30FF per tent/car. A bed at the cheerful *Refuge-Auberge L'Embaradère* (☎ 05 59 05 41 88, 13 ave de la Gare) costs 60FF while half-board is 140FF. It's closed on Monday except in school holidays.

The spotless and spruce *Hôtel de France* (☎ 05 59 05 33 71, fax 05 59 05 43 83, ave de la Gare) has basic rooms for 190FF (from 230FF with bathroom). *Hôtel le Lorry* (☎ 05 59 05 31 22, route des Cols) has singles/doubles with shower costing from 205/238FF (from 228/358FF with bathroom) and offers a range of *menus* from 68FF.

Gabas
postcode 64440 • pop 36
• elevation 1027m
Tiny Gabas, 13km south of Laruns, is mainly a trekking base. Notice its equally small-scale 12th-century chapel, the only vestige of what was once the last Compostela pilgrim hostel before the Spanish frontier at Col du Pourtalet.

A bunk at the cheery Club Alpin Français (CAF) *refuge* (☎ 05 59 05 33 14), 0.5km south of Gabas, costs 50FF while half-board costs 140FF. It opens daily June to September and during other school holidays (weekends only for the rest of the year; closed November to mid-December). Basic rooms at *Hôtel-Restaurant Vignau* (☎ 05 59 05 34 06, fax 05 59 05 46 12) start at

150FF (200FF with bathroom) while *menus* cost between 55FF and 120FF. A good alternative for a modest meal is *Restaurant Le Pic du Midi* (☎ 05 59 05 33 00).

From the CAF refuge, a steepish 3.5km walk brings you to the Lac de Bious-Artigues reservoir (1420m) and a superb view south-east to Pic du Midi d'Ossau and south-west to Pic d'Ayous. Allow two hours for the round trip.

Le Petit Train d'Artouste
Winter skiers and summer holidaymakers converge upon charmless, lakeside Artouste-Fabrèges (1250m), 6km by road south of Gabas, to squeeze into the cable car which soars up the flanks of the 2032m Pic de la Sagette. From there, an open-topped train built for dam workers in the 1920s, runs for 10km along a line as far as Lac d'Artouste (1991m). The train (☎ 05 59 05 36 99 for information) runs June to September. The complicated price structure for the return journey by cable car and train ranges from 69/57/49FF for adults/under 15s/under 10s in June to 99/85/72FF in August. Allow a good four hours. For walkers, the return cable car fare is 21FF.

FOIX
postcode 09000 • pop 10,000
• elevation 380m
Foix is distinguished by its castle, 11th-century church and streets lined with medieval, half-timbered houses, and has been the county-seat of the Ariege département since the French Revolution.

Orientation
Foix sits in the crook of the confluence of the Rivers Ariege and Arget. Its oldest, most attractive quarter is on the western bank of the Ariege. Cours Gabriel Fauré, the principal thoroughfare, runs past the main square and tourist office.

Information
The tourist office (☎ 05 61 65 12 12, fax 05 61 65 64 63), 45 Cours Gabriel Fauré, opens 9 am to noon and 2 to 6 pm Monday to Saturday (7 pm continuously plus

PYRENEES

Sunday – with shorter hours – between July and mid-September).

Château des Comtes de Foix

This imposing castle with its three crenellated, gravity-defying towers stands guard over the town. Constructed in the 10th century as a stronghold for the Counts of Foix, it served as a prison from the 16th century onwards; graffiti scratched into the stones by some hapless prisoner is still visible. Today it houses an archaeological museum. From May to September, the chateau opens 9.45 am to noon and 2 to 6 pm daily (continuously in July and August). For the rest of the year, it opens 10.30 am to noon and 2 to 5.30 pm, Wednesday to Sunday. Admission costs 25FF.

Places to Stay

On the RN20 just north of Foix, *Camping du Lac* (☎ 05 61 65 11 58, fax 05 61 05 32 62) charges 65FF for two adults, tent and car. It has a small pool and opens April to October.

The three star *Hôtel Lons* (☎ 05 61 65 52 44, fax 05 61 02 68 18, 6 Place Duthil) has good value rooms with bathroom from 250FF (ask for one overlooking the river). The more modest *Hotel La Barbacane* (☎ 05 61 65 50 44, fax 05 61 02 74 33, 1 ave de Lerida) has an entrance flanked by a pair of chubby cherubs/ It has rooms costing from 180FF and opens April to October.

Places to Eat

Bright and airy *Vanille et Chocolat* (19 rue des Marchands) serves delicious salads and grills starting at 40FF and has an excellent *menu* for 55FF. *La Bodega* (7 rue Lafaurie) specialises in tapas and hearty Spanish cuisine. *Grand Café Gros* (27 cours Gabriel Fauré) opens 11.30 am to 11 pm and you can plough your way through their self-service selection for a bargain 45FF.

Getting There & Away

There are trains between Toulouse and Foix (73FF, one hour, 11 daily) and a couple of buses are operated by Salt Autocars (☎ 05 61 65 08 40).

Around Foix

Beneath **Labouiche**, 6km from Foix on the D1, flows Europe's longest navigable underground river, along which you can take a spectacular 1500m, 75-minute boat trip (45FF). Boats operate from 10 am to noon and 2 to 6 pm daily between April and September (afternoons only in April and May; 9.30 am to 6 pm continuously in July and August).

ST-BERTRAND DE COMMINGES

postcode 31510 • pop 220 • elevation 560

On an isolated hillock, St-Bertrand and its **Cathédrale Ste-Marie** loom protectively over the Garonne valley and the much pillaged remains of the Gallo-Roman town of Lugdunum Convenarum, where you can wander at will for free.

The splendourous Renaissance oak choir stalls, snug below the soaring Gothic eastern end, are a blend of the serene and spiritual tempered by earthy realism. They were carved in 1535 by local artisans.

The cathedral opens 9 am to 7 pm daily, May to September (Sundays, afternoons only). Core hours for the rest of the year are 10 am to midday and 2 to 5 pm. Admission costs 25FF (children and students 10FF) and the adjacent tourist office (☎ 05 61 95 44 44) has a detailed pamphlet in English.

Unless you've got wheels, the final 9km from the train station at Montréjeau, which has frequent connections to Toulouse (103FF, two hours) and Pau (109FF), are a problem. If you're reluctant to hoof it, call Allo Taxi on ☎ 05 61 95 66 36.

BAGNÈRES DE LUCHON

postcode 31110 • pop 2900
• elevation 630m

Bagnères de Luchon, a trim little town with gracious 19th-century buildings, expanded to accommodate the *curistes* who came to take the waters at its splendid Thermes (health spa). Nowadays, the Thermes offer relaxation and fitness sessions for weary skiers and walkers, mainstay of the town's tourism-based economy. Invest, for example, 75FF to loll in the scented steam of its 150m-long underground *vaporarium* then

PYRENEES

dunk yourself in the caressing 32°C waters of its pool. Follow this with a little flutter in elegant surroundings of the town's Casino and you've had a right good night out.

The stylish allées d'Étigny, flanked by cafes and restaurants, links place Joffre with the Thermes. Just off it to the west is the base of the cabin lift, which in 10 minutes hauls you up to Superbagnères, at 1800m the starting point for winter skiing and summer walking. The lift operates daily in the ski season and during July and August (weekends only during most other months). The fare is 25FF one-way or 40FF for a round trip.

Information
The tourist office (☎ 05 61 79 21 21, fax 05 61 79 11 23, ✉ luchon@luchon.com) at 18 allées d'Étigny opens 9 am to 7 pm daily, April to October (with a lunch break during the rest of the year).

Activities
Cycling Although you'll huff and puff, the area is rich in opportunities for mountain biking. Pick up a free copy of *Guide des Circuits VTT*, prepared by the local VTT club, from the tourist office. To rent a bike, see Getting There & Around below.

Walking Threading from Luchon and Superbagnères are an amazing 250km of waymarked trails, which range from gentle valley-bottom strolls to more demanding high mountain treks. Among the latter is the soul-stirring walk from Superbagnères to Lac d'Espingo and on to Lac du Portillon (5 hours one way). Ask at the tourist office for the pamphlet *Sentiers Balisés du Pays de Luchon*, pick up IGN 1:25,000 map No 1848OT, *Bagnères de Luchon*, pull on your boots and you're away.

Other Activities The open skies above Superbagnères are magnificent for parapenting. Contact École Soaring (☎/fax 05 61 79 29 23) at 14 rue Sylvie. More down-to-earth, both Pyrénées Aventure (☎ 05 61 79 20 59) at 9 rue Dr Germès and Virgule 7 (☎/fax 05 61 79 01 97), 4 place du Comminges, arrange canyon clambering, while the former also does rafting and canoeing on the River Garonne.

Getting There & Around
There are SNCF train or bus services between Luchon and Montréjeau (36FF, 50 minutes, five to six daily), which has frequent connections to Toulouse (103FF, two hours) and Pau (109FF).

There's extensive free parking around the Casino and cabin lift station.

For bicycle hire, contact Liberty Cycles – Cycles Bailey Demiguel (☎ 05 61 79 12 87) at 82 avenue Foch – look for the Statue of Liberty sign. Mountain bikes cost 50/80/350FF per half-day/day/week (60/90/450FF in July and August) and tourers, 25/40/150FF (30/45/200FF in high season).

Toulouse Area

The Toulouse area is in something of a geographical limbo. When France's new regional boundaries were mapped out in the 1960s, Languedoc's traditional centre, Toulouse, was excluded from Languedoc-Roussillon. Thus it is no longer Languedoc and not quite the Pyrenees. Despite its identity problems, it's a fascinating region with heaps of historical sights and activities.

Central to the area is Toulouse itself, one of France's fastest-growing cities, a vibrant centre with a large student population. To its south lie the Pyrenees while within easy reach are four towns with strong historical connections: Albi, 75km to the north-east; Montauban, 53km northwards; Condom, 110km to the north-west; and Auch, 77km west.

West of Toulouse city, the historical region of Gascony (Gasgogne) rolls all the way to the Atlantic. Famous for its lush, rolling countryside, sleepy *bastides* (fortified villages), fine wines, foie gras and Armagnac liqueur, slow-pace Gascony is ideal for experiencing some of France's finest examples of medieval and Renaissance architecture.

Getting Around
For train timetables and fares throughout the region, ring ☎ 06 36 35 35 35. Calls are charged at 2.25FF per minute and waiting time, once you're connected, can be long.

TOULOUSE
postcode 31000 • pop 690,000
• elevation 147m
Toulouse, capital of the Midi-Pyrénées region, is France's fourth-largest city (after Paris, Lyons and Marseilles), renowned for its high-tech industries, especially its advanced aerospace facilities. It's also a major centre of higher education: the city's universities, founded in the 13th century to combat Catharism (see the boxed text 'The Cathars' in the Languedoc-Roussillon chapter), and its 14 *grandes écoles* (presti-

Highlights

- **Space Age** – Aérospatiale and the Cité de l'Espace museum, Toulouse
- **Toulouse-Lautrec** – the Musée Toulouse-Lautrec in his home town, Albi
- **After Dark** – Toulouse's vibrant nightlife

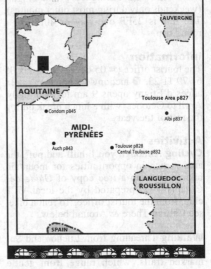

gious training institutions) and other institutes have 110,000 students, more than any other French provincial city.

With no quarries nearby, most older buildings in the city centre are in rose-red brick, earning the city the nickname *la ville rose* (the pink city).

History
Toulouse, known to the Romans as Tolosa, was the Visigoth capital from 419 to 507. It was unsuccessfully besieged by the Saracens in 721. In the 12th and 13th centuries the counts of Toulouse supported the Cathars. However, three centuries later, during the Wars of Religion, the city sided with the Catholic League. Many Toulouse

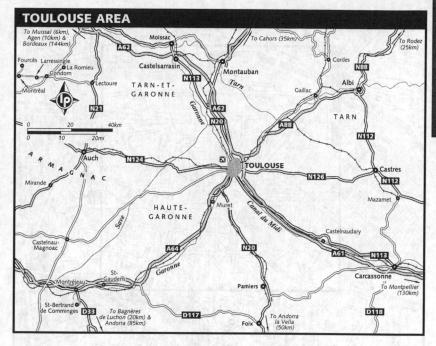

TOULOUSE AREA

merchants grew rich in the 16th and 17th centuries from the woad (blue dye) trade, which collapsed when the Portuguese began importing indigo from India. The Toulouse Parliament ruled Languedoc from 1420 until the 1789 revolution.

During WWI, Toulouse became a centre for the manufacture of arms and aircraft. In the 1920s, Antoine de St-Exupéry, author of *Le Petit Prince* (The Little Prince), and other daring pilots pioneered mail flights to north-western Africa and South America. After WWII, Toulouse became the nucleus of the country's aerospace industry. Passenger planes built here have included the Caravelle, Concorde and Airbus and local factories also produce the Ariane rocket.

Orientation

The heart of Toulouse is bounded to the east by blvd de Strasbourg and its continuation, blvd Lazare Carnot, and, to the west, by the Garonne River. Its two principal squares are

place du Capitole and, 200m eastwards, place Wilson. From the latter, the wide allées Jean Jaurès lead to the main bus station and Gare Matabiau, the train station, both just across the Canal du Midi.

Rue du Taur runs north from place du Capitole to the Basilique St-Sernin. The pedestrianised rue St-Rome and rue des Changes lead south to the transport hub of place Esquirol.

Information

Tourist Offices In the base of the Donjon du Capitole, a 16th-century tower on square Charles de Gaulle, is the tourist office (☎ 05 61 11 02 22, fax 05 61 22 03 63, ✉ ottoulouse@mipnet.fr). It's open 9 am to 6 pm weekdays (shorter hours and a lunch break at weekends), October to April. The rest of the year it opens 9 am to 7 pm, Monday to Saturday, plus 10 am to 1 pm and 2 to 5 pm on Sunday. It has quite a lot of material in English, both free and for sale.

TOULOUSE AREA

TOULOUSE

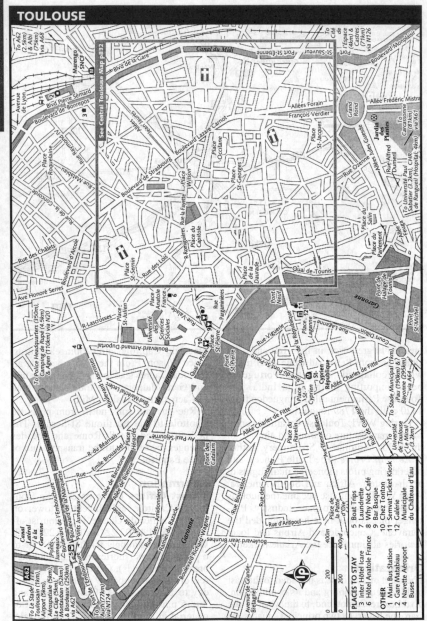

PLACES TO STAY
3 Inter Hôtel Icare
6 Hôtel Anatole France

OTHER
1 Main Bus Station
2 Gare Matabiau
4 Navette Aéroport
   Buses

5 Boat Trips
7 Laundrette
8 Why Not Café
9 Bar Basque
10 Chez Tonton
11 Semvat Ticket Kiosk
12 Galerie
    Municipale
    du Château d'Eau

Post & Communications Online time at Résomania cybercafe (☎ 05 62 30 25 64, ✉ resomania@wanadoo.fr, 85 rue Pargaminières) is 40FF an hour, costed by the minute. It's open 11.30 am to midnight, Monday to Saturday (2 to 7 pm on Sunday). France Telecom has several public access points, payable with a *télécarte* (see Email & Internet Access in the Facts for the Visitor chapter), including 11 place du Capitole, its showroom in the south-eastern corner of place Esquirol and a 24-hour kiosk on allées du Président Roosevelt.

Bookshops Toulouse, as befits a city with so many students, has scores of bookshops, many clustered near place du Capitole. The Bookshop (☎ 05 61 22 99 92) at 17 rue Lakanal has an excellent selection of English-language books and runs an info board. Librairie Étrangère (☎ 05 61 21 67 21), 16 rue des Lois, also carries a good range of English titles and is a wonderful place to browse if languages are your scene (fancy a French-Hausa dictionary? Or an anthology of contemporary Arabic short stories? This is your place). The equally engaging Ombres Blanches (☎ 05 34 45 53 33), 48–50 rue Gambetta, specialises in travel guides and maps and can detain you for hours if you're a cartophile.

Laundry Central laundrettes include those at 5 rue Maury, 10 rue de Stalingrad and 29 rue Pargaminières. All are open at least 7 am to 9 pm daily.

Place du Capitole

Bustling, pedestrianised place du Capitole is the city's main square. On the ceiling of the arcades on its western side are 29 vivid illustrations of the city's history by contemporary artist Raymond Moretti.

On the eastern side is the 128m-long facade of Toulouse's city hall, the **Capitole**, a name related to the ancient city council (*capitol* in Occitan). Built in the early 1750s, it's a focus of civic pride. Within it is the Théâtre du Capitole (☎ 05 61 63 13 13), one of France's most prestigious opera and operetta venues.

The interior of the Capitole, including its over-the-top, late-19th-century **Salle des Illustres** (Hall of the Illustrious), can be visited on weekdays for free (closed at weekends). On its eastern side is the green square Charles de Gaulle, or Jardin du Capitole.

Vieux Quartier

The small 18th-century Old Quarter is a web of narrow lanes and plazas south of place du Capitole and place Wilson. Typical is place St-Georges, rich in cafes and restaurants. Place de la Daurade is the city's 'beach' beside the Garonne, peaceful by day and romantic by night, overlooking the floodlit Pont Neuf.

Basilique St-Sernin

Once a Benedictine abbey church, St-Sernin was an important stop on the Santiago de Compostela pilgrimage route. The chancel of this vast, 115m-long brick basilica, France's largest and most complete Romanesque structure, was built between 1080 and 1096 and the nave was added in the 12th century. The basilica is topped by a magnificent eight-sided 13th-century **tower** and spire, erected during the 15th century.

Inside, the ambulatory is bordered by chapels rich in gilded 17th-century reliquaries. Directly above the double-level **crypt** is the 18th-century **tomb of St-Sernin** beneath a sumptuous canopy. In the north transept is a well-preserved **12th-century fresco** of Christ's Resurrection.

The basilica is open 8.30 to 11.45 am and 2 to 5.45 pm Monday to Saturday (without a lunchbreak – plus 9 am to 7.30 pm on Sunday – in July and August). The ambulatory chapels and crypt (admission 10FF) are open 10 to 11.30 am and 2 to 5 pm daily (except Sunday morning). Between July and September crypt and chapel visiting hours are 10 am (12.30 pm on Sunday) to 6 pm daily.

Église Notre Dame du Taur

The 14th-century Église Notre Dame du Taur was constructed to honour St-Sernin, patron of the basilica that bears his name. At the end of the nave are three chapels, the middle one housing a 16th-century Black Madonna known as Notre Dame du Rempart. It is open 10 am to noon and 2 to 7.15 pm daily, and admission is free.

Église des Jacobins

The Dominican or Jacobin order was founded by St Dominic in 1215 to preach Church doctrine to the Cathars. The Church of the Jacobins, the order's mother church, was begun soon afterwards and completed in 1385.

Inside, the Gothic structure seems to defy gravity. A single row of seven 22m-high columns, running smack down the middle of the nave and looking for all the world like palm trees as they spread their fan vaulting, manages to support the roof. The remains of St Thomas Aquinas (1225–74), an early head of the Dominican order, are interred below the modern, grey-marble altar on the northern side, having been moved from the Basilique St-Sernin. From outside, admire the 45m-high octagonal 13th-century belfry. The church was used as an artillery barracks during the 19th century. It's open 9 am to 7 pm daily. Admission to the tranquil cloister costs 10FF.

The 14th-century refectory, entered through the Église des Jacobins, nowadays houses temporary art exhibitions.

Hôtel d'Assézat & Hôtels Particuliers

Toulouse boasts about 50 handsome *hôtels particuliers* – grand, private mansions mostly dating from the 16th century.

The Hôtel d'Assézat on rue de Metz, built by a rich woad merchant, is one of the finest. It now houses the eclectic paintings, bronzes and *objets d'art* assembled by Georges Bemberg, a cosmopolitan Argentinean collector, and donated to the city. The collection is open 10 am to 6 pm, Tuesday to Sunday (to 9 pm on Thursday). Admission costs 30FF (students 18FF).

Musée des Augustins

The Musée des Augustins (☎ 05 61 22 21 82), 21 rue de Metz, houses a superb collection of paintings and stone artefacts, many seized by the Revolutionary government or gathered from vandalised monuments. The stone carvings, which include a particularly fine collection of Romanesque sculpture, include religious statuary, capitals, keystones, sarcophagi, gargoyles, tombstones and inscriptions. The museum occupies a former Augustinian monastery. The gardens of its two 14th-century **cloisters** are among the prettiest in southern France.

The museum is open 10 am to 6 pm daily except Tuesday (to 9 pm on Wednesday), and to 10 pm daily between June and September. Admission costs 12FF (students free) or 20FF when there's a special exhibition.

Cathédrale St-Étienne

The Cathedral of St Stephen has a bizarre layout. The vast, 12th-century nave is out of kilter with the huge choir, built in northern French Gothic style as part of an ambitious (and unfinished) late-13th-century plan to realign the cathedral along a different axis (note the improvised Gothic vaulting that links the two sections).

The western rose window dates from 1230 while the layer-cake belfry has a Romanesque base, a Gothic middle and a 16th-century top. The western portal was added about 1450, the northern entrance not until 1929.

The cathedral, located just south of rue de Metz, is open to visitors 7.30 am to 7 pm daily.

Musée Paul Dupuy

The Paul Dupuy Museum (☎ 05 61 14 65 50), 13 rue de la Pléau, in the 18th-century Hôtel de Besson, has a fine collection of glasswork, medieval religious art, china, armaments, and rare clocks and watches. The **pharmacy**, which dates from the mid-17th century, came from Toulouse's Jesuit college. Admission costs 10FF (20FF if there's a special exhibition). It's open 10 am to 5 pm (to 6 pm in summer) daily except Tuesday.

Galerie Municipale du Château d'Eau

Occupying a 19th-century *château d'eau* (water tower), this municipal photography museum (☎ 05 61 77 09 40) at the western end of Pont Neuf puts on superb exhibitions by the world's finest photographers. Its documentation centre is unique in France and it has a great collection of posters and postcards for sale.

The gallery is open 1 to 7 pm daily except Tuesday and holidays. Admission costs 15FF (students 10FF).

Cité de l'Espace

Space City (☎ 05 62 71 48 71) is a mind-boggling space museum and planetarium. On ave Jean Gonord on the eastern outskirts of the city, it's marked by a 55m-high space rocket. The museum includes interactive attractions and fascinating displays on satellites and future life aboard space stations. It's open 9.30 am to 7 pm daily during school holidays (to 6 pm, closed Monday the rest of the year). Admission costs 69FF (children 49FF). Take bus No 15 from allées Jean Jaurès to the end of the line, then walk about 600m, aiming for that rocket.

Aérospatiale

From Monday to Saturday, the aerospace company Aérospatiale (based in Colomiers, about 10km west of the city centre) runs 1½-hour tours (55FF, students 45FF) of its huge Clément Ader aircraft factory, where Airbuses are assembled.

To book a tour, call ☎ 05 61 15 44 00 at least a week in advance. In July and August you can book through the tourist office. Be sure to take a passport or ID.

Canal & Boat Trips

The city's many canalside paths are peaceful places to walk, run or cycle. Port de l'Embouchure is the meeting point of the Canal du Midi (1681; linking Toulouse with the Mediterranean), the Canal Latéral à la Garonne (1856; flowing to the Atlantic) and the Canal de Brienne (1776).

Several Toulouse operators run short trips on the canals and/or the Garonne, leaving from Quai de la Daurade or Ponts Jumeaux. Prices are typically 50FF for a 1½-hour cruise and 125FF for a half-day outing.

Special Events

Major annual events include:

- Festival Garonne: a riverside celebration of music, dance and theatre (July).
- Musique d'Été: jazz, classical, choral and other music at 9 pm on Tuesday and Thursday all around town (July & August).
- Jazz sur Son 31: an international jazz festival (October).

Places to Stay

Most of Toulouse's hotels cater for businesspeople so rooms are easiest to find at weekends, when there are great discounts and, surprisingly, during most of the July and August holiday period. Many midrange places offer much better value for money than budget alternatives.

Places to Stay – Budget

Camping Open year-round, the often packed *Camping de Rupé* (☎ 05 61 70 07 35, 21 chemin du Pont de Rupé), 6km north-west of the train station, charges 72FF for two people with a tent and car. From place Jeanne d'Arc take bus No 59 (last departure 7.25 pm) to the Rupé stop.

Hostels Strangely for such a major city, Toulouse has no youth hostel.

Hotels Most cheap hotels near the train station and the nearby red-light district around place de Belfort are dirty, noisy and disagreeable. If you arrive by rail, walk to allées Jean Jaurès or take the metro into town.

The exceptionally friendly *Hôtel Beauséjour* (☎/fax 05 61 62 77 59, 4 rue Caffarelli) is great value with basic rooms from 110FF and doubles/triples with bathroom at 150/190FF. At *Hôtel Splendid* (☎/fax 05 61 62 43 02), nearly opposite at No 13, basic rooms start at 90FF while singles/doubles/triples with bathroom are 130/150/210FF. Hall showers at both cost 10FF.

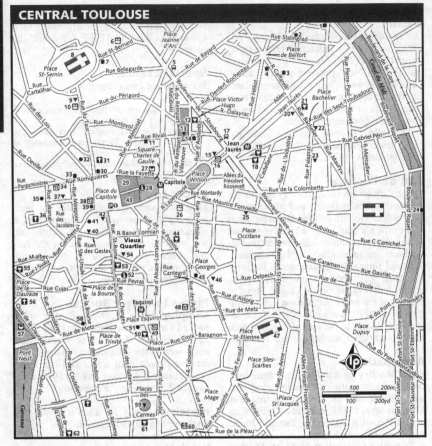

CENTRAL TOULOUSE

You can't beat the central location of *Hôtel du Grand Balcon* (☎ 05 61 21 48 08, fax 05 61 21 59 98, 8 rue Romiguières). In the 1920s, aviator-author Antoine de St-Exupéry would hole up in room No 32 between flights in this faded yet still elegant place and the lobby is a veritable shrine to him. Prices range from 160FF to 210FF for basic rooms to between 230FF and 270FF for those with bathroom.

Hôtel des Arts (☎ 05 61 23 36 21, 1 bis rue Cantegril) is also well situated. Singles/doubles cost 120/140FF with washbasin, 150/170FF with shower and 155/180FF

with bathroom. Showers are 10FF per person or 15FF for an intimate twosome. *Hôtel Anatole France* (☎ 05 61 23 19 96, 46 place Anatole France) has doubles with washbasin for 120FF, with shower for 140FF and with bathroom for 175FF.

Places to Stay – Mid-Range

Inter Hôtel Icare (☎ 05 61 63 66 55, fax 05 61 63 00 53, 11 blvd Bonrepos) has spacious, soundproofed singles/doubles/ triples with bathroom from 200/220/390FF. The family-run *Hôtel La Chartreuse* (☎ 05 61 62 93 39, fax 05 61 62 58 17, 4 bis blvd

CENTRAL TOULOUSE

PLACES TO STAY	OTHER	
1 Hôtel La Chartreuse	2 Laundrette	36 Église des Jacobins
3 Hôtel Beauséjour	5 Navette Aéroport	38 France Telecom Internet
4 Hôtel Splendid	Buses; Semvat Kiosk	Kiosk
7 Hôtel Saint Sernin	6 Cinéma ABC	39 Semvat Information Point;
11 Hôtel Albert 1er	8 Basilique St-Sernin	Octave
14 Hôtel de France	10 La Cinémathèque de	41 Ombres Blanches
30 Hôtel du Taur	Toulouse	43 Théâtre du Capitole
33 Hôtel du Grand Balcon	12 L'Hugo Club	44 Shanghai Express
45 Hôtel des Arts	16 France Telecom	47 Cathédrale St-
	Internet Kiosk	Étienne
PLACES TO EAT	17 Navette Aéroport Buses; Air	48 Musée des Augustins
9 La Salade Gasconne	France Office	49 France Telecom Showroom &
13 Les Halles Victor	18 La Strada	Internet Kiosk
Hugo	19 Bodega Bodega	50 Pub Les 2-G
15 Octave	21 Opus	51 Espace Transport
20 Shun	24 Rev'Moto	Semvat
22 Restaurant L'Indochine	26 Cinéma Utopia	52 SNCF Information Office
23 Restaurant le Taj Mahal	27 Main Post Office	53 L'Ubu
25 Restaurant Saveur Bio	28 Tourist Office	55 Café des Artistes
37 Au Gascon	29 Capitole	56 Église Notre Dame de la
40 Restaurant Benjamin	31 Église Notre Dame du	Daurade
42 Brasserie St-André	Taur	57 Boat Trips
46 Bistrot Van Gogh	32 Librairie Étrangère	58 Hôtel d'Assézat
54 Les Caves de la Maréchale	34 Résomania	60 Musée Paul Dupuy
59 Covered Food Market	35 The Bookshop	61 Pub-Disco B-Machine
		62 La Tantina de Burgos

Bonrepos) has smaller rooms equipped with bathroom and cable TV for 168FF and 190FF.

The area around place Victor Hugo abounds in two-star hotels. **Hôtel de France** (☎ 05 61 21 88 24, fax 05 61 21 99 77, 5 rue d'Austerlitz) has spotless doubles/ quads with bathroom and air-con from 195/390FF. **Hôtel Albert 1er** (☎ 05 61 21 17 91, fax 05 61 21 09 64, ✉ hotel.albert .1er@wanadoo.fr, 8 rue Rivals) has comfortable singles with bathroom and air-con costing between 230FF and 340FF (doubles 290FF to 410FF).

Hôtel du Taur (☎ 05 61 21 17 54, 2 rue du Taur) has quiet, fairly spacious singles/ doubles with bathroom for 230FF to 315FF (triples 320FF to 350FF). Equally peaceful is **Hôtel St-Sernin** (☎ 05 61 21 73 08, fax 05 61 22 49 61, 2 rue St-Bernard) with fully equipped singles/doubles/triples from 250/290/390FF and garage parking (40FF).

Places to Eat

Most restaurants in Toulouse offer what the French call *bon rapport qualité-prix* – good value for money. Among the best value of all are the small, spartan, lunchtime-only *restaurants* on the first floor of Les Halles Victor Hugo. Fast, packed and no-nonsense, catering for market vendors and shoppers alike, they serve up generous, delicious quantities of hearty fare for 55FF to 85FF per *menu*.

Place St-Georges is almost entirely taken over by cafe tables; at night it's one of the liveliest outdoor spots in town. Both blvd de Strasbourg and the perimeter of place du Capitole are lined with restaurants and cafes. Lots of places around town have lunch *menus* for 50FF to 60FF.

Restaurants – French Specialising in regional cuisine, *Les Caves de la Maréchale* (☎ 05 61 23 89 88, 3 rue Jules Chalande), closed Monday lunchtime and Sunday, occupies the magnificently vaulted brick cellar of a pre-Revolution convent. Lunch/ dinner menus start at 85/135FF and there's a lunchtime 56FF *formule rapide* (*menu* with a choice of courses). *Restaurant Benjamin* (☎ 05 61 22 92 66, 7 rue des Gestes), where classical columns blend with modern decor, serves excellent *nouvelle cuisine*. Lunch/dinner *menus* start at 65/93FF.

Intimate *Au Gascon* (☎ 05 61 21 67 16, 9 rue des Jacobins), with generous *menus* between 59FF and 128FF, is the perfect place for duck, duck and yet more duck. *Bistrot Van Gogh* (☎ 05 61 21 03 15, 21 place St-Georges) with its huge outdoor terrace has lunch/dinner *menus* at 65/120FF. Alternatively, go a la carte and try their generous *cassoulet* (rich meat and bean stew) for 94FF or *parillade* (grill) of eight different kinds of fish (134FF).

The 75FF and 95FF *menus* and main courses (35FF to 80FF) at *Brasserie St-André* (☎ 05 61 22 56 37, 39 rue St-Rome) attract a mainly young crowd to its cellar, where the barrel-vaulted ceiling resembles the upper half of a brick submarine. Meals are served from 7.45 pm throughout the night; it's closed on Sunday.

Octave (☎ 05 62 27 05 21), with branches at 9 place du Capitole and 11 allées du Président Roosevelt, serves rich ice cream. Avoid Breathalyser tests after eating the Armagnac *pruneaux* (prune) or Grand Marnier flavours.

Restaurants – Other Serving tasty vegetarian food, including a 40FF lunchtime mixed plate, a great-value 60FF buffet and three 85FF *menus*, is *Restaurant Saveur Bio* (☎ 05 61 12 15 15, 22 rue Maurice Fonvieille), closed Saturday evening and Sunday. *La Salade Gasconne* (75 rue du Taur) serves tasty salads (40FF to 50FF) plus pasta and grills.

The Indian *Restaurant Le Tajmahal* (☎ 05 61 99 26 80, 24 rue Palaprat), open evenings only and mainly carnivore, offers some vegetarian dishes, such as the *spécialité thali* (85FF).

At *Shun* (☎ 05 61 99 39 20, 35 rue Bachelier), Japanese and elegant, lunch/dinner *menus* start at 80/145FF; it's closed on Monday. Nearby is *Restaurant L'Indochine* (☎ 05 61 62 17 46, 46 place Bachelier), one of several Asian eateries in the

area, offering copious 48FF and 67FF Chinese and Vietnamese *menus*.

Self-Catering For fresh produce, visit *Les Halles Victor Hugo* (the large covered food market at place Victor Hugo) or the *market* on place des Carmes. Both are open until 1 pm daily except Monday. Another small *market* sells organically grown food at place du Capitole on Tuesday and Saturday mornings.

Entertainment

For what's on where, pick up a copy of *Toulouse Hebdo* (3FF), *Le Flash* (6FF) (both weekly) or *Intramuros* (free from the tourist office and cinemas).

Pubs & Bars Almost every square in the Vieux Quartier has at least one cafe, busy day and night, while rue des Blanchers has several 'alternative' joints. Those clustered around place St-Pierre beside the Garonne pull in a predominantly young crowd. *Chez Tonton* at No 16 and Spanish-flavoured *Bar Basque* (No 7) are sports bars. Nearby are the *Why Not Café* (5 rue Pargaminières), with its beautiful terrace, and *Café des Artistes* (13 place de la Daurade), an art-student hang-out.

La Tantina de Burgos (27 ave de la Garonnette) and *Bodega Bodega* (1 rue Gabriel Péri), both popular *bodegas* (wine bars), have live music at weekends. *Opus* (24 rue Bachelier) offers food until 1.30 am and dancing all night, while *L'Hugo Club* (18 place Victor Hugo) is another dance-bar.

Discos & Clubs Toulouse has discos in double figures. Two hot spots near the centre are *La Strada* (4 rue Gabriel Péri), closed Sunday and Monday, which may still be undergoing extensive renovation, and *L'Ubu* (16 rue St-Rome), closed on Sunday. Connoisseurs of bizarre names may like to risk *Le Clap* (146 chemin des Étroits); take exit 24 off the A64.

Gay Venues Toulouse is a very gay city – it ain't called *la ville rose* just for those pink bricks. Try the popular *Pub Les 2-G* on rue des Tourneurs, *Pub-Disco B-Machine* on place des Carmes or *Shanghai Express (12 rue de la Pomme)*.

Cinemas The three-screen *Cinéma Utopia* (☎ 05 61 23 66 20, 24 rue Montardy) and *Cinéma ABC* (☎ 05 61 29 81 00, 13 rue St Bernard) both show nondubbed foreign films. *Cinémathèque de Toulouse (☎ 05 62 30 25 35, 69 rue du Taur)* also frequently has nondubbed screenings.

Shopping

Toulouse's main shopping district, rich in department stores and expensive boutiques, embraces rue du Taur, rue d'Alsace-Lorraine, rue de la Pomme, rue des Arts and nearby streets. Place St-Georges too is surrounded by fashionable shops. Place du Capitole hosts a huge flea market each Wednesday and you'll find an antiquarian book-market on place St-Étienne on Saturday.

Getting There & Away

Air Toulouse-Blagnac international airport (☎ 05 61 42 44 00) is 8km north-west of the city centre. Air France and Air Liberté between them have over 30 flights a day to/from Paris (mainly Orly). There are also daily or almost-daily flights from many other cities in France and Europe. Among the no-frills airlines, Ryanair flies daily and Buzz at weekends only to/from London Stansted.

Bus Toulouse's modern bus station (☎ 05 61 61 67 67) is just north of the train station. Destinations include Agen (66FF, three hours, two daily on weekdays only), Albi (60FF, 1½ hours, five to eight daily), Auch (58FF, 1½ hours, one to three daily), Castres (56FF, 1½ hours, three daily), Montauban (38FF, 1¼ hours, five to eight daily), Millau (135FF, four hours, two daily), Foix (52FF, 1½ hours, two daily) and Andorra (75FF, four hours, one to two daily).

Semvat's Arc-en-Ciel buses, serving local destinations in Haute-Garonne and

nearby *départements*, also use the station, as do Intercars (☎ 05 61 58 14 53) and Eurolines (☎ 05 61 26 40 04). Both offices are closed on Sunday.

Train Toulouse's train station, Gare Matabiau, is on blvd Pierre Sémard, about 1km north-east of the city centre.

Local destinations served by many daily direct trains include Albi (64FF, 1¼ hours), Auch (72FF, 1½ hours), Bayonne (196FF, 3¾ hours), Bordeaux (165FF, 2½ hours), Cahors (87FF, 1½ hours), Carcassonne (74FF, one hour), Castres (73FF, 1¼ hours), Foix (69FF, 1¼ hours), Lourdes (125FF, two hours), Montauban (47FF, 40 minutes) and Pau (145FF, 2½ hours).

The fare to Paris is 356FF by Corail (6½ hours, Gare d'Austerlitz) and 447FF by TGV (5½ hours, Gare Montparnasse via Bordeaux).

At 5 rue Peyras, SNCF has an information and ticketing office, open 9.30 am to 6.30 pm weekdays (9.30 am to 12.30 pm and 1.30 to 5.45 pm on Saturday).

Car Hire companies include ADA (☎ 05 61 48 55 55 in town, ☎ 05 61 30 00 33 at the airport), Budget (☎ 05 61 63 18 18 in town, ☎ 05 61 71 85 80 at the airport) and Europcar (☎ 05 61 62 52 89).

Getting Around

To/From the Airport The Navette Aéroport bus (☎ 05 34 60 64 00) links town and airport every 20 minutes and costs 23FF. The last run to the airport is at 8.20 pm, Sunday to Friday (7.40 pm on Saturday). Pick it up at the bus station, near Jean Jaurès metro station, place Jeanne d'Arc or blvd Lascrosses. From the airport, the last bus leaves at 11.30 pm daily.

An airport taxi costs about 100FF.

Bus & Metro The local bus network and 15-station metro line are run by Semvat (☎ 05 61 41 70 70). A ticket for either costs 7.50FF (9FF to the suburbs). A 10-ticket carnet is 62FF (70FF to the suburbs) and a daily pass costs 45FF. Most bus lines run daily until 8 or 9 pm. The seven 'night' bus lines all start at the train station and run from 10 pm to just after midnight.

The fully automated metro runs northeast to south-west from Jolimont to Basso Cambo. Major city stops are Jean Jaurès, Capitole, Esquirol and Marengo SNCF (the train station). These last two are also important metro/bus interchanges.

Semvat has ticket and information kiosks at Marengo and Jean Jaurès metro stations and 9 place du Capitole. There's also an Espace Transport Semvat office at 7 place Esquirol. All supply route maps, as does the tourist office.

Car Parking is tight in the city centre. There are huge car parks under place du Capitole, beneath ave Jean Jaurès, just off place Wilson and above the covered market at place Victor Hugo. At place St-Sernin you can park for free (except Sunday) – if you can find a spot.

Taxi There are 24-hour taxi stands at the train station (☎ 05 61 21 00 72), place Wilson (☎ 05 61 21 55 46) and place Esquirol (☎ 05 61 80 36 36).

Bicycle Specialists Rev'Moto (☎ 05 62 47 07 08, ✉ info@revmoto.com, 14 blvd de la Gare) rent out just about every kind of bike (50/80/420FF per half-day/day/week) plus scooters and motorbikes.

ALBI
postcode 81000 • pop 47,000
• elevation 169m

Almost all of central Albi, including the huge, fortress-like Gothic cathedral, is built from bricks of reddish clay, dug from the nearby Tarn River. Albi is best known for the so-called Albigensian heresy of the 12th and 13th centuries and the violent crusade that crushed it (see the boxed text 'The Cathars' in the Languedoc-Roussillon chapter).

One of Albi's most famous natives was the artist Henri de Toulouse-Lautrec, renowned for his posters and lithographs of the bars, brothels and music halls of Montmartre in *belle époque* Paris. Albi's Musée

Toulouse-Lautrec has the most extensive collection of his work anywhere.

Orientation
Cathédrale Ste-Cécile dominates the heart of the old quarter. From it, a web of narrow, pedestrianised streets stretches south-east to place du Vigan, Albi's commercial hub. The train station is about 1km south-west of the city centre.

Information
The tourist office (☎ 05 63 49 48 80, fax 05 63 49 48 98, ✉ otsi.albi@wanadoo.fr) on place Ste Cécile is open 9 am to 12.30 pm and 2 to 6 pm Monday to Saturday (9 am to 7.30 pm in July and August).

The tourist office, in an excellent initiative that ought to be followed by many more Midi towns with pedestrianised old quarters, has developed three signed walks. Ask for its free guide pamphlet in English, *Three Cultural Heritage Routes*.

The main post office on place du Vigan has Cyberposte. You can check your emails at Les Royaumes Virtuels (☎ 05 63 43 24 88), 55 rue Croix Verte. Open 11 am to midnight daily (from 2 pm on Sunday), it charges 42FF per hour, billed by the minute.

The Lavomatique laundrette at 10 rue Émile Grand is open 7 am to 9 pm daily.

Cathédrale Ste-Cécile
As much a fortress as a church, this mighty cathedral was begun in 1282, not long after the Cathar movement was crushed. Built to impress and subdue and constructed of red brick in the southern (or Meridional) Gothic style, it was finished around a century later. Not everybody's idea of attractive – indeed, the cathedral's dominant feature is its sheer bulk – it's breathtaking when illuminated at night.

When you step inside, the contrast with the plain, sunburned exterior is total. No surface was left untouched by the Italian artists who in the early 16th-century painted their way along its vast nave. An intricately carved, lacy **rood screen**, many of its statues smashed in the Revolution, spans the

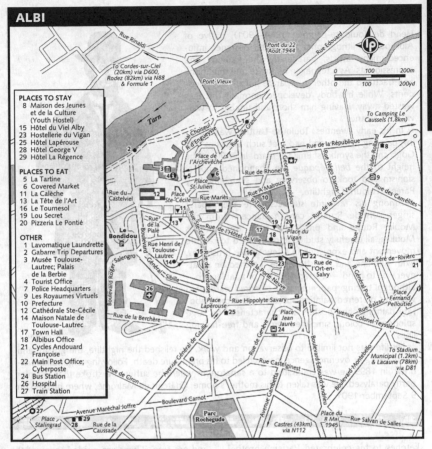

ALBI

PLACES TO STAY
8 Maison des Jeunes
   et de la Culture
   (Youth Hostel)
15 Hôtel du Viel Alby
23 Hostellerie du Vigan
25 Hôtel Lapérouse
28 Hôtel George V
29 Hôtel La Régence

PLACES TO EAT
5 La Tartine
9 Covered Market
11 La Calèche
13 La Tête de l'Art
16 Le Tournesol
19 Lou Secret
20 Pizzeria Le Pontié

OTHER
1 Lavomatique Laundrette
2 Gabarre Trip Departures
3 Musée Toulouse-
   Lautrec; Palais
   de la Berbie
4 Tourist Office
7 Police Headquarters
9 Les Royaumes Virtuels
10 Prefecture
12 Cathédrale Ste-Cécile
14 Maison Natale de
   Toulouse-Lautrec
17 Town Hall
18 Albibus Office
21 Cycles Andouard
   Françoise
22 Main Post Office;
   Cyberposte
24 Bus Station
26 Hospital
27 Train Station

sanctuary. The **stained-glass windows** in the apse and choir date from the 14th to the 16th centuries. On no account miss the **grand chœur** (great choir; 5FF) with its frescoes, chapels and 30 fine biblical polychrome figures carved in stone. At the western end, behind today's main altar, is *Le Jugement Dernier* (The Last Judgement; 1490), a particularly vivid Doomsday horror-show of the damned being boiled in oil, tortured, beheaded or gobbled by demons and monsters.

The cathedral opens 9 am to noon and 2.30 to 6.30 pm daily (8.30 am to 7 pm from mid-June to mid-September). From June to September the tourist office runs tours of the cathedral twice daily (except Saturday) costing 27FF (students 13.50FF).

Musée Toulouse-Lautrec
Just beside the tourist office, the Toulouse-Lautrec Museum (☎ 05 63 49 48 70) occupies the **Palais de la Berbie**, a vast, fortress-like 13th- to 15th-century archbishop's palace.

It boasts over 500 examples of the artist's work – everything from simple pencil

In Toulouse-Lautrec: Of Cancan Dancers & Prostitutes

NICKY CAVEN

Henri de Toulouse-Lautrec (1864–1901), native of Albi, painter, lithographer and poster designer, influenced many artists, particularly the Fauvists and expressionists. As a teenager, he broke one thighbone and fractured the other in separate horse-riding accidents. While his body developed normally, his legs wasted away, leaving him short and unable to walk without a cane.

In his early twenties, Toulouse-Lautrec was studying painting in Paris and had met such artists as Van Gogh and the symbolist Émile Bernard. In 1890, at the height of the *belle époque*, he abandoned impressionism and took to observing and sketching 'gay Paree's' colourful nightlife.

Among his favourite subjects were the cabaret singer Aristide Bruant, cancan dancers from the Moulin Rouge and prostitutes from the rue des Moulins, all carefully studied and sketched to capture movement and expression in a few simple brushlines. With sure line and fast strokes he sketched on whatever was to hand – a scrap of paper or a tablecloth – although tracing paper or buff-coloured cardboard were his preferred painting surfaces. His more elaborate paintings and posters are characterised by large splodges of colour, simplified forms and free-flowing lines.

His life was not limited to observation and work. He relished the nightlife, the gossip, and the drinking – overindulgence in which led to his premature death. Following a mental breakdown in 1899 he was committed to a sanatorium where he suffered a stroke that left him partly paralysed. He was taken to his mother's home, Château de Malromé, where he died on 9 September 1901.

---

sketches to his celebrated Parisian brothel scenes such as the *Salon de la rue des Moulins*. On the top floor are works by, among other artists, Degas, Matisse and Rodin.

Admission costs 25FF (students 12FF) and you can hire an audioguide taped commentary in English.

The museum's core hours are 10 am to noon and 2 to 5 pm (longer as the days become lighter). It closes on Tuesday between October and March. In July and August it's open 9 am to 6 pm.

The ornamental palace gardens and courtyard keep to much the same schedule

and are free. There are guided tours of the museum in French (25FF) twice daily from mid-June to mid-September.

A short walk away, at 14 rue Henri de Toulouse-Lautrec, a plaque on the wall of the privately owned **Maison Natale de Toulouse-Lautrec** marks the house where the artist was born.

River Trips

From mid-June to September you can take a 35-minute trip (20FF) on a *gabarre*, a flat-bottomed sailing barge of the kind that used to haul goods down the Garonne to Bordeaux. They depart from just below the

Palais de la Berbie every half-hour, 10 am to 12.30 pm and 2 to 6.30 pm.

Special Events

The biggest events in Albi's calendar are Festival Albi-Jazz in late June and a three-day series of ancient-music concerts at the end of July. Carnaval, at the beginning of Lent, is also a lively time to be in town.

Places to Stay

Camping Just off Route de Millau, 2km north-east of place du Vigan, is *Camping Le Caussels* (☎/fax 05 63 60 37 06). Open April to mid-October, it charges 65FF for two people with tent/caravan and car. Take bus No 5 from place du Vigan to the terminus.

Hostels The youth hostel, more commonly known as the *Maison des Jeunes et de la Culture* (☎ 05 63 54 53 65, fax 05 63 54 61 55, 13 rue de la République), is 400m north-east of place du Vigan. Open year-round, dorm beds cost 48FF. Take bus No 1 from the train station to the République stop.

Hotels Near the bus and train stations is the friendly, recommended *Hôtel George V* (☎ 05 63 54 24 16, fax 05 63 49 90 78, ✉ hotel.georgev@ilink.fr, 29 ave Maréchal Joffre). It has shower-equipped doubles at 190FF and rooms with full bathroom from 240FF. Neighbouring *Hôtel La Régence* (☎ 05 63 54 01 42) at No 27 has basic rooms from 130FF (from 160FF with shower, 200FF with bathroom).
Hôtel Lapérouse (☎ 05 63 54 69 22, fax 05 63 38 03 69, 21 place Lapérouse) has a pool and cosy rooms with shower for 160FF (210FF to 350FF with bathroom).

More central and above a great restaurant is *Hôtel du Vieil Alby* (☎ 05 63 54 14 69, fax 05 63 54 96 75, 25 rue Henri de Toulouse-Lautrec), where – a rarity in France – every bedroom is non-smoking. Rooms cost 250FF to 280FF with shower and 300FF to 350FF with bathroom. Parking, difficult hereabouts, costs 45FF. The hotel closes during the second half of January and late June/early July. *Hostellerie du*

Vigan (☎ 05 63 54 01 23, fax 05 63 47 05 42, 16 place du Vigan), also central, has spacious, modern doubles from 300FF (triples at 390FF) and a popular brasserie below.

Albi's *Formule 1* hotel (☎ 05 63 47 59 27, fax 05 63 77 65 79) is in the Cantepau district, beside an Intermarché restaurant. Doubles cost 155FF. Take bus No 1 from the train or bus station or place du Vigan.

Places to Eat

Restaurants For something quick, *La Tartine* (☎ 05 63 54 50 60), with its large terrace opposite the tourist office, offers a 65FF *menu* and main courses from 55FF. The traffic noise – not to mention the fumes – may drive you inside.

Intimate *La Tête de l'Art* (☎ 05 63 38 44 75, 7 rue de la Piale) has *menus* from 75FF. Opposite is *La Calèche* (☎ 05 63 54 15 52, 6 rue de la Piale), with similar fare from 85FF.

Lou Secret (☎ 05 63 38 26 40) is tucked away down an alley at the north-western corner of place du Vigan. Friendly and bustling, it serves delightful regional cuisine in addition to a strong a la carte choice. It's closed Sunday lunchtime. A more up-market venue for local food is the *restaurant* of the Hôtel du Vieil Alby, where mouthwatering *menus* cost from 95FF to 240FF and a lunchtime special is 75FF.

Le Tournesol (☎ 05 63 38 38 14, 11 rue de l'Ort-en-Salvy) is a small vegetarian restaurant that serves a plat du jour for 48FF; salad platters start at the same price. It's open for lunch Tuesday to Saturday plus 7.15 to 9.30 pm on Friday evening.

Place du Vigan, ripped up for massive roadworks at the time of writing, should again become the prime nightlife area. On it, *Pizzéria Le Pontié* (☎ 05 63 54 16 34) has a pleasant terrace and pizzas from 39FF, while Hostellerie du Vigan has a popular *brasserie*.

Self-Catering Fresh fare can be picked up from the architecturally stylish *covered market* (closed Monday) north-east of the cathedral. An animated Saturday morning farmers' market overflows from place Ste-Cécile into the surrounding streets.

Getting There & Away

Bus The bus station, little more than a parking area and known as the Halte des Autobus, is on the south-western corner of place Jean Jaurès. The tourist office has timetable information. Services include Cordes (25FF, 45 minutes, two per day on weekdays only), Castres (32FF, 50 minutes, up to 10 daily) and Toulouse (50FF, one hour, eight daily).

Train The train station (☎ 05 63 54 50 50) is at place Stalingrad, 1km south-west of the tourist office. For town, take bus No 1 (last departure 7.15pm).

There are multiple trains to/from Rodez (69FF, 1¼ hours), Millau (via Rodez, 112FF, 2½ hours), Toulouse (64FF, 1¼ hours) and Cordes (37FF, one hour). For Montauban (94FF), change in Toulouse.

Getting Around

Car Leave your vehicle in the large car park at Le Bondidou, near the cathedral.

Bus Local buses are run by Albibus (☎ 05 63 38 43 43), which has an information office next to the town hall. Single tickets cost 5FF; a carnet of 10 costs 43FF. There's no Sunday service.

Taxi You can order a taxi on ☎ 05 63 47 99 99 or ☎ 05 63 54 85 03.

Bicycle Cycles Andouard Françoise (☎ 05 63 38 44 47) at 7 rue Séré de Rivière rents out mountain bikes for 100/500FF per day/week and tourers for 80/350FF.

MONTAUBAN
postcode 82000 • pop 55,000
• elevation 80m

On the right bank of the Tarn River, Montauban was founded in 1144 by Count Alphonse Jourdain of Toulouse who, legend has it, was so charmed by its trailing willow trees (*alba* in Occitan) that he named the place Mont Alba.

Montauban, southern France's second-oldest bastide, sustained significant damage during the Albigensian crusade. It became a Huguenot stronghold around 1570. The Edict of Nantes (1598) brought royal concessions to the Huguenots but, after its repeal by Louis XIV in 1685, the town's Protestants again suffered persecution.

Montauban's many classical town-houses date from the prosperous decades following the Catholic reconquest.

Orientation

Place Nationale, surrounded by arcaded 17th-century brick buildings, is the heart of the old city but today's hub is more place Franklin Roosevelt to its south. The bus and train stations are across the Tarn River at the western end of ave de Mayenne.

Information

The tourist office (☎ 05 63 63 60 60, fax 05 63 63 65 12, @ officetourisme@montauban .com) on place Prax-Paris is open 9 am to noon and 2 to 7 pm Monday to Saturday. During July and August, it's open continuously on weekdays and also 10 am to noon and 3 to 6 pm on Sunday. Ask for its exhaustive pamphlet in English, *Discovering Montauban on Foot*.

There's a laundrette at 26 rue de l'Hôtel de Ville.

Musée Ingres

Jean Auguste Dominique Ingres (1780–1867), the neoclassical painter and accomplished violinist, was a native of Montauban. Many of his works, plus canvases by Tintoretto, Van Dyck, Courbet and others, are exhibited in the Musée Ingres (☎ 05 63 22 12 92) at 19 rue de l'Hôtel de Ville, a former bishop's palace.

It's open 10 am to noon and 2 to 6 pm Tuesday to Saturday and on Sunday afternoon (daily in July and August). Admission costs 20FF but for 25FF you can buy a pass admitting you to the small nearby museums of Histoire Naturelle (natural history), Terroir (local costumes and traditions) and Résistance et Déportation (mementoes of WWII) as well.

euro currency converter 10FF = €1.52

Ingres' Hobby

The artist Jean Auguste Dominique Ingres (1780–1867) was born in Montauban. A leading exponent of the neoclassical style, tempered by steamy sensuality, he confronted the often-soppy romanticism prevailing in France at the time. His most celebrated works include the *Odalisque* series of fleshy female nudes and highly detailed portraits, including several of Napoleon.

While Ingres is celebrated for the purity and grace of his drawing and has taken his rightful place in the pantheon of great painters, most French people know of him in a different context altogether. Away from his easel, Monsieur Ingres would relax by playing the violin. Today, the French phrase for 'hobby' is still *violon d'Ingres*.

Churches

The 18th-century **Cathédrale Notre Dame de l'Assomption** on place Franklin Roosevelt, with its clean, classical lines, contains one of Ingres' masterpieces, *Le Vœu de Louis XIII*, depicting the king pledging France to the Virgin. The hexagonal belfry of 13th-century **Église St-Jacques** still bears cannonball marks from Louis XIII's 1621 siege of the town.

Special Events

Alors Chante in May is a festival of French song. Jazz à Montauban is a giant jam in the third week of July. The Fête des Quatre-Cent Coups (400 Blows) is a weekend street festival in September. It commemorates the moment when, says local lore, a fortune-teller told Louis XIII, besieging Montauban in 1621, to blast off 400 cannons simultaneously against the town, which still failed to fall.

Places to Stay

Open year-round is *Camping la Forge* (☎ 05 63 31 00 44) in Albias, 10km to the north-east on the N20. The charge for a tent, car and two people is 68FF.

Central and popular, *Hôtel du Commerce* (☎ 05 63 66 31 32, fax 05 63 03 18 46, 9 place Franklin Roosevelt) has basic singles/doubles/triples/quads for a bargain 120/130/175/240FF. Rooms with bathroom go for between 175FF and 310FF. It also offers a very generous 30FF buffet breakfast.

Hôtel Le Lion d'Or (☎ 05 63 20 04 04, fax 05 63 66 77 39, 22 ave de Mayenne) has singles with washbasin and toilet for 130FF and singles/doubles with shower for 230/250FF. Almost next door, and a notch up, *Hôtel d'Orsay* (☎ 05 63 66 06 66, fax 05 63 66 19 39, ave Roger Salengro) offers comfortable doubles with toilet and shower for 280FF to 350FF. Both places are near the train station.

Places to Eat

Probably Montauban's best value for money is the 64FF lunch *menu* at smoky *Bistrot du Faubourg* (☎ 05 63 63 49 89, 111 Faubourg Lacapelle), closed on Saturday evening and Sunday. Place Nationale has several brasseries, including the *Agora Café* (☎ 05 63 63 05 74), closed on Sunday, and the popular *Brasserie des Arts* (☎ 05 63 20 20 90), open lunchtime only from November to March, which has a daily special for 42FF and *menus* at 82FF and 120FF.

Restaurant Au Fil de l'Eau (☎ 05 63 66 11 85, 14 quai du Dr Lafforgue), closed on Sunday evening and Monday, offers tempting *menus* between 130FF and 295FF and is plastered with merited recommendations from Gallic gastronomic guides. Rivalling it is *La Cuisine d'Alain*, restaurant of the Hôtel d'Orsay, with *menus* at 130FF, 180FF and 280FF and free wine and coffee with lunch.

There's a Saturday *farmers' market* in place Prax-Paris and a smaller one up to 1 pm daily in place Nationale.

Getting There & Away

Bus Several daily buses for Toulouse

(40FF) and Auch leave from the bus station on place Lalaque, 350m north-east of the train station. Those to/from Moissac and Agen (two hours) stop at place Prax-Paris three times daily. From the train station, two or three SNCF buses run to Albi (70FF, 1¼ hours, daily except Saturday).

Train There are regular trains to Paris' Gare d'Austerlitz (337FF, six hours) and TGVs to Gare Montparnasse (426FF, five hours, four daily), Toulouse (47FF, 30 minutes, at least hourly), Bordeaux (139FF, two hours, frequent) via Agen (60FF, 45 minutes) and locally to Moissac (29FF, 20 minutes, up to six daily).

Getting Around

Bus Transports Montalbanais' (☎ 05 63 63 52 52) eight local lines run Monday to Saturday until around 8 pm. Tickets cost 5.50FF each or 41FF for a book of 10. Bus No 3 connects the train and bus stations with the town centre.

Car Use the free parking under Pont Vieux or Parking Occitan in place Prax-Paris, where the above-ground section – markedly cheaper than the adjacent underground park – charges 10FF for up to six hours.

Taxi Ring Radio Taxis on ☎ 05 63 66 99 99.

Bicycle Denayrolles Garage (☎ 05 63 03 62 02), north-east of the town centre at 878 ave Jean Moulin, rents out mountain bikes for 100/200/450FF per day/three days/week.

AROUND MONTAUBAN
Moissac

Moissac, an easy day-trip from Montauban or Toulouse, was once a major stop for Santiago de Compostela pilgrims. Its church, **Abbaye St-Pierre**, resplendent with France's finest Romanesque sculpture, became a model for more modest ecclesiastical buildings all over southern France.

Above the **south portal**, completed around 1130, is a superb tympanum depicting St John's Vision of the Apocalypse, with Christ in majesty flanked by the apostles, angels and 24 awestruck elders.

In the **cloister** 116 delicate marble columns support wedge-shaped, deeply carved capitals, each a little masterpiece of foliage, earthy figures or biblical scenes. The Revolution's toll is sickening – nearly every face is smashed.

You enter the cloister through the tourist office (☎ 05 63 04 01 85) on place Durand de Bredon, behind the church. Both are open 9 am to noon and 2 to 5 pm daily (to 6 pm between mid-March and mid-October; to 7 pm in July and August). The tourist office shows a free 10-minute video (available in English) and sells a detailed guidebook, also in English. Admission (30FF) includes the cloister, a museum of folk art and furnishings, and a library containing replicas of the monastery's beautiful illuminated manuscripts.

There are up to six trains daily to/from Montauban (29FF), the majority also serving Toulouse (66FF). You can park for free in place des Récollets (the market square) and just above (north of) the tourist office.

AUCH

postcode 32000 • **pop 25,000**
• **elevation 166m**

Auch has been an important trade crossroads ever since the Romans conquered a Celtic tribe called the Auscii and established Augusta Auscorum on the flats east of the Gers River. Auch had its heyday in the Middle Ages when it was run by the counts of Armagnac (and their archbishops), who built the city's cathedral. Its second flowering was in the late 18th century, following the building of new roads to Toulouse and into the Pyrenees. A slide into rural obscurity followed the Revolution in 1789.

Auch is the place to enjoy genuine Gascon cuisine and makes a convenient base for exploring the Gers region's underrated gentle countryside.

Orientation

Hilltop Auch, with place de la Libération, place de la République and the cathedral at its heart, contains most of the sights, restau-

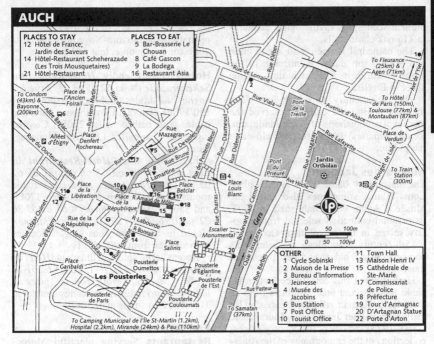

AUCH

PLACES TO STAY	PLACES TO EAT
12 Hôtel de France; Jardin des Saveurs	5 Bar-Brasserie Le Chouan
14 Hôtel-Restaurant Scheherazade (Les Trois Mousquetaires)	8 Café Gascon
21 Hôtel-Restaurant	9 La Bodega
	16 Restaurant Asia

OTHER
1 Cycle Sobinski
2 Maison de la Presse
3 Bureau d'Information Jeunesse
4 Musée des Jacobins
6 Bus Station
7 Post Office
10 Tourist Office
11 Town Hall
13 Maison Henri IV
15 Cathédrale de Ste-Marie
17 Commissariat de Police
18 Préfecture
19 Tour d'Armagnac
20 D'Artagnan Statue
22 Porte d'Arton

rants, shops and hotels. Pedestrianised rue Dessoles is its principal shopping street. The old town, tumbling away to the south, is a web of lanes, steps and little courtyards. Across the Gers River is 'new' Auch and the train station.

Information

Tourist Offices The tourist office (☎ 05 62 05 22 89, fax 05 62 05 92 04) at 1 rue Dessoles occupies a handsomely restored 15th-century building, the Maison Fedel. It's open 9 am to noon and 2 to 6 pm Monday to Saturday (also on Sunday morning, Easter to mid-September). Hours in July and August are 9.30 am to 6.30 pm.

Its town map indicates a couple of signed walking tours. An English version of the exhaustively detailed accompanying pamphlet is in preparation.

Post & Communications The main post office on rue Gambetta has Cyberposte.

You can also access the Web (20FF per hour) at Auch's Bureau d'Information Jeunesse, 17 rue Rouget de Lisle, which is usually open in the afternoon to 5.30 pm Monday to Saturday.

Cathédrale de Ste-Marie

This magnificent building, a UNESCO World Heritage Site, moved Napoleon II to exclaim, 'A cathedral like this should be put in a museum!' Constructed over two centuries, from 1489 to 1680, it ranges in style from pure Gothic to Italian Renaissance. To appreciate the contrast, take a look at the doorway in the external north wall; the lower part is lacy Gothic while the upper, unadorned arch is purest Florentine.

Though the heavy western facade impresses by its sheer bulk – and looks very grand illuminated at night – what people come to see is inside: 18 vivid 16th-century Renaissance stained-glass windows and the astonishing **grand chœur** (great choir), featuring over 1500 individual carvings of biblical scenes and mythological creatures in 113 oak choir-stalls.

The cathedral is open 9.30 am to noon and 2 to 5 pm daily. Admission to the grand chœur costs 8FF, including a guide sheet in English.

The 14th-century, 40m-high **Tour d'Armagnac** behind the cathedral served the medieval archbishops of Auch (and, later, Revolutionaries) as a prison. It's closed to the public.

Musée des Jacobins

The museum (☎ 05 62 05 74 79) at 4 place Louis Blanc, sometimes also called the Musée d'Auch, was established in 1793, its original collection selected from property seized in the Revolution. Occupying a 15th-century Dominican monastery, it's one of France's oldest and best provincial museums.

Highlights of this eclectic collection include frescoes and other artefacts from an early Gallo-Roman villa, landscapes by locally born painter Jean-Louis Rouméguère (1863–1925) and one of the country's finest collections of the ethnography of the Americas, from pre-Colombian pottery to 18th-century religious art.

It's open 10 am to noon and 2 to 6 pm Tuesday to Sunday (to 5 pm, October to April). Admission costs 20FF (10FF if you produce an entry ticket to the cathedral's grand chœur).

Escalier Monumental

The 370-step, 19th-century Monumental Stairway, now undergoing a much-needed face-lift, drops to the river from place Salinis. Near the bottom swaggers a statue of d'Artagnan, the fictional swashbuckling Gascon hero immortalised by Alexandre Dumas in *Les Trois Mousquetaires* (The Three Musketeers). Nearby, a series of narrow, stepped alleyways, collectively called Les Pousterles, also plunge to the plain.

Places to Stay

Camping The spartan, riverside *Camping*

Municipal de l'Île St-Martin (☎ 05 62 05 00 22), 1.2km south of the town centre, is open mid-April to mid-November and costs 40FF for two people, tent and car.

Hotels The friendly *Hôtel-Restaurant Scheherazade* (☎ 05 62 05 13 25, 7 rue Espagne) has singles/doubles with shower for 150/170FF (190/210FF with bathroom) and triples with bathroom for 230FF. Confusingly, it's also called Les Trois Mousquetaires.

East of the river, *Hôtel-Restaurant du Lion d'Or* (☎ 05 62 63 66 00, fax 05 62 63 00 38, 7 rue Pasteur) has comfortable rooms with bathroom for between 170FF and 350FF. *Hôtel de Paris* (☎ 05 62 63 26 22, fax 05 62 60 04 27, 38 ave de la Marne), closed in November, has singles/doubles with shower from 230/250FF.

Rooms at the splendid three-star *Hôtel de France* (☎ 05 62 61 71 71, fax 05 62 61 71 81, ✉ auchgarreau@intercom.fr, 2 place de la Libération) range from singles/doubles at 315/385FF to suites at 1850FF.

Places to Eat

Restaurants Serving plentiful Moroccan dishes for 55FF to 80FF is *Hôtel-Restaurant Scheherazade* (see Places to Stay). *Restaurant Asia* (☎ 05 62 05 93 17, 3 rue Arnaud de Môles), open daily except Monday, offers Chinese and Vietnamese dishes from 30FF to 60FF. *La Bodega* (☎ 05 62 05 69 17, 7 rue Dessoles), closed Sunday lunchtime, serves tapas or full meals and attracts a young crowd.

The bar at *Bar-Brasserie Le Chouan* (☎ 05 62 05 08 47, rue Mazagran), closed on Sunday, does baguette sandwiches (14FF to 20FF) and offers a good 45FF *buffet des entrées* – a glorified salad bar. In the brasserie upstairs, salads, omelettes and Gascon dishes start at 70FF or you can select from *menus* at 68FF and 89FF. Another inexpensive introduction to regional fare is the 75FF *menu* at the charming *Café Gascon* (☎ 05 62 61 88 08, 5 rue Lamartine); it is closed on Wednesday.

If you're serious about Gascon food, relax in the elegant *Jardin des Saveurs*

(☎ 05 62 61 71 71) at Hôtel de France, where chef Roland Garreau is an acknowledged specialist. It needn't bust your budget: enticing *menus* begin at only 110FF, rising to the gastronomic revelation of his *découvertes de Gascogne* (explore Gascony) menu at 380FF.

Self-Catering There's a *market* on Thursday around Jardin Ortholan and on Saturday in front of the cathedral.

Getting There & Away
Useful bus connections include Condom (34FF, 40 minutes, two to four daily), Montauban (53FF, 1¾ hours, three services daily – one by SNCF – on Monday, Wednesday and Friday) and Tarbes (63FF, two hours, three daily). These services stop at both the bus station (☎ 05 62 05 76 37) and train station (☎ 05 62 60 62 12).

Up to eight SNCF buses daily connect Auch's train station with Toulouse (72FF, 1¾ hours) and Agen (60FF, 1½ hours).

Getting Around
There's extensive free parking the length of allées d'Étigny. Cycles Sobinski (☎ 05 62 63 60 56) at 35 ave de l'Yser rents out both VTTs and touring bikes for 40/70/300FF per half-day/day/week.

CONDOM
postcode 32100 • pop 7500
• elevation 80m

Poor Condom, whose name has made it the butt of so many nudge-snigger English-language jokes (the French don't even use the word, preferring *préservatif* or, more familiarly, *capote anglaise*, an 'English hood' – touché!).

Some tourists only stop to be photographed beside the sign 'Bienvenue à Condom, Ville Propre' (Welcome to Condom,

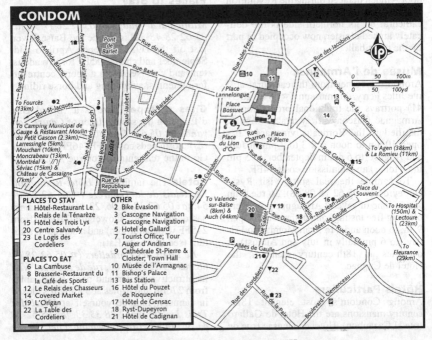

PLACES TO STAY
1 Hôtel-Restaurant Le Relais de la Ténarèze
15 Hôtel des Trois Lys
20 Centre Salvandy
23 Le Logis des Cordeliers

PLACES TO EAT
6 La Cambuse
8 Brasserie-Restaurant du la Café des Sports
12 Le Relais des Chasseurs
14 Covered Market
19 L'Origan
22 La Table des Cordeliers

OTHER
2 Bike Évasion
3 Gascogne Navigation
4 Gascogne Navigation
5 Hôtel de Gallard
7 Tourist Office; Tour Auger d'Andiran
9 Cathédrale St-Pierre & Cloister; Town Hall
10 Musée de l'Armagnac
11 Bishop's Palace
13 Bus Station
16 Hôtel du Pouzet de Roquepine
17 Hôtel de Gensac
18 Ryst-Dupeyron
21 Hôtel de Cadignan

the Clean Town). But if you penetrate more deeply, you'll find that this self-confident – and indeed very clean – town beside the Baïse River is worth a visit for its cathedral, some fine restaurants and a clutch of sober neoclassical mansions.

Information
The tourist office (☎ 05 62 28 00 80, fax 05 62 28 45 46, ⓔ otsi@condom.org) is in the 13th-century Tour Auger d'Andiran at place Bossuet, just west of the cathedral. It's open 9.30 am to noon and 2 to 5.30 pm Monday to Saturday (9 am to 12.30 pm and 2.30 to 7 pm daily in July and August). It carries a couple of useful walking guides, in French, to the heart of town (2FF each).

Cathédrale St-Pierre
Condom's 16th-century cathedral with its lofty nave and elaborately carved chancel is a rich example of southern flamboyant Gothic architecture. Its most richly sculpted door – much defaced during the Revolution – gives onto place St-Pierre. Abutting the cathedral on its northern side is the delicately arched cloister, now occupied in part by the town hall.

Musée de l'Armagnac
Around the corner from the cathedral at 2 rue Jules Ferry, this museum (☎ 05 62 28 31 41) portrays the traditional production of Armagnac, Gascony's fiery rival to Cognac, distilled in the Bordeaux vineyards. It's open 10 am to noon and 3 to 7 pm in July and August (to 6 pm in September, to 5 pm in October) and admission costs 14FF.

To sample the real stuff, visit **Ryst-Dupeyron** (☎ 05 62 28 08 08), 36 rue Jean Jaurès, one of several Armagnac producers offering free tastings and cellar tours. Open 9 am to noon and 2 to 5 pm Monday to Friday (to 6 pm daily in July and August), it occupies an 18th-century mansion, the Hôtel de Cugnac.

Hôtels Particuliers
Among Condom's most elegant 18th-century mansions are the Hôtel de Gallard (rue H Cazaubon), Hôtel de Gensac (rue de

Roquepine), Hôtel du Pouzet de Roquepine (rue Jean Jaurès) and Hôtel de Cadignan (allées de Gaulle). None is open to the public.

River Cruises
During July and August, Gascogne Navigation (☎ 05 62 28 46 46) runs 1½-hour cruises (45FF) every afternoon except Sunday at 3 and 4.30 pm from its quayside base, La Captainerie. It also rents out small boats by the day and bigger ones by the week, and has another office on rue Maréchal Foch.

Special Events
On the second weekend in May, Bandas à Condom brings marching and brass bands from all over Europe for 48 hours of nonstop oompah. Les Théatrales, a theatre festival highlighting young actors, is held from 16 to 21 July – immediately followed by Rockin' Condom, two days of rock around the clock.

Places to Stay
Camping The well-equipped *Camping Municipal de Gauge (☎ 05 62 28 17 32, fax 05 62 28 48 32)* is beside the Baïse River, just off the D931. It's open April to mid-September and charges 55FF for two adults, tent and car. Nearby is a sports centre offering tennis, swimming and horse riding.

Gîtes d'Étape There is a 16-bed Gîte d'Étape on the second floor of *Centre Salvandy (☎ 05 62 28 23 80, 20 rue Jean Jaurès)*; dorm beds cost 41FF (46FF in winter). Go to the rear entrance on rue St-Exupéry.

Hotels The family-run *Hôtel-Restaurant Le Relais de la Ténarèze (☎ 05 62 28 02 54, fax 05 62 28 46 96, 22 ave d'Aquitaine)* has doubles with shower for 210FF (from 245FF with bathroom) and a bargain restaurant (see Places to Eat).

Le Logis des Cordeliers (☎ 05 62 28 03 68, fax 05 62 68 29 03, rue de la Paix), with its attractive garden and pool, has doubles from 270FF and triples at 390FF. It's closed in January. Indulge yourself at *Hôtel des Trois Lys (☎ 05 62 28 33 33, fax 05 62 28 41 85, ⓔ hoteltroislys@minitel.net, 38 rue*

Gambetta); in an 18th-century mansion, it has basic rooms from 260FF and ones with bathroom costing between 420FF and 650FF. Both these hotels have pools.

Places to Eat

Restaurants For a small town, Condom is disproportionately rich in good-value restaurants.

Two hotel restaurants, two dining experiences that couldn't be more different; the one at *Hotel-Restaurant Le Relais de la Ténarèze* (see Places to Stay) serves a wonderfully hearty three-course dinner for 65FF; it's closed on Saturday evening and Sunday. There's no menu and you take what Madame has simmering in the pot. In contrast, the recently revamped restaurant at *Hôtel des Trois Lys* offers the finest Gascon cuisine with lipsmacking a la carte dishes for around 80FF and a *menu terroir* (regional menu) at 160FF.

La Cambuse (☎ 05 62 68 48 95), beside the tourist office, spills onto place Bossuet in summertime. Try their *formule crêpe* package: one sweet pancake, one savoury, salad, 0.25L of cider, and coffee, all for 45FF. It also does salads (32FF) and sandwiches (from 15FF). Another top choice for budget travellers is *L'Origan* (☎ 05 62 68 24 84, 4 rue Cadéo), closed on Sunday and Monday, offering a choice of robust Italian dishes. Both places also do takeaways. At the unpretentious *Le Relais des Chasseurs* (☎ 05 62 28 20 14, 3 blvd de la Libération), *menus* start at 55FF. It's closed in the evening, on Sunday and on Monday.

Brasserie-Restaurant du Café des Sports (☎ 05 62 28 15 26, 11 rue Charron) offers primarily regional cuisine in its rich *menus*, starting at 95FF. Another excellent, if pricier, choice for local specialities is *La Table des Cordeliers* (☎ 05 62 68 28 36), closed on Thursday. In a 14th-century chapel near Le Logis des Cordeliers (see Places to Stay), it has *menus* from 140FF to 320FF.

Restaurant Moulin du Petit Gascon (☎ 05 62 28 28 42) enjoys an unparalleled site on the river close to Camping Municipal de Gauge. *Menus* cost between 75FF (lunch only) and 145FF.

Self-Catering There's a *farmers' market*, rich in local produce, on Wednesday and Saturday mornings in the covered market.

Getting There & Away

ATR (☎ 05 62 05 46 24) has three to five daily buses to Auch (33FF, 50 minutes), including one that continues to Toulouse (81FF, 2½ hours) and one early-bird run daily to Bordeaux (101FF, three hours).

Citram Pyrénées (☎ 05 59 27 22 22) has a weekday bus to Pau (130FF, 2½ hours) at 11.15 am (9.10 am at weekends) and to Agen (46FF, 45 minutes). A return bus leaves Condom for Pau at 5.15 pm Monday to Saturday and at 3 pm on Sunday.

Getting Around

Bike Évasion (☎ 05 62 28 00 47) at 14 blvd St-Jacques, open Tuesday to Saturday, rents out bikes for 50/70/450FF per half-day/day/week.

AROUND CONDOM

Condom makes a good base for exploring the gentle Armagnac countryside and its attractive villages. Bus services, except to/from Lectoure, are nonexistent but the mild undulation makes it ideal cycling country.

Château de Cassaigne

Enjoy a free visit to this 13th-century chateau (☎ 05 62 28 04 02), the ancient country house of the bishops of Condom, and sample Armagnac from its 18th-century distillery. About 7km south-west of Condom, just off the D931 to Eauze, it's open 9 am to noon and 2 to 7 pm year-round.

Fourcès

Fourcès (pronounce that 's'), 13km north-west of Condom, is a picturesque bastide on the Auzoue river. Uniquely circular, it retains the shape of the original chateau that once occupied today's main 'square'. Well-restored medieval houses still ring its shady expanse. You can sip a drink or have a not-too-copious lunch on the terrace of *L'Auberge*, with *menus* at 85FF and 105FF. Opposite is the tiny, dusty, one-room Musée des Vieux Métiers (Museum of Ancient Crafts); admission is free.

There's an audioguide in English (15FF), available from the office of Multiple Rural at the entrance to the village.

Larressingle

Larressingle, 5km west of Condom on the D15, is probably France's cutest fortified village. It's certainly the most besieged, bravely withstanding armies of Compostela pilgrims and tourists.

It's well worth joining the throngs invading this textbook bastion, which bears witness to the troubled times of medieval Gascony. Within the largely intact original walls are the remains of a castle-keep, once the principal residence of the bishops of Condom, and the sturdy Romanesque Église St-Sigismond. More recent is **La Halte du Pèlerin** (The Pilgrims Waystage; ☎ 05 62 28 11 58), a rather naff waxwork museum of medieval village life (17FF) with an optional English commentary, open 10.30 am to 6.30 pm daily, June to September (from 2.30 pm during other school holidays).

Beyond the fortifications is **Cité des Machines du Moyen-Âge** (30FF), a display of working reproductions of medieval war engines, open 11 am to 5 pm from Easter to November (to 7 pm in July and August).

During July and August, there are afternoon guided tours in French (25FF, daily except Monday). Ring ☎ 05 62 28 39 83 for information.

Montréal & Séviac

Montréal, established in 1255, was one of Gascony's first bastides. Its chunky Gothic church squats at the edge of place Hôtel de Ville, the arcaded main square, scene of a bustling Friday market.

At Séviac, 1.5km south-west of Montréal, are the remarkable excavated remains of a 4th-century Gallo-Roman villa. Discovered by the local parish priest in 1868, the site is still being excavated. What archaeologists have revealed are the remains of a luxurious villa, including baths and outbuildings, on the agricultural estate of a 4th-century Roman aristocrat. Large areas

of its spectacular mosaic floors – over 450 mosaics have so far been uncovered – have survived.

Admission costs 20FF and includes entry to the museum at Montréal's tourist office where artefacts from Séviac are displayed. The site is open 10 am to noon and 2 to 6 pm daily, March to November (to 7 pm with no lunch break in July and August), and you can borrow a detailed explanatory sheet in English.

Montréal's tourist office and museum (☎ 05 62 29 42 85) on place Hôtel de Ville are both open 10 am to noon and 2 to 6 pm daily between June and October (weekdays only during the rest of the year, closed in January).

La Romieu

La Romieu, 11km from Condom and once an important stopover on the Santiago de Compostela route, takes its name from the Occitan *roumieu*, meaning pilgrim. It's dominated by the magnificent 14th-century collegiate church of St-Pierre (admission 20FF). Staff from the tourist office, just opposite the entrance, will let you into the fine Gothic cloister that gives onto the church. Left of the altar is the **sacristy** where original medieval frescoes include arcane biblical characters, black angels and esoteric symbols. Climb the 136 steps of the double-helix stairway to the top of the octagonal tower for a good view over the countryside.

The tourist office (☎ 05 62 28 86 33) and church are open 10 am to noon and 2 to 6 pm daily except Sunday morning (to 7 pm between June and September, closed in January).

In the six-hectare **Arboretum Coursiana** (☎ 05 62 68 22 80) west of the village, over 650 trees and rare plants flourish. The initiative of a local agricultural engineer, it's open 9 am to 7 pm daily, mid-March to November, and admission costs 25FF.

Lectoure

Lectoure's main claim to fame is its superb **Musée Lapidaire** (☎ 05 62 68 70 22) in the cellars of the former episcopal palace, today the town hall. It displays finds from several local Gallo-Roman sites, including some fine Roman jewellery, mosaics and an early Christian marble sarcophagus. Hours are 10 am to noon and 2 to 6 pm daily (closed on Tuesday, October to February); admission costs 15FF.

Rearing over the museum is the heavyweight bulk of the 15th-century **Cathédrale St-Gervais et St-Protais** with its curious, ornate tower.

The tourist office (☎ 05 62 68 76 98), beside the cathedral, is open 9 am to noon and 2 to 6 pm daily, except Saturday afternoon and Sunday (9 am to 12.30 pm and 2.30 to 7 pm daily in July and August).

Lectoure is 36km north of Auch. SNCF's Auch-Agen buses stop here eight times daily Monday to Friday, less often at weekends (Auch 35FF, 40 minutes; Agen 36FF, 50 minutes).

Andorra

The Catalan-speaking principality of Andorra (population 66,000), whose mountainous territory comprises only 464 sq km, nestles in the Pyrenees between Catalunya and France. Although it *is* tiny, this political anomaly contains some of the most dramatic scenery and best skiing in the Pyrenees. And in summer there's plenty of good walking in the higher, more remote parts of the principality. A handful of Romanesque churches give a glimpse of Andorra's history.

Facts about Andorra

HISTORY

By tradition, Andorra's independence is credited to Charlemagne, who captured the region from the Muslims in AD 803. In 843, Charlemagne's grandson, Charles II, granted the Valls d'Andorra (Valleys of Andorra) to Sunifred, Count of Urgell, whose base was La Seu d'Urgell, in Catalunya. From the counts, Andorra later passed to the bishops of La Seu d'Urgell. In the 13th century, after a successional dispute between the bishops and the French counts of Foix, to the north, Andorra's first constitutional documents, the Pareatges, established a system of shared sovereignty between the two rivals. This feudal set up created a peculiar political equilibrium that saved Andorra from being swallowed by its powerful neighbours.

Since the 1950s, Andorra has developed as a centre for skiing and duty-free shopping – the latter growing out of the smuggling of French goods to Spain during the Spanish Civil War and Spanish goods to France in WWII (Andorra remained neutral in both). These activities have brought not only wealth, foreign workers and eight million visitors a year, but also some unsightly development and heavy traffic within and around the capital, Andorra la Vella.

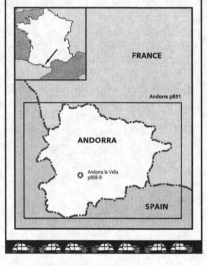

FRANCE

Andorra p851

ANDORRA

Andorra la Vella
p858-9

SPAIN

GEOGRAPHY

Andorra, is essentially a pair of major Pyrenean valleys and their surrounding mountains. It measures 25km from north to south at its maximum and 29km from east to west. Most of its 40 or so towns and hamlets – some with just a few dozen people – are in the valleys.

The main river, the Gran Valira, is formed near the capital, Andorra la Vella, by the confluence of the Rivers Valira d'Orient and Valira del Nord.

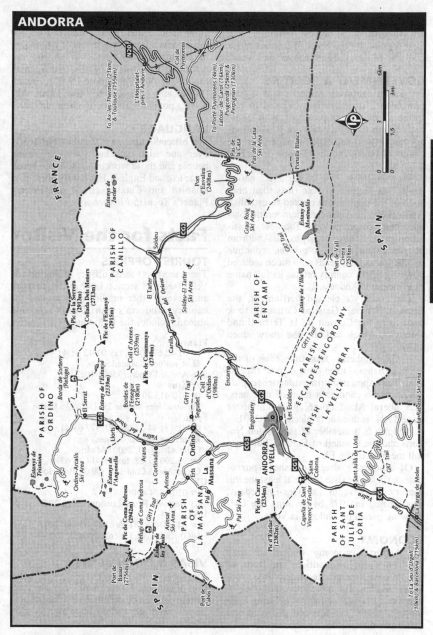

ANDORRA

Pic de Coma Pedrosa (2942m), in western Andorra, is the highest mountain. The lowest point, on the Spanish frontier at La Farga de Moles, is 838m above sea level.

GOVERNMENT & POLITICS

For seven centuries Andorra was a 'co-princedom', its sovereignty vested in two 'princes': the French president, who inherited the job from France's pre-Revolutionary kings (who had taken it over from the counts of Foix), and the bishops of La Seu d'Urgell.

Then in 1993, 75% of the 9123 native Andorrans eligible to vote (less than one-sixth of the population) elected to establish Andorra as an independent, democratic 'parliamentary co-princedom'. The new constitution gave full sovereignty to the Andorran people, although the 'co-princes' continue to function as joint heads with much reduced powers, and the country retains its full name of Principat d'Andorra.

The country's elected parliament, the Consell General (General Council), took over from the Consell de la Terra (Land Council), which had run the show since 1419.

Its 28 members – four from each of the seven parishes – meet three or four times a year. They appoint a prime minister *(cap de govern)* who chooses a team of ministers. The liberal Marc Forné, prime minister since 1994, is due for re-election in 2001.

Andorra is a member of the United Nations and the Council of Europe, but not a full member of the EU.

Of Andorra's seven parishes *(parròquies)*, six have existed since at least the 9th century. The seventh, Escaldes-Engordany, was created in 1978 by dividing the fast-growing parish of Andorra la Vella.

ECONOMY

The Andorran economy is based on cheap tax-free shopping, tourism (millions of people pass through the principality every year) banking. The most important components of the small and ever-declining agricultural sector are tobacco growing and cattle raising.

POPULATION & PEOPLE

Only about a quarter of Andorra's 66,000 inhabitants, almost two-thirds of whom live in Andorra la Vella and its suburbs, are Andorran nationals. The rest are Spanish (about 30,000), Portuguese (5000), French (5000) and others. Until the 1950s Andorra's population was only around 6000.

LANGUAGE

The official language is Catalan, but nearly everyone also speaks Spanish. Young people and those working in tourism speak basic to good English. For handy phrases in Spanish and Catalan check out Lonely Planet's *Spanish Phrasebook*.

Facts for the Visitor

TOURIST OFFICES

There are two tourist offices in Andorra la Vella (see that section later in the chapter) and several other smaller ones around the country. Andorra's tourist representation abroad includes the following:

France
(☎ 01 42 61 50 55, fax 01 42 61 41 91,
🖃 ot_andorra@wanadoo.fr)
26 Ave de l'Opéra, 75001 Paris
Germany
(☎ 030-415 49 14)
Finsterwalder Strasse 28, D-13435 Berlin
Spain
(☎ 91 431 74 53, fax 91 577 63 41,
🖃 turisme.andorra@ctv.es)
Calle Alcalá 73, 28001 Madrid
(☎ 93 200 07 87, fax 93 414 18 63)
Carrer Marià Cubí 159, 08021 Barcelona
UK
(☎ 020-8874 4806)
63 Westover Road, London SW18 2RF
USA
(☎ 847-674 30 91, fax 847-329 94 70)
6800 Knox Ave, Lincolnwood, IL 60646

VISAS & DOCUMENTS

Visas aren't necessary, but bring your passport or national ID card with you. The relevant regulations for France or Spain should be followed, depending on which is travelled through to reach Andorra.

EMBASSIES & CONSULATES
Andorran Embassies

Andorra has embassies in France and Spain:

France
(☎ 01 40 06 03 30, fax 01 40 06 03 64)
30 Rue d'Astorg, 75008 Paris
Spain
(☎ 91 431 7453, fax 91 577 63 41,
✉ ambaixada@emb-principado-andorra.es)
Calle Alcalá 73, 28001 Madrid

Embassies & Consulates in Andorra

France and Spain maintain reciprocal diplomatic missions in Andorra:

France
Embassy: (☎ 82 08 09) Carrer les Canals 38–40
Consulate: (☎ 86 91 96) Carrer de la Sobrevia
Spain
Embassy: (☎ 80 00 30) Carrer Prat de la Creu 34

CUSTOMS

For information about duty-free allowances for goods entering Spain or France from Andorra, pick up the leaflet *Traveller's Duty Free Allowance* from a tourist office. Allowances include 5L of still wine; either 1.5L of spirits or 3L of lighter spirits or sparkling wine and 300 cigarettes. Checks for smugglers are rigorous on the Spanish border.

MONEY

Andorra, which has no currency of its own, will continue to use pesetas (ptas) and French francs (FF) until euro notes and coins are issued on 1 January 2002.

Exchange Rates

country	unit		franc		peseta
Australia	A$1	=	4.04FF	=	102 ptas
Canada	C$1	=	5.02FF	=	127 ptas
euro	€1	=	6.56FF	=	166 ptas
France			10FF	=	254 ptas
Germany	DM1	=	3.35FF	=	85 ptas
Ireland	IR£1	=	8.32FF	=	211 ptas
Japan	¥100	=	6.87FF	=	174 ptas
Netherlands	NLG1	=	2.97FF	=	76 ptas
New Zealand	NZ$1	=	3.05FF	=	77 ptas
Spain			3.94FF	=	100 ptas
UK	£1	=	10.96FF	=	278 ptas
USA	US$1	=	7.50FF	=	190 ptas

POST & COMMUNICATIONS
Post

Andorra has no postal service of its own. France and Spain each operate a separate postal system with their own Andorran stamps. They're valid only for items posted within Andorra – and needed only for international mail since letters for destinations within the country go free.

International mail (except letters to Spain) is better routed through the French postal system.

Letters to Andorra la Vella marked 'Poste Restante' go to the town's French post office. It costs about 3FF per letter.

Telephone

International Andorra's country code is ☎ 376. The cheap rate for international calls applies between 9 pm and 7 am plus all day Sunday. During off-peak hours, a three-minute call to Europe costs 210 ptas (306 ptas to the US or Australia). Dial ☎ 111 for directory assistance.

Public Telephones Public telephones take pesetas (francs in Pas de la Casa) or an Andorran *teletarja*. These are telephone cards worth 50, 100 and 150 units are widely sold and cost 500/900/1350 ptas.

Email and Internet Access

You can log on at Punt Internet (☎ 86 36 71) on the fifth floor of Carrer Bonaventura Riberaygua 39, near the bus station, in Andorra la Vella. It opens 10 am to 1 pm and 3.30 to 9 pm weekdays (plus 4 to 8 pm Saturday in August and September). It costs 1000 ptas per hour.

MEDIA

Andorra has three radio stations: the government-run Ràdio Nacional Andorra (RNA; 94.2MHz); Ràdio Valira (93.3MHz) and Radio Andorra Uno (96.0MHz), both private. You can see Spanish and French TV, along with the local ATV station.

The principality's main daily paper is the conservative, Catalan language *Diari d'Andorra*. The other daily is the *Periodic d'Andorra*; *Poble Andorra* is published weekly.

TIME

Andorra is two hours ahead of GMT/UTC from the last Sunday in March to the last Sunday in October, and one hour at other times.

ELECTRICITY

The electric current is 220V at 50Hz.

USEFUL ORGANISATIONS

For information on weather and snow conditions in winter, call ☎ 84 88 52 (Spanish) or ☎ 84 88 53 (French). Ring ☎ 84 88 84 for information about road conditions in Spanish, French and Catalan.

DANGERS & ANNOYANCES

There's only minimal legislation to protect the consumer. And there's no grading system for hotels, which sometimes fail to post their prices. Some have tariffs that differ wildly between low and high season.

Long traffic jams can clog Andorra la Vella's main arteries and Andorran drivers must rank among Europe's most reckless. Without respect for zebra crossings, they hurtle around the tight mountain bends as if propelled by some collective death wish.

Emergency telephone numbers include:

Police	☎ 110
Medical emergency	☎ 116
Fire or ambulance	☎ 118
Mountain rescue service	☎ 112

BUSINESS HOURS & PUBLIC HOLIDAYS

Shops in Andorra la Vella are generally open 9.30 am to 1 pm and 3.30 to 8 pm daily except (in most cases) Sunday afternoon.

ACTIVITIES

Skiing

Downhill Andorra, with five downhill ski resorts, boasts the Pyrenees' best skiing and snowboarding with ski passes that are considerably cheaper than those of most other European resorts. For up-to-the-minute information, contact one of the capital's two tourist offices or Ski Andorra (☎ 86 43 89, fax 86 59 10, @ skiand@andornet.ad).

Best resorts are Soldeu-El Tarter and Pas de la Casa-Grau Roig in the east. In the north-west, Arinsal, Pal and Ordino-Arcalís are more limited and often windier.

Skiing is good for all levels. The season normally lasts from December to April, depending on snow conditions (all resorts have snow-making machines if nature lets them down).

Prices for lift passes and ski school (and often accommodation too) rise at peak times: all weekends, 23 December to 7 January, 10 February to early March (when French schools enjoy their winter break) and Easter week.

You can buy a five-day pass for all resorts for 15,450 ptas (low season) or 18,300 ptas (high season).

Skiing tuition costs 3600–4250 ptas an hour for individuals, or 10,100–12,500 ptas for 15 hours of group classes.

You can hire ski gear for around 1500 ptas daily (5200–7250 ptas for five days). Snowboards cost 2500–3000 ptas a day (10,500–13,500 ptas for five days).

Cross-Country Skiing La Rabassa in the south is a cross-country skiing centre with 15km of marked forest trails.

Walking

Andorra's tranquil, unspoiled back country hides more than 50 lakes beneath its soaring mountains. Best season for walking is June to September, when temperatures reach well above 20°C, dropping to around 10°C at night. June can be wet.

Walkers can sleep for free in any of Andorra's 26 mountain refuges (*refugis*; see following Accommodation section).

The most up-to-date and accurate maps are a series of four covering the whole of this small country. Produced at 1:25000 by the Spanish IGN, *Llorts*, No 183-I, and *Andorra La Vella*, No 183-III, are available while Nos 183-II and 183-IV were in the pipeline at the time of writing.

Tourist offices stock a very useful booklet (*Sport Activities* in English) with 52 recommended walks and over a dozen mountain bike routes.

ACCOMMODATION

Andorra, which lives from touroeuros, is tough for budget accommodation. Most visitors come within organised tours – indeed, if you're happy to stay in one place, the cheapest option, especially during the ski season, is to take a package holiday.

Hotels fill up in July and August and from December to March, when many places increase prices substantially and others don't take independent travellers.

Andorra's 26 refuges (essentially for walkers) do not require reservations. All are some distance from the road and all except one are unstaffed and free. Most have bunks, fireplaces and drinkable water but no cooking facilities. Invest 200 ptas in the *Mapa de Refugis i Grans Recorreguts*, a map which pinpoints them all.

Tourist offices stock a comprehensive free brochure, *Hotels, Restaurants, Apartaments i Càmpings*. Be warned, however, that, while the rest of the information is reliable, the prices it quotes are merely suggestions.

SHOPPING

With low customs duties and no sales tax, Andorra is famous for luxury goods shopping. Emporia cluster in Andorra la Vella, Pas de la Casa and near the Spanish border; even though potential savings are no longer what they were, shopping around, you could pay up to 25% less than in Spain or France.

Getting There & Away

The only way into Andorra – unless you trek across the mountains – is by road. One of the two roads in climbs from La Seu d'Urgell in Spain, 20km south of Andorra la Vella. The other enters Andorra at Pas de la Casa on the eastern border with France, then crosses the spectacular 2408m Port d'Envalira, the Pyrenees' highest road pass, en route to Andorra la Vella. Both entry routes have bus services.

The nearest major airports are in Barcelona (225km south) and Toulouse (180km north). Both are linked to Andorra by bus or train and bus combinations.

Schedules for some of the following bus and train services are subject to seasonal change.

BUS & TRAIN
France

Autocars Nadal (☎ 82 11 38), with the French company Espace Fram, link Toulouse's bus station and Andorra la Vella (2750 ptas, four hours, two buses daily on Monday, Wednesday, Friday and Sunday). Services to Toulouse continue to the town's airport, starting point for the evening bus to Andorra, which departs at 6 pm, then calls by the Toulouse bus station.

By rail, the most convenient option is to take a train from Toulouse to either L'Hospitalet (2¼ to 2¾ hours) or Latour-de-Carol (2½ to 3¼ hours), both in France. From Latour de Carol station, Hispano Andorrana buses (1125 ptas, 10.30 am and 1.15 pm daily) go on to Andorra la Vella. Two daily buses make the return journey (7.30 am and 10.30 am). The early one allows you to connect with trains to Toulouse and Barcelona and, if you hang around, Perpignan.

From L'Hospitalet, two buses leave for Andorra la Vella (7.35 am and 7.45 pm, daily). Returning buses from the Andorran capital also run daily (5.45 am, 1.30 pm in summer, and 5 pm).

In high summer, there's a supplementary daily service from L'Hospitalet (5 pm). Five buses run from L'Hospitalet as far as Pas de la Casa on Saturdays.

If you're picking up a bus mid-route – at Soldeu for instance – get to the stop in good time, as they sometimes go through earlier than scheduled.

See also the Spain section below.

Spain

La Hispano Andorrana (☎ 82 13 72) buses run between La Seu d'Urgell and Carrer Doctor Nequi in Andorra la Vella (345 ptas, 30 minutes, five to eight daily).

ANDORRA

Alsina Graells (☎ 82 73 79) buses link Barcelona's Estació del Nord and Andorra la Vella's bus station, Carrer Bonaventura Riberaygua (2435 ptas to 2715 ptas, four hours, up to seven buses daily).

Novatel Autocars (☎ 86 48 87, ❷ novatel @andornet.ad) has services from Andorra la Vella's bus station to Barcelona's El Prat airport (3500 ptas, three daily). Eurolines (☎ 86 00 10) buses run between Andorra la Vella (departing from the car park of Hotel Diplomàtic opposite the bus station) and Barcelona's Sants bus station (2800 ptas, four daily). Three buses originate from/ continue to Barcelona's El Prat airport (3300 ptas).

Samar/Andor-Inter (☎ 82 62 89) buses link Andorra la Vella and Madrid (4700 ptas, 9 hours, three times weekly) via Zaragoza (2300 ptas).

A fun alternative is to take the 9.18 am train from Barcelona's Sants station to Latour-de-Carol in France, from where a connecting bus leaves for Andorra at 1.15 pm (total journey costs 2500 ptas, 5½ hours). In the reverse direction, there's no such convenient connection; it's better to take a direct bus to Barcelona.

Getting Around

BUS
Buses run along the principality's three main roads; the CG1, CG2 and CG3. Ask at a tourist office for the free brochure, Línies Regulars de Transport Públic de Passatgers, which gives current timetables for the eight bus routes radiating from the capital.

CAR & MOTORCYCLE
The speed limit is 40km/h in populated areas and 90km/h elsewhere. Two problems are the recklessness of local drivers (see Dangers & Annoyances) and Andorra la Vella's horrendous traffic jams. It's possible to bypass the worst of the latter by taking Avinguda de Salou, which becomes Avinguda de Tarragona, around the southern side of town. If you're travelling between the parishes of Ordino or La Massana and Encamp or Canillo, avoid this motorist's nightmare by taking the scenically striking route over the Coll d'Ordino. However, snow blocks this alternative for much of the winter.

Andorra la Vella

pop 23,000 • elevation 1029m
Andorra la Vella (Vella, meaning 'old', is pronounced 'vey-yah'), capital and only real town of the principality, lies in the valley of the River Gran Valira, surrounded by mountains of up to 2400m.

The town is mainly engaged in retailing duty-free electronics and luxury goods. With the mountains, constant din of jackhammers and 'mall' architecture, you could almost be in Hong Kong, were it not for the snowcapped peaks and lack of noodle shops!

Orientation
Andorra la Vella is strung out along one main street, whose name changes from Avinguda Príncep Benlloch to Avinguda Meritxell to Avinguda Carlemany. The little Barri Antic (Historic Quarter) is split by this traffic filled artery. The town merges with the once separate villages of Les Escaldes and Engordany to the east and Santa Coloma to the south-west.

Information
Tourist Offices The municipal tourist office (☎/fax 82 71 17), Plaça de la Rotonda, opens 9 am to 1 pm and 4 to 8 pm daily (to 7 pm on Sunday, continuously to 9 pm in July and August).

The national tourist office (☎ 82 02 14, fax 82 58 23) is just off Plaça Rebés. It's open 10 am (9 am, July to September) to 1 pm and 3 to 7 pm Monday to Saturday plus Sunday morning.

Money Crédit Andorrà, Avinguda Meritxell 80, has a 24-hour banknote exchange machine that accepts 15 currencies.

American Express is represented by the Viatges Relax travel agency (☎ 82 20 44, fax 82 70 55, ✉ relaxtravel@viatgesrelax .com), Carrer Mossén Tremosa 2.

Post & Communications The French post office, La Poste (☎ 82 04 08), Carrer Pere d'Urg 1, opens 8.30 am to 2.30 pm weekdays and 9 am to noon Saturday. It takes only French francs. Conversely, the Spanish post office, Correus i Telègrafs, (☎ 82 02 57), Carrer Joan Maragall 10, accepts only pesetas. This particular piece of Ruritanian silliness – they're the only institutions not to deal in both currencies – will cease in 2002, when both will use euros. It at least observes the same hours as its counterpart.

You can make international telephone calls from street pay phones or from the Servei de Telecomunicacions d'Andorra (STA; ☎ 86 01 23), Avinguda Meritxell 110, which also has a fax service. It opens 9 am to 9 pm daily.

For information on email and Internet access see Facts for the Visitor earlier in the chapter.

Bookshops Casa del Llibre, Carrer Fiter Rossell 3, has a reasonable selection of books, some in English. For readers of Spanish, French or Catalan, Llibreria Jaume Caballé (☎ 82 94 54), Avinguda Fiter Rossell 31, has a splendid collection of second hand and new travel books and maps, but few titles in English.

Barri Antic

The small Barri Antic was the heart of Andorra la Vella when it was little more than a village. The **Casa de la Vall**, constructed in 1580, has served as Andorra's parliament building since 1702. Downstairs is **El Tribunal de Corts**, the country's only courtroom. The **Sala del Consell**, upstairs, is one of the cosiest parliament chambers in the world. The **Chest of the Seven Locks** (Set Panys) once held Andorra's most important official documents; it could be opened only if a key-bearing representative from each of the seven parishes was present.

Free, heavily subscribed guided tours (available in English) are given Monday to

Saturday (daily in August). In summer it's advisable to book at least a week ahead (☎ 82 91 29) to ensure a place. This said, individuals can often be squeezed in at the last minute.

Plaça del Poble

This large public square, just south of Plaça Rebés, occupies the roof of the Edifici Administratiu Govern d'Andorra, a modern government building. Affording good views, it's a popular local gathering place. The lift in the south-eastern corner whisks you down to the car park below.

Caldea

In Les Escaldes, what looks like a large, futuristic cathedral is actually the Caldea spa complex (☎ 80 09 95), Europe's largest. Fed by hot springs, its heart is a 600 sq m lagoon kept at a constant 32°C. Other pools, plus Turkish baths, saunas, jacuzzis and hydromassage are included in the three-hour admission ticket (2950 ptas).

Caldea is a 10 minute walk upstream from Plaça de la Rotonda. It opens daily from 10 am until 11 pm (the last admission is at 9 pm).

Places to Stay – Budget

Camping At the southern edge of town, *Camping Valira* (☎ 82 23 84, *Avinguda de Salou*) charges 525 ptas per person/tent/car and has a small pool. It opens year round. *Camping Riberaygua* (☎ 82 66 99) and *Camping Santa Coloma* (☎ 82 88 99), both in Santa Coloma, about 2.5km south-west of Plaça Guillemó, also open year round and have similar prices.

Pensiones, Hostels & Hotels For excellent value try *Residència Benazet* (☎ 82 06 98, *Carrer la Llacuna 21*) where large rooms (with washbasin), for up to four people, cost 1400 ptas a person.

Nearby, the friendly *Hostal del Sol* (☎ 82 37 01, *Plaça Guillemó*) has spruce singles/ doubles with shower for 2000/3900 ptas.

In the Barri Antic, *Pensió La Rosa* (☎ 82 18 10, *Antic Carrer Major 18*) has plain singles/doubles for 2000/3500 ptas plus

ANDORRA

ANDORRA

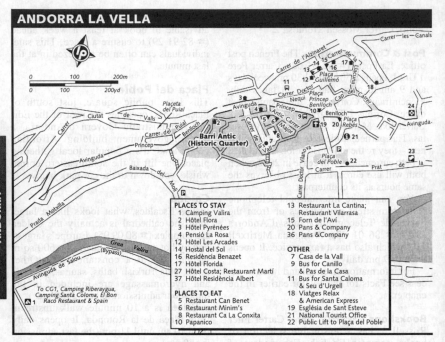

ANDORRA LA VELLA

0	100	200m
0	100	200yd

Barri Antic (Historic Quarter)

PLACES TO STAY
1   Càmping Valira
2   Hôtel Flora
3   Hôtel Pyrénées
4   Pensió La Rosa
12 Hôtel Les Arcades
14 Hostal del Sol
16 Residència Benazet
17 Hôtel Florida
27 Hôtel Costa; Restaurant Martí
37 Hôtel Residència Albert

PLACES TO EAT
5   Restaurant Can Benet
6   Restaurant Minim's
8   Restaurant Ca La Conxita
10 Papanico

13 Restaurant La Cantina;
    Restaurant Vilarrasa
15 Forn de l'Aví
20 Pans & Company
36 Pans &Company

OTHER
7   Casa de la Vall
9   Bus for Canillo
    & Pas de la Casa
11 Bus for Santa Caloma
    & Seu d'Urgell
18 Viatges Relax
    & American Express
19 Església de Sant Esteve
21 National Tourist Office
22 Public Lift to Plaça del Poble

To CG1, Camping Riberaygua,
Camping Santa Coloma, El Bon
Racó Restaurant & Spain

triples, quads and a veritable dormitory sleeping six for 1500 ptas per person.

Hotel Costa (☎ 82 14 39, *Avinguda Meritxell 44*) has basic but clean rooms for 1700/3000 ptas. Recently renovated *Hotel Residència Albert* (☎ 82 01 56, *Avinguda Doctor Mitjavila 16*) has good value singles/doubles/triples, the majority with bathroom, for 2700/4500/6000 ptas.

Places to Stay – Mid-Range & Top End

The delightful *Hotel Florida* (☎ 82 01 05, fax 86 19 25, 🖃 *aran@solucions.ad, Calle la Lacuna 15*), one block from Plaça Guillemó, has modern singles/doubles for 5425/7850 ptas (6750/9500 ptas at weekends), including breakfast. *Hotel Les Arcades* (☎ 82 13 55, *Plaça Guillemó 5*) has rooms with bathroom and TV for 5000 ptas.

At *Hotel Pyrénées* (☎ 86 00 06, fax 82 02 65, 🖃 *ph@mypic.ad, Avinguda Príncep Benllock 20*), rooms cost 5000/8250 ptas;

half-board is obligatory in the high season. *Hotel Flora* (☎ 82 15 08, fax 86 20 85, 🖃 *flora@andornet.ad, Antic Carrer Major 25*) has immaculate singles/doubles/triples for 6500/9500/13,000 ptas, including breakfast. Both hotels have a tennis court, a swimming pool and private garage (1000–1300 ptas per night).

Nearly all hotels in this category hike up their prices by 20% or more in the high season (including August and major Spanish or French public holidays), when advance reservations are essential.

Places to Eat

Restaurants The friendly *Restaurant La Cantina* (*Plaça Guillemó*) is a place where you can expect huge servings. An *amanida variada* (mixed salad) as an entrée is almost big enough to make you forget about the main course. These start at around 800 ptas or you can choose from their 1200 ptas *menu*. Next door, try welcoming

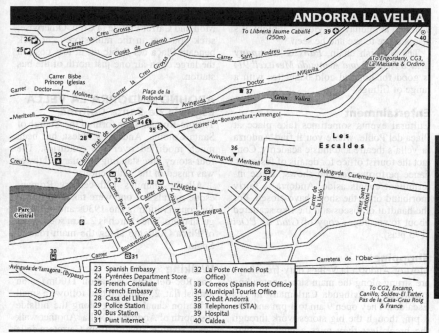

ANDORRA LA VELLA

23 Spanish Embassy	32 La Poste (French Post
24 Pyrénées Department Store	Office)
25 French Consulate	33 Correos (Spanish Post Office)
26 French Embassy	34 Municipal Tourist Office
28 Casa del Llibre	35 Crèdit Andorrà
29 Police Station	38 Telephones (STA)
30 Bus Station	39 Hospital
31 Punt Internet	40 Caldea

Vilarrasa, which has good value two/three course *menus* at 950/1450 ptas. Just off Plaça Guillemó, **Forn de l'Aví** has an excellent *menu* for 850 ptas and does hunky *platos combinados* (725 ptas to 850 ptas). With its wide selection of breads and sticky cakes, plus great coffee, it's a good place to start the day.

There is a trio of great places in the heart of the Barri Antic. **Restaurant Ca La Conxita** (☎ 82 99 48, *Placeta de Monjó 3*) is a bustling little family business where you can see the staff cooking. You can eat well for around 2500 ptas. **Restaurant Can Benet** (☎ 82 89 22, *Antic Carrer Major 9*), where main dishes cost between 1600 ptas and 2300 ptas, is also delightful. A couple of doors away and in the same price bracket, **Restaurant Minim's** also serves primarily French dishes in an equally pleasant ambience.

The restaurant of **Hotel Pyrénées** (see Places to Stay) serves Catalan, French and Spanish dishes amid sparkling chandeliers and two-tone tablecloths. Platos combinados go from a very reasonable 625 ptas to 1400 ptas.

Restaurant Martí, (☎ 82 43 84, *Avinguda Meritxell 44*), has *menus* for 1200 ptas and 1550 ptas and platos combinados from 650 ptas.

The best place for real Catalan cooking is the decidedly upmarket **El Bon Racó** (☎ 82 20 85, *Avinguda de Salou 86*), Santa Coloma's main street, about a kilometre west of Camping Valira. Meat – especially *xai* (lamb) – roasted in an open hearth is the speciality, but you might also try *escudella*, a stew of chicken, sausage and vegetables and almost the Andorran national dish. Expect to part with close to 3000 ptas for a full meal with wine.

Fast Food & Snacks Lively **Papanico** (☎ 86 73 33, *Avinguda Príncep Benlloch 4*) has tasty *tapas* from 250 ptas each and does a range of sandwiches and platos combinados. Fun at midday and vibrant at night, it's also a place to see and be seen.

The Spanish chain, **Pans & Company** (*Plaça Rebés 2 and Avinguda Meritxell 91*) is good for hot and cold baguettes with a range of fillings.

Entertainment
Cultural events sometimes take place at Plaça del Poble, where you'll find Andorra la Vella's theatre and music academy. Contact the tourist office for details of festivals, dance performances and shows. These intermittent events aside, Andorra is fairly moribund once the shops have closed. For the handful of discos and the like scattered about town, buy a copy of *Guia de l'Oci* (175 ptas).

Shopping
Most of Andorra la Vella's duty-free shops are strung along the main street, extending eastwards to Avinguda Carlemany in Les Escaldes. They open 9 am to 1 pm and 4 to 8 pm, though the big stores work through the break lest they miss a buck or two. When the eager hordes pour in on Saturdays and in July and August, the shops open from 9 am to 9 pm (until 7 pm on Sunday).

Getting There & Around
Buses to La Seu d'Urgell via Santa Coloma and Sant Julià leave from the stop on Carrer Doctor Nequi. Those for all other Andorran destinations and French railway stations just over the border (see Getting There & Away earlier in this chapter) pass by the bus stop on Avinguda Príncep Benlloch. Long distance buses pull in at the main bus station.

Call ☎ 86 30 00 to order a taxi in Andorra la Vella. To hire a car, ring Europcar (☎ 82 00 91, fax 82 06 42), Avis (☎ 87 18 55, fax 87 18 45) or Hertz (☎ 82 64 04, fax 86 70 40).

Parking Andorra la Vella is a traffic nightmare; you're much better off walking. Vehicles with non-Andorran number plates can stay without charge for up to 48 hours in the car park at the junction of Baixada del Moli and Carrer Prat de la Creu. Otherwise, stick your car in the multistorey car park beneath Plaça del Poble or, at less cost, in the large open-air one just north of the bus station.

AROUND ANDORRA LA VELLA
Església de Santa Coloma
The pre-Romanesque form of the Church of Santa Coloma, Andorra's oldest, has been much modified over the centuries. The four-storey, free standing circular bell tower was raised in the 12th century.

All the church's 12th-century Romanesque murals but one were taken to Berlin for conservation in the 1930s and still languish there. The church is 2.5km south-west of Plaça Guillemó along the main road to Spain.

Walking
The **Rec del Solà** (elevation 1100m) is an almost flat, 2.5km path that follows a small irrigation canal running along the hillside just north of Andorra la Vella. Another walk heads south-eastwards from Carretera de la Comella up to the **Refugi de Prat Primer** (2250m). The ascent takes about three hours from Andorra la Vella.

From Carrer dels Barrers in Santa Coloma, a path leads north-westwards up the hill to **Capella de Sant Vicenç d'Enclar** (20 minutes), former site of a castle. A trail continues up the valley to **Bony de la Pica** (2405m) on the Spanish border, from which you can follow the crest north-east to **Pic d'Enclar** (2382m) and **Pic de Carroi** (2334m), which overlooks Santa Coloma from the north – a fairly exacting circular day's walk.

North-Western Andorra

La Massana, 6km north of Andorra la Vella, is the gateway to the ski centres of Arinsal and Pal. From here the CG3 continues north into the mountainous Parish of Ordino, arguably the country's most beautiful area, with its slate and fieldstone farmhouses, gushing streams and picturesque old bridges. It has plenty of fine walks and, in winter, skiing at the Ordino-Arcalís ski area.

LA MASSANA

pop 3000 • elevation 1253m

The village of La Massana, much less attractive than its smaller neighbours a few kilometres north, has a number of hotels and some good restaurants.

The tourist office (☎ 83 56 93), Plaça del Quart, is at the junction of the CG3 and the road to Arinsal and Pal. It opens 9 am to 1 pm and 3 to 7 pm daily.

Places to Stay

La Massana is a little too brash and noisy and not close enough to either the skiing or walking action to make a great base. It can be a backup if places farther into the mountains are full.

Camping Santa Catarina (☎ 83 50 65) is in a grassy field next to a stream just outside La Massana by the CG3. It opens late-June to mid-September. Charges are 385 ptas per person and 350 ptas each per tent and car. The rather dreary *Hotel Palanques (☎ 83 50 07)* is La Massana's cheapest option. On the corner of the CG3 and Carrer Major, it has singles/doubles with shower for 3000/4500 ptas.

Places to Eat

You can get pizzas from 800 ptas at *Pizzeria el Vesuvio* on the main road just north of Hotel La Massana. *Restaurant Cal Cristobal*, much more gastronomically exciting, specialises in grills with main dishes between 1000 ptas and 1500 ptas. To get there, climb the steps opposite the Esso garage on the CG3, a little north of the Pizzeria.

Just outside the village are two of Andorra's better restaurants; *La Borda de l'Aví*, half a kilometre north of the tourist office on the road to Arinsal, and *La Borda Raubert*, 1km beyond. Both are rustic places with open hearths and offer grills, Andorran specialities and a range of good wines.

Getting There & Away

Buses between Andorra la Vella and Ordino pass through La Massana about every half-hour from 7 am to 9 pm.

ARINSAL & PAL SKI AREAS

Arinsal (☎ 83 58 22, fax 83 62 42), 5km north-west of La Massana, has good skiing and snowboarding for beginners and intermediates and a lively après-ski scene. Pal (☎ 83 62 36, fax 83 59 04), 7km from La Massana, has gentler slopes that make it ideal for families.

Both of the more exposed ski areas of Pal and Ordino-Arcalís (see later in this section) can be considerably colder than those of eastern Andorra.

Skiing

Arinsal has 28km of pistes, a vertical drop of 1010m and 13 lifts – including a smart new cabin lift to hurtle you up from the village. Lift passes cost 2800/3300 ptas a day in the low/high season. For three days it costs 7500/9000 ptas.

Pal has 35km of pistes, a vertical drop of 578m and 12 lifts. Lift passes cost 3000/3700 ptas a day in the low/high season. Three day passes cost 7500/9000 ptas.

Walking

From Aparthotel Crest at Arinsal's northern extremity, a trail leads north-westwards then westwards to **Estany de les Truites** (2260m). *Refugi de Coma Pedrosa (☎ 32 79 55)*, Andorra's only staffed mountain refuge, is just above this natural lake. The cost per night is 1100 ptas, and it does snacks and meals (dinner is 1800 ptas). It opens June to late September. The steepish walk up to the lake takes around 1½ hours. From here, it's about a further 1½ to 2 hours to **Pic de la Coma Pedrosa** (2942m), Andorra's highest point.

Places to Stay

The large, well equipped *Camping Xixerella (☎ 83 66 13)* near Erts is open year round and has an outdoor swimming pool. Charges are 500 ptas to 600 ptas each per adult, tent and car.

ANDORRA

In Arinsal, the friendly and recently renovated *Hostal Pobladó* (☎ *83 51 22,* **ⓔ** *hospoblado@andornet.ad)* is situated beside the new cabin lift. Its lively bar also offers Internet access on the side. Rooms cost 4400 ptas (6100 ptas with bathroom), including breakfast. *Hotel Coma Pedrosa* (*☎/fax 83 51 23)*, also welcoming and popular with skiers and summer walkers, has rooms for 5500 ptas.

More upmarket, *Hotel Solana* (☎ *83 51 27, fax 83 73 95)* has large rooms with bathroom for 6500/9000 ptas. Pal has no accommodation.

Places to Eat

As a change from the plentiful snack and sandwich joints, try Arinsal's *Refugi de la Fondue*, up the hill towards the main chair lift, which does cheese or meat *fondue* dishes. Although *Restaurant el Moli* bills itself as Italian – and indeed offers the usual staple pastas and pizzas (both 900 ptas to 1200 ptas) – it also has more exotic fare such as pork stir fry (1575 ptas) and Thai green coconut chicken curry (1650 ptas).

Entertainment

In winter, Arinsal fairly throbs after sunset. In summer, it can be almost mournful. When the snow's around, call by *Surf* near the base of the cabin lift. This pub, dance venue and restaurant, specialises in Argentinian dishes of juicy grilled meat (1250 ptas to 2200 ptas). *Rocky Mountain*, similarly all-embracing, has a gringo menu with dishes such as T-bone steak and 'New York style cheesecake'. *Quo Vadis*, a late-night bar popular with English skiers, occasionally has live music.

Getting There & Away

Daily buses run between Andorra la Vella and Arinsal via La Massana (185 ptas, 9.30 am, 1 and 6.15 pm). Buses also link La Massana and Arinsal (10 daily), and La Massana and Pal (four daily). In winter, Skibus runs between La Massana and Arinsal (325 ptas, five daily), and Arinsal and Pal (five daily). For some of these services, you need to change in Erts.

ORDINO
pop 1000 • elevation 1300m

Ordino is large as local villages go. Despite recent development it retains its Andorran character, as most buildings are still constructed using local stone. The tourist office (☎ 73 70 80) is within the Centre Esportiu d'Ordino sports complex beside the CG3. It opens 9 am to 1 pm and 3 to 7 pm daily (morning only on Sunday).

Museu d'Areny i Plandolit and Museo Postal de Andorra

This ancestral home of one of Andorra's great families, the Areny Plandolits, was built in 1633. Modified in the mid-19th century, it's now a museum (☎ 83 69 08) which offers half-hour guided visits of its richly furnished interior in Spanish or Catalan.

Within the same grounds, the Museo Postal de Andorra is far from nerdy. It has an interesting 15-minute audiovisual programme (available in English) and a comprehensive collection of stamps issued by France and Spain specifically for Andorra (see Post & Communications in the Facts for the Visitor section earlier in the chapter).

Admission to each museum costs 300 ptas. Both are open 9.30 am to 1.30 pm and 3 to 6.30 pm Tuesday to Saturday plus Sunday morning.

Walking

From the hamlet of Segudet, just east of Ordino, a path goes up through fir woods to the **Coll d'Ordino** (1980m), reached in about 1½ hours. **Pic de Casamanya** (2740m), where you can enjoy expansive panoramas, is some two hours north from the col.

Places to Stay & Eat

The cavernous *Hotel Casamanya* (☎ *83 50 11, fax 83 84 76)* has singles/doubles for 4000/7000 ptas. Better value for money is the small, family-run *Hotel Santa Bàrbara de la Vall d'Ordino* with singles/doubles for 5500/8000 ptas. Rooms at the splendid top-end *Hotel Coma* fluctuate from 4500/9000 ptas in low season to 9000/13,000 ptas in high season.

Bar Restaurant Quim has a basic *menu* for 1350 ptas. Next door, *Restaurant Armengol* offers a *menu* for 1500 ptas and a wide range of plentiful a la carte meat dishes.

Getting There & Away
Daily buses run to/from Andorra la Vella (130 ptas, 7 am to 9 pm, about every half-hour).

VALL D'ORDINO
The tiny, partly Romanesque Església de Sant Martí in **La Cortinada** has 12th-century frescoes in remarkably good condition. Opposite is a small working water powered flour- and sawmill. It opens June to November.

Exhilarating trails lead from the small settlements that nestle beside the CG3, north of Ordino.

Walking
A track leads west from Llorts (1413m) up the River de l'Angonella valley to a group of lakes, the Estanys de l'Angonella, at about 2300m. Count on three hours to get there.

From slightly north of the even smaller settlement of **El Serrat** (1600m), a secondary road leads 4km east to the Borda de Sorteny mountain refuge (1969m), from where trails lead on into the high mountain area from where you can undertake a circular route embracing Pic de l'Estanyó and Pic de la Serrera.

From a little north of **Arans** (1385m), a trail goes north-eastwards to Bordes de l'Ensegur (2180m), where there is an old shepherd's hut.

Places to Stay
Some 200m north of Llorts, *Camping Els Pardassos* (☎ 85 00 22), one of the most beautiful campsites in Andorra, has its own spring. It opens mid-June to mid-September. *Hotel Vilaró* (☎ 85 02 25), just south of the village, has singles/doubles with washbasin and bidet for 2200/4000 ptas.

Hotel Sucará in La Cortinada has singles/doubles for 3500/5200 ptas outside

high season, when half-board (7200 ptas per person) is obligatory. Renowned locally for its rich Catalan and Andorran cuisine, it has excellent value *menus* at 1600 ptas and 2500 ptas.

Getting There & Away
Buses to El Serrat leave Andorra la Vella at 1 and 8.30 pm daily (240 ptas), with a return journey departing El Serrat at 1.45 am and 2.45 pm. The small communities in the valley are also served by buses linking Ordino and Arcalís (see the next section).

ORDINO-ARCALÍS SKI AREA
The slopes of the Ordino-Arcalís ski area (☎ 85 01 21, fax 85 04 40) in Andorra's far north-western corner are good for beginners and intermediates. A number of the rugged peaks in this beautiful area reach 2700m and provide challenging, spectacular summer walking. There's no accommodation in Arcalís.

Orientation & Information
Restaurant La Coma (2200m) at the end of the paved road (closed in winter) is a useful landmark. From it, the Creussans chair lift, opened in 2000 and the highest in Andorra, whisks you up to 2625m.

Skiing
In winter, Ordino-Arcalís has a decent selection of runs but can be cold and windy. There are 14 lifts covering 26km of pistes at altitudes between 1940m and 2625m. A lift pass costs 2950/7350 ptas for one/three days in the low season (3700/9200 ptas, high season).

Walking
The trail behind Restaurant La Coma leads eastwards across the hill, then north and over the ridge to a group of beautiful mountain lakes, **Estanys de Tristaina.** The walk to the first lake takes about 30 minutes.

Places to Eat
The *Restaurant La Coma* opens 10 am to 6 pm daily, from December to early May and late June to early September. During

these months, it offers both snacks and a full menu.

Getting There & Away
In the ski season buses link Ordino and the ski station (125 ptas, 10 daily). In summer, buses go as far as El Serrat and continue to Arcalís on request (four daily, except Sunday).

Eastern Andorra

Andorra's best skiing is here, at Soldeu-El Tarter and Pas de la Casa-Grau Roig.

ENCAMP
Encamp houses the **Museu Nacional de l'Automòbil** (National Automobile Museum; ☎ 83 22 66). Beside the CG2, it has about 100 vintage cars plus antique motorcycles and bicycles. It opens 9.30 am to 1.30 pm and 3 to 6 pm Tuesday to Saturday plus 10 am to 2 pm Sunday. Admission costs 300 ptas.

Most of the **Església Sant Romà de les Bons**, about 1km north of Encamp, dates from the 12th century. The Romanesque frescoes in the apse are reproductions of the originals, now in Barcelona's Museu Nacional d'Art de Cataluña.

To the right of the CG2, 3km north of Encamp, the austere **Santuari de Nostra Senyora de Meritxell** looms over the highway. Designed by internationally renowned Catalan architect, Ricardo Bofill, it replaces the original shrine to Andorra's patron, destroyed by fire in 1972.

Buses run daily from Andorra la Vella to Encamp (110 ptas, 7 am to 9.30 pm, every 20 or 30 minutes).

In winter, Funicamp, the long bubble lift at the northern end of Encamp, gives access to the Grau Roig and Pas de la Casa snowfields, thus saving you a 25km drive over the Port d'Envalira.

Information
The tourist office (☎ 73 10 00, fax 83 18 78), beside the CG2, 100m south of Encamp's town hall, is a striking smoked-glass cube. It opens 9 am to 1 pm and 3.30 to 6 pm, Monday to Saturday.

CANILLO
Canillo, about 7km west of Soldeu and El Tarter and considerably more tranquil than either, makes a good base for a skiing or summer activity holiday. It offers canyon clambering, guided walks, a climbing gully (*vía ferrata*) and climbing wall, the year-round Palau de Gel with ice rink and swimming pool, and endless possibilities for hiking (including an easy signed nature walk that follows the valley downstream from Soldeu). The tourist office (☎ 85 10 02) is on the main road at the eastern end of the village. A little beyond is the splendid 11th-century Romanesque church of Sant Joan de Caselles.

Places to Stay
For the moment – although the introduction of a bubble lift giving direct access to the Soldeu-El Tarter ski slopes may bring a change – accommodation in Canillo is markedly less expensive than higher up the valley. And in contrast with accommodation in the bigger resorts, prices of the hotels we've selected remain constant year round.

Of Canillo's five camp sites, *Camping Santa Creu* (☎ 85 14 62) is the greenest and, since it's the farthest from the highway, the quietest. *Hotel Casa Nostra* (☎ 85 10 23) has simple rooms for 2500 ptas (3250 ptas with shower, 3750 ptas with full bathroom). *Hotel Pellissé* (☎ 85 12 05, fax 85 18 75), east of town opposite the church of Sant Joan de Caselles, has decent singles/doubles for 2750/4400 ptas while *Hotel Canigó* (☎ 85 10 24, fax 85 18 24) does comfortable singles/doubles for 3000/5000 ptas.

SOLDEU-EL TARTER SKI AREA
Soldeu and El Tarter, both popular with British skiers, are separate villages 2km apart joined by interconnecting ski lift systems. Each has a small tourist office at the base of the ski lifts (Soldeu ☎ 85 24 92, El Tarter ☎ 89 05 01,). They are open

Whitewash-and-wood houses line the ports of St-Jean de Luz and its quiet twin Ciboure.

Deep in thought at Toulouse's Café des Artistes

The 14th-century Cathédrale Ste-Cécile, Albi

Traditional timbered houses grace Bayonne, the cultural capital of the French Basque Country.

St-Jean de Luz has a colourful past of piracy – today its spoils are tuna, anchovies and sardines.

Interesting architectural details adorn pretty Turenne, the Dordogne.

Medieval Sarlat-La-Canéda

December to April, plus July and August. For skiing information, ring ☎ 85 11 51. Soldeu has the bulk of the accommodation and facilities.

Skiing

The skiing here gets better every time we visit. With the grafting on of a new bubble lift and ski area above Canillo in 2001, 23 lifts will connect 86km of runs with a vertical drop of 850m. The slopes, wooded in their lower reaches, are often warmer than the more exposed ski areas of Pas de la Casa and Grau Roig.

Lift passes for a day/three days cost 3650/8580 ptas in low season, 4200/10,050 ptas in high season.

Walking

You'll find a week's worth of walks based around Canillo and Soldeu in Lonely Planet's *Walking in France*.

Places to Stay & Eat

Most places in Soldeu are full to bursting with groups and expensive for the independent traveller. Cosy *Hotel Naudi* (☎ 85 11 48, fax 85 20 22) with its welcoming bar and restaurant has singles/doubles for 6000/8500 ptas, year round.

Residència Supervalira (☎ 85 10 82, fax 85 10 62), 2.5km north of Soldeu, has offhand service and singles/doubles for 3500/5000 ptas outside the ski season, when rooms cost 6250 ptas.

At the top end, *Sport Hotel* (☎ 87 86 00, fax 87 06 66, @ sporthotels@andorra .ad) charges 9000 ptas per person in low season (11,000 ptas, high season), including breakfast.

On the main street, the cheerful restaurant of *Hotel Bruxelles* does well-filled sandwiches (450 ptas to 575 ptas), whopping burgers and a tasty *menu* for 1175 ptas. *Restaurant Fontanella* does a range of Italian specialities, plus the usual pizzas and pastas. *Snack-Bar Bonell*, 50m south of the cabin lift station, has rather overpriced platos combinados and pizzas, and more reasonably priced daily specials (575 ptas to 825 ptas).

Entertainment

The night scene at Soldeu buzzes in winter. *Pussy Cat* and its neighbour, *Fat Albert*, both one block from the main street, rock until far too late for impressive skiing the next day. *Piccadilly Pub* by the Sport Hotel is a clone of a British pub that occasionally has bands. *Capital Discoteca*, with free admission on Tuesday, Wednesday and at the weekend, is a busy dance hangout.

Getting There & Around

Buses run daily from Andorra la Vella to El Tarter and Soldeu (375 ptas, 40 minutes, 9 am to 8 pm hourly). In winter, there are free shuttle buses (just flash your ski pass) between Canillo and the two upper villages (with a break from noon to 3 pm, about every hour until 11 pm).

All three villages are also on the route of buses between Andorra la Vella and the French railheads of Latour de Carol and L'Hospitalet (see the main Getting There & Away section earlier in this chapter).

PAS DE LA CASA-GRAU ROIG SKI AREA

The linked ski stations of Pas de la Casa and Grau Roig lie either side of the Port d'Envalira pass. Pas de la Casa, on the French border and largest of the Andorran ski resorts, is an architecturally bleak place with numerous shops, principally catering for French visitors. In high season (especially the French winter school holiday from mid-February to early March), it's nearly impossible to get a bed and lift queues can be frustratingly long.

Grau Roig, with just one hotel, is on the western side of the col, 2km south of the CG2.

Information

Pas de la Casa's tourist office (☎ 85 52 92, fax 85 62 75), opposite the Andorran customs station, opens 9 am to 7 pm daily, except Sunday afternoon.

Skiing

Skiing and snowboarding here are well suited to all levels. The combined ski area

ANDORRA

(☎ 87 19 00) has 100km of pistes and a network of 29 lifts. Lift passes cost 3700/8800 ptas for a day/three days in low season, and 4200/10,000 ptas in high season.

Other Activities

In winter, for a magnificent bird's eye view of the Pyrenees and Andorra in its entirety, take a 10 minute helicopter flight from Grau Roig with Helitrans (☎ 86 65 66). At 6000 ptas, a chopper doesn't come cheap, and they require a minimum of 4 people.

Places to Stay

During the winter ski season and, to a lesser extent, July and August, it's almost impossible to find reasonably priced accommodation in Pas de la Casa since so many hotels are occupied partially or fully by tour companies.

One of the most reasonable places – all is relative – is *Hotel/Aparthotel Condor* (☎ 85 57 08, fax 85 55 78, Carrer Bearn 14), where, according to season, singles/doubles/triples cost from 4400/6600/8500 ptas (low season) to 6850/11,750/14,000 ptas (high season).

At *Hotel la Montanya* (☎ 85 53 18, fax 85 58 98, ✉ pimand@hotmail.com, Carrer Cataluña 12), singles/doubles with breakfast start at 6300/7600 ptas (low season) and 8900/12,800 ptas (high season).

Hotel Casado (☎ 85 52 19, fax 85 54 98, Carrer Cataluña 23) has rooms including

breakfast for 7000/9000 ptas in the low season, and 10,300/13,000 ptas in the high season.

Places to Eat

In Pas de la Casa, you can eat sandwiches and burgers until they ooze out of your ears. For more substantial fare, try the battery of restaurants around the base of the ski slopes.

If you fancy something more subtle, visit *Restaurant La Cabanya*, co-located with Hotel/Aparthotel Condor, which has *menus* for 1300 ptas and 2150 ptas. *Bar Restaurant Cava Roca*, beside the Parking Central, does a great *menu* for 1400 ptas and has a wide selection of a la carte meat dishes.

Entertainment

During the ski season, Pas de la Casa, considerably larger than its Andorran competitors, throbs after dark. Dance away your bruises at *West End* and *Billboard*. *Milwaukee* packs in the après ski crowd too.

Getting There & Away

From Andorra la Vella, one daily bus goes to and from Pas de la Casa (620 ptas, 9 am returning at 11.30 am). Pas de la Casa is also on the bus routes between Andorra la Vella and the French railheads of L'Hospitalet and Latour-de-Carol, each no more than 12km away (see the main Getting There & Away section earlier in this chapter).

Languedoc-Roussillon

The region of Languedoc-Roussillon was formed in the 1960s by merging two historic provinces. It stretches in an arc along the coast from Provence to the Pyrenees with its northern flanks bordering the Massif Central. The region has everything a traveller could want: mountains, sea, great towns – such as Montpellier, its vibrant capital – and a lot of history.

Languedoc

Languedoc takes its name from the *langue d'oc*, a language closely related to today's Catalan and quite distinct from the *langue d'oïl*, the forerunner of modern French, spoken to the north (the words *oc* and *oïl* meant 'yes'). When France's new regional boundaries were mapped out, Languedoc's traditional centre, Toulouse to the south-west, was excluded from Languedoc-Roussillon.

History

Languedoc was settled as early as 450,000 BC. Phoenicians, Greeks, Romans, Visigoths and Moors all passed through the region before it came under Frankish control in about the 8th century. The Franks were generally happy to leave affairs in the hands of local rulers, and around the 12th-century Occitania (today's Languedoc) reached its zenith. At the time, Occitan was the language of the troubadours and the cultured speech of southern France. However, the Albigensian Crusade, launched to suppress the 'heresy' of Catharism in 1208, led to Languedoc's annexation by the French kingdom. The treaty of Villers-Cotterêts (1539), which made the langue d'oïl the realm's official language, sounded the death knell for Occitan, though a revival spearheaded by the poet Frédéric Mistral in the 19th century breathed new life into the language now called Provençal. You'll see a fair few street signs in Provençal, even in Montpellier.

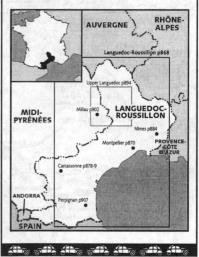

Geography

Languedoc has two distinct areas: the plains of Lower Languedoc (Bas Languedoc), and the rugged, mountainous terrain of Upper Languedoc (Haut Languedoc) to the north. From the plains rise the region's towns and cities, including Montpellier, a leading university centre. Bordering Provence to the east is the sun-baked old Roman town of Nîmes. Follow the coast south-westwards

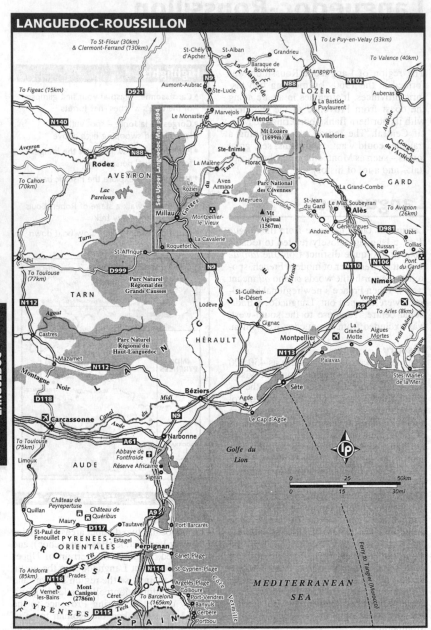

LANGUEDOC-ROUSSILLON

and you come to the attractive port of Sète. Just inland lie the cities of Béziers and Narbonne. Farther inland, the walled city of Carcassonne hovers over the hot plain like a medieval mirage.

The coastline of Lower Languedoc is broken by a string of lagoons (*étangs* in French, literally 'ponds'), separated from the sea by sandy beaches. A number of ugly modern resorts have been built, the most well known being the futuristic La Grande Motte, near Montpellier.

Away from the coast are ruined castles crowning rocky outcrops, and the countless vineyards that make Languedoc the largest wine-producing area of France.

Upper Languedoc is quite distinct from the sun-soaked lowlands or the Auvergne region of the Massif Central. Its isolation appeals to visitors in search of the great outdoors. It includes Lozère, France's most sparsely populated region, which takes in the Parc National des Cévennes, a wild, mountainous area long the refuge of hermits and exiles.

Farther westwards loom the Grands Causses, bare limestone plateaus rising above deep canyons like the Gorges du Tarn. The small towns of Mende, Florac, Alès and Millau are like little oases sprinkled through this wilderness.

Getting Around

Travel between cities by rail or bus is no problem. Getting to remote hilltop castles will pose a challenge for those without their own wheels, as will travelling around most of Upper Languedoc (eg, Lozère, the Grands Causses and the Cévennes).

For train timetables and fares throughout the region, ring ☎ 06 36 35 35 35. Calls are charged at 2.25FF per minute and waiting time, once you're connected, can be long.

MONTPELLIER
postcode 34000 • pop 228,000

The 17th-century philosopher John Locke may have had one glass of Minervois wine too many when he wrote: 'I find it much better to go twise (sic) to Montpellier than once to the other world'. Paradise it ain't,

but Montpellier continues to attract visitors with its reputation for innovation and vitality.

Until recently, Languedoc's largest city simply slumbered in the Midi sun. Things began changing in the 1960s, however, when many *pieds noirs* (Algerian-born French) left North Africa and settled here, swelling the population. Later a dynamic left-wing local government came to power, promoting the pedestrianisation of the old city, designing an unusual central housing project and attracting high-tech industries. The result is that it is one of France's fastest-growing, most self-confident cities.

Students form nearly a quarter of the city's population and the university is particularly celebrated for its medical faculties; Europe's first medical school was founded here early in the 12th century. Though little qualifies as a 'must see', the pedestrianised old city remains charming – with its narrow alleys, stone arches, fine *hôtels particuliers* (private mansions) and decaying splendour.

Montpellier hosts a popular theatre festival in June and a two-week international dance festival in June/July.

Orientation

Montpellier's Centre Historique is surrounded by wide boulevards, with place de la Comédie, an enormous pedestrianised square, at its heart.

North-east of the square is Esplanade Charles de Gaulle, a pleasant tree-lined promenade. To the east is Le Polygone, a modern shopping complex, and Antigone, a mammoth housing project.

Westwards sprawls the city's oldest quarter, a web of pedestrianised lanes between rue de la Loge and Grand rue Jean Moulin. Bus and train stations are an easy walk south of place de la Comédie.

Information

Tourist Offices Montpellier's main tourist office (☎ 04 67 60 60 60, fax 04 67 60 60 61, ✆ office.tourisme@mirt.fr) is at the southern end of Esplanade Charles de Gaulle. It opens from 9 am to 6.30 pm

LANGUEDOC

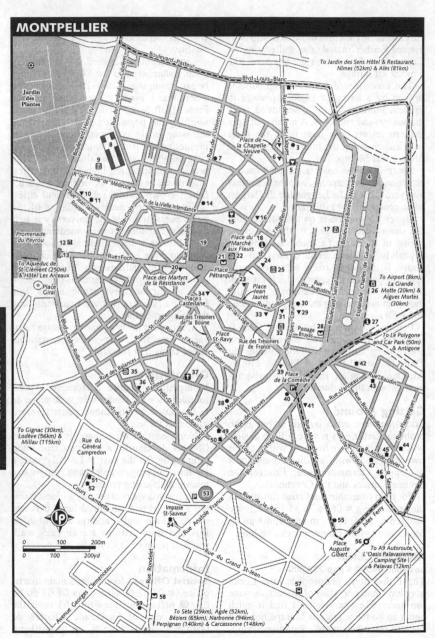

MONTPELLIER

Jardin des Plantes

Boulevard Pasteur

Blvd-Louis-Blanc

To Jardin des Sens Hôtel & Restaurant, Nîmes (52km) & Alès (81km)

Rue des Écoles Laïques

Boulevard Henri IV

Rue du Cardinal de Cabrières

Rue de l'Université

Place de la Chapelle Neuve

R de l'École de Médecine

Rue Jean Jacques Rousseau

R Ste-Croix

R de la Vieille Intendance

Rue Lamballerès

L'Aiguillerie

Boulevard Bonne Nouvelle

Esplanade Charles de Gaulle

Promenade du Peyrou

To Aqueduc de St-Clément (250m) & Hôtel Les Arceaux

Place Giral

Rue Foch

Place des Martyrs de la Résistance

Place Pétrarque

Place du Marché aux Fleurs

Rue des Augustins

Boulevard Sarrail

To Airport (8km), La Grande Motte (20km) & Aigues Mortes (30km)

Place Jean Jaurès

Place Castellane

Place la Loge

Rue Collot

Blvd-Ledru-Rollin

Rue St-Guilhem

Rue des Trésoriers de la Bourse

Rue de l'Ancien Courrier

Place St-Ravy

Rue des Trésoriers de France

Rue du Cauzit

Passage Bruyas

To Le Polygone and Car Park (50m) & Antigone

Rue des Balances

Rd-Pout des Flammes

Petit-St-Jean

Rue En Gondeau

Rue Jean-Moulin

Rue des Étuves

Place de la Comédie

Rue Vanneau

Rue Baudin

Rue Boussairolles

Blvd-du-Jeu-de-Paume

To Gignac (30km), Lodève (56km) & Millau (115km)

Rue du Général Campredon

Grand-Rue-Jean-Moulin

Rue Loys

Blvd-Victor-Hugo

Rue de Verdun

R-Aristide-Olivier

Rue Flaugergues

Rue Joffre

Rue Sérane

Cours Gambetta

Impasse St-Sauveur

Rue Anatole France

Rue de la République

Rue Jules Ferry

Place Auguste Gibert

To A9 Autoroute, L'Oasis Palavasienne, Camping Site & Palavas (12km)

Rue Ronddelet

Rue du Grand St-Jean

Avenue Georges Clemenceau

0   100   200m
0   100   200yd

To Sète (29km), Agde (52km), Béziers (65km), Narbonne (94km), Perpignan (140km) & Carcassonne (148km)

euro currency converter 10FF = €1.52

MONTPELLIER

PLACES TO STAY		
1 Auberge de Jeunesse	31 Simple Simon	19 Prefecture
11 Hôtel Le Guilhem	33 Restaurant Cerdan	21 Post Office
42 Hôtel de la Comédie	34 Halles Castellane Market	22 St@tion Internet
43 Hôtel des Touristes	36 La Tomate	25 Musée du Vieux Montpellier;
44 Hôtel Mistral	39 Chez Fels	Musée Fougau; Hôtel de
45 Hôtel le Paris	41 Monoprix Supermarket	Varennes
47 Hôtel Édouard VII	48 Restaurant Verdi	26 Pavillon du Musée Fabre
49 Hôtel Majestic	53 Halles Laissac Market	27 Main Tourist Office
50 Hôtel des Étuves		28 Post Office
51 Hôtel Cosmos	OTHER	30 Les Cinq Continents
52 Hôtel Abysse	3 Laundrette	Bookshop
54 Hôtel du Littoral	4 Le Corum	32 Musée Languedocien; Hôtel
	5 Volt Face	des Trésoriers de France
PLACES TO EAT	7 Bill's Book Company	35 Dimension 4 Cybercafé
2 Chez Marceau	8 Cathédrale St-Pierre	37 Église St-Roche
6 Le Vieil Écu	9 Musée Atger; Muséed'	38 Hôtel St-Côme
10 Le Petit Jardin	Anatomie; Medical Faculty	40 Opéra-Comédie
16 L'Heure Bleue	12 Palais de Justice	46 Laundrette
20 Le Menestrel	13 Arc de Triomphe	55 SMTU Bus Information Office
23 Salmon Shop	14 Bookshop	56 Train Station
24 La Diligence	15 Mash Disco Bar	57 Bus Station; Villà Vélo
29 Tripti Kulai	17 Musée Fabre	58 Main Post Office; Cyberposte
	18 Maison de la Lozère	59 Laundrette

daily (reduced hours at weekends, later closing in summer).

The TIC annexe (☎ 04 67 92 90 03), at the train station, opens 9 am to 1 pm and 3 to 7 pm weekdays, May to September.

For information on the Parc National des Cévennes, Gorges du Tarn and Grands Causses in neighbouring Lozère, go to Maison de la Lozère (☎ 04 67 66 36 10, fax 04 67 60 33 22), 27 rue de l'Aiguillerie. Open 9.30 am to 12.30 pm and 2 to 6 pm (closed Sunday and Monday).

Post & Communications The main post office, 13 place Rondelet, has Cyberposte.

At France Telecom's high-tech St@tion Internet, 6–8 place du Marché aux Fleurs, billing (50FF per hour, 40FF for under 26s) is by the minute. It's open 10 am to 8 pm daily except Sunday (from 2 pm Monday).

To nibble while you surf, visit Dimension 4 Cybercafé (☎ 04 67 60 57 57), 11 rue des Balances. Open midday to midnight daily, they charge 1FF per minute for accessing emails or a bargain 35FF per hour.

Bookshops Rue de l'Université is lined with specialist bookshops, including Book-

shop (☎ 04 67 66 09 08) at No 4, which stocks novels and travel guides in English. Along the street at No 44, Bill's Book Company (☎ 04 67 66 37 11) also carries new and second-hand titles in English.

Les Cinq Continents, 20 rue Jacques Cœur, an excellent specialist travel bookshop, has a good stock of maps, Lonely Planet guides and a few other English-language books.

Laundry There are laundrettes at 8 rue des Écoles Laïques, near the Auberge de Jeunesse, 11 rue Sérane and 12 rue St-Denis, opposite the main post office (leave your smalls to spin as you check your emails). All open 7.30 am to at least 9 pm daily.

Hôtels Particuliers
During the 17th and 18th centuries, Montpellier's wealthier merchants built tasteful private mansions with large inner courtyards. Fine examples are **Hôtel de Varennes**, place Pétrarque, a harmonious blend of Romanesque and Gothic, and **Hôtel St-Côme**, Grand rue Jean Moulin, the city's first anatomy theatre for medical

LANGUEDOC

students and nowadays the Chambre de Commerce. The 17th-century **Hôtel des Trésoriers de France**, 7 rue Jacques Cœur, today houses the Musée Languedocien.

Museums

The city's cultural showpiece is **Musée Fabre** (☎ 04 67 14 83 00), 39 blvd Bonne Nouvelle. Founded in 1825, it has one of France's richest collections of French, Italian, Flemish and Dutch works from the 16th century onwards. A small room is devoted to the 19th-century realist painter Gustave Courbet; the top floor has more contemporary works. The museum hosts temporary exhibitions in the nearby **Pavillon du Musée Fabre**. The main museum opens 9 am to 5.30 pm (5 pm at weekends, closed Monday). Admission costs 20FF (students 10FF).

The **Musée Languedocien** (☎ 04 67 52 93 03), 7 rue Jacques Cœur, displays the region's archaeological finds as well as *objets d'art* from the 17th to 19th centuries. It opens 2 to 5 pm (3 to 6 pm in July and August, closed Sunday). Admission costs 20FF (students 10FF).

There are four other museums, all free. Two are upstairs in the Hôtel de Varennes: **Musée du Vieux Montpellier** (☎ 04 67 66 02 94), a storehouse of the city's memorabilia from the Middle Ages to the Revolution, opens 9.30 am to noon and 1.30 to 5 pm (closed Sunday and Monday); **Musée Fougau**, which deals with traditional Occitan life, only opens 3 to 6 pm, Wednesday and Thursday.

In the medical faculty, 2 rue de l'École de Médecine, **Musée Atger** (☎ 04 67 66 27 77) houses a striking collection of French, Italian and Flemish drawings. It opens 1.30 to 5.45 pm Monday, Wednesday and Friday. The **Musée d'Anatomie** (☎ 04 67 60 73 71), worth a visit if you're into looking at body parts in jars, opens 2.30 to 5 pm, Wednesday only. The medical faculty is closed during university holidays.

Around Promenade du Peyrou

This large, tree-lined square is dominated by the **Arc de Triomphe** (1692) at one end,

and the **Château d'Eau** – a hexagonal water tower – at the other. Stretching away from the latter is the 18th-century **Aqueduc de St-Clément**, under which there's a bustling flea market on Saturday and *pétanque* (bowling) most afternoons. To the north, off blvd Henri IV, is the **Jardin des Plantes**, France's oldest botanic garden, founded in 1593. Opposite the garden is **Cathédrale St-Pierre**, with a strange, oversized 15th-century porch.

Beaches

The closest beach – at **Palavas-les-Flots**, 12km south of the city – is backed by an ugly concrete skyline. Take bus No 17 or 28 from the bus station.

About 20km south-east of Montpellier is **La Grande Motte**, a resort famous for its futuristic, wacky architecture. Aigues Mortes, on the western edge of the Camargue (see the Provence chapter), is a further 11km to the north-east.

For bus details, see Getting There & Away later in this section.

Organised Tours

Contact Vill'à Vélo (see Bicycle in Getting Around) for details of bike tours of the city (80FF, price including one day's cycle hire), organised in collaboration with the tourist office.

For those who prefer ambling, the main tourist office offers two-hour walking tours in French (39FF) at 3 pm on Wednesday and Saturday.

Places to Stay – Budget

Camping The closest camp sites are around the suburb of Lattes, some 4km south of the city centre. *L'Oasis Palavasienne* (☎ *04 67 15 11 61, fax 04 67 15 10 62, route de Palavas*), open April to September, charges between 97FF and 141FF for two people, car and tent, according to season. Take bus No 17 from Montpellier bus station to the Oasis.

Hostels The *Auberge de Jeunesse* (☎ *04 67 60 32 22, fax 04 67 60 32 30, 2 impasse de la Petite Corraterie*) is just off rue des Écoles Laïques. The grandiose mosaic entrance contrasts with its basic dorms but who can complain when there's a friendly bar and a bed costs just 48FF a night? From bus and train stations, the tram and Le Rabelais night bus (see Getting Around later in the chapter) pass nearby.

Hotels At *Hôtel des Touristes (☎ 04 67 58 42 37, fax 04 67 92 61 37, 10 rue Baudin)*, good-sized singles/doubles/triples with shower start at 150/180/260FF. Close by, *Hôtel Le Paris (☎ 04 67 58 37 11, fax 04 67 92 79 72, 15 rue Aristide Olivier)*, an unpretentious joint, has basic but bright singles/doubles for 125/180FF (230/300FF with shower).

Hôtel Mistral (☎ 04 67 58 45 25, fax 04 67 58 23 95, 25 rue Boussairolles) is rather a grand place for the price with basic singles for 160FF and singles/doubles with bathroom from 220/230FF. Since there's no hall shower, fastidious travellers go for the latter option. The more modern *Hôtel Édouard VII (☎ 04 67 58 42 13, fax 04 67 58 93 66, 10 rue Aristide Olivier)* has basic rooms for 155FF, and with bathroom from 205FF.

Friendly *Hôtel des Étuves (☎ 04 67 60 78 19, 24 rue des Étuves)*, creeping up like a vine around a spiral staircase, has singles/doubles with bathroom starting at 130/160FF. Close by, *Hôtel Majestic (☎ 04 67 66 26 85, 4 rue du Cheval Blanc)*, off Grand rue Jean Moulin, provides basic singles/doubles for 110/140FF and doubles/triples/quads with bathroom for 200/300/350FF.

The quiet *Hôtel du Littoral (☎ 04 67 92 28 10, fax 04 67 58 93 41, 3 impasse St-Sauveur)*, off rue Anatole France, has large, basic singles/doubles costing from 145/155FF (from 185/175FF with shower, from 200/210FF with bathroom). Hall showers cost 15FF.

Three blocks away, at *Hôtel Abysse (☎ 04 67 92 39 05, 13 rue du Général Campredon)* basic but pleasant singles start at 110FF and singles/doubles with shower from 140/160FF. A few doors away, welcoming *Hôtel Cosmos (☎ 04 67 92 43 97, 7 rue du Général Campredon)* has singles/doubles from 140/160FF (200/240FF with shower). Street parking – rare in Montpellier – is available nearby.

Places to Stay – Mid-Range & Top End

At *Hôtel de la Comédie (☎ 04 67 58 43 64, fax 04 67 58 58 43, 1 bis rue Baudin)* fully equipped singles range from 210FF to 280FF and doubles from 310FF to 400FF.

Hôtel Les Arceaux (☎ 04 67 92 03 03, fax 04 67 92 05 09, 33 blvd des Arceaux), opposite the Aqueduc de St-Clément, has attractive singles/doubles for 280/300FF.

Hôtel Le Guilhem (☎ 04 67 52 90 90, fax 04 67 60 67 67, @ hotel-leguilhem@ mnet.fr, 18 rue Jean-Jacques Rousseau) occupies a 16th-century building. The welcome is warm and its spacious, airy rooms, which start at 360FF, are very tastefully furnished.

Places to Eat

Restaurants Eating places abound in every nook and cranny of Montpellier's crammed old quarter. Barrel-vaulted *Tripti Kulai (☎ 04 67 66 30 51, 20 rue Jacques Cœur)* is a popular vegetarian place which does salads from 49FF and *menus* for 69FF and 85FF. It opens noon to 9.30 pm. It's closed Sunday. The brasserie-style *Restaurant Cerdan (☎ 04 67 60 86 96, 8 rue Collot)* has five different *menus* of mostly local fare ranging from 71FF to 190FF. It's closed Sunday.

La Tomate (☎ 04 67 60 49 38, 6 rue Four des Flammes), renowned primarily for its *cassoulet* (rich bean, pork and duck stew) and other regional dishes, does salads the size of a kitchen garden plus dessert for 50FF and *menus* from 50FF upwards. It's closed Sunday and Monday.

The rear patio of *La Diligence (☎ 04 67 66 12 21, 2 place Pétrarque)* is spanned by one of the Hôtel de Varennes' Gothic-style galleries. An 89/155FF *menu* is served at lunch/dinner. Close by, *Maison de la Lozère (27 rue de l'Aiguillerie)* is home to a truly superb restaurant with innovative *menus*, rich in local fare, at 140FF, 225FF and 265FF.

LANGUEDOC

At vaulted **Le Menestrel** (☎ 04 67 60 62 51, impasse Périer), just off Rue Foch, lunch/dinner menus start at 78/95FF; their menu gastronomique at 155FF is worth every centime. It's open from Tuesday to Saturday.

For delicious Italian fare, try the cosy **Restaurant Verdi** (☎ 04 67 58 68 55, rue Aristide Olivier); menus start at 75FF. It opens Monday to Saturday.

Place de la Chapelle Neuve is bordered by little restaurants including the prestigious **Vieil Écu** (☎ 04 67 66 39 44), which has a three-course menu for 120FF and an excellent a la carte choice. More modest but scarcely less pleasurable, **Chez Marceau** (☎ 04 67 66 08 09), in the same square, has a varied 62FF menu. If you prefer greener surroundings, try **Le Petit Jardin** (☎ 04 67 60 78 78, 20 rue Jean-Jacques Rousseau) which overlooks a small fairy-tale garden. Lunch and dinner menus cost 90/125FF.

Sybarites with a healthy bank balance will drool over the menu at the **restaurant** of the **Jardin des Sens** hotel (☎ 04 67 79 63 38), run by twin chefs Jacques and Laurent Pourcel. Sadly, our budget could not stretch to testing the 350FF to 530FF menus at this Michelin three-star place. Reservations are required.

For something fishy, head for the welcoming **Salmon Shop** (5 rue de la Petite Lodge) with its mock log cabin decor. It has a salmon-based plat du jour (50FF), smoked salmon sandwiches (29FF) and salmon salads (36FF).

For a midday takeaway sandwich, try one of the crunchy baguettes, filled with salad and Alsacien goodies, at **Chez Fels** (off place de la Comédie).

Cafes All summer long, place de la Comédie is alive with cafes where you can grab a quick bite and watch street entertainers perform. Smaller, more intimate squares include place Jean Jaurès and place St-Ravy.

L'Heure Bleue (☎ 04 67 66 41 65, rue de la Carbonnerie) is a tea salon where you can sip Earl Grey to a background of classical music. **Simple Simon** (☎ 04 67 66 03 43, 1 rue des Trésoriers de France) is an English tearoom serving cheese-and-onion pies, 25 types of tea and other British delights. It's open midday (from 3 pm in winter) to 7 pm (closed Sunday).

Self-Catering Food markets, operating daily until about noon, include a small one on place Jean Jaurès, the adjoining **Halles Castellane** and **Halles Laissac** occupying the ground floor of a multistorey car park. **Le Polygone** shopping complex is bursting with food shops.

Luxury local food products – cheeses, honey with almonds, sweet chestnuts, truffles and the like – are sold at the **Maison de la Lozère** (see Tourist Offices under Information earlier in the chapter).

Entertainment

Montpellier has a busy cultural calendar. To find out what's on where, pick up the free weekly Agenda guide at the tourist office.

Tickets for performances held at Montpellier's numerous theatres are sold at the **Opéra-Comédie** box office (☎ 04 67 60 05 45, place de la Comédie). Concerts are also held at **Le Corum** (☎ 04 67 61 67 61) at the northern end of esplanade Charles de Gaulle.

For a drink, a handful of local haunts flank rue En-Gondeau, off rue Grand Jean Moulin.

Mash Disco Bar (☎ 04 67 60 37 15, 5 rue de Girone) opens 7 pm to 1 am (closed Sunday and Monday). It's very much a student hangout. Call by on Wednesday when the international Erasmus Students Association hold their weekly moot. Gay bars include **Volt Face** (☎ 04 67 52 86 89, 4 rue des Écoles Laïques).

Getting There & Away

Air Montpellier's airport (☎ 04 67 20 85 00) is 8km south-east of town. There are several flights daily to Paris and the cut-price airline Buzz has a weekend-only service to/from London Stansted.

Bus The bus station (☎ 04 67 92 01 43), at place du Bicentenaire, is immediately

LANGUEDOC

south-west of the train station. Courriers du Midi (☎ 04 67 06 03 67) runs hourly buses to La Grande Motte (24FF, 35 minutes). A few continue to Aigues Mortes (35FF, 1½ hours, six daily) and, in summer, Stes-Maries de la Mer in the Camargue (66FF, two hours). It operates 10 or so daily services to Béziers (70FF, 1¾ hours) and Sète (32FF, 1¼ hours).

Over 15 local SMTU buses run daily between the bus station and the beach at Palavas (7FF, 35 minutes).

Eurolines (☎ 04 67 58 57 59) has buses to most European destinations including Barcelona (190FF, five hours), London (590FF, 17 hours) and Amsterdam (580FF, 21 hours). Linebus (☎ 04 67 58 95 00) mainly operates services to destinations in Spain.

Train The two-storey train station is on place Auguste Gibert.

Major destinations include Paris, Gare de Lyon by TGV (379/452FF weekdays/weekends, four to five hours, about 10 daily), Carcassonne (113FF, 1¾ hours, 10+ daily), Millau (130FF, three hours, three daily) and Perpignan (115FF, two hours, 10+ daily).

Over 20 trains daily go northwards to Nîmes (47FF, 30 minutes) and southwards to Narbonne (80FF, one hour) via Sète (30FF), Agde (47FF) and Béziers (61FF).

Car Europcar (☎ 04 67 06 89 00), Budget (☎ 04 67 92 69 00) and Avis (☎ 04 67 92 92 00) have offices at the airport and train station.

Getting Around

To/From the Airport Courriers du Midi runs a shuttle bus between airport and bus station (30FF, 15 minutes, up to 15 daily).

Bus & Tram Take a ride, even just for fun, on the spanking new, high-tech, high-speed leave-your-car-at-home tram, inaugurated in late 2000. Like city buses, it's run by SMTU (☎ 04 67 22 87 87), 27 rue Maguelone. The office opens 7 am to 7 pm, Monday to Saturday (it's scheduled to move round the corner to rue Jules Ferry in 2001).

Regular buses run until about 8.30 pm daily, while Petibus gas-powered minibuses circulate through the restricted old city, until 7.30 pm Monday to Saturday. At night, a service called Le Rabelais takes over. It makes an hourly loop around the old city from the train station, and the last bus departs at 12.30 am. Individual bus tickets cost 7FF. A one-day pass costs 20FF and a 10-ticket carnet, 53FF.

Taxi There's a rank outside the train station. To call a cab, ring Taxi Tram (☎ 04 67 58 10 10) or Taxi 2000 (☎ 04 67 03 45 45).

Bicycle Montpellier, with over 100km of cycle track, actively encourages biking. Vill'à Vélo (☎ 04 67 92 92 67), an admirable urban initiative, rents cycles for 10/20/40FF per hour/half day/full day and tandems for 50/80FF per half/full day. Based in the bus station at the time of writing, it was expected to move to the SMTU bus information office, 27 rue Maguelone (see Bus & Tram earlier in the section). It opens 9 am to 8.30 pm, Monday to Saturday (10 am to 8 pm Sunday), April to October (daily with shorter hours during the rest of the year).

SÈTE

postcode 34200 • pop 42,000

Sète, 26km south-west of Montpellier, is France's largest Mediterranean fishing port and biggest commercial port after Marseille. Established by Louis XIV in the 17th century as Cette, it prospered as the harbours of Aigues Mortes and Narbonne were cut off from the sea by sand and silt deposits.

Huddled east of Mont St-Clair (from where there are great views of town and port), it has lots in its favour: waterways and canals, beaches, outdoor cafes and shoals of fish and seafood restaurants.

The tourist office (☎ 04 67 74 71 71, fax 04 67 46 17 54, @ tourisme@ville_sete.fr), 60 Grand'Rue Mario Roustan, opens 9 am to noon and 2 to 6 pm, Monday to Saturday (9 am to 8 pm daily, July and August). Take bus No 2 from the train station.

euro currency converter €1 = 6.56FF

Sète was the birthplace of poet Paul Valéry (1871–1945) and childhood home of singer Georges Brassens (1921–81). Both are buried here and there is a small **Valéry museum** (☎ 04 67 46 20 98), rue François Desnoyer. Admission costs 10FF. It's open 10 am to noon and 2 to 6 pm daily, except Tuesday (daily in July and August).

On the first weekend in July, Sète celebrates La Fête de la St-Pierre, or Fête des Pêcheurs (Fisherfolk's Festival). The Fête de la St-Louis fills six frantic days around 25 August with *joutes nautiques* (jousting contests), where participants try to knock each other into the water from rival boats, spurred on by musical bands.

The *Auberge de Jeunesse* (☎ 04 67 53 46 68, fax 04 67 51 34 01) is on rue du Général Revest, 1.5km north-west of the tourist office.

Compagnie Marocaine de Navigation (COMNAV) runs ferries to the Moroccan port of Tangier (Tanger) from quai d'Alger. For tickets, schedules and information, call by SNCM (☎ 04 67 46 68 00, fax 04 67 74 93 05), 4 quai d'Alger. Also see the Sea section in the Getting There & Away chapter.

AGDE
postcode 34300 • pop 22,000
Originally a Phoenician, then a Greek settlement at the mouth of the Hérault River, Agde (from *agathos*, the Greek for 'good') is a picturesque fishing port with narrow streets. The train station, on the west bank of the Hérault River, has services to/from Montpellier, Sète and Béziers.

The tourist office (☎ 04 67 94 29 68, fax 04 67 94 03 50), 1 place Molière, opens 9 am to noon and 2 to 6 pm (9 am to 7 pm in July and August).

The fortress-like **Cathédrale St-Étienne**, its foundations those of a 5th-century Roman church, dates mainly from the 12th century. Like many other buildings in town, it's constructed in dark grey basalt.

Regular shuttle buses ply the 5km route to the modern tourist resort of **Le Cap d'Agde**, famed for its long beaches and large nudist colony. It has a small tourist office (☎ 04 67 01 04 04, fax 04 67 26 22 99).

BÉZIERS
postcode 34500 • pop 72,000
The graceful town of Béziers, 23km west of Agde, was first settled by the Phoenicians and became an important military post in Roman times. It was almost completely destroyed in 1209 during the Albigensian Crusade when some 20,000 people, many of whom had taken refuge in the cathedral, were slaughtered. In happier times, the local tax collector, Paul Riquet (1604–80), moved heaven and earth to build the Canal du Midi, a 240km-long piece of engineering (including aqueducts and over 100 locks) which enabled cargo vessels to sail from the Atlantic to the Mediterranean without having to circumnavigate Spain.

Today Béziers is the wine capital of Languedoc and *dégustation* (wine tasting) tops the agenda of many tourists, particularly during the wine harvest festival in October.

The tourist office (☎ 04 67 76 47 00, fax 04 67 76 50 80) is in the Palais des Congrès, 28 ave St-Saens.

Cathédrale St-Nazaire, on a hill overlooking town, is a fortified church typical of the region, with massive towers, an imposing facade and a huge 14th-century rose window.

Bullfighting is very popular; opponents would be wise to stay away during the four day *féria* (bullfighting festival) in early August.

Regional buses leave from the bus station on place Général de Gaulle. The train station is on blvd de Verdun, south of the centre.

NARBONNE
postcode 11100 • pop 47,100
Once a coastal port but now 13km inland because of silting-up, Narbonne is a quiet provincial town with a long history. As capital of Gallia Narbonensis, it was among the principle centres of Roman rule in Gaul. With the collapse of Rome, it became the Visigoth capital before passing to the Moors, then Franks. It was incorporated into France in 1507.

Massive **Cathédrale St-Just** dominates

LANGUEDOC

the town. Although construction stopped in the early 14th century, its unfinished Gothic choir is still, at 41m, one of France's highest. The **treasury** has a beautiful Flemish tapestry of the Creation; the delicate **cloister** dates from the 15th and 16th centuries. You can climb the 105 steps to the top of the north tower.

Adjoining the cathedral to the south and facing place de l'Hôtel de Ville, the fortified **Palais des Archevêques** (Archbishops' Palace) includes the **Donjon Gilles Aycelin**, a large, square 13th-century tower, and the town hall, with its exuberant 19th-century facade by Viollet-le-Duc, which houses the **Musée d'Art** and **Musée Archéologique**.

The tourist office (☎ 04 68 65 15 60, fax 04 68 65 59 12), place Roger Salengro, is just north-west of the cathedral. It's open 8.30 am to noon and 2 to 6 pm, Monday to Saturday (8.30 am to 7 pm plus Sunday morning in summer).

Just off the N9, 15km south of Narbonne, is the **Réserve Africaine de Sigean** (☎ 04 68 48 20 20), where lions, tigers and other 'safari' specimens live in semi-liberty. It's open daily and admission costs 105FF. For those who arrive by bike or on foot, there's free – in a manner of speaking – transport around the reserve.

CARCASSONNE
postcode 11000 • pop 45,000
From afar, Carcassonne looks like some fairy-tale medieval city. Bathed in late-afternoon sunshine and highlighted by dark clouds, the Cité (as the old walled city is known) is truly breathtaking.

Once inside the fortified walls, Carcassonne is far less magical. Luring some 200,000 visitors in July and August alone, it can be a tourist hell in high summer.

Today's Cité defences are the culmination of centuries of fortifications built by Gauls, Romans, Visigoths, Moors and Franks. In the 13th century, they served as one of the major strongholds of the Cathars (see the boxed text 'The Cathars' later in the chapter). After 1659, when Roussillon was annexed to France, Carcassonne, now no longer a frontier town, began its slow

decline. By the 18th century the Cité was 'little more than a slum' and only the 1850 intervention of Viollet-le-Duc prevented the remaining fortifications being demolished. Elaborate restoration work, for which he was largely responsible, was completed in 1910.

Carcassonne is not just the Cité, however. The Ville Basse (lower town), a more modest stepsister to camp Cinderella up the hill, established in the 13th century, also merits a browse.

Orientation
The River Aude separates the Ville Basse – a perfect grid of one-way streets – from the Cité, up on a hill 500m south-east. Pedestrianised rue Georges Clemenceau leads from the train station and Canal du Midi southwards through the heart of this lower town.

Information
The main tourist office (☎ 04 68 10 24 30, fax 04 68 10 24 38), square Gambetta, opens 9 am to 12.15 pm and 1.45 to 6.30 pm Monday to Saturday (9 am to 7 pm daily in July and August). In the Cité, there's a small tourist office annexe (☎ 04 68 10 24 36) in the Tour Narbonnaise, open 9 am to 6 pm daily (to 7 pm in summer).

Alerte Rouge (Red Alert) is a cybercafe (☎ 04 68 25 20 39), 73 rue Verdun, where you can plug in all day, every day, 10 am to 1 am, for a bargain 30FF an hour.

Librairie Loubatières, a bookshop on place du Château, in the Cité, sells an excellent range of maps and guidebooks, as well as quality art and history books on the region.

Laundrettes, La Lavandière, 31 rue Aimé Ramon, and Laverie-Self at No 63, both spin 9 am to 9 pm daily.

La Cité
Just beside the main entrance to the Cité a magnificent reconditioned 19th-century roundabout (carrousel) spins to old Julie Andrews numbers. It's emblematic of the blend of tack and charm within.

The Cité, dramatically illuminated at

LANGUEDOC

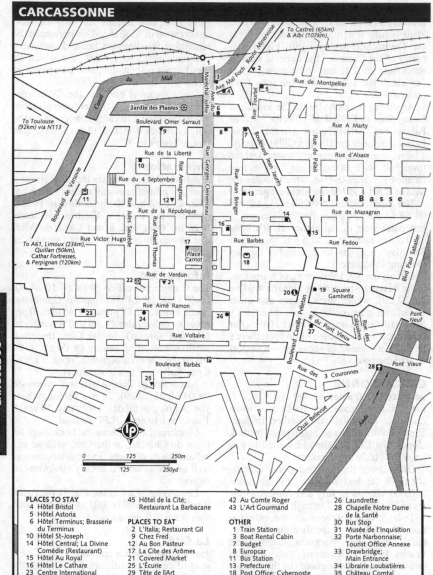

CARCASSONNE

PLACES TO STAY
4 Hôtel Bristol
5 Hôtel Astoria
6 Hôtel Terminus; Brasserie du Terminus
10 Hôtel St-Joseph
14 Hôtel Central; La Divine Comédie (Restaurant)
15 Hôtel Au Royal
16 Hôtel Le Cathare
23 Centre International de Séjour
27 Relais du Square; Le Gargantua Restaurant
40 Auberge de Jeunesse

45 Hôtel de la Cité; Restaurant La Barbacane

PLACES TO EAT
2 L'Italia; Restaurant Gil
9 Chez Fred
12 Au Bon Pasteur
17 La Cite des Arômes
21 Covered Market
25 L'Écurie
29 Tête de l'Art
36 Le Château
39 L'Écu d'Or
41 Les Fontaines du Soleil
42 Au Comte Roger
43 L'Art Gourmand

OTHER
1 Train Station
3 Boat Rental Cabin
7 Budget
8 Europcar
11 Bus Station
13 Prefecture
18 Post Office; Cyberposte
19 CART (Local Bus) Kiosk
20 Main Tourist Office
22 L'Alerte Rouge (cybercafe)
24 Laundrette

26 Laundrette
28 Chapelle Notre Dame de la Santé
30 Bus Stop
31 Musée de l'Inquisition
32 Porte Narbonnaise; Tourist Office Annexe
33 Drawbridge; Main Entrance
34 Librairie Loubatières
35 Château Comtal
38 Post Office
44 Porte d'Aude
46 Basilique St-Nazaire
47 Grand Théâtre

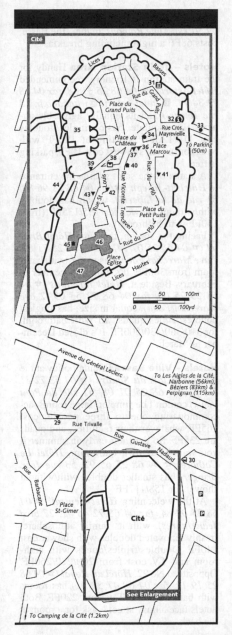

night, is Carcassonne's only major sight. Enclosed by two walls – the inner one 1.3km long, the outer 1.7km – it's one of Europe's largest city fortifications, punctuated by 52 stone towers.

In fact, only the lower sections of the Cité walls are original. The rest, including the anachronistic witch's hat roofs (the originals were flatter and weren't covered with slate), were stuck on by Viollet-le-Duc in the 19th century.

From square Gambetta, it's an attractive walk to the Cité across Pont Vieux, along rue Barbacane, then up and in through Porte d'Aude. Alternatively, take bus No 2, which runs about every 40 minutes, to the Cité's main entrance. There's also a *navette* (shuttle service) between the Cité, square Gambetta and train station, its frequency varying according to season. Leave your vehicle in the large car park (20/30FF for cars/caravans) beside the main entrance.

Once across the drawbridge, you're faced with a massive bastion, the **Porte Narbonnaise** and, just inside, the tourist office annexe. Rue Cros Mayrevieille, suffocating in kitschy souvenir shops, leads up to place du Château, heart of the Cité.

Within the walls, there's a rash of small, hole-in-the-wall private museums, each eager to extract your money. In the rear of a souvenir shop sprouts 'Les Cathares: Leur Fabuleuse Histoire' (The Cathars: Their Fantastic History), not far from Monuments in Miniature, a Hat Museum, a Schooldays Museum and a particularly repellent exhibition of torture devices. All are very resistible.

Through another archway and across a second dry moat is the 12th-century **Château Comtal**. A 40-minute guided tour of castle and ramparts – and you have to be guided – costs 35FF (students 23FF). Tours in English depart between two and five times per day, according to season. The chateau opens 9 am to 7.30 pm daily between June and September (until 5 or 6 pm the rest of the year).

South of place du Château is **Basilique St-Nazaire**. The rounded arches of the nave are Romanesque while the graceful transept

LANGUEDOC

arms and choir, with its curtain of exquisite stained glass, are purest Gothic. Next to the basilica is the **Grand Théâtre**, an open-air stage used for summer performances.

Falconry

Birds of prey dive and swoop at **Les Aigles de la Cité** (☎ 04 68 47 88 89, admission 45FF), 800m south of the Cité walls. The park opens 2.30 pm daily between April and October and there's a 45-minute demonstration at 3 pm (continuously 3 to 7 pm in July and August).

Special Events

On 14 July at 10.30 pm, L'Embrasement de la Cité (Setting the Cité Ablaze) celebrates Bastille Day with a firework display which is rivalled only by Paris' pyrotechnics.

Throughout July, the Festival de la Cité brings music, opera, dance and theatre to town. The dynamic and concurrent Festival Off is an alternative, fringe celebration with street theatre and a host of events, both free and paying.

Carcassonne: Terre d'Histoire, celebrated in the first three weeks of August, brings more music and theatre to the Cité while in October the Fête des Vendanges marks the grape harvest.

Places to Stay

Camping The *Camping de la Cité* (☎ 04 68 25 11 77, route de St-Hilaire), about 3.5km south of the main tourist office, opens March to early October, and charges between 75FF and 95FF for two people with tent and car, depending on the season. Take bus No 5 (hourly until 6.40 pm) from square Gambetta to the route de Cazilhac stop.

Hostels In the heart of the Cité, the large, cheery *Auberge de Jeunesse* (☎ 04 68 25 23 16, fax 04 68 71 14 84, ✉ carcassonne@ fuaj.org, rue Vicomte Trencavel) has dorm beds for 74FF, including breakfast. There's a snack bar offering light meals and a great outside terrace. It's closed mid-December to the end of January.

B&B at the *Centre International de Séjour* (☎ 04 68 11 17 00, fax 04 68 11 17 09, 91 rue Aimé Ramon), in the Ville Basse, costs 68FF a night including breakfast.

Hotels – Train Station Area Handy for the train station is friendly, recommended *Hôtel Astoria* (☎ 04 68 25 31 38, fax 04 68 71 34 14, ✉ hotel-astoria@wanadoo.fr, 18 rue Tourtel) and its equally agreeable annexe. Immaculate basic singles/doubles cost 110/130FF (starting at 190FF with bathroom). Hall showers cost 10FF, parking is free.

A statue of the saint guards the entrance to *Hôtel St-Joseph* (☎/fax 04 68 71 96 89, 81 rue de la Liberté), which has doubles with/without shower for 155/135FF (from 180FF with bathroom).

Facing the station, the huge *Hôtel Bristol* (☎ 04 68 25 07 24, fax 04 68 25 71 89, 7 ave Maréchal Foch) has rooms with bathroom from 300FF. It's closed December to February. Beside it, *Hôtel Terminus* (☎ 04 68 25 25 00, fax 04 68 72 53 09, 2 ave Maréchal Foch), equal in size, has singles/ doubles/triples/quads, all with bathroom, for 310/360/430/500FF. It's closed December to March.

Hotels – Ville Basse Pricing policy at the amiable *Relais du Square* (☎ 04 68 72 31 72, fax 04 68 25 01 08, 51 rue du Pont Vieux) couldn't be simpler: large rooms, accommodating one to three people, cost 165FF, whatever their facilities, and quads are 235FF. So get their early in summer if you want your own bathroom. *Hôtel Le Cathare* (☎ 04 68 25 65 92, 53 rue Jean Bringer) has smaller doubles with/without shower for 158/117FF.

At the welcoming *Hôtel Central* (☎ 04 68 25 03 84, fax 04 68 72 46 41, 27 blvd Jean Jaurès), with its family atmosphere, freshly renovated doubles with shower cost 140FF. Doubles/triples/quads with bathroom and TV cost from 200/220/260FF. Opposite at No 22, *Hôtel au Royal* (☎ 04 68 25 19 12, fax 04 68 47 33 01) has rooms with bathroom and TV from 220FF. Both hotels face a busy street – ask for a room at the back.

Hotels – Cité The *Hôtel de la Cité* (☎ 04 68 71 98 71, fax 04 68 71 50 15, @ *reservations@hoteldelacite.com, place de l'Église*) has rooms fit for royalty (literally so: 'a favourite hideaway for Europe's crowned heads, film stars, writers and intellectuals', proclaims its glossy brochure). If you fancy a retreat in such august company, a room will set you back between 950FF and 3200FF (closed January and February).

Places to Eat

Restaurants – Ville Basse Cosy *Au Bon Pasteur* (☎ 04 68 25 46 58, 29 rue Armagnac) has nine different seafood dishes, yummy cassoulet and *menus* from 72FF. It closes Sunday evening and Monday.

Equally popular is *Chez Fred* (☎ 04 68 72 02 23, 31 blvd Omer Sarraut) with its rustic decor and great outside terrace. The weekday lunchtime *menu bistro* (75FF) is good value; other *menus* start at 110FF.

Also handy for the station, *L'Italia* (☎ 04 68 47 08 64, 32 route Minervoise) is a pizza-plus joint that also does takeaways. Next door is the more stylish *Restaurant Gil* (☎ 04 68 47 85 23) with Catalan-influenced *menus* from 100FF. *Brasserie du Terminus* (☎ 94 68 71 15 45), where the waiters dash around like sprinters, is justifiably popular at all hours.

Le Gargantua, restaurant of *Relais du Square* (see Places to Stay earlier in the section), has a weekday *menu du jour* at 69FF and others from 128FF. *La Divine Comédie* (☎ 04 68 72 59 66), beside Hôtel Central, serves both pizzas and good regional cuisine on its pleasant outside terrace.

L'Écurie (☎ 04 68 72 04 04, 1 rue d'Alembert) serves hearty local cuisine, primarily a la carte but also with a *menu* at 135FF.

Restaurants – Cité It's wise to reserve in advance if you're planning to eat in the Cité, particularly at lunchtime. *Le Château* (☎ 04 68 25 05 16, 4 place du Château) is an upscale place with *menus* starting at 98FF. Next door, the more casual *Auberge de Dame Carcas* (☎ 04 68 71 23 23) has *menus* costing from 85FF and a fine selection of local wines at reasonable prices.

Just round the corner, *Les Fontaines du Soleil* (☎ 04 68 47 87 06, 32 rue du Plô) has tempting *menus* to whet every appetite, with prices ranging from 60FF to 300FF. *L'Écu d'Or* (☎ 04 68 25 49 03, 7 rue Porte d'Aude) serves various cassoulet dishes and *menus* from 130FF).

At the chic *Barbacane*, the restaurant Hôtel de la Cité, its chef Franck Putelat weaves the magic that has earned a Michelin star.

Cafes The cafes overlooking place Carnot in the Ville Basse spill out onto the fountain-clad square in summer. In the north-western corner, *La Cité des Arômes* indeed wafts out scents of rich Arabica and has a mind-boggling choice of coffees.

In the Cité, place Marcou is one big outside cafe when the sun shines. At the foot of the Cité walls is *Tête de l'Art* (☎ 04 68 47 36 36, 37 bis rue Trivalle). Live bands play here some nights and house specialities are 'pork dishes and good humour'. It opens 8 am to 2 am.

Self-Catering The *covered market (rue de Verdun)* opens daily except Sunday; there's an *open-air market (place Carnot)* every Tuesday, Thursday and Saturday.

Chocolate fiends should head straight for the irresistible *L'Art Gourmand (13 rue St-Louis)*, which sells a creative range of calorie-laced goodies. The ice cream is pretty hot too – all 30 varieties of it.

Getting There & Away

Air Carcassonne-Salvaza airport (☎ 04 68 71 96 46) is just west of town near the Carcassonne Ouest A61 motorway exit. Air Liberté has three weekday flights (one/two at weekends) to Orly, Paris. Ryanair (☎ 04 68 71 96 65) flies daily to/from London Stansted (see Getting There & Away section at the beginning of this book).

Bus We can only reiterate the advice of the tourist office: take the train. The

LANGUEDOC

few destinations served by the slow and rare regional buses include Narbonne and Toulouse. Buses and Eurolines stop on blvd de Varsovie, 500m south-west of the train station.

Train Carcassonne is on the important line linking Toulouse (74FF, 50 minutes, 10+ trains daily) with Béziers (70FF, 50 minutes, five daily), Narbonne (55FF, 30–45 minutes, up to 15 daily) and Montpellier (113FF, 1½ hours, 10+ daily, direct or changing in Narbonne). For Perpignan (93FF), change in Narbonne.

Getting Around

To/From the Airport CART bus No 7 runs between square Gambetta and the airport (20 minutes, seven daily).

Bus Local buses are run by CART (☎ 04 68 47 82 22), which has an information kiosk on square Gambetta, the central bus hub. A single ticket costs 5.50FF; a carnet of 10 costs 47.50FF. Buses run until about 7 pm, Monday to Saturday.

Car Europcar (☎ 04 68 25 05 09), 7 blvd Omer Sarraut, and Budget (☎ 04 68 72 31 31) at No 5 are a two-minute walk from the train station. Cars are forbidden in the Cité during the day. Leave your vehicle in the huge car park (20FF per day) just east of the main entrance.

Taxi Taxis loiter outside the train station. Alternatively, order one on ☎ 04 68 71 50 50.

Boat Motorboats and houseboats can be hired under the bridge just south of the train station. For information call Nautic (☎ 04 68 71 88 95, fax 04 67 94 05 41), ave Maréchal Foch.

The Cathars

In Languedoc you'll come across the term *le Pays Cathar* (the Cathar Land), recalling the cruel Albigensian Crusade – the hounding and extermination of a religious sect called the Cathars.

Cathars (from the Greek word *katharos* meaning 'pure') believed that God's kingdom was locked in battle with Satan's evil world. Humans were evil at heart, having been inspired by Satan to revolt against God after being driven out of heaven. But, Cathars believed, a pure life, followed by several reincarnations, would free the spirit from its satanical body. The ascetic *parfaits* (the perfect ones) followed strict vegetarian diets and abstained from sex.

Catharism spread from the Balkans to Toulouse, Albi and Carcassonne during the 11th to 13th centuries. Reacting against worldly Rome and preaching in *langue d'oc*, the local tongue, the sect found many followers among all classes.

In 1208, Pope Innocent III preached a crusade against the Cathars, who were closely associated with the Albigenses, a sect based in the city of Albi. The Albigensian Crusade was a chance for northern rulers to expand their territory into Languedoc, supported spiritually by St-Dominic of Toulouse and in the field by the cruel Simon de Montfort.

After long sieges, the major Cathar centres at Béziers, Carcassonne, the village of Minerve and the dramatically sited fortresses of Montségur, Quéribus and Peyrepertuse were taken and hundreds of 'perfects' were burned as heretics. One of the more notorious episodes of the Albigensian Crusade took place in Béziers in 1209 when some 20,000 of the faithful were slaughtered. The final massacre was at Montségur in 1244, as 200 Cathars, refusing to renounce their faith when the castle was captured after a 10-month siege, were burned alive in a mass funerary pyre. In 1321, the burning of the last perfect, Guillaume Bélibaste, in the chateau of Villerouge-Terménès (a village on the D613, which runs between Narbonne and Couiza), marked the end of Catharism in Languedoc.

AROUND CARCASSONNE
Cathar Fortresses

Over a century before the Albigensian Crusade forced the Cathars into the arid mountains which once marked the frontier
between France and Aragon, the inaccessible fortresses where they sought refuge had
been erected, stone by stone. The two most
famous ones, **Peyrepertuse** and **Quéribus**,
are about halfway between Carcassonne
and Perpignan, off the D117. Both, alas, are
all but inaccessible without your own
wheels.

Peyrepertuse, the larger, squatting high
on a ridge with a drop of several hundred
metres on all sides, occupies one of the
most dramatic sites of any castle anywhere.
The fortress opens 10 am to 7 pm daily,
April to September (9 am to 8 pm in July
and August). Admission costs 20FF.

Quéribus, perched precariously at 728m
on a rocky spur, marked the Cathars' last
stand in 1255. It opens 10 am to 6 pm daily,
April to October (9 am to 8 pm in July and
August). Admission costs 25FF. You can
also ramble over the castle weekends and
school holidays during the rest of the year.

It's wild country and views from both
make the pulse race. They can be hot as hell
in high summer so be sure to pack extra
water.

Contact the tourist office in the small
town of Quillan (☎ 04 68 20 07 78), 51km
west of Quéribus, for up-to-date details of
buses from Perpignan, which pass within
8km, and information on hiking routes to
the fortresses.

NÎMES
postcode 30000 • pop 135,000

Nîmes, a little bit Provençal (Avignon is
only 47km to the north-east) but with a soul
as Languedocien as cassoulet, is graced by
some of Europe's best-preserved Roman
buildings. Most famous are Les Arènes, an
amphitheatre reminiscent of the Colosseum
in Rome, and the Maison Carrée, a 1st-
century temple. Founded by the Emperor
Augustus, the Roman Colonia Nemausensis
reached its zenith during the 2nd century
AD, receiving its water from a Roman

aqueduct system that included the Pont du
Gard, an awesome arched bridge 23km
north-east of town (see Around Nîmes later
in the chapter). The sacking of the city by
the Vandals in the early 5th century began a
downward spiral from which it has never
recovered. Mind you, lazy, laid-back Nîmes
does get more than 300 days of sunshine
every year.

Nîmes becomes more Spanish than
French during its *férias*. Encircled by vineyards and *garrigue*, scrub and headily
scented rosemary, lavender and thyme,
Nîmes is a good base from which to explore
the nearby limestone hills, the picturesque
village of Uzès and the Pont du Gard.

Orientation

Almost everything, including traffic, revolves around Les Arènes. North of
the amphitheatre, the fan-shaped, largely
pedestrianised old city is bounded by blvd
Victor Hugo, blvd Amiral Courbet and blvd
Gambetta. The main squares are place de la
Maison Carrée, place du Marché and place
aux Herbes, just north of which lies Îlot Littré, the old dyer's quarter where Nîmes
serge (better known as denim – see the
boxed text 'Denim de Nîmes' later in the
section) used to be made.

From esplanade Charles de Gaulle, ave
Feuchères strikes south to the train and bus
stations.

Information

Tourist Offices The main tourist office
(☎ 04 66 67 29 11, fax 04 66 21 81 04, **@**
info@ot-nimes.fr), 6 rue Auguste, opens
8 am to 7 pm daily (from 8.30 am, November to March; until 8 pm, July and August;
shorter hours, Saturday and Sunday).

Its train station annexe (☎ 04 66 84 18
13) opens 9.30 am to 12.30 pm and 2 to
6 pm (from 10 am to 3 pm Sunday, closed
winter weekends).

For information on the Gard department,
visit the Maison du Tourisme (☎ 04 66 36
96 30, fax 04 66 36 13 14), 3 place des
Arènes. It's open 8.45 am to 6 pm weekdays
and 9 am to noon, Saturday (9 am to 6 pm,
Monday to Saturday, in July and August).

LANGUEDOC

NÎMES

PLACES TO STAY
7 New Hôtel la Baume
11 Hôtel Central
12 Cat Hôtel
13 Hôtel du Temple
24 Hôtel de la Maison Carrée
29 Hôtel de la Mairie
33 Hôtel Amphithéâtre
34 Hôtel Le Lisita
35 Hôtel Concorde
39 Hôtel Le France

PLACES TO EAT
5 Côte Bleue
6 Covered Market
14 Le Pétrin (Boulangerie)
15 Le Menestrel
17 Cafés Nadal
20 Le Portofino
21 L'Assiette
26 La Truye qui Filhe
31 Lakayna
32 Le Sandaga
40 Grand Café de la Bourse
41 Goulbarge
42 Les Parasols
46 Les Olivades;
   La Vinothèque
47 La Fournaise

OTHER
1 Post Office; Cyberposte
2 La Coupole des Halles
   Shopping Centre; FNAC
3 Laundrette
4 Main Tourist Office
8 Laundrette
9 PC Gamer
10 Église St-Baudille
16 Cathédrale de St-Castor
18 Maison Carré
19 Carré d'Art

OTHER (continued)
22 Netgames
25 Théâtre de Nîmes
27 Musée du Vieux Nîmes
28 Musées d'Archéologie;
   d'Histoire Naturelle
30 Town Hall
36 TCN bus kiosk
37 Palais de Justice
38 Boutique des Arènes
43 Les Arènes
44 Matador Statue
45 Bureau de Locations
   des Arènes
48 Maison du Tourisme
49 Chez Edgar
50 Post Office; Cyberposte
51 Musée des Beaux Arts
52 TCN bus stops
53 Train Station
54 Bus Station

Post & Communications The central post office, blvd de Bruxelles, has Cyberposte.

Nîmes is well endowed with cybercafes. Netgames (☎ 04 66 36 36 16), right beside the Maison Carrée, opens 10 am to 9 pm (from 3 pm/noon on Sunday/Monday) and charges 25FF per hour. Equally central, PC Gamer (☎ 04 66 76 27 85), 2 rue Nationale, opens 11 am to 1 am, Monday to Saturday (from 2 pm on Sunday) and charges 30FF per hour. Friendly, casual – and much quieter – Le Vauban (☎ 04 66 76 09 71), 34 ter rue Clérisseau, functions 9.30 am to

9.30 pm, charging 50FF per hour or 1FF per minute. It's at the intersection with rue Menard, the continuation of rue du Grand Couvent.

Laundry Laundrettes at 20 rue de l'Agau and 14 rue Nationale open 7 am to 9 pm daily.

Les Arènes
This superb Roman amphitheatre, built around AD 100 to seat 24,000 spectators, is better preserved than any similar structure in France. It even retains its upper storey,

unlike its counterpart in Arles. The interior has four tiers of seats and a system of exits and passages (called, engagingly, *vomitoires*), designed so that patricians attending animal and gladiator combats never had to rub shoulders with the plebs up top.

Covered by a removable roof in winter, Les Arènes lives on as a sporting and cultural venue – for theatre performances, concerts, bullfights and the like. Unless there's something on, it opens from 9 am to 6 pm (6.30 pm in summer). Tickets (28FF) are sold at the Boutique des Arènes, tucked into its northern walls.

Maison Carrée

This remarkably preserved rectangular Roman temple, today called the Maison Carrée (Square House), was constructed around AD 5 to honour Augustus' two adopted sons and has survived the centuries as a meeting hall (during the Middle Ages), private residence, stable (in the 17th century), church and, after the Revolution, archive.

Entered through six symmetrical Corinthian columns, it opens 9 am to noon and 2.30 to 7 pm (2 to 6 pm in winter). Admission is free.

The striking glass and steel building across the square, completed in 1993, is the **Carrée d'Art** (Square of Art), which houses the municipal library and Musée d'Art Contemporain (see Museums later in the section). The work of British architect Sir Norman Foster, who designed the seminal Hongkong & Shanghai Bank building in Hong Kong and London's Stansted airport, it harmonises well with the Maison Carrée. It's everything modern architecture should be: innovative, complementary and beautiful – a wonderful, airy building just to float around.

Jardins de la Fontaine

The Fountain Gardens, home to Nîmes' other major Roman monuments, spread around the Source de la Fontaine (the site of a spring, temple and baths in Roman times). They retain a rather elegant air, with statue-adorned paths running around inky water-

---

Denim de Nîmes

During the 18th century, Nîmes' sizeable Protestant middle class – banned from government posts and various other ways of earning a living – turned its energies to trade and manufacturing. Among the products of Protestant-owned factories was a twilled fabric known as *serge*. This soft but durable fabric became very popular among workers and, stained blue, was the uniform of the fishermen of Genoa.

When a Bavarian-Jewish immigrant to the USA, Levi Strauss (1829–1902), began producing trousers in California during and after the gold rush of 1849, he soon realised that miners needed garments that would last. After trying tent canvas, he began importing the *serge de Nîmes*, now better known as denim.

---

ways. **Temple de Diane** – 'it is strictly forbidden to escalade this monument', says the sign in English rather quaintly – is left (west) through the main entrance.

A 10- to 15-minute uphill walk brings you to the crumbling shell of the 30m high **Tour Magne** (15FF), raised around 15 BC and largest of the series of towers that once ran along the city's 7km-long Roman ramparts. From here, there's a magnificent view of Nîmes and the surrounding countryside. A combination ticket, also allowing admission to Les Arènes, costs 34FF. The tower opens 9 am to 7 pm (until 5 pm in winter).

The gardens are a mere five minutes' walk from La Maison Carrée. Head northwestwards along rue Gaston Boissier then left along quai de la Fontaine. They close at 10 pm (6.30 pm in winter).

Museums

Nîmes' half-dozen museums open 11 am to 6 pm daily except Monday. Each charges 28FF admission. Most are in sore need of a new broom. Museum buffs can save by picking up from the tourist office a three-day pass (60FF) giving entry to most sites.

The **Musée du Vieux Nîmes** in the

17th-century episcopal palace just south of **Cathédrale de St-Castor** is a rather tedious museum which portrays key elements of Nîmes' history.

The **Musée d'Archéologie**, 13 blvd Amiral Courbet, brings together Roman and pre-Roman artefacts unearthed around Nîmes. Exhibits are disgracefully underdocumented, the majority bearing nothing more than a peeling paper label with an enigmatic number. It also houses a hotchpotch of artefacts from Africa, piled high in bazaar-like style and still bearing yellowing captions such as 'Abyssinia' and 'Dahomey'. In the same building, the **Musée d'Histoire Naturelle** has a musty collection of stuffed animals gazing bleakly out and row upon row of bulls' horns. Only the custodians, protected from importune visitors within their own glass case, have any vitality.

The **Musée des Beaux-Arts**, rue de la Cité Foulc, has a fairly pedestrian collection of Flemish, Italian and French works as well as a Roman mosaic.

Bustling, refreshing **Musée d'Art Contemporain** in the Carrée d'Art is a complete contrast. Housing both permanent and rotating exhibitions of modern art, it merits a visit, even if only to wonder at the innards of this striking building.

Organised Tours

The tourist office (see Information earlier in the section) arranges various two-hour city tours (28FF) in French at 10 am on Tuesday, Thursday and Saturday in summer (2.30 pm on Saturday during the rest of the year).

Taxi TRAN (☎ 04 66 29 40 11) offers a one-hour tour of the city (150FF for up to six people) with cassette commentary in English.

Special Events

In March, Nîmes hosts the week-long Printemps du Jazz festival. July and August bring forth an abundance of dance, theatre, rock, pop and jazz events. The tourist office has a free yearly calendar of events.

Férias & Bullfights The three férias – the three-day Féria Primavera (Spring Festival)

in February, the five-day Féria de Pentecôte (Whitsuntide Festival) in June, and the three-day Féria des Vendanges coinciding with the grape harvest on the third weekend in September – revolve around the daily or twice-daily *corridas* (bullfights). Tickets cost between 100FF and 500FF; it's prudent to reserve well in advance through the Bureau de Locations des Arènes (☎ 04 66 67 28 02), on the south-western side of Les Arènes, which accepts telephone bookings.

Bloodless bullfights, in which tokens or acorns are plucked from between the bull's horns, are called *courses Camarguaises* or *courses à la cocarde*. They're generally held the weekend before a féria and at other times during the bullfighting season. Tickets cost between 50FF and 100FF. The best bulls are rewarded with a couple of bars from the opera *Carmen* as they leave the arena.

Places to Stay

During Nîmes' three férias, some hotels raise their prices and accommodation can be hard to find.

Places to Stay – Budget

Camping At *Domaine de la Bastide* (☎ 04 66 38 09 21), open all year and 4km south of town on route de Générac (the D13), two people with tent and car pay 66FF. From the station, take bus No 1, direction Caremeau. At the Jean Jaurès stop, change to bus D and get off at La Bastide, the terminus.

Hostels The *Auberge de Jeunesse* (☎ 04 66 23 25 04, fax 04 66 23 84 27, ✉ nimes@ fuaj.org, chemin de la Cigale) is 3.5km north-west of the train station. Dorm beds cost 52FF. From the train station, take bus No 2, towards Alès or Villeverte, and get off at the Stade stop. The hostel rents mountain bikes to guests (see Getting Around later in the section).

Hotels Surprisingly, Nîmes has plenty of cheap, decent hotels, many conveniently situated in the old city.

For excellent views of Les Arènes (provided that the wooden window shutters will creak open, that is), **Hôtel Le France** (☎ *04 66 67 23 05, fax 04 66 67 76 93, 4 blvd des Arènes)* has rather dreary rooms and a pricing policy similar to that of the Romans at the amphitheatre: the higher you go, the cheaper the room. Singles/doubles with washbasin on the 4th floor (there's no lift) cost 110/175FF, 3rd-floor rooms with bathroom, 130/190FF, and others, nearer ground level, cost between 150FF and 280FF.

Hôtel Concorde (☎ *04 66 67 91 03, 3 rue des Chapeliers)* has smallish singles/doubles starting at 115/135FF. Those with bathroom start at 165/190FF.

Rooms with washbasin/shower start at 135/180FF (200FF with full bathroom) at the two-star **Hôtel de La Mairie** (☎ *04 66 67 65 91, 11 rue des Greffes)*. Triples/quads cost 210/260FF with washbasin/shower.

The welcoming **Hôtel de la Maison Carrée** (☎ *04 66 67 32 89, fax 04 66 76 22 57, 14 rue de la Maison Carrée)* is highly recommended. Singles with washbasin start at 145FF (160FF with shower), singles/doubles with bathroom and TV cost 180/220FF, and triples/quads 330/350FF.

Around Église St-Baudille are several bargain-basement hotels. **Hôtel Central** (☎ *04 66 67 27 75, fax 04 66 21 77 79, 2 place du Château)*, with its creaky floorboards and bunches of wild flowers painted on each bedroom door, oozes charm. Singles/doubles/triples with bathroom and TV start at 190/210/230FF. Rooms at **Hôtel du Temple** (☎ *04 66 67 54 61, fax 04 66 36 04 36)*, just opposite, are spick and span, even if some of the wallpaper – different in every room – might induce biliousness. Room prices are – more than coincidentally – almost the same as those of Hôtel Central.

Places to Stay – Mid-Range

Next door to Hôtel Le France and equally well situated, **Le Lisita** (☎ *04 66 67 66 20, fax 04 66 76 22 30)* is altogether cheerier than its neighbour. Doubles with bathroom begin at 235FF. Around the corner, **Hôtel Amphithéâtre** (☎ *04 66 67 28 51, fax 04 66 67 07 79, 4 rue des Arènes)* is one of the city's loveliest options with singles/doubles/triples starting at 185/240/305FF.

Cat Hôtel (☎ *04 66 67 22 85, fax 04 66 21 57 51, 22 blvd Amiral Courbet)* has one or two basic singles with toilet for 140FF. The majority, singles/doubles with bathroom, cost 205/230FF.

Places to Stay – Top End

Most of Nîmes' multistarred hotels belong to chains and are scattered around the city's periphery. A touch more individual in both setting and decor is **New Hôtel La Baume** (☎ *04 66 76 28 42, fax 04 66 76 28 45,* **@** *nimeslabaume@new-hotel.com, 21 rue Nationale)* just north of the old city. Singles/doubles equipped with everything your heart could desire (including air-con) start at 450/510FF.

Places to Eat

Nîmes' gastronomy owes as much to Provence as it does to Languedoc. Aïoli, *rouille* and other spicy southern delights are as abundant in this city as cassoulet. Sample the Costières de Nîmes wines from the pebbly vineyards to the south. If you're teetotal, your water couldn't come fresher: Perrier, the famous fizzy French mineral water, comes from nearby Vergèze (see Around Nîmes later in the chapter).

Restaurants Just west of place des Arènes is **Les Olivades** (☎ *04 66 21 71 78, 18 rue Jean Reboul)*, usually packed and specialising in local wines. It has *menus* for 85FF and 120FF plus a popular lunchtime special for 65FF. Risking resting on its laurels, it's closed Saturday lunchtime and all Sunday and Monday.

Le Portofino (☎ *04 66 36 16 14, 3 rue Corneille)* and its neighbour, **L'Assiette** (☎ *04 66 21 03 03)*, both offer arresting views of the Carrée d'Art. The Portofino serves great home-made dishes; the *carbonara* topped with a raw egg (49FF) is particularly tasty. The more upmarket Assiette serves local cuisine and does great salads – pick and mix your own from over 25 ingredients. Both offer a lunchtime *menu* for 60FF and have summer terraces that spill onto the pedestrianised street.

The small **Restaurant Le Menestrel**

(☎ 04 66 67 54 45, 6 rue École Vieille) is the place for rich local cuisine. Observe yourself in the giant overhead mirror as you tuck away one of its imaginative *menus* at 60FF, 85FF and 125FF. It closes Tuesday lunchtime and Monday.

Equally small and charming is the all-blue *Côte Bleue* (corner of rue Littré and rue du Grand Couvent). It serves mostly local dishes, both inside and outside on its straw-covered terrace.

Beneath the vaults of a restored 14th-century inn, *La Truye qui Filhe* (☎ 04 66 21 76 33) achieves the near-impossible, blending a self-service format with a warm, homely atmosphere. It's almost worth planning your day around their changing daily *menu* – superb value at 52FF. Indeed, you almost have to: it only opens between noon and 1.30 pm and closes Sunday and throughout August. Another great midday – and only midday – place is *Bistrot de Tatie Agnès* (☎ 04 66 21 00 81), beside Hôtel de la Maison Carrée. Its toasted sandwiches (45FF) are as original as its name and you can make a meal out of the giant salads (45FF to 55FF).

Nîmes is also a great place to sample more exotic cuisines. *Lakayna* (☎ 04 66 21 10 96, 18 rue de l'Étoile) has couscous and *tajines* prepared in the manner of the Kabyles of eastern Algeria for around 80FF. A truly generous *couscous royal* – just one of 13 variations – costs 135FF.

Rue Porte de France is rich in ethnic cooking. *Goulbarge* (☎ 04 66 67 37 53, 15, rue Porte de France) is an Indian place while *La Fournaise* (38 rue Porte de France) offers dishes from the Indian Ocean island of Réunion. It opens Tuesday to Saturday. Around the corner, *Les Parasols* (☎ 04 66 21 74 99, 11 rue Bigot) has Sicilian specialities, tons of pizza and spaghetti dishes and *menus* for 89FF and 125FF. Nearby, *Le Sandaga* (☎ 04 66 67 11 98, 2 rue Bec de Lièvre) serves a range of Senegalese dishes (60–80FF). It opens Tuesday to Saturday.

Cafes Place aux Herbes is one communal outside cafe in summer. Equally bustling,

beneath the huge palm tree that sprawls in its centre, is place du Marché.

Grand Café de la Bourse (☎ 04 66 67 21 91), bang opposite Les Arènes, is great for breakfast or a quick coffee on the terrace or inside.

Self-Catering Nîmes plays host to colourful *markets* in the old city on Thursday in July and August. The large, modern covered *food market* opens until midday daily. *Le Pétrin* (rue de la Curaterie) sells traditional breads of all shapes, sizes and grains.

The quaint *Cafés Nadal*, overlooking place aux Herbes, specialises in local herbs, oils and spices. Knowledgeable staff at *La Vinothéque*, which shares premises with Restaurant Les Olivades, can guide you through their unbeatable choice of local wines.

Entertainment

Nîmescope, a free fortnightly entertainment listing, is available at the tourist office and major hotels. Year round, music concerts, theatre performances and movie screenings are held in Les Arènes – less frequently in summer, however.

The *Théâtre de Nîmes* (☎ 04 66 36 02 04, place de la Calade) has drama, music and opera performances throughout the year.

Chez Edgar (3 rue de la Cité Foulc) puts on live music and cabaret most weekends.

Getting There & Away

Air Nîmes' airport (☎ 04 66 70 49 49), 10km south-east of the city on the A54 to Arles, has five flights a day (three at weekends) to/from Paris Orly. Ryanair flies daily to/from London Stansted.

Bus The bus station, rue Ste-Félicité, is behind the train station. Beside the information office (☎ 04 66 29 52 00) is an interactive terminal where you can call up information about all routes served from the bus station.

Regional destinations include Pont du Gard (35FF, 45 minutes, five/six daily –

two of which continue to Collias on the Gard River), Uzès (37FF, 45 minutes, seven to 10 daily) and Alès (42FF, 1¼ hours, four to five daily). There are also buses to/from Avignon (44FF, 1½ hours, six to eight daily) and Arles (34FF, 30–45 minutes, four to eight daily).

Long-haul operators have their offices at the far, eastern end of the bus station. Eurolines (☎ 04 66 29 49 02) covers most European destinations including London (650FF, 20 hours) and Amsterdam (580FF, 20 hours). Line Buses (☎ 04 66 29 50 62) operate services to/from Spain.

Train The train station is at the southeastern end of ave Feuchères. Major destinations include Paris' Gare de Lyon by TGV (366FF to 431FF, four hours, seven daily), Alès (47FF, 40 minutes, 12 daily), Arles (41FF, 30 minutes, 10+ daily), Avignon (65FF, 30 minutes, 10+ daily), Marseilles (76FF, 1¼ hours, 12 daily) and Montpellier (66FF, 30 minutes, 15+ daily). Three SNCF buses head for Aigues Mortes in the Camargue (39FF, 1¼ hours).

Car Rental companies include ADA (☎ 04 66 84 25 60), Europcar (☎ 04 66 21 31 35) and Budget (☎ 04 66 70 49 42). Europcar and Budget also have a kiosk at the airport.

Getting Around
To/From the Airport Airport buses (28FF, 40 minutes) go from the bus station via esplanade Charles de Gaulle three to five times daily to coincide with flights. For current times, ring ☎ 04 66 29 27 29.

Bus Local buses are run by TCN (☎ 04 66 38 15 40), whose ticket and information kiosk is in the north-eastern corner of esplanade Charles de Gaulle, the main bus hub. Many buses stop on ave Feuchères and blvd Talabot (to the right as you exit the train station). A single ticket/carnet of 10 costs 7/48FF.

Taxi Taxis hover around esplanade Charles de Gaulle. To order one by phone, call ☎ 04 66 29 40 11.

Bicycle The Auberge de Jeunesse (see Hostels under Places to Stay – Budget earlier in the section) rents mountain bikes (50FF per day) to hostellers staying there. Piaggio Center (☎ 04 66 21 91 03), 23 blvd Talabot, 300m east of the train station, hires bikes for 80FF per day, March to November.

AROUND NÎMES
The Perrier Plant
Ever wondered how they get the bubbles into a bottle of Perrier water? Or why it's that stubby shape? Visit the spring and bottling plant at Vergèze, on the RN113, 13km south-west of Nîmes. It's open 9.30 to 10.30 am and 1 to 4 pm weekdays (afternoons only at weekends, longer hours in summer). Admission costs 20FF – and we trust their tongue is firmly in their cheek when they advertise 'dégustation gratuite' (free tasting)!

Pont du Gard
The exceptionally well-preserved, three-tiered Roman aqueduct known as the Pont du Gard was once part of a 50km-long system of canals built about 19 BC by Agrippa, Augustus' powerful deputy and son-in-law, to bring water from near Uzès to Nîmes. The 35 small arches of the 275m-long upper tier, which runs 49m above the River Gard, contain a watercourse designed to carry 20,000 cubic metres of water a day. The Romans built the aqueduct with stone from the nearby Vers quarry. The largest boulders weigh over five tonnes.

From car parks either side of the Gard River, you can walk along the road bridge, built in 1743 and running parallel with the top of the aqueduct's lower tier. The best view of the Pont du Gard is from upstream, beside the river, where you can swim on hot days. The Pont du Gard is frequented by two million people a year (averaging a horrendous 5000-plus visitors per day).

Information The Maison de Tourisme (☎ 04 66 37 00 02), near the aqueduct on the southern side (right bank), is only open 9 am to 7 pm, June to September.

LANGUEDOC

Places to Stay The nearest camp site is *Camping International des Gorges du Verdon* (☎ 04 66 22 81 81), on the bridge's northern side. Go west along the D981 towards Uzès for 1.75km and turn left along chemin Barque Vieille. On the southern side (right bank), *Camping Municipal La Sousta* (☎ 04 66 37 12 80) is no more than a five-minute walk from the bridge. Both open mid-March to mid-October and charge around 70FF for two people, a car and tent.

On the northern side, *Le Vieux Moulin* (☎ 04 66 37 14 35, fax 04 66 37 26 48), an attractive inn with some truly splendid views of the Pont du Gard, was undergoing extensive renovations when we passed. It's expected to reopen in 2001, probably from mid-March to early November.

Getting There & Away The Pont du Gard is 23km north-east of Nîmes, 26km west of Avignon and 12km south-east of Uzès. Buses to/from each stop 1km north of the bridge beside the Auberge Blanche. There are five buses daily from Nîmes, two of which continue to Collias, and three from Avignon.

The extensive car parks on the northern/southern side of the river cost 22/17FF.

River Gard

The wild River Gard descends from the Cévennes Mountains. It's known for its unpredictability; torrential rains can raise the water level by as much as 5m in almost no time. During long dry spells, by contrast, it sometimes almost disappears.

The River Gard has cut itself a long, meandering 20km gorge (Les Gorges du Gardon) through the hills from **Russan** to the village of **Collias**, about 6km upstream from the Pont du Gard. The GR6 runs beside it most of the way.

Boating In Collias, Kayak Vert (☎ 04 66 22 84 83, fax 04 66 22 88 78, ✉ kayak .vert@wanadoo.fr), and Canoë Le Tourbillon (☎ 04 66 22 85 54), both based under the village bridge, plus Eurocanoë (☎ 04 66 22 91 25), just a little downstream, rent kayaks and canoes (50/35FF per hour; 145/90FF per day).

You can paddle down to the Pont du Gard (180/105FF for a canoe/kayak for two) in half a day or arrange to be dropped off 22km upstream at Russan, from where there's a great descent back through the Gorges du Gardon. The latter, a full-day trip, is usually possible only between March

JANE SMITH

A 2000-year-old feat of engineering: the Roman Pont du Gard

and mid-June, when the river is high enough.

Cycling Both Kayak Vert and Canoë Le Tourbillon rent mountain bikes for 80/110FF per half day/day.

Uzès
postcode 30700 • pop 7700

Uzès, a laid-back little hill town 25km north of Nîmes, proved the perfect location for the 1990 film *Cyrano de Bergerac*, starring Gérard Depardieu. With its faithfully restored Renaissance facades, impressive Duché (Ducal Palace), narrow streets and ancient towers, it's a charming place to wander around.

Orientation & Information Within the small, near-circular pedestrianised old town, are the Duché and, a short distance south-west, place aux Herbes. West of this shady square on ave de la Libération is the grandly named *gare routiére* – in fact, a bus stop.

The tourist office (☎ 04 66 22 68 88, fax 04 66 22 95 19), place Albert I, is just north of the Duché. It opens 9 am to 6 pm daily (10 am to noon and 2 to 5 pm at weekends) between June and September (shorter hours during the rest of the year).

Things to See The Duché, or Château Ducal (☎ 04 66 22 18 96), a privately-owned medieval fortress, was altered and expanded almost continuously from the 11th to 18th century. Together with some fine period furniture, tapestries and paintings, there's a bizarre Salle du Fantôme (Ghost Room), a late-20th-century graft-on like something left over from Halloween.

Visitable only by guided tour (one hour, in French), the Duché opens 10 am to 1 pm and 2 to 6.30 pm daily, July to September (shorter hours during the rest of the year). Admission costs a hefty 55FF.

Close by, just off rue Port Royal, is the beautifully landscaped **Jardin Médiéval** (Medieval Garden), open 3 to 7 pm in July and August (2 to 4 pm, April to June, September and October). Admission costs 10FF.

Special Events Uzès is big on festivals and fairs – one of the more animated is the Foire à l'Ail (Garlic Fair), held on 24 June. On Saturday mornings from November to March, there's a truffle market in place aux Herbes, while on the third Sunday in January there is a full-blown Truffle Fair. The town is also renowned for its Nuits Musicales d'Uzès, an international festival of Baroque music held in the second half of July.

Places to Stay Uzès makes a pleasant day trip from either Nîmes or Avignon. If you decide to stay the night, the least expensive hotel is *Hostellerie Provençale* (☎ 04 66 22 11 06, 1 rue Grande Bourgade). Rooms cost 165/195FF without/with bathroom and the restaurant does *menus* from 79FF. It closes Sunday and Monday except in July and August.

The nearest camp site is *Camping du Mas du Rey* (☎ 04 66 22 18 27) in Arpaillargues, 4km west on the D120.

Getting There & Away Buses running between Avignon and Alès on the Cévennes border call by Uzès three times daily. There are also seven to 10 services daily to/from Nîmes.

ALÈS & AROUND
postcode 30100 • pop 41,000

Alès-en-Cévennes, 45km from Nîmes, 70km from Montpellier and snuggled against the River Gard, is the Gard department's second largest town. Coal was mined here from the 13th century, when monks first dug into the surrounding hills, until 1986, when the last pit closed. A little opencast mining is the last vestige of this long tradition.

The pedestrianised heart of town, having long ago shed its sooty past, is pleasant, if unexciting, to stroll through. Gateway to the Cévennes mountains and bright with flowers in summer, Alès is a convenient base for visiting three unique exhibitions close by.

The tourist office (☎ 04 66 52 32 15, fax 04 66 52 57 09), beside the Gard at place

Gabriel Peri, opens 9 am to noon and 1.30 to 6.30 pm daily in summer (closed Sunday during the rest of the year).

Mine Témoin

No museum, this. Don a safety helmet and visit an actual mine where, until recently, mining apprentices learnt and applied their trade. Preceded by a video (in French), the one-hour guided tour leads you along 650m of underground galleries. Functioning from April to November, it opens 10 am to 7.30 pm daily, June to August (reduced hours in other months). Admission costs 38FF, including a free explanatory pamphlet in English. The show mine (☎ 04 66 30 45 15), chemin de la Cité Ste-Marie, is a 1km walk from the tourist office.

Bambouseraie de Prafrance

If any place in France deserves an award for self-promotion, it's the huge Bamboo Grove and Nursery (☎ 04 66 61 70 47) in Générargues, 12km south-west of Alès. Founded in 1855 by a spice merchant, it contains over 150 bamboo species as well as aquatic gardens and an Asian village. Come in early winter and you might experience a rare sight: bamboo with a light dusting of snow.

The Bambouseraie (35FF) opens 9.30 am to 7 pm daily, March to mid-November. A fun way to get there is on the Cévennes steam train (see Getting There & Away later in the section).

Musée du Désert

The Musée du Désert (☎ 04 66 85 02 72) portrays the clandestine way of life of the Camisards (see the boxed text 'The Camisard Revolt'). Set in the charming hamlet of Le Mas Soubeyran, 5km north of the Bambouseraie, it opens 9.30 am to noon and 2.30 to 6 pm (continuously to 7 pm in July and August). Admission costs 22FF.

To reach Le Mas Soubeyran from the Bambouseraie, head west along the D50 then turn right onto the D509 after Luziers village.

Places to Stay

Try *Camping la Croix Clémentine* (☎ 04 66 86 52 69), in Cendras, 4km north-west of Alès. It's open April to mid-September. In high season, it charges 112FF for two people, tent and car (66FF off-peak).

Between June and August, the *Foyer Mixte de Jeunes Travailleurs* (☎ 04 66 86 19 80, 2 ave Jean-Baptiste Dumas), 1km north-west of the train station, accepts travellers. A bed for the night costs 80FF.

The Camisard Revolt

Early in the 18th century, the Cévennes region was the setting of what has been called the first guerrilla war in modern history, fought by Protestants against Louis XIV's army. The revocation of the Edict of Nantes in 1685 took away rights that the Huguenots had enjoyed as Protestants since 1598. Many emigrated, while others fled deep into the wild Cévennes, from where a local leader named Roland, only 22 at the time, led the resistance against the French army sent to crush them in 1702.

Poorly equipped but knowing the countryside intimately, the outlaws resisted for two years. They fought in their shirts – *camiso* in langue d'oc; thus their popular name, Camisards. The royal army slowly gained the upper hand, and on the king's orders the local population was either massacred or forced to flee. Roland was killed and most villages were methodically destroyed.

Each year, on the first Sunday of September, thousands of French Protestants meet at Roland's village in Le Mas Soubeyran, a sleepy hamlet near the village of Mialet, just off the Corniche des Cévennes. His birthplace is now the Musée du Désert, which details the persecution of Protestantism in the Cévennes between 1685 and the reintroduction of religious freedom with Louis XVI's 1787 Edict of Tolerance. The museum's name is that by which this entire period was known: *le Désert* (the desert).

Highly recommended, as much for its fine restaurant as for its pleasant rooms, is **Hôtel Le Riche** (☎ 04 66 86 00 33, fax 04 66 30 02 63), opposite the train station. Modern singles/doubles start at 170/250FF. It's closed August. About 100m northwards, **Hôtel Durand** (☎ 04 66 86 28 94, 3 blvd Anatole France) has trim singles/doubles with bathroom for 170/190FF.

Getting There & Away
Bus From the bus station, place Pierre Sémard, at least one bus daily heads into the Cévennes to Florac (61FF, 1½ hours), and three to Uzès (39FF, one hour), continuing to Avignon. For the Bambouseraie take the St-Jean du Gard service (32FF, one hour, two or three daily – up to 10 during the school year), some of which go via Anduze. From either town, you can take the Cévennes steam train (see the following section) onwards.

Train There are up to 10 trains daily to/from Montpellier (81FF, 1¼ to 1½ hours), some require a change in Nîmes (47FF, 45 minutes, 12+ daily). Four trains daily link Alès and Mende (89FF, 2¼ hours).

From April to October the little Cévennes steam train (train à vapeur; ☎ 04 66 85 13 17) takes 40 minutes to chug the 13km between St-Jean du Gard and Anduze via the Bambouseraie. It makes four return trips daily, April to August (not Monday in April and May), slimming down its schedule as winter approaches. One-way/return fares cost 45/58FF.

PARC NATIONAL DES CÉVENNES
The diverse Parc National des Cévennes (elevation 378m to 1699m), a UNESCO World Biosphere Reserve, is home to isolated hamlets and a wide variety of fauna and flora (an astounding 2250 plant species have been recorded). Several of its animals, including red deer, beavers and vultures, have been reintroduced over the last two decades.

There are four main areas: Mont Lozère, much of the Causse Méjean, the Cévennes

valleys (Vallées Cévenoles) and Mont Aigoual. Florac makes a good base for exploration while Alès, Anduze and St-Jean du Gard to the south-east also serve as gateways.

The park has three **ecomuseums**: the Écomusées du Mont Lozère, de la Cévenne and du Causse, each one of which has several different sites. For details, ask at the Maison du Parc (see Information in the later Florac section).

History
The 910 sq km park was created in 1970 to bring ecological stability to a region that, because of religious and later economic upheavals, has long had a destabilising human presence. Population influxes, which saw the destruction of forests for logging and pastures, were followed by mass desertions as people gave up the fight against the inhospitable climate and terrain. Emigration led to the abandonment of hamlets and farms, many of which were snapped up in the 1960s by wealthy Parisians and foreigners.

Mont Lozère
This 1699m-high lump of granite in the north of the park is shrouded in cloud and ice in winter and covered with heather and blueberries, peat bogs and flowing streams in summer. The Écomusée du Mont Lozère has a permanent exhibition in the Maison du Mont Lozère (☎ 04 66 45 80 73) at Pont de Montvert, 20km north-east of Florac. The museum opens 10.30 am to 12.30 pm and 2.30 to 6.30 pm, mid-April to September. Admission costs 20FF.

Cévennes Valleys
Sweet chestnut trees (châtaigniers), first planted back in the Middle Ages, carpet the Cévennes valleys, the park's central region of inaccessible ravines and jagged ridges, along one of which runs the breathtaking Corniche des Cévennes (see Getting There & Away later in the section). Chestnuts, once staple to the local diet, were eaten raw, roasted or dried after the flesh had been separated from the burr by walking over them

LANGUEDOC

UPPER LANGUEDOC

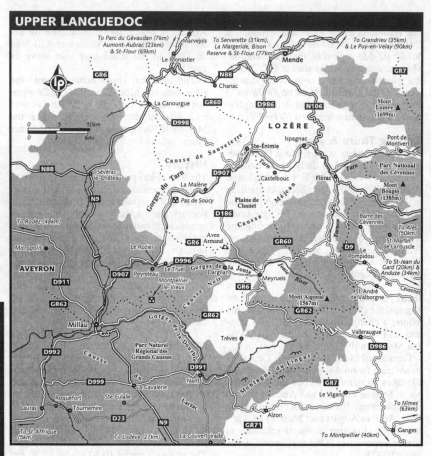

in shoes fitted with long serrated spikes. These days they are the preferred food of the valleys' wild boars, though they are still used in certain sauces and desserts.

Mont Aigoual

Only 70km from the coast, Mont Aigoual (1567m) and the neighbouring Montagne du Lingas region are known more for searing winds and heavy snowfall than Mediterranean climes. The area is thick with beech trees thanks to a successful reforestation program begun in 1875 to counteract years of uncontrolled logging.

The meteorological station on Mont Aigoual (☎ 04 67 82 60 01) offers a stunning 360° view over the Cévennes.

Activities

There's cross-country skiing (over 100km of marked trails) on Mont Aigoual and Mont Lozère in winter, and donkey treks are popular in the area in warmer months (see Activities in the later Florac section). There are 600km of donkey and horse-riding trails and 200km marked out for VTT enthusiasts. An equally well-developed network of footpaths attracts walkers year round. The free pamphlet in French, *Itinéraires et Sentiers Pédestres*, summarises the dozen GR trails which criss-cross the park. In addition, there are 22 shorter signed walks of between two and seven hours' duration and 20 easy, educational trails. Maps and booklets are available at the Maison du Parc in Florac, where you can also pick up a free *gîtes d'étape* brochure listing some 100 places to spend the night. Ask too about the Festival Nature held between June and October when various outdoor activities, lectures and field trips are conducted.

Getting There & Away

If you don't have your own transport, the region is practically as impenetrable as it was centuries ago. For the very limited bus service between Florac and Alès, see Getting There & Away in the later Florac section. By car, the most spectacular route between the two towns is the Corniche des Cévennes, a ridge road that winds along the mountain crests of the Cévennes for 56km from St-Jean du Gard to Florac.

FLORAC

postcode 48400 • pop 2100
• elevation 542m

Florac, 79km north-west of Alès and 38km south-east of Mende, is a pleasant little town and a great base for exploring the Parc National des Cévennes and the upper reaches of the Gorges du Tarn. At the northern end of the wild Corniche des Cévennes, Florac is draped along the River Tarnon, one of the tributaries of the Tarn, while the fortress-like cliffs of the Causse Méjean loom 1000m overhead.

Orientation

The town has one main road, ave Jean Monestier, running parallel to the Tarnon River. The main squares are tiny place de la Mairie and esplanade Marceau Farelle.

Information

The tourist office (☎ 04 66 45 01 14, fax 04 66 45 25 80, ❷ otsi@ville-florac.fr), ave Jean Monestier, opens 9 am to 12.30 pm and 2 to 7.30 pm daily except Sunday, April to September (weekdays during the rest of the year). It also functions on Sunday morning in high summer.

Walkers down from the hills will appreciate the small laundrette, 11 rue du Pêcher, spinning 8.30 am to 7.30 pm. It opens Monday to Saturday.

Maison du Parc National des Cévennes Occupying the handsome restored 17th-century Château de Florac, the Maison du Parc (☎ 04 66 49 53 01, fax 04 66 49 53 02, ❷ pnc@bsi.fr) has a wealth of information, guides to the park, maps and wildlife books. Most are in French but

---

Travels with a Donkey

The Cévennes were even wilder and more untamed back in October 1878, when Scottish writer Robert Louis Stevenson crossed them with only a donkey for company.

'I was looked upon with contempt, like a man who should project a journey to the moon, but yet with a respectful interest, like one setting forth for the inclement Pole', Stevenson wrote in *Travels with a Donkey in the Cévennes*, published the following year.

Accompanied by the mouse-coloured Modestine, bought for 65FF and a glass of brandy, Stevenson took a respectable 12 days to travel the 220km on foot (Modestine carried his gear) from Le Monastier to St-Jean du Gard. Afterwards, he sold his ass – and wept.

The Stevenson trail, first retraced and marked with the cross of St-Andrew by a Scottish woman in 1978, today follows the GR70, crossing Mont du Goulet (1497m) and Mont Lozère (1699m) en route. Donkeys, which can be hired in Florac, carry between 30 to 50kg and cover 10 to 25km per day.

there's an English version of the good guidebook, *Parc National des Cévennes* (99FF).

The best overall map of the park is the IGN's *Parc National des Cévennes* (46FF) at 1:100,000. Six IGN Top 25 maps (57FF each) cover the area at 1:25,000: Nos 2641ET, 2641OT, 2640OT, 2739OT, 2740ET and 2741ET.

The Maison du Parc opens 9 am to 7 pm daily in July and August; 9 am to noon and 2 to 6 pm the rest of the year (closed weekends, November to Easter).

Activities

The tourist office has details on a whole summer's worth of outdoor activities, which include caving, canyon clambering, mountain climbing, gliding, horse-riding, kayaking and canoeing. For information on the Park's rich walking potential, contact the Maison du Parc (see also Activities in the earlier Parc National des Cévennes section).

Donkey Treks Why not follow the lead of Robert Louis Stevenson (see the boxed text 'Travels with a Donkey' earlier in the chapter) and hire a pack animal? Several companies are in the donkey business. They include Gentiane (☎ 04 66 41 04 16, fax 04 66 41 03 23) in Pont de Montvert and Tramontane (☎ 04 66 45 92 44) in St-Martin de Lansuscle. Typical prices are 200FF to 250FF per day and 1200FF to 1400FF per week. Both outfits can reserve en-route accommodation and provide an optional guide (an additional 600FF to 800FF per day). Though each is outside Florac, they'll transport the dumb creatures to Florac for a fee (around 5FF/km).

Whether you're swaying on a donkey or simply walking, you'll find *The Robert Louis Stevenson Trail* by Alan Castle (Cicerone Press) an excellent, practica, well-informed companion. Pick up the free pamphlet *Suivre les Traces de R. L. Stevenson* (Follow in The Footsteps of RLS), which details accommodation along the trail, too.

Cycling To rent a bike, try Cévennes Évasion (☎/fax 04 66 45 18 31, ℮ cevennes

.evasion@wanadoo.fr) at 5 place Boyer, to be found at the northern end of Florac's esplanade. Rates are 70/110FF for a half day/day. In summer, they'll take you for free up to the Causse Méjean, from where you can coast back down.

Climbing & Caving Cévennes Évasion arranges caving (230FF), rock climbing (230FF) and canyon clambering (280FF) expeditions. They also run canoe and kayak trips (prices, inclusive of transport, are as those for Ste-Énimie – see the Gorges du Tarn section).

Places to Stay

Camping There are a pair of riverside municipal camp sites 1.5km from town. Northwards, *Le Pont du Tarn* (☎ 04 66 45 18 26), off the N106, charges 56FF for two adults, car and tent. It opens April to mid-October. To the south, *La Tière* (☎ 04 66 45 00 53) on the D907 is marginally cheaper at 51FF. It's open July and August.

Gîtes d'Étape A trekker's favourite is *L'Ancien Presbytère* (☎ 04 66 45 24 54, 18 rue du Pêcher). The town-run *gîte communal* (☎ 04 66 45 14 93, 7 bis rue du Four) opens all year. Beds at each cost 50/55FF.

Hotels The cheapest option is *Chez Bruno* (☎ 04 66 45 11 19, 21 l'Esplanade), which has musty rooms from 110FF to 170FF. The frayed *Hôtel Central de La Poste* (☎ 04 66 45 00 01, fax 04 66 45 14 04, 4 ave Maurice Tour) has rooms with bathroom between 180FF and 230FF.

Hôtel Les Gorges du Tarn (☎ 04 66 45 00 63, fax 04 66 45 10 56, 48 rue du Pêcher) has decent enough rooms costing 180FF with washbasin (260FF with shower). It opens Easter to October.

Better value is *Grand Hôtel du Parc* (☎ 04 66 45 03 05, fax 04 66 45 11 81, ℮ grandhotelduparc@wanadoo.fr, 47 ave Jean Monestier). With spacious rooms, a pool and delightful gardens, it's a great spot to recharge your batteries. Rooms cost between 250FF and 300FF with bathroom. It's open mid-March to November.

Once a stop for medieval pilgrims, the Pyrenees town of Borce is a popular start for high-altitude walks.

It's a hard life – eating grass, soaking up sunshine and breathing the fresh Pyrenees air.

Nîmes' sunshine makes it popular with artists.

Sir Norman Foster's Carrée d'Art, Nîmes

Languedoc is France's largest wine-growing region.

Nîmes boasts some impressive Roman architecture: Les Arènes is still used for concerts today.

The modern, rather soulless *Hôtel Le Pont Neuf* (☎ 04 66 45 01 67), on the roundabout at the southern end of town, opens year round. Rooms start at 260FF (triples cost from 340FF), all with bathrooms.

Places to Eat

Most Florac hotels have restaurants. *La Source du Pêcher* (☎ 04 66 45 03 01) has a wonderful open-air terrace, perched above the little River Pêcher. *Menus* range between 85FF and 170FF. It opens April to October.

Le Chapeau Rouge (☎ 04 66 45 23 40), beside the tourist office, may be little more than a shed but the food, with regional *menus* starting at 78FF and a good wine selection, is excellent.

Maison du Pays Cévenol (3 rue du Pêcher) sells local specialities – liqueurs, jams, Pélardon cheese and chestnuts in all their guises.

Getting There & Away

It's not easy. There are two buses a day to/from Alès in summer (60FF, 1½ hours) and one during the rest of the year, leaving from the Salle des Fêtes car park off ave Jean Monestier. That's it for public transport, so keep your hitching thumb supple.

MENDE

postcode 48000 • pop 12,500
• elevation 731m

Mende, a quiet little place straddling the River Lot, is the capital of Lozère, France's least populous department. It makes a good base for exploring the northern part of Upper Languedoc, the Lot Valley and the Gorges du Tarn.

Orientation & Information

Mende's oval-shaped centre is ringed by a one-way road. The tourist office (☎/fax 04 66 65 02 69) is in the town hall annexe, just off place Charles de Gaulle. It's open 8.30 am to 8 pm daily (except Sunday morning in July and August) and 8.30 am to 12.30 pm and 2 to 6 pm weekdays (plus Saturday morning) the rest of the year.

Things to See & Do

You can wander through Mende in a matter of minutes but if you have time on your hands, pick up the tourist office brochure in English, *Mende: Heritage Visit of the City*, describing every nook and cranny of historical interest. The most outstanding feature is the 14th-century, twin-towered *Cathédrale Notre Dame* on place Urbain V. The highest of its two towers, the *Clocher de l'Évêque* (84m), offers a fine view of the town and Lot Valley.

Places to Stay

Camping Try *Camping Le Tivoli* (☎ 04 66 65 00 38), 2km west of town, on the N88 to Florac. It charges 77FF for two people with tent and car and opens all year.

Hotels Cheapest option is *Hôtel du Gévaudan* (☎ 04 66 65 14 74, 2 rue d'Aigues Passes). Small, nondescript singles/doubles cost 120/130FF with washbasin and 150/160FF with shower. *Hôtel des Remparts* (☎ 04 66 65 02 29, place Théophile Roussel) has spartan singles/doubles for 160/185FF. Ask for a room away from the busy road.

Opposite place du Foirail on the busy ring road, *Hôtel du Commerce* (☎ 04 66 65 13 73, 2 blvd Henri Bourrillon) is a labyrinthine place. Modern singles/doubles with bathroom go for 180/220FF and triples for 300FF.

Hôtel de France (☎ 04 66 65 00 04, fax 04 66 49 30 47, 9 blvd Lucien Arnault), a Logis de France, has pleasing singles/doubles with bathroom for 220/240FF.

Places to Eat

Le Mazel (☎ 04 66 65 05 33, 25 rue du Collège), with good value *menus* between 79FF and 140FF, is a recognised gourmet venue. Or else drop into the nearby *Bodega Casa del Sol* (☎ 04 66 49 20 00, 13 rue Basse) which serves a variety of tapas dishes from 10FF each. For a swift half, nip into the packed *Irish Pub* (place de la République).

Local foodies with fat wallets don't dine out in town. They follow their stomachs 57km east to the *Balme* hotel and restaurant

LANGUEDOC

(☎ 04 66 46 80 14, fax 04 66 46 85 26) in Villefort or 42km north-west to Aumont-Aubrac, where the **Prouhèze** (☎ 04 66 42 80 07, fax 04 66 42 87 78) cooks up various gastronomic feasts and is honoured with one star by Michelin.

Getting There & Away
Bus Buses leave from both place du Foirail and the train station. One bus daily goes to Rodez (three hours) and Marvejols (50 minutes) while two head for Le Puy-en-Velay (two hours, weekdays only).

Train The train station is 1km north of the town across the River Lot. There are four trains daily to Montpellier (142FF, 3½ hours) via Alès (89FF, 2¼ hours) and Nîmes (116FF, three hours). Northbound, two SNCF buses and one train run daily to/from Clermont-Ferrand in Massif Central (155FF, three hours).

Getting Around
Bicycle Espace Bike (☎/fax 04 66 65 01 81, 1 blvd du Soubeyran) rents out bikes for 50/70/350FF per half day/day/week. It opens Tuesday to Saturday.

AROUND MENDE
Wolf Reserve
Wolves once roamed freely through the Lozère forests but today you'll see them only in the Parc du Gévaudan (☎ 04 66 32 09 22), Ste-Lucie, 7km north of Marvejols. The reserve is the initiative of a local enthusiast with a love for wolves, supported by the Brigitte Bardot Foundation. Over 100 Mongolian, Canadian, Siberian and Polish wolves live here in semi-liberty. Admission costs 33FF and the park opens 10 am to 4.30 pm daily (to 6 pm, June to September).

Trains run from Mende (36FF, 45 minutes, three daily) to Marvejols, 30km to the west. From Marvejols, you have to walk.

La Margeride
La Margeride, one of the most isolated areas of Lozère, is a granite range running north-south from the Massif Central to-

wards Mende. This high plateau, cloaked in pine forests and dotted with occasional old stone villages, is ideal outdoor activities terrain. In winter there are snowshoe and cross-country ski trails.

A good base for exploring La Margeride is **Les Bouviers** (1418m). *Bouviers* is the name for the local herders who bring their flocks to the high summer pasture. Around one of their seasonal shelters has grown a small activities centre (☎ 04 66 47 41 54), open year round. It's an excellent base for hiking (there are over 100km of signed trails), mountain biking, rock climbing and cross-country skiing. You can hire equipment and stay in its *gîte d'étape* for 60FF a night.

To get there, take the N106 northwards from Mende and turn north-eastwards on the D5 at Serverette.

Bison Reserve Above the village of Ste-Eulalie en Margeride, 8km north-west of Les Bouviers, is the Réserve de Bisons d'Europe (☎ 04 66 31 40 40), established in 1992 with 25 European bison transferred from the Bialowieza forest in Poland.

Within their 200-hectare reserve, the bison roam freely. Visitors, by contrast, must follow a guided tour, either by horse-drawn carriage (62FF) or along a defined walking path (30FF). The reserve opens 10 am to noon and 2 to 5 pm daily (to 7 pm continuously, mid-June to mid-September).

GORGES DU TARN
From the village of Ispagnac, 9km north-west of Florac, the spectacular Gorges du Tarn wind south-westwards for about 50km, ending just north of Millau. En route are two villages: medieval Ste-Énimie (a good base for canoeing and walking along the gorges) and, 13km downstream, the equally attractive La Malène.

The gorge, 400 to 600m deep, marks the boundary between the Causse de Sauveterre to the north and the Causse Méjean to the south. From these plateaus, it looks like a white, limestone abyss, its green waters dotted here and there with bright canoes and kayaks. In summer, the riverside road (the

D907 bis) is often jammed with cars, buses and caravans (over 3000 cars a summer's day grind through Ste-Énimie).

Information
Ste-Énimie's tourist office (☎ 04 66 48 53 44), just north of the bridge, opens 9.30 am to 1 pm and 2.30 to 5 pm between May and mid-September (to 7 pm in July and August). It's open 10 am to 12.15 pm and 1.45 to 5 pm the rest of the year (closed weekends). It stocks maps and walking guides, including IGN Top 25 map, *Gorges du Tarn* (No 2640OT; 58FF).

Ste-Énimie
postcode 48210 • pop 500 • elevation 470m
Ste-Énimie, 27km from Florac and 56km from Millau, is named after a Merovingian princess who founded a monastery here in the 6th century after bathing in a local spring and recovering from leprosy. Like an avalanche of grey-brown stone on the northern side of the Tarn, the village blends perfectly into the steep, once-terraced slope behind it. Long isolated, it's now a popular destination for day-trippers from Millau, Mende and Florac and one of the starting points for descending the Tarn by canoe or kayak.

The little Romanesque **Église de Ste-Énimie** in the centre of the village dates from the 12th century. Just behind it on place du Presbytère, the tiny **Écomusée Le Vieux Logis** (☎ 04 66 48 53 44) has one vaulted room in a reconstructed old house full of antique local furniture, lamps, tableware and costumes. Admission costs 10FF. It's open April to September.

Boating & Canoeing
Riding the River Tarn is at its best in high summer when the river is usually low and the descent a lazy trip over mostly calm water. You can get as far as the impassable Pas de Soucy, a barrier of boulders about 9km downriver from La Malène.

A handful of companies organise canoe and kayak descents. These include Canoë Paradan (☎ 04 66 48 56 90) and Locanoë

Castelbouc (☎ 04 66 48 55 57) in Ste-Énimie, Au Moulin de la Malène (☎ 04 66 48 51 14) in La Malène, and Cévennes Évasion in Florac (see the Florac section earlier in this chapter).

Prices per person are roughly the same. They include Ste-Énimie to La Malène (13km, 3½ hours) at 120FF or to the Pas de Soucy (23km, 6½ hours) for 150FF.

The Ste-Énimie tourist office sells the useful guide, *Découvertes en Canoë-Kayak – Gorges du Tarn* (40FF), and also has information on companies offering rafting and descents of the River Tarn.

Walking & Cycling
The Sentier de la Vallée du Tarn trail, blazed in yellow and green, runs for around 250km, from Pont de Montvert on Mont Lozère, down the Gorges and all the way to Albi. The GR60 follows an old drovers' route, winding down from the Causse de Sauveterre to Ste-Énimie, crossing the bridge and continuing southwards up to the Causse Méjean in the direction of Mont Aigoual.

Less strenuously, there are 23 circular, signed walks, each between four and seven hours duration, in the stretch between Ispagnac and La Malène.

VT Tour le Chambonnet (☎ 04 66 44 22 99), in Ispagnac, rents mountain bikes, as does La Périgouse (see Horse Riding later in the section). Both charge 70/110FF per half day/day.

The Ste-Énimie tourist office sells the useful *Vallée et Gorges du Tarn – Balades à Pied et à VTT* (98FF) guide, which details various walking and cycling routes in the region.

Horse-Riding
Centre Équestre La Périgouse (☎ 04 66 48 53 71, fax 04 66 48 81 20), in Ste-Énimie, hires horses for 75FF an hour or 180/250FF per half day/day. It opens Easter to October.

Places to Stay
Camp sites along the riverside road can be expensive, but *Camping Les Gorges du Tarn* (☎ 04 66 48 50 51), about 800m above

LANGUEDOC

the village on the road to Florac, costs only 42FF for two people, tent and car. It opens March to mid-October.

The tourist office in Ste-Énimie has details of B&B accommodation in local homes and gîtes d'étape. Many houses in La Malène have chambre d'hôte signs outside. Hotels in Ste-Énimie and La Malène, mostly open April to September, are usually full. Try **Hôtel Le Central** (☎ 04 66 48 50 23, *rue Basse*), facing the Tarn, or **Hôtel du Commerce** (☎/fax 04 66 48 50 01) across the little bridge. The Central has singles/doubles for 140/200FF; the Commerce for 130/250FF.

A fabulous place to stay if you have the cash is 15th-century **Château de la Caze** (☎ 04 66 48 51 01, fax 04 66 48 55 75, ⓔ chateau.de.la.caze@wanadoo.fr), on the banks of the Tarn 2km north of La Malène. Luxury rooms start at 500FF and the hotel/restaurant opens mid-March to mid-November.

Getting There & Away

Public transport along the Gorges du Tarn is virtually nonexistent, so small wonder the traffic snarl-ups are so intense. In July and August there's one bus a day from Millau which takes an extremely roundabout route – and that's all.

PARC NATUREL RÉGIONAL DES GRANDS CAUSSES

The Parc Naturel Régional des Grands Causses, west of the Cévennes, embraces an area of harsh limestone plateaus on the southern rim of the Massif Central. Scorched in summer and windswept in winter, their stony surfaces hold little moisture; water filters through the limestone to form an underground world ideal for cavers.

The Rivers Tarn, Jonte and Dourbie have sliced deep gorges through the 5000 sq km plateau, creating four distinct *causses* ('plateaus' in the local patois): Sauveterre, Méjean, Noir and Larzac. Each is different in its delicate geological forms. One may look like a dark lunar surface, another like a Scottish moor covered with the thinnest layer of grass, while the next is gentler and

more fertile. But all are eerie and empty except for the occasional shepherd wandering with his flock – and all offer magnificent walking and mountain biking.

Millau, at the heart of the park, is a good base for venturing into this wild region. The southern part of the park, home to France's 'king of cheeses' (see the boxed text 'The King of Cheeses' later in the chapter), is known as Le Pays du Roquefort (the Land of Roquefort). The Gorges de la Jonte, populated by myriad swooping birds of prey and rivalling the neighbouring Gorges du Tarn in beauty, skim the park's eastern boundary.

Causse de Sauveterre

This northernmost *causse* is a gentle, hilly plateau dotted with a few compact, isolated farms resembling fortified villages. Every possible patch of fertile earth is cultivated, creating irregular, intricately patterned wheat fields.

Causse Méjean

Causse Méjean, the highest, with an average altitude nudging 1000m, is also the most barren and isolated. Occasional fertile depressions dot poor pasture and streams gurgle down into the limestone through sinkholes, funnels and fissures.

Underground, this combination of water and limestone has created some spectacular scenery. The cavern of **Aven Armand** (☎ 04 66 45 61 31) on the plateau's south-western side lies about 75m below the surface. Stretching some 200m, it bristles with a subterranean forest of stalagmites and stalactites. The one-hour guided visit costs 48FF while a combination ticket, including admission to the Chaos de Montpellier-le-Vieux (see the Causse Noir section later in the chapter), costs 60FF. It opens April to October.

Nearby is the equally spectacular, even larger cavern of **Dargilan** (☎/fax 04 66 45 60 20). A one-hour tour culminates in a sudden exit to a ledge with a dizzying view of the Gorges de la Jonte (see later in the section) way below. Admission costs 41FF. It opens mid-March to October.

Causse Noir

Rising immediately east of Millau, this 'black' causse is encircled by gorges. It's best known for **Montpellier-le-Vieux** (☎ 05 65 60 66 30), an area of jagged rocks called *chaos*, 18km north-east of Millau overlooking the Gorges de la Dourbie. Water erosion has created over 120 hectares of weird limestone formations with fanciful names such as the Sphinx and the Elephant. Three trails, lasting one to three hours, cover the site, as does a tourist train.

Officially, Montpellier-le-Vieux opens 9 am to 7 pm, mid-March to October but when it's closed, nothing stops you wandering around freely. Admission costs 30FF and the little train, 12FF.

Causse du Larzac

The Causse du Larzac (800 to 1000m) is the largest of the four causses. An endless sweep of distant horizons and rocky steppes broken by medieval villages, it's known as the 'French Desert'. To its west lies the Roquefort region, to the north, Millau.

It's known in particular for old, fortified villages such as **Ste-Eulalie**, long the capital of the Larzac region, and **La Couvertoirade**, both built by the Knights Templar, a religious military order that distinguished itself during the Crusades.

Gorges de la Jonte

The dramatic Gorges de la Jonte cut east-west from Meyrueis to Le Rozier, below the north-western slopes of the Aigoual massif. Just west of Le Truel on the D996 is **Belvédère des Vautours** (Vulture Viewing Point) above which the birds nest, high in the cliffs. Vultures had all but disappeared from the Causses skies but the descendants of a colony of 20 which was reintroduced into the gorges now wheel and plane.

The vulture centre (☎ 05 65 62 69 69) has an impressive multimedia exhibition, including live video transmission from the nesting sites of what must be the world's most heavily researched vultures. The centre organises half-day birding treks (40FF) to the surrounding gorges. It opens 10 am to 6 pm (7 pm in summer), mid-March to mid-November. Admission costs 33FF.

Getting There & Away

For the limited public transport access to the Parc, see Getting There & Away under Millau.

MILLAU

postcode 12100 • pop 22,500 • elevation 370m

Millau (pronounced mee-yo) sits between the Causse Noir and Causse du Larzac at the confluence of the Rivers Tarn and Dourbie. In fact just over the border in the Midi-Pyrénées department of Aveyron, it's tied to Languedoc historically and culturally. A prosperous town, famous for glove-making, it nowadays enjoys the benefits of being the main centre for the Parc Naturel Régional des Grand Causses.

Convenient take-off points and good thermals have made Millau a thriving hang-gliding and parapente centre.

Information

The tourist office (☎ 05 65 60 02 42, fax 05 65 61 36 08) is in the impressive Hôtel du Districte building on rue Droite. It's open 9 am to 12.30 pm and 2 to 6.30 pm (closed Sunday) and 9 am to 7 pm continuously (shorter hours on Sunday) in July and August. Ask for a copy, in English, of the pamphlet giving ideas for six day trips by car from Millau.

The Parc Naturel Régional des Grands Causses office (☎ 05 65 61 35 50) is at 71 blvd de l'Ayrolle.

The main post office, 12 ave Alfred Merle, has Cyberposte.

The laundrette beside Ailes Passion Aveyron on ave Gambetta, opens 7 am to 9 pm daily.

Le Beffroi

This 42m-tall belfry, rue Droite, has a square base dating from the 12th century, tapering into a 17th-century octagonal tower from which there's a great view. It opens 10 am to noon and 3.30 to 6 pm, mid-July to mid-September. Admission costs 15FF.

LANGUEDOC

MILLAU

PLACES TO STAY
5 Grand Hôtel de Paris
    et de la Poste
7 Hôtel Emma Calvé
11 Hôtel La Capelle

PLACES TO EAT
12 La Mangeoire
13 La Marmite
14 Au Bec Fin
15 Les Vitrines du Terroir
17 Le Buron
19 Covered Market
20 La Braconne
25 Auberge Occitane
26 Le Chien à la Fenêtre
27 Le Square

OTHER
1 Train Station
2 Bus Station
3 À Venir Car Rental
4 Main Post Office;
    Cyberposte
6 Millau Évasion
8 Église Sacré Cœur
9 Ailes Passion Aveyron
10 Laundrette
16 Cycle Espace
18 Le Beffroi (Belfry)
21 Église Notre Dame de
    l'Espinasse
22 Musée de Millau
23 Horizon Loisirs Sportifs
24 Tourist Office; Hôtel du
    Districte
28 Parc Naturel Régional des
    Grandscausses Park Office

Musée de Millau

The **Millau Museum** (☎ 05 65 59 01 08) in Hôtel de Pégayrolles, place du Maréchal Foch, has a rich collection of fossils, including mammoth molars and a dinosaur skeleton from the Causse du Larzac. In the cellar is a huge array of plates and vases from **La Graufesenque**, once Gallo-Roman pottery workshops just south of the River Tarn on the route de Montpellier. The first-floor leather and glove section illustrates Millau's tanneries and their products through the ages.

The museum opens 10 am to noon and 2 to 6 pm daily (closed Sunday between October and March, no lunch break in summer). Admission costs 27FF or you can buy a combined ticket, which includes admission to La Graufesenque, for 35FF.

Hang-Gliding & Parapente

Several companies run introductory courses (average cost: 2000FF for five or six days) as well as tandem flights (400FF). Millau Évasion (☎ 05 65 59 15 30, fax 05 65 61 26 22, ✉ evasion@millau-evasion.com), 21 ave de la République, has English-speaking instructors and operates year round.

Two similar outfits are Ailes Passion Aveyron (☎ 05 65 61 20 96, fax 05 65 60 04 59), 12 ave Gambetta, and Horizon Loisirs Sportifs (☎ 05 65 59 78 60, fax 05 65 59 78 59), just off place du Maréchal Foch.

Rock Climbing

The 50 to 200m-high cliffs of the Gorges de la Jonte are a renowned venue for climbers of all levels (in 2000 Millau hosted the world climbing championships). To join a group, contact Horizon Loisirs Sportifs (see Hang-Gliding & Parapente earlier in the chapter).

Walking & Cycling

Walkers, spoilt for choice, can select from a wealth of local circuits. Just about every hamlet has one and probably several signed trails radiating from it. *Randonnée Pédestre* (45FF) describes 22 walks around Millau, the Gorges du Tarn and the Grands Causses, all waymarked and varying from 1½ to six hours. Even if you don't read French, it's worth picking up – you can navigate by its explicit maps. *Randonnée VTT-Cyclos* is a comparable and equally practical manual for bikers, detailing 10 VTT and 10 touring-bike routes. The tourist office sells both.

For more demanding trekking, the GR60 traverses the Gorges du Tarn at Ste-Énimie and crosses the Causse Méjean, the GR62 goes over the Causse Noir, passing Montpellier-le-Vieux before winding down to Millau, while the GR71 and its spurs thread across the Causse du Larzac and through its Templar villages.

Special Events

In mid-August, the four-day pétanque world series is held in Millau. Its 16 competitions (including just one for women in this male-dominated sport) attract some 6000 players and even more spectators. Millau hosts a jazz festival in mid-July.

Places to Stay

Camping There are several huge riverside camp sites just east of town. Closest is *Deux Rivières* (☎ 05 65 60 00 27), 1.25km from the train station. It charges 70FF for two people with car and tent. It opens April to October.

About 500m farther along ave de Millau Plage, a pitch at *La Graufesenque* (☎ 05 65 61 18 83) is 60FF (98FF in July and August). It's open mid-April to September.

A more peaceful summer-only option is the small *camp site* beside Gîte de la Maladerie (see Gîte d'Étape later in the chapter). It's basic, fairly isolated and charges about 15FF per person.

Hostels The year-round *Auberge de Jeunesse* (☎ 05 65 61 27 74, 26 rue Lucien Costes), opposite the fire station, charges 51FF. The warden knocks off at 6 pm so arrive early.

Gîte d'Étape Also open year round and 2.5km from the train station, *Gîte de la Maladerie* (☎ 05 65 61 06 57, fax 05 65 60 41 84, chemin de la Graufesenque) has a more pleasant atmosphere and charges 50FF a night for a dorm bed. To get there, cross Pont Lerouge and follow the river to the left (eastwards).

Hotels Many hotels are closed between October and Easter. One that isn't is *Grand Hôtel de Paris et de la Poste* (☎ 05 65 60 00 52, 10 ave Alfred Merle). Not as grandiose as the name would have you believe, it's a friendly, informal place where rooms with toilet/shower cost 140/160FF (220FF with full bathroom).

The stylish *Hôtel Emma Calvé* (☎ 05 65 60 13 49, 28 ave Jean Jaurès) opens year round. In summer it's a riot of flowers; airy rooms, all with bathroom, range between 280FF and 350FF.

Central but quiet, *Hôtel La Capelle* (☎ 05 65 60 14 72, place de la Fraternité) occupies a wing of a one-time leather factory. Its large terrace with views towards the Causse Noir makes for a perfect breakfast spot. Fairly basic doubles start at 160FF, rising to 260FF with full bathroom. Parking is free. *Hôtel des Causses* (☎ 05 65 60 03 19, fax 05 65 60 86 90, 56 ave Jean Jaurès) has pleasant rooms between 245FF and 450FF. Both hotels close in winter.

LANGUEDOC

Places to Eat

Restaurants Cosy *La Braconne* (☎ 05 65 60 30 93, 7 place du Maréchal Foch) has excellent regional *menus* from 98FF and is famed for its grilled trotters. It has a good selection of Faugères wines and its outside seating overlooks an attractive square. It's closed Sunday night and Monday. More modestly, *Au Bec Fin* (☎ 05 65 60 13 20, 20 rue de la Capelle) also serves regional dishes with *menus* costing from 60FF to 155FF. It's open June to September.

Long-established *La Mangeoire* (☎ 05 65 60 13 16, 8 blvd de la Capelle), in the vaults beneath the former city walls, serves delightful mainly regional dishes. *Menus* go from a midday special at 60FF to a mouth-watering gourmet blow-out at 265FF. A few doors down, *La Marmite* (☎ 05 65 61 20 44, 14 blvd de la Capelle) also has hearty regional *menus* and much the same price range. Don't miss its delicious *salade au Roquefort et chataîgnes* (Roquefort and chestnut salad).

Various Roquefort concoctions are also dished up at the cosy *Auberge Occitane* (☎ 05 65 60 45 54, 15 rue Peyrollerie). Its *médaillon de bœuf au Roquefort* (78FF) is definitely worth sinking your teeth into. *Menus* cost 70FF and 110FF. Opposite, the creperie *Le Chien à la Fenêtre* (10 rue Peyrollerie) offers 23 types of crepe and a *menu* – based on pancakes, naturally! – at 57FF.

Close by is *Le Square* (☎ 05 65 61 26 00, 10 rue St-Martin), which has tempting *menus* for 92FF and 148FF.

Self-Catering Market mornings are Wednesday and Friday in place du Maréchal Foch, place Emma Calvé and the covered market. *Les Vitrines du Terroir* (17 blvd de l'Ayrolle) and *Le Buron* (rue Droite), opposite the belfry, are fromageries selling local specialities including Roquefort and Perail du Larzc cheeses.

Getting There & Away

Bus The bus station (☎ 05 65 59 89 33) is beside the train station at the end of ave Alfred Merle. Buses go to Montpellier (95FF, 2¼ hours, five daily), Rodez (63FF, 1¾ hours, at least six daily) and Toulouse (four hours, two daily except Sunday) via Albi (80FF, 2½ hours).

Local scheduled services are extremely limited in summer. Generally there's only one bus daily to Le Rozier (33FF, 30 minutes), the closest stop for Montpellier-le-Vieux (10km south). Two services daily run between Millau and Meyrueis (60FF, 1¼ hours), the nearest a bus approaches Aven Armand (5.5km off route) and Dargilan (1km off route).

For Roquefort, take the Toulouse bus (departures at 7 am and 12.45 pm) and get off at Lauras (30FF), from where it's a pleasant enough 3km uphill walk.

In July and August, a special tourist bus runs from Millau to the Templar villages plus Montpellier-le-Vieux while another goes to Roquefort (each 60FF, running Monday, Wednesday and Friday). There's also a daily circuit embracing the Gorges de la Jonte (calling by Aven Armand) and Gorges du Tarn. Each allows viewing time at all the major sites and you can hop off at any point en route – but check first when the next one's due or you might be stuck for a couple of days!

Train Connections from Millau's train station (☎ 05 65 60 11 65) include Paris' Gare de Lyon (349FF, 9½ hours, two daily), Béziers (90FF, 1½ hours, three daily), Clermont-Ferrand (173FF, 4¾ hours, one daily), Montpellier (130FF, 1¾ hours, two daily) and Toulouse (153FF, 3½ hours, one daily). Via Rodez (63FF, 1¼ hours), there are trains to Albi (112FF, 2½ hours on the direct 7.27 am train).

The train station closest to Roquefort is at Tournemire (27FF, 30 minutes, five daily, all at inconvenient times), a 3km walk away.

Car À Venir (☎ 05 65 61 20 77), 7 ave Alfred Merle, is an agent for Budget. Europcar (☎ 05 65 59 19 19) is at 3 place Frédéric Bompaire.

Getting Around

Bicycle 'Le Vélo est Mon Métier' ('Bikes are my Business') is the cheery slogan of the young owner of Cycle Espace (☎ 05 65 61 14 29), 21 blvd de l'Ayrolle, who supplies chat in plenty for free and VTTs at 90/450FF per day/week (70/390FF for a tourer).

La Barbotte (☎ 05 65 62 66 26) in Le Rozier (from where you can cycle to Montpellier-le-Vieux, 10km away) rents VTTs for 130/550FF per day/week.

AROUND MILLAU
Roquefort
In the heart of the Parc Naturel Régional des Grands Causses and 25km south-west of Millau is the village of Roquefort-sur-Soulzon (population 780) where ewe's milk is turned into France's most famous blue cheese. Clinging to a hillside, its steep, narrow streets – permeated with a cheesy smell – are crammed with tourists heading for the cool natural caves where a dozen different producers ripen some 22,000 tonnes of Roquefort cheese a year.

La Société (☎ 05 65 59 93 30) has one-hour guided tours (15FF) that include a rather feeble sound-and-light show in the caves and a sampling of the three very distinct varieties that the company produces. Established in 1842, it's the largest Roquefort producer, churning out 70% of the world's supply, 30% of which is exported. The caves open 9.30 to 11.30 am and 1.30 to 5 pm daily and 9.30 am to 6 pm in July and August. Tours of the equally pungent *caves* of Le Papillon (☎ 05 65 58 50 08), rue

de la Fontaine, established in 1906 are free and follow a similar timetable.

After enduring a dégustation session of 10 different Roqueforts at Le Moderne (see Places to Stay & Eat later in the section), this author's palate reeled in ecstasy over the buttery Roquefort made by Le Vieux Berger (☎ 05 65 59 91 48), smallest of the Roquefort producers.

It's also possible to visit farms in the region, from which some 130 million litres of ewe's milk are collected annually. Contact the tourist office (☎ 05 65 58 56 00, fax 05 65 58 56 01, ✉ info@roquefort.com) at the western entry to the village. It's open 9 am to 6 pm daily in July and August (Monday to Saturday between April and October, weekdays in winter).

Places to Stay & Eat There are no hotels in Roquefort. The closest is *Le Combalou* (☎ *05 65 59 91 70, fax 05 65 59 98 18)*, a popular truckers' overnight stop, 2.5km west towards St-Affrique. Singles/doubles cost 180/210FF.

Better value and tasteful (in every sense) is *Le Moderne (☎ 05 65 49 20 44, fax 05 65 49 36 55)*, opposite the train station in St-Affrique, 13km from Roquefort. Comfortable rooms with a bathroom in the main building cost 250FF to 320FF. More basic rooms in its *Annexe Les Tilleuls* cost 95/150FF with washbasin/shower. Roquefort-based *menus* in its fantastic restaurant, start at 100FF and allow you to

LANGUEDOC

The King of Cheeses
The mouldy blue-green veins running through Roquefort are, in fact, the spores of microscopic mushrooms, picked in the caves at Roquefort then cultivated on leavened bread.

During the cheese's ripening process – which takes place in the same natural caves cut in the mountainside – delicate draughts of air called *fleurines* sweep through the cave like a sieve, encouraging the blue *penicillium roqueforti* to eat its way through the white cheese curds. The word 'fleurine' is derived from the langue d'oc word *flarina*, meaning 'to blow'.

At around 100FF a kilogram, Roquefort ranks as one of France's priciest and most noble cheeses. In 1407, Charles VI granted exclusive Roquefort cheese-making rights to the villagers of Roquefort. In the 17th century, the Sovereign Court of the Parliament of Toulouse imposed severe penalties against fraudulent cheese makers trading under the Roquefort name.

select from 10 different Roquefort cheeses – they're well worth making a detour for.

Equally fine if less refined are the hearty portions of local fodder dished out at **Hôtel de La Gare** (☎ 05 65 59 91 06, fax 05 65 58 91 94) in Tournemire, 3km east of Roquefort. *Menus* start at 89FF, rooms at 160FF for two.

Getting There & Away Roquefort is hard to get to without a car. For train and bus information, see the Millau section earlier in the chapter.

Micropolis

Micropolis (☎ 05 65 73 01 15, *e* resa@ micropolis-cite-des-insectes.tm.fr), 'La Cité des Insectes' (Insect City), is just outside the village of St-Léons, off the D11 19km north-west of Millau.

Ever felt small? This mindboggling high-tech experience (as much as exhibition) happens in a building shaped like a giant caterpillar. Here, grass grows six metres tall. The facts and statistics of insect life, all compellingly presented, seem equally tall, but all are true.

It's open 10 am to 4 pm daily, March to December (until 6 pm in June and September or 7 pm in July and August). There's a whole range of prices (the biggest determining factor, this being France, is the kind of lunch your package includes!). Basic admission costs 53FF (68FF including the impressive multimedia presentation).

Roussillon

Roussillon, sometimes known as French Catalonia, sits on Spain's doorstep at the eastern end of the Pyrenees. It's the land of the Tramontane, a violent wind which howls down from the mountains, chilling to the bone in winter and in summer strong enough to upturn a caravan. The main city is Perpignan, capital of the department of Pyrénées-Orientales.

Long part of Catalonia (nowadays confined to the autonomous region in north-eastern Spain), Roussillon has kept many symbols of Catalan unity. The *sardane* folk dance is still performed and the Catalan language, closely related to Occitan (also know as Provençal), is widely spoken.

History

Roussillon was inhabited in prehistoric times, and one of Europe's oldest skulls was found in a cave near Tautavel (see the Around Perpignan section later in the chapter). In 1172, Roussillon came under the control of trans-Pyrenean Catalonia-Aragon. Although Perpignan was the capital of the kingdom of Majorca for most of the next two centuries, Roussillon spent much of the late Middle Ages under Aragonese rule.

In 1640, the Catalans revolted against the Castilian kings in Madrid, who had engulfed Aragon. After a two-year siege, Perpignan was relieved with the help of the French to the north. The subsequent 1659 Treaty of the Pyrenees defined the border between Spain and France once and for all, ceding the northern section of Catalonia, Roussillon, to the French, much to the indignation of the locals.

Geography

The southern end of the Lower Languedoc plain is dominated by Perpignan, to the west of which rises Mont Canigou (2786m), a peak revered by the Catalan people. All around is a mosaic of vineyards, olive and fig groves and vegetable fields. The flat coastline ends abruptly at the rocky foothills of the Pyrenees, backdrop to the Côte Vermeille, a coastal area of deep red rocks and soil which inspired Fauvist artists such as Matisse and Dérain.

PERPIGNAN
postcode 66000 • pop 116,000

As much Catalan as French, Perpignan (Perpinyà in Catalan) was, from 1278 to 1344, capital of the kingdom of Majorca, which stretched northwards as far as Montpellier and included the Balearic Islands. The town later became an important commercial centre and remains the third largest Catalan city after Barcelona and Lleida in Spain.

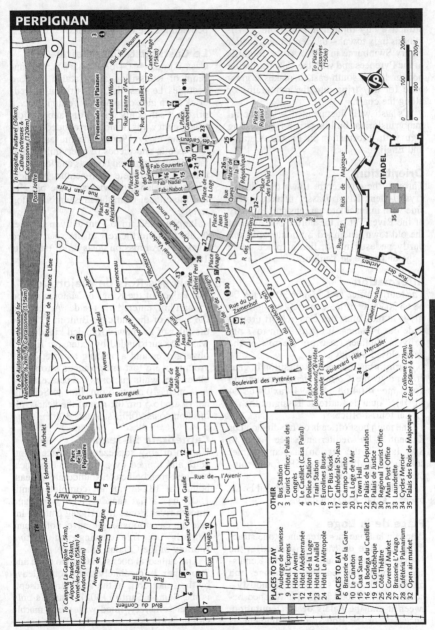

PERPIGNAN

PLACES TO STAY
1 Auberge de Jeunesse
9 Hôtel L'Express
11 Hôtel Avenir
14 Hôtel Méditerranée
14 Hôtel de la Loge
23 Hôtel Le Maillol
24 Hôtel Le Métropole

PLACES TO EAT
6 Brasserie de la Gare
10 Le Caneton
15 Casa Sansa
16 La Bodega du Castillet
19 La Grillothèque
25 Côté Théâtre
26 Covered Market
27 Brasserie L'Arago
28 Cafétéria Palmarium
32 Open air market

OTHER
3 Bus Station
4 Tourist Office; Palais des Congrès
4 Le Castillet (Casa Pairal)
5 Police Station
7 Train Station
8 Eurolines Buses
13 CTP Bus Kiosk
17 Cathédrale St-Jean
18 Campo Santo
20 La Loge de Mer
21 Town Hall
22 Palais de la Députation
29 Palais de Justice
30 Regional Tourist Office
31 Main Post Office
33 Laundrette
34 Cycles Mercier
35 Palais des Rois de Majorque

ROUSSILLON

Perpignan isn't southern France's most attractive city though it's far from a 'villainous ugly town' – the verdict of traveller Henry Swinburne in 1775. At the foothills of the Pyrenees and with the Côte Vermeille not far to the south-east, it makes a great base for day trips into the mountains or along the coast.

It's also well documented – outside all major historical buildings is a freestanding sign with information in French, Catalan and English.

Orientation

Through the city centre flows the narrow, crystal-clear River Basse, banked either side with immaculate gardens and tributary of the River Têt to the north. The heart of the old town, encircled by boulevards and partly pedestrianised, lies at place de la Loge and place de Verdun.

Information

The tourist office (☎ 04 68 66 30 30, fax 04 68 66 30 26, ✪ office-contact@smi-telecom .fr) is in the Palais des Congrès off promenade des Platanes. It opens 9 am to 7 pm daily in summer (to 6 pm the rest of the year, closed Sunday).

For information about Roussillon in general, go to the Comité Départemental du Tourisme (☎ 04 68 34 29 94, fax 04 68 34 71 01), 7 quai de Lattre de Tassigny, the regional tourist office.

The main post office is on rue du Docteur Zamenhof. La Méditerranée (see Places to Stay later in the section) has an internet cafe, open to all, charging 15FF for 15 minutes, 40FF per hour).

The laundrette, 23 rue du Maréchal Foch, opens 7 am to 8.30 pm daily.

Place de la Loge

Place de la Loge has three fine stone structures. La Loge de Mer, constructed in the 14th century and rebuilt during the Renaissance, once housed the exchange and maritime tribunal. It's now – scandalously – home to a fast-food joint. Sandwiched between it and the Palais de la Députation, once seat of the Roussillon parliament, is

the town hall with its typically Roussillon pebbled facade of river stones.

Le Castillet & Casa Païral

Casa Païral, (☎ 04 68 35 42 05), the museum of Roussillon and Catalan folklore occupies Le Castillet, a 14th-century red-brick town gate on place de Verdun. Once a prison, it's the only vestige of Vauban's fortified town walls, which surrounded the city until the early 1900s. The museum now houses bits and pieces of everything Catalan – from traditional bonnets and lace mantillas to a complete 17th-century kitchen. There are also great views of the old city and the citadel from the museum's rooftop terrace.

It opens 9.30 am to 7 pm daily in summer (9 am to 6 pm the rest of the year, closed Tuesday). Admission costs 25FF (students 10FF).

Palais des Rois de Majorque

The Palace of the Kings of Majorca sits on a small hill, entered via rue des Archers, to the south of the old city. Built in 1276 for the ruler of the newly founded kingdom, it was once surrounded by extensive fig and olive groves and a hunting reserve. These grounds were lost once Vauban's formidable citadel walls enclosed the palace.

It opens 10 am to 6 pm, June to September (9 am to 5 pm the rest of the year). Admission costs 20FF (students 10FF).

Cathédrale St-Jean

Uncomfortably squeezed into place Gambetta and topped by a typically Provençal wrought-iron bell cage, Cathédrale St-Jean, begun in 1324 and not completed until 1509, has a flat facade of red brick and smooth river stones in a zigzag pattern. Inside the cavernous single nave, notice particularly the fine carving and relative sobriety of the Catalan altarpiece.

The cathedral opens 7.30 am to noon and 3 to 7 pm. Immediately to its south (leave by the small door in the southern transept) is the Campo Santo (1302), France's only cloister-cemetery, lined with white-marble Gothic porticoes.

Special Events

As befits a town so close to the Spanish border, Perpignan is rich in fiestas. For Tio Tio, part of the pre-Lent carnival celebrations, white-robed merrymakers mob the streets dragging bathtubs filled with flour, which they toss over everyone in sight. Carnival closes with the 'burning of the king' on the banks of the River Basse.

For the Good Friday Procession de la Sanch, penitents wearing *caperutxa* (traditional hooded red or black robes) parade silently through the old city. A 'sacred' flame is brought down from Mont Canigou amid much singing and dancing during the week-long Fête de la St-Jean, marking midsummer. It coincides with the Marché Médiéval (Medieval Market), when half the town dons tights and wimples.

Perpignan hosts a two-week jazz festival in mid-October and, on the third Thursday in October, a wine festival during which a barrel of the year's new wine is ceremonially borne to Cathédrale St-Jean to be blessed.

Places to Stay – Budget

Camping Year-round, *Camping La Garrigole* (☎ 04 68 54 66 10, *2 rue Maurice Lévy*), 1.5km west of the train station, charges 76FF for two people with tent and vehicle. Take bus No 19 from the station or place Gabriel Peri and get off at the Garrigole terminus.

Hostels At the *Auberge de Jeunesse* (☎ 04 68 34 63 32, fax 04 68 51 16 02, *end of rue Claude Marty*), just north of Parc de la Pépinière, dorm beds cost 70FF, including breakfast.

Hotels There's a string of hotels along ave Général de Gaulle. *Hôtel L'Express* (☎ 04 68 34 89 96, *No 3*) has smallish rooms without shower for 90FF and singles/doubles/triples with shower for 120/150/180FF. *La Méditerranée* (☎ 04 68 34 87 48, *No 62 bis*) has nicer but still basic singles/doubles at 120/150FF (from 190/225FF with full bathroom). Hall showers cost 15FF.

Friendly *Hôtel Avenir* (☎ 04 68 34 20 30,

fax 04 68 34 15 63, *11 rue de l'Avenir*), comes highly recommended. It has basic singles/doubles costing from 90/120FF, doubles/triples quads with shower for 190/220/250FF and rooms with full bathroom at 190FF. Most rooms have a small terrace and each is uniquely and charmingly decorated by the proprietor.

Dingy *Hôtel Le Métropole* (☎ 04 68 34 43 34, *3 rue des Cardeurs*) ranks as the cheapest option in the old town. Basic rooms at 75FF and 95FF and ones with shower for 135FF are good value for what they are.

A room at *Hôtel Formule 1* (☎ 04 68 56 96 00) on the western side of town, just beneath the A9, costs 155FF. Take bus No 19 from the CTP kiosk on place Gabriel Peri.

Places to Stay – Mid-Range

The *Hôtel Le Maillol* (☎ 04 68 51 10 20, fax 04 68 51 20 29), in an attractive 17th-century building, barely 15m from Hôtel Le Métropole, has singles/doubles with bathroom for 190/220FF.

Hôtel de La Loge (☎ 04 68 34 41 02, fax 04 68 34 25 13, ✉ hoteldelaloge@ wanadoo.fr, *1 rue des Fabriques d'En Nabot*) has fully equipped singles/doubles starting at 235/285FF.

Places to Eat

Restaurants On place Arago, there is something for everyone at the stylish *Brasserie l'Arago*. Sample their fine local wines, sold by the glass or bottle, or pick from a whole page of sexy, if expensive, cocktails. They do pizzas (around 40FF) and have a strong a la carte menu (main dishes, 65FF to 100FF). More modestly, *Cafétéria Palmarium*, a long-standing Perpignan favourite, is a spacious, self-service place with character, open 7 am until 9.30 pm daily.

For great food with a strong Catalan bias, *Casa Sansa* (☎ 04 68 34 21 84, *2 rue des Fabriques Nadal*) is a popular restaurant-cum-art gallery where main dishes range from 38FF to 100FF. It's closed Sunday and Monday. *La Bodega du Castillet* (☎ 04 68 34 88 98, *rue des Fabriques Couvertes*),

Dalí's Train of Thought

Few travellers finding themselves in Perpignan will be able to agree with Salvador Dalí's (no doubt chemically induced) assessment that the city's train station is the centre of the universe. According to local lore (and a plaque in front of the building), the Catalan surrealist painter (1904–89) was visiting the capital of French Catalunya in 1965 when, emerging from a taxi in front of the train station, he experienced an epiphany. 'Suddenly, before me, everything appeared with the clarity of lightning,' he wrote. 'I found myself in the centre of the universe'. Dalí went on to describe this nondescript place as 'la source d'illuminations' and 'la cathédrale d'intuitions' – no doubt putting a smile on the faces of local tourism authorities and most Perpignanais. Two years later, this centre of the universe was the subject of yet another Dalí painting (he produced tens of thousands of them in his lifetime – or at least signed the canvases). It now hangs in a museum in Düsseldorf, Germany.

with its friendly, unmistakably Catalan ambience, is one street east. Expect to pay between 150FF to 200FF for a push-back-your-plate-and-groan a la carte three-course dinner.

To fill your stomach most agreeably while emptying your purse, indulge yourself with the subtle cuisine at *Côté Théatre* (*☎/fax 04 68 34 60 00, 7 rue du Théatre*). It has *menus* from 148FF (lunchtime only) to 330FF. It closes Monday midday and Sunday.

La Grillothèque (*☎ 04 68 34 06 99, 7 rue des Cardeurs*) has a 70FF *menu* and specialises in mussels – prepared seven different ways.

Near the train station are plenty of cheap and cheerful places, including Arab, Turkish and Alsacien joints. Cheery *Brasserie de la Gare*, for example, does *menus* at 65FF and 85FF. *Le Caneton (12 rue Victor Hugo)* must be one of France's best value and tiniest restaurants. Open weekdays only, it's little more than a room in a private house but the three-course 30FF *menu* will fill you up.

Self-Catering There's a morning *food market (place des Poilus)* and a *covered market (place de la République)* open 7 am to 1 pm and 4 to 7.30 pm. Both are closed Monday.

Getting There & Away

Air Perpignan's airport (*☎ 04 68 52 60 70*), 5km north-west of the town centre, has six flights a day to/from Paris Orly. Ryanair has a daily flight to/from London Stansted.

Bus The bus station (*☎ 04 63 35 29 02*) is on ave Général Leclerc. For coastal resorts, there are seven services daily to/from Collioure (32FF) and Port Vendres (35FF), five of which continue to Banyuls (42FF, one hour). For Canet-Plage (13FF), take CTP bus No 1 (13FF, 35 minutes), which runs about every half hour from place de Catalogne or place Gabriel Peri.

Seven buses daily run along the Têt Valley to Vernet-les-Bains (53FF, 1½ hours) via Prades (45FF). Up the Tech valley, there are nine buses daily to Céret (35FF, 50 minutes).

For long distance buses, the Eurolines office (*☎ 04 68 34 11 46*), ave Général de Gaulle, is just east of the train station.

Train Perpignan's small train station – centre of the universe according to Salvador Dalí (see the boxed text 'Dalí's Train of Thought') – is served by bus Nos 2 and 19.

Major destinations include Barcelona (100FF, three hours, two daily) and Montpellier (115FF, two hours, 7+ daily) via Narbonne (57FF, 45 minutes, 12+ daily). For Paris (461FF), change in Montpellier; for Carcassonne (93FF), in Narbonne.

Closer to home are Cerbère/Portbou on the Spanish border (43FF, 40 minutes, 8+ daily) via Collioure, Port-Vendres and Banyuls.

The nearest you can get to Andorra by train is La Tour de Carol (117FF, four hours, twice daily) – from where there are connecting buses – via Prades (40FF, 40 minutes) and Villefranche (5+ daily).

Car Rental companies include ADA (☎ 04 68 35 69 80) and Budget (☎ 04 68 34 25 43).

Getting Around

The local bus company, CTP, has an information kiosk (☎ 04 68 61 01 13) on place Gabriel Peri. Last buses leave at 8 pm and Sunday services are curtailed drastically. Single tickets cost 6.50FF, a one-day pass, 25FF and a 10-ticket carnet costs 50FF.

In the old town, free minibuses ply a circular route around major landmarks. Bright yellow and signed *Le P'tit Bus*, they run until 7 pm daily except Sunday and except – come on now, we're in France! – between 12.30 and 1.30 pm.

For a taxi, call Accueil Perpignan Taxis (☎ 04 68 35 15 15). You can rent mountain bikes at Cycles Mercier (☎ 04 68 85 02 71), 20 ave Gilbert Brutus.

AROUND PERPIGNAN
Coastal Beaches

The nearest beach – all 5km of it – is at **Canet-Plage**, backed by a sprawl of hotels and apartment blocks. There's a small tourist office (☎ 04 68 73 61 00, @ infos@ ot-canet.fr). Rent a bicycle (80FF per day) from Sun Bike 66 (☎ 04 68 73 88 65) and cruise the promenade or ride around the Étang de Canet, a small inland lake and nature reserve.

From **Argèles-Plage** southwards, wide, sandy beaches give way to rocky coastline as the Pyrenees tumble to the sea, their steep flanks terraced with vineyards.

From late June to mid-July and late August to early September, Bus Interplages (☎ 04 68 35 67 51) links the coast from Canet-Plage to Port-Vendres. Buses leave 10 am and 2.30 pm, Monday to Saturday. Buses from Canet-Plage to Cerbère operate 9.30 am, 2 and 4.30 pm, daily, mid-July to the end of August.

Côte Vermeille

Near the Spanish border, where the Pyrenees foothills reach the sea, is the Côte Vermeille (Vermilion Coast). Against a backdrop of vineyards, it's riddled with small, rocky bays and little ports that once engaged in sardine and anchovy fishing but now have economies based on tourism.

One such port is picturesque **Collioure** where pleasure craft and fishing boats bob together below houses washed in soft pastel colours. Known to the Phoenicians and once Perpignan's port, Collioure found fame early this century when it inspired the Fauvist art of Henri Matisse and André Dérain. The port's castle, **Château Royal**, once the summer residence of the kings of Majorca, is now a museum (☎ 04 68 82 06 43). The tourist office (☎ 04 68 82 15 47, @ collioure@little-france.com) is across the creek at place 18 Juin.

Three kilometres south, **Port-Vendres**, the only natural harbour and deep water port hereabouts, has been exploited ever since Greek mariners roamed the rocky coastline. A significant entrepot until the independence of France's North African territories in the 1960s, it remains an important coastal fishing and leisure port. The small tourist office (☎ 04 68 82 07 54) is in its north-western corner.

Banyuls, a further 7km south, has a small pebble beach and, at its southern limit, beyond the tourist office (☎ 04 68 88 31 58), a fine **aquarium** (☎ 04 68 88 73 39, admission 25FF). Much more than yet another commercial enterprise with smiling dolphins, it also functions as the oceanographic research station of Paris' Université Pierre et Marie Curie. It's open 9 am to midday and 2 to 6.30 pm daily.

Céret

It's mainly the **Musée d'Art Moderne** (☎ 04 68 87 27 76,), 8 blvd Maréchal Joffre, Céret's Museum of Modern Art, which draws visitors to this town of 8000 souls, perched snug in the Pyrenean foothills just off the Tech valley. Superbly endowed for such a small community, its collection owes much to an earlier generation of visitors and

ROUSSILLON

residents, including Picasso, Braque, Chagall, Matisse, Juan Gris and Manolo, all of whom donated works (53 by Picasso alone). Admission costs 35FF. It opens 10 am to 6 pm daily (it closes one hour later in high summer, closed Tuesday, October to April).

Firmly Catalan, Céret is also splendidly disproportionate in the number and vigour of its festivals. Famous for its juicy cherries (the first pickings of the season are packed off to the French president), it kicks off with the Fête de la Cerise (cherry festival) in late-May. Summer sees the féria with bullfights and roistering and La Fête de la Sardane, celebrating the *sardane*, folk dance par excellence of the Catalans – and, of course, yet more bullfights. More sedately, **Les Méennes** is a festival of primarily classical music. The tourist office (☎ 04 68 87 00 53) is on ave Clemenceau.

Tautavel
Some 30km north-west of Perpignan, the village of Tautavel has what is thought to be Europe's oldest human skull. Estimated at 450,000 years old, it's in the **Musée de la Préhistoire** (☎ 04 68 29 07 76), along with many other prehistoric items that were found in the Arago Cave, a few kilometres north of town.

The museum (36FF) opens 10 am to 12.30 pm and 2 to 6 pm (continuously, April to June and September; 9 am to 9 pm in July and August).

Vernet-les-Bains
A thermal town beloved by wrinkled Brits, Vernet-les-Bains (population 1500, elevation 650m) is a base for climbing **Mont Canigou** (2786m), the Pyrenees' easternmost major peak. Three tracks wind up from Vernet. To do it the easy way, take a jeep (☎ 04 68 05 51 14 for information), costing about 150FF, from Vernet to Les Cortalets (2175m) and walk the rest of the way (three hours return).

The tourist office (☎ 04 68 05 55 35) is on rue Jules Ferry.

Provence

For the vast majority of the year, Provence is bathed in the most glorious southern sunshine, with a warmth and intensity of light unknown in other parts of France. Along the coast, the Mediterranean reflects and refracts the sun's rays, making for sharp, distinct colours. Inland, the hues are more subtle: the red tile roofs and blue skies are softened by an infinite variety of greens and by the looming presence of limestone hills, often wrapped in a gentle haze.

Many Provençal cities and towns date from at least Roman times and offer a wonderful array of cultural treasures, ranging from Roman theatres (still used for music and other festivals) and medieval fortifications to outstanding art museums. The region's population centres boast generous public spaces – just as they did under Augustus – and the locals spend a good part of their lives outdoors, sipping *pastis* (a liquorice-flavoured aperitif) in cafes or playing *pétanque*, a type of bowls using heavy metal balls, under the shade of the region's plane trees.

History

Provence was settled over the centuries by the Ligurians, the Celts and the Greeks, but it was only after its conquest by Julius Caesar in the mid-1st century BC and its integration into the Roman Empire that the region really began to flourish. Many exceptionally well preserved Roman theatres, aqueducts, baths and other ancient buildings can still be seen in towns such as Arles, Orange and Vaison-la-Romaine. After the collapse of the empire in the late 5th century, Provence suffered invasions by the Visigoths, Burgundians and the Ostrogoths. The Arabs – who for some time held the Iberian Peninsula and parts of France – were defeated in the 8th century.

During the 14th century, the Catholic Church – under a series of French-born popes – moved its headquarters from feud-riven Rome to Avignon, thus beginning the

Highlights

- **Avignon** – tour the immense Palais des Papes
- **Gordes** or **Les Baux de Provence** – stroll the streets of these remarkable *villages perchés* (perched villages)
- **Activities** – climb Mont Ventoux or go white-water rafting along the Gorges du Verdon
- **Arles** – follow in the footsteps of Van Gogh, see sketches by Picasso in the Musée Réattu and watch a bullfight in the Roman amphitheatre
- **Digne-les-Bains** – travel by narrow-gauge train to Nice
- **Carpentras market** – shop for local specialities like truffles, fruits, vegetables, olives and lavender marmalade

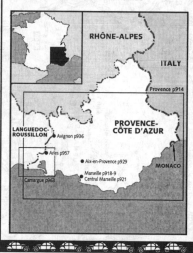

most resplendent period in that city's history. Provence became part of France in 1481, but Avignon and Comtat Venaissin, with its seat at Carpentras, remained under papal control until the Revolution.

PROVENCE

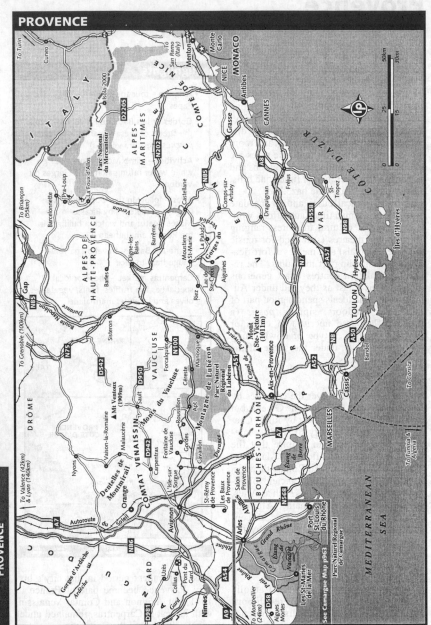

The Perfume of Provence

If there's any one aroma associated with Provence, it's lavender *(lavande)*. Lavender fields – once seen, never forgotten – include those at the Abbaye de Sénanque near Gordes, the Musée de la Lavande (Lavender Museum; ☎ 04 90 76 91 23) in Coustellet and those which carpet the arid Sault region, east of Mont Ventoux on the Vaucluse plateau.

The sweet purple flower is harvested between 15 July and 15 August. Lavender farms, distilleries and ornamental gardens open to visitors are listed in the English-language brochure *Les Routes de la Lavande* (free from tourist offices).

The Maison de l'Environment et de la Chasse (☎ 04 90 64 13 96), Ave de l'Oratoire, Sault, organises lavender tours, which take in the lavender farms where the crop is grown and the essence extracted.

Geography

Provence stretches along both sides of the River Rhône from just north of Orange down to the Mediterranean, and along France's southern coast from the Camargue salt marshes in the west to Marseilles in the east. Beyond Marseilles is the Côte d'Azur, which, though historically part of Provence, appears in a separate chapter in this book along with Monaco.

South of Arles, the Camargue marshlands – actually the delta of the Rhône – are within a triangle formed by the Grand Rhône to the east and the Petit Rhône to the west.

East of the Rhône are most of the region's mountains and hills: the Baronnies; 1909m Mont Ventoux; the Vaucluse plateau; the rugged Lubéron range; and the little Alpilles. Farther east is Europe's most spectacular canyon, the Gorges du Verdon.

Climate

Provence's weather is bright, sunny and dry for much of the year. Indeed, the region's extraordinary light served as an important inspiration for such painters as Van Gogh, Cézanne and Picasso. But the cold, dry winds of the mistral gain surprising fury – with little warning – as they blow southwards down the narrow Rhône Valley, and can turn a fine spring day into a bone-chilling wintry one.

The mistral tends to blow continuously for several days and can reach speeds of more than 100km per hour, damaging crops, whipping up forest fires and generally driving everybody around the bend. It is caused by the coincidence of a high-pressure area over central France and a low-pressure area over the Mediterranean, and is most common in winter and spring.

Language

The various dialects of Provençal – whose grammar is more closely related to Catalan and Spanish than French – are still spoken every day by hundreds of thousands of people across southern France, especially by older residents of rural areas.

From the 12th to the 14th century, Provençal was the literary language of France and northern Spain, and was used as far afield as Italy. During that period, it was the principal language of the medieval troubadours, poets – often courtiers and nobles – whose melodies and elegant poems were motivated by the ideal of courtly love.

A movement for the revival of Provençal literature, culture and identity began in the mid-19th century. Its most prominent member was the poet Frédéric Mistral (1830–1914), recipient of the Nobel prize for literature in 1904. In recent years, the language has again enjoyed something of a revival, and in many areas signs are written in Provençal and French.

Getting There & Away

For information on ferry services from Marseilles to Sardinia and Tunisia, see Sea in the introductory Getting There & Away

PROVENCE

euro currency converter €1 = 6.56FF

chapter. For details on ferries from Marseilles to Corsica, see Getting There & Away in the Corsica chapter.

Marseilles Region

MARSEILLES
pop 798,430

The cosmopolitan port of Marseilles (Marseille in French) is France's second city and its third-largest metropolitan area, with some 1.23 million inhabitants. The city has not in any way been made quaint for the benefit of tourists, its urban geography and atmosphere – utterly atypical of Provence, by the way – being a function of the diversity of its inhabitants, the majority of whom are immigrants from the Mediterranean basin, West Africa and Indochina.

Marseilles is notorious for organised crime and racial tensions, but, regardless of the city's dubious political leaning, visitors who enjoy exploring on foot will be rewarded with more sights, sounds, smells and big-city commotion than almost anywhere else in the country. There really is no other city quite like it in France; you'll either love it or hate it.

History

Around 600 BC, a trading post known as Massilia was founded at what is now Marseilles' old port by Greek mariners from Phocaea, a city in Asia Minor. In the 1st century BC, the city backed Pompey the Great rather than Julius Caesar, whose forces captured Massilia in 49 BC and exacted commercial revenge by confiscating the fleet and directing Roman trade elsewhere. Massilia retained its status as a free port and was, for a while, the last western centre of Greek learning, but the city soon declined and became little more than a collection of ruins. It was revived in the early 10th century by the counts of Provence.

Marseilles was pillaged by the Aragonese in 1423, but the greatest calamity in its history took place in 1720, when the plague (carried by a merchant vessel from Syria) killed around 50,000 of the city's 90,000 inhabitants.

Marseilles became part of France in the 1480s but the city soon acquired a reputation for rebelling against the central government. The local population enthusiastically embraced the Revolution, and in 1792 some 500 volunteers were sent to defend Paris. As the troops made their way northwards, they took to singing a catchy new march composed a few months earlier in Strasbourg. The song, which was soon dubbed *La Marseillaise*, subsequently became France's national anthem (see the boxed text 'La Marseillaise' in the Alsace chapter).

In the 19th century, Marseilles grew prosperous from colonial trade. Commerce with North Africa grew rapidly after the French occupation of Algeria in 1830, and maritime opportunities expanded further when the Suez Canal opened in 1869. During WWII, Marseilles was bombed by the Germans and Italians in 1940, and by the Allies in 1943–44.

Today, Marseilles is renowned as France's most important seaport and the second largest port in Europe after Rotterdam. When the TGV Méditerranée rail line is finally completed, Marseilles will be linked by high-speed train to Avignon, Lyons and Paris.

Orientation

The city's main thoroughfare, the wide boulevard called La Canebière, stretches eastwards from the Vieux Port (Old Port). The train station is north of La Canebière at the northern end of blvd d'Athènes. Just a few blocks south of La Canebière is bohemian cours Julien, a large pedestrianised square dominated by a water garden, fountains and palm trees, and lined with some of Marseilles' hippest cafes, restaurants and theatres. The city's commercial heart is around rue Paradis, which gets more fashionable as you move south. The new ferry terminal is west of place de la Joliette, a few minutes walk north of the Nouvelle Cathédrale.

Marseilles is divided into 15 arrondissements; however, most travellers will only be concerned with three or four. Places

PROVENCE

mentioned in the text have the arrondisse-ment (1er, 2e, etc) listed after the street address.

Information

Tourist Offices The tourist office (☎ 04 91 13 89 00, fax 04 91 13 89 20, ✆ destination-Marseilles@wanadoo.fr), 4 La Canebière (1er), opens 9 am to 7 pm (10 am to 5 pm on Sunday). From mid-June to mid-September, it opens daily until 7.30pm. Staff can make hotel reservations.

The tourist office annexe (☎ 04 91 50 59 18), at the main train station, opens 10 am to 1 pm and 1.30 to 5 pm (closed at the weekend); during July and August it opens 9 am to 6 pm Monday to Saturday.

Money The Banque de France on place Es-trangin Pastré, a block west of place de la Préfecture, opens 8.45 am to 12.30 pm and 1.30 to 3.30 pm (closed at the weekend).

There are a number of banks and ex-change bureaus on La Canebière near the old port. American Express (☎ 04 91 13 71 21), 39 La Canebière (1er), opens 8 am to 6 pm Monday to Friday (8 am to noon and 2 to 5 pm Saturday).

Post & Communications The main post office, 1 place de l'Hôtel des Postes (1er), opens 8 am to 7 pm (Saturday till noon; closed Sunday). Exchange services are available.

Near the train station, the crowded branch post office (☎ 04 91 50 89 25), 11 rue Honnorat (3e) – which does not change money – opens 8.30 am to 6.30 pm (Satur-day until noon; closed Sunday).

Marseilles' postcodes are '130' plus the arrondissement number – postcode 13001 for addresses in the 1st arrondissement (1er) etc.

Internet Café (☎ 04 91 42 09 37), 25 rue de Village (6e), charges 30/50FF for 30 minutes/one hour of access. It opens 10 am to 8 pm (until 4.30 pm on Friday and from 2.30 pm on Sunday). Definitely more 'in' is Le Rezo Cybercafé (☎ 04 91 42 70 02, ✆ lerezo@lerezo.com), 68 cours Julien (6e). It charges the same rates and opens 9.30 am

to 8 pm Monday, 9.30 am to 10 pm Tues-day to Friday and 10 am to 11 pm Saturday.

Bookshops The northern end of rue Par-adis (1er) is lined with bookshops, includ-ing Librairie Lamy (☎ 04 91 33 57 91) at No 21, which has a very good selection of English-language novels. It opens 9 am to 12.30 pm and 1.45 to 6.45 pm Monday to Saturday.

For the best range of maps, travel books and Lonely Planet guides in the whole of Provence, look no further than Librairie de la Bourse (☎ 04 91 33 63 06), 8 rue Paradis (1er). Lonely Planet guides are also sold by FNAC (☎ 04 91 39 94 00), on the top floor of the Centre Bourse shopping centre off cours Belsunce (1er).

Laundry Laverie Self-Service, 5 rue Jus-tice Breteuil (1er), opens 6.30 am to 8 pm. Laverie des Allées at 15 allées Léon Gam-betta, near place des Capucins, opens 8 am to 9 pm.

Medical Services & Emergency Hôpital de la Timone (☎ 04 91 38 60 00) is at 264 rue St-Pierre (5e).

The Préfecture de Police (☎ 04 91 39 80 00), place de la Préfecture (1er), is open 24 hours.

Dangers & Annoyances Despite its fear-some reputation for crime, Marseilles is no more dangerous than other French cities. As elsewhere, street crime is best avoided by keeping your wits about you and your valuables hard to get at. *Never* leave any-thing you value in a parked car.

At night, avoid walking alone in the Bel-sunce area, a poor neighbourhood south-west of the train station bounded by La Canebière, cours Belsunce and rue d'Aix, rue Bernard du Bois and blvd d'Athènes.

Walking Tours

Old Port Area Marseilles grew up around the old port, where ships have docked for at least 26 centuries. The main commercial docks were transferred to the Joliette area on the coast north of here in the 1840s, but

PROVENCE

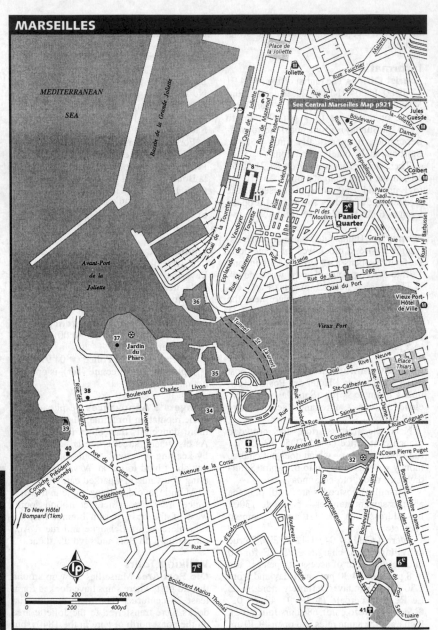

MARSEILLES

MEDITERRANEAN

SEA

Bassin de la Grande Joliette

Avant-Port
de la
Joliette

Place de
la Joliette

Joliette

Rue Fauchier

Rue de la République

Rue de la Joliette

Rue de Mazenod

Avenue Robert Schuman

See Central Marseilles Map p921

Jules
la-Joliette

Boulevard des Dames

Jules
Guesde

Colbert

Place
Sadi-Carnot

Rue

Rue H Barbusse

Panier
Quarter

Pl des
Moulins

Grand' Rue

Rue de la Loge

Quai du Port

Vieux Port-
Hôtel
de Ville

Quai de la Tourette

Ave Vaudoyer

Esplanade de la Tourette

Rue St Laurent

Rue de la Tourette

Rue de l'Evêché

Rue Caisserie

36

Tunnel St Laurent

Jardin
du
Pharo

37

35

34

Vieux Port

Quai de Rive Neuve

Place
Thiars

Rue fort N-Dame

Ste-Catherine

Rue Neuve

Rue Fort N-Dame

Sainte

Rue Grignan

Boulevard Charles Livon

Rue des Catalans

38

39

40

Corniche Président
John F Kennedy

Rue Cap Dessemond

Ave de la Corse

Avenue Pasteur

Boulevard de la Corderie

Cours Pierre Puget

32

Boulevard André Aune

Rue Vauvenargues

Boulevard Notre Dame

Rue Jules Moulet

33

Avenue de la Corse

7e

6e

Rue du Fort

To New Hôtel
Bompard (1km)

Rue d'Endoume

Boulevard

Teilline

Rue

Boulevard Marius Thomas

41

Sanctuaire

0   200   400m
0   200   400yd

PROVENCE

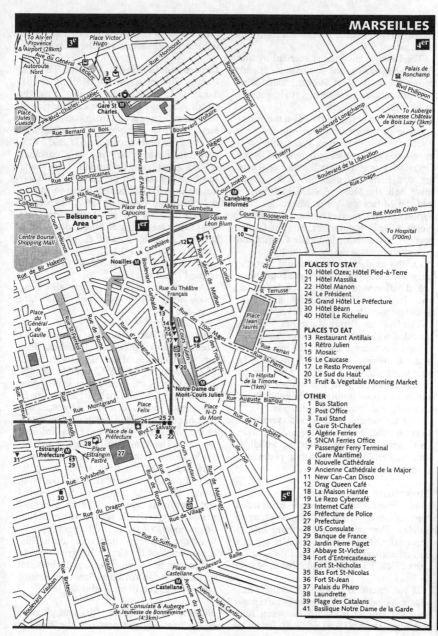

MARSEILLES

PLACES TO STAY
10 Hôtel Ozea; Hôtel Pied-à-Terre
21 Hôtel Massilia
22 Hôtel Manon
24 Le Président
25 Grand Hôtel Le Préfecture
30 Hôtel Béarn
40 Hôtel Le Richelieu

PLACES TO EAT
13 Restaurant Antillais
14 Rétro Julien
15 Mosaic
16 Le Caucase
17 Le Resto Provençal
20 Le Sud du Haut
31 Fruit & Vegetable Morning Market

OTHER
1 Bus Station
2 Post Office
3 Taxi Stand
4 Gare St-Charles
5 Algérie Ferries
6 SNCM Ferries Office
7 Passenger Ferry Terminal
    (Gare Maritime)
8 Nouvelle Cathédrale
9 Ancienne Cathédrale de la Major
11 New Can-Can Disco
12 Drag Queen Café
18 La Maison Hantée
19 Le Rezo Cybercafé
23 Internet Café
26 Préfecture de Police
27 Prefecture
28 US Consulate
29 Banque de France
32 Jardin Pierre Puget
33 Abbaye St-Victor
34 Fort d'Entrecasteaux;
    Fort St-Nicholas
35 Bas Fort St-Nicolas
36 Fort St-Jean
37 Palais du Pharo
38 Laundrette
39 Plage des Catalans
41 Basilique Notre Dame de la Garde

PROVENCE

euro currency converter €1 = 6.56FF

the old port is still active as a harbour for fishing craft, pleasure yachts and ferries to the Château d'If.

The harbour entrance is guarded by **Bas Fort St-Nicolas** (on the southern side) and, across the water, **Fort St-Jean**, founded in the 13th century by the Knights Hospitaller of St John of Jerusalem.

In 1943, the neighbourhood on the northern side of the quai du Port – at the time a seedy area with a strong Resistance presence – was systematically dynamited by the Germans. It was rebuilt after the war. There are two museums near the 17th-century **town hall**: the Musée des Docks Romains and the Musée du Vieux Marseilles. The **Panier Quarter**, most of whose residents are North African immigrants, is a bit farther north. The Centre de la Vieille Charité and its museums sit at the top of the hill.

On the southern side of the old port, the large and lively **place Thiars** and **cours Honoré d'Estienne d'Orves** pedestrian zone, with its late-night restaurants and cafes, stretches south from quai de Rive Neuve.

The liveliest part of Marseilles – always crowded with people of all ages and ethnic groups – is situated around the intersection of La Canebière and cours Belsunce. The area just north of La Canebière and east of cours Belsunce, which is known as **Belsunce**, is a poor immigrant neighbourhood currently undergoing rehabilitation.

The fashionable **6th arrondissement** is worth a stroll, especially the area between La Canebière and the **Prefecture building**. Rue St-Ferréol is a bustling pedestrian shopping street.

Museums

Unless noted otherwise, the museums listed here are open 10 am to 5 pm Tuesday to Sunday. They open 11 am to 6 pm June to September. Admission to each museum's permanent/temporary exhibitions usually costs 12/18FF (students and those aged over 65 free).

If you intend to visit all Marseilles' museums, consider investing in a *passeport pour les musées* (available between June and September; ☎ 04 91 14 58 80 for information). It costs 50FF (students and children 25FF), is valid for 15 days, and allows unlimited admission to all the museums.

Centre de la Vieille Charité The Old Charity Cultural Centre (☎ 04 91 56 28 38), 2 rue de la Charité (2e), is in the mostly North African Panier Quarter. The superb permanent exhibits and imaginative temporary exhibitions are housed in a workhouse and hospice built between 1671 and 1745, and restored after serving as a barracks (1905), a rest home for soldiers (WWI) and low-cost housing for people who lost their homes in WWII. It is also home to **Musée d'Archéologie** (Museum of Archaeology; ☎ 04 91 14 58 80) and **Musée des Arts Africains, Océaniens & Amérindiens** (Museum of African, Oceanic & American Indian Art; ☎ 04 91 14 58 38). The centre opens 9 am to noon and 1.30 to 4.45 pm (closed at the weekend).

A combined ticket covering all of the above costs 30FF; individual tickets are available too.

Musée d'Histoire de Marseilles Roman history buffs should visit the History of Marseilles Museum (☎ 04 91 90 42 22), just north of La Canebière on the ground floor of the Centre Bourse shopping centre (1er). Exhibits include the remains of a merchant vessel – discovered by chance in the old port in 1974 – that plied the waters of the Mediterranean in the early 3rd century AD. The 19m-long timbers, which include five different kinds of wood, show evidence of having been repaired repeatedly. To preserve the soaked and decaying wood, the whole thing was freeze-dried right where it now sits – hidden behind glass in a dimly lit room. The museum opens noon to 7 pm (closed Tuesday).

Roman buildings, uncovered during the construction of the Centre Bourse shopping centre, can be seen just outside the museum in the **Jardin des Vestiges** (Garden of Ruins), which fronts rue Henri Barbusse (1er).

Musée de la Mode Glitz and glamour is the name of the game at the Fashion

CENTRAL MARSEILLES

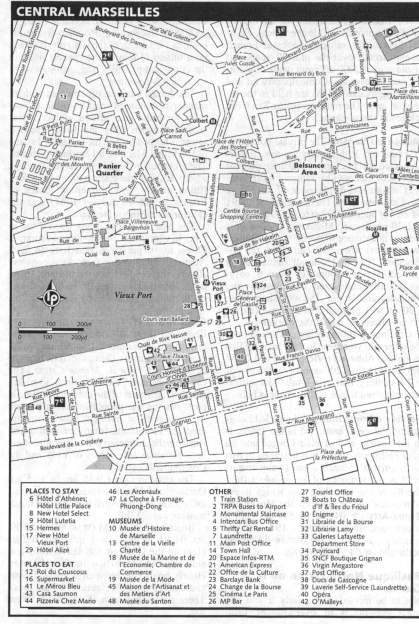

PLACES TO STAY
6   Hôtel d'Athénes;
    Hôtel Little Palace
8   New Hotel Select
9   Hôtel Lutetia
15 Hermes
17 New Hôtel
    Vieux Port
29 Hôtel Alizé

PLACES TO EAT
12 Roi du Couscous
16 Supermarket
41 Le Mérou Bleu
43 Casa Saumon
44 Pizzeria Chez Mario

46 Les Arcenaulx
47 La Cloche à Fromage;
    Phuong-Dong

MUSEUMS
10 Musée d'Histoire
    de Marseille
13 Centre de la Vieille
    Charité
18 Musée de la Marine et de
    l'Economie; Chambre de
    Commerce
19 Musée de la Mode
45 Maison de l'Artisanat et
    des Metiers d'Art
48 Musée du Santon

OTHER
1   Train Station
2   TRPA Buses to Airport
3   Monumental Staircase
4   Intercars Bus Office
5   Thrifty Car Rental
7   Laundrette
11 Main Post Office
14 Town Hall
20 Espace Infos-RTM
21 American Express
22 Office de la Culture
23 Barclays Bank
24 Change de la Bourse
25 Cinéma Le Paris
26 MP Bar

27 Tourist Office
28 Boats to Château
    d'If & Îles du Frioul
30 Énigme
31 Librairie de la Bourse
32 Librairie Lamy
33 Galeries Lafayette
    Department Store
34 Puyricard
35 SNCF Boutique Grignan
36 Virgin Megastore
37 Post Office
38 Ducs de Gascogne
39 Laverie Self-Service (Laundrette)
40 Opéra
42 O'Malleys

PROVENCE

euro currency converter €1 = 6.56FF

Museum (☎ 04 91 56 59 57), 11 La Canebière (1er). Housed in Marseilles' superb Espace Mode Méditerranée (Mediterranean Fashion Space), the museum looks at French fashion trends over the past 30 years and displays over 2000 different items of clothing and accessories. Contemporary art and photography exhibitions are held in the reception area. The museum opens 2 to 6 pm (closed at the weekend).

Musée du Santon The private collection of 18th- and 19th-century *santon* (fingernail-sized nativity figures that are typical of Provence) gathered by santon-maker Marcel Carbonnel is displayed at 47 rue Neuve Ste-Catherine (7e). The museum (☎ 04 91 54 26 58) opens 9.30 am to 12.30 pm and 2 to 6.30 pm (closed Monday). Admission is free, as is entrance to the adjoining *ateliers* (workshops) where you can watch the minuscule 2.5cm to 15cm-tall figures being crafted. Guided tours (in French only) are usually conducted on Tuesday and Thursday at 2.30 pm. The workshops open 8.30 am to 1 pm and 2 to 5.30 pm (closed Friday afternoon and at the weekend).

Continuing 100m farther up the hill from the museum, you come to the imposing Romanesque **Abbaye St-Victor** (☎ 04 91 05 84 48), built in the 12th century on the site of a 4th-century martyr's tomb. Marseilles' annual sacred music festival is held here.

Palais de Longchamp Colonnaded Longchamp Palace, constructed in the 1860s, is at the eastern end of blvd Longchamp on blvd Philippon (4e). It was designed in part to disguise a *château d'eau* (water tower) built at the terminus of an aqueduct from the River Durance. The two wings house Marseilles' oldest museum, the **Musée des Beaux-Arts** (☎ 04 91 14 59 30; 10FF), which specialises in 15th- to 19th-century paintings, as well as the **Musée d'Histoire Naturelle** (☎ 04 91 62 30 78).

Basilique Notre Dame de la Garde

Not to be missed, particularly if you like great panoramas or overwrought 19th-century architecture, is a hike up to the Basilique Notre Dame de la Garde (☎ 04 91 13 40 80), an enormous Romano-Byzantine basilica 1km south of the old port. It stands on a hilltop (162m) – the highest point in the city – and provides staggering views of sprawling Marseilles.

The domed basilica, ornamented with all manner of coloured marble, intricate mosaics, murals and gilded objects, was erected between 1853 and 1864. The bell tower is topped by a 9.7m-tall gilded statue of the Virgin Mary on a 12m-high pedestal. The great bell inside is 2.5m tall and weighs a hefty 8324kg (the clapper alone is 387kg). Bullet marks from Marseilles' Battle of Liberation (15–25 August 1944) scar the cathedral's northern facade.

The basilica and its crypt open 7 am to 7 pm in winter and 7 am to 8 pm in summer (7 am to 10 pm from mid-June to mid-August). Admission is free; dress conservatively. Bus No 60 links the old port (from cours Jean Ballard) with the basilica. Count on 30 minutes each way by foot.

Château d'If

Château d'If (☎ 04 91 59 02 30), the 16th-century fortress-turned-prison made infamous by Alexandre Dumas' classic work of fiction, *Le Comte de Monte Cristo* (The Count of Monte Cristo), is on a 30-sq-km island 3.5km west of the entrance to the old port. Among the people incarcerated here were all sorts of political prisoners, hundreds of Protestants (many of whom perished in the dungeons), the Revolutionary hero Mirabeau, the rebels of 1848 and the Communards of 1871.

The chateau opens 9.15 am to 5.15 pm October and March (closed Monday) and daily 9 am to 7 pm April to September. Admission costs 22FF.

Boats run by GACM (☎ 04 91 55 50 09, fax 04 91 55 60 23), 1 quai des Belges (1er), to the Château d'If leave from outside the GACM office in the old port. Hourly boats run between 9 am and noon and 2 and 5 pm (50FF return, 20 minutes). There are sailings at 6.45 am and 6.30 pm too.

PROVENCE

Îles du Frioul

The islands of Ratonneau and Pomègues, each of which is about 2.5km long, are a few hundred metres west of the Château d'If. They were linked by a dike in the 1820s. From the 17th to 19th centuries the islands were used as a place of quarantine for people suspected of carrying plague or cholera.

Today, the rather barren islands (total area about 200 hectares) shelter sea birds, rare plants and bathers, and are dotted with fortifications (used by German troops during WWII), the ruins of the old quarantine hospital, **Hôpital Caroline**, and Fort Ratonneau.

Boats to the Château d'If also serve the Îles du Frioul (50FF return; 80FF if you want to stop at Château d'If too).

Markets

Marseilles is home to a colourful array of markets, the most 'aromatic' being the daily fresh fish market, held from 8 am to 1 pm on quai des Belges.

Cours Julien hosts a variety of morning markets. Shop here for fresh flowers on Wednesday and Saturday, fruit and vegetables on Friday, antique books every second Saturday and stamps or antique books on Sunday. Stalls laden with everything from second-hand clothing to pots and pans fill nearby place Jean Jaurès 8 am to 1 pm on Saturday.

Organised Tours

The tourist office offers various guided tours, including a walking tour of the city (40FF) departing from outside the tourist office at 2 or 2.30 pm on Sunday.

In summer, GACM (☎ 04 91 55 50 09) runs boat trips from the old port to Cassis and back (120FF), which pass by the stunning Calanques, dramatic formations of coastal rock that attract unusual wildlife.

Places to Stay

Marseilles has some of France's cheapest hotels – as cheap as 50FF a night! The bad news is that many are filthy dives in dodgy areas whose main business is renting out rooms by the hour. Some don't even have any showers. Establishments mentioned here are relatively clean and reputable.

Places to Stay – Budget

Camping Tents can usually be set up on the grounds of the *Auberge de Jeunesse Château de Bois Luzy* (see Hostels) for 26FF per person.

Hostels The *Auberge de Jeunesse de Bonneveine* (☎ 04 91 73 21 81, fax 04 91 73 97 23, ✆ *Marseilles@fuaj.org, impasse du Docteur Bonfils, 8e*), is about 4.5km south of the centre and charges 72FF, including breakfast. It opens year round (closed January). Take bus No 44 from the Rond Point du Prado metro stop and get off at the place Bonnefons stop.

Auberge de Jeunesse Château de Bois Luzy (☎/fax 04 91 49 06 18, allées des Primevères, 12e), is 4.5km east of the centre in the Montolivet neighbourhood. A bed costs 45FF; breakfast costs 18FF. A hostelling card is mandatory. Take bus No 6 from near the Réformés metro stop.

Hotels – Train Station Area The hotels around the train station are convenient if you arrive by train, but you'll find better value elsewhere. There's a cluster of small, extremely cheap hotels of less than stellar reputation along rue des Petites Maries (1er).

Two star *Hôtel d'Athènes (Central Marseilles map; ☎ 04 91 90 12 93, fax 04 91 90 72 03, 37–39 blvd d'Athènes, 1er)*, is at the foot of the grand staircase leading from the train station into town. Average but well-kept singles and doubles with shower and toilet cost 220FF to 300FF. Rooms in its adjoining one-star annexe called *Hôtel Little Palace* go from 120FF to 180FF.

Hotels – North of La Canebière Hotels listed in this section appear on both the Central Marseilles and Marseilles map.

Overlooking the bustling old port, the *New Hôtel Vieux Port (☎ 04 91 90 51 42, fax 04 91 90 76 24, ✆ Marseillesvieux-port@ new-hotel.com, 3 bis rue Reine Elisabeth,*

PROVENCE

1er), is a large renovated complex with modern singles/doubles costing 260/350FF. At the weekend and from 7 July to 1 September, the rate for all doubles drops to 335FF, making it good value for couples on a weekend visit to the city.

Rooms at the very pleasant *New Hotel Select* (☎ 04 91 50 65 50, fax 04 91 50 45 56, ✉ *Marseillesselect@new-hotel.com, 4 allées Léon Gambetta, 1er)* run by the same company cost 350/380FF for rooms (about 20% cheaper at the weekend and in July/August).

Not far from the New Select is homely, very clean *Hôtel Lutetia* (☎ 04 91 50 81 78, fax 04 91 50 23 52, *38 allées Léon Gambetta, 1er)* with smallish rooms equipped with TV and phone for 230/260FF.

Hôtel Ozea (☎ 04 91 47 91 84, *12 rue Barbaroux, 1er)* welcomes new guests 24 hours a day (at night just ring the bell to wake up the night clerk). Clean, old-fashioned doubles without/with shower cost 120/150FF. There are no hall showers.

There are well-kept singles and doubles at *Hôtel Pied-à-Terre* (☎ 04 91 92 00 95, *18 rue Barbaroux, 1er)* costing 120/150FF without/with shower. There are no hall showers. Reception opens until 1 am.

Hotels – Prefecture Area All the hotels in this section are on the Marseilles map. Blvd Louis Salvator (6e), located in a decent neighbourhood, has a number of clean and renovated two-star hotels touting bright rooms with modern decor. Take the metro to Estrangin Préfecture station to reach all these hotels.

Grand Hôtel Le Préfecture (☎ 04 91 54 31 60, fax 04 91 54 24 95, *9 blvd Louis Salvator, 6e)* has perfectly respectable rooms with shower, toilet and TV for 190FF and ones with a bath for 220FF.

Le Président (☎ 04 91 48 67 29, fax 04 91 94 24 44, *12 blvd Louis Salvator, 6e)* has rooms with shower, toilet and TV for 190FF and ones with a bath for 240FF.

Continuing up the hill you come to the one star *Hôtel Massilia* (☎ 04 91 54 79 28, *25 blvd Louis Salvator, 6e)*, which has doubles with shower and toilet for 160FF,

doubles with shower only for 150FF and shower-equipped singles for 130FF. Almost opposite is the more upmarket *Hôtel Manon* (☎ 04 91 48 67 01, fax 04 91 47 23 04, *36 blvd Louis Salvator, 6e)*, which has bright singles/doubles with all mod-cons starting at 195/230FF.

Hôtel Béarn (☎ 04 91 37 75 83, fax 04 91 47 27 91, *63 rue Sylvabelle, 6e)* is quiet with colourfully decorated singles/doubles costing 100/120FF with shower, and starting at 180/200FF with shower and toilet. Guests can watch TV in the common room. Reception closes at 11 pm or midnight and access after 11 pm is via security code.

Places to Stay – Mid-Range & Top End

Hôtel Alizé (*Central Marseilles map;* ☎ 04 91 33 66 97, fax 04 91 54 80 06, *35 quai des Belges, 1er)* is an elegant old pile overlooking the old port. It has pleasant singles/doubles with air-con and soundproofed windows from 285/395FF.

Built into the rocks and offering fantastic sea and beach views is idyllic, two-star *Hôtel Le Richelieu* (*Marseilles map;* ☎ 04 91 31 01 92, *52 Corniche Président John F Kennedy, 7e)*, next to the plage des Catalans. Singles or doubles cost 190FF with shower, 185FF to 215FF with shower and toilet, and 220FF to 240FF with TV as well. Rooms facing the street can be quite noisy.

Recommended by the Marseilles Tourist office itself is *Hermes* (*Central Marseilles map;* ☎ 04 96 11 63 63, fax 04 96 11 63 64, ✉ *hotel.hermes@wanadoo.fr, 2 rue de la Bonneterie)*. This tastefully renovated establishment overlooks the old port and has a great view from its top floor solarium. Rates start at 260FF to 300FF for a single/double room.

New Hôtel Bompard (☎ 04 91 52 10 93, fax 04 91 31 02 14, ✉ *Marseillesbompard @new-hotel.com, 1 rue des Flots Bleues, 7e)*, just off Corniche Président John F Kennedy, sports three stars thanks to its elegant sea views, swimming pool and extensive grounds. Singles/doubles with all the gadgets cost 420/460FF in July and August.

Places to Eat

Marseilles' restaurants offer an incredible variety of cuisines, but no trip to Marseilles is complete without sampling bouillabaisse – a seafood stew with onions, white wine and tomatoes, flavoured with fennel and saffron. Unless noted otherwise, the places listed below are on the Central Marseilles map.

Restaurants – French Fish is the predominant dish in Marseilles, be it soup, *huîtres* (oysters), *moules* (mussels) or other shellfish, all of which are plentiful in this port city. The length of quai de Rive Neuve (1er) is plastered with outside cafes and touristy restaurants touting bouillabaisse on its menu boards; those along quai du Port on the northern side of the old port are pricier. To the south, the pedestrian streets around place Thiars are packed with terrace cafes and restaurants in the warmer months.

The upmarket *Casa Saumon (☎ 04 91 54 22 89, 22 rue de la Paix, 1er)*, serves salmon in a rustic but refined atmosphere. It opens noon to 2.30 pm and 7.30 to 10.30 pm Monday to Saturday. Its main menu costs around 128FF.

Le Mérou Bleu (☎ 04 91 54 23 25, 32–36 rue St-Saëns, 1er), is a popular restaurant with a lovely terrace. It has bouillabaisse (75FF to 145FF), other seafood dishes (72FF to 125FF), first courses (38FF to 78FF) and pasta.

Pizzeria Chez Mario (☎ 04 91 54 48 54, 8 rue Euthymènes, 1er) is more than just a plain old pizzeria. Chez Mario has fish and grilled meats (85FF to 110FF) and pasta (starting at 60FF) too. It opens noon to 2.30 pm and 7.30 to 11.30 pm.

La Cloche à Fromage (27 cours Honoré d'Estienne d'Orves, 1er), has cheese, cheese and more cheese – 70 types in fact. Various *plateaux* (trays) are available starting at 92FF and there is a lunchtime *menu* costing 59FF. Close by is the delightful restaurant and *salon de thé* inside the unusual *Les Arcenaulx (27 cours Honoré d'Estienne d'Orves, 1er)* a beautifully restored complex wrapped around cours des Arcenaulx. Booking is recommended.

There is a colourful choice of French eateries on cours Julien near the Notre Dame du Mont-Cours Julien metro station (Marseilles map). Particularly tasty places include *Le Resto Provençal (☎ 04 91 48 85 12, 64 cours Julien, 1er)*, which has a very pleasant outside dining terrace. It has a *menu* offering (predominantly fishy) regional fare for 115FF, a *plat du jour* for 43FF and a good-value lunchtime *menu* for 65FF.

Le Sud du Haut (☎ 04 91 92 66 64, 80 cours Julien, 1er) is painted bright blue and yellow on the outside and furnished with an eclectic collection of obscure items inside. Strictly Provençal dishes are served here too. Their *assiette du sud* menu costs 50FF.

Restaurants – North African & Asian Given its number of North African immigrants, it's not surprising that couscous reigns supreme in certain parts of Marseilles. *Roi du Couscous (☎ 04 91 91 45 46, 63 rue de la République, 2e)* – the 'king of couscous' – dishes up the steamed semolina with meats and vegetables for 35FF to 60FF, while a three course lunchtime *menu* costs just 50FF, including 0.25L of wine.

For Vietnamese and Chinese fare, the many restaurants on, or just off, rue de la République are worth a visit. One good and popular Vietnamese eatery on the southern side of the Old Port is *Phuong-Dong (☎ 04 91 54 28 01, 25 cours Honoré d'Estienne d'Orves, 1er)*. Try the Vietnamese beef with onions or their vegetarian spring rolls. An all-in menu costs 58FF.

Restaurants – Other Ethnic Cours Julien (Marseilles map), previously mentioned for its French cuisine, is lined with fun and funky restaurants offering a tantalising variety of ethnic food: Indian, Antillean, Pakistani, Thai, Armenian, Lebanese, Tunisian, Italian and so on.

Noteworthy options include the upstairs Caribbean *Restaurant Antillais (☎ 04 91 48 71 89, 10 cours Julien, 1er)*. It is run by a congenial couple from the West Indies who offer a 100FF *menu* (including a carafe of house wine), plus a colourful range of

PROVENCE

starters (starting at 20FF) and main dishes (starting at 40FF).

An excellent value Caribbean-themed eatery with 'student dishes' costing 29FF is *Mosaic* (☎ 04 91 47 35 98, 38 cours Julien). Their *plat du jour* only costs 49FF.

Armenian restaurant *Le Caucase* (☎ 04 91 48 36 30, 62 cours Julien), serves all sorts of unpronounceable (to non-Hayaren speakers, that is) dishes that are as tasty as they are unrecognisable. The *menu* costs 88FF. Le Caucase only opens in the evening.

Cafes Cafes crowd quai de Rive Neuve and cours Honoré d'Estienne d'Orves (1er), a large, long, open square two blocks south of the quay. There is another cluster overlooking place de la Préfecture, at the southern end of rue St-Ferréol (1er).

The *salon de thé* inside the Virgin Megastore *(75 rue St-Ferréol, 1er)* opens 10 am to 8 pm (until midnight on Saturday; closed Sunday).

Dressed to kill? Then head for elitist *Café de la Mode (11 La Canebière, 1er)* inside Musée de la Mode, open noon to 7 pm Tuesday to Sunday.

Cours Julien has a colourful cluster of great cafes at its northern end, including bright yellow *Rétro Julien (22 Cours Julien, 1er)* serving *crêpes*.

Self-Catering Fresh fruit and vegetables are sold at *Marché des Capucins (place des Capucins, 1er)*, one block north of La Canebière, and the *fruit and vegetable market (cours Pierre Puget, 6e)*. Both open Monday to Saturday.

Entertainment

Cultural event listings appear in the monthly *Vox Mag* and weekly *Taktik* and *Sortir*, all distributed for free at the tourist office, cinemas and the ticket offices mentioned below. Comprehensive listings also appear in the weekly *L'Officiel des Loisirs* (2FF at newspaper kiosks).

Tickets for most cultural events are sold at *billetteries* (ticket counters; ☎ 04 91 39 94 00); in FNAC (☎ 04 91 39 94 00) on the top floor of the Centre Bourse shopping centre; the Virgin Megastore (☎ 04 91 55 55 00), 75 rue St-Ferréol (1er); Arcenaulx (☎ 04 91 59 80 37), 25 cours Honoré d'Estienne d'Orves (1er); and the Office de la Culture (☎ 04 91 33 33 79), 42 La Canebière (1er).

Clubs & Bars For a good selection of rock, reggae, country and other live music, try *La Maison Hantée* (☎ 04 91 92 09 40, 10 rue Vian, 6e), a very hip street between cours Julien and rue des Trois Rois. One of Marseilles' two Irish pubs, *O'Malleys (quai de Rive Neuve, 1er)*, overlooks the old port on the corner of rue de la Paix.

Popular gay bars include *Énigme (22 rue Beauvau, 1er)*, and *MP Bar (10 rue Beauvau, 1er)* further along. Camper than a row of tents and full of fun is lively *Drag Queen Café (2 rue Sénac de Meilhan, 1er)*, which hosts live bands and opens until 5.30 am at the weekend. Opposite is equally hectic *New Can-Can Disco (3 rue Sénac de Meilhan, 1er)*, open until 6 am.

Shopping

For a mouthwatering selection of *foie gras* (goose liver pâté), Provençal wines and other culinary delights, shop at Ducs de Gascogne (39 rue Paradis, 1er). Puyricard (25 rue Francis Davso, 1er), a *chocolatier*, is more suited to those with a sweet tooth.

A rich array of coffee, tea and chocolate is sold at Maison Debout, 46 rue Francis Davso (1er), a traditional and very quaint shop.

Getting There & Away

Air The Marseilles-Provence airport (☎ 04 42 14 14 14), also known as the Marseilles-Marignane airport, is 28km north-west of the city in Marignane.

Bus The bus station (*gare des autocars*; ☎ 04 91 08 16 40), 3 place Victor Hugo (3e), is 150m to the right as you exit the train station. The information counter (☎ 04 91 08 16 40) opens 7 am to 6 pm (9 am to noon and 2 to 6 pm on Sunday). It doubles as a left-luggage office (10FF per bag per day). Tickets are sold either at company ticket counters (closed most of the time) or

PROVENCE

on the bus. Scrappy handwritten schedules are stuck up on a noticeboard outside the bus station building.

There are buses to Aix-en-Provence (28FF, 35 minutes via the autoroute/one hour via the N8, every 5 to 10 minutes), Avignon (92FF, 35 minutes, seven daily), Cannes (126FF, two hours), Carpentras (75FF), Cassis (25FF), Cavaillon (55FF), Digne-les-Bains (84FF, 2½ hours, four daily), Nice (140FF, 2¾ hours), Nice airport, Orange, Salon-de-Provence and other destinations. There is an infrequent service to Castellane (see Getting There & Away in the Gorges du Verdon section).

Eurolines (☎ 04 91 50 57 55, fax 04 91 08 32 21) has buses to Spain, Belgium, the Netherlands, Italy, Morocco, the UK and other countries. Its counter in the bus station opens 9 am to noon and 2 to 6 pm (7.30 am to noon and 1 to 5 pm on Saturday; closed Sunday).

Intercars (☎ 04 91 50 08 66, fax 04 91 06 72 34, ✉ intercars.Marseilles@wanadoo.fr), office next to Eurolines in the bus station, has buses to the UK, Spain, Portugal, Morocco, Poland and Slovakia. The office opens 9.15 am to noon and 2 to 5.30 or 6 pm on alternate days (closed Sunday).

Train Marseilles' passenger train station, served by both metro lines, is called Gare St-Charles (☎ 0 836 35 35 35). The information and ticket reservation office, one level below the tracks next to the metro entrance, opens 9 am to 8 pm (closed Sunday). Luggage may be left at the left-luggage office off platform 1. The office opens 6 am to 10 pm and it costs 20FF per piece of luggage per day. In town, train tickets can be bought in advance at the SNCF Boutique Grignan, 17 rue Grignan (1er), which opens 9 am to 4.30 pm (closed at the weekend).

From Marseilles there are trains to more or less any destination in France. Some sample destinations are Paris' Gare de Lyon (379FF, 4¼ hours by TGV, 10 daily), Avignon (92FF, one hour), Lyons (209FF, 3¼ hours), Nice (149FF, 1½ hours), Barcelona (342FF, 8½ hours) and Geneva (262FF, 6½ hours).

The volunteer retirees in the SOS Voyageurs office (☎ 04 91 62 12 80), across the corridor from the police post, help problem-plagued passengers.

Car Rental agencies offering better rates include Thrifty (☎ 04 91 05 92 18; metro Gare St-Charles), 8 blvd Voltaire (1er), and Europcar (☎ 04 91 99 40 90; metro Gare St-Charles), next to the train station at 7 blvd Maurice Bourdet (1er).

Boat Marseilles' passenger ferry terminal (*gare maritime*; ☎ 04 91 56 38 63, fax 04 91 56 38 70) is 250m west of place de la Joliette (2e). It's modern and spacious, but facilities for foot passengers are fairly sparse. There is a poorly-stocked snack bar, no ATMs and little to keep you amused while waiting for a boat.

The Société Nationale Maritime Corse Méditerranée (SNCM; ☎ 0 836 67 95 00, fax 04 91 56 35 86) links Marseilles with Corsica (see Getting There & Away in the Corsica chapter), Sardinia and Tunisia. It serves the ports of Algiers, Annaba, Bejaia, Oran and Skikda in Algeria, though services are prone to disruption/cancellation because of the political troubles there. SNCM's office, 61 blvd des Dames (2e), opens 8 am to 6 pm (8.30 am to noon and 2 to 5.30 pm Saturday; closed Sunday).

Algérie Ferries (☎ 04 91 90 64 70), 29 blvd des Dames (2e), opens 8.15 to 11.45 am and 1 to 4.45 pm (closed at the weekend). Ticketing and reservations for the Tunisian and Moroccan ferry companies, Compagnie Tunisienne de Navigation (CTN) and Compagnie Marocaine de Navigation (COMANAV; departures from 4 quai d'Alger in Sète; ☎ 04 67 46 68 00), are handled by SNCM.

For more information on ferry services to/from North Africa and Sardinia, see the Sea section in the introductory Getting There & Away chapter.

Getting Around
To/From the Airport Navette shuttle buses operated by TRPA (☎ 04 91 50 59 34 in Marseilles; ☎ 04 42 14 31 27 at the

PROVENCE

airport) link Marseilles-Provence airport (47FF, one hour) with Marseilles train station. Buses to the airport leave from outside the train station's main entrance every 20 minutes between 5.30 am and 9.50 pm; buses from the airport depart between 6.30 am and 10.50 pm.

Bus & Metro Marseilles has two fast, well-maintained metro lines (Métro 1 and Métro 2), a tram line and an extensive bus network.

The metro, which began operation in 1977, trams and most buses run from about 5 am to 9 pm. From 9.25 pm to 12.30 am, metro and tram routes are covered every 15 minutes by buses M1 and M2 and Tramway 68; stops are marked with fluorescent green signs reading *métro en bus* (metro by bus). Most of the 11 Fluobus night buses (☎ 04 91 91 92 10 for information) begin their runs in front of the Espace Infos-RTM office, 6 rue des Fabres (1er), which distributes route maps.

Bus/metro tickets (9FF) can be used on any combination of metro, bus and tram for one hour after they've been time-stamped (no return trips). A carnet of six costs 42FF; a day pass 25FF. Tram stops have modern blue ticket *composteurs* (cancelling machines) that should be used to time-stamp your ticket before you board.

For information on Marseilles' public transport system, drop into Espace Infos-RTM (☎ 04 91 91 92 10), rue des Fabres. It opens 8.30 am to 6 pm (9 am to 5.30 pm Saturday). Tickets can be purchased here from as early as 6.10 am until 7.50 pm.

Taxi There's a taxi stand to the right as you exit the train station through the main entrance. Marseilles Taxi (☎ 04 91 02 20 20) and Taxis France (☎ 04 91 49 91 00) dispatch taxis 24 hours a day.

AIX-EN-PROVENCE
postcode 13100 • pop 134,222
Aix-en-Provence, which most people just call Aix (pronounced like the letter 'x'), is one of France's most graceful – and popular – cities, prompting one reader to slam it

as '...a waste because it is too touristy' and another to say '...the nearest thing to traffic hell'. Either way, its harmonious fusion of majestic public squares, shaded avenues and mossy fountains, many of which have gurgled since the 18th century, cannot be disputed. Some 200 elegant mansions date from the 17th and 18th centuries, many exhibiting the unmistakable influence of Italian baroque, and coloured that distinctive Provençal yellow.

The city is enlivened by the University of Aix-Marseilles, whose forerunner was established in 1409. It counts a student body of about 30,000, many of whom are foreigners undertaking intensive French-language courses.

History
Aix was founded as a military camp under the name of Aquae Sextiae (Waters of Sextius) in 123 BC on the site of thermal springs, which are still flowing to this day. Fortunately for stuck-up Aix, the settlement became known as Aix – not Sex.

The town was established after Roman forces under the proconsul Sextius Calvinus had destroyed the Ligurian Celtic stronghold of Entremont, 3km to the north, and enslaved its inhabitants. In the 12th century, the counts of Provence made Aix their capital.

The city reached its zenith as a centre of art and learning under the enlightened King René (1409–80), a brilliant polyglot who brought painters to his court from around Europe (especially Flanders) and instituted administrative reforms for the benefit of his subjects.

Orientation
Cours Mirabeau, Aix's main boulevard, stretches from La Rotonde, a roundabout with a huge fountain and also called place du Général de Gaulle, eastwards to place Forbin. The oldest part of the city, Vieil Aix, is north of cours Mirabeau; most of the streets, alleys and public squares in this part of town are closed to traffic.

South of cours Mirabeau is the Quartier Mazarin, whose regular street grid was laid

PROVENCE

AIX-EN-PROVENCE

PLACES TO STAY
- 15 Hôtel des Arts-Le Sully
- 22 Hôtel du Globe
- 32 Grand Hôtel Nègre Coste
- 36 Hôtel de France
- 41 Hôtel St-Christophe
- 51 Hôtel Cardinal
- 52 Hôtel Cardinal (Annexe)
- 55 Hôtel des Quatre Dauphins

PLACES TO EAT
- 1 Spar Supermarket
- 7 La Boulangerie du Coin
- 9 L'Arbre à Pain
- 11 Le Platanos
- 13 University Restaurant

- 25 Restaurant Nem d'Asie
- 26 La Fontaine
- 27 Les Bacchanales
- 28 Fromagerie des Augustins
- 30 Boulangerie
- 31 Les Deux Garçons
- 33 Monoprix Department Store
- 37 Mondial Café
- 42 Yôji
- 47 Gu et Fils

OTHER
- 2 Cathédrale St-Sauveur
- 3 Université d'Aix-Marseilles III (Foreign student language department)
- 4 Museé du Vieil Aix

- 5 Galerie du Festival; Galerie Mosca
- 6 Musée des Tapisseries
- 8 Laundrette
- 10 Hub Lot Cybercafé
- 12 Église de la Madeleine
- 14 Laundrette
- 16 Studio Keaton Cinema
- 17 Théâtre
- 18 Rich Art
- 19 Palais de Justice
- 20 Town Hall
- 21 Cave du Felibrige
- 23 Laundrette
- 24 Laundrette
- 29 Change Nazareth
- 34 Galerie d'Art du Conseil Général

- 35 Change L'Agence
- 38 La Rotonde
- 39 Post Office
- 40 Tourist Office
- 43 Le Cézanne
- 44 Cinéma Mazarin
- 45 Banque Nationale de Paris
- 46 Bechard Fabrique de Calissons
- 48 Musée Paul Arbaud
- 49 Banque de France
- 50 Paradox Librairie Internationale
- 53 Église St-Jean de Malte
- 54 Musée Granet
- 56 Pétanque Course
- 57 Boulodrome Municipal
- 58 Train Station

PROVENCE

euro currency converter €1 = 6.56FF

out in the 17th century. The entire city centre is ringed by a series of one-way boulevards.

Aix's chic shops are clustered along pedestrian rue Marius Reinaud, which winds its way behind the Palais de Justice on place de Verdun.

Information

Tourist Office Aix's highly efficient – and very busy – tourist office (☎ 04 42 16 11 61, fax 04 42 16 11 62), 2 place du Général de Gaulle, opens 8.30 am to 8 pm (10 pm in July and August; Sunday year round from 10 am to 1 pm and 2 to 6 pm). Email them on ✉ infos@aixenprovencetourism.com.

Hotel bookings cost 5FF, which is set against the cost of the room. See their Web site at www.aixenprovencetourism.com.

Money Near the graceful place des Quatre Dauphins, Banque de France, 18 rue du Quatre Septembre, opens 9.15 am to 12.15 pm and 1.30 to 3 pm (closed at the weekend).

Commercial banks mass along cours Mirabeau and cours Sextius, which runs north–south to the west of La Rotonde. Local American Express agent, Change L'Agence (☎ 04 42 26 84 77), is at 15 cours Mirabeau. The Change Nazareth (☎ 04 42 38 28 28) exchange bureau, 7 rue Nazareth, opens 9 am to 7 pm (5 pm on Sunday) in July and August.

Post & Communications The post office, on the corner of ave des Belges and rue Lapierre, opens 8.30 am to 7 pm (Saturday until noon; closed Sunday).

The hourly rate at Aix's lone cybercafe, the Hub Lot Cybercafé (☎ 04 42 21 37 31, ✉ hub1@mail.vif.fr), 15–27 rue Paul Bert, is 45FF until 7 pm, and 25FF after 7 pm. It opens at 9 am.

Bookshop Paradox Librairie Internationale (☎ 04 42 26 47 99), 15 rue du Quatre Septembre, sells English-language novels and guidebooks, including Lonely Planet guides. It buys/sells second-hand books too, and opens 9 am to 12.30 pm and 2 to 6.30 pm Monday to Saturday.

Laundry Laundrettes abound – at 3 rue de la Fontaine, 34 cours Sextius, 3 rue de la Fonderie and 60 rue Boulegon. All open 7 or 8 am to 8 pm.

Walking Tour

Aix's social scene centres on shaded **Cours Mirabeau**, a wide avenue laid out during the latter half of the 1600s and named after the heroic revolutionary Comte de Mirabeau. Trendy cafes spill out onto the pavements on the sunny northern side of the street, which is crowned by a leafy rooftop of plane trees. The shady southern side shelters a string of elegant Renaissance *hôtels particuliers*; **Hôtel d'Espargnet** (1647) at No 38 being among the most impressive (today it houses the university's economics department). The Marquis of Entrecasteaux murdered his wife in their family home, **Hôtel d'Isoard de Vauvenarges** (1710), at No 10.

The large, cast-iron fountain at the western end of cours Mirabeau, **Fontaine de la Rotonde**, dates from 1860. At the avenue's eastern end, the fountain at place Forbin is decorated with a 19th-century statue of King René holding a bunch of Muscat grapes, a varietal he is credited with introducing to the region. Moss-covered **Fontaine d'Eau Thermale** at the intersection of cours Mirabeau and rue du Quatre Septembre spouts water at a temperature of 34°C.

Other streets and squares lined with hôtels particuliers include **rue Mazarine**, one block south of cours Mirabeau; **place des Quatre Dauphins**, two blocks farther south, whose fountain dates from 1667; the eastern continuation of cours Mirabeau, **rue de l'Opéra** (at Nos 18, 24 and 26); and the pretty, fountain-clad **place d'Albertas** just west of place St-Honoré, where live music is sometimes performed on balmy summer evenings. Sunday strollers should not miss a jaunt to **place de l'Hôtel de Ville**, where the city brass band entertains the crowds most Sunday mornings.

South of Aix's historic centre is the pleasing **parc Jourdan**, a spacious green park dominated by Aix's largest fountain

PROVENCE

and home to the town's **Boulodrome Municipal**, where old men gather beneath the shade of the trees to play pétanque on sunny days. Pétanque is also the name of the game on the tree-studded court opposite the park entrance on ave du Parc. Spectators are welcome.

Museums

The tourist office sells a Passeport Musées for 60FF that gets you into Atelier Cézanne, Musée Granet, Musée des Tapisseries, Musée d'Histoire Naturelle and Pavillon de Vendôme.

Aix's finest is **Musée Granet** (☎ 04 42 38 14 70), place St-Jean de Malte, housed in a 17th-century priory of the Knights of Malta. Exhibits include Celtic statues from Entremont as well as Roman artefacts, while the museum's collection of paintings boasts 16th- to 19th-century Italian, Dutch and French works as well as some of Aix-born Cézanne's lesser known paintings and watercolours. The museum opens 10 am to noon and 2 to 6 pm daily except Tuesday. Admission costs 10FF for adults (students aged under 25 free).

The **Musée des Tapisseries** (Tapestry Museum; ☎ 04 42 23 09 91), in the Ancien Archevêché (Former Archbishop's Palace), 28 place des Martyrs de la Résistance, reopened in May 1998 after months of renovation. It opens 10 am to noon and 2 to 5.45 pm (closed Sunday); admission costs 15FF. **Musée Paul Arbaud** (☎ 04 42 38 38 95), 2a rue du Quatre Septembre, displays books, manuscripts and a collection of Provençal faïence – tin-glazed earthenware; it opens 2 to 5 pm Monday to Saturday. Admission costs 15FF (students 10FF).

Art lovers should not miss the **Petit Musée Cézanne** (☎ 04 42 23 42 53, fax 04 42 21 60 30) inside the Galerie du Festival straddling rue de Littera at 24 rue Gaston de Saporta. Next door at No 22 is the chic **Galerie Mosca** (☎ 04 42 21 07 51), which hosts interesting and unusual art exhibitions. The **Galérie d'Art du Conseil Général** (☎ 04 42 93 03 67), 21 bis cours Mirabeau, also has exhibitions and opens 10.30 am to 6 pm Tuesday to Saturday.

Cathédrale St-Sauveur

Aix's cathedral incorporates the architectural features of every major period from the 5th to 18th centuries. The main Gothic structure, built between 1285 and 1350, includes the Romanesque nave of a 12th-century church as part of its southern aisle; the chapels were added in the 14th and 15th centuries, and there is a 5th-century sarcophagus in the apse.

The cathedral opens 8 am to noon and 2 to 6 pm. Mass is held here at 8 am (Saturday at 6.30 pm, Sunday at 9 and 10.30 am and 7 pm). Gregorian chants are often sung here at 4.30 pm on Sunday – an experience not to be missed.

The 15th-century *Triptyque du Buisson Ardent* (Triptych of the Burning Bush) in the nave is by Nicolas Froment; it is usually only opened for groups. Near it is a triptych panel illustrating Christ's passion. The tapestries encircling the choir date from the 18th century and the fabulous gilt organ is baroque. There's a *son et lumière* (sound and light) show at 9.30 pm most nights in summer.

Cézanne Trail

Paul Cézanne (1839–1906), Aix's most celebrated son (at least after his death), did much of his painting in and around the city. If you're interested in the minutiae of his day-to-day life – where he ate, drank, played and worked – just follow the **Circuit de Cézanne**, marked by round bronze markers in the pavement that begin at the tourist office. The markers are coordinated with a trilingual guide called *In the Footsteps of Paul Cézanne*, available free from the tourist office.

Cézanne's last studio, now opened to the public as **Atelier Paul Cézanne** (☎ 04 42 21 06 53), is atop a hill about 1.5km north of the tourist office at 9 Ave Paul Cézanne. It has been left exactly as it was when he died and though none of his works hang here, his tools do. It opens 10 am to noon and 2 to 5 pm (2.30 to 6 pm from June to September) daily except Tuesday. Admission costs 16FF (students 10FF). Take bus No 1 to the Cézanne stop.

PROVENCE

Markets

Aix is the premier market town in Provence. A mass of fruit and vegetable stands are set up each morning on **place Richelme**, just as they have been for centuries. Depending on the season, you can buy olives, chèvre (goat's cheese), garlic, lavender, honey, peaches, melons and a whole host of other sun-kissed products. Another grocery market is set up on **place des Prêcheurs** on Tuesday, Thursday and Saturday mornings.

A **flower market** is set up on place des Prêcheurs on Sunday mornings, and on Tuesday, Thursday and Saturday mornings on place de l'Hôtel de Ville. There's a **flea market** (marché aux puces) on place de Verdun.

Language Courses

In summer Aix teems with young Americans attempting to twist their tongues round those fiddly French r's and the like. See courses in the Facts for the Visitor chapter for details on language courses at the American University Center in Aix.

Organised Tours

Between April and October, the tourist office runs a packed schedule of guided bus tours around the region in English and in French. Ask for the free brochure entitled Excursions en Provence at the tourist office or study the noticeboard outside.

Special Events

Aix has a sumptuous cultural calendar. The most sought-after tickets are for the week-long Festival Provençal d'Aix et du Pays d'Aix, which brings the most refined classical music, opera and ballet each July to such city venues as the Cathédrale St-Sauveur and the old Théâtre Municipal, 17 rue de l'Opéra. Fortunately, practitioners of more casual musical expression – buskers – bring the festival spirit to cours Mirabeau.

Other festivals include the two day Festival du Tambourin (Tambourine Festival) in mid-April, the Aix Jazz Festival in early July and the Fête Mistralienne marking the birthday of Provençal hero Frédéric Mistral

on 13 September. For detailed information contact the Comité Officiel des Fêtes (☎ 04 42 63 06 75) or the tourist office.

Places to Stay

Despite being a student town, Aix is not cheap. In July and August, when hotel prices rise precipitously, it may be possible to stay in the university dorms – contact the tourist office for details or you can call the student accommodation outfit CROUS (☎ 04 42 26 47 00), ave Jules Ferry, in the Cité des Gazelles.

The tourist office has comprehensive details of chambres d'hôtes and gîtes ruraux in and around Aix; it also has a list (updated weekly) of all types of accommodation – including farmhouses – to rent on a long-term basis. Hotel bookings are now coordinated via one email address (✉ resex @aixenprovencetourism.com) and there are more choices than the representative samples listed here.

Places to Stay – Budget

Camping Two kilometres south-east of town, *Camping Arc-en-Ciel* (☎ 04 42 26 14 28, route de Nice), open from April to September, is at Pont des Trois Sautets. It costs 90FF for a person with tent site and opens mid-March to mid-October. Take bus No 3 to Les Trois Sautets stop.

Hostels The *Auberge de Jeunesse du Jas de Bouffan* (☎ 04 42 20 15 99, fax 04 42 59 36 12, 3 ave Marcel Pagnol) is almost 2km west of the centre. Bed and breakfast costs 68FF and sheet hire costs 11FF a night. Rooms are locked between 12 pm and 5 pm. Take bus line No 4 from La Rotonde to the Vasarely stop.

Hotels On the city centre's eastern fringe, laid-back and friendly *Hôtel des Arts-Le Sully* (☎ 04 42 38 11 77, fax 04 42 26 77 31, 69 blvd Carnot) (second entrance at 5 rue de la Fonderie), is strategically situated a touch away from the milling crowds. It has decent singles/doubles with shower and toilet for 149/175FF and TV-equipped doubles for 220FF.

Just north of blvd Jean Jaurès, *Hôtel Paul* (☎ *04 42 23 23 89, fax 04 42 63 17 80, 10 ave Pasteur*), has rooms for one or two with shower and toilet for 190FF. The hotel is a 10-minute walk from the tourist office; alternatively take minibus No 2 from La Rotonde or the bus station.

Places to Stay – Mid-Range

Hôtel Cardinal (☎ *04 42 38 32 30, fax 04 42 26 39 05, 24 rue Cardinale*), is a charming place in a charming street and has large rooms with shower, toilet and a mix of modern and period furniture. Year-round prices are 220FF to 300FF for a single, 260FF to 320FF for a double and 350FF to 420FF for a small self-catering suite in its annexe at 12 rue Cardinale.

Similar *Hôtel de France* (☎ *04 42 27 90 15, fax 04 42 26 11 47, 63 rue Espariat*), has serviceable singles/doubles with washbasin from 210/240FF and with shower for 280/310FF.

Just out of the pedestrianised area, *Hôtel du Globe* (☎ *04 42 26 03 58, fax 04 42 26 13 68, 74 cours Sextius*), has pleasant singles with toilet starting at 170FF and doubles/triples with shower and toilet starting at 230/400FF. Garage parking costs 45FF a night.

Places to Stay – Top End

Aix is well endowed with three- and four-star hotels, though many are on the outskirts of town.

Those close to the centre include charming, highly recommended *Hôtel des Quatre Dauphins* (☎ *04 42 38 16 39, fax 04 42 38 60 19, 54 rue Roux Alpheran*), which charges 295/335FF for singles/doubles with period furnishings and shower.

Hôtel St-Christophe (☎ *04 42 26 01 24, fax 04 42 38 53 17, 2 ave Victor Hugo*), sporting a pleasant breakfast terrace, has singles/doubles with shower for 390/430FF.

Three star *Grand Hôtel Nègre Coste* (☎ *04 42 27 74 22, fax 04 42 26 80 93, 33 cours Mirabeau*), has rooms overlooking what many consider to be France's most beautiful main street for around 450/750FF. Garage parking is available.

Places to Eat

Aix has lots of lovely places to dine, but the prices do little to moderate the town's up-market gastronomic image. Fortunately, ethnic cuisines are both plentiful and of high quality. Aix's cheapest dining street is rue Van Loo, which is lined with tiny restaurants offering Italian, Chinese, Thai and other Asian cuisines.

Aix's pastry speciality is the *calisson*, a sweet biscuit made with almond paste comprising 40% almonds and 60% fruit syrup.

Restaurants The area around rue de la Verrerie and rue Félibre Gaut offers various options, though Vietnamese and Chinese eateries abound. *Restaurant Nem d'Asie* (☎ *04 42 26 53 06, 22 rue Félibre Gaut*) is one of the cheapest places, with lunchtime *menus* starting at 50FF. Numerous cafes, brasseries and restaurants can be found nearby in the heart of the city on place des Cardeurs and place de l'Hôtel de Ville.

La Fontaine (☎ *04 42 27 53 35, 5 rue de la Fontaine d'Argent*) is named after the pretty little fountain that plays on its outside terrace. Strictly Provençal cuisine is cooked up here, as is the case at upmarket *Les Bacchanales* (☎ *04 42 27 21 06, 10 rue de la Couronne*), which offers a delectable *menu gourmand* for 295FF and a cheaper, less rich *menu* for 145FF (children 95FF).

For Greek food, *Le Platanos* (☎ *04 42 21 33 19, 13 rue Rifle-Rafle*) hidden away down a crooked side street, offers a 55FF *menu* for lunch and an 85FF *menu* for dinner. *Yôji* (☎ *04 42 38 84 48, 7 ave Victor Hugo*) is an upmarket Japanese place that offers succulent *menus* for 125FF to 205FF in the evening and starting at 80FF at lunchtime.

L'Arbre à Pain (☎ *04 42 96 99 95, 12 rue Constantin*) is a vegetarian place that prides itself on its low-calorie, full-flavoured dishes. Its home-made ice cream, which comes in such flavours as melon, violet and lavender, is particularly enticing.

If you're on the Peter Mayle trail, head straight for *Gu et Fils* (☎ *04 42 26 75 12, 3 rue Frédéric Mistral*), or rather 'Chez Gu' as the author of *A Year in Provence*

PROVENCE

described the place before launching into verbal raptures about the patron's moustache and culinary skills. It serves purely Provençal dishes.

For those after a very cheap meal, there's a *restaurant universitaire* (☎ 04 42 38 03 68, 10 cours des Arts et Métiers). You may have to buy a ticket from a student for about 15FF. It generally opens 11.15 am to 1.15 pm and 6.30 to 7.30 pm.

Cafes No visit to Aix is complete without a quick pose behind your shades at Aix's most renowned cafe, *Les Deux Garçons* (☎ 04 42 26 00 51, 53 cours Mirabeau), on the sunny side of the street. Dating from 1792, this pricey brasserie (a former intellectual hang-out) is just one of many people-watching spots along this street.

Not quite so conspicuous are the plentiful open-air cafes that sprawl across squares such as place des Cardeurs, forum des Cardeurs, place de Verdun and place de l'Hôtel de Ville. *Mondial Café* (☎ 04 42 26 05 44, 1 cours Mirabeau), overlooking La Rotunde at the western end of the street, specialises in shellfish dishes and supersized salads (starting at 60FF).

Self-Catering The next best thing to bread from the *market* is the fresh and often warm loaves sold at *La Boulangerie du Coin (4 rue Boulegon)*. It is also one of the few *boulangeries* to bake on Sunday, along with the one on rue Tournefort that never closes.

Monoprix Department Store (cours Mirabeau) has groceries in the basement supermarket, and opens 8.30 am to 8 pm Monday to Saturday. For late-night supplies, try *Spar (4 rue Jacques de la Roque)*.

Entertainment

Pick up a free copy of the monthly *Le Mois à Aix* at the tourist office to find out what's on where and when.

Cinema The people of Aix are particularly fond of what the French call *le septième art* (the seventh art), and two cinemas are dedicated solely to screening nondubbed films: *Cinéma Mazarin* (☎ 04 42 26 99 85, 6 rue

Laroque), and small *Studio Keaton* (☎ 04 42 26 86 11, 45 rue Manuel). Massive 12-screen *Le Cézanne* (☎ 04 36 68 04 06, 3 rue Marcel Guillaume), has both dubbed and nondubbed films.

Shopping

A splendid array of local wines – some *very* expensive – are sold at the Cave du Felibrige at 18 rue des Cordeliers. For fresh, soft, hard, high or creamy cheeses of all shapes, sizes and smells, head for Fromagerie des Augustins at rue Espariat.

And what sweeter way to end that sunny summer picnic than with a couple of calissons from Bechard Fabrique de Calissons, 12 cours Mirabeau, a classy *pâtisserie* and *confiseur*. Aix's traditional almond confections weigh in here at 17FF per 100g (50FF per 100g including ornate packaging). Designer chocolates are sold at Rich Art, 6 rue Thiers, open 9.30 am to 12.30 pm and 3 to 7 pm.

Getting There & Away

Bus Aix's bus station is located on the southern side of ave de l'Europe, a 10-minute walk south-west from La Rotonda (off map). It is served by numerous companies. The information office (☎ 04 42 27 17 91) opens 7.30 am to 6.30 pm Monday to Saturday. In July and August it also opens 9 am to 5.30 pm on Sunday.

There are buses to Marseilles (28FF, 35 minutes via the autoroute/one hour via the N8, every five to 10 minutes), Arles (68FF, 1¾ hours, two daily); Avignon via the autoroute (87FF, one hour, six daily) or via the national road (72FF, 1½ hours, four daily) and Toulon (84FF, one hour, four daily).

Sumian buses serve Apt, Castellane and the Gorges du Verdon via La Palud (see the Gorges du Verdon section for details).

Train Aix's tiny train station, at the southern end of ave Victor Hugo, opens 5.45 am to 9.45 pm. The information office (☎ 0 836 35 35 35) opens daily 9 am to 5.30 pm. Luggage lockers (15FF to 20FF) are accessible between 5 am and 10 pm. There are frequent services to Briançon (175FF, 3½ hours), Gap (134FF, two hours) and, of course, Marseilles (38FF, 35 minutes, at least 18 daily), from where there are connections to just about everywhere.

Getting Around

Bus The city's 14 bus and three minibus lines are operated by Aix en Bus (☎ 04 42 26 37 28), whose information desk inside the tourist office opens 10 am to 6 pm (10 am to 12.30 pm Saturday; closed Sunday).

La Rotonde is the main bus hub. Most services run until 8 pm. A single/carnet of 10 bus tickets costs 7/44FF. Minibus No 1 links the train and bus stations with La Rotonde and cours Mirabeau. Minibus 2 starts at the bus station and then follows much the same route.

Taxi Taxis can usually be found outside the bus station. To order one, call Taxi Radio Aixois (☎ 04 42 27 71 11) or Taxi Mirabeau (☎ 04 42 21 61 61).

The Vaucluse

The Vaucluse is Provence at its most picturesque. Many of the area's towns date from Roman times and still boast impressive Gallo-Roman structures. The villages, which spring to life on market days, are surrounded by some of France's most attractive countryside, brightened by the rich hues of wild herbs, lavender and vines. The Vaucluse is watched over by Mont Ventoux, which at 1909m is Provence's highest peak.

Geography

The Vaucluse is shaped like a fan, with Avignon, the region's capital, at the hinge. Orange, famed for its Roman theatre, and the smaller Roman town of Vaison-la-Romaine are north of Avignon and west of Mont Ventoux. Carpentras, near the centre of the Vaucluse, also dates from Roman times but is better known for its ancient Jewish community. Just to the south is Fontaine de Vaucluse, to the east of which are Gordes and Roussillon, enticing Provençal villages overlooking a fertile valley. Farther east

still is Apt, one of the best bases for exploring the Lubéron range to the south.

Getting Around

If you don't have access to a car, it is possible to get from town to town by local bus, but the frequency and pace of services are very much in keeping with the relaxed tempo of Provençal life.

AVIGNON

postcode 84000 • pop 85,935

Avignon entered this millennium as the European Capital of Culture. It acquired its ramparts and its reputation as a city of art and culture during the 14th century, when Pope Clement V and his court fled political turmoil in Rome and established themselves near Avignon. From 1309 to 1377, the Holy See was based in the city under seven French-born popes, and huge sums of money were invested in building and decorating the papal palace and other important church edifices. Under the popes' tolerant rule, the city became a place of asylum for Jews and political dissidents.

Opponents of the move to Avignon – many of them Italians, like the celebrated poet Petrarch, who lived in Fontaine de Vaucluse at the time – called Avignon 'the second Babylonian captivity' and charged that the city had become a den of criminals and brothel-goers, and was unfit for papal habitation. Pope Gregory XI left Avignon in 1376, but his death two years later led to the Great Schism (1378–1417), during which rival popes – up to three at one time, each with his own College of Cardinals – resided at Rome and Avignon and spent most of their energies denouncing and excommunicating one another. They also expended great efforts on gaining control of church revenues, among whose sources was the sale of indulgences.

Even after the schism was settled and a pope – Martin V – acceptable to all factions established himself in Rome, Avignon remained under papal rule and continued to serve as an important cultural centre. The city and the nearby Comtat Venaissin (now the department of Vaucluse) were ruled by

PROVENCE

AVIGNON

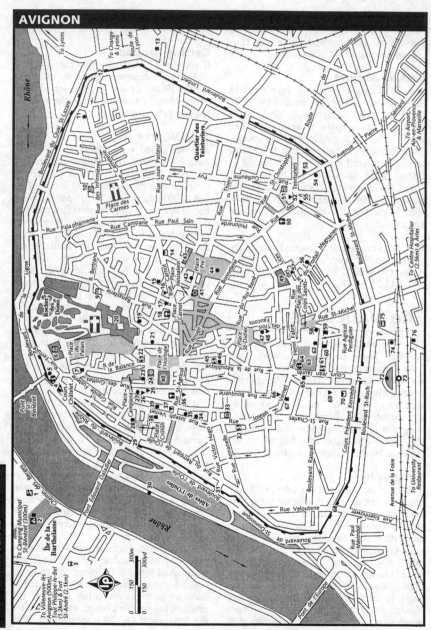

AVIGNON

PLACES TO STAY		69	Restaurant Le St-Louis
2	Camping Bagatelle; Auberge Bagatelle		
7	Hôtel du Palais des Papes		**OTHER**
13	Avignon Squash Club	1	Swimming Pool
15	Hôtel Médiéval	3	La Barthelasse Bus Stop
19	Hôtel de la Mirande	4	Pont St-Bénézet Tourist Office
28	Hôtel L'Europe	5	Tour de Châtelet; Entrance to Pont St-Bénézet
38	Hôtel Mignon		
39	Hôtel Le Provençal	6	Musée du Petit Palais
59	Hôtel Colbert	8	Cathédrale Notre Dame des Doms
60	Hôtel Splendid		
62	Hôtel du Parc	9	La Manutention (Cinéma Utopia)
67	Hôtel Innova		
76	Hôtel Monclar	10	CyberHighway
		11	Shakespeare Bookshop
PLACES TO EAT		12	Porte St-Lazare
16	Restaurant Song Long	14	Branch Post Office
17	Le Belgocargo	18	Église St-Pierre
25	Natural Café; La Fourchette	20	Palais des Papes
26	Simple Simon Tea Lunch	21	Bureau du Festival
36	Boulangerie Pâtisserie	22	Banque de France
37	Casino Grocery	23	Maison des Pays de Vaucluse
48	Le Caveau du Théâtre; Les Caulisses		
		24	Opéra d'Avignon
52	Sindabad	27	Le Val d'Arômes
53	Restaurant Au 19éme	29	Porte de l'Oulle
55	Woolloomooloo	30	Mireio Embarcadère
57	Le Petit Comptoir	31	Porte St-Dominique
66	La Cuisine de Reine	32	Caixa Bank

33	Musée Calvet
34	Université d'Avignon
35	Puyricard
40	Town Hall
41	Synagogue
42	TCRA Bus Information Kiosk
43	Palais de Justice
44	Les Halles
45	Lyonnais de Banque
46	FNAC
47	Maison des Vins
49	École des Beaux-Arts
50	Chapelle des Pénitents Gris
51	Cyberdrome
54	Cycles Peugeot
56	Laundrette
58	Laundrette
61	Change Chaix Conseil
63	Square Agricol Perdiguier
64	Tourist Office
65	Maison de la Presse
68	Porte St-Roch
70	Main Post Office; Bus No 10 stop
71	Porte de la République; Local Bus Information Office
72	Pont d'Argent
73	Train Station
74	Car Rental Agencies
75	Bus Station

papal legates until 1791, when they were annexed to France.

Today, Avignon continues its traditional role as a patron of the arts, most notably through its annual performing arts festival. Avignon's other attractions include the pont d'Avignon, a bustling walled city, and a number of interesting museums.

Orientation

The main avenue within the walled city (intra-muros) runs northwards from the train station to place de l'Horloge; it's called cours Jean Jaurès south of the tourist office and rue de la République north of it.

Place de l'Horloge is 300m south of place du Palais, which abuts the Palais des Papes. The city gate nearest the train station is Porte de la République, while the city gate next to pont Édouard Daladier, which leads to Villeneuve-lès-Avignon, is Porte de l'Oulle. The rehabilitated Quartier des Teinturiers (old dyers' quarter), centred around rue des Teinturiers, south-east of place Pie, is Avignon's bohemian – and increasingly trendy – part of town.

Information

Tourist Offices The tourist office (☎ 04 32 74 32 74, fax 04 90 82 95 03, @ information @ot-avignon.fr), 41 cours Jean Jaurès, is 300m north of the train station. It opens 9 am to 6 pm (5 pm on Saturday, 10 am to midday on Sunday). During the Avignon Festival it opens 10 am to 8 pm daily (5 pm on Sunday).

Between 1 April and 31 October, two-hour city tours (in English and French; 50FF, children 30FF) depart from the tourist office on Tuesday and Thursday at 10 am.

At the pont St-Bénézet, the Espace St-Bénézet tourist office annexe opens 9 am to 7 pm daily May to September.

PROVENCE

Money The Banque de France, at the northern end of place de l'Horloge, opens Monday to Friday 8.35 am to 12.05 pm and 1.35 to 3.35 pm.

There are 24-hour currency exchange machines at the Lyonnais de Banque, 13 rue de la République, and at the Caixa Bank, 67 rue Joseph Vernet. There is a convenient ATM in the train station forecourt.

The Change Chaix Conseil (☎ 04 90 27 27 89), 43 cours Jean Jaurès, opens 10 am to 1 pm and 3 to 7 pm April to October. In July and August it opens 8.30 am to 8.30 pm.

Post & Communications The main post office, on cours Président Kennedy, opens 8 am to 7 pm (Saturday until noon; closed Sunday). Currency exchange stops at 5 pm on weekdays and 11 am on Saturday. The branch on the corner of rue Carnot and rue Général Leclerc opens 8.30 am to noon and 1.30 to 6.30 pm (Saturday until noon; closed Sunday).

Cyberdrome (☎ 04 90 16 05 15, fax 04 90 16 05 14, ✆ cyberdrome@wanadoo.fr) charges 25FF for 30 minutes on-line access or 400FF for 10 hours and opens 7 am to 1 am.

CyberHighway (☎ 04 90 27 02 09, ✆ CyberHighway@wanadoo.fr) at 30 rue des Infirmières, between place des Carmes and rue Cabassole charges 30FF an hour or offers five-hour bulk rates for 120FF.

Bookshops Maison de la Presse (☎ 04 90 86 57 42), opposite the tourist office at 34 cours Jean Jaurès, has a good selection of maps and French-language regional guides. Alternatively, try Shakespeare (☎ 04 90 27 38 50), 155 rue Carreterie, an English bookshop and *salon de thé* open 9.30 am to 12.30 pm and 2 to 6.30 pm Tuesday to Saturday.

Laundry Lavmatic, 27 rue du Portail Magnanen, opens 7 am to 7.30 pm. Laverie La Fontaine, 66 place des Corps Saints, opens 7 am to 8 pm.

Medical Services The Centre Hospitalier (☎ 04 90 80 12 90), 2.5km south of the train station on rue Raoul Follereau, is at the southern terminus of bus line Nos 1 and 3 (marked on bus maps as 'Hôpital Sud').

Pont St-Bénézet (Le Pont d'Avignon)

St Bénézet's bridge (☎ 04 90 85 60 16) was built between 1177 and 1185 to link Avignon with the settlement across the Rhône that later became Villeneuve-lès-Avignon. By tradition, the construction of the bridge is said to have begun when Bénézet (Benedict the Bridge Builder), a pastor from Ardèche, was told in three visions to get the Rhône spanned at any cost. Yes, this is also the **Pont d'Avignon** mentioned in the French nursery rhyme. In actual fact, people did not dance *sur le pont d'Avignon* (on the bridge of Avignon) but *sous* (under) it in between the arches.

The 900m-long wooden structure was repaired and rebuilt several times before all but four of its 22 spans – over both channels of the Rhône and the island in the middle, Île de la Barthelasse – were washed away once and for all in the mid-1600s.

Admission to the bridge via cours Châtelet costs 17FF (students 9FF). It opens 9 am to 7 pm daily. Between 1 October and 31 March it opens 9.30 am to 5.30 pm. Many people find a distant view of the bridge from the Rocher des Doms or Pont Édouard Daladier much more interesting. And it is, of course, free.

Walled City

Avignon's most interesting bits are within the roughly oval walled city, which is surrounded by almost 4.5km of ramparts built between 1359 and 1370. The ramparts were restored during the 19th century, but the original moats were not, leaving the crenellated fortifications looking purposeless and certainly less imposing than they once did. Even in the 14th century this defence system was hardly state-of-the-art: the towers were left open on the side facing the city, and machicolations (openings in the parapets for dropping things like boiling oil or for shooting arrows at attackers) are lacking in many sections.

Doctor, Philosopher & Prophet

It has been over 440 years since the first publication of *The Centuries* by Nostradamus. This 10-volume collection of verse predicted the entire future history from the time of Nostradamus until the end of all time.

Nostradamus was born Michel de Nostradame on 15 December 1403 in the Provençal town of St-Rémy. He was the son of Jewish converts to Christianity who had fled the Spanish Inquisition. In his time he was known as a great thinker, a physician and *chef de cuisine*.

For many years he ran a successful practice as a doctor while indulging in his passion for cooking. His recipes for health-giving jams were widely popular among the people of St-Rémy. But his reputation as a physician eventually fell into disrepute when the plague swept Europe decimating even his own family – something which Michel could not prevent. He moved to Salon-de Provence near Aix-en-Provence, called himself Nostradamus and took to star-gazing and dabbling in astrology, eventually producing his first *Almanac* in 1550. This consisted of 12 four-line poems, or quatrains, which predicted events for each month of the year ahead. These were so popular that he began to write one for each year.

By 1558 he had completed the last volume of his monumental work *The Centuries*. When he correctly predicted the death of the King of France in 1559, his star as a seer was at its ascendancy. He was seen as a genius among the intelligentsia of his time, but as a demon by the under-educated peasant class. His works are still in print and still widely read and among the prophesies allegedly made and proved correct by subsequent history is the rise of Hitler and the death of President Kennedy.

Palais des Papes The huge Gothic Palace of the Popes (☎ 04 90 27 50 74), place du Palais, was built during the 14th century as a fortified palace for the pontifical court. It is mainly of interest because of the dramatic events that took place here, since the undecorated stone halls, though impressive, are nearly empty except for occasional art exhibits. The best view of the Palais des Papes complex is from across the river along the chemin des Berges on the Île de la Barthelasse. The fabulous cours d'Honneur – the palace's main courtyard – has played host to the Avignon theatre festival since 1947. Tickets range in price from 120FF to 200FF.

The Palais des Papes opens 9 am to 7 pm (9 pm in July and 8 pm in August and September). Admission to the palace's interior costs 45FF (36FF with the Pass, students 37FF); this includes hire of a very user-friendly audioguide in English. One-hour guided tours are available in English from April to October, usually at 11.30 am and 2.30 and 4.45 pm. Occasionally, special exhibits may raise the admission charges by 10FF or more.

Musée du Petit Palais This museum (☎ 04 90 86 44 58), which served as a bishop's and archbishop's palace during the 14th and 15th centuries, is at the far northern end of place du Palais. It houses an outstanding collection of 13th- to 16th-century Italian religious paintings. It opens 9.30 am to noon and 2 to 6 pm (closed Tuesday). It opens 10 am to 6 pm in July and August. Admission costs 30FF (15FF with Pass and for students).

Rocher des Doms Just up the hill from the cathedral is the Rocher des Doms, a delightful bluff-top park that affords great views of the Rhône, Pont St-Bénézet, Villeneuve-lès-Avignon and the Alpilles. A semicircular viewpoint indicator tells you what you're looking at.

Musée Calvet Musée Calvet (☎ 04 90 86 33 84), 65 rue Joseph Vernet, housed in the elegant Hôtel de Villeneuve-Martignan (1741–54), has a large archaeological collection of artefacts from prehistory to Roman times and paintings from the 16th

PROVENCE

to 20th centuries. Admission costs 30FF (students and seniors 15FF). It opens 10 am to 1 pm and 2 to 6 pm (closed Tuesday; 10 am to 7 pm from June to September).

Boat Excursions

Les Grands Bateaux de Provence (☎ 04 90 85 62 25, fax 04 90 85 61 14), based at the Mireio Embarcadère on allées de l'Oulle, opposite the Porte de l'Oulle, runs excursions from Avignon down the Rhône to Arles, vineyard towns and even the Camargue (160FF to 345FF including a meal, four to seven hours).

Bateau Bus (same contact details) makes less ambitious trips seven times daily in July and August to Villeneuve-lès-Avignon (near the Tour de Philippe le Bel) and back (35FF, children 18FF, 1½ hours).

Organised Tours

Autocars Lieutard (☎ 04 90 86 36 75, fax 04 90 85 57 07, ✉ cars.lieutard@wanadoo.fr), based at the bus station, offers a variety of thematic bus tours between April and October, including to Nîmes and the Pont du Gard (100FF, 4½ hours), Vaison-la-Romaine and Orange (100FF, 4½ hours), the Lubéron (100FF, 4½ hours) and to the wine cellars at Châteauneuf-du-Pape (100FF, three hours).

Special Events

The world-famous Festival d'Avignon, founded in the late 1940s, is held every year from early July to early August. It attracts many hundreds of performance artists (actors, dancers and musicians) who put on some 300 *spectacles* of all sorts each day in every imaginable venue. There are, in fact, two simultaneous events: the prestigious, expensive and government-subsidised official festival, and the fringe one called Festival Off.

Tickets for official festival performances in the Palais des Papes' cours d'Honneur cost 130FF to 190FF. A Carte Public Adhérent (65FF) gets you a 30% discount on all Festival Off performances.

Information on the official festival can be obtained by contacting the Bureau du Festival (☎ 04 90 27 66 50, fax 04 90 27 66 83), 8 bis rue de Mons, F-84000 Avignon. Tickets can be reserved from mid-June.

Places to Stay

During the festival, it's practically impossible to find a hotel room unless you've reserved months in advance. The tourist office has information on special dormitory accommodation. Hotel rooms are readily available in August, however, when places in the rest of the Vaucluse department are at a premium. Hotel and gîtes reservations anywhere in Vaucluse can be made through the Maison des Pays de Vaucluse (☎ 04 90 82 05 81, fax 04 90 86 54 77), place Campana.

Places to Stay – Budget

Camping Three-star *Camping Bagatelle* (☎ 04 90 86 30 39, *Île de la Barthelasse*) open year round, is an attractive, shaded camp site just north of pont Édouard Daladier, 850m from the walled city. High season charges are 23.80FF per adult, 11FF to pitch a tent and 7FF for parking. Reception opens 8 am to 9 pm, but you can arrive any time. Take bus No 10 from in front of the main post office to the La Barthelasse stop. Follow the river to the camp site.

Four-star *Camping Municipal St-Bénézet* (☎ 04 90 82 63 50, *chemin de la Barthelasse*), is a bit farther north. It opens 1 March to 31 October, and costs 52/70.50FF in the low/high season for two people plus a tent site and parking.

Hostels The 210-bed *Auberge Bagatelle* (☎ 04 90 85 78 45, fax 04 90 27 16 23) is part of a large, park-like area on Île de la Barthelasse that includes Camping Bagatelle. A bed in a rather cramped room costs 60FF.

From April to September a bunk in a converted squash court at the *Avignon Squash Club* (☎ 04 90 85 27 78, *32 blvd Limbert*) costs 60FF. Reception opens 9 am to 10 pm (closed Sunday from September to June; open 8 to 11 am and 5 to 11 pm in July and August). Take bus No 7 from the train station to the Université stop.

Hotels – Within the Walls There are three hotels all close to each other on the same street; if one is full, try the next one. One-star **Hôtel Le Parc** (☎ 04 90 82 71 55, 18 rue Agricol Perdiguier), offers singles/doubles without shower for 145/175FF and 195/215FF with shower.

Friendly, one-star **Hôtel Splendid** (☎ 04 90 86 14 46, fax 04 90 85 38 55, 17 rue Agricol Perdiguier), has rooms with shower for 130/200FF and with shower and toilet for 170/280FF. The hotel rents bikes too (see the Getting Around section).

The third in the trio, two-star **Hôtel Colbert** (☎ 04 90 86 20 20, fax 04 90 85 97 00, 7 rue Agricol Perdiguier), smells of disinfectant but has well-priced singles with shower for 160FF and doubles/triples with shower and toilet for 210/260FF.

Always busy one-star **Hôtel Innova** (☎ 04 90 82 54 10, fax 04 90 82 52 39, 100 rue Joseph Vernet), has bright, comfortable and soundproofed rooms ranging in price from 140FF to 220FF. Breakfast costs 25FF.

One-star **Hôtel Mignon** (☎ 04 90 82 17 30, fax 04 90 85 78 46, 12 rue Joseph Vernet), has spotless, well kept and soundproofed singles with shower costing 150FF and doubles with shower and toilet costing 220FF.

Hotels – Outside the Walls The noisy, family-run **Hôtel Monclar** (☎ 04 90 86 20 14, fax 04 90 85 94 94, ✆ hmonclar84@ aol.com, 13 Ave Monclar), is in an 18th-century building just across the tracks from the train station. Eminently serviceable doubles start at 165FF with sink and bidet. The hotel has its own car park (30FF) and a pretty little back garden.

Places to Stay – Mid-Range

Two-star **Hôtel Le Provençal** (☎ 04 90 85 25 24, fax 04 90 82 75 81, 13 rue Joseph Vernet), has singles/doubles with toilet for 180FF and rooms with shower, toilet and TV for 240FF.

Very charming, old-world **Hôtel du Palais des Papes** (☎ 04 90 86 04 13, fax 04 90 27 91 17, 1 rue Gérard Philippe), has doubles with shower, TV and toilet for 280FF to 480FF; the pricier rooms sport a view of the Palais des Papes. Triples start at 520FF and dogs cost an extra 50FF.

Splendid two-star **Hôtel Médiéval** (☎ 04 90 86 11 06, fax 04 90 82 08 64, 15 rue Petite Saunerie), housed in a restored 17th-century house down a quiet street not far from the Palais des Papes, has singles/doubles with all the trimmings from 240FF to 320FF. It also has studios to rent on a weekly, monthly or long-term basis.

Places to Stay – Top End

'A place of pilgrimage for men and women of taste' is how the French newspaper Le Figaro summed up four-star **Hôtel de la Mirande** (☎ 04 90 85 93 93, fax 04 90 86 26 85, 4 place de la Mirande), Avignon's most exclusive hotel, housed in a former 14th-century cardinal's palace behind the Palais des Papes. Exquisitely furnished rooms start at 1700FF (1850FF April to October). The hotel has its own cooking school.

Four star **Hôtel L'Europe** (☎ 04 90 14 76 76, fax 04 90 14 76 71, ✆ reservations@ hotel-d-europe.fr, 12 place Crillon), is cheap in comparison – rooms cost 690FF to 2000FF (dogs an extra 50FF), breakfast costs 98FF and menus in its restaurant cost 285FF and 420FF.

Places to Eat

From Easter until mid-November, half of place de l'Horloge is taken over by tourist restaurants and cafes. Menus start at about 75FF. Many restaurants open just for the festival; most have special festival menus.

Restaurants – place de l'Horloge & Around For hearty and healthy fodder in a rustic setting (tree trunks for benches etc) look no farther than atmospheric **Natural Café** (☎ 04 90 85 90 82, 17 rue Racine); it opens Tuesday to Saturday. Adjoining it is more conventional **La Fourchette** (☎ 04 90 85 20 93, 17 rue Racine), a Michelin-recommended place with menus for 150FF. 'The Fork' is open Monday to Friday.

Nearby, **Simple Simon Tea Lunch** (☎ 04 90 86 62 70, 26 rue Petite Fusterie), is an endearing, très anglais place for an afternoon

PROVENCE

cuppa (20FF to 23FF) with cake, pie, scones or cheesecake (27FF). Light meals (45FF to 85FF) are available all afternoon. Simple Simon closes on Sunday and in August.

South of the square is *Le Caveau du Théâtre* (☎ 04 90 82 60 91, 16 rue des Trois Faucons). It has a lunchtime *formule* comprising a *tarte salée* (savoury tart) and dessert costing 65FF and 110FF evening *menus*. You can also taste wine here, also possible at less formal *Les Caulisses* next door.

Both open noon to 2 pm and 7.30 to 10.30 pm, and are closed Saturday and Sunday lunchtime.

Heading east from place de l'Horloge, you come to rue Carnot, home to a handful of Vietnamese and Chinese places. *Restaurant Song Long* (☎ 04 90 86 35 00, 1 rue Carnot) offers a wide variety of excellent Vietnamese dishes, including 16 *plats végétariens* (vegetarian soups, salads, starters and main dishes from 28FF to 40FF). Lunch/dinner *menus* are 35FF, 40FF and 45FF. Song Long opens daily.

Le Belgocargo (☎ 04 90 85 72 99, 7 rue Armand de Pontmartin), a Belgian place tucked behind Église St-Pierre, serves mussels 16 different ways for 49FF to 68FF and *waterzooi de volaille* (a creamy Belgian stew of chicken, leeks and herbs) costing 58FF. Swill it down with a glass of cherry-flavoured kriek beer, served on tap.

Restaurants – Quartier des Teinturiers

Rue des Teinturiers is one of Avignon's most fun streets by both day and night. Pleasant bohemian-style restaurants and bistros include small *Sindabad* (☎ 04 90 14 69 45, 53 rue des Teinturiers), which offers good Tunisian, Asian and Provençal home cooking. It has a 50FF *plat du jour* and opens from noon and from 6 pm Monday to Saturday.

The highlight is *Woolloomooloo* (☎ 04 90 85 28 44, 16 rue des Teinturiers), next to a large working water wheel. Each week the jumble of eclectic antique and contemporary furnishings is rearranged to create a 'new look' for this eccentric restaurant. *Menus* cost around 67FF to 89FF and there

are vegetarian and Antillean dishes too. Woolloomooloo opens from noon and from 7.30 pm (closed Sunday and Monday).

On the western fringe of the old dyers' quarter is *Le Petit Comptoir* (☎ 04 90 86 10 94, 52 rue des Lices), opposite the crumbling arched facade of *très belle* École des Beaux-Arts. This tiny, eight-table place offers diners the choice of a main course and dessert or entrée for 40FF, or all three for 70FF. The pork kebab marinated in lemon and ginger is particularly tasty.

For a more classical approach, try the very refined *Restaurant Au 19éme* (☎ 04 90 27 16 00, 75 rue Guillaume Puy), housed in the 19th-century townhouse where absinthe beverage inventor Jules Pernod once lived. It hosts live jazz on Saturday evening, harp recitals on Friday evening, and has lunchtime/evening *menus* costing from 95/130FF (closed Saturday lunchtime and Monday evening).

Restaurants – Top End

Elegant restaurant and *salon de thé La Cuisine de Reine* (☎ 04 90 85 99 04, 83 rue Joseph Vernet) opposite the Hôtel Innova inside Le Cloître des Arts, is wrapped around an 18th-century courtyard. *Menus* start at 120FF and include a surprise *pique-nique à la maison* comprising smoked meats, olives and crusty bread. Calorie-killer cakes and pastries are served in its heavenly art cafe. It is open Tuesday to Saturday.

Equally worth the cash are the gastronomic feasts served at *Restaurant Le St-Louis* (☎ 04 90 27 55 55, 20 rue du Portail Boquier), overlooking a fabulous 16th-century cloister courtyard dominated by a huge moss-covered fountain. Lunch/dinner *menus* start at 99/140FF.

The *restaurant universitaire* of the Faculté de Droit (Law Faculty), south-west of the train station on ave du Blanchissage, opens October to June except during university holidays. Meals are served from 11.30 am to 1.30 pm and 6.30 to 7.30 pm (closed Saturday evening and Sunday). People with student cards can buy tickets (about 15FF or 30FF) at the CROUS office (☎ 04 90 82 42 18), 29 blvd Limbert, open

PROVENCE

10.30 am to 12.30 pm Monday, Tuesday, Wednesday and Friday.

Self-Catering Les Halles on place Pie has a *food market* open 7 am to 1 pm Tuesday to Sunday. The complex opens 6 am to 1.30 pm.

Near place de l'Horloge, the *Boulangerie Pâtisserie (17 rue St-Agricol)* opens 7.45 am to 7.30 pm (closed Sunday). *Casino* grocery, 22 rue St-Agricol, opens 8 am to 12.45 pm and 3 to 7.30 pm Monday to Saturday.

Entertainment

For information on the Festival d'Avignon and Festival Off, see Special Events earlier in this section. Tickets for many cultural events and performances are sold at the tourist office.

Events listings are included in the free *César* weekly magazine and in the tourist office's fortnightly newsletter, *Rendez-vous d'Avignon*. Tickets for most events are sold at FNAC (☎ 04 90 14 35 35), 19 rue de la République, open 10 am to 7 pm Monday to Saturday.

The **Opéra d'Avignon** (☎ 04 90 82 23 44), housed in an imposing structure built in 1847, place de l'Horloge, stages operas, operettas, plays, symphonic concerts, chamber music concerts and ballet from June. The box office opens 11 am to 6 pm Monday to Saturday.

Cinemas The Cinéma Utopia (☎ 04 90 82 65 36), 4 rue des Escaliers Ste-Anne, La Manutention complex (follow the 'Promenade des Papes' signs east from place du Palais), is a student entertainment/cultural centre with a jazz club, cafe and four cinemas screening nondubbed films (30FF). Its programme is featured in the free weekly *Utopia*.

Shopping

Luxury local foods in jars, tins and bottles are sold at upmarket Le Val d'Arômes, 28 rue Petite Fusterie. Puyricard, 33 rue Joseph Vernet, is the place for designer chocolate.

Getting There & Away

Air Avignon-Caumont airport (☎ 04 90 81 51 51) is 8km south-east of Avignon.

Bus The bus station (*halte routière*; ☎ 04 90 82 07 35) is in the basement of the building down the ramp to the right as you exit the train station on blvd St-Roch. The information window opens 8 am to noon and 1.30 to 6 pm Saturday until noon; it is closed Sunday. You can leave luggage here (10FF). Tickets are sold on the buses, which are run by about 20 different companies.

Places you can get to by bus include Aix-en-Provence (90FF for the one-hour trip via the highway, 82FF for the 1½-hour trip along secondary roads, four to six daily), Arles (40FF, 1½ hours, four or five direct daily), Carpentras (23FF, 45 minutes, about 15 daily), Marseilles (92FF, 35 minutes by direct bus, seven daily), Montélimar (68FF, two hours), Nice (168FF, one daily), Nîmes (43FF, 1¼ hours, five daily) and Orange (31FF, 40 minutes, about 20 daily). Most lines operate on Sunday at reduced frequency.

Long-haul bus companies Linebus (☎ 04 90 85 30 48) and Eurolines (☎ 04 90 85 27 60) have offices at the far end of the bus platforms.

Train The train station (☎ 0 836 35 35 35) is across blvd St-Roch from Porte de la République. The information counters open 9 am to 6.15 pm (closed Sunday). The left-luggage room, to the left as you exit the station, opens 6 am to 9.30 pm. Luggage left in the automatic lockers (security-controlled) costs 15FF to 30FF depending on size. Luggage left with the luggage guardian costs a standard 30FF per 24 hours or part thereof.

There are frequent trains to Arles (36FF, 20 minutes, 14 to 18 daily), Marseilles (92FF, one hour), Nice (206FF, 2½ hours), Nîmes (46FF, 30 minutes, 15 daily), Orange (29FF, 20 minutes, 17 daily) and, by TGV, Paris' Gare de Lyon (370FF, 3¼ hours).

Car Most car rental agencies are signposted from the train station. Europcar (☎ 04 90 85 01 40) is in the Ibis building. Budget (☎ 04 90 27 34 95) is down the ramp to the right

PROVENCE

as you exit the station, and Hertz (☎ 04 90 82 37 67) is at 4 blvd St-Michel.

Getting Around

Bus Local TCRA bus tickets cost 6.50FF each if bought from the driver; a carnet of five tickets (good for 10 rides) costs 48FF at TCRA offices. Buses run from 7 am to about 7.40 pm (8 am to 6 pm and less frequently on Sunday). The two most important bus transfer points are the Poste stop at the main post office and place Pie.

Carnets and free bus maps *(plan du réseau)* are available at the Point d'Accueil-Vente (☎ 04 90 82 68 19) in the tower wall (La Tourelle) of the old city at Porte de la République across from the train station, and from the Espace Bus kiosk (☎ 04 90 85 44 93), place Pie. Both open 8.15 am to noon and 1.45 to 6.30 pm (8.45 am to noon on Saturday).

Villeneuve-lès-Avignon is linked with Avignon by bus No 10, which stops in front of Avignon's main post office and on the western side of the walled city near Porte de l'Oulle.

Taxi Pick up a taxi outside the train station or call the place Pie taxi stand (☎ 04 90 82 20 20), open 24 hours.

Bicycle Cycles Peugeot (☎ 04 90 86 32 49), 80 rue Guillaume Puy, has three-speeds and 10-speeds for 60/130/240FF for one day/three days/a week (plus 1000FF deposit). It opens 8 am to noon and 2 to 7 pm Monday to Saturday.

Hôtel Splendid (☎ 04 90 23 96 08), 17 rue Agricol Perdiguier, rents mountain bikes for 100/180/650FF per day/weekend/week (plus 2500FF deposit).

AROUND AVIGNON

Twenty-five kilometres south of Avignon, past the small town of **St-Rémy de Provence** (population 9340), is **Les Baux de Provence** (population 468), vividly immortalised on canvas by van Gogh during his stay in an asylum in 1889–90. This fortified village, named after the 245m-high *baou* (rocky spur) on which it is perched, pulls in some 2.5 million tourists a year (putting it on a par with Mont St-Michel in Normandy as one of France's biggest tourist attractions outside of Paris).

The most pleasant time to visit the Château des Baux (☎ 04 90 54 55 56), a former feudal home of Monaco's Grimaldi royal family, is early evening after the caterpillar of tourist coaches has evacuated the village for the day. It opens 7 am to 7.30 pm, until 8.30 pm in July and August. Admission costs 47FF.

The tourist office (☎ 04 90 54 34 39, fax 04 90 54 51 51) has information on Les Baux's few accommodation options. Note, there is no free parking within 800m of the village. Park for free at the carpark of the **Cathédrale d'Images** – a rather uninspiring and very overpriced (47FF) sound and light show set in a former quarry cave just north of the village. From here you can easily walk back to Les Baux.

Villeneuve-lès-Avignon

Villeneuve-lès-Avignon is across the Rhône from Avignon (and in a different department), was founded in the late 13th century. It became known as the City of Cardinals because many primates affiliated with the papal court built large residences in the town, despite the fact that it was in territory ruled by the French crown and not the pope. Avignon's picturesque sister city also has a few interesting sights, all of which are included in a 45FF combined ticket sold at the major sights. From Avignon, Villeneuve can be reached by foot or bus No 10 (from the main post office).

Chartreuse du Val de Bénédiction, 60 rue de la République, was once the largest and most important Carthusian monastery in France (32/21FF). **Musée Pierre de Luxembourg** on rue de la République has a fine collection of religious paintings; it's open from Tuesday to Sunday (20/12FF; closed February).

Tour Philippe-le-Bel, a defensive tower built in the 14th century at what was then the north-western end of pont St-Bénézet, has great views of Avignon's walled city, the river and the surrounding countryside.

Admission costs 10FF. Another Provençal panorama can be enjoyed from 14th-century **Fort St-André** (25FF, students 15FF).

ORANGE

postcode 84100 • pop 27,989

Through a 16th-century marriage with the German House of Nassau, the House of Orange (the princely dynasty that had ruled Orange since the 12th century) became active in the history of the Netherlands and later, through William III (William of Orange), also in England. Orange (Arenja in Provençal), which had earlier been a stronghold of the Reformation, was ceded to France in 1713 by the Treaty of Utrecht, but to this day many members of the royal house of the Netherlands are known as the princes and princesses of Orange-Nassau.

Orientation

The train station is just over 1km east of place de la République, the city centre, along ave Frédéric Mistral and rue de la République. Rue St-Martin links place de la République and nearby place Clemenceau with the tourist office, which is 250m to the west. **Théâtre Antique**, Orange's magnificent Roman theatre, is two blocks south of place de la République. The tiny River Meyne lies north of the centre. From the train station, bus No 2 from rue Jean Reboul (first left after exiting the station) goes to the Théâtre Antique or République stop.

Information

Tourist Office Orange's tourist office (☎ 04 90 34 70 88, fax 04 90 34 99 62, ✉ officetourisme@infonie.fr), 5 cours Aristide Briand, opens 9 am to 6 pm Monday to Saturday (from April to September 9 am to 7 pm and 10 am to 6 pm on Sunday).

Money The Banque de France at 5 rue Frédéric Mistral opens 8.30 am to noon and 1.30 to 3.30 pm weekdays.

Post The post office, opposite the bus station on blvd Édouard Daladier, opens 8.30 am to 6.30 pm (8 am to noon Saturday; closed Sunday).

Laundry The laundrette at 5 rue St-Florent opens 7 am to 8 pm.

Théâtre Antique

Orange's magnificent Roman theatre (☎ 04 90 51 17 60), designed to seat about 10,000 spectators, was probably built during the time of Augustus Caesar (ruled 27 BC to 14 AD). Its **stage wall** *(mur de scène)*, the only such Roman structure still standing in its entirety (minus a few mosaics and the roof), is 103m wide and almost 37m high. Its plain exterior can be viewed from adjacent place des Frères Mounets to the north.

For a panoramic view of the Roman masterpiece, follow Montée Philbert de Chalons or Montée Lambert to the top of **Colline St-Eutrope** (St-Eutrope Hill; elevation 97m), where a circular viewing table explains what's what. En route you pass the ruins of a 12th-century **chateau**, the former residence of the princes of Orange.

Those not into walking can always hop aboard the 54-seat **Orangeois tourist train** that departs every 30 minutes or so from outside the Théâtre Antique. The city tour (25FF) lasts one hour and takes in all the major sights as well as scaling the Colline St-Eutrope.

The theatre opens 9 am to 6.30 pm from April to early October, (9 am to noon and 1.30 to 5 pm during the rest of the year). Admission costs 30FF (students 25FF).

Arc de Triomphe

Orange's Roman triumphal arch, one of the most remarkable of its kind in France, is at the northern end of plane tree-lined ave de l'Arc de Triomphe about 450m from the centre of town. Probably built around 20 BC, it is 19m in height and width, and 8m thick. The exceptional friezes commemorate Julius Caesar's victories over the Gauls in 49 BC, triumphs of which the Romans wished to remind every traveller approaching the city. The arch has been restored several times since 1825.

Overlooking the eastern side of the arch is the local **pétanque court** where old men gather under the shade of the trees on sunny days to play Provençal *boules* (bowls).

PROVENCE

Special Events

In June and August, Théâtre Antique comes alive with all-night concerts, cinema screenings and various musical events during Les Nuits du Théâtre Antique. During the last fortnight in July, it plays host to Les Chorégies d'Orange, a series of weekend operas, classical concerts and choral performances. Seats (50FF to 900FF) for this prestigious festival have to be reserved months beforehand; it is possible to catch a free glimpse of the action from the lookout atop Colline St-Eutrope. Orange also plays host to a week-long jazz festival in June.

Tickets for events held in the Théâtre Antique can be reserved at the Location Théâtre Antique (☎ 04 90 34 24 24, fax 04 90 11 00 85), 14 place Silvain, which opens 9 am to noon and 2 to 5 pm weekdays. To buy tickets for other cultural events (including those held at the modern Palais des Princes, cours Pourtoules), go next door to the Service Culturel (☎ 04 90 51 57 57, fax 04 90 51 60 51), open 8.30 am to 5.30 pm weekdays.

Places to Stay

Camping Three-star *Camping Le Jonquier* (☎ 04 90 34 49 48, fax 04 90 34 16 97, 1321 rue Alexis Carrel), near the Arc de Triomphe, opens 1 April to 30 September. It charges 28FF per person and 30FF for a tent.

Take bus No 1 from the République stop (on ave Frédéric Mistral, 600m from the train station) to the Arc de Triomphe. From there, walk 100m back, turn right onto rue des Phocéens and right again onto rue des Étudiants. The camp site is across the football field.

Hotels The cheapest joint in town is *Bar Hôtel* (☎ 04 90 34 13 31, 22 rue Caristie), which has basic singles or doubles with shower for 140FF or with shower and toilet for 145FF. The reception is the bar downstairs.

Also cheap is the *Hôtel de la Gare* (☎ 04 90 34 00 23, fax 04 90 34 91 72, 60 ave Frédéric Mistral), next to the train station, where rooms start at 170FF.

A block north of the Théâtre Antique, the welcoming *Hôtel Arcotel* (☎ 04 90 34 09 23, fax 04 90 51 61 12, 8 place aux Herbes), has singles/doubles from 110FF to 300FF.

Around the corner, the atmospheric *Hôtel St-Florent* (☎ 04 90 34 18 53, fax 04 90 51 17 25, 4 rue du Mazeau), has great rooms with giant murals painted on the walls and fantastic antique wooden beds adorned with crushed and studded velvet. Rooms cost 170/210FF with shower.

Places to Eat

East of place Clemenceau, there are a number of moderately priced restaurants. The food at *Le Bambou* (☎ 04 90 51 65 19, 17 rue du Pont Neuf) is said to be particularly tasty.

La Sangria (☎ 04 90 34 31 96, 3 place de la République), has *menus* for 50FF (lunch only), 70FF and 105FF. Close by, *Chez Daniel* (☎ 04 90 34 63 48, rue Second Weber), dishes out oysters, mussels and other shellfish by the dozen. Daniel also offers inspirational fish platters costing 120FF to 180FF, to eat in or take away.

For a taste of India, head to the Indian *New Kasmir* (☎ 04 90 34 90 09, rue de Tourre), just west of the Théâtre Antique, which has spicy *menus* for 80FF and 95FF. Highly recommended for its local fare is *Le Yaca* (☎ 04 90 34 70 03, 24 place Silvain), close by. It has a 65FF regional *menu*. Don't miss the *soupe au pistou* at *Le Provençal* (☎ 04 90 34 01 89, 27 rue de la République).

For a real treat, head for *Le Garden* (☎ 04 90 34 64 47, 6 place de Langes), a block west of place Clemenceau. The restaurant is furnished in 1930s style and specialises in truffles. Its *brouillade aux truffes* with salad (180FF) is a veritable feast of pricey (and local) black fungi.

Thursday is market day in Orange.

Getting There & Away

Bus The bus station (☎ 04 90 34 15 59 or ☎ 04 90 34 13 39) is south-east of the centre of the city on cours Pourtoules. Buses from here go to Avignon, Carpentras, Marseilles and Vaison-la-Romaine.

PROVENCE

Train Orange's tiny train station (☎ 04 90 11 88 64), at the eastern end of Ave Frédéric Mistral, is 1.5km east of the tourist office.

Trains go in two directions: northwards to Lyons (137FF, 2¼ hours, 13 daily) and Paris' Gare de Lyon (385FF, 3¼ hours), and southwards to Avignon (29FF, 15 minutes, 17 daily), Marseilles (130FF, 1½ hours, 10 daily) and beyond.

VAISON-LA-ROMAINE
postcode 84110 • pop 5904

Vaison-la-Romaine, 23km and 47km north-east of Orange and Avignon, respectively, is endowed with extensive Roman ruins, a picturesque medieval old city and plenty of tourists.

In the 2nd century BC, the Romans conquered an important Celtic city on this site and renamed it Vasio Vocontiorum. The Roman city flourished, in part because it was granted considerable autonomy, but around the 6th century the Great Migrations forced the population to move to the hill across the river, which was easier to defend. The counts of Toulouse built a castle on top of the hill in the 12th century. The resettlement of the original site began in the 17th century.

The Roman remains discovered at Vaison include villas decorated with mosaics, colonnaded streets, public baths, a theatre and an aqueduct; the latter brought water down from Mont Ventoux.

The two-week Choralies, a choral festival held each year in August in the Roman theatre, is said to be the largest of its kind in Europe.

Vaison, like Malaucène and Carpentras, 10km and 27km to the south, is a good base for exploring the Mont Ventoux region.

Orientation
Vaison is bisected by the ever flooding Ouvèze River. The Roman city centre, on top of which the modern city centre has been built, is on the river's right (northern) bank; the medieval Haute Ville is on the left (southern) bank.

In the modern city, pedestrianised Grand' rue heads north-westwards from the pont Romain bridge, changing its name near the Roman ruins to ave du Général de Gaulle.

To get from the bus station to the tourist office, turn left as you leave the station then left into rue Colonel Parazols, which leads past the Fouilles de Puymin excavations along rue Burrhus to the tourist office.

Information
Tourist Office The tourist office (☎ 04 90 36 02 11, fax 04 90 28 76 04, ✉ ot-vaison@axit.fr), inside the Maison du Tourisme et des Vins, is just off ave du Général de Gaulle on place du Chanoine Sautel. It opens 9 am to noon and 2 to 5.45 pm (open on Sunday from 9 am to 1 pm from Easter to September). It opens 9 am to midday and 2 to 6.45 pm in July and August.

Post The post office, which has an exchange service, is diagonally opposite place du 11 Novembre. It opens 8.30 am to noon and 2 to 5 pm (until noon Saturday; closed Sunday).

Gallo-Roman Ruins
The Gallo-Roman ruins that have been unearthed in Vaison can be visited at two sites: **Fouilles de Puymin**, the excavations on the eastern side of ave du Général de Gaulle, and **Fouilles de la Villasse**, which are to the west of the same road.

Fouilles de Puymin, whose entrance is opposite the tourist office, is the more interesting of the pair. It includes houses, mosaics and a theatre (designed to accommodate some 6000 people) built around 20 AD under the reign of Tiberius. **Musée Archéologique** displays some of the artefacts found. Its collection of statues includes the silver bust of a 3rd-century patrician and likenesses of Hadrian and his wife Sabina. At Fouilles de la Villasse, you can visit the mosaic- and fresco-decorated house in which the silver bust was discovered.

Both sites open 10 am to 12.30pm and 2 to 6.30 pm daily, November to February. It opens 9 or 9.30 am to 12.30 pm and 2 to 6 or 7 pm from March to October. Admission to both sites costs 41FF (students/children

PROVENCE

22/14FF). From April to October, there are guided tours (10FF) in English; check the schedule at the tourist office.

Medieval Quarter

Across the much repaired **pont Romain**, on the southern bank of the Ouvèze, lies the **Haute Ville**, which dates from the 13th and 14th centuries. Narrow, cobblestone alleyways lead up the hill past restored houses. At the summit, which affords a nice view, is an imposing 12th-century **chateau**, modernised in the 15th century only to be later abandoned.

Places to Stay

The tourist office has comprehensive accommodation lists, including details on chambres d'hôtes and self-catering places in the surrounding region.

Camping Opposite Théâtre Antique in the northern section of the Fouilles de Puymin, *Camping du Théâtre Romain* (☎ 04 90 28 78 66, fax 04 90 28 78 76, chemin de Brusquet), opens from 15 March to 31 October and charges 86/105FF for two people with a tent and car in June/July.

Larger *Camping Carpe Diem* (☎ 04 90 36 02 02, fax 04 90 36 36 90, route de St-Marcellin) south-east of the centre opens 30 March to 5 November. Charges are 110/120FF in June/July. Both sites have swimming pools.

Hostels Quiet but expensive *Centre International de Séjour à Cœur Joie* (☎ 04 90 36 00 78, fax 04 90 36 09 89, ✉ centracj .france@wanadoo.fr, ave César Geoffray) 500m south-east of town along the river, has views of Mont Ventoux. Weekly full-board rates are 1855FF per person.

Hotels Hotels are few and far between. Twenty-four room *Hôtel Le Burrhus* (☎ 04 90 36 00 11, fax 04 90 36 39 05, 2 place Montfort)*, and eight-room *Hôtel des Lis* (same ☎/fax, 20 cours Henri Fabre), practically next door and owned by the same people, charge from 240FF and 350FF, respectively, for a double with shower and

toilet. Both close from 12 November to 20 December and on Sunday in January and February.

Shopping

Wine such as *Gigondas*, *Châteauneuf-du-Pape* and *Villages des Côtes du Rhône*, honey and honey nougat are all local specialities, but nothing can compare with the delectable black truffles harvested around Vaison-la-Romain. Sure they don't come cheap (95FF for 12.5g), but just a few shavings of the costly black fungus will turn the most prosaic plate of pasta into a bite-sized helping of heaven itself.

Local wines and local food products can be tasted and bought at the Maison des Vins, in the basement of the Maison du Tourisme et des Vins.

Getting There & Away

The bus station, where Lieutard buses (☎ 04 90 36 09 90 in Vaison, ☎ 04 90 86 36 75 in Avignon) has an office, is east of the modern town on ave des Choralies. There are limited services from Vaison to Orange (45 minutes), Avignon (1¼ hours) and Carpentras (45 minutes). The office opens 9 am to noon and 2 to 7 pm.

MONT VENTOUX

The narrow ridge running east to west known as Mont Ventoux is the most prominent geographical feature in northern Provence, thanks to its height (1909m) and its isolation. The radar and antenna-studded summit, accessible by road, affords spectacular views of Provence, the southern Alps and – when it's especially clear – even the Pyrenees.

Mont Ventoux marks the boundary between the fauna and flora of northern France and that of southern France. Some species – including the snake eagle, numerous spiders and a variety of butterflies – are found only here. The mountain's forests were felled 400 years ago to build ships, but since 1860 some areas have been reforested with a variety of species, including the majestic cedar of Lebanon. The mix of deciduous trees makes the mountain especially colourful in autumn.

Since the summit is considerably cooler than the surrounding plains – there can be a difference of up to 20°C – and receives twice as much precipitation, bring warm clothes and rain gear at any time of the year. Areas above 1300m are usually snow-covered from December to April.

Mont Ventoux is regularly included in the route of the Tour de France, and it was here that British cyclist Tommy Simpson collapsed and died during the 1967 event. There is a memorial to him.

Just west of Mont Ventoux rise the sharp pinnacles of the limestone **Dentelles de Montmirail**; the surrounding area makes great hiking terrain. Near the eastern end of the Mont Ventoux massif is the village of **Sault** (800m), surrounded in summer by a patchwork of purple lavender. **Malaucène**, 10km south of Vaison-la-Romaine and the former summer residence of the Avignon popes, is where most people begin their forays into the surrounds of Mont Ventoux, which is 21km to the east. Come winter, **Mont Serein** (1445m), 16km east of Malaucène and 5km from Mont Ventoux's summit on the D974, is transformed into a bustling ski station.

Information

Tourist Offices The Malaucène tourist office (☎/fax 04 90 65 22 59), place de la Mairie, opens 10 am (9 am in summer) to noon and 3.30 pm (3 pm in summer) to 5.30 pm Monday to Saturday. Its efficient counterpart on ave de la Promenade in Sault (☎ 04 90 64 01 21, fax 04 90 64 15 03, ⓔ ot-sault@axit.fr) opens 10 am to noon and 2 to 6 pm daily from 1 April to 30 September, 9 am to 1 pm and 2 to 7 pm in July and August, and from 10 am to noon and 2.30 to 4.30 pm from 1 October to 31 March (closed on Sunday and Monday).

There is an information chalet on Mont Serein (☎ 04 90 63 42 02).

Maps Didier-Richard's 1:50,000 scale map No 27, entitled *Massif du Ventoux*, includes Mont Ventoux, the Monts du Vaucluse and the Dentelles de Montmirail. It is available at some of the area's larger tourist offices, and many bookshops and newsagents. More detailed is IGN's Série Bleue 1:25,000 *Mont Ventoux* (No 3140ET; 58FF).

Walking

The GR4, running from the River Ardèche to the west, crosses the Dentelles de Montmirail before climbing up the northern face of Mont Ventoux. It then joins the GR9, and both trails follow the bare, white ridge before parting ways, with the GR4 winding eastwards to the Gorges du Verdon. The GR9, which takes you to most of the area's ranges (including the Monts du Vaucluse and Lubéron range), is arguably the most spectacular trail in Provence.

Getting There & Around

If you've got a car, the summit of Mont Ventoux can be reached from Sault via the D164 or – in summer – from Malaucène or St-Estève via the switchback D974, built in the 1930s. This mountain road is often snow-blocked until as late as April. For information on bus services in the area, see Getting There & Away under Carpentras.

EgoBike Shop (☎ 04 90 65 22 15) in Malaucène rents mountain bikes.

CARPENTRAS
postcode 84200 • pop 26,090

The drowsy agricultural town of Carpentras was an important trading centre in Greek times and later a Gallo-Roman city before becoming the capital of the papal territory of the Comtat Venaissin in 1320. It flourished in the 14th century, when it was visited frequently by Pope Clement V (who preferred it to Avignon) and numerous cardinals. During the same period, Jews expelled from territory controlled by the French crown (especially in Languedoc and Provence) sought refuge in the Comtat Venaissin, where they could live – subject to certain restrictions – under the protection of the pope. Today, Carpentras' 14th century synagogue is the oldest such structure in France still in use.

Carpentras is equidistant (25km) from Avignon to the south-west and Orange to the north-west. The town is small, easy to

PROVENCE

navigate on foot, and best known for its bustling Friday markets. It hosts the eclectic Estivales de Carpentras, a two-week music, dance and theatre festival, in July.

Orientation

In the 19th century, the city's fortifications and walls were replaced by a ring of boulevards: ave Jean Jaurès, blvd Alfred Rogier, blvd du Nord, blvd Maréchal Leclerc, blvd Gambetta and blvd Albin Durand. The partly pedestrianised old city lies inside.

If you arrive by bus, walk northeastwards to place Aristide Briand, a major traffic intersection at the southernmost point on the almost heart-shaped ring of boulevards. Ave Jean Jaurès leads to the tourist office, while pedestrian-only rue de la République, which heads due north, takes you straight to the cathedral and the 17th-century Palais de Justice. The town hall is a few blocks north-east of the cathedral.

Information

Tourist Office The tourist office (☎ 04 90 63 00 78, fax 04 90 60 41 02, @ tourist .carpentras@axit.fr), 170 allée Jean Jaurès, sells a good range of regional maps and guides, and organises guided city tours (25FF; children 10FF). Ask for the free English-language brochure *The Discover Carpentras Tour* if you prefer to do it yourself. The office opens 9 am to 12.30 pm and 2 to 6.30 pm (6 pm on Saturday; closed Sunday). It opens 9 am to 7 pm in July and August (9.30 am to 12.30 pm on Sunday). Staff exchange foreign currency when the banks are closed.

Money The Banque de France at 161 blvd Albin Durand opens 9 am to noon and 1.30 to 3.30 pm Monday to Friday. Commercial banks are on central place Aristide Briand and blvd Albin Durand.

Post The post office, 65 rue d'Inguimbert, opens 8.30 am to 7 pm (until noon Saturday).

Laundry The laundrette, 118 rue Porte de Monteux (the road linking place du Général de Gaulle and blvd Albin Durand), opens 7 am to 8 pm.

Synagogue

Carpentras' wonderful synagogue was founded on this site in 1367, rebuilt in 1741–43 and restored in 1929 and 1954. For centuries, it served as the focal point of the town's 1000-strong Jewish community. The sanctuary on the 1st floor is decorated with wood panelling and liturgical objects from the 18th century. Down below, there's an oven that was used until 1904 to bake matzo, the unleavened bread eaten at Passover.

The synagogue, opposite the town hall on place Juiverie, can be identified by a stone plaque, positioned high on the wall, which is inscribed with Hebrew letters. About 100 Jewish families live in Carpentras today. It opens 10 am to noon and 3 to 5 pm (4 pm on Friday; closed at the weekend). The tourist office sells the informative English booklet *The Road to Jewish Heritage in the South of France* (15FF).

Cathedral

Carpentras' one-time cathedral, now officially known as Église St-Siffrein, was built in the Méridional (southern French) Gothic style between 1405 and 1519. The doorway, whose design is classical and badly in need of renovation, was added in the 17th century. The bell tower is modern. **Trésor d'Art Sacré** (Treasury of Religious Art) displays various liturgical objects and reliquaries from the 14th to 19th centuries, including the **St-Mors**, the Holy Bridle bit supposedly made by St Helen for her son Constantine from a nail taken from the True Cross. The cathedral opens 10 am to noon and 2 to 4 pm (until 6 pm in summer; closed Tuesday year round).

Museums

Carpentras' museums open 10 am to noon and 2 to 4 pm (until 6 pm in summer; closed Tuesday year round). **Musée Comtadin**, which displays artefacts related to local history and folklore, and **Musée Duplessis**, whose paintings are from the personal collection of Monseigneur d'Inguimbert, are both on the western side of the old city at 234 blvd Albin Durand. The same 18th-century building houses the **Bibliothèque Inguimbertine**, a large library with numerous rare books, incunabula and manuscripts.

Musée Sobirats, one block west of the cathedral at 112 rue du Collège, is an 18th-century private residence decorated and crammed with furniture, faïence and *objets d'art* in the Louis XV and Louis XVI styles.

The hospital in the 18th-century **Hôtel Dieu**, place Aristide Briand, has an old-time pharmacy, complete with pharmaceutical ceramics. It opens to the public (10FF) 9 to 11.30 am on Monday, Wednesday and Thursday. The hospital's chapel is also of interest, but you must make arrangements with the tourist office to visit it.

Markets

Friday is market day in Carpentras, and is one of the most colourful in Provence. Place Aristide Briand and rue de la République have the usual knock-off jeans, generic T-shirts and junk, but rue d'Inguimbert and most of ave Jean Jaurès are laden with tables covered with nougat, strong local cheeses, orange and lavender marmalade, cauldrons of paella, buckets of olives and fresh fruit (especially the wonderful local melons). From November to the beginning of March, truffles are sold on place Aristide Briand 8 to 10 am every Friday. Carpentras' biggest fair is held on the Fête de St-Siffrein (Feast of St Siffrein) on 27 November. In July and August, there's a wine market in front of the tourist office.

Places to Stay

Camping Outside town on the Route de St-Didier is *Camping Lou Comtadou en Provence* (☎ 04 90 67 03 16, fax 04 90 67 04 62, ave Pierre de Coubertin), open Easter to October. It charges 22FF per person and 29FF for a tent or car. *Camping Le Brégoux* (☎ 04 90 62 62 50, fax 04 90 62 65 21, Chemin du Vas) at Aubignan, 5km north of Carpentras, opens 15 March to 31 October. Camping fees start from 16FF per person.

Hotels Arguably the best budget place in town is one-star *Hôtel du Théâtre* (☎ 04 90 63 02 90, 7 blvd Albin Durand), a very friendly establishment overlooking place Aristide Briand. Large, quiet (the windows are double-glazed) rooms for one or two start at 160FF; triples cost 260FF.

At the northern end of town, the eight-room *Hôtel La Lavande* (☎ 04 90 63 13 49, 282 blvd Alfred Rogier), has doubles without/with shower costing 155/205FF. From the tourist office, follow blvd Jean Jaurès north-east into blvd Alfred Rogier; the hotel is on the left just past the intersection of rue Porte de Mazan.

Le Fiacre (☎ 04 90 63 03 15, fax 04 90 60 49 73, 153 rue Vigne), a short distance north of the tourist office, has single/double rooms starting at 240/250FF.

Places to Eat

Regional fare rules at *Le Marijo* (☎ 04 90 60 42 65, 73 rue Raspail), which serves up superb three- and four-course locally inspired *menus* from around 80FF. For the cheese course, order the goat's cheese marinated for 15 days in herbs and olive oil and sprinkled with *marc*, a local *eau de vie*. This place is closed on Sunday.

Equally palatable are the truffles served in season (January to March) at *Le Vert Galant* (☎ 04 90 67 15 50, 12 rue de Clapiès). Expect to pay at least 120FF a head, plus a lot more if you intend sampling the precious bits of black fungi. Le Vert Galant, honoured with one Michelin star, closes during the last three weeks of August. *L'Oriental* (☎ 04 90 63 19 57, 26 rue de la Monnaie), specialises in Moroccan couscous starting at 69FF.

Getting There & Away

The train station is served by goods trains only, so buses operated by Cars Comtadins and Cars Arnaud provide Carpentras' only intercity public transport. The bus station, place Terradou, is 150m south-west of place Aristide Briand.

Schedules are available from the Cars Comtadins office (☎ 04 90 67 20 25) across the square at 38 ave Wilson. It opens 8 am

PROVENCE

to noon and 2 to 6 pm Monday to Friday. The tourist office can also help.

There are hourly services to Avignon (45 minutes) and less frequent runs to Orange (40 minutes), Cavaillon (45 minutes) and L'Isle-sur-Sorgue (20 minutes), 7km west of Fontaine de Vaucluse. Even less frequent are buses (weekdays only) to Vaison-la-Romaine (45 minutes) via Malaucène, Bédoin (40 minutes) at the southwestern foot of Mont Ventoux, and Sault (1½ hours) on the south-eastern side of Mont Ventoux.

FONTAINE DE VAUCLUSE
postcode 84800 • pop 610
The mighty spring for which Fontaine de Vaucluse (Vau-Cluso La Font in Provençal) is named is actually the spot where the River Sorgue ends its subterranean course and gushes to the surface. At the end of winter and in early spring, up to 200 cubic metres of water per second spill forth magnificently from the base of the cliff, forming one of the world's most powerful springs.

During drier periods, the much reduced flow simply seeps through the rocks at various points downstream from the cliff, and the spring itself becomes little more than a still, very deep pond. Following numerous unsuccessful human and roboticised attempts to reach the bottom, an unmanned submarine touched base – 315m-deep – in 1985.

Some 1.5 million visitors descend upon pretty Fontaine de Vaucluse each year to stroll its streets and throw pebbles into its deep, deep pond.

Information
The tourist office (☎ 04 90 20 32 22, fax 04 90 20 21 37, ✉ officetourisme.vaucluse@ wanadoo.fr) is on pedestrianised chemin de la Fontaine, south-east of central place de la Colonne on the way to the spring. It opens 10 am to 6 pm Monday to Saturday.

If you come by car, you will have no choice but to fork out 15FF for the privilege of parking. There is no free parking to be found *anywhere*.

Museums
For its size, the attractive village of Fontaine de Vaucluse has an inordinate number of small museums, dealing with such diverse subjects as the Résistance movement (**Musée d'Histoire 1939–1945**; ☎ 04 90 20 24 00; adjoining the tourist office; 20FF), speleology, and even justice and punishment (**Musée Historique de la Justice et des Châtiments**; ☎ 04 90 20 24 58; Chemin de la Fontaine; 20FF).

Moulin à Papier on the river banks opposite the tourist office is an impressive reconstruction of a paper mill, built on the site of Fontaine de Vaucluse's old mill, whose wheel turned and whose pinewood mallets steadily beat away from 1522 until 1968. It opens 9 am to 12.30 pm and 2 to 6 pm (Sunday from 10.30 am). It opens 9 am to 7 pm in July and August; admission is free. Beautiful flower-encrusted paper, made as it was in the 16th century, is sold in the adjoining boutique and art gallery.

The Italian Renaissance poet Petrarch lived in Fontaine de Vaucluse from 1337 to 1353, immortalising his true love, Laura, wife of Hugues de Sade, in verse. **Musée Pétrarque** (☎ 04 90 20 37 20; 10FF) on the left bank of the Sorgue is devoted to his work, sojourn and broken heart.

Places to Stay
Camping Municipal Les Prés (☎ 04 90 20 32 38, route du Cavaillon) is west of the village centre near the large public carpark and the Sorgue. The *Auberge de Jeunesse* (☎ 04 90 20 31 65, fax 04 90 20 26 20, Chemin de la Vignasse), is south of the Fontaine de Vaucluse in the direction of Lagnes (walk uphill from the bus stop). A bed for the night costs 48FF.

The tourist office has a list of chambres d'hôtes in the village. Fontaine de Vaucluse has three hotels, the best of the three being the 16-room *Font de Lauro* (☎ 04 90 20 31 49, fax 04 90 20 31 49, plan de Saumane). Doubles start at 170FF.

Getting There & Away
Fontaine de Vaucluse is 21km south-east of Carpentras and some 7km east of L'Isle-

PROVENCE

sur-Sorgue, the nearest 'real' town. From Avignon, Voyages Arnaud runs a bus (25FF, one hour, two or three daily) with a stop at Fontaine de Vaucluse, from where it's a short walk to the spring. There are Arnaud buses from Carpentras to L'Isle-sur-Sorgue (20 minutes).

GORDES
postcode 84220 • pop 2092

On the white, rocky southern face of the Vaucluse plateau, the tiered village of Gordes forms an amphitheatre overlooking the Sorgue and Calavon rivers. The top of the village is crowned by a sturdy chateau built between the 11th and 16th centuries. In summer, this once typical Provençal village is frighteningly overrun with tourists, but it's still worth a wander around if you've got the wheels to get you there.

Information

The tourist office (☎ 04 90 72 02 75, fax 04 90 72 04 39), in the chateau's Salle des Gardes (Guards' Hall), place du Château, opens 9 am to noon and 2 to 6 pm.

Getting There & Away

Gordes is some 18km east of Fontaine de Vaucluse and about 20km west of Apt. The closest town is Cavaillon, 16km to the south-west, which is served by train (☎ 04 90 71 04 40 for information) and bus (☎ 04 90 78 32 39) from many cities and towns in Provence. Buses run by Les Express de la Durance (☎ 04 90 71 03 00 in Cavaillon) link Gordes with Cavaillon twice a day except Sunday.

AROUND GORDES

The main reason people come to Gordes is to visit the walled Village des Bories (☎ 04 90 72 03 48), 4km south-west of Gordes, just off the D2 heading for Cavaillon. Bories are one or two-storey beehive-shaped huts constructed without mortar using thin wedges of limestone. They were first built in the area in the Bronze Age and were continuously lived in, renovated and even built anew until as

late as the 18th century. It is not known what purpose they first served, but over the centuries they have been used as shelters, workshops, wine cellars and storage sheds. The 'village' contains about 20 such structures, restored to their appearance of about 150 years ago. Some people say the bories remind them of Ireland's *clochán*. The site opens 9 am to 7.30 pm daily. Admission costs 35FF (aged under 17 20FF).

Some 4km north-west of Gordes and off the D177 is Cistercian Abbaye de Sénanque (Sénanque Abbey; ☎ 04 90 72 05 72) which, in summer, is framed by fields of lilac lavender. The abbey, founded in 1148 and today inhabited by just five monks, opens 10 am to noon and 2 to 6 pm (2 to 5 pm only between November and March). It opens 2 to 6 pm on Sunday year round (morning Mass at 9 am). Admission costs 25FF (students 20FF).

ROUSSILLON
postcode 84220 • pop 1200

Roussillon lies in the valley between the Vaucluse plateau and the Lubéron range. Some two millennia ago, the Romans used its distinctive ochre earth for producing pottery glazes. These days the whole village – even the gravestones in the cemetery – is built of the reddish local stone, making it a popular place for painters eager to try out the range of their palettes. The red and orange hues are especially striking given the yellow-white bareness of the surrounding area and the green conifers sprinkled around town.

Information

The tourist office (☎/fax 04 90 05 60 25), in the centre of Roussillon on place de la Poste, opens 10 am to noon and 2 to 6.30 pm (closed on Sunday in winter). It changes money from 10 to 11.30 am and 2 to 6 pm. A complete list of hotels, chambres d'hôtes and restaurants in and around Roussillon is pinned up outside the office.

Sentier des Ocres

The 1km-long Ochre Trail begins about 100m north of Roussillon's centre and will

PROVENCE

lead you through fairy-tale groves of chestnuts, maritime pines and scrub to the bizarre and beautiful ochre formations created by erosion and fierce winds over the centuries. It can be steep at times, but there are lead ropes to hold onto.

Don't wear white; you'll return smudged from head to toe in rust-coloured dust. It opens 10 am to 5 pm. Admission costs 10FF.

Getting There & Away
Roussillon, 9km east of Gordes in the direction of Apt (11km east again), is inaccessible by public transport. The GR6 walking trail passes through here.

APT & THE LUBÉRON
The Lubéron hills stretch from Cavaillon in the west to Manosque in the east, and from Apt southwards to the River Durance. The area is named after the main range, a compact massif with a gentle, 1100m-high summit. Its oak-covered northern face is steep and uneven, while its southern face is drier and more Mediterranean in both climate and flora. Much of the Lubéron is within the boundaries of the Parc Naturel Régional du Lubéron. The area has some great walking trails and is an excellent place for bicycling.

The Lubéron area is dotted with bories (see Around Gordes). The town of Apt, a very good base for exploring the Lubéron, is largely unexceptional except for its grapes, cherries and *fleurions*, candied or crystallised fruits, which are sold everywhere. It celebrates its Cherry Festival each year in May.

Information
Tourist Offices As you enter Apt from Cavaillon, the tourist office (☎ 04 90 74 03 18, fax 04 90 04 64 30, ✉ tourisme.apt@ pacwan.fr) is just over the bridge at 20 ave Philippe de Girard. It opens 9 am to noon and 2 to 6 pm (closed Sunday). In July and August it opens until 7 pm and 9 am to noon on Sunday.

Ask for the leaflet entitled *Apt – à Découvrir*, which details, in English as well as French, two one-hour city tours signposted around town with colour-coded markers.

The tourist office sells regional maps such as the Top 25 (3242OT) *Map of Apt and the Parc Naturel Régional du Lubéron*, or the *Cavaillon* map (3142OT). Both cost 58FF each.

Park Offices Information on the Parc Naturel Régional du Lubéron, including details of the park's two dozen *gîtes d'étape*, is available in Apt from the Maison du Parc (☎ 04 90 04 42 00, fax 04 90 04 81 15), 60 place Jean Jaurès.

The centre has plenty of information on hiking and cycling in the park, and sells an excellent range of guides including the recommended topoguide *Le Parc Naturel Régional du Lubéron à Pied* (75FF), which details 24 walks including the GR9, GR92 and GR97 trails.

The park office opens 8.30 am to noon and 1.30 to 7 pm (closed Saturday afternoon and Sunday; open until 6 pm from October to March).

Parc Naturel Régional du Lubéron
The Lubéron Regional Park's 1200 sq km encompass numerous villages, desolate forests, unexpected gorges and abandoned farmhouses, well on the way to falling into ruin – or perhaps restoration by fans of Peter Mayle, whose purchase and renovation of a house just outside the pretty village of **Ménerbes** in the late 1980s formed the basis of his witty, best-selling books *A Year in Provence* and *Toujours Provence*.

Places to Stay
Camping By the river, just out of town, *Camping Municipal Les Cèdres* (☎/fax 04 90 74 14 61, route de Rustrel), opens 15 February to 15 November.

It charges 12FF per person and 10FF for a tent or car.

Three-star *Camping Le Lubéron* (☎ 04 90 04 85 40, fax 04 90 74 12 19, route de Saignon), south-east of Apt, opens 1 April to 30 September. Rates for two persons, a tent and a car are about 100FF.

Hostels The *Auberge de Jeunesse* (☎ 04 90 74 39 34), 6km south-east of Apt in the village of Saignon, offers bed and breakfast for 75FF. The hostel closes mid-January to mid-February. To get there without a car, use your feet or thumb.

Hotels In Apt, welcoming *Hôtel du Palais* (☎ 04 90 04 89 32, place Gabriel Péri) provides fairly basic doubles with washbasin costing 160FF, 180FF with shower and 200FF with shower and toilet; triples with shower cost 210FF, with bath and toilet 260FF. *Menus* in its popular streetside restaurant start at 89FF.

Hôtel L'Aptois (☎ 04 90 74 02 02, fax 04 90 74 64 79, 289 cours Lauze de Perret), has doubles starting at 170/320FF with washbasin/shower and toilet. It closes 14 February to 15 March.

Part of the Logis de France chain is the cosy *Auberge du Lubéron* (☎ 04 90 74 12 50, fax 04 90 04 79 49, 8 place Faubourg du Ballet), on the opposite side of the river. Comfortable singles/doubles in the low season cost 240/290FF, rising to 290/450FF in July and August.

Getting There & Away

Buses to Aix-en-Provence (45FF, 1½ hours, two daily) leave from the bus station (☎ 04 90 74 20 21) east of the centre at 250 ave de la Libération. The trip to Avignon (42FF, three or four daily) takes 1¼ hours. There is also a service to/from Digne-les-Bains (63FF, two hours, two daily), Cavaillon (27FF, 40 minutes, two daily), Manosque (one hour, twice daily) and Marseilles (56FF, 2½ hours, two daily). The station opens 8 am to noon and 2.30 to 4.45 pm daily.

Getting Around

Hire a mountain bike from Cycles Agnel (☎ 04 90 74 17 16), along the river east of place de la Bouquerie at 86 Quai Général Leclerc, or Cycles Ricaud (☎ 04 90 74 16 43), 44 quai Général Leclerc. Rates are 80/400FF a day/week.

Arles & the Camargue

ARLES

postcode 13200 • pop 50,513

The attractive city of Arles sits on the northern tip of the Camargue alluvial plain on the Grand Rhône River, just south of where the Petit Rhône splits off from it. Avignon is 36km to the north-east, while Nîmes (see the Languedoc-Roussillon chapter) is 31km to the north-west.

Arles began its ascent to prosperity and political importance in 49 BC, when the victorious Julius Caesar – to whom the city had given its support – captured and plundered Marseilles, which had backed Caesar's rival, the general and statesman Pompey the Great. Arles soon replaced Marseilles as the region's major port and became the sort of Roman provincial centre that, within a century and a half, needed a 20,000-seat amphitheatre and a 12,000-seat theatre to entertain its citizens. These days, the two structures are still used to stage cultural events and bullfights.

Arles' most famous resident was Vincent van Gogh (1853–90), who settled in the town for a year in 1888 and immortalised on canvas many of the city's most picturesque streets and surrounding rural areas.

Orientation

The centre of Arles is enclosed by the Grand Rhône River to the north-west, blvd Émile Combes to the east and, to the south, blvd des Lices and blvd Georges Clemenceau. It is shaped somewhat like a foot, with the train station, place de la Libération and place Lamartine (where Van Gogh once lived) at the ankle, the Arènes at the anklebone and the tourist office squashed under the arch. Covering a relatively small area, it's easily explored on – what else? – foot.

Information

Tourist Offices The central tourist office (☎ 04 90 18 41 20, fax 04 90 18 41 29,

@ ot-arles@visitprovence.com), Esplanade Charles de Gaulle, a short trip along blvd des Lices, opens 9 am to 6 pm (7 pm from April to September). It opens 10 am to noon on Sunday (9 am to 1 pm from April to September). The tourist office annexe (☎ 04 90 49 36 90) at the train station opens 9 am to 1 pm and 1.30 to 5 pm (closed Sunday). It opens 9 am to 1 pm and 2 to 6 pm from April to September (closed Sunday).

Both offices make accommodation bookings (☎ 04 90 18 41 22) and exchange foreign currency. They also sell a discounted combination ticket to all of Arles' sights for 65FF (students and children 50FF); museums sell the pass too.

From mid-June to mid-September, the tourist office runs several thematic city tours.

Money The Banque de France, 35 ter rue du Docteur Fanton, opens 8.30 am to 12.10 pm and 1.50 to 3.30 pm (closed at the weekend). There are several banks along rue de la République and an easily-spotted BNP Bank ATM on place de la République

Post The central post office, 5 blvd des Lices, opens 8.30 am to 7 pm (Saturday until noon; closed Sunday).

Bookshops Librairie Van Gogh (☎ 04 90 96 86 65), wrapped around the courtyard of Espace Van Gogh at 1 place Félix Rey, is a fantastic bookshop sporting an extensive range of English-language art and history books, as well as books and guides about the region. It opens 10 am to 12.30 pm and 2 to 6.30 pm Tuesday to Saturday. Reading matter can also be found at Actes Sud (☎ 04 90 49 56 77), 47 rue du Docteur Fanton.

Laundry The laundrette at 6 rue de la Cavalerie opens 7 am to 7 pm. The Miel Matic laundrette at 12 rue Portagnel opens 7.45 am to noon and 1.45 to 6.30 pm (closed Wednesday and Sunday).

Les Arènes

Arles' Roman amphitheatre, built in the late 1st or early 2nd century AD, measures 136m by 107m, making it marginally larger than its counterpart in Nîmes. Like other such structures around the Roman Empire, it was built to stage sporting contests, chariot races and the wildly popular and bloody spectacles so beloved by the Roman public. Wild animals were pitted against other animals or gladiators (usually slaves or criminals), who fought each other until one was either killed or surrendered (in the latter case his throat was usually then slit). Executions were carried out either by the executioner or by pushing the victim into the arena with a wild animal.

In the early medieval period, during the Arab invasions, the Arènes was transformed into a fortress; three of the four defensive towers can still be seen around the structure. These days, the Arènes has a capacity of more than 12,000 and still draws a full house during the bullfighting season (see the boxed text 'Bullfighting').

The Arènes, which is hidden away in the web of narrow streets in the city centre, opens 9 am to 6.30 pm from 16 June to 15 September. At other times there is a break between 12 and 2 pm, and closing is usually one hour earlier. The Arènes' *bureau de location* (ticket office; ☎ 04 90 96 03 70) is

Bullfighting

In mise à mort bullfighting (*corrida*), which is popular in Spain, Latin America and parts of southern France, a bull bred to be aggressive is killed in a colourful and bloody ceremony involving picadors, toreadors, matadors and horses. But not all bullfighting ends with a dead animal. In a *course Camarguaise* (Camargue-style bullfight), white-clad *razeteurs* try to remove ribbons tied to the bull's horns with hooks held between their fingers.

In Arles, the bullfighting season begins around Easter with a bullfighting festival known as the Feria (or Féria) and runs until September. The Feria incorporates both the course Camarguaise and corrida, and is held in the Arènes.

PROVENCE

ARLES

PLACES TO STAY
3 Hôtel de France et de la Gare
4 Hôtel Terminus et Van Gogh
6 Hôtel Régence
8 Hôtel de Paris
9 Hôtel Mirador
10 Hôtel Voltaire
11 Hôtel Gauguin;
     Hôtel Le Rhône
15 Hôtel du Musée
23 Hôtel de la Muette

PLACES TO EAT
5 Monoprix Supermarket
12 La Giraudière
17 La Paillotte
19 L'Entrevue
21 La Dame Jeanne
22 El Quinto Toro
26 L'Hostellerie
30 Café Van Gogh
31 Le Bistrot Arlésien
32 Spa Supermarket

OTHER
1 Bus Station
2 Train Station
7 Laundrette

13 Miel Matic Laundrette
14 Musée Réattu
16 Thermes de Constantin
18 Actes Sud Bookshop
20 Banque de France
24 Rencontres Internationales de
     la Photographie
25 Les Arènes Bureau
     de Location
27 Les Arènes
28 Fondation Vincent Van Gogh
29 Destination Camargue
33 La Farandole
34 Museon Arlaten
35 Cryptoporticus du Forum
36 Town Hall
37 Église St-Trophime
38 Entrance to Théâtre
     Antique
39 Théâtre Antique
40 Cloître St-Trophime
41 BNP Bank ATM
42 Puyricard
43 Espace Van Gogh; Le Jardin
     des Délices
44 Regional Bus Office
45 Tourist Office
46 Main Post Office

To Tarascon & Avignon

Avenue Paulin Talabot

Avenue Lamartine

Place Lamartine

Place de la Libération

Porte de la Cavalerie

Grand Rhône

*To Musée Camarguais (10km),
Aéroport de Nîmes-Arles-
Camargue (20km), Nîmes (31km),
Les St-Maries (37km),
& Montpellier (73km)*

Pont de Trinquetaille

Quai Max Dormoy

Rue du Bac

Rue de la Liberté

Rue de la République

R. Porcelets

Rue Jean Granaud

Rue Jean Gambetta

Rue du 4 Septembre

Rue du Quatre Septembre

Rue du Grand Prieuré

Rue Réattu

Rue de la Calade

Rue de la Cavalerie

Rue de l'Amphithéâtre

Rue du Refuge

Rue Voltaire

Rue Augustin Tardieu

Rue Portagnel

Place Voltaire

Rue du Docteur Fanton

R des Suisses

Rue des Arènes

Rue de l'Hôtel de Ville

Place du Forum

Rue des Pénitents Bleus

Rue Balze

Place Balechou

Rue Diderot

Boulevard Émile Combes

Place de la République

Rue Balechon

Rue Truchet

R. Chavary

Place Félix Rey

Rue Molière

Rue Jean Jaurès

Rue du Cloître

Jardin d'Été

Boulevard des Lices

Blvd Georges Clemenceau

Rue Émile Fassin

Avenue du Général Leclerc

Blvd Émile Zola

Blvd Victor Hugo

*To Camping City,
Aix-en-Provence (63km)
& Marseille (80km)*

*To Van Gogh Bridge (2km)
& Port St-Louis (40km)*

*To Musée
Archéologique
d'Arles (130m);
Auberge de
Jeunesse (2km)*

0   100   200m
0   100   200yd

PROVENCE

euro currency converter €1 = 6.56FF

on the northern side of the amphitheatre on Rond Point des Arènes.

Théâtre Antique

The Roman theatre (☎ 04 90 96 93 30), which dates from the end of the 1st century BC, was used for many hundreds of years as a convenient source of construction materials, so little of the original structure – measuring 102m in diameter – remains, except for two imposing columns. Entered through the Jardin d'Été (Summer Garden) on blvd des Lices, it hosts open-air dance, film and music festivals in summer. The Théâtre Antique has the same opening hours as the Arènes and charges the same admission.

Église St-Trophime

This austere Provençal Romanesque-style church was once a cathedral, as Arles was an archbishopric from the 4th century until 1790. It stands on the site of several earlier churches, and was built in the late 11th and 12th centuries – perhaps using stone cut from the Théâtre Antique. The church is named after St Trophimus, a late 2nd or early 3rd century bishop of Arles.

Across the courtyard is serene **Cloître St-Trophime** (☎ 04 90 49 36 36), surrounded by superbly sculptured columns. The two Romanesque galleries date from the 1100s, while the two Gothic galleries are from the 14th century. The cloister opens the same hours as the Arènes and charges 20FF admission (students 15FF).

Other Roman Sites

The partly preserved **Thermes de Constantin**, near the river on rue du Grand Prieuré, were built in the 4th century. The Roman baths keep the same opening hours as Les Arènes. Admission costs 20FF (students 15FF).

Cryptoporticus du Forum are underground storerooms, most of which were carved out in the 1st century BC. To gain access you need to go through a 17th-century Jesuit chapel on rue Balze, they also keep the same hours as the Arènes and cost 20FF (students 15FF).

Museums

Housed in a strikingly modern building, the **Musée d'Archéologique d'Arles** (also called Musée de l'Arles Antique; ☎ 04 90 18 88 88 or ☎ 04 90 18 88 89) brings together the rich collections of the former Musée d'Art Païen (Museum of Pagan Art) and Musée d'Art Chrétien (Museum of Christian Art). Exhibits include Roman statues, artefacts, marble sarcophagi and an assortment of early Christian sarcophagi from the 4th century. The archaeology museum is 1.5km south-west of the tourist office at ave de la 1ère Division Française Libre on the Presqu'île du Cirque Romain. It opens 10 am to 6 pm (closed Tuesday); and 9 am to 8 pm April to September. Admission costs 35FF (students 25FF).

Museon Arlaten (☎ 04 90 96 08 23), rue de la République, founded by the Nobel prize-winning poet Frédéric Mistral (see Language at the beginning of this chapter), is dedicated to preserving and displaying everyday objects related to traditional Provençal life: furniture, crafts, costumes, ceramics, wigs, a model of the Tarasque (a people-eating amphibious monster of Provençal legend) etc. It occupies a 16th-century townhouse constructed around Roman ruins, and opens 9 am to noon and 2 to 5 pm (6 pm in April, May and September, 6.30 pm in June and 7 pm in July and August). The museum closes on Monday between October and June. Admission costs 25FF (students 20FF).

Musée Réattu (☎ 04 90 96 37 68), housed in a former 15th-century priory at 10 rue du Grand Prieuré, exhibits works by some of the world's finest photographers, modern and contemporary works of art, and paintings by 18th- and 19th-century Provençal artists. The museum also has 57 Picasso drawings, sketched by the eccentric artist between December 1970 and November 1971. His more conventional portrait of his mother Maria, painted in Côte d'Antibes in 1923, is particularly fine. The museum opens 9 am to 12.30 pm and 2 to 5.30 pm daily (9 am to noon and 2 to 7 pm from April to September). Admission costs 20FF (students 15FF).

PROVENCE

Vincent van Gogh

When Vincent van Gogh (1853–90) arrived in Provence in 1888, the quality of the light and colours were a great revelation to him. He spent an intensely productive year at Arles, during which he painted all sorts of local scenes, among them the pont de Langlois, a little bridge that has been rebuilt 3km south of Arles (from town, take bus No 1 to the Pont Van Gogh terminus). His famous painting of the bridge entitled *The Bridge at Arles* is on display in the Netherlands at the Kröller-Müller National Museum in Otterlo. Some of van Gogh's other best known canvases – *Sunflowers, Van Gogh's Chair* and *Café at Night* – were all painted in Arles.

In 1888, van Gogh's friend and fellow artist Gauguin came to stay with him for several months. But their different temperaments and approaches to art soon led to a quarrel, after which van Gogh – overcome with despair – chopped off part of his left ear. In May 1889, because of recurrent bouts of madness, he voluntarily entered an asylum in St-Rémy de Provence (25km north-east of Arles over the Alpilles). He stayed there for a year, during which time he continued to be amazingly productive. In 1890, while staying in Auvers-sur-Oise (just north of Paris), van Gogh – lonely to the point of desperation and afraid his madness was incurable – shot and killed himself.

There are few tangible remains of Vincent van Gogh's stay in Arles. All traces of his rented yellow house and the nearby cafe on Place Lamartine – both of which appear in his paintings – were wiped out during WWII. Despite this being his most prolific period – he produced some 200 canvases in the space of a year – not a single piece of van Gogh's work remains in Arles today.

van Gogh Trail

Fondation Vincent van Gogh (☎ 04 90 49 94 04, fax 04 90 49 55 49), inside the Palais de Luppé at 24 bis Rond Point des Arènes, markets itself as a 'tribute to van Gogh through international artists'. It displays a wealth of paintings by other artists inspired by Arles' most famous resident. The centre opens 9.30 am to noon and 2 to 5.30 pm (10 am to 7 pm between April and October). Admission costs 30FF (students 20FF).

Gallery **La Rose des Vents** (☎ 04 90 93 25 96), 18 rue Diderot, displays various van Gogh reproductions as well as copies of letters written by the artist to his brother Theo. It opens 10.30 am to 12.30 pm and 3 to 7 pm (closed Sunday morning and Monday).

Various art exhibitions take place at **Espace van Gogh** (☎ 04 90 49 39 39, fax 04 90 43 80 85), housed in the old Hôtel Dieu and former hospital on place Félix Rey, where van Gogh spent some time.

Organised Tours

Tours of the Camargue by jeep are organised by many companies, including Provence Camargue Tours (☎ 04 90 49 85 58), 1 rue Émile Fassin; Havas Voyages (☎ 04 90 96 13 25), 4 blvd des Lices; and Destination Camargue (☎ 04 90 96 94 44, fax 04 90 49 84 31), 29 rue Balechou. The latter organises half-day trips (180FF; children 100FF), departing daily from Arles at 3 pm in summer. Reservations can also be made at La Boutique Provençal (☎ 04 90 49 84 31), 8 Rond Point des Arènes. For more information see the Camargue section.

Special Events

Arles has a full calendar of summertime cultural events. In early July, Les Rencontres Internationales de la Photographie (International Photography Festival) and its exhibits attract photographers and aficionados from around the world. The two-week Fêtes d'Arles, which usually kicks off at the end of June, brings dance, theatre, music and poetry readings to the city. For more information contact the Festiv'Arles office (☎ 04 90 96 47 00 or ☎ 04 90 96 81 18, fax 04 90 96 81 17), 35 place de la République. Other fascinating events include the Festival Mosaïque Gitane in mid-July, which celebrates Gypsy (Romany people) culture, and the week-long Fête des

PROVENCE

Prémices du Riz in mid-August, marking the start of the rice harvest.

Places to Stay

Except during festivals, bullfights and July and August, Arles has plenty of reasonably priced accommodation. There are lots of gîtes ruraux (☎ 04 90 59 49 40 for reservations) in the surrounding countryside, especially the Camargue. Ask the tourist office for the list.

Places to Stay – Budget

Camping The nearest camping ground to Arles is two-star *Camping City* (☎ 04 90 93 08 86, fax 04 90 93 91 07, 67 route de Crau), 1km south-east of the city centre on the road to Marseilles. It opens 1 April to 30 September and charges 24FF (children 17FF) plus 25FF for a tent and car. Take bus No 2 to the Hermite stop.

Hostels The 100-bed *Auberge de Jeunesse* (☎ 04 90 96 18 25, fax 04 90 96 31 26, 20 ave Maréchal Foch), 2km from the centre, charges 75FF including breakfast. It opens 5 February to 20 December. Take bus No 3 or 8 from blvd Georges Clemenceau (No 8 from place Lamartine) to the Fournier stop.

Hotels Close to the train station, one-star *Hôtel de France et de la Gare* (☎ 04 90 96 01 24, fax 04 90 96 90 87, 1–3 place Lamartine), has singles and doubles with shower and toilet for between 165FF and 220FF. Next door, renovated and also one-star *Hôtel Terminus et Van Gogh* (☎/fax 04 90 96 12 32, 5 place Lamartine) has similar singles and doubles with washbasin, for between 200FF and 240FF.

Heading into town you come to a few more cheapies. No-star *Hôtel Voltaire* (☎ 04 90 96 13 58, 1 place Voltaire), has serviceable rooms, some overlooking the pretty square, starting at 120/140FF with washbasin/shower.

Old-fashioned and cluttered one-star *Hôtel Le Rhône* (☎ 04 90 96 43 70, 11 place Voltaire), has rooms with washbasin starting at 130FF, rooms with shower starting at 170FF, and rooms with shower and toilet starting at 210FF.

One-star *Hôtel de Paris* (☎ 04 90 96 05 88, 8 rue de la Cavalerie), above a cheap cafe, also has cheap rooms (170FF). Nearby two-star *Hôtel Régence* (☎ 04 90 96 39 85, fax 04 90 96 67 64, 5 rue Marius Jouveau) overlooks the Rhône and has uninspiring singles/doubles starting at 140/175FF.

Places to Stay – Mid-Range

Renovated, two-star *Hôtel Gauguin* (☎ 04 90 96 14 35, fax 04 90 18 98 87, 5 place Voltaire), has doubles equipped with alarm clocks and showers for 180FF (with toilet too for 210FF). Nearby, singles or doubles at 15-room *Hôtel Mirador* (☎ 04 90 96 28 05, fax 04 90 96 59 89, 3 rue Voltaire), cost 215/245FF with toilet and shower/bath. Cheaper rooms with no toilet – just shower – cost 190FF.

Appealing, 20-room two-star *Hôtel du Musée* (☎ 04 90 93 88 88, fax 04 90 49 98 15, 11 rue du Grand Prieuré), occupies a fine 12th- to 13th-century building. It is spacious and has a rear terrace garden. Doubles with shower/bath and toilet start at 230/350FF.

Family-run, two-star *Hôtel de la Muette* (☎ 04 90 96 15 39, fax 04 90 49 73 16, 15 rue des Suisses) is part of the Logis de France chain and has appropriately prettily furnished rooms with toilet and shower/bath starting at 220/300FF. Breakfast costs 37FF.

Places to Eat

Blvd Georges Clemenceau and blvd des Lices are lined with plane trees and brasseries with terraces. The latter are fine for a meal if you don't mind dining à la traffic fumes.

Restaurants Place du Forum, an intimate square shaded by eight large plane trees, turns into one big dining table at lunch and dinner. Most of the restaurants here are mid-range, though *Le Bistrot Arlésien* (place du Forum) has salads for 20FF to 60FF and reasonably priced plats du jour for 55FF to 60FF. *El Quinto Toro* (☎ 04 90 49 62 29, 12 rue de la Liberté), a cosy and popular Spanish restaurant nearby, is slightly cheaper than its counterparts on the square. Unpretentious *La Dame Jeanne* (☎ 04 90 96 37 09, 4 rue des Pénitents Bleus), offers a three-course *menu* for 78FF and a four-course one for 100FF.

Calm and cool *L'Entrevue* (☎ 04 90 93 37 28, 23 quai Max Dormoy) down by the riverfront in a cinema and bookshop complex, doesn't in fact offer a view of the water (it is blocked by high river ramparts), but is a stylish, laid-back place serving Asian and Caribbean-inspired cuisine, including a fantastic *couscous royal* (98FF) and wonderfully refreshing mint and pine kernel tea.

L'Hostellerie (☎ 04 90 96 13 05, 62 rue du Refuge) has a terrace with an excellent view towards the amphitheatre. It offers a good selection of salads (25FF to 69FF) and a *menu* for 78FF. It closes on Tuesday. Decked out with wooden blue shutters, *La Giraudière* (☎ 04 90 93 27 52, 53–55 rue Condorcet), is an attractive place overlooking place Voltaire. It also offers a tempting regional *menu* for 85FF. *La Paillotte* (☎ 04 90 96 33 15, 26 rue du Docteur Fanton) is very popular with locals and dishes up great *aïoli Provençal* for 78FF, and an excellent *petite bouillabaisse* for 108FF.

Cafes Arles' most idyllic cafe is *Le Jardin des Délices* at Espace van Gogh, overlooking ornamental gardens inspired by van Gogh's painting *The Hospital Garden at Arles*. A variety of salads and light meals are served here, costing between 40FF and 50FF for a set formule.

Also paying homage to Vincent's Arles roots is very yellow *Café Van Gogh*, (place du Forum), reminiscent of the yellow house on place Lamartine that van Gogh chose as the subject for his canvas *Café at Night*. Café Van Gogh, which is a busy bar by night, has *menus* for 75FF and 95FF.

Self-Catering The *Spar Supermarket* (19 rue de la République) opens 8.30 am to 12.15 pm and 3.30 to 7.30 pm. *Monoprix* (place Lamartine) opens 8.30 am to 7.25 pm. Both close on Sunday.

On Wednesday, *market stalls* sprawl the length of blvd Émile Combes along the outside of the city walls. The food section is at the northern end. On Saturday morning, the market moves to blvd des Lices and blvd Georges Clemenceau.

Shopping

Locally made *saucisson d'Arles* (Arles sausage) is sold at sausage-makers La Farandole, (11 rue des Porcelets). The sweet-toothed can purchase exquisite Provençal chocolates from Puyricard, (54 rue de la République).

Getting There & Away

Air Nîmes-Arles-Camargue airport (also called Garons airport; ☎ 04 66 70 49 49) is 20km north-west of the city on the A54.

Bus The bus station, at the end of ave Paulin Talabot, is about 1km north of the Arènes. The information office (☎ 04 90 49 38 01) opens 7.30 am to 4 pm Monday to Saturday. Most intercity buses stop here. Some also stop at 24 blvd Georges Clemenceau, where the regional bus company Les Cars de Camargue (☎ 04 90 96 94 78) has an office; it also has an office at 4 rue Jean Mathieu Artaud. It runs services to Nîmes (33FF, 50 minutes, six daily) and Marseilles (87FF, 2½ hours, two daily) via Aix-en-Provence (68FF, 1¾ hours).

Les Cars de Camargue buses also link Arles with various parts of the Camargue, including Les Stes-Maries de la Mer (37FF, one hour, two daily in winter and six to nine daily in summer), Port St-Louis (38.50FF, 65 minutes, six daily) and many places en route such as Mas du Pont de Rousty, Pioch Badet and Pont de Gau. If you'll be staying in the Camargue for a few days, it might be worth purchasing a Passe Camargue (140FF), which gives you three days of unlimited travel on the two main bus routes.

Eurolines (☎ 04 90 96 94 78), the long-haul bus company, sells tickets at 24 blvd Georges Clemenceau.

Train Arles train station (☎ 0 836 35 35 35) is opposite the bus station. The information

PROVENCE

office opens 9 am to 12.30 pm and 2 to 6.30 pm (closed Sunday). Major rail destinations include Nîmes (41FF, 30 minutes), Montpellier (75FF, one hour), Marseilles (71FF, 40 minutes) and Avignon (36FF, 20 minutes).

Getting Around

To/From the Airport CTM (☎ 04 90 93 74 90) runs bus regular services to Nîmes-Arles-Camargue airport from blvd Georges Clemenceau.

Bus Local buses are run by STAR (☎ 04 90 96 87 47). The information office at 16 blvd Georges Clemenceau, west of the tourist office, opens 8.30 am to 12.30 pm and 1.30 to 6 pm (2 pm in summer; closed at the weekend). This is the main bus hub, though most buses also stop at place Lamartine, a short walk south of the train station. In general, STAR buses run from 7 am to 7 pm (5 pm on Sunday). A single ticket costs 5FF; a 10-ticket carnet 42FF. In addition to its 11 bus lines, STAR runs minibuses called Starlets that circle most of the old city every half-hour from 7.15 am to 7.40 pm Monday to Saturday. Best of all, they're free.

Taxi To order a taxi, ring ☎ 04 90 49 69 59.

CAMARGUE

The sparsely-populated, 780-sq-km delta of the River Rhône known as the Camargue is famed for its desolate beauty and the incredibly varied bird life that its wetlands support. Over 400 species of land and water birds inhabit the region, including storks, bee-eaters and some 160 other migratory species.

Most impressive of all are the huge flocks of pink flamingos that come here to nest during the spring and summer; many set up house near the Étang de Vaccarès and Étang du Fangassier lakes.

The Camargue has been formed over the ages by sediment deposited by the Rhône as it flows into the Mediterranean. In southern Camargue, the areas between the sea-wall embankments that line water channels are taken up by shallow salt marshes, inland

Camargue Cowboys

Gardians are Camargue cowboys who herd the region's cattle and, during the bullfighting season, bulls. The Fête des Gardians, held in Arles on the first weekend of May, honours these mounted herdsmen who, clad in leather hats, chequered shirts and cowboy boots, usher the horned beasts through town on horseback to the Arènes. Traditionally, *gardians* live in *cabanes de gardians*, tiny white-washed cottages crowned with a thatched roof and sealed with a strip of mortar.

lakes and lagoons whose brackish waters positively shimmer in the Provençal sun.

The northern part of the delta consists of dry land, and in the years following WWII huge tracts were desalinated as part of a costly drainage and irrigation programme designed to make the area suitable for large-scale agriculture, especially the cultivation of rice. Rice production is a very important part of the Camarguais economy.

Most of the Camargue wetlands are within the Parc Naturel Régional de Camargue, which was set up in 1970 to preserve the area's fragile ecosystems by maintaining a balance between ecological considerations and the region's economic mainstays of agriculture, salt production, hunting, grazing and tourism.

In certain areas, the Camargue's famous herds of cream-coloured horses can still be seen, along with the black bulls that are raised for bullfighting and roam free under the watchful eyes of a mounted *gardian* (see the boxed text 'Camargue Cowboys'). But you're much more likely to see bulls grazing in fenced-in fields and horses that are saddled and tethered, waiting in rows under the blazing sun for tourists willing to pay for a ride.

At least one traditional Camargue phenomenon is alive and well: the area's savage mosquitoes are flourishing, feeding on the blood of hapless passers-by just as they have for countless aeons. Pack *plenty* of insect repellent – then pack more.

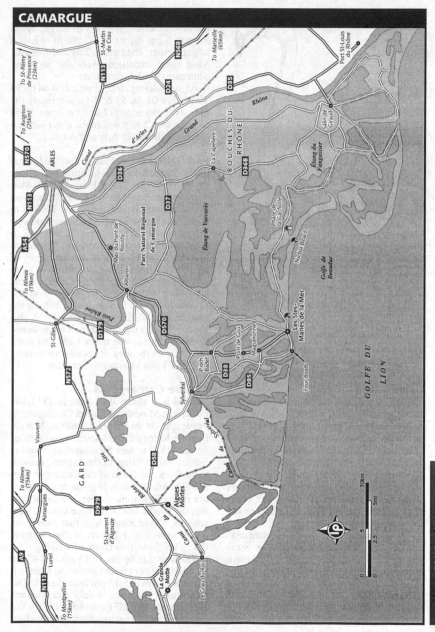

CAMARGUE

JANE SMITH

Impressive flocks of flamingos gather in the Camargue wetlands each spring.

fax 04 90 97 71 15, ✉ saintes-maries@ enprovence.com), 5 ave Van Gogh, opens 9 am to 6 pm daily (until 7 pm from Easter to September, and8 pm in July and August). Visit their excellent Web site at www .saintesmariesdelamer.com.

Aigues Mortes' tourist office (☎ 04 66 53 73 00, fax 04 66 53 65 94), just inside the old city at Porte de la Gardette, opens 9 am to noon and 2 to 6 pm (until 8 pm with no lunchtime break in July and August).

Park Offices The Parc Naturel Régional de Camargue has an information centre (☎ 04 90 97 86 32) at Pont de Gau, 4km north of Les Stes-Maries. Exhibits focus on environmental issues. From the glassed-in foyer you can watch birds through powerful binoculars. The centre opens 9 am to 6 pm (9.30 am to 5 pm from October to March; closed Friday). It also has plenty of information on walking and bird-watching.

The Réserve Nationale de Camargue has an office (☎ 04 90 97 00 97) at La Capelière, which is along the D36B on the eastern side of Étang de Vaccarès. It also has exhibits on the Camargue's ecosystems, flora and fauna, and many trails and paths fan out from the area. It opens 9 am to noon and 2 to 5 pm Monday to Saturday.

Orientation

Shaped like a croissant with the Étang de Vaccarès in the centre, the 850-sq-km Parc Naturel Régional de Camargue is enclosed by the Petit Rhône and Grand Rhône rivers. The Étang de Vaccarès and nearby peninsulas and islands form the Réserve Nationale de Camargue, a 135-sq-km nature reserve.

Rice is cultivated in the northern sections of the delta. There are enormous salt evaporation pools around Salin de Giraud on the Camargue's south-eastern tip.

The Camargue's two most important centres are the seaside resort of Les Stes-Maries de la Mer and the tiny walled town of Aigues Mortes to the north-west.

Information

Tourist Offices Les Stes-Maries de la Mer's tourist office (☎ 04 90 97 82 55,

Musée Camarguais

Housed in a sheep shed built in 1812, the Camargue Museum (Museon Camarguen in Provençal; ☎ 04 90 97 10 82) at Mas du Pont de Rousty (10km south-west of Arles on the D570 to Les Stes-Maries) is an excellent introduction to the history, ecosystems, flora and fauna of the Camargue river delta. Much attention is given to traditional life in the Camargue (sheep and cattle raising, salt production at Salin de Giraud, local arts). A 3.5km nature trail that ends at an observation tower begins at the museum. Count on about two hours of walking.

The museum opens 10.15 am to 4.45 pm (closed Tuesday) from October to March. It opens 9.15 am to 5.45 pm from April to October (until 6.45 pm in July and August). Admission costs 25FF (students 13FF). The museum can be reached from Arles by bus;

PROVENCE

The Gitan Pilgrimage

Every year for three days at the end of May, *Gitans* (Romany people, formerly called gypsies) from all over Europe gather at the Camargue fishing village of Les Stes-Maries de la Mer to honour their patron saint, Sarah. According to a Provençal legend, Sarah (along with Mary Magdelene, Mary Jacob, Mary Salome and other Biblical figures) fled the Holy Land in a small boat, drifting around for a while before landing near the River Rhône.

In 1448, skeletal remains believed to have belonged to Sarah, Mary Jacob and Mary Salome were found in a crypt in Les Stes-Maries. Gitans have been making the pilgrimage here ever since, though these days they make a few concessions to modernity. In the old days pilgrims arrived by horse or carriage; today they pull into town by car and camper van. But there's still plenty of dancing and music performed in the streets, and a statue of Sarah is carried through the town accompanied by men and women in traditional dress and tossed into the sea. *Courses Camarguaises* (non-lethal bull-fights) are also held. The Festival Mosaïque Gitane, a celebration of Gitan culture with theatre, music, film and dance, is held in Arles every year in mid-July.

see Getting There & Away in that section for details.

Aigues Mortes
postcode 30220 • pop 4999
On the western edge of the Camargue, 28km north-west of Les Stes-Maries, is the curiously named walled town of Aigues Mortes (which could be translated as Dead Waters'). Aigues Mortes was established on marshy flat land in the mid-13th century by Louis IX (St Louis) so the French crown would have a Mediterranean port under its direct control. (At the time, the area's other ports were controlled by various rival powers, including the counts of Provence.) In 1248, Louis IX's ships – all 1500 of them – gathered here before setting sail to the Holy Land for the Sixth Crusade.

Aigues Mortes' sturdy, rectangular ramparts, the tops of which afford great views over the marshlands, can be easily circumambulated from Tour de Constance. Inside the walls, there's a fair bit of tourist hype, though the restored Église Notre Dame des Sablons is worth a look.

Les Stes-Maries de la Mer
postcode 13732 • pop 2478
This coastal resort is known for its nearby beaches and fortified Romanesque church (12th to 15th centuries), a pilgrimage site for centuries.

Les Stes-Maries is most animated during the annual Gitan pilgrimage (see the boxed text 'The Gitan Pilgrimage') on 24–25 May. There is a **Musée des Gitanes** (☎ 04 90 97 52 85), also known as the 'Panorama du Voyage', next to the Auberge de Jeunesse in Pioch Badet.

Tickets for **bullfights** held in Les Stes-Maries' Arènes on ave Van Gogh are sold at the ticket office, tucked into its outer walls, between 3 and 7 pm Monday to Saturday. Reservations can also be made by phoning ☎ 04 90 97 10 60.

Beaches
The coast near Les Stes-Maries is lined with around 30km of uninterrupted fine-sand beaches. The area around **Phare de la Gacholle**, the lighthouse 11km east of town, is frequented by *naturalistes* (nudists).

Walking
There are numerous walking paths and trails in the Parc Naturel Régional and the Réserve Nationale, on the embankments and along the coast. Both park offices sell detailed walking maps of the area, including the 1:25,000 IGN Série Bleue maps Nos 2944E and 2944O.

Boat Excursions
Several companies with offices in Les

PROVENCE

Stes-Maries have boat excursions of the Camargue, including Camargue Bateau de Promenade (☎ 04 90 97 84 72), 5 rue des Launes, and Quatre Maries (☎ 04 90 97 70 10), 36 ave Théodore Aubanel. Both depart from the Port Gardian in the centre of Les Stes-Maries.

Le Tiki III (☎ 04 90 97 81 68) is a beat-up old paddleboat that plies the delta's shallow waters and charges 60FF for a 1½-hour tour. Le Tiki is docked at the mouth of the Petit Rhône 1.5km west of Les Stes-Maries.

Other Activities

There are numerous horse farms offering *promenade à cheval* (horse riding) along the D570 (Route d'Arles) leading into Les Stes-Maries. Expect to pay about 75/350FF an hour/day.

For detailed info on equestrian activities in the Camargue contact the Association Camarguaise de Tourisme Équestre (☎ 04 90 97 86 32, fax 04 90 97 70 82), Centre de Gines, Pont de Gau.

Kayak Vert Camargue (☎ 06 09 56 06 47 or ☎ 04 90 97 88 89, fax 04 90 97 80 32), Mas des Baumelles, 8km north of Les Stes-Maries off the D38, arranges canoeing and kayaking on the Petit Rhône.

Organised Tours

La Maison du Guide (☎ 06 12 44 73 52, fax 04 66 73 52 30, ✆ guide.camargue@wanadoo.fr), at Montcalm, between Aigues-Mortes and Les Stes-Maries on the D58, organises a variety of guided tours on foot, by boat and by bike.

Many companies in Arles organise tours of the Camargue by jeep (see Organised Tours in the Arles section). In Les Stes-Maries, Safari Photo du Delta (☎ 04 66 70 09 65, fax 04 66 70 22 47), on the seafront at 13 ave de la Plage, organises jeep safaris.

Places to Stay

Camping Three-star *Camping La Brise* (☎ 04 90 97 84 67, fax 04 90 97 72 01, ave Marcle Carrière), is north-east of the centre of Les Stes-Maries. One person plus tent costs 50FF in high season.

Four-star *Camping Le Clos du Rhône* (☎ 04 90 97 85 99, fax 04 90 97 78 85) is on the Route d'Aigues Mortes. Both sites have swimming pools and you can also rent four-person bungalows. The charge for one person plus tent is 70FF in high season.

Hostels There's an *Auberge de Jeunesse* (☎ 04 90 97 51 72, fax 04 90 97 54 88) in the hamlet of Pioch Badet, 8km north of Les Stes-Maries on the D570 to Arles. Bed and breakfast costs 65FF. Reception opens 7.30 to 10.30 am and 5 to 11 pm (5 pm to midnight in July and August).

Les Cars de Camargue buses from Arles to Les Stes-Maries (36.50FF, one hour, six to nine daily) drop you at the door (see Bus under Getting There & Away in the Arles section for details).

Farmhouses Numerous old *mas* (farmhouses) surround Les Stes-Maries; many have rooms to let. Particularly good value is *Mas de la Grenouillère* (☎ 04 90 97 90 22, fax 04 90 97 70 94, 1.5km down a dirt track signposted 1km north of Les Stes-Maries off the D570. The small but comfortable rooms have a terrace overlooking open fields full of frogs which sing guests to sleep each night. Doubles/triples start at 260/380FF. La Grenouillère (literally, 'the frog farm') has a swimming pool and stables, and organises horse riding.

Even more idyllic is nearby *Étrier Camarguais* (☎ 04 90 97 81 14, fax 04 90 97 88 11), a farmhouse-hotel built from 'a dream, flowers and the sun' 500m before La Grenouillère along the same dirt track. Doubles cost 400/540FF in the low/high season. The reception of the 'Camargue Stirrup' is in a traditional *cabane de gardian* (see the boxed text 'Camargue Cowboys' earlier in this section).

Hotels Heaps of hotels – mostly three or four stars, in the low-rise 'farmhouse style' and costing at least 300FF per night – line the D570, the main road from Arles into Les Stes-Maries. Hotels in town are equally expensive.

PROVENCE

The cheapest rooms can be had at *Les Vagues* (☎/fax 04 90 97 84 40, 12 ave Théodore Aubanel), on the road that runs along the port west of the tourist office, or *Le Delta* (☎ 04 90 97 81 12, fax 04 90 97 72 85, 1 place Mireille) on the right as you enter Les Stes-Maries from the north. Doubles at Les Vagues start at 190FF. Le Delta offers shower-equipped singles/doubles for 185/205FF.

The cheapest place to stay in Aigues Mortes' historical centre is *Hôtel Carrière* (☎ 04 66 53 73 07, fax 04 66 53 84 75, 18 rue Pasteur), where rooms start at 200FF.

A cut above it is *Hôtel St-Louis* (☎ 04 66 53 72 68, fax 04 66 53 75 92, 10 rue Amiral Courbet), with rooms from 280FF to 490FF. The St-Louis closes from January to mid-March. Both hotels have good restaurants with *menus* from 79FF and 98FF, respectively.

Getting There & Away

For details about bus connections to/from Arles (via Pont de Gau and Mas du Pont de Rousty) and the three day Passe Camargue ticket, see Bus under Getting There & Away in the Arles section. In the high season, there are two buses a day from Les Stes-Maries to Nîmes (1¼ hours) via Aigues Mortes.

Getting Around

As long as you can put up with the ubiquitous insect pests and stiff sea breezes, bicycles are a fine way to explore the Camargue which is, of course, very flat. East of Les Stes-Maries, areas along the seafront and farther inland are reserved for walkers and cyclists.

For a list of cycling routes (in English) go to Le Vélo Saintois (☎/fax 04 90 97 74 56), 19 ave de la République, which hires out mountain bikes for 80/200FF per day/three days. It also has tandems and delivers bikes to your hotel door.

The Pioch Badet hostel and Le Vélociste (☎ 04 90 97 83 26), place des Remparts, both rent bikes too. The latter offers bike, horse and canoe packages.

North-Eastern Provence

DIGNE-LES-BAINS

postcode 04000 • pop 16,064

Provence hits the Alps, and the land of snow and melted cheese meets the land of sun and olives, around Digne-les-Bains, which is 106km north-east of Aix-en-Provence and 152km north-west of Nice. This laid-back town is named after its thermal springs, visited annually by 11,000 people in search of a water cure for rheumatism, respiratory ailments and other medical conditions.

The area is also known for the production of lavender, which is harvested in August and honoured in Digne with the five-day festival, Corso de la Lavande, starting on the first weekend of the month, and with Les Journées Lavande throughout the region in mid-August. In summer, you'll smell the little purple flower everywhere. In spring, flowering poppies sprinkle the green fields with buttons of bright red.

Digne itself is unremarkable, though it was the home of a very remarkable woman, Alexandra David-Néel, an adventurer whose travels to Tibet brought her wide acclaim. The shale around Digne is rich in fossils.

The route Napoléon (now the N85 in these parts), which Bonaparte followed in 1815 on his way to Paris after his escape from Elba, passes through Digne and Castellane, the gateway to the Gorges du Verdon.

Orientation

Digne is built on the eastern bank of the shallow Bléone River. The major roads into town converge at the Point Rond du 11 Novembre 1918, a roundabout 400m north-east of the train station. The main street is plane tree-lined blvd Gassendi, which heads north-eastwards from the Point Rond and passes the large place du Général de Gaulle, the town's main public square.

PROVENCE

Information

Tourist Offices The tourist office (☎ 04 92 31 42 73, fax 04 92 36 62 62, ❷ info@ ot-dignelesbains.fr) inside the Maison du Tourisme, 11 Point Rond du 11 Novembre 1918, opens 8.45 am to noon and 2 to 6 pm Monday to Saturday. It opens 8.45 am to 12.30 pm and 2 to 7 pm from May to October (10.30 am to noon and 3 to 7 pm on Sunday). The office has information on a variety of guided tours in the region.

The Relais Départemental des Gîtes de France (☎ 04 92 31 52 39, fax 04 92 32 32 63), also in the Maison du Tourisme, books accommodation at gîtes in the area. It opens 8 am to noon and 2 to 6 pm (5 pm on Friday; closed at the weekend). Bookings are only made between 9 and 11 am and 1 to 4 pm.

Money The Banque de France, 16 blvd Soustre, opens 8.45 am to noon and 1.45 to 3.45 pm Monday to Friday.

Post & Communications Digne's main post office, east of the tourist office at 4 rue André Honnorat, opens 8 am to 7 pm (Saturday until noon; closed Sunday). The Abrite le Cybercafe (☎ 04 92 30 87 17, ❷ cybercafe@mairie-digneslesbains.fr) is in the centre of the town.

Laundry The laundrette in the old city, 4 place du Marché, opens 8 am to 7 pm (closed Sunday). The one at 99 blvd Gassendi opens 9 am to 7 pm.

Fondation Alexandra David-Néel

Paris-born writer and philosopher Alexandra David-Néel, who spent her last years in Digne, is known for the incognito voyage she made early in the 1900s to Tibet. Her memory – and her interest in Tibet – are kept enthusiastically alive by the Fondation Alexandra David-Néel (☎ 04 92 31 32 38), which occupies her erstwhile residence at 27 ave Maréchal Juin, as well as by the Journées Tibétaines, an annual celebration of Tibetan culture held at the end of August. Fondation Alexandra David-Néel is just over 1km from town on the road to Nice.

From October to June, free tours (with headphones for English speakers) start at 10.30 am and 2 and 4 pm; from April to September, tours begin at 10.30 am and 2, 3.30 and 5 pm. To get there take TUD bus No 3 to the Stade Rolland stop.

Museums

In the old city, the **Musée d'Art Religieux** (☎ 04 92 36 75 00), place des Récollets, south-east of the cathedral in the Chapelle des Pénitents, displays liturgical objects and religious art. It opens from 10 am to 6 pm July to October.

Réserve Naturelle Géologique

Digne is in the middle of the Réserve Naturelle Géologique, whose spectacular fossil deposits include the footprints of prehistoric birds as well as ammonites, spiral shells that look something like a ram's horn. You'll need a detailed regional map or a topoguide to the Digne and Sisteron areas (sold at the tourist office) and your own transport (or a patient thumb) to get to the 18 sites, most of which are around **Barles** (24km north of Digne) and **Barrême** (28km south-east of Digne). There's an impressive limestone slab with some 500 ammonites 3km north of Digne on the road to Barles (and 1km north of the Centre de Géologie).

The Réserve Naturelle's headquarters, the **Centre de Géologie** (☎ 04 92 36 70 70, fax 04 92 36 70 71) at St-Benoît, is 2km north of town off the road to Barles. Its exhibits on matters mineral and geological open 9 am to noon and 2 to 5.30 pm (4.30 pm on Friday; closed at the weekend from November to March). Admission costs 25FF (students/children 18/15FF). Take TUD bus No 2, get off over the bridge at the Champourcin stop, then take the road to the left.

Thermal Spa

You can take to the waters from February to early December at the Établissement Thermal (☎ 04 92 32 32 92) 2km east of Digne's centre. The cost of a good soak starts at 35FF and goes up to 155FF for a spa bath and massage. Voyeurs rather than *curistes*

PROVENCE

can join the weekly free tour on Thursday at 2 pm from March to August.

Places to Stay

In July and August you may be required to take half-board at many of Digne's hotels.

Camping The *Camping du Bourg* (☎ 04 92 31 04 87, route de Barcelonnette), nearly 2km north-east of Digne, opens April to October and costs 65FF for two people with a car and tent or caravan (60FF if you're taking a cure). Take bus No 2 towards Barcelonnette and get off at the Notre Dame du Bourg stop. From there it's a 600m walk.

Camping des Eaux Chaudes (☎ 04 92 32 31 04, route des Thermes), near the Établissement Thermal about 1.5km from Digne, charges 75FF for two people with a car and tent or caravan (67FF for curistes). Both sites open from 1 April to 31 October each year.

Gîtes d'Étape Walkers can avail themselves of the *Gîte du Château des Sièyes* (☎ 04 92 31 20 30, ave Georges Pompidou), nearly 2km north-west of the town centre off the road to Sisteron. Dorm beds cost 55FF. Take bus No 1 headed for Sisteron, and get off at the Pompidou stop.

The peaceful *Centre de Géologie* (☎ 04 92 36 70 70) at St-Benoît has rooms for one, two and four people and charges 60FF per person.

Hotels Overlooking the central place du Général de Gaulle, the *Hôtel Petit St-Jean* (☎ 04 92 31 30 04, fax 04 92 36 05 80, 14 cours des Arès), has good-value double rooms from 150FF to 190FF. *Menus* in its terrace restaurant start at 67FF.

In the old city, little *Hôtel L'Origan* (☎/fax 04 92 31 62 13, 6 rue Pied de Ville), has an upmarket restaurant (*menus* for 70FF, 98FF, 125FF and 170FF) but affordable singles with washbasin starting at 90FF and doubles with shower starting at 140FF.

Two-star *Hôtel Central* (☎ 04 92 31 31 91, fax 04 92 31 49 78, 26 blvd Gassendi), has doubles starting at 150FF to 315FF. Also with two stars, *Hôtel Le Coin Fleuri*

(☎ 04 92 31 04 51, 9 blvd Victor Hugo), has doubles with washbasin/shower starting at 220/300FF and a great garden to relax in.

For something a bit more upmarket there's *Hostellerie de L'Aiglon* (☎ 04 92 31 02 70, fax 04 92 32 45 83, @ aiglon@ alpes-net.fr, 1 rue de Provence), whose entrance attached to the Chapelle St-Esprit leads to calm, pastel rooms starting at 240FF. It costs 15FF to park in the private garage. Its restaurant, La Chapelle, serves good regional fare.

Places to Eat

Restaurants One of the cheapest places in town for lunch is the *Restaurant-Cafétéria Le Victor Hugo* (☎ 04 92 31 57 23, 8–10 blvd Victor Hugo), with *plats du jour* from around 35FF. *Le Point Chaud* (☎ 04 92 31 30 71, 95 blvd Gassendi), is a dark, cheap and local haunt.

Away from the terraces on place du Général de Gaulle, *La Braisière* (☎ 04 92 31 59 63, 19 place de l'Évêché), has a good lunch *menu* for 68FF, a dinner *menu* for 90FF and a fine view over the town. It does excellent *tartiflette* (85FF) and *raclette* (95FF).

Self-Catering A *food market* takes over place du Général de Gaulle on Wednesday and Saturday mornings. Luxury local products are sold at *Saveurs et Couleurs* (7 blvd Gassendi). *Casino Supermarket* (42 blvd Gassendi) opens 7.30 am to 12.30 pm and 3.30 to 7.30 pm.

Getting There & Away

Bus The bus station (☎ 04 92 31 50 00) is behind the tourist office on place du Tampinet. Some 11 regional companies operate buses to Nice (150FF, 2¼ hours, at 1.45 pm) via Castellane (near the Gorges du Verdon, 64FF, 1¼ hours, one daily) as well as Marseilles (80FF, 2½ hours, four daily) and Apt (61.50FF, two hours, two daily). The bus station opens 8.40 am to 12.30 pm and 2.30 to 6.30 pm Monday to Saturday.

Train The train station (☎ 04 92 31 00 67) is a 10-minute walk westwards from the

PROVENCE

tourist office on ave Pierre Sémard. The ticket windows open 8.15 am to 12.30 pm and 1 to 8 pm (8.15 am to 12.30 pm and 1.45 to 4.45 pm on Saturday). There are four trains daily to Marseilles (138FF, 2¼ hours) and three to Briançon (153FF) via St-Auban.

The two-car diesel trains operated by the government-owned Chemins de Fer de la Provence (☎ 04 92 31 01 58 in Digne; ☎ 04 93 82 10 72 in Nice) run along a scenic and winding narrow-gauge line to Nice's Gare du Sud (☎ 04 93 82 10 17) via St-Martin du Var, 26km north-east of Nice. The entire trip takes about 3¼ hours and costs 109FF one way. There are four runs in each direction a day.

GORGES DU VERDON

The gorgeous 25km-long Gorges du Verdon (also known as the Grand Canyon du Verdon), the largest canyon in Europe, slice through the limestone plateau midway between Avignon and Nice. They begin at Rougon (near the confluence of the Verdon and Jabron rivers) and continue westwards until the river flows into Lac de Ste-Croix. The village of Castellane (population 1349) is east of Rougon and is the main gateway for the gorges.

Carved by the greenish waters of the Verdon River, the gorges are 250m to 700m deep. The bottom is 8m to 90m wide, while the rims are 200m to 1500m apart.

Information

Tourist Offices The best source of information for the Gorges du Verdon is the Castellane tourist office (☎ 04 92 83 61 14, fax 04 92 83 76 89, ✉ office@castellane. org), rue Nationale, or its counterpart in Moustiers Ste-Marie (☎ 04 92 74 67 84, fax 04 92 74 60 65). The Castellane office opens 9 am to 1 pm and 2 to 7 pm (closed on Sunday afternoon). Moustiers opens 10 am to noon and 2 to 7 pm.

There's a small tourist office in the centre of La Palud-sur-Verdon (☎/fax 04 92 77 32 02 or ☎ 04 92 77 38 02), and a Syndicat d'Initiative (☎/fax 04 94 85 68 40) in Trigance.

The Canyon

The bottom of the gorges can be visited only on foot or by raft, but motorists and cyclists can enjoy spectacular (if dizzying) views from two cliff-side roads.

The Northern Rim The D952 follows the northern rim and passes the **Point Sublime** viewpoint at the canyon's entrance, from where the GR4 trail leads to the bottom of the gorge. The best view from the northern side is from **Belvédère de l'Escalès** along the currently blocked **route de Crêtes** (D23). Drive to the third bend and hold your breath since the drop-off down into the gorge is quite stunning. Retrace your steps to the D952.

Another stunning view is offered by **La Corniche Sublime** (the D19 to the D71), which goes along the southern rim and takes you to such landmarks as the **Balcons de la Mescla** (Mescla Terraces) and **pont de l'Artuby** (Artuby Bridge), the highest bridge in Europe.

A complete circuit of the Gorges du Verdon via Moustiers Ste-Marie involves about 140km of driving; the tourist office in Castellane has the good English-language brochure *Driving Tours* with 11 itineraries. The only real village en route is **Palud-sur-Verdon** (930m), 2km north-east of the northern bank of the gorges. In summer, heavy traffic often slows travel to a crawl.

The bottom of the canyon, first explored in its entirety in 1905, presents walkers and white-water rafters with an overwhelming series of cliffs and narrows. You can walk most of it along the often difficult GR4, which is covered by Didier-Richard's 1:50,000 scale map No 19, *Haute Provence-Verdon* (72FF). It is also included in the excellent English-language book, *Canyon du Verdon – The Most Beautiful Hikes* (27FF at Castellane or Moustiers tourist offices), which lists 28 walks in the gorges. The full GR4 takes two days, though short descents into the canyon are possible from a number of points. Bring along a torch (flashlight) and drinking water. Camping rough on gravel beaches along the way is illegal, but people do it.

PROVENCE

Activities

Castellane's tourist office has a complete list of companies offering rafting, canyoning, horse riding, mountaineering, biking and other outdoor pursuits. Aboard Rafting (☎/fax 04 92 83 76 11), 8 place Marcel Sauvaire, runs white-water rafting trips (180FF to 440FF) as well as canyoning (200FF to 350FF), hot-dogging (200FF), windsurfing, paragliding and mountain biking. It is open from April to September.

Places to Stay & Eat

Camping *Camping de Bourbon* (☎ 04 92 77 38 17), just east of La Palud, charges about 14FF per person and 6FF for a tent. It is open from May to September. Near Castellane, the river is lined with some 15 seasonal camp sites that tend to be crowded and pricey. *Domaine de Chasteuil Provence* (☎ 04 92 83 61 21, fax 04 92 83 75 62), just south of Castellane and sporting a swimming pool is open from June to mid-October and charges 60/73FF for two people with a car and tent in the low/high season.

Hostels The *Auberge de Jeunesse Le Trait d'Union* (☎ 04 92 77 38 72, fax 04 92 77 30 48), 500m south of La Palud at the beginning of La Route des Crêtes (here called Route de la Maline), opens from April to October. Bed and breakfast costs 66FF.

Gîte d'Étape de Fontaine Basse (☎ 04 94 85 68 36, fax 04 94 85 68 50), 16km south-east of Castellane in Trigance, charges 100FF for bed and breakfast. In Castellane, a bed at *L'Oustaou* gîte d'étape (☎ 04 92 83 77 27, chemin des Listes), costs 60FF a night.

Hotels If you're not looking for something expensive, Castellane is the place for you. Numerous hotels line the central square, place Marcel Sauvaire, and adjoining place de l'Église. For particularly good value there's the *Grand Hôtel du Levant* (☎ 04 92 83 60 05, fax 04 92 83 72 14), an impressive pile on place Marcel Sauvaire, which offers singles/doubles with shower and toilet for 150/180FF.

Shower-equipped doubles with toilet at

Hôtel La Forge (☎ 04 92 83 62 61, place de l'Église) start at 200FF, while *Hostellerie du Roc* (04 92 83 62 65, place de l'Église) has doubles/triples starting at 225/300FF.

Off place Marcel Sauvaire, *Hôtel du Verdon* (☎ 04 92 83 62 02, fax 04 92 83 73 80, rue de la République) has doubles with washbasin/shower for 160/180FF. On the same street, *Ma Petite Auberge* (☎ 04 92 83 62 06, fax 04 92 83 68 49, rue de la République) has doubles with shower that cost 190FF and ones with toilet too for 240FF.

A 10-minute walk from town is the excellent-value *Stadi Hôtel* (☎ 04 92 83 76 47, fax 04 94 84 63 36), on the N85 out of Castellane (direction Digne-les-Bains). It has a swimming pool, shows English-language films every evening and has doubles for 220FF. A week's stay in a two- to four-person studio costs 2700FF.

If you are looking for something expensive head for the three-star *Château de Trigance* (☎ 04 94 76 91 18, fax 04 94 85 68 99), 16km south-east of Castellane in the hilltop village of Trigance. Rooms in the restored 10th century castle start at 600FF.

Getting There & Away

Public transport to, from and around the Gorges du Verdon is limited. Autocars Sumian (☎ 04 42 67 60 34 in Jouques) runs buses from Marseilles to Castellane via Aix-en-Provence (109FF), La Palud and Moustiers. VFD (☎ 04 76 47 77 77 in Grenoble; ☎ 04 93 85 24 56 in Nice) runs a daily bus from Grenoble to Nice via Digne and Grasse, stopping in Castellane en route. The tourist offices have schedules.

Getting Around

Bus In July and August, Navettes Autocar (☎ 04 92 83 40 27) runs shuttle buses around the gorges daily except Sunday, linking Castellane with the Point Sublime, La Palud and La Maline. Ask at the tourist office in Castellane for schedules and fares.

Bicycle The Stadi Hôtel (see Places to Stay) rents mountain bikes for 50/75FF a

PROVENCE

half/full day. L'Arc-en-Ciel (☎ 04 92 77 37 40), a restaurant and gîte near central place de l'Église in La Palud, rents bikes too.

PRA-LOUP

The ski resort of Pra-Loup (elevation 1600m), 8.5km south-west of Barcelonnette and 70km south-east of Gap, is connected by a lift system across the Vallon des Agneliers with another ski resort called La Foux d'Allos. The upper part of the Pra-Loup has been built up with many apartment blocks, while the lower part has chalet-style accommodation.

There is a large variety of runs for all levels of skiers and snowboarders, but the majority are for intermediates and advanced. Cross-country skiing is limited around Pra-Loup and is better in the Ubaye Valley. St-Paul-sur-Ubaye, in a valley below and to the north-east of Pra-Loup, has 25km of cross-country runs at 1400m to 1500m and Larche has 30km of runs at 1700m to 2000m.

Pra-Loup's 53 lifts are between 1600m and 2600m, with 160km of runs and a vertical drop of almost 1000m.

Information

The tourist office (☎ 04 92 84 10 04, fax 04 92 84 02 93, ✉ praloup@karatel.fr), École de Ski Français (ESF; ☎ 04 92 84 11 05) and post office, where you can change money too, are all inside the Maison de Pra-Loup.

Places to Stay

Studios and apartments are the best option and cost from 1090FF per week for two during the low season. At the bottom end of the hotel range is *Auberge de Pra-Loup* (☎ 04 92 84 10 05) in the eastern part of the village, which has doubles from 170FF plus 25FF for breakfast. Mid-range *Hôtel Manon* (☎ 04 92 84 17 82, fax 04 92 84 15 08) in the western part of the village has decent rooms from 295FF to 335FF. *Hôtel Les Airelles* (☎ 04 92 84 13 24, fax 04 92 84 64 09) in the centre of the village is at the top end with rooms from 335/500FF in the low/high season.

Getting There & Away

The nearest train station is Gap, from where there are a couple of buses daily to Pra-Loup (53FF, 1¾ hours) via Barcelonnette.

LA FOUX D'ALLOS

La Foux d'Allos (1800m) is connected by a lift system to Pra-Loup. By road, Pra-Loup is 23.5km to the north, but there is no public transport available between the two resorts. The tourist office (☎ 04 92 83 80 70, fax 04 92 83 86 27) is in the Maison de la Foux, on the main square.

Places to Stay

The *Auberge de Jeunesse* (☎ 04 92 83 81 08, fax 04 92 83 83 70, ✉ la-foux-allos@ fuaj.org) is in the upper part of the village near the major lift stations. In summer, a bed in a room for two, four, six or eight people costs around 84FF including breakfast. In winter, only weekly packages are usually available.

Apartments are the main type of accommodation here and studios for two start at 1300FF per week during the low season and 2800FF in the high season. One of the few hotels at La Foux is the *Hôtel Le Toukal* (☎ 04 92 83 82 76) on the main square, which has rooms costing from 180/330FF, depending on the season. Fine rooms at three-star *Hôtel Le Sestrière* (☎ 04 92 83 81 70, fax 04 92 83 11 62) near the main square cost between 300FF and 400FF.

Getting There & Away

Buses link the village of La Foux d'Allos, which is 9km south-east of the resort, with Digne-les-Bains and Avignon.

It is possible to get to La Foux d'Allos from Nice by train departing from Nice's Gare des Chemins de Fer de Provence (☎ 04 93 88 34 72), 4 bis rue Alfred-Binet. Take a train to La Vœsubie-Plan-du-Var. The rest of the trip is by bus, with a change required at Thorame.

Another option is to take an Autocars Girieud bus (☎ 04 92 83 40 27) from Nice and Digne, changing buses in Thorame.

Côte d'Azur & Monaco

The Côte d'Azur (Azure Coast), also known as the French Riviera, stretches along France's Mediterranean coast from Toulon to the Italian border. Technically part of Provence, it also includes most of the departments of Alpes-Maritimes and Var. Many towns along the coast – Nice, Monaco, Antibes, Cannes, St-Tropez – are well known as the playgrounds of the rich, famous and tanned, and publicised in films and in the tabloids and glossy magazines. The reality is rather less glamorous, but the Côte d'Azur still has a great deal to attract visitors: sun, 40km of beach, sea water as warm as 25°C, all sorts of cultural activities and, sometimes, even a sprinkle of glitter.

The capital of the Côte d'Azur is Nice, whose plentiful hotels and excellent rail links make it a good base for exploring the region. As you follow the coast westwards, you come to the attractive town of Antibes, the wealthy resort of Cannes and, just west of the stunning red mountain known as the Massif de l'Estérel, the twin towns of St-Raphaël and Fréjus. Inland, the hills overlooking the coast are dotted with towns and villages such as Grasse (renowned for its perfumes), Vence, St-Paul de Vence and Bormes-les-Mimosas.

The forested Massif des Maures stretches from St-Raphaël to Hyères. West of the fashionable port town of St-Tropez you'll find the region's most unspoiled coastline, where capes and cliffs alternate with streams and beaches, many of the latter sheltered from the open sea by the Îles d'Hyères – three large islands (and a couple of tiny ones) some 10km offshore. Workaday Toulon, best known for its role as a naval base, is at the western edge of the Côte d'Azur.

East of Nice, the foothills of the Alps plummet precipitously into the Mediterranean. Three roads, known as *corniches*, take you eastwards from Nice past a number of villages overlooking the sea to Menton and the Italian border. The tiny

Highlights

- **Nice** – hang out in the Côte d'Azur's liveliest and happening city
- **Grasse** – learn what it takes to be a *nez* (nose) at the *parfumeries*
- **Cannes** – go for a stroll along blvd de la Croisette or lay on Cannes' sandy beach
- **Monaco** – see how royalty lives in the Palais du Prince, or watch the world-famous Formula 1 Grand Prix race
- **Îles de Lérins** and **Îles d'Hyères** – explore these fascinating and tranquil islands

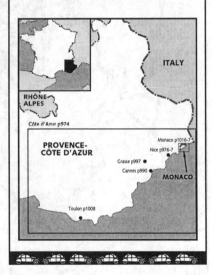

Principality of Monaco, with its centre at Monte Carlo, is roughly midway between Nice and Menton.

History

Occupied by the Ligurians from the 1st millennium BC, the eastern part of France's Mediterranean coast was colonised around 600 BC by Greeks from Asia Minor, who

CÔTE D'AZUR

CÔTE D'AZUR

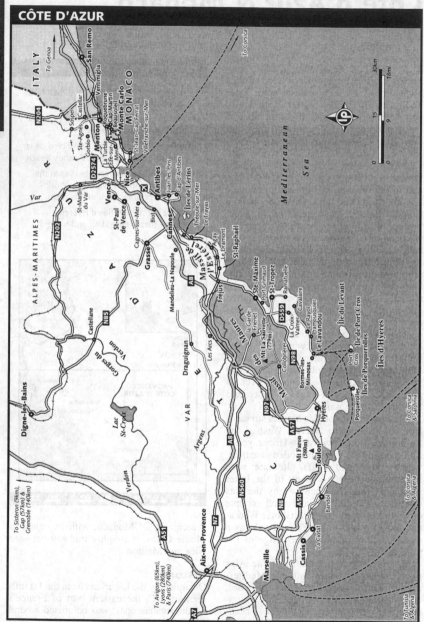

settled in Massalia (modern-day Marseille). The colony soon expanded to other points along the coast, including what are now Hyères, St-Tropez, Antibes and Nice. Called in to help Massalia against the threat of invasion by Celto-Ligurians from Entremont in 125 BC, the Romans defeated the Celts and Ligurians and created the Provincia Romana – the area between the Alps, the sea and the River Rhône – from which the name Provence is derived.

In 1388 Nice and its hinterland, also known as the County of Nice, were incorporated into the lands of the House of Savoy. The rest of Provence became part of the French kingdom in 1482; the centralist policies of the French kings saw the region's autonomy greatly reduced. In 1860, after an agreement between Napoleon III and the House of Savoy helped drive the Austrians from northern Italy, France took possession of Savoy and the area around Nice.

In the 19th century, wealthy French, English, American and Russian tourists discovered the Côte d'Azur. Primarily a winter resort, the area attracted an increasing number of affluent visitors thanks to its beauty and temperate climate. The intensity and clarity of the region's colours and light appealed to many painters – particularly the impressionists – including Cézanne, Van Gogh, Matisse and Picasso. Writers and other celebrities were also attracted to the region and contributed to its fame. Little fishing ports became exclusive resorts, and in no time the most beautiful spots were occupied by private villas that looked more like castles. With improved rail and road access and the advent of paid holidays for all French workers in 1936, even more tourists flocked to the region, leading to its development as a summer resort.

Radio

The Monte Carlo-based Riviera Radio, an English-language radio station that broadcasts 24 hours a day, can be picked up on 106.3 MHz FM in Monaco, and on 106.5 MHz FM and 98.8 MHz FM along the rest of the Côte d'Azur. The BBC World Service news is broadcast every hour.

Dangers & Annoyances

Theft – from backpacks, pockets, cars and even laundrettes – is a serious problem along the Côte d'Azur. Keep a very sharp eye on your bags, especially at train and bus stations, on overnight trains (the Rome–Nice–Barcelona line is notorious for thefts), in tourist offices, in fast-food restaurants, and on the beaches.

Getting There & Away

For information on ferry services from Nice and Toulon to Corsica, see the Getting There & Away section in the Corsica chapter.

Getting Around

SNCF trains shuttle back and forth along the coast between St-Raphaël and the Italian border, making Nice (Nizza in Italian) a great base for exploring the eastern half of the Côte d'Azur. The area between St-Raphaël – where the train line veers inland – and Toulon can be reached by bus.

If you're planning to drive along the coast in summer, be prepared for some mighty slow going. It can sometimes take hours to move just a few kilometres, no doubt the reason why the well heeled have taken to reaching their seaside properties by helicopter.

However, except for the traffic-plagued high season, the Côte d'Azur is easily accessible by car. The fastest way to get around is by the boring A8 autoroute which, travelling west to east, starts near Aix-en-Provence, approaches the coast at Fréjus, skirts the Estérel range and runs more or less parallel to the coast from Cannes all the way to the Italian border at Ventimiglia (Vintimille in French).

Nice to Toulon

NICE

postcode 06000 & 06300 • pop 342,738

The fashionable but relaxed and fun city of Nice, considered the capital of the Riviera, makes a great base from which to explore the rest of the Côte d'Azur. The city has lots of relatively cheap places to stay and is only

CÔTE D'AZUR

NICE

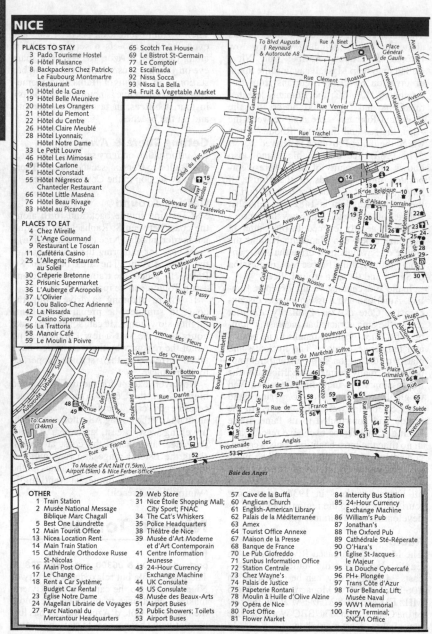

PLACES TO STAY
3 Pado Tourisme Hostel
6 Hôtel Plaisance
8 Backpackers Chez Patrick;
   Le Faubourg Montmartre
   Restaurant
10 Hôtel de la Gare
19 Hôtel Belle Meunière
20 Hôtel Les Orangers
21 Hôtel du Piemont
22 Hôtel du Centre
26 Hôtel Claire Meublé
28 Hôtel Lyonnais;
   Hôtel Notre Dame
33 Le Petit Louvre
46 Hôtel Les Mimosas
49 Hôtel Carlone
54 Hôtel Cronstadt
55 Hôtel Négresco &
   Chantecler Restaurant
66 Hôtel Little Maséna
76 Hôtel Beau Rivage
83 Hôtel au Picardy

65 Scotch Tea House
69 Le Bistrot St-Germain
77 Le Comptoir
82 Escalinada
92 Nissa Socca
93 Nissa La Bella
94 Fruit & Vegetable Market

PLACES TO EAT
4 Chez Mireille
7 L'Ange Gourmand
9 Restaurant Le Toscan
11 Cafétéria Casino
25 L'Allegria; Restaurant
   au Soleil
30 Crêperie Bretonne
32 Prisunic Supermarket
36 L'Auberge d'Acropolis
37 L'Olivier
40 Lou Balico-Chez Adrienne
42 La Nissarda
47 Casino Supermarket
56 La Trattoria
58 Manoir Café
59 Le Moulin à Poivre

OTHER
1 Train Station
2 Musée National Message
   Biblique Marc Chagall
5 Best One Laundrette
12 Main Tourist Office
13 Nicea Location Rent
14 Main Train Station
15 Cathédrale Orthodoxe Russe
   St-Nicolas
16 Main Post Office
17 Le Change
18 Rent a Car Système;
   Budget Car Rental
23 Église Notre Dame
24 Magellan Librairie de Voyages
27 Parc National du
   Mercantour Headquarters

29 Web Store
31 Nice Étoile Shopping Mall;
   City Sport; FNAC
34 The Cat's Whiskers
35 Police Headquarters
38 Théâtre de Nice
39 Musée d'Art Moderne
   et d'Art Contemporain
41 Centre Information
   Jeunesse
43 24-Hour Currency
   Exchange Machine
44 UK Consulate
45 US Consulate
48 Musée des Beaux-Arts
51 Airport Buses
52 Public Showers; Toilets
53 Airport Buses

57 Cave de la Buffa
60 Anglican Church
61 English-American Library
62 Palais de la Méditerranée
63 Amex
64 Tourist Office Annexe
67 Maison de la Presse
68 Banque de France
70 Le Pub Giofreddo
71 Sunbus Information Office
72 Station Centrale
73 Chez Wayne's
74 Palais de Justice
78 Papeterie Rontani
78 Moulin à Huille d'Olive Alzine
79 Opéra de Nice
80 Post Office
81 Flower Market

84 Intercity Bus Station
85 24-Hour Currency
   Exchange Machine
86 William's Pub
87 Jonathan's
88 The Oxford Pub
89 Cathédrale Sté-Réperate
90 O'Hara's
91 Église St-Jacques
   le Majeur
95 La Douche Cybercafé
96 PH+ Plongée
97 Trans Côte d'Azur
98 Tour Bellanda; Lift;
   Musée Naval
99 WW1 Memorial
100 Ferry Terminal;
   SNCM Office

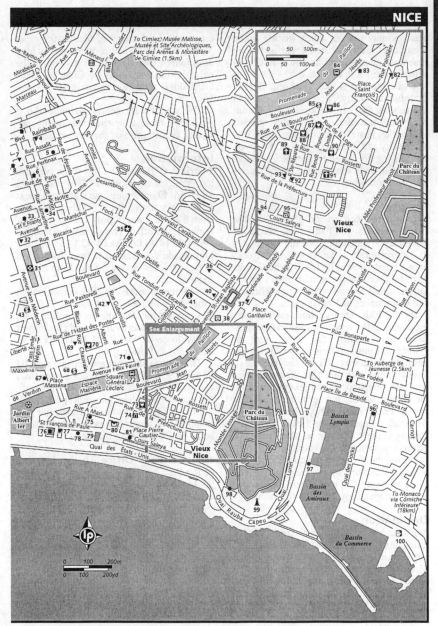

NICE

CÔTE D'AZUR

a short train or bus ride from Monaco, Cannes and other Riviera hot spots. Nice's beaches may not be worth writing home about, but the city is blessed with as fine an ensemble of museums as you'll find anywhere in the south of France.

While Menton is gentrified and Cannes graceful and classy, Nice is brash and bold and in your face. It is enormously popular with young travellers, as the proliferation of backpacker hostels aptly demonstrates. It is a large city and is quite spread out. So if you are looking for serenity and peace, move on. If you want some action, then Nice is the place to find it.

History

Nice was founded around 350 BC by the Greek seafarers who had settled Marseille. They named the colony Nikaia, apparently to commemorate a victory (*nike* in Greek) over a nearby town. In 154 BC the Greeks were followed by the Romans, who settled farther uphill around what is now Cimiez, site of a number of Roman ruins.

By the 10th century, Nice was ruled by the counts of Provence. In 1388 the town refused to recognise the new count of Provence, Louis of Anjou, and turned instead to Amadeus VII of the House of Savoy. In the 18th and 19th centuries Nice was temporarily occupied several times by the French, but did not definitively become part of France until 1860, when Napoleon III struck a deal with the House of Savoy. The agreement (known as the Treaty of Turin) was ratified by a vote.

During the Victorian period Nice became popular with the English aristocracy, who came to enjoy the city's mild winter climate. European royalty soon followed.

Orientation

Ave Jean Médecin runs south from near the train station to place Masséna. The modern city centre, the area north and west of place Masséna, includes the upmarket pedestrianised streets of rue de France and rue Masséna. The Station Centrale and intercity bus station are three blocks east of place Masséna.

The famous promenade des Anglais follows the gently curved beachfront from the city centre to the airport, 6km to the west. Vieux Nice (Old Nice) is delineated by blvd Jean Jaurès, quai des États-Unis and, to the east, the hill known as Le Château. Place Garibaldi is at the north-eastern tip of Vieux Nice.

The wealthy residential neighbourhood of Cimiez, home to several outstanding museums, is just north of the city centre.

Information

Tourist Offices The most convenient tourist office (☎ 04 93 87 07 07, fax 04 93 16 85 16, ✉ otc@nice.coteazur.org) is next to the train station on ave Thiers. It opens from 8 am to 7 pm (8 pm from July to September). Another (less crowded) office (☎ 04 92 14 48 00, fax 04 92 14 49 03) at 5 promenade des Anglais is open from 8 am to 6 pm (closed Sunday; 8 pm from May to September).

Near the airport is the Nice Ferber branch office (☎ 04 93 83 32 64, fax 04 93 72 08 27), promenade des Anglais (towards town from the airport terminal). Inside the airport is an info desk (☎ 04 93 21 44 11, fax 04 93 21 44 50) at Terminal 1.

The Centre Information Jeunesse (☎ 04 93 80 93 93), 19 rue Gioffredo, is open from 8.45 am to 6.45 pm (closed at the weekend). An excellent-value museum pass (140/70FF), available at tourist offices and participating museums, gives free admission to some 60 Côte d'Azur museums.

National Park Office The headquarters of the Parc National du Mercantour (☎ 04 93 16 78 88, fax 04 93 88 79 05), 23 rue d'Italie, is open from 9 am to 6 pm on weekdays. It stocks numerous guides including the free *Les Guides Randoxygène* series, which details 25 canyoning routes, 40 mountain biking (VTT) trails and hiking trails in the park (see Around Menton for more details).

Money The Banque de France, 14 ave Félix Faure, opens 8.45 am to 12.15 pm and 1.30 to 3.30 pm (closed at the weekend).

Amex (☎ 04 93 16 53 53), 11 promenade des Anglais, is open 9 am to 8 pm daily from October to May and 9 am to 9 pm from May to September (10 am to 6 pm on holidays). Barclays Bank on rue Alphonse Karr is open from 8.40 to 11.45 am and 1.30 to 4.45 pm (closed at the weekend).

Opposite the train station, Le Change (☎ 04 93 88 56 80) at 17 ave Thiers (to the right as you exit the terminal building) offers decent rates and is open from 7 am to midnight. Hours are the same at its other branch at 64 ave Jean Médecin (☎ 04 93 13 45 44).

The Banque Populaire de la Côte d'Azur, 17 ave Jean Médecin, has a 24-hour currency exchange machine, as does its branch just north of Vieux Nice at 20 blvd Jean Jaurès.

Post & Communications The main post office, in a fantastic red brick building at 23 ave Thiers, exchanges foreign currency and is open from 8 am to 7 pm (Saturday until noon; closed Sunday).

In Vieux Nice the post office at 2 rue Louis Gassin is open from 8.30 am to 12.30 pm and 2 to 6.30 pm (Saturday from 8 am to noon; closed Sunday). Poste restante services are also available at Amex (see Money).

The Web Store (☎ 04 93 87 87 99, ✆ info@webstore.fr), 12 rue de Russie, charges 30/50FF for 30 minutes/one hour on-line. It opens 10 am to noon and 2 to 7 pm (closed Sunday).

For a drink while you surf, log in at the La Douche Cybercafé, (☎ 04 93 62 81 31, ✆ ladouche@wanadoo.fr), 32 Cours Saleya. It opens from 2 pm onwards daily.

Bookshops New and second-hand guides and English-language novels are available from The Cat's Whiskers (☎/fax 04 93 80 02 66), 26 rue Lamartine, which is open from 9.30 am to 12.15 pm and 2 to 6.45 pm (Saturday from 9.30 am to 12.15 pm and 3 to 6 pm; closed Sunday).

The Magellan Librairie de Voyages (☎ 04 93 82 31 81), 3 rue d'Italie, has an excellent selection of IGN maps, Didier-Richard walking maps, topoguides and other walking information, most of it in French. It also stocks travel guides – including Lonely Planet in English. Papeterie Rontani (☎ 04 93 62 32 43), 5 rue Alexandre Mari, and the Maison de la Presse, place Masséna, are two other great map and guide places.

Library The English-American library, 12 rue de France, is open from 10 to 11 am and 3 to 5 pm, Tuesday to Thursday. Short-term memberships are welcomed. Cut through the passageway opposite 17 rue de France and walk straight ahead down the steps.

Laundry Self-service laundrettes are plentiful. Near the train station, head for 8 rue de Belgique (open 7 am to 11 pm), 14 rue de Suisse or 16 rue d'Angleterre (both open 7 am to 9 pm). Nearer to the beach, try 39 rue de la Buffa (open 7 am to 9 pm) or Top Speed, 12 rue de la Buffa (open 8 am to 8 pm).

Emergency The police headquarters (☎ 04 92 17 22 22; foreign tourist department ☎ 04 92 17 20 31) is at 1 ave Maréchal Foch.

Promenade des Anglais

The palm-lined 'English promenade', established by Nice's English colony in 1822 as a seaside walking path, provides a fine stage for a stroll along the beach and the Baie des Anges (Bay of Angels). Don't miss the facade of the Art Deco **Palais de la Méditerranée**, crumbling in all its magnificence at 13–17 promenade des Anglais; it was gutted by the local council in the 1980s.

Other pleasant places for a walk include **Quai des États-Unis**, the promenade leading east to Vieux Nice that honours US President Wilson's decision in 1917 for the USA to join WWI (a colossal memorial commemorating the 4000 people from Nice who died during the war is carved in the rock at the eastern end of the quay); the **Jardin Albert 1er**, laid out in the late 19th century; **Espace Masséna**, a public square enlivened by fountains; **Place Masséna**, whose early-19th-century, neoclassical arcaded buildings are painted in various shades of ochre and red; **Ave Jean Médecin**, Nice's main commercial street; and **Cimiez**, the most exclusive quarter in Nice.

Vieux Nice

This area of narrow, winding streets between quai des États-Unis and the Musée d'Art Moderne et d'Art Contemporain has looked pretty much the same since the 1700s. Arcade-lined **Place Garibaldi**, built during the latter half of the 18th century, is named after Giuseppe Garibaldi (1807–82), one of the great heroes of Italian unification, who was born in Nice and is also buried in the cemetery in the Parc du Château.

Interesting churches in Vieux Nice include the baroque **Cathédrale Ste-Réparate** at place Rossetti, built around 1650; the blue-grey and yellow **Église St-Jacques Le Majeur** at place du Gésu (close to rue Rossetti), whose baroque ornamentation dates from the mid-17th century; as well as the mid-18th-century **Chapelle de la Miséricorde**, next to place Pierre Gautier.

Rue Benoît Bunico, which runs perpendicular to rue Rossetti, served as Nice's Jewish ghetto after a 1430 law restricted where Jews could live. Gates at each end were locked at sunset.

Parc du Château

At the eastern end of quai des États-Unis, atop a 92m-high hill, is this shady public park, where local families come to stroll, admire the panoramic views of Nice and the sparkling Baie des Anges, or visit the artificial waterfall. It's a great place to escape the heat on a summer afternoon. It opens 7 am to 8 pm.

The chateau after which the hill and park are named was established in the 12th century but was razed by Louis XIV in 1706. In the one remaining tower, the 16th-century **Tour Bellanda**, above the eastern end of quai des États-Unis, is the **Musée Naval** (☎ 04 93 80 47 61). It opens from 10 am to noon and 2 to 5 pm (7 pm in summer; closed Monday and Tuesday). The

cemetery where Garibaldi (see Vieux Nice) is buried covers the north-west of the park.

To get to the top of the chateau, take the *ascenseur* (lift; 3.50/5FF single/return, children 1.80/3.60FF) from under the Tour Bellanda. It operates from 9 am to 5.50 pm (7.50 pm in summer). Alternatively, walk up Montée Lesage or up the steps at the eastern end of rue Rossetti.

Musée d'Art Moderne et d'Art Contemporain

The Museum of Modern & Contemporary Art (☎ 04 93 62 61 62) – Nice's pride and joy in the architectural stakes – specialises in French and American avant-garde works from the 1960s to the present. Glass walkways connect the four marble-coated towers, on top of which is a must-see rooftop garden and gallery featuring pieces by Nice-born Yves Klein (1928–62). Other highlights include Andy Warhol's *Campbell's Soup Can* (1965), a shopping trolley wrapped by Christo, and a pea-green Model T Ford compressed into a 1.6m-high block by Marseille-born French sculptor César.

The museum, at ave St-Jean Baptiste, is open from 10 am to 6 pm (closed Tuesday). Admission is 25/15FF for adults/students. Art films and cult movies are screened most Thursdays at 3 and 8.30 pm in the auditorium. Take bus No 17 from the train station to the Station Centrale, from where the museum is a three minute walk north-east.

Musée National Message Biblique Marc Chagall

The Marc Chagall Biblical Message Museum (☎ 04 93 53 87 20), whose main exhibit is in five small rooms, is across the street from 4 ave Docteur Ménard, close to blvd de Cimiez. Don't miss the mosaic of the rose window at Metz Cathedral viewed through a plate-glass window across a small pond. The museum is open from 10 am to 5 pm (6 pm from July to October; closed Tuesday year round). Admission costs 30/20FF for adults/students (38/28FF in summer). Take bus No 15 from place Masséna to the stop in front of the museum or walk.

Musée des Beaux-Arts

The Fine Arts Museum (☎ 04 92 15 28 28), 33 ave des Baumettes, is housed in a fantastic, yellow and ochre-coloured late-19th-century villa – the former residence of a Ukrainian princess – just off rue de France. The six-column terrace around the back that overlooks the small, pretty public garden, is worth a glance too.

Opening hours are 10 am to noon and 2 to 6 pm (closed Monday). Admission costs 25FF (students 15FF). The one-hour guided tour at 3 pm on Wednesday (in French only) costs an extra 20FF. Bus No 38 from the Station Centrale stops outside.

Musée Matisse

The Matisse Museum (☎ 04 93 81 08 08), 164 ave des Arènes de Cimiez, which houses a fine collection of works by Henri Matisse, is 2.5km north-east of the train station in the bourgeois district of Cimiez. The museum's permanent collection is displayed in a red-ochre, 17th-century Genoese mansion overlooking an olive grove and the **Parc des Arènes**. Temporary exhibitions are hosted in the futuristic basement building that leads through to the stucco-decorated villa. Well known pieces in the permanent collection include Matisse's blue paper cutouts of *Blue Nude IV* and *Woman with Amphora*.

Matisse is buried in the cemetery of the **Monastère de Cimiez** (Cimiez Monastery; ☎ 04 93 81 00 04), which today houses a small museum run by – and unravelling the history of – the monastery's Franciscan monks. The artist's grave is signposted *sépulture Henri Matisse* from the cemetery's main entrance (next to the monastery church on ave Bellanda). A flight of stairs leads from the eastern end of the olive grove to ave Bellanda.

The museum opens from 10 am to 5 pm (from 10 am to 6 pm April to September; closed Tuesday year round). Admission costs 25FF (students 15FF). Guided tours (in French) take place on Wednesday at 3 pm; you can arrange tours in English. Take bus No 15, 17, 20, 22 or 25 from the Station Centrale to the Arènes stop.

Musée et Site Archéologiques

Behind the Musée Matisse, on the eastern side of the Parc des Arènes, lie the ruins of the Roman city of Cemenelum – the focus of the Archaeology Museum (☎ 04 93 81 59 57), 160 ave des Arènes de Cimiez. The public baths and the amphitheatre – the venue for outdoor concerts during the Nice Jazz Festival – can both be visited.

Opening hours and admission fees for the Musée et Site Archéologiques are the same as the Musée Matisse. Admission costs 25FF (student 15FF). To get here from the latter, turn left out of the main park entrance on ave des Arènes de Cimiez, walk 100m, then turn left again onto ave Monte Croce, where the main entrance to the archaeological site is located.

Cathédrale Orthodoxe Russe St-Nicolas

The multicoloured Russian Orthodox Cathedral of St-Nicolas (☎ 04 93 96 88 02), crowned by six onion domes, was built between 1902 and 1912 in early-17th-century style and is an easy 15 minute walk from the train station. Step inside and you're transported to Imperial Russia. It is on ave Nicolas II opposite 17 blvd du Tzaréwich and is open from 9 or 9.30 am to noon and 2.30 to 5.30 pm (closed Sunday morning). Admission costs 15/10FF. Shorts, miniskirts and sleeveless shirts are forbidden.

Activities

If you don't like the feel of sand between your toes, Nice's **beaches** are for you: they are covered with smooth round pebbles. Sections of beach open to the public without charge alternate with 15 **plages concédées** (private beaches), for which you have to pay by renting a chair (around 60FF a day) or mattress (around 55FF).

Along the beach you can hire catamaran paddleboats (80FF to 90FF an hour) or sailboards and jet skis (300FF for a half-hour), go parascending (220FF for 15 minutes) and water-skiing (100FF to 130FF for 10 minutes) or try paragliding (200FF for 10 minutes).

There are public indoor showers (15FF)

and toilets (2FF) opposite 50 promenade des Anglais.

PH+ Plongée (☎ 04 93 26 09 03), 3 quai des Deux Emmanuel, and l'Odyssée (☎ 04 93 89 42 44), 14 quai des Docks, both offer **diving courses**, organise diving expeditions and rent equipment. An introductory dive costs around 160FF; equipment is extra.

Trans Côte d'Azur (☎ 04 92 00 42 30), quai Lunel, organises **glass-bottomed boat trips** around the Baie des Anges (60/40FF for adults/children) and to the Îles de Lérins (see the Cannes section later in the chapter), St-Tropez and Monaco. The ticket office is open from 8 am to 7 pm (until 11.45 pm on Saturday; closed Sunday).

For details of **walking** and **mountain-biking** trails in the region, go to the head-quarters of the Parc National du Mercantour (see Information) or the Club Alpin Français (☎ 04 93 62 59 99), 14 ave Mirabeau.

Inline Skating The promenade des Anglais is *the* place to skate. City Sport, inside the Nice Étoile shopping centre, ave Jean Médecin, rents inline skates and protective kneepads.

Special Events

The colourful Carnaval de Nice, held every spring around Mardi Gras (Shrove Tuesday), fills the streets with floats and musicians. The week-long Nice Jazz Festival sets the town jiving in July; the fabulous main venue is the olive grove behind the Musée Matisse in the Cimiez district.

Places to Stay

Nice has a surfeit of reasonably priced places to stay. During the Easter university holidays, lots of American students descend on Nice for a transatlantic 'College Week', making cheap accommodation hard to find after 10 or 11 am. Nice is also crowded with budget travellers during July and August. Inexpensive places fill up by late morning.

Hôtels meublés (literally, 'furnished hotels') are rooms with cooking facilities in 'hotels' (often just private flats) where little or no service is provided.

In summer, many young people sleep on the beach. This is theoretically illegal and public beaches are supposed to be closed between midnight and 6 am, but the Nice (and nice) police usually look the other way. However, watch out for thieves.

The information desk at the bus station (see the Getting There & Away section) has information on Logis de France hotels and other rural properties in the region.

Places to Stay – Budget

Hostels Touting a great tree-studded garden decked out with tables and chairs for guests to lounge on is the busy *Hôtel Belle Meunière* (☎ 04 93 88 66 15, 21 ave Durante), which has dorm beds for 76FF (96FF with shower and 101FF with shower and toilet), including breakfast.

Equally popular is the rambling *Hôtel Les Orangers* (☎ 04 93 87 51 41, fax 04 93 82 57 82, 10 bis ave Durante) almost opposite in a turn-of-the-century townhouse. A bed in a snug four, five or six-bed room with shower and fantastic, huge windows costs 85FF. The cheerful owner Marc speaks excellent English after dealing with Anglophone backpackers for over 20 years.

Heading into town along ave Jean Médecin, you come to the popular 21-bed *Backpackers Chez Patrick* (☎ 04 93 80 30 72, 32 rue Pertinax). A dorm bed costs 80FF a night, there's no curfew or daytime closure and Patrick, who runs the place, is great at directing party-mad backpackers to the hot spot of the moment. The hotel is above the Faubourg Montmartre restaurant (see the Places to Eat section).

The *Pado Tourisme* hostel (☎ 04 93 80 98 00, 26 blvd Raimbaldi), charges 60FF for a bed in a mixed dorm. Reception is open from 8 am to noon and 6 to 9 pm; there is a daytime closure between noon and 6 pm.

Nice's *Auberge de Jeunesse* (☎ 04 93 89 23 64, fax 04 92 04 03 10, route Forestière de Mont Alban), is 4km east of the train station. Bed and breakfast costs 68.50FF. Curfew is at midnight and rooms are locked from midday to 5 pm. Take bus No 14 (last one at 8.20 pm) from the Station Centrale bus terminal on place Général Leclerc, which is linked to the train station by bus Nos 15 and 17, and get off at the L'Auberge stop.

Hotels – Train Station Area The quickest way to get to all these hotels is to walk straight down the steps opposite the train station onto ave Durante. The first place you hit is the clean, warm and welcoming *Hôtel Belle Meunière* (see Hostels), always packed with backpackers. As well as dorms, it has large doubles/triples with high ceilings, some with century-old decor, from 182/243FF (with shower and toilet). It is closed in December and January.

The highly recommended *Hôtel Les Orangers* (see Hostels) has great doubles and triples with shower and a balcony overlooking palm-tree gardens, for 210FF. Rooms are gloriously sunlit thanks to their great century-old windows and come with fridge (and hotplate on request). The clean and attractive *Hôtel de la Gare* (☎/fax 04 93 88 75 07, 35 rue d'Angleterre), has modern singles/doubles with washbasin/shower and toilet for 115/200FF.

The spotless *Hôtel Claire Meublé* (☎ 04 93 87 87 61, fax 04 93 16 85 28, ✆ hotel_ clair_meuble@hotmail.com, 6 rue d'Italie) has had glowing reports from readers. Their compact fully-equipped studios for two to five persons range in price from 200FF to 220FF and are particularly suited for families and couples who wish to self cater.

Rue d'Alsace-Lorraine is dotted with more upmarket two-star hotels: one of the cheapest is the *Hôtel du Piemont* (☎ 04 93 88 25 15, fax 04 93 16 15 18, 19 rue d'Alsace-Lorraine), which has bargain singles/ doubles with washbasin from 110/130FF. Singles/doubles with shower start at 140/ 170FF.

Hotels – City Centre The reception of the friendly *Hôtel Little Masséna* (☎ 04 93 87 72 34, 22 rue Masséna), on the 5th floor, is open until 8 pm. Doubles with washbasin/shower/toilet and shower cost 140/ 180/220FF. Rooms come with a hot plate and fridge.

The relaxed, family-style *Hôtel Les Mimosas* (☎ 04 93 88 05 59, 26 rue de la Buffa) is two blocks north-east of the (currently closed) Musée Masséna. Utilitarian rooms of a good size for one/two people cost 120/190FF. Showers cost 10FF.

Midway between the sea and the station is the colourful *Le Petit Louvre* (☎ 04 93 80 15 54, fax 04 93 62 45 08, 10 rue Emma Tiranty), run by a humorous musician and his wife, for 17 years. A faceless Mona Lisa greets guests as they enter, and corridors are adorned with an eclectic bunch of paintings. Singles/doubles with shower, washbasin, fridge and hotplate are 180/205FF.

On a side street off ave Jean Médecin is the one-star *Hôtel Lyonnais* (☎ 04 93 88 70 74, fax 04 93 16 25 56, 20 rue de Russie), which has singles/doubles with washbasin for 110/145FF. Nightly rates increase by about 30FF in the high season.

Hotels – Vieux Nice The *Hôtel au Picardy* (☎ 04 93 85 75 51, 10 blvd Jean Jaurès) has single/double rooms from 120/ 150FF; there are also pricier rooms that include toilet and shower. Hall showers cost 10FF.

Places to Stay – Mid-Range

Near the train station there are lots of two-star hotels along rue d'Angleterre, rue d'Alsace-Lorraine, rue de Suisse, rue de Russie and ave Durante.

In the centre, the *Hôtel Plaisance* (☎ 04 93 85 11 90, fax 04 93 80 88 92, 20 rue de Paris), is a pleasing old two-star place with air-conditioned singles/doubles from 260FF to 440FF.

Named after its location near the Église Notre Dame is the very clean and modern *Hôtel Notre Dame* (☎ 04 93 88 70 44, fax 04 93 82 20 38, 22 rue de Russie), which has spacious doubles/triples with private shower and toilet for 240/300FF. Its 17 rooms fill quickly so get there early. Another good-value place, little publicised, is the modest, 28 room *Hôtel du Centre* (☎ 04 93 88 83 85, fax 04 93 82 29 80, ✆ hotel-centre@webstore.fr, 2 rue de Suisse), which has very neat rooms with shared/private shower for 144/174FF.

A stone's throw from the sea and from the Musée des Beaux-Arts is the good-value *Hôtel Carlone* (☎/fax 04 93 44 71 61, *2 blvd François Grosso*). Light and airy rooms for one or two with washbasin/shower and toilet start at 190/230FF.

Fabulously like home and equally close to the sea is the welcoming *Hôtel Cronstadt* (☎ 04 93 82 00 30, fax 04 93 16 87 40, *3 rue Cronstadt*). Exceptionally quiet and graceful rooms cost 270/310FF for singles/doubles including breakfast.

Places to Stay – Top End
Matisse stayed at the *Hôtel Beau Rivage* (☎ 04 93 80 80 70, fax 04 93 80 55 77, @ nicebeaurivage@new-hotel.com, *24 rue St-François de Paule*), when he was in town in 1916. Before that, in 1891, Russian playwright Anton Chekhov (1860–1904) graced the place with his presence. Sea views from the hotel, which today touts four-stars, remain superb. The cheapest rooms cost 650/850FF in the low/high season, breakfast costs a mere 95FF.

The pink-domed, green-shuttered, four-star *Hôtel Négresco* (☎ 04 93 16 64 00 or ☎ 04 93 88 00 58, fax 04 93 88 35 68, @ negresco@nicematin.fr, *37 promenade des Anglais*), built in the *belle époque* style. This is Nice's fanciest hotel. It dates from the early 1900s and is a protected historic monument. Rooms with a sea/sea and garden view start at 1350FF, and a continental/American-style breakfast is only another 130/190FF. The Négresco's restaurant is also considered the best in town.

Places to Eat
Restaurants – Train Station Area
The *Restaurant Le Toscan* (☎ 04 93 88 40 54, *1 rue de Belgique*), is a family-run Italian place offering large portions of tripe or home-made pasta from noon to 2 pm and 6.45 to 10 pm (closed Sunday). *Menus* cost from 65FF to 115FF

Corsican chants and energetic guitar duets are some of the Île de Beauté delights performed every Thursday, Friday and Saturday evening at the Corsican *L'Allegria* (☎ 04 93 87 42 00, *7 rue d'Italie*). If it's a chilly day, ask for a filling bowl of *soupe course*, a large portion of Corsica's more staple soups. Next door is the unpretentious and very friendly *Restaurant au Soleil* (☎ 04 93 88 77 44, *9 rue d'Italie*), which offers good local cuisine at unbeatable prices, including an all-day omelette breakfast for 35FF.

Adorned with fat contented cherubs on its outside walls is the atmospheric *L'Ange Gourmand* (*47 rue Lamartine*). Its *carte*, which changes daily and is handwritten, includes an 89FF *menu*. Close by, on the corner of blvd Raimbaldi and rue Miron is the handsome *Chez Mireille* (☎ 04 93 85 27 23), which specialises in paella, paella and more paella for a 120FF a pop. It is closed Monday and Tuesday in June and early July.

Bursting with hungry backpackers is the cheap and cheerful *Le Faubourg Montmartre* (☎ 04 93 62 55 03, *32 rue Pertinax*). The house speciality is bouillabaisse (120FF for two) and there's a 68FF *menu*. It opens for lunch at noon and for dinner from 5.30 pm.

Restaurants – City Centre
The rue Masséna pedestrian mall and nearby streets and squares, including rue de France and place Magenta, are crammed with touristy outdoor cafes and restaurants, although most don't offer particularly good value.

One worth sampling is *La Trattoria* (*rue Dalpozzo*), whose terrace restaurant fills the entire southern stretch of the street. It specialises in pizza *au feu de bois* (cooked with a wood fire). Nearby is the small and homely *Le Moulin à Poivre* (*rue de France*) a couple of doors west of the Manoir Café. The 'Pepper Mill' has a *plat du jour* for 50FF, a 120FF *menu* and plenty of home-made pasta dishes.

Near the port, *L'Olivier* (☎ 04 93 26 89 09, *2 place Garibaldi*), is a small, simple and very local place. A meal guaranteed to fill you up costs around 100FF. It is closed Wednesday evening, Sunday and during August.

La Nissarda (☎ 04 93 85 26 29, *17 rue Gubernatis*), serves specialities of Nice and Normandy. The *menus* are reasonably priced at 60FF (lunch only), 78FF, 98FF and 138FF (closed on Sunday and during August). Nearby, *Le Bistrot Saint Germain* (☎ 04 93 13 45 12, *9 rue Chauvain*), brings a touch of Paris to Nice, with walls decorated with photos of Parisian scenes.

Graceful and very local is *Le Comptoir* (☎ 04 93 92 08 80, *20 rue St-François de Paule*), close to the seashore. The restaurant, which has an adjoining nightclub, is decked out in Art Deco style and has a terrace too. A lunchtime/evening meal will be around 120/250FF. It is closed on Monday.

For a mind-blowing traditional French meal in a luxurious setting, try the Michelin two-star *Chantecler* (☎ 04 93 16 64 00) inside the Hôtel Négresco. Impeccable service and tantalising cuisine add up to a hefty 500FF-per-head (at least) bill.

Restaurants – Vieux Nice Many of the narrow streets of Vieux Nice are lined with restaurants, cafes, pizzerias and so on that draw locals and visitors alike. There are dozens of cafes and restaurants on Cours Saleya, place Rossetti and place Pierre Gautier, many of which buzz until well past midnight (later during the summer).

A perennial favourite with locals is *Nissa Socca* (☎ 04 93 80 18 35, *5 rue Ste-Réparate*), which specialises in delicious Niçois dishes such as *socca* (a thin layer of chickpea flour and olive oil batter fried on a griddle), *salade Niçoise, farcis* (stuffed vegetables) and *ratatouille*. Nissa Socca is closed in January and June.

If you don't want to stand in line (inevitable), try *Nissa La Bella* (☎ 04 93 62 10 20, *6 rue Ste-Réparate*), opposite, which serves similar (but not as good) dishes.

A short distance north of Vieux Nice *Lou Balico-Chez Adrienne* (☎ 04 93 85 93 71, *20 ave St-Jean Baptiste*), serves excellent Niçois specialities, as well as bouillabaisse (250FF), really a Marseille speciality. Mains range from 80FF to 125FF.

Nearby is the equally local *L'Auberge d'Acropolis*, *(9 rue Penchienatti)*, which has a regional plat du jour for 45FF, a wholesome lunch *menu* for 60FF and evening ones for 95FF and 120FF.

The house speciality at the enchanting (smiling staff, candlelit terrace etc) *Escalinada* (☎ 04 93 62 11 71, *22 rue Pairolière*), is *testicules de mouton panés* (sheep's testicles in batter).

Cafes For home-made cakes and hearty tarts like grandma bakes, look no farther than the cosy *Scotch Tea House* (☎ 04 93 87 75 62, *4 ave de Suède*), tucked in between designer clothing shops. It opens 9 am to 7 pm and is *the* place to go for good old-fashioned afternoon tea.

Cool, chic and always packed is the refined *Manoir Café* (☎ 04 93 16 36 16, *32 rue de France*). Jazz bands play here on Wednesday evenings. Reserve a table in advance if you want to dine.

Sweet *crêpes*, savoury *galette*, punchy ciders and a great range of ice creams are beautifully presented at the busy *Crêperie Bretonne* (☎ 04 93 16 02 98, *3 rue de Russie*). It is closed on Monday.

Cafeterias Dirt-cheap places near the train station include the *Flunch Cafétéria* (☎ 04 93 88 41 35), to the left as you exit the station building. It opens 11 am to 10 pm.

The *Cafétéria Casino* (☎ 04 93 82 44 44, *7 ave Thiers*), serves breakfast (10FF to 17FF) from 8 to 11 am and other meals until 9.30 pm. Its good-value 29FF *formule* comprises its plat du jour plus an entrée, cheese or dessert.

Self-Catering There's a *fruit & vegetable market* in front of the prefecture, cours Saleya, from 7 am to 1 pm. The fresh *fish market* is on place St-François every morning from 6 am to 1 pm. Both markets are closed on Monday. The *Prisunic Supermarket* (*33 ave Jean Médecin*) opens from 8.30 am to 8.30 pm (closed Sunday); the branch at place Garibaldi closes at 8 pm. The *Casino Supermarket* (*27 blvd Gambetta*), on the western side of the city, has the same hours as the latter.

Entertainment

The tourist office has detailed information on Nice's abundant cultural activities, many of which are listed in its free monthly brochure, *Le Mois à Nice*. More useful is the weekly *L'Officiel des Loisirs Côte d'Azur* (2FF) available from newsstands on Wednesday. Tickets to events of all sorts can be purchased at FNAC (☎ 04 92 17 77 77), 24 ave Jean Médecin (inside the Nice Étoile shopping mall).

Cinema Nice has two cinemas offering nondubbed films, many of them in English. The *Cinéma Nouveau Mercury* (☎ 04 93 55 32 31 for a recorded message in French, 16 place Garibaldi), and the *Cinéma Rialto* (☎ 04 93 88 08 41, 4 rue de Rivoli). Art films (usually in French or with French subtitles) are screened in the auditorium inside the Musée d'Art Moderne et d'Art Contemporain.

Classical Music Operas and orchestral concerts are held at the ornate *Opéra de Nice* (☎ 04 92 17 40 40, 4–6 rue St-François de Paule), built in 1885 and undergoing a face-lift (it is around the corner from quai des États-Unis). The box office opens 10 am to 6 pm (closed Sunday). The best tickets for operas/concerts and ballets cost 50/20FF; the opera house is closed between mid-June and September.

Theatre The superbly modern *Théâtre de Nice* (☎ 04 93 80 52 60), whose entrance on promenade des Arts faces the Musée d'Art Moderne et d'Art Contemporain, is one block west of place Garibaldi. The two halls host a wide variety of first-rate theatre performances and concerts. Ticket prices range from 60FF to 170FF. The information desk opens 1 to 7 pm (closed Sunday and Monday) and one hour before each performance.

Pubs & Bars Terraced cafes and bars – perfect for quaffing beers and sipping pastis – abound in Nice. For a taste of some excellent Belgian brew or one of 70-plus types of beer, try *Le Pub Gioffredo* (rue Chauvain).For a pint of Guinness head straight for the *O'Haras* (☎ 04 93 80 43 22, 22 rue Droite) in Vieux Nice.

Nice boasts a rash of pubs run by Anglophones, with happy hours and live music. Best known is *Chez Wayne's* (☎ 04 93 13 46 99, 15 rue de la Préfecture), which hosts a bilingual quiz on Tuesday, a ladies' night on Wednesday, karaoke on Sunday, and live bands on Friday and Saturday. Wayne's is open from 3 pm to midnight (later at the weekend). Happy hour is until 9 pm. The *Oxford* (☎ 04 93 92 24 54, 4 rue Mascoïnat) is a striking-looking pub that does a wide range of English and Irish draft beers and is open until 4 am.

Another hot spot is *Jonathan's* (☎ 04 93 62 57 62, 1 rue de la Loge), also a *bar à musique*. Live bands (country, boogie-woogie, Irish folk etc) play every night in summer.

William's Pub (☎ 04 93 85 84 66, 4 rue Centrale), has live music from around 9 pm except on Sunday; the pub is open from 6 pm to 2.30 am. There's pool, darts and chess in the basement.

Shopping

Cours Saleya hosts a wonderful flower market from 6 am to 5.30 pm Tuesday to Saturday and on Sunday morning. There are a number of vendors selling *fruits glacés* (glazed or candied fruits), a speciality of the region. The figs, tangerine slices and pears have to be tasted to be believed. The best-value place for wine-tasting and buying is the traditional wine cellar, and a good one is the Cave de la Buffa (☎ 04 93 88 10 26), 49 rue de la Buffa. Olive oil is sold in excess at the quaint Moulin à Huile d'Olive Alziari shop, 14 rue St-François de Paule.

Designer names abound above the beautiful fashion boutiques languishing along rue Paradis, rue de Suède, rue Alphonse Karr and rue du Maréchal Joffre. Shop for unusual handmade art, crafts and jewellery at the *marché nocturne* (night market), held from 6.30 pm to midnight on Cours Saleya between July and September.

Getting There & Away

Air Nice's international airport, Aéroport International Nice-Côte d'Azur (☎ 04 93 21 30 30), is 6km west of the city centre.

Bus Lines operated by some two dozen bus companies stop at the intercity bus station (☎ 04 93 85 61 81), 5 blvd Jean Jaurès. The busy information counter (☎ 04 93 85 03 90) opens 8 am to 6.30 pm (closed Sunday).

There are slow but frequent services until about 7.30 pm daily to Antibes (25.50FF, 1¼ hours), Cannes (32FF, 1½ hours), Grasse (38FF, 1¼ hours), Menton (28.50FF, 1¼ hours), Monaco (20FF return, 45 minutes) and St-Raphaël (51FF, two hours). Hourly buses run to Vence (22FF, 50 minutes). To Castellane, the gateway to the Gorges du Verdon, there's one bus a day at 7.30 am (102FF, 1½ hours). Buses run to the ski resort of Isola 2000 four times a day (90FF, 2¼ hours).

For long-haul travel, Intercars (☎ 04 93 80 08 70), at the bus station, takes you to various European destinations; it sells Eurolines tickets for buses to London, Brussels and Amsterdam. The counter is open from 9 am to 12 pm and from 2.30 to 6 pm.

Train Nice's main train station, Gare Nice Ville (or Gare Thiers), ave Thiers, is 1200m north of the beach. The information office is open from 8 am to 6.30 pm (closed Sunday).

There are fast, frequent services (up to 40 trains a day in each direction) to towns along the coast between St-Raphaël and Ventimiglia across the Italian border, including Antibes (22FF, 25 minutes), Cannes (32FF, 40 minutes), Menton (26FF, 35 minutes), Monaco (20FF, 20 minutes) and St-Raphaël (56FF, 45 minutes).

The two or three TGVs that link Nice with Paris' Gare de Lyon (455FF, seven hours) are infrequent, so you may find it more convenient to go via Marseilles.

The luggage lockers (15FF to 30FF depending on bag size), are open from 7 am to 9.30 pm. You can also store bags at the left-luggage office (☎ 04 93 86 57 49; 30FF a bag), open from 7 am to 10 pm. Reimbursements for train tickets are available in the office (☎ 04 93 82 62 11) near the left-luggage window, open from 9 am to noon and 1 to 4 pm (closed at the weekend). Lost luggage and other problems are handled by

SOS Voyageurs (☎ 04 93 82 62 11), open 9 am to noon and 3 to 6 pm (closed at the weekend).

The ever-popular two-car diesel trains operated by Les Chemins de Fer de la Provence (☎ 04 93 88 34 72 in Nice; ☎ 04 92 31 01 58 in Digne-les-Bains) make the scenic trip four times daily from Nice's Gare du Sud (☎ 04 93 82 10 17), 4 bis rue Alfred Binet, to Digne-les-Bains (109FF, 3¼ hours).

Boat The fastest and least expensive SNCM ferries from mainland France to Corsica depart from Nice (see Getting There & Away at the start of the Corsica chapter).

The SNCM office (☎ 04 93 13 66 66), ferry terminal, quai du Commerce, issues tickets (otherwise try a travel agency in town). It is open from 8 am to 7 pm (until 11.45 am on Saturday; open two hours before a scheduled departure on Sunday). From ave Jean Médecin take bus No 1 or 2 to the Port stop.

Getting Around
To/From the Airport Sunbus route No 23 (8FF), which runs to the airport every 20 or 30 minutes from about 6 am to 8 pm, can be picked up at the train station or on blvd Gambetta, rue de France or rue de la Californie.

From the intercity bus station or promenade des Anglais (near the Hôtel Négresco), you can also take the yellow ANT bus (21FF; ☎ 04 93 56 35 40), which bears a symbol of an aeroplane pointing upwards (every 20 minutes; 30 minutes on Sunday). Buses also make the run from the train station.

A taxi from the airport to the centre of Nice will cost between 85FF and 125FF, depending on the time of day and whether you're at Terminal 1 or 2.

Bus Local buses, run by Sunbus, cost 8/68FF for a single/10 rides. After you time-stamp your ticket, it's valid for one hour and can be used for one transfer. The Nice by Bus pass, valid for one/five/seven days costs 22/85/110FF and includes a return trip to the airport. Passes are sold at the Sun Bus information office (☎ 04 93 16 52 10), 10 ave Félix Faure, which is open from 7.15 am to 7 pm (until 6 pm Saturday; closed Sunday).

The Station Centrale, Sunbus' main hub, takes up three sides of Square Général Leclerc, which is between ave Félix Faure and blvd Jean Jaurès (near Vieux Nice and the intercity bus station). The Sunbus kiosk at Station Centrale is open from 6.15 am to 7.30 pm.

Bus No 12 links the train station with promenade des Anglais and the beach. To get from the train station to Vieux Nice and the intercity bus station, take bus No 2, 5 or 17. At night, four Noctambuses run north, east and west from place Masséna.

Car & Motorcycle Rent a Car Système (☎ 04 93 88 69 69, fax 04 93 88 43 36), in the same building as Budget car rental opposite the train station at 38 ave Aubert (corner of ave Thiers), offers the best rates. Around the corner, JML (☎ 04 93 16 07 00, fax 04 93 16 07 48), 36 ave Aubert, is another cheapie. Budget (☎ 04 97 03 35 03) has another office in town at 1 bis ave Gustave V.

Nicea Location Rent (☎ 04 93 82 42 71, fax 04 93 87 76 36), 9 ave Thiers, rents mopeds from 250FF a day (extra for petrol and a helmet), 50cc scooters for 390FF a day, and 125cc motorcycles for 465FF a day. The office is open from 9 am to 6 pm (closed Sunday).

Taxi There are taxi stands right outside the train station and on ave Félix Faure near place Masséna; otherwise you can order one on ☎ 04 93 13 78 78.

ANTIBES AREA
Cagnes-sur-Mer
postcode 06804 • pop 41,000
Cagnes-sur-Mer is made up of Le Haut de Cagnes, the old hill town; Le Cros de Cagnes, the former fishing village by the beach; and Cagnes Ville, a fast-growing modern quarter. The old city with its ram-

parts is dominated by the 14th-century Château Grimaldi (☎ 04 93 20 85 57), place Grimaldi, which houses a museum of contemporary Mediterranean art and stages an annual international art festival.

Near Cagnes Ville is the **Musée Renoir** (☎ 04 93 20 61 07), Chemin des Collettes, the home and studio of Renoir from 1907 to 1919. It has retained its original decor and has several of the artist's works on display. The villa is set within a magnificent olive grove.

Both museums are open from 10 am to noon and 2 to 6 pm (closed Tuesday year round); it opens 10.30 am to 12.30 pm and 1.30 to 6 pm May to September. Admission to each costs 20FF (children 10FF).

The tourist office (☎ 04 93 20 61 64, fax 04 93 20 52 63), 6 blvd Maréchal Juin, Cagnes Ville, is just off the A8.

Biot
postcode 06410 • pop 5500
This charming *village perché* (perched village) was once an important pottery-manufacturing centre specialising in large earthenware oil and wine containers. Metal containers brought an end to this industry, but Biot is still active in the production of handicrafts. The village streets are a pleasant place for a stroll, but you will have to get there early to beat the hordes.

The attractive **Place des Arcades** dates from the 13th and 14th centuries. At the foot of the village is a **glass factory** where you can watch glass-blowers at work.

The tourist office (☎ 04 93 65 05 85) is at place de la Chapelle. Biot can be reached by bus from Antibes.

The **Musée National Fernand Léger** (☎ 04 92 91 50 30), Chemin du Val de Pôme, is dedicated to the artist Fernand Léger (1881–1955) and contains 360 of his works, including paintings, mosaics, ceramics and stained-glass windows. A huge, colourful mosaic decorates the museum's facade.

It opens from 10 am to 12.30 pm and 2 to 5.30 pm daily except Tuesday (open from 11 am to 6 pm between July and October). Admission costs 28/18FF.

Antibes
postcode 06600 • pop 71,000
Directly across the Baie des Anges from Nice, Antibes has as many attractions as its larger neighbour but is not as crowded. It has beautiful sandy beaches, 16th-century ramparts that run right along the shore, an attractive pleasure-boat harbour (Port Vauban) and an old city with narrow, winding streets and flower-bedecked houses.

The city was first settled around the 4th century BC by Greeks from Marseilles, who named it Antipolis. It was later taken over by the Romans and then by the Grimaldi family, who ruled it from 1384 to 1608. Because of its position on the border of France and Savoy, it was fortified in the 17th and 18th centuries, but these fortifications were torn down in 1894 to give the city room to expand. Antibes has appealed to many artists over the years, most notably Picasso, Max Ernst and Nicolas de Staël.

Juan-les-Pins
postcode 06160
Juan-les-Pins, contiguous to Antibes, is known for both its beautiful 2km-long sandy beach, backed by pine trees, and its outrageous nightlife – a legacy of the 1920s when Americans swung into town with their jazz music and oh-so-brief swimsuits. Party town it might be, but it's an expensive place to sleep – stay in Antibes and commute by bus, train or on foot. The tourist office (☎ 04 92 90 53 05), 51 blvd Guillaumont, opens 9 am to 12.30 pm and 2 to 7 pm (Saturday until noon and 6 pm; closed Sunday) Hours in July and August are 9 am to 8 pm (Sunday from 10 am to 1 pm).

A jazz festival – Jazz à Juan – is held here each year in the second half of July, attracting musicians and music-lovers from around the world.

Between April and September, six daily ferries go from the Embarcadère Courbet (☎ 04 93 68 98 98) in Juan-les-Pins to Îles de Lérins (see the Cannes section).

Cap d'Antibes
Luxurious villas and the Hôtel du Cap, Côte d'Azur's top hotel, are well hidden behind a thick screen of plants and trees on this select peninsula, south-east of Juan-les-Pins. The **Jardin Thuret** (☎ 04 93 67 88 00), 41 blvd du Cap, was established in 1856 and is home to a wide variety of exotic plants. Opening hours are 8.30 am to 5.30 pm (closed at the weekend).

The lovely gardens at the **Villa Eilenroc** (☎ 04 93 67 74 33), right on the tip of Cap d'Antibes, are open from 1.30 to 5 pm on Wednesday (9 am to 5 pm in summer).

CANNES
postcode 06400 • pop 69,363
It's the money of the affluent, spent with fashionable nonchalance, that continues to keep Cannes' many expensive hotels, fancy restaurants and exorbitant boutiques in business and its yachts as big as ocean liners afloat. But the harbour, the bay, the hill west of the port called Le Suquet, the beachside promenade, the beaches and the people sunning themselves provide more than enough natural beauty to make at least a day trip here well worth the effort.

Cannes is famous for its cultural activities and many festivals, the most renowned being the 10-day International Film Festival in mid-May, which sees the city's population treble overnight. Cannes has just one museum and, since its speciality is ethnography, the only art you're likely to come across is in the many rather pretty galleries scattered around town. Cannes' town motto may be 'Life is a festival', but the main tourist season only runs from May to October.

Still, Cannes is a pretty town and comes to life on a sunny day at any time of the year. The view of Cannes from the Corniche de l'Estérel with its background of the snow-capped Alpes Maritimes in late winter is a magnificent sight.

Orientation
Don't expect to be struck down by glitz and glamour the minute you step foot in Cannes: seedy sex shops and peep shows abound around the train station on rue Jean Jaurès. Things get better along rue d'Antibes, the main shopping street a couple of

CÔTE D'AZUR

Cannes

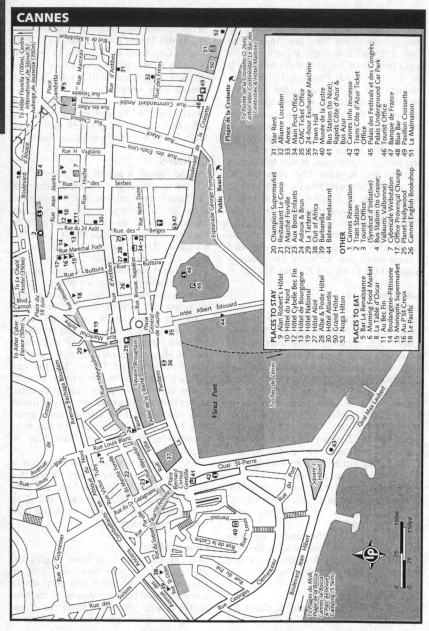

CANNES

PLACES TO STAY
9 Alan Robert's Hôtel
10 Hôtel du Nord
12 Hôtel Cybelle Bec Fin
13 Hôtel de Bourgogne
19 Hôtel National
27 Hôtel Alizé
28 Albe & Poste Hôtel
30 Hôtel Atlantis
50 Grand Hôtel
52 Noga Hilton

PLACES TO EAT
5 Bar La Renaissance
6 Morning Food Market
8 La Table d'Oscar
11 Au Bec Fin
14 Boulangerie-Pâtisserie
15 Monoprix Supermarket
16 Au P'tit Creux
18 Le Pacific

20 Champion Supermarket
21 Restaurant Le Croco
22 Marché Forville
23 Aux Bons Enfants
24 Astoux & Brun
29 La Tarterie
38 Out of Africa
39 Barbarella
44 Bateau Restaurant

OTHER
1 Cannes Réservation
2 Train Station
3 Tourist Office
   (Syndicat d'Initiative)
4 Bus Station (to Grasse;
   Vallauris; Valbonne)
17 Cybercafe Webstation
25 Planet Hollywood
26 Cannes English Bookshop

31 Star Rent
32 Alliance Location
33 Amex
34 Main Post Office
35 CNIC Ticket Office
36 24-hr Exchange Machine
37 Town Hall (Mairie)
40 Musée de la Castre
41 Bus Station (to Nice);
   Rapids Côte d'Azur &
   Bus Azur
42 Cannes Info Jeunesse
43 Trans Côte d'Azur Ticket
   Office
45 Palais des Festivals et des Congrès;
   Palais Underground Car Park
46 Tourist Office
47 Banque de France
48 Blue Bar
49 Pavillon Croisette
51 La Malmaison

blocks south of here. Several blocks farther south still is the huge Palais des Festivals et des Congrès, just east of the Vieux Port (old port).

Cannes' most famous promenade, the magnificent, hotel-lined blvd de la Croisette, begins at the Palais des Festivals and continues eastwards along the Baie de Cannes to Pointe de la Croisette. Place Bernard Cornut Gentille, where the bus station is located, is on the north-western corner of the Vieux Port.

Information

Tourist Offices The tourist office (☎ 04 93 39 24 53, fax 04 92 99 84 23, @ semoftou@palais-festivals-cannes.fr) on the ground floor of the Palais des Festivals is open from 9 am to 7 pm Monday to Friday and 10 am to 6 pm at the weekend (9 am to 8 pm daily in July and August).

The tourist office annexe (☎ 04 93 99 19 77), 1st floor of the train station, is open from 9 am to noon and 2 to 6 pm (closed at the weekend). The office is signposted 'Syndicat d'Initiative' – exit the train station, turn left and walk up the flight of stairs.

The Cannes Info Jeunesse office (☎ 04 93 06 31 31, fax 04 93 06 31 59), 5 quai St-Pierre, is open from 9 am to noon and 2 to 6 pm (closed at the weekend).

Money The Banque de France at 8 blvd de la Croisette is open from 8.30 am to noon and 1.30 to 3.30 pm. There are banks along rue d'Antibes and on rue Buttura.

Amex (☎ 04 93 38 15 87), 8 rue des Belges, is open from 9 am to 6 pm (until noon on Saturday; closed Sunday). Office Provençal Change (☎ 04 93 39 34 37) is inside the Maison de la Chance, corner of rue Maréchal Foch and rue Jean Jaurès.

There is a 24-hour currency exchange machine behind the port building on La Pantiero. The main post office offers foreign currency exchange and an ATM.

Post & Communications The main post office, 22 rue Bivouac Napoléon, is open from 8 am to 7 pm (until noon on Saturday; closed Sunday).

Asher Cyber Espace (☎ 04 92 99 03 01, @ asher@riviera.net), 44 blvd Carnot, is open from 9.30 am to 7 pm (from 9 am to midnight Friday and Saturday; closed Sunday). Cybercafe Webstation (☎/fax 04 93 68 72 37, @ webstation@cannescityshop.com) at 26 rue Hoche is closer to the town centre and handy for the train station. It opens from 10 to 12.30 am Monday to Saturday. One-hour/30-minutes access time costs 45/30FF.

Bookshops English-language novels are available at the Cannes English Bookshop (☎ 04 93 99 40 08), 11 rue Bivouac Napoléon, open from 9.30 am to 1 pm and 2 to 7 pm (closed Sunday).

Musée de la Castre

The Musée de la Castre (☎ 04 93 38 55 26), housed in the chateau atop Le Suquet, has a diverse collection of Mediterranean and Middle Eastern antiquities as well as objects of ethnographic interest from all over the world. It is open from 10 am to noon and 2 to 5 pm (closed Tuesday). Afternoon hours are 2 to 6 pm from April to June and 3 to 7 pm in July and August. Admission costs 10FF (free for students and children).

Walking

Since people-watching is the main reason to come to Cannes, and people are best watched while strolling, and strolling is one of the few activities in Cannes that doesn't cost anything, taking a leisurely walk is highly recommended.

The best places to walk are not far from the water. The pine- and palm-shaded walkway along **blvd de la Croisette** is probably the classiest promenade on the whole Riviera; **La Malmaison** (1863), tucked between the awesome Grand Hôtel and the flashy Noga Hilton at No 47, hosts various art exhibitions.

Some of the biggest yachts you'll ever see are likely to be bobbing gently in the **Vieux Port**, which was once Cannes' inner fishing harbour. The nearby streets are particularly pleasant on a summer's night, when the many cafes and restaurants – overflowing

Starring at Cannes

The Festival International du Film is a closed shop: unless you're John Travolta, Brigitte Bardot or simply damn rich, beautiful and worth a tabloid splash, you have absolutely no chance of scoring a ticket to the legendary Cannes film festival.

The Festival International du Film was created in 1939 to counter Mussolini's fascist propaganda film festival in Venice. It was not until 1946, however, after WWII, that the first festival starred at Cannes.

The 10-day festival revolves around the 60,000 sq m Palais des Festivals, likened to an Egyptian tomb by Liza Minnelli and called 'the bunker' by the local population. Around its stark concrete base, it is adorned with the hand imprints and autographs of celebrities – Timothy Dalton, Brooke Shields, Bardot, David Lynch, Johnny Halliday and the like. The largest of the Film Palace's 12 theatres seats 2300 people.

At the centre of the competition is the prestigious Palme d'Or, awarded by the jury and its president to the winning film – generally not a box office hit. Notable exceptions include Coppola's *Apocalypse Now* (1979), Steven Soderbergh's *Sex, Lies & Video Tape* (1989), David Lynch's *Wild at Heart* (1990) and Tarentino's *Pulp Fiction* (1994).

An equally integral part of the annual festival is the Marché du Film (Film Market) where an estimated US$200 million worth of business takes place.

Around 7000 'names' – trailed by 3000 journalists – attend the star-studded spectacle. Most stay at the Carlton, Majestic or Noga Hilton hotels. They eat at Roger Vergé's *Le Moulin de Mougins* (☎ 04 93 75 78 24), a converted 16th-century mill 8km north of Cannes. The festival's annual US$2000-a-head Cinema Against AIDS charity dinner is often held here. In 1997 Hollywood star Sharon Stone auctioned off her belly-button ring over dinner.

with laughing patrons in the latest fashions – light up the area with coloured neon signs.

Just west of the Vieux Port, **Le Suquet** hill affords quite spectacular views of Cannes, especially in the late afternoon and on clear nights.

Beaches
Unlike Nice, Cannes is endowed with a beach of the sandy variety, most of which is sectioned off for guests of the fancy hotels lining blvd de la Croisette. Here, sun worshippers lap up the beachside equivalent of room service (65FF for a less-than-generous tomato salad delivered to your deck chair; strips of carpet leading to the water's edge etc). This arrangement leaves only a relatively small strip of sand near the Palais des Festivals for the bathing pleasure of picnicking hoi polloi. However, free public beaches, **Plages du Midi** and **Plages de la Bocca**, stretch for several kilometres westwards from the Vieux Port along blvd Jean Hibert and blvd du Midi.

Places to Stay
Hotel prices in Cannes fluctuate wildly according to seasonal demand. Tariffs can be up to 50% higher in July and August – when you're lucky to find a room at any price – than they are in winter. Don't even consider staying in Cannes during the film festival in May unless you have booked months in advance (a year in advance at the budget places). Most upmarket places only accept 12-day bookings during this period.

If you are still keen to try, then get in touch with Cannes Réservation (☎ 0 810 06 12 12, fax 04 93 99 06 60, @ cannes-reservation@en-france.com). They are at 8 blvd d'Alsace.

Places to Stay – Budget
Camping In Cannes, camping is not cheap. *Parc Bellevue* (☎ 04 93 47 28 97, fax 04 93 48 66 25, 67 ave Maurice Chevalier), Cannes-La Bocca, about 5.5km west of the centre of town, is open from April to October. It charges 105FF for two people with a

Amphitheatre-shaped Gordes looks over Provence.

Shhh! The Basilique Notre Dame, Marseilles

The aroma of lavender permeates Provence.

The port of Marseilles is France's second city.

The 'fragrant' fish market, Vieux Port, Marseilles

The medieval village of Èze, Côte d'Azur, offers fabulous views along the coast.

Chance your arm at Monte Carlo's casino.

The bustling life of glamorous Port de Monaco

tent and car. Bus No 9 from the bus station on place Bernard Cornut Gentille stops about 400m away.

Hostels Cannes' modern *Centre International de Séjour et de la Jeunesse* (☎/fax 04 93 99 26 79, ✉ centre.sejour.youth.hostel .cannes@wanadoo.fr, 35 ave de Vallauris), is about 400m north-east of the train station. A bed in a four- to six-person dorm costs between 70FF and 80FF (depending on season) including breakfast. If you don't have a HI card (available for 70/100FF for those under/over 26) you can buy a 2FF card for one night. Each of the three floors has a kitchen, and there's a laundry room. Reception opens 8 am to 12.30 pm and 2.30 to 10.30 pm (3 to 10 pm at the weekend). Curfew is at midnight (2 am at the weekend).

The very pleasant private hostel, *Le Chalit* (☎ 06 15 28 07 09, fax 04 93 99 22 11, ✉ le_chalit@libertysurf.fr, 27 ave du Maréchal Galliéni), is 300m north-west of the station. It charges 90FF for a bed in rooms for four to eight people. Sheets cost extra. There is one kitchen with a food and drinks machine. Le Chalit is open year round and there is no curfew. Reservations (via credit card in summer) are highly recommended from March to October.

Hotels Cannes has a handful of handy hotels for budget travellers that won't break the bank. Directly opposite the train station is the uninspiring, but cheap, *Hôtel du Nord* (☎ 04 93 38 48 79, fax 04 92 99 28 20, 6 rue Jean Jaurès). Basic one-star singles/doubles with washbasin cost 170/190FF. Close by, *Hôtel Cybelle Bec Fin* (☎ 04 93 38 31 33, fax 04 93 38 43 47, 14 rue du 24 Août), has rooms with washbasin for 120/140FF, and 150/180FF with shower.

Heading towards the Auberge de Jeunesse, you pass the excellent-value but little-known *Hôtel Florella* (☎/fax 04 93 38 48 11, 55 blvd de la République). Rooms just like home for one/two people with washbasin cost 120/190FF; doubles with shower and TV cost 200FF.

The large *Hôtel Atlantis* (☎ 04 93 39 18 72, fax 04 93 68 37 65, 4 rue du 24 Août),

may have a two-star rating, but its cheapest singles/doubles with TV and minibar cost only 155/195FF during the low season. This rises to 195/220FF during festival periods and in July and August. The hotel also has a mini gym, spa and sauna for guests' use.

The *Hôtel de Bourgogne* (☎ 04 93 38 36 73, fax 04 92 99 28 41, 11 rue du 24 Août), has rooms with washbasin for 143/186FF and doubles with shower/shower and toilet for 223/286FF. The *Hôtel National* (☎ 04 93 39 91 92, fax 04 92 98 44 06, 8 rue Maréchal Joffre), has rooms from 130/220FF. Doubles/triples with shower and toilet cost 250/300FF.

Places to Stay – Mid-Range
Opposite the main post office, the neat and modern *Albe & Poste Hôtel* (☎ 04 97 06 21 21, fax 04 97 06 21 27, ✉ albe-et-poste-hotel@wanadoo.fr, 31 rue Bivouac Napoléon), has rooms with shower from 200FF to 500FF.

Next door, the *Hôtel Alizé* (☎ 04 93 39 62 17, fax 04 93 39 64 32, ✉ hotelalizecannes @compuserve.com, 29 rue Bivouac Napoléon) has singles/doubles with all mod-cons for 300/340FF.

Opposite the train station, *Alan Robert's Hôtel* (☎/fax 04 93 38 06 07, ✉ roberts-hotel@wanadoo.fr, 16 rue Jean Jaurès), has singles/doubles with shower and toilet from 250/280FF.

Places to Stay – Top End
During the film festival, Cannes' horribly expensive hotels buzz with the frantic comings-and-goings of journalists, paparazzi and stars. Fortunately for their fans – who can only dream of staying in such a place during Cannes' most precious days of May – all of the top-end hotels are along blvd de la Croisette.

The best known ones include the *Carlton Inter-Continental* (☎ 04 93 06 40 06, fax 04 93 06 40 25, ✉ cannes@interconti.com, 58 blvd de la Croisette), the Art Deco *Hôtel Martinez* (☎ 04 92 98 73 00, fax 04 93 39 67 82, 73 la Croisette), the *Grand Hôtel* (☎ 04 93 38 15 45, fax 04 93 68 97 45, 45 la Croisette) and the *Noga Hilton* (☎ 04 92

CÔTE D'AZUR

99 70 00, fax 04 92 99 70 11, **e** *salescannes @hilton.com, 50 la Croisette).* Guests pay at least 2000FF for a double.

Places to Eat

Restaurants There are a few inexpensive restaurants around rue du Marché Forville and lots of little, though not necessarily cheap, restaurants along rue St-Antoine and rue du Suquet. One of the cheapest restaurants in Cannes is **Restaurant Le Croco** (**☎** *04 93 68 60 55, 11 rue Louis Blanc).* Pizzas, grilled meat and fish, and shish kebabs are the main items for sale. The plat du jour is 49FF and *menus* are 59FF (lunch) and 105FF.

Up in Le Suquet, try the beautifully furnished **Out of Africa** (**☎** *04 93 68 98 06, 6 rue St-Dizier),* or the less tame **Barbarella** (**☎** *04 92 99 17 33, 14–16 rue St-Dizier),* a couple of doors down the hill.

Near the train station, **La Table d'Oscar** (**☎** *04 93 38 42 46, 26 rue Jean Jaurès),* has daily specialities – *aïoli garni* (boiled fish with garlic mayonnaise), rabbit, *farcis* for 50FF to 75FF, and a 98FF *menu* in summer. It is closed on Sunday night and on Monday. Nearby, **Au Bec Fin** (**☎** *04 93 38 35 86, 12 rue du 24 Août),* is often filled with regulars. You can choose from two excellent plats du jour for 55FF to 69FF or a 105FF *menu.* Try the *daube de bœuf* (beef stew) *à la Provençale.* It is closed Saturday evening and Sunday.

For fish, dine at **Astoux & Brun** (**☎** *04 93 39 21 87, 21 rue Félix Faure).* Every type and size of oyster is available by the dozen here, as well as elaborate fish platters, scallops, and mussels stuffed with garlic and parsley. In summer, chefs draw the crowds by preparing the shellfish out front. It opens from 10 am to 1 am. For dinner afloat, try the **Bateau Restaurant** (**☎** *04 93 68 98 88, rue Commandant André),* moored on the Jetée Albert Édouard. Try one of their 17 varieties of pizza.

In the centre of town, **Le Pacific** (**☎** *04 93 39 46 71, 14 rue Vénizélos)* is a favourite with local Cannois – its generous, three-course 65FF *menu* is the major draw card. It is closed Friday evening and on Saturday.

Another good choice is the popular **Aux Bons Enfants** *(80 rue Meynadier).* It offers regional dishes like aïoli garni and *mesclun* (a rather bitter salad of dandelion greens and other roughage) in a convivial atmosphere. It has a 94FF *menu* and is open for lunch and dinner on weekdays and for lunch on Saturday (open Saturday evenings in June and July). There are several other small restaurants at this end of rue Meynadier.

Cafes Coffee houses, cafes and *salons de thé* abound in upmarket Cannes. One very down-to-earth place worth a bite (or at least a pastis before dining) is the small and cosy **Bar La Renaissance**, overlooking the bustling place Gambetta market from the corner of rue Teisseire and rue Marceau. Black-and-white photos of yesterday's stars and glamour queens line the walls – a pleasant contrast to the simple wooden tables and chairs.

La Tarterie (**☎** *04 93 39 67 43, 33 rue Bivouac Napoléon)* has a range of salads from 30FF, but it's the house specialities – sweet/savoury tarts costing no more than 18/35FF a slice – that bring in the crowds.

Self-Catering The **food market**, place Gambetta, is held every morning (closed Monday in winter). The **Marché Forville**, a fruit and vegetable market on rue du Marché Forville, two blocks north of place Bernard Cornut Gentille, is open every morning except Monday (when a flea market takes pride of place).

Square Brougham, next to the Vieux Port, is a great place for a picnic – buy filled baguettes and other lunchtime snacks from the **Boulangerie-Pâtisserie** *(12 rue Maréchal Foch)* or from **Au P'tit Creux**, which is opposite. Large supermarkets include **Monoprix** *(9 rue Maréchal Foch)* – take the second entrance on the corner of rue Jean Jaurès and rue Buttura and **Champion** *(6 rue Meynadier).*

Entertainment

Ask the tourist office for a copy of the monthly *Le Mois à Cannes*, which lists what's on and where. Nondubbed films are screened from time to time at the cinemas along rue Félix Faure and its continuation, rue d'Antibes.

Hot spots guaranteed to draw a crowd (and various stars when they roll into town) include the *Blue Bar*, opposite Christian Dior on the corner of la Croissette and rue Commandant André; the *Pavillon Croisette (42 la Croisette)*, which has oyster platters for 135FF; *Planet Hollywood* (☎ 04 93 06 78 27, 1 Allée de la Liberté), where actors and supermodels are rumoured to hang out at Festival time and *Le Bar des Célébrités* (☎ 04 93 06 40 06, 58 la Croisette) at the Carlton Inter-Continental, named after the people sufficiently rich to afford its 2000FF bottles of champagne.

Getting There & Away

Bus Buses to Nice (32FF, 1½ hours, every 20 minutes), Nice airport (75FF for the 40 minute trip via the autoroute, 48.50FF for the 1½ hour trip via the regular road, hourly from 8 am to 7 pm) and other destinations leave from place Bernard Cornut Gentille, next to the Hôtel de Ville in Cannes centre. Most are operated by Rapides Côte d'Azur. The information office (☎ 04 93 39 11 39) is open from 6 am to 6 pm (closed Sunday).

Buses to Grasse (line No 600, 45 minutes), Vallauris (line No 640), Valbonne (line No 630) and elsewhere depart from the bus station to the left as you exit the train station.

Train The information desk at the train station (☎ 04 93 99 50 35), rue Jean Jaurès, is open from 8.30 am to 6 pm (7 pm from mid-July to September).

Destinations within easy reach include St-Raphaël (34FF, 25 minutes, two an hour), from where you can get buses to St-Tropez and Toulon. Other destinations include Nice (32FF, 40 minutes) and Marseilles (133FF, two hours).

Getting Around

Helicopter Héli-Inter (☎ 04 93 21 46 46, fax 04 93 21 46 47) can whirl high-fliers

from Nice airport to the Palm Beach helipad on La Pointe de la Croisette in Cannes in a mere six minutes. The one-way fare is around 400FF.

Bus Bus Azur serves Cannes and destinations up to 7km from town. Its office (☎ 04 93 39 18 71), place Bernard Cornut Gentille (same building as Rapides Côte d'Azur), is open from 7 am to 7 pm. Single/10 tickets cost 7.70/51FF. A weekly Carte Palm'Hebdo/ monthly Carte Croisette is 57/195FF. Bus No 8 runs along the coast from place Bernard Cornut Gentille to the port and Palm Beach Casino on La Pointe de la Croisette.

Car & Motorcycle Star Rent (☎ 04 93 38 13 48), 92 rue d'Antibes, and Excellence (☎ 04 93 94 67 67, @ sales@excellence.fr) rent out cars fit for a star (Ferraris for 13,900FF a day etc). If you prefer something a little more economical, try Thrifty (☎ 04 93 94 61 00), 16 rue du 14 Juillet, which has simple a Fiat Cinquecento from 250FF a day.

Street parking can be a nightmare in Cannes, but there are plenty of pay car parks, which charge at least 10FF an hour. The easiest park to get to is the Palais underground Car Park right next to the Tourist Office. The easy-to-spot entry is off La Croisette.

Alliance Location (☎ 04 93 38 62 62), 19 rue des Frères, rents motorcycles (from 260FF a day) and scooters (160/200FF for one/two people) as well as mobile phones (70FF plus calls). The shop is open from 9 am to 7 pm.

Taxi Call ☎ 04 93 38 91 91 or ☎ 04 93 49 59 20 to order a taxi.

AROUND CANNES
Îles de Lérins

The eucalyptus and pine-covered Île Ste-Marguerite, where the enigmatic Man in the Iron Mask – immortalised by Alexandre Dumas in his novel *Le Vicomte de Bragelonne* (The Viscount of Bragelonne) and in the more recent 1998 Hollywood release *The Man in the Iron Mask* – was held during the late 17th century, lies 1km from the mainland.

The island, home to 20 families and measuring only 3.25km by 1km, is encircled and crisscrossed by trails and paths. The **Musée de la Mer** in the Fort Royal has interesting exhibits dealing with the fort's history and various ships that have been wrecked off the island's coast. The door to the left as you enter leads to the old state prisons, built under Louis XIV and the home in 1685 to Huguenots imprisoned for their refusal to renounce their Protestant faith. The inventor of the steam boat, Claude François Dorothée, is said to have come up with the idea while in prison here in 1773. The museum and cells are open from 10.30 am to 12.15 pm and 2 to 5.40 pm (closed Tuesday). It closes at 5.30 pm between April and June and at 6.30 pm from July to September. Admission costs 10FF.

The smaller, forested **Île St-Honorat**, which is just 1.5km long and 400m wide, was once the site of a renowned and powerful monastery founded in the 5th century. Today it is home to Cistercian monks who own the island but welcome people to visit their monastery and seven small chapels dotted around the island.

Neither island has a fantastic beach; in some places, sunbathers lie on mounds of dried seaweed. Camping, cycling and smoking (theoretically – people still light up) are forbidden on both islands. There are no hotels, *gîtes* or camp sites.

The Compagnie Maritime Cannoise (CMC; ☎ 04 93 38 66 33, fax 04 93 38 66 44) runs ferries to Île St-Honorat (50FF return, 20 minutes) and Île Ste-Marguerite (50FF return, 15 minutes). Both islands can be visited for 75FF. The ticket office (☎ 04 93 38 66 33), at the Vieux Port across Jetée Albert Édouard from the Palais des Festivals, is open from 8.30 am to 6 pm daily.

Trans Côte d'Azur (☎ 04 92 98 71 30, fax 04 93 38 69 02, ☺ trans-cote-azur@wanadoo.fr) charges from 60FF to 90FF for trips to/from both islands. Its office is opposite the Hôtel Sofitel on quai St-Pierre. It also runs boats to St-Tropez (180FF return), Monaco (180FF), Île de Porquerolles (270FF) and San Remo (250FF) in Italy.

For part of the year there are boats to the Îles de Lérins from Juan-les-Pins. See Juan-les-Pins under Antibes Area for more information.

GRASSE
postcode 06130 • pop 42,000
• elevation 333m

If it weren't for the scents wafting through Grasse – just 17km north of Cannes and the Mediterranean – your olfactories might detect a sea breeze. But for centuries, Grasse, with its distinct red and orange tile roofs rising up the slopes of the pre-Alps, has been one of France's most important centres of perfume production, along with Paris and Montpellier.

These days there are five master perfumers – or *nez* (noses), as they're called – in the world. Combining their natural gift with seven years of study, they are able to identify, from no more than a whiff, about 6000 scents. Somewhere between 200 and 500 of these fragrances are used to make just one perfume. Compelling reading associated with Grasse is *Perfume*, a novel by Patrick Süskind about the fantastic life and amazing nose of Jean-Baptiste Grenouille.

Grasse and the surrounding region also produce some of France's most highly prized flowers, including lavender (which you'll see growing profusely in the countryside), jasmine, centifolia roses, mimosa, orange blossom and violets.

History
Founded by the Romans, Grasse became a small republic by the early Middle Ages, exporting tanned skins and oil (from which it may have earned its name – *gras* or *matière grasse* means 'fat' in French). It was taken over by the counts of Provence in 1226 and became part of France in the 16th century. Already a strong trading centre, Grasse grew even richer with the advent of perfumed gloves in the 1500s. Once established, the glove-makers split from the tanners, setting up a separate industry that eventually led to the creation of

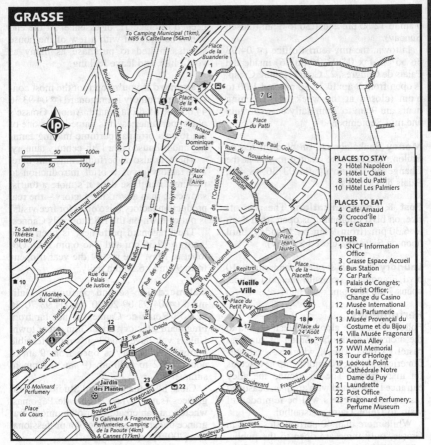

GRASSE

To Camping Municipal (1km),
N85 & Castellane (56km)

Place de la Buanderie

Place de la Foux

Place du Patti

Place Aux Aires

Rue M. Isnard
Rue Dominique Comte

Rue du Rouachier

Rue Paul Goby

To Sainte Thérèse (Hotel)

Place Jean Jaurès

Place de la Placette

Vieille Ville

Rue du Palais de Justice

To Molinard Perfumery

Place du Petit Puy

Place du 24 Août

Jardin des Plantes

To Galimard & Fragonard Perfumeries, Camping de la Paoute (4km) & Cannes (17km)

Boulevard Carnot

Jacques Crouet

Boulevard Fragonard

0   50   100m
0   50   100yd

Boulevard Eugène Charabot

Avenue Thiers

Boulevard Gambetta

Avenue Yves Emmanuel Baudoin

Rue de l'Oratoire

Rue du Peyreguas

Rue Droite

Rue Amiral de Grasse

Rue des Augustins

Boulevard du Jeu de Ballon

Rue Marcel Journet

Rue Repitrel

Rue Gazan

Rue Jean Ossola

Rue Mirabeau

Rue du Barri

Tracastel

Cours H. Crespi

PLACES TO STAY
2 Hôtel Napoléon
5 Hôtel L'Oasis
8 Hôtel du Patti
10 Hôtel Les Palmiers

PLACES TO EAT
4 Café Arnaud
9 Crocod'Île
16 Le Gazan

OTHER
1 SNCF Information Office
3 Grasse Espace Accueil
6 Bus Station
7 Car Park
11 Palais de Congrès; Tourist Office; Change du Casino
12 Musée International de la Parfumerie
13 Musée Provençal du Costume et du Bijou
14 Villa Musée Fragonard
15 Aroma Alley
16 WWI Memorial
17 WWI Memorial
18 Tour d'Horloge
19 Lookout Point
20 Cathédrale Notre Dame du Puy
21 Laundrette
22 Post Office
23 Fragonard Perfumery; Perfume Museum

perfumeries. These in turn flourished in the 18th century, when perfume became fashionable, and members of high society never went anywhere without leaving a distinct aroma in their wake. Of course, it was a fashion necessity, not accessory – people seldom, if ever, took a bath in the 18th century.

Orientation

While the town of Grasse and its suburbs sprawl over a wide area of hill and valley, the old city is a small area, densely packed into the hillside like so many of the towns

across the border in Italy. Its steep, cobbled stairways and roads (some with impossibly tight hairpin bends) are best explored on foot. The N85, better known as the Route Napoléon, which leads north to Castellane and Digne-les-Bains and south to Cannes, runs right through Grasse, where it becomes the town's main (and often very congested) thoroughfare, blvd du Jeu de Ballon.

Information

Tourist Office The tourist office marked Grasse Espace Accueil (☎ 04 93 40 13 13, fax 04 93 40 12 82), two minutes from the bus station at place de la Foux, is open from 9 am to 12.30 pm and 1.30 to 6 pm (closed Sunday).

In town, the tiny tourist office (☎ 04 93 36 66 66, fax 04 93 36 86 36) inside the Palais de Congrès, 22 Cours Honoré Cresp, is open from 9 am to 12.30 pm and 1.30 to 6 pm (closed at the weekend). Opening hours are 9 am to 7 pm daily between July and mid-September.

Money Banks abound on blvd du Jeu de Ballon. You can also change money at the Change du Casino (☎ 04 93 36 48 48), Palais de Congrès.

Post & Communications The post office, on blvd Fragonard, is open from 8 am to 6.30 pm (from 9 am on Monday, until noon on Saturday, closed Sunday).

Laundry The self-service laundrette at 10 blvd Fragonard, opposite the post office, opens 7 am to 9 pm.

Perfumeries

Follow your nose along rue Jean Ossola to the archway at the beginning of rue Tracastel (Aroma Alley), where several perfumeries have been conjuring up new scents for many years. The air around the alley entrance is saturated with aromas. Seasoned (as it were) travellers will be reminded of visits to Delhi, Cairo or Istanbul.

While more than 40 perfumeries exist in Grasse, only three are open to the public. It's unlikely that you'll know any of the perfumeries by name, as the perfumes are sold only from their factories or by mail order. The names the world knows are the big brands that buy the perfumers' essence and reap considerable profit from it.

During a tour you'll be taken through every stage of perfume production, from extraction and distillation to the work of the 'noses'.

The guides will explain the differences between perfume, which contains 20% pure essence, and its weaker partners, eau de toilette and eau de Cologne, which contain 2% to 6% concentrate. You'll also hear about the extraordinary quantity of flowers needed to make 1L of essence. At the end you'll be squirted with a few of the house scents, invited to purchase as many as you'd like, and leave reeking.

Fragonard If you're on foot the most convenient perfumery is Fragonard (☎ 04 93 36 44 65), 20 blvd Fragonard. Among Grasse's oldest perfumeries, it is named after one of the town's original perfume-making families and is housed in a 17th-century tannery.

There is also a perfume museum here. The factory gives a brief introduction to perfume, but these days it's more a tourist showcase than a working factory. The real production factory (also open for free visits) is out of town on the N85 towards Cannes.

The Fragonard perfumery is open from 9 am to 12.30 pm and 2 to 6 pm from October to May. The rest of the year it opens from 9 am to 6.30 pm daily.

Galimard The second perfumery, Galimard (☎ 04 93 09 20 00, fax 04 93 70 36 22), 73 Route de Cannes, is not far from Fragonard's factory, about 3km out of town. Unless you have wheels it's not a feasible option. The factory is open from 9 am to noon and 2 to 5.30 pm (9 am to 6 pm in summer).

Close by is the Galimard Studio des Fragrances (same ☎/fax), Route de Pégomas, where you can create your own unique fragrance under the guidance of a professional nez (200FF, two hours).

Molinard Housed in a turreted, Provençal-style villa surrounded by immaculate lawns and a blaze of flowers, Molinard (☎ 04 93 36 01 62, fax 04 93 36 03 91), 60 blvd Victor Hugo, is a much ritzier affair than Fragonard.

Molinard also offers 'create your own perfume' sessions (200FF, 1¼ hours) as well as a seminar about the history of perfume (150FF, one hour), after which participants walk away with a Molinard diploma. The perfumery is open from 9 am to 12.30 pm and 2 to 6 pm daily except Sunday (9 am to 6.30 pm from July to September).

Villa Musée Fragonard

Named after the artist Jean-Honoré Fragonard, who was born in Grasse in 1732, this
villa (☎ 04 93 40 32 64), 23 blvd Fragonard,
now a museum, is where the artist lived for
a year in 1790. The artist's paintings, famous for their licentious scenes, are on display in the museum. It opens 10 am to noon
and 2 to 5 pm (closed Monday and Tuesday). From June to September it opens
10 am to 1 pm and 2 to 7 pm daily. Admission is free.

Musée Provençal du Costume et du Bijou

Visiting Grasse's colourful costume and
jewellery museum comes as a breath of
fresh air after touring the town's perfumeries. The museum (☎ 04 93 36 44 65),
2 rue Jean Ossola, is housed inside the
stately Hôtel de Clapiers Cabris, the private
mansion of the sister of revolutionary
Mirabeau – the Marquise de Cabris – who
lived in Grasse from 1769. It opens 10 am to
1 pm and 2 to 6 pm. Admission is free.

Musée International de la Parfumerie

Opened in 1989, the International Perfume
Museum (☎ 04 93 36 80 20), 8 blvd Fragonard, examines every detail of perfume production, from extraction techniques to sales
and publicity, and traces its 400 years of
history in Grasse. One of the most appealing sections of the museum is the rooftop
conservatory, where lavender, mint, thyme
and jasmine are grown in a heady mix of
aromatic scents. It opens 10 am to
noon and 2 to 5 pm daily except Monday
and Tuesday (10 am to 7 pm from June to
September). Admission costs 25FF (students 12.50FF).

Cathédrale Notre Dame du Puy

Although rather uninteresting in itself, the
former cathedral, built in Provençal Romanesque style in the 12th and 13th centuries and reworked in the 18th century,
contains a painting by Fragonard entitled
Washing of the Feet and several early paintings by Rubens, including *The Crown of*
Thorns and *Christ Crucified*. The cathedral
is open from 9.30 am (8.30 am on Saturday)
to 11.30 am and 2.30 to 6 pm (3 to 7 pm on
Saturday).

Special Events

Grasse's two main events – related to flowers and scents, naturally – are Exporose in
May and La Jasminade, held during the first
weekend in August.

Places to Stay

Camping The two-star *Camping Municipal* (☎ 04 93 36 28 69, blvd Alice de Rothschild) (continuation of ave Thiers), is 1km
north-east of the bus station. It charges
59FF for one person with tent and car. It is
closed in January. Bus No 8, marked
'Piscine', leaves from the bus station and
stops at the front of the camping ground.
Another site is *Camping de la Paoute* (☎ 04
93 09 11 42, 160 Route de Cannes), 4km
south of Grasse.

Hotels The cheapest option in town is the
Hôtel Napoléon (☎ 04 93 36 05 87, 6 ave
Thiers). Singles/doubles with washbasin
start at 140/160FF. The hotel is closed from
the end of December to the end of January.
Opposite is the small, rather run-down
Hôtel L'Oasis (☎ 04 93 36 02 72, place de
la Buanderie), which has rooms with washbasin for 170/180FF and singles/doubles
with shower for 190/225FF.

If you have a car or don't mind an uphill
amble, the two-star *Sainte Thérèse* (☎ 04
93 36 10 29, fax 04 93 36 11 73, 39 ave Yves
Emmanuel Baudoin), just over 1km from
the tourist office, is a good choice. From the
hotel you get a panoramic view of the
valley and the dusty, orange-roofed town.
Singles/doubles start at 160/220FF and private parking is available. The hotel is
closed from October to mid-November.
Another option on the same road is *Hôtel
Les Palmiers* (☎/fax 04 93 36 07 24, 17 ave
Yves Emmanuel Baudoin). Prices in winter/
summer start at 130/190FF.

For something more upmarket, try the
modern, rather unattractive two-star *Hôtel
du Patti* (☎ 04 93 36 01 00, fax 04 93 36 36

40, place du Patti), in the heart of the old city. It has pleasant singles/doubles with private bath and toilet from 330/420FF. Parking is available.

Places to Eat

Easy to find and easy on the pocket is **Croc-od'Île** (☎ 04 93 36 71 02, 12 blvd du Jeu de Ballon) where mussels, pommes frites and a beer will cost you no more than 55FF, crêpes from 38FF to 50FF or a small pizza from 30FF to 46FF. It opens all day and every day. Somewhat more expensive is the popular **Café Arnaud** (☎ 04 93 36 44 88, 10 place de la Foux) where lively owner Maryse Cannetto will serve you an expansive Alsatian menu for 125FF or cheaper menus at 78FF. Tucked away in the old town is **Le Gazan** (☎ 04 93 36 22 88, rue Gazan), offering good-value 65FF lunchtime menus or good fish dishes.

Getting There & Away

Bus The ticket office at the bus station (☎ 04 93 36 08 43), place de la Buanderie, closes at 5.15 pm. Several companies operate from here. Rapides Côte d'Azur (☎ 04 92 96 88 88) has buses to Nice (38.50FF, 1¼ hours) via Cannes (20.50FF, 45 minutes) every half-hour (hourly on Sunday). VFD has a morning bus to Grenoble (six hours), which stops in Castellane (near the Gorges du Verdon) and Digne-les-Bains, and from Grenoble continues on to Chambéry, Annecy and Geneva.

Train The train line does not reach Grasse but SNCF has an information office (☎ 04 93 36 06 13) at the bus station, open from 8.30 am to 5.30 pm (closed Sunday).

MASSIF DE L'ESTÉREL

The most stunning natural feature of the entire Côte d'Azur (apart from the azure-blue sea) is the lump of red porphyry rock known as the Massif de l'Estérel. Covered by pine, oak and eucalyptus trees until devastating fires in 1985 and 1986 and now beginning to return to life, this range lies between St-Raphaël and Mandelieu-La Napoule, which is inland from Cannes.

A drive or walk along the Corniche de l'Estérel (also known as the Corniche d'Or and the N98) – the coastal road that runs along the base of the range – is not to be missed as the views are spectacular. Along the way you'll find many small summer resorts and inlets where you can swim. Some of the places worth visiting include **Le Dramont**, where the 36th US Division landed on 15 August 1944; **Agay**, a sheltered bay with an excellent beach; the resorts of **Le Trayas** and **Théoule-sur-Mer**; and **Mandelieu-La Napoule**, a pleasant resort with a large pleasure-boat harbour near a fabulously restored 14th-century castle. In summer, when the Corniche de l'Estérel gets very crowded, choose the inland N7, which runs through the hills and feels like a whole different world.

There are all sorts of walks you can go on in the Massif de l'Estérel, but for the more difficult trails you will need to come equipped with a good map, such as IGN's Série Bleue (1:25,000) No 3544ET. Many of the walks, such as those up to the Pic de l'Ours (496m) and the Pic du Cap Roux (452m), are signposted.

Places to Stay

There are camping grounds at various places along the coast, including Le Dramont, Agay, Anthéor, Le Trayas and Mandelieu-La Napoule.

The **Auberge de Jeunesse** (☎ 04 93 75 40 23, fax 04 93 75 43 45, 9 ave de la Véronèse), Le Trayas, midway between Cannes and Fréjus (about 20km from each), is on a beautiful site overlooking the sea. The hostel is 1.5km up the hill from the Auberge Blanche bus stop. The hostel is closed from 10 am to 5 pm and during January. Bed and breakfast is 68FF. You must have an HI card. Telephone reservations are not accepted. You can camp for 44FF (including breakfast).

FRÉJUS & ST-RAPHAËL

Fréjus (population 41,000), first settled by Massiliots (the Greeks who founded Marseilles) and colonised by Julius Caesar around 49 BC as Forum Julii, is known for its Roman ruins. Once an important port, the town was sacked by various invaders, including the Saracens in the 10th century. Much of the town's commercial activity ceased after its harbour silted up in the 16th century.

At the foot of the Massif de l'Estérel is St-Raphaël (population 26,500), a beachside resort town a couple of kilometres south-east of Fréjus. This was one of the main landing bases of US and French troops in August 1944.

Orientation

Although St-Raphaël is 2km south-east of Fréjus, the suburbs of the two have now become so intertwined that they seem almost to form a single town. Fréjus comprises the hillside Fréjus Ville, about 3km from the seafront, and Fréjus Plage, on the Gulf of Fréjus. The Roman remains are almost all in Fréjus Ville.

Information

Tourist Offices The Fréjus tourist office (☎ 04 94 51 83 83, fax 04 94 51 00 26, ℮ frejus.tourisme@wanadoo.fr), 325 rue Jean Jaurès, is open from 9 am to noon and 2 to 6 pm Monday to Saturday (from 10 am on Sunday). Staff make hotel reservations and distribute an excellent map of Fréjus locating its archaeological treasures.

From June to mid-September the tourist office kiosk (☎ 04 94 51 48 42) by the beach (opposite 11 blvd de la Libération) is open from 10 am to noon and 3 to 7 pm daily.

St-Raphaël's tourist office (☎ 04 94 19 52 52, fax 04 94 83 85 40, ℮ touroff@ clubinternet.fr), rue Waldeck Rousseau, across the street from the train station, is open from 9 am to noon and 2 to 6 pm daily except Sunday (9 am to 7 pm daily in July and August). Their Web site is at www.st-raphael.com.

Money The Banque National de Paris (BNP) is just west of the Fréjus Ville tourist office on rue Jean Jaurès and is open from 8.30 am to noon and 1.45 to 5 pm (closed at the weekend).

Post & Communications In Fréjus (postcode 83600), the post office on ave Aristide Briand is open from 8.30 am to 7 pm (until noon on Saturday; closed Sunday). There's another on blvd de la Libération opposite the tourist office.

In St-Raphaël (postcode 83700), the post office is east of the tourist office on ave Victor Hugo.

Roman Ruins

West of Fréjus' old city on rue Henri Vadon (past the Porte des Gaules) is the mostly rebuilt 1st- and 2nd-century **arènes** (amphitheatre; ☎ 04 94 17 19 19). It once seated an audience of 10,000 and is today used for rock concerts and bullfights. It opens from 9 or 9.30 am to noon and 2 to 6 or 6.30 pm (closed Tuesday).

At the south-eastern end of rue des Moulins is the **Porte d'Orée**, the only arcade of the thermal baths still standing. North of the old town on rue du Théâtre Romain are the remains of a **Roman theatre**, open from 9 or 9.30 am to 5 or 6.30 pm (closed Tuesday).

Le Groupe Épiscopal

In the centre of town on place Formigé, on the site of a Roman temple, is an episcopal ensemble, comprising an 11th- and 12th-century **cathedral** (☎ 04 94 51 26 30), one of the first Gothic buildings in the region, though it retains certain Roman features. The carved-wood doors at the main entrance were added during the Renaissance.

To the left of the cathedral is the octagonal 5th-century **baptistry**, with a Roman column on each of its eight corners. Stairs from the narthex lead up to the stunning 12th- and 13th-century **cloister**, whose features include some of the columns of the Roman temple and painted wooden ceilings from the 14th and 15th centuries. It looks onto a beautiful courtyard with a well tended garden and a well.

In the cathedral's cloister is the Musée Archéologique (Archaeological Museum), which has a marble statue of Hermes, a head of Jupiter, and a magnificent 3rd-century mosaic depicting a leopard. The museum is open from 9 am to noon and 2 to 5 pm daily except Tuesday (9 am to 7 pm daily from April to October). Admission, which includes entry to the baptistry and cloister, costs 20FF (students 15FF).

Beaches

Fréjus Plage, lined with buildings from the 1950s, and St-Raphaël have excellent sandy beaches.

St-Raphaël is a leading **diving** centre, thanks in part to the **WWII shipwrecks** off the coast. Most diving clubs in town organise dives to the wrecks, which range from a 42m-long US minesweeper to a landing craft destroyed by a rocket in 1944 during the Allied landings. Plongée 83 (☎ 04 94 95 27 18), 29 ave de la Gare, and CIP St-Raphaël Odyssée (☎ 04 94 83 66 65), Vieux Port, organise night and day dives and courses for beginners.

Les Bateaux de St-Raphaël (☎ 04 94 95 17 46, fax 04 94 82 71 45), Gare Maritime, organises daily **boat excursions** in summer from St-Raphaël to the Îles de Lérins (160FF return), and the Fréjus and St-Tropez gulfs (60FF return). It also runs daily boats to St-Tropez and Port Grimaud (see Getting There & Away in the St-Tropez section).

Places to Stay

Accommodation in Fréjus and St-Raphaël is not cheap.

Camping Fréjus has 15 camp sites, one of the best being the four-star *Holiday Green* (☎ 04 94 19 88 30, fax 04 94 19 88 31), on the road to Bagnols, open from 28 March to 24 October. It's 7km from the beach but has its own large pool. Nightly rates are 40/25FF per adult/child and 44/62FF per tent in the low/high season.

Closest to the beach is the *Parc de Camping de Saint Aygulf Plage* (☎ 04 94 17 62 49, fax 04 94 81 03 16, 270 ave Salvarelli), in St-Aygulf, south of Fréjus. This huge camp site – with space for 1100-plus tents – is open from 27 April to 31 October.

Hostels The *Auberge de Jeunesse Fréjus-St-Raphaël* (☎ 04 94 52 93 93, fax 04 94 53 25 86, @ youth.hostel.frejus.st.raphael@wanadoo.fr, chemin du Counillier), near Fréjus Ville, is set in a seven hectare park. Dorm beds cost 67FF, including breakfast, or 82FF in the *New Hostel* nearby. You can camp here for 32FF a night.

If you arrive by train get off at St-Raphaël, take bus No 7 and walk up the hill. In July and August bus No 6 goes directly to the hostel. From Fréjus' train station or from place Paul Vernet bus No 3 is the best option.

Hotels In Fréjus, the 11-room, no-star *Hôtel Bellevue* (☎ 04 94 51 39 04, fax 04 94 51 35 20, place Paul Vernet), has basic singles/doubles from 149/170FF (doubles with shower for 280FF).

The two-star *Auberge du Vieux Four* (☎ 04 94 51 56 38, fax 04 94 53 82 85, 49 rue Grisolle) has well-kept rooms with shower and toilet for 200/250FF – and a good restaurant too.

Next door, the two-star *Hôtel Le Flore* (☎ 04 94 51 38 35, fax 04 94 52 28 20, 35 rue Grisolle), has rooms from 190FF.

At Fréjus Plage, the 27-room *Hôtel L'Oasis* (☎ 04 94 51 50 44, fax 04 94 53 01 04, impasse Jean-Baptiste Charcot), set amid pine trees, has comfortable rooms with TV for 350FF. It is closed from November to mid-February.

Also at Fréjus Plage is the *Hôtel Sable et Soleil* (☎ 04 94 51 08 70, fax 04 94 53 49 12, 158 ave Paul Arène), facing an ugly carpark, where singles/doubles cost 280/350FF. The 'Sand and Sun' has facilities for disabled people.

Getting There & Away

Bus No 5, run by Forum Cars (☎ 04 94 95 16 71 in Fréjus), links Fréjus' train station and place Paul Vernet with St-Raphaël. Both Fréjus and St-Raphaël are on the train line from Nice to Marseilles. For information, call ☎ 0 836 35 35 35.

There's an especially frequent service from Nice to Gare de St-Raphaël-Valescure, south-east of the centre. The information office here is open from 9.15 am to 1 pm and 2.30 to 6 pm.

ST-TROPEZ

postcode 83990 • pop 5700

In 1956 St-Tropez was the setting for the film *Et Dieu Créa la Femme* (And God Created Woman) starring Brigitte Bardot. Its stunning success brought about St-Tropez's rise to stardom – or destruction, depending on your point of view. But one thing is clear: the peaceful little fishing village of St-Tropez, somewhat isolated from the rest of the Côte d'Azur at the end of its own peninsula, suddenly became the favourite of the jet set. Ever since, St-Tropez has lived on its sexy image.

Attempts to keep St-Tropez small and exclusive have created at least one tangible result: you'll probably have to wait in huge traffic queues to drive into town. Yachts, way out of proportion to the size of the old harbour and irritatingly blocking the view, chased away the simple fishing boats a long time ago. And while painters and their easels jostle each other for space along the harbour quay, in summer there's little of the intimate village air that artists such as the pointillist Paul Signac found so alluring. Still, sitting in a cafe on place des Lices in late May, watching the locals engage in a game of *pétanque* (bowls) in the shade of the age-old plane trees, you could be in any little Provençal village.

Orientation

St-Tropez lies at the southern end of the narrow Bay of St-Tropez, opposite the Massif des Maures. The old city, with its narrow streets, is packed between quai Jean Jaurès (the main quay of the Vieux Port), place des Lices (a lovely shady rectangular 'square' a few blocks inland) and what's left of the 16th-century citadel overlooking the town from the north-east.

Information

Tourist Offices The tourist office (☎ 04 94 97 45 21, fax 04 94 97 82 66, @ tourisme@nova.fr), quai Jean Jaurès, opens 9.30 am to 1 pm and 3 to 10.30 pm in high season. Hours vary slightly at other times of the year. It organises guided city tours in French and English (20/10FF adults/children).

Money At the port, the Crédit Lyonnais, 21 quai Suffren, is open from 8 am to noon and 1.30 to 4.45 pm (closed on weekends). It has a 24-hour exchange machine.

Post & Communications The post office, place Celli, one block from the port, is open from 9 am to noon and 2 to 5 pm (until noon on Saturday; closed Sunday). There is an exchange service.

Laundry The Laverie du Port, on quai de Lépi, close to the beginning of the big car park near the port, is open from 7 am to 10 pm. A small load costs an expensive 32FF.

Musée de l'Annonciade

The Musée de l'Annonciade (☎ 04 94 97 04 01), in a disused chapel on place Grammont, Vieux Port, contains an impressive collection of modern art, including works by Matisse, Bonnard, Dufy, Derain and Rouault. Signac, who set up his home and studio in St-Tropez, is well represented. The museum is open from 10 am to noon and 2 to 6 pm daily except Tuesday (10 am to noon and 3 to 7 pm from June to September; closed in November). Admission costs 30FF (students 15FF).

Musée Naval

If you're really bored with watching the antics of the rich and (maybe not so) famous, visit the Naval Museum (☎ 04 94 97 59 43) in the dungeon of the citadel at the end of Montée de la Citadelle. It is open from 10 am to 5 or 6 pm (closed Tuesday). Apart from displays concerning the town's maritime history, it also has information about the Allied landings that took place here in August 1944. The best photographs of St-Tropez can be taken from the citadel grounds. Admission costs 25/15FF.

Beaches

About 4km south-east of the town is the start of a magnificent sandy beach, Plage de Tahiti, and its continuation, Plage de Pampelonne. It runs for about 9km between Cap du Pinet and the rocky Cap Camarat. To get there on foot, head out of town along ave de la Résistance (south of place des Lices) to Route de la Belle Isnarde and then Route de Tahiti. Otherwise, the bus to Ramatuelle, a village south of St-Tropez, stops at various points along a road that runs about 1km inland from the beach.

The coastline east of Toulon, from Le Lavandou to the St-Tropez peninsula (including spots around the peninsula), is well endowed with *naturiste* (nudist) beaches. It's also legal in some other places, mostly in secluded spots or along sheltered streams farther inland.

On the southern side of Cap Camarat is a secluded nudist beach, **Plage de l'Escalet**. Several streams around here also attract bathers in the buff. To get there you can take the bus to Ramatuelle, but you'll have to walk or, if lucky, hitch the 4km southeast to the beach. Closer to St-Tropez is **La Moutte**, a naturiste beach 4.5km east of town – take Route des Salins, which runs between two of the houses owned by BB (as Bardot is known in France).

Walks

The Sentier Littoral (coastal path) goes all the way from St-Tropez south to the beach of Cavalaire along some 35km of splendid rocky outcrops and hidden bays. In parts the setting is reminiscent of the tropics minus the coconut palms. If the distance is too great, you can walk as far as Ramatuelle and return on the bus.

If you can read French, invest in the pocket-sized *Promenez-vous à Pied – Le Golfe de St-Tropez* (47FF), which details 26 walks around St-Tropez; buy a copy from the Maison de la Presse on quai Jean Jaurès.

Places to Stay – Budget & Mid-Range

Surprise, surprise! There's not a cheap hotel to be found in St-Tropez. To the south-east along Plage de Pampelonne there are plenty of multi-star camping grounds.

St-Tropez's cheapest hotel is the dingy *Hôtel La Méditerranée* (☎ 04 94 97 00 44, fax 04 94 97 47 83, 21 blvd Louis Blanc). Doubles start at 200FF. One rung up the

price ladder is the *Hôtel Les Chimères* (☎ 04 94 97 02 90, fax 04 94 97 63 57, Port du Pilon), at the south-western end of ave du Général Leclerc. Singles/doubles with shower and breakfast cost 328/358FF.

Well worth the cash is the calm and quiet *Le Baron* (☎ 04 94 97 06 57, fax 04 94 97 58 72, 23 rue de l'Aïoli). Rooms – all with TV and private bath – overlook the citadel and cost between 350FF and 600FF.

Places to Stay – Top End

St-Tropez's top-end hotels are mostly open from early April to mid-October. The town's most expensive offering is the four-star *La Bastide de Saint-Tropez* (☎ 04 94 97 58 16, fax 04 94 97 21 71, route des Carles) on the southern side of town. This plush establishment is fully equipped to cater for every taste. Low-season room prices start at 980FF and jump to 1680/2080FF in the high season. This place is open year round. View the hotel on-line before taking the plunge at www.nova.fr/bastide.

Places to Eat

Restaurants Quai Jean Jaurès is lined with restaurants, most with *menus* from 100FF or 150FF and with a strategic view of the silverware and crystal of those dining on the decks of their yachts.

Extremely tasteful and not too expensive is the informal *Café Sud* (☎ 04 94 97 71 72, 12 rue Étienne Berny), tucked down a narrow street off places des Lices. It has a *menu* for 140FF and tables are outside in a star-topped courtyard. Close by, the *Bistrot des Lices* (☎ 04 94 97 29 00, 3 places des Lices) serves traditional Provençal cuisine, including wonderful *ratatouille*, with dishes from 120FF to 190FF.

Le Petit Charron (☎ 04 94 97 73 78, 5 rue Charrons), off place des Lices is another delicious bet. For locals, the top place to eat is the *Auberge des Maures* (☎ 04 94 97 01 50, 8 rue due Docteur Boutin) off rue Allard, not far from the port.

Cafes Former haunts of BB and her glam friends and foes include *Le Café* (☎ 04 94 97 44 69, place des Lices), which is St-

Tropez's most historic cafe. Formally called the Café des Arts, it is not to be confused with the place of the same name on the corner of place des Lices and ave du Mai Foch. Another good people-watching spot and hard to miss with its bright red decor, is *Sénéquier (quai Jean Jaurès)*, by the old harbour. *Le Gorille*, on the opposite corner, is open 24 hours and is a perfect place for breakfast after dancing the night away.

Self-Catering The *Prisunic Supermarket (9 ave du Général Leclerc)* is open from 8 am to 8 pm (closed Sunday). The place des Lices *market* is held on Tuesday and Saturday mornings. There's also one on place aux Herbes behind quai Jean Jaurès, open until about noon daily.

Getting There & Away

Bus St-Tropez bus station, ave Général de Gaulle, is on the south-western edge of town on the one main road out. The information office (☎ 04 94 54 62 36) is open from 8 am to noon and 2 to 6 pm (until noon Saturday; closed Sunday). Buses to Ramatuelle (five a day) leave from the bus station and run parallel to the coast about 1km inland. Sodetrav (☎ 04 94 12 55 12 in Hyères) has eight buses daily to/from St-Raphaël-Valescure train station to St-Tropez bus station, via Fréjus (48FF, 1¼ hours). Buses from St-Tropez to Toulon (95FF, 2¼ hours) go inland before joining the coast at Cavalaire; they also stop at Le Lavandou and Hyères.

Boat In July and August, MMG (☎ 04 94 95 17 46 in Ste-Maxime) operates a shuttle boat service from St-Tropez to Ste-Maxime (34FF, 30 minutes, 26 daily) and Port Grimaud (28FF, 20 minutes, 11 daily). Between April and July, Les Bateaux de St-Raphaël (☎ 04 94 95 17 46, fax 04 94 83 88 55 in St-Raphaël) runs two boats daily from St-Tropez to St-Raphaël (52FF, 50 minutes).

Car If you go to St-Tropez by car be prepared for long delays, both getting in and out the town. Here is a tip to minimise the frustration of waiting: avoid the coastal roads. Instead approach from the Provençale Autoroute and exit at Le Muy (exit 35). Take the D558 road across the Massif des Maures and via La Garde Freinet to Port Grimaud. Park your car (easily) here and take the regular shuttle boat to St-Tropez. Exit the same way.

Getting Around

MAS (☎/fax 04 94 97 00 60), 3–5 rue Joseph Quaranta, rents mountain bikes (80FF per day, plus 2000FF deposit) and scooters (190FF to 290FF, plus 2500FF deposit).

Several hire places line ave du Général Leclerc. To order a taxi ring ☎ 04 94 97 05 27. To order a taxi boat call Taxi de Mer (☎ 06 09 53 15 47), 5 Quartier Neuf.

ST-TROPEZ TO TOULON
Massif des Maures

Stretching from Hyères to Fréjus, this arc-shaped massif is covered with pine, chestnut and cork oak trees. The vegetation makes it appear almost black and gives rise to its name, which comes from the Provençal word *mauro* (dark pine wood).

The Massif des Maures offers superb walking and cycling opportunities. There are four roads you can take through the hills, the northernmost being a ridge road, the 85km-long **Route des Crêtes**, which runs close to La Sauvette (779m), the massif's highest peak. It continues east through the village of **La Garde Freinet**, a perfect getaway from the summer hordes. Within the massif are a number of places worth visiting.

If you like chestnuts, the place to go is **Collobrières**, a small town renowned for its chestnut purée and *marrons glacés* (chestnuts cooked in syrup and glazed). About 12km east of Collobrières are the ruins of a 12th- to 13th-century monastery, **La Chartreuse de la Verne**. North-east of the monastery is the village of **Grimaud**, notable for its castle ruins, small Roman church, windmill and pretty streets.

The tourist office in St-Tropez distributes a map/guide called *Tours in the Golfe of St-*

Tropez – Pays des Maures, which describes four driving, cycling or walking itineraries.

Bormes-les-Mimosas
postcode 83230 • pop 5000

Within the Massif des Maures is the 12th-century village of Bormes-les-Mimosas, famous for its great diversity of flora. This beautiful village has attracted lots of artists and craftspeople, many of whom you will see at work as you wander through the tiny streets. With stretches of fine sand and numerous inlets, the seafront offers lots of water sports. Various festivals are held here throughout the year – if you're around in September, don't miss the Fête des Vendanges (Grape Harvest Festival). The tourist office (☎ 04 94 71 15 17, fax 04 94 64 79 57) is on place Gambetta.

Le Lavandou
postcode 83980 • pop 5200

Once a fishing village, Le Lavandou, about 5km south-east of Bormes-les-Mimosas, has become a very popular destination, thanks mainly to its 12km-long sandy beach. Although the town itself may not have much to offer, it is a good base for exploring the nearby Massif des Maures, especially if you are interested in doing some cycling. The resort is also close to the three idyllic Îles d'Hyères, which you can reach easily by boat.

Le Lavandou's tourist office (☎ 04 94 71 00 61, fax 04 94 64 73 79) is on quai Gabriel Péri.

Corniche des Maures

This 26km-long coastal road (part of the D559) stretches from Le Lavandou north-east to La Croix-Valmer. All along here you can enjoy breathtaking views. There are also lots of great beaches for swimming, sunbathing or windsurfing. Among the towns that the road passes through are Cavalière, Pramousquier and Le Rayol.

Îles d'Hyères

The oldest and largest naturiste colony in the region is on Île du Levant, the eastern-most of the three Hyères Islands. Indeed, half of this 8km-long island is reserved for naturists.

Vedettes Îles d'Or (☎ 04 94 71 01 02), which has an office at the ferry terminal in Le Lavandou, operates boats to Île du Levant and Port Cros (both cost 124/68FF return for adults/children, 35 minutes). There are at least four boats a day in the warmer months (hourly in summer) but only four a week in winter. To Porquerolles there is a boat three times a week (daily in July and August) and the return fare is 142/100FF. Boats also sail from Hyères (one hour) in the high season.

Parc National de Port Cros Created in 1963 to protect at least one small part of the Côte d'Azur from overdevelopment, Port Cros is France's smallest national park, encompassing just 700 hectares of land – essentially the island of Port Cros – as well as an 1800-hectare zone of water around it. The middle island of the Îles d'Hyères, Port Cros is a marine reserve, but is also known for its rich variety of insects and butterflies. Keeping the water around it clean (compared with the rest of the coast) is one of the reserve's big problems.

The park's head office (☎ 04 94 12 82 30) is on the mainland at 50 rue St Claire in Hyères. The island can be visited year round, but walkers must stick to the marked paths. Fishing, camping and fires are not allowed.

Getting There & Away Boats to the Îles d'Hyères leave from various towns along the coast, including Le Lavandou and Hyères. Boats from Toulon run only from Easter to September (see Boat under Getting There & Away in the Toulon section).

TOULON
postcode 83000 • pop 168,000

Toulon is France's most important naval port, serving as a base for the French navy's Mediterranean fleet. As a result of heavy bombing in WWII, the city's run-down centre looks very grim when compared to Nice, Cannes or even Marseilles.

Initially a Roman colony, Toulon only became part of France in 1481 – the city grew in importance after Henri IV founded an arsenal here. In the 17th century the port was enlarged by Vauban. The young Napoleon Bonaparte first made a name for himself in 1793 during a siege in which the English, who had taken over Toulon, were expelled.

As in any large port, there's a lively quarter with heaps of bars where locals and sailors seem to spill out of every door. Women travelling on their own may wish to avoid some of the old city streets at night, particularly around rue Chevalier Paul and the western end of rue Pierre Sémard.

All in all, it's a city like no other on the Côte d'Azur, though it's unclear why anyone would want to spend much time here when pulsating Marseilles, fine beaches and the tranquil Îles d'Hyères are so close. Still, the old city is pleasant enough for a stroll and the promenade is unpretentious. On top of that the accommodating tourist office does try hard to promote what is otherwise an ordinary workaday French town.

Orientation

Toulon is built around the *rade*, a sheltered bay lined with quays. To the west is the naval base and to the east the ferry terminal, from where boats set sail for Corsica. The city is at its liveliest along quai de la Sinse and quai Stalingrad (from where ferries depart for the Îles d'Hyères) and in the old city. North-west of the old city is the train station.

Separating the old city from the northern section is a multilane, multinamed thoroughfare (known as ave du Maréchal Leclerc and blvd de Strasbourg as it runs through the centre), which teems with traffic. It continues west to Marseilles and east to the French Riviera.

Immediately north-west of here, off rue Chalucet, is a pleasant city park. Toulon's central square is the enormous place de la Liberté.

Information

Tourist Offices The main tourist office (☎ 04 94 18 53 00, fax 04 94 18 53 09, @ toulon.tourisme@wanadoo.fr), place

Raimu, is open from 9 am to 6 pm (from 10 am to noon on Sunday). The Maison de l'Étudiant (☎ 04 94 93 14 21), rue de la Glacière, is also a handy information source.

Money The Banque de France on ave Vauban is open from 8.30 am to noon and 1.30 to 3.30 pm (closed at the weekend). Commercial banks line blvd de Strasbourg.

Post & Communications The post office on rue Bertholet (second entrance on rue Ferrero) is open from 8 am to 7 pm (until 6 pm on Tuesday; until noon on Saturday; closed Sunday). For an Internet connection, try Cyber Espace (☎ 04 94 41 06 05), 10 place Pasteur. It opens 10 am to 8 pm.

Laundry There are several laundrettes in the old city, including Lav'Ipso at 25 rue Baudin (open from 7 am to 9 pm) where a 6kg load will cost 16FF.

Musée de Toulon

The Toulon Museum (☎ 04 94 93 15 54), 113 ave du Maréchal Leclerc, houses an unexceptional **art museum** and a rather moth-eaten **natural history museum** in a Renaissance-style building. The museum is open from 9 am to 6 pm. Admission is free.

Musée de la Marine

The Naval Museum (☎ 04 94 02 02 01), in the lovely old arsenal building on place Monsenergue, is open from 9.30 am to noon and 2 to 6 pm daily except Tuesday (9.30 am to noon and 3 to 7 pm daily in July and August). Admission costs 29FF (students and children 19FF).

Mont Faron

Overlooking the old city from the north is Mont Faron (580m), from which you can see Toulon's port in its true magnificence. Near the summit is the **Tour Beaumont Mémorial du Débarquement**, commemorating the Allied landings that took place along the coast here in August 1944. The steep road up to the summit is also used for the Tour de Méditerranée (February) and Paris-Nice (March) professional cycling races.

CÔTE D'AZUR

TOULON

PLACES TO STAY
3   Hôtel Terminus
4   Hôtel La Résidence
6   Hôtel Maritima
11 Hôtel d'Europe
19 Hôtel de Provence
21 Hôtel Molière
24 Hôtel Little Palace

PLACES TO EAT
7   Maharajah
9   Al Dente
10 La Muraille de Chine
12 Cafétéria du Centre
13 Mini Casino
    Supermarket
15 8 à Huit Grocery
22 Le Petit Prince
23 Les Enfants Gâtés
25 Constantinoise
28 Covered Food Market
35 Food Market

OTHER
1   Train Station
2   Sodetrav
5   Entrance to City Park
8   Banque de France
14 Musée de Toulon
16 RMTT (Bus) Kiosk
17 Cinéma Le Royal
18 Post Office
20 Théâtre Municipal
26 Maison de l'Étudiant
27 Lav'Ipso (Laundrette)
29 Tourist Office
30 Musée de la Marine
31 Le Batelier de la Rade
    Boat Trips
32 RMTT Sitcat Boats
33 Statue
34 Town Hall
36 Scubazur (Diving Shop)
37 Le Batelier de la Rade
    Boat Trips
38 Cyber Espace

Boulevard Louvois
To Mont Faron & Téléphérique
Boulevard Commandant Nicolas
Boulevard Pierre Toesca
Place de l'Europe
Rue Mirabeau
Rue Gimelli
Place Albert 1er
Rue Peiresc
Rue Chalucet
Rue Revel
Avenue Vauban
Rue Dumont d'Urville
Rue Gimelli
Boulevard de Tessé
Place de la Liberté
Rue de Chabannes
Rue V Clappier
Rue Picot
Avenue Colbert
Ave du Maréchal Leclerc
Boulevard de Strasbourg
To Marseille (60km) & Aix-en-Provence (78km)
Ave du Moulin
Ave A Guiol
Rue Berthelot
Rue Ferrero
Rue Jean Jaurès
Rue Louis Jourdan
Rue Pastoureau
To Hyères (18km), Le Lavandou (30km), St-Tropez (69km), Nice & Cannes (124km)
Rue Racine
Rue Molière
Rue Conseile
Rue de l'Humilité
Rue Berthelot
Place des Trois Dauphins
Place V. Hugo
Place Puget
Avenue Général Magnan
Place d'Armes
Rue Anatole France
Vieille Ville
Rue Pierre Sémard
Rue Lamalgue
Rue de Pomet
Rue Andrieu
Rue Hoche
Rue Alezard
Rue Baudin
Place Monsenergue
Rue Aubau
Camile
Rue des Savonniers
Rue Chevalier Paul
Rue N Laugier
Place Camille Ledeau
Rue de la Glacière
Place Vincent Raspail
Rue Michelet
Rue Zola
Place Gustave Lambert
Place de la Cathédrale
Place Raimu
Place d'Alger
Cours Lafayette
Place Louis Blanc
Rue Merle
Ave de Besagne
Quai Stalingrad
Avenue de la République
Qual de la Sinse
Petite Rade
To Camping Le Beauregard (6km)
To La Seyne (8km)
To Cablettes (18km)
To St-Mandrier-sur-Mer (28km)
To Îles d'Hyères
To Ferry Terminal & SNCM Office (100m)
Place Pasteur

0   100   200m
0   100   200yd

euro currency converter 10FF = €1.52

A *téléphérique* (cableway; ☎ 04 94 92 68 25) climbs the mountain from ave de Vence. It runs from 9 am to noon and 2 to 5.30 pm (closed Monday) and costs 38/26FF return for adults/children. Take bus No 40 from place de la Liberté.

Boat Excursions

Excursions around the rade, with a commentary (in French only) on the events that took place here during WWII, leave from quai Stalingrad or quai de la Sinse. Trips cost an average of 45FF for one hour. Les Batelier de la Rade (☎ 04 94 46 24 65), quai de la Sinse, also does three-hour tours of the Îles d'Hyères (120FF).

Between June and September, SNRTM (☎ 04 94 93 07 56) runs several trips, some with a meal on board, to Cannes and St-Tropez.

Sitcat boats (☎ 04 94 46 35 46) run by RMTT, the local transport company, link quai Stalingrad with the towns on the peninsula across the harbour, including La Seyne (line 8M), St-Mandrier-sur-Mer (line 28M) and Sablettes (line 18M). The 20-minute ride costs the same as a bus ticket: 8FF (10FF if you buy your ticket aboard). The ticket office is open from 8 am to 12.15 pm and 2 to 5.15 pm. Boats run from around 6 am to 8 pm.

Scubazur (☎ 04 94 92 19 29, fax 04 94 92 24 13), ave de la République, is a first-class diving shop that has plenty of information on all the **diving clubs and schools** along the Côte d'Azur.

Places to Stay

Camping The closest camping ground to Toulon, *Le Beauregard* (☎ 04 94 20 56 35), is on the coast some 6km east in Quartier Ste-Marguerite. It costs 25/13FF per adult/child and 21FF for a tent. Take bus No 7 from the train station to the La Terre Promise stop.

Hotels There are plenty of cheap options in the old city, though some – particularly those at the western end of rue Jean Jaurès – are less than salubrious. They're better avoided.

Immediately opposite the train station is the cheap and unsmiling *Hôtel Terminus* (☎ 04 94 89 23 54, 7 blvd de Tessé), which has singles/doubles costing upwards of 115/260FF. It flogs 59FF *menus* in its adjoining restaurant.

Another one, conveniently close to the bus and train stations, is *Hôtel La Résidence* (☎ 04 94 92 92 81, 18 rue Gimelli). The rooms are not as impressive as the lobby, with its enormous gilt mirror and balding Oriental carpets, but they're a bargain. Simple singles/doubles cost 120/130FF and those with shower cost 190FF. It's easy to park around here.

Heading into town, the *Hôtel Maritima* (☎ 04 94 92 39 33, 9 rue Gimelli), has equally simple single/double rooms for 125/140FF. Rooms with a shower are 180FF and ones with a toilet too are 220FF. The pleasant *Hôtel Little Palace* (☎ 04 94 92 26 62, fax 04 94 89 13 77, 6 rue Bertholet), has simple rooms from 80/100FF and from 150FF with shower.

Beside the opera house, the one-star *Hôtel Molière* (☎ 04 94 92 78 35, fax 04 94 62 85 82, 12 rue Molière), has rooms from 95/110FF.

Hôtel de Provence (☎ 04 94 93 19 00, 53 rue Jean Jaurès) is welcoming but often full. Basic rooms start at around 110/125FF, or 150/175FF with shower.

East of the train station is the *Hôtel d'Europe* (☎ 04 94 92 37 44, fax 04 94 62 37 50, 7 rue de Chabannes), which has rooms for one or two people for 230FF, 250FF and 310FF. Photos of each room category accompany the price list displayed in reception. Some of the rooms have little balconies.

Places to Eat

Pricey restaurants, terraces and bars with occasional live music are abundant along the quays; *menus* start at 100FF and a tiny bouillabaisse or aïoli garni will set you back 80FF to 100FF. Another lively area is place Victor Hugo and neighbouring place Puget. Cheaper fare can be found in the old city's more dilapidated streets around rue Chevalier Paul.

CÔTE D'AZUR

Restaurants You can have a hearty meal in the humble Algerian restaurant *Constantinoise* (☎ 04 94 09 28 69, *rue Pierre Sémard*). It's mainly frequented by local men, but friendly outsiders – particularly in these tense times in Toulon – are more than welcome. A generous serving of couscous with salad costs as little as 30FF and the coffee is black, thick and sweet.

Another very popular and modern place is *Les Enfants Gâtés* (☎ 04 94 09 14 67, *7 rue Corneille*). The 'Spoiled Children' is run by a young crowd and is one of the most pleasant places in town to dine without breaking the bank. The plat du jour is 55FF. Close by is the equally charming *Le Petit Prince* (*10 rue de l'Humilité*), named after Antoine de St-Exupéry's book for children.

There are some decent restaurants near the train station: *La Muraille de Chine* (☎ 04 94 92 04 21, *32 rue Gimelli*) has Chinese *menus* for 58FF and 85FF. It's closed on Sunday.

Nearby is *Al Dente* (☎ 04 94 93 02 50, *30 rue Gimelli*), a cool and elegant Italian place serving 11 types of home-made pasta for 44FF to 66FF and salads for 38FF to 48FF. The lunch/evening *menu* is 60/104FF. Al Dente is open for lunch daily except Sunday and for dinner to 10.30 or 11 pm. *Maharajah* (☎ 04 94 91 93 46, *15 rue Gimelli*), an Indian eatery, has lunch/dinner *menus* for 60/129FF and *thalis* (trays with an assortment of dishes) for 149FF. It is closed on Monday.

Cafétéria du Centre (☎ 04 94 92 68 57, *27–29 rue Gimelli*), has cheap three-course *menus* for 39.50FF. It opens 11 am to 2.30 pm and 6.30 to 10 pm (closed Sunday).

Self-Catering The southern half of Cours Lafayette is one long *open-air food market* held, in typical Provençal style, under the plane trees. There's a *covered food market* on place Vincent Raspail. Both are open daily except Monday.

Near the train station, there is a small *Mini Casino Supermarket* (*7 ave Vauban*), and *8 à Huit* grocery (*ave du Maréchal Leclerc*).

Getting There & Away

Bus Intercity buses leave from the bus terminal on place de l'Europe, to the right as you exit the train station. Information and bus tickets for the several companies that serve the region are available from Sodetrav (☎ 04 94 28 93 40), 4 blvd Pierre Toesca (opposite the terminal), open from 6.15 am to 7 pm (6.20 to 9.20 am, 11.15 am to 12.30 pm and 2 to 6.25 pm at the weekend).

There are buses to Hyères (35FF, 40 minutes) every 15 minutes, of which a further eight continue eastwards along the coast, stopping at Le Lavandou (60FF, 1¼ hours) and other towns, before arriving in St-Tropez (94FF, 2¼ hours). Francelignes Comett (☎ 04 91 61 83 00 in Marseilles) has buses to Aix-en-Provence (88/138FF one way/return, 1¼ hours, four daily; two on Sunday in July and August). Phocéens Cars (☎ 04 93 85 66 61 in Nice) goes to Nice (130FF, 2½ hours) via Hyères and Cannes (122FF, two hours) twice daily (except Sunday).

Train The train station (☎ 0 836 35 35 35) is at place Albert 1er, near blvd Pierre Toesca. The information office is open from 8 am to 7 pm (closed Sunday). There are frequent connections to cities along the coast, including Marseilles (58FF, 40 minutes), Cannes (96FF, 1¾ hours, hourly) and Nice (114FF, 1½ hours, hourly). Trains to Paris' Gare de Lyon (403FF, 5¾ hours) go via Marseilles.

Boat Ferries to Corsica and Sardinia are run by the SNCM (☎ 04 94 16 66 66), which has an office at 49 ave de l'Infanterie de Marine (opposite the ferry terminal). It opens 8.30 am to noon (11.30 am on Saturday) and 2 to 5.45 pm daily except Sunday. For more information, see the introductory Getting There & Away section of the Corsica chapter.

Boats from Toulon to the Îles d'Hyères only run from Easter to September and are operated by several companies, such as Trans Med 2000 (☎ 04 94 92 55 88). All depart from quai Stalingrad. The trip to Porquerolles (105FF return) takes one hour.

It's another 40 minutes to Port Cros, from where it's a 20 minute hop to Île du Levant (165FF return to tour all three islands).

Getting Around

Bus Local buses are run by RMTT (☎ 04 94 03 87 03), which has an information kiosk at the main local bus hub on place de la Liberté. It is open from 7.30 am to noon and 1.30 to 6.30 pm (closed at the weekend). Single/10 tickets cost 8/54FF. Buses generally run until around 7.30 or 8.30 pm. Sunday service is limited.

Bus Nos 7 and 13 link the train station with quai Stalingrad.

Nice to Menton

THE CORNICHES

Nice and Menton (and the 30km of towns in between) are linked by three corniches (coastal roads), each one higher up the hill than the last. If you're in a hurry and don't mind missing the scenery, you can drive a bit farther inland and take the A8.

Corniche Inférieure

The Corniche Inférieure (also known as the Basse Corniche or Lower Corniche; the N98) sticks pretty close to the villa-lined waterfront and the nearby train line, passing (as it goes from Nice eastwards to Menton) through Villefranche-sur-Mer, St-Jean-Cap Ferrat, Beaulieu-sur-Mer, Èze-sur-Mer, Cap d'Ail (where there's a seaside hostel; ☎ 04 93 78 18 58) and Monaco.

Villefranche-sur-Mer Set in one of the Côte d'Azur's most charming harbours, this little port (population 8000) overlooks the Cap Ferrat peninsula. It has a well preserved 14th-century old city with a 16th-century citadel and a church dating from 100 years later. Steps break up the tiny streets that weave through the old city, the most interesting of which is rue Obscure. Keep a lookout for occasional glimpses of the sea as you wander through the streets that lead down to the fishing port. Villefranche was a particular favourite of Jean Cocteau, who painted the frescoes (1957) in the 17th-century **Chapelle St-Pierre**.

St-Jean-Cap Ferrat Once a fishing village, the seaside resort of St-Jean-Cap Ferrat (population 2250) lies on the spectacular wooded peninsula of Cap Ferrat, which conceals a bounty of millionaires' villas. On the narrow isthmus of Cap Ferrat is the **Musée de Béatrice Ephrussi de Rothschild** (☎ 04 93 01 33 09), housed in the Villa Île de France, which was built in the style of the great houses of Tuscany for the Baroness de Rothschild in 1912. It abounds with antique furniture, paintings, tapestries and porcelain and is surrounded by beautiful gardens. It opens 10 am to 6 pm from mid-February to October (to 7 pm in July and August). During the rest of the year its hours are 2 to 6 pm (10 am to 6 pm at the weekend). Admission costs 46FF (students 35FF) and includes entry to the gardens and the collections on the *rez-de-chaussée* (ground floor). It costs an extra 15FF to view those on the 1st floor.

Moyenne Corniche

The Moyenne Corniche – the middle coastal road (the N7) – clings to the hillside, affording great views if you can find somewhere to pull over. It takes you from Nice past the Col de Villefranche, Èze and Beausoleil, the French town up the hill from Monte Carlo.

Èze Perched on a rocky peak at an altitude of 427m is the picturesque village of Èze (population 2450), once occupied by Ligurians and Phoenicians. Below is its coastal counterpart, Èze-sur-Mer. Make your way to the exotic garden for fabulous views up and down the coast. The German philosopher Friedrich Nietzsche (1844–1900) spent some time here, during which time he started to write *Thus Spoke Zarathustra*. The path that links Èze-sur-Mer and Èze is named after him.

Grande Corniche

The Grande Corniche – whose panoramas are by far the most spectacular – leaves

CÔTE D'AZUR

Nice as the D2564. It passes the **Col d'Èze**, where there's a great view; **La Turbie**, which is on a promontory directly above Monaco and offers a stunning night-time vista of the principality; and **Le Vistaëro**.

Roquebrune Dominating this appealing hilltop village (population 12,300), which lies just between Monaco and Menton, is a medieval dungeon that is complete with a re-created manor house. Roquebrune's tortuous little streets, which lead up to the castle, are lined with shops selling handicrafts and souvenirs and are overrun with tourists in the high season.

Carved out of the rock is the impressive rue Moncollet, with arcaded passages and stairways.

For more information, contact the tourist office (☎ 04 93 35 62 87, fax 04 93 28 57 00), 20 ave Paul Doumer, in nearby **Cap Martin**, an exclusive suburb of Menton known for its sumptuous villas and famous past residents (Winston Churchill and the architect Le Corbusier among them).

MENTON
postcode 06500 • pop 29,000
Menton, reputed to be the warmest spot on the Côte d'Azur (especially during winter), is only a few kilometres from the Italian border. In part because of the weather, Menton is popular with older holiday-makers, whose way of life and preferences have made the town's after-dark entertainment a tad tranquil compared to other spots along the coast. Guy de Maupassant, Robert Louis Stevenson, Gustave Flaubert and Katherine Mansfield all found solace in Menton. Today, the town draws Italians from across the border, retaining a magnetic charm free of the airs and pretensions found in other areas of the Côte d'Azur.

Menton is famed for its cultivation of lemons. Giant, larger-than-life sculptures made from lemons, lemons and more lemons take over the town for two weeks during Menton's fabulous Fête des Citrons (Lemon Festival) in February. The festival kicks off on Mardi Gras.

Orientation
Promenade du Soleil runs south-west to north-east along the beach; the train line runs approximately parallel about 500m inland. Ave Édouard VII links the train station with the beach. Ave Boyer, where the tourist office is, is 350m to the east. From the station, walk along ave de la Gare and take the second right off what appears to be a two-way divided promenade. The tourist office is about halfway down ave Boyer.

The Vieille Ville is on and around the hill at the north-eastern end of promenade du Soleil. The Vieux Port lies just beyond it.

Information
Tourist Office The tourist office (☎ 04 92 41 76 76, fax 04 92 41 76 78, ☺ ot@ villedementon.com), inside the Palais de l'Europe at 8 ave Boyer, is open from 8.30 am to 12.30 pm and 1.30 to 6 pm (Saturday from 9 am to noon and 2 to 6 pm; closed Sunday).

Thematic organised tours (Menton and the *belle époque*, artists, gardens etc) are arranged by the Maison du Patrimoine (☎ 04 92 10 33 66, fax 04 93 28 46 85), 5 rue Ciapetta. It has a more central information office (☎ 04 92 10 97 10) at 24 rue St-Michel. Tours cost 30FF per person.

Money There are plenty of banks along rue Partouneaux. Barclays Bank (☎ 04 93 28 60 00) at 39 ave Félix Faure is open from 8.30 am to noon and 1.50 to 4.30 pm (closed at the weekend). It has an automatic exchange machine outside. Another 24-hour currency machine is outside the Crédit Lyonnais that is two doors down from the tourist office on ave Boyer.

Post & Communications The post office, Cours George V, is open from 8 am to 6.30 pm (to 6 pm on Thursday; until noon on Saturday; closed Sunday).

Bookshop A fine range of guides, travel books and foreign-language newspapers are available at the Maison de la Presse at 25 ave Félix Faure.

Église St-Michel
The early 17th-century Church of St-Michael, the grandest baroque church in this part of France, sits perched in the centre of the Vieille Ville, which has many narrow, winding passageways. The church is usually open from 10 am to noon and 3 to 6 pm (closed Saturday morning). The ornate interior is Italian in inspiration.

Musée Jean Cocteau
The Jean Cocteau Museum (☎ 04 93 57 72 30), quai Napoléon III, south-west of the Vieux Port, displays work by Jean Cocteau (1889–1963) – poet, dramatist and film director – in a seafront bastion dating from 1636. Cocteau's work includes drawings, tapestries, ceramics and mosaics such as the pebble designs that decorate the fort's outside walls.

The museum is open from 10 am to noon and 2 to 6 pm (closed Tuesday). Admission is free. Don't miss Cocteau's frescoes in the **Salle des Mariages** (Marriage Hall) in the Hôtel de Ville, place Ardoïno, open 8.30 am to 12.30 pm and 1.30 to 5 pm (closed at the weekend). Admission costs 5FF.

Beach
The beach along promenade du Soleil is public but, like its counterpart in Nice, it's covered with smooth little rocks. There are more beaches directly north of the Vieux Port, including Plages des Sablettes with sand and clean water, and east of Port de Garavan, the main pleasure-boat harbour.

The Centre Nautique (☎ 04 93 35 49 70, fax 04 93 35 77 05), promenade de la Mer, rents laser boats/catamarans/kayaks for 105/125/55FF an hour. The **sailing school** also runs two-hour courses and arranges water-skiing (126FF).

The Compagnie de Navigation et de Tourisme de Menton (☎ 04 93 35 51 72), Vieux Port, organises boat trips to Monaco (63FF) and the Italian Riviera (93FF).

Places to Stay
Camping The two-star *Camping Saint Michel* (☎ 04 93 35 81 23, route des Ciappes de Castellar), open from 1 April to 15 October, is 1km north-east of the train station up Plateau St-Michel. It costs 18/18/19FF per person/tent/car. The two-star *Camping Fleur de Mai* (☎ 04 93 57 22 36, 67 Route de Gorbio), just 2km north-west of the train station, is open from 1 April to 30 September.

Hostels The *Auberge de Jeunesse* (☎ 04 93 35 93 14, fax 04 93 35 93 07, plateau St-Michel), is 500m from Camping St-Michel. Bed and breakfast is 68FF. It's closed from 12 to 5 pm (10 am to 5 pm in winter) and closes at again midnight. The walk from the train station is quite a hike uphill, and there are lots of steps. Otherwise take a Line 6 bus and get off at the camp site.

Hotels Just next door to the train station, the no-star *Hôtel Le Chouchou* (☎/fax 04 93 57 69 87, place de la Gare) has basic singles/doubles above the bar for 150/250FF. Opposite, the also no-star *Hôtel Le Terminus* (☎ 04 93 35 77 00, fax 04 92 10 49 81, place de la Gare) has a few rooms starting at 165/225FF. Hall showers are free. Reception is closed after 11 am on Saturday and after 5 pm on Sunday, but you can always find someone to help you in the bar-restaurant areas during opening times.

The one-star *Hôtel de Belgique* (☎ 04 93 35 72 66, fax 04 93 41 44 77, @ hotel-de-belgique@wannadoo.fr, 1 ave de la Gare) has rooms from 145/280FF; rooms with a private shower start at 260FF. The hotel is closed in November. Also close by, two-star *Hôtel Claridges* (☎ 04 93 35 72 53, fax 04 93 35 42 90, 39 ave de Verdun) has comfortable rooms starting at 160/220FF. The two-star *Hôtel Le Globe* (☎ 04 92 10 59 70, fax 04 92 10 59 71, 21 ave de Verdun), opposite the tourist office, is part of the Logis de France chain. Rooms are around 250/350FF.

In town, the two-star *Hôtel des Arcades* (☎ 04 93 35 70 62, fax 04 93 35 35 97, 41 ave Félix Faure), under the arches, is one of Menton's most picturesque options. Rooms with washbasin cost 180/380FF. The best sea views are to be found at *Saint Michel* (☎ 04 93 57 46 33, fax 04 93 57 71 19,

1684 promenade du Soleil). Rooms cost 220/480FF in summer.

Places to Eat

Restaurants There are places to eat galore – at any time of day – along ave Félix Faure and its pedestrianised continuation, rue St-Michel. Place Clemenceau and place aux Herbes in the Vieille Ville are equally popular. There are more pricey restaurants with terraces fanned by cool breezes along promenade du Soleil.

Notable places include *Le Chaudron* (☎ *04 93 35 90 25, 28 rue St-Michel)*, which has filling salads from 32FF to 68FF and *menus* for 92FF and 126FF; and *Ulivo* (☎ *04 93 35 45 65, place du Cap)*, which is run by an Italian family and specialises in mussel dishes. Some 10 different types, all for 48FF, are on offer. Pasta dishes start at 42FF and giant salads kick off at 25FF.

Slightly cheaper places, including pizzerias, line quai de Monléon in the Vieille Ville. Along pedestrianised rue St-Michel delicious takeaway crêpes or *gauffres* (waffles) are available for between 10FF and 25FF, depending on the topping.

Self-Catering In the Vieille Ville, the *Marché Municipal* (also known as Les Halles) on quai de Monléon sells all kinds of food. It opens from 5 am to 1 pm (closed Monday morning).

The *Marché U Supermarket* at 38 rue Partouneaux is open from 8.30 am to 7.15 pm (until 7 pm on Saturday; closed Sunday). The *Comtesse du Barry* shop, next door, serves luxury *foie gras* products.

Getting There & Away

Bus The bus station (☎ 04 93 28 43 27) is next to 12 promenade Maréchal Leclerc, the northern continuation of ave Boyer. The information office (☎ 04 93 35 93 60 or ☎ 04 93 28 43 27 for international services) is open from 8 am to noon and 2 to 6 pm (closed Saturday afternoon and on Sunday).

There are buses to Monaco (12.50FF return, 30 minutes), Nice (28FF return, 1¼ hours), Ste-Agnès (43FF return, 45 minutes) and Sospel (60FF return, 45 minutes).

There are also buses to the Nice-Côte d'Azur airport (95FF, 1½ hours) via Monaco run by Bus RCA (☎ 04 93 21 30 83).

Train The information office (☎ 0 836 35 35 35) at the train station is open from 8.45 am to noon and 2 to 6 pm (from 8.30 am to noon and 2 to 6 pm on Saturday; closed Sunday). The station is open from 5 am to 11.30 pm. Trains to Ventimiglia cost 14FF and take 10 minutes. For more information on rail services along the Côte d'Azur see Trains under Getting There & Away in the Nice section.

Getting Around

TUM (Transports Urbains de Menton) (☎ 04 93 35 93 60) runs nine bus lines in and around the city. Lines one and two link the train station with the old town. Tickets cost 6.50FF.

AROUND MENTON

There are many interesting places to visit near Menton, including the Vallée de la Roya, the Vallée des Merveilles (Valley of Wonders) and the Parc National du Mercantour (see Information in the Nice section). Nearby villages worth visiting include Gorbio and Ste-Agnès (9km and 10km to the north-west, respectively), and Castellar and Sospel (7km and 19km north of Menton). There are good walking and hiking areas near each of these places as well as some great views over the Riviera.

The **Vallée de la Roya** once served as a hunting ground for King Victor Emmanuel II of Italy and only became part of France in 1947. In this valley is the pretty village of **Breuil-sur-Roya**. Overlooking the valley is the fortified village of **Saorge**, set in a natural amphitheatre and remarkable for its maze of narrow, stepped streets and its 15th- to 17th-century houses. A good map for walks in the area, particularly in the Parc National du Mercantour, is the Didier & Richard No 9. IGN's Série Bleue maps Nos 3741OT *(Vallée de la Vesubie, Parc National du Mercantour)* and 3841OT *(Vallée de la Roya, Vallée des Merveilles)* cover the areas in a scale of 1:25,000.

Monaco (Principauté de Monaco)

postcode 98000 • pop 30,000

The tiny Principality of Monaco, which has been under the rule of the Grimaldi family for most of the period since 1297, is a sovereign state whose territory, surrounded by France, covers only 1.95 sq km. It has been ruled since 1949 by Prince Rainier III (born in 1923), whose sweeping constitutional powers make him much more then a mere figurehead. For decades, the family has been featured on the front pages of the tabloids, though since the death in 1982 of the beloved Princess Grace (remembered from her Hollywood days as the actress Grace Kelly), the media has concentrated on the not-so-successful love lives of the couple's two daughters, Caroline and Stephanie.

Glamorous Monte Carlo is famed for its casino and its role, since 1911, as host to the annual Formula One Grand Prix in May, which sees drivers from around the world tear round a track that winds its way through the town and around the port.

The citizens of Monaco (known as Monégasques), of whom there are only about 5000 out of the total population, pay no taxes. They have their own flag (red and white), own national holiday (19 November), own country telephone code and own traditional Monégasque dialect. The official language is French although many street signs, particularly in Monaco Ville, are in French and Monégasque. The official religion is Roman Catholic. There are no border formalities upon entering Monaco. The principality was admitted to the UN as a full member in 1993.

Orientation

Monaco consists of six principal areas: Monaco Ville (also known as the old city and the Rocher de Monaco), a 60m-high, 800m long outcrop of rock on the southern side of the Port de Monaco where the Palais du Prince (Prince's Palace) is; Monte Carlo, famous for its casino, which is north of the port and the annual Formula One Grand Prix; La Condamine, the flat area southwest of the port; Fontvieille, the industrial area south-west of Monaco Ville; Moneghetti, the hillside suburb west of La Condamine; and Larvotto, the beach area north of Monte Carlo. The French town of Beausoleil is just three streets up the hill from Monte Carlo.

Information

Tourist Offices The Direction du Tourisme et des Congrès de la Principauté de Monaco (☎ 92 16 61 66, fax 92 16 60 00, @ dtc@monaco-congres.com), 2a blvd des Moulins, is across the public gardens from the casino. It opens 9 am to 7 pm (from 10 am to noon on Sunday). From mid-June to mid-September there are several tourist information kiosks open around the principality. See the Web site at www.monaco-congres.com.

Money Monaco uses the French franc. Both French and Monégasque franc coins are in circulation, but the latter are difficult to find and not widely accepted outside the principality. The entire Monégasque collection of currency dating from 1640 can be seen in the Musée des Timbres et des Monnaies (Stamp & Money Museum; ☎ 93 15 41 50, fax 93 15 41 45), 11 Terrasses de Fontvieille.

In Monte Carlo there are numerous banks in the vicinity of the casino. In La Condamine, try blvd Albert 1er. Amex (☎ 93 25 74 45), 35 blvd Princesse Charlotte, is open from 9.30 am to 12.30 pm and 2 to 6 pm Monday to Friday.

Post & Communications Monégasque stamps are valid only within Monaco. Postal rates are the same as those in France. Monaco's public telephones accept Monégasque or French *télécartes*.

Telephone numbers in Monaco only have eight digits. Calls between Monaco and the rest of France are treated as international

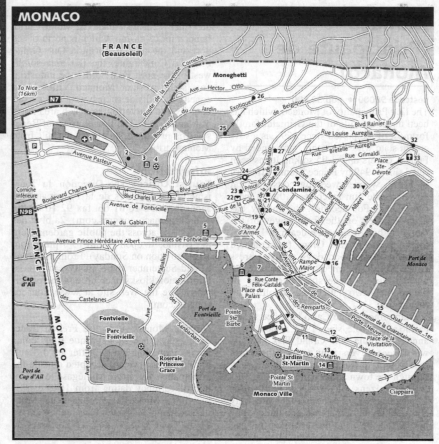

MONACO

calls. Dial 00 followed by Monaco's country code (377) when calling Monaco from the rest of France or abroad. To call France from Monaco, dial 00 and France's country code (33). This applies even if you are only making a call from the eastern side of blvd de France (in Monaco) to its western side (in France)!

The main post office is in Monte Carlo at 1 ave Henri Dunant inside the Palais de la Scala. It is open from 8 am to 7 pm (until noon Saturday; closed Sunday), but it does not exchange foreign currency. There are post offices in each of the other four areas,

including those at place de la Visitation in Monaco Ville, and across the road from the train station in La Condamine (open 8 am to 7 pm; until noon Saturday; closed Sunday).

There is a cybercorner inside Stars 'n' Bars (☎ 93 50 95 95, ✉ info@starsnbars .com), 6 quai Antoine 1er, open 11 am to midnight. Half an hour on-line costs 40FF.

Bookshop Scruples (☎ 93 50 43 52), 9 rue Princesse Caroline, is an English-language bookshop open from 9.30 am to noon and 2.30 to 7 pm (6.30 pm on Saturday; closed Sunday).

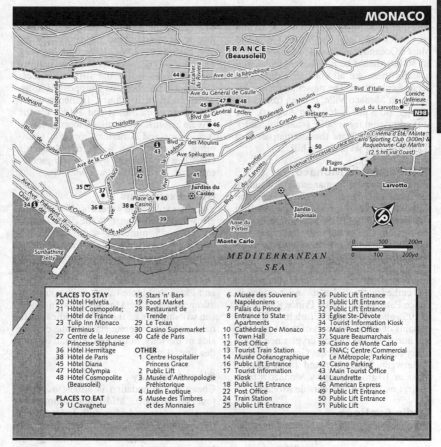

MONACO

PLACES TO STAY
20 Hôtel Helvetia
21 Hôtel Cosmopolite;
   Hôtel de France
23 Tulip Inn Monaco
   Terminus
27 Centre de la Jeunesse
   Princesse Stéphanie
36 Hôtel Hermitage
38 Hôtel de Paris
45 Hôtel Diana
47 Hôtel Olympia
48 Hôtel Cosmopolite
   (Beausoleil)

PLACES TO EAT
9 U Cavagnetu

15 Stars 'n' Bars
19 Food Market
28 Restaurant de
   Trende
29 Le Texan
30 Casino Supermarket
40 Café de Paris

OTHER
1 Centre Hospitalier
  Princesse Grace
2 Public Lift
3 Musée d'Anthropologie
  Préhistorique
4 Jardin Exotique
5 Musée des Timbres
  et des Monnaies

6 Musée des Souvenirs
  Napoléoniens
7 Palais du Prince
8 Entrance to State
  Apartments
10 Cathédrale De Monaco
11 Town Hall
12 Post Office
13 Tourist Train Station
14 Musée Océanographique
16 Public Lift Entrance
17 Tourist Information
   Kiosk
18 Public Lift Entrance
22 Post Office
24 Train Station
25 Public Lift Entrance

26 Public Lift Entrance
31 Public Lift Entrance
32 Public Lift Entrance
33 Église Ste-Dévote
34 Tourist Information Kiosk
35 Main Post Office
37 Square Beaumarchais
39 Casino de Monte Carlo
41 FNAC; Centre Commercial
   Le Métropole; Parking
42 Casino Parking
43 Main Tourist Office
44 Laundrette
46 American Express
49 Public Lift Entrance
50 Public Lift Entrance
51 Public Lift

Laundry In Beausoleil, on the border between Monaco and France, there is the Self Laverie laundrette at 1 rue Jean Jaurès. It is open from 7 am to 9 pm daily.

Palais du Prince & Musée des Souvenirs Napoléoniens

The changing of the guard takes place daily outside the Prince's Palace (☎ 93 25 18 31), at the southern end of rue des Remparts in Monaco Ville, at precisely 11.55 am.

The guards, who carry out their duties of state in spiffy dress uniform (white in summer, black in winter), are apparently resigned to the comic-opera nature of their duties.

You can visit the palace's **state apartments**, open from 9.30 am to 6.30 pm from June to October (to 5 pm in October) and from 10.30 am to 12.30 pm and from 2 to 5 pm from December to May.

Half-hour guided visits in English begin every 15 or 20 minutes. Admission costs 30FF (children 15FF). A combined ticket for admission to the **Musée des Souvenirs Napoléoniens** – a display of Napoleon's personal effects in the southern wing of the palace – costs 40FF (children 20FF).

Musée Océanographique

If you're planning to see just one aquarium on your whole trip, the world-renowned Musée Océanographique de Monaco (☎ 93 15 36 00) should be it. It has 90 tanks, and upstairs there are all sorts of exhibits on ocean exploration. The museum, on ave St-Martin in Monaco Ville, is open from 9 am to 7 pm (to 8 pm in July and August). The stiff admission fee is 60FF (students 30FF). Bus Nos 1 and 2 are the alternatives to a relatively long walk up the hill.

Cathédrale de Monaco

The unspectacular Romanesque–Byzantine cathedral (1875), 4 rue Colonel, has one draw: the grave of former Hollywood film star Grace Kelly (1929–82), which lies on the western side of the cathedral choir. Her modest tombstone, inscribed with the Latin words *Gratia Patricia Principis Rainerii III*, is heavily adorned with flowers. Tourists usually do a quick march around the cathedral in order to see her grave. Grace Patricia Kelly wed Prince Rainier III in 1956 and died in a car crash in 1982. The remains of other members of the royal family, buried in the church crypt since 1885, today rest behind Princess Grace's grave.

Between September and June, Sunday Mass at 10 am is sung by Monaco's boys choir, Les Petits Chanteurs de Monaco.

Jardin Exotique

The steep slopes of the wonderful Jardin Exotique (☎ 93 15 29 80), 62 blvd du Jardin Exotique, are home to some 7000 varieties of cacti and succulents from all over the world. The spectacular view alone is worth at least half the admission fee of 40FF (students 19FF), which also gets you into the Musée d'Anthropologie Préhistorique and includes a half-hour guided visit to the Observatory Caves, a network of stalactite and stalagmite caves 279 steps down the hillside. The Jardin Exotique opens 9 am to 6 pm (or dusk) from mid-September to mid-May and until 7 pm the rest of the year. From the tourist office, take bus No 2 to the Jardin Exotique terminus. The Web site is at www.monte-carlo.mc/jardinexotique.

Casino

The drama of watching people risk their money in Monte Carlo's spectacularly ornate casino (☎ 92 96 20 20), built between 1878 and 1910, makes visiting the gaming rooms almost worth the stiff entry fees: 50FF for admission the European Rooms, which has slot machines, French roulette and *trente et quarante*; and 100FF for the Private Rooms, which offer baccarat, blackjack, craps and American roulette. Gambling accounts for 4.3% of Monaco's GDP. See the Web site www.casino-monte-carlo.com for the full lowdown.

Boat Excursions

You can explore the waters off Monaco in a glass-bottomed boat (70/50FF for adults/students, 55 minutes) with Aquavision (☎ 92 16 15 15, ✉ CNTM@atlantis.mc), quai des États-Unis. Boats depart at 11 am, 2.30 and 4 pm.

The nearest beaches, Plages du Larvotto and Plage de Monte Carlo, are a couple of kilometres east of Monte Carlo. In town, sun worshippers lie their oiled bodies out to bake on giant concrete slabs on the eastern side of the jetty, at the northern end of quai des États-Unis.

Places to Stay

Cheap accommodation is almost nonexistent in Monaco. Mid-range rooms are equally scarce and often full. Indeed, over three-quarters of Monaco's hotel rooms are classified as 'four-star deluxe'. Fortunately, Nice is not too far away.

Places to Stay – Budget & Mid-Range

Hostel The *Centre de la Jeunesse Princesse Stéphanie* (☎ 93 50 83 20, fax 93 25 29 82, 24 ave Prince Pierre de Monaco), is 120m up the hill from the train station. Only travellers aged between 16 and 31 can stay here – for 70FF per person, including breakfast, shower and sheets. Stays are usually limited to three nights during the summer. Beds are given out each morning on a first-come first-served basis; numbered tickets are distributed from 9 am (or even earlier) near the front gate. Registration begins at 11 am.

Hotels In La Condamine, the clean and pleasant *Hôtel Cosmopolite* (☎ *93 30 16 95, fax 93 30 23 05,* ✉ *hotel-cosmopolite@ monte-carlo.mc, 4 rue de la Turbie),* the only one-star hotel in Monaco, has decent singles/doubles with shower for 282/314FF and doubles without shower for 228FF.

The two-star *Hôtel de France* (☎ *93 30 24 64, fax 92 16 13 34,* ✉ *hotel-france@ monte-carlo.mc, 6 rue de la Turbie),* has rooms with shower, toilet and TV starting at 350/390FF, including breakfast. The two-star *Hôtel Helvetia* (☎ *93 30 21 71, fax 92 16 70 51,* ✉ *hotel-helvetia@monte-carlo.mc, 1 bis rue Grimaldi),* has a few singles/ doubles without shower for 290/320FF, or 320/370FF with shower.

Refurbished in 1999, the three-star *Tulip Inn Monaco Terminus* (☎ *92 05 63 00, fax 92 05 20 10,* ✉ *tulipinn-terminus@ monte-carlo.mc, 9 ave Prince Pierre)* has upped its single/double rates to reflect its facelift to 475/640FF.

In French Beausoleil, there are three hotels virtually in a row, three streets up from the casino and close to the Beausoleil market. When calling these hotels from Monaco (eg from the train station), dial ☎ 00 33, then the 10 digit number (dropping the first 0). First up the *Hôtel Diana* (☎ *04 93 78 47 58, fax 04 93 41 88 94, 17 blvd du Général Leclerc)* has rooms for one or two with shower/bath for 290/360FF. The *Hôtel Cosmopolite* (☎ *04 93 78 36 00, 19 blvd du Général Leclerc),* unrelated to the hotel of the same name in La Condamine, has rooms with shower and TV for 195FF (330/350FF with toilet for one/two people). Between them is the *Hôtel Olympia* (☎ *04 93 78 12 70, 17 bis blvd du Général Leclerc),* which has rooms with shower, TV and toilet for 270/300FF.

Places to Stay – Top End

World-famous places include the *Hôtel de Paris* (☎ *92 16 30 00, fax 92 16 38 50,* ✉ *hp@sbm.mc, place du Casino),* where writer Colette spent the last years of her life, and the four-star *Hôtel Hermitage* (☎ *92 16 40 00, fax 93 16 38 52,* ✉ *hh@ sbm.mc, square Beaumarchais).* Prices reflect the luxurious, *belle époque* ambience of both hotels – expect to pay between 1910FF and 2240FF for a 'standard' double. If you arrive in a Fiat or a Ford, park them well away from these hotels: the forecourt is littered only with Bentleys and Rollers.

Places to Eat

Restaurants There are over 132 listed restaurants in Monaco so finding a place to eat will not be hard. The trick is to do it at a price you can afford. Grab a copy of the free *Restaurants – Monaco* booklet from the tourist office when you arrive and go for it. In the meantime here are a few starters.

There are a few cheap restaurants in La Condamine along rue de la Turbie and simple sandwich bars along quai Albert 1er.

On the southern side of the port is the flashy *Stars 'n' Bars* (☎ *93 50 95 95, 6 quai Antoine 1er),* open from noon to 3 am (closed Monday). Billed as a blues bar and restaurant, it is more like a huge country and western saloon. Here you can eat main dishes of American-sized portions and excellent salads (65FF to 75FF), listen to live music and watch the staff strut their stuff in starred-and-striped leather shorts and boots.

The same Texan businessman runs *Le Texan* (☎ *93 30 34 54, 4 rue Suffren Reymond)* where you can sample Tex-Mex fajitas for 110FF, or a tuck into Heap Big T-Bone for a hefty 145FF.

One of the few affordable restaurants specialising in Monégasque dishes is *U Cavagnetu* (☎ *93 30 35 80, 14 rue Comte Félix-Gastaldi)* where a lunchtime menu is 85FF and in the evening jumps to between 115FF and 140FF. Very traditional and cosy is the small *Restaurant de Trende* (☎ *93 30 37 72, 19 rue de la Turbie).* The decor is totally 1930s and the food absolutely Provençal.

Cafes In Monte Carlo, the place to people-watch and spot the limo is from the sprawling terrace of the *Café de Paris* (☎ *92 16 20 20, place du Casino).*

Self-Catering In La Condamine, there's a *food market (place d'Armes)*, open from 7 am Monday to Saturday, and a *Casino supermarket (blvd Albert 1er)*, which is open from 8.45 am to 12.30 pm and 2.45 to 7.30 pm (no break on Friday or Saturday; closed Sunday). Summer hours are 8.30 am to 8 pm (closed Sunday).

Entertainment

Tickets for most cultural events are sold at FNAC (☎ 93 10 81 81), Centre Commercial le Métropole, 17 ave Spélugues.

Cinema In summer, films are screened at the open-air **Cinéma d'Été** (☎ 93 25 86 80) in the Monte Carlo Sporting Club, ave Princesse Grace, Larvotto. Nondubbed films with French subtitles are shown at 9.30 pm daily and admission costs 50FF to 90FF.

Theatre A charming spot to while away a summer evening is the 18th-century fortress **Théâtre du Fort Antoine** (☎ 93 50 80 00, fax 93 50 66 94), ave de la Quarantaine, which is now used as an outside theatre. Plays are staged here at 9.30 pm on Monday in July and August, and admission costs 50FF to 70FF.

Shopping

The 168-page, pocket-size *Monaco Shopping* guide, published annually and distributed for free (upon request) by the tourist office, is indispensable to serious shoppers. The Galerie Riccadonna (☎ 93 50 84 46, fax 92 16 06 78), 7 rue Grimaldi, sells seriously funky designer furniture for very serious amounts of money.

Getting There & Away

Bus There is no bus station in Monaco. Intercity buses leave from various stops around the city.

Train Trains to/from Monaco are run by the French SNCF. The information desk at Monaco train station, ave Prince Pierre, is open from 9.30 am to noon and 2.30 to 6.30 pm.

Taking the train along the coast is highly recommended – the sea and the mountains provide a truly magnificent sight. There are frequent trains eastwards to Menton (13FF, 10 minutes), Nice (20FF, 20 minutes) and the first town across the border in Italy, Ventimiglia (Vintimille in French; 21FF, 25 minutes).

Car Parking facilities are good in Monaco with some 25 official pay car parks scattered around the principality. One of the most convenient parks is the Casino Parking from where you exit directly to the door of the Tourist office.

Driving around Monaco is not recommended (or really necessary) and you cannot take your car up to the Monaco Ville unless you have Monaco or 06 (Alpes-Maritimes) licence plates.

Getting Around

Bus Monaco's urban bus system has six lines, though in practice you are unlikely to ever need to use the bus since Monaco is so compact. The most useful bus is Line No 4, which links the train station with the tourist office, the casino and the Larvotto district. A ticket costs 8.50FF.

Full bus route details are in the free Monaco map given out at the Tourist Office or at car park pay points.

Tourist Train If the hills of Monaco are too much for you the slightly tacky *Azur Express* **tourist train** (☎ 92 05 64 38) starts from opposite the Musée Océanographique. The 35-minute city tour costs 35FF and it runs every day from 10.30 am to 6 pm (5 pm in winter). Commentaries are in English, French, Italian and German.

Lifts Some 15 public lifts (*ascenseurs publics*) run up and down the hillside, all marked on the free town brochure distributed by the tourist. Most operate 24 hours, others run between 6 am and midnight or 1 am only.

Taxi To order a taxi, call ☎ 93 15 01 01.

Corsica (Corse)

Corsica is the most mountainous and geographically diverse of the Mediterranean islands, earning it the perfectly justified title of *l'île de beauté* (the island of beauty). Although it covers only 8720 sq km, Corsica in many ways resembles a miniature continent, with 1000km of coastline lapped by azure seas, soaring granite mountains that stay snowcapped until July, a huge national park (Parc Naturel Régional de la Corse), flatland marshes (along the east coast), an uninhabited desert (Désert des Agriates) in the north-west and a 'continental divide' running down the middle of the island. Much of the land is covered with *maquis*, a typically Corsican form of vegetation whose low, dense shrubs provide many of the spices used in Corsican cooking. During WWII, the fighters of the French Resistance became known as 'maquis' because the movement was very active in Corsica.

HISTORY

From the 11th to the 13th century Corsica was ruled by the Italian city-state of Pisa, which sent Tuscan architects and stonemasons to build numerous Romanesque churches on the island. Pisa's supremacy was contested – and in 1284 ended – by its commercial rival, Genoa, whose authority was in turn challenged by Aragon. In the mid-15th century the Genoese handed over the governing of Corsica – beset at the time by near anarchy, in part because of Muslim raids on coastal areas – to the Office de St-Georges, a powerful financial organisation with its own army. To prevent seaborne raids from North Africa, the office built a massive early-warning and defence system that included hilltop watchtowers along the coast (many of which can be seen to this day) and several citadels.

On a number of occasions, Corsican discontent with foreign rule led to open revolt. In 1755, after 25 years of intermittent warfare against the Genoese, the Corsicans declared their island independent. They were

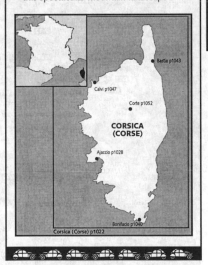

led by the extraordinary Pasquale Paoli (1725–1807), under whose enlightened rule they established a National Assembly and adopted the most democratic constitution in Europe.

The Corsicans chose inland Corte as their capital, set up a system of justice to replace the vendetta method of retribution, founded a school system and established a university.

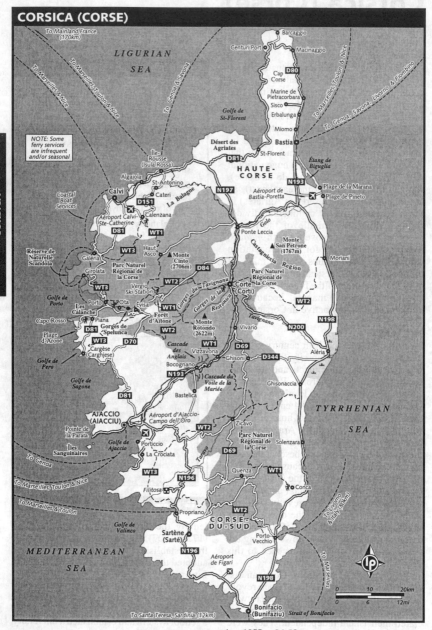

CORSICA (CORSE)

To Mainland France (170km)

LIGURIAN SEA

To Marseilles, Toulon & Nice

To Genoa & Savona

To Marseilles, Toulon, Livorno & Piombino

Barcaggio

Centuri Port

Macinaggio

Cap Corse **D80**

Marine de Pietracorbara

Sisco

Erbalunga

Miomo

Bastia

Golfe de St-Florent

Désert des Agriates

St-Florent

D812

Étang de Biguglia

HAUTE-CORSE

N193

Plage de la Marana

Aéroport de Bastia-Poretta

Plage de Pineto

Île-Rousse (Isula Rossa)

Algajola

St-Antonino

N197

Calvi

Cateri

D151

La Balagne

Calenzana

Aéroport Calvi-Ste-Catherine

D81

WT1

Ponte Leccia

Golo

Coastal Boat Services

Réserve de Naturelle Scandola

Galéria

WT3

Haut Asco

Monte Cinto (2706m)

D84

Castagniccia

Monte San Petrone (1767m)

Moriani

Castagniccia Region

Golfe de Porto

WT3

Girolata

Porto

Les Calanche

Parc Naturel Régional de la Corse

Vergio Ski Station

Gorges du Tavignanu

Corte (Corti)

Parc Naturel Régional de la Corse

WT2

Ota

Evisa

WT1

Gorges de la Restonica

Tavignano

N198

Capo Rosso

Piana

Forêt d'Aïtone

Monte Rotondo (2622m)

Vivario

N200

Plage d'Arone

Gorges de Spelunca

D81

WT2

WT1

Vizzavona

D69

Aléria

D70

WT3

Cargèse (Carghjese)

Cascade des Anglais

Bocognano

D344

Golfe de Pero

N193

Ghisoni

Golfe de Sagone

D81

Cascade du Voile de la Mariée

Bastelica

Ghisonaccia

TYRRHENIAN SEA

AJACCIO (AIACCIU)

Aéroport d'Ajaccio-Campo dell'Oro

WT2

Zicavo

Parc Naturel Régional de la Corse

Solenzara

Pointe de la Parata

Golfe d'Ajaccio

Porticcio

La Crociata

Taravo

D69

Îles Sanguinaires

To Genoa

Quenza

WT1

To Marseilles, Toulon & Nice

WT3

N196

Corica

To Marseilles, Toulon

Filitosa

WT2

To Livorno & Italy (80km)

Propriano

CORSE-DU-SUD

Golfe de Valinco

Sartène (Sarté)

Porto-Vecchio

MEDITERRANEAN SEA

N196

Aéroport de Figari

To Marseilles

N198

0   10   20km
0   6   12mi

Bonifacio (Bunifaziu)

To Santa Teresa, Sardinia (12km)

Strait of Bonifacio

euro currency converter 10FF = €1.52

However, the island's independence was short-lived: in 1768 the Genoese ceded Corsica – over which they had no effective control – to their ally the French King Louis XV, whose troops defeated Paoli's army in 1769.

France has ruled the island ever since, except for a period in 1794–96, when it was under English domination, and during the German and Italian occupation of 1940–43. Corsica's most famous native son was Napoleon Bonaparte, emperor of the French and, in the early years of the 19th century, ruler of much of Europe.

GOVERNMENT & POLITICS

Despite having spent only 14 years as an autonomous country, the people of Corsica have retained a fiercely independent streak. Though very few Corsicans support the Front de Libération Nationale de la Corse (FLNC) – whose initials and nationalist slogans are spray-painted all over the island – or other violent separatist organisations, they remain very proud of their language, culture and traditions.

Since the assassination of Corsica's *préfet* (prefect), Claude Erignac, in Ajaccio (Ajacciu in Corsican) in February 1998, the French government has adopted a tougher approach towards the corruption that has dogged the island for decades. An undercover investigation into the activities of French bank Crédit Agricole on the island in March 1998 uncovered losses of US$150 million in agricultural loans that had never been repaid.

LANGUAGE

The Corsican language (Corsu), which was almost exclusively oral until recently, is more closely related to Italian than French. It constitutes an important component of Corsican identity, and many people (especially at the university in Corte) are working to ensure its survival. Street signs in most towns are now bilingual or exclusively in Corsican. You'll see lots of French highway signs 'edited' with spray paint into their *nomi Corsi* (Corsican names).

The Moor's Head

La Tête de Maure (Moor's Head) – a black head wearing a white bandanna and a hooped earring – is the emblem of Corsica. It has stood as a symbol of victory since the time of the Crusades, but it was not until 1297 during the reign of the Kings of Aragon that it first showed its face in Corsica.

Following the island's declaration of independence in 1755, Pasquale Paoli declared the emblem his country's own. According to legend, the white bandanna originally covered the eyes of the black head, and was raised to the forehead to symbolise the island's glorious liberation.

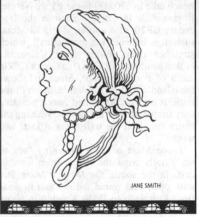

JANE SMITH

WHEN TO GO

The best time of year to visit Corsica is in May and June, when the sun is shining, the olives are ripening, the wildflowers are blooming – and tourists few. Hay fever sufferers might prefer to visit in September and October when, though the countryside might be less green and the days shorter, they can be sure they won't sneeze their way round the island. Before Easter, there are practically no tourists – or tourist infrastructure for that matter; most hotels, camp sites and restaurants operate seasonally. During summer school holidays, Corsica is transformed into a circus of holiday-makers. Prices for everything rocket skywards.

CORSICA

DANGERS & ANNOYANCES

When Corsica makes the headlines, it's often because nationalist militants seeking Corsican independence have engaged in some act of violence, such as bombing a public building, robbing a bank, blowing up a vacant holiday villa or murdering the prefect. But the violence, which in 1997 included 290 bombings and 22 murders (some inter-factional), is *not* targeted at tourists, and there is no reason for visitors to fear for their safety.

ACTIVITIES
Walking

Corsica's superb hiking trails – most of which take in 330,000-hectare Parc Naturel Régional de la Corse – include the legendary **GR20**, also known as Frà Li Monti (literally, 'between the mountains'), which stretches over 160km from Calenzana (10km south-east of Calvi) to Conca (20km north of Porto Vecchio). Since it follows the island's continental divide, much of the route is above 2000m and hence passable only from mid-June to October. Walking the entire length of the trail takes at least two weeks.

Three Mare à Mare (meaning 'sea to sea') trails cross the island from west to east. In the south, the **Mare à Mare Sud** trail, open year round, allows you to walk from Propriano to Porto Vecchio in about five days. In the centre of the island, the seven-day **Mare à Mare Centre** trail links La Crociata (about 25km south of Ajaccio) with Ghisonaccia; it opens from about May to November.

The **Mare à Mare Nord** trail, which connects Cargèse (via Évisa) with Moriani (40km south of Bastia), takes seven to 12 days (depending on your route) and is passable only from about May to November. On the north-west coast, the **Mare è Monti** (sea and mountains) trail from Cargèse to Calenzana (via Évisa, Ota, Girolata and Galéria) takes about 10 days. It is open all year but is at its best in spring and autumn.

Some 600km of trails, including the GR20, are covered in *Walks in Corsica*

Corsican Polyphony

Corsican band Les Nouvelles Polyphonies Corses won the heart of a nation – and not just Corsicans – with its magnetic polyphonic performance at the opening ceremony of the 1992 Winter Olympics in Albertville, mainland France.

Bewitching in their simplicity, *polyphonies* (Corsican chants) are traditionally sung by a choir of voices *a capella* (without musical accompaniment). *Paghjellas* are sung by three male voices – a tenor, baritone and bass – and mark the passage of life: the *O Culomba* paghjella celebrates women's beauty and its power over men; *A Mio Ghjallinuccia Nera* features a farmer who, eager to travel the world, asks one of his black hens to lend him her wings.

Equally compelling are the sacred chants sung in village churches in the mountainous Castagniccia region east of Corte. In Pigna, south of L'Île-Rousse, polyphonic evenings are held in summer in the Casa Musicale (☎ 04 95 61 77 31). Calvi hosts the five-day Rencontres Polyphoniques festival each year in mid-September.

The recordings of the Sartène Male Voice Choir and contemporary bands I Muvrini, Canta U Populu Corsu and Les Nouvelles Polyphonies Corses are widely available on CD. In Corsica, tune into Radio Corse-Frequenza Mora (100.5 MHz FM in Ajacciu, 101.7 MHz FM in Bastia, 97.7 MHz FM in Corte and 91.7 MHz FM in Calvi).

(120FF), an invaluable topoguide published in London by Robertson McCarta. Lonely Planet's *Corsica* also contains detailed descriptions of the GR20 hike.

ORGANISED TOURS

Objectif Nature (☎/fax 04 95 32 54 34, ✉ objectif-nature@wanadoo.fr), 3 rue Notre Dame de Lourdes, Bastia, arranges guided cycling, walking, horse riding and fishing trips to the island's interior (eg, along parts of the GR20) as well as sea kayaking and diving.

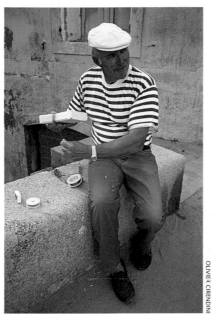

Corsican fisherman – it's all in the preparation...

Corsica's Mediterranean sunshine colours.

Stroll around Calvi's old winding streets.

Take the scenic route from Calvi to Île Rousse.

Sun and clear water: Anse de Ficajola, Corsica

TONY WHEELER

Corsica's majestic scenery and superb trails make it a paradise for walkers.

SALLY DILLON

Sartène: 'the most Corsican of Corsica's towns'

OLIVIER CIRENDINI

Houses teeter atop limestone cliffs in Bonifacio.

In Ajaccio, contact Maison d'Informations Randonées du Parc Naturel Régional de la Corse (see Information in the Ajaccio section) or Muntagne Corse (☎ 04 95 20 53 14) at 2 ave de la Grande Armée.

PLACES TO STAY
Camping

Most of Corsica's many camp sites open only from June to September. Camping outside recognised camp sites is prohibited, in part because of the danger of fires (especially in the maquis). In remote areas hikers can bivouac in *refuge* grounds for 20FF a night.

Refuges & Gîtes d'Étape

Maison d'Informations Randonées du Parc Naturel Régional de la Corse provides hikers with lists of mountain *refuges* and *gîtes d'étape* along the GR20 and other hiking trails (see Walking in the previous Activities section). A night's accommodation in a park *refuge* costs around 50FF. Nightly rates in a gîte d'étape are 40FF to 80FF; most offer half-board too (145FF to 185FF a night).

Gîtes

Depending on how far away the beach is, *gîtes ruraux* (country cottages, also called *meublés ruraux*) with shower and toilet for two or more people can be rented for 1000FF to 2200FF a week; prices double or triple between June and September when most places are booked up months in advance. In Ajaccio, Relais des Gîtes Ruraux (☎ 04 95 51 72 82, fax 04 95 51 72 89), 1 rue du Général Fiorella, provides information on available cottages.

Hotels

Corsica's budget hotel rooms are more expensive than their mainland counterparts; virtually nothing is available for less than 140FF. Outside of Bastia, Ajaccio and Corte, the vast majority of hotels close between November and Easter.

Corse-Corsica Hotels-Restaurants published by the Logis de France (✉ info@logis-de-france.fr) lists comfortable hotels in Corsica. Book through the Association des Logis de France office in Bastia (☎ 04 95 54 44 30), BP 210, F-20293, or in Porto Vecchio (☎ 04 95 70 05 93, fax 04 95 70 47 82), 12 rue Jean Jaurès, F-20137.

GETTING THERE & AWAY

Visitors are charged a 'regional tax' of 30FF upon arrival *and* departure. It is not included in the prices quoted below but will usually be included in your quoted air or ferry fare.

Air

Corsica's four main airports are at Ajaccio, Bastia, Figari (near Bonifacio) and Calvi. Return airfares to Corsica from Marseilles/Nice/Paris cost approximately 800/700/1200FF. People under 25 or over 60 may qualify for a 700/600/800FF return fare.

Boat

Details on ferry services are available from many French travel agents. During the summer – especially from mid-July to early September – reservations for vehicles and couchettes (sleeping berths) on *all* routes must be made well in advance.

In addition to the basic fares listed below, each port levies an additional tax on visitors and vehicles, ranging from 24FF to 44FF for a passenger and 35FF to 64FF for a vehicle, depending on which port you are coming from and arriving at.

To/From Mainland France Almost all ferry services between the French mainland (Nice, Marseilles and Toulon) and Corsica (Ajaccio, Bastia, Calvi, Île Rousse, Porto Vecchio and Propriano) are handled by the state-owned Société Nationale Maritime Corse-Méditerranée (SNCM; ☎ 0 836 67 95 00, fax 04 92 56 35 86, ✉ correspondance@sncm.fr). You can also make on-line bookings at www.sncm.fr.

Schedules and fares are comprehensively listed in the SNCM pocket timetable, free from tourist offices, some hotels and SNCM offices. In the height of summer there are up to eight ferries daily; in winter there are as few as eight a week and fares are substantially cheaper.

euro currency converter €1 = 6.56FF

CORSICA

A one-way ticket costs 210FF (240FF from late June to early September) to and from Nice, and 256FF (292FF in summer) to and from Marseilles or Toulon. Daytime crossings take about 6½ hours. For overnight trips, the cheapest couchette/most comfortable cabin costs an additional 72/288FF (low season).

For people aged under 25 and seniors, one-way fares are 184/210FF in winter/summer for all sailings to/from Nice and 224/256FF to/from Marseilles and Toulon. Children under 12 pay 50% of the adult fare.

Transporting a small car costs between 214FF and 612FF (from Marseilles or Toulon) and 161FF and 509FF (from Nice) depending on the season. Motorcycles under/over 100cc cost 136/149FF to 437FF and bicycles cost 91FF.

Corsica Ferries and SNCM also run a 70km/h express NGV (Navire à Grande Vitesse) service from Nice to Calvi (2½ hours), Bastia (3½ hours) and Île Rousse (three hours). Fares on these zippy NGVs, which carry 500 passengers and 148 vehicles, are similar to those charged for passage on the regular ferries, though the supplement with Corsica ferries is between 50FF and 70FF.

To/From Italy Corsica Ferries (☎ 04 95 32 95 95, fax 04 95 32 14 71 in Bastia; ☎ 019 216 0041, fax 019 216 0043 in Savona; ☎ 0586 88 13 80, fax 0586 89 61 03 in Livorno) has year-round car ferry services to Bastia from Savona (Savone), 32km west of Genoa (Gênes), and Livorno (Livourne). Except for overnight runs, which take eight hours, the crossing takes about six hours on the regular day ferry, or three hours on the *Corsica Express* NGV. From 1 June to 30 September the company also runs ferries from Savona to Île Rousse.

Depending on which route you take and when you travel, individuals pay between 99FF and 170FF to Livorno, or 114FF and 180FF to Savona (no student or senior discounts). Small cars cost between 260FF and 660FF each way; bicycles are free. Cabins for two people start at 200FF (from Bastia).

Port taxes of around 44FF are also payable. Bookings can be made on-line at www.corsicaferries.com.

From mid-April to October, Moby Lines (☎ 04 95 34 84 94, fax 04 95 32 17 94 in Bastia; ☎ 0586 82 68 23, fax 0586 82 68 24 in Livorno) links Bastia with the Italian ports of Genoa (6½ hours) and Livorno (four hours). From July to early September, Moby Lines' car ferries also link Bastia with Piombino (3½ hours). Depending on when you travel, the one-way fare is 110FF to 175FF for passengers and 235FF to 615FF for a small car. Cabins with two couchettes start at 105FF.

Between 21 April and 17 September, Corsica Marittima (☎/fax 04 95 54 66 99 in Bastia; ☎ 0586 21 05 07, fax 0586 21 05 15 in Livorno) runs twice-daily express NGV ferries from Bastia to Livorno (two hours). Two adults plus one vehicle cost from 448FF one-way in low (orange) season to 760FF in high (blue) season. Book on-line at www.corsica-marittima.com.

For information on ferries from Sardinia to Bonifacio, see Getting There & Away in the Bonifacio section.

Getting Around

Bus Bus transport around the island is slow, infrequent, relatively expensive and handled by a network of independent companies. On longer routes, most of which are operated by Eurocorse, there are only one, two or at most four runs daily. Except during July and August, only a handful of intercity buses operate on Sunday and holidays.

Train This is the most interesting, fun and comfortable way to tour the island – despite Corsica's metre-gauge single-track rail system being a good century behind the TGV. The two- and four-car trains screech and crawl their way through the stunning mountain scenery of the interior, stopping at tiny rural stations and, when necessary, for sheep, goats and cows. At higher elevations, special snowploughs keep the tracks passable in winter.

The 232km network consists of two lines that meet to exchange passengers at Ponte

Leccia. Between September and July, the Ajaccio–Corte–Bastia line is served by four trains a day (two on Sunday and holidays). Services are slightly reduced in winter and increased in August. Two daily trains year-round (coordinated with the Ajaccio–Corte–Bastia service) link Bastia with Ponte Leccia, Île Rousse and Calvi. Printed schedules are available at train stations.

Fares range from 59FF (Bastia–Corte) to 145FF (Ajaccio–Calvi). Children aged under 12 are entitled to half-price tickets; those under four travel for free.

Transporting a bicycle costs a flat 76FF no matter how far you're going. The surcharge for bulky hand luggage (6FF) is rarely applied. Leaving luggage at train station ticket windows costs 20FF for 24 hours. For further information contact Chemins de Fer de la Corse (CFC) in Bastia (☎ 04 95 32 80 57, fax 04 95 34 09 15).

Rail Passes Most rail passes are not valid on the CFC system, though holders of Inter-Rail passes get 50% off.

If you are making a return journey of less than 200km within 48 hours, you are eligible for a *billet touristique* (tourist ticket) which is 25% cheaper than a regular return ticket. These tickets are not available in July, August or the first half of September.

Year-round, the CFC sells its own rail pass – La Carte Zoom – which is well worth buying if you intend making more than a couple of train journeys within Corsica. The Carte Zoom costs a flat 290FF and is valid for seven days, entitling you to unlimited travel on the entire CFC rail network.

Car & Motorcycle Travelling by road is a convenient but occasionally taxing way to explore Corsica. Most of the roads are spectacular but narrow and harrowing: the hairpin curves are not preceded by any sort of warning, and guard rails are usually little more than low stone walls. Shoulders are narrow or non-existent and bridges are often single lane. Count on averaging 50km/h.

The most beautiful roads in Corsica include the D84 from Porto to the Vergio ski station via Évisa and the Forêt d'Aïtone,

and the D69 from the N193 (near Vivario) via the forests of the Parc Régional to Ghisoni (linked to the east coast by the D344) and Sartène. The fastest road on the island is the N198, which runs along the flat east coast from Bastia to Bonifacio. A good road map (such as Michelin's yellow-jacketed 1:200,000 map No 90) will be indispensable.

Ajaccio to Porto

Corsica's wildest, most spectacularly scenic coast runs from Ajaccio northwards to Calvi. The entries in this section are listed from south to north.

AJACCIO
postcode 20000 • pop 60,000
The port city of Ajaccio, birthplace of Napoleon Bonaparte (1769–1821), is a great place to begin a visit to Corsica. This pastel-shaded Mediterranean town is a fine place for strolling, but spending some time here can also be educational: Ajaccio's several museums and many statues dedicated to Bonaparte speak volumes, not about Napoleon himself, but about how the people of his native town prefer to think of him.

Orientation
Ajaccio's main street is cours Napoléon, which stretches from place de Gaulle northwards to the train station and beyond. The old city is south of place Foch. The city is easily negotiated on foot.

Information
Tourist Offices The tourist office (☎ 04 95 51 53 03, fax 04 95 51 53 01, ✉ ajaccio .tourisme@wanadoo.fr), 1 place Foch, opens 8 am to 6 pm (8 am to noon and from 2 to 5 pm on Saturday). It opens 8 am to 8.30 pm and 9 am to 1 pm on Sunday from July to mid-September. It closes at 7 pm from April to June and in October.

At the airport, the information counter (☎ 04 95 23 56 56) opens 6 am to 10.30 pm.

Maison d'Informations Randonées du Parc Naturel Régional de la Corse (☎ 04 95

CORSICA

AJACCIO (AJACCIU)

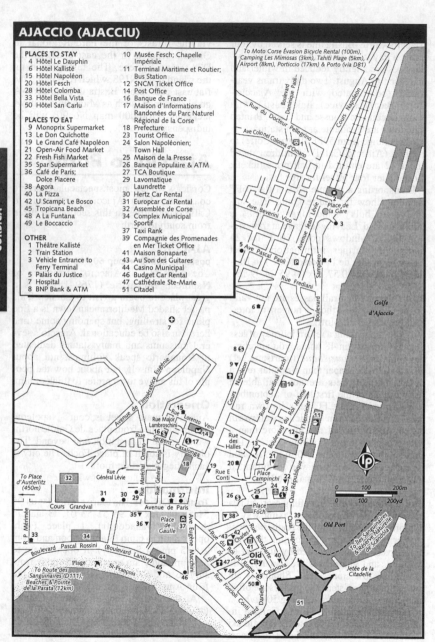

PLACES TO STAY
4   Hôtel Le Dauphin
6   Hôtel Kallisté
15 Hôtel Napoléon
20 Hôtel Fesch
28 Hôtel Colomba
33 Hôtel Bella Vista
50 Hôtel San Carlu

PLACES TO EAT
9   Monoprix Supermarket
13 Le Don Quichotte
19 Le Grand Café Napoléon
21 Open-Air Food Market
22 Fresh Fish Market
35 Spar Supermarket
36 Café de Paris;
    Dolce Piacere
38 Agora
40 La Pizza
42 U Scampi; Le Bosco
45 Tropicana Beach
48 A La Funtana
49 Le Boccaccio

OTHER
1   Théâtre Kallisté
2   Train Station
3   Vehicle Entrance to
    Ferry Terminal
4   Palais du Justice
7   Hospital
8   BNP Bank & ATM

10 Musée Fesch; Chapelle
    Impériale
11 Terminal Maritime et Routier;
    Bus Station
12 SNCM Ticket Office
14 Post Office
16 Banque de France
17 Maison d'Informations
    Randonées du Parc Naturel
    Régional de la Corse
18 Prefecture
23 Tourist Office
24 Salon Napoléonien;
    Town Hall
25 Maison de la Presse
26 Banque Populaire & ATM
27 TCA Boutique
29 Lavomatique
    Laundrette
30 Hertz Car Rental
31 Europcar Car Rental
32 Assemblée de Corse
34 Complex Municipal
    Sportif
37 Taxi Rank
39 Compagnie des Promenades
    en Mer Ticket Office
41 Maison Bonaparte
43 Au Son des Guitares
44 Casino Municipal
46 Budget Car Rental
47 Cathédrale Ste-Marie
51 Citadel

To Moto Corse Évasion Bicycle Rental (100m),
Camping Les Mimosas (3km), Tahiti Plage (5km),
Airport (8km), Porticcio (17km) & Porto (via D81)

Boulevard Dominique Paoli
Rue du Docteur Pellegrino
Cours Napoléon
Ave Colonel Colonna d'Ornano
Ave Beverini Vico
Avenue Jean Lévie
Sampiero
Place de la Gare
5 Ave Pascal Paoli
Rue Frediani
Boulevard
Golfe d'Ajaccio

Avenue de l'Impératrice Eugénie
Rue Lorenzo Vero
Rue Major Lambroschini
Rue Sergent Casalonga
Rue Maréchal Ornano
Rue Général Campi
Rue Général Lévie
Rue E Conti
Place Campinchi
Rue des Halles
Rue du Cardinal Fesch
Boulevard du Roi Jérôme
Quai l'Herminier
Quai Napoléon
Quai République

To Place d'Austerlitz (450m)
Cours Grandval
Avenue de Paris
R P. Mérimée
Boulevard Pascal Rossini
(Boulevard Lantivy)
Place de Gaulle
Ave Eugène Macchini
St-François
Plage
To Route des Sanguinaires (D111), Beaches & Pointe de la Parata (12km)
Place François

Ave. St-Charles
Rue St-Roi de Rome
Rue Bonaparte
Old City
Rue Forcioli Conti
Rue Danielle Casanova
Boulevard
Old Port
To Îles Sanguinaires & réserve Naturelle de Scandola
Jetée de la Citadelle

0   100   200m
0   100   200yd

51 79 10, fax 04 95 21 88 17), 2 rue Major Lambroschini, provides information on the Parc Naturel Régional de Corse and its walking trails. It opens 8.30 am to 12.30 pm and 2 to 6 pm (5 pm on Friday; closed at the weekend).

Money Banque de France, 8 rue Sergent Casalonga, opens 8.45 am to noon and 1.45 to 3.30 pm (closed at the weekend). There are several banks in the tan buildings that abut place de Gaulle. There are handy ATMs at BNP bank on cours Napoléon and at Banque Populaire on place Foch, as well as at the post office.

Post The central post office, 13 cours Napoléon, opens 8 am to 6.30 pm (Saturday until noon; closed Sunday). Exchange services are available.

Bookshops Maison de la Presse, 2 place Foch, sells maps and topoguides.

Napoleonic Museums

Maison Bonaparte (☎ 04 95 21 43 89), rue St-Charles, is housed in the building in the old city where Napoleon was born and raised until the age of nine. The house was sacked by Corsican nationalists in 1793 but rebuilt (with a grant from the government in Paris) later in the decade. It opens 9 am to noon and 2 to 6 pm (10 am to 4.45 pm, from October to April, closed Sunday afternoon and Monday morning). Admission costs 22FF (students and seniors 15FF); it includes a guided tour in French.

Salon Napoléonien (☎ 04 95 21 90 15), on the 1st floor of the town hall, place Foch, exhibits Napoleonic medals, paintings and busts. It opens 9 to 11.45 am and 2 to 4.45 pm Monday to Friday, and until 5.45 pm on Saturday between 15 June and 15 September. Admission costs 5FF.

Impressive **Musée Fesch** (☎ 04 95 21 48 17), 50–52 rue du Cardinal Fesch, named after Napoleon's maternal uncle, has a fine collection of 14th- to 19th-century Italian primitive paintings. It opens 9.15 am to 12.15 pm and 2.15 to 5.15 pm (closed Sunday and Monday) mid-September to

mid-June, and 10 am to 5.30 pm (Friday night from 9.30 pm to midnight; closed Tuesday) the rest of the year. Admission costs 25FF (students 15FF). There is a separate fee of 10FF (students 5FF) for the Renaissance **Chapelle Impériale**, built in the 1850s as a sepulchre for members of the Bonaparte family. Napoleon himself is buried in the Invalides in Paris.

Napoleonic Cathedral

Ajaccio's Venetian, Renaissance-style **Cathédrale Ste-Marie**, built during the latter half of the 16th century, is in the old city on the corner of rue Forcioli Conti and rue St-Charles. It contains Napoleon's marble baptismal font, to the right of the entrance, and the painting **Vierge au Sacré-Cœur** by Eugène Delacroix (1798–1863), in the back corner on the left-hand wall of the chapel. It opens 7 to 11.30 am and 3 to 6.30 pm (6 pm in winter; closed Sunday afternoon year round).

Pointe de la Parata

Pointe de la Parata, a wild, black-granite promontory 12km west of the city on Route des Sanguinaires (D111), is famed for its sunsets, which can be contemplated from the base of a crenellated, early 17th-century Genoese watchtower. To get there, take bus No 5, which runs six to eight times daily in winter and every 20 minutes in July and August.

Îles Sanguinaires, a group of small islands visible offshore, turn a deep red as the sun sets – hence the name Bloody Islands. Nothing but a huge squawking colony of seagulls inhabits these islands. From mid-April to October, they can be visited on two-hour boat excursions that set sail from the Compagnie des Promenades en Mer ticket office (☎ 04 95 51 31 31, fax 04 95 23 23 27) on the quayside opposite place Foch (old port), usually at 5.30 pm. Admission costs 100FF (children 50FF) rising to 120FF (children 60FF) in July and August.

The same company also runs boat trips to the UNESCO-protected **Réserve Naturelle de Scandola** (see Boat Excursions in the Porto section later in the chapter for

CORSICA

details). A boat sets sail from Ajaccio's old port at 9 am and returns at 6 pm (220FF; children 110FF).

Beaches
Ajaccio's beaches are nothing special. Plage de Ricanto, popularly known as **Tahiti Plage**, is about 5km east of town on the way to the airport; it is served by bus No 1. The small, segmented beaches between Ajaccio and Pointe de la Parata (Ariane, Neptune, Palm Beach and Marinella) are served by bus No 5. Both buses run from place du Général de Gaulle. The ritzy resort town of **Porticcio**, 17km south of Ajaccio across the bay, has a great – if somewhat crowded – beach. Between mid-April and October, there are two boats daily from Ajaccio, departing from Ajaccio's quayside opposite place Foch at 2.30 and 6 pm (30/50FF single/return, 30 minutes).

Places to Stay – Budget
Camping About 3km north of the centre of town, *Camping Les Mimosas* (☎ 04 95 20 99 85, fax 04 95 10 01 77, route d'Alata) opens 1 April to 15 October. It costs 29/12/12FF per adult/car/tent. Prices drop by 10% out of season. Take bus No 4 from place de Gaulle or cours Napoléon to the roundabout at the western end of cours Jean Nicoli and walk up route d'Alata for 1km.

Hotels Nine-room *Hôtel Colomba* (☎ 04 95 21 12 66, 8 ave de Paris) has clean, pleasant singles/doubles starting at 140/200FF; doubles with shower cost 180FF. Reservations (by phone or post) must be in French.

Hôtel Bella Vista (☎ 04 95 21 07 97, fax 04 95 21 81 88, blvd Lantivy) overlooks the bay and has stunning views of the palm tree-studded beach and the sea. Simple but tasteful rooms with shower and toilet cost from 190FF to 260FF according to the season. The hotel opens year round.

Places to Stay – Mid-Range
Also well-located, close to the centre of Ajaccio, is the colourful, three-star *Hôtel Fesch* (☎ 04 95 51 62 62, fax 04 95 21

83 36, 7 rue Cardinal Fesch). Good value singles/doubles with shower start at 295/315FF.

For great views of the bay, look no farther than the simple but friendly *Hôtel Le Dauphin* (☎ 04 95 21 12 94, fax 04 95 21 88 69, 11 blvd Sampiero). Rooms start at 230/260FF in low season, rising to 250/290FF in July and August.

Friendly, English-speaking and efficiently run *Hôtel Kallisté* (☎ 04 95 51 34 45, fax 04 95 21 79 00, @ hotelkalliste@cyrnos.com, 51 cours Napoléon) offers classy rooms with shower and toilet for 240/280FF in low season (320/360FF in June, July and September; 380/430FF in August). Most rooms have air-conditioning and TV and are well-equipped for PC users wishing to connect to the Internet. Breakfast (38FF) is served in your room. The hotel also lets self-catering studios.

Places to Stay – Top End
Calm *Hôtel San Carlu* (☎ 04 95 21 13 84, fax 04 95 21 09 99, 8 blvd Danielle Casanova) overlooking the citadel in a quiet and graceful part of town, has spacious singles/doubles with all the perks from 360/450FF.

Modern *Hôtel Napoléon* (☎ 04 95 51 54 00, fax 04 95 21 80 40, 4 rue Lorenzo Vero) has three-star rooms warranting no complaints for 340/400FF.

Places to Eat
Restaurants Ajaccio's restaurants, while good to better outside the tourist season, can feel the pinch in high summer with often less than satisfactory service and food quality.

Cafes can be found along blvd du Roi Jérôme, quai Napoléon and the northern side of place de Gaulle; *Café de Paris* and neighbouring *Dolce Piacere* (place de Gaulle) both have giant terraces offering good square and sea views.

In the old city, rue St-Charles and rue Conventionnel Chiappe are lined with eating places. Popular *U Scampi* (☎ 04 95 21 38 09, 11 rue Conventionnel Chiappe) serves fish and other Corsican specialities (including octopus stew) on a fine, flower-filled terrace. Lunch and dinner *menus* start at 85FF. It opens year round (closed Friday night and Saturday lunchtime). *Le Bosco* (☎ *04 95 21 25 06, 11 rue Conventionnel Chiappe*) opposite shares the same terrace as U Scampi and offers pretty much the same sort of *menus*, including a 195FF shellfish platter.

Le Boccaccio (☎ *04 95 21 16 77, 19 rue du Roi de Rome*) serves high-quality Italian cuisine; spaghetti costs from 58FF to 62FF and mains (meat and fish) 74FF to 130FF. Le Boccaccio opens noon to 2 pm and 7 to 10 pm (closed Monday in winter).

Just off place Foch is arty *Agora* (☎ *04 95 21 08 29, rue Emmanuel Arène*), a modern place with crepes, couscous and light snacks that adjoins a small book and music boutique. *Le Don Quichotte* (☎ *04 95 21 27 30, rue des Halles*) has pizzas costing from 40FF to 50FF and *menus* starting at 73FF.

The best pizza in town can be had at *La Pizza* (☎ *04 95 21 30 71, 2 rue des Anciens Fosées*). Prices range from 45FF to 59FF. Try the *quatre saisons* pizza, liberally sprinkled with chilli-laced olive oil.

For an unsurpassable sea view, try *Tropicana Beach* (☎ *04 95 51 12 98, blvd Pascal Rossini*), which is home to an elegant indoor restaurant as well as a fantastic terrace built on stilts above the lapping waves. *Menus* start at 75FF; ice cream and light snacks are served on the veranda. *Le Grand Café Napoléon* (☎ *04 95 21 42 54, 10 cours Napoléon*), opposite the prefecture, is considered the queen of cours Napoléon's terrace cafes.

For a splurge in the old city, consider *A La Funtana* (☎ *04 95 21 78 04, 7 rue Notre Dame*), with an evening *menu* for 150FF and fish dishes costing from 110FF to 140FF. It opens noon to 2 pm and 8 to 11 pm (closed Sunday, Monday lunchtime and in June).

Self-Catering An *open-air food market* (*place Campinchi*) operates until 1 pm (closed Monday except between June and September). There is a *fresh fish market* (*between place Foch and quai République*) every morning in the tan-painted building behind the food market.

Near place de Gaulle, the **Spar Supermarket** (*opposite 4 cours Grandval*) opens 8.30 am to 12.30 pm and 3 to 7.30 pm Monday to Saturday. *Monoprix Supermarket* (*opposite 40 cours Napoléon*) opens 8.30 am to 7.15 pm Monday to Saturday.

Entertainment

Music, dance and dramas are hosted at Ajaccio's municipal *Théâtre Kallisté* (☎ *04 95 22 78 54, 6 ave Colonel Colonna d'Ornano*). For traditional music, try *Au Son des Guitares* (☎ *04 95 51 15 47, 7 rue du Roi de Rome*), which hosts local guitar bands every evening from 10 pm onwards.

If you fancy a flutter, *Casino Municipal* (☎ *04 95 50 40 60, blvd Pascal Rossini*) opens 3pm to 3 am. There are poker machines, roulette and blackjack to soak up your cash, or you can simply relax in the piano bar.

Getting There & Away

Air Aéroport d'Ajaccio-Campo dell'Oro (☎ 04 95 23 56 56) is 8km east of the city.

Bus Terminal Maritime et Routier on quai l'Herminier houses Ajaccio's bus station. About a dozen companies have services from here, daily except Sunday and holidays, to Bastia (110FF, two daily), Bonifacio (110FF, two or three daily), Calvi (120FF, with a change at Ponte Leccia), Corte (60FF, two daily), Porto and Ota (70FF, two daily) Sartène (70FF, two or three daily) and many small villages.

The bus station's information counter (☎ 04 95 51 55 45), which can provide schedules, opens 7 am to 7 or 8 pm daily. Eurocorse (☎ 04 95 21 06 30 or ☎ 04 95 51 05 08), responsible for most of the long-distance lines, keeps its kiosk open 8.30 am to 4 pm Monday to Saturday.

Train The train station (☎ 04 95 23 11 03), blvd Sampiero (place de la Gare), is staffed 6.15 or 7.30 am to 6.30 pm daily (8 pm from late May to late September).

CORSICA

Car About a dozen car-rental companies have airport bureaus that open whenever there are incoming flights. The tourist office has a complete list.

Hôtel Kallisté (see Places to Stay – Mid-Range) rents cars, offering rates that undercut all the major car-rental companies; it opens seven days a week. A three-door vehicle costs 300/1560FF per day/week, including unlimited mileage. Prices rise in July and August.

Leading car rental companies in town include Hertz (☎ 04 95 21 70 94, fax 04 95 21 72 50), 8 cours Grandval; Europcar (☎ 04 95 21 05 49, fax 04 95 51 39 38), 16 cours Grandval; and Budget (☎ 04 95 21 17 18, fax 04 95 21 00 07), 1 blvd Lantivy.

Boat The ferry terminal is in the Terminal Maritime et Routier on quai l'Herminier. SNCM's ticketing office (☎ 04 95 29 66 99), across the street at 3 quai l'Herminier, opens 8 to 11.45 am and 2 to 6 pm (closed Saturday afternoon and Sunday). When there's an evening ferry, the SNCM bureau in the ferry terminal sells tickets for pedestrian passengers two or three hours before departure time; tickets for vehicles are available at the port's vehicle entrance.

From mid-April to October, Compagnie des Promenades en Mer (☎ 04 95 51 31 31 or ☎ 04 95 23 23 38, fax 04 95 23 23 27) runs boats from Ajaccio's old port to Bonifacio (240FF return; children 120FF).

Getting Around

To/From the Airport Transports Corse d'Ajaccio (TCA) bus No 1 (or, late at night, the No 6) links the airport with Ajaccio train and bus stations; tickets cost 20FF. The downside is there's only one bus an hour (departing on the hour from the airport, and on the half-hour from town). Buses run 6.30 am to 10.30 pm, depending on flight schedules.

A taxi from the airport to the centre of Ajaccio costs around 120FF (140FF at night), including the 10FF airport surcharge.

Bus Local bus maps and timetables can be picked up at the TCA Boutique (☎ 04 95 51

43 23), 2 ave de Paris, open from 8 am to noon and 2.30 to 6 pm Monday to Saturday. A single bus ticket/carnet of 10 costs 7.50/58FF. Buses mainly run from place Général de Gaulle and cours Napoléon.

Taxi There's a taxi rank (☎ 04 95 21 00 87) on the eastern side of place de Gaulle or you can call Radio Taxis Ajacciens on ☎ 04 95 25 09 13.

Moped Hôtel Kallisté (see Places to Stay – Mid-Range) rents mopeds for 195/986FF per day/week. Prices drop between October and April.

About 500m north of the train station on montée St-Jean, Moto Corse Évasion (☎ 04 95 20 52 05, fax 04 95 22 48 11) rents mountain bikes for 50/85FF per half-day/day.

CARGÈSE (CARGHJESE)
postcode 20130 • pop 900

Perched on a steep promontory between the Golfe de Sagone (to the south) and Golfe de Pero (to the north), Cargèse – founded just over two centuries ago by Greek settlers – retains the appearance and ambience of a Greek village.

In 1676, about 600 Greeks from Itilo in the southern Peloponnese fled their Ottoman-controlled homeland and were given refuge on Corsica by the Republic of Genoa. Loyal to the Genoese and relatively prosperous, the Greek settlers soon became objects of hostility for their Corsican neighbours. After suffering repeated attacks elsewhere on the island, the descendants of the original settlers founded Cargèse, also known as Cargèse-la-Grecque because of its Greek foundation, in 1774. Each year on Easter Monday and 15 August, a colourful religious procession led by Cargèse's Greek Catholic congregation wends its way through the village.

Orientation

The D81, Cargèse's main street, is known as both ave de la République (towards Ajaccio from the post office) and rue Colonel Fieschi (towards Porto from the post office). The square stone object 250m up rue Colonel Fieschi from the post office is an old *lavoir*, traditionally used for washing clothes.

Information
The tourist office (☎ 04 95 26 41 31) on rue du Docteur Dragacci opens 9 am to noon and 4 to 7 pm daily between June and September, and 4 to 6 pm Monday to Friday the rest of the year.

Churches
Cargèse is well known for its two churches – one eastern (Orthodox) rite, the other western (Catholic) – which face each other across a patchwork of neatly tended hillside vegetable plots. Both afford fine views of the town and of the turquoise Golfe de Sagone.

The 19th-century **Catholic church** is painted white and cream and has a square white bell tower on the side of the structure, while the **Greek Orthodox church** has stone buttresses and a polygonal bell tower on top of the building. The interior of the Greek church – constructed from 1852 to 1870 by the faithful, who worked on Sunday after attending Divine Liturgy – is adorned with a number of icons brought from Greece in the 1670s by the original settlers. Services are held in Greek using prayer books that include both a transliteration of the Greek text and a French translation.

Beaches
The Genoese towers atop Pointe d'Omigna (accessible by a footpath) and Pointe de Cargèse overlook **Plage de Pero**, a long, wide stretch of sand about 1km north of the town centre. Take the road leading down the hill from the lavoir on rue Colonel Fieschi.

Places to Stay & Eat
M'hôtel Punta e Mare (☎ 04 95 26 44 33, fax 04 95 26 49 54, route de Paomia) has pleasant doubles with shower and toilet costing from 200FF to 300FF. On the main through road, *Hôtel de France 'Chez Mimimo'* (☎ 04 95 26 41 07, rue Colonel Fieschi), open from April to October only,

offers doubles with shower and toilet for 160FF. In July and August, only half-board (230FF per person) is available.

About 100m towards Porto from the lavoir, elegant *Hôtel Le St-Jean* (☎ 04 95 26 46 68, fax 04 95 26 43 93, place St-Jean) has doubles with a sea view starting at 250FF.

For eating try *Le Sélect* (04 95 26 43 41, rue du Docteur Dragacci), a neat little cafe that does unassuming *menus* such as chicken wings and chips. At the southern end of the same street is *A Volta* (04 95 26 41 96, rue du Docteur Dragacci), where you can eat a varied *menu* for 98FF with a great view of the sea.

Getting There & Away
Two daily buses from Ota (37km north-east) via Porto (32km north) to Ajaccio (50km south) stop in front of the post office.

PIANA
postcode 20115 • pop 500
• elevation 438m

The hillside village of Piana affords breathtaking views of the Golfe de Porto and the soaring mountains of the interior. It is a good base for walks to nearby Les Calanques, and has somehow managed to remain admirably untouched by the hordes of summer tourists it attracts. The eve of Good Friday is marked by La Granitola, a traditional festival during which hooded penitents, bearing crosses and dressed in white gowns and blue capes, parade through the village to Piana's Église Ste-Marie.

The village's *syndicat d'initiative* (tourist office; ☎ 04 95 27 80 28) has hiking information and distributes the free leaflet *Piana Randonnées*. Nearby beaches include **Anse de Ficajola**, right below Piana and reached by an extremely narrow 4km road (signposted 'Marine de Figajola'), and **Plage d'Arone**, 11km south-west of town via the scenic D824. From the D824, a trail leads westwards to the tower-topped **Capo Rosso**.

Places to Stay & Eat
One-star, 17-room *Hôtel Continental* (☎ 04 95 27 83 12), 100m up the hill from the

church, has spacious doubles with wash-basin and bidet costing from 180FF to 250FF (270FF with shower or bath and toilet). It opens April to September. On the D81 towards Cargèse, two-star *Hôtel Le Scandola* (☎ 04 95 27 80 07, fax 04 95 27 83 88) has doubles/triples with balconies for around 250/300FF. It opens April to mid-October.

Below the D81 on the other side of the village, grand old 30-room *Hôtel des Roches Rouges* (☎ 04 95 27 81 81, fax 04 95 27 81 76), dating from 1912 is one of Corsica's most romantic places to stay. Spacious and renovated double rooms with a view of Les Calanques, Piana and Anse de Ficajola, and with shower, toilet and balcony, cost 320FF (340FF for half-board). The 'Red Rocks' opens April to mid-November.

Getting There & Away
Buses between Porto and Ajaccio stop near the church and the post office.

LES CALANQUES
The most stunning natural sight in Corsica is Les Calanques de Piana (E Calanche in Corsican), a spectacular mountain landscape of red, orange and grey granite cliffs, spikes and outcrops. Created by the rock's uneven response to the forces of erosion, these amazing formations, some of which resemble animals, buildings, and the like, have been made even more intricate by *taffoni*, spherical cavities carved out of the rock face by the dissolving action of water. Less rocky areas support pine and chestnut forests, whose dark green foliage contrasts dramatically with the coloured granite.

The multicoloured spires of Les Calanques tower 300m above the deep blue waters of the sea below. When it's clear, the D81 and various walking paths afford breathtaking views. To get to Les Calanques take the marked walking trail off the D81 about 1.5km north of Piana. Another trail leads from the signposted Tête du Chien 1km or so further north.

Calanche is the plural of the Corsican word *calanca*, pronounced 'kah-**lahnk**', the same as its French equivalent, *calanques*.

Walking
Piana's syndicat d'initiative (see under Piana) has information on walking in the region. About 8km south-west of Porto on the D81 is **Le Chalet des Roches Bleues**, a modern wood and granite souvenir shop that serves as a useful landmark. Four trails begin in the immediate vicinity:

La Corniche This is a steep, forested 40-minute walk that leads up to a fantastic view of Les Calanche. It begins on the inland side of the bridge situated 50m down the hill (towards Porto) from the chalet. Trail markings are yellow.

Chemin du Château Fort This one-hour trail to a solid block of rock that looks like a fortress affords stunning views of the Golfe de Porto. It begins 700m down the hill (towards Porto) from the chalet; the trailhead is on the seaward side of the D81 to the right of the rock that looks like a *tête de chien* (dog's head). Trail markings are blue.

Chemin des Muletiers The steep, one-hour Mule-Drivers' Trail begins 400m up the hill (towards Piana) from the chalet on the inland side of the D81; the trailhead is 15m down the hill from the roadside sanctuary dedicated to the Virgin Mary. Trail markings are blue.

La Châtaigneraie A three-hour circuit through chestnut groves that begins 25m up the hill and across the road from the chalet.

Getting There & Away
Buses from Ajaccio to Porto will drop you off at the chalet.

PORTO (PORTU)
postcode 20150 • pop 460
The pleasant (if somewhat purpose-built and touristy) seaside village of Porto (Portu in Corsican), nestled among huge outcrops of red granite and renowned for its sunsets, is an excellent base for exploring some of Corsica's most beautiful sights, including Les Calanche, Girolata and the Gorges de Spelunca.

Information
The tourist office (☎ 04 95 26 10 55, fax 04 95 26 14 25), built into the wall separating the marina's upper and lower car parks, has lots of walking information, some of it free and in English. It opens 9 am to 8 pm

Monday to Saturday in July and August, and 9.30 am to noon and 2.30 to 6.30 pm Monday to Friday the rest of the year. The only ATM between Ajaccio and Calvi is here at Porto.

Parc Naturel Régional de la Corse has an office inside Maison de Porto (☎ 04 95 26 15 14), just around the corner from the tourist office.

Things to See & Do
The overdeveloped **marina** is surrounded by hotels and places to eat. A short trail leads to a **Genoese tower** (10FF), open 10 am to 6 pm between April and October. From the marina, the estuary of the Porto River is behind the line of buildings to the left as you face the sea. On the far side of the river, reached by a footbridge, there's a modest **beach** of grey gravel and sand, a small harbour and one of Corsica's best-known **eucalyptus groves**.

From mid-April to October, Compagnie des Promenades en Mer (☎ 04 95 26 15 16) has excursions by regular or glass-bottomed boat (170FF) to the fishing village of **Girolata**. The boats sail by the **Réserve Naturelle de Scandola** (Scandola Nature Reserve), home to numerous rare birds and listed as a UNESCO World Heritage List site for its unique seagull and fishing eagle populations. It may be possible to catch another boat from Girolata to Calvi – see Boat Excursions in the Calvi section. From Porto there are also excursions to Les Calanche (80FF). Ask at the tourist office for booking information.

Places to Stay
Camping Pricey *Camping Les Oliviers* (☎ 04 95 26 14 49, fax 04 95 26 12 49) is a few hundred metres down the D81, next to the bridge over the Porto River, on an olive-treed hillside. *Funtana al' Ora* (☎ 04 95 26 11 65, fax 04 95 26 15 48), 2km east of Porto on the road to Évisa, charges 28FF per person and 11FF for a tent or car. It opens May to November.

Hotels On the eastern edge of town towards Ota, *Hôtel Le Maquis* (☎ 04 95 26 12 19, fax 04 95 26 12 77) has singles/doubles from 130/180FF. On the left-hand side of the marina (as you face the sea), one-star, 10-room *Hôtel du Golfe* (☎ 04 95 26 13 33) provides shower-equipped doubles without/with toilet for 160/180FF. Prices rise by 20FF per person in July and August.

Also at the marina, two-star *Hôtel Monte Rosso* (☎ 04 95 26 11 50, fax 04 95 26 12 30), in the third building from the Genoese tower, offers decent doubles with bath and toilet for 240FF (300FF in July and August). It opens April to mid-October. *Hôtel Le Riviera* (☎ 04 95 26 13 61, fax 04 95 26 10 15) next door has doubles with shower and toilet costing from 200FF.

Getting There & Around
Bus Autocars SAIB (☎ 04 95 22 41 99) has two buses daily linking Porto and nearby Ota with Ajaccio (2½ hours). From mid-May to mid-October the company also runs a return bus from Porto to Calvi (three hours).

Car & Motorcycle From May to late September, two and four wheels can be hired from Porto Locations (☎/fax 04 95 26 10 13), across the street from the supermarket down the hill from the pharmacy. Daily rates for a moped are around 300FF.

OTA
postcode 20150 • pop 200
• elevation 310m
Ota, a tiny village of stone houses perched above the Porto River, is 5km inland from Porto. It is blessed with some of the best budget accommodation on the island and is not far from the trail climbing up to the celebrated Gorges de Spelunca.

Walking
Pont de Pianella, an especially graceful Genoese bridge, is just under 2km east of Ota along the D124. About 300m away, the two single-lane ponts d'Ota span the Onca and Aïtone rivers, which meet here to form the Porto River.

The trail (once a mule track) up the **Gorges de Spelunca** to Évisa (three hours) via the **pont de Zaglia** (another Genoese bridge) begins on the left bank of the Aïtone (ie on the far side of the farther of the two ponts d'Ota if you're coming from Ota). The trail markings are orange. If you'd like to walk one way and ride the other, Gîte d'Étape Chez Félix (see Places to Stay & Eat) can supply a taxi for 220FF one way.

Places to Stay & Eat

Spanking-clean *Gîte d'Étape Chez Marie* (☎ 04 95 26 11 37) opens year round and charges 60FF for a bed in a very modern dormitory room, and 120FF for a double. There is a large, pleasant communal kitchen too. Reception is in *Bar-Restaurant Chez Marie*.

Gîte d'Étape Chez Félix (☎ 04 95 26 12 92) offers beds in four- and six-person rooms for 50FF. Doubles/triples with shower and toilet cost 200/240FF. Kitchen facilities are available. Reception is in *Restaurant Chez Félix* on place de la Fontaine.

Both restaurants offer wholesome Corsican home cooking aimed primarily at a backpacking budget.

Getting There & Away

Place de la Fontaine in Ota, 5km east of Porto's pharmacy via the D124, is linked to both Porto and Ajaccio by a bus in the morning and a minibus in the afternoon (service on Sunday and holidays from July to mid-September only).

ÉVISA

postcode 20126 • pop 250
• elevation 830m

Surrounded by chestnut groves (*les châtaigneraies*), the peaceful highland village of Évisa – between the Gorges de Spelunca and majestic Forêt d'Aïtone – is something of a hill station, with fresh, crisp mountain air and a wealth of worthy walking trails.

Forêt d'Aïtone

The Aïtone Forest (800m to 2057m), which surrounds the upper reaches of the River Aïtone, has some of Corsica's most impressive stands of laricio pines, perfectly straight trees, two centuries old, rising up to 60m tall. This forest once provided beams

---

> ## Chestnut Bread & Beer
>
> The Corsicans have been planting and tending *châtaigniers* (chestnut trees) since the 16th century at least, when the island's Genoese rulers started requisitioning Corsica's grain crop for use back home. The tree became known as *l'arbre à pain* (the bread tree) because of the many uses the Corsicans found for chestnut flour (*farine de châtaigne*). These days the flour is primarily used to make pastries.
>
> The meat of pigs raised on chestnuts is famous for its flavour. Other chestnutty delights worth a nibble include *falculelli* (pressed and frittered Corsican *brocciu* cheese served on a chestnut leaf), *beignets au brocciu à la farine de châtaigne* (brocciu cheese frittered in chestnut flour), *délice à la châtaigne* (Corsican chestnut cake) and, last but not least, *bière à la châtaigne* (chestnut beer).

and masts for Genoese ships. The forest begins a few kilometres east of Évisa and stretches to 1477m-high **Col de Vergio** (Bocca di Verghju). **Cascades d'Aïtone** (Aïtone Falls) are 4km north-east of Évisa via the D84 and a 500m footpath.

Places to Stay

Hostels Open early April to October, the *Gîte d'Étape* (☎ 04 95 26 21 88), charges 60FF for a bed. From the post office, follow the concrete path down the stairs to the road, turn left, and walk 100m to the white building with brown shutters.

Hotels Pleasant doubles with bath/shower go for 200/180FF at aptly named *La Châtaigneraie* (Chestnut Grove; ☎ 04 95 26 24 47), on the western edge of the village. In the village centre, *Hôtel Restaurant du Centre* (☎ 04 95 26 20 92) offers doubles with shower and toilet for 200FF.

Two-star *Hôtel L'Aïtone* (☎ 04 95 26 20 04, fax 04 95 26 24 18), closed in mid-November and mid-January, is on the upper outskirts of town. Rustic shower-equipped rooms without/with toilet cost between 180/

220FF and 200/320FF, depending on the season. Don't miss out on a swim in the pool while you're here; the hotel restaurant offers a fantastic panorama stretching as far as the Golfe de Porto.

Getting There & Away

The D84, which links Porto with Évisa, Vergio and Corte, is one of the most spectacular roads in Corsica – and one of the most frightening to drive.

There are two buses daily from Évisa to Ajaccio. A taxi (☎ 04 95 26 20 22) to Ota costs around 200FF.

South of Ajaccio

FILITOSA

Corsica's most important prehistoric site, Filitosa (☎ 04 95 74 00 91) is about 25km north-west of Propriano; take the N196 and then follow the D57 for 9km.

Inhabited from 5850 BC until the Roman period, its fortifications, buildings, megaliths and statue-menhirs – armed with swords and daggers – have been the subject of intense study since their accidental discovery in 1946. The hilltop site, shaded by olive trees (some up to 1000 years old), and the small **museum** open 8 am until sunset daily. Admission costs 22FF.

SARTÈNE (SARTÈ)

postcode 20100 • pop 3500

The sombre and introverted hillside town of Sartène, built mostly of grey stone, has long been suspicious of outsiders, and with good reason. In 1583, pirates from Algiers raided the town and carried 400 local people off into slavery in North Africa; such raids did not end until the 18th century. The town was long notorious for its banditry and bloody vendettas, and in the early 19th century a violent struggle between rival landowners deteriorated into house-to-house fighting, forcing most of the population to flee. Today's Sartène, whose unofficial slogan is 'the most Corsican of Corsica's towns', is a fascinating place to spend half a day.

Orientation & Information

From place de la Libération, Sartène's main square, cours Sœur Amélie leads south towards Bonifacio the hill, while cours Général de Gaulle heads north down the hill and back to Ajaccio. The old Santa Anna quarter is north of place de la Libération.

The tourist office (☎ 04 95 77 15 40), 6 rue Borgo, is 30m up the hill from place de la Libération. It opens 9 am to noon and 3 to 6 pm Monday to Friday, and until 7 pm Monday to Saturday in July and August; from October to April it opens mornings only.

Things to See

Near the WWI **memorial** in the middle of place de la Libération is granite-built **Église Ste-Marie**. Inside, on the wall to the left of the entrance, hang the 32kg oak cross and 14kg chain that are carried and dragged by the red-robed penitent in the annual Procession du Catenacciu (see the boxed text 'Procession du Catenacciu'). The baroque marble altar was crafted in Italy in the 17th century. The arch through the middle of the **town hall** (formerly the Palace of the Genoese Governors), on the northern side of the square, leads to the **Santa Anna quarter**, a residential neighbourhood of austere, grey, granite houses and sombre, almost medieval alleyways and staircases.

Musée de la Préhistoire Corse (Museum of Corsican Prehistory; ☎ 04 95 77 01 09), housed in a three-storey stone building built as a prison in the 1840s, opens 10 am to noon and 2 to 5 pm (6 pm from mid-June to mid-September; closed at the weekend year round). Admission costs 10FF (children and students 5FF).

Places to Stay

In a quiet, shaded gully a few kilometres towards Ajaccio, *Camping U Farrandu* (☎ 04 95 73 41 69), opens year round. Adults pay 35FF.

The only hotel in central Sartène is two-star *Hôtel Les Roches* (☎ 04 95 77 07 61, fax 04 95 77 19 93), off ave Jean Jaurès just below the Santa Anna quarter. From April to October, singles/doubles with shower and

CORSICA

CORSICA

Procession du Catenacciu

On the eve of Good Friday, the people of Sartène perform an ancient ritual known as the Procession du Catenacciu. In a colourful re-enactment of the Passion, the Catenacciu (literally, 'the chained one'), an anonymous, barefoot penitent covered from head to foot in a red robe and cowl, carries a huge cross through the town while dragging a heavy chain shackled to the ankle. The Catenacciu is followed by a procession of other penitents, members of the clergy and local notables. As the chain clatters by on the cobblestones, local people look on in great (if rather humourless) excitement. Needless to say, everyone is curious to find out the identity of the penitent, who is selected by the parish priest from among applicants seeking to expiate a grave sin.

toilet cost 240/260FF; a valley view costs a little more. Nightly rates rise in July and August. A very pleasant alternative is two-star, 31-room *Hôtel La Villa Piana* (☎ *04 95 77 07 04, fax 04 95 73 45 65*), part of the Logis de France chain on the N196 about 1.5km towards Ajaccio and Propriano. The cheapest doubles with shower and toilet cost 225FF, although those with a private terrace and valley view for 340FF are worth the splurge. The hotel opens April to mid-October.

Places to Eat

Sartène's top eating spot is small, simple *Aux Gourmets* (☎ *04 95 77 16 08, 10 cours Sœur Amélie*). It not only serves delicious Corsican specialities such as courgettes stuffed with *brocciu frais*, a soft, white ewe's-milk cheese unique to Corsica, made between October and June (58FF), but also is excellent value, with *menus* costing between 70FF and 98FF.

La Chaumière (☎ *04 95 77 07 13, 39 rue Médecin-Capitaine Louis Bénédetti*) another Corsican restaurant 200m up the hill from the tourist office, offers a *menu* for 90FF. Several other Corsican restaurants can be found in the Santa Anna quarter.

Getting There & Away

Sartène, on the bus line linking Ajaccio (86km) with Bonifacio (53km), is served by at least two buses daily in each direction; Sunday buses only run in July and August.

Buses operated by Eurocorse stop at the Ollandini travel agency (☎ 04 95 77 18 41), cours Gabriel Péri (near the bottom of cours Sœur Amélie). Buses run by Ricci (☎ 04 95 51 08 19) stop at Bar Le Cyrnos (☎ 04 95 77 11 22), 14 cours Général de Gaulle.

BONIFACIO (BUNIFAZIU)

postcode 20169 • pop 2700

The Citadel of Bonifacio sits 70m above the turquoise waters of the Mediterranean atop a long, narrow and eminently defensible promontory sometimes referred to as 'Corsica's Gibraltar'.

On all sides, white limestone cliffs sculpted by the wind and the waves – topped in places with precariously perched, multistorey apartment houses – drop almost vertically to the sea. The northern side of the promontory looks out on Bonifacio Sound (Goulet de Bonifacio), a 1.5km-long fjord only 100m to 150m wide, while the Citadel's southern ramparts afford views of the coast of Sardinia 12km to the south across the Strait of Bonifacio (Bouches de Bonifacio). Not surprisingly, the city is overflowing with tourists and the shops that cater to them.

Given the geographical details supplied by Homer about Ulysses' encounter with the cannibalistic Laestrygonians, it is possible that this episode of the *Odyssey* was set in Bonifacio Sound.

Orientation

Bonifacio consists of two main areas: the marina, at the south-eastern corner of Bonifacio Sound, and the Citadel – also known as the Vieille Ville (old city) or the Ville Haute (upper city) – which occupies the middle section of the 250m-wide promontory.

The Citadel, linked to the marina by ave Charles de Gaulle, has three gates: Porte de Gênes, open only to pedestrians; Porte de France, a one-way exit for cars (with a

Bread of the Dead & Other Treats

Bonifacio's pastry speciality is *paides morts*, a nut and raisin bread, which delightfully translates as 'bread of the dead'. Other sweet Corsican delights include *fougazi* (big, flat, sugar-covered, aniseed-flavoured biscuits), *canistrelli* (sugar-crusted biscuits, often flavoured with lemon, almonds or even white wine), *canistrone* (cheese tarts) and *moustachole* (bread with big sugar crystals on top).

In the Citadelle, all these breads are baked at *Boulangerie-Pâtisserie Faby*, 4 rue St-Jean Baptiste, open 8 am to 12.30 pm and 4 to 7 pm daily (8 pm in July and August, when there's no midday closure). At the marina, try *Boulangerie-Pâtisserie Michel Sorba*, 1-3 rue St-Érasme, which opens 8 am to 12.30 pm and 4.30 to 7 pm (closed Sunday afternoon and Monday); it opens 6 am to 8 pm in July and August.

nearby pedestrian exit); and the entrance-only road under Fort St-Nicolas that ends up at the Foreign Legion monument.

The ferry terminal is below the Citadel on the southern side of Bonifacio Sound.

Information
Tourist Offices In the Citadel, the tourist office (☎ 04 95 73 11 88, fax 04 95 73 14 97), 2 rue Fred Scamaroni, opens 9 am to 8 pm daily in summer and 9 am to noon and 2 to 6 pm Monday to Friday the rest of the year.

Money Société Générale, outside the Citadel at 38 rue St-Érasme, exchanges currency for a 25FF commission (closed at the weekend), and sports the only ATM in town; check its rates. In summer, there are several exchange bureaus along the marina.

Post The post office is on place Carrega in the Citadel, and opens 9 am to noon and 2 to 5 pm (Saturday until noon; closed Sunday). From July to mid-September, weekday hours are 8.30 am to 6 pm.

Laundry The Lavoir de la Marine at 1 quai Jerôme Comparetti opens most of the day. A 7kg load costs 40FF.

Citadel
Bonifacio Sound is linked to the Citadel via two sets of stairs. One – known as Montée Rastello and, farther up, Montée St-Roch – links rue St-Érasme with Porte de Gênes. The other one connects the ferry terminal with the Porte de France. The old city has

something of a medieval ambience, in part because of the cramped alleyways, which are lined with tall, narrow stone houses. The flying buttresses overhead carry rainwater to cisterns. **Rue des Deux Empereurs** is aptly named because Charles V and Napoleon once slept in the houses at Nos 4 and 7, respectively. Charles V spent three days in Bonifacio on his way to Algiers in 1541, while Lieutenant Colonel Bonaparte was based here for several months in early 1793 while planning an expedition to Sardinia.

Église Ste-Marie Majeure, a Romanesque structure built in the 14th century but significantly modified later, is known for its square campanile and its loggia (roofed porch), under which is a large communal cistern, a vital asset in time of siege. The cistern is now used as a conference hall. The marble altar inside dates from the early 17th century.

Impressive **Porte de Gênes**, reached by a drawbridge dating from 1598, was the only entrance to the Citadel until the Porte de France was built in 1854. A visit to the **Grand Bastion**, above Porte de Gênes, costs 10FF; it opens April to mid-October. There are great sea views from nearby **place du Marché** and **place Manichella**. The two holes in the ground topped by twin glass pyramids in the centre of place Manichella were used during the 13th century to store grain, salted meats and other food supplies to feed the town's inhabitants in case of siege.

From the south-western corner of the Citadel, the **Escalier du Roi d'Aragon** (Staircase of the King of Aragon), whose 187

CORSICA

CORSICA

BONIFACIO (BUNIFAZIU)

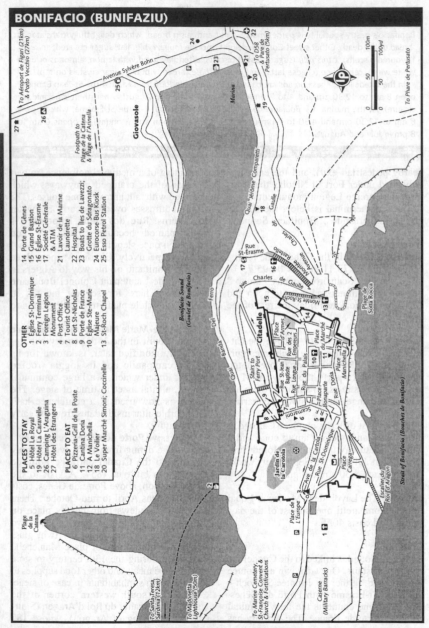

To Aéroport de Figari (21km)
& Porto Vecchio (27km)

To D58
& Pare de Pertusato (5km)

To Phare de Pertusato

Avenue Sylvère Bohn

Giovasole

Marina

Footpath to
Plage de la Catena
& Plage de l'Arinella

Quai Jérôme Comparetti

Quai de Gaulle

Bonifacio Sound
(Goulet de Bonifacio)

Quai Banda

Quai Nord

Rue St-Erasme

Rue Charles de Gaulle

Montée St-Roch

Plage de
Sotta Rocca

Citadelle

Place
de Armes
Rue des 2
Empereurs

Place
du Marché

Place
Manichella

Stairs to
Ferry Port

Rue St-Jean
Baptiste
Rue Longue
Rue du Palais
Rue Doria

Place
10
Bonaparte

Rue Scaramoni

Jardin de
la Carotola

Ave de la Cartola

Rue St-Dominique

Place
Carrega

Place de
L'Europe

Escalier du
Roi d'Aragon

Strait of Bonifacio (Bouches de Bonifacio)

Plage
de la
Catena

To Santa Teresa,
Sardinia (12km)

To Madonetta
Lighthouse (50m)

To Marine Cemetery,
St-François Convent &
Church & Fortifications

Caserne
(Military Barracks)

PLACES TO STAY
5 Hôtel Le Royal
19 Hôtel La Caravelle
26 Camping L'Araguina
27 Hôtel des Étrangers

PLACES TO EAT
6 Pizzeria-Grill de la Poste
11 Cantina Doria
12 A Manichella
18 Le Voilier
20 Super Marché Simoni; Coccinelle

OTHER
1 Église St-Dominique
2 Ferry Terminal
3 Foreign Legion
   Monument
4 Post Office
7 Tourist Office
8 Fort St-Nicholas
9 Porte de France
10 Église Ste-Marie
   Majeure
13 St-Roch Chapel
14 Porte de Gênes
15 Grand Bastion
16 Église St-Erasme
17 Société Générale
   & ATM
21 Lavoir de la Marine
   Laundrette
22 Hospital
23 Boats to Îles de Lavezzi;
   Grotte du Sdragonato
24 Eurocorse Bus Kiosk
25 Esso Petrol Station

100m
100yd

steps were built, according to legend, by Aragonese troops during the siege of 1420, leads down the cliff. Unless it's windy or stormy, the staircase can be visited from June to September (10FF).

Beaches

To get to **plage de Sotta Rocca**, a small bit of rocky coast below the south-eastern corner of the Citadel, walk down the steps that lead down the hill from the hairpin curve on ave Charles de Gaulle.

There are several sandy coves on the northern side of Bonifacio Sound, including **plage de la Catena** and **plage de l'Arinella**. On foot, follow the trail that begins on ave Sylvère Bohn a bit up the hill from the Esso petrol station.

Walking

There are at least four marked walks that are in various stages of signposting and development.

The easiest is the 2km, 30-minute stroll along the cliff tops to see the views back to Bonifacio with its clifftop houses seemingly dangling in the air over the water.

Phare de Pertusato, a lighthouse 5.6km south-east of the Citadel on Capo Pertusato (Cape Pertusato), can be reached in about 30 minutes.

These and another two longer marked walks start at the top of Montée Rastello.

Boat Excursions

From June to September, marina-based Vedettes Christina (☎ 04 95 73 09 77) and a bunch of other companies including Thalassa (☎ 04 95 73 10 17, ✉ thalassa@ bonifacio.com) run trips to Îles de Lavezzi, an island nature reserve where you can swim and picnic; tickets cost around 100FF. The company also offers one-hour excursions to **Grotte du Sdragonato**, whose roof is pierced by a hole that is said to resemble a backwards silhouette of Corsica.

Places to Stay

Camping Shaded by olive trees, *Camping L'Araguina* (☎ 04 95 73 02 96, ave Sylvère Bohn) is 400m north of the marina and

opens mid-March to October. It charges 31/34FF per person in the low/high season, plus 11FF for a tent and 11FF to park a car.

Hotels The 32-room *Hôtel des Étrangers* (☎ 04 95 73 01 09, fax 04 95 73 16 97, ave Sylvère Bohn), 500m north of the marina, opens early April to October. Doubles with shower and toilet cost 220FF (280FF to 390FF from July to September).

In the Citadel, two-star *Hôtel Le Royal* (☎ 04 95 73 00 51, fax 04 95 73 04 68, rue Fred Scamaroni) has rooms for 225FF, 250FF and 290FF from October to April; prices double in July and August.

At the marina, three-star *Hôtel La Caravelle* (☎ 04 95 73 00 03, fax 04 95 73 00 41, 35 quai Jérôme Comparetti) offers doubles for 450FF to 750FF (including breakfast). It opens April to mid-October.

Places to Eat

Restaurants In the Citadel, *Pizzeria-Grill de la Poste* (☎ 04 95 73 13 31, 5 rue Fred Scamaroni), offers Corsican dishes as well as pizza and pasta (45FF to 69FF). *Cantina Doria* (☎ 04 95 73 50 49, 27 rue Doria) is a neat, rustic, hole-in-the-wall place where you dine on wooden benches, surrounded by old farming utensils. Their *soupe Corse*, costing 40FF is enormous (enough for two people) while their *spaghetti au prisuttu* (50FF) is also recommended.

A Manichella (☎ 04 95 73 12 75, place du Marché) is a pleasant snack bar offering light lunches and fine panoramic sea views.

There are lots of touristy restaurants along the southern side of the marina: waterside *Le Voilier* (☎ 04 95 73 07 06, quai Jérôme Comparetti), offers a tempting 'island of beauty' *menu* costing 110FF, a sea fish *menu* for 190FF and a *menu de Voilier* for 170FF.

Self-Catering At the marina, *Super Marché Simoni* (93 quai Jérôme Comparetti), opens 8 am to 12.30 pm and 3.30 to 7.30 pm (closed Sunday afternoon). *Coccinelle* supermarket next door has a fresh bakery counter.

CORSICA

Getting There & Away

Air Bonifacio's international airport, Aéroport de Figari (☎ 04 95 71 10 10), is 21km north of town.

Bus Eurocorse (☎ 04 95 70 13 83 in Porto Vecchio) has buses to Ajaccio (10FF) via Sartène. To get to Bastia, change buses at Porto Vecchio, which is served by two daily buses (four in summer). All buses leave from the car park next to the Eurocorse kiosk (open in summer only).

Boat Saremar (☎ 04 95 73 00 96 in Bonifacio; ☎ 0789 754 156 in Santa Teresa) and Moby Lines (☎ 04 95 73 00 29 in Bonifacio; ☎ 0789 751 449 in Santa Teresa) both offer a daily car and passenger ferry service year round from Bonifacio's ferry port to Santa Teresa, Sardinia (50 minutes, two to seven daily).

Saremar charges 45/65FF for a one-way passenger fare in low/high season, while Moby Lines charges 50/65FF. Cars cost between 129FF and 183FF one way, depending on the season. There is an additional 18.50FF port tax on top of the ticket price.

Bastia Area

BASTIA

postcode 20200 • pop 37,800

Bustling Bastia is Corsica's main centre of business and commerce, and has an Italian atmosphere found nowhere else on the island. It was the seat of the Genoese governors of Corsica from the 15th century, when construction of the *bastiglia* (fortress), from which the city's name comes, was begun. You can easily spend a day wandering around, the old port being Bastia's definite highlight; but most visitors move on pretty quickly.

If you have a car, Bastia is a convenient base for exploring Cap Corse, the 40km-long peninsula north of Bastia.

Orientation

The focal point of the modern city centre is 300m-long place St-Nicolas. Bastia's principal thoroughfares are east–west ave Maréchal Sebastiani, which links the south ferry terminal with the train station, and north–south blvd Paoli, a fashionable shopping street one block west of place St-Nicolas.

South of place St-Nicolas are the town's three older neighbourhoods: Terra Vecchia (which is centred around place de l'Hôtel de Ville, also known as place du Marché), the old port and the Citadel.

Information

Tourist Offices The tourist office (☎ 04 95 55 96 85, fax 04 95 55 96 00), place St-Nicolas, opens 8 am to noon and 2 to 6 pm (closed Sunday afternoon). It opens 8 am to 8 pm daily in July and August.

Money Banque de France, 2 bis cours Henri Pierangeli, opens 8.45 am to 12.10 pm and 1.55 to 3.30 pm (closed at the weekend). Commercial banks are dotted along the western side of place St-Nicolas, along rue César Campinchi and rue du Conventionnel Salicetti. Most have ATMs. There is also an exchange counter at the south ferry terminal.

Post The post office on ave Maréchal Sebastiani opens 8 am to 7 pm weekdays (Saturday until noon). Exchange services are available.

Bookshops Walking maps and topoguides are available at Librairie Jean-Patrice Marzocchi (☎ 04 95 34 02 95), 2 rue du Conventionnel Salicetti, open 9.30 am to noon and 2.30 to 7 pm (closed all day Sunday and Monday morning).

Laundry Le Lavoir du Port, in the car park at the northern end of rue du Commandant Luce de Casabianca, opens 7 am to 9 pm daily.

Walking Tour

Much of Bastia can be seen in a half-day stroll starting with **place St-Nicolas**, an esplanade almost as long as three football pitches, laid out in the late 19th century.

BASTIA

Inset

Jardin Romieu

Same Scale as Main Map

Jetée du Dragon

45

Place du Donjon 46

Citadelle (Terra Nova)

Rue de l' Évêché

Place Dominique Vincetti

47

48

To Hospital; Plage de l'Arinella (2km), Camping Le San Damiano (10km), Plage de la Marana (12km) & Airport (24km)

To Géant Port Toga Centre Commercial, Hôtel Cyrnea (2km), Camping Les Orangers (4km) & Cap Course

Toga Marina

R. de l'Impératrice Eugénie

LIGURIAN SEA

0   100   200m
0   100   200yd

R Notre Dame de Lourdes

Avenue Emile Sari

Rue de Castabianca

Rue du Chanoine Lecchi

Rue du Commandant Luce de Casabianca

Rue Capanelle

Rue César Campinchi

Rue Général Graziani

Rue du Nouveau Port

Blvd du Fango

Square Mal Leclerc

Avenue Maréchal Sébastiani

Square St-Victor

Ave F Pietri

Rue Gabriel Péri

Rue du Conventionnel Salicetti

Rue César Campinchi

Boulevard Paoli

Boulevard Général de Gaulle

Place St-Nicolas

Place St-Nicolas

Pedestrian Bridge

Rue Miot

Rue St-François

Rue Napoléon

Cours Henri Pierangeli

Quai des Martyrs de la Libération

Terra Vecchia

Place de l'Hôtel de Ville

Rue des Zéphyrs

Rue St-Jean

Blvd Hyacinthe de Montera

Rue des Terrasses

Rue de la Marine

Rue Favalelli

Boulevard Paoli

Rue Général Carbuccia

Quai du Sud

Tunnel Under the Old Port

Old Port

See Inset

PLACES TO STAY
9 Hôtel Bonaparte
16 Hôtel Le Riviera
25 Hôtel Napoléon
27 Hôtel d'Univers
28 Hôtel Les Voyageurs
32 Hôtel Central
39 Hôtel Posta Vecchia

PLACES TO EAT
6 La Voûte
10 Spar Supermarket
35 Café Pannini
40 Chez Mémé
41 Café Wha
42 Chez Lavezzi
43 Le Colomba

OTHER
1 North Ferry Terminal
2 Vehicle Entrance for Car Ferries
3 Le Lavoir du Port Laundrette
4 Police Nationale
5 Corsica Ferries Office
7 Objectif Nature
8 Cave Seddas
11 Prefecture Building
12 Buses for Airport
13 Post Office
14 Short-Haul Bus Terminal
15 Taxi Rank
17 Moby Lines Office
18 South Ferry Terminal; SNCM Office
19 Fountain
20 Town Hall
21 Buses to Sisco, Plage de la Marana & Cap Corse
22 Tourist Office
23 Cap Corse Mattei
24 Librairie Jean-Patrice Marzocchi
26 Rapides Bleus Bus Office
29 Buses for Calvi
30 Train Station
31 Statue of Napoleon
33 Banque de France
34 Oratoire
36 Former Town Hall
37 Oratoire de l'Immaculée Conception
38 Église St-Jean Baptiste
44 Palais de Justice
45 Palais des Gouverneurs; Musée d'Ethnographic Corse
46 Main Entrance to Citadelle
47 Église Ste-Marie
48 Citadelle Entrance

CORSICA

A statue of **Napoleon Bonaparte** dressed as a Roman emperor proudly stands guard at the southern end. Cafes line the western side of the square.

Between place St-Nicolas and the old port lies the historic neighbourhood of **Terra Vecchia**, a neighbourhood of old houses (some 18th century), towering tenements and narrow streets. It is centred around shady **place de l'Hôtel de Ville**, now an open-air marketplace and car park.

The **old port** is a jumble of boats, restaurants, and crumbling tenement buildings. The entrance to the port is guarded by two beacons. **Jetée du Dragon**, the jetty that leads to the southern (red) beacon, affords great views of the harbour, where pleasure craft mingle with the local fleet of bright blue and white wooden boats.

Farther south still is the **Citadel**, also known as Terra Nova, built by the Genoese between the 15th and 17th centuries. It can be reached by climbing the stairs through **Jardin Romieu**, the hillside park on the southern side of the old port.

Inside the double gates of the Citadel, at place du Donjon, is mustard-yellow **Palais des Gouverneurs** (Governors' Palace). It houses a rather dusty and dull anthropology museum, **Musée d'Ethnographic Corse** (☎ 04 95 31 09 12), and an old **Genoese prison**.

It opens 9 or 10 am to noon and 2 to 6 pm (5 pm at the weekend out-of-season, 7 pm May to September); there is no midday closure April to October. Admission costs 15FF (including the prison).

Activities

Objectif Nature (☎/fax 04 95 32 54 34, ✉ objectif-nature@wanadoo.fr), 3 rue Notre Dame de Lourdes, organises a host of outdoor activities including kayaking expeditions (250FF a day), day and night sea fishing trips (from 350FF per person for groups of six or more), walking, mountaineering, horse riding (350FF a day including lunch) and diving (180FF for a first-time dive).

Its office opens 9 am to 6 pm Monday to Saturday.

Places to Stay

Most of Bastia's hotels are open year round. The tourist office can provide a comprehensive list of all available accommodation.

Places to Stay – Budget

Camping Small *Camping Les Orangers* (☎ 04 95 33 24 09), open April to mid-October, is about 4km north of Bastia in Miomo. It costs 25/10/13FF per adult/car/tent. Take the bus to Sisco from opposite the tourist office.

Camping Le San Damiano (☎ 04 95 33 68 02), open April to October, is about 5km south of Bastia. It costs 32/12/12FF per adult/car/tent. Take the airport bus to get there.

Hotels One-star *Hôtel Le Riviera* (☎ 04 95 31 07 16, fax 04 95 34 17 39, 1 bis rue du Nouveau Port), has doubles with shower and toilet costing 200/250FF in the low/high season. Reception is on the 1st floor. Family-run *Hôtel Central* (☎ 04 95 31 71 12, fax 04 95 31 82 40, 3 rue Miot), has basic singles/doubles with shower and toilet costing from 180/200FF and better-equipped rooms with TV starting at 230/250FF.

One of the most convenient hotels in Bastia is 20-room *Hôtel d'Univers* (☎ 04 95 31 03 38, fax 04 95 31 19 91, 3 ave Maréchal Sebastiani). Renovated rooms cost 250/280FF in the low season or 300/350FF in the high season.

Nearby is three-star *Hôtel Les Voyageurs* (☎ 04 95 34 90 80, fax 04 95 34 00 65, 9 ave Maréchal Sebastiani). Doubles with shower and toilet here are very good value and start at 250/280FF in the low/high season. Breakfast costs 30FF.

Places to Stay – Mid-Range

The very central *Hôtel Napoléon* (☎ 04 95 31 60 30, fax 04 95 31 77 83, 43 blvd Paoli) has small but comfortable doubles equipped with all the amenities for around 290FF to 590FF. Prices rise precipitously from early July to early September. From April to October, the two-star, 23-room *Hôtel Bonaparte* (☎ 04 95 34 07 10, fax 04 95 32 35 62,

45 blvd Général Graziani), has doubles with shower and toilet costing from 300FF to 450FF; breakfast costs an additional 40FF.

Overlooking the sea is *Hôtel Posta Vecchia* (☎ 04 95 32 32 38, fax 04 95 46 07 37, quai des Martyrs de la Libération), which has excellent-value singles/doubles with shower and toilet costing 220/250FF. Rates rise by 30/50FF in July and August.

Motorists looking for a safe place to park and a quiet location should look no further than *Hôtel Cyrnea* (☎ 04 95 31 41 71, fax 04 95 31 72 65, route de Cap) 2km north of Bastia at Pietranera. Quiet double rooms with balconies overlooking gardens and the sea start at around 350FF.

Places to Eat
Restaurants & Cafes Cafes and brasseries line the western side of place St-Nicolas. Many more restaurants and cafes can be found along the northern side of the old port, on quai des Martyrs de la Libération and on place de l'Hôtel de Ville in Terra Vecchia, where *Café Pannini* on the north-western corner of the square is popular for its jumbo sandwiches.

In the new town, *La Voûte* (☎ 04 95 32 47 11, 6 bis rue du Commandant Luce de Casabianca) is the most inspiring option, offering some French cuisine but mainly pizzas, under brick vaults and on a terrace overlooking the port. Mains cost 65FF to 99FF and the *menu* costs 125FF.

The old port area is better supplied with eateries and is crammed with small, cosy restaurants that ooze charm. Many boast fabulous port views too, such as pricey, but delicious *Chez Lavezzi* (☎ 04 95 31 05 73, 8 rue St-Jean), which serves exquisitely presented dishes on its pink waterfront terrace. Expect to pay at least 150FF a head.

Le Colomba (☎ 04 95 32 79 14, Vieux Port) is a large pizzeria serving an impressive range of 32 pizzas costing from 39FF to 57FF. The *Brazilian pizza* is the house speciality. It opens daily year round and there is live Corsican music on Thursday night.

For a cheap and cheerful approach, head straight for fun-loving *Café Wha* (☎ 04 95 34 25 79, Vieux Port), which also has a terrace facing the water. It serves a range of fast-food Mexican dishes and is always packed. Dishes cost from 50FF to 60FF.

Facing the seafront, with a large open-air terrace in warmer weather, is *Chez Mémé* (☎ 04 95 31 44 12, quai des Martyrs de la Libération), a no-nonsense eatery with ample portions of good food. Try paella (70FF) or mussels and chips (60FF) and wash it down with the excellent house rosé.

Self-Catering A bustling *food market* is held at place de l'Hôtel de Ville in Terra Vecchio every morning except Monday.

There is a large *Spar supermarket* on the corner of rue César Campinchi and rue Capanelle. The huge Géant Port Toga Centre Commercial houses a *Casino supermarket*.

Shopping
For Corsican wines, look no farther than richly stocked Cave Seddas at 3 ave Emile Sari. The local liqueur, Cap Corse, is sold at the atmospheric Cap Corse Mattei, 15 blvd Général de Gaulle, which hosts a permanent exhibition on the Corsican aperitif.

Getting There & Around
Air Bastia-Poretta airport (☎ 04 95 54 54 54) is 24km south of the city. Municipal buses to the airport (50FF, around eight to nine a daily) depart from the prefecture building across the roundabout from the train station. The tourist office has schedules. A taxi to the airport will cost from 125FF to 185FF.

Bus Rapides Bleus (☎ 04 95 31 03 79), 1 ave Maréchal Sebastiani, runs buses to Porto Vecchio and Bonifacio (via Porto Vecchio), and handles tickets for the Eurocorse service to Corte and Ajaccio. The afternoon bus to Calvi run by Les Beaux Voyages (☎ 04 95 65 11 35) leaves at 4.30 pm from outside the train station.

Rue du Nouveau Port, north of the tourist office, has been turned into a bus terminal for short-haul buses serving villages south and west of Bastia. Buses to Cap Corse leave from ave François Pietri, across the street from the tourist office.

euro currency converter €1 = 6.56FF

Train The train station (☎ 04 95 32 80 61), ave Maréchal Sebastiani, opens 6.30 am to 8 pm; it opens 7 am to noon and 2 to 7 pm on Sunday.

Boat The south ferry terminal for foot passengers is at the eastern end of ave François Pietri; the left-luggage office, open 8 to 11.30 am and 2 to 7 pm, charges 10FF per bag. The north ferry terminal entrance for vehicles is 600m to the north.

The SNCM office (☎ 04 95 54 66 81) inside the south terminal opens 8 to 11.45 am and 2 to 5.45 pm (Saturday until noon; closed Sunday). Tickets are sold two hours before departure in the Corsica Marittima ticket section of the terminal building.

Moby Lines (☎ 04 95 34 84 94, fax 04 95 32 17 94), 4 rue du Commandant Luce de Casabianca, opens 8 am to noon and 2 to 6 pm (until noon Saturday; closed Sunday). The company's bureau in the ferry terminal opens two hours before each sailing.

Corsica Ferries (☎ 04 95 32 95 95, fax 04 95 32 14 71), 15 bis rue Chanoine Leschi, opens 8.30 am to noon and 2 to 6.30 pm (closed Sunday and, except in summer, on Saturday afternoon); there's no midday closure from mid-June to mid-September.

CAP CORSE

The long, narrow peninsula at Corsica's northern tip stretches about 40km northwards from Bastia. Cap Corse's 15km-wide strip of valleys and mountains (up to 1300m high) affords spectacular views of the sea, particularly along the steep and rocky west coast.

Once intensively cultivated, the areas where grapevines, olive trees and fruit orchards once flourished have now been reclaimed by the maquis. Cap Corse can be visited as a car or bus excursion from Bastia; the tourist office has details.

On the east coast, there are sandy beaches at **Marine de Pietracorbara**, about 10km north of **Erbalunga**; and slightly north of **Macinaggio**, a small fishing village near the northern tip of Cap Corse. The west coast has many sandy coves.

The North Coast

CALVI

postcode 20260 • pop 4800

The prosperous citadel town of Calvi sits atop a promontory at the western end of a beach-lined, half-moon-shaped bay. Seaside sunbathers can either admire the iridescent turquoise waters of the Golfe de Calvi or, if they turn around, ponder Monte Cinto (2706m) and its soaring neighbours only 20km inland, snowcapped during all but the hottest months.

In 1794, a British expeditionary fleet assisting Pasquale Paoli's Corsican nationalist forces, who had fallen out with the island's post-Revolutionary government, besieged and bombarded Calvi. In the course of the battle, one Captain Horatio Nelson was wounded by rock splinters and lost the use of his right eye.

Orientation

The Citadel – also known as the Haute Ville (upper city) – is on a rocky promontory north-east of the Basse Ville (lower city). Blvd Wilson, which is the major thoroughfare in the commercial centre, is up the hill from quai Landry and the marina (*port de plaisance*).

Information

Tourist Offices The tourist office (☎ 04 95 65 16 67, fax 04 95 65 14 09), near the marina, opens 9 am to 1.30 pm and 2 to 7 pm (closed Saturday afternoon and Sunday).

From mid-June to mid-September, the tourist office has an annexe inside the gate to the Citadel (closed Saturday afternoon and Sunday).

Money Crédit Lyonnais, blvd Wilson, opens until 4.30 pm (closed at the weekend) and sports a handy ATM. There are several banks and exchange places (mostly seasonal) along blvd Wilson and quai Landry.

Post The post office, where blvd Wilson meets ave de la République, opens 8.30 am

CALVI

PLACES TO STAY
12 Hôtel du Centre
19 Hôtel Le Rocher
26 Auberge de Jeunesse
   BVJ Corsotel

PLACES TO EAT
9 Callelu Restaurant
10 Île de Beauté
11 Covered Market
17 Alimentation du Golfe
18 Best Of
28 Super-U Supermarket

OTHER
1 Église St-Jean Baptiste
2 Caserne Sampiero
   (Palais des Gouverneurs)
3 Monument aux Morts;
   Buses for Calenzana &
   & Porto
4 Hall de la Presse
5 Gate to Citadelle;
   Tourist Office Annexe
6 Chez Tao
7 Ferry Terminal
8 Tour de Sel
13 Crédit Lyonnais & ATM
14 Église Ste-Marie Majeure
15 Tramar
16 Croisières Colombo Line
20 Post Office
21 Les Beaux Voyages
22 Buses for Bastia &
   Calenzana
23 Taxi Rank
24 Tourist Office
25 Train Station
27 Laundrette

CORSICA

Calvi

---

to 5 pm (Saturday until noon; closed Sunday). Exchange services are available.

Bookshops Topoguides and walking maps are sold at Hall de la Presse (☎ 04 95 65 05 14), 13 blvd Wilson.

Citadel

Set atop an 80m-high granite promontory surrounded by massive Genoese fortifications, the Citadel affords great views. The town's renowned loyalty to Genoa is recalled by the motto *Civitas Calvi Semper Fidelis* (the city of Calvi, forever faithful),

accorded to the town by the Republic of Genoa in 1562 and carved over the gate to the Citadel.

The imposing **Palais des Gouverneurs** (Governors' Palace) on place d'Armes was built in the 13th century and enlarged in the mid-16th century. It now serves – under the name Caserne Sampiero – as a barracks and mess hall for officers of the Foreign Legion.

Up the street from Caserne Sampiero is **Église St-Jean Baptiste**, built in the 13th century and rebuilt in 1570; the main altar dates from the 17th century. The women of the local elite used to sit in the screened boxes, whose grilles served to shelter them from the inquisitive gaze of the rabble. To the right of the altar is *Christ des Miracles*, an ebony statue of Jesus that was paraded around town in 1553 shortly before the besieging Turkish forces fell back. Credited with saving Calvi from the Saracens, the statue has since been the object of great veneration.

In the northern part of the Citadel, a marble plaque marks the site of the house where, according to local tradition, the navigator Christopher Columbus was born.

Beaches

Calvi's 4km-long beach begins at the marina and stretches east around the Golfe de Calvi. See the later Getting There & Away section for details of Tramways de la Balagne and travelling along the coast.

Boat Excursions

From April to October, Croisières Colombo Line (☎ 04 95 65 32 10, fax 04 95 65 03 40) offers six-hour, glass-bottomed boat excursions (260FF) from Calvi's marina to the seaside hamlets of Galéria and Girolata via the Réserve de Naturelle Scandola.

Places to Stay

Camping Three-star *Camping Les Castors* (☎ 04 95 65 13 30, route de Pietra Maggiore), open from April to mid-October, is 800m south-east of the town centre. Charges are 30/12/12FF per adult/car/tent. In July and August these prices are higher.

Farther south, two-star *Camping La Clé des Champs* (☎ 04 95 65 00 86, route de Pietra Maggiore), open April to October, charges 25/12/10FF per adult/car/tent. Reception opens 9 am to 10.30 pm.

There are a handful of other camping grounds farther along this street.

Hostels The 130-bed *Auberge de Jeunesse BVJ Corsotel* (☎ 04 95 65 14 15, fax 04 95 65 33 72, ave de la République) opens late March to October. Beds in rooms for two to eight people cost 120FF per person, which

includes a filling breakfast. Reception opens 7 am to 1.30 pm and 5 to 10 pm.

Hotels The cheapest place after the Auberge de Jeunesse is *Hôtel du Centre* (☎ 04 95 65 02 01, 14 rue Alsace-Lorraine). Open only from 1 June to 13 September, rooms with showers go for between 180FF and 250FF depending on the season.

Hôtel Le Rocher (☎ 04 95 65 20 04, fax 04 95 65 36 71, blvd Wilson) provides mini-apartments with kitchenettes, fridges and air-con for two/four people costing from 355/550FF to 740/980FF, depending on the season. From November to early April ring ☎ 04 95 65 11 35 for advance bookings.

Open year round, *Hotel Meridiana* (☎ 04 95 65 31 38, fax 04 95 65 32 72, ave Santa Maria) is set back a bit from the main town area, but is a good bet for people with their own vehicles. Large and airy rooms, all with a sea view, range in price from 300FF for a standard room to 900FF for a deluxe room depending on the season.

Places to Eat

Restaurants Calvi's restaurants generally offer excellent quality, but you won't find many *menus* for under 70FF or 80FF. From May to September, quai Landry in the Basse Ville and, one block up the hill, rue Clemenceau buzz night and day with well-heeled visitors browsing for a place to eat.

For a snack on the move, head for sandwich bar *Best Of (rue Clemenceau)*, which sells a huge variety of sandwiches (around 25FF) including some with Corsican fillings.

One place definitely worth a nibble among the waterfront's line-up of romantic waterfront cafes and restaurants is *Île de Beauté* (☎ 04 95 65 00 46, quai Landry), which specialises in fish and Corsican cuisine and has *menus* costing 100FF and 150FF.

A couple of doors away is cosy *Callelu Restaurant* (☎ 04 95 65 22 18, quai Landry), which specialises in fish dishes from between 110FF and 120FF. Their comprehensive *menu* goes for 110FF.

Self-Catering The tiny *Marché Couvert,* (covered market) near Église Ste-Marie Majeure opens 8 am to noon Monday to Saturday. There's a large **Super-U Supermarket** *(ave Christophe Colomb)* south of the train station. Alternatively, try **Alimentation du Golfe** *(southern end of rue Clemenceau).*

Entertainment

Within the Citadel walls, *Chez Tao* (☎ 04 95 65 60 73) is *the* place to go, particularly because, as any local will proudly tell you, the owners are said to be direct descendants of Rasputin. Rock idol Bono from U2 is just one of the more contemporary celebrities who have popped into this fun piano bar for a drink when passing through town. Chez Tao opens June to September.

Getting There & Away

Air Calvi-Ste-Catherine airport (☎ 04 95 65 88 88) is 7km south-east of Calvi. Sample return prices to/from the mainland with Air Littoral are Nice (785FF, twice daily), Marseilles (825FF, two to three times daily) and Montpellier (1380FF, twice daily).

Bus The tourist office has bus information and can supply photocopied time tables. Buses to Bastia and Calenzana (only in summer) are run by Les Beaux Voyages (☎ 04 95 65 15 02), place de la Porteuse d'Eau. From mid-May to mid-October, Autocars SAIB (☎ 04 95 26 13 70) has a bus down the island's spectacular north-west coast from Calvi's Monument aux Morts (war memorial) to Galéria (1¼ hours) and Porto (three hours).

Train Calvi's train station (☎ 04 95 65 00 61), just off ave de la République, opens until 7.30 pm. There are two departures daily to Ajaccio, Bastia, Corte and stations in between.

From mid-April to mid-October, the one-car diesel *navettes* (shuttle trains) of CFC's Le Tramway de la Balagne make 19 stops along the coast between Calvi and Île Rousse (22km, 45 minutes). The line is divided into three sectors – you need one

ticket (available on board for 10FF) for each sector. Carnets of six tickets are sold at stations.

Boat The ferry terminal is below the southern side of the Citadel; schedules are posted at the tourist office. From Calvi there are express NGV ferries to Nice (2½ hours, five a week); see the earlier Getting There & Away section for details.

Ferry tickets can only be bought at the port two hours before departure. At all other times, SNCM tickets are handled by Tramar (☎ 04 95 65 01 38), quai Landry, open 8.25 am to noon and 1 to 5.30 pm (Saturday until noon; closed Sunday). Les Beaux Voyages (☎ 04 95 65 15 02), place de la Porteuse d'Eau, is an agent for Corsica Ferries (closed Sunday and, except from May to October, on Saturday too).

For information on getting from Calvi to Porto by sea, see Boat Excursions in the Calvi and Porto sections.

Getting Around

To/From the Airport There is no bus service from Calvi to the airport. Taxis (☎ 04 95 65 03 10), 24 hours a day from place de la Porteuse d'Eau, cost 75FF (105FF after 7 pm and on Sunday).

AROUND CALVI
La Balagne

The Balagne region is an area of low hills between the Monte Cinto massif and the sea. Its coastline stretches north-east from Galéria, all the way to **Désert des Agriates**, the desert area that begins 18km east of Île Rousse. The coast between Calvi and Île Rousse is dotted with a string of fine-sand beaches (eg at **Algajola**), many of them served by Le Tramway de la Balagne (see Getting There & Away under Calvi).

Inland, La Balagne, known as the 'Garden of Corsica', is renowned for the fertility of its soil, whose bounty once made the region among Corsica's wealthiest.

The main inland town, **Calenzana**, is 10km south-east of Calvi, to which it is linked by bus during the summer. Calenzana is the northern terminus of the GR20 and Mare è Monti trails.

From Calenzana, the D151 to Île Rousse is a particularly picturesque drive.

After the village of **Cateri**, bear right along the D413 for 2.5km to the beautiful, crumbling village of **St-Antonino**, dramatically perched on a hilltop and offering stunning views of the region.

ÎLE ROUSSE (ISULA ROSSA)
postcode 20220 • pop 2300

The bustling port and beach resort of Île Rousse, 24km north-east of Calvi, was founded by the Corsican nationalist leader Pasquale Paoli in 1758 to compete with fiercely pro-Genoese Calvi.

Its name is derived from the red granite of Île de la Pietra, a rocky island (now connected to the mainland) whose Genoese watchtower presides over an active passenger and freight port.

Orientation & Information

The ferry port is on a peninsula about 500m north of the train station, which is 400m north-west of place Paoli, the main square. The old city is between place Paoli and the train station.

The very friendly tourist office (☎ 04 95 60 04 35, fax 04 95 60 24 74, @ info@ ot-ile-rousse.fr) on the southern side of place Paoli operates year round.

It opens 9 am to noon and 2 to 6 pm Monday to Saturday. In summer it opens 9 am to 7 pm daily.

Things to See

Beachfront **promenade Marinella** runs along the coast between the train tracks and the sand.

There's more sandy coastline east of town past the rocks, near pricey **Musée Océanographique** (☎ 04 95 60 27 81).

The area of narrow streets north of place Paoli is known as the **Vieille Ville**.

On **Île de la Pietra**, the reddish island-turned-peninsula where the ferry port is located, there's a **Genoese tower** and, at the far end, a **lighthouse**, from which there are views of nearby islets.

Places to Stay & Eat

Hôtel Le Grillon (☎ 04 95 60 00 49, fax 04 95 60 43 69, 10 ave Paul Doumer) offers decent singles/doubles with shower and toilet for 180/200FF in the low season and 200/250FF in July.

Twenty-room, two-star **Hôtel L'Isola Rossa** (☎ 04 95 60 01 32, fax 04 95 60 33 02) is just one of a handful of overpriced hotels lining promenade du Port, the street running towards the port from the train station. L'Isola Rossa has doubles costing 280FF to 300FF in May, with prices rising to around 400FF for the same rooms in July and August.

Rue Paoli has quite a few decent eateries. **Chez Paco** (☎ 04 95 60 03 76, rue Paoli) is a reasonable place to dine. Mussels and chips (55FF) and bouillabaisse royale (85FF) are among the daily items on offer.

Getting There & Away

Bus Buses on the Calvi–Bastia run stop in front of Café de la Paix, 3 ave Piccioni (just south of place Paoli).

Train The quaint train station (☎ 04 95 60 00 50) is midway between place Paoli and the ferry port. Île Rousse makes an easy day trip from Calvi.

Boat Tramar (☎ 04 95 60 09 56), 200m south-east of place Paoli on ave Joseph Calizi, handles SNCM, Corsica Ferries and Moby Lines ticketing. It opens 8.30 am to noon and 2 to 5.30 pm (closed Saturday afternoon and Sunday).

Corte Area

CORTE (CORTI)
postcode 20250 • pop 5700
• elevation 400m

When Pasquale Paoli led Corsica to independence in 1755, one of his first acts was to make this fortified town at the geographical centre of the island the country's capital.

To this day, Corte remains a potent symbol of Corsican independence.

CORSICA

Paoli, whose world-view was steeped in the ideas of the Enlightenment, founded a national university here in 1765, but it was closed four years later when the short-lived Corsican republic was taken over by France. Università di Corsica Pasquale Paoli was reopened in 1981 and now has about 3000 students; it is they who make Corte the island's youngest, liveliest and least touristy town.

Ringed with mountains snow-kissed until as late as early June, Corte is an excellent base for walking; some of the island's highest peaks are a bit west of town. To the east lies the Castagniccia region.

Orientation

Corte's main street is shop-lined cours Paoli. At its southern end is place Paoli, from where the narrow streets of the Ville Haute wend their way west up to the Citadel.

The train station, on ave Jean Nicoli, is 1km south-east (down the hill) of cours Paoli.

Information

Tourist Offices The tourist office (☎ 04 95 46 26 70, fax 04 95 46 34 05, **@** Cort .Tourisme@wanadoo.fr), La Citadel, opens 9 am to noon and 2 to 5 pm Monday to Friday. In July and August, it opens 9 am to 8 pm.

Money There are several banks along the northern part of cours Paoli. Caisse d'Épargne and Crédit Agricole banks both have ATMs close to each other on cours Paoli. The post office also has an ATM.

Post & Communications The post office, ave du Baron Mariani, opens 8 am to noon and 2 to 5 pm (Saturday until noon only; closed Sunday). There is one Internet terminal in the post office.

Bookshops Maison de la Presse, 24 cours Paoli, has an excellent stock of maps, topoguides, mountain-biking and walking guides, as well as quality books on Corsican history, flora and fauna, cuisine and so on.

Laundry Speed Laverie, in the same shopping complex as the Casino Supermarket, opens 8 am to 9 pm daily.

Citadel

Corte's partly derelict citadel, the only such fortress in the interior of the island, towers above the town from a rocky promontory overlooking the alleyways of the Ville Haute (to the east) and the Tavignanu and Restonica rivers (to the south and west). The highest part is the **chateau** (also known as the Nid d'Aigle, eagle's nest), which was built in 1419 by a Corsican nobleman allied with the Aragonese and was considerably expanded by the French during the 18th and 19th centuries. The citadel served as a Foreign Legion base from 1962 until 1983.

Impressive **Museu di a Corsica** (Musée de la Corse; ☎ 04 95 45 25 45, fax 04 95 45 25 36, **@** museu@sitec.fr) houses an outstanding exhibition on Corsican folk traditions, crafts, agriculture, economy and anthropology. It has a small cinema too and hosts temporary art and music exhibitions on the ground floor. Captions are in French and Corsican. The museum opens 10 am to 8 pm in July and August (until 6 pm between April and June, closed Monday, and until 5 pm between September and March closed Sunday and Monday). Admission costs 35FF (students 20FF).

Outside the ramparts, a staircase leads from just below the **belvédère** (viewing platform) down to the river.

Palazzu Naziunale

The Genoese-built National Palace, down the hill from the citadel gate, served as the seat of Corsica's government during the island's short-lived independence. Today, the structure is occupied by a Corsican studies centre affiliated with the university. The basement, which once served as a prison, is used to house temporary exhibitions.

Farther down the hill at place Gaffory is the location of mid-15th-century **Église de l'Annonciation**. The walls of nearby houses are pocked with numerous bullet marks from Corsica's mid-18th-century war of independence.

CORSICA

CORSICA

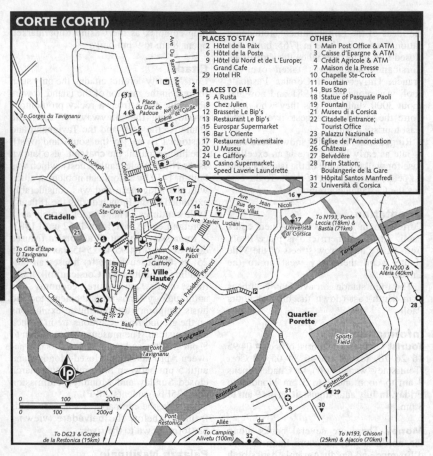

CORTE (CORTI)

PLACES TO STAY
2 Hôtel de la Paix
6 Hôtel de la Poste
9 Hôtel du Nord et de L'Europe;
   Grand Cafe
29 Hôtel HR

PLACES TO EAT
5 A Rusta
8 Chez Julien
12 Brasserie Le Bip's
13 Restaurant Le Bip's
15 Eurospar Supermarket
16 Bar L'Oriente
17 Restaurant Universitaire
20 U Museu
24 Le Gaffory
30 Casino Supermarket;
   Speed Laverie Laundrette

OTHER
1 Main Post Office & ATM
3 Caisse d'Epargne & ATM
4 Crédit Agricole & ATM
7 Maison de la Presse
10 Chapelle Ste-Croix
11 Fountain
14 Bus Stop
18 Statue of Pasquale Paoli
19 Fountain
21 Museu di a Corsica
22 Citadelle Entrance;
   Tourist Office
23 Palazzu Nazionale
25 Église de l'Annonciation
26 Château
27 Belvédère
28 Train Station;
   Boulangerie de la Gare
31 Hôpital Santos Manfredi
32 Università di Corsica

Places to Stay

Camping Attractive, olive-shaded *Camping Alivetu* (☎ 04 95 46 11 09, fax 04 95 46 12 34, faubourg de St-Antoine), open 1 April to 15 October, is just south of pont Restonica. It charges 32/15/15FF per adult/car/tent. You can camp under the trees at *Gîte d'Étape U Tavignanu* (see Hostels) for 10FF per tent plus 20FF per person.

Hostels Sixteen-bed *Gîte d'Étape U Tavignanu* (☎ 04 95 46 16 85, fax 04 95 61 14 01, chemin de Baliri) is quiet – except for birds and rushing water. It opens year round

and charges 80FF for bed and breakfast. From pont Tavignanu, walk west along chemin de Baliri and follow the signs. The gîte is about 500m over the small bridge and 250m from the end of the narrow road.

For details on staying in the university dorms during July and August, contact the CROUS secrétariat (☎ 04 95 45 21 00), Résidence Pasquale Paoli, on the university's main campus.

Hotels Clean, utilitarian, 135-room *Hôtel HR* (☎ 04 95 45 11 11, fax 04 95 61 02 85, 6 allée du 9 Septembre) has singles/doubles costing 135/250FF in low season and 135/400FF in high season.

From mid-May to mid-October, the one-star, 12-room *Hôtel de la Poste* (☎ *04 95 46 01 37, 2 place du Duc de Padoue)* has spacious, simply furnished rooms with toilet for 140FF and 170FF with shower. Some rooms don't have much of a window. Family-run, 11-room *Hôtel du Nord et de L'Europe* (☎ *04 95 46 00 68, fax 04 95 47 40 72, 22 cours Paoli)* accommodates students in winter but accepts travellers from April to October. Rooms with shower range in price from 180FF to 270FF.

Very comfortable, two-star *Hôtel de la Paix* (☎ *04 95 46 06 72, fax 04 95 46 23 84, ave du Général de Gaulle)* has 60 neat, airy rooms ranging in price between 180FF and 340FF depending on size and season. The hotel opens year round.

Places to Eat

Restaurants There are a number of student-oriented sandwich and pizza takeaways on place Paoli and along cours Paoli. *Grand Cafe* (☎ *04 95 46 00 68, 22 cours Paoli)* under the Hotel du Nord and under the same ownership is one cosy student hangout where you can also leave your backpacks for free. *Bar L'Oriente* (☎ *04 95 61 11 17, ave Jean Nicoli)* opposite the university, is another popular hangout; its terrace cafe is particularly pleasant.

Restaurant Universitaire (ave Jean Nicoli) on the main campus of the Università di Corsica, in Résidence Pasquale Paoli, opens 11.30 am to 1.30 pm and 6.30 to 9 pm Monday to Friday October to June. Meal tickets (20FF) are sold from 11 am to 1 pm to students only.

Corsican cuisine is on offer at *A Rusta* (☎ *04 95 46 28 56, 19 cours Paoli)*, whose *menu* costs 75FF and mains 45FF to 65FF. Further south on the opposite side of the same street is rustic *Chez Julien* (☎ *04 95 46 02 90, 24 cours Paoli)*, which serves a good value 68FF *menu*.

Local fare is also served at *Restaurant Le Bip's* (☎ *04 95 46 06 26, 14 cours Paoli)*, a cellar restaurant at the bottom of the flight of stairs 20m down the hill from

Brasserie Le Bip's (☎ *04 95 46 04 48)*. The restaurant's 80FF *menu* changes daily; fish dishes cost 50FF to 120FF. Heading uphill to the citadel, there is *Le Gaffory* (☎ *04 95 61 05 58, place Gaffory)*, which has 60FF lunchtime *menus*.

By popular vote, Corte's best restaurant is *U Museu* (☎ *04 95 61 08 36, rampe Ribanelle)* which has an excellent range of tasty local fare. Among the recommended dishes are *civet de sanglier aux myrtes sauvages* (wild boar in myrtle) costing 65FF and *soissons Corses* (Corsican lima beans) for 49FF.

Self-Catering Corte's top boulangerie is the *Boulangerie de la Gare*, which is inside the main train station building – and does a roaring trade as a result!

There is a *Eurospar Supermarket (7 ave Xavier Luciani)* and a *Casino Supermarket (allée du 9 Septembre)*.

Getting There & Away

Bus Corte is on Eurocorse's Bastia–Ajaccio route, served by two buses daily in each direction (no Sunday service). The stop is at 3 ave Xavier Luciani, where a schedule is posted.

Train The train station (☎ 04 95 46 00 97) is staffed 8 am to noon and 2 to 6.30 pm (closed Sunday after 11 am early September to late June). You can leave luggage for free at the Grand Cafe (see Places to Eat).

AROUND CORTE

South-west of Corte, the clear, greenish-blue waters of the Restonica River flow past pine and chestnut groves as they tumble down **Gorges de la Restonica**, a deep valley whose grey-white granite walls are studded with bushes and trees. Some of the area's choicest trails begin about 16km south-west of Corte at **Bergeries de Grotelle** (1375m), which can be reached by car via the narrow D623.

Trails from here lead to a number of glacial lakes, including **Lac de Mello (Melu)** (1711m), a one-hour walk from the Bergeries (sheepfolds), and **Lac de Capitello**

(Capitellu) (1930m), 40 minutes beyond Lac de Mello near the GR20. Both are ice-covered half the year.

West of Corte, there are some arduous hiking trails in and around the **Tavignanu River Valley**, including one to **Lac Nino (Ninu)** (1743m; a 9½-hour walk from Corte). About 20km south of Corte lies fine

1526-hectare **Forêt de Vizzavona** (Vizzavona Forest; 800m to 1650m), cut through with 43km of forest trails. Magnificent **Cascade des Anglais**, accessible on foot from Vizzavona village, and the equally fantastic **Cascade du Voile de la Mariée**, farther south-west near Bocognano, are both worth the hike.

Language

Modern French developed from the *langue d'oïl*, a group of dialects spoken north of the Loire River that grew out of the vernacular Latin used during the late Gallo-Roman period. The langue d'oïl – particularly the Francien dialect spoken in the Île de France – eventually displaced the *langue d'oc*, the dialects spoken in the south of the country and from which the Mediterranean region of Languedoc got its name.

Standard French is taught and spoken in France, but its various accents and sub-dialects are an important source of identity in certain regions. In addition, some of the peoples subjected to French rule many centuries ago have preserved their traditional languages. These include Flemish in the far north; Alsatian in Alsace; Breton (a Celtic tongue similar to Cornish and Welsh) in Brittany; Basque (a language unrelated to any other) in the Basque Country; Catalan in Roussillon (Catalan is the official language of nearby Andorra and the first language of many in the Spanish province of Catalonia); Provençal in Provence; and Corsican on the island of Corsica.

Around 122 million people worldwide speak French as their first language; it is an official language in Belgium, Switzerland, Luxembourg, the Canadian province of Quebec and over two dozen other countries, most of them former French colonies in Africa. It is also spoken in the Val d'Aosta region of north-western Italy. Various forms of Creole are used in Haiti, French Guiana and parts of Louisiana. France even has a special government ministry (Ministère de la Francophonie) to deal with the country's relations with the French-speaking world.

While the French rightly or wrongly have a reputation for assuming that all human beings should speak French – until WWI it was *the* international language of culture and diplomacy – you'll find that any attempt to communicate in French will be much appreciated. Probably your best bet is always to approach people politely in French, even if the only sentence you know is *Pardon, madame/monsieur/mademoiselle, parlez-vous anglais?* (Excuse me, madam/sir/miss, do you speak English?).

For a more comprehensive guide to the French language get hold of Lonely Planet's *French phrasebook*.

Grammar

An important distinction is made in French between *tu* and *vous*, which both mean 'you'. *Tu* is only used when addressing people you know well, children or animals. When addressing an adult who is not a personal friend, *vous* should be used unless the person invites you to use *tu*. In general, younger people insist less on this distinction, and they may use *tu* from the beginning of an acquaintance.

All nouns in French are either masculine or feminine and adjectives reflect the gender of the noun they modify. The feminine form of many nouns and adjectives is indicated by a silent *e* added to the masculine form, as in *étudiant* and *étudiante*, the masculine and feminine for 'student'. In the following phrases we have indicated both masculine and feminine forms where necessary. The masculine form comes first, separated from the feminine by a slash. The gender of a noun is often indicated by a preceding article: 'the/a/some', *le/un/du* (m), *la/une/de la* (f); or a possessive adjective, 'my/your/his/her', *mon/ton/son* (m), *ma/ta/sa* (f). With French, unlike English, the possessive adjective agrees in number and gender with the thing possessed: 'his/her mother', *sa mère*.

Pronunciation

Most letters in French are pronounced more or less the same as their English equivalents. A few which may cause confusion are:

j   as the 's' in 'leisure', eg *jour* (day)

c   before e and i, as the 's' in 'sit';
     before a, o and u it's pronounced as
     the English 'k'. When underscored
     with a 'cedilla' (ç) it's always pro-
     nounced as the 's' in 'sit'.

French has a number of sounds that are difficult for Anglophones to produce. These
include:

- The distinction between the 'u' sound (as
  in *tu*) and 'oo' sound (as in *tout*). For both
  sounds, the lips are rounded and projected
  forwards, but for the 'u' the tongue is
  towards the front of the mouth, its tip
  against the lower front teeth, whereas for
  the 'oo' the tongue is towards the back of
  the mouth, its tip behind the gums of the
  lower front teeth.

- The nasal vowels. With nasal vowels the
  breath escapes partly through the nose and
  partly through the mouth. There are no
  nasal vowels in English; in French there
  are three, as in *bon vin blanc* (good white
  wine). These sounds occur where a sylla-
  ble ends in a single n or m; the n or m is
  silent but indicates the nasalisation of the
  preceding vowel.

- The r. The standard r of Parisian French is
  produced by moving the bulk of the tongue
  backwards to constrict the air flow in the
  pharynx while the tip of the tongue rests
  behind the lower front teeth. It's similar to
  the noise made by some people before spitting, but with much less friction.

Basics

Yes.	*Oui.*
No.	*Non.*
Maybe.	*Peut-être.*
Please.	*S'il vous plaît.*
Thank you.	*Merci.*
You're welcome.	*Je vous en prie.*
Excuse me.	*Excusez-moi.*
Sorry/Forgive me.	*Pardon.*

Greetings

Hello/Good morning.	*Bonjour.*
Good evening.	*Bonsoir.*
Good night.	*Bonne nuit.*
Goodbye.	*Au revoir.*

Small Talk

How are you?	*Comment allez-vous?* (polite) *Comment vas-tu?/ Comment ça va?* (informal)
Fine, thanks.	*Bien, merci.*
What's your name?	*Comment vous appelez-vous?*
My name is ...	*Je m'appelle ...*
I'm pleased to meet you.	*Enchanté* (m)/ *Enchantée.* (f)
How old are you?	*Quel âge avez-vous?*
I'm ... years old.	*J'ai ... ans.*
Do you like ...?	*Aimez-vous ...?*
Where are you from?	*De quel pays êtes-vous?*
I'm from ...	*Je viens ...*
Australia	*d'Australie*
Canada	*du Canada*
England	*d'Angleterre*
Germany	*d'Allemagne*
Ireland	*d'Irlande*
New Zealand	*de Nouvelle Zélande*
Scotland	*d'Écosse*
Wales	*du Pays de Galle*
the USA	*des États-Unis*

Language Difficulties

I understand.	*Je comprends.*
I don't understand.	*Je ne comprends pas.*
Do you speak English?	*Parlez-vous anglais?*
Could you please write it down?	*Est-ce que vous pouvez l'écrire?*

Getting Around

I want to go to ...	*Je voudrais aller à ...*
I'd like to book a seat to ...	*Je voudrais réserver une place pour ...*
What time does the ... leave/arrive?	*À quelle heure part/arrive ...?*
aeroplane	*l'avion*
bus (city)	*l'autobus*
bus (intercity)	*l'autocar*
ferry	*le ferry(-boat)*
train	*le train*
tram	*le tramway*

Where is (the) ...?	*Où est ...?*
bus stop	*l'arrêt d'autobus*
metro station	*la station de métro*
train station	*la gare*
tram stop	*l'arrêt de tramway*
ticket office	*le guichet*

I'd like a ... ticket.	*Je voudrais un billet ...*
one-way	*aller-simple*
return	*aller-retour*
1st class	*première classe*
2nd class	*deuxième classe*

| How long does the trip take? | *Combien de temps dure le trajet?* |

The train is ...	*Le train est ...*
delayed	*en retard*
on time	*à l'heure*
early	*en avance*

Do I need to ...?	*Est-ce que je dois ...?*
change trains	*changer de train*
change platform	*changer de quai*

left-luggage locker	*consigne automatique*
platform	*quai*
timetable	*horaire*

I'd like to hire ...	*Je voudrais louer ...*
a bicycle	*un vélo*
a car	*une voiture*
a guide	*un guide*

Signs

ENTRÉE	ENTRANCE
SORTIE	EXIT
OUVERT	OPEN
FERMÉ	CLOSED
CHAMBRES LIBRES	ROOMS AVAILABLE
COMPLET	NO VACANCIES
RENSEIGNEMENTS	INFORMATION
INTERDIT	PROHIBITED
(COMMISSARIAT DE) POLICE	POLICE STATION
TOILETTES, WC	TOILETS
HOMMES	MEN
FEMMES	WOMEN

Around Town

I'm looking for ...	*Je cherche ...*
a bank/ exchange office	*une banque/ un bureau de change*
the city centre	*le centre-ville*
the ... embassy	*l'ambassade de ...*
the hospital	*l'hôpital*
my hotel	*mon hôtel*
the market	*le marché*
the police	*la police*
the post office	*le bureau de poste/ la poste*
a public phone	*une cabine téléphonique*
a public toilet	*les toilettes*
the tourist office	*l'office de tourisme*

Where is (the) ...?	*Où est ...?*
beach	*la plage*
bridge	*le pont*
castle/mansion	*le château*
cathedral	*la cathédrale*
church	*l'église*
island	*l'île*
lake	*le lac*
main square	*la place centrale*
mosque	*la mosquée*
old city (town)	*la vieille ville*
the palace	*le palais*
quay/bank	*le quai/la rive*
ruins	*les ruines*
sea	*la mer*
square	*la place*
tower	*la tour*

| What time does it open/close? | *Quelle est l'heure d'ouverture/ de fermeture?* |
| I'd like to make a telephone call. | *Je voudrais téléphoner.* |

I'd like to change ...	*Je voudrais changer ...*
some money	*de l'argent*
travellers cheques	*chèques de voyage*

Directions

| How do I get to ...? | *Comment dois-je faire pour arriver à ...?* |
| Is it near/far? | *Est-ce près/loin?* |

LANGUAGE

Can you show me on the map/ city map?	*Est-ce que vous pouvez me le montrer sur la carte/le plan?*
Go straight ahead.	*Continuez tout droit.*
Turn left.	*Tournez à gauche.*
Turn right.	*Tournez à droite.*
at the traffic lights	*aux feux*
at the next corner	*au prochain coin*
behind	*derrière*
in front of	*devant*
opposite	*en face de*
north	*nord*
south	*sud*
east	*est*
west	*ouest*

Accommodation

I'm looking for ...	*Je cherche ...*
the youth hostel	*l'auberge de jeunesse*
the campground	*le camping*
a hotel	*un hôtel*
Where can I find a cheap hotel?	*Où est-ce que je peux trouver un hôtel bon marché?*
What's the address?	*Quelle est l'adresse?*
Could you write it down, please?	*Est-ce vous pourriez l'écrire, s'il vous plaît?*
Do you have any rooms available?	*Est-ce que vous avez des chambres libres?*
I'd like to book ...	*Je voudrais réserver ...*
a bed	*un lit*
a single room	*une chambre pour une personne*
a double room	*une chambre double*
a room with a shower and toilet	*une chambre avec douche et WC*
I'd like to stay in a dormitory.	*Je voudrais coucher dans un dortoir.*
How much is it ...?	*Quel est le prix ...?*
per night	*par nuit*
per person	*par personne*

Is breakfast included?	*Est-ce que le petit déjeuner est compris?*
Can I see the room?	*Est-ce que je peux voir la chambre?*
Where is ...?	*Où est ...?*
the bathroom	*la salle de bains*
the shower	*la douche*
Where is the toilet?	*Où sont les toilettes?*
I'm going to stay ...	*Je resterai ...*
one day	*un jour*
a week	*une semaine*

Shopping

How much is it?	*C'est combien?*
It's too expensive for me.	*C'est trop cher pour moi.*
Can I look at it?	*Est-ce que je peux le/la voir?* (m/f)
I'm just looking.	*Je ne fais que regarder.*
Do you accept credit cards?	*Est-ce que je peux payer avec ma carte de crédit?*
Do you accept travellers cheques?	*Est-ce que je peux payer avec des chèques de voyage?*
It's too big/small.	*C'est trop grand/petit.*
more/less	*plus/moins*
cheap	*bon marché*
cheaper	*moins cher*
bookshop	*la librairie*
chemist/pharmacy	*la pharmacie*
laundry/laundrette	*la laverie*
market	*le marché*
newsagency	*l'agence de presse*
stationers	*la papeterie*
supermarket	*le supermarché*

Time & Dates

What time is it?	*Quelle heure est-il?*
It's (two) o'clock.	*Il est (deux) heures.*
When?	*Quand?*
today	*aujourd'hui*
tonight	*ce soir*
tomorrow	*demain*

day after tomorrow	après-demain
yesterday	hier
all day	toute la journée
in the morning	du matin
in the afternoon	de l'après-midi
in the evening	du soir

Monday	lundi
Tuesday	mardi
Wednesday	mercredi
Thursday	jeudi
Friday	vendredi
Saturday	samedi
Sunday	dimanche

January	janvier
February	février
March	mars
April	avril
May	mai
June	juin
July	juillet
August	août
September	septembre
October	octobre
November	novembre
December	décembre

Numbers

1	un
2	deux
3	trois
4	quatre
5	cinq
6	six
7	sept
8	huit
9	neuf
10	dix
11	onze
12	douze
13	treize
14	quatorze
15	quinze
16	seize
17	dix-sept
20	vingt
100	cent
1000	mille

| one million | un million |

Emergencies

Help!	Au secours!
Call a doctor!	Appelez un médecin!
Call the police!	Appelez la police!
Leave me alone!	Fichez-moi la paix!
I've been robbed.	On m'a volé.
I've been raped.	On m'a violée.
I'm lost.	Je me suis égaré/ égarée. (m/f)

Health

I'm sick.	Je suis malade.
I need a doctor.	Il me faut un médecin.
Where is the hospital?	Où est l'hôpital?
I have diarrhoea.	J'ai la diarrhée.
I'm pregnant.	Je suis enceinte.

I'm ...	Je suis ...
diabetic	diabétique
epileptic	épileptique
asthmatic	asthmatique
anaemic	anémique

I'm allergic ...	Je suis allergique ...
to antibiotics	aux antibiotiques
to penicillin	à la pénicilline
to bees	aux abeilles

antiseptic	antiseptique
aspirin	aspirine
condoms	préservatifs
contraceptive	contraceptif
medicine	médicament
nausea	nausée
sunblock cream	crème solaire haute protection
tampons	tampons hygiéniques

FOOD

breakfast	le petit déjeuner
lunch	le déjeuner
dinner	le dîner
grocery store	l'épicerie

| I'd like the set menu. | Je prends le menu. |

I'm a vegetarian.	*Je suis végétarien/ végétarienne.*
I don't eat meat.	*Je ne mange pas de viande.*

Starters (Appetisers)

assiette anglaise
plate of cold mixed meats and sausages
assiette de crudités
plate of raw vegetables with dressings
entrée
starter
fromage de tête
pâté made with pig's head set in jelly
soufflé
a light, fluffy dish made with egg yolks,
stiffly beaten egg whites, flour and cheese
or other ingredients

Soup

bouillon
broth or stock
croûtons
fried or roasted bread cubes, often added
to soups
potage
thick soup made with puréed vegetables
soupe de poisson
fish soup
soupe du jour
soup of the day

Meat, Chicken & Poultry

agneau	lamb
aiguillette	thin slice of duck fillet
andouille or *andouillette*	sausage made from pork or veal tripe
bifteck	steak
bœuf	beef
bœuf haché	minced beef
boudin noir	blood sausage (black pudding)
brochette	kebab
canard	duck
caneton	duckling
cervelle	brains
charcuterie	cooked or prepared meats (usually pork)
cheval	horse meat
chèvre	goat
chevreau	kid (goat)
chevreuil	venison

côte	chop of pork, lamb or mutton
côtelette	cutlet
cuisses de grenouilles	frogs' legs
entrecôte	rib steak
dinde	turkey
épaule d'agneau	shoulder of lamb
escargot	snail
faisan	pheasant
faux-filet	sirloin steak
filet	tenderloin
foie	liver
foie gras de canard	duck liver pâté
foie gras d'oie	goose liver pâté
gibier	game
gigot d'agneau	leg of lamb
jambon	ham
langue	tongue
lapin	rabbit
lard	bacon
lardon	pieces of chopped bacon
lièvre	hare
mouton	mutton
oie	goose
pieds de porc	pigs' trotters
pigeonneau	squab (young pigeon)
pintade	guinea fowl
porc	pork
poulet	chicken
rillettes	pork pâté
rognons	kidneys
sanglier	wild boar
saucisson	large sausage
saucisson fumé	smoked sausage
steak	steak
tournedos	thick slices of fillet
tripes	tripe
veau	veal
venaison	venison
viande	meat
volaille	poultry

Common Meat & Poultry Dishes

blanquette de veau or *d'agneau*
veal or lamb stew with white sauce
chapon
capon
chou farci
stuffed cabbage

civet
  game stew
fricassée
  stew with meat that has first been fried
grillade
  grilled meats
marcassin
  young wild boar
steak tartare
  raw ground meat mixed with onion, raw
  egg yolk and herbs

Ordering a Steak

bleu
  nearly raw
saignant
  very rare (literally 'bleeding')
à point
  medium rare but still pink
bien cuit
  literally 'well cooked', but usually like
  medium rare

Fish & Seafood

anchois	anchovy
anguille	eel
bouzigues	mussels
brème	bream
brochet	pike
cabillaud	cod
calmar	squid
carrelet	plaice
chaudrée	fish stew
colin	hake
coquille Saint-Jacques	scallop
crabe	crab
crevette grise	shrimp
crevette rose	prawn
écrevisse	small, freshwater crayfish
fruits de mer	seafood
gambas	king prawns
goujon	gudgeon (small freshwater fish)
hareng	herring
homard	lobster
huître	oyster
langouste	crayfish
langoustine	very small saltwater 'lobster' (Dublin Bay prawn)

maquereau	mackerel
merlan	whiting
morue	cod
moules	mussels
oursin	sea urchin
palourde	clam
poisson	fish
raie	ray
rouget	mullet
sardine	sardine
saumon	salmon
sole	sole
thon	tuna
truite	trout

Vegetables, Herbs & Spices

ail	garlic
aïoli or *ailloli*	garlic mayonnaise
aneth	dill
anis	aniseed
artichaut	artichoke
asperge	asparagus
aubergine	aubergine (eggplant)
avocat	avocado
basilic	basil
betterave	beetroot
cannelle	cinnamon
carotte	carrot
céleri	celery
cèpe	cep (boletus mushroom)
champignon	mushroom
champignon de Paris	button mushroom
chou	cabbage
citrouille	pumpkin
concombre	cucumber
cornichon	gherkin (pickle)
courgette	courgette (zucchini)
crudités	small pieces of raw vegetables
échalotte	shallot
épice	spice
épinards	spinach
estragon	tarragon
fenouil	fennel
fève	broad bean
genièvre	juniper
gingembre	ginger
haricots	beans
haricots blancs	white beans

haricots rouge	kidney beans
haricots verts	French (string) beans
herbe	herb
laitue	lettuce
légume	vegetable
lentilles	lentils
maïs	sweet corn
menthe	mint
navet	turnip
oignon	onion
olive	olive
origan	oregano
panais	parsnip
persil	parsley
petit pois	pea
poireau	leek
poivron	green pepper
pomme de terre	potato
riz	rice
salade	salad or lettuce
sarrasin	buckwheat
seigle	rye
tomate	tomato
truffe	truffle

Cooking Methods

à la broche	spit-roasted
à la vapeur	steamed
au feu de bois	cooked over a wood-burning stove
au four	baked
en croûte	in pastry
farci	stuffed
fumé	smoked
gratiné	browned on top with cheese
grillé	grilled
pané	coated in bread-crumbs
rôti	roasted
sauté	sautéed (shallow fried)

Sauces & Accompaniments

béchamel
 basic white sauce
huile d'olive
 olive oil
mornay
 cheese sauce
moutarde
 mustard

pistou
 pesto (pounded mix of basil, hard cheese, pine-nuts, olive oil and garlic)
provençale
 tomato, garlic, herb and olive oil dressing or sauce
rouille
 spicy condiment made from red chillis, garlic, olive oil and fish stock
tartare
 mayonnaise with herbs
vinaigrette
 salad dressing made with oil, vinegar, mustard and garlic

Fruit & Nuts

abricot	apricot
amande	almond
ananas	pineapple
arachide	peanut
banane	banana
cacahuète	peanut
cassis	blackcurrant
cerise	cherry
citron	lemon
datte	date
figue	fig
fraise	strawberry
framboise	raspberry
grenade	pomegranate
groseille	red currant/gooseberry
mangue	mango
marron	chestnut
melon	melon
mirabelle	type of plum
myrtille	bilberry (blueberry)
noisette	hazelnut
noix de cajou	cashew
orange	orange
pamplemousse	grapefruit
pastèque	watermelon
pêche	peach
pistache	pistachio
poire	pear
pomme	apple
prune	plum
pruneau	prune
raisin	grape

Desserts & Sweets

crêpe (also known as *krampouez*)
 thin pancake

crêpes suzettes
 orange-flavoured crepes flambéed in liqueur
dragée
 sugared almond
éclair
 pastry filled with cream
farine de semoule
 semolina flour
flan
 egg-custard dessert
frangipane
 pastry filled with cream and flavoured with almonds or a cake mixture containing ground almonds
galette
 wholemeal or buckwheat pancake; also a type of biscuit
gâteau
 cake
gaufre
 waffle
gelée
 jelly
glace
 ice cream
glace au chocolat
 chocolate ice cream
île flottante
 literally 'floating island'; beaten egg-white lightly cooked, floating on a creamy sauce
sablé
 shortbread biscuit
tarte
 tart (pie)
tarte aux pommes
 apple tart

yaourt
 yoghurt

Snacks
croque-monsieur
 a grilled ham and cheese sandwich
croque-madame
 a croque-monsieur with a fried egg
frites
 chips (French fries)
quiche
 quiche; savoury egg, bacon and cream tart

Basics
beurre	butter
chocolat	chocolate
confiture	jam
crème fraîche	cream
farine	flour
huile	oil
lait	milk
miel	honey
œufs	eggs
poivre	pepper
sel	salt
sucre	sugar
vinaigre	vinegar

Utensils
bouteille	bottle
carafe	carafe
pichet	jug
verre	glass
couteau	knife
cuillère	spoon
fourchette	fork
serviette	serviette (napkin)

Glossary

(m) indicates masculine gender, (f) feminine gender and (pl) plural

accueil (m) – reception

alimentation (f) – grocery store

arrondissement (m) – administrative division of large city; abbreviated on signs as 1er (1st arrondissement), 2e or 2ème (2nd) etc

auberge de jeunesse (f) – youth hostel

baie (f) – bay

bastide (f) – medieval settlement in southwestern France, usually built on a grid plan and surrounding an arcaded square

belle époque (f) – literally 'beautiful age'; era of elegance and gaiety characterising fashionable Parisian life in the period preceding WWI

billet (m) – ticket

billet jumelé (m) – combination ticket, good for more than one site, museum etc

billeterie (f) – ticket office or counter

boulangerie (f) – bakery, bread shop

boules (f pl) – a game not unlike lawn bowls played with heavy metal balls on a sandy pitch; also called *pétanque*

brasserie (f) – restaurant usually serving food all day (original meaning: brewery)

bureau de change (m) – exchange bureau

bureau de poste (m) or *poste* (f) – post office

capitainerie (f) – harbour master's office

carnet (m) – a book of five or 10 bus, tram or metro tickets sold at a reduced rate

carrefour (m) – crossroads

carte (f) – card; menu; map

caserne (f) – military barracks

cave (f) – wine cellar

chambre (f) – room

chambre de bonne (f pl) – maids' quarters

chambre d'hôte (f) – B&B

charcuterie (f) – pork butcher's shop and delicatessen

chars à voile (m pl) – sand yachts

cimetière (m) – cemetery

coffre (m) – hotel safe

col (m) – mountain pass

consigne (f) – left-luggage office

consigne automatique (f) – left-luggage locker

consigne manuelle (f) – left-luggage office

correspondance (f) – linking tunnel or walkway, eg, in the metro; rail or bus connection

couchette (f) – sleeping berth on a train or ferry

cour (f) – courtyard

crémerie (f) – dairy, cheese shop

cyclisme (m) – cycling

dégustation (f) – tasting

demi (m) – 330mL glass of beer

demi-pension (f) – half-board (B&B with either lunch or dinner)

département (m) – administrative division of France

douane (f) – customs

église (f) – church

embarcadère (m) – pier, jetty

épicerie (f) – small grocery store

fauteuil (m) – seat on trains, ferries or at the theatre

fête (f) – festival

forêt (f) – forest

formule or **formule rapide** (f) – similar to a *menu* but allows choice of whichever two of three courses you want (eg, starter and main course or main course and dessert)

fouilles (f pl) – excavations at an archaeological site

foyer (m) – workers' or students' hostel

fromagerie (f) – cheese shop

funiculaire (m) – funicular railway

galerie (f) – covered shopping centre or arcade

gare or gare SNCF (f) – railway station
gare maritime (f) – ferry terminal
gare routière (f) – bus station
gaufre (f) – waffle with various toppings, usually eaten as a snack
gendarmerie (f) – police station; police force
gîte d'étape (m) – walkers' accommodation, usually in a village
gîte rural (m) – country cottage
golfe (m) – gulf
grande école (f) – prestigious educational institution offering training in such fields as business management, engineering and the applied sciences

halles (f pl) – covered market, central food market
halte routière (f) – bus stop
horaire (m) – timetable or schedule
hôte payant (m) – paying guest
hôtel de ville (m) – city or town hall
hôtes payants (m pl) or *hébergement chez l'habitant* (m) – homestays
hydroglisseur (m) – hydrofoil or hydroplane

intra-muros – old city (literally 'within the walls')

jardin (m) – garden
jardin botanique (m) – botanic garden
jours fériés (m pl) – public holidays

laverie (f) or *lavomatique* (m) – laundrette

mairie (f) – city or town hall
maison de la presse (f) – newsagent
maison du parc (f) – a national park's headquarters and/or visitors' centre
mandat postal (m) – postal money order
marché (m) – market
marché aux puces (m) – flea market
marché couvert (m) – covered market
mas (m) – farmhouse; tiny hamlet
menu (m) – fixed-price meal with two or more courses
mistral (m) – incessant north wind in southern France said to drive people crazy
Mobylette (f) – moped

musée (m) – museum

navette (f) – shuttle bus, train or boat

Occitan – a language also known as *langue d'oc* or sometimes Provençal, related to Catalan

palais de justice (m) – law courts
parlement (m) – parliament
pâtisserie (f) – cake and pastry shop
pensions de famille (f pl) – similar to B&Bs
pétanque (f) – see *boules*
pied noir (m) – literally, 'black feet'; the name given to Algerian-born French people
piste cyclable (f) – bicycle path
place (f) – square, plaza
plage (f) – beach
plan (m) – city map
plan du quartier (m) – map of nearby streets (hung on the wall near metro exits)
plat du jour (m) – daily special in a restaurant
pont (m) – bridge
port (m) – harbour, port
port de plaisance (m) – pleasure-boat harbour or marina
porte (f) – gate in a city wall
poste (f) or *bureau de poste* (m) – post office
poste (m) – telephone extension
préfecture (f) – prefecture (capital of a *département*)
presqu'île (f) – peninsula
pression (f) – draught beer

quai (m) – quay, railway platform
quartier (m) – quarter, district

refuge (m) – mountain hut, basic shelter for walkers
rez-de-chausée (m) – ground floor
rive (f) – bank of a river
riverain (m) – local resident
rond point (m) – roundabout
routier (m) – trucker or truckers' restaurant

sentier (m) – trail
service des urgences (f) – casualty ward

sortie (f) – exit
spectacle (m) – performance, play, theatrical show
square (m) – public garden
supplément (m) – supplement, additional cost
syndicat d'initiative (m) – tourist office

tabac (m) – tobacconist (also selling bus tickets, phonecards etc)
table d'orientation (f) – viewpoint indicator
taxe de séjour (f) – municipal tourist tax
télécarte (f) – phonecard
téléphérique (m) – cableway or cable car
télésiège (m) – chair lift
téléski (m) – ski lift, tow
tour (f) – tower
tour d'horloge (f) – clock tower

vallée (f) – valley
v.f. (f) – *version française*; a film dubbed in French
vieille ville (f) – old town or city
ville neuve (f) – new town or city
v.o. (f) – *version originale*; a nondubbed film with French subtitles
voie (f) – train platform

ACRONYMS

The French love acronyms as much as the British and Americans do. Many transport companies are known by acronyms whose derivations are entirely unknown by the average passenger.

BP – *boîte postale* (post office box)
FN – Front National (National Front)
GR – *grande randonnée* (long-distance hiking trail)
ONU – Organisation des Nations Unies (the UN)
PC – Parti Communiste
PS – Parti Socialiste
RPR – Rassemblement pour la République (right-wing political party)
SMIC – *salaire minimum interprofessionel de croissance* (minimum wage)
SNCF – Société Nationale des Chemins de Fer (state-owned railway company)
SNCM – Société Nationale Maritime Corse-Méditerranée (state-owned ferry company linking Corsica and mainland France)
TGV – *train à grande vitesse* (high-speed train, bullet train)
UDF – Union pour la Démocratie Française (right-wing political party)
VTT – *vélo tout terrain* (mountain bike)

Regional Dishes Glossary

Abbreviations

A&L – Alsace and Lorraine
AC – Atlantic Coast
B – Brittany
BU – Burgundy
C – Champagne
CA&M – Côte d'Azure and Monaco
CO – Corsica
FA&J – French Alps and the Jura
FBC – French Basque Country
FNF – Far Northern France
L – Lyons
L-R – Languedoc-Roussillon
LDQ – Limousin, the Dordogne and Quercy
LV – Loire Valley
MC – Massif Central
N – Normandy
P – Paris
PR – Provence
T&P – Toulouse and the Pyrenees

à la Languedocienne (L-R) – dishes with a garlicky garnish of tomatoes, aubergines and *cèpes*

à la Provençale (PR) – dish with garlic-seasoned tomatoes

agneau chilindron (FBC) – sautéed lamb with potatoes and garlic

aïoli garni (CA&M) – boiled fish with garlic mayonnaise

alouêttes sans têtes (CO) – beef olives

anchoïade (PR) – anchovy-paste dipping sauce

assiette Provençale (PR) – a mixture of regional savouries

baeckeoffe (A&L) – stew made of several meats (often pork, mutton and beef) and vegetables that have been marinated for two days; traditionally prepared at home before being cooked in the oven of a nearby bakery

bergamote (A&L) – tiny golden squares made with essence of bergamot, a pear-shaped citrus fruit grown in southern Europe

bleu des causses (L-R) – cheese

bœuf bourguignon (BU) – beef marinat-ed and cooked in red wine with mushrooms, onions and bacon

boles de picolat (L-R) – spicy pork meat-balls in a casserole

bonhomme Normand (N) – duck in a cider and cream sauce

bouillabaisse (PR) – at least three kinds of fresh fish cooked in broth with onions, tomatoes, saffron and various herbs, in-cluding bay leaves, sage and thyme

bouilliture (AC) – eel stew with wine, mushrooms and prunes

bourride (CA&M) – a rich fish soup

brebis (FBC) – ewe's milk cheese

brocciu (CO) – soft white cheese

calisson (PR) – a small confection made with almond paste

Calvados (N) – apple-flavoured brandy

Camembert (N) – a soft creamy cheese

canard à la Montmorency (P) – duck with cherries

canard flambé au Calvados (N) – duck with Calvados

cargolade (L-R) – grilled snails

cassis (BU) – liqueur made with blackcur-rants

cassoulet (T&P) – a rich casserole con-taining beans, knuckle of pork, preserved goose, bacon and sausage

cèpes (L-R) – boletus mushrooms

charcuterie (A&L) – bacon, little Stras-bourg sausages, knackwurst, smoked ham and smoked pork chops

chaudrée (AC) – fish stew

chèvre (PR) – goat's cheese that has been marinated for 15 days in herbs and olive oil and then sprinkled with *marc*

choucroute (L) – sauerkraut served with meat

choucroute Alsacienne or **choucroute garnie** (A&L) – sauerkraut served hot with charcuterie

choux au lard (A&L) – cabbage with bacon

civet (L-R) – spiny lobster cooked in wine

confit de canard (LDQ) – preserved duck

confit d'oie (LDQ) – preserved goose

coq à la bière (FNF) – carbonade-like chicken stew

coq au vin (BU) – chicken cooked in wine

corniottes (BU) – cheese cake

cotriade (B) – fish and potato stew

cou d'oie farci (LDQ) – goose's neck stuffed with pork and veal mince

couscous – a spicy North African dish consisting of steamed semolina and a meat stew

crème de cassis – blackcurrant-flavoured liqueur

crêpe au buerre (B) – buttered *crêpe*

crêpes Languedociennes (L-R) – rum-flambéed pancakes filled with vanilla cream

daube de bœuf (PR) – beef stew with red wine, cooked in a pot-bellied casserole called a *daubière*

diots au vin blanc (FA&J) – little spicy sausages cooked with white wine

douillon (N) – pear cooked in pastry

esqueixade de bacallà (L-R) – salt cod salad

estocaficado (PR) – salt cod and tomato stew

faire chabrot (LDQ) – the addition of wine to soup just before consumption

faisan au verjus (LDQ) – pheasant cooked in verjuice (unripe grape juice)

far breton (B) – prune and custard flan

feuilleté (LDQ) – light, triangular pastries filled with salmon, mussels etc

figatelli (CO) – a rich liver sausage

flammeküche or **tarte flambée** (A&L) – a thin layer of pastry topped with cream, onion, bacon and sometimes cheese or mushrooms and cooked in a wood-fired oven

fleichkechele (A&L) – mixed grilled meats

fondue au chocolat (T&P) – melted chocolate with fruits

fondue Auvergnate (MC) – cheese fondue made with Cantal

fondue bourguignonne (BU) – meat fondue with sauces

fondue Savoyarde (FA&J) – cheese fondue

fricandeau (L-R) – fresh tuna braised in a fish stock with olives or anchovies

fromage de chèvre (LV) – goat's milk cheese

fruits glacés (CA&M) – glazed or candied fruits

garbure (FBC) – a filling cabbage and bean soup

garbure (T&P) – a thick soup made with fresh vegetables, beans, cabbage and ham

gochuak (FBC) – hazelnut biscuits

gougère (BU) – salted soft cheese balls

jambon de Bayonne (FBC) – Bayonne ham

jambon en croûte (A&L) – ham wrapped in a crust of bread

jambon persillé (BU) – ham and parsley in aspic

jambonneau braisé (A&L) – ham

kanouga (FBC) – cubes of rich, chewy chocolate or coffee candy, wrapped in metallic paper

kir (BU) – sweet blackcurrant liqueur combined with white wine as an aperitif

kougelhopf (A&L) – sultana and almond cake easily identified by its ribbed, dome-like shape; traditionally eaten at breakfast and popular in France thanks to Marie-Antoinette, who tasted it for the first time when on a visit to Alsace

kouing-aman (B) – heavy buttery cake

Lyon mustard (L) – sharp mustard

macarons (AC) – soft biscuits made from almond flour, egg whites and sugar; brought to Saint Émilion in the 17th century by Ursuline nuns

madeleines (A&L) – small lemon tea-cakes adored by Proust

marc (PR) – spirit distilled from the debris left after the final pressing of grapes for wine

mesclun (CA&M) – a rather bitter salad of dandelion greens and other leaves

michettes (CA&M) – savoury bread stuffed with cheese, olives, anchovies and onions

miroton Lyonnais (L) – beef with onion

mojhettes (AC) – white beans

morue pochée (PR) – poached cod

mouchous (FBC) – almond biscuits

mouclade rochelaise (AC) – mussels in a cream and curry sauce

moules marinières (FBC) – mussels cooked in their own juice with onions

moutarde (BU) – mustard, flavoured with anything from tarragon to honey and ranging in taste from delicate to fiery

Munster (A&L) – strong-smelling soft cheese

pain brié (N) – thick white bread

pain d'épice (BU) – gingerbread made with honey and spices that traditionally takes six to eight weeks to prepare

Paris-Brest (P) – stuffed choux pastry ring

pescajoun aux fruits (LDQ) – egg pancake with fruit

pibales (AC) – baby eels

piccata (FA&J) – veal escalope in batter

pierrade (T&P) – meats that you grill yourself

pierre à feu (C) – meat that you cook for yourself on a hot volcanic rock

piperade (FBC) – a rich stew of tomatoes and peppers mixed with eggs and then scrambled

pochouse (BU) – freshwater fish stew

potage Saint-Germain (P) – garden pea soup

poule au pot (T&P) – chicken stuffed with vegetables and prepared with tomato sauce, a favourite of King Henri IV

poulet au vinaigre (L) – chicken in sour cream and vinegar

poulet Basquaise (FBC) – Basque-style chicken

poulet vallée d'Auge (N) – chicken in cream and cider

quenelles (L) – light fish dumplings, often made with pike

raclette (T&P) – melted cheese with cold cuts and pickles

ragoût de mouton (B) – lamb baked for five hours under a layer of roots and herbs

ratafia (C) – an aperitif liqueur flavoured with almonds

ratatouille (PR) – tomatoes, eggplant and squash, stewed together along with green peppers, garlic and various kinds of aromatic herb

salade fécampoise (N) – salad of potatoes, smoked herring and eggs

salade Lyonnaise (L) – green salad with croutons, bacon and egg

salmis de palombe (FBC) – wood pigeon partially roasted and then simmered in a rich sauce made with wine and vegetable purée

socca (CA&M) – a thin layer of chickpea flour and olive oil batter fried on a griddle

sole Normande (N) – sole with mussels, shrimps and mushrooms

soupe au pistou (PR) – a soup made with vegetables, noodles, beans, basil and garlic

spaetzle (A&L) – Alsatian noodles

tajines – slow cooked stews of meat and vegetables flavoured with herbs and spices from North Africa

tarte Alsacienne (A&L) – a custard tart made with local fruits, especially Alsatian plums called *quetsches*

tarte Lyonnaise (L) – custard tart with Kirsch and almonds

tartiflette (FA&J) – a filling concoction of oven-cooked potatoes and *reblochon* cheese

teurgoule (N) – a sweet, cinnamon-flavoured rice pudding typical of the Bayeux region

toro à la gardianne (L-R) – a rich stew of beef, herbs and red wine

tourte (A&L) – raised pie with ham, bacon or ground pork, eggs and leeks

tripes à la mode de Caen (N) – a heavily spiced tripe stew

tripoux (LDQ) – lamb's tripe with herbs

tripoux (MC) – mutton and veal tripe cooked in a white wine sauce

trois viandes sur pierre chaude
(FA&J) – thinly sliced pieces of beef, veal
and duck that you fry yourself on a hot
ceramic plate
truffade (MC) – potatoes prepared with
very young Cantal cheese
ttorro (FBC) – Basque fish soup

vacherin (L) – strawberry meringue tart

Welsh rarebit (FNF) – fondue prepared
with dark beer

zwiebelküche or **tarte à l'oignon**
(A&L) – an onion tart

Acknowledgments

Many thanks to the following travellers who wrote to us with helpful hints, useful advice and interesting anecdotes:

A Hobbs, Abbie Wilson, Adrian Rys, Adrienne Hogg, Adrienne Shaw, Ai Leen, Ailsa Townley, Albert Lo, Alex Aeachus, Alex Lennox, Alex Marcovitch, Alexander Winter, Alison Johnston, Alka Shingwekar, Allan Hough, Amanda Shaw, Andrea Rogge, Andrew Berger, Andy Semmler, Ann Read, Anna Angelsmark, Anne K Gulsvik, Antje Vogler, Antonella Rosati, Antonia Mitchell, Aysha Schurmann, Ayunsa Tani

Barry & Joanne Ducolon, BD Pollard, Benjamin Shinewald, Bettina Buesselmann, Bill & Jeannie Boyle, Bob Hammon, Braeme Brock, Brian Batley, Brian Hagen, Bruno Geoffrin, Bruno Morel

Cam Woolcock, Carmel Davidson, Cathryn Jones, Cato Kjarvik, Charles Mellor, Chris & Ginie Udy, Christine M Newcombe, Christoph Hediger, Claudia Turner, Cliff Ellen, Colin Cha Fong, Curt Pack

D Falkener, Daniel Guthrie, Dave Bullock, Dave Gelbert, David Adami, David Beauchamp, David Goodey, David Harris, David Smith, Denise Carter Evans, Dick Scotton, Didier van er Brule, Dina Paulsrud, Doug Drysdale, Dr P Henschke

Elaine Ellsworth, Elizabeth Compton, Elodie Boisson Kheng, Elodie Foucat, Emily Reardon, Eric Berg, Eric Bertrand, Eric Carlson, Erica Pelino, Ernest Enchelmeyer, Essi Suikkanen

Felix Chong, Fiona Enright, Fiona Radcliff, Fiona Trafford-Walker, Francois Szymanski, Frank Chai, Frederic Pichon

Geoff Brown, Giles Dawe, Gill Maddox, Glynn Bowen, Gordon Smith, Graeme Brock, Graham A Singh, Graham Ferreira, Graham Thompson, Guillaume Dijoux

H Belanger, Heather Phillips, Helen Motte, Hollis Gardner

Ian Deacon, Ian McColm

J McBride, J McDonogh, J Thom, J Wilsher, James AM Phillips, James Carty, James Prescott, James Rodger, Jan Bohuslav, Jane Johnston, Janine Brooks, Jay Smith, JE Wilson, Jennifer Cropley, Jenny Cross, Jeremy Petersen, Jessie Handoll, Jim Breen, Jim Havill, JM Curbieres, Joelie Key, John Cock, John, Tina & Rachel Sparks, Josephine Hsieh, Judith Kadouch, Judith Lovdokken, Julian Bryers, Julie Harper, June & Iain Eddy, June Wright

Karen Culley, Karen Kepke, Karen Pearce, Kate Perkins, Katherine Coventry, Katie Do, Katrina Vanin, Kay Bellingham, Ken Shaw, Kuo-ken Tai, Kylie Cox

Laura Thornton, Lawrence Webb, Libby Hankins, Linda Butler, Lindsay Inwood, Lindy Gaze, Lisa Dooley, Lisa Tait, Liz Freebairn, Louise Fogarty, Lyn Hoffman, Lynn McDonald

Malcolm Pearson, Malcolm Wallace, Malte Killisch, Manon Kok, Margaret & Michael Clark, Marge Gruzen, Marianne Pallotti, Marie-Nancy Bourques, Martha Bays, Martin Garvey, Marvin Baer, Masako Kakui, Matt Burgess, Matt Neil, May Backhouse, MB Maunsell, Melanie Lowe, Meredith Roe, Meredith Thompson, Michael Fougeres, Michael McLindon, Michael Tyler, Michelle Calderwood, Miriam Pizzoferrato, Mohammed A El-Kuwaiz

Nicole Topfer, Norman Pruter

Osa Kauffman, Oystein R Kvisla

Paolo Polini, Paul & Laura Wren, Paul Hockaday, Paul Tyler, Paula Seaton, Peter Butler, Peter Cocks, Peter Dickson, Phil Case, Philip Barker, Phyl Shimfield, Pieter Beelen

R Nalewajk, Reg Quelch, Richard Bush, Richard Oates, Richard Parr, Richard Stallard, Robert Canter, Robert Dorin, Robert Leonard, Rod Harris, Roderick White, Roger Gardiner, Ron Lamothe,

Ronen Kowalsky, Rosemary Craig, Ross McGregor, Ross Yarwood, Ryan Summers

Sally Carter, Samantha Walker, Sarah Earl, Scott T Sanders, Stephen Lead, Steve Risby, Sue Walker, Susan Morris, Susana Fortini, Susannah Witty, Sylvia Grant, Sylvie Delobel

Tamara Somers, Tatiana Blackington, The Hipperson family, Theresa Sweeny, Thierry Joly, Thng Hui Hong, Thomas Fuchs, Thomas Lim, Thomas

Rau, Tim Godby, Tim Hughes, Tom Ivancic, Tony Blackmore, Triin Rohtmae

Vaidyanathan Ganesh Ramachandran, Vanessa Hammond, Victor Dolcourt

Wayne McCallum

Yasmin Dalati

Zane Katsikis

LONELY PLANET

You already know that Lonely Planet publishes more than this one guidebook, but you might not be aware of the other products we have on this region. Here is a selection of titles that you may want to check out as well:

Corsica
ISBN 0 86442 792 1
US$15.95 • UK£9.99 • 120FF

Cycling France
ISBN 1 86450 036 0
US$19.99 • UK£12.99 • 149FF

French phrasebook
ISBN 0 86442 450 7
US$5.95 • UK£3.99 • 40FF

The Loire
ISBN 1 86450 097 2
US$17.99 • UK£11.99 • 140FF

Out to Eat Paris
ISBN 1 86450 107 3
US$14.99 • UK£7.99 • 99FF

Paris
ISBN 1 86450 125 1
US$15.99 • UK£9.99 • 119FF

Paris City Map
ISBN 1 86450 011 5
US$5.95 • UK£3.99 • 39FF

Paris condensed
ISBN 1 86450 044 1
US$9.95 • UK£5.99 • 59FF

Provence & the Côte d'Azur
ISBN 1 86450 196 0
US$17.99 • UK£11.99 • 139FF

South-West France
ISBN 0 86442 794 8
US$16.95 • UK£11.99 • 130FF

Walking in France
ISBN 0 86442 601 1
US$19.99 • UK£12.99 • 149FF

Available wherever books are sold.

LONELY PLANET

Guides by Region

Lonely Planet is known worldwide for publishing practical, reliable and no-nonsense travel information in our guides and on our Web site. The Lonely Planet list covers just about every accessible part of the world. Currently there are 16 series: Travel guides, Shoestring guides, Condensed guides, Phrasebooks, Read This First, Healthy Travel, Walking guides, Cycling guides, Watching Wildlife guides, Pisces Diving & Snorkeling guides, City Maps, Road Atlases, Out to Eat, World Food, Journeys travel literature and Pictorials.

AFRICA Africa on a shoestring • Cairo • Cairo City Map • Cape Town • Cape Town City Map • East Africa • Egypt • Egyptian Arabic phrasebook • Ethiopia, Eritrea & Djibouti • Ethiopian (Amharic) phrasebook • The Gambia & Senegal • Healthy Travel Africa • Kenya • Malawi • Morocco • Moroccan Arabic phrasebook • Mozambique • Read This First: Africa • South Africa, Lesotho & Swaziland • Southern Africa • Southern Africa Road Atlas • Swahili phrasebook • Tanzania, Zanzibar & Pemba • Trekking in East Africa • Tunisia • Watching Wildlife East Africa • Watching Wildlife Southern Africa • West Africa • World Food Morocco • Zimbabwe, Botswana & Namibia
Travel Literature: Mali Blues: Traveling to an African Beat • The Rainbird: A Central African Journey • Songs to an African Sunset: A Zimbabwean Story

AUSTRALIA & THE PACIFIC Auckland • Australia • Australian phrasebook • Australia Road Atlas • Bush-walking in Australia •Cycling New Zealand • Fiji • Fijian phrasebook • Healthy Travel Australia, NZ and the Pacific • Islands of Australia's Great Barrier Reef • Melbourne • Melbourne City Map • Micronesia • New Cale-donia • New South Wales & the ACT • New Zealand • Northern Territory • Outback Australia • Out to Eat – Melbourne • Out to Eat – Sydney • Papua New Guinea • Pidgin phrasebook • Queensland • Rarotonga & the Cook Islands • Samoa • Solomon Islands • South Australia • South Pacific • South Pacific phrasebook • Sydney • Sydney City Map • Sydney Condensed • Tahiti & French Polynesia • Tasmania • Tonga • Tramping in New Zealand • Vanuatu • Victoria • Walking in Australia • Watching Wildlife Australia • Western Australia
Travel Literature: Islands in the Clouds: Travels in the Highlands of New Guinea • Kiwi Tracks: A New Zealand Journey • Sean & David's Long Drive

CENTRAL AMERICA & THE CARIBBEAN Bahamas, Turks & Caicos • Baja California • Bermuda • Central America on a shoestring • Costa Rica • Costa Rica Spanish phrasebook • Cuba • Dominican Republic & Haiti • Eastern Caribbean • Guatemala • Guatemala, Belize & Yucatán: La Ruta Maya • Healthy Travel Central & South America • Jamaica • Mexico • Mexico City • Panama • Puerto Rico • Read This First: Central & South America • World Food Mexico • Yucatán
Travel Literature: Green Dreams: Travels in Central America

EUROPE Amsterdam • Amsterdam City Map • Amsterdam Condensed • Andalucía • Austria • Baltic States phrasebook • Barcelona • Barcelona City Map • Berlin • Berlin City Map • Britain • British phrasebook • Brus-sels, Bruges & Antwerp • Brussels City Map • Budapest • Budapest City Map • Canary Islands • Central Europe • Central Europe phrasebook • Corfu & the Ionians • Corsica • Crete • Crete Condensed • Croatia • Cycling Britain • Cycling France • Cyprus • Czech & Slovak Republics • Denmark • Dublin • Dublin City Map • Eastern Europe • Eastern Europe phrasebook • Edinburgh • Estonia, Latvia & Lithuania • Europe on a shoestring • Finland • Florence • France • Frankfurt Condensed • French phrasebook • Georgia, Armenia & Azerbaijan • Germany • German phrasebook • Greece • Greek Islands • Greek phrasebook • Hungary • Iceland, Greenland & the Faroe Islands • Ireland • Istanbul • Italian phrasebook • Italy • Krakow • Lisbon • The Loire • London • London City Map • London Condensed • Madrid • Malta • Mediterranean Europe • Mediterranean Europe phrasebook • Moscow • Mozambique • Munich • the Netherlands • Norway • Out to Eat – London • Paris • Paris City Map • Paris Condensed • Poland • Portugal • Portuguese phrasebook • Prague • Prague City Map • Provence & the Côte d'Azur • Read This First: Europe • Romania & Moldova • Rome • Rome City Map • Russia, Ukraine & Belarus • Russian phrasebook • Scandinavian & Baltic Europe • Scandinavian Europe phrase-book • Scotland • Sicily • Slovenia • South-West France • Spain • Spanish phrasebook • St Petersburg • St Petersburg City Map • Sweden • Switzerland • Trekking in Spain • Tuscany • Ukrainian phrasebook • Venice • Vienna • Walking in Britain • Walking in France • Walking in Ireland • Walking in Italy • Walking in Spain • Walking in Switzerland • Western Europe • Western Europe phrasebook • World Food France • World Food Ireland • World Food Italy • World Food Spain
Travel Literature: Love and War in the Apennines • The Olive Grove: Travels in Greece • On the Shores of the Mediterranean • Round Ireland in Low Gear • A Small Place in Italy • After Yugoslavia

LONELY PLANET

Mail Order

Lonely Planet products are distributed worldwide. They are also available by mail order from Lonely Planet, so if you have difficulty finding a title please write to us. North and South American residents should write to 150 Linden St, Oakland, CA 94607, USA; European and African residents should write to 10a Spring Place, London NW5 3BH, UK; and residents of other countries to Locked Bag 1, Footscray, Victoria 3011, Australia.

INDIAN SUBCONTINENT Bangladesh • Bengali phrasebook • Bhutan • Delhi • Goa • Healthy Travel Asia & India • Hindi & Urdu phrasebook • India • Indian Himalaya • Karakoram Highway • Kerala • Mumbai (Bombay) • Nepal • Nepali phrasebook • Pakistan • Rajasthan • Read This First: Asia & India • South India • Sri Lanka • Sri Lanka phrasebook • Tibet • Tibetan phrasebook • Trekking in the Indian Himalaya • Trekking in the Karakoram & Hindukush • Trekking in the Nepal Himalaya
Travel Literature: The Age of Kali: Indian Travels and Encounters • Hello Goodnight: A Life of Goa • In Rajasthan • A Season in Heaven: True Tales from the Road to Kathmandu • Shopping for Buddhas • A Short Walk in the Hindu Kush • Slowly Down the Ganges

ISLANDS OF THE INDIAN OCEAN Madagascar & Comoros • Maldives • Mauritius, Réunion & Seychelles

MIDDLE EAST & CENTRAL ASIA Bahrain, Kuwait & Qatar • Central Asia • Central Asia phrasebook • Dubai • Hebrew phrasebook • Iran • Israel & the Palestinian Territories • Istanbul • Istanbul City Map • Istanbul to Cairo on a shoestring • Jerusalem • Jerusalem City Map • Jordan • Lebanon • Middle East • Oman & the United Arab Emirates • Syria • Turkey • Turkish phrasebook • World Food Turkey • Yemen
Travel Literature: Black on Black: Iran Revisited • The Gates of Damascus • Kingdom of the Film Stars: Journey into Jordan

NORTH AMERICA Alaska • Boston • Boston City Map • California & Nevada • California Condensed • Canada • Chicago • Chicago City Map • Deep South • Florida • Great Lakes • Hawaii • Hiking in Alaska • Hiking in the USA • Honolulu • Las Vegas • Los Angeles • Los Angeles City Map • Louisiana & The Deep South • Miami • Miami City Map • New England • New Orleans • New York City • New York City City Map • New York City Condensed • New York, New Jersey & Pennsylvania • Oahu • Out to Eat – San Francisco • Pacific Northwest • Puerto Rico • Rocky Mountains • San Francisco • San Francisco City Map • Seattle • Southwest • Texas • USA • USA phrasebook • Vancouver • Virginia & the Capital Region • Washington DC • Washington, DC City Map • World Food Deep South, USA • World Food New Orleans
Travel Literature: Caught Inside: A Surfer's Year on the California Coast • Drive Thru America

NORTH-EAST ASIA Beijing • Beijing City Map • Cantonese phrasebook • China • Hiking in Japan • Hong Kong • Hong Kong City Map • Hong Kong Condensed • Hong Kong, Macau & Guangzhou • Japan • Japanese phrasebook • Korea • Korean phrasebook • Kyoto • Mandarin phrasebook • Mongolia • Mongolian phrasebook • Seoul • Shanghai • South-West China • Taiwan • Tokyo
Travel Literature: In Xanadu: A Quest • Lost Japan

SOUTH AMERICA Argentina, Uruguay & Paraguay • Bolivia • Brazil • Brazilian phrasebook • Buenos Aires • Chile & Easter Island • Colombia • Ecuador & the Galapagos Islands • Healthy Travel Central & South America • Latin American Spanish phrasebook • Peru • Quechua phrasebook • Read This First: Central & South America • Rio de Janeiro • Rio de Janeiro City Map • Santiago • South America on a shoestring • Santiago • Trekking in the Patagonian Andes • Venezuela
Travel Literature: Full Circle: A South American Journey

SOUTH-EAST ASIA Bali & Lombok • Bangkok • Bangkok City Map • Burmese phrasebook • Cambodia • Hanoi • Healthy Travel Asia & India • Hill Tribes phrasebook • Ho Chi Minh City • Indonesia • Indonesian phrasebook • Indonesia's Eastern Islands • Jakarta • Java • Lao phrasebook • Laos • Malay phrasebook • Malaysia, Singapore & Brunei • Myanmar (Burma) • Philippines • Pilipino (Tagalog) phrasebook • Read This First: Asia & India • Singapore • Singapore City Map • South-East Asia on a shoestring • South-East Asia phrasebook • Thailand • Thailand's Islands & Beaches • Thailand, Vietnam, Laos & Cambodia Road Atlas • Thai phrasebook • Vietnam • Vietnamese phrasebook • World Food Thailand • World Food Vietnam

ALSO AVAILABLE: Antarctica • The Arctic • The Blue Man: Tales of Travel, Love and Coffee • Brief Encounters: Stories of Love, Sex & Travel • Chasing Rickshaws • The Last Grain Race • Lonely Planet Unpacked • Not the Only Planet: Science Fiction Travel Stories • Lonely Planet On the Edge • Sacred India • Travel with Children • Travel Photography: A Guide to Taking Better Pictures

LONELY PLANET

Mail Order

Lonely Planet products are distributed worldwide. They are also available by mail order from Lonely Planet, so if you have difficulty finding a title please write to us. North and South American residents should write to Embarcadero West, 155 Filbert St, Suite 251, Oakland, CA 94607, USA; European and African residents should write to 10a Spring Place, London NW5 3BH; and residents of other countries to PO Box 617, Hawthorn, Victoria 3122, Australia.

Index

Text

A

Abbaye de Cîteaux 554–5
Abbaye de Fontenay 567
accommodation 106–11
Accous 819–20
activities, see individual
  activities
Agde 876
Aigies Mortes 965
Aiguille du Midi 617
air travel 137–42, 150
  airports & airlines 137
  Australia 142
  buying tickets 137–9
  Canada 141
  Continental Europe 141–2
  Ireland 142
  New Zealand 142
  North Africa 142
  UK 140
  USA 140–1
  within France 150
Aix-en-Provence 928–35
Aix-les-Bains 636
Ajaccio 1027–32, **1028**
Albert 326
Albertville 636
Albi 836–40, **837**
Alençon 381–2
Alès-en-Cévennes 891–3
Alpe d'Huez 652
Alps, the 29, 608–57, **609**
Alsace 454–482, **455**
Ambleteuse 316
Amboise 526–9, **527**
Amiens 328–32, **329**
Andlau 470
Andorra 850–66, **851**
  accommodation 855
  geography 850–2
  getting around 856
  getting there & away 855–6
  history 850
Andorra la Vella 856–60, **858–9**
Angers 534–8, **535**
Anjou 534–41
Annecy 626–31, **628**

Antibes 989
Apt 954–5
Arcachon 769–72, **770**
architecture 44–9
Arinsal 861–2
Arles 955–62, **957**
Arras 321–4, **322**
Arreau 811
Arromanches 369–72
Arthur, King 385, 429
Atlantic Coast 733–4, **734**
Aubazime 699
Aubusson 697-8
Auch 842–5, **843**
Audinghen 315
Autoire 731
Autun 576–80, **577**
Auxerre 560–5, **562**
Avallon 567–71, **568**, **569**
Avignon 935–44, **936**

B

Baccarat 489
Bagnères de Luchon 824–5
Baldaccini, César 52
Ballon d'Alsace 480
ballooning 102
  Loire Valley 505
Barbie, Klaus 589
bars 131
Basilique St-Denis 281–2
Basilique St-Sernin 829
Bastia 1042–6, **1043**
Bastille Day 96–7
Battle of Normandy 369, 370
Battle of the Somme 324–8, **325**
Baudelaire, Charles 43
Baume-les-Messieurs 663
Bayeux 363–9, **364**
  Tapestry 365
Bayonne 777–84, **778–9**
beaches
  Cannes 992
  Corsica 1041
  Fréjus 1002
  Menton 1013
  St-Raphaël 1002
  St-Tropez 1003–04
Beaujolais 604–5
Beaulieu-sur-Dordogne 701–2

Beaune 556–60, **557**
Beauvais 332–4, **333**
Bedous 819
Belfort 663–4
Belle Île 423–4
Bergerac 719–20
Berlioz, Hector 40
Bernadotte, Jean-Baptiste 802
Besançon 657–62, **659**
Besse-en-Chandesse 682
Béziers 876
Biarritz 784–8, **785**
bicycle travel, see cycling
Bidarray 797
Biot 988
bird-watching 101
Blésois 510–17
Blois 510–17, **511**
boating, see also canoeing
  Burgundy 544
  Languedoc 899
  Provence 940, 965–6
boat travel 145–9
  Canada 149
  Channel Islands 148
  Ireland 148
  Italy 148
  North Africa 148–9
  UK 145–8
  USA 149
Bonaparte, Napoleon, see
  Napoleon
Bonifacio 1038–42, **1040**
books 77–9, see also
  literature
Borce 820–2
Bordeaux 755–64, **756**
  wine 764–5
Bormes-les-Mimosas 1006
Boulogne-sur-Mer 316–20, **317**
Bouziès 725–6
Brest 404–6
Breton flag 386
Briançon 653–6, 654
Briare 509
Brittany 383–434, **384**
Brive-la-Gaillarde 698–9
bullfighting 956
Bunifaziu, see Bonifacio
Burgundy 542–83, **543**

Bold indicates maps.

Boxed Text

MAP LEGEND

BOUNDARIES

━·━·━·━·━ International
━··━··━··━ Regional

HYDROGRAPHY

Coastline
River, Creek
Lake
Canal
Spring, Rapids
Waterfalls
Swamp
Cemetery

PARIS .... National Capital
Nantes .... Large City
Lorient .... City
Redon .... Large Town
Janzé .... Town
La Goutas .... Village
Place to Stay
Camping Ground
Caravan Park
Chalet or Hut
Place to Eat
Pub or Bar
Airport
Ancient or City Wall
Archaeological Site
Bank
Beach

ROUTES & TRANSPORT

Freeway
Highway
Major Road
Minor Road
Unsealed Road
City Freeway
City Highway
City Road
City Street, Lane

Pedestrian Mall
Tunnel
Train Route & Station
Metro & Station
Tramway
Cable Car or Chairlift
Walking Track
Walking Tour
Ferry Route

AREA FEATURES

Building
Park, Gardens
Market
Beach, Desert

MAP SYMBOLS

Border Crossing
Bus Stop, Station
Castle or Fort
Cathedral or Church
Cave
Cliff or Escarpment
Dive Site
Embassy
Ferry or Boat Terminal
Hospital
Internet Cafe
Monument
Mountain or Hill
Museum
National Park

One Way Street
Parking
Pass
Police Station
Post Office
Shopping Centre
Ski Field
Stately Home or Palace
Surf Beach
Swimming Pool
Telephone
Temple
Toilet
Tourist Information
Transport
Vineyard or Winery
Zoo

Note: not all symbols displayed above appear in this book

LONELY PLANET OFFICES

Australia
Locked Bag 1, Footscray, Victoria 3011
☎ 03 9689 4666 fax 03 9689 6833
email: talk2us@lonelyplanet.com.au

USA
150 Linden St, Oakland, CA 94607
☎ 510 893 8555 TOLL FREE: 800 275 5555
fax 510 893 8572
email: info@lonelyplanet.com

UK
10a Spring Place, London NW5 3BH
☎ 020 7428 4800 fax 020 7428 4828
email: go@lonelyplanet.co.uk

France
1 rue du Dahomey, 75011 Paris
☎ 01 55 25 33 00 fax 01 55 25 33 01
email: bip@lonelyplanet.fr
www.lonelyplanet.fr

World Wide Web: www.lonelyplanet.com or AOL keyword: lp
Lonely Planet Images: lpi@lonelyplanet.com.au